ROTHMANS FOOTBALL YEARBOOK 1994-95

EDITOR: JACK ROLLIN

First published in 1994
by HEADLINE BOOK PUBLISHING

10 9 8 7 6 5 4 3 2 1

Cover photographs *Action Images.* **Front** Ryan Giggs (Manchester United)

British Library Cataloguing in Publication Data
Rothmans Football Yearbook.—1994–95
1. Association Football—Serials
796.334′05

ISBN 0 7472 1030 6 (hardback)
0 7472 7857 1 (softback)

Typeset by BPC Whitefriars Ltd,
Tunbridge Wells

Printed and bound in Great Britain by
BPC Hazell Books Ltd
Member of BPC Ltd

HEADLINE BOOK PUBLISHING
A division of Hodder Headline PLC
338 Euston Road
London NW1 3BH

CONTENTS

INTERNATIONAL FOOTBALL

EUROPEAN FOOTBALL

NON-LEAGUE FOOTBALL

INFORMATION AND RECORDS

INTRODUCTION

The 25th edition of Rothmans Football Yearbook provides a comprehensive list of all results in the World Cup including the qualifying competition. For the finals, there are results, goalscorers, times and attendances plus referees.

On the domestic scene there are again six pages for each English club in the FA Carling Premiership and Endsleigh Insurance League. Though squad numbers were used in the Premier and by some clubs in the Football League, the more familiar 1 to 11 and 12 and 14 numbers have been utilised.

There are complete new entries for the 92 English clubs under the 'Did you know' section, coverage of amateur, schools, university and women's football. The performances of British clubs in Europe are monitored and special articles include those on the Football Trust, Football and the law, Referees and the involvement of the Chaplains in the game.

Transfer fees are again listed, but there remains a wide variation in what can be determined as an accurate figure, when net fees, tribunal decisions and complicated additional payments are concerned. Also the date when a player is signed often varies from the one given as his registration. Again players notified as being transferred between non-league clubs are also quoted without an indication of fees.

The Editor would like to thank Alan Elliott for the Scottish section, Norman Barrett for the Milestones Diary and Ian Vosper for the Obituaries. Thanks are also dues to John English who provided his usual painstaking and conscientious reading of the proofs. Appreciation, too, for the fine editorial assistance of Glenda Meeson and Christine Forrest.

The Editor would also like to pay tribute to the various organisations who have helped to make this edition complete, especially Sheila Murphy of the Football League, Mike Foster of the FA Premier League and the secretaries of all the Football League and Scottish League clubs for their kind co-operation. The ready availability of Football League secretary David Dent and his staff to answer queries was as usual most appreciated especially Ian Cotton and Chris Hull and thanks are due in equal measure to the Scottish Football League as well as Adrian Cook and Neil Harrison of the FA Premier League.

ACKNOWLEDGEMENTS

The Editor would also like to express his appreciation of the following individuals and organisations for their co-operation: Glynis Firth, Sandra Whiteside, Lorna Parnell, Debbie Birch (all from the Football League), David C. Thompson of the Scottish League, Alan Dick, Malcolm Brodie, Bob Hennessy, Peter Hughes (English Schools FA), W.P. Goss (AFA), Ken Scott for GM Vauxhall Conference information, Rev. Nigel Sands, Edward Grayson, Ken Goldman, Andy Howland and Don Aldridge.

Special thanks are due to Lorraine Jerram of Headline Book Publishing Ltd for her unflagging patience, sincerity, understanding and appreciation plus excellent support from Fiona Matthews.

Finally sincere thanks to Allan Wyatt, Trevor Stevens and the production staff at BPC Whitefriars for their efforts in the production of this book which was much appreciated throughout the year.

EDITORIAL

Much of the focus of attention during the World Cup was on the alleged yellow peril of cautions issued and its implications for the domestic game. This was, in reality, a red herring.

Reference to Football and the Law on Page 986 clearly shows that the crackdown on players kicking opponents from behind is something which should not have been allowed to develop anyway.

That said, much of what was seen in the World Cup was positive and might yet prevent those in authority, who had become nervous over the negative trends which were apparent in the 1990 World Cup, from implementing drastic changes. Larger goals, abolition of offside and kicks-in were among the ideas being freely discussed. The kick-in has yet to be kicked out.

A more liberal view of the offside law was again nothing new. According to Law XI, a player shall not be declared off-side merely by being in an off-side position. The interpretation of interfering with play, is open to argument and abuse in varying proportions and countless wiseacres have been quoted as enquiring what was a player doing there if he was not being so involved.

The penalty shoot-out ending to Brazil's victory over Italy was the greatest disappointment, but success went to the most accomplished team. Yet surely this must be the last time players will be required to decide the symbol of world professional football supremacy by a lottery.

Awarding three points for a win did not have any factual effect on the group tables. With two points, the placings would have all been the same. Does attitude depend on incentive or vice versa?

Domestically, crowds were again on the up and up, the overall increase for the four leading divisions being more than a million. Premiership champions Manchester United were the best supported team in the country with an average crowd of 44,244. But they did not have the highest attendance in League games. That honour went to Aston Villa when 45,347 turned up for the last viewing of the Holte End terracing before ground alterations removed it. Such nostalgia is to be applauded and for a similar reason, Huddersfield Town's last home game at their ground before moving a few yards away, brought in another sentimental gathering.

For the first time squad numbers were used in the FA Carling Premiership and by some teams in the Endsleigh Insurance League. We decided that the more familiar 1 to 11 was in keeping with our requirements. In five or ten years time the No. 40 as used by goalkeeper Jon Sheffield on loan to Swindon Town will mean little or nothing. Similarly the No.1 as used by Charlton Athletic's defender Stuart Balmer might confuse him with a goalkeeper. Playing for Blackburn against Shrewsbury in a Coca-Cola Cup replay on 9 November, Ian Pearce wore no number at all...The defence rests.

Numbers have gradually meant little or nothing in the game for many years, probably since the demise of the WM formation in the early 1960s. In fact it is interesting to note that the goalscoring record was established in 1960–61 when 6985 goals were scored in the same number of matches as last season. Thirty or more years ago the average was 3.44, last season it was slightly down on 1992–93 at 2.67 with 5418 goals scored.

A sour note was reached with the number of dismissals which totalled 288 at the end of the full League programme and included cup games but not the play-offs, which alas increased the overall total.

ROTHMANS 25TH ANNIVERSARY AWARDS

1970 **GORDON BANKS** Stoke City and England goalkeeper. Touched memorable heights with his World Cup performances in Mexico.

1971 **FRANK McLINTOCK** Arsenal and Scotland defender. His commanding presence and inspiring leadership fired the Gunners League and Cup double.

1972 **BRIAN CLOUGH** Charismatic and controversial manager of Derby County who insisted on and delivered entertaining football.

1973 **BOBBY CHARLTON** Manchester United and England forward who retired after an illustrious career which epitomised the Busby era.

1974 **BILLY BREMNER** Ebullient midfield dynamo of the successful Leeds United team and a Scottish international of renown. Five Rothmans awards in a row.

1975 **ALAN MULLERY** Fulham and England midfield player. Industrious, skilful yet part of the club's football with a smile approach. Player of the Year.

1976 **LAWRIE McMENEMY** Canny manager of unfashionable Southampton the Second Division team who beat Manchester United in the FA Cup final.

1977 **JACK TAYLOR** England and FIFA referee, respected all over the world for his integrity and impartiality as a first-class official.

1978 **PETER SHILTON** Cost a then record £250,000 for a goalkeeper and conceded just 18 goals in 37 matches as Nottingham Forest won the title.

1979 **TREVOR FRANCIS** the first domestic £1 million transfer. Shrugged off this expensive tag and graced Forest and England attacks.

1980 **TREVOR BROOKING** West Ham United's majestic midfield maestro turned goalscorer in their successful FA Cup Final at Wembley.

1981 **GLENN HODDLE** Midfield general of Tottneham Hotspur whose flair and vision shone through the season for Spurs and England.

1982 **KENNY DALGLISH** the influential Scottish attack organiser in Liverpool's 13th League championship and League Cup success.

1983 **GRAHAM TAYLOR** Manager of homespun Watford who against the odds took the club to runners-up place in the First Division.

1984 **JOHN HOLLINS** Chelsea and England midfield player who bowed out after displaying exemplary conduct and consistency in over 700 League games.

1985 **PAT JENNINGS** Arsenal's gentle giant of a goalkeeper in his testimonial season and at 40 was still a first choice for Northern Ireland.

1986 **GARY LINEKER** Everton and England striker. Emerged as a world class player and finished as leading scorer in the World Cup finals.

1987 **CLIVE ALLEN** Tottenham Hotspur and England forward. Maintained an impressive scoring rate in the top flight with 49 League and cup goals.

1988 **STEVE BULL** Wolverhampton Wanderers centre-forward who became the first player to achieve more than 50 goals in a season for 27 years.

1989 **GEORGE GRAHAM** Arsenal manager who showed shrewd tactical awareness in masterminding the League title for the Highbury club.

1990 **ALAN HANSEN** Elegant Scottish international central defender of Liverpool who made light of persistent injury in their 18th League championship.

1991 **STUART PEARCE** Nottingham Forest and England left-back, the first defender to score as many as 16 League and Cup goals without the aid of a penalty kick.

1992 **GORDON STRACHAN** Sprightly Leeds United and Scotland veteran whose example and stamina befitted a player half his age.

1993 **ALEX FERGUSON** The manager who brought the chamionship back to Manchester United after 26 years in a eye-catching style appreciated at Old Trafford.

1994 **ALAN SHEARER** Missed early weeks of the season with injury but still scored nearly half of Blackburn Rovers goals in their chase for the title.

MILESTONES DIARY 1993–94

June 1993

Ardiles takes over at Spurs ... Beardsley returns to Newcastle ... Marseille accused of match-fixing

13 England salvage some pride in Washington with a 1-1 draw against Brazil, David Platt scoring soon after coming on at the start of the second half, but a Brazilian equalizer 14 minutes from time denies England a first victory for 3 months. In Italy, three days' of rioting in Perugia greets the news that the local club may be denied promotion to Serie B because of bribery allegations.

14 Terry Venables loses his legal battle with Alan Sugar to remain Spurs' chief executive as the High Court upholds their right to sack him, their focal point being the background to Teddy Sheringham's transfer from Nottm Forest last summmer. England U-15 Schoolboys beat Germany 3-0 at Don Valley, Sheffield.

15 England U-21s beat France 1-0 to win the Toulon Tournament for the third time in four years.

16 A Steve Staunton free-kick gives Ireland a 1-0 win in Lithuania, taking them top of World Cup Group 3.

18 Forest pay Millwall £1.5m for defender Colin Cooper. UEFA ban Poland from staging internationals in Chorzow as a result of violence when England played there earlier this month.

19 W.Germany beat England 2-1 at the Pontiac Silverdome, the first major international to be played indoors on grass, and win US Cup '93, English finishing last. West Brom threaten to sue as manager Ossie Ardiles leaves them to take over the hot seat at Spurs; they appoint his assistant, former Spurs boss Keith Burkinshaw, in his place.

22 Neil Ruddock refuses Spurs' new deal.

23 Southend sell Stan Collymore to Nottm Forest for £2m. Peter Beardsley returns to Newcastle, signed for £1.4m from Everton.

24 Valenciennes striker Christophe Robert is arrested over allegations of match fixing in Marseille's crucial end-of-season fixture.

25 FA chief executive Graham Kelly is to head their probe into allegations of corruption in the game.

28 Carlton Palmer, 27, signs a new 5-year contract with Sheffield Wed.

29 Marseille are now accused of attempting to bribe CSKA Moscow players in last season's European Cup.

30 Edwin Stein resigns as manager of Barnet to join former boss Barry Fry as assistant at Southend.

July

Premier League to be known as FA Carling Premiership ... Rangers break British record with £4m for Duncan Ferguson ... Man Utd pay £3.75m for Roy Keane ... Football League to be known as Endsleigh Insurance League

1 Police detain 12 Marseille players for questioning re the growing bribes scandal, after Argentinian Jorge Burruchaga of Valenciennes becomes the third player charged with corruption.

2 A Football League commission clears 12 Barnet players to receive free transfers. French police question Marseille general manager Jean-Pierre Bernès over his alleged part in bribery scandal.

4 Zambia, less than 10 weeks after losing all but three of their first-choice players in an air crash, beat Morocco 2-1 in Lusaka in a World Cup qualifying match.

5 UEFA are to hold an inquiry into the Marseille bribery scandal, even though CSKA Moscow have suddenly withdrawn their allegations.

6 Ossie Ardiles sacks Ray Clemence and appoints Steve Perryman as his assistant and Pat Jennings as Spurs goalkeeper coach; Doug Livermore, who shared the first-team running with Clemence last season, will remain to handle first-team coaching and scouting.

9 Glenn Roeder leaves Gillingham to become Watford manager, replacing Steve Perryman, who resigned before joining Spurs earlier this week.

10 The Polish FA strip Legia Warsaw of the League title after a match-rigging scandal.

12 Leeds pay a club record £2.9m for striker Briane Deane, and Sheffield Utd directors Derek Dooley and Bernard Proctor resign in protest after chairman Reg Brealey accepts the increased offer. The Premier League will be known as the FA Carling Premiership next season. Marseille's Jean-Jacques Eydelie confesses to offering bribes to three Valenciennes players, after his wife accuses general manager Bernès of instigating the bribes.

13 Hearts become Scotland's third club in the UEFA Cup after Polish teams Legia Warsaw and LKS Lodz are banned for match-fixing in the Polish championship.

14 Sampdoria sign England captain David Platt from fellow Italian club Juventus for an estimated £5.2m, bringing his career transfer aggregate to £17.4m. Rangers sign Dundee Utd striker Duncan Ferguson for a British record £4m. Des Walker of Sampdoria agrees to sign for Sheffield Wed in a £2.7m deal. Huddersfield manager Ian Ross resigns.

15 Neil Warnock takes over at Huddersfield, their 6th manager in 8 years.

19 Manchester Utd sign Roy Keane from Nottm Forest for £3.75m. United's young Welsh star Ryan Giggs signs a 3-year sponsorship deal for an estimated £325,000 with boot manufacturers Reebok. The Football League recommendation to expel Barnet fails to get the 75% of votes necessary. Neil Ruddock's transfer to Liverpool is put on hold when Spurs refuse to pay him a £100,000 'loyalty bonus' for his year at the club.

20 Spurs reach a compromise with Ruddock and his £2.5m transfer to Liverpool will be completed tomorrow. Liverpool must pay Forest £2.275m for Nigel Clough, signed 6 weeks ago, less than the £3m asking price.
21 Chelsea sign Newcastle midfielder Gavin Peacock for £1.25m. Former Barnet chairman Stan Flashman sells his 67% interest in the club for a nominal £1.
22 The Football League will be known as the Endsleigh Insurance League next season, having completed a £3.5m, 3-year sponsorship deal with the Gloucester-based company. Robbie Fowler (Liverpool) hits 3 for England U-18s, who beat Spain 5-1 at Walsall to reach Euro final.
23 Julie Hemsley of the Women's Football Alliance, is the first woman to sit on the FA Council.
25 England U-18s win the European Youth Championship for a record 9th time, beating holders Turkey 1-0 in the final in front of 23,381 at the City Ground, Nottm. Arsenal beat Manchester Utd at Ellis Park, Johannesburg, in front of a 70,000 crowd, and Bryan Robson is controversially sent off for "foul and abusive language" and will miss two matches at the start of the season. Brazil lose 2-0 to Bolivia in La Paz, their first World Cup qualifying defeat for 40 years. Marseille general manager Jean-Pierre Bernès resigns. Mexico beat USA 4-0 at the Azteca Stadium, Mexico City, to retain the Concacaf Gold Cup.
27 Southampton protest to the Football League over Neil Ruddock's £2.5m transfer from Spurs to Liverpool, having had their £1.5m valuation of the defender halved by a tribunal when they sold him to Spurs a year ago.
29 Terry Venables must put up £300,000 "security for costs" if he is to proceed with his High Court bid to seize control of Spurs.
31 Paul Gascoigne scores for Lazio but they lose 3-2 to Spurs at White Hart Lane in the Makita Tournament. Chelsea beat Ajax on penalties.

August

£13m star in car crash ... Manchester United win Charity Shield on penalties ... Manchester City sack Peter Reid

1 Chelsea slam Spurs 4-0 at White Hart Lane to win the Makita Tournament, Tony Cascarino hitting 3. Australia lose keeper Mark Bosnich's stand-in Robert Zabica after 16 minutes for foul play and go down 2-1 to Canada in the first leg of the World Cup play-off, in Edmonton. Norwich beat Swedish Fifth Division side Krylbo IF 15-0, a record British win in Scandinavia, Efan Ekoku scoring 8.
3 AC Milan's £13m star Gianluigi Lentini crashes his car and suffers a fractured skull, but the injury is not expected to threaten his career. Spurs sign midfielder Jason Dozzell from Ipswich.
4 Millwall open their shining New Den with a game against Sporting Lisbon, but lose 2-1 in front of a 17,887 crowd. Double Cup winners Arsenal reveal pre-tax profits of £2.53m last season despite a wage bill of £6.92m. Portsmouth striker Guy Whittingham signs for Aston Villa in a £1.2m deal.
7 Manchester Utd beat Arsenal 5-4 on penalties, after a 1-1 draw, to win the FA Charity Shield. The opening day of the Scottish season sees 4 draws in the Premier League, only Rangers and Kilmarnock winning.
8 Blackburn's Alan Shearer scores twice in a friendly as a late substitute, to make a positive step in his comeback from injury.
9 Spurs' Nick Barmby (shin-splints operation) and Newcastle's Peter Beardsley, whose cheekbone is fractured in three places in a clash with Liverpool's Neil Ruddock in a friendly, will both miss the start of the season.
10 A tribunal orders Spurs to pay £1.25m for central defender Colin Calderwood, three times what they offered Swindon. Kilmarnock lose 2-1 at home to Morton in the Scottish League Cup.
11 Partick beat Div 2 side Albion 11-1 (at Motherwell) in the Scottish League Cup.
14 The English season opens with 6 away wins out of 10 Premiership matches, including a shock 3-0 defeat for Arsenal at Highbury, with Mick Quinn scoring all Coventry's goals. New boy Nigel Clough scores both Liverpool's goals in their 2-0 defeat of Sheffield Wed at Anfield, where the visitors' Carlton Palmer is sent off for a reckless tackle after only 13 minutes. Wimbledon owner Sam Hammam admits writing obscene graffiti on the West Ham dressing-room walls with the purpose of making them think it was done by the home side, and a police report is sent to the FA. In the Endsleigh Insurance League Division 1, Sunderland look set for another season of struggle, going down 5-0 at Derby. In the Scottish Premier, Rangers, 2-1 victors at St Johnstone, are the only 100% side after only two games.
15 Manchester Utd make a great start to their defence of the Premiership title with a 2-0 win at Norwich. Australia beat Canada 2-1 at Sydney (3-3 aggregate) and win the penalty shoot-out 4-1 and will meet a South American runner-up for a place in next year's World Cup. This could be Argentina, who lose 2-1 in Colombia, their first defeat in 33 matches since the 1990 World Cup final.
17 Ipswich and Everton chalk up their second Premiership wins, the former going top. League new boys Wycombe Wanderers win 2-0 at Leyton Orient in the 1st leg of the Coca-Cola Cup 1st round. Lazio doctor Claudio Bartolini slams Paul Gascoigne's fitness at the start of the season.
18 Coventry, Manchester Utd and Liverpool record their second wins in the Premiership, United going top on goal difference as Roy Keane scores 2 on his home debut. Barnet win 2-0 at Southend in the 1st round 1st leg of the Coca-Cola Cup to embarrass former manager Barry Fry.
19 Sheffield Wed sign England winger Andy Sinton from QPR for £2.7m.
20 Former Villa manager Tony Barton, 57, dies.
21 Everton beat Sheffield Utd 4-2, with Tony Cottee getting 3, and go top of the Premiership on goal difference from Ipswich. Norwich win 4-0 at Leeds. In Div 1, Middlesbrough, now the only 100%

club, beat Derby 3-0 to go top with a game in hand and goals over Charlton, who lose 4-0 at Sunderland. Crowd trouble in the Div 2 match at Craven Cottage involving visiting Cardiff fans causes referee Ian Hemley to take the players off for 22 minutes soon after the start; Cardiff win 3-1. After losing Peter Billing in 10 minutes, 10-man Port Vale slam Barnet 6-0 with a hat-trick in each half from Bernie Slaven and Martin Foyle, respectively. In the Scottish Premier, Motherwell win 1-0 at Kilmarnock to go top on goal difference over Rangers, whose 100% record is spoilt with a 0-0 draw at Celtic Park. First Division Stirling have three men sent off in their 2-0 defeat at Falkirk.

22 Liverpool win 5-0 at Swindon and take over at the top of the Premiership from Everton on goal difference.

23 Manchester Utd win 2-1 at Villa Park to take over at the top of the Premiership.

24 Middlesbrough maintain their 100% record in Div 1 with a 4-1 win at Barnsley.

25 The three 100% Premiership clubs all lose - Liverpool 2-1 at home to Spurs, Everton and Ipswich 1-0 at Newcastle and Norwich, respectively - leaving Manchester Utd still top by a point. Bradford beat Darlington 6-0 to win 11-1 in the Coca-Cola Cup, while in the 3rd round of the Scottish League Cup Celtic win 9-1 at Arbroath.

26 Manchester City player-manager Peter Reid is sacked along with assistant Sam Ellis on the recommendation of new general manager John Maddock; Reid was nearly 3 years in the job. A transfer tribunal rules that Spurs must pay Ipswich £1.75m for Jason Dozzell.

27 Oxford manager Brian Horton is the surprise new appointment at Manchester City as police quell an angry demonstration against chairman Peter Swales, but caretaker Tony Book remains in charge as they are held 1-1 at home by Coventry.

28 Manchester Utd win 3-1 at Southampton to stay 1 point ahead of 2-0 home winners Arsenal and Liverpool in the Premiership, while Swindon gain their first point with a 0-0 draw at Carrow Road and halt Norwich's march. Ian Rush scores his 200th League goal for Liverpool in their 2-0 win over Leeds, who fail to score at Anfield for the 7th successive match and haven't won there since 1972. Another away win for Middlesbrough in Div 1, 3-2 at Wolves, leaves them as the only 100% side in England. In Scotland, Motherwell beat Raith 4-1 to go 2 points clear of Rangers, beaten 2-1 at home by Kilmarnock.

29 David Platt marks his debut for Sampdoria with a goal in their 2-1 win over Napoli, the third time he has done this in Italy (Bari and Juventus were the others). Frank Hill, 87, former Aberdeen, Arsenal and Scotland half-back who managed several League clubs, dies in the USA.

31 Newcastle manager Kevin Keegan is struck on the head in an incident with a fan during their 1-1 draw at Ipswich. The FA find Manchester Utd and Leeds guilty of misconduct for withdrawing players from a summer youth tour to Scandinavia, but unrepentant Leeds manager Howard Wilkinson warns the FA that too much soccer can ruin the health of young players, and Man Utd's Alex Ferguson agrees. FIFA president Joao Havelange warns France they will be suspended from international soccer if they don't resolve the Marseille bribery scandal by 23 September.

September

Dynamo Tbilisi expelled from European Cup for bribery ... Marseille banned for a year ... England beat Poland at Wembley ... Andy Roxburgh quits as Scotland coach

1 Manchester Utd beat West Ham 3-0 to take a 3-point lead in the Premiership. Sheffield Wed, who score 3 goals in 11 second-half minutes, are denied their first victory of the season when Norwich score 3 in the next 13 minutes. Rangers beat Aberdeen 2-1 after extra time in the 4th round of the Scottish League Cup. The FA merely reprimand Leeds and Manchester Utd for withdrawing their youth players from the Scandinavian tour.

2 Terry Venables, resigning from the Spurs board after selling the majority of his 23.3% shareholding for over £3m, makes it clear he is available for work. Spurs chairman Alan Sugar agrees to settle out of court with West Brom over the alleged breach of contract by Ossie Ardiles.

3 Three weeks after signing a 4-year contract with Sheffield Wed, Paul Warhurst goes to Blackburn for £2.7m. UEFA expel Linfield's European Cup conquerors Dynamo Tbilisi for allegedly bribing the match officials in the first leg.

4 With England's vital World Cup match next Wednesday, there is no Saturday Premiership football. Charlton's 2-2 draw at Watford takes them to the top of Div 1 as Middlesbrough are without a game. In Scotland, Motherwell retain top place despite their 3-0 defeat at St Johnstone. Nigeria beat holders Ghana 2-1 in the final of the World U-17 Cup in Tokyo.

5 Colombia shatter Argentina 5-0 in Buenos Aires to clinch their own World Cup place next year and leave Argentina to play off against Australia.

6 UEFA expel European Cup holders Marseille from the competition for a year, after deciding there is sufficient evidence to confirm bribery allegations, and the French Football Federation are given two days to nominate a replacement club; the ban means Marseille are also out of the Toyota Cup (World Club Championship) and the European Super Cup.

8 England beat Poland 3-0 at Wembley, but will probably need to win in Rotterdam next month to qualify for the World Cup finals. Ireland record a fourth successive win for the first time in their history, 2-0 over Lithuania, and stay top of Group 3, 1 point ahead of Denmark. Monaco, 3rd in the French League last season, will replace Marseille in the European Cup, the 2nd-placed Paris St Germain having opted to stay in the Cup-Winners Cup.

9 Linfield are reinstated in the European Cup as UEFA reject Tbilisi's appeal. The FA clamp down on Cup Final ticket recipients whose tickets found their way on to the black market; among those banned from receiving tickets are Portsmouth manager Jim Smith (5 years) and former England keeper Ray Clemence (3).

10 Manchester City chairman Peter Swales says he will sell his shares "for the right price".

11 Manchester Utd lose their unbeaten record, going down 1-0 to Chelsea at Stamford Bridge, their first defeat in 17 League matches. Arsenal join them on 16 points, beating Ipswich 4-0 thanks to a Kevin Campbell hat-trick. Leeds end their sequence of 24 away matches in the League without a win, beating Southampton 2-0 at the Dell. There is crowd trouble at the Valley in Charlton's goalless draw with Millwall; police have to quell fighting between opposing fans and make 10 arrests, two players are sent off, and Charlton chairman Roger Alwen is attacked by a fan. But, with Middlesbrough suffering their first defeat, 1-0 at Southend, Charlton stay top. Motherwell beat Hearts 2-0 to go 1 point clear in the Scottish Premier.

13 Andy Roxburgh quits as Scottish coach, having equalled Jock Stein's record of 61 internationals.

14 Scottish clubs enjoy a satisfactory night in Europe, Aberdeen winning 3-0 at Valur in the 1st round 1st leg of the Cup-Winners' Cup, with Hearts beating Atletico Madrid 2-1 and Celtic drawing 0-0 at Young Boys in the UEFA Cup. Eintracht Frankfurt win 6-0 at Dynamo Moscow in the UEFA Cup. Tranmere beat Luton 4-1 and go top of the Endsleigh League Division 1.

15 Manchester Utd celebrate their return to the European Cup after 25 years with a 3-2 win over Honved in Hungary, and Rangers edge Levski Sofia by the same score at Ibrox. In the Cup-Winners' Cup, Arsenal recover from a poor start to beat Odense 2-1 in Denmark, but Cardiff crash 5-2 to Standard Liege in Belgium after leading 2-1, and riot police detain 150 Cardiff followers (eventually deporting 77). Norwich make a brilliant European debut, beating Vitesse Arnhem 3-0 at Carrow Road in the UEFA Cup.

16 The reprieved Linfield beat FC Copenhagen 3-0 at Windsor Park in the 1st leg of their European Cup 1st round tie. The *Panorama* programme on BBC TV makes serious allegations about the business dealings of former Spurs chief executive Terry Venables. Duncan Ferguson, Glasgow Rangers' £4m striker, is given a year's probation at the Sheriff's Court for punching a stranger in a hotel bar last November, is told to "grow up" and must accept counselling. The FA instruct Premiership clubs to highlight interval substitutions by having the subs enter the field after the others on a signal from the referee, thus avoiding the confusion caused by squad numbering.

17 Liverpool sign left-back Julian Dicks from West Ham in a £1.6m straight swap for David Burrows and Mike Marsh. Manchester City sign Irish defender Alan Kernaghan from Middlesbrough for £1.6m.

18 Blackburn lose 2-0 at home to West Ham, missing their chance to top the Premiership as leaders Manchester Utd and Arsenal play tomorrow. Liverpool's Bruce Grobbelaar and Steve McManaman almost come to blows over Everton's first goal in their 2-0 defeat. Crystal Palace win 4-1 at West Brom and oust Charlton, held 0-0 at Bristol City, from the top of Div 1. More trouble for Cardiff as 17 fans are arrested after their 1-0 defeat at Blackpool. Hibs are new leaders of the Scottish Premier, winning 3-1 at St Johnstone.

19 A goal from Eric Cantona before half-time gives Man Utd victory over Arsenal and a 3-point lead in the Premiership. Brazil beat Uruguay 2-0 to maintain their 100% record of World Cup finals appearances, finishing above Bolivia, who draw 1-1 with Ecuador, and thus eliminating Uruguay.

21 In 2nd round 1st leg Coca-Cola Cup ties, holders Arsenal win 5-0 at Huddersfield, Ian Wright scoring 3, Blackpool beat Sheffield Utd, who have Adrian Littlejohn sent off, 3-0, Sunderland revive 20-year-old Wembley memories with a 2-1 win over Leeds. Craig Hignett notches 4 in Middlesbrough's 5-0 defeat of Brighton, Pat Nevin 3 as Tranmere beat Oxford 5-1. Hibs beat Dundee Utd 1-0 to reach the final of the Scottish League Cup.

22 In World Cup qualifying matches, Holland win 7-0 at San Marino and Norway beat Poland 1-0 to make England's task that little bit harder in Group 2; Norwegian keeper Erik Thorstvedt of Spurs and a Polish player are sent off. In the Coca-Cola Cup 1st leg, Man Utd and Norwich go down 2-1 at Stoke and Bradford respectively, Man City are held 1-1 at home by Reading, while West Ham slam Chesterfield 5-1. Rangers beat Celtic 1-0 to reach the Scottish League Cup final. The French Football Federation strip Marseille of last season's League title and indefinitely suspend all players and officials facing corruption charges. Winless Northampton sack player-manager Phil Chard.

23 Ex-England striker Steve Bull of Wolves is found guilty of bringing the game into disrepute for punching Wrexham's Mel Pejic in a pre-season friendly and is banned for three matches.

24 Linesman John Griffiths is found guilty by the FA of misconduct and warned about his future conduct for his part in the "prank" played during fitness testing. Disgruntled Marseille fans invade the pitch 3 minutes from time and cause the abandonment of their match against Metz, who are leading 3-0, Marseille having had two players dismissed in the first half.

25 Efan Ekoku hits 4 as Norwich slam 4th-placed Everton 5-1 at Goodison after going a goal down. Man Utd beat Swindon 4-2 and stay 3 points ahead of Arsenal. Tranmere edge past non-playing Palace in Div 1. Aberdeen, the only one of the four Scottish Premier leaders to win, go top.

26 A 0-0 draw at Charlton is enough to lift Palace back to the top of Div 1. Former Everton chairman Sir John Moores, 97, dies.

27 Nottingham Forest are the subject of a *World in Action* programme alleging irregularities over the disposal of tickets for the 1992 League Cup final with Man Utd.

28 More grief for Cardiff in the Cup-Winners Cup, a 3-1 home reverse leaving them beaten 8-3 by Standard Liege, while Hearts and Dundee Utd both go out of the UEFA Cup, the latter on away goals after extra time. The shock of the night is Torpedo Moscow's 3-1 defeat in Israel by Maccabi Haifa, who win the tie 3-2. Liverpool's Neil Ruddock is found guilty of misconduct in the brawl with Blackburn and can expect an appropriate ban. Nottm Forest admit that "an apparent discrepancy between ticket sales and cash banked" had led them to call in the police fraud squad.

29 Two headers from Steve Bruce at Old Trafford ease Man Utd through 5-3 on aggregate over Honved to the 2nd round of the European Cup, but an injury-time strike by Levski Sofia at Ibrox Park puts Rangers out on away goals, and it's heartbreak too for Linfield, who see the last of their 3-0 lead disappear in an extended injury time in Copenhagen and lose in extra time. Arsenal, not

convincingly, and Aberdeen consolidate 1st-leg away wins to come through safely in the Cup-Winners' Cup, and Villa, Norwich and, after extra time, Celtic come safely through in the UEFA Cup. In the only League match in England, Middlesbrough beat Leicester 2-0 to go top of the Endsleigh Div 1 on goals scored.

October

Paul Warhurst breaks leg ... Liam Brady resigns at Celtic ... Barnet win their first point ... England beaten in Holland and virtually out of World Cup ... Bobby Gould resigns at Coventry ... Rangers win Scottish League Cup ... Manchester Utd go 11 points clear in the Premiership

2 Manchester Utd win 3-2 at Sheffield Wed to open up a 5-point lead in the Premiership over Arsenal. Liverpool end their run of four successive defeats by drawing 0-0 with Arsenal at Anfield, but it is their 5th game without a goal. Paul Warhurst breaks his leg in Blackburn's 3-1 win at Swindon. A John Salako hat-trick in Palace's 4-1 defeat of Stoke helps them stay top of Div 1, ahead of Tranmere on goals. Arthur Cox resigns through ill health after 9 years as Derby manager, and will be replaced by Roy McFarland, who has been in charge during Cox's 6-week absence with back trouble.

3 Spurs beat Everton 3-2 to go 5th in the Premiership despite being behind with only 2 minutes of normal time left.

4 Darlington manager Billy McEwan resigns after they drop to the bottom of the League, without a win in any competition. Former Scotland, Man Utd and Coventry defender Jim Holton, 42, dies at the wheel of his car, apparently from a heart attack.

5 In the 2nd round of the Coca-Cola Cup, Blackpool lose 2-0 at Bramall Lane but knock out Sheffield Utd 3-2 on aggregate. Wycombe claw back their 3-0 deficit against Coventry, whom they eliminated last year, and go ahead in extra time before 2 goals in the last 10 minutes see the Premiership side through. Star of the night is 18-year-old Liverpool striker Robbie Fowler, who scores all 5 goals against Fulham at Anfield, while Andy Cole hits 3 in Newcastle's 7-1 triumph at Notts County. Hibs beat Raith 3-2 to take over at the top of the Scottish Premier on goal difference from Aberdeen, who are held at home by Hearts.

6 Defeat in the Coca-Cola Cup at Third Division Shrewsbury by 2-0 (2-1 agg) puts more pressure on beleaguered Southampton manager Ian Branfoot, who sees central defender Ken Monkou sent off when the scores are level. Leeds are another Premiership side to go out to lesser opposition, losing 2-1 at Elland Road to Sunderland, who win the tie 4-2. Spurs have Darren Caskey sent off in the second half against Burnley with the tie at 1-1, but score 2 late goals to go through; manager Ossie Ardiles confirms he will fine Gordon Durie the maximum for his abusive reaction on being substituted. Millwall beat Watford 4-3 in a thriller at the Den, after a goalless 1st leg, and three players are dismissed. Dougie Arnott scores 2 late goals at Ibrox as Motherwell beat Rangers 2-1 to join the Scottish Premier leaders.

7 Liam Brady resigns after two unsuccessful years as Celtic manager, his assistant Joe Jordan taking temporary charge. Kevin Keegan ends speculation that he will take over the England job should they fail to qualify for the World Cup finals, signing a new 3-year contract with Newcastle, and Manchester United's young stars Ryan Giggs and Lee Sharpe agree to sign improved 5-year contracts with the Premiership leaders. Birmingham manager Terry Cooper is reported to the FA by referee Gerald Ashby for comments made during the Coca-Cola Cup tie against Villa.

8 *The Daily Express* publishes "fresh documentary evidence" relating to Paul Gascoigne's controversial move from Spurs to Lazio, suggesting that chairman Alan Sugar was not only unaware that Lazio had faxed an improved conditional offer the day before he and Terry Venables took over the club in June 1991, but had given Lazio a second charge over White Hart Lane in the event of the player not recovering fitness. Joe Jordan, declining the caretaker job at Celtic, feels obliged to add his resignation to Liam Brady's. Nigeria draw 1-1 in Algeria to qualify for the World Cup finals.

9 No Premiership matches because of England's World Cup preparation. Palace, also without a game, lose the Division 1 leadership to Tranmere, 2-1 victors over Bolton. Hibs win 2-0 at Motherwell to go 2 points clear in the Scottish Premier. Former Bolton left-back Ralph Banks dies at 73.

10 Brave Zambia fail to qualify for the World Cup, going down 1-0 in Morocco, who will go to the finals. Cameroon beat Zimbabwe 3-1 and also qualify. Barnet win their first point of the season, holding Cardiff 0-0 at Underhill in their 11th match.

12 Dutch police arrest at least 140 English soccer fans in Amsterdam for tomorrow's crucial World Cup tie. Graham Taylor produces a controversial England side, choosing Carlton Palmer ahead of Andy Sinton to fill in for the suspended Paul Gascoigne, and Paul Merson, not guaranteed an Arsenal place, rather than club-mate Ian Wright; he clashes vehemently with the Press over the composition of the team.

13 Holland beat England 2-0, leaving them with little chance of World Cup qualification. Norway clinch their World Cup place with a 3-0 win in Poland. About 1,400 football fans are arrested in Holland, most of them reported to be English, 600 of them detained for not having tickets. Ireland go down 3-1 at home to Spain and, with Denmark beating N. Ireland 1-0, are now struggling to qualify for the USA. Wales beat Cyprus 2-0 and are still in with a chance. Scotland lose 3-1 in Italy and aren't. The biggest shock of the night is France's 3-2 defeat at home by Israel, who score twice in the last 8 minutes. Sweden's 3-2 defeat of Finland clinches their World Cup place.

14 The bookies install Leeds manager Howard Wilkinson as 7-2 favourite to succeed Graham Taylor as England supremo.

15 Spurs manager Ossie Ardiles, dissatisfied with Gordon Durie's commitment, puts the Scottish striker up for sale. Ireland manager Jack Charlton rules himself out of contention for the England

job, as do Glenn Hoddle and Ron Atkinson. Argentina coach Alfio Basile gives Diego Maradona the captaincy.

16 Manchester Utd go 7 points clear in the Premiership with a 2-1 win over Spurs, as Arsenal are held 0-0 at Highbury by Man City and Norwich, 2-1 victors at Stamford Bridge, go 2nd on goal difference. Crewe score twice in the last 4 minutes to win 2-1 at Scarborough and take over from Preston at the top of Div 3. There are hat-tricks for Matthew Carmichael in Scunthorpe's 7-0 drubbing of Northampton and Chris Pike in Hereford's 5-0 defeat of Colchester, who make League history by losing both keepers - John Keeley and Nathan Munson - for "professional fouls".

17 The FA charge Spurs with misconduct over the appointment of West Brom's Ardiles as manager in June.

18 Spurs announce profits of £3.3m. Scarborough sack manager Phil Chambers after 6 months.

19 Norwich shock Bayern Munich in the UEFA Cup, winning 2-1 in Germany in the 1st leg of their 2nd round tie. A great result for Villa, too, 1-1 against Deportivo La Coruna in Spain. FIFA suspend German referee Assenmacher, whose handling of the Holland-England game caused so much controversy.

20 Manchester Utd, two up in 13 minutes against Galatasaray in the European Cup, concede 3 goals and need a late Cantona strike to salvage a 3-3 draw from the Turkish champions, while AC Milan win 6-0 at FC Copenhagen. In the Cup-Winners' Cup, Arsenal beat Standard Liege 3-0 at Highbury, but Aberdeen lose a two-goal lead to come away from Italy 3-2 down to Torino. In the UEFA Cup, Celtic beat Sporting Lisbon 1-0 at Parkhead. Portsmouth city council pass the club's plans for a £25m stadium at Farlington to replace Fratton Park in 1996-97.

21 The FA charge Birmingham manager Terry Cooper with misconduct relating to comments made to referee Gerald Ashby in a Coca-Cola Cup game.

22 Villa winger Tony Daley agrees to join Udinese in Italy in a £2m deal. A Premier League committee views TV re-runs of 44 questionable goals from last season, and strips credited goalscorers of 10 of them. All 32 Premiership referees will meet next month at Birmingham in a "weekend of education" to review the season so far. The Belgian cabinet give the go-ahead for renovation to start on the Heysel Stadium next year.

23 A single Lee Sharpe goal at Everton is enough to send Manchester Utd 9 points clear in the Premiership as their challengers Norwich and Arsenal can do no better than goalless draws. Alan Shearer gives notice he is back to his best with a hat-trick for Blackburn at Elland Road, but Leeds twice come back from two down to draw 3-3. QPR move into 5th place with a comprehensive 5-1 demolition of Coventry, whose manager Bobby Gould promptly resigns.

24 Back-from-injury Ally McCoist, coming on as sub, scores his first goal of the season with a spectacular overhead kick to give Rangers an 81st-minute winner as they beat Hibs 2-1 at Parkhead in the final of the Scottish League Cup.

26 In the 3rd round of the Coca-Cola Cup, Blackburn are held 0-0 at home by 3rd Division Shrewsbury, Swindon lose 2-0 at Portsmouth, and Crystal Palace draw 2-2 at Everton, who scrape a last-minute equalizer. Leeds and England midfielder David Batty signs for Blackburn for £2.75m. Lou Macari is finally confirmed as the new Celtic manager.

27 An Ian Rush hat-trick, doubling his season's goal tally, gives Liverpool a 3-2 win at Anfield over Ipswich in the Coca-Cola Cup, while Manchester Utd crush Leicester 5-1 at Old Trafford. Newcastle manager Kevin Keegan walks out of a Press conference after their 2-1 defeat at Wimbledon when asked about the missing Andy Cole. Liverpool, hoping to sign Southampton keeper Tim Flowers for an agreed £2.5m (including £1m "makeweight" David James), must hold fast while the England keeper waits for Blackburn's offer. Former Hartlepool manager Alan Murray takes over at Darlington, and former Chelsea defender Steve Wicks at Scarborough.

28 Saudi Arabia and South Korea win their final matches in Qatar to qualify for the World Cup finals, while an Iraq equalizer with the last kick denies Japan a place. Chelsea sign Stoke striker Mark Stein for £1.5m, but Villa winger Tony Daley's move to Udinese is in doubt as the Italian club renege and now want him on loan. The FA, using freeze-frame TV evidence for the first time, clear Liverpool centre-back Neil Ruddock of punching Blackburn's Mike Newell. West Ham director and one-time chairman Len Cearns dies at 79.

29 Keegan and Premiership leading scorer Andy Cole make peace at Newcastle. Paul Gascoigne, in London for an Achilles' tendon examination, is ordered by doctors to rest for 3 weeks and will miss England's match in San Marino. Sheffield Utd manager Dave Bassett and former Coventry boss Bobby Gould escape with warnings for criticizing referees.

30 Manchester Utd extend their Premiership lead to 11 points, coming back from a goal down to beat QPR 2-1 at Old Trafford, while nearest rivals Arsenal and Norwich draw 0-0 at Highbury. Robbie Fowler scores a hat-trick in Liverpool's 4-2 defeat of Southampton, and Newcastle avenge Wednesday's Coca-Cola Cup defeat, beating Wimbledon 4-0 with a hat-trick from the inspired Peter Beardsley and one from the contrite Andy Cole. A late Duncan Shearer goal at Pittodrie takes Aberdeen to the top of the Scottish Premier and denies bottom club Dundee their first away point.

31 Australia hold Argentina 1-1 in Sydney in the first leg of their World Cup play-off, equalizing a Maradona-made goal just before half-time.

November

United out of European Cup, beaten by Galatasaray ... Norwich beat Bayern Munich in UEFA Cup .. . Blackburn pay £2m for keeper Flowers ... San Marino 9-second shock for England as Holland and Ireland clinch World Cup places ... Graham Taylor resigns England post ... Villa inflict Arsenal's first defeat in 26 cup ties

1 Manchester Utd get a hostile greeting from Galatasaray fans when they arrive in Turkey, "Welcome to Hell" the message on banners at Istanbul airport. The FA confirm the 1996 European

Championship venues as Wembley, Aston Villa, Leeds, Liverpool, Manchester United, Newcastle, Sheffield Wednesday and either Arsenal or Nottm Forest.

2 Charlton lose ground at the top of Div 1, a 2-1 home defeat by Derby cutting their lead to 2 points over Palace. Div 2 produces two high-scoring matches: Exeter recover from 2-0 down to beat Fulham 6-4, helped by a hat-trick from Micky Ross, and Blackpool beat Hull 6-2. But the most sensational scoring is produced in Div 3, by the bottom club in the League, Darlington, hitherto winless and with only 7 goals from 13 games, a tally that is doubled in their 7-3 hammering of Colchester.

3 A lack-lustre performance by Manchester Utd in Turkey allows Galatasaray the 0-0 draw they need to go through to the lucrative league stage of the European Cup, and to compound their misery Eric Cantona is sent off after the final whistle and he and Bryan Robson are struck by police in the players' tunnel. By contrast, goal-starved Arsenal slam 7 past Standard Liege in Belgium to record a 10-0 victory in the Cup-Winners' Cup and Norwich hold Bayern Munich 1-1 at Carrow Road to go through to the 3rd round of the UEFA Cup 3-2 on aggregate. Spurs are found guilty of misconduct for approaching Ossie Ardiles without permission from his club, West Brom, earlier in the year, and are fined £25,000 plus costs and severely censured and warned regarding their future conduct.

4 Southampton finally allow goalkeeper Tim Flowers to go to Blackburn for £2m, thanks to acquiring a replacement, Dave Beasant, from Chelsea. The Premier League launch an inquiry into the dealings of agents, with a commission comprising chief executive Rick Parry, former Palace manager Steve Coppell and a leading QC. After yesterday's elimination from Europe, Manchester United's share price slips 57p to £5.30.

6 With Manchester Utd playing tomorrow, two of their four "chasers" take the opportunity of reducing the gap to 8 points, Villa beating another of them, Arsenal, 2-1 at Highbury - the Gunners' goal saving them from a record fifth League match in succession without one - and Norwich winning 2-1 at Sheffield Utd. Division 1 has new leaders, Leicester, whose 3-0 defeat of Southend takes them ahead on goals of Charlton.

7 Manchester Utd restore their 11-point Premiership lead with a stirring 3-2 win at Maine Road after Man City had taken a 2-0 half-time lead through Niall Quinn, Eric Cantona atoning for his lapse in Turkey with two goals and Roy Keane hitting an 87th-minute winner. Derby, hitherto 100% in the League at home, miss their chance to go top, in a big way, succumbing 4-0 to Wolves, Steve Bull hitting a hat-trick.

8 Arthur Rowe, manager of the "push and run" Spurs of the early 1950s, dies at 85. Graham Taylor includes Blackburn winger Stuart Ripley in his squad for the San Marino match. UEFA contact Man Utd regarding Eric Cantona's reported bribery allegations against the referee of their European Cup tie in Istanbul.

9 Blackburn recover from 3-1 down at Shrewsbury in the Coca-Cola Cup 3rd round replay to win 4-3 in extra time. FIFA rule that players feigning injury in the World Cup finals will be automatically cautioned - another test of the referee's mind-reading abilities - and referees will also be instructed to have injured players removed from the pitch immediately, unless they have serious head injuries or cuts - a test of the referee's medical knowledge. FIFA general secretary Sepp Blatter says British football is 30 years behind the times, with the emphasis on developing the athletic aspect of the game at the expense of technique. Watford are fined £10,000 and ordered to pay Gillingham £30,000 compensation for poaching their manager Glen Roeder.

10 In Coca-Cola Cup replays, Everton win 4-1 at the Palace after going a goal down, Arsenal win 3-0 at Norwich. Joe Jordan is appointed manager of Stoke.

11 UEFA clear Man United's Eric Cantona of making bribery allegations against the referee in Istanbul. PFA chief executive Gordon Taylor calls for a major shake-up of the country's coaching system and threatens - the FA call it blackmail - to initiate an alternative scheme.

12 UEFA slap a 4-match suspension on Eric Cantona in European club competition and fine Man Utd £2,500 for "incorrect conduct" (3 bookings and Cantona's dismissal) and Galatasaray £7,000 for use of fireworks in the stadium and £2,500 for inadequate security.

13 With no Premiership programme, Charlton steal the limelight and return to the top of Div 1 with their 5-1 thrashing of Notts County after going behind in 5 minutes. In the first round of the FA Cup, Sutton United are once more the non-League heroes; they win 4-3 at Colchester with a goal 2 minutes from time, having lost a 2-0 lead. Other non-Leaguers to overcome League opponents are Bromsgrove, 2-1 winners at Northampton, and Macclesfield, who beat Hartlepool 2-0, while Nuneaton concede a last-minute equalizer at Swansea.

14 Newly non-League Halifax beat West Brom 2-1 in the 1st round of the FA Cup, while new boys Wycombe win 2-1 at 2nd Division Bristol Rovers.

15 2nd Division Fulham go out of the Cup at Yeovil to a last-minute goal. A jarred back muscle rules Alan Shearer out of England's squad for Wednesday's game with San Marino, which England must win by 7 goals to have a chance of qualifying for the World Cup finals. The Football Managers' Association (FMA) deliver a plan to the Premier League that includes recommendations for a reduction in teams to 18 (again), a midwinter break, transfers to be conducted only in the summer and a short period in January, and the League Cup to be completed in the first half of the season.

17 With Holland winning 3-1 in Poland, England's result is purely academic, but they sensationally go behind in under 9 seconds to San Marino, the quickest goal in international football, and stay that way for 22 minutes, before they equalize; Ian Wright scores 4 and they run out 7-1 winners, which would not have been enough. Jack Charlton's Ireland qualify for the United States, drawing 1-1 with N. Ireland in Belfast. Fortunately for the Irish, Spain, who have their keeper sent off, beat Denmark 1-0 to go top of the group, and Ireland's superior goals record (19-6) over Denmark (15-2) takes them through. For the first time since British countries entered the World Cup (1950), they

have no team in the finals, Wales going down 2-1 to Romania in Cardiff, when a win would have seen them through, the RCS managing only a 0-0 draw in Belgium. Paul Bodin will remember his penalty that hits the bar at a crucial time for Wales, but the real tragedy of the match occurs at the end, when a rocket fired across the pitch kills a man in the North Stand. The sensational result of the night is France's 2-1 home defeat by Bulgaria, who score the winner in injury time and qualify instead of them. Argentina are the last qualifiers, scraping through with a 1-0 win over Australia and a 2-1 aggregate. Craig Brown is confirmed as Scotland's new manager and he gets off to a successful start with a 2-0 win in Malta that has no effect on their position (4th) in Group 1.

20 After the midweek traumas, business is as usual in the Premiership, with Manchester Utd's 3-1 defeat of Wimbledon keeping them 11 points clear of Villa. Charlton forge ahead again in Div 1, a 1-0 win at Peterborough taking them 4 points clear of Tranmere, 3-1 losers at Millwall. Aberdeen's match at Raith is postponed and they are knocked off the top of the Scottish Premier by Motherwell, 2-0 victors over Dundee Utd, and Rangers, 1-0 at Hibs.

21 Newcastle beat Liverpool 3-0, Andy Cole scoring all 3 goals. Saudi Arabia appoint former Holland manager Leo Beenhakker coach for the World Cup finals.

22 A goalless draw at home to Man City brings Chelsea their first point in 7 games. The FA's controversial Director of Coaching Charles Hughes, in a rare appearance before the Press to promote the FA's new policy of reducing the number of games played by 9–16-year-olds (from some 150 to a maximum 60), takes the opportunity to defend himself against the widely spread assumption that he is the "high priest" of the long-ball game, as well as taking a sideswipe at England manager Graham Taylor for picking too many players and repeatedly altering the team's shape. Rangers complete the signing of Gordon Durie from Spurs for £1.2m.

23 Graham Taylor resigns the post of England manager, and his assistant Lawrie McMenemy also steps down. PFA chief executive Gordon Taylor reckons coaching supremo Charles Hughes should go as well. The FA hope to make a caretaker appointment before Christmas. The chairman of the FA's International Committee, Manchester City chairman Peter Swales, refutes any criticism and says he will not resign. Former Liverpool star Phil Neal, caretaker for a month, is confirmed as Coventry manager in time to see his team go down 2-1 at Blackburn, for whom Shearer scores both goals again and who go 2nd in the Premiership. In FA Cup replays, Nuneaton, a goal down in 9 minutes, beat Swansea 2-1, but Telford go down 1-0 at Huddersfield despite dominating for long stretches. Five replays are postponed because of severe weather.

24 Norwich lose the 1st leg of their 3rd round UEFA Cup tie 1-0 to Inter-Milan at Carrow Road, Dennis Bergkamp converting a late penalty, and will be without the services in the 2nd leg of the three Ians - Butterworth, Crook and Culverhouse, who are all booked for a second time in the campaign. Man Utd are held 0-0 at home by Ipswich, but increase their Premiership lead to 12 points as Villa lose 2-0 at home to Southampton, Le Tissier's goals taking the Saints out of the last three. Bottom club Swindon chalk up their first Premiership victory, after 16 games, 1-0 over QPR, despite having Dutch defender Luc Nijholt sent off in the 16th minute. England keeper David Seaman is sent off for a "professional foul" near the end of Arsenal's goalless draw at West Ham. Spurs captain Gary Mabbutt sustains a badly fractured cheekbone in a clash with Wimbledon's John Fashanu in a bruising 1-1 draw at White Hart Lane and will be out for several weeks. Don Howe, the favourite to take over as caretaker England manager, rules himself out. English coaching receives a boost from Switzerland's English manager Roy Hodgson and Norway's Egil Olsen, both on their way to the USA, who claim it is still the most respected in Europe. The FA nominate six men to investigate the structure of their organizaion, League president Gordon McKeag and five County FA representatives. Hartlepool sack manager Viv Busby.

25 The FA hold a conference Quality Education Opportunities for all Young Footballers in which they stress the importance of learning skills and enjoying playing rather than the quest for medals. Former Sunderland defender John MacPhail is the new Hartlepool manager.

26 Sunderland sack manager Tery Butcher, replacing him with coach Mick Buxton till the end of the season, and Bob Murray resigns as chairman. John Fashanu and Wimbledon owner Sam Hammam slam Spurs for calling Gary Mabbutt's cheekbone injury a "fractured skull". Spurs have further problems as striker Teddy Sheringham undergoes a cartilage operation. The FA fine Aston Villa £20,000 with £15,000 costs for a breach of rules over the signing of Australian keeper Mark Bosnich, and Notts County receive similar penalties for the signing of two other Australians.

27 Manchester Utd win 1-0 at Coventry and stretch their Premiership lead to 14 points as Blackburn lose 1-0 at Ipswich. Out of the 19 Scottish fixtures, 10 are postponed.

28 Birmingham, despite 5 defeats in 6 games, decline manager Terry Cooper's offer to resign.

29 Man City chairman Peter Swales resigns after 20 years, citing death threats against his family as the reason, but he will stay on the board and continue to resist Francis Lee's takeover attempts. Terry Cooper resigns from Birmingham after all, following verbal abuse from fans. The PFA launch a crusade to rid the game of the "lethal elbow", chiefly by having any challenge in which the elbow is wielded regarded as dangerous play, whether it is intentional or not.

30 The FA invest former England captain Jimmy Armfield, now a sports journalist and broadcaster, with the task of finding the next England manager, appointing him, in effect, as a headhunter. Peter Swales states he will not seek re-election as chairman of the International Committee next June after his 4-year term is completed and will take no part in the search for the new England supremo. Man City's Irish striker Niall Quinn has severed cruciate knee ligaments and will miss the World Cup finals. Holders Arsenal suffer their first defeat in 26 Cup ties as Aston Villa beat them 1-0 at Highbury to knock them out of the Coca-Cola Cup. Motherwell go back to the top of the Scottish Premier with a 1-0 victory over Partick. Spurs decide to officially report the Mabbutt-Fashanu incident to the FA, supplying video evidence of what they claim was a "dangerous

challenge", while Wimbledon point out again that the referee, Keith Hackett, did not award a foul and saw no reason to regret his decision even after studying a video.

December

New format and more money for European Cup ... Everton manager Howard Kendall resigns ... Danny Blanchflower dies ... 16-team World Club Cup for 1995 ... Havelange bans Pelé from World Cup draw ... FA leave Fashanu unpunished ... Manchester Utd end year with 14-point lead ... Paul Gascoigne injures groin getting out of bed ... OBE for Lion of Vienna

1 Stand-in striker Sol Campbell scores a late winner for Spurs who knock Blackburn out in the 4th round of the Coca-Cola Cup at White Hart Lane. Mark Hateley scores twice to send Rangers to the top of the Scottish Premier with a 2-0 victory over Aberdeen. Brighton survive another High Court winding-up petition, settling debts of £600,000.

2 Ex-Scotland manager Andy Roxburgh becomes UEFA's first European Technical Director and warns that Scotland will struggle to reach the finals of major competitions if they continue to play so much club football and allow the national side so little preparation time.

3 Spurs' injured captain Gary Mabbutt accuses Wimbledon's John Fashanu of playing without due care and attention, referring to the challenge that almost cost him his right eye and has put him out of action. The Premiership chairmen vote 20-2 against reducing the competition to 18 teams. Referee Joe Worrall decides, on seeing a video, that he was wrong to book Leeds' John Pemberton for a foul on Spurs' Nick Barmby on 20 November, and the FA have removed the booking, the first time this has been done on video evidence. Tranmere beat Peterborough 2-1 and return to the top of Div 1.

4 Everton manager Howard Kendall resigns after watching his side gain their first Premiership victory at Goodison for 10 weeks. Man Utd are held 2-2 at home by Norwich (who score their 24th away goal to only 3 at home). Charlton beat Luton 1-0 to leapfrog back to the top of Div 1. Sutton enhance their giantkilling reputation with a 1-0 away victory over Torquay in the 2nd round of the FA Cup, and Nuneaton draw 1-1 at Bournemouth. Rangers win 2-0 at Motherwell to go 2 points clear of them and Celtic in the Scottish Premier. Brighton manager Barry Lloyd leaves by "mutual consent" after 7 years. Wimbledon striker John Fashanu takes up his new role as Unicef "special ambassador".

5 Non-League Bath beat Hereford 2-1 in the Cup.

6 The FA are to allow professional clubs unlimited access to young players from the age of 9 and will limit the number of matches they play.

7 Manchester Utd take a 15-point lead in the Premiership with a 3-0 win over Sheffield Utd at Bramall Lane. Nearly 39 years after beating Honved 3-2 in that famous floodlit friendly, Wolves, thanks to president Sir Jack Hayward, celebrate the completion of the £15m redevelopment of Molineux with a 1-1 draw against the same club. Southend manager Barry Fry is given permission to have talks with Birmingham.

8 In the UEFA Cup 3rd round, Norwich go down to a late Bergkamp goal in Milan and Inter win 2-0 on aggregate, but the "unfashionable" English club receive many plaudits for the way they have played in Europe. QPR, beaten 3-2 at Anfield, finish with 9 men as Simon Barker and Les Ferdinand are sent off. Arsenal will not, after all, stage European Championship games in 1996 because the Highbury pitch is 4m too short.

9 Danny Blanchflower, the inspirational captain and original thinker who led Spurs to their 1961 double, dies at 67.

10 Former England manager Bobby Robson is sacked by Sporting Lisbon after their unexpected exit from the UEFA Cup, despite sharing top spot in the Portuguese League with Benfica. The FA set up an inquiry into the Fashanu-Mabbutt incident. FIFA announce plans for a biennial 16-team World Club Cup to start in 1995. Barry Fry takes over at Birmingham, bringing assistant Edwin Stein and coach David Howell with him from Southend.

11 An equalizer from League top scorer Andy Cole earns Newcastle a draw at St James' Park with Man Utd, who nevertheless increase their Premiership lead to 13 points over Leeds. Bottom club Swindon are denied a historic win at Anfield when Mark Wright makes it 2-2 with 4 minutes to go. Tranmere's 1-0 win at Luton takes them above no-game Charlton again. In Div 3, Wycombe, the only side in the League unbeaten away, lose 3-1 at Chester. Rangers, who go 3 down midway through the first half at home to Dundee Utd, lose both central defenders with injuries before the interval and Ian Ferguson in injury time, sent off for spitting after being elbowed in the face. They lose 3-0, but no one takes advantage of their slip-up and they remain top of the Scottish Premier by a point from Celtic. In the 1st round of the Scottish Cup, 2nd Div leaders Stranraer, 3-1 down at home to Whitehill Welfare and with their goalkeeper dismissed, score twice in the last 13 minutes to force a replay. In other ties, Ross County beat St Cuthbert 11-0, Grant scoring 5, and Forfar, 2 places and 2 points above Queen of the South in Div 2, beat them 8-3. Steve Coppell is to take up an appointment next Tuesday as chief executive of the League Managers' Association.

12 Holders Sao Paulo retain the World Club Championship in Tokyo, beating AC Milan 3-2. FIFA rule that players may play for any country they qualify for provided they have not played in competitive matches for another country.

13 A *World in Action* TV programme makes allegations regarding loans Spurs made to players several years ago, focusing especially on dealings with present manager Ossie Ardiles when he was a player, although there is nothing to say that he ever acted improperly.

14 In their Coca-Cola Cup 4th round replay, Liverpool force extra time at Wimbledon with a last-

minute own goal from keeper Hans Segers, but he redeems himself by saving a John Barnes penalty 5 minutes into the first period and then two more in the shoot-out to put his side into the quarter-finals for the first time. In the rearranged fixture postponed on Saturday, Aberdeen beat Partick 2-1 at Pittodrie and edge past Rangers at the top of the Scottish Premier League on goal difference. FIFA president Joao Havelange attempts to exclude countryman Pelé from taking part in the upcoming World Cup draw ceremony, as the President of the Brazilian Federation, Ricardo Teixiera, who happens to be Havelange's son-in-law, is suing Pelé for defamation over charges Pelé has made of corruption in the Federation. Brentford manager Dave Webb tenders his resignation after being ordered by a League appeals committee to reinstate Micky Bennett, whom he had dismissed for breaking team-mate Joe Allon's jaw in a training incident.

15 Liam Brady takes over struggling 2nd Division Brighton, whose new chairman Greg Stanley staves off another High Court action by increasing his stake in the club and settling various tax debts. Brentford chairman Martin Lange stands by manager Dave Webb and declines his resignation.

16 The FA of Wales reject national team manager Terry Yorath's increased salary demand when his current contract expires at the end of the month.

17 FIFA announce the new World Cup seeding, made on a geographical and ethnic basis, but after a rehearsal and an attempted explanation by general secretary Sepp Blatter, he resigns himself to the fact that no one is going to understand it. One change in the finals is that there will be 3 points for a win. Former Orient, Arsenal, Forest and Millwall centre-forward Len Julians dies from cancer at 60.

18 Home wins for Leeds and Blackburn, over Arsenal and Man City respectively, keep up the slight pressure on Man Utd, who play tomorrow. Barcelona manager Johan Cruyff will not, after all, be in charge of Holland in the World Cup finals, the Dutch FA rejecting his "excessive" fee requirements, and Dick Advocaat is expected to remain as coach.

19 The shameful banning of Pelé's participation casts a shadow over the World Cup draw in Las Vegas, in which Ireland are drawn to play Italy in their first match, with Mexico and Norway to follow. Leading Aston Villa 1-0 after 89 minutes, Manchester Utd achieve a result that more closely reflects their superiority - 3-1 - to restore their 13-point lead in the Premiership. Crystal Palace win 1-0 at Tranmere to take over from them at the top of Div 1 on goals scored.

20 As heavy betting on Terry Venables becoming the new England manager reduces the odds from the original 25-1 to 5-2, the leading bookies suspend betting. England's scheduled friendly against Germany in Hamburg on 20 April may be postponed because it turns out to be the anniversary of Hitler's birth and officials fear neo-Nazi problems. Harry Cavan, 77, retires after 35 years as president of the Irish FA.

22 Crowd trouble again at Cardiff delays the kick-off with Swansea for 40 minutes as hundreds of fans brawl on the pitch, and after Cardiff score what turns out to be the only goal of the game, soon after half-time, Swansea fans rip out seats and hurl scraps of wood and metal at their rivals.

23 An FA commission of inquiry into the Fashanu-Mabbutt incident spend $4\frac{1}{2}$ hours interviewing witnesses, studying video tapes and speaking to the two men involved, but require more time to sift through the evidence before deciding whether to charge the Wimbledon striker with misconduct.

24 As Gary Mabbutt, who suffered four fractures of the cheekbone and three of an eye-socket, prepares to face more surgery on his injuries, the FA commission decide not to charge John Fashanu because they are not convinced there was "sufficient intent", even though referee Keith Hackett has now said he felt there was a "measure of intent" and would have cautioned Fashanu for dangerous play had he seen the incident clearly at the time.

26 A Paul Ince goal 2 minutes from time saves Man United's unbeaten home record, earning them a draw against challengers Blackburn at Old Trafford, and takes them 13 points clear of Leeds.

27 Southampton beat Chelsea 3-1 to leapfrog over them and leave the London club, without a win in 11 matches, in deep trouble, just a point above bottom Premiership team Swindon. The latter are crushed 4-0 at home by Arsenal, Kevin Campbell hitting a hat-trick. In Div 1, Palace go 2 points clear with a 3-1 success at Oxford. Aberdeen's 1-0 win at Dundee Utd takes them to the top of the Scottish Premier again as Rangers are held at home by Hearts. Franz Beckenbauer returns to club management with his old side Bayern Munich.

28 A Mark Stein goal in 11 minutes gives Chelsea their first Premiership win in 14 matches, 1-0 over Newcastle, takes them out of the relegation zone and eases the mounting pressure on manager Glenn Hoddle.

29 Man Utd finish the year with a flourish - and a 14-point Premiership lead - after winning 5-2 at Oldham. Jimmy Gabriel is to continue in his caretaker role at Goodison, as Everton, who have not scored since he took over at the start of the month, cannot name a new manager until their takeover battle is settled. Manager of bottom club Peterborough, Lil Fuccillo, resigns, and will be replaced till the end of the season by former manager Chris Turner, who gives up the chairmanship but remains chief executive and part owner. Terry Venables, apparently on short lists for both the England and Wales supremo jobs, is offered £100,000 to coach Nigeria in the World Cup finals. Paul Gascoigne continues his Lazio record of more injuries than appearances, returning to Rome from a Christmas break with a groin strain.

30 Former Bolton and England centre-forward Nat Lofthouse, the "Lion of Vienna", receives an OBE in the New Year Honours List, and battered Spurs captain Gary Mabbutt gets an MBE to alleviate the pain. Another elbow in the face that goes unpunished by the referee, Villa's Neil Cox on Norwich keeper Bryan Gunn last night, has PFA chief executive Gordon Taylor up in arms, his point being that if players continue to get away with such challenges they will proliferate - again, the referee felt there was no intent and said Gunn had asked him not to book Cox. Former Southampton manager Lawrie McMenemy, who resigned as England's No.2 when Graham Taylor left, has rejoined the club as a director and pledged his full support for manager Ian Branfoot.

Meanwhile the Hampshire FA appoint a woman, former international Sue Lopez, 48, as their chief coach.

31 Ireland are among the 8 seeds for the European Championships to be held in England in 1996. The others are Denmark, France, Germany, Holland, Italy, Russia and Sweden. Doncaster sack manager Steve Beaglehole. Chairman of Aberdeen since 1970, Dick Donald, dies at 82, and will be succeeded by his son, Ian.

January 1994

Everton accused of poaching Norwich manager . . . Sir Matt Busby dies . . . Bristol City win at Anfield . . . Venables is England's new 'coach' . . . Souness leaves Liverpool . . . Lee takeover at Maine Road

1 Man United are held again at home, 0-0 by Leeds, and Blackburn, 1-0 winners at Villa, reduce their Premiership lead to 12 points. In Div 1, Millwall beat leaders Crystal Palace 3-0 to go 3rd, while Tranmere move to within a point of Palace with a 2-1 win over Watford. With Aberdeen's game being one of 4 Scottish Premier games off, Rangers go top again thanks to their 4-2 win over Celtic at Parkhead, where the home directors are showered with abuse and missiles from the fans.

3 Monday's programme suffers some postponements, including Blackburn's home game with Wimbledon. Norwich reject Everton's approach for their manager Mike Walker. Former England and Man City back Jimmy Meadows dies at 62.

4 Liverpool salvage their pride with a remarkable 3-3 draw, coming back from 3 down against leaders Man Utd at Anfield.

7 Norwich chairman Robert Chase accuses Everton of poaching as manager Mike Walker resigns and signs a 3½-year contract with the Goodison club worth about £650,000.

8 The 3rd round of the FA Cup produces its usual shocks, notably non-League Kidderminster's 2-1 victory at Birmingham and Stockport's home triumph by the same score over Premier club QPR. There are notable performances, too, from non-League Bath, who hold Stoke to a goalless draw at the Victoria Ground; 1st Division Portsmouth, who three times come back through hat-trick hero Alan McLoughlin to hold high-flyers Blackburn 3-3 at Ewood Park; Barnet, who play their home tie at Stamford Bridge and still hold Chelsea 0-0; Port Vale, who hold Southampton 1-1 at the Dell and Forest who accomplish the same against Wednesday at Hillsborough. Big guns who live to fight another day are Liverpool, whose match at Bristol City is abandoned through floodlight failure with the score 1-1, and Spurs, who scrape an 86th-minute equalizer at Peterborough. Barnsley leave it late at non-League Bromsgrove, notching two goals in the last 3 minutes for a 2-1 victory. Rangers go 2 points clear in the Scottish Premiership with a 3-0 defeat of Kilmarnock. In the 2nd round of the Scottish FA Cup Highland League club Ross County demolish 2nd Division Forfar 4-0 away from home, Grant scoring a hat-trick. Elfed Ellis, president of the FA of Wales, dies at 72.

9 Man Utd win their Cup match 1-0 at Sheffield Utd, but scorer Mark Hughes is sent off for a second yellow card near the end.

10 A last-minute goal from captain Tony Adams gives holders Arsenal a 1-0 win at Millwall. The Barnet player-manager, keeper Gary Philips, steps down to become assistant to new manager Ray Clemence as a court winding-up order is postponed for 2 months.

11 Much-abused Southampton manager Ian Branfoot 'relinquishes' the job after 2½ years. Last season's beaten finalists Sheffield Wed reach the Coca-Cola semi-finals again with a 2-1 victory at Wimbledon thanks to a spectacular late goal from Mark Bright. Aberdeen use their game in hand to win 1-0 at Dundee and draw level with Scottish Premier leaders Rangers. Wales are fined £7,000 by FIFA for the fatal rocket incident last November at the international at Cardiff Arms Park.

12 Portsmouth produce another outstanding Cup performance, this time in the Coca-Cola quarter-finals, twice coming back with goals from Paul Walsh to hold Man Utd 2-2 at Old Trafford. Villa reach the semi-finals with a 2-1 win at Tottenham. Norwich appoint caretaker John Deehan manager while the League ask Everton, alleged poachers of former Norwich boss Mike Walker, to explain their actions. Former Birmingham and Oxford manager Arthur Turner dies at 84. Highland League clubs Ross County and Caledonian Thistle are elected to the Scottish League, expanded to 4 divisions of 10 for next season.

13 Much travelled former Scottish international Tommy Hutchison, 46, hangs up his boots but will remain on Merthyr Tydfil's coaching staff.

15 Man Utd retain their 13-point lead in the Premiership with a 1-0 win at Spurs while Blackburn win 2-1 at Bramall Lane helped by a Shearer double and a Sheffield double dismissal. Everton ease their problems with a 6-2 win over bottom club Swindon, Tony Cottee hitting 3. Palace's Div 1 lead evaporates with a 2-0 defeat at Wolves, Millwall moving 2nd on goals with a 1-0 win over Bolton. At the other end Paul Furlong scores a hat-trick as Watford notch a 5-2 win over Birmingham who have Steve Claridge and Gary Cooper sent off. In Scotland, Rangers scrape a 1-1 draw at bottom club Dundee, but they go 1 point ahead of Aberdeen, whose match at Celtic is abandoned goalless through fog after 61 minutes. In the Cup, Highland League Huntley beat Albion Rovers 5-3 in their first round tie, which is played at the 11th attempt.

16 The Division 1 race hots up as 5th-placed Leicester beat 4th-placed Charlton 2-1 to go top. Terry Venables moves closer to the England job as he is cleared by police of any impropriety in his business ventures as alleged in recent TV documentaries.

18 In FA Cup replays, veteran Bernie Slaven scores to give Port Vale a 1-0 win over Southampton, still managerless, but Stoke win 4-1 at Bath. Tottenham present a winding-up petition to the High Court against Terry Venables' company Edennote in an effort to regain an estimated £350,000 costs incurred in a previous action by him, while Sugar emerges from a Premier League inquiry into transfer dealings and gives qualified backing for Venables as the next England manager. Celtic sign

Man Utd back Lee Martin, the fee to be decided. Clyde, homeless since 1976 and sharing Hamilton's ground since 1991, unveil their new ground, Broadwood Stadium, in Cumbernauld.

19 England's scheduled friendly with Germany in Hamburg on Hitler's birthday, 20 April, already moved from Munich because of fears of disruption by neo-Nazis, is cancelled for security reasons, while the FA continue to prevaricate about the England appointment, cancelling scheduled Press conferences but insisting on the side that Venables will be appointed the new manager. In the FA Cup 3rd round replays, Bolton, who humbled Liverpool last season, shock Everton 3-2 at Goodison in extra time after being 2-0 down, but Spurs beat Peterborough 5-4 on penalties after the bottom 1st Division club hold them to 1-1.

20 Sir Matt Busby, Manchester United president, former Scottish international, and father figure of English football, dies at 84 after a long illness. Alan Ball leaves Exeter to take charge at Southampton, where he will be reunited with Lawrie McMenemy, who becomes general manager.

21 Liverpool's young striker Robbie Fowler has a cracked bone in his leg and will be out for about 6 weeks. Leeds' back Mel Sterland is to retire at 32 after a vain 2-year battle with Achilles' tendon trouble. Blackburn report a £6.3m loss in their last financial year (to 30 June 1993).

22 Man Utd, after a moving tribute to Matt Busby, beat Everton 1-0, a scoreline that does little justice to a display he would have been proud of, and go 16 points clear of Blackburn who play tomorrow. Alan Ball has immediate success at Southampton, who win 2-1 at Newcastle and move out of the relegation zone, while Spurs must start to worry after going down 2-1 at bottom club Swindon. Crystal Palace, inspired by Paul Stewart on loan from Liverpool, stem their run of three defeats, beating leaders Leicester 2-1 to go back on top of Div 1, while bottom club Peterborough record their first away win, 2-0 at Cup contenders Portsmouth. All 6 Scottish Premier matches are drawn. Ireland's two national teams are drawn in the same group for the 4th time in 16 years and will have Portugal and Austria as their chief opponents in the qualifying competition for the European Championships to be played in England in 1996.

23 Blackburn beat Leeds 2-1, both goals scored by Alan Shearer, the winner in the last minute of a match blemished before the start by the disgraceful display of the Leeds fans during the one-minute silence for Sir Matt Busby. Swindon ban a fan for the rest of the season for swearing during their minute's silence on Saturday.

24 Terry Cooper, on holiday, agrees to take over at Exeter.

25 Liverpool go down at Anfield in a Cup replay to a non-Premiership team for the second season running, losing 1-0 to Bristol City. The programme for the match contains an apology by John Barnes demanded by manager Grame Souness for a piece in a Sunday paper by Barnes criticizing his manager's 'abrasive manner'. Terry Venables has a 4-hour meeting with FA chief executive Graham Kelly during which it is assumed he has been offered the England job.

26 Man Utd win their Coca-Cola Cup replay 1-0 at Portsmouth and will play Sheff Wed in the semi-finals. Venables and Kelly have further talks and the long-awaited announcement is scheduled for 2 pm on Friday. England are to play Germany on 20 April (Hitler's birthday) after all, at Berlin's Olympic Stadium.

27 Former Fulham chairman Ernie Clay dies at 76.

28 The expected comings and goings materialize with the official appointment of Terry Venables as England's new 'coach', as the manager's job will now be called; the resignation of Graeme Souness after 33 months in charge at Anfield; and the appointment of John Toshack as the new 'technical director' of Wales. It is clear at the Venables press conference that there is a get-out clause in the event of unforeseen circumstances; Liverpool's assistant manager Roy Evans is expected to take charge till the end of the season; and Toshack also signs an extended contract with his Spanish club, Real Sociedad, until June 1998.

29 GM Vauxhall Conference leaders Kidderminster beat Preston, 3rd in Div 3, 1-0 to reach the 5th round of the FA Cup. Man City are also victims of 4th-round giant-killing, outplayed by 2nd Division Cardiff, missing a penalty, and going down 1-0 at Ninian Park just as the Francis Lee takeover is completed. Lee, the former City and England star, having bought 29.9 per cent of the club's shares from former chairman Peter Swales for £3m, will be officially installed as chairman when he returns from holiday this week to a club in ever-deepening crisis. In the Coca-Cola Cup replay, Tranmere beat Forest 2-0 to earn a semi-final place against Villa.

30 Man Utd win 2-0 at Norwich to earn a 5th-round tie at Wimbledon in the Cup and keep their treble hopes alive - the odds are now only 5-1 against. After the game, manager Alex Ferguson makes a verbal attack on the BBC and Jimmy Hill in particular for his criticism of Eric Cantona's reckless fouls.

31 Liverpool go back to the tried and tested Boot Room to appoint caretaker Roy Evans manager with a 2½-year contract.

February

Cup shocks for Premier sides Arsenal, Blackburn, Leeds, Newcastle and Villa from Division 1 clubs ... FIFA red-card 'tackles from behind'

1 Crystal Palace, a goal down at half time to bottom club Peterborough, win 3-2 to extend their Div 1 lead to 4 points. Wolves' former England striker Steve Bull will be out for the rest of the season as an op reveals the extent of the knee injury incurred in Saturday's Cup tie at Port Vale. Diego Maradona is sacked by Argentinian club Newell's Old Boys after repeatedly failing to attend training.

2 Newcastle sign Norwich City striker Ruel Fox for £2,25m. The FA of Wales hold a Press conference, with new part-time technical director John Toshack and his full-time partner Mike Smith on show. Toshack will not be paid and has no contract, but his Spanish club Real Sociedad will receive a facility fee each time he is released.

3 Maradona is in more trouble, said to have been smuggled out of Argentina in a pick-up truck after an incident in which he is alleged to have shot at journalists with an air-gun.

5 Man Utd win 3-2 at QPR to maintain their 13-point Premiership lead over Blackburn, who beat Wimbledon 3-0. At the other end of the table, only 2 points now separate the last 5 clubs, with Swindon notching their 4th win of the season, 3-1 over Coventry, thanks to a Jan Fjortoft hat-trick, and drawing level with gameless Sheffield Utd. Reading lose their first home game in Div 2, but maintain their 8-point advantage. Rangers spring into a 2-point lead in Scotland with a comprehensive 5-1 defeat of Partick. In Div 1, a capacity crowd of 6,200 sees Clyde open their new stadium with a 2-0 defeat by former landlords Hamilton.

8 Charlton, 2nd in Div 1, shock Blackburn, their counterparts in the Premiership, 1-0 at Ewood Park in the FA Cup 4th round replay

9 Three more Premiership giants sensationally fall in the Cup to Div 1 sides, in 4th-round replays - holders Arsenal go down at home 3-1 to Bolton after extra time; Leeds, despite drawing level with two goals in the last 3 minutes, lose 3-2 to Oxford after extra time, also at home; and Newcastle crash 2-0 at Luton. Chelsea beat last year's finalists Sheffield Wed 3-1 after extra time at Hillsborough. In the tie that was postponed, Bristol City notch a convincing 4-0 win at Stockport, Wayne Allison scoring a second-half hat-trick in 18 minutes.

10 Gary Mabbutt, wearing a protective 'Phantom' face mask, makes a typically courageous comeback in Spurs' reserves 80 days after sustaining his horrific injuries. Marseille chairman Bernard Tapie, former government minister, is released on bail after being charged with corruption, and is ordered to give up ownership of the club.

12 Blackburn win 2-0 at Spurs and are now 10 points behind Premiership leaders Man Utd with a game still in hand. In Div 1, another Birmingham defeat, 2-1 at Millwall, sees them drop into the last three. Rangers maintain their 2-point advantage over Aberdeen and Motherwell in the Scottish Premier with a controversial 2-0 victory over in-form Hibs, whose captain Gordon Hunter is sent off for a 'professional foul'.

13 A Ryan Giggs goal after 19 minutes is the only score at Old Trafford in Man United's first leg of the Coca-Cola Cup semi-final against Sheffield Wed.

14 On a snow-covered pitch at the Dell, a Matthew Le Tissier hat-trick, including 2 from the spot, celebrates Alan Ball's first home game as manager as Southampton beat Liverpool 4-2 and move out of the bottom three.

15 All 4 Endsleigh League matches are postponed.

16 Tranmere take their home leg of the Coca-Cola Cup semi-final against Villa 3-1. Bryan Hamilton is the surprise choice for the new N.Ireland supremo to take the place of Billy Bingham, who retired last month. The Football League find Birmingham guilty of poaching manager Barry Fry and colleagues from Southend, but fail to agree on a punishment at this time.

17 Birmingham are fined a record £55,000, with £75,000 compensation to Southend, for luring manager Barry Fry and company from Roots Hall.

18 Terry Venables recruits Bryan Robson and Don Howe as coaches to assist with the senior England side and Dave Sexton to run the Under-21s. Newcastle manager Kevin Keegan reluctantly drops out-of-form Mike Hooper because of a hate campaign from supporters, but threatens to leave the club if there is any repeat.

19 No surprises so far in the 5th round of the FA Cup, but Kidderminster hold out till the 69th minute in front of 8,000 at their Aggborough Stadium before Lee Chapman scores to give West Ham a 1-0 victory. Blackburn beat Newcastle 1-0 in the Premiership to cut Man United's lead to just 7 points. In the Scottish Cup, Rangers slam Alloa 6-0, Ally McCoist hitting 3 in his first full game since November.

20 An Alan Stubbs free-kick 8 minutes from time takes Bolton into the last eight of the Cup, 1-0 at the expense of Villa, their third Premiership scalp, this time without an away replay. Hot favourites Man Utd clear a tricky hurdle in classic style, winning 3-0 at Wimbledon, and are now 6-5 on favourites to win the Cup. In the Scottish Cup, Hearts' 2-1 win at Hibs is their 21st game without defeat against their Edinburgh rivals and leaves them with a quarter-final tie against Rangers at Ibrox.

21 Saudi Arabia sack Dutch coach Leo Beenhakker because his training methods were "not suitable". Luton chairman David Kohler makes allegations regarding crowd disurbances at their Cup tie in Cardiff.

22 Blackburn can only draw 2-2 at Carrow Road despite playing against 10 men for 45 minutes, so although they trail Man Utd by only 6 points they have played a game more. Palace extend their Div 1 lead to 6 points with a 4-1 win over Bristol City. Several Endsleigh League games are postponed because of the weather.

23 The Sheffield Wed v Man Utd Coca-Cola Cup semi-final second leg is postponed because of snow on access roads, even though the Hillsborough pitch is playable. In the Premiership, Andy Cole scores a hat-trick as Newcastle beat Coventry to go above Arsenal and Leeds into 3rd place. Spurs striker Teddy Sheringham, sidelined already for over 4 months, needs another knee operation.

25 FIFA general secretary Sepp Blatter indicates that tackles from behind where there is no hope of getting the ball are to be punished with compulsory red cards. Celtic directors reveal a plan for a 40,000-seater stadium at Cambuslang, on the outskirts of Glasgow, to be financed by a public share flotation - the package put together to foil two serious takeover attempts.

26 Man Utd scrape a 2-2 draw with West Ham at Upton Park with a Paul Ince goal 3 minutes from time, but their Premiership lead is stretched to 7 points and their title hopes strengthened by Blackburn's 1-0 defeat at Highbury, where a fractured leg sustained by striker Kevin Gallacher will probably keep him out for the rest of the season. Many matches are called off around the country,

and in Scotland, where only two Premier League matches are played, Rangers win 2-1 at Raith and now lead the field by 4 points.

27 Aston Villa reach the Coca-Cola Cup final, beating Tranmere 5-4 on penalties when Villa keeper Mark Bosnich, who is controversially not sent off earlier, makes three saves from the spot. And it's a last-minute Mark Stein penalty at Stamford Bridge that gives Chelsea a 4-3 win over Spurs, who now find themselves dangerously close to the Premiership relegation zone after a 7th consecutive defeat.

28 Terry Venables' first England squad, for the friendly against Denmark next week, includes three uncapped players, left-back Graeme Le Saux (Blackburn), winger Darren Anderton (Spurs) and striker Matthew Le Tissier (Southampton), and the recalled Peter Beardsley. Notable absentees are Arsenal's Ian Wright, Paul Merson and Lee Dixon, Sheffield Wednesday's Andy Sinton and Carlton Palmer, and Liverpool's Nigel Clough, while Chris Waddle and Lee Sharpe are unfit.

March

Chelsea win at Old Trafford . . . Platt England's new captain . . . First blood to Venables . . . Toshack comes and goes for Wales . . . Cantona off twice in four days . . . Villa end United's treble dream . . .Graham Taylor takes over at Wolves

1 Dundee Utd win their Scottish Cup 4th round replay at Motherwell 1-0. In the Premier Division, in a protest against the Celtic board, thousands of fans boycott the match with Kilmarnock.

2 Man Utd, with only a one-goal lead from the first leg, cruise past Sheffield Wed 4-1 at Hillsborough to reach the Coca-Cola Cup final. In FA Cup replays, Wolves take another scalp for the Endsleigh League, beating Ipswich 2-1 at Portman Road. In the Premiership, Spurs end a run of 7 consecutive defeats when Ronny Rosenthal hits a second-half equalizer against Villa at White Hart Lane, but they have two penalties saved by spot-kick expert Mark Bosnich.

3 Five Celtic directors call for the resignation of vice-chairman David Smith and secretary Chris White for withholding information about the club's financial plight.

4 Matters come to a head at Celtic, who are saved from the brink of receivership by Fergus McCann, a Canadian multi-millionaire who failed with an £18m rescue package last year, and Brian Dempsey, a former director of the club. With the ousting of three directors marking the end of 'dynastic' control, McCann will take over next week as full-time chief executive and the new consortium is expected to refurbish Parkhead at a cost of £16m instead of going ahead with the move to Cambuslang and floating the club on the Stock Market. The FA fine Man Utd manager Alex Ferguson £250 for remarks made to the referee of an A-team Lancashire League match in December.

5 Man Utd suffer their first home defeat of the season, and only their second Premiership defeat - and it's Chelsea again who inflict it, with Gavin Peacock again the scorer, as they complete a 1-0 Premiership double over the leaders. Blackburn take advantage, beating Liverpool 2-0 to move within 4 points of United. Ian Wright scores a hat-trick in Arsenal's 5-1 win at Ipswich. In Div 1, Palace win 1-0 at Portsmouth to stretch their lead to 7 points over Charlton, beaten 3-2 at Bolton for whom John McGinlay hits 3. Birmingham slip deeper into the mire. In the Scottish Premier, a last-minute Hateley penalty gives Rangers a 2-1 win over Motherwell and stretches their lead to 6 points over Aberdeen. Teams in the World Cup finals will be permitted to use 3 substitutes, including one goalkeeper

6 Paul Gascoigne, playing for Lazio against Roma, is helped off the pitch in tears with suspected fractured rib and arm, injuries that would keep him out of England's friendly against Denmark on Wednesday, Venables' first game as coach.

7 Terry Venables makes Sampdoria midfdielder David Platt the new England captain. Paul Gascoigne's injuries are not fractures, but he remains doubtful for the Denmark match. Cardiff must pay their suspended £25,000 fine because of their fans' behaviour in matches against Swansea in December and Luton last month. Swansea have a suspended £30,000 fine slapped on them for their part in the trouble.

9 A Platt goal gives Terry Venables' England a 1-0 victory over Denmark in an encouraging performance at Wembley that pleases a capacity 72,000 crowd. Alan Shearer plays as a lone striker, well supported from a midfield in which Ince and a partly fit Gascoigne lay deep. Graeme Le Saux and Darren Anderton enjoy promising dbuts. John Toshack has an unhappy start to international management as Wales go down 3-1 to Norway at Ninian Park.

10 Crystal Palace sign Watford's 18-year-old striker Bruce Dyer for £1.25m.

11 Gunnar Halle, Oldham's Norwegian back, needs another knee operation and will be out of the World Cup finals.

12 Bolton's great Cup run comes to an end in the 6th round as Oldham beat them 1-0 at Burnden Park with an 84th-minute goal from Darren Beckford, while favourites Man Utd take a step nearer the treble at Old Trafford, beating another Div 1 side Charlton 3-1 despite having keeper Schmeichel dismissed just before half-time with the score 0-0. Their Premiership challengers Blackburn are without a game, and Newcastle steal the limelight with a 7-1 victory over Swindon, the surprise being that Andy Cole fails to score. Div 3 leaders Crewe have keeper Mark Smith sent off after 19 seconds - a Football League record - and lose 1-0 at lowly Darlington.

13 Chelsea beat Wolves 1-0 at Stamford Bridge and will play either West Ham or Luton in the Cup semi-finals.

14 Luton keep the Endsleigh League flag flying in the FA Cup with a goalless draw at Upton Park in the quarter-finals. Scunthorpe manager Richard Money resigns, physio David Moore taking over as caretaker-manager.

15 A goal from skipper Tony Adams after 66 minutes gives Arsenal a 1-0 aggregate win over Torino and takes them into the Cup-Winners Cup semi-finals. In Division 1, Leicester's 3-0 victory at Birmingham takes them to within 5 points of leaders Palace, while Birmingham drop to bottom. Long-time runaway leaders of both Divs 2 and 3, Reading and Crewe, respectively, are brought back to the pack and overtaken by Plymouth and Chester, respectively. English-born Bolton midfielder Jason McAteer plumps for Ireland and is called up by Jack Charlton for next week's game against Russia.

16 John Toshack resigns as Wales technical director after one match in charge, citing an 'atmosphere' he did not particularly like and implying that he was shocked at the political and administrative infighting at the FA of Wales. His action promps calls for the resignation of Alun Evans, chief executive of the FAW. Man Utd put on a show of class at Old Trafford, again brushing aside Sheff Wed, this time 5-0, to restore their 7-point lead over Blackburn in the Premiership. After 8 years as manager, Graham Turner resigns from Wolves, who have dropped out of the promotion race, and there is speculation that former England supremo Graham Taylor will take his place. Coca-Cola, sponsors of the Football League Cup, sign a £3m deal to sponsor the Scottish League Cup. Everton dismiss England U-21 midfielder Billy Kenny for 'gross misbehaviour'.

17 Wales appoint London-born former manager Mike Smith (1974-79) as their new technical director.

19 Eric Cantona is sent off for stamping on an opponent, the second Man Utd dismissal in 8 days, and bottom club Swindon later score to draw 2-2 with the Premiership leaders, who now go 8 points clear of Blackburn, playing tomorrow. Ian Wright hits another hat-trick for Arsenal in their 4-0 victory at Southampton. Reading go back on top in Div 2.

20 A goal 2 minutes from time by Mike Newell gives Blackburn a 2-1 win at Sheff Wed and sustains the pressure on Man Utd, now only 5 points clear at the top of the Premiership. Palace beat Charlton 2-0 to extend their Div 1 lead also to 5 points.

21 Norwich, without a Premiership win since the defection of manager Mike Walker 10 weeks ago, choose an opportune moment to break the run, beating Walker's new side Everton 3-0 at Carrow Road. The Scottish League announce a sponsorship deal with Bell's, the whisky firm, for £6m over 4 years. Leeds complain to Rangers over chairman David Murray's blatant use of the media to publicize their interest in Gary McAllister.

22 Eric Cantona is sent off for the second time in 4 days as Man Utd are held 2-2 by Arsenal at Highbury, this time for a second bookable offence, and will now miss another game in addition to his 3-match ban, while Roy Keane will also miss the Cup semi-final after collecting a booking that takes him over the limit. United, now 6 points ahead of Blackburn, who have a game in hand, can take solace from the return of Lee Sharpe, scorer of both their goals, after a hernia operation kept him out for 17 matches.

23 Scott Oakes, 21, is a hat-trick hero as Luton beat West Ham 3-2 in their Cup replay to reach a Wembley semi-final against Chelsea. Div 1 leaders Crystal Palace slip up badly, losing 1-0 to Middlesbrough, only their second home defeat this season, and although they retain their 5-point lead, Forest now have 2 games in hand.

24 Transfer deadline day sees record sales, over £7m, including three £1m plus deals - defender Darren Peacock from QPR to Newcastle for a club record £2.7m, with Hereford earning £250,000 from a sell-on agreement; Swedish winger Anders Limpar, who has been unable to sustain a first-team place at Highbury, from Arsenal to Everton for £1.6m; and acrobatic Peter Beagrie from Everton to Man City for £1.1m. Much-travelled striker Clive Allen, 32, leaves West Ham for Millwall, his 7th London club.

26 With Man Utd involved in tomorrow's Coca-Cola Cup final. Blackburn take advantage of their game in hand to beat poor Swindon 3-1 and reduce the gap at the top of the Premiership to a mere 3 points - it was once 16. Spurs record their first win in 11 games, 1-0 at Everton. Palace stride away again 8 points ahead in Div 1 with a 2-0 win at Stoke. An Andy Saville goal 2 minutes from time against Middlesbrough gives Birmingham their first win in 15 games, but they remain bottom. In Scotland, it is now a three-horse race, Rangers leading Motherwell by 4 points and Aberdeen by 5. In Div 1, Hamilton beat bottom club Brechin 9-1, Duffield scoring 4.

27 Villa end Man United's treble dream with a fine 3-1 victory in the Coca-Cola Cup final at Wembley, and Andrei Kanchelskis becomes the 4th United player dismissed in 5 games, handling on the line in the last minute.

28 Sheff Utd give themselves a lifeline, coming from two down to beat West Ham 3-2 at Bramall Lane, but remain 3rd from bottom. Fulham, lurking just above the Div 2 relegation zone, sack manager Don Mackay, putting assistant Ray Lewington in charge. Marseille owner Bernard Tapie is charged with fraud regarding the club accounts.

29 Arsenal make a good start in the Cup-Winners Cup semi-finals, drawing 1-1 in Paris. Blackburn's challenge to Man Utd in the Premiership is torpedoed by Wimbledon, who beat them 4-1 after being a goal down at half-time. Graham Taylor is confirmed as manager of 1st Division Wolves and they celebrate with a 3-1 win at Bolton. The former England manager, on a 3-year contract worth £500,000, offers to meet in person the fans who have expressed disapproval of his appointment. Palace draw at Peterborough to go 9 points clear in Div 1, but have played 3 or 4 games more than their challengers. In Scotland, Brechin City, losing 2-0 at home to Airdrie, are the first team to be relegated to Div 2 - with 8 games still to play.

30 Man United reestablish their 6-point Premiership lead with a shaky 1-0 win over Liverpool at Old Trafford. Barcelona beat Galatasaray 3-0 and, with Monaco, progress into the European Cup semi-finals. In the other group, AC Milan, held 0-0 at home by Anderlecht, nevertheless qualify for the semi stage, while Bobby Robson's Porto win 5-0 at Werder Bremen, the heaviest home defeat suffered by a German club for 39 years, and look set to join them.

April

England-Germany match cancelled ... another serious injury for Gascoigne ... Hughes cracker keeps United in Cup ... Blackburn close 16-point gap ... Palace up, Swindon down ... Everton guilty of inducement ... Cole's Newcastle record

1 Sports Minister Iain Sproat is reconsidering requirements of the 1989 Football Spectators Act regarding all-seater stadiums for Premiership and Div 1 clubs and may extend the deadline in certain cases.

2 Two dazzling Alan Shearer goals put Blackburn right back in the Championship reckoning as they beat Man Utd 2-0 and move just 3 points behind again with 7 games left. In the relegation zone only Southampton lose. Sheffield Utd beat Liverpool 2-1, their first win at Anfield for 26 years. Teddy Sheringham marks his return after 5 months with a goal soon after coming on 7 minutes after the interval as Spurs win 2-1 at Norwich to ease their relegation fears, but Everton's 5-1 drubbing at Sheffield Wed leaves them in danger of the drop. Graham Taylor enjoys a winning home debut in Div 1 as Wolves beat Tranmere 2-1. In Scotland, Aberdeen hold Rangers 1-1 at Ibrox, but the excitement is at Central Park, where the day's smallest crowd, 225, see Div 2 bottom club Cowdenbeath beat Arbroath 1-0 with a goal from Willie Callaghan after 76 minutes to chalk up their first home win for 39 games and nearly two years.

4 The Bank Holiday programme brings no change in the Championship position but while Man Utd gain a shaky 3-2 victory against relegation strugglers and Cup semi-final opponents Oldham at Old Trafford, Blackburn notch a convincing 3-0 away win over Everton, who now find themselves in deep trouble. Spurs, with a 4-1 home defeat by West Ham, have not won at home in 14 Premiership matches. In Div 1, Graham Taylor's honeymoon is quickly over as Wolves go down 4-0 at Oxford. A 5-0 defeat at Burnley condemns Barnet to the 3rd Division next season. Exeter could join them after losing 5-0 at home to Cambridge whose goals are all scored by Steve Butler, making it 8 in 3 days after his hat-trick against Orient on Saturday.

6 With police intelligence building up of massive demonstrations being planned, the FA controversially call off England's friendly with Germany planned for 20 April, Hitler's birthday, but Terry Venables will pick a squad for an international get-together.

7 Paul Gascoigne sustains a career-threatening double fracture of his right leg in a Lazio 5-a-side training game. FIFA president Joao Havelange announces that he wants an extra 8 teams in the 1998 World Cup finals in France, making 32 in all. Leyton Orient sack manager Peter Eustace.

9 Chelsea beat Luton 2-0 at Wembley with 2 Gavin Peacock goals to reach the FA Cup final. As the Premiership fixtures focus on relegation, Southampton move up to 3rd from bottom with a tremendous 5-4 win at Norwich after going 3-1 down, Matthew Le Tissier scoring a hat-trick and making a last-minute winner for Ken Monkou. The position at the top of Div 1 becomes even clearer, as leaders Palace beat play-off hopefuls Millwall 1-0 with a Chris Armstrong goal after 62 minutes and Forest, 10 points behind, win 1-0 at the Valley. Barry Fry enjoys a rare bright moment as Birmingham beat his old team Southend 3-1. In Div 2, Hartlepool join Barnet in relegation misery, hammered into Div 3 7-0 at Rotherham, Shaun Goater scoring 4. In the Scottish Cup semi-finals, an 88th-minute goal from Brian Welsh earns Dundee Utd a draw against Aberdeen. Paul Gascoigne is operated on in London and his career prognosis is much happier.

10 Mark Hughes saves double-chasing Man Utd from defeat in the FA Cup semi-final at Wembley with a brilliant and spectacular opportunist volley a minute from the end of extra time after full-back Neil Pointon had given Oldham a deserved lead a minute into the second period. Scottish treble chasers Rangers are also lucky to survive their Cup semi-finals in a goalless draw with Kilmarnock.

11 Blackburn beat Villa 1-0 with a goal from Alan Shearer after 10 minutes to draw level with Man Utd on 79 points - having closed a one-time 16-point gap - but have a poorer goal difference and have played a game more. England coach Terry Venables names his 24-man training squad and gives Chris Bart-Williams (Sheff Wed), Andy Cole (Newcastle), Jamie Redknapp (Liverpool), Chris Sutton (Norwich) and Jason Wilcox (Blackburn) their first taste of the senior squad.

12 Arsenal reach the Cup-Winners Cup final, beating Paris St Germain 1-0 (2-1) with a goal after only 5 minutes by Kevin Campbell, but their joy is tempered by the booking of Ian Wright which rules him out of the final. In the first Scottish Cup final replay, Dundee Utd beat Aberdeen 1-0 in with a 70th-minute goal by Jim McInally. Shrewsbury take over from Chester at the top of Div 3 with a 2-1 win at Rochdale.

13 It's a different story at Maine Road, where Man Utd, inspired by the return of Russian winger Andrei Kanchelskis, overwhelm Oldham 4-1 in the FA Cup semi-final replay and equal Arsenal's record of reaching 12 finals. Oldham's only complaint is the price of the tickets. Rangers stay on course for the Scottish treble, coming from behind with 2 second-half goals from Mark Hateley to beat Kilmarnock 2-1.

14 FIFA are to use video evidence in the World Cup for the first time, for disciplinary purposes and not during the game. The FA increase the Cup finalists' share of tickets from 52% to 60% just as the government announce legislation giving the police power to arrest touts selling tickets outside grounds at inflated prices. It's "Don't mention the war" again as the more recently departed Rudolph Hess's birthday causes the German authorities to declare that their game with Wales in April next year cannot be played in Berlin.

16 The Premiership race is still wide open as first Blackburn slip, losing 3-1 at Southampton, and then, kicking off at 5 pm, Man Utd fail to take advantage and lose 1-0 to a John Fashanu goal at Wimbledon. Crystal Palace virtually clinch promotion to the Premiership, their 1-0 win at Luton taking them out of reach of the three 3rd-placed sides with only 7th-placed Millwall able to catch them by winning their last 7 matches.

17 Spurs lose 2-0 at Leeds and it's crisis time - 5th from bottom with 4 games remaining, they play the two clubs below them, Oldham and Southampton, in the next few days. Palace's promotion is

confirmed as Millwall are held 2-2 at the Den by Forest, who have a solid 2nd place. Britain's most expensive player, Duncan Ferguson, is in trouble again, video evidence showing what the referee missed in Rangers' game on Saturday, a head-butt on Raith's John McStay. In Italy, AC Milan clinch their 3rd successive championship title.

20 N.Ireland open their European Championship qualifying campaign with an easy 4-1 win over all-amateur dbutants Liechtenstein. In friendly internationals, Scotland win 2-1 in Austria with Bolton's 30-year-old John McGinlay scoring on his dbut; Ireland do something England couldn't, they win 1-0 in Holland with a goal from lone striker Tommy Coyne; and Wales are beaten at home 2-0 by Sweden. Spurs' vital relegation clash at Oldham is washed out, leaving the losing Cup semi-finalists with a frightening fixture pile-up. The Premier League find Everton guilty of "indirectly inducing" Mike Walker to leave Norwich, by means of media leaks not clandesine approaches, and fine them £75,000 with another £50,000 in compensation and costs. Arsenal's Danish international John Jensen is injured in the 3-1 win against Hungary and will miss the Cup-Winners Cup final.

22 The French Football Federation, after nearly a year of deliberation, rule on the Marseille bribery scandal, relegating the European champions to the Second Division and suspending club president Bernard Tapie and three players - Eydlie of Marseille and Robert and Argentine international Burruchaga of Valenciennes - until 1996. (Marseille's former general manager Jean-Pierre Bernes has already been banned from football for life.)

23 Eric Cantona, returning from suspension, scores both goals in Man United's 2-0 defeat of Man City at Old Trafford, and the champions regain their 3-point lead over Blackburn, who play tomorrow. Wimbledon seal Swindon's fate with a 4-2 victory at the County Ground that dispatches them back to Div 1 after just one season in the Premiership. Spurs finally take steps to shake off the relegation threat, their fluent 3-0 win over Southampton being their first at White Hart Lane since October. Peterborough are relegated from Div 1 after their 5-1 defeat at Charlton for whom Garry Nelson hits 3, but Oxford, who take a point from Leicester, and Birmingham, mounting a belated revival with a 2-0 victory at Portsmouth, are not finished yet. New Scottish cap John McGinlay completes a great week with a hat-trick in Bolton's 4-1 win over Middlesbrough. In Div 2, Reading win 4-0 at Blackpool and with a lead of 9 points are assured of at least a play-off place. In Div 3, home wins for leaders Shrewsbury, 2-1 over Northampton, and Chester, 3-1 over Hereford, earn them promotion. In Scotland, Rangers beat their their Cup final opponents Dundee Utd 2-1 at Ibrox with goals by Gordon Durie and retain their 7 point lead in the Premier League. In Div 2, Stranraer win 3-2 at E.Stirling to clinch promotion. Tranmere chairman Peter Johnson is set to assume complete control of Everton in the summer now that he has the backing of Lady Grantchester, daughter of the late John Moores.

24 Blackburn virtually kill their chances of the Premiership title with their failure to beat QPR at Ewood Park. With 3 matches left, they are 2 points behind Man Utd, who have a home game in hand.

26 Dean Holdsworth hits his first Premiership hat-trick for Wimbledon as they hammer another nail into Oldham's relegation coffin with a 3-0 defeat at Selhurst Park. Motherwell beat Rangers 2-1 to to reduce their Scottish Premier lead over them to 5 points with 4 games each to play. Bundesliga leaders Bayern Munich must replay their 2-1 win over Nuremberg because the linesman gave one of their goals when the ball did not cross the line. A 1978 precedent was cited, but this opens up a Pandora's box of possibilities where TV evidence is available, apart from being in blatant contravention of the laws of the game..

27 Man Utd score an important 2-0 win at Leeds as Blackburn keep up the Premiership pressure with a 2-1 victory at West Ham. The European Cup semis result in 3-0 wins for the favourites, Milan over Monaco and Barcelona over Bobby Robson's Porto. Milan's central defenders Baresi, who is cautioned, and Costacurta, sent off, will both miss the final. Andy Cole's goal in Newcastle's impressive 5-0 Premiership defeat of Villa is his 40th League and Cup goal of the season, a Newcastle record. In Div 1,Birmingham's late revival continues with a 4-2 win at West Brom that takes them out of the bottom 3 for the first time since February and leaves West Brom 2nd from bottom.

28 Oldham make official complaints to the FA and PFA about incidents in Tuesday's defeat by Wimbledon, citing, after studying a video of the game, several illegal uses of the elbow and one instance of a punch.

30 With the big guns of the Premiership not playing, all the drama takes place at the other end of the table and Everton find themselves 3rd from bottom and staring relegation in the face with one match left. Their 3-0 defeat at Leeds is compounded by wins by Sheff Utd and Southampton over Newcastle (2-0) and Villa (4-1) respectively. Oldham can only draw at home to Sheff Wed and are 3 points behind Everton but with 2 games in hand, while Tottenham's 2-1 defeat at Wimbledon leaves them only 1 point (but 4 places) above Everton. Two long runs are broken, Swindon winning away for the first time in their last game, 3-1 at QPR, and Arsenal, who have their eyes on next week's Cup-Winners Cup final, losing their first Premiership game in 20, 2-0 at home to West Ham. It's a sad day at Anfield as Norwich beat Liverpool 1-0 to spoil their farewell to the Kop before the bulldozers move in. Forest secure promotion from Div 1 with a 3-2 win at already relegated Peterborough despite going two down in 7 minutes. West Brom beat Grimsby 1-0 and move out of the last 3 at the expense of Oxford and Birmingham, who draw at Bolton. All but one of the Div 2 promotion and play-off positions are settled: Reading go up as champions, while Plymouth, Port Vale and Stockport still dispute the other automatic promotion spot, York and Burnley having qualified for the last two play-off places. Exeter join Hartlepool and Barnet in the drop to Div 3, with either Blackpool or Fulham to follow. Steve Butler, who scored all 5 in Cambridge's win at Exeter, hits another 3 in Cambridge's 7-2 win at Cardiff. Shrewsbury tie up the Div 3 championship with a 4-1 win at Scunthorpe, and Chester also gain promotion despite losing to Northampton. Crewe beat Wycombe 2-1 to go above them into 3rd, but the two still dispute this last automatic promotion place. Preston and Torquay reach the play-offs, but the last place is up for grabs.

Bottom club Darlington win 3-0 at Mansfield and can still catch Northampton and avoid dropping out of the League. Five red cards in Premiership and Endsleigh League matches today take the seasonal tally to 281, a new record. In Scotland, Rangers are held at Ibrox by Celtic and, with Motherwell beating Kilmarnock 1-0 in the only Premier game not drawn, lead by 4 points with 3 games still to play. Motherwell secure their UEFA Cup place for next season. Ruud Gullit will return to AC Milan next season after a year with Sampdoria.

May

Double for United . . . Rangers 6th title in row . . . Arsenal's Cup-Winners Cup triumph . . . AC Milan win European Cup in style . . . crowd violence at Millwall . . . Dundee United at last . . . Ireland win in Germany . . . Gullit walks out on Dutch squad

1 Man United take a step closer to retaining the Championship with a 2-1 win at Portman Road, but Schmeichel is injured and may miss the Cup final. United are 5 points ahead of Blackburn with only 2 games each to play. Crystal Palace take their long-awaited chance to clinch the Division 1 title with a 3-2 win at Ayresome Park which torpedoes Middlesbrough's faint play-off chances.

2 Blackburn finally concede the Premiership title to Manchester United, going down 2-1 at Coventry. This is United's 9th Championship and they are hot favourites to complete their 1st League and Cup double when they meet Chelsea at Wembley in 12 days' time. Two unsuccessful managers lose their jobs, Lennie Lawrence parting company with Middlesbrough by mutual consent and Frank Stapleton getting the sack from Bradford City. FIFA will not intervene over the Bundesliga decision to replay a game because of a refereeing error.

3 Millwall's 1-0 win at Barnsley and Leicester's home draw with Bolton clinch both clubs a Div 1 play-off place, but Wolves' failure to beat Sunderland at home condemns them to another season in Div 1. Luton, without a win for 8 matches, beat West Brom 3-2 to ensure 1st Division football next season. Scottish Premier leaders Rangers lose 1-0 at Hibs but retain their 4-point lead over Motherwell, who blow their chances with a 2-1 home defeat by Dundee Utd. Barring the loss of their last 2 matches and 2 wins for Motherwell, together with a 20-goal turnaround, Rangers can celebrate their 6th Scottish Championship on the trot. Bayern Munich convert their 2-1 win over Nuremberg into 5-0 victory in the controversial replayed Bundesliga match.

4 An inspired Alan Smith strike is enough to give underdogs Arsenal a 1-0 triumph over holders Parma in the European Cup-Winners Cup final at Copenhagen. Champions Man Utd celebrate with a 2-0 home win over Southampton, who remain in relegation trouble. Newcastle sign manager Kevin Keegan for 10 years and star striker Andy Cole for 4. Rangers £4m striker Duncan Ferguson is charged by the police with assault in connection with the alleged head-butting of Raith player John McStay on 16 April.

5 Spurs win 2-0 at battle-weary Oldham to save themselves from possible relegation and all but condemn their opponents to Div 1.

7 The last Saturday of the League season sees Everton produce a Houdini act to survive in the Premiership, as they come from 2-0 down at home to wreckers Wimbledon and achieve an improbable 3-2 win with a goal from Stuart in the 81st minute. Their success, Ipswich's goalless draw at Blackburn and Southampton's 3-3 draw at West Ham leave Sheffield Utd to go down, the Blades losing 3-2 to Cup-finalists Chelsea as Mark Stein scores 2 in the last 15 minutes. Oldham's miracle does not materialize, although they manage a 1-1 draw at Norwich, and they are also relegated, along with long-gone Swindon, whose farewell is a cruel 5-0 home defeat by Leeds. Newcastle consolidate 3rd place by beating Arsenal 2-0, another goal for Andy Cole giving him a club record of 41 and the highest Premiership tally of 34. All Division 1 matches are being played tomorrow to accommodate TV schedules, but there is violence in Portsmouth when 300 West Brom fans arrive for their vital relegation game, including a stabbing during a fight in a pub. In Div 2, Plymouth's 8-1 victory at Hartlepool is in vain, and they will have to fight out the play-offs as Port Vale win 3-1 at Brighton to secure the 2nd automatic promotion spot, Stockport blowing it by failing to beat Hull at home. Blackpool beat Orient 4-1 to stay in Div 2 at the expense of Fulham, beaten 2-1 at Swansea. Crewe gain the 3rd automatic promotion spot in Div 3 with a 2-1 win at already promoted Chester after going a goal down. Darlington beat Bury 1-0 to claim Endsleigh League survival at the expense of Northampton, whose fans disgrace themselves before, during and after the match and whose 4-0 defeat at Chesterfield condemns them to non-League football - unless, as now seems likely, GMV Conference winners Kidderminster are prevented from taking up the position they have won because ground improvements have not been completed in time. On Scotland's penultimate Saturday, Rangers are confirmed Scottish champions again.

8 The English season - bar play-offs - finishes with bouts of violence at Portsmouth, where there are arrests and a delayed start, and at Southend, where opposing fans fight on the pitch. West Brom win 1-0 at Portsmouth to save their 1st Division skins and sentence Birmingham (on goals), whose brave, last-gasp 2-1 win at Tranmere for a 7th game without defeat is in vain, to at least a year in Div 2. The last Premiership match takes place at Old Trafford, where Bryan Robson bids a final farewell to Man Utd fans on his 340th appearance for the club, but party-poopers Coventry hold them to a goalless draw.

9 Coventry defender Phil Babb, who hopes to make the Irish World Cup squad, accuses Eric Cantona of stamping on him in yesterday's game at Old Trafford, although the referee took no action after the challenge in question. PFA chief executive Gordon Taylor is named president of the European PFA.

11 Terry Venables names England B captain Steve Bould (Arsenal) and Villa skipper Kevin Richardson, both 31 and uncapped, in his 20-man squad for friendlies against Greece and Norway, while 30-year-old Chelsea defender Steve Clarke, who last played for Scotland 6 years ago, is named in their 18 for the match against Holland. Inter Milan unexpectedly struggle to beat Salzburg 1-0 at San Siro in the second leg of the UEFA Cup final to win 2-0 on aggregate. Man Utd

keeper Peter Schmeichel is declared fit to play in the Cup final, and right-winger Andrei Kanchelskis signs a new 5-year contract. Liverpool give keeper Bruce Grobbelaar and former captain Ronnie Whelan free transfers.

12 The FA charge Spurs with misconduct regarding alleged unauthorized loans to players between 1985 and 1989. The Scottish FA ban Rangers' Duncan Ferguson for 12 games for the incident against Raith. He can appeal, and his lawyers are also considering action against the SFA, who have refused to defer their action even though the matter is sub judice. Arsenal beat Millwall 3-0 at Highbury to take the FA Youth Cup 5-3 on aggregate. England's World Cup referee Philip Don has been chosen to take charge of the European Cup final.

14 Manchester United complete the double with a 4-0 triumph over Chelsea at Wembley, although the score is a cruel reflection on the London club's contribution to a match they control up to half-time, and in which they stand level for an hour before Eric Cantona converts 2 penalties in 7 minutes, the second a highly controversial award. St Johnstone's 1-0 victory at Motherwell is not enough to keep them in the Scottish Premier Division as Kilmarnock stay above them on goal difference after drawing 0-0 at Hibs. In Div 1, George O'Boyle scores 4 as Dunfermline beat Clyde 5-0, but they are pipped for promotion by Falkirk, whose 1-1 draw at Clydebank is all they need.

15 In the first round of the League play-offs, Derby will take a 2-0 lead over Millwall to the New Den in Div 1, Torquay the same over Preston to Deepdale in Div 3, and most impressive of all new boys Wycombe win their away leg against Carlisle 2-0. The shock of the day occurs in Wales, however, where Abacus League champions Barry Town beat Cardiff 2-1 in the Welsh Cup final to win a place in Europe next season. Colchester sack player-manager Roy McDonough.

16 Man United's Danish keeper Peter Schmeichel signs a new 4-year contract worth £1.5m. Lincoln sack manager Keith Alexander.

17 Terry Venables enjoys another encouraging night at Wembley as England comprehensively beat a below-strength Greece 5-0 with a 'Christmas tree' formation featuring Alan Shearer as a lone striker.

18 AC Milan put on a masterly display in Athens to beat fancied Barcelona 4-0 in the final of the European Cup. Derby beat Millwall 3-1 at the New Den (5-1 on aggregate) in the Div 1 play-offs amid disgraceful scenes of crowd violence, pitch invasions, and racism directed at the visitors' black players. Derby's opponents in the Wembley decider will be Leicester, who beat Tranmere 2-1 (2-1) with a David Speedie goal 5 minutes from time, although the controversial striker, on as a substitute, is sent off along with Tranmere keeper Eric Nixon in injury time. In the Div 2 play-offs, Burnley win 3-1 at Plymouth after being held at home and will meet Stockport, 1-0 victors over York. In Div 3, Preston neutralize their 2-0 deficit and beat Torquay 4-3 on aggregate after extra time, although the visitors are severely handicapped by the sending-off of Darren Moore after 36 minutes. Preston will play Wycombe, who have little trouble in disposing of Carlisle, and are no strangers to Wembley, having won the FA Trophy there in 1991 and 1993.

19 The FA charge Millwall over crowd misconduct during yesterday's match with Derby, which has prompted calls to end the play-offs. Ipswich reinstall John Lyall as team manager, with Mick McGiven becoming football development manager.

20 QPR give England striker Les Ferdinand a lucrative new 2-year contract but release veteran captain Ray Wilkins. GMV Conference champions Kidderminster abandon their campaign for entry into the League Division 3.

21 After 6 final defeats, Dundee Utd, in Ivan Golac's first season as manager, at last win the Scottish FA Cup, beating and outplaying hot favourites Rangers 1-0 at Hampden Park and ruining the Gers' chance to complete an unprecedented back-to-back domestic treble.

22 Terry Venables' honeymoon is over as Norway again hold England to a draw at Wembley in a goalless friendly.

23 Keeper Neville Southall becomes the most-capped Welsh player with 74, overtaking Peter Nicholas, as Wales beat Estonia 2-1 in a friendly in Tallinn.

24 Ireland beat Bolivia 1-0 in a friendly in Dublin, Packie Bonner keeping a clean sheet as he equals Liam Brady's Irish Republic record of 72 caps. ITV clinch a multi-million-pound deal with UEFA for rights to screen 11 European Cup fixtures next season including the final. In the High Court case that began yesterday in which Dean Saunders is accused of deliberately causing the career-wrecking injury to Paul Elliott, evidence given for the prosecution includes opinions from players Terry Butcher and Dennis Wise and former referee Anthony Ward, who all accuse Saunders of an "over the top" challenge.

25 As Spurs are about to submit their response to charges of misconduct over irregular loans to players, the FA rule that, in the event of their being punished by relegation, Sheffield Utd will retain their place in the Premiership instead of being relegated. Chelsea pay a club record £2.3m for Watford striker Paul Furlong to replace Tony Cascarino, who has been given a free transfer. Wimbledon striker John Fashanu is cleared for the second time of illegal use of the elbow, the FA deciding to take no action on Oldham's complaints concerning an incident in last month's clash. Wimbledon's Vinnie Jones, formerly of Chelsea, subpoenaed to give evidence in the Elliott-Saunders case, says only Saunders knows whether there was any malicious intent in his challenge, while Chelsea chairman Ken Bates is sure that Saunders launched himself into a two-footed tackle through the air that "landed on Elliott's knee". Lennie Lawrence, recently sacked by Middlesbrough, is appointed manager of 2nd Div Bradford.

26 Ireland's Geordie manager, Jack Charlton, is granted the Freedom of the City of Dublin. Derby, Grimsby, Middlesbrough, Portsmouth and Sunderland are granted limited deadlines for conversion to all-seater stadiums because of their plan to move to new ones, but National Heritage Secretary Peter Brooke warns Barnsley, Chelsea, Man City, Newcastle, Oldham and Swindon that they will probably have to start the new season with reduced capacities, using seated areas only. Spurs will face an FA inquiry on 14 June regarding their alleged irregular payments to players, but rumours of

continued on page 1022

LEAGUE REVIEW

Manchester United retained their FA Premier League title under its sponsorship as the FA Carling Premiership. They fully deserved this honour, as on their day they were easily the most accomplished team in the division.

Only once in the season when a league table was reproduced, did they not appear in first place. That was after the third match when, by being held to a 1-1 draw at home by Newcastle United, they were placed third.

Chelsea succeeded in beating United twice by 1-0, the scorer on each occasion being Gavin Peacock. United managed to avoid the hat-trick, with a convincing 4-0 win in the FA Cup Final.

The Old Trafford Club suffered only two other defeats, both of them late in the season when Blackburn Rovers, their nearest challengers, threatened to make inroads into United's lead at the top. Blackburn produced arguably their best performance of the season on 2 April at Ewood Park, when they won 2-0. Rovers had also gone close to setting up a double of their own when at Old Trafford on Boxing Day, they came within two minutes of a 1-0 win until Paul Ince equalized for United.

Manchester United also lost 1-0 at Wimbledon, two weeks after the Blackburn defeat, but from then on, convincingly recovered. Their team selection problems were hampered in the closing weeks by suspensions. Eric Cantona was suspended for five matches and the attack never quite looked as potent in his absence.

The controversial Frenchman finished as the club's leading goalscorer and converted two penalties in the Cup Final. He worked well with Mark Hughes and Ryan Giggs, both of whom finished with double scoring figures.

The defence was generally sound, only Liverpool managing to score more than twice against them in one match. In between the Chelsea defeats, United went 22 matches without defeat in the league, and it came as no real surprise when they clinched the title.

For their part, Blackburn, who had spent heavily on new players, were unfortunately hit by injuries, but relied overmuch on the scoring ability of Alan Shearer. Oddly enough they appeared more of a threat when some distance from United, only for the pressure to tell on them as they closed in.

Newly promoted Newcastle had an excellent first season back in the top flight. Andy Cole scored freely and was well supported by a rejuvenated Peter Beardsley transferred from Everton. Their 82 goals was a Premier record and they equalled the biggest win by beating Swindon Town 7-1.

Arsenal, who had difficulty scoring goals in the previous season, still did not appear entirely happy up front, but the defence conceded only 28 goals, another Premier record, after the worst possible start when they were beaten 3-0 at home by Coventry. Consolation for the Gunners was a spirited run in the Cup-Winners' Cup, in which they beat the Italian club Parma 1-0 in the final.

For Aston Villa, their season was one of mixed fortune. They ended it merely in mid-table, but only after beating Manchester United in the Coca-Cola Cup Final; a victory which prevented a possible United treble.

Despite finishing fifth, the challenge from Leeds never materialized after the half-way stage, but Wimbledon's sixth place was their highest in the new Premier setup and they were able to beat both Manchester United and Blackburn in the closing weeks.

Sheffield Wednesday never adequately replaced the departed Paul Warhurst and the injured David Hirst and though Liverpool finished eighth, it was another disappointing season at Anfield. The famous Kop disappeared at the end of the season in ground alterations and the other significant change was the replacement of Graeme Souness by Roy Evans, another of Liverpool's backroom boys.

Queens Park Rangers frequently looked a better team than their results suggested, but they lacked consistency and rumours affecting the possible transfer of Les Ferdinand, did not help.

Coventry were unable to sustain their fine start, a club best for 56 years and Norwich hit a sterile patch, when manager Mike Walkerleft for Everton midway through the season.

For West Ham, thirteenth place was considered satisfactory, as they consolidated their position after promotion, but Chelsea were never able to sustain any momentum to take them into the top half of the table and they had to be content with their successes over Manchester United.

Wretched form at home kept Tottenham on the brink of the relegation area and the financial scandals which were about to surface were unhelpful to events on the field. Distractions of a different nature at Manchester City culminated in a takeover by former

Maine Road idol Franny Lee and resulted in many personnel changes.

Everton were involved in one of the great escapes of all time. Trailing by 2-0 after only twenty minutes of the last match against Wimbledon, they recovered to win 3-2 and with other results going their way, survived. Southampton also avoided the drop and were indebted to Matthew Le Tissier, who scored 25 of their 49 league goals. The third lucky team proved to be Ipswich, who were saved themselves on the last day when Mark Stein's injury time goal for Chelsea put Sheffield United down. Ipswich scored only 35 goals.

United were accompanied by Oldham, whose long flirtation with danger ended at Norwich, where they could only draw, but even a win would not in the end have saved them.

Swindon were the first to be relegated and were never able to get off the bottom, though they did score four times against Manchester United over two games. But they let in 100 goals and obtained only 30 points.

In the Endsleigh Insurance First Division, Crystal Palace returned to the Premiership at the first opportunity and proved to be the most consistent team in the closing weeks with one defeat in the last nine matches and that after the title was secured. For manager Alan Smith, it was a reward in his first season in charge.

Automatically promoted with them were Nottingham Forest who had also spent just one season out of the top. They, too, were under new management with Frank Clark, a one-time disciple of Brian Clough and they produced effective, attractive football.

Despite finishing third, Millwall had goalscoring problems and lost in the play-offs to Derby, who again showed their erratic streak.

Fourth placed Leicester edged out Tranmere to meet Derby at Wembley and their jinx at the ground was finally ended. Tranmere came close to causing an upset in the Coca-Cola Cup semi-final when they were minutes away from eliminating Aston Villa.

Notts County's away form improved too late and Wolves might well have been better advised to replace the injured Steve Bull at a crucial time. Manager Graham Taylor took over late in the season from Graham Turner, but was unable to push Wolves higher.

Top scorer in the country last season was Andy Cole (Newcastle United). He has averaged almost a goal a game since joining the Tyneside club. (Colorsport).

Alan Shearer (right) scores for Blackburn Rovers against Manchester United. Paul Parker attempts to intervene. (Action Images).

Failure to clinch a play-off place cost Manager Lennie Lawrence his job at Middlesbrough and Stoke City were never as threatening after Stein's departure to Chelsea. Charlton appeared handily poised at the end of February in second place, but lost 11 of their remaining matches. Sunderland spent the season in the bottom half of the table, Bristol City produced their best by beating Liverpool at Anfield in the FA Cup and Bolton's League form also suffered from their cup run in which they splendidly accounted for Everton, Arsenal and Aston Villa.

Southend were never the same outfit losing manager Barry Fry to Birmingham and Grimsby were the division's draw specialists with 20, including 14 at home.

For a time, Gerry Creaney's arrival from Celtic boosted Portsmouth's goalscoring, but a spate of injuries cost them dearly towards the end of the season. A late revival for Barnsley avoided relegation and Watford celebrated their similar survival with a win at Crystal Palace.

Reaching the semi-final of the FA Cup was almost a distraction for Luton needing to pile up points, but they managed it, while West Bromwich saved themselves on the last day by winning 1-0 atPortsmouth.

Not so fortunate were Birmingham, who used 40 players during the season and were beaten by Kidderminster in the FA Cup. They were relegated with Oxford who had beaten Leeds in the cup and Peterborough, whose better performances were all too few.

Reading had the best goal difference in the Endsleigh League and veteran striker Jimmy Quinn was a prolific scorer. They won automatic promotion from the Second Division with Port Vale, who had just missed out last season.

Plymouth were the high scorers in the league with 88 goals including an 8-1 win at luckless Hartlepool on the last day, but Burnley beat them in the play-offs. Fourth placed Stockport beat York, but lost 2-1 to Burnley at Wembley.

Frank Stapleton was a casualty at Bradford. He lost his managerial seat after failure to reach the play-offs and Bristol Rovers failed to live up to their pre-season tip as promotion favourites.

Hull must have been disappointed not to get into the frame and an uncharacteristic free-scoring spell by Cambridge was too late in the season. Steve Butler scored five goals in one game for them. Huddersfield were rarely out of danger until remaining unbeaten in the last twelve matches.

Wrexham stayed in mid table after promotion and Swansea ended an indifferent season by winning the Autoglass Trophy. Brighton improved steadily after Liam Brady took over, but Rotherham managed three wins in a row just once in early season.

Brentford's fortunes changed dramatically; they had one run of 15 games without defeat, another of 16 without a win, while Bournemouth were as high as second after six games, but were unable to sustain such heady achievement.

A season of frustration cost manager Peter Eustace his job at Leyton Orient and only a late revival pulled Cardiff clear. The Welsh club had constrasting cup results: beating Manchester City in the FA Cup and losing to Barry Town in the Welsh Cup.

Blackpool salvaged themselves on the last day, beating ten-man Orient 4-1, but Fulham, Exeter, Hartlepool and Barnet went down. Fulham's defeat at Swansea caused their downfall, Exeter had stayed third from bottom for months and Hartlepool's defence conceded goals freely. Barnet never recovered from losing their first ten matches.

Shrewsbury were full value for their championship in Division Three, after just missing out in 1992–93 and were joined by Chester and Crewe. Chester bounced back smartly after relegation and Crewe made it despite faltering in the closing weeks. There was much satisfaction for newcomers Wycombe, who finished fourth, then accounted for Carlisle and Preston in the play-offs. Preston had looked safe enough for automatic promotion. Torquay were handicapped by a tendency to draw games, 16 in all and Preston edged them out of the play-offs. Chesterfield drew seven of their last 10 to miss out on them and Rochdale who topped the division in September, fell away badly. Losing four of their last five ruined Walsall's chances and inconsistency proved Scunthorpe's downfall.

Mansfield tightened their defence after early problems, but remained in mid-table and Bury's improvement was not maintained. They did not win one of their last ten.

Scarborough only once managed as many as three wins in a row as did Doncaster, while Gillingham were never out of the bottom half. Colchester's defence improved but their attack lost its edge. Roy McDonough left Colchester and there was a similar dismissal for Keith Alexander following disappointments at Lincoln.

Wigan had a poor season as did Hereford, until a brief respite in mid-April. Darlington won three of their last four to avoid last place, but Northampton was saved from relegation to the GM Vauxhall Conference by Kidderminster's failure to have their ground in satisfactory condition for the Football League.

Steve Walsh (9) scores Leicester City's second goal to ensure promotion to the FA Carling Premiership during the play-off final against Derby County. (Colorsport).

INTRODUCTION TO THE CLUB SECTION

The full page team photographs which appear on the first of each club's six pages in this section of the yearbook were taken at the beginning of the 1993–94 season, and therefore relate to the season covered by this edition's statistics.

The third and fourth pages of each club's section give a complete record of the League season for the club concerned, including date, venue, opponents, result, half-time score, League position, goalscorers, attendance and complete line-ups, including substitutes where used, for every League game in the 1993–94 season. Squad numbers have been ignored; those used are familiar ones 1–11, 12 and 14. These two pages also include consolidated lists of goalscorers for the club in League, Coca-Cola and FA Cup matches and a summary of results in the two main domestic cups. The full League history of the club, a complete list of major honours won and best placings achieved, and a note of the team's first and second choice colours appears on the sixth page of this section. The colours are checked with the clubs at the time of going to press, but please note that second choice colours may vary during the season.

Note also that the League position shown after each League result is recalculated as at every Saturday night plus full holiday programmes, but the position after mid-week fixtures will not normally be updated. Please be advised that the attendance figures quoted for each Endsleigh Insurance League game are those which appeared in the Press at the time. But those in the FA Carling Premiership are official. The attendance statistics published on pages 610 and 611 are those issued officially by the Football League after the season has been completed. However, the figures for each League game are those used by the Football League in its weekly bulletin, in conjunction with the *Daily Telegraph* and Jack Rollin's Monday morning statistics in that newspaper.

On the fourth page of each club's section, the total League appearances for the season are listed at the top of each player's column. Substitutes are inserted as numbers 12 and 14 where they actually came on to play. The players taken off are now respectively given a light type figure and an italic one, replacing the * and +. This has enabled more players to be listed in the columns available. Where only one substitute has been used, the number 12 is listed.

In the totals at the top of each column, substitute appearances are listed separately by the '+' sign, but have been amalgamated in the totals which feature in the player's historical section on the final page for each club. Thus these appearances include those as substitute.

The final pages for each club list all the players included on the FA Premier League and Football League's 'Retained' list, which is published at the end of May. Here you will find each player's height and weight, where known, plus birthplace, birthdate and source, together with total League appearances and goals for each club he has represented. Full names of all other players retained including trainees, non-contract players and schoolboys are also given. In addition more club information is added on these pages including items of interest from the club's history and a list of previous managers, plus new items in the 'Did you know' series.

The player's details remain under the club which retained him at the end of the season. An asterisk * by a player's name on the fifth and sixth pages means that he was given a free transfer at the end of the 1993–94 season, a dagger † against a name means that he is a non-contract player, and a double dagger ‡ indicates that the player's registration was cancelled during the season. An § indicates either a Trainee or an Associated Schoolboy who has made Football League appearances.

The play-offs in the Football League are listed separately on pages 586 and 587. Appearances made by players in these play-offs will *not* be included in their career totals.

ARSENAL 1993–94 *Back row (left to right):* Pat Rice (Youth Team Coach), Gary Lewin (First Team Physio), Martin Keown, Paul Merson, Alan Smith, Steve Bould, David Seaman, Alan Miller, Tony Adams, Andy Linighan, Paul Davis, Lee Dixon, Stewart Houston (First Team Coach), George Armstrong (Reserve Team Coach).
Front row: Ray Parlour, Mark Flatts, David Hillier, Steve Morrow, Eddie McGoldrick, Ian Selley, Neil Heaney, George Graham (Manager), Ian Wright, John Jensen, Kevin Campbell, Jimmy Carter, Anders Limpar, Pal Lydersen, Nigel Winterburn.

FA Premiership **ARSENAL**

Arsenal Stadium, Highbury, London N5 1BU. Telephone 071–226 0304. Box office direct line 071–354 5404. Commercial and Marketing 071– 359 0808. Recorded information on 071–359 0131. Clubline: 0891 20 20 20. Mail Order 071–354 8397.

Ground capacity: 38,500 all seated.

Record attendance: 73,295 v Sunderland, Div 1, 9 March 1935.

Record receipts: £233,595 v Everton, Littlewoods Cup semi-final, 24 February 1988.

Pitch measurements: 110yd × 71yd.

Chairman: P. D. Hill-Wood. ***Vice-chairman:*** D. Dein.

Directors: Sir Robert Bellinger CBE, DSC, R. G. Gibbs, C. E. B. L. Carr, R. C. S. Carr, D. D. Fiszman.

Managing Director: K. J. Friar.

Manager: George Graham. ***Assistant Manager/Coach:*** Stewart Houston.

Physio: Gary Lewin. ***Reserve Coach:*** George Armstrong. ***Youth Coach:*** Pat Rice.

Secretary: K. J. Friar. ***Assistant Secretary:*** David Miles. ***Commercial Manager:*** John Hazell. ***Marketing Manager:*** Phil Carling.

Year Formed: 1886. ***Turned Professional:*** 1891. ***Ltd Co.:*** 1893.

Previous Names: 1886, Dial Square; 1886–91, Royal Arsenal; 1891–1914, Woolwich Arsenal.

Club Nickname: 'Gunners'.

Previous Grounds: 1886–87, Plumstead Common; 1887–88, Sportsman Ground; 1888–90, Manor Ground; 1890–93, Invicta Ground; 1893–1913, Manor Ground; 1913, Highbury.

Record League Victory: 12–0 v Loughborough T, Division 2, 12 March 1900 – Orr; McNichol, Jackson; Moir, Dick (2), Anderson (1); Hunt, Cottrell (2), Main (2), Gaudie (3), Tennant (2).

Record Cup Victory: 11–1 v Darwen, FA Cup, 3rd rd, 9 January 1932 – Moss; Parker, Hapgood; Jones, Roberts, John; Hulme (2), Jack (3), Lambert (2), James, Bastin (4).

Record Defeat: 0–8 v Loughborough T, Division 2, 12 December 1896.

Most League Points (2 for a win): 66, Division 1, 1930–31.

Most League Points (3 for a win): 83, Division 1, 1990–91.

Most League Goals: 127, Division 1, 1930–31.

Highest League Scorer in Season: Ted Drake, 42, 1934–35.

Most League Goals in Total Aggregate: Cliff Bastin, 150, 1930–47.

Most Capped Player: Kenny Sansom, 77 (86), England.

Most League Appearances: David O'Leary, 558, 1975–93.

Record Transfer Fee Received: £2,000,000 from Leeds U for David Rocastle.

Record Transfer Fee Paid: £2,500,000 to Crystal Palace for Ian Wright, September 1991.

Football League Record: 1893 Elected to Division 2; 1904–13 Division 1; 1913–19 Division 2; 1919–92 Division 1; 1992– FA Premier League.

Honours: *Football League:* Division 1 – Champions 1930–31, 1932–33, 1933–34, 1934–35, 1937–38, 1947–48, 1952–53, 1970–71, 1988–89, 1990–91; Runners-up 1925–26, 1931–32, 1972–73; Division 2 – Runners-up 1903–04. *FA Cup:* Winners 1929–30, 1935–36, 1949–50, 1970–71, 1978–79, 1992–93; Runners-up 1926–27, 1931–32, 1951–52, 1971–72, 1977–78, 1979–80. *Double Performed:* 1970–71. *Football League Cup:* Winners 1986–87, 1992–93; Runners-up 1967–68, 1968–69, 1987–88. **European Competitions:** *Fairs Cup:* 1963–64, 1969–70 (winners), 1970–71; *European Cup:* 1971–72, 1991–92; *UEFA Cup:* 1978–79, 1981–82, 1982–83; *European Cup-Winners' Cup:* 1979–80 (runners-up), 1993–94 (winners).

ARSENAL 1993—94 LEAGUE RECORD

Match No.	Date	Venue	Opponents	Result		H/T Score	Lg. Pos.	Goalscorers	Attendance
1	Aug 14	H	Coventry C	L	0-3	0-1	—		26,397
2	16	A	Tottenham H	W	1-0	0-0	—	Wright	28,355
3	21	A	Sheffield W	W	1-0	1-0	9	Wright	26,023
4	24	H	Leeds U	W	2-1	1-0	—	Newsome (og), Merson	29,042
5	28	H	Everton	W	2-0	0-0	3	Wright 2	29,063
6	Sept 1	A	Blackburn R	D	1-1	0-1	—	Campbell	14,410
7	11	H	Ipswich T	W	4-0	2-0	2	Wright, Campbell 3	28,563
8	19	A	Manchester U	L	0-1	0-1	—		44,009
9	25	H	Southampton	W	1-0	1-0	2	Merson	26,902
10	Oct 2	A	Liverpool	D	0-0	0-0	2		42,750
11	16	H	Manchester C	D	0-0	0-0	3		29,567
12	23	A	Oldham Ath	D	0-0	0-0	3		12,105
13	30	H	Norwich C	D	0-0	0-0	3		30,516
14	Nov 6	H	Aston Villa	L	1-2	0-0	6	Wright	31,773
15	20	A	Chelsea	W	2-0	2-0	6	Smith, Wright (pen)	26,839
16	24	A	West Ham U	D	0-0	0-0	—		20,279
17	27	H	Newcastle U	W	2-1	1-0	3	Wright, Smith	36,091
18	Dec 4	A	Coventry C	L	0-1	0-0	4		12,632
19	6	H	Tottenham H	D	1-1	0-1	—	Wright	35,669
20	12	H	Sheffield W	W	1-0	0-0	—	Wright	22,026
21	18	A	Leeds U	L	1-2	1-1	5	Campbell	37,289
22	27	A	Swindon T	W	4-0	2-0	4	Campbell 3, Wright	17,214
23	29	H	Sheffield U	W	3-0	2-0	4	Campbell 2, Wright	27,035
24	Jan 1	A	Wimbledon	W	3-0	2-0	3	Campbell, Parlour, Wright	16,584
25	3	H	QPR	D	0-0	0-0	3		34,935
26	15	A	Manchester C	D	0-0	0-0	3		25,642
27	22	H	Oldham Ath	D	1-1	1-1	3	Wright (pen)	26,524
28	Feb 13	A	Norwich C	D	1-1	1-0	—	Campbell	17,667
29	19	A	Everton	D	1-1	0-0	3	Merson	19,760
30	25	H	Blackburn R	W	1-0	0-0	3	Merson	35,030
31	Mar 5	A	Ipswich T	W	5-1	3-0	3	Wright 3 (1 pen), Youds (og), Parlour	18,803
32	19	A	Southampton	W	4-0	2-0	4	Wright 3 (1 pen), Campbell	16,790
33	22	H	Manchester U	D	2-2	1-1	—	Pallister (og), Merson	36,203
34	26	H	Liverpool	W	1-0	0-0	3	Merson	35,556
35	Apr 2	H	Swindon T	D	1-1	1-1	4	Smith	31,635
36	4	A	Sheffield U	D	1-1	0-0	4	Campbell	20,019
37	16	H	Chelsea	W	1-0	0-0	4	Wright	34,314
38	19	H	Wimbledon	D	1-1	0-1	—	Bould	21,292
39	23	A	Aston Villa	W	2-1	1-0	4	Wright 2 (1 pen)	31,580
40	27	A	QPR	D	1-1	0-1	—	Merson	11,442
41	30	H	West Ham U	L	0-2	0-0	4		33,700
42	May 7	A	Newcastle U	L	0-2	0-0	4		32,216

Final League Position: 4

GOALSCORERS

League (53): Wright 23 (5 pens), Campbell 14, Merson 7, Smith 3, Parlour 2, Bould 1, own goals 3.
Coca-Cola Cup (10): Wright 6, Merson 2, Campbell 1, Smith 1.
FA Cup (4): Adams 2, Smith 1, Wright 1.

Seaman 39	Dixon 32 + 1	Winterburn 34	Davis 21 + 1	Linighan 20 + 1	Adams 35	Jensen 27	Wright 39	Campbell 28 + 9	Merson 24 + 9	Limpar 9 + 1	McGoldrick 23 + 3	Keown 23 + 10	Parlour 24 + 3	Selley 16 + 2	Hillier 11 + 4	Smith 21 + 4	Heaney 1	Bould 23 + 2	Morrow 7 + 4	Miller 3 + 1	Flatts 2 + 1	Dickov — + 1	Match No.
1	2	3	4	5	6	*7*	8	9	10	11	12	14											1
1		3	4	5	6	7	8	9			11	2	10										2
1		3	4	5	6	7	8	9	12		11	2	10										3
1		3	4	5			8	9	10		11	2	7	6	12								4
1		3		5	6	7	8	9	12		11	2	10		4								5
1		3		5	6	7	8	9	10		11	2	4	12									6
1		3	4	5	6	*7*	8	9	*10*	14	11	2			12								7
1		3	12	5	6	7	8	9	*10*		11	2			4	14							8
1		3	4	5	6	7	8	9	10		11	2			12								9
1	2	3	4	5	6	7	8	9	10		11												10
1	2	3	4	5	6		8	12			7		10			9	11						11
1	2	3	4	5	6		8	12	10		11				7	9							12
1	2	*3*	4		6	7	8	12	10	11		14				9		5					13
1	2	3			6	7	8	9	10	11		5		4									14
1	2	3	4	5			8		10			11		7		9		6	12				15
1	2	3		5			*8*	12	10	11		7				9		6	4	14			16
1	2	3				7	8		10		11	6				9		5	4				17
1	2	3	4		*6*		8	12	10		11	5		7		9		14					18
1	2				6	7	8	12	10	11		3		4		9		5					19
	2				6	7	8	12	10	11		*5*		4		9		14	3	1			20
1	2	3			6	7	8	10		11			14	4		*9*		5	12				21
1	2	3			*6*	7	8	9	12		11	14	10		4			5					22
1	2	3			6	7	*8*	9	12		11	14	10		4			5					23
1	*2*	3			6	7	8	9	12		11	14	10		4			5					24
1	2	3			6	7	8	9			11	12	10		4			5					25
1	2	3			6	*7*	8	9	12		11	14	10		4			5					26
1	2	3			6	*7*	8	9	12		11	14	10		4			5					27
1	2	3	4		6	7		8	10				11			9		5					28
1	2	3	4		*6*	7		8	10			14	11		12	9		5					29
1	2	3	4		6	7		8	10				11			9		5					30
1	2	3			6		8		12	11		14	10	7	*4*	9		5					31
1	2	3		5	6		8	9		11		4	10	7		12							32
1	2	3	4		6	7	8	12	10					11		9		5					33
1	2			6		*7*	8	9	10			3	4	11		12		5	14				34
1	2		4	5	6	*7*	8	12	10		14	3	11			9							35
1	14	3			6		8	10	12		11	*2*	4	7		9		5					36
1	2				6		8	9			11	5	10	7	4	12			3				37
1	2		4		6		8	7				3	10	11		9		5			12		38
1	2		4	6			8	10				7	12			9		5	3		11		39
1	2			5	6		8		10		12	3	11	14		9			4		*7*		40
		3	4	6			8	9	*10*		2		7	11				5	12	1		14	41
	2	3	4	14	6		8				11		12	10		9		5	7	1			42

Coca-Cola Cup	Second Round	Huddersfield T (a)	5-0
		(h)	1-1
	Third Round	Norwich C (h)	1-1
		(a)	3-0
	Fourth Round	Aston Villa (h)	0-1
FA Cup	Third Round	Millwall (a)	1-0
	Fourth Round	Bolton W (a)	2-2
		(h)	1-3

ARSENAL

Player and Position	Ht	Wt	Birth Date	Birth Place	Source	Clubs	League App	League Gls
Goalkeepers								
Allan Miller	6 3	14 07	29 3 70	Epping	Trainee	Arsenal	8	—
						Plymouth Arg (loan)	13	—
						WBA (loan)	3	—
						Birmingham C (loan)	15	—
David Seaman	6 4	14 10	19 9 63	Rotherham	Apprentice	Leeds U	—	—
						Peterborough U	91	—
						Birmingham C	75	—
						QPR	141	—
						Arsenal	158	—
James Will*	6 2	13 13	7 10 72	Turiff	Trainee	Arsenal	—	—
						Sheffield U (loan)	—	—
Defenders								
Tony Adams	6 3	13 11	10 10 66	London	Apprentice	Arsenal	319	20
Steve Bould	6 4	14 02	16 11 62	Stoke	Apprentice	Stoke C	183	6
						Torquay U (loan)	9	—
						Arsenal	161	5
Stuart Campbell*	5 9	10 07	2 1 75	Bexley	Trainee	Arsenal	—	—
Lee Dixon	5 8	11 08	17 3 64	Manchester	Local	Burnley	4	—
						Chester	57	1
						Bury	45	5
						Stoke C	71	5
						Arsenal	215	15
Martin Keown	6 1	12 04	24 7 66	Oxford	Apprentice	Arsenal	22	—
						Brighton (loan)	16	—
						Brighton (loan)	7	1
						Aston Villa	112	3
						Everton	96	—
						Arsenal	49	—
Ryan Kirby*	5 11	12 00	6 9 74	Chingford	Trainee	Arsenal	—	—
Andy Linighan	6 4	13 10	18 6 62	Hartlepool	Smiths BC	Hartlepool U	110	4
						Leeds U	66	3
						Oldham Ath	87	6
						Norwich C	86	8
						Arsenal	69	2
Pal Lydersen	6 0	14 01	10 9 65	Odense	IK Start.	Arsenal	15	—
Scott Marshall	6 1	12 05	1 5 73	Edinburgh	Trainee	Arsenal	2	—
						Rotherham U (loan)	10	1
						Oxford U (loan)	—	—
Steve Morrow	5 11	12 02	2 7 70	Belfast	Trainee	Arsenal	29	—
						Reading (loan)	10	—
						Watford (loan)	8	—
						Reading (loan)	3	—
						Barnet (loan)	1	—
Roy O'Brien	6 1	12 00	27 11 74	Cork	Trainee	Arsenal	—	—
Ken Webster*	5 8	13 02	2 3 73	Hammersmith	Trainee	Arsenal	—	—
Nigel Winterburn	5 8	11 04	11 12 63	Coventry	Local	Birmingham C	—	—
						Oxford U	—	—
						Wimbledon	165	8
						Arsenal	233	5
Midfield								
Jimmy Carter	5 10	11 01	9 11 65	London	Apprentice	Crystal Palace	—	—
						QPR	—	—
						Millwall	110	10
						Liverpool	5	—
						Arsenal	22	2
						Oxford U (loan)	5	—
Paul Davis	5 10	10 13	9 12 61	London	Apprentice	Arsenal	347	29
Mark Flatts	5 06	9 08	14 10 72	Haringay	Trainee	Arsenal	13	—
						Cambridge U (loan)	5	1
						Brighton (loan)	10	1
David Hillier	5 10	12 05	19 12 69	Blackheath	Trainee	Arsenal	88	2
John Jensen	5 10	12 06	3 5 65	Denmark	Brondby	Arsenal	59	—
Chris McDonald			14 10 75	Edinburgh	Trainee	Arsenal	—	—
Eddie McGoldrick	5 10	12 00	30 4 65	London	Kettering T	Northampton T	107	9
						Crystal Palace	147	11
						Arsenal	26	—

ARSENAL

Colours: Red shirts with white sleeves, white shorts, red and white hooped stockings. **Change colours:** Navy shirts with teal sleeves, navy shorts, navy and teal hooped stockings.

Foundation: Formed by workers at the Royal Arsenal, Woolwich in 1886 they began as Dial Square (name of one of the workshops) and included two former Nottingham Forest players Fred Beardsley and Morris Bates. Beardsley wrote to his old club seeking help and they provided the new club with a full set of red jerseys and a ball. The club became known as the "Woolwich Reds" although their official title soon after formation was Woolwich Arsenal.

First Football League game: 2 September, 1893, Division 2, v Newcastle U (h) D 2-2 – Williams; Powell, Jeffrey; Devine, Buist, Howat; Gemmell, Henderson, Shaw (1), Elliott (1), Booth.

Did you know: Arsenal recorded their 100th goal in European football against Odense in the 35th minute of their European Cup-Winners' Cup match on 15 September during a 2-1 win. It was also Ian Wright's first goal in such a competition.

Managers (and Secretary-Managers)
Sam Hollis 1894–97, Tom Mitchell 1897–98, George Elcoat 1898–99, Harry Bradshaw 1899–1904, Phil Kelso 1904–08, George Morrell 1908–15, Leslie Knighton 1919–25, Herbert Chapman 1925–34, George Allison 1934–47, Tom Whittaker 1947–56, Jack Crayston 1956–58, George Swindin 1958–62, Billy Wright 1962–66, Bertie Mee 1966–76, Terry Neill 1976–83, Don Howe 1984–86, George Graham May 1986– .

Player and Position	*Ht*	*Wt*	*Birth Date*	*Birth Place*	*Source*	*Clubs*	*League App*	*League Gls*
Gavin McGowan	5 11	12 03	16 1 76	Blackheath	Trainee	Arsenal	2	—
Ray Parlour	5 10	11 12	7 3 73	Romford	Trainee	Arsenal	54	4
Ian Selley	5 9	10 01	14 6 74	Chertsey	Trainee	Arsenal	27	—
Forwards								
Kevin Campbell	6 1	13 08	4 2 70	Lambeth	Trainee	Arsenal	143	42
						Leyton Orient (loan)	16	9
						Leicester C (loan)	11	5
Adrian Clarke	5 10	11 00	28 9 74	Suffolk	Trainee	Arsenal	—	—
Tony Connolly*	5 8	11 07	17 6 75	Cork	Trainee	Arsenal	—	—
Paul Dickov	5 5	11 05	1 11 72	Glasgow	Trainee	Arsenal	4	2
						Luton T (loan)	15	1
						Brighton (loan)	8	5
Paul Merson	6 0	13 02	20 3 68	London	Apprentice	Arsenal	233	63
						Brentford (loan)	7	—
Paul Read	5 11	12 06	25 9 73	Harlow	Trainee	Arsenal	—	—
Paul Shaw	5 11	12 02	4 9 73	Burnham	Trainee	Arsenal	—	—
Alan Smith	6 3	12 13	21 11 62	Birmingham	Alvechurch	Leicester C	191	73
						Leicester C (loan)	9	3
						Arsenal	245	84
Ian Wright	5 9	11 08	3 11 63	Woolwich	Greenwich Borough	Crystal Palace	225	89
						Arsenal	100	62
Soner Zumrutel	5 6	11 00	6 10 74	Islington	Trainee	Arsenal	—	—

Trainees
Black, Michael J; Clarke, Anthony A; Dennis, Kevin J; Drake, Robbie; Griggs, Timothy; Hall, Graeme B; Howell, Jamie; Hughes, Stephen J; Imber, Noel S. P; McGowan, Gavin G; Rawlins, Matthew; Rose, Matthew; Talor, Ross E.

Associated Schoolboys
Bowes, Terry D; Crowe, Jason; Day, Jamie R; Lopez, Rik; Richardson, Lee; Wicks, Matthew.

Associated Schoolboys who have accepted the Club's offer of a Traineeship/Contract
Hollingsworth, Orlando; Rankin, Isaiah; Tello, Gregory; Wynter, Jermaine.

ASTON VILLA 1993–94 *Back row (left to right):* Matthias Breitkreutz, Shaun Teale, Dwight Yorke, Neil Cox, Paul McGrath, Dariusz Kubicki, Earl Barrett, Stephen Staunton.
Centre row: Colin Clarke, Jim Walker, Andy Townsend, Stefan Beinlich, Garry Parker, Nigel Spink, Mark Bosnich, David Farrell, Ugo Ehiogu, Stephen Froggatt, Dave Sexton.
Front row: Ray Houghton, Gordon Cowans, Kevin Richardson, Ron Atkinson, Jim Barron, Dean Saunders, Dalian Atkinson, Tony Daley.

FA Premiership **ASTON VILLA**

Villa Park, Trinity Rd, Birmingham B6 6HE. Telephone 021–327 2299. Fax 021–322 2107. Commercial Dept. 021–327 5399. Clubcall: 0898 121148. Ticketline: 0898 121848. Ticket office: 021–327 5353. Club shop: 021–327 2800.

Ground capacity: 46,000.

Record attendance: 76,588 v Derby Co, FA Cup 6th rd, 2 March 1946.

Record receipts: £385,678 Everton v Norwich C, FA Cup semi-final, 15 April 1989.

Pitch measurements: 115yd × 75yd.

President: H. J. Musgrove. ***Chairman:*** H. D. Ellis.

Directors: J. A. Alderson, Dr D. H. Targett, P. D. Ellis.

Manager: Ron Atkinson. ***Assistant Manager:*** Jim Barron. ***First Team Coach:*** Dave Sexton.

Secretary: Steven Stride. ***Director of Youth:*** Dave Richardson.

Physio: Jim Walker. ***Youth Coach:*** Colin Clarke. ***Chief Scout:*** Brian Whitehouse. ***Fitness Consultant:*** Paul Barron.

Commercial Manager: Abdul Rashid.

Year Formed: 1874. ***Turned Professional:*** 1885. ***Ltd Co.:*** 1896.

Previous Grounds: 1874–76, Aston Park; 1876–97, Perry Barr; 1897, Villa Park.

Club Nickname: 'The Villans'.

Record League Victory: 12–2 v Accrington S, Division 1, 12 March 1892 – Warner; Evans, Cox; Harry Devey, Jimmy Cowan, Baird; Athersmith (1), Dickson (2), John Devey (4), L. Campbell (4), Hodgetts (1).

Record Cup Victory: 13–0 v Wednesbury Old Ath, FA Cup, 1st rd, 30 October 1886 – Warner; Coulton, Simmonds; Yates, Robertson, Burton (2); R. Davis (1), A. Brown (3), Hunter (3), Loach (2), Hodgetts (2).

Record Defeat: 1–8 v Blackburn R, FA Cup, 3rd rd, 16 February 1889.

Most League Points (2 for a win): 70, Division 3, 1971–72.

Most League Points (3 for a win): 78, Division 2, 1987–88.

Most League Goals: 128, Division 1, 1930–31.

Highest League Scorer in Season: 'Pongo' Waring, 49, Division 1, 1930–31.

Most League Goals in Total Aggregate: Harry Hampton, 215, 1904–15.

Most Capped Player: Paul McGrath, 38, Republic of Ireland.

Most League Appearances: Charlie Aitken, 561, 1961–76.

Record Transfer Fee Received: £5,500,000 from Bari for David Platt, August 1991.

Record Transfer Fee Paid: £2,300,000 to Liverpool for Dean Saunders, September 1992.

Football League Record: 1888 Founder Member of the League; 1936–38 Division 2; 1938–59 Division 1; 1959–60 Division 2; 1960–67 Division 1; 1967–70 Division 2; 1970–72 Division 3; 1972–75 Division 2; 1975–87 Division 1; 1987–88 Division 2; 1988–92 Division 1; 1992– FA Premier League.

Honours: *FA Premier League:* – Runners-up 1992–93. *Football League:* Division 1 – Champions 1893–94, 1895–96, 1896–97, 1898–99, 1899–1900, 1909–10, 1980–81; Runners-up 1888–89, 1902–03, 1907–08, 1910–11, 1912–13, 1913–14, 1930–31, 1932–33, 1989–90; Division 2 – Champions 1937–38, 1959–60; Runners-up 1974–75, 1987–88; Division 3 – Champions 1971–72. *FA Cup:* Winners 1887, 1895, 1897, 1905, 1913, 1920, 1957; Runners-up 1892, 1924. *Double Performed:* 1896–97. *Football League Cup:* Winners 1961, 1975, 1977, 1994; Runners-up 1963, 1971. **European Competitions:** *European Cup:* 1981–82 (winners), 1982–83; *UEFA Cup:* 1975–76, 1977–78, 1983–84, 1990–91, 1993–94. *World Club Championship:* 1982–83; *European Super Cup:* 1982–83 (winners).

ASTON VILLA 1993—94 LEAGUE RECORD

Match No.	Date	Venue	Opponents	Result		H/T Score	Lg. Pos.	Goalscorers	Attendance
1	Aug 14	H	QPR	W	4-1	1-1	—	Atkinson 2, Saunders, Staunton	32,944
2	18	A	Sheffield W	D	0-0	0-0	—		28,450
3	21	A	Wimbledon	D	2-2	1-1	10	Richardson, McGrath	7564
4	23	H	Manchester U	L	1-2	1-1	—	Atkinson	39,624
5	28	H	Tottenham H	W	1-0	0-0	10	Staunton (pen)	32,498
6	31	A	Everton	W	1-0	1-0	—	Whittingham	24,067
7	Sept 11	H	Coventry C	D	0-0	0-0	5		31,181
8	18	A	Ipswich T	W	2-1	1-1	3	Saunders, Townsend	16,858
9	25	A	Oldham Ath	D	1-1	0-1	3	Saunders	12,836
10	Oct 2	H	Newcastle U	L	0-2	0-0	7		37,336
11	16	A	West Ham U	D	0-0	0-0	7		20,416
12	23	H	Chelsea	W	1-0	1-0	7	Atkinson	29,706
13	30	A	Swindon T	W	2-1	1-1	5	Teale, Atkinson	16,332
14	Nov 6	A	Arsenal	W	2-1	0-0	3	Whittingham, Townsend	31,773
15	20	H	Sheffield U	W	1-0	0-0	2	Whittingham	24,686
16	24	H	Southampton	L	0-2	0-0	—		16,180
17	28	A	Liverpool	L	1-2	0-1	—	Atkinson	38,484
18	Dec 4	A	QPR	D	2-2	1-2	5	Richardson, Parker	14,915
19	8	H	Sheffield W	D	2-2	1-1	—	Cox, Saunders (pen)	20,304
20	11	H	Wimbledon	L	0-1	0-0	7		17,940
21	19	A	Manchester U	L	1-3	0-1	—	Cox	44,499
22	29	A	Norwich C	W	2-1	0-1	8	Houghton, Saunders	20,650
23	Jan 1	H	Blackburn R	L	0-1	0-1	10		40,903
24	15	H	West Ham U	W	3-1	2-1	9	Richardson, Atkinson 2	28,869
25	22	A	Chelsea	D	1-1	1-0	10	Saunders	18,348
26	Feb 6	H	Leeds U	W	1-0	0-0	—	Townsend	26,919
27	12	H	Swindon T	W	5-0	1-0	6	Saunders 3 (2 pens), Froggatt, Richardson	27,637
28	22	H	Manchester C	D	0-0	0-0	—		19,254
29	Mar 2	A	Tottenham H	D	1-1	1-0	—	Parker	17,452
30	6	A	Coventry C	W	1-0	1-0	—	Daley	14,323
31	12	H	Ipswich T	L	0-1	0-1	5		23,732
32	16	A	Leeds U	L	0-2	0-1	—		33,126
33	19	H	Oldham Ath	L	1-2	0-0	7	Redmond (og)	21,214
34	30	H	Everton	D	0-0	0-0	—		36,044
35	Apr 2	A	Manchester C	L	0-3	0-2	10		26,075
36	4	H	Norwich C	D	0-0	0-0	9		25,416
37	11	A	Blackburn R	L	0-1	0-1	—		19,287
38	16	A	Sheffield U	W	2-1	2-1	9	Richardson, Fenton	18,402
39	23	H	Arsenal	L	1-2	0-1	10	Houghton	31,580
40	27	A	Newcastle U	L	1-5	1-3	—	Beinlich	32,217
41	30	A	Southampton	L	1-4	0-2	10	Saunders	18,803
42	May 7	H	Liverpool	W	2-1	0-1	10	Yorke 2	45,347

Final League Position: 10

GOALSCORERS

League (46): Saunders 10 (3 pens), Atkinson 8, Richardson 5, Townsend 3, Whittingham 3, Cox 2, Houghton 2, Parker 2, Staunton 2 (1 pen), Yorke 2, Beinlich 1, Daley 1, Fenton 1, Froggatt 1, McGrath 1, Teale 1, own goal 1.
Coca-Cola Cup (16): Atkinson 6, Saunders 4 (1 pen), Houghton 2, Richardson 2, Barrett 1, Teale 1.
FA Cup (3): Houghton 1, Saunders 1 (pen), Yorke 1.

Spink 14 + 1	Barrett 39	Staunton 24	Teale 37 + 1	McGrath 30	Richardson 40	Houghton 25 + 5	Townsend 32	Saunders 37 + 1	Atkinson 29	Daley 19 + 8	Cowans 9 + 2	Froggatt 8 + 1	Small 8 + 1	Parker 17 + 2	Whittingham 13 + 5	Cox 16 + 4	Bosnich 28	Ehiogu 14 + 3	Kubicki 1 + 1	Beinlich 6 + 1	Yorke 2 + 10	Farrell 4	Fenton 9 + 3	Breitkreutz 1 + 1	*Match No.*
1	2	3	4	5	6	*7*	8	9	10	11	12														1
1	2	3	4	5	6		8	9	10	7	12	11													2
1	2	3	4	5	6	7		9	10		8	11													3
1	2	*3*	4	5	6	*7*		9	10			14	11	8	12										4
1	2	3	4	5	6	7		9	10	11				8	12										5
1	2	3	4	5	6		8	9	10		7				11	12									6
1	2	3	4	5	6	12	8	9	10		7				11										7
1	2	3	4	5	6	12	8	9	10	14	7				*11*										8
		3	4	5	6	7	8	9			10				11	2	1								9
1		3	4	5	6	12	8	9	10	14	7				*11*	2									10
			4	5	6	7	8	9	10	11			3			2	1								11
	2		4		6		8	9	5	11	7			12	10		1	3							12
1	2		4		6	9	*8*		5	12		11		10	7			3	14						13
14	2		4	5	6	*7*	8	9	10	11			3		12		*1*								14
	2		4	5	*6*		8	9	10	11			3	12	7		1	14							15
	2		4	5	6	12	8	9		11				10	7		1		3						16
	2			5	6	7	8	9	10				3	11	12	4	1								17
	2		4	5	6	7	8	9	10	12				11		3	1								18
	3		4	5		7		9	10		6			8		2	1			11					19
	3		4	5		*7*		9	10		6			8	12	2	1	14		11					20
	2		4	5	6			9	10	12			7	8	11	3	1								21
	2	3	4	5	6	7	8	9							10	11	1				12				22
	2	3	12	5	6	7	8	9							10	4	1				14	*11*			23
	2	3	4	5	6	7	8	9	10	11						12	1								24
	2	3	4	5	6	7	8	9	10	11							1								25
	2	3	4	5	6	*7*	8	9	10	11						12	1				14				26
	2			5	6	4	*8*	9	10	11		7				3	1	12			14				27
	2		4		6		8	12					3	10	11		1	5			7		9		28
	2		4	5	6			9	10	7		11		8		3	1			12					29
	3		4		6		8	9		7				11		2	1	5					10		30
	3		4		6		*8*	9	10	7				11		2	1	5			12		14		31
	3		4	5	6			9	*10*			11	*7*	8		2	1				12		14		32
	2	3	4	5	6	7		9				11		8			1				12		10		33
	2	3	4		6	7		9				11		8			1	5			10		12		34
	2	3	4		6		8	9		7				11			1	5			12		10		35
	2	3	4		6		8	9	10	7							1	5			12		11		36
	2	3	4		6	12	8	9	10	11							1	5					7		37
1	2	3	4		6	7	8			12								5		10		11	9		38
1	3		4		6	7	8		10							2		5				11	9		39
1	2	3	4		6	7	8			12								5		10		11	*9*	14	40
1	2	3		*5*	6	7	8	9		12						14		4		10				11	41
	2	3		5	6	7	8	9		11			14				1	4		*10*	12				42

Coca-Cola Cup	Second Round	Birmingham C (a)	1-0
		(h)	1-0
	Third Round	Sunderland (a)	4-1
	Fourth Round	Arsenal (a)	1-0
	Fifth Round	Tottenham H (a)	2-1
	Semi-final	Tranmere R (a)	1-3
		(h)	3-1
	Final at Wembley	Manchester U	3-1
FA Cup	Third Round	Exeter C (a)	1-0
	Fourth Round	Grimsby T (a)	2-1
	Fifth Round	Bolton W (a)	0-1

ASTON VILLA

Player and Position	Ht	Wt	Birth Date	Birth Place	Source	Clubs	League App	League Gls
Goalkeepers								
Mark Bosnich	6 1	13 07	13 1 72	Fairfield	Croatia Sydney	Manchester U	3	—
						Aston Villa	46	—
Michael Oakes	6 1	12 07	30 10 73	Northwich	Trainee	Aston Villa	—	—
						Scarborough (loan)	1	—
						Tranmere R (loan)	—	—
Nigel Spink	6 2	14 08	8 8 58	Chelmsford	Chelsmford C	Aston Villa	346	—
Defenders								
Earl Barrett	5 11	11 00	28 4 67	Rochdale	Apprentice	Manchester C	3	—
						Chester C (loan)	12	—
						Oldham Ath	183	7
						Aston Villa	94	1
Chris Boden	5 09	11 00	13 10 73	Wolverhampton	Trainee	Aston Villa	—	—
						Barnsley (loan)	4	—
Paul Browne	6 1	12 00	17 2 75	Glasgow	Trainee	Aston Villa	—	—
Ugo Ehiogu	6 2	13 03	3 11 72	London	Trainee	WBA	2	—
						Aston Villa	29	—
Darren Evans	5 10	11 00	30 9 74	Wolverhampton	Trainee	Aston Villa	—	—
Dariusz Kubicki	5 10	11 07	6 6 63	Warsaw	Legia Warsaw	Aston Villa	25	—
						Sunderland (loan)	15	—
Paul McGrath	6 2	14 00	4 12 59	Greenford	St Patrick's Ath	Manchester U	163	12
						Aston Villa	183	7
Andrew Mitchell	5 10	11 06	12 9 76	Rotherham	Trainee	Aston Villa	—	—
John Murphy			9 9 75	Cork		Aston Villa	—	—
Riccardo Scimeca	6 1	12 09	13 6 75	Leamington Spa	Trainee	Aston Villa	—	—
Bryan Small	5 9	11 09	15 11 71	Birmingham	Trainee	Aston Villa	31	—
Steve Staunton	6 0	12 04	19 1 69	Drogheda	Dundalk	Liverpool	65	—
						Bradford C (loan)	8	—
						Aston Villa	103	8
Shaun Teale	6 0	13 10	10 3 64	Southport	Weymouth	Bournemouth	100	4
						Aston Villa	119	2
Daniel West			17 4 75	Poole		Aston Villa	—	—
Midfield								
Matthias Breitkreutz	5 9	11 03	12 5 71	Crivitz	Bergmann Borsig	Aston Villa	13	—
Lee Burchell	5 7	10 06	12 11 76	Birmingham	Trainee	Aston Villa	—	—
Steven Cowe	5 7	10 02	29 9 74	Gloucester	Trainee	Aston Villa	—	—
Neil Cox	6 00	12 10	8 10 71	Scunthorpe	Trainee	Scunthorpe U	17	1
						Aston Villa	42	3
Richard Crisp‡	5 7	10 05	23 5 72	Wordsley	Trainee	Aston Villa	—	—
						Scunthorpe U (loan)	8	—
Gareth Farrelly	6 0	12 07	28 8 75	Dublin	Home Farm	Aston Villa	—	—
Steve Froggatt	5 10	11 00	9 3 73	Lincoln	Trainee	Aston Villa	35	2
Lee Hendrie			18 5 77	Birmingham	Trainee	Aston Villa	—	—
Ray Houghton	5 7	10 10	9 1 62	Glasgow	Amateur	West Ham U	1	—
						Fulham	129	16
						Oxford U	83	10
						Liverpool	153	28
						Aston Villa	69	5
Garry Parker	5 11	12 05	7 9 65	Oxford	Apprentice	Luton T	42	3
						Hull C	84	8
						Nottingham F	103	17
						Aston Villa	81	12
Kevin Richardson	5 7	11 07	4 12 62	Newcastle	Apprentice	Everton	109	16
						Watford	39	2
						Arsenal	96	5
					Real Sociedad	Aston Villa	124	13
Andy Townsend	5 11	12 13	23 7 63	Maidstone	Weymouth	Southampton	83	5
						Norwich C	71	8
						Chelsea	110	12
						Aston Villa	32	3

ASTON VILLA

Colours: Claret shirts with sky collar and thin blue stripes, white shorts with claret and sky trim, white stockings with claret trim. **Change colours:** Black, green and red striped shirts, black shorts with green trim, black stockings with green trim.

Foundation: Cricketing enthusiasts of Villa Cross Wesleyan Chapel, Aston, Birmingham decided to form a football club during the winter of 1873–74. Football clubs were few and far between in the Birmingham area and in their first game against Aston Brook St. Mary's Rugby team they played one half rugby and the other soccer. In 1876 they were joined by a Scottish soccer enthusiast George Ramsay who was immediately appointed captain and went on to lead Aston Villa from obscurity to one of the country's top clubs in a period of less than 10 years.

First Football League game: 8 September, 1888, Football League, v Wolverhampton W, (a) D 1-1 – Warner; Cox, Coulton; Yates, H. Devey, Dawson; A. Brown, Green (1), Allen, Garvey, Hodgetts.

Did you know: The highest League attendance of the 1993–94 season was 45,347 recorded at Villa Park on 7 May for the visit of Liverpool. It was the last day of the Holte End terracing before ground reconstruction.

Managers (and Secretary-Managers)
George Ramsay 1884–1926*, W. J. Smith 1926–34*, Jimmy McMullan 1934–35, Jimmy Hogan 1936–44, Alex Massie 1945–50, George Martin 1950–53, Eric Houghton 1953–58, Joe Mercer 1958–64, Dick Taylor 1965–67, Tommy Cummings 1967–68, Tommy Docherty 1968–70, Vic Crowe 1970–74, Ron Saunders 1974–82, Tony Barton 1982–84, Graham Turner 1984–86, Billy McNeill 1986–87, Graham Taylor 1987–90, Dr. Jozef Venglos 1990–91, Ron Atkinson June 1991– .

Player and Position	Ht	Wt	Birth Date	Birth Place	Source	Clubs	League App	League Gls
Forwards								
Dalian Atkinson	6 0	13 10	21 3 68	Shrewsbury		Ipswich T	60	18
						Sheffield W	38	10
						Real Sociedad	26	12
						Aston Villa	71	20
Stefan Beinlich	5 11	11 02	13 1 72	Berlin	Bergmann Borsig	Aston Villa	16	1
Trevor Berry	5 07	10 08	1 8 74	Surrey	Bournemouth	Aston Villa	—	—
Darren Byfield	5 10	11 00	29 9 76	Birmingham	Trainee	Aston Villa	—	—
Tony Daley	5 8	10 08	18 10 67	Birmingham	Apprentice	Aston Villa	233	31
Neil Davis	5 8	11 00	15 8 73	Bloxwich	Redditch U	Aston Villa	—	—
David Farrell	5 11	11 02	11 11 71	Birmingham	Redditch U	Aston Villa	6	—
						Scunthorpe U (loan)	5	1
Graham Fenton	5 10	11 03	22 5 74	Wallsend	Trainee	Aston Villa	12	1
						WBA (loan)	7	3
Scott Murray	5 10	11 00	26 5 74	Aberdeen	Fraserburgh	Aston Villa	—	—
Dennis Pearce	5 9	11 00	10 9 74	Wolverhampton	Trainee	Aston Villa	—	—
Dean Saunders	5 8	10 06	21 6 64	Swansea	Apprentice	Swansea C	49	12
						Cardiff C (loan)	4	—
						Brighton	72	21
						Oxford U	59	22
						Derby Co	106	42
						Liverpool	42	11
						Aston Villa	73	22
Guy Whittingham	5 10	11 12	10 11 64	Evesham	Yeovil	Portsmouth	160	88
						Aston Villa	18	3
						Wolverhampton W (loan)	13	8
Dwight Yorke	5 11	11 13	3 12 71	Tobago	Tobago	Aston Villa	91	21

Trainees
Aston, Lee A; Brock, Stuart A; Brown, Ian S; Hines, Leslie D; Impey, James J; Moore, David; Peters, Mark P; Rachel, Adam; Senior, Marc A.

Associated Schoolboys
Appleby, Mark; Barret, Neil R; Blackwood, Michael; Deacon, Robert A; Hadland, Guy W; Halliday, James S; Hickman, John A; Jones, Jonathan B; Jones, Mark A; Lescott, Aaron A; Lonsdale, David; Miles, Nicholas; Petty, Ben J; Read, Lewis T; Reece, Dominic M. A; Serrie, David J.

Associated Schoolboys who have accepted the Club's offer of a Traineeship/Contract
Burgess, Richard D; Collins, Lee D; Hughes, Robert D; Jaszczun, Antony J; Miley, Jonathan H; Walker, Richard M.

BARNET 1993–94 *Back row (left to right):* Mark Hall, Tony Lynch, Andy Pape, Kelly Haag, Nicky Evans.
Centre row: Barry Frankham (Physio), Roger Thompson, Tony Finnigan, Tim Alexander, Greg Rioch, Alan Walker, David Barnett, Carl Hoddle, Ben Barnett, Gordon Ogbourne, Phil Edwards.
Front row: Gary Smith, Louis Affor, Shaun Close, Gary Phillips (Player/Manager), Mark Newson, Geoff Cooper, Paul Wilson.
(Photograph: Sue Morgan)

Division 3 **BARNET**

Underhill Stadium, Barnet Lane, Barnet, Herts EN5 2BE. Telephone 081–441 6932. Fax 081–447 0655. Credit Card Bookings: 081–441 1677. Clubcall: 0891 121544.

Ground capacity: Not yet known.

Record attendance: 11,026 v Wycombe Wanderers. FA Amateur Cup 4th Round 1951–52.

Record Receipts: £31,202 v Portsmouth FA Cup 3rd Round 5th January 1991.

Pitch measurements: 112yd × 72yd.

Chairman: D. J. Buchler. FCA. ***Chief Executive:*** D. B. Edwards OBE.

Directors: S. Glynne, F. Higgins FCA.

General Manager: Ray Clemence OBE. ***Player-manager:*** Gary Phillips. ***Physio:*** Barry Frankham.

Coach: Terry Bullivant. ***Secretary:*** Bryan Ayres. ***Commercial Manager:*** John Linton. ***Marketing Manager:*** Tessa Bills.

Year Formed: 1888. ***Turned Professional:*** 1965. ***Ltd Co:***

Club Nickname: The Bees.

Previous Names: 1906–19 Barnet Alston FC.

Previous Grounds: Queens Road (1888–1901) Totteridge Lane (1901–07).

Record League Victory: 6–0 v Lincoln C (away), Division 4, 4 September 1991 – Pape; Poole, Naylor, Bodley, Howell, Evans (1), Willis (1), Murphy (1), Bull (2), Lowe, Showler (1 og).

Record Defeat: 1–5 v York C, Division 3, 13 March 1993.

Most League Points (3 for a win): 79, Division 3, 1992–93.

Most League Goals: 81, Division 4, 1991–92.

Highest League Scorer in Season: Gary Bull, 20, Division 4, 1991–92.

Most League Goals in Total Aggregate: Gary Bull 37, 1991–93.

Most League Appearances: Gary Phillips, 90, 1991–94.

Record Transfer Fee Received: £350,000 from Wimbledon for Andy Clarke, February 1991.

Record Transfer Fee Paid: £40,000 to Barrow for Kenny Lowe, January 1991 and £40,000 to Runcorn for Mark Carter, February 1991.

Football League Record: Promoted to Division 4 from GMVC 1991; 1991–92 Division 4; 1992–93 Division 3; 1993–94 Division 2; 1994– Division 3.

Honours: *Football League:* best season 24th, Division 2, 1993–94. *FA Amateur Cup:* Winners 1945–46. *GM Vauxhall Conference:* Winners 1990–91. *FA Cup:* best season; never past 3rd rd. *League Cup:* never past 2nd rd.

BARNET 1993—94 LEAGUE RECORD

Match No.	Date	Venue	Opponents	Result		H/T Score	Lg. Pos.	Goalscorers	Attendance
1	Aug 14	H	Hull C	L	1-2	1-2	—	Walker	2129
2	21	A	Port Vale	L	0-6	0-3	23		7538
3	28	H	Swansea C	L	0-1	0-0	24		1996
4	Sept 1	A	Reading	L	1-4	1-2	—	Haag	4971
5	4	A	Blackpool	L	1-3	1-1	24	Evans	4328
6	11	H	Bournemouth	L	1-2	0-2	24	Evans	2979
7	14	H	Fulham	L	0-2	0-2	—		3066
8	18	A	Leyton Orient	L	2-4	0-0	24	Haag (pen), Barnett D	4812
9	25	A	Wrexham	L	0-4	0-1	24		3767
10	Oct 2	H	Bristol R	L	1-2	0-0	24	Haag	3158
11	10	H	Cardiff C	D	0-0	0-0	—		2084
12	16	A	Huddersfield T	W	2-1	0-0	24	Finnigan, Haag	5614
13	23	H	Cambridge U	L	2-3	1-1	24	Cooper 2	2997
14	30	A	Brentford	L	0-1	0-0	24		5873
15	Nov 2	A	Hartlepool U	L	1-2	0-1	—	Evans	1960
16	6	H	Bradford C	L	1-2	0-1	24	Close	2350
17	20	A	York C	D	1-1	0-1	24	Haag (pen)	2966
18	27	H	Rotherham U	W	2-1	0-0	24	Haag, Rowe	1938
19	Dec 11	H	Port Vale	L	2-3	1-0	24	Haag, Rowe	3100
20	18	A	Hull C	D	4-4	2-1	24	Lynch 2, Hoddle, Scott	4115
21	27	A	Brighton & HA	L	0-1	0-1	24		10,053
22	29	H	Burnley	D	1-1	0-0	24	Close	2360
23	Jan 1	A	Stockport Co	L	1-2	1-1	24	Haag (pen)	5121
24	15	H	Huddersfield T	L	0-1	0-1	24		3022
25	22	A	Cardiff C	D	0-0	0-0	24		5698
26	29	H	Brentford	D	0-0	0-0	24		2502
27	Feb 5	A	Cambridge U	D	1-1	1-1	24	Gibson	3473
28	12	H	Plymouth Arg	D	0-0	0-0	24		2854
29	18	A	Swansea C	L	0-2	0-2	—		3278
30	25	H	Blackpool	L	0-1	0-0	24		2448
31	Mar 5	A	Bournemouth	D	1-1	0-1	24	Cooper	3407
32	8	A	Plymouth Arg	L	0-1	0-0	—		7595
33	12	H	Leyton Orient	W	3-1	2-1	24	Lynch, Gibson, Newson	2717
34	15	A	Fulham	L	0-3	0-1	—		3326
35	19	H	Wrexham	L	1-2	1-0	24	Scott	1853
36	22	H	Exeter C	W	2-1	0-1	—	Dolby, Gibson	1604
37	26	A	Bristol R	L	2-5	0-4	24	Wilson (pen), Edwards	3802
38	29	A	Exeter C	D	0-0	0-0	—		2269
39	Apr 2	H	Brighton & HA	D	1-1	0-1	24	Dichio	2733
40	4	A	Burnley	L	0-5	0-0	24		10,412
41	9	H	Stockport Co	D	0-0	0-0	24		1798
42	12	H	Reading	L	0-1	0-1	—		2289
43	26	H	Hartlepool U	W	3-2	1-2	—	Wilson 2 (2 pens), Dichio	1351
44	30	H	York C	L	1-3	1-2	24	Gibson	2363
45	May 3	A	Bradford C	L	1-2	0-0	—	Dolby	3472
46	7	A	Rotherham U	D	1-1	1-0	24	Newson	3674

Final League Position: 24

GOALSCORERS

League (41): Haag 8 (3 pens), Gibson 4, Cooper 3, Evans 3, Lynch 3, Wilson 3 (3 pens), Close 2, Dichio 2, Dolby 2, Newson 2, Rowe 2, Scott 2, Barnett D 1, Edwards 1, Finnigan 1, Hoddle 1, Walker 1.
Coca-Cola Cup (4): Lynch 2, Haag 1, Walker 1.
FA Cup (4): Close 1, Haag 1, Hoddle 1, Rowe 1.

Pape 4	Newson 29	Cooper 24 + 12	Smith 8 + 1	Walker 38	Barnett D 19	Marwood 18 + 5	Carter 4 + 1	Haag 31 + 7	Hoddle 43 + 1	Lynch 11 + 11	Evans 4 + 8	Close 21 + 6	Phillips 42	Alexander 27 + 5	Wilson 34	Affor — + 3	Hall 3	Barnett B — + 2	Rioch 3	Haylock 18 + 2	Finnigan 5 + 1	Rowe 9 + 1	Scott 30	Mutchell 14	Gibson 20	Dolby 13 + 3	Edwards 5	Tomlinson 10 + 1	McDonald 10	Dichio 9	*Match No.*
1	2	3	4	5	6	7	*8*	9	10	11	12	14																			1
	2	3	4	*5*	6	7	14	9	10	11	12	8	1																		2
	2	3	4	5	6	*7*	8	9	*10*		12	11	1	14																	3
1	2	3	*4*	5	6		8	9	10	11	12	7		14																	4
1	2	3		5	6		8	9	10	14	*11*	12		*7*	4																5
		3	12	5	6	7		9	10		11	8	1	2	4	14															6
		3		5		7		9	10		11	*8*	1	2	4	12	6	14													7
		14		5	6	*7*		9	4	12		10	1	11	2		*8*		3												8
1		8		5	6			9	4		12	10		11	2	14	*7*		3												9
		8	*11*	6	3	7		9	14		10	12	1		2				4	5											10
		8		5	6	7		9	4				1	11	2					3	10										11
		8		5	6	7		9	4				1	11	2					3	10										12
		8		5		*7*		9	4		12	6	1	11	2					3	10										13
		8	*6*	5		7		9	4		12	10	1	11	2			14		3											14
		8	2	5	6	7		9	4		12	10	1	11						*3*	14										15
		12		5	6	7		9	4			10	1	2						3		8	11								16
		12		*5*	6	*7*		9	4			10	1	14	2					3		8	11								17
		12		5	6	7		9	4			10	1		2					3		8	11								18
	3			5		7		9	4	12		10	1	6						2		8	11								19
	3	12		5		*7*		9	4	8		10	1	6						14			11	2							20
	5	12		6		*7*		9	4	14		10	1	2								8	11	3							21
	3	12		5				*9*	4	14		10	1	6	7							8	11	2							22
	5	12		6				9	4	14		10	1	2						7		8	11	*3*							23
	6			5				9	4	8		10	1	2	7							12	11	3							24
	6		2	5				*9*	4	14			1	12	7						10	8	11	3							25
	6	12		5	2			*9*	4			14	1		7						10	8	11	3							26
	6	8		5	*2*	12			4			10	1		7					14			11	3	9						27
		8		5	6			9		12		4	1		7					2			11	3	10						28
		7		5	6			9	4	12			1							2			10	3	8	11					29
	6							9	4	7			1	3	5					2			10		8	11					30
	6	8				14		12	4	7			1	3	5					*2*			10		9	11					31
	6	8		5		14		12	4	*7*			1		3					2			11		9	10					32
	6	8		5		14		12	4	7			1		3					2			11		*9*	10					33
	6	8		5				12	4	7			1		3					2			11		9	10					34
	6			5		12		8	4	7			1		2								11	3	9	10					35
		12						8	4	14			1	6	3								11	2	*9*	10	5	*7*			36
				5									1	12	8								11	3	9	4	6	7	2	10	37
	6			5					4				1	7	3								11		9	12		10	2	8	38
	6			5				12	4				1	3	8								11		9			7	2	10	39
	6			5				12	4				1	*3*	8								11		9	7		14	2	10	40
	6	12		5					4			14	1	3	8								11		9	*7*		10	2		41
	6	8						12	4				1	3									11		9	14	5	*10*	2	7	42
	6	3							4			14	1		8								11		*9*	12	5	10	2	7	43
	6	12							4				1		8								11		9	3	5	10	2	7	44
	6								4				1	5	8								11		9	3		10	2	7	45
	6	3							4	12			1	5	8									11	9			10	2	7	46

Coca-Cola Cup	First Round	Southend U (a)	2-0
		(h)	1-1
	Second Round	QPR (h)	1-2
		(a)	0-4
FA Cup	First Round	Carshalton Ath (h)	2-1
	Second Round	Crawley (a)	2-1
	Third Round	Chelsea (at Stamford Bridge)	0-0
		(a)	0-4

BARNET

Player and Position	Ht	Wt	Birth Date	Birth Place	Source	Clubs	League App	League Gls
Goalkeepers								
Andy Pape‡	6 0	12 00	22 3 62	London	Enfield	Barnet	40	—
Gary Phillips	6 0	14 00	20 9 61	St Albans		WBA	—	—
					Barnet	Brentford	143	—
						Reading	24	—
						Hereford U	6	—
						Barnet	90	—
Defenders								
Tim Alexander	6 0	12 00	29 3 74	Chertsey	Wimbledon	Barnet	32	—
Russell Edwards*	6 2	12 07	21 12 73	Beckenham	Local	Crystal Palace	—	—
						Barnet	5	1
Tony Finnigan‡	5 10	11 09	17 10 62	Wimbledon	Crystal Palace	Fulham	—	—
						Crystal Palace	105	10
						Blackburn R	36	—
						Hull C	18	1
						Swindon T	3	—
						Brentford	3	—
						Barnet	6	1
Paul Haylock*	5 9	11 10	24 3 63	Lowestoft	Apprentice	Norwich C	155	3
						Gillingham	152	—
						Maidstone U	48	1
						Shrewsbury T	18	1
						Barnet	20	—
David McDonald	5 11	11 07	2 1 71	Dublin	Trainee	Tottenham H	2	—
						Gillingham (loan)	10	—
						Bradford C (loan)	7	—
						Reading (loan)	11	—
						Peterborough U	29	—
						Barnet	10	—
Robert Mutchell	5 10	11 02	2 1 74	Solihull	Trainee	Oxford U	—	—
						Barnet	14	—
Mark Newson	5 10	12 06	7 12 60	Stepney	Apprentice	Charlton Ath	—	—
					Maidstone U	Bournemouth	177	23
						Fulham	102	4
						Barnet	29	2
Darren Oxbrow‡	6 1	12 06	1 9 69	Ipswich	Trainee	Ipswich T	—	—
						Maidstone U	85	2
						Colchester U	16	4
						Barnet	1	—
Alan Walker	6 2	12 11	17 12 59	Mossley	Telford U	Lincoln C	75	4
						Millwall	92	8
						Gillingham	151	7
						Plymouth Arg	2	1
						Mansfield T	22	1
						Barnet	38	1
Paul Wilson	5 9	11 04	26 9 64	London	Barking	Barnet	68	4
Midfield								
Geoff Cooper*	5 10	11 00	27 12 60	Kingston	Bognor Regis	Brighton	7	—
					Barnet	Barnet	31	1
						Wycombe W	—	—
						Barnet	36	3
Nicky Evans*	6 0	11 10	6 7 58	Bedford	Wycombe W	Barnet	39	8
Carl Hoddle	6 4	11 00	8 3 67	Harlow	Bishop's Stortford	Leyton Orient	28	2
						Barnet	62	3
Brian Marwood*	5 7	11 06	5 2 60	Seaham Harbour	Apprentice	Hull C	158	51
						Sheffield W	128	27
						Arsenal	52	16
						Sheffield U	22	3
						Middlesbrough (loan)	3	—
						Swindon T	11	1
						Barnet	23	—
Peter Scott	5 9	11 12	1 10 63	London	Apprentice	Fulham	277	27
						Bournemouth	10	—
						Barnet	30	2

BARNET

Colours: Amber and black striped shirts, black shorts, amber stockings. **Change colours:** Sky blue shirts, sky blue shorts, sky blue stockings.

Foundation: Barnet Football Club was formed in 1888, disbanded in 1901. A club known as Alston Works FC was then formed and in 1906 changed its name to Barnet Alston FC. In 1912 it combined with The Avenue to become Barnet and Alston.

First Football League game: 17 August, 1991, Division 4, v Crewe Alex (h) L 4-7 – Phillips; Blackford, Cooper (Murphy), Horton, Bodley (Stein), Johnson, Showler, Carter (2), Bull (2), Lowe, Evans.

Did you know: When Barnet played Carshalton Athletic in a first round FA Cup tie on 13 November 1993, goalkeeper Gary Phillips was the only survivor from the team beaten 4-0 by the same opposition on 20 November 1982. This time Barnet won 2-1.

Managers: (since 1946) Lester Finch, George Wheeler, Dexter Adams, Tommy Coleman, Gerry Ward, Gordon Ferry, Brian Kelly, Bill Meadows, Barry Fry, Roger Thompson, Don McAllister, Barry Fry, Edwin Stein, Gary Phillips (player-manager) August 1993–

Player and Position	*Ht*	*Wt*	*Birth Date*	*Place*	*Source*	*Clubs*	*League App*	*Gls*
Gary Smith	5 10	12 09	3 12 68	Harlow	Apprentice	Fulham	1	—
						Colchester U	11	—
					Enfield, Wycombe W, Welling U	Barnet	9	—
Michael Tomlinson	5 9	11 00	15 9 72	Lambeth	Trainee	Leyton Orient	14	1
						Barnet	11	—
Forwards								
Louis Affor	5 4	11 07	29 8 72	London	Southend U	Barnet	3	—
Ben Barnett‡			18 12 69	London	Heybridge S	Barnet	2	—
Shaun Close*	5 8	10 01	8 9 66	Islington	Trainee	Tottenham H	9	—
						Bournemouth	39	8
						Swindon T	44	1
						Barnet	27	2
Terry Gibson	5 5	10 00	23 12 62	Walthamstow	Apprentice	Tottenham H	18	4
						Coventry C	98	43
						Manchester U	23	1
						Wimbledon	86	22
						Swindon T (loan)	9	1
						Peterborough U	1	—
						Barnet	20	4
Kelly Haag*	6 0	12 03	6 10 70	Enfield	Trainee	Brentford	5	—
						Fulham	67	9
						Barnet	38	8
Tony Lynch*	5 8	10 08	20 1 66	Paddington	Maidstone U	Brentford	45	6
					Wealdstone	Barnet	36	4

BARNSLEY 1993–94 *Back row (left to right):* David Currie, Adrian Moses, Gareth Williams, David Watson, Lee Butler, Jamie Robinson, Andy Rammell, Charlie Bishop.
Centre row: Colin Walker (Youth Team Coach), Eric Winstanley (First Team Coach), Mark Feeney, Ian Bryson, Robert Hanby, Brendan O'Connell, Deiniol Graham, Gary Fleming, Mark Burton, Gerry Taggart, Wayne Biggins, Martin Bullock, Steve Stafford (Physio).
Front row: John Gregg, Owen Archdeacon, Andrew Liddell, Danny Wilson (Player/Coach), Viv Anderson (Manager), Glynn Snodin, Nicky Eaden, Neil Redfearn, Greg Morgan.

Division 1 BARNSLEY

Oakwell Ground, Grove St, Barnsley, South Yorkshire S71 1ET. Telephone Barnsley (0226) 295353. Clubcall: 0891 121152. Commercial Office: 0226 286718. Fax: 0226 201000.

Ground capacity: 27,398 (15,000 under cover).

Record attendance: 40,255 v Stoke C, FA Cup 5th rd, 15 February 1936.

Record receipts: Not disclosed.

Pitch measurements: 110yd × 75yd.

President: Arthur Raynor. ***Chairman:*** J. A. Dennis.

Directors: C. B. Taylor (Vice-chairman), C. H. Harrison, M. R. Hayselden, J. N. Kelly, S. Manley, I. D. Potter.

Player-Manager: Danny Wilson.

First Team Coach: Eric Winstanley. ***Physio:*** Steve Stafford.

General Manager/Secretary: Michael Spinks. ***Lotteries Manager:*** Gerry Whewall. ***Marketing Manager:*** Ian Davies.

Year Formed: 1887. ***Turned Professional:*** 1888. ***Ltd Co.:*** 1899.

Previous Name: Barnsley St Peter's, 1887–97.

Club Nickname: 'The Tykes', 'Reds' or 'Colliers'.

Record League Victory: 9–0 v Loughborough T, Division 2, 28 January 1899 – Greaves; McCartney, Nixon; Porteous, Burleigh, Howard; Davis (4), Hepworth (1), Lees (1), McCullough (1), Jones (2). 9–0 v Accrington S, Division 3 (N), 3 February 1934 – Ellis; Cookson, Shotton; Harper, Henderson, Whitworth; Spence (2), Smith (1), Blight (4), Andrews (1), Ashton (1).

Record Cup Victory: 6–0 v Blackpool, FA Cup, 1st rd replay, 20 January 1910 – Mearns; Downs, Ness; Glendinning, Boyle (1), Utley; Bartrop, Gadsby (1), Lillycrop (2), Tufnell (2), Forman. 6–0 v Peterborough U, League Cup, 1st rd, 2nd leg, 15 September 1981 – Horn; Joyce, Chambers, Glavin (2), Banks, McCarthy, Evans, Parker (2), Aylott (1), McHale, Barrowclough (1).

Record Defeat: 0–9 v Notts Co, Division 2, 19 November 1927.

Most League Points (2 for a win): 67, Division 3 (N), 1938–39.

Most League Points (3 for a win): 74, Division 2, 1988–89.

Most League Goals: 118, Division 3 (N), 1933–34.

Highest League Scorer in Season: Cecil McCormack, 33, Division 2, 1950–51.

Most League Goals in Total Aggregate: Ernest Hine, 123, 1921–26 and 1934–38.

Most Capped Player: Gerry Taggart, 28, Northern Ireland.

Most League Appearances: Barry Murphy, 514, 1962–78.

Record Transfer Fee Received: £1,500,000 from Nottingham F for Carl Tiler, May 1991.

Record Transfer Fee Paid: £250,000 to Oldham Ath for David Currie, September 1991.

Football League Record: 1898 Elected to Division 2; 1932–34 Division 3 (N); 1934–38 Division 2; 1938–39 Division 3 (N); 1946–53 Division 2; 1953–55 Division 3 (N); 1955–59 Division 2; 1959–65 Division 3; 1965–68 Division 4; 1968–72 Division 3; 1972–79 Division 4; 1979–81 Division 3; 1981–92 Division 2; 1992– Division 1.

Honours: *Football League:* best season: 3rd, Division 2, 1914–15, 1921–22; Division 3 (N) – Champions 1933–34, 1938–39, 1954–55; Runners-up 1953–54; Division 3 – Runners-up 1980–81; Division 4 – Runners-up 1967–68; Promoted 1978–79. *FA Cup:* Winners 1912; Runners-up 1910. *Football League Cup:* best season: 5th rd, 1981–82.

BARNSLEY 1993—94 LEAGUE RECORD

Match No.	Date	Venue	Opponents	Result		H/T Score	Lg. Pos.	Goalscorers	Attendance
1	Aug 14	H	WBA	D	1-1	0-0	—	Anderson	12,940
2	17	A	Peterborough U	L	1-4	0-2	—	Currie	5875
3	21	A	Watford	W	2-0	2-0	7	Biggins, Bryson	5937
4	24	H	Middlesbrough	L	1-4	1-1	—	Anderson	10,597
5	28	H	Birmingham C	L	2-3	1-0	10	Redfearn, Anderson	7241
6	Sept 4	A	Millwall	L	0-2	0-1	19		8010
7	11	H	Nottingham F	W	1-0	1-0	14	Archdeacon (pen)	13,280
8	18	A	Tranmere R	W	3-0	1-0	10	Rammell, Redfearn, O'Connell	6755
9	25	H	Leicester C	L	0-1	0-1	15		10,392
10	Oct 2	A	Luton T	L	0-5	0-2	18		6201
11	9	H	Charlton Ath	L	0-1	0-1	19		5186
12	16	A	Bristol C	W	2-0	1-0	17	Bryson, Redfearn	6923
13	23	H	Southend U	L	1-3	0-3	21	Redfearn (pen)	5240
14	30	A	Stoke C	L	4-5	3-2	22	Redfearn, O'Connell, Bryson, Archdeacon	14,679
15	Nov 2	A	Oxford U	D	1-1	0-1	—	Redfearn	4065
16	7	H	Grimsby T	L	1-2	1-1	—	O'Connell	5797
17	13	A	Wolverhampton W	D	1-1	1-0	23	Biggins	18,355
18	20	H	Crystal Palace	L	1-3	1-1	23	Redfearn	5384
19	27	H	Bolton W	D	1-1	1-1	23	Jackson	6755
20	Dec 4	A	Grimsby T	D	2-2	2-0	23	Payton, Redfearn	8123
21	11	H	Peterborough U	W	1-0	1-0	18	Payton	6209
22	19	A	WBA	D	1-1	0-0	—	Payton	16,062
23	27	H	Derby Co	L	0-1	0-1	22		11,565
24	Jan 1	H	Portsmouth	W	2-0	1-0	22	O'Connell, Redfearn	6328
25	3	A	Sunderland	L	0-1	0-1	22		19,302
26	15	H	Bristol C	D	1-1	1-0	23	Rammell	5222
27	22	A	Charlton Ath	L	1-2	0-0	23	Payton	7072
28	Feb 5	A	Southend U	W	3-0	0-0	22	Eaden, Redfearn, Rammell	4101
29	12	H	Stoke C	W	3-0	1-0	21	Rammell, Redfearn, Taggart	7561
30	Mar 1	A	Notts Co	L	1-3	1-2	—	Payton	6297
31	5	A	Birmingham C	W	2-0	0-0	21	O'Connell, Rammell	15,382
32	12	H	Tranmere R	W	1-0	0-0	20	Payton	6203
33	16	A	Nottingham F	L	1-2	0-1	—	Taggart	20,491
34	19	A	Leicester C	W	1-0	0-0	20	Payton	15,640
35	26	H	Luton T	W	1-0	0-0	19	Payton	6289
36	29	H	Sunderland	W	4-0	2-0	—	Eaden, Liddell, Payton, Rammell	10,042
37	Apr 2	A	Derby Co	L	0-2	0-1	19		14,968
38	4	H	Notts Co	L	0-3	0-1	19		6827
39	9	A	Portsmouth	L	1-2	0-0	19	Redfearn (pen)	7005
40	12	H	Watford	L	0-1	0-0	—		4380
41	16	H	Oxford U	W	1-0	0-0	20	Williams	4874
42	23	A	Crystal Palace	L	0-1	0-0	18		20,326
43	26	A	Middlesbrough	L	0-5	0-3	—		6368
44	30	H	Wolverhampton W	W	2-0	0-0	18	O'Connell, Payton	11,329
45	May 3	H	Millwall	L	0-1	0-0	—		5059
46	8	A	Bolton W	W	3-2	1-0	18	Bishop, Payton 2	11,661

Final League Position: 18

GOALSCORERS

League (55): Payton 12, Redfearn 12 (2 pens), O'Connell 6, Rammell 6, Anderson 3, Bryson 3, Archdeacon 2 (1 pen), Biggins 2, Eaden 2, Taggart 2, Bishop 1, Currie 1, Jackson 1, Liddell 1, Williams 1.
Coca-Cola Cup (2): Archdeacon 1 (pen), Bryson 1.
FA Cup (5): Archdeacon 1, O'Connell 1, Payton 1, Rammell 1, Taggart 1.

Butler 37	Fleming 46	Snodin 7 + 4	Wilson 43	Taggart 38	Anderson 20	O'Connell 38	Redfearn 46	Bryson 16	Biggins 12 + 1	Archdeacon 41 + 1	Graham 1 + 1	Currie — + 3	Robinson — + 1	Bishop 37 + 1	Watson 9	Eaden 36 + 1	Rammell 31 + 3	Liddell 11 + 11	Jackson 2 + 2	Boden 4	Williams 4 + 5	Payton 25	Sheridan 2 + 1	*Match No.*
1	2	3	4	5	6	7	8	9	10	11	12													1
1	2	3	4	5	6	7	8		10	11	9	12												2
1	2	3	4	5	6	7	8	9	10	11			12											3
1	2	3	4	5	6	7	8	9	10	11		12												4
1	2	3	4	5	6	7	8	9	10	11				12										5
	2		4		6	7	8	9	10	11				5	1	3	12							6
	2		4	5	6	7	8		10	11				3	1		9							7
	2		4	5	6	7	10	9		11				3	1		8							8
	2		4	5	6	7	10	9		11				3	1		8	12						9
	2		4	5	6	7	10	9		11				3	1	14	8	12						10
	2		4	5	6	7	10	9	12	11				3	1			8	14					11
	2		4		6	7	8	9	10					5	1	11		12		3				12
	2		4			7	8	9	10					5	1	6	12	11		3				13
1	2		4		6	7	10	9		12				5		11	8	14		3				14
1	2		4			7	10	9		11				6		5		8		3	12			15
1	2				6	7	8	9	10	11				4		5		12			3			16
1	2		4		6	7	8	9	10	11				5		3								17
1	2		4		6	7	8	9	10	11				5		3		12			14			18
1	2		4	5		7	8			11		12		6		3			9			10		19
1	2		4	5		7	8			11				6		3	12		9			10		20
1	3		4	5		7	8			11				6		2	9					10		21
1	3		4	5		7	8			11				6		2	9					10		22
1	3		4	5		7	8			11				6		2	9					10		23
1	3		4	5		7	8			11				6		2	9					10		24
1	3			5		7	8			11				6		2	9	12				10	4	25
1	3		4	5		7	8			11				6		2	9					10		26
1	3		4	5		7	8			11				6		2	9					10		27
1	3		4	5		7	8			11				6		2	9					10		28
1	3		4	5		7	8			11				6		2	9					10		29
1	3	14	4	5		7	8			11				6		2	9	12				10		30
1	3		4	5	6	7	8			11						2	9					10		31
1	3		4	5	6	7	8			11						2	9					10		32
1	3		4	5		7	8			11				6		2	9					10		33
1	3		4	5		7	8			11				6		2	9	12				10		34
1	3		4	5			8			11				6		2	9	7				10		35
1	3		4	5			8			11				6		2	9	7				10		36
1	3	12	4	5			8			11				6		2	9	7				10		37
1	3	11	4	5			8							6		2	9	7				10	12	38
1	3	11		5	6	7	8									2	9	12			14	10	4	39
1	3	14	4	5	6		8			11						2	9	7			12	10		40
1	3		4	5			8			11				6		2	9	7			10			41
1	3		4	5			8			11				6		2	9	7	12		10			42
1	3		4	5		7	8			11				6		2	9					10		43
1	3		4	5		7	8			11				6		2	9					10		44
1	3		4	5		7	8			11				6		2	9	12			10			45
	3	14	4	5			8			11				6	1	2	9	7			12	10		46

Coca-Cola Cup	Second Round	Peterborough U (h)	1-1
		(a)	1-3
FA Cup	Third Round	Bromsgrove R (a)	2-1
	Fourth Round	Plymouth Arg (a)	2-2
		(h)	1-0
	Fifth Round	Oldham Ath (a)	0-1

BARNSLEY

Player and Position	*Ht*	*Wt*	*Birth Date*	*Birth Place*	*Source*	*Clubs*	*League App*	*League Gls*
Goalkeepers								
Lee Butler	6 2	14 02	30 5 66	Sheffield	Haworth Colliery	Lincoln C	30	—
						Aston Villa	8	—
						Hull C (loan)	4	—
						Barnsley	108	—
David Watson	5 11	12 00	10 11 73	Barnsley	Trainee	Barnsley	14	—
Defenders								
Viv Anderson	6 1	12 02	29 8 56	Nottingham	Apprentice	Nottingham F	328	15
						Arsenal	120	9
						Manchester U	54	2
						Sheffield W	70	8
						Barnsley	20	3
Charlie Bishop	6 0	12 01	16 2 68	Nottingham	Stoke C	Watford	—	—
						Bury	114	6
						Barnsley	109	1
Steve Davis*	6 0	12 07	26 7 65	Birmingham	Stoke C	Crewe Alex	145	1
						Burnley	147	11
						Barnsley	20	—
Nicky Eaden	6 0	12 00	12 12 72	Sheffield	Trainee	Barnsley	39	2
Gary Fleming	5 9	11 03	17 2 67	Londonderry	Apprentice	Nottingham F	74	—
						Manchester C	14	—
						Notts Co (loan)	3	—
						Barnsley	190	—
Robert Hanby	5 10	11 10	24 12 74	Pontefract	Trainee	Barnsley	—	—
Scott Jones	5 10	11 08	1 5 75	Sheffield	Trainee	Barnsley	—	—
Adrian Moses	6 1	12 08	4 5 75	Doncaster	School	Barnsley	—	—
Gerry Taggart	6 1	12 03	18 10 70	Belfast	Trainee	Manchester C	12	1
						Barnsley	171	13
Midfield								
Owen Archdeacon	5 7	10 08	4 3 66	Greenock	Gourock U	Celtic	76	7
						Barnsley	186	19
Troy Bennett			25 12 75	Barnsley	Trainee	Barnsley	2	—
David Brooke	5 11	11 03	23 11 75	Barnsley	Trainee	Barnsley	—	—
Mark Burton	5 8	11 07	7 5 73	Barnsley	Trainee	Barnsley	5	—
Mark Feeney	5 7		26 7 74	Derry	Trainee	Barnsley	2	—
Warren Godfrey‡	5 11	11 02	31 3 73	Liverpool	Trainee	Liverpool	—	—
						Barnsley	8	—
John Gregg*	5 9	11 00	26 3 75	Manchester	Trainee	Barnsley	—	—
Andrew Liddell	5 8	10.05	28 6 73	Leeds	Trainee	Barnsley	44	3
Gregory Morgan	5 7	10 00	12 10 73	Batley	Trainee	Barnsley	—	—
Andy Payton	5 9	10 06	23 10 66	Burnley	Apprentice	Hull C	144	55
						Middlesbrough	19	3
						Celtic	36	15
						Barnsley	25	12
Neil Redfearn	5 10	12 09	20 6 65	Dewsbury	Nottingham F	Bolton W	35	1
						Lincoln C (loan)	10	1
						Lincoln C	90	12
						Doncaster R	46	14
						Crystal Palace	57	10
						Watford	24	3
						Oldham Ath	62	16
						Barnsley	128	19
Darren Sheridan	5 6	10 12	8 12 67	Manchester	Winsford	Barnsley	3	—
Glynn Snodin	5 6	9 05	14 2 60	Rotherham	Apprentice	Doncaster R	309	61
						Sheffield W	59	1
						Leeds U	94	10
						Oldham Ath (loan)	8	1
						Rotherham U	3	—
						Hearts	34	—
						Barnsley	11	—

BARNSLEY

Colours: Red shirts, white shorts, red stockings. **Change colours:** Navy and turquoise striped shirts, black shorts, black stockings.

Foundation: Many clubs owe their inception to the church and Barnsley are among them, for they were formed in 1887 by the Rev. T. T. Preedy, curate of Barnsley St. Peter's and went under that name until it was dropped in 1897 a year before being admitted to the Second Division of the Football League.

First Football League game: 1 September, 1898, Division 2, v Lincoln C (a) L 0-1 – Fawcett; McArtney, Nixon; King, Burleigh, Porteous; Davis, Lees, Murray, McCullough, McGee.

Did you know: Despite an ordinary season in 1913–14 in which they finished fifth in Division 2, Barnsley used only 18 players, their fewest in a League competition. Unusually, too, they drew only one of their games.

Managers (and Secretary-Managers)
Arthur Fairclough 1898–1901*, John McCartney 1901–04*, Arthur Fairclough 1904–12, John Hastie 1912–14, Percy Lewis 1914–19, Peter Sant 1919–26, John Commins 1926–29, Arthur Fairclough 1929–30, Brough Fletcher 1930–37, Angus Seed 1937–53, Tim Ward 1953–60, Johnny Steele 1960–71 (continued as GM), John McSeveney 1971–72, Johnny Steele (GM) 1972–73, Jim Iley 1973–78, Allan Clarke 1978–80, Norman Hunter 1980–84, Bobby Collins 1984–85, Allan Clarke 1985–89, Mel Machin 1989–93, Viv Anderson 1993–94, Danny Wilson June 1994–

Player and Position	Ht	Wt	Birth Date	Birth Place	Source	Clubs	League App	League Gls
Danny Wilson	5 6	11 00	1 1 60	Wigan	Wigan Ath	Bury	90	8
						Chesterfield	100	13
						Nottingham F	10	1
						Scunthorpe U (loan)	6	3
						Brighton	135	33
						Luton T	110	24
						Sheffield W	98	11
						Barnsley	43	—
Forwards								
Martin Bullock	5 5	10 07	5 3 75	Derby	Eastwood T	Barnsley	—	—
David Currie*	5 11	12 09	27 11 62	Stockton	Local	Middlesbrough	113	31
						Darlington	76	33
						Barnsley	80	30
						Nottingham F	8	1
						Oldham Ath	31	3
						Barnsley	75	12
						Rotherham U (loan)	5	2
						Huddersfield T (loan)	7	1
Deniol Graham*	5 10	10 05	4 10 69	Cannock	Trainee	Manchester U	2	—
						Barnsley	38	2
						Preston NE (loan)	8	—
						Carlisle U (loan)	2	1
Chris Jackson	6 0	12 00	16 1 76	Barnsley	Trainee	Barnsley	7	1
Brendan O'Connell	5 10	10 09	12 11 66	London		Portsmouth	—	—
						Exeter C	81	19
						Burnley	64	17
						Huddersfield T (loan)	11	1
						Barnsley	170	27
Andy Rammell	5 10	11 07	10 2 67	Nuneaton	Atherstone U	Manchester U	—	—
						Barnsley	141	33
Gareth Williams	5 10	11 08	12 3 67	Isle of Wight	Gosport Borough	Aston Villa	12	—
						Barnsley	34	6
						Hull C (loan)	4	—
						Hull C (loan)	16	2

Trainees
Arkle, Paul I; Beckett, Luke J; Bochenski, Simon; Cannon, Richard P; Clyde, Darran E. J; Gregory, Andrew; Jebson, Carl M; Perry, Jonathan M; Shelley, Steven P; Sollitt, Adam J; Yates, Kevin.

****Non-Contract**
Widdowson, Steven

Associated Schoolboys
Baker, Damian; Clarkson, Mark R; Davenport, Marc S; Fearon, Dean A; Holmes, Robin S; Hylson, Shane E; Jackson, Darren; Leach, Kevin R; Lee, Robin; O'Connor, Craig; Owen, Daniel J. M; Ravenscroft, Andrew S; Richardson, Lee W; Shenton, Daniel R; Swallow, Christopher J; Taylor, David J; Webster, Stephen.

Associated Schoolboys who have accepted the Club's offer of a Traineeship/Contract
Clayton, Steven; Hayes, Shaun A; Hume, Mark A; Jones, Dean S; McClare, Sean P; Morgan, Christopher P; Shaw, Ian.
**Non-Contract Players who are retained must be re-signed before they are eligible to play in League matches.

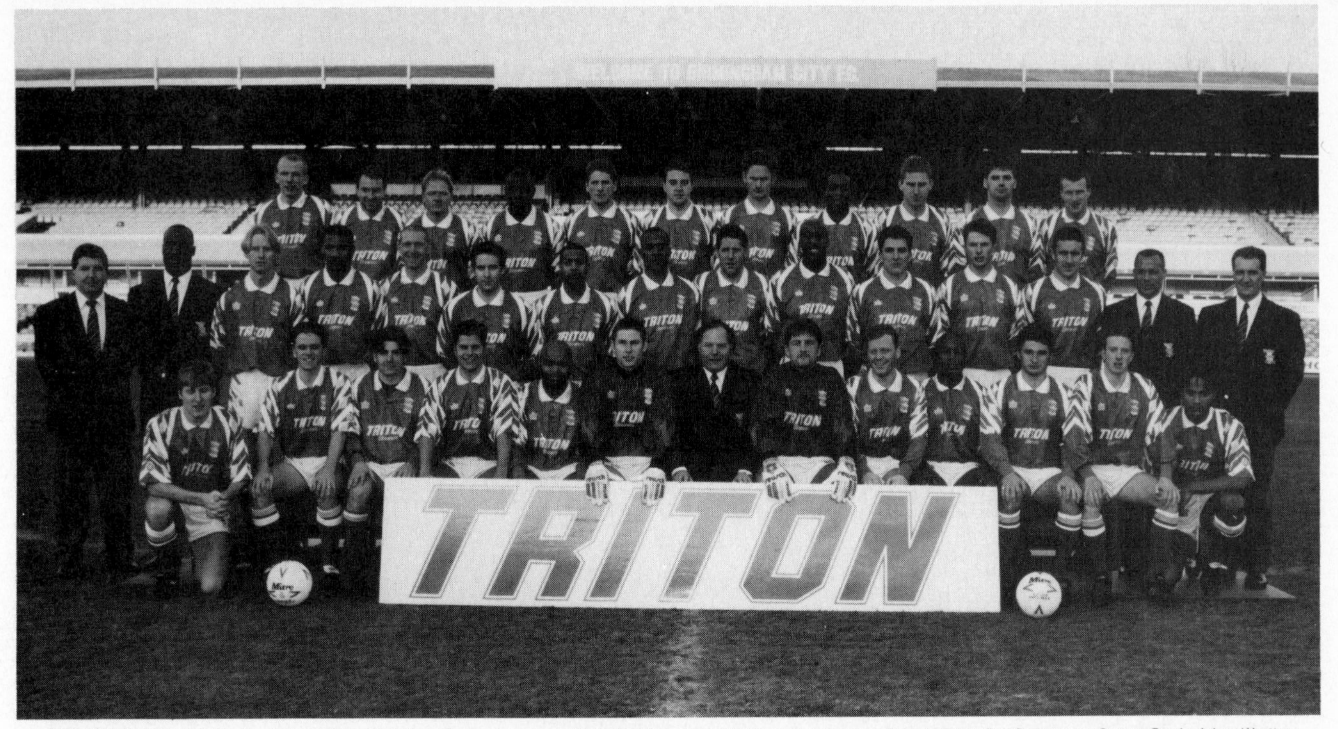

BIRMINGHAM CITY 1993–94 *Back row (left to right):* Kenny Lowe, John Frain, Keith Downing, Jason Beckford, Paul Harding, Richard Scott, Ben Sedgemore, George Parris, Adam Wratten, Darren Rogers, Steve Claridge.
Centre row: Phil Edwards (Physio), Dave Howell (Coach), Paul Tait, Roger Willis, Andy Saville, Paul Moulden, Louie Donowa, Peter Shearer, Ted McMinn, Chris Whyte, Richard Dryden, Paul Fenwick, Liam Daish, Edwin Stein (Coach), Lil Fuccillo (Chief Scout).
Front row: Steve McGavin, David Smith, Paul Peschisolido, Scott Hiley, Danny Wallace, Ian Bennett, Barry Fry, Kevin Miller, Gary Cooper, Lyndon Hooper, Vasili Kalogeracos, Steve Robinson, Juan Miguel Desouza.

Division 2 **BIRMINGHAM CITY**

St Andrews, Birmingham B9 4NH. Telephone 021–772 0101. Lottery office/Souvenir shop: 021–772 1245. Clubcall: 0891 121188. Fax: 021–766 7866. Club Soccer Shop: 021–766 8274.

Ground capacity: 28,235.

Record attendance: 66,844 v Everton, FA Cup 5th rd, 11 February 1939.

Record receipts: £230,000 v Aston Villa, Coca Cola Cup 2nd rd 1st leg, 21 September 1993.

Pitch measurements: 115yd × 75yd.

Directors: J. F. Wiseman (Chairman), K. R. Brady (Managing Director), D. Sullivan, D. Gold, R. Gold, B. Gold, H. Brandman, A. G. Jones.

Manager: Barry Fry. ***Assistant Manager:*** Edwin Stein. ***Coach:*** David Howell. ***Physio:*** Cate Janes. ***Commercial Manager:*** Allan Robson.

Secretary: A. G. Jones BA, MBA.

Year Formed: 1875. ***Turned Professional:*** 1885. ***Ltd Co.:*** 1888.

Previous Names: 1875–88, Small Heath Alliance; 1888, dropped 'Alliance'; became Birmingham 1905; became Birmingham City 1945.

Club Nickname: 'Blues'.

Previous Grounds: 1875, waste ground near Arthur St; 1877, Muntz St, Small Heath; 1906, St Andrews.

Record League Victory: 12–0 v Walsall T Swifts, Division 2, 17 December 1892 – Charnley; Bayley, Jones; Ollis, Jenkyns, Devey; Hallam (2), Walton (3), Mobley (3), Wheldon (2), Hands (2). 12–0 v Doncaster R, Division 2, 11 April 1903 – Dorrington; Goldie, Wassell; Beer, Dougherty (1), Howard; Athersmith (1), Leonard (3), McRoberts (1), Wilcox (4), Field (1). Aston. (1 og).

Record Cup Victory: 9–2 v Burton W, FA Cup, 1st rd, 31 October 1885 – Hedges; Jones, Evetts (1); F. James, Felton, A. James (1); Davenport (2), Stanley (4), Simms, Figures, Morris (1).

Record Defeat: 1–9 v Sheffield W, Division 1, 13 December 1930 and v Blackburn R, Division 1, 5 January 1895.

Most League Points (2 for a win): 59, Division 2, 1947–48.

Most League Points (3 for a win): 82, Division 2, 1984–85.

Most League Goals: 103, Division 2, 1893–94 (only 28 games).

Highest League Scorer in Season: Joe Bradford, 29, Division 1, 1927–28.

Most League Goals in Total Aggregate: Joe Bradford, 249, 1920–35.

Most Capped Player: Malcolm Page, 28, Wales.

Most League Appearances: Frank Womack, 491, 1908–28.

Record Transfer Fee Received: £975,000 from Nottingham F for Trevor Francis, February 1979.

Record Transfer Fee Paid: £350,000 to Derby Co for David Langan, June 1980.

Football League Record: 1892 elected to Division 2; 1894–96 Division 1; 1896–1901 Division 2; 1901–02 Division 1; 1902–03 Division 2; 1903–08 Division 1; 1908–21 Division 2; 1921–39 Division 1; 1946–48 Division 2; 1948–50 Division 1; 1950–1955 Division 2; 1955–65 Division 1; 1965–72 Division 2; 1972–79 Division 1; 1979–80 Division 2; 1980–84 Division 1; 1984–1985 Division 2; 1985–86 Division 1; 1986–89 Division 2; 1989–92 Division 3; 1992–94 Division 1; 1994– Division 2.

Honours: *Football League:* Division 1 best season: 6th, 1955–56; Division 2 – Champions 1892–93, 1920–21, 1947–48, 1954–55; Runners-up 1893–94, 1900–01, 1902–03, 1971–72, 1984–85. Division 3 Runners-up 1991–92. *FA Cup:* Runners-up 1931, 1956. *Football League Cup:* Winners 1963. *Leyland Data Cup:* Winners 1991. **European Competitions:** *European Fairs Cup:* 1955–58, 1958–60 (runners-up), 1960–61 (runners-up), 1961–62.

BIRMINGHAM CITY 1993—94 LEAGUE RECORD

Match No.	Date	Venue	Opponents	Result		H/T Score	Lg. Pos.	Goalscorers	Attendance
1	Aug 14	A	Charlton Ath	L	0-1	0-1	—		7708
2	22	H	Wolverhampton W	D	2-2	0-2	—	Peschisolido, Saville	15,117
3	28	A	Barnsley	W	3-2	0-1	13	Smith 2, Shutt	7241
4	31	H	Crystal Palace	L	2-4	1-2	—	Peschisolido 2	13,856
5	Sept 4	H	Derby Co	W	3-0	3-0	7	Saville 2, Frain	14,582
6	12	A	Leicester C	D	1-1	0-0	—	Peschisolido	10,366
7	18	H	Grimsby T	D	1-1	1-1	11	Donowa	11,302
8	25	H	Luton T	D	1-1	1-0	12	Shutt	11,081
9	Oct 2	A	Middlesbrough	D	2-2	0-1	11	Peschisolido 2	13,801
10	9	A	Sunderland	L	0-1	0-1	15		19,265
11	16	H	Watford	W	1-0	0-0	12	Wallace	12,823
12	19	H	Bolton W	W	2-1	0-0	—	Shutt, Phillips (og)	12,071
13	23	A	Peterborough U	L	0-1	0-1	10		7575
14	31	H	Millwall	W	1-0	1-0	—	Shutt	9377
15	Nov 2	A	Bristol C	L	0-3	0-1	—		9192
16	6	H	Nottingham F	L	0-3	0-1	12		16,996
17	20	H	Portsmouth	L	0-1	0-0	16		11,896
18	27	H	Tranmere R	L	0-3	0-1	18		9915
19	Dec 4	A	Nottingham F	L	0-1	0-1	18		22,061
20	11	A	Crystal Palace	L	1-2	1-2	20	Saville	11,295
21	18	H	Charlton Ath	W	1-0	0-0	17	Lowe	13,714
22	26	A	Stoke C	L	1-2	0-1	—	Peschisolido	16,584
23	28	H	WBA	W	2-0	2-0	17	Saville (pen), Peschisolido	28,228
24	Jan 1	A	Southend U	L	1-3	0-1	19	Peschisolido	10,729
25	3	H	Oxford U	D	1-1	0-1	17	Donowa	15,142
26	11	A	Notts Co	L	1-2	0-1	—	Cooper	7212
27	15	A	Watford	L	2-5	0-3	20	Willis, McGavin	7636
28	22	H	Sunderland	D	0-0	0-0	20		15,884
29	Feb 5	H	Peterborough U	D	0-0	0-0	21		15,140
30	12	A	Millwall	L	1-2	0-1	22	Saville	9438
31	19	H	Notts Co	L	2-3	0-1	22	Frain (pen), Saville	12,913
32	22	A	Wolverhampton W	L	0-3	0-1	—		24,931
33	25	A	Derby Co	D	1-1	0-0	22	Claridge	16,624
34	Mar 5	H	Barnsley	L	0-2	0-0	23		15,382
35	12	A	Grimsby T	L	0-1	0-0	23		5405
36	15	H	Leicester C	L	0-3	0-2	—		14,681
37	19	A	Luton T	D	1-1	0-1	24	Claridge	7690
38	26	H	Middlesbrough	W	1-0	0-0	24	Saville	12,409
39	29	A	Oxford U	L	0-2	0-2	—		8344
40	Apr 2	H	Stoke C	W	3-1	1-1	23	Claridge, Ward, Willis	13,568
41	9	H	Southend U	W	3-1	1-0	23	Doherty, Saville, Willis	14,307
42	16	H	Bristol C	D	2-2	0-2	23	Claridge (pen), Donowa	20,316
43	23	A	Portsmouth	W	2-0	1-0	22	Willis, Claridge (pen)	11,101
44	27	A	WBA	W	4-2	1-1	—	Claridge 2, Donowa, Saville	20,316
45	30	A	Bolton W	D	1-1	1-1	22	Willis	13,602
46	May 8	A	Tranmere R	W	2-1	1-0	22	Donowa, Garnett (og)	15,210

Final League Position: 22

GOALSCORERS

League (52): Saville 10 (1 pen), Peschisolido 9, Claridge 7 (2 pens), Donowa 5, Willis 5, Shutt 4, Frain 2 (1 pen), Smith 2, Cooper 1, Doherty 1, Lowe 1, McGavin 1, Wallace 1, Ward 1, own goals 2.
Coca-Cola Cup (3): Frain 1, Parris 1, Peschisolido 1.
FA Cup (1): Harding 1.

Miller 24	Hiley 28	Frain 26	Parris 22 + 2	Dryden 34	Downing 1	Mardon 5 + 3/Ward 9	Black 2	Saville 38 + 1	Smith 22 + 3/Rogers 1	McMinn 19 + 3	Donowa 14 + 7	Fenwick 6 + 3	Whyte 33	Peschisolido 21 + 3	Moulden 5 + 2	Shutt 18 + 8	Tait 9 + 1	Scott 5 + 1	Hooper 1 + 4	Potter 7	Wallace 8 + 2	Morgan — + 1	Jenkinson 2 + 1	Harding 14 + 2	Cooper 16 + 2	Lowe 10 + 2	Barnett 8 + 1	Bennett 22	Willis 11 + 5	Daish 19	Claridge 17 + 1	McGavin 6 + 2	Shearer 2	De Souza 1 + 6	Doherty 12 + 1	Huxford 5	Dominguez 3 + 2	*Match No.*
1	2	3	4	5	6	7	*8*	9	10	11	12	14																										1
1	2	3	4	5		7		10	8	11	12		6	*9*	14																							2
1	2	3	4	5		7		9	10		12		6		8	11																						3
1	2	3	4	5				10	8		7		6	9		11																						4
1	2	3	4	5				10	8		7		6	9		11																						5
1	2	3	4	5				10	8		7		6	9		11																						6
1	2	3	4	5				10	8	12	7		6	9		11																						7
1	2	3		5		14		9	10	8	7		6	12		11	*4*																					8
1	2	3		5				10	8		7		6	9		11	4																					9
1		3		5		4			8	12	7		6	*9*		11	10	2	14																			10
1				5		12			10	7			6	*9*		11	4	2	14	3	8																	11
1	2		4	5		12		9	10	7			6			11			14	3	*8*																	12
1	2		4	5			*8*	9	10	11			6					12	*7*	3		14																13
1	2		4	5				9	8	10	7	12	6			11				3																		14
1	2		4	5				9	8		7	6				11				3	12		10															15
1	2		4	5		8		12	10	7						11	14			3	*9*		6															16
1	2		4	5				9	10	7				12	8	11	6			3																		17
1			4	5				10	3			2	6	9	11	7	8						12															18
1			2	5				10	3	*7*		14	6	9		11	4				12			8														19
1			4	5				10	3	7	12	2	6	9					14		8			*11*														20
1				5				10	14	*7*		2	6	9		12					8			11	3	4												21
1				5				10		7		*2*	6	9		12					8			11	3	4	14											22
			2	5				10	14	7			6	9		12					*8*				3	11	4	1										23
			2	5				10	12	*7*			6	9							8				3	11	4	1	14									24
	2			5				10	11	7	12		6	9											3	8		1	4									25
	2		12	5				9		14			6											*11*	3	7		1		4	8	10						26
	2			5						*7*			6				9							12	3	11		1	14	4	8	10						27
	2		3	5					8	7			6													11		1	12	4	9	10						28
	2	3	4	5										9										7				1		8		10	6	12	11			29
	2	3	12	5				10						9			6							*7*				1		8			4	14	11			30
		3	4	5				10		*7*		2		9											6	8		1				12		14	11			31
		3		5				10						9											7	6	4	1			8	12		14	*11*	2		32
1			3	5				9																	7	12	6			4	8	10			11	2		33
1		3		5				10						9											7	12	6			4	8	*11*			14	2		34
		3											6	12	9	*7*								10	4			1	14	5	8					2	11	35
		3						9					6		*8*	7								10	4			1	14	5	12					2	11	36
		3						9					6		14	12		2						10	*4*			1	7	5	8						11	37
		3				7		9			12		6					2						*11*	4			1	10	5	8						14	38
		3				7		9			12		6					2						*11*	4			1	10	5	8						14	39
	2	3				7		9																4			5	1	10	6	8				11			40
	2	3				7		9																4			5	1	10	6	8			12	11			41
	2					7			3		4					12											5	1	10	6	8			9	11			42
	2	3				7		9			4		5															1	10	6	8			12	11			43
	2	3				7		*9*			4		5			12								14				1	10	6	8				11			44
	2	3				7		*9*			4		5			12									14			1	10	6	8				11			45
	2	3				7		9			*4*		5			12									14			1	10	6	8				11			46

Coca-Cola Cup	First Round	Plymouth Arg (h)	3-0
		(a)	0-2
	Second Round	Aston Villa (h)	0-1
		(a)	0-1
FA Cup	Third Round	Kidderminster H (h)	1-2

BIRMINGHAM CITY

Player and Position	Ht	Wt	Birth Date	Birth Place	Source	Clubs	League App	League Gls
Goalkeepers								
Ian Bennett	6 0	12 00	10 10 71	Worksop	Newcastle U	Peterborough U	72	—
						Birmingham C	22	—
Kevin Miller	6 1	12 10	15 3 69	Falmouth	Newquay	Exeter C	163	—
						Birmingham C	24	—
Defenders								
Dave Barnett	6 0	12 08	16 4 67	London	Windsor & Eton	Colchester U	20	—
						WBA	—	—
						Walsall	5	—
					Kidderminster H	Barnet	59	3
						Birmingham C	9	—
Gary Cooper	5 8	11 03	20 11 65	Edgware	Fisher Ath	Maidstone U	60	7
						Peterborough U	88	10
						Birmingham C	18	1
Liam Daish	6 2	13 05	23 9 68	Portsmouth	Apprentice	Portsmouth	1	—
						Cambridge U	139	4
						Birmingham C	19	—
Richard Dryden	6 0	11 02	14 6 69	Stroud		Bristol R	13	—
						Exeter C	51	7
						Manchester C (loan)	—	—
						Notts Co	31	1
						Plymouth Arg (loan)	5	—
						Birmingham C	45	—
Paul Fenwick	6 1	12 01	25 8 69	London	Winnipeg Fury	Birmingham C	19	—
George Parris	5 9	13 00	11 9 64	Ilford	Apprentice	West Ham U	239	12
						Birmingham C	37	—
Darren Rogers*	5 10	11 02	9 4 71	Birmingham	Trainee	WBA	14	1
						Birmingham C	18	—
						Wycombe W (loan)	1	—
Richard Scott	5 9	10 10	29 9 74	Dudley	Trainee	Birmingham C	7	—
Chris Whyte	6 1	11 10	2 9 61	London	Amateur	Arsenal	90	8
						Crystal Palace (loan)	13	—
					Los Angeles R	WBA	84	7
						Leeds U	113	5
						Birmingham C	33	—
Roger Willis	6 1	11 06	17 6 67	Sheffield		Grimsby T	9	—
					Barnet	Barnet	44	13
						Watford	36	2
						Birmingham C	16	5
Adam Wratten	6 0		30 11 74	Coventry	Trainee	Birmingham C	—	—
Midfield								
Simon Black§			9 11 75	Marston Green	Trainee	Birmingham C	2	—
Neil Doherty	5 9		21 2 69	Barrow	Trainee	Watford	—	—
					Barrow	Birmingham C	13	1
Keith Downing	5 8	11 00	23 7 65	Oldbury	Mile Oak R	Notts Co	23	1
						Wolverhampton W	191	8
						Birmingham C	1	—
John Frain	5 7	11 10	8 10 68	Birmingham	Apprentice	Birmingham C	243	23
Paul Harding	5 9	12 05	6 3 64	Mitcham	Barnet	Notts Co	54	1
						Southend U (loan)	5	—
						Watford (loan)	2	—
						Birmingham C	16	—
Scott Hiley	5 9	10 07	27 9 68	Plymouth	Trainee	Exeter C	210	12
						Birmingham C	35	—
Lyndon Hooper	5 4		30 5 66	Guyana	Toronto Blizzard	Birmingham C	5	—
Kenny Lowe	6 1	11 04	6 11 64	Sedgefield	Apprentice	Hartlepool U	54	3
					Barrow	Scarborough	4	—
					Barrow	Barnet	72	5
						Stoke C	9	—
						Birmingham C	12	1
Steven Robinson	5 4	10 11	17 1 75	Nottingham	Trainee	Birmingham C	—	—
Ben Sedgemore	5 10	13 11	5 8 75	Wolverhampton	Trainee	Birmingham C	—	—
Paul Tait	6 1	10 00	31 1 71	Sutton Coldfield	Trainee	Birmingham C	92	7
						Millwall (loan)	—	—

BIRMINGHAM CITY

Colours: All blue. **Change colours:** All red.

Foundation: In 1875 cricketing enthusiasts who were largely members of Trinity Church, Bordesley, determined to continue their sporting relationships throughout the year by forming a football club which they called Small Heath Alliance. For their earliest games played on waste land in Arthur Street, the team included three Edden brothers and two James brothers.

First Football League game: 3 September, 1892, Division 2, v Burslem Port Vale (h) W5-1 – Charsley; Bayley, Speller; Ollis, Jenkyns, Devey; Hallam (1), Edwards (1), Short (1), Wheldon (2), Hands.

Did you know: Full-back Frank Womack's record of 491 League appearances for Birmingham City would have been substantially increased but for the period between 1915 and 1918, when he added a further 92 in wartime regional matches.

Managers (and Secretary-Managers)
Alfred Jones 1892–1908*, Alec Watson 1908–1910, Bob McRoberts 1910–15, Frank chRichards 1915–23, Bill Beer 1923–27, Leslie Knighton 1928–33, George Liddell 1933–39, Harry Storer 1945–48, Bob Brocklebank 1949–54, Arthur Turner 1954–58, Pat Beasley 1959–60, Gil Merrick 1960–64, Joe Mallett 1965, Stan Cullis 1965–70, Fred Goodwin 1970–75, Willie Bell 1975–77, Jim Smith 1978–82, Ron Saunders 1982–86, John Bond 1986–87, Garry Pendrey 1987–89, Dave Mackay 1989–1991, Lou Macari 1991, Terry Cooper 1991–93, Barry Fry December 1993–

Player and Position	Ht	Wt	Birth Date	Birth Place	Source	Clubs	League App	League Gls
Forwards								
Jason Beckford*	5 9	12 04	14 2 70	Manchester	Trainee	Manchester C	20	1
						Blackburn R (loan)	4	—
						Port Vale (loan)	5	1
						Birmingham C	7	2
						Bury (loan)	3	—
Steve Claridge	5 11	11 08	10 4 66	Portsmouth	Fareham	Bournemouth	7	1
					Weymouth	Crystal Palace	—	—
						Aldershot	62	19
						Cambridge U	79	28
						Luton T	16	2
						Cambridge U	53	18
						Birmingham C	18	7
Juan De Souza	6 1		11 2 70	Newham	Dagenham	Birmingham C	7	—
Jose Dominguez	5 3		16 2 74	Lisbon	Benfica	Birmingham C	5	—
Lou Donowa	5 9	11 00	24 9 64	Ipswich	Apprentice	Norwich C	62	11
						Stoke C (loan)	4	1
					Coruna, Willem II Tilburg	Ipswich T	23	1
						Bristol C	24	3
						Birmingham C	68	9
						Crystal Palace (loan)	—	—
						Burnley (loan)	4	—
						Shrewsbury T (loan)	4	—
Vasili Kalogeracos	5 7		21 3 75	Perth	Floreat Athena	Birmingham C	—	—
Steve McGavin	5 8	11 00	24 1 69	North Walsham	Sudbury	Colchester U	58	17
						Birmingham C	8	1
Trevor Morgan†	6 2	13 04	30 9 56	Forest Gate	Leytonstone	Bournemouth	53	13
						Mansfield T	12	6
						Bournemouth	88	33
						Bristol C	32	8
						Exeter C	30	9
						Bristol R	55	24
						Bristol C	19	8
						Bolton W	77	17
						Colchester U	32	12
						Exeter C	17	3
					Hong Kong	Birmingham C	1	—

Continued on Page 103

Trainees
Black, Simon A; Bunch, James P. G; Cross, Robert B; Hickman, Ryan; Hiles, Paul M; Hughes, Lee R; Jones, Ian; Prince, Simon P; Rea, Simon; Round, Steven C; Steadman, Richard D; Webb, Matthew L; Weston, Richard J.

Associated Schoolboys
Bryan, Simon M; Burden, Neil; Crockett, Daniel J; Douglas, Nathan L; Fieldhouse, Sean P; Hatton, Paul M; Marsh, CHristopher D; Powell, Jason D; Robinson, Anthony A; Sandland, Paul N; Simcox, Neil R; White, Paul; Worrall, Dean J.

Associated Schoolboys who have accepted the Club's offer of a Traineeship/Contract
Bass, Jonathan D. M; Challinor, Paul D; Dandy, Richard; Dyer, Wayne; Hinton, Craig; McKenzie, Christy; Unitt, David T.

BLACKBURN ROVERS 1993–94 *Back row (left to right):* Tony Dobson, Nicky Marker, Richard Brown, David May, Frank Talia, Bobby Mimms, Matt Dickins, Colin Hendry, Andy Scott, Henning Berg, Mark Atkins.
Centre row: Tony Parkes, Alan Shearer, Kevin Moran, Stuart Ripley, Mike Newell, Bob Dewhurst, Patrik Andersson, Tim Sherwood, Peter Thorne, Paul Ainscough, Andy Morrison, Ray Harford.
Front row: Asa Hartford, Lee Makel, Steve Grunshaw, Joshua Metcalf, Kevin Gallacher, Kenny Dalglish, Simon Ireland, Graeme Le Saux, Gary Tallon, Jason Wilcox, Mike Pettigrew.

FA Premiership **BLACKBURN ROVERS**

Ewood Park, Blackburn BB2 4JF. Telephone Blackburn (0254) 698888. Fax 0254 671042. Ticket Office: (0254) 696767. Club Shop: (0254) 672137.

Ground capacity: 30,000.

Record attendance: 61,783 v Bolton W, FA Cup 6th rd, 2 March, 1929.

Record receipts: £156,000 v Newcastle U, FA Cup 5th rd, 13 February 1993.

Pitch measurements: 115yd × 76yd.

Chairman: R. D. Coar BSC. ***Vice-chairman:*** T. W. Ibbotson. ***Directors:*** K. C. Lee, I. R. Stanners, G. R. Root FCMA, R. L. Matthewman.

Manager: Kenny Dalglish MBE. ***Assistant Manager:*** Ray Harford. ***Physio:*** Mike Pettigrew. ***Coach:*** Tony Parkes.

Commercial Manager: Ken Beamish.

Secretary: John W. Howarth FAAI.

Year Formed: 1875. ***Turned Professional:*** 1880. ***Ltd Co.:*** 1897.

Club Nickname: Rovers.

Previous Grounds: 1875/6, all matches played away; 1876, Oozehead Ground; 1877, Pleasington Cricket Ground; 1878, Alexandra Meadows; 1881, Leamington Road; 1890, Ewood Park.

Record League Victory: 9–0 v Middlesbrough, Division 2, 6 November 1954 – Elvy; Suart, Eckersley; Clayton, Kelly, Bell; Mooney (3), Crossan (2), Briggs, Quigley (3), Langton (1).

Record Cup Victory: 11–0 v Rossendale, FA Cup 1st rd, 13 October 1884 – Arthur; Hopwood, McIntyre; Forrest, Blenkhorn, Lofthouse; Sowerbutts (2), J. Brown (1), Fecitt (4), Barton (3), Birtwistle (1).

Record Defeat: 0–8 v Arsenal, Division 1, 25 February 1933.

Most League Points (2 for a win): 60, Division 3, 1974–75.

Most League Points (3 for a win): 84, FA Premier League, 1993–94.

Most League Goals: 114, Division 2, 1954–55.

Highest League Scorer in Season: Ted Harper, 43, Division 1, 1925–26.

Most League Goals in Total Aggregate: Simon Garner, 168, 1978–92.

Most Capped Player: Bob Crompton, 41, England.

Most League Appearances: Derek Fazackerley, 596, 1970–86.

Record Transfer Fee Received: £720,000 (net) from Leeds U for Scott Sellars, September 1992.

Record Transfer Fee Paid: £3,300,000 to Southampton for Alan Shearer, July 1992.

Football League Record: 1888 Founder Member of the League; 1936–39 Division 2; 1946–48 Division 1; 1948–58 Division 2; 1958–66 Division 1; 1966–71 Division 2; 1971–75 Division 3; 1975–79 Division 2; 1979–80 Division 3; 1980–92 Division 2; 1992– FA Premier League.

Honours: *FA Premier League:* – Runners-up 1993–94. *Football League:* Division 1 – Champions 1911–12, 1913–14; Division 2 – Champions 1938–39; Runners-up 1957–58; Division 3 – Champions 1974–75; Runners-up 1979–80. *FA Cup:* Winners 1884, 1885, 1886, 1890, 1891, 1928; Runners-up 1882, 1960. *Football League Cup:* Semi-final 1961–62, 1992–93. *Full Members' Cup:* Winners 1986–87.

BLACKBURN ROVERS 1993—94 LEAGUE RECORD

Match No.	Date	Venue	Opponents	Result	H/T Score	Lg. Pos.	Goalscorers	Attendance
1	Aug 14	A	Chelsea	W 2-1	0-0	—	Ripley, Newell	29,189
2	18	H	Norwich C	L 2-3	1-1	—	Atkins, Wilcox	14,260
3	21	H	Oldham Ath	W 1-0	1-0	7	Moran	14,397
4	24	A	Manchester C	W 2-0	1-0	—	Newell, Gallacher	25,185
5	29	A	Newcastle U	D 1-1	0-0	—	Shearer	33,987
6	Sept 1	H	Arsenal	D 1-1	1-0	—	Gallacher	14,410
7	12	A	Liverpool	W 1-0	0-0	—	Newell	37,355
8	18	H	West Ham U	L 0-2	0-1	7		14,437
9	25	H	Sheffield W	D 1-1	0-0	7	Shearer	14,495
10	Oct 2	A	Swindon T	W 3-1	1-1	5	Shearer 2, Ripley	15,847
11	18	H	Sheffield U	D 0-0	0-0	—		14,276
12	23	A	Leeds U	D 3-3	1-0	6	Shearer 3	37,827
13	30	H	Tottenham H	W 1-0	1-0	4	Shearer	17,462
14	Nov 6	A	QPR	L 0-1	0-0	8		17,636
15	20	H	Southampton	W 2-0	1-0	7	Shearer 2 (1 pen)	17,343
16	23	H	Coventry C	W 2-1	1-0	—	Shearer 2	16,376
17	27	A	Ipswich T	L 0-1	0-1	—		14,436
18	Dec 5	H	Chelsea	W 2-0	1-0	—	Le Saux, Shearer	16,756
19	11	A	Oldham Ath	W 2-1	1-1	3	Shearer 2	13,887
20	18	H	Manchester C	W 2-0	1-0	3	Gallacher, Shearer	19,479
21	26	A	Manchester U	D 1-1	1-0	—	Gallacher	44,511
22	29	H	Everton	W 2-0	2-0	2	Shearer 2	22,061
23	Jan 1	A	Aston Villa	W 1-0	1-0	2	Shearer	40,903
24	15	A	Sheffield U	W 2-1	1-1	2	Shearer 2	19,124
25	23	H	Leeds U	W 2-1	1-0	—	Shearer 2	17,475
26	Feb 5	H	Wimbledon	W 3-0	3-0	2	Shearer (pen), Wilcox, Ripley	17,264
27	12	A	Tottenham H	W 2-0	0-0	2	Shearer, Gallacher	30,236
28	19	H	Newcastle U	W 1-0	0-0	2	May	20,798
29	22	A	Norwich C	D 2-2	1-1	—	Gallacher 2	15,124
30	25	A	Arsenal	L 0-1	0-0	2		35,030
31	Mar 5	H	Liverpool	W 2-0	1-0	2	Wilcox, Sherwood	20,831
32	20	A	Sheffield W	W 2-1	1-1	—	Wilcox, Newell	24,655
33	26	H	Swindon T	W 3-1	2-1	2	Shearer 2 (1 pen), Sherwood	20,046
34	29	A	Wimbledon	L 1-4	1-0	—	Wilcox	10,537
35	Apr 2	H	Manchester U	W 2-0	0-0	2	Shearer 2	20,866
36	4	A	Everton	W 3-0	1-0	2	Newell 2, Wilcox	27,463
37	11	H	Aston Villa	W 1-0	1-0	—	Shearer	19,287
38	16	A	Southampton	L 1-3	0-2	2	Ripley	19,105
39	24	H	QPR	D 1-1	1-0	—	Shearer	19,913
40	27	A	West Ham U	W 2-1	1-0	—	Berg, Pearce	22,186
41	May 2	A	Coventry C	L 1-2	1-1	—	Le Saux	16,646
42	7	H	Ipswich T	D 0-0	0-0	2		20,633

Final League Position: 2

GOALSCORERS

League (63): Shearer 31 (3 pens), Gallacher 7, Newell 6, Wilcox 6, Ripley 4, Le Saux 2, Sherwood 2, Atkins 1, Berg 1, May 1, Moran 1, Pearce 1.
Coca-Cola Cup (5): Newell 2 (1 pen), May 1, Pearce 1, Shearer 1.
FA Cup (6): Shearer 2, Gallacher 1, May 1, Sherwood 1, Wilcox 1.

Mimms 13	May 40	Le Saux 40 + 1	Sherwood 38	Moran 19	Marker 16 + 7	Ripley 40	Atkins 8 + 7	Newell 27 + 1	Gallacher 27 + 3	Wilcox 31 + 2	Berg 38 + 3	Shearer 34 + 6	Andersson 1	Warhurst 4 + 5	Hendry 22 + 1	Wright 7 + 5	Batty 26	Flowers 29	Pearce 1 + 4	Morrison 1 + 4	Makel — + 2	*Match No.*
1	2	3	4	5	6	7	8	9	10	11	12											1
1	2	3	4	5	6	7	8	9	*10*	11	12	14										2
1	2	3	4	5	6	7		9	10	11	8	12										3
1	2	3	4	5	6	7	12	9	*10*	11	8	14										4
1	2	3	4		5	*7*	12	9	10	11	6	14	8									5
1	2	3	4	5	6	7	12	9	*10*	11	8	14										6
1	2	3	4	5	12	7		9	10	11	8			6								7
1	2	3	4	5	12	7		9	10	*11*	8	14		6								8
1	2	3	8		4	7		12	10	*11*	14	9		6	5							9
1	2	3	4	5	12	7	14		*10*	11	8	9		6								10
1	2	3	4		6	7		10	11		8	9			5							11
1	2	3	4		6	7	12	10	*11*		8	9			5	14						12
1			8		6	7	12	10	11		2	9			5	3	4					13
	6	12	8			7		10	11		2	9			5	3	4	1				14
	2	6	8		5	7		10	12		11	9				3	4	1				15
	2	6	8		5	7		10	12		11	9				3	4	1				16
	2	6	8			7		10	12		11	9			5	3	4	1				17
	3	6	8			7		10	11		2	9			5		4	1				18
	2	3	8			7		10	11		6	9			5		4	1				19
	2	3	8			7		10	11	12	6	9			5		4	1				20
	2	3	8			7		10	11	12	6	9			5		4	1				21
	2	3	8			7			10	11	6	9			5		4	1				22
	2	3	8			7			10	11	6	9			5		4	1				23
	2	3	8	6		7			10	11		9			5		4	1	12			24
	6	3	8	5	12	7			*10*	11	2	9					4	1	14			25
		3	*8*	5	6	7			10	11	2	9					4	1	12	14		26
	2	3		5	6	7	8		10	11	4	9						1				27
	2	3		5		7	8		10	11	6	9				12	4	1				28
	6	3		5		7	8		10	11	2	9					4	1				29
	2	3		*5*	6	7	12		10	11	8	9					4	1		14		30
	2	3	8	5	10	7				11	6	9			12		4	1				31
	2	3	8			7		10		11	6	9			5		4	1				32
	2	3	8		14	7		10		11	6	9		12	5		*4*	1				33
	2	3	8	5		7		10		11	6	9		12			4	1				34
	2	3	8		12	7		10		11	6	9			5		4	1				35
	2	3	8			7		10		11	6	9			5	12	4	1				36
	2	3	8			*7*		10		11	6	9		12	5	14	4	1				37
	2	3	8	5		7		10		11	6	9		12			*4*	1		14		38
	2	3	8			7		10		11	6	9		12	5		4	1				39
	2	3	4			*7*	8			11	6	9			5	10		1	12	14		40
	2	3	4		12		*8*			11	6	9			5	10		1		7	14	41
	2	3	8	*4*			10			11	6	9			5	12		1	7		14	42

Coca-Cola Cup	Second Round	Bournemouth (h)	1-0
		(a)	0-0
	Third Round	Shrewsbury T (h)	0-0
		(a)	4-3
	Fourth Round	Tottenham H (a)	0-1
FA Cup	Third Round	Portsmouth (h)	3-3
		(a)	3-1
	Fourth Round	Charlton Ath (a)	0-0
		(h)	0-1

BLACKBURN ROVERS

Player and Position	Ht	Wt	Birth Date	Birth Place	Source	Clubs	League App	League Gls
Goalkeepers								
Matt Dickins	6 4	14 00	3 9 70	Sheffield	Trainee	Sheffield U	—	—
						Leyton Orient (loan)	—	—
						Lincoln C	27	—
						Blackburn R	1	—
						Blackpool (loan)	19	—
						Lincoln C (loan)	—	—
Tim Flowers	6 2	14 01	3 2 67	Kenilworth	Apprentice	Wolverhampton W	63	—
						Southampton (loan)	—	—
						Southampton	192	—
						Swindon T (loan)	2	—
						Swindon T (loan)	5	—
						Blackburn R	29	—
Bobby Mimms	6 2	12 13	12 10 63	York	Halifax T	Rotherham U	83	—
						Everton	29	—
						Notts Co (loan)	2	—
						Sunderland (loan)	4	—
						Blackburn R (loan)	6	—
						Manchester C (loan)	3	—
						Tottenham H	37	—
						Aberdeen (loan)	6	—
						Blackburn R	122	—
Frank Talia			20 7 72	Melbourne	Sunshine George Cross	Blackburn R	—	—
						Hartlepool U (loan)	14	—
Defenders								
Patrik Andersson (To Moenchengladbach November 1993)			18 8 71	Borgeby	Malmo	Blackburn R	12	—
Mark Atkins	6 1	12 00	14 8 68	Doncaster		Scunthorpe U	48	2
						Blackburn R	219	29
Henning Berg			1 9 69	Eidsvell	Lillestrom	Blackburn R	45	1
Richard Brown	5 10	11 02	13 1 67	Nottingham	Ilkeston T	Sheffield W	—	—
					Kettering T	Blackburn R	28	—
						Maidstone U (loan)	3	—
Colin Hendry	6 1	12 00	7 12 65	Keith	Islavale	Dundee	41	2
						Blackburn R	102	22
						Manchester C	63	5
						Blackburn R	94	5
Graeme Le Saux	5 9	12 00	17 10 68	Jersey		Chelsea	90	8
						Blackburn R	50	2
Nick Marker	6 1	13 00	3 5 65	Exeter	Apprentice	Exeter C	202	3
						Plymouth Arg	202	13
						Blackburn R	38	—
David May	6 0	11 07	24 6 70	Oldham	Trainee	Blackburn R	123	3
Kevin Moran	5 11	12 09	29 4 56	Dublin	Pegasus	Manchester U	231	21
					Sporting Gijon	Blackburn R	147	10
Ian Pearce	6 1	12 04	7 5 74	Bury St Edmunds	School	Chelsea	4	—
						Blackburn R	5	1
Andrew Scott			27 6 75	Manchester	Trainee	Blackburn R	—	—
Paul Warhurst	6 1	12 07	26 9 69	Stockport	Trainee	Manchester C	—	—
						Oldham Ath	67	2
						Sheffield W	66	6
						Blackburn R	9	—
Midfield								
Paul Ainscough	5 11	10 08	22 8 75	Blackburn	Trainee	Blackburn R	—	—
David Batty	5 7	10 07	2 12 68	Leeds	Trainee	Leeds U	211	4
						Blackburn R	26	—
Paul Harford	6 4	13 12	21 10 74	Kent	Trainee	Blackburn R	—	—
Lee Makel	5 10	9 10	11 1 73	Sunderland	Trainee	Newcastle U	12	1
						Blackburn R	3	—
Joshua Metcalf*	5 8	11 05	8 10 74	Dublin	Trainee	Blackburn R	—	—
Thomas Morgan			30 3 77	Dublin	Trainee	Blackburn R	—	—
Andy Morrison	5 11	12 00	30 7 70	Inverness	Trainee	Plymouth Arg	113	6
						Blackburn R	5	—

BLACKBURN ROVERS

Colours: Blue and white halved shirts, white shorts with blue trim, blue stockings with white trim. **Change colours:** Black shirts with red stripe, red shorts, black stockings with red trim.

Foundation: It was in 1875 that some Public School old boys called a meeting at which the Blackburn Rovers club was formed and the colours blue and white adopted. The leading light was John Lewis, later to become a founder of the Lancashire FA, a famous referee who was in charge of two FA Cup Finals, and a vice-president of both the FA and the Football League.

First Football League game: 15 September, 1888, Football League, v Accrington (h) D 5-5 – Arthur; Beverley, James Southworth; Douglas, Almond, Forrest; Beresford (1), Walton, John Southworth (1), Fecitt (1), Townley (2).

Did you know: Fred Blackburn, born near Blackburn, made 204 League and Cup appearances for the club as a winger around the turn of the century. His brother Arthur also had a spell with Rovers.

Managers (and Secretary-Managers)
Thomas Mitchell 1884–96*, J. Walmsley 1896–1903*, R. B. Middleton 1903–25, Jack Carr 1922–26 (TM under Middleton to 1925), Bob Crompton 1926–30 (Hon. TM), Arthur Barritt 1931–36 (had been Sec. from 1927), Reg Taylor 1936–38, Bob Crompton 1938–41, Eddie Hapgood 1944–47, Will Scott 1947, Jack Bruton 1947–49, Jackie Bestall 1949–53, Johnny Carey 1953–58, Dally Duncan 1958–60, Jack Marshall 1960–67, Eddie Quigley 1967–70, Johnny Carey 1970–71, Ken Furphy 1971–73, Gordon Lee 1974–75, Jim Smith 1975–78, Jim Iley 1978, John Pickering 1978–79, Howard Kendall 1979–81, Bobby Saxton 1981–86, Don Mackay 1987–91, Kenny Dalglish October 1991–

Player and Position	*Ht*	*Wt*	*Birth Date*	*Birth Place*	*Source*	*Clubs*	*League App*	*League Gls*
Tim Sherwood	6 1	11 04	6 2 69	St Albans	Trainee	Watford	32	2
						Norwich C	71	10
						Blackburn R	88	5
Alan Wright	5 4	9 04	28 9 71	Ashton-under-Lyme	Trainee	Blackpool	98	—
						Blackburn R	69	1
Forwards								
Kevin Gallacher	5 7	9 11	23 11 66	Clydebank	Duntocher BC	Dundee U	131	27
						Coventry C	100	28
						Blackburn R	39	12
Steven Grunshaw*	5 9	12 01	7 1 75	Blackburn	Trainee	Blackburn R	—	—
Simon Ireland	5 11	11 12	23 11 71	Barnstaple	School	Huddersfield T	19	—
						Wrexham (loan)	5	—
						Blackburn R	1	—
						Mansfield T (loan)	9	1
Chris Malone			29 12 75	Drogheda		Blackburn R	—	—
Mike Newell	6 1	11 00	27 1 65	Liverpool	Liverpool	Crewe Alex	3	—
						Wigan Ath	72	25
						Luton T	63	18
						Leicester C	81	21
						Everton	68	15
						Blackburn R	88	25
Stuart Ripley	5 11	12 06	20 11 67	Middlesbrough	Apprentice	Middlesbrough	249	26
						Bolton W (loan)	5	1
						Blackburn R	80	11
Alan Shearer	5 11	11 03	13 8 70	Newcastle	Trainee	Southampton	118	23
						Blackburn R	61	47
Gary Tallon	5 10	11 02	5 9 73	Drogheda	Trainee	Blackburn R	—	—
Peter Thorne	6 0	12 10	21 6 73	Manchester	Trainee	Blackburn R	—	—
						Wigan Ath (loan)	11	—
Jason Wilcox	5 10	11 06	15 7 71	Bolton	Trainee	Blackburn R	123	14

Trainees
Bardsley, Christopher J; Gaston, Karl S; Gifford, Andrew J; Gill, Wayne J; Goodall, Daniel J; Grassby, Darren P; Hitchen, Steven J; Holt, Michael A; McCrone, Christopher P; Ormerod, Brett R; Sinnott, Adam J; Sweeney, Damian C; Thornton, Scott L; Whealing, Anthony J.

Associated Schoolboys
Borg, John C. A; Cairns, Paul S; Dunn, David J. I; Forbes, Christopher; Harding, John M; Jones, Gareth; Krupa, Michael P; McLean, James L; Owler, Lee; Rimmer, Martin J; Stewart, Gareth J; Trudgill, Paul C; Watkins, Steven L.

Associated Schoolboys who have accepted the Club's offer of a Traineeship/Contract
Beattie, James S; Broomes, Marlon C; Hope, Richard P; Morron, Keith J; Taylor, Philip M; Williams, Karl A.

BLACKPOOL 1993–94 *Back row (left to right):* Glynn Little, Mark Bonner, Mark Murray, David Robinson, Tony Rodwell, Chris Beech, Neil Mitchell, Andy Watson.
Centre row: Gary Briggs, Jamie Murphy, Melvin Capleton, Mitch Cook, Steve McIlhargey, Dave Bamber, Lee Martin, Phil Horner, Chris Speak, James Quinn, Paul Stoneman.
Front row: Ian Gore, Bryan Griffiths, Kevin Sheedy, Mike Davies, Neil Bailey (Youth Team Manager), Billy Ayre (Team Manager), Steve Redmond (Physio), Andy Gouck, Grant Leitch, Jonathon Irvine, Andrew Trickett.

Division 2 BLACKPOOL

Bloomfield Rd Ground, Blackpool FY1 6JJ. Telephone Blackpool (0253) 404331. Fax: 0253 405011. Clubcall: 0891 121648.

Ground capacity: 9654.

Record attendance: 38,098 v Wolverhampton W, Division 1, 17 September 1955.

Record receipts: £72,949 v Tottenham H, FA Cup 3rd rd, 5 January 1991.

Pitch measurements: 112yd × 74yd.

President: C. A. Sagar BEM.

Chairman: Owen J. Oyston. ***Deputy chairman:*** Mrs V. Oyston.

Managing Director: Mrs G. Bridge.

Directors: G. Warburton, J. Wilde MBE, W. Bingham MBE.

Manager: —.

Secretary: D. J. Allan.

Commercial Manager: Geoffrey Warburton.

Coach: Neil Bailey. ***Physio:*** Stephen Redmond.

Year Formed: 1887. ***Turned Professional:*** 1887. ***Ltd Co.:*** 1896.

Previous Name: 'South Shore' combined with Blackpool in 1899, twelve years after the latter had been formed on the breaking up of the old 'Blackpool St John's' club.

Club Nickname: 'The Seasiders'.

Previous Grounds: 1887, Raikes Hall Gardens; 1897, Athletic Grounds; 1899, Raikes Hall Gardens; 1899, Bloomfield Road.

Record League Victory: 7–0 v Preston NE (away), Division 1, 1 May 1948 – Robinson; Shimwell, Crosland; Buchan, Hayward, Kelly; Hobson, Munro (1), McIntosh (5), McCall, Rickett (1).

Record Cup Victory: 7–1 v Charlton Ath, League Cup, 2nd rd, 25 September 1963 – Harvey; Armfield, Martin; Crawford, Gratrix, Cranston; Lea, Ball (1), Charnley (4), Durie (1), Oakes (1).

Record Defeat: 1–10 v Small Heath, Division 2, 2 March 1901 and v Huddersfield T, Division 1, 13 December 1930.

Most League Points (2 for a win): 58, Division 2, 1929–30.

Most League Points (3 for a win): 86, Division 4, 1984–85.

Most League Goals: 98, Division 2, 1929–30.

Highest League Scorer in Season: Jimmy Hampson, 45, Division 2, 1929–30.

Most League Goals in Total Aggregate: Jimmy Hampson, 247, 1927–38.

Most Capped Player: Jimmy Armfield, 43, England.

Most League Appearances: Jimmy Armfield, 568, 1952–71.

Record Transfer Fee Received: £750,000 from QPR for Trevor Sinclair, August 1993.

Record Transfer Fee Paid: £116,666 to Sunderland for Jack Ashurst, October 1979.

Football League Record: 1896 Elected to Division 2; 1899 Failed re-election; 1900 Re-elected; 1900–30 Division 2; 1930–33 Division 1; 1933–37 Division 2; 1937–67 Division 1; 1967–70 Division 2; 1970–71 Division 1; 1971–78 Division 2; 1978–81 Division 3; 1981–85 Division 4; 1985–90 Division 3; 1990–92 Division 4; 1992– Division 2.

Honours: *Football League:* Division 1 – Runners-up 1955–56; Division 2 – Champions 1929–30; Runners-up 1936–37, 1969–70; Division 4 – Runners-up 1984–85. *FA Cup:* Winners 1953; Runners-up 1948, 1951. *Football League Cup:* Semi-final 1962. *Anglo-Italian Cup:* Winners 1971; Runners-up 1972.

BLACKPOOL 1993—94 LEAGUE RECORD

Match No.	Date	Venue	Opponents	Result		H/T Score	Lg. Pos.	Goalscorers	Attendance
1	Aug 14	A	Cambridge U	L	2-3	1-2	—	Griffiths (pen), Quinn	4903
2	21	H	Brentford	D	1-1	0-1	19	Watson	4024
3	28	A	Wrexham	W	3-2	2-1	12	Sheedy, Bonner, Beech	4957
4	31	H	Plymouth Arg	W	2-1	0-0	—	Griffiths (pen), Watson	3865
5	Sept 4	H	Barnet	W	3-1	1-1	5	Bonner, Griffiths, Bamber	4328
6	11	A	Bradford C	L	1-2	1-1	7	Griffiths	6869
7	14	A	Hartlepool U	L	0-2	0-0	—		2114
8	18	H	Cardiff C	W	1-0	1-0	6	Griffiths	4767
9	25	H	Bournemouth	W	2-1	1-1	5	Watson, Bonner	4489
10	Oct 2	A	Rotherham U	W	2-0	0-0	6	Bonner, Watson	3770
11	9	A	Swansea C	D	4-4	2-3	4	Griffiths, Watson, Mitchell 2	3775
12	16	H	Port Vale	L	1-3	0-1	9	Griffiths	8969
13	23	A	Exeter C	L	0-1	0-0	9		3421
14	30	H	Brighton & HA	W	2-0	0-0	8	Watson, Griffiths	4468
15	Nov 2	H	Hull C	W	6-2	2-1	—	Watson 2, Griffiths 2, Quinn, Beech	3968
16	6	A	Reading	D	1-1	1-0	5	Griffiths	6559
17	20	H	Huddersfield T	W	2-1	0-0	4	Watson, Horner	4704
18	27	A	Leyton Orient	L	0-2	0-1	7		3369
19	Dec 4	H	Hartlepool U	W	2-1	1-0	4	Griffiths 2 (1 pen)	3130
20	11	A	Brentford	L	0-3	0-2	6		4769
21	19	H	Cambridge U	L	2-3	1-2	—	Watson 2	4576
22	28	H	York C	L	0-5	0-2	9		4501
23	Jan 1	A	Burnley	L	1-3	1-1	11	Robinson	18,165
24	3	H	Bristol R	L	0-1	0-1	11		3311
25	8	H	Fulham	L	2-3	0-1	12	Griffiths, Bamber	3374
26	15	A	Port Vale	L	0-2	0-2	12		7915
27	22	H	Swansea C	D	1-1	0-0	13	Gouck	7080
28	29	A	Brighton & HA	L	2-3	1-1	14	Briggs, Robinson	7800
29	Feb 1	A	Stockport Co	L	0-1	0-0	—		5288
30	5	H	Exeter C	W	1-0	1-0	13	Bamber	3747
31	12	A	Fulham	L	0-1	0-0	13		4259
32	19	H	Wrexham	W	4-1	1-1	12	Bonner, Watson 3	4069
33	22	A	Plymouth Arg	L	1-2	0-0	—	Rodwell	7102
34	25	A	Barnet	W	1-0	0-0	12	Watson	2448
35	Mar 5	H	Bradford C	L	1-3	0-1	12	Gouck	5276
36	12	A	Cardiff C	W	2-0	1-0	12	Watson, Griffiths	5186
37	19	A	Bournemouth	L	0-1	0-1	15		3335
38	26	H	Rotherham U	L	1-2	0-0	16	Mitchell	3588
39	30	A	Bristol R	L	0-1	0-1	—		4231
40	Apr 2	H	Stockport Co	W	2-0	0-0	17	Bonner, Watson	5235
41	4	A	York C	L	1-2	1-2	17	Watson	5740
42	9	H	Burnley	L	1-2	0-2	17	Griffiths	7956
43	16	A	Hull C	D	0-0	0-0	19		6211
44	23	H	Reading	L	0-4	0-1	20		4529
45	30	A	Huddersfield T	L	1-2	1-1	21	Watson	16,195
46	May 7	H	Leyton Orient	W	4-1	1-1	20	Horner, Bonner, Bamber, Watson	5458

Final League Position: 20

GOALSCORERS

League (63): Watson 20, Griffiths 16 (3 pens), Bonner 7, Bamber 4, Mitchell 3, Beech 2, Gouck 2, Horner 2, Quinn 2, Robinson 2, Briggs 1, Rodwell 1, Sheedy 1.
Coca-Cola Cup (10): Watson 5, Bamber 3, Quinn 1, own goal 1.
FA Cup (0):

Martin 43	Davies 24	Cook 45	Horner 41	Stoneman 9 + 1	Gore 29	Watson 40	Leitch 1 + 1	Bamber 20 + 2	Bonner 39 + 1	Griffiths 42 + 1	Quinn 1 + 13	Beech 24 + 11	Briggs 32	Gouck 25 + 2	Sheedy 25 + 1	Mitchell 8 + 16	Robinson 9 + 3	Rodwell 28	McIlhargey 3 + 1	Bailey 1	Murphy 14 + 2	Whitworth 3	Symons — + 1	Thorpe — + 1	Match No.
1	2	3	4	5	6	7	8	9	10	*11*	12	14													1
1	2	3	4	6		7		9	8	11	12	14	5	*10*											2
1	2	3			6	7		9	8	11		4	5		10										3
1	2	3			6	7		9	8	*11*	12	4	5		10	14									4
1	2	3		5	6	7		9	8	*11*	12	4			10	14									5
1	2	3			6	7		9	8	11		4	5		10										6
1	2	3		12	6	7			8	*11*		4	5		10	14	9								7
1	2	3	4		6	7			8	11		9	5		10										8
1	2	3	4			7		9	8	11		6	5		10										9
1	2	3	4			7			8	11		6	5		10			9							10
1	2	3	4			7			8	11			5	6	10	12		9							11
	2		4					9	8	11	12	14	5	6		10		7	1	*3*					12
1	2	3	4			7			8	11			5	6	10			9							13
1	2	3	4			7			8	11	12	14	5	6	10			*9*							14
1	2	3	4			7			8	11	12	10	5	6				9							15
1	2	3	4			7			8	11	12	10	5	6				9							16
1	2	3	4			7			8	11	12		5	6		10					9				17
1		3	4		5	7			8	11	12			6	9	10					2				18
1		3	4	5		7	12		8	11	9	6			10						2				19
1		3	4		6	7			8	11	12				10	9					2	5			20
1	2	3	4		6	7			8	11	14				*10*	12					9	5			21
1	2	3	4			7				11	14	8		6	*10*	12					9	5			22
1	2	3	4			7		12		11		8	5	10			9				6				23
1	2	3	4			*7*		12		11		8	5	10		14	9				6				24
1	2	3	4			7		8		11		12	5		10		9				6				25
1	2	3	4		6			9		11			5		10	12	8	7	14						26
	2	3	4		6			9		11			5	12	10		8	7	1						27
1		3	4		6			9	8	11		14	5	2	*10*		12	7							28
1		3	4		6			9	12	*11*		2	5	10		14	8	7							29
1		3	4		6			9	2	*11*		12	5	10		14	8	7							30
1		3	4	5	6	8		9	2	*11*		14			10		12	7							31
1		3	4		6	8		9	2	11		10	5					7							32
1		3	4		6	8		9	2			11	5	10				7							33
1		3	4		6	8		9	2	11		12	5	10				7							34
1		3	4		6	8		9	2	11			5	10			12	7							35
1		3	4		6	8			2	*11*		12	5	10	9	14		7							36
1		3	4		6	8			2	11		*12*	5	10	9	14		7							37
1		3	4		6	8			2	11				10	9	12		7			5				38
1		3	4		6	8			2	11				10		9		7			5				39
1		3	4	6		8			2	11		9		10				7			5				40
		3	4	6		8			2	*11*		9		10	12	14		7	1		5				41
1		3	4		6	8			2	12		*9*	5	14	10	11		7							42
1		3	4		6	8			2	11		9	*5*	10		14		7			12				43
1		3	4		6	8			2	11		9	5			12		7			10				44
1		3	4	5	6	8			2			9				11	10	7					12		45
1		3	4	5	6	*8*		9	2			10				11		7			12			14	46

Coca-Cola Cup	First Round	Doncaster R (a)	1-0
		(h)	3-3
	Second Round	Sheffield U (h)	3-0
		(a)	0-2
	Third Round	Peterborough U (h)	2-2
		(a)	1-2
FA Cup	First Round	Port Vale (a)	0-2

BLACKPOOL

Player and Position	Ht	Wt	Birth Date	Birth Place	Source	Clubs	League App	League Gls
Goalkeepers								
Mel Capleton	5 11	12 00	24 10 73	London	Trainee	Southend U	—	—
						Blackpool	—	—
Steve McIlhargey*	6 0	11 07	28 8 63	Ferryhill	Blantyre Celtic	Walsall	—	—
						Blackpool	101	—
						Chester C (loan)	1	—
Lee Martin	6 0	13 00	9 9 68	Huddersfield	Trainee	Huddersfield T	54	—
						Blackpool	67	—
Defenders								
Neil Bailey			26 9 58	Wigan	Apprentice	Burnley	—	—
						Newport Co	134	7
						Wigan Ath	41	2
						Stockport Co	51	—
						Newport Co (loan)	9	1
					Retired	Blackpool	9	—
Gary Briggs	6 3	12 10	8 5 58	Leeds	Apprentice	Middlesbrough	—	—
						Oxford U	420	18
						Blackpool	136	4
Michael Davies	5 8	10 07	19 1 66	Stretford	Apprentice	Blackpool	309	16
Jamie Murphy	6 1	13 00	25 2 73	Manchester	Trainee	Blackpool	49	—
Mark Murray*	5 8	10 12	13 6 73	Manchester	Trainee	Blackpool	3	—
Paul Stoneman	6 1	13 06	26 2 73	Whitley Bay	Trainee	Blackpool	39	—
Andy Watson	5 9	11 02	1 4 67	Huddersfield	Harrogate T	Halifax T	83	15
						Swansea C	14	1
						Carlisle U	56	22
						Blackpool	55	22
Midfield								
Mark Bonner	5 10	11 00	7 6 74	Ormskirk	Trainee	Blackpool	58	7
Mitch Cook	6 0	12 0	15 10 61	Scarborough	Scarborough	Darlington	34	4
						Middlesbrough	6	—
						Scarborough	81	10
						Halifax T	54	2
						Scarborough (loan)	9	1
						Darlington (loan)	9	—
						Darlington	27	3
						Blackpool	62	—
Ian Gore	5 11	12 04	10 1 68	Liverpool		Birmingham C	—	—
					Southport	Blackpool	196	—
Andy Gouck	5 9	11 02	8 6 72	Blackpool	Trainee	Blackpool	93	9
Mark Kelly‡	5 9	10 05	7 10 66	Blackpool		Shrewsbury T	—	—
						Cardiff C	105	2
						Fulham	64	2
						Blackpool	—	—
Neil Mitchell			7 11 74	Lytham	Trainee	Blackpool	37	4
Kevin Sheedy	5 9	10 11	21 10 59	Builth Wells	Apprentice	Hereford U	51	4
						Liverpool	3	—
						Everton	274	67
						Newcastle U	37	4
						Blackpool	26	1
Andrew Trickett*	5 10	11 07	24 1 75	Burnley	Trainee	Blackpool	—	—
Forwards								
Dave Bamber	6 3	13 10	1 2 59	St. Helens	Manchester Univ	Blackpool	86	29
						Coventry C	19	3
						Walsall	20	7
						Portsmouth	4	1
						Swindon T	106	31
						Watford	18	3
						Stoke C	43	8
						Hull C	28	5
						Blackpool	111	60
Chris Beech			16 9 74	Blackpool	Trainee	Blackpool	36	2
Brian Griffiths	5 9	11 00	26 1 65	Prescot	St Helens T	Wigan Ath	189	44
						Blackpool	43	16

BLACKPOOL

Colours: Tangerine shirts with navy and white trim, white shorts, tangerine stockings with navy blue tops. **Change colours:** Navy and sky blue stripes, navy shorts, navy stockings.

Foundation: Old boys of St. John's School who had formed themselves into a football club decided to establish a club bearing the name of their town and Blackpool FC came into being at a meeting at the Stanley Arms Hotel in the summer of 1887. In their first season playing at Raikes Hall Gardens, the club won both the Lancashire Junior Cup and the Fylde Cup.

First Football League game: 5 September, 1896, Division 2, v Lincoln C (a) L 1-3 – Douglas; Parr, Bowman; Stuart, Stirzaker, Norris; Clarkin, Donnelly, R. Parkinson, Mount (1), J. Parkinson.

Did you know: On 22 January 1994 spectators were granted free admission to Bloomfield Road for the visit of Swansea City. The crowd was recorded at 7080, but was not the highest at the ground during the season. It was believed to be the first non-paying occasion in Football League history.

Managers (and Secretary-Managers)
Tom Barcroft 1903–33* (Hon. Sec.), John Cox 1909–11, Bill Norman 1919–23, Maj. Frank Buckley 1923–27, Sid Beaumont 1927–28, Harry Evans 1928–33 (Hon. TM), Alex "Sandy" Macfarlane 1933–35, Joe Smith 1935–58, Ronnie Suart 1958–67, Stan Mortensen 1967–69, Les Shannon 1969–70, Bob Stokoe 1970–72, Harry Potts 1972–76, Allan Brown 1976–78, Bob Stokoe 1978–79, Stan Ternent 1979–80, Alan Ball 1980–81, Allan Brown 1981–82, Sam Ellis 1982–89, Jimmy Mullen 1989–90, Graham Carr 1990, Bill Ayre 1990–94.

Player and Position	Ht	Wt	Birth Date	Birth Place	Source	Clubs	League App	League Gls
Philip Horner	6 1	12 07	10 11 66	Leeds	Lincoln C	Leicester C	10	—
						Rotherham U (loan)	4	—
						Halifax T	72	4
						Blackpool	153	20
Grant Leitch*	6 1	12 05	31 10 72	South Africa		Blackpool	25	1
James Quinn			15 12 74	Coventry	Trainee	Birmingham C	4	—
						Blackpool	14	2
						Stockport Co (loan)	1	—
David Robinson*	6 0	13 02	27 11 69	Newcastle	Trainee	Newcastle U	8	—
						Peterborough U (loan)	7	3
						Reading	8	—
						Blackpool	26	4
Tony Rodwell	5 11	11 02	26 8 62	Southport	Colne Dynamoes	Blackpool	133	17
Chris Speak*	6 0	12 04	20 8 73	Preston	Trainee	Blackpool	1	—
Paul Symons§			20 4 76	North Shields		Blackpool	1	—
Lee Thorpe§			14 12 75	Wolverhampton		Blackpool	1	—

Trainees
Birkman, Darren M; Capocci, Daniel; Carroll, David; Craggs, Graham; Croasdale, Peter J; Gawthorpe, Neil J; Lowery, Ian; Maclean, Fraser R; Parkinson, Stuart G; Shaw, Richard E; Sheppard, James H; Sunderland, Jonathan; Symons, Paul; Thompson, Paul D; Thorpe, Lee A; Torre, Stephen R; Ward, Robert D; Williams, Scott M.

****Non-Contract**
Bailey, Neil.

Associated Schoolboys
Ashcroft, Paul R; Birkman, Peter L; Black, Peter I. J; Blacow, Iain C; Carden, Paul; Cross, James R; Day, David R; Ellis, Thomas D; Foulds, Mark A; Haddow, Paul A; Hall, Gary A; Hartley, Michael G; Humphreys, Michael L; Hunt, Kris; Jones, Liam; Linklater, Paul; Mairs, Paul S. A; Perkes, Barry J; Ramsdale, Stephen; Shockledge, Lee S; Smith, Leigh I.

Associated Schoolboys who have accepted the Club's offer of a Traineeship/Contract
Hall, Lee D; Hills, John D.

**Non-Contract Players who are retained must be re-signed before they are eligible to play in League matches.

BOLTON WANDERERS 1993–94 *Back row (left to right):* Jason Lydiate, Andy Mason, Phil Brown, Alan Stubbs, Jimmy Phillips, Gary Parkinson.
Third row: Neil Fisher, Darren Oliver, Mark Patterson, Keith Branagan, Chris Clarke, Aidan Davison, Mark Winstanley, Mark Seagraves, David Burke.
Second row: Steve Carroll, Stuart Whittaker, Alan Thompson, Jason McAteer, Owen Coyle, Andy Roscoe, Andy Walker, David Lee, Ewan Simpson.
Front row: Scott Green, John McGinlay, Julian Darby, Bruce Rioch, Colin Todd, Steve Fulton, Tony Kelly, Nicky Spooner.

Division 1 BOLTON WANDERERS

Burnden Park, Bolton BL3 2QR. Telephone Bolton (0204) 389200. Fax (0204) 382334. Information Service: Bolton 21101. Commercial Dept. (0204) 24518.

Ground capacity: 22,500.

Record attendance: 69,912 v Manchester C, FA Cup 5th rd, 18 February 1933.

Record receipts: £158,364 v Everton, FA Cup 3rd rd, 8 January 1994.

Pitch measurements: 113yd × 76yd.

President: Nat Lofthouse.

Chairman: G. Hargreaves.

Directors: P. A. Gartside, G. Ball, G. Seymour, G. Warburton, W. B. Warburton, B. Scowcroft.

Team Manager: Bruce Rioch. ***Assistant Manager:*** Colin Todd. ***Physio:*** E. Simpson.

Chief Executive & Secretary: Des McBain. ***Commercial Manager:*** T. Holland.

Year Formed: 1874. ***Turned Professional:*** 1880. ***Ltd Co.:*** 1895.

Previous Name: 1874–77, Christ Church FC; 1877 became Bolton Wanderers.

Club Nickname: 'The Trotters'.

Previous Grounds: Park Recreation Ground and Cockle's Field before moving to Pike's Lane ground 1881; 1895, Burnden Park.

Record League Victory: 8–0 v Barnsley, Division 2, 6 October 1934 – Jones; Smith, Finney; Goslin, Atkinson, George Taylor; George T. Taylor (2), Eastham, Milsom (1), Westwood (4), Cook. (1 og).

Record Cup Victory: 13–0 v Sheffield U, FA Cup, 2nd rd, 1 February 1890 – Parkinson; Robinson (1), Jones; Bullough, Davenport, Roberts; Rushton, Brogan (3), Cassidy (5), McNee, Weir (4).

Record Defeat: 1–9 v Preston NE, FA Cup 2nd rd, 10 December 1887.

Most League Points (2 for a win): 61, Division 3, 1972–73.

Most League Points (3 for a win): 90, Division 2, 1992–93.

Most League Goals: 96, Division 2, 1934–35.

Highest League Scorer in Season: Joe Smith, 38, Division 1, 1920–21.

Most League Goals in Total Aggregate: Nat Lofthouse, 255, 1946–61.

Most Capped Player: Nat Lofthouse, 33, England.

Most League Appearances: Eddie Hopkinson, 519, 1956–70.

Record Transfer Fee Received: £340,000 from Birmingham C for Neil Whatmore, August 1981.

Record Transfer Fee Paid: £350,000 to WBA for Len Cantello, May 1979.

Football League Record: 1888 Founder Member of the League; 1899–1900 Division 2; 1900–03 Division 1; 1903–05 Division 2; 1905–08 Division 1; 1908–09 Division 2; 1909–10 Division 1; 1910–11 Division 2; 1911–33 Division 1; 1933–35 Division 2; 1935–64 Division 1; 1964–71 Division 2; 1971–73 Division 3; 1973–78 Division 2; 1978–80 Division 1; 1980–83 Division 2; 1983–87 Division 3; 1987–88 Division 4; 1988–92 Division 3; 1992–93 Division 2; 1993– Division 1.

Honours: *Football League:* Division 1 best season: 3rd, 1891–92, 1920–21, 1924–25; Division 2 – Champions 1908–09, 1977–78; Runners-up 1899–1900, 1904–05, 1910–11, 1934–35, 1992–93; Division 3 – Champions 1972–73. *FA Cup:* Winners 1923, 1926, 1929, 1958; Runners-up 1894, 1904, 1953. *Football League Cup:* Semi-final 1976–77. *Freight Rover Trophy:* Runners-up 1986. *Sherpa Van Trophy:* Winners 1989.

BOLTON WANDERERS 1993—94 LEAGUE RECORD

Match No.	Date	Venue	Opponents	Result		H/T Score	Lg. Pos.	Goalscorers	Attendance
1	Aug 14	A	Grimsby T	D	0-0	0-0	—		8593
2	21	H	Stoke C	D	1-1	0-0	17	Coyle	11,328
3	28	A	Charlton Ath	L	0-3	0-1	24		7573
4	31	H	Oxford U	W	1-0	1-0	—	McGinlay	8230
5	Sept 11	A	Luton T	W	2-0	1-0	11	McGinlay 2	7199
6	18	H	Leicester C	L	1-2	0-0	17	McGinlay (pen)	12,049
7	26	H	Nottingham F	W	4-3	1-2	—	Lee 2, Thompson, Patterson	10,578
8	Oct 2	A	Bristol C	L	0-2	0-1	16		7704
9	9	A	Tranmere R	L	1-2	1-1	18	Brown	10,128
10	16	H	Millwall	W	4-0	2-0	13	McGinlay 2, McAteer, Lee	9386
11	19	A	Birmingham C	L	1-2	0-0	—	Thompson	12,071
12	23	A	Watford	L	3-4	2-0	16	McAteer, Lee, Thompson	7492
13	30	H	Derby Co	L	0-2	0-0	19		11,464
14	Nov 2	H	Peterborough U	D	1-1	1-0	—	McGinlay	7058
15	6	A	WBA	D	2-2	0-2	20	Green, McAteer	15,709
16	21	A	Middlesbrough	W	1-0	1-0	—	McGinlay	6828
17	24	H	Crystal Palace	W	1-0	0-0	—	McGinlay	7486
18	27	A	Barnsley	D	1-1	1-1	14	Coyle	6755
19	Dec 7	H	WBA	D	1-1	0-0	—	Coyle	9277
20	11	A	Oxford U	W	2-0	0-0	13	Kelly, Thompson	5559
21	18	H	Grimsby T	D	1-1	1-1	13	Coyle	9431
22	27	H	Sunderland	D	0-0	0-0	13		18,496
23	28	A	Portsmouth	D	0-0	0-0	13		14,276
24	Jan 1	H	Notts Co	W	4-2	2-0	13	Fleck, Green, Thompson, Draper (og)	11,041
25	3	A	Wolverhampton W	L	0-1	0-1	14		24,053
26	12	A	Southend U	W	2-0	1-0	—	Stubbs, McGinlay	4969
27	15	A	Millwall	L	0-1	0-0	13		9772
28	23	H	Tranmere R	W	2-1	1-0	—	McGinlay 2	11,550
29	Feb 5	H	Watford	W	3-1	0-0	10	Coyle, Watson (og), McGinlay (pen)	10,150
30	12	A	Derby Co	L	0-2	0-1	11		16,698
31	22	A	Stoke C	L	0-2	0-1	—		14,257
32	25	A	Crystal Palace	D	1-1	0-1	13	Coyle	17,245
33	Mar 5	H	Charlton Ath	W	3-2	1-0	11	McGinlay 3 (1 pen)	13,027
34	19	A	Nottingham F	L	2-3	1-2	16	Brown, Green	23,846
35	26	H	Bristol C	D	2-2	2-1	16	Lee, Coyle	10,221
36	29	H	Wolverhampton W	L	1-3	0-1	—	McGinlay	12,405
37	Apr 2	A	Sunderland	L	0-2	0-0	18		18,574
38	4	H	Portsmouth	D	1-1	0-0	17	McGinlay	9560
39	9	A	Notts Co	L	1-2	0-1	17	McGinlay	7270
40	12	H	Southend U	L	0-2	0-2	—		7140
41	16	A	Peterborough U	W	3-2	0-1	17	Walker 2, Welsh (og)	6616
42	23	H	Middlesbrough	W	4-1	0-0	17	McGinlay 3, Green	9220
43	30	H	Birmingham C	D	1-1	1-1	17	Walker	13,602
44	May 3	A	Leicester C	D	1-1	1-0	—	McGinlay	18,145
45	5	H	Luton T	W	2-1	0-1	—	McGinlay, Thompson	7102
46	8	H	Barnsley	L	2-3	0-1	14	Seagraves, McGinlay	11,661

Final League Position: 14

GOALSCORERS

League (63): McGinlay 25 (3 pens), Coyle 7, Thompson 6, Lee 5, Green 4, McAteer 3, Walker 3, Brown 2, Fleck 1, Kelly 1, Patterson 1, Seagraves 1, Stubbs 1, own goals 3.
Coca-Cola Cup (3): Coyle 1, Kelly 1 (pen), McGinlay 1.
FA Cup (16): Coyle 5, McGinlay 3 (1 pen), McAteer 2, Stubbs 2, Brown 1, Patterson 1, Thompson 1, Walker 1.

Branagan 10	Brown 42	Phillips 41 + 1	Kelly 35	Burke 11 + 1	Winstanley 19 + 2	Lee 35 + 6	McAteer 45 + 1	Coyle 25 + 5	McGinlay 39	Thompson 19 + 8	Green 11 + 11	Stubbs 41	Patterson 34 + 1	Darby 3 + 2	Seagraves 32 + 3	Davison 30 + 1	Hoult 3 + 1	Fleck 6 + 1	Parkinson 1	Walker 7 + 4	Lydiate 5	Fulton 4	Roscoe 2 + 1	Walton 3	Fisher — + 2	Spooner 1	Whittaker 2	*Match No.*
1	2	3	4	5	6	7	8	9	10	11	12																	1
1	2	3	4	5		7	8	9	10	11		6	12															2
1	2	3	4	5		7	8	9	10	12		6	11															3
1	2	3	4	5		7	8	*9*	10	12		6	11	14														4
1	2	3	4			7	8	9	10	12		6	*11*	5	14													5
1	2	3	4			7	8	9	10	12		6	11	5														6
1	2	3	4			7	8	9		10	12	6	11	*5*	14													7
1	2	3	*4*			7	8		10	9	12	6	11	14	5													8
1	2	3	4			7	8		10	9	12	6	11		5													9
	2	3	4		6	7	8		10	9	12		11		5	1												10
	2	3	4			7	8		10	9		6	11		5	1												11
	2	3	4			7	8		10	9		6	11		5	1												12
1	2	3	4			7	8	12	10	9		6	11		5	14												13
	2	3	4			7	8		10		9	6	11		5	1												14
	2	3	*4*			7	8	12	10		9	6	11		5	1	14											15
	2	3	4		6	12	7	9	10	11		8			5		1											16
	2	3	4		6		7	9	10	11		8			5		1											17
	2	3	4		6		7	9	10	11		8			5		1											18
	2	3	4		6	12	7	9	10	11		8			5	1												19
	2	3	4		6	12	7	9	10	*11*	14	8			5	1												20
	2	3	4		6	10	7	9		11	12	8			*5*	1		14										21
	2			3	6	7	4	9			5	8	11		12	1		10										22
			4	3	6		7				9	8	11		5	1		10	2									23
	2	14		*3*	6	7	4	9		12	5	8	11			1		10										24
	2	3	4		6		7			12	9	8	11		5	1		10										25
	2			3		7	4		10		6	8	11		5	1		9										26
	2		4	3	6	7	5		10		12	8	11			1		9										27
	2	3	4		6	7	5	9	10	12		8	11			1												28
	2	3	4	12	6	7	5	9	10			8	*11*			1				14								29
	2	3	4			7	5	9	10			8	11		6	1				12								30
		3	4	8		14	5	9	10	*7*			11		6	1				12	2							31
		3	4	2		7	8	9	10				11		6	1					5							32
	2	3	4			7	8	9	10			6	11		5	1												33
	2	3	4		14	7	8	9	*10*		12	6	11		5	1												34
	2	3	4		14	7	8	9			12	6	11		5	1				*10*								35
	2	3			6	12	8	9	10	7		4	11		5	1												36
	2	3	*4*		6	7	8	9	10	14			11		5	1				12								37
	2	3					8		10		12	4			5	1				9	6	7	11					38
	2	3				12	8		10		9	4			5						6	7	11	1				39
	2	3	4			7	8		10			6	11		5					9				1				40
	2	3	*4*			7	8	12	10			6	11		5					9				1	14			41
	2	3				7	8	12	10		4	6	11		5	1				9								42
	2	3			5	7	8	12	10		4	6	11			1				9								43
	2	3			5	7	12		10		4	6	11			1				9	8							44
		3				7	8		10	11		6			5	1						4				2	9	45
	2	3				7	8		10	*11*		6			5	1						4	12		14		9	46

Coca-Cola Cup	First Round	Bury (h)	0-2
		(a)	2-0
	Second Round	Sheffield W (h)	1-1
		(a)	0-1
FA Cup	First Round	Gretna (a)	3-2
	Second Round	Lincoln C (a)	3-1
	Third Round	Everton (h)	1-1
		(a)	3-2
	Fourth Round	Arsenal (h)	2-2
		(a)	3-1
	Fifth Round	Aston Villa (h)	1-0
	Sixth Round	Oldham Ath (h)	0-1

BOLTON WANDERERS

Player and Position	Ht	Wt	Birth Date	Birth Place	Source	Clubs	League App	League Gls
Goalkeepers								
Keith Branagan	6 1	13 00	10 7 66	Fulham		Cambridge U	110	—
						Millwall	46	—
						Brentford (loan)	2	—
						Gillingham (loan)	1	—
						Fulham (loan)	—	—
						Bolton W	56	—
Chris Clarke*			1 5 74	Barnsley	Trainee	Bolton W	—	—
Aidan Davison	6 2	13 11	11 5 68	Sedgefield	Billingham Syn	Notts Co	1	—
						Leyton Orient (loan)	—	—
						Bury	—	—
						Chester C (loan)	—	—
						Blackpool (loan)	—	—
						Millwall	34	—
						Bolton W	31	—
Mark Walton‡	6 2	13 13	1 6 69	Merthyr	Swansea C	Luton T	—	—
						Colchester U	40	—
						Norwich C	22	—
						Wrexham (loan)	6	—
						Dundee	—	—
						Bolton W	3	—
Defenders								
Phil Brown*	5 11	11 06	30 5 59	South Shields	Local	Hartlepool U	217	8
						Halifax T	135	19
						Bolton W	256	14
David Burke*	5 10	11 00	6 8 60	Liverpool	Apprentice	Bolton W	69	1
						Huddersfield T	189	3
						Crystal Palace	81	—
						Bolton W	106	—
Jason Lydiate	5 11	12 07	29 10 71	Manchester	Trainee	Manchester U	—	—
						Bolton W	12	—
Andrew McKay	5 10	11 10	16 1 75	Bolton	Trainee	Bolton W	—	—
Jimmy Phillips	6 0	12 00	8 2 66	Bolton	Apprentice	Bolton W	108	2
						Rangers	25	—
						Oxford U	79	8
						Middlesbrough	139	6
						Bolton W	42	—
Mark Seagraves	6 1	12 10	22 10 66	Bootle		Liverpool	—	—
						Norwich C (loan)	3	—
						Manchester C	42	—
						Bolton W	144	7
Nicky Spooner	5 8	11 00	5 6 71	Manchester	Trainee	Bolton W	22	2
Alan Stubbs	6 2	12 12	6 10 71	Kirkby	Trainee	Bolton W	138	4
Mark Winstanley	6 1	12 04	22 1 68	St. Helens	Trainee	Bolton W	220	3
Midfield								
Neil Fisher	5 8	11 00	7 11 70	St Helens	Trainee	Bolton W	13	1
Stephen Fulton	5 10	11 00	10 8 70	Greenock	Celtic BC	Celtic	76	2
						Bolton W	4	—
						Peterborough U (loan)	3	—
Tony Kelly	5 10	11 09	1 10 64	Prescot	Liverpool	Derby Co	—	—
						Wigan Ath	101	15
						Stoke C	36	4
						WBA	26	1
						Chester C (loan)	5	—
						Colchester U (loan)	13	2
						Shrewsbury T	101	15
						Bolton W	102	5
Dave Lee	5 8	10 02	5 11 67	Manchester	Schools	Bury	208	35
						Southampton	20	—
						Bolton W	73	10
Jason McAteer	5 10	10 05	18 6 71	Liverpool	Marine	Bolton W	67	3
Andrew Roscoe	5 11	12 00	4 6 73	Liverpool	Trainee	Liverpool	—	—
						Bolton W	3	—
Alan Thompson	6 0	12 05	22 12 73	Newcastle	Trainee	Newcastle U	16	—
						Bolton W	27	6

BOLTON WANDERERS

Colours: White shirts, navy blue shorts, red stockings, blue and white tops. **Change colours:** Red and blue striped shirts, white shorts, red stockings.

Foundation: In 1874 boys of Christ Church Sunday School, Blackburn Street, led by their master Thomas Ogden, established a football club which went under the name of the school and whose president was Vicar of Christ Church. Membership was 6d (two and a half pence). When their president began to lay down too many rules about the use of church premises, the club broke away and formed Bolton Wanderers in 1877, holding their earliest meetings at the Gladstone Hotel.

First Football League game: 8 September, 1888, Football League, v Derby C (h), L 3-6 – Harrison; Robinson, Mitchell; Roberts, Weir, Bullough, Davenport (2), Milne, Coupar, Barbour, Brogan (1).

Did you know: On 13 November 1993, 100 years to the day that Bolton had previously played a Scottish team and beaten Third Lanark 3-2, they beat Gretna 3-2 in another FA Cup tie.

Managers (and Secretary-Managers)
Tom Rawthorne 1874–85*, J. J. Bentley 1885–86*, W. G. Struthers 1886–87*, Fitzroy Norris 1887*, J. J. Bentley 1887–95*, Harry Downs 1895–96*, Frank Brettell 1896–98*, John Somerville 1898–1910, Will Settle 1910–15, Tom Mather 1915–19, Charles Foweraker 1919–44, Walter Rowley 1944–50, Bill Ridding 1951–68, Nat Lofthouse 1968–70, Jimmy McIlroy 1970, Jimmy Meadows 1971, Nat Lofthouse 1971 (then admin. man. to 1972), Jimmy Armfield 1971–74, Ian Greaves 1974–80, Stan Anderson 1980–81, George Mulhall 1981–82, John McGovern 1982–85, Charlie Wright 1985, Phil Neal December 1985–92, Bruce Rioch May 1992–

Player and Position	Ht	Wt	Birth Date	Birth Place	Source	Clubs	League App	League Gls
Forwards								
Owen Coyle	5 11	10 5	14 7 66	Glasgow	Renfrew YM	Dumbarton	103	36
						Clydebank	63	33
						Airdrieonians	123	50
						Bolton W	30	7
Scott Green	6 0	11 12	15 1 70	Walsall	Trainee	Derby Co	—	—
						Bolton W	146	20
John McGinlay	5 9	11 06	8 4 64	Inverness	Elgin C	Shrewsbury T	60	27
						Bury	25	9
						Millwall	34	10
						Bolton W	73	41
Gary Martindale	5 11	11 09	24 6 71	Liverpool	Burscough	Bolton W	—	—
Andrew Mason	5 11	11 08	22 11 74	Bolton	Trainee	Bolton W	—	—
Mark Patterson	5 6	10 10	24 5 65	Darwen	Apprentice	Blackburn R	101	20
						Preston NE	55	19
						Bury	42	10
						Bolton W	127	7
Andy Walker	5 8	10 07	6 4 65	Glasgow	Baillieston J	Motherwell	76	17
						Celtic	108	30
						Newcastle U (loan)	2	—
						Bolton W	67	44
Stuart Whittaker	5 7	9 03	2 1 75	Liverpool	Liverpool	Bolton W	2	—

Trainees
Antrobus, Wayne A; Cumberbatch, Grant; Evans, Robert T. D; Fist, Dean T; Hamilton, Robin J; Harrison, Craig A; Hughes, Lee A; Leather, Ian; Osmand, Marc; Redmond, Brendan R; Wall, Ryan J; Whittle, Paul A; Wiggans, Andrew R.

Associated Schoolboys
Atkinson, Ian J; Chiswala, Tendai J; Darby, Philip; Doherty, Martin A; Fagan, Steven J; Feeney, Gareth T; Glennon, Mathew W; Hallatt, Christopher; Holden, Dean; Irwin, Nicholas J; Jordan, Richard; Lewis, Gary S; Lloyd, Steven M; McGaw, Daniel; Murray, Lee; Potter, Lee; Purslow, David J; Westhead, Mark L.

Associated Schoolboys who have accepted the Club's offer of a Traineeship/Contract
Bowman, Matthew S; Gregory, Christopher; Martin, Shaun A; Proctor, Daniel R.

AFC BOURNEMOUTH 1993–94 *Back row (left to right):* Mike Trusson (Youth Manager), Adrian Pennock, Steve Fletcher, Mark Morris, Alex Watson, Peter Shearer, Stuart Kerr, John Williams (Youth and Community Officer).

Centre row: Michael McElhatton, Keith Rowland, Joe Parkinson, Vince Bartram, Neil Moss, Neil Masters, Robert Murray, David Williams (Assistant Manager).

Front row: Steve Hardwick (Physio), Mark O'Connor, Paul Wood, Russell Beardsmore, Tony Pulis (Manager), Scott Mean, Brian McGorry, Paul Mitchell, Sean O'Driscoll (Community Officer/Physio).

Division 2 **AFC BOURNEMOUTH**

Dean Court Ground, Bournemouth, Dorset BH7 7AF. Telephone Bournemouth (0202) 395381. Fax: (0202) 309797.

Ground capacity: 11,880.

Record attendance: 28,799 v Manchester U, FA Cup 6th rd, 2 March 1957.

Record receipts: £33,723 v Manchester U, FA Cup 3rd rd, 7 January 1984.

Pitch measurements: 112yd × 75yd.

Chairman: N Hayward.

Directors: B. E. Willis (vice-chairman), E. G. Keep, G. M. C. Hayward, C. W. Legg, K. Gardiner.

Secretary: K. R. J. MacAlister.

Manager: Tony Pulis. ***First Team Coach:*** Mike Trusson. ***Youth team coach:*** John Williams. ***Physio: Steve Hardwick.***

Year Formed: 1899. ***Turned Professional:*** 1912. ***Ltd Co.:*** 1914.

Previous Names: Boscombe St Johns, 1890–99; Boscombe FC, 1899–1923; Bournemouth & Boscombe Ath FC, 1923–71.

Club Nickname: 'Cherries'.

Previous Grounds: 1899–1910, Castlemain Road, Pokesdown; 1910, Dean Court.

Record League Victory: 7–0 v Swindon T, Division 3 (S), 22 September 1956 – Godwin; Cunningham, Keetley; Clayton, Crosland, Rushworth; Siddall (1), Norris (2), Arnott (1), Newsham (2), Cutler (1). 10–0 win v Northampton T at start of 1939–40 expunged from the records on outbreak of war.

Record Cup Victory: 11–0 v Margate, FA Cup, 1st rd, 20 November 1971 – Davies; Machin (1), Kitchener, Benson, Jones, Powell, Cave (1), Boyer, MacDougall (9 incl. 1p), Miller, Scott (De Garis).

Record Defeat: 0–9 v Lincoln C, Division 3, 18 December 1982.

Most League Points (2 for a win): 62, Division 3, 1971–72.

Most League Points (3 for a win): 97, Division 3, 1986–87.

Most League Goals: 88, Division 3 (S), 1956–57.

Highest League Scorer in Season: Ted MacDougall, 42, 1970–71.

Most League Goals in Total Aggregate: Ron Eyre, 202, 1924–33.

Most Capped Player: Gerry Peyton, 7 (33), Republic of Ireland.

Most League Appearances: Sean O'Driscoll, 413, 1984–94.

Record Transfer Fee Received: £800,000 from Everton for Joe Parkinson, March 1994.

Record Transfer Fee Paid: £210,000 to Gillingham for Gavin Peacock, August 1989.

Football League Record: 1923 Elected to Division 3 (S). Remained a Third Division club for record number of years until 1970; 1970–71 Division 4; 1971–75 Division 3; 1975–82 Division 4; 1982–87 Division 3; 1987–90 Division 2; 1990– 92 Division 3; 1992– Division 2.

Honours: *Football League:* Division 3 – Champions 1986–87; Division 3 (S) – Runners-up 1947–48. Promotion from Division 4 1970–71 (2nd), 1981–82 (4th). *FA Cup:* best season: 6th rd, 1956–57. *Football League Cup:* best season: 4th rd, 1962, 1964. *Associate Members' Cup:* Winners 1984.

BOURNEMOUTH 1993—94 LEAGUE RECORD

Match No.	Date	Venue	Opponents	Result		H/T Score	Lg. Pos.	Goalscorers	Attendance
1	Aug 14	A	Bristol R	W	1-0	0-0	—	Fletcher	7234
2	21	H	Bradford C	D	1-1	0-0	8	Cotterill	4769
3	28	A	Hartlepool U	D	1-1	0-0	10	Parkinson	2482
4	31	H	York C	W	3-1	1-0	—	McGorry 2, Cotterill	4113
5	Sept 4	H	Burnley	W	1-0	1-0	4	Cotterill	5574
6	11	A	Barnet	W	2-1	2-0	2	Masters (pen), Fletcher	2979
7	18	H	Cambridge U	L	1-2	1-1	4	Cotterill	5200
8	25	A	Blackpool	L	1-2	1-1	9	Aspinall	4489
9	Oct 2	H	Stockport Co	D	1-1	0-1	12	Cotterill	4274
10	9	A	Fulham	W	2-0	0-0	10	Pennock, Fletcher	4004
11	16	H	Brighton & HA	W	2-1	1-0	8	Masters, McGorry	5896
12	23	A	Leyton Orient	D	0-0	0-0	7		3896
13	30	H	Exeter C	D	1-1	1-1	9	Wood	5102
14	Nov 6	A	Wrexham	L	1-2	0-1	11	Wood	4023
15	20	H	Hull C	L	0-2	0-2	15		4124
16	27	A	Reading	L	0-3	0-0	16		5549
17	Dec 7	H	Port Vale	W	2-1	1-0	—	Cotterill, Wood	2954
18	11	A	Bradford C	D	0-0	0-0	11		4407
19	18	H	Bristol R	W	3-0	3-0	10	Pennock, Wood, Cotterill	4811
20	27	H	Brentford	L	0-3	0-2	12		5744
21	Jan 1	H	Plymouth Arg	L	0-1	0-0	14		6990
22	3	A	Huddersfield T	D	1-1	0-0	14	Murray	6047
23	15	A	Brighton & HA	D	3-3	1-1	14	Murray 2, Aspinall	9689
24	22	H	Fulham	L	1-3	1-1	14	Murray	5464
25	29	A	Exeter C	W	2-0	1-0	13	Wood, Chivers	3602
26	Feb 5	H	Leyton Orient	D	1-1	1-1	14	O'Connor	4084
27	12	A	Swansea C	D	1-1	0-1	14	Cotterill	3255
28	19	H	Hartlepool U	D	0-0	0-0	14		3201
29	25	A	Burnley	L	0-4	0-2	14		10,383
30	Mar 5	H	Barnet	D	1-1	1-0	16	Aspinall	3407
31	8	A	Rotherham U	W	2-1	1-0	—	Aspinall, Cotterill	2884
32	12	A	Cambridge U	L	2-3	1-2	14	O'Connor 2	2836
33	15	H	Cardiff C	W	3-2	2-0	—	Cotterill 2, Chivers	2385
34	19	H	Blackpool	W	1-0	1-0	12	Cotterill	3335
35	22	A	York C	L	0-2	0-1	—		3648
36	26	A	Stockport Co	W	2-0	1-0	13	Cotterill, Burns	5277
37	29	H	Huddersfield T	L	1-2	0-1	—	Watson	3104
38	Apr 2	A	Brentford	D	1-1	1-0	14	Fletcher	4305
39	5	H	Rotherham U	D	0-0	0-0	—		3097
40	9	A	Plymouth Arg	L	0-2	0-1	15		7971
41	16	A	Port Vale	L	1-2	0-0	16	Pennock	7603
42	19	H	Swansea C	L	0-1	0-1	—		2465
43	21	A	Cardiff C	L	1-2	0-2	—	Fletcher	3838
44	23	H	Wrexham	L	1-2	0-1	18	Aspinall	2522
45	30	A	Hull C	D	1-1	1-0	19	Russell	4926
46	May 5	H	Reading	W	2-1	1-1	—	Fletcher, Cotterill	6739

Final League Position: 17

GOALSCORERS

League (51): Cotterill 14, Fletcher 6, Aspinall 5, Wood 5, Murray 4, McGorry 3, O'Connor 3, Pennock 3, Chivers 2, Masters 2 (1 pen), Burns 1, Parkinson 1, Russell 1, Watson 1.
Coca-Cola Cup (4): Beardsmore 1, Fletcher 1, Masters 1, Parkinson 1.
FA Cup (7): Aspinall 1 (pen), Cotterill 1, McGorry 1, Masters 1, Pennock 1, Watson 1, Wood 1.

Bartram 41	Pennock 40	Masters 18	Morris 38	Watson 45	Parkinson 30	O'Connor 45	McGorry 16	Fletcher 31 + 5	Cotterill 36 + 1	Beardsmore 15 + 9	Wood 11 + 5	Murray 5 + 15	Mean 1 + 4	Leadbitter 20 + 7	Aspinall 22 + 2	O'Driscoll 7 + 1	Chivers 24 + 2	McElhatton 6 + 4	Mitchell 4	Moss 5 + 1	Russell 17	Skinner 16	Burns 13 + 1	Kevan — + 1	Town — + 1	Match No.
1	2	3	4	5	6	7	8	9	10	11	12	14														1
1	2	3	4	5	6	7	8	9	10	11			12	14												2
1	2	3	4	5	6	7	8	9	10	11					12											3
1	2	3	4	5	6	7	8	9	10	11					12											4
1	2	3	4	5	6	7		9	10	11				12	8											5
1	2	3	4	5	6	7		9	10	11				12	8											6
1	2	3	4	5	6	7		9	10	11	12			14	8											7
1	2	3	4	5	6	7	8	9		14	12			11	10											8
1	2	3	4	5	6		8	9	10	11	12			7												9
1	2	3	4	5	6	7	8	9	10	12				11												10
1	2	3	4	5	6	7	8	9	10	11				12												11
1	2	3	4	5	6	7	8	9		11	12			10												12
1	2		4	5	6	7		9		11	10		8	3		12										13
1	2	3	4	5	6	7		9		12	10			11			8									14
1	2	3	4	5	6	7	8			12	11			10			9									15
1		3	4	5	6	7	8			12	11			10		9	2	14								16
1		3		5	6	7	8		10		9	12		11		2	4									17
1	11	3	4	5	6	7	8		10		9						2									18
1	2	3	4	5	6	7	8	9	10		11	12					14									19
1	2			5	6	7	8	9	10		11	12		3			14		4							20
1	2			5	6	7	8	9	10			12			11		4		3							21
1	2			5	6	7		9	10	12		14		3	8		4	11								22
1	9			5	6	7			10			11		3	8		4		2	12						23
	9			5		7		10		6		11	12	3	8		4		2	1						24
	2			5		7		14	10	12	9	11		3	8	6	4			1						25
	2			5	6	7		12	10		9	11		3	8		4			1						26
1	11		4	5	6	7			10		9	12		3	8		2									27
1			4	5	6	7		9	10	11		12		3	8		2									28
1			4	5	6	7		9	10	11		12	14	3	8		2									29
1	9		4	5	6	7		10		12		14		3	8		2				11					30
1	9		4	5		7			10			14		12	8		2	6			11	3				31
1	9		4			7			10			12			8		2	6			11	3	5			32
	8		4	5		7		9	10								2	12		1	11	3	6			33
1	2		4	5	9	7		8	10	12											11	3	6			34
1	2		4	5	8	7		9		10		12									11	3	6			35
1	9		4	5		7		12	10						8		2	14			11	3	6			36
1	9		4	5		7		12	10						8		2				11	3	6			37
1	9		4	5		7		8	10					12			2				11	3	6			38
1			4	5		7		9	10			12		8			2				11	3	6			39
1			4	5		7			10			9	12				2	8			11	3	6			40
1	6		4	5		7		9	10								2	8			11	3				41
1	6		4	5		7			10			12			9			8			11	3	2			42
1	2		4	5		7		12	10						8	9					11	3	6			43
1	2		4	5		7		9	12						10	6					11	3	8	14		44
1	2		4	5		7		9	10						8	6					11	3	12			45
	2		4	5		7		9	10							6		12		1	11	3	8		14	46

Coca-Cola Cup	First Round	Cardiff C (h)	3-1
		(a)	1-1
	Second Round	Barnsley (a)	0-1
		(h)	0-0
FA Cup	First Round	Brighton & HA (h)	4-2
	Second Round	Nuneaton (h)	1-1
		(a)	1-0
	Third Round	Preston NE (a)	1-2

AFC BOURNEMOUTH

Player and Position	Ht	Wt	Birth Date	Birth Place	Source	Clubs	League App	League Gls
Goalkeepers								
Vince Bartram	6 2	13 04	7 8 68	Birmingham	Local	Wolverhampton W	5	—
						Blackpool (loan)	9	—
						WBA (loan)	—	—
						Bournemouth	132	—
Neil Moss	6 1	12 11	10 5 75	New Milton	Trainee	Bournemouth	7	—
Defenders								
Gary Chivers†	5 11	11 05	15 5 60	Stockwell	Apprentice	Chelsea	133	4
						Swansea C	10	—
						QPR	60	—
						Watford	14	—
						Brighton	217	13
						Bournemouth	26	2
Michael McElhatton	6 0	12 08	16 4 75	Co.Kerry	Trainee	Bournemouth	11	—
Paul Morrell‡	5 11	13 05	23 3 61	Poole	Weymouth	Bournemouth	343	8
Mark Morris	6 1	13 08	26 9 62	Morden	Apprentice	Wimbledon	168	9
						Aldershot (loan)	14	—
						Watford	41	1
						Sheffield U	56	3
						Bournemouth	124	4
Adrian Pennock	5 11	12 01	27 3 71	Ipswich	Trainee	Norwich C	1	—
						Bournemouth	83	4
Alex Watson	6 0	11 09	5 4 68	Liverpool	Apprentice	Liverpool	4	—
						Derby Co (loan)	5	—
						Bournemouth	129	5
John Williams	6 1	13 12	3 10 60	Liverpool	Amateur	Tranmere R	173	13
						Port Vale	50	2
						Bournemouth	117	9
						Wigan Ath (loan)	4	—
						Cardiff C	6	—
						Bournemouth	—	—
Tim Wooding‡	6 00	12 00	5 7 73	Wellingborough	Trainee	Norwich C	—	—
						Bournemouth	—	—
Midfield								
Russell Beardsmore	5 6	8 10	28 9 68	Wigan	Apprentice	Manchester U	56	4
						Blackburn R (loan)	2	—
						Bournemouth	24	—
David Kevan*	5 8	10 12	31 8 68	Wigtown	Apprentice	Notts Co	89	3
						Cardiff C (loan)	7	—
						Stoke C	81	2
						Maidstone U (loan)	3	—
						Bournemouth	1	—
Scott Mean	5 11	11 11	13 12 73	Crawley	Trainee	Bournemouth	20	1
Mark O'Connor	5 7	10 02	10 3 63	Rochdale	Apprentice	QPR	3	—
						Exeter C (loan)	38	1
						Bristol R	80	10
						Bournemouth	128	12
						Gillingham	116	8
						Bournemouth	45	3
Sean O'Driscoll	5 8	11 03	1 7 57	Wolverhampton	Alvechurch	Fulham	148	13
						Bournemouth (loan)	19	1
						Bournemouth	394	18
Tony Pulis	5 10	11 08	16 1 58	Newport	Apprentice	Bristol R	85	3
					Happy Valley	Bristol R	45	2
						Newport Co	77	—
						Bournemouth	74	3
						Gillingham	16	—
						Bournemouth	16	1
David Williams‡	5 10	11 08	11 3 55	Cardiff	Clifton Ath	Bristol R	352	66
						Norwich C	60	11
						Bournemouth	1	—

AFC BOURNEMOUTH

Colours: Red shirts with white V shape & reverse V shape 3"pattern, black shorts with white piping, black stockings with red/white turnback. **Change colours:** Purple shirts with green & navy V shape & reverse V shape 3' pattern, white shorts, white stockings.

Foundation: There was a Bournemouth FC as early as 1875, but the present club arose out of the remnants of the Boscombe St John's club (formed 1890). The meeting at which Boscombe FC came into being was held at a house in Gladstone Road in 1899. They began by playing in the Boscombe and District Junior League.

First Football League game: 25 August, 1923, Division 3(S), v Swindon T (a), L 1-3 – Heron; Wingham, Lamb; Butt, C. Smith, Voisey; Miller, Lister (1), Davey, Simpson, Robinson.

Did you know: Bournemouth's best defensive record was established in 1981–82 when they conceded just 30 goals in 46 Division 4 matches. This helped immeasurably towards fourth place which ensured promotion. They also drew a club record 19 games that season.

Managers (and Secretary-Managers)
Vincent Kitcher 1914–23*, Harry Kinghorn 1923–25, Leslie Knighton 1925–28, Frank Richards 1928–30, Billy Birrell 1930–35, Bob Crompton 1935–36, Charlie Bell 1936–39, Harry Kinghorn 1939–47, Harry Lowe 1947–50, Jack Bruton 1950–56, Fred Cox 1956–58, Don Welsh 1958–61, Bill McGarry 1961–63, Reg Flewin 1963–65, Fred Cox 1965–70, John Bond 1970–73, Trevor Hartley 1974–78, John Benson 1975–78, Alec Stock 1979–80, David Webb 1980–82, Don Megson 1983, Harry Redknapp 1983–92, Tony Pulis 1992–

Player and Position	*Ht*	*Wt*	*Birth Date*	*Birth Place*	*Source*	*Clubs*	*League App*	*League Gls*
Forwards								
Warren Aspinall	5 8	11 00	13 9 67	Wigan	Apprentice	Wigan Ath	10	1
						Everton	7	—
						Wigan Ath (loan)	41	21
						Aston Villa	44	14
						Portsmouth	132	21
						Swansea C (loan)	5	—
						Bournemouth	24	5
Steve Cotterill	6 1	12 05	20 7 64	Cheltenham	Burton A	Wimbledon	17	6
						Brighton (loan)	11	4
						Bournemouth	37	14
Steve Fletcher	6 2	14 00	26 6 72	Hartlepool	Trainee	Hartlepool U	32	4
						Bournemouth	67	10
Stuart Kerr*	6 0	12 00	3 10 74	Bournemouth	Trainee	Bournemouth	—	—
Chris Leadbitter	5 9	10 07	17 10 67	Middlesbrough	Apprentice	Grimsby T	—	—
						Hereford U	36	1
						Cambridge U	176	18
						Bournemouth	27	—
Robert Murray	5 11	11 07	31 10 74	Hammersmith	Trainee	Bournemouth	45	8
Kevin Russell	5 8	10 12	6 12 66	Portsmouth	Brighton	Portsmouth	4	1
						Wrexham	84	43
						Leicester C	43	10
						Peterborough U (loan)	7	3
						Cardiff C (loan)	3	—
						Hereford U (loan)	3	1
						Stoke C (loan)	5	1
						Stoke C	40	5
						Burnley	28	6
						Bournemouth	17	1
David Town§			9 12 76	Bournemouth	Trainee	Bournemouth	1	—

Trainees
Barfoot, Stuart J; Carcary, Murray J; Champion, Neil B; Eastland, Robert L; Ferrett, Christopher A; Hearn Matthew C; Jones, Mark D; Reeve, James M; Town, David E.

****Non-Contract**
Chivers, Gary P. S.

Associated Schoolboys
Camfield, Adam J; Cox, Robin A; Daniel, Gareth; Griffin, Anthony R; Howe, Edward J; Kemp, Steven; Preston, Jonathan R; Taylor, Robert A; Vivian, Stuart L; Wyatt, Richard.

Associated Schoolboys who have accepted the Club's offer of a Traineeship/Contract
Benson, David; Dean, Michael J; Smith, Mark L; Strong, Steven G; Unwin, Trevor D; Wells, David.
**Non-Contract Palyers who are retained must be re-signed before they are eligible to play in League matches.

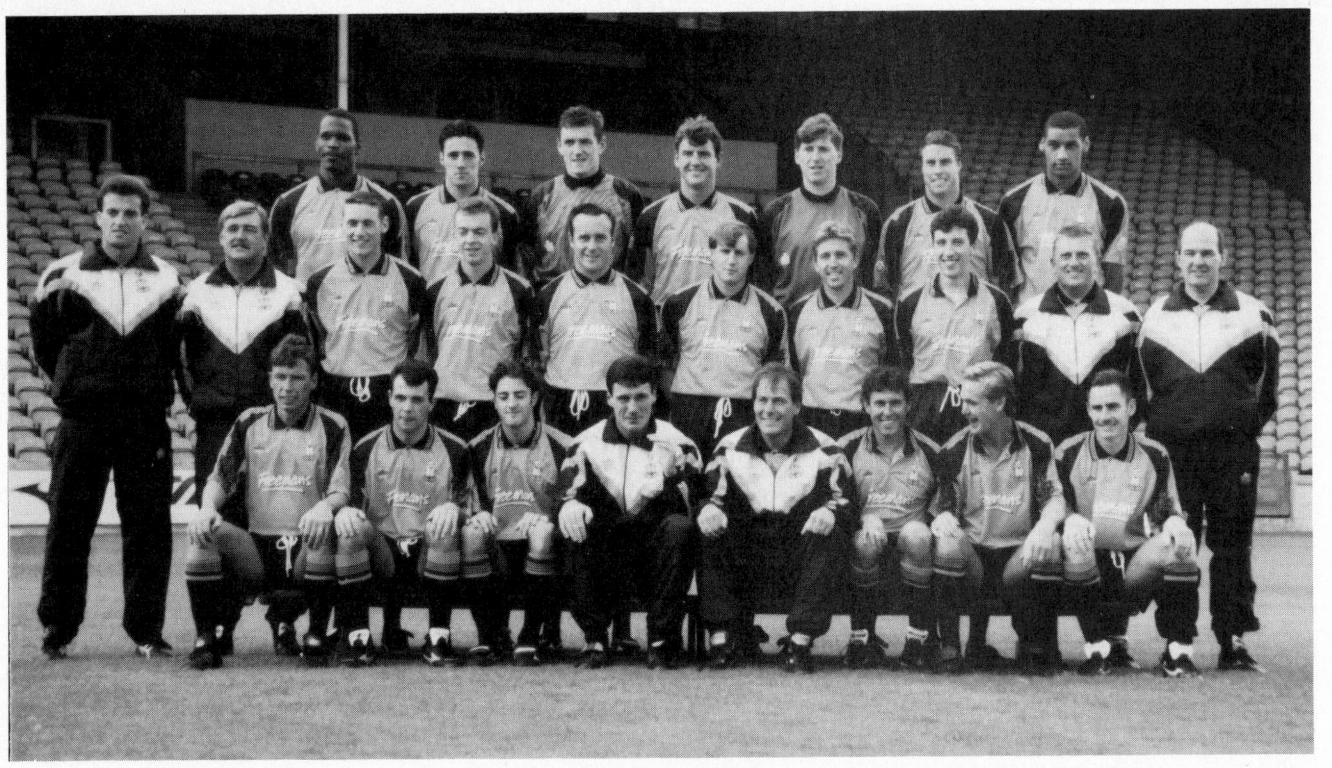

BRADFORD CITY 1993–94 *Back row (left to right):* Noel Blake, Colin Hoyle, Ian Bowling, Gavin Oliver, Paul Tomlinson, Sean McCarthy, Dean Richards.
Centre row: Steve Foster (Physio), Steve Smith (Youth Coach), Richard Wilson, Michael McHugh, Wayne Heseltine, Paul Jewell, Gary Robson, Tim Steele, Andy Hanson (Chief Scout), Alan Jackson (Reserve Physio).
Front row: Michael Duxbury, Craig Lawford, Scott Partridge, Frank Stapleton (Manager), Stuart Pearson (Assistant Manager), Gary Williams, Lee Duxbury, Paul Reid.

Division 2 **BRADFORD CITY**

Valley Parade Ground, Bradford BD8 7DY. Telephone Bradford (0274) 306062 (Office); Fax (0274) 307457.

Ground capacity: 14,387.

Record attendance: 39,146 v Burnley, FA Cup 4th rd, 11 March 1911.

Record receipts: £59,250 v Tottenham H, FA Cup 3rd rd, 7 January 1989.

Pitch measurements: 110yd × 76yd.

Chairman: Geoffrey Richmond. ***Vice-chairman:*** David Thompson FCA.

Directors: Elizabeth Richmond, David Richmond, Terry Goddard.

Manager: Lennie Lawrence. ***Assistant Manager:*** —.

Youth Coach: Steve Smith. ***Physio:*** Leena Stocks.

Secretary: Shaun Harvey. ***Commercial Manager: Allan Gilliver.***

Year Formed: 1903. ***Turned Professional:*** 1903. ***Ltd Co.:*** 1908.

Club Nickname: 'The Bantams'.

Record League Victory: 11–1 v Rotherham U, Division 3 (N), 25 August 1928 – Sherlaw; Russell, Watson; Burkinshaw (1), Summers, Bauld; Harvey (2), Edmunds (3), White (3), Cairns, Scriven (2).

Record Cup Victory: 11–3 v Walker Celtic, FA Cup, 1st rd (replay), 1 December 1937 – Parker; Rookes, McDermott; Murphy, Mackie, Moore; Bagley (1), Whittingham (1), Deakin (4 incl. 1p), Cooke (1), Bartholomew (4).

Record Defeat: 1–9 v Colchester U, Division 4, 30 December 1961.

Most League Points (2 for a win): 63, Division 3 (N), 1928–29.

Most League Points (3 for a win): 94, Division 3, 1984–85.

Most League Goals: 128, Division 3 (N), 1928–29.

Highest League Scorer in Season: David Layne, 34, Division 4, 1961–62.

Most League Goals in Total Aggregate: Bobby Campbell, 121, 1981–84, 1984–86.

Most Capped Player: Harry Hampton, 9, Northern Ireland.

Most League Appearances: Cec Podd, 502, 1970–84.

Record Transfer Fee Received: £850,000 from Everton for Stuart McCall, June 1988.

Record Transfer Fee Paid: £290,000 to Newcastle U for Peter Jackson, October 1988.

Football League Record: 1903 Elected to Division 2; 1908–22 Division 1; 1922–27 Division 2; 1927–29 Division 3 (N); 1929–37 Division 2; 1937–61 Division 3; 1961–69 Division 4; 1969–72 Division 3; 1972–77 Division 4; 1977–78 Division 3; 1978–82 Division 4; 1982–85 Division 3; 1985–90 Division 2; 1990–92 Division 3; 1992– Division 2.

Honours: *Football League:* Division 1 best season: 5th, 1910–11; Division 2 – Champions 1907–08; Division 3 – Champions 1984–85; Division 3 (N) – Champions 1928–29; Division 4 – Runners-up 1981–82. *FA Cup:* Winners 1911 (first holders of the present trophy). *Football League Cup:* best season: 5th rd, 1965, 1989.

BRADFORD CITY 1993—94 LEAGUE RECORD

Match No.	Date	Venue	Opponents	Result		H/T Score	Lg. Pos.	Goalscorers	Attendance
1	Aug 14	H	Brighton & HA	W	2-0	2-0	—	McCarthy, Jewell	6074
2	21	A	Bournemouth	D	1-1	0-0	6	Reid (pen)	4769
3	28	H	Exeter C	W	6-0	3-0	1	McCarthy 2, Reid 2, Jewell 2	5866
4	31	A	Stockport Co	L	1-4	1-1	—	McCarthy	4236
5	Sept 4	A	Fulham	D	1-1	1-0	8	McCarthy	4221
6	11	H	Blackpool	W	2-1	1-1	5	McCarthy, Richards	6869
7	15	H	Reading	L	2-4	0-1	—	McCarthy 2	4853
8	18	A	Swansea C	L	0-2	0-1	12		3373
9	25	H	Cambridge U	W	2-0	0-0	7	Duxbury L, McCarthy	5666
10	Oct 2	A	Hull C	L	1-3	1-2	13	McCarthy	9492
11	9	A	Bristol R	L	3-4	1-0	14	Showler, Duxbury L 2	5323
12	16	H	Burnley	L	0-1	0-1	16		9501
13	23	A	Hartlepool U	W	2-1	1-1	15	Duxbury L, McCarthy	2536
14	30	H	York C	D	0-0	0-0	15		6729
15	Nov 2	H	Huddersfield T	W	3-0	0-0	—	Starbuck (og), McCarthy 2	8096
16	6	A	Barnet	W	2-1	1-0	9	Showler, Duxbury L	2350
17	20	H	Plymouth Arg	L	1-5	0-3	9	Nicholls (og)	5204
18	27	A	Cardiff C	D	1-1	0-0	10	McCarthy	4213
19	Dec 11	H	Bournemouth	D	0-0	0-0	12		4407
20	18	A	Brighton & HA	W	1-0	0-0	11	Williams (pen)	6535
21	27	H	Rotherham U	W	2-1	1-0	10	Reid, Duxbury L	7765
22	29	A	Brentford	L	0-2	0-1	10		6059
23	Jan 1	H	Wrexham	W	1-0	0-0	8	Robson	5829
24	8	H	Leyton Orient	D	0-0	0-0	11		5260
25	15	A	Burnley	W	1-0	0-0	10	Showler	13,517
26	22	H	Bristol R	L	0-1	0-1	10		6122
27	29	A	York C	D	1-1	1-1	10	Showler	5985
28	Feb 5	H	Hartlepool U	W	2-1	2-0	9	Robson, Tolson	7907
29	12	A	Leyton Orient	L	1-2	1-1	10	Reid	3690
30	19	A	Exeter C	D	0-0	0-0	11		2758
31	Mar 1	A	Port Vale	D	0-0	0-0	—		7294
32	5	A	Blackpool	W	3-1	1-0	10	Showler, Tomlinson G, Duxbury L	5276
33	12	H	Swansea C	W	2-1	0-0	9	Duxbury L, Power	8220
34	15	A	Reading	D	1-1	0-1	—	Power	5293
35	19	A	Cambridge U	L	1-2	1-0	10	Tomlinson G	3095
36	26	H	Hull C	D	1-1	0-1	10	Tomlinson G	9419
37	29	H	Port Vale	W	2-1	0-1	—	Jewell, Tolson	5776
38	Apr 2	A	Rotherham U	L	1-2	1-1	10	Tomlinson G	4604
39	4	H	Brentford	W	1-0	0-0	9	Reid	6703
40	9	A	Wrexham	W	3-0	2-0	9	Reid 2 (1 pen), Jewell	3406
41	13	H	Fulham	D	0-0	0-0	—		5015
42	17	A	Huddersfield T	D	1-1	1-0	—	Williams (pen)	9342
43	26	H	Stockport Co	L	1-2	0-0	—	Duxbury L	5720
44	30	A	Plymouth Arg	L	1-3	1-1	10	Tomlinson G	10,985
45	May 3	H	Barnet	W	2-1	0-0	—	Hamilton, Tomlinson G	3472
46	7	H	Cardiff C	W	2-0	0-0	7	Reid, Richards	6642

Final League Position: 7

GOALSCORERS

League (61): McCarthy 14, Duxbury L 9, Reid 9 (2 pens), Tomlinson G 6, Jewell 5, Showler 5, Power 2, Richards 2, Robson 2, Tolson 2, Williams 2 (2 pens), Hamilton 1, own goals 2.
Coca-Cola Cup (13): McCarthy 7, Jewell 3, Reid 1, Showler 1, Steele 1.
FA Cup (0):

Tomlinson P 23	Hoyle 22 + 7	Heseltine 11 + 1	Duxbury L 43	Richards 46	Oliver 35	Steele 8 + 3	Robson 46	McCarthy 18	Jewell 28 + 2	Reid 36 + 2	Stapleton 16 + 12	Showler 26 + 6	Williams 31 + 1	Blake 7	Lawford 8 + 3	Ford 5	McHugh 3 + 2	Bowling 23	Partridge — + 1	Tomlinson G 12 + 5	Barlow 2	Sinnott 18	Duxbury M 12 + 1	Tolson 16 + 6	Wilson 5	Power 2 + 1	Grayston 2	Hamilton 2	*Match No.*
1	2	3	4	5	6	7	8	9	10	11																			1
1	2	3	4	5	6	*7*	8	9	10	11	12	14																	2
1		3	4	5	6	*7*	8	9	10	11	12	14	2																3
1		3	4	5	6	*7*	8	9	10	11	12	14	2																4
1		3		6		7	8	9	10	4	12	11	2	5															5
1		3		5	6		8	9	7	10	4	11	2		12														6
1		3		5	6	12	8	9	7	10	4	11			2														7
1			4	5	6	12	8	9	7		10	11			3	2													8
1			4	5	6	10	8	9	7			11			3	2	12												9
			4	5	6		8	9	7			11			3	2	10	1											10
		12	4	5	6		8	9	*7*			11	10		3	2		1	14										11
		3	4	5	*6*	12	8	9	7			11	10		14	2		1											12
1		3	4	6			8	9	12			11	2	5	10		7												13
1		3	4	6			8	9	*7*	12		11	2	5	10					14									14
1			4	6			8	9	7	10		11	2	5							3								15
			4	6			8	9	7	10		11	2	5				1			3								16
			4	6			8	9		10	2	11		5	3		7	1											17
	14	3	4	6			8	9	*10*	11	12	7	2	5				1											18
	14		4	5	6		8			11	*10*	12	2					1				3	7	9					19
	14		4	5	6		8			11	*10*	12	2					1				3	7	9					20
	14		7	5	6		8			10	12	11	*2*					1				3	4	9					21
	2		7	5	6		8			11	10	12						1				3	4	9					22
	2		4	5	6	7	8			10	12	11						1				3		9					23
	2		4	5	6	7	8			10	12	11						1				3		9					24
	2		4	5	6		8					11						1				3	7	9	10				25
	2		4	5	6		8					11						1				3	7	9	10				26
	2		4	5	6		8			12		11						1				3	7	9	10				27
	2		4	5	6		8			7		11						1				3		9	10				28
	2		4	5	6		8			7	12	11	14					1				*3*		9	10				29
	2		4	5	6		8		12	7	10	11	3					1						9					30
	2		4	5	6		8		10	7	9	11	3					1		12									31
	2		4	5	6		8		10	7	*9*	11	3					1		14			12						32
	2		4	5	6		8		10	7		11	3					1		12						9			33
	2		4	5	6		8		10	7	12		3					1		14			11			*9*			34
	2		4	5	6		8		7	11	9		3				12	1		10									35
1	2		4	5	6		8		10	11	12		*3*		14					9			7						36
1	2		4	5	6		8		7	11	10		3							9				12					37
1	2		4	5	6		8		7	11	10		3							9				12					38
1	2		4	5	6		8		7	11			3							9				10					39
1	14		4	5	6		8		7	11	10		*2*							9		3		12					40
1	14		4	5	6		8		7	11	10		*2*							9		3		12					41
1			4	5	6		8		7	11			2							9		3	10	12					42
1	3		4	6			8			11	12		2							9		5	10	7					43
1	2		4	6			8			11	10		3							9		5	*7*	12		14			44
1			4	6			8			11			2							9		5		10			3	7	45
1	12		4	6			8			11			2							9		5		10			3	7	46

Coca-Cola Cup	First Round	Darlington (a)	5-1
		(h)	6-0
	Second Round	Norwich C (h)	2-1
		(a)	0-3
FA Cup	First Round	Chester C (h)	0-0
		(a)	0-1

BRADFORD CITY

Player and Position	Ht	Wt	Birth Date	Birth Place	Source	Clubs	League App	League Gls
Goalkeepers								
Ian Bowling	6 3	14 08	27 7 65	Sheffield	Gainsborough T	Lincoln C	59	—
						Hartlepool U (loan)	1	—
						Bradford C (loan)	7	—
						Bradford C	23	—
Paul Tomlinson	6 2	13 12	22 2 64	Brierley Hill	Middlewood R	Sheffield U	37	—
						Birmingham C (loan)	11	—
						Bradford C	256	—
Defenders								
Wayne Benn	5 10	11 00	7 8 76	Pontefract	Trainee	Bradford C	—	—
Noel Blake (To Dundee December 1993)	6 0	13 11	12 1 62	Jamaica	Sutton Coldfield	Aston Villa	4	—
						Shrewsbury T (loan)	6	—
						Birmingham C	76	5
						Portsmouth	144	10
						Leeds U	51	4
						Stoke C	75	3
						Bradford C (loan)	6	—
						Bradford C	39	3
Mike Duxbury*	5 9	11 02	1 9 59	Accrington	Apprentice	Manchester U	299	6
						Blackburn R	27	—
						Bradford C	65	—
Neil Grayston§	5 8	10 09	25 11 75	Keighley	Trainee	Bradford C	2	—
Wayne Heseltine*	5 9	11 06	3 12 69	Bradford	Trainee	Manchester U	—	—
						Oldham Ath	1	—
						Bradford C	54	1
Craig Lawford*	5 10	11 10	25 11 72	Dewsbury	Trainee	Bradford C	20	1
Gavin Oliver	6 0	12 10	6 9 62	Felling	Apprentice	Sheffield W	20	—
						Tranmere R (loan)	17	1
						Brighton (loan)	16	—
						Bradford C	302	9
Dean Richards	6 0	12 00	9 6 74	Bradford	Trainee	Bradford C	56	3
Wayne Scargill	5 10	11 09	30 4 68	Barnsley	Frickley Ath	Bradford C	—	—
Lee Sinnott	6 1	12 07	12 7 65	Pelsall	Apprentice	Walsall	40	2
						Watford	78	2
						Bradford C	173	6
						Crystal Palace	55	—
						Bradford C	18	—
Gary Williams*	5 9	11 12	17 6 60	Wolverhampton	Apprentice	Aston Villa	240	—
						Walsall (loan)	9	—
						Leeds U	39	3
						Watford	42	—
						Bradford C	85	5
Richard Wilson‡			12 3 75	Bradford	Trainee	Bradford C	—	—
Midfield								
Lee Duxbury	5 10	11 07	7 10 69	Skipton	Trainee	Bradford C	189	25
						Rochdale (loan)	10	—
Derrick Hamilton§	5 11	11 10	15 8 76	Bradford	Trainee	Bradford C	2	1
Paul Reid	5 8	10 08	19 1 68	Warley	Apprentice	Leicester C	162	21
						Bradford C (loan)	7	—
						Bradford C	82	15
Gary Robson	5 7	10 12	6 7 65	Durham	Apprentice	WBA	218	28
						Bradford C	46	2
Paul Showler	5 10	11 06	10 10 66	Doncaster	Altrincham	Barnet	71	12
						Bradford C	32	5
Forwards								
Colin Hoyle*	5 11	12 03	15 1 72	Derby	Trainee	Arsenal	—	—
						Chesterfield (loan)	3	—
						Barnsley	—	—
						Bradford C	62	1
Paul Jewell	5 8	11 10	28 9 64	Liverpool	Apprentice	Liverpool	—	—
						Wigan Ath	137	35
						Bradford C	213	39

BRADFORD CITY

Colours: Claret and amber shirts, black shorts, black stockings. **Change colours:** Blue shirts, blue shorts, blue stockings.

Foundation: Bradford was a rugby stronghold around the turn of the century but after Manningham RFC held an archery contest to help them out of financial difficulties in 1903, they were persuaded to give up the handling code and turn to soccer. So they formed Bradford City and continued at Valley Parade. Recognising this as an opportunity of spreading the dribbling code in this part of Yorkshire, the Football League immediately accepted the new club's first application for membership of the Second Division.

First Football League game: 1 September, 1903, Division 2, v Grimsby T (a), L 0-2 – Seymour; Wilson, Halliday; Robinson, Millar, Farnall; Guy, Beckram, Forrest, McMillan, Graham.

Did you know: Bradford City hold the record for most consecutive cup games without conceding a goal. From the third round in 1910–11 to the third round replay the following season they completed 12 matches in such a manner.

Managers (and Secretary-Managers)
Robert Campbell 1903–05, Peter O'Rourke 1905–21, David Menzies 1921–26, Colin Veitch 1926–28, Peter O'Rourke 1928–30, Jack Peart 1930–35, Dick Ray 1935–37, Fred Westgarth 1938–43, Bob Sharp 1943–46, Jack Barker 1946–47, John Milburn 1947–48, David Steele 1948–52, Albert Harris 1952, Ivor Powell 1952–55, Peter Jackson 1955–61, Bob Brocklebank 1961–64, Bill Harris 1965–66, Willie Watson 1966–69, Grenville Hair 1967–68, Jimmy Wheeler 1968–71, Bryan Edwards 1971–75, Bobby Kennedy 1975–78, John Napier 1978, George Mulhall 1978–81, Roy McFarland 1981–82, Trevor Cherry 1982–87, Terry Dolan 1987–89, Terry Yorath 1989–90, John Docherty 1990–91, Frank Stapleton 1991–94, Lennie Lawrence May 1994–

Player and Position	*Ht*	*Wt*	*Birth Date*	*Place*	*Source*	*Clubs*	*League App*	*Gls*
Lee Power	5 11	11 02	30 6 72	Lewisham	Trainee	Norwich C	44	10
						Charlton Ath (loan)	5	—
						Sunderland (loan)	3	—
						Portsmouth (loan)	2	—
						Bradford C	3	2
Frank Stapleton	6 0	13 01	10 7 56	Dublin	Apprentice	Arsenal	225	75
						Manchester U	223	60
						Ajax	4	—
						Derby Co	10	1
					Le Havre	Blackburn R	81	13
						Aldershot	—	—
						Huddersfield T	5	—
						Bradford C	68	2
Neil Tolson	6 1	10 07	25 10 73	Wordley	Trainee	Walsall	9	1
						Oldham Ath	3	—
						Bradford C	22	2
Graeme Tomlinson	5 9	11 07	10 12 75	Keighley	Trainee	Bradford C	17	6

Trainees
Benn, Wayne; Blair, David A; Carss, Anthony J; Grayston, Neil J; Hamilton, Derrik V; Jackson, Scott; Lowe, Anthony S; Lynch, Michael; Midgley, Craig S; Murphy, Brendan F; Proctor, James A; Richardson, Christopher; Stabb, Christopher J; Stuttard, Andrew J; Tomlinson, Graeme M.

Associated Schoolboys
Airdrie, Stewart W; Aldred, Andrew J; Bates, Craig A; Bolland, Paul G; Briggs, Ian M; Brown, Paul M; Cannon, Alex; Davies, Robert A; Edwards, Gavin P; Edwards, Ian D; Feltwell, Peter A; Freeman, Wesley G; Goff, Leslie A; Harrison, Spencer K; Helliwell, Jonathan L; Jama, Paul M; Kearns, Marc J; Kitchen, Simon J; Long, Alistair D; McLean, Ian J; Nichols, Stuart J; O'Brien, Andrew J; Palmer, Dean; Patten, Carl B; Serrant, Wesley P; Stead, Nathan M; Symonds, David K; Thirkhill, James M; Wardman, Paul J; Yates, David A.

Associated Schoolboys who have accepted the Club's offer of a Traineeship/Contract
Davey, Ben J. N; Holmes, Richard M; Mazurke, Shane.

BRENTFORD 1993–94 *Back row (left to right):* Keith Millen, Marcus Gayle, Graham Benstead, Terry Evans, Tamer Fernandes, Jamie Bates, Shane Westley, Dean Williams.
Centre row: David Webb (Manager), Kevin Lock (Assistant Manager), Joe Allon, Danny Sains, Carl Hutchings, Simon Ratcliffe, Scott Morgan, Stuart Morgan (Youth Team Manager), Roy Clare (Physio).
Front row: Micky Bennett, Paul Stephenson, Brian Statham, Grant Chalmers, Billy Manuel, Paul Buckle, Rob Peters, Paul Smith, Craig Ravenscroft.

Division 2 BRENTFORD

Griffin Park, Braemar Rd, Brentford, Middlesex TW8 0NT. Telephone 081–847 2511. Fax 081–568 9940. Commercial Dept: 081–560 6062. Press Office: 081–574 3047. Clubcall: 0898 121108.

Ground capacity: 13,870.

Record attendance: 39,626 v Preston NE, FA Cup 6th rd, 5 March 1938.

Record receipts: £79,838 v Tottenham H, Coca Cola Cup 2nd rd 2nd leg, 7 October 1992.

Pitch measurements: 111yd × 74yd.

President: W. Wheatley. ***Life Vice-president:*** F. Edwards.

Chairman: M. M. Lange. ***Vice-chairman:*** G. V. Potter.

Directors: B. Evans, J. Herting, E. J. Radley-Smith MS, FRCS, LRCP, D. Tana.

Managing Director: Keith Loring.

Manager: David Webb. ***Assistant Manager:*** Kevin Lock.

Physio: Roy Johnson.

Youth Team Manager: Peter Nicholas.

Community Officer: Lee Doyle.

Secretary: Polly Kates.

Press Officer/Programme Editor: Eric White (081–574 3047). ***Promotions Manager:*** Royce Dickinson. ***Safety officer:*** Jill Dawson.

Year Formed: 1889. ***Turned Professional:*** 1899. ***Ltd Co.:*** 1901.

Club Nickname: 'The Bees'.

Previous Grounds: 1889–91, Clifden Road; 1891–95, Benns Fields, Little Ealing; 1895–98, Shotters Field; 1898–1900, Cross Road, S. Ealing; 1900–04, Boston Park; 1904, Griffin Park.

Record League Victory: 9–0 v Wrexham, Division 3, 15 October 1963 – Cakebread; Coote, Jones; Slater, Scott, Higginson; Summers (1), Brooks (2), McAdams (2), Ward (2), Hales (1). (1 og).

Record Cup Victory: 7–0 v Windsor & Eton (away), FA Cup, 1st rd, 20 November 1982 – Roche; Rowe, Harris (Booker), McNichol (1), Whitehead, Hurlock (2), Kamara, Bowles, Joseph (1), Mahoney (3), Roberts.

Record Defeat: 0–7 v Swansea T, Division 3 (S), 8 November 1924 and v Walsall, Division 3 (S), 19 January 1957.

Most League Points (2 for a win): 62, Division 3 (S), 1932–33 and Division 4, 1962–63.

Most League Points (3 for a win): 82, Division 3, 1991–92.

Most League Goals: 98, Division 4, 1962–63.

Highest League Scorer in Season: Jack Holliday, 38, Division 3 (S), 1932–33.

Most League Goals in Total Aggregate: Jim Towers, 153, 1954–61.

Most Capped Player: John Buttigieg, (53), Malta.

Most League Appearances: Ken Coote, 514, 1949–64.

Record Transfer Fee Received: £720,000 from Wimbledon for Dean Holdsworth, August 1992.

Record Transfer Fee Paid: £275,000 to Chelsea for Joe Allon, November 1992.

Football League Record: 1920 Original Member of Division 3; 1921–33 Division 3 (S); 1933–35 Division 2; 1935–47 Division 1; 1947–54 Division 2; 1954–62 Division 3 (S); 1962–63 Division 4; 1963–66 Division 3; 1966–72 Division 4; 1972–73 Division 3; 1973–78 Division 4; 1978–92 Division 3; 1992–93 Division 1; 1993– Division 2.

Honours: *Football League:* Division 1 best season: 5th, 1935–36; Division 2 – Champions 1934–35; Division 3 – Champions 1991–92; Division 3 (S) – Champions 1932–33; Runners-up 1929–30, 1957–58; Division 4 – Champions 1962–63. *FA Cup:* best season: 6th rd, 1938, 1946, 1949, 1989. *Football League Cup:* best season: 4th rd, 1982–83. *Freight Rover Trophy* – Runners-up 1985.

BRENTFORD 1993—94 LEAGUE RECORD

Match No.	Date	Venue	Opponents	Result		H/T Score	Lg. Pos.	Goalscorers	Attendance
1	Aug 14	H	Exeter C	W	2-1	1-1	—	Allon, Gayle	5537
2	21	A	Blackpool	D	1-1	1-0	7	Allon	4024
3	28	H	Reading	W	1-0	1-0	5	Allon	6848
4	31	A	Hull C	L	0-1	0-1	—		4517
5	Sept 4	A	Rotherham U	L	0-2	0-2	12		4333
6	11	H	Swansea C	D	1-1	0-1	15	Ratcliffe	5042
7	14	H	Leyton Orient	L	0-1	0-0	—		5149
8	18	A	Brighton & HA	L	1-2	1-0	21	Williams DA	5734
9	25	H	Port Vale	L	1-2	0-0	22	Gayle	5106
10	Oct 2	A	Cambridge U	D	1-1	1-0	22	Benjamin	3612
11	9	A	Hartlepool U	W	1-0	0-0	19	Benjamin	1802
12	16	H	Wrexham	W	2-1	1-0	15	Ratcliffe, Allon	5801
13	23	A	York C	W	2-0	0-0	14	Smith, Allon	3513
14	30	H	Barnet	W	1-0	0-0	10	Allon	5873
15	Nov 2	H	Cardiff C	D	1-1	1-0	—	Allon	4756
16	6	A	Plymouth Arg	D	1-1	0-1	12	Allon	6407
17	20	H	Burnley	D	0-0	0-0	11		6085
18	27	A	Huddersfield T	W	3-1	2-0	9	Mundee 2 (2 pens), Ravenscroft	4544
19	Dec 11	H	Blackpool	W	3-0	2-0	9	Gayle, Mundee 2	4769
20	18	A	Exeter C	D	2-2	1-2	9	Gayle, Mundee (pen)	4250
21	27	A	Bournemouth	W	3-0	2-0	7	Mundee (pen), Harvey, Bartram (og)	5744
22	29	H	Bradford C	W	2-0	1-0	6	Ratcliffe, Smith	6059
23	Jan 1	A	Fulham	D	0-0	0-0	7		9797
24	3	H	Stockport Co	D	1-1	0-0	6	Miller (og)	6410
25	8	H	Bristol R	L	3-4	1-3	8	Mundee 3	6841
26	15	A	Wrexham	W	2-1	1-1	8	Gayle, Bates	3701
27	22	H	Hartlepool U	W	1-0	1-0	5	Bates	6334
28	29	A	Barnet	D	0-0	0-0	6		2502
29	Feb 5	H	York C	D	1-1	0-1	6	Mundee	5710
30	12	A	Bristol R	W	4-1	3-0	5	Gayle, Allon 3	5685
31	19	A	Reading	L	1-2	1-1	7	Thompson	9056
32	22	H	Hull C	L	0-3	0-1	—		4361
33	25	H	Rotherham U	D	2-2	1-0	6	Mundee, Allon	4980
34	Mar 5	A	Swansea C	D	1-1	0-1	8	Harvey	3187
35	12	H	Brighton & HA	D	1-1	0-1	8	Ratcliffe	6728
36	15	A	Leyton Orient	D	1-1	0-0	—	Allon	3185
37	19	A	Port Vale	L	0-1	0-0	9		8269
38	26	H	Cambridge U	D	3-3	3-2	9	Taylor, Statham, Grainger	5052
39	29	A	Stockport Co	L	1-3	1-2	—	Annon	4361
40	Apr 2	H	Bournemouth	D	1-1	0-1	9	Grainger	4305
41	4	A	Bradford C	L	0-1	0-0	11		6703
42	9	H	Fulham	L	1-2	1-2	11	Taylor	6638
43	16	A	Cardiff C	D	1-1	1-1	11	Harvey	5268
44	23	H	Plymouth Arg	D	1-1	1-0	13	Smith	6173
45	30	A	Burnley	L	1-4	1-2	14	Ashby	11,363
46	May 7	H	Huddersfield T	L	1-2	1-0	16	Harvey	4483

Final League Position: 16

GOALSCORERS

League (57): Allon 13, Mundee 11 (4 pens), Gayle 6, Harvey 4, Ratcliffe 4, Smith 3, Bates 2, Benjamin 2, Grainger 2, Taylor 2, Annon 1, Ashby 1, Ravenscroft 1, Statham 1, Thompson 1, Williams D A 1, own goals 2.
Coca-Cola Cup (3): Westley 2, Peters 1.
FA Cup (4): Allon 2 (1 pen), Gayle 2.

Benstead 5	Statham 31	Manuel 17 + 1	Bates 45	Westley 31	Ratcliffe 41 + 2	Stephenson 25	Hutchings 20 + 9	Bennett 6 + 2	Allon 21	Gayle 35	Peters 8 + 4	Mundee 37 + 2	Williams DA 2 + 1	Williams DP 6 + 1	Ravenscroft 4 + 3	Tilson 2	Cornwell 4	Benjamin 12 + 2	Metcalf 3 + 4	Morgan 1	Dearden 35	Smith 32	Grainger 31	Harvey 23 + 3	Thompson 9 + 1	Annon 5 + 4	Taylor 5	Watson 2 + 1	Ashby 8	Fernandes — + 1	Match No.
1	2	3	4	5	6	7	8	9	10	11																					1
1	2	3	4	5	6	7	8	9	10		11																				2
1	2	3	4	5	6	7		9	10	8	11	12																			3
1		3	4	5	6	7		9	10	2	11	8	12																		4
1		3	4	5	6	7	12		10	2	11	8	9	14																	5
		3	4	5	6	7		9	10	2	11	8		1	12																6
		3	4	5	6	7	14	9	10	2	11	8		1	12																7
		3	4	5	6	7				2	12	8	9	1		10	11														8
		3	4	5	6	7				2	12	8		1		10	11	9	14												9
			4	5	6	7	3	14		2	12	8		1			11	9	10												10
				5	6	7	3			2		8		1			11	9	10	4											11
			4	5	6	7	3		10	2		8						9	12		1	11									12
			4	5	6	7	3		10	8		12						9			1	11	2								13
			4	5	6	7	3		10	9	12								8		1	11	2								14
			4	5	6	7	3		10	8	9										1	11	2								15
			4	5	6	7	3	12	10	11	9										1	8	2								16
			4	5	6	7	3			9		10			12						1	8	2	11							17
	2		4	5	6					8		10			9						1	7	3	11							18
	2		4	5	6	7				8		11						9			1	10	3	12							19
	2		4	5	6					8		11						9			1	10	3	7							20
	2		4	5	6					8		11						9			1	10	3	7							21
	2		4	5	6					8		11						9			1	10	3	7							22
	2		4	5	6					8		11						9			1	10	3	7							23
	2		4	5	6		12			8		11						9			1	10	3	7							24
	2		4	5	6					8		11						9	12		1	10	3	7							25
	2	11	4	5	6		7			8		9			10			12			1		3								26
	2	11	4	5	6		7			8		9			10			12	14		1		3								27
	2	11	4	5	6	7	12		10	8		9									1		3								28
	2		4	5	6	7				8		9									1	10	3	11							29
	2		4		6	7			10	8		9									1	11	3		5						30
	2		4		6	7			10	8		9									1	11	3	12	5						31
	2		4	5	6	7	12		10	8		9									1	11	3	14							32
	2		4	5	6	7	12		10			9									1	8	3	11							33
	2		4		6				10	8		9									1	7	3	11	5						34
	2		4		6		3		10	8		9									1	7		11	5	12					35
	2		4		6				10	8		9									1	7	3	11	5	12					36
	2		4		6		3		10	8		9									1	7		11	5	12					37
	2		4		6		12					9									1	7	3	11	5	8	10	14			38
			4				2					9									1	7	3	11		8	10	6	5		39
	2		4		6		12					9									1	7	3	11		8	10		5		40
	2	3	4		6		8														1	7	9	11			10		5		41
	2	14	4		6	7	12					9									1	8	3	11			10		5		42
	2	3	4		12		8					9									1	7		11	5			10	6		43
	2	10	4		12		8														1	7	3	11	5	9			6		44
	2	3	4				8					9									1	7	6	11		10			5	12	45
	2	3	4				8					9			10						1	7	6	11	12	14			5		46

Coca-Cola Cup	First Round	Watford (h)	2-2
		(a)	1-3
FA Cup	First Round	VS Rugby (a)	3-0
	Second Round	Cardiff C (h)	1-3

BRENTFORD

Player and Position	Ht	Wt	Birth Date	Birth Place	Source	Clubs	League App	League Gls
Goalkeepers								
Graham Benstead†	6 2	12 04	20 8 63	Aldershot	Apprentice	QPR	—	—
						Norwich C (loan)	1	—
						Norwich C	15	—
						Colchester U (loan)	18	—
						Sheffield U (loan)	8	—
						Sheffield U	39	—
						Brentford	112	—
Kevin Dearden	5 11	12 08	8 3 70	Luton	Trainee	Tottenham H	1	—
						Cambridge U (loan)	15	—
						Hartlepool U (loan)	10	—
						Oxford U (loan)	—	—
						Swindon T (loan)	1	—
						Peterborough U (loan)	7	—
						Hull C (loan)	3	—
						Rochdale (loan)	2	—
						Birmingham C (loan)	12	—
						Portsmouth (loan)	—	—
						Brentford	35	—
Tamer Fernandes	6 3	13 07	7 12 74	London	Trainee	Brentford	1	—
Dean P Williams	6 1	12 08	5 1 72	Lichfield	Tamworth	Brentford	7	—
Defenders								
Barry Ashby	6 2	12 03	21 11 70	London	Trainee	Watford	114	3
						Brentford	8	1
Jamie Bates	6 1	12 12	24 2 68	London	Trainee	Brentford	241	8
Martin Grainger	5 11	12 00	23 8 72	Enfield	Trainee	Colchester U	46	7
						Brentford	31	2
Billy Manuel	5 5	10 00	28 6 69	Hackney	Apprentice	Tottenham H	—	—
						Gillingham	87	5
						Brentford	94	1
Scott Morgan	6 1	11 06	22 3 75	Colchester	Bournemouth	Brentford	1	—
Rob Peters	5 8	11 02	18 5 71	Kensington	Trainee	Brentford	30	1
Simon Ratcliffe	5 11	11 09	8 2 67	Davyhulme	Apprentice	Manchester U	—	—
						Norwich C	9	—
						Brentford	189	13
Brian Statham	5 11	11 00	21 5 69	Zimbabwe	Apprentice	Tottenham H	24	—
						Reading (loan)	8	—
						Bournemouth (loan)	2	—
						Brentford (loan)	18	—
						Brentford	76	1
David Thompson	6 3	12 07	20 11 68	Ashington	Trainee	Millwall	92	6
						Bristol C	17	—
						Brentford	10	1
Shane Westley	6 2	13 08	16 6 65	Canterbury	Apprentice	Charlton Ath	8	—
						Southend U	144	10
						Norwich C (loan)	—	—
						Wolverhampton W	50	2
						Brentford	48	1
Midfield								
Bob Booker‡	6 3	13 03	25 1 58	Watford	Bedmond Sports	Brentford	251	41
						Sheffield U	109	13
						Brentford	19	2
Carl Hutchings	5 11	11 00	24 9 74	London	Trainee	Brentford	29	—
Paul Smith	5 11	14 00	18 9 71	Lenham	Trainee	Southend U	20	1
						Brentford	32	3
Tony Sorrell‡	5 11	12 04	17 10 66	London	Bishop's Stortford	Maidstone U	55	8
						Peterborough U	—	—
						Colchester U	5	1
						Barnet	8	2
						Brentford	—	—
Forwards								
Darren Annon			17 2 72	London	Carshalton Ath	Brentford	9	1
Ian Benjamin	5 11	13 01	11 12 61	Nottingham	Apprentice	Sheffield U	5	3
						WBA	2	—
						Notts Co	—	—
						Peterborough U	80	14
						Northampton T	150	59
						Cambridge U	25	2
						Chester C	22	2
						Exeter C	32	4
						Southend U	122	33
						Luton T	13	2
						Brentford	14	2

BRENTFORD

Colours: Red and white vertical striped shirts, black shorts, red stockings. **Change colours:** Blue shirts, dark blue shorts, dark blue stockings.

Foundation: Formed as a small amateur concern in 1889 they were very successful in local circles. They won the championship of the West London Alliance in 1893 and a year later the West Middlesex Junior Cup before carrying off the Senior Cup in 1895. After winning both the London Senior Amateur Cup and the Middlesex Senior Cup in 1898 they were admitted to the Second Division of the Southern League.

First Football League game: 28 August, 1920, Division 3, v Exeter C (a), L 0-3 – Young; Rosier, Hodson; Amos, Levitt, Elliott; Henery, Morley, Spredbury, Thompson, Smith.

Did you know: Between 2 October and 12 February in 1993–94, Brentford completed a club record 11 away matches without defeat.

Managers (and Secretary-Managers)
Will Lewis 1900–03*, Dick Molyneux 1903–06, W. G. Brown 1906–08, Fred Halliday 1908–26 (only secretary to 1922), Ephraim Rhodes 1912–15, Archie Mitchell 1921–22, Harry Curtis 1926–49, Jackie Gibbons 1949–52, Jimmy Blain 1952–53, Tommy Lawton 1953, Bill Dodgin Snr 1953–57, Malcolm Macdonald 1957–65, Tommy Cavanagh 1965–66, Billy Gray 1966–67, Jimmy Sirrel 1967–69, Frank Blunstone 1969–73, Mike Everitt 1973–75, John Docherty 1975–76, Bill Dodgin Jnr 1976–80, Fred Callaghan 1980–84, Frank McLintock 1984–87, Steve Perryman 1987–90, Phil Holder 1990–93, David Webb May 1993–

Player and Position	*Ht*	*Wt*	*Birth Date*	*Birth Place*	*Source*	*Clubs*	*League App*	*League Gls*
Paul Birch	6 0	12 05	3 12 68	Reading	Trainee	Arsenal	—	—
						Portsmouth	—	—
						Brentford	18	2
Lee Harvey	5 11	11 07	21 12 66	Harlow	Local	Leyton Orient	184	23
						Nottingham F	2	—
						Brentford	26	4
Murray Jones‡	6 4	14 00	7 10 64	Bexley	Carshalton	Crystal Palace	—	—
						Bristol C	—	—
						Doncaster R (loan)	—	—
						Exeter C	20	3
						Grimsby T	28	3
						Brentford	16	—
Matthew Metcalf	5 10	12 01	28 7 69	Norwich	Braintree	Brentford	7	—
Denny Mundee	5 10	11 00	10 10 68	Swindon	Apprentice	QPR	—	—
						Swindon T	—	—
						Bournemouth	100	6
						Torquay U (loan)	9	—
						Brentford	39	11
Craig Ravenscroft	5 6	9 07	20 12 74	London	Trainee	Brentford	7	1
Paul Stephenson	5 10	12 02	2 1 68	Wallsend	Apprentice	Newcastle U	61	1
						Millwall	98	6
						Gillingham (loan)	12	2
						Brentford	36	—
Robert Taylor	6 0	11 07	30 4 71	Norwich	Trainee	Norwich C	—	—
						Leyton Orient (loan)	3	1
						Birmingham C	—	—
						Leyton Orient	73	20
						Brentford	5	2
Dean A Williams	6 1	13 00	14 11 70	Hampstead	St Albans	Brentford	3	1

Trainees
Beer, Jamie T; Campbell, Corey A; Cleary, Kevin J; Cooper, Paul; Edgley, David C; Evans, Luke D; Flitter, Matthew A. H; Gibson, Robert W; Hoare, Andrew S; Houhgton, Anthony J; Lacey, Scott A; Marskell, Ben; McGhee, David; Miller, Barry S; North, Tyrone L; Potter, Andrew J.

****Non-Contract**
Hurdle, Agustus A. J.

Associated Schoolboys
Bourne, David A; Brown, Dominic; Clare, Lewis; Cotter, John M; Green, Darren, J; Hamblin, Leigh C; Mitchell, Terence F; O'Neill, Stephen M; Paul, Ricky; Ravenscroft, Alexander V; Stockwell, Mark R.

Associated Schoolboys who have accepted the Club's offer of a Traineeship/Contract
Lecky, Marcus; Mills, Paul.
**Non-Contract Players who are retained must be re-signed before they are eligible to play in League matches.

BRIGHTON AND HOVE ALBION 1993–94 *Back row (left to right):* Larry May (Reserve Team Coach), Stuart Myall, John Crumplin, Nicky Bissett, Andy Kennedy, Steve Foster, Paul McCarthy, Colin Pates, Ted Streeter (Youth Development Officer).
Centre row: Malcolm Stuart (Physio), Mark Farrington, Danny Simmonds, Mark Ormerod, Robert Codner, Nicky Rust, Simon Funnell, Stuart Tuck, Martin Hinshelwood (First Team Coach).
Front row: Stuart Munday, Darron Wilkinson, Kurt Nogan, Dean Wilkins, Barry Lloyd (Manager), Ian Chapman, Matthew Edwards, Bradley Wosahlo, Gavin Geddes.

Division 2 BRIGHTON & HOVE ALBION

Goldstone Ground, Old Shoreham Rd, Hove, Sussex BN3 7DE. Telephone Brighton (0273) 778855. Fax (0273) 321095. Commercial Dept: (0273) 778230. Ticket office (0273) 778855. Shop (0273) 326412. Recorded information (team & ticket news etc): Seagull Line 0891 800609.

Ground capacity: 17,607.

Record attendance: 36,747 v Fulham, Division 2, 27 December 1958.

Record receipts: £109,615.65 v Crawley T, FA Cup 3rd rd, 4 January 1992.

Pitch measurements: 112yd × 75yd.

Directors: G. A. Stanley (Chairman), W. Archer, R. A. Bloom, J. L. Campbell, B. E. Clarke, P. Kent, D. Sizen, D. Stanley, D. Sullivan.

Manager: Liam Brady. ***Assistant Manager:*** Gerry Ryan.

Secretary: Ron Pavey. ***Chief Executive/Deputy Chairman:*** David Bellotti.

Coach: Jimmy Case. ***Physio:*** Malcolm Stuart.

Marketing Manager: Terry Gill.

Year Formed: 1901. ***Turned Professional:*** 1901. ***Ltd Co.:*** 1904.

Previous Grounds: 1901, County Ground; 1902, Goldstone Ground.

Club Nickname: 'The Seagulls'.

Record League Victory: 9–1 v Newport C, Division 3 (S), 18 April 1951 – Ball; Tennant (1p), Mansell (1p); Willard, McCoy, Wilson; Reed, McNichol (4), Garbutt, Bennett (2), Keene (1). 9–1 v Southend U, Division 3, 27 November 1965 – Powney; Magill, Baxter; Leck, Gall, Turner; Gould (1), Collins (1), Livesey (2), Smith (3), Goodchild (2).

Record Cup Victory: 10–1 v Wisbech, FA Cup, 1st rd, 13 November 1965 – Powney; Magill, Baxter; Collins (1), Gall, Turner; Gould, Smith (2), Livesey (3), Cassidy (2), Goodchild (1). (1 og).

Record Defeat: 0–9 v Middlesbrough, Division 2, 23 August 1958.

Most League Points (2 for a win): 65, Division 3 (S), 1955–56 and Division 3, 1971–72.

Most League Points (3 for a win): 84, Division 3, 1987–88.

Most League Goals: 112, Division 3 (S), 1955–56.

Highest League Scorer in Season: Peter Ward, 32, Division 3, 1976–77.

Most League Goals in Total Aggregate: Tommy Cook, 114, 1922–29.

Most Capped Player: Steve Penney, 17, Northern Ireland.

Most League Appearances: 'Tug' Wilson, 509, 1922–36.

Record Transfer Fee Received: £900,000 from Liverpool for Mark Lawrenson, August 1981.

Record Transfer Fee Paid: £500,000 to Manchester U for Andy Ritchie, October 1980.

Football League Record: 1920 Original Member of Division 3; 1921–58 Division 3 (S); 1958–62 Division 2; 1962–63 Division 3; 1963–65 Division 4; 1965–72 Division 3; 1972–73 Division 2; 1973–77 Division 3; 1977–79 Division 2; 1979–83 Division 1; 1983–87 Division 2; 1987–88 Division 3; 1988– Division 2.

Honours: *Football League:* Division 1 best season: 13th, 1981–82; Division 2 – Runners-up 1978–79; Division 3 (S) – Champions 1957–58; Runners-up 1953–54, 1955–56; Division 3 – Runners-up 1971–72, 1976–77, 1987–88; Division 4 – Champions 1964–65. *FA Cup:* Runners-up 1982–83. *Football League Cup:* best season: 5th rd, 1978–79.

BRIGHTON & HOVE ALBION 1993—94 LEAGUE RECORD

Match No.	Date	Venue	Opponents	Result		H/T Score	Lg. Pos.	Goalscorers	Attendance
1	Aug 14	A	Bradford C	L	0-2	0-2	—		6074
2	21	H	Hartlepool U	D	1-1	1-1	21	Kennedy	5230
3	28	A	Cardiff C	D	2-2	0-1	20	Nogan, Munday	7687
4	Sept 1	H	Bristol R	L	0-2	0-0	—		5675
5	4	H	Huddersfield T	D	2-2	0-1	22	Edwards, Funnell	4518
6	11	A	York C	L	1-3	0-1	23	Nogan	3446
7	14	A	Burnley	L	0-3	0-2	—		8837
8	18	H	Brentford	W	2-1	0-1	23	Nogan 2	5734
9	25	A	Leyton Orient	W	3-1	1-1	20	McCarthy, Edwards 2	4737
10	Oct 2	H	Exeter C	D	0-0	0-0	19		5230
11	9	H	Stockport Co	D	1-1	1-1	20	Nogan	5330
12	16	A	Bournemouth	L	1-2	0-1	20	Chapman	5896
13	23	H	Rotherham U	L	0-2	0-2	20		5104
14	30	A	Blackpool	L	0-2	0-0	22		4468
15	Nov 2	H	Wrexham	D	1-1	1-0	—	Geddes	5530
16	6	A	Fulham	W	1-0	0-0	22	Nogan	4383
17	20	H	Reading	L	0-1	0-1	22		6309
18	27	A	Port Vale	L	0-4	0-3	23		7261
19	Dec 11	A	Hartlepool U	D	2-2	0-1	22	Codner, Bissett	1558
20	18	H	Bradford C	L	0-1	0-0	23		6535
21	27	H	Barnet	W	1-0	1-0	22	Chapman (pen)	10,053
22	Jan 1	H	Cambridge U	W	4-1	1-0	20	Nogan 3, Funnell	9753
23	3	A	Plymouth Arg	D	1-1	1-0	21	Nogan	15,334
24	8	A	Hull C	D	0-0	0-0	21		5386
25	15	H	Bournemouth	D	3-3	1-1	21	Edwards, Chapman, McCarthy	9689
26	22	A	Stockport Co	L	0-3	0-1	22		6657
27	29	H	Blackpool	W	3-2	1-1	20	Flatts, Nogan 2	7800
28	Feb 5	A	Rotherham U	W	1-0	0-0	20	Codner	3773
29	12	H	Hull C	W	3-0	2-0	17	Wilkins, Nogan, Codner	8251
30	23	A	Bristol R	L	0-1	0-1	—		4776
31	25	A	Huddersfield T	W	3-1	1-1	16	Foster, Farrington, Codner	5088
32	Mar 5	H	York C	W	2-0	1-0	15	Codner, Nogan	8302
33	8	A	Swansea C	L	0-3	0-1	—		2893
34	12	A	Brentford	D	1-1	1-0	17	Nogan	6728
35	16	H	Burnley	D	1-1	0-1	—	Nogan	8021
36	19	H	Leyton Orient	W	2-0	1-0	17	Codner, Kennedy	8202
37	26	A	Exeter C	D	1-1	1-0	17	Nogan	3107
38	30	H	Plymouth Arg	W	2-1	0-0	—	Nogan, Dickov	9500
39	Apr 2	A	Barnet	D	1-1	1-0	16	Nogan	2733
40	6	H	Swansea C	W	4-1	2-0	—	Dickov, Codner, Foster, Nogan	9303
41	9	A	Cambridge U	L	1-2	0-0	13	Crumplin	4425
42	12	H	Cardiff C	L	3-5	1-3	—	McCarthy, Nogan 2 (1 pen)	7653
43	16	A	Wrexham	W	3-1	1-0	12	Dickov, Crumplin, Codner	2613
44	23	H	Fulham	W	2-0	1-0	11	Dickov 2	10,606
45	30	A	Reading	L	0-2	0-1	13		11,840
46	May 7	H	Port Vale	L	1-3	0-2	14	Wilkins	15,423

Final League Position: 14

GOALSCORERS

League (60): Nogan 22 (1 pen), Codner 8, Dickov 5, Edwards 4, Chapman 3 (1 pen), McCarthy 3, Crumplin 2, Foster 2, Funnell 2, Kennedy 2, Wilkins 2, Bissett 1, Farrington 1, Flatts 1, Munday 1, Geddes 1.
Coca-Cola Cup (3): Nogan 2, Kennedy 1.
FA Cup (2): Kennedy 2.

Rust 46	Myall 12 + 1	Chapman 45	Wilkins 20 + 1	Bissett 12	Pates 34	Edwards 25 + 2	Kennedy 8 + 4	Nogan 41	Codner 40	Wilkinson 8 + 3	Crumplin 29 + 3	Funnell 14 + 10	Munday 33 + 1	Geddes 7 + 5	Foster 34	Farrington 4 + 2	McCarthy 37	Tuck 5 + 6	Simmonds 6 + 8	Wosahlo 1	Flatts 9 + 1	Case 21	Fox M 4 + 8	Dickov 8	Johnson 1 + 1	Andrews 1 + 4	Fox S — + 1	McGarrigle 1	Match No.
1	2	3	4	5	6	7	8	9	10	11	12	14																	1
1		3	4	5	6	7	8	9	10		11		2																2
1	12	3	4	5	6	7	8	9	10		11		2																3
1	2	3	4	5	6		7		8		10	11	9	12															4
1	2	3	4	6		7			10		11	8	9		5														5
1	2	3			6	7		9	10		11	8	4		5	12													6
1	2	3	4		6	7		9	10	11	8				5														7
1	2	3	4	5	6	7	8	9	10		12						11												8
1	2	3	4	5		7		9	10	11	8		12				6												9
1	2	3	4			7		9	10	11	8	12	5					6	14										10
1	2	3				7		9	10			8	5				4	6	11										11
1	2	3				7		9	10	12		8		14	5		4	6	11										12
1	2	3				4		9	10	7		12		6	5	8		11	14										13
1		3				7		9	10					6	5	8	4	11	2										14
1		3			6	7		9	10			12	2	11	5	8	4	14											15
1		3			6	7	8	9	10				2	11	5		4												16
1		3		5	6	7	8		10		9		2	11		12	4												17
1	2	3		5	6	7			10			9	8	11			4		12										18
1		3		5	6	7			10				2	11	4		8			9									19
1		3		2	6	7		9	10	11			8		5		4		12										20
1		3		4	6	7		9		11	8	12	2		5		10		14										21
1		3			4	11		9			2	10			5		6		12		7	8							22
1		2			4	11		9				10		12	5		6		3		7	8							23
1		2			4	11		9				10		12	5		6		3		7	8							24
1		2			4	11		9				10		12	5		6	14	3		7	8							25
1		3			4	11		9				10	2		5		6	12			7	8							26
1		3			4			9	10		11	12	2		5		6				7	8							27
1		3			4			9	10		11	12	2		5		6	14			7	8							28
1		11	4		3			9	10		12	14	2		5		6				7	8							29
1		11	4		3			9	10			12	2		5		6				7	8	14						30
1		11	4		3			9	10	12	7		2		5	8	6				14								31
1		11	4		3	12		9	10		7	8	2		5		6	14											32
1		11	4		3			9	10	2	7	12			5		6	14				8							33
1		11			3			9	10		7	8	2		5		6					4							34
1		11			3	12		9	10		7	8	2		5		6					4	14						35
1		11	12		3		8	9	10		7		2		5		6					4	14						36
1		11	4		3		12	9	10		7		2		5		6							8					37
1		11	4		3		12	9	10		7		2		5		6						14	8					38
1		3	11		5		12	9	10		7		2				6					4	14	8					39
1			11		3		12	9	10		7		2		5		6					4	14	8					40
1		11			3			9	10		7				5		6					4	14	8	2	12			41
1		3						9	10		7		2		5		6					4	11	8	12	14			42
1		3						9	10	12	7		2		5		6					4	11	8		14			43
1		3						9	10		7		2		5		6		12			4	11	8			14		44
1		3	8					9	10		7		2		5		6		12			4	11			14			45
1		3	8					9	10		7		2				6					4	12			11		5	46

Coca-Cola Cup	First Round	Gillingham (a)	0-1
		(h)	2-0
	Second Round	Middlesbrough (a)	0-5
		(h)	1-3
FA Cup	First Round	Bournemouth (a)	2-4

BRIGHTON & HOVE ALBION

Player and Position	Ht	Wt	Birth Date	Birth Place	Source	Clubs	League App	League Gls
Goalkeepers								
Nicky Rust	6 0	13 01	25 9 74	Cambridge	Arsenal	Brighton	46	—
Defenders								
Nicky Bissett	6 2	12 10	5 4 64	Fulham	Barnet	Brighton	85	8
Ian Chapman	5 9	12 05	31 5 70	Brighton		Brighton	205	7
Steve Foster	6 1	14 00	24 9 57	Portsmouth		Portsmouth	109	6
						Brighton	172	6
						Aston Villa	15	3
						Luton T	163	11
						Oxford U	95	9
						Brighton	69	6
Ross Johnson§			1 2 76	Brighton	Trainee	Brighton	2	—
Paul McCarthy	6 0	13 06	4 8 71	Cork	Trainee	Brighton	111	3
Stuart Munday	5 11	11 00	28 9 72	London	Trainee	Brighton	55	2
Stuart Myall	5 10	12 12	12 11 74	Eastbourne	Trainee	Brighton	20	—
Colin Pates	6 0	13 00	10 8 61	Mitcham	Apprentice	Chelsea	281	10
						Charlton Ath	38	—
						Arsenal	21	—
						Brighton (loan)	17	—
						Brighton	34	—
Danny Simmonds	5 11	11 05	17 12 74	Eastbourne	Trainee	Brighton	14	—
Stuart Tuck	5 11	11 02	1 10 74	Brighton	Trainee	Brighton	11	—
Midfield								
Philip Andrews§			14 9 76	Andover	Trainee	Brighton	5	—
Jimmy Case	5 9	12 08	18 5 54	Liverpool	South Liverpool	Liverpool	186	23
						Brighton	127	10
						Southampton	215	10
						Bournemouth	40	1
						Halifax T	21	2
						Wrexham	4	—
						Darlington	1	—
					Sittingbourne	Brighton	21	—
Robert Codner	5 11	11 08	23 1 65	Walthamstow	Barnet	Brighton	243	35
John Crumplin	5 8	11 10	26 5 67	Bath	Bognor Regis	Brighton	207	7
Matthew Edwards*	5 10	11 00	15 6 71	Hammersmith	Trainee	Tottenham H	—	—
						Reading (loan)	8	—
						Brighton	60	6
Mark Fox§			17 11 75	Basingstoke	Trainee	Brighton	12	—
Gavin Geddes	5 10	11 08	7 10 72	Brighton		Brighton	12	1
Kevin McGarrigle			9 4 77	Newcastle	Trainee	Brighton	1	—
Dean Wilkins	5 10	12 04	12 7 62	Hillingdon	Apprentice	QPR	6	—
						Brighton	2	—
						Orient (loan)	10	—
					PEC Zwolle	Brighton	261	22
Darron Wilkinson*	5 11	12 08	24 11 69	Reading	Wokingham	Brighton	38	3
Bradley Wosahlo*	5 10	10 06	14 2 75	Ipswich	Trainee	Brighton	1	—
Forwards								
Mark Farrington*	5 10	11 12	15 6 65	Liverpool	Everton	Norwich C	14	2
						Cambridge U	10	1
						Cardiff C	31	3
					Feyenoord	Brighton	28	4
Simon Fox§			28 8 77	Basingstoke	Trainee	Brighton	1	—
Simon Funnell	6 0	12 08	8 8 74	Brighton	Trainee	Brighton	27	2
Andy Kennedy*	6 2	13 00	8 10 64	Stirling	Sauchie Ath	Rangers	15	3
						Birmingham C	76	18
						Sheffield U (loan)	9	1
						Blackburn R	59	23
						Watford	25	4
						Bolton W (loan)	1	—
						Brighton	42	10
Kurt Nogan	5 11	12 07	9 9 70	Cardiff	Trainee	Luton T	33	3
						Peterborough U	—	—
						Brighton	71	42
John Ryan			7 12 75	Cork	Cork C	Brighton	—	—

BRIGHTON & HOVE ALBION

Colours: Royal blue shirts with white pin stripe, royal blue sleeves, royal blue shorts with white and royal trim, royal blue stockings with red/white trim. **Change colours:** White shirts with red/royal trim, white shorts with royal trim, white stockings with royal and red band on turnover.

Foundation: A professional club Brighton United was formed in November 1897 at the Imperial Hotel, Queen's Road, but folded in March 1900 after less than two seasons in the Southern League at the County Ground. An amateur team, Brighton & Hove Rangers was then formed by some prominent United supporters and after one season at Withdean, decided to turn semi-professional and play at the County Ground. Rangers were accepted into the Southern League but then also folded June 1901. John Jackson the former United manager organised a meeting at the Seven Stars public house, Ship Street on 24 June 1901 at which a new third club Brighton & Hove United was formed. They took over Rangers' place in the Southern League and pitch at County Ground. The name was changed to Brighton & Hove Albion before a match was played because of objections by Hove FC.

First Football League game: 28 August, 1920, Division 3, v Southend U (a), L 0-2 – Hayes; Woodhouse, Little; Hall, Comber, Bentley; Longstaff, Ritchie, Doran, Rodgerson, March.

Did you know: Simon Fox, an 85th minute substitute against Fulham at 16 years 241 days, became Brighton's youngest debutant on 23 April 1994. His brother Mark had been replaced six minutes earlier.

Managers (and Secretary-Managers)
John Jackson 1901–05, Frank Scott-Walford 1905–08, John Robson 1908–14, Charles Webb 1919–47, Tommy Cook 1947, Don Welsh 1947–51, Billy Lane 1951–61, George Curtis 1961–63, Archie Macaulay 1963–68, Fred Goodwin 1968–70, Pat Saward 1970–73, Brian Clough 1973–74, Peter Taylor 1974–76, Alan Mullery 1976–81, Mike Bailey 1981–82, Jimmy Melia 1982–83, Chris Cattlin 1983–86, Alan Mullery 1986–87, Barry Lloyd 1987–93, Liam Brady December 1993–

Trainees
Andrews, Phillip D; Fox, Mark S; Henderson, Nicholas J; (h) Kember, Paul M. J; Macaulay, Lee; McGarrigle, Kevin; Ormerod, Mark I; Scott, Steven; Smith, Daniel K; Thompson, Ian; Tilley, Anthony J; Whitehouse, Timothy J; (h) Wood, David; Yorke-Johnson, Ross.

****Non-Contract**
Brady, William L.

Associated Schoolboys
Campbell, Stuart; Carter, Richard A. J; Kennett, Paul J; Kirkland, Joel M; Morse, Christopher; Richardson, Paul M; Russell, Matthew D; Virgo, James; Westcott, John P. J.

Associated Schoolboys who have accepted the Club's offer of a Traineeship/Contract
Mayo, Kerry; Pickering, Jay T.
**Non-Contract Players who are retained must be re-signed before they are eligible to play in League matches.

Birmingham City players continued from Page 61

Paul Moulden	5 8	11 03	6 9 67	Farnworth	Apprentice	Manchester C	64	18
						Bournemouth	32	13
						Oldham Ath	38	4
						Brighton (loan)	11	5
						Birmingham C	20	5
Alan O'Neill‡			27 8 73	Cork	Cobh Ramblers	Birmingham C	4	—
Paul Peschisolido	5 4	10 05	25 5 71	Canada	Toronto Blizzard	Birmingham C	43	16
Andrew Saville	6 0	12 06	12 12 64	Hull	Local	Hull C	100	18
						Walsall	38	5
						Barnsley	82	21
						Hartlepool U	37	13
						Birmingham C	49	17
Peter Shearer	6 0	11 06	4 2 67	Birmingham	Apprentice	Birmingham C	4	—
						Rochdale	1	—
					Cheltenham T	Bournemouth	85	10
						Birmingham C	2	—
Carl Shutt	5 10	11 13	10 10 61	Sheffield	Spalding U	Sheffield W	40	16
						Bristol C	46	10
						Leeds U	79	17
						Birmingham C	26	4
						Manchester C (loan)	6	—
Danny Wallace	5 4	10 04	21 1 64	London	Apprentice	Southampton	255	64
						Manchester U	47	6
						Millwall (loan)	3	—
						Birmingham C	10	1

BRISTOL CITY 1993–94 *Back row (left to right):* Martin Scott, Gerry Harrison, Dariusz Dziekanowski, Wayne Allison, David Thompson, Rob Edwards, Matt Bryant, Jim McIntyre.
Centre row: Leroy Rosenoir (First Team Coach), Russell Osman (Manager), Andy Llewellyn, Nicky Morgan, Mark Gavin, Keith Welch, Mark Aizelwood, Andy Leaning, Ray Atteveld, Steve Benton, Junior Bent, Clive Whitehead (Reserve Team Coach), Dave Bell (Youth Team Coach).
Front row: Gary Shelton, Glenn Pennyfather, Brian Tinnion, Ian Baird, Dave Martin, Stuart Munro, Mark Shail, Ian Brown, Liam Robinson.

Division 1 BRISTOL CITY

Ashton Gate, Bristol BS3 2EJ. Telephone Bristol (0272) 632812 (5 lines). Fax 0272 639574. Commercial: 0272 633876. Shop: 0272 538566. Clubcall: 0891 121176. Supporters Club: (0272) 665554. Community Dept: (0272) 664685.

Ground capacity: 20,000 approx.

Record attendance: 43,335 v Preston NE, FA Cup 5th rd, 16 February 1935.

Record receipts: £132,325 v Liverpool, FA Cup 3rd rd, 8 January 1994.

Pitch measurements: 115yd × 75yd.

Chairman: D. Russe. ***Vice-chairman:*** M. Fricker.

Directors: D. Coller, J. Clapp, G. Williams. ***Commercial Manager:*** John Cox.

Manager: Russell Osman. ***Assistant Manager:*** . ***Coach:*** Leroy Rosenior.

Physio: H. Footman. ***Secretary:*** Jean Harrison. ***Commercial Manager:*** John Cox.

Year Formed: 1894. ***Turned Professional:*** 1897. ***Ltd Co.:*** 1897. BCFC (1982) PLC.

Previous Name: Bristol South End 1894–97.

Club Nickname: 'Robins'.

Previous Grounds: 1894, St John's Lane; 1904, Ashton Gate.

Record League Victory: 9–0 v Aldershot, Division 3 (S), 28 December 1946 – Eddols; Morgan, Fox; Peacock, Roberts, Jones (1); Chilcott, Thomas, Clark (4 incl. 1p), Cyril Williams (1), Hargreaves (3).

Record Cup Victory: 11–0 v Chichester C, FA Cup, 1st rd, 5 November 1960 – Cook; Collinson, Thresher; Connor, Alan Williams, Etheridge; Tait (1), Bobby Williams (1), Atyeo (5), Adrian Williams (3), Derrick. (1 og).

Record Defeat: 0–9 v Coventry C, Division 3 (S), 28 April 1934.

Most League Points (2 for a win): 70, Division 3 (S), 1954–55.

Most League Points (3 for a win): 91, Division 3, 1989–90.

Most League Goals: 104, Division 3 (S), 1926–27.

Highest League Scorer in Season: Don Clark, 36, Division 3 (S), 1946–47.

Most League Goals in Total Aggregate: John Atyeo, 314, 1951–66.

Most Capped Player: Billy Wedlock, 26, England.

Most League Appearances: John Atyeo, 597, 1951–66.

Record Transfer Fee Received: £1,750,000 from Newcastle United for Andy Cole, March 1993.

Record Transfer Fee Paid: £500,000 to Arsenal for Andy Cole, July 1992.

Football League Record: 1901 Elected to Division 2; 1906–11 Division 1; 1911–22 Division 2; 1922–23 Division 3 (S); 1923–24 Division 2; 1924–27 Division 3 (S); 1927–32 Division 2; 1932–55 Division 3 (S); 1955–60 Division 2; 1960–65 Division 3; 1965–76 Division 2; 1976–80 Division 1; 1980–81 Division 2; 1981–82 Division 3; 1982–84 Division 4; 1984–90 Division 3; 1990–92 Division 2; 1992– Division 1.

Honours: *Football League:* Division 1 – Runners-up 1906–07; Division 2 – Champions 1905–06; Runners-up 1975–76; Division 3 (S) – Champions 1922–23, 1926–27, 1954–55; Runners-up 1937–38; Division 3 – Runners-up 1964–65, 1989–90. *FA Cup:* Runners-up 1909. *Football League Cup:* Semi-final 1970–71, 1988–89. *Welsh Cup:* Winners 1934. *Anglo-Scottish Cup:* Winners 1977–78. *Freight Rover Trophy:* Winners 1985–86; Runners-up 1986–87.

BRISTOL CITY 1993—94 LEAGUE RECORD

Match No.	Date	Venue	Opponents	Result		H/T Score	Lg. Pos.	Goalscorers	Attendance
1	Aug 14	A	Wolverhampton W	L	1-3	0-1	—	Scott	21,052
2	21	H	Crystal Palace	W	2-0	0-0	13	Baird, Allison	12,068
3	28	A	Derby Co	L	0-1	0-0	21		15,643
4	Sept 4	H	Southend U	W	2-1	1-0	12	Tinnion (pen), Osman	7396
5	11	A	Oxford U	L	2-4	1-2	19	Baird 2	5464
6	14	H	Leicester C	L	1-3	0-0	—	Scott	7899
7	18	H	Charlton Ath	D	0-0	0-0	20		7484
8	25	A	Portsmouth	D	0-0	0-0	20		10,702
9	Oct 2	H	Bolton W	W	2-0	1-0	15	Allison, Scott	7704
10	5	A	Luton T	W	2-0	0-0	—	Tinnion (pen), Baird	5956
11	9	A	Notts Co	L	0-2	0-0	10		6418
12	16	H	Barnsley	L	0-2	0-1	15		6923
13	23	A	Tranmere R	D	2-2	1-1	—	Shail, Allison	7123
14	30	H	Sunderland	W	2-0	0-0	12	Allison, Baird	8162
15	Nov 2	H	Birmingham C	W	3-0	1-0	—	Allison 3	9192
16	6	A	Middlesbrough	W	1-0	1-0	9	Tinnion (pen)	9687
17	13	H	Millwall	D	2-2	1-0	8	Allison 2	8416
18	20	A	Watford	D	1-1	0-1	10	Martin	6045
19	27	A	Peterborough U	W	2-0	2-0	8	Robinson 2	5084
20	Dec 4	H	Middlesbrough	D	0-0	0-0	8		8441
21	11	A	Leicester C	L	0-3	0-2	10		13,394
22	18	H	Wolverhampton W	W	2-1	1-0	9	Allison, Brown I	15,151
23	27	A	WBA	W	1-0	1-0	9	Tinnion	22,888
24	28	H	Nottingham F	L	1-4	0-0	11	Edwards	20,725
25	Jan 1	A	Grimsby T	L	0-1	0-0	11		5469
26	3	H	Stoke C	D	0-0	0-0	12		11,132
27	15	A	Barnsley	D	1-1	0-1	11	Scott	5222
28	22	H	Notts Co	L	0-2	0-1	11		7538
29	Feb 5	H	Tranmere R	W	2-0	0-0	11	Tinnion, Allison	8171
30	12	A	Sunderland	D	0-0	0-0	12		16,816
31	22	A	Crystal Palace	L	1-4	1-1	—	Shail	11,508
32	25	A	Southend U	W	1-0	1-0	11	Allison	4615
33	Mar 5	H	Derby Co	D	0-0	0-0	12		8723
34	15	H	Oxford U	L	0-1	0-1	—		6635
35	19	H	Portsmouth	W	1-0	0-0	11	Allison	6352
36	26	A	Bolton W	D	2-2	1-2	14	Allison 2	10,221
37	30	A	Stoke C	L	0-3	0-1	—		13,208
38	Apr 2	H	WBA	D	0-0	0-0	16		8624
39	4	A	Nottingham F	D	0-0	0-0	16		24,162
40	9	H	Grimsby T	W	1-0	0-0	14	Scott (pen)	5480
41	16	A	Birmingham C	D	2-2	2-0	15	Partridge 2	20,316
42	19	H	Luton T	W	1-0	1-0	—	Edwards	5350
43	23	H	Watford	D	1-1	1-0	13	Partridge	8324
44	30	A	Millwall	D	0-0	0-0	13		11,189
45	May 3	A	Charlton Ath	L	1-3	1-1	—	Partridge	6727
46	8	H	Peterborough U	W	4-1	2-0	13	Bent 2, Robinson 2	7790

Final League Position: 13

GOALSCORERS

League (47): Allison 15, Baird 5, Scott 5 (1 pen), Tinnion 5 (3 pens), Partridge 4, Robinson 4, Bent 2, Edwards 2, Shail 2, Brown I 1, Martin 1, Osman 1.
Coca-Cola Cup (1): Robinson 1.
FA Cup (7): Allison 4, Tinnion 2, Shail 1.

Welch 45	Munro 43 + 1	Scott 45	Aizlewood 5	Shail 35 + 1	Hewlett 11 + 1	Wyatt 8 + 2	Shelton 3	Baird 16 + 3	Robinson 31 + 10	Tinnion 40 + 1	Allison 35 + 4	Kamara — + 1	Edwards 31 + 7	Bent 17 + 3	Brown I 5 + 6	Harrison 1	Osman 4 + 1	Gavin 6 + 2	Rosenior 1 + 4	Borrows 6	Bryant 27 + 1	Martin 33 + 1	Llewellyn 15	Pennyfather 7 + 5	Fowler — + 1	Harriott 17	Hoyland 6	Partridge 7 + 2	Milsom 1 + 2	McKop 2 + 2	Barclay 2	Brown W 1	*Match No.*
1	2	3	4	5	*6*	*7*	8	9	10	11	12	14																					1
1	2	3	4	5	6	7	8	9	10	11	12																						2
1	2	3	4	5			11	9		10	12		6	*7*	8																		3
1	2	3		5				9	8	10			11	7	12	4	6																4
1	2	3	4	5				9		10	8		11	*7*			6	12	14														5
1	2	3	4	5				9	*7*	10	8						6	11	12														6
1	3	*6*		4				9	12	*10*	8		14					11		2	5	7											7
1	3			4				9	10		8		6				12	11		2	5	*7*											8
1	3	6		4				9	10	11	8		14					12		2	5	*7*											9
1	3	6		4				9	10	11			12					8		2	5	7											10
1	3	6		4				9	10	11	12							*8*		2	5	7											11
1	3	6		4				9	12	11	8		14						*10*	2	5	*7*											12
1	3	6		4				9	12	11	10		14	*8*							5	*7*	2										13
1	3	6		4				9	12	11	10		14	8							5	*7*	2										14
1	3	6		4					9	11	10			8							5	7	2										15
1		3		4					9	11	10		6	8							5	7	2	12									16
1		3		4					9	11	10		6	8							5	7	2	12									17
1	12	3		4					9	11	10		6	8							5	7	2										18
1	4	3							9	11	10		6	8							5	7	2										19
1	4	3							9	11	10		6	*8*	14						5	7	2	12									20
1	4	3							9	11	10		6		8						5		2	7	12								21
1	4	3							9	11	10		6	12	8						5		2	7									22
1	4	3						12	9	11	10		6		8						5		2	7									23
1	4	3						12	*9*	11	10		6		8						5	14	2	7									24
1	*4*	3		14				9	12		10		11					8			5	7	2	6									25
1	2	3		4				9	8	11	10		6		12						5	7											26
1	2	3		4					9	11	10		6	8			5					7											27
1	5	3		4					9	11	10		6	8					12			7	*2*	14									28
1	5	3		4					9	6	10		11		12							7	2	8									29
1	5	3		4					9	11	10		6		12						14	*7*		8		2							30
1	8	3		4					9	11	10		6		12						5	7				2							31
1	8	3		4					9	11	10		6								5	7		12		2							32
1	4	3								11	10		6	*9*					12		5	*7*				2	8	14					33
1	*7*	3			8				9	11	10		6	12							5					2	4	14					34
1	6	3		4	8			12	9	11	10										5					2	7						35
1	3	6		4	8				9	11	10										5					2	7		12				36
1	3	6		4	8				12	11	10										5	9				2	*7*		14				37
1	5	3		4	8				9	11	10		12									7				2	6						38
1	5	3		4		8				11	10		6									7				2			9				39
1	5	3		4	12	8					10		11									7				2		9		6			40
1	4	3			6	*8*			12		10		11									7				2		9		5			41
1	4	3			6	8			5				11	12								7				2		9			10		42
1	6	3		4	8	14			5	12			11									7				2		9			*10*		43
1	5	3		4	*8*	14			12	6			11	10								7				2		9					44
1	5	3		4		*8*			12	6			11	10								7				2		9		14			45
	5	3		4		*8*			12	6			11	10								7				2		9		14		1	46

Coca-Cola Cup	First Round	Swansea C (a)	1-0
		(h)	0-2
FA Cup	Third Round	Liverpool (h) abandoned	1-1
		(h)	1-1
		(a)	1-0
	Fourth Round	Stockport Co (a)	4-0
	Fifth Round	Charlton Ath (h)	1-1
		(a)	0-2

BRISTOL CITY

Player and Position	Ht	Wt	Birth Date	Birth Place	Source	Clubs	League App	League Gls
Goalkeepers								
Wayne Brown§			14 1 77	Southampton	Trainee	Bristol C	1	—
Simon Rudgley	5 11	11 10	25 9 73	London	Fulham	Bristol C	—	—
Keith Welch	6 0	12 0	3 10 68	Bolton	Trainee	Bolton W	—	—
						Rochdale	205	—
						Bristol C	116	—
Defenders								
Stephen Benton*	5 10	12 03	20 12 73	Bristol	Trainee	Bristol C	—	—
Matthew Bryant	6 1	12 11	21 9 70	Bristol	Trainee	Bristol C	134	4
						Walsall (loan)	13	—
Robert Edwards	6 0	11 06	1 7 73	Kendal		Carlisle U	48	5
						Bristol C	76	3
Marvin Harriott			20 4 74	Dulwich	West Ham U	Oldham Ath	—	—
						Barnsley	—	—
						Leyton Orient (loan)	8	—
						Bristol C	17	—
Nathan Hicks	6 2		23 9 74	Plymouth	Trainee	Bristol C	—	—
Andy Llewellyn*	5 7	11 00	26 2 66	Bristol	Apprentice	Bristol C	301	3
						Exeter C (loan)	15	—
Henry McKop	5 11	12 00	8 7 67	Zimbabwe	Bonner SC	Bristol C	4	—
Stuart Munro	5 8	10 05	15 9 62	Falkirk	Bo'ness U	St Mirren	1	—
						Alloa	60	6
						Rangers	179	3
						Blackburn R	1	—
						Bristol C	60	—
Russell Osman	5 11	12 01	14 2 59	Repton	Apprentice	Ipswich	294	17
						Leicester C	108	8
						Southampton	96	6
						Bristol C	70	3
Mark Shail	6 1	13 03	15 10 63	Sweden	Yeovil	Bristol C	40	2
Robert Skidmore*	6 0	12 09	22 8 74	Bristol	Trainee	Bristol C	—	—
Brian Tinnion	5 11	11 05	23 2 68	Stanley	Apprentice	Newcastle U	32	2
						Bradford C	145	22
						Bristol C	52	7
Midfield								
Ray Atteveld‡	5 10	12 00	8 9 66	Amsterdam	Haarlem	Everton	51	1
						West Ham U (loan)	1	—
						Bristol C	14	1
Gary Durbin*	5 9	12 04	16 12 74	Bristol	Trainee	Bristol C	—	—
Jason Fowler	6 1	11 06	20 8 74	Bristol	Trainee	Bristol C	2	—
Matthew Hewlett	6 2	10 11	25 2 76	Bristol	Trainee	Bristol C	12	—
Abdul Kamara*	5 9	11 00	10 2 74	Southampton	Southampton	Bristol C	1	—
Colin Loss	5 11	11 04	15 8 73	Brentwood	Trainee	Norwich C	—	—
						Derby Co	—	—
					Gresley R	Bristol C	—	—
David Martin	6 1	13 01	25 4 63	East Ham	Apprentice	Millwall	140	6
						Wimbledon	35	3
						Southend U	221	19
						Bristol C	34	1
Glenn Pennyfather‡	5 8	11 05	11 2 63	Billericay	Apprentice	Southend U	238	36
						Crystal Palace	34	1
						Ipswich T	15	1
						Bristol C	26	1
Martin Scott	5 8	10 10	7 1 68	Sheffield	Apprentice	Rotherham U	94	3
						Nottingham F (loan)	—	—
						Bristol C	153	12
Gary Shelton*	5 7	10 12	21 3 58	Nottingham	Apprentice	Walsall	24	—
						Aston Villa	24	7
						Notts Co (loan)	8	—
						Sheffield W	198	18
						Oxford U	65	1
						Bristol C	150	24
						Rochdale (loan)	3	—
Forwards								
Wayne Allison	6 1	12 06	16 10 68	Huddersfield		Halifax T	84	23
						Watford	7	—
						Bristol C	158	35

BRISTOL CITY

Colours: Red shirts, white shorts, red and white stockings. **Change colours:** Purple shirts, green shorts, white stockings with purple top.

Foundation: The name Bristol City came into being in 1897 when the Bristol South End club, formed three years earlier, decided to adopt professionalism and apply for admission to the Southern League after competing in the Western League. The historic meeting was held at The Albert Hall, Bedminster. Bristol City employed Sam Hollis from Woolwich Arsenal as manager and gave him £40 to buy players. In 1901 they merged with Bedminster, another leading Bristol club.

First Football League game: 7 September, 1901, Division 2, v Blackpool (a) W 2-0 – Moles; Tuft, Davies; Jones, McLean, Chambers; Bradbury, Connor, Boucher, O'Brien (2), Flynn.

Did you know: When Bristol City won their first and only Welsh Cup in 1933–34, their victims were Cardiff City, New Brighton, Port Vale and Tranmere Rovers 3-0 in a replayed final at Chester.

Managers (and Secretary-Managers)
Sam Hollis 1897–99, Bob Campbell 1899–1901, Sam Hollis 1901–05, Harry Thickett 1905–10, Sam Hollis 1911–13, George Hedley 1913–15, Jack Hamilton 1915–19, Joe Palmer 1919–21, Alex Raisbeck 1921–29, Joe Bradshaw 1929–32, Bob Hewison 1932–49 (under suspension 1938–39), Bob Wright 1949–50, Pat Beasley 1950–58, Peter Doherty 1958–60, Fred Ford 1960–67, Alan Dicks 1967–80, Bobby Houghton 1980–82, Roy Hodgson 1982, Terry Cooper 1982–88 (Director from 1983), Joe Jordan 1988–90, Jimmy Lumsden 1990–92, Denis Smith 1992–93, Russell Osman March 1993–

Ian Baird	6 2	12 12	1 4 64	Rotherham	Apprentice	Southampton	22	5
						Cardiff C (loan)	12	6
						Newcastle U (loan)	5	1
						Leeds U	85	33
						Portsmouth	20	1
						Leeds U	77	17
						Middlesbrough	63	19
						Hearts	64	15
						Bristol C	19	5
Dominic Barclay§			5 9 76	Bristol	Trainee	Bristol C	2	—
Junior Bent	5 5	10 06	1 3 70	Huddersfield	Trainee	Huddersfield T	36	6
						Burnley (loan)	9	3
						Bristol C	78	9
						Stoke C (loan)	1	—
Ian Brown	5 10	11 05	11 9 65	Ipswich	Chelmsford C	Bristol C	11	1
						Colchester U (loan)	4	1
Raphael Burke	5 8	10 07	3 7 74	Bristol	Trainee	Manchester U	—	—
						Bristol C	—	—
Stuart Duffin	5 9	11 07	27 6 75	Glasgow		Bristol C	—	—
Dariusz Dziekanowski‡	6 1	12 13	30 9 62	Warsaw	Legia Warsaw	Celtic	49	10
						Bristol C	43	7
James McIntyre‡	5 11	11 05	24 5 72	Dumbarton	Duntocher Boys	Bristol C	1	—
						Exeter C (loan)	15	3
Paul Milsom	6 1	13 03	5 10 74	Bristol	Trainee	Bristol C	3	—
Scott Partridge	5 9	10 09	13 10 74	Leicester	Trainee	Bradford C	5	—
						Bristol C	9	4
Liam Robinson	5 7	11 05	29 12 65	Bradford	Nottingham F	Huddersfield T	21	2
						Tranmere R (loan)	4	3
						Bury	262	89
						Bristol C	41	4
Leroy Rosenior	6 1	11 10	24 3 64	London	School	Fulham	54	16
						QPR	38	7
						Fulham	34	20
						West Ham U	53	15
						Fulham (loan)	11	3
						Charlton Ath (loan)	3	—
						Bristol C	51	12
Michael Wyatt	5 11	11 03	12 9 74	Bristol	Trainee	Bristol C	10	—

Trainees
Ayres, Timothy; Barclay, Dominic A; Brown, Wayne L; Carey, Louis A; De Ste Croix, Lee; Donaldson, Michael I; Farrow, Marcus W; Gitsham, Scott A; Haines, Daniel C; Huggins, Dean S; (h) Lewis, Krishnan C; Licata, Guiseppe; Parrott, Lee; Peach, Daniel J; Pettitt, David M; Saunders, Marc A; Westlake, Andrew E.

Associated Schoolboys
Anderson, Paul; Badman, Mark; Budd, Christopher R; Clarke, Robert; Doherty, Thomas E; Fowler, Paul; Greaves, James; Hale, Matthew; Hobbs, Darren J; Jacobs, Kristen; Rich, Stephen J; Ridge, Neil; Saunders, Mark; Sloan, Christopher J; Smith, Dwayne; Vanes, Michael; Wilmot, Ellis J.

Associated Schoolboys who have accepted the Club's offer of a Traineeship/Contract
Alderman, Scott; Carree, Nicholas W; Dibble, Anthony J; Kentish, Neil A; Langan, Kevin; Loydon, Gareth; Perry, Richard; Plummer, Dwayne; Ponfield, Stuart.

BRISTOL ROVERS 1993–94 *Back row (left to right):* Bill Clark, David Mehew, Lee Maddison, Justin Skinner, Justin Channing, Richard Evans, Andy Tillson, Ian Alexander, Paul Hardyman.

Third row: Roy Dolling (Youth Development Manager), Carl Saunders, Tony Pounder, Ian Wright, Gareth Taylor, Brian Parkin, Marcus Browning, John Taylor, Ian McLean, Gary Waddock, Keith James (Physio).

Second row: Steve Cross (Reserve Team Manager), Ray Kendall (Kit Manager), Vernon Stokes (Director), Ron Craig (Director), Denis Dunford (Chairman), John Ward (Manager), Geoff Dunford (Vice Chairman), Ian Wilson (Club Secretary), Tony Gill (Youth Coach), Dennis Booth (Assistant Manager).

Front row: Marcus Stewart, Lee Archer, Paul Tovey, Scott Crossey, Andy Gurney, Martin Paul, Marco Micciche, Worrell Sterling.

Division 2 BRISTOL ROVERS

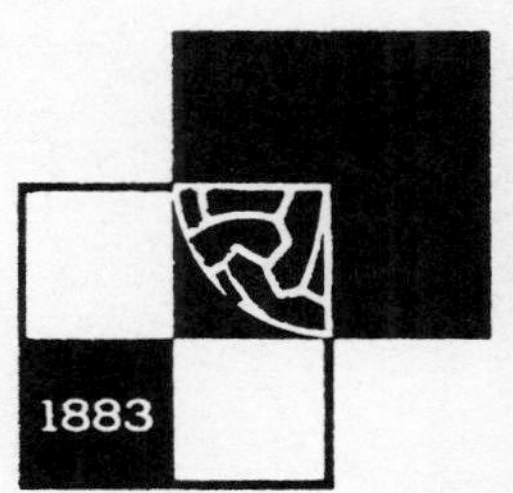

Twerton Park, Twerton, Bath, BA2 1DB. Telephone: 0272 352508. Fax: 0272 353477. Training ground: 0272 861743. Match day ticket office: 0225 312327. Offices: 199 Two Mile Road, Kingswood, Bristol BS15 1AZ. 0272 352303. Pirates Hotline 0891 338345. Fax 0272 352303.

Ground capacity: 8880.

Record attendance: 9464 v Liverpool, FA Cup 4th rd, 8 February 1992 (Twerton Park). 38,472 v Preston NE, FA Cup 4th rd, 30 January 1960 (Eastville).

Record receipts: £62,480 v Liverpool, FA Cup 4th rd, 8 February 1992.

Pitch measurements: 110yd × 75yd.

President: Marquis of Worcester.

Vice-Presidents: Dr W. T. Cussen, A. I. Seager, H. E. L. Brown, R. Redmond.

Chairman: D. H. A. Dunford. ***Vice-chairman:***G. M. H. Dunford.

Directors: R. Craig, V. Stokes (director in charge of administration), R. Andrews.

Manager: John Ward. ***Assistant Manager:*** Dennis Booth.

Coach: Steve Cross. ***Physio:*** Keith James. ***Youth team coach:*** Tony Gill. ***Commercial Manager:*** Tony Wood.

Secretary: Ian Wilson. ***Assistant Secretary:*** I. I. Wilson. ***Office Manager:*** Mrs Angela Mann.

Year Formed: 1883. ***Turned Professional:*** 1897. ***Ltd Co.:*** 1896.

Previous Names: 1883, Black Arabs; 1884, Eastville Rovers; 1897, Bristol Eastville Rovers; 1898, Bristol Rovers.

Club Nickname: 'Pirates'.

Previous Grounds: Purdown, Three Acres, Ashley Hill, Rudgeway, Eastville.

Record League Victory: 7–0 v Brighton & HA, Division 3 (S), 29 November 1952 – Hoyle; Bamford, Geoff Fox; Pitt, Warren, Sampson; McIlvenny, Roost (2), Lambden (1), Bradford (1), Peterbridge (2). (1 og). 7–0 v Swansea T, Division 2, 2 October 1954 – Radford; Bamford, Watkins; Pitt, Muir, Anderson; Petherbridge, Bradford (2), Meyer, Roost (1), Hooper (2). (2 og). 7–0 v Shrewsbury T, Division 3, 21 March 1964 – Hall; Hillard, Gwyn Jones; Oldfield, Stone (1), Mabbutt; Jarman (2), Brown (1), Biggs (1p), Hamilton, Bobby Jones (2).

Record Cup Victory: 6–0 v Merthyr Tydfil, FA Cup, 1st rd, 14 November 1987 – Martyn; Alexander (Dryden), Tanner, Hibbitt, Twentyman, Jones, Holloway, Meacham (1), White (2), Penrice (3) (Reece), Purnell.

Record Defeat: 0–12 v Luton T, Division 3 (S), 13 April 1936.

Most League Points (2 for a win): 64, Division 3 (S), 1952–53.

Most League Points (3 for a win): 93, Division 3, 1989–90.

Most League Goals: 92, Division 3 (S), 1952–53.

Highest League Scorer in Season: Geoff Bradford, 33, Division 3 (S), 1952–53.

Most League Goals in Total Aggregate: Geoff Bradford, 245, 1949–64.

Most Capped Player: Neil Slatter, 10 (22), Wales.

Most League Appearances: Stuart Taylor, 545, 1966–80.

Record Transfer Fee Received: £1,000,000 from Crystal Palace for Nigel Martyn, November 1989.

Record Transfer Fee Paid: £370,000 to QPR for Andy Tillson, November 1992.

Football League Record: 1920 Original Member of Division 3; 1921–53 Division 3 (S); 1953–62 Division 2; 1962–74 Division 3; 1974–81 Division 2; 1981–90 Division 3; 1990– 92 Division 2. 1992–93 Division 1; 1993– Division 2.

Honours: *Football League:* Division 2 best season: 6th, 1955–56, 1958–59; Division 3 (S) – Champions 1952–53; Division 3 – Champions 1989–90; Runners-up 1973–74. *FA Cup:* best season: 6th rd, 1950–51, 1957–58. *Football League Cup:* best season: 5th rd, 1970–71, 1971–72.

BRISTOL ROVERS 1993—94 LEAGUE RECORD

Match No.	Date	Venue	Opponents	Result		H/T Score	Lg. Pos.	Goalscorers	Attendance
1	Aug 14	H	Bournemouth	L	0-1	0-0	—		7234
2	21	A	Leyton Orient	L	0-1	0-0	24		4155
3	28	H	Fulham	W	2-1	1-0	17	Taylor 2	5261
4	Sept 1	A	Brighton & HA	W	2-0	0-0	—	Taylor 2	5675
5	4	A	Hull C	L	0-3	0-1	15		5362
6	11	H	Port Vale	W	2-0	2-0	13	Taylor, Skinner	4908
7	15	H	Exeter C	D	1-1	0-0	—	Browning	5001
8	18	A	Rotherham U	D	1-1	0-1	15	Archer	4000
9	25	H	Burnley	W	3-1	3-0	10	Taylor, McLean, Sterling	5732
10	Oct 2	A	Barnet	W	2-1	0-0	7	Browning, Taylor	3158
11	9	H	Bradford C	W	4-3	0-1	5	Stewart 2 (2 pens), Taylor, Sterling	5323
12	16	A	Cardiff C	W	2-1	1-0	4	Taylor 2	5563
13	23	H	Plymouth Arg	D	0-0	0-0	4		7758
14	30	A	Huddersfield T	L	0-1	0-0	7		5612
15	Nov 2	A	York C	W	1-0	0-0	—	Taylor	3758
16	6	H	Hartlepool U	D	1-1	0-1	4	Skinner	5308
17	20	A	Stockport Co	W	2-0	1-0	3	Archer, Taylor	5250
18	27	H	Cambridge U	W	2-1	0-1	3	Skinner, Taylor	4477
19	Dec 11	H	Leyton Orient	D	1-1	1-1	3	Taylor	4604
20	18	A	Bournemouth	L	0-3	0-3	5		4811
21	Jan 1	H	Swansea C	L	1-2	0-0	10	Browning	6285
22	3	A	Blackpool	W	1-0	1-0	8	Archer	3311
23	8	A	Brentford	W	4-3	3-1	5	Browning, Taylor 2, Skinner	6841
24	15	H	Cardiff C	W	2-1	1-0	4	Taylor, McLean	5683
25	22	A	Bradford C	W	1-0	1-0	4	Archer	6122
26	26	H	Reading	D	1-1	1-0	—	Clark	7694
27	29	H	Huddersfield T	D	0-0	0-0	2		5127
28	Feb 5	A	Plymouth Arg	D	3-3	3-2	3	Skinner, Archer, Sterling	13,318
29	12	H	Brentford	L	1-4	0-3	6	Stewart	5685
30	19	A	Fulham	W	1-0	1-0	3	Taylor	5063
31	23	H	Brighton & HA	W	1-0	1-0	—	Taylor	4776
32	25	H	Hull C	D	1-1	1-1	2	Taylor	5703
33	Mar 5	A	Port Vale	L	0-2	0-1	4		8682
34	12	H	Rotherham U	L	0-2	0-2	5		4224
35	15	A	Exeter C	L	0-1	0-0	—		4399
36	19	A	Burnley	L	1-3	0-1	5	Hardyman	10,651
37	22	A	Wrexham	L	2-3	1-1	—	Waddock, Channing	3184
38	26	H	Barnet	W	5-2	4-0	6	Channing 3 (1 pen), Walker (og), Stewart	3802
39	30	H	Blackpool	W	1-0	1-0	—	Sterling	4231
40	Apr 2	A	Reading	L	0-2	0-1	6		8035
41	4	H	Wrexham	W	3-1	3-0	6	Pounder 2, Stewart	4708
42	9	A	Swansea C	L	0-2	0-0	7		3961
43	16	H	York C	L	0-1	0-0	8		5007
44	23	A	Hartlepool U	L	1-2	0-1	8	Taylor	1409
45	30	H	Stockport Co	D	1-1	0-0	8	Sterling	4189
46	May 7	A	Cambridge U	W	3-1	2-0	8	Taylor 2, Channing	4402

Final League Position: 8

GOALSCORERS

League (60): Taylor 23, Archer 5, Channing 5 (1 pen), Skinner 5, Sterling 5, Stewart 5 (2 pens), Browning 4, McLean 2, Pounder 2, Clark 1, Hardyman 1, Waddock 1, own goal 1.
Coca-Cola Cup (1): Sterling 1.
FA Cup (1): Archer 1.

Parkin 43	Alexander 15 + 3	Hardyman 17 + 8	Waddock 39	Clark 34 + 2	Yates 1	Sterling 43	Taylor 44 + 1	Stewart 23 + 6	Browning 30 + 1	Archer 37	Maddison 36 + 1	Davis 2 + 8	Channing 28 + 1	Tillson 12 + 1	Skinner 27 + 2	Saunders 4 + 3	Pounder 8 + 2	McLean 17 + 10	Wright 29	Paul — + 4	Margetson 2 + 1	Evans 1 + 1	Kelly 1	Pritchard 11	Gurney 2 + 1	Tovey — + 1	*Match No.*
1	2	3	4	5	6	7	8	9	*10*	11	12	14															1
1			4	5		7	8	9	12	11	3		2	6	10												2
1	12		4	5			8	*9*	7	11	3	14	2	6	10												3
1	12		4	5		7	8			11	3	14	2	6	10	*9*											4
1	12		4	5		7	8			11	3	14	2	6	10	*9*											5
1	2			5		7	8		4	11	3			6	10	9	12										6
1	2			5		7	8	12	4	11	3				10	9		6									7
1	2			5		7	8	9	4	11	3				10	12		6									8
1	2	14				7	8	9	4	11	3				*10*	12		6	5								9
1	2		10				8	9	4	11	3					12	7	6	5								10
1	2		10			7	8	9	4	11	3	12						6	5								11
1			10			7	8	9	4	11	3		2					6	5								12
1			10	12		7	8	9	4	11	3		2					6	5								13
1			10	14		7	8	9	4	11	3		2		12			*6*	5								14
1		11	10	6		7	8		4		3	9	2		12				5								15
1			10	5		7	8		4	11	3	12	2		9				6								16
1			10	5		7	8		4	11	3		2		9				6								17
1			10	5		7	8		4	11	3		2		9			12	6								18
1				5		7	8	9	4	11	3			2	10				6	12							19
1			10	5		7	8		4	11	3		2		9				6		12						20
	2			5		7	8	*10*	4	11	3		12		9				6	14	1						21
1	2	12	10	5			8		4	11	3				9			14	*6*			7					22
	2	12	10	5		7	*8*		4	11	3			14	9			6			1						23
1	2	12	10	5		7	8		4	11	3				9			6									24
1	2	12	10	5		7	8		4	11	3				9			6									25
1	2	12	10	5		7	8		4	11	3				9			6									26
1	2		10	5		7	8		4	11	3				9			6									27
1	*2*	12	10	5		7	8	14	4	11	3				9			6									28
1		12	10	5		7	*8*	4		11	3	14	2		9			6									29
1		4	10	5		7	8	9		11	3		2					12	6								30
1		4	10	5		7	8	*9*		11	3		2				14	12	6								31
1		9	10	5		7	8	12	4	11	3		2						6								32
		9	10	5		7	8		4	11	3		2						6				1				33
1		11	10	5		7	8	9	4		3		2						6			12					34
1				5		7	8	9		*11*	3	12	4		10			14	6					2			35
1		10	4	5		7	8	12			3		9				11	14	6					*2*			36
1		10	4	5		7	8	12			3		9				11		6					2			37
1		3	4	5		7	8	9					10				11		6					2			38
1		3	4	5		7	8	10					*9*	6			11			12				2			39
1		3	4	5		7	8	9						6	10		11	12							2		40
1		3	4			7		9				*8*		6	10		11	12	5	14				2			41
1		3	4			7	8						9	6	10		11	12	5					*2*		14	42
1		3	4			7	12		8	11			9	6	10				5					2			43
1		3	4			7	8	14	9	11			*10*	6				12	5					*2*			44
1		3	4			7	8	9		11			10					6	5					2	12		45
1			4			7	8	9		11			10					6	5					2	3		46

Coca-Cola Cup	First Round	WBA (h)	1-4
		(a)	0-0
FA Cup	First Round	Wycombe W (h)	1-2

BRISTOL ROVERS

Player and Position	Ht	Wt	Birth Date	Birth Place	Source	Clubs	League App	League Gls
Goalkeepers								
Gavin Kelly*	6 0	12 13	29 9 68	Beverley		Hull C	11	—
						Bristol R (loan)	—	—
						Bristol R	30	—
Brian Parkin	6 1	12 00	12 10 65	Birkenhead	Local	Oldham Ath	6	—
						Crewe Alex (loan)	12	—
						Crewe Alex	86	—
						Crystal Palace (loan)	—	—
						Crystal Palace	20	—
						Bristol R	181	—
Defenders								
Ian Alexander	5 8	10 07	26 1 63	Glasgow	Leicester J	Rotherham U	11	—
						Motherwell	24	2
						Morton	7	1
					Pezoporikos	Bristol R	291	6
Justin Channing	5 11	11 07	19 11 68	Reading	Apprentice	QPR	55	5
						Bristol R	54	8
Billy Clark	6 0	12 03	19 5 67	Christchurch	Local	Bournemouth	4	—
						Bristol R	140	5
Steve Cross*	5 10	11 05	22 12 59	Wolverhampton	Apprentice	Shrewsbury T	262	34
						Derby Co	73	3
						Bristol R	43	2
Andrew Gurney	5 7	10 08	25 1 74	Bristol	Trainee	Bristol R	3	—
Paul Hardyman	5 8	11 07	11 3 64	Portsmouth	Local	Portsmouth	117	3
						Sunderland	106	9
						Bristol R	62	5
Ian McLean	6 2	13 02	13 8 66	Paisley	Metroford	Bristol R	27	2
Lee Maddison	5 11	11 00	5 10 72	Bristol	Trainee	Bristol R	59	—
David Pritchard	5 7	11 04	27 5 72	Wolverhampton	Telford	Bristol R	11	—
Gareth Taylor	6 2	12 05	25 2 73	Weston-Super-Mare	Southampton	Bristol R	1	—
Andy Tillson	6 2	12 07	30 6 66	Huntingdon	Kettering T	Grimsby T	105	5
						QPR	29	2
						Grimsby T (loan)	4	—
						Bristol R	42	—
Ian Wright	6 1	12 08	10 3 72	Lichfield	Trainee	Stoke C	6	—
						Bristol R	29	—
Midfield								
Lee Archer	5 6	9 06	6 11 72	Bristol	Trainee	Bristol R	44	6
Scott Crossey‡	5 6	9 07	18 2 75	Somerset	Trainee	Bristol R	—	—
Richard Evans*	5 11	11 07	12 4 68	Ebbw Vale	Weymouth	Bristol R	15	1
						Exeter C (loan)	5	2
Justin Skinner	6 0	11 03	30 1 69	London	Apprentice	Fulham	135	23
						Bristol R	83	8
Worrell Sterling	5 7	10 11	8 6 65	Bethnal Green	Apprentice	Watford	94	14
						Peterborough U	193	29
						Bristol R	43	5
Paul Tovey	5 8	11 07	5 12 73	Wokingham	Trainee	Bristol R	1	—
Gary Waddock	5 10	11 12	17 3 62	Alperton	Apprentice	QPR	203	8
					Charleroi	Millwall	58	2
						QPR	—	—
						Swindon T (loan)	6	—
						Bristol R	70	1
Forwards								
Marcus Browning	5 11	12 00	22 4 71	Bristol	Trainee	Bristol R	62	5
						Hereford U (loan)	7	5
Mike Davis	6 0	12 00	19 10 74	Bristol	Yate T	Bristol R	11	1
David Mehew*	5 11	12 06	29 10 67	Camberley		Leeds U	—	—
						Bristol R	222	63
						Exeter C (loan)	7	—
Martin Paul	5 8	9 07	2 2 75	Whalley	Trainee	Bristol R	4	—
Tony Pounder*	5 8	11 00	11 3 66	Yeovil	Weymouth	Bristol R	113	10

BRISTOL ROVERS

Colours: Blue and white quartered shirts, white shorts, blue stockings. **Change colours:** Green, black, white shadow striped shirts, black shorts, white stockings.

Foundation: Bristol Rovers were formed at a meeting in Stapleton Road, Eastville, in 1883. However, they first went under the name of the Black Arabs (wearing black shirts). Changing their name to Eastville Rovers in their second season, they won the Gloucestershire Senior Cup in 1888–89. Original members of the Bristol & District League in 1892, this eventually became the Western League and Eastville Rovers adopted professionalism in 1897.

First Football League game: 28 August, 1920, Division 3, v Millwall (a) L 0-2 – Stansfield; Bethune, Panes; Boxley, Kenny, Steele; Chance, Bird, Sims, Bell, Palmer.

Did you know: On 7 January 1956, Bristol Rovers beat Manchester United 4-0 in a third round FA Cup tie in front of a crowd of 35,872 at Eastville. World Cup referee Ken Aston was the official in charge.

Managers (and Secretary-Managers)
Alfred Homer 1899–1920 (continued as secretary to 1928), Ben Hall 1920–21, Andy Wilson 1921–26, Joe Palmer 1926–29, Dave McLean 1929–30, Albert Prince-Cox 1930–36, Percy Smith 1936–37, Brough Fletcher 1938–49, Bert Tann 1950–68 (continued as GM to 1972), Fred Ford 1968–69, Bill Dodgin Snr 1969–72, Don Megson 1972–77, Bobby Campbell 1978–79, Harold Jarman 1979–80, Terry Cooper 1980–81, Bobby Gould 1981–83, David Williams 1983–85, Bobby Gould 1985–87, Gerry Francis 1987–91, Martin Dobson 1991, Dennis Rofe 1992, Malcolm Allison 1992–93, John Ward March 1993–

Player and Position	*Ht*	*Wt*	*Birth Date*	*Birth Place*	*Source*	*Clubs*	*League App*	*League Gls*
Philip Purnell‡	5 6	9 08	16 9 64	Bristol		Bristol R	153	22
						Swansea C (loan)	5	1
Marcus Stewart	5 10	10 03	7 11 72	Bristol	Trainee	Bristol R	100	21
John Taylor	6 2	11 12	24 10 64	Norwich	Local	Colchester U	—	—
					Sudbury	Cambridge U	160	46
						Bristol R	95	44

Trainees
Barton, Jonathan; Dale, Dylan R. J; Dibble, Jamie L. A; Francis, Marlon B; French, Jonathan C; Goddard, Timothy P; Harrington, Mark P; Hayfield, Matthew A; Hope, Matthew P; Law, Marcus W; Levett, Simon; Micciche, Marco; Mills, Nicholas C; Parkinson, Matthew S; Rofe, Daniel; White, Thomas M; Wiltshire, John M.

Associated Schoolboys
De-Long, Nicholas M; Gitson, Lee A; Hope, David J; Lloyd, Andrew P; Low, Joshua D; Morgan, Gavin S; Nelson, Ricky O; Sanderson, Jonathan; Spring, Andrew J; Westlake, Tristan M; Williams, Leigh M.

Associated Schoolboys who have accepted the Club's offer of a Traineeship/Contract
Serjeant, Philip R.

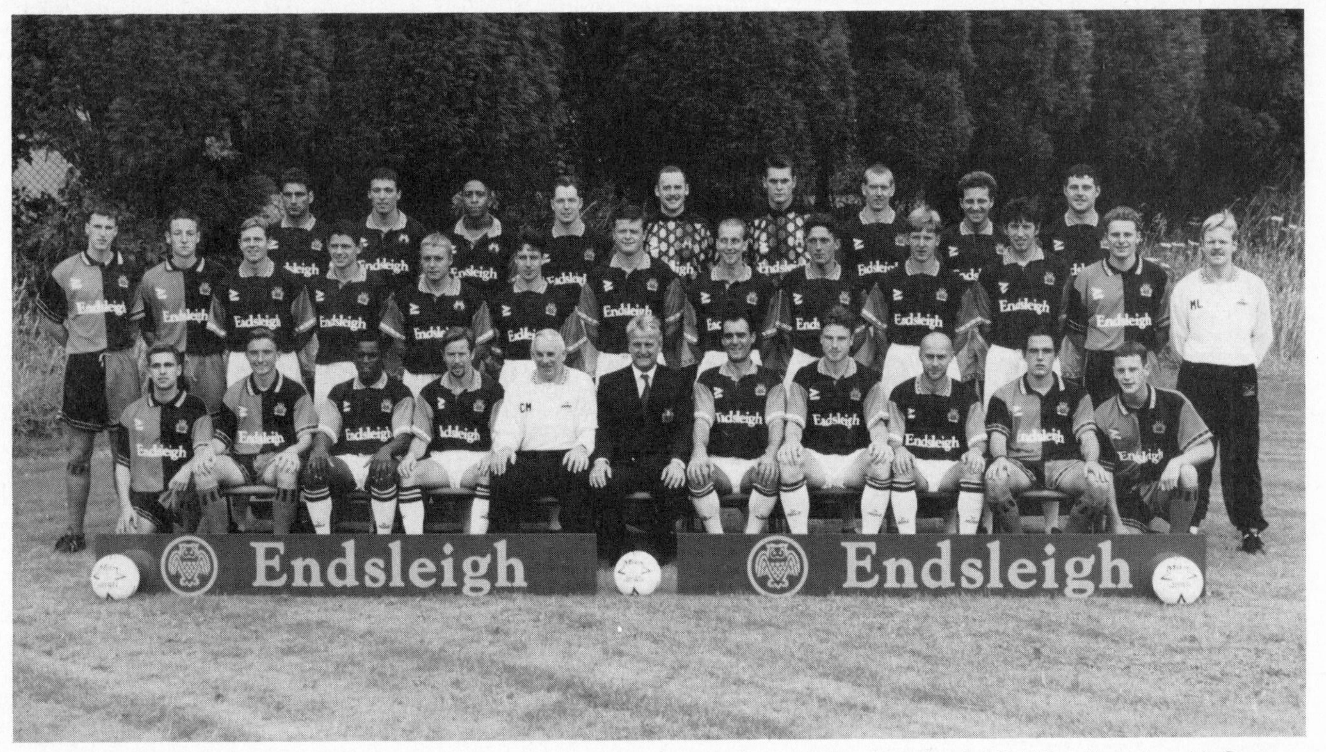

BURNLEY 1993–94 *Back row (left to right):* Adrian Randall, Mark Monington, Roger Eli, Robbie Painter, David Williams, Marlon Beresford, Paul Wilson, Warren Joyce, John Deary.
Centre row: Neil Howarth, John Mullin, Ian Measham, Steve Harper, Les Thompson, Steve Penney, John Pender, David Campbell, David Eyres, Andy Farrell, John Clayton, Wayne Dowell, Mark Leather (Physio).
Front row: Graham Lancashire, Chris Brass, John Francis, Adrian Heath, Clive Middlemass (Assistant Manager), Jimmy Mullen (Manager), Mike Conroy, Steve Davis, Kevin Russell, Brian Welch, Richard Livingstone.

Division 1 BURNLEY

Turf Moor, Burnley BB10 4BX. Telephone Burnley (01282) 427777. Fax (01282) 428938. Clubcall: 0891 121153.

Ground capacity: 22,085.

Record attendance: 54,775 v Huddersfield T, FA Cup 3rd rd, 23 February 1924.

Record receipts; £63,988 v Sheffield W, FA Cup 6th rd, 12 March 1983.

Pitch measurements: 115yd × 73yd.

Chairman: F. J. Teasdale.

Vice-chairman: Dr R. D. Iven MRCS (Eng), LRCP (Lond), MRCGP.

Directors: B. Dearing LLB, B. Rothwell JP, C. Holt,R. Blakeborough.

Manager: Jimmy Mullen. ***Assistant Manager:*** Clive Middlemass.

Secretary: Mark Blackbourne. ***Youth Team Coach:*** Harry Wilson.

Commercial Manager: T. Skelly. ***Physio:*** M. Leather.

Year Formed: 1882. ***Turned Professional:*** 1883. ***Ltd Co.:*** 1897.

Previous Name: 1881–82, Burnley Rovers.

Club Nickname: 'The Clarets'.

Previous Grounds: 1881, Calder Vale; 1882, Turf Moor.

Record League Victory: 9–0 v Darwen, Division 1, 9 January 1892 – Hillman; Walker, McFettridge, Lang, Matthews, Keenan, Nicol (3), Bowes, Espie (1), McLardie (3), Hill (2).

Record Cup Victory: 9–0 v Crystal Palace, FA Cup, 2nd rd (replay) 10 February 1909 – Dawson; Barron, McLean; Cretney (2), Leake, Moffat; Morley, Ogden, Smith (3), Abbott (2), Smethams (1). 9–0 v New Brighton, FA Cup, 4th rd, 26 January 1957 – Blacklaw; Angus, Winton; Seith, Adamson, Miller; Newlands (1), McIlroy (3), Lawson (3), Cheesebrough (1), Pilkington (1). 9–0 v Penrith FA Cup, 1st rd, 17 November 1984 – Hansbury; Miller, Hampton, Phelan, Overson (Kennedy), Hird (3 incl. 1p), Grewcock (1), Powell (2), Taylor (3), Biggins, Hutchison.

Record Defeat: 0–10 v Aston Villa, Division 1, 29 August 1925 and v Sheffield U, Division 1, 19 January 1929.

Most League Points (2 for a win): 62, Division 2, 1972–73.

Most League Points (3 for a win): 83, Division 4, 1991–92.

Most League Goals: 102, Division 1, 1960–61.

Highest League Scorer in Season: George Beel, 35, Division 1, 1927–28.

Most League Goals in Total Aggregate: George Beel, 178, 1923–32.

Most Capped Player: Jimmy McIlroy, 51 (55), Northern Ireland.

Most League Appearances: Jerry Dawson, 522, 1907–28.

Record Transfer Fee Received: £300,000 from Everton for Martin Dobson, August 1974, and from Derby Co for Leighton James, November 1975.

Record Transfer Fee Paid: £165,000 to QPR for Leighton James, September 1978.

Football League Record: 1888 Original Member of the Football League; 1897–98 Division 2; 1898–1900 Division 1; 1900–13 Division 2; 1913–30 Division 1; 1930–47 Division 2; 1947–71 Division 1; 1971–73 Division 2; 1973–76 Division 1; 1976–80 Division 2; 1980–82 Division 3; 1982–83 Division 2; 1983–85 Division 3; 1985–92 Division 4; 1992–94 Division 2; 1994– Division 1.

Honours: *Football League:* Division 1 – Champions 1920–21, 1959–60; Runners-up 1919–20, 1961–62; Division 2 – Champions 1897–98, 1972–73; Runners-up 1912–13, 1946–47; Division 3 – Champions 1981–82. Division 4 – Champions 1991–92. Record 30 consecutive Division 1 games without defeat 1920–21. *FA Cup:* Winners 1913–14; Runners-up 1946–47, 1961–62. *Football League Cup:* semi-final 1960–61, 1968–69, 1982–83. *Anglo Scottish Cup:* Winners 1978–79. *Sherpa Van Trophy:* Runners-up 1988. **European Competitions;** *European Cup:* 1960–61. *European Fairs Cup:* 1966–67.

BURNLEY 1993—94 LEAGUE RECORD

Match No.	Date	Venue	Opponents	Result		H/T Score	Lg. Pos.	Goalscorers	Attendance
1	Aug 14	H	Port Vale	W	2-1	1-1	—	Joyce 2	12,594
2	21	A	Reading	L	1-2	0-2	12	Eyres (pen)	5855
3	28	H	Leyton Orient	W	4-1	2-1	7	Eyres, Deary, Farrell, Heath	10,133
4	31	A	Rotherham U	L	2-3	1-2	—	Law (og), Francis	5533
5	Sept 4	A	Bournemouth	L	0-1	0-1	13		5574
6	11	H	Fulham	W	3-1	1-0	12	Randall, Eyres, Deary	9021
7	14	H	Brighton & HA	W	3-0	2-0	—	Russell 2, Davis	8837
8	18	A	Stockport Co	L	1-2	0-1	9	Francis	5122
9	25	A	Bristol R	L	1-3	0-3	12	Russell	5732
10	Oct 2	H	Hartlepool U	W	2-0	1-0	8	Eyres, Heath	9532
11	9	H	Plymouth Arg	W	4-2	1-1	8	Eyres, Monington, Peel 2	10,488
12	16	A	Bradford C	W	1-0	1-0	6	Heath	9501
13	23	H	Huddersfield T	D	1-1	0-0	6	Eyres (pen)	12,011
14	30	A	Cambridge U	W	1-0	1-0	3	Eyres	4826
15	Nov 2	A	Swansea C	L	1-3	1-2	—	Francis	3358
16	6	H	York C	W	2-1	1-0	3	Eyres 2 (1 pen)	10,236
17	20	A	Brentford	D	0-0	0-0	6		6085
18	27	H	Exeter C	W	3-2	2-1	4	Russell, Eyres (pen), Francis	9040
19	Dec 11	H	Reading	L	0-1	0-1	7		11,650
20	18	A	Port Vale	D	1-1	0-0	7	Mullin	10,710
21	27	H	Wrexham	W	2-1	0-1	5	Russell, Davis	15,357
22	29	A	Barnet	D	1-1	0-0	5	Heath	2360
23	Jan 1	H	Blackpool	W	3-1	1-1	4	Farrell, Russell, Francis	18,165
24	3	A	Hull C	W	2-1	1-1	4	Davis, Deary	11,232
25	15	H	Bradford C	L	0-1	0-0	5		13,517
26	22	A	Plymouth Arg	L	2-3	0-2	6	Heath, Philliskirk	10,595
27	29	H	Cambridge U	W	3-0	1-0	5	Randall, Eyres (pen), Heath	10,659
28	Feb 5	A	Huddersfield T	D	1-1	0-0	5	Deary	10,634
29	12	H	Cardiff C	W	2-0	0-0	4	Philliskirk, Francis	11,276
30	19	A	Leyton Orient	L	1-3	1-0	5	Parkinson	5201
31	25	H	Bournemouth	W	4-0	2-0	5	Eyres, Philliskirk, Joyce, Davis	10,383
32	Mar 1	A	Cardiff C	L	1-2	1-0	—	Davis	5469
33	5	A	Fulham	L	2-3	2-1	6	Eyres, Randall	4943
34	12	H	Stockport Co	D	1-1	0-0	7	McMinn	13,130
35	16	A	Brighton & HA	D	1-1	1-0	—	Davis	8021
36	19	H	Bristol R	W	3-1	1-0	5	Philliskirk, Heath, McMinn	10,651
37	26	A	Hartlepool U	L	1-4	1-2	7	Eyres	2879
38	29	H	Hull C	W	3-1	1-0	—	Pender, Eyres 2 (1 pen)	10,574
39	Apr 2	A	Wrexham	L	0-1	0-0	7		7253
40	4	H	Barnet	W	5-0	0-0	7	Philliskirk 3, Heath, Eyres	10,412
41	9	A	Blackpool	W	2-1	2-0	4	Eyres, Francis	7956
42	16	H	Swansea C	D	1-1	0-1	6	Davis	10,694
43	23	A	York C	D	0-0	0-0	6		8642
44	26	H	Rotherham U	D	0-0	0-0	—		10,806
45	30	H	Brentford	W	4-1	2-1	6	Eyres, McMinn, Heath, Randall	11,363
46	May 7	A	Exeter C	L	1-4	0-1	6	Joyce	3155

Final League Position: 6

GOALSCORERS

League (79): Eyres 19 (6 pens), Heath 9, Davis 7, Francis 7, Philliskirk 7, Russell 6, Deary 4, Joyce 4, Randall 4, McMinn 3, Farrell 2, Peel 2, Monington 1, Mullin 1, Parkinson 1, Pender 1, own goal 1.
Coca-Cola Cup (7): Eyres 3 (1 pen), Davis 1, Deary 1, Francis 1, Russell 1.
FA Cup (7): Eyres 4, Heath 1, Joyce 1, own goal 1.

Beresford 46	Measham 6	Thompson 36	Davis 42	Pender 42	Joyce 19 + 3	Francis 31 + 12	Deary 43	Heath 41	Russell 26 + 2	Eyres 45	Monington 16 + 4	Farrell 13 + 9	Randall 31 + 6	Mullin 1 + 5	Patterson — + 1	Peel 4 + 9	Wilson 11	Philliskirk 19	Parkinson 20	McMinn 14	Lancashire — + 1	Smith — + 1	Match No.
1	2	3	4	5	6	7	8	9	10	11	12												1
1	2	3	4	5	6	7	8	9	10	11	12												2
1	2	3	4	5		7	8	9	10	11		6											3
1	2	3	4	5		7	8	9	10	11	12	6	14										4
1	2	3	4	5		7	8	9	10	11	12	6	14										5
1	2	3	4	5		7	8	9	10	11			6										6
1		3	4	5		7	8	9	10	11		2	6	12									7
1		3	4	5		7	8	9	10	11		2	6										8
1		3	4	5		7	8	9	10	11		2	6	12	14								9
1		3	4	5		7	8	9	10	11	2	12	6			14							10
1		3	4	5		7	8	9	10	11	2		6			12							11
1		3	4	5		12	8	9	10	11	2		6			7							12
1		3	4	5		12	8	9	10	11	2		6			7							13
1		3	4	5		7	8	9	10	11	2		6										14
1		3	4	5	14	7	8	9	10	11	2		6			12							15
1		3	4	5	6	7	8	9	10	11	2					12							16
1		3	4	5	6	7	8	9	10	11	2		12										17
1		3	4	5	6	7	8	9	10	11	2												18
1		3	4	5	6	7	8	9	10	11	2		12	14									19
1		3	4	5	2	7	8	9	10	11		12	6	14									20
1			4	5	2	7	8		10	11			6			9	3						21
1			4	5	2	7	8	9	10	11		12	6			14	3						22
1		3	4	5	2	7	8	9	10	11		6											23
1		3	4	5	2	7	8	9	10			6					11						24
1		3	4	5	2	7	8	9	10	11		12	6			14							25
1		3	4	5	2	14	8	9	10	11	6	12						7					26
1		3		5	12	7	8	9		11	4		6					10	2				27
1		3		5		7	8	9	12	11	4		6					10	2				28
1				5		7	8	9		11	4		6				3	10	2				29
1				5		7	8	9	12	11	4		6				3	10	2				30
1			4	5	8	7		9		11			6			12	3	10	2				31
1			4	5	8	12		9		11	7	14	6				3	10	2				32
1			4	5		12	8	9		11			6				3	10	2	7			33
1			4	5		12	8	9		11			6				3	10	2	7			34
1			4	5		12	8	9		11			6				3	10	2	7			35
1			4	5		12	8	9		11			6				3	10	2	7			36
1		3	4	5		12	8	9		11			6					10	2	7			37
1		3	4	5		12	8	9		11		14	6					10	2	7			38
1		3	4	5		12	8	9		11		6						10	2	7			39
1		3	4	5		12	8	9		11			6					10	2	7			40
1		3	4		6	9	8			11		5	12					10	2	7			41
1		3	4		6		8			11		5	12	9		14		10	2	7			42
1		3	4		10		8			11		5	6			12		9	2	7			43
1		3	4		12		8			11		5	6	14		9		10	2	7			44
1		3	4	5		10	8	9		11		12	6						2	7	14		45
1		3	4	5	8	10		9		11		12	6						2	7		14	46

Coca-Cola Cup	First Round	Preston NE (a)	2-1
		(h)	4-1
	Second Round	Tottenham H (h)	0-0
		(a)	1-3
FA Cup	First Round	York C (h)	0-0
		(a)	3-2
	Second Round	Rochdale (h)	4-1
	Third Round	Charlton Ath (a)	0-3

BURNLEY

Player and Position	Ht	Wt	Birth Date	Birth Place	Source	Clubs	League App	League Gls
Goalkeepers								
Marlon Beresford	6 1	12 06	2 9 69	Lincoln	Trainee	Sheffield W	—	—
						Bury (loan)	1	—
						Ipswich T (loan)	—	—
						Northampton T (loan)	13	—
						Crewe Alex (loan)	3	—
						Northampton T (loan)	15	—
						Burnley	90	—
Wayne Russell	6 2	13 07	29 11 67	Cardiff	Ebbw Vale	Burnley	—	—
David Williams	6 0	12 00	18 9 68	Liverpool	Trainee	Oldham Ath	—	—
						Burnley	24	—
						Rochdale (loan)	6	—
						Crewe Alex (loan)	—	—
Defenders								
Chris Brass	5 9	11 03	24 7 75	Easington	Trainee	Burnley	—	—
Steve Davis	6 2	12 08	30 10 68	Hexham	Trainee	Southampton	7	—
						Burnley (loan)	9	—
						Notts Co (loan)	2	—
						Burnley	119	15
Wayne Dowell	5 10	11 02	28 12 73	Co Durham	Trainee	Burnley	—	—
Roger Eli*	5 11	11 03	11 9 65	Bradford	Apprentice	Leeds U	2	—
						Wolverhampton W	18	—
						Cambridge U	—	—
						Crewe Alex	27	1
						York C	4	1
						Bury	2	—
					Northwich Vic	Burnley	99	11
Andy Farrell	6 0	11 00	7 10 65	Colchester	School	Colchester U	105	5
						Burnley	257	19
Neil Howarth‡	6 2	12 06	15 11 71	Farnworth	Trainee	Burnley	1	—
Paul McKay	5 8	10 05	28 1 71	Banbury	Trainee	Burnley	12	—
Gary Parkinson	5 10	11 06	10 1 68	Middlesbrough	Everton	Middlesbrough	202	5
						Southend U (loan)	6	—
						Bolton W	3	—
						Burnley	20	1
John Pender	6 0	12 03	19 11 63	Luton	Apprentice	Wolverhampton W	117	3
						Charlton Ath	41	—
						Bristol C	83	3
						Burnley	165	8
Les Thompson	5 10	11 00	23 9 68	Cleethorpes		Hull C	35	4
						Scarborough (loan)	3	1
						Maidstone U	38	—
						Burnley	39	—
Paul Wilson	5 10	13 00	2 8 68	Bradford	Trainee	Huddersfield T	15	—
						Norwich C	—	—
						Northampton T	141	6
						Halifax T	45	7
						Burnley	31	—
Midfield								
Dave Campbell*	5 10	11 02	2 6 65	Eglinton	Oxford BC	Nottingham F	41	3
						Notts Co (loan)	18	2
						Charlton Ath	30	1
						Plymouth Arg (loan)	1	—
						Bradford C	35	4
						Shamrock R (loan)	31	5
						WBA	—	—
						Rotherham U	1	—
						Burnley	8	—
						Lincoln C (loan)	4	1
John Deary	5 10	12 04	18 10 62	Ormskirk	Apprentice	Blackpool	303	43
						Burnley	199	22
Warren Joyce	5 9	11 11	20 1 65	Oldham	Local	Bolton W	184	17
						Preston NE	177	34
						Plymouth Arg	30	3
						Burnley	22	4
Paul McKenzie	5 9	11 10	4 10 69	Aberdeen	Peterhead	Burnley	4	—
Mark Monington	6 1	13 00	21 10 70	Bilsthorpe	Schoolboy	Burnley	84	5

BURNLEY

Colours: Claret shirts with sky blue sleeves, white shorts and stockings. **Change colours:** Jade/black halved shirts and shorts, jade stockings.

Foundation: The majority of those responsible for the formation of the Burnley club in 1881 were from the defunct rugby club Burnley Rovers. Indeed, they continued to play rugby for a year before changing to soccer and dropping "Rovers" from their name. The changes were decided at a meeting held in May 1882 at the Bull Hotel.

First Football League game: 8 September, 1888, Football League, v PNE (a), L 2-5 – Smith; Lang, Bury, Abrams, Friel, Keenan, Brady, Tait, Poland (1), Gallocher (1), Yates.

Did you know: When Burnley beat Loughborough Town 9-3 in a Division 2 match on 28 March 1898, Jimmy Ross scored a hat-trick in the first 14 minutes and went on to claim five of their goals.

Managers (and Secretary-Managers)
Arthur F. Sutcliffe 1893–96*, Harry Bradshaw 1896–99*, Ernest Magnall 1899–1903*, Spen Whittaker 1903–10, R. H. Wadge 1910–11*, John Haworth 1911–25, Albert Pickles 1925–32, Tom Bromilow 1932–35, Alf Boland 1935–39*, Cliff Britton 1945–48, Frank Hill 1948–54, Alan Brown 1954–57, Billy Dougall 1957–58, Harry Potts 1958–70 (GM to 1972), Jimmy Adamson 1970–76, Joe Brown 1976–77, Harry Potts 1977–79, Brian Miller 1979–83, John Bond 1983–84, John Benson 1984–85, Martin Buchan 1985, Tommy Cavanagh 1985–86, Brian Miller 1986–89, Frank Casper 1989–91, Jimmy Mullen October 1991–

Player and Position	Ht	Wt	Birth Date	Birth Place	Source	Clubs	League App	League Gls
Steve Penney‡	5 8	10 07	16 1 64	Ballymena	Ballymena U	Brighton Hearts Burnley	138 9 11	15 — 3
Nick Pickering*	6 0	11 10	4 8 63	Newcastle	Apprentice	Sunderland Coventry C Derby Co Darlington Burnley	179 78 45 57 4	18 9 3 7 —
Brian Welch*	5 08	11 11	17 7 73	South Shields	Hebburn	Burnley	—	—
Paul Weller	5 8	10 10	6 3 75	Brighton	Trainee	Burnley	—	—
Forwards								
John Clayton	5 11	11 07	20 8 61	Elgin	Apprentice Bulova, Hong Kong	Derby C Chesterfield Tranmere R Plymouth Arg Fortuna Sittard Volendam Burnley	24 33 47 77 47 61 3	4 5 35 21 16 18 1
David Eyres	5 10	11 00	26 2 64	Liverpool	Rhyl	Blackpool Burnley	158 45	38 19
John Francis	5 8	11 02	21 11 63	Dewsbury	Emley	Halifax T Sheffield U Burnley Cambridge U Burnley	4 42 101 29 52	— 6 26 3 8
Adrian Heath	5 6	10 01	11 1 61	Stoke	Apprentice Espanol	Stoke C Everton Aston Villa Manchester C Stoke C Burnley	95 226 9 75 6 84	16 71 — 4 — 29
Graham Lancashire	5 10	11 12	19 10 72	Blackpool	Trainee	Burnley Halifax T (loan) Chester C (loan)	30 2 11	8 — 7

Continued on Page 133

Trainees
Allen, Nicholas S; Artur, Paul M; Bannister, Andrew P; Borland, John R; Chadkirk, Paul G; Davies, Glen; Evers, Robert L; Lowey, Simon P; McCluskey, Anthony; Oakes, Andrew M; Pickup, Stephen; Powell, Francis M; Smith, Ian P; Taylor, Matthew J.

Associated Schoolboys
Carr-Lawton, Colin; Ciaraldi, Craig; Cotton, David P; Gierke, Leon K; Gray, Adam R; Hefferman, Jason; Hill, Gareth R; Hill, James R; King, James M; Knight, Danny; Magowan, Laurie T; Mawson, Craig J; Mutton, Thomas J; O'Leary, Daniel W; Pates, Bradley J; Quinn, Mark P; Scott, Christopher; Sherran, Antony A; Smith, Carl P; Stansfield, Paul; Watson, Michael A.

Associated Schoolboys who have accepted the Club's offer of a Traineeship/Contract
Duerden, Ian C.

BURY 1993–94 *Back row (left to right):* Tony Rigby, Ian Stevens, Peter Valentine, Mark Kearney, Andrew Reid, Nick Daws.
Centre row: Cliff Roberts (Coach), Mandy Johnson, Derek Ward, Paul Williamson, Alan Knill, Darryl Sloane, Ian Hughes, John King (Assistant Manager).
Front row: David Esdaile, Lee Anderson, Ronnie Mauge, Mike Walsh (Manager), David Adekola, Kenny Woods, Roger Stanislaus.

Division 3 **BURY**

Gigg Lane, Bury BL9 9HR. Telephone 061–764 4881. Fax 061–764 5521. Commercial Dept. 061–705 2144. Clubcall: 0898 121197. Community Programme: 061–797 5423. Social Club: 061–764 6771.

Ground capacity: 12,000 (unofficial).

Record attendance: 35,000 v Bolton W, FA Cup 3rd rd, 9 January 1960.

Record receipts: £37,000 v Bolton W, Division 3 play-off, 19 May 1991.

Pitch measurements: 112yd × 72yd.

Chairman: T. Robinson. ***Vice-chairman:*** Canon J. R. Smith MA.

Directors: C. H. Eaves, J. Smith, F. Mason.

Manager: Mike Walsh. ***Coaches:*** Stan Ternent and Cliff Roberts. ***Physio:*** Alan Raw. ***Youth Development:*** W. Joyce.

Assistant Secretary: J. Neville. ***Commercial Manager:*** Neville Neville.

Year Formed: 1885. ***Turned professional:*** 1885. ***Ltd Co.:*** 1897. ***Club Nickname:*** 'Shakers'.

Club Sponsors: MacPherson Paints.

Record League Victory: 8–0 v Tranmere R, Division 3, 10 January 1970 – Forrest; Tinney, Saile; Anderson, Turner, McDermott; Hince (1), Arrowsmith (1), Jones (4), Kerr (1), Grundy. (1 og).

Record Cup Victory: 12–1 v Stockton, FA Cup, 1st rd (replay), 2 February 1897 – Montgomery; Darroch, Barbour; Hendry (1), Clegg, Ross (1); Wylie (3), Pangbourn, Millar (4), Henderson (2), Plant. (1 og).

Record Defeat: 0–10 v Blackburn R, FA Cup, preliminary round, 1 October 1887 and v West Ham U, Milk Cup, 2nd rd, 2nd leg, 25 October 1983.

Most League Points (2 for a win): 68, Division 3, 1960–61.

Most League Points (3 for a win): 84, Division 4, 1984–85.

Most League Goals: 108, Division 3, 1960–61.

Highest League Scorer in Season: Craig Madden, 35, Division 4, 1981–82.

Most League Goals in Total Aggregate: Craig Madden, 129, 1978–86.

Most Capped Player: Bill Gorman, 11 (13), Republic of Ireland and (4), Northern Ireland.

Most League Appearances: Norman Bullock, 506, 1920–35.

Record Transfer Fee Received: £375,000 from Southampton for David Lee, October 1991.

Record Transfer Fee Paid: £175,000 to Shrewsbury T for John McGinlay, July 1990.

Football League Record: 1894 Elected to Division 2; 1895–1912 Division 1; 1912–24 Division 2; 1924–29 Division 1; 1929–57 Division 2; 1957–61 Division 3; 1961–67 Division 2; 1967–68 Division 3; 1968–69 Division 2; 1969–71 Division 3; 1971–74 Division 4; 1974–80 Division 3; 1980–85 Division 4; 1985– Division 3.

Honours: *Football League:* Division 1 best season: 4th, 1925–26; Division 2 – Champions 1894–95; Runners-up 1923–24; Division 3 – Champions 1960–61; Runners-up 1967–68. *FA Cup:* Winners 1900, 1903. *Football League Cup:* Semi-final 1963.

BURY 1993—94 LEAGUE RECORD

Match No.	Date	Venue	Opponents	Result		H/T Score	Lg. Pos.	Goalscorers	Attendance
1	Aug 14	H	Northampton T	D	0-0	0-0	—		2540
2	21	A	Scunthorpe U	D	1-1	0-0	15	Reid	3375
3	28	H	Crewe Alex	W	1-0	0-0	10	Rigby	2708
4	31	A	Preston NE	L	1-3	0-0	—	Rigby	5886
5	Sept 4	A	Shrewsbury T	L	0-1	0-1	16		2669
6	11	H	Wycombe W	L	1-2	0-1	17	Blissett	2559
7	18	A	Lincoln C	D	2-2	1-1	17	Carter, Rigby	2469
8	25	A	Colchester U	L	1-4	0-2	20	Kearney	2702
9	Oct 2	H	Mansfield T	D	2-2	1-1	20	Carter 2	2317
10	9	H	Wigan Ath	W	3-0	1-0	17	Kelly T, Mauge, Rigby	2729
11	16	A	Doncaster R	W	3-1	1-1	15	Stevens, Adekola 2	2613
12	23	H	Hereford U	W	5-3	2-1	13	Carter, Stevens, Mauge, Daws, Rigby	2354
13	30	A	Scarborough	L	0-1	0-1	15		1879
14	Nov 2	A	Chester C	L	0-3	0-1	—		2540
15	6	H	Chesterfield	W	2-1	1-1	15	Carter 2	2340
16	20	A	Rochdale	L	1-2	0-2	16	Mulligan	3758
17	27	H	Darlington	W	5-1	3-0	14	Kelly T 2, Rigby, Carter 2	2052
18	Dec 11	H	Scunthorpe U	W	1-0	1-0	11	Carter	2389
19	18	A	Northampton T	W	1-0	0-0	9	Rigby	2369
20	27	A	Walsall	W	1-0	0-0	7	Carter	6248
21	Jan 1	A	Gillingham	L	0-1	0-0	10		3440
22	4	H	Preston NE	D	1-1	0-0	—	Carter	4164
23	15	H	Doncaster R	W	4-0	3-0	8	Carter 2 (1 pen), Lucketti, Stevens	2383
24	22	A	Wigan Ath	L	1-3	1-2	10	Carter	2476
25	25	A	Carlisle U	W	2-1	2-1	—	Stevens, Kelly T	4430
26	29	H	Scarborough	L	0-2	0-0	8		3040
27	Feb 5	A	Hereford U	L	0-3	0-2	9		1805
28	12	H	Carlisle U	W	2-1	0-0	9	Stevens, Carter	2807
29	19	A	Crewe Alex	W	4-2	1-0	7	Kelly T 2, Carter 2	4276
30	25	H	Shrewsbury T	L	2-3	2-0	7	Carter (pen), Kelly T	3443
31	Mar 5	A	Wycombe W	L	1-2	1-1	9	Carter (pen)	4737
32	12	H	Lincoln C	W	1-0	0-0	7	Mauge	2214
33	19	H	Colchester U	L	0-1	0-0	9		2108
34	26	A	Mansfield T	D	2-2	2-1	9	Carter, Stevens	2496
35	29	H	Torquay U	D	1-1	0-1	—	Adekola	2018
36	Apr 2	H	Walsall	L	1-2	1-0	10	Smith (og)	2263
37	5	A	Torquay U	D	0-0	0-0	—		4111
38	16	H	Chester C	D	1-1	0-1	13	Adekola	3142
39	19	H	Gillingham	D	0-0	0-0	—		1687
40	23	A	Chesterfield	D	1-1	0-1	12	Stevens	2906
41	30	H	Rochdale	L	0-1	0-0	12		3270
42	May 7	A	Darlington	L	0-1	0-1	13		3039

Final League Position: 13

GOALSCORERS

League (55): Carter 20 (3 pens), Kelly 7, Rigby 7, Stevens 7, Adekola 4, Mauge 3, Blissett 1, Daws 1, Kearney 1, Lucketti 1, Mulligan 1, Reid 1, own goal 1.
Coca-Cola Cup (2): Blissett 1, Powell 1.
FA Cup (0):

Kelly G 1	Anderson 11	Stanislaus 35	Daws 33 + 4	Jackson 37 + 2	Knill 8	Rigby 33	Hughes 38	Blissett 8 + 2	Stevens 28 + 5	Powell 4 + 1	Reid 2 + 2	Collings 1	Jones 4	Hanson 1	Woods — + 2	Bracey 40	Adekola 7 + 12	Ward 2 + 1	Kearney 7 + 2	Carter 36	Kelly T 34 + 1	Luckett 27	Mauge 25 + 1	Mulligan 2 + 1	Cross 16 + 1	Johnrose 11 + 3	Worsley — + 1	Ryan 8 + 1	Beckford 3	Match No.
1	2	3	4	5	6	7	8	9	10	11	12																			1
	2	3	4	5	6		8	9		11	12	1	7	10	14															2
		3	4	5	6	7	8	9	12	11			2			1	10	14												3
	2	3	4	5	6	7	8	9		11	10					1	12													4
	2	3	4	5	6	7	8	9	10						12	1	11													5
	2	3	4	5	6	7		9	11							1			8	10										6
		3	4	5	6	7		9	12							1		2	8	10	11									7
	5	3	4	6		7		10								1		2	8	11	9									8
		3	4	5		7	8		10							1			12	11	9	6	2							9
		3	4	5		7	8	12	10							1			14	11	9	6	2							10
		3		5		7	8		10							1	12		4	11	9	6	2							11
		3	12	5		7	8		10							1			4	11	9	6	2							12
		3	4		6	7	8		10							1	12		2	11	9	5								13
			4	6		7	8						2			1	9		3	11	10	5								14
		3	4	6		7	8									1	9			11	10	5	2	12						15
		3	4	5		7	8						6			1				11	9		2	10						16
		3	4	6		9	2			12	5					1				10	7		8	11						17
		3	4	5		7	2									1	12			10	11		8		6	9	14			18
		3	4	6		7	2									1				10	11		8		5	9				19
		3	4	5		10	2		12							1				9	7		8		6	11				20
		3	4	5			2		9							1	12			10	7				6	11		8		21
		3	4	5		8	2		9							1				10	7	6			11					22
		3	4	5			2		9							1				10	7	6			11			8		23
		3	4	5			11		9							1	12			10	7	6			2			8		24
		3	4	5			11		9							1				10	7	6	12		2			8		25
		3	4	5			11		9							1	12			10	7	6	8		2			14		26
		3	4	5			10		9							1	12				7	6	8		2	11				27
		3	4	5		8	10		9							1				11	7	6	2							28
		3	4	5		8	10		9							1				11	7	6	2							29
		3	4			8	6		9							1				10	7	5	11		2	12				30
		3	4	5		8	2		9							1				10	7	6	11		12					31
		3	4	5		8	2		9							1				10	7	6	11							32
		3		5		8	4	12	9							1				10	7	6	11		2	14				33
		3		12		8	4		9							1				10	7	5	6		2	14			11	34
		3	12	5		8	4		9							1	14			10	7	6			2				11	35
		3	12	5		8			9							1	14			10	7	6	11		2				4	36
	2		4	5			8		9							1	12			10	7	6	3			11				37
	3		4	5		8	2		9							1	12			10	7	6				11				38
	3					8	2		12							1	9			10	7	6	5			11		4		39
	3		12	14		8	2		9							1	7			10		6	5			11		4		40
	3			5		8	2		12							1	9			10	7		6			11		4		41
			4	5			2		9							1				10	12	6	7		3	11		8		42

Coca-Cola Cup	First Round	Bolton W (a)	2-0
		(h)	0-2
FA Cup	First Round	Scarborough (a)	0-1

BURY

Player and Position	Ht	Wt	Birth Date	Birth Place	Source	Clubs	League App	League Gls
Goalkeepers								
Lee Bracey	6 1	12 08	11 9 68	Ashford	Trainee	West Ham U	—	—
						Swansea C	99	—
						Halifax T	73	—
						Bury	40	—
Paul Collings‡	6 2	12 00	30 9 68	Liverpool		Tranmere R	4	—
						Bury	1	—
Andy Gorton†	5 11	11 04	23 9 66	Salford		Oldham Ath	26	—
						Stockport Co (loan)	14	—
						Tranmere R (loan)	1	—
						Stockport Co	34	—
						Lincoln C	20	—
					Glossop	Oldham Ath	—	—
						Crewe Alex	3	—
						Bury	—	—
Gary Kelly	5 11	12 03	3 8 66	Fulwood	Apprentice	Newcastle U	53	—
						Blackpool (loan)	5	—
						Bury	173	—
						West Ham U (loan)	—	—
Barry Siddall†	6 1	14 02	12 9 54	Ellesmere Port	Apprentice	Bolton W	137	—
						Sunderland	167	—
						Darlington (loan)	8	—
						Port Vale	81	—
						Blackpool (loan)	7	—
						Stoke C	20	—
						Tranmere R (loan)	12	—
						Manchester C (loan)	6	—
						Blackpool	110	—
						Stockport Co	21	—
						Hartlepool U	11	—
						WBA	—	—
						Carlisle U	24	—
						Chester C	9	—
						Preston NE	1	—
						Bury	—	—
Defenders								
Lee Anderson	5 8	10 08	4 10 73	Bury	Trainee	Bury	29	—
Ryan Cross	6 1	13 06	11 10 72	Plymouth	Trainee	Plymouth Arg	19	—
						Hartlepool U	50	2
						Bury	17	—
Ian Hughes	5 11	12 00	2 8 74	Bangor	Trainee	Bury	85	—
Michael Jackson	5 11	11 10	4 12 73	West Cheshire	Trainee	Crewe Alex	5	—
						Bury	39	—
Phil Jones†	5 8	10 09	1 12 69	Liverpool	Trainee	Everton	1	—
						Blackpool (loan)	6	—
						Wigan Ath	88	2
						Bury	4	—
Chris Lucketti	6 0	12 10	28 9 71	Littleborough	Trainee	Rochdale	1	—
						Stockport Co	—	—
						Halifax T	78	2
						Bury	27	1
Ron Mauge	5 10	10 06	10 3 69	Islington	Trainee	Charlton Ath	—	—
						Fulham	50	2
						Bury	90	10
						Manchester C (loan)	—	—
Paul Morris‡			6 2 75	Bolton	Trainee	Bury	1	—
John Ryan*	5 10	11 07	18 2 62	Ashton	Apprentice	Oldham Ath	77	8
						Newcastle U	28	1
						Sheffield W	8	1
						Oldham Ath	23	—
						Mansfield T	62	1
						Chesterfield	82	6
						Rochdale	70	2
						Bury	9	—
Roger Stanislaus	5 9	12 06	2 11 68	Hammersmith	Trainee	Arsenal	—	—
						Brentford	111	4
						Bury	143	5
Midfield								
Nick Daws	5 11	13 02	15 3 70	Manchester	Altrincham	Bury	73	2

BURY

Colours: White shirts, navy blue shorts, navy stockings. **Change colours:** Green/purple shirts, purple shorts, purple stockings.

Foundation: A meeting at the Waggon & Horses Hotel, attended largely by members of Bury Wesleyans and Bury Unitarians football clubs, decided to form a new Bury club. This was officially formed at a subsequent gathering at the Old White Horse Hotel, Fleet Street, Bury on April 24, 1885.

First Football League game: 1 September, 1894, Division 2, v Manchester C (h) W 4-2 – Lowe; Gillespie, Davies; White, Clegg, Ross; Wylie, Barbour (2), Millar (1), Ostler (1), Plant.

Did you know: When Bury beat Doncaster 3-1 on 16 October 1993, goalkeeper Lee Bracey saved two penalties. It helped Rovers to record the team's first away win of the season.

Managers (and Secretary-Managers)
T. Hargreaves 1887*, H. S. Hamer 1887–1907*, Archie Montgomery 1907–15, William Cameron 1919–23, James Hunter Thompson 1923–27, Percy Smith 1927–30, Arthur Paine 1930–34, Norman Bullock 1934–38, Jim Porter 1944–45, Norman Bullock 1945–49, John McNeil 1950–53, Dave Russell 1953–61, Bob Stokoe 1961–65, Bert Head 1965–66, Les Shannon 1966–69, Jack Marshall 1969, Les Hart 1970, Tommy McAnearney 1970–72, Alan Brown 1972–73, Bobby Smith 1973–77, Bob Stokoe 1977–78, David Hatton 1978–79, Dave Connor 1979–80, Jim Iley 1980–84, Martin Dobson 1984–89, Sam Ellis 1989–90, Mike Walsh December 1990–

Player and Position	*Ht*	*Wt*	*Birth Date*	*Birth Place*	*Source*	*Clubs*	*League App*	*League Gls*
David Esdaille‡	5 8	11 00	22 7 63	Manchester		Wrexham	4	—
						Bury	6	—
Mark Kearney*	5 10	11 00	12 6 62	Ormskirk	Marine	Everton	—	—
						Mansfield T	250	29
						Bury (loan)	13	1
						Bury	100	4
John Norman			26 6 71	Birkenhead		Bury	2	—
Andrew Reid‡	6 0	13 01	4 7 62	Manchester	Altrincham	Bury	33	1
Tony Rigby	5 10	12 01	10 8 72	Ormskirk	Barrow	Bury	54	9
Derek Ward*	5 10	11 03	17 5 72	Birkenhead		Bury	28	—
Forwards								
David Adekola	5 11	12 02	18 5 68	Nigeria		Bury	35	12
						Exeter C (loan)	3	1
Luther Blissett*	5 10	12 03	1 2 58	W. Indies	Juniors	Watford	246	95
						AC Milan	30	5
						Watford	127	44
						Bournemouth	121	56
						Watford	42	10
						WBA (loan)	3	1
						Bury	10	1
						Mansfield T (loan)	5	1
Mark Carter	5 9	11 06	17 12 60	Liverpool	Runcorn	Barnet	82	30
						Bury	36	20
David Christie†	6 1	12 00	26 2 73	Salford	Trainee	Preston NE	4	—
						Halifax T	9	—
						Bury	—	—
Dave Hanson†			19 11 68	Huddersfield	Farsley Celtic	Bury	1	—
Lenny Johnrose	5 11	12 00	29 11 69	Preston	Trainee	Blackburn R	42	11
						Preston NE (loan)	3	1
						Hartlepool U	66	11
						Bury	14	—

Continued on Page 193

Trainees
Adams, Daniel B; Berry, Damian J; Chadwick, Craig A; Cowburn, Gary; Dale, Geoffrey A; Devine, David J; Dooner, Paul B; George, Lee J; Higgens, Saul J; Radcliffe, Matthew S; Shuttleworth, Barry; Steele, Winfield; Swailes, Matthew; Taylor, Paul A; Wallace, Richard E; Williamson, Paul J.

****Non-Contract**
Birks, Stephen J; Fahy, Alan; Gorton, Andrew W; Nixon, Craig G; Pickering, Christopher G; Siddall, Barry.

Associated Schoolboys
Andrew, Steven P; Clarke, Russell S; Cocker, David R. S; Denney, Philip M; Flood, Richard T; Forrest, Martyn W; Fraser, Christopher J. W; Gatter, Andrew A; Green, Alexanfer J; Grogan, Jon P. G; Horne, Matthew S. M; Horton, Steven A; Hutchinson, Christopher P; Jarrett, Jason L. M; Kane, Marvin A; Kenyon, Phillip; Matthews, Andrew J; McNally, Daniel S; Menzies, Anton M; Nuttall, Mark; Phillipson, Barry J; Rawlinson, Craig A; Scholes, Matthew J; Stevens, Richard A; Winrow, Brian; Young, Ian T.

**Non-Contract Players who are retained must be re-signed before they are eligible to play in League matches.

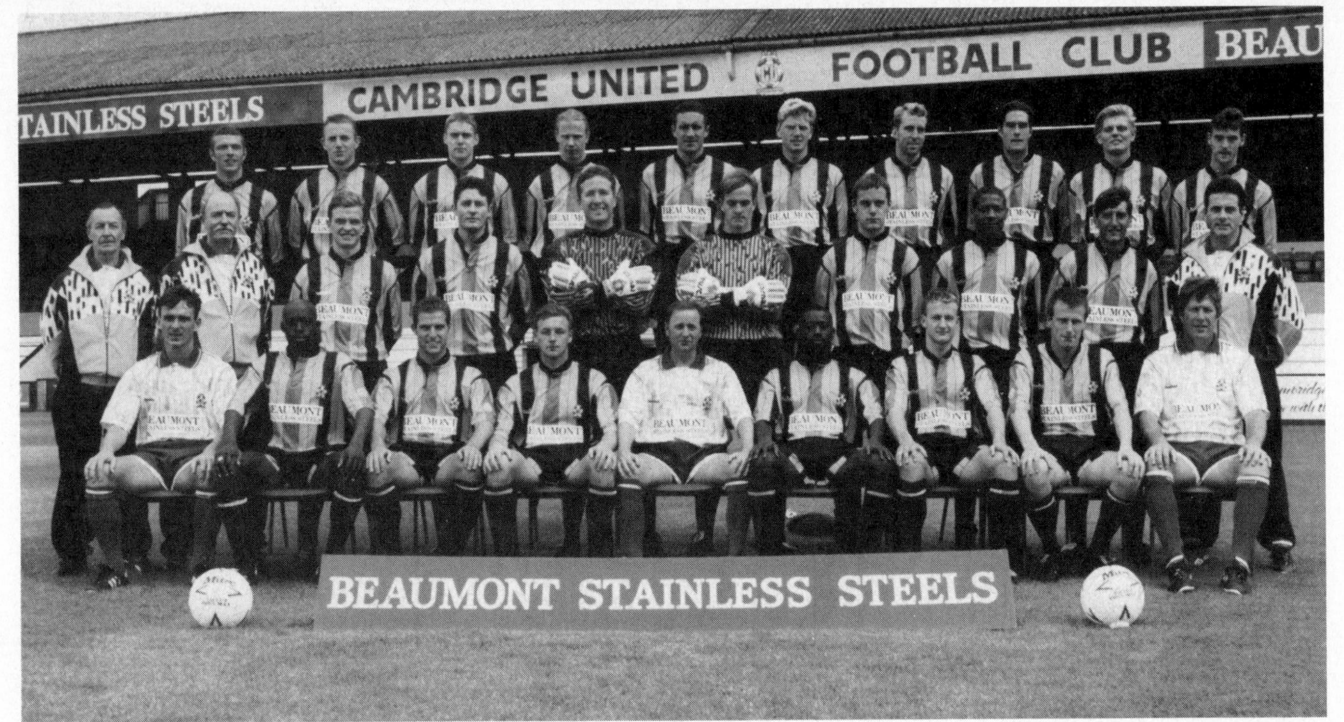

CAMBRIDGE UNITED 1993–94 *Back row (left to right):* John Fowler, Gary Rowett, Danny Granville, Jody Craddock, Liam Daish, Steve Butler, Michael Heathcote, Michael Danzey, Neil Lyne, Craig Middleton.

Centre row: Roger Parker (Kit Manager), John Griffin (Chief Scout), Michael Cheetham, Richard Wilkins, John Filan, Jon Sheffield, Jamie Smeeth, Micah Hyde, Gary Clayton, Ken Steggles (Physio).

Front row: Danny O'Shea (Player/Coach), Kofi Nyamah, Andy Fensome, Dean Barrick, Gary Johnson (Manager), Junior Hunter, Andrew Jeffrey, Steve Claridge, Tommy Taylor (Youth Team Manager).

Division 2 CAMBRIDGE UNITED

Abbey Stadium, Newmarket Rd, Cambridge, CB5 8LN. Telephone (0223) 566500. Clubcall: 0891 121141. Fax 0223 566502.

Ground capacity: 10,206.

Record attendance; 14,000 v Chelsea, Friendly, 1 May 1970.

Record receipts: £86,308 v Manchester U, Rumbelows Cup 2nd rd 2nd leg, 9 October 1991.

Pitch measurements: 110yd × 74yd.

Chairman: R. H. Smart. ***Vice-chairman:*** R. F. Hunt. ***Directors:*** G. Harwood, J. Howard, R. Hunt, G. Lowe, R. Smith.

Manager: Gary Johnson. ***Youth Manager:*** Tommy Taylor.

Physio: Ken Steggles. ***Player-coach:*** Danny O'Shea.

Secretary: Steve Greenall. ***Commercial Manager:*** John Holmes. ***Stadium Manager:*** Ian Darler.

Year Formed: 1919. ***Turned Professional:*** 1946. ***Ltd Co.:*** 1948.

Club Nickname: The 'U's'.

Previous Name: Abbey United until 1949.

Record League Victory: 6–0 v Darlington, Division 4, 18 September 1971 – Roberts; Thompson, Akers, Guild, Eades, Foote, Collins (1p), Horrey, Hollett, Greenhalgh (4), Phillips. (1 og). 6–0 v Hartlepool, Division 4, 11 February 1989 – Vaughan; Beck, Kimble, Turner, Chapple (1), Daish, Clayton, Holmes, Taylor (3 incl. 1p), Bull (1), Leadbitter (1).

Record Cup Victory: 5–1 v Bristol C, FA Cup, 5th rd, second replay, 27 February 1990 – Vaughan; Fensome, Kimble, Bailie (O'Shea), Chapple, Daish, Cheetham (Robinson), Leadbitter (1), Dublin (2), Taylor (1), Philpott (1).

Record Defeat: 0–6 v Aldershot, Division 3, 13 April 1974 and v Darlington, Division 4, 28 September 1974 and v Chelsea, Division 2, 15 January 1983.

Most League Points (2 for a win): 65, Division 4, 1976–77.

Most League Points (3 for a win): 86, Division 3, 1990–91.

Most League Goals: 87, Division 4, 1976–77.

Highest League Scorer in Season: David Crown, 24, Division 4, 1985–86.

Most League Goals in Total Aggregate: Alan Biley, 74, 1975–80.

Most Capped Player: Tom Finney, 7 (15), Northern Ireland.

Most League Appearances: Steve Spriggs, 416, 1975–87.

Record Transfer Fee Received: £1,000,000 from Manchester U for Dion Dublin, August 1992.

Record Transfer Fee Paid: £190,000 to Luton T for Steve Claridge, November 1992.

Football League Record: 1970 Elected to Division 4; 1973–74 Division 3; 1974–77 Division 4; 1977–78 Division 3; 1978–84 Division 2; 1984–85 Division 3; 1985–90 Division 4; 1990–91 Division 3; 1991–92 Division 2; 1992–93 Division 1; 1993– Division 2.

Honours: *Football League:* Division 2 best season: 5th, 1991–92; Division 3 – Champions 1990–91; Runners-up 1977–78; Division 4 – Champions 1976–77. *FA Cup:* best season: 6th rd, 1989–90, 1990–91. *Football League Cup:* 5th rd, 1992–93.

CAMBRIDGE UNITED 1993—94 LEAGUE RECORD

Match No.	Date	Venue	Opponents	Result		H/T Score	Lg. Pos.	Goalscorers	Attendance
1	Aug 14	H	Blackpool	W	3-2	2-1	—	Heathcote, Danzey, Butler	4903
2	21	A	Stockport Co	L	1-3	0-1	11	Danzey	3782
3	28	H	Hull C	L	3-4	2-2	15	Daish 2, Butler (pen)	3861
4	31	A	Port Vale	D	2-2	1-0	—	Claridge, Danzey	6484
5	Sept 4	A	Reading	L	1-3	0-1	20	Claridge	5007
6	11	H	Rotherham U	L	0-1	0-0	22		3804
7	14	H	Swansea C	W	2-0	0-0	—	Clayton, Cheetham	3338
8	18	A	Bournemouth	W	2-1	1-1	16	Claridge, Rowett	5200
9	25	A	Bradford C	L	0-2	0-0	18		5666
10	Oct 2	H	Brentford	D	1-1	0-1	17	Claridge (pen)	3612
11	9	A	Wrexham	D	1-1	1-0	17	Claridge	4220
12	16	H	Hartlepool U	W	1-0	0-0	14	Clayton	3318
13	23	A	Barnet	W	3-2	1-1	12	Heathcote, Claridge, Flatts	2997
14	30	H	Burnley	L	0-1	0-1	16		4826
15	Nov 2	H	Plymouth Arg	W	2-0	1-0	—	Claridge, Rowett	3135
16	6	A	Huddersfield T	D	1-1	0-0	13	Nyamah	4767
17	19	H	Cardiff C	D	1-1	1-0	—	Claridge	3076
18	27	A	Bristol R	L	1-2	1-0	14	Heathcote	4477
19	Dec 11	H	Stockport Co	D	0-0	0-0	16		3239
20	19	A	Blackpool	W	3-2	2-1	—	Hyde, Butler, Claridge	4576
21	27	A	Leyton Orient	L	1-2	0-1	15	Corazzin	6300
22	29	H	Exeter C	W	3-0	1-0	12	Claridge, Corazzin, Butler	3744
23	Jan 1	A	Brighton & HA	L	1-4	0-1	13	Claridge	9753
24	3	H	Fulham	W	3-0	1-0	12	Clayton 2, Nyamah	4557
25	8	H	York C	L	0-2	0-2	13		3534
26	15	A	Hartlepool U	W	2-0	2-0	11	Rowett, Corazzin	1690
27	22	H	Wrexham	D	2-2	0-1	11	Rowett, Butler	3353
28	29	A	Burnley	L	0-3	0-1	12		10,659
29	Feb 5	H	Barnet	D	1-1	1-1	12	Heathcote	3473
30	12	A	York C	L	0-2	0-0	12		3334
31	19	A	Hull C	L	0-2	0-0	13		4090
32	22	H	Port Vale	W	1-0	0-0	—	Rowett	2543
33	25	H	Reading	L	0-1	0-0	13		4029
34	Mar 5	A	Rotherham U	L	0-3	0-1	13		3266
35	12	H	Bournemouth	W	3-2	2-1	13	Butler 2, Middleton	2836
36	15	A	Swansea C	L	2-4	1-3	—	Sloan, Butler (pen)	2699
37	19	H	Bradford C	W	2-1	0-1	13	Corazzin, Cheetham	3095
38	26	A	Brentford	D	3-3	2-3	14	Granville 2, Corazzin	5052
39	29	A	Fulham	W	2-0	1-0	—	Granville, Corazzin	3444
40	Apr 2	H	Leyton Orient	W	3-1	1-0	12	Butler 3 (1 pen)	3762
41	4	A	Exeter C	W	5-0	3-0	10	Butler 5 (1 pen)	2258
42	9	H	Brighton & HA	W	2-1	0-0	10	Heathcote, Granville	4425
43	16	A	Plymouth Arg	W	3-0	1-0	9	Joseph, Corazzin 2	8872
44	26	H	Huddersfield T	L	4-5	1-3	—	Middleton, Hyde, Butler 2 (1 pen)	3901
45	30	A	Cardiff C	W	7-2	1-0	9	Granville, Butler 3, Corazzin 2, Joseph	5175
46	May 7	H	Bristol R	L	1-3	0-2	10	Barrick	4402

Final League Position: 10

GOALSCORERS

League (79): Butler 21 (5 pens), Claridge 11 (1 pen), Corrazin 10, Granville 5, Heathcote 5, Rowett 5, Clayton 4, Danzey 3, Cheetham 2, Daish 2, Hyde 2, Joseph 2, Middleton 2, Nyamah 2, Barrick 1, Flatts 1, Sloan 1.
Coca-Cola Cup (3): Claridge 3 (1 pen).
FA Cup (2): Heathcote 1, Nyamah 1.

Filan 46	Jeffrey 37 + 3	Barrick 44	O'Shea 36 + 2	Heathcote 40	Daish 18	Middleton 17 + 2	Danzey 10 + 4	Butler 33	Clayton 20 + 5	Claridge 24	Lyne — + 3	Fowler 16 + 4	Rowett 24 + 5	Hunter 3 + 11	Fensome 1 + 1	Cheetham 8 + 5	Nyamah 4 + 10	Hyde 13 + 5	Livett 10	Flatts 5	Craddock 19 + 1	Corazzin 28	Joseph 27	Skelly 2	Wilkins 7	Sloan 4	Granville 10 + 1	Hay — + 3	Match No.
1	2	3	4	5	6	7	8	9	10	11	12																		1
1	2	3	4	5	6		8	9	10	11	12	7	14																2
1	2	3	4	5	6		8	9	10	11		7	12	14															3
1	2	3	4	5	6		8	9	10	11		7		12															4
1	2	3	4	5	6		8	9	10	11		7	14	12															5
1	5	3	4		6	7	8	9	10	11	12				2	14													6
1	5	3	4		6			9	10	8		7	2			11	12												7
1	5	3	4		6			9	10	8		7	2			11		12											8
1	5	3	4		6		14	9	10	8		7	2		12	11													9
1	5	3	4		6		9		10	8			2	11			12		7										10
1	5	3	4		6				10	8		2	9	11			12		7										11
1	2	3	4	5	6				10	8			9				12		7	11									12
1	9	3	4	5	6				10	8			2						7	11									13
1	9	3	4	5	6		14		10	8		12	2						7	11									14
1	2	3	4	5	6		10			8		9	12				14		7	11									15
1	2	3	4	5	6		10			8		9	12				14		7	11									16
1	2	3	4	5	6		14			8		9	10				11	12	7										17
1	2	3	4	5	6		14			8		9	10				11	12	7										18
1	2	3	4	5				9		8			10	12				7			6	11							19
1		3	4	5				9	12	8			10					7			6	11	2						20
1	14	3	4	5				9	12	8			10					7			6	11	2						21
1	7	3	4	5				9	12	8			10								6	11	2						22
1	7	3	4	5				9	12	8			10	14							6	11	2						23
1		3	4	5			9		7	8			10				12				6	11	2						24
1	8	3	4	5				9	7				10	14			12				6	11	2						25
1	12	8		5				9	7			4	10								6	11	2	3					26
1	6	3		5				9	7			4	10	12				14				11	2	8					27
1		3	4	5		12			7				10						9		6	11	2		8				28
1		3	4	5		9			7				10	12			14				6	11	2		8				29
1	2	3	4	5					12				10	9			14				6	11	7		8				30
1	2	3	4	5				9					10	12			7					11	6		8				31
1	2	3	4	5		12		9					10				7					11	6		8				32
1	2	3	4	5		7		9													12	11	6		8	10			33
1	2	3	4	5		7		9								12						11	6		8	10			34
1	2		4	5		8		9								7		6				11	3			10			35
1	2		4	5		8		9								7		6				11	3			10	12	14	36
1		3	4	5		8		9								7		10				11	2				6	12	37
1		3	4	5		8		9								7		10				11	2				6	12	38
1	14	3		5		8		9						12		7		10			4	11	2				6		39
1	7	3		5		8		9				12		14				10			4	11	2				6		40
1	7	3		5		8		9				14				12		10			4	11	2				6		41
1	7	3		5		8		9										10			4	11	2				6		42
1	7	3		5		8		9								12		10			4	11	2				6		43
1	7	3		5		8		9				14				12		10			4	11	2				6		44
1	7	3	12	5		8		9				10									4	11	2				6		45
1	7	3	12	5		8		9				10						14			4	11	2				6		46

Coca-Cola Cup	First Round	Luton T (h)	1-0
		(a)	1-0
	Second Round	Ipswich T (a)	1-2
		(h)	0-2
FA Cup	First Round	Reading (h)	0-0
		(a)	2-1
	Second Round	Wycombe W (a)	0-1

CAMBRIDGE UNITED

Player and Position	Ht	Wt	Birth Date	Birth Place	Source	Clubs	League App	League Gls
Goalkeepers								
John Filan	5 11	12 10	8 2 70	Sydney	Budapest St George	Cambridge U	52	—
Jon Sheffield	5 11	11 07	1 2 69	Bedworth		Norwich C	1	—
						Aldershot (loan)	11	—
						Ipswich T (loan)	—	—
						Aldershot (loan)	15	—
						Cambridge U (loan)	2	—
						Cambridge U	26	—
						Colchester U (loan)	6	—
						Swindon T (loan)	2	—
Defenders								
Jody Craddock	6 0	11 10	25 7 75	Redditch	Christchurch	Cambridge U	20	—
Mike Heathcote	6 2	12 05	10 9 65	Durham	Spennymoor U	Sunderland	9	—
						Halifax T (loan)	7	1
						York C (loan)	3	—
						Shrewsbury T	44	6
						Cambridge U	104	12
Andrew Jeffrey	5 10	12 02	15 1 72	Bellshill	Cambridge C	Cambridge U	40	—
Matthew Joseph	5 7	10 02	30 9 72	Bethnal Green	Trainee	Arsenal	—	—
						Gillingham	—	—
						Cambridge U	27	2
Danny O'Shea	6 0	12 08	26 3 63	Kennington	Apprentice	Arsenal	6	—
						Charlton Ath (loan)	9	—
						Exeter C	45	2
						Southend U	118	12
						Cambridge U	172	1
Jamie Smeeth‡	6 1	13 00	7 9 74	Hackney		Cambridge U	—	—
Midfield								
Dean Barrick	5 9	12 00	30 9 69	Hemsworth	Trainee	Sheffield W	11	2
						Rotherham U	99	7
						Cambridge U	44	1
Michael Cheetham*	5 11	11 05	30 6 67	Amsterdam	Army	Ipswich T	4	—
						Cambridge U	132	22
John Fowler	5 10	11 10	27 10 74	Preston	Trainee	Cambridge U	23	—
						Preston NE (loan)	6	—
Danny Granville	5 11	12 05	19 1 75	Islington	Trainee	Cambridge U	11	5
Micah Hyde	5 9	10 05	10 11 74	Newham	Trainee	Cambridge U	18	2
Simon Livett	5 10	12 02	8 1 69	Newham	Trainee	West Ham U	1	—
						Leyton Orient	24	—
						Cambridge U	10	—
Richard Skelly†			24 3 72	Norwich		Cambridge U	2	—
Richard Wilkins*	6 0	12 00	28 5 65	London	Haverhill R	Colchester U	152	22
						Cambridge U	81	7
Forwards								
Kevin Bartlett	5 8	11 01	12 10 62	Portsmouth	Apprentice Fareham	Portsmouth	3	—
						Cardiff C	82	25
						WBA	37	10
						Notts Co	99	33
						Port Vale (loan)	5	1
						Cambridge U	8	1
Steve Butler	6 2	13 00	27 1 62	Birmingham	Wokingham	Brentford	97	44
					Maidstone U (1986)	Watford	62	9
						Bournemouth (loan)	1	—
						Cambridge U	56	27
Carlo Corazzin	5 9	12 05	25 12 71	Canada	Vancouver 86ers	Cambridge U	28	10
Michael Danzey*	6 1	12 00	8 2 71	Widnes	Trainee	Nottingham F	—	—
						Chester C (loan)	2	—
						Peterborough U	1	—
					St Albans	Cambridge U	16	3
						Scunthorpe U (loan)	3	1
Darran Hay†			12 12 69	Hitchin		Cambridge U	3	—
Junior Hunter	5 7	11 00	1 2 75	Lambeth	Trainee	Cambridge U	14	—
Neil Lyne	6 1	12 04	4 4 70	Leicester	Leicester U	Nottingham F	—	—
						Walsall (loan)	7	—
						Shrewsbury T (loan)	16	6
						Shrewsbury T	64	11
						Cambridge U	17	—
						Chesterfield	6	1

CAMBRIDGE UNITED

Colours: Amber & black striped shirts, black shorts with amber & black trim, black & amber stockings.
Change colours: Patterned white & sky blue shirts, royal blue shorts, royal blue stockings.

Foundation: The football revival in Cambridge began soon after World War II when the Abbey United club (formed 1919) decided to turn professional and in 1949 changed their name to Cambridge United. They were competing in the United Counties League before graduating to the Eastern Counties League in 1951 and the Southern League in 1958.

First Football League game: 15 August, 1970, Division 4, v Lincoln C (h) D 1-1 – Roberts; Thompson, Meldrum (1), Slack, Eades, Hardy, Leggett, Cassidy, Lindsey, McKinven, Harris.

Did you know: When Cambridge United won 7-2 at Cardiff City on 30 April 1994, it was their highest score in a League game. Steve Butler scored three goals, taking his total to 13 in six matches including five at Exeter.

Managers (and Secretary-Managers)
Bill Whittaker 1949–55, Gerald Williams 1955, Bert Johnson 1955–59, Bill Craig 1959–60, Alan Moore 1960–63, Roy Kirk 1964–66, Bill Leivers 1967–74, Ron Atkinson 1974–78, John Docherty 1978–83, John Ryan 1984–85, Ken Shellito 1985, Chris Turner 1985–90, John Beck 1990–1992, Ian Atkins 1992–93, Gary Johnson June 1993–

Player and Position	*Ht*	*Wt*	*Birth Date*	*Place*	*Source*	*Clubs*	*League App*	*Gls*
Craig Middleton	5 9	11 00	10 9 70	Nuneaton	Trainee	Coventry C	3	—
						Cambridge U	19	2
Kofi Nyamah	5 8	10 07	20 6 75	Islington	Trainee	Cambridge U	14	2
Philip Parkhill‡			22 2 74	Harrogate		Cambridge U	—	—
Scott Sloan (on loan from Falkirk (on loan from Falkirk))	5 10	11 06	14 12 67	Wallsend		Cambridge U	4	1

Trainees
Barry, Mark S; Beresford, Paul R; (h) Collard, Alan; Gutzmore, Leon J. F; Hamilton, Colin; Joseph, Marc E; Kyd, Michael R; Lake, Edward J; Pack, Lenny J; Parker, Scott J; Rattle, Jonathan P; Stock, Russell J; Toombs, David J; Walker, Richard K; Williams, Stuart R.

****Non-Contract**
Atkins, Frank; Hay, Darran A; Skelly, Richard B.

Associated Schoolboys
Dolby, Lee R; Greig, Neil; Haniver, Adam M; King, Edward; King, Stuart; Maguire, Derek M. H; McDermott, Liam; Webb, Darren; Youngs, Thomas A. J.

Associated Schoolboys who have accepted the Club's offer of a Traineeship/Contract
Beall, Matthew H; Hassan, Hassan; Hayes, Adrian M; Howes, Shaun.
**Non-Contract Players who are retained must be re-signed before they are eligible to play in League matches.

Burnley players continued from Page 121

Player	Ht	Wt	Date	Place	Source	Clubs	App	Gls
Richard Livingstone	5 10	11 02	10 4 74	Aberdeen	Trainee	Burnley	—	—
Ted McMinn	5 11	11 02	28 9 62	Castle Douglas	Glenafton Athletic	Queen of the S	62	5
						Rangers	63	4
					Seville	Derby Co	123	9
						Birmingham C	22	—
						Burnley	14	3
John Mullin	6 0	11 05	11 8 75	Bury	School	Burnley	6	1
Nathan Peel	6 1	12 07	17 5 72	Blackburn	Trainee	Preston NE	10	1
						Sheffield U	1	—
						Halifax T (loan)	3	—
						Burnley	13	2
Tony Philliskirk	6 1	12 02	10 2 65	Sunderland	Amateur	Sheffield U	80	20
						Rotherham U (loan)	6	1
						Oldham Ath	10	1
						Preston NE	14	6
						Bolton W	141	51
						Peterborough U	43	15
						Burnley	19	7
Adrian Randall	5 11	10 11	10 11 68	Amesbury	Apprentice	Bournemouth	3	—
						Aldershot	107	12
						Burnley	78	7
Paul Smith			22 1 76	Burnley	Trainee	Burnley	1	—

CARDIFF CITY 1993–94 *Back row (left to right):* Gary Thompson, Paul Millar, Mark Aizlewood, Nick Richardson.
Centre row: Anthony Bird, Lee Baddeley, Phil Kite, Mark Grew, Steve Williams, Phil Stant, Derek Brazil.
Front row: Cohen Griffiths, Damon Searle, Carl Dale, Roger Gibbins (Coach), Eddie May (Manager), Jason Perry, Nathan Wigg, Nathan Blake.

Division 2 CARDIFF CITY

Ninian Park, Cardiff CF1 8SX. Telephone Cardiff (0222) 398636. Fax (0222) 341148. Newsline (0891) 888603.

Ground capacity: 20,284.

Record attendance: 61,566, Wales v England, 14 October 1961.

Club record: 57,893 v Arsenal, Division 1, 22 April 1953.

Record receipts: £141,756 v Manchester C, FA Cup 4th rd, 29 January 1994.

Pitch measurements: 114yd × 78yd.

Directors: R. Wright, M. Boyce, W. Dixon, D. Henderson, J. Oliver, S. Williams.

Secretary: Jim Finney.

Manager: Eddie May. ***Commercial Manager:***

Physio: Jimmy Goodfellow. ***Coach:*** Eddie May.

Year Formed: 1899. ***Turned Professional:*** 1910. ***Ltd Co.:*** 1910.

Previous Names: 1899–1902, Riverside; 1902–08, Riverside Albion; 1908, Cardiff City.

Club Nickname: 'Bluebirds'.

Previous Grounds: Riverside, Sophia Gardens, Old Park and Fir Gardens. Moved to Ninian Park, 1910.

Record League Victory: 9–2 v Thames, Division 3 (S), 6 February 1932 – Farquharson; E. L. Morris, Roberts; Galbraith, Harris, Ronan; Emmerson (1), Keating (1), Jones (1), McCambridge (1), Robbins (5).

Record Cup Victory: 8–0 v Enfield, FA Cup, 1st rd, 28 November 1931 – Farquharson; Smith, Roberts; Harris (1), Galbraith, Ronan; Emmerson (2), Keating (3); O'Neill (2), Robbins, McCambridge.

Record Defeat: 2–11 v Sheffield U, Division 1, 1 January 1926.

Most League Points (2 for a win): 66, Division 3 (S), 1946–47.

Most League Points (3 for a win): 86, Division 3, 1982–83.

Most League Goals: 93, Division 3 (S), 1946–47.

Highest League Scorer in Season: Stan Richards, 30, Division 3 (S), 1946–47.

Most League Goals in Total Aggregate: Len Davies, 128, 1920–31.

Most Capped Player: Alf Sherwood, 39 (41), Wales.

Most League Appearances: Phil Dwyer, 471, 1972–85.

Record Transfer Fee Received: £300,000 from Sheffield U for Nathan Blake, February 1994.

Record Transfer Fee Paid: £180,000 to San Jose Earthquakes for Godfrey Ingram, September 1982.

Football League Record: 1920 Elected to Division 2; 1921–29 Division 1; 1929–31 Division 2; 1931–47 Division 3 (S); 1947–52 Division 2; 1952–57 Division 1; 1957–60 Division 2; 1960–62 Division 1; 1962–75 Division 2; 1975–76 Division 3; 1976–82 Division 2; 1982–83 Division 3; 1983–85 Division 2; 1985–86 Division 3; 1986–88 Division 4; 1988–90 Division 3; 1990–92 Division 4; 1992–93 Division 3; 1993– Division 2.

Honours: *Football League:* Division 1 – Runners-up 1923–24; Division 2 – Runners-up 1920–21, 1951–52, 1959–60; Division 3 (S) – Champions 1946–47; Division 3 – Champions 1992–93. Runners-up 1975–76, 1982–83; Division 4 – Runners-up 1987–88. *FA Cup:* Winners 1926–27 (only occasion the Cup has been won by a club outside England); Runners-up 1925. *Football League Cup:* Semi-final 1965–66. *Welsh Cup:* Winners 21 times. *Charity Shield:* 1927. European Competitions: *European Cup-Winners' Cup:* 1964–65, 1965–66, 1967–68, 1968–69, 1969–70, 1970–71, 1971–72, 1973–74, 1974–75, 1976–77, 1977–78, 1988–89, 1991–92, 1992–93, 1993–94.

CARDIFF CITY 1993—94 LEAGUE RECORD

Match No.	Date	Venue	Opponents	Result	H/T Score	Lg. Pos.	Goalscorers	Attendance
1	Aug 14	H	Leyton Orient	W 2-0	0-0	—	Blake, Griffith	9920
2	21	A	Fulham	W 3-1	1-0	2	Blake 2, Thompson	5696
3	28	H	Brighton & HA	D 2-2	1-0	3	Blake, Cornwell	7687
4	31	A	Exeter C	D 2-2	1-0	—	Griffith, Cornwell	3049
5	Sept 4	A	Port Vale	D 2-2	2-0	6	Blake, Griffith	8140
6	11	H	Hull C	L 3-4	2-1	11	Thompson, Richardson 2 (1 pen)	7421
7	18	A	Blackpool	L 0-1	0-1	17		4767
8	25	H	Plymouth Arg	L 2-3	0-2	19	Stant, Millar	6362
9	Oct 2	A	York C	L 0-5	0-3	20		3762
10	10	A	Barnet	D 0-0	0-0	—		2084
11	16	H	Bristol R	L 1-2	0-1	22	Richardson (pen)	5563
12	23	A	Wrexham	L 1-3	0-0	22	Bird	4245
13	30	H	Hartlepool U	D 2-2	0-2	21	Bird, Blake (pen)	3710
14	Nov 2	A	Brentford	D 1-1	0-1	—	Blake	4756
15	6	H	Stockport Co	W 3-1	0-0	21	Blake 3 (1 pen)	4738
16	19	A	Cambridge U	D 1-1	0-1	—	Bird	3076
17	27	H	Bradford C	D 1-1	0-0	19	Stant	4213
18	Dec 11	H	Fulham	W 1-0	0-0	18	Blake	5120
19	18	A	Leyton Orient	D 2-2	1-0	18	Stant, Thompson	3691
20	22	H	Swansea C	W 1-0	0-0	—	Thompson	9815
21	Jan 1	H	Reading	W 3-0	0-0	15	Griffith, Aizlewood, Richardson	10,257
22	3	A	Rotherham U	L 2-5	0-4	16	Millar 2 (2 pens)	3395
23	15	A	Bristol R	L 1-2	0-1	17	Blake	5683
24	22	H	Barnet	D 0-0	0-0	17		5698
25	Feb 5	H	Wrexham	W 5-1	2-1	18	Adams, Richardson, Bird, Blake 2	10,847
26	12	A	Burnley	L 0-2	0-0	20		11,276
27	Mar 1	H	Burnley	W 2-1	0-1	—	Thompson, Stant	5469
28	5	A	Hull C	L 0-1	0-1	21		4998
29	12	H	Blackpool	L 0-2	0-1	21		5186
30	15	A	Bournemouth	L 2-3	0-2	—	Dale, Griffith	2385
31	19	A	Plymouth Arg	W 2-1	2-1	21	Stant 2	9587
32	22	A	Hartlepool U	L 0-3	0-1	—		1077
33	26	H	York C	D 0-0	0-0	21		4806
34	29	H	Rotherham U	W 1-0	1-0	—	Bird	3583
35	Apr 2	A	Swansea C	L 0-1	0-0	21		3711
36	4	H	Huddersfield T	D 2-2	1-2	21	Brock, Perry	5525
37	9	A	Reading	D 1-1	0-1	21	Hopkins (og)	7129
38	12	A	Brighton & HA	W 5-3	3-1	—	Millar 3 (2 pens), Stant, Fereday	7653
39	16	H	Brentford	D 1-1	1-1	21	Brock	5268
40	19	A	Huddersfield T	L 0-2	0-1	—		6267
41	21	H	Bournemouth	W 2-1	2-0	—	Stant, Millar (pen)	3838
42	23	A	Stockport Co	D 2-2	0-1	19	Stant, Flynn (og)	5455
43	26	H	Exeter C	W 2-0	1-0	—	Aizlewood, Dale	4631
44	30	H	Cambridge U	L 2-7	0-1	18	Griffith, Dale	5175
45	May 3	H	Port Vale	L 1-3	0-1	—	Stant	4705
46	7	A	Bradford C	L 0-2	0-0	19		6642

Final League Position: 19

GOALSCORERS

League (66): Blake 14 (2 pens), Stant 10, Millar 7 (5 pens), Griffith 6, Bird 5, Richardson 5 (2 pens), Thompson 5, Dale 3, Aizlewood 2, Brock 2, Cornwell 2, Adams 1, Fereday 1, Perry 1, own goals 2.
Coca-Cola Cup (2): Bird 1, own goal 1.
FA Cup (10): Stant 4, Blake 3, Bird 1, Thompson 1, own goal 1.

Grew 11	James 9	Searle 41 + 1	Brazil 31	Perry 40	Ratcliffe 6	Bird 25 + 10	Richardson 38 + 1	Thompson 28 + 2	Blake 20	Griffith 39 + 3	Kite 17 + 1	Cornwell 5	Millar 28 + 9	Baddeley 25 + 5	Wigg 8 + 11	Stant 34 + 2	Jones 2	Knill 4	Williams 18	Aizlewood 22	Young 3 + 3	Evans T 4 + 1	Adams 9 + 5	Dale 7 + 8	Brock 14	Fereday 17	Walker 1	Graham — + 1	Evans A — + 1	*Match No.*
1	2	3	4	5	6	7	8	9	10	11	12																			1
	2	3	4	5	6	11	8	9	10		1	*7*	12	14																2
	2	3	4	5		*6*	8	9	10	11	1	7		12	14															3
	2	3	4	5			8	9	10	11	1	7	6																	4
	2	3		5	6		8	9	10	11	1	7	4	12																5
	2	3		5	6		8	11	10	7	1	4				9														6
	2	12		5	6	14	*8*	10		11	1		7	4		9	3													7
	2	3	8	4	6	7		10			1		11			9		5												8
	2		6	4		8		10		11					7	9	3	5	1											9
		3	4	2		*7*		8	10	11	1		12	6	14	9		5												10
		3	4	2			8	9	10	11	1		7	14		12		*5*		6										11
		3	4	2		14	8	9	10	11	1		7	5		12				6										12
			3	2		7	8	12	10	11	1		4	5		9				6										13
		3	2	6		7	8		10	11			4	5		9			1											14
		3	2	6		7	8		10	11			4	5	12	*9*			1		14									15
1		3	2	6		7	8		10	11				5		9				4										16
1		3	2	6		7	8		10	11			12	5		9				4										17
1		3	2	6		7	8		10	11			12	5		9				4										18
1		3	2	6		7	8	12		11			10	5		9				4										19
1		3	2	6		14	8	*7*	10	11			12	5		9				4										20
1		3	2	6			8	7		11			10	5		9				4										21
		3	2	6		12	8	7		11			10	5		9			1	4										22
1		3	2	5		12	8	*7*	10	11			6		14	9						4								23
1		3	2	5		*11*	8	7	10	9			6	12						4			14							24
1		3	2			7	8		10	11				5	6					4		12	*9*	14						25
1		3	2	6		12	8	*7*	10	11			4	5									9	14						26
		3	2	6		11	8	7					10	5		9			1					12	4					27
		3	2	6		*11*	8	7		14			10	5		9			1					12	4					28
		3	*2*	6			8	7		11			14	5		9			1					12	4	10				29
		3		6		9	8			11			7	5					1				12	10	4	2				30
		3		6		7	8			11					5	9			1					10	4	2				31
		3		6		*7*	8			11				5	12	9			1				14	10	4	2				32
		3		6		14	8			11				5	12	9			1	4				*10*	7	2				33
		3	2	6		10				7			12	5		9			1	4					8	11				34
		3	2	6		*9*	12			10			14	5	7				1	4					8	11				35
		3	2	6		*10*				7			12	5		9			1	4			14		8	11				36
		3	2	5			8			12	1		6		14	9				4			*10*		7	11				37
		3	2	5			8			10	1		6		12	9				4					7	11				38
		3		5			8	10		11	1		6		4	9							12		7	2				39
		3		5		12	8	10		*11*	1		6		4	9							*7*	14		2				40
		3		5			8	7		11			6		12	9			1	4			*10*	14		2				41
		3				14	8	7		11			6		12	9			1		5		*4*	10		2				42
						12		7		11			6			9			1	4	14	2	5	10	*8*	3				43
						8		*7*		12			6		14	9			1	4	5	2	11	10		3				44
		3					8	7		11	1		6	5	10	9				*4*	14			12		2				45
		3				10	8				1		6		4	9					5	2	11				*7*	12	14	46

Coca-Cola Cup	First Round	Bournemouth (a)	1-3
		(h)	1-1
FA Cup	First Round	Enfield (a)	0-0
		(h)	1-0
	Second Round	Brentford (a)	3-1
	Third Round	Middlesbrough (h)	2-2
		(a)	2-1
	Fourth Round	Manchester C (h)	1-0
	Fifth Round	Luton T (h)	1-2

CARDIFF CITY

Player and Position	Ht	Wt	Birth Date	Birth Place	Source	Clubs	League App	League Gls
Goalkeepers								
Mark Grew*	5 11	12 08	15 2 58	Bilston	Amateur	WBA	33	—
						Wigan Ath (loan)	4	—
						Notts Co (loan)	—	—
						Leicester C	5	—
						Oldham Ath (loan)	5	—
						Ipswich T	6	—
						Fulham (loan)	4	—
						WBA (loan)	1	—
						Derby Co (loan)	—	—
						Port Vale	184	—
						Blackburn R (loan)	13	—
						Cardiff C	21	—
Phil Kite	6 1	14 07	26 10 62	Bristol	Apprentice	Bristol R	96	—
						Tottenham H (loan)	—	—
						Southampton	4	—
						Middlesbrough (loan)	2	—
						Gillingham	70	—
						Bournemouth	7	—
						Sheffield U	11	—
						Mansfield T (loan)	11	—
						Plymouth Arg (loan)	2	—
						Rotherham U (loan)	1	—
						Crewe Alex (loan)	5	—
						Stockport Co (loan)	5	—
						Cardiff C	18	—
Steven Williams	6 3	12 12	16 10 74	Aberystwyth	Coventry C	Cardiff C	18	—
Defenders								
Mark Aizlewood	6 1	13 12	1 10 59	Newport	Apprentice	Newport Co	38	1
						Luton T	98	3
						Charlton Ath	152	9
						Leeds U	70	3
						Bradford C	39	1
						Bristol C	101	3
						Cardiff C	22	2
Lee Baddeley	6 1	12 06	12 7 74	Cardiff	Trainee	Cardiff C	58	—
Derek Brazil	5 11	10 05	14 12 68	Dublin	Rivermount BC	Manchester U	2	—
						Oldham Ath (loan)	1	—
						Swansea C (loan)	12	1
						Cardiff C	65	—
Terry Evans§			8 1 76	Pontypridd	Trainee	Cardiff C	5	—
Benjamin Graham§			23 9 75	Pontypool	Trainee	Cardiff C	1	—
Ian Jones§			26 8 76	Germany	Trainee	Cardiff C	2	—
Jason Perry	5 11	10 04	2 4 70	Newport		Cardiff C	198	4
Paul Ramsey (To St Johnstone July 1993)	5 11	13 00	3 9 62	Londonderry	Apprentice	Leicester C	290	13
						Cardiff C	69	7
Damon Searle	5 11	10 04	26 10 71	Cardiff	Trainee	Cardiff C	161	2
Midfield								
Wayne Fereday	5 9	11 08	16 6 63	Warley	Apprentice	QPR	197	21
						Newcastle U	33	—
						Bournemouth	23	—
						WBA	48	3
						Cardiff C	17	1
Nick Richardson	6 0	12 07	11 4 67	Halifax	Local	Halifax T	101	17
						Cardiff C	78	9
Lee Walker§			27 6 76	Pontypool	Trainee	Cardiff C	1	—
Nathan Wigg	5 9	10 05	27 9 74	Cardiff	Trainee	Cardiff C	19	—
Forwards								
Darren Adams	5 7	10 07	12 1 74	Newham	Danson Furnace	Cardiff C	14	1
Anthony Bird	5 10	11 09	1 9 74	Cardiff	Trainee	Cardiff C	44	6
Carl Dale	6 0	12 00	29 4 66	Colwyn Bay	Bangor C	Chester C	116	41
						Cardiff C	76	33
David A Evans§			25 11 75		Trainee	Cardiff C	1	—
Cohen Griffith	5 10	11 07	26 12 62	Georgetown	Kettering T	Cardiff C	196	35

CARDIFF CITY

Colours: Blue shirts, white shorts, blue stockings. **Change colours:** All red.

Foundation: Credit for the establishment of a first class professional football club in such a rugby stronghold as Cardiff, is due to members of the Riverside club formed in 1899 out of a cricket club of that name. Cardiff became a city in 1905 and in 1908 the local FA granted Riverside permission to call themselves Cardiff City.

First Football League game: 28 August, 1920, Division 2, v Stockport C (a) W 5-2 – Kneeshaw; Brittain, Leyton; Keenor (1), Smith, Hardy; Grimshaw (1), Gill (2), Cashmore, West, Evans (1).

Did you know: In 1961–62 and despite being a Welsh club, Cardiff City played in the Anglo-French Friendship Cup, beating Racing Club Lens 4-2 and 2-0.

Managers (and Secretary-Managers)
Davy McDougall 1910–11, Fred Stewart 1911–33, Bartley Wilson 1933–34, B. Watts-Jones 1934–37, Bill Jennings 1937–39, Cyril Spiers 1939–46, Billy McCandless 1946–48, Cyril Spiers 1948–54, Trevor Morris 1954–58, Bill Jones 1958–62, George Swindin 1962–64, Jimmy Scoular 1964–73, Frank O'Farrell 1973–74, Jimmy Andrews 1974–78, Richie Morgan 1978–82, Len Ashurst 1982–84, Jimmy Goodfellow 1984, Alan Durban 1984–86, Frank Burrows 1986–89, Len Ashurst 1989–91, Eddie May July 1991–

Player and Position	*Ht*	*Wt*	*Birth Date*	*Place*	*Source*	*Clubs*	*League App*	*Gls*
Robbie James	5 11	13 0	23 3 57	Swansea	Apprentice	Swansea C	394	99
						Stoke C	48	6
						QPR	87	4
						Leicester C	23	—
						Swansea C	90	16
						Bradford C	89	6
						Cardiff C	51	2
Paul Millar	6 2	12 07	16 11 66	Belfast	Portadown	Port Vale	40	5
						Hereford U (loan)	5	2
						Cardiff C	85	10
Phil Stant	6 1	12 07	13 10 62	Bolton	Camberley Army	Reading	4	2
						Hereford U	89	38
						Notts Co	22	6
						Blackpool (loan)	12	5
						Lincoln C (loan)	4	—
						Huddersfield T (loan)	5	1
						Fulham	19	5
						Mansfield T	57	32
						Cardiff C	60	21
						Mansfield T (loan)	4	1
Garry Thompson	6 1	14 00	7 10 59	Birmingham	Apprentice	Coventry C	134	38
						WBA	91	39
						Sheffield W	36	7
						Aston Villa	60	17
						Watford	34	8
						Crystal Palace	20	3
						QPR	19	1
						Cardiff C	30	5
Scott Young§			14 1 76	Pontypridd	Trainee	Cardiff C	6	—

Trainees
Bartley, Kevin D; Davis, Christopher; Evans, David A; Evans, Terry; Graham, Benjamin; Haworth, Simon O; Ingram, Christopher D; Jones, Ian M; Keepin, Matthew W; Mountain, Patrick D; Quoi, Anthony J; Street, Daniel C; Walker, Lee; Young, Scott.

Associated Schoolboys
Cadette, Nathan D; Davies, Craig; Hicks, Mike; Hill, John; James, Anthony; McCarthy, James; Parsons, James; Phillips, Lee; Powell, Dave; Rees, Steven; Rendell, John; Rowland, James; Tobutt, Richard.

Associated Schoolboys who have accepted the Club's offer of a Traineeship/Contract
Jarman, Lee; Pugh, Richard; Street, Lee J; Vick, Leigh.

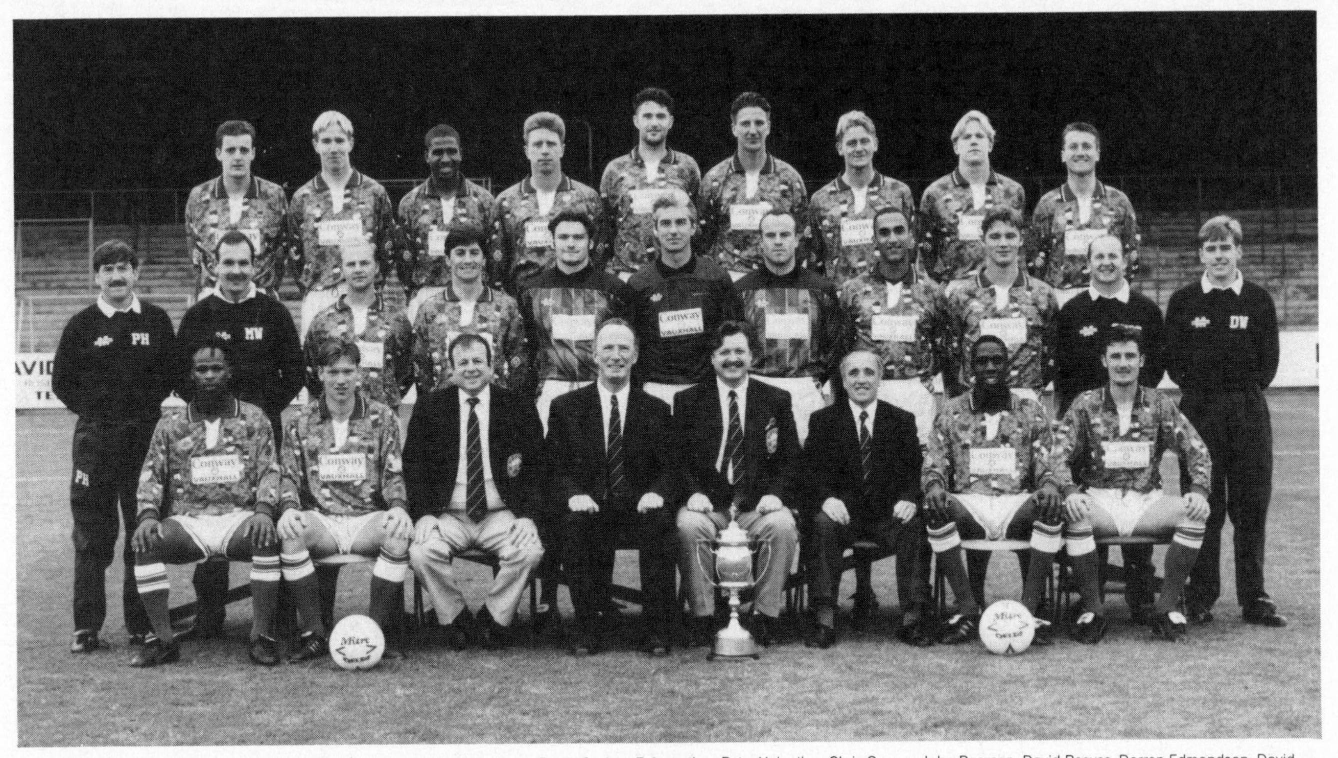

CARLISLE UNITED 1993–94 *Back row (left to right):* Paul Conway, Jason Prins, Carlton Fairweather, Peter Valentine, Chris Curran, John Pearson, David Reeves, Darren Edmondson, David Burgess.

Centre row: Peter Hampton (Physio), Mick Wadsworth (Director of Coaching), Ian Arnold, Joe Joyce, Tony Craig, Mervyn Day (Player Coach), Tony Elliott, George Oghani, Tony Gallimore, David McCreery (Player Coach), David Wilkes (Youth Team Coach).

Front row: Rod Thomas, Simon Davey, Albert Doweck (Director), Barry Chaytow (Vice Chairman), Michael Knighton (Chairman), Bob McKnight (Director), Dean Walling, Shane Reddish.

Division 3 CARLISLE UNITED

Brunton Park, Carlisle CA1 1LL. Telephone Carlisle (0228) 26237. Fax (0228) 30138. Promotions Dept: (0228) 24014. Commercial Dept: (0228) 24014.

Record attendance: 27,500 v Birmingham C, FA Cup 3rd rd, 5 January 1957 and v Middlesbrough, FA Cup 5th rd, 7 February 1970.

Record receipts: £104,410 v Sunderland, FA Cup 3rd rd replay, 18 January 1994.

Ground capacity: 12,771.

Pitch measurements: 117yd × 78yd.

President: J. C. Monkhouse. ***Vice-presidents:*** H. A. Jenkins, R. S. Liddell, J. R. Sheffield, T. A. Bingley, Dr. T. Gardner.

Directors: M Knighton (Chairman), B. Chaytow (Vice-chairman), R. McKnight, A. Doweck.

Director of Coaching: Mick Wadsworth ***Player-coaches:*** David McCreery and Mervyn Day. ***Assistant Manager:*** Peter Hampton.

Physio: Peter Hampton.

Commercial Managers: Martin Hudson and Donna Wenn.

Acting Secretary: Jim Thoburn.

Year Formed: 1903. ***Ltd Co.:*** 1921.

Previous Grounds: 1903–5, Milholme Bank; 1905–9, Devonshire Park; 1909– Brunton Park.

Previous Name: Shaddongate United.

Club Nickname: 'Cumbrians' or 'The Blues'.

Record League Victory: 8–0 v Hartlepools U, Division 3 (N), 1 September 1928 – Prout; Smiles, Cook; Robinson (1) Ross, Pigg; Agar (1), Hutchison (1), McConnell (4), Ward (1), Watson. 8–0 v Scunthorpe United, Division 3 (N), 25 December 1952 – MacLaren; Hill, Scott; Stokoe, Twentyman, Waters; Harrison (1), Whitehouse (5), Ashman (2), Duffett, Bond.

Record Cup Victory: 6–1 v Billingham Synthonia, FA Cup, 1st rd, 17 November 1956 – Fairley; Hill, Kenny; Johnston, Waters, Thompson; Mooney, Broadis (1), Ackerman (2), Garvie (3), Bond.

Record Defeat: 1–11 v Hull C, Division 3 (N), 14 January 1939.

Most League Points (2 for a win): 62, Division 3 (N), 1950–51.

Most League Points (3 for a win): 80, Division 3, 1981–82.

Most League Goals: 113, Division 4, 1963–64.

Highest League Scorer in Season: Jimmy McConnell, 42, Division 3 (N), 1928–29.

Most League Goals in Total Aggregate: Jimmy McConnell, 126, 1928–32.

Most Capped Player: Eric Welsh, 4, Northern Ireland.

Most League Appearances: Alan Ross, 466, 1963–79.

Record Transfer Fee Received: £275,000 from Vancouver Whitecaps for Peter Beardsley, April 1981.

Record Transfer Fee Paid: £120,000 to York C for Gordon Staniforth, October 1979.

Football League Record: 1928 Elected to Division 3 (N); 1958–62 Division 4; 1962–63 Division 3; 1963–64 Division 4; 1964–65 Division 3; 1965–74 Division 2; 1974–75 Division 1; 1975–77 Division 2; 1977–82 Division 3; 1982–86 Division 2; 1986–87 Division 3; 1987–92 Division 4; 1992– Division 3.

Honours: *Football League:* Division 1 best season: 22nd, 1974–75; Promoted from Division 2 (3rd) 1973–74; Division 3 – Champions 1964–65; Runners-up 1981–82; Division 4 – Runners-up 1963–64. *FA Cup:* 6th rd 1974–75. *Football League Cup:* Semi-final 1969–70.

CARLISLE UNITED 1993—94 LEAGUE RECORD

Match No.	Date	Venue	Opponents	Result		H/T Score	Lg. Pos.	Goalscorers	Attendance
1	Aug 14	H	Wycombe W	D	2-2	1-1	—	Thomas, Curran	7752
2	21	A	Doncaster R	D	0-0	0-0	13		2575
3	28	H	Rochdale	L	0-1	0-1	17		5438
4	31	A	Torquay U	D	1-1	0-1	—	Gallimore	3331
5	Sept 4	A	Scarborough	W	3-0	2-0	12	Fairweather, Davey 2	2044
6	11	H	Chesterfield	W	3-0	2-0	9	Thomas 2, Walling	5335
7	18	A	Scunthorpe U	L	1-2	1-1	12	Burgess	3361
8	25	A	Chester C	D	0-0	0-0	13		2911
9	Oct 2	H	Gillingham	L	1-2	0-0	15	Valentine	6449
10	9	A	Shrewsbury T	L	0-1	0-1	18		3254
11	16	H	Mansfield T	D	1-1	1-0	19	Davey	4480
12	23	A	Northampton T	D	1-1	0-0	18	Edmondson	2877
13	30	H	Walsall	W	2-1	1-1	18	Reeves, Davey	4216
14	Nov 2	H	Lincoln C	D	3-3	2-1	—	Walling, Edmondson, Arnold (pen)	5098
15	6	A	Wigan Ath	W	2-0	0-0	16	Reeves, Flounders	2411
16	20	H	Preston NE	L	0-1	0-0	17		10,279
17	27	A	Colchester U	L	1-2	1-1	17	Thomas	2316
18	Dec 11	H	Doncaster R	W	4-2	1-2	16	Davey, Walling, Edmondson, Thomas	4245
19	18	A	Wycombe W	L	0-2	0-2	16		5044
20	27	A	Darlington	W	3-1	3-1	15	Reeves 2, Graham	4800
21	28	H	Crewe Alex	L	1-2	1-1	16	Reeves	7073
22	Jan 1	A	Hereford U	D	0-0	0-0	16		2204
23	3	H	Torquay U	D	1-1	1-1	15	Davey (pen)	4872
24	15	A	Mansfield T	W	1-0	1-0	12	Reeves	2378
25	25	H	Bury	L	1-2	1-2	—	Reeves	4430
26	29	A	Walsall	W	1-0	0-0	12	Reeves	4833
27	Feb 5	H	Northampton T	L	0-1	0-0	14		4535
28	12	A	Bury	L	1-2	0-0	15	Reddish	2807
29	19	A	Rochdale	W	1-0	1-0	14	Davey	2927
30	25	H	Scarborough	W	2-0	1-0	11	Davey, Walling	4270
31	Mar 5	A	Chesterfield	L	0-3	0-0	13		2475
32	12	H	Scunthorpe U	W	3-1	0-0	12	Conway 2, Valentine	4076
33	19	H	Chester C	W	1-0	0-0	11	Reeves	4193
34	26	A	Gillingham	L	0-2	0-1	13		2586
35	Apr 2	H	Darlington	W	2-0	0-0	11	Walling, Thomas	4088
36	4	A	Crewe Alex	W	3-2	2-1	10	Thomas 2, Robinson	3679
37	9	H	Hereford U	L	1-2	1-0	11	Conway	4065
38	16	A	Lincoln C	D	0-0	0-0	12		2738
39	23	H	Wigan Ath	W	3-0	3-0	11	Thomas, Arnold, Reeves	3796
40	30	A	Preston NE	W	3-0	1-0	10	Reeves, Arnold 2	11,363
41	May 3	H	Shrewsbury T	W	2-1	2-0	—	Davey, Arnold	8007
42	7	H	Colchester U	W	2-0	1-0	7	Kinsella (og), Conway	9305

Final League Position: 7

GOALSCORERS

League (57): Reeves 11, Davey 9 (1 pen), Thomas 9, Arnold 5 (1 pen), Walling 5, Conway 4, Edmondson 3, Valentine 2, Burgess 1, Curran 1, Fairweather 1, Flounders 1, Gallimore 1, Graham 1, Reddish 1, Robinson 1, own goal 1.
Coca-Cola Cup (2): Davey 1, Thomas 1.
FA Cup (8): Arnold 3, Edmondson 2, Davey 1, Gallimore 1, Reeves 1.

Day 16	Burgess 36 + 4	Gallimore 40	Holden 1	Curran 4 + 2	Edmondson 21 + 1	Thomas 37 + 1	Reddish 33 + 2	Oghani 8 + 6	Davey 42	Fairweather 11 + 1	Arnold 7 + 7	Walling 40	Valentine 18 + 2	Joyce 28 + 1	Pearson 5 + 2	McCreery 6 + 7	Reeves 34	Prins 2 + 3	Flounders 6 + 2	Conway 16 + 2	Elliott 6	Graham 2	McMahon 2	Murray 2 + 6	Barnes 2	Caig 20	Robinson 16	Rouse 1 + 4	Delap — + 1	Peacock — + 1	Match No.
1	2	3	4	5	6	7	8	9	10	11	12																				1
1	2	3			6	7	8	9	10	11		4	5																		2
1	2	3			6	7	8	9	10	11	12	4	5	14																	3
1	2	3			6	7	8		10	11	9	4	5		12																4
1	2	3			6	7	8		10	11		4	5		9	12															5
1	2	3			6	7	8	9	10	11		4	5			12															6
1	2	3			6	7	8	12	10	11		4	5		9	14															7
1	2	3			6	9	8	7	10	11		4	5			12															8
1	2	3			6	7	8		10	11		4	5			12	9	14													9
1	2	3			6	7	8		10	11		4	5				9	12													10
1	2	3			6	7	8	11	10			4	5				9	12													11
1	2	3			6	7			10	12	11	4	5			8	9														12
1	2	3			6	7			10	11	12	4	5				9		8	14											13
1	2	3			6	7	11		10		12	4	5				9		8												14
	2	3			6	7	11		10			4		5			9		8		1										15
1	2	3			6	7	11		10		12	4		5			9		8												16
1	2	3			6	7	11		10			4		5		12	9		8												17
	2	3			6	7	11	12	10		8	4		5		14	9				1										18
	2	3			6	7		12	10			4		5		11	9				1	8									19
	2			6			12		10			4		5		11	9	8			1	7	3	14							20
	2	3		12	6	7	11		10			4		5			9	8			1			14							21
	2	3		6				12	10			4		5		11	9			7	1				8						22
	2	3		11	6			12	10			4		5			9			8				14	7	1					23
	2	3				14	6	11	10		12	4		5			9			7			8			1					24
	2	3		14		7	11	6	10		12	4		5			9			8						1					25
	2	3				7			10			4		5		11	9			8						1	6				26
	2					7			10			4	12	5		11	9			8				3		1	6				27
	2	3				7	11	12	10			4		5	14		9		8							1	6				28
	2	3				7	11		10			4		5	8		9							12		1	6				29
	2	7					6		10			4		5	8		9		12					11		1	3	14			30
	2	3				7	11		10			4	6	5	8		9		12							1		14			31
		3				7	11		10			4	5	2			9			12						1	6	8			32
		3				7	11		10			4	5	2			9			8						1	6				33
	12	3				7	11		10			4	5	2			9			8						1	6	14			34
	2	3				7	11		10			4		5			9			8				12		1	6				35
	2	3				7	11		10			4	12	5			9			8						1	6				36
	2	3			12	7	11		10			4		5			9			8						1	6		14		37
	2	3				7	11		10			4		5			9			8						1	6	12			38
	12	3				7	4		10		11		5	2			9			8						1	6			14	39
	2	3				7	12		10		11	4		5			9			8				14		1	6				40
	12	3				7	5		10		11	4		2			9			8						1	6				41
	12	3				7	5		10		11	4		2			9			8						1	6				42

Coca-Cola Cup	First Round	Chesterfield (a)	1-3
		(h)	1-1
FA Cup	First Round	Knowsley U (a)	4-1
	Second Round	Stalybridge C (h)	3-1
	Third Round	Sunderland (a)	1-1
		(h)	0-1

CARLISLE UNITED

Player and Position	Ht	Wt	Birth Date	Birth Place	Source	Clubs	League App	League Gls
Goalkeepers								
Anthony Caig	6 1	13 05	11 4 74	Whitehaven	Trainee	Carlisle U	21	—
Mervyn Day	6 2	15 01	26 6 55	Chelmsford	Apprentice	West Ham U	194	—
						Orient	170	—
						Aston Villa	30	—
						Leeds U	227	—
						Coventry C (loan)	—	—
						Luton T (loan)	4	—
						Sheffield U (loan)	1	—
						Carlisle U	16	—
Tony Elliott	6 0	12 12	30 11 69	Nuneaton		Birmingham C	—	—
						Hereford U	75	—
						Huddersfield T	15	—
						Carlisle U	6	—
Defenders								
Dave Burgess	5 10	11 04	20 1 60	Liverpool.	Local	Tranmere R	218	1
						Grimsby T	69	—
						Blackpool	101	1
						Carlisle U (loan)	6	—
						Carlisle U	40	1
Darren Edmondson	6 0	12 02	4 11 71	Coniston	Trainee	Carlisle U	114	5
Tony Hopper§			31 5 76	Carlisle	Trainee	Carlisle U	1	—
Joe Joyce	5 10	11 07	18 3 61	Consett	School	Barnsley	334	4
						Scunthorpe U	91	2
						Carlisle U	29	—
						Darlington (loan)	4	—
Steven McMahon‡	6 4	14 03	22 4 70	Glasgow	Ferguslie	Swansea C	2	—
						Carlisle U	2	—
Paul Murray§			31 8 76	Carlisle	Trainee	Carlisle U	8	—
Craig Potts‡	5 10	11 00	25 2 74	Carlisle	Trainee	Carlisle U	14	—
Jamie Robinson	6 0	12 03	26 2 72	Liverpool	Trainee	Liverpool	—	—
						Barnsley	9	—
						Carlisle U	16	1
Peter Valentine	5 10	12 00	16 6 63	Huddersfield	Apprentice	Huddersfield T	19	1
						Bolton W	68	1
						Bury	319	16
						Carlisle U	20	2
Dean Walling	6 0	12 00	17 4 69	Leeds		Leeds U	—	—
						Rochdale	65	8
					Guiseley	Carlisle U	100	10
Midfield								
Simon Davey	5 10	11 02	1 10 70	Swansea	Trainee	Swansea C	49	4
						Carlisle U	80	14
Rory Delap§			6 7 76	Coldfield	Trainee	Carlisle U	2	—
Tony Gallimore	5 10	11 10	21 2 72	Crewe	Trainee	Stoke C	11	—
						Carlisle U (loan)	16	—
						Carlisle U (loan)	8	1
						Carlisle U	40	1
David McCreery*	5 6	10 07	16 9 57	Belfast	Apprentice	Manchester U	87	7
						QPR	57	4
					Tulsa R	Newcastle U	243	2
						Hearts	29	—
						Hartlepool U	30	—
						Carlisle U	35	—
Shane Reddish	5 10	11 10	5 5 71	Bolsover	Trainee	Doncaster R	60	3
						Carlisle U	35	1
Shaun Rouse†	5 9	11 02	28 2 72	Gt Yarmouth	Rangers	Bristol C	—	—
						Carlisle U	5	—
Jeff Thorpe	5 10	12 06	17 11 72	Whitehaven	Trainee	Carlisle U	69	1
Derek Walsh	5 7	11 05	24 10 67	Hamilton	Apprentice	Everton	1	—
						Hamilton A.	2	—
						Carlisle U	121	7
Forwards								
Ian Arnold	5 9	11 00	4 7 72	Durham City	Trainee	Middlesbrough	3	—
						Carlisle U	43	11
Richie Bond‡	5 11	11 06	27 10 65	Blyth	Blyth S	Blackpool	1	—
						Carlisle U	—	—
Paul Conway†			17 4 70	London	Oldham Ath	Carlisle U	18	4
Chris Curran‡	6 1	12 06	6 1 71	Manchester	Trainee	Crewe Alex	5	—
						Scarborough	40	4
						Carlisle U	6	1

CARLISLE UNITED

Colours: Blue shirts, white shorts, blue stockings. **Change colours:** Green top shirts with white and red stripes, green shorts, green stockings.

Foundation: Carlisle United came into being in 1903 through the amalgamation of Shaddongate United and Carlisle Red Rose. The new club was admitted to the Second Division of the Lancashire Combination in 1905–06, winning promotion the following season.

First Football League game: 25 August, 1928, Division 3(N), v Accrington S (a) W 3-2 – Prout; Coulthard, Cook; Harrison, Ross, Pigg; Agar, Hutchison, McConnell (1), Ward (1), Watson. 1 o.g.

Did you know: Carlisle United reached the Northern Area semi-final of the Autoglass Trophy in 1993–94 beating Mansfield Town after extra time on 11 January, attracting a crowd of 8686, the highest attendance at that stage of the competition.

Managers (and Secretary-Managers)
H. Kirkbride 1904–05*, McCumiskey 1905–06*, J. Houston 1906–08*, Bert Stansfield 1908–10, J. Houston 1910–12, D. Graham 1912–13, George Bristow 1913–30, Billy Hampson 1930–33, Bill Clarke 1933–35, Robert Kelly 1935–36, Fred Westgarth 1936–38, David Taylor 1938–40, Howard Harkness 1940–45, Bill Clark 1945–46*, Ivor Broadis 1946–49, Bill Shankly 1949–51, Fred Emery 1951–58, Andy Beattie 1958–60, Ivor Powell 1960–63, Alan Ashman 1963–67, Tim Ward 1967–68, Bob Stokoe 1968–70, Ian MacFarlane 1970–72, Alan Ashman 1972–75, Dick Young 1975–76, Bobby Moncur 1976–80, Martin Harvey 1980, Bob Stokoe 1980–85, Bryan "Pop" Robson 1985, Bob Stokoe 1985–86, Harry Gregg 1986–87, Cliff Middlemass 1987–91, Aidan McCaffery 1991–92, David McCreery 1992–93, Mick Wadsworth (Director of coaching) August 1993–

Carlton Fairweather‡	5 11	11 00	22 9 61	London	Tooting & Mitcham	Wimbledon	138	26
						Carlisle U	12	1
Steve Holden	6 0	11 13	4 9 72	Luton	Trainee	Leicester C	1	—
						Carlisle U	22	1
George Oghani*	5 11	12 01	2 9 60	Manchester	Hyde	Bolton W	99	27
						Wrexham (loan)	7	—
						Burnley	74	21
						Stockport Co	8	2
						Hereford U	8	2
						Scarborough	50	18
					Evagoras	Carlisle U	53	15
Lee Peacock§			9 10 76	Paisley	Trainee	Carlisle U	1	—
John Pearson	6 3	13 00	1 9 63	Sheffield	Apprentice	Sheffield W	105	24
						Charlton Ath	61	15
						Leeds U	99	12
						Rotherham U (loan)	11	5
						Barnsley	32	4
						Hull C (loan)	15	—
						Carlisle U	7	—
Paul Proudlock‡	5 10	11 00	25 10 65	Hartlepool	Local	Hartlepool U	15	—
						Middlesbrough	5	1
						Carlisle U	155	20
						Hartlepool U (loan)	6	—
David Reeves	6 0	11 05	19 11 67	Birkenhead	Heswall	Sheffield W	17	2
						Scunthorpe U (loan)	4	2
						Scunthorpe U (loan)	6	4
						Burnley (loan)	16	8
						Bolton W	134	29
						Notts Co	13	2
						Carlisle U	34	11
Rod Thomas	5 6	10 10	10 10 70	London	Trainee	Watford	84	9
						Gillingham (loan)	8	1
						Carlisle U	38	9

Trainees
Dalton, Neil J; Delap, Rory J; Doyle, Nikki; Ellwood, James T; Fryer, Andrew M; Gill, Gary P; Hopper, Tony; Murray, Paul; Peacock, Lee A; Prokas, Richard; Varty, John W; Wilson, Darren L; Wilson, Graeme J.

****Non-Contract**
Conway, Paul J; Wilkes, David A.

Associated Schoolboys
Andrews, Brett P; Bird, Shane L; Doswell, Lee A; Edgar, Robbie; Edwards, Richard; Green, Mark; Hewitt, Steven P; Holt, Steven; Kirk, Nigel B. J; Lawson, Wayne; Lewis, Graeme; Livingstone, Gareth; McMahon, Ronan J; Mellon, Marc R; Palmer, Daniel R; Thurstan, Matthew; Thurston, Mark R.

Associated Schoolboys who have accepted the Club's offer of a Traineeship/Contract
Armstrong, Gavin; Hodgson, Michael; Jansen, Matthew B; Sandwith, Kevin; Taylor, Lee R.
**Non-Contract Players who are retained must be re-signed before they are eligible to play in League matches.

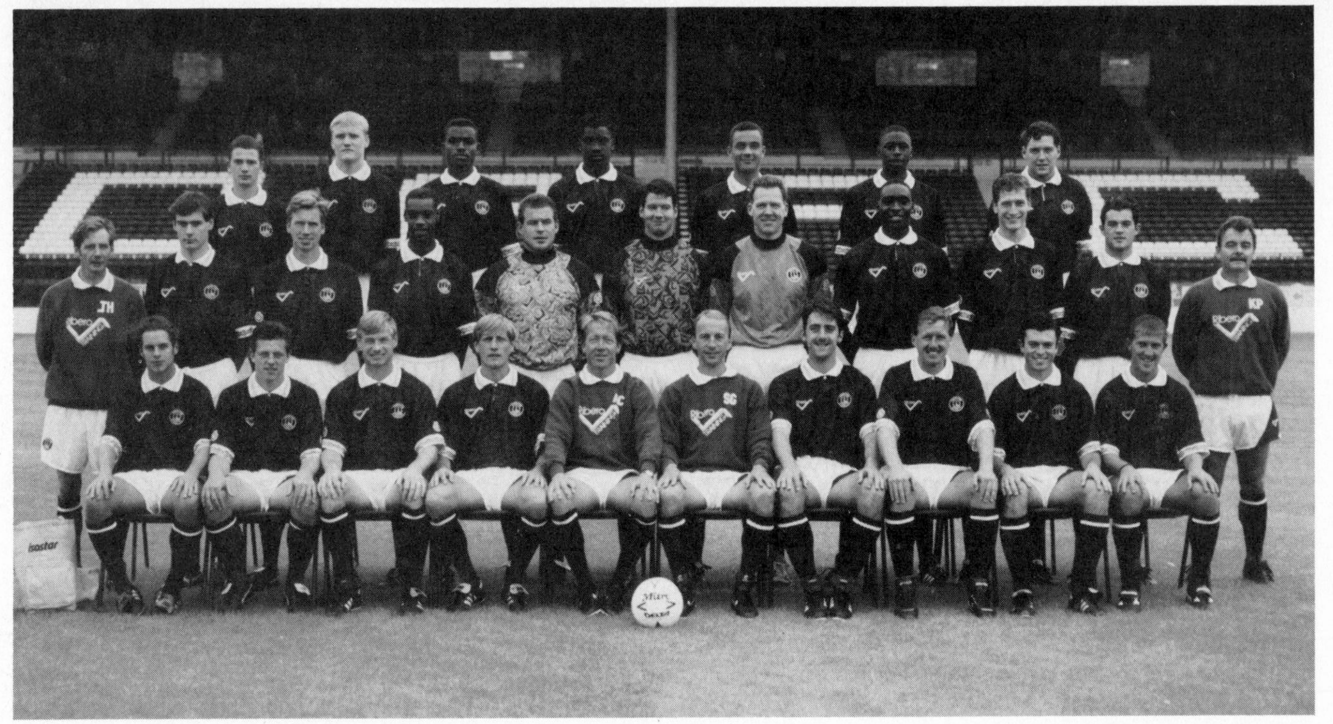

CHARLTON ATHLETIC 1993–94 *Back row (left to right):* Paul Linger, Danny Mills, Sam Appiah, Linvoy Primus, Kim Grant, Shaun Newton, Peter Garland.
Centre row: Jimmy Hendry (Physio), Steve Brown, Alan Pardew, Richard Rufus, John Vaughan, Mike Salmon, Bob Bolder, Carl Leaburn, Phil Chapple, Paul Sturgess, Keith Peacock (Reserve Team Coach).
Front row: Scott Minto, Paul Gorman, Garry Nelson, Alan McLeary, Alan Curbishley (Player/Manager), Steve Gritt (Player/Manager), Stuart Balmer, Colin Walsh, Darren Pitcher, John Robinson.
(Photograph: Tom Morris)

Division 1 **CHARLTON ATHLETIC**

The Valley, Floyd Road, Charlton, London SE7 8BL. Telephone 081–293 4567. Fax 081–293 5143. Clubcall (0891) 121146.

Ground: The Valley, London SE7 8BL.

Ground capacity: 15,000.

Record attendance: 75,031 v Aston Villa, FA Cup 5th rd, 12 February 1938 (at The Valley).

Record receipts: £114,618.70 v Liverpool (at Selhurst Park), Division 1, 23 January 1988.

Pitch measurements: 112yd × 73yd.

President: R. D. Collins.

Chairman: R. N. Alwen. ***Deputy Chairmen:*** R. A. Murray and M. A. Simons.

Directors: S. T. Clarke, R. D. Collins, M. C. Stevens, D. G. Ufton, G. Bone.

General Manager: Jonathan Fuller.

Joint Managers: Steve Gritt and Alan Curbishley.

Reserve team manager: Keith Peacock. ***Youth team manager:*** John Cartwright. ***Youth Development officer:*** Neil Banfield. ***Physio:*** Jimmy Hendry.

Secretary: Chris Parkes.

Marketing Manager: Steve Dixon.

Year Formed: 1905. ***Turned Professional:*** 1920. ***Ltd Co.:*** 1919.

Club Nickname: 'Addicks'.

Previous Grounds: 1906, Siemen's Meadow; 1907, Woolwich Common; 1909, Pound Park; 1913, Horn Lane; 1920, The Valley; 1923, Catford (The Mount); 1924, The Valley; 1985 Selhurst Park; 1991 Upton Park; 1992 The Valley.

Record League Victory: 8–1 v Middlesbrough, Division 1, 12 September 1953 – Bartram; Campbell, Ellis; Fenton, Ufton, Hammond; Hurst (2), O'Linn (2), Leary (1), Firmani (3), Kiernan.

Record Cup Victory: 7–0 v Burton A, FA Cup, 3rd rd, 7 January 1956 – Bartram; Campbell, Townsend; Hewie, Ufton, Hammond; Hurst (1), Gauld (1), Leary (3), White, Kiernan (2).

Record Defeat: 1–11 v Aston Villa, Division 2, 14 November 1959.

Most League Points (2 for a win): 61, Division 3 (S), 1934–35.

Most League Points (3 for a win): 77, Division 2, 1985–86.

Most League Goals: 107, Division 2, 1957–58.

Highest League Scorer in Season: Ralph Allen, 32, Division 3 (S), 1934–35.

Most League Goals in Total Aggregate: Stuart Leary, 153, 1953–62.

Most Capped Player: John Hewie, 19, Scotland.

Most League Appearances: Sam Bartram, 583, 1934–56.

Record Transfer Fee Received: £750,000 from Newcastle U for Robert Lee, September 1992.

Record Transfer Fee Paid: £600,000 to Chelsea for Joe McLaughlin, August 1989.

Football League Record: 1921 Elected to Division 3 (S); 1929–33 Division 2; 1933–35 Division 3 (S); 1935–36 Division 2; 1936–57 Division 1; 1957–72 Division 2; 1972–75 Division 3; 1975–80 Division 2; 1980–81 Division 3; 1981–86; Division 2; 1986–90 Division 1; 1990–92 Division 2; 1992– Division 1.

Honours: *Football League:* Division 1 – Runners-up 1936–37; Division 2 – Runners-up 1935–36, 1985–86; Division 3 (S) – Champions 1928–29, 1934–35; Promoted from Division 3 (3rd) 1974–75, 1980–81. *FA Cup:* Winners 1947; Runners-up 1946. *Football League Cup:* best season: 4th rd, 1962–63, 1965–66, 1978–79. *Full Members Cup:* Runners-up 1987.

CHARLTON ATHLETIC 1993—94 LEAGUE RECORD

Match No.	Date	Venue	Opponents	Result		H/T Score	Lg. Pos.	Goalscorers	Attendance
1	Aug 14	H	Birmingham C	W	1-0	1-0	—	Chapple	7708
2	17	A	Portsmouth	W	2-1	2-0	—	Nelson, Walsh	15,701
3	21	A	Sunderland	L	0-4	0-0	2		17,647
4	24	H	Tranmere R	W	3-1	1-0	—	Newton, Leaburn, Minto (pen)	6666
5	28	H	Bolton W	W	3-0	1-0	2	Walsh, Nelson, Garland	7573
6	Sept 4	A	Watford	D	2-2	1-1	1	Nelson, Minto	6925
7	11	H	Millwall	D	0-0	0-0	1		8416
8	18	A	Bristol C	D	0-0	0-0	2		7484
9	26	H	Crystal Palace	D	0-0	0-0	—		7947
10	Oct 2	A	Wolverhampton W	D	1-1	0-0	5	Chapple	16,907
11	9	A	Barnsley	W	1-0	1-0	3	Pardew (pen)	5186
12	16	H	Leicester C	W	2-1	1-0	2	Chapple, Pitcher (pen)	8316
13	23	A	Grimsby T	W	1-0	1-0	1	Grant	5118
14	30	H	Oxford U	W	1-0	1-0	1	Nelson	7811
15	Nov 2	H	Derby Co	L	1-2	1-1	—	Nelson	8123
16	7	A	Luton T	L	0-1	0-1	—		6327
17	13	H	Notts Co	W	5-1	1-1	1	Leaburn, Nelson 2, Newton, Walsh	7078
18	20	A	Peterborough U	W	1-0	0-0	1	Nelson	6273
19	Dec 4	H	Luton T	W	1-0	0-0	1	Chapple	7121
20	12	H	Portsmouth	L	0-1	0-1	—		6975
21	18	A	Birmingham C	L	0-1	0-0	2		13,714
22	27	A	Southend U	L	2-4	1-2	4	Leaburn, Pardew	10,123
23	29	H	Stoke C	W	2-0	1-0	3	Leaburn, McLeary	8416
24	Jan 1	A	Nottingham F	D	1-1	0-0	4	McLeary	26,543
25	3	H	WBA	W	2-1	0-0	3	Pardew, Leaburn	8316
26	16	A	Leicester C	L	1-2	0-0	—	Balmer	12,577
27	22	H	Barnsley	W	2-1	0-0	2	Robinson, Robson	7072
28	Feb 5	H	Grimsby T	L	0-1	0-0	2		7598
29	12	A	Oxford U	W	4-0	1-0	2	Leaburn 2, Pardew (pen), Nelson	7126
30	22	H	Sunderland	D	0-0	0-0	—		7904
31	25	H	Watford	W	2-1	2-0	2	Pardew 2 (1 pen)	7546
32	Mar 5	A	Bolton W	L	2-3	0-1	2	Pardew, Robson	13,027
33	15	A	Millwall	L	1-2	0-0	—	Nelson	13,320
34	20	A	Crystal Palace	L	0-2	0-1	—		14,408
35	26	H	Wolverhampton W	L	0-1	0-1	7		8416
36	30	A	WBA	L	0-2	0-0	—		14,091
37	Apr 2	H	Southend U	W	4-3	0-0	7	Gorman, Leaburn, Pardew 2	9117
38	4	A	Stoke C	L	0-1	0-1	8		13,569
39	9	H	Nottingham F	L	0-1	0-1	10		12,330
40	16	A	Derby Co	L	0-2	0-0	12		15,784
41	19	A	Middlesbrough	L	0-2	0-2	—		6982
42	23	H	Peterborough U	W	5-1	3-0	11	Nelson 3, Leaburn, Pardew	8626
43	26	A	Tranmere R	L	0-2	0-0	—		8170
44	30	A	Notts Co	D	3-3	1-2	12	Leaburn, McLeary, Bennett	7019
45	May 3	H	Bristol C	W	3-1	1-1	—	Nelson, Chapple, Scott (og)	6727
46	8	H	Middlesbrough	L	2-5	0-2	11	Walsh, Nelson	8905

Final League Position: 11

GOALSCORERS

League (61): Nelson 15, Leaburn 10, Pardew 10 (3 pens), Chapple 5, Walsh 4, McLeary 3, Minto 2 (1 pen), Newton 2, Robson 2, Balmer 1, Bennett 1, Garland 1, Gorman 1, Grant 1, Pitcher 1 (pen), Robinson 1, own goal 1.
Coca-Cola Cup (1): Leaburn 1.
FA Cup (8): Grant 2, Leaburn 2, Pitcher 2 (1 pen), Pardew 1, Robson 1.

Salmon 41	Pitcher 42	Minto 42	Garland 21 + 6	McLeary 44	Balmer 25 + 6	Robinson 27	Gorman 7 + 7	Leaburn 39	Chapple 40 + 4	Walsh 32 + 3	Nelson 34 + 9	Newton 11 + 8	Curbishley — + 1	Linger — + 5	Grant 18 + 12	Sturgess 5 + 3	Pardew 24 + 2	Vaughan 5 + 1	Brown 18 + 1	Bailey — + 4	Robson 20 + 3	Small 1 + 1	Bennett 10	Match No.
1	2	3	4	5	*6*	7	8	9	10	11	12	14												1
1	2	3	4	5		7		9	6	11	10	8	12											2
1	2	3	4	5		7	12	9	6	11	10	8												3
1	2	3	4	5		7	12	9	6	11	10	*8*		14										4
1	2	*3*	4	5		7		9	6	11	10	8			12	14								5
1	2	3	4	5	12	7		9	6	11	10	8												6
1	2	3	4	5		7		9	6	11	10	8			12									7
1	2	3	4	5	12	7	9		6	11		8			10									8
1	2	3		5	6	7	14		8	11	*10*	12			9		4							9
1	2	3		5	6	7		9	8	*11*	10	12			14		4							10
1	2	3		5	6	7		9	11		10	8			12		4							11
	2	3		5		7		9	6	11	10			12	8		*4*	1	14					12
1	2	3			6	7			5	*11*	10	8		12	9	14			4					13
1	2	3		*6*	4	7		9	5	11	10	12			8					14				14
1	2	3		6	4	7		*9*	5	11	10	12			8					14				15
1	2	3		6	4	7		9	5	11	10	*8*			12					14				16
1	2	3	*4*	6	7			9	5	11	10	12			8					14				17
1	2	3	4	6	8	7		9	5	11	10										12			18
1	2	3	4	6	8	7		9	5	*11*	10	12									14			19
1	2	3	*4*	5	6	7		9	8	11	10	12									14			20
1	2	3	4	5	6	7		9	8		10						12				11			21
1	2	3		5	4	7		9	6	11	*10*				14		12				8			22
1	8	3		5				9	6	11	12				10		4		2		7			23
1	8	3	14	5				9	6	11	12				*10*		4		2		7			24
1	8	3		5				9	6	11	12				10		4		2		7			25
1		3	4	5	6	7		9			12				10		8		2		11			26
1		3	4	5	12	7		9	6		14				*10*		8		2		11			27
1	8	3		5	14			9	*6*		12	11			10		4		2		7			28
1	4	3	14	5	6			9	12		10				8		11		2		*7*			29
1	8		14	5	6		9		12		11				10	3	4		2		*7*			30
1	8	3	10		6		*9*		5		11			14		12	4		2		7			31
	8	3		5	6			9	12		11				*10*		4	1	2		7	14		32
	8			5	6					11	10				12	3	4	1	2		7	9		33
	8	3		5	6			9	14	11	10				12		4	1	2		*7*			34
1	8	3	4	5	14			9	6	11	10				12				2		*7*			35
1	8	3	4	5	2			9	6	11	10				12						*7*			36
1		3	14	5	2		10	9	6	*11*	12						4				7		8	37
1		3	4	5	2		9		6	14	10				12	*8*	11						7	38
1	8	3		5	*2*		10	9	6	14	12						4				11		7	39
1	8	3		5				9	6					12	10		4		2		11		7	40
1	8	3		5			12	9	6	14					10		4		2		11		*7*	41
1	8	3	14	5		7	12	9	6	*11*	10						4						2	42
1	2	3		5		7	12	9	6	11	10						4						8	43
1	8	3	14	5			12	9	6	11	10						*4*		2				7	44
1	8		4	5		11		9	6		10				12	3		14	2				7	45
	8		4	5	12	7		9	6	11	10					3		1					2	46

Coca-Cola Cup	Second Round	Crystal Palace (a)	1-3
		(h)	0-1
FA Cup	Third Round	Burnley (h)	3-0
	Fourth Round	Blackburn R (h)	0-0
		(a)	1-0
	Fifth Round	Bristol C (a)	1-1
		(h)	2-0
	Sixth Round	Manchester U (a)	1-3

CHARLTON ATHLETIC

Player and Position	Ht	Wt	Birth Date	Birth Place	Source	Clubs	League App	League Gls
Goalkeepers								
Bob Bolder*	6 3	14 06	2 10 58	Dover	Dover	Sheffield W	196	—
						Liverpool	—	—
						Sunderland	22	—
						Luton T (loan)	—	—
						Charlton Ath	249	—
Mike Salmon	6 2	13 00	14 7 64	Leyland	Local	Blackburn R	1	—
						Chester C (loan)	16	—
						Stockport Co	118	—
						Bolton W	26	—
						Wrexham (loan)	17	—
						Wrexham	83	—
						Charlton Ath	67	—
John Vaughan*	5 10	13 01	26 6 64	Isleworth	Apprentice	West Ham U	—	—
						Charlton Ath (loan)	6	—
						Bristol R (loan)	6	—
						Wrexham (loan)	4	—
						Bristol C (loan)	2	—
						Fulham	44	—
						Bristol C (loan)	3	—
						Cambridge U	178	—
						Charlton Ath	6	—
Defenders								
Stuart Balmer	6 1	13 00	20 6 69	Falkirk	Celtic BC	Celtic	—	—
						Charlton Ath	118	3
Steve Brown	6 1	12 08	13 5 72	Brighton	Trainee	Charlton Ath	20	—
Dean Chandler	6 0	11 05	6 5 76	London	Trainee	Charlton Ath	—	—
Phil Chapple	6 2	12 07	26 11 66	Norwich		Norwich C	—	—
						Cambridge U	187	19
						Charlton Ath	44	5
Andy Gray*	5 9	10 00	22 11 74	Essex	Trainee	Charlton Ath	—	—
Alan McLeary	6 0	11 11	6 10 64	London	Apprentice	Millwall	307	5
						Sheffield U (loan)	3	—
						Wimbledon (loan)	4	—
						Charlton Ath	44	3
Scott Minto	5 10	10 00	6 8 71	Cheshire	Trainee	Charlton Ath	180	7
Darren Pitcher	5 9	12 02	12 10 69	London	Trainee	Charlton Ath	173	8
						Galway (loan)	—	—
Linvoy Primus*	5 10	12 04	14 9 73	Stratford	Trainee	Charlton Ath	4	—
Richard Rufus	6 1	11 02	12 1 75	Lewisham	Trainee	Charlton Ath	—	—
Midfield								
Mickey Bennett	5 10	11 11	27 7 69	London	Apprentice	Charlton Ath	35	2
						Wimbledon	18	2
						Brentford	46	4
						Charlton Ath	10	1
Lee Bowyer	5 9	9 11	3 1 77	London	Trainee	Charlton Ath	—	—
Alan Curbishley	5 11	11 10	8 11 57	Forest Gate	Apprentice	West Ham U	85	5
						Birmingham C	130	11
						Aston Villa	36	1
						Charlton Ath	63	6
						Brighton	116	13
						Charlton Ath	28	—
Peter Garland	5 9	12 00	20 1 71	Croydon	Trainee	Tottenham H	1	—
						Newcastle U	2	—
						Charlton Ath	40	2
Steve Gritt	5 9	10 10	31 10 57	Bournemouth	Apprentice	Bournemouth	6	3
						Charlton Ath	347	24
						Walsall	20	1
						Charlton Ath	33	1
Paul Linger	5 8	10 01	20 12 74	Tower Hamlets	Trainee	Charlton Ath	7	—
Danny Mills	6 0	11 05	13 2 75	Sidcup	Trainee	Charlton Ath	—	—
Shaun Newton	5 8	10 04	20 8 75	Camberwell	Trainee	Charlton Ath	21	2
Alan Pardew	5 10	11 00	18 7 61	Wimbledon	Yeovil	Crystal Palace	128	8
						Charlton Ath	80	21
John Robinson	5 10	11 05	29 8 71	Bulawayo, Rhodesia	Apprentice	Brighton	62	6
						Charlton Ath	42	3

CHARLTON ATHLETIC

Colours: Red shirts, white shorts, red stockings. **Change colours:** White shirts, red shorts, white stockings.

Foundation: The club was formed on 9 June 1905, by a group of 14 and 15-year-old youths living in streets by the Thames in the area which now borders the Thames Barrier. The club's progress through local leagues was so rapid that after the First World War they joined the Kent League where they spent a season before turning professional and joining the Southern League in 1920. A year later they were elected to the Football League's Division 3 (South).

First Football League game: 27 August, 1921, Division 3(S), v Exeter C (h) W 1-0 – Hughes; Mitchell, Goodman; Dowling (1), Hampson, Dunn; Castle, Bailey, Halse, Green, Wilson.

Did you know: In 1933–34 Charlton Athletic's average attendance in Division 3 (South) was 10,574. Their first season in Division 1 during 1936–37 produced crowds averaging 31,086.

Managers (and Secretary-Managers)
Bill Rayner 1920–25, Alex McFarlane 1925–27, Albert Lindon 1928, Alex McFarlane 1928–32, Jimmy Seed 1933–56, Jimmy Trotter 1956–61, Frank Hill 1961–65, Bob Stokoe 1965–67, Eddie Firmani 1967–70, Theo Foley 1970–74, Andy Nelson 1974–79, Mike Bailey 1979–81, Alan Mullery 1981–82, Ken Craggs 1982, Lennie Lawrence 1982–91, Steve Gritt/Alan Curbishley July 1991–

Player and Position	*Ht*	*Wt*	*Birth Date*	*Birth Place*	*Source*	*Clubs*	*League App*	*League Gls*
Paul Sturgess	5 11	12 05	4 8 75	Dartford	Trainee	Charlton Ath	12	—
Colin Walsh	5 9	10 11	22 7 62	Hamilton	Apprentice	Nottingham F	139	32
						Charlton Ath	208	20
						Peterborough U (loan)	5	1
						Middlesbrough (loan)	13	1
Forwards								
Sam Appiah*	5 10	11 08	14 4 75	Ghana	Trainee	Charlton Ath	—	—
Paul Gorman*	5 9	12 02	18 9 68	Macclesfield		Doncaster R	16	2
					Fisher Ath	Charlton Ath	40	8
Kim Grant	5 10	10 12	25 9 72	Ghana	Trainee	Charlton Ath	67	5
Carl Leaburn	6 3	11 03	30 3 69	Lewisham	Apprentice	Charlton Ath	197	30
						Northampton T (loan)	9	—
Garry Nelson	5 10	11 04	16 1 61	Braintree	Amateur	Southend U	129	17
						Swindon T	79	7
						Plymouth Arg	74	20
						Brighton	144	46
						Notts Co (loan)	2	—
						Charlton Ath	128	27
Mark Robson	5 7	10 05	22 5 69	Newham	Trainee	Exeter C	26	7
						Tottenham H	8	—
						Reading (loan)	7	—
						Watford (loan)	1	—
						Plymouth Arg (loan)	7	—
						Exeter C (loan)	8	1
						West Ham U	47	8
						Charlton Ath	23	2

Trainees
Blain, Dean R; Burt, Leslie; Chadwick, Neil; Colman, Leigh T; Dowson, Keith S; Edwards, Daniel J; Garnish, James F; Jackson, James T; Lawson, John W; Lee, Dean J; Magloire, Christopher; Morley, Darren M. R; (h) Morris, David J; Reynolds, Stuart; (h) Ross, Leo K; Rufus, Marvin M; Stuart, Jamie C.

Associated Schoolboys
Bell, Ryan W; Bright, Gavin A; Carey, Matthew D. R; Carnegie, Daniel I; Cella, Nicholas D; Constantinou, Anthony; Cooley, Danny; Craggy, Jamie J; Foster, Daniel C; Goldup, Robert; Jones, Paul A; King, Aaron S; Lee, Matthew A; Lomakin, Justin A; Mbuya, Modisa; Moore, Anthony; Nicholls, Kevin J. R; Walsh, Paul D; Warren, Kevin; Watkins, Jake A.

Associated Schoolboys who have accepted the Club's offer of a Traineeship/Contract
Crane, Paul S; Kyte, Jamie R; Larkin, Andrew K; Matthews, Patrick W; Oakey, Stephen R; Tindall, Jason; Way, James W.

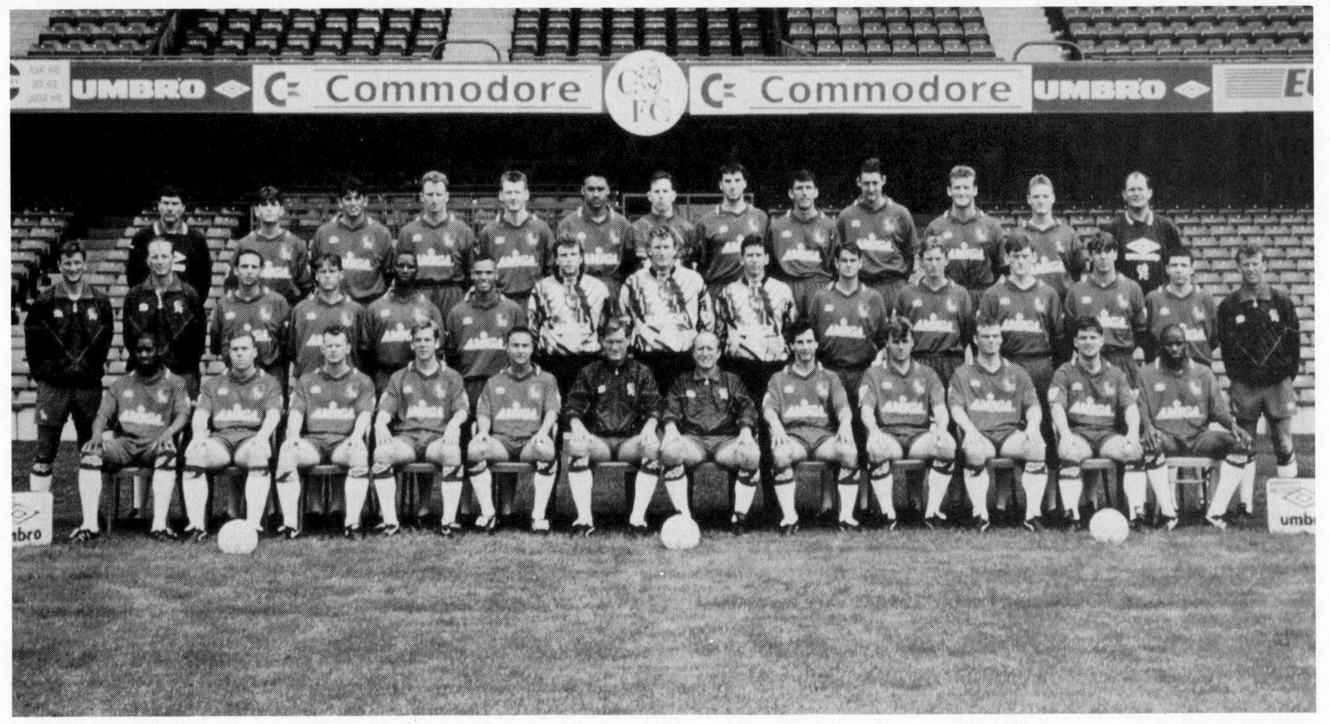

CHELSEA 1993–94 *Back row (left to right):* Dave Collyer (Youth Development Manager), Anthony Barness, Neil Shipperley, Steve Livingstone, Nigel Spackman, Paul Elliott, Nick Colgan, Ian Pearce, Tony Cascarino, David Lee, Erland Johnsen, Craig Norman, Gwyn Williams.

Centre row: Eddie Niedzwiecki (Reserve Team Manager), Bob Ward (Physio), Damian Matthew, Darren Barnard, Zeke Rowe, Andy Myers, Dmitri Kharine, Dave Beasant, Kevin Hitchcock, Steve Clarke, Terry Skiverton, David Hopkin, Craig Burley, Mussie Izzet, Graham Rix (Youth Team Manager).

Front row: Eddie Newton, Gareth Hall, Graham Stuart, Andy Dow, Dennis Wise, Glenn Hoddle (Team Manager), Peter Shreeves (Assistant Manager), Gavin Peacock, Mal Donaghy, Robert Fleck, John Spencer, Frank Sinclair.

FA Premiership CHELSEA

Stamford Bridge, London SW6 1HS. Telephone 071–385 5545. Clubcall: 0891 121159. Ticket News and Promotions: 0891 121011. Ticket credit card service: 071–386 7799. Fax: 071 381 4831.

Ground capacity: 29,700 (during ground development); 41,000 (eventually).

Record attendance: 82,905 v Arsenal, Division 1, 12 Oct 1935.

Record receipts: £465,324 v Manchester U, FA Premier League, 11 September 1993.

Pitch measurements: 110yd × 72yd.

President: G. M. Thomson.

Chairman: K. W. Bates. ***Vice-chairman:***

Directors: C. Hutchinson (Managing), Y. S. Todd, M. Harding.

Team Manager: Glenn Hoddle. ***Assistant Manager:*** Peter Shreeves.

Physio: Bob Ward. ***Reserve Team Manager:*** Eddie Niedzwiecki.

Company Secretary/Director: Yvonne Todd. ***Match Secretary:*** Keith Lacy. ***Commercial Manager:*** Carole Phair.

Year Formed: 1905. ***Turned Professional:*** 1905. ***Ltd Co.:*** 1905.

Club Nickname: 'The Blues'.

Record League Victory: 9–2 v Glossop N E, Division 2, 1 September 1906 – Byrne; Walton, Miller; Key (1), McRoberts, Henderson; Moran, McDermott (1), Hilsdon (5), Copeland (1), Kirwan (1).

Record Cup Victory: 13–0 v Jeunesse Hautcharage, ECWC, 1st rd 2nd leg, 29 September 1971 – Bonetti; Boyle, Harris (1), Hollins (1p), Webb (1), Hinton, Cooke, Baldwin (3), Osgood (5), Hudson (1), Houseman (1).

Record Defeat: 1–8 v Wolverhampton W, Division 1, 26 September 1953.

Most League Points (2 for a win): 57, Division 2, 1906–07.

Most League Points (3 for a win): 99, Division 2, 1988–89.

Most League Goals: 98, Division 1, 1960–61.

Highest League Scorer in Season: Jimmy Greaves, 41, 1960–61.

Most League Goals in Total Aggregate: Bobby Tambling, 164, 1958–70.

Most Capped Player: Ray Wilkins, 24 (84), England.

Most League Appearances: Ron Harris, 655, 1962–80.

Record Transfer Fee Received: £2,200,000 from Tottenham H for Gordon Durie, July 1991.

Record Transfer Fee Paid: £2,100,000 to Norwich C for Robert Fleck, July 1992.

Football League Record: 1905 Elected to Division 2; 1907–10 Division 1; 1910–12 Division 2; 1912–24 Division 1; 1924–30 Division 2; 1930–62 Division 1; 1962–63 Division 2; 1963–75 Division 1; 1975–77 Division 2; 1977–79 Division 1; 1979–84 Division 2; 1984–88 Division 1; 1988–89 Division 2; 1989–92 Division 1; 1992– FA Premier League.

Honours: *Football League:* Division 1 – Champions 1954–55; Division 2 – Champions 1983–84, 1988–89; Runners-up 1906–7, 1911–12, 1929–30, 1962–63, 1976–77. *FA Cup:* Winners 1970; Runners-up 1915, 1967, 1994. *Football League Cup:* Winners 1964–65; Runners-up 1971–72. *Full Members' Cup:* Winners 1985–86. *Zenith Data Systems Cup:* Winners 1989–90.**European Competitions:** *European Fairs Cup:* 1958–60, 1965–66, 1968–69; *European Cup-Winners' Cup:* 1970–71 (winners), 1971–72.

CHELSEA 1993—94 LEAGUE RECORD

Match No.	Date	Venue	Opponents	Result		H/T Score	Lg. Pos.	Goalscorers	Attendance
1	Aug 14	H	Blackburn R	L	1-2	0-0	—	Peacock	29,189
2	17	A	Wimbledon	D	1-1	0-0	—	Wise	11,263
3	21	A	Ipswich T	L	0-1	0-1	16		17,355
4	25	H	QPR	W	2-0	1-0	—	Peacock, Cascarino	20,191
5	28	H	Sheffield W	D	1-1	1-1	14	Lee	16,652
6	Sept 1	A	Tottenham H	D	1-1	1-0	—	Cascarino	27,567
7	11	H	Manchester U	W	1-0	1-0	13	Peacock	37,064
8	18	A	Coventry C	D	1-1	1-0	14	Peacock	13,586
9	25	H	Liverpool	W	1-0	0-0	12	Shipperley	31,271
10	Oct 2	A	West Ham U	L	0-1	0-1	14		18,917
11	16	H	Norwich C	L	1-2	0-1	15	Peacock	16,923
12	23	A	Aston Villa	L	0-1	0-1	15		29,706
13	30	H	Oldham Ath	L	0-1	0-1	16		15,372
14	Nov 6	A	Leeds U	L	1-4	0-0	18	Shipperley	35,050
15	20	H	Arsenal	L	0-2	0-2	18		26,839
16	22	H	Manchester C	D	0-0	0-0	—		10,128
17	27	A	Sheffield U	L	0-1	0-1	20		16,119
18	Dec 5	A	Blackburn R	L	0-2	0-1	—		16,756
19	11	H	Ipswich T	D	1-1	1-0	20	Peacock	13,208
20	27	A	Southampton	L	1-3	1-1	21	Stein	14,221
21	28	H	Newcastle U	W	1-0	1-0	19	Stein	23,133
22	Jan 1	A	Swindon T	W	3-1	2-0	17	Shipperley, Stein, Wise	16,261
23	3	H	Everton	W	4-2	2-0	17	Burley, Stein 2 (1 pen), Shipperley	18,338
24	15	A	Norwich C	D	1-1	1-0	17	Stein	19,472
25	22	H	Aston Villa	D	1-1	0-1	17	Stein	18,348
26	Feb 5	A	Everton	L	2-4	1-3	17	Stein 2 (1 pen)	18,201
27	12	A	Oldham Ath	L	1-2	0-1	17	Spencer	12,002
28	27	H	Tottenham H	W	4-3	3-2	—	Donaghy, Stein 2 (1 pen), Spencer	19,398
29	Mar 5	A	Manchester U	W	1-0	0-0	17	Peacock	44,745
30	16	H	Wimbledon	W	2-0	1-0	—	Fashanu (og), Burley	11,903
31	19	A	Liverpool	L	1-2	0-2	16	Burley	38,629
32	26	H	West Ham U	W	2-0	1-0	14	Barnard, Hoddle	19,545
33	30	A	Sheffield W	L	1-3	0-2	—	Spencer	20,433
34	Apr 2	H	Southampton	W	2-0	1-0	12	Spencer, Johnsen	19,801
35	4	A	Newcastle U	D	0-0	0-0	14		32,218
36	13	A	QPR	D	1-1	0-0	—	Wise	15,735
37	16	A	Arsenal	L	0-1	0-0	14		34,314
38	23	H	Leeds U	D	1-1	0-1	14	Spencer	18,544
39	27	H	Swindon T	W	2-0	2-0	—	Wise (pen), Peacock	11,180
40	30	A	Manchester C	D	2-2	2-2	14	Fleck, Cascarino	33,594
41	May 4	H	Coventry C	L	1-2	1-2	—	Cascarino	8923
42	7	H	Sheffield U	W	3-2	0-1	14	Kjeldbjerg, Stein 2	21,782

Final League Position: 14

GOALSCORERS

League (49): Stein 13 (3 pens), Peacock 8, Spencer 5, Cascarino 4, Shipperley 4, Wise 4 (1 pen), Burley 3, Barnard 1, Donaghy 1, Fleck 1, Hoddle 1, Johnsen, 1, Kjeldbjerg 1, Lee 1, own goal 1.
Coca-Cola Cup (3): Wise 2, Shipperley 1.
FA Cup (13): Peacock 6, Burley 3, Spencer 2, Shipperley 1, Stein 1.

Kharine 40	Clarke 39	Sinclair 35	Dow 13 + 1	Johnsen 27 + 1	Donaghy 24 + 4	Hoddle 16 + 3	Spencer 13 + 6	Cascarino 16 + 4	Peacock 37	Wise 35	Fleck 7 + 2	Lee 3 + 4	Myers 6	Kjeldbjerg 29	Newton 33 + 3	Shipperley 18 + 6	Hall 4 + 3	Hopkin 12 + 9	Hitchcock 2	Barnard 9 + 3	Stein 18	Burley 20 + 3	Spackman 5 + 4	Duberry 1	Match No.
1	2	3	4	5	6	7	8	9	10	11	12	14													1
1	2	3			6	7	12	9	10	11	8		5	4											2
1	2			5	6	7		9	10	11	8	12	3	4	14										3
1	2			5	6	7		9	10	11		4	3		8										4
1	2			5	6	7		9	10	11		12	3	4	8	14									5
1	2	3	5		6	7		9	10	11		12		4	8	14									6
1	2	3	5		6	7		9	10	11				4	8	12	14								7
1	2	3	5		6	7	12		10	11				4	8	9									8
1	2	3	5		6	7		10		11				4	8	9	12								9
1	2	3	5		6	7	12		10	11				4	8	9	14								10
1	2	3	5			7		10	8		12			4	11	9	6								11
1	2	3	5	14	6	7		12			8			4	11	9		10							12
	2	3			6	5		10		11				4	8	12		14	1	7	9				13
		3		6	14	5		10	8	11				4	7	12		2	1		9				14
1	2	3		5	6				8	11		4			12	10		14		7	9				15
1	2	3			6				8	11				4	7	10				5	9				16
1	2	3			6			12	8	11				4	5	10		7			9	14			17
1		3		5	6			12	8	11					7	10	2	4			9	14			18
1		3		5	6			10	8	11					7		2	4			9	12			19
1	2	6							10	11				4	8	12	3	7			9	5			20
1	2	3	4	5			12		8	11					7	10					9	6	14		21
1	2	3	4	5			12		8	11					7	10					9	6	14		22
1	2	3	4	5					8	11					7	10					9	6			23
1	2	3	12	5					8				4		7	10					9	11	6		24
1	2	3	4	5	14		12		8							10		7			9	11	6		25
1	2	3		5	6				8						12	10		7		14	9	11	4		26
1	2	3		5			7		10				6		8			12		4	9	11			27
1	2			5	3		7		10	11				4	8			12			9	6			28
1	2	3		5			7		10	11				4	8			12			9	6			29
1	2	3		5		12			10	11				4	8	9		7				6			30
1	2		3	5		7			10	11				4	8	9		12				6			31
1	2			5	14	12	7		10	11				4	8	9				3		6			32
1	2	5			6	7	9		10	11				4				12		3		8			33
1	2	3		5			9	12	10	11				4	8			7		14		6			34
1	2	3		5	6		9	10		11				4						12		7	8		35
1	2	3		5			9	10	8	11				4	7			12		6					36
1	2	3			6		9		10	11		5		4	8			7							37
1	2	3			6		9		10	11	8			4	7					5			12		38
1	2	3		5			9		10	11	8			4	7							6	12		39
1	2			5	3			9	10	11	8			4				12				6	7		40
1	2	3		5	12			9			10				8			7		6		11		4	41
1	2	3		5		12	7		10	11				4	8						9	6			42

Coca-Cola Cup	Second Round	WBA (a)	1-1
		(h)	2-1
	Third Round	Manchester C (a)	0-1
FA Cup	Third Round	Barnet (at Stamford Bridge)	0-0
		(h)	4-0
	Fourth Round	Sheffield W (h)	1-1
		(a)	3-1
	Fifth Round	Oxford U (a)	2-1
	Sixth Round	Wolverhampton W (h)	1-0
	Semi-final at Wembley	Luton T	2-0
	Final at Wembley	Manchester U	0-4

CHELSEA

Player and Position	Ht	Wt	Birth Date	Birth Place	Source	Clubs	League App	League Gls
Goalkeepers								
Nick Colgan	6 1	12 00	19 9 73	Eire	Drogheda	Chelsea	—	—
						Crewe Alex (loan)	—	—
Kevin Hitchcock	6 1	12 02	5 10 62	Custom House	Barking	Nottingham F	—	—
						Mansfield T (loan)	14	—
						Mansfield T	168	—
						Chelsea	57	—
						Northampton T (loan)	17	—
						West Ham U (loan)	—	—
Dmitri Kharine	6 2	12 04	16 8 68	Moscow	CSKA Moscow	Chelsea	45	—
Defenders								
Darren Barnard	5 10	12 00	30 11 71	Rinteln	Wokingham	Chelsea	29	2
Anthony Barness	5 10	13 01	25 3 72	London	Trainee	Charlton Ath	27	1
						Chelsea	2	—
						Middlesbrough (loan)	—	—
Stephen Clarke	5 10	10 02	29 8 63	Saltcoats	Beith J	St Mirren	151	6
						Chelsea	222	6
Mal Donaghy*	5 9	10 00	13 9 57	Belfast	Larne	Luton T	410	16
						Manchester U	89	—
						Luton T (loan)	5	—
						Chelsea	68	3
Michael Duberry	6 1	12 13	14 10 75	Enfield	Trainee	Chelsea	1	—
Paul Elliott	6 2	11 11	18 3 64	London	Apprentice	Charlton Ath	63	1
						Luton T	66	4
						Aston Villa	57	7
					Bari	Celtic	54	2
						Chelsea	42	3
Gareth Hall	5 8	10 07	20 3 69	Croydon		Chelsea	127	3
Erland Johnsen	6 0	12 10	5 4 67	Fredrikstad (Norway)	Bayern Munich	Chelsea	72	1
Jakob Kjeldbjerg	6 2	13 08	21 10 69	Denmark	Silkeborg	Chelsea	29	1
David Lee	6 3	13 12	26 11 69	Kingswood	Trainee	Chelsea	104	9
						Reading (loan)	5	5
						Plymouth Arg (loan)	9	1
Craig Norman	5 10	11 09	21 3 75	Perivale	Trainee	Chelsea	—	—
Frank Sinclair	5 8	11 02	3 12 71	Lambeth	Trainee	Chelsea	79	1
						WBA (loan)	6	1
Terry Skiverton	6 0	12 04	20 6 75	Mile End	Trainee	Chelsea	—	—
Midfield								
Craig Burley	6 1	11 07	24 9 71	Ayr	Trainee	Chelsea	35	3
Andrew Dow	5 9	10 07	7 2 73	Dundee	Sporting Club 85	Dundee	18	1
						Chelsea	14	—
Glenn Hoddle	6 0	11 06	27 10 57	Hayes	Apprentice	Tottenham	377	88
					Monaco	Chelsea	—	—
						Swindon T	64	1
						Chelsea	19	1
David Hopkin	5 9	10 03	21 8 70	Greenock	Pt Glasgow R BC	Morton	18	—
						Chelsea	25	—
Mustafa Izzet	5 10	10 03	31 10 74	Mile End	Trainee	Chelsea	—	—
Andy Myers	5 8	9 10	3 11 73	Hounslow	Trainee	Chelsea	23	1
Gavin Peacock	5 8	11 08	18 11 67	Kent		QPR	17	1
						Gillingham	70	11
						Bournemouth	56	8
						Newcastle U	105	35
						Chelsea	37	8
Zeke Rowe	5 6	9 08	30 10 73	Stoke Newington	Trainee	Chelsea	—	—
						Barnet (loan)	10	2
Nigel Spackman	6 1	13 02	2 12 60	Romsey	Andover	Bournemouth	119	10
						Chelsea	141	12
						Liverpool	51	—
						QPR	29	1
						Rangers	100	1
						Chelsea	15	—

CHELSEA

Colours: Royal blue shirts and shorts, white stockings. **Change colours:** Graphite, tangerine and navy shirts, tangerine, navy and graphite shorts, tangerine, navy and graphite stockings.

Foundation: Chelsea may never have existed but for the fact that Fulham rejected an offer to rent the Stamford Bridge ground from Mr. H. A. Mears who had owned it since 1904. Fortunately he was determined to develop it as a football stadium rather than sell it to the Great Western Railway and got together with Frederick Parker, who persuaded Mears of the financial advantages of developing a major sporting venue. Chelsea FC was formed in 1905, and when admission to the Southern League was denied, they immediately gained admission to the Second Division of the Football League.

First Football League game: 2 September, 1905, Division 2, v Stockport C (a) L 0-1 – Foulke; Mackie, McEwan; Key, Harris, Miller; Moran, J.T. Robertson, Copeland, Windridge, Kirwan.

Did you know: On 29 January 1994, Chelsea met Sheffield Wednesday for the 14th time in the FA Cup, the most games they had played against any opposition in the competition. They drew 1-1, but won the replay 3-1.

Managers (and Secretary-Managers)
John Tait Robertson 1905–07, David Calderhead 1907–33, A. Leslie Knighton 1933–39, Billy Birrell 1939–52, Ted Drake 1952–61, Tommy Docherty 1962–67, Dave Sexton 1967–74, Ron Suart 1974–75, Eddie McCreadie 1975–77, Ken Shellito 1977–78, Danny Blanchflower 1978–79, Geoff Hurst 1979–81, John Neal 1981–85 (Director to 1986), John Hollins 1985–88, Bobby Campbell 1988–91, Ian Porterfield 1991–93, David Webb 1993, Glenn Hoddle June 1993–

Player and Position	*Ht*	*Wt*	*Birth Date*	*Birth Place*	*Source*	*Clubs*	*League App*	*League Gls*
Forwards								
Tony Cascarino*	6 2	13 12	1 9 62	St Paul's Cray	Crockenhill	Gillingham	219	78
						Millwall	105	42
						Aston Villa	46	11
						Celtic	24	4
						Chelsea	40	8
Robert Fleck	5 10	10 03	11 8 65	Glasgow	Possil YM	Partick T	2	1
						Rangers	85	29
						Norwich C	143	40
						Chelsea	40	3
						Bolton W (loan)	7	1
Eddie Newton	5 11	11 02	13 12 71	Hammersmith	Trainee	Chelsea	71	6
						Cardiff C (loan)	18	4
Graham Rix	5 9	11 00	23 10 57	Doncaster	Apprentice	Arsenal	351	41
						Brentford (loan)	6	—
					Caen, Le Havre	Dundee	14	2
						Chelsea	—	—
Neil Shipperley	6 1	13 12	30 10 74	Chatham	Trainee	Chelsea	27	5
John Spencer	5 6	10 00	11 9 70	Glasgow	Rangers Am BC	Rangers	—	—
						Morton (loan)	4	1
					Lisbung, HK	Rangers	13	2
						Chelsea	42	12
Mark Stein	5 6	11 02	28 1 66	S. Africa		Luton T	54	19
						Aldershot (loan)	2	1
						QPR	33	4
						Oxford U	82	18
						Stoke C	94	50
						Chelsea	18	13
Dennis Wise	5 6	9 05	15 12 66	Kensington	Southampton	Wimbledon	135	27
						Chelsea	133	27

Trainees
Baker, Joseph P. J; Bowder, Stanley R; Brown, Kevin; Carroll, Lee G; Christie, Terry W; Ellis, Clinton; Hall, David G; Hughes, Andrew J; Kelly, Russell; McCann, Christian; Mendes, Hillyard A; Nicholls, Mark; Yates, Paul S.

****Non-Contract**
Rix, Graham.

Associated Schoolboys
Aggrey, Jimmy; Allen, Kristian; Bedeau, Anthony C; Beech, Tom W; Brannan, Francis; Brookes, Ross; Carlin, Philip L; Harley, Jonathan; Harrison, Gavin A; Jones, Lee; Limbert, Peter A; Morris, Jody; Neufville, Marvin; Quinn, Paul J; Sheerin, Joe.

Associated Schoolboys who have accepted the Club's offer of a Traineeship/Contract
Dennis, Daniel G; Hanlon, Ritchie K; Hughes, John P; Ullah, Ainsley C.
**Non-Contract Players who are retained must be re-signed before they are eligible to play in League matches.

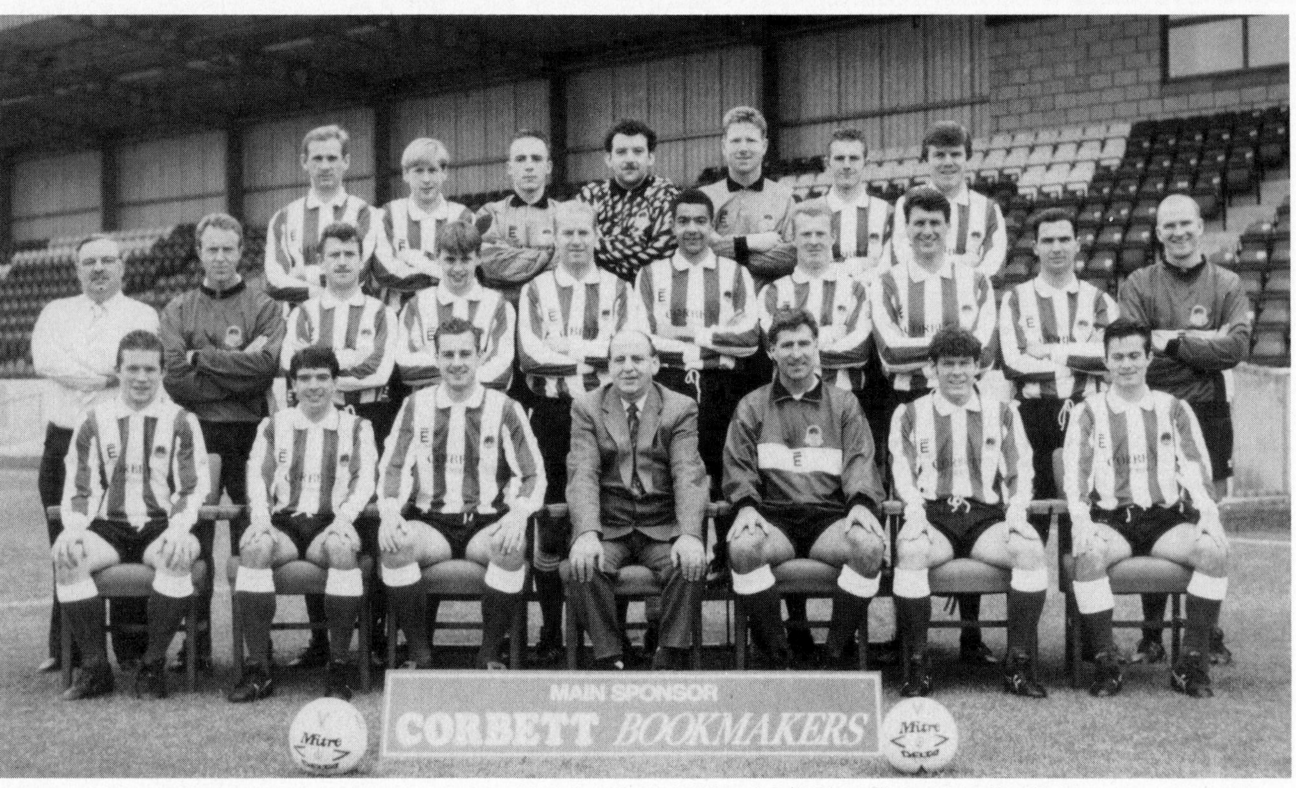

CHESTER CITY 1993–94 *Back row (left to right):* David Pugh, Paul Wheeler, John Bagnall, David Felgate, Billy Stewart, Lee Moss, Mark Leonard.
Centre row: Derek Barber (Secretary), Jim Harvey, Joe Jakub, Ian Berry, Colin Greenall, Spencer Whelan, David Thompson, Mark Came, Darren Donnelly, Joe Hinnigan (Physio).
Front row: Mark Limbert, Stuart Rimmer, Chris Lightfoot, R. H. Crofts (Chairman), Graham Barrow, Iain Jenkins, Roger Preece.

Division 2 CHESTER CITY

The Deva Stadium, Bumpers Lane, Chester, CH1 4LT. Telephone Chester (0244) 371376, 371809. Fax: (0244) 390265. Commercial: (0244) 390243.

Ground capacity: 6000.

Record attendance: 20,500 v Chelsea, FA Cup 3rd rd (replay), 16 January, 1952 (at Sealand Road).

Record receipts: £30,609 v Sheffield W, FA Cup 4th rd, 31 January 1987.

Pitch measurements: 115yd × 78yd.

Club Patron: Duke of Westminster.

Manager: Graham Barrow.

Secretary: Derek Barber JP, AMITD. ***Physio:*** Joe Hinnigan. ***Commercial Manager:*** Miss A. Walker.

Year Formed: 1884. ***Turned Professional:*** 1902. ***Ltd Co.:*** 1909.

Previous Name: Chester until 1983.

Club Nickname: 'Blues' and 'City'.

Previous Grounds: Faulkner Street; Old Showground; 1904, Whipcord Lane; 1906, Sealand Road; 1990, Moss Rose Ground, Macclesfield; 1992, The Stadium, Bumpers Lane.

Record League Victory: 12–0 v York C, Division 3 (N), 1 February 1936 – Middleton; Common, Hall; Wharton, Wilson, Howarth; Horsman (2), Hughes, Wrightson (4), Cresswell (2), Sargeant (4).

Record Cup Victory: 6–1 v Darlington, FA Cup, 1st rd, 25 November 1933 – Burke; Bennett, Little; Pitcairn, Skitt, Duckworth; Armes (3), Whittam, Mantle (2), Cresswell (1), McLachlan.

Record Defeat: 2–11 v Oldham Ath, Division 3 (N), 19 January 1952.

Most League Points (2 for a win): 56, Division 3 (N), 1946–47 and Division 4, 1964–65.

Most League Points (3 for a win): 84, Division 4, 1985–86.

Most League Goals: 119, Division 4, 1964–65.

Highest League Scorer in Season: Dick Yates, 36, Division 3 (N), 1946–47.

Most League Goals in Total Aggregate: Stuart Rimmer, 108, 1985–88, 1991–94.

Most Capped Player: Bill Lewis, 7 (30), Wales.

Most League Appearances: Ray Gill, 408, 1951–62.

Record Transfer Fee Received: £300,000 from Liverpool for Ian Rush, May 1980.

Record Transfer Fee Paid: £94,000 to Barnsley for Stuart Rimmer, August 1991.

Football League Record: 1931 Elected Division 3 (N); 1958–75 Division 4; 1975–82 Division 3; 1982–86 Division 4; 1986–92 Division 3; 1992–93 Division 2; 1993–94 Division 3; 1994– Division 2.

Honours: *Football League:* Division 3 – Runners-up 1993–94; Division 3 (N) – Runners-up 1935–36; Division 4 – Runners-up 1985–86. *FA Cup:* best season: 5th rd, 1976–77, 1979–80. *Football League Cup:* Semi-final 1974–75. *Welsh Cup:* Winners 1908, 1933, 1947. *Debenhams Cup:* Winners 1977.

CHESTER CITY 1993—94 LEAGUE RECORD

Match No.	Date	Venue	Opponents	Result		H/T Score	Lg. Pos.	Goalscorers	Attendance
1	Aug 14	H	Doncaster R	L	0-1	0-0	—		2752
2	21	A	Wycombe W	L	0-1	0-1	21		5607
3	28	H	Chesterfield	W	3-1	0-1	14	Lightfoot, Rimmer, Thompson	2283
4	31	A	Lincoln C	W	3-0	0-0	—	Pugh, Leonard, Rimmer	4038
5	Sept 4	A	Rochdale	L	0-2	0-2	13		3063
6	11	H	Scunthorpe U	L	0-2	0-1	15		2195
7	18	A	Scarborough	W	1-0	0-0	13	Leonard	1510
8	25	H	Carlisle U	D	0-0	0-0	14		2911
9	Oct 2	A	Wigan Ath	L	3-6	1-3	16	Leonard (pen), Wheeler 2	1889
10	9	A	Darlington	W	2-1	1-1	12	Rimmer, Wheeler (pen)	1767
11	16	H	Shrewsbury T	W	1-0	1-0	10	Rimmer	3052
12	23	A	Mansfield T	W	4-0	0-0	8	Wheeler 3, Rimmer	2545
13	30	H	Torquay U	D	1-1	0-0	7	Bishop	2563
14	Nov 2	H	Bury	W	3-0	1-0	—	Lightfoot 2, Rimmer	2540
15	6	A	Hereford U	W	5-0	2-0	3	Anderson (og), Wheeler, Lightfoot 2, Pugh	2092
16	20	H	Northampton T	W	1-0	0-0	3	Pugh	2650
17	27	A	Crewe Alex	L	1-2	1-0	5	Lightfoot	4749
18	Dec 11	H	Wycombe W	W	3-1	0-0	3	Rimmer, Leonard, Pugh	3195
19	17	A	Doncaster R	W	4-3	0-1	—	Leonard 2, Pugh, Bishop	1914
20	27	A	Preston NE	D	1-1	1-1	3	Nebbeling (og)	12,790
21	Jan 1	A	Colchester U	D	0-0	0-0	4		3170
22	15	A	Shrewsbury T	L	0-3	0-2	7		5365
23	22	H	Darlington	D	0-0	0-0	7		2777
24	29	A	Torquay U	W	3-1	1-1	5	Greenall, Flitcroft, Thompson	2959
25	Feb 1	H	Lincoln C	D	1-1	0-1	—	Lancashire	2648
26	5	H	Mansfield T	D	1-1	1-0	5	Lancashire	2664
27	12	A	Walsall	D	1-1	1-0	6	Pugh (pen)	4602
28	19	A	Chesterfield	W	2-1	1-1	5	Lancashire, Leonard	2847
29	25	H	Rochdale	W	3-1	0-1	4	Pugh 2 (1 pen), Rimmer	3472
30	Mar 1	H	Gillingham	W	1-0	1-0	—	Pugh	3128
31	5	A	Scunthorpe U	D	1-1	1-0	2	Lightfoot	2669
32	12	H	Scarborough	W	4-1	3-1	2	Thompson 3, Came	2882
33	15	H	Walsall	W	2-1	1-0	—	Lightfoot, Thompson	3324
34	19	A	Carlisle U	L	0-1	0-0	1		4193
35	26	H	Wigan Ath	W	2-1	2-1	1	Pugh (pen), Preece	3542
36	Apr 2	H	Preston NE	W	3-2	1-2	1	Lancashire 2, Leonard	5638
37	4	A	Gillingham	D	2-2	1-1	1	Pugh, Green (og)	3165
38	9	H	Colchester U	W	2-1	1-1	1	Lightfoot 2	3394
39	16	A	Bury	D	1-1	1-0	2	Lancashire	3142
40	23	H	Hereford U	W	3-1	1-0	2	Pugh, Lancashire, Preece	3845
41	30	A	Northampton T	L	0-1	0-1	2		6432
42	May 7	H	Crewe Alex	L	1-2	1-1	2	Lightfoot	5550

Final League Position: 2

GOALSCORERS

League (69): Pugh 12 (3 pens), Lightfoot 11, Leonard 8 (1 pen), Rimmer 8, Lancashire 7, Wheeler 7 (1 pen), Thompson 6, Bishop 2, Preece 2, Came 1, Flitcroft 1, Greenall 1, own goals 3.
Coca-Cola Cup (1): Rimmer 1.
FA Cup (3): Leonard 1, Lightfoot 1, Preece 1.

Stewart 7	Preece 38 + 1	Jakub 35 + 1	Bishop 9 + 9	Came 30	Greenall 42	Thompson 40 + 1	Lightfoot 37	Rimmer 26 + 9	Leonard 28 + 4	Pugh 36 + 1	Jenkins 30 + 4	Donnelly — + 9	Wheeler 23 + 2	Whelan 22	Barrow 10 + 3	McIlhargey 1	Felgate 34	Flitcroft 4 + 4	Lancashire 10 + 1	*Match No.*
1	2	3	4	5	6	*7*	8	9	10	11	12	14								1
1	2	3	4	5	6	7	8	*9*	10	11	12	14								2
1	2	3		5	6	7	8	9	10	11	4		12							3
1	2	3			6	7	8	9	10	11	4	12		5						4
1	2	3			6	7	8	9	10	11	4			5						5
1	*2*	3	14	5	6	7	8	9	10	11	4	12								6
1	2	3		5	6	7	8	9	10	11	4				12					7
	2	3		*5*	6	7	8	9	10	11	4	14			12	1				8
	2	3	14	5	6	7	8	9	*10*	12	4		11				1			9
	2	3		5	6	7	8	9		10	4		11		12		1			10
	2	3		5	6	7	8	9		10	4		11				1			11
	2	3		5	6	7	8	9			4		11		10		1			12
	2	3	12	5	6	7	8	9			4	14	11		10		1			13
	2	3		5	6	7	8	9		10	4		11				1			14
	2	3	12		6	7	8	9		10	4		11	5			1			15
	2	3			6	7	8	9		10	4		11	5			1			16
	2	3	10	5	6	7	8		9		4		11				1			17
	2	3	7	5	6			9	10	11	4		8				1			18
	2	3	12	5	6	14	8	*9*	10	11	4		7				1			19
	2	3		5	6	7	8		10	11	4		9				1			20
	2	3		5	6	7	8	12	10	11	4		9				1			21
	2	3	12	5	6	7	8	9	10		4		11				1	14		22
	2	3	8		6	7		9	10		4	14	*11*	5			1	12		23
		3	10		6	7		9		11	2	12		5	8		1	4		24
	2	3	8		6	7		9		11	4			5			1	10	12	25
		3	4		6	*7*	8		12	11	2	14		5			1	10	9	26
	2	3			6	7	10		12	11	4			5	8		1		9	27
	2				6	7	4	12	3	11			10	5	8		1		9	28
	2			5	6	7	4	12		11			10	3	8		1		9	29
	2		14	5	6	7	4	9	12	11			*10*	3			1	8		30
	2			5	6	7	4	9	12	11			10	3	8		1			31
	14		12	5	6	7	4		9	11	3		10	2	*8*		1			32
	4	14	10	*5*	6	7	8	12	9	11	3			2			1			33
	2		14		6	7	4	12	9	11	3		*10*	5	8		1			34
	8	3			6	7	4		9	11	2			5			1		10	35
	4	3		5	6	7		12	9	11				2	8		1		10	36
	8	3		5	6	7	4	12	*9*	11			14	2			1		10	37
	2	3		5	6	7	8	12	9	11			4				1		10	38
		2		5	6	7	*8*	12	9	11	14		3	4			1		10	39
	4	3		5	6	7	8		9	11				2			1		10	40
	4	*3*		5	6	7	8	9	10	11	12			2			1	14		41
	4	3		5	6	7	8	9	10	11	2						1	12		42

Coca-Cola Cup	First Round	Sunderland (a)	1-3
		(h)	0-0
FA Cup	First Round	Bradford C (a)	0-0
		(h)	1-0
	Second Round	Hull C (h)	2-0
	Third Round	Plymouth Arg (a)	0-1

CHESTER CITY

Player and Position	Ht	Wt	Birth Date	Birth Place	Source	Clubs	League App	League Gls
Goalkeepers								
John Bagnall†	6 0	12 00	23 11 73	Southport	Preston NE	Chester C	—	—
David Felgate	6 2	13 06	4 3 60	Blaenau Ffestiniog	Blaenau Ffestiniog	Bolton W	—	—
						Rochdale (loan)	35	—
						Bradford C (loan)	—	—
						Crewe Alex (loan)	14	—
						Rochdale (loan)	12	—
						Lincoln C	198	—
						Cardiff C (loan)	4	—
						Grimsby T (loan)	12	—
						Grimsby T	12	—
						Bolton W	238	—
						Rotherham U (loan)	—	—
						Bury	—	—
						Wolverhampton W	—	—
						Chester C	34	—
Billy Stewart*	5 11	11 07	1 1 65	Liverpool	Apprentice	Liverpool	—	—
						Wigan Ath	14	—
						Chester C	272	—
Defenders								
Ian Berry‡			18 1 75	Bury	Blackburn R	Chester C	—	—
Mark Came*	6 0	12 13	14 9 61	Exeter	Winsford U	Bolton W	195	7
						Chester C	47	1
Colin Greenall	5 10	11 06	30 12 63	Billinge	Apprentice	Blackpool	183	9
						Gillingham	62	4
						Oxford U	67	2
						Bury (loan)	3	—
						Bury	68	5
						Preston NE	29	1
						Chester C	42	1
Joe Hinnigan*	6 0	12 00	3 21 55	Liverpool	S Liverpool	Wigan Ath	66	10
						Sunderland	63	4
						Preston NE	52	8
						Gillingham	103	7
						Wrexham	29	1
						Chester C	54	2
Iain Jenkins	5 11	11 07	24 11 72	Prescot	Trainee	Everton	5	—
						Bradford C (loan)	6	—
						Chester C	34	—
Mark Limbert*	5 9	12 06	3 10 73	Hawarden	Trainee	Chester C	14	—
Spencer Whelan	6 1	11 13	17 9 71	Liverpool	Liverpool	Chester C	93	—
Midfield								
Graham Barrow*	6 2	13 07	13 6 54	Chorley	Altrincham	Wigan Ath	179	36
						Chester C	248	17
Eddie Bishop*	5 8	11 07	28 11 62	Liverpool	Runcorn	Tranmere R	76	19
						Chester C	87	19
						Crewe Alex (loan)	3	—
Joe Jakub*	5 6	9 06	7 12 56	Falkirk	Apprentice	Burnley	42	—
						Bury	265	27
					AZ Alkmaar	Chester C	42	1
						Burnley	163	8
						Chester C	36	—
Chris Lightfoot	6 1	12 00	1 4 70	Wimwick	Trainee	Chester C	249	29
Lee Moss‡			3 9 74	Blackburn	Blackburn R	Chester C	—	—
Roger Preece	5 9	10 12	9 6 69	Much Wenlock	Coventry C	Wrexham	110	12
						Chester C	126	2
David Pugh	5 10	11 02	19 9 64	Liverpool	Runcorn	Chester C	179	23
Forwards								
Darren Donnelly*	5 10	11 06	28 12 71	Liverpool	Trainee	Blackburn R	2	—
						Chester C	9	—
David Flitcroft	6 0	13 09	14 1 74	Bolton	Trainee	Preston NE	8	2
						Lincoln C (loan)	2	—
						Chester C	8	1

CHESTER CITY

Colours: Blue and white striped shirts, black shorts, blue stockings. **Change colours:** All white.

Foundation: All students of soccer history have read about the medieval games of football in Chester, but the present club was not formed until 1884 through the amalgamation of King's School Old Boys with Chester Rovers. For many years Chester were overshadowed in Cheshire by Northwich Victoria and Crewe Alexandra who had both won the Senior Cup several times before Chester's first success in 1894–95.

First Football League game: 2 September, 1931, Division 3(N), v Wrexham (a) D 1-1 – Johnson; Herod, Jones; Keeley, Skitt, Reilly; Thompson, Ranson, Jennings (1), Cresswell, Hedley.

Did you know: On 28 August 1993 Chester City beat Chesterfield 3-1. This victory ended a run of 14 League and Cup games without a win dating back to the previous season.

Managers (and Secretary-Managers)
Charlie Hewitt 1930–36, Alex Raisbeck 1936–38, Frank Brown 1938–53, Louis Page 1953–56, John Harris 1956–59, Stan Pearson 1959–61, Bill Lambton 1962–63, Peter Hauser 1963–68, Ken Roberts 1968–76, Alan Oakes 1976–82, Cliff Sear 1982, John Sainty 1982–83, John McGrath 1984, Harry McNally 1985–92, Graham Barrow 1992–94.

Player and Position	*Ht*	*Wt*	*Birth Date*	*Place*	*Source*	*Clubs*	*League App*	*Gls*
Mark Leonard	5 11	11 10	27 9 62	St Helens	Witton Albion	Everton	—	—
						Tranmere R (loan)	7	—
						Crewe Alex	54	15
						Stockport Co	73	24
						Bradford C	157	29
						Rochdale	9	1
						Preston NE	22	1
						Chester C	32	8
Stuart Rimmer	5 8	11 00	12 10 64	Southport	Apprentice	Everton	3	—
						Chester C	114	67
						Watford	10	1
						Notts Co	4	2
						Walsall	88	31
						Barnsley	15	1
						Chester C	122	41
David Thompson	5 11	12 10	27 5 62	Manchester	Local	Rochdale	155	13
						Manchester U (loan)	—	—
						Notts Co	55	8
						Wigan Ath	108	14
						Preston NE	46	4
						Chester C	80	9
Paul Wheeler*	5 9	11 00	3 1 65	Caerphilly	Apprentice	Bristol R	—	—
					Aberaman	Cardiff C	101	10
						Hull C	5	—
						Hereford U	54	12
						Stockport Co	23	5
						Scarborough (loan)	7	1
						Chester C	39	7

Trainees
Bold, Ian N; Millar, Scott G; Murphy, John J; Spence, Steven J; Wood, Philip W.

Associated Schoolboys
Ashford, Mark A; Crane, Brian; Hayes, Oliver; Hayward, Mark; Parsonage, Wayne; Peers, Simon M; Quinn, Phillip; Savage, Carl A; Seaton, James A; Smith, Paul; Stockton, Anthony P; Thompson, Andrew J; Webb, Mark.

Associated Schoolboys who have accepted the Club's offer of a Traineeship/Contract
Briggs, Gregory M; Brown, Greg; Cannon, Ian; Moss, Steven J; Pemberton, Michael A; Sweeney, Roy J; Tudor, Mark A; Turner, David J.

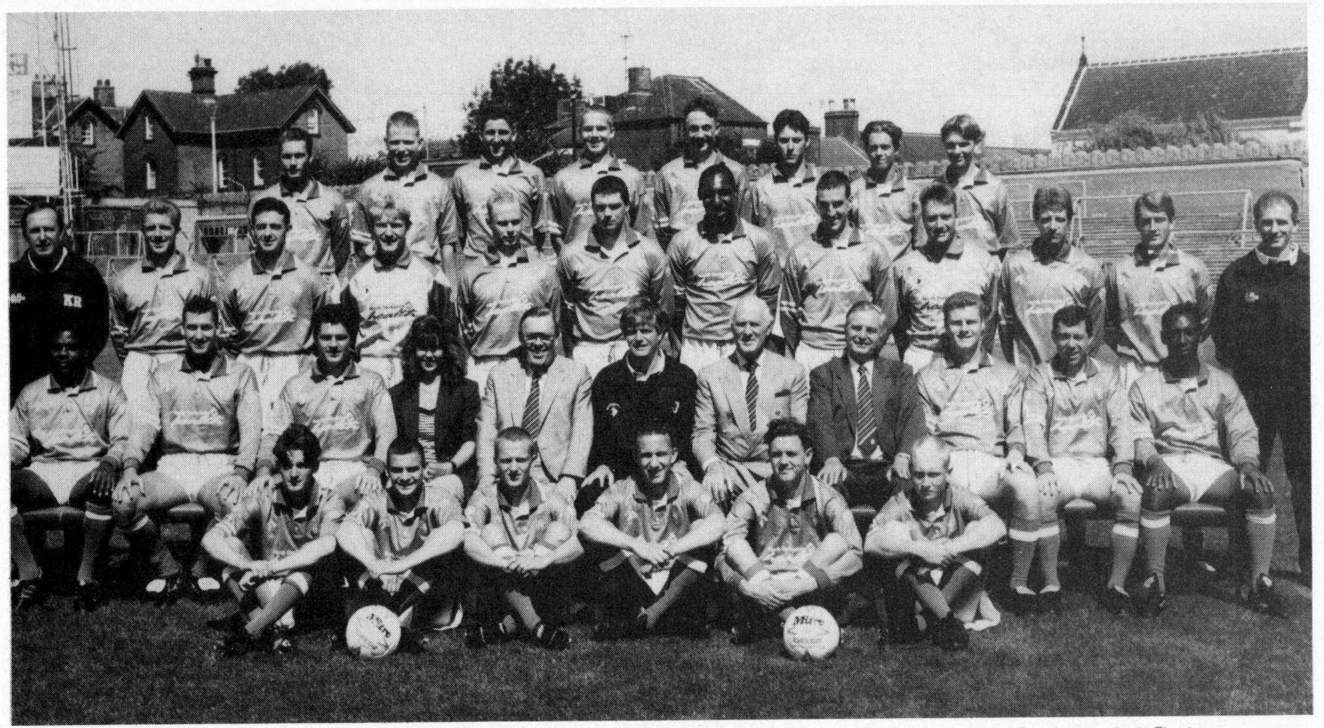

CHESTERFIELD 1993–94 *Back row (left to right):* Scott Whitehead, Mark Smith, Rob Clarke, Kevin Davies, Mark Jones, Lee Ashton, Paul Ledger, Jamie Thacker.
Third row: Kevin Randall (Assistant Manager), Stuart Cash, Lee Rogers, Chris Marples, Steve Williams, Paul McGugan, Andy Morris, Darren Carr, Mick Leonard, Trevor Hebberd, Steve Norris, Dave Rushbury (Physio).
Second row: Tony Dennis, Lee Turnbull, Tony Brien, Nicola Hodgson (Secretary), Barrie Hubbard (Vice-Chairman), John Duncan (Team Manager), Norton Lea (Chairman), Bob Pepper (Director), Sean Dyche, Cliff Carr, Mark Jules.
Front row: Chris Elson, Jamie Sorrell, Adam Aylward, Jamie Bettney, Nick Otter, Richard Hopkinson.

Division 3 CHESTERFIELD

Recreation Ground, Chesterfield S40 4SX. Telephone Chesterfield (0246) 209765. Fax 0246 556799. Commercial Dept: (0246) 231535.

Ground capacity: 11,279.

Record attendance: 30,968 v Newcastle U, Division 2, 7 April 1939.

Record receipts: £32,410 v Sheffield U, Division 3, 25 March 1989.

Pitch measurements: 113yd × 73yd.

President: His Grace the Duke of Devonshire MC, DL, JP.

Chairman: J. N. Lea. ***Vice-chairman:*** B. W. Hubbard.

Directors: R. F. Pepper, M. L. Warner, J. S. Mowatt.

Manager: John Duncan.

Physio: Dave Rushbury. ***Assistant Manager:*** Kevin Randall.

Secretary: Mrs N. J. Bellamy. ***Commercial Manager:*** Jim Brown.

Year Formed: 1866. ***Turned Professional:*** 1891. ***Ltd Co:*** 1871.

Previous Names: Chesterfield Town.

Club Nickname: 'Blues' or 'Spireites'.

Record League Victory: 10–0 v Glossop, Division 2, 17 January 1903 – Clutterbuck; Thorpe, Lerper; Haig, Banner, Thacker; Tomlinson (2), Newton (1), Milward (3), Munday (2), Steel (2).

Record Cup Victory: 5–0 v Wath Ath (away), FA Cup, 1st rd, 28 November 1925 – Birch; Saxby, Dennis; Wass, Abbott, Thompson; Fisher (1), Roseboom (1), Cookson (2), Whitfield (1), Hopkinson.

Record Defeat: 0–10 v Gillingham, Division 3, 5 September 1987.

Most League Points (2 for a win): 64, Division 4, 1969–70.

Most League Points (3 for a win): 91, Division 4, 1984–85.

Most League Goals: 102, Division 3 (N), 1930–31.

Highest League Scorer in Season: Jimmy Cookson, 44, Division 3 (N), 1925–26.

Most League Goals in Total Aggregate: Ernie Moss, 161, 1969–76, 1979–81 and 1984–86.

Most Capped Player: Walter McMillen, 4 (7), Northern Ireland.

Most League Appearances: Dave Blakey, 613, 1948–67.

Record Transfer Fee Received: £200,000 from Wolverhampton W for Alan Birch, August 1981.

Record Transfer Fee Paid: £150,000 to Carlisle U for Phil Bonnyman, March 1980.

Football League Record: 1899 Elected to Division 2; 1909 failed re-election; 1921–31 Division 3 (N); 1931–33 Division 2; 1933–36 Division 3 (N); 1936–51 Division 2; 1951–58 Division 3 (N); 1958–61 Division 3; 1961–70 Division 4; 1970–83 Division 3; 1983–85 Division 4; 1985–89 Division 3; 1989–92 Division 4; 1992– Division 3.

Honours: *Football League:* Division 2 best season: 4th, 1946–47; Division 3 (N) – Champions 1930–31, 1935–36; Runners-up 1933–34; Division 4 – Champions 1969–70, 1984–85. *FA Cup:* best season: 5th rd, 1932–33, 1937–38, 1949–50. *Football League Cup:* best season: 4th rd, 1964–65. *Anglo-Scottish Cup:* Winners 1980–81.

CHESTERFIELD 1993—94 LEAGUE RECORD

Match No.	Date	Venue	Opponents	Result		H/T Score	Lg. Pos.	Goalscorers	Attendance
1	Aug 14	A	Gillingham	W	2-0	1-0	—	Morris, Jules	3485
2	21	H	Hereford U	W	3-1	2-1	1	Norris 2, Turnbull	2718
3	28	A	Chester C	L	1-3	1-0	6	Norris	2283
4	31	H	Mansfield T	L	0-2	0-0	—		5712
5	Sept 4	H	Darlington	D	1-1	0-1	10	Norris	2982
6	11	A	Carlisle U	L	0-3	0-2	14		5335
7	18	H	Walsall	L	0-1	0-0	16		2800
8	25	A	Rochdale	L	1-5	1-5	19	Norris	2481
9	Oct 2	H	Wycombe W	L	2-3	0-1	19	Morris, Turnbull (pen)	2956
10	9	A	Preston NE	L	1-4	1-0	20	Lyne	6581
11	16	H	Torquay U	W	3-1	0-0	20	Moss, Hewitt, Norris	2393
12	23	A	Lincoln C	W	2-1	1-0	16	Norris 2	3591
13	30	H	Crewe Alex	W	2-0	0-0	16	Morris, Norris	3501
14	Nov 2	H	Wigan Ath	W	1-0	1-0	—	Norris	2758
15	6	A	Bury	L	1-2	1-1	17	Morris	2340
16	20	H	Scarborough	W	1-0	0-0	11	Trotter	2110
17	27	A	Northampton T	D	2-2	0-0	13	Norris, Morris	1866
18	Dec 18	H	Gillingham	W	3-2	1-1	11	Law, Moss, Morris	2348
19	28	A	Scunthorpe U	D	2-2	2-1	13	Hewitt, Norris	3266
20	Jan 1	H	Shrewsbury T	L	1-2	1-1	13	Morris	3614
21	3	A	Mansfield T	W	2-1	1-0	11	Moss 2	4272
22	15	A	Torquay U	L	0-1	0-1	13		3188
23	22	H	Preston NE	D	1-1	0-0	12	Curtis	3804
24	25	H	Doncaster R	D	1-1	0-1	—	Norris	2606
25	29	A	Crewe Alex	W	1-0	1-0	11	Curtis	3846
26	Feb 5	H	Lincoln C	D	2-2	1-0	11	Norris (pen), Law	3104
27	12	A	Colchester U	W	2-0	1-0	10	Morris 2	2783
28	19	H	Chester C	L	1-2	1-1	10	Gregory	2847
29	Mar 5	H	Carlisle U	W	3-0	0-0	10	Norris 2, Davies	2475
30	8	A	Darlington	D	0-0	0-0	—		2655
31	12	A	Walsall	W	1-0	1-0	9	Carr D	4157
32	15	A	Hereford U	W	3-0	2-0	—	Davies, Morris 2	1806
33	19	H	Rochdale	D	1-1	0-0	7	Moss	3282
34	26	A	Wycombe W	W	1-0	1-0	7	Norris (pen)	5752
35	29	H	Colchester U	D	0-0	0-0	—		3089
36	Apr 2	A	Doncaster R	D	0-0	0-0	8		2748
37	4	H	Scunthorpe U	D	1-1	1-1	7	Norris (pen)	3629
38	9	A	Shrewsbury T	D	0-0	0-0	7		4846
39	16	A	Wigan Ath	L	0-1	0-0	7		1998
40	23	H	Bury	D	1-1	1-0	7	Moss	2906
41	30	A	Scarborough	D	1-1	1-0	9	Norris	2631
42	May 7	H	Northampton T	W	4-0	2-0	8	Hewitt, Davies 2, Curtis	5285

Final League Position: 8

GOALSCORERS

League (55): Norris 19 (3 pens), Morris 11, Moss 6, Davies 4, Curtis 3, Hewitt 3, Law 2, Turnbull 2 (1 pen), Carr D 1, Gregory 1, Jules 1, Lyne 1, Trotter 1.
Coca-Cola Cup (5): Norris 2, Jules 1, Morris 1, Turnbull 1 (pen).
FA Cup (0):

Leonard 31 + 1	Rogers 32	Carr C 20 + 3	Brien 9	Carr D 28	Dennis 4 + 6	Dyche 19 + 1	Norris 30 + 9	Jules 28 + 5	Turnbull 8	Morris 32 + 2	Curtis 35 + 1	Hebberd 14 + 4	McGugan 2 + 3	Knowles 1	Taylor 1	Cash 4 + 2	Davies 16 + 8	Lyne 5 + 1	Marples 11	Madden 26	Law 31	Moss 26	Hewitt 28 + 1	Spooner 5	Trotter 14 + 1	Gregory 2 + 1	Stringfellow — + 1	Pearson — + 1	*Match No.*
1	2	3	4	5	6	7	8	9	10	11																			1
1	2	3	4	5		7	8	9	10	*11*	6	12	14																2
1	2	3	4	5		7	8	9	10		6	12		11															3
1	2	3	4	5	12	11	8	9	10		*6*		14		7														4
1	2	3	4	5		7	8	9	10		6	11	12																5
1	2	3	4	5	11	7	8	9	10		6																		6
1	2	3	4	5		7	8	9	*10*		11		6			12	14												7
1		10	4	5	12	7	8	11			14	2	*6*			3		9											8
1	*2*	3	4	5		7	8	12	10	11	6					14		9											9
		3			4		8	11			7	2					12	9	1	5	6	10	14						10
					4	12	8	11		9	7	3							1	5	6	10	2						11
		3		5		7	8			10	4						12		1		6	9	2	11					12
		3		5		7	8			9	4								1		6	10	2	11					13
		3				7	8			9	4					11			1	5	6	10	2						14
		12				7	8			9	4					3	14		1	*5*	6	10	2	11					15
	3			5		7	8			9		11							1	4	6		2		10				16
	10			5		7	8			9		11							1	3	6		2		4				17
	11			5		7	8			9									1	3	6	10	2		4				18
		11		5		7	8			9									1	3	6	10	2		4		12		19
14	3				12		8	11		9	6	7							*1*	5		10	2		4				20
1	3				14		*8*	12		9	6	7				11				5		10	2		4				21
1	3				12		*8*	11		9	7						14			5	6	10	2		4				22
1	3						8	12		9	7	11					14			5	6	10	2		*4*				23
1	3						8	12		9	7	*11*					14			5	6	10	2		4				24
1	3	12						11		9	7	5					8				6	10	2		4				25
1	3						8	11		9	7	5					10				6		2		4				26
1	3				12			11		9	7						8			5	6	10	2		4				27
1	3	14					12	11		9	7						8			5	6		2		*4*	10			28
1	3			5			12	11		9	7						8			4	6		2			10			29
1	3			5			12	11		9	7						8			4	6		2		10				30
1	3			5				11		9	7	12					8			4	6	10	2						31
1	2	3		5			12	11		9	7						8			4	6	*10*			14				32
1	2	3		5			12	11		9	7						8			4	6	10							33
1	3	4		5			12	11		9	7						8				6	10	2						34
1	3			5			8	11			7						4	9			6	10	2			12			35
1	3			5			12	11		9	7						8			4	6	10	2						36
1		3					8	11		9	7	2					4	12		5	6	10							37
1		3		5		11	12			9	7	2					8			4	6	*10*						14	38
1	3	10		5		*11*	12	14		9	7						8			4	6		2						39
1	3			5			8	11		12	7	14						9		*4*	6	10	2						40
1	3			5			8	11		9							12			4	6	10	2	7					41
1	3			5			8	11		12	4						9				6	10	2	7					42

Coca-Cola Cup	First Round	Carlisle U (h)	3-1
		(a)	1-1
	Second Round	West Ham U (a)	1-5
		(h)	0-2
FA Cup	First Round	Rochdale (h)	0-1

CHESTERFIELD

Player and Position	Ht	Wt	Birth Date	Birth Place	Source	Clubs	League App	League Gls
Goalkeepers								
Mick Leonard	5 11	11 00	9 5 59	Carshalton	Epson & Ewell	Halifax T	69	—
						Notts Co	204	—
						Chesterfield	176	—
						Halifax T (loan)	3	—
Chris Marples	6 0	13 03	3 8 64	Chesterfield	Goole	Chesterfield	84	—
						Stockport Co	57	—
						York C	138	—
						Scunthorpe U (loan)	1	—
						Chesterfield	36	—
Jon Thomson†	5 10	12 00	23 12 73	Newcastle	Trainee	Derby Co	—	—
						Chesterfield	—	—
Defenders								
Darren Carr	6 2	13 00	4 9 68	Bristol		Bristol R	30	—
						Newport Co	9	—
						Sheffield U	13	1
						Crewe Alex	104	5
						Chesterfield	28	1
Stuart Cash*	5 10	11 11	5 9 65	Tipton	Halesowen	Nottingham F	—	—
						Rotherham U (loan)	8	1
						Brentford (loan)	11	—
						Shrewsbury T (loan)	8	1
						Chesterfield	29	—
Jamie Hewitt	5 11	11 07	17 5 68	Chesterfield	School	Chesterfield	249	14
						Doncaster R	33	—
						Chesterfield	29	3
Nicky Law	6 1	12 07	8 9 61	London	Apprentice	Arsenal	—	—
						Barnsley	114	1
						Blackpool	66	1
						Plymouth Arg	38	5
						Notts Co	47	4
						Scarborough (loan)	12	—
						Rotherham U	128	4
						Chesterfield	31	2
Paul McGugan‡	6 2	12 00	17 7 64	Glasgow	Eastercraigs	Celtic	49	2
						Barnsley	49	2
						Chesterfield	77	6
Lawrie Madden*	5 11	13 01	28 9 55	London	Arsenal Manchester Univ	Mansfield T	10	—
						Charlton Ath	113	7
						Millwall	47	2
						Sheffield W	212	2
						Leicester C (loan)	3	—
						Wolverhampton W	67	1
						Darlington	5	—
						Chesterfield	26	—
Lee Rogers	5 11	12 01	21 10 66	Doncaster	Doncaster R	Chesterfield	254	1
Midfield								
Cliff Carr*	5 8	10 12	19 6 64	London	Apprentice	Fulham	145	14
						Stoke C	124	1
						Shrewsbury T	1	1
						Mansfield T	20	—
						Chesterfield	65	1
Tommy Curtis	5 8	11 04	1 3 73	Exeter	School	Derby Co	—	—
						Chesterfield	36	3
Tony Dennis	5 7	10 02	1 12 63	Eton	Slough	Cambridge U	111	10
						Chesterfield	10	—
Sean Dyche	6 0	11 07	28 6 71	Kettering	Trainee	Nottingham F	—	—
						Chesterfield	132	8
Trevor Hebberd*	6 0	11 04	19 6 58	Winchester	Apprentice	Southampton	97	7
						Bolton W (loan)	6	—
						Leicester C (loan)	4	1
						Oxford U	260	37
						Derby Co	81	10
						Portsmouth	4	—
						Chesterfield	74	1
Cameron Knowles†			19 9 69	Ripon		Chesterfield	1	—
David Moss	6 0	13 04	15 11 68	Doncaster	Boston U	Doncaster R	18	5
						Chesterfield	26	6

CHESTERFIELD

Colours: Blue shirts, white shorts, blue stockings. **Change colours:** Green and white striped shirts, navy shorts, navy stockings.

Foundation: Chesterfield are fourth only to Stoke, Notts County and Nottingham Forest in age for they can trace their existence as far back as 1866, although it is fair to say that they were somewhat casual in the first few years of their history playing only a few friendlies a year. However, their rules of 1871 are still in existence showing an annual membership of 2s (10p), but it was not until 1891 that they won a trophy (the Barnes Cup) and followed this a year later by winning the Sheffield Cup, Barnes Cup and the Derbyshire Junior Cup.

First Football League game: 2 September, 1899, Division 2, v Sheffield W (a) L 1-5 – Hancock; Pilgrim, Fletcher; Ballantyne, Bell, Downie; Morley, Thacker, Gooing, Munday (1), Geary.

Did you know: On 5 October 1993 Kevin Davies became the youngest player to make his debut in the Coca-Cola Cup when he played against West Ham United at 16 years 104 days.

Managers (and Secretary-Managers)
E. Russell Timmeus 1891–95*, Gilbert Gillies 1895–1901, E. F. Hind 1901–1902, Jack Hoskin 1902–1906, W. Furness 1906–07, George Swift 1907–10, G. H. Jones 1911–13, R. L. Weston 1913–17, T. Callaghan 1919, J. J. Caffrey 1920–22, Harry Hadley 1922, Harry Parkes 1922–27, Alec Campbell 1927, Ted Davison 1927–32, Bill Harvey 1932–38, Norman Bullock 1938–45, Bob Brocklebank 1945–48, Bobby Marshall 1948–52, Ted Davison 1952–58, Duggie Livingstone 1958–62, Tony McShane 1962–67, Jimmy McGuigan 1967–73, Joe Shaw 1973–76, Arthur Cox 1976–80, Frank Barlow 1980–83, John Duncan 1983–87, Kevin Randall 1987–88, Paul Hart 1988–91, Chris McMenemy 1991–93, John Duncan February 1993– .

Laurie Pearson†	6 0	13 00	2 7 65	Newcastle	Gateshead	Hull C	59	—
						Bristol C	—	—
						Port Vale	3	—
					Scotland	Darlington	28	4
						Chesterfield	1	—
Steve Spooner†	5 10	12 00	25 1 61	London	Apprentice	Derby Co	8	—
						Halifax T	72	13
						Chesterfield	93	14
						Hereford U	84	19
						York C	72	11
						Rotherham U	19	1
						Mansfield T	58	3
						Blackpool	2	—
						Chesterfield	5	—
Scott Whitehead	5 9	11 10	20 4 74	Doncaster	Trainee	Chesterfield	9	—
Steven Williams*	5 11	10 06	18 7 70	Mansfield	Trainee	Mansfield T	11	—
						Chesterfield	98	12
Forwards								
Kevin Davies	6 0	12 12	26 3 77	Sheffield	Trainee	Chesterfield	24	4
Ricardo Gabbiadini†	5 11	13 06	11 3 70	Newport	Trainee	York C	1	—
						Sunderland	1	—
						Blackpool (loan)	5	3
						Brighton (loan)	1	—
						Grimsby T (loan)	3	1
						Crewe Alex (loan)	2	—
						Hartlepool U	14	2
						Scarborough	7	1
						Carlisle U	24	3
						Chesterfield	—	—
Mark Jules	5 10	11 01	5 9 71	Bradford	Trainee	Bradford C	—	—
						Scarborough	77	16
						Chesterfield	33	1
Andy Morris	6 4	15 07	17 11 67	Sheffield		Rotherham U	7	—
						Chesterfield	192	40
						Exeter C (loan)	7	2
Steve Norris	5 10	10 10	22 9 61	Coventry	Telford	Scarborough	45	13
						Notts Co (loan)	1	—
						Carlisle U	29	5
						Halifax T	56	35
						Chesterfield	90	40
Steve Taylor†			18 12 73	Chesterfield		Chesterfield	1	—

Trainees
Ashton, Lee J; Aylward, Adam C; Bettney, Jamie D; Clarke, Robert I; Elson, Christopher B; Hopkinson, Richard; Ledger, Paul M; Otter, Nicholas A; Smith, Mark; Sorrell, James A.

****Non-Contract**
Brown, James G; Spooner, Stephen A.

Associated Schoolboys
Kuchta, Andrew S; Needham, Darren M; Needham, Gavin P; Pugh, Mark A; Shaw, Neil A.
**Non-Contract Players who are retained must be re-signed before they are eligible to play in League matches.

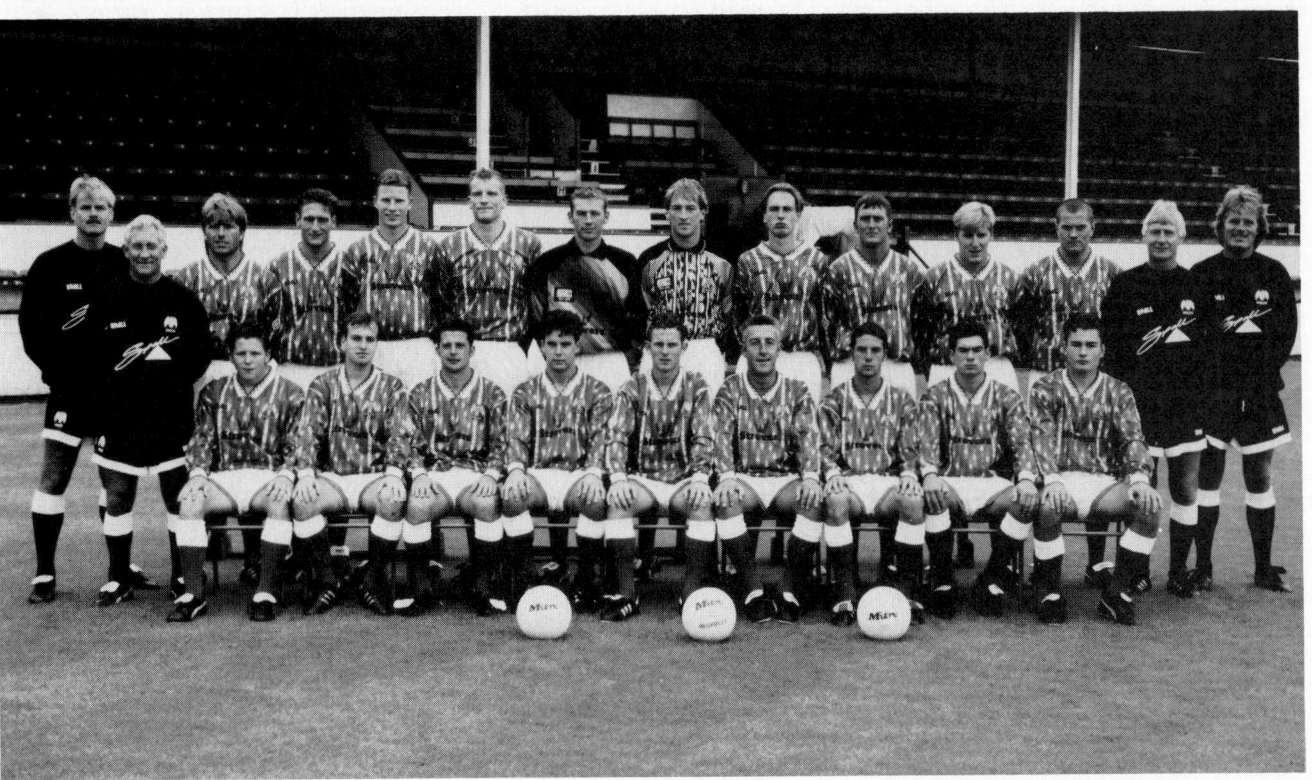

COLCHESTER UNITED 1993–94 *Back row (left to right):* Roy McDonough (Manager), Terry Price (First Team Coach), Paul Roberts, Tony English, Andrew Partner, Peter Cawley, Nathan Munson, John Keeley, Paul Flowers, Steven Ball, Steve McGavin, Martin Grainger, Brian Owen (Physio), Steve Foley (Youth Team Coach).
Front row: Scott Ridgers, Gary Bennett, Jason Cook, Simon Betts, Mark Kinsella, Nicky Smith, Sean Campbell, Paul Abrahams, Eamon Mongan.

Division 3 COLCHESTER UNITED

Layer Rd Ground, Colchester, Essex CO2 7JJ.

Telephone (0206) 574042. Fax: (0206) 48700. Club Shop (0206) 561180. Soccer Centre: (0206) 571581. Commercial Dept: (0206) 574042.

Ground capacity: 7944.

Record attendance: 19,072 v Reading, FA Cup 1st rd, 27 Nov, 1948.

Record receipts: £26,330 v Barrow, GM Vauxhall Conference, 2 May 1992.

Pitch measurements: 110yd × 71yd.

Patron: Mrs Mary Frank, Mayor of Colchester.

Directors: Gordon Parker (Chairman), Peter Heard (vice-chairman), John Worsp, Peter Powell.

Manager: George Burley. ***Player-coach:*** Steve Whitton. ***Youth coach:*** Steve Foley.

Physio: Brian Owen. ***Consultant Physio:*** C. Simpson.

Secretary: Sue Smith.

Commercial Manager: Marie Partner. ***Lottery Manager:*** Jackie McDonough.

Year Formed: 1937. ***Turned Professional:*** 1937. ***Ltd Co.:*** 1937.

Club Nickname: 'The U's'.

Record League Victory: 9–1 v Bradford C, Division 4, 30 December 1961 – Ames; Millar, Fowler; Harris, Abrey, Ron Hunt; Foster, Bobby Hunt (4), King (4), Hill (1), Wright.

Record Cup Victory: 7–1 v Yeovil T (away), FA Cup, 2nd rd (replay), 11 December 1958 – Ames; Fisher, Fowler; Parker, Milligan, Hammond; Williams (1), McLeod (2), Langman (4), Evans, Wright.

Record Defeat: 0–8 v Leyton Orient, Division 4, 15 October 1989.

Most League Points (2 for a win): 60, Division 4, 1973–74.

Most League Points (3 for a win): 81, Division 4, 1982–83.

Most League Goals: 104, Division 4, 1961–62.

Highest League Scorer in Season: Bobby Hunt, 37, Division 4, 1961–62.

Most League Goals in Total Aggregate: Martyn King, 131, 1959–65.

Most Capped Player: None.

Most League Appearances: Micky Cook, 613, 1969–84.

Record Transfer Fee Received: £100,000 from Birmingham C for Steve McGavin, January 1994.

Record Transfer Fee Paid: £40,000 to Lokeren for Dale Tempest, August 1987.

Football League Record: 1950 Elected to Division 3(S); 1958–61 Division 3; 1961–62 Division 4; 1962–65 Division 3; 1965–66 Division 4; 1966–68 Division 3; 1968–74 Division 4; 1974–76 Division 3, 1976–77 Division 4; 1977–81 Division 3; 1981–90 Division 4; 1990–92 GM Vauxhall Conference; 1992– Division 3.

Honours: *Football League:* Division 3(S) best season: 3rd , 1956–57; Division 4 – Runners-up 1961–62. *FA Cup* best season: 1970–71, 6th rd (record for a Fourth Division club shared with Oxford United and Bradford City). *Football League Cup:* best season 5th rd 1974–75. *GM Vauxhall Conference winners* 1991–92. *FA Trophy winners* 1991–92.

COLCHESTER UNITED 1993—94 LEAGUE RECORD

Match No.	Date	Venue	Opponents	Result		H/T Score	Lg. Pos.	Goalscorers	Attendance
1	Aug 14	H	Lincoln C	W	1-0	0-0	—	Kinsella	3198
2	21	A	Crewe Alex	L	1-2	0-1	11	Ball	2700
3	28	H	Northampton T	W	3-2	2-2	7	Grainger (pen), English, Kinsella	2874
4	31	H	Shrewsbury T	D	3-3	3-1	—	McGavin 2, Brown S	2723
5	Sept 4	A	Torquay U	D	3-3	2-0	7	Brown S, McGavin, Curran (og)	2989
6	11	H	Rochdale	L	2-5	2-2	11	McDonough, Brown S	2776
7	18	A	Wycombe W	W	5-2	1-1	8	Kinsella, McDonough, McGavin, Grainger, Brown S	6025
8	25	H	Bury	W	4-1	2-0	5	Brown S 3, McGavin	2702
9	Oct 2	A	Preston NE	L	0-1	0-0	6		6412
10	9	H	Scunthorpe U	W	2-1	1-1	5	Kinsella, Brown S	3405
11	16	A	Hereford U	L	0-5	0-2	7		1848
12	23	H	Wigan Ath	W	3-1	1-1	4	McDonough 2, Kinsella	2814
13	30	A	Gillingham	L	0-3	0-2	6		3964
14	Nov 2	A	Darlington	L	3-7	1-3	—	Dickens, McGavin, Kinsella	1299
15	6	H	Walsall	L	0-1	0-1	12		2736
16	20	A	Doncaster R	L	1-2	0-0	15	McGavin	2034
17	27	H	Carlisle U	W	2-1	1-1	12	English 2	2316
18	Dec 11	H	Crewe Alex	L	2-4	1-1	14	English, Brown S	2647
19	27	H	Mansfield T	D	0-0	0-0	16		3476
20	28	A	Scarborough	W	2-0	0-0	12	McDonough, McGavin	1226
21	Jan 1	H	Chester C	D	0-0	0-0	11		3170
22	3	A	Shrewsbury T	L	1-2	1-0	12	Ball	4245
23	15	H	Hereford U	W	1-0	0-0	11	Dickens	2439
24	22	A	Scunthorpe U	D	1-1	0-0	11	Cawley	2854
25	29	H	Gillingham	L	1-2	0-0	13	Watts	3436
26	Feb 5	A	Wigan Ath	W	1-0	0-0	12	Dickens	1695
27	12	H	Chesterfield	L	0-2	0-1	12		2783
28	19	A	Northampton T	D	1-1	1-1	13	McDonough	3185
29	25	H	Torquay U	L	1-2	0-0	14	Betts	2573
30	Mar 5	A	Rochdale	D	1-1	1-0	15	Watts	2202
31	12	H	Wycombe W	L	0-2	0-0	15		3932
32	15	A	Lincoln C	L	0-2	0-0	—		1631
33	19	A	Bury	W	1-0	0-0	15	McDonough	2108
34	26	H	Preston NE	D	1-1	0-1	14	Brown I	2950
35	29	A	Chesterfield	D	0-0	0-0	—		3089
36	Apr 2	A	Mansfield T	D	1-1	1-1	16	Gray (og)	2117
37	4	H	Scarborough	L	1-2	0-2	18	Meyer (og)	2501
38	9	A	Chester C	L	1-2	1-1	18	Brown S	3394
39	16	H	Darlington	L	1-2	1-1	18	Kinsella	2332
40	23	A	Walsall	W	2-1	1-0	17	Watkiss (og), Kinsella	2980
41	30	H	Doncaster R	W	3-1	0-1	16	Whitton 2, Brown S	2378
42	May 7	A	Carlisle U	L	0-2	0-1	17		9305

Final League Position: 17

GOALSCORERS

League (56): Brown S 11, Kinsella 8, McGavin 8, McDonough 7, English 4, Dickens 3, Ball 2, Grainger 2 (1 pen), Watts 2, Whitton 2, Betts 1, Brown I 1, Cawley 1, own goals 4.
Coca-Cola Cup (2): Kinsella 1, McDonough 1.
FA Cup (3): Brown S 1, English 1, McGavin 1.

Keeley 15	Betts 31 + 2	Roberts 21	Kinsella 42	English 42	Grainger 5 + 3	Ball 27 + 5	Bennett 3 + 1	McDonough 36 + 2	McGavin 20 + 1	Smith 29 + 10	Cook J — + 1	Abrahams 1 + 3	Allpress 21 + 2	Campbell 1 + 3	Morrow — + 1	Brown S 30 + 4	Cawley 36	Dickens 28 + 4	Richardson 1 + 7	Locke 4	Munson 2 + 1	Desborough 1	Basham 1	Sheffield 6	Fry 12 + 5	Watts 8 + 4	Booty — + 1	Cheesewright 17	Hyslop 8	Brown I 4	Whitton 8	Barada 1	Gentle — + 2	Cook A 1 + 1	Match No.
1	2	3	4	5	6	7	8	9	10	11	12	14																							1
1	2	3	4	5	6	7	8	9	10	11			12	14																					2
1		3	4	5	6	7	8	9	10	11			2		12	14																			3
1		3	4	5	6	7		9	10	11			2			8																			4
1		3	4	5	12	7		9	10	11			2			8	6	14																	5
1		3	4	5	6	7	12	9	10	11			2			8		14																	6
1	2	3	4	5	12			9	10	11						8	6	7																	7
1	2	3	4	5	12			9	10	11						8	6	7	14																8
1	2	3	4	5				9	10	11						8	6	7	12																9
1		3	4	5				9	10	11						8	6	7		2															10
1		3	4	5		12		9	10	11						8	6	7		2	14														11
1		3	4	5		12		9	10	11			2			8	6	7																	12
		3	4	5		7		9	10	11						8	6		12	2		1													13
1		3	4	5		2		9	10	11							6	7	12	8															14
1	2	3	4	5				9	10	11		12					6	7	8																15
1	2		4	5		14		9	10	11						8	6	7	12				3												16
	2	3	4	5		7		9	10	11		14				8	6		12		1														17
	2	3	4	5		7		9		11		10				8	6	12	14		1														18
	2	3	4	5		7		9	10	11						8	6	12						1	14										19
	2	3	4	5		14		9	12	11						8	6	7						1	10										20
	2	3	4	5				9	10	11						8	6	7						1	12										21
	2	3	4	5		12		9	10	11			14			8	6	7						1											22
	2		4	5		11		9					3				6	7						1	10	8	12								23
	2		4	5		11		9		12			3			8	6	7						1	10	14									24
	2		4	5		8		9		12			3			11	6	7							10	14		1							25
	2		4	5		8		9					3	12			6	7							10	11		1							26
	2		4	5		8		9		12			3	10			6	7							14	11		1							27
	2		4	5				9		12			3			11	6	8							14	10		1	7						28
	6		4	2				9		10			3			11	5	8							12			1	7						29
	14		4	2		8				12			3			9	5	7							11	10		1	6						30
	14		4	2		8				12			3			9	5	7							11	10		1	6						31
	2		4	5		8				12			3			9	6	7								11		1	10						32
	2		4	5		11		9		12			3	14		8		7								10		1	6						33
	2		4	5		11		9		12						8	6	7										1	3	10					34
	2		4	5		11		9		12						14	6	7										1	3	10	8				35
	2		4	5		11		12		3						9	6	7								14		1		10	8				36
	2		4	5		10		9		3						12	6	7								14		1		11	8				37
	2		4	5		11				3			6			9	7								10			1			8				38
	2		4	5				12		11			3			9	6	7							10			1			8				39
	2		4	5		7		9		11			3				6								10			1			8				40
	2		4	5				9		11			3			12	6								10						8	1	14	7	41
	2		4	5		7		9					3			11	6								10			1			8		14	12	42

Coca-Cola Cup	First Round	Fulham (a)	1-2
		(h)	1-2
FA Cup	First Round	Sutton U (h)	3-4

COLCHESTER UNITED

Player and Position	Ht	Wt	Birth Date	Birth Place	Source	Clubs	League App	League Gls
Goalkeepers								
John Cheesewright	6 0	11 05	12 1 73	Hornchurch	Tottenham H	Southend U	—	—
						Birmingham C	1	—
					Braintree T	Colchester U	17	—
Mickey Desborough†			28 11 69	London	Chelmsford C	Colchester U	1	—
Nathan Munson‡			10 11 74	Colchester	Trainee	Colchester U	4	—
Defenders								
Tim Allpress	6 0	12 00	27 1 71	Hitchin	Trainee	Luton T	1	—
						Preston NE (loan)	9	—
					Bayer Uerdingen	Colchester U	23	—
Simon Betts	5 8	10 07	3 3 73	Middlesbrough	Trainee	Ipswich T	—	—
						Scarborough	—	—
						Colchester U	56	1
Peter Cawley	6 4	13 00	15 9 65	London	Chertsey	Wimbledon	1	—
						Bristol R (loan)	10	—
						Fulham (loan)	5	—
						Bristol R	3	—
						Southend U	7	1
						Exeter C	7	—
						Barnet	3	—
						Colchester U	60	4
Tony English	6 0	12 04	19 10 66	Luton	Coventry C	Colchester U	297	40
Paul Flowers‡	5 11	12 06	7 9 74	London	Trainee	Colchester U	3	—
Christian Hyslop	5 11	11 07	14 6 72	Watford	Trainee	Southend U	19	—
						Northampton T (loan)	8	—
						Colchester U	8	—
Andy Partner	6 1	12 10	21 10 74	Colchester	Trainee	Colchester U	1	—
Paul Roberts*	5 9	11 13	27 4 62	London	Apprentice	Millwall	146	—
						Brentford	62	—
						Swindon T	27	—
						Southend U	38	—
						Aldershot	39	—
						Exeter C	3	—
						Southend U	54	—
					Fisher Ath	Colchester U	63	1
Midfield								
Steve Ball	6 0	12 01	2 9 69	Colchester	Trainee	Arsenal	—	—
						Colchester U	4	—
						Norwich C	2	—
						Colchester U	56	6
Neal Butler			11 9 75	Newport Pagnall	Luton T	Colchester U	—	—
Anthony Cook			17 9 76	Hemel Hempstead	Trainee	Colchester U	2	—
Jason Cook	5 7	10 06	29 12 69	Edmonton	Trainee	Tottenham H	—	—
						Southend U	30	1
						Colchester U	35	1
Alan Dickens*	5 11	12 05	3 9 64	Plaistow	Apprentice	West Ham U	192	23
						Chelsea	48	1
						WBA (loan)	3	1
						Brentford	15	1
						Colchester U	32	3
Warren Donald	5 7	10 03	7 10 64	Hillingdon	Apprentice	West Ham U	2	—
						Northampton T (loan)	11	2
						Northampton T	177	11
						Colchester U	10	—
Mark Kinsella	5 9	11 00	12 8 72	Dublin	Home Farm	Colchester U	86	14
Scott Ridgers‡			9 9 74	Colchester	Trainee	Colchester U	—	—
Nicky Smith	5 7	10 00	28 1 69	Berkley		Southend U	60	6
						Colchester U	81	4
Forwards								
Paul Abrahams	5 8	10 06	31 10 73	Colchester	Trainee	Colchester U	27	6
Justin Booty§			2 6 76	Colchester	Trainee	Colchester U	1	—

COLCHESTER UNITED

Colours: Blue and white striped shirts, white shorts, white stockings. **Change colours:** White shirts, black shorts black stockings white trim.

Foundation: Colchester United was formed in 1937 when a number of enthusiasts of the much older Colchester Town club decided to establish a professional concern as a limited liability company. The new club continued at Layer Road which had been the amateur club's home since 1909.

First Football League game: 19 August, 1950, Division 3(S), v Gillingham (a) D 0-0 – Wright; Kettle, Allen; Bearryman, Stewart, Elder; Jones, Curry, Turner, McKim, Church.

Did you know: In 1971 Colchester United won three trophies: the Harwich Charity Cup, the Watney Cup and the The Giant-Killers Cup for their successful exploits in the FA Cup.

Managers (and Secretary-Managers)
Ted Fenton 1946–48, Jimmy Allen 1948–53, Jack Butler 1953–55, Benny Fenton 1955–63, Neil Franklin 1963–68, Dick Graham 1968–72, Jim Smith 1972–75, Bobby Roberts 1975–82, Allan Hunter 1982–83, Cyril Lea 1983–86, Mike Walker 1986–87, Roger Brown 1987–88, Jock Wallace 1989, Mick Mills 1990. Ian Atkins 1990–91, Roy McDonough 1991–94, George Burley June 1994–

Player and Position	*Ht*	*Wt*	*Birth Date*	*Place*	*Source*	*Clubs*	*League App*	*Gls*
Steve Brown	5 11	11 10	6 12 73	Southend	Trainee	Southend U	10	2
						Scunthorpe U	—	—
						Colchester U	34	11
Sean Campbell*			31 12 74	Bristol	Trainee	Colchester U	4	—
Chris Fry	5 9	9 06	23 10 69	Cardiff	Trainee	Cardiff C	55	1
						Hereford U	90	10
						Colchester U	17	—
Justin Gentle	5 7	10 09	6 6 74	Enfield	Trainee	Luton T	—	—
						Colchester U	2	—
Roy McDonough	6 1	13 07	16 10 58	Solihull	Apprentice	Birmingham C	2	1
						Walsall	82	15
						Chelsea	—	—
						Colchester U	93	24
						Southend U	22	4
						Exeter C	20	1
						Cambridge U	32	5
						Southend U	186	30
						Colchester U	63	16
Grant Morrow‡	5 10	11 07	4 10 70	Glasgow	Rowntree Mackintosh	Doncaster R	64	7
						Colchester U	1	—
John Richardson‡			28 7 66	Durham	Chesham U	Colchester U	8	—
Scott Walters			23 9 75	Hemel Hempstead	Watford	Colchester U	—	—
Steve Whitton	6 1	13 06	4 12 60	East Ham	Apprentice	Coventry C	74	21
						West Ham U	39	6
						Birmingham C (loan)	8	2
						Birmingham C	95	28
						Sheffield W	32	4
						Ipswich T	88	15
						Colchester U	8	2

Trainees
Andress, Simon; Booty, Justin; Cardy, Jonathan D; Champ, Paul J; Cook, Anthony M; Dowdeswell, David J; Francis, Dean E; Henderson, Gary D; Jordan, Alan; King, Matthew J; Lawrence, Robert; Lewis, Ben; Lock, Anthony C; Partner, Lloyd; Rees, Benjamin D; Roberts, Danny; Schultz, David H; Seal, Richard; Siddons, James.

Associated Schoolboys
Bailey, Ryan; Fielding, Stuart P; O'Donnell, Daniel J; Stevens, Christopher J.

Associated Schoolboys who have accepted the Club's offer of a Traineeship/Contract
Duguid, Karl A; Green, Sean M.

COVENTRY CITY 1993–94 *Back row (left to right):* Bert Edwards (Youth Manager), Tim Exeter (Fitness Coach), Stewart Robson, John Williams, Mick Harford, Jonathan Gould, Lee Hirst, Steve Ogrizovic, Jason Smith, David Busst, Phil Babb, Trevor Gould (Youth Team Coach).
Centre row: Joe Roach (PT Instructor), Brian Roberts (Reserve Team Coach), Martyn Booty, Lee Hurst, Brian Borrows, David Rennie, Roy Wegerle, Leigh Jenkinson, Ray Woods, Paul O'Brien, Lloyd McGrath, George Dalton (Physio), Peter Hill (Kit Manager).
Front row: Peter Ndlovu, Sean Flynn, Tony Sheridan, Peter Atherton, Phil Neal (Assistant Manager), Bobby Gould (Team Manager), Mick Quinn, Steve Morgan, Willie Boland, David Carmichael.

FA Premiership COVENTRY CITY

Highfield Road Stadium, King Richard Street, Coventry CV2 4FW. Telephone (General Enquiries): (0203) 223535. Ticket office: (0203) 225545. Fax: 0203 630318.

Ground capacity: 22,600.

Record attendance: 51,455 v Wolverhampton W, Division 2, 29 April 1967.

Record receipts: £177,271.55 v Nottingham F, Littlewoods Cup Semi-final 2nd leg, 25 February 1990.

Pitch measurements: 110yd × 75yd.

Life President: Derrick H. Robbins.

Chairman: B. A. Richardson. ***Deputy chairman:*** M. C. McGinnity.

Directors: G. W. Curtis, E. W. Grove, A. M. Jepson, J. F. W Reason, P. D. H. Robins.

Secretary: Graham Hover.

Team Manager: Phil Neal. ***Assistant Manager:*** Mick Brown. ***Physio:*** George Dalton. ***Sales & Marketing Manager:*** Mark Jones.

Year Formed: 1883. ***Turned Professional:*** 1893. ***Ltd Co.:*** 1907.

Previous Names: 1883–98, Singers FC; 1898, Coventry City FC.

Club Nickname: 'Sky Blues'.

Previous Grounds: Binley Road, 1883–87; Stoke Road, 1887–99; Highfield Road, 1899–.

Record League Victory: 9–0 v Bristol C, Division 3 (S), 28 April 1934 – Pearson; Brown, Bisby; Perry, Davidson, Frith; White (2), Lauderdale Bourton (5), Jones (2), Lake.

Record Cup Victory: 7–0 v Scunthorpe U, FA Cup, 1st rd, 24 November 1934 – Pearson; Brown, Bisby; Mason, Davidson, Boileau; Birtley (2), Lauderdale (2), Bourton (1), Jones (1), Liddle (1).

Record Defeat: 2–10 v Norwich C, Division 3 (S), 15 March 1930.

Most League Points (2 for a win): 60, Division 4, 1958–59 and Division 3, 1963–64.

Most League Points (3 for a win): 63, Division 1, 1986–87.

Most League Goals: 108, Division 3 (S), 1931–32.

Highest League Scorer in Season: Clarrie Bourton, 49, Division 3 (S), 1931–32.

Most League Goals in Total Aggregate: Clarrie Bourton, 171, 1931–37.

Most Capped Player: Dave Clements, 21 (48), Northern Ireland.

Most League Appearances: George Curtis, 486, 1956–70.

Record Transfer Fee Received: £1,500,000 from Blackburn R for Kevin Gallacher, March 1993.

Record Transfer Fee Paid: £900,000 to Dundee U for Kevin Gallacher, January 1990.

Football League Record: 1919 Elected to Division 2; 1925–26 Division 3 (N); 1926–36 Division 3 (S); 1936–52 Division 2; 1952–58 Division 3 (S); 1958–59 Division 4; 1959–64 Division 3; 1964–67 Division 2; 1967–92 Division 1; 1992– FA Premier League.

Honours: *Football League:* Division 1 best season: 6th, 1969–70; Division 2 – Champions 1966–67; Division 3 – Champions 1963–64; Division 3 (S) – Champions 1935–36; Runners-up 1933–34; Division 4 – Runners-up 1958–59. *FA Cup:* Winners 1986–87. *Football League Cup:* best season: Semi-final 1980–81, 1989–90. **European Competitions:** *European Fairs Cup:* 1970–71.

COVENTRY CITY 1993—94 LEAGUE RECORD

Match No.	*Date*	*Venue*	*Opponents*	*Result*		*H/T Score*	*Lg. Pos.*	*Goalscorers*	*Attendance*
1	Aug 14	A	Arsenal	W	3-0	1-0	—	Quinn 3 (1 pen)	26,397
2	18	H	Newcastle U	W	2-1	0-1	—	Ndlovu, Harford	15,763
3	21	H	West Ham U	D	1-1	0-1	4	Wegerle	12,864
4	24	A	Oldham Ath	D	3-3	1-1	—	Williams J, Ndlovu, Wegerle (pen)	10,817
5	27	A	Manchester C	D	1-1	0-1	—	Wegerle	21,537
6	Sept 1	H	Liverpool	W	1-0	1-0	—	Babb	16,735
7	11	A	Aston Villa	D	0-0	0-0	3		31,181
8	18	H	Chelsea	D	1-1	0-1	6	Morgan	13,586
9	25	H	Leeds U	L	0-2	0-1	10		13,933
10	Oct 2	A	Norwich C	L	0-1	0-1	11		16,239
11	16	H	Southampton	D	1-1	0-0	13	Babb	9837
12	23	A	QPR	L	1-5	0-3	13	Ndlovu	12,979
13	31	H	Sheffield U	D	0-0	0-0	—		10,439
14	Nov 6	H	Everton	W	2-1	1-0	13	Quinn 2	11,550
15	20	A	Sheffield W	D	0-0	0-0	11		23,379
16	23	A	Blackburn R	L	1-2	0-1	—	Ndlovu	16,376
17	27	H	Manchester U	L	0-1	0-0	—		17,009
18	Dec 4	H	Arsenal	W	1-0	0-0	13	Quinn	12,632
19	11	A	West Ham U	L	2-3	1-2	16	Darby 2	17,243
20	18	H	Oldham Ath	D	1-1	1-0	16	Wegerle	11,792
21	26	A	Wimbledon	W	2-1	1-1	—	Ndlovu, Williams J	4739
22	Jan 1	A	Tottenham H	W	2-1	1-1	13	Babb, Wegerle	26,015
23	3	H	Swindon T	D	1-1	0-0	12	Wegerle	15,869
24	15	A	Southampton	L	0-1	0-1	13		12,397
25	22	H	QPR	L	0-1	0-1	14		12,065
26	Feb 2	H	Ipswich T	W	1-0	1-0	—	Flynn	11,244
27	5	A	Swindon T	L	1-3	0-2	12	Darby	14,635
28	12	A	Sheffield U	D	0-0	0-0	13		15,394
29	19	H	Manchester C	W	4-0	0-0	11	Rennie, Quinn, Williams J, Ndlovu	11,739
30	23	A	Newcastle U	L	0-4	0-0	—		32,210
31	25	A	Liverpool	L	0-1	0-1	11		38,547
32	Mar 6	H	Aston Villa	L	0-1	0-1	—		14,323
33	19	A	Leeds U	L	0-1	0-0	13		30,023
34	26	H	Norwich C	W	2-1	1-0	12	Flynn, Quinn	13,515
35	Apr 2	H	Wimbledon	L	1-2	0-2	13	Ndlovu	11,312
36	4	A	Ipswich T	W	2-0	0-0	12	Flynn, Ndlovu	12,782
37	9	H	Tottenham H	W	1-0	0-0	12	Ndlovu (pen)	14,487
38	16	H	Sheffield W	D	1-1	1-0	12	Ndlovu (pen)	13,052
39	23	A	Everton	D	0-0	0-0	12		23,352
40	May 2	H	Blackburn R	W	2-1	1-1	—	Darby 2	16,646
41	4	A	Chelsea	W	2-1	2-1	—	Ndlovu, Morgan	8923
42	8	A	Manchester U	D	0-0	0-0	—		44,717

Final League Position: 11

GOALSCORERS

League (43): Ndlovu 11 (2 pens), Quinn 8 (1 pen), Wegerle 6 (1 pen), Darby 5, Babb 3, Flynn 3, Williams J 3, Morgan 2, Harford 1, Rennie 1.
Coca-Cola Cup (5): Morgan 3, Babb 1, Quinn 1.
FA Cup (0):

Gould 9	Sheridan 4 + 4	Babb 40	Atherton 39 + 1	Rennie 34	Williams J 27 + 5	Robson 1	Ndlovu 40	Wegerle 20 + 1	Quinn 28 + 4	Flynn 33 + 3	Morgan 39 + 1	Harford — + 1	Williams P 3 + 6	Boland 24 + 3	Borrows 29	McGrath 10 + 1	Busst 2 + 1	Booty 2	Jenkinson 10 + 6	Ogrizovic 33	Kruszynski 1 + 1	Gayle 3	Darby 25 + 1	Marsden 5 + 2	Robertson — + 3	Pickering 1 + 3	Match No.
1	2	3	4	5	6	*7*	8	9	10	11	12																1
1	2	3	4	5	7		8	9	10	11	*6*	12	14														2
1	*2*	3	4	5	7		8	9	10	11	6		12	14													3
1		3	4	5	6		8	9	*10*		7		12	14	2	11											4
1			4	5	7		8	9					3	11		2	6	10	12								5
1	14	3	4	5	6		8	9	*10*		2		12	11		7											6
	14	3	4	5	6		8	*9*	10		2		12	11		7				1							7
	12	3	4	5	6		8	9	10		2			11		7				1							8
	12	3	4	5	14			9	10		2			11				*7*		1	6	8					9
	7	5	4		6			9	10	12	3		2	11					8	1	14						10
1		5	4		7		8	9	10	12	3			11		2	*6*		14								11
1		5	4				8	14	10	7	3		12	11	2	9			*6*								12
		5		6	12		8	9	10	4	3			11	2	7				1							13
		5		4			8	9	10	6	3			11	2	7				1			12				14
		5	12	4	6		8		10	9	3			11	2	7				1							15
		5	4	6	7		8		10	12	3			11	2					1				9			16
		5	2	6	12		8	9	10	4	3			*11*						1			7	14			17
		5	2	6			8	9	10	4	3			11						1			7				18
		5	2	6	12		8	9	10	4	3			*11*						1			7	14			19
		5	4		12		8	9	10	11	3				2					1			7	6			20
		5	4		7		8	9		6	3				2					1			11	10			21
		5	4		7		8	9	12	6	3				2					1			11	10			22
		5	4		7		8	9	12	6	3				2					1			11	10			23
		5	4	6	7		8		10	11			3		2				12	1			9				24
		5	4	6	7		8		10	11	3				2					1			9		12		25
		5	4	6	7		8		12	11	3				2					1		10	9				26
		5	4	6	*7*		8		12	11	3				2					1		10	9		14		27
		5	4	6	7		8		10	11	3				2					1			9				28
		5	4	6	7		8		10	11	3				2				12	1			9				29
		5	4	6	7		8			11	3				2		14		10	1			9		12		30
			4	5	7		8		10	6	3			11	2					1			9			12	31
		5	4	6	7		8		10	11	3				2					1			9				32
		5	4		*7*		8		10	6	3			11	2				12	1			9			14	33
		5	4	6	7		8		10	11	3			12	2					1			9				34
		5	4	6	7		8		10	11	3				2				12	1			9				35
		5	4	6			8			7	3			11	2				10	1			9				36
		5	4	6			8			9	3			11	2	12			10	1						7	37
		5	4	6			8			9	3			11	2				10	1			7				38
		5	4	6			8			9	3			11	2				10	1			7			12	39
		5	4	6			8			9	3			11	2				10	1			7				40
1		5	4	6			8			9	3			11	2				10				7				41
		5	4	6			8			9	3			11	2				10	1			7				42

Coca-Cola Cup	Second Round	Wycombe W (h)	3-0
		(a)	2-4
	Third Round	Oldham Ath (a)	0-2
FA Cup	Third Round	Newcastle U (a)	0-2

COVENTRY CITY

Player and Position	Ht	Wt	Birth Date	Birth Place	Source	Clubs	League App	League Gls
Goalkeepers								
Martin Davies	6 2	13 07	28 6 74	Swansea	Trainee	Coventry C	—	—
Jonathan Gould	6 1	12 07	18 7 68	Paddington		Halifax T	32	—
						WBA	—	—
						Coventry C	18	—
Steve Ogrizovic	6 5	15 00	12 9 57	Mansfield	ONRYC	Chesterfield	16	—
						Liverpool	4	—
						Shrewsbury T	84	—
						Coventry C	382	1
Defenders								
Peter Atherton	5 11	12 03	6 4 70	Orrell	Trainee	Wigan Ath	149	1
						Coventry C	114	—
Phil Babb	6 0	12 03	30 11 70	Lambeth		Millwall	—	—
						Bradford C	80	14
						Coventry C	74	3
Brian Borrows	5 10	10 12	20 12 60	Liverpool	Amateur	Everton	27	—
						Bolton W	95	—
						Coventry C	330	11
						Bristol C (loan)	6	—
Dave Busst	6 1	12 10	30 6 67	Birmingham	Moor Green	Coventry C	13	—
Lorcan Costello	5 9	11 02	11 11 76	Dublin	Trainee	Coventry C	—	—
Julian Darby	6 0	11 04	3 10 67	Bolton		Bolton W	270	36
						Coventry C	26	5
Lee Hirst*	6 2	12 07	26 1 69	Sheffield		Scarborough	108	6
						Coventry C	—	—
						Lincoln C (loan)	7	—
Steve Morgan	5 11	13 00	19 9 68	Oldham	Apprentice	Blackpool	144	10
						Plymouth Arg	121	6
						Coventry C	40	2
Ally Pickering	5 11	11 01	22 6 67	Manchester	Buxton	Rotherham U	88	2
						Coventry C	4	—
David Rennie	6 0	12 00	29 8 64	Edinburgh	Apprentice	Leicester C	21	1
						Leeds U	101	5
						Bristol C	104	8
						Birmingham C	35	4
						Coventry C	43	1
Brian Roberts	5 8	11 07	6 11 55	Manchester	Apprentice	Coventry C	215	1
						Hereford U (loan)	5	—
						Birmingham C	187	—
						Wolverhampton W	21	—
						Coventry C	—	—
Jason Smith	6 2	12 04	6 9 74	Bromsgrove	Tiverton	Coventry C	—	—
Midfield								
Willie Boland	5 9	11 02	6 8 75	Ennis	Trainee	Coventry C	28	—
Sean Flynn	5 8	11 08	13 3 68	Birmingham	Halesowen T	Coventry C	65	5
Lee Hurst	6 0	11 09	21 9 70	Nuneaton	Trainee	Coventry C	49	2
Detsi Kruszynski‡	6 0	12 12	14 10 61	Divschav	Homburg	Wimbledon	71	4
						Brentford (loan)	8	—
						Brentford	6	—
					Saarbrucken, Homburg	Peterborough U	3	—
						Coventry C	2	—
Lloyd McGrath*	5 5	11 06	24 2 65	Birmingham	Apprentice	Coventry C	214	4
Gavin O'Toole	5 9	11 01	19 9 75	Dublin	Trainee	Coventry C	—	—
Sandy Robertson	5 9	10 07	26 4 71	Edinburgh	S Form	Rangers	26	1
						Coventry C	3	—
Stewart Robson	5 11	12 04	6 11 64	Billericay	Apprentice	Arsenal	151	16
						West Ham U	69	4
						Coventry C (loan)	4	—
						Coventry C	53	3
John Williams	6 2	12 04	11 5 68	Birmingham	Cradley T	Swansea C	39	11
						Coventry C	73	11
Simon Wood	5 9	11 08	24 9 76	Hull	Trainee	Coventry C	—	—
Forwards								
David Carmichael*			5 3 75	Immingham	Trainee	Coventry C	—	—
Alistair Farquhar	5 8	10 12	15 8 76	Aberfeldy	Trainee	Coventry C	—	—

COVENTRY CITY

Colours: All Sky blue. **Change colours:** Green and black striped shirts, green shorts, green stockings.

Foundation: Workers at Singer's cycle factory formed a club in 1883. The first success of Singers' FC was to win the Birmingham Junior Cup in 1891 and this led in 1894 to their election to the Birmingham and District League. Four years later they changed their name to Coventry City and joined the Southern League in 1908 at which time they were playing in blue and white quarters.

First Football League game: 30 August, 1919, Division 2, v Tottenham H (h) L 0-5 – Lindon; Roberts, Chaplin, Allan, Hawley, Clarke, Sheldon, Mercer, Sambrooke, Lowes, Gibson.

Did you know: Coventry City were unbeaten in their first eight FA Carling Premiership matches in 1993–94, the best start made by the club since 1937–38 when they completed 15 without defeat.

Managers (and Secretary-Managers)
H. R. Buckle 1909–10, Robert Wallace 1910–13*, Frank Scott-Walford 1913–15, William Clayton 1917–19, H. Pollitt 1919–20, Albert Evans 1920–24, Jimmy Kerr 1924–28, James McIntyre 1928–31, Harry Storer 1931–45, Dick Bayliss 1945–47, Billy Frith 1947–48, Harry Storer 1948–53, Jack Fairbrother 1953–54, Charlie Elliott 1954–55, Jesse Carver 1955–56, Harry Warren 1956–57, Billy Frith 1957–61, Jimmy Hill 1961–67, Noel Cantwell 1967–72, Bob Dennison 1972, Joe Mercer 1972–75, Gordon Milne 1972–81, Dave Sexton 1981–83, Bobby Gould 1983–84, Don Mackay 1985–86, George Curtis 1986–87 (became MD), John Sillett 1987–90, Terry Butcher 1990–92, Don Howe 1992, Bobby Gould 1992–93, Phil Neal November 1993–

John Gayle	6 4	13 01	30 7 64	Birmingham	Burton Alb	Wimbledon	20	2
						Birmingham C	44	10
						Walsall (loan)	4	1
						Coventry C	3	—
Mick Harford	6 3	14 05	12 2 59	Sunderland	Lambton St BC	Lincoln C	115	41
						Newcastle U	19	4
						Bristol C	30	11
						Birmingham C	92	25
						Luton T	139	57
						Derby Co	58	15
						Luton T	29	12
						Chelsea	28	9
						Sunderland	11	2
						Coventry C	1	1
Leigh Jenkinson	6 0	12 02	9 7 69	Thorne	Trainee	Hull C	130	13
						Rotherham U (loan)	7	—
						Coventry C	21	—
						Birmingham C (loan)	3	—
Andrew Lovelock	5 9	10 12	20 12 76	Swindon	Trainee	Coventry C	—	—
Peter Ndlovu	5 8	10 02	25 2 73	Zimbabwe	Highlanders	Coventry C	95	20
Mick Quinn	5 9	13 00	2 5 62	Liverpool	Derby Co	Wigan Ath	69	19
						Stockport Co	63	39
						Oldham Ath	80	34
						Portsmouth	121	54
						Newcastle U	115	59
						Coventry C	58	25
Tony Sheridan	6 0	11 08	21 10 74	Dublin		Coventry C	9	—
Michael Stephenson	5 9	12 00	6 10 73	Coventry	Trainee	Coventry C	—	—
Roy Wegerle	5 11	11 00	19 3 64	South Africa	Tampa Bay R	Chelsea	23	3
						Swindon T (loan)	7	1
						Luton T	45	10
						QPR	75	29
						Blackburn R	34	6
						Coventry C	27	6
Paul Williams	5 7	10 00	11 9 69	Leicester	Trainee	Leicester C	—	—
						Stockport Co	70	4
						Coventry C	9	—
						WBA (loan)	5	—
Ray Woods*	5 11	10 00	7 6 65	Birkenhead	Apprentice	Tranmere R	7	2
					Colne D.	Wigan Ath	28	3
						Coventry C	21	1
						Wigan Ath (loan)	13	—
						Shrewsbury T (loan)	9	1

Trainees
Barnwell-Edinboro, Jamie; Blake, Timothy A; Bowman, Robert J. J; Christie, Iyseden; Hall, Marcus T. J; Jones, Richard, J; Keeling, Tommy L; Lenton, James A; Rogers, Lee; Williams, James D; Willis, Adam P.

Associated Schoolboys
Birks, Gregg; McGregor, Scott C; Morgan, Leon R; Nugent, Matthew; Slater, Lee; Smith, Dean; Sutton, Christopher W.

Associated Schoolboys who have accepted the Club's offer of a Traineeship/Contract
Ducros, Andrew J; Harrison, Neil S; Healy, Brett W; Nolan, Carl N; Robinson, Mark T.

CREWE ALEXANDRA 1993–94 *Back row (left to right)*: Phil Clarkson, Michael Jackson, Darran Rowbotham, Andrew Woodward, Stewart Evans, Mark Smith, Graham Abel, Dele Adebola, Anthony Hughes, Steve Macauley.

Front row: Wayne Collins, Mark Gardiner, Andy Lyons, Steve Walters, Dario Gradi (Manager), Steve Garvey, Neil Lennon, Terry Naylor, Gareth Whalley.

Division 2 CREWE ALEXANDRA

Football Ground, Gresty Rd, Crewe, CW2 6EB. Telephone Crewe (0270) 213014. (0270) 55657.

Ground capacity: 7200.

Record attendance: 20,000 v Tottenham H, FA Cup 4th rd, 30 January 1960.

Record receipts: £41,093 v Liverpool, FA Cup 3rd rd, 6 January 1992.

Pitch measurements: 112yd × 74yd.

President: N. Rowlinson.

Chairman: J. Bowler. ***Vice-chairman:*** N. Hassall.

Directors: K. Potts, D. Rowlinson, R. Clayton, J. McMillan, E. Weetman, J. R. Holmes.

Manager: Dario Gradi.

Secretary/Commercial Manager: Mrs Gill Palin.

Year Formed: 1877. ***Turned Professional:*** 1893. ***Ltd Co.:*** 1892.

Club Nickname: 'Railwaymen'.

Record League Victory: 8–0 v Rotherham U, Division 3 (N), 1 October 1932 – Foster; Pringle, Dawson; Ward, Keenor (1), Turner (1); Gillespie, Swindells (1), McConnell (2), Deacon (2), Weale (1).

Record Cup Victory: 5–0 v Druids, FA Cup, 1st rd, 15 October 1887 – Hickton; Conde, Cope; Bayman, Halfpenny, Osborne (1); Pearson, Payne (1), Price (1), Tinsley, Ellis. (2 scorers unknown.)

Record Defeat: 2–13 v Tottenham H, FA Cup 4th rd replay, 3 February 1960.

Most League Points (2 for a win): 59, Division 4, 1962–63.

Most League Points (3 for a win): 78, Division 4, 1988–89.

Most League Goals: 95, Division 3 (N), 1931–32.

Highest League Scorer in Season: Terry Harkin, 35, Division 4, 1964–65.

Most League Goals in Total Aggregate: Bert Swindells, 126, 1928–37.

Most Capped Player: Bill Lewis, 12 (30), Wales.

Most League Appearances: Tommy Lowry, 436, 1966–78.

Record Transfer Fee Received: £600,000 from Liverpool for Rob Jones, October 1991.

Record Transfer Fee Paid: £80,000 to Barnsley for Darren Foreman, March 1990.

Football League Record: 1892 Original Member of Division 2; 1896 Failed re-election; 1921 Re-entered Division 3 (N); 1958–63 Division 4; 1963–64 Division 3; 1964–68 Division 4; 1968–69 Division 3; 1969–89 Division 4; 1989–91 Division 3; 1991–92 Division 4; 1992–94 Division 3; 1994– Division 2.

Honours: *Football League:* Division 2 best season: 10th, 1892–93. *FA Cup:* best season: semi-final 1888. *Football League Cup:* best season: 3rd rd, 1974–75, 1975–76, 1978–79, 1992–93. *Welsh Cup:* Winners 1936, 1937.

CREWE ALEXANDRA 1993—94 LEAGUE RECORD

Match No.	Date	Venue	Opponents	Result	H/T Score	Lg. Pos.	Goalscorers	Attendance
1	Aug 14	A	Preston NE	W 2-0	1-0	—	Walters, Clarkson	6879
2	21	H	Colchester U	W 2-1	1-0	2	Ward 2	2700
3	28	A	Bury	L 0-1	0-0	8		2708
4	31	H	Northampton T	W 3-1	1-1	—	Ward, Clarkson, Annan	3002
5	Sept 4	H	Mansfield T	W 2-1	0-0	2	Evans, Abel	3155
6	11	A	Walsall	D 2-2	2-2	3	Ward, Evans	4404
7	18	H	Darlington	W 2-1	2-0	2	Smith S (pen), Naylor	3295
8	25	A	Torquay U	D 3-3	2-0	2	Collins, Rowbotham, Ward	4009
9	Oct 2	H	Lincoln C	D 2-2	2-1	3	Rowbotham, Brown (og)	3361
10	9	H	Hereford U	W 6-0	4-0	2	Naylor 3, Rowbotham, Ward 2	3509
11	16	A	Scarborough	W 2-1	0-1	1	Evans, Smith S	1551
12	23	H	Gillingham	W 1-0	0-0	1	Smith S (pen)	3611
13	30	A	Chesterfield	L 0-2	0-0	2		3501
14	Nov 2	A	Shrewsbury T	D 2-2	1-1	—	Collins, Rowbotham	5585
15	6	H	Rochdale	W 2-1	1-0	2	Jones, Butler (og)	4049
16	20	A	Wycombe W	L 1-3	1-2	2	Rowbotham	6137
17	27	H	Chester C	W 2-1	0-1	2	Rowbotham, Booty	4749
18	Dec 11	A	Colchester U	W 4-2	1-1	1	Rowbotham 2, Gardiner, Whalley	2647
19	17	H	Preston NE	W 4-3	2-1	—	Naylor, Rowbotham 2, Murphy	6035
20	28	A	Carlisle U	W 2-1	1-1	1	Evans 2	7073
21	Jan 1	H	Doncaster R	W 2-0	1-0	1	Rowbotham, Evans	4480
22	3	A	Northampton T	D 2-2	1-2	1	Smith S, Naylor	3404
23	15	H	Scarborough	D 1-1	1-1	1	Smith S (pen)	3594
24	22	A	Hereford U	W 2-1	1-0	1	Rowbotham, Lennon	2638
25	29	H	Chesterfield	L 0-1	0-1	1		3846
26	Feb 5	A	Gillingham	W 3-1	0-0	1	Lennon, Macauley, Smith S	3713
27	12	H	Scunthorpe U	D 3-3	2-2	1	Tierney, Edwards, Naylor	3507
28	19	H	Bury	L 2-4	0-1	1	Rowbotham, Edwards	4276
29	25	A	Mansfield T	W 2-1	2-1	1	Rowbotham, Macauley	3509
30	Mar 5	H	Walsall	L 1-2	0-1	1	Ward	4358
31	12	A	Darlington	L 0-1	0-1	1		2373
32	15	A	Scunthorpe U	L 1-2	1-2	—	Smith S (pen)	2122
33	19	H	Torquay U	L 2-3	1-2	4	Ward, Naylor	3484
34	26	A	Lincoln C	W 2-1	1-0	2	Evans, Lennon	3007
35	Apr 2	A	Wigan Ath	D 2-2	1-1	4	Naylor, Murphy	2335
36	4	H	Carlisle U	L 2-3	1-2	4	Naylor 2	3679
37	9	A	Doncaster R	D 0-0	0-0	4		1820
38	16	H	Shrewsbury T	D 0-0	0-0	4		5251
39	19	H	Wigan Ath	W 4-1	1-0	—	Ward, Macauley, Rowbotham, Lennon	3396
40	23	A	Rochdale	L 1-2	0-1	4	Naylor	3096
41	30	H	Wycombe W	W 2-1	1-1	3	Ward 2	6182
42	May 7	A	Chester C	W 2-1	1-1	3	Naylor, Ward	5550

Final League Position: 3

GOALSCORERS

League (80): Rowbotham 15, Naylor 13, Ward 13, Evans 7, Smith S 7 (4 pens), Lennon 4, Macauley 3, Clarkson 2, Collins 2, Edwards 2, Murphy 2, Abel 1, Annan 1, Booty 1, Gardiner 1, Jones 1, Tierney 1, Walters 1, Whalley 1, own goals 2.
Coca-Cola Cup (3): Lyons 1, Rowbotham 1, Ward 1.
FA Cup (7): Edwards 1, Gardiner 1, Lennon 1, Naylor 1, Rowbotham 1, Smith S 1 (pen), Whalley 1.

Smith M 32	Collins 27 + 8	Gardiner 31 + 3	Evans 39 + 1	Smith S 36 + 1	Hughes 4 + 2	Ward 24 + 1	Naylor 30 + 7	Clarkson 6 + 1	Rowbotham 39 + 1	Walters 20	Lennon 31 + 2	Whalley 12 + 3	Wilson 16 + 2	Lyons 1 + 1	Woodward 9 + 3	Abel 18 + 2	Annan 9 + 1	Jones 4 + 4	Booty 30 + 1	Macauley 17	Edwards 8 + 4	Tierney 4 + 4	Murphy 5 + 7	Wilkinson 2 + 1	Gayle 8	Match No.
1	2	3	4	5	*6*	7	8	9	10	11	12	14														1
1	2	*3*	4		6	9		8	7	11	12	10	5	14												2
1		3	4			9		8	11		7	12	6	10	2	5										3
1		3	4			9		8	10	11	7		6		12	5	2									4
1		3	4			9		8	10	11	7		6		12	*5*	2	14								5
1	14	3	4	6		9	12		10	11	7					5	*2*	8								6
1	2	3	4	6		9	8	12	10	11	7					5										7
1	2	3	4	6		9	8	10	11		7	12				*5*		14								8
1	2	3	4	6	5	9	*8*		11		7	10			12			14								9
1	7	3	4	6		9	8		11			10	12			5		14	*2*							10
1	7	3	4	6			8		10	11		9							2	5	12					11
1	7	3	4	5			8		10	11		9	12						2	6						12
1	7	3	4	5			12		10	11		9						8	2	6						13
1	7	*3*	4	5	14		12		10	11		9						8	2	6						14
1	7	3	4	6			8		10			9				5		11	2		12					15
1	*7*	3	4	5	12		8		11		10								2	6	9	14				16
1		3	4		5		8		11		10	7	6			12			2		9					17
1	9	3	4	12			8		11	*10*		7	6			5			2				14			18
1	2	3	4	10			8		11	9		7	6			5							12			19
1	2	3	4	10			8		11	*9*		7	6			5			12				14			20
1		3	4	10			8		11	9	7		6			5			2							21
1	12	3	4	10			8		11	9	7		6			5			2							22
1	9	3	4	10			8		11		6					5			2		12		7			23
1	12	3	4	6			8		11	9	7					5			2				10			24
1	12	3	4	6			8		11	9	7					5			2		14	*10*				25
1		14		6		9	12		8	10	*4*						3		2	5	11	7				26
1				6		9	12		8	10	4						3		2	5	11	7				27
1	10	14	12	6			8		9		4						3		*2*	5	11	7				28
1	2	10	6	3			8		9		7				4					5	11	12				29
1	7		6	3		12	*8*		9		10				4				2	5	11		14			30
1	7		6	3		9					10				4	5			2		11	12	*8*	14		31
	7	14	*6*	3		9	12		11		10				4	5			2				8	1		32
	7	5	6	3		9	12		*11*		10				4		14		2				8	1		33
	7	5	6	3		9	8		11		10				4				2				12		1	34
	7	5	6	3		9	8		11		10				4				2				12		1	35
	7	5	6	3		9	8		12		10				*4*				2	11			14		1	36
	7	5	6	3		9	8				10		4						2	11					1	37
	7		6	3		9	8		11		10		4						2	5		12			1	38
	12		6	3		9	8		11		10		4				7		2	5					1	39
	12		6	3		9	8		11		10		4			14	*7*		2	5					1	40
	12		6	3		9	8		11		10		4				7		2	5					1	41
1	12		6	3		9	8		11	7	10		4						2	5						42

Coca-Cola Cup	First Round	Wrexham (h)	0-1
		(a)	3-3
FA Cup	First Round	Darlington (h)	4-2
	Second Round	Macclesfield (h)	2-1
	Third Round	Leeds U (a)	1-3

CREWE ALEXANDRA

Player and Position	Ht	Wt	Birth Date	Birth Place	Source	Clubs	League App	League Gls
Goalkeepers								
Mark Gayle	6 0	12 00	21 10 69	Bromsgrove	Trainee	Leicester C	—	—
						Blackpool	—	—
					Worcester C	Walsall	75	—
						Crewe Alex	8	—
						Liverpool (loan)	—	—
Mark Smith‡	6 1	13 09	2 1 73	Birmingham	Trainee	Nottingham F	—	—
						Crewe Alex	39	—
Ian Wilkinson	5 11	12 00	2 7 73	Warrington	Trainee	Manchester U	—	—
						Stockport Co	—	—
						Crewe Alex	3	—
Defenders								
Graham Abel*	6 2	13 00	17 9 60	Runcorn	Runcorn	Chester C	296	29
						Crewe Alex	20	1
Richard Annan	5 8	10 00	4 12 68	Leeds	Guiseley	Crewe Alex	19	1
Martyn Booty	5 8	12 01	30 5 71	Kirby Muxloe	Trainee	Coventry C	5	—
						Crewe Alex	31	1
Martin Clark*	5 10	10 06	12 9 70	Accrington	Accrington S	Crewe Alex	—	—
Anthony Hughes	6 0	12 05	3 10 73	Liverpool	Trainee	Crewe Alex	23	1
Neil Lennon	5 9	11 06	25 6 71	Lurgan	Trainee	Manchester C	1	—
						Crewe Alex	91	7
Steve Macauley	6 1	12 00	4 3 69	Lytham	Fleetwood	Crewe Alex	51	7
Mark Rivers			26 11 75	Crewe	Trainee	Crewe Alex	—	—
Paul Rushton*	5 10	11 10	25 1 74	Buckley	Trainee	Crewe Alex	—	—
Shaun Smith	5 10	11 00	9 4 71	Leeds	Trainee	Halifax T	7	—
						Crewe Alex	83	11
Gus Wilson	5 11	12 00	11 4 63	Manchester	Runcorn	Crewe Alex	94	—
Andy Woodward	5 10	10 12	23 9 73	Stockport	Trainee	Crewe Alex	18	—
Midfield								
Shaun Brooks	5 7	11 00	9 10 62	London	Apprentice	Crystal Palace	54	4
						Orient	148	26
						Bournemouth	128	13
						Stockport Co (loan)	—	—
						Crewe Alex	—	—
Chris Byrne*	5 9	10 08	9 2 75	Manchester	Trainee	Crewe Alex	—	—
Phil Clarkson	5 10	10 08	13 11 68	Hambleton	Fleetwood	Crewe Alex	70	21
Wayne Collins	6 0	12 00	4 3 69	Manchester	Winsford U	Crewe Alex	35	2
William Hudson*			8 9 75	Wandsworth		Crewe Alex	—	—
Danny Murphy	5 9	10 03	18 3 77	Chester	Trainee	Crewe Alex	12	2
Darren Rowbotham	5 10	11 05	22 10 66	Cardiff	Trainee	Plymouth Arg	46	2
						Exeter C	118	47
						Torquay U	14	3
						Birmingham C	36	6
						Hereford U (loan)	8	2
						Mansfield T (loan)	4	—
						Crewe Alex	40	15
Francis Tierney	5 10	10 12	10 9 75	Liverpool	Trainee	Crewe Alex	9	1
Gareth Whalley	5 10	11 00	19 12 73	Manchester	Trainee	Crewe Alex	40	2
Forwards								
Dele Adebola	6 3	12 06	23 6 75	Liverpool	Trainee	Crewe Alex	6	—
Mark Ceraolo			10 11 75	Birkenhead		Crewe Alex	—	—
Robert Edwards	5 8	11 07	23 2 70	Manchester	Trainee	Crewe Alex	106	27
Stewart Evans*	6 4	11 05	15 11 60	Maltby	Apprentice	Rotherham U	—	—
					Gainsborough T	Sheffield U	—	—
						Wimbledon	175	50
						WBA	14	1
						Plymouth Arg	45	10
						Rotherham U	65	14
						Torquay U (loan)	15	5
						Crewe Alex	83	12

CREWE ALEXANDRA

Colours: Red shirts, white shorts, red stockings. **Change colours:** Blue shirts, white shorts, blue stockings.

Foundation: Crewe Alexandra played cricket and probably rugby before they decided to form a football club in 1877. Whether they took the name "Alexandra" from a pub where they held their meetings, or whether it was after Princess Alexandra, is a matter of conjecture. Crewe's first trophy was the Crewe and District Cup in 1887 and it is worth noting that they reached the semi-finals of the FA Cup the following year.

First Football League game: 3 September, 1892, Division 2, v Burton Swifts (a) L 1-7 – Hickton; Moore, Cope; Linnell, Johnson, Osborne; Bennett, Pearson (1), Bailey, Barnett, Roberts.

Did you know: When Neil Lennon was capped by Northern Ireland at the end of the 1993–94 season, he became the first honoured at full international level at the club since Fred Keenor, who won his last appearance for Wales while with Crewe against Scotland in the 1932–33 season.

Managers (and Secretary-Managers)
W. C. McNeill 1892–94*, J. G. Hall 1895–96*, 1897 R. Roberts* (1st team sec.), J. B. Bromerley 1898–1911* (continued as Hon. Sec. to 1925), Tom Bailey 1925–38, George Lillicrop 1938–44, Frank Hill 1944–48, Arthur Turner 1948–51, Harry Catterick 1951–53, Ralph Ward 1953–55, Maurice Lindley 1955–58, Harry Ware 1958–60, Jimmy McGuigan 1960–64, Ernie Tagg 1964–71 (continued as secretary to 1972), Dennis Viollet 1971, Jimmy Melia 1972–73, Ernie Tagg 1974, Harry Gregg 1975–78, Warwick Rimmer 1978–79, Tony Waddington 1979–81, Arfon Griffiths 1981–82, Peter Morris 1982–83, Dario Gradi June 1983–

Player and Position	*Ht*	*Wt*	*Birth Date*	*Birth Place*	*Source*	*Clubs*	*League App*	*League Gls*
Mark Gardiner	5 10	10 07	25 12 66	Cirencester	Apprentice	Swindon T	10	—
						Torquay U	49	4
						Crewe Alex	182	33
Steve Garvey	5 9	11 01	22 11 73	Tameside	Trainee	Crewe Alex	22	1
Tony Naylor	5 8	10 08	29 3 67	Manchester	Droylsden	Crewe Alex	122	45
Steve Walters	5 10	11 08	9 1 72	Plymouth	Trainee	Crewe Alex	135	9
Ashley Ward	6 1	11 07	24 11 70	Manchester	Trainee	Manchester C	1	—
						Wrexham (loan)	4	2
						Leicester C	10	—
						Blackpool (loan)	2	1
						Crewe Alex	45	17
Carwyn Williams*			21 10 74	Pwllheli	Trainee	Crewe Alex	—	—

Trainees
Chapman, Iain A; Corcoran, Matthew L; Ellis, Duncan J; Fraser, Stuart A; Hawtin, Dale C; Murray, Thomas O; Ouslem, Joseph A; Pope, Steven A; Simpson, Wesley L.

****Non-Contract**
Turpin, Simon A.

Associated Schoolboys
Blinston, Gareth T; Brice, Paul A; Bullock, Darren J; Burke, Andrew J; Chadwick, Gareth; Connors, Christopher J; Cox, Lee A; Critchley, Neil; Gannon, Michael J; Hill, Kevin W; Hulse, Robert W; Johnson, Seth M; Jones, Andrew J; Knight, Darren P; Longman, David P; Lunt, Kenny V; Mason, Philip; Morse, Peter R; Mottram, Paul G; Owen, Gareth J; Parker, Justin N; Richardson, Paul M; Smith, Peter L; Spearritt, Paul; Sumner, Martin D; Webster, Colin J. L; Whittaker, David A.

Associated Schoolboys who have accepted the Club's offer of a Traineeship/Contract
Bell, Christopher G; Collins, James I; Dungey, James A; Edwards, Gareth J; Hibbs, John R; Humphray, Darren J; Murray, David R; Percival, Christopher; Street, Kevin; Wolstenhulme, Michael D.
**Non-Contract Players who are retained must be re-signed before they are eligible to play in League matches.

CRYSTAL PALACE 1993–94 *Back row (left to right):* John Salako, Grant Watts, Simon Rodger, Bobby Bowry, Paul Mortimer.
Third row: Lee Sinnott, Darren Patterson, Chris Armstrong, Andy Barnes, David Whyte, George Ndah, Gareth Southgate.
Second row: David Kemp (Coach), John Humphrey, Stuart Massey, Andy Woodman, Nigel Martyn, Andy Thorn, Eric Young, Steve Harrison (Coach).
Front row: Simon Osborn, Ricky Newman, Dean Gordon, Alan Smith (Manager), Richard Shaw, Chris Coleman, Martin O'Connor.

FA Premiership **CRYSTAL PALACE**

Selhurst Park, London SE25 6PU. Telephone 081–653 1000. Lottery Office: 081–771 9502. Club Shop: 081–653 5584. Dial-A-Seat Ticketline 081–771 8841. Palace Publications: 081–771 8299. Fax: 081–653 6312. Palace clubline: 0891 400 333. Palace Ticket Line: 0891 400 334 (normal 0891 charges apply for these services).

Ground capacity: 18,300.

Record attendance: 51,482 v Burnley, Division 2, 11 May 1979.

Record receipts: £327,124 v Manchester U, FA Premier League, 21 April 1993 (League); £336,583 v Chelsea, Coca Cola Cup 5th rd, 6 January 1993.

Pitch measurements: 110yd × 74yd.

President: S. Stephenson.

Chairman: R. G. Noades.

Directors: R. G. Noades (Chairman and Managing), B. Coleman, A. S. C. De Souza, M. E. Lee, S. Hume-Kendall, P. H. J. Norman, R. E. Anderson, V. E. Murphy, C. L. Noades.

Team Manager: Alan Smith. ***Coaches:*** Steve Harrison, David Kemp and Dave Garland. ***Physio:*** Peter McClean.

Company Secretary: Doug Miller. ***Club Secretary:*** Mike Hurst. ***Assistant Secretary:*** Terry Byfield. ***Sales and Marketing Manager:*** Mike Ryan.

Year Formed: 1905. ***Turned Professional:*** 1905. ***Ltd Co.:*** 1905.

Club Nickname: 'The Eagles'.

Club Sponsor: TDK.

Commercial Manager: Graham Drew.

Previous Grounds: 1905, Crystal Palace; 1915, Herne Hill; 1918, The Nest; 1924, Selhurst Park.

Record League Victory: 9–0 v Barrow, Division 4, 10 October 1959 – Rouse; Long, Noakes; Truett, Evans, McNichol; Gavin (1), Summersby (4 incl. 1p), Sexton, Byrne (2), Colfar (2).

Record Cup Victory: 8–0 v Southend U, Rumbelows League Cup, 2nd rd (1st leg), 25 September 1990 – Martyn; Humphrey (Thompson (1)), Shaw, Pardew, Young, Thorn, McGoldrick, Thomas, Bright (3), Wright (3), Barber (Hodges (1)).

Record Defeat: 0–9 v Burnley, FA Cup, 2nd rd replay, 10 February 1909 and 0–9 v Liverpool, Division 1, 12 September 1990.

Most League Points (2 for a win): 64, Division 4, 1960–61.

Most League Points (3 for a win): 90, Division 1, 1993–94.

Most League Goals: 110, Division 4, 1960–61.

Highest League Scorer in Season: Peter Simpson, 46, Division 3 (S), 1930–31.

Most League Goals in Total Aggregate: Peter Simpson, 153, 1930–36.

Most Capped Player: Eric Young, 19 (20), Wales.

Most League Appearances: Jim Cannon, 571, 1973–88.

Record Transfer Fee Received: £2,500,000 from Arsenal for Ian Wright, September 1991.

Record Transfer Fee Paid: £1,800,000 to Sunderland for Marco Gabbiadini, September 1991.

Football League Record: 1920 Original Members of Division 3; 1921–25 Division 2; 1925–58 Division 3 (S); 1958–61 Division 4; 1961–64 Division 3; 1964–69 Division 2; 1969–73 Division 1; 1973–74 Division 2; 1974–77 Division 3; 1977–79 Division 2; 1979–81 Division 1; 1981–89 Division 2; 1989–92 Division 1; 1992–93 FA Premier League; 1993–94 Division 1; 1994– FA Premier League.

Honours: *Football League:* Division 1 best season: 3rd 1990–91; Division 2 – Champions 1978–79; Runners-up 1968–69; Division 3 – Runners-up 1963–64; Division 3 (S) – Champions 1920–21; Runners-up 1928–29, 1930–31, 1938–39; Division 4 – Runners-up 1960–61. *FA Cup:* best season: Runners-up 1989–90. *Football League Cup:* best season; semi-final 1992–93. *Zenith Data System Cup:* Winners: 1991.

CRYSTAL PALACE 1993—94 LEAGUE RECORD

Match No.	Date	Venue	Opponents	Result		H/T Score	Lg. Pos.	Goalscorers	Attendance
1	Aug 14	H	Tranmere R	D	0-0	0-0	—		14,785
2	21	A	Bristol C	L	0-2	0-0	22		12,068
3	24	H	Nottingham F	W	2-0	1-0	—	Young, Gordon	15,048
4	28	H	Portsmouth	W	5-1	2-1	6	Armstrong 3, Gordon, Southgate	14,428
5	31	A	Birmingham C	W	4-2	2-1	—	Williams, Armstrong 2, Shaw	13,856
6	Sept 12	H	Sunderland	W	1-0	1-0	—	Armstrong	11,318
7	18	A	WBA	W	4-1	0-1	1	Coleman, Whyte, Southgate, Armstrong	17,873
8	26	A	Charlton Ath	D	0-0	0-0	—		7947
9	Oct 2	H	Stoke C	W	4-1	3-0	1	Southgate, Salako 3	12,880
10	17	H	Wolverhampton W	D	1-1	1-1	—	Humphrey	13,056
11	23	A	Derby Co	L	1-3	0-2	4	Armstrong	16,586
12	30	H	Grimsby T	W	1-0	1-0	3	Southgate	12,202
13	Nov 2	H	Luton T	W	3-2	3-2	—	Young, Shaw, Whyte	10,925
14	6	A	Notts Co	L	2-3	2-1	4	Armstrong 2	6904
15	20	A	Barnsley	W	3-1	1-1	3	Armstrong, Williams 2	5384
16	24	A	Bolton W	L	0-1	0-0	—		7486
17	28	A	Watford	W	3-1	1-0	—	Williams, Southgate, Salako	7485
18	Dec 5	H	Notts Co	L	1-2	0-1	—	Osborn	12,642
19	8	A	Leicester C	D	1-1	0-1	—	Williams	16,706
20	11	H	Birmingham C	W	2-1	2-1	3	Southgate, Salako	11,295
21	19	A	Tranmere R	W	1-0	0-0	—	Williams	7011
22	27	A	Oxford U	W	3-1	1-0	1	Armstrong 2, Salako	10,356
23	29	H	Southend U	W	1-0	0-0	1	Rodger	18,255
24	Jan 1	A	Millwall	L	0-3	0-0	1		16,779
25	15	A	Wolverhampton W	L	0-2	0-1	1		23,851
26	22	H	Leicester C	W	2-1	1-1	1	Coleman, Armstrong	17,045
27	Feb 1	H	Peterborough U	W	3-2	0-1	—	Salako, Rodger, Armstrong	12,426
28	5	H	Derby Co	D	1-1	0-0	1	Gordon	15,615
29	12	A	Grimsby T	D	1-1	1-0	1	Southgate	6302
30	19	A	Nottingham F	D	1-1	0-0	1	Matthew	24,232
31	22	H	Bristol C	W	4-1	1-1	—	Gordon (pen), Salako, Armstrong 2	11,508
32	25	H	Bolton W	D	1-1	1-0	1	Southgate	17,245
33	Mar 5	A	Portsmouth	W	1-0	0-0	1	Young	13,508
34	12	H	WBA	W	1-0	1-0	1	Stewart	16,576
35	16	A	Sunderland	L	0-1	0-0	—		15,892
36	20	H	Charlton Ath	W	2-0	1-0	—	Armstrong, Stewart	14,408
37	23	H	Middlesbrough	L	0-1	0-1	—		12,811
38	26	A	Stoke C	W	2-0	0-0	1	Gordon (pen), Williams	18,071
39	29	A	Peterborough U	D	1-1	1-0	—	Rodger	8412
40	Apr 2	H	Oxford U	W	2-1	0-0	1	Armstrong, Stewart	15,510
41	6	A	Southend U	W	2-1	1-0	—	Young, Armstrong	9776
42	9	H	Millwall	W	1-0	0-0	1	Armstrong	23,142
43	16	A	Luton T	W	1-0	1-0	1	Coleman	9880
44	23	H	Barnsley	W	1-0	0-0	1	Young	20,326
45	May 1	A	Middlesbrough	W	3-2	2-2	—	Southgate, Whyte, Armstrong	8638
46	8	H	Watford	L	0-2	0-0	1		28,749

Final League Position: 1

GOALSCORERS

League (73): Armstrong 22, Southgate 9, Salako 8, Williams 7, Gordon 5 (2 pens), Young 5, Coleman 3, Rodger 3, Stewart 3, Whyte 3, Shaw 2, Humphrey 1, Matthew 1, Osborn 1.
Coca-Cola Cup (7): Southgate 3, Armstrong 1, Gordon 1, Thorn 1, Whyte 1.
FA Cup (0):

Martyn 46	Humphrey 32	Coleman 46	Southgate 46	Young 46	Thorn 10	Osborn 5 + 1	Bowry 17 + 4	Armstrong 43	Williams 21 + 3	Gordon 39 + 6	Whyte 10 + 6	Rodger 37 + 5	Shaw 30 + 4	Massey 1	Salako 34 + 4	O'Connor 2	Newman 10 + 1	Stewart 18	Ndah — + 1	Matthew 11 + 1	Dyer 2 + 9	Match No.
1	2	3	4	5	6	7	8	9	10	11	12											1
1	2	3	4	5	6		8	9	10	12	7	11	14									2
1	2	3	4	5	6		8	9	10	12		11	7									3
1	2	6	4	5			8	9	10	3		11	7									4
1	2	6	4	5			8	9	10	3		11	7									5
1	2	6	4	5				9	10	3		11	7	8								6
1	2	3	4	5	6		8	9	10	14	12	11	7									7
1	2	3	4	5	6		8		10	12	9	11	7		14							8
1	2	3	4	5	6		8		12		9	11	7		10							9
1	2	3	4	5	6		8	9		12	10	14	7		11							10
1	2	3	4	5	6			9		12	10	8	7		11							11
1	2	3	4	5	6			9		11	10	8	7									12
1	2	3	4	5	6			9		11	10	8	7		12							13
1	2	6	4	5			14	9	12	3	10	8	7		11							14
1		6	4	5		7		9	10	3		8	12		11	2						15
1		6	4	5		7		9	10	3	14	8	12		11	2						16
1		6	4	5		7		9	10	3		8	2		11							17
1		6	4	5		7	12	9	10	3	14	8	2		11							18
1		6	4	5			7	9	10	3			2		11		8					19
1		6	4	5			7	9	10	3			2		11		8					20
1		6	4	5			7	9	10	3		12	2		11		8					21
1		6	4	5			7	9	10	3		12	2		11		8					22
1		6	4	5			7	9	10	3		12	2		11		8					23
1		6	4	5		14	7	9	10	3		12	2		11		8					24
1		6	4	5				9	10	3	12	7	2		11		8					25
1		6	4	5				9		3		7	2		11		8	10				26
1		6	4	5			12	9		3		7	2		11		8	10				27
1		6	4	5			12	9		3		7	2		11		8	10	14			28
1	2	6	4	5				9		3		7			11			10		8		29
1	2	6	4	5				9		3		7			11			10		8		30
1	2	6	4	5				9		3	12		7		11			10		8		31
1	2	6	4	5				9		3		7			11			10		8		32
1	2	6	4	5				9		3		7			11			10		8		33
1	2	6	4	5				9		3		7			11			10		8	12	34
1	2	6	4	5				9		3		7			11			10		8	12	35
1	2	6	4	5			8	9		3		7			11			10			12	36
1	2	6	4	5			8	9		3		7	14		11			10			12	37
1	2	6	4	5				9	14	3		7	8		12			10			11	38
1	2	6	4	5					9	3		7	8		12			10			11	39
1	2	6	4	5				9		3		7	8		11			10			12	40
1	2	6	4	5				9	10	3		7	8		11						12	41
1	2	6	4	5				9		3		7	8		11			10		12		42
1	2	6	4	5				9		3		7			11			10		8		43
1	2	6	4	5				9		3		7			11			10		8	12	44
1	2	6	4	5				9		3	10	7			11		14			8	12	45
1	2	6	4	5				9		3	10	7			11					8	12	46

Coca-Cola Cup	Second Round	Charlton Ath (h)	3-1
		(a)	1-0
	Third Round	Everton (a)	2-2
		(h)	1-4
FA Cup	Third Round	Wolverhampton W (a)	0-1

CRYSTAL PALACE

Player and Position	Ht	Wt	Birth Date	Birth Place	Source	Clubs	League App	League Gls
Goalkeepers								
James Glass	6 1	11 10	1 8 73	Epsom	Trainee	Crystal Palace	—	—
Nigel Martyn	6 2	14 00	11 8 66	St Austell	St Blazey	Bristol R	101	—
						Crystal Palace	189	—
Andy Woodman*	6 1	12 04	11 8 71	Denmark Hill	Apprentice	Crystal Palace	—	—
Defenders								
Chris Coleman	6 2	12 10	10 6 70	Swansea	Apprentice	Swansea C	160	2
						Crystal Palace	102	12
Sean Daly*			18 11 74	Lambeth	Trainee	Crystal Palace	—	—
Dean Gordon	6 0	11 05	10 2 73	Croydon	Trainee	Crystal Palace	59	5
John Humphrey	5 10	11 03	31 1 61	Paddington	Apprentice	Wolverhampton W	149	3
						Charlton Ath	194	3
						Crystal Palace	139	2
						Reading (loan)	8	—
Darren Patterson	6 2	11 10	15 10 69	Belfast	Trainee	WBA	—	—
						Wigan Ath	97	6
						Crystal Palace	—	—
Simon Rodger	5 9	11 07	3 10 71	Shoreham	Trainee	Crystal Palace	87	5
Richard Shaw	5 9	11 08	11 9 68	Brentford	Apprentice	Crystal Palace	151	3
						Hull C (loan)	4	—
Eric Smith	6 2	12 08	20 10 75	Dublin	Trainee	Crystal Palace	—	—
Gareth Southgate	5 10	11 12	3 9 70	Watford	Trainee	Crystal Palace	110	12
Paul Sparrow	6 0	11 04	24 3 75	London	Trainee	Crystal Palace	—	—
Andy Thorn	6 0	11 05	12 11 66	Carshalton	Apprentice	Wimbledon	107	2
						Newcastle U	36	2
						Crystal Palace	128	3
Jamie Vincent	5 10	11 09	18 6 75	London	Trainee	Crystal Palace	—	—
Eric Young	6 2	13 00	25 3 60	Singapore	Slough T	Brighton	126	10
						Wimbledon	99	9
						Crystal Palace	148	15
Midfield								
Bobby Bowry	5 8	10 00	19 5 71	Croydon		Crystal Palace	32	1
Tim Clark*			30 1 75	Croydon	Trainee	Crystal Palace	—	—
Ian Cox	6 0	12 02	25 3 71	Croydon	Carshalton Ath	Crystal Palace	—	—
Mark Hawthorne‡	5 9	10 12	31 10 73	Glasgow	Trainee	Crystal Palace	—	—
Mark Holman‡	5 11	12 04	29 10 73	Croydon	Trainee	Crystal Palace	—	—
Stuart Massey*	5 10	10 10	17 11 64	Crawley	Sutton U	Crystal Palace	2	—
Damian Matthew	5 11	10 10	23 9 70	Islington, London	Trainee	Chelsea	21	—
						Luton T (loan)	5	—
						Crystal Palace	12	1
Paul Mortimer	5 11	11 03	8 5 68	London	Fulham	Charlton Ath	113	17
						Aston Villa	12	1
						Crystal Palace	22	2
						Brentford (loan)	6	—
George Ndah	6 1	10 00	23 12 74	Camberwell	Trainee	Crystal Palace	14	—
Ricky Newman	5 10	11 00	5 8 70	Guildford		Crystal Palace	13	—
						Maidstone U (loan)	10	1
Simon Osborn	5 10	11 04	19 1 72	New Addington	Apprentice	Crystal Palace	55	5
Paul Stokoe‡			19 7 75	Sidcup	Trainee	Crystal Palace	—	—
Forwards								
Chris Armstrong	6 0	11 00	19 6 71	Newcastle		Wrexham	60	13
						Millwall	28	5
						Crystal Palace	78	37
Andy Barnes*	5 11	12 06	31 3 67	Croydon	Sutton U	Crystal Palace	1	—
						Carlisle U (loan)	2	—
Bruce Dyer	5 10	11 02	13 4 75	Ilford	Trainee	Watford	31	6
						Crystal Palace	11	—
Brian Launders	5 10	11 12	8 6 76	Dublin	Trainee	Crystal Palace	—	—
John Salako	5 9	11 00	11 2 69	Nigeria.	Trainee	Crystal Palace	176	18
						Swansea C (loan)	13	3

CRYSTAL PALACE

Colours: Red and blue shirts, red shorts, red stockings. **Change colours:** Yellow shirts, sky blue shorts, white stockings.

Foundation: There was a Crystal Palace club as early as 1861 but the present organisation was born in 1905 after the formation of a club by the company that controlled the Crystal Palace (the building that is), had been rejected by the FA who did not like the idea of the Cup Final hosts running their own club. A separate company had to be formed and they had their home on the old Cup Final ground until 1915.

First Football League game: 28 August, 1920, Division 3, v Merthyr T (a) L 1-2 – Alderson; Little, Rhodes; McCracken, Jones, Feebury; Bateman, Conner, Smith, Milligan (1), Whibley.

Did you know: Crystal Palace when members of the Southern League, beat Division 2 Chelsea 7-1 in a third qualifying round tie in the FA Cup on 18 November 1905, the year of Chelsea's formation.

Managers (and Secretary-Managers)
John T. Robson 1905–07, Edmund Goodman 1907–25 (had been secretary since 1905 and afterwards continued in this position to 1933). Alec Maley 1925–27, Fred Maven 1927–30, Jack Tresadern 1930–35, Tom Bromilow 1935–36, R. S. Moyes 1936, Tom Bromilow 1936–39, George Irwin 1939–47, Jack Butler 1947–49, Ronnie Rooke 1949–50, Charlie Slade and Fred Dawes (joint managers) 1950–51, Laurie Scott 1951–54, Cyril Spiers 1954–58, George Smith 1958–60, Arthur Rowe 1960–62, Dick Graham 1962–66, Bert Head 1966–72 (continued as GM to 1973), Malcolm Allison 1973–76, Terry Venables 1976–80, Ernie Walley 1980, Malcolm Allison 1980–81, Dario Gradi 1981, Steve Kember 1981–82, Alan Mullery 1982–84, Steve Coppell 1984–93, Alan Smith June 1993–

Player and Position	*Ht*	*Wt*	*Birth Date*	*Place*	*Source*	*Clubs*	*League App*	*Gls*
Anthony Scully	5 7	11 12	12 6 76	Dublin	Trainee	Crystal Palace	—	—
Niall Thompson‡	5 11	11 00	16 4 74	Birmingham	Trainee	Crystal Palace	—	—
Grant Watts*	6 0	11 02	5 11 73	Croydon	Trainee	Crystal Palace	4	—
						Colchester U (loan)	12	2
David Whyte	5 9	10 06	20 4 71	Greenwich		Crystal Palace	27	4
						Charlton Ath (loan)	8	2
Paul Williams	5 7	10 03	16 8 65	London	Woodford T	Charlton Ath	82	23
						Brentford (loan)	7	3
						Sheffield W	93	25
						Crystal Palace	42	7

Trainees
Boxall, Daniel J; Charlton Paul; Dixon, Edward J; Fenner, Richard S; Hall, Kevin R; Harris, Jason A. S; Keadell, Mark P; Little, Glen; Mannering, Peter C; McCluskie, Mark M; Roberts, Christopher; Rourke, Marcus P; White, Craig S.

Associated Schoolboys
Barnard, Dean; Cowie, Stuart; Field, Gary; Henderson, Mark; Hibbert, James; Hoo, James A; Ivett, James G; Martin, Andrew P; Neville, Ben A. W; Pattimore, Michael R; Small-King, Shane O. P; Smith, Paul I. D; Spencer, Marcus W; Stevens, David P; Symons, Shaun P; Wastell, James.

Associated Schoolboys who have accepted the Club's offer of a Traineeship/Contract
Freeman, Andrew; Parry, David M; Sherling, William.

Bury players continued from Page 127

Player	Ht	Wt	Birth Date	Place	Source	Clubs	App	Gls
Tony Kelly	5 9	11 06	14 2 66	Meridan		Bristol C	6	1
					St Albans C	Stoke C	58	5
						Hull C (loan)	6	1
						Cardiff C (loan)	5	1
						Bury	35	7
Darren Lyons	6 1	12 00	9 11 66	Manchester	Ashton U	Bury	36	7
Gary Powell‡	5 10	10 02	2 4 69	Holylake	Trainee	Everton	—	—
						Lincoln C (loan)	11	—
						Scunthorpe U (loan)	4	1
						Wigan Ath (loan)	14	4
						Wigan Ath	70	13
						Bury	5	—
John Russell			13 8 70	Bellshill	Winsford U	Bury	—	—
Ian Stevens	5 9	12 00	21 10 66	Malta	Trainee	Preston NE	11	2
						Stockport Co	2	—
					Lancaster C	Bolton W	47	7
						Bury	110	38
Kenny Woods‡	5 10	11 07	15 4 74	Liverpool	Trainee	Everton	—	—
						Bury	2	—

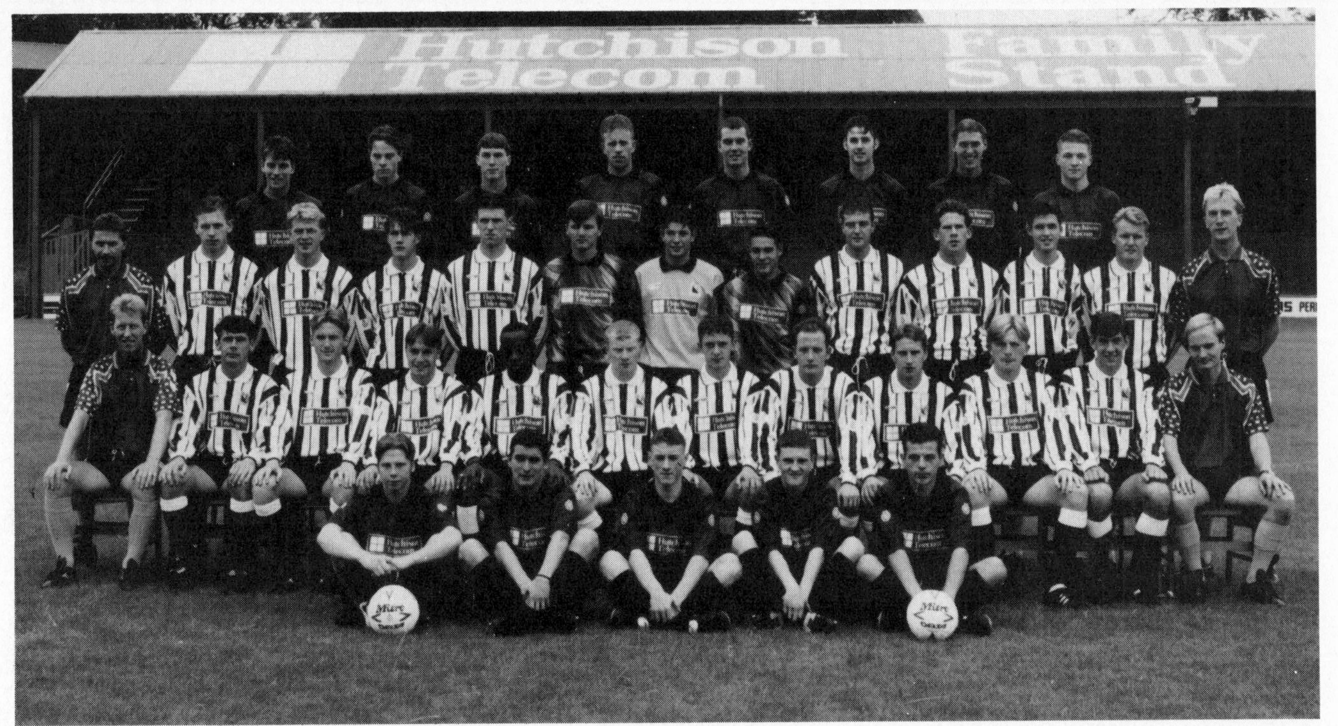

DARLINGTON 1993–94 *Back row (left to right):* Andrew Ripley, Stuart Carter, David Reed, David McGlynn, Matthew Cinnerman, Kevin Brown, Mark Casey, Neil Taylor.
Third row: Gerry Forrest (Coach), Paul Cooper, Mark Sunley, Ashley Fickling, Sean Gregan, Darren Collier, Peter May, Ryan Scott, Steve O'Shaughnessy, Stephen Gaughan, Adam Reed, Ian Juryeff, Tim Parkin (Coach).
Second row: Billy McEwan (Manager), Andy Toman, Simon Shaw, Steven Ball, Gary Chapman, George Switzer, Carl Robinson, Anthony Isaacs, Gary Himsworth, Lee Ellison, Kevin Maddick, Nigel Carnell (Physio).
Front row: James Middleton, Justin Theakston, Peter May, Michael Kew, Robert Blake.

Division 3 DARLINGTON

Feethams Ground, Darlington, DL1 5JB. Telephone Darlington (0325) 465097. Fax (0325) 381377.

Ground capacity: 4939.

Record attendance: 21,023 v Bolton W, League Cup 3rd rd, 14 November 1960.

Record receipts: £32,300 v Rochdale, Division 4, 11 May 1991.

Pitch measurements: 110yd × 74yd.

President: A. Noble.

Chairman: J. Brockbank. ***Vice-chairman:*** S. Weeks.

Directors: B. Lowery, G. Hodgson, G. Hampton, E. Bennett, R. Tonks.

Manager: Alan Murray. ***Coach*** Eddie Kyle.

Chief Executive: T. D. Hughes.

Secretary: T. D. Hughes. ***Physio:*** Nigel Carnell.

Year Formed: 1883. ***Turned Professional:*** 1908. ***Ltd Co.:*** 1891.

Club Nickname: 'The Quakers'.

Record League Victory: 9–2 v Lincoln C, Division 3 (N), 7 January 1928 – Archibald; Brooks, Mellen; Kelly, Waugh, McKinnell; Cochrane (1), Gregg (1), Ruddy (3), Lees (3), McGiffen (1).

Record Cup Victory: 7–2 v Evenwood T, FA Cup, 1st rd, 17 November 1956 – Ward; Devlin, Henderson; Bell (1p), Greener, Furphy; Forster (1), Morton (3), Tulip (2), Davis, Moran.

Record Defeat: 0–10 v Doncaster R, Division 4, 25 January 1964.

Most League Points (2 for a win): 59, Division 4, 1965–66.

Most League Points (3 for a win): 85, Division 4, 1984–85.

Most League Goals: 108, Division 3 (N), 1929–30.

Highest League Scorer in Season: David Brown, 39, Division 3 (N), 1924–25.

Most League Goals in Total Aggregate: Alan Walsh, 90, 1978–84.

Most Capped Player: None.

Most League Appearances: Ron Greener, 442, 1955–68.

Record Transfer Fee Received: £200,000 from Leicester C for Jim Willis, December 1991.

Record Transfer Fee Paid: £95,000 to Motherwell for Nick Cusack, January 1992.

Football League Record: 1921 Original Member Division 3 (N); 1925–27 Division 2; 1927–58 Division 3 (N); 1958–66 Division 4; 1966–67 Division 3; 1967–85 Division 4; 1985–87 Division 3; 1987–89 Division 4; 1989–90 GM Vauxhall Conference; 1990–91 Division 4; 1991– Division 3.

Honours: *Football League:* Division 2 best season: 15th, 1925–26; Division 3 (N) – Champions 1924–25; Runners-up 1921–22; Division 4 Champions 1990–91 – Runners-up 1965–66. *FA Cup:* best season: 3rd rd, 1910–11, 5th rd, 1957–58. *Football League Cup:* best season: 5th rd, 1967–68. GM Vauxhall Conference Champions 1989–90.

DARLINGTON 1993—94 LEAGUE RECORD

Match No.	Date	Venue	Opponents	Result	H/T Score	Lg. Pos.	Goalscorers	Attendance
1	Aug 14	H	Rochdale	D 1-1	0-0	—	Himsworth	2327
2	21	A	Lincoln C	D 1-1	1-1	14	Gaughan	2699
3	28	H	Torquay U	L 1-2	1-1	16	Ball	1738
4	31	H	Scarborough	L 0-2	0-1	—		1910
5	Sept 4	A	Chesterfield	D 1-1	1-0	20	Gaughan	2982
6	11	H	Shrewsbury T	L 0-2	0-2	21		1702
7	18	A	Crewe Alex	L 1-2	0-2	21	White	3295
8	25	H	Walsall	D 0-0	0-0	21		1613
9	Oct 2	A	Northampton T	L 0-1	0-1	22		2153
10	9	H	Chester C	L 1-2	1-1	22	Gaughan	1767
11	16	A	Gillingham	L 1-2	1-1	22	Isaacs	3063
12	23	H	Wycombe W	D 0-0	0-0	22		2057
13	30	A	Scunthorpe U	L 0-3	0-1	22		3025
14	Nov 2	H	Colchester U	W 7-3	3-1	—	Ellison 2, Painter 2, Chapman 2, Himsworth	1299
15	6	A	Preston NE	L 2-3	0-1	22	Gregan, Painter	6711
16	20	H	Mansfield T	W 2-0	1-0	21	Pearson, Chapman	2043
17	27	A	Bury	L 1-5	0-3	21	Appleby	2052
18	Dec 11	H	Lincoln C	W 3-2	2-1	21	Himsworth, Painter 2	1936
19	18	A	Rochdale	D 0-0	0-0	21		2205
20	27	H	Carlisle U	L 1-3	1-3	21	Cross	4800
21	28	A	Doncaster R	W 3-1	1-0	19	Chapman, Ellison, Painter	2194
22	Jan 3	A	Scarborough	L 0-3	0-1	20		1793
23	8	A	Hereford U	D 1-1	0-0	20	Chapman	1710
24	15	H	Gillingham	W 2-1	0-0	19	Painter, Ellison	2111
25	22	A	Chester C	D 0-0	0-0	19		2777
26	25	H	Wigan Ath	D 0-0	0-0	—		1837
27	29	H	Scunthorpe U	W 2-1	1-0	19	Pearson, Painter	2142
28	Feb 12	H	Hereford U	L 1-3	1-2	20	Pearson	2111
29	19	A	Torquay U	L 1-2	1-0	20	Painter	3039
30	Mar 5	A	Shrewsbury T	D 1-1	1-0	21	Pearson	4011
31	8	H	Chesterfield	D 0-0	0-0	—		2655
32	12	H	Crewe Alex	W 1-0	1-0	21	Painter (pen)	2373
33	19	A	Walsall	L 0-3	0-2	21		2983
34	26	H	Northampton T	L 0-1	0-1	22		2700
35	29	A	Wycombe W	L 0-2	0-0	—		4491
36	Apr 2	A	Carlisle U	L 0-2	0-0	22		4088
37	4	H	Doncaster R	L 1-3	1-0	22	Slaven	1978
38	9	A	Wigan Ath	L 0-2	0-0	22		1709
39	16	A	Colchester U	W 2-1	1-1	22	Shaw, Chapman	2332
40	23	H	Preston NE	L 0-2	0-1	22		2739
41	30	A	Mansfield T	W 3-0	1-0	22	Painter, Chapman, Cross	2734
42	May 7	H	Bury	W 1-0	1-0	21	Slaven	3039

Final League Position: 21

GOALSCORERS

League (42): Painter 11 (1 pen), Chapman 7, Ellison 4, Pearson 4, Gaughan 3, Himsworth 3, Cross 2, Slaven 2, Appleby 1, Ball 1, Gregan 1, Isaacs 1, Shaw 1, White 1.
Coca-Cola Cup (1): Juryeff 1.
FA Cup (2): Ellison 1, Painter 1.

Collier 42	Gaughan 32	Switzer 12 + 2	Isaacs 16 + 4	Sunley 17 + 1	O'Shaughnessy 32	Shaw 18 + 12	Himsworth 28	Chapman 38 + 3	Juryeff 1	Ball 15 + 5	Ellison 18 + 11	Gregan 21 + 2	White 4	Pearson 26 + 2	Cooper 1	Maddick 1 + 1	Reed 11 + 2	Madden 5	Fickling 1	McNab 4	Painter 35 + 1	Joyce 4	Ripley — + 2	Case 1	Kirkham 2 + 7	Cross 26	Appleby 10	Crosby 25	Scott — + 1	Kavanagh 5	Slaven 11	*Match No.*
1	2	3	4	5	6	7	8	9	10	11	12																					1
1	2	3	4		6	7	8	9		11		5	10																			2
1	11	*3*	4		6	2	8	9		7	12	5	10	14																		3
1	11	3	4		6	2	8			7		5		12	*9*	10	14															4
1	2		8		5	7	11	9		3				10			4	6														5
1	2		7		5	8		9		3	12		10	11				6	4													6
1	2		*4*		5	7	8	14		12			9	3				6		10	11											7
1	4	3		5			8	9						7				6		10	11	2										8
1	4	3		5		12	8	9				14		7				*6*		10	11	2										9
1	4	3	12	5			8	9				6		*7*						10	11	2	14									10
1	2		4	5		*7*	8	9		3	12	6		10			14				11											11
1	7		10	5		12	8	*9*		14		6		3							11	2		4								12
1		14	4	5		12	8	9		*7*	10	6		3			2				11											13
1			4	5		12	8	9		14	10	6		3			2				11				*7*							14
1			4	5			8	9		7	10	6		3			2				11				12							15
1	2		4			5	8	9		12	10	*6*		7							11				14	3						16
1			4		6	2	5	9		12	10			7							11					3	8					17
1					6	12	8	*9*		7	10			4							11				14	3	2	5				18
1					6	12	8	9		7	10			4							11					3	2	5				19
1	7				11		4	10			9			6							8				12	3	2	5				20
1	7			6	11	12	4	10			9										8					3	2	5	14			21
1	7			6	11	12	4	10			*9*										8				14	3	2	5				22
1	7				11	8	4	10			9			6							12					3	2	5				23
1	7			2	11	12	4	*10*			9			6							8		14			3		5				24
1	7				11	12	4	10			9			6							8					3	2	5				25
1	7				11		4	10			9	6				12					8					3	2	5				26
1	7		14		11	12	*4*	10			9			6							8					3	2	5				27
1		12		2	11	7	4	10			9			6							8					3		5				28
1			12	2	11		4	10			9			6			7				8					3		5				29
1					11	2		10			12	9		6							8					3		5		4	7	30
1					11	2		10			12	9		6							8					3		5		4	7	31
1	2				11			10			12	9		6							8					3		5		4	7	32
1	2		14		11			10			12	*9*		6							8					3		5		4	7	33
1	4			6	11	2		12		10											8					3		5		9	7	34
1	4		7	2	11			9		*10*	12	6									8				14	3		5				35
1	4		7	2	11			9		*10*	12	6									8				14	3		5				36
1	4				11	10		12				6					2				8				9	3		5			7	37
1	4	*3*			11	12		10		6	9	14					2				8							5			7	38
1	4	3			11	9		10									2				8					6		5			7	39
1	4	3				10		9			12	11					2				8					6		5			7	40
1	4	3			11			9				10					2				8					6		5			7	41
1	4	3		12	11			9				10					2				8					6		5			7	42

Coca-Cola Cup	First Round	Bradford C (h)	1-5
		(a)	0-6
FA Cup	First Round	Crewe Alex (a)	2-4

DARLINGTON

Player and Position	*Ht*	*Wt*	*Birth Date*	*Birth Place*	*Source*	*Clubs*	*League App*	*League Gls*
Goalkeepers								
Darren Collier	5 11	11 09	1 12 67	Stockton	Middlesbrough	Blackburn R	27	—
						Darlington	42	—
Adrian Swan†			31 7 73	Middlesbrough		Darlington	—	—
						Leicester C (loan)	—	—
Defenders								
Steve Ball*	5 6	10 10	22 11 73	Leeds	Leeds U	Darlington	42	3
Andy Crosby	6 2	13 00	3 3 73	Rotherham	Leeds U	Doncaster R	51	—
						Darlington	25	—
Alan Dowson‡	5 10	11 02	17 6 70	Gateshead	Trainee	Millwall	1	—
						Fulham (loan)	4	—
						Bradford C	18	—
						Darlington	32	—
Sean Gregan	6 2	13 7	29 3 74	Cleveland	Trainee	Darlington	57	2
Steve O'Shaughnessy	6 2	13 01	13 10 67	Wrexham		Leeds U	—	—
						Bradford C	1	—
						Rochdale	109	16
						Exeter C	3	—
						Darlington	88	2
Adam Reed	6 0	12 00	18 2 75	Bishop Auckland	Trainee	Darlington	14	—
Ryan Scott§			20 3 76	Saltburn	Trainee	Darlington	1	—
Mark Sunley*	6 1	12 07	13 10 71	Stockton		Middlesbrough	—	—
						Darlington	35	—
George Switzer*	5 6	9 10	13 10 73	Salford	Trainee	Manchester U	—	—
						Darlington	14	—
Midfield								
Paul Cross	5 7	9 06	31 10 65	Barnsley	Apprentice	Barnsley	118	—
						Preston NE (loan)	5	—
						Hartlepool U	74	1
						Darlington	26	2
Steve Gaughan	5 11	11 02	14 4 70	Doncaster		Doncaster R	67	3
						Sunderland	—	—
						Darlington	89	4
Anthony Isaacs*	5 8	10 07	8 4 73	Middlesbrough		Darlington	51	2
Peter Kirkham	6 0	11 04	28 10 74	Newcastle	Newcastle U	Darlington	9	—
Neil McNab	5 7	11 00	4 6 57	Greenock		Morton	14	—
						Tottenham H	72	3
						Bolton W	35	4
						Brighton	103	4
						Leeds U (loan)	5	—
						Portsmouth (loan)	—	—
						Manchester C	221	16
						Tranmere R	105	6
						Huddersfield T (loan)	11	—
						Darlington	4	—
Robert Painter	5 11	11 00	26 1 71	Ince	Trainee	Chester C	84	8
						Maidstone U	30	5
						Burnley	26	2
						Darlington	36	11
Andrew Ripley	5 8	11 10	10 12 75	Middlesbrough	Trainee	Darlington	2	—
Simon Shaw	6 0	12 00	21 9 73	Teeside	Trainee	Darlington	54	5
Forwards								
Gary Chapman	5 8	11 07	1 5 64	Bradford	Local	Bradford C	5	—
						Notts Co	25	4
						Mansfield T (loan)	6	—
						Exeter C	24	5
						Torquay U	8	—
						Darlington	41	7
Paul Cooper‡			24 12 75	Darlington	Trainee	Darlington	1	—
Mark Dobie	5 11	11 07	8 11 63	Carlisle	Gretna	Cambridge U	—	—
						Torquay U	20	2
						Darlington	36	8

DARLINGTON

Colours: Black and white. **Change colours:** All red.

Foundation: A football club was formed in Darlington as early as 1861 but the present club began in 1883 and reached the final of the Durham Senior Cup in their first season, losing to Sunderland in a replay after complaining that they had suffered from intimidation in the first. The following season Darlington won this trophy and for many years were one of the leading amateur clubs in their area.

First Football League game: 27 August, 1921, Division 3(N), v Halifax T (h) W 2-0 – Ward; Greaves, Barbour; Dickson (1), Sutcliffe, Malcolm; Dolphin, Hooper (1), Edmunds, Wolstenholme, Winship.

Did you know: On 2 November 1993 Darlington beat Colchester United 7-3. It was their first League win of the season. It was reported that Darlington had had 12 shots on target during the game compared with six by Colchester.

Managers (and Secretary-Managers)
Tom McIntosh 1902–11, W. L. Lane 1911–12*, Dick Jackson 1912–19, Jack English 1919–28, Jack Fairless 1928–33, George Collins 1933–36, George Brown 1936–38, Jackie Carr 1938–42, Jack Surtees 1942, Jack English 1945–46, Bill Forrest 1946–50, George Irwin 1950–52, Bob Gurney 1952–57, Dick Duckworth 1957–60, Eddie Carr 1960–64, Lol Morgan 1964–66, Jimmy Greenhalgh 1966–68, Ray Yeoman 1968–70, Len Richley 1970–71, Frank Brennan 1971, Ken Hale 1971–72, Allan Jones 1972, Ralph Brand 1972–73, Dick Conner 1973–74, Billy Horner 1974–76, Peter Madden 1976–78, Len Walker 1978–79, Billy Elliott 1979–83, Cyril Knowles 1983–87, Dave Booth 1987–89, Brian Little 1989–91, Frank Gray 1991–92, Ray Hankin 1992, Billy McEwan 1992–93, Alan Murray October 1993–

Player and Position	*Ht*	*Wt*	*Birth Date*	*Place*	*Source*	*Clubs*	*League App*	*Gls*
Tony Ellison*	6 0	12 00	13 1 73	Bishop Auckland	Trainee	Darlington	72	17
						Hartlepool U (loan)	4	1
Gary Himsworth	5 7	9 08	19 12 69	Appleton	Trainee	York C	88	8
						Scarborough	92	6
						Darlington	28	3
Kevin Maddick*	6 0	12 04	18 9 74	Durham	Trainee	Darlington	3	—
Bernie Slaven	5 11	12 00	13 11 60	Paisley		Morton	22	1
						Airdrie	2	—
						Queen of the South	2	—
						Albion R	42	27
						Middlesbrough	307	118
						Port Vale	33	9
						Darlington	11	2

Trainees
Blake, Robert J; Carter, Stuart; Casey, Mark; Cimmermann, Mathew J; May, Peter G; McGlynn, David; Middleton, James; Pugh, Michael S; Scott, Ryan; Taylor, Neil V; Theakston, Justin; Trees, Steven R.

Associated Schoolboys
Dann, Steven W; Darke,Peter; Gibbon, Adam C; Goodwin, Marc T; Robinson, Benjamin M; Roxby, John P; Tarrant, Neil K.

Associated Schoolboys who have accepted the Club's offer of a Traineeship/Contract
Elliott, Stuart M; Key, Daniel C.

DERBY COUNTY 1993–94 *Back row (left to right):* Billy McEwan (Coach), Lee Carsley, Paul Williams, Mark Stallard, Shane Nicholson, Richard Goulooze, Martin Taylor, Craig Short, Steve Sutton, Michael Forsyth, John Harkes, Darren Wassall, Gary Charles, Alan Durban (Chief Scout), Gordon Guthrie (Physio).
Front row: Martyn Chalk, Dean Sturridge, Paul Simpson, Craig Ramage, Tommy Johnson, Paul Kitson, Roy McFarland (Team Manager), Marco Gabbiadini, Martin Kuhl, Steve Hayward, Jason Kavanagh, Mark Pembridge, Mel Sage.

Division 1 **DERBY COUNTY**

Baseball Ground, Shaftesbury Crescent, Derby DE3 8NB. Telephone Derby (0332) 340105. Fax 0332 293514. Ramtique Sports Shop: (0332) 292081. Clubcall: 0891 121187.

Ground capacity: 19,500 (15,000 seated).

Record attendance: 41,826 v Tottenham H, Division 1, 20 September 1969.

Record receipts: £146,651 v Aston Villa, FA Cup 4th rd, 5 February 1992.

Pitch measurements: 110yd × 71yd.

President:

Chairman: B. E. Fearn. ***Vice-chairman:*** L. V. Pickering.

Directors: C. W. McKerrow, W. Hart, J. N. Kirkland, M. Mills, M. Horton.

Manager: Roy McFarland. ***Chief Scout:*** Alan Durban.

Coach: Billy McEwan. ***Physio:*** Gordon Guthrie.

General Manager/Secretary: Michael Dunford. ***Commercial Manager:*** Colin Tunnicliffe.

Year Formed: 1884. ***Turned Professional:*** 1884. ***Ltd Co.:*** 1896.

Club Nickname: 'The Rams'.

Previous Grounds: 1884–95, Racecourse Ground; 1895, Baseball Ground.

Record League Victory: 9–0 v Wolverhampton W, Division 1, 10 January 1891 – Bunyan; Archie Goodall, Roberts; Walker, Chalmers, Roulston (1); Bakewell, McLachlan, Johnny Goodall (1), Holmes (2), McMillan (5). 9–0 v Sheffield W, Division 1, 21 January 1899 – Fryer; Methven, Staley; Cox, Archie Goodall, May; Oakden (1), Bloomer (6), Boag, McDonald (1), Allen. (1 og).

Record Cup Victory: 12–0 v Finn Harps, UEFA Cup, 1st rd 1st leg, 15 September 1976 – Moseley; Thomas, Nish, Rioch (1), McFarland, Todd (King), Macken, Gemmill, Hector (5), George (3), James (3).

Record Defeat: 2–11 v Everton, FA Cup 1st rd, 1889–90.

Most League Points (2 for a win): 63, Division 2, 1968–69 and Division 3 (N), 1955–56 and 1956–57.

Most League Points (3 for a win): 84, Division 3, 1985–86 and Division 3, 1986–87.

Most League Goals: 111, Division 3 (N), 1956–57.

Highest League Scorer in Season: Jack Bowers, 37, Division 1, 1930–31 and Ray Straw, 37 Division 3 (N), 1956–57.

Most League Goals in Total Aggregate: Steve Bloomer, 292, 1892–1906 and 1910–14.

Most Capped Player: Peter Shilton, 34 (125), England.

Most League Appearances: Kevin Hector, 486, 1966–78 and 1980–82.

Record Transfer Fee Received: £2,900,000 from Liverpool for Dean Saunders, July 1991.

Record Transfer Fee Paid: £2,500,000 to Notts Co for Craig Short, September 1992.

Football League Record: 1888 Founder Member of the Football League; 1907–12 Division 2; 1912–14 Division 1; 1914–15 Division 2; 1915–21 Division 1; 1921–26 Division 2; 1926–53 Division 1; 1953–55 Division 2; 1955–57 Division 3 (N); 1957–69 Division 2; 1969–80 Division 1; 1980–84 Division 2; 1984–86 Division 3; 1986–87 Division 2; 1987–91 Division 1; 1991–92 Division 2; 1992– Division 1.

Honours: *Football League:* Division 1 – Champions 1971–72, 1974–75; Runners-up 1895–96, 1929–30, 1935–36; Division 2 – Champions 1911–12, 1914–15, 1968–69, 1986–87; Runners-up 1925–26; Division 3 (N) Champions 1956–57; Runners-up 1955–56. *FA Cup:* Winners 1945–46; Runners-up 1897–98, 1898–99, 1902–03. *Football League Cup:* Semi-final 1967–68. *Texaco Cup:* 1971–72. **European Competitions:** *European Cup:* 1972–73, 1975–76; *UEFA Cup:* 1974–75, 1976–77. *Anglo-Italian Cup:* Runners-up 1992–93.

DERBY COUNTY 1993—94 LEAGUE RECORD

Match No.	Date	Venue	Opponents	Result		H/T Score	Lg. Pos.	Goalscorers	Attendance
1	Aug 14	H	Sunderland	W	5-0	3-0	—	Pembridge 2 (1 pen), Gabbiadini, Kitson, Short	18,027
2	18	A	Nottingham F	D	1-1	0-0	—	Forsyth	26,682
3	21	A	Middlesbrough	L	0-3	0-2	4		15,168
4	28	H	Bristol C	W	1-0	0-0	7	Gabbiadini	15,643
5	Sept 4	A	Birmingham C	L	0-3	0-3	9		14,582
6	11	H	Peterborough U	W	2-0	0-0	6	Gabbiadini, Johnson	14,779
7	18	A	Millwall	D	0-0	0-0	9		9881
8	25	A	Notts Co	L	1-4	0-3	11	Gabbiadini	11,005
9	Oct 3	H	WBA	W	5-3	0-0	—	Kitson, Simpson 2, Pembridge (pen), Short	13,370
10	9	H	Luton T	W	2-1	1-0	6	Kitson, Johnson	15,885
11	16	A	Portsmouth	L	2-3	1-1	7	Johnson, Kitson	12,404
12	23	H	Crystal Palace	W	3-1	2-0	6	Harkes, Kitson, Pembridge	16,586
13	30	A	Bolton W	W	2-0	0-0	6	Pembridge, Simpson	11,464
14	Nov 2	A	Charlton Ath	W	2-1	1-1	—	Simpson, Pembridge	8123
15	7	H	Wolverhampton W	L	0-4	0-1	—		14,310
16	13	A	Oxford U	L	0-2	0-1	6		7151
17	20	H	Grimsby T	W	2-1	2-1	5	Short, Pembridge (pen)	13,498
18	27	H	Southend U	L	1-3	1-1	7	Simpson	14,458
19	Dec 5	A	Wolverhampton W	D	2-2	1-1	—	Gabbiadini 2	16,900
20	18	A	Sunderland	L	0-1	0-1	10		16,001
21	27	A	Barnsley	W	1-0	1-0	11	Kitson	11,565
22	28	H	Leicester C	W	3-2	2-0	9	Pembridge, Gabbiadini, Johnson	17,372
23	Jan 1	A	Stoke C	L	1-2	1-1	10	Gabbiadini	20,307
24	3	H	Tranmere R	W	4-0	3-0	9	Gabbiadini 3, Williams	16,874
25	15	H	Portsmouth	W	1-0	0-0	6	Johnson	15,645
26	22	A	Luton T	L	1-2	0-1	7	Forsyth	9371
27	29	H	Watford	L	1-2	1-0	7	Kitson	15,308
28	Feb 5	A	Crystal Palace	D	1-1	0-0	7	Charles	15,615
29	12	H	Bolton W	W	2-0	1-0	7	Pembridge, Gabbiadini	16,698
30	19	A	Watford	W	4-3	1-2	5	Watson (og), Kitson, Johnson, Gabbiadini	8277
31	22	H	Middlesbrough	L	0-1	0-1	—		14,716
32	25	H	Birmingham C	D	1-1	0-0	4	Johnson	16,624
33	Mar 5	A	Bristol C	D	0-0	0-0	5		8723
34	12	H	Millwall	D	0-0	0-0	6		15,303
35	16	A	Peterborough U	D	2-2	0-1	—	Johnson, Nicholson	7371
36	26	A	WBA	W	2-1	1-0	5	Johnson, Simpson	17,437
37	29	A	Tranmere R	L	0-4	0-2	—		7114
38	Apr 2	H	Barnsley	W	2-0	1-0	5	Johnson, Harkes	14,968
39	5	A	Leicester C	D	3-3	3-3	—	Kitson 2, Willis (og)	20,050
40	9	H	Stoke C	W	4-2	2-0	6	Simpson, Cranson (og), Pembridge, Kitson	16,593
41	16	H	Charlton Ath	W	2-0	0-0	4	Johnson, Kitson	15,784
42	20	H	Notts Co	D	1-1	0-0	—	Dijkstra (og)	18,602
43	23	A	Grimsby T	D	1-1	0-0	4	Kitson	7451
44	27	H	Nottingham F	L	0-2	0-1	—		19,300
45	30	H	Oxford U	W	2-1	0-0	5	Pembridge (pen), Johnson	16,206
46	May 8	A	Southend U	L	3-4	2-4	6	Simpson 2, Johnson	8119

Final League Position: 6

GOALSCORERS

League (73): Gabbiadini 13, Johnson 13, Kitson 13, Pembridge 11 (4 pens), Simpson 9, Short 3, Forsyth 2, Harkes 2, Charles 1, Williams 1, Nicholson 1, own goals 4.
Coca-Cola Cup (5): Gabbiadini 2, Johnson 1, Kitson 1, Simpson 1.
FA Cup (1): Johnson 1.

Taylor 46	Charles 43	Forsyth 27 + 1	Kuhl 27	Short 43	Wassall 25	Simpson 27 + 7	Williams 30 + 4	Kitson 41	Gabbiadini 33 + 6	Pembridge 39 + 2	Harkes 31 + 2	Ramage 3 + 2	Johnson 31 + 6	Kavanagh 9 + 10	Coleman 2	Hayward 2 + 3	Nicholson 22	Ratcliffe 6	Cowans 19	Match No.
1	2	3	4	5	6	7	8	9	10	11										1
1	2	3	4	5	6		8	9	10	11	7									2
1	2	3	4	5	6			*9*	10	11	7	8	12	14						3
1	2	3	4	5	6		8	9	10	11	7									4
1	2	3	4	5		11	8	9	10		7				6					5
1	2	3	4	5	6	11	8	9	10				7							6
1	2	3	4	5	6	7	8	9	10	11										7
1	2	3	4	5	6	7	8	9	10	11			12							8
1	2	3	4	5	6	7	*8*	9	10	11	14		12							9
1		3		5	6	11		9	10	4	7		8	2						10
1	2	3		5	6	11		9	*10*	4	7		8	12		14				11
1		3	4	5	6	11		9		10	7		8	2						12
1	8	3	4	5	6	11	12	9		10	7			2						13
1	8	3	4	5	6	11		9		10	7			2						14
1	2	3	4	5		11	12	9		10	7		8	6						15
1	2	3		5		11	10	9			7		8	12	*6*	14	4			16
1	2	3		5	6	11	12	9	10	4	7		8							17
1	2	3		5	6	11		9	10	4	7		8							18
1	2	3	4	5	6	11		9	10	8	7									19
1	2	3	4	5	6	11	14	9	10	*8*	7		12							20
1	2	3	4	5	6		11	9	*10*	8	7	14	12							21
1	2	3	4	5	6		11		10	8	7	12	9							22
1	2	3	4	5	6	12	11		10		7	*8*	9	14						23
1	2	3	4	5	6	12	11		10	8	7		9							24
1	2	3	4	5	6		11	9	10	8			7							25
1	2	3	4		6	12		9	10	8			7	14			5	*11*		26
1	2	*3*	4		6	12		9	10	8		11	7	14			5			27
1	2		4				3		10	8			9	6			5	11	7	28
1	2		*4*	5		12	6	9	10	8			11	14			3		7	29
1	2			5		12	6	9	10	8			11			4	3		7	30
1	2		4	5		12	6	9	10	8			11				3		7	31
1	2		4	5			6	9	10	8			11				3		7	32
1	2		4	5			6	9	10	8			12				3	11	7	33
1	2			5				9	10	8	12		11	4			3	6	7	34
1	2			5				9	10		8		11	4			3	6	7	35
1	2			5		11	6	9	10	12	4		8				3		7	36
1	2			5		11	6	9	10	12	4		8				3		7	37
1	2			5		11	6	9		10	4		8				3		7	38
1	2			5			6	9	12	10	4		8				3	11	7	39
1	2			5		11	6	9		10	4		8				3		7	40
1	2			5		11	6	9	12	10	4		8				3		7	41
1	2			5		11	6	9	12	10	4		8				3		7	42
1	2			5		11	6	9	12	10	4		8	14			*3*		7	43
1	2			5		11	6	9	8	10	4			12		14	*3*		7	44
1	2			5		11	6	*9*	14	10	4		8	12			3		7	45
1		12		5	6	11			14	10	4		8	2		9	3		*7*	46

Coca-Cola Cup	Second Round	Exeter C (a)	3-1
		(h)	2-0
	Third Round	Tottenham H (h)	0-1
FA Cup	Third Round	Oldham Ath (a)	1-2

DERBY COUNTY

Player and Position	Ht	Wt	Birth Date	Birth Place	Source	Clubs	League App	League Gls
Goalkeepers								
Steve Sutton	6 1	13 07	16 4 61	Hartington	Apprentice	Nottingham F	199	—
						Mansfield T (loan)	8	—
						Derby Co (loan)	14	—
						Coventry C (loan)	1	—
						Luton T (loan)	14	—
						Derby Co	35	—
Martin Taylor	5 11	12 04	9 12 66	Tamworth	Mile Oak R	Derby Co	82	—
						Carlisle U (loan)	10	—
						Scunthorpe U (loan)	8	—
Defenders								
Lee Carsley	5 10	11 11	28 2 74	Birmingham	Trainee	Derby Co	—	—
Gary Charles	5 9	10 13	13 4 70	London		Nottingham F	56	1
						Leicester C (loan)	8	—
						Derby Co	43	1
Mike Forsyth	5 11	12 02	20 3 66	Liverpool	Apprentice	WBA	29	—
						Northampton T (loan)	—	—
						Derby Co	303	8
Richard Goulooze	5 11	13 06	16 11 67	Holland	SC Heerenveen	Derby Co	12	—
Shane Nicholson	5 10	11 00	3 6 70	Newark	Trainee	Lincoln C	133	6
						Derby Co	39	1
Justin Phillips*	6 3	14 07	17 12 71	Derby	Trainee	Derby Co	3	—
Kevin Ratcliffe†	5 11	12 07	12 11 60	Mancot	Apprentice	Everton	359	2
						Dundee	4	—
						Everton	—	—
						Cardiff C	25	1
						Nottingham F	—	—
						Derby Co	6	—
Steve Round	5 10	11 00	9 11 70	Buxton	Trainee	Derby Co	9	—
Mel Sage*	5 8	10 04	24 3 64	Gillingham	Apprentice	Gillingham	132	5
						Derby Co	140	4
Craig Short	6 2	12 03	25 6 68	Bridlington	Pickering T	Scarborough	63	7
						Notts Co	128	6
						Derby Co	81	6
Wayne Sutton			1 10 75	Derby	Trainee	Derby Co	—	—
Andrew Tretton			9 10 76	Derby	Trainee	Derby Co	—	—
Darren Wassall	5 11	11 09	27 6 68	Edgbaston		Nottingham F	27	—
						Hereford U (loan)	5	—
						Bury (loan)	7	1
						Derby Co	49	—
Midfield								
Kevin Cooper	5 6	9 10	8 2 75	Derby	Trainee	Derby Co	—	—
Gordon Cowans	5 7	9 8	27 10 58	Durham	Apprentice	Aston Villa	286	42
						Bari	94	3
						Aston Villa	117	7
						Blackburn R	50	2
						Aston Villa	11	—
						Derby Co	19	—
John Harkes	5 10	11 10	8 3 67	New Jersey	USSF	Sheffield W	81	7
						Derby Co	33	2
Steve Hayward	5 10	11 07	8 9 71	Walsall	Trainee	Derby Co	23	1
Jason Kavanagh	5 9	11 00	23 11 71	Birmingham	Birmingham C	Derby Co	65	—
Martin Kuhl	5 11	11 13	10 1 65	Frimley	Apprentice	Birmingham C	111	5
						Sheffield U	38	4
						Watford	4	—
						Portsmouth	157	27
						Derby Co	59	1
Mark Pembridge	5 7	11 01	29 11 70	Methyr Tydfil	Trainee	Luton T	60	6
						Derby Co	83	19
Stephen Powell			14 12 76	Derby	Trainee	Derby Co	—	—
Paul Williams	5 11	12 00	26 3 71	Burton	Trainee	Derby Co	123	23
						Lincoln C (loan)	3	—

DERBY COUNTY

Colours: White shirts with black sleeves, black shorts, white stockings. **Change colours:** Black cyan and white striped shirts, cyan shorts, black stockings.

Foundation: Derby County was formed by members of the Derbyshire County Cricket Club in 1884, when football was booming in the area and the cricketers thought that a football club would help boost finances for the summer game. To begin with, they sported the cricket club's colours of amber, chocolate and pale blue, and went into the game at the top immediately entering the FA Cup.

First Football League game: 8 September, 1888, Football League, v Bolton W (a) W 6-3 – Marshall; Latham, Ferguson, Williamson; Monks, W. Roulstone; Bakewell (2), Cooper (2), Higgins, H. Plackett, L. Plackett (2).

Did you know: When Derby County beat Sunderland 5-0 in a Division 1 match on 14 August 1993, it was their best win on the opening day of the season for 79 years.

Managers (and Secretary-Managers)
Harry Newbould 1896–1906, Jimmy Methven 1906–22, Cecil Potter 1922–25, George Jobey 1925–41, Ted Magner 1944–46, Stuart McMillan 1946–53, Jack Barker 1953–55, Harry Storer 1955–62, Tim Ward 1962–67, Brian Clough 1967–73, Dave Mackay 1973–76, Colin Murphy 1977, Tommy Docherty 1977–79, Colin Addison 1979–82, Johnny Newman 1982, Peter Taylor 1982–84, Roy McFarland 1984, Arthur Cox 1984–93, Roy McFarland October 1993–

Player and Position	*Ht*	*Wt*	*Birth Date*	*Birth Place*	*Source*	*Clubs*	*League App*	*League Gls*
Forwards								
Martyn Chalk	5 6	10 00	30 8 69	Louth	Louth U	Derby Co	7	1
Marco Gabbiadini	5 10	12 04	20 1 68	Nottingham	Apprentice	York C	60	14
						Sunderland	157	74
						Crystal Palace	15	5
						Derby Co	103	28
Tommy Johnson	5 10	11 02	15 1 71	Newcastle	Trainee	Notts Co	118	47
						Derby Co	84	23
Paul Kitson	5 11	10 12	9 1 71	Co Durham	Trainee	Leicester C	50	6
						Derby Co	97	34
Paul Simpson	5 7	11 04	26 7 66	Carlisle	Apprentice	Manchester C	121	18
						Oxford U	144	43
						Derby Co	85	28
Mark Stallard	6 0	12 06	24 10 74	Derby	Trainee	Derby Co	8	—
Dean Sturridge	5 7	10 10	26 7 73	Birmingham	Trainee	Derby Co	11	—

Trainees
Ashbee, Ian; Cunningham, Carl M; Davies, William; Franklin, Nicholas; Green, Matthew R; Henson, Christopher P; Johnson, Brian A; Matthews, Martin; McAra, Ian; McGann, Thomas G; (h) McKeever, Nigel R; Smith, Craig; Ward, Michael J; Warren, Matthew T. J; Wrack, Darren; Wright, Nicholas J.

****Non-Contract**
Quy, Andrew J.

Associated Schoolboys
Barnett, Chris; Boyes, Iain; Dutton, Stuart; Gittus, Mark G; Green, Steven A; Hofford, Mark F. M; McHugh, Edward T; McHugh, Philip; Price, Jonathan; Rowntree, Martyn E; White, Robert; Wright, Andrew; Wright, Matthew R; Yates, Tom W.

Associated Schoolboys who have accepted the Club's offer of a Traineeship/Contract
Brown, Duane C; Clarke, Bret; Connolly, Stuart T; Kozluk, Robert; Lyons, Patrick M; Marshall, Andrew J; Murphy, Shaun P; Owen, Steve.

**Non-Contract Players who are retained must be re-signed before they are eligible to play in League matches.

DONCASTER ROVERS 1993–94 *Back row (left to right):* Andy Beasley, Chris Swailes, Kevin Hulme, Danny Williamson, Graeme Jones, Stuart Ford.
Centre row: Phil McLaughlin (Physio), Paul Williams, Lee Turnbull, Mark Yates, David Roche, Russ Wilcox, Steve Harper, Dr C. Head, Jim Golze (Youth Coach).
Front row: Ian Measham, Lee Thew, Charles Dunn (Director), Steve Beaglehole, Paul Whitmarsh, Clive Freeman.
(Photograph: Paul Gilligan)

Division 3 DONCASTER ROVERS

Belle Vue Ground, Doncaster, DN4 5HT. Telephone Doncaster (0302) 539441. Fax (0302) 539679.

Ground capacity: 7794.

Record attendance: 37,149 v Hull C, Division 3 (N), 2 October 1948.

Record receipts: £22,000 v QPR, FA Cup 3rd rd, 5 January 1985.

Pitch measurements: 110yd × 76yd.

Chairman: J. J. Burke. ***Vice-chairman:*** K. Chappell.

Directors: R. Kennan, C. Dunn, K. Haron, L. Mabbett, J. A. Richardson, T. Sedgewick.

Manager: Sammy Chung. ***Coach:*** John Bird.

Secretary: Mrs K. J. Oldale. ***Physio:*** Phil McLoughlin. ***Youth Team Coach:*** Jim Golze. ***Commercial Executive:*** Terry Burdass. ***Commercial Manager:*** Gary Godden.

Year Formed: 1879. ***Turned Professional:*** 1885. ***Ltd Co.:*** 1905 and 1920.

Club Nickname: 'Rovers'.

Previous Grounds: 1880–1916, Intake Ground; 1920–22, Benetthorpe Ground; 1922, Low Pasture, Belle Vue.

Record League Victory: 10–0 v Darlington, Division 4, 25 January 1964 – Potter; Raine, Meadows; Windross (1), White, Ripley (2); Robinson, Book (2), Hale (4), Jeffrey, Broadbent (1).

Record Cup Victory: 7–0 v Blyth Spartans, FA Cup, 1st rd, 27 November 1937 – Imrie; Shaw, Rodgers; McFarlane, Bycroft, Cyril Smith; Burton (1), Kilourhy (4), Morgan (2), Malam, Dutton.

Record Defeat: 0–12 v Small Heath, Division 2, 11 April 1903.

Most League Points (2 for a win): 72, Division 3 (N), 1946–47.

Most League Points (3 for a win): 85, Division 4, 1983–84.

Most League Goals: 123, Division 3 (N), 1946–47.

Highest League Scorer in Season: Clarrie Jordan, 42, Division 3 (N), 1946–47.

Most League Goals in Total Aggregate: Tom Keetley, 180, 1923–29.

Most Capped Player: Len Graham, 14, Northern Ireland.

Most League Appearances: Fred Emery, 417, 1925–36.

Record Transfer Fee Received: £250,000 from QPR for Rufus Brevett, February 1991.

Record Transfer Fee Paid: £60,000 to Stirling Albion for John Philliben, March 1984.

Football League Record: 1901 Elected to Division 2; 1903 Failed re-election; 1904 Re-elected; 1905 Failed re-election; 1923 Re-elected to Division 3 (N); 1935–37 Division 2; 1937–47 Division 3 (N); 1947–48 Division 2; 1948–50 Division 3 (N); 1950–58 Division 2; 1958–59 Division 3; 1959–66 Division 4; 1966–67 Division 3; 1967–69 Division 4; 1969–71 Division 3; 1971–81 Division 4; 1981–83 Division 3; 1983–84 Division 4; 1984–88 Division 3; 1988– 92 Division 4; 1992– Division 3.

Honours: *Football League:* Division 2 best season: 7th, 1901–02; Division 3 (N) Champions 1934–35, 1946–47, 1949–50; Runners-up 1937–38, 1938–39; Division 4 – Champions 1965–66, 1968–69; Runners-up 1983–84. Promoted 1980–81 (3rd). *FA Cup:* best season: 5th rd, 1951–52, 1953–54, 1954–55, 1955–56. *Football League Cup:* best season: 5th rd, 1975–76.

DONCASTER ROVERS 1993—94 LEAGUE RECORD

Match No.	Date	Venue	Opponents	Result		H/T Score	Lg. Pos.	Goalscorers	Attendance
1	Aug 14	A	Chester C	W	1-0	0-0	—	Moss	2752
2	21	H	Carlisle U	D	0-0	0-0	7		2575
3	28	A	Walsall	W	2-1	1-0	4	Bottomley, Moss	2965
4	31	A	Gillingham	D	0-0	0-0	—		2923
5	Sept 4	H	Wigan Ath	W	3-1	1-0	3	Hulme, Jeffrey, Harper	3075
6	11	A	Preston NE	L	1-3	0-1	6	Freeman	7294
7	17	H	Mansfield T	L	0-1	0-0	—		4340
8	25	A	Wycombe W	L	0-1	0-0	11		4905
9	Oct 2	H	Rochdale	W	2-1	1-1	10	Roche, Jones	3103
10	9	A	Lincoln C	L	1-2	0-1	11	Roche	3901
11	16	H	Bury	L	1-3	1-1	14	Jones	2613
12	23	A	Shrewsbury T	W	1-0	1-0	11	Jones	2675
13	30	H	Northampton T	W	2-1	1-0	9	Freeman, Roche	2227
14	Nov 1	H	Scunthorpe U	W	3-1	1-0	—	Hulme, Williamson, Jones	4439
15	6	A	Scarborough	L	0-2	0-1	7		2057
16	20	H	Colchester U	W	2-1	0-0	6	Yates, Page	2034
17	27	A	Hereford U	L	1-2	1-2	8	Whitmarsh	1817
18	Dec 11	A	Carlisle U	L	2-4	2-1	10	Hulme, Page	4245
19	17	H	Chester C	L	3-4	1-0	—	Wilcox, Hulme, Turnbull (pen)	1914
20	28	H	Darlington	L	1-3	0-1	15	Page	2194
21	Jan 1	A	Crewe Alex	L	0-2	0-1	17		4480
22	3	H	Gillingham	D	0-0	0-0	16		1830
23	8	H	Torquay U	L	0-2	0-1	17		1685
24	15	A	Bury	L	0-4	0-3	17		2383
25	22	H	Lincoln C	W	1-0	0-0	15	Harper	2374
26	25	A	Chesterfield	D	1-1	1-0	—	Page	2606
27	29	A	Northampton T	D	0-0	0-0	16		2900
28	Feb 5	H	Shrewsbury T	D	0-0	0-0	15		2047
29	12	A	Torquay U	L	1-2	0-1	17	Hulme	3080
30	19	H	Walsall	W	4-0	2-0	16	Roche (pen), Cunningham, Hulme, Yates	2029
31	Mar 4	H	Preston NE	D	1-1	0-0	—	Hulme	3321
32	12	A	Mansfield T	L	1-2	0-1	17	Kitchen	2763
33	19	H	Wycombe W	L	0-3	0-3	18		2358
34	22	A	Wigan Ath	D	0-0	0-0	—		1438
35	26	A	Rochdale	W	1-0	0-0	17	Yates	2165
36	Apr 2	H	Chesterfield	D	0-0	0-0	18		2748
37	4	A	Darlington	W	3-1	0-1	16	Worthington, Lawrence, Hulme	1978
38	9	H	Crewe Alex	D	0-0	0-0	15		1820
39	16	A	Scunthorpe U	W	3-1	1-0	15	Worthington, Yates, Roche	4151
40	23	H	Scarborough	L	0-4	0-2	16		1854
41	30	A	Colchester U	L	1-3	1-0	17	Wilcox	2378
42	May 7	H	Hereford U	W	1-0	1-0	15	Thew	1603

Final League Position: 15

GOALSCORERS

League (44): Hulme 8, Roche 5 (1 pen), Jones 4, Page 4, Yates 4, Freeman 2, Harper 2, Moss 2, Wilcox 2, Worthington 2, Bottomley 1, Cunningham 1, Jeffrey 1, Kitchen 1, Lawrence 1, Thew 1, Turnbull 1 (pen), Whitmarsh 1, Williamson 1.
Coca-Cola Cup (3): Harper 1, Hulme 1, Wilcox 1.
FA Cup (2): Williamson 2.

Beasley 37	Hewitt 5 + 1	Freeman 23 + 2	Yates 33 + 1	Bottomley 10	Wilcox 40	Harper 25 + 6	Hulme 33 + 1	Jones 24 + 4	Moss 9	Jeffrey 8	Cunningham 19 + 6	Brentano 1	Prindiville — + 1	Measham 21	France — + 1	Roche 30	Whitmarsh 2 + 4	Turnbull 10 + 1	Williamson 10 + 3	Dunphy 1	Williams — + 1	Ford 4 + 2	Page 18 + 4	Swailes 17	Thew 6 + 5	Fowler 7 + 4	Clarke D 15 + 1	Kitchen 14	Luscombe 5 + 3	Marquis 9	Lawrence 2 + 7	Atkins 7	Limber 3 + 1	Worthington 8	Ingham 1	Clarke N 5	Match No.
1	2	3	4	5	6	7	8	9	10	11	12																									1
1		3	4	5	6	7	8	9	10	11	12	2																								2
1	2	3	4	5	6	7	8	9	10	11																										3
1	2	3	4	5	6	7	8	9	10	11	12																									4
1	2	3	4	5	6	7	8	12	10	11	9																									5
1	2	3	4	5	6	7	8	12	10	11	9		14																							6
1		3	4	5	6	7	8	12	10	11	9			2																						7
1	12	3	4	5	6	7	8	9	10	11				2	14																					8
1		3	4	5	6	7	8	9	11					2		10	12																			9
1		3	4	5	6		8	9			14			2		7	12	10	11																	10
1		3	4		5	11	8	9			12			2		7		10	14	6																11
1		3	4		5		8	9			6			2		7		10	11		12															12
1		3	4		5		8	9			6			2		7	10		11																		13
1		3	4		5		8	9			6			2		7		10	11			12														14
1		3	4		5		8	9			6			2		7	12	10	11																		15
		3	8		5	4		9						2		7		10	11			1	6														16
1		3	8		5						6					7	9	10	11			12	4	2	14											17
1		3	4		5	2	8	12			6					7		10	11				9		14											18
		12	4		5	14	8	9						2		7		10				1	11			3									6	19
1		12	4		5	9	8							2				10	7				11			3									6	20
1			7		5	12	8	9			6			2					14				10		11	3									4	21
1					5	12	8	9			6			2		7			14				10		11	3									4	22
1					5	12	8	9			6			2		7		14	3				10		11										4	23
1		3			5	7	8	9			6			2									10		11		4										24
1		11			5	7		9						2		8							10	6	4	12	3										25
1		11	4		5	7		9			12			2		8							10	6		14	3										26
1		11	4			7	5				9			2		8							10	6		12	3										27
1		11	4			7	9				5			2		8	12						10	6			3										28
1			4		5		9				11			2		8							10	6			3	7	12								29
1			4		5		9				11					8							12	6	14	10	3	2	7								30
1			4		5		9				11					8							12	6	14	10	3	2	7								31
1			4		5	14	9				11					8							12	6		10	3	2	7								32
1			4		5	11	9	10								8								6		12	2	7	3	14						33	33
1					5	7	9	10								8								6			3	2	12		14	4	11				34
1			12		5		9	10								8								6			3	2	14	4		11		7			35
1					5		9									8								6			3	2	10	4	12	11		7			36
1					5	7	12	9								8								6			3	2		4	14	11		10			37
1					5	12	9									8							7	6			3	2		4	14	11		10			38
1			6		5	9										8							7				3	2		4	14	11	12	10			39
			6		5	9										8						1	7		12			2		4	14	11	3	10			40
			5		9	11										8						1	12	6				2		4	7		3	10			41
			4		5	11																	9	6	8	12		2		3	7			10	1		42

Coca-Cola Cup	First Round	Blackpool (h)	0-1
		(a)	3-3
FA Cup	First Round	Shrewsbury T (a)	1-1
		(h)	1-2

DONCASTER ROVERS

Player and Position	Ht	Wt	Birth Date	Birth Place	Source	Clubs	League App	League Gls
Goalkeepers								
Andy Beasley	6 2	13 06	5 2 64	Sedgley	Apprentice	Luton T.	—	—
						Mansfield T (loan)	—	—
						Gillingham (loan)	—	—
						Mansfield T	94	—
						Peterborough U (loan)	7	—
						Scarborough (loan)	4	—
						Bristol R (loan)	1	—
						Doncaster R	37	—
Stuart Ford‡	5 11	11 13	20 7 71	Sheffield	Trainee	Rotherham U	5	—
						Scarborough (loan)	6	—
						Scarborough	22	—
						Bury	—	—
						Doncaster R	6	—
Gary Ingham†			9 10 64	Rotherham	Rotherham U	Doncaster R	1	—
Defenders								
Paul Bottomley (on loan from Bridlington T)			11 9 65	Harrogate	Bridlington T	Doncaster R	10	1
Steve Brentano†			9 11 61	Hull	North Ferriby U	Hull C	12	—
					Bridlington T	Doncaster R	1	—
Jon Cullen‡			10 1 73	Durham	Trainee	Doncaster R	9	—
Clive Freeman	5 8	12 08	12 9 62	Leeds	Altrincham	Doncaster R	—	—
					Bridlington T	Swansea C	14	—
						Carlisle U (loan)	4	—
					Altrincham	Doncaster R	25	2
Sam Kitchen	5 9	11 00	11 6 67	Germany	Frickley Ath	Leyton Orient	43	1
						Doncaster R	14	1
Paul Marquis	6 1	12 00	29 8 72	Enfield	Trainee	West Ham U	1	—
						Doncaster R	9	—
Ian Measham	5 11	11 08	14 12 64	Barnsley	Apprentice	Huddersfield T	17	—
						Lincoln C (loan)	6	—
						Rochdale (loan)	12	—
						Cambridge U	46	—
						Burnley	182	2
						Doncaster R	21	—
Colin Miller (To St Johnstone)	5 8	11 07	4 10 64	Lanark	Toronto Blizzard	Rangers	2	—
						Doncaster R	61	3
					Hamilton Steelers	Hamilton A	198	5
David Roche	5 11	12 01	13 12 70	Newcastle	Trainee	Newcastle U	36	—
						Peterborough U (loan)	4	—
						Doncaster R	30	5
Chris Swailes	6 2	12 07	19 10 70	Gateshead	Bridlington T	Doncaster R	17	—
Russell Wilcox	6 0	11 10	25 3 64	Hemsworth	Apprentice	Doncaster R	1	—
					Cambridge U, Frickley Ath.	Northampton T	138	9
						Hull C	100	7
						Doncaster R	40	2
Graeme Worsley†	5 10	11 02	4 1 69	Liverpool	Bootle	Shrewsbury T	105	4
						Bury	1	—
						Doncaster R	—	—
Midfield								
Ian Atkins†	6 0	12 03	16 1 57	Birmingham	Apprentice	Shrewsbury T	278	58
						Sunderland	77	6
						Everton	7	1
						Ipswich T	77	4
						Birmingham C	93	6
						Colchester U	—	—
						Birmingham C	8	—
						Cambridge U	2	—
						Sunderland	—	—
						Doncaster R	7	—
Kieron Brady‡	5 9	11 13	17 9 71	Glasgow	Trainee	Sunderland	33	7
						Doncaster R (loan)	4	3
						Doncaster R	—	—

DONCASTER ROVERS

Colours: White shirts with red lightning stripes, red shorts, red stockings. **Change colours:** White shirts with red & green stripes over shoulder and above waist, green shorts, green stockings.

Foundation: In 1879 Mr. Albert Jenkins got together a team to play a game against the Yorkshire Institution for the Deaf. The players stuck together as Doncaster Rovers joining the Midland Alliance in 1889 and the Midland Counties League in 1891.

First Football League game: 7 September, 1901, Division 2, v Burslem Port Vale (h) D 3-3 – Eggett; Simpson, Layton; Longden, Jones, Wright; Langham, Murphy, Price, Goodson (2), Bailey (1).

Did you know: Tom Keetley scored six goals at Ashington on 16 February 1929 in a 7-4 win. He finished with 40 League goals to his credit for Doncaster Rovers that season.

Managers (and Secretary-Managers)
Arthur Porter 1920–21*, Harry Tufnell 1921–22, Arthur Porter 1922–23, Dick Ray 1923–27, David Menzies 1928–36, Fred Emery 1936–40, Bill Marsden 1944–46, Jackie Bestall 1946–49, Peter Doherty 1949–58, Jack Hodgson and Sid Bycroft (joint managers) 1958, Jack Crayston 1958–59 (continued as Sec-Man to 1961), Jackie Bestall (TM) 1959–60, Norman Curtis 1960–61, Danny Malloy 1961–62, Oscar Hold 1962–64, Bill Leivers 1964–66, Keith Kettleborough 1966–67, George Raynor 1967–68, Lawrie McMenemy 1968–71, Maurice Setters 1971–74, Stan Anderson 1975–78, Billy Bremner 1978–85, Dave Cusack 1985–87, Dave Mackay 1987–89, Billy Bremner July 1989–91, Steve Beaglehole 1991–93, Ian Atkins 1994, Sammy Chung July 1994–

Player and Position	*Ht*	*Wt*	*Birth Date*	*Birth Place*	*Source*	*Clubs*	*League App*	*League Gls*
Grant Chalmers‡	5 10	11 10	12 9 69	Guernsey	Northerners	Brentford	11	1
						Doncaster R	—	—
David Clarke*	5 10	11 00	3 12 64	Nottingham	Apprentice	Notts Co	123	7
						Lincoln C	147	9
						Doncaster R	16	—
Eddie Gormley‡	5 7	10 07	23 10 68	Dublin	Bray W	Tottenham H	—	—
						Chesterfield (loan)	4	—
						Motherwell (loan)	—	—
						Shrewsbury T (loan)	—	—
						Doncaster R	118	16
Mark Hine‡	5 8	10 08	18 5 64	Middlesbrough	Local	Grimsby T	22	1
						Darlington	128	8
						Peterborough U	55	8
						Scunthorpe U	22	2
						Doncaster R	25	1
Nicholas Limber	5 9	11 01	23 1 74	Doncaster	Trainee	Doncaster R	13	1
						Manchester C	—	—
						Peterborough U (loan)	2	—
						Doncaster R	4	—
Lee Thew	5 10	11 05	23 10 74	Sunderland	Trainee	Doncaster R	11	1
Paul Williams	6 0	12 02	25 9 70	Liverpool	Trainee	Sunderland	9	—
						Swansea C (loan)	12	1
						Doncaster R	1	—
Mark Yates	5 11	11 09	24 1 70	Birmingham	Trainee	Birmingham C	54	6
						Burnley	18	1
						Lincoln C (loan)	14	—
						Doncaster R	34	4
Forwards								
Craig Bennett	6 0	12 00	29 8 73	Doncaster	Trainee	Doncaster R	8	—

Continued on Page 229

Trainees
Buxton, Nicholas G; Fint, Carl; Harmer, Russell D; Kennerdale, Nick A; Lee, Christian; Maxfield, Scott; Pallant, Sean P; Pask, Darren L; Saunders, Lee J; Sibson, Andrew; Taylor, James M; Webb, Paul A.

****Non-Contract**
Atkins, Ian L; Ingham, Gary.

Associated Schoolboys
Abbotts, Scott P; Birkinshaw, Daniel; Cave, Darren; Cawthorne, Ian; Chapman, James S; Corry, David; Cowlam, Paul; Decent, Philip A; George, Mathew A; Gill, Andrew; Higginbottom, Matthew J; Hodgkinson, James A; Johnson, Ian; Jones, David J; Nixon, Russell S; Pyke, Otis S; Scattergood, Andrew J; Seaston, Mark A; Somerville, John F; Wake, Alexander D; Wren, Simon D.

Associated Schoolboys who have accepted the Club's offer of a Traineeship/Contract
Elliott, Craig D.

**Non-Contract Players who are retained must be re-signed before they are eligible to play in League matches.

EVERTON 1993–94 *Back row (left to right):* John Ebbrell, Neil Moore, Andy Hinchcliffe, Neville Southall, Stephen Reeves, Jason Kearton, Brett Angell, Matthew Jackson.
Centre row: David Williams (First Team Coach), Jimmy Gabriel, Paul Rideout, Gary Ablett, Graham Stuart, Robert Warzycha, Stuart Barlow, David Unsworth, Paul Holmes, Tony Grant, Les Helm (Physio), Jim Martin (Kit Manager).
Front row: Tony Cottee, Predrag Radosavljevic, Barry Horne, Peter Beagrie, Mike Walker (Manager), Dave Watson, Ian Snodin, Billy Kenny, Mark Ward.

FA Premiership **EVERTON**

Goodison Park, Liverpool L4 4EL. Telephone 0151–521 2020. Fax 0151–523 9666. Ticket Infoline: 0891 121599. Clubcall 0891 121199. Dial-a-seat service: 0151–525 1231.

Ground capacity: 40,180.

Record attendance: 78,299 v Liverpool, Division 1, 18 September 1948.

Record receipts: £207,780 v Liverpool, FA Cup, 5th rd, 21 February 1988.

Pitch measurements: 112yd × 78yd.

Chairman: Dr D. M. Marsh.

Directors: Sir Desmond Pitcher, K. M. Tamlin, Sir Philip Carter CBE, D. A. B. Newton, W. Kenright.

Manager: Mike Walker. ***Assistant Manager:*** David Williams. ***Coach:*** Jimmy Gabriel.

Physio: Les Helm.

Chief Executive & Secretary: Jim Greenwood.

Commercial Manager: Derek Johnston. ***Sales Promotion Manager:*** Colum Whelan.

Year Formed: 1878. ***Turned Professional:*** 1885. ***Ltd Co.:*** 1892.

Previous Name: St Domingo FC, 1878–79.

Club Nickname: 'The Toffees'.

Previous Grounds: 1878, Stanley Park; 1882, Priory Road; 1884, Anfield Road; 1892, Goodison Park.

Record League Victory: 9–1 v Manchester C, Division 1, 3 September 1906 – Scott; Balmer, Crelley; Booth, Taylor (1), Abbott (1); Sharp, Bolton (1), Young (4), Settle (2), George Wilson. 9–1 v Plymouth Arg, Division 2, 27 December 1930 – Coggins; Williams, Cresswell; McPherson, Griffiths, Thomson; Critchley, Dunn, Dean (4), Johnson (1), Stein (4).

Record Cup Victory: 11–2 v Derby Co, FA Cup, 1st rd, 18 January 1890 – Smalley; Hannah, Doyle; Kirkwood (3), Holt, Parry; Latta, Brady (3), Geary (2), Chadwick, Millward (3).

Record Defeat: 4–10 v Tottenham H, Division 1, 11 October 1958.

Most League Points (2 for a win): 66, Division 1, 1969–70.

Most League Points (3 for a win): 90, Division 1, 1984–85.

Most League Goals: 121, Division 2, 1930–31.

Highest League Scorer in Season: William Ralph 'Dixie' Dean, 60, Division 1, 1927–28 (All-time League record).

Most League Goals in Total Aggregate: William Ralph 'Dixie' Dean, 349, 1925–37.

Most Capped Player: Neville Southall, 74, Wales.

Most League Appearances: Ted Sagar, 465, 1929–53.

Record Transfer Fee Received: £2,750,000 from Barcelona for Gary Lineker, July 1986.

Record Transfer Fee Paid: £2,000,000 to West Ham U for Tony Cottee, July 1988.

Chairman: B. E. Fearn. ***Vice-chairman:*** L. V. Pickering.
Football League Record: 1888 Founder Member of the Football League; 1930–31 Division 2; 1931–51 Division 1; 1951–54 Division 2; 1954–92 Division 1; 1992– FA Premier League.

Honours: *Football League:* Division 1 – Champions 1890–91, 1914–15, 1927–28, 1931–32, 1938–39, 1962–63, 1969–70, 1984–85, 1986–87; Runners-up 1889–90, 1894–95, 1901–02, 1904–05, 1908–09, 1911–12, 1985–86; Division 2 Champions 1930–31; Runners-up 1953–54. *FA Cup:* Winners 1906, 1933, 1966, 1984; Runners-up 1893, 1897, 1907, 1968, 1985, 1986, 1989. *Football League Cup:* Runners-up 1976–77, 1983–84. *League Super Cup:* Runners-up 1986. *Simod Cup:* Runners-up 1989. *Zenith Data System Cup:* Runner-up 1991. **European Competitions:** *European Cup:* 1963–64, 1970–71. *European Cup-Winners' Cup:* 1966–67, 1984–85 (winners). *European Fairs Cup:* 1962–63, 1964–65, 1965–66. *UEFA Cup:* 1975–76, 1978–79, 1979–80.

EVERTON 1993—94 LEAGUE RECORD

Match No.	Date	Venue	Opponents	Result		H/T Score	Lg. Pos.	Goalscorers	Attendance
1	Aug 14	A	Southampton	W	2-0	2-0	—	Beagrie, Ebbrell	14,051
2	17	H	Manchester C	W	1-0	1-0	—	Rideout	26,025
3	21	H	Sheffield U	W	4-2	2-1	1	Cottee 3, Ebbrell	24,177
4	25	A	Newcastle U	L	0-1	0-1	—		34,490
5	28	A	Arsenal	L	0-2	0-0	8		29,063
6	31	H	Aston Villa	L	0-1	0-1	—		24,067
7	Sept 11	A	Oldham Ath	W	1-0	1-0	7	Cottee	13,666
8	18	H	Liverpool	W	2-0	1-0	4	Ward, Cottee	38,157
9	25	H	Norwich C	L	1-5	1-1	8	Rideout	20,631
10	Oct 3	A	Tottenham H	L	2-3	1-0	—	Rideout, Cottee (pen)	27,487
11	16	A	Swindon T	D	1-1	1-0	12	Beagrie	14,437
12	23	H	Manchester U	L	0-1	0-0	12		35,455
13	30	A	Ipswich T	W	2-0	1-0	11	Barlow, Whelan (og)	15,078
14	Nov 6	A	Coventry C	L	1-2	0-1	12	Rideout	11,550
15	20	H	QPR	L	0-3	0-1	13		17,326
16	23	H	Leeds U	D	1-1	0-0	—	Cottee	17,102
17	27	A	Wimbledon	D	1-1	1-0	12	Barlow	6934
18	Dec 4	H	Southampton	W	1-0	1-0	11	Cottee	13,265
19	8	A	Manchester C	L	0-1	0-1	—		20,513
20	11	A	Sheffield U	D	0-0	0-0	13		15,135
21	18	H	Newcastle U	L	0-2	0-1	15		25,362
22	27	H	Sheffield W	L	0-2	0-0	16		16,471
23	29	A	Blackburn R	L	0-2	0-2	16		22,061
24	Jan 1	H	West Ham U	L	0-1	0-1	16		19,602
25	3	A	Chelsea	L	2-4	0-2	16	Cottee, Barlow	18,338
26	15	H	Swindon T	W	6-2	2-0	16	Ebbrell, Cottee 3 (1 pen), Ablett, Beagrie	20,760
27	22	A	Manchester U	L	0-1	0-1	16		44,750
28	Feb 5	H	Chelsea	W	4-2	3-1	15	Ebbrell, Rideout 2, Angell	18,201
29	12	H	Ipswich T	D	0-0	0-0	15		19,641
30	19	H	Arsenal	D	1-1	0-0	15	Cottee	19,760
31	Mar 5	H	Oldham Ath	W	2-1	1-1	14	Radosavljevic, Stuart	18,881
32	13	A	Liverpool	L	1-2	1-2	—	Watson	44,281
33	21	A	Norwich C	L	0-3	0-1	—		16,432
34	26	H	Tottenham H	L	0-1	0-0	17		23,460
35	29	A	Aston Villa	D	0-0	0-0	—		36,044
36	Apr 2	A	Sheffield W	L	1-5	0-2	17	Cottee	24,080
37	4	H	Blackburn R	L	0-3	0-1	18		27,463
38	9	A	West Ham U	W	1-0	0-0	17	Cottee	20,243
39	16	A	QPR	L	1-2	0-0	17	Cottee	13,330
40	23	H	Coventry C	D	0-0	0-0	18		23,352
41	30	A	Leeds U	L	0-3	0-0	20		35,487
42	May 7	H	Wimbledon	W	3-2	1-2	17	Stuart 2 (1 pen), Horne	31,233

Final League Position: 17

GOALSCORERS

League (42): Cottee 16 (2 pens), Rideout 6, Ebbrell 4, Barlow 3, Beagrie 3, Stuart 3 (1 pen), Ablett 1, Angell 1, Horne 1, Radosavljevic 1, Ward 1, Watson 1, own goal 1.
Coca-Cola Cup (14): Rideout 4, Cottee 3, Watson 3, Beagrie 1, Snodin 1, Ward 1 (pen), own goal 1.
FA Cup (3): Barlow 2, Rideout 1.

Southall 42	Holmes 15	Jackson 37 + 1	Snodin 28 + 1	Watson 27 + 1	Ablett 32	Ward 26 + 1	Ebbrell 39	Cottee 36 + 3	Rideout 21 + 3	Beagrie 29	Radosavljevic 9 + 14	Barlow 6 + 16	Hinchcliffe 25 + 1	Stuart 26 + 4	Horne 28 + 4	Angell 13 + 3	Warzycha 3 + 4	Unsworth 7 + 1	Moore 4	Limpar 9	Rowett — + 2	Match No.
1	2	3	4	5	6	7	8	9	10	11												1
1	2	3	4	*5*	6	7	8	9	10	11	12	14										2
1	2	5			6	7	4	9	10	11	12	14	3	*8*								3
1	*2*	5			6	7	4	9	10	11	12	14	3	8								4
1	2	5			6	7	4	*9*	10		12	14	3	8	11							5
1		5			6	7	4	9	*10*	11	12	14	3	8	2							6
1	2	5			6	7	4	9	*10*	11	8	14	3		12							7
1	2	5			6	7	4	9	10	11	12		3		8							8
1	*2*	5			6	7	4	9	10	11	12		3		8	14						9
1	2	5			6	7	4	*9*	10	11	12	14	3		8							10
1		2		5	6	7	4	9	*10*	11	12	14	3		8							11
1	2	14		5	6	*7*	4	9		11	12	10	3		8							12
1	2		12	5	6	7	4	9		11		10	3		8							13
1	2			5	6	7	4	9	10	11		12	3		8							14
1	2	3		5	6	7	4	9		*11*	8	10		14	12							15
1		2	*11*	5	6	7	4	9			10	12	3	14	8							16
1		2	11	5	6	7	4	9			12	*10*	3	14	8							17
1		2	6	5	3	7	4	9		11				10	8		12					18
1		2	6	5	3	7	4	9		11				10	8		12					19
1		2	6	5	3	7	4	9		11				8			10					20
1		2	6	5	3	7	4	9			12	10		8			11					21
1		2	6	5	3	7	4			11	*12*	10		9	8		14					22
1		5	2		6	7	4	9		11			3		8		12	10				23
1	2	5	3		6	*7*	4	9	10	11		12		14	8							24
1	2	*5*	6		3	7		9	10	11		12		8	4			14				25
1		5	2		6	7	4	9		11		12	3		8	10						26
1		2	6		3		4	9		11		12	14	8		10	*7*		5			27
1		2	5		6		4		9	11	7		3	8		10						28
1		2	6	14			4	12	9	11	*7*		3	8		10			5			29
1		2	4	5				12	9	11	*7*		3	8	14	10			6			30
1		2	6	5		14		9	12	11	*7*		3	8	4	10						31
1		2	6	5			4	9	12	11	*7*		3	8	14	10						32
1		2	6	5			4	9	10	11	7		3	8		12						33
1		2	6	5			4	9	10				3	7	8	12				11		34
1		2	6	5			4						3	7	8	10		9		11		35
1		2	6	5			4	12						7	8	*10*		3	9	11	14	36
1		2	6	5			4	9				12		7	8	10		3		11		37
1		2	3	5	6		4	9	12					7	8	10				11		38
1		2	3	5	6		4	9						7	8	10				11		39
1		2		5			4	9			12		3	7	8	10		6		11		40
1			3	5	6		4	9	10					7	8			2		11	12	41
1			3	5	6		4	9	10			12		7	8			2		11		42

Coca-Cola Cup	Second Round	Lincoln C (a)	4-3
		(h)	4-2
	Third Round	Crystal Palace (h)	2-2
		(a)	4-1
	Fourth Round	Manchester U (h)	0-2
FA Cup	Third Round	Bolton W (a)	1-1
		(h)	2-3

EVERTON

Player and Position	Ht	Wt	Birth Date	Birth Place	Source	Clubs	League App	League Gls
Goalkeepers								
Jason Kearton	6 1	11 10	9 7 69	Ipswich (Australia)	Brisbane Lions	Everton	5	—
						Stoke C (loan)	16	—
						Blackpool (loan)	14	—
Steve Reeves	6 0	11 09	24 9 74	Dagenham	Trainee	Everton	—	—
Neville Southall	6 1	12 01	16 9 58	Llandudno	Winsford	Bury	39	—
						Everton	453	—
						Port Vale (loan)	9	—
Defenders								
Gary Ablett	6 0	11 04	19 11 65	Liverpool	Apprentice	Liverpool	109	1
						Derby Co (loan)	6	—
						Hull C (loan)	5	—
						Everton	89	2
John Doolan*	5 11	11 09	7 5 73	Liverpool	Trainee	Everton	—	—
Andy Hinchcliffe	5 10	12 10	5 2 69	Manchester	Apprentice	Manchester C	112	8
						Everton	90	2
Paul Holmes	5 10	11 03	18 2 68	Wortley	Apprentice	Doncaster R	47	1
						Torquay U	138	4
						Birmingham C	12	—
						Everton	19	—
Matthew Jackson	6 1	12 12	19 10 71	Leeds	School	Luton T	9	—
						Preston NE (loan)	4	—
						Everton	95	4
Neil Moore	6 1	12 02	21 9 72	Liverpool	Trainee	Everton	5	—
Joe Parkinson	5 11	12 02	11 6 71	Eccles	Trainee	Wigan Ath	119	6
						Bournemouth	30	1
						Everton	—	—
Mark Powell*	5 9	10 08	8 5 75	Ellesmere Port	Trainee	Everton	—	—
Dave Watson	6 0	11 12	20 11 61	Liverpool	Amateur	Liverpool	—	—
						Norwich C	212	11
						Everton	268	19
Midfield								
John Ebbrell	5 7	9 12	1 10 69	Bromborough		Everton	159	9
Tony Grant	5 7	9 06	14 11 74	Liverpool	Trainee	Everton	—	—
Mark Grugel	5 8	10 01	9 3 76	Liverpool	Local	Everton	—	—
Barry Horne	5 10	12 02	18 5 62	St Asaph	Rhyl	Wrexham	136	17
						Portsmouth	70	7
						Southampton	112	6
						Everton	66	2
Terry Jones*	5 7	9 12	3 12 74	Liverpool	Trainee	Everton	—	—
Billy Kenny	5 07	10 10	19 9 73	Liverpool	Trainee	Everton	17	1
Jonathan O'Connor	5 10	11 03	29 10 76	Darlington	Trainee	Everton	—	—
Chris Priest	5 9	10 10	18 10 73	Leigh	Trainee	Everton	—	—
Jim Quigley	5 8	11 02	21 9 76	Derry	Trainee	Everton	—	—
Carl Ruffer*	5 8	10 04	20 12 74	Chester	Trainee	Everton	—	—
Ian Snodin	5 7	9 01	15 8 63	Rotherham	Apprentice	Doncaster R	188	25
						Leeds U	51	6
						Everton	145	3
Mark Ward	5 6	9 12	10 10 62	Prescot	Northwich Vic	Oldham Ath	84	12
						West Ham U	165	12
						Manchester C	55	14
						Everton	83	6
						Birmingham C (loan)	9	1
Forwards								
Brett Angell	6 1	12 00	20 8 68	Marlborough	Cheltenham T	Derby Co	—	—
						Stockport Co	70	28
						Southend U	115	47
						Everton (loan)	1	—
						Everton	15	1
Stuart Barlow	5 10	11 02	16 7 68	Liverpool		Everton	57	8
						Rotherham U (loan)	—	—

EVERTON

Colours: Royal blue shirts with white collar, white shorts, blue stockings. **Change colours:** White shirts with black and grey trim, black shorts, black stockings.

Foundation: St. Domingo Church Sunday School formed a football club in 1878 which played at Stanley Park. Enthusiasm was so great that in November 1879 they decided to expand membership and changed the name to Everton playing in black shirts with a white sash and nicknamed the "Black Watch". After wearing several other colours, royal blue was adopted in 1901.

First Football League game: 8 September, 1888, Football League, v Accrington (h) W 2-1 – Smalley; Dick, Ross; Holt, Jones, Dobson; Fleming (2), Waugh, Lewis, E. Chadwick, Farmer.

Did you know: Graham Stuart's successful 24th minute penalty against Wimbledon when trailing 2-0 on 7 May 1994 was only his second spot kick. His first attempt had failed while with Chelsea. Stuart added a second goal and Everton recovered to beat Wimbledon 3-2, thus avoiding relegation.

Managers (and Secretary-Managers)
W. E. Barclay 1888–89*, Dick Molyneux 1889–1901*, William C. Cuff 1901–18*, W. J. Sawyer 1918–19*, Thomas H. McIntosh 1919–35*, Theo Kelly 1936–48, Cliff Britton 1948–56, Ian Buchan 1956–58, Johnny Carey 1958–61, Harry Catterick 1961–73, Billy Bingham 1973–77, Gordon Lee 1977–81, Howard Kendall 1981–87, Colin Harvey 1987–90, Howard Kendall 1990–93, Mike Walker January 1994–

Player and Position	Ht	Wt	Birth Date	Birth Place	Source	Clubs	League App	League Gls
Tony Cottee	5 7	11 03	11 7 65	West Ham	Apprentice	West Ham U	212	92
						Everton	181	72
Mo Johnston (To Hearts October 1993)	5 9	10 06	30 4 63	Glasgow	Milton Battlefield	Partick T	85	41
						Watford	38	23
						Celtic	99	52
						Nantes	66	22
						Rangers	76	31
						Everton	34	10
Anders Limpar	5 8	11 07	24 9 65	Solna	Cremonese	Arsenal	96	17
						Everton	9	—
Predrag Radosavljevic*	5 11	12 10	24 6 63	Belgrade	St Louis Storms	Everton	46	4
Paul Rideout	5 11	12 01	14 8 64	Bournemouth	Apprentice	Swindon T	95	38
						Aston Villa	54	19
						Bari	99	23
						Southampton	75	19
						Swindon T (loan)	9	1
						Notts Co	11	3
						Rangers	12	1
						Everton	48	9
Gary Rowett	6 0	12 10	6 3 74	Bromsgrove	Trainee	Cambridge U	63	9
						Everton	2	—
Graham Stuart	5 8	11 06	24 10 70	Tooting, London	Trainee	Chelsea	87	14
						Everton	30	3
Paul Tait*	5 8	10 10	24 10 74	Newcastle	Trainee	Everton	—	—
David Unsworth	5 11	12 02	16 10 73	Preston	Trainee	Everton	13	1
Robert Warzycha	5 8	11 10	20 6 63	Poland	Gornik Zabrze	Everton	72	6
Nicky Young*	5 7	10 01	24 4 73	Liverpool	Trainee	Everton	—	—

Trainees
Allen, Graham; Ashley, David P; Hayes, Phillip J; Hennigan, Gerard J; Holcroft, Peter I; Price, Christopher; Singleton, Benjamin P; Smith, Alexander P; Speare, James; Weathers, Andrew W; Woods, Matthew J.

Associated Schoolboys
Ali, Thomas A; Ball, Michael J; Barton, Joseph S; Branch, Paul M; Davies, Paul; Denton, Adam M; Gabrielson, Daniel J; Hardman, Christopher S; Haynes, John W; Holmes, N; Hulbert, Robin J; Lane, Christopher; Lynch, Paul E; McDermott, Wayne; Milligan, Jamie; Moore, David G; O'Toole, John; Obrien, Michael G; West, Andrew.

Associated Schoolboys who have accepted the Club's offer of a Traineeship/Contract
Hussin, Edward W; Knight, Christopher D; Maguire, John; McCann, Gavin P; McHugh, Bartholomew; Moore, Richard; Roscoe, Christopher J; Townsend, Richard P; Tynan, Robert L; Wood, Robert D. M.

EXETER CITY 1993–94 *Back row (left to right):* Scott Daniels, Toby Redwood, Stuart Storer, Peter Fox, Chris White, Jason Minett, Andy Harris.
Centre row: Peter Whiston, Ronnie Robinson, Gary Worthington, Russell Coughlin, Jon Brown, Mark Brown, Craig Taylor, David Cooper.
Front row: Danny Bailey, Ronnie Jepson, Mike Chapman (Physio), Alan Ball, Mike Radford (Youth Development Officer), George Kent (Community Officer), Alan Tonge, Jason Percival.

Division 3 EXETER CITY

St James Park, Exeter EX4 6PX. Telephone Exeter (0392) 54073. Fax (0392) 425885. Training ground: (0395) 232784.

Ground capacity: 10,570.

Record attendance: 20,984 v Sunderland, FA Cup 6th rd (replay), 4 March 1931.

Record receipts: £59,862.98 v Aston Villa, FA Cup 3rd rd 8 January 1994.

Pitch measurements: 114yd × 73yd.

Honorary President: W. C. Hill.

Chairman: A. I. Doble.

Directors: P. Carter, M. Couch, S. W. Dawe, L. G. Vallance.

Manager: Terry Cooper. ***Assistant Manager/Coach:*** Trevor Morgan. ***Physio:*** Mike Chapman.

Secretary: Margaret Bond. ***Company Secretary:*** P. Carter.

Commercial Manager: Steve Birley.

Year Formed: 1904. ***Turned Professional:*** 1908. ***Ltd Co.:*** 1908.

Club Nickname: 'The Grecians'.

Record League Victory: 8–1 v Coventry C, Division 3 (S), 4 December 1926 – Bailey; Pollard, Charlton; Pullen, Pool, Garrett; Purcell (2), McDevitt, Blackmore (2), Dent (2), Compton (2). 8–1 v Aldershot, Division 3 (S), 4 May 1935 – Chesters; Gray, Miller; Risdon, Webb, Angus; Jack Scott (1), Wrightson (1), Poulter (3), McArthur (1), Dryden (1). (1 og).

Record Cup Victory: 9–1 v Aberdare, FA Cup 1st rd, 26 November 1927 – Holland; Pollard, Charlton; Phoenix, Pool, Gee; Purcell (2), McDevitt, Dent (4), Vaughan (2), Compton (1).

Record Defeat: 0–9 v Notts Co, Division 3 (S), 16 October 1948 and v Northampton T, Division 3 (S), 12 April 1958.

Most League Points (2 for a win): 62, Division 4, 1976–77.

Most League Points (3 for a win): 89, Division 4, 1989–90.

Most League Goals: 88, Division 3 (S), 1932–33.

Highest League Scorer in Season: Fred Whitlow, 33, Division 3 (S), 1932–33.

Most League Goals in Total Aggregate: Tony Kellow, 129, 1976–78, 1980–83, 1985–88.

Most Capped Player: Dermot Curtis, 1 (17), Eire.

Most League Appearances: Arnold Mitchell, 495, 1952–66.

Record Transfer Fee Received: £500,000 from Rangers for Chris Vinnicombe, November 1989.

Record Transfer Fee Paid: £65,000 to Blackpool for Tony Kellow, March 1980.

Football League Record: 1920 Elected Division 3; 1921–58 Division 3 (S); 1958–64 Division 4; 1964–66 Division 3; 1966–77 Division 4; 1977–84 Division 3; 1984–90 Division 4; 1990–92 Division 3; 1992–94 Division 2; 1994– Division 3.

Honours: *Football League:* Division 3 best season: 8th, 1979–80; Division 3 (S) – Runners-up 1932–33; Division 4 – Champions 1989–90; Runners-up 1976–77. *FA Cup:* best season: 6th rd replay, 1931. *Football League Cup:* never beyond 4th rd. *Division 3 (S) Cup:* Winners 1934.

EXETER CITY 1993—94 LEAGUE RECORD

Match No.	Date	Venue	Opponents	Result		H/T Score	Lg. Pos.	Goalscorers	Attendance
1	Aug 14	A	Brentford	L	1-2	1-1	—	Daniels	5537
2	21	H	York C	L	1-2	0-1	22	Jepson (pen)	2807
3	28	A	Bradford C	L	0-6	0-3	23		5866
4	31	H	Cardiff C	D	2-2	0-1	—	Jepson, Storer	3049
5	Sept 4	H	Hartlepool U	W	2-1	1-1	21	Worthington, Jepson	2644
6	11	A	Huddersfield T	W	1-0	1-0	16	Ross	5266
7	15	A	Bristol R	D	1-1	0-0	—	Alexander (og)	5001
8	18	H	Wrexham	W	5-0	3-0	13	Jepson 4 (1 pen), Wigley	3982
9	25	H	Swansea C	W	1-0	0-0	8	Jepson (pen)	3655
10	Oct 2	A	Brighton & HA	D	0-0	0-0	11		5230
11	9	H	Reading	L	4-6	1-4	12	Jepson 2, Ross 2	4725
12	16	A	Stockport Co	L	0-4	0-3	13		4349
13	23	H	Blackpool	W	1-0	0-0	13	Ross	3421
14	30	A	Bournemouth	D	1-1	1-1	13	Jepson	5102
15	Nov 2	H	Fulham	W	6-4	3-2	—	Ross 3, Robinson, Daniels, Jepson	2919
16	6	A	Leyton Orient	D	1-1	1-1	10	Whiston	3798
17	20	H	Port Vale	D	1-1	0-0	10	Storer	3908
18	27	A	Burnley	L	2-3	1-2	12	Monington (og), Jepson	9040
19	Dec 11	A	York C	L	0-3	0-3	15		2409
20	18	H	Brentford	D	2-2	2-1	15	Davies, Worboys	4250
21	29	A	Cambridge U	L	0-3	0-1	16		3744
22	Jan 1	H	Hull C	L	0-1	0-1	18		3547
23	22	A	Reading	L	0-1	0-0	21		7174
24	29	H	Bournemouth	L	0-2	0-1	22		3602
25	Feb 5	A	Blackpool	L	0-1	0-1	22		3747
26	12	H	Rotherham U	D	1-1	1-0	22	Ross	3113
27	19	H	Bradford C	D	0-0	0-0	22		2758
28	25	A	Hartlepool U	W	2-1	1-0	22	Cooper M, Morgan	1695
29	Mar 2	H	Plymouth Arg	L	2-3	1-0	—	Cooper M, Adekola	6601
30	5	H	Huddersfield T	L	2-3	2-1	22	Cooper M (pen), Morgan	2939
31	12	A	Wrexham	D	1-1	0-0	22	Morgan	3053
32	15	H	Bristol R	W	1-0	0-0	—	Ross (pen)	4399
33	19	A	Swansea C	L	0-2	0-0	22		2512
34	22	A	Barnet	L	1-2	1-0	—	Cooper M	1604
35	26	H	Brighton & HA	D	1-1	0-1	22	Morgan	3107
36	29	H	Barnet	D	0-0	0-0	—		2269
37	Apr 2	A	Plymouth Arg	L	0-1	0-0	22		12,986
38	4	H	Cambridge U	L	0-5	0-3	22		2258
39	9	A	Hull C	L	1-5	1-2	22	Cooper M	4663
40	16	A	Fulham	W	2-0	2-0	22	Minett, Cooper M (pen)	4602
41	19	A	Rotherham U	L	0-3	0-1	—		2804
42	23	H	Leyton Orient	W	1-0	1-0	22	Turner	1933
43	26	A	Cardiff C	L	0-2	0-1	—		4631
44	30	A	Port Vale	L	0-3	0-0	22		10,377
45	May 2	H	Stockport Co	L	1-2	1-1	—	Turner	1992
46	7	H	Burnley	W	4-1	1-0	22	Cooper M 2, Pears, Turner	3155

Final League Position: 22

GOALSCORERS

League (52): Jepson 13 (3 pens), Ross 9 (1 pen), Cooper M 8 (2 pens), Morgan 4, Turner 3, Daniels 2, Storer 2, Adekola 1, Davies 1, Minett 1, Pears 1, Robinson 1, Whiston 1, Wigley 1, Worboys 1, Worthington 1, own goals 2.
Coca-Cola Cup (3): Jepson 2 (1 pen), Storer 1.
FA Cup (6): Bailey 1, Harris 1, Jepson 1, Ross 1, Storer 1, Worthington 1.

Fox 25 + 1	White 7 + 1	Robinson 21 + 1	Bailey 29 + 5	Daniels 39 + 2	Whiston 22	Storer 44	Coughlin 35	Ross 26 + 1	Worthington 8 + 7	Wigley 22 + 1	Minett 34 + 4	Jepson 16	Bond 1	Percival — + 4	Thirlby 7 + 3	Cooper D — + 1	Redwood 11 + 2	Brown 18 + 5	Gosney 1	Veysey 11 + 1	Harris 4	Worboys 4	Davies 5 + 1	Pears 6 + 5	Cecere 2	Tonge — + 1	Turner 22	Morgan 12	Gavin 12	Adekola 1 + 2	Llewellyn 15	Richardson 4 + 3	Mehew 5 + 2	McKnight 9 + 1	Phillips 7 + 2	Cooper M 21	*Match No.*
1	2	3	4	5	6	7	8	9	10	11	12																										1
1	2	3	4	5	6	7	8	10		11	12	9																									2
1	2	3	4	5	6	7	8				11	9	10	12																							3
1	2	3	4	5	6	7	8		10	11		9			12																						4
1	*2*	3	4	5	6	7	8		10	11		9		12		14																					5
1		3	4	5	6	7	8	10		11	2	9																									6
1		3	*4*	5	6	7	8	10	12	11	2	9					14																				7
1		3	4	5	6	7	8	10		11	2	9																									8
1		3	4	5		7	8	10		11	2	9						6																			9
1		3	4	5	6	7	8	10	12	11	2	9																									10
14		3	4	5	6	7	8	10		11	2	9						12	*1*																		11
	2		4	5	6	7	8	10	12	11		9					3			1																	12
		3	4	5	6	7	8	10		11		9					2			1																	13
		3	4	5	6	7	8	10		11	2	9								1																	14
		3	4	5	6	7	8	10		11	2	9								1																	15
		3	4	5	6	7	8	9	10	11	2									1																	16
1			4	5	6	7	8	10	12	11	2	9						3																			17
1	14		*4*	5	6	7	8		10		2	9		12				3			11																18
1	2	12	4	5	6	7			10	11	8							3				9															19
1				5	6	7	8	10	12	11	2							3				9	4														20
1		3	14	5		7	8	10	12	*11*	2							4				9	6														21
1		3	11	5	6	7	8	10			2							12				*9*	4	14													22
			4	5		7			10		2			12			3	6		1	8		11		9												23
			4	5		7		12	10		2						3	6		1	*8*		11		9	14											24
1				5		7	4			11	2						3	6			8		12				9	10									25
1			14	5		7	8	6	12		2						3										9	10	11							*4*	26
1		3	12	5		7	8	6			2																9	10	11							4	27
1		3		5		7	8	*6*			2							12									9	10	11	14						4	28
1		3		5		7	8	6			2							12									9	*10*	11	14						4	29
1		3	14	5		7	8				2							12									9	10	11	*6*						4	30
1						7	8	6			12						*3*	5									9	10	11		2	14				4	31
1							8	6		7							3	5									9	10	11		2					4	32
1			6			7	8			12							3	5		14							9	10	11		2					4	33
				12		7	8										3	5		1				6			9	10	11		2					4	34
				12		7	8										3	5		1				*6*			9	10	11		2		14			4	35
				5			8	6		11	12							3									9	10			2		*7*	1	14	4	36
			8	5		7		*6*			10							3									9		11		2		12	1	14	4	37
			8			7		6			3				14									12			9		11		2	5		1	10	*4*	38
			6			7	8				3				14									12			9				2	5	10	1	11	4	39
			8	5		7					3				6					1							9				2		10	12	11	4	40
			8	5		7					3				6					1				12			9				2		10		11	4	41
			14	5	6	7	*8*				3				11									12			9				2		10	1		4	42
			8	5		7					3				11			6						10			9				2	12		1		4	43
				5	6	7					3				8									10			9				2	12		1	11	4	44
				5		7					3				8		12							10			9				2	6		1	11	4	45
				5		7					3				8			2						10			9					6		1	11	4	46

Coca-Cola Cup	First Round	Walsall (a)	0-0
		(h)	2-1
	Second Round	Derby Co (h)	1-3
		(a)	0-2
FA Cup	First Round	Farnborough T (a)	3-1
	Second Round	Leyton Orient (a)	1-1
		(h)	2-2
	Third Round	Aston Villa (h)	0-1

EXETER CITY

Player and Position	Ht	Wt	Birth Date	Birth Place	Source	Clubs	League App	League Gls
Goalkeepers								
Peter Fox	5 10	12 04	5 7 57	Scunthorpe	Apprentice	Sheffield W	49	—
						West Ham U (loan)	—	—
						Barnsley (loan)	1	—
						Stoke C	409	—
						Wrexham (loan)	—	—
						Exeter C	26	—
Andy Gosney‡	6 4	13 02	8 11 63	Southampton	Apprentice	Portsmouth	48	—
						York C (loan)	5	—
						Birmingham C	21	—
						Exeter C	1	—
Allen McKnight†	6 1	13 07	27 1 64	Antrim	Distillery	Celtic	12	—
						Albion R (loan)	36	—
						West Ham U	23	—
						Airdrieonians	2	—
						Stockport Co	—	—
						Rotherham U	3	—
						Walsall	8	—
						Exeter C	10	—
Ken Veysey*	5 11	11 08	8 6 67	Hackney	Arsenal	Torquay U	72	—
						Oxford U	57	—
						Sheffield U (loan)	—	—
						Exeter C	12	—
Defenders								
Kevin Bond†	6 2	13 10	22 6 57	London	Bournemouth	Norwich C	142	12
					Seattle S	Manchester C	110	11
						Southampton	140	6
						Bournemouth	126	4
						Exeter C	19	—
Jon Brown	5 10	11 03	8 9 66	Barnsley	Denaby U	Exeter C	127	1
David Cooper	6 0	12 00	7 3 73	Welwyn	Luton T	Exeter C	34	—
Scott Daniels	6 1	11 09	22 11 69	Benfleet	Trainee	Colchester U	73	—
						Exeter C	110	7
Toby Redwood*	5 11	11 08	7 10 73	Newton Abbot	Trainee	Exeter C	20	—
Ronnie Robinson	5 9	11 05	22 10 66	Sunderland		Ipswich T	—	—
					Vaux Breweries	Leeds U	27	—
						Doncaster R	78	5
						WBA	1	—
						Rotherham U	86	2
						Peterborough U	47	—
						Exeter C	22	1
						Huddersfield T (loan)	2	—
Craig Taylor‡	6 1	12 00	24 1 74	Plymouth	Trainee	Exeter C	5	—
Alan Tonge*	5 8	11 11	25 2 72	Bury	Trainee	Manchester U	—	—
						Exeter C	19	1
Chris White*	5 11	11 10	11 12 70	Chatham	Trainee	Portsmouth	—	—
						Peterborough U	13	—
						Doncaster R (loan)	6	—
						Exeter C	19	—
Midfield								
Danny Bailey	5 9	12 07	21 5 64	Leyton	Apprentice	Bournemouth	2	—
					Local	Torquay U	1	—
					Wealdstone	Exeter C	64	2
						Reading	50	2
						Fulham (loan)	3	—
						Exeter C	61	—
Mark Brown*			8 7 75	Jersey	Trainee	Exeter C	—	—
Mark Cooper	5 8	11 04	18 12 68	Wakefield	Trainee	Bristol C	—	—
						Exeter C	50	12
						Southend U (loan)	5	—
						Birmingham C	39	4
						Fulham	14	—
						Huddersfield T (loan)	10	4
						Wycombe W	2	1
						Exeter C	21	8

EXETER CITY

Colours: Red and white striped shirts, white shorts, red stockings. **Change colours:** Blue and white striped shirts, blue shorts, blue stockings.

Foundation: Exeter City was formed in 1904 by the amalgamation of St. Sidwell's United and Exeter United. The club first played in the East Devon League and then the Plymouth & District League. After an exhibition match between West Bromwich Albion and Woolwich Arsenal was held to test interest as Exeter was then a rugby stronghold, Exeter City decided at a meeting at the Red Lion Hotel to turn professional in 1908.

First Football League game: 28 August, 1920, Division 3, v Brentford (h) W 3-0 – Pym; Coleburne, Feebury (1p); Crawshaw, Carrick, Mitton; Appleton, Makin, Wright (1), Vowles (1), Dockray.

Did you know: Exeter City were unbeaten in their opening 13 matches during 1986–87. Because of a record 23 drawn games, their finishing position was no higher than 14th in Division 4.

Managers (and Secrětary-Managers)
Arthur Chadwick 1910–22, Fred Mavin 1923–27, Dave Wilson 1928–29, Billy McDevitt 1929–35, Jack English 1935–39, George Roughton 1945–52, Norman Kirkman 1952–53, Norman Dodgin 1953–57, Bill Thompson 1957–58, Frank Broome 1958–60, Glen Wilson 1960–62, Cyril Spiers 1962–63, Jack Edwards 1963–65, Ellis Stuttard 1965–66, Jock Basford 1966–67, Frank Broome 1967–69, Johnny Newman 1969–76, Bobby Saxton 1977–79, Brian Godfrey 1979–83, Gerry Francis 1983–84, Jim Iley 1984–85, Colin Appleton 1985–87, Terry Cooper 1988–91, Alan Ball 1991–94, Terry Cooper January 1994–

Player and Position	*Ht*	*Wt*	*Birth Date*	*Birth Place*	*Source*	*Clubs*	*League App*	*League Gls*
Russell Coughlin	5 8	11 12	15 2 60	Swansea	Apprentice	Manchester C	—	—
						Blackburn R	24	—
						Carlisle U	130	13
						Plymouth Arg	131	18
						Blackpool	102	8
						Shrewsbury T (loan)	5	—
						Swansea C	101	2
						Exeter C	35	—
Mark Gavin	5 8	10 07	10 12 63	Bailleston	Apprentice	Leeds U	30	3
						Hartlepool U (loan)	7	—
						Carlisle U	13	1
						Bolton W	49	3
						Rochdale	23	6
						Hearts	9	—
						Bristol C	69	6
						Watford	13	—
						Bristol C	41	2
						Exeter C	12	—
Andy Harris	5 10	12 02	17 11 70	Birmingham	Trainee	Birmingham C	1	—
						Oxford U (loan)	1	—
						Exeter C	38	1
Jason Minett	5 10	10 02	12 8 71	Peterborough	Trainee	Norwich C	3	—
						Exeter C (loan)	12	—
						Exeter C	38	1
Jason Percival‡	5 7	10 11	20 9 73	Nuneaton	Trainee	Stoke C	—	—
						Exeter C	4	—
Jon Richardson§			29 8 75	Nottingham		Exeter C	7	—
Anthony Thirlby§			4 3 76	Germany	Trainee	Exeter C	10	—
Robert Turner	6 3	14 01	18 9 66	Durham	Apprentice	Huddersfield T	1	—
						Cardiff C	39	8
						Hartlepool U (loan)	7	1
						Bristol R	26	2
						Wimbledon	10	—
						Bristol C	52	12
						Plymouth Arg	66	17
						Notts Co	8	1
						Shrewsbury T (loan)	9	—
						Exeter C	22	3

Continued on Page 247

Trainees
Ball, James A; Barnes, Paul T; Darch, Kevin J; Hare, Matthew; Harris, Matthew; Hutchings, Mark; Lafferty, Philip R; McConnell, Barry; Medlin, Nicholas R. M; Noon, Philip B; Pears, Richard J; Phillips, Martin J; Rice, Gary J; Richardson, Jonathan D. P' Rollason, Andrew J; Thirlby, Anthony D.

Associated Schoolboys
Beavis, Ian J; Bell, Daniel A; Bennett, Troy M; Derham, Roger K; Dodge, William J; Green, Brendan S; Harris, Daniel; Harris, Nathan G; Holmes, Mark; McTighe, Daniel P; Shearer, Adam; Steer, Richard; Thomas, Nigel W; Vittles, James M. S; Walker, Scott; Wilkinson, John C; Wright Brett M.

Associated Schoolboys who have accepted the Club's offer of a Traineeship/Contract
Edwards, Wayne A; Grant, Christopher S; Littley, James M; Moxey, Matthew J.

FULHAM 1993–94 *Back row (left to right):* Julian Hails, John Richards, Mark Cooper, Sean Farrell, Peter Baah, Duncan Jupp, Glen Thomas.
Centre row: Martin Ferney, Collin Omogbehin, Terry Angus, Jim Stannard, Lee Harrison, Mark Munds, Udo Onwere, John Marshall.
Front row: Chris Smith (Physio), Paul Kelly, Jeff Eckhardt, Lee Tierling, Don Mackay (Manager), Simon Morgan, Martin Pike, Gary Brazil, Ray Lewington (Assistant Manager).

Division 3 **FULHAM**

Craven Cottage, Stevenage Rd, Fulham, London SW6 6HH. Telephone 071–736 6561. Call Line: 0891 440044.

Ground capacity: 14,542.

Record attendance: 49,335 v Millwall, Division 2, 8 October 1938.

Record receipts: £80,247 v Chelsea, Division 2, 8 October 1983.

Pitch measurements: 110yd × 75yd.

Chief Executive: R.J. Summers.

Chairman: Jimmy Hill.

Directors: W. F. Muddyman (Vice-chairman), C. A. Swain, A. Muddyman, T. Wilson, D. E. Shrimpton.

Manager: Ian Branfoot. ***Assistant Manager:*** Len Walker.

Physio: Chris Smith. ***Community Officer:*** Gary Mulcahey.

Club Secretary: Mrs Janice O'Doherty.

Commercial Manager: Ken Myers.

Year Formed: 1879. ***Turned Professional:*** 1898. ***Ltd Co.:*** 1903. ***Reformed:*** 1987.

Club Nickname: 'Cottagers'.

Previous Name: 1879–88, Fulham St Andrew's.

Previous Grounds: 1879 Star Road, Fulham; c.1883 Eel Brook Common, 1884 Lillie Road; 1885 Putney Lower Common; 1886 Ranelagh House, Fulham; 1888 Barn Elms, Castelnau; 1889 Purser's Cross (Roskell's Field), Parsons Green Lane; 1891 Eel Brook Common; 1891 Half Moon, Putney; 1895 Captain James Field, West Brompton; 1896 Craven Cottage.

Record League Victory: 10–1 v Ipswich T, Division 1, 26 December 1963 – Macedo; Cohen, Langley; Mullery (1), Keetch, Robson (1); Key, Cook (1), Leggat (4), Haynes, Howfield (3).

Record Cup Victory: 6–0 v Wimbledon (away), FA Cup, 1st rd (replay), 3 December 1930 – Iceton; Gibbon, Lilley; Oliver, Dudley, Barrett; Temple, Hammond (1), Watkins (1), Gibbons (2), Penn (2). 6–0 v Bury, FA Cup, 3rd rd, 7 January 1938 – Turner; Bacuzzi, Keeping; Evans, Dennison, Tompkins; Higgins, Worsley, Rooke (6), O'Callaghan, Arnold.

Record Defeat: 0–10 v Liverpool, League Cup 2nd rd, 1st leg, 23 September 1986.

Most League Points (2 for a win): 60, Division 2, 1958–59 and Division 3, 1970–71.

Most League Points (3 for a win): 78, Division 3, 1981–82.

Most League Goals: 111, Division 3 (S), 1931–32.

Highest League Scorer in Season: Frank Newton, 43, Division 3 (S), 1931–32.

Most League Goals in Total Aggregate: Gordon Davies, 159, 1978–84, 1986–91.

Most Capped Player: Johnny Haynes, 56, England.

Most League Appearances: Johnny Haynes, 594, 1952–70.

Record Transfer Fee Received: £333,333 from Liverpool for Richard Money, May 1980.

Record Transfer Fee Paid: £150,000 to Orient for Peter Kitchen, February 1979, and to Brighton & HA for Teddy Maybank, December 1979.

Football League Record: 1907 Elected to Division 2; 1928–32 Division 3 (S); 1932–49 Division 2; 1949–52 Division 1; 1952–59 Division 2; 1959–68 Division 1; 1968–69 Division 2; 1969–71 Division 3; 1971–80 Division 2; 1980–82 Division 3; 1982–86 Division 2; 1986–92 Division 3; 1992–94 Division 2; 1994– Division 3.

Honours: *Football League:* Division 1 best season: 10th, 1959–60; Division 2 – Champions 1948–49; Runners-up 1958–59; Division 3 (S) – Champions 1931–32; Division 3 – Runners-up 1970–71. *FA Cup:* Runners-up 1974–75. *Football League Cup:* best season: 5th rd, 1967–68, 1970–71.

FULHAM 1993—94 LEAGUE RECORD

Match No.	Date	Venue	Opponents	Result		H/T Score	Lg. Pos.	Goalscorers	Atten-dance
1	Aug 14	A	Hartlepool U	W	1-0	1-0	—	Brazil	3133
2	21	H	Cardiff C	L	1-3	0-1	14	Baddeley (og)	5696
3	28	A	Bristol R	L	1-2	0-1	16	Hails	5261
4	31	H	Wrexham	D	0-0	0-0	—		3685
5	Sept 4	H	Bradford C	D	1-1	0-1	19	Farrell	4221
6	11	A	Burnley	L	1-3	0-1	21	Brazil	9021
7	14	A	Barnet	W	2-0	2-0	—	Baah 2	3066
8	18	H	York C	L	0-1	0-1	20		3595
9	25	A	Huddersfield T	L	0-1	0-1	23		5616
10	Oct 2	H	Leyton Orient	L	2-3	1-1	23	Farrell, Brazil	4417
11	9	H	Bournemouth	L	0-2	0-0	23		4004
12	16	A	Hull C	D	1-1	1-0	23	Farrell	6089
13	23	H	Stockport Co	L	0-1	0-1	23		3615
14	30	A	Reading	L	0-1	0-0	23		7020
15	Nov 2	A	Exeter C	L	4-6	2-3	—	Hails, Farrell, Eckhardt, Brazil	2919
16	6	H	Brighton & HA	L	0-1	0-0	23		4383
17	20	A	Rotherham U	W	2-1	1-1	23	Brazil 2	2667
18	27	H	Swansea C	W	3-1	1-0	22	Morgan, Hails, Brazil	3282
19	Dec 11	A	Cardiff C	L	0-1	0-0	23		5120
20	17	H	Hartlepool U	W	2-0	1-0	—	Brazil, Farrell	2998
21	27	H	Port Vale	D	0-0	0-0	21		5760
22	28	A	Plymouth Arg	L	1-3	1-1	21	Morgan	15,609
23	Jan 1	H	Brentford	D	0-0	0-0	22		9797
24	3	A	Cambridge U	L	0-3	0-1	22		4557
25	8	A	Blackpool	W	3-2	1-0	22	Baah, Morgan, Farrell	3374
26	15	H	Hull C	L	0-1	0-0	22		4407
27	22	A	Bournemouth	W	3-1	1-1	20	Angus, Brazil (pen), Eckhardt	5464
28	30	H	Reading	W	1-0	0-0	—	Hails	6911
29	Feb 5	A	Stockport Co	W	4-2	2-1	16	Eckhardt 2, Brazil 2	5488
30	12	H	Blackpool	W	1-0	0-0	15	Bedrossian	4259
31	19	H	Bristol R	L	0-1	0-1	16		5063
32	22	A	Wrexham	L	0-2	0-0	—		2094
33	Mar 5	H	Burnley	W	3-2	1-2	17	Morgan, Eckhardt, Brazil	4943
34	12	A	York C	L	0-2	0-0	19		3572
35	15	H	Barnet	W	3-0	1-0	—	Brazil, Marshall, Baah	3326
36	19	H	Huddersfield T	D	1-1	1-1	18	Angus	3624
37	26	A	Leyton Orient	D	2-2	0-1	18	Herrera, Farrell	5096
38	29	H	Cambridge U	L	0-2	0-1	—		3444
39	Apr 2	A	Port Vale	D	2-2	2-1	20	Pike, Farrell	7380
40	4	H	Plymouth Arg	D	1-1	1-0	20	Morgan	5819
41	9	A	Brentford	W	2-1	2-1	20	Morgan, Haworth	6638
42	13	A	Bradford C	D	0-0	0-0	—		5015
43	16	H	Exeter C	L	0-2	0-2	20		4602
44	23	A	Brighton & HA	L	0-2	0-1	21		10,606
45	30	H	Rotherham U	W	1-0	0-0	20	Farrell	5217
46	May 7	A	Swansea C	L	1-2	0-1	21	Brazil	4355

Final League Position: 21

GOALSCORERS

League (50): Brazil 14 (1 pen), Farrell 9, Morgan 6, Eckhardt 5, Baah 4, Hails 4, Angus 2, Bedrossian 1, Haworth 1, Herrera 1, Marshall 1, Pike 1, own goal 1.
Coca-Cola Cup (5): Farrell 3, Brazil 1, own goal 1.
FA Cup (0):

Stannard 46	Morgan 36 + 1	Pike 31 + 2	Ferney 22 + 1	Jupp 28 + 2	Thomas 37	Hails 37	Cooper 2 + 3	Farrell 34	Brazil 46	Marshall 21	Baah 26 + 7	Angus 28 + 8	Onwere 20 + 2	Eckhardt 33 + 2	Kelly 1 + 2	Mahorn 1 + 2	Tierling 5 + 9	Herrera 23	Bedrossian 24 + 6	Haworth 4 + 7	Mison 1 + 3	Match No.
1	2	3	4	5	6	7	8	9	10	11	12	14										1
1	2	3	4	5	6	7	8	9	10	11	12		14									2
1	2	3	4	5		7	14	9	10	11	12	6	8									3
1	2	3	4		6	7	12	9	10	5	11		8									4
1	2	3	4	8	6	7	12	9	10	5	11											5
1	2	3	4		6	7		9	10	5	11		8	12								6
1	2	3	4		6	7			10	5	11		8	9								7
1	2	3		12		7		9	10	5	11	6	8	4	14							8
1	2	3	4	5	6	7		9	10		11	12	8			14						9
1	2	3	4	5	6			9	10		14	12	8		7	11						10
1	2	3	4	8	6	7		9	10			5		11		12						11
1		3	4	2	6	7		9	10		11	5		8			12					12
1	2	3	4	8	6	7		9	10			5		11	12		14					13
1	2		4		6	7		9	10			5	12	11				3	8			14
1			4		6	7		9	10		12	5	8	2			14	3	11			15
1			3	2	6	7		9	10		12	5	11	4			14		8			16
1			8	2	6	7		9	10		12	5		4				3	11			17
1	2			6		7		9	10		11	5		4				3	8			18
1	2			5	6	7		9	10		11			4				3	8			19
1	2			5	6	7		9	10		11			4				3	8			20
1	2			5	6	7		9	10		11	12		4				3	8			21
1	2			5		7		9	10		11	6	4				12	3	8	14		22
1	2			5	6	7		9	10		11	12	4					3	8			23
1	2			5	6	7		9	10		11	3	4				12		8	14		24
1	2			5	6	7		9	10		11		4					3	8	12		25
1				2	6	7		9	10		11	5	4	12				3	8	14		26
1		12		2	6	7			10		11	5	4	9				3	8			27
1		12		2	6	7			10		11	5	4	9				3	8			28
1		3		2	6	7			10		11	5	4	9					8		12	29
1		3		2	6	7			10		11	5	4	9			12		8			30
1	12	3			6	7			10	2	11	5	4	9			14		8			31
1	8	3			6	7			10	2	11	5	4	9					12			32
1	8	3			6	7			10	2	11	5		9					4			33
1	8	3		12	6	7			10	2	11	5		9					4			34
1	8	3		6		7		9	10	2	11	5		4								35
1	8	3		6		7		9	10	2	11	5		4					12			36
1	8	3			6			9	10	2		5		4			12	11	7			37
1	8	3			6			9	10	2		5		4				11	7	12		38
1	8	3	7	5	6			9	10	2		14		4				11	12			39
1	2	3	8	5	6			9	10			14		4			7	11	12			40
1	2	3	8					9	10			5		4			7	6		11	12	41
1	2	3	8						10			5		4			7	6		11	9	42
1	2	3	8						10	11		5		4			7	6	12	9	14	43
1	2	3	8		6				10	11		14		4			7	5	12	9		44
1	2	3			6	7		9	10	11				4				5	8	12		45
1	2	3	14		6	7		9	10	11				4				5	8	12		46

Coca-Cola Cup	First Round	Colchester U (h)	2-1
		(a)	2-1
	Second Round	Liverpool (h)	1-3
		(a)	0-5
FA Cup	First Round	Yeovil (a)	0-1

FULHAM

Player and Position	Ht	Wt	Birth Date	Birth Place	Source	Clubs	League App	League Gls
Goalkeepers								
Lee Harrison	6 2	12 02	12 9 71	Billericay	Trainee	Charlton Ath	—	—
						Fulham (loan)	—	—
						Gillingham (loan)	2	—
						Fulham (loan)	—	—
						Fulham	—	—
Jim Stannard	6 2	14 12	6 10 62	London	Local	Fulham	41	—
						Charlton Ath (loan)	1	—
						Southend U (loan)	17	—
						Southend U	92	—
						Fulham	312	1
Defenders								
Terry Angus	6 0	12 00	14 1 66	Coventry	VS Rugby	Northampton T	116	6
						Fulham	36	2
Jeff Eckhardt	6 0	11 07	7 10 65	Sheffield		Sheffield U	74	2
						Fulham	249	25
Martin Ferney	5 11	12 04	8 11 71	Lambeth	Trainee	Fulham	53	1
Roberto Herrera	5 7	10 06	12 6 70	Torbay	Trainee	QPR	6	—
						Torquay U (loan)	11	—
						Torquay U (loan)	5	—
						Fulham	23	1
Duncan Jupp	6 0	12 02	25 1 75	Guildford	Trainee	Fulham	33	—
John Marshall	5 10	12 01	18 8 64	Surrey	Apprentice	Fulham	368	26
Simon Morgan	5 10	11 07	5 9 66	Birmingham		Leicester C	160	3
						Fulham	144	17
Colin Omogbehin‡	6 0		10 9 74	Croydon	Trainee	Fulham	—	—
Martin Pike*	5 11	11 07	21 10 64	South Shields	Apprentice	WBA	—	—
						Peterborough U	126	8
						Sheffield U	129	5
						Tranmere R (loan)	2	—
						Bolton W (loan)	5	1
						Fulham	190	14
Glen Thomas	6 1	12 07	6 10 67	Hackney	Apprentice	Fulham	244	6
Midfield								
Ara Bedrossian†	5 9	10 00	2 6 67	Cyprus		Fulham	39	1
Sean Farrell	6 1	12 08	28 2 69	Watford	Apprentice	Luton T	25	1
						Colchester U (loan)	9	1
						Northampton T (loan)	4	1
						Fulham	94	31
Paul Kelly*	5 7	10 13	24 2 74	Hillingdon	Trainee	Fulham	6	—
Michael Mison§	6 3	13 02	8 11 75	London	Trainee	Fulham	4	—
Mark Munoz‡	5 11		16 10 74	Lambeth	Trainee	Fulham	—	—
Udo Onwere*	6 0	11 07	9 11 71	Hammersmith	Trainee	Fulham	85	7
Forwards								
Peter Baah*	5 9	10 04	1 5 73	Littleborough	Trainee	Blackburn R	1	—
						Fulham	49	4
Gary Brazil	5 11	10 02	19 9 62	Tunbridge Wells	Crystal Palace	Sheffield U	62	9
						Port Vale (loan)	6	3
						Preston NE	166	58
						Newcastle U	23	2
						Fulham	163	39
Julian Hails	5 10	11 01	20 11 67	Lincoln		Fulham	101	11
Robert Haworth§	6 2	12 12	21 11 75	Edgware	Trainee	Fulham	11	1
Jonathan Richards‡			3 10 74	Southend	Trainee	Fulham	—	—
Lee Tierling*	5 7	11 08	25 10 72	Wegberg	Trainee	Portsmouth	—	—
						Fulham	19	—

FULHAM

Colours: White shirts, red and black trim, black shorts, white stockings red and black trim. **Change colours:** Red/black striped shirts, white shorts, red stockings.

Foundation: Churchgoers were responsible for the foundation of Fulham, which first saw the light of day as Fulham St. Andrew's Church Sunday School FC in 1879. They won the West London Amateur Cup in 1887 and the championship of the West London League in its initial season of 1892–93. The name Fulham had been adopted in 1888.

First Football League game: 3 September, 1907, Division 2, v Hull C (h) L 0-1 – Skene; Ross, Lindsay; Collins, Morrison, Goldie; Dalrymple, Freeman, Bevan, Hubbard, Threlfall.

Did you know: Fulham, the only club to beat a team who went on to reach the FA Cup Final, achieved the feat on 7 January 1946 in a second leg FA Cup tie 2-1 against Charlton Athletic. Moreover they had lost left-back Cliff Lloyd with an ankle injury after 12 minutes.

Managers (and Secretary-Managers)
Harry Bradshaw 1904–09, Phil Kelso 1909–24, Andy Ducat 1924–26, Joe Bradshaw 1926–29, Ned Liddell 1929–31, Jim MacIntyre 1931–34, Jim Hogan 1934–35, Jack Peart 1935–48, Frank Osborne 1948–64 (was secretary-manager or GM for most of this period), Bill Dodgin Snr 1949–53, Duggie Livingstone 1956–58, Bedford Jezzard 1958–64 (GM for last two months), Vic Buckingham 1965–68, Bobby Robson 1968, Bill Dodgin Jnr 1969–72, Alec Stock 1972–76, Bobby Campbell 1976–80, Malcolm Macdonald 1980–84, Ray Harford 1984–86, Ray Lewington 1986–90, Alan Dicks 1990–91, Don Mackay 1991–94, Ian Branfoot June 1994–

Trainees
Abbott, Stuart R. C; Andrews, Nicholas T; Bartley, Carl A; Bolt, Daniel A; Bower, Daniel N; Brooker, Paul; Carey, John D. T; Girdler, Stuart; Gregory, John G; Hawkins, Benjamin J; Haworth, Robert J; Mison, Michael; O'Brien, Alexander J. E. S; Power, James S; Power, Raymond O; (h) Ray, Kevin P; Shevlin, Malcolm P; Smith, David P; Williams, Carl J. P.

****Non-Contract**
Bedrossian, Ara

Associated Schoolboys
Bartlett, Richard J; Cox, Kevin M; Cully, Paul S; Jennings, Gary B; Perkins, Mark S; White, Dean B; Whitthread, Paul.

Associated Schoolboys who have accepted the Club's offer of a Traineeship/Contract
Grover, Adam A; Probets, Clayton.
**Non-Contract Players who are retained must be re-signed before they are eligible to play in League matches.

Doncaster Rovers players continued from Page 211

Tony Cullen‡	5 6	11 07	30 9 69	Newcastle	Local	Sunderland	29	—
						Carlisle U (loan)	2	1
						Rotherham U (loan)	3	1
						Bury (loan)	4	—
						Swansea C	27	3
						Doncaster R	—	—
Lee Fowler*	5 8	11 07	26 1 69	Nottingham	Trainee	Stoke C	49	—
						Preston NE	32	2
						Doncaster R	11	—
Darren France‡	6 0	14 02	8 8 67	Hull	North Ferriby	Hull C	43	7
						Doncaster R	1	—
Steve Harper	5 10	11 05	3 2 69	Stoke	Trainee	Port Vale	28	2
						Preston NE	77	10
						Burnley	69	8
						Doncaster R	31	2
Peter Heritage‡	6 1	13 00	8 11 60	Bexhill	Hythe Town	Gillingham	57	11
						Hereford U	57	9
						Doncaster R	31	2
Kevin Hulme	5 10	11 09	2 12 67	Farnworth	Radcliffe Borough	Bury	110	21
						Chester C (loan)	4	—
						Doncaster R	34	8
Graeme Jones	6 0	12 12	13 3 70	Gateshead	Bridlington T	Doncaster R	28	4
Jamie Lawrence	5 10	12 03	8 3 70	Balham	Cowes	Sunderland	4	—
						Doncaster R	9	1
Lee Luscombe	6 0	12 04	16 7 71	Guernsey	Trainee	Southampton	—	—
						Brentford	42	6
						Millwall	2	—
						Doncaster R	8	—
Don Page	5 10	11 03	18 1 64	Manchester	Runcorn	Wigan Ath	74	15
						Rotherham U	55	13
						Rochdale (loan)	4	1
						Doncaster R	22	4
Paul Whitmarsh	5 8	10 12	18 9 73	London	Trainee	West Ham U	—	—
						Doncaster R	6	1

GILLINGHAM 1993–94 *Back row (left to right):* Lawrence Osbourne, Andy Arnott, Liburd Henry, Gary Breen, Tony Butler, Paul Hague, Paul Baker, Robin Trott.
Centre row: Paul Clark, Richard Carpenter, Nick Forster, Steve Banks, Neil Smillie (Reserve and Youth Team Manager), Javed Mughal (Physio), Malcolm Machin (Youth Development Officer), Scott Barrett, Lee Palmer, Robert Reinelt, Neil Smith.
Front row: Joe Dunne, Paul Watson, Tony Eeles, Steve Crane, Mike Flanagan (Manager), Richard Green, Eliot Martin, Mark Dempsey, Gary Micklewhite.

Division 3 GILLINGHAM

Priestfield Stadium, Gillingham, ME7 4DD. Telephone Medway (0634) 851854/576828. Fax (0634) 850986. Commercial Office: 851462.

Ground capacity: 10,412.

Record attendance: 23,002 v QPR, FA Cup 3rd rd 10 January 1948.

Record receipts: £49,377 v Swindon T, play-offs, 22 May 1987.

Pitch measurements: 114yd × 75yd.

President: J. W. Leech. ***Vice-presidents:*** G. B. Goodere, G. V. W. Lukehurst.

Chairman: B. R. Baker. ***Vice-chairman:*** Rt. Hon. Earl Henry Sondes.

Managing Director: A. Smith.

Directors: M. G. Lukehurst, Mrs. V. Smith.

Manager: Mike Flanagan. ***Coach:*** Mike Ling.

Physio: Javed Mughal.

Secretary: Bill Williams. ***Commercial Manager:***

Year Formed: 1893. ***Turned Professional:*** 1894. ***Ltd Co.:*** 1893.

Club Nickname: 'The Gills'.

Previous Name: New Brompton, 1893–1913.

Record League Victory: 10–0 v Chesterfield, Division 3, 5 September 1987 – Kite; Haylock, Pearce, Shipley (2) (Lillis), West, Greenall (1), Pritchard (2), Shearer (2), Lovell, Elsey (2), David Smith (1).

Record Cup Victory: 10–1 v Gorleston, FA Cup, 1st rd, 16 November 1957 – Brodie; Parry, Hannaway; Riggs, Boswell, Laing; Payne, Fletcher (2), Saunders (5), Morgan (1), Clark (2).

Record Defeat: 2–9 v Nottingham F, Division 3 (S), 18 November 1950.

Most League Points (2 for a win): 62, Division 4, 1973–74.

Most League Points (3 for a win): 83, Division 3, 1984–85.

Most League Goals: 90, Division 4, 1973–74.

Highest League Scorer in Season: Ernie Morgan, 31, Division 3 (S), 1954–55 and Brian Yeo, 31, Division 4, 1973–74.

Most League Goals in Total Aggregate: Brian Yeo, 135, 1963–75.

Most Capped Player: Tony Cascarino, 3 (51), Republic of Ireland.

Most League Appearances: John Simpson, 571, 1957–72.

Record Transfer Fee Received: £300,000 from Tottenham H for Peter Beadle, June 1992.

Record Transfer Fee Paid: £102,500 to Tottenham H for Mark Cooper, October 1987.

Football League Record: 1920 Original Member of Division 3; 1921 Division 3 (S); 1938 Failed re-election; Southern League 1938–44; Kent League 1944–46; Southern League 1946–50; 1950 Re-elected to Division 3 (S); 1958–64 Division 4; 1964–71 Division 3; 1971–74 Division 4; 1974–89 Division 3; 1989–92 Division 4; 1992– Division 3.

Honours: *Football League:* Division 3 best season: 4th, 1978–79, 1984–85; Division 4 – Champions 1963–64; Runners-up 1973–74. *FA Cup:* best season: 5th rd, 1969–70. *Football League Cup:* best season: 4th rd, 1964.

GILLINGHAM 1993—94 LEAGUE RECORD

Match No.	Date	Venue	Opponents	Result		H/T Score	Lg. Pos.	Goalscorers	Attendance
1	Aug 14	H	Chesterfield	L	0-2	0-1	—		3485
2	21	A	Rochdale	L	0-3	0-2	22		2092
3	28	H	Scarborough	D	2-2	1-1	20	Baker, Forster	2526
4	31	H	Doncaster R	D	0-0	0-0	—		2923
5	Sept 4	A	Wycombe W	D	1-1	0-0	21	Forster	6226
6	11	H	Torquay U	D	2-2	1-0	19	Forster, Green (pen)	2927
7	18	A	Shrewsbury T	D	2-2	1-1	18	Baker, Green (pen)	2811
8	25	H	Scunthorpe U	W	1-0	1-0	16	Smillie	2872
9	Oct 2	A	Carlisle U	W	2-1	0-0	14	Forster 2	6449
10	9	A	Walsall	L	0-1	0-0	16		4639
11	16	H	Darlington	W	2-1	1-1	13	Arnott, Smith	3063
12	23	A	Crewe Alex	L	0-1	0-0	15		3611
13	30	H	Colchester U	W	3-0	2-0	14	Green, Forster, Reinelt	3964
14	Nov 2	H	Hereford U	W	2-0	1-0	—	Arnott, Forster	3168
15	6	A	Mansfield T	L	1-2	1-0	14	Forster	2421
16	20	H	Wigan Ath	D	2-2	1-1	14	Forster, Baker	2727
17	27	A	Lincoln C	L	1-3	1-1	16	Baker	2979
18	Dec 11	H	Rochdale	L	1-2	0-1	17	Forster	2493
19	18	A	Chesterfield	L	2-3	1-1	17	Micklewhite, Forster	2348
20	27	H	Northampton T	W	1-0	1-0	17	Terry (og)	4648
21	Jan 1	H	Bury	W	1-0	0-0	14	Smillie	3440
22	3	A	Doncaster R	D	0-0	0-0	14		1830
23	15	A	Darlington	L	1-2	0-0	16	Henry	2111
24	22	H	Walsall	D	1-1	0-1	17	Baker	3211
25	29	A	Colchester U	W	2-1	0-0	15	Smith, Forster	3436
26	Feb 5	H	Crewe Alex	L	1-3	0-0	16	Forster	3713
27	12	A	Preston NE	D	0-0	0-0	16		6167
28	19	A	Scarborough	D	1-1	0-0	18	Baker	1527
29	25	H	Wycombe W	L	0-1	0-0	18		4292
30	Mar 1	A	Chester C	L	0-1	0-1	—		3128
31	5	A	Torquay U	W	1-0	0-0	18	Green	3353
32	12	H	Shrewsbury T	L	0-2	0-0	18		3038
33	19	A	Scunthorpe U	D	1-1	1-0	17	Baker	2386
34	26	H	Carlisle U	W	2-0	1-0	16	Carpenter (pen), Forster	2586
35	Apr 2	A	Northampton T	W	2-1	0-0	15	Carpenter, Forster	4579
36	4	H	Chester C	D	2-2	1-1	15	Baker, Butler	3165
37	12	H	Preston NE	D	2-2	1-2	—	Forster 2	2453
38	16	A	Hereford U	L	0-2	0-1	17		1964
39	19	A	Bury	D	0-0	0-0	—		1687
40	23	H	Mansfield T	W	1-0	0-0	15	Forster	2390
41	30	A	Wigan Ath	L	0-2	0-0	15		1346
42	May 7	H	Lincoln C	D	1-1	1-0	16	Carpenter (pen)	2840

Final League Position: 16

GOALSCORERS

League (44): Forster 18, Baker 8, Green 4 (2 pens), Carpenter 3 (2 pens), Arnott 2, Smillie 2, Smith 2, Butler 1, Henry 1, Micklewhite 1, Reinelt 1, own goal 1.
Coca-Cola Cup (1): Reinelt 1.
FA Cup (3): Baker 1, Micklewhite 1, Smith 1.

Barrett 13	Martin 8 + 1	Watson 14	Clark 11 + 2	Butler 25 + 2	Smith 31 + 4	Micklewhite 28 + 1	Carpenter 40	Arnott 6 + 4	Forster 35 + 6	Smillie 38	Green 38 + 1	Crane 1 + 5	Reinelt 16 + 9	Dunne 37	Palmer 28	Baker 30 + 3	Banks 29	Breen 20 + 2	Hague 1	Henry 12 + 2	Trott 1	Match No.
1	2	3	4	5	6	7	8	*9*	10	11	12	14										1
1	2	3	12	5	8	7	4		10	11	6	14	*9*									2
1			*4*		8	7	6	10	12	11	5		14	2	3	9						3
			4		10	7	6			11	5	8	12	2	3	9	1					4
			4		10	7	6		8	11	5	12		2	3	9	1					5
			4		10	7	6		8	11	5			2	3	9	1					6
				4	10	7	6		8	11	5		12	2	3	9	1					7
	6			4	10				8	11	5		7	2	3	9	1					8
			12	4	10		6		8	11	5		7	2	3	9	1					9
				4	10		6	12	8	11	5		7	2	3	9	1					10
1				4	8		6	9	10	11	5	12	7	2	3							11
1				*4*	8	7	6	9	10	11	5	12		2	3			14				12
1				4	8	7	6	9	10	11	5		12	2	3							13
1				4	8	*7*	6	9	10	11	5			2	3	12		14				14
1	6			4	8		7		10	11	5		12	2	3	9						15
	2			4	8	11	7		10					6	3	9	1	5				16
	2			4	8	11	7		10					6	3	9	1	5				17
			4	5		7	6		10	11			8	2	3	9	1					18
						7	6		10	11	5		8	2	3	9	1		4			19
	12		4			7	6		10	11	5		8	2	3		1			9		20
			4		8	7	6		10	11	5		12	2	3		1			9		21
			4		8	7	6		10	11	5		12		3		1	2		9		22
			4		10	7	6		8	11	5				3		1	2		9		23
				4	10	7	6		12	11	5			2	3	8	1			9		24
				4	10	7			12	11	5		6	2	3	8	1			9		25
				4	10	7	6		12	11	5			2	3	8	1			9		26
				4	10	7	6		8	11	5				3	12	1	2		9		27
					10	7	6		8	11	5			2	3	12	1	4		9		28
					10	*7*	6		8	11	5		12	2	3	9	1	4		14		29
		3			10		6		12	7	5		11	2		9	1	4		8		30
		3		14	10		6		12	7	5		11	2		9	1	4		8		31
		3		12	10		6		8	7	5		11	2		9	1	4				32
		3			8		6		10	7	5		12	2		9	1	4		11		33
		3		10			6		8	7	5		11	2		9	1	4				34
	11	3		10			6		8	7	5			2		9	1	4				35
	11	3		10			6		8		5		7	2		9	1	4		12		36
		3		10			6		8	7	5		11	2		9	1	4				37
1		3		10	12	11	6	14	8	7	5			2		*9*		4				38
1		3		10	12	11	6		8	7	5			2		9		4				39
1		3		10	11	12	6		8		5		7	2		9		4				40
1		3			12	11	6	14	8	7	5			2		*9*		4			10	41
1			10		12	7	6	14	8	11	5			2	3	*9*		4				42

Coca-Cola Cup	First Round	Brighton & HA (h)	1-0
		(a)	0-2
FA Cup	First Round	Yeading (a)	0-0
		(h)	3-1
	Second Round	Plymouth Arg (a)	0-2

GILLINGHAM

Player and Position	Ht	Wt	Birth Date	Birth Place	Source	Clubs	League App	League Gls
Goalkeepers								
Steven Banks	6 0	13 02	9 2 72	Hillingdon	Trainee	West Ham U	—	—
						Gillingham	29	—
Scott Barrett	5 11	13 08	2 4 63	Derby	Ilkeston T	Wolverhampton W	30	—
						Stoke C	51	—
						Colchester U (loan)	13	—
						Stockport Co (loan)	10	—
						Colchester U	—	—
						Gillingham	47	—
Alan Gough‡	5 11	12 13	10 3 71	Watford	Shelbourne	Portsmouth	—	—
						Fulham	3	—
						Gillingham	—	—
Defenders								
Gary Breen	6 1	12 07	12 12 73	London	Charlton Ath	Maidstone U	19	—
						Gillingham	51	—
Tony Butler	6 2	11 12	28 9 72	Stockport	Trainee	Gillingham	79	1
Richard Green	6 1	13 11	22 11 67	Wolverhampton		Shrewsbury T	125	5
						Swindon T	—	—
						Gillingham	90	11
Paul Hague	6 2	12 06	16 9 72	Durham	Trainee	Gillingham	9	—
Rob Hindmarch†	6 1	13 04	27 4 61	Stannington	Apprentice	Sunderland	115	2
						Portsmouth (loan)	2	—
						Derby Co	164	9
						Wolverhampton W	40	2
						Gillingham	—	—
Eliot Martin	5 6	10 00	27 9 72	Plumstead	Trainee	Gillingham	53	1
Lee Palmer	5 11	13 00	19 9 70	Gillingham	Trainee	Gillingham	110	4
Robin Trott	6 1	13 04	17 8 74	Orpington	Trainee	Gillingham	1	—
Paul Watson	5 8	10 10	4 1 75	Hastings	Trainee	Gillingham	15	—
Midfield								
Paul Baker	6 1	13 06	5 1 63	Newcastle	Bishop Auckland	Southampton	—	—
						Carlisle U	71	11
						Hartlepool U	197	67
						Motherwell	9	1
						Gillingham	54	14
Richard Carpenter	5 10	13 00	30 9 72	Sheppey	Trainee	Gillingham	80	4
Paul Clark*	5 9	13 07	14 9 58	Benfleet	Apprentice	Southend U	33	1
						Brighton	79	9
						Reading (loan)	2	—
						Southend U	276	3
						Gillingham	90	1
Mark Dempsey*	5 8	11 02	10 12 72	Dublin	Trainee	Gillingham	48	2
Joe Dunne	5 8	11 06	25 5 73	Dublin	Trainee	Gillingham	78	—
Tony Eeles*	5 6	10 08	15 11 70	Chatham	Trainee	Gillingham	73	5
Andrew Ramage	5 11	12 02	3 10 74	Hornchurch	Dagenham	Gillingham	—	—
Neil Smith	5 9	12 00	30 9 71	London	Trainee	Tottenham H	—	—
						Gillingham	100	7
Forwards								
Andy Arnott	6 1	12 00	18 10 73	Chatham	Trainee	Gillingham	44	10
						Manchester U (loan)	—	—
Steve Crane*	5 9	12 00	3 6 72	Essex	USA	Gillingham	13	1
Nick Forster	5 9	11 05	8 9 73	Oxted	Horley T	Gillingham	67	24
Liburd Henry*	5 11	12 09	29 8 67	Dominica	Leytonstone/ Ilford	Watford	10	1
						Halifax T (loan)	5	—
						Maidstone U	67	9
						Gillingham	42	2
Gary Micklewhite	5 7	10 04	21 3 61	Southwark	Apprentice	Manchester U	—	—
						QPR	106	11
						Derby Co	240	31
						Gillingham	29	1

GILLINGHAM

Colours: Blue shirts, white shorts, white stockings. **Change colours:** All red.

Foundation: The success of the pioneering Royal Engineers of Chatham excited the interest of the residents of the Medway Towns and led to the formation of many clubs including Excelsior. After winning the Kent Junior Cup and the Chatham District League in 1893, Excelsior decided to go for bigger things and it was at a meeting in the Napier Arms, Brompton, in 1893 that New Brompton FC came into being as a professional concern, securing the use of a ground in Priestfield Road.

First Football League game: 28 August, 1920, Division 3, v Southampton (h) D 1-1 – Branfield; Robertson, Sissons; Battiste, Baxter, Wigmore; Holt, Hall, Gilbey (1), Roe, Gore.

Did you know: In 1963–64 Gillingham achieved more points (60) than they scored goals (59), but their Division 4 championship owed much to their defence which only conceded a club record 30 goals.

Managers (and Secretary-Managers)
W. Ironside Groombridge 1896–1906* (previously financial secretary), Steve Smith 1906–08, W. I. Groombridge 1908–19*, George Collins 1919–20, John McMillan 1920–23, Harry Curtis 1923–26, Albert Hoskins 1926–29, Dick Hendrie 1929–31, Fred Maven 1932–37, Alan Ure 1937–38, Bill Harvey 1938–39, Archie Clark 1939–58, Harry Barratt 1958–62, Freddie Cox 1962–65, Basil Hayward 1966–71, Andy Nelson 1971–74, Len Ashurst 1974–75, Gerry Summers 1975–81, Keith Peacock 1981–87, Paul Taylor 1988, Keith Burkinshaw 1988–89, Damien Richardson 1989–93, Mike Flanagan July 1993–

Player and Position	*Ht*	*Wt*	*Birth Date*	*Birth Place*	*Source*	*Clubs*	*League App*	*League Gls*
Lawrence Osborne‡	5 10	11 11	20 10 67	London	Apprentice	Arsenal	—	—
						Newport Co	15	—
					Redbridge Forest	Maidstone U	37	4
					Redbridge Forest	Maidstone U	53	8
						Gillingham	6	1
Robert Reinelt	5 10	11 13	11 3 74	Epping	Trainee	Aldershot	5	—
						Gillingham	25	1
Neil Smillie	5 6	10 07	19 7 58	Barnsley	Apprentice	Crystal Palace	83	7
						Brentford (loan)	3	—
						Brighton	75	2
						Watford	16	3
						Reading	39	—
						Brentford	172	18
						Gillingham	38	2

Trainees
Carney, John L; Christou, Christopher B; Comer, Sam M. J; Corbyn, Richard; Emerick, Karl S; Francis, Daniel J; Hake, Kevin S; Hills, Marc; Maxted, Daniel R; Osborne, Lee; Smart, Matthew; Smith, Gary J; Sykes, Pauil J; Verrall, Damon F; Wilson, Paul A. F.

Associated Schoolboys
Barton, Jason L; Cullum, Andrew J; Lander, Daniel M; Roser, Craig M; Williams, Lee M.

Associated Schoolboys who have accepted the Club's offer of a Traineeship/Contract
Clifford, Kevin D; Spiller, Lee M.

GRIMSBY TOWN 1993–94 *Back row (left to right):* Simon Dunlop, Neil Woods, Peter Handyside, Paul Crichton, Rhys Wilmot, Graham Rodger, Mark Lever, Paul Futcher.
Centre row: Ken Reed (Physio), Tony Ford, Craig Shakespeare, Craig Maddison, Paul Agnew, Paul Groves, Clive Mendonca, Jim Dobbin, Richard O'Kelly (Youth Coach).
Front row: Kevin Jobling, Tony Rees, Tommy Watson, Gary Childs, Arthur Mann (Reserve Coach), Alan Buckley (Manager), Tony Daws, Dave Gilbert, John McDermott, Gary Croft.

Division 1 GRIMSBY TOWN

Blundell Park, Cleethorpes, South Humberside DN35 7PY. Telephone Cleethorpes (0472) 697111. Fax (0472) 693665. Clubcall: 0898 121576.

Ground capacity: 16,116.

Record attendance: 31,651 v Wolverhampton W, FA Cup 5th rd, 20 February 1937.

Record receipts: £119,758 v Aston Villa, FA Cup 4th rd, 29 January 1994.

Pitch measurements: 111yd × 75yd.

Presidents: T. J. Lindley, T. Wilkinson.

Chairman: P. W. Furneaux. ***Vice-chairman:*** W. H. Carr.

Directors: T. Aspinall, G. Lamming, J. Mager.

Manager: Alan Buckley. ***Assistant Manager:*** Arthur Mann.

Youth team coach: Richard O'Kelly.

Company Secretary: Ian Fleming. ***Commercial Manager:*** Anthony Richardson. ***Lottery Manager:*** T. E. Harvey.

Physio: Ken Reed.

Year Formed. 1878. ***Turned Professional:*** 1890. ***Ltd Co.:*** 1890.

Previous Name: Grimsby Pelham.

Club Nickname: 'The Mariners'.

Previous Grounds: Clee Park; Abbey Park.

Record League Victory: 9–2 v Darwen, Division 2, 15 April 1899 – Bagshaw; Lockie, Nidd; Griffiths, Bell (1), Nelmes; Jenkinson (3), Richards (1), Cockshutt (3), Robinson, Chadburn (1).

Record Cup Victory: 8–0 v Darlington, FA Cup, 2nd rd, 21 November 1885 – G. Atkinson; J. H. Taylor, H. Taylor; Hall, Kimpson, Hopewell; H. Atkinson (1), Garnham, Seal (3), Sharman, Monument (4).

Record Defeat: 1–9 v Arsenal, Division 1, 28 January 1931.

Most League Points (2 for a win): 68, Division 3 (N), 1955–56.

Most League Points (3 for a win): 83, Division 3, 1990–91.

Most League Goals: 103, Division 2, 1933–34.

Highest League Scorer in Season: Pat Glover, 42, Division 2, 1933–34.

Most League Goals in Total Aggregate: Pat Glover, 182, 1930–39.

Most Capped Player: Pat Glover, 7, Wales.

Most League Appearances: Keith Jobling, 448, 1953–69.

Record Transfer Fee Received: £650,000 from Sunderland for Shaun Cunnington, July 1992.

Record Transfer Fee Paid: £150,000 to Blackpool for Paul Groves, August 1992.

Football League Record: 1892 Original Member Division 2; 1901–03 Division 1; 1903 Division 2; 1910 Failed re-election; 1911 re-elected Division 2; 1920–21 Division 3; 1921–26 Division 3 (N); 1926–29 Division 2; 1929–32 Division 1; 1932–34 Division 2; 1934–48 Division 1; 1948–51 Division 2; 1951–56 Division 3 (N); 1956–59 Division 2; 1959–62 Division 3; 1962–64 Division 2; 1964–68 Division 3; 1968–72 Division 4; 1972–77 Division 3; 1977–79 Division 4; 1979–80 Division 3; 1980–87 Division 2; 1987–88 Division 3; 1988–90 Division 4; 1990–91 Division 3; 1991– 92 Division 2; 1992– Division 1.

Honours: *Football League:* Division 1 best season: 5th, 1934–35; Division 2 – Champions 1900–01, 1933–34; Runners-up 1928–29; Division 3 (N) – Champions 1925–26, 1955–56; Runners-up 1951–52; Division 3 – Champions 1979–80; Runners-up 1961–62; Division 4 – Champions 1971–72; Runners-up 1978–79; 1989–90. *FA Cup:* Semi-finals, 1936, 1939. *Football League Cup:* best season: 5th rd, 1979–80, 1984–85. *League Group Cup:* Winners 1981–82.

GRIMSBY TOWN 1993—94 LEAGUE RECORD

Match No.	Date	Venue	Opponents	Result		H/T Score	Lg. Pos.	Goalscorers	Attendance
1	Aug 14	H	Bolton W	D	0-0	0-0	—		8593
2	21	A	Nottingham F	L	3-5	1-2	19	Mendonca 2, Dobbin	23,225
3	24	H	Portsmouth	D	1-1	0-1	—	Mendonca (pen)	5259
4	28	H	Tranmere R	D	0-0	0-0	18		4793
5	Sept 4	A	Peterborough U	W	2-1	0-0	11	Mendonca, Groves	5962
6	11	H	Watford	D	2-2	1-0	13	Jemson (pen), Groves	4783
7	18	A	Birmingham C	D	1-1	1-1	16	Gilbert	11,302
8	25	H	Wolverhampton W	W	2-0	1-0	10	Childs, Mendonca	6310
9	28	A	Sunderland	D	2-2	2-0	—	Groves, Gray Martin (og)	15,488
10	Oct 2	A	Oxford U	D	2-2	1-0	7	Jemson, Childs	4301
11	9	H	Southend U	W	4-0	2-0	7	Mendonca 2 (1 pen), Childs 2	4726
12	16	A	Stoke C	L	0-1	0-0	8		14,696
13	23	H	Charlton Ath	L	0-1	0-1	12		5118
14	30	A	Crystal Palace	L	0-1	0-1	15		12,202
15	Nov 2	H	Leicester C	D	0-0	0-0	—		6344
16	7	A	Barnsley	W	2-1	1-1	—	Mendonca 2 (1 pen)	5797
17	20	A	Derby Co	L	1-2	1-2	14	Mendonca (pen)	13,498
18	27	A	Millwall	L	0-1	0-0	16		7691
19	Dec 4	H	Barnsley	D	2-2	0-2	16	Dobbin, Watson	8123
20	18	A	Bolton W	D	1-1	1-1	19	Dobbin	9431
21	27	H	Notts Co	D	2-2	1-1	18	Livingstone, Walker (og)	7781
22	29	A	Luton T	L	1-2	1-0	21	Groves	7234
23	Jan 1	H	Bristol C	W	1-0	0-0	17	Groves	5469
24	3	A	Middlesbrough	L	0-1	0-1	18		10,441
25	15	H	Stoke C	D	0-0	0-0	19		8577
26	22	A	Southend U	W	2-1	1-1	18	Dobbin, Livingstone	4367
27	Feb 1	H	WBA	D	2-2	0-0	—	Shakespeare, Groves	4740
28	5	A	Charlton Ath	W	1-0	0-0	18	Mendonca	7598
29	12	H	Crystal Palace	D	1-1	0-1	18	Mendonca	6302
30	19	A	Portsmouth	L	1-3	0-2	17	Groves	7794
31	Mar 5	A	Tranmere R	W	2-1	2-1	18	Childs, Shakespeare	6454
32	8	H	Peterborough U	W	3-2	1-1	—	Groves, Livingstone, Childs	4504
33	12	H	Birmingham C	W	1-0	0-0	14	Croft	5405
34	15	A	Watford	W	3-0	1-0	—	Gilbert (pen), Groves, Shakespeare	5109
35	19	A	Wolverhampton W	D	0-0	0-0	13		20,224
36	26	H	Oxford U	W	1-0	0-0	11	Mendonca	5025
37	29	H	Middlesbrough	D	1-1	0-1	—	Groves	5709
38	Apr 2	A	Notts Co	L	1-2	0-1	14	Rodger	7205
39	4	H	Luton T	W	2-0	1-0	11	Gilbert 2	5542
40	9	A	Bristol C	L	0-1	0-0	12		5480
41	12	H	Sunderland	L	0-1	0-0	—		4732
42	16	A	Leicester C	D	1-1	1-0	14	Mendonca	15,859
43	23	H	Derby Co	D	1-1	0-0	15	Groves	7451
44	30	A	WBA	L	0-1	0-1	15		16,870
45	May 3	H	Nottingham F	D	0-0	0-0	—		11,930
46	8	H	Millwall	D	0-0	0-0	16		5355

Final League Position: 16

GOALSCORERS

League (52): Mendonca 14 (4 pens), Groves 11, Childs 6, Dobbin 4, Gilbert 4 (1 pen), Livingstone 3, Shakespeare 3, Jemson 2 (1 pen), Croft 1, Rodger 1, Watson 1, own goals 2.
Coca-Cola Cup (6): Dobbin 2, Mendonca 2, Groves 1, Okorie 1.
FA Cup (2): Croft 1, Groves 1.

Crichton 46	McDermott 26	Croft 31 + 5	Futcher 39	Lever 21 + 1	Groves 46	Watson 6 + 5	Gilbert 37	Daws 9 + 1	Mendonca 39	Shakespeare 21 + 12	Dobbin 27 + 2	Rodger 20 + 4	Ford 27 + 2	Woods 3 + 8	Crosby 2 + 1	Jobling 4 + 7	Handyside 11 + 2	Childs 30 + 1	Jemson 6	Agnew 21 + 2	Okorie — + 5	Livingstone 27	Rees 7 + 9	*Match No.*
1	2	3	4	5	6	*7*	8	*9*	10	11	12	14												1
1	2		4	5	9	12	*8*		10	3	6	14	*7*	11										2
1	2	3	4	12	9		8		10		6	5		11	7									3
1	2	*3*		5	9	12	8		10		6	4		11	*7*	14								4
1	2	3			11		8	9	10	12	6	4					5	7						5
1	2	3			11		8	9		12	6	4			14		5	*7*	10					6
1	2	3			11	7	8	9			6						5		10	4				7
1	2	3	4	5	9		8		10	12	6							7	11					8
1	2		4	5	11				9	8	6							7	10	3	12			9
1	2		4	5	11				9	8	6	12						7	10	3				10
1	2		4		11		8		9	12	6	5				14		7	10	*3*				11
1	2		4	5	11		8	*9*	10	12	6					14		7		3				12
1	2		4	*5*	11	12		9	10	8	6					14		7		3				13
1	2		4	5	11	12			10		6					8		7		*3*	14	9		14
1		3	4	5	11				10		6		2			8		7			12	9		15
1		3	4	5	11		8		10		*6*		2			14		7				9	12	16
1	2	3	4	5	11		*8*	9	10	6			12			14		7						17
1		3	4	5	11	12	8	*10*		*7*	6					2						9	14	18
1		3	4	5	11	*7*	8	*10*		12	6					2						9	14	19
1	2	3	4	5	11	7	8		10	12	6											9		20
1	2	3	4	*5*	11	7	8		10	12	6											9	14	21
1	2	3	4		11		*8*		10	12	6		7				5					9	14	22
1	2	3	4		11		8		10		6		7				5					9		23
1	2	3	4		11				10	12	*6*		7				5			8		9	14	24
1		3	4		9	*7*	*8*		10	11	6		2				5			12			14	25
1		3	4		11		8		*10*	7	6	14	2				5	12				9		26
1		3	4	5	11		*8*		10	12	6		2					7				9	14	27
1		3	4		11				10	8	6	5	2					7				9		28
1		3	4		11		8	14	10	12	6	5	2					7					*9*	29
1	2	3	4		11				10	6		5	8					*7*		12	14		*9*	30
1		12	4		11		8		10	6		5	2					7		3	14		*9*	31
1	2		4		11		8		10			5	6					7		3		9		32
1	2	12	4		11		8					5	6	14				7		3		9	*10*	33
1	2		4		11		8			6		5	7							3		9	10	34
1	2	3	4		11		8			6		5	7	12								9	10	35
1	*2*	12	4		11		8		10	6		5	14					7		3		9		36
1			4		11		8		10	6		5	2					7		3		9		37
1		*3*			11		8		10	6		5	2	14			12	7		4		9		38
1		12			11		8		*10*	6		5	2	14			4	7		3		9		39
1		12			11		8		10	6		5	2	14			4	7		3		*9*		40
1		2	4		11		8		10			5	6	12				7		3		9		41
1		2	4	6	11				10			5	8					7		3		9		42
1		2	4	5	11		8		10				6	12				7		3		9		43
1		2	4	5	11		8		10				6	12			14	7		*3*		9		44
1		3	4	5	11		8		10	6			2					7				9	12	45
1		3	4		11		8		10	6	12		2			14	5	*7*					9	46

Coca-Cola Cup	Second Round	Hartlepool U (h)	3-0
		(a)	2-0
	Third Round	Tranmere R (a)	1-4
FA Cup	Third Round	Wigan Ath (h)	1-0
	Fourth Round	Aston Villa (h)	1-2

GRIMSBY TOWN

Player and Position	Ht	Wt	Birth Date	Birth Place	Source	Clubs	League App	League Gls
Goalkeepers								
Paul Crichton	6 1	12 05	3 10 68	Pontefract	Apprentice	Nottingham F	—	—
						Notts Co (loan)	5	—
						Darlington (loan)	5	—
						Peterborough U (loan)	4	—
						Darlington (loan)	3	—
						Swindon T (loan)	4	—
						Rotherham U (loan)	6	—
						Torquay U (loan)	13	—
						Peterborough U	47	—
						Doncaster R	77	—
						Grimsby T	46	—
Rhys Wilmot	6 1	12 00	21 2 62	Newport	Apprentice	Arsenal	8	—
						Hereford U (loan)	9	—
						Orient (loan)	46	—
						Swansea C (loan)	16	—
						Plymouth Arg (loan)	17	—
						Plymouth Arg	116	—
						Grimsby T	33	—
Defenders								
Paul Agnew	5 9	10 07	15 8 65	Lisburn	Cliftonville	Grimsby T	231	3
Gary Croft	5 9	10 08	17 2 74	Burton-on-Trent	Trainee	Grimsby T	69	1
Paul Futcher	6 0	12 03	25 9 56	Chester	Apprentice	Chester	20	—
						Luton T	131	1
						Manchester C	37	—
						Oldham Ath	98	1
						Derby Co	35	—
						Barnsley	230	—
						Halifax T	15	—
						Grimsby T	125	—
Joby Gowshall			7 8 75	Louth	Trainee	Grimsby T	—	—
Peter Handyside	6 1	12 03	31 7 74	Dumfries	Trainee	Grimsby T	24	—
Mark Lever	6 3	12 08	29 3 70	Beverley	Trainee	Grimsby T	188	7
John McDermott	5 7	10 00	3 2 69	Middlesbrough		Grimsby T	264	4
Graham Rodger	6 2	11 13	1 4 67	Glasgow	Apprentice	Wolverhampton W	1	—
						Coventry C	36	2
						Luton T	28	2
						Grimsby T	70	8
Midfield								
Gary Childs	5 7	10 08	19 4 64	Birmingham	Apprentice	WBA	3	—
						Walsall	131	17
						Birmingham C	55	2
						Grimsby T	146	18
Jim Dobbin	5 9	10 07	17 9 63	Dunfermline	Whitburn BC	Celtic	2	—
						Motherwell (loan)	2	—
						Doncaster R	64	13
						Barnsley	129	12
						Grimsby T	100	16
Simon Dunlop*	5 11	12 00	24 11 74	Grimsby	Trainee	Grimsby T	—	—
David Gilbert	5 4	10 04	22 6 63	Lincoln	Apprentice	Lincoln C	30	1
						Scunthorpe U	1	—
					Boston U	Northampton T	120	21
						Grimsby T	219	35
Paul Groves	5 11	11 05	28 2 66	Derby	Burton Alb	Leicester C	16	1
						Lincoln C (loan)	8	1
						Blackpool	107	21
						Grimsby T	92	23
Kevin Jobling	5 9	10 11	1 1 68	Sunderland	Apprentice	Leicester C	9	—
						Grimsby T	186	8
						Scunthorpe U (loan)	—	—
Craig Shakespeare	5 10	12 05	26 10 63	Birmingham	Apprentice	Walsall	284	45
						Sheffield W	17	—
						WBA	112	12
						Grimsby T	33	3
Tommy Watson	5 8	10 10	29 9 69	Liverpool	Trainee	Grimsby T	149	21

GRIMSBY TOWN

Colours: Black and white vertical striped shirts, black shorts with red triangular panel on side, white stockings with red band on turnover. **Change colours:** Red and royal blue striped shirts, red shorts, red stockings.

Foundation: Grimsby Pelham FC as they were first known, came into being at a meeting held at the Wellington Arms in September 1878. Pelham is the family name of big landowners in the area, the Earls of Yarborough. The receipts for their first game amounted to 6s. 9d. (approx. 39p). After a year, the club name was changed to Grimsby Town.

First Football League game: 3 September, 1892, Division 2, v Northwich Victoria (h) W 2-1 – Whitehouse; Lundie, T. Frith; C. Frith, Walker, Murrell; Higgins, Henderson, Brayshaw, Riddoch (2), Ackroyd.

Did you know: Grimsby Town achieved a club record in 1993–94 when they registered 20 drawn matches. Their previous highest had been 17 in 1964–65 when they finished 10th in Division 3.

Managers (and Secretary-Managers)
H. N. Hickson 1902–20*, Haydn Price 1920, George Fraser 1921–24, Wilf Gillow 1924–32, Frank Womack 1932–36, Charles Spencer 1937–51, Bill Shankly 1951–53, Billy Walsh 1954–55, Allenby Chilton 1955–59, Tim Ward 1960–62, Tom Johnston 1962–64, Jimmy McGuigan 1964–67, Don McEvoy 1967–68, Bill Harvey 1968–69, Bobby Kennedy 1969–71, Lawrie McMenemy 1971–73, Ron Ashman 1973–75, Tom Casey 1975–76, Johnny Newman 1976–79, George Kerr 1979–82, David Booth 1982–85, Mike Lyons 1985–87, Bobby Roberts 1987–88, Alan Buckley June 1988–

Player and Position	Ht	Wt	Birth Date	Birth Place	Source	Clubs	League App	League Gls
Forwards								
Tony Ford*	5 9	12 02	14 5 59	Grimsby	Apprentice	Grimsby T	354	54
						Sunderland (loan)	9	1
						Stoke C	112	13
						WBA	114	14
						Grimsby T	68	3
						Bradford C (loan)	5	—
Steve Livingstone	6 1	11 04	8 9 69	Middlesbrough	Trainee	Coventry C	31	5
						Blackburn R	30	10
						Chelsea	1	—
						Port Vale (loan)	5	—
						Grimsby T	27	3
Clive Mendonca	5 10	10 07	9 9 68	Tullington	Apprentice	Sheffield U	13	4
						Doncaster R (loan)	2	—
						Rotherham U	84	27
						Sheffield U	10	1
						Grimsby T (loan)	10	3
						Grimsby T	81	24
Tony Rees	5 9	11 13	1 8 64	Merthyr Tydfil	Apprentice	Aston Villa	—	—
						Birmingham C	95	12
						Peterborough U (loan)	5	2
						Shrewsbury T (loan)	2	—
						Barnsley	31	3
						Grimsby T	141	33
Neil Woods	6 0	12 11	30 7 66	York	Apprentice	Doncaster R	65	16
						Rangers	3	—
						Ipswich T	27	5
						Bradford C	14	2
						Grimsby T	122	24

Trainees
Barratt, Mark A; Black, Steven G. G; Brookes, Mark; Buckley, Simon J; Cook, John; Lambert, Darren K; Martin, Paul A; McPhee, Kevin W; Miller, David; Mulhall, Sean; Neil, James D; Petchey, Stewart L; Rushby, Mathew S; Wilkinson, David A.

****Non-Contract**
Trinder, Jason L.

Associated Schoolboys
Applegate, James M; Bell, Richard P; Bloomer, Matthew B; Brown, James K; Ellerby, James M; Gresham, Stewart J; Hanslip, Nicholas; Love, Andrew M; Oster, John M; Oswin, Matthew S. W; Rockhill, Anthony J.

Associated Schoolboys who have accepted the Club's offer of a Traineeship/Contract
Burdon, Andrew J; Carinci, Pietro; Fraser, Steven M; Hamnett, John C; Harsley, Paul; Lester, Jack W; Mundell, Andrew A; Savage, Christopher I; Welton, Guy E.
**Non-Contract Players who are retained must be re-signed before they are eligible to play in League matches.

HARTLEPOOL UNITED 1993–94 *Back row (left to right):* Darren Hannah, Chris Creamer, Keith Oliver, Chris Lynch, Nicky Southall, Steve Jones, Tim Carter, Paul Linyard, Phil Gilchrist, Paul Thompson, Stephen Halliday, Anthony March, Mark Dawkins.
Centre row: Eric Gates, Jack Watson, Micky Gallagher, Chris Homer, Darren Grimes, Neil Maughan, Keith Nobbs, Paul Olsson, Ian McGuckin, Ryan Cross, Andrew Fletcher, Keith Houchen, Mick Tait, Matty Hyson, Denny Ingram, Jason Porteous, Viv Busby, Gary Henderson (Physio).
Front row: Simon Anderson, Paul Wardle, Paul Lowery, Paul Cross, Brian Honour, Dean Emerson, John MacPhail (Player/Manager), Paul Wratten, Nicky Peverell, Colin West, John Gallacher, Anthony Skedd, Craig Hyndman.

Division 3 **HARTLEPOOL UNITED**

The Victoria Ground, Clarence Road, Hartlepool, TS24 8BZ. Telephone Hartlepool (0429) 272584. Commercial Dept: (0429) 222077. Fax: (0429) 863007. Football in the Community: (0429) 862595.

Ground capacity: 6721.

Record attendance: 17,426 v Manchester U, FA Cup 3rd rd, 5 January 1957.

Record receipts: £42,300 v Tottenham H, Rumbelows Cup, 2nd rd 2nd leg, 9 October 1990.

Pitch measurements: 110yd × 75yd.

President: E. Leadbitter.

Chairman: G. Gibson. ***Vice-chairman:*** A. Bamford.

Directors: G. Gibson, A. Elliott.

Manager: John MacPhail. ***Coach*** :Billy Horner.

Youth/Reserve Coach: Eric Gates. ***Physio:*** Gary Henderson. ***Commercial Manager:*** G. McDonnell. ***Assistant Secretary:*** John Elliott.

Year Formed: 1908. ***Turned Professional:*** 1908. ***Ltd Co.:*** 1908.

Club Nickname: 'The Pool'.

Previous Names: Hartlepools United until 1968; Hartlepool until 1977.

Record League Victory: 10–1 v Barrow, Division 4, 4 April 1959 – Oakley; Cameron, Waugh; Johnson, Moore, Anderson; Scott (1), Langland (1), Smith (3), Clark (2), Luke (2). (1 og).

Record Cup Victory: 6–0 v North Shields, FA Cup, 1st rd, 30 November 1946 – Heywood; Brown, Gregory; Spelman, Lambert, Jones; Price, Scott (2), Sloan (4), Moses, McMahon.

Record Defeat: 1–10 v Wrexham, Division 4, 3 March 1962.

Most League Points (2 for a win): 60, Division 4, 1967–68.

Most League Points (3 for a win): 82, Division 4, 1990–91.

Most League Goals: 90, Division 3 (N), 1956–57.

Highest League Scorer in Season: William Robinson, 28, Division 3 (N), 1927–28 and Joe Allon, 28, Division 4, 1990–91.

Most League Goals in Total Aggregate: Ken Johnson, 98, 1949–64.

Most Capped Player: Ambrose Fogarty, 1 (11), Republic of Ireland.

Most League Appearances: Wattie Moore, 447, 1948–64.

Record Transfer Fee Received: £300,000 from Chelsea for Joe Allon, August 1991.

Record Transfer Fee Paid: £60,000 to Barnsley for Andy Saville, March 1992.

Football League Record: 1921 Original Member of Division 3 (N); 1958–68 Division 4; 1968–69 Division 3; 1969–91 Division 4; 1991–92 Division 3; 1992–94 Division 2; 1994– Division 3.

Honours: *Football League:* Division 3 best season: 22nd, 1968–69; Division 3 (N) – Runners-up 1956–57. *FA Cup:* best season: 4th rd, 1954–55, 1977–78, 1988–89, 1992–93. *Football League Cup,* best season: 4th rd, 1974–75.

HARTLEPOOL UNITED 1993—94 LEAGUE RECORD

Match No.	Date	Venue	Opponents	Result		H/T Score	Lg. Pos.	Goalscorers	Attendance
1	Aug 14	H	Fulham	L	0-1	0-1	—		3133
2	21	A	Brighton & HA	D	1-1	1-1	20	Gallacher	5230
3	28	H	Bournemouth	D	1-1	0-0	21	Honour	2482
4	31	A	Leyton Orient	W	2-1	0-0	—	West, Southall	3399
5	Sept 4	A	Exeter C	L	1-2	1-1	18	Southall	2644
6	11	H	Stockport Co	W	1-0	1-0	14	Thompson	2473
7	14	H	Blackpool	W	2-0	0-0	—	West, Honour	2114
8	18	A	Port Vale	L	0-1	0-1	14		7279
9	25	H	York C	L	0-2	0-1	17		3050
10	Oct 2	A	Burnley	L	0-2	0-1	18		9532
11	9	H	Brentford	L	0-1	0-0	21		1802
12	16	A	Cambridge U	L	0-1	0-0	21		3318
13	23	H	Bradford C	L	1-2	1-1	21	Johnrose	2536
14	30	A	Cardiff C	D	2-2	2-0	20	Johnrose, West	3710
15	Nov 2	H	Barnet	W	2-1	1-0	—	Houchen, Johnrose	1960
16	6	A	Bristol R	D	1-1	1-0	20	West	5308
17	20	H	Wrexham	L	1-2	1-2	21	Southall	1530
18	27	A	Plymouth Arg	L	0-2	0-1	21		5881
19	Dec 4	A	Blackpool	L	1-2	0-1	21	Stoneman (og)	3130
20	11	H	Brighton & HA	D	2-2	1-0	21	Southall, Honour (pen)	1558
21	17	A	Fulham	L	0-2	0-1	—		2998
22	27	H	Huddersfield T	L	1-4	1-2	23	Southall (pen)	3286
23	28	A	Hull C	L	0-1	0-0	23		4607
24	Jan 1	H	Rotherham U	W	2-0	0-0	23	Houchen 2	2101
25	8	A	Reading	L	0-4	0-2	23		6217
26	15	H	Cambridge U	L	0-2	0-2	23		1690
27	22	A	Brentford	L	0-1	0-1	23		6334
28	28	A	Swansea C	D	1-1	0-0	—	Thompson	2573
29	Feb 5	A	Bradford C	L	1-2	0-2	23	Thompson	7907
30	12	H	Reading	L	1-4	1-0	23	McGuckin	2218
31	19	A	Bournemouth	D	0-0	0-0	23		3201
32	25	H	Exeter C	L	1-2	0-1	23	McGuckin	1695
33	Mar 5	A	Stockport Co	L	0-5	0-3	23		4076
34	8	H	Leyton Orient	D	1-1	0-0	—	Southall	1251
35	12	H	Port Vale	L	1-4	1-2	23	MacPhail	1798
36	19	A	York C	L	0-3	0-1	23		3191
37	22	H	Cardiff C	W	3-0	1-0	—	Olsson, Southall (pen), Houchen	1077
38	26	H	Burnley	W	4-1	2-1	23	Houchen 2, Southall, Thompson	2879
39	29	H	Swansea C	W	1-0	1-0	—	Houchen	1354
40	Apr 2	A	Huddersfield T	D	1-1	0-0	23	West	5717
41	4	H	Hull C	L	0-1	0-1	23		2448
42	9	A	Rotherham U	L	0-7	0-4	23		2792
43	23	H	Bristol R	W	2-1	1-0	23	Houchen, Peverell	1409
44	26	A	Barnet	L	2-3	2-1	—	Southall, Olsson	1351
45	30	A	Wrexham	L	0-2	0-1	23		2013
46	May 7	L	Plymouth Arg	L	1-8	0-4	23	Peverell	2382

Final League Position: 23

GOALSCORERS

League (41): Southall 9 (2 pens), Houchen 8, West 5, Thompson 4, Honour 3 (1 pen), Johnrose 3, McGuckin 2, Olsson 2, Peverell 2, Gallacher 1, MacPhail 1, own goal 1.
Coca-Cola Cup (3): Honour 1, Tait 1, West 1.
FA Cup (0):

Carter 18	Cross R 17	Cross P 16	McGuckin 33 + 2	MacPhail 29 + 3	Emerson 12 + 1	Gallacher 2	Wratten 42	West 29 + 7	Honour 17	Peverell 6 + 10	Southall 38 + 2	Gilchrist 30 + 5	Tait 25 + 1	Thompson 20 + 6	Johnrose 9 + 4	Houchen 34	Olsson 29 + 3	Ingram 13	Halliday 7 + 4	Skedd 21 + 1	Jones 28	Lynch 17 + 2	Garrett 14	Oliver — + 1	Match No.
1	2	3	4	5	6	7	8	9	10	*11*	12	14													1
1	2	3	4	5	12	7	8	9	10		11		6												2
1	2	3		5	6		8	9	10	14	11	*4*	7	12											3
1	2	3	4	5	6		8	9	10	12	11			7											4
1	2	3	4	5	6		8	9	10	12	11			7											5
1	2	3	4	5	6		8	9	10		11			7	12										6
1	2	3	4	5	6		8	9	10		11			7	12										7
1	2	3	4	5	6		8	9	10		11			7	12										8
1	2	3	4	5	6		8	9	10		11			7	12										9
1	2	3	4	5	6		8	7	10			12			11	9									10
1	2	3	4	5	6		8	*7*	10			12			11	9	14								11
1	2	3		5	6		8			14	12	4	7		*10*	9	11								12
1	2	3	4	5	6		8			12			7		10	9	11								13
1	2	3	4	5			8	11		12			7		10	9	6								14
1	2	3	4	5			8	11				12	7		10	9	6								15
1	2	3	4	5			8	11				7			10	9	6								16
1			4	5							7	3	6		8	9	12	2	10	11					17
1	2			5			11	12	10		7	6	4		8	9				3					18
			12	5			8	*11*	10		7	6	4			9	14	2		3	1				19
			5				8	11	10		7	6	4			9		2		3	1				20
				5			8	11	10		7	6	4	12		9		*2*		3	1	14			21
				5			8	11	*10*		7		4	12		9	6	2		14	1	3			22
				5			8	11			7	6	2			9	4			10	1	3			23
				5			8	11			7	6	2			9	4			10	1	3			24
				5			8	11			7	6	2			9	4			10	1	3			25
				5			*8*	11		12	7	6	2	9			4		14	10	1	3			26
			5	12			8				7	6	11	*9*			4	2	14	10	1	3			27
			5	12			8				7		6	14		9	4	2	*11*	10	1	3			28
			5				8				7	11	6	12		9	4	2	14	10	1	*3*			29
			5				8				7	11	6	12		9	4	2	14	10	1	*3*			30
			5				8				2	11	6	7		9	4			10	1	3			31
			5	12			8	14	10		2	6		7		9	4		*11*		1	3			32
			5	6			8	10		12	*11*	3		7		9	4				1		2	14	33
			5	4			8	10			11	3		7		9				6	1		2		34
			5	4				10		12	11	3		*7*		9	8			6	1		2		35
			5	4				10			11	3		7		9	8			6	1		2		36
			5				10				11	4		7		9	8			6	1	3	2		37
			5				10	12			11	4		7		9	8			6	1	3	2		38
			5				10	12		14	11	4		7		9	8			6	1	*3*	2		39
			5				10	6			11	4		7		9	8				1	3	2		40
			5				10	6			11	4		7		9	8				1	3	2		41
			5				10	6		9	11	4	12	7			8				1	3	2		42
							6			8	11	4	5			9	7	3	10		1		2		43
			14				*6*	12		8	11	4	5			9	7	3	10		1		2		44
			5				6	12		8	11	14	4			9	7	3	10		1		2		45
								12		8	11	5	4			9	7	3	10	*6*	1	14	2		46

Coca-Cola Cup	First Round	Stockport Co (a)	1-1
		(h)	2-1
	Second Round	Grimsby T (a)	0-3
		(h)	0-2
FA Cup	First Round	Macclesfield (a)	0-2

HARTLEPOOL UNITED

Player and Position	Ht	Wt	Birth Date	Birth Place	Source	Clubs	League App	League Gls
Goalkeepers								
Steven Jones	5 11	12 03	31 1 74	Teeside	Trainee	Hartlepool U	37	—
Paul Linyard§	6 1	12 00	18 7 77	Keighley	Trainee	Hartlepool U	—	—
Defenders								
Scott Garrett			9 1 74	Gateshead	Trainee	Hartlepool U	14	—
Philip Gilchrist	6 0	11 12	25 8 73	Stockton	Trainee	Nottingham F	—	—
						Middlesbrough	—	—
						Hartlepool U	59	—
Denny Ingram§	5 10	11 08	27 6 76	Sunderland	Trainee	Hartlepool U	13	—
Thomas McGuckin	6 2	12 02	24 4 73	Middlesbrough	Trainee	Hartlepool U	56	3
John MacPhail†	6 0	12 03	7 12 55	Dundee	St. Columba's	Dundee	68	—
						Sheffield U	135	7
						York C	142	24
						Bristol C	26	1
						Sunderland	130	22
						Hartlepool U	157	4
Keith Nobbs‡	5 10	11 10	19 9 61	Bishop Auckland	Apprentice	Middlesbrough	1	—
						Halifax T	87	1
					Bishop Auckland	Hartlepool U	280	1
Midfield								
Brian Honour	5 7	12 05	16 2 64	Horden	Apprentice	Darlington	74	4
					Peterlee	Hartlepool U	318	25
Keith Oliver§	5 8	10 03	15 1 76	South Shields	Trainee	Hartlepool U	1	—
Paul Olsson*	5 8	10 11	24 12 65	Hull	Apprentice	Hull C	—	—
						Exeter C (loan)	8	—
						Exeter C	35	2
						Scarborough	48	5
						Hartlepool U	171	13
Tony Skedd	5 5	10 00	19 5 75	North Cleveland	Trainee	Hartlepool U	23	—
Mick Tait*	5 11	12 05	30 9 56	Wallsend	Apprentice	Oxford U	64	23
						Carlisle U	106	20
						Hull C	33	3
						Portsmouth	240	30
						Reading	99	9
						Darlington	79	2
						Hartlepool U	61	1
Paul Wratten*	5 7	10 00	29 11 70	Middlesbrough	Trainee	Manchester U	2	—
						Hartlepool U	57	1
Forwards								
Andrew Fletcher	6 0	13 00	12 8 71	Saltburn	Trainee	Middlesbrough	—	—
						Scarborough	48	11
					Billingham	Hartlepool U	—	—
John Gallacher (To Falkirk January 1994)	5 10	10 08	26 1 69	Glasgow		Falkirk	18	5
						Newcastle U	29	6
						Hartlepool U	23	2
Stephen Halliday§	5 10	11 02	3 5 76	Sunderland	Charlton Ath	Hartlepool U	11	—
Keith Houchen	6 2	12 08	25 7 60	Middlesbrough	Chesterfield	Hartlepool U	170	65
						Orient	76	20
						York C	67	19
						Scunthorpe U	9	3
						Coventry C	54	7
						Hibernian	57	11
						Port Vale	49	10
						Hartlepool U	34	8
Chris Lynch	6 0	11 00	18 11 74	Middlesbrough	Halifax T	Hartlepool U	20	—
Nick Peverell*	5 11	11 10	28 4 73	Middlesbrough	Trainee	Middlesbrough	—	—
						Hartlepool U	35	3
Nicky Southall	5 10	11 02	28 1 72	Teeside	Trainee	Hartlepool U	101	18
Paul Thompson	5 11	11 10	17 4 73	Newcastle	Trainee	Hartlepool U	28	5
Colin West*	5 8	11 10	19 9 67	Middlesbrough	Apprentice	Chelsea	16	4
						Partick T (loan)	24	10
						Swansea C (loan)	14	3
						Dundee	35	6
						Hartlepool U	36	5

HARTLEPOOL UNITED

Colours: Navy/sky blue. **Change colours:** All yellow.

Foundation: The inspiration for the launching of Hartlepool United was the West Hartlepool club which won the FA Amateur Cup in 1904–05. They had been in existence since 1881 and their Cup success led in 1908 to the formation of the new professional concern which first joined the North-Eastern League. In those days they were Hartlepools United and won the Durham Senior Cup in their first two seasons.

First Football League game: 27 August, 1921, Division 3(N), v Wrexham (a) W 2-0 – Gill; Thomas, Crilly; Dougherty, Hopkins, Short; Kessler, Mulholland (1), Lister (1), Robertson, Donald.

Did you know: On 15 March 1971 Hartlepool United entertained Brentford in a 0-0 draw. It was the one-millionth game to have been played since the formation of the Football League in 1888.

Managers (and Secretary-Managers)
Alfred Priest 1908–12, Percy Humphreys 1912–13, Jack Manners 1913–20, Cecil Potter 1920–22, David Gordon 1922–24, Jack Manners 1924–27, Bill Norman 1927–31, Jack Carr 1932–35 (had been player-coach since 1931), Jimmy Hamilton 1935–43, Fred Westgarth 1943–57, Ray Middleton 1957–59, Bill Robinson 1959–62, Allenby Chilton 1962–63, Bob Gurney 1963–64, Alvan Williams 1964–65, Geoff Twentyman 1965, Brian Clough 1965–67, Angus McLean 1967–70, John Simpson 1970–71, Len Ashurst 1971–74, Ken Hale 1974–76, Billy Horner 1976–83, Johnny Duncan 1983, Mike Docherty 1983, Billy Horner 1984–86, John Bird 1986–88, Bobby Moncur 1988–89, Cyril Knowles 1989–91, Alan Murray 1991–93, Viv Busby 1993, John MacPhail November 1993–

Trainees
Anderson, Simon C; Dawkins, Mark A; Gallagher, Michael A; Grimes, Darren; Halliday, Stephen W; Hannah, Darren J; Homer, Christopher; Hyndman, Craig N; Hyson, Matthew A; Ingram, Stuart D; Linyard, Paul M; March, Anthony; Maughan, Neil G; Oliver, Keith; Porteous, Jason; Wardle, Paul.

****Non-Contract**
Macphail, John.

Associated Schoolboys who have accepted the Club's offer of a Traineeship/Contract
Allinson, Jamie; Gallagher, Ian; Hyson, Daniel J.
**Non-Contract Players who are retained must be re-signed before they are eligible to play in League matches.

Exeter City players continued from Page 223
Forwards

Michele Cecere	6 0	11 04	4 1 68	Chester	Apprentice	Oldham Ath	52	8
						Huddersfield T	54	8
						Stockport Co (loan)	1	—
						Walsall	112	32
						Exeter C	2	—
Eamonn Dolan‡	5 10	12 01	20 9 67	Dagenham	Apprentice	West Ham U	15	3
						Bristol C (loan)	3	—
						Birmingham C	12	1
						Exeter C	26	4
Nicky Morgan‡	5 10	13 10	30 10 59	East Ham	Apprentice	West Ham U	21	2
						Portsmouth	95	32
						Stoke C	88	21
						Bristol C	80	23
						Bournemouth (loan)	6	1
						Exeter C	12	4
Richard Pears§			16 7 76	Exeter	Trainee	Exeter C	11	1
Martin Phillips§			13 3 76	Exeter	Trainee	Exeter C	15	—
Mike Ross	5 6	9 13	2 9 71	Southampton		Portsmouth	4	—
						Exeter C	27	9
Stuart Storer	5 11	11 08	16 1 67	Harborough	Local	Mansfield T	1	—
						Birmingham C	8	—
						Everton	—	—
						Wigan Ath (loan)	12	—
						Bolton W	123	12
						Exeter C	54	6
Peter Whiston	6 0	11 06	4 1 68	Widnes		Plymouth Arg	10	—
						Torquay U (loan)	8	1
						Torquay U	32	—
						Exeter C	85	7
Steve Wigley*	5 9	10 05	15 10 61	Ashton	Curzon Ashton	Nottingham F	82	2
						Sheffield U	28	1
						Birmingham C	87	4
						Portsmouth	120	12
						Exeter C	23	1
Gary Worthington	5 10	10 05	10 11 66	Cleethorpes	Apprentice	Manchester U	—	—
						Huddersfield T	—	—
						Darlington	40	15
						Wrexham	72	18
						Wigan Ath	63	20
						Exeter C	15	1
						Doncaster R (loan)	8	2

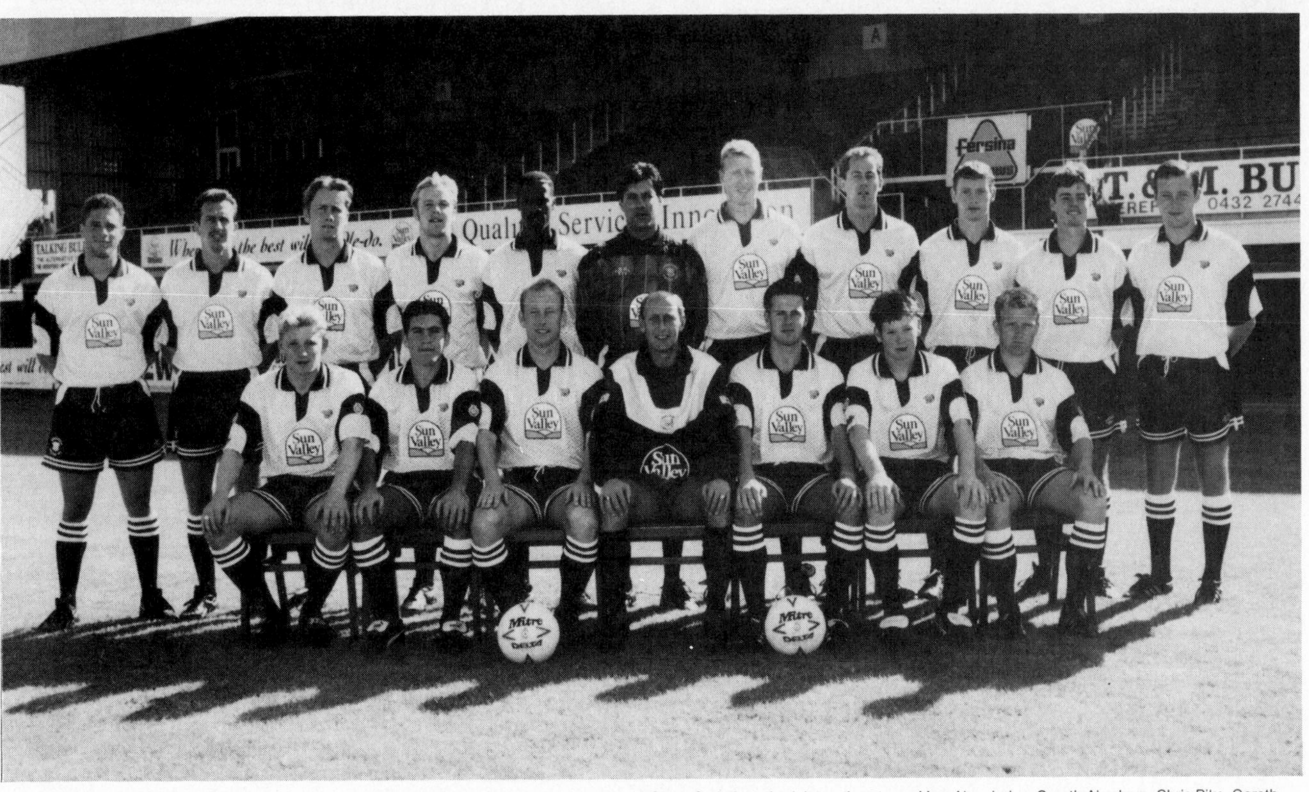

HEREFORD UNITED 1993–94 *Back row (left to right):* David Morris, Colin Anderson, Howard Clark, Craig Langford, Leroy Armstrong-May, Alan Judge, Gareth Abraham, Chris Pike, Gareth Davies, Chris Fry, Steve Clements.
Front row: Max Nicholson, Steve Walker, Derek Hall, Greg Downs (Manager), Owen Pickard, Paul Eversham, Simon Brain.

Division 3 **HEREFORD UNITED**

Edgar Street, Hereford, HR4 9JU. Telephone Hereford (0432) 276666. Fax (0432) 341359. Commercial Dept: (0432) 273155.

Ground capacity: 13,777.

Record attendance: 18,114 v Sheffield W, FA Cup 3rd rd, 4 January 1958.

Record receipts: £72,840 v Manchester U, FA Cup 4th rd, 28 January 1990.

Pitch measurements: 111yd × 74yd.

Chairman: P. S. Hill FRICS. ***Vice-chairman:*** M. B. Roberts.

Directors: D. H. Vaughan, J. W. T. Duggan, D. A. Jones, R. A. Fry (Managing).

Manager: Greg Downs.

Physio: Colin Taylor.

Secretary: David Vaughan.

Year Formed: 1924. ***Turned Professional:*** 1924. ***Ltd Co.:*** 1939.

Club Nickname: 'United'.

Record League Victory: 6–0 v Burnley (away), Division 4, 24 January 1987 – Rose; Rodgerson, Devine, Halliday, Pejic, Dalziel, Harvey (1p), Wells, Phillips (3), Kearns (2), Spooner.

Record Cup Victory: 6–1 v QPR, FA Cup, 2nd rd, 7 December 1957 – Sewell; Tomkins, Wade; Masters, Niblett, Horton (2p); Reg Bowen (1), Clayton (1), Fidler, Williams (1), Cyril Beech (1).

Record Defeat: 0–6 v Rotherham U, Division 4, 29 April 1989.

Most League Points (2 for a win): 63, Division 3, 1975–76.

Most League Points (3 for a win): 77, Division 4, 1984–85.

Most League Goals: 86, Division 3, 1975–76.

Highest League Scorer in Season: Dixie McNeil, 35, 1975–76.

Most League Goals in Total Aggregate: Stewart Phillips, 93, 1980–88, 1990–1.

Most Capped Player: Brian Evans, 1 (7), Wales.

Most League Appearances: Mel Pejic, 412, 1980–92.

Record Transfer Fee Received: £200,000 from QPR for Darren Peacock, December 1990.

Record Transfer Fee Paid: £50,000 to Halifax T for Ian Juryeff, December 1989.

Football League Record: 1972 Elected to Division 4; 1973–76 Division 3; 1976–77 Division 2; 1977–78 Division 3; 1978–92 Division 4; 1992– Division 3.

Honours: *Football League:* Division 2 best season: 22nd, 1976–77; Division 3 – Champions 1975–76; Division 4 – Runners-up 1972–73. *FA Cup:* best season: 4th rd, 1971–72, 1976–77, 1981–82, 1989–90. *Football League Cup:* best season: 3rd rd, 1974–75. *Welsh Cup:* Winners, 1990.

HEREFORD UNITED 1993—94 LEAGUE RECORD

Match No.	Date	Venue	Opponents	Result		H/T Score	Lg. Pos.	Goalscorers	Attendance
1	Aug 14	H	Scarborough	L	0-1	0-1	—	—	2157
2	21	A	Chesterfield	L	1-3	1-2	20	Pickard	2718
3	28	H	Lincoln C	L	1-2	0-1	21	Pickard	1900
4	31	H	Wycombe W	L	3-4	2-2	—	Pike 2, Hall	2847
5	Sept 4	A	Scunthorpe U	W	2-1	1-0	19	Pike, Hall	3091
6	11	H	Northampton T	D	1-1	1-0	18	Nicholson	2276
7	18	A	Rochdale	L	0-2	0-2	20		2645
8	25	H	Wigan Ath	W	3-0	1-0	18	Nicholson, Abraham, May	1813
9	Oct 2	A	Walsall	D	3-3	0-0	18	Fry, Hall, Morris	3725
10	9	A	Crewe Alex	L	0-6	0-4	19		3509
11	16	H	Colchester U	W	5-0	2-0	17	Pike 3 (1 pen), Fry, Hall	1848
12	23	A	Bury	L	3-5	1-2	19	Fry, Pike 2 (1 pen)	2354
13	30	H	Preston NE	L	2-3	0-2	20	Pickard, Clark H	3383
14	Nov 2	A	Gillingham	L	0-2	0-1	—		3168
15	6	H	Chester C	L	0-5	0-2	20		2092
16	20	A	Torquay U	D	1-1	0-0	20	Pike	2846
17	27	H	Doncaster R	W	2-1	2-1	20	Pickard, Clark H	1817
18	Dec 18	A	Scarborough	W	1-0	1-0	18	Nicholson	1209
19	27	H	Shrewsbury T	L	0-1	0-1	18		4333
20	Jan 1	H	Carlisle U	D	0-0	0-0	19		2204
21	3	A	Wycombe W	L	2-3	0-2	19	Clark H, Eversham	5528
22	8	H	Darlington	D	1-1	0-0	19	Clark H (pen)	1710
23	15	A	Colchester U	L	0-1	0-0	20		2439
24	18	A	Mansfield T	L	1-2	1-0	—	Hall	1802
25	22	H	Crewe Alex	L	1-2	0-1	21	Reece	2638
26	Feb 5	H	Bury	W	3-0	2-0	21	Hall 2, Akinbiyi	1805
27	12	A	Darlington	W	3-1	2-1	21	Pike 2, Hall	2111
28	19	A	Lincoln C	L	1-3	0-2	21	Akinbiyi	2277
29	Mar 1	A	Preston NE	L	0-3	0-0	—		6641
30	5	A	Northampton T	W	1-0	0-0	20	Pike	5394
31	12	H	Rochdale	W	5-1	2-0	19	Pike 2, Clark H, Steele, Anderson	1964
32	15	H	Chesterfield	L	0-3	0-2	—		1806
33	19	A	Wigan Ath	W	4-3	2-1	19	Roberts 2, Pike, Hall	1542
34	26	H	Walsall	L	0-1	0-0	19		2744
35	29	H	Scunthorpe U	L	1-2	0-2	—	Nicholson	1707
36	Apr 2	A	Shrewsbury T	L	0-2	0-0	19		5310
37	4	H	Mansfield T	L	2-3	0-2	19	Pike, Roberts	1996
38	9	A	Carlisle U	W	2-1	0-1	19	Roberts 2	4065
39	16	H	Gillingham	W	2-0	1-0	19	Pike 2 (2 pens)	1964
40	23	A	Chester C	L	1-3	0-1	19	Clark H	3845
41	30	H	Torquay U	D	2-2	1-1	20	Steele, Pickard	2726
42	May 7	A	Doncaster R	L	0-1	0-1	20		1603

Final League Position: 20

GOALSCORERS

League (60): Pike 18 (4 pens), Hall 9, Clark H 6, Pickard 5, Roberts 5, Nicholson 4, Fry 3, Akinbiyi 2, Steele 2, Abraham 1, Anderson 1, Eversham 1, May 1, Morris 1, Reece 1.
Coca-Cola Cup (3): Hall 2 (1 pen), May 1.
FA Cup (2): Hall 1, Pike 1.

Judge 39	Downs 27	Preddy 9 + 4	Davies 30 + 1	Langford 3 + 1	Clark H 35 + 2	Hall 42	Clements 2 + 5	Pickard 30 + 6	Pike 34	Nicholson 22 + 5	Fry 12 + 4	Morris 23 + 6	Anderson 32 + 3	Abraham 29 + 1	May 5 + 2	Eversham 3 + 5	Smith 17 + 1	Thomas 3	Brain 2 + 1	Reece 28	Harrison 6	Steele 20	Akinbiyi 3 + 1	Roberts 5 + 1	Williams 1 + 1	Clark D — + 1	*Match No.*
1	2	*3*	4	5	6	7	8	9	10	11	12	14															1
1	2			4	8	7		9	10		12	6	3	5	11												2
1			2	*4*		7	14	12	10	11	8	6	3	5	9												3
1			4		2	7		9	10	11	8	6	3	5		12											4
1	2		4			7		9	10	11	8	6	3	5			12										5
1	2		4			7		9	10	11	8	6	3		12		5										6
1	3		4		2	7	*8*	9	10	11	12	6			14		5										7
1	3		4			7	12			11	10	6		2	9	8	5										8
	3		*2*		8	7		12		11	10	6	14	5	9		4	1									9
	3				2	7		10		11	8	6	4		9		5	1	12								10
1	3		2			7			10	11	8	6	12	4			5		9								11
1	3		2		14	7			10	11	8	6	12	4			5		*9*								12
1	3		2		10	7		9		12	8	6	11	4			5										13
1	3			12	9	7				11	8	6	10	4		2	5										14
1	3		4		14	7			9	11	*8*	2	10	12			5			6							15
1	4				2	7		9	10	11			3				5			6	8						16
1	4				2	7		9	10	11	12		3				5			6	8						17
1		3	4		2	7		9	10	11							5			6	8						18
1		3	4		2	7	12	9	10	11							5			6	8						19
1		3	4		2	7		9	10	12			11				5			6	8						20
1		*3*	4		2	7		9	10	12		14	11			8	5			6							21
1		3	4		2	7		10		12		9	11			14	5			6	*8*						22
1			4		2	7		9	10	11			3	5						6		8					23
1		11	4		2	7		9	10				3	5						6		8					24
1		11			2	7		9	10			4	3	5						6		8	12				25
1		11			2	7		12	10			4	3	5						6		8	9				26
1					2	7		11	10			4	3	5						6		8	9				27
1			4		2	7		11	10				3	5		12				6		8	9				28
1	3	14	4		2	7		9	10	*11*		12		5						6		8					29
1	11		4		2	7		9	10			12	3	5						6		8					30
1	11	12	4		2	7		9	10				3	5						6		8					31
1	11	12	4		2	7		9	*10*				3	5		14				6		8					32
1	3		*4*		2	7		12	9	11		14		5						6		8		10			33
1	3				2	7		12	9			4	11	5						6		8		10			34
1					2	7			9	11		4	3	5						6		8		10			35
1	3				2	7		12	9			4	11	5						6		8		10			36
1			14		2	7		9	10	11		4	3	*5*						6		8		12			37
1	3		4		2	7		10		12			11	5						6		8		9			38
1	3		4		2	7	12	9	10				11	5						6		8					39
	3		4		2	7	12	*9*	10			5	11			14		1		6		8					40
1	3		4		2	7		9	10			12	11	5						6		*8*			14		41
1	3	12	4		2	7		10					11	5						6		8			*9*	14	42

Coca-Cola Cup	First Round	Torquay U (h)	0-2
		(a)	2-0
	Second Round	Wimbledon (h)	0-1
		(a)	1-4
FA Cup	First Round	Cambridge C (a)	1-0
	Second Round	Bath C (a)	1-2

HEREFORD UNITED

Player and Position	Ht	Wt	Birth Date	Birth Place	Source	Clubs	League App	League Gls
Goalkeepers								
Ron Green‡	6 2	14 00	3 10 56	Birmingham	Alvechurch	Walsall	163	—
						WBA (loan)	—	—
						Shrewsbury T	19	—
						Bristol R (loan)	18	—
						Bristol R	38	—
						Scunthorpe U	78	—
						Wimbledon	4	—
						Shrewsbury T (loan)	17	—
						Manchester C (loan)	—	—
						Walsall	67	—
					Local	Colchester U	4	—
						Cambridge U	—	—
						Shrewsbury T	—	—
						Walsall	—	—
						Hereford U	—	—
Alan Judge*	5 11	11 06	14 5 60	Kingsbury	Amateur	Luton T	11	—
						Reading (loan)	33	—
						Reading	44	—
						Oxford U	80	—
						Lincoln C (loan)	2	—
						Cardiff C (loan)	8	—
						Hereford U	105	—
Brian Thomas§			7 6 76	Neath	Trainee	Hereford U	3	—
Defenders								
Gareth Abraham*	6 4	12 11	13 2 69	Merthyr Tydfil	Trainee	Cardiff C	87	4
						Hereford U	49	2
Howard Clark	5 11	11 01	19 9 68	Coventry	Apprentice	Coventry C	20	1
						Darlington (loan)	5	—
						Shrewsbury T	56	—
						Hereford U	37	6
Gareth Davies			11 12 73	Hereford	Trainee	Hereford U	67	1
Greg Downs	5 9	10 07	13 12 58	Carlton	Apprentice	Norwich C	169	7
						Torquay U (loan)	1	1
						Coventry C	146	4
						Birmingham C	17	—
						Hereford U	105	2
Craig Langford*	6 1		12 3 75	Solihull	Trainee	Hereford U	5	—
Phil Preddy§			20 11 75	Hereford	Trainee	Hereford U	13	—
Kevan Smith*	6 3	12 07	13 12 59	Eaglescliffe	Stockton	Darlington	245	11
						Rotherham U	59	4
						Coventry C	6	—
						York C	31	5
						Darlington	98	5
						Hereford U (loan)	6	—
						Hereford U	18	—
Midfield								
Colin Anderson*	5 10	10 08	26 4 62	Newcastle	Apprentice	Burnley	6	—
						Torquay U	109	11
						QPR (loan)	—	—
						WBA	140	10
						Walsall	26	2
						Hereford U	70	1
Steve Clements*	5 10	11 10	26 9 72	Slough	Trainee	Arsenal	—	—
						Hereford U	7	—
Paul Eversham	5 9	11 07	28 1 75	Hereford	Trainee	Hereford U	8	1
Derek Hall	5 8	12 03	5 1 65	Manchester	Apprentice	Coventry C	1	—
						Torquay U (loan)	10	2
						Torquay U	45	4
						Swindon T	10	—
						Southend U	123	15
						Halifax T	49	4
						Hereford U	103	18
Adrian Heathcock‡			26 1 75	Dudley	Trainee	Hereford U	2	—
David Morris*	5 11	12 00	19 11 71	Plumstead	Trainee	Bournemouth	1	—
						Hereford U	40	1

HEREFORD UNITED

Colours: White shirts, black shorts, white stockings. **Change colours:** Red and black diamond shirts, white shorts, white and black stockings.

Foundation: A number of local teams amalgamated in 1924 under the chairmanship of Dr. E. W. Maples to form Hereford United and joined the Birmingham Combination. They graduated to the Birmingham League four years later.

First Football League game: 12 August, 1972, Division 4, v Colchester U (a) L 0-1 – Potter; Mallender, Naylor; Jones, McLaughlin, Tucker; Slattery, Hollett, Owen, Radford, Wallace.

Did you know: Chris Pike scored a hat-trick against Colchester United on 16 October 1993 and achieved it by beating three different players. Colchester had two goalkeepers sent off for professional fouls.

Managers (and Secretary-Managers)
Eric Keen 1939, George Tranter 1948–49, Alex Massie 1952, George Tranter 1953–55, Joe Wade 1956–62, Ray Daniels 1962–63, Bob Dennison 1963–67, John Charles 1967–71, Colin Addison 1971–74, John Sillett 1974–78, Mike Bailey 1978–79, Frank Lord 1979–82, Tommy Hughes 1982–83, Johnny Newman 1983–87, Ian Bowyer 1987–90, Colin Addison 1990–91, John Sillett 1991–92, Greg Downs May 1992–

Player and Position	*Ht*	*Wt*	*Birth Date*	*Birth Place*	*Source*	*Clubs*	*League App*	*League Gls*
Andy Reece	5 11	12 04	5 9 62	Shrewsbury	Willenhall	Bristol R	239	17
						Walsall (loan)	9	1
						Walsall (loan)	6	—
						Hereford U	28	1
Steve Walker*	5 7	11 02	7 10 74	Worcester	Wolverhampton W	Hereford U	—	—
Forwards								
Simon Brain*	5 6	10 08	31 3 66	Evesham	Cheltenham T	Hereford U	87	20
Dean Clarke§			28 7 77	Hereford	Trainee	Hereford U	1	—
Mark Cross§			6 5 76	Abergavenny	Trainee	Hereford U	1	—
Leroy May‡	6 1	11 07	12 8 69	Wolverhampton	Tividale	Walsall	4	—
					Tividale	Hereford U	21	3
Max Nicholson*	5 10	12 03	3 10 71	Leeds	Trainee	Doncaster R	27	2
						Hereford U	63	7
Owen Pickard	5 10	11 03	18 11 69	Barnstaple	Trainee	Plymouth Arg	16	1
						Hereford U	73	14
Chris Pike	6 2	13 07	19 10 61	Cardiff	Barry T	Fulham	42	4
						Cardiff C (loan)	6	2
						Cardiff C	148	65
						Hereford U	34	18
Tim Steele	5 9	11 00	1 2 67	Coventry	Apprentice	Shrewsbury T	61	5
						Wolverhampton W	75	7
						Stoke C (loan)	7	1
						Bradford C	11	—
						Hereford U	20	2
Chris Williams§			21 9 76	Neath	Trainee	Hereford U	2	—

Trainees
Brown, Stewart S; Brownrigg, Andrew D; Clarke, Dean B; Cross, Mark; Gambling, Benjamin R; Hulbert, Nolan; Lees, Michael J; Mackenzie, Neil D; Preedy, Phillip; Taylor, Clive A; Thomas, Brian; Tivey, Robert; Warner, Robert M; Watkins, Edward J; Williams, Christopher J.

****Non-Contract**
Edwards, Michael S; Watkins, Andrew J.
**Non-Contract Players who are retained must be re-signed before they are eligible to play in League matches.

HUDDERSFIELD TOWN 1993–94 *Back row (left to right):* Scot Whitehead, Richard Ward, Rodney Rowe, Simon Baldry, Kevin Blackwell, Steve Francis, Chris Billy, Gary Clayton, Gerry Harrison, Simon Collins.
Centre row: Mick Jones (Assistant Manager), Richard Logan, Ronnie Jepson, Ifem Onuora, Pat Scully, Peter Jackson, Andrew Booth, Graham Mitchell, Jon Dyson, Dave Wilson (Physio).
Front row: Michael Midwood, Simon Trevitt, Tom Cowan, Phil Starbuck, Neil Warnock (Manager), Darren Bullock, Iain Dunn, Phil Robinson, Mark Wells.

Division 2 HUDDERSFIELD TOWN

Leeds Rd, Huddersfield HD1 6PX. Telephone (0484) 420335. Fax (0484) 515122. Club Shop: 0484 534867. Recorded Information: (0891) 121635.

Ground capacity: 16,000 rising to 20,000.

Record attendance: 67,037 v Arsenal, FA Cup 6th rd, 27 February1932.

Record receipts: £89,081 v Arsenal, Coca-Cola Cup, 2nd rd lst leg, 21 September 1993.

Pitch measurements: 115yd × 76yd.

Chairman: T. S. Fisher. ***Vice-chairman:*** D. G. Headey.

Directors: M. Asquith, D. Taylor, R. Whiteley.

Associate Director: T. J. Cherry.

Manager: Neil Warnock. ***Assistant Manager:*** Mick Jones.

Secretary: Alan D. Sykes. ***Commercial Manager:*** Alan Stevenson. ***Chief Executive:*** Paul Fletcher.

Physio: Dave Wilson.

Year Formed: 1908. ***Turned Professional:*** 1908. ***Ltd Co.:*** 1908.

Club Nickname: 'The Terriers'.

Record League Victory: 10–1 v Blackpool, Division 1, 13 December 1930 – Turner; Goodall, Spencer; Redfern, Wilson, Campbell; Bob Kelly (1), McLean (4), Robson (3), Davies (1), Smailes (1).

Record Cup Victory: 7–1 v Chesterfield (away), FA Cup, 3rd rd, 12 January 1929 – Turvey; Goodall, Wadsworth; Evans, Wilson, Naylor: Jackson (1), Kelly, Brown (3), Cumming (2), Smith. (1 o.g).

Record Defeat: 1–10 v Manchester C, Division 2, 7 November 1987.

Most League Points (2 for a win): 66, Division 4, 1979–80.

Most League Points (3 for a win): 82, Division 3, 1982–83.

Most League Goals: 101, Division 4, 1979–80.

Highest League Scorer in Season: Sam Taylor, 35, Division 2, 1919–20; George Brown, 35, Division 1, 1925–26.

Most League Goals in Total Aggregate: George Brown, 142, 1921–29 and Jimmy Glazzard, 142, 1946–56.

Most Capped Player: Jimmy Nicholson, 31 (41), Northern Ireland.

Most League Appearances: Billy Smith, 520, 1914–34.

Record Transfer Fee Received: £308,000 from Southampton for Simon Charlton, June 1993.

Record Transfer Fee Paid: £245,000 to Watford for Iwan Roberts, July 1990.

Football League Record: 1910 Elected to Division 2; 1920–52 Division 1; 1952–53 Division 2; 1953–56 Division 1; 1956–70 Division 2; 1970–72 Division 1; 1972–73 Division 2; 1973–75 Division 3; 1975–80 Division 4; 1980–83 Division 3; 1983–88 Division 2; 1988–92 Division 3; 1992– Division 2.

Honours: *Football League:* Division 1 – Champions 1923–24, 1924–25, 1925–26; Runners-up 1926–27, 1927–28, 1933–34; Division 2 – Champions 1969–70; Runners-up 1919–20, 1952–53; Division 4 – Champions 1979–80. *FA Cup:* Winners 1922; Runners-up 1920, 1928, 1930, 1938. *Football League Cup:* Semi-final, 1967–68. *Autoglass Trophy:* Runners-up 1993–94.

HUDDERSFIELD TOWN 1993—94 LEAGUE RECORD

Match No.	Date	Venue	Opponents	Result		H/T Score	Lg. Pos.	Goalscorers	Attendance
1	Aug 14	H	Reading	L	0-3	0-2	—		6415
2	21	A	Rotherham U	W	3-2	1-1	13	Onuora, Roberts, Wells	5540
3	28	H	Stockport Co	D	1-1	0-1	13	Onuora	7053
4	31	A	Swansea C	L	0-1	0-1	—		4318
5	Sept 4	A	Brighton & HA	D	2-2	1-0	17	Wells, Onuora	4518
6	11	H	Exeter C	L	0-1	0-1	20		5266
7	14	H	Port Vale	D	1-1	0-0	—	Dunn	5154
8	18	A	Hull C	L	1-2	0-1	22	Starbuck	7570
9	25	H	Fulham	W	1-0	1-0	21	Hicks	5616
10	Oct 2	A	Plymouth Arg	L	0-2	0-1	21		6646
11	9	A	York C	W	2-0	1-0	18	Wells, Roberts	6363
12	16	H	Barnet	L	1-2	0-0	19	Wells	5614
13	23	A	Burnley	D	1-1	0-0	19	Starbuck	12,011
14	30	H	Bristol R	W	1-0	0-0	19	Roberts	5612
15	Nov 2	A	Bradford C	L	0-3	0-0	—		8096
16	6	H	Cambridge U	D	1-1	0-0	19	Rowe	4767
17	20	A	Blackpool	L	1-2	0-0	19	Roberts	4704
18	27	H	Brentford	L	1-3	0-2	20	Starbuck (pen)	4544
19	Dec 11	H	Rotherham U	W	2-1	1-0	19	Starbuck (pen), Onuora	4994
20	18	A	Reading	D	0-0	0-0	20		5675
21	27	A	Hartlepool U	W	4-1	2-1	16	Jepson, Onuora, Bullock, Trevitt	3286
22	Jan 1	A	Leyton Orient	L	0-1	0-0	19		4599
23	3	H	Bournemouth	D	1-1	0-0	19	Starbuck (pen)	6047
24	15	A	Barnet	W	1-0	1-0	16	Robinson P	3022
25	22	H	York C	W	3-2	1-1	16	Jepson 3	6802
26	29	A	Bristol R	D	0-0	0-0	15		5127
27	Feb 5	H	Burnley	D	1-1	0-0	15	Onuora	10,634
28	12	A	Wrexham	L	1-3	0-2	19	Bullock	4011
29	19	A	Stockport Co	L	0-3	0-2	19		5071
30	22	H	Swansea C	D	1-1	1-0	—	Currie	3854
31	25	H	Brighton & HA	L	1-3	1-1	19	Clayton	5088
32	Mar 5	A	Exeter C	W	3-2	1-2	19	Dunn, Booth, Bullock	2939
33	12	H	Hull C	L	0-2	0-0	20		6675
34	15	A	Port Vale	L	0-1	0-0	—		7010
35	19	A	Fulham	D	1-1	1-1	20	Booth	3624
36	26	H	Plymouth Arg	W	1-0	0-0	20	Booth	5619
37	29	A	Bournemouth	W	2-1	1-0	—	Starbuck, Booth	3104
38	Apr 2	H	Hartlepool U	D	1-1	0-0	19	Booth	5717
39	4	A	Cardiff C	D	2-2	2-1	18	Starbuck, Baldry	5525
40	9	H	Leyton Orient	W	1-0	1-0	19	Booth	4995
41	12	H	Wrexham	W	3-0	1-0	—	Starbuck (pen), Jepson, Booth	4191
42	17	H	Bradford C	D	1-1	0-1	—	Dunn	9342
43	19	H	Cardiff C	W	2-0	1-0	—	Booth 2	6267
44	26	A	Cambridge U	W	5-4	3-1	—	Dunn, Starbuck 3 (1 pen), Booth	3901
45	30	H	Blackpool	W	2-1	1-1	11	Baldry, Starbuck	16,195
46	May 7	A	Brentford	W	2-1	0-1	11	Dunn 2	4483

Final League Position: 11

GOALSCORERS

League (58): Starbuck 12 (5 pens), Booth 10, Dunn 6, Onuora 6, Jepson 5, Roberts 4, Wells 4, Bullock 3, Baldry 2, Clayton 1, Currie 1, Hicks 1, Robinson P 1, Rowe 1, Trevitt 1.
Coca-Cola Cup (4): Dunn 3, Roberts 1.
FA Cup (2): Jackson 1, Rowe 1.

Francis 46	Trevitt 31	Billy 34	Dyson 19 + 3	Mitchell 20 + 2	Jackson 30 + 3	Barnett 1	Marsden 2	Roberts 14 + 1	Onuora 12 + 10	Starbuck 45 + 1	Dunn 20 + 14	Booth 18 + 8	Hicks 20 + 2	Robinson P 39	Wells 21 + 1	Williams 4 + 2	Harkness 5	Whitney 14	Rowe 7 + 6	Collins 1	Logan 9 + 7	Bullock 20	Jepson 19 + 4	Currie 7	Robinson R 2	Clayton 15 + 2	Cowan 10	Scully 11	Baldry 10	Blackwell — + 1	Match No.
1	2	3	4	5	6	7	8	9	10	11	12	14																			1
1	2	3			6			9	10	4	7		5	8	11																2
1	2	3			6			9	10	4	7		5	8	11																3
1	2	3		12	6			9	10	4	7	14	5	8	11																4
1	2	3		12	6			9	10	4	7	14	5	8	11																5
1	2	3	12		6			9	10	4	7	14	5	8	11																6
1	2	3			6			9		4	7		5	8	11	10															7
1	2	3	14		6			9	12	4	7		5	8	11	10															8
1	2		6		14		10			4	12	9	5	8	11	7	3														9
1	2		5		6			12		4	7	9	14	8	11	10	3														10
1	2		5		6			9		4	7		10	8	11	12	3														11
1	2		5		6			9		4	7	14	10	8	11	12	3														12
1	2			5	6			9		4	7		10	8	11		3														13
1	2			5	6			9	12	4	7		10	8	11			3	14												14
1	2			5	6			9	12	4			10	8	11			3	7												15
1	2				6					4		10	5	8	11			3	9	7	12										16
1	2		14	5	6			9		12	10		4	8				3	7			11									17
1	2			4	6					9	10	12	5		11			3	7		14	8									18
1	2	7	5		6				10	11				8				3	12			4	9								19
1		2	5		6				10	11				8				3	7			4	9								20
1	7	2	5		6				10	11	12	14		8				3				4	9								21
1	7	2	5		6				10	11	12			8	4			3					9								22
1	7	2	5		6				10	11	12			8	4			3	14				9								23
1	7	2	5		6					11				8				3				4	9	10							24
1	7	2	5		6					11	12			8				3				4	9	10							25
1	2	7	5							11	12		6	8							14	4	9	10	3						26
1	2	7	5						12	11			6	8					14			4	9	10	3						27
1	2	7	5		6					11	12			8	14			3				4	9	10							28
1	2	7	5		6				10	11	12		14	8	3								9			4					29
1		7	5						12	11		14	6	8	3				4				9	10		2					30
1		7	5						12	11	14		6	8	3				4				9	10		2					31
1		3		2	6				12	11	10	9		4				5			7	8				14					32
1	5	3		2	6				12	11	10	9		4							7	8				14					33
1		3		2	6				12	11	10	9		4							7	8	14			5					34
1		3		2	6				12	11	10	9		4							7	8	14			5					35
1		2		6						4	12	9										8	10			7	3	5	11		36
1		2		6						10		9									4	8				7	3	5	11		37
1		2		6						10		9							14		4	8	12			7	3	5	11		38
1		2		6	12					10		9		3							4	8				7		5	11		39
1		2		6						4		9		8									10			7	3	5	11		40
1		2		6						4		9		8							12		10			7	3	5	11		41
1		2		6						4	12	9		8							14		10			7	3	5	11		42
1		2		6	14					4	12	9		8							7	10					3	5	11		43
1	2		6							4	11	9							12		14	8	10			7	3	5			44
1		2		6						4	12	9		8							14		10			7	3	5	11		45
1	2			6						4	10	9									8		12			7	3	5	11	14	46

Coca-Cola Cup	First Round	Scarborough (h)	0-0
		(a)	3-0
	Second Round	Arsenal (h)	0-5
		(a)	1-1
FA Cup	First Round	Telford U (a)	1-1
		(h)	1-0
	Second Round	Port Vale (a)	0-1

HUDDERSFIELD TOWN

Player and Position	Ht	Wt	Birth Date	Birth Place	Source	Clubs	League App	League Gls
Goalkeepers								
Kevin Blackwell	5 11	12 10	21 12 58	Luton	Barnet	Scarborough	44	—
						Notts Co	—	—
						Torquay U	18	—
						Huddersfield T	1	—
Steve Francis	5 11	11 05	29 5 64	Billericay	Apprentice	Chelsea	71	—
						Reading	216	—
						Huddersfield T	46	—
Defenders								
Jon Dyson	6 1	12 00	18 12 71	Mirfield	School	Huddersfield T	37	—
Peter Jackson	6 0	12 07	6 4 61	Bradford	Apprentice	Bradford C	278	24
						Newcastle U	60	3
						Bradford C	58	5
						Huddersfield T	155	3
Richard Logan	6 0	13 03	24 5 69	Barnsley	Gainsborough T	Huddersfield T	16	—
Graham Mitchell	6 0	11 05	16 2 68	Shipley	Apprentice	Huddersfield T	232	2
Stephen Payne	5 11	12 00	1 8 75	Pontefract	Trainee	Huddersfield T	—	—
Pat Scully	6 1	13 02	23 6 70	Dublin		Arsenal	—	—
						Preston NE (loan)	13	1
						Northampton T (loan)	15	—
						Southend U	115	6
						Huddersfield T	11	—
Simon Trevitt	5 11	11 02	20 12 67	Dewsbury	Apprentice	Huddersfield T	204	3
Scot Whitehead	5 8	11 09	13 8 75	Doncaster	Trainee	Huddersfield T	—	—
Jonathan Whitney	5 10		23 12 70	Nantwich	Winsford	Huddersfield T	14	—
Midfield								
Anthony Brennan‡	5 7	10 12	1 12 73	Dublin	Trainee	Huddersfield T	—	—
Darren Bullock	5 8	12 04	12 2 69	Worcester	Nuneaton	Huddersfield T	20	3
Gary Clayton	5 11	12 08	2 2 63	Sheffield	Burton Alb	Doncaster R	35	5
						Cambridge U	179	17
						Peterborough U (loan)	4	—
						Huddersfield T	17	1
Simon Collins	6 0	11 02	16 12 73	Pontefract	Trainee	Huddersfield T	2	—
Gerry Harrison*	5 10	12 12	15 4 72	Lambeth	Trainee	Watford	9	—
						Bristol C	38	1
						Cardiff C (loan)	10	1
						Hereford U (loan)	6	—
						Huddersfield T	—	—
Tom Mooney‡	5 11	11 02	14 12 73	Newry	Trainee	Huddersfield T	1	—
Phil Robinson	5 10	10 10	6 1 67	Stafford	Apprentice	Aston Villa	3	1
						Wolverhampton W	71	8
						Notts Co	66	5
						Birmingham C (loan)	9	—
						Huddersfield T	75	5
Richard Ward	5 8	11 00	17 11 73	Scarborough	Trainee	Notts Co	—	—
						Huddersfield T	—	—
						Scarborough	—	—
Mark Wells	5 9	10 10	15 10 71	Leicester	Trainee	Notts Co	2	—
						Huddersfield T	23	4
Forwards								
Simon Baldry§	5 10		12 2 76	Huddersfield	Trainee	Huddersfield T	10	2
Chris Billy	5 11	11 08	2 1 73	Huddersfield	Trainee	Huddersfield T	57	2
Andrew Booth	5 10	10 03	17 3 73	Huddersfield	Trainee	Huddersfield T	34	12
Iain Dunn	5 11	10 10	1 4 72	Derwent	School	York C	77	11
						Chesterfield	13	1
					Goole T	Huddersfield T	62	9
Ron Jepson	6 1	13 02	12 5 63	Stoke	Nantwich	Port Vale	22	—
						Peterborough U (loan)	18	5
						Preston NE	38	8
						Exeter C	54	21
						Huddersfield T	23	5

HUDDERSFIELD TOWN

Colours: Blue and white striped shirts, blue shorts, blue stockings with red and white hoops on turnover.
Change colours: White shirts with black sleeves, black shorts, black and white stockings.

Foundation: A meeting, attended largely by members of the Huddersfield & District FA, was held at the Imperial Hotel in 1906 to discuss the feasibility of establishing a football club in this rugby stronghold. However, it was not until a man with both the enthusiasm and the money to back the scheme came on the scene, that real progress was made. This benefactor was Mr. Hilton Crowther and it was at a meeting at the Albert Hotel in 1908, that the club formally came into existence with a capital of £2,000 and joined the North-Eastern League.

First Football League game: 3 September, 1910, Division 2, v Bradford PA (a) W 1-0 – Mutch; Taylor, Morris; Beaton, Hall, Bartlett; Blackburn, Wood, Hamilton (1), McCubbin, Jee.

Did you know: On 30 April 1994 Huddersfield Town's best crowd of the season numbering 16,195 witnessed a 2-1 win over Blackpool. It was the club's final match at Leeds Road after 86 years prior to a move to new headquarters.

Managers (and Secretary-Managers)
Fred Walker 1908–10, Richard Pudan 1910–12, Arthur Fairclough 1912–19, Ambrose Langley 1919–21, Herbert Chapman 1921–25, Cecil Potter 1925–26, Jack Chaplin 1926–29, Clem Stephenson 1929–42, David Steele 1943–47, George Stephenson 1947–52, Andy Beattie 1952–56, Bill Shankly 1956–59, Eddie Boot 1960–64, Tom Johnston 1964–68, Ian Greaves 1968–74, Bobby Collins 1974 1–75 (GM), Tom Johnston 1975–7/1977–78, Mike Buxton 1978–86, Steve Smith 1986–87, Malcolm Macdonald 1987–88, Eoin Hand 1988–92, Ian Ross 1992–93, Neil Warnock July 1993–

Player and Position	*Ht*	*Wt*	*Birth Date*	*Birth Place*	*Source*	*Clubs*	*League App*	*League Gls*
Iffy Onuora	5 10	11 10	28 7 67	Glasgow	British Universities	Huddersfield T	165	30
Rodney Rowe	5 8	12 08	30 7 75	Huddersfield	Trainee	Huddersfield T	13	1
Philip Starbuck	5 10	10 13	24 11 68	Nottingham	Apprentice	Nottingham F	36	2
						Birmingham C (loan)	3	—
						Hereford U (loan)	6	—
						Blackburn R (loan)	6	1
						Huddersfield T	128	35

Trainees
Baldry, Simon; Collins, Sam J; (h) Crompton, Glen S; Crowther, Matthew J; Crowther, Paul; Doherty, Gerald A; Donaldson, Stephen; Garside, Liam; Illingworth, Jeremy M; Kelly, Mark A; Midwood, Michael A; Taylor, Craig L; Wood, Nicholas I.

Associated Schoolboys
Beardow, Nigel C; Bemrose, Daniel S; Butler, Neil J; Cooke, Peter J; Fearnley, Robert A; Fearnley, Thomas E; Good, Nicholas A; Halstead, Miles R; Heddon, Matthew P; Hutchinson, James M; Ingham, Andrew W; Jones, Gavin; Scott, Paul; Smith, Steve D; Stansfield, James E; Tully, Jamie P; Whitehead, Kristian M. J; Williams, Adam R; Woodcock, Thomas.

Associated Schoolboys who have accepted the Club's offer of a Traineeship/Contract
Gonsalves, Ryan M; Jones, Geoffrey A; Lawson, Ian J; Stott, Michael J; Sweet, Benjamin J; Sykes, James A.

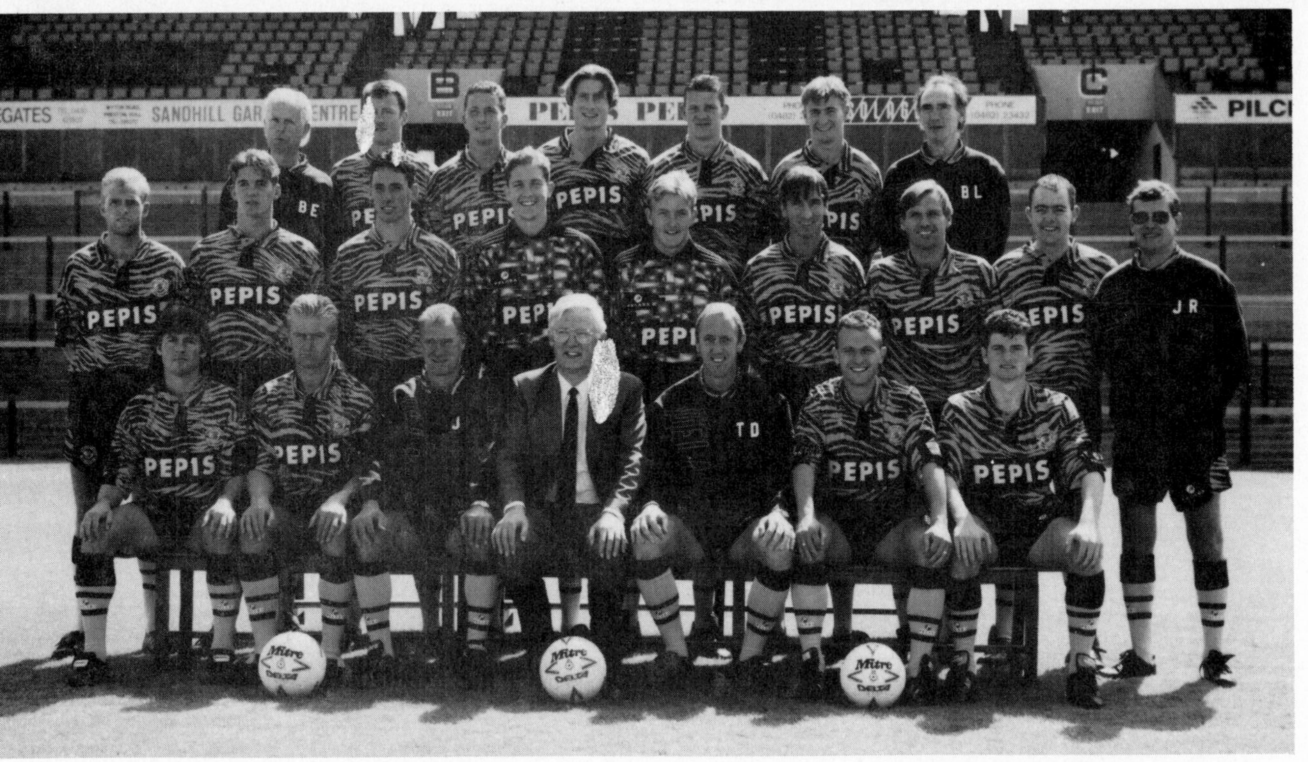

HULL CITY 1993–94 *Back row (left to right):* Bernard Ellison (Youth Team Coach/Chief Scout), Greg Abbott, Graeme Atkinson, Chris Hargreaves, Dean Windass, Matty Hopkin, Billy Legg (U16s Coach).
Centre row: Lee Warren, Neil Allison, Gary Hobson, Alan Fettis, Steve Wilson, Brian Mitchell, David Mail, Rob Miller, Jeff Radcliffe (Physio).
Front row: Steve Moran, Linton Brown, Jeff Lee (Assistant Manager), Martin Fish (Chairman), Terry Dolan (Manager), David Norton, Adam Lowthorpe.

Division 2 HULL CITY

Boothferry Park, Hull HU4 6EU. Telephone Hull (0482) 51119. Commercial Manager: (0482) 566050. Football in the Community Office: 0482 565088. Fax: 0482 565752.

Ground capacity: 17,528.

Record attendance: 55,019 v Manchester U, FA Cup 6th rd, 26 February 1949.

Record receipts: £79,604 v Liverpool FA Cup, 5th rd, 18 February 1989.

Pitch measurements: 112yd × 73yd.

President: T. C. Waite FIMI, MIRTE.

Honorary Vice-president: D. Robinson, H. Bermitz, J. Johnson BA, DPA.

Vice-presidents: R. Beercock, K. Davis, N. Howe, R. Booth, A. Fetiveau, W. Law.

Chairman: M. W. Fish MCA. ***Vice-chairman:*** R. M. Chetham.

Directors: G. H. C. Needler MA, FCA, .

Manager: Terry Dolan. ***Assistant Manager:*** Jeff Lee.

Secretary: M. W. Fish. ***Physio:*** Jeff Radcliffe MCSP, SRP.

Commercial Manager: Simon Cawkhill. ***Stadium Manager:*** John Cooper.

Ticket Office/Gate Manager: Wilf Rogerson. ***Hon, Medical Officers:*** G. Hoyle, MBCHB, FRCS, Dr. B. Kell, MBBS.

Year Formed: 1904. ***Turned Professional:*** 1905. ***Ltd Co.:*** 1905.

Club Nickname: 'The Tigers'.

Previous Grounds: 1904, Boulevard Ground (Hull RFC); 1905, Anlaby Road (Hull CC); 1944/5 Boulevard Ground; 1946, Boothferry Park.

Record League Victory: 11–1 v Carlisle U, Division 3 (N), 14 January 1939 – Ellis; Woodhead, Dowen; Robinson (1), Blyth, Hardy; Hubbard (2), Richardson (2), Dickinson (2), Davies (2), Cunliffe (2).

Record Cup Victory: 8–2 v Stalybridge Celtic (away), FA Cup, 1st rd, 26 November 1932 – Maddison; Goldsmith, Woodhead; Gardner, Hill (1), Denby; Forward (1), Duncan, McNaughton (1), Wainscoat (4), Sargeant (1).

Record Defeat: 0–8 v Wolverhampton W, Division 2, 4 November 1911.

Most League Points (2 for a win): 69, Division 3, 1965–66.

Most League Points (3 for a win): 90, Division 4, 1982–83.

Most League Goals: 109, Division 3, 1965–66.

Highest League Scorer in Season: Bill McNaughton, 39, Division 3 (N), 1932–33.

Most League Goals in Total Aggregate: Chris Chilton, 195, 1960–71.

Most Capped Player: Terry Neill, 15 (59), Northern Ireland.

Most League Appearances: Andy Davidson, 520, 1952–67.

Record Transfer Fee Received: £750,000 from Middlesbrough for Andy Payton, November 1991.

Record Transfer Fee Paid: £200,000 to Leeds U for Peter Swan, March 1989.

Chairman: B. E. Fearn. ***Vice-chairman:*** L. V. Pickering.
Football League Record: 1905 Elected to Division 2; 1930–33 Division 3 (N); 1933–36 Division 2; 1936–49 Division 3 (N); 1949–56 Division 2; 1956–58 Division 3 (N); 1958–59 Division 3; 1959–60 Division 2; 1960–66 Division 3; 1966–78 Division 2; 1978–81 Division 3; 1981–83 Division 4; 1983–85 Division 3; 1985–91 Division 2; 1991– 92 Division 3; 1992– Division 2.

Honours: *Football League:* Division 2 best season: 3rd, 1909–10; Division 3 (N) – Champions 1932–33, 1948–49; Division 3 – Champions 1965–66; Runners-up 1958–59; Division 4 – Runners-up 1982–83. *FA Cup:* best season: Semi-final, 1930. *Football League Cup:* best season: 4th, 1973–74, 1975–76, 1977–78. *Associate Members' Cup:* Runners-up 1984.

HULL CITY 1993—94 LEAGUE RECORD

Match No.	Date	Venue	Opponents	Result		H/T Score	Lg. Pos.	Goalscorers	Attendance
1	Aug 14	A	Barnet	W	2-1	2-1	—	Abbott, Brown	2129
2	21	H	Plymouth Arg	D	2-2	1-1	5	Brown, Windass (pen)	3580
3	28	A	Cambridge U	W	4-3	2-2	2	Windass 3 (1 pen), Brown	3861
4	31	H	Brentford	W	1-0	1-0	—	Windass (pen)	4517
5	Sept 4	H	Bristol R	W	3-0	1-0	2	Windass 3	5362
6	11	A	Cardiff C	W	4-3	1-2	1	Lee 2, Moran, Bound	7421
7	14	A	Wrexham	L	0-3	0-0	—		4345
8	18	H	Huddersfield T	W	2-1	1-0	1	Brown, Atkinson	7570
9	25	A	Reading	D	1-1	0-1	2	Brown	6453
10	Oct 2	H	Bradford C	W	3-1	2-1	1	Windass, Abbott (pen), Brown	9492
11	9	A	Port Vale	L	1-2	1-1	3	Allison	9459
12	16	H	Fulham	D	1-1	0-1	3	Peacock	6089
13	23	A	Swansea C	L	0-1	0-0	3		3774
14	30	H	Leyton Orient	L	0-1	0-0	6		5246
15	Nov 2	A	Blackpool	L	2-6	1-2	—	Abbott 2	3968
16	6	H	Rotherham U	W	4-1	3-1	6	Brown, Moran 3	4860
17	20	A	Bournemouth	W	2-0	2-0	5	Brown, Atkinson	4124
18	27	H	Stockport Co	L	0-1	0-0	8		7119
19	Dec 11	A	Plymouth Arg	L	1-2	0-2	8	Windass	6460
20	18	H	Barnet	D	4-4	1-2	8	Windass 3 (1 pen), Moran	4115
21	27	A	York C	D	0-0	0-0	9		8481
22	28	H	Hartlepool U	W	1-0	0-0	6	Windass	4607
23	Jan 1	A	Exeter C	W	1-0	1-0	6	Windass	3547
24	3	H	Burnley	L	1-2	1-1	7	Abbott	11,232
25	8	H	Brighton & HA	D	0-0	0-0	7		5386
26	15	A	Fulham	W	1-0	0-0	7	Windass	4407
27	22	H	Port Vale	D	0-0	0-0	8		6918
28	29	A	Leyton Orient	L	1-3	1-0	8	Williams	4355
29	Feb 5	H	Swansea C	L	0-1	0-0	8		4668
30	12	A	Brighton & HA	L	0-3	0-2	9		8251
31	19	H	Cambridge U	W	2-0	0-0	8	Atkinson, Windass	4090
32	22	A	Brentford	W	3-0	1-0	—	Windass, Brown, Atkinson	4361
33	25	A	Bristol R	D	1-1	1-1	7	Atkinson	5703
34	Mar 5	H	Cardiff C	W	1-0	1-0	7	Windass (pen)	4998
35	12	A	Huddersfield T	W	2-0	0-0	6	Dewhurst, Windass	6675
36	15	H	Wrexham	D	0-0	0-0	—		5749
37	19	H	Reading	L	1-2	0-1	6	Windass (pen)	7107
38	26	A	Bradford C	D	1-1	1-0	8	Williams	9419
39	29	A	Burnley	L	1-3	0-1	—	Lee	10,574
40	Apr 2	H	York C	D	1-1	0-0	8	Windass	8190
41	4	A	Hartlepool U	W	1-0	1-0	8	Norton	2448
42	9	H	Exeter C	W	5-1	2-1	8	Atkinson 2, Dewhurst, Norton, Windass	4663
43	16	H	Blackpool	D	0-0	0-0	7		6211
44	23	A	Rotherham U	L	0-1	0-0	7		4944
45	30	H	Bournemouth	D	1-1	0-1	7	Abbott	4926
46	May 7	A	Stockport Co	D	0-0	0-0	9		7666

Final League Position: 9

GOALSCORERS

League (62): Windass 23 (6 pens), Brown 9, Atkinson 7, Abbott 6 (1 pen), Moran 5, Lee 3, Dewhurst 2, Norton 2, Williams 2, Allison 1, Bound 1, Peacock 1.
Coca-Cola Cup (3): Abbott 1, Atkinson 1, Windass 1.
FA Cup (2): Brown 1, Hargreaves 1.

Wilson 9	Mitchell 9	Hobson 36	Warren 28 + 5	Allison 27 + 1	Abbott 40	Norton 44	Moran 11 + 6	Brown 38 + 4	Windass 43	Atkinson 36 + 4	Lee 37 + 6	Bound 7	Miller 2 + 1	Mann 2 + 3	Fettis 37	Lowthorpe 3	Hargreaves 21 + 7	Peacock 4 + 7	Mail 21 + 3	Dewhurst 27	Williams 16	Dakin 8 + 1	Match No.
1	2	3	4	5	6	7	8	9	10	11													1
1	2	3	4	5	6	7	8	9	10	11	12												2
1	2	3		5	6	7		9	10	11	8	4											3
1	2	3		5	6	7		9	10	11	8	4											4
1	2	3		5	6	7		9	10	11	8	4											5
1		3		5	6	7	2	9	10	11	8	4											6
1			12	5	6	7	2	9	10	11	8	4	3	14									7
	2	3		5	6	7		9	10	11	8	4			1								8
	2	3	12	5	6	7	14	9	10	11	8	4			1								9
		3	4	5	6	7		9	10	11	8		12		1	2							10
		3	4	5	6	7		9	10	11	8				1	2							11
		3	4	5	6	7	10	9		11	8				1	2	12	14					12
	2	3	4	5	6	7	12	9	10	11					1		8						13
	2	3	4	5	6		12	9	10	11	7				1		8	14					14
		3	4	5	6		12	9	10	11	8				1		7	2	14				15
			4	12	6	2	8	9	10	11	14				1		7		3	5			16
			4	2	6	7	12	9	10	11	14		3		1		8			5			17
			4	2	6	7	12	9	10	11					1		8		3	5			18
1			4	2	6	7	8	9	10	11	3						12			5			19
1		5	4	2	6	7	8	9	10	11	3						12		14				20
		3	4	2		7	8		10		6			11	1		9	12	5				21
		3	4			7		9	10		6			11	1		8	12	5	2			22
		3	12		6	7		9	10	11	2				1		8		4	5			23
		3	12		6	7		9	10	11	2				1		8	14	4	5			24
		3			6	7		9	10	11	2				1		12		4	5	8		25
		3	11		6	7		9	10		2				1				4	5	8		26
		3	11		6	7		9	10		2				1			12	4	5	8		27
		3	11		6	7			10		2				1		9		4	5	8		28
		3	11		6	7		9	10	12	2				1				4	5	8		29
		3	5		6	7	8	9		11	2				1		12		4		10		30
		3	5		6	2	8		10	7	12				1		9		4		11		31
		3	7		6	2		9	10	12	8				1				4	5	11		32
			7		6	2		9	10	3	8				1				4	5	11		33
			7		6	2		9	10	3	8				1		12		4	5	11		34
			7		6	2		9	10	3	8				1				4	5	11		35
			7		6	2		9	10	3	8				1				4	5	11		36
			7		6	2		9	10	3	8				1		12		4	5	11		37
		3	7		6	2		9			8			12	1		10		4	5	11	14	38
		3	12			2		9	10	14	8				1		7		4	5	11	6	39
		3		4	6	2		9	10	12	8			14	1		11			5		7	40
		3		4		6			10	7	8				1		9			5	11	2	41
		3		4		6		12	10	11	8				1		9	7		5		2	42
		3		4		6		12	10	11	8				1		9	7		5		2	43
		3		4	6	7		12	10	11	8				1		9		14	5		2	44
		3		4	6	7		12	10	11	14				1		9	8		5		2	45
		3		4	6	7		9	10	11	12				1		8	14		5		2	46

Coca-Cola Cup	First Round	Notts Co (a)	0-2
		(h)	3-1
FA Cup	First Round	Runcorn (a) abandoned	1-0
		(a)	2-0
	Second Round	Chester C (a)	0-2

HULL CITY

Player and Position	Ht	Wt	Birth Date	Birth Place	Source	Clubs	League App	League Gls
Goalkeepers								
Alan Fettis	6 1	11 04	1 2 71	Newtonards	Ards	Hull C	100	—
Steve Wilson	5 11	11 00	24 4 74	Hull	Trainee	Hull C	40	—
Defenders								
Neil Allison	6 2	11 10	20 10 73	Hull	Trainee	Hull C	47	1
Simon Dakin	5 11	11 07	30 11 74	Nottingham	Derby Co	Hull C	9	—
Robert Dewhurst	6 3	13 01	10 9 71	Keighley	Trainee	Blackburn R	13	—
						Darlington R (loan)	11	1
						Huddersfield T (loan)	7	—
						Hull C	27	2
Gary Hobson	6 2	12 10	12 11 72	North Ferriby	Trainee	Hull C	77	—
Adam Lowthorpe	5 10	11 00	7 8 75	Hull	Trainee	Hull C	3	—
David Mail	5 11	11 12	12 9 62	Bristol	Apprentice	Aston Villa	—	—
						Blackburn R	206	4
						Hull C	136	2
Brian Mitchell	6 1	13 01	16 7 63	Stonehaven	King St	Aberdeen	65	1
						Bradford C	178	9
						Bristol C	16	—
						Hull C	9	—
Midfield								
Greg Abbott	5 9	10 10	14 12 63	Coventry	Apprentice	Coventry C	—	—
						Bradford C	281	38
						Halifax T	28	1
					Guiseley	Hull C	67	7
Linton Brown	5 9	11 00	12 4 68	Driffield	Guiseley	Halifax T	3	—
						Hull C	65	10
Darren Cairns‡	5 10	11 02	1 9 74	Glasgow	Trainee	Hull C	—	—
Matthew Hopkin*	5 10	11 00	17 10 74	Hull	Trainee	Hull C	—	—
Chris Lee	5 10	11 07	18 6 71	Halifax	Trainee	Bradford C	—	—
						Rochdale	26	2
						Scarborough	78	3
						Hull C	43	3
Neil Mann	5 10	12 00	9 11 72	Nottingham	Grimsby T	Hull C	5	—
Robert Millar*	6 0	11 10	3 11 72	Manchester	Trainee	Oldham Ath	—	—
						Hull C	28	—
David Norton	5 7	11 03	3 3 65	Cannock	Apprentice	Aston Villa	44	2
						Notts Co	27	1
						Rochdale (loan)	9	—
						Hull C (loan)	15	—
						Hull C	134	5
Richard Peacock	5 11	11 00	29 10 72	Sheffield	Sheffield FC	Hull C	11	1
Dean Stowe*	5 9	11 02	27 3 75	Burnley	Trainee	Hull C	1	—
Lee Warren*	6 0	11 13	28 2 69	Manchester	Trainee	Leeds U	—	—
						Rochdale	31	1
						Hull C	153	1
						Lincoln C (loan)	3	1
Dean Windass	5 9	12 03	1 4 69	Hull		Hull C	116	36
Forwards								
Graeme Atkinson	5 8	10 08	11 11 71	Hull	Trainee	Hull C	140	22
Matthew Edeson§	5 10	11 00	11 8 76	Beverley	Trainee	Hull C	2	—
Christian Hargreaves	5 11	11 00	12 5 72	Cleethorpes	Trainee	Grimsby T	51	5
						Scarborough (loan)	3	—
						Hull C	28	—
David Jones	6 4	13 10	3 7 64	Harrow		Chelsea	—	—
						Bury	1	—
						Leyton Orient	2	—
						Burnley	4	—
						Ipswich T	—	—
						Doncaster R	40	14
						Bury	9	—
						Hull C	12	1

HULL CITY

Colours: Black and amber striped shirts, black shorts, amber stockings with two black hoops and black turnover. **Change colours:** White and jade.

Foundation: The enthusiasts who formed Hull City in 1904 were brave men indeed. More than that they were audacious for they immediately put the club on the map in this Rugby League fortress by obtaining a three-year agreement with the Hull Rugby League club to rent their ground! They had obtained quite a number of conversions to the dribbling code, before the Rugby League forbade the use of any of their club grounds by Association Football clubs. By that time, Hull City were well away having entered the FA Cup in their initial season and the Football League, Second Division after only a year.

First Football League game: 2 September, 1905, Division 2, v Barnsley (h) W 4-1 – Spendiff; Langley, Jones; Martin, Robinson, Gordon (2); Rushton, Spence (1), Wilson (1), Howe, Raisbeck.

Did you know: Between 13 February and 20 March 1982, Les Mutrie scored in a club record nine consecutive League games for Hull City. His total was 14 during this spell.

Managers (and Secretary-Managers)
James Ramster 1904–05*, Ambrose Langley 1905–13, Harry Chapman 1913–14, Fred Stringer 1914–16, David Menzies 1916–21, Percy Lewis 1921–23, Bill McCracken 1923–31, Haydn Green 1931–34, John Hill 1934–36, David Menzies 1936, Ernest Blackburn 1936–46, Major Frank Buckley 1946–48, Raich Carter 1948–51, Bob Jackson 1952–55, Bob Brocklebank 1955–61, Cliff Britton 1961–70 (continued as GM to 1971), Terry Neill 1970–74, John Kaye 1974–77, Bobby Collins 1977–78, Ken Houghton 1978–79, Mike Smith 1979–82, Bobby Brown 1982, Colin Appleton 1982–84, Brian Horton 1984–88, Eddie Gray 1988–89, Colin Appleton 1989, Stan Ternent 1989–91, Terry Dolan February 1991– .

Player and Position	*Ht*	*Wt*	*Birth Date*	*Birth Place*	*Source*	*Clubs*	*League App*	*League Gls*
Steve Moran	5 8	11 03	10 1 61	Croydon	Amateur	Southampton	180	78
						Leicester C	43	14
						Reading	116	30
						Exeter C	57	27
						Hull C	17	5

Trainees
Armstrong, Gary; Beddard, Elliot J; Cass, Jamie M; Chambers, David; Doughty, Mark J; Edeson, Matthew K; Haigh, Gavin S; Kirk, Wayne K; Knight, Paul M; Lobley, Hayden S; Mitchell, Alexander S; Plant, Ian R; Saxton, Warren C; Skewis, Darren A; Stead, Nathan D; Watson, Michael P; White, Richard C.

Associated Schoolboys
Galvin, Matthew J.

Associated Schoolboys who have accepted the Club's offer of a Traineeship/Contract
Fewings, Paul J; Ogle, Gareth D; Shore, Philip A; Wilkinson, Ian J.

IPSWICH TOWN 1993–94 *Back row (left to right):* Lee Honeywood, Paul Mason, David Gregory, Eddie Youds, Bontcho Guentchev, Neil Gregory, Simon Milton, David Pirie.
Centre row: Lee Durrant, Paul Goddard, Gavin Johnson, Steve Palmer, Clive Baker, Philip Morgan, Steve Whitton, Adam Tanner, Gary Thompson, Graham Connell.
Front row: Mick Stockwell, Phil Whelan, Geraint Williams, David Linighan, Jason Dozzell, Neil Thompson, Chris Kiwomya, John Wark.

FA Premiership — IPSWICH TOWN

Portman Road, Ipswich, Suffolk IP1 2DA. Telephone Ipswich (0473) 219211 (4 lines). Ticket office: (0473) 221133. Sales & Marketing Dept: (0473) 212202.

Ground capacity: 23,000.

Record attendance: 38,010 v Leeds U, FA Cup 6th rd, 8 March 1975.

Record receipts: £105,950 v AZ 67 Alkmaar, UEFA Cup Final 1st leg, 6 May 1981.

Pitch measurements: 112yd × 70yd.

Chairman: J. Kerr MBE.

President: P. M. Cobbold. ***Vice-President:*** J. M. Sangster.

Directors: H. R. Smith, K. H. Brightwell, J. Kerridge, D. Sheepshanks, P. M. Cobbold.

Team Manager: Mick McGiven. ***Manager:*** John Lyall. ***Assistant Manager:*** Charlie Woods. ***Reserve Coach:*** Bryan Klug. ***Youth Team Coach:*** Peter Trevivian.

Physio: D. Bingham.

Secretary: David C. Rose.

Commercial Manager: Richard Powell. ***Sales & Promotions Manager:*** Mike Noye.

Year Formed: 1878. ***Turned Professional:*** 1936. ***Ltd Co.:*** 1936.

Club Nickname: 'Blues' or 'Town'.

Record League Victory: 7–0 v Portsmouth, Division 2, 7 November 1964 – Thorburn; Smith, McNeil; Baxter, Bolton, Thompson; Broadfoot (1), Hegan (2), Baker (1), Leadbetter, Brogan (3). 7–0 v Southampton, Division 1, 2 February 1974 – Sivell; Burley, Mills (1), Morris, Hunter, Beattie (1), Hamilton (2), Viljoen, Johnson, Whymark (2), Lambert (1) (Woods). 7–0 v WBA, Division 1, 6 November 1976 – Sivell; Burley, Mills, Talbot, Hunter, Beattie (1), Osborne, Wark (1), Mariner (1) (Bertschin), Whymark (4), Woods.

Record Cup Victory: 10–0 v Floriana, European Cup, Prel. rd, 25 September 1962 – Bailey; Malcolm, Compton; Baxter, Laurel, Elsworthy (1); Stephenson, Moran (2), Crawford (5), Phillips (2), Blackwood.

Record Defeat: 1–10 v Fulham, Division 1, 26 December 1963.

Most League Points (2 for a win): 64, Division 3 (S), 1953–54 and 1955–56.

Most League Points (3 for a win): 84, Division 1, 1991–92.

Most League Goals: 106, Division 3 (S), 1955–56.

Highest League Scorer in Season: Ted Phillips, 41, Division 3 (S), 1956–57.

Most League Goals in Total Aggregate: Ray Crawford, 203, 1958–63 and 1966–69.

Most Capped Player: Allan Hunter, 47 (53), Northern Ireland.

Most League Appearances: Mick Mills, 591, 1966–82.

Record Transfer Fee Received: £1,900,000 from Tottenham Hotspur for Jason Dozzell, August 1993.

Record Transfer Fee Paid: £800,000 to Celtic for Stuart Slater, October 1993.

Football League Record: 1938 Elected to Division 3 (S); 1954–55 Division 2; 1955–57 Division 3 (S); 1957–61 Division 2; 1961–64 Division 1; 1964–68 Division 2; 1968–86 Division 1; 1986–92 Division 2; 1992– FA Premier League.

Honours: *Football League:* Division 1 – Champions 1961–62; Runners-up 1980–81, 1981–82; Division 2 – Champions 1960–61, 1967–68, 1991–92; Division 3 (S) – Champions 1953–54, 1956–57. *FA Cup:* Winners 1977–78. *Football League Cup:* best season: Semi-final 1981–82, 1984–85, *Texaco Cup:* 1972–73. **European Competitions:** *European Cup:* 1962–63. *European Cup-Winners' Cup:* 1978–79. *UEFA Cup:* 1973–74, 1974–75, 1975–76, 1977–78, 1979–80, 1980–81 (winners), 1981–82, 1982–83.

IPSWICH TOWN 1993—94 LEAGUE RECORD

Match No.	Date	Venue	Opponents	Result		H/T Score	Lg. Pos.	Goalscorers	Attendance
1	Aug 14	A	Oldham Ath	W	3-0	2-0	—	Marshall, Palmer, Mason	12,074
2	17	H	Southampton	W	1-0	0-0	—	Marshall	14,958
3	21	H	Chelsea	W	1-0	1-0	2	Marshall	17,355
4	25	A	Norwich C	L	0-1	0-1	—		18,976
5	28	A	Sheffield U	D	1-1	0-1	5	Whitton	17,932
6	31	H	Newcastle U	D	1-1	0-0	—	Kiwomya	19,126
7	Sept 11	A	Arsenal	L	0-4	0-2	11		28,563
8	18	H	Aston Villa	L	1-2	1-1	12	Marshall	16,858
9	26	H	Tottenham H	D	2-2	0-1	—	Milton, Marshall	19,437
10	Oct 2	A	QPR	L	0-3	0-0	15		12,292
11	17	H	Leeds U	D	0-0	0-0	—		17,532
12	25	A	Wimbledon	W	2-0	0-0	—	Mason, Stockwell	7756
13	30	H	Everton	L	0-2	0-1	13		15,094
14	Nov 6	H	Sheffield W	L	1-4	0-1	14	Marshall	14,767
15	20	A	Swindon T	D	2-2	1-1	15	Wark 2 (1 pen)	13,860
16	24	A	Manchester U	D	0-0	0-0	—		43,300
17	27	H	Blackburn R	W	1-0	1-0	—	Youds	14,436
18	Dec 4	H	Oldham Ath	D	0-0	0-0	16		11,789
19	8	A	Southampton	W	1-0	0-0	—	Kiwomya	9028
20	11	A	Chelsea	D	1-1	0-1	12	Kiwomya	13,208
21	18	H	Norwich C	W	2-1	1-1	10	Wark (pen), Megson (og)	19,751
22	27	H	West Ham U	D	1-1	1-0	11	Linighan	20,988
23	Jan 1	H	Liverpool	L	1-2	0-0	14	Marshall	22,270
24	15	A	Leeds U	D	0-0	0-0	14		31,317
25	22	H	Wimbledon	D	0-0	0-0	13		11,849
26	Feb 2	A	Coventry C	L	0-1	0-1	—		11,244
27	5	A	Manchester C	L	1-2	1-1	14	Marshall	28,188
28	12	A	Everton	D	0-0	0-0	14		19,641
29	22	H	Sheffield U	W	3-2	3-1	—	Linighan, Marshall, Slater	11,468
30	Mar 5	H	Arsenal	L	1-5	0-3	15	Dixon (og)	18,803
31	12	A	Aston Villa	W	1-0	1-0	—	Johnson	23,732
32	19	A	Tottenham H	D	1-1	1-0	12	Kiwomya	26,653
33	23	A	Newcastle U	L	0-2	0-1	—		32,234
34	26	H	QPR	L	1-3	0-0	13	Guentchev	14,653
35	29	H	Manchester C	D	2-2	1-1	—	Linighan, Guentchev (pen)	12,871
36	Apr 2	A	West Ham U	L	1-2	0-1	15	Mason	18,307
37	4	H	Coventry C	L	0-2	0-0	15		12,782
38	9	A	Liverpool	L	0-1	0-0	16		30,485
39	16	H	Swindon T	D	1-1	0-1	16	Marshall	14,760
40	23	A	Sheffield W	L	0-5	0-2	17		23,854
41	May 1	H	Manchester U	L	1-2	1-1	—	Kiwomya	22,478
42	7	A	Blackburn R	D	0-0	0-0	19		20,633

Final League Position: 19

GOALSCORERS

League (35): Marshall 10, Kiwomya 5, Linighan 3, Mason 3, Wark 3 (2 pens), Guentchev 2 (1 pen), Johnson 1, Milton 1, Palmer 1, Slater 1, Stockwell 1, Whitton 1, Youds 1, own goals 2.
Coca-Cola Cup (6): Marshall 2, Kiwomya 1, Mason 1 (pen), Milton 1, Whitton 1.
FA Cup (8): Marshall 3, Johnson 1, Palmer 1, Stockwell 1, Thompson 1, Wark 1.

Baker 15	Stockwell 42	Thompson N 32	Mason 18 + 4	Wark 38	Linighan 38	Williams 34	Whelan 28 + 1	Palmer 31 + 5	Marshall 28 + 1	Kiwomya 34 + 3	Guentchev 9 + 15	Whitton 7 + 4	Milton 11 + 4	Yallop 2 + 5	Forrest 27	Goddard 3 + 1	Slater 28	Youds 18 + 5	Johnson 16	Durrant 3 + 4	Match No.
1	2	3	4	5	6	7	8	9	10	11											1
1	2	3	4	5	6	7	8	9	10	11	12										2
1	2	3	4	5	6	7	8	9	*10*	11	12	14									3
1	2	3		5	6	7	4	10		11	*8*	9	12	14							4
	4	3		5	6	7		8		11	12	9	14	*2*	1	10					5
	2	3		5	6	7		*4*		11	12	9	8	14	1	10					6
	2	3		5	6	7	8	4		11		9			1	10					7
	2	3	4	5	6	7	8	*9*	10	11	12	14			1						8
	2	3	4	5	6	7			10	11		9	8		1						9
	2	3	4	5	6	7			10	11			9		1		8				10
	2	3	4	5	6		7	9		11		12	10		1		8				11
	2	3	4	5	6	7	10	12	9	*11*			14		1		8				12
1	2	3	4	5	*6*		11		10		12	9	7				8	14			13
1	2	3	4	5	6		*11*	12	10			7	9				8	14			14
1	2	3		5			8	9	6	11			7	10				4			15
	2	3	4	5	6		8	9	10	11				12	1			7			16
	2	3	4	5	6		11	9	10						1		8	7			17
	2	3		5	6		4	*9*	10	11		12	14		1		8	7			18
	2	3		5	6	10	4	9		11					1	12	8	7			19
	2	3		5	6	4	10	9		11	12				1		8	7			20
	2	3		5	6	4	10	9		11	12				1		8	7			21
	4	3		5	6	7	10	9	12	11					1		8	2			22
	4	3		5	6	7	8		9	11	12			14	1			*2*	10		23
	4	3		5	6	7		12	9		8				1		11	2	10		24
	4	3	14	5	6	7			9	12	8				1		11	*2*	10		25
	4	3		5	6	7		14	9	12	8				1		11	2	*10*		26
	4	3		5	6	7		14	9	12	8				1		*11*	2	10		27
	4	3		*5*	6	7	14	9	10	11	12				1		8	2			28
	4	3	14	5	6	7		*9*	10	11	12				1		8	2			29
1	4	3	12	5	6	7		9	10	11							8	2			30
1	2		4	5			6	9	10	11							8		3	7	31
1	2		4	5		7	6	9	10	11							8		3		32
1	2		4	5		7	6	9	10	11							8		3	12	33
1	2	3	4		5	7	6			11	10						8		9	12	34
1	2				5	4	6	9		11	10						8		3	7	35
1	2		12		5	4	6	9		11	10						8	14	3	*7*	36
1	8		4		5	7	6	9			10						11	2	3	12	37
	4			5	6	7	3	9		11	12				1		8	2	10		38
	2			5	6	4		*9*	10	11			7		1		8	12	3	14	39
	2			5	6	*4*		9	10	11	12		7	14	1		8		3		40
	2			5	6	4	3	9	10	11	12		7		1			14	*8*		41
	2	3	4	5	6	7		9	10	11	12		8		1						42

Coca-Cola Cup	Second Round	Cambridge U (h)	2-1
		(a)	2-0
	Third Round	Liverpool (a)	2-3
FA Cup	Third Round	Swindon T (a)	1-1
		(h)	2-1
	Fourth Round	Tottenham H (h)	3-0
	Fifth Round	Wolverhampton W (a)	1-1
		(h)	1-2

IPSWICH TOWN

Player and Position	Ht	Wt	Birth Date	Birth Place	Source	Clubs	League App	League Gls
Goalkeepers								
Clive Baker	5 9	11 00	14 3 59	North Walsham	Amateur	Norwich C	4	—
						Barnsley	291	—
						Coventry C	—	—
						Ipswich T	46	—
Craig Forrest	6 5	14 00	20 9 67	Vancouver	Apprentice	Ipswich T	200	—
						Colchester U (loan)	11	—
Philip Morgan	6 1	13 00	18 12 74	Stoke	Trainee	Ipswich T	—	—
Defenders								
Leo Cotterell	5 9	10 00	2 9 74	Cambridge	Trainee	Ipswich T	—	—
Lee Honeywood*	5 8	10 10	3 8 71	Chelmsford	Trainee	Ipswich T	—	—
Gavin Johnson	5 11	11 12	10 10 70	Eye	Trainee	Ipswich T	115	11
David Linighan	6 2	13 00	9 1 65	Hartlepool	Local	Hartlepool U	91	5
						Leeds U (loan)	—	—
						Derby Co	—	—
						Shrewsbury T	65	1
						Ipswich T	243	12
Neil Thompson	5 11	13 08	2 10 63	Beverley	Nottingham F	Hull C	31	—
					Scarborough	Scarborough	87	15
						Ipswich T	191	18
John Wark	5 11	12 12	4 8 57	Glasgow	Apprentice	Ipswich T	296	94
						Liverpool	70	28
						Ipswich T	89	23
						Middlesbrough	32	2
						Ipswich T	112	12
Phil Whelan	6 4	14 01	7 8 72	Stockport		Ipswich T	69	2
Frank Yallop	5 11	12 00	4 4 64	Watford	Apprentice	Ipswich T	268	6
Edward Youds	6 1	13 03	3 5 70	Liverpool	Trainee	Everton	8	—
						Cardiff C (loan)	1	—
						Wrexham (loan)	20	2
						Ipswich T	40	1
Midfield								
Andy Bernal‡	5 10	12 05	16 7 66	Canberra		Ipswich T	9	—
Vlado Bozinoski†	5 10	11 03	30 3 64	Macedonia	Sporting Lisbon	Ipswich T	9	—
Graham Connell	5 10	11 05	31 10 74	Glasgow	Trainee	Ipswich T	—	—
Lee Durrant	5 10	11 07	18 12 73	Gt Yarmouth	Trainee	Ipswich T	7	—
David Gregory	5 11	11 10	23 1 70	Sudbury	Trainee	Ipswich T	31	2
Paul Mason	5 8	11 09	3 9 63	Liverpool	Groningen	Aberdeen	158	27
						Ipswich T	22	3
Simon Milton	5 10	11 05	23 8 63	London	Bury St Edmunds	Ipswich T	176	37
						Exeter C (loan)	2	3
						Torquay U (loan)	4	1
Steve Palmer	6 1	12 13	31 3 68	Brighton	Cambridge University	Ipswich T	94	2
Mick Stockwell	5 9	11 04	14 2 65	Chelmsford	Apprentice	Ipswich T	300	20
Adam Tanner	6 0	12 01	25 10 73	Maldon	Trainee	Ipswich T	—	—
Geraint Williams	5 7	10 06	5 1 62	Treorchy	Apprentice	Bristol R	141	8
						Derby Co	277	9
						Ipswich T	71	—
Forwards								
Paul Goddard*	5 7	12 00	12 10 59	Harlington	Apprentice	QPR	70	23
						West Ham U	170	54
						Newcastle U	61	19
						Derby Co	49	15
						Millwall	20	1
						Ipswich T	72	13
Neil Gregory	5 11	11 10	7 10 72	Zambia	Trainee	Ipswich T	—	—
						Chesterfield (loan)	3	1
Bontcho Guentchev	5 10	11 07	7 7 64	Bulgaria	Sporting Lisbon	Ipswich T	45	5
Chris Kiwomya	5 10	10 12	2 12 69	Huddersfield		Ipswich T	210	48

IPSWICH TOWN

Colours: Blue shirts, white sleeves, white shorts, blue stockings. **Change colours:** Red and black striped shirts, black shorts, red and black stockings.

Foundation: Considering that Ipswich Town only reached the Football League in 1938, many people outside of East Anglia may be surprised to learn that this club was formed at a meeting held in the Town Hall as far back as 1878 when Mr. T. C. Cobbold, MP, was voted president. Originally it was the Ipswich Association FC to distinguish it from the older Ipswich Football Club which played rugby. These two amalgamated in 1888 and the handling game was dropped in 1893.

First Football League game: 27 August, 1938, Division 3(S), v Southend U (h) W 4-2 – Burns; Dale, Parry; Perrett, Fillingham, McLuckie; Williams, Davies (1), Jones (2), Alsop (1), Little.

Did you know: On 20 November 1993 John Wark celebrated his 600th appearance for Ipswich Town, in three separate spells, with two goals in a 2-2 draw at Swindon Town.

Managers (and Secretary-Managers)
Mick O'Brien 1936–37, Scott Duncan 1937–55 (continued as secretary), Alf Ramsey 1955–63, Jackie Milburn 1963–64, Bill McGarry 1964–68, Bobby Robson 1969–82, Bobby Ferguson 1982–87, Johnny Duncan 1987–90, John Lyall May 1990– .

Player and Position	*Ht*	*Wt*	*Birth Date*	*Birth Place*	*Source*	*Clubs*	*League App*	*League Gls*
Ian Marshall	6 1	12 12	20 3 66	Oxford	Apprentice	Everton	15	1
						Oldham Ath	170	36
						Ipswich T	29	10
David Pirie	5 9	11 05	15 4 75	Glasgow	Trainee	Ipswich T	—	—
Stuart Slater	5 9	10 04	27 3 69	Sudbury	Apprentice	West Ham U	141	11
						Celtic	43	3
						Ipswich T	28	1
Gary Thompson	6 0	11 04	7 9 72	Ipswich		Ipswich T	—	—

Trainees
Coates, Scott L; Dolby, Gavin P; Eaton, Daniel J; Ellis, Kevin E; Graham, Stephen G; Hood, Paul; Mansfield, Graham P; McCrindle, Scott; Mortley, Peter R; Norfolk, Lee R; Portrey, Simon D; Scowcroft, James B; Vaughan, Anthony J; Weston, Kenneth; Weston, Matthew.

Associated Schoolboys
Allis, Robert T; Armitage, Gavin L; Burgess, Mark P; Dyer, Kieron; Fitch, Matthew S; Keeble, Christopher; Kennedy, John N; Lee, Jonathan J; Matthews, Jamie L; Midgley, Neil; Miller, Thomas W; Naylor, Richard A; Oates, Ryan; Scott, Jason; Stiff, Matthew P; Strong, Grant; Sutton, Brian; Theobald, David J; Wolton, Dominic J.

Associated Schoolboys who have accepted the Club's offer of a Traineeship/Contract
Bell, Leon C; Brown, Wayne L; Elsworth, Patrick D; Hollman, James; May, Robert D; Miller, Marc P; Pearson, Craig D; Wright, Richard I.

LEEDS UNITED 1993–94 *Back row (left to right):* Ray Wallace, Jon Newsome, Frank Strandli, David Wetherall, Mark Beeney, John Lukic, Gary McAllister, Brian Deane, Steve Hodge.
Centre row: Mike Hennigan (Coach), David O'Leary, Noel Whelan, Mark Tinkler, Kevin Sharp, Gary Kelly, David Rocastle, Chris Fairclough, Tony Dorigo, Mel Sterland, Geoff Ladley (Physio).
Front row: Gary Speed, David Kerslake, David Batty, Howard Wilkinson (Manager), Gordon Strachan, Jamie Forrester, Rod Wallace.
(Photograph: Varley Picture Agency)

LEEDS UNITED

Elland Road, Leeds LS11 0ES. Telephone Leeds (0532) 716037 (4 lines). Ticket Office: (0532) 710710. Fax: (0532) 720370. Clubcall: 0891 121181.

Ground capacity: 40,000.

Record attendance: 57,892 v Sunderland, FA Cup 5th rd (replay), 15 March 1967.

Record receipts: £291,549 v Manchester U, Rumbelows Cup semi-final 2nd leg, 24 February 1991.

Pitch measurements: 117yd × 72yd.

President: The Right Hon The Earl of Harewood LLD.

Executive Directors: L. H. Silver OBE (Chairman); P. J. Gilman (Vice-chairman); W. J. Fotherby (Managing).

Directors: J. W. G. Marjason, R. Barker, M. Bedford, E. Carlile, F. Feldman, A. Hudson, G. M. Holmes, P. Ridsdale, K. J. Woolmer.

Manager: Howard Wilkinson. ***Assistant Manager:*** Mick Hennigan.

Company/Club Secretary: Nigel Pleasants.

General Manager: Alan Roberts.

Coaches: Paul Hart, Peter Gunby.

Physios: Geoff Ladley, Alan Sutton.

Commercial Manager: Bob Baldwin.

Year Formed: 1919, as Leeds United after disbandment (by FA order) of Leeds City (formed in 1904). ***Turned Professional:*** 1920. ***Ltd Co.:*** 1920.

Club Nickname: 'United'.

Record League Victory: 8–0 v Leicester C, Division 1, 7 April 1934 – Moore; George Milburn, Jack Milburn; Edwards, Hart, Copping; Mahon (2), Firth (2), Duggan (2), Furness (2), Cochrane.

Record Cup Victory: 10–0 v Lyn (Oslo), European Cup, 1st rd 1st leg, 17 September 1969 – Sprake; Reaney, Cooper, Bremner (2), Charlton, Hunter, Madeley, Clarke (2), Jones (3), Giles (2) (Bates), O'Grady (1).

Record Defeat: 1–8 v Stoke C, Division 1, 27 August 1934.

Most League Points (2 for a win): 67, Division 1, 1968–69.

Most League Points (3 for a win): 85, Division 2, 1989–90.

Most League Goals: 98, Division 2, 1927–28.

Highest League Scorer in Season: John Charles, 42, Division 2, 1953–54.

Most League Goals in Total Aggregate: Peter Lorimer, 168, 1965–79 and 1983–86.

Most Capped Player: Billy Bremner, 54, Scotland.

Most League Appearances: Jack Charlton, 629, 1953–73.

Record Transfer Fee Received: £2,700,000 from Blackburn Rovers for David Batty, October 1993.

Record Transfer Fee Paid: £2,700,000 to Sheffield United for Brian Deane, July 1993.

Football League Record: 1920 Elected to Division 2; 1924–27 Division 1; 1927–28 Division 2; 1928–31 Division 1; 1931–32 Division 2; 1932–47 Division 1; 1947–56 Division 2; 1956–60 Division 1; 1960–64 Division 2; 1964–82 Division 1; 1982–90 Division 2; 1990–92 Division 1; 1992– FA Premier Division.

Honours: *Football League:* Division 1 – Champions 1968–69, 1973–74, 1991–92; Runners-up 1964–65, 1965–66, 1969–70, 1970–71, 1971–72; Division 2 – Champions 1923–24, 1963–64, 1989–90; Runners-up 1927–28, 1931–32, 1955–56. *FA Cup:* Winners 1972; Runners-up 1965, 1970, 1973. *Football League Cup:* Winners 1967–68. **European Competitions:** *European Cup:* 1969–70, 1974–75 (runners-up), 1992–93. *European Cup-Winners' Cup:* 1972–73 (runners-up). *European Fairs Cup:* 1965–66, 1966–67 (runners-up), 1967–68 (winners), 1968–69, 1970–71 (winners). *UEFA Cup:* 1971–72, 1973–74, 1979–80.

LEEDS UNITED 1993—94 LEAGUE RECORD

Match No.	Date	Venue	Opponents	Result		H/T Score	Lg. Pos.	Goalscorers	Attendance
1	Aug 14	A	Manchester C	D	1-1	0-0	—	Deane	32,366
2	17	H	West Ham U	W	1-0	0-0	—	Speed	34,588
3	21	H	Norwich C	L	0-4	0-2	12		32,008
4	24	A	Arsenal	L	1-2	0-1	—	Strachan	29,042
5	28	A	Liverpool	L	0-2	0-2	18		44,068
6	30	H	Oldham Ath	W	1-0	1-0	—	Strachan	28,717
7	Sept 11	A	Southampton	W	2-0	0-0	12	Deane, Speed	13,511
8	18	H	Sheffield U	W	2-1	2-1	8	McAllister, Strachan	33,879
9	25	A	Coventry C	W	2-0	1-0	4	Wallace Rod 2	13,933
10	Oct 2	H	Wimbledon	W	4-0	2-0	3	Speed 2, McAllister 2	30,255
11	17	A	Ipswich T	D	0-0	0-0	—		17,532
12	23	H	Blackburn R	D	3-3	0-1	4	McAllister (pen), Newsome, Sherwood (og)	37,827
13	30	A	Sheffield W	D	3-3	1-2	6	Fairclough, Wallace Rod, Speed	31,892
14	Nov 6	H	Chelsea	W	4-1	0-0	4	Deane, Wallace Rod 2, Rocastle	35,050
15	20	A	Tottenham H	D	1-1	0-0	10	Deane	31,275
16	23	A	Everton	D	1-1	0-0	—	Wallace Rod	17,102
17	27	H	Swindon T	W	3-0	0-0	2	Deane, Wallace Rod, Speed	32,630
18	Dec 4	H	Manchester C	W	3-2	2-0	2	Wallace Rod, Speed, Deane	33,820
19	8	A	West Ham U	W	1-0	0-0	—	Wallace Rod	20,468
20	13	A	Norwich C	L	1-2	0-1	—	Wallace Rod	16,586
21	18	H	Arsenal	W	2-1	1-1	2	McAllister, Adams (og)	37,289
22	22	A	Newcastle U	D	1-1	0-0	—	Fairclough	36,388
23	29	H	QPR	D	1-1	0-0	3	Hodge	39,124
24	Jan 1	A	Manchester U	D	0-0	0-0	4		44,724
25	15	H	Ipswich T	D	0-0	0-0	4		31,317
26	23	A	Blackburn R	L	1-2	0-1	—	Speed	17,475
27	Feb 6	A	Aston Villa	L	0-1	0-0	—		26,919
28	19	H	Liverpool	W	2-0	1-0	4	Wetherall, McAllister	40,029
29	28	A	Oldham Ath	D	1-1	1-0	—	McAllister	11,136
30	Mar 5	H	Southampton	D	0-0	0-0	5		30,829
31	13	A	Sheffield U	D	2-2	1-0	—	Speed, Deane	19,425
32	16	H	Aston Villa	W	2-0	1-0	—	Wallace Rod, Deane	33,126
33	19	H	Coventry C	W	1-0	0-0	5	Wallace Rod	30,023
34	26	A	Wimbledon	L	0-1	0-1	5		9035
35	Apr 1	H	Newcastle U	D	1-1	0-1	—	Fairclough	40,005
36	4	A	QPR	W	4-0	2-0	5	Deane, Wallace Rod, White 2	15,365
37	17	H	Tottenham H	W	2-0	0-0	—	Wallace Rod 2	33,658
38	23	A	Chelsea	D	1-1	1-0	5	Speed	18,544
39	27	H	Manchester U	L	0-2	0-0	—		41,127
40	30	H	Everton	W	3-0	0-0	5	McAllister, Watson (og), White	35,487
41	May 3	H	Sheffield W	D	2-2	0-1	—	White, Wallace Rod	33,575
42	7	A	Swindon T	W	5-0	2-0	5	Deane 2, White, Wallace Rod, Fairclough	17,228

Final League Position: 5

GOALSCORERS

League (65): Rod Wallace 17, Deane 11, Speed 10, McAllister 8 (1 pen), White 5, Fairclough 4, Strachan 3, Hodge 1, Newsome 1, Rocastle 1, Wetherall 1, own goals 3.
Coca-Cola Cup (2): Speed 1, Whelan 1.
FA Cup (7): Forrester 2, Deane 1, Speed 1, Strachan 1, Wetherall 1, White 1.

Lukic 20	Kelly 42	Dorigo 37	Batty 8 + 1	Fairclough 40	O'Leary 10	Strachan 32 + 1	Whelan 6 + 10	Deane 41	McAllister 42	Speed 35 + 1	Wallace Rod 34 + 3	Newsome 25 + 4	Beeney 22	Wetherall 31 + 1	Strandli — + 4	Rocastle 6 + 1	Hodge 7 + 1	Pemberton 6 + 3	Forrester 2 + 1	Sharp 7 + 3	Wallace Ray — + 1	White 9 + 6	Tinkler — + 3	Ford — + 1	Match No.
1	2	3	4	5	6	7	8	9	10	11	12														1
1	2	3	4	5	6	7	8	9	10	11	12	14													2
1	2	3	4	5	6	7	8	9	10	11		12													3
1	2	3	4	5		7	8	9	10	11	12	6													4
1	2	3	4	5		7	12	9	10	11	8	6													5
	2	3	4			7		9	10	11	8	6	1	5											6
	2	3	4			7		9	10	11	8	6	1	5	12										7
	2	3	4	5		7		9	10	11	8		1	6	12										8
	2	3		5		7		9	10	11	8	6	1	4											9
	2	3		5		7		9	10	11	8	6	1	4	12										10
	2	3		5				9	10	11	8	6	1	4	12	7									11
	2	3	12	5			14	9	10	11	8	6	1	4		7									12
	2	3		5				9	10	11	8	6	1	4		7	12								13
	2	3		5				9	10	11	8	6	1	4		7									14
	2	3		5			12	9	10	11	8		1	6		7		4							15
	2	3		5			12	9	10	11	8		1	6		7		4							16
	2	3		5		7		9	10	11	8		1	6				4	12						17
	2	3		5		7	12	9	10	11	8		1	6						4	14				18
	2	3		5		7		9	10	11	8		1	6				12		4					19
	2	3		5		7	12	9	10		8		1	6			11			4					20
	2	3		5		7		9	10		8	6	1	4		12	11								21
	2	3		5			7	9	10		8	4	1				11	6		12					22
	2	3		5		7		9	10		8	4	1				6			12		11			23
	2	3		5		8		9	10			4	1				11	6		12		7			24
	2	3		5		8		9	10	12		4	1	14			6		11			7			25
	2	3		5		8	12	9	10	11		4	1					14	6			7			26
	2	3		5		8	12	9	10	11		4	1				6					7			27
1	2	3		5	6	7		9	10	11	8	14		4								12			28
1	2	3		5		7		9	10	11	8	4		6											29
1	2	3		5	6	7		9	10	11	8			4								12			30
1	2	3		5	6	7		9	10	11	8			4											31
1	2	3		5	6	7		9	10	11	8	12		4											32
1	2	3		5		7		9	10	11	8	4		6											33
1	2	3		5		7		9	10	11	8	4		6								12			34
1	2	3		5		7		9	10	11	8	4		6								12			35
1	2	3		5				9	10	11	8	4		6								7	12		36
1	2			5				9	10	11	8	4		6						3		7			37
1	2			5		12		9	10	11	8	4		6						3		7			38
1	2	3		5		7	12	9	10	11	8	4		6				14							39
1	2			5	6	7	9		10	11	8			4						3		12	14		40
1	2			5	6	7		9	10	11	8			4						3		12	14		41
1	2			5	6	11	12	9	10		8			4				3				7		14	42

Coca-Cola Cup	Second Round	Sunderland (a)	1-2
		(h)	1-2
FA Cup	Third Round	Crewe Alex (h)	3-1
	Fourth Round	Oxford U (a)	2-2
		(h)	2-3

LEEDS UNITED

Player and Position	Ht	Wt	Birth Date	Birth Place	Source	Clubs	League App	League Gls
Goalkeepers								
Mark Beeney	6 4	14 07	30 12 67	Pembury		Gillingham	2	—
						Maidstone U	50	—
						Aldershot (loan)	7	—
						Brighton & HA	69	—
						Leeds U	23	—
Scott Cousin			31 1 75	Leeds	Trainee	Leeds U	—	—
John Lukic	6 4	13 13	11 12 60	Chesterfield	Apprentice	Leeds U	146	—
						Arsenal	223	—
						Leeds U	139	—
Paul Pettinger			1 10 75	Sheffield	Barnsley	Leeds U	—	—
Defenders								
Robert Bowman			21 11 75	Durham	Trainee	Leeds U	4	—
Andrew Couzens	5 9	11 07	4 6 75	Shipley	Trainee	Leeds U	—	—
Tony Dorigo	5 10	10 09	31 12 65	Australia	Apprentice	Aston Villa	111	1
						Chelsea	146	11
						Leeds U	108	4
Chris Fairclough	5 11	11 02	12 4 64	Nottingham	Apprentice	Nottingham F	107	1
						Tottenham H	60	5
						Leeds U	188	21
Mark Humphries	5 10	12 12	23 12 71	Glasgow	Cove R	Aberdeen	2	—
						Leeds U	—	—
Gary Kelly	5 8	10 12	9 7 74	Drogheda	Home Farm	Leeds U	44	—
Jon Newsome	6 2	13 11	6 9 70	Sheffield	Trainee	Sheffield W	7	—
						Leeds U	76	3
Gary O'Hara‡			13 12 73	Belfast	Trainee	Leeds U	—	—
David O'Leary	6 1	13 09	2 5 58	London	Apprentice	Arsenal	558	10
						Leeds U	10	—
John Pemberton	5 11	12 03	18 11 64	Oldham	Chadderton	Rochdale	1	—
						Crewe Alex	121	1
						Crystal Palace	78	2
						Sheffield U	68	—
						Leeds U	9	—
Mel Sterland‡	6 0	13 05	1 10 61	Sheffield	Apprentice	Sheffield W	279	37
						Rangers	9	3
						Leeds U	114	16
Ray Wallace	5 6	10 02	2 10 69	Lewisham	Trainee	Southampton	35	—
						Leeds U	7	—
						Swansea C (loan)	2	—
						Reading (loan)	3	—
David Wetherall	6 3	12 00	14 3 71	Sheffield	School	Sheffield W	—	—
						Leeds U	46	2
Midfield								
Mark Ford	5 7	10 03	10 10 75	Pontefract	Trainee	Leeds U	1	—
Steve Hodge	5 8	9 11	25 10 62	Nottingham	Apprentice	Nottingham F	123	30
						Aston Villa	53	12
						Tottenham H	45	7
						Nottingham F	82	20
						Leeds U	54	10
Gary McAllister	6 1	10 11	25 12 64	Motherwell	Fir Park BC	Motherwell	59	6
						Leicester C	201	47
						Leeds U	154	20
Kevin Sharp	5 9	10 07	19 9 74	Ontario	Auxerre	Leeds U	14	—
Matthew Smithard			13 6 76	Leeds	Trainee	Leeds U	—	—
Gary Speed	5 9	10 06	8 9 69	Hawarden	Trainee	Leeds U	180	34
Gordon Strachan	5 6	10 06	9 2 57	Edinburgh		Dundee	60	13
						Aberdeen	183	55
						Manchester U	160	33
						Leeds U	191	37
Mark Tinkler‡	5 10	10 02	24 10 74	Bishop Auckland	Trainee	Leeds U	10	—

LEEDS UNITED

Colours: All white with yellow and blue trim. **Change colours:** Yellow and blue striped shirts, blue shorts, yellow stockings.

Foundation: Immediately the Leeds City club (founded in 1904) was wound up by the FA in October 1919, following allegations of illegal payments to players, a meeting was called by a Leeds solicitor, Mr. Alf Masser, at which Leeds United was formed. They joined the Midland League playing their first game in that competition in November 1919. It was in this same month that the new club had discussions with the directors of a virtually bankrupt Huddersfield Town who wanted to move to Leeds in an amalgamation. But Huddersfield survived even that crisis.

First Football League game: 28 August, 1920, Division 2, v Port Vale (a) L 0-2 – Down; Duffield, Tillotson; Musgrove, Baker, Walton; Mason, Goldthorpe, Thompson, Lyon, Best.

Did you know: Leeds United's first season in the FA Cup during 1920–21 saw them beat Boothtown 5-2 and Leeds Steelworks 7-0 in preliminary round matches. They then withdrew from the competition!

Managers (and Secretary-Managers)
Dick Ray 1919–20, Arthur Fairclough 1920–27, Dick Ray 1927–35, Bill Hampson 1935–47, Willis Edwards 1947–48, Major Frank Buckley 1948–53, Raich Carter 1953–58, Bill Lambton 1958–59, Jack Taylor 1959–61, Don Revie 1961–74, Brian Clough 1974, Jimmy Armfield 1974–78, Jock Stein 1978, Jimmy Adamson 1978–80, Allan Clarke 1980–82, Eddie Gray 1982–85, Billy Bremner 1985–88, Howard Wilkinson October 1988– .

Player and Position	*Ht*	*Wt*	*Birth Date*	*Place*	*Source*	*Clubs*	*League App*	*Gls*
Forwards								
Brian Deane	6 3	12 07	7 2 68	Leeds	Apprentice	Doncaster R	66	12
						Sheffield U	197	82
						Leeds U	41	11
Jamie Forrester	5 7	10 00	1 11 74	Bradford	Auxerre	Leeds U	9	—
Ryan Nicholls‡			10 5 73	Cardiff	Trainee	Leeds U	—	—
Frank Strandli	5 10	12 07	16 5 72	Norway	IK Start	Leeds U	14	2
Steven Tobin‡			24 3 75	Manchester	Trainee	Leeds U	—	—
Rodney Wallace	5 7	10 01	2 10 69	Lewisham	Trainee	Southampton	128	45
						Leeds U	103	35
Noel Whelan	5 11	10 07	30 12 74	Leeds	Trainee	Leeds U	17	—
David White	6 1	12 09	30 10 67	Manchester		Manchester C	285	79
						Leeds U	15	5

Trainees
Blunt, Jason; Connor, David; Fawell, Nicky; Grant, Anthony; Harte, Ian P; Hoyle, Michael S; Kavanagh, Sean; Littlewood, Martin; Lowndes, Nathan P; Lynam, Gary; Marks, Jamie; O'Shea, Alan; Wharton, Paul; Willetts, Harvey A.

Assopciated Schoolboys
Elliott, Steven W; Fairham, Steven J; Fidler, Richard M; Fitzgerald, Lee A; Greene, Neil T; Holliday, Kevin; Hudson, Daniel R; Jackson, Daniel M. D; Matthews, Lee J; McCulloch, Andrew J; Morgan, Simon R; Obrien, Kieron J; Otter, Simon A; Owen, Craig; Porter, Darren; Smith, Mark R; Trower, Kevin J.

Associated Schoolboys who have accepted the Club's offer of a Traineeship/Contract
Brown, Matthew; Davies, Lawrence; Foster, Martin; Gray, Andrew D; Heath, Stephen D; Jackson, Mark G; Jaques, Daniel; Moody, James D; Shepherd, Paul.

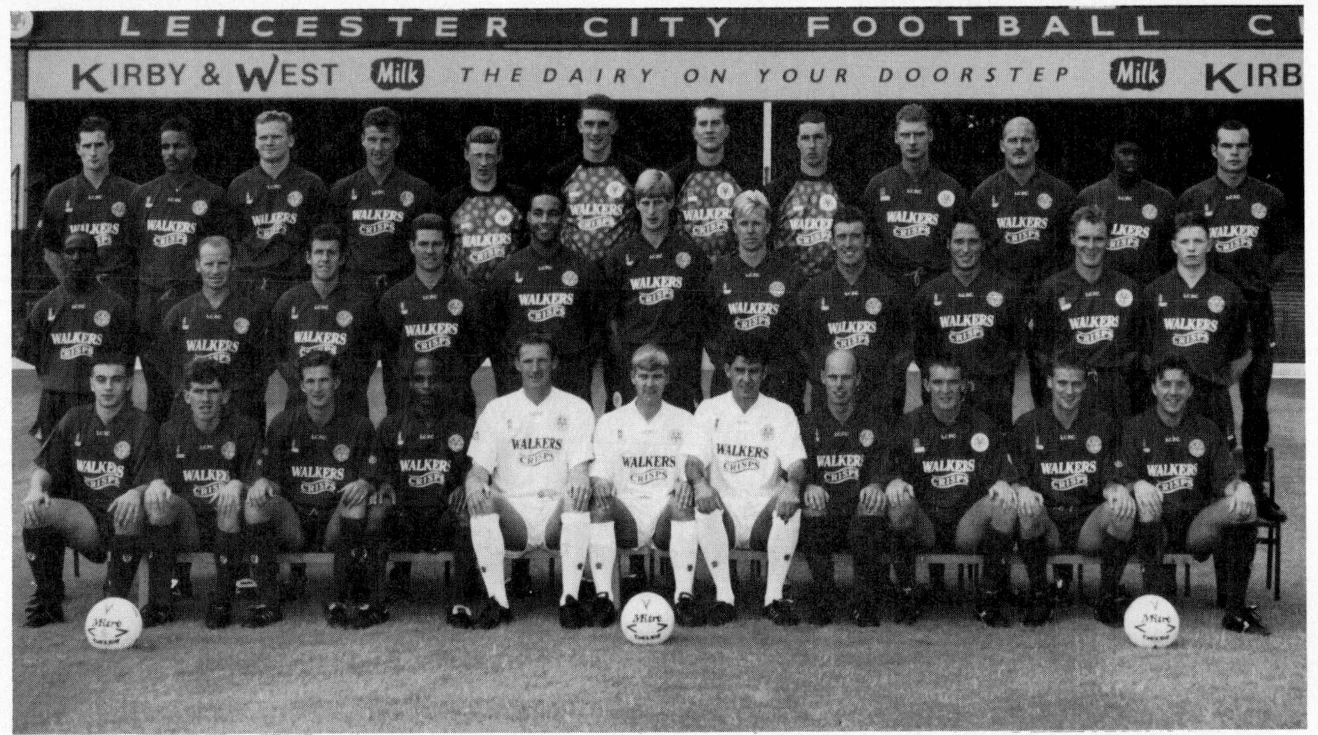

LEICESTER CITY 1993–94 *Back row (left to right):* Jimmy Willis, Scott Eustace, Brian Carey, Steve Walsh, Kevin Poole, Russell Hoult, Gavin Ward, Carl Muggleton, Michael Trotter, Gary Coatsworth, Ian Thompson, Richard Smith.

Centre row: Neil Lewis, David Speedie, Colin Gibson, Gary Mills, Tony James, Ian Ormondroyd, David Oldfield, Steve Thompson, Lee Philpott, Colin Hill, Adrian Crane.

Front row: Matt Bedder, David Lowe, Simon Grayson, Warren Haughton, Allan Evans (Assistant Manager), Brian Little (Manager), John Gregory (First Team Coach), Steve Agnew, Mike Whitlow, Phil Gee, Bobby Davison.

FA Premiership **LEICESTER CITY**

City Stadium, Filbert St, Leicester LE2 7FL. Telephone Leicester (0533) 555000. Fax (0533) 470585. Ticket Office: (0533) 553313. Club Store: 0533 559455. Ticket line: 0891 121028. Clubcall: 0891 121185. Marketing: (0533) 854000. Shop: (0533) 559455.

Ground capacity: 22,517.

Record attendance: 47,298 v Tottenham H, FA Cup 5th rd, 18 February 1928.

Record receipts: £189,426 v Tranmere Rovers, Division 1 play-off semi-final, 18 May 1994.

Pitch measurements: 112yd × 75yd.

President: K. R. Brigstock.

Chairman: Martin George. ***Vice-Chairman:*** Tom Smeaton.

Chief Executive: Barrie Pierpoint.

Directors: J. M. Elsom FCA, R. W. Parker, J. E. Sharp, T. W. Shipman, W. K. Shooter FCA.

Manager: Brian Little. ***Assistant Manager*** :Allan Evans. ***First Team Coach:*** John Gregory. ***Youth team coach:*** Tony McAndrew.

Football Secretary: Ian Silvester.

Company Secretary: Steve Kind.

Head of Publicity/Press Officer: Paul Mace.

Physio: Alan Smith. ***Commercial Manager:*** Karen Finney.

Year Formed: 1884.

Club Nickname: 'Fiberts' or 'Foxes'.

Previous Grounds: 1884, Victoria Park; 1887, Belgrave Road; 1888, Victoria Park; 1891, Filbert Street.

Previous Name: 1884–1919, Leicester Fosse.

Record League Victory: 10–0 v Portsmouth, Division 1, 20 October 1928 – McLaren; Black, Brown; Findlay, Carr, Watson; Adcock, Hine (3), Chandler (6), Lochhead, Barry (1).

Record Cup Victory: 8–1 v Coventry C (away), League Cup, 5th rd, 1 December 1964 – Banks; Sjoberg, Norman (2); Roberts, King, McDerment; Hodgson (2), Cross, Goodfellow, Gibson (1), Stringfellow (2). (1 og).

Record Defeat: 0–12 (as Leicester Fosse) v Nottingham F, Division 1, 21 April 1909.

Most League Points (2 for a win): 61, Division 2, 1956–57.

Most League Points (3 for a win): 77, Division 2, 1991–92.

Most League Goals: 109, Division 2, 1956–57.

Highest League Scorer in Season: Arthur Rowley, 44, Division 2, 1956–57.

Most League Goals in Total Aggregate: Arthur Chandler, 259, 1923–35.

Most Capped Player: John O'Neill, 39, Northern Ireland.

Most League Appearances: Adam Black, 528, 1920–35.

Record Transfer Fee Received: £1,350,000 from Derby Co for Paul Kitson, March 1992.

Record Transfer Fee Paid: £360,000 to Portsmouth for Mark Blake, March 1994.

Football League Record: 1894 Elected to Division 2; 1908–09 Division 1; 1909–25 Division 2; 1925–35 Division 1; 1935–37 Division 2; 1937–39 Division 1; 1946–54 Division 2; 1954–55 Division 1; 1955–57 Division 2; 1957–69 Division 1; 1969–71 Division 2; 1971–78 Division 1; 1978–80 Division 2; 1980–81 Division 1; 1981–83 Division 2; 1983–87 Division 1; 1987–92 Division 2; 1992–94 Division 1; 1994– FA Premier League.

Honours: *Football League:* Division 1 – Runners-up 1928–29; Division 2 – Champions 1924–25, 1936–37, 1953–54, 1956–57, 1970–71, 1979–80; Runners-up 1907–08. *FA Cup:* Runners-up 1949, 1961, 1963, 1969. *Football League Cup:* Winners 1964; Runners-up 1965. **European Competitions:** *European Cup-Winners' Cup:* 1961–62.

LEICESTER CITY 1993—94 LEAGUE RECORD

Match No.	Date	Venue	Opponents	Result		H/T Score	Lg. Pos.	Goalscorers	Attendance
1	Aug 14	H	Peterborough U	W	2-1	2-1	—	Thompson (pen), James	13,671
2	21	A	Tranmere R	L	0-1	0-0	15		8766
3	28	H	Millwall	W	4-0	0-0	8	Agnew, Walsh 2, Joachim	12,219
4	Sept 12	H	Birmingham C	D	1-1	0-0	—	Walsh	10,366
5	14	A	Bristol C	W	3-1	0-0	—	Speedie 2, Walsh	7899
6	18	A	Bolton W	W	2-1	0-0	5	Speedie 2	12,049
7	25	A	Barnsley	W	1-0	1-0	3	Oldfield	10,392
8	29	A	Middlesbrough	L	0-2	0-1	—		11,871
9	Oct 2	H	Notts Co	W	3-2	1-2	3	Speedie 2, Thompson (pen)	16,319
10	16	A	Charlton Ath	L	1-2	0-1	4	Agnew	8316
11	24	H	Nottingham F	W	1-0	1-0	—	Speedie	17,624
12	30	A	Luton T	W	2-0	1-0	2	Thompson (pen), Speedie	8813
13	Nov 2	A	Grimsby T	D	0-0	0-0	—		6344
14	6	H	Southend U	W	3-0	2-0	1	Joachim, Oldfield, Thompson (pen)	15,387
15	14	A	Stoke C	L	0-1	0-1	—		15,984
16	20	H	Oxford U	L	2-3	1-0	6	Thompson (pen), Whitlow	14,070
17	27	H	Wolverhampton W	D	2-2	0-2	5	Roberts 2	18,395
18	Dec 5	A	Southend U	D	0-0	0-0	—		6114
19	8	H	Crystal Palace	D	1-1	1-0	—	Roberts	16,706
20	11	H	Bristol C	W	3-0	2-0	5	Speedie 2, Joachim	13,394
21	19	A	Peterborough U	D	1-1	0-0	—	Bradshaw (og)	8595
22	27	H	Watford	D	4-4	1-0	6	Thompson (pen), Oldfield 2, Ormondroyd	21,744
23	28	A	Derby Co	L	2-3	0-2	5	Joachim, Roberts	17,372
24	Jan 1	H	Sunderland	W	2-1	0-0	6	Speedie, Joachim	19,615
25	12	H	WBA	W	4-2	2-1	—	Roberts 2, Whitlow, Mardon (og)	15,640
26	16	H	Charlton Ath	W	2-1	0-0	—	Grayson, Roberts	12,577
27	22	A	Crystal Palace	L	1-2	1-1	4	Thompson	17,045
28	Feb 6	A	Nottingham F	L	0-4	0-2	—		26,616
29	12	H	Luton T	W	2-1	1-0	4	Coatsworth, Roberts	16,149
30	19	A	WBA	W	2-1	1-1	2	Roberts, Ormondroyd	18,513
31	23	H	Tranmere R	D	1-1	0-1	—	McGreal (og)	14,028
32	Mar 6	A	Millwall	D	0-0	0-0	—		8085
33	12	H	Middlesbrough	W	2-0	1-0	2	Joachim, Speedie	16,116
34	15	A	Birmingham C	W	3-0	2-0	—	Joachim, Ormondroyd, Roberts	14,681
35	19	H	Barnsley	L	0-1	0-0	3		15,640
36	26	A	Notts Co	L	1-4	1-2	3	Ormondroyd	11,907
37	30	H	Portsmouth	L	0-3	0-3	—		15,146
38	Apr 2	A	Watford	D	1-1	0-0	3	Agnew	8645
39	5	H	Derby Co	D	3-3	3-3	—	Roberts 3	20,050
40	9	A	Sunderland	W	3-2	1-1	3	Joachim 2, Kerr (pen)	17,198
41	16	H	Grimsby T	D	1-1	0-1	3	Joachim	15,859
42	23	A	Oxford U	D	2-2	1-1	6	Blake, Joachim	8818
43	26	A	Portsmouth	W	1-0	1-0	—	Kerr	7869
44	30	H	Stoke C	D	1-1	0-0	4	Willis	19,291
45	May 3	H	Bolton W	D	1-1	0-1	—	Gee	18,145
46	8	A	Wolverhampton W	D	1-1	1-0	4	Coatsworth	27,229

Final League Position: 4

GOALSCORERS

League (72): Roberts 13, Speedie 12, Joachim 11, Thompson 7 (6 pens), Oldfield 4, Ormondroyd 4, Walsh 4, Agnew 3, Coatsworth 2, Kerr 2 (1 pen), Whitlow 2, Blake 1, Gee 1, Grayson 1, James 1, Willis 1, own goals 3.
Coca-Cola Cup (9): Ormondroyd 2, Hill 1, Joachim 1, Oldfield 1, Speedie 1, Thompson 1, Walsh 1, Whitlow 1.
FA Cup (1): Oldfield 1.

Ward 32	Hill 30 + 1	Whitlow 31	Carey 24 + 3	Walsh 9 + 1	James 4 + 5	Mills 21 + 2	Thompson 30	Speedie 37	Agnew 36	Philpott 10 + 9	Joachim 27 + 9	Smith 2 + 6	Poole 14	Gibson 11 + 4	Ormondroyd 30 + 1	Oldfield 24 + 3	Grayson 39 + 1	Lewis 24	Willis 9	Gee 6 + 6	Roberts 26	Coatsworth 15 + 4	Eustace — + 1	Lowe 1 + 4	Blake 10 + 1	Kerr 4 + 3	Match No.
1	2	*3*	4	5	6	7	8	9	10	11	12	14															1
	2	3	4	5	6	7	8	9	10		11	12	1														2
1	6	3		5	12	2	8	9	10		7			4	11												3
1	6	3		5		2	8	9	10		7			4	11												4
1	6	3	4	5		2	8	9	10						11	7											5
1	6	3	4	5		*2*	8	9	10		12				11	7	14										6
1	6	3		5			8	9	10		12	4			11	7	2										7
1	6	3		5		14	8	9	10		12	*4*			11	7	2										8
1	6	5					8	9	10	12	7				11	4	2	3									9
1	6	3					8	9	10	12	7				*11*	4	2		5	14							10
1	6	5				12	8	9	10		7				11	4	2	3									11
1	6	3	5			4	8	9	10		7	12			11		2										12
1	6	3	5			4	8	9	10		7				11		2										13
1	6	3	5			4	8	9	10		7			14	*11*	12	2										14
1	6	3	5			*4*	8	9		12	7	14		11		10	2										15
1	6	3	5			4	8	9		11	7	12				10	2										16
1	6		*5*			4	8	9	11	12	7	14					2	3			10						17
1		6	5			4	8	9	7	11							2	3		12	10						18
1		6	14			*4*	8	9	5	11	7						2	3		12	10						19
1	6						8	9	5	11	7					12	2	3			10	*4*	14				20
1	*6*	4					8	9	5	11	7					12	2	3			10	14					21
1	6						8	*9*	5	11				3	12	7	2				10	4		14			22
1	6						8	9	5		12				11	7	2	3			10	4					23
	6						8	*9*	5	12	7		1			11	2	3			10	4		14			24
	6	3				4	8	9	5				1	11		7	2				10						25
	6	3	14			4	8	*9*	5				1	11		7	2				10			12			26
	6	3	14			4	8						1	11		7	2			12	10	5		*9*			27
	6	3				4	8		5		9		1			7	2	11			10			12			28
1		6	4			7	8	9							11		2	3			10	5					29
1	12	6	4			7	8	9		14					11		2	*3*			10	5					30
1		6	4			*7*		9			12				11	8	2	3			10	5					31
1	7	6	4					9	5		12			14	11	8		*3*			10	2					32
1	6	3	4					*9*	5		7			14	11	8	2				10	12					33
1	6	3	4					9	5		7				11	8	2				10						34
1	*6*	3	4					9	5		7			14	11	8	2				10	12					35
1			4		6			9	5	7	12				11		2				10	3			8		36
1		6	4	12				*9*	5		7				11		2	3			10				8	14	37
				5	11			*9*	6		12		1				2	3	4	14	10				8	7	38
					12				6		7		1		11	*5*	2	3	4	9	10				8	14	39
					14				6		7		1		11		2	3	*4*	9	10	12			8	5	40
									6	12	7		1		11		2	3	4	9	10	5			8		41
			5		14					12	7		1	6	11		2	3	4	*9*	10				8		42
			5								7		1	6	11		2	3	4			9			8	10	43
			5							12	7		1	*6*	11		2	3	4	10		9			8	14	44
								9	6	10			1		11	7	2	3	4	12		5			8		45
1			4		14					10				6	11	7	2	3		*9*		5		12	8		46

Coca-Cola Cup	Second Round	Rochdale (a)	6-1
		(h)	2-1
	Third Round	Manchester U (a)	1-5
FA Cup	Third Round	Manchester C (a)	1-4

LEICESTER CITY

Player and Position	Ht	Wt	Birth Date	Birth Place	Source	Clubs	League App	League Gls
Goalkeepers								
Russell Hoult	6 3	14 01	22 11 72	Leicester	Trainee	Leicester C	10	—
						Lincoln C (loan)	2	—
						Blackpool (loan)	—	—
						Bolton W (loan)	4	—
Carl Muggleton (To Celtic January 1994)	6 2	13 07	13 9 68	Leicester	Apprentice	Leicester C	46	—
						Chesterfield (loan)	17	—
						Blackpool (loan)	2	—
						Hartlepool U (loan)	8	—
						Stockport Co (loan)	4	—
						Liverpool (loan)	—	—
						Stoke C (loan)	6	—
						Sheffield U (loan)	—	—
Kevin Poole	5 10	12 06	21 7 63	Bromsgrove	Apprentice	Aston Villa	28	—
						Northampton T (loan)	3	—
						Middlesbrough	34	—
						Hartlepool U (loan)	12	—
						Leicester C	75	—
Gavin Ward	6 2	12 12	30 6 70	Sutton Coldfield	Aston Villa	Shrewsbury T	—	—
						WBA	—	—
						Cardiff C	59	—
						Leicester C	32	—
Defenders								
Ian Blyth*			21 10 74	Coventry	Trainee	Leicester C	—	—
Brian Carey	6 3	11 13	31 5 68	Cork	Cork C	Manchester U	—	—
						Wrexham (loan)	3	—
						Wrexham (loan)	13	1
						Leicester C	27	—
Gary Coatsworth	6 0	13 02	7 10 68	Sunderland		Barnsley	6	—
						Darlington	22	2
						Leicester C	32	4
Colin Gibson*	5 8	11 01	6 4 60	Bridport	Apprentice	Aston Villa	185	10
						Manchester U	79	9
						Port Vale (loan)	6	2
						Leicester C	59	4
Simon Grayson	5 11	12 13	16 12 69	Ripon	Trainee	Leeds U	2	—
						Leicester C	77	2
Colin Hill	5 11	12 08	12 11 63	Hillingdon	Apprentice	Arsenal	46	1
						Brighton (loan)	—	—
					Maritimo	Colchester U	69	—
						Sheffield U	82	1
						Leicester C (loan)	10	—
						Leicester C	77	—
Tony James*	6 3	14 02	27 6 67	Sheffield	Gainsborough T	Lincoln C	29	—
						Leicester C	107	11
Neil Lewis	5 7	10 09	28 6 74	Wolverhampton	Trainee	Leicester C	31	—
Richard Smith	5 11	12 10	3 10 70	Leicester	Trainee	Leicester C	85	1
						Cambridge U (loan)	4	—
Steve Walsh	6 2	13 13	3 11 64	Fulwood	Local	Wigan Ath	126	4
						Leicester C	245	41
Mike Whitlow	5 11	12 03	13 1 68	Northwich	Witton Alb	Leeds U	77	4
						Leicester C	60	3
Jimmy Willis	6 0	12 02	12 7 68	Liverpool	Blackburn R	Halifax T	—	—
						Stockport Co	10	—
						Darlington	90	6
						Leicester C	19	1
						Bradford C (loan)	9	1
Midfield								
Steve Agnew	5 8	11 10	9 11 65	Shipley	Apprentice	Barnsley	194	29
						Blackburn R	2	—
						Portsmouth (loan)	5	—
						Leicester C	45	4
Mark Blake	5 11	12 07	16 12 70	Nottingham	Trainee	Aston Villa	31	2
						Wolverhampton W (loan)	2	—
						Portsmouth	15	—
						Leicester C	11	1
Adrian Crane*	5 9	11 00	6 9 74	Leicester	Trainee	Leicester C	—	—
Warren Haughton*	5 7	10 02	13 9 73	Birmingham	Trainee	Leicester C	—	—
David Oldfield	5 11	13 02	30 5 68	Perth, Australia	Apprentice	Luton T	29	4
						Manchester C	26	6
						Leicester C	174	25
Ian Thompson			17 2 75	Leicester	Trainee	Leicester C	—	—

LEICESTER CITY

Colours: All blue. **Change colours:** All gold.

Foundation: In 1884 a number of young footballers who were mostly old boys of Wyggeston School, held a meeting at a house on the Roman Fosse Way and formed Leicester Fosse FC. They collected 9d (less than 4p) towards the cost of a ball, plus the same amount for membership. Their first professional, Harry Webb from Stafford Rangers, was signed in 1888 for 2s 6d (12p) per week, plus travelling expenses.

First Football League game: 1 September, 1894, Division 2, v Grimsby T (a) L 3-4 – Thraves; Smith, Bailey; Seymour, Brown, Henrys; Hill, Hughes, McArthur (1), Skea (2), Priestman.

Did you know: Versatile Graham Cross appeared in nearly 600 matches for Leicester City between 1960 and 1976. He made 498 League appearances, 59 in the FA Cup and a further 40 in the League Cup.

Managers (and Secretary-Managers)
William Clark 1896–97, George Johnson 1898–1907*, James Blessington 1907–09, Andy Aitken 1909–11, J. W. Bartlett 1912–14, Peter Hodge 1919–26, William Orr 1926–32, Peter Hodge 1932–34, Andy Lochhead 1934–36, Frank Womack 1936–39, Tom Bromilow 1939–45, Tom Mather 1945–46, Johnny Duncan 1946–49, Norman Bullock 1949–55, David Halliday 1955–58, Matt Gillies 1959–68, Frank O'Farrell 1968–71, Jimmy Bloomfield 1971–77, Frank McLintock 1977–78, Jock Wallace 1978–82, Gordon Milne 1982–86, Bryan Hamilton 1986–87, David Pleat 1987–91, Brian Little May 1991–

Steve Thompson	5 10	12 00	2 11 64	Oldham	Apprentice	Bolton W	335	49
						Luton T	5	—
						Leicester C	108	18
Michael Trotter*	6 0	12 12	27 10 69	Hartlepool	Trainee	Middlesbrough	—	—
						Doncaster R (loan)	3	—
						Darlington	29	2
						Leicester C	3	—
						Chesterfield (loan)	15	1
Forwards								
Scott Eustace	6 0	12 04	13 6 75	Leicester	Trainee	Leicester C	1	—
Phil Gee	6 0	12 01	19 12 64	Pelsall	Gresley R	Derby Co	124	26
						Leicester C	44	7
Julian Joachim	5 6	11 10	20 9 74	Peterborough	Trainee	Leicester C	62	21
David Lowe	5 10	11 10	30 8 65	Liverpool	Apprentice	Wigan Ath	188	40
						Ipswich T	134	37
						Port Vale (loan)	9	2
						Leicester C	37	11
						Port Vale	19	5
Gary Mills	5 9	11 10	11 11 61	Northampton	Apprentice	Nottingham F	58	8
					Seattle S	Derby Co	18	1
					Seattle S	Nottingham F	79	4
						Notts Co	75	8
						Leicester C	199	15
Ian Ormondroyd	6 4	13 05	22 9 64	Bradford	Thackley	Bradford C	87	20
						Oldham Ath (loan)	10	1
						Aston Villa	56	6
						Derby Co	25	8
						Leicester C	71	7
Lee Philpott	5 9	12 00	21 2 70	Barnet	Trainee	Peterborough U	4	—
						Cambridge U	134	17
						Leicester C	46	3
Iwan Roberts	6 3	12 06	26 6 68	Bangor		Watford	63	9
						Huddersfield T	142	50
						Leicester C	26	13
David Speedie	5 7	11 01	20 2 60	Glenrothes	Amateur	Barnsley	23	—
						Darlington	88	21
						Chelsea	162	47
						Coventry C	122	31
						Liverpool	12	6
						Blackburn R	36	23
						Southampton	11	—
						Birmingham C (loan)	10	2
						WBA (loan)	7	2
						West Ham U (loan)	11	4
						Leicester C	37	12

Trainees
Bedder, Paul M; Chivers, David J; Clay, Richard D; Clowes, Gavin D; Finney, Nicki D. J; Halford, Dean C; Hallam, Craig D; James, Scott, A; Linton, Martin; Livingstone, Maurice A; Maisey, Neil K; McMahon, Sam K; Morgans, Ryland D; Murphy, Gerald J; Poole, Richard J; Stewart, Tony; Warner, Timothy V.

Associated Schoolboys
Arcos-Diaz, Migeul; Aris, Greg; Austen, Jonathan; Beckford-Quailey, Damion A; Bent, Gavin R; Branston, Guy; Ekins, David; Farrell, Lee; Fox, Martin R; Goodwin, Tommy N; Hamblin, Paul; Jackson, Matthew; Kennedy, Andrew; Kew, Adam; King, Neil I; Mason, James D; Middleton, Carl; Neil, Gary D. C; Oakes, Stefan T; Ord, Tony; Payne, Dean; Wilson, Stevie J.

Associated Schoolboys who have accepted the Club's offer of a Traineeship/Contract
Campbell, Stuart; Heskey, Emile; Johnson, Owen R; Oram, Kevin F; Quincey, Lee P; Wenlock, Stephen; Wilson, Stuart K.

LEYTON ORIENT 1993–94 *Back row (left to right):* Vaughan Ryan, Mark Warren, Terry Howard, Robert Taylor, Nathan Beckett, Ian Hendon, Simon Livett, Nicky Sweetman.
Centre row: Pat Dellar (Kit Manager), Chris Turner (Assistant Manager), Sam Kitchen, Mark Cooper, Gary Bellamy, Paul Heald, Paul Newell, Warren Hackett, Colin West, Danny Carter, John Sitton (Coach), Andy Taylor (Physio).
Front row: Bradley Gamble, Danny Benstock, Mickey Tomlinson, Peter Eustace (Manager), Trevor Putney, Bernie Dixon (Chief Scout/Youth Development Officer), Barry Lakin, Steve Okai, Dominic Ludden.

Division 2 — LEYTON ORIENT

Leyton Stadium, Brisbane Road, Leyton, London E10 5NE. Telephone 081–539 2223/4. Fax 081–539 4390. Clubcall: 0898 121150.

Ground capacity: 17,065 (7,171 seats).

Record attendance: 34,345 v West Ham U, FA Cup 4th rd, 25 January 1964.

Record receipts: £87,867.92 v West Ham U, FA Cup 3rd rd, 10 January 1987.

Pitch measurements: 110yd × 80yd.

Chairman: T. Wood OBE.

Directors: D. L. Weinrabe, H. Linney, V. Marsh, J. Goldsmith FR, BA.

Team Manager: Peter Eustace. ***Assistant Manager:*** Chris Turner. ***Physio:*** A. Taylor.

Secretary: Miss Carol Stokes. ***Asst. Sec.:*** Mrs Sue Tilling. ***Commercial Manager:*** Frank Woolf.

Year Formed: 1881. ***Turned Professional:*** 1903. ***Ltd Co.:*** 1906.

Club Nickname: 'The O's'.

Previous Names: 1881–86, Glyn Cricket and Football Club; 1886–88, Eagle Football Club; 1888–98, Orient Football Club; 1898–1946, Clapton Orient; 1946–66, Leyton Orient; 1966–87, Orient.

Previous Grounds: Glyn Road, 1884–96; Whittles Athletic Ground, 1896–1900; Millfields Road, 1900–30; Lea Bridge Road, 1930–37.

Record League Victory: 8–0 v Crystal Palace, Division 3 (S), 12 November 1955 – Welton; Lee, Earl; Blizzard, Aldous, McKnight; White (1), Facey (3), Burgess (2), Heckman, Hartburn (2). 8–0 v Rochdale, Division 4, 20 October 1987 – Wells; Howard, Dickenson (1), Smalley (1), Day, Hull, Hales (2), Castle (Sussex), Shinners (2), Godfrey (Harvey), Comfort (2). 8–0 v Colchester U, Division 4, 15 October 1988 – Wells; Howard, Dickenson, Hales (1p), Day (1). Sitton (1), Baker (1), Ward, Hull (3). Juryeff, Comfort (1).

Record Cup Victory: 9–2 v Chester, League Cup, 3rd rd, 15 October 1962 – Robertson; Charlton, Taylor; Gibbs, Bishop, Lea; Deeley (1), Waites (3), Dunmore (2), Graham (3), Wedge.

Record Defeat: 0–8 v Aston Villa, FA Cup 4th rd, 30 January 1929.

Most League Points (2 for a win): 66, Division 3 (S), 1955–56.

Most League Points (3 for a win): 75, Division 4, 1988–89.

Most League Goals: 106, Division 3 (S), 1955–56.

Highest League Scorer in Season: Tom Johnston, 35, Division 2, 1957–58.

Most League Goals in Total Aggregate: Tom Johnston, 121, 1956–58, 1959–61.

Most Capped Player: John Chiedozie, 8 (10), Nigeria.

Most League Appearances: Peter Allen, 432, 1965–78.

Record Transfer Fee Received: £600,000 from Notts Co for John Chiedozie, August 1981.

Record Transfer Fee Paid: £175,000 to Wigan Ath for Paul Beesley, October 1989.

Football League Record: 1905 Elected to Division 2; 1929–56 Division 3 (S); 1956–62 Division 2; 1962–63 Division 1; 1963–66 Division 2; 1966–70 Division 3; 1970–82 Division 2; 1982–85 Division 3; 1985–89 Division 4; 1989–92 Division 3; 1992– Division 2.

Honours: *Football League:* Division 1 best season: 22nd, 1962–63; Division 2 – Runners-up 1961–62; Division 3 – Champions 1969–70; Division 3 (S) – Champions 1955–56; Runners-up 1954–55. *FA Cup:* Semi-final 1977–78. *Football League Cup:* best season: 5th rd, 1963.

LEYTON ORIENT 1993—94 LEAGUE RECORD

Match No.	Date	Venue	Opponents	Result		H/T Score	Lg. Pos.	Goalscorers	Attendance
1	Aug 14	A	Cardiff C	L	0-2	0-0	—		9920
2	21	H	Bristol R	W	1-0	0-0	15	Taylor	4155
3	28	A	Burnley	L	1-4	1-2	18	West	10,133
4	31	H	Hartlepool U	L	1-2	0-0	—	Howard	3399
5	Sept 4	H	York C	W	2-0	1-0	14	West 2	3698
6	11	A	Plymouth Arg	L	1-3	1-1	17	Barnett	5657
7	14	A	Brentford	W	1-0	0-0	—	Carter	5149
8	18	H	Barnet	W	4-2	0-0	11	Barnett, Okai, Bellamy, Carter	4812
9	25	H	Brighton & HA	L	1-3	1-1	15	Hackett	4737
10	Oct 2	A	Fulham	W	3-2	1-1	10	Putney, Hendon 2	4417
11	9	H	Rotherham U	D	1-1	0-0	11	Howard	3304
12	16	A	Reading	L	1-2	0-1	11	West	6066
13	23	H	Bournemouth	D	0-0	0-0	17		3896
14	30	A	Hull C	W	1-0	0-0	12	West	5246
15	Nov 2	A	Stockport Co	L	0-3	0-1	—		4323
16	6	H	Exeter C	D	1-1	1-1	15	Cooper	3798
17	20	A	Swansea C	D	1-1	0-1	16	Cooper	3160
18	27	H	Blackpool	W	2-0	1-0	11	West, Cooper	3369
19	Dec 11	A	Bristol R	D	1-1	1-1	13	Cooper	4604
20	18	H	Cardiff C	D	2-2	0-1	14	Cooper, Cockerill	3691
21	27	H	Cambridge U	W	2-1	1-0	11	Cockerill, Okai	6300
22	29	A	Port Vale	L	1-2	1-1	13	Barnett	8978
23	Jan 1	H	Huddersfield T	W	1-0	0-0	12	Carter	4599
24	3	A	Wrexham	L	2-4	1-3	13	West, Hackett	3567
25	8	A	Bradford C	D	0-0	0-0	11		5260
26	15	H	Reading	D	1-1	0-1	12	West	6253
27	22	A	Rotherham U	L	1-2	0-1	12	West	3392
28	29	H	Hull C	W	3-1	0-1	11	West 2, Barnett	4355
29	Feb 5	A	Bournemouth	D	1-1	1-1	11	Pennock (og)	4084
30	12	H	Bradford C	W	2-1	1-1	11	Bogie, Carter	3690
31	19	H	Burnley	W	3-1	0-1	9	Bogie, Carter, Putney	5201
32	25	A	York C	L	0-3	0-2	10		3414
33	Mar 5	H	Plymouth Arg	W	2-1	2-0	9	Bogie, Carter	5334
34	8	A	Hartlepool U	D	1-1	0-0	—	Barnett	1251
35	12	A	Barnet	L	1-3	1-2	11	West	2717
36	15	H	Brentford	D	1-1	0-0	—	Barnett	3185
37	19	A	Brighton & HA	L	0-2	0-1	11		8202
38	26	H	Fulham	D	2-2	1-0	12	Thomas, Carter	5096
39	29	H	Wrexham	D	2-2	1-0	—	Cooper, Barnett	2643
40	Apr 2	A	Cambridge U	L	1-3	0-1	13	Cooper	3762
41	4	H	Port Vale	L	2-3	1-2	13	Thomas, Cooper	3412
42	9	A	Huddersfield T	L	0-1	0-1	16		4995
43	16	H	Stockport Co	D	0-0	0-0	15		3984
44	23	A	Exeter C	L	0-1	0-1	17		1933
45	30	H	Swansea C	W	2-1	1-0	17	West 2 (1 pen)	3529
46	May 7	A	Blackpool	L	1-4	1-1	18	Hackett	5458

Final League Position: 18

GOALSCORERS

League (57): West 14 (1 pen), Cooper 8, Barnett 7, Carter 7, Bogie 3, Hackett 3, Cockerill 2, Hendon 2, Howard 2, Okai 2, Putney 2, Thomas 2, Bellamy 1, Taylor 1, own goal 1.
Coca-Cola Cup (0):
FA Cup (5): Hackett 2, Carter 1, Cooper 1, Lakin 1.

Turner 6	Hendon 35 + 1	Howard 20 + 5	Hackett 32 + 1	Bellamy 27 + 2	Ryan 16 + 1	Carter 35 + 1	Lakin 11 + 4	Taylor 12 + 11	Tomlinson 4	Putney 20 + 2	Ludden 29 + 5	Kitchen 7 + 4	Barnett 32 + 4	West 42 + 1	Benstock 9 + 3	Newell 40	Austin 30	Okai 5 + 6	Cooper 20 + 9	Livett — + 1	Harriott 8	Bogie 34	Cockerill 19	Gamble 1	Warren 5 + 1	Purse 2 + 3	Thomas 5	*Match No.*
1	2	3	4	5	6	7	8	9	10	11	12																	1
1	2	3	4		6	7		9	10	11	8	5	12															2
1	2	3	4			7	12	9		11	8	5	*6*	10	14													3
1	2	3	4			7	6	9			8	5	11	10														4
1	2	3	4	6		7	12	9		11	*8*	5	14	10														5
1	2	*3*	4	6		7	12	9		11		5	8	10	14													6
	2		4	6		7	5			11			9	10		1	3	8										7
	2	12	4	6		7	5			11			9	10		1	3	*8*	14									8
	2		4	*6*		7	5			11			9	10		1	3	8	12	14								9
	2		4	6	8	7		12		11				10		1	3		9		5							10
	2	4		6	*8*	7		12		11	14			10		1	3		9		5							11
	2		4		8	*7*	14	12			11			10		1	3		9		5	6						12
	2	*11*	4		8	7		9			14			10		1	3		12		5	6						13
	2		4		8	7	11	9						10		1	3		12		5	6						14
	2		4		8		*11*	9	7			14		10		1	3		12		5	6						15
	2		4		8		11		7					10		1	3		9		5	6						16
	2		4	12	8		11							10		1	3	6	9		5	7						17
	2		4	5			11	12					8	10		1	3	6	9			7						18
	2	12	4	5		7							8	10		1	3		9			11	6					19
	2		4	5		7					3	12	8	10		1			9			11	6					20
	2	12	4	5			7				3		8	10		1		14				11	6	*9*				21
	2	9	4	5							3	7	8	10		1		12				11	6					22
	2	8	4	5		7							9	10		1	3					11	6					23
	2	*9*	4	5		7					3	12	8	10		1		14				11	6					24
	2	9	4	5		7					3		8	10		1						11	6					25
	2	9	4	5		7		12			3	14	8	10		1						11	6					26
		9	4	5	14	7		12			3	*2*	8	10		1						11	6					27
	3	4		5		8		9			2		7	10	12	1						11	6					28
	3	4		5		*8*		9		14	2		7	10		1			12			11	6					29
	2	4		5		7		12			3		8		9	1			10			11	6					30
	2			5		7				*8*	3		14	12	9	1	4		10			11	6					31
	2			5		7				8	3		14	10	*9*	1	4		12			11	6					32
	2	3				7		12		*8*	14		6	5	9	1	4		10			11						33
		3				7		12		8	14		6	5	9	1	4		*10*			11			2			34
					6	7		9			3		8	5		1	4	12	10			11			2			35
				6		7		12			3		8	5	9	1	4		10			11			2			36
				2	6	7		12			3		8	5	9	1	*4*		10			11				14		37
				6		7				*2*	3		8	5		1	4	12	10			11				14	9	38
				12		7				2	3		8	5	11	1	4		10							6	9	39
			12			7					3		8	5	6	1	4	14	10			11				*2*	9	40
			4	6	2						3		8	9		1	5		10			11					7	41
		5	4		2					12	3			9		1	6		*10*			11	8			14	7	42
	14		4		2	*7*				6	3		9	10		1	5		12			11	8					43
	7		4		*2*					6	3		9	10		1	5		12			11	8		14			44
	7	12	4							6	3		9	10		1	5					11	8		2			45
	7	12	4			14				6	3		*9*	10		1	5					11	8		2			46

Coca-Cola Cup	First Round	Wycombe W (h)	0-2
		(a)	0-1
FA Cup	First Round	Gravesend (h)	2-1
	Second Round	Exeter C (h)	1-1
		(a)	2-2

LEYTON ORIENT

Player and Position	Ht	Wt	Birth Date	Birth Place	Source	Clubs	League App	League Gls
Goalkeepers								
Paul Heald	6 2	12 05	20 8 68	Wath-on-Dearne	Trainee	Sheffield U	—	—
						Leyton Orient	131	—
						Coventry C (loan)	2	—
						Crystal Palace (loan)	—	—
						Swindon T (loan)	2	—
Paul Newell	6 1	11 05	23 2 69	Greenwich	Trainee	Southend U	15	—
						Leyton Orient	61	—
						Colchester U (loan)	14	—
Chris Turner	5 11	11 12	15 9 58	Sheffield	Apprentice	Sheffield W	91	—
						Lincoln C (loan)	5	—
						Sunderland	195	—
						Manchester U	64	—
						Sheffield W	75	—
						Leeds U (loan)	2	—
						Leyton Orient	57	—
Defenders								
Kevin Austin	5 9	10 12	12 2 73	London	Saffron Walden	Leyton Orient	30	—
Nathan Beckett	6 2	13 00	31 5 75	Hertford	Trainee	Leyton Orient	—	—
Gary Bellamy	6 2	11 05	4 7 62	Worksop	Apprentice	Chesterfield	184	7
						Wolverhampton W	136	9
						Cardiff C (loan)	9	—
						Leyton Orient	68	5
Danny Benstock*			10 7 70	London	Barking	Leyton Orient	21	—
Warren Hackett*	5 9	11 12	16 12 71	Newham	Tottenham H	Leyton Orient	72	3
Ian Hendon	6 0	12 10	5 12 71	Ilford	Trainee	Tottenham H	4	—
						Portsmouth (loan)	4	—
						Leyton Orient (loan)	6	—
						Barnsley (loan)	6	—
						Leyton Orient	36	2
Terry Howard	6 1	11 07	26 2 66	Stepney	Apprentice	Chelsea	6	—
						C Palace (loan)	4	—
						Chester C (loan)	2	—
						Leyton Orient	301	30
Darren Purse			14 2 77	London	Trainee	Leyton Orient	5	—
Chris Zoricich	5 11	11 10	3 5 69	New Zealand		Leyton Orient	62	1
Midfield								
Ian Bogie	5 7	12 00	6 12 67	Newcastle	Apprentice	Newcastle U	14	—
						Preston NE	79	12
						Millwall	51	1
						Leyton Orient	34	3
Danny Carter	5 11	11 12	29 6 69	Hackney	Billericay	Leyton Orient	159	22
Glenn Cockerill	5 10	12 03	25 8 59	Grimsby	Louth U	Lincoln C	71	10
						Swindon T	26	1
						Lincoln C	115	25
						Sheffield U	62	10
						Southampton	287	32
						Leyton Orient	19	2
Bradley Gamble*	5 7	9 12	4 2 75	London	Trainee	Leyton Orient	1	—
Barry Lakin			19 9 73	Dartford	Trainee	Leyton Orient	24	2
Dominic Ludden	5 7	10 09	30 3 74	Basildon	Trainee	Leyton Orient	58	1
Stephen Okai*	5 8	10 12	3 12 73	Ghana	Schoolboy	Leyton Orient	25	4
Trevor Putney	5 9	11 08	11 2 61	Harold Hill	Brentwood & W	Ipswich T	103	8
						Norwich C	82	9
						Middlesbrough	48	1
						Watford	52	2
						Leyton Orient	22	2
Vaughan Ryan	5 8	10 12	2 9 68	Westminster		Wimbledon	82	3
						Sheffield U (loan)	3	—
						Leyton Orient	37	—
Martin Thomas†	5 8	10 08	12 9 73	Lyndhurst	Trainee	Southampton	—	—
						Leyton Orient	5	2
Mark Warren	5 9	10 05	12 11 74	Clapton	Trainee	Leyton Orient	21	—
						West Ham U (loan)	—	—

LEYTON ORIENT

Colours: Red shirts with white pinstripe, white shorts, red stockings. **Change colours:** White shirts with blue pinstripe, blue shorts, blue stockings.

Foundation: There is some doubt about the foundation of Leyton Orient, and, indeed, some confusion with clubs like Leyton and Clapton over their early history. As regards the foundation, the most favoured version is that Leyton Orient was formed originally by members of Homerton Theological College who established Glyn Cricket Club in 1881 and then carried on through the following winter playing football. Eventually many employees of the Orient Shipping Line became involved and so the name Orient was chosen in 1888.

First Football League game: 2 September, 1905, Division 2, v Leicester Fosse (a) L 1-2 – Butler; Holmes, Codling; Lamberton, Boden, Boyle; Kingaby (1), Wootten, Leigh, Evenson, Bourne.

Did you know: When Clapton Orient beat Charlton Athletic 3-0 on 11 January 1936 in a third round FA Cup tie, the attendance of 18,658 and receipts amounting to 1040 were records at the Lea Bridge Road ground.

Managers (and Secretary-Managers)
Sam Omerod 1905–06, Ike Ivenson 1906, Billy Holmes 1907–22, Peter Proudfoot 1922–29, Arthur Grimsdell 1929–30, Peter Proudfoot 1930–31, Jimmy Seed 1931–33, David Pratt 1933–34, Peter Proudfoot 1935–39, Tom Halsey 1939–39, Billy Wright 1939–45, Billy Hall 1945, Billy Wright 1945–46, Charlie Hewitt 1946–48, Neil McBain 1948–49, Alec Stock 1949–56, 1956–58, 1958–59, Johnny Carey 1961–63, Benny Fenton 1963–64, Dave Sexton 1965, Dick Graham 1966–68, Jimmy Bloomfield 1968–71, George Petchey 1971–77, Jimmy Bloomfield 1977–81, Paul Went 1981, Ken Knighton 1981, Frank Clark May 1982–-91 (MD), Peter Eustace 1991–94, Chris Turner/John Sitton April 1994–

Player and Position	Ht	Wt	Birth Date	Birth Place	Source	Clubs	League App	League Gls
Forwards								
Gary Barnett	5 6	9 13	11 3 63	Stratford	Apprentice	Coventry C	—	—
						Huddersfield T	22	1
						Oxford U	45	9
						Wimbledon (loan)	5	1
						Fulham (loan)	2	1
						Fulham	180	30
						Huddersfield T	100	11
						Leyton Orient	36	7
Mark Cooper*	6 2	13 04	5 4 67	Cambridge	Apprentice	Cambridge U	71	17
						Tottenham H	—	—
						Shrewsbury T	6	2
						Gillingham	49	11
						Leyton Orient	150	45
Andy Jones‡	5 11	13 06	9 1 63	Wrexham	Rhyl	Port Vale	90	49
						Charlton Ath	66	15
						Port Vale (loan)	17	3
						Bristol C (loan)	4	1
						Bournemouth	40	8
						Leyton Orient	59	13
Nicky Sweetman	5 8	11 00	21 10 74	Herts	Trainee	Leyton Orient	—	—
Colin West	6 0	13 11	13 11 62	Wallsend	Apprentice	Sunderland	102	21
						Watford	45	20
						Rangers	10	2
						Sheffield W	45	8
						WBA	73	22
						Port Vale (loan)	5	1
						Swansea C	33	12
						Leyton Orient	43	14

Trainees
Bird, Robert J; Cawte, Tony D; Collinson, David J; Gabrielli, Antony; Huckstep, Andrew; Loomes, Jody D; Munyenya, Daniel N; Pallecaros, George; Perifimou, Christopher; Quinn, John P; Smith, Marcus P; Wedlock, Grant; Weir, Andrew J; Wilkie, Glen.

Associated Schoolboys
Aboram, Jeffrey; Antoine, Marlon A; Blogg, James D; Brazier, Jeffery C; Cockerill, David; Everingham, William L; Fuhr, Matthew; Haylock, James R; Honeyball, Scott R; Jones, Anthony S; Kinseley, Mark; Landsman, Paul S; Nash, Daniel T; Neal, George J; Straight, Arron A; Weaver, Luke D. S; Young, Colin N.

Associated Schoolboys who have accepted the Club's offer of a Traineeship/Contract
Doe, Steven R; Haynes, Jason D; Martin, Gary D; Pike, David A; Shearer, Lee S; Sopp, Darryl J; Sugg, Darren W.

LINCOLN CITY 1993–94 *Back row (left to right):* Paul Ward, Matthew Carbon, Sean Dunphy, Michael Pollitt, Jason Lee, Jason Kabia, Anthony Lormor.
Centre row: Steve Stoutt (Youth Team Coach), David Clarke, Peter Costello, Stephen Parkinson, Grant Brown, Ian Baraclough, Neil Matthews, Paul Smith, Neil McDiarmid (Physio).
Front row: Ben Dixon, Darren Chapman, Steve Mardenborough, Keith Alexander (Manager), David Puttnam, David Hill, John Schofield.

Division 3 LINCOLN CITY

Sincil Bank, Lincoln LN5 8LD. Telephone Lincoln (0522) 522224. Fax: (0522) 520564. Executive Club: (0522) 532634. Centre spot: (0522) 536438.

Ground capacity: 11,039.

Record attendance: 23,196 v Derby Co, League Cup 4th rd, 15 November 1967.

Record receipts: £44,184.46 v Everton, Coca-Cola Cup 2nd rd 1st leg, 21 September 1993.

Pitch measurements: 110yd × 75yd.

Hon. Life Presidents: V. C. Withers, D. W. L. Bocock.

President: H. Dove.

Chairman: K. J. Reames. ***Vice-chairman:*** G. R. Davey (and Managing).

Directors: H. C. Sills, J. Hicks.

Hon. Consultant Surgeon: Mr Brian Smith. ***Hon. Club Doctor:*** Nick Huntley.

Secretary: Phil Hough.

Manager: Sam Ellis. ***Physio:*** Neil McDiarmid GRAD DIP (Phys), MCSP, SRP.

Year Formed: 1883. ***Turned Professional:*** 1892. ***Ltd Co.:*** 1892.

Club Nickname: 'The Red Imps'.

Previous Grounds: 1883, John O'Gaunt's; 1894, Sincil Bank.

Record League Victory: 11–1 v Crewe Alex, Division 3 (N), 29 September 1951 – Jones; Green (1p), Varney; Wright, Emery, Grummett (1); Troops (1), Garvey, Graver (6), Whittle (1), Johnson (1).

Record Cup Victory: 8–1 v Bromley, FA Cup, 2nd rd, 10 December 1938 – McPhail; Hartshorne, Corbett; Bean, Leach, Whyte (1); Hancock, Wilson (1), Ponting (3), Deacon (1), Clare (2).

Record Defeat: 3–11 v Manchester C, Division 2, 23 March 1895.

Most League Points (2 for a win): 74, Division 4, 1975–76.

Most League Points (3 for a win): 77, Division 3, 1981–82.

Most League Goals: 121, Division 3 (N), 1951–52.

Highest League Scorer in Season: Allan Hall, 42, Division 3 (N), 1931–32.

Most League Goals in Total Aggregate: Andy Graver, 144, 1950–55 and 1958–61.

Most Capped Player: David Pugh, 3 (7), Wales and George Moulson, 3, Republic of Ireland.

Most League Appearances: Tony Emery, 402, 1946–59.

Record Transfer Fee Received: £250,000 plus increments from Blackburn R for Matt Dickins, March 1992.

Record Transfer Fee Paid: £63,000 to Leicester City for Grant Brown, January 1990.

Football League Record: 1892 Founder member of Division 2. Remained in Division 2 until 1920 when they failed re-election but also missed seasons 1908–09 and 1911–12 when not re-elected. 1921–32 Division 3 (N); 1932–34 Division 2; 1934–48 Division 3 (N); 1948–49 Division 2; 1949–52 Division 3 (N); 1952–61 Division 2; 1961–62 Division 3; 1962–76 Division 4; 1976–79 Division 3; 1979–81 Division 4; 1981–86 Division 3; 1986–87 Division 4; 1987–88 GM Vauxhall Conference; 1988–92 Division 4; 1992– Division 3.

Honours: *Football League:* Divison 2 best season: 5th, 1901–02; Division 3 (N) – Champions 1931–32, 1947–48, 1951–52; Runners-up 1927–28, 1930–31, 1936–37; Division 4 – Champions 1975–76; Runners-up 1980–81. *FA Cup:* best season: 1st rd of Second Series (5th rd equivalent), 1886–87, 2nd rd (5th rd equivalent), 1889–90, 1901–02. *Football League Cup:* best season: 4th rd, 1967–68. GM Vauxhall Conference Champions – 1987–88.

LINCOLN CITY 1993—94 LEAGUE RECORD

Match No.	Date	Venue	Opponents	Result		H/T Score	Lg. Pos.	Goalscorers	Attendance
1	Aug 14	A	Colchester U	L	0-1	0-0	—		3198
2	21	H	Darlington	D	1-1	1-1	16	Baraclough (pen)	2699
3	28	A	Hereford U	W	2-1	1-0	12	Baraclough, Johnson D	1900
4	31	H	Chester C	L	0-3	0-0	—		4038
5	Sept 4	H	Preston NE	L	0-2	0-1	18		3793
6	11	A	Mansfield T	L	0-1	0-0	20		2678
7	18	H	Bury	D	2-2	1-1	19	Johnson D, Jones	2469
8	25	H	Northampton T	W	4-3	1-2	15	West, Johnson D, Jones, Puttnam	2705
9	Oct 2	A	Crewe Alex	D	2-2	1-2	17	Clarke, Brown	3361
10	9	H	Doncaster R	W	2-1	1-0	13	West 2	3901
11	16	A	Wycombe W	W	3-2	3-1	12	West, Baraclough (pen), Matthews	5623
12	23	H	Chesterfield	L	1-2	0-1	14	Johnson D	3591
13	30	A	Rochdale	W	1-0	0-0	11	Loughlan	2551
14	Nov 2	A	Carlisle U	D	3-3	1-2	—	West, Lormor, Smith M	5098
15	6	H	Torquay U	W	1-0	0-0	10	Hill	3244
16	20	A	Walsall	L	2-5	2-3	10	Hill, Brown	4580
17	27	H	Gillingham	W	3-1	1-1	10	Baraclough (pen), Matthews, Schofield	2979
18	Dec 11	A	Darlington	L	2-3	1-2	12	Johnson D, Matthews	1936
19	27	H	Scunthorpe U	W	2-0	1-0	11	Johnson D, West	6030
20	Jan 1	H	Scarborough	L	0-1	0-1	12		3812
21	15	H	Wycombe W	L	1-3	1-0	14	Williams	3735
22	22	A	Doncaster R	L	0-1	0-0	18		2374
23	29	H	Rochdale	D	1-1	1-1	18	Schofield	2703
24	Feb 1	A	Chester C	D	1-1	1-0	—	Mardenborough	2648
25	5	A	Chesterfield	D	2-2	0-1	18	Brown, Loughlan	3104
26	12	H	Wigan Ath	L	0-1	0-0	18		2534
27	19	H	Hereford U	W	3-1	2-0	17	Campbell, Matthews 2	2277
28	25	A	Preston NE	L	0-2	0-0	17		5941
29	Mar 1	A	Shrewsbury T	W	2-1	0-0	—	Hill, Huckerby	4706
30	5	H	Mansfield T	L	1-2	1-1	16	Baraclough (pen)	3384
31	12	A	Bury	L	0-1	0-0	16		2214
32	15	H	Colchester U	W	2-0	0-0	—	Mardenborough, Matthews	1631
33	19	A	Northampton T	D	0-0	0-0	14		3868
34	26	H	Crewe Alex	L	1-2	0-1	15	Daws	3007
35	29	A	Wigan Ath	W	1-0	0-0	—	Skipper (og)	1349
36	Apr 2	A	Scunthorpe U	L	0-2	0-1	14		3571
37	4	H	Shrewsbury T	L	0-1	0-0	17		2823
38	9	A	Scarborough	D	2-2	2-0	16	Matthews, Calvert (og)	1314
39	16	H	Carlisle U	D	0-0	0-0	16		2738
40	23	A	Torquay U	L	2-3	0-2	18	Johnson D 2	3270
41	30	H	Walsall	L	1-2	0-1	18	Daws	2665
42	May 7	A	Gillingham	D	1-1	0-1	18	Daws	2840

Final League Position: 18

GOALSCORERS

League (52): Johnson D 8, Matthews 7, West 6, Baraclough 5 (4 pens), Brown 3, Daws 3, Hill 3, Jones 2, Loughlan 2, Mardenborough 2, Schofield 2, Campbell 1, Clarke 1, Huckerby 1, Lormor 1, Puttnam 1, Smith M 1, Williams 1, own goals 2.
Coca-Cola Cup (7): Johnson D 2, Lormor 2, Baraclough 1 (pen), Brown 1, Matthews 1.
FA Cup (3): Johnson D 1, Lormor 1, West 1.

Pollitt 30	Smith P 33 + 3	Clarke 7	Hill 27 + 5	Smith M 20	Brown 38	Schofield 40	Mardenborough 14 + 7	Baraclough 34 + 3	Costello 6 + 5	Puttnam 13	Dunphy 14 + 3	Dixon 5 + 3	Lormor 5 + 5	Johnson D 38 + 3	Matthews 31 + 5	Carbon 9	Parkinson 1 + 2	Jones — + 4	Flitcroft 2	West 13 + 5	Loughlan 4 + 8	Burridge 4	Hirst 7	Williams 4 + 4	Platnauer 13	Campbell 2 + 2	Johnson A 16	Daws 14	Ridings 10	Huckerby — + 6	Leaning 8	*Match No.*
1	2	3	4	5	6	7	8	9	*10*	11	12	14																				1
1	2	3	4	6		7	8	9	*10*	11	5		12	14																		2
1	2	3	4		6	7	8	*9*	10	11	5			12	14																	3
1	2	3	*4*		6	7	8		10	11	5		12	9	14																	4
1	2		4		6	7	8		12	11	5	*10*		9	14	3																5
1	2	3	4	6		7	8		12		*5*			9	10	11	14															6
1	2		4	5	6	*7*		8	12	11				9	10	*3*		14														7
1				5	6	2		8	12	11				9	10	*3*		14	4	7												8
1	2	3			6	4		8	12	*11*				9	10	5		14		*7*												9
1	2	3	12		6	4		8		11				9	10	5				7												10
1	2		14	5	6			8		11				9	10	4		12	*3*	7												11
1	2		14	5	6	4	12	*8*		11				9	10	3				7												12
1	2		3	5	6	4		8					12	9	10					7	11											13
1	2		3	5	6	4	14	8					12	9	10					*7*	11											14
1	2		3	5	6	4	12	8					11	9	10					7												15
1	2		3		5	4	12	8					7	9	10					6	11											16
1	2		3	5	6	4		8					11	9	10					7	12											17
1	2		4	5	6	7	12	8					*11*	9	10	3					14											18
	2		3	5	6	7		8		11				9	10					12		1	4									19
	2		3	6	4	7	12	8				14		*9*	10					11		1	5									20
1	2		3	5	6	7		8		*11*				9	12					14			4	10								21
	2		3	5	6	7		8			4		*11*	9	12					14		1		10								22
	2		3	*5*	6	7		8				11	12	9	10						14	1	4									23
1	2		*3*		6	4	7	8			12	11		9	10						14		5									24
1	2				6	4	7	11	8		12			9	*10*						14		5		3							25
1	2		3		6		*7*	8	10			14		9			12				11		5			4						26
1	2		3		6	7		8						9	10											4	5	11				27
1	2		3		6	4		8						9	10						12						5	11	7			28
1	2		3	5	6	7		8						*9*	10											12	4		11	14		29
1	2		*3*	5	6	7		8						9	10											12	4		11	14		30
1	2		12		6	4	7	8						9	10										3		5	*11*		14		31
1	2			5		4	7	8						9	10						12				3		6	11				32
1			12			4	7	*2*			5			9	10						14				3		6	11	8			33
	12				2	4	7	8			5			9	*10*										3		6	11		14	1	34
	12				4	2	*7*	8			5			9	10									14	3		6	11			1	35
	12				4	2		8			5			9	10									14	3		6	11	*7*		1	36
					4	8		12			5	*2*		9	10									14	3		6	11	7		1	37
					4	8		12			5	*2*		9	10										3		6	11	7	14	1	38
			2		*4*	8		9			5			12						14				10	3		6	11	7		1	39
1			2		4	8		12			5			9						14				10	3		6	11	*7*			40
	2		10		5	4								9						8				12	3		6	11	7		1	41
	2				5	4	12							9	10		*8*			7					3		6	11		14	1	42

Coca-Cola Cup	First Round	Port Vale (a)	2-2
		(h)	0-0
	Second Round	Everton (h)	3-4
		(a)	2-4
FA Cup	First Round	Witton A (a)	2-0
	Second Round	Bolton W (h)	1-3

LINCOLN CITY

Player and Position	Ht	Wt	Birth Date	Birth Place	Source	Clubs	League App	League Gls
Goalkeepers								
John Burridge (To Aberdeen March 1994)	5 11	13 03	3 12 51	Workington	Apprentice	Workington	27	—
						Blackpool	134	—
						Aston Villa	65	—
						Southend U (loan)	6	—
						Crystal Palace	88	—
						QPR	39	—
						Wolverhampton W	74	—
						Derby Co (loan)	6	—
						Sheffield U	109	—
						Southampton	62	—
						Newcastle U	67	—
						Hibernian	65	—
						Newcastle U	—	—
						Scarborough	3	—
						Lincoln C	4	—
Andy Leaning	6 1	14 07	18 5 63	York	Rowntree Mackintosh	York C	69	—
						Sheffield U	21	—
						Bristol C	75	—
						Lincoln C	8	—
Michael Pollitt	6 4	14 00	29 2 72	Bolton	Trainee	Manchester U	—	—
						Oldham Ath (loan)	—	—
						Bury	—	—
						Lincoln C	57	—
Defenders								
Grant Brown	6 0	11 12	19 11 69	Sunderland	Trainee	Leicester C	14	—
						Lincoln C	181	8
Matthew Carbon	6 2	11 13	8 6 75	Nottingham	Trainee	Lincoln C	10	—
Sean Dunphy	6 3	13 05	5 11 70	Rotherham	Trainee	Barnsley	6	—
						Lincoln C	53	2
						Doncaster R (loan)	1	—
Alan Johnson	5 11	11 12	19 2 71	Ince	Trainee	Wigan Ath	180	13
						Lincoln C	16	—
Nicky Platnauer	5 11	12 10	10 6 61	Leicester	Bedford T	Bristol R	24	7
						Coventry C	44	6
						Birmingham C	28	2
						Reading (loan)	7	—
						Cardiff C	115	6
						Notts Co	57	1
						Port Vale (loan)	14	—
						Leicester C	35	—
						Scunthorpe U	14	2
						Mansfield T	25	—
						Lincoln C	13	—
Mark Smith	6 2	13 11	21 3 60	Sheffield	Apprentice	Sheffield W	282	16
						Plymouth Arg	82	6
						Barnsley	104	10
						Notts Co	5	—
						Chesterfield (loan)	6	1
						Huddersfield T (loan)	5	—
						Port Vale (loan)	6	—
						Lincoln C	20	1
Dean West	5 10	11 07	5 12 72	Wakefield	Leeds U	Lincoln C	70	13
Midfield								
Ian Baraclough*	6 1	12 00	4 12 70	Leicester	Trainee	Leicester C	—	—
						Wigan Ath (loan)	9	2
						Grimsby T (loan)	4	—
						Grimsby T	1	—
						Lincoln C	73	10
David Hill	5 11	12 04	6 6 66	Nottingham	Local	Scunthorpe U	140	10
						Ipswich T	61	—
						Scunthorpe U	65	6
						Lincoln C	32	3
Darren Huckerby§			23 4 76	Nottingham	Trainee	Lincoln C	6	1
Steve Parkinson	5 11	11 11	27 8 74	Lincoln	Trainee	Lincoln C	5	—
David Puttnam	5 10	11 09	3 2 67	Leicester	Leicester U	Leicester C	7	—
						Lincoln C	155	16

LINCOLN CITY

Colours: Red and white striped shirts, black shorts, red stockings with white trim. **Change colours:** Jade shirts, black shorts, jade stockings.

Foundation: Although there was a Lincoln club as far back as 1861, the present organisation was formed in 1883 winning the Lincolnshire Senior Cup in only their fourth season. They were Founder members of the Midland League in 1889 and that competition's first champions.

First Football League game: 3 September, 1892, Division 2, v Sheffield U (a) L 2-4 – W. Gresham; Coulton, Neill; Shaw, Mettam, Moore; Smallman, Irving (1), Cameron (1), Kelly, J. Gresham.

Did you know: Debutant Darren Huckerby, a 78th minute substitute for Lincoln City on 1 March 1994, scored after six minutes to end Shrewsbury Town's run of 16 matches without defeat. Lincoln won 2-1.

Managers (and Secretary-Managers)
David Calderhead 1900–07, John Henry Strawson 1907–14 (had been secretary), George Fraser 1919–21, David Calderhead Jnr. 1921–24, Horace Henshall 1924–27, Harry Parkes 1927–36, Joe McClelland 1936–46, Bill Anderson 1946–65 (GM to 1966), Roy Chapman 1965–66, Ron Gray 1966–70, Bert Loxley 1970–71, David Herd 1971–72, Graham Taylor 1972–77, George Kerr 1977–78, Willie Bell 1977–78, Colin Murphy 1978–85, John Pickering 1985, George Kerr 1985–87, Peter Daniel 1987, Colin Murphy 1987–90, Allan Clarke 1990, Steve Thompson 1990–93, Keith Alexander 1993–94, Sam Ellis May 1994–

Player and Position	*Ht*	*Wt*	*Birth Date*	*Place*	*Source*	*Clubs*	*League App*	*Gls*
David Ridings	6 0	12 00	27 2 70	Farnworth	Cutzon Ashton	Halifax T	21	4
						Lincoln C	10	—
Jon Schofield	5 11	11 03	16 5 65	Barnsley	Gainsborough T	Lincoln C	219	10
Paul Ward‡	5 11	12 05	15 9 63	Sedgefield	Apprentice	Chelsea	—	—
						Middlesbrough	76	1
						Darlington	124	9
						Leyton Orient	31	1
						Scunthorpe U	55	6
						Lincoln C	39	—
Forwards								
Keith Alexander†	6 4	13 06	14 11 58	Nottingham	Barnet	Grimsby T	83	26
						Stockport Co	11	—
						Lincoln C	45	4
Peter Costello‡	6 0	12 00	31 10 69	Halifax	Trainee	Bradford C	20	2
						Rochdale	34	10
						Peterborough U	8	—
						Lincoln C (loan)	3	—
						Lincoln C	38	7
Tony Daws	5 8	11 10	10 9 66	Sheffield	Apprentice	Notts Co	8	1
						Sheffield U	11	3
						Scunthorpe U	183	63
						Grimsby T	16	1
						Lincoln C	14	3
Ben Dixon	6 1	11 00	16 9 74	Lincoln	Trainee	Lincoln C	13	—
David Johnson	6 2	14 03	29 10 70	Rother Valley	Trainee	Sheffield W	6	—
						Hartlepool U (loan)	7	2
						Hartlepool U (loan)	3	—
						Lincoln C	41	8
Jason Kabia‡	5 11	12 00	28 5 69	Sutton in Ashfield	Oakham United	Lincoln C	28	4
						Doncaster R (loan)	5	—

Continued on Page 307

Trainees
Allen, Dean L; Coles, Christopher J; Dimech, Luke A; Don-Duncan, Ross; Evans, Dion M; Frecklington, David M; Gilliatt, Jamie R; Graham, Steven E; Hercock, David L; Huckerby, Darren C; Irlam, Ashley J; Morgan, James; Oseni, Kaseem; Rawlinson, CHristopher; Sewell, Steven J; Williams, Steven R.

****Non-Contract**
Alexander, Keith.

Associated Schoolboys
Birkett, Peter E; Cyster, Daniel T; Davie, Lee T; Joseph, Christopher D; McGill, Andrew J; Murphy, Benjamin C; Rankin, Mark; Tavender, Matthew J.

Associated Schoolboys who have accepted the Club's offer of a Traineeship/Contract
Bartlett, Darren S; Brown, Kevin; Davis, Matthew D; Dixon, Andrew S; Gresham, Robert K; Walters, Gary A; Wilkins, Adam L.
**Non-Contract Players who are retained must be re-signed before they are eligible to play in League matches.

LIVERPOOL 1993–94 *Back row (left to right):* David Burrows, Nicky Tanner, Jan Molby, David James, Mike Hooper, Mark Wright, Paul Stewart, Torben Piechnik.
Centre row: Ronnie Moran, Roy Evans, Steve Harkness, Mike Marsh, John Barnes, Stig Bjornebye, Ronny Rosenthal, Rob Jones, Phil Boersma.
Front row: Nigel Clough, Mark Walters, Ian Rush, Steve Nicol, Graeme Souness, Jamie Redknapp, Steve McManaman, Don Hutchison, Michael Thomas.
(Photograph: John Cocks)

FA Premiership

LIVERPOOL

Anfield Road, Liverpool L4 0TH. Telephone 0151–263 2361. Clubcall: 0891 121184. Ticket and Match Information: 0151–260 9999 (24-hour service) or 0151–260 8680 (office hours) Credit Card bookings.

Ground Capacity: 40,500.

Record attendance: 61,905 v Wolverhampton W, FA Cup 4th rd, 2 February 1952.

Record receipts: £342,000 v Genoa, UEFA Cup, 4th rd 2nd leg, 18 March 1992.

Pitch measurements: 110yd × 75yd.

Chairman: D. R. Moores.

Directors: Sir J. W. Smith CBE, JP, DL, HON. LLD, J. T. Cross, N. White FSCA, T. D. Smith, P. B. Robinson, T. Saunders.

Vice-presidents: C. J. Hill, H. E. Roberts, W. D. Corkish FCA, R. Paisley OBE, HON MSC.

Team Manager: Roy Evans. ***Coach:*** Ron Moran.

Chief Executive/General Secretary: Peter Robinson. ***Commercial Manager:*** M. L. Turner.

Year Formed: 1892. ***Turned Professional:*** 1892. ***Ltd Co.:*** 1892.

Club Nickname: 'Reds' or 'Pool'.

Record League Victory: 10–1 v Rotherham T, Division 2, 18 February 1896 – Storer; Goldie, Wilkie; McCarthy, McQueen, Holmes; McVean (3), Ross (2), Allan (4), Becton (1), Bradshaw.

Record Cup Victory: 11–0 v Stromsgodset Drammen, ECWC 1st rd 1st leg, 17 September 1974 – Clemence; Smith (1), Lindsay (1p), Thompson (2), Cormack (1), Hughes (1), Boersma (2), Hall, Heighway (1), Kennedy (1), Callaghan (1).

Record Defeat: 1–9 v Birmingham C, Division 2, 11 December 1954.

Most League Points (2 for a win): 68, Division 1, 1978–79.

Most League Points (3 for a win): 90, Division 1, 1987–88.

Most League Goals: 106, Division 2, 1895–96.

Highest League Scorer in Season: Roger Hunt, 41, Division 2, 1961–62.

Most League Goals in Total Aggregate: Roger Hunt, 245, 1959–69.

Most Capped Player: Ian Rush, 60 (66), Wales.

Most League Appearances: Ian Callaghan, 640, 1960–78.

Record Transfer Fee Received: £2,750,000 from Juventus for Ian Rush, June 1986.

Record Transfer Fee Paid: £2,900,000 to Derby Co for Dean Saunders, July 1991.

Football League Record: 1893 Elected to Division 2; 1894–95 Division 1; 1895–96 Division 2; 1896–1904 Division 1; 1904–05 Division 2; 1905–54 Division 1; 1954–62 Division 2; 1962–92 Division 1; 1992– FA Premier Division.

Honours: *Football League:* Division 1 – Champions 1900–01, 1905–06, 1921–22, 1922–23, 1946–47, 1963–64, 1965–66, 1972–73, 1975–76, 1976–77, 1978–79, 1979–80, 1981–82, 1982–83, 1983–84, 1985–86, 1987–88, 1989–90 (Liverpool have a record number of 18 League Championship wins); Runners-up 1898–99, 1909–10, 1968–69, 1973–74, 1974–75, 1977–78, 1984–85, 1986–87, 1988–89, 1990–91; Division 2 – Champions 1893–94, 1895–96, 1904–05, 1961–62. *FA Cup:* Winners 1965, 1974, 1986, 1989, 1992; Runners-up 1914, 1950, 1971, 1977, 1988; *Football League Cup:* Winners 1981, 1982, 1983, 1984; Runners-up 1977–78, 1986–87. *League Super Cup:* Winners 1985–86. **European Competitions:** *European Cup:* 1964–65, 1966–67, 1973–74, 1976–77 (winners), 1977–78 (winners), 1978–79, 1979–80, 1980–81 (winners), 1981–82, 1982–83, 1983–84 (winners), 1984–85 (runners-up); *European Cup-Winners' Cup:* 1965–66 (runners-up), 1971–72, 1974–75, 1992–93; *European Fairs Cup:* 1967–68, 1968–69, 1969–70, 1970–71; *UEFA Cup:* 1972–73 (winners), 1975–76 (winners), 1991–92; *Super Cup:* 1977 (winners), 1978, 1984; *World Club Championship:* 1981 (runners-up).

LIVERPOOL 1993—94 LEAGUE RECORD

Match No.	Date	Venue	Opponents	Result		H/T Score	Lg. Pos.	Goalscorers	Attendance
1	Aug 14	H	Sheffield W	W	2-0	1-0	—	Clough 2	43,792
2	18	A	QPR	W	3-1	3-1	—	Rush, Nicol, Clough	19,625
3	22	A	Swindon T	W	5-0	2-0	—	Ruddock, McManaman 2, Whelan, Marsh	17,364
4	25	H	Tottenham H	L	1-2	1-2	—	Clough	42,456
5	28	H	Leeds U	W	2-0	2-0	2	Rush, Molby (pen)	44,068
6	Sept 1	A	Coventry C	L	0-1	0-1	—		16,735
7	12	H	Blackburn R	L	0-1	0-0	—		37,355
8	18	A	Everton	L	0-2	0-1	9		38,157
9	25	A	Chelsea	L	0-1	0-0	13		31,271
10	Oct 2	H	Arsenal	D	0-0	0-0	13		42,750
11	16	H	Oldham Ath	W	2-1	0-0	10	Fowler, Barlow (og)	32,661
12	23	A	Manchester C	D	1-1	0-0	9	Rush	30,403
13	30	H	Southampton	W	4-2	2-1	7	Fowler 3, Rush	32,818
14	Nov 6	H	West Ham U	W	2-0	0-0	5	Clough, Martin (og)	42,254
15	21	A	Newcastle U	L	0-3	0-3	—		36,246
16	28	H	Aston Villa	W	2-1	1-0	—	Fowler, Redknapp	38,484
17	Dec 4	A	Sheffield W	L	1-3	1-1	9	Fowler	32,177
18	8	H	QPR	W	3-2	2-1	—	Barnes, Rush, Molby (pen)	24,561
19	11	H	Swindon T	D	2-2	0-0	8	Barnes, Wright	32,739
20	18	A	Tottenham H	D	3-3	0-1	7	Fowler 2 (1 pen), Redknapp	31,394
21	26	A	Sheffield U	D	0-0	0-0	—		22,932
22	28	H	Wimbledon	D	1-1	1-1	8	Scales (og)	32,232
23	Jan 1	A	Ipswich T	W	2-1	0-0	7	Ruddock, Rush	22,270
24	4	H	Manchester U	D	3-3	2-3	—	Clough 2, Ruddock	42,795
25	15	A	Oldham Ath	W	3-0	0-0	6	Dicks, Fowler, Redknapp	14,573
26	22	H	Manchester C	W	2-1	1-1	5	Rush 2	41,872
27	Feb 5	A	Norwich C	D	2-2	0-1	5	Culverhouse (og), Barnes	19,746
28	14	A	Southampton	L	2-4	0-3	—	Dicks (pen), Rush	18,306
29	19	A	Leeds U	L	0-2	0-1	7		40,029
30	25	H	Coventry C	W	1-0	1-0	5	Rush	38,547
31	Mar 5	A	Blackburn R	L	0-2	0-1	6		20,831
32	13	H	Everton	W	2-1	2-1	—	Rush, Fowler	44,281
33	19	H	Chelsea	W	2-1	2-0	6	Rush, Burley (og)	38,629
34	26	A	Arsenal	L	0-1	0-0	6		35,556
35	29	A	Manchester U	L	0-1	0-1	—		44,751
36	Apr 2	H	Sheffield U	L	1-2	1-0	6	Rush	36,642
37	4	A	Wimbledon	D	1-1	0-0	7	Redknapp	13,819
38	9	H	Ipswich T	W	1-0	0-0	7	Dicks (pen)	30,485
39	16	H	Newcastle U	L	0-2	0-1	7		44,601
40	23	A	West Ham U	W	2-1	1-1	7	Fowler, Rush	26,106
41	30	H	Norwich C	L	0-1	0-1	8		44,339
42	May 7	A	Aston Villa	L	1-2	1-0	8	Fowler	45,347

Final League Position: 8

GOALSCORERS

League (59): Rush 14, Fowler 12 (1 pen), Clough 7, Redknapp 4, Barnes 3, Dicks 3 (2 pens), Ruddock 3, McManaman 2, Molby 2 (2 pens), Marsh 1, Nicol 1, Whelan 1, Wright 1, own goals 5.
Coca-Cola Cup (14): Fowler 6, Rush 4, Clough 1, Molby 1 (pen), Ruddock 1, own goal 1.
FA Cup (1): Rush 1.

Grobbelaar 29	Jones R 38	Bjornebye 6 + 3	Nicol 27 + 4	Wright 31	Ruddock 39	Clough 25 + 2	Molby 11	Rush 41 + 1	Whelan 23	Walters 7 + 10	Redknapp 29 + 6	McManaman 29 + 1	Marsh — + 2	Burrows 3 + 1	Hutchison 6 + 5	Rosenthal — + 3	Dicks 24	Stewart 7 + 1	Fowler 27 + 1	Matteo 11	Harkness 10 + 1	Piechnik 1	Barnes 24 + 2	Thomas 1 + 6	James 13 + 1	Match No.
1	2	3	4	5	6	7	8	9	10	11	12															1
1	2	3	4	5	6	7	8	9	10		12	11														2
1	2	*3*	4	5	6	7	8	9	10			11	12	14												3
1	2		4	5	6	7	8	9	10	12		11		3												4
1	2			5	6	7	8	9	10			11	12	3	4											5
1	2		4	5	6	7	8	9	10	12		11		3												6
1	2	*3*	4	5	6	7	8	9	10		12	11				14										7
1			2	5	6	7		9	4	10	8	*11*				12	3	14								8
1	2			5	6	7		9			10	12			4		3	8	11							9
1	2			5	6	7		9			10				4		3	8	11							10
1	2		14	5	6	7		9		12	10				*4*		3	8	11							11
1	2	3	4	5	6			9		10	12				14			*8*	11	7						12
1	2	3	4	5	6			9								12		7	11	8	10					13
1	2	14	*4*	5	6	7		9			12							8	11	10	3					14
1			2		6	7		9			4							8	11	10	3	5	12			15
1			2	5	6		8	9		12	4								11	7	3		10			16
1	2		*4*	5	6	7	8	12		14									11	9	3		10			17
1	2		12	5	6		8	9			4	7							11		3		10			18
1	2		12	5	6		8	9			4	7							11		3		10			19
1	2		4	5		12		9		14	6	7							11	*8*	3		10			20
1	2		4	5	6	7		9		12	8	10					3		11							21
1	2		3	5	6	7		9		12	4	10							11	8						22
1	2	14		5	6	7		9			4	10							11	*8*	3		12			23
1	2	12		5	6	7		9			4	8					3		11				10			24
1	2		4		5	7		9			6	11					3		8				10	12		25
1	2		4		5	7		9		8	6	11					3						10			26
1	2			5		7		9	6	8		11					3			4			10			27
1	2		4	5		7		9	6	8	12	11					3						10			28
1	2			5	6			9	8	12	4	11					3			7			10		14	29
	2			5	6	12		9	8	11	4	7					3						10		1	30
	2			5	6	7		9	8	12	4	11					3						10		1	31
	2			5	6			9	8		4	7					3		11				10	12	1	32
	2			5	6			9	8		4	7					3		11				10	12	1	33
	2		14	*5*	6			9	8		4	7					3		11				10	12	1	34
	2		5		6			9	8		4	11					3		12				10	7	1	35
	2		5		6			9	8		4	7			14		3		11				*10*	12	1	36
	2		5		6			9	8		4	7					3		11				10		1	37
	2		5		6			9	8		4	7			12		3		11				10		1	38
	2		5		6			9	8		4	*7*			12		3		11				10	14	1	39
			5		6	7		9			8				4		3		11		2		10		1	40
	2		5		6	7		9	8		4				12		3		11				10		1	41
	2		5		6			9	8		4				7		3		11		12		10		1	42

Coca-Cola Cup	Second Round	Fulham (a)	3-1
		(h)	5-0
	Third Round	Ipswich T (h)	3-2
	Fourth Round	Wimbledon (h)	1-1
		(a)	2-2
FA Cup	Third Round	Bristol C (a) abandoned	1-1
		(a)	1-1
		(h)	0-1

LIVERPOOL

Player and Position	Ht	Wt	Birth Date	Birth Place	Source	Clubs	League App	League Gls
Goalkeepers								
Daniel Embleton*	5 11	11 04	27 3 75	Liverpool	Trainee	Liverpool	—	—
Bruce Grobbelaar*	6 1	13 00	6 10 57	Durban	Vancouver Whitecaps	Crewe Alex	24	1
					Vancouver Whitecaps	Liverpool	440	—
						Stoke C (loan)	4	—
David James	6 4	14 13	1 8 70	Welwyn	Trainee	Watford	89	—
						Liverpool	43	—
Anthony Warner	6 4	13 09	11 5 74	Liverpool	School	Liverpool	—	—
Defenders								
Stig Inge Bjornebye	5 10	11 09	11 12 69	Norway	Rosenborg	Liverpool	20	—
Iain Brunskill	5 10	12 05	5 11 76	Ormskirk	Trainee	Liverpool	—	—
Lee Bryden	5 11	11 00	15 11 74	Stockton	Trainee	Liverpool	—	—
Julian Dicks	5 10	13 00	8 8 68	Bristol	Apprentice	Birmingham C	89	1
						West Ham U	159	29
						Liverpool	24	3
Andrew Harris			26 2 77	Springs	Trainee	Liverpool	—	—
Rob Jones	5 8	11 00	5 11 71	Wrexham	Trainee	Crewe Alex	75	2
						Liverpool	96	—
Rodney McAree*	5 7	10 02	19 8 74	Dungannon	Trainee	Liverpool	—	—
Dominic Matteo	6 1	11 10	28 4 74	Dumfries	Trainee	Liverpool	11	—
Torben Piechnik	6 0	12 04	21 5 63	Copenhagen	Copenhagen	Liverpool	17	—
Neil Ruddock	6 2	12 06	9 5 68	London	Apprentice	Millwall	—	—
						Tottenham H	9	—
						Millwall	2	1
						Southampton	107	9
						Tottenham H	38	3
						Liverpool	39	3
John Scott*	5 8	10 09	9 3 75	Aberdeen	Trainee	Liverpool	—	—
Nick Tanner	6 2	13 07	24 5 65	Bristol	Mangotsfield	Bristol R	107	3
						Liverpool	40	1
						Norwich C (loan)	6	—
						Swindon T (loan)	7	—
Mark Wright	6 2	13 03	1 8 63	Dorchester	Amateur	Oxford U	10	—
						Southampton	170	7
						Derby Co	144	10
						Liverpool	85	3
Midfield								
Phil Charnock	5 11	11 02	14 2 75	Southport	Trainee	Liverpool	—	—
Ian Frodsham	5 09	11 00	22 12 75	Liverpool	Trainee	Liverpool	—	—
Steve Harkness	5 10	11 02	27 8 71	Carlisle	Trainee	Carlisle U	13	—
						Liverpool	32	—
						Huddersfield T (loan)	5	—
Istvan Kozma (To Ujpesti July 1993)	5 9	12 00	3 12 64	Paszto, Hungary	Bordeaux	Dunfermline Ath	90	8
						Liverpool	6	—
Jan Molby	6 1	14 07	4 7 63	Kolding	Ajax	Liverpool	204	42
Ashley Neal	6 00	11 10	16 12 74	Liverpool	Trainee	Liverpool	—	—
Terry Nestor*	5 10	11 04	22 10 74	Warrington	Trainee	Liverpool	—	—
Steve Nicol	5 10	12 00	11 12 61	Irvine	Ayr U BC	Ayr U	70	7
						Liverpool	339	36
Paul O'Donnell	5 10	11 03	6 10 75	Limerick	Trainee	Liverpool	—	—
Scott Paterson*	5 11	12 00	13 5 72	Aberdeen	Cove Rangers	Liverpool	—	—
Jamie Redknapp	6 0	12 00	25 6 73	Barton on Sea	Trainee	Bournemouth	13	—
						Liverpool	70	7
Mark Stalker*	5 10	11 05	24 9 74	Liverpool	Trainee	Liverpool	—	—
Michael Thomas	5 9	12 06	24 8 67	Lambeth	Apprentice	Arsenal	163	24
						Portsmouth (loan)	3	—
						Liverpool	32	4
Ronnie Whelan*	5 9	10 13	25 9 61	Dublin	Home Farm	Liverpool	362	46

LIVERPOOL

Colours: All red with white markings. **Change colours:** Racing green with white markings.

Foundation: But for a dispute between Everton FC and their landlord at Anfield in 1892, there may never have been a Liverpool club. This dispute persuaded the majority of Evertonians to quit Anfield for Goodison Park, leaving the landlord, Mr. John Houlding, to form a new club. He originally tried to retain the name "Everton" but when this failed, he founded Liverpool Association FC on 15 March, 1892.

First Football League game: 2 September, 1893, Division 2, v Middlesbrough Ironopolis (a) W 2-0 – McOwen; Hannah, McLean; Henderson, McQue (1), McBride; Gordon, McVean (1), M. McQueen, Stott, H. McQueen.

Did you know: On 28 August 1993, Ian Rush scored his 200th League goal of his Liverpool career against John Lukic the Leeds United goalkeeper. His first goal achieved 12 years earlier had been scored against Arsenal and their goalkeeper John Lukic.

Managers (and Secretary-Managers)
W. E. Barclay 1892–96, Tom Watson 1896–1915, David Ashworth 1920–22, Matt McQueen 1923–28, George Patterson 1928–36 (continued as secretary), George Kay 1936–51, Don Welsh 1951–56, Phil Taylor 1956–59, Bill Shankly 1959–74, Bob Paisley 1974–83, Joe Fagan 1983–85, Kenny Dalglish 1985–91, Graeme Souness 1991–94, Roy Evans January 1994–

Player and Position	*Ht*	*Wt*	*Birth Date*	*Birth Place*	*Source*	*Clubs*	*League App*	*League Gls*
Forwards								
John Barnes	5 11	12 07	7 11 63	Jamaica	Sudbury Court	Watford	233	65
						Liverpool	205	70
Nigel Clough	5 9	11 04	19 3 66	Sunderland	ACT Hunters	Nottingham F	311	101
						Liverpool	27	7
Sean Fallon*	6 0	12 08	11 5 76	New Zealand	Trainee	Liverpool	—	—
Robbie Fowler	5 9	11 08	9 4 75	Liverpool	Trainee	Liverpool	28	12
Don Hutchison	6 2	11 08	9 5 71	Gateshead	Trainee	Hartlepool U	24	2
						Liverpool	45	7
Lee Jones	5 8	10 08	29 5 73	Wrexham	Trainee	Wrexham	39	10
						Liverpool	—	—
						Crewe Alex (loan)	8	1
Steve McManaman	6 0	10 06	11 2 72	Liverpool	School	Liverpool	93	11
Ian Rush	6 0	12 06	20 10 61	St. Asaph	Apprentice	Chester	34	14
						Liverpool	224	139
						Juventus	29	7
						Liverpool	189	73
Paul Stewart	5 11	11 03	7 10 64	Manchester	Apprentice	Blackpool	201	56
						Manchester C	51	26
						Tottenham H	131	28
						Liverpool	32	1
						Crystal Palace (loan)	18	3
Mark Walters	5 9	11 08	12 1 64	Birmingham	Apprentice	Aston Villa	181	39
						Rangers	106	32
						Liverpool	76	14
						Stoke C (loan)	9	2

Trainees
Brenchley, Scott A; Clegg, David L; Gouldbourne, Ronald; Kinney, Westley M; Li, Christian; McAuley, Hugh F; Morley, Dominic A; Morris, Stephen; Robinson, Paul J; Snape, Paul F; Wilkinson, Martin D; Wyke, Stanley.

****Non-Contract**
Robinson, David.

Associated Schoolboys
Burghall, Terence R; Cartwright, Lee C; Culshaw, Thomas A; Friars, Sean M; Hamilton, Glen; Howard, Michael A; Jones, Wyn V; Koumas, Jason; Lyonette, Paul M; Maxwell, Layton J; Newby, Jon P. R; Parkinson, Andrew J; Stannard, John F; Todd, Luke G; Williams, Daniel I. L; Wright, Anthony A; Wright, Stephen J; Yates, Michael A.

Associated Schoolboys who have accepted the Club's offer of a Traineeship/Contract
Brazier, Philip; Carragher, James L; Cassidy, Jamie; Larmour, David J; Moore, Michael A; Prior, Lee J; Proctor, Paul; Quinn, Mark P; Quinn, Stuart; Roberts, Gareth W; Thompson, David A.
**Non-Contract Players who are retained must be re-signed before they are eligible to play in League matches.

LUTON TOWN 1993–94 *Back row (left to right):* Tony Thorpe, Jamie Campbell, Juergen Sommer, Andy Petterson, Des Linton, Paul Telfer.
Centre row: John Moore (First Team Coach), Andy McDade (Physio), Scott Oakes, Ceri Hughes, Marvin Johnson, David Greene, John Dreyer, Julian James, Terry Westley (Youth Team Coach), Wayne Turner (Reserve Team Coach).
Front row: Jason Rees, Ian Benjamin, Trevor Peake, David Pleat (Manager), David Preece, Martin Williams, Richard Harvey.

Division 1 LUTON TOWN

Kenilworth Road Stadium, 1 Maple Rd, Luton, Beds. LU4 8AW. Telephone, Offices: Luton (0582) 411622; Ticket Office: (0582) 416976. Credit Hotline (0582) 30748 (24 hrs); Banqueting: (0582) 411526. Special Loupe system for deaf and blind in our handicapped area. Soccer Line 0839 664466.

Ground capacity: 10,499.

Record attendance: 30,069 v Blackpool, FA Cup 6th rd replay, 4 March 1959.

Record receipts: £115,541.20 v West Ham U, FA Cup 6th rd, 23 March 1994.

Pitch measurements: 110yd × 72yd.

President: E. Pearson.

Chairman & Managding Director: D. A. Kohler BSC (HONS), ARICS.

Directors: C. S. Bassett, C. T. F. Green, P. Collins, N. Terry.

Secretary: J. K. Smylie.

Directors: P. Collins, E. S. Pearson, H. Richardson, N. Terry.

Commercial Manager: Kathy Leather.

Manager: David Pleat. ***Assistant Manager:*** John Moore.

Reserve team coach: Wayne Turner. ***Youth team coach:*** Terry Westley.

Physio: Andy McDade.

Year Formed: 1885. ***Turned Professional:*** 1890. ***Ltd Co.:*** 1897.

Club Nickname: 'The Hatters'.

Previous Grounds: 1885, Excelsior, Dallow Lane; 1897, Dunstable Road; 1905, Kenilworth Road.

Record League Victory: 12–0 v Bristol R, Division 3 (S), 13 April 1936 – Dolman; Mackey, Smith; Finlayson, Nelson, Godfrey; Rich, Martin (1), Payne (10), Roberts (1), Stephenson.

Record Cup Victory: 9–0 v Clapton, FA Cup, 1st rd (replay after abandoned game), 30 November 1927 – Abbott; Kingham, Graham; Black, Rennie, Fraser; Pointon, Yardley (4), Reid (2), Woods (1), Dennis (2).

Record Defeat: 0–9 v Small Heath, Division 2, 12 November 1898.

Most League Points (2 for a win): 66, Division 4, 1967–68.

Most League Points (3 for a win): 88, Division 2, 1981–82.

Most League Goals: 103, Division 3 (S), 1936–37.

Highest League Scorer in Season: Joe Payne, 55, Division 3 (S), 1936–37.

Most League Goals in Total Aggregate: Gordon Turner, 243, 1949–64.

Most Capped Player: Mal Donaghy, 58 (91), Northern Ireland.

Most League Appearances: Bob Morton, 494, 1948–64.

Record Transfer Fee Received: £1,500,000 from Nottingham F for Kingsley Black, August 1991.

Record Transfer Fee Paid: £850,000 to Odense for Lars Elstrup, August 1989.

Football League Record: 1897 Elected to Division 2; 1900 Failed re-election; 1920 Division 3; 1921–37 Division 3 (S); 1937–55 Division 2; 1955–60 Division 1; 1960–63 Division 2; 1963–65 Division 3; 1965–68 Division 4; 1968–70 Division 3; 1970–74 Division 2; 1974–75 Division 1; 1975–82 Division 2; 1982– Division 1.

Chairman: B. E. Fearn. ***Vice-chairman:*** L. V. Pickering.
Honours: *Football League:* Division 1 best season: 7th, 1986–87; Division 2 – Champions 1981–82; Runners-up 1954–55, 1973–74; Division 3 – Runners-up 1969–70; Division 4 – Champions 1967–68; Division 3 (S) – Champions 1936–37; Runners-up 1935–36. *FA Cup:* Runners-up 1959. *Football League Cup:* Winners 1987–88; Runners-up 1988–89. *Simod Cup:* Runners-up 1988.

LUTON TOWN 1993—94 LEAGUE RECORD

Match No.	Date	Venue	Opponents	Result		H/T Score	Lg. Pos.	Goalscorers	Attendance
1	Aug 14	H	Watford	W	2-1	0-0	—	Telfer, Dixon	9149
2	21	A	Portsmouth	L	0-1	0-1	16		12,248
3	28	H	Nottingham F	L	1-2	1-1	22	Hartson	9788
4	Sept 11	H	Bolton W	L	0-2	0-1	24		7199
5	14	A	Tranmere R	L	1-4	0-1	—	Benjamin	5871
6	18	A	Middlesbrough	D	0-0	0-0	23		12,487
7	25	A	Birmingham C	D	1-1	0-1	23	Telfer	11,081
8	Oct 2	H	Barnsley	W	5-0	2-0	21	Hartson, Oakes 2, James, Houghton	6201
9	5	H	Bristol C	L	0-2	0-0	—		5956
10	9	A	Derby Co	L	1-2	0-1	23	Williams	15,885
11	16	H	Notts Co	W	1-0	1-0	21	Dickov	6366
12	20	A	Sunderland	L	0-2	0-2	—		13,760
13	23	A	Oxford U	W	1-0	1-0	19	Hughes	5161
14	30	H	Leicester C	L	0-2	0-1	21		8813
15	Nov 2	A	Crystal Palace	L	2-3	2-3	—	Aunger, Hughes	10,925
16	7	H	Charlton Ath	W	1-0	1-0	—	Telfer	6327
17	13	A	Southend U	L	1-2	0-1	18	Dixon	5567
18	27	H	Stoke C	W	6-2	3-2	15	Dixon 3, Hughes, Oakes, Hartson	7384
19	Dec 4	A	Charlton Ath	L	0-1	0-0	17		7121
20	11	H	Tranmere R	L	0-1	0-0	19		7045
21	19	A	Watford	D	2-2	0-2	—	Preece, Dreyer (pen)	7567
22	27	A	Peterborough U	D	0-0	0-0	20		9522
23	29	H	Grimsby T	W	2-1	0-1	18	Harper, Hughes	7234
24	Jan 1	A	WBA	D	1-1	1-0	18	Preece	16,138
25	15	A	Notts Co	W	2-1	0-0	17	Dixon 2	6589
26	22	H	Derby Co	W	2-1	1-0	17	Telfer, Oakes	9371
27	Feb 5	H	Oxford U	W	3-0	2-0	16	Oakes, Thomas, Thorpe	7366
28	12	A	Leicester C	L	1-2	0-1	17	James	16,149
29	22	H	Portsmouth	W	4-1	2-0	—	Telfer, Preece, Hughes, Oakes	6533
30	25	H	Sunderland	W	2-1	2-0	14	Hughes, Oakes	9367
31	Mar 5	A	Nottingham F	L	0-2	0-0	16		22,249
32	8	H	Middlesbrough	D	1-1	0-0	—	Dreyer (pen)	6741
33	19	H	Birmingham C	D	1-1	1-0	18	Telfer	7690
34	26	A	Barnsley	L	0-1	0-0	18		6289
35	30	A	Millwall	D	2-2	1-1	—	Dreyer, Hartson	9235
36	Apr 2	H	Peterborough U	W	2-0	1-0	17	Dixon 2	8398
37	4	A	Grimsby T	L	0-2	0-1	18		5542
38	12	H	Wolverhampton W	L	0-2	0-1	—		8545
39	16	H	Crystal Palace	L	0-1	0-1	20		9880
40	19	A	Bristol C	L	0-1	0-1	—		5350
41	23	A	Wolverhampton W	L	0-1	0-1	20		25,479
42	26	H	Millwall	D	1-1	0-0	—	Preece	8257
43	30	H	Southend U	D	1-1	0-0	20	Hartson	7504
44	May 3	H	WBA	W	3-2	1-0	—	Preece, James, Hartson	10,053
45	5	A	Bolton W	L	1-2	1-0	—	Hughes	7102
46	8	A	Stoke C	D	2-2	0-2	20	Oakes, Telfer (pen)	15,911

Final League Position: 20

GOALSCORERS

League (56): Dixon 9, Oakes 8, Hughes 7, Telfer 7 (1 pen), Hartson 6, Preece 5, Dreyer 3 (2 pens), James 3, Aunger 1, Benjamin 1, Dickov 1, Harper 1, Houghton 1, Thomas 1, Thorpe 1, Williams 1.
Coca-Cola Cup (0):
FA Cup (9): Oakes 5, Hartson 1, Preece 1, Telfer 1, Thorpe 1.

Sommer 43	Johnson 17	James 29 + 4	Williams 5 + 10	Peake 36	Dreyer 40	Telfer 44 + 1	Oakes 33 + 3	Dixon 27 + 2	Rees 8 + 2	Preece 28 + 1	Houghton 6 + 9	Petterson 2 + 3	Hughes 42	Benjamin 2 + 1	Hartson 21 + 13	Harper 40 + 1	Linton 32 + 1	Dickov 8 + 7	Campbell 4 + 12	Aunger 5	Thomas 17 + 3	Thorpe 4 + 10	Burke 2 + 1	Greene 10	Davis 1	McLaren — + 1	Match No.
1	2	3	4	5	6	7	8	9	10	11	12	14															1
1	2	3	4	5	6	7	*8*	9		11	12		10	14													2
1	2	3	12	5	6	4		9	14	11	10		*8*		7												3
1	2	*3*	12	5	6	4	14	9		11	10		8		*7*												4
1	3		12	5	6	4	9		10	11			8	7		2											5
1	3	12		5	6	4	8		9	11			10	*7*	14	2											6
1	2	3	12	5	6	4	8		9				10		11	7											7
1	2	3	4	5	6	7	8				12		*10*		9	11	14										8
1	2	3	4	5	6	7	8				12		10		9	11											9
1	3		12	5	6	7	8						10		9	*4*	2	11	14								10
1	3		12	5	6	7	8						10		9	4	2	*11*	14								11
1	3		12	5	6	7	8		10				4		9		2	*11*	14								12
1	3			5	6	7	12	*9*			10		8			4	2	11	14								13
1	3			5	6	7	8	12			14		10		9	*4*	2	11									14
1	3			5	6	7	*8*	9					10			4	2	14	12	11							15
1	3		12	5	6	7	8	9					10			4	2	14		*11*							16
1				5	6	7		9			8		*10*			4	2	14	12	11	3						17
1				5			8	9	*10*				7		12	4	2	11	6		3	14					18
1				5		12	8	9	*7*				10		14	4	2	*11*	6		3						19
1				5		7	12	9		10			8		14	4	2	*11*	6		3						20
1				5	6	7	*8*	9		11	14		10			4	2	12			3						21
1		14		5	6	7		9		11	10		8			4	*2*	12			3						22
1		14		5	6	7	*8*	9					10		11	4	2	12			3						23
1		14		5	6	7		9		11	10		*8*			4	2	12			3						24
1		3		5	6	7	8	9		*11*			10		14	4	2		12								25
1		3		5	6	7	8	9					10		12	4	2		11								26
1		3		5	6	7	*8*			10	14				9	4	2				11	12					27
1		3		5	6	7	8			11	14		10		9	4	*2*		12								28
1		3		5	6	7	*8*	9		11			10		12	4	2					14					29
1		3		5	6	7	*8*	9		11			10		12	4	2					14					30
1	5	3			6	7		9		11		12	8			4	2					*10*	14				31
1		3	14		6	7		9		10			8		12	4	*2*						11	5			32
		3	12		6	7	8			11		1			9	4	2					14	*10*	5			33
1		3	2	5	6	7	8	9		*11*			10		12	4					14						34
1		3		5	6	7	8			11			10		9	4			12		2						35
1		3		5	6	7	8	9	14	11					*10*	4			12		2						36
1		4			6	7			*10*				8		9	14	2		12	11	3			5			37
1		3			6	7	8	*9*		11			10		12	4	2				14			5			38
1		6				7	*8*	12		11			10		9	4	2				3	14		5			39
1		3			6	7		9		11			8		12	4	2			*10*		14		5			40
1		6				7		9		11	12		8			4	2				3	10		5			41
1		2			6	7		9		11			8		12	4					3	10		5			42
1		3			6	7	*8*			11			10		9	4	2				12	14		5			43
1		2		5	6	7	8			11		14	10		9	4					3	12					44
		3		5	6	7	8			12		1	*10*		9	4	2				11	14					45
		3		5		7	8						10		9	*4*	2		12			11		6	1	14	46

Coca-Cola Cup	First Round	Cambridge U (a)	0-1
		(h)	0-1
FA Cup	Third Round	Southend U (h)	1-0
	Fourth Round	Newcastle U (a)	1-1
		(h)	2-0
	Fifth Round	Cardiff C (a)	2-1
	Sixth Round	West Ham U (a)	0-0
		(h)	3-2
	Semi-final at Wembley	Chelsea	0-2

LUTON TOWN

Player and Position	Ht	Wt	Birth Date	Birth Place	Source	Clubs	League App	League Gls
Goalkeepers								
Kelvin Davis§	6 1	13 06	29 9 76	Bedford	Trainee	Luton T	1	—
Andrew Petterson	6 1	14 10	26 9 69	Fremantle		Luton T	19	—
						Swindon T (loan)	—	—
						Ipswich T (loan)	—	—
						Ipswich T (loan)	1	—
Jurgen Sommer	6 4	15 12	27 2 64	New York		Luton T	43	—
						Brighton (loan)	1	—
						Torquay U (loan)	10	—
Defenders								
John Dreyer*	6 1	11 06	11 6 63	Alnwick	Wallingford T	Oxford U	60	2
						Torquay U (loan)	5	—
						Fulham (loan)	12	2
						Luton T	214	13
David Greene	6 2	13 05	26 10 73	Luton	Trainee	Luton T	11	—
Alan Harper	5 8	10 09	1 11 60	Liverpool	Apprentice	Liverpool	—	—
						Everton	127	4
						Sheffield W	35	—
						Manchester C	50	1
						Everton	51	—
						Luton T	41	1
Richard Harvey	5 10	11 10	17 4 69	Letchworth	Apprentice	Luton T	105	2
						Blackpool (loan)	5	—
Marvin Johnson	6 0	12 03	29 10 68	Wembley	Apprentice	Luton T	120	3
Des Linton	6 1	13 02	5 9 71	Birmingham	Trainee	Leicester C	11	—
						Luton T	56	1
Paul McLaren	6 0	12 06	17 11 76	Wycombe	Trainee	Luton T	1	—
Trevor Peake*	6 0	12 10	10 2 57	Nuneaton	Nuneaton Bor	Lincoln C	171	7
						Coventry C	278	6
						Luton T	114	—
Richard Philip*	5 11	11 07	20 10 74	Surrey	Trainee	Luton T	—	—
Greg Rioch	5 11	10 09	24 6 75	Sutton Coldfield	Trainee	Luton T	—	—
						Barnet (loan)	3	—
Mitchell Thomas	6 2	12 00	2 10 64	Luton	Apprentice	Luton T	107	1
						Tottenham H	157	6
						West Ham U	38	3
						Luton T	20	1
Midfield								
Scott Houghton	5 5	11 06	22 10 71	Hitchin	Trainee	Tottenham H	10	2
						Ipswich T (loan)	8	1
						Cambridge U (loan)	—	—
						Gillingham (loan)	3	—
						Charlton Ath (loan)	6	—
						Luton T	15	1
Ceri Hughes	5 10	11 05	26 2 71	Pontypridd	Trainee	Luton T	107	10
Julian James	5 10	11 10	22 3 70	Tring	Trainee	Luton T	145	9
						Preston NE (loan)	6	—
David Preece	5 6	11 05	28 5 63	Bridgnorth	Apprentice	Walsall	111	5
						Luton T	294	17
Jason Rees*	5 5	9 10	22 12 69	Pontypridd	Trainee	Luton T	82	—
						Mansfield T (loan)	15	1
Neil Ryan*	5 10	11 08	27 1 75	Luton	Trainee	Luton T	—	—
Aaron Skelton	5 10	11 05	22 11 74	Welwyn Garden	Trainee	Luton T	—	—
Paul Telfer	5 9	11 06	21 10 71	Edinburgh	Trainee	Luton T	98	10
Forwards								
Geoff Aunger	5 8	11 10	4 2 68	Red Deer	Vancouver 86ers	Luton T	5	1
Jamie Campbell	6 1	11 03	21 10 72	Birmingham	Trainee	Luton T	36	1
Kerry Dixon	6 0	14 01	24 7 61	Luton	Dunstable	Reading	116	51
						Chelsea	335	147
						Southampton	9	2
						Luton T (loan)	17	3
						Luton T	29	9

LUTON TOWN

Colours: White shirts with navy vertical pinstripe, navy blue collar with orange flash, navy blue shorts with orange and white trim on bottom of legs, white stockings with navy and orange turnover. **Change colours:** Navy shorts with white vertical pinstripe, white collar and orange flash, white shorts with navy and orange trim on bottom of legs, navy stockings with white and orange turnover.

Foundation: Formed by an amalgamation of two leading local clubs, Wanderers and Excelsior a works team, at a meeting in Luton Town Hall in April 1885. The Wanderers had three months earlier changed their name to Luton Town Wanderers and did not take too kindly to the formation of another Town club but were talked around at this meeting. Wanderers had already appeared in the FA Cup and the new club entered in its inaugural season.

First Football League game: 4 September, 1897, Division 2, v Leicester Fosse (a) D 1-1 – Williams; McCartney, McEwen; Davies, Stewart, Docherty; Gallacher, Coupar, Birch, McInnes, Ekins (1).

Did you know: Luton Town were unbeaten in their opening ten matches in Division 3 (South) during 1928–29. Their final position was seventh.

Managers (and Secretary-Managers)
Charlie Green 1901–28*, George Thomson 1925, John McCartney 1927–29, George Kay 1929–31, Harold Wightman 1931–35, Ted Liddell 1936–38, Neil McBain 1938–39, George Martin 1939–47, Dally Duncan 1947–58, Syd Owen 1959–60, Sam Bartram 1960–62, Bill Harvey 1962–64, George Martin 1965–66, Allan Brown 1966–68, Alec Stock 1968–72, Harry Haslam 1972–78, David Pleat 1978–86, John Moore 1986–87, Ray Harford 1987–89, Jim Ryan 1900–91, David Pleat June 1991–

Player and Position	*Ht*	*Wt*	*Birth Date*	*Birth Place*	*Source*	*Clubs*	*League App*	*League Gls*
John Hartson	5 11	11 13	5 4 75	Swansea	Trainee	Luton T	34	6
Scott Oakes	5 11	11 04	5 8 72	Leicester	Trainee	Leicester C	3	—
						Luton T	101	15
Darren Salton*	6 2	13 00	16 3 72	Edinburgh	Trainee	Luton T	18	—
Tony Thorpe	5 9	12 00	10 4 74	Leicester		Luton T	14	1
Neil Watkins*			23 8 75	Cardiff		Luton T	—	—
Martin Williams	5 9	11 12	12 7 73	Luton	Leicester C	Luton T	38	2

Trainees
Campbell, Lee A; Chenery, Ben R; Davis, Kelvin G; Gibb, Darren W; Goodridge, Steven J; Issott, Gary D; Jukes, Andrew; Palmer, Stephen; Power, Daniel J; Simpson, Gary J; Woodsford, Jamie M; Woolgar, Matthew.

Associated Schoolboys
Barr, Andrew R; Beverstock, Paul R; Boyce, Emerson; Doherty. Gary M; Dowsing, Cliwt L; Flinn, Gary; French, James R; George, Liam B; Jenner, Roger A; Jones, Ian; Kester, Matthew J; Quince, Jason; Sneddon, Thomas; Webb, Nicholas M.

Associated Schoolboys who have accepted the Club's offer of a Traineeship/Contract
Douglas, Stuart A; Evers, Sean A; Turner, Samuel; Willmott, Christopher A.

Lincoln City players continued from Page 295

Tony Lormor*	6 1	12 03	29 10 70	Ashington	Trainee	Newcastle U	8	3
						Norwich C (loan)	—	—
						Lincoln C	100	30
Tony Loughlan*			19 1 70	Croydon	Leicester U	Nottingham F	2	1
						Lincoln C	12	2
Steve Mardenborough	5 8	11 09	11 9 64	Birmingham	Apprentice	Coventry C	—	—
						Wolverhampton W	9	1
						Cambridge U (loan)	6	—
						Swansea C	36	7
						Newport Co	64	11
						Cardiff C	32	1
						Hereford U	27	—
						Darlington	106	18
						Lincoln C	21	2
Neil Matthews	6 0	12 12	19 9 66	Grimsby		Grimsby T	11	1
						Scunthorpe U (loan)	1	—
						Halifax T (loan)	9	2
						Bolton W (loan)	1	—
						Halifax T	105	29
						Stockport Co	43	15
						Halifax T (loan)	3	—
						Lincoln C	60	18
Paul Smith	5 10	10 09	9 11 64	Rotherham	Apprentice	Sheffield U	36	1
						Stockport Co (loan)	7	5
						Port Vale	44	7
						Lincoln C	215	27
Steven Williams§			3 11 75	Sheffield	Trainee	Lincoln C	8	1

MANCHESTER CITY 1993–94 *Back row (left to right):* David Kerr, Paul Lake, Niall Quinn, David Brightwell, Garry Flitcroft, Ian Brightwell.
Centre row: Eamonn Salmon (Physio), Tony Book (First Team Coach), David White, Michel Vonk, Alfons Groenendijk, Andy Dibble, Martyn Margetson, Tony Coton, Mike Sheron, Steve Lomas, Michael Quigley, David Moss (Assistant Manager), Les Chapman (Reserve Team Coach).
Front row: Richard Edghill, Rick Holden, Terry Phelan, Keith Curle, Brian Horton (Manager), Steve McMahon, Adie Mike, Andy Hill, Fitzroy Simpson.
(Photograph: *Manchester Evening News*)

FA Premiership **MANCHESTER CITY**

Maine Road, Moss Side, Manchester M14 7WN. Telephone 061–226 1191/2. Fax: 061–227 9418. Ticket Office: 061–226 2224. Dial-a-Seat: 061–227 9229. Development Office: 061–226 3143. Clubcall: 0891 121191. Ticketcall: 0891 121591.

Ground capacity: 21,500 (subject to official FLA agreement).

Record attendance: 84,569 v Stoke C, FA Cup 6th rd, 3 March 1934 (British record for any game outside London or Glasgow).

Record receipts: £512,235 Manchester U v Oldham Ath, FA Cup semi-final replay, 13 April 1994.

Pitch measurements: 118yd × 76yd.

Chairman: F. H. Lee. ***Vice-charman:*** F. Pye.***Managing Director:*** C. J. Barlow.

Directors: I. L. G. Niven, A. Thomas, J. G. Dunkerley, W. A. Miles, G. Doyle, B. Turnbull, J. Greibach, C. B. Muir OBE, D. A. Holt, A. M. Lewis.

General Secretary: J. B. Halford. ***Commercial Manager:*** P. Critchley.

Manager: Brian Horton. ***Assistant Manager:*** David Moss. ***First team coach:*** Tony Book. ***Physio:*** Eamonn Salmon. ***Youth team coach:*** Neil McNab.

Year Formed: 1887 as Ardwick FC; 1894 as Manchester City.

Turned Professional: 1887 as Ardwick FC. ***Ltd Co.:*** 1894. ***Club Nickname:*** Blues/The Citizens.

Previous Names: 1887–94, Ardwick FC (formed through the amalgamation of West Gorton and Gorton Athletic, the latter having been formed in 1880).

Previous Grounds: 1880–81, Clowes Street; 1881–82, Kirkmanshulme Cricket Ground; 1882–84, Queens Road; 1884–87, Pink Bank Lane; 1887–1923, Hyde Road (1894–1923, as City); 1923, Maine Road.

Record League Victory: 10–1 Huddersfield T, Division 2, 7 November 1987 – Nixon; Gidman, Hinchcliffe, Clements, Lake, Redmond, White (3), Stewart (3), Adcock (3), McNab (1) Simpson.

Record Cup Victory: 10–1 v Swindon T, FA Cup, 4th rd, 29 January 1930 – Barber; Felton, McCloy; Barrass, Cowan, Heinemann; Toseland, Marshall (5), Tait (3), Johnson (1), Brook (1).

Record Defeat: 1–9 v Everton, Division 1, 3 September 1906.

Most League Points (2 for a win): 62, Division 2, 1946–47.

Most League Points (3 for a win): 82, Division 2, 1988–89.

Most League Goals: 108, Division 2, 1926–27.

Highest League Scorer in Season: Tommy Johnson, 38, Division 1, 1928–29.

Most League Goals in Total Aggregate: Tommy Johnson, 158, 1919–30.

Most Capped Player: Colin Bell, 48, England.

Most League Appearances: Alan Oakes, 565, 1959–76.

Record Transfer Fee Received: £1,700,000 from Tottenham H for Paul Stewart, June 1988.

Record Transfer Fee Paid: £2,500,000 to Wimbledon for Keith Curle, August 1991.

Football League Record: 1892 Ardwick elected founder member of Division 2; 1894 Newly-formed Manchester C elected to Division 2; Division 1 1899–1902, 1903–09, 1910–26, 1928–38, 1947–50, 1951–63, 1966–83, 1985–87, 1989–92; Division 2 1902–03, 1909–10, 1926–28, 1938–47, 1950–51, 1963–66, 1983–85, 1987–89; 1992– FA Premier League.

Honours: *Football League:* Division 1 – Champions 1936–37, 1967–68; Runners-up 1903–04, 1920–21, 1976–77; Division 2 – Champions 1898–99, 1902–03, 1909–10, 1927–28, 1946–47, 1965–66; Runners-up 1895–96, 1950–51, 1987–88. *FA Cup:* Winners 1904, 1934, 1956, 1969; Runners-up 1926, 1933, 1955, 1981. *Football League Cup:* Winners 1970, 1976; Runners-up 1973–74. **European Competitions:** *European Cup:* 1968–69. *European Cup-Winners' Cup:* 1969–70 (winners), 1970–71. *UEFA Cup:* 1972–73, 1976–77, 1977–78, 1978–79.

MANCHESTER CITY 1993—94 LEAGUE RECORD

Match No.	Date	Venue	Opponents	Result		H/T Score	Lg. Pos.	Goalscorers	Attendance
1	Aug 14	H	Leeds U	D	1-1	0-0	—	Flitcroft	32,366
2	17	A	Everton	L	0-1	0-1	—		26,025
3	21	A	Tottenham H	L	0-1	0-0	18		24,535
4	24	H	Blackburn R	L	0-2	0-1	—		25,185
5	27	H	Coventry C	D	1-1	1-0	—	Sheron	21,537
6	Sept 1	A	Swindon T	W	3-1	0-0	—	Vonk, Quinn, Mike	16,067
7	11	H	QPR	W	3-0	2-0	15	Quinn, Sheron, Flitcroft	24,445
8	20	A	Wimbledon	L	0-1	0-0	—		8533
9	25	A	Sheffield U	W	1-0	0-0	14	Sheron	20,067
10	Oct 4	H	Oldham Ath	D	1-1	0-0	—	Sheron	21,401
11	16	A	Arsenal	D	0-0	0-0	14		29,567
12	23	H	Liverpool	D	1-1	0-0	14	White	30,403
13	Nov 1	A	West Ham U	L	1-3	0-2	—	Curle (pen)	16,605
14	7	H	Manchester U	L	2-3	2-0	—	Quinn 2	35,155
15	20	A	Norwich C	D	1-1	0-0	16	Quinn	16,626
16	22	A	Chelsea	D	0-0	0-0	—		10,128
17	27	H	Sheffield W	L	1-3	0-0	17	Sheron	23,416
18	Dec 4	A	Leeds U	L	2-3	0-2	17	Sheron, Griffiths	33,820
19	8	H	Everton	W	1-0	1-0	—	Griffiths	20,513
20	11	H	Tottenham H	L	0-2	0-0	17		21,566
21	18	A	Blackburn R	L	0-2	0-1	—		19,479
22	28	H	Southampton	D	1-1	1-1	17	Phelan	24,712
23	Jan 1	A	Newcastle U	L	0-2	0-2	19		35,585
24	15	H	Arsenal	D	0-0	0-0	19		25,642
25	22	A	Liverpool	L	1-2	1-1	20	Griffiths	41,872
26	Feb 5	H	Ipswich T	W	2-1	1-1	18	Griffiths, Flitcroft	28,188
27	12	H	West Ham U	D	0-0	0-0	19		29,118
28	19	A	Coventry C	L	0-4	0-0	20		11,739
29	22	A	Aston Villa	D	0-0	0-0	—		19,254
30	25	H	Swindon T	W	2-1	1-1	18	Horlock (og), Rocastle	26,360
31	Mar 5	A	QPR	D	1-1	0-1	19	Rocastle	13,474
32	12	H	Wimbledon	L	0-1	0-1	19		23,981
33	19	H	Sheffield U	D	0-0	0-0	19		25,448
34	26	A	Oldham Ath	D	0-0	0-0	19		16,462
35	29	A	Ipswich T	D	2-2	1-1	—	Walsh, Rosler	12,871
36	Apr 2	H	Aston Villa	W	3-0	2-0	19	Beagrie, Walsh, Rosler	26,075
37	4	A	Southampton	W	1-0	0-0	17	Karl	16,377
38	9	H	Newcastle U	W	2-1	1-1	15	Walsh, Brightwell D	33,774
39	16	H	Norwich C	D	1-1	0-1	15	Rosler	28,020
40	23	A	Manchester U	L	0-2	0-2	15		44,333
41	30	H	Chelsea	D	2-2	2-2	15	Rosler, Walsh	33,594
42	May 7	A	Sheffield W	D	1-1	0-1	16	Rosler	33,589

Final League Position: 16

GOALSCORERS

League (38): Sheron 6, Quinn 5, Rosler 5, Griffiths 4, Walsh 4, Flitcroft 3, Rocastle 2, Beagrie 1, Brightwell D 1, Curle 1 (pen), Karl 1, Mike 1, Phelan 1, Vonk 1, White 1, own goal 1.
Coca-Cola Cup (5): White 2, Lomas 1, Quinn 1, Vonk 1.
FA Cup (4): Ingebrigtsen 3, Kernaghan 1.

Coton 31	Hill 15 + 2	Phelan 30	McMahon 35	Curle 29	Vonk 34 + 1	White 16	Sheron 29 + 4	Simpson 12 + 3	Flitcroft 19 + 2	Holden 9	Reid 1 + 3	Brightwell D 19 + 3	Groenendijk 9	Quinn 14 + 1	Mike 1 + 8	Edghill 22	Kernaghan 23 + 1	Lomas 17 + 6	Dibble 11	Griffiths 11 + 5	Ingebrigtsen 2 + 6	Kerr 2	Quigley 2	Rocastle 21	Shutt 5 + 1	Foster 1	Rosler 12	Walsh 11	Karl 4 + 2	Brightwell I 6 + 1	Beagrie 9	Match No.
1	2	3	4	*5*	6	7	8	9	10	11	12	14																				1
1	2	3	4		6	7	8		10	11	12	5	9																			2
1	2	3	4		6	7	8		10	11	9	5		12																		3
1	*2*	3	4	5	6		8		10	11	12	14	7	9																		4
1		3	4	5	6	7	8		10	11			2	9																		5
1			4	5	6	*7*	8	12	10	11		3	2	9	14																	6
1		3	4	5		7	8		10	11		6	2	9	12																	7
1			4	5			8	7	10			3	11	9	12	2	6															8
1			4	5			8			11		3	7	9		2	6	10														9
		3	4	5			8		10	11			*7*	9	12	2	6	14	1													10
1		3	4	5			8	7	10					9		2	6	11														11
1		3	4	5		7	8	11	10					9		2	6	12														12
1		3	4	5	12	7	*8*		10					9		2	6	11		14												13
1		3	4	5	11	7	8		10					9		2	6															14
1		3	4	5		7	8	10						9		2	6	11		12												15
1		3	4	5	2	7	8	10						9			6	11		12												16
1		3	4	5	2	7	8	10						9	12		6	11														17
1		3	4	5	2	7	8	9							10		*6*	11		12	14											18
1		3	4	5	6	7	8		10									11		9	12	2										19
1		3		5	6	7	8		10			12						11		9	14	2	*4*									20
1		3		5	6	7	8									2	4	11		9	12		10									21
1		3		5	10		8	12				6				2	4	*11*		9	14			7								22
1					10		8	9				3				2	6	11			12			4	7	5						23
1	11				10		12		14			5	*6*			2	4	3		9	8			7								24
1	11				10				7			6				2	5	3		9	8			4								25
1	11			5	6		8		10							2		3		9				4	7							26
1		3	4	5	6		8		10							2	12	14		9				7	*11*							27
1		3	4		6		8	12							14	2	5	10		*9*				7	11							28
1	12	3	4		6		8	9								2	5	10						7	11							29
	14	3	4		6		8	11	10							2	5		1	9				*7*	12							30
	11	3	4		6		8								12	2	5		1	9				7			10					31
1	*11*	3	4		6			9							12	2	5							7			8	10	14			32
1	2	11	4		6							3					5			12				7			8	10	9			33
1	2		4	5	6		12					3												7			9	10		8	11	34
	2		4	5	6							3							1					7			9	10		8	11	35
	2		4	5	6		12					3							1					7			9	10		8	11	36
	2		4	5	6		12					3							1					*7*			9	10	14	8	11	37
	2		4	5	6							3						12	1					7			9	10	8		11	38
	2		4	5	6							3						12	1					7			9	10	8		11	39
	2		4	5	6							3							1					7			9	10	8	12	11	40
	2		4		6							3				5			1					7			9	10		8	11	41
		3	4		6				12							2	5	14	1					*7*			9	10		8	11	42

Coca-Cola Cup	Second Round	Reading (h)	1-1
		(a)	2-1
	Third Round	Chelsea (h)	1-0
	Fourth Round	Nottingham F (a)	0-0
		(h)	1-2
FA Cup	Third Round	Leicester C (h)	4-1
	Fourth Round	Cardiff C (a)	0-1

MANCHESTER CITY

Player and Position	Ht	Wt	Birth Date	Birth Place	Source	Clubs	League App	League Gls
Goalkeepers								
Tony Coton	6 2	13 07	19 5 61	Tamworth	Mile Oak	Birmingham C	94	—
						Hereford U (loan)	—	—
						Watford	233	—
						Manchester C	141	—
Andy Dibble	6 2	13 07	8 5 65	Cwmbran	Apprentice	Cardiff C	62	—
						Luton T	30	—
						Sunderland (loan)	12	—
						Huddersfield T (loan)	5	—
						Manchester C	87	—
						Aberdeen (loan)	5	—
						Middlesbrough (loan)	19	—
						Bolton W (loan)	13	—
						WBA (loan)	9	—
						Oldham Ath (loan)	—	—
Martyn Margetson	6 0	13 10	8 9 71	West Glamorgan	Trainee	Manchester C	6	—
						Bristol R (loan)	3	—
						Bolton W (loan)	—	—
Defenders								
Jim Bentley	6 1	13 00	11 6 76	Liverpool	Trainee	Manchester C	—	—
Keith Curle	6 0	12 07	14 11 63	Bristol	Apprentice	Bristol R	32	4
						Torquay U	16	5
						Bristol C	121	1
						Reading	40	—
						Wimbledon	93	3
						Manchester C	108	9
Richard Edghill	5 9	10 01	23 9 74	Oldham	Trainee	Manchester C	22	—
Gary Flitcroft	5 11	11 08	6 11 72	Bolton	Trainee	Manchester C	53	8
						Bury (loan)	12	—
John Foster	5 10	11 01	19 9 73	Manchester	Trainee	Manchester C	1	—
Joe Harkin	5 10	11 04	9 12 75	Derry	Trainee	Manchester C	—	—
Andy Hill	5 10	12 00	20 1 65	Maltby	Apprentice	Manchester U	—	—
						Bury	264	10
						Manchester C	85	6
Kare Ingebrigtsen	5 7	10 03	11 11 65	Rosenborg	Rosenborg	Manchester C	15	—
Rae Ingram	5 11	12 02	6 12 74	Manchester	Trainee	Manchester C	—	—
Alan Kernaghan	6 2	13 00	25 4 67	Otley	Apprentice	Middlesbrough	212	16
						Charlton Ath (loan)	13	—
						Manchester C	24	—
Terry Phelan	5 8	10 00	16 3 67	Manchester		Leeds U	14	—
						Swansea C	45	—
						Wimbledon	159	1
						Manchester C	67	1
Ian Smith§			28 11 76	Bury	Trainee	Manchester C	—	—
Michael Vonk	6 3	13 03	28 10 68	Holland	SVV/Dordrecht	Manchester C	70	3
Midfield								
Peter Beagrie	5 8	9 10	28 11 65	Middlesbrough	Local	Middlesbrough	33	2
						Sheffield U	84	11
						Stoke C	54	7
						Everton	114	11
						Sunderland (loan)	5	1
						Manchester C	9	1
David Brightwell	6 1	13 05	7 1 71	Lutterworth	Trainee	Manchester C	34	1
						Chester C (loan)	6	—
Ian Brightwell	5 10	11 07	9 4 68	Lutterworth	Congleton T	Manchester C	204	16
Alphonse Groenendijk	6 1	12 11	17 5 64	Leiden	Ajax	Manchester C	9	—
Stefan Karl			3 2 70	Hohenm-Oelsen	Dortmund	Manchester C	6	1
David Kerr	5 11	11 00	6 9 74	Dumfries	Trainee	Manchester C	3	—
Paul Lake	6 0	12 02	28 10 68	Manchester	Trainee	Manchester C	110	7
Steve Lomas	6 0	12 08	18 1 74	Hanover	Trainee	Manchester C	23	—
Steve McMahon	5 9	11 08	20 8 61	Liverpool	Apprentice	Everton	100	11
						Aston Villa	75	7
						Liverpool	204	29
						Manchester C	80	1
Mike Quigley	5 6	9 04	2 10 70	Manchester	Trainee	Manchester C	12	—
John Sharpe	5 11	11 06	9 8 75	Birmingham	Trainee	Manchester C	—	—

MANCHESTER CITY

Colours: Sky blue shirts, white shorts, sky blue stockings. **Change colours:** Red and black striped shirts, black shorts, black stockings with white top.

Foundation: Manchester City was formed as a Limited Company in 1894 after their predecessors Ardwick had been forced into bankruptcy. However, many historians like to trace the club's lineage as far back as 1880 when St. Mark's Church, West Gorton added a football section to their cricket club. They amalgamated with Gorton Athletic in 1884 as Gorton FC. Because of a change of ground they became Ardwick in 1887.

First Football League game: 3 September, 1892, Division 2, v Bootle (h) W 7-0 – Douglas; McVickers, Robson; Middleton, Russell, Hopkins; Davies (3), Morris (2), Angus (1), Weir (1), Milarvie.

Did you know: Manchester City's first FA Cup tie was a qualifying round match against Liverpool Stanley in 1890–91 and resulted in a 12-0 win. But when due to meet Halliwell in the next round they scratched from the competition.

Managers (and Secretary-Managers)
Joshua Parlby 1893–95*, Sam Omerod 1895–1902, Tom Maley 1902–06, Harry Newbould 1906–12, Ernest Magnall 1912–24, David Ashworth 1924–25, Peter Hodge 1926–32, Wilf Wild 1932–46 (continued as secretary to 1950), Sam Cowan 1946–47, John "Jock" Thomson 1947–50, Leslie McDowall 1950–63, George Poyser 1963–65, Joe Mercer 1965–71 (continued as GM to 1972), Malcolm Allison 1972–73, Johnny Hart 1973, Ron Saunders 1973–74, Tony Book 1974–79, Malcolm Allison 1979–80, John Bond 1980–83, John Benson 1983, Billy McNeill 1983–86, Jimmy Frizzell 1986–87 (continued as GM), Mel Machin 1987–89, Howard Kendall 1990, Peter Reid 1990–93, Brian Horton August 1993–

Player and Position	Ht	Wt	Birth Date	Birth Place	Source	Clubs	League App	League Gls
Mike Sheron	5 9	11 03	11 1 72	Liverpool	Trainee	Manchester C	100	24
						Bury (loan)	5	1
Fitzroy Simpson	5 8	10 07	26 2 70	Trowbridge	Trainee	Swindon T	105	9
						Manchester C	55	2
Scott Thomas	5 9	10 08	30 10 74	Bury	Trainee	Manchester C	—	—
Greg Thomson‡	5 10	10 10	13 9 75	Edinburgh	Trainee	Manchester C	—	—
Jim Whitley	5 9	11 00	14 4 75	Zambia	Trainee	Manchester C	—	—
Forwards								
Chris Beech			5 11 75	Congleton	Trainee	Manchester C	—	—
David Crawley	6 0		10 6 77	Dundalk	Dundalk	Manchester C	—	—
Stephen Finney	5 10	12 00	31 10 73	Hexham	Trainee	Preston NE	6	1
						Manchester C	—	—
Carl Griffiths	5 9	10 06	15 7 71	Coventry	Trainee	Shrewsbury T	143	54
						Manchester C	16	4
Michael Hughes	5 6	10 08	2 8 71	Larne	Carrick R	Manchester C	26	1
Adie Mike	6 0	11 06	16 11 73	Manchester	Trainee	Manchester C	14	2
						Bury (loan)	7	1
Niall Quinn	6 3	13 10	6 10 66	Dublin		Arsenal	67	14
						Manchester C	136	50
David Rocastle	5 9	11 12	2 5 67	Lewisham	Apprentice	Arsenal	218	24
						Leeds U	25	2
						Manchester C	21	2
Uwe Rosler	6 0	12 04	15 11 68	Attenburg	Dynamo Dresden	Manchester C	12	5
Paul Walsh	5 7	10 08	1 10 62	Plumstead	Apprentice	Charlton Ath	87	24
						Luton T	80	24
						Liverpool	77	25
						Tottenham H	128	19
						QPR (loan)	2	—
						Portsmouth	73	14
						Manchester C	11	4

Trainees

Brennan, Steven J; Brown, Michael R; Crawley, David; Evans, Gareth J; Kielty, Gerrard T; McDonnell, Matthew J; Roe, David A; Samuel, Gavin; Tarpey, Gerard E; Turner, David E; Walker, David A.

Associated Schoolboys

Bailey, Alan; Barrass, Nathan C; Brisco, Neil A; Burrows, Benjamin A; Collings, Stephen P; Edwards, Paul; Ford, Andrew; Hunter, Glenn W. P; Maddocks, Marc N; Morley, Neal T; Muir, Alex; Rimmer, Stephen A; Rishworth, Stephen P; Sailesman, Neil A; Smith, Steven J; Wardley, Andrew; Whitley, Jeffrey; Wills, David J.

Associated Schoolboys who have accepted the Club's offer of a Traineeship/Contract

Blore, Darren L; Callaghan, Anthony S; Crooks, Lee R; Greenacre, Christopher M; Harris, Samuel R; Morley, David T; Nurse, David J; Pridham, Christopher; Rowlands, Aled J. R.

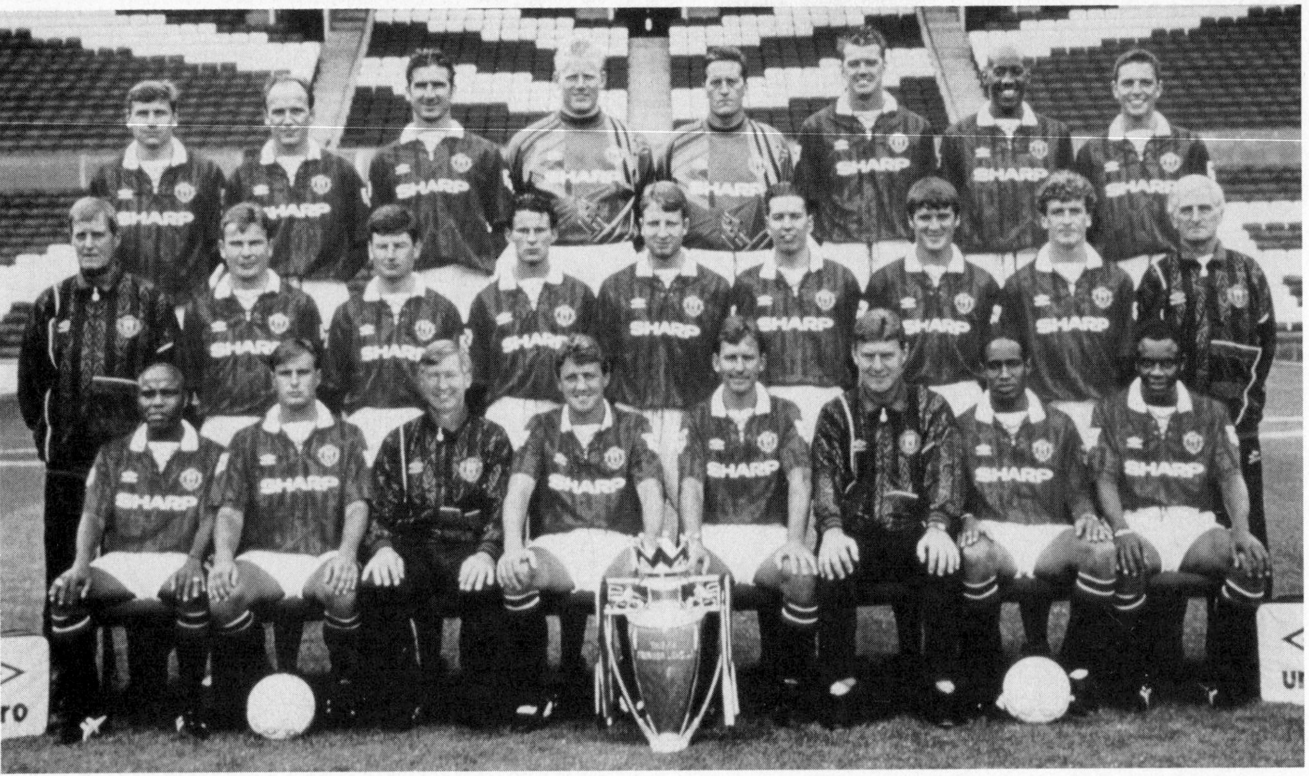

MANCHESTER UNITED 1993–94 *Back row (left to right):* Andrei Kanchelskis, Mike Phelan, Eric Cantona, Peter Schmeichel, Les Sealey, Gary Pallister, Dion Dublin, Lee Sharpe. *Centre row:* Norman Davies (Kit Manager), Brian McClair, Denis Irwin, Ryan Giggs, Lee Martin, Darren Ferguson, Roy Keane, Mark Hughes, Jim McGregor (Physio). *Front row:* Danny Wallace, Clayton Blackmore, Alex Ferguson (Manager), Steve Bruce, Bryan Robson, Brian Kidd (Assistant Manager), Paul Ince, Paul Parker.

FA Premiership MANCHESTER UNITED

Old Trafford, Manchester M16 0RA. Telephone 061–872 1661. Fax 061–876 5502. Ticket and Match Information: 061–872 0199. Membership enquiries: 061–872 5208. Souvenir shop: 061–872 3398.

Ground capacity: 43,500 (all-seater).

Record attendance: 76,962 Wolverhampton W v Grimsby T, FA Cup semi-final. 25 March 1939.

Club record: 70,504 v Aston Villa, Division 1, 27 December 1920.

Record receipts: £476,294 v Charlton Ath, FA Cup 6th rd, 12 March 1994.

Pitch measurements: 116yd × 76yd.

Chairman/Chief Executive: C. M. Edwards.

Directors: J. M. Edelson, R. Charlton CBE, E. M. Watkins LL.M., R. L. Olive, R. P. Launders.

Manager: Alex Ferguson. ***Assistant Manager:*** Brian Kidd.

Secretary: Kenneth Merrett. ***Commercial Manager:*** D. A. McGregor.

Year Formed: 1878 as Newton Heath LYR; 1902, Manchester United.

Turned Professional: 1885. ***Ltd Co.:*** 1907.

Previous Name: Newton Heath, 1880–1902.

Club Nickname: 'Red Devils'.

Previous Grounds: 1880–93, North Road, Monsall Road; 1893, Bank Street; 1910, Old Trafford (played at Maine Road 1941–49).

Record League Victory: 10–1 v Wolverhampton W, Division 1, 15 October 1892 – Warner; Mitchell, Clements; Perrins, Stewart (3), Erentz; Farman (1), Hood (1), Donaldson (3), Carson (1), Hendry (1).

Record Cup Victory: 10–0 v RSC Anderlecht, European Cup, Prel. rd (2nd leg), 26 September 1956 – Wood; Foulkes Byrne; Colman, Jones, Edwards; Berry (1), Whelan (2), Taylor (3), Viollet (4), Pegg.

Record Defeat: 0–7 v Blackburn R, Division 1, 10 April 1926 and v Aston Villa, Division 1, 27 December 1930 and v Wolverhampton W. Division 2, 26 December 1931.

Most League Points (2 for a win): 64, Division 1, 1956–57.

Most League Points (3 for a win): 92, FA Premier League, 1993–94.

Most League Goals: 103, Division 1, 1956–57 and 1958–59.

Highest League Scorer in Season: Dennis Viollet, 32, 1959–60.

Most League Goals in Total Aggregate: Bobby Charlton, 199, 1956–73.

Most Capped Player: Bobby Charlton, 106, England.

Most League Appearances: Bobby Charlton, 606, 1956–73.

Record Transfer Fee Received: £1,800,000 from Barcelona for Mark Hughes, August 1986.

Record Transfer Fee Paid: £3,750,000 to Nottingham F for Roy Keane, July 1993.

Football League Record: 1892 Newton Heath elected to Division 1; 1894–1906 Division 2; 1906–22 Division 1; 1922–25 Division 2; 1925–31 Division 1; 1931–36 Division 2; 1936–37 Division 1; 1937–38 Division 2; 1938–74 Division 1; 1974–75 Division 2; 1975–92 Division 1; 1992– FA Premier League.

Honours: *FA Premier League:* – Champions 1992–93, 1993–94. *Football League:* Division 1 – Champions 1907–8, 1910–11, 1951–52, 1955–56, 1956–57, 1964–65, 1966–67; Runners-up 1946–47, 1947–48, 1948–49, 1950–51, 1958–59, 1963–64, 1967–68, 1979–80, 1987–88, 1991–92. Division 2 – Champions 1935–36, 1974–75; Runners-up 1896–97, 1905–06, 1924–25, 1937–38. *FA Cup:* Winners 1909, 1948, 1963, 1977, 1983, 1985, 1990, 1994; Runners-up 1957, 1958, 1976, 1979. *Football League Cup:* Winners 1991–92, 1982–83 (Runners-up), 1990–91 (Runners-up), 1993–94 (Runners-up). **European Competitions:** *European Cup:* 1956–57 (s-f), 1957–58 (s-f), 1965–66 (s-f), 1967–68 (winners), 1968–69 (s-f), 1993–94. *European Cup-Winners' Cup:* 1963–64, 1977–78, 1983–84, 1990–91 (winners). 1991–92. *European Fairs Cup:* 1964–65. *UEFA Cup:* 1976–77, 1980–81, 1982–83, 1984–85, 1992–93. *Super Cup:* 1991 (winners).

MANCHESTER UNITED 1993—94 LEAGUE RECORD

Match No.	Date	Venue	Opponents	Result		H/T Score	Lg. Pos.	Goalscorers	Attendance
1	Aug 15	A	Norwich C	W	2-0	1-0	—	Giggs, Robson	19,705
2	18	H	Sheffield U	W	3-0	2-0	—	Keane 2, Hughes	41,949
3	21	H	Newcastle U	D	1-1	1-0	3	Giggs	41,829
4	23	A	Aston Villa	W	2-1	1-1	—	Sharpe 2	39,624
5	28	A	Southampton	W	3-1	2-1	1	Sharpe, Cantona, Irwin	16,189
6	Sept 1	H	West Ham U	W	3-0	2-0	—	Sharpe, Cantona (pen), Bruce	44,613
7	11	A	Chelsea	L	0-1	0-1	1		37,064
8	19	H	Arsenal	W	1-0	1-0	—	Cantona	44,009
9	25	H	Swindon T	W	4-2	2-0	1	Kanchelskis, Cantona, Hughes 2	44,583
10	Oct 2	A	Sheffield W	W	3-2	0-0	1	Hughes 2, Giggs	34,548
11	16	H	Tottenham H	W	2-1	0-0	1	Keane, Sharpe	44,655
12	23	A	Everton	W	1-0	0-0	1	Sharpe	35,455
13	30	H	QPR	W	2-1	0-1	1	Cantona, Hughes	44,663
14	Nov 7	A	Manchester C	W	3-2	0-2	—	Cantona 2, Keane	35,155
15	20	H	Wimbledon	W	3-1	0-0	1	Pallister, Hughes, Kanchelskis	44,748
16	24	H	Ipswich T	D	0-0	0-0	—		43,300
17	27	A	Coventry C	W	1-0	0-0	—	Cantona	17,009
18	Dec 4	H	Norwich C	D	2-2	2-1	1	Giggs, McClair	44,694
19	7	A	Sheffield U	W	3-0	2-0	—	Hughes, Sharpe, Cantona	26,744
20	11	A	Newcastle U	D	1-1	0-0	1	Ince	36,332
21	19	H	Aston Villa	W	3-1	1-0	—	Cantona 2, Ince	44,499
22	26	H	Blackburn R	D	1-1	0-1	—	Ince	44,511
23	29	A	Oldham Ath	W	5-2	3-2	1	Kanchelskis, Cantona (pen), Bruce, Giggs 2	16,708
24	Jan 1	H	Leeds U	D	0-0	0-0	1		44,724
25	4	A	Liverpool	D	3-3	3-2	—	Bruce, Giggs, Irwin	42,795
26	15	A	Tottenham H	W	1-0	0-0	1	Calderwood (og)	31,343
27	22	H	Everton	W	1-0	1-0	1	Giggs	44,750
28	Feb 5	A	QPR	W	3-2	2-1	1	Kanchelskis, Cantona, Giggs	21,267
29	25	A	West Ham U	D	2-2	1-0	1	Hughes, Ince	28,832
30	Mar 5	H	Chelsea	L	0-1	0-0	1		44,745
31	16	H	Sheffield W	W	5-0	4-0	—	Giggs, Hughes, Ince, Cantona 2	43,669
32	19	A	Swindon T	D	2-2	1-1	1	Keane, Ince	18,102
33	22	A	Arsenal	D	2-2	1-1	—	Sharpe 2	36,203
34	30	H	Liverpool	W	1-0	1-0	—	Ince	44,751
35	Apr 2	A	Blackburn R	L	0-2	0-0	1		20,866
36	4	H	Oldham Ath	W	3-2	1-0	1	Giggs, Dublin, Ince	44,686
37	16	A	Wimbledon	L	0-1	0-1	1		28,553
38	23	H	Manchester C	W	2-0	2-0	1	Cantona 2	44,333
39	27	A	Leeds U	W	2-0	0-0	—	Kanchelskis, Giggs	41,127
40	May 1	A	Ipswich T	W	2-1	1-1	—	Cantona, Giggs	22,478
41	4	H	Southampton	W	2-0	0-0	—	Kanchelskis, Hughes	44,705
42	8	H	Coventry C	D	0-0	0-0	—		44,717

Final League Position: 1

GOALSCORERS

League (80): Cantona 18 (2 pens), Giggs 13, Hughes 11, Sharpe 9, Ince 8, Kanchelskis 6, Keane 5, Bruce 3, Irwin 2, Dublin 1, McClair 1, Pallister 1, Robson 1, own goal 1.
Coca-Cola Cup (19): Hughes 5, McClair 4, Giggs 3, Bruce 2, Sharpe 2, Cantona 1, Dublin 1, Kanchelskis 1.
FA Cup (18): Cantona 4 (2 pens), Hughes 4, Kanchelskis 3, Irwin 2, Giggs 1, Ince 1, Keane 1, McClair 1, Robson 1.

Schmeichel 40	Parker 39 + 1	Irwin 42	Bruce 41	Kanchelskis 28 + 3	Pallister 41	Robson 10 + 5	Ince 39	Keane 34 + 3	Hughes 36	Giggs 32 + 6	McClair 12 + 14	Sharpe 26 + 4	Cantona 34	Butt — + 1	Martin 1	Phelan 1 + 1	Ferguson 1 + 2	Dublin 1 + 4	Thornley — + 1	Walsh 2 + 1	Neville 1	McKee 1	*Match No.*
1	2	3	4	5	6	7	8	9	10	11													1
1	2	3	4	5	6	*7*	8	9	10	11	12												2
1	*2*	3	4	*5*	6	7	8	9	10	11	12	14											3
1	2	3	4	5	6		8	9	10	7		11											4
1	2	3	4	14	6		8	*9*	10	11	12	5	7										5
1	2	3	4	*10*	6	14	8	9		11	12	5	7										6
1	2	3	4		6	10	8	9		11	12	5	7										7
1	2	3	4		6		8	9	10	11	12	5	7										8
1	2	3	4	*11*	6		8	9	10	14	12	5	7										9
1	2	3	4	12	6		8	9	10	11		5	7										10
1	2	3	4		6	*7*		9	10	*11*	12	5	8	14									11
1		3	4		6		8	11	10		9	5	7		2								12
1	2	3	4				8	9	10	11		5	7			6							13
1	2	3	4	11	6		8	9	10	12		5	7										14
1	2	3	4	11	6	9	8		10			5	7			12							15
1	2	3	4	11	6	*9*	8		10	12		5	7				14						16
1	2	3	4		6		8		10	11		5	7				9						17
1	2	3	4	5	6		8		10	11	9	12	7										18
1	2	3	4		6		8	12	10	11	9	5	7										19
1	2	3	4	14	6		8	12	*10*	11	9	5	7										20
1	2	3	4	11	6		8	9	10	12		5	7										21
1	2	3	4		6		8	9	*10*	11	12	5	7				14						22
1	2	3	4	10	6	14	*8*	9		11	12	5	7										23
1	2	3	4	5	6	8		10		11	9		7										24
1	2	3	4	5	6		8	10		11	9		7										25
1	2	3	4	5	6		8	9	10	11	12		7										26
1	2	3	4	5	6		8	9	10	11			7										27
1	2	3	4	5	6		8	9	10	11			7										28
1	2	*3*	4	5	6		8	11	10		9		7					12	14				29
1	2	3	4	5	6	14	8	7	10	11	*9*							12					30
1	2	3	4	*5*	6	14	8	9	10	11	12		7										31
1	2	3	4		6		8	5	10	11	9		7										32
1	2	3	4		6		8	9	10	11	12	5	7										33
1	2	3	4	11	6	14	8	9	10	12		5	*7*										34
1	2	3	4	7	6		8	9	10	11	12	5											35
1		2	4	7	6		8	5	10	11	9	3						12					36
1	*2*	3	4	5	6	*7*	8		10	11	9	12						14					37
1	2	3	4	5	6		8	9	10	12		11	7										38
1	2	3	4	5	6		8	9	10	11			7										39
1	2	3	4	5	6		8	9	10	11		12	7							14			40
	4	2		5	6		8	9	10	11		3	7							1			41
	12	3	4		6	8		14			9	5	7					10		1	2	*11*	42

Coca-Cola Cup	Second Round	Stoke C (a)	1-2
		(h)	2-0
	Third Round	Leicester C (h)	5-1
	Fourth Round	Everton (a)	2-0
	Fifth Round	Portsmouth (h)	2-2
		(a)	1-0
	Semi-final	Sheffield W (h)	1-0
		(a)	4-1
	Final at Wembley	Aston Villa	1-3
FA Cup	Third Round	Sheffield U (a)	1-0
	Fourth Round	Norwich C (a)	2-0
	Fifth Round	Wimbledon (a)	3-0
	Sixth Round	Charlton Ath (h)	3-1
	Semi-final at Wembley	Oldham Ath	1-1
	Replay at Maine Road		4-1
	Final at Wembley	Chelsea	4-0

MANCHESTER UNITED

Player and Position	Ht	Wt	Birth Date	Birth Place	Source	Clubs	League App	League Gls
Goalkeepers								
Jim Leighton (To Hibernian)	6 1	12 09	24 7 58	Johnstone	Dalry Thistle	Aberdeen	300	—
						Manchester U	73	—
						Arsenal (loan)	—	—
						Reading (loan)	8	—
						Dundee	21	—
						Sheffield U (loan)	—	—
Kevin Pilkington	6 0	12 00	5 3 74	Hitchin	Trainee	Manchester U	—	—
Peter Schmeichel	6 4	13 06	18 11 68	Glodsone	Brondby	Manchester U	122	—
Les Sealey*	6 1	13 06	29 9 57	Bethnal Green	Apprentice	Coventry C	158	—
						Luton T	207	—
						Plymouth Arg (loan)	6	—
						Manchester U (loan)	2	—
						Manchester U	31	—
						Aston Villa	18	—
						Coventry C (loan)	2	—
						Birmingham C (loan)	12	—
						Manchester U	—	—
Gary Walsh	6 1	13 01	21 3 68	Wigan		Manchester U	40	—
						Airdrie (loan)	3	—
						Oldham Ath (loan)	6	—
Defenders								
Steve Bruce	6 0	12 6	31 12 60	Newcastle	Apprentice	Gillingham	205	29
						Norwich C	141	14
						Manchester U	244	33
Chris Casper	5 11	10 09	28 4 75	Burnley	Trainee	Manchester U	—	—
Denis Irwin	5 8	11 00	31 70 65	Cork	Apprentice	Leeds U	72	1
						Oldham Ath	167	4
						Manchester U	154	11
Patrick McGibbon	6 0	11 07	6 9 73	Lurgan	Portadown	Manchester U	—	—
Lee Martin (To Celtic March 1994)	5 11	11 05	5 2 68	Hyde		Manchester U	73	1
Colin Murdock	6 1	12 00	2 7 75	Ballymena	Trainee	Manchester U	—	—
Gary Neville	5 10	11 04	18 2 75	Bury	Trainee	Manchester U	1	—
John O'Kane	5 10	11 04	15 11 74	Nottingham	Trainee	Manchester U	—	—
Gary Pallister	6 4	13 04	30 6 65	Ramsgate		Middlesbrough	156	5
						Darlington (loan)	7	—
						Manchester U	194	6
Paul Parker	5 7	10 13	4 4 64	Essex	Apprentice	Fulham	153	2
						QPR	125	1
						Manchester U	97	1
Mike Phelan*	5 11	11 01	24 9 62	Nelson	Apprentice	Burnley	168	9
						Norwich C	156	9
						Manchester U	102	2
Steven Riley*	5 9	10 09	6 2 75	Manchester	Trainee	Manchester U	—	—
Neil Whitworth	6 2	12 06	12 4 72	Ince	Trainee	Wigan Ath	2	—
						Manchester U	1	—
						Preston NE (loan)	6	—
						Barnsley (loan)	11	—
						Rotherham U (loan)	8	1
						Blackpool (loan)	3	—
Midfield								
David Beckham	5 11	10 09	2 5 75	Leytonstone	Trainee	Manchester U	—	—
Clayton Blackmore*	5 9	11 06	23 9 64	Neath	Apprentice	Manchester U	186	19
Karl Brown*	5 5	9 09	7 2 75	Unsworth	Trainee	Manchester U	—	—
Nicky Butt	5 10	11 00	21 1 75	Manchester	Trainee	Manchester U	2	—
Simon Davies	5 11	10 02	23 4 74	Winsford	Trainee	Manchester U	—	—
						Exeter C (loan)	6	1
Craig Dean	5 10	11 07	1 7 75	Nuneaton	Trainee	Manchester U	—	—
Paul Ince	5 10	11 07	21 10 67	Ilford	Trainee	West Ham U	72	7
						Manchester U	170	19
Andrei Kanchelskis	5 10	12 04	23 1 69	Kirowgrad	Donezts	Manchester U	93	14
Roy Keane	5 10	11 03	10 8 71	Cork	Cobh Ramblers	Nottingham F	114	22
						Manchester U	37	5
Craig Lawton*	5 7	10 03	5 1 72	Mancot	Trainee	Manchester U	—	—
Mark Rawlinson	5 8	11 11	9 6 75	Bolton	Trainee	Manchester U	—	—

MANCHESTER UNITED

Colours: Red shirts, white shorts, black stockings. **Change colours:** Black shirts, black shorts, black stockings.

Foundation: Manchester United was formed as comparatively recently as 1902 after their predecessors, Newton Heath, went bankrupt. However, it is usual to give the date of the club's foundation as 1878 when employees of the Lancashire and Yorkshire Railway Company formed Newton Heath L and YR. Cricket and Football Club. They won the Manchester Cup in 1886 and as Newton Heath FC were admitted to the Second Division in 1892.

First Football League game: 3 September, 1892, Division 1, v Blackburn R (a) L 3-4 – Warner; Clements, Brown; Perrins, Stewart, Erentz; Farman (1), Coupar (1), Donaldson (1), Carson, Mathieson.

Did you know: Steve Bruce became the first Englishman to captain the League and Cup double winners in the present century when he led Manchester United to their triumph last season.

Managers (and Secretary-Managers)
Ernest Magnall 1900–12, John Robson 1914–21, John Chapman 1921–26, Clarence Hildrith 1926–27, Herbert Bamlett 1927–31, Walter Crickmer 1931–32, Scott Duncan 1932–37, Jimmy Porter 1938–44, Walter Crickmer 1944–45*, Matt Busby 1945–69 (continued as GM then Director), Wilf McGuinness 1969–70, Frank O'Farrell 1971–72, Tommy Docherty 1972–77, Dave Sexton 1977–81, Ron Atkinson 1981–86, Alex Ferguson November 1986–

Bryan Robson*	5 10	11 11	11 1 57	Chester-le-Street	Apprentice	WBA	197	39
						Manchester U	345	74
Lee Sharpe	5 11	11 04	25 7 71	Halesowen	Trainee	Torquay U	14	3
						Manchester U	134	14
Forwards								
Eric Cantona	6 1	12 10	24 5 66	Paris		Auxerre	13	2
						Martigues	—	—
						Auxerre	68	21
						Marseille	22	5
						Bordeaux	11	6
						Montpellier	33	10
						Marseille	18	8
						Nimes	17	2
						Leeds U	28	9
						Manchester U	56	27
Dion Dublin	6 0	12 04	22 4 69	Leicester		Norwich C	—	—
						Cambridge U	156	52
						Manchester U	12	2
Ryan Giggs	5 11	10 10	29 11 73	Cardiff	School	Manchester U	119	27
Keith Gillespie	5 9	11 00	18 2 75	Larne	Trainee	Manchester U	—	—
						Wigan Ath (loan)	8	4
Mark Hughes	5 9	11 12	1 11 63	Wrexham	Apprentice	Manchester U	89	37
					Barcelona, Bayern Munich	Manchester U	222	74
Richard Irving	5 8	10 07	10 9 75	Halifax	Trainee	Manchester U	—	—
Brian McClair	5 9	12 00	8 12 63	Bellshill	Apprentice	Aston Villa	—	—
						Motherwell	39	15
						Celtic	145	99
						Manchester U	261	80
Colin McKee	5 10	11 00	22 8 73	Glasgow	Trainee	Manchester U	1	—
						Bury (loan)	2	—
Giuliano Maiorana*	5 9	11 08	18 4 69	Cambridge	Histon	Manchester U	7	—
Joe Roberts*	5 8	10 10	12 9 74	Crewe	Trainee	Manchester U	—	—
Robert Savage*	5 11	10 01	18 10 74	Wrexham	Trainee	Manchester U	—	—
Paul Scholes	5 8	10 07	16 11 74	Salford	Trainee	Manchester U	—	—
Ben Thornley	5 8	10 07	21 4 75	Bury	Trainee	Manchester U	1	—

Trainees
Appleton, Michael A; Baker, Desmond L; Barnes, Lee M; Clegg, Michael J; Cooke, Terence J; Flash, Richard G; Gardner, David S; Gibson, Paul R; Hall, Daniel J; Hall, Stephen; Hart, Ian M; Heckingbottom, Paul; Hudson, Vincent, J; Johnson, David A; Lyons, Paul; McDonald, Robert F; Mitten, Paul J; Monaghan, Matthew S; Mustoe, Neil J; Neville, Philip J; Parkin, Daniel J; Pierce, David E; Ryan, Mark; Twynham, Gary S; Westwood, Ashley M; Whittam, Philip R.

Associated Schoolboys
Bickerton, Gary; Brightwell, Stuart; Byers, James A; Calderone, Christopher J; Crossland, Mark D; Curtis, John C. K; Devenney, Michael P; Dickman, Elliott; Fitzpatrick, Lee G; Ford, Ryan; Higginbotham, Daniel J; Kaye, Peter J; Lamb, Kris A; Marston, Neil J; McLoughlin, Clinton A; Michael, James D; Millard, Ross J; Mills, Leon J; Naylor, Gavin E; Phillips, Paul D; Ryan, Michael S. P; Wilson, Mark A; Wood, Jamie.

Associated Schoolboys who have accepted the Club's offer of a Traineeship/Contract
Duncan, Andrew; Hilton, David; Macken, Jonathan P; Maxon, Heath R; Mulryne, Philip P; Smith, Thomas; Teather, Paul; Trees, Robert V; Twiss, Michael J; Wallwork, Ronald.

MANSFIELD TOWN 1993–94 *Back row (left to right):* Dominic Crooks, Steve Foster, Chris Timons, Darren Ward, Stephen Brown, Jason Pearcey, Kevin Gray, Paul McLoughlin.
Third row: Bill Dearden (Assistant Manager), Rob Musson, Steve Wilkinson, Ian Stringfellow, Paul Holland, Nicky Clarke, Alex Sykes, Kevin Noteman, Wayne Stark, John Newman (Chief Scout), Dennis Pettitt (Physio).
Second row: Dean Marrows, Steve Parkin, Chris Perkins, Paul Fleming, George Foster (Manager), Lee Wilson, Gary Castledine, Wayne Fairclough, Michael Williams, Michael Baines.
Front row: Bryan Rafferty, Jamie Morgan, Paul Handford, Lee Wilkinson, Jamie Hague, Chris Kerry, Lea Whyman, Mark Wood.

Division 3 MANSFIELD TOWN

Field Mill Ground, Quarry Lane, Mansfield, NG18 5DA. Telepone Manfield (0623) 23567. Commercial Office/Shop: 0623 658070. Fax: 0623 25014

Ground capacity: 10,468.

Record attendance: 24,467 v Nottingham F, FA Cup 3rd rd, 10 January 1953.

Record receipts: £46,915 v Sheffield W, FA Cup 3rd rd, 5 January 1991.

Pitch measurements: 115yd × 70yd.

Chairman/Chief Executive: Keith Haslam.

Directors: K. Walker, Mrs M. Haslam.

Manager: Andy King. ***Assistant Manager:*** Bill Dearden.

Physio: Barry Statham.

Community Scheme Organiser: D. Bentley Tel: 0623 25197.

Secretary: Mick Horton. ***Marketing Manager:*** L. Smith.

Year Formed: 1910. ***Turned Professional:*** 1910. ***Ltd Co.:*** 1921.

Previous Name: Mansfield Wesleyans 1891–1910.

Club Nickname: 'The Stags'.

Record League Victory: 9–2 v Rotherham U, Division 3 (N), 27 December 1932 – Wilson; Anthony, England; Davies, S. Robinson, Slack; Prior, Broom, Readman (3), Hoyland (3), Bowater (3).

Record Cup Victory: 8–0 v Scarborough (away), FA Cup, 1st rd, 22 November 1952 – Bramley; Chessell, Bradley; Field, Plummer, Lewis; Scott, Fox (3), Marron (2), Sid Watson (1), Adam (2).

Record Defeat: 1–8 v Walsall, Division 3 (N), 19 January 1933.

Most League Points (2 for a win): 68, Division 4, 1974–75.

Most League Points (3 for a win): 81, Division 4, 1985–86.

Most League Goals: 108, Division 4, 1962–63.

Highest League Scorer in Season: Ted Harston, 55, Division 3 (N), 1936–37.

Most League Goals in Total Aggregate: Harry Johnson, 104, 1931–36.

Most Capped Player: John McClelland, 6 (53), Northern Ireland.

Most League Appearances: Rod Arnold, 440, 1970–83.

Record Transfer Fee Received: £500,000 from Middlesbrough for Simon Coleman, September 1989.

Record Transfer Fee Paid: £80,000 to Leicester C for Steve Wilkinson, September 1989.

Football League Record: 1931 Elected to Division 3 (S); 1932–37 Division 3 (N); 1937–47 Division 3 (S); 1947–58 Division 3 (N); 1958–60 Division 3; 1960–63 Division 4; 1963–72 Division 3; 1972–75 Division 4; 1975–77 Division 3; 1977–78 Division 2; 1978–80 Division 3; 1980–86 Division 4; 1986–91 Division 3; 1991–92 Division 4; 1992–93 Division 2; 1993– Division 3.

Honours: *Football League:* Division 2 best season: 21st, 1977–78; Division 3 – Champions 1976–77; Division 4 – Champions 1974–75; Division 3 (N) – Runners-up 1950–51. *FA Cup:* best season: 6th rd, 1968–69. *Football League Cup:* best season: 5th rd, 1975–76. *Freight Rover Trophy:* Winners 1986–87.

MANSFIELD TOWN 1993—94 LEAGUE RECORD

Match No.	Date	Venue	Opponents	Result		H/T Score	Lg. Pos.	Goalscorers	Attendance
1	Aug 14	H	Shrewsbury T	W	1-0	0-0	—	Noteman	2983
2	28	H	Scunthorpe U	L	0-1	0-1	15		2751
3	31	A	Chesterfield	W	2-0	0-0	—	Clarke, Wilson	5712
4	Sept 4	A	Crewe Alex	L	1-2	0-0	14	Stant	3155
5	11	H	Lincoln C	W	1-0	0-0	10	Wilkinson	2678
6	17	A	Doncaster R	W	1-0	0-0	—	Noteman	4340
7	25	H	Preston NE	D	2-2	0-1	8	Noteman, Wilkinson	3762
8	Oct 2	A	Bury	D	2-2	1-1	9	Reed, Stringfellow	2317
9	9	H	Scarborough	W	4-2	1-0	7	Young (og), Gray, Noteman (pen), Stringfellow	2589
10	12	A	Northampton T	L	1-5	1-1	—	McLoughlin	2462
11	16	A	Carlisle U	D	1-1	0-1	6	Stringfellow	4480
12	23	H	Chester C	L	0-4	0-0	9		2545
13	30	A	Wigan Ath	L	1-4	0-2	12	Clarke	1434
14	Nov 2	A	Rochdale	D	1-1	1-1	—	Reed	2042
15	6	H	Gillingham	W	2-1	0-1	11	Holland, Clarke	2421
16	20	A	Darlington	L	0-2	0-1	12		2043
17	27	H	Walsall	L	1-2	0-1	15	Wilkinson	2875
18	Dec 11	H	Northampton T	W	1-0	1-0	13	Holland	2491
19	17	A	Shrewsbury T	D	2-2	1-0	—	Wilkinson, McLoughlin	3392
20	27	A	Colchester U	D	0-0	0-0	12		3476
21	Jan 1	A	Torquay U	L	0-1	0-0	15		3496
22	3	H	Chesterfield	L	1-2	0-1	17	Wilkinson	4272
23	15	H	Carlisle U	L	0-1	0-1	18		2378
24	18	H	Hereford U	W	2-1	0-1	—	Gray, Blissett	1802
25	22	A	Scarborough	D	1-1	0-0	13	Holland	1557
26	25	A	Wycombe W	L	0-1	0-0	—		4424
27	29	H	Wigan Ath	L	2-3	0-0	17	Timons, Fairclough	2285
28	Feb 5	A	Chester C	D	1-1	0-1	17	Wilkinson	2664
29	12	H	Wycombe W	W	3-0	1-0	14	Fairclough, Hadley, Wilkinson	3009
30	19	A	Scunthorpe U	W	3-2	0-0	11	Hadley 2, Holland	3089
31	25	H	Crewe Alex	L	1-2	1-2	12	Holland	3509
32	Mar 5	A	Lincoln C	W	2-1	1-1	11	Johnson A (og), Noteman	3384
33	12	H	Doncaster R	W	2-1	1-0	11	Parkin, Rees	2763
34	19	A	Preston NE	L	1-3	0-1	12	Wilkinson	6747
35	26	H	Bury	D	2-2	1-2	12	Holland, Hadley	2496
36	Apr 2	H	Colchester U	D	1-1	1-1	13	Holland	2117
37	4	A	Hereford U	W	3-2	2-0	12	Wilkinson 2, Hadley	1996
38	9	H	Torquay U	W	2-1	2-1	10	Ireland, Boothroyd	2260
39	16	H	Rochdale	L	0-1	0-0	11		2362
40	23	A	Gillingham	L	0-1	0-0	14		2390
41	30	H	Darlington	L	0-3	0-1	14		2734
42	May 7	A	Walsall	W	2-0	1-0	12	Sykes, Lampkin	4304

Final League Position: 12

GOALSCORERS

League (53): Wilkinson 10, Holland 7, Hadley 5, Noteman 5 (1 pen), Clarke 3, Stringfellow 3, Fairclough 2, Gray 2, McLoughlin 2, Reed 2, Blissett 1, Boothroyd 1, Ireland 1, Lampkin 1, Parkin 1, Rees 1, Stant 1, Sykes 1, Timons 1, Wilson 1, own goals 2.
Coca-Cola Cup (3): McLoughlin 1, Noteman 1, Stant 1.
FA Cup (1): Wilkinson 1.

Pearcey 9	Perkins 2 + 1	Platnauer 25	Stringfellow 10 + 4	Gray 42	Clarke 14 + 1	Noteman 29 + 4	Holland 38	Stant 4	McLoughlin 19 + 4	Castledine 14 + 7	Wilkinson 36 + 6	Foster S 2 + 3	Fairclough 27 + 2	Wilson 9 + 5	Fleming 25 + 3	Ward 33	Reed 12 + 1	Parkin 21 + 2	Boothroyd 22 + 1	Rees 15	Blissett 4 + 1	Sykes 1 + 1	Timons 15 + 1	Hadley 14	Lampkin 11 + 2	Ireland 8 + 1	Kerry 1 + 1	Stark — + 1	Match No.
1	2	3	4	5	6	7	8	9	10	11	12																		1
1		3		5	6	7	8	9	11	14	12	2	*4*	10															2
1		3		5	6	7	8	9	11		10		4	12	2														3
1		3		5	6	7	*8*	9	11	14	12		4	10	2														4
		3	12	5	*6*	7	8		9	14	11		4	10	2	1													5
		3		5	6	7	8		9		10		4	11	2	1													6
		3	12	5	6	7	8		9		10		4	*11*	2	1	14												7
1		3	8	5		7			9	6	10	12	4		2		11												8
1		3	8	5	14	7	10		9	6	12		*4*		2		11												9
1		3	8	5	6		10		9		7		4		2		11												10
		3	8	5	6		10		9	7	12		*4*		2	1	11	14											11
		3	8	5	6	7	10		9	4	12				2	1	11												12
		3		5	6	4			9	7	10			8	2	1	11	12											13
				5	6	10	4			7	9	2		8	12	1	11	3											14
		3	*4*	5	6	7	8		12		9		14		2	1	11	10											15
		3	4	5	6		8				9	12	7		2	1	11	10											16
		3	*4*	5			8		12	6	9	14	7		2	1	11	10											17
	14	3	12	5			4		6		9		7	8		1	*11*	10	2										18
		3		5			8		6		9		7		2	1	11	10	4										19
		3		5		7	4		8		9			12	2	1		10	11	6									20
		3		5		7	4		*8*		9			12	2	1		10	11	6	14								21
		3		5		*7*	4		12		9		11	14	2	1		10		6	8								22
	3			5		7	4			10	9		11			1			2	6	8	12							23
		3		5		7	4		8		9		6		12	1			2	11	10								24
		3		5		7	4		8	14	9		6		2	1			12	11	*10*								25
		3	8	5		12	4			10	9		6		2	1				11			7						26
		3	12	5		8	4			10	9		6		14	1			2	11			7						27
				5		12	6				9		4	10	2	1		8	3	11			7						28
				5		12	4				9		6	14	2	1		8	3	11			7	*10*					29
				5			4				9		6			1		8	3	11			7	10	2				30
				5		12	4				9		6			1		8	3	11			7	10	2				31
				5		6	4				9					1		8	3	11			7	10	2				32
				5		6	4		12		9					1		8	3	11			7	10	2				33
				5		*6*	4			12	9					1		8	3	11			7	10	2	14			34
				5		6	4			8	9					1			3				7	10	2	11			35
				5		6	4			8	9		12			1			3				7	10	2	11			36
				5		6	4			12	9					1		8	3				7	10	2	11			37
				5		6	4				9					1		8	3				7	10	2	11			38
				5		7	4			12	9		6			1		8	3				14	10	*2*	11			39
1				5		*7*					9		6		2			8	3				4	10	12	11	14		40
1				5			4			7	9		6		2			8	3					10	12	11			41
				5							9				2	1			3			4	6	10	8	11	7	12	42

Coca-Cola Cup	First Round	Stoke C (a)	2-2
		(h)	1-3
FA Cup	First Round	Preston NE (h)	1-2

MANSFIELD TOWN

Player and Position	Ht	Wt	Birth Date	Birth Place	Source	Clubs	League App	League Gls
Goalkeepers								
Jason Pearcey	6 1	13 06	2 7 71	Leamington Spa	Trainee	Mansfield T	74	—
Darren Ward	5 11	12 09	11 5 74	Worksop	Trainee	Mansfield T	46	—
Defenders								
Adrian Boothroyd	5 8	10 12	8 2 71	Bradford	Trainee	Huddersfield T	10	—
						Bristol R	16	—
						Hearts	4	—
						Mansfield T	23	1
Nicky Clarke‡	5 11	13 11	20 8 67	Walsall	Apprentice	Wolverhampton W	81	1
						Mansfield T	43	5
						Chesterfield (loan)	7	—
						Doncaster R (loan)	5	—
					Bromsgrove R	Preston NE (loan)	—	—
Wayne Fairclough*	5 10	12 02	27 4 68	Nottingham	Apprentice	Notts Co	71	—
						Mansfield T	141	12
Paul Fleming	5 7	11 08	6 9 67	Halifax		Halifax T	139	1
						Mansfield T	66	—
George Foster‡	5 10	11 02	26 9 56	Plymouth	Apprentice	Plymouth Arg	212	6
						Torquay U (loan)	6	3
						Exeter C (loan)	28	—
						Derby Co	30	—
						Mansfield T	373	—
Stephen Foster‡			3 12 74	Mansfield	Trainee	Mansfield T	5	—
Simeon Hodson	5 10	11 06	5 3 66	Lincoln	Apprentice	Notts Co	27	—
						Charlton Ath	5	—
						Lincoln C	56	—
						Newport Co	34	1
						WBA	83	—
						Doncaster R	15	—
						Mansfield T	17	—
Steve Parkin	5 6	11 07	7 11 65	Mansfield	Apprentice	Stoke C	113	5
						WBA	48	2
						Mansfield T	39	1
Chris Perkins*	5 11	10 09	9 1 74	Nottingham	Trainee	Mansfield T	8	—
Chris Timons			8 12 74	Nottingham	Clipstone W	Mansfield T	16	1
Midfield								
Kevin Gray	6 0	13 08	7 1 72	Sheffield	Trainee	Mansfield T	141	3
Paul Holland	5 11	12 05	8 7 73	Lincoln	School	Mansfield T	116	16
Kevin Lampkin	5 10	11 08	20 12 72	Liverpool	Trainee	Liverpool	—	—
						Huddersfield T	13	—
						Mansfield T	13	1
Wayne Stark§			14 10 76	Derby	Trainee	Mansfield T	1	—
Forwards								
Gary Castledine	5 8	11 04	27 3 70	Dumfries		Mansfield T	56	3
Stewart Hadley	6 0	13 02	30 12 73	Dudley	Halesowen	Derby Co	—	—
						Mansfield T	14	5
Chris Kerry§			15 4 76	Chesterfield	Trainee	Mansfield T	2	—
Paul McLoughlin	5 10	11 11	23 12 63	Bristol	Bristol C	Cardiff C	49	4
					Gisborne C	Hereford U	74	14
						Wolverhampton W	28	4
						Walsall (loan)	9	4
						York C (loan)	1	—
						Mansfield T	61	9
Kevin Noteman	5 10	11 12	15 10 69	Preston	Trainee	Leeds U	1	—
						Doncaster R	106	20
						Mansfield T	63	9
Ian Stringfellow‡	5 9	11 04	8 5 69	Nottingham	Apprentice	Mansfield T	167	28
						Blackpool (loan)	3	1
						Chesterfield (loan)	1	—
Alex Sykes*	5 4	11 07	2 4 74	Mansfield	School	Mansfield T	2	1

MANSFIELD TOWN

Colours: All yellow with navy blue trim. **Change colours:** White shirts, black shorts, black stockings all with red trim.

Foundation: Many records give the date of Mansfield Town's formation as 1905. But the present club did not come into being until 1910 when the Mansfield Wesleyans (formed 1891) and playing in the Notts and District League, decided to spread their wings and changed their name to Mansfield Town, joining the new Central Alliance in 1911.

First Football League game: 29 August, 1931, Division 3(S), v Swindon T (h) W 3-2 – Wilson; Clifford, England; Wake, Davis, Blackburn; Gilhespy, Readman (1), Johnson, Broom (2), Baxter.

Did you know: Mansfield Town won a friendly against a Netherlands FA XI on 23 September 1931 played under floodlights in Holland. John Jepson scored both goals in a 2-1 win four days after his only League game for them.

Managers (and Secretary-Managers)
John Baynes 1922–25, Ted Davison 1926–28, Jack Hickling 1928–33, Henry Martin 1933–35, Charlie Bell 1935, Harold Wightman 1936, Harold Parkes 1936–38, Jack Poole 1938–44, Lloyd Barke 1944–45, Roy Goodall 1945–49, Freddie Steele 1949–51, George Jobey 1952–53, Stan Mercer 1953–55, Charlie Mitten 1956–58, Sam Weaver 1958–60, Raich Carter 1960–63, Tommy Cummings 1963–67, Tommy Eggleston 1967–70, Jock Basford 1970–71, Danny Williams 1971–74, Dave Smith 1974–76, Peter Morris 1976–78, Billy Bingham 1978–79, Mick Jones 1979–81, Stuart Boam 1981–83, Ian Greaves 1983–89, George Foster 1989–93, Andy King November 1993–

Player and Position	*Ht*	*Wt*	*Birth Date*	*Birth Place*	*Source*	*Clubs*	*League App*	*League Gls*
Steve Wilkinson	6 0	11 02	1 9 68	Lincoln	Apprentice	Leicester C	9	1
						Rochdale (loan)	—	—
						Crewe Alex (loan)	5	2
						Mansfield T	191	61
Lee Wilson*	5 10	11 03	23 5 72	Mansfield	Clipstone W	Mansfield T	18	1

Trainees
Baines, Michael; Hague, Jamie; Handford, Paul M; Kerry, Christopher B; Marrows, Dean; Morgan, James K; Musson, Robert J; Stark, Wayne R; Turner, Martin; Wilkinson, Lee A; Williams, Michael J; Wood, Mark J.

****Non-Contract**
Lampkin, Kevin

Associated Schoolboys
Baughan, Russell M; Burley, Dean A; Johnson, Craig A; Jones, Ryan; Leech, James; Rankin, Darrel A; Sedlan, Jason M; Sisson, Michael A; Storer, David J; Whitehead, James R; Williams, Ryan N; Winter, David M; Wright, Darren.

Associated Schoolboys who have accepted the Club's offer of a Traineeship/Contract
Clarke, Darrell J; Hopley, Dean C; Spink, Neil D.

**Non-Contract Players who are retained must be re-signed before they are eligible to play in League matches.

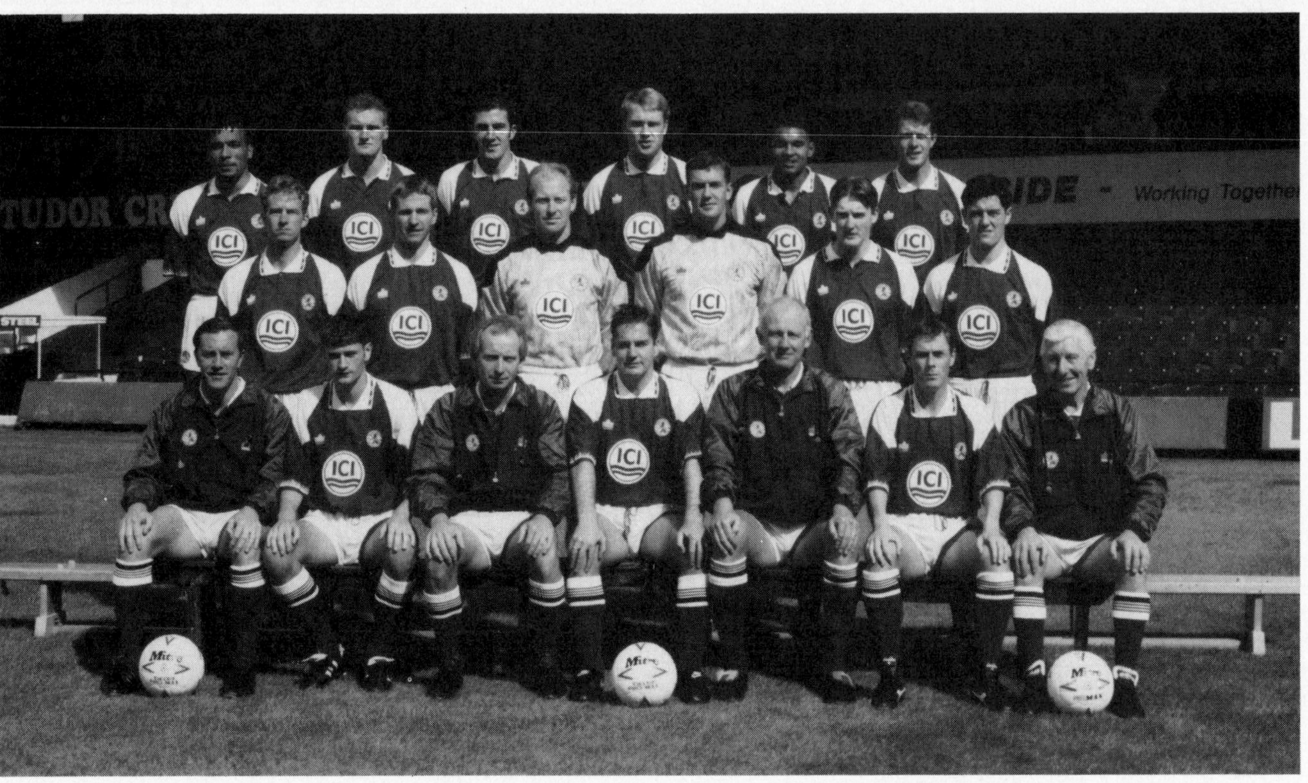

MIDDLESBROUGH 1993–94 *Back row (left to right):* Craig Fleming, Nicky Mohan, Paul Wilkinson, Alan Kernaghan, Richard Liburd, Derek Whyte.
Centre row: Robbie Mustoe, Chris Morris, Steve Pears, Ian Ironside, Jamie Pollock, Graham Kavanagh.
Front row: Mark Nile (Physio), Alan Moore, Lennie Lawrence (Manager), John Hendrie, John Pickering (Assistant Manager), Tommy Wright, Tommy Johnson (Physio).

Division 1 **MIDDLESBROUGH**

Ayresome Park, Middlesbrough, Cleveland TS1 4PB. Telephone Middlesbrough (0642) 819659. Commercial Dept. (0642) 826664. Ticket office: (0642) 815996. Fax (0642) 820244. Clubcall: 0891 121181.

Ground capacity: 26,629.

Record attendance: 53,596 v Newcastle U, Division 1, 27 December 1949.

Record receipts: £200,351 v Newcastle U, Coca Cola Cup 2nd rd 2nd leg, 7 October 1992.

Pitch measurements: 114yd × 74yd.

Chairman: S. Gibson.

Directors: G. Cooke, R. Corbidge, G. Fordy.

Chief Executive/Secretary: Keith Lamb.

Manager:Bryan Robson. ***Assistant Manager:*** Viv Anderson.

Physio: Mark Nile. ***Commercial Director:*** G. Fordy.

Youth Development Officer: Ron Bone.

Year Formed: 1876. ***Turned Professional:*** 1889; became amateur 1892, and professional again, 1899. ***Ltd Co:*** 1892.

Club Nickname: 'The Boro'.

Previous Grounds: 1877, Old Archery Ground, Linthorpe Road; 1903, Ayresome Park.

Record League Victory: 9–0 v Brighton & HA, Division 2, 23 August 1958 – Taylor; Bilcliff, Robinson; Harris (2 pens), Phillips, Walley; Day, McLean, Clough (5), Peacock (2), Holliday.

Record Cup Victory: 9–3 v Goole T, FA Cup, 1st rd, 9 January 1915 – Williamson; Haworth, Weir; Davidson, Cook, Malcolm; Wilson, Carr (3), Elliott (3), Tinsley (3), Davies.

Record Defeat: 0–9 v Blackburn R, Division 2, 6 November 1954.

Most League Points (2 for a win): 65, Division 2, 1973–74.

Most League Points (3 for a win): 94, Division 3, 1986–87.

Most League Goals: 122, Division 2, 1926–27.

Highest League Scorer in Season: George Camsell, 59, Division 2, 1926–27 (Second Division record).

Most League Goals in Total Aggregate: George Camsell, 326, 1925–39.

Most Capped Player: Wilf Mannion, 26, England.

Most League Appearances: Tim Williamson, 563, 1902–23.

Record Transfer Fee Received: £2,300,000 from Manchester United for Gary Pallister, August 1989.

Record Transfer Fee Paid: £900,000 to Celtic for Derek Whyte, August 1992.

Football League Record: 1899 Elected to Division 2; 1902–24 Division 1; 1924–27 Division 2; 1927–28 Division 1; 1928–29 Division 2; 1929–54 Division 1; 1954–66 Division 2; 1966–67 Division 3; 1967–74 Division 2; 1974–82 Division 1; 1982–86 Division 2; 1986–87 Division 3; 1987–88 Division 2; 1988–89 Division 1; 1989–92 Division 2; 1992–93 FA Premier League; 1993– Division 1.

Honours: *Football League:* Division 1 best season: 3rd, 1913–14. Division 2 – Champions 1926–27, 1928–29, 1973–74; Runners-up 1901–02, 1991–92. Division 3 – Runners-up 1966–67, 1986–87. *FA Cup:* best season: 6th rd, 1935–36, 1946–47, 1969–70, 1974–75, 1976–77, 1977–78; old last eight 1900–01, 1903–04. *Football League Cup:* Semi-final 1975–76. *Amateur Cup:* Winners 1895, 1898, *Anglo-Scottish Cup:* Winners 1975–76.

MIDDLESBROUGH 1993—94 LEAGUE RECORD

Match No.	Date	Venue	Opponents	Result		H/T Score	Lg. Pos.	Goalscorers	Attendance
1	Aug 14	A	Notts Co	W	3-2	2-0	—	Wilkinson, Moore 2	9392
2	21	H	Derby Co	W	3-0	2-0	1	Kernaghan, Short (og), Hendrie	15,168
3	24	A	Barnsley	W	4-1	1-1	—	Moore 2, Hendrie 2	10,597
4	28	A	Wolverhampton W	W	3-2	1-2	1	Hendrie 2, Pollock	21,061
5	Sept 11	A	Southend U	L	0-1	0-0	2		6495
6	14	H	Stoke C	L	1-2	1-2	—	Hignett	13,189
7	18	H	Luton T	D	0-0	0-0	4		12,487
8	25	A	WBA	D	1-1	0-0	5	Whyte	15,766
9	29	H	Leicester C	W	2-0	1-0	—	Wilkinson, Hendrie	11,871
10	Oct 2	H	Birmingham C	D	2-2	1-0	4	Hendrie, Moore	13,801
11	10	A	Watford	L	0-2	0-0	—		7582
12	17	H	Sunderland	W	4-1	3-1	—	Hignett, Hendrie, Wilkinson 2	12,772
13	24	A	Millwall	D	1-1	1-1	—	Barber (og)	6686
14	30	H	Peterborough U	D	1-1	1-1	5	Mustoe	10,704
15	Nov 2	A	Portsmouth	L	0-2	0-0	—		12,503
16	6	H	Bristol C	L	0-1	0-1	10		9687
17	21	H	Bolton W	L	0-1	0-1	—		6828
18	Dec 4	A	Bristol C	D	0-0	0-0	13		8441
19	11	A	Stoke C	L	1-3	0-2	15	Peake	13,777
20	18	H	Notts Co	W	3-0	3-0	14	Moore, Kavanagh 2	7869
21	27	A	Nottingham F	D	1-1	0-0	14	Moore	26,901
22	29	H	Tranmere R	D	0-0	0-0	14		12,351
23	Jan 1	A	Oxford U	D	1-1	0-0	14	Pollock	5763
24	3	H	Grimsby T	W	1-0	1-0	13	Wilkinson	10,441
25	16	A	Sunderland	L	1-2	0-0	—	Vickers	16,473
26	22	H	Watford	D	1-1	1-0	16	Moore	8089
27	Feb 6	H	Millwall	W	4-2	1-2	—	Hignett 2, Vickers, Wilkinson	6286
28	12	A	Peterborough U	L	0-1	0-0	16		7020
29	22	A	Derby Co	W	1-0	1-0	—	Vickers	14,716
30	Mar 5	H	Wolverhampton W	W	1-0	0-0	14	Wilkinson	12,092
31	8	A	Luton T	D	1-1	0-0	—	Mustoe	6741
32	12	A	Leicester C	L	0-2	0-1	15		16,116
33	15	H	Southend U	W	1-0	1-0	—	Wilkinson	7378
34	19	H	WBA	W	3-0	2-0	10	Wilkinson, Pollock, Hendrie	10,516
35	23	A	Crystal Palace	W	1-0	1-0	—	Hignett	12,811
36	26	A	Birmingham C	L	0-1	0-0	9		12,409
37	29	A	Grimsby T	D	1-1	1-0	—	Pollock	5709
38	Apr 2	H	Nottingham F	D	2-2	1-1	10	Pollock 2	17,056
39	4	A	Tranmere R	L	0-4	0-2	12		8225
40	9	H	Oxford U	W	2-1	1-0	8	Moore, Wilkinson	8586
41	16	H	Portsmouth	L	0-2	0-2	11		10,041
42	19	H	Charlton Ath	W	2-0	2-0	—	Moore, Hendrie	6982
43	23	A	Bolton W	L	1-4	0-0	10	Wilkinson	9220
44	26	H	Barnsley	W	5-0	3-0	—	Taggart (og), Pollock 2, Wilkinson 2 (1 pen)	6368
45	May 1	H	Crystal Palace	L	2-3	2-2	—	Liburd, Wilkinson	8638
46	8	A	Charlton Ath	W	5-2	2-0	9	Wilkinson, Hendrie 3, Pollock	8905

Final League Position: 9

GOALSCORERS

League (66): Wilkinson 15 (1 pen), Hendrie 13, Moore 10, Pollock 9, Hignett 5, Vickers 3, Kavanagh 2, Mustoe 2, Kernaghan 1, Liburd 1, Peake 1, Whyte 1, own goals 3.
Coca-Cola Cup (10): Hignett 5, Hendrie 3, Mustoe 1, Wilkinson 1.
FA Cup (3): Kavanagh 1, Moore 1, Wilkinson 1.

Pears 46	Morris 14 + 1	Liburd 41	Pollock 34	Kernaghan 6	Whyte 42	Hendrie 28 + 1	Hignett 25 + 4	Wilkinson 45	Mustoe 38	Moore 42	Fleming 35 + 5	Wright 9 + 7	Mohan 22 + 4	Kavanagh 5 + 6	Stamp 8 + 2	Barron 1 + 1	Johnson 1 + 1	Gannon 6 + 1	Illman — + 1	Peake 30	Forrester — + 1	Vickers 25 + 1	Todd 2 + 1	Winnie 1	Match No.
1	2	3	4	5	6	7	8	9	10	11	12														1
1	2	3	4	5	6	7	8	9	10	11															2
1	2	3	4	5	6	10	8	9	11	7	12														3
1	2	3	4	5	6	7	8	9	10	11	12														4
1	2	3	4	5	6	7	8	9	10	11															5
1	2	3	4	5	6	7	8	9	10	11		12													6
1	2	3	4		6	7	8	9	10	11	12		5	14											7
1	2	3	4		6		8	9	10	11	7		5	12											8
1	2	3	4		6	7	8	9	10	11	12		5												9
1	2	3	4		6	7	8	9	10	11			5	12											10
1	2	3			6	7	8	9	10	11			5		4										11
1	2	3	4		6	7	8	9	10	11			5												12
1	2	3			6	7	8	9	10	11	4		5	12											13
1	2	3			6	7	8	9	10	11	4		5												14
1		3			6		11	9	4		7		5	8		2	10								15
1		3			6		8	9	10	11	2		5	7		12		4	14						16
1	12	3			6		8		4	11	2		5	7	9					10	14				17
1		3			6		8	9	4	11	2		5		7					10		12			18
1		3			6	12	8	9	10	11	2		5					14		7		4			19
1		3			6			9	4	11	2		5	8			12	7		10			14		20
1		3	8		6			9	4	11	2		5					7		10					21
1		3	8		6			9	4	11	2		5					7		10					22
1		3	8					9	4	11	2		5					7		10		6			23
1		3	4					9	7	11	2		5					8		10		6			24
1		3	4				12	9	10	11	2		5		7					8		6			25
1			4		3		8	9		11	2		5	7						10		6			26
1		3			6		8	9	10	11	2	7								4		5			27
1		3			6		8	9	10	11	2	7		12						4		5			28
1		3			6	8		9	10	11	2	12			7					4		5			29
1		3	4		6	7		9	8	11	2	12	14							10		5			30
1			4		6	7		9	8	11	2		3							10		5			31
1			4		6	7	14	9	8	11	2	12	3							10		5			32
1		3	4		6	7		9	8	11	2									10		5			33
1		3	4		6	7		9	8	11	2	12								10		5			34
1		3	7		6		8	9	4	11	2									10		5			35
1		3	4		6		8	9	7	11	2	12								10		5			36
1		3	4		6		8	9		11	2				7					10		5			37
1		3	4		6	7		9		11	2	8	12							10		5			38
1			4		6	7		9		11	2	8	12		14					10		5		3	39
1		3	4		6	7		9		11	2	8			12					10		5			40
1		3	4		6	7	12	9		11	2	8								10		5			41
1		3	4		6	7	12	9		11	2				8					10		5			42
1		3	4		6	7		9		11	2	12			8					10		5			43
1		3	4			7		9	8		2	11								10		5	6		44
1		3	4		6	7		9	8		2	11								10		5			45
1			4		6	7		9	8		2	11	12	14						10		5	3		46

Coca-Cola Cup	Second Round	Brighton & HA (h)	5-0
		(a)	3-1
	Third Round	Sheffield W (h)	1-1
		(a)	1-2
FA Cup	Third Round	Cardiff C (a)	2-2
		(h)	1-2

MIDDLESBROUGH

Player and Position	Ht	Wt	Birth Date	Birth Place	Source	Clubs	League App	League Gls
Goalkeepers								
Andy Collett	5 11	12 00	28 10 73	Middlesbrough	Trainee	Middlesbrough	2	—
Steve Pears	6 0	12 11	22 1 62	Brandon	Apprentice	Manchester U	4	—
						Middlesbrough (loan)	12	—
						Middlesbrough	322	—
Ben Roberts	6 0	12 06	22 6 75	Bishop Auckland	Trainee	Middlesbrough	—	—
Defenders								
Michael Barron	5 10	11 03	22 12 74	Chester le Street	Trainee	Middlesbrough	2	—
Wesley Byrne			9 2 77	Dublin	Trainee	Middlesbrough	—	—
Curtis Fleming	5 8	11 04	8 10 68	Manchester	St Patrick's Ath	Swindon T	—	—
					St Patrick's Ath	Middlesbrough	92	—
Robert Lake‡			13 10 71	Stockton	Trainee	Middlesbrough	—	—
Richard Liburd	5 9	11 01	26 9 73	Nottingham	Forest Ath	Middlesbrough	41	1
David McKinlay			20 11 75	Kinross	Trainee	Middlesbrough	—	—
Nicky Mohan	6 2	12 00	6 10 70	Middlesbrough	Trainee	Middlesbrough	99	4
						Hull C (loan)	5	1
Chris Morris	5 10	10 08	24 12 63	Newquay		Sheffield W	74	1
						Celtic	163	8
						Middlesbrough	40	1
Andrew Todd	5 10	10 11	21 9 74	Derby	Trainee	Middlesbrough	3	—
Steve Vickers	6 2	12 00	13 10 67	Bishop Auckland	Spennymoor U	Tranmere R	311	11
						Middlesbrough	26	3
Richard Ward			6 1 77	Middlesbrough	Trainee	Middlesbrough	—	—
Derek Whyte	5 11	11 05	31 8 68	Glasgow	Celtic BC	Celtic	216	7
						Middlesbrough	77	1
David Winnie (on loan from Aberdeen)	5 1	10 07	26 10 66	Glasgow		Middlesbrough	1	—
Midfield								
Craig Hignett	5 10	11 00	12 1 70	Whiston		Crewe Alex	121	42
						Middlesbrough	50	9
Graham Kavanagh	5 10	11 00	3 12 73	Dublin	Home Farm	Middlesbrough	21	2
						Darlington (loan)	5	—
Stephen McGargle			24 10 75	Gateshead	Trainee	Middlesbrough	—	—
Alan Moore	5 10	11 00	25 11 74	Dublin	Rivermount	Middlesbrough	44	10
Robbie Mustoe	5 10	10 08	28 8 68	Oxford		Oxford U	91	10
						Middlesbrough	132	9
Michael Oliver	5 10	12 04	2 8 75	Cleveland	Trainee	Middlesbrough	—	—
Andy Peake	5 10	12 00	1 11 61	Market Harborough	Apprentice	Leicester C	147	13
						Grimsby T	39	4
						Charlton Ath	177	5
						Middlesbrough	86	1
Jamie Pollock	6 0	11 12	16 2 74	Stockton	Trainee	Middlesbrough	83	11
Philip Stamp	5 9	11 09	12 12 75	Middlesbrough	Trainee	Middlesbrough	10	—
Forwards								
Nicholas Agiadis			18 11 75	Middlesbrough	Trainee	Middlesbrough	—	—
Paul Forrester‡	5 8	12 00	3 11 72	Edinburgh		Middlesbrough	1	—
John Hendrie	5 7	11 07	24 10 63	Lennoxtown	Apprentice	Coventry C	21	2
						Hereford U (loan)	6	—
						Bradford C	173	46
						Newcastle U	34	4
						Leeds U	27	5
						Middlesbrough	140	28
Neil Illman‡	5 7	11 05	29 4 75	Doncaster	Trainee	Middlesbrough	1	—
Ian Johnson			1 9 75	Sunderland	Trainee	Middlesbrough	2	—
Carl Saunders	5 8	11 02	26 11 64	Marston Green	Local	Stoke C	164	23
						Bristol R	142	42
						Oxford U	5	—
						Walsall	2	—
						Middlesbrough	—	—
Mark Taylor	6 2	13 03	8 11 74	Saltburn	Trainee	Middlesbrough	—	—

MIDDLESBROUGH

Colours: Red and white. **Change colours:** Jade and hunter green stripes.

Foundation: The story of how the idea of a Middlesbrough football club was first mooted at a tripe supper at the Corporation Hotel in 1875 is well known locally. But the club was formally established at a meeting in the Talbot Hotel the following year and is one of the oldest clubs in the North East.

First Football League game: 2 September, 1899, Division 2, v Lincoln C (a) L 0-3 – Smith; Shaw, Ramsey; Allport, McNally, McCracken; Wanless, Longstaffe, Gettins, Page, Pugh.

Did you know: On 18 November 1933, Middlesbrough beat Sheffield United 10-3. George Camsell scored four times, his first effort, in which he beat four opponents before scoring, was arguably his finest ever.

Managers (and Secretary-Managers)
John Robson 1899–1905, Alex Massie 1905–06, Andy Aitken 1906–09, J. Gunter 1908–10*, Andy Walker 1910–11, Tom McIntosh 1911–19, James Howie 1920–23, Herbert Bamlett 1923–26, Peter McWilliam 1927–34, Wilf Gillow 1934–44, David Jack 1944–52, Walter Rowley 1952–54, Bob Dennison 1954–63, Raich Carter 1963–66, Stan Anderson 1966–73, Jack Charlton 1973–77, John Neal 1977–81, Bobby Murdoch 1981–82, Malcolm Allison 1982–84, Willie Maddren 1984–86, Bruce Rioch 1986–90, Colin Todd 1990–91, Lennie Lawrence 1991–94, Bryan Robson May 1994–

Player and Position	*Ht*	*Wt*	*Birth Date*	*Birth Place*	*Source*	*Clubs*	*League App*	*League Gls*
Paul Wilkinson	6 0	11 09	30 10 64	Louth	Apprentice	Grimsby T	71	27
						Everton	31	7
						Nottingham F	34	5
						Watford	134	52
						Middlesbrough	132	43
Tommy Wright	5 7	9 10	10 1 66	Dunfermline	Apprentice	Leeds U	81	24
						Oldham Ath	112	23
						Leicester C	129	22
						Middlesbrough	52	5

Trainees
Bagayoko, Salif; Creamer, Christopher P; Dwyer, Paul J; Mils, Andrew D; Richardson, Paul; Skingsley, Ross A; Smith, Steven; Summerbell, Mark; White, Alan; Whittaker, Stewart J.

Associated Schoolboys
Baker, Steven R; Campbell, Andrew P; Carter, Graeme J; Connor, Paul; Dunn, Thomas; Fielding, Kyle W; Haley, Craig; Jones, Thomas A. M; Ormerod, Anthony; Reeve, Christopher J; Slater, Darren; Spark, Philip J; Swalwell, Andrew D; White, Darren.

Associated Schoolboys who have accepted the Club's offer of a Traineeship/Contract
Brumpton, David M; Cosgrove, Antony; Harrison, Paul; Howarth, Andrew J; Payne, Lee J; Riggall, Paul J

MILLWALL 1993–94 *Back row (left to right):* Paul Holsgrove, Etienne Verveer, Jamie Moralee, Mark Foran, Tony McCarthy, Lee Luscombe, Richard Huxford, Tony Dolby.
Centre row: Keith Johnstone (Physio), Paul Manning, Keith Stevens, Jon Goodman, James Saddington, Kasey Keller, Carl Emberson, John Byrne, John Kerr, Kenny Cunningham, John Humphrey, Peter Melville (Physio).
Front row: Andy May, Andy Roberts, Ian Bogie, Alex Rae, Ian McDonald (Reserve Coach), Mick McCarthy (Manager), Ian Evans (First Team Coach), Phil Barber, Gavin Maguire, Ian Dawes, Malcolm Allen.

Division 1 **MILLWALL**

The Den, Zampa Road, Bermondsey SE16 3LN. Telephone 071–232 1222. Ticket Office: 071–231 9999. Club Shop: 071–231 5881. Fax: 071–231 3663.

Ground capacity: 20,146.

Record Attendance: 20,093 v Arsenal, FA Cup 3rd rd, 10 January 1994.

Record Receipts: (to be advised).

Pitch measurements: 100metres × 68m.

President: Lord Mellish of Bermondsey.

Chairman: Reg Burr. ***Vice-chairman:*** Peter Mead. ***Directors:*** Brian Mitchell, Jeff Burnige, Cllr. David Sullivan, J. M. R. Berardo.

Chief Executive Secretary: Graham Hortop. ***Assistant Secretary:*** Yvonne Haines.

Manager: Mick McCarthy. ***First team coach:*** Ian Evans.

Reserve team coach: Ian McDonald. ***Youth team coach:*** Tom Walley. ***Chief Scout:*** Ron Howard. ***Youth Development Officer:*** Allen Batsford. ***Physios:*** Peter Melville, Keith Johnstone. ***Hon. Medical Officer:*** Dr. Daniel Baron.

Sales & Promotions Manager: Mike Sullivan. ***Commercial Manager:*** Billy Neil.

Year Formed: 1885. ***Turned Professional:*** 1893. ***Ltd Co.:*** 1894.

Previous Names: 1885, Millwall Rovers; 1889, Millwall Athletic.

Club Nickname: 'The Lions'.

Previous Grounds: 1885, Glengall Road, Millwall; 1886, Back of 'Lord Nelson'; 1890, East Ferry Road; 1901, North Greenwich; 1910, The Den, Cold Blow Lane; 1993, The Den, Bermondsey.

Record League Victory: 9–1 v Torquay U, Division 3 (S), 29 August 1927 – Lansdale; Tilling, Hill; Amos, Bryant (3), Graham; Chance, Hawkins (3), Landells (1), Phillips (2), Black. 9–1 v Coventry C, Division 3 (S), 19 November 1927 – Lansdale; Fort, Hill; Amos, Collins (1), Graham; Chance, Landells (4), Cock (2), Phillips (2), Black.

Record Cup Victory: 7–0 v Gateshead, FA Cup, 2nd rd, 12 December 1936 – Yuill; Ted Smith, Inns; Brolly, Hancock, Forsyth; Thomas (1), Mangnall (1), Ken Burditt (2), McCartney (2), Thorogood (1).

Record Defeat: 1–9 v Aston Villa, FA Cup 4th rd, 28 January 1946.

Most League Points (2 for a win): 65, Division 3 (S), 1927–28 and Division 3, 1965–66.

Most League Points (3 for a win): 90, Division 3, 1984–85.

Most League Goals: 127, Division 3 (S), 1927–28.

Highest League Scorer in Season: Richard Parker, 37, Division 3 (S), 1926–27.

Most League Goals in Total Aggregate: Teddy Sheringham, 93, 1984–91.

Most Capped Player: Eamonn Dunphy, 22 (23), Republic of Ireland.

Most League Appearances: Barry Kitchener, 523, 1967–82.

Record Transfer Fee Received: £2,000,000 from Nottingham F for Teddy Sheringham, July 1991.

Record Transfer Fee Paid: £800,000 to Derby Co for Paul Goddard, December 1989.

Football League Record: 1920 Original Members of Division 3; 1921 Division 3 (S); 1928–34 Division 2; 1934–38 Division 3 (S); 1938–48 Division 2; 1948–58 Division 3 (S); 1958–62 Division 4; 1962–64 Division 3; 1964–65 Division 4; 1965–66 Division 3; 1966–75 Division 2; 1975–76 Division 3; 1976–79 Division 2; 1979–85 Division 3; 1985–88 Division 2; 1988–90 Division 1; 1990–92 Division 2; 1992– Division 1.

Honours: *Football League:* Division 1 best season: 7th 1992–93; Division 2 – Champions 1987–88; Division 3 (S) – Champions 1927–28, 1937–38; Runners-up 1952–53; Division 3 – Runners-up 1965–66, 1984–85; Division 4 – Champions 1961–62; Runners-up 1964–65. *FA Cup:* Semi-final 1900, 1903, 1937 (first Division 3 side to reach semi-final). *Football League Cup:* best season: 5th rd, 1973–74, 1976–77. *Football League Trophy:* Winners 1982–83.

MILLWALL 1993—94 LEAGUE RECORD

Match No.	Date	Venue	Opponents	Result	H/T Score	Lg. Pos.	Goalscorers	Attendance
1	Aug 14	A	Stoke C	W 2-1	1-1	—	Bogie, Murray	18,766
2	22	H	Southend U	L 1-4	1-1	—	Kerr	10,273
3	25	A	Wolverhampton W	L 0-2	0-1	—		19,570
4	28	A	Leicester C	L 0-4	0-0	23		12,219
5	Sept 4	H	Barnsley	W 2-0	1-0	13	Kerr, Rae	8010
6	11	A	Charlton Ath	D 0-0	0-0	16		8416
7	18	H	Derby Co	D 0-0	0-0	18		9881
8	25	A	Peterborough U	D 0-0	0-0	17		6219
9	Oct 2	H	Watford	W 4-1	2-0	10	Goodman 3, Roberts	7707
10	9	H	WBA	W 2-1	1-0	8	Goodman, Rae (pen)	11,010
11	16	A	Bolton W	L 0-4	0-2	11		9386
12	20	H	Notts Co	W 2-0	0-0	—	Rae (pen), Verveer	5887
13	24	H	Middlesbrough	D 1-1	1-1	—	Whyte (og)	6686
14	31	A	Birmingham C	L 0-1	0-1	—		9377
15	Nov 3	A	Nottingham F	W 3-1	1-0	—	Goodman, Murray, Stevens	17,584
16	6	H	Oxford U	D 2-2	1-0	11	Kennedy 2	7794
17	13	A	Bristol C	D 2-2	0-1	10	Rae, Beard	8416
18	20	H	Tranmere R	W 3-1	2-0	9	Mitchell, Goodman, Kennedy	8653
19	27	H	Grimsby T	W 1-0	0-0	6	Mitchell	7691
20	Dec 4	A	Oxford U	W 2-0	0-0	5	Jackson (og), Verveer	5540
21	11	A	Notts Co	W 3-1	0-0	4	Rae 3	6516
22	19	H	Stoke C	W 2-0	0-0	—	Rae, Kennedy	8930
23	27	H	Portsmouth	D 0-0	0-0	3		12,104
24	28	A	Sunderland	L 1-2	1-1	3	Roberts	19,283
25	Jan 1	H	Crystal Palace	W 3-0	0-0	3	Goodman, Verveer, Rae (pen)	16,779
26	15	H	Bolton W	W 1-0	0-0	2	Rae	9772
27	22	A	WBA	D 0-0	0-0	3		15,172
28	Feb 6	A	Middlesbrough	L 2-4	2-1	—	Rae (pen), Moralee	6286
29	12	H	Birmingham C	W 2-1	1-0	3	Verveer 2	9438
30	Mar 2	A	Southend U	D 1-1	1-1	—	Mitchell	4615
31	6	H	Leicester C	D 0-0	0-0	—		8085
32	12	A	Derby Co	D 0-0	0-0	5		15,303
33	15	H	Charlton Ath	W 2-1	0-0	—	Rae 2	13,320
34	22	H	Peterborough U	W 1-0	0-0	—	Greenman (og)	8518
35	26	A	Watford	L 0-2	0-1	4		9036
36	30	H	Luton T	D 2-2	1-1	—	Moralee, Berry	9235
37	Apr 2	A	Portsmouth	D 2-2	0-1	4	Cunningham, Mitchell	11,591
38	6	H	Sunderland	W 2-1	2-0	—	Mitchell 2	10,244
39	9	A	Crystal Palace	L 0-1	0-0	5		23,142
40	17	H	Nottingham F	D 2-2	1-0	—	Moralee, Mitchell	12,543
41	20	H	Wolverhampton W	W 1-0	0-0	—	Mitchell	11,883
42	23	A	Tranmere R	L 2-3	0-2	5	Moralee, Kerr	9141
43	26	A	Luton T	D 1-1	0-0	—	Kerr	8257
44	30	H	Bristol C	D 0-0	0-0	6		11,189
45	May 3	A	Barnsley	W 1-0	0-0	—	Mitchell	5059
46	8	A	Grimsby T	D 0-0	0-0	3		5355

Final League Position: 3

GOALSCORERS

League (58): Rae 13 (4 pens), Mitchell 9, Goodman 7, Verveer 5, Kennedy 4, Kerr 4, Moralee 4, Murray 2, Roberts 2, Beard 1, Berry 1, Bogie 1, Cunningham 1, Stevens 1, own goals 3.
Coca-Cola Cup (4): Huxford 1, Moralee 1, Murray 1, Verveer 1.
FA Cup (0):

Keller 44	Cunningham 39	Dawes 20 + 1	Maguire 3	McCarthy 2	Stevens 44	Roberts 42	Bogie 4	Murray 7 + 6	Kerr 13 + 10	Dolby 13 + 4	Byrne 1 + 3	Huxford 25 + 6	Luscombe — + 2	Barber 32 + 3	Thatcher 8	Rae 34 + 2	Verveer 22 + 8	Moralee 25 + 5	Van Den Hauwe 23	Goodman 18 + 1	Beard 8 + 6	May 1 + 2	Mitchell 26 + 1	Patmore — + 1	Kennedy 9 + 3	Emblen 12	Carter 2	Hurlock 13	Allen 11 + 1	Berry 5 + 5	*Match No.*
1	2	3	4	5	6	7	8	9	10	11	12																				1
1	2	3	4	5	6	7	8	9	10	*11*	12	14																			2
1	2	3	5		6	4	*8*	9	10		12	7	14	11																	3
1	2	3			6	4	8	12	10		*9*	7	14	11	5																4
1	2	3			6	4		12	10	14		5		11		7	8	*9*													5
1	2	3			6	4			10	14		12		11		7	8	*9*	5												6
1	2	3			6	4			10			14		11		7	*8*	9	5	12											7
1	2	3			6	4		14	10	12		7		11			*8*	9	5												8
1	*6*					4		12		3		7		11			8	9	5	10	2	14									9
1	5				6	4		12		3		2		11		7	8	9		10											10
1	5				6	4		9		3		2		11		7	8			*10*	12		14								11
1	2				6	4				3				11		7	8		5	9			10	12							12
1	2				6	4				3		12		*11*		7	8		5		14		10		9						13
1	2				6	4		8		3		7		*11*				12	5	10	14				9						14
1	2				6	4		8		3		7		14				12	5	10	11				*9*						15
1	2				6	4		*8*		3		7		14				12	5	10	11				9						16
1	2				6	4				3		8		14		7			*5*	10	11		9		12						17
1	2				6	4						12		11		7				10	3		9		8	5					18
1					6	4								11		7	12		3	10	2		9		8	5					19
1					6	4						11		3		7	12			10	2		9		8	5					20
1					6	4				14		11		3		7	12			10	*2*		9		8	5					21
1					6	4				2		11		3		7	8			*10*	14		9		12	5					22
1					6	4				*2*		11		3		7	12			10	14		9		8	5					23
1					6	4						11		3	*2*	7	8	12		10	14		9			5					24
1					6	4						11		3	2	7	8	12		10			9			5					25
	3				6	4						2		11		7	8	*9*	5	10		12			14		1				26
	2				6				10			12		11	3	7	8	9	5			4					1				27
1	5				6	4		12	10			2		11	3	7	8	9													28
1	2	12			6	4			10					11	3	7	8	9	5												29
1	2	3			6	4								11		7	12	9	5				10					8			30
1	2	3			6	4			14					11		7	12	9	5				*10*					8			31
1	2	3			6	4			12					11		7	5	9					10					8			32
1	2	3			6	4			12					11		7	5	9					10					8			33
1	2	3			6	4			12			5		11		7	8	9					10								34
1	2	3			6	4						5		11		7	*8*	9					10						12	14	35
1	2	3			6	4						5					8	9					10						7	11	36
1	2	3			6	4										12		9	5				10					7	8	11	37
1	2	3			6	4			9							12			5				10					7	8	11	38
1	2	3							12							7	14	*9*	5				10			6		4	8	11	39
1	2	3			6	4										7	11	9	5				10						8		40
1	2	3			6				12							7	14	9	5				10					4	8	*11*	41
1	2				6				12					11	3	7		9	*5*				10					4	8	14	42
1	2				6	11			10						3	7		9								5		4	8	12	43
1	2				6	11			12			3				*7*		9	5				10					4	8	14	44
1	2				6	11			12			3				7		9					10			5		4	8		45
1	2				6	4			12			3		11		*7*				9						5		8	10	14	46

Coca-Cola Cup	Second Round	Watford (a)	0-0
		(h)	4-3
	Third Round	QPR (a)	0-3
FA Cup	Third Round	Arsenal (h)	0-1

MILLWALL

Player and Position	Ht	Wt	Birth Date	Birth Place	Source	Clubs	League App	League Gls
Goalkeepers								
Tim Carter	6 2	13 11	5 10 67	Bristol	Apprentice	Bristol R	47	—
						Newport Co (loan)	1	—
						Carlisle U (loan)	4	—
						Sunderland	37	—
						Bristol C (loan)	3	—
						Birmingham C (loan)	2	—
						Hartlepool U	18	—
						Millwall	2	—
Carl Emberson	6 1	13 11	13 7 73	Epsom	Trainee	Millwall	—	—
						Colchester U (loan)	13	—
Kasey Keller	6 1	13 07	27 11 69	Washington	Portland Univ	Millwall	90	—
David Wietecha	6 4		1 11 74	Colchester		Millwall	—	—
						Crewe Alex (loan)	—	—
						Rotherham U (loan)	—	—
Defenders								
Mark Beard	5 10	10 12	8 10 74	Roehampton	Trainee	Millwall	14	1
Ken Cunningham	6 0	11 08	28 6 71	Dublin		Millwall	121	1
Ian Dawes	5 10	11 10	22 2 63	Croydon	Apprentice	QPR	229	3
						Millwall	211	5
Neil Emblen			19 6 71	Bromley	Sittingbourne	Millwall	12	—
Mike Harle			31 10 72	Lewisham	Sittingbourne	Millwall	—	—
Richard Huxford	5 10	11 06	25 7 69	Scunthorpe	Kettering T	Barnet	33	1
						Millwall	31	—
						Birmingham C (loan)	5	—
Mick McCarthy	6 2	13 12	7 2 59	Barnsley	Apprentice	Barnsley	272	7
						Manchester C	140	2
						Celtic	48	—
					Lyon	Millwall	35	2
Tony McCarthy	6 1	12 03	9 11 69	Dublin	Shelbourne	Millwall	9	1
Matthew Middleton			22 1 75	Lambeth	Trainee	Millwall	—	—
James Saddington	6 0	11 13	12 9 72	Cambridge	Cambridge C	Millwall	—	—
Keith Stevens	6 0	12 10	21 6 64	Merton	Apprentice	Millwall	390	7
Ben Thatcher	5 10	11 10	30 11 75	Swindon		Millwall	8	—
Pat Van Den Hauwe	5 11	11 10	16 12 60	Dendermonde	Apprentice	Birmingham C	123	1
						Everton	135	2
						Tottenham H	116	—
						Millwall	23	—
Midfield								
Daniel Chapman			21 11 74	Deptford	Trainee	Millwall	—	—
James Connor			22 8 74	Middlesbrough		Millwall	—	—
Paul Holsgrove*	6 2	12 11	26 8 69	Wellington	Trainee	Aldershot	3	—
						Wimbledon (loan)	—	—
						WBA (loan)	—	—
					Wokingham	Luton T	2	—
					Heracles	Millwall	11	—
Terry Hurlock*	5 9	13 03	22 9 58	Hackney	Leytonstone/ Ilford	Brentford	220	18
						Reading	29	—
						Millwall	104	8
						Rangers	29	2
						Southampton	61	—
						Millwall	13	—
Gavin Maguire	5 10	11 08	24 11 67	Hammersmith	Apprentice	QPR	40	—
						Portsmouth	91	—
						Newcastle U (loan)	3	—
						Millwall	12	—
						Scarborough (loan)	2	—
Paul Manning‡	5 10	11 04	21 1 74	Lewisham	Trainee	Millwall	1	—
Andy May	5 8	11 10	26 2 64	Bury	Apprentice	Manchester C	150	8
						Huddersfield T	114	5
						Bolton W (loan)	10	2
						Bristol C	90	4
						Millwall	38	1
Geoffrey Pitcher			15 8 75	Sutton	Trainee	Millwall	—	—
Alex Rae	5 9	11 05	30 9 69	Glasgow	Bishopbriggs	Falkirk	83	20
						Millwall	143	40

MILLWALL

Colours: Blue shirts, white shorts, blue stockings. **Change colours:** Yellow shirts, black shorts, black stockings.

Foundation: Formed in 1885 as Millwall Rovers by employees of Morton & Co, a jam and marmalade factory in West Ferry Road. The founders were predominantly Scotsmen. Their first headquarters was the The Islanders pub in Tooke Street, Millwall. Their first trophy was the East End Cup in 1887.

First Football League game: 28 August, 1920, Division 3, v Bristol R (h) W 2-0 – Lansdale; Fort, Hodge; Voisey (1), Riddell, McAlpine; Waterall, Travers, Broad (1), Sutherland, Dempsey.

Did you know: Millwall as a Southern League club beat Aston Villa the Football League champions in a third round second replayed FA Cup tie on 5 March 1900. After 1-1 and 0-0 draws the third match was played at Reading.

Managers (and Secretary-Managers)
William Henderson 1894–99*, E. R. Stopher 1899–1900, George Saunders 1900–11, Herbert Lipsham 1911–19, Robert Hunter 1919–33, Bill McCracken 1933–36, Charlie Hewitt 1936–40, Bill Voisey 1940–44, Jack Cock 1944–48, Charlie Hewitt 1948–56, Ron Gray 1956–57, Jimmy Seed 1958–59, Reg Smith 1959–61, Ron Gray 1961–63, Billy Gray 1963–66, Benny Fenton 1966–74, Gordon Jago 1974–77, George Petchey 1978–80, Peter Anderson 1980–82, George Graham 1982–86, John Docherty 1986–90, Bob Pearson 1990, Bruce Rioch 1990–92, Mick McCarthy March 1992–

Andy Roberts	5 10	13 00	20 3 74	Dartford	Trainee	Millwall	94	2
Etienne Verveer	5 11	11 12	22 9 67	Surinam	Chur	Millwall	56	7

Forwards

Clive Allen	5 10	12 03	20 5 61	London	Apprentice	QPR	49	32
						Arsenal	—	—
						Crystal Palace	25	9
						QPR	87	40
						Tottenham H	105	60
					Bordeaux	Manchester C	53	16
						Chelsea	16	7
						West Ham U	38	17
						Millwall	12	—
Phil Barber	5 11	12 06	10 6 65	Tring	Aylesbury	Crystal Palace	234	35
						Millwall	110	12
Greg Berry	5 10	12 00	5 3 71	Essex	East Thurrock	Leyton Orient	80	14
						Wimbledon	7	1
						Millwall	10	1
Tony Dolby	5 10	12 02	16 4 74	Greenwich	Trainee	Millwall	35	1
						Barnet (loan)	16	2
Jon Goodman	5 11	12 11	2 6 71	Walthamstow	Bromley	Millwall	94	27
Mark Kennedy	5 11	11 09	15 5 76	Dublin	Trainee	Millwall	13	4
John Kerr	5 8	11 05	6 3 65	Toronto	Harrow Borough	Portsmouth	4	—
						Peterborough U (loan)	10	1
					San Diego Sockers	Millwall	29	5
David Mitchell	6 1	12 07	13 6 62	Glasgow		Rangers	26	6
					Feyenoord	Chelsea	7	—
						Newcastle U (loan)	2	1
						Swindon T	68	16
					Altay Izmir	Millwall	27	9
Jamie Moralee	5 11	11 05	2 12 71	Wandsworth	Trainee	Crystal Palace	6	—
						Millwall	67	19
Bruce Murray	6 3	13 08	25 1 66	Washington	USSF	Millwall	13	2
						Stockport Co (loan)	3	—
Jermaine Wright			21 10 75	Greenwich	Trainee	Millwall	—	—

Trainees
Collins, Michael M; Francis, Dean; Gordon, Neville; Hatcher, Kevin T; Irving, Paul R; Jones, Steven M. C; Luckett, Colin A; Morey, Robert B; Morgan, Vaughan A; Mulraney, Mark A. J; Perkins, Steven; Roberts, Michael; Walley, Simon J; Williams, Richard.

****Non-Contract**
Cronin, Adrian; Morrisey, Robert E.

Associated Schoolboys
Armstrong, Dean; Bannister, Jonathan P; Canoville, Dean; Dale, Sammy D; Dann, James; Day, John P; Edwards, Daniel; Godbold, Marc; Hockton, Danny J; Nightingale, Lewis; Prankard, Paul; Stevens, Shaun; Thompson, Sam; White, Darren J.

Associated Schoolboys who have accepted the Club's offer of a Traineeship/Contract
Aris, Steven; Bircham, Marc; Dillon, Warren; Hirst, Matthew; Johnson, Steven L; Kelly, Steven; Keown, Darren; O'Neil, Phil.

NEWCASTLE UNITED 1993–94 *Back row (left to right):* Danny Anderson, David Roche, Alun Armstrong, Steve Watson, Kevin Brock, Steve Harper, Scott Sellars, John Beresford, Robert Lee, Richard Appleby.

Centre row: Derek Fazackerley (First Team Coach), Peter Cormack, Liam O'Brien, Alan Neilson, Tommy Wright, Pavel Srnicek, Matty Appleby, Rob Elliott, Tony Dinning, Nathan Murray.

Front row: Andy Cole, Alex Mathie, Steve Howey, Lee Clark, Barry Venison, Terry McDermott (Assistant Manager), Kevin Keegan (Manager), Brian Kilcline, Kevin Scott, Niki Papavasiliou, Peter Beardsley, Paul Bracewell.

NEWCASTLE UNITED

St James' Park, Newcastle-upon-Tyne NE1 4ST. Telephone 091–232 8361. Lottery Office: 091–230 2861. Commercial Dept: 091–232 0406. Ticket Office Hotline: 091–261 1571. Club Shop: 091–261 6357. Club Shop Answering Service: 091–232 4080. Football in the Community Scheme: 091–261 9715. Conference and Banqueting: 091–222 1860. Club Fax: 091–232 9875. Clubcall: 0891 121590. Clubcall Ticket Line: 0891 121190. Club Shop numbers: St James' Park Club Shop: 091–261 6357. Metro Centre Club Shop: 091–461 0000. Eldon Square Club Shop: 091–230 0808. Haymarket Club Shop: 091–232 2473.

Ground capacity: 32,536.

Record attendance: 68,386 v Chelsea, Division 1, 3 Sept 1930.

Record receipts: £157,153 v Sunderland, Division 2 play-off, semi-final, 16 May 1990.

Pitch measurements: 110yd × 73yd (subject to alteration).

President: T. L. Bennett.

Chairman: Sir John Hall.

Vice-chairman: W. F. Shepherd. ***Chief Executive:*** A. O. Fletcher.

Directors: D. S. Hall, R. Jones, T. L. Bennett.

Manager: Kevin Keegan. ***Assistant Manager:*** Terry McDermott.

Coaches: Arthur Cox, Chris McMenemy and Derek Fazackerley. ***Physio:*** Derek Wright.

General Manager/Secretary: R. Cushing.

Assistant Secretary: A. Toward. ***Marketing Control:*** Trevor Garwood.

Year Formed: 1881. ***Turned Professional:*** 1889. ***Ltd Co.:*** 1890.

Club Nickname: 'Magpies'.

Previous Names: Stanley 1881; Newcastle East End 1882–1892.

Previous Grounds: South Byker, 1881; Chillingham Road, Heaton, 1886 to 1892.

Record League Victory: 13–0 v Newport Co, Division 2, 5 October 1946 – Garbutt; Cowell, Graham; Harvey, Brennan, Wright; Milburn (2), Bentley (1), Wayman (4), Shackleton (6), Pearson.

Record Cup Victory: 9–0 v Southport (at Hillsborough) FA Cup, 4th rd, 1 February 1932 – McInroy; Nelson, Fairhurst; McKenzie, Davidson, Weaver (1); Boyd (1), Jimmy Richardson (3), Cape (2), McMenemy (1), Lang (1).

Record Defeat: 0–9 v Burton Wanderers, Division 2, 15 April 1895.

Most League Points (2 for a win): 57, Division 2, 1964–65.

Most League Points (3 for a win): 96, Division 1, 1992–93.

Most League Goals: 98, Division 1, 1951–52.

Highest League Scorer in Season: Hughie Gallacher, 36, Division 1, 1926–27.

Most League Goals in Total Aggregate: Jackie Milburn, 178, 1946–57.

Most Capped Player: Alf McMichael, 40, Northern Ireland.

Most League Appearances: Jim Lawrence, 432, 1904–22.

Record Transfer Fee Received: £2,000,000 from Tottenham H for Paul Gascoigne, July 1988.

Record Transfer Fee Paid: £2,700,000 to QPR for Darren Peacock, March 1994.

Football League Record: 1893 Elected to Division 2; 1898–1934 Division 1; 1934–48 Division 2; 1948–61 Division 1; 1961–65 Division 2; 1965–78 Division 1; 1978–84 Division 2; 1984–89 Division 1; 1989–92 Division 2; 1992–93 Division 1; 1993– FA Premier League.

Honours: *Football League:* Division 1 – Champions 1904–05, 1906–07, 1908–09, 1926–27, 1992–93; Division 2 – Champions 1964–65; Runners-up 1897–98, 1947–48. *FA Cup:* Winners 1910, 1924, 1932, 1951, 1952, 1955; Runners-up 1905, 1906, 1908, 1911, 1974. *Football League Cup:* Runners-up 1975–76. *Texaco Cup:* Winners 1973–74, 1974–75. **European Competitions:** *European Fairs Cup:* 1968–69 (winners), 1969–70, 1970–71 *UEFA Cup:* 1977–78. *Anglo-Italian Cup:* Winners 1973.

NEWCASTLE UNITED 1993—94 LEAGUE RECORD

Match No.	Date	Venue	Opponents	Result		H/T Score	Lg. Pos.	Goalscorers	Attendance
1	Aug 14	H	Tottenham H	L	0-1	0-1	—		34,565
2	18	A	Coventry C	L	1-2	1-0	—	Atherton (og)	15,763
3	21	A	Manchester U	D	1-1	0-1	17	Cole	41,829
4	25	H	Everton	W	1-0	1-0	—	Allen	34,490
5	29	H	Blackburn R	D	1-1	0-0	—	Cole	33,987
6	31	A	Ipswich T	D	1-1	0-0	—	Cole	19,126
7	Sept 13	H	Sheffield W	W	4-2	1-1	—	Cole 2, Mathie, Allen	33,519
8	18	A	Swindon T	D	2-2	2-0	13	Clark, Allen (pen)	15,393
9	25	H	West Ham U	W	2-0	0-0	11	Cole 2	34,179
10	Oct 2	A	Aston Villa	W	2-0	0-0	6	Allen (pen), Cole	37,366
11	16	H	QPR	L	1-2	0-1	11	Allen	33,801
12	24	A	Southampton	L	1-2	0-0	—	Cole	13,804
13	30	H	Wimbledon	W	4-0	1-0	9	Beardsley 3 (1 pen), Cole	33,371
14	Nov 8	A	Oldham Ath	W	3-1	0-1	—	Cole 2, Beardsley	13,821
15	21	H	Liverpool	W	3-0	3-0	—	Cole 3	36,246
16	24	H	Sheffield U	W	4-0	2-0	—	Ward (og), Beardsley 2 (1 pen), Cole	35,029
17	27	A	Arsenal	L	1-2	0-1	—	Beardsley	36,091
18	Dec 4	A	Tottenham H	W	2-1	0-0	3	Beardsley 2	30,780
19	11	H	Manchester U	D	1-1	0-0	4	Cole	36,332
20	18	A	Everton	W	2-0	1-0	4	Cole, Beardsley	25,362
21	22	H	Leeds U	D	1-1	0-0	—	Cole	36,388
22	28	A	Chelsea	L	0-1	0-1	5		23,133
23	Jan 1	H	Manchester C	W	2-0	2-0	5	Cole 2	35,585
24	4	A	Norwich C	W	2-1	1-1	—	Beardsley, Cole	19,564
25	16	A	QPR	W	2-1	1-1	—	Clark, Beardsley	15,774
26	22	H	Southampton	L	1-2	1-1	4	Cole	32,067
27	Feb 12	A	Wimbledon	L	2-4	0-2	4	Beardsley 2 (2 pens)	13,358
28	19	A	Blackburn R	L	0-1	0-0	5		20,798
29	23	H	Coventry C	W	4-0	0-0	—	Cole 3, Mathie	32,210
30	Mar 5	A	Sheffield W	W	1-0	0-0	4	Cole	33,153
31	12	H	Swindon T	W	7-1	2-0	3	Beardsley 2 (1 pen), Lee 2, Watson 2, Fox	32,219
32	19	A	West Ham U	W	4-2	1-0	3	Lee 2, Cole, Mathie	23,132
33	23	H	Ipswich T	W	2-0	1-0	—	Sellars, Cole	32,234
34	29	H	Norwich C	W	3-0	1-0	—	Cole, Lee, Beardsley	32,228
35	Apr 1	A	Leeds U	D	1-1	1-0	—	Cole	40,005
36	4	H	Chelsea	D	0-0	0-0	3		32,218
37	9	A	Manchester C	L	1-2	1-1	3	Sellars	33,774
38	16	A	Liverpool	W	2-0	1-0	3	Lee, Cole	44,601
39	23	H	Oldham Ath	W	3-2	1-1	3	Fox, Beardsley, Lee	32,214
40	27	H	Aston Villa	W	5-1	3-1	—	Bracewell, Beardsley 2 (1 pen), Cole, Sellars	32,217
41	30	A	Sheffield U	L	0-2	0-0	3		29,013
42	May 7	H	Arsenal	W	2-0	0-0	3	Cole, Beardsley (pen)	32,216

Final League Position: 3

GOALSCORERS

League (82): Cole 34, Beardsley 21 (7 pens), Lee 7, Allen 5 (2 pens), Mathie 3, Sellars 3, Clark 2, Fox 2, Watson 2, Bracewell 1, own goals 2.
Coca-Cola Cup (12): Cole 6, Allen 2 (1 pen), Beardsley 1, Bracewell 1, Lee 1, Sellars 1.
FA Cup (3): Beardsley 2 (1 pen), Cole 1.

Srnicek 21	Venison 36 + 1	Beresford 34	Bracewell 32	Scott 18	Howey 13 + 1	Lee 41	Allen 9	Cole 40	Clark 29	Papavasiliou 7	O'Brien 4 + 2	Watson 29 + 3	Wright 2 + 1	Neilson 10 + 4	Mathie — + 16	Beardsley 35	Hooper 19	Sellars 29 + 1	Elliott 13 + 2	Jeffrey 2	Robinson 12 + 4	Kilcline 1	Fox 14	Appleby 1	Holland 2 + 1	Peacock 9	Match No.
1	2	3	4	5	6	7	*8*	9	10	11	12	14															1
1	2	3	4	5		7		9	10	11	6	8	12														2
1	2	3	4	5		7		9	10	11	6	8															3
1	2	3	4	5			8	9	10	11	6	7															4
1	2	3	4	5		7		9	10	11	6	8															5
1	2	3	4	5		7	8	9	10	*11*	12	6		14													6
	2	3	4	5		7	8	9	10	11		6	1		12												7
	2	3	4	5		7	11	9	10			6	1			8											8
	2	3	4	5		7	11	9	10			6				8	1										9
	2	3	4	5		7	11	9	10			6				8	1										10
	2	3	4	5		7	11	9	10			6				8	1										11
	2	3	4	5		7	*11*	9	10			6			12	8	1	14									12
	2	3	4	5		7		9	10			6				8	1	11									13
	2		4	5		7		9	10			6				8	1	11	3								14
	2		4	5		7		9	10			6				8	1	11	3								15
	2		4	5		7		9	10			6			12	8	1	11	3								16
	2		4	5	14	7		9	*10*			6			12	8	1	11	3								17
	2		4		5	7		9	10			6				8	1		3	11							18
	2		4		5	7		9	10			6				8	1	11	3								19
	2	3	4		5	7		9	10			6				8	1	11	12								20
	2	3	4		5	7		9	10			6			12	8	1	11									21
	2	3	4		5	7		9	10			*6*			12	8	1	11			14						22
		3	*4*		6	7		9	10			14			12	8	1	11			2	5					23
		3		5	6	7		9	10							8	1	11	4		2						24
	2	3	4		6	7		9	10							8	1	11			5						25
	2	3	4		6	7		9	10							8	1	11			5						26
	2	3			5	9			10			6			12	8	1	11	4				7				27
1	2	3			5	9			10			6				8		11	4				7				28
1						*7*		9	10			2		5	12	8		11	3		14		6	4			29
1		3			4	7		9				6		5		8		11	12		2		10				30
1	4	3				7		9				6				8		11	5		2		10				31
1	4	3				7		9				*6*		14	12	8		11	5		2		10				32
1	4	3				7		9				6		14	12	8		11	*5*		2				10		33
1		3	*4*			7		9						6	12	8		11			2		10		14	5	34
1	12	3	4			7		9						6		8		11			2		10			5	35
1	6	*3*	4			7		9						14	12	8		11			2				10	5	36
1	3					7		9						6	12	8		11		10	2		4			5	37
1	*2*	3	4			7		9						6	12	8		11			14		10			5	38
1	2	3	4			7		9						6		8		11					10			5	39
1	2	3	*4*			7		9				14		6	12	8		11					10			5	40
1	2	3	4			7		9						6		8		11					10			5	41
1	2	3				7		9				4		6		8		11			12		10			5	42

Coca-Cola Cup	Second Round	Notts Co (h)	4-1
		(a)	7-1
	Third Round	Wimbledon (a)	1-2
FA Cup	Third Round	Coventry C (h)	2-0
	Fourth Round	Luton T (h)	1-1
		(a)	0-2

NEWCASTLE UNITED

Player and Position	Ht	Wt	Birth Date	Birth Place	Source	Clubs	League App	League Gls
Goalkeepers								
Steve Harper			3 2 70	Easington		Newcastle U	—	—
Michael Hooper	6 2	13 05	10 2 64	Bristol		Bristol C	1	—
						Wrexham (loan)	20	—
						Wrexham	14	—
						Liverpool	51	—
						Leicester C (loan)	14	—
						Newcastle U	19	—
Pavel Srnicek	6 2	14 09	10 3 68	Ostrava	Banik Ostrava	Newcastle U	73	—
Defenders								
Matthew Appleby	5 10	11 02	16 4 72	Middlesbrough	Trainee	Newcastle U	20	—
						Darlington (loan)	10	1
Peter Cormack*	6 0	11 05	8 6 74	Liverpool	Hutcheson Vale	Meadowbank T	2	—
						Newcastle U	—	—
Tony Dinning*			12 4 75	Wallsend		Newcastle U	—	—
Robbie Elliott	5 10	10 13	25 12 73	Newcastle	Trainee	Newcastle U	30	—
Darron McDonough‡	5 11	12 12	7 11 62	Antwerp	Apprentice	Oldham Ath	183	14
						Luton T	105	5
						Newcastle U	3	—
Nathan Murray			10 9 75	South Shields	Trainee	Newcastle U	—	—
Alan Neilson	5 11	11 07	26 9 72	Wegburg	Trainee	Newcastle U	36	1
Darren Peacock	6 2	12 06	3 2 68	Bristol	Apprentice	Newport Co	28	—
						Hereford U	59	4
						QPR	126	6
						Newcastle U	9	—
Brian Reid (on loan from Rangers)	6 2	11 12	15 6 70	Paisley		Newcastle U	—	—
Barry Venison	5 10	11 09	16 8 64	Consett	Apprentice	Sunderland	173	2
						Liverpool	110	1
						Newcastle U	81	—
Steve Watson	6 0	12 07	1 4 74	North Shields	Trainee	Newcastle U	86	3
Midfield								
Richie Appleby			18 9 75	Middlesbrough	Trainee	Newcastle U	—	—
John Beresford	5 5	10 04	4 9 66	Sheffield	Apprentice	Manchester C	—	—
						Barnsley	88	5
						Portsmouth	107	8
						Newcastle U	76	1
Paul Bracewell	5 8	10 09	19 7 62	Stoke	Apprentice	Stoke C	129	5
						Sunderland	38	4
						Everton	95	7
						Sunderland	113	2
						Newcastle U	57	3
Kevin Brock*	5 9	10 12	9 9 62	Middleton Stoney	Apprentice	Oxford U	246	26
						QPR	40	2
						Newcastle U	145	15
						Cardiff C (loan)	14	2
Lee Clark	5 7	11 07	27 10 72	Wallsend	Trainee	Newcastle U	123	18
Ruel Fox	5 6	10 00	14 1 68	Ipswich	Apprentice	Norwich C	172	22
						Newcastle U	14	2
Chris Holland	5 9	11 05	11 9 75	Whalley	Trainee	Preston NE	1	—
						Newcastle U	3	—
Steve Howey	6 1	10 05	26 10 71	Sunderland	Trainee	Newcastle U	88	3
Nicos Papavasiliou	5 8	10 02	31 8 70	Limassol	Ofi Crete	Newcastle U	7	—
Mark Robinson	5 9	11 08	21 11 68	Manchester	Trainee	WBA	2	—
						Barnsley	137	6
						Newcastle U	25	—
Scott Sellars	5 7	9 10	27 11 65	Sheffield	Apprentice	Leeds U	76	12
						Blackburn R	202	35
						Leeds U	7	—
						Newcastle U	43	5

NEWCASTLE UNITED

Colours: Black and white striped shirts, black shorts, black stockings. **Change colours:** All blue.

Foundation: It stemmed from a newly formed club called Stanley in 1881. In October 1882 they changed their name to Newcastle East End to avoid confusion with Stanley in Co. Durham. Shortly afterwards another club Rosewood merged with them. Newcastle West End had been formed in August 1882 and they played on a ground which is now St. James' Park. In 1889, West End went out of existence after a bad run and the remaining committee men invited East End to move to St. James' Park. They accepted and at a meeting in Bath Lane Hall in 1892, changed their name to Newcastle United.

First Football League game: 2 September, 1893, Division 2, v Royal Arsenal (a) D 2-2 – Ramsay; Jeffery, Miller; Crielly, Graham, McKane; Bowman, Crate (1), Thompson, Sorley (1), Wallace. Graham and not Crate scored according to some reports.

Did you know: On 22 January 1994, Andy Cole equalled George Robledo's race to 30 goals in a season which had been achieved on 26 January 1952. Both achieved the feat in 29 League and Cup games in exactly 161 days.

Managers (and Secretary-Managers)
Frank Watt 1895–32 (continued as secretary to 1932), Andy Cunningham 1930–35, Tom Mather 1935–39, Stan Seymour 1939–47 (Hon-manager), George Martin 1947–50, Stan Seymour 1950–54 (Hon-manager), Duggie Livingstone 1954–56, Stan Seymour (Hon-manager 1956–58), Charlie Mitten 1958–61, Norman Smith 1961–62, Joe Harvey 1962–75, Gordon Lee 1975–77, Richard Dinnis 1977, Bill McGarry 1977–80, Arthur Cox 1980–84, Jack Charlton 1984, Willie McFaul 1985–88, Jim Smith 1988–91, Ossie Ardiles 1991–92, Kevin Keegan February 1992–

Player and Position	*Ht*	*Wt*	*Birth Date*	*Birth Place*	*Source*	*Clubs*	*League App*	*League Gls*
Forwards								
Malcolm Allen	5 8	11 08	21 3 67	Dioniolen	Apprentice	Watford	39	5
						Aston Villa (loan)	4	—
						Norwich C	35	8
						Millwall	81	24
						Newcastle U	9	5
Alun Armstrong			22 2 75	Gateshead	School	Newcastle U	—	—
Peter Beardsley	5 8	11 07	18 1 61	Newcastle	Wallsend BC	Carlisle U	102	22
					Vancouver Whitecaps	Manchester U	—	—
					Vancouver Whitecaps	Newcastle U	147	61
						Liverpool	131	46
						Everton	81	25
						Newcastle U	35	21
Andy Cole	5 11	11 02	15 10 71	Nottingham	Trainee	Arsenal	1	—
						Fulham (loan)	13	3
						Bristol C (loan)	12	8
						Bristol C	29	12
						Newcastle U	52	46
Mike Jeffrey	5 11	11 06	11 8 71	Liverpool	Trainee	Bolton W	15	—
						Doncaster R (loan)	11	6
						Doncaster R	38	13
						Newcastle U	2	—
Robert Lee	5 10	11 13	1 2 66	West Ham	Hornchurch	Charlton Ath	298	59
						Newcastle U	77	17
Alex Mathie	5 10	10 07	20 12 68	Bathgate		Celtic	11	—
						Morton	74	31
						Port Vale (loan)	3	—
						Newcastle U	16	3

Trainees
Baldwin, Shaun T; Elliott, Stuart T; Keen, Peter; McAlindon, Gareth E; Pepper, Graham A; Pouton, Alan; Stokoe, Graham; Thornton, Mark.

Associated Schoolboys
Asiamah, Anthony; Beharall, David; Burt, Jamie P; Craig, Ian; Gibson, Barry J; Gibson, David E; Hoggarth, Philip M; McClen, James D; McClen, Steven P; Metcalfe, Craig D; Milbourne, Ian; Muir, Karl J; Shutt, Matthew J; Tait, Jordan A; Talbot, Paul M; Underwood, Matthew R.

Associated Schoolboys who have accepted the Club's offer of a Traineeship/Contract
Barrett, Paul D; Brayson, Paul; Burt, David C; Garrity, James K; Main, Paul; Winskill, Neil.

NORTHAMPTON TOWN 1993–94 *Back row (left to right):* Lee Colkin, Jason Burnham, Martin Aldridge, Mark Parsons.
Centre row: Denis Casey (Physio), Kevin Wilkin, Steve Terry, Barry Richardson, Steve Sherwood, Phil Chard, Ken Gillard, Paul Curtis (Youth Coach).
Front row: Ian Gilzean, Terry Fleming, Steve Brown, John Barnwell (Manager), Les Phillips, Micky Bell, Darren Harmon.
(Photograph: Pete Norton)

Division 3 NORTHAMPTON TOWN

Sixfields Stadium, Upton Way, Northampton NN1 4PS.

Telephone Northampton (0604) 234100. Fax (0604) 604176. Commercial Dept: (0604) 234100. Soccer Line: 0839 664477.

Ground capacity: 7673.

Record attendance (at County Ground): 24,523 v Fulham, Division 1, 23 April 1966.

Record receipts (at County Ground): £47,292.40 v Coventry C, FA Cup 3rd rd, 6 January 1990.

Pitch measurements: 112yd × 75yd.

Chairman: B. J. Ward.

Directors: B. Stonhill, B. Hancock, M. Church, B. Church, D. Kerr, B. Collins, B. Lomax.

Secretary: Barry Collins.

Manager: John Barnwell. ***Assistant Manager:*** Peter Morris.

Physio: Dennis Casey. ***Commercial Manager: Bob Gorrill.***

Year Formed: 1897. ***Turned Professional:*** 1901. ***Ltd Co.:*** 1901.

Previous Ground: County Ground.

Club Nickname: 'The Cobblers'.

Record League Victory: 10–0 v Walsall, Division 3 (S), 5 November 1927 – Hammond; Watson, Jeffs; Allen, Brett, Odell; Daley, Smith (3), Loasby (3), Hoten (1), Wells (3).

Record Cup Victory: 10–0 v Sutton T FA Cup pr rd, 7 December 1907 – Cooch; Drennan, Lloyd Davies, Tirrell (1), McCartney, Hickleton, Badenock (3), Platt (3), Lowe (1), Chapman (2), McDiarmid.

Record Defeat: 0–11 v Southampton, Southern League, 28 December 1901.

Most League Points (2 for a win): 68, Division 4, 1975–76.

Most League Points (3 for a win): 99, Division 4, 1986–87.

Most League Goals: 109, Division 3, 1962–63 and Division 3 (S), 1952–53.

Highest League Scorer in Season: Cliff Holton, 36, Division 3, 1961–62.

Most League Goals in Total Aggregate: Jack English, 135, 1947–60.

Most Capped Player: E. Lloyd Davies, 12 (16), Wales.

Most League Appearances: Tommy Fowler, 521, 1946–61.

Record Transfer Fee Received: £265,000 from Watford for Richard Hill, July 1987.

Record Transfer Fee Paid: £85,000 to Manchester C for Tony Adcock, January 1988.

Football League Record: 1920 Original Member of Division 3; 1921 Division 3 (S); 1958–61 Division 4; 1961–63 Division 3; 1963–65 Division 2; 1965–66 Division 1; 1966–67 Division 2; 1967–69 Division 3; 1969–76 Division 4; 1976–77 Division 3; 1977–87 Division 4; 1987–90 Division 3; 1990–92 Division 4; 1992– Division 3.

Honours: *Football League:* Division 1 best season: 21st, 1965–66; Division 2 – Runners-up 1964–65; Division 3 – Champions 1962–63; Division 3 (S) – Runners-up 1927–28, 1949–50; Division 4 – Champions 1986–87; Runners-up 1975–76. *FA Cup:* best season: 5th rd, 1933–34, 1949–50, 1969–70. *Football League Cup:* best season: 5th rd, 1964–65, 1966–67.

NORTHAMPTON TOWN 1993—94 LEAGUE RECORD

Match No.	Date	Venue	Opponents	Result		H/T Score	Lg. Pos.	Goalscorers	Attendance
1	Aug 14	A	Bury	D	0-0	0-0	—		2540
2	28	A	Colchester U	L	2-3	2-2	19	Brown, Gilzean	2874
3	31	A	Crewe Alex	L	1-3	1-1	—	Gilzean	3002
4	Sept 4	H	Walsall	L	0-1	0-1	22		3266
5	11	A	Hereford U	D	1-1	0-1	22	Gilzean	2276
6	18	H	Wigan Ath	L	0-2	0-0	22		2235
7	25	A	Lincoln C	L	3-4	2-1	22	Aldridge, Brown, Harmon	2705
8	Oct 2	H	Darlington	W	1-0	1-0	21	Aldridge	2153
9	9	H	Wycombe W	D	1-1	0-0	21	Aldridge	5197
10	12	H	Mansfield T	W	5-1	1-1	—	Gilzean, Harmon, Terry, Brown 2 (1 pen)	2462
11	16	A	Scunthorpe U	L	0-7	0-4	5		2184
12	23	H	Carlisle U	D	1-1	0-0	21	Aldridge	2877
13	30	A	Doncaster R	L	1-2	0-1	21	Gilzean	2227
14	Nov 2	A	Torquay U	L	0-2	0-0	—		2704
15	6	H	Shrewsbury T	L	0-3	0-1	21		2650
16	20	A	Chester C	L	0-1	0-0	22		2650
17	27	H	Chesterfield	D	2-2	0-0	22	Gilzean, Aldridge	1866
18	Dec 11	A	Mansfield T	L	0-1	0-1	22		2491
19	18	H	Bury	L	0-1	0-0	22		2369
20	27	A	Gillingham	L	0-1	0-1	22		4648
21	Jan 1	A	Rochdale	L	2-6	0-3	22	Gilzean, Harmon	2453
22	3	H	Crewe Alex	D	2-2	2-1	22	Gilzean, Colkin	3404
23	8	A	Scarborough	L	1-2	1-1	22	Gilzean	1703
24	22	A	Wycombe W	L	0-1	0-1	22		6737
25	29	H	Doncaster R	D	0-0	0-0	22		2900
26	Feb 5	A	Carlisle U	W	1-0	0-0	22	Chard	4535
27	12	H	Scarborough	W	3-2	1-2	22	Harmon, Fitzpatrick, Gilzean	2974
28	19	H	Colchester U	D	1-1	1-1	22	Wilkin	3185
29	25	A	Walsall	W	3-1	0-0	22	Harmon, Wilkin, Patmore	4533
30	Mar 5	H	Hereford U	L	0-1	0-0	22		5394
31	8	H	Scunthorpe U	W	4-0	1-0	—	Harmon, Fleming (pen), Aldridge, Wilkin	3192
32	12	A	Wigan Ath	D	1-1	0-0	22	Cornwell	1855
33	15	H	Preston NE	W	2-0	1-0	—	Fensome (og), Aldridge	3845
34	19	H	Lincoln C	D	0-0	0-0	22		3868
35	26	A	Darlington	W	1-0	1-0	20	Warburton	2700
36	Apr 2	H	Gillingham	L	1-2	0-0	21	Patmore	4579
37	4	A	Preston NE	D	1-1	1-0	20	Harmon	7517
38	9	H	Rochdale	L	1-2	0-1	21	Aldridge	3330
39	16	H	Torquay U	L	0-1	0-0	21		3519
40	23	A	Shrewsbury T	L	1-2	1-1	21	Wilkin	6512
41	30	H	Chester C	W	1-0	1-0	21	Wilkin	6432
42	May 7	A	Chesterfield	L	0-4	0-2	22		5285

Final League Position: 22

GOALSCORERS

League (44): Gilzean 10, Aldridge 8, Harmon 7, Wilkin 5, Brown 4 (1 pen), Patmore 2, Chard 1, Colkin 1, Cornwell 1, Fitzpatrick 1, Fleming 1 (pen), Terry 1, Warburton 1, own goal 1.
Coca-Cola Cup (0):
FA Cup (1): Aldridge 1.

Richardson 27	Parsons 19	Gillard 13 + 1	Phillips 26	Terry 39	Wood 1	Fleming 26 + 5	Wilkin 24	Gilzean 29 + 4	Brown 24	Bell 37 + 1	Harmon 28 + 3	Chard 25 + 3	Colkin 17 + 3	Sherwood 15 + 1	Francis — + 1	Burnham 15 + 2	Aldridge 23 + 6	Stackman — + 1	Preston 1	Hyslop 8	Sampson 8	Patmore 11 + 6	Harrison 2	Gallacher 5	Elad 8 + 2	Warburton 17	Fitzpatrick 1 + 1	Cornwell 13	Match No.
1	2	3	4	5	6	7	8	9	10	11	12																		1
1	2	3	4	5		7		9	10	11		6	8																2
1	2	3	4	5		7		9	10	11		6	8	12															3
	2	3	4	5		7		9	10	11		6	8	1	12														4
	2		4	5		7		9	10	11	12	6	8	1		3													5
	2	12	4	5				9	10	11	7	6	8	1		3													6
	2		4	5		12		9	10	11	7		6	1		3	8												7
	2	3	4	5				9	10	11	7	6		1		12	8												8
	2	3	4	5				9	10	11	7	6		1			8												9
	2	3	4	5				9	10	11	7	6		1		12	8												10
	2	3	4	5		12		9	10	11	7	6		1			8												11
1	2	3	4	5		12		9	10	11	7	6					8												12
1	2		4	5		12		9	10	11	7		3			6	8												13
1	2		4	5		8		9	10	11		6	7			3	12	14											14
1			4	5		12		9	10	11		6	7			3	8		2										15
	2	3	4	5				9		11	7	6	12	1		10	8												16
	2	3	4	5				9		11		6	7	1		10	8												17
	2		4	5					10	11		7		1			8			3	6	9							18
	2		4	5					10	11		7	14	1			12			3	6	9	8						19
			4	5			7		10			2	11	1			12			3	6	9	8						20
	2		4	5			7	12	10		14		11	1			8			3	6	9							21
			4	5			7	9	10		2		11	1			8			3	6								22
1				5		4	7	9	10	12	2		11				8			3	6								23
1			4	5		2	7	9	10	11			12				8			3	6	14							24
1			4	5		2	7	9	10	11							8				6			3	12				25
1						2	7	12	10	11	4	6								3		9			8	5			26
1		3				2	7	9		11	4	6													8	5	10		27
1		3				2	7	9		11	4	6										12			8	5		10	28
1				6		2	7	12		11	4	3										9			8	5		10	29
1				6		2	7	12		11	4					3						9			8	5		10	30
1				6		2	7	9		11	4					3	12								8	5		10	31
1				6		2	7	9		11	4					3	8									5	12	10	32
1				6		2	7	9		11	4					3	8									5		10	33
1				6		2	7	9		11	4					3	8					12				5		10	34
1				6		2	7	9		11	4	12				3	8									5		10	35
1				6		2	7	9		11	4	12				3	8					14				5		10	36
1				6		2	7			11	4	3					8					9				5		10	37
1				6		2	7			11	4	3					8					9				5		10	38
1				6		2	7			11	4	8					12					9		3		5		10	39
1				6		2	7			11	4	8	9									12		3	14	5		10	40
1			9	6		2	7			11	4		10									12		3	8	5			41
1			9	6		2	7				4	14	10				12					11		3	8	5			42

Coca-Cola Cup	First Round	Reading (a)	0-3
		(h)	0-2
FA Cup	First Round	Bromsgrove R (h)	1-2

NORTHAMPTON TOWN

Player and Position	Ht	Wt	Birth Date	Birth Place	Source	Clubs	League App	League Gls
Goalkeepers								
Barry Richardson	6 0	12 00	5 8 69	Willington Key	Trainee	Sunderland	—	—
						Scunthorpe U	—	—
						Scarborough	30	—
						Northampton T	96	—
Steve Sherwood*	6 4	14 07	10 12 53	Selby	Apprentice	Chelsea	16	—
						Brighton (loan)	—	—
						Millwall (loan)	1	—
						Brentford (loan)	16	—
						Brentford (loan)	46	—
						Watford	211	1
						Grimsby T	183	—
						Northampton T	16	—
Defenders								
James Benton‡			9 4 75	Wexford	Trainee	Northampton T	10	1
Jason Burnham*	5 10	11 07	8 5 73	Mansfield	Notts County	Northampton T	88	2
Lee Colkin	5 11	12 00	15 7 74	Nuneaton	Trainee	Northampton T	36	1
Bernard Gallacher†	5 9	11 00	22 3 67	Johnstone	Apprentice	Aston Villa	57	—
						Blackburn R (loan)	4	—
						Doncaster R	2	—
						Brighton	45	1
						Northampton T	5	—
Ken Gillard*	5 9	11 08	30 4 72	Dublin	Trainee	Luton T	—	—
						Northampton T	23	—
Mark Parsons*			24 2 75	Luton		Northampton T	51	—
Richard Preston§	5 11	11 02	7 5 76	Basildon	Trainee	Northampton T	1	—
Scott Stackman§	5 11	12 06	16 11 75	Arizona	Trainee	Northampton T	1	—
Steve Terry*	6 1	13 05	14 6 62	Clapton	Apprentice	Watford	160	14
						Hull C	62	4
						Northampton T	181	17
Darren Wood‡	6 1	12 08	22 10 68	Derby	Trainee	Chesterfield	67	3
						Reading	32	2
						Northampton T	4	1
Midfield								
Michael Bell	5 8	10 04	15 11 71	Newcastle	Trainee	Northampton T	141	9
Phil Chard*	5 8	11 03	16 10 60	Corby	Nottingham F	Peterborough U	172	18
						Northampton T	115	27
						Wolverhampton W	34	5
						Northampton T	163	19
Paul Fitzpatrick†	6 4	12 00	5 10 65	Liverpool		Tranmere R	—	—
						Liverpool	—	—
						Preston NE	—	—
						Bolton W	14	—
						Bristol C	44	7
						Carlisle U	109	4
						Preston NE (loan)	2	—
						Leicester C	27	4
						Birmingham C	7	—
						Bury (loan)	9	—
						Hamilton A	18	1
						Northampton T	2	1
Darren Harmon	5 5	9 12	30 1 73	Northampton	Trainee	Notts Co	—	—
						Shrewsbury T	6	2
						Northampton T	56	8
Paul Lamb‡			12 9 74	Plumstead	Trainee	Northampton T	3	—
Warren Patmore			14 8 71	Kingsbury		Cambridge U	1	—
						Millwall	1	—
						Northampton T	17	2
Les Phillips	5 8	10 06	7 1 63	Lambeth	Apprentice	Birmingham C	44	3
						Oxford U	179	9
						Northampton T	26	—
Forwards								
Martin Aldridge			6 12 74	Northampton	Trainee	Northampton T	43	10
Efon Elad†	5 10	12 00	5 9 70	Hillingdon	Cologne	Northampton T	10	—

NORTHAMPTON TOWN

Colours: Claret and white. **Change colours:** Yellow and black.

Foundation: Formed in 1897 by school teachers connected with the Northampton and District Elementary Schools' Association, they survived a financial crisis at the end of their first year when they were £675 in the red and became members of the Midland League – a fast move indeed for a new club. They achieved Southern League membership in 1901.

First Football League game: 28 August, 1920, Division 3, v Grimsby T (a) L 0-2 – Thorpe; Sproston, Hewison; Jobey, Tomkins, Pease; Whitworth, Lockett, Thomas, Freeman, MacKechnie.

Did you know: Steve Sherwood became the oldest player to appear for Northampton Town when he played against Chesterfield on 27 November 1993 when 13 days short of his 40th birthday.

Managers (and Secretary-Managers)
Arthur Jones 1897–1907*, Herbert Chapman 1907–12, Walter Bull 1912–13, Fred Lessons 1913–19, Bob Hewison 1920–25, Jack Tresadern 1925–30, Jack English 1931–35, Syd Puddefoot 1935–37, Warney Cresswell 1937–39, Tom Smith 1939–49, Bob Dennison 1949–54, Dave Smith 1954–59, David Bowen 1959–67, Tony Marchi 1967–68, Ron Flowers 1968–69, Dave Bowen 1969–72 (continued as GM and secretary to 1985 when joined the board), Billy Baxter 1972–73, Bill Dodgin Jnr 1973–76, Pat Crerand 1976–77, Bill Dodgin Jnr 1977, John Petts 1977–78, Mike Keen 1978–79, Clive Walker 1979–80, Bill Dodgin Jnr 1980–82, Clive Walker 1982–84, Tony Barton 1984–85, Graham Carr 1985–90, Theo Foley 1990–92, Phil Chard 1992–93, John Barnwell September 1993–

Player and Position	Ht	Wt	Birth Date	Birth Place	Source	Clubs	League App	League Gls
Terry Fleming	5 9	11 00	5 1 73	Marston Green	Trainee	Coventry C	13	—
						Northampton T	31	1
Sean Francis	5 10	11 09	1 8 72	Birmingham	Trainee	Birmingham C	6	—
						Northampton T	1	—
Ian Gilzean*	6 1	12 10	10 12 69	London	Trainee	Tottenham H	—	—
						Dundee	24	5
						Doncaster R (loan)	3	—
						Northampton T	33	10
Gary Harrison	5 9	11 05	12 3 75	Northampton	Aston Villa	Northampton T	2	—
Kevin Wilkin			1 10 67	Cambridge	Cambridge C	Northampton T	74	11

Trainees
Dalby, Craig A; Elekes, Stefan; Hewes, Nigel; Justin, Steven M; King, Darryl J; Musgrove, Neil S; Preddie, Delroy E; Preston, Richard J; Scott, Martin A; Stackman, Harry S; Willoughby, Damian.

Associated Schoolboys
Caine, John; Dady, Steven; Gascoyne, Murray; Preekel, Garry; Wright, David A; Wright, Scott.

Associated Schoolboys who have accepted the Club's offer of a Traineeship/Contract
Boxford, Edward M. C; Jakes, Simon C.

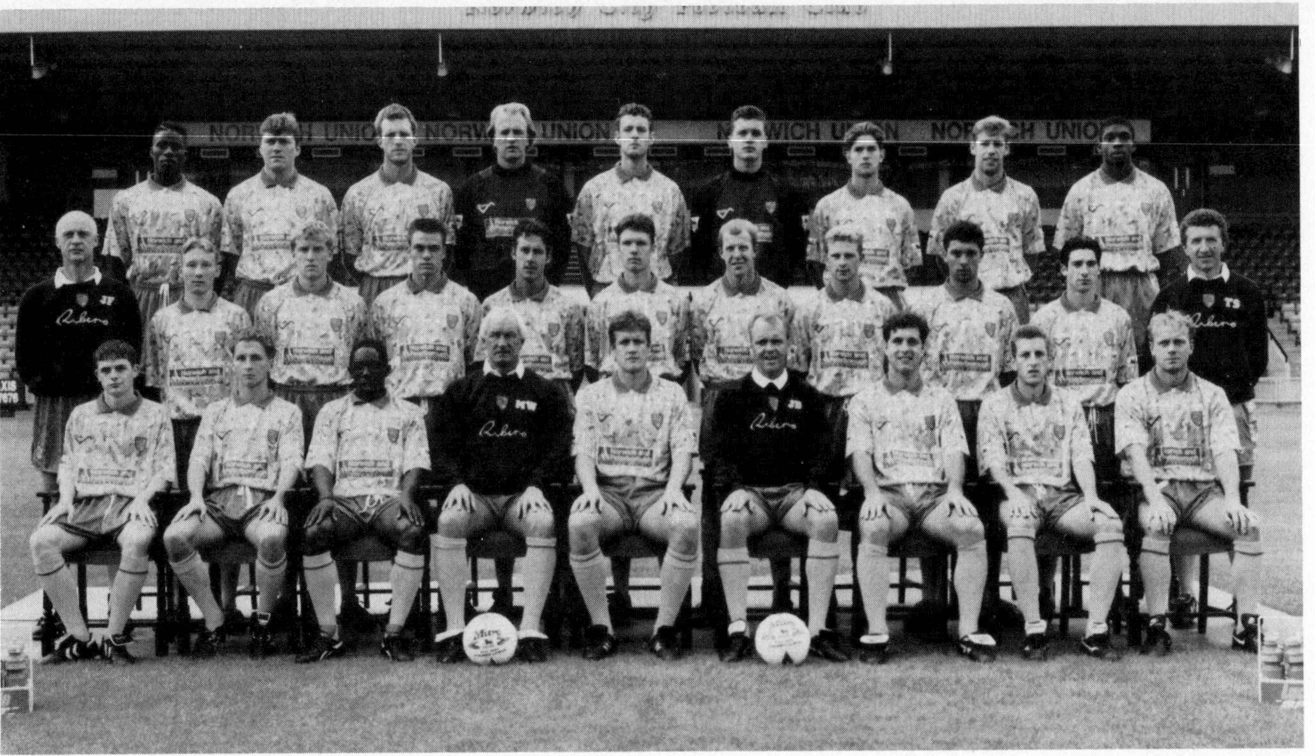

NORWICH CITY 1993–94 *Back row (left to right):* Ade Akinbiyi, Rob Newman, Spencer Prior, Bryan Gunn, Chris Sutton, Andy Marshall, Andy Johnson, John Polston, Efan Ekoku.
Centre row: John Faulkner (Reserve Team Manager), Deryn Brace, Lee Power, Daryl Sutch, Ian Culverhouse, Colin Woodthorpe, Gary Megson, Mark Robins, David Smith, Robert Ullathorne, Tim Sheppard (Physio).
Front row: Jamie Cureton, Darren Eadie, Ruel Fox, Mike Walker (Manager), Ian Butterworth, John Deehan (Assistant Manager), Mark Bowen, Ian Crook, Jeremy Goss.

FA Premiership **NORWICH CITY**

Chairman: B. E. Fearn. ***Vice-chairman:*** L. V. Pickering.
Carrow Road, Norwich NR1 1JE. Telephone Norwich (0603) 760760. Fax (0603) 665510. Box Office: (0603) 761661. Canary Call: 0891 424212. Clubcall: 0891 121144. Match Information Line: 0891 121514.

Ground capacity: 21,272.

Record attendance: 43,984 v Leicester C, FA Cup 6th rd, 30 March 1963.

Record receipts: £261,918 v Internazionale, UEFA Cup 3rd rd 1st leg, 24 November 1993.

Pitch measurements: 114yd × 74yd.

President: G. C. Watling.

Chairman: Robert T. Chase JP. ***Vice-chairman:*** J. A. Jones.

Directors: B. W. Lockwood, G. A. Paterson.

Manager: John Deehan. ***Coach:*** Gary Megson. ***Reserve team coach:*** John Faulkner.

Commercial Manager: Ray Cossey.

Physio: Tim Sheppard MCSP, SRP.

Secretary: A. R. W. Neville.

Year Formed: 1902. ***Turned Professional:*** 1905. ***Ltd Co.:*** 1905.

Club Nickname: 'The Canaries'.

Previous Grounds: 1902, Newmarket Road; 1908–35, The Nest, Rosary Road.

Record League Victory: 10–2 v Coventry C, Division 3 (S), 15 March 1930 – Jarvie; Hannah, Graham; Brown, O'Brien, Lochhead (1); Porter (1), Anderson, Hunt (5), Scott (2), Slicer (1).

Record Cup Victory: 8–0 v Sutton U, FA Cup, 4th rd, 28 January 1989 – Gunn; Culverhouse, Bowen, Butterworth, Linighan, Townsend (Crook), Gordon, Fleck (3), Allen (4), Phelan, Putney (1).

Record Defeat: 2–10 v Swindon T, Southern League, 5 September 1908.

Most League Points (2 for a win): 64, Division 3 (S), 1950–51.

Most League Points (3 for a win): 84, Division 2, 1985–86.

Most League Goals: 99, Division 3 (S), 1952–53.

Highest League Scorer in Season: Ralph Hunt, 31. Division 3 (S), 1955–56.

Most League Goals in Total Aggregate: Johnny Gavin, 122, 1945–54, 1955–58.

Most Capped Player: Mark Bowen, 24 (26), Wales; David Phillips, 24 (52), Wales.

Most League Appearances: Ron Ashman, 592, 1947–64.

Record Transfer Fee Received: £2,250,000 from Newcastle U for Ruel Fox, February 1994.

Record Transfer Fee Paid: £925,000 to Port Vale for Darren Beckford, June 1991.

Football League Record: 1920 Original Member of Division 3; 1921 Division 3 (S): 1934–39 Division 2; 1946–58 Division 3 (S); 1958–60 Division 3; 1960–72 Division 2; 1972–74 Division 1; 1974–75 Division 2; 1975–81 Division 1; 1981–82 Division 2; 1982–85 Division 1; 1985–86 Division 2; 1986–92 Division 1; 1992– FA Premier League.

Honours: *FA Premier League* best season: 3rd 1992–93. *Football League:* Division 2 – Champions 1971–72, 1985–86. Division 3 (S) – Champions 1933–34; Division 3 – Runners-up 1959–60. *FA Cup:* Semi-finals 1959, 1989, 1992. *Football League Cup:* Winners 1962, 1985; Runners-up 1973, 1975. **European Competitions:** *UEFA Cup:* 1993–94.

NORWICH CITY 1993—94 LEAGUE RECORD

Match No.	Date	Venue	Opponents	Result		H/T Score	Lg. Pos.	Goalscorers	Attendance
1	Aug 15	H	Manchester U	L	0-2	0-1	—		19,705
2	18	A	Blackburn R	W	3-2	1-1	—	Sutton 2, Newman	14,260
3	21	A	Leeds U	W	4-0	2-0	6	Fox 2, Sutton, Goss	32,008
4	25	H	Ipswich T	W	1-0	1-0	—	Goss	18,976
5	28	H	Swindon T	D	0-0	0-0	4		17,614
6	Sept 1	A	Sheffield W	D	3-3	0-0	—	Bowen, Ekoku, Sutton	25,175
7	11	H	Wimbledon	L	0-1	0-0	8		14,851
8	18	A	QPR	D	2-2	2-1	10	McDonald (og), Eadie	13,359
9	25	A	Everton	W	5-1	1-1	5	Ekoku 4, Sutton	20,631
10	Oct 2	H	Coventry C	W	1-0	1-0	4	Fox	16,239
11	16	A	Chelsea	W	2-1	1-0	2	Fox, Sutton	16,923
12	23	H	West Ham U	D	0-0	0-0	2		20,175
13	30	A	Arsenal	D	0-0	0-0	2		30,516
14	Nov 6	A	Sheffield U	W	2-1	1-1	2	Goss, Eadie	18,254
15	20	H	Manchester C	D	1-1	0-0	3	Fox	16,626
16	27	A	Oldham Ath	L	1-2	0-0	21	Sutton	10,198
17	Dec 4	A	Manchester U	D	2-2	1-2	7	Sutton, Fox (pen)	44,694
18	13	H	Leeds U	W	2-1	1-0	—	Sutton, Ekoku	16,586
19	18	A	Ipswich T	L	1-2	1-1	6	Bowen	19,751
20	27	A	Tottenham H	W	3-1	2-0	6	Sutton 2, Ekoku	31,130
21	29	H	Aston Villa	L	1-2	1-0	7	Sutton	20,650
22	Jan 1	A	Southampton	W	1-0	1-0	6	Sutton	16,556
23	4	H	Newcastle U	L	1-2	1-1	—	Bowen	19,564
24	15	H	Chelsea	D	1-1	0-1	7	Ekoku	19,472
25	24	A	West Ham U	D	3-3	1-1	—	Sutton 2, Fox	20,738
26	Feb 5	H	Liverpool	D	2-2	1-0	8	Sutton 2	19,746
27	13	H	Arsenal	D	1-1	0-1	—	Ekoku	17,667
28	19	A	Swindon T	D	3-3	2-2	9	Sutton, Newman, Goss	15,341
29	22	H	Blackburn R	D	2-2	1-1	—	Sutton 2 (1 pen)	15,124
30	25	H	Sheffield W	D	1-1	0-0	9	Sutton	18,311
31	Mar 5	A	Wimbledon	L	1-3	1-1	9	Ekoku	7206
32	12	H	QPR	L	3-4	1-0	9	Ekoku 2, Bowen	16,499
33	21	H	Everton	W	3-0	1-0	—	Culverhouse, Sutton, Bowen	16,432
34	26	A	Coventry C	L	1-2	0-1	9	Eadie	13,515
35	29	A	Newcastle U	L	0-3	0-1	—		32,228
36	Apr 2	H	Tottenham H	L	1-2	0-0	11	Sutton	21,181
37	4	A	Aston Villa	D	0-0	0-0	11		25,416
38	9	H	Southampton	L	4-5	1-1	11	Robins, Goss, Sutton 2	17,150
39	16	A	Manchester C	D	1-1	1-0	11	Ullathorne	28,020
40	23	H	Sheffield U	L	0-1	0-1	11		18,474
41	30	A	Liverpool	W	1-0	1-0	11	Goss	44,339
42	May 7	H	Oldham Ath	D	1-1	0-1	12	Ullathorne	20,394

Final League Position: 12

GOALSCORERS

League (65): Sutton 25 (1 pen), Ekoku 12, Fox 7 (1 pen), Goss 6, Bowen 5, Eadie 3, Newman 2, Ullathorne 2, Culverhouse 1, Robins 1, own goal 1.
Coca-Cola Cup (5): Fox 2, Crook 1, Ekoku 1, Sutton 1.
FA Cup (2): Sutton 2.

Gunn 41	Culverhouse 42	Bowen 41	Butterworth 23 + 2	Polston 24	Goss 34	Crook 38	Newman 32	Robins 9 + 4	Fox 25	Sutton 41	Ekoku 20 + 7	Megson 21 + 1	Prior 13	Eadie 9 + 6	Sutch 1 + 2	Ullathorne 11 + 5	Power 2 + 3	Woodthorpe 18 + 2	Smith 5 + 2	Johnson — + 2	Howie 1 + 1	Adams 11 + 3	Akinbiyi — + 2	Match No.
1	2	3	4	5	6	7	8	9	10	11	12													1
1	2	3	4	5	6	7	8	9	10	11														2
1	2	3	4	5	6	7	8	9	10	11	12													3
1	2	3	4	5	6	7	8	9	10	11														4
1	2	3	*4*	5	6	7	8	9	10	11	12	14												5
1	2	3		5	6	7	8	9	10	11	12		4											6
1	2	3		5	6	7	8	12	10	11	9		4											7
1	2	3		5	6	7	4		10	11	9			8										8
1	2	3	4	5	6	7	8		10	11	9													9
1	2	3		5	6	7	8		10	11	9	4												10
1	2	3	4		6	7	8	9	10	11			5											11
1	2	3	4		6	7	5		10	11		8		12	9									12
1	2	3	4			7	8		10	11		6	5	9										13
1	2		4	5	6	7	8		10	11				9		3								14
1	2	3	4	5	6	7	8		10	9		11			12									15
1	2	3	4	5	6	7	8		10	11						12	9							16
1	2	3	*4*		6		8		10	11		7		12	14		9	5						17
1	2	3					8		10	11	9	4	*5*			14	12	6	7					18
1	2	3	4				5		10	11	9	7					12	6	8					19
1	2	3	4			7	6		10	11	9	8				12		5						20
1	2	3	*4*			7	6		10	11	9					12		5	8	14				21
1	2	3	4			7	8		10	11	9	6						5						22
1	2	3	4			7	6		10	11	9	8						5						23
1	2	3	4			7	8		10	11	9	6						5		12				24
1	2	3	4		11	7	8		10	9	12	6						5						25
1	2	3		5	11	7	8			9	10	4		*12*				6			14			26
1	2	3		5	6	7	8			11	9	*10*		12			14	4						27
	2	3		5	6	7	8			10	9			12				4			1	11		28
1	2	3	12	5	11	4	8			10	*9*			14		6						*7*		29
1	2	3	12	5	6	7	8			10	9					4						11		30
1	2	3	4		6	7	5			10	9					8						11		31
1	2	3			6	4	*8*			10	9					12		5	11			7	14	32
1	2	3	4	5	6	7				9		8		10					12			11		33
1	2	3	4	5	6	7				9		8		10				12				11		34
1	2	3			6	7						8	5	9		10		4				11	12	35
1	2	3			6	7		12		9		8	5	10				4				11		36
1	2	3			6	7				9		8	5	*10*		11		4	12			14		37
1	2	3			6	7		12		9		8	5	*10*		4	14					11		38
1	2	3		5	11	7		10		9	12		6			4			*8*			14		39
1	2	3		5	6	7		10		9	12		4			8						11		40
1	2	3		5	11	7				9	10		6			8		4						41
1	2	3		5	11			12		9	10	8	*6*			7		4				14		42

Coca-Cola Cup	Second Round	Bradford C (a)	1-2
		(h)	3-0
	Third Round	Arsenal (a)	1-1
		(h)	0-3
FA Cup	Third Round	Wycombe W (a)	2-0
	Fourth Round	Manchester U (h)	0-2

NORWICH CITY

Player and Position	Ht	Wt	Birth Date	Birth Place	Source	Clubs	League App	League Gls
Goalkeepers								
Bryan Gunn	6 2	13 13	22 12 63	Thurso	Invergordon BC	Aberdeen	15	—
						Norwich C	283	—
Scott Howie	6 2	13 07	4 1 72	Glasgow	Ferguslie U	Clyde	55	—
						Norwich C	2	—
Andy Marshall	6 2	13 03	14 4 75	Bury	Trainee	Norwich C	—	—
Defenders								
Mark Bowen	5 8	11 13	7 12 63	Neath	Apprentice	Tottenham H	17	2
						Norwich C	253	20
Ian Butterworth	6 1	12 10	25 1 65	Crewe	Apprentice	Coventry C	90	—
						Nottingham F	27	—
						Norwich C	235	4
Ian Culverhouse	5 10	11 02	22 9 64	Bishop's Stortford	Apprentice	Tottenham H	2	—
						Norwich C	296	1
Rob Newman	6 0	13 00	13 12 63	Bradford-on-Avon	Apprentice	Bristol C	394	52
						Norwich C	91	11
John Polston	5 11	11 03	10 6 68	London	Apprentice	Tottenham H	24	1
						Norwich C	104	6
Spencer Prior	6 1	12 09	22 4 71	Rochford	Trainee	Southend U	135	3
						Norwich C	13	—
Robert Ullathorne	5 8	10 00	11 10 71	Wakefield	Trainee	Norwich C	38	5
Colin Woodthorpe	5 11	11 08	13 1 69	Ellesmere Pt	Apprentice	Chester C	155	6
						Norwich C	43	1
Midfield								
Ian Crook	5 8	10 06	18 1 63	Romford	Apprentice	Tottenham H	20	1
						Norwich C	242	14
Jeremy Goss	5 9	10 09	11 5 65	Cyprus	Amateur	Norwich C	147	11
Andrew Johnson	5 11	11 06	2 5 74	Bath	Trainee	Norwich C	6	1
Gary Megson	5 10	12 00	2 5 59	Manchester	Apprentice	Plymouth Arg	78	10
						Everton	22	2
						Sheffield W	123	13
						Nottingham F	—	—
						Newcastle U	24	1
						Sheffield W	110	12
						Manchester C	82	2
						Norwich C	45	1
David Smith	5 9	11 12	26 12 70	Liverpool	Trainee	Norwich C	18	—
Daryl Sutch	6 0	12 00	11 9 71	Lowestoft	Trainee	Norwich C	38	2
Forwards								
Neil Adams	5 8	10 08	23 11 65	Stoke	Local	Stoke C	32	4
						Everton	20	—
						Oldham Ath (loan)	9	—
						Oldham Ath	129	23
						Norwich C	14	—
Adeola Akinbiyi	6 1	12 08	10 10 74	Hackney	Trainee	Norwich C	2	—
						Hereford U (loan)	4	2
Jamie Cureton	5 8	10 05	28 8 75	Bristol	Trainee	Norwich C	—	—
Darren Eadie	5 7	10 00	10 6 75	Chippenham	Trainee	Norwich C	15	3
Efan Ekoku	6 1	12 00	8 6 67	Manchester	Sutton U	Bournemouth	62	21
						Norwich C	31	15
Mark Robins	5 7	10 04	22 12 69	Ashton-under-Lyme.	Apprentice	Manchester U	48	11
						Norwich C	50	16
Chris Sutton	6 3	12 01	10 3 73	Nottingham	Trainee	Norwich C	102	35

NORWICH CITY

Colours: Yellow shirts, green trim, green shorts, yellow trim, yellow stockings. **Change colours:** All blue.

Foundation: Formed in 1902, largely through the initiative of two local schoolmasters who called a meeting at the Criterion Cafe, they were shocked by an FA Commission which in 1904 declared the club professional and ejected them from the FA Amateur Cup. However, this only served to strengthen their determination. New officials were appointed and a professional club established at a meeting in the Agricultural Hall in March 1905.

First Football League game: 28 August, 1920, Division 3, v Plymouth A (a) D 1-1 – Skermer; Gray, Gadsden; Wilkinson, Addy, Martin; Laxton, Kidger, Parker, Whitham (1), Dobson.

Did you know: Efan Ekoku set a FA Premier League record by scoring four goals for Norwich City at Everton on 25 September 1993 in a 5-1 win.

Managers (and Secretary-Managers)
John Bowman 1905–07, James McEwen 1907–08, Arthur Turner 1909–10, Bert Stansfield 1910–15, Major Frank Buckley 1919–20, Charles O'Hagan 1920–21, Albert Gosnell 1921–26, Bert Stansfield 1926, Cecil Potter 1926–29, James Kerr 1929–33, Tom Parker 1933–37, Bob Young 1937–39, Jimmy Jewell 1939, Bob Young 1939–45, Cyril Spiers 1946–47, Duggie Lochhead 1945–50, Norman Low 1950–55, Tom Parker 1955–57, Archie Macaulay 1957–61, Willie Reid 1961–62, George Swindin 1962, Ron Ashman 1962–66, Lol Morgan 1966–69, Ron Saunders 1969–73, John Bond 1973–80, Ken Brown 1980–87, Dave Stringer 1987–92, Mike Walker 1992–94, John Deehan January 1994–

Trainees
Carey, Shaun P; Carus, Joshua; Crowfoot, Darren L; Gibb, Alistair S; Harrington, Justin D; Kreft, Stacey; Levin, Gavin; Lewis, Paul; Liffen, Neil; Mellon, Richard C; Mills, Daniel; Mitchell, James; Morgan, Christian W; O'Neill, Keith P; Oldbury, Marcus J; Simpson, James R; Woodman, Clayton K; Wright, Jonathan.

Associated Schoolboys
Baines, Wesley; Bellamy, Craig D; Broughton, Drewe O; Chapman, Andrew L; Collins, Darren J; Coote, Adrian; Jones, Owen R; Karim, Alexis W; Lewis, Craig K; Morgan, Ryan S; Roche, Stewart D. C; Tipple, Gaven L; Wilson, Che C. A.

Associated Schoolboys who have accepted the Club's offer of a Traineeship/Contract
Hobbs, Paul; Shore, Jamie.

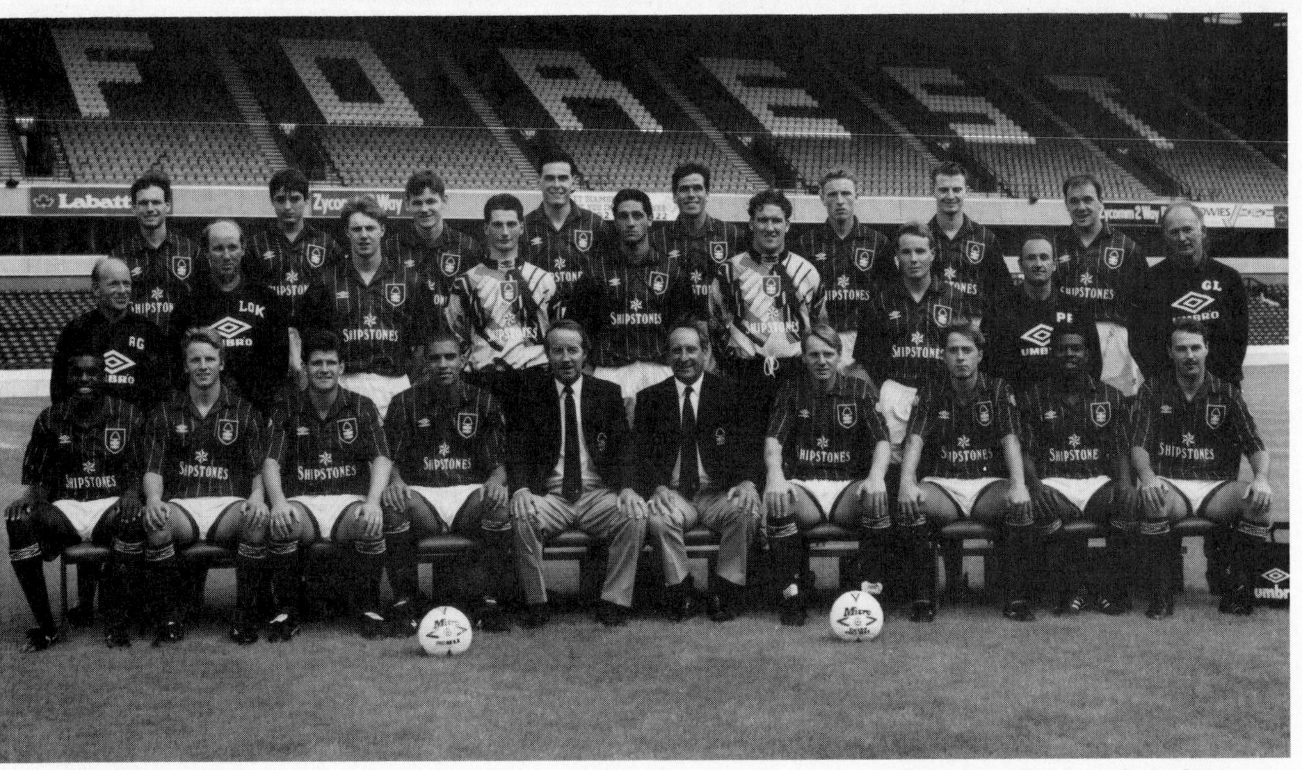

NOTTINGHAM FOREST 1993–94 *Back row (left to right):* Gary Crosby, Ray McKinnon, Lee Glover, Stephen Chettle, Neil Webb, Scot Gemmill, Colin Cooper, Stephen Stone.
Centre row: Archie Gemmill (Coach), Liam O'Kane (Coach), Carl Tiler, Andrew Marriott, Robert Rosario, Mark Crossley, Kingsley Black, Peter Edwards (Fitness Coach), Graham Lyas (Physio).
Front row: Vance Warner, Gary Bull, Brian Laws, Stanley Collymore, Frank Clark (Manager), Alan Hill (Assistant Manager), Stuart Pearce, Ian Woan, Des Lyttle, Brett Williams.

FA Premiership NOTTINGHAM FOREST

City Ground, Nottingham NG2 5FJ. Telephone Nottingham (0602) 526000. Fax (0602) 526003. Information Desk: 526016. Commercial Office: 526006. Commercial office fax (0602) 526007. Ticket office: (0602) 526002. Souvenir shop: (0602) 526026. Junior Reds: 526001. Lottery Office: 526005. Youth & Community Foundation: 810089.

Ground capacity: 28,231 (22,898 seats).

Record attendance: 49,945 v Manchester U, Division 1, 28 October 1967.

Record receipts: £236,593 v Middlesbrough, FA Cup 4th rd, 23 January 1993.

Pitch measurements: 115yd × 78yd.

Chairman: F. Reacher. *Vice-chairman:* I. I. Korn.

Directors: G. E. Macpherson, J. F. Hickling, J. M. Smith, Dr. G. W. Waterhouse, C. Wootton.

Manager: Frank Clark. *Assistant Manager:* Alan Hill.

Secretary: P. White. *Commercial Manager:* Dave Pullan.

Coach: Liam O'Kane. *Physio:* G. Lyas.

Year Formed: 1865. *Turned Professional:* 1889. *Ltd Co.:* 1982.

Club Nickname: 'Reds'.

Previous Grounds: 1865, Forest Racecourse; 1879, The Meadows; 1880, Trent Bridge Cricket Ground; 1882, Parkside, Lenton; 1885, Gregory, Lenton; 1890, Town Ground; 1898, City Ground.

Record League Victory: 12–0 v Leicester Fosse, Division 1, 12 April 1909 – Iremonger; Dudley, Maltby; Hughes (1), Needham, Armstrong; Hooper (3), Marrison, West (3), Morris (2), Spouncer (3 incl. 1p).

Record Cup Victory: 14–0 v Clapton (away), FA Cup, 1st rd, 17 January 1891 – Brown; Earp, Scott; A. Smith, Russell, Jeacock; McCallum (2), 'Tich' Smith (1), Higgins (5), Lindley (4), Shaw (2).

Record Defeat: 1–9 v Blackburn R, Division 2, 10 April 1937.

Most League Points (2 for a win): 70, Division 3 (S), 1950–51.

Most League Points (3 for a win): 83, Division 1, 1993–94.

Most League Goals: 110, Division 3 (S), 1950–51.

Highest League Scorer in Season: Wally Ardron, 36, Division 3 (S), 1950–51.

Most League Goals in Total Aggregate: Grenville Morris, 199, 1898–1913.

Most Capped Player: Stuart Pearce, 56, England.

Most League Appearances: Bob McKinlay, 614, 1951–70.

Record Transfer Fee Received: £3,750,000 from Manchester U for Roy Keane, July 1993.

Record Transfer Fee Paid: £2,000,000 to Millwall for Teddy Sheringham, July 1991 and £2,000,000 to Southend U for Stan Collymore, June 1992.

Football League Record: 1892 Elected to Division 1; 1906–07 Division 2; 1907–11 Division 1; 1911–22 Division 2; 1922–25 Division 1; 1925–49 Division 2; 1949–51 Division 3 (S); 1951–57 Division 2; 1957–72 Division 1; 1972–77 Division 2; 1977–92 Division 1; 1992–93 FA Premier League; 1993–94 Division 1; 1994– FA Premier League.

Honours: Football League: Division 1 – Champions 1977–78; Runners-up 1966–67, 1978–79; Division 2 – Champions 1906–07, 1921–22; Runners-up 1956–57; Division 3 (S) – Champions 1950–51. *FA Cup:* Winners 1898, 1959; Runners-up 1991. *Anglo-Scottish Cup:* Winners 1976–77; *Football League Cup:* Winners 1977–78, 1978–79, 1988–89, 1989–90; Runners-up 1979–80. *Simod Cup:* Winners 1989. *Zenith Data Systems Cup:* Winners: 1991–92. **European Competitions:** *Fairs Cup:* 1961–62, 1967–68. *European Cup:* 1978–79 (winners), 1979–80 (winners), 1980–81. *Super Cup:* 1979–80 (winners), 1980–81 (runners-up). *World Club Championship:* 1980–81 (runners-up). *UEFA Cup:* 1983–84, 1984–85.

NOTTINGHAM FOREST 1993—94 LEAGUE RECORD

Match No.	Date	Venue	Opponents	Result		H/T Score	Lg. Pos.	Goalscorers	Attendance
1	Aug 15	A	Southend U	D	1-1	1-1	—	Pearce (pen)	8609
2	18	H	Derby Co	D	1-1	0-0	—	Woan	26,682
3	21	H	Grimsby T	W	5-3	2-1	3	Black, Futcher (og), Glover, Woan, Rosario	23,225
4	24	A	Crystal Palace	L	0-2	0-1	—		15,048
5	28	A	Luton T	W	2-1	1-1	3	Black, Woan	9788
6	Sept 11	A	Barnsley	L	0-1	0-1	9		13,280
7	19	H	Stoke C	L	2-3	0-2	—	Phillips, Pearce	20,843
8	26	A	Bolton W	L	3-4	2-1	—	Collymore 2, Phillips	10,578
9	Oct 2	H	Portsmouth	D	1-1	0-0	19	Stone	20,727
10	16	H	Tranmere R	W	2-1	1-0	19	Collymore, Gemmill	20,771
11	20	H	Oxford U	D	0-0	0-0	—		18,462
12	24	A	Leicester C	L	0-1	0-1	—		17,624
13	30	H	Notts Co	W	1-0	0-0	16	Collymore	26,721
14	Nov 3	H	Millwall	L	1-3	0-1	—	Glover	17,584
15	6	A	Birmingham C	W	3-0	1-0	12	Collymore, Glover 2	16,996
16	10	A	Wolverhampton W	D	1-1	0-1	—	Collymore	21,621
17	21	A	WBA	W	2-0	2-0	—	Collymore 2	15,581
18	27	A	Sunderland	W	3-2	2-1	11	Gemmill, Collymore 2	16,968
19	Dec 4	H	Birmingham C	W	1-0	1-0	9	Whyte (og)	22,061
20	19	H	Southend U	W	2-0	1-0	—	Cooper, Black	21,641
21	27	H	Middlesbrough	D	1-1	0-0	10	Collymore	26,901
22	28	A	Bristol C	W	4-1	0-0	8	Collymore 2, Webb, Woan	20,725
23	Jan 1	H	Charlton Ath	D	1-1	0-0	8	Lyttle	26,543
24	3	A	Watford	W	2-1	0-1	7	Cooper, Gemmill	14,539
25	16	A	Tranmere R	W	2-1	0-1	—	Cooper, Gemmill	8500
26	23	H	Wolverhampton W	D	0-0	0-0	—		23,008
27	Feb 6	H	Leicester C	W	4-0	2-0	—	Gemmill 2, Glover, Woan	26,616
28	12	A	Notts Co	L	1-2	0-0	6	Phillips	18,655
29	19	H	Crystal Palace	D	1-1	0-0	6	Bohinen	24,232
30	25	A	Oxford U	L	0-1	0-0	8		9346
31	Mar 2	H	Peterborough U	W	2-0	1-0	—	Gemmill 2	19,329
32	5	H	Luton T	W	2-0	0-0	3	Cooper, Pearce (pen)	22,249
33	12	A	Stoke C	W	1-0	1-0	3	Webb	20,550
34	16	H	Barnsley	W	2-1	1-0	—	Cooper, Phillips	20,491
35	19	H	Bolton W	W	3-2	2-1	2	Chettle, Pearce, Collymore	23,846
36	26	A	Portsmouth	L	1-2	0-1	2	Collymore	12,578
37	30	H	Watford	W	2-1	2-0	—	Stone, Webb	23,044
38	Apr 2	A	Middlesbrough	D	2-2	1-1	2	Lee, Rosario	17,056
39	4	H	Bristol C	D	0-0	0-0	2		24,162
40	9	A	Charlton Ath	W	1-0	1-0	2	Lee	12,330
41	17	A	Millwall	D	2-2	0-1	—	Collymore, Stone	12,543
42	24	H	WBA	W	2-1	1-0	—	Stone, Cooper	24,018
43	27	A	Derby Co	W	2-0	1-0	—	Cooper, Stone	19,300
44	30	A	Peterborough U	W	3-2	1-2	2	Collymore 2, Pearce	14,010
45	May 3	A	Grimsby T	D	0-0	0-0	—		11,930
46	8	H	Sunderland	D	2-2	1-0	2	Pearce (pen), Collymore	27,010

Final League Position: 2

GOALSCORERS

League (74): Collymore 19, Gemmill 8, Cooper 7, Pearce 6 (3 pens), Glover 5, Stone 5, Woan 5, Phillips 4, Black 3, Webb 3, Lee 2, Rosario 2, Bohinen 1, Chettle 1, Lyttle 1, own goals 2.
Coca-Cola Cup (11): Collymore 5, Black 2, Cooper 1, Crosby 1, Gemmill 1, Webb 1.
FA Cup (1): Cooper 1.

Crossley 36 + 1	Lyttle 37	Pearce 42	Cooper 36 + 1	Chettle 46	Stone 45	Black 30 + 7	Webb 17 + 4	Rosario 15 + 1	Glover 15 + 3	Woan 23 + 1	Harvey — + 2	Laws 6 + 1	Phillips 40 + 3	Collymore 27 + 1	Warner 1	Blatherwick 3	Gemmill 30 + 1	Wright 10	Kilford — + 1	Howe 2 + 2	Crosby 4 + 2	Bohinen 22 + 1	Bull 3 + 8	Haaland 3	Lee 10 + 3	Tiler 3	*Match No.*
1	2	3	4	5	6	7	8	9	*10*	11	12	14															1
1	2	3	4	5	6	7	8	9	10	11	12																2
1	2	3	4	5	6	7	8	9	10	11			12														3
1	2	3	4	5	6	7	8	9	14	11			12	*10*													4
1	2	3		5	6	7	8	9	10	11			12		4												5
1	2	3		5	6	7	8	9	12	11				10		4											6
1	2	3		5	6			9	8	11			7	10		4	12										7
	2			5		7		9		*11*		3	6	10		4	8	1	12	14							8
	3			5	6	11						2	7	10			8	1		9	4						9
		3		5	6	11		9				2	7	10			8	1		12	4						10
		3	12	5	6	11		9				2	7				8	1		10	4						11
		3	*4*	5	6	11	12	9				2	7	10			8	1			14						12
		3	4	5	6	11			9			2	7	10			8	1									13
	2	3	4	5	6	11	12		9				7	10			8	1									14
	2		4	5	6	11	12		9				7	10			8	1				3					15
	2	3	4	5	6				9				7	10			8	1			11						16
1	2	3	4	5	6	11							7	10			8					9					17
12	2	3	4	5	6	11							7	10			8	1				9					18
1		3	4	5	6	11			12				2	10			8					9	7				19
1	2	3	4	5	6	11							7	10			8					9					20
1	2	3	4	5	6	11							7	10			8					9					21
1	2		4	5	6		3			11			7	10			8					9					22
1	2	3	4	5	6	12	8			11			7	10								9					23
1	2	3	4	5	6	12	9			11			7	*10*			8						14				24
1	2	3	4	5	*6*	12	9		10	11			7				8						14				25
1		3	4	5	6		8		10	11			7				2					9	12				26
1	2	3		5	6				10	11			7				8					9		4			27
1	2	3	4	5	6	11			10				7				8					9	12				28
1	2	3	4	5	6				10	11			7				8					9	12				29
1	2	3	4	5	6				10	11			7				8					9	12				30
1	2	3	4	5	6	11							7				8					9	10				31
1	2	3	4	5	6	11	12						7				8					9			10		32
1	2	3	4	5	6	11	10						7									8			9		33
1	2	3	4	5	6	11	8						7									9	12		10		34
1	2	3		5	*6*	11	8						7	12							14		9	4	10		35
1	*2*	3	4	5	6	11	8	14					7	10								9			12		36
1		3	4	5	6	11	8						7	10										2	9		37
1	2	3	4	5	6	11	8	9					7										12		10		38
1	2	3	4	5	6	11		10		12			7									8			9		39
1	2	3	4	5	6	11		9		8			7									12			10		40
1	2	3		5	6					11			7	10			8								9	4	41
1	2	3	4	5	6	12				11			7	10			8								9		42
1	2	3	4	5	6					11			7	10			8					9					43
1	2	3	4	5	6	12		*9*		11			7	10			8								14		44
1		3	4	5	6	12				11			7	10			8					*9*			14	2	45
1		3	4	5	6	12				11			7	10			8					9				2	46

Coca-Cola Cup	Second Round	Wrexham (a)	3-3
		(h)	3-1
	Third Round	West Ham U (h)	2-1
	Fourth Round	Manchester C (h)	0-0
		(a)	2-1
	Fifth Round	Tranmere R (h)	1-1
		(a)	0-2
FA Cup	Third Round	Sheffield W (a)	1-1
		(h)	0-2

NOTTINGHAM FOREST

Player and Position	Ht	Wt	Birth Date	Birth Place	Source	Clubs	League App	League Gls
Goalkeepers								
Richard Clark	5 11	12 04	6 4 77	Nuneaton	Trainee	Nottingham F	—	—
Mark Crossley	6 0	13 09	16 6 69	Barnsley		Nottingham F	158	—
						Manchester U (loan)	—	—
Mark Statham*	6 2	12 02	11 11 75	Barnsley	Trainee	Nottingham F	—	—
Tommy Wright	6 1	13 05	29 8 63	Belfast	Linfield	Newcastle U	73	—
						Hull C (loan)	6	—
						Nottingham F	10	—
Defenders								
Steve Blatherwick	6 1	12 12	20 9 73	Nottingham	Notts Co	Nottingham F	3	—
						Wycombe W (loan)	2	—
Gary Bowyer	6 0	12 13	26 6 71	Manchester		Hereford U	14	2
						Nottingham F	—	—
Ray Byrne*	6 1	11 02	4 7 72	Newry	Newry	Nottingham F	—	—
Steve Chettle	6 1	12 00	27 9 68	Nottingham	Apprentice	Nottingham F	215	7
Colin Cooper	5 11	11 05	28 2 67	Durham		Middlesbrough	188	6
						Millwall	77	6
						Nottingham F	37	7
Nathan Drury	6 0	11 02	15 1 76	Leeds	Trainee	Nottingham F	—	—
Craig Gilmore	5 10	11 00	8 12 76	Leeds	Trainee	Nottingham F	—	—
Paul Haywood	5 11	10 02	4 10 75	Barnsley	Trainee	Nottingham F	—	—
Danny Hinshelwood	5 9	10 11	4 12 75	Bromley	Trainee	Nottingham F	—	—
Ian Kilford	5 10	10 05	6 10 73	Bristol	Trainee	Nottingham F	1	—
						Wigan Ath (loan)	8	3
Brian Laws	5 10	11 05	14 10 61	Wallsend	Apprentice	Burnley	125	12
						Huddersfield T	56	1
						Middlesbrough	107	12
						Nottingham F	147	4
Des Lyttle	5 9	12 00	24 9 71	Wolverhampton	Worcester C	Swansea C	46	1
						Nottingham F	37	1
Ray McKinnon (To Aberdeen Febrary 1994)	5 8	9 11	5 8 70	Dundee	S Form	Dundee U	53	6
						Nottingham F	6	1
Stuart Pearce	5 10	12 09	24 4 62	London	Wealdstone	Coventry C	51	4
						Nottingham F	301	47
Richard Smith	5 11	11 10	24 1 74	Lichfield	Trainee	Nottingham F	—	—
Stuart Thom	6 2	11 08	27 12 76	Dewsbury	Trainee	Nottingham F	—	—
Carl Tiler	6 2	13 00	11 2 70	Sheffield	Trainee	Barnsley	71	3
						Nottingham F	66	1
Vance Warner	5 11	11 05	3 9 74	Leeds	Trainee	Nottingham F	1	—
Darren Watkins	5 11	11 02	17 3 77	Middlesbrough	Trainee	Nottingham F	—	—
Brett Williams*	5 10	11 12	19 3 68	Dudley	Apprentice	Nottingham F	43	—
						Stockport Co (loan)	2	—
						Northampton T (loan)	4	—
						Hereford U (loan)	14	—
						Oxford U (loan)	7	—
						Stoke C (loan)	2	—
Dale Wright	6 00	12 05	21 12 74	Middlesbrough	Trainee	Nottingham F	—	—
Midfield								
Craig Armstrong	5 11	12 04	23 5 75	South Shields	Trainee	Nottingham F	—	—
Kingsley Black	5 8	10 11	22 6 68	Luton	School	Luton T	127	26
						Nottingham F	86	12
Lars Bohinen	5 11	12 02	8 9 66	Vadso	Young Boys Berne	Nottingham F	23	1
Anthony Carbone	5 10	11 06	13 10 74	Perth	Perth Italia	Nottingham F	—	—
Gary Crosby	5 7	9 11	8 5 64	Sleaford	Lincoln U Grantham	Lincoln C	7	—
						Nottingham F	152	12
						Grimsby T (loan)	3	—
John Finnigan	5 8	10 05	29 3 76	Wakefield	Trainee	Nottingham F	—	—
Scot Gemmill	5 10	10 01	2 1 71	Paisley	School	Nottingham F	107	17
Alf-Inge Haaland	5 10	12 12	23 11 72	Stavanger	Bryne	Nottingham F	3	—
Stephen Howe	5 7	10 04	6 11 73	Annitsford	Trainee	Nottingham F	4	—
David Phillips	5 10	11 02	29 7 63	Wegberg	Apprentice	Plymouth Arg	73	15
						Manchester C	81	13
						Coventry C	100	8
						Norwich C	152	18
						Nottingham F	43	4

NOTTINGHAM FOREST

Colours: Red shirts, white shorts, red stockings. **Change colours:** Blue shirts, green shorts, blue stockings.

Foundation: One of the oldest football clubs in the world, Nottingham Forest was formed at a meeting in the Clinton Arms in 1865. Known originally as the Forest Football Club, the game which first drew the founders together was "shinney" a form of hockey. When they determined to change to football in 1865, one of their first moves was to buy a set of red caps to wear on the field.

First Football League game: 3 September, 1892, Division 1, v Everton (a) D 2-2 – Brown; Earp, Scott; Hamilton, A. Smith, McCracken; McCallum, W. Smith, Higgins (2), Pike, McInnes.

Did you know: The only Nottingham Forest player to have been an ever present in League games for four consecutive seasons was George Needham, a defender, who appeared in every match from 1911–12 to 1914–15 inclusive.

Managers (and Secretary-Managers)
Harry Radford 1889–97*, Harry Haslam 1897–1909*, Fred Earp 1909–12, Bob Masters 1912–25, John Baynes 1925–29, Stan Hardy 1930–31, Noel Watson 1931–36, Harold Wightman 1936–39, Billy Walker 1939–60, Andy Beattie 1960–63, John Carey 1963–68, Matt Gillies 1969–72, Dave Mackay 1972, Allan Brown 1973–75, Brian Clough 1975–93, Frank Clark June 1993–

Steven Stone	5 9	11 03	20 8 71	Gateshead	Trainee	Nottingham F	58	6
Lee Stratford	5 10	10 08	11 11 75	Barnsley	Trainee	Nottingham F	—	—
Justin Walker	5 10	11 08	6 9 75	Nottingham	Trainee	Nottingham F	—	—
Neil Webb	6 0	13 07	30 7 63	Reading	Apprentice	Reading	72	22
						Portsmouth	123	34
						Nottingham F	146	47
						Manchester U	75	8
						Nottingham F	30	3
Ross Wilson	5 8	10 00	29 9 76	Chatham	Trainee	Nottingham F	—	—
Terry Wilson‡	6 0	10 10	8 2 69	Broxburn	Apprentice	Nottingham F	105	9
						Newcastle U (loan)	2	—
Ian Woan	5 10	11 09	14 12 67	Wirrall	Runcorn	Nottingham F	85	16
Forwards								
Gary Bull	5 9	11 07	12 6 66	West Bromwich		Southampton	—	—
						Cambridge U	19	4
					Barnet	Barnet	83	37
						Nottingham F	11	—
Stan Collymore	6 2	14 00	22 1 71	Stone	Stafford R	Crystal Palace	20	1
						Southend U	30	15
						Nottingham F	28	19
Lee Glover	5 10	12 01	24 4 70	Kettering	Trainee	Nottingham F	76	9
						Leicester C (loan)	5	1
						Barnsley (loan)	8	—
						Luton T (loan)	1	—
Stephen Guinan	6 1	12 12	24 12 75	Birmingham	Trainee	Nottingham F	—	—
Luke Hughes	5 10	10 04	17 9 75	Sunderland	Trainee	Nottingham F	—	—
Jason Kaminsky‡			5 12 73	Leicester	Trainee	Nottingham F	1	—
Jason Lee	6 3	13 08	9 5 71	Newham	Trainee	Charlton Ath	1	—
						Stockport Co (loan)	2	—
						Lincoln C	93	21
						Southend U	24	3
						Nottingham F	13	2
Paul McGregor	5 10	10 04	17 12 74	Liverpool	Trainee	Nottingham F	—	—
Lee Marshall	5 9	9 12	1 8 75	Nottingham	Trainee	Nottingham F	—	—
Craig Mendum	5 9	10 08	13 4 77	Saltburn	Trainee	Nottingham F	—	—
Carl Rookyard	5 9	10 05	3 9 75	Burton on Trent	Trainee	Nottingham F	—	—
Robert Rosario	6 3	12 01	4 3 66	Hammersmith	Hillingdon Bor	Norwich C	126	18
						Wolverhampton W (loan)	2	1
						Coventry C	59	8
						Nottingham F	26	3
Mark Walley	5 10	10 06	17 9 76	Barnsley	Trainee	Nottingham F	—	—
Stephen Woolford	5 10	11 00	24 11 76	Leeds	Trainee	Nottingham F	—	—

Associated Schoolboys
Anderson, Dale R; Barber, Andrew J; Bough, Gareth G; Cooper, David M; Cooper, Richard A; Dawson, Andrew; Douglass, Russell B; Elder, Mark; Fitchett, Scott; Follett, Richard J; George, Daniel; Girolami, Daniel R; Goodlad, Mark; Grim, Robert J; Harewood, Marlon A; Henders, Mark R. A; Henshaw, Carl H; Hodgson, Richard J; Melton, Stephen; Simonsen, Steven P. A; Simpson, Mark; Sinden, Richard P. G; Swanson, Kevin; Taylor, Neil; Turner, Barry.

Associated Schoolboys who have accepted the Club's offer of a Traineeship/Contract
Archer, Paul; Atkinson, Craig; Cowling, Lee; Morgan, Ian; O'Neill, Shane; Orr, Stephen; Poole, Darren; Redden, Damion; Turner, Darren.

NOTTS COUNTY 1993–94 *Back row (left to right):* Tony Agana, David Smith, Paul Cox, Steve Slawson, Dean Yates, Andy Williams, Robbie Turner, Dave Robinson, David Reeves. *Centre row:* Richard Walker, Chris Short, Meindert Dijkstra, Mark Smith, Shaun Murphy, Bob Catlin, Steve Cherry, Gary Lund, Paul Harding, Charlie Palmer, Gavin Warboys, Alan Paris. *Front row:* Russell Slade (Assistant Manager), Mark Draper, Andy Legg, Gary McSwegan, Dean Thomas, Derek Pavis (Chairman), Mick Walker (Manager), Phil Turner, Kevin Wilson, Paul Devlin, Michael Johnson, Dave Lawson (Physio).
(Photograph: Empics)

Division 1 NOTTS COUNTY

County Ground, Meadow Lane, Nottingham NG2 3HJ. Telephone Nottingham (0602) 861155 or 529000. Fax: (0602) 866442. Ticket office: (0602) 850632. Clubline: 0891 888684. Football in the Community: 863656. Supporters Club: 866802.

Ground capacity: 20,336.

Record attendance: 47,310 v York C, FA Cup 6th rd, 12 March 1955.

Record receipts: £124,539.10 v Manchester C, FA Cup 6th rd, 16 February 1991.

Pitch measurements: 114yd × 74yd.

Chairman: D. C. Pavis. ***Vice-chairman:*** J. Mounteney.

Directors: W. A. Hopcroft, D. Ward, F. Sherwood (President).

Manager: Mick Walker. ***Assistant Manager:*** Russell Slade. ***Commerical Manager:*** Elaine Howes.

Coach: Wayne Jones. ***Chief Executive:*** Neal Hook MCIM. AMLD.

Physio: Dennis Pettitt.

Year Formed: 1862 *(*see Foundation*).

Turned Professional: 1885. ***Ltd Co.:*** 1888.

Club Nickname: 'Magpies'.

Previous Grounds: 1862, The Park; 1864, The Meadows; 1877, Beeston Cricket Ground; 1880, Castle Ground; 1883, Trent Bridge; 1910, Meadow Lane.

Record League Victory: 11–1 v Newport C, Division 3 (S), 15 January 1949 – Smith; Southwell, Purvis; Gannon, Baxter, Adamson; Houghton (1), Sewell (4), Lawton (4), Pimbley, Johnston (2).

Record Cup Victory: 15–0 v Rotherham T (at Trent Bridge), FA Cup, 1st rd, 24 October 1885 – Sherwin; Snook, H. T. Moore; Dobson (1), Emmett (1), Chapman; Gunn (1), Albert Moore (2), Jackson (3), Daft (2), Cursham (4). (1 og).

Record Defeat: 1–9 v Blackburn R, Division 1, 16 November, 1889 and v Aston Villa, Division 1, 29 September, 1888 and v Portsmouth, Division 2, 9 April, 1927.

Most League Points (2 for a win): 69, Division 4, 1970–71.

Most League Points (3 for a win): 87, Division 3, 1989–90.

Most League Goals: 107, Division 4, 1959–60.

Highest League Scorer in Season: Tom Keetley, 39, Division 3 (S), 1930–31.

Most League Goals in Total Aggregate: Les Bradd, 124, 1967–78.

Most Capped Player: Kevin Wilson, 15 (40), Northern Ireland.

Most League Appearances: Albert Iremonger, 564, 1904–26.

Record Transfer Fee Received: £2,500,000 from Derby Co for Craig Short, September 1992.

Record Transfer Fee Paid: £685,000 to Sheffield U for Tony Agana, November 1991.

Football League Record: 1888 Founder Member of the Football League; 1893–97 Division 2; 1897–1913 Division 1; 1913–14 Division 2; 1914–20 Division 1; 1920–23 Division 2; 1923–26 Division 1; 1926–30 Division 2; 1930–31 Division 3 (S); 1931–35 Division 2; 1935–50 Division 3 (S); 1950–58 Division 2; 1958–59 Division 3; 1959–60 Division 4; 1960–64 Division 3; 1964–71 Division 4; 1971–73 Division 3; 1973–81 Division 2; 1981–84 Division 1; 1984–85 Division 2; 1985–90 Division 3; 1990–91 Division 2; 1991– Division 1.

Honours: *Football League:* Division 1 best season: 3rd, 1890–91, 1900–01; Division 2 – Champions 1896–97, 1913–14, 1922–23; Runners-up 1894–95, 1980–81; Division 3 (S) – Champions 1930–31, 1949–50; Runners-up 1936–37; Division 3 – Runners-up 1972-73; Division 4 – Champions 1970–71; Runners-up 1959–60. *FA Cup:* Winners 1893–94; Runners-up 1890–91. *Football League Cup:* best season: 5th rd, 1963–64, 1972–73, 1975–76. *Anglo-Italian Cup:* Runners-up 1994.

NOTTS COUNTY 1993—94 LEAGUE RECORD

Match No.	Date	Venue	Opponents	Result		H/T Score	Lg. Pos.	Goalscorers	Attendance
1	Aug 14	H	Middlesbrough	L	2-3	0-2	—	Draper (pen), Lund	9392
2	21	A	Peterborough U	D	1-1	0-0	18	Draper	6890
3	28	H	Sunderland	W	1-0	0-0	15	Draper	9166
4	Sept 4	A	Tranmere R	L	1-3	0-0	21	Simpson	6317
5	11	H	WBA	W	1-0	0-0	15	Draper	9870
6	18	A	Watford	L	1-3	0-2	21	Draper	6959
7	25	H	Derby Co	W	4-1	3-0	14	McSwegan 3, Turner P	11,005
8	Oct 2	A	Leicester C	L	2-3	2-1	17	Draper (pen), McSwegan	16,319
9	9	H	Bristol C	W	2-0	0-0	11	McSwegan (pen), Draper	6418
10	16	A	Luton T	L	0-1	0-1	16		6366
11	20	A	Millwall	L	0-2	0-0	—		5887
12	23	H	Portsmouth	D	1-1	0-1	18	Walker	6681
13	30	A	Nottingham F	L	0-1	0-0	20		26,721
14	Nov 2	A	Wolverhampton W	L	0-3	0-1	—		15,989
15	6	H	Crystal Palace	W	3-2	1-2	17	McSwegan 2 (1 pen), Lund	6904
16	13	A	Charlton Ath	L	1-5	1-1	17	Agana	7078
17	20	H	Stoke C	W	2-0	0-0	15	Robinson, Turner P	9815
18	28	H	Oxford U	W	2-1	1-1	—	Devlin, Agana	5302
19	Dec 5	A	Crystal Palace	W	2-1	1-0	—	Devlin 2	12,642
20	11	H	Millwall	L	1-3	0-0	14	Lund	6516
21	18	A	Middlesbrough	L	0-3	0-3	15		7869
22	27	A	Grimsby T	D	2-2	1-1	18	Lund, Devlin	7781
23	Jan 1	A	Bolton W	L	2-4	0-2	15	Turner P, Lund	11,041
24	3	H	Southend U	W	2-1	1-0	15	Draper, Dijkstra	6503
25	11	H	Birmingham C	W	2-1	1-0	—	Devlin, McSwegan	7212
26	15	H	Luton T	L	1-2	0-0	14	Agana	6589
27	22	A	Bristol C	W	2-0	1-0	14	Legg, Agana	7538
28	Feb 5	A	Portsmouth	D	0-0	0-0	14		9359
29	12	H	Nottingham F	W	2-1	0-0	13	McSwegan, Palmer	18,655
30	19	A	Birmingham C	W	3-2	1-0	10	McSwegan, Wilson, Legg	12,913
31	22	H	Peterborough U	W	2-1	1-0	—	McSwegan 2	6106
32	Mar 1	H	Barnsley	W	3-1	2-1	—	Draper 2, Lund	6297
33	5	A	Sunderland	L	0-2	0-1	8		16,269
34	12	H	Watford	W	1-0	1-0	7	Lund	6378
35	16	A	WBA	L	0-3	0-1	—		14,594
36	26	H	Leicester C	W	4-1	2-1	6	McSwegan, Matthews, Lund 2	11,907
37	30	A	Southend U	L	0-1	0-0	—		3758
38	Apr 2	H	Grimsby T	W	2-1	1-0	6	Matthews 2	7205
39	4	A	Barnsley	W	3-0	1-0	4	Devlin, Lund, McSwegan	6827
40	9	H	Bolton W	W	2-1	1-0	4	Murphy, Devlin	7270
41	12	H	Tranmere R	D	0-0	0-0	—		6318
42	16	H	Wolverhampton W	L	0-2	0-0	6		13,438
43	20	A	Derby Co	D	1-1	0-0	—	Draper	18,602
44	23	A	Stoke C	D	0-0	0-0	7		16,470
45	30	H	Charlton Ath	D	3-3	2-1	7	Draper (pen), Lund, McSwegan	7019
46	May 8	A	Oxford U	L	1-2	0-1	7	Draper	8475

Final League Position: 7

GOALSCORERS

League (65): McSwegan 15 (2 pens), Draper 13 (3 pens), Lund 11, Devlin 7, Agana 4, Matthews 3, Turner P 3, Legg 2, Dijkstra 1, Murphy 1, Palmer 1, Robinson 1, Simpson 1, Walker 1, Wilson 1.
Coca-Cola Cup (5): Cox 1, Draper 1, Lund 1, McSwegan 1, own goal 1.
FA Cup (4): Agana 1, Devlin 1, Draper 1, Lund 1.

Cherry 45	Wilson 27 + 2	Johnson 33 + 1	Turner P 40	Cox 15 + 4	Walker 21	Devlin 40 + 1	Draper 44	McSwegan 28 + 9	Reeves 1 + 3	Legg 29 + 1	Lund 45 + 1	Williams 1 + 1	Catlin 1	Short 5 + 1	Simpson 5 + 1	Slawson 4	Dijkstra 16 + 2	Thomas 5 + 2	Agana 18 + 2	Gallagher 13	Palmer 22	King 6	Goater 1	Matthews 6 + 6	Robinson 2	Sherlock 6 + 1	Foster 9	Gannon 2	Reid 5	Murphy 11	Yates — + 1	Match No.
1	2	3	4	5	6	7	8	9	10	11	12	14																				1
	2	3	4	5	6	7	8		12	11	9	10	1																			2
1	2	3			6	7	8			11	9			4	5	10																3
1	2	3			6	7	8		12	11	9			4	5	10																4
1	2	3	5		6	7	8	12		11	9			4		10																5
1	2	3	5		6	7	8	9	12		10			14		11	4															6
1			4		5	7	8	9		11	10			2			6	3	12													7
1			4	5	6	7	8	9		11	10			2				3														8
1			4		5	7	8	9		11	10							3		2	6											9
1	14	3		12	5	7	8	9		11	10				4					2	6											10
1	8	3	4	5	6	7		12		11	10								9	2												11
1			4	5	6	7		9		11	10							8	12	2		3										12
1		11	4		5	7	8	12			10							6	9	2		3										13
1		4	6	12	5	7	8	9			10							14	11	2		3										14
1		4	5	6		7	8	9			10				12			14	11	2		3										15
1		5	6		4	7	8				10								11	2		3	9	12								16
1	10	5	6			7	8				9								11	2		3			4							17
1	10	3	6		5	7	8				9								11	2					4							18
1	10	3	6		5	7	8				9								11	2	4											19
1	10	3	6		5	7	8	12			9								11	2	4											20
1	10	3	6	2	5	7	8	12			9								11		4											21
1		3	4	2	6	7	8	10			9						5		11													22
1	2	5	6	3		7	8	10			9				11		4							12								23
1	2	5	6	4		7	8	10			9						3							11								24
1		4				7	8	12		10	9				6		3							11		2	5					25
1		4	6			7	8	12		10	9						3		11								5	2				26
1			6			7	8			10	9								11		4					3	5	2				27
1			4			7	8				9						6		11		2					3	5		10			28
1		6	4			7	8	11		12	9						14				2					3	5		10			29
1	14	6	4	12			8	10		11	9						3				2						5		7			30
1	11		4	12			8	10		7	9						3				2					6	5					31
1			4	2		7	8	10		11	9						3				6					12	5					32
1	4			2		7	8	10		11	9						3							12		6	5					33
1			4	6	5	7	8	10		3	9									2									11			34
1	2	5	4	6		7	8	10		3	9													12					11			35
1	2	5	4				8	10		11	9										6			7						3		36
1	2	5	4				8	10		11	9						12				6			7						3		37
1	2	5	4			12	8	10		11	9										6			7						3		38
1	2	5	4			7	8	10		11	9										6									3		39
1	2	5	4			7	8	10		11	9										6									3		40
1	2	5	4			7	8	10		11	9										6			12						3		41
1	2		4			7	8	12		11	9						5				6			10						3		42
1			4	6		7	8	12		11	9						5		10		2									3		43
1	2	12	4			7	8	11			9						5		10		6									3		44
1	2	5	4			7	8	10			9								11		6									3		45
1	2	5					8	10		11	9						4		7		6			12						3	14	46

Coca-Cola Cup	First Round	Hull C (h)	2-0
		(a)	1-3
	Second Round	Newcastle U (a)	1-4
		(h)	1-7
FA Cup	Third Round	Sutton U (h)	3-2
	Fourth Round	West Ham U (h)	1-1
		(a)	0-1

NOTTS COUNTY

Player and Position	Ht	Wt	Birth Date	Birth Place	Source	Clubs	League App	League Gls
Goalkeepers								
Taylor Baradat†			14 8 72	Charlottesville		Notts Co	—	—
						Colchester U (loan)	1	—
Bob Catlin*	6 2	14 00	22 6 65	London	Marconi	Notts Co	3	—
						Birmingham C (loan)	8	—
Steve Cherry	6 1	13 00	5 8 60	Nottingham	Apprentice	Derby Co	77	—
						Port Vale (loan)	4	—
						Walsall	71	—
						Plymouth Arg	73	—
						Chesterfield (loan)	10	—
						Notts Co	241	—
Paul Dolan	6 4	13 05	16 4 66	Ottawa	Vancouver W	Notts Co	—	—
Defenders								
Paul Cox	5 11	11 12	1 1 72	Nottingham	Trainee	Notts Co	41	1
Meindert Dijkstra	5 11	12 00	28 2 67	Eindhoven	Willem II	Notts Co	29	1
Tommy Gallagher	5 10	10 08	25 8 74	Nottingham	Trainee	Notts Co	13	—
Brian Horseman*			16 10 74	Cleveland	Trainee	Notts Co	—	—
Michael Johnson	5 11	11 00	4 7 73	Nottingham	Trainee	Notts Co	76	—
Shaun Murphy	6 0	12 00	5 11 70	Sydney	Perth Italia	Notts Co	19	2
Charlie Palmer	6 0	12 03	10 7 63	Aylesbury	Apprentice	Watford	10	1
						Derby Co	51	2
						Hull C	70	1
						Notts Co	182	7
Alan Paris*	6 0	11 10	15 8 64	Slough	Slough T	Watford	—	—
						Peterborough U	137	2
						Leicester C	88	3
						Notts Co	42	1
David Robinson‡	6 0	13 00	14 1 65	Cleveland		Hartlepool U	66	1
						Halifax T	72	1
						Peterborough U	95	9
						Notts Co	3	1
Paul Sherlock	5 11	11 05	17 11 73	Wigan	Trainee	Notts Co	7	—
Chris Short	5 10	12 02	9 5 70	Munster		Scarborough	43	1
						Manchester U (loan)	—	—
						Notts Co	79	2
Dean Thomas	5 10	11 08	19 12 61	Bedworth	Nuneaton Borough	Wimbledon	57	8
					Fortuna Dusseldorf	Northampton T	74	11
						Notts Co	134	8
Richard Walker	6 0	12 00	9 11 71	Derby	Trainee	Notts Co	33	4
Dean Yates	6 1	12 00	26 10 67	Leicester	Apprentice	Notts Co	293	33
Midfield								
Mark Draper	5 10	11 00	11 11 70	Derby	Trainee	Notts Co	222	40
Michael Galloway			13 10 74	Nottingham	Trainee	Notts Co	—	—
Neil Glasser*	5 9	11 03	17 10 74	Johannesbury	Trainee	Nottingham F	—	—
						Notts Co	—	—
Andy Legg	5 8	10 07	28 7 66	Neath	Briton Ferry	Swansea C	163	29
						Notts Co	30	2
Peter Reid*	5 8	10 07	20 6 56	Huyton	Apprentice	Bolton W	225	23
						Everton	159	8
						QPR	29	1
						Manchester C	103	1
						Southampton	7	—
						Notts Co	5	—
Michael Simpson	5 9	10 08	28 2 74	Nottingham	Trainee	Notts Co	6	1
Eddie Snook	5 7	10 01	18 10 68	Washington	Apprentice	Notts Co	—	—
Phil Turner	5 9	10 13	12 2 62	Sheffield	Apprentice	Lincoln C	241	19
						Grimsby T	62	8
						Leicester C	24	2
						Notts Co	187	14
Forwards								
Tony Agana	6 0	12 02	2 10 63	London	Weymouth	Watford	15	1
						Sheffield U	118	42
						Notts C	13	1
						Leeds U (loan)	2	—
						Notts Co	49	6

NOTTS COUNTY

Colours: Black and white striped shirts, white shorts, black stockings. **Change colours:** Tartan shirts, black shorts, tartan stockings.

Foundation: For many years the foundation date of the Football League's oldest club was given as 1862 and the club celebrated its centenary in 1962. However, the researches of Keith Warsop have since shown that the club was on a very haphazard basis at that time, playing little more than practice matches. The meeting which put it on a firm footing was held at the George IV Hotel in December 1864, when they became known as the Notts Football Club.

First Football League game: 15 September, 1888, Football League, v Everton (a) L 1-2 – Holland; Guttridge, McLean; Brown, Warburton, Shelton; Hodder, Harker, Jardine, Moore (1), Wardle.

Did you know: Henry Cursham scored a record 48 goals in FA Cup matches for Notts County between 1880 and 1887 in the competition proper, though in those days more of the early rounds were regionalized.

Managers (and Secretary-Managers)
Edwin Browne 1883–93*, Tom Featherstone 1893*, Tom Harris 1893–13*, Albert Fisher 1913–27, Horace Henshall 1927–34, Charlie Jones 1934–35, David Pratt 1935, Percy Smith 1935–36, Jimmy McMullan 1936–37, Harry Parkes 1938–39, Tony Towers 1939–42, Frank Womack 1942–43, Major Frank Buckley 1944–46, Arthur Stollery 1946–49, Eric Houghton 1949–53, George Poyser 1953–57, Tommy Lawton 1957–58, Frank Hill 1958–61, Tim Coleman 1961–63, Eddie Lowe 1963–65, Tim Coleman 1965–66, Jack Burkitt 1966–67, Andy Beattie (GM 1967), Billy Gray 1967–68, Jimmy Sirrel 1969–75, Ron Fenton 1975–77, Jimmy Sirrel 1978–82 (continues as GM to 1984), Howard Wilkinson 1982–83, Larry Lloyd 1983–84, Richie Barker 1984–85, Jimmy Sirrel 1985–87, John Barnwell 1987–88, Neil Warnock 1989–93, Mick Walker January 1993–

Player and Position	*Ht*	*Wt*	*Birth Date*	*Birth Place*	*Source*	*Clubs*	*League App*	*League Gls*
Paul Devlin	5 8	10 05	14 4 72	Birmingham	Stafford R	Notts Co	75	10
Philip Hill*	5 8	11 00	14 6 74	Scarborough	Trainee	Notts Co	—	—
Gary Lund	6 0	11 00	13 9 64	Grimsby	School	Grimsby T	60	24
						Lincoln C	44	13
						Notts Co	225	57
						Hull C (loan)	11	3
Gary McSwegan	5 7	10 09	24 9 70	Glasgow	Rangers Amateur BC	Rangers	18	4
						Notts Co	37	15
Rob Matthews	6 0	12 05	14 10 70	Slough	Loughborough Univ	Notts Co	25	8
Stephen Slawson	6 0	12 06	13 11 72	Nottingham	Trainee	Notts Co	33	4
						Burnley (loan)	9	2
David Smith‡	5 11	12 00	25 6 61	Sidcup	Welling U	Gillingham	104	10
						Bristol C	97	10
						Plymouth Arg	18	2
						Notts Co	37	8
Kevin Wilson	5 7	10 10	18 4 61	Banbury	Banbury U	Derby Co	122	30
						Ipswich T	98	34
						Chelsea	152	42
						Notts Co	69	3
						Bradford C (loan)	5	—
Gavin Worboys	6 0	11 00	14 7 74	Doncaster	Trainee	Doncaster R	7	2
						Notts Co	—	—
						Exeter C (loan)	4	1

Trainees
Burke, Anthony G; Chadbourne, Martyn A; Dodson, Matthew J; Giles, Damon P; Henry, Alvin M; Hunt, James M; (h) King, Jon M; Lawley, Edward W. H; Lewis, Gavin; Ludlow, Lee; Marshall, Daniel J; Needham, Benjamin D; Pawley, Ian D; Pearson, Christopher D; Redmile, Matthew I; Ridgeway, Ian D; Rigby, Matthew R.

****Non-Contract**
Withington, Andrew P.

Associated Schoolboys
Bateman, Neal S; Bryan, Courtney; Burns, Colin C; Dudley, Craig B; Gee, Christopher; Ghilsanzoni, Jay; Hackett, Mark; Hennessy, Simon; Henshaw, Terrence R; Hurst, Liam J. J; Jones, Kevin P; Lazar, Edmund; Leggett, Karl R; Marshall, Ben; Mitchell, Paul; Moroziuk, Stefan; Mundell, Toby; Newton, Richard J; Patton, Nigel; Russell, Matthew L; Smith, Neil S; Smith, Steven L; Todd, Andrew J; Wright, Scott.

Associated Schoolboys who have accepted the Club's offer of a Traineeship/Contract
Derry, Shaun P; Eaton, Jamie; Fitzgerald, Louie; Folwell, John A; Marshall, Jamie; Wilkes, Timothy C; Wilson, Scott R.

**Non-Contract Players who are retained must be re-signed before they are eligible to play in League matches.

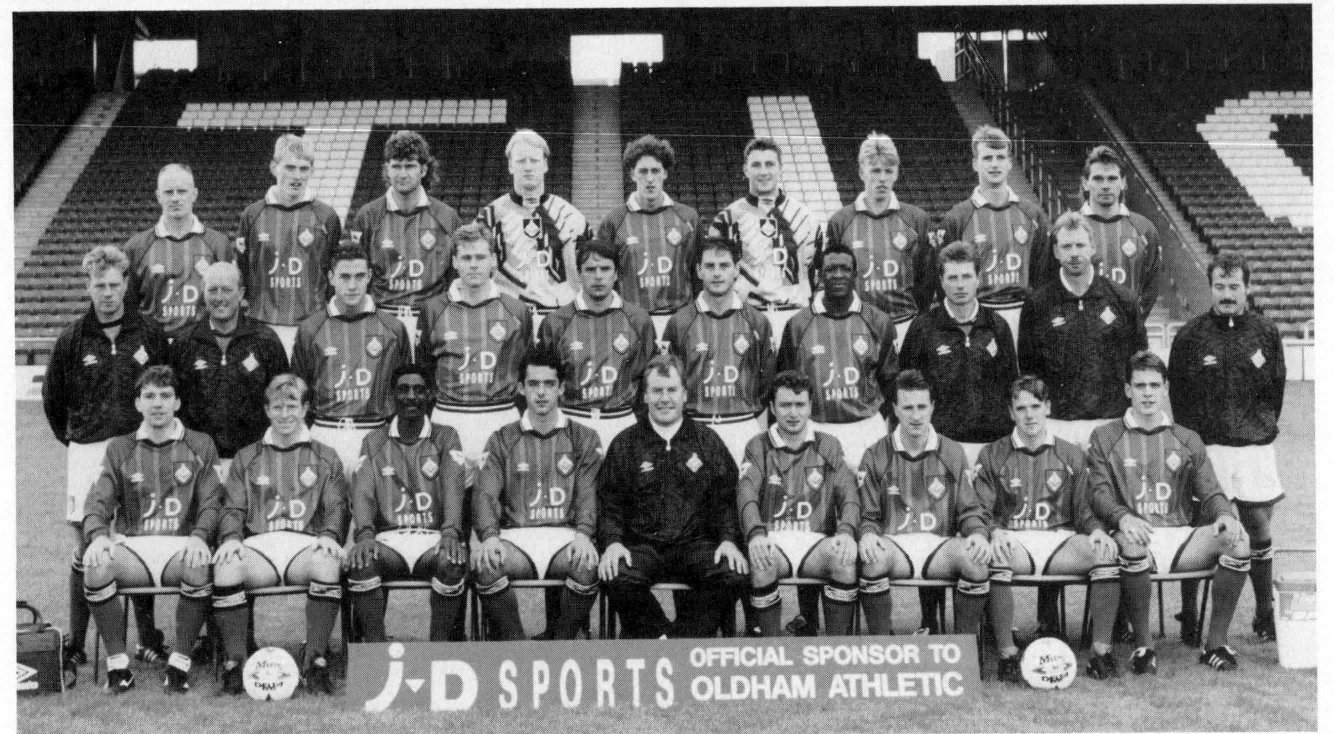

OLDHAM ATHLETIC 1993–94 *Back row (left to right):* Andy Ritchie, Neil Tolson, Ian Marshall, Jon Hallworth, Ian Olney, Paul Gerrard, Gunnar Halle, Richard Jobson, Neil Pointon. *Centre row:* Ronnie Evans (Kit Manager), Bill Urmson (Youth Team Coach), Chris Makin, Neil McDonald, Graeme Sharp, Steve Redmond, Darren Beckford, Willie Donachie (Assistant Manager/First Team Coach), Andy Holden (Reserve Team Coach), Ian Liversedge (Physio).
Front row: Mark Brennan, Andy Barlow, Roger Palmer, Craig Fleming, Joe Royle (Team Manager), Mike Milligan, Neil Adams, Nick Henry, Paul Bernard.

Division 1 **OLDHAM ATHLETIC**

Boundary Park, Oldham OL1 2PA. Telephone 0161–624 4972. Ticket office: 0891 121582. Commercial Office: 0161–627 1802. Clubcall: 0891 121142.

Ground capacity: 13,544 (all seated).

Record attendance: 47,671 v Sheffield W, FA Cup 4th rd. 25 January 1930.

Record receipts: £138,680 v Manchester U, FA Premier League, 29 December 1993.

Pitch measurements: 110yd × 74yd.

President: R. Schofield.

Chairman & Chief Executive: I. H. Stott, ***Vice-chairman:*** D. A. Brierley.

Directors: G. T. Butterworth, R. Adams, D. R. Taylor, P. Chadwick, J. Slevin, N. Holden.

Manager: Joe Royle.

Secretary: Terry Cale. ***Commercial Manager:*** Alan Hardy. ***Public Relations Office:*** Gordon A. Lawton.

Coaches: Willie Donachie, Billy Urmson, Andy Hoden. ***Physio:*** Ian Liversedge.

Year Formed: 1895. ***Turned Professional:*** 1899. ***Ltd Co.:*** 1906.

Previous Name: 1895, Pine Villa; 1899, Oldham Athletic.

Club Nickname: 'The Latics'.

Previous Ground: Sheepfoot Lane; 1905, Boundary Park.

Record League Victory: 11–0 v Southport, Division 4, 26 December 1962 – Hollands; Branagan, Marshall; McCall, Williams, Scott; Ledger (1), Johnstone, Lister (6), Colquhoun (1), Whitaker (3).

Record Cup Victory: 10–1 v Lytham, FA Cup, 1st rd, 28 November 1925 – Gray; Wynne, Grundy; Adlam, Heaton, Naylor (1), Douglas, Pynegar (2), Ormston (2), Barnes (3), Watson (2).

Record Defeat: 4–13 v Tranmere R, Division 3 (N), 26 December 1935.

Most League Points (2 for a win): 62, Division 3, 1973–74.

Most League Points (3 for a win): 88, Division 2, 1990–91.

Most League Goals: 95, Division 4, 1962–63.

Highest League Scorer in Season: Tom Davis, 33, Division 3 (N), 1936–37.

Most League Goals in Total Aggregate: Roger Palmer, 141, 1980–94.

Most Capped Player: Gunnar Halle, (38), Norway.

Most League Appearances: Ian Wood, 525, 1966–80.

Record Transfer Fee Received: £1,700,000 from Aston Villa for Earl Barrett, February 1992.

Record Transfer Fee Paid: £700,000 to Aston Villa for Ian Olney, June 1992.

Football League Record: 1907 Elected to Division 2; 1910–23 Division 1; 1923–35 Division 2; 1935–53 Division 3 (N); 1953–54 Division 2; 1954–58 Division 3 (N); 1958–63 Division 4; 1963–69 Division 3; 1969–71 Division 4; 1971–74 Division 3; 1974–91 Division 2; 1991–92 Division 1; 1992–94 FA Premier League; 1994– Division 1.

Honours: *Football League:* Division 1 – Runners-up 1914–15; Division 2 – Champions 1990–91; Runners-up 1909–10; Division 3 (N) – Champions 1952–53; Division 3 – Champions 1973–74; Division 4 – Runners-up 1962–63. *FA Cup:* Semi-final 1913, 1990. *Football League Cup:* Runners-up 1990.

OLDHAM ATHLETIC 1993—94 LEAGUE RECORD

Match No.	Date	Venue	Opponents	Result		H/T Score	Lg. Pos.	Goalscorers	Attendance
1	Aug 14	H	Ipswich T	L	0-3	0-2	—		12,074
2	18	A	Swindon T	W	1-0	0-0	—	Bernard	11,940
3	21	A	Blackburn R	L	0-1	0-1	14		14,397
4	24	H	Coventry C	D	3-3	1-1	—	Bernard, Ritchie (pen), Olney	10,817
5	28	H	Wimbledon	D	1-1	1-0	15	Bernard	9633
6	30	A	Leeds U	L	0-1	0-1	—		28,717
7	Sept 11	H	Everton	L	0-1	0-1	18		13,666
8	18	A	Tottenham H	L	0-5	0-3	20		24,614
9	25	H	Aston Villa	D	1-1	1-0	20	Halle	12,836
10	Oct 4	A	Manchester C	D	1-1	0-0	—	Sharp	21,401
11	16	A	Liverpool	L	1-2	0-0	20	Beckford	32,661
12	23	H	Arsenal	D	0-0	0-0	20		12,105
13	30	A	Chelsea	W	1-0	1-0	19	Beckford	15,372
14	Nov 8	H	Newcastle U	L	1-3	1-0	—	Jobson	13,821
15	20	A	West Ham U	L	0-2	0-1	21		17,211
16	24	A	Sheffield W	L	0-3	0-2	—		18,509
17	27	H	Norwich C	W	2-1	0-0	21	Sharp, Makin	10,198
18	Dec 4	A	Ipswich T	D	0-0	0-0	19		11,789
19	7	H	Swindon T	W	2-1	1-0	—	Holden, Redmond	9771
20	11	H	Blackburn R	L	1-2	1-1	18	Holden	13,887
21	18	A	Coventry C	D	1-1	0-1	18	Bernard	11,792
22	27	A	QPR	L	0-2	0-0	18		13,218
23	29	H	Manchester U	L	2-5	2-3	18	Sharp, Holden	16,708
24	Jan 1	A	Sheffield U	L	1-2	1-2	20	Jobson	17,066
25	15	H	Liverpool	L	0-3	0-0	21		14,573
26	22	A	Arsenal	D	1-1	1-1	21	Sharp	26,524
27	Feb 5	H	Southampton	W	2-1	2-1	20	McCarthy, Bernard	9982
28	12	H	Chelsea	W	2-1	1-0	18	Jobson, Sharp	12,002
29	28	H	Leeds U	D	1-1	0-1	—	Beckford	11,136
30	Mar 5	A	Everton	L	1-2	1-1	20	Sharp	18,881
31	19	A	Aston Villa	W	2-1	0-0	20	Beckford, Holden	21,214
32	26	H	Manchester C	D	0-0	0-0	20		16,462
33	30	A	Southampton	W	3-1	2-0	—	Sharp, Benali (og), Holden	14,101
34	Apr 2	H	QPR	W	4-1	1-1	18	Jobson, Beckford, McCarthy, McCarthy (og)	10,440
35	4	A	Manchester U	L	2-3	0-1	19	McCarthy, Sharp	44,686
36	16	H	West Ham U	L	1-2	1-2	20	Holden (pen)	11,669
37	23	A	Newcastle U	L	2-3	1-1	21	Jobson, Sharp	32,214
38	26	A	Wimbledon	L	0-3	0-1	—		6766
39	30	H	Sheffield W	D	0-0	0-0	21		12,973
40	May 3	H	Sheffield U	D	1-1	1-1	—	Beckford	14,779
41	5	H	Tottenham H	L	0-2	0-1	—		14,283
42	7	A	Norwich C	D	1-1	1-0	21	McCarthy	20,394

Final League Position: 21

GOALSCORERS

League (42): Sharp 9, Beckford 6, Holden 6 (1 pen), Bernard 5, Jobson 5, McCarthy 4, Halle 1, Makin 1, Olney 1, Redmond 1, Ritchie 1 (pen), own goals 2.
Coca-Cola Cup (5): Sharp 2, Beckford 1, Bernard 1, Halle 1.
FA Cup (7): Beckford 3, Pointon 2, Holden 1, Ritchie 1.

Gerrard 15 + 1	Fleming 37	Pointon 23 + 2	Henry 22	Jobson 37	Redmond 31 + 2	Halle 22 + 1	Ritchie 13 + 9	Olney 10	Milligan 39	Bernard 32	Adams 7 + 6	Sharp 31 + 3	Beckford 13 + 9	Barlow 3 + 3	McDonald 3	Brennan 11	Hallworth 19	Palmer 1 + 7	Holden 28 + 1	Makin 26 + 1	Key 2	Eyre 1 + 1	Walsh 6	Beresford — + 1	McCarthy 19 + 1	Pedersen 7 + 3	Graham 4 + 1	Match No.
1	2	3	4	5	6	7	8	9	10	11	12	14																1
1	2	3	4	5	6	7		9	10	11	8																	2
1	2	3	4	5	6	7	12	9	10	11	8																	3
1	2	3	4	5	6	7	8	9	10	11																		4
1	2	3	4	5	6	7	8	9	10	11			12															5
1	2	3	4	5	6	7	12	9	10	11			8	14														6
1	2		4	5	6	7	8	9	10		12	14			3	11												7
1	3		4	5	6	2	8	9	10	11		12				7												8
	2			5	6	4	8		10	11	7	9	12	3			1	14										9
14	2		4	5	6	7			10	11	12	9	8	3			1											10
1	2		4		6	5			10	7		9	8	3					11									11
1	2				6	5			10	7		9	8	12		4			11	3								12
	2	14			6	5			10	7		9	8			4			11	3	1	12						13
	2			5	6			8	10	11	12	9				4		7		3	1							14
	2	14		5	6	7	12	8	10	11		9				4				3			1					15
	2			5	6	3	8		10	11	7	9								12		4	1	14				16
	2			5	6	4	8			10	7	9						12	11	3			1					17
	2	3		5	6	4			10	7		9							11				1		8			18
	2	3		5	6	4	12		10	7		9							11				1		8	14		19
	2	3		5	6	8	12		10	7	14	9							11				1			4		20
	2	3			6	4	12		10	8	7	9					1		11							5		21
	2			5			12		10	8	7	9					1		11	3						4	6	22
	2			5		4			10	7	12	9					1		11	3						6	8	23
	2			5		4	8		10	7		9					1		11	3						6		24
	2			5	6		8			7		9	10				1		11	3					12		4	25
	2	4		5	6				10	7		8					1	14	11	3					9	12		26
	2	4		5					10	7		8			6		1	12	11	3					9			27
	2	4		5					10	7		8	14		6		1		11	3					9	12		28
	2		6	5	14				10	7		8	12				1		11	3					9	4		29
			2	5	6				10	7		8	12				1		11	3					9	4		30
		2	4		5		7		10				8				1	12	11	3					9		6	31
		2	4	5	6		7		10				8				1		11	3					9			32
		2	4	5	6		12		10			8	7				1		11	3					9		14	33
		2		5	6				10			8	7			4	1	12	11	3					9			34
	4	3		5	6				10			8	12			7	1	14	11	2					9			35
	6	3	4	5					10	7		8	12				1		11	2					9			36
	2		4	5	6				10	11		8				7	1		12	3					9			37
1	2		4	5	6	14			10			8	12			7			11	3					9			38
1	6	3	4	5					10	7		8	12						11	2					9			39
1	6	3	4	5					10			8	7						11	2					9			40
1	6	3	4	5	14		12		10			8	7						11	2					9			41
1	6	3	4	5			8						7	12		10			11	2					9			42

Coca-Cola Cup	Second Round	Swansea C (a)	1-2
		(h)	2-0
	Third Round	Coventry C (h)	2-0
	Fourth Round	Tranmere R (a)	0-3
FA Cup	Third Round	Derby Co (h)	2-1
	Fourth Round	Stoke C (h)	0-0
		(a)	1-0
	Fifth Round	Barnsley (h)	1-0
	Sixth Round	Bolton W (a)	1-0
	Semi-final at Wembley	Manchester U	1-1
	Replay at Maine Road		1-4

OLDHAM ATHLETIC

Player and Position	Ht	Wt	Birth Date	Birth Place	Source	Clubs	League App	League Gls
Goalkeepers								
Paul Gerrard	6 1	12 06	22 1 73	Heywood	Trainee	Oldham Ath	41	—
Jon Hallworth	6 1	14 03	26 10 65	Stockport	School	Ipswich T	45	—
						Swindon T (loan)	—	—
						Fulham (loan)	—	—
						Bristol R (loan)	2	—
						Oldham Ath	153	—
Defenders								
Andy Barlow	5 9	11 01	24 11 65	Oldham		Oldham Ath	259	5
						Bradford C (loan)	2	—
Willie Donachie*	5 9	11 05	5 10 51	Glasgow	Juniors	Manchester C	351	2
					Portland T	Norwich C	11	—
					Portland T	Burnley	60	3
						Oldham Ath	169	3
Craig Fleming	6 0	11 07	6 10 71	Calder	Trainee	Halifax T	57	—
						Oldham Ath	93	1
David Hall*			19 10 73	Manchester	Trainee	Oldham Ath	—	—
Gunnar Halle‡	5 11	11 02	11 8 65	Oslo	Lillestrom	Oldham Ath	91	6
Andy Holden	6 1	13 10	14 9 62	Flint	Rhyl	Chester C	100	17
						Wigan Ath	49	4
						Oldham Ath	21	4
Richard Jobson	6 1	13 05	9 5 63	Hull	Burton Alb	Watford	28	4
						Hull C	221	17
						Oldham Ath	157	10
Chris Makin	5 11	11 00	8 5 73	Manchester	Trainee	Oldham Ath	27	1
						Wigan Ath (loan)	15	2
Tore Pedersen‡			29 9 69	Norway	Brann	Oldham Ath	10	—
Neil Pointon	5 10	11 00	28 11 64	Church Warsop	Apprentice	Scunthorpe U	159	2
						Everton	102	5
						Manchester C	74	2
						Oldham Ath	59	3
Stephen Price*			13 11 75	Hannover	Trainee	Oldham Ath	—	—
Steven Redmond	5 11	12 13	2 11 67	Liverpool	Apprentice	Manchester C	235	7
						Oldham Ath	64	1
Midfield								
David Beresford§			11 11 76	Middlesbrough	Trainee	Oldham Ath	1	—
Paul Bernard	5 11	11 08	30 12 72	Edinburgh	Trainee	Oldham Ath	88	15
Mark Brennan	5 10	10 13	4 10 65	Rossendale	Apprentice	Ipswich T	168	19
						Middlesbrough	65	6
						Manchester C	29	6
						Oldham Ath	25	3
Richard Graham			28 11 74	Dewsbury	Trainee	Oldham Ath	5	—
Nick Henry	5 6	9 08	21 2 69	Liverpool	Trainee	Oldham Ath	203	16
Rick Holden	5 11	12 07	9 9 64	Skipton		Burnley	1	—
						Halifax T	67	12
						Watford	42	8
						Oldham Ath	129	19
						Manchester C	50	3
						Oldham Ath	29	6
Patrick McDonagh*			14 3 76	Dublin	Trainee	Oldham Ath	—	—
Neil McDonald	5 11	11 04	2 11 65	Wallsend	Wallsend BC	Newcastle U	180	24
						Everton	90	4
						Oldham Ath	24	1
Mike Milligan	5 8	11 00	20 2 67	Manchester		Oldham Ath	162	17
						Everton	17	1
						Oldham Ath	117	6
Paul Rickers			9 5 75	Pontefract	Trainee	Oldham Ath	—	—
Forwards								
Darren Beckford	6 1	11 01	12 5 67	Manchester	Apprentice	Manchester C	11	—
						Bury (loan)	12	5
						Port Vale (loan)	11	4
						Port Vale	167	68
						Norwich C	38	8
						Oldham Ath	29	9

OLDHAM ATHLETIC

Colours: All blue with red piping. **Change colours:** Red and white shirts, white shorts, white stockings.

Foundation: It was in 1895 that John Garland, the landlord of the Featherstall and Junction Hotel, decided to form a football club. As Pine Villa they played in the Oldham Junior League. In 1899 the local professional club Oldham County, went out of existence and one of the liquidators persuaded Pine Villa to take over their ground at Sheepfoot Lane and change their name to Oldham Athletic.

First Football League game: 9 September, 1907, Division 2, v Stoke (a) W 3-1 – Hewitson; Hodson, Hamilton; Fay, Walders, Wilson; Ward, W. Dodds (1), Newton (1), Hancock, Swarbrick (1).

Did you know: Seventeen years after leading the Newton-le-Willows attack at Oldham Athletic in an 11-0 defeat, Billy Hibbert joined the Latics. In the interim period he had been capped by England while at Bury.

Managers (and Secretary-Managers)
David Ashworth 1906–14, Herbert Bamlett 1914–21, Charlie Roberts 1921–22, David Ashworth 1923–24, Bob Mellor 1924–27, Andy Wilson 1927–32, Jimmy McMullan 1933–34, Bob Mellor 1934–45 (continued as secretary to 1953), Frank Womack 1945–47, Billy Wootton 1947–50, George Hardwick 1950–56, Ted Goodier 1956–58, Norman Dodgin 1958–60, Jack Rowley 1960–63, Les McDowall 1963–65, Gordon Hurst 1965–66, Jimmy McIlroy 1966–68, Jack Rowley 1968–69, Jimmy Frizzell 1970–82, Joe Royle July 1982–

Player and Position	*Ht*	*Wt*	*Birth Date*	*Birth Place*	*Source*	*Clubs*	*League App*	*League Gls*
John Eyre			9 10 74	Humberside	Trainee	Oldham Ath	2	—
Sean McCarthy	6 0	12 05	12 9 67	Bridgend	Bridgend	Swansea C	91	25
						Plymouth Arg	70	19
						Bradford C	131	60
						Oldham Ath	20	4
Ian Olney	6 1	11 00	17 12 69	Luton	Trainee	Aston Villa	88	16
						Oldham Ath	44	13
Roger Palmer	5 10	11 00	30 1 59	Manchester	Apprentice	Manchester C	31	9
						Oldham Ath	466	141
Andy Ritchie	5 10	11 11	28 11 60	Manchester	Apprentice	Manchester U	33	13
						Brighton	89	23
						Leeds U	136	40
						Oldham Ath	184	70
Graeme Sharp	6 1	11 09	16 10 60	Glasgow	Eastercraigs	Dumbarton	40	17
						Everton	322	111
						Oldham Ath	97	28

Trainees
Adams, Christian; Beresford, David; Berry, Matthew; Boden, Liam T; Booth, Matthew J; Evans, Richard L; Feltham, Paul D; Frost, John A; Hilton, Robert C; Kay, Simon P; Knapman, Stephen C; Pemberton, Martin C; Serrant, Carl; Smith, Howard W; Southern-Quinn, Dean; Speak, Matthew I; Thorp, Matthew C; Wood, Jamie M; Woods, Andrew N.

Associated Schoolboys
Agg, Nathan; Brown, David A; Clitheroe, Lee; Ford, Robert J; Harris, Gareth H; Hotte, Mark S; Jablonski, Mark P; Jeffries, Paul; Martin, Dean J; Mather, Gregg R; McGrath, Ryan K; Selfe, Oliver; Walsh, Daniel G; Yorke-Robinson, David; Zarac, Neil.

Associated Schoolboys who have accepted the Club's offer of a Traineeship/Contract
Allott, Mark S; Darnborough, Lee; Gorman, Darren A; Holt, Andrew; Hughes, Andrew J; Levendis, Andrew; McNiven, David J; McNiven, Scott A; Ramsden, Gavin S; Richardson, Lloyd M; Stott, Lee.

OXFORD UNITED 1993–94 *Back row (left to right):* David Collins, Matthew Murphy, Nick Cusack, Paul Kee, Anton Rogan, Darren Jackson, Paul Reece, Paul Wanless, Mark Druce, Steve Tavinor.

Centre row: Peter Rhoades-Brown (Football Community Officer), Steve McClaren (Reserve/Youth Team Coach), John Clinkard (Physio), Keith Holmes, Alex Dyer, Tristan Didcock, Robert Mutchell, Matthew Keeble, Robert Ford, Chris Allen, Andrew Wallbridge, David Moss (First Team Coach), Maurice Evans (General Manager), Malcolm Elias (Youth Development Officer).

Front row: Joey Beauchamp, David Penney, Les Robinson, Jim Magilton, Brian Horton (Manager), Mike Ford, Mickey Lewis, Jon Narbett, Garry Smart.

Division 2 **OXFORD UNITED**

Manor Ground, Headington, Oxford, OX3 7RS. Telephone Oxford (0865) 61503. Fax: (0865) 741820. Supporters Club: (0865) 63063. Clubcall (information): 0891 121029. Clubcall (match commentary) 0891 121172. Fax: (0865) 741820.

Ground capacity: 11,071.

Record attendance: 22,750 v Preston NE, FA Cup 6th rd, 29 February 1964.

Record receipts: £103,411 v Leeds U, FA Cup 4th rd, 29 January 1994.

Pitch measurements: 110yd × 75yd.

President: The Duke of Marlborough.

Directors: K. A. Cox (Managing), D. M. Clitheroe, G. E. Coppock, P. L. Lowe.

Manager: Denis Smith. ***Coach:*** Malcolm Crosby. ***Physio:*** John Clinkard.

Secretary: Mick Brown. ***Commercial manager:*** Tony Watson.

Year Formed: 1893. ***Turned Professional:*** 1949. ***Ltd Co.:*** 1949.

Club Nickname: 'The U's'.

Previous Names: 1893, Headington; 1894, Headington United; 1960, Oxford United.

Previous Grounds: 1893–94 Headington Quarry; 1894–98 Wootten's Field; 1898–1902 Sandy Lane Ground; 1902–09 Britannia Field; 1909–10 Sandy Lane; 1910–14 Quarry Recreation Ground; 1914–22 Sandy Lane; 1922–25 The Paddock Manor Road; 1925– Manor Ground.

Record League Victory: 7–0 v Barrow, Division 4, 19 December 1964 – Fearnley; Beavon, Quartermann; Ron Atkinson (1), Kyle, Jones; Morris, Booth (3), Willey (1), Graham Atkinson (1), Harrington (1).

Record Cup Victory: 6–0 v Gillingham, League Cup, 2nd rd (1st leg), 24 September 1986 – Judge; Langan, Trewick, Phillips (Brock), Briggs, Shotton, Houghton (1), Aldridge (4 incl. 1p), Charles (Leworthy), Hebberd, Slatter. (1 og).

Record Defeat: 0–6 v Liverpool, Division 1, 22 March 1986.

Most League Points (2 for a win): 61, Division 4, 1964–65.

Most League Points (3 for a win): 95, Division 3, 1983–84.

Most League Goals: 91, Division 3, 1983–84.

Highest League Scorer in Season: John Aldridge, 30, Division 2, 1984–85.

Most League Goals in Total Aggregate: Graham Atkinson, 77, 1962–73.

Most Capped Player: Jim Magilton, 18 (22), Northern Ireland.

Most League Appearances: John Shuker, 478, 1962–77.

Record Transfer Fee Received: £1,190,000 from Derby Co for Dean Saunders, October 1988.

Record Transfer Fee Paid: £487,500 to Swansea C for Andy Melville, July 1990.

Football League Record: 1962 Elected to Division 4; 1965–68 Division 3; 1968–76 Division 2; 1976–84 Division 3; 1984–85 Division 2; 1985–88 Division 1; 1988–92 Division 2; 1992–94 Division 1; 1994– Division 2.

Honours: *Football League:* Division 1 best season: 18th, 1985–86, 1986–87; Division 2 – Champions 1984–85; Division 3 – Champions 1967–68, 1983–84; Division 4 – Promoted 1964–65 (4th). *FA Cup:* best season: 6th rd, 1963–64 (record for 4th Division club). *Football League Cup:* Winners 1985–86.

OXFORD UNITED 1993—94 LEAGUE RECORD

Match No.	Date	Venue	Opponents	Result		H/T Score	Lg. Pos.	Goalscorers	Attendance
1	Aug 14	H	Portsmouth	W	3-2	2-2	—	Symons (og), Allen, Magilton (pen)	8550
2	21	A	WBA	L	1-3	1-1	9	Robinson	17,227
3	28	H	Watford	L	2-3	2-1	17	Robinson, Beauchamp	5159
4	31	A	Bolton W	L	0-1	0-1	—		8230
5	Sept 11	H	Bristol C	W	4-2	2-1	17	Allen, Magilton 2 (2 pens), Dyer	5464
6	18	A	Peterborough U	L	1-3	1-0	22	Rogan	5148
7	25	A	Tranmere R	L	0-2	0-0	22		6056
8	Oct 2	H	Grimsby T	D	2-2	0-1	24	Magilton (pen), Ford M	4301
9	10	H	Stoke C	W	1-0	1-0	—	Penney	6489
10	16	A	Southend U	L	1-6	0-4	23	Penney	4432
11	20	A	Nottingham F	D	0-0	0-0	—		18,462
12	23	H	Luton T	L	0-1	0-1	24		5161
13	30	A	Charlton Ath	L	0-1	0-1	22		7811
14	Nov 2	H	Barnsley	D	1-1	1-0	—	Cusack	4065
15	6	A	Millwall	D	2-2	0-1	24	Beauchamp, Cusack	7794
16	13	H	Derby Co	W	2-0	1-0	22	Elliott, Magilton	7151
17	20	A	Leicester C	W	3-2	0-1	18	Cusack, Rogan, Dyer	14,070
18	28	A	Notts Co	L	1-2	1-1	—	Elliott	5302
19	Dec 4	H	Millwall	L	0-2	0-0	21		5540
20	11	H	Bolton W	L	0-2	0-0	22		5559
21	18	A	Portsmouth	D	1-1	0-1	21	Beauchamp	8980
22	27	H	Crystal Palace	L	1-3	0-1	23	Dyer	10,356
23	28	A	Wolverhampton W	L	1-2	0-0	23	Elliott	25,908
24	Jan 1	H	Middlesbrough	D	1-1	0-0	23	Byrne	5763
25	3	A	Birmingham C	D	1-1	1-0	23	Dyer	15,142
26	11	H	Sunderland	L	0-3	0-2	—		5877
27	15	H	Southend U	W	2-1	0-0	22	Cusack 2	6613
28	22	A	Stoke C	D	1-1	0-1	22	Beauchamp	14,689
29	Feb 5	A	Luton T	L	0-3	0-2	23		7366
30	12	H	Charlton Ath	L	0-4	0-1	24		7126
31	25	H	Nottingham F	W	1-0	0-0	23	Dyer	9346
32	Mar 5	A	Watford	L	1-2	1-1	24	Cusack	7049
33	12	H	Peterborough U	L	1-2	0-0	24	Moody	5789
34	15	A	Bristol C	W	1-0	1-0	—	Byrne	6635
35	19	H	Tranmere R	W	1-0	0-0	21	Beauchamp	4506
36	26	A	Grimsby T	L	0-1	0-0	23		5025
37	29	H	Birmingham C	W	2-0	2-0	—	Moody (pen), Byrne	8344
38	Apr 2	A	Crystal Palace	L	1-2	0-0	22	Byrne	15,510
39	4	H	Wolverhampton W	W	4-0	3-0	21	Byrne, Venus (og), Moody, Elliott	10,423
40	9	A	Middlesbrough	L	1-2	0-1	22	Moody (pen)	8586
41	12	H	WBA	D	1-1	0-1	—	Moody	9028
42	16	A	Barnsley	L	0-1	0-0	22		4874
43	23	H	Leicester C	D	2-2	1-1	23	Elliott, Moody	8818
44	26	A	Sunderland	W	3-2	1-2	—	Moody 2 (1 pen), Allen	14,712
45	30	A	Derby Co	L	1-2	0-0	23	Byrne	16,206
46	May 8	H	Notts Co	W	2-1	1-0	23	Byrne, Beauchamp	8475

Final League Position: 23

GOALSCORERS

League (54): Moody 8 (3 pens), Byrne 7, Beauchamp 6, Cusack 6, Dyer 5, Elliott 5, Magilton 5 (4 pens), Allen 3, Penney 2, Robinson 2, Rogan 2, Ford M 1, own goals 2.
Coca-Cola Cup (2): Beauchamp 1, Wanless 1.
FA Cup (8): Byrne 2, Elliott 2, Allen 1, Beauchamp 1, Dyer 1, Magilton 1.

Kee 3	Smart 22 + 1	Ford M 41	Lewis 46	Collins 18 + 8	Rogan 29	Magilton 29	Beauchamp 43 + 2	Dyer 30 + 8	Robinson 36	Allen 34 + 11	Cusack 18 + 2	Druce 5 + 14	Reece 4	Narbett 1	Penney 13 + 3	Wanless 1 + 8	Whitehead 39	Ford R 12 + 2	Keeble — + 1	Elliott 32	Byrne 27 + 3	Jackson 1 + 1	Saunders 2 + 3	Moody 15	Carter 5	*Match No.*
1	2	3	4	5	6	7	8	9	10	11																1
1	2	3	4	5	6	7	8	9	10	11	12															2
1	2	3	4	5	6	7	8	9	10	11		12														3
	2	3	4	5		7	8	9	10	12		11	1	6												4
	2	3	4	12	6	7	*8*	14	5	11	9		1		10											5
	2		4	3	6	7	8	9	5	11			1		10	12										6
		3	4	2	6	7	8	9	5	11		12	1		10											7
		3	4	2	6	7	8	9	5	11		12			*10*	14	1									8
		3	4	2	6	7	8		5	11		*9*			10	12	1	14								9
		3	4	2	6	*7*	8		5	11		9			10	12	1	14								10
		3	4	2	6	7	8	12	5	11					10	9	1									11
		3	4	2	6	7	8	9	5	11					*10*	12	1		14							12
		3	*4*	2	6	7	8	12	5	11	9	14			10		1									13
		3	4	2	6	7	8	12	5	11	9	14			*10*		1									14
		3	4	14	6	7	8		*5*	11	9				12		1			2	10					15
		3	4		6	7	8		5	11	9				12		1			2	10					16
		3	4	14	6	7	8	12	5	11	*9*						1			2	10					17
		3	4	5	6	7	8	12		11	9						1			2	10					18
			4	14	6	7	8	12	*5*	11	9						1			2	10	3				19
			4	5	6	7	8	3		11	9	12			10		1			2						20
			4	5	6	7	8	3		11	9	12			*10*		1			2		14				21
		3	4		6	7	8	11	5	12	9						1			2	*10*		14			22
		3	4		6	7	8	11	5		9						1			2	10					23
		3	4		6	7	8	11	5	12		14					1			2	10		*9*			24
		3	4		6	7	8	11	5	12		14					1			2	*10*		9			25
		3	4		6	7	8	11	5	12	*9*						1			2	10		14			26
		3	4		6	7	8	11	5	12	9						1			2	10					27
		3	4		6	7	8	11	5	12	*9*						1			2	10		14			28
		3	4		6	7	8	11	5	12	*9*				14		1			2	10					29
	14	3	*7*		6		8		5	11	12				9		1	4		2	10					30
	2	4	7	12			8	3		11		14					1	5		6	*10*			9		31
	5	2	7	6				12		11	10	14					1	4		3	8			9		32
	5	3	7	14			8	6		11	10						1	*4*		2	12			9		33
	5	3	7				8	6		11							1	4		2	10			9		34
	5	3	7				8	6		11							1	4		2	10			9		35
	5	3	7				12	6		11							1	4		2	10			9	8	36
	5	3	7				12	6		11		14					1	4		2	*10*			9	8	37
	5	3	7				9	6	4	11						12	1			2	10				8	38
	5	3	7				11	6	4	12						14	1			2	10			*9*	8	39
	5	3	*7*				11	6	4	12						14	1			2	10			9	8	40
	5	3	7				11	6	4	8							1			2	10			9		41
	5		7	3			11	6	*4*	12		14					1	8		2	10			9		42
	5	3	7				11	6	4	8		12					1			2	10			9		43
	5	3	7				11		4	10		6					1	8		2	12			9		44
	5	3	7	14			11		4	10		6					1	*8*		2	12			9		45
	5	3	7	12			11		4	10							1	8		2	6			9		46

Coca-Cola Cup	Second Round	Tranmere R (a)	1-5
		(h)	1-1
FA Cup	Third Round	Tranmere R (h)	2-0
	Fourth Round	Leeds U (h)	2-2
		(a)	3-2
	Fifth Round	Chelsea (h)	1-2

OXFORD UNITED

Player and Position	Ht	Wt	Birth Date	Birth Place	Source	Clubs	League App	League Gls
Goalkeepers								
Paul Kee*	6 3	12 05	8 11 69	Belfast	Ards	Oxford U	56	—
						Reading (loan)	—	—
Paul Reece	5 11	12 07	16 7 68	Nottingham	Kettering T	Grimsby T	54	—
						Doncaster R	1	—
						Oxford U	39	—
Philip Whitehead	6 3	13 07	17 12 69	Halifax	Trainee	Halifax T	42	—
						Barnsley	16	—
						Halifax T (loan)	9	—
						Scunthorpe U (loan)	8	—
						Scunthorpe U (loan)	8	—
						Bradford C (loan)	6	—
						Oxford U	39	—
Defenders								
David Collins	6 1	12 10	30 10 71	Dublin	Trainee	Liverpool	—	—
						Wigan Ath (loan)	9	—
						Oxford U	39	—
Matthew Elliott	6 3	14 05	1 11 68	Surrey	Epsom & Ewell	Charlton Ath	—	—
						Torquay U	124	15
						Scunthorpe U (loan)	8	1
						Scunthorpe U	53	7
						Oxford U	32	5
Ceri Evans	6 1	14 02	2 10 63	Christchurch	Otago Univ	Oxford U	116	3
Mike Ford	6 0	11 02	9 2 66	Bristol	Apprentice	Leicester C	—	—
					Devizes	Cardiff C	145	13
						Oxford U	163	10
Darren Jackson*	6 1	12 08	24 9 71	Bristol	Trainee	Oxford U	14	—
						Reading (loan)	5	—
Les Robinson	5 8	11 01	1 3 67	Mansfield	Local	Mansfield T	15	—
						Stockport Co	67	3
						Doncaster R	82	12
						Oxford U	123	2
Anton Rogan	5 11	12 06	25 3 66	Belfast	Distillery	Celtic	127	4
						Sunderland	46	1
						Oxford U	29	2
Gary Smart*	5 9	11 03	29 4 64	Totnes	Wokingham	Oxford U	175	—
Steve Tavinor*	5 10	11 06	28 1 74	Oxford	Trainee	Oxford U	—	—
Andy Wallbridge‡	6 0	12 00	14 11 73	Croydon	Trainee	Oxford U	—	—
Midfield								
Tristan Didcock‡	5 9	10 00	19 9 73	Chipping Norton	Trainee	Oxford U	—	—
Alex Dyer	5 11	11 12	14 11 65	West Ham	Watford	Blackpool	108	19
						Hull C	60	14
						Crystal Palace	17	2
						Charlton Ath	78	13
						Oxford U	38	5
Bobby Ford	5 8	10 06	22 9 74	Oxford	Trainee	Oxford U	14	—
Mickey Lewis	5 6	10 10	15 2 65	Birmingham	School	WBA	24	—
						Derby Co	43	1
						Oxford U	242	6
Steve McClaren‡	5 7	9 04	3 5 61	Fulford	Apprentice	Hull C	178	16
						Derby Co	25	—
						Lincoln C (loan)	8	—
						Bristol C	61	2
						Oxford U	33	—
Jon Narbett‡	5 10	10 08	21 11 68	Birmingham	Apprentice	Shrewsbury T	26	3
						Hereford U	149	31
						Leicester C (loan)	—	—
						Oxford U	15	—
Paul Wanless	6 1	13 04	14 12 73	Banbury	Trainee	Oxford U	22	—
Forwards								
Chris Allen	5 11	12 02	18 11 72	Oxford	Trainee	Oxford U	90	7
Joe Beauchamp	5 10	11 10	13 3 71	Oxford	Trainee	Oxford U	124	20
						Swansea C (loan)	5	2

OXFORD UNITED

Colours: Gold shirts with blue sleeves, blue shorts, gold stockings. **Change colours:** Red and blue mix shirts, red shorts, red stockings.

Foundation: There had been an Oxford United club around the time of World War I but only in the Oxfordshire Thursday League and there is no connection with the modern club which began as Headington in 1893, adding "United" a year later. Playing first on Quarry Fields and subsequently Wooton's Fields, they owe much to a Dr. Hitchings for their early development.

First Football League game: 18 August, 1962, Division 4, v Barrow (a) L 2-3 – Medlock; Beavon, Quartermain; R. Atkinson, Kyle, Jones; Knight, G. Atkinson (1), Houghton (1), Cornwell, Colfar.

Did you know: In 1953–54 while still known as Headington United, the club went from the first qualifying round to the fourth round proper, ten matches in all. They were beaten by Bolton Wanderers 4-2. That season Headington played 62 games.

Managers (and Secretary-Managers)
Harry Thompson 1949–58 (Player Manager 1949-51), Arthur Turner 1959–69 (continued as GM to 1972), Ron Saunders 1969, George Summers 1969–75, Mike Brown 1975–79, Bill Asprey 1979–80, Ian Greaves 1980–82, Jim Smith 1982–85, Maurice Evans 1985–88, Mark Lawrenson 1988, Brian Horton 1988–93, Denis Smith September 1993–

Player and Position	*Ht*	*Wt*	*Birth Date*	*Birth Place*	*Source*	*Clubs*	*League App*	*League Gls*
John Byrne	5 11	13 01	1 2 61	Manchester	Apprentice	York C	175	55
						QPR	126	30
					Le Havre	Brighton	51	14
						Sunderland	33	8
						Millwall	17	1
						Brighton (loan)	7	2
						Oxford U	30	7
Nick Cusack	6 0	11 13	24 12 65	Rotherham	Alvechurch	Leicester C	16	1
						Peterborough U	44	10
						Motherwell	77	17
						Darlington	21	6
						Oxford U	59	10
						Wycombe W (loan)	4	—
Mark Druce	5 11	11 11	3 3 74	Oxford	Trainee	Oxford U	25	1
Keith Holmes*	5 10	10 10	4 3 74	Oxford	Trainee	Oxford U	—	—
Matthew Keeble‡	5 9	10 00	8 9 72	Chipping Norton		Oxford U	2	—
Paul Moody	6 3	14 03	13 6 67	Portsmouth	Waterlooville	Southampton	12	—
						Reading (loan)	5	1
						Oxford U	15	8
Matthew Murphy	5 10	11 00	20 8 71	Northampton	Corby	Oxford U	2	—
David Penney	5 8	10 07	17 8 64	Wakefield	Pontefract	Derby Co	19	—
						Oxford U	110	15
						Swansea C (loan)	12	3
						Swansea C (loan)	11	2

Trainees
Bastable, Gary J; Border, Benjamin J; (h) Bowen, Wayne; Byles, Paul J; Cantwell, Sean M; Cullip, Daniel; Forinton, Howard L; Foster, Dale; Godfrey, Russell L; Goodall, Grant S; Gordon, Ian P; Greig, Neil S; Maciak, Jason; Mann, Alan S; Marsh, Simon T; Sterling, Leon W; Turner, Simon J; Watts, Darren W.

Associated Schoolboys
Anderson, Simon P; Concannon, Ian D; Cook, James; Davies, Nathan W; Davies, Simon L; Davis, Paul; Deacon, Tom; Edwards, Christian; Evans, David A; Gesner, Stevie J; Hunt, Timothy; Macmuiris, Paul; Medford, Jamie W. K; Redknap, Benjamin M; Smith, Jonathan P; Smith, Kirk A; Stanway, Mark R; Stone, Paul; Tregurtha, David M; Twine, Richard; Whittingham, James; Wilson, Neil A.

Associated Schoolboys who have accepted the Club's offer of a Traineeship/Contract
Bowen, Jamie; Hammond, Paul J; Hayter, Jonathon R; McGregor, Marc R; Powell, Paul; Robertson, Andrew.

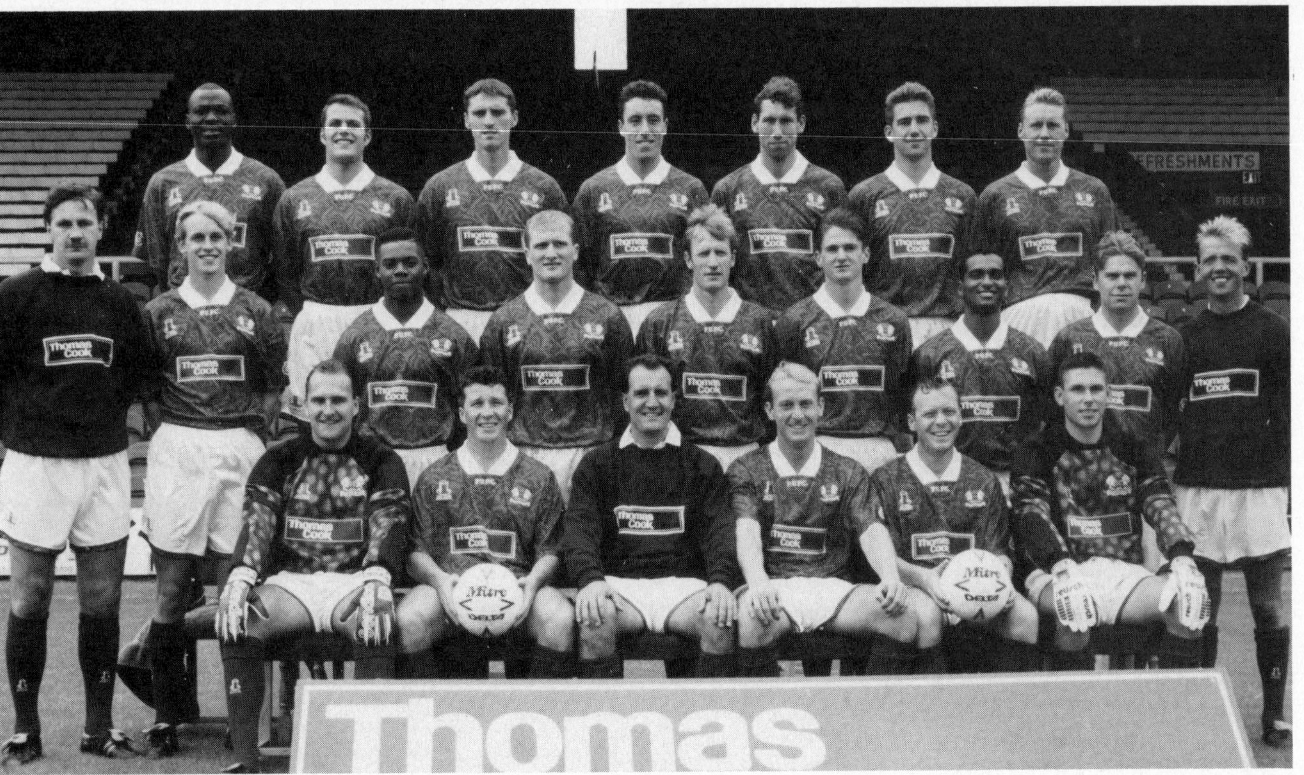

PETERBOROUGH UNITED 1993–94 *Back row (left to right):* Domenico Iorfa, Craig Boardman, Lee Howarth, Steve Welsh, John McGlashan, Mark Peters, Tony Philliskirk.
Centre row: Keith Oakes (Assistant Manager/Physio), Darren Edey, Jason Brissett, Marcus Ebdon, Tony Adcock, Chris Greenman, Bobby Barnes, Andrew Curtis, Mick Halsall.
Front row: Fred Barber, Tony Spearing, Lil Fuccillo (Manager), Darren Bradshaw, Gary Cooper, Ian Bennett.

Division 2 PETERBOROUGH UNITED

London Road Ground, Peterborough PE2 8AL. Telephone Peterborough (0733) 63947. Fax 0733 557210.

Ground capacity: 18,978.

Record attendance: 30,096 v Swansea T, FA Cup 5th rd, 20 February 1965.

Record receipts: £51,315 v Brighton & HA, 5th rd, 15 February 1986.

Pitch measurements: 112yd × 75yd.

Chairman: A. H. Hand.

Directors: N. Hard, P. Sagar. ***Company Secretary:*** Miss Caroline Hand.

Chief Executive: Chris Turner.

Manager: John Still. ***Assistant Manager:*** Mick Halsall. ***Coach:*** Mick Halsall.

Physio: Keith Oakes.

Commercial Manager: Michael Vincent.

Year Formed: 1934. ***Turned Professional:*** 1934. ***Ltd Co.:*** 1934.

Club Nickname: 'The Posh'.

Record League Victory: 8–1 v Oldham Ath, Division 4, 26 November 1969 – Drewery; Potts, Noble; Conmy, Wile, Wright; Moss (1), Price (3), Hall (4), Halliday, Robson.

Record Cup Victory: 6–0 v Redditch, FA Cup, 1st rd (replay), 22 November 1971 – Drewery; Carmichael, Brookes; Oakes, Turner, Wright; Conmy, Price (1), Hall (2), Barker (2), Robson (1).

Record Defeat: 1–8 v Northampton T, FA Cup 2nd rd (2nd replay), 18 December, 1946.

Most League Points (2 for a win): 66, Division 4, 1960–61.

Most League Points (3 for a win): 82, Division 4, 1981–82.

Most League Goals: 134, Division 4, 1960–61.

Highest League Scorer in Season: Terry Bly, 52, Division 4, 1960–61.

Most League Goals in Total Aggregate: Jim Hall, 122, 1967–75.

Most Capped Player: Tony Millington, 8 (21), Wales.

Most League Appearances: Tommy Robson, 482, 1968–81.

Record Transfer Fee Received: £400,000 from Notts Co for David Robinson, October 1992.

Record Transfer Fee Paid: £100,000 to Halifax T for David Robinson, July 1989 and to Millwall for John McGlashan, February 1993.

Football League Record: 1960 Elected to Division 4; 1961–68 Division 3, when they were demoted for financial irregularities; 1968–74 Division 4; 1974–79 Division 3; 1979–91 Division 4; 1991–92 Division 3; 1992–94 Division 1; 1994– Division 2.

Honours: *Football League:* Division 1 best season: 10th Division 1 1992–93; Division 4 – Champions 1960–61, 1973–74. *FA Cup:* best season: 6th rd, 1965. *Football League Cup:* Semi-final 1966.

PETERBOROUGH UNITED 1993—94 LEAGUE RECORD

Match No.	Date	Venue	Opponents	Result	H/T Score	Lg. Pos.	Goalscorers	Attendance
1	Aug 14	A	Leicester C	L 1-2	1-2	—	Cooper (pen)	13,671
2	17	H	Barnsley	W 4-1	2-0	—	Iorfa 2, Adcock, Barnes	5875
3	21	H	Notts Co	D 1-1	0-0	5	Welsh	6890
4	28	A	Southend U	L 0-3	0-0	11		5075
5	Sept 4	H	Grimsby T	L 1-2	0-0	18	Cooper	5962
6	11	A	Derby Co	L 0-2	0-0	22		14,779
7	18	H	Oxford U	W 3-1	0-1	19	Philliskirk 3	5148
8	25	H	Millwall	D 0-0	0-0	19		6219
9	Oct 2	A	Sunderland	L 0-2	0-1	22		17,846
10	9	H	Portsmouth	D 2-2	1-2	22	McGlashan, Adcock	6538
11	16	A	WBA	L 0-3	0-0	24		15,134
12	23	H	Birmingham C	W 1-0	1-0	23	Philliskirk (pen)	7575
13	30	A	Middlesbrough	D 1-1	1-1	23	Iorfa	10,704
14	Nov 2	A	Bolton W	D 1-1	0-1	—	Rush	7058
15	6	H	Tranmere R	D 0-0	0-0	21		5519
16	20	H	Charlton Ath	L 0-1	0-0	24		6273
17	27	H	Bristol C	L 0-2	0-2	24		5084
18	Dec 3	A	Tranmere R	L 1-2	0-2	—	Adcock (pen)	6294
19	11	A	Barnsley	L 0-1	0-1	24		6209
20	19	H	Leicester C	D 1-1	0-0	—	Adcock	8595
21	27	H	Luton T	D 0-0	0-0	24		9522
22	28	A	Watford	L 1-2	0-1	24	Adcock	7155
23	Jan 1	H	Wolverhampton W	L 0-1	0-0	24		10,298
24	15	H	WBA	W 2-0	0-0	24	Strodder (og), Charlery	7757
25	22	A	Portsmouth	W 2-0	1-0	24	Adcock 2	19,534
26	Feb 1	A	Crystal Palace	L 2-3	1-0	—	Charlery 2	12,426
27	5	A	Birmingham C	D 0-0	0-0	24		15,140
28	12	H	Middlesbrough	W 1-0	0-0	23	Charlery	7020
29	19	H	Stoke C	D 1-1	1-1	23	Bradshaw	7428
30	22	A	Notts Co	L 1-2	0-1	—	Iorfa	6106
31	Mar 2	A	Nottingham F	L 0-2	0-1	—		19,329
32	5	H	Southend U	W 3-1	2-0	22	Charlery, Adcock, Spearing	5878
33	8	A	Grimsby T	L 2-3	1-1	—	Adcock, Iorfa	4504
34	12	A	Oxford U	W 2-1	0-0	22	McGorry, Iorfa	5789
35	16	H	Derby Co	D 2-2	1-0	—	Charlery, Iorfa	7371
36	22	A	Millwall	L 0-1	0-0	—		8518
37	26	H	Sunderland	L 1-3	1-2	22	Adcock (pen)	8753
38	29	H	Crystal Palace	D 1-1	0-1	—	Iorfa	8412
39	Apr 2	A	Luton T	L 0-2	0-1	24		8398
40	5	H	Watford	L 3-4	1-1	—	McGlashan, Adcock 2 (1 pen)	7734
41	9	A	Wolverhampton W	D 1-1	1-1	24	McGlashan	23,676
42	13	A	Stoke C	L 0-3	0-2	—		10,181
43	16	H	Bolton W	L 2-3	1-0	24	Hackett, McGorry	6616
44	23	A	Charlton Ath	L 1-5	0-3	24	Charlery	8626
45	30	H	Nottingham F	L 2-3	2-1	24	McGorry, Charlery	14,010
46	May 8	A	Bristol C	L 1-4	0-2	24	Furnell	7790

Final League Position: 24

GOALSCORERS

League (48): Adcock 12 (3 pens), Charlery 8, Iorfa 8, Philliskirk 4 (1 pen), McGorry 3, McGlashan 3, Cooper 2 (1 pen), Barnes 1, Bradshaw 1, Furnell 1, Hackett 1, Rush 1, Spearing 1, Welsh 1, own goal 1.
Coca-Cola Cup (8): Adcock 1, Bradshaw 1, Brissett 1, Hackett 1, McGlashan 1, Oliver 1, Philliskirk 1, Rush 1.
FA Cup (2): Brissett 1, Charlery 1.

Bennett 19	McDonald 28 + 1	Spearing 33 + 1	McGlashan 26 + 2	Peters 17 + 2	Welsh 45	Iorfa 24 + 10	Cooper 13 + 1	Adcock 40 + 2	Ebdon 10	Barnes 5 + 3	Brissett 23 + 7	Philliskirk 6 + 5	Bradshaw 38 + 1	Hackett 18 + 4	Howarth 24 + 1	Rush 2 + 2	Greenman 24 + 1	Furnell 5 + 5	Gibson 1	Barber 24	Charlery 26	Fulton 3	Halsall — + 1	Carter 9 + 2	Kruszynski 2 + 1	Anthrobus 2	Williams 16 + 2	McGorry 14 + 4	McGee 5 + 1	Cooksey 3	Clark 1	*Match No.*
1	2	3	4	5	6	7	8	9	10	11																						1
1	2	3	4	5	6	7	8	9	10	11	12																					2
1	2	3	4	5	6	7	8	9	10	11		12																				3
1	2	3	4	5	6	7	8	9	10	*11*		12	14																			4
1	2	3	4	5	6	*7*	10	9			12	14	8	11																		5
1	2	3	4	5	6	7	10	9				12	8	11																		6
1	2	3		5	6	7	10	12		11		9	4	8																		7
1	2	3		5	6	7	10	12			11	9	4	8																		8
1	2	3		5	6		10	7			11	9	4	8																		9
1	2		10	5	6	12		7			11	9	4	8	3																	10
1	2		10	5	6	12		7			11	9	4	8	3																	11
1	2	3	10		6	12	14	7			*11*	9	4	8	5																	12
1	2	3	10		6	7	11	9					4	8	5	12																13
1	2	3	10		6	*7*	11	9			14		4	8	5	12																14
1		3	10		6		11	7			12		4	8	5	9	2															15
1	3		10	14	6			7		12	*11*		4	8	5	9	2															16
1	3		9		6		11	*7*	10	12			4	8	5		2	14														17
1		3	10	12	6			7			11		4	8	5		2	9														18
1		3	8		6			7	10		11		4		5		2	12	9													19
	2	3	8		6			7	11		12		4		5			9		1	10											20
	2	*3*			6			7	8	14		12	4		5			9		1	10	11										21
	2		8	3	6	12		7					4		5			9		1	10	11	14									22
	2				6			7	9		11		4				5			1	10	8		3								23
	2	12	4		6	*7*		9			11				5		3	14		1	10				8							24
	2	3			6			7	8		11				5		4	12		1	10					9						25
		3			6	*9*		7			11		2	12	5		4			1	10			14	8							26
	2				6	12		7			11		8		5		4			1	10			3		9						27
					6	12		9			11		2		5		4			1	10			3			7	8				28
					6			9			11		2		5		4			1	10			3			7	8				29
		3			6	12		9			11		2		5		4			1	10				14		7	*8*				30
	14	3			*6*	12		9					2	11	5		4			1	10						7	8				31
	2	3			6			9			12		5				4			1	10			11			7	8				32
	2	3			6	12		9			11				5		4			1	10						7	8				33
	2	3			6	7		9			11		5				4			1	10							8				34
	2	3			6	7		9			11		5				4			1	10						12	8				35
	2	3			6	7		9			*11*		5				4			1	10			12			14	8				36
		3	12		6	7		9					5				4			1	10						2	8	11			37
		3	12		6	7		9					5	14			4			1	10						2	8	*11*			38
		3	8		6	7		9					5	*11*			4			1	10						2	12	14			39
			8		6	7		9			12		2		5					1	10			3			4		11			40
			8	5	6	7		*9*					2	14						1	10			3			4	12	11			41
			8	5	6	*7*							2	14				9		1	10			3			4	12	11			42
		3	8	5	6	14		*9*			11			7			2			1	10						4	12				43
		3	8	5	6	*9*							2	7	14		12				10						4	11		1		44
		3		5	6	9					11		8				2				10						4	7		1		45
		3	10			9					11		8		5			12						2			4	7		1	6	46

Coca-Cola Cup	Second Round	Barnsley (a)	1-1
		(h)	3-1
	Third Round	Blackpool (a)	2-2
		(h)	2-1
	Fourth Round	Portsmouth (h)	0-0
		(a)	0-1
FA Cup	Third Round	Tottenham H (h)	1-1
		(a)	1-1

PETERBOROUGH UNITED

Player and Position	Ht	Wt	Birth Date	Birth Place	Source	Clubs	League App	League Gls
Goalkeepers								
Fred Barber	5 10	12 00	26 8 63	Ferryhill	Apprentice	Darlington	135	—
						Everton	—	—
						Walsall	153	—
						Peterborough U (loan)	6	—
						Chester (loan)	8	—
						Blackpool (loan)	2	—
						Peterborough U	63	—
						Colchester U (loan)	10	—
						Chesterfield (loan)	—	—
Scott Cooksey	6 0		24 6 72	Birmingham	Bromsgrove R	Peterborough U	3	—
Defenders								
Craig Boardman‡	6 0	11 08	30 11 70	Barnsley	Trainee	Nottingham F	—	—
						Peterborough U	—	—
Ian Carter			20 9 67	Birmingham		Peterborough U	11	—
Simon Clark†			12 3 67	Boston	Stevenage Bor	Peterborough U	1	—
Chris Greenman	5 10	11 06	22 12 68	Bristol	School	Coventry C	6	—
						Peterborough U	34	—
Lee Howarth	6 1	12 06	3 1 68	Bolton	Chorley	Peterborough U	62	—
Mark Peters	6 0	11 03	6 7 72	St Asaph	Trainee	Manchester C	—	—
						Norwich C	—	—
						Peterborough U	19	—
Tony Spearing	5 9	10 12	7 10 64	Romford	Apprentice	Norwich C	69	—
						Stoke C (loan)	9	—
						Oxford U (loan)	5	—
						Leicester C	73	1
						Plymouth Arg	35	—
						Peterborough U	56	1
Steve Welsh	6 0	12 03	19 4 68	Glasgow	Army	Cambridge U	1	—
						Peterborough U	132	2
Midfield								
Darren Bradshaw	5 11	11 04	19 3 67	Sheffield	Matlock T	Chesterfield	18	—
						York C	59	3
						Newcastle U	38	—
						Peterborough U	73	1
Andy Curtis‡	5 10	11 07	2 12 72	Doncaster	Trainee	York C	12	—
						Peterborough U	11	1
Marcus Ebdon	5 9	11 00	17 10 70	Pontypool	Trainee	Everton	—	—
						Peterborough U	53	6
Mick Halsall	5 10	11 04	21 7 61	Bootle	Apprentice	Liverpool	—	—
						Birmingham C	36	3
						Carlisle U	92	11
						Grimsby T	12	—
						Peterborough U	249	28
Brian McGorry	5 10	11 00	16 4 70	Liverpool	Weymouth	Bournemouth	61	11
						Peterborough U	18	3
David Morrison			30 11 74	Waltham Forest	Chelmsford C	Peterborough U	—	—
Graham Retallick‡	5 10	11 13	8 2 70	Cambridge	Histon	Peterborough U	5	—
Lee Williams	5 7	11 00	3 2 73	Birmingham	Trainee	Aston Villa	—	—
						Shrewsbury T (loan)	3	—
						Peterborough U	18	—
Forwards								
Tony Adcock	5 10	11 09	27 2 63	Bethnal Green	Apprentice	Colchester U	210	98
						Manchester C	15	5
						Northampton T	72	30
						Bradford C	38	6
						Northampton T	35	10
						Peterborough U	111	35
Bobby Barnes (To Partick T January 1944)	5 7	10 09	17 12 62	Kingston	Apprentice	West Ham	43	5
						Scunthorpe U (loan)	6	—
						Aldershot	49	26
						Swindon T	45	13
						Bournemouth	14	—
						Northampton T	98	37
						Peterborough U	49	9

PETERBOROUGH UNITED

Colours: Royal blue shirts, white shorts, white stockings. **Change colours:** All red.

Foundation: The old Peterborough & Fletton club, founded in 1923, was suspended by the FA during season 1932–33 and disbanded. Local enthusiasts determined to carry on and in 1934 a new professional club Peterborough United was formed and entered the Midland League the following year.

First Football League game: 20 August, 1960, Division 4, v Wrexham (h) W 3-0 – Walls; Stafford, Walker; Rayner, Rigby, Norris; Halls, Emery (1), Bly (1), Smith, McNamee (1).

Did you know: In 1991–92 Peterborough United completed 67 first class matches, reaching the semi-final of the Autoglass Trophy and winning promotion through the play-offs. They also accounted for Wimbledon, Newcastle United and Liverpool in the League Cup.

Managers (and Secretary-Managers)
Jock Porter 1934–36, Fred Taylor 1936–37, Vic Poulter 1937–38, Sam Madden 1938–48, Jack Blood 1948–50, Bob Gurney 1950–52, Jack Fairbrother 1952–54, George Swindin 1954–58, Jimmy Hagan 1958–62, Jack Fairbrother 1962–64, Gordon Clark 1964–67, Norman Rigby 1967–69, Jim Iley 1969–72, Noel Cantwell 1972–77, John Barnwell 1977–78, Billy Hails 1978–79, Peter Morris 1979–82, Martin Wilkinson 1982–83, John Wile 1983–86, Noel Cantwell 1986–88 (continued as GM), Mick Jones 1988–89, Mark Lawrenson 1989–90, Chris Turner 1991–92, Lil Fuccillo 1992–93, John Still May 1994–

Player and Position	*Ht*	*Wt*	*Birth Date*	*Birth Place*	*Source*	*Clubs*	*League App*	*League Gls*
Jason Brissett			7 9 74	Redbridge	Arsenal	Peterborough U	30	—
Ken Charlery	6 1	12 07	28 11 64	Stepney	Beckton U	Maidstone U	59	11
						Peterborough U	51	19
						Watford	48	13
						Peterborough U	26	8
Darren Edey‡			4 5 72	Tidworth	Stamford U	Peterborough U	—	—
Andy Furnell§			13 2 77	Peterborough	Trainee	Peterborough U	10	1
Gary Hackett	5 7	11 03	11 10 62	Stourbridge	Bromsgrove R	Shrewsbury T	150	17
						Aberdeen	15	—
						Stoke C	73	7
						WBA	44	3
						Peterborough U	22	1
Dominic Iorfa	6 1	12 12	1 10 68	Lagos	Antwerp	QPR	8	—
						Peterborough U	60	9
John McGlashan	6 1	12 00	3 6 67	Dundee	Dundee Violet	Montrose	68	11
						Millwall	16	—
						Cambridge U (loan)	1	—
						Fulham (loan)	5	1
						Peterborough U	46	3

Trainees
Adams, Mark J; Clapham, Paul F; Fuff, Glen B; Furnell, Andrew P; Peaty, Andrew K; Semple, Ryan E. J; Stanhope, Andrew P; Thomas, David W; Tyler, Mark R.

****Non-Contract**
Clark, Simon; Curtis, Andrew.

Associated Schoolboys
Davies, Simon; Deadman, Aaron J; Edwards, Michael R; French, Daniel J; Griffin, Scott; Houston, Norman N; Lewis, Stuart K; Miles, Lee; Miller, Neil; Owen, Lee G; Redding, Christopher; Sinclair, Brett K; Thomas, Gareth R; Ward, Scott R; Williamson, Ian P.

Associated Schoolboys who have accepted the Club's offer of a Traineeship/Contract
Coleman, Andrew D; Drury, Adam J; Knowles, Christopher J.

**Non-Contract Players who are retianed must be re-signed before they are eligible to play in League matches.

PLYMOUTH ARGYLE 1993–94 *Back row (left to right):* Marcus Crocker, Michael Evans, Adrian Burrows, Paul Boardman, Wayne Burnett, Keith Hill, Marc Edworthy.
Centre row: Craig Skinner, Kevin Nugent, Richard Landon, Ray Newland,, Alan Nicholas, Matthew Smith, Andy Comyn, Darren Garner, Paul Sumner (Physio).
Front row: Dominic Naylor, Dwight Marshall, Mark Patterson, Steve Castle, Peter Shilton (Manager), John McGovern (Assistant Manager), Steve McCall, Paul Dalton, Martin Barlow.

Division 2 **PLYMOUTH ARGYLE**

Home Park, Plymouth, Devon PL2 3DQ. Telephone Plymouth (0752) 562561. Fax: (0752) 606167. Marketing Department:(0752) 569597. Lottery Shop: (0752) 561041. Pilgrim Shop: (0752) 558292.

Ground capacity: 19,640.

Record attendance: 43,596 v Aston Villa, Division 2, 10 October1936.

Record receipts: £128,000 v Burnley, Division 2 play-off, 18 May 1994.

Pitch measurements: 110yd × 72yd.

President: S. J. Rendell.

Chairman: D. McCauley. ***Vice-chairman:*** P. Bloom.

Directors: D. Angilley, G. Jasper, I. Jones.

Manager: Peter Shilton. ***Assistant Manager:*** John McGovern. ***Youth team coach:*** Ian Bowyer. ***Physio:*** Paul Sumner.

Secretary: Michael Holladay. ***Commercial Manager:*** Roger Williams.

Year Formed: 1886. ***Turned Professional:*** 1903. ***Ltd Co.:*** 1903.

Club Nickname: 'The Pilgrims'.

Previous Name: 1886–1903, Argyle Athletic Club.

Record League Victory: 8–1 v Millwall, Division 2, 16 January 1932 – Harper; Roberts, Titmuss; Mackay, Pullan, Reed; Grozier, Bowden (2), Vidler (3), Leslie (1), Black (1). (1 og). 8–1 v Hartlepool U (a), Division 2, 7 May 1994 – Nicholls; Patterson (Naylor), Hill, Burrows, Comyn, McCall, Barlow, Castle, Landon, Marshall, Dalton.

Record Cup Victory: 6–0 v Corby T, FA Cup, 3rd rd, 22 January 1966 – Leiper; Book, Baird; Williams, Nelson, Newman; Jones (1), Jackson (1), Bickle (3), Piper (1), Jennings.

Record Defeat: 0–9 v Stoke C, Division 2, 17 December 1960.

Most League Points (2 for a win): 68, Division 3 (S), 1929–30.

Most League Points (3 for a win): 87, Division 3, 1985–86.

Most League Goals: 107, Division 3 (S), 1925–26 and 1951–52.

Highest League Scorer in Season: Jack Cock, 32, Division 3 (S), 1925–26.

Most League Goals in Total Aggregate: Sammy Black, 180, 1924–38.

Most Capped Player: Moses Russell, 20 (23), Wales.

Most League Appearances: Kevin Hodges, 530, 1978–92.

Record Transfer Fee Received: £350,000 from Southend U for Gary Poole, July 1993.

Record Transfer Fee Paid: £250,000 to Hartlepool U for Paul Dalton, June 1992.

Football League Record: 1920 Original Member of Division 3; 1921–30 Division 3 (S); 1930–50 Division 2; 1950–52 Division 3 (S); 1952–56 Division 2; 1956–58 Division 3 (S); 1958–59 Division 3; 1959–68 Division 2; 1968–75 Division 3; 1975–77 Division 2; 1977–86 Division 3; 1986– Division 2.

Honours: *Football League:* Division 2 best season: 4th, 1931–32, 1952–53; Division 3 (S) – Champions 1929–30, 1951–52; Runners-up 1921–22, 1922–23, 1923–24, 1924–25, 1925–26, 1926–27 (record of six consecutive years); Division 3 – Champions 1958–59; Runners-up 1974–75, 1985–86. *FA Cup:* best season: semi-final 1983–84. *Football League Cup:* Semi-final 1965, 1974.

PLYMOUTH ARGYLE 1993—94 LEAGUE RECORD

Match No.	Date	Venue	Opponents	Result		H/T Score	Lg. Pos.	Goalscorers	Attendance
1	Aug 14	H	Stockport Co	L	2-3	0-1	—	Evans, Comyn	6863
2	21	A	Hull C	D	2-2	1-1	17	Castle 2	3580
3	28	H	Port Vale	W	2-0	0-0	11	Marshall, Castle	6072
4	31	A	Blackpool	L	1-2	0-0	—	Castle	3865
5	Sept 4	A	Swansea C	W	1-0	0-0	10	Dalton	4616
6	11	H	Leyton Orient	W	3-1	1-1	8	Castle 2, Hill	5657
7	14	H	Rotherham U	W	4-2	4-2	—	Nugent, Comyn, Castle, Dalton	6293
8	18	A	Reading	L	2-3	0-1	5	Nugent, Castle (pen)	6209
9	25	A	Cardiff C	W	3-2	2-0	4	Nugent 2, Comyn	6362
10	Oct 2	H	Huddersfield T	W	2-0	1-0	4	Castle, Trevitt (og)	6646
11	9	A	Burnley	L	2-4	1-1	6	Castle, Dalton	10,488
12	16	H	York C	W	2-1	1-1	5	Dalton, Comyn	5982
13	23	A	Bristol R	D	0-0	0-0	5		7758
14	30	H	Wrexham	D	1-1	0-0	4	Barlow	6977
15	Nov 2	A	Cambridge U	L	0-2	0-1	—		3135
16	6	H	Brentford	D	1-1	1-0	8	Dalton	6407
17	20	A	Bradford C	W	5-1	3-0	7	Comyn, Marshall 3, Nugent	5204
18	27	H	Hartlepool U	W	2-0	1-0	5	Castle, Nugent	5881
19	Dec 11	H	Hull C	W	2-1	2-0	5	Burnett, Castle	6460
20	17	A	Stockport Co	W	3-2	0-0	—	Castle 3	4174
21	28	H	Fulham	W	3-1	1-1	2	Nugent, Dalton, Onwere (og)	15,609
22	Jan 1	A	Bournemouth	W	1-0	0-0	2	Marshall	6990
23	3	H	Brighton & HA	D	1-1	0-1	2	Castle	15,334
24	15	A	York C	D	0-0	0-0	2		4115
25	22	H	Burnley	W	3-2	2-0	2	Marshall, Nugent 2	10,595
26	Feb 5	H	Bristol R	D	3-3	2-3	4	Marshall, Dalton, Evans	13,318
27	12	A	Barnet	D	0-0	0-0	3		2854
28	19	A	Port Vale	L	1-2	1-1	4	Marshall	9093
29	22	H	Blackpool	W	2-1	0-0	—	Marshall, Nugent	7102
30	25	H	Swansea C	W	2-1	1-1	3	Evans, McCall	8930
31	Mar 2	A	Exeter C	W	3-2	0-1	—	Gavin (og), Burnett, Evans	6601
32	5	A	Leyton Orient	L	1-2	0-2	2	Castle	5334
33	8	H	Barnet	W	1-0	0-0	—	Evans	7595
34	12	H	Reading	W	3-1	1-1	2	Nugent 2, Dalton	14,953
35	15	A	Rotherham U	W	3-0	0-0	—	Nugent, Evans 2	2982
36	19	H	Cardiff C	L	1-2	1-2	2	Evans	9587
37	26	A	Huddersfield T	L	0-1	0-0	2		5619
38	30	A	Brighton & HA	L	1-2	0-0	—	Evans	9500
39	Apr 2	H	Exeter C	W	1-0	0-0	2	Dalton	12,986
40	4	A	Fulham	D	1-1	0-1	2	Nugent	5819
41	9	H	Bournemouth	W	2-0	1-0	2	Marshall, Castle	7971
42	16	H	Cambridge U	L	0-3	0-1	2		8872
43	23	A	Brentford	D	1-1	0-1	2	Landon	6173
44	26	A	Wrexham	W	3-0	2-0	—	Barlow, Marshall, Dalton	2518
45	30	H	Bradford C	W	3-1	1-1	2	Castle 2, Landon	10,985
46	May 7	A	Hartlepool U	W	8-1	4-0	3	Marshall, McCall, Landon 3, Dalton 2, Castle	2382

Final League Position: 3

GOALSCORERS

League (88): Castle 21 (1 pen), Nugent 14, Dalton 12, Marshall 12, Evans 9, Comyn 5, Landon 5, Barlow 2, Burnett 2, McCall 2, Hill 1, own goals 3.
Coca-Cola Cup (2): Barlow 1, Marshall 1.
FA Cup (7): Dalton 3, Nugent 3, Marshall 1.

Newland 4 + 1	Patterson 41	Naylor 42 + 1	Hill 28 + 1	Comyn 46	McCall 44 + 1	Burnett 30 + 2	Castle 44	Nugent 39	Marshall 28 + 3	Dalton 40	Evans 16 + 6	Edworthy 7 + 5	Barlow 22 + 4	Nicholls 38	Boardman — + 1	Shilton 4	Burrows 20 + 2	Skinner 9 + 7	Crocker — + 1	Landon 3 + 3	McCarthy 1 + 1	Match No.
1	2	3	4	5	6	7	8	9	10	11	12											1
1	2	3	4	5	12		8	9	10		11	6	7									2
	2	3	4	5	6		8	9	10	11	12		7	1								3
1	2	3	4	5	6		8		10	11	*9*	12	7		14							4
	2	3		5	6		8		10	11	9	4	7			1	12					5
	2	3	4	5	6		8	9	10	11		12	7			1						6
	2	3	4	5	6		8	9		11	10		7	1								7
	2	3	4	5	6		8	9		11	10		7	1								8
	2	3	4	5	6		8	9		11			7	1				10				9
	2	3	4	5	6		8	9	10	11		12	7			1						10
	2	3		5	6		8	9	10	11			7			1	4	12				11
	2	3		5	6	10	8	9	12	11			7	1			4					12
	2	3		5	6		8	9		11			7	1			4	10				13
	2	3		5	6		8	9	12	11			7	1			4	10				14
	2	3		5	6	14	*8*	9	12	11			7	1			4	10				15
	2	3		5	6	7	8	9		11				1			4	10	12			16
		3		5	6	7	8	9	10	11		2		1			4					17
	2	3		5	6	7	8	9	10					1			4	11				18
	2	3		5	6	7	8	9	10					1			4	11				19
	2	3	12	5	6	7	8	9	10	11				1			4					20
	2	3	4	5	6	7	8	9	10	11				1								21
	2	3	4	5	6	7	8	9	10	11		12		1								22
		3	4	5	6	7	8	9	10	11	12	2		1								23
		3	4	5	6	7	8	9	10	11		2	12	1								24
		3	4	5	6	7	8	9	10	11		2		1								25
	2	3	4	5	6	7	8		10	11	9			1								26
14	2	3	4	5	6	*7*	8		10	11	12			1						9		27
	2	3	4	5	6	7	8		10	11	12		14	1							*9*	28
	2	3	4	5	6	7	8	9	10		12		11	1								29
1	2	3	4	5	6	7	8	9	10		11							12				30
	2	3	4	5	6	7	8	9			10			1				11			12	31
	2	3		5	6	7	8	9		11	10			1			4	12				32
	2	3		5	6	7	8	9		11	10			1			4	12				33
	2	3		5	6	7	8	9		11	10			1			4					34
	2	3		5	6	7	8	9		11	10			1			4	12				35
	2	3		5		7	8	9		11	10		12	1			4	6				36
	2	3		5	6	7	8	9		11	10			1			4	12				37
	2	3		5	6	7	8	9		11	10			1			4					38
	2	3	4	5	6	7	8	9		11	10		12	1								39
	2	3	4	5	6	7	8	9		11			10	1						12		40
	2		4	5	3	7	8	9	10	11		12	6	1								41
		3	4	5	6	7		9	*10*	11		2	8	1				12		14		42
	2	3	4	5	6	*7*		9	10	11			8	1			12			14		43
	2		3	5	6		8	9	10	11			7	1			4					44
	2		3	5	6	12	8		10	11			7	1			4			9		45
	2	12	3	5	6		8		10	11			7	1			4			9		46

Coca-Cola Cup	First Round	Birmingham C (a)	0-3
		(h)	2-0
FA Cup	First Round	Marlow (a)	2-0
	Second Round	Gillingham (h)	2-0
	Third Round	Chester C (h)	1-0
	Fourth Round	Barnsley (h)	2-2
		(a)	0-1

PLYMOUTH ARGYLE

Player and Position	*Ht*	*Wt*	*Birth Date*	*Place*	*Source*	*Clubs*	*League App*	*Gls*
Goalkeepers								
Ray Newland*	6 1	12 01	19 7 71	Liverpool	Everton	Plymouth Arg	26	—
Alan Nicholls	6 0		28 8 73	Birmingham	Cheltenham T	Plymouth Arg	38	—
Peter Shilton	6 0	14 00	18 9 49	Leicester	Apprentice	Leicester C	286	1
						Stoke C	110	—
						Nottingham F	202	—
						Southampton	188	—
						Derby Co	175	—
						Plymouth Arg	34	—
Defenders								
Adrian Burrows*	5 11	11 12	16 1 59	Sutton	Local	Mansfield T	78	5
						Northampton T	88	4
						Plymouth Arg	277	14
						Southend U (loan)	6	—
Andy Comyn	6 1	12 00	2 6 68	Manchester	Alvechurch	Aston Villa	15	—
						Derby Co	63	1
						Plymouth Arg	46	5
Keith Hill	6 0	11 03	17 5 69	Bolton	Apprentice	Blackburn R	96	3
						Plymouth Arg	65	1
Dominic Naylor	5 9	11 07	12 8 70	Watford	Trainee	Watford	—	—
						Halifax T	6	1
					Barnet	Barnet	51	—
						Plymouth Arg	43	—
Mark Patterson	5 10	11 05	13 9 68	Leeds	Trainee	Carlisle U	22	—
						Derby Co	51	3
						Plymouth Arg	41	—
Matthew Smith*	5 11		28 8 73	Derby	Derby Co	Plymouth Arg	—	—
Midfield								
Martin Barlow	5 7	10 03	25 6 71	Barnstable	Trainee	Plymouth Arg	110	7
Wayne Burnett	5 9	10 11	4 9 71	London	Trainee	Leyton Orient	40	—
						Blackburn R	—	—
						Plymouth Arg	32	2
Steve Castle	5 11	12 05	17 5 66	Barkingside	Apprentice	Orient	243	55
						Plymouth Arg	75	32
Paul Dalton	5 11	11 07	25 4 67	Middlesbrough	Brandon	Manchester U	—	—
						Hartlepool U	151	37
						Plymouth Arg	72	21
Mark Edworthy	5 7	9 08	24 12 72	Barnstaple	Trainee	Plymouth Arg	42	—
Darren Garner*	5 6	10 01	10 12 71	Plymouth	Trainee	Plymouth Arg	27	1
Steve McCall	5 11	12 06	15 10 60	Carlisle	Apprentice	Ipswich T	257	7
						Sheffield W	29	2
						Carlisle U (loan)	6	—
						Plymouth Arg	89	4
Jamie Morgan§	5 11	11 00	1 10 75	Plymouth	Trainee	Plymouth Arg	3	—
Forwards								
Paul Boardman*	6 0	11 02	6 11 67	Tottenham		Plymouth Arg	3	1
Marcus Crocker	5 10	11 05	8 10 74	Plymouth	Trainee	Plymouth Arg	5	—
Mike Evans	6 0	11 02	1 1 73	Plymouth	Trainee	Plymouth Arg	62	10
						Blackburn R (loan)	—	—
Richard Landon	6 3		22 3 70	Barnsley	Bedworth U	Plymouth Arg	6	5
Dwight Marshall	5 7	10 10	3 10 65	Jamaica	Grays Ath	Plymouth Arg	99	27
						Middlesbrough (loan)	3	—
Kevin Nugent	6 1	12 04	10 4 69	Edmonton	Trainee	Leyton Orient	94	20
						Cork C (loan)	—	—
						Plymouth Arg	88	25
Craig Skinner	5 8	11 00	21 10 70	Bury	Trainee	Blackburn R	16	—
						Plymouth Arg	29	1

PLYMOUTH ARGYLE

Colours: Green and black striped shirts, black shorts, black stockings. **Change colours:** All white.

Foundation: The club was formed in September 1886 as the Argyle Football Club by former public and private school pupils who wanted to continue playing the game. The meeting was held in a room above the Borough Arms (a Coffee House), Bedford Street, Plymouth. It was common then to choose a local street/terrace as a club name and Argyle or Argyll was a fashionable name throughout the land due to Queen Victoria'great interest in Scotland.

First Football League game: 28 August, 1920, Division 3, v Norwich C (h) D 1-1 – Craig; Russell, Atterbury; Logan, Dickinson, Forbes; Kirkpatrick, Jack, Bowler, Heeps (1), Dixon.

Did you know: When Plymouth won 8-1 at Hartlepool United on 7 May 1994 in a Division 2 match, it was the highest win in the four English Leagues during the season and equalled the club's biggest victory in the competition.

Managers (and Secretary-Managers)
Frank Brettell 1903–05, Bob Jack 1905–06, Bill Fullerton 1906–07, Bob Jack 1910–38, Jack Tresadern 1938–47, Jimmy Rae 1948–55, Jack Rowley 1955–60, Neil Dougall 1961, Ellis Stuttard 1961–63, Andy Beattie 1963–64, Malcolm Allison 1964–65, Derek Ufton 1965–68, Billy Bingham 1968–70, Ellis Stuttard 1970–72, Tony Waiters 1972–77, Mike Kelly 1977–78, Malcolm Allison 1978–79, Bobby Saxton 1979–81, Bobby Moncur 1981–83, Johnny Hore 1983–84, Dave Smith 1984–88, Ken Brown 1988–90, David Kemp 1990–92, Peter Shilton March 1992–

Trainees
Albery, Matthew D; Baker, Kevin C; Bass, Sam T; Bevan, Richard D; Dawe, Simon; Hutchinson, James; Morgan, James A; O'Hagan, Daniel A. N; Payne, Ian N; Rutkowski, Yan M; Twiddy, Christopher; Wotton, Paul A.

****Non-Contract**
Shilton, Peter L.

Associated Schoolboys
Ahearn, Jamie P; Ashton, Jon; Atkinson, David J; Beswetherick, Jonathan B; Birt, Andrew J; Bushby, Ryan; Ford, Liam A; Francis, Kevin; Garland, Philip L; Hellier, Ryan W; Henwood, Mark D; Hoare, Steven J; Hockley, Wayne; Latham, Matthew J; Le Tissier, Justin; Lockyer, Adam J; Neno, Richard J; Richardson, Dominic K; Sargent, Andrew D; Shilton, Sam; Sweeney, Terry N; Tucker, Matthew J; Turpin, Paul; Williams, Jeremy J.

**Non-Contract Players who are retained must be re-signed before they are eligible to play in League matches.

PORTSMOUTH 1993–94 *Back row (left to right):* Mark Chamberlain, Mark Blake, Lee Russell, Andy Awford, Mark Kelly, Darryl Powell, Ray Daniel.
Centre row: Mike Bailey (Reserve Team Manager), Graham Paddon (Assistant Manager), Chris Burns, Shaun Gale, Brian Horne, Alan Knight, Guy Butters, Kit Symons, Neil Sillett (Physio), Gordon Neave (Kit Manager).
Front row: Paul Hall, Mark Stimson, Shaun Murray, Paul Walsh, Bjorn Kristensen, Jim Smith (Manager), Lee Chapman, Warren Neill, Alan McLoughlin, Roy Young, John Durnin, Jon Gittens.

Division 1 PORTSMOUTH

Fratton Park, Frogmore Rd, Portsmouth PO4 8RA. Telephone Portsmouth (0705) 731204. Fax (0705) 734129. Commercial Dept: (0705) 827111. Ticket Office: (0705) 750825. Lottery Office: (0705) 825016. Clubcall: 0891 338383.

Ground capacity: 26,452.

Record attendance: 51,385 v Derby Co, FA Cup 6th rd, 26 February 1949.

Record receipts: £214,000 v Manchester U, Coca-Cola Cup 5th rd replay, 26 January 1994.

Pitch measurements: 116yd × 73yd.

Chairman: J. A. Gregory. ***Vice-chairman:*** D. K. Deacon.

Directors: M. H. Gregory, B. A. V. Henson, J. S. Hutchison.

Manager: Jim Smith. ***Coach:*** Graham Paddon.

Secretary: Paul Weld. ***Marketing Manager:*** Julie Baker.

Physio: Neil Sillett. ***Youth Team Coach:*** K. Todd.

Year Formed: 1898. ***Turned Professional:*** 1898. ***Ltd Co.:*** 1898.

Club Nickname: 'Pompey'.

Record League Victory: 9–1 v Notts Co, Division 2, 9 April 1927 – McPhail; Clifford, Ted Smith; Reg Davies (1), Foxall, Moffat; Forward (1), Mackie (2), Haines (3), Watson, Cook (2).

Record Cup Victory: 7–0 v Stockport Co, FA Cup, 3rd rd, 8 January 1949 – Butler; Rookes, Ferrier; Scoular, Flewin, Dickinson; Harris (3), Barlow, Clarke (2), Phillips (2), Froggatt.

Record Defeat: 0–10 v Leicester C, Division 1, 20 October 1928.

Most League Points (2 for a win): 65, Division 3, 1961–62.

Most League Points (3 for a win): 91, Division 3, 1982–83.

Most League Goals: 91, Division 4, 1979–80.

Highest League Scorer in Season: Guy Whittingham, 42, Division 1, 1992–93.

Most League Goals in Total Aggregate: Peter Harris, 194, 1946–60.

Most Capped Player: Jimmy Dickinson, 48, England.

Most League Appearances: Jimmy Dickinson, 764, 1946–65.

Record Transfer Fee Received: £2,000,000 from Tottenham H for Darren Anderton, May 1992.

Record Transfer Fee Paid: £650,000 to Celtic for Gerry Creaney, January 1994.

Football League Record: 1920 Original Member of Division 3; 1921 Division 3 (S); 1924–27 Division 2; 1927–59 Division 1; 1959–61 Division 2; 1961–62 Division 3; 1962–76 Division 2; 1976–78 Division 3; 1978–80 Division 4; 1980–83 Division 3; 1983–87 Division 2; 1987–88 Division 1; 1988–92 Division 2; 1992– Division 1.

Chairman: B. E. Fearn. ***Vice-chairman:*** L. V. Pickering.
Honours: *Football League:* Division 1 – Champions 1948–49, 1949–50; Division 2 – Runners-up 1926–27, 1986–87; Division 3 (S) – Champions 1923–24; Division 3 – Champions 1961–62, 1982–83. *FA Cup:* Winners 1939; Runners-up 1929, 1934. *Football League Cup:* best season: 5th rd, 1960–61, 1985–86.

PORTSMOUTH 1993—94 LEAGUE RECORD

Match No.	Date	Venue	Opponents	Result		H/T Score	Lg. Pos.	Goalscorers	Attendance
1	Aug 14	A	Oxford U	L	2-3	2-2	—	Chapman 2	8550
2	17	H	Charlton Ath	L	1-2	0-2	—	Symons (pen)	15,701
3	21	H	Luton T	W	1-0	1-0	10	Hall	12,248
4	24	A	Grimsby T	D	1-1	1-0	—	McLoughlin	5259
5	28	A	Crystal Palace	L	1-5	1-2	12	Neill	14,428
6	Sept 4	H	Stoke C	D	3-3	3-1	14	Durnin, Walsh, Gittens	12,552
7	11	A	Wolverhampton W	D	1-1	0-0	18	Durnin	19,019
8	18	H	Southend U	W	2-1	1-1	12	Durnin, Powell	11,093
9	25	H	Bristol C	D	0-0	0-0	13		10,702
10	Oct 2	A	Nottingham F	D	1-1	0-0	13	Powell	20,727
11	9	A	Peterborough U	D	2-2	2-1	13	McLoughlin, Walsh	6538
12	16	H	Derby Co	W	3-2	1-1	9	Walsh, Durnin, Symons (pen)	12,404
13	23	A	Notts Co	D	1-1	1-0	13	Dobson	6681
14	30	H	Tranmere R	W	2-0	0-0	8	Dobson, Walsh	12,462
15	Nov 2	H	Middlesbrough	W	2-0	0-0	—	Hall, Durnin	12,503
16	6	A	Sunderland	W	2-1	2-0	6	Walsh, Doling	17,146
17	20	A	Birmingham C	W	1-0	0-0	7	Stimson	11,896
18	27	A	WBA	L	1-4	0-2	9	McLoughlin	13,867
19	Dec 4	H	Sunderland	L	0-1	0-1	11		11,891
20	7	H	Watford	W	2-0	1-0	—	Durnin, Butters	8242
21	12	A	Charlton Ath	W	1-0	1-0	—	Neill	6975
22	18	H	Oxford U	D	1-1	1-0	6	McLoughlin	8980
23	27	A	Millwall	D	0-0	0-0	8		12,104
24	28	H	Bolton W	D	0-0	0-0	7		14,276
25	Jan 1	A	Barnsley	L	0-2	0-1	9		6328
26	15	A	Derby Co	L	0-1	0-0	12		15,645
27	22	H	Peterborough U	L	0-2	0-1	12		19,534
28	Feb 5	H	Notts Co	D	0-0	0-0	13		9359
29	11	A	Tranmere R	L	1-3	0-2	—	McLoughlin	6914
30	19	H	Grimsby T	W	3-1	2-0	14	Creaney 3 (1 pen)	7794
31	22	A	Luton T	L	1-4	0-2	—	Symons	6533
32	25	A	Stoke C	L	0-2	0-1	15		14,506
33	Mar 5	H	Crystal Palace	L	0-1	0-0	17		13,508
34	12	A	Southend U	L	1-2	1-1	18	Creaney	4437
35	15	H	Wolverhampton W	W	3-0	1-0	—	Chamberlain, Creaney 2	7840
36	19	A	Bristol C	L	0-1	0-0	17		6352
37	26	H	Nottingham F	W	2-1	1-0	17	Creaney, Hall	12,578
38	30	A	Leicester C	W	3-0	3-0	—	Creaney, Hall, McLoughlin	15,146
39	Apr 2	H	Millwall	D	2-2	1-0	15	Powell, Creaney (pen)	11,591
40	4	A	Bolton W	D	1-1	0-0	15	Creaney	9560
41	9	H	Barnsley	W	2-1	0-0	13	Wood, Powell	7005
42	16	A	Middlesbrough	W	2-0	2-0	10	Creaney, Powell	10,041
43	23	H	Birmingham C	L	0-2	0-1	14		11,101
44	26	H	Leicester C	L	0-1	0-1	—		7869
45	30	A	Watford	L	0-1	0-1	14		10,141
46	May 8	H	WBA	L	0-1	0-1	17		17,629

Final League Position: 17

GOALSCORERS

League (52): Creaney 11 (2 pens), Durnin 6, McLoughlin 6, Powell 5, Walsh 5, Hall 4, Symons 3 (2 pens), Chapman 2, Dobson 2, Neill 2, Butters 1, Chamberlain 1, Doling 1, Gittens 1, Stimson 1, Wood 1.
Coca-Cola Cup (10): Walsh 4, Durnin 2, Burns 1, Kristensen 1, McLoughlin 1, Stimson 1.
FA Cup (4): McLoughlin 4.

Knight 43	Awford 35	Butters 12 + 3	McLoughlin 37 + 1	Symons 29	Stimson 28 + 1	Neill 35	Chamberlain 12 + 7	Chapman 5	Blake 15	Kristensen 31 + 5	Burns 8 + 4	Powell 17 + 11	Walsh 30	Hall 16 + 12	Price 1 + 4	Aspinall — + 5	Horne 3	Russell 5 + 5	Durnin 23 + 5	Gittens 30	Daniel 14 + 2	Dobson 23 + 1	Pethick 14 + 4	Power 1 + 1	Doling 9 + 4	Creaney 18	Wood 7 + 5	Boere 4 + 1	Burton 1 + 1	Match No.
1	2	3	4	5	6	7	8	9	*10*	11	12	14																		1
1	2	3	4	5	6	7	*8*	9	11		12		10	14																2
1	2		*4*	5	6	7		9	11		3		10	8	12	14														3
	2		4	5	6	7		9	11		3		10	*8*	12		1	14												4
	2		4	5	6	7		9	*8*	11			10		12		1	3	14											5
	2	11	4			7			8		3	14	*10*		12		1		9	5	6									6
1			4	5	6	7			8	11	3		10	12					9	2										7
1	6		4	5		7				11	3	12	10	8					9	2										8
1	6		4	5	8	7			3	11		12	10						9	2										9
1	6		4	5						11		9	10	8	7	12				2		3								10
1	6		4		5					11	7	*8*	10			12			9	2		14	3							11
1	6		4	5	8					11			10						9	2		7	3	12						12
1	6		4	5	8								10	12					9	2		*7*	3	11	14					13
1	6		4	5	*8*	7	11						10						9	2		3	14		12					14
1	6			5	8	7	11						*10*	12					9	2		4	14		3					15
1	6	2	4	5	8	7						12	10						9			11	14		*3*					16
1	6		*4*	5	8	7			3	14			10						9	2	12	11								17
1	6		4	5	8	7				*11*			10			14			9	2	12	3								18
1	6	5	4			*7*				11			10	12		14			9	2	3				8					19
1	6	14	4	5		7				11			10	12					9	2	*8*				3					20
1	6	3	4	5		7				11			10					12	9	2					8					21
1	6	3	4	5		7	*8*			11			10	14				12	9			2								22
1		3	4	5		7	12			11			10					8	9		6	2								23
1	6		4	5		7			*8*	11		14	10	12					9		3	2								24
1	6		4	5	12		*8*			14		9	10					11			3	2	7							25
1	6	5	*4*		7	2	12			11		9	10						8		3				14					26
1	6		4			7			8	11	14	9	10					3	12			*5*			2					27
1	6		4	5		7	8			11	14	12	10						*2*		3					9				28
1	*6*		4	5		7			8	11		12	10							2	3		14			9				29
1				5		7			8	11		10		4						2	3	6				9	12			30
1				5		*7*			8	11		10		4					12	2	3	6				9	14			31
1	6	3		5	*2*	7				11	4	12	10						8							9	14			32
1	6	5	4		3					14	*8*		10	11					12	2			7			9				33
1	6	14	4		*3*				8	11				12						2	5		7			9	10			34
1			4		11		*8*			7		12		14						5	3	6	2			9	10			35
1	6		4		3		8					12		14				11			5	2	*7*			9	10			36
1	2		12		11	7	8					*3*		4				14		5		6				9		10		37
1	2	6	4		11	7	14			12		3		*8*						5						9		10		38
1	2		4			7	8			12		3		11						5		6				9	14	*10*		39
1	*2*		4			7				11		3		12						5		6	8			9	14	10		40
1			4	5		7	12			11		3		8						2		6				9	10			41
1			4		6	7	12			11		3		8						2			5			9	10			42
1					6	7				11		3		8					4	2			5		14	9	*10*	12		43
1				*4*	6		12			11		3		8					14	2			5		7	9			10	44
1					6	7	12			11		3		8				14	*4*			2	5		10	9				45
1		12			6		7			11		3		8						4		2	5		*9*		10		14	46

Coca-Cola Cup	Second Round	Rotherham U (a)	0-0
		(h)	5-0
	Third Round	Swindon T (h)	2-0
	Fourth Round	Peterborough U (a)	0-0
		(h)	1-0
	Fifth Round	Manchester U (a)	2-2
		(h)	0-1
FA Cup	Third Round	Blackburn R (a)	3-3
		(h)	1-3

PORTSMOUTH

Player and Position	Ht	Wt	Birth Date	Birth Place	Source	Clubs	League App	League Gls
Goalkeepers								
Aaron Flahavan	6 1	12 10	15 12 75	Southampton	Trainee	Portsmouth	—	—
Brian Horne*	5 11	13 13	5 10 67	Billericay	Apprentice	Millwall	163	—
						Watford (loan)	—	—
						Middlesbrough (loan)	4	—
						Stoke C (loan)	1	—
						Portsmouth	3	—
Alan Knight	6 0	13 00	3 6 61	Balham	Apprentice	Portsmouth	535	—
Defenders								
Andy Awford	5 9	11 09	14 7 72	Worcester	Worcester C	Portsmouth	142	—
Guy Butters	6 3	13 00	30 10 69	Hillingdon	Trainee	Tottenham H	35	1
						Southend U (loan)	16	3
						Portsmouth	86	4
Tony Dobson	6 1	12 10	5 2 69	Coventry	Apprentice	Coventry C	54	1
						Blackburn R	41	—
						Portsmouth	24	2
Shaun Gale*	6 0	11 06	8 10 69	Reading	Trainee	Portsmouth	3	—
Jon Gittens	6 0	12 06	22 1 64	Moseley	Paget R	Southampton	18	—
						Swindon T	126	6
						Southampton	19	—
						Middlesbrough (loan)	12	1
						Middlesbrough	13	—
						Portsmouth	30	1
Bjorn Kristensen	6 1	12 05	10 10 63	Malling	Aarhus	Newcastle U	80	4
						Bristol C (loan)	4	—
						Portsmouth	46	1
Warren Neill	5 9	11 05	21 11 62	Acton	Apprentice	QPR	181	3
						Portsmouth	211	2
Robbie Pethick	5 10	11 07	8 9 70	Tavistock	Weymouth	Portsmouth	18	—
Chris Price*	5 7	10 02	30 3 60	Hereford	Apprentice	Hereford U	330	27
						Blackburn R	83	11
						Aston Villa	110	2
						Blackburn R	19	3
						Portsmouth	18	—
Lee Russell	5 11	11 04	3 9 69	Southampton	Trainee	Portsmouth	57	1
Mark Stimson	5 11	11 00	27 12 67	Plaistow	Trainee	Tottenham H	2	—
						Leyton Orient (loan)	10	—
						Gillingham (loan)	18	—
						Newcastle U	86	2
						Portsmouth (loan)	4	—
						Portsmouth	29	1
Kit Symons	6 1	10 10	8 3 71	Basingstoke	Trainee	Portsmouth	120	6
Midfield								
Chris Burns	6 0	12 00	9 11 67	Manchester	Cheltenham T	Portsmouth	90	9
						Swansea C (loan)	4	—
						Bournemouth (loan)	14	1
Ray Daniel	5 8	11 09	10 12 64	Luton	Apprentice	Luton T	22	4
						Gillingham (loan)	5	—
						Hull C	58	3
						Cardiff C	56	1
						Portsmouth	78	4
Stuart Doling	5 6	10 06	28 10 72	Newport, IOW	Trainee	Portsmouth	32	3
Samuel Igoe			30 9 75	Spelthorne	Trainee	Portsmouth	—	—
Alan McLoughlin	5 8	10 00	20 4 67	Manchester	Local	Manchester U	—	—
						Swindon T	9	—
						Torquay U	24	4
						Swindon T	97	19
						Southampton	24	1
						Aston Villa (loan)	—	—
						Portsmouth	98	17
Forwards								
Michael Birmingham‡			25 7 75	Portsmouth	Trainee	Portsmouth	—	—
Deon Burton			25 10 76	Ashford	Trainee	Portsmouth	2	—

PORTSMOUTH

Colours: Blue shirts, white shorts, red stockings. **Change colours:** red and black halved shirts, red shorts, black stockings.

Foundation: At a meeting held in his High Street, Portsmouth offices in 1898, solicitor Alderman J. E. Pink and five other business and professional men agreed to buy some ground close to Goldsmith Avenue for £4,950 which they developed into Fratton Park in record breaking time. A team of professionals was signed up by manager Frank Brettell and entry to the Southern League obtained for the new club's September 1899 kick-off.

First Football League game: 28 August, 1920, Division 3, v Swansea T (h) W 3-0 – Robson; Probert, Potts; Abbott, Harwood, Turner; Thompson, Stringfellow (1), Reid (1), James (1), Beedie.

Did you know: During the period from 1913 to 1923 Shirley Abbott captained Portsmouth as a defender, his career spanned the Southern League, wartime football and Football League matches. Signed from Derby County he later played for Queens Park Rangers.

Managers (and Secretary-Managers)
Frank Brettell 1898–1901, Bob Blyth 1901–04, Richard Bonney 1905–08, Bob Brown 1911–20, John McCartney 1920–27, Jack Tinn 1927–47, Bob Jackson 1947–52, Eddie Lever 1952–58, Freddie Cox 1958–61, George Smith 1961–70, Ron Tindall 1970–73 (GM to 1974), John Mortimore 1973–74, Ian St. John 1974–77, Jimmy Dickinson 1977–79, Frank Burrows 1979–82, Bobby Campbell 1982–84, Alan Ball 1984–89, John Gregory 1989–90, Frank Burrows 1990–1991, Jim Smith May 1991–

Player and Position	*Ht*	*Wt*	*Birth Date*	*Place*	*Source*	*Clubs*	*League App*	*Gls*
Mark Chamberlain*	5 9	10 07	19 11 61	Stoke	Apprentice	Port Vale	96	17
						Stoke C	112	17
						Sheffield W	66	8
						Portsmouth	167	20
Colin Clarke‡	6 0	13 06	30 10 62	Newry	Apprentice	Ipswich T	—	—
						Peterborough	82	18
						Gillingham (loan)	8	1
						Tranmere R	45	22
						Bournemouth	46	26
						Southampton	82	36
						Bournemouth (loan)	4	2
						QPR	46	11
						Portsmouth	85	18
Gerry Creaney	5 10	10 07	13 4 70	Coatbridge	Celtic BC	Celtic	113	36
						Portsmouth	18	11
Aaron Cunningham			11 11 73	New Jersey	Trainee	Portsmouth	—	—
John Durnin	5 10	11 04	18 8 65	Bootle	Waterloo Dock	Liverpool	—	—
						WBA (loan)	5	2
						Oxford U	161	44
						Portsmouth	28	6
Paul Hall	5 9	10 02	3 7 72	Manchester	Trainee	Torquay U	93	1
						Portsmouth	28	4
Mark Kelly*	5 8	9 10	27 11 69	Sutton		Portsmouth	49	2
						Tottenham H (loan)	—	—
Darryl Powell	6 0	12 03	15 1 71	Lambeth	Trainee	Portsmouth	98	11
Paul Wood	5 9	10 01	1 11 64	Middlesbrough	Apprentice	Portsmouth	47	6
						Brighton	92	8
						Sheffield U	28	3
						Bournemouth (loan)	21	—
						Bournemouth	78	18
						Portsmouth	12	1
Roy Young*	5 9	11 00	28 10 73	Romsey	Trainee	Portsmouth	—	—

Trainees
Braybrook, Kevin P; Burden, Steven L; Gardner, Christopher D; Hounsell, Daniel J; Hussey, Matthew R; Mosedale, Anthony J; Rowe, David J; Spake, Daniel; Stewart, Paul T; Totten, Alexander R; Wakefield, David; Waterman, David G.

****Non-Contract**
Barnard, Simon R.

Associated Schoolboys
Barnes, Ashley R; Brackley, Peter; Burrows, Marc P; Chapman, David R; Clarke, Jonathon M; Dewey, Kevin L; Fitzgerald, Philip J; Foster, Mark J; Guile, Neil R; Holland, Perry D; Jukes, Nathan B; Karimzadeh, Ashkan; Macdonald, Gary; Marshall, John P; Miller, Joseph; Neary, Andrew J; O'Brien, Paul A; Porter, Daniel J; Ramsay, Peter E; Weston, Lee P; Williams, Adam L; Willis, Jonathan M; Wright, David S; Wyatt, Nicky.
**Non-Contract Players who are retained must be re-signed before they are eligible to play in League matches.

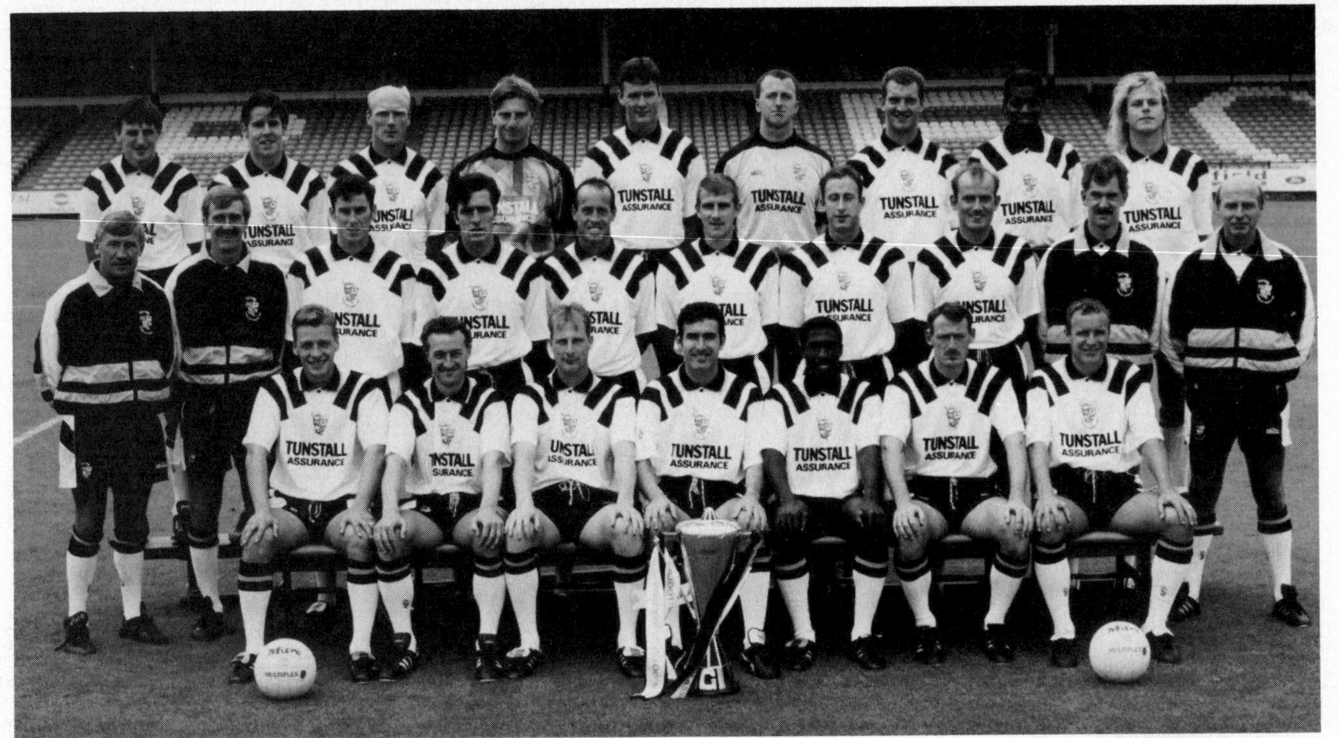

PORT VALE 1993–94 *Back row (left to right):* Peter Billing, Mike Harrison, Neil Aspin, Paul Musselwhite, Gareth Griffiths, Trevor Wood, Peter Swan, Ian Taylor, Robin van der Laan.
Centre row: Bobby Downes (Coach), Ian Miller (Youth Coach), Allen Tankard, Bernie Slaven, Martin Foyle, Dean Glover, Darren Hughes, Simon Mills, Jim Joyce (Physio), John Rudge (Manager).
Front row: Andy Porter, Kevin Kent, Bradley Sandeman, John Jeffers, Dean Stokes, Nicky Cross, Paul Kerr.
(Photograph: *Stoke Evening Sentinel*)

Division 1 **PORT VALE**

Vale Park, Burslem, Stoke-on-Trent ST6 1AW. Telephone Stoke-on-Trent (0782) 814134. Commercial Dept: (0782) 835524. Clubcall: 0898 121636. Fax: 834981. Commercial Fax (0782) 836875. Valiant Leisure shop: (0782) 818718.

Ground capacity: 22,359.

Record attendance: 50,000 v Aston Villa, FA Cup 5th rd, 20 February 1960.

Record receipts: £170,022 v Liverpool, Rumbelows Cup 3rd rd replay, 20 November 1991.

Pitch measurements: 116yd × 76yd.

President: J. Burgess.

Chairman: W. T. Bell TECH. ENG, MIMI.

Directors: N. C. Tizley, I. McPherson, A. Belfield (vice-chairman).

Manager: John Rudge. ***Secretary:*** R. A. Allan. ***Commercial Executive:*** Richard Burley.

Coach: Bobby Downes. ***Physio:*** J. Joyce MCSP, SRP, GRAD.DIP (Phys). ***Medical Officer:*** Dr. G. Gardner MB, CHB. ***Stadium manager:*** F. W. Lodey. ***Groundsman:*** R. Fairbanks. ***Community scheme officer:*** Jim Cooper (0782 575594).

Year Formed: 1876. ***Turned Professional:*** 1885. ***Ltd Co.:*** 1911.

Club Nickname: 'Valiants'.

Previous Name: Burslem Port Vale; became Port Vale, 1911.

Previous Grounds: 1876, Limekin Lane, Longport; 1881, Westport; 1884, Moorland Road, Burslem; 1886, Athletic Ground, Cobridge; 1913, Recreation Ground, Hanley; 1950, Vale Park.

Record League Victory: 9–1 v Chesterfield, Division 2, 24 September 1932 – Leckie; Shenton, Poyser; Sherlock, Round, Jones; McGrath, Mills, Littlewood (6), Kirkham (2), Morton (1).

Record Cup Victory: 7–1 v Irthlingborough (away), FA Cup, 1st rd, 12 January 1907 – Matthews; Dunn, Hamilton; Eardley, Baddeley, Holyhead; Carter, Dodds (2), Beats, Mountford (2), Coxon (3).

Record Defeat: 0–10 v Sheffield U, Division 2, 10 December 1892 and v Notts Co, Division 2, 26 February 1895.

Most League Points (2 for a win): 69, Division 3 (N), 1953–54.

Most League Points (3 for a win): 89, Division 2, 1992–93.

Most League Goals: 110, Division 4, 1958–59.

Highest League Scorer in Season: Wilf Kirkham 38, Division 2, 1926–27.

Most League Goals in Total Aggregate: Wilf Kirkham, 154, 1923–29, 1931–33.

Most Capped Player: Sammy Morgan, 7 (18), Northern Ireland.

Most League Appearances: Roy Sproson, 761, 1950–72.

Record Transfer Fee Received: £925,000 from Norwich C for Darren Beckford, June 1991.

Record Transfer Fee Paid: £375,000 from Oxford U for Martin Foyle, June 1991.

Football League Record: 1892 Original Member of Division 2, Failed re-election in 1896; Re-elected 1898; Resigned 1907; Returned in Oct, 1919, when they took over the fixtures of Leeds City; 1929–30 Division 3 (N); 1930–36 Division 2; 1936–38 Division 3 (N); 1938–52 Division 3 (S); 1952–54 Division 3 (N); 1954–57 Division 2; 1957–58 Division 3 (S); 1958–59 Division 4; 1959–65 Division 3; 1965–70 Division 4; 1970–78 Division 3; 1978–83 Division 4; 1983–84 Division 3; 1984–86 Division 4; 1986–89 Division 3; 1989–94 Division 2; 1994– Division 1.

Honours: *Football League:* Division 2 – Runners-up 1993–94; Division 3 (N) – Champions 1929–30, 1953–54; Runners-up 1952–53; Division 4 – Champions 1958–59; Promoted 1969–70 (4th). *FA Cup:* Semi-final 1954, when in Division 3. *Football League Cup:* never past 2nd rd. *Autoglass Trophy:* Winners: 1992–93.

PORT VALE 1993—94 LEAGUE RECORD

Match No.	Date	Venue	Opponents	Result		H/T Score	Lg. Pos.	Goalscorers	Attendance
1	Aug 14	A	Burnley	L	1-2	1-1	—	Taylor	12,594
2	21	H	Barnet	W	6-0	3-0	9	Slaven 3, Foyle 3	7538
3	28	A	Plymouth Arg	L	0-2	0-0	14		6072
4	31	H	Cambridge U	D	2-2	0-1	—	Cross, Kerr	6484
5	Sept 4	H	Cardiff C	D	2-2	0-2	16	Slaven 2	8140
6	11	A	Bristol R	L	0-2	0-2	18		4908
7	14	A	Huddersfield T	D	1-1	0-0	—	Slaven	5154
8	18	H	Hartlepool U	W	1-0	1-0	18	Kerr	7279
9	25	A	Brentford	W	2-1	0-0	13	Van der Laan, Cross	5106
10	Oct 2	H	Wrexham	W	3-0	0-0	9	Kerr, Cross 2	8722
11	9	H	Hull C	W	2-1	1-1	9	Cross 2	9459
12	16	A	Blackpool	W	3-1	1-0	7	Cross 2, Taylor	8969
13	23	H	Reading	L	0-4	0-0	8		9252
14	30	A	Rotherham U	W	2-0	2-0	5	Taylor, Foyle	4786
15	Nov 6	H	Swansea C	W	3-0	2-0	7	Taylor, Cook (og), Glover	7854
16	20	A	Exeter C	D	1-1	0-0	8	Van der Laan	3908
17	27	H	Brighton & HA	W	4-0	3-0	6	Foyle 2, Cross, Taylor	7261
18	Dec 7	A	Bournemouth	L	1-2	0-1	—	Jeffers	2954
19	11	A	Barnet	W	3-2	0-1	4	Foyle, Kerr, Taylor	3100
20	18	H	Burnley	D	1-1	0-0	4	Slaven	10,710
21	27	A	Fulham	D	0-0	0-0	4		5760
22	29	H	Leyton Orient	W	2-1	1-1	4	Van der Laan, Foyle	8978
23	Jan 1	A	York C	L	0-1	0-0	5		5903
24	15	H	Blackpool	W	2-0	2-0	6	Briggs (og), Cross	7915
25	22	A	Hull C	D	0-0	0-0	7		6918
26	Feb 5	A	Reading	W	2-1	2-0	7	Foyle, Kent	7645
27	12	H	Stockport Co	D	1-1	0-0	7	Foyle	10,628
28	19	H	Plymouth Arg	W	2-1	1-1	6	Taylor, Lowe	9093
29	22	A	Cambridge U	L	0-1	0-0	—		2543
30	Mar 1	H	Bradford C	D	0-0	0-0	—		7294
31	5	H	Bristol R	W	2-0	1-0	5	Taylor 2	8682
32	12	A	Hartlepool U	W	4-1	2-1	4	Gilchrist (og), Lowe, Cross, Aspin	1798
33	15	H	Huddersfield T	W	1-0	0-0	—	Kent	7010
34	19	H	Brentford	W	1-0	0-0	4	Taylor	8269
35	26	A	Wrexham	L	1-2	0-1	4	Van der Laan	7202
36	29	A	Bradford C	L	1-2	1-0	—	Foyle	5776
37	Apr 2	H	Fulham	D	2-2	1-2	4	Allon 2	7380
38	4	A	Leyton Orient	W	3-2	2-1	4	Foyle 3	3412
39	12	H	Rotherham U	W	2-1	1-1	—	Griffiths 2	6804
40	16	H	Bournemouth	W	2-1	0-0	3	Taylor, Cross	7603
41	19	A	Stockport Co	L	1-2	0-1	—	Lowe	5910
42	21	H	York C	W	2-1	1-0	—	Lowe, Glover	8703
43	26	A	Swansea C	W	1-0	1-0	—	Taylor	4252
44	30	H	Exeter C	W	3-0	0-0	3	Foyle 2, Kent	10,377
45	May 3	A	Cardiff C	W	3-1	1-0	—	Taylor, Lowe, Kent	4705
46	7	A	Brighton & HA	W	3-1	2-0	2	Glover, Foyle 2	15,423

Final League Position: 2

GOALSCORERS

League (79): Foyle 18, Taylor 13, Cross 12, Slaven 7, Lowe 5, Kent 4, Kerr 4, Van der Laan 4, Glover 3, Allon 2, Griffiths 2, Aspin 1, Jeffers 1, own goals 3.
Coca-Cola Cup (2): Slaven 1, Taylor 1.
FA Cup (5): Foyle 1, Kerr 1, Porter 1, Slaven 1, Tankard 1.

Musselwhite 46	Kent 23 + 7	Tankard 22 + 4	Aspin 40	Billing 7 + 1	Glover 46	Slaven 20 + 3	Porter 28 + 9	Foyle 36 + 1	Kerr 24 + 1	Taylor 42	Jeffers 21 + 4	Van der Laan 29 + 4	Swan 40	Cross 29 + 8	Livingstone 4 + 1	Sandeman 4 + 5	Stokes 21	Newhouse — + 2	Griffiths 3 + 1	Lowe 18 + 1	Allon 3 + 1	*Match No.*
1	2	3	4	5	6	7	8	9	*10*	11	12	14										1
1	2	3	4	5	6	7		9	10	11		8										2
1	2	3	4	12	6	7			10	11		8	5	9								3
1	2	3	4		6	7			10	11		8	5	9								4
1	2	3	4		6	7	12		10	11		8	5	*9*	14							5
1	2	3		4	6	7	10			11	12	8	5		9							6
1	2	3		4	6	7				11	10	8	5		9							7
1		3		2	6	7	12		4	11	10	8	5		9							8
1		3		2	6	7	14		*4*	11	10	8	5	12	9							9
1		3	2		6	*7*	12	14	4	11	10	8	5	9								10
1	12	3	5	2	6			10	4	11	7	8		9								11
1		3	2		6			10	4	11	7	8	5	9								12
1	12	3	2		6			10	4	11	7	8	5	9								13
1		12	2		6	7	3	10		11	4	8	5	9								14
1		3	2		6	7	4	10	12	11		8	5	9								15
1		3	2		6	14	12	10	4	11	*7*	8	5	9								16
1		3	2		6	14	12	10	4	11	7	8	5	*9*								17
1		3	2		6	14	12	10	4	11	7	8	5	*9*								18
1			2		6	7		10	4	11	9	8	5			3						19
1			2		6	7	12	10	4	11	9	8	5				3					20
1			2		6	7		10	4	11	9	8	5	12		3						21
1			2		6	7	12	10	4	11	9	8	5				3					22
1	14		2		6	7	*11*	10	4		9	8	5	12			3					23
1	12		2		6		7		4	11	10	8	5	9			3					24
1	4		2		6	7	10				11	8	5	*9*		12	3	14				25
1	4		2		6	7	11	10			12	*8*	5	9			3	14				26
1	4		2		5	7	8	10		11				9			3		6			27
1	4		2		6		8	10		11			5	9			3			7		28
1	4		2		6		8	10		11			5	9			3			7		29
1	*4*		2		6		8	9	10	11		14	5	12			3			7		30
1			2		6		4	9	10	11		12	5	8			3			7		31
1			2		6		4	9	10	11		12	5	8			3			7		32
1	12		2		*6*		4	9	10			11	5	8		14	3			7		33
1			2		6		4	9		11		10	5	8			3			7		34
1	12		2		6		*4*	9		11		10	5	8			3			7	14	35
1	12		2		6		4	8		11		*10*	5	14			3			7	9	36
1	10		2		6		4	*8*		11			5	12		14	3			7	9	37
1	7		2		6		4	8		11			5	10			3			12	9	38
1	10	12	2		6		4	8		11				9			3		5	7		39
1	10	12	2		6		4	8		11				9			3		5	7		40
1	10	12	2		6		4	8		11			5	*9*			3		14	7		41
1	9	3	2		6		4	8		11	10		5	12						7		42
1	9	3	2		6		4	8		11			5	10		12				7		43
1	9	3	*2*		6		4	8		11	12		5	10		14				7		44
1	9	3			6		4	8		11	10		5	12		2				7		45
1	9	3			6		4	8		11	10		5			2				7		46

Coca-Cola Cup	First Round	Lincoln C (h)	2-2
		(a)	0-0
FA Cup	First Round	Blackpool (h)	2-0
	Second Round	Huddersfield T (h)	1-0
	Third Round	Southampton (a)	1-1
		(h)	1-0
	Fourth Round	Wolverhampton W (h)	0-2

PORT VALE

Player and Position	Ht	Wt	Birth Date	Birth Place	Source	Clubs	League App	League Gls
Goalkeepers								
Paul Musselwhite	6 2	12 07	22 12 68	Portsmouth		Portsmouth	—	—
						Scunthorpe U	132	—
						Port Vale	87	—
Trevor Wood*	5 11	13 00	3 11 68	Jersey	Apprentice	Brighton	—	—
						Port Vale	42	—
Defenders								
Neil Aspin	6 0	12 06	12 4 65	Gateshead	Apprentice	Leeds U	207	5
						Port Vale	200	2
Peter Billing	6 2	13 00	24 10 64	Liverpool	South Liverpool	Everton	1	—
						Crewe Alex	88	1
						Coventry C	58	1
						Port Vale (loan)	12	—
						Port Vale	8	—
Dean Glover	5 10	11 13	29 12 63	West Bromwich	Apprentice	Aston Villa	23	—
						Sheffield U (loan)	10	—
						Middlesbrough	50	5
						Port Vale	238	12
Gareth Griffiths	6 4	14 00	10 4 70	Winsford	Rhyl	Port Vale	4	2
Darren Hughes	5 11	10 11	6 10 65	Prescot	Apprentice	Everton	3	—
						Shrewsbury T	37	1
						Brighton	26	2
						Port Vale	184	4
Simon Mills*	5 8	11 04	16 8 64	Sheffield	Apprentice	Sheffield W	5	—
						York C	99	5
						Port Vale	184	8
Dean Stokes			23 5 70	Birmingham	Halesowen	Port Vale	21	—
Allen Tankard	5 10	11 07	21 5 69	Fleet	Trainee	Southampton	5	—
						Wigan Ath	209	4
						Port Vale	26	—
Midfield								
Andy Porter	5 9	11 02	17 9 68	Manchester	Trainee	Port Vale	183	4
Bradley Sandeman	5 10	10 08	24 2 70	Northampton	Trainee	Northampton T	58	3
						Maidstone U	57	8
						Port Vale	31	1
Ian Taylor	6 1	12 00	4 6 68	Birmingham	Moor Green	Port Vale	83	28
Ray Walker	5 10	11 12	28 9 63	North Shields	Apprentice	Aston Villa	23	—
						Port Vale (loan)	15	1
						Port Vale	276	32
Forwards								
Joe Allon	5 11	12 02	12 11 66	Gateshead		Newcastle U	9	2
						Swansea C	34	11
						Hartlepool U	112	50
						Chelsea	14	2
						Port Vale (loan)	6	—
						Brentford	45	19
						Southend U (loan)	3	—
						Port Vale	4	2
Nicky Cross*	5 9	11 12	7 2 61	Birmingham	Apprentice	WBA	105	15
						Walsall	109	45
						Leicester C	58	15
						Port Vale	144	39
Martin Foyle	5 10	11 02	2 5 63	Salisbury	Amateur	Southampton	12	1
						Blackburn R (loan)	—	—
						Aldershot	98	35
						Oxford U	126	36
						Port Vale	96	33
Michael Harrison*	6 1	12 02	19 1 73	Cannock	Trainee	Port Vale	—	—
Oliver Heald			13 3 75	Vancouver		Port Vale	—	—
John Jeffers	5 10	11 10	5 10 68	Liverpool	Trainee	Liverpool	—	—
						Port Vale	170	9
Kevin Kent	5 11	11 00	19 3 65	Stoke	Apprentice	WBA	2	—
						Newport Co	33	1
						Mansfield T	229	36
						Port Vale	91	5

PORT VALE

Colours: White shirts, black shorts, black and white stockings. **Change colours:** All yellow.

Foundation: Formed in 1876 as Port Vale, adopting the prefix 'Burslem' in 1884 upon moving to that part of the city. It was dropped in 1911.

First Football League game: 3 September, 1892, Division 2, v Small Heath (a) L 1-5 – Frail; Clutton, Elson; Farrington, McCrindle, Delves; Walker, Scarratt, Bliss (1), Jones. (Only 10 men).

Did you know: An 89th minute goal from left-back Alan Tankard enabled Port Vale to beat Huddersfield Town 1-0 in an FA Cup second round tie on 3 December 1993. It set up a tie against Southampton the player's former club, which also proved successful for Port Vale.

Managers (and Secretary-Managers)
Sam Gleaves 1896–1905*, Tom Clare 1905–11, A. S. Walker 1911–12, H. Myatt 1912–14, Tom Holford 1919–24 (continued as trainer), Joe Schofield 1924–30, Tom Morgan 1930–32, Tom Holford 1932–35, Warney Cresswell 1936–37, Tom Morgan 1937–38, Billy Frith 1945–46, Gordon Hodgson 1946–51, Ivor Powell 1951, Freddie Steele 1951–57, Norman Low 1957–62, Freddie Steele 1962–65, Jackie Mudie 1965–67, Sir Stanley Matthews (GM) 1965–68, Gordon Lee 1968–74, Roy Sproson 1974–77, Colin Harper 1977, Bobby Smith 1977–78, Dennis Butler 1978–79, Alan Bloor 1979, John McGrath 1980–83, John Rudge March 1984–

Player and Position	*Ht*	*Wt*	*Birth Date*	*Place*	*Source*	*Clubs*	*League App*	*Gls*
Paul Kerr	5 8	11 03	9 6 64	Portsmouth	Apprentice	Aston Villa	24	3
						Middlesbrough	125	13
						Millwall	44	14
						Port Vale	63	15
						Leicester C (loan)	7	2
Peter Swan	6 0	12 00	29 9 66	Leeds	Local	Leeds U	49	11
						Hull C	80	24
						Port Vale	111	5
Robin Van der Laan	5 11	12 05	5 9 68	Schiedam	Wageningen	Port Vale	132	19

Trainees
Abbey, Paul A; Boswell, Matthew H; Brammeld, Criag G; Burton, Matthew; Christopher, Anton; Corden, Simon W; Coyne, Kevin; Cunningham, Dean; Day, Myles A. J; Eyre, Richard P; Jackson, Michael I; Morris, Adam J; Patrick, Matthew; Shaw, Gareth R.

Associated Schoolboys
Commander, Andrew P; Heath, Dominic; Smolenski, Andrew; Stevens, David; Whitmore, Paul; Wilson, Kenneth J.

Associated Schoolboys who have accepted the Club's offer of a Traineeship/Contract
Brown, Mark; Butler, Robert J; Davis, Neal N.

PRESTON NORTH END 1993–94 *Back row (left to right):* Eddie Baranowski (Fitness Consultant), Paul Masefield, Jamie Squires, Trevor Matthewson, Kelham O'Hanlon, Steve Berryman, Steve Woods, Steve Holmes, Mickey Norbury, Gavin Nebbeling, Glenn Bonnell (Chief Scout).

Centre row: Brian Hickson (Kit Man), Kevin Magee, Ryan Kidd, Greg Challender, Mike Conroy, David Moyes, Stuart Hicks, Tony Ellis, Neil Whalley, Richard Lucas, Sam Allardyce (Youth Team Coach), Alex Moreno (Physio).

Front row: Farrell Kilbane, Ian Bryson, Chris Sulley, Liam Watson, Gary Peters (Assistant Manager), John Beck (Manager), Lee Cartwright, Gareth Ainsworth, Paul Raynor, Andy Fensome.

(Photograph: Karen Pearson)

Division 3 **PRESTON NORTH END**

Deepdale, Preston PR1 6RU. Telephone Preston (0772) 795919 (club). (0772) 795465 (Commercial). (0772) 704275 (Community office). Fax (0772) 653266 (club). (0772) 703800 (Commercial).

Ground capacity: 16,249.

Record attendance: 42,684 v Arsenal, Division 1, 23 April 1938.

Record receipts: £68,650 v Sheffield W, FA Cup 3rd rd, 4 January 1992.

Pitch measurements: 110yd × 71yd.

President: Tom Finney OBE, JP.

Vice President: T. C. Nicholson JP, FCIOB.

Chairman: Keith W. Leeming.

Directors: M. J. Woodhouse (snr) (vice-chairman), D. Shaw (Managing), J. E. Starkie LL.B (Lond), M. J. Woodhouse (jnr).

Manager: John Beck. ***Assistant Manager:*** Gary Peters.

Coach: Sam Allardyce.

Secretary: Audrey Shaw. ***Physio:*** Alexis Moreno MCSP.

Commercial Manager: Paul Agnew.

Year Formed: 1881. ***Turned Professional:*** 1885. ***Ltd Co.:*** 1893.

Club Nicknames: 'The Lilywhites' or 'North End'.

Record League Victory: 10–0 v Stoke, Division 1, 14 September 1889 – Trainer; Howarth, Holmes; Kelso, Russell (1), Graham; Gordon, Jimmy Ross (2), Nick Ross (3), Thomson (2), Drummond (2).

Record Cup Victory: 26–0 v Hyde, FA Cup, 1st rd, 15 October 1887 – Addision; Howarth, Nick Ross; Russell (1), Thomson (5), Graham (1); Gordon (5), Jimmy Ross (8), John Goodall (1), Dewhurst (3), Drummond (2).

Record Defeat: 0–7 v Blackool, Division 1, 1 May 1948.

Most League Points (2 for a win): 61, Division 3, 1970–71.

Most League Points (3 for a win): 90, Division 4, 1986–87.

Most League Goals: 100, Division 2, 1927–28 and Division 1, 1957–58.

Highest League Scorer in Season: Ted Harper, 37, Division 2, 1932–33.

Most League Goals in Total Aggregate: Tom Finney, 187, 1946–60.

Most Capped Player: Tom Finney, 76, England.

Most League Appearances: Alan Kelly, 447, 1961–75.

Record Transfer Fee Received: £765,000 from Manchester C for Michael Robinson, June 1979.

Record Transfer Fee Paid: £125,000 to Norwich C for Mike Flynn, December 1989.

Football League Record: 1888 Founder Member of League; 1901–04 Division 2; 1904–12 Division 1; 1912–13 Division 2; 1913–14 Division 1; 1914–15 Division 2; 1919–25 Division 1; 1925–34 Division 2; 1934–49 Division 1; 1949–51 Division 2; 1951–61 Division 1; 1961–70 Division 2; 1970–71 Division 3; 1971–74 Division 2; 1974–78 Division 3; 1978–81 Division 2; 1981–85 Division 3; 1985–87 Division 4; 1987–92 Division 3; 1992–93 Division 2; 1993– Division 3.

Honours: *Football League:* Division 1 – Champions 1888–89 (first champions), 1889–90; Runners-up 1890–91, 1891–92, 1892–93, 1905–06, 1952–53, 1957–58; Division 2 – Champions 1903–04, 1912–13, 1950–51; Runners-up 1914–15, 1933–34; Division 3 – Champions 1970–71; Division 4 – Runners-up 1986–87. *FA Cup:* Winners 1889, 1938; Runners-up 1888, 1922, 1937, 1954, 1964. *Double Performed:* 1888–89. *Football League Cup:* best season: 4th rd, 1963, 1966, 1972, 1981.

PRESTON NORTH END 1993—94 LEAGUE RECORD

Match No.	Date	Venue	Opponents	Result		H/T Score	Lg. Pos.	Goalscorers	Attendance
1	Aug 14	H	Crewe Alex	L	0-2	0-1	—		6879
2	21	A	Scarborough	W	4-3	2-1	9	Ellis 2, Ainsworth 2	2329
3	28	H	Shrewsbury T	W	6-1	5-0	5	Ainsworth 2, Conroy 3, Nebbeling	4941
4	31	H	Bury	W	3-1	0-0	—	Nebbeling, Conroy, Ellis	5886
5	Sept 4	A	Lincoln C	W	2-0	1-0	1	Ellis, Raynor	3793
6	11	H	Doncaster R	W	3-1	1-0	1	Conroy, Matthewson, Raynor	7294
7	18	A	Torquay U	L	3-4	1-1	3	Conroy, Ellis, Ainsworth	3912
8	25	A	Mansfield T	D	2-2	1-0	3	Ellis 2	3762
9	Oct 2	H	Colchester U	W	1-0	0-0	1	Ellis	6412
10	9	H	Chesterfield	W	4-1	0-1	1	Raynor, Ellis 3 (1 pen)	6581
11	16	A	Wigan Ath	D	2-2	2-2	2	Conroy, Challender	3741
12	23	H	Rochdale	W	2-1	0-0	2	Ellis 2 (1 pen)	8491
13	30	A	Hereford U	W	3-2	2-0	1	Moyes, Ellis 2	3383
14	Nov 2	A	Walsall	L	0-2	0-1	—		4446
15	6	H	Darlington	W	3-2	1-0	1	Nebbeling 2, Cartwright	6711
16	20	A	Carlisle U	W	1-0	0-0	1	Ellis	10,279
17	27	H	Wycombe W	L	2-3	0-1	1	Ainsworth, Challender	9265
18	Dec 11	H	Scarborough	D	2-2	0-2	2	Bryson, Ellis (pen)	6290
19	17	A	Crewe Alex	L	3-4	1-2	—	Moyes, Conroy, Raynor	6035
20	27	H	Chester C	D	1-1	1-1	2	Ellis	12,790
21	Jan 1	H	Scunthorpe U	D	2-2	0-0	2	Conroy, Norbury	7669
22	4	A	Bury	D	1-1	0-0	—	Norbury	4164
23	15	H	Wigan Ath	W	3-0	0-0	2	Ellis 2, Conroy	7728
24	22	A	Chesterfield	D	1-1	0-0	3	Moyes	3804
25	Feb 5	A	Rochdale	L	1-2	1-1	4	Conroy	4317
26	12	H	Gillingham	D	0-0	0-0	4		6167
27	19	A	Shrewsbury T	L	0-1	0-0	6		5391
28	25	H	Lincoln C	W	2-0	0-0	6	Conroy, Raynor	5941
29	Mar 1	H	Hereford U	W	3-0	0-0	—	Ellis 2, Bryson	6641
30	4	A	Doncaster R	D	1-1	0-0	—	Yates (og)	3321
31	12	H	Torquay U	W	3-1	1-0	5	Ellis 2, Sulley	6641
32	15	A	Northampton T	L	0-2	0-1	—		3845
33	19	H	Mansfield T	W	3-1	1-0	5	Norbury 2, Ainsworth	6747
34	26	A	Colchester U	D	1-1	1-0	5	Norbury	2950
35	Apr 2	A	Chester C	L	2-3	2-1	5	Ainsworth, Ellis	5638
36	4	H	Northampton T	D	1-1	0-1	5	Ainsworth	7517
37	9	A	Scunthorpe U	L	1-3	1-1	5	Ainsworth	3790
38	12	A	Gillingham	D	2-2	2-1	—	Moyes, Green (og)	2453
39	16	H	Walsall	W	2-0	1-0	5	Ainsworth, Fensome	7020
40	23	A	Darlington	W	2-0	1-0	5	Raynor, Ellis	2739
41	30	H	Carlisle U	L	0-3	0-1	5		11,363
42	May 7	A	Wycombe W	D	1-1	1-1	5	Kidd	7442

Final League Position: 5

GOALSCORERS

League (79): Ellis 26 (3 pens), Conroy 12, Ainsworth 11, Raynor 6, Norbury 5, Moyes 4, Nebbeling 4, Bryson 2, Challender 2, Cartwright 1, Fensome 1, Kidd 1, Matthewson 1, Sulley 1, own goals 2.
Coca-Cola Cup (2): Cartwright 1, Ellis 1.
FA Cup (5): Ellis 2 (1 pen), Conroy 1, Moyes 1, Raynor 1.

O'Hanlon 23	Callaghan 1	Sulley 21	Nebbeling 22	Kidd 35 + 1	Raynor 36 + 3	Ainsworth 34 + 4	Whalley 17 + 4	Norbury 11 + 10	Ellis 36 + 1	Burton 2 + 1	Masefield 6	Cartwright 36 + 3	Conroy 28 + 4	Matthewson 12	Lucas 21 + 3	Moyes 29	Bamber — + 1	Challender 5 + 5	Woods 19 + 1	Fensome 31	Holland — + 1	Bryson 24 + 1	Watson 1	Magee 5 + 2	Kilbane — + 1	Hicks 3 + 1	Squires 4	Match No.
1	2	3	4	5	6	7	8	9	10	11																		1
1		3	4	5	6	7	11	9	10		2	8	12															2
1		3	5		11	7	4	12	10		2	8	9	6														3
1		3	5		11	7	4		10		2	8	9	6														4
1		3	5	12	11	7	4		10		2	8	9	6														5
1		3	5	2	11	7	4		10			8	9	6														6
1		3	5	*2*	11	7	4	12	10			8	9	6	14													7
1			5		11	7	4		10			8	9	6	3	2	12											8
1		3	5		11	7		12	10		2	8	9	6	*4*			14										9
		3	5		11	7			10		2	8	9	6				4	1									10
			5	3	11	7			10			8	9	6				4	1	2	12							11
1			5	3	11	*7*	4	12	10			8	9			6		14		2								12
1			5	3	11		4	9	10			8	7			6				2								13
1			5	3	11		*4*	9	10	12		8	7			6		14		2								14
1			5	3	11		4	12		10		8	9		7	6				2								15
1			5	3	11	7	12		10			8	9		4	6				2								16
1				3	11	7	4		10				9		5	6		8	12	2								17
				3	11	7	4	12	10				9		5	6		*8*	1	2		14						18
1		3		5	11	7	4		10			14	12		8	6				*2*		9						19
1			5	3	11	*7*	*4*		10			14	12		8	6				2		9						20
1			5	3	11			12	10			4	9		8	6				2		7						21
1			5	3	11	*7*		12				4	9		8	6				2		10						22
1		3	5		11	12			10			8	9		4	6				2		7						23
1			5	3	11	12			10			8	9		4	6				2		7						24
			5	3	11	12		14	10			8	9		4	6			1	2		7						25
		3		5	11	12	14		10			*8*	9		4	6			1	2		7						26
				5	11	3	9		10			8	12		4	6			1	2		7						27
		3		5	11	7			10			12	9		4	6			1	2		8						28
		3		5	11	7			10			4	9			6			1	2		8						29
				3	12	*7*	14					4	9	5		6			1	2		8	10	*11*				30
		3		2	11	7		9	10			4		5		6			1			8			12			31
				3	*11*	7	12	9	10			4		5		6			1	2		8		14				32
1		3		5	11	7		9	10			4				6				2		8						33
1		3		5	12	7		9				4				6		10		2		8		11				34
		3		6	11	7		9	10			4							1	2		8				5		35
		3		6		7		9	10			4			12				1	2		8		11		5		36
		3		6		7		14	10			4	*9*		12				1	2		8		11		5		37
		3		5		7			10			4	9		8	6			1	2		11		12				38
				5	12	7		9	10			4			8	6			1	2		11					3	39
				5	*10*	7			12			4	9		8	6		14	1	2		11					3	40
				5	9	7			10			4			8	6			1	2		11					3	41
				5	9	7						4			8	6		14	1	2		10		*11*		12	3	42

Coca-Cola Cup	First Round	Burnley (h)	1-2
		(a)	1-4
FA Cup	First Round	Mansfield T (a)	2-1
	Second Round	Shrewsbury T (a)	1-0
	Third Round	Bournemouth (h)	2-1
	Fourth Round	Kidderminster H (a)	0-1

PRESTON NORTH END

Player and Position	Ht	Wt	Birth Date	Birth Place	Source	Clubs	League App	League Gls
Goalkeepers								
Lee Bambert†			31 10 68	Burnley	Chorley	Preston NE	1	—
Stephen Berryman†			26 12 66	Blackburn		Hartlepool U	1	—
						Exeter C	—	—
						Cambridge U	1	—
						Barnet	—	—
						Preston NE	—	—
Glenn Johnstone‡	6 3	14 07	5 6 67	Kenya	Lancaster C	Preston NE	10	—
Kelham O'Hanlon	6 1	13 01	16 5 62	Saltburn	Apprentice	Middlesbrough	87	—
						Rotherham U	248	—
						Carlisle U	83	—
						Preston NE	23	—
Steve Woods	6 1	13 00	23 2 70	Glasgow	Kilpatrick BC	Hibernian	—	—
						Clydebank	47	—
						Preston NE	20	—
Defenders								
Craig Allardyce‡	6 3	13 09	9 6 75	Bolton	Trainee	Preston NE	1	—
Sam Allardyce†	6 2	14 00	19 10 54	Dudley	Apprentice	Bolton W	184	21
						Sunderland	25	2
						Millwall	63	2
						Coventry C	28	1
						Huddersfield T	37	—
						Bolton W	14	—
						Preston NE	90	2
						WBA	1	—
					Ireland	Preston NE	3	—
Aaron Callaghan‡	5 11	11 02	8 10 66	Dublin	Apprentice	Stoke C	7	—
						Crewe Alex (loan)	8	—
						Oldham Ath	16	2
						Crewe Alex	158	6
						Preston NE	36	2
Greg Challlender	6 0	12 08	5 2 73	Rochdale	Mossley	Preston NE	10	2
Jonathan Davidson‡	5 8	11 11	1 3 70	Cheadle	Trainee	Derby Co	12	2
						Preston NE	21	1
						Chesterfield (loan)	1	—
Stuart Hicks	6 1	13 00	30 5 67	Peterborough	Wisbech	Colchester U	64	—
						Scunthorpe U	67	1
						Doncaster R	36	—
						Huddersfield T	22	1
						Preston NE	4	—
Steve Holmes	6 2	13 00	13 1 72	Middlesbrough	Guisborough T	Preston NE	—	—
Ryan Kidd	6 0	11 07	6 10 71	Heywood	Trainee	Port Vale	1	—
						Preston NE	51	1
Farrell Kilbane	6 0	13 00	21 10 74	Preston	Cambridge U	Preston NE	1	—
Paul Masefield‡	6 1	12 12	21 10 70	Birmingham	Trainee	Birmingham C	—	—
						Preston NE	—	—
						Exeter C	1	—
						Stockport Co	7	—
						Doncaster R	9	—
						Preston NE	6	—
Trevor Matthewson	6 1	12 05	12 2 63	Sheffield	Apprentice	Sheffield W	3	—
						Newport Co	75	—
						Stockport Co	80	—
						Lincoln C	83	8
						Birmingham C	168	12
						Preston NE	12	1
David Moyes	6 1	12 10	25 4 63	Glasgow	Drumchapel A	Celtic	24	—
						Cambridge U	79	1
						Bristol C	83	6
						Shrewsbury T	96	11
						Dunfermline Ath	105	13
						Hamilton A	5	—
						Preston NE	29	4
Gavin Nebbeling	6 0	12 10	15 5 63	Johannesburg	Arcadia Shepherds	Crystal Palace	151	8
						Northampton T (loan)	11	—
						Fulham	88	2
						Hereford U (loan)	3	—
						Preston NE	22	4
Jamie Squires	6 1	12 00	15 11 75	Preston	Trainee	Preston NE	4	—

PRESTON NORTH END

Colours: White and navy shirts, navy shorts, navy stockings. **Change colours:** Yellow and blue shirts, blue shorts, blue stockings.

Foundation: North End Cricket and Rugby Club which was formed in 1863, indulged in most sports before taking up soccer in about 1879. In 1881 they decided to stick to football to the exclusion of other sports and even a 16–0 drubbing by Blackburn Rovers in an invitation game at Deepdale, a few weeks after taking this decision, did not deter them for they immediately became affiliated to the Lancashire FA.

First Football League game: 8 September, 1888, Football League, v Burnley (h) W 5-2 – Trainer; Haworth, Holmes; Robertson, W. Graham, J. Graham; Gordon (1), Ross (2), Goodall, Dewhurst (2), Drummond.

Did you know: Between 12 September 1891 and 2 January 1892, Preston NE won 13 consecutive matches during a season in which they finished as runners-up in Division 1.

Managers (and Secretary-Managers)
Charlie Parker 1906–15, Vincent Hayes 1919–23, Jim Lawrence 1923–25, Frank Richards 1925–27, Alex Gibson 1927–31, Lincoln Hayes 1931–1932 (run by committee 1932–36), Tommy Muirhead 1936–37, (run by committee 1937–49), Will Scott 1949–53, Scot Symon 1953–54, Frank Hill 1954–56, Cliff Britton 1956–61, Jimmy Milne 1961–68, Bobby Seith 1968–70, Alan Ball Sr 1970–73, Bobby Charlton 1973–75, Harry Catterick 1975–77, Nobby Stiles 1977–81, Tommy Docherty 1981, Gordon Lee 1981–83, Alan Kelly 1983–85, Tommy Booth 1985–86, Brian Kidd 1986, John McGrath 1986–90, Les Chapman 1990–92, John Beck December 1992–

Player and Position	*Ht*	*Wt*	*Birth Date*	*Birth Place*	*Source*	*Clubs*	*League App*	*League Gls*
Chris Sulley	5 8	10 00	3 12 59	Camberwell	Apprentice	Chelsea	—	—
						Bournemouth	206	3
						Dundee U	7	—
						Blackburn R	134	3
						Port Vale	40	1
						Preston NE	21	1
Midfield								
Gareth Ainsworth	5 10	12 05	10 5 73	Blackburn	Blackburn R	Preston NE	5	—
						Cambridge U	4	1
						Preston NE	64	11
Ian Bryson	5 11	11 11	26 11 62	Kilmarnock		Kilmarnock	215	40
						Sheffield U	155	36
						Barnsley	16	3
						Preston NE	25	2
Lee Cartwright	5 8	10 06	19 9 72	Rawtenstall	Trainee	Preston NE	120	9
Peter Craven			30 6 68	Hanover	Park Avenue	Bury	—	—
						Halifax T	7	—
						Preston NE	—	—
Andy Fensome	5 8	11 02	18 2 69	Northampton	Trainee	Norwich C	—	—
						Newcastle U (loan)	—	—
						Cambridge U	126	1
						Preston NE	31	1
Richard Lucas	5 10	11 04	22 9 70	Sheffield	Trainee	Sheffield U	10	—
						Preston NE	50	—
Neil Whalley	6 0	12 09	29 10 65	Liverpool	Warrington T	Preston NE	35	—
Forwards								
Simon Burton*	5 10	10 04	29 12 73	Bolton	Trainee	Preston NE	24	3
Mike Conroy	6 0	11 00	31 12 65	Glasgow	Apprentice	Coventry C	—	—
						Clydebank	114	38
						St Mirren	10	1
						Reading	80	7
						Burnley	77	30
						Preston NE	32	12

Continued on Page 421

Trainees
Banks, Andrew M; Borwick, Christopher S; Brandes, Christopher M; Brooks, Gilbert I; Calligan, John K; Corcoran, Damian P; Ellis, Richard G; Farragher, Kieran T; Kilbane, Kevin D; Linford, Paul R; McMenemy, Paul J; Powell, Anthony.

Associated Schoolboys
Almond, Timothy J; Barnes, Stephen W; Bolton, David J; Bolton, James L; Broadbent, Lee; Cruse, Paul M; Keenan, Christopher J; Kilshaw, Mark J; Knapp, David A; McCann, David; Smith, Gary A; Smith, Kevin J; Southworth, Brian J; Subachus, Anthony V; Swarbrick, Michael J.

Associated Schoolboys who have accepted the Club's offer of a Traineeship/Contract
Hayton, Kyle; Lucas, David A; McKenna, Paul S; Potts, Colin E; Stewart, Simon D. S.

QUEENS PARK RANGERS 1993–94 *Back row (left to right):* Les Ferdinand, Stephen Gallen, Daniele Dichio, Tony Witter, Richard Hurst, Devon White, Alan McDonald, Peter Caldwell, Darren Peacock, Karl Ready, Brian Croft, Trevor Sinclair.

Centre row: Les Boyle (Kit Manager), Des Bulpin (Youth Team Manager), Bradley Allen, Steve Yates, Michael Meaker, Alan McCarthy, Jan Stejskal, Mark Graham, Doug Freedman, Kevin Gallen, Marvin Bryan, Roger Cross (Reserve Team Manager), Brian Morris (Physio).

Front row: Clive Wilson, David Bardsley, Ian Holloway, Rufus Brevett, Ray Wilkins, Frank Sibley (Coach), Gerry Francis (Manager), Simon Barker, Darren Finlay, Maurice Doyle, Andrew Impey, Gary Penrice.

(Photograph: Action Images)

FA Premiership **QUEENS PARK RANGERS**

South Africa Road, W12 7PA. Telephone 081–743 0262. Fax: 081–749 0994. Box Office: 081–749 5744 (24 hour information service 081 749 7798). Supporters Club: 081–749 6771. Club Shop: 081–749 6862. Marketing: 081–740 8737.

Ground capacity: 19,300.

Record attendance: 35,353 v Leeds U, Division 1, 27 April 1974.

Record receipts: £218,475 v Manchester U, FA Premier League, 5 February 1994.

Pitch measurements: 112yd × 72yd.

Chairman: R. C. Thompson.

Directors: (Corporate): R. B. Copus (Club); P. D. Ellis, A. Ingham, A. Ellis.

Manager: Gerry Francis. ***Assistant Manager/Coach:*** Frank Sibley.

Secretary: Miss S. F. Marson. ***Marketing Executive: Lynne Davie.***

Reserve Team Coach: Roger Cross.

Physio: Brian Morris.

Year Formed: 1885 *(*see Foundation*). ***Turned Professional:*** 1898. ***Ltd Co.:*** 1899.

Club Nicknames: 'Rangers' or 'Rs'. ***Previous Name:*** 1885–87, St Jude's.

Previous Grounds: 1885 *(*see Foundation*), Welford's Fields; 1888–99; London Scottish Ground, Brondesbury, Home Farm, Kensal Rise Green, Gun Club Wormwood Scrubs, Kilburn Cricket Ground; 1899, Kensal Rise Athletic Ground; 1901, Latimer Road, Notting Hill; 1904, Agricultural Society, Park Royal; 1907, Park Royal Ground; 1917, Loftus Road; 1931, White City; 1933, Loftus Road; 1962, White City; 1963, Loftus Road.

Record League Victory: 9–2 v Tranmere R, Division 3, 3 December 1960 – Drinkwater; Woods, Ingham; Keen, Rutter, Angell; Lazarus (2), Bedford (2), Evans (2), Andrews (1), Clark (2).

Record Cup Victory: 8–1 v Bristol R (away), FA Cup, 1st rd, 27 November 1937 – Gilfillan; Smith, Jefferson; Lowe, James, March; Cape, Mallett, Cheetham (3), Fitzgerald (3) Bott (2). 8–1 v Crewe Alex, Milk Cup, 1st rd, 3 October 1983 – Hucker; Neill, Dawes, Waddock (1), McDonald (1), Fenwick, Micklewhite (1), Stewart (1), Allen (1), Stainrod (3), Gregory.

Record Defeat: 1–8 v Mansfield T, Division 3, 15 March 1965 and v Manchester U, Division 1, 19 March 1969.

Most League Points (2 for a win): 67, Division 3, 1966–67.

Most League Points (3 for a win): 85, Division 2, 1982–83.

Most League Goals: 111, Division 3, 1961–62.

Highest League Scorer in Season: George Goddard, 37, Division 3 (S), 1929–30.

Most League Goals in Total Aggregate: George Goddard, 172, 1926–34.

Most Capped Player: Alan McDonald, 43, Northern Ireland.

Most League Appearances: Tony Ingham, 519, 1950–63.

Record Transfer Fee Received: £2,750,000 from Sheffield Wednesday for Andy Sinton, August 1993.

Record Transfer Fee Paid: £1,000,000 to Luton T for Roy Wegerle, December 1989.

Football League Record: 1920 Original Members of Division 3; 1921–48 Division 3 (S); 1948–52 Division 2; 1952–58 Division 3 (S); 1958–67 Division 3; 1967–68 Division 2; 1968–69 Division 1; 1969–73 Division 2; 1973–79 Division 1; 1979–83 Division 2; 1983–92 Division 1; 1992– FA Premier League.

Honours: *Football League:* Division 1 – Runners-up 1975–76; Division 2 – Champions 1982–83; Runners-up 1967–68, 1972–73; Division 3 (S) – Champions 1947–48; Runners-up 1946–47; Division 3 – Champions 1966–67. *FA Cup:* Runners-up 1982. *Football League Cup:* Winners 1966–67; Runners-up 1985–86. (In 1966–67 won Division 3 and Football League Cup). **European Competition:** *UEFA Cup:* 1976–77, 1984–85.

QUEENS PARK RANGERS 1993—94 LEAGUE RECORD

Match No.	Date	Venue	Opponents	Result		H/T Score	Lg. Pos.	Goalscorers	Attendance
1	Aug 14	A	Aston Villa	L	1-4	1-1	—	Ferdinand	32,944
2	18	H	Liverpool	L	1-3	1-3	—	Wilkins	19,625
3	21	H	Southampton	W	2-1	1-0	15	Penrice, Wilson (pen)	10,613
4	25	A	Chelsea	L	0-2	0-1	—		20,191
5	28	A	West Ham U	W	4-0	1-0	13	Peacock, Ferdinand 2, Penrice	18,084
6	Sept 1	H	Sheffield U	W	2-1	1-1	—	Sinclair, Wilson (pen)	11,113
7	11	A	Manchester C	L	0-3	0-2	14		24,445
8	18	H	Norwich C	D	2-2	1-2	15	Sinclair, Ferdinand	13,359
9	27	A	Wimbledon	D	1-1	1-1	—	McDonald	9478
10	Oct 2	H	Ipswich T	W	3-0	0-0	12	White 2, Barker	12,292
11	16	A	Newcastle U	W	2-1	1-0	8	Ferdinand, Allen	33,801
12	23	H	Coventry C	W	5-1	3-0	5	Ferdinand, Allen 2, Impey, Barker	12,979
13	30	A	Manchester U	L	1-2	1-0	8	Allen	44,663
14	Nov 6	H	Blackburn R	W	1-0	0-0	7	Hendry (og)	17,636
15	20	A	Everton	W	3-0	1-0	4	Allen 3	17,326
16	24	A	Swindon T	L	0-1	0-1	—		14,674
17	27	H	Tottenham H	D	1-1	1-0	8	Ferdinand	17,694
18	Dec 4	H	Aston Villa	D	2-2	2-1	8	McGrath (og), Penrice	14,915
19	8	A	Liverpool	L	2-3	1-2	—	Ferdinand, Barker	24,561
20	11	A	Southampton	W	1-0	1-0	6	Ferdinand	11,946
21	27	H	Oldham Ath	W	2-0	0-0	7	White, Penrice	13,218
22	29	A	Leeds U	D	1-1	0-0	6	Meaker	39,124
23	Jan 1	H	Sheffield W	L	1-2	0-0	8	Ferdinand	16,858
24	3	A	Arsenal	D	0-0	0-0	9		34,935
25	16	H	Newcastle U	L	1-2	1-1	—	Penrice	15,774
26	22	A	Coventry C	W	1-0	1-0	8	White	12,065
27	Feb 5	H	Manchester U	L	2-3	1-2	9	Wilson (pen), Ferdinand	21,267
28	Mar 5	H	Manchester C	D	1-1	1-0	10	Penrice	13,474
29	12	A	Norwich C	W	4-3	0-1	10	Barker, Peacock, Penrice, White	16,499
30	16	A	Sheffield U	D	1-1	1-0	—	Barker	14,183
31	19	H	Wimbledon	W	1-0	0-0	8	Peacock	11,368
32	26	A	Ipswich T	W	3-1	0-0	7	Impey 2, Ferdinand	14,653
33	Apr 2	A	Oldham Ath	L	1-4	1-1	9	Ferdinand	10,440
34	4	H	Leeds U	L	0-4	0-2	10		15,365
35	9	A	Sheffield W	L	1-3	0-3	10	White	22,437
36	13	H	Chelsea	D	1-1	0-0	—	Ferdinand	15,735
37	16	H	Everton	W	2-1	0-0	10	White, Ferdinand	13,330
38	24	A	Blackburn R	D	1-1	0-1	—	Ready	19,913
39	27	H	Arsenal	D	1-1	1-0	—	Penrice	11,442
40	30	H	Swindon T	L	1-3	0-0	9	Ferdinand	9875
41	May 3	H	West Ham U	D	0-0	0-0	—		10,850
42	7	A	Tottenham H	W	2-1	1-1	9	Sinclair 2	26,105

Final League Position: 9

GOALSCORERS

League (62): Ferdinand 16, Penrice 8, Allen 7, White 7, Barker 5, Sinclair 4, Impey 3, Peacock 3, Wilson 3 (3 pens), McDonald 1, Meaker 1, Ready 1, Wilkins 1, own goals 2.
Coca-Cola Cup (10): Allen 3, Barker 2, Ferdinand 2, Impey 1, Meaker 1, Sinclair 1.
FA Cup (1): Barker 1.

Roberts 16	Ready 19 + 3	Wilson 42	Wilkins 39	Peacock 30	Witter 1	Impey 31 + 2	Holloway 19 + 6	Ferdinand 35 + 1	Allen 14 + 7	Barker 35 + 2	White 12 + 6	Yates 27 + 2	Penrice 23 + 3	Sinclair 30 + 2	Brevett 3 + 4	Bardsley 32	McDonald 12	Doyle 1	Stejskal 26	Meaker 11 + 3	McCarthy 4	Match No.
1	2	3	4	5	6	7	8	9	10	11	12											1
1	2	3	4	5		7		9		11	12	6	10	8								2
1	2	3	4	5		7		9		11	12	6	10	8	14							3
1	2	3	4	5		7		9		8		6	10	12	11							4
1	14	3	4	5		7		9	12	11			10	8		2	6					5
1	12	3	4	5		7		9		11			10	8		2	6					6
1		3	4	5		7		9	12				10	11		2	6	8				7
		3	4	5		7		9		8			10	11		2	6		1			8
	14	3	4	5		7		9		8	12		10	11		2	6		1			9
		3	4	5		7			10	8	9			11	12	2	6		1			10
		3	4	5		7		9	10	8		12		11		2	6		1			11
		3	4	5		7	12	9	10	8				11		2	6		1			12
		3	4	5		7	12	9	10	8				11		2	6		1			13
		3	4	5		7	12	9	10	8				11		2	6		1			14
		3	4	5		7		9	10	8		6		11		2			1			15
		3		5		7	8	9	10	4		6		11		2			1			16
		3		5		7	8	9	10	4						2	6		1	11		17
	5	3	4			7	12		10	8			9			2	6		1	11		18
	6	3	4	5		7		9	10	8			12			2			1	11		19
	6	3	4	5		7	12	9	10	8		14		11		2			1			20
		3	4	5			8				9	6	10	11	12	2			1	7		21
		3	4	5		12	8	9				6	10	11		2			1	7		22
		3	4	5				9				6	10	11	8	2			1	7		23
		3	4	5				9		8		6	10	11		2			1	7		24
1		3	4	5		7		9		8		6	10	11		2				12		25
		3	4	5			7			8	9	6	10	11		2			1	12		26
		3	4	5			7	9		8		6	10	11		2			1	12		27
		3	4	5		7		9		8		6	10	11		2			1			28
		3	4	5			12			8	9	6	10	11		2			1	7		29
		3	4	5				12		8	9	6	10	11		2			1	7		30
	2	3	4	5			8	9			10	6		11					1	7		31
	2	3	4			7	8	9	14	11	10	6	12						1		5	32
	2	3	4			7	8	9		11	10	6	12						1		5	33
	2	3	4			7	8	9	12	11		6	10			5			1			34
1	5	3				7	8	9	10	4	12	6				2				11		35
1	5	3	4			7	8	9		11	10	6		12		2						36
1	5	3	4			7	8	9		12	10	6		11		2						37
1	5	3	4			7	8	9		12	10	6		11		2						38
1	5	3	4			7	8		12	11	9	6	10			2						39
1	5	3	4			7	8	9	12	11		6	10								2	40
1	5	3	4				7	9	12	8		6	10	11	14						2	41
1	5	3	4			14	8	9	7	10	12	6		11	2							42

Coca-Cola Cup	Second Round	Barnet (a)	2-1
		(h)	4-0
	Third Round	Millwall (h)	3-0
	Fourth Round	Sheffield W (h)	1-2
FA Cup	Third Round	Stockport Co (a)	1-2

QUEENS PARK RANGERS

Player and Position	Ht	Wt	Birth Date	Birth Place	Source	Clubs	League App	League Gls
Goalkeepers								
Peter Caldwell	6 1	13 00	5 6 72	Dorchester	Trainee	QPR	—	—
Tony Roberts	6 0	12 00	4 8 69	Bangor	Trainee	QPR	63	—
Jan Stejskal	6 3	12 00	15 1 62	Czechoslovakia	Sparta Prague	QPR	108	—
Defenders								
David Bardsley	5 10	11 00	11 9 64	Manchester	Apprentice	Blackpool	45	—
						Watford	100	7
						Oxford U	74	7
						QPR	182	4
Rufus Brevett	5 8	11 00	24 9 69	Derby	Trainee	Doncaster R	109	3
						QPR	39	—
Darren Finlay*	5 4	10 00	19 12 73	Belfast	Trainee	QPR	—	—
Stephen Gallen*	6 00	12 00	21 11 73	London	Trainee	QPR	—	—
Alan McCarthy	5 11	12 10	11 1 72	London	Trainee	QPR	9	—
						Watford (loan)	9	—
						Plymouth Arg (loan)	2	—
Alan McDonald	6 2	12 07	12 10 63	Belfast	Apprentice	QPR	298	9
						Charlton Ath (loan)	9	—
Danny Maddix	5 10	11 07	11 10 67	Ashford	Apprentice	Tottenham H	—	—
						Southend U (loan)	2	—
						QPR	139	6
Karl Ready	6 1	12 00	14 8 72	Neath		QPR	26	1
Tony Witter	6 1	12 07	12 8 65	London	Grays Ath	Crystal Palace	—	—
						QPR	1	—
						Millwall (loan)	—	—
						Plymouth Arg (loan)	3	1
						Reading (loan)	4	—
Steve Yates	5 11	11 00	29 1 70	Bristol	Trainee	Bristol R	197	—
						QPR	29	—
Midfield								
Simon Barker	5 9	11 00	4 11 64	Farnworth	Apprentice	Blackburn R	182	35
						QPR	184	17
Brian Croft	5 9	10 10	27 9 67	Chester		Chester C	59	3
						Cambridge U	17	2
						Chester C	114	3
						QPR	—	—
						Shrewsbury T (loan)	4	—
Ian Holloway	5 8	10 10	12 3 63	Kingswood	Apprentice	Bristol R	111	14
						Wimbledon	19	2
						Brentford (loan)	13	2
						Brentford	16	—
						Torquay U (loan)	6	—
						Bristol R	179	26
						QPR	89	2
Michael Meaker	5 11	11 05	18 8 71	Greenford	Trainee	QPR	26	1
						Plymouth Arg (loan)	4	—
Trevor Sinclair	5 10	11 02	2 3 73	Dulwich	Trainee	Blackpool	112	15
						QPR	32	4
Ray Wilkins	5 8	11 02	14 9 56	Hillingdon	Apprentice	Chelsea	179	30
						Manchester U	160	7
						AC Milan	73	2
					Paris St Germain	Rangers	70	2
						QPR	154	7
Clive Wilson	5 7	10 00	13 11 61	Manchester	Local	Manchester C	98	9
						Chester (loan)	21	2
						Chelsea	81	5
						Manchester C (loan)	11	—
						QPR	136	10
Forwards								
Bradley Allen	5 7	10 00	13 9 71	Harold Wood	School	QPR	68	24
Dennis Bailey	5 10	11 06	13 11 65	Lambeth	Farnborough T	Crystal Palace	5	1
						Bristol R (loan)	17	9
						Birmingham C	75	23
						Bristol R (loan)	6	1
						QPR	39	10
						Charlton Ath (loan)	4	—
						Watford (loan)	8	4

QUEENS PARK RANGERS

Colours: Blue and white hooped shirts, white shorts, white stockings. **Change colours:** All red with black trim.

Foundation: There is an element of doubt about the date of the foundation of this club, but it is believed that in either 1885 or 1886 it was formed through the amalgamation of Christchurch Rangers and St. Jude's Institute FC. The leading light was George Wodehouse, whose family maintained a connection with the club until comparatively recent times. Most of the players came from the Queen's Park district so this name was adopted after a year as St. Jude's Institute.

First Football League game: 28 August, 1920, Division 3, v Watford (h) L 1-2 – Price; Blackman, Wingrove; McGovern, Grant, O'Brien; Faulkner, Birch (1), Smith, Gregory, Middlemiss.

Did you know: In a South-East Counties League match against Charlton Athletic on 4 September 1993, Kevin Gallen scored eight goals in a 9-1 win for Queens Park Rangers youth team.

Managers (and Secretary-Managers)
James Cowan 1906–13, James Howie 1913–20, Ted Liddell 1920–24, Will Wood 1924–25 (had been secretary since 1903), Bob Hewison 1925–30, John Bowman 1930–31, Archie Mitchell 1931–33, Mick O'Brien 1933–35, Billy Birrell 1935–39, Ted Vizard 1939–44, Dave Mangnall 1944–52, Jack Taylor 1952–59, Alec Stock 1959–65 (GM to 1968), Jimmy Andrews 1965, Bill Dodgin Jnr 1968, Tommy Docherty 1968, Les Allen 1969–70, Gordon Jago 1971–74, Dave Sexton 1974–77, Frank Sibley 1977–78, Steve Burtenshaw 1978–79, Tommy Docherty 1979–80, Terry Venables 1980–84, Gordon Jago 1984, Alan Mullery 1984, Frank Sibley 1984–85, Jim Smith 1985–88, Trevor Francis 1988–90, Don Howe 1990–91, Gerry Francis June 1991–

Player and Position	*Ht*	*Wt*	*Birth Date*	*Birth Place*	*Source*	*Clubs*	*League App*	*League Gls*
Marvin Bryan	6 0	12 02	2 8 75	Paddington	Trainee	QPR	—	—
Daniele Dichio	6 3	11 00	19 10 74	London	Trainee	QPR	—	—
						Barnet (loan)	9	2
Maurice Doyle	5 8	10 07	17 10 69	Ellesmere Port	Trainee	Crewe Alex	8	2
						QPR	6	—
						Crewe Alex (loan)	7	2
						Wolverhampton W (loan)	—	—
Les Ferdinand	5 11	13 05	18 12 66	London	Hayes	QPR	126	56
						Brentford (loan)	3	—
						Besiktas (loan)	—	—
Doug Freedman	5 9	11 00	21 1 74	Glasgow	Trainee	QPR	—	—
Kevin Gallen	5 11	12 03	21 9 75	Hammersmith	Trainee	QPR	—	—
Mark Graham	5 6	10 00	24 10 74	Newry	Trainee	QPR	—	—
Andrew Impey	5 8	10 06	13 9 71	Hammersmith	Yeading	QPR	86	5
Gary Penrice	5 8	10 06	23 3 64	Bristol	Bristol C	Bristol R	188	54
						Watford	43	18
						Aston Villa	20	1
						QPR	60	17
Devon White	6 3	14 00	2 3 64	Nottingham	Arnold T	Lincoln C	29	4
					Boston U	Bristol R	202	53
						Cambridge U	22	4
						QPR	25	9

Trainees
Brazier, Matthew R; Challis, Trevor M; Cross, John R; Goodwin, Lee; Goodwin, Paul A; Hurst, Richard A; Mahoney-Johnson, Michael A; Monteath, Jonathan; Plummer, Christopher S; Power, Graeme R; White, Dene; Wood, Kristian J.

Associated Schoolboys
Camilleri, Colin F; Currie, Michael J; Evelyn, Mark J; Franklin, Damien M; Holloway, Grant J; Langley, Richard; Perry, Mark J; Powell, Barry J; Purser, Wayne M; Robinson, Nicky J; Roostan, Benjamin L; Spiller, Richard B; Toms, Frazer P; Webb, Luke A.

Associated Schoolboys who accepted the Club's offer of a Traineeship/Contract
Bruce, Paul M; Harris, Jonathan; Holman, Lee C; Mernagh, Gavin C; Motton, Matthew P. J; Quashie, Nigel F.

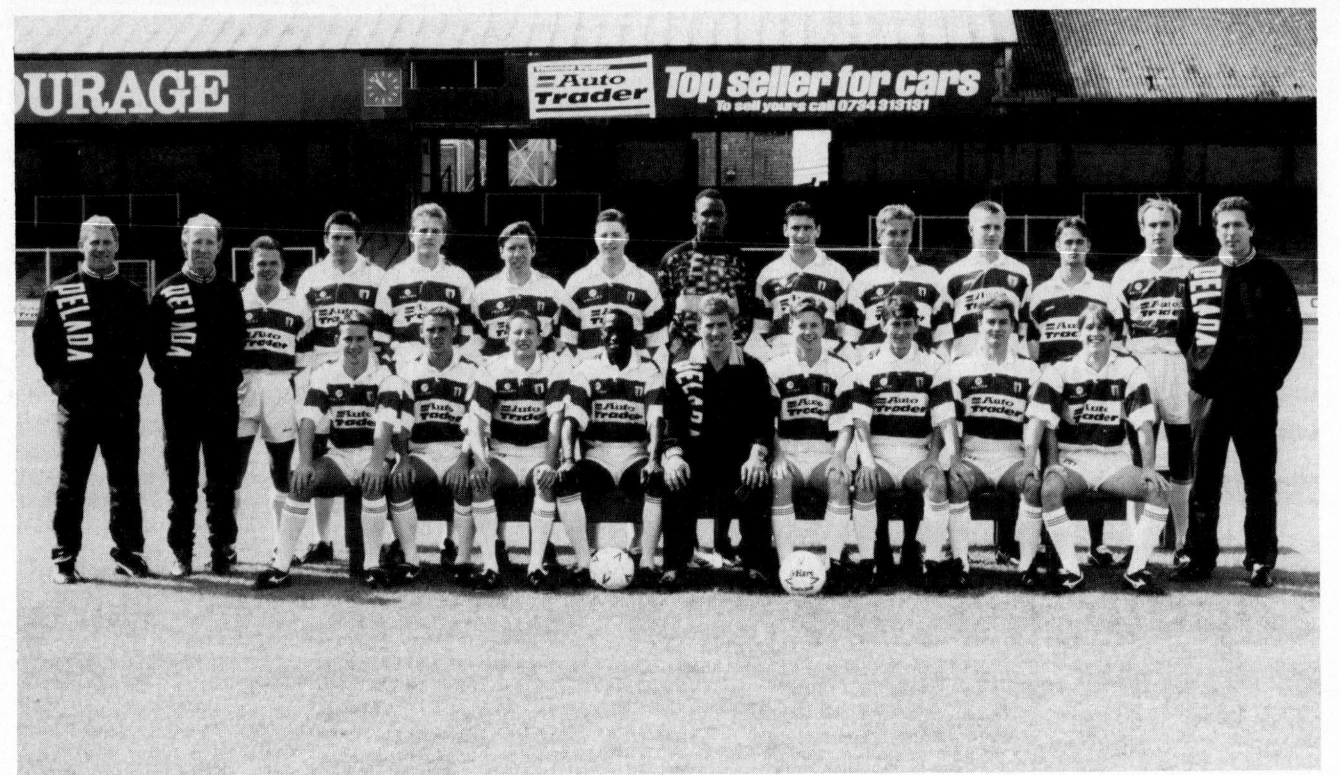

READING 1993–94 *Back row (left to right):* Mike Hickman (Youth Development Officer), John Haselden (Physio), Mark Holzman, Jeff Hopkins, Phil Parkinson, Ray Ranson, Darren McCance, Shaka Hislop, Adrian Williams, Kevin Dillon, David Bass, Lea Barkus, Jimmy Quinn, Colin Lee (Assistant Manager).
Front row: Stuart Lovell, Andy Gray, Scott Taylor, Keith McPherson, Mark McGhee (Manager), Dylan Kerr, Tom Jones, Mick Gooding, James Lambert.

Division 1 READING

Elm Park, Norfolk Road, Reading RG3 2EF. Telephone Reading (0734) 507878.

Ground capacity: 12,061.

Record attendance: 33,042 v Brentford, FA Cup 5th rd, 19 February 1927.

Record receipts: £70,693.79 v Arsenal, FA Cup 3rd rd, 10 January 1987.

Pitch measurements: 112yd × 77yd.

Life President: J. H. Brooks.

Chairman: John Madejski. ***Managing Director:*** M. J. Lewis.

Directors: G. Denton.

Manager: Mark McGhee.

Coach: Colin Lee. ***Youth development officer:*** Mike Hickman.

Physio: John Haselden.

Commercial Manager: Kevin Girdler.

Secretary: Jayne E. Hill.

Year Formed: 1871. ***Turned Professional:*** 1895. ***Ltd Co.:*** 1895.

Club Nickname: 'The Royals'.

Previous Grounds: 1871, Reading Recreation; Reading Cricket Ground; 1882, Coley Park; 1889, Caversham Cricket Ground; 1896, Elm Park.

Record League Victory: 10–2 v Crystal Palace, Division 3 (S), 4 September 1946 – Groves; Glidden, Gulliver; McKenna, Ratcliffe, Young; Chitty, Maurice Edelston (3), McPhee (4), Barney (1), Deverell (2).

Record Cup Victory: 6–0 v Leyton, FA Cup, 2nd rd, 12 December 1925 – Duckworth; Eggo, McConnell; Wilson, Messer, Evans; Smith (2), Braithwaite (1), Davey (1), Tinsley, Robson (2).

Record Defeat: 0–18 v Preston NE, FA Cup 1st rd, 1893–94.

Most League Points (2 for a win): 65, Division 4, 1978–79.

Most League Points (3 for a win): 94, Division 3, 1985–86.

Most League Goals: 112, Division 3 (S), 1951–52.

Highest League Scorer in Season: Ronnie Blackman, 39, Division 3 (S), 1951–52.

Most League Goals in Total Aggregate: Ronnie Blackman, 158, 1947–54.

Most Capped Player: Jimmy Quinn, 12, Northern Ireland.

Most League Appearances: Martin Hicks, 500, 1978–91.

Record Transfer Fee Received: £500,000 from Wimbledon for Keith Curle, October 1988.

Record Transfer Fee Paid: £250,000 to Leicester C for Steve Moran, November 1987 and £250,000 to Huddersfield T for Craig Maskell, August 1990.

Football League Record: 1920 Original Member of Division 3; 1921–26 Division 3 (S); 1926–31 Division 2; 1931–58 Division 3 (S); 1958–71 Division 3; 1971–76 Division 4; 1976–77 Division 3; 1977–79 Division 4; 1979–83 Division 3; 1983–84 Division 4; 1984–86 Division 3; 1986–88 Division 2; 1988–92 Division 3; 1992–94 Division 2; 1994– Division 1.

Honours: *Football League:* Division 2 – Champions 1993–94; Division 3 – Champions 1985–86. Division 3 (S) – Champions 1925–26; Runners-up 1931–32, 1934–35, 1948–49, 1951–52; Division 4 – Champions 1978–79. *FA Cup:* Semi-final 1927. *Football League Cup:* best season: 4th rd, 1965, 1966, 1978. *Simod Cup:* Winners 1987–88.

READING 1993—94 LEAGUE RECORD

Match No.	Date	Venue	Opponents	Result		H/T Score	Lg. Pos.	Goalscorers	Attendance
1	Aug 14	A	Huddersfield T	W	3-0	2-0	—	Gooding, Quinn, Lovell	6415
2	21	H	Burnley	W	2-1	2-0	3	Quinn, McPherson	5855
3	28	A	Brentford	L	0-1	0-1	8		6848
4	Sept 1	H	Barnet	W	4-1	2-1	—	Gooding, Parkinson, Quinn, Gilkes	4971
5	4	H	Cambridge U	W	3-1	1-0	3	Quinn 2, Parkinson	5007
6	11	A	Wrexham	L	2-3	1-2	4	Jones (og), Lovell	3941
7	15	A	Bradford C	W	4-2	1-0	—	Parkinson, Lovell, Quinn 2 (1 pen)	4853
8	18	H	Plymouth Arg	W	3-2	1-0	3	Quinn 2, Gooding	6209
9	25	H	Hull C	D	1-1	1-0	3	Hopkins	6453
10	Oct 1	A	Swansea C	D	1-1	0-0	—	Hartenberger	4245
11	9	A	Exeter C	W	6-4	4-1	2	Quinn 2, Lovell 2, Taylor 2	4725
12	16	H	Leyton Orient	W	2-1	1-0	2	Quinn 2	6066
13	23	A	Port Vale	W	4-0	0-0	2	Lovell, Taylor, Quinn 2 (1 pen)	9252
14	30	H	Fulham	W	1-0	0-0	2	Quinn	7020
15	Nov 2	A	Rotherham U	D	2-2	1-0	—	Lovell 2	3171
16	6	H	Blackpool	D	1-1	0-1	2	Quinn	6559
17	20	A	Brighton & HA	W	1-0	1-0	1	Taylor	6309
18	27	H	Bournemouth	W	3-0	0-0	1	Quinn 2, Gooding	5549
19	Dec 11	A	Burnley	W	1-0	1-0	1	Gooding	11,650
20	18	H	Huddersfield T	D	0-0	0-0	1		5675
21	28	H	Stockport Co	W	2-0	2-0	1	Lovell 2	11,240
22	Jan 1	A	Cardiff C	L	0-3	0-0	1		10,257
23	3	H	York C	W	2-1	1-1	1	Quinn 2	7199
24	8	H	Hartlepool U	W	4-0	2-0	1	Quinn, Lovell, Gooding, Taylor	6217
25	15	A	Leyton Orient	D	1-1	1-0	1	Lovell	6253
26	22	H	Exeter C	W	1-0	0-0	1	Hartenberger	7174
27	26	A	Bristol R	D	1-1	0-1	—	Quinn (pen)	7694
28	30	A	Fulham	L	0-1	0-0	—		6911
29	Feb 5	H	Port Vale	L	1-2	0-2	1	Quinn (pen)	7645
30	12	A	Hartlepool U	W	4-1	0-1	1	Lovell 2, Taylor, Quinn	2218
31	19	H	Brentford	W	2-1	1-1	1	Hopkins, Quinn	9056
32	25	A	Cambridge U	W	1-0	0-0	1	Quinn	4029
33	Mar 5	H	Wrexham	L	0-1	0-0	1		6311
34	12	A	Plymouth Arg	L	1-3	1-1	1	Kerr	14,953
35	15	H	Bradford C	D	1-1	1-0	—	Lovell	5293
36	19	A	Hull C	W	2-1	1-0	1	Quinn 2	7107
37	26	H	Swansea C	W	2-1	0-0	1	Quinn (pen), Lovell	6464
38	29	A	York C	L	0-1	0-1	—		5558
39	Apr 2	H	Bristol R	W	2-0	1-0	1	Quinn, Lovell	8035
40	9	H	Cardiff C	D	1-1	1-0	1	Gilkes	7129
41	12	A	Barnet	W	1-0	1-0	—	Lovell	2289
42	16	H	Rotherham U	D	0-0	0-0	1		6295
43	23	A	Blackpool	W	4-0	1-0	1	Kerr, Lovell 2, Quinn	4529
44	28	A	Stockport Co	D	1-1	0-1	—	Gooding	7221
45	30	H	Brighton & HA	W	2-0	1-0	1	Quinn 2 (1 pen)	11,840
46	May 5	A	Bournemouth	L	1-2	1-1	—	Quinn	6739

Final League Position: 1

GOALSCORERS

League (81): Quinn 35 (6 pens), Lovell 20, Gooding 7, Taylor 6, Parkinson 3, Gilkes 2, Hartenberger 2, Hopkins 2, Kerr 2, McPherson 1, own goal 1.
Coca-Cola Cup (7): Lovell 2, Quinn 2, Dillon 1, Gray 1, Parkinson 1.
FA Cup (1): Gooding 1.

Hislop 46	Ranson 22 + 2	Kerr 45	McPherson 19 + 1	Williams 41	Parkinson 42	Gilkes 29 + 10	Dillon 31 + 1	Quinn 46	Lovell 43 + 2	Gooding 41	Taylor 34 + 4	Hopkins 40 + 2	Jones 11 + 6	Gray — + 5	Hartenberger — + 9	Lambert 1 + 5	Humphrey 8	Bass — + 1	Witter 4	Carey — + 1	Wallace 3	*Match No.*
1	2	3	4	5	6	7	8	9	10	11												1
1	2	3	4	5	6	7	8	9	10	11												2
1	2	3	4	5	6	7	8	9	10		*11*	12	14									3
1	2	3	4	5	6	7	8	9	10	*11*		12	14									4
1	2	3	12	5	6	7	8	9	10	11		4										5
1	2	3	4		6	7	8	9	10	11		5		12								6
1		3	4	5	6	7	8	9	10	11		2										7
1		3	4	5	6	7	8	9	10	11		2		12								8
1	*2*	3	4		6	7	8	9	10	11	14	5		12								9
1	2	3		5	6	7	8	9	10	11		4			12							10
1	2	3	4		6		8	9	10	11	7	5										11
1	2	3		5	6	12	8	9	10	11	7	4										12
1	2	3		5	6	12	8	9	10	11	7	4										13
1	2	3	4		6	12	8	9	10	11	7	5										14
1	2	3		5	6	12	8	9	10	11	7	4										15
1		3	4	5	6	7	8	9	10	*11*	12	2			14							16
1	2	3		5	6	7		9	10	11	8	4										17
1		3		5	6	7	8	9	10	2	11	4				12						18
1		3		5	6	7	8	9		11	10	4			12		2					19
1		3		5	6	7	8	9	12	11	10	4					2					20
1		3		5	6	7	8	9	10	2	11	4										21
1	2	3		5		7	8	9	10	6	11	4				12						22
1	2	3		5			8	9	10	6	11	4				7						23
1		3		5	*6*		8	9	10	7	11	4		12			2	14				24
1		3		5	6		8	9	10	7	11	4			12		2					25
1		3		5	6	8		9	10	7	11	4			12		2					26
1		3		5	6	8		9	10	7	11	4			12		2					27
1		3		5	6	*7*	8	9	10	11	12	4			14		2					28
1		3	5		6		8	9	*10*	11	7	4	12		14		2					29
1	2	3		*5*	6	12	8	9	14	11	7		10						4			30
1		3	8	5	6			9	10		7	2	11						4			31
1		3	8	5	6	12		*9*	10		7	2	11			14			4			32
1	2	3		10		*8*		9	6		7	5	11			12			4	14		33
1		3		5		8		9	10	6	7	4	11			12					2	34
1		3		5	6	7		9	10	8	12	4	11								2	35
1		3		5	6	7		9	10	8	11	4									2	36
1		3		5	6	7	8	9	10	2	11	4										37
1	14	3		5	6	*7*	*8*	9	10	2	11	4	12									38
1	2	3		5	6	7		9	10	8	11	4										39
1	2	3		5	6	7		9	*10*	8	11	4	12	14								40
1	2	3		5	6	12	8	9	10		11	4	7									41
1	2		4	5	6	*7*	8	9	10	3	11		12		14							42
1	12	3	4	5	6			9	10	8	11	2	7									43
1		3	4	5	6	12		9	10	8	11	2	7									44
1		3	4	5	6	12		9	10	8	11	2	7									45
1		3	4	5	6	12	14	9	10	8	*11*	2	7									46

Coca-Cola Cup	First Round	Northampton T (h)	3-0
		(a)	2-0
	Second Round	Manchester C (a)	1-1
		(h)	1-2
FA Cup	First Round	Cambridge U (a)	0-0
		(h)	1-2

READING

Player and Position	Ht	Wt	Birth Date	Birth Place	Source	Clubs	League App	League Gls
Goalkeepers								
Neil Hislop	6 6	12 02	22 2 69	London		Reading	58	—
Defenders								
Alan Carey§			21 8 75	Greenwich	Trainee	Reading	1	—
Mark Holzman*	5 7	10 07	22 2 73	Bracknell	Trainee	Reading	32	1
Jeff Hopkins	6 0	12 12	14 4 64	Swansea	Apprentice	Fulham	219	4
						Crystal Palace	70	2
						Plymouth Arg (loan)	8	—
						Bristol R	6	—
						Reading	78	3
Dylan Kerr	5 11	12 05	14 1 67	Valetta	Arcadia Shepherds	Leeds U	13	—
						Doncaster R (loan)	7	1
						Blackpool (loan)	12	1
						Reading	45	2
Daren McCance†	6 0	10 12	13 9 73	Consett	Trainee	Reading	1	—
Keith McPherson	5 11	10 11	11 9 63	Greenwich	Apprentice	West Ham U	1	—
						Cambridge U (loan)	11	1
						Northampton T	182	8
						Reading	154	6
Ray Ranson	5 9	11 12	12 6 60	St. Helens	Apprentice	Manchester C	183	1
						Birmingham C	137	—
						Newcastle U	83	1
						Manchester C	17	—
						Reading	24	—
Adrian Williams	5 10	11 00	16 8 71	Reading	Trainee	Reading	143	10
Midfield								
Kevin Dillon*	6 0	12 07	18 12 59	Sunderland	Apprentice	Birmingham C	186	15
						Portsmouth	215	45
						Newcastle U	62	—
						Reading	101	4
Tommy Jones	5 10	11 07	7 10 64	Aldershot	Weymouth	Aberdeen	28	3
						Swindon T	168	12
						Reading	38	1
Stuart Lovell	5 10	10 06	9 1 72	Sydney	Trainee	Reading	121	34
Philip Parkinson	6 0	11 06	1 12 67	Chorley	Apprentice	Southampton	—	—
						Bury	145	5
						Reading	81	7
Scott Taylor	5 9	11 00	23 11 70	Portsmouth	Trainee	Reading	163	16
Forwards								
Lea Barkus	5 7	10 02	7 12 74	Reading	Trainee	Reading	15	1
David Bass	5 11	12 07	29 11 74	Frimley	Trainee	Reading	9	—
Michael Gilkes	5 8	10 02	20 7 65	Hackney		Reading	277	34
						Chelsea (loan)	1	—
						Southampton (loan)	6	—
Mick Gooding	5 7	10 13	12 4 59	Newcastle	Bishop Auckland	Rotherham U	102	10
						Chesterfield	12	—
						Rotherham U	156	33
						Peterborough U	47	21
						Wolverhampton W	44	4
						Reading	192	23
Andy Gray	5 6	10 10	25 10 73	Southampton		Reading	17	3
Uwe Hartenberger			1 2 68	Lauterecken	Bayer Uerdingen	Reading	9	2
James Lambert	5 7	10 04	14 9 73	Henley	School	Reading	33	3
Mark McGhee†	5 10	12 00	25 5 57	Glasgow	Apprentice	Bristol C	—	—
						Morton	64	37
						Newcastle U	28	5
						Aberdeen	164	63
						SV Hamburg	30	7
						Celtic	88	27
						Newcastle U	67	24
						Reading	45	7

READING

Colours: Navy and white hooped shirts, white shorts, white stockings. **Change colours:** Yellow and navy blue hooped shirts, blue shorts, blue stockings.

Foundation: Reading was formed as far back as 1871 at a public meeting held at the Bridge Street Rooms. They first entered the FA Cup as early as 1877 when they amalgamated with the Reading Hornets. The club was further strengthened in 1889 when Earley FC joined them. They were the first winners of the Berks and Bucks Cup in 1878–79.

First Football League game: 28 August, 1920, Division 3, v Newport C (a) W 1-0 – Crawford; Smith, Horler; Christie, Mavin, Getgood; Spence, Weston, Yarnell, Bailey (1), Andrews.

Did you know: Adrian Williams completed every shirt number for Reading on 5 March 1994 when he wore the No. 10 against Wrexham. He had even deputised for an injured goalkeeper two years earlier.

Managers (and Secretary-Managers)
Thomas Sefton 1897–1901*, James Sharp 1901–02, Harry Matthews 1902–20, Harry Marshall 1920–22, Arthur Chadwick 1923–25, H. S. Bray 1925–26 (secretary only since 1922 and 26–35), Andrew Wylie 1926–31, Joe Smith 1931–35, Billy Butler 1935–39, John Cochrane 1939, Joe Edelston 1939–47, Ted Drake 1947–52, Jack Smith 1952–55, Harry Johnston 1955–63, Roy Bentley 1963–69, Jack Mansell 1969–71, Charlie Hurley 1972–77, Maurice Evans 1977–84, Ian Branfoot 1984–89, Ian Porterfield 1989–91, Mark McGhee May 1991–

Player and Position	*Ht*	*Wt*	*Birth Date*	*Birth Place*	*Source*	*Clubs*	*League App*	*League Gls*
Jimmy Quinn	6 0	12 07	18 11 59	Belfast	Oswestry T	Swindon T	49	10
						Blackburn R	71	17
						Swindon T	64	30
						Leicester C	31	6
						Bradford C	35	14
						West Ham U	47	18
						Bournemouth	43	19
						Reading	88	52

Trainees
Brown, Philip R; Carey, Alan W; Champion, Marc G; Conway, Martin J; Curran, James M; Holzman, Gary R; Montgomery, Noel T; Randall, Gareth E; Sharp, James; Staples, Stephen J; Stowell, Matthew D; Thorpe, Michael S; Wilkinson, Robert H.

****Non-Contract**
McGhee, Mark.

Associated Schoolboys
Barnes, Stuart R; Curtis, Richard; Deeks, Steven G. G; Didcock, Lee; Dugdale, Andrew; Forbes, Andrew J; Frith, Alastair S; Gibbs, Jason D; Holloway, Neil S; Jerome, Mark R; Kostiw, Richard; Leach, James P; Lunn, Michael J; Lynch, Giles S; Lyttle, Clive A; May, Steven J; McLeod, Stuart C; Norris, Jordan; Oleinik, Gary J; Potter, Christopher J; Roach, Neville; Rooke, Maxwell J; Szymonik, Ben; Warrington, Lee J; Young, Stuart J. G.

Associated Schoolboys who have accepted the Club's offer of a Traineeship/Contract
Jones, Matthew; Jones, Russell; Richards, Scott.
**Non-Contract Players who are retained must be re-signed before they are eligible to play in League matches.

Preston North End players continued from Page 409

Player	Ht	Wt	Date	Place	Source	Clubs	App	Gls
Tony Ellis	5 11	11 00	20 10 64	Salford	Northwich Vic	Oldham Ath	8	—
						Preston NE	86	26
						Stoke C	77	19
						Preston NE	72	48
Paul Heavey*	6 0	11 09	24 11 74	Billinge	Trainee	Preston NE	—	—
Kevin Magee	5 10	11 04	10 4 71	Bangour	Armadale Th	Partick T	11	—
						Preston NE	7	—
John Muir	6 2	14 06	26 4 63	Sedgley	Dudley T	Doncaster R	75	18
						Stockport Co	13	3
						Torquay U (loan)	12	—
						Preston NE	—	—
Mike Norbury	6 1	11 10	22 1 69	Hemsworth	Bridlington	Cambridge U	26	3
						Preston NE	42	13
Paul Raynor	6 0	11 04	29 4 66	Nottingham	Apprentice	Nottingham F	3	—
						Bristol R (loan)	8	—
						Huddersfield T	50	9
						Swansea C	191	27
						Wrexham (loan)	6	—
						Cambridge U	49	2
						Preston NE	39	6
Liam Watson	5 11	11 10	21 5 70	Liverpool	Warrington T	Preston NE	9	3

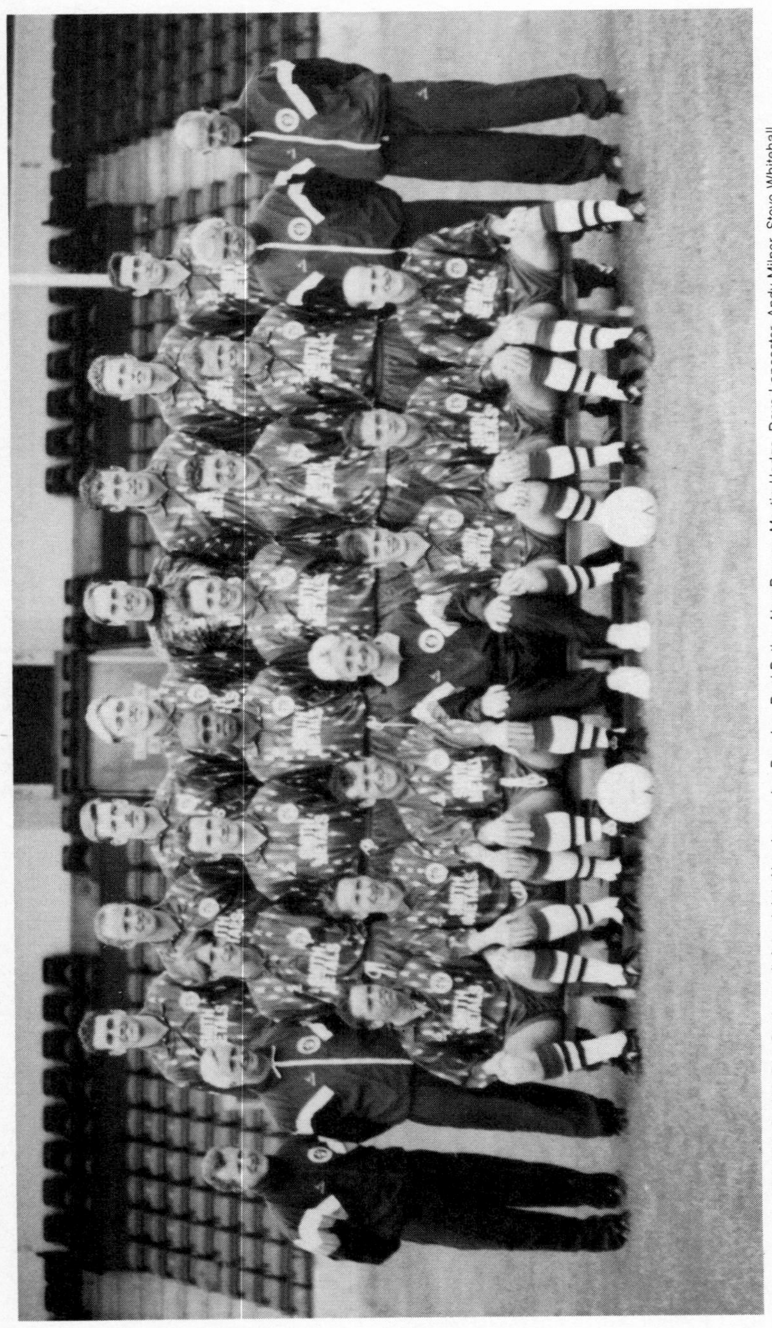

ROCHDALE 1993–94 *Back row (left to right):* Alec Jones, Jon Bowden, Paul Butler, Alan Reeves, Martin Hodge, Dave Lancaster, Andy Milner, Steve Whitehall.
Centre row: Mick Docherty (Assistant Manager), John Dawson (Physio), Jason Anders, Mark Stuart, Steve Mulrain, John Ryan, Tony Beever, Steve Doyle, Trevor Jones (Youth Team Coach), Jimmy Robson (Youth and Reserve Team Manager).
Front row: Trevor Snowdon, Andy Flounders, Shaun Reid, Dave Sutton (Manager), Andy Howard, Andy Thackeray, Jimmy Graham.

Division 3 ROCHDALE

Spotland, Sandy Lane, Rochdale OL11 5DS. Telephone Rochdale (0706) 44648. Fax: (0706) 48466. Commercial: (0706) 47521.

Ground capacity: 6700.

Record attendance: 24,231 v Notts Co, FA Cup 2nd rd, 10 December 1949.

Record receipts: £46,000 v Burnley, Division 4, 5 May 1992.

Pitch measurements: 114yd × 76yd.

President: Mrs L. Stoney.

Chairman: D. F. Kilpatrick.

Directors: G. R. Brierley, T. Butterworth, C. Dunphy, M. Mace, J. Marsh, G. Morris.

Manager: Dave Sutton.

Secretary: Keith Clegg. ***Coach:*** Mick Docherty. ***Commercial Manager:*** S. Walmsley. ***Advertising & Sponsorship Manager:*** L. Duckworth.

Physio: J. Dawson.

Year Formed: 1907. ***Turned Professional:*** 1907. ***Ltd Co.:*** 1910.

Club Nickname: 'The Dale'.

Record League Victory: 8–1 v Chesterfield, Division 3 (N), 18 December 1926 – Hill; Brown, Ward; Hillhouse, Parkes, Braidwood; Hughes, Bertram, Whitehurst (5), Schofield (2), Martin (1).

Record Cup Victory: 8–2 v Crook T, FA Cup, 1st rd, 26 November 1927 – Moody; Hopkins, Ward; Braidwood, Parkes, Barker; Tompkinson, Clennell (3) Whitehurst (4), Hall, Martin (1).

Record Defeat: 0–8 v Wrexham, Division 3 (N), 28 December 1929, 0–8 v Leyton Orient, Division 4, 20 October 1987, and 1–9 v Tranmere R, Division 3 (N), 25 December 1931.

Most League Points (2 for a win): 62, Division 3 (N), 1923–24.

Most League Points (3 for a win): 67, Division 4, 1991–92.

Most League Goals: 105, Division 3 (N), 1926–27.

Highest League Scorer in Season: Albert Whitehurst, 44, Division 3 (N), 1926–27.

Most League Goals in Total Aggregate: Reg Jenkins, 119, 1964–73.

Most Capped Player: None.

Most League Appearances: Graham Smith, 317, 1966–74.

Record Transfer Fee Received: £200,000 from Bristol C for Keith Welch, July 1991.

Record Transfer Fee Paid: £80,000 to Scunthorpe U for Andy Flounders, August 1991.

Football League Record: 1921 Elected to Division 3 (N); 1958–59 Division 3; 1959–69 Division 4; 1969–74 Division 3; 1974–92 Division 4; 1992– Division 3.

Football League: Division 3 best season: 9th, 1969–70; Division 3 (N) – Runners-up 1923–24, 1926–27. *FA Cup:* best season: 5th rd, 1989–90. *Football League Cup:* Runners-up 1962 (record for 4th Division club).

ROCHDALE 1993—94 LEAGUE RECORD

Match No.	Date	Venue	Opponents	Result		H/T Score	Lg. Pos.	Goalscorers	Attendance
1	Aug 14	A	Darlington	D	1-1	0-0	—	Thackeray	2327
2	21	H	Gillingham	W	3-0	2-0	3	Butler, Whitehall, Stuart	2092
3	28	A	Carlisle U	W	1-0	1-0	1	Reeves	5438
4	31	H	Wigan Ath	L	1-2	1-0	—	Whitehall	2628
5	Sept 4	H	Chester C	W	2-0	2-0	4	Whitehall, Doyle	3063
6	11	A	Colchester U	W	5-2	2-2	2	Lancaster 2, Butler, Reeves, Whitehall	2776
7	18	H	Hereford U	W	2-0	2-0	1	Lancaster 2	2645
8	25	H	Chesterfield	W	5-1	5-1	1	Reid, Whitehall 2, Lancaster, Stuart	2481
9	Oct 2	A	Doncaster R	L	1-2	1-1	2	Lancaster	3103
10	9	A	Torquay U	D	1-1	1-0	3	Stuart	3874
11	16	H	Walsall	D	0-0	0-0	3		2923
12	23	A	Preston NE	L	1-2	0-0	3	Stuart	8491
13	30	H	Lincoln C	L	0-1	0-0	4		2551
14	Nov 2	H	Mansfield T	D	1-1	1-1	—	Howard	2042
15	6	A	Crewe Alex	L	1-2	0-1	8	Williams	4049
16	20	H	Bury	W	2-1	2-0	7	Bowden, Williams	3758
17	27	A	Scunthorpe U	L	1-2	0-0	9	Stuart (pen)	3106
18	Dec 11	A	Gillingham	W	2-1	1-0	7	Lancaster 2	2493
19	18	H	Darlington	D	0-0	0-0	8		2205
20	Jan 1	H	Northampton T	W	6-2	3-0	7	Lancaster 3, Whitehall, Stuart, Taylor	2453
21	4	A	Wigan Ath	D	0-0	0-0	—		1912
22	15	A	Walsall	L	0-1	0-1	10		4437
23	22	H	Torquay U	W	4-1	1-1	8	Thackeray, Lancaster 2, Whitehall	2319
24	29	A	Lincoln C	D	1-1	1-1	9	Milner	2703
25	Feb 5	H	Preston NE	W	2-1	1-1	8	Stuart, Whitehall	4317
26	12	A	Shrewsbury T	D	1-1	0-1	8	Whitehall	4882
27	19	H	Carlisle U	L	0-1	0-1	9		2927
28	25	A	Chester C	L	1-3	1-0	9	Milner	3472
29	Mar 1	H	Scarborough	W	2-1	1-0	—	Reid, Stuart	1827
30	5	H	Colchester U	D	1-1	0-1	8	Stuart	2202
31	12	A	Hereford U	L	1-5	0-2	10	Whitehall	1964
32	19	A	Chesterfield	D	1-1	0-0	10	Whitehall	3282
33	26	H	Doncaster R	L	0-1	0-0	10		2165
34	Apr 2	A	Scarborough	L	1-2	0-0	12	Thackeray	1448
35	4	H	Wycombe W	D	2-2	1-0	13	Whitehall, Bowden	2575
36	9	A	Northampton T	W	2-1	1-0	12	Stuart, Bowden	3330
37	12	H	Shrewsbury T	L	1-2	0-0	—	Reid	5402
38	16	A	Mansfield T	W	1-0	0-0	10	Thackeray	2362
39	19	A	Wycombe W	D	1-1	0-1	—	Stuart	5226
40	23	H	Crewe Alex	W	2-1	1-0	8	Stuart, Whitehall	3096
41	30	A	Bury	W	1-0	0-0	7	Stuart	3270
42	May 7	H	Scunthorpe U	L	2-3	2-2	9	Reeves, Lancaster	3118

Final League Position: 9

GOALSCORERS

League (63): Lancaster 14, Whitehall 14, Stuart 13 (1 pen), Thackeray 4, Bowden 3, Reeves 3, Reid 3, Butler 2, Milner 2, Williams 2, Doyle 1, Howard 1, Taylor 1.

Coca-Cola Cup (4): Flounders 1 (pen), Lancaster 1, Stuart 1, own goal 1.

FA Cup (2): Stuart 1 (pen), Whitehall 1 (pen).

Hodge 42	Thackeray 35 + 2	Graham 28 + 1	Reid 39	Reeves 41	Butler 38	Stuart 41 + 1	Doyle 32 + 2	Flounders 9 + 2	Whitehall 37 + 2	Lancaster 37 + 3	Bowden 11 + 18	Milner 14 + 11	Ryan 10 + 2	Mulrain — + 2	Oliver 14 + 5	Jones 3 + 1	Matthews 5 + 1	Howard — + 5	Williams 9 + 2	Snowden — + 1	Taylor 1 + 9	Finley 1	Shelton 3	Peake 10	Formby 2 + 3	Match No.
1	2	3	4	5	6	7	8	9	10	11	12															1
1	2	3	4	5	6	7	8	9	10	11		12														2
1	2	3	4	5	6	7	8	9	*10*	11	12	14														3
1	2	3	4	5	6	7	8	9	10	*11*	12	14														4
1	2	3	4	5	6	7	8	9	10	11			12													5
1	2	3	4	5	*6*	7		9	10	11	8	14	12													6
1	2	3	4	5	6	7	8		10	9		14	11	*12*												7
1	2	3	4	5	6	7	8	12	*10*	9		14	11													8
1	2	3	4	5	6	7	8	12	10	9		14	*11*													9
1	2	3	4	5	6	7			10	*9*		14	11		8	12										10
1	2	3	4	5	6	7	8		10	9			11		12											11
1	2		4	5	6	7	8		*10*	9		14	11		3		12									12
1	2	3	4	5	6	7	12		*10*	9		11			14		8									13
1	*12*		4	5	6	7	8		10	9		11			3		2	14								14
1				5	6	7	8		10	*9*	4			12	3		2	14	11							15
1	2	12		5	6	7	8			9	4		11		3				10							16
1	14	9		5	6	7	8			12	4		11		*3*	2			10							17
1			4	5	*6*	11		8	10	9			7		3		2			12	14					18
1	2		4	5		11	12	*8*	10	9	6		7		3						14					19
1	2		4	5		11	8		10	9	12	*7*			3						14	6				20
1	2		4	5	6	11	8		*10*	9	12	7			3						14					21
1	2		4	5	6	11	8		*10*	9	12	7			3						14					22
1	2		4	5	6	11	8		12	9	14	7			3						*10*					23
1	2	3	4	5	6	11			10	9	8	7						12								24
1	2	3	4	5		11			10	9	8	7				6		12								25
1	2	3	4	5		11			12	9	14	7				*6*			10				8			26
1	2	3	4	5	6	*11*			10	12	14	7							9				8			27
1	*2*	3	4	5	6	11			10		14	7						12	9				8			28
1		3	4	5	6	7	8		10	12		*11*			14		2		9							29
1	2	3	4	5	6	7	8		*10*	9	14	11							12							30
1		3	4	5	6	7	*8*	11	10	9	2	12			14											31
1	2	3	4	5	6	7	8		11	9	10				12											32
1	2		4	5	6	7	*8*		10		12				3				9					11	14	33
1	2		4	5	6	12	8			9		7			3				*10*		14			11		34
1	2	3	4	5	6	7	8		*10*	9	12										14			11		35
1	2	3	4	5	6	7	8		*10*	9	12										14			11		36
1	2	3	4	5	6	7	8		10	9	12										14			*11*		37
1	2	3	4	5	6	7	8		10	9	12													*11*	14	38
1	2	3	4		6	7	8		10	9	5													11	12	39
1	2	3	4	5	6	*7*	8		10	9	12	14												11		40
1			4	5	6	7	8		10	9	2													11	3	41
1	2		4	5	6	7	*8*		10	9	12								14					11	3	42

Coca-Cola Cup	First Round	York C (h)	2-0
		(a)	0-0
	Second Round	Leicester C (h)	1-6
		(a)	1-2
FA Cup	First Round	Chesterfield (a)	1-0
	Second Round	Burnley (a)	1-4

ROCHDALE

Player and Position	Ht	Wt	Birth Date	Birth Place	Source	Clubs	League App	League Gls
Goalkeepers								
Martin Hodge	6 1	14 06	4 2 59	Southport	Apprentice	Plymouth Arg	43	—
						Everton	25	—
						Preston NE (loan)	28	—
						Oldham Ath (loan)	4	—
						Gillingham (loan)	4	—
						Preston NE (loan)	16	—
						Sheffield W	197	—
						Leicester C	75	—
						Hartlepool U	69	—
						Rochdale	42	—
Defenders								
Paul Butler	6 2	13 00	2 11 72	Manchester	Trainee	Rochdale	81	4
Jimmy Graham	5 11	11 00	15 11 69	Glasgow	Trainee	Bradford C	7	—
						Rochdale (loan)	11	—
						Rochdale	126	1
Alex Jones‡	6 2	12 08	27 11 64	Blackburn	Apprentice	Oldham Ath	9	—
						Stockport Co (loan)	3	—
						Preston NE	101	3
						Carlisle U	62	4
						Rochdale	13	—
						Motherwell	12	1
						Rochdale	33	2
Neil Matthews	6 0	11 07	3 12 67	Manchester	Apprentice	Blackpool	76	1
						Cardiff C	66	2
						Rochdale	6	—
Darren Oliver	5 8	10 05	1 11 71	Liverpool		Bolton W	3	—
						Peterborough U (loan)	—	—
						Rochdale	19	—
Alan Reeves	6 0	12 00	19 11 67	Birkenhead		Norwich C	—	—
						Gillingham (loan)	18	—
						Chester C	40	2
						Rochdale	116	9
Jason Smart‡	6 0	12 10	15 2 69	Rochdale	Trainee	Rochdale	117	4
						Crewe Alex	89	2
						Rochdale	—	—
Midfield								
Jon Bowden	6 10	11 07	21 1 63	Stockport	Local	Oldham Ath	82	5
						Port Vale	70	7
						Wrexham	147	20
						Rochdale	95	17
Steve Doyle	5 9	11 01	2 6 58	Neath	Apprentice	Preston NE	197	8
						Huddersfield T	161	6
						Sunderland	100	2
						Hull C	47	2
						Rochdale	110	1
Andy Howard*	5 6	10 02	15 3 72	Southport	Liverpool	Blackpool	—	—
					Fleetwood	Rochdale	20	3
Jason Peake	5 9	11 05	29 9 71	Leicester	Trainee	Leicester C	8	1
						Hartlepool U (loan)	6	1
						Halifax T	33	1
						Rochdale	10	—
Shaun Reid	5 8	11 10	13 10 65	Huyton	Local	Rochdale	133	4
						Preston NE (loan)	3	—
						York C	106	7
						Rochdale	79	7
Trevor Snowden*	5 8	11 00	4 10 73	Sunderland	Seaham Red Star	Rochdale	14	—
Andy Thackeray	5 9	11 00	13 2 68	Huddersfield		Manchester C	—	—
						Huddersfield T	2	—
						Newport Co	54	4
						Wrexham	152	14
						Rochdale	78	10
Forwards								
Jason Anders*	5 10	10 06	13 3 74	Rochdale	Trainee	Rochdale	17	1
Anthony Beever*	6 0	12 05	18 9 74	Huddersfield	Trainee	Rochdale	1	—

ROCHDALE

Colours: Blue with red and white chevrons. **Change colours:** All green.

Foundation: Considering the love of rugby in their area, it is not surprising that Rochdale had difficulty in establishing an Association Football club. The earlier Rochdale Town club formed in 1900 went out of existence in 1907 when the present club was immediately established and joined the Manchester League, before graduating to the Lancashire Combination in 1908.

First Football League game: 27 August, 1921, Division 3(N), v Accrington Stanley (h) W 6-3 – Crabtree; Nuttall, Sheehan; Hill, Farrer, Yarwood; Hoad, Sandiford, Dennison (2), Owens (3), Carney (1).

Did you know: During 1926–27, Rochdale's most successful season in Division 3 (North), they scored in every home game and the average attendance of 7095 has never been bettered by the club.

Managers (and Secretary-Managers)
Billy Bradshaw 1920, (run by committee 1920–22), Tom Wilson 1922–23, Jack Peart 1923–30, Will Cameron 1930–31, Herbert Hopkinson 1932–34, Billy Smith 1934–35, Ernest Nixon 1935–37, Sam Jennings 1937–38, Ted Goodier 1938–52, Jack Warner 1952–53, Harry Catterick 1953–58, Jack Marshall 1958–60, Tony Collins 1960–68, Bob Stokoe 1967–68, Len Richley 1968–70, Dick Conner 1970–73, Walter Joyce 1973–76, Brian Green 1976–77, Mike Ferguson 1977–78, Doug Collins 1979, Bob Stokoe 1979–80, Peter Madden 1980–83, Jimmy Greenhoff 1983–84, Vic Halom 1984–86, Eddie Gray 1986–88, Danny Bergara 1988–89, Terry Dolan 1989–91, Dave Sutton February 1991–

Player and Position	*Ht*	*Wt*	*Birth Date*	*Birth Place*	*Source*	*Clubs*	*League App*	*League Gls*
Andy Flounders‡	5 11	11 06	13 12 63	Hull	Apprentice	Hull C	159	54
						Scunthorpe U	196	87
						Rochdale	85	31
						Rotherham U (loan)	6	2
						Carlisle U (loan)	8	1
Kevin Formby	5 11	12 00	22 7 71	Ormskirk	Burscough	Rochdale	5	—
Dave Lancaster	6 3	14 00	8 9 61	Preston	Colne Dynamoes	Blackpool	8	1
						Chesterfield (loan)	12	4
						Chesterfield	69	16
						Rochdale	40	14
Andy Milner	5 11	11 07	10 2 67	Kendal	Netherfield	Manchester C	—	—
						Rochdale	127	25
Steve Mulrain	5 10	11 07	23 10 72	Lambeth	Trainee	Leeds U	—	—
						Rochdale	8	2
Mark Stuart	5 10	11 03	15 12 66	Hammersmith	QPR	Charlton Ath	107	28
						Plymouth Arg	57	11
						Ipswich T (loan)	5	2
						Bradford C	29	5
						Huddersfield T	15	3
						Rochdale	42	13
Jamie Taylor	5 6	9 12	11 1 77	Bury	Trainee	Rochdale	10	1
Steve Whitehall	5 9	10 11	8 12 66	Bromborough	Southport	Rochdale	115	36
Paul A Williams	6 3	14 06	8 9 63	Sheffield	Nuneaton	Preston NE	1	—
						Newport Co	26	3
						Sheffield U	8	—
						Hartlepool U	8	—
						Stockport Co	24	14
						WBA	44	5
						Coventry C (loan)	2	—
						Stockport Co	16	3
						Rochdale	11	2

Trainees
Bayliss, David A; Chadwick, Gavin R. D; Crowe, Asa A; Fishwick, Alexander J; Holden, Martin J; Jordan, Steven; McCartney, William; McCormick, Matthew P; Meehan, Andrew T. V; Ross, Jason T; Walsh, Lee.

****Non-Contract**
Creighton, Mark G; Dunford, Neil.

Associated Schoolboys
Adams, Paul; Hill, Paul S; Jones, Stuart J; Leitheiser, Franc J; Ogden, John; Stansfield, Colin A; Swettenham, Andrew B.

**Non-Contract Players who are retained must be re-signed before they are eligible to play in League matches.

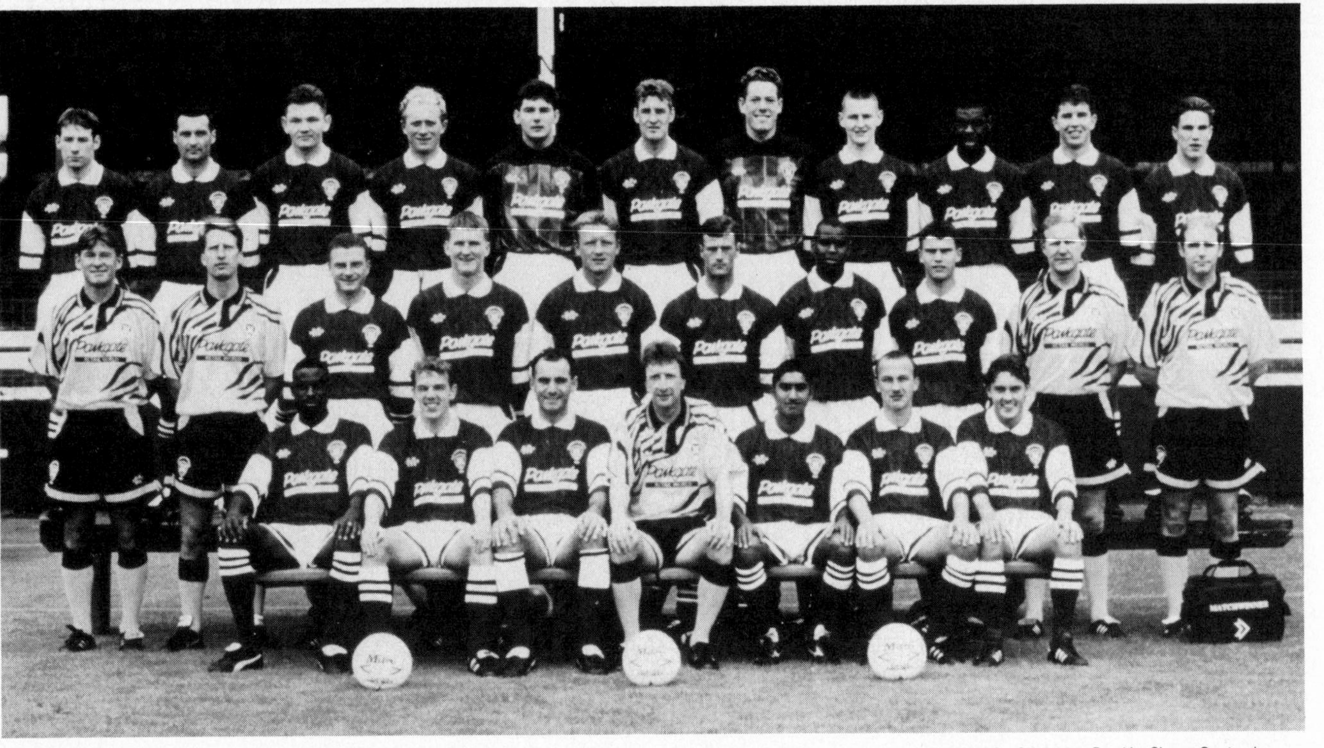

ROTHERHAM UNITED 1993–94 *Back row (left to right):* Jon Howard, Ian Banks, Neil Richardson, Nicky Law, Billy Mercer, Nigel Johnson, Matthew Clarke, Ian Breckin, Shaun Goater, Len Curtis, Glyn Roberts.
Centre row: Chris Hutchings (Player Coach), Billy Russell (Youth Team Coach), Wayne Jacobs, Karl Marginson, Chris Wilder, Ally Pickering, Des Hazel, Scott Smith, John Breckin (Assistant Manager), Ian Bailey (Physio).
Front row: Don Page, Mark Todd, Imre Varadi, Phil Henson (Manager), Chris Dolby, Shaun Goodwin, Paul Hurst.

Division 2 ROTHERHAM UNITED

Millmoor Ground, Rotherham S60 1HR. Telephone Rotherham (0709) 562434. Fax (0709) 563336.

Ground Capacity: 11,533.

Record attendance: 25,000 v Sheffield U, Division 2, 13 December 1952 and v Sheffield W, Division 2, 26 January 1952.

Record receipts: £79,155 v Newcastle U, FA Cup 4th rd, 23 January 1993.

Pitch measurements. 115yd × 75yd.

President: Sir J. Layden.

Chairman: K. F. Booth.

Directors: R. Hull (Vice-chairman), C. A. Luckock, J. A. Webb.

Manager: Phil Henson. ***Assistant Manager:*** John Breckin. ***Coach:*** Billy Russell. ***Physio:*** Ian Bailey.

Secretary: N. Darnill.

Commercial Manager: D. Nicholls.

Year Formed: 1884. ***Turned Professional:*** 1905. ***Ltd Co.:*** 1920.

Club Nickname: 'The Merry Millers'.

Previous Names: 1884, Thornhill United; 1905, Rotherham County; 1925, amalgamated with Rotherham Town under Rotherham United.

Previous Ground: Red House Ground; 1907, Millmoor.

Record League Victory: 8–0 v Oldham Ath, Division 3 (N), 26 May 1947 – Warnes; Selkirk, Ibbotson; Edwards, Horace Williams, Danny Williams; Wilson (2), Shaw (1), Ardron (3), Guest (1), Hainsworth (1).

Record Cup Victory: 6–0 v Spennymoor U, FA Cup, 2nd rd, 17 December 1977 – McAlister; Forrest, Breckin, Womble, Stancliffe, Green, Finney, Phillips (3), Gwyther (2) (Smith), Goodfellow, Crawford (1). 6–0 v Wolverhampton W, FA Cup, 1st rd, 16 November 1985 – O'Hanlon; Forrest, Dungworth, Gooding (1), Smith (1), Pickering, Birch (2), Emerson, Tynan (1), Simmons (1), Pugh.

Record Defeat: 1–11 v Bradford C, Division 3 (N), 25 August 1928.

Most League Points (2 for a win): 71, Division 3 (N), 1950–51.

Most League Points (3 for a win): 82, Division 4, 1988–89.

Most League Goals: 114, Division 3 (N), 1946–47.

Highest League Scorer in Season: Wally Ardron, 38, Division 3 (N), 1946–47.

Most League Goals in Total Aggregate: Gladstone Guest, 130, 1946–56.

Most Capped Player: Harold Millership, 6, Wales.

Most League Appearances: Danny Williams, 459, 1946–62.

Record Transfer Fee Received: £200,000 from Bristol C for Martin Scott, December 1990.

Record Transfer Fee Paid: £100,000 to Cardiff C for Ronnie Moore, August 1980.

Football League Record: 1893 Rotherham Town elected to Division 2; 1896 Failed re-election; 1919 Rotherham County elected to Division 2; 1923–51 Division 3 (N); 1951–68 Division 2; 1968–73 Division 3; 1973–75 Division 4; 1975–81 Division 3; 1981–83 Division 2; 1983–88 Division 3; 1988–89 Division 4; 1989–91 Division 3; 1991–92 Division 4; 1992– Division 2.

Honours: *Football League:* Division 2 best season: 3rd, 1954–55 (equal points with champions and runners-up); Division 3 – Champions 1980–81; Division 3 (N) – Champions 1950–51; Runners-up 1946–47, 1947–48, 1948–49; Division 4 – Champions 1988–89; Runners-up 1991–92. *FA Cup:* best season: 5th rd, 1953, 1968. *Football League Cup:* Runners-up 1961.

ROTHERHAM UNITED 1993—94 LEAGUE RECORD

Match No.	Date	Venue	Opponents	Result		H/T Score	Lg. Pos.	Goalscorers	Attendance
1	Aug 14	A	Wrexham	D	3-3	1-1	—	Banks, Goater, Goodwin	5570
2	21	H	Huddersfield T	L	2-3	1-1	16	Varadi, Wilder (pen)	5540
3	28	A	York C	D	0-0	0-0	19		4674
4	31	H	Burnley	W	3-2	2-1	—	Helliwell, Varadi 2	5533
5	Sept 4	H	Brentford	W	2-0	2-0	9	Hazel 2	4333
6	11	A	Cambridge U	W	1-0	0-0	6	Varadi	3804
7	14	A	Plymouth Arg	L	2-4	2-4	—	Varadi 2	6293
8	18	H	Bristol R	D	1-1	1-0	10	Varadi	4000
9	25	A	Stockport Co	L	0-2	0-0	14		4903
10	Oct 2	H	Blackpool	L	0-2	0-0	15		3770
11	9	A	Leyton Orient	D	1-1	0-0	15	Varadi	3304
12	16	H	Swansea C	D	1-1	1-0	17	Goodwin	3178
13	23	A	Brighton & HA	W	2-0	2-0	16	Pickering, Goodwin	5104
14	30	H	Port Vale	L	0-2	0-2	17		4786
15	Nov 2	H	Reading	D	2-2	0-1	—	Hazel, Whitworth	3171
16	6	A	Hull C	L	1-4	1-3	18	Varadi	4860
17	20	H	Fulham	L	1-2	1-1	18	Todd	2667
18	27	A	Barnet	L	1-2	0-0	18	Goodwin	1938
19	Dec 11	A	Huddersfield T	L	1-2	0-1	20	Varadi	4994
20	17	H	Wrexham	W	2-1	1-0	—	Brien, Marshall	2664
21	27	A	Bradford C	L	1-2	0-1	20	Goodwin	7765
22	Jan 1	A	Hartlepool U	L	0-2	0-0	21		2101
23	3	H	Cardiff C	W	5-2	4-0	20	Varadi 3, Goater, Goodwin	3395
24	14	A	Swansea C	D	0-0	0-0	—		3271
25	22	H	Leyton Orient	W	2-1	1-0	18	Wilder, Goater	3392
26	Feb 5	H	Brighton & HA	L	0-1	0-0	21		3773
27	12	A	Exeter C	D	1-1	0-1	21	Helliwell	3113
28	19	H	York C	W	2-1	1-0	20	Jacobs, Goodwin	3816
29	25	A	Brentford	D	2-2	0-1	20	Varadi, Jacobs	4980
30	Mar 5	H	Cambridge U	W	3-0	1-0	20	Banks (pen), Goater, Brien	3266
31	8	H	Bournemouth	L	1-2	0-1	—	Helliwell	2884
32	12	A	Bristol R	W	2-0	2-0	18	Barras, Roberts	4224
33	15	H	Plymouth Arg	L	0-3	0-0	—		2982
34	19	H	Stockport Co	L	1-2	0-1	19	Goater	3755
35	26	A	Blackpool	W	2-1	0-0	19	Goater 2	3588
36	29	A	Cardiff C	L	0-1	0-1	—		3583
37	Apr 2	H	Bradford C	W	2-1	1-1	18	Williams, Goater	4604
38	5	A	Bournemouth	D	0-0	0-0	—		3097
39	9	H	Hartlepool U	W	7-0	4-0	18	Goater 4, Goodwin, Varadi 2	2792
40	12	A	Port Vale	L	1-2	1-1	—	Banks	6804
41	16	A	Reading	D	0-0	0-0	18		6295
42	19	H	Exeter C	W	3-0	1-0	—	Goater, Williams, Varadi	2804
43	23	H	Hull C	W	1-0	0-0	15	Varadi	4944
44	26	A	Burnley	D	0-0	0-0	—		10,806
45	30	A	Fulham	L	0-1	0-0	15		5217
46	May 7	H	Barnet	D	1-1	0-1	15	Varadi	3674

Final League Position: 15

GOALSCORERS

League (63): Varadi 19, Goater 13, Goodwin 8, Banks 3 (1 pen), Hazel 3, Helliwell 3, Brien 2, Jacobs 2, Wilder 2 (1 pen), Williams 2, Barras 1, Marshall 1, Pickering 1, Roberts 1, Todd 1, Whitworth 1.
Coca-Cola Cup (5): Banks 1, Hazel 1, Law 1, Varadi 1, own goal 1.
FA Cup (1): Wilder 1 (pen).

Mercer 17	Pickering 12	Jacobs 40 + 2	Banks 31	Richardson 27	Law 10	Hazel 26 + 3	Goodwin 38	Helliwell 37 + 3	Goater 25 + 14	Wilder 35 + 2	Varadi 38 + 1	Hutchings 5 + 2	Clarke 29 + 1	Marginson 6	Kiwomya 4 + 3	Whitworth 8	Brien 25 + 1	Dolby — + 1	Williams 34	Todd 9 + 2	Howard 4 + 4	Marshall 10	Hurst 3 + 1	Roberts 11 + 3	Barras 5	Breckin 10	Smith 7	*Match No.*
1	2	3	4	5	6	7	8	9	10	11																		1
1	2	3	4	5	6	7	8	9		11	10																	2
1	2	3	4	5	6	7	8	9	12	11	10																	3
1	2	3	4	5	6	7	8	9	12	11	10																	4
1	2	3	4	5	6	7	8	9		11	10																	5
1	2	3	4	5	6	7	8	9		11	10																	6
1	2	3	4	5	6	7	8	9		11	10																	7
1	2	3	4	5	6	7	8	9	12	*11*	10	14																8
	2	3	4	5	6		8	9	7		10	12	1	11														9
1		3	4	5	6		8	9	12	2	10	7			11													10
1	2	3	4	5			8	9		11	10			7		6												11
1	2	3		5			8	9	12	11	10			*7*		6	4	14										12
	2	3		5			8	9			10		1	11		6	4		7									13
1		3		*5*		2	8	9	12		10			11		6	4		7	14								14
1		3				7	8	9	12		10			11		6	5		2	4								15
1		3				11	8	9	12	2	10					6	5		7	4								16
1		3					8		9	2					11	6	5		7	4	10							17
1			4			12	8	14	9	2		3			*11*	6	5		7		10							18
1						7	8	9	12	2	10	3	14				5		4			6	11					19
		14				7	8		*9*	2	10	3	1		12		5		4	11		6						20
		14				7	8		9	2	10	*3*	1		12		5		4	11		6						21
		3				7	8		12	2	10		1		9		5		4	11		6						22
		3	7				8		9	2	10		1		12		5		4			6		11				23
		3	7				8	12	9	2	10		1				5		4			6		11				24
		3					8		9	2	10		1				5		4	7		6		11				25
		3					8	12	9	2	10		1				5		4	*7*		6		11				26
		3	7				8	9	12	2	10		1				5		4			6		11				27
		3	7				8	9	12	2	10		1				5		4	14		*6*		11				28
		3	7				8	9	12	2	10		1				5		4					11	6			29
		3	7				8	9	10	2			1				5		4		12			11	6			30
		3	7				8	9	10	2			1				5		4	11	12				6			31
		3	7				8	9	10	2			1				5		4					11	6			32
		3	7			14	8	9	10	2	12		1				5		*4*					11	6			33
		3	7	6			8	9	12	2	10		1				5		4					11				34
		3	7	6		14	*8*	9	11	2	10		1				5		4					12				35
		3	7	6		8		9		2	10		1				5		4		11		12					36
		3		6		7	8	9	11	2	10		1						4		12					5		37
		3		6		7	8	9	11	2	10		1						4					12		5		38
		3		6		7	*8*	9	11	2	10		1				14		4		12					5		39
			8	6		7		9	11				1						4		10		3	12		5	2	40
			8	6		7		9	11		10		1						4				3			5	2	41
		3	8	6		7		9	11		10		1						4							5	2	42
		3	8	6		7		9	11		10		1						4							5	2	43
		3	8	6		7		9	11		10		1						4							5	2	44
		3	8	6		7		9	11	12	10		1						4							5	2	45
		3	8	6		7		9	11	12	10		1						4							5	2	46

Coca-Cola Cup	First Round	Wigan Ath (a)	1-0
		(h)	4-2
	Second Round	Portsmouth (h)	0-0
		(a)	0-5
FA Cup	First Round	Stockport Co (h)	1-2

ROTHERHAM UNITED

Player and Position	Ht	Wt	Birth Date	Birth Place	Source	Clubs	League App	League Gls
Goalkeepers								
Matthew Clarke	6 3	11 07	3 11 73	Sheffield	Trainee	Rotherham U	39	—
William Mercer	6 1	13 05	22 5 69	Liverpool	Trainee	Liverpool	—	—
						Rotherham U	103	—
Defenders								
Ian Breckin	6 1	12 09	24 2 75	Rotherham	Trainee	Rotherham U	10	—
Tony Brien	5 11	11 09	10 2 69	Dublin	Apprentice	Leicester C	16	1
						Chesterfield	204	8
						Rotherham U	26	2
Len Curtis‡	5 11	13 00	2 1 73	Dublin	Leeds U	Rotherham U	—	—
Paul Hurst	5 7	10 04	25 9 74	Sheffield	Trainee	Rotherham U	4	—
Chris Hutchings*	5 10	11 06	5 7 57	Winchester	Harrow Bor	Chelsea	87	3
						Brighton	153	4
						Huddersfield T	110	10
						Walsall	40	—
						Rotherham U	78	4
Wayne Jacobs	5 9	10 02	3 2 69	Sheffield	Apprentice	Sheffield W	6	—
						Hull C	129	4
						Rotherham U	42	2
Nigel Johnson*	6 2	13 13	23 6 64	Rotherham	Apprentice	Rotherham U	89	1
						Nottingham F (loan)	—	—
						Manchester C	4	—
						Rotherham U	175	9
Neil Richardson	5 11	13 02	3 3 68	Sunderland	Brandon U	Rotherham U	77	4
Billy Russell*	5 10	11 03	14 9 59	Glasgow	Apprentice	Everton	—	—
					Celtic	Doncaster R	244	15
						Scunthorpe U	117	7
						Rotherham U	104	2
Scott Smith	5 8	11 06	6 3 75	Christchurch	Trainee	Rotherham U	7	—
Chris Wilder	5 11	11 02	23 9 67	Wortley	Apprentice	Southampton	—	—
						Sheffield U	93	1
						Walsall (loan)	4	—
						Charlton Ath (loan)	1	—
						Charlton Ath (loan)	2	—
						Leyton Orient (loan)	16	1
						Rotherham U	69	10
Midfield								
Ian Banks	5 10	13 05	9 1 61	Mexborough	Apprentice	Barnsley	164	37
						Leicester C	93	14
						Huddersfield T	78	17
						Bradford C	30	3
						WBA	4	—
						Barnsley	96	7
						Rotherham U	76	8
Shaun Goodwin	5 8	10 11	14 6 69	Rotherham	Trainee	Rotherham U	223	27
Des Hazel	5 11	10 13	15 7 67	Bradford	Apprentice	Sheffield W	6	—
						Grimsby T (loan)	9	2
						Rotherham U	217	29
Karl Marginson	6 0	11 00	11 11 70	Manchester		Rotherham U	7	—
Glyn Roberts	5 11	12 02	19 10 74	Ipswich	Norwich C	Rotherham U	14	1
Mark Todd	5 8	10 04	4 12 67	Belfast	Trainee	Manchester U	—	—
						Sheffield U	70	5
						Wolverhampton W (loan)	7	—
						Rotherham U	50	7
Andy Williams	6 0	11 09	29 7 62	Birmingham	Solihull B	Coventry C	9	—
						Rotherham U	87	13
						Leeds U	46	3
						Port Vale (loan)	5	—
						Notts Co	39	2
						Huddersfield T (loan)	6	—
						Rotherham U	34	2

ROTHERHAM UNITED

Colours: Red and white. **Change colours:** Yellow and black.

Foundation: This club traces its history back to the formation of Thornhill United in 1878 (reformed 1884). They changed their name to Rotherham County in 1905. Confusion exists because of the existence of the Rotherham Town club (founded c. 1885) and in the Football League as early as 1893 but this club was not the one previously mentioned. The Town amalgamated with Rotherham County to form Rotherham United in 1925.

First Football League game: 2 September, 1893, Division 2, Rotherham T v Lincoln C (a) D 1-1 – McKay; Thickett, Watson; Barr, Brown, Broadhead; Longden, Cutts, Leatherbarrow, McCormick, Pickering. 1 o.g. 30 August, 1919, Division 2, Rotherham C v Nottingham F (h) W 2-0 – Branston; Alton, Baines; Bailey, Coe, Stanton; Lee (1), Cawley (1), Glennon, Lees, Lamb.

Did you know: On 23 October 1993 at Brighton, Billy Mercer was unable to play in goal having been taken ill overnight. His deputy Matthew Clarke was sent off for handling the ball outside his area, but Rotherham won 2-0.

Managers (and Secretary-Managers)
Billy Heald 1925–29 (secretary only for long spell), Stanley Davies 1929–30, Billy Heald 1930–33, Reg Freeman 1934–52, Andy Smailes 1952–58, Tom Johnston 1958–62, Danny Williams 1962–65, Jack Mansell 1965–67, Tommy Docherty 1967–68, Jimmy McAnearney 1968–73, Jimmy McGuigan 1973–79, Ian Porterfield 1979–81, Emlyn Hughes 1981–83, George Kerr 1983–85, Norman Hunter 1985–87, Dave Cusack 1987–88, Billy McEwan 1988–91, Phil Henson January 1991–

Player and Position	*Ht*	*Wt*	*Birth Date*	*Birth Place*	*Source*	*Clubs*	*League App*	*League Gls*
Forwards								
John Buckley‡	5 9	11 00	10 5 62	Glasgow	Celtic	Partick T	45	5
						Doncaster R	84	11
						Leeds U	10	1
						Leicester C (loan)	5	—
						Doncaster R (loan)	6	—
						Rotherham U	105	13
						Partick Th	26	5
						Scunthorpe U	43	8
						Rotherham U	4	—
Chris Dolby	5 8	9 12	4 9 74	Dewsbury	Trainee	Rotherham U	1	—
Shaun Goater	6 1	12 00	25 2 70	Bermuda		Manchester U	—	—
						Rotherham U	120	33
						Notts Co (loan)	1	—
Ian Helliwell	6 3	14 02	7 11 62	Rotherham	Matlock T	York C	160	40
						Scunthorpe U	80	22
						Rotherham U	40	3
Jonathan Howard	6 0	12 02	7 10 71	Sheffield	Trainee	Rotherham U	36	5
Andrew Kiwomya*	5 9	10 10	1 10 67	Huddersfield		Barnsley	1	—
						Sheffield W	—	—
					Retired injury	Dundee	21	1
						Rotherham U	7	—
Imre Varadi	5 10	12 00	8 7 59	Paddington	Letchworth GC	Sheffield U	10	4
						Everton	26	6
						Newcastle U	81	39
						Sheffield W	76	33
						WBA	32	9
						Manchester C	65	26
						Sheffield W	22	3
						Leeds U	26	5
						Luton T (loan)	6	1
						Oxford U (loan)	5	—
						Rotherham U	50	23

Trainees
Ayrton, Matthew R; Barnard, Mark; Boucken, Kriss; Colley, Chad; Duffty, Gary H; Fitzpatrick, David; Green, Paul W; Handbury, Lee A; Haran, Mark P; Hilton, Christopher; Hoe, Michael J; Hogg, Stuart S; Thomas, Steven M; Viljoen, Nik; Wake, Ryan; Wilkinson, Damian D; Wood, Marcus.

Associated Schoolboys
Bagshaw, Neil D; Darby, Richard; Dart, Luke S; Garlick, Christopher J; Garlick, Richard P; Gordon, James D; Green, Matthew E; Hunt, Liam D; Levers, Roger; McKenzie, Robert A; Mill, Christopher; Parkin, Philip D; Partridge, Paul G; Roberts, Martin J; Safhill, Steffan P. D; Shultz, Daniel P; Smith, Jamie M; Smith, Peter J; Sutcliffe, Wayne C.

SCARBOROUGH 1993–94 *Back row (left to right):* Hughie Carroll (Team Assistant), Mark Calvert, Stuart Young, Jason Rockett, Paul Robinson, Geoffrey Horsfield, Damian Henderson, Adie Meyer, Dr Andrew Davidson.

Centre row: Stephen Swales, Andrew Mockler, Simon Thompson, Steve Charles, Phil Chambers (Assistant Manager), Darren Foreman, John Ashdjian, Darren Knowles.

Front row: Lee Harper, Paul Cawthorn, Andrew Hudson.

Division 3 SCARBOROUGH

The McCain Stadium, Seamer Road, Scarborough YO12 4HF.

Telephone (0723) 375094. Fax (0723) 378733.

Ground capacity: 6899.

Record Attendance: 11,130 v Luton T, FA Cup 3rd rd, 8 January 1938. Football League: 7314 v Wolverhampton W, Division 4, 15 August 1987.

Record receipts: £37,609.50 v Arsenal, Coca-Cola Cup 4th rd, 6 January 1993.

Pitch measurements: 120yd × 75yd.

President and Chief Executive: John Birley.

Chairman: J. Russell.

Directors: Mrs G. Russell.

Manager: Steve Wicks. ***Assistant Manager:*** Phil Chambers.

Secretary: Eric J. Hall.

Commercial Manager: T. Jasper. ***Physio:*** K. Warner.

Year Formed: 1879. ***Turned Professional:*** 1926. ***Ltd Co.:*** 1933.

Club Nickname: 'The Boro'.

Previous Grounds: 1879–87, Scarborough Cricket Ground; 1887–98, Recreation Ground; 1898– Athletic Ground.

Record League Victory: 4–0 v Bolton W, Division 4, 29 August 1987 – Blackwell; McJannet, Thompson, Bennyworth (Walker), Richards (1) (Cook), Kendall, Hamill (1), Moss, McHale, Mell (1), Graham. (1 og). 4–0 v Newport Co (away), Division 4, 12 April 1988 – Ironside; McJannet, Thompson, Kamara, Richards (1), Short (1), Adams (Cook 1), Brook, Outhart (1), Russell, Graham.

Record Cup Victory: 6–0 v Rhyl Ath, FA Cup, 1st rd, 29 November 1930 – Turner; Severn, Belton; Maskell, Robinson, Wallis; Small (1), Rand (2), Palfreman (2), A. D. Hill (1), Mickman.

Record Defeat: 1–16 v Southbank, Northern League, 15 November 1919.

Most League Points (3 for a win): 77, Division 4, 1988–89.

Most League Goals: 69, Division 4, 1990–91.

Highest League Scorer in Season: Darren Foreman, 27, Division 4, 1992–93.

Most League Goals in Total Aggregate: Darren Foreman, 34, 1991–94.

Most Capped Player: None.

Most League Appearances: Steve Richards, 119, 1987–90.

Record Transfer Fee Received: £240,000 from Notts Co for Chris Short, September 1990.

Record Transfer Fee Paid: £102,000 to Leicester C for Martin Russell, March 1989.

Football League Record: Promoted to Division 4 1987; 1992– Division 3.

Honours: *Football League:* Division 4 best season: 5th, 1988–89. *FA Cup:* best seasons: 3rd rd, 1931, 1938, 1976, 1978. *Football League Cup:* best season: 4th rd 1993. *FA Trophy:* Winners 1973, 1976, 1977. *GM Vauxhall Conference:* Winners 1987.

SCARBOROUGH 1993—94 LEAGUE RECORD

Match No.	Date	Venue	Opponents	Result		H/T Score	Lg. Pos.	Goalscorers	Attendance
1	Aug 14	A	Hereford U	W	1-0	1-0	—	Young	2157
2	21	H	Preston NE	L	3-4	1-2	8	Young, Knowles, Charles (pen)	2329
3	28	A	Gillingham	D	2-2	1-1	11	Henderson, Young	2526
4	31	A	Darlington	W	2-0	1-0	—	Young, Henderson	1910
5	Sept 4	H	Carlisle U	L	0-3	0-2	9		2044
6	11	A	Wigan Ath	W	2-1	1-0	8	Henderson, Calvert	1682
7	18	H	Chester C	L	0-1	0-0	11		1510
8	25	H	Shrewsbury T	L	1-3	1-2	12	Thompson	1137
9	Oct 2	A	Scunthorpe U	D	1-1	1-1	13	Calvert	2910
10	9	A	Mansfield T	L	2-4	0-1	14	Henderson, Young	2589
11	16	H	Crewe Alex	L	1-2	1-0	18	Charles	1551
12	23	A	Walsall	L	0-1	0-0	20		3941
13	30	H	Bury	W	1-0	1-0	19	Young	1879
14	Nov 2	A	Wycombe W	L	0-4	0-4	—		3975
15	6	H	Doncaster R	W	2-0	1-0	18	Henderson, Young	2057
16	20	A	Chesterfield	L	0-1	0-0	18		2110
17	27	H	Torquay U	L	1-2	0-1	18	Murray	1460
18	Dec 11	A	Preston NE	D	2-2	2-0	18	White, Whitington	6290
19	18	H	Hereford U	L	0-1	0-1	19		1209
20	28	H	Colchester U	L	0-2	0-0	20		1226
21	Jan 1	A	Lincoln C	W	1-0	1-0	18	White	3812
22	3	H	Darlington	W	3-0	1-0	18	Whitington 2, White	1793
23	8	H	Northampton T	W	2-1	1-1	16	Toman, Whitington	1703
24	15	A	Crewe Alex	D	1-1	1-1	15	White	3594
25	22	H	Mansfield T	D	1-1	0-0	16	White	1557
26	29	A	Bury	W	2-0	0-0	14	Whitington, Meyer	3040
27	Feb 5	H	Walsall	W	1-0	1-0	13	Davis	1851
28	12	A	Northampton T	L	2-3	2-1	13	Whitington, Murray	2974
29	19	H	Gillingham	D	1-1	0-0	15	Cawthorn	1527
30	25	A	Carlisle U	L	0-2	0-1	15		4270
31	Mar 1	A	Rochdale	L	1-2	0-1	—	Young	1827
32	5	H	Wigan Ath	W	4-1	1-1	12	Charles (pen), White, Whitington 2	1390
33	12	A	Chester C	L	1-4	1-3	13	White	2882
34	19	A	Shrewsbury T	L	0-2	0-1	16		3901
35	26	H	Scunthorpe U	L	0-1	0-0	18		1571
36	Apr 2	H	Rochdale	W	2-1	0-0	17	White, Charles	1448
37	4	A	Colchester U	W	2-1	2-0	14	Thompson, Young	2501
38	9	H	Lincoln C	D	2-2	0-2	14	White, Murray	1314
39	16	H	Wycombe W	W	3-1	2-0	14	Charles, Whitington, Murray	2090
40	23	A	Doncaster R	W	4-0	2-0	13	Murray, Whitington, Charles, Calvert	1854
41	30	H	Chesterfield	D	1-1	0-1	13	Charles (pen)	2631
42	May 7	A	Torquay U	L	0-2	0-2	14		3470

Final League Position: 14

GOALSCORERS

League (55): Whitington 10, White 9, Young 9, Charles 7 (3 pens), Henderson 5, Murray 5, Calvert 3, Thompson 2, Cawthorn 1, Davis 1, Knowles 1, Meyer 1, Toman 1.
Coca-Cola Cup (0):
FA Cup (1): Young 1.

Evans 26	Thompson 29 + 3	Davis 24 + 1	Mockler 6	Meyer 36	Rockett 33 + 1	Charles 37	Knowles 42	Henderson 17	Calvert 42	Young 21 + 7	Ashdjian 2 + 5	Robinson 3 + 1	Swales 24 + 2	Cawthorn 6 + 2	Horsfield 6	Harper — + 2	Burridge 3	Murray 29	Whitington 26 + 1	Oakes 1	White 24	Toman 12 + 1	Dineen 1 + 1	Sheppard 9	Maguire 2	McHugh 1 + 2	Foreman — + 3	Hawke — + 1	*Match No.*
1	2	3	4	5	6	7	8	9	10	11	12																		1
1	2	3	4	5	6	7	8	9	10	11	12																		2
	2	3	4	5	6	7	8	9	10	11		1	12																3
	2	3	4	5	6	7	8	9	10	11		1	12																4
	2	3	4	5	6	7	8	9	10	11	12	1																	5
1	2	3	4	5	6	7	8	9	10	11	12																		6
1	2	3		5	6	7	8	9	10	11	4			12															7
1	8	3		5	6	7	4	9	10	11			2	12															8
1		*6*		5		7	2	9	4	11	12		3	8	10	14													9
1		6		5		7	2	9	4	11			3	8	10	12													10
1		6		5	12	7	2	9	4	11			3	8	10														11
1				5	6	7	2	9	4	11	8		3		10														12
		5			6	7	2	9	4	11			3	8	10		1												13
		5			6	7	2	9	4	11			3		10		1	8											14
	10	5			6	7	2	9	4	11			3				1	8											15
1	10	5			6	7	2	9	4	11			3					8	12										16
	11	14		5	*6*	7	2	9	4	12			3					8	10	1									17
1		5			6	7	2		4				3					8	10		9	11							18
1		5			6	7	2		4				3					8	10		9	11						12	19
1	14	5		6		7	2		4	12			3					8	10		9	*11*							20
1	7			5	6		2		4				3					8	10		9	11							21
1	7			5	6		2		4				3					8	10		9	11							22
1	7			5	6		2		4				3					8	10		9	11							23
1	7			5	6		2		4				3					8	10		9	11							24
1	7			5	6		2		4			12	3					8	10		9	11							25
1	7	6		5		3	2		4									8	10		9	11							26
1		6		5		3	2		4									8	10		9	11	7						27
1	7	6		5		3	2		4									8	10		9	11	12						28
1				5	6	11	2		4				3	7				8	10		9								29
1	14			5	6	11	2		4	12			3	*7*				8	10			9							30
1	7			5	6	11	2		4	12			3					8	10		9								31
1	7			5	6	11	2		4				3					8	10		9								32
1	7			5	6	11	2		4				3					8	10		9	12							33
	7	6		5		11	2		4				3					8	10		9			1					34
	12	6		*5*		3	2		4	14								8	10		9			1	7	11			35
	7			5	6	3	2		4	12								8	10		9			1	11				36
	3	11		5	6	7	2		4	12								8	10		9			1					37
	3			5	6	7	2		4	11								8	10		9			1					38
	3			5	6	7	2		4	11								8	10		9			1					39
	3			5	6	7	2		4	11								8	*10*		9			1		12	14		40
	3			5	6	7	2		4	11								8	10		9			1		12	14		41
	3			5	6	7	2		4	11								8	10		9			1			12		42

Coca-Cola Cup	First Round	Huddersfield T (a)	0-0
		(h)	0-3
FA Cup	First Round	Bury (h)	1-0
	Second Round	Wigan Ath (a)	0-1

SCARBOROUGH

Player and Position	Ht	Wt	Birth Date	Birth Place	Source	Clubs	League App	League Gls
Goalkeepers								
Mark Evans	6 0	11 08	24 8 70	Leeds	Trainee	Bradford C	12	—
						Scarborough	46	—
Paul Robinson*			2 1 74	Scarborough	Trainee	Sheffield W	—	—
						Scarborough	4	—
Defenders								
Darren Davis	6 0	11 00	5 2 67	Sutton-in-Ashfield	Apprentice	Notts Co	92	1
						Lincoln C	102	4
						Maidstone U	31	2
					Frickley Ath	Scarborough	25	1
Craig Gaunt	5 11	12 02	31 3 73	Nottingham	Trainee	Arsenal	—	—
						Huddersfield T	—	—
						Chesterfield	—	—
						Scarborough	—	—
Lee Harper	5 11	12 05	24 3 75	Bridlington	York C	Scarborough	2	—
Owen McGee	5 5	10 08	29 4 70	Teesside	Trainee	Middlesbrough	21	1
						Scarborough	24	—
Adrian Meyer	6 0	14 00	22 9 70	Bristol	Trainee	Scarborough	101	9
Steve Swales	5 8	10 00	26 12 73	Whitby	Trainee	Scarborough	33	—
Simon Thompson	5 9	10 06	27 2 70	Sheffield	Trainee	Rotherham U	28	—
						Scarborough	92	5
Midfield								
Paul Cawthorn‡	5 6	10 00	26 5 75	Pontefract	Trainee	Scarborough	11	1
Steve Charles	5 9	10 07	10 5 60	Sheffield	Sheffield Univ	Sheffield U	123	10
						Wrexham	113	37
						Mansfield T	237	39
						Scunthorpe U (loan)	4	—
						Scarborough	53	10
Jack Dineen	5 7	10 10	29 9 70	Brighton	Torsby	Scarborough	2	—
Martin Gill			7 9 73	Sunderland	Hartlepool U	Scarborough	—	—
Warren Hawke	5 10	10 11	20 9 70	Durham	Trainee	Sunderland	25	1
December 1993						Chesterfield (loan)	7	1
						Carlisle U (loan)	8	2
						Northampton T (loan)	7	1
						Raith R	2	—
						Scarborough	1	—
Geoff Horsfield‡	5 10	10 07	1 11 73	Barnsley		Scarborough	12	1
Darren Knowles	5 6	10 01	8 10 70	Sheffield	Trainee	Sheffield U	—	—
						Stockport Co	63	—
						Scarborough	42	1
Andrew Mockler‡	5 11	11 13	18 11 70	Stockton	Trainee	Arsenal	—	—
						Scarborough	74	10
Jason Rockett	5 11	12 00	26 9 69	London		Rotherham U	—	—
						Scarborough	34	—
Andy Toman	5 10	11 07	7 3 62	Northallerton	Bishop Auckland	Lincoln C	24	4
						Hartlepool U	112	28
						Darlington	115	10
						Scarborough (loan)	6	—
						Scunthorpe U	15	5
						Scarborough	13	1
Forwards								
John Ashdjian‡	5 10	10 07	13 9 72	Hackney	Northampton T	Scarborough	67	14
Mark Calvert	5 9	11 05	11 9 70	Consett	Trainee	Hull C	30	1
						Scarborough	42	3
Darren Foreman	5 10	10 08	12 2 68	Southampton		Barnsley	47	8
						Crewe Alex	23	4
						Scarborough	83	34
Michael McHugh	5 11	11 00	3 4 71	Donegal		Bradford C	31	4
						Scarborough	3	—

SCARBOROUGH

Colours: Red and white. **Change colours:** Yellow and black.

Foundation: Scarborough came into being as early as 1879 when they were formed by members of the town's cricket club and went under the name of Scarborough Cricketers' FC with home games played on the North Marine Road Cricket Ground.

First Football League game: 15 August, 1987, Division 4, v Wolverhampton W (h) D 2-2 – Blackwell; McJannet, Thompson, Bennyworth, Richards, Kendall, Hamill, Moss, McHale (1), Mell (1), Graham.

Did you know: On 30 October 1993 Scarborough beat Bury 1-0 at home in a League game. On 13 November they repeated the score against the same team in a first round FA Cup tie and again Stuart Young was the scorer.

Managers (and Secretary-Managers)
B. Chapman 1945–47*, George Hall 1946–47, Harold Taylor 1947–48, Frank Taylor 1948–50, A. C. Bell (Director & Hon. TM) 1950–53, Reg Halton 1953–54, Charles Robson (Hon. TM) 1954–57, George Higgins 1957–58, Andy Smailes 1959–61, Eddie Brown 1961–64, Albert Franks 1964–65, Stuart Myers 1965–66, Graham Shaw 1968–69, Colin Appleton 1969–73, Ken Houghton 1974–75, Colin Appleton 1975–81, Jimmy McAnearney 1981–82, John Cottam 1982–84, Harry Dunn 1984–86, Neil Warnock 1986–88, Colin Morris 1989, Ray McHale 1989–93, Phil Chambers 1993, Steve Wicks October 1993–

Player and Position	*Ht*	*Wt*	*Birth Date*	*Place*	*Source*	*Clubs*	*League App*	*Gls*
Shaun Murray	5 8	11 02	7 2 70	Newcastle	Trainee	Tottenham H	—	—
						Portsmouth	34	1
						Millwall (loan)	—	—
						Scarborough	29	5
Jason White	6 0	12 10	19 10 71	Meriden	Derby Co	Scunthorpe U	68	16
						Darlington (loan)	4	1
						Scarborough	24	9
Craig Whitington	5 11	12 04	3 9 70	Brighton	Crawley T	Scarborough	27	10
Stuart Young	5 11	12 00	16 12 72	Hull	Arsenal	Hull C	19	2
						Northampton T	8	2
						Scarborough	28	9

Trainees
Hudson, Andrew.

****Non-Contract**
Willgrass, Alexandre P.
**Non-Contract Players who are retained must be re-signed before they are eligible to play in League matches.

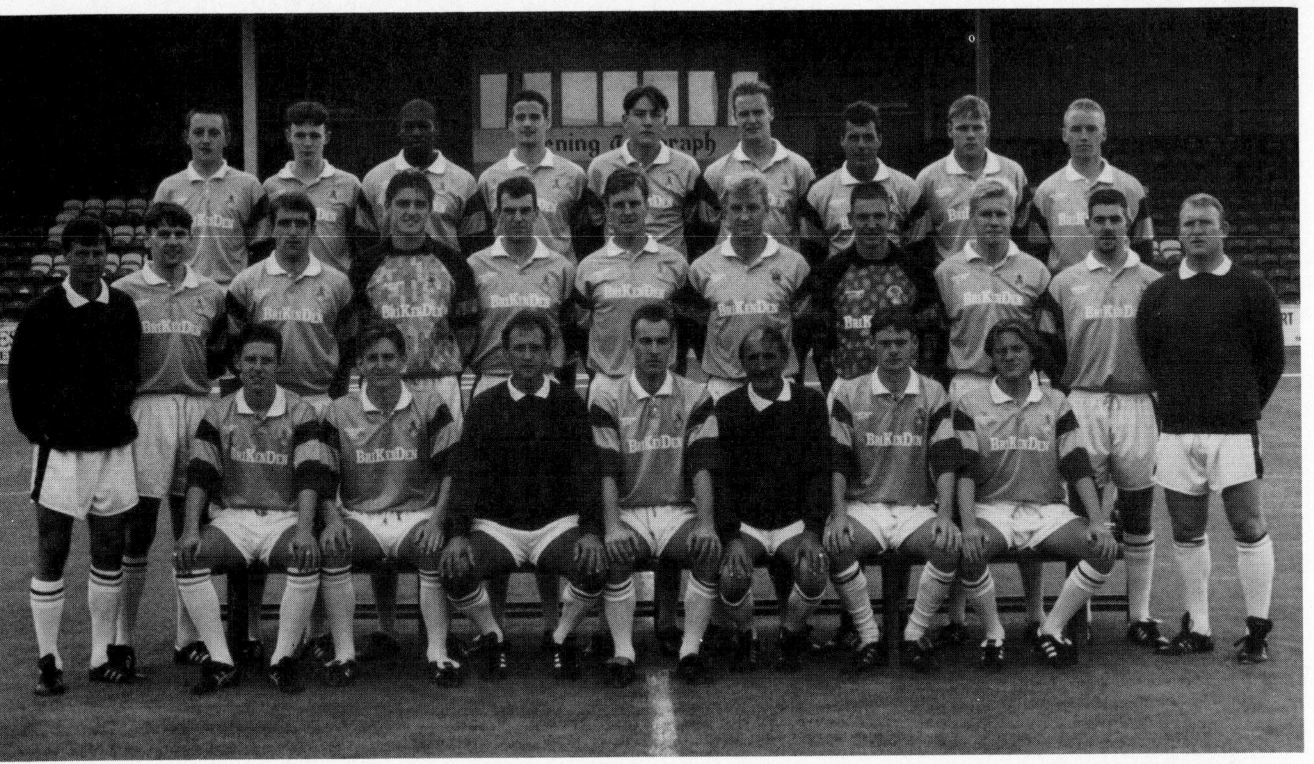

SCUNTHORPE UNITED 1993–94 *Back row (left to right):* James McNeil, Tim Ryan, Jason White, Chris Hope, Paul Ellender, Ian Thompstone, Mark Smith, Gary Nixon, Steve Thornber.
Centre row: Ian Whyte (Youth Development Officer), David Foy, Matt Carmichael, Richard Wilmot, Neil Trebble, Ian Helliwell, Matthew Elliott, Mark Samways, Russell Bradley, Steven Brown, David Moore (Physio).
Front row: John Watson, Paul Mudd, Richard Money (Manager), Dean Martin, Colin Morris (Chief Coach), Graham Alexander, Sammy Goodacre.

Division 3 — SCUNTHORPE UNITED

Glanford Park, Scunthorpe, South Humberside DN15 8TD. Telephone Scunthorpe (0724) 848077. Fax (0724) 857986.

Ground capacity: 9183.

Record attendance: Old Showground: 23,935 v Portsmouth, FA Cup 4th rd, 30 January 1954. Glanford Park: 8775 v Rotherham U, Division 4, 1 May 1989.

Record receipts: £44,481.50 v Leeds U, Rumbelows Cup 2nd rd lst leg, 24 September 1991.

Pitch measurements: 110yd × 71yd.

Vice-presidents: I. T. Botham, G. Johnson, A. Harvey, G. J. Alston, R. Ashman.

Chairman: K. Wagstaff.

Vice-chairman: R. Garton.

Directors: J. B. Borrill, C. Plumtree, S. Wharton, B. Collen.

Team Manager: David Moore.

Chief Executive/Secretary: A. D. Rowing. ***Commercial Manager:*** A. D. Rowing.

Year Formed:1899. ***Turned Professional:*** 1912. ***Ltd Co.:*** 1912.

Club Nickname: 'The Iron'.

Previous Names: Amalgamated with Brumby Hall: North Lindsey United to become Scunthorpe & Lindsey United, 1910; dropped '& Lindsey' in 1958.

Previous ground: Old Showground to 1988.

Record League Victory: 8–1 v Luton T, Division 3, 24 April 1965 – Sidebottom; Horstead, Hemstead; Smith, Neale, Lindsey; Bramley (1), Scott, Thomas (5), Mahy (1), Wilson (1).

Record Cup Victory: 9–0 v Boston U, FA Cup, 1st rd, 21 November 1953 – Malan; Hubbard, Brownsword; Sharpe, White, Bushby; Mosby (1), Haigh (3), Whitfield (2), Gregory (1), Mervyn Jones (2).

Record Defeat: 0–8 v Carlisle U, Division 3 (N), 25 December 1952.

Most League Points (2 for a win): 66, Division 3 (N), 1956–57, 1957–58.

Most League Points (3 for a win): 83, Division 4, 1982–83.

Most League Goals: 88, Division 3 (N), 1957–58.

Highest League Scorer in Season: Barrie Thomas, 31, Division 2, 1961–62.

Chairman: B. E. Fearn. ***Vice-chairman:*** L. V. Pickering.
Most League Goals in Total Aggregate: Steve Cammack, 110, 1979–81, 1981–86.

Most Capped Player: None.

Most League Appearances: Jack Brownsword, 595, 1950–65.

Record Transfer Fee Received: £350,000 from Aston Villa for Neil Cox, February 1991.

Record Transfer Fee Paid: £80,000 to York City for Ian Helliwell, August 1991.

Football League Record: 1950 Elected to Division 3 (N); 1958–64 Division 2; 1964–68 Division 3; 1968–72 Division 4; 1972–73 Division 3; 1973–83 Division 4; 1983–84 Division 3; 1984–92 Division 4; 1992– Division 3.

Honours: *Football League:* Division 2 best season: 4th, 1961–62; Division 3 (N) – Champions 1957–58. *FA Cup:* best season: 5th rd, 1957–58, 1969–70. *Football League Cup:* never past 3rd rd.

SCUNTHORPE UNITED 1993—94 LEAGUE RECORD

Match No.	Date	Venue	Opponents	Result		H/T Score	Lg. Pos.	Goalscorers	Attendance
1	Aug 14	A	Wigan Ath	W	2-0	0-0	—	Mudd, Smith	2353
2	21	H	Bury	D	1-1	0-0	4	Thompstone	3375
3	28	A	Mansfield T	W	1-0	1-0	3	Toman	2751
4	31	A	Walsall	D	0-0	0-0	—		2519
5	Sept 4	H	Hereford U	L	1-2	0-1	8	Thompstone	3091
6	11	A	Chester C	W	2-0	1-0	5	Toman, Juryeff	2195
7	18	H	Carlisle U	W	2-1	1-1	4	Carmichael 2	3361
8	25	A	Gillingham	L	0-1	0-1	7		2872
9	Oct 2	H	Scarborough	D	1-1	1-1	5	Thompstone	2910
10	9	A	Colchester U	L	1-2	1-1	10	Carmichael	3405
11	16	H	Northampton T	W	7-0	4-0	5	Carmichael 3, Thompstone, Smith, Toman, Elliott	2184
12	23	A	Torquay U	D	1-1	1-0	7	Toman	3241
13	30	H	Darlington	W	3-0	1-0	3	Carmichael (pen), Alexander, Trebble	3025
14	Nov 1	A	Doncaster R	L	1-3	0-1	—	Trebble	4439
15	6	H	Wycombe W	D	0-0	0-0	6		3604
16	20	A	Shrewsbury T	D	0-0	0-0	8		2436
17	27	H	Rochdale	W	2-1	0-0	6	Toman, Thompstone	3106
18	Dec 11	A	Bury	L	0-1	0-1	9		2389
19	18	H	Wigan Ath	W	1-0	0-0	7	Carmichael	2873
20	27	A	Lincoln C	L	0-2	0-1	8		6030
21	28	H	Chesterfield	D	2-2	1-2	8	Carmichael (pen), Mudd	3266
22	Jan 1	A	Preston NE	D	2-2	0-0	8	Knill, Carmichael	7669
23	3	H	Walsall	W	5-0	0-0	7	Martin, Smith, Bullimore, Carmichael, Henderson	3417
24	22	H	Colchester U	D	1-1	0-0	9	Carmichael	2854
25	29	A	Darlington	L	1-2	0-1	10	Carmichael	2142
26	Feb 5	H	Torquay U	L	1-3	1-1	10	Carmichael	2755
27	12	A	Crewe Alex	D	3-3	2-2	11	Martin, Carmichael, Danzey	3507
28	19	H	Mansfield T	L	2-3	0-0	12	Carmichael 2	3089
29	Mar 5	H	Chester C	D	1-1	0-1	14	Mudd	2669
30	8	A	Northampton T	L	0-4	0-1	—		3192
31	12	A	Carlisle U	L	1-3	0-0	14	Goodacre	4076
32	15	H	Crewe Alex	W	2-1	2-1	—	Alexander, Thornber	2122
33	19	H	Gillingham	D	1-1	0-1	13	Juryeff	2386
34	26	A	Scarborough	W	1-0	0-0	11	Smith	1571
35	29	A	Hereford U	W	2-1	2-0	—	Carmichael, Juryeff	1707
36	Apr 2	H	Lincoln C	W	2-0	1-0	9	Alexander, Goodacre	3571
37	4	A	Chesterfield	D	1-1	1-1	9	Alexander	3629
38	9	H	Preston NE	W	3-1	1-1	9	Smith, Bradley, Bullimore	3790
39	16	H	Doncaster R	L	1-3	0-1	9	Goodacre	4151
40	23	A	Wycombe W	D	2-2	0-0	10	Smith, Bullimore (pen)	5755
41	30	H	Shrewsbury T	L	1-4	0-1	11	Juryeff	4587
42	May 7	A	Rochdale	W	3-2	2-2	11	Thornber, Juryeff, Lancaster (og)	3118

Final League Position: 11

GOALSCORERS

League (64): Carmichael 18 (2 pens), Smith 6, Juryeff 5, Thompstone 5, Toman 5, Alexander 4, Bullimore 3 (1 pen), Goodacre 3, Mudd 3, Martin 2, Thornber 2, Trebble 2, Bradley 1, Danzey 1, Elliott 1, Henderson 1, Knill 1, own goal 1.
Coca-Cola Cup (1): Martin 1.
FA Cup (4): Goodacre 2, Carmichael 1, Toman 1.

Samways 41	Alexander 40 + 1	Mudd 31 + 2	Carmichael 42	Elliott 14	Bradley 34	Thompstone 29 + 1	Martin 26	Trebble 8 + 6	Thornber 21 + 3	Smith 26 + 4	Goodacre 10 + 8	Hope 37 + 4	Juryeff 20 + 3	Toman 15	Watson 1 + 4	White 2 + 7	Knill 25	Henderson 15 + 5	Sansam 4 + 6	Bullimore 17 + 1	Danzey 3	Ryan — + 1	Heath 1 + 1	Match No.
1	2	3	4	5	6	7	8	*9*	10	11	12	14												1
1	14	3	*2*	5		7	4	12		11	8	6	9	10										2
1	2	3	4	5		7	8			11	12	6	9	10										3
1	2	3	4	5		7	8	12	11			6	9	10										4
1	2	3	4	5		7	8	12	14	*11*		6	9	10										5
1	2	3	11	5	6	7	8	12				4	9	10										6
1	2	*3*	11	5	6	7	8			12		4	9	10	14									7
1	2	3	11	5	6	*7*	8	14	10	12		4				9								8
1	2	3	4	5	6	7	8	10				12		11		9								9
1	2	3	9	5	6	7	8	14		11		4		*10*		12								10
1	2	3	9	5	6	7	*8*			11		4	14	10		12								11
1	2	3	9	5	6	*7*	8	11				4		10	14	12								12
1	2	3	9	5	6	*7*		11	8			4		10	14	12								13
1	2	3	9	5	6	7		11	*8*			4		10	14	12								14
1	2	3	9		6	7			8	14		4		10	*11*	12	5							15
1	2	3	9		6	7	8			11	12	4		10			5							16
1	2	3	9		6	7	8			11	*12*	4		10		14	5							17
1	2	3	9		6	7	8			11		4					5	10						18
1	2	3	9		6		8		*11*		14	4	12				5	10	7					19
1	2	3	9		6		8		10	7		4	11				5	12						20
1	2	3	9		6		8					4	12				5	11	7	10				21
1	2	14	9		6		8	3				4	10				5	11	*7*	12				22
1		12	9		6		8	*7*		11		4	3				5	10	14	2				23
1	2	3	9		6	7				11		4					5	8	12	10				24
1	2	3	9		6	7	8					4					5	11		10				25
1	2	3	9		6		8					4					5	11	12	10	7			26
1	2	3	9		6		8		12	11		4					5	7			10			27
1	2	3	9		6	12	8		14	11		4					5	7			*10*			28
1	2	3	9		*6*	7	8	11	10	14	12	4					5							29
1	2	3	9			7	8			11		4					5	10	6					30
1	2	3	6						10	11	*7*	4	9				5	12	14	8				31
1	2	3	6						10	11	7	4	*9*				5	12	14	8				32
1	2	3	6						10	11	7	4	9				*5*	12	14	8				33
1	2		6		5	3			10	11	7	4	9							8				34
1	2		6		5	3			10	11	7	4	9							8		12		35
1	2		6		5	3			10	11	7	4	9							8				36
1	2		6		5	3			10		7	4	9				11	12		*8*			14	37
1	2		6		5	3			10	11			9				4	7		8				38
1	2		6		5	3			10	11	9	12					4	7		8				39
	2		6		5				10	11	12	3	9				4	7		8			1	40
1	2		6		5				10	11	12	3	9				4	7		8				41
1	2		6		5	3			10	11	7	12	9				4			8				42

Coca-Cola Cup	First Round	Shrewsbury T (a)	0-1
		(h)	1-1
FA Cup	First Round	Accrington S (a)	3-2
	Second Round	Walsall (a)	1-1
		(h)	0-0
	Third Round	Wimbledon (a)	0-3

SCUNTHORPE UNITED

Player and Position	Ht	Wt	Birth Date	Birth Place	Source	Clubs	League App	League Gls
Goalkeepers								
Michael Heath†	5 9	11 00	7 2 74	Hull	Trainee	Tottenham H	—	—
						Scunthorpe U	2	—
Mark Samways	6 2	13 10	11 11 68	Doncaster	Trainee	Doncaster R	121	—
						Scunthorpe U (loan)	8	—
						Scunthorpe U	72	—
Richard Wilmott‡	6 4	13 07	29 8 69		Stevenage	Scunthorpe U	3	—
Defenders								
Graham Alexander	5 10	11 08	10 10 71	Coventry	Trainee	Scunthorpe U	119	14
Paul Ellender*	6 1	12 07	21 10 74	Scunthorpe	Trainee	Scunthorpe U	—	—
Chris Hope	6 0	11 01	14 11 72	Sheffield	Darlington	Nottingham F	—	—
						Scunthorpe U	41	—
Alan Knill	6 2	11 07	8 10 64	Slough	Apprentice	Southampton	—	—
						Halifax T	118	6
						Swansea C	89	3
						Bury	144	8
						Cardiff C (loan)	4	—
						Scunthorpe U	25	1
Paul Longden	5 7	11 00	28 9 62	Wakefield	Apprentice	Barnsley	5	—
						Scunthorpe U	368	—
Paul McCullagh‡	5 11	11 04	6 2 74	Brigg	Trainee	Scunthorpe U	5	1
Paul Mudd	5 8	11 02	13 11 70	Hull	Trainee	Hull C	1	—
						Scarborough	98	2
						Scunthorpe U	33	3
Tim Ryan			10 12 74	Stockport	Trainee	Scunthorpe U	2	—
Midfield								
Russell Bradley	6 0	12 05	28 3 66	Birmingham	Dudley T	Nottingham F	—	—
						Hereford U (loan)	12	1
						Hereford U	77	3
						Halifax T	56	3
						Scunthorpe U	34	1
Wayne Bullimore	5 9	10 06	12 9 70	Sutton-in-Ashfield	Trainee	Manchester U	—	—
						Barnsley	35	1
						Stockport Co	—	—
						Scunthorpe U	18	3
David Foy‡	6 1	12 00	20 10 72	Coventry	Trainee	Birmingham C	3	—
						Scunthorpe U	3	—
Steven Housham			24 2 76	Gainsborough T	Trainee	Scunthorpe U	—	—
James McNeil‡			1 10 74	Scunthorpe	Trainee	Scunthorpe U	—	—
Dean Martin	5 11	11 10	9 9 67	Halifax	Local	Halifax T	153	7
						Scunthorpe U	101	7
Christian Sansam			26 12 75	Hull	Trainee	Scunthorpe U	10	—
Ian Thompstone	6 1	13 02	17 1 71	Manchester	Trainee	Manchester C	1	1
						Oldham Ath	—	—
						Exeter C	15	3
						Halifax T	31	9
						Scunthorpe U	41	7
Stephen Thornber	5 10	11 02	11 10 65	Dewsbury	Local	Halifax T	104	4
						Swansea C	117	6
						Blackpool	24	—
						Scunthorpe U	24	2
John Watson‡	5 9	10 10	14 4 74	South Shields	Trainee	Newcastle U	1	—
						Scunthorpe U	5	—
Forwards								
Matt Carmichael	6 2	11 07	13 5 64	Singapore	Army	Lincoln C	133	18
						Scunthorpe U	42	18
Sam Goodacre	5 7	10 12	1 12 70	Sheffield	School	Sheffield W	—	—
						Scunthorpe U	39	12
Damian Henderson	6 2	13 07	12 5 73	Leeds	Trainee	Leeds U	—	—
						Scarborough	17	5
						Scunthorpe U	20	1

SCUNTHORPE UNITED

Colours: White shirts, claret and blue trim collar and sleeves, sky blue shorts, claret and white trim, sky blue stockings with claret and white trim. **Change colours:** Red with green, yellow and claret flashes.

Foundation: The year of foundation for Scunthorpe United has often been quoted as 1910, but the club can trace its history back to 1899 when Brumby Hall FC, who played on the Old Showground, consolidated their position by amalgamating with some other clubs and changing their name to Scunthorpe United. The year 1910 was when that club amalgamated with North Lindsey United as Scunthorpe and Lindsey United. The link is Mr. W. T. Lockwood whose chairmanship covers both years.

First Football League game: 19 August, 1950, Division 3(N), v Shrewsbury T (h) D 0-0 – Thompson; Barker, Brownsword; Allen, Taylor, McCormick; Mosby, Payne, Gorin, Rees, Boyes.

Did you know: Matt Carmichael set a club record when he scored in eight consecutive League games for Scunthorpe United between 28 December and 19 February 1994.

Managers (and Secretary-Managers)
Harry Allcock 1915–53*, Tom Crilly 1936–37, Bernard Harper 1946–48, Leslie Jones 1950–51, Bill Corkhill 1952–56, Ron Suart 1956–58, Tony McShane 1959, Bill Lambton 1959, Frank Soo 1959–60, Dick Duckworth 1960–64, Fred Goodwin 1964–66, Ron Ashman 1967–73, Ron Bradley 1973–74, Dick Rooks 1974–76, Ron Ashman 1976–81, John Duncan 1981–83, Allan Clarke 1983–84, Frank Barlow 1984–87, Mick Buxton 1987–91, Bill Green 1991–93, Richard Money 1993–94, David Moore June 1994–

Player and Position	*Ht*	*Wt*	*Birth Date*	*Birth Place*	*Source*	*Clubs*	*League App*	*League Gls*
Ian Juryeff	5 11	12 0	24 11 62	Gosport	Apprentice	Southampton	—	—
					Sweden	Southampton	2	—
						Mansfield T (loan)	12	5
						Reading (loan)	7	1
						Orient	111	44
						Ipswich T (loan)	2	—
						Halifax T	17	7
						Hereford U	28	4
						Halifax T	72	13
						Darlington	34	6
						Scunthorpe U	23	5
Mark Smith	5 9	12 02	19 12 61	Sheffield		Sheffield U	—	—
					Worksop, Gainsborough T	Scunthorpe U	1	—
					Kettering	Rochdale	27	7
						Huddersfield T	96	11
						Grimsby T	77	4
						Scunthorpe U	30	6
Neil Trebble†			16 2 69	Hitchin	Stevenage Bor	Scunthorpe U	14	2
Jason Yates*	5 11	12 11	10 12 74	Walsall	Trainee	Scunthorpe U	—	—

Trainees
Cox, Jason; Field, Lee; Hughes, Richard G; Phillips, Adam P; Price, Gregory T; Storey, Neil M; Walsh, Michael S.

****Non-Contract**
Heath, Michael; Moore, David.

Associated Schoolboys
Carmody, Michael; Gunn, Jonathan P; Smith, Robert C; Vickers, Ryan A.

Associated Schoolboys who have accepted the Club's offer of a Traineeship/Contract
Collins, Gavin M; Exley, John J.
**Non-Contract Players who are retained must be re-signed before they are eligible to play in League matches.

SHEFFIELD UNITED 1993–94 *Back row (left to right):* Willie Falconer, Jonas Wirmola, David Tuttle, Chris Kamara, Brian Gayle, Alan Kelly, Jostein Flo, David Walton, Paul Beesley, Alan Cork, John Pemberton.

Centre row: Derek French (Physio), John Gannon, Carl Bradshaw, Paul Rogers, Glyn Hodges, Simon Tracey, Charlie Hartfield, Andy Scott, David Barnes, Kevin Gage, Geoff Taylor (Assistant Manager).

Front row: Franz Carr, Tom Cowan, Dane Whitehouse, Dave Bassett (Team Manager), Mitch Ward, John Reed, Adrian Littlejohn.

Division 1 SHEFFIELD UNITED

Bramall Lane Ground, Sheffield S2 4SU. Telephone Sheffield (0742) 738955. Fax: (0742) 723030. Ticket Office: (0742) 766771. Pools Office: (0742) 727901. Club Shop: (0742) 750596. Community Scheme: (0742) 769314. Executive Suite: (0742) 755277. Blades Clubcall: 0891 332950.

Ground capacity: 23,500.

Record attendance: 68,287 v Leeds U, FA Cup 5th rd, 15 February 1936.

Record receipts: £261,758 v Manchester U, FA Cup 5th rd, 14 February 1993.

Pitch measurements: 110yd × 72yd.

Chairman: R. L. Brealey.

Directors: A. H. Laver, D. Dooley, B. Proctor, J. A. Plant JP.

Team Manager: Dave Bassett. ***Assistant Manager:*** Geoff Taylor. ***Coaches:*** Brian Eastick, Wally Downes. ***Youth Coach:*** Keith Mincher.

Physios: Derek French, D. Circuit.

Secretary: D. Capper AFA. ***Commercial Manager:*** Andy R. Daykin.

Youth Development Officer: John Dungworth.

Community Programme Organiser: Tony Currie, Tel: 769314.

Year Formed: 1889. ***Turned Professional:*** 1889. ***Ltd Co.:*** 1899.

Club Nickname: 'The Blades'.

Record League Victory: 10–0 v Burslem Port Vale (away), Division 2, 10 December 1892 – Howlett; Witham, Lilley; Howell, Hendry, Needham; Drummond (1), Wallace (1), Hammond (4), Davies (2), Watson (2).

Record Cup Victory: 5–0 v Newcastle U (away), FA Cup, 1st rd, 10 January 1914 – Gough; Cook, English; Brelsford, Howley, Sturgess; Simmons (2), Gillespie (1), Kitchen (1), Fazackerley, Revill (1). 5–0 v Corinthians, FA Cup, 1st rd, 10 January 1925 – Sutcliffe; Cook, Milton; Longworth, King, Green; Partridge, Boyle (1), Johnson 4), Gillespie, Tunstall. 5–0 v Barrow, FA Cup, 3rd rd, 7 January 1956 – Burgin; Coldwell, Mason; Fountain, Johnson, Iley; Hawksworth (1), Hoyland (2), Howitt, Wragg (1), Grainger (1).

Record Defeat: 0–13 v Bolton W, FA Cup 2nd rd, 1 February 1890.

Most League Points (2 for a win): 60, Division 2, 1952–53.

Most League Points (3 for a win): 96, Division 4, 1981–82.

Most League Goals: 102, Division 1, 1925–26.

Highest League Scorer in Season: Jimmy Dunne, 41, Division 1, 1930–31.

Most League Goals in Total Aggregate: Harry Johnson, 205, 1919–30.

Most Capped Player: Billy Gillespie, 25, Northern Ireland.

Most League Appearances: Joe Shaw, 629, 1948–66.

Record Transfer Fee Received: £2,700,000 from Leeds U for Brian Deane, July 1993.

Record Transfer Fee Paid: £700,000 to Ipswich T for Brian Gayle, September 1991.

Football League Record: 1892 Elected to Division 2; 1893–1934 Division 1; 1934–39 Division 2; 1946–49 Division 1; 1949–53 Division 2; 1953–56 Division 1; 1956–61 Division 2; 1961–68 Division 1; 1968–71 Division 2; 1971–76 Division 1; 1976–79 Division 2; 1979–81 Division 3; 1981–82 Division 4; 1982–84 Division 3; 1984–88 Division 2; 1988–89 Division 3; 1989–90 Division 2; 1990–92 Division 1; 1992–94 FA Premier League; 1994– Division 1.

Honours: *Football League:* Division 1 – Champions 1897–98; Runners-up 1896–97, 1899–1900; Division 2 – Champions 1952–53; Runners-up 1892–93, 1938–39, 1960–61, 1970–71, 1989–90; Division 4 – Champions 1981–82. *FA Cup:* Winners 1899, 1902, 1915, 1925; Runners-up 1901, 1936. *Football League Cup:* best season: 5th rd, 1961–62, 1966–67, 1971–72.

SHEFFIELD UNITED 1993—94 LEAGUE RECORD

Match No.	Date	Venue	Opponents	Result		H/T Score	Lg. Pos.	Goalscorers	Attendance
1	Aug 14	H	Swindon T	W	3-1	1-0	—	Falconer, Bradshaw, Rogers	20,904
2	18	A	Manchester U	L	0-3	0-2	—		41,949
3	21	A	Everton	L	2-4	1-2	13	Whitehouse, Cork	24,177
4	24	H	Wimbledon	W	2-1	1-0	—	Flo, Falconer	15,555
5	28	H	Ipswich T	D	1-1	1-0	11	Flo	17,932
6	Sept 1	A	QPR	L	1-2	1-1	—	Flo	11,113
7	11	H	Tottenham H	D	2-2	0-1	16	Littlejohn 2	21,325
8	18	A	Leeds U	L	1-2	1-2	17	Kelly (og)	33,879
9	25	H	Manchester C	L	0-1	0-0	17		20,067
10	Oct 2	A	Southampton	D	3-3	0-1	18	Falconer, Flo 2	11,619
11	18	A	Blackburn R	D	0-0	0-0	—		14,276
12	23	H	Sheffield W	D	1-1	1-1	18	Hodges	30,044
13	31	A	Coventry C	D	0-0	0-0	—		10,439
14	Nov 6	H	Norwich C	L	1-2	1-1	19	Whitehouse (pen)	18,254
15	20	A	Aston Villa	L	0-1	0-0	19		24,686
16	24	A	Newcastle U	L	0-4	0-2	—		35,029
17	27	H	Chelsea	W	1-0	1-0	18	Clarke (og)	16,119
18	Dec 4	A	Swindon T	D	0-0	0-0	18		12,882
19	7	H	Manchester U	L	0-3	0-2	—		26,744
20	11	H	Everton	D	0-0	0-0	19		15,135
21	18	A	Wimbledon	L	0-2	0-0	18		6728
22	26	H	Liverpool	D	0-0	0-0	—		22,932
23	29	A	Arsenal	L	0-3	0-2	21		27,035
24	Jan 1	H	Oldham Ath	W	2-1	2-1	18	Whitehouse (pen), Ward	17,066
25	3	A	West Ham U	D	0-0	0-0	18		20,365
26	15	H	Blackburn R	L	1-2	1-1	18	Hendry (og)	19,124
27	22	A	Sheffield W	L	1-3	0-0	18	Whitehouse (pen)	34,959
28	Feb 12	H	Coventry C	D	0-0	0-0	21		15,394
29	22	A	Ipswich T	L	2-3	1-3	—	Cork, Carr	11,468
30	Mar 5	A	Tottenham H	D	2-2	0-0	21	Gayle, Blake	25,741
31	13	H	Leeds U	D	2-2	0-1	—	Flo, Gayle	19,425
32	16	H	QPR	D	1-1	0-1	—	Blake	14,183
33	19	A	Manchester C	D	0-0	0-0	21		25,448
34	26	H	Southampton	D	0-0	0-0	21		19,522
35	28	H	West Ham U	W	3-2	1-2	—	Whitehouse, Gayle, Rogers	13,646
36	Apr 2	A	Liverpool	W	2-1	0-1	20	Flo 2	36,642
37	4	H	Arsenal	D	1-1	0-0	20	Rogers	20,019
38	16	H	Aston Villa	L	1-2	1-2	21	Littlejohn	18,402
39	23	A	Norwich C	W	1-0	1-0	20	Blake	18,474
40	30	H	Newcastle U	W	2-0	0-0	19	Blake 2	29,013
41	May 3	A	Oldham Ath	D	1-1	1-1	—	Cork	14,779
42	7	A	Chelsea	L	2-3	1-0	20	Flo, Hodges	21,782

Final League Position: 20

GOALSCORERS

League (42): Flo 9, Blake 5, Whitehouse 5 (3 pens), Cork 3, Falconer 3, Gayle 3, Littlejohn 3, Rogers 3, Hodges 2, Bradshaw 1, Carr 1, Ward 1, own goals 3.
Coca-Cola Cup (2): Davison 1, Ward 1.
FA Cup (0):

Kelly 29 + 1	Ward 20 + 2	Beesley 22 + 3	Falconer 21 + 2	Tuttle 31	Pemberton 8	Bradshaw 39 + 1	Rogers 24 + 1	Cork 7 + 12	Scott 12 + 3	Whitehouse 35 + 3	Gage 16 + 5	Littlejohn 12 + 7	Cowan 4	Hoyland 17 + 1	Flo 32 + 1	Wirmola 8	Kamara 15 + 1	Tracey 13 + 2	Hodges 19 + 12	Barnes 2	Hartfield 3 + 2	Davison 8 + 1	Nilsen 21 + 1	Carr 10	Gayle 13	Gannon 14	Blake 7 + 5	*Match No.*
1	2	3	4	5	6	7	8	9	10	*11*	12	14																1
1	2		4	5	6	7	8	14	10	11	12		3	*9*														2
1	2	12	4	5	6	*7*	8	14	10	11			3		9													3
1		3	4		6	7		10		11	2				9	5	8											4
1	12	3	4		6	7		14	*10*	11	2				9	5	8											5
1	2	3	4		6	7			*10*	11	12	14			9	5	8											6
1			4		6	7		12		11	2	10	3		9	5	8	14										7
1	2		4		6	7				11		10	3		9	5	8		12									8
		6	4	5		7	8	12		11	*2*	14			9			1	10	3								9
		6	4	5		7	8			12	2	10			9			1	*11*	3	14							10
		3	4			2	8	12		*11*				6	9	5		1	7		14	10						11
	3		4	5		2	8	10		12				6	9			1	11		7	14						12
	3		4	5		2	8	12		11		9		6				1	7		10							13
			4	5		2	8	12		11		10		6	9			1	14				3	7				14
1	14		4	5		7	*8*	12		11	2	10		6					9				3					15
1	2		4	5		7	8		12	11				6			14				10	*9*	3					16
1	8	6	4	5		7			10	11	2			9					12				3					17
1	8	6	4	5		7			10	11	2			9					12				3					18
1	8	*6*	4	5		7	14		10		2			9	12				11				3					19
1			4	5		*7*	8	12	14		2			6	9				11			10	3					20
1		3	4	5		7		10		11	2				9	6	8		12									21
1	*4*	5	12			2			14	11	3			6	9		8		7			10						22
1		6				2	8	12	10	11				4	9	*5*			14			7	3					23
1	8	3	12	5		2				11		14		6	9		4		7			*10*						24
1	8	3		5		2				11		12		6	9		4		7			10						25
1	*8*	3		5		2		9	10	11	12	14		6			4		7									26
1	8	3		5		2			10	11				6	9		4		7				12					27
1	8			5					10	11	2	12			9		4		7				3		6			28
1				5		2		9		12		*10*					8		11				3	7	6	4	14	29
1				5		2				3	12	*10*			9		4		11					7	6	8	14	30
1		12		5		2									9		4		11			10	3	*7*	6	8	14	31
1		14		5		7	8	12			2				9								*3*	11	6	4	10	32
1		3		5			8			11	2				9									7	6	4	10	33
1				5		12	8			11	2				9				14				3	7	6	*4*	10	34
1				5		2	8			11		10			9			14	12				3	7	6	4		35
				5		2	8			11		10			9			1					3	7	6	4		36
		6		5		2	8			11		10			9			1	7				3			4	12	37
				5		2	8			11		10			9			1	14				3	7	6	*4*	12	38
	7	5				2	8			11					9			1	12				3		6	4	10	39
	7	6		5		2	8			11					9			1	12				3			4	10	40
14		5				2	8	7		11					*9*			1	12				3		6	4	10	41
	7					2	8			3				12	9			1	11				5		6	4	10	42

Coca-Cola Cup	Second Round	Blackpool (a)	0-3
		(h)	2-0
FA Cup	Third Round	Manchester U (h)	0-1

SHEFFIELD UNITED

Player and Position	Ht	Wt	Birth Date	Birth Place	Source	Clubs	League App	League Gls
Goalkeepers								
Sal Bibbo	6 2	13 00	24 8 74	Basingstoke	Bournemouth	Sheffield U	—	—
Alan Kelly	6 2	12 05	11 8 68	Preston		Preston NE	142	—
						Sheffield U	63	—
Simon Tracey	6 0	12 00	9 12 67	Woolwich	Apprentice	Wimbledon	1	—
						Sheffield U	138	—
Defenders								
Paul Beesley	6 1	11 11	21 7 65	Wigan	Marine	Wigan Ath	155	3
						Leyton Orient	32	1
						Sheffield U	141	5
Tom Cowan	5 8	10 08	28 8 69	Bellshill	Netherdale BC	Clyde	16	2
						Rangers	12	—
						Sheffield U	45	—
						Stoke C (loan)	14	—
						Huddersfield T (loan)	10	—
Ross Davidson	5 8	11 04	13 11 73	Chertsey	Walton & Hersham	Sheffield U	—	—
Ashley Fickling	5 10	11 08	15 11 72	Sheffield	Trainee	Sheffield U	—	—
						Darlington (loan)	15	—
Mark Foran	6 4	13 12	30 10 73	Aldershot	Trainee	Millwall	—	—
						Sheffield U	—	—
Matthew Foreman	6 0		15 2 75	Gateshead	Trainee	Sheffield U	—	—
Kevin Gage	5 9	11 02	21 4 64	Chiswick	Apprentice	Wimbledon	168	15
						Aston Villa	115	8
						Sheffield U	70	2
Brian Gayle	6 1	12 07	6 3 65	London		Wimbledon	83	3
						Manchester C	55	3
						Ipswich T	58	4
						Sheffield U	77	8
Charles Hartfield	6 0	12 02	4 9 71	London	Trainee	Arsenal	—	—
						Sheffield U	29	—
Roger Nilsen	5 9	11 08	8 8 69	Norway	Viking St	Sheffield U	22	—
Martin Thomson	5 10	11 08	3 10 74	Bradford	Trainee	Sheffield U	—	—
David Tuttle	5 9	12 10	6 2 72	Reading	Trainee	Tottenham H	13	—
						Peterborough U (loan)	7	—
						Sheffield U	31	—
Lee Wainwright‡	5 11		9 1 75	Sheffield	Trainee	Sheffield U	—	—
Mitch Ward	5 8	10 12	18 6 71	Sheffield	Trainee	Sheffield U	58	3
						Crewe Alex (loan)	4	1
Jonas Wirmola			17 7 69	Sweden	Sparvagens	Sheffield U	8	—
Midfield								
Graham Anthony	5 10	10 08	9 8 75	Jarrow	Trainee	Sheffield U	—	—
Mark Blount	5 10	12 00	5 1 74	Derby	Gresley R	Sheffield U	—	—
Tim Butterfield‡	5 11		18 10 74	Sheffield	Trainee	Sheffield U	—	—
Franz Carr	5 7	10 12	24 9 66	Preston	Apprentice	Blackburn R	—	—
						Nottingham F	131	17
						Sheffield W (loan)	12	—
						West Ham U (loan)	3	—
						Newcastle U	25	3
						Sheffield U	18	4
Matthew Cherrill	5 10	11 12	10 10 73	Sheffield	Trainee	Sheffield U	—	—
Willie Falconer (To Celtic)	6 1	11 09	5 4 66	Aberdeen	Lewis U	Aberdeen	77	13
						Watford	98	12
						Middlesbrough	53	10
						Sheffield U	23	3
John Gannon	5 8	10 10	18 12 66	Wimbledon	Apprentice	Wimbledon	16	2
						Crewe Alex (loan)	15	—
						Sheffield U (loan)	16	1
						Sheffield U	134	5
						Middlesbrough (loan)	7	—
Craig Hellewell*			9 7 75	Doncaster		Sheffield U	—	—

SHEFFIELD UNITED

Colours: Red/white striped shirts, black shorts, black stockings. **Change colours:** Jade/navy trim shirts, navy/jade trim shorts, navy/jade trim stockings.

Foundation: In March 1889, Yorkshire County Cricket Club formed Sheffield United six days after an FA Cup semi-final between Preston North End and West Bromwich Albion had finally convinced Charles Stokes, a member of the cricket club, that the formation of a professional football club would prove successful at Bramall Lane. The United's first secretary, Mr. J. B. Wostinholm was also secretary of the cricket club.

First Football League game: 3 September, 1892, Division 2, v Lincoln C (h) W 4-2 – Lilley; Witham, Cain; Howell, Hendry, Needham (1); Wallace, Dobson, Hammond (3), Davies, Drummond.

Did you know: On 16 March 1954 Sheffield United played their first floodlight game since the 19th century, beating Rotherham United 2-1 in a friendly at Bramall Lane. The first had been in 1878.

Managers (and Secretary-Managers)
J. B. Wostinholm 1889–1899*, John Nicholson 1899–1932, Ted Davison 1932–52, Reg Freeman 1952–55, Joe Mercer 1955–58, Johnny Harris 1959–68 (continued as GM to 1970), Arthur Rowley 1968–69, Johnny Harris (GM resumed TM duties) 1969–73, Ken Furphy 1973–75, Jimmy Sirrel 1975–77, Harry Haslam 1978–81, Martin Peters 1981, Ian Porterfield 1981–86, Billy McEwan 1986–88, Dave Bassett January 1988–

Player and Position	*Ht*	*Wt*	*Birth Date*	*Place*	*Source*	*Clubs*	*League App*	*Gls*
Jamie Hoyland	6 0	12 08	23 1 66	Sheffield	Apprentice	Manchester C	2	—
						Bury	172	35
						Sheffield U	87	6
						Bristol C (loan)	6	—
Chris Kamara*	6 1	12 00	25 12 57	Middlesbrough	Apprentice	Portsmouth	63	7
						Swindon T	147	21
						Portsmouth	11	—
						Brentford	152	28
						Swindon T	87	6
						Stoke C	60	5
						Leeds U	20	1
						Luton T	49	—
						Sheffield U (loan)	8	—
						Middlesbrough (loan)	5	—
						Sheffield U	16	—
Paul Rogers	6 0	12 05	21 3 65	Portsmouth	Sutton U	Sheffield U	65	6
Andy Scott	6 1	11 05	2 8 72	Epsom	Sutton U	Sheffield U	17	1
Danny Smith*	5 9		8 1 75	Sheffield	Manchester C	Sheffield U	—	—
Dane Whitehouse	5 9	10 13	14 10 70	Sheffield	Trainee	Sheffield U	107	18
Forwards								
Tony Battersby	5 10	11 08	30 8 75	Doncaster	Trainee	Sheffield U	—	—
Nathan Blake	5 10	12 00	27 1 72	Cardiff	Chelsea	Cardiff C	131	35
						Sheffield U	12	5
Carl Bradshaw	6 0	11 00	2 10 68	Sheffield	Apprentice	Sheffield W	32	4
						Barnsley (loan)	6	1
						Manchester C	5	—
						Sheffield U	147	8
David Brocklehurst	5 10	10 08	7 3 74	Chesterfield	Trainee	Sheffield U	—	—
Alan Cork*	6 0	12 00	4 3 59	Derby	Amateur	Derby C	—	—
						Lincoln C (loan)	5	—
						Wimbledon	430	145
						Sheffield U	54	7

Trainees
Anane, David O; Andison, Gary; Beech, Neil; Collins, Eric; Dickman, Lewis L; Evans, Thomas; Hill, Matthew; Holt, Craig; Innes, Lee M; Johnston, Derek J. G. J. M; Kennedy, Steven; Letts, Simon C; Pearson, Gary; Pearson, Gregg; Powell, Craig; Quinn, Wayne; Rixon, James; Storey, Brett; Tee, Jason K; Thorpe, Andrew; Vine, Darren, Zivkovic, Barry L.

Associated Schoolboys
Bamforth, Liam A; Briggs, SImon J; Capper, David A; Davies, Kevin J; Doane, Ben N. D. C; Eastwood, Mark; Heritage, Paul W; Humble, Steven J; James, Owen; Lewin, Karlda D; Ludlam, Ryan; Mays, Ross A; Stephenson, Liam; Thompson, Brian C; Webber, Richard P. J.

Associated Schoolboys who have accepted the Club's offer of a Traineeship/Contract
Bettney, Christopher J; Dyer, Liam D; Elton, Paul; Hawes, Steven R; Hocking, Matthew J; Innes, Gary J; Litten, Thomas N; Metcalf, Ian R; Spooner, Daniel; Summerell, StewartD; Wood, Paul J.

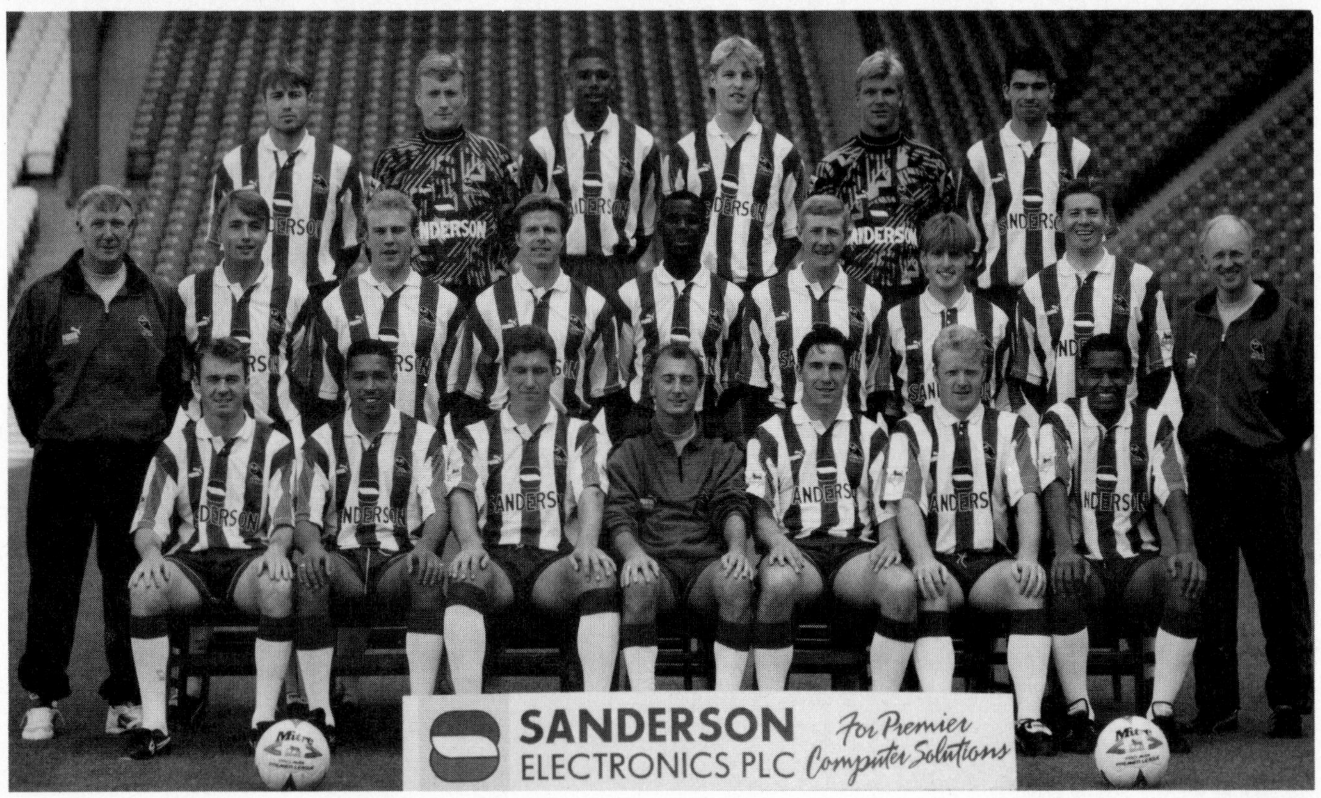

SHEFFIELD WEDNESDAY 1993–94 *Back row (left to right):* Paul Warhurst, Kevin Pressman, Carlton Palmer, Andy Pearce, Chris Woods, Julian Watts.
Centre row: Richie Barker (Assistant Manager), Nigel Jemson, Gordon Watson, Roland Nilsson, Chris Bart-Williams, Nigel Worthington, Graham Hyde, Chris Waddle, Alan Smith (Physio).
Front row: John Sheridan, Des Walker, Nigel Pearson, Trevor Francis (Manager), David Hirst, Phil King, Mark Bright.

FA Premiership **SHEFFIELD WEDNESDAY**

Hillsborough, Sheffield, S6 1SW. Telephone Sheffield (0742) 343122. Box Office: Sheffield 337233. Clubcall: 0898 121186.

Ground capacity: 36,020.

Record attendance: 72,841 v Manchester C, FA Cup 5th rd, 17 February 1934.

Record receipts: £533,918 Sunderland v Norwich C, FA Cup semi-final, 5 April 1992.

Pitch measurements: 115yd × 77yd.

Chairman: D. G. Richards. ***Vice-chairman:*** K. T. Addy.

Directors: C. Woodward, E. Barron, G. K. Hulley, R. M. Grierson FCA, J. Ashton MP.

Manager: Trevor Francis. ***Assistant Manager:*** Richie Barker.

Physio: D. Galley.

Secretary: G. H. Mackrell FCCA. ***Commercial Manager:*** S. T. O'Toole.

Year Formed: 1867 (fifth oldest League club).

Turned Professional: 1887. ***Ltd Co.:*** 1899.

Former Names: The Wednesday until 1929.

Club Nickname: 'The Owls'.

Previous Grounds: 1867, Highfield; 1869, Myrtle Road; 1877, Sheaf House; 1887, Olive Grove; 1899, Owlerton (since 1912 known as Hillsborough). Some games were played at Endcliffe in the 1880s. Until 1895 Bramall Lane was used for some games.

Record League Victory: 9–1 v Birmingham, Division 1, 13 December 1930 – Brown; Walker, Blenkinsop; Strange, Leach, Wilson; Hooper (3), Seed (2), Ball (2), Burgess (1), Rimmer (1).

Record Cup Victory: 12–0 v Halliwell, FA Cup, 1st rd, 17 January 1891 – Smith; Thompson, Brayshaw; Harry Brandon (1), Betts, Cawley (2); Winterbottom, Mumford (2), Bob Brandon (1), Woolhouse (5), Ingram (1).

Record Defeat: 0–10 v Aston Villa, Division 1, 5 October 1912.

Most League Points (2 for a win): 62, Division 2, 1958–59.

Most League Points (3 for a win): 88, Division 2, 1983–84.

Most League Goals: 106, Division 2, 1958–59.

Highest League Scorer in Season: Derek Dooley, 46, Division 2, 1951–52.

Most League Goals in Total Aggregate: Andy Wilson, 199, 1900–20.

Most Capped Player: Nigel Worthington, 50, Northern Ireland.

Most League Appearances: Andy Wilson, 502, 1900–20.

Record Transfer Fee Received: £2,650,000 from Blackburn R for Paul Warhurst, September 1993.

Record Transfer Fee Paid: £2,750,000 to Sampdoria for Des Walker, July 1993 and £2,750,000 to QPR for Andy Sinton, August 1993.

Football League Record: 1892 Elected to Division 1; 1899–1900 Division 2; 1900–20 Division 1; 1920–26 Division 2; 1926–37 Division 1; 1937–50 Division 2; 1950–51 Division 1; 1951–52 Division 2; 1952–55 Division 1; 1955–56 Division 2; 1956–58 Division 1; 1958–59 Division 2; 1959–70 Division 1; 1970–75 Division 2; 1975–80 Division 3; 1980–84 Division 2; 1984–90 Division 1; 1990–91 Division 2; 1991–92 Division 1; 1992– FA Premier League.

Honours: *Football League:* Division 1 – Champions 1902–03, 1903–04, 1928–29, 1929–30; Runners-up 1960–61; Division 2 – Champions 1899–1900, 1925–26, 1951–52, 1955–56, 1958–59; Runners-up 1949–50, 1983–84. *FA Cup:* Winners 1896, 1907, 1935; Runners-up 1890, 1966, 1993. *Football League Cup:* Winners 1990–91; Runners-up 1992–93. **European Competitions:** *Fairs Cup:* 1961–62, 1963–64, 1992–93.

SHEFFIELD WEDNESDAY 1993—94 LEAGUE RECORD

Match No.	Date	Venue	Opponents	Result		H/T Score	Lg. Pos.	Goalscorers	Atten-dance
1	Aug 14	A	Liverpool	L	0-2	0-1	—		43,792
2	18	H	Aston Villa	D	0-0	0-0	—		28,450
3	21	H	Arsenal	L	0-1	0-1	20		26,023
4	25	A	West Ham U	L	0-2	0-0	—		19,441
5	28	A	Chelsea	D	1-1	1-1	21	Bright	16,652
6	Sept 1	H	Norwich C	D	3-3	0-0	—	Bart-Williams, Bright, Sinton	25,175
7	13	A	Newcastle U	L	2-4	1-1	—	Sinton 2	33,519
8	18	H	Southampton	W	2-0	0-0	19	Sheridan (pen), Hirst	22,503
9	25	A	Blackburn R	D	1-1	0-0	19	Hyde	14,495
10	Oct 2	H	Manchester U	L	2-3	0-0	19	Bart-Williams, Bright	34,548
11	16	H	Wimbledon	D	2-2	1-0	19	Waddle, Jones	21,752
12	23	A	Sheffield U	D	1-1	1-1	19	Palmer	30,044
13	30	H	Leeds U	D	3-3	2-1	20	Waddle, Jones, Bright	31,892
14	Nov 6	A	Ipswich T	W	4-1	1-0	17	Jemson 2, Bright, Palmer	14,767
15	20	H	Coventry C	D	0-0	0-0	17		23,379
16	24	H	Oldham Ath	W	3-0	2-0	—	Watson 2, Jemson	18,509
17	27	A	Manchester C	W	3-1	0-0	—	Jones 2, Jemson	23,416
18	Dec 4	H	Liverpool	W	3-1	1-1	12	Ruddock (og), Wright (og), Bright	32,177
19	8	A	Aston Villa	D	2-2	1-1	—	Bart-Williams, Teale (og)	20,304
20	12	A	Arsenal	L	0-1	0-0	—		22,026
21	18	H	West Ham U	W	5-0	1-0	13	Marsh (og), Bright, Waddle, Jemson, Palmer	26,350
22	27	A	Everton	W	2-0	0-0	10	Bright, Palmer	16,471
23	29	H	Swindon T	D	3-3	1-2	10	Bright, Watson 2	30,570
24	Jan 1	A	QPR	W	2-1	0-0	9	Bright, Watson	16,858
25	3	H	Tottenham H	W	1-0	1-0	6	Bright	32,514
26	15	A	Wimbledon	L	1-2	0-2	8	Pearce	5536
27	22	H	Sheffield U	W	3-1	0-0	7	Bright, Pearce, Watson	34,959
28	Feb 5	A	Tottenham H	W	3-1	1-0	6	Coleman, Bright 2	23,078
29	25	A	Norwich C	D	1-1	0-0	8	Watson	18,311
30	Mar 5	H	Newcastle U	L	0-1	0-0	8		33,153
31	12	A	Southampton	D	1-1	0-0	8	Bart-Williams	16,391
32	16	A	Manchester U	L	0-5	0-4	—		43,669
33	20	H	Blackburn R	L	1-2	1-1	—	Watson	24,655
34	30	H	Chelsea	W	3-1	2-0	—	Bart-Williams, Palmer, Sheridan (pen)	20,433
35	Apr 2	H	Everton	W	5-1	2-0	7	Jones, Bart-Williams, Worthington, Bright 2	24,080
36	4	A	Swindon T	W	1-0	0-0	6	Watson	13,927
37	9	H	QPR	W	3-1	3-0	6	Bright 2, Sheridan (pen)	22,437
38	16	A	Coventry C	D	1-1	0-1	6	Jones	13,052
39	23	H	Ipswich T	W	5-0	2-0	6	Linighan (og), Watson, Pearce, Bart-Williams, Bright	23,854
40	30	A	Oldham Ath	D	0-0	0-0	7		12,973
41	May 3	A	Leeds U	D	2-2	1-0	—	Bart-Williams, Watson	33,575
42	7	H	Manchester C	D	1-1	1-0	7	Watson	33,589

Final League Position: 7

GOALSCORERS

League (76): Bright 19, Watson 12, Bart-Williams 8, Jones 6, Jemson 5, Palmer 5, Pearce 3, Sheridan 3 (3 pens), Sinton 3, Waddle 3, Coleman 1, Hirst 1, Hyde 1, Worthington 1, own goals 5.
Coca-Cola Cup (10): Bright 2, Palmer 2, Watson 2, Bart-Williams 1, Hirst 1, Jemson 1, Jones 1.
FA Cup (5): Bright 2, Bart-Williams 1, Hyde 1, Pearce 1.

Woods 10	Nilsson 38	King 7 + 3	Palmer 37	Pearce 29 + 3	Walker 42	Sheridan 19 + 1	Warhurst 4	Hirst 6 + 1	Bart-Williams 30 + 7	Worthington 30 + 1	Bright 36 + 4	Hyde 27 + 9	Sinton 25	Waddle 19	Pearson 4 + 1	Watson 15 + 8	Jones 24 + 3	Pressman 32	Williams 4	Poric 2 + 4	Jemson 10 + 8	Francis — + 1	Coleman 10 + 5	Linighan B 1	Briscoe — + 1	Watts 1	Match No.
1	2	3	4	5	6	7	8	9	*10*	11	12	14															1
1	2	3	4	5	6	7	8	9		11	12	10															2
1		*2*	4	5	6	7	8	9	14	3	12	10	11														3
1	2		4		6		5	*9*	10	3	12	7	11	8	14												4
1	2				6	7			4	3	9	10	11	8	5												5
1	2				6	7			4	3	9	10	11	8	5												6
1	2				6	7			4	3	9	10	11	8	5	12											7
1	2		4		6	7		9	14	*3*	10	12	11	8	5												8
1	2	3		5	6	7			4	12	9	*10*	11	8			14										9
1	2	3	4		5	7			6		9	10	11	8													10
			2	5	6				4		9	10	11	8			7	1	3	12							11
	2		4	5	6						9	10	3	8			7	1		11	12						12
	2		4	5	6	12				3	9		11	8			7	1			10						13
	2		4	5	6					3	9	12	11	8			7	1			10						14
	2		4	5	6					3		9	11	8			7	1			10	12					15
	2		4	*5*	6				14	3		12	11	8		9	7	1			10						16
	2		4		5				12	3	9	10	11	8			6	1			7						17
	2		4		5				6	3	9	10		8			11	1		12	*7*		14				18
	2		4		5				6	3	9	10		8			11	1			7		12				19
	2		4	12	5				11	3	9	10					8	1		14	*7*		6				20
	2		4	5	6				11	3	9	10		8				1			7						21
	2		4	5	6				11	3	9	10		8		14	12	1			*7*						22
	2		4	*5*	6				12	3	10	7	11	8		9	14	1									23
	2		4	14	5				*6*	3	10	8	11			9	7	1			12						24
	2		4	14	5				6	3	10	8	*11*			9	7	1			12						25
			4	5	6				12		10	8	11			9	7	1					3	2			26
	2		4	5	6				12		10	8	11			9	7	1					3				27
	2		4	5	6			12	11		10	8				9	*7*	1					3		14		28
	2		4	5	6			9	*7*		10	8	11			12		1		14			3				29
	2	14	4	5	6				7		10	*8*	11			9		1			12		3				30
	2	3	4	5	6				7		10		11			9		1					8				31
	2	3		5	6				10		9		11			12		1		7			8			4	32
	2	14	4		5	*7*			6		10	8	11			9		1			12		3				33
	2		4	5	6	11			*7*	3	9	14				12	8	1	10								34
	2	14	4	5	6	*11*			7	3	9					12	8	1	10								35
	2		4	5	6	11			7	3	*9*					12	8	1	10				14				36
	2		4	5	6	11			7	3	10					9	8	1					12				37
	2		4	5	6	11			10	3	9	8				12	7	1					14				38
	2		4	5	6	*11*			8	3	10	14				9	7	1			12						39
	2		4	5	6	*11*			8	3	10	14				9	7	1			12						40
			4	5	6	*11*			8	3	10	14				9	7	1			12		2				41
	2		4	5	6	11			8	3	10	12				9	7	1									42

Coca-Cola Cup	Second Round	Bolton W (a)	1-1
		(h)	1-0
	Third Round	Middlesbrough (a)	1-1
		(h)	2-1
	Fourth Round	QPR (a)	2-1
	Fifth Round	Wimbledon (a)	2-1
	Semi-final	Manchester U (a)	0-1
		(h)	1-4
FA Cup	Third Round	Nottingham F (h)	1-1
		(a)	2-0
	Fourth Round	Chelsea (a)	1-1
		(h)	1-3

SHEFFIELD WEDNESDAY

Player and Position	Ht	Wt	Birth Date	Birth Place	Source	Clubs	League App	League Gls
Goalkeepers								
Stewart Kearn			1 12 75	Salisbury		Sheffield W	—	—
Lance Key	6 2	14 13	13 5 68	Kettering	Histon	Sheffield W	—	—
						York C (loan)	—	—
						Oldham Ath (loan)	2	—
						Portsmouth (loan)	—	—
Kevin Pressman	6 1	14 02	6 11 67	Fareham	Apprentice	Sheffield W	94	—
						Stoke C (loan)	4	—
Chris Woods	6 2	14 05	14 11 59	Boston	Apprentice	Nottingham F	—	—
						QPR	63	—
						Norwich C (loan)	10	—
						Norwich C	206	—
						Rangers	173	—
						Sheffield W	90	—
Defenders								
David Faulkner			8 10 75	Sheffield	Trainee	Sheffield W	—	—
Phil King	5 8	13 00	28 12 67	Bristol	Apprentice	Exeter C	27	—
						Torquay U	24	3
						Swindon T	116	4
						Sheffield W	129	2
						Notts Co (loan)	6	—
Brian Linighan			2 11 73	Hartlepool	Trainee	Sheffield W	1	—
John Linighan*			2 11 73	Hartlepool	Trainee	Sheffield W	—	—
Roland Nilsson	5 10	12 00	27 11 63	Helsingborg	IFK Gothenburg	Sheffield W	151	2
Carlton Palmer	6 2	12 04	5 12 65	West Bromwich	Trainee	WBA	121	4
						Sheffield W	205	14
Andy Pearce	6 4	13 00	20 4 66	Bradford	Halesowen	Coventry C	71	4
						Sheffield W	32	3
Nigel Pearson	6 1	14 11	21 8 63	Nottingham	Heanor T	Shrewsbury T	153	5
						Sheffield W	180	14
Simon Stewart	6 1	12 00	1 11 73	Leeds	Trainee	Sheffield W	6	—
Des Walker	5 10	11 05	26 11 65	Hackney	Apprentice	Nottingham F	264	1
						Sampdoria	30	—
						Sheffield W	42	—
Julian Watts	6 3	12 01	17 3 71	Sheffield		Rotherham U	20	1
						Sheffield W	5	—
						Shrewsbury T (loan)	9	—
Nigel Worthington	5 11	12 05	4 11 61	Ballymena	Ballymena U	Notts Co	67	4
						Sheffield W	338	12
Midfield								
Chris Bart-Williams	5 11	11 00	16 6 74	Freetown	Trainee	Leyton Orient	36	2
						Sheffield W	86	14
Steven Brown	5 9	10 05	15 10 74	Sheffield	Trainee	Sheffield W	—	—
Simon Coleman	6 0	10 08	13 3 68	Worksop		Mansfield T	96	7
						Middlesbrough	55	2
						Derby Co	70	2
						Sheffield W	15	1
Darren Holmes	5 8	11 03	30 1 75	Sheffield	Trainee	Sheffield W	—	—
Graham Hyde	5 7	11 07	10 11 70	Doncaster	Trainee	Sheffield W	69	2
Ryan Jones	6 1	13 10	23 7 73	Sheffield	Trainee	Sheffield W	36	6
Michael McVeigh*	5 9	11 05	24 9 74	Rotherham	Trainee	Sheffield W	—	—
Adem Poric	5 9	11 13	22 4 73	London	St George's	Sheffield W	6	—
John Sheridan	5 9	12 00	1 10 64	Manchester	Local	Leeds U	230	47
						Nottingham F	—	—
						Sheffield W	142	24
Ronald Simpson‡			12 3 74	Easington	Trainee	Sheffield W	—	—
Andy Sinton	5 8	10 10	19 3 66	Newcastle.	Apprentice	Cambridge U	93	13
						Brentford	149	28
						QPR	160	22
						Sheffield W	25	3
Mike Williams	5 10	11 02	21 11 69	Bradford	Maltby	Sheffield W	7	—
						Halifax T (loan)	9	1

SHEFFIELD WEDNESDAY

Colours: Blue and white striped shirts, blue shorts, blue stockings. **Change colours:** All black with yellow and grey trim.

Foundation: Sheffield, being one of the principal centres of early Association Football, this club was formed as long ago as 1867 by the Sheffield Wednesday Cricket Club (formed 1825) and their colours from the start were blue and white. The inaugural meeting was held at the Adelphi Hotel and the original committee included Charles Stokes who was subsequently a founder member of Sheffield United.

First Football League game: 3 September, 1892, Division 1, v Notts C (a) W 1-0 – Allan; T. Brandon (1), Mumford; Hall, Betts, H. Brandon; Spiksley, Brady, Davis, R.N. Brown, Dunlop.

Did you know: In December 1934 Sheffield Wednesday beat FK Austria 3-0 to end the visitors unbeaten tour of England. Ellis Rimmer (2) and Walter Millership scored the goals, watched by 12,445.

Managers (and Secretary-Managers)
Arthur Dickinson 1891–1920*, Robert Brown 1920–33, Billy Walker 1933–37, Jimmy McMullan 1937–42, Eric Taylor 1942–58 (continued as GM to 1974), Harry Catterick 1958–61, Vic Buckingham 1961–64, Alan Brown 1964–68, Jack Marshall 1968–69, Danny Williams 1969–71, Derek Dooley 1971–73, Steve Burtenshaw 1974–75, Len Ashurst 1975–77, Jackie Charlton 1977–83, Howard Wilkinson 1983–88, Peter Eustace 1988–89, Ron Atkinson 1989–91, Trevor Francis June 1991–

Player and Position	*Ht*	*Wt*	*Birth Date*	*Birth Place*	*Source*	*Clubs*	*League App*	*League Gls*
Forwards								
Richard Barker	6 0	11 08	30 5 75	Sheffield	Trainee	Sheffield W	—	—
Mark Bright	6 0	13 00	6 6 62	Stoke	Leek T	Port Vale	29	10
						Leicester C	42	6
						Crystal Palace	227	92
						Sheffield W	70	30
Lee Briscoe§	5 7	10 09	30 9 75	Pontefract	Trainee	Sheffield W	1	—
Trevor Francis†	5 10	11 07	19 4 54	Plymouth	Apprentice	Birmingham C	271	115
					Detroit E	Birmingham C	9	3
						Nottingham F	20	6
					Detroit E	Nottingham F	50	22
						Manchester C	26	12
						Sampdoria	68	17
						Atalanta	21	1
						Rangers	18	—
						QPR	32	12
						Sheffield W	76	5
Matthew Hardwick	5 10	11 5	12 9 74	Rotherham	School	Sheffield W	—	—
David Hirst	5 11	13 01	7 12 67	Barnsley	Apprentice	Barnsley	28	9
						Sheffield W	218	84
Nigel Jemson	5 10	12 10	10 8 69	Preston	Trainee	Preston NE	32	8
						Nottingham F	47	13
						Bolton W (loan)	5	—
						Preston NE (loan)	9	2
						Sheffield W	51	9
						Grimsby T (loan)	6	2
Michael Rowntree‡			18 11 73	Hartlepool	Trainee	Sheffield W	—	—
Chris Waddle	6 2	12 13	14 12 60	Hepworth	Tow Law T	Newcastle U	170	46
						Tottenham H	138	33
						Marseille	107	22
						Sheffield W	52	4
Gordon Watson	5 7	13 03	20 3 71	Kent	Trainee	Charlton Ath	31	7
						Sheffield W	43	13

Trainees
Aldous, Richard; Bailey, Gavin J; Jackson, Kirk S. S; Ludlam, Craig; Mason, Richard M; Pass, Steven D; Scargill, Jonathan M; Sykes, Paul K.

Associated Schoolboys
Batty, Mark P; Cadet, Ryan L; Harkin, Thomas E; Harrison, Andrew J; Haslam, Steven R; Hutchinson, Sean A; James, Mark B; Kotylo, Krystof J; Milley, Christopher; Platts, Mark A; Powell, Vill W; Quinn, Andrew J; Simpkins, James M; Simpkins, Michael J; Smith, Andrew A; Thirlwell, Paul; Wood, James; Wood, Scott R.

Associated Schoolboys who have accepted the Club's offer of a Traineeship/Contract
Bowler, Martin S; Humphreys, Ritchie J; Kirkpatrick, Matthew R; Pringle, Alan J; Sharman, Samuel J; Smith, Daniel J; Stevens, Andrew E; Thorpe, Steven M; Weaver, Simon D.

SHREWSBURY TOWN 1993–94 *Back row (left to right):* Fred Davies (Caretaker Manager), Gary Patterson, Kevin Summerfield, Tommy Lynch, Dean Spink, James Mulvey, Paul Edwards, Mark Williams, Jason Yates, John Brough, Steve MacKenzie, Malcolm Musgrove (Physio).
Front row: O'Neill Donaldson, Mark Smith, Nicholas Brookman, Paul Evans, Michael Brown, Carl Griffiths, Kevin Seabury, Joe Gallen, Mark Taylor.

Division 2 SHREWSBURY TOWN

Gay Meadow, Shrewsbury SY2 6AB. Telephone Shrewsbury (0743) 360111. Commercial Dept: 56316. Clubcall: 0898 121194.

Ground capacity: 7500.

Record attendance: 18,917 v Walsall, Division 3, 26 April 1961.

Record receipts: £36,240 v Ipswich T, FA Cup 5th rd, 13 February 1982.

Pitch measurements: 116yd × 76yd.

Vice-president: Dr J. Millard Bryson.

Chairman: R. Bailey.

Directors: F. C. G. Fry, M. J. Starkey, G. W. Nelson, W. H. Richards, K. R. Woodhouse.

Manager: Fred Davies. ***Commercial Manager:*** M. Thomas.

Physio: Malcolm Musgrove.

Secretary: M. J. Starkey.

Club Nickname: 'Town' or 'Shrews'.

Year Formed: 1886. ***Turned Professional:*** 1905 (approx). ***Ltd Co.:*** 1936.

Previous Ground: Old Shrewsbury Racecourse.

Record League Victory: 7–0 v Swindon T, Division 3 (S), 6 May 1955 – McBride; Bannister, Keech; Wallace, Maloney, Candlin; Price, O'Donnell (1), Weigh (4), Russell, McCue (2).

Record Cup Victory: 7–1 v Banbury Spencer, FA Cup, 1st rd, 4 November 1961 – Gibson; Walters, Skeech; Wallace, Pountney, Harley; Kenning (2), Pragg, Starkey (1), Rowley (2), McLaughlin (2).

Record Defeat: 1–8 v Norwich C, Division 3 (S), 1952–53 and v Coventry C, Division 3, 22 October 1963.

Most League Points (2 for a win): 62, Division 4, 1974–75.

Most League Points (3 for a win): 79, Division 3, 1993–94.

Most League Goals: 101, Division 4, 1958–59.

Highest League Scorer in Season: Arthur Rowley, 38, Division 4, 1958–59.

Most League Goals in Total Aggregate: Arthur Rowley, 152, 1958–65 (thus completing his League record of 434 goals).

Most Capped Player: Jimmy McLaughlin, 5 (12), Northern Ireland and Bernard McNally, 5, Northern Ireland.

Most League Appearances: Colin Griffin, 406, 1975–89.

Record Transfer Fee Received: £385,000 from WBA for Bernard McNally, July 1989.

Record Transfer Fee Paid: £100,000 to Aldershot for John Dungworth, November 1979 and £100,000 to Southampton for Mark Blake, August 1990.

Football League Record: 1950 Elected to Division 3 (N); 1951–58 Division 3 (S); 1958–59 Division 4; 1959–74 Division 3; 1974–75 Division 4; 1975–79 Division 3; 1979–89 Division 2; 1989–94 Division 3; 1994– Division 2.

Honours: *Football League:* Division 2 best season: 8th, 1983–84, 1984–85; Division 3 – Champions 1978–79, 1993–94; Division 4 – Runners-up 1974–5. *FA Cup:* best season: 6th rd, 1978–79, 1981–82. *Football League Cup:* Semi-final 1961. *Welsh Cup:* Winners 1891, 1938, 1977, 1979, 1984, 1985; Runners-up 1931, 1948, 1980.

SHREWSBURY TOWN 1993—94 LEAGUE RECORD

Match No.	Date	Venue	Opponents	Result		H/T Score	Lg. Pos.	Goalscorers	Attendance
1	Aug 14	A	Mansfield T	L	0-1	0-0	—		2983
2	21	H	Walsall	L	1-2	0-0	19	Brown	3681
3	28	A	Preston NE	L	1-6	0-5	22	Brown	4941
4	31	A	Colchester U	D	3-3	1-3	—	Lynch, Summerfield, Spink	2723
5	Sept 4	H	Bury	W	1-0	1-0	17	Donaldson	2669
6	11	A	Darlington	W	2-0	2-0	13	Clarke 2	1702
7	18	H	Gillingham	D	2-2	1-1	14	Griffiths, Summerfield	2811
8	25	A	Scarborough	W	3-1	2-1	10	Griffiths 3	1137
9	Oct 2	H	Torquay U	W	3-2	0-1	8	Kelly (og), Spink, Summerfield	2725
10	9	H	Carlisle U	W	1-0	1-0	6	Griffiths	3254
11	16	A	Chester C	L	0-1	0-1	10		3052
12	23	H	Doncaster R	L	0-1	0-1	10		2675
13	30	A	Wycombe W	D	1-1	0-1	10	Brown	5064
14	Nov 2	H	Crewe Alex	D	2-2	1-1	—	Donaldson, Spink	5585
15	6	A	Northampton T	W	3-0	1-0	9	Spink 2, Lynch	2650
16	20	H	Scunthorpe U	D	0-0	0-0	9		2436
17	27	A	Wigan Ath	W	5-2	1-0	7	Clarke 2 (1 pen), Spink 3	1498
18	Dec 11	A	Walsall	W	1-0	1-0	6	Spink	4979
19	17	H	Mansfield T	D	2-2	0-1	—	Walton, Clarke	3392
20	27	A	Hereford U	W	1-0	1-0	6	Clarke	4333
21	Jan 1	A	Chesterfield	W	2-1	1-1	5	Spink 2	3614
22	3	H	Colchester U	W	2-1	0-1	2	Walton, Spink	4245
23	15	H	Chester C	W	3-0	2-0	3	Clarke 2 (1 pen), Williams	5365
24	29	H	Wycombe W	W	1-0	0-0	3	Spink	5967
25	Feb 5	A	Doncaster R	D	0-0	0-0	3		2047
26	12	H	Rochdale	D	1-1	1-0	3	Reeves (og)	4882
27	19	H	Preston NE	W	1-0	0-0	2	Lynch	5391
28	25	A	Bury	W	3-2	0-2	2	Clarke (pen), Spink, Brown	3443
29	Mar 1	H	Lincoln C	L	1-2	0-0	—	Walton	4706
30	5	H	Darlington	D	1-1	0-1	3	Taylor	4011
31	12	A	Gillingham	W	2-0	0-0	3	Walton, Spink	3038
32	19	H	Scarborough	W	2-0	1-0	2	Gallen, Spink	3901
33	26	A	Torquay U	D	0-0	0-0	3		4085
34	Apr 2	H	Hereford U	W	2-0	0-0	2	Spink, Lynch	5310
35	4	A	Lincoln C	W	1-0	0-0	2	Brown	2823
36	9	H	Chesterfield	D	0-0	0-0	2		4846
37	12	A	Rochdale	W	2-1	0-0	—	Spink, Walton	5402
38	16	A	Crewe Alex	D	0-0	0-0	1		5251
39	23	H	Northampton T	W	2-1	1-1	1	Woods, Clarke	6512
40	30	A	Scunthorpe U	W	4-1	1-0	1	Patterson, Brown, Clarke, Taylor	4587
41	May 3	A	Carlisle U	L	1-2	0-2	—	Brown	8007
42	7	H	Wigan Ath	D	0-0	0-0	1		7686

Final League Position: 1

GOALSCORERS

League (63): Spink 18, Clarke 11 (3 pens), Brown 7, Griffiths 5, Walton 5, Lynch 4, Summerfield 3, Donaldson 2, Taylor 2, Gallen 1, Patterson 1, Williams 1, Woods 1, own goals 2.
Coca-Cola Cup (7): Summerfield 3, Brown 1, Evans 1, Griffiths 1, MacKenzie 1 (pen).
FA Cup (3): Gallen 1, Spink 1, Walton 1.

Edwards 42	Hockaday 30 + 2	Lynch 32 + 3	Evans 11 + 2	Spink 38 + 2	Blake 15	Patterson 35 + 4	Clarke 27 + 1	Summerfield 18 + 15	Griffiths 8 + 1	MacKenzie 3	Brown 40 + 1	Withe 23 + 3	Taylor 41	Williams 35 + 1	Donaldson 6 + 3	Gallen 4 + 2	Smith 4 + 4	Walton 27	Brough 1 + 1	Croft 4	Donowa 4	Rutherford 7 + 7	Woods 7 + 2	*Match No.*
1	2	3	4	5	6	*7*	8	9	10	11	12	14												1
1	2	3		7	5		8	9	10	11	6	12	4											2
1	2		10	*9*	6	11	8	5			7	3	4	12	14									3
1	2	3	*11*	12	6	14	8	10			7		4	5	9									4
1	2	3	11		6	12	8	10			7		4	5	9									5
1	2		11		6		8	10	12		7	3	4	5	9									6
1		3	11	5	6	12	8	9	10		7	*2*	4			14								7
1	*2*	3	11	9	6	4	12		10		7	14	8	5										8
1			11	12	6	4	8	9	10		7	3	2	5										9
1	12		11	8	6	4		9	10		7	3	2	5										10
1	12	14	*11*	8	6	4		9	10		7	3	2	5										11
1	2	3	11	8	6	14		*9*	10		7		4	5	12									12
1	2	5		10	6	11		8			7	3	4		9									13
1	2	5	12	10	6	11		8			7	3	4		*9*		14							14
1	2	5		10		11		8			7	3	4				9	6						15
1	2	3		10		11				8	7		4	5				6	9					16
1	2	3		9		11	8				7	10	4	5				6						17
1	2			9		10	8	12			7	3	4	5				6		11				18
1	2			9		10	8	12			7	3	4	5				6		11				19
1	2			9		11	8	12			7	6	4	5				10		3				20
1	2	14		9		11	8				7	3	4	5			12	6		*10*				21
1	2	14		9		11	8	12			7	3	4	5			*10*	6						22
1		2		9		11	8	12			7	3	4	5			10	6						23
1		2		9		10	8				7	3	4	5				6			11			24
1		3		9		10	8	12			7	2	4	5				6			11			25
1		3	12	9	6	10	*8*				7	2	4	5					14		11			26
1		2		9		10	8				7	3	4	5			12	6			11			27
1		2		9		10	8	12			7	3	4	5			*11*	6				14		28
1		2		9		10		12			7	3	4	5	11			6				8		29
1		2		9		10	8	*7*				3	4	5		14	12	6				11		30
1	2	3		9		10		12			7		4	5		8		6				11		31
1	2	3		9				10			7		4	5	12	8		6				11		32
1	2	3		9		10					7		4	5		8		6				11	12	33
1	2	3		9		10		12			7		4	5		8		6				14	*11*	34
1	2	3		9		10	8	12			7		4	5				6					11	35
1	2	3		9		10	8				7		4	5				6				12	11	36
1	2	3		9		10		8			7		4	5				6				11		37
1	2	3		9		10		8			7		4	5				6				11	12	38
1	2	3		9		10	8	12			7		4	5				6				14	*11*	39
1	2	3		*9*		10	8	12			7		4	5				6				14	11	40
1	2	3		9		*10*	8	12			7		4	5				6				14	11	41
1	2	3		9		10	8	12			7		4	5				6				14	*11*	42

Coca-Cola Cup	First Round	Scunthorpe U (h)	1-0
		(a)	1-1
	Second Round	Southampton (a)	0-1
		(h)	2-0
	Third Round	Blackburn R (a)	0-0
		(h)	3-4
FA Cup	First Round	Doncaster R (h)	1-1
		(a)	2-1
	Second Round	Preston NE (h)	0-1

SHREWSBURY TOWN

Player and Position	Ht	Wt	Birth Date	Birth Place	Source	Clubs	League App	League Gls
Goalkeepers								
Tim Clarke	6 3	13 07	19 9 68	Stourbridge	Halesowen	Coventry C	—	—
						Huddersfield T	70	—
						Rochdale (loan)	2	—
					Halesowen	Shrewsbury T	—	—
Paul Edwards	5 11	11 05	22 2 65	Liverpool	St. Helens T	Crewe Alex	29	—
						Shrewsbury T	84	—
Defenders								
Mark Blake*	6 1	12 08	19 12 67	Portsmouth	Apprentice	Southampton	18	2
						Colchester U (loan)	4	1
						Shrewsbury T (loan)	10	—
						Shrewsbury T	132	3
David Hockaday	5 9	11 02	9 11 57	Billingham	Amateur	Blackpool	147	24
						Swindon T	245	6
						Hull C	72	2
						Stoke C (loan)	7	—
						Shrewsbury T	32	—
David Walton	6 2	13 04	10 4 73	Bedlingham	Trainee	Sheffield U	—	—
						Shrewsbury T	27	5
Mark S Williams	6 0	13 00	28 9 70	Cheshire	Newtown	Shrewsbury T	67	2
Chris Withe	5 10	11 12	25 9 62	Liverpool	Apprentice	Newcastle U	2	—
						Bradford C	143	2
						Notts Co	80	3
						Bury	31	1
						Chester C (loan)	2	—
						Mansfield T (loan)	11	—
						Mansfield T	65	5
						Shrewsbury T	26	—
Midfield								
Nick Brookman‡	5 9	10 07	28 10 68	Manchester	Trainee	Bolton W	57	10
						Stockport Co	6	—
					Shrewsbury T	Shrewsbury T	—	—
Paul Evans	5 6	10 08	1 9 74	Oswestry	Trainee	Shrewsbury T	19	—
Tommy Lynch	6 0	12 06	10 10 64	Limerick	Limerick	Sunderland	4	—
						Shrewsbury T	175	10
Steve MacKenzie*	5 11	12 05	23 11 61	Romford	Apprentice	Crystal Palace	—	—
						Manchester C	58	8
						WBA	148	23
						Charlton Ath	100	7
						Sheffield W	15	2
						Shrewsbury T	24	1
Gary Patterson	5 11	11 05	27 11 72	Newcastle	Trainee	Notts Co	—	—
						Shrewsbury T	39	1
Kevin Seabury	5 9	11 06	24 11 73	Shrewsbury	Trainee	Shrewsbury T	1	—
Mark Smith	5 9	10 04	16 12 64	Bellshill	St Mirren BC	Queen's Park	82	7
						Celtic	6	—
						Dunfermline Ath	53	6
						Stoke C (loan)	2	—
						Nottingham F	—	—
						Reading (loan)	3	—
						Shrewsbury T	39	1
Kevin Summerfield	5 11	11 00	7 1 59	Walsall	Apprentice	WBA	9	4
						Birmingham C	5	1
						Walsall	54	17
						Cardiff C	10	1
						Plymouth Arg	139	26
						Exeter C (loan)	4	—
						Shrewsbury T	144	22
Mark Taylor	5 8	11 08	22 2 66	Walsall	Local	Walsall	113	4
						Sheffield W	9	—
						Shrewsbury T (loan)	19	2
						Shrewsbury T	112	9
Forwards								
John Brough*	6 1	12 07	8 1 73	Heanor	Trainee	Notts Co	—	—
						Shrewsbury T	16	1

SHREWSBURY TOWN

Colours: Amber/blue trim shirts, blue shorts, amber stockings, blue trim. **Change colours:** Red shirts, white shorts, red stockings.

Foundation: Shrewsbury School having provided a number of the early England and Wales internationals it is not surprising that there was a Town club as early as 1876 which won the Birmingham Senior Cup in 1879. However, the present Shrewsbury Town club was formed in 1886 and won the Welsh FA Cup as early as 1891.

First Football League game: 19 August, 1950, Division 3(N), v Scunthorpe U (a) D 0-0 – Eggleston; Fisher, Lewis; Wheatley, Depear, Robinson; Griffin, Hope, Jackson, Brown, Barker.

Did you know: On 12 February 1994 Shrewsbury Town set up a club record 14th League game without defeat and Fred Davies became the longest serving caretaker-manager in League football, having been appointed as such in May 1993.

Managers (and Secretary-Managers)
W. Adams 1905–12*, A. Weston 1912–34*, Jack Roscamp 1934–35, Sam Ramsey 1935–36, Ted Bousted 1936–40, Leslie Knighton 1945–49, Harry Chapman 1949–50, Sammy Crooks 1950–54, Walter Rowley 1955–57, Harry Potts 1957–58, Johnny Spuhler 1958, Arthur Rowley 1958–68, Harry Gregg 1968–72, Maurice Evans 1972–73, Alan Durban 1974–78, Richie Barker 1978, Graham Turner 1978–84, Chic Bates 1984–87, Ian McNeill 1987–90, Asa Hartford 1990–91, John Bond 1991–93, Fred Davies February 1994 (previously caretaker-manager from May 1993)–

Player and Position	*Ht*	*Wt*	*Birth Date*	*Birth Place*	*Source*	*Clubs*	*League App*	*League Gls*
Mike Brown	5 9	10 12	8 2 68	Birmingham	Apprentice	Shrewsbury T	190	9
						Bolton W	33	3
						Shrewsbury T	58	8
Wayne Clarke	6 0	11 08	28 2 61	Wolverhampton	Apprentice	Wolverhampton W	148	30
						Birmingham C	92	38
						Everton	57	18
						Leicester C	11	1
						Manchester C	21	2
						Shrewsbury T (loan)	7	6
						Stoke C (loan)	9	3
						Wolverhampton W (loan)	1	—
						Walsall	39	21
						Shrewsbury T	28	11
O'Neill Donaldson*	6 0	11 04	24 11 69	Birmingham	Hinckley	Shrewsbury T	28	4
Joe Gallen	5 11	11 08	2 9 72	Hammersmith	Trainee	Watford	—	—
						Exeter C (loan)	6	—
						Shrewsbury T	6	1
Paul Kinnaird (To Partick T)	5 8	10 10	11 11 66	Glasgow	Apprentice	Norwich C	—	—
						Dundee U	18	—
						Motherwell	34	—
						St Mirren	57	4
						Partick T	33	3
						Shrewsbury T	4	1
						St Johnstone	8	—
Mark Rutherford	5 11	11 00	25 3 72	Birmingham	Trainee	Birmingham C	5	—
					Shelbourne	Shrewsbury T (loan)	14	—
Dean Spink	5 11	13 08	22 1 67	Birmingham	Halesowen	Aston Villa	—	—
						Scarborough (loan)	3	2
						Bury (loan)	6	1
						Shrewsbury T	159	31

Trainees
Berry, Craig S; Evans, Paul D; Grenham, Tony A; Hitchman, Neil D; Jefferis, Martin; King, Nathan P; Martin, Lee C; Reed, Ian P; Whatmore, Jody; Woodvine, Andrew T.

Associated Schoolboys
Currier, Damian J; Stephens, Philip P.

Associated Schoolboys who have accepted the Club's offer of a Traineeship/Contract
Green, Adam B; Pemberton, Stephen.

SOUTHAMPTON 1993–94 *Back row (left to right):* Paul McDonald, Nicky Banger, Jason Dodd, Jeff Kenna, Tommy Widdrington, Derek Allan, Simon Charlton.
Centre row: Francis Benali, Iain Dowie, Steve Wood, Paul Moody, Tim Flowers, Kenneth Monkou, Ian Andrews, Matthew Bound, Richard Hall, Neil Maddison, Perry Groves.
Front row: Lew Chatterley (First Team Coach), Stuart Gray, Micky Adams, Kevin Moore, Ian Branfoot (Manager), Glenn Cockerill, Terry Hurlock, Matthew Le Tissier, Don Taylor (Physio).

FA Premiership **SOUTHAMPTON**

The Dell, Milton Road, Southampton SO9 4XX. Telephone Southampton (0703) 220505. Fax 0703 330360. Ticket enquiries: (0703) 228575.

Ground capacity: 15,000.

Record attendance: 31,044 v Manchester U, Division 1, 8 October 1969.

Record receipts: £163,204 v Blackburn R, FA Premier League, 16 April 1994.

Pitch measurements: 110yd × 72yd.

Chairman: F. G. L. Askham FCA.

Vice-Chairman: K. St. J. Wiseman.

Directors: I. L. Gordon, B. H. D. Hunt, L. McMenemy, M. R. Richards FCA.

President: J. Corbett. ***Vice-president:*** E. T. Bates.

Manager: Alan Ball. ***Joint Assistant Managers:*** John Mortimore, Lew Chatterley.

Coach: Lew Chatterley. ***Physio:*** Don Taylor.

Secretary: Brian Truscott. ***Commercial Manager:***

Year Formed: 1885. ***Turned Professional:*** 1894. ***Ltd Co.:*** 1897.

Club Nickname: 'The Saints'.

Previous Name: Southampton St Mary's until 1885.

Previous Grounds: 1885, Antelope Ground; 1897, County Cricket Ground; 1898, The Dell.

Record League Victory: 9–3 v Wolverhampton W, Division 2, 18 September 1965 – Godfrey; Jones, Williams; Walker, Knapp, Huxford; Paine (2), O'Brien (1), Melia, Chivers (4), Sydenham (2).

Record Cup Victory: 7–1 v Ipswich T, FA Cup, 3rd rd, 7 January 1961 – Reynolds; Davies, Traynor; Conner, Page, Huxford; Paine (1), O'Brien (3 incl. 1p), Reeves, Mulgrew (2), Penk (1).

Record Defeat: 0–8 v Tottenham H, Division 2, 28 March 1936 and v Everton, Division 1, 20 November 1971.

Most League Points (2 for a win): 61, Division 3 (S), 1921–22 and Division 3, 1959–60.

Most League Points (3 for a win): 77, Division 1, 1983–84.

Most League Goals: 112, Division 3 (S), 1957–58.

Highest League Scorer in Season: Derek Reeves, 39, Division 3, 1959–60.

Most League Goals in Total Aggregate: Mike Channon, 185, 1966–77, 1979–82.

Most Capped Player: Peter Shilton, 49 (125), England.

Most League Appearances: Terry Paine, 713, 1956–74.

Record Transfer Fee Received: £3,300,000 from Blackburn R for Alan Shearer, July 1992.

Record Transfer Fee Paid: £1,000,000 to Swindon T for Alan McLoughlin, December 1990.

Football League Record: 1920 Original Member of Division 3; 1921–22 Division 3 (S); 1922–53 Division 2; 1953–58 Division 3 (S); 1958–60 Division 3; 1960–66 Division 2; 1966–74 Division 1; 1974–78 Division 2; 1978–92 Division 1; 1992– FA Premier League.

Honours: *Football League:* Division 1 – Runners-up 1983–84; Division 2 – Runners-up 1965–66, 1977–78; Division 3 (S) – Champions 1921–22; Runners-up 1920–21; Division 3 – Champions 1959–60. *FA Cup:* Winners 1975–76; Runners-up 1900, 1902. *Football League Cup:* Runners-up 1978–79. *Zenith Data Systems Cup:* Runners-up 1991–92. **European Competitions:** *European Fairs Cup:* 1969–70. *UEFA Cup:* 1971–72, 1981–82, 1982–83, 1984–85. *European Cup-Winners' Cup:* 1976–77.

SOUTHAMPTON 1993—94 LEAGUE RECORD

Match No.	Date	Venue	Opponents	Result		H/T Score	Lg. Pos.	Goalscorers	Attendance
1	Aug 14	H	Everton	L	0-2	0-2	—		14,051
2	17	A	Ipswich T	L	0-1	0-0	—		14,958
3	21	A	QPR	L	1-2	0-1	22	Dowie	10,613
4	25	H	Swindon T	W	5-1	1-0	—	Le Tissier 2, Kenna, Dowie, Maddison	12,505
5	28	H	Manchester U	L	1-3	1-2	19	Maddison	16,189
6	31	A	Wimbledon	L	0-1	0-1	—		6036
7	Sept 11	H	Leeds U	L	0-2	0-0	20		13,511
8	18	A	Sheffield W	L	0-2	0-0	21		22,503
9	25	A	Arsenal	L	0-1	0-1	21		26,902
10	Oct 2	H	Sheffield U	D	3-3	1-0	21	Monkou, Maddison, Kenna	11,619
11	16	A	Coventry C	D	1-1	0-0	21	Charlton	9837
12	24	H	Newcastle U	W	2-1	0-0	—	Le Tissier 2	13,804
13	30	A	Liverpool	L	2-4	1-2	21	Le Tissier 2	32,818
14	Nov 6	H	Tottenham H	W	1-0	0-0	20	Maddison	16,017
15	20	A	Blackburn R	L	0-2	0-1	20		17,343
16	24	A	Aston Villa	W	2-0	0-0	—	Le Tissier 2	16,180
17	29	H	West Ham U	L	0-2	0-2	—		13,258
18	Dec 4	A	Everton	L	0-1	0-1	21		13,265
19	8	H	Ipswich T	L	0-1	0-0	—		9028
20	11	H	QPR	L	0-1	0-1	21		11,946
21	18	A	Swindon T	L	1-2	1-1	21	Le Tissier	13,565
22	27	H	Chelsea	W	3-1	1-1	20	Widdrington, Dowie, Bennett	14,221
23	28	A	Manchester C	D	1-1	1-1	20	Dowie	24,712
24	Jan 1	H	Norwich C	L	0-1	0-1	21		16,556
25	15	H	Coventry C	W	1-0	1-0	20	Le Tissier (pen)	12,397
26	22	A	Newcastle U	W	2-1	1-1	18	Maddison, Le Tissier	32,067
27	Feb 5	A	Oldham Ath	L	1-2	1-2	19	Le Tissier	9982
28	14	H	Liverpool	W	4-2	3-0	—	Le Tissier 3 (2 pens), Maskell	18,306
29	25	H	Wimbledon	W	1-0	0-0	17	Le Tissier	14,790
30	Mar 5	A	Leeds U	D	0-0	0-0	18		30,829
31	12	H	Sheffield W	D	1-1	0-0	18	Monkou	16,391
32	19	H	Arsenal	L	0-4	0-2	18		16,790
33	26	A	Sheffield U	D	0-0	0-0	18		19,522
34	30	H	Oldham Ath	L	1-3	0-2	—	Le Tissier	14,101
35	Apr 2	A	Chelsea	L	0-2	0-1	21		19,801
36	4	H	Manchester C	L	0-1	0-0	21		16,377
37	9	A	Norwich C	W	5-4	1-1	20	Ullathorne (og), Le Tissier 3 (1 pen), Monkou	17,150
38	16	H	Blackburn R	W	3-1	2-0	19	Dowie, Allen, Le Tissier (pen)	19,105
39	23	A	Tottenham H	L	0-3	0-1	19		25,959
40	30	H	Aston Villa	W	4-1	2-0	17	Le Tissier 2, Monkou, Maddison	18,803
41	May 4	A	Manchester U	L	0-2	0-0	—		44,705
42	7	A	West Ham U	D	3-3	1-1	18	Le Tissier 2 (1 pen), Maddison	26,952

Final League Position: 18

GOALSCORERS

League (49): Le Tissier 25 (6 pens), Maddison 7, Dowie 5, Monkou 4, Kenna 2, Allen 1, Bennett 1, Charlton 1, Maskell 1, Widdrington 1, own goal 1.
Coca-Cola Cup (1): Moore 1.
FA Cup (1): Dowie 1.

Andrews 5	Kenna 40 + 1	Adams 17 + 2	Charlton 29 + 4	Hall 4	Monkou 35	Le Tissier 38	Cockerill 12 + 2	Dowie 39	Maddison 41	Banger 4 + 10	Benali 34 + 3	Bennett — + 8	Flowers 12	Widdrington 11	Powell 1	Bartlett 4 + 3	Moore 14	Wood 27	Allen 29 + 3	Moody 3 + 2	Reid 7	Beasant 25	Hurlock 2	Dodd 5 + 5	Cramb — + 1	Hughes — + 2	Magilton 15	Maskell 6 + 4	Heaney 2	Bound 1	Match No.
1	2	3	4	5	6	7	8	9	10	*11*	12	14																			1
	2	3		5	6	7	8	9	10	12	11		1	4																	2
	2	3	12	5	6	*7*	8	9	10		4		1		11	14															3
	2	3	4	*5*	6	7	8	9	10	12	14		1			11															4
	2	3	14		6	7	8	9	10	12	4		1			11	*5*														5
	2	3	14		6	7	8	9	10	12	4		1			*11*	5														6
	2		14		*6*	7	8	9	10	11	3	12	1			4	5														7
	2		4			7	8	9	10	12	3		1			14	5	6	*11*												8
	2	3			6		8	*9*	10	14	12		1				4	5	11	7											9
	2	3			6		12	9	10		4		1				5		11	7	8										10
	2	3	4		6			9	10				1				5		11	7	8										11
	2	3				7		9	10		4		1				5	6	11	12	8										12
	2	3			6	7	12	9	10		4		1				5		11		8										13
1	2	3			6	7		9	10		4							5	11		8										14
1	2	12	*4*		6	7	8	9	10		3	14						5	11												15
1	2		4		6	7	8	9	10		3							5	11												16
1	2	12	4		6	7	*8*	9	10		3	14						5	11												17
	2	3	6			7		*9*	10		4							5	11			1	8	12	14						18
	2	3	4			7			10		6							5	11	12		1	8	9							19
	2		4		6	7		9	10		3					12		5	11			1		8							20
	2		4		6	7			10		3	12		9				5	11		8	1									21
		3				7		9	10		6	12		8				5	11		4	1		2							22
	2	3				7		9	10		4	12		8			6	5	11			1									23
	14	3				7		9	10		4	12		8			6	5	11			1		*2*							24
	2		4		6	7		9	10					8				5	11			1		3							25
	2		3		6	7		9	10	8							4	5	11			1									26
	2		3		6	7		9	10	8							4	5	11			1				12					27
	2		4		6	7		9	10		3							5				1					8	11			28
	2		4		6	7		9	10		3							5	12			1					8	11			29
	2		4		6	7		9	10		3							5				1					8	11			30
	2		4		6	7		9	10	14	3							*5*	12			1					8	11			31
	2		4		6	7		9	10	12	3							*5*	14			1					8	11			32
	2		4		6	7		9	10		3							5				1					8		11		33
	2		4		6	7		9			3							5	11			1		12		14	8	*10*			34
	2		4		6	7		9	10		3							5	11			1		14			8	12			35
	2		4		6	7		9	10	12	3							5	11			1					8				36
	2		4		6	7		9	10		3								11			1					8			5	37
	2		4		6	7		9	*10*		3			5					11			1		14			8	12			38
	2		3		6				9	14				10			4	*5*	7			1					8	12	11		39
	2		4		6	7		9	10		3			5					11			1		12			8				40
	2		4		6	7		9	10		3			5					11			1					8	12			41
	2		4		6	7		9	10		3			5					11			1					8				42

Coca-Cola Cup	Second Round	Shrewsbury T (h)	1-0
		(a)	0-2
FA Cup	Third Round	Port Vale (h)	1-1
		(a)	0-1

SOUTHAMPTON

Player and Position	Ht	Wt	Birth Date	Birth Place	Source	Clubs	League App	League Gls
Goalkeepers								
Ian Andrews	6 2	13 07	1 12 64	Nottingham	Apprentice	Leicester C	126	—
						Swindon T (loan)	1	—
						Celtic	5	—
						Leeds U (loan)	1	—
						Southampton	10	—
Dave Beasant	6 4	14 01	20 3 59	Willesden	Edgware T	Wimbledon	340	—
						Newcastle U	20	—
						Chelsea	133	—
						Grimsby T (loan)	6	—
						Wolverhampton W (loan)	4	—
						Southampton	25	—
Defenders								
Derek Allan	6 0	12 00	24 12 74	Irving	Ayr United BC	Ayr U	5	—
						Southampton	1	—
Matthew Bound	6 2	13 12	9 11 72	Trowbridge	Trainee	Southampton	5	—
						Hull C (loan)	7	1
Simon Charlton	5 7	10 11	25 10 71	Huddersfield	Trainee	Huddersfield T	124	1
						Southampton	33	1
Jason Dodd	5 10	11 13	2 11 70	Bath		Southampton	109	1
Gary Ferguson‡	5 11	11 08	16 9 74	Belfast	Reading	Southampton	—	—
Stuart Gray‡	5 10	11 09	19 4 60	Withernsea	Local	Nottingham F	49	3
						Bolton W (loan)	10	—
						Barnsley	120	23
						Aston Villa	106	9
						Southampton	12	—
Richard Hall	6 2	13 01	14 3 72	Ipswich	Trainee	Scunthorpe U	22	3
						Southampton	59	7
Jeff Kenna	5 11	11 09	27 8 70	Dublin	Trainee	Southampton	86	4
Kenneth Monkou	6 3	14 05	29 11 64	Surinam	Feyenoord	Chelsea	94	2
						Southampton	68	5
Kevin Moore*	6 0	13 00	29 4 58	Grimsby	Local	Grimsby T	400	27
						Oldham Ath	13	1
						Southampton	148	10
						Bristol R (loan)	7	—
						Bristol R (loan)	4	1
Chris Pickering‡	5 11	11 08	18 12 74	Stockport	Trainee	Southampton	—	—
Steve Wood*	6 1	12 04	2 2 63	Bracknell	Apprentice	Reading	219	9
						Millwall	110	—
						Southampton	46	—
Midfield								
Paul Allen	5 7	10 10	28 8 62	Aveley	Apprentice	West Ham U	152	6
						Tottenham H	292	23
						Southampton	32	1
Neal Bartlett	5 10	11 12	7 4 75	Southampton	Trainee	Southampton	8	—
David Hughes	5 9	10 10	30 12 72	St Albans	Trainee	Southampton	2	—
Neil Maddison	5 10	10 07	2 10 69	Darlington	Trainee	Southampton	95	13
Jim Magilton	5 10	12 07	6 5 69	Belfast	Apprentice	Liverpool	—	—
						Oxford U	150	34
						Southampton	15	—
Matthew Robinson	5 11	10 07	23 12 74	Exeter	Trainee	Southampton	—	—
Paul Sheerin	5 10	10 13	28 8 74	Edinburgh	Whitehill Welfare	Alloa	9	—
						Southampton	—	—
Paul Tisdale	5 9	10 08	14 1 73	Malta	School	Southampton	—	—
						Northampton T (loan)	5	—
Tommy Widdrington	5 10	11 07	21 11 71	Newcastle	Trainee	Southampton	26	1
						Wigan Ath (loan)	6	—
Forwards								
Nicky Banger	5 9	11 07	25 2 71	Southampton	Trainee	Southampton	51	6
Francis Benali	5 10	11 00	30 12 68	Southampton	Apprentice	Southampton	138	—
Frankie Bennett	5 8	11 11	3 1 69	Birmingham	Halesowen	Southampton	8	1

SOUTHAMPTON

Colours: Red and white striped shirts, black shorts, black stockings. **Change colours:** Turquoise/royal blue striped shirts, turquoise shorts, royal blue stockings.

Foundation: Formed largely by players from the Deanery FC, which had been established by school teachers in 1880. Most of the founders were connected with the young men's association of St. Mary's Church. At the inaugural meeting held in November 1885 the club was named Southampton St. Mary's and the church's curate was elected president.

First Football League game: 28 August, 1920, Division 3, v Gillingham (a) D 1-1 – Allen; Parker, Titmuss; Shelley, Campbell, Turner; Barratt, Dominy (1), Rawlings, Moore, Foxall.

Did you know: Matthew Le Tissier scored his 100th League goal for Southampton with a penalty kick in a 3-3 draw against West Ham United on 7 May 1994, to ensure the Saints retained their FA Carling Premiership status.

Managers (and Secretary-Managers)
Cecil Knight 1894–95*, Charles Robson 1895–97, E. Arnfield 1897–1911* (continued as secretary), George Swift 1911–12, E. Arnfield 1912–19, Jimmy McIntyre 1919–24, Arthur Chadwick 1925–31, George Kay 1931–36, George Gross 1936–37, Tom Parker 1937–43, J. R. Sarjantson stepped down from the board to act as secretary-manager 1943–47 with the next two listed being team managers during this period), Arthur Dominy 1943–46, Bill Dodgin Snr 1946–49, Sid Cann 1949–51, George Roughton 1952–55, Ted Bates 1955–73, Lawrie McMenemy 1973–85, Chris Nicholl 1985–91, Ian Branfoot 1991–94, Alan Ball January 1994–

Player and Position	*Ht*	*Wt*	*Birth Date*	*Birth Place*	*Source*	*Clubs*	*League App*	*League Gls*
Colin Cramb	6 0	11 09	23 6 74	Lanark	Hamilton A. BC	Hamilton Acad	48	10
						Southampton	1	—
Kevin Doherty	5 9	11 00	2 9 75	Londonderry	Trainee	Southampton	—	—
Iain Dowie	6 1	13 07	9 1 65	Hatfield	Hendon	Luton T	66	16
						Fulham (loan)	5	1
						West Ham U	12	4
						Southampton	105	25
Perry Groves	5 10	12 08	19 4 65	London	Apprentice	Colchester U	156	26
						Arsenal	156	21
						Southampton	15	2
Neil Heaney	5 9	11 09	3 11 71	Middlesbrough	Trainee	Arsenal	7	—
						Hartlepool U (loan)	3	—
						Cambridge U (loan)	13	2
						Southampton	2	—
Matthew Le Tissier	6 1	12 10	14 10 68	Guernsey	Trainee	Southampton	251	100
Paul McDonald	5 6	9 07	20 4 68	Motherwell	Merry Street BC	Hamilton Acad	215	26
						Southampton	—	—
Craig Maskell	5 10	11 04	10 4 68	Aldershot	Apprentice	Southampton	6	1
						Swindon T (loan)	—	—
						Huddersfield T	87	43
						Reading	72	26
						Swindon T	47	22
						Southampton	10	1
Lee Powell‡	5 5	9 00	2 6 73	Newport	Trainee	Southampton	7	—

Trainees
Allen, Peter; Blamey, Nathan; Carr, Neil; Elliott, Lee; Everest, Anthony D; Hamill, Rory; Harper, Paul W; Hooks, John; Hopper, Neil; Jansen, Nicholas J; Joseph, Urias; Liney, Andrew; McNally, Aron A; Oakley, Matthew; Phillips, Daniel; Rowe, Richard.

Associated Schoolboys
Agamasu, Victor; Bartys, James; Batchelor, Adam; Bevan, Scott; Blake, Dean; Bradley, Shane; Cairns, Kwesi; Catley, Andrew; Collar, Stuart; Conaty, Steven; Davis, Neil; Deegan, Christopher M; Desborough, Daniel; Hayward, Daniel; Henderson, Justin; Homer, Gareth; Jenkins, Stephen M; Kelly, Jay; McCarthy, Craig; Page, David; Roberts, Daniel; Skinner, Darren M; Smith, Christopher G; Smith, Neil; Sullivan, Andrew; Swan, James; Warner, Philip.

Associated Schoolboys who have accepted the Club's offer of a Traineeship/Contract
Basham, Steven; Care, Simon J; Carter, John; Flahavan, Darryl J; Hazlehurst, Daniel R; McAllister, Craig; Phillips, Sam; Piper, David; Spedding, Duncan; Williams, Andrew P.

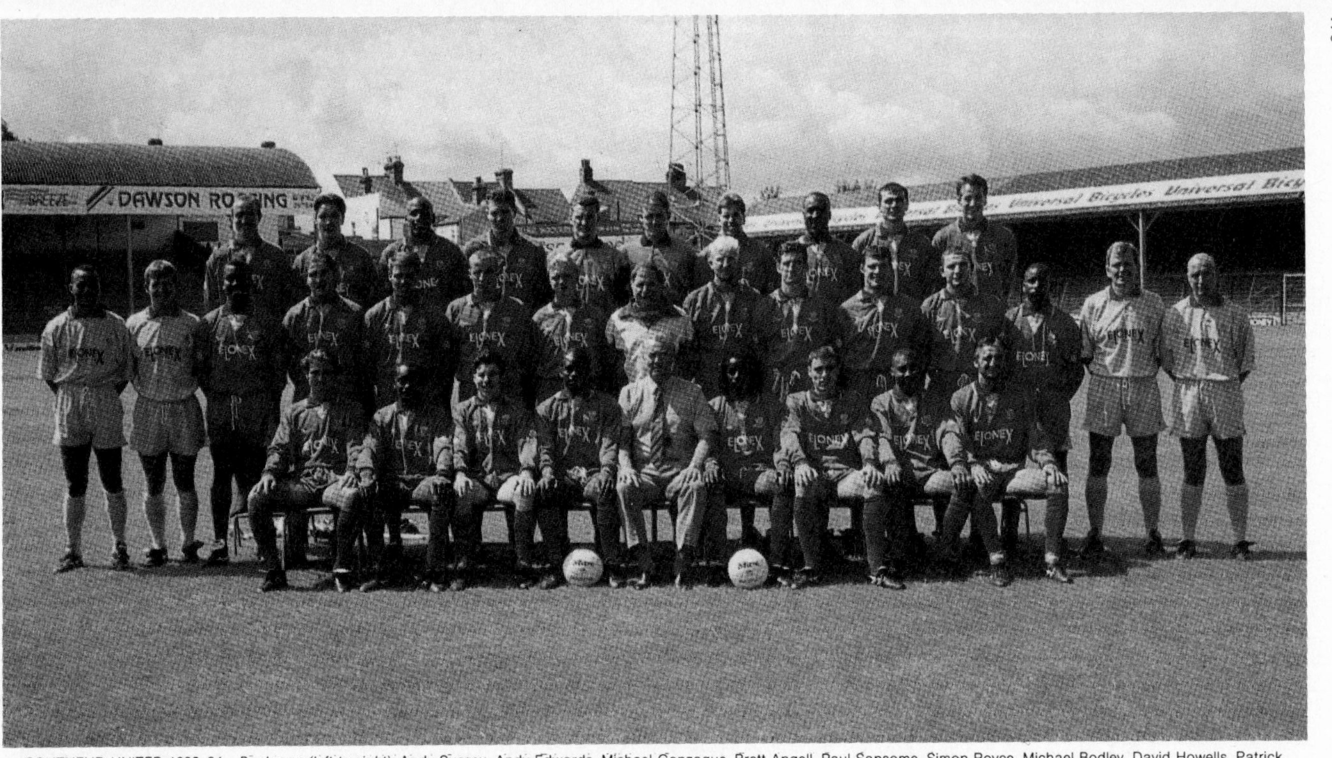

SOUTHEND UNITED 1993–94 *Back row (left to right):* Andy Sussex, Andy Edwards, Michael Gonzague, Brett Angell, Paul Sansome, Simon Royce, Michael Bodley, David Howells, Patrick Scully, Graham Bressington.

Centre row: Edwin Stein, John Gowens, Chris Powell, Gary Poole, Steve Tilson, Jamie Southon, Christian Hyslop, Barry Fry, John Cornwell, Gary Jones, Tommy Mooney, Craig Davidson, Mark Hall, Alan Raw, Danny Greaves.

Front row: Neil Rowbury, Andy Ansah, Derek Payne, Keith Jones, Vic Jobson (Chairman), Ricky Otto, Jonathon Hunt, Jae Martin, Adam Locke.

Division 1 SOUTHEND UNITED

Roots Hall Football Ground, Victoria Avenue, Southend-on-Sea SS2 6NQ. Telephone Southend (0702) 340707. Fax 0702 330164. Commercial Dept: (0702) 437154/6. Soccerline: 0839 664444. Ticket Office: (0702) 435602. Infoline: 0839 664443.

Ground capacity: 11,758.

Record attendance: 31,090 v Liverpool FA Cup 3rd rd, 10 January 1979.

Record receipts: £83,999 v West Ham U, Division 1, 7 April 1993.

Pitch measurements: 110yd × 74yd.

President: N. J. Woodcock.

Chairman and Managing Director: V. T. Jobson. ***Vice-chairman and Chief Executive:*** J. W. Adams.

Secretary: J. W. Adams.

Directors: J. Bridge, B. R. Gunner, W. R. Kelleway, D. M. Markscheffel, C. V. Murphy, N. J. Woodcock (President). ***Associate Directors:*** A. W. Jobson, R. J. Osborne.

Manager: Peter Taylor. ***Assistant Manager:*** Phil Holder. ***Youth Team Coach: Danny Greaves.***

Physio: John Cowens. ***Commercial Manager:*** John Carter. ***Stadium Manager:*** David Jobson.

Club Nickname: 'The Blues or The Shrimpers'.

Year Formed: 1906. ***Turned Professional:*** 1906. ***Ltd Co.:*** 1919.

Previous Grounds: 1906, Roots Hall, Prittlewell; 1920, Kursaal; 1934, Southend Stadium; 1955, Roots Hall Football Ground.

Record League Victory: 9–2 v Newport Co, Division 3 (S), 5 September 1936 – McKenzie; Nelson, Everest (1); Deacon, Turner, Carr; Bolan, Lane (1), Goddard (4), Dickinson (2), Oswald (1).

Record Cup Victory: 10–1 v Golders Green, FA Cup, 1st rd, 24 November 1934 – Moore; Morfitt, Kelly; Mackay, Joe Wilson, Carr (1); Lane (1), Johnson (5), Cheesmuir (2), Deacon (1), Oswald. 10–1 v Brentwood, FA Cup, 2nd rd, 7 December 1968 – Roberts; Bentley, Birks; McMillan (1) Beesley, Kurila; Clayton, Chisnall, Moore (4), Best (5), Hamilton. 10–1 v Aldershot, Leyland Daf Cup, Pr rd, 6 November 1990 – Sansome; Austin, Powell, Cornwell, Prior (1), Tilson (3), Cawley, Butler, Ansah (1), Benjamin (1), Angell (4).

Record Defeat: 1–9 v Brighton & HA, Division 3, 27 November 1965.

Most League Points (2 for a win): 67, Division 4, 1980–81.

Most League Points (3 for a win): 85, Division 3, 1990–91.

Most League Goals: 92, Division 3 (S), 1950–51.

Highest League Scorer in Season: Jim Shankly, 31, 1928–29 and Sammy McCrory, 1957–58, both in Division 3 (S).

Most League Goals in Total Aggregate: Roy Hollis, 122, 1953–60.

Most Capped Player: George Mackenzie, 9, Eire.

Most League Appearances: Sandy Anderson, 451, 1950–63.

Record Transfer Fee Received: £2,000,000 from Nottingham F for Stan Collymore, June 1993.

Record Transfer Fee Paid: £350,000 to Plymouth Arg for Gary Poole, June 1993.

Football League Record: 1920 Original Member of Division 3; 1921–58 Division 3 (S); 1958–66 Division 3; 1966–72 Division 4; 1972–76 Division 3; 1976–78 Division 4; 1978–80 Division 3; 1980–81 Division 4; 1981–84 Division 3; 1984–87 Division 4; 1987–89 Division 3; 1989–90 Division 4; 1990–91 Division 3; 1991–92 Division 2; 1992– Division 1.

Honours: *Football League:* Best season: 15th, Division 1, 1993–94. Division 3 – Runners-up 1990–91; Division 4 – Champions 1980–81; Runners-up 1971–72, 1977–78. *FA Cup:* best season: old 3rd rd, 1920–21, 5th rd, 1925–26, 1951–52, 1975–76, 1992–93. *Football League Cup:* never past 3rd rd.

SOUTHEND UNITED 1993—94 LEAGUE RECORD

Match No.	Date	Venue	Opponents	Result		H/T Score	Lg. Pos.	Goalscorers	Attendance
1	Aug 15	H	Nottingham F	D	1-1	1-1	—	Sussex	8609
2	22	A	Millwall	W	4-1	1-1	—	Lee, Otto, Mooney, Ansah	10,273
3	28	H	Peterborough U	W	3-0	0-0	5	Angell 2, Ansah	5075
4	Sept 1	A	WBA	D	2-2	0-0	—	Angell 2	14,482
5	4	A	Bristol C	L	1-2	0-1	4	Sussex	7396
6	11	H	Middlesbrough	W	1-0	0-0	3	Otto	6495
7	18	A	Portsmouth	L	1-2	1-1	7	Jones K	11,093
8	25	A	Stoke C	W	1-0	0-0	6	Mooney	16,145
9	Oct 2	H	Tranmere R	L	1-2	0-1	6	Higgins (og)	5860
10	9	A	Grimsby T	L	0-4	0-2	9		4726
11	16	H	Oxford U	W	6-1	4-0	6	Mooney 3, Otto 2, Edwards	4432
12	23	A	Barnsley	W	3-1	3-0	5	Angell, Otto 2	5240
13	30	H	Wolverhampton W	D	1-1	0-0	7	Jones K	8071
14	Nov 3	H	Watford	W	2-0	2-0	—	Hunt, Poole (pen)	4584
15	6	A	Leicester C	L	0-3	0-2	7		15,387
16	13	H	Luton T	W	2-1	1-0	4	Otto, Hunt	5567
17	20	A	Sunderland	W	2-0	1-0	4	Angell, Bressington (pen)	15,452
18	27	A	Derby Co	W	3-1	1-1	3	Hunt, Jones G, Otto	14,458
19	Dec 5	H	Leicester C	D	0-0	0-0	—		6114
20	11	H	WBA	L	0-3	0-0	6		6807
21	19	A	Nottingham F	L	0-2	0-1	—		21,641
22	27	H	Charlton Ath	W	4-2	2-1	5	Jones K, Lee, Otto, Bressington (pen)	10,123
23	29	A	Crystal Palace	L	0-1	0-0	6		18,255
24	Jan 1	H	Birmingham C	W	3-1	1-0	5	Jones K, Hunt, Lee	10,729
25	3	A	Notts Co	L	1-2	0-1	5	Jones K	6503
26	12	H	Bolton W	L	0-2	0-1	—		4969
27	15	A	Oxford U	L	1-2	0-0	9	Jones G	6613
28	22	H	Grimsby T	L	1-2	1-1	10	Otto	4367
29	Feb 5	H	Barnsley	L	0-3	0-0	12		4101
30	12	A	Wolverhampton W	W	1-0	1-0	8	Jones G	22,774
31	25	H	Bristol C	L	0-1	0-1	12		4615
32	Mar 2	H	Millwall	D	1-1	1-1	—	Sussex	4615
33	5	A	Peterborough U	L	1-3	0-2	13	Poole	5878
34	12	H	Portsmouth	W	2-1	1-1	10	Beadle, Sussex	4437
35	15	A	Middlesbrough	L	0-1	0-1	—		7378
36	19	H	Stoke C	D	0-0	0-0	12		4542
37	25	A	Tranmere R	D	1-1	0-1	—	Sussex	5526
38	30	H	Notts Co	W	1-0	0-0	—	Otto	3758
39	Apr 2	A	Charlton Ath	L	3-4	0-0	13	Hunt, Ansah 2	9117
40	6	H	Crystal Palace	L	1-2	0-1	—	Hunt	9776
41	9	A	Birmingham C	L	1-3	0-1	16	Bressington (pen)	14,307
42	12	A	Bolton W	W	2-0	2-0	—	Bodley, Ansah	7140
43	16	A	Watford	L	0-3	0-3	16		7694
44	23	H	Sunderland	L	0-1	0-0	16		4734
45	30	A	Luton T	D	1-1	0-0	16	Otto	7504
46	May 8	H	Derby Co	W	4-3	4-2	15	Ansah 2, Sussex (pen), Otto	8119

Final League Position: 15

GOALSCORERS

League (63): Otto 13, Ansah 7, Angell 6, Hunt 6, Sussex 6 (1 pen), Jones K 5, Mooney 5, Bressington 3 (3 pens), Jones G 3, Lee 3, Poole 2 (1 pen), Beadle 1, Bodley 1, Edwards 1, own goal 1.
Coca-Cola Cup (1): Angell 1.
FA Cup (0):

Sansome 42	Edwards 41 + 1	Powell 46	Jones K 19 + 1	Scully 8	Bressington 27 + 1	Ansah 23 + 4	Payne 32 + 3	Sussex 18 + 3	Otto 44 + 1	Angell 17	Jones G 14 + 8	Hunt 36 + 6	Locke 7 + 1	Lee 18 + 6	Mooney 9 + 5	Harding 2 + 3	Bodley 16	Poole 38	Howell 6	Allon 2 + 1	Martin 1 + 3	Gridelet 21 + 8	Royce 4 + 2	Tilson 3 + 7	Beadle 8	Nogan 4 + 1	Match No.
1	2	3	4	*5*	6	*7*	8	9	10	11	12	14															1
1	4	3			6	7	8	5	10	11		14	*2*	9	12												2
1	4	3			6	7	8	5	10	11		14	*2*	9		12											3
1	4	3			*6*	7	8	5	10	11		14	2	9		12											4
1	5	3				7	8	6	*10*	11		14	2	9		12	4										5
1		3	4		6	7	8		10					9		11		2	5								6
1		3	4		6	7	8		10					9		11		2	5	12							7
1		3	4		6	7	8		10					9	12			2	5	11							8
1	12	3	4		6	7	8		10						9			2	5	*11*	14						9
1		3			6		8		10	11		7		9	12			2	*5*			4	14				10
1	4	3		5		*7*			10	11		6		12	9			2			14	8					11
	4	3	14	5		*7*			10	11		6		12	9			2				8	1				12
	6	3	4	5			8		10	11	14	7			*9*			2				12	1				13
1	6	3	4	5			8		10	11		7			9			2				12					14
1	5	3	4		*6*		8		10	11	14	7			9			2				12					15
1	5	3	4		6		8		10	11	9	7						2									16
1	5	3	4		6		8		10	11	9	7							2			12					17
1	5	3	4		6		8		10	11	9	7						2									18
1	5	3			6		8		10	11	*9*	7		12	14			2				4					19
1	5	3	4		*6*		8		10	11	9	7		12				2				14					20
1	5	3	4						10	11		*7*		12	9		6	2				8		14			21
1	5	3	4		12				10		9	7		11			6	2				8					22
1	5	3	4						10		9	7		11	12		6	2				8					23
1	5	3	4		6		12		10		*9*	7		11				2				8		14			24
1	5	3	4		6				10		9	7		11				2				8		12			25
1	5	3	4		6		8	14	10			7		*11*	9			2				12					26
1	5	3	4		6			14	10		9	*7*		11			8	2					12				27
	5	3					8		10		11	7		12	9		6	2				4	1				28
	5	3			4		8		10		9	7	12	11			6	2					1				29
1	5	3			6		8		10		9	7		11				2				4					30
1	5	3			6	12	14	8	10		9	7	2	11								*4*					31
1	5	3			6	12	8	9	10			*7*	4	11				2						14			32
1	5	3			6	12	8	11	10			7	4					2							9		33
1	6	3		5		4	8	11	10			7						2							9		34
1	6	3		5		4	8	11	10			*7*						2				12		14	9		35
1	6	3		5		*7*	8	4	10			14						2				12			9	11	36
1	5	3				7		4				10					6	2			12	8		14	*9*	11	37
1	5	3				*7*	8	9	12			10					6	2				4				11	38
1	5	3				12	8	9	10			7					6	2				4				11	39
1	5	3			8	11		9	10		12	7					6	2				4					40
1	5	3			6	11	14	*8*	10		12	7						2				4			9		41
1	5	3				11	8		10		12	7					6	2				4			9		42
1	5	3				11	8		10		12	7					6	2				*4*		14	9		43
1	5	3			2	11	4	14	10		12	7					6				9			*8*			44
1	5	3				11		9	10			7					6	2				8		4			45
1	5	3				11		9	10			7					6	2				4		8		12	46

Coca-Cola Cup	First Round	Barnet (h)	0-2
		(a)	1-1
FA Cup	Third Round	Luton T (a)	0-1

SOUTHEND UNITED

Player and Position	Ht	Wt	Birth Date	Birth Place	Source	Clubs	League App	League Gls
Goalkeepers								
Ron Fearon‡	6 0	11 12	19 11 60	Romford	QPR	Reading	61	—
					Sutton	Ipswich T	28	—
						Brighton (loan)	7	—
						Leyton Orient	—	—
						Ipswich T	—	—
						Walsall (loan)	1	—
						Southend U	—	—
Simon Royce	6 2	11 07	9 9 71	Forest Gate	Heybridge Swifts	Southend U	10	—
Paul Sansome	6 0	13 07	6 10 61	N. Addington	Crystal Palace	Millwall	156	—
						Southend U	272	—
Defenders								
Mick Bodley	5 11	12 00	14 9 67	Hayes	Apprentice	Chelsea	6	1
						Northampton T	20	—
						Barnet	69	3
						Southend U	16	1
Graham Bressington	6 0	12 00	8 7 66	Eton	Wycombe W	Lincoln C	141	7
						Southend U	28	3
Craig Davidson	5 11	11 08	2 5 74	Harold Wood	Trainee	Southend U	—	—
Michael Gonzaque‡	6 1	12 03	27 3 75	Canning Town	Trainee	Southend U	—	—
David Howell	6 0	12 00	10 10 58	London	Enfield	Barnet	57	3
						Southend U	6	—
Gary Poole	6 0	11 00	11 9 67	Stratford	Arsenal	Tottenham H	—	—
						Cambridge U	43	—
					Barnet	Barnet	40	2
						Plymouth Arg	39	5
						Southend U	38	2
Chris Powell	5 8	11 03	8 9 69	Lambeth		Crystal Palace	3	—
						Aldershot (loan)	11	—
						Southend U	177	3
Midfield								
John Cornwell	6 4	13 00	13 10 64	Bethnal Green	Apprentice	Orient	202	35
						Newcastle U	33	1
						Swindon T	25	—
						Southend U	101	5
						Cardiff C (loan)	5	2
						Brentford (loan)	4	—
						Northampton T (loan)	13	1
Andy Edwards	6 2	13 06	17 9 71	Epping	Trainee	Southend U	103	2
Phil Gridelet	5 11	12 00	30 4 67	Edgware	Barnet	Barnsley	6	—
						Rotherham U (loan)	9	—
						Southend U	29	—
Mark Hall	5 6	10 12	13 1 73	London	Tottenham H	Southend U	12	—
						Barnet (loan)	3	—
Keith Jones	5 9	11 02	14 10 64	Dulwich	Apprentice	Chelsea	52	7
						Brentford	169	13
						Southend U	83	11
Adam Locke	5 10	12 02	20 8 70	Croydon	Trainee	Crystal Palace	—	—
						Southend U	73	4
						Colchester U (loan)	4	—
Ricky Otto	5 10	11 00	9 11 67	London	Dartford	Leyton Orient	56	13
						Southend U	45	13
Derek Payne	5 7	10 01	26 4 67	Edgware	Hayes	Barnet	51	6
						Southend U	35	—
Neil Rowbury*	5 11	11 04	27 12 74	Barking	Trainee	Southend U	—	—
Jamie Southon	5 9	11 09	13 10 74	Hornchurch	Trainee	Southend U	1	—
Forwards								
Andy Ansah	5 9	10 02	19 3 69	Lewisham	Crystal Palace	Brentford	8	2
						Southend U	144	33
Jonathan Hunt	5 10	11 00	2 11 71	London		Barnet	33	—
						Southend U	42	6

SOUTHEND UNITED

Colours: Blue shirts, yellow trim, blue shorts, blue trim, blue stockings. **Change colours:** All yellow.

Foundation: The leading club in Southend around the turn of the century was Southend Athletic, but they were an amateur concern. Southend United was a more ambitious professional club when they were founded in 1906, employing Bob Jack as secretary-manager and immediately joining the Second Division of the Southern League.

First Football League game: 28 August, 1920, Division 3, v Brighton & HA (a) W 2-0 – Capper; Reid, Newton; Wileman, Henderson, Martin; Nicholls, Nuttall, Fairclough (2), Myers, Dorsett.

Did you know: On 6 April 1994 Paul Sansome played his 500th first team match in goal for Southend United. It was against Crystal Palace, the club he first joined as an apprentice.

Managers (and Secretary-Managers)

Bob Jack 1906–10, George Molyneux 1910–11, O. M. Howard 1911–12, Joe Bradshaw 1912–19, Ned Liddell 1919–20, Tom Mather 1920–21, Ted Birnie 1921–34, David Jack 1934–40, Harry Warren 1946–56, Eddie Perry 1956–60, Frank Broome 1960, Ted Fenton 1961–65, Alvan Williams 1965–67, Ernie Shepherd 1967–69, Geoff Hudson 1969–70, Arthur Rowley 1970–76, Dave Smith 1976–83, Peter Morris 1983–84, Bobby Moore 1984–86, Dave Webb 1986–87, Dick Bate 1987, Paul Clark 1987–88, Dave Webb (GM) 1988–92, Colin Murphy 1992–93, Barry Fry 1993, Peter Taylor December 1993–

Gary Jones	6 0	12 08	6 4 69	Huddersfield	Rossington Main	Doncaster R	20	2
					Boston U	Southend U	22	3
						Lincoln C (loan)	4	2
Jae Martin	5 10	12 04	5 2 76	London	Trainee	Southend U	4	—
Tommy Mooney	5 10	12 05	11 8 71	Teesside North	Trainee	Aston Villa	—	—
						Scarborough	107	30
						Southend U	14	5
						Watford (loan)	10	2
Andy Sussex	6 0	13 11	23 11 64	Enfield	Apprentice	Orient	144	17
						Crewe Alex	102	24
						Southend U	59	13
Steve Tilson	5 11	12 05	27 7 66	Essex	Burnham	Southend U	157	20
						Brentford (loan)	2	—

Trainees

Blunden, Larry; Derry, Dasvid J; Johnson, Carl; Kent, Matthew J; Kinnear, Anthony D; Lockwood, Matthew D; Longman, Kenneth G; McGlew, Neil; Nesling, Jon; O'Meara, Lee P; Parmenter, Steven J; Perkins, Declan O; Scott, Daniel L; Stone, Damon T; Warwick, Mark J; Whitehouse, Christopher J.

****Non-Contract**

Oliver, Stephen J.

**Non-Contract Players who are retained must be re-signed before they are eligible to play in League matches.

Sheffield United players continued from Page 451

Bobby Davison*	5 9	11 09	17 7 59	South Shields	Seaham CW	Huddersfield T	2	—
						Halifax T	63	29
						Derby Co	206	83
						Leeds U	91	31
						Derby Co (loan)	10	8
						Sheffield U (loan)	11	4
						Leicester C	25	6
						Sheffield U	9	—
Peter Duffield (To Hamilton A September 1993)	5 6	10 07	4 2 69	Middlesbrough		Middlesbrough	—	—
						Sheffield U	58	14
						Halifax T (loan)	12	6
						Rotherham U (loan)	17	4
						Blackpool (loan)	5	1
						Bournemouth (loan)	—	—
						Stockport Co (loan)	7	4
						Crewe Alex (loan)	2	—
Jostein Flo	6 4	14 00	3 10 64	Norway	Sogndal	Sheffield U	33	9
Glyn Hodges	6 0	12 03	30 4 63	Streatham	Apprentice	Wimbledon	232	49
						Newcastle U	7	—
						Watford	86	15
						Crystal Palace	7	—
						Sheffield U	100	12
Adrian Littlejohn	5 10	10 04	26 9 70	Wolverhampton	WBA	Walsall	44	1
						Sheffield U	53	11
John Reed	5 10	10 11	27 8 72	Rotherham	Trainee	Sheffield U	1	—
						Scarborough (loan)	14	6
						Scarborough (loan)	6	—
						Darlington (loan)	10	2
						Mansfield T (loan)	13	2
Rob Scott	6 1	11 08	15 8 73	Epsom	Sutton U	Sheffield U	—	—

STOCKPORT COUNTY1993–94 *Back row (left to right):* Michael Hym, Jim Gannon, Paul A. Williams, Alan Finley, Tony Barras, Bill Williams, Jim Carstairs.
Centre row: Martin James, Sean Connelly, Neil Edwards, Ian Ironside, Ian Wilkinson, Dave Miller, Chris Beaumont, Darren Ryan.
Front row: Kevin Francis, David Frain, Michael Wallace, Danny Bergara (Manager), Peter Ward, Lee Todd, Andy Preece.

Division 2 **STOCKPORT COUNTY**

Edgeley Park, Hardcastle Road, Stockport, Cheshire SK3 9DD. Telephone 061–480 8888. Fax: 061–480 0230. Club Shop: 061–480 8117. Lottery Office: 061–480 1247. Clubcall: 0891 121638.

Ground capacity: 8020.

Record attendance: 27,833 v Liverpool, FA Cup 5th rd, 11 February 1950.

Record receipts: £66,807 v Bristol C, FA Cup 4th rd, 9 February 1994.

Pitch measurements: 110yd × 72yd.

Hon. Vice-presidents: Mike Yarwood OBE, Freddie Pye, Andrew Barlow.

Chairman: Brendan Elwood. ***Vice-chairman:*** Grahame White.

Directors: Mike Baker, Michael Rains, Brian Taylor, Vincent Snell, David Jolley, John D. Simpson FCA.

Secretary: Gary Glendenning BAACCA. Dave Coxon.

Manager: Danny Bergara. ***Assistant Manager:*** John Sainty.

Coach: Dave Jones. ***Physio:*** Rodger Wylde.

Assistant Secretary: Andrea Welborn. ***Commercial Manager:*** John Rutter. ***Marketing Manager and programme editor:*** Steve Bellis.

Year Formed: 1883. ***Turned Professional:*** 1891. ***Ltd Co.:*** 1908.

Club Nicknames: 'County' or 'Hatters'.

Previous Names: Heaton Norris Rovers, 1883–88; Heaton Norris, 1888–90.

Previous Grounds: 1883 Heaton Norris Recreation Ground; 1884 Heaton Norris Wanderers Cricket Ground; 1885 Chorlton's Farm, Chorlton's Lane; 1886 Heaton Norris Cricket Ground; 1887 Wilkes' Field, Belmont Street; 1889 Nursery Inn, Green Lane; 1902 Edgeley Park.

Record League Victory: 13–0 v Halifax T, Division 3 (N), 6 January 1934 – McGann; Vincent (1p), Jenkinson; Robinson, Stevens, Len Jones; Foulkes (1), Hill (3), Lythgoe (2), Stevenson (2), Downes (4).

Record Cup Victory: 6–2 v West Auckland T (away), FA Cup, 1st rd, 14 November 1959 – Lea; Betts (1), Webb; Murray, Hodder, Porteous; Wilson (1), Holland, Guy (2), Ritchie (1), Davock (1).

Record Defeat: 1–8 v Chesterfield, Division 2, 19 April 1902.

Most League Points (2 for a win): 64, Division 4, 1966–67.

Most League Points (3 for a win): 85, Division 2, 1993–94.

Most League Goals: 115, Division 3 (N), 1933–34.

Highest League Scorer in Season: Alf Lythgoe, 46, Division 3 (N), 1933–34.

Most League Goals in Total Aggregate: Jack Connor, 132, 1951–56.

Most Capped Player: Harry Hardy, 1, England.

Most League Appearances: Andy Thorpe, 489, 1978–86, 1988–92.

Record Transfer Fee Received: £250,000 from WBA for Paul A. Williams, March 1991.

Record Transfer Fee Paid: £125,000 to Preston NE for Mike Flynn, March 1993.

Football League Record: 1900 Elected to Division 2; 1904 Failed re-election; 1905–21 Division 2; 1921–22 Division 3 (N); 1922–26 Division 2; 1926–37 Division 3 (N); 1937–38 Division 2; 1938–58 Division 3 (N); 1958–59 Division 3; 1959–67 Division 4; 1967–70 Division 3; 1970–91 Division 4; 1991–92 Division 3; 1992– Division 2.

Honours: *Football League:* Division 2 best season: 10th, 1905–06; Division 3 (N) – Champions 1921–22, 1936–37; Runners-up 1928–29, 1929-30; Division 4 – Champions 1966–67; Runners-up 1990–91. *FA Cup:* best season: 5th rd, 1935, 1950. *Football League Cup:* best season: 4th rd, 1972–73. *Autoglass Trophy:* Runners-up 1991–92, 1992–93.

STOCKPORT COUNTY 1993—94 LEAGUE RECORD

Match No.	Date	Venue	Opponents	Result		H/T Score	Lg. Pos.	Goalscorers	Attendance
1	Aug 14	A	Plymouth Arg	W	3-2	1-0	—	Francis 2, Preece	6863
2	21	H	Cambridge U	W	3-1	1-0	1	Preece 2, Francis	3782
3	28	A	Huddersfield T	D	1-1	1-0	4	Preece	7053
4	31	H	Bradford C	W	4-1	1-1	—	Richards (og), Francis, Ryan, Preece	4236
5	Sept 4	H	Wrexham	W	1-0	1-0	1	Ryan	4886
6	11	A	Hartlepool U	L	0-1	0-1	3		2473
7	14	A	York C	W	2-1	2-0	—	Ryan, Preece	3606
8	18	H	Burnley	W	2-1	0-1	2	Preece, Ryan	5122
9	25	H	Rotherham U	W	2-0	0-0	1	Preece, Ward	4903
10	Oct 2	A	Bournemouth	D	1-1	1-0	2	Francis	4274
11	9	A	Brighton & HA	D	1-1	1-1	1	Preece	5330
12	16	H	Exeter C	W	4-0	3-0	1	Ryan, Francis, Frain, Ward	4349
13	23	A	Fulham	W	1-0	1-0	1	Preece	3615
14	30	H	Swansea C	W	4-0	2-0	1	Francis (pen), Preece 3	4641
15	Nov 2	H	Leyton Orient	W	3-0	1-0	—	Beaumont, Francis, Ryan	4323
16	6	A	Cardiff C	L	1-3	0-0	1	Frain	4738
17	20	H	Bristol R	L	0-2	0-1	2		5250
18	27	A	Hull C	W	1-0	0-0	2	Francis	7119
19	Dec 11	A	Cambridge U	D	0-0	0-0	2		3239
20	17	H	Plymouth Arg	L	2-3	0-0	—	Preece, Frain	4174
21	28	A	Reading	L	0-2	0-2	3		11,240
22	Jan 1	H	Barnet	W	2-1	1-1	3	Francis 2	5121
23	3	A	Brentford	D	1-1	0-0	3	Francis	6410
24	22	H	Brighton & HA	W	3-0	1-0	3	Preece 3	6657
25	Feb 1	H	Blackpool	W	1-0	0-0	—	Francis	5288
26	5	H	Fulham	L	2-4	1-2	2	Francis, Preece	5488
27	12	A	Port Vale	D	1-1	0-0	2	Francis	10,628
28	19	H	Huddersfield T	W	3-0	2-0	2	Robinson P (og), Francis 2	5071
29	Mar 5	H	Hartlepool U	W	5-0	3-0	3	Francis 3, Gannon, Flynn	4076
30	8	A	Wrexham	W	1-0	1-0	—	Wallace	4756
31	12	A	Burnley	D	1-1	0-0	3	Preece	13,130
32	15	H	York C	L	1-2	0-2	—	Gannon	3899
33	19	A	Rotherham U	W	2-1	1-0	3	Gannon, Francis	3755
34	26	H	Bournemouth	L	0-2	0-1	3		5277
35	29	H	Brentford	W	3-1	2-1	—	Ward, Francis 2 (1 pen)	4361
36	Apr 2	A	Blackpool	L	0-2	0-0	3		5235
37	9	A	Barnet	D	0-0	0-0	3		1798
38	12	A	Swansea C	W	2-1	1-0	—	Wallace, Preece	2483
39	16	A	Leyton Orient	D	0-0	0-0	4		3984
40	19	H	Port Vale	W	2-1	1-0	—	Francis 2	5910
41	23	H	Cardiff C	D	2-2	1-0	4	Williams B, Gannon	5455
42	26	A	Bradford C	W	2-1	0-0	—	Wallace, Preece	5720
43	28	H	Reading	D	1-1	1-0	—	Francis	7221
44	30	A	Bristol R	D	1-1	0-0	4	Pritchard (og)	4189
45	May 2	A	Exeter C	W	2-1	1-1	—	Francis 2	1992
46	7	H	Hull C	D	0-0	0-0	4		7666

Final League Position: 4

GOALSCORERS

League (74): Francis 28 (2 pens), Preece 21, Ryan 6, Gannon 4, Frain 3, Wallace 3, Ward 3, Beaumont 1, Flynn 1, Williams B 1, own goals 3.
Coca-Cola Cup (2): Francis 1, Ryan 1.
FA Cup (9): Francis 3, Preece 2, Beaumont 1, Frain 1, Todd 1, Wallace 1.

Edwards 26	Connelly 30 + 2	Wallace 36 + 1	Frain 32 + 1	Flynn 46	Finley 7	James 9 + 15	Ward 34 + 1	Francis 45	Ryan 26 + 6	Preece 43	Beaumont 26 + 6	Miller 36 + 2	Gannon 31 + 4	Ironside 10 + 1	Todd 31 + 2	Emerson 7 + 1	Williams B 16	Barras 3	Quinn — + 1	Murray 2 + 1	Cantona — + 3	Keeley 10	Match No.
1	2	3	4	5	6	7	8	9	10	11	12												1
1		3	4	5	6	7	8	9	10	11		2	12										2
1		3	4	5	6	7	8	9	10	11			2										3
1		3	4	5	6	7	8	9	10	11			2										4
1		3	4	5	6	7	8	9	10	11			2										5
1	14	3	4	5	6	*7*	8	9	10	11	12		2										6
1	12	3	4	5	6	14	8	9	*10*	11		7	2										7
1	6	3	4	5		12	8	9	10	11		7	2										8
1	6	3	4	5			8	9	10	11		7	2										9
1	6	3	4	5			8	9	10	11		7	2	12									10
1	6	3	4	5		12	8	9	10	11		7	2										11
1	6		4	5		12	8	9	10	11	2	7			3								12
1	6		4	5			8	9	10	11	2	7			3								13
1	6		4	5			8	9	10	11	2	7	12		3								14
1	6		4	5		14	8	9	*10*	11	2	7	12		3								15
1	6		4	5		14	8	9	*10*	11	2	7	12		3								16
1	6	14	4	5			8	9	*10*	11	2	12	7		3								17
1	6		4	5		10	8	9		11	2	7			3								18
1		3	4	5				9	12	11	10	7	6		2	8							19
1		3	4	5			12	9	14	11	10	7	*6*		2	8							20
1		3	4	5		12	8	9		11	10	7			2	6							21
1		3	4	5		12	8	9	6	11	10	7					2						22
1		3	4	5			8	9	12	11	10	7			2		6						23
1		3	4	5		12	8	9		11	10	7			2			6					24
1		3	4	5			8	9		11	10	7			2			6					25
1		3	4	5		12	8	9		11	10	7			2			6					26
	7	3	4	5			8	9	12	11	10			1	2		6						27
	2		4	5			8	9	12	11	10		7	1	3		6						28
	10	3		5			8	*9*		11	12	6	7	1	2	4			14				29
	2	3		5			8	9		11	10	6	7	1		4							30
	2	3		5			8	9		11	10	6	7	1	12	4							31
		3		5			8	9		11	10	6	7	1	12	4	*2*			14			32
		3	4	5		12	8	9			10	6	7	1	2					11			33
	3		4	5		12	8	9			10	6	7	1	2					*11*	14		34
	6	3	4	5		11	8	9			10	12	7	1	2								35
	6	3		5		*9*	8			11	10		7	1	2	12	4				14		36
	2		4	5		12		9		11	10	6	7		3		8					1	37
	2	8		5				9	10	11		4	7		3		6					1	38
	2	8		5				9	12	11	10	4	7		3		6					1	39
	2	8		5		12		9	10	11		4	7		3		6					1	40
	2	8	14	5		12		9	10	11		4	7		3		*6*					1	41
	2	8		5				9	10	11		4	7		3		6					1	42
	2	8		5				9	10	11		4	7		3		6					1	43
	2	8		5				9	10	11	12	4	7		3		6					1	44
	2	8		5				*9*	10	11	12	4	7		3		6				14	1	45
	2	8		5				9	10	11	12	4	7		3		6					1	46

Coca-Cola Cup	First Round	Hartlepool U (h)	1-1
		(a)	1-2
FA Cup	First Round	Rotherham U (a)	2-1
	Second Round	Halifax T (h)	5-1
	Third Round	QPR (h)	2-1
	Fourth Round	Bristol C (h)	0-4

STOCKPORT COUNTY

Player and Position	Ht	Wt	Birth Date	Birth Place	Source	Clubs	League App	League Gls
Goalkeepers								
Neil Edwards	5 8	11 02	5 12 70	Aberdare	Trainee	Leeds U	—	—
						Huddersfield T (loan)	—	—
						Stockport Co	100	—
Ian Ironside	6 2	13 00	8 3 64	Sheffield	N. Ferriby U	Scarborough	88	—
						Middlesbrough	13	—
						Scarborough (loan)	7	—
						Stockport Co	11	—
John Keeley	6 1	14 02	27 7 61	Plaistow	Apprentice	Southend U	54	—
					Chelmsford C	Brighton	138	—
						Oldham Ath	2	—
						Oxford U (loan)	6	—
						Reading (loan)	6	—
						Chester C (loan)	4	—
						Colchester U	15	—
						Stockport Co	10	—
Defenders								
Jim Carstairs*	6 0	12 05	29 1 71	St. Andrews	Trainee	Arsenal	—	—
						Brentford (loan)	8	—
						Cambridge U	—	—
						Stockport C	34	1
Sean Connelly	5 10	11 10	26 6 70	Sheffield	Hallam	Stockport Co	39	—
Alan Finley*	6 3	14 03	10 12 67	Liverpool	Marine	Shrewsbury T	63	2
						Stockport Co	66	5
						Carlisle U (loan)	1	—
						Rochdale (loan)	1	—
Mike Flynn	6 0	11 00	23 2 69	Oldham	Trainee	Oldham Ath	40	1
						Norwich C	—	—
						Preston NE	136	7
						Stockport Co	56	1
Jim Gannon	6 2	13 00	7 9 68	London	Dundalk	Sheffield U	—	—
						Halifax T (loan)	2	—
						Stockport Co	172	39
						Notts Co (loan)	2	—
Lee Todd	5 5	10 03	7 3 72	Hartlepool	Hartlepool U	Stockport Co	105	—
Bill Williams	5 10	12 11	7 10 60	Rochdale	Local	Rochdale	95	2
						Stockport Co	104	1
						Manchester C	1	—
						Stockport Co	156	7
Midfield								
Joel Cantona	5 10		26 10 67	Paris	Ujpest Dozsa	Stockport Co	3	—
Dean Emerson	5 9	12 11	27 12 62	Salford	Local	Stockport Co	156	7
						Rotherham U	55	8
						Coventry C	114	—
						Hartlepool U	45	1
						Stockport Co	8	—
Andrew Gibson (on loan from Aberdeen))	5 8	11 04	2 2 69	Dechmont		Stockport	—	—
Martin James	5 10	11 07	18 5 71	Formby	Trainee	Preston NE	98	11
						Stockport Co	32	—
Brian McCord	5 10	11 06	24 8 68	Derby	Apprentice	Derby Co	5	—
						Barnsley	43	2
						Mansfield T (loan)	11	1
						Stockport Co	8	—
David Miller	5 11	11 12	8 1 64	Burnley	Apprentice	Burnley	32	3
						Crewe Alex (loan)	3	—
						Tranmere R	29	1
						Preston NE	58	2
						Burnley (loan)	4	—
						Carlisle U	109	7
						Stockport Co	78	1
Phil Owen			11 1 75	Bangor	Trainee	Manchester C	—	—
						Stockport Co	—	—
Andy Preece	6 1	12 00	27 3 67	Evesham		Northampton T	1	—
					Worcester C.	Wrexham	51	7
						Stockport Co	97	42

STOCKPORT COUNTY

Colours: Royal and pale blue shirts, red horizontal zig zag, white shorts, white stockings, blue trim. **Change colours:** Jade shirts, jade shorts, jade stockings.

Foundation: Formed at a meeting held at Wellington Road South by members of Wycliffe Congregational Chapel in 1883, they called themselves Heaton Norris Rovers until changing to Stockport County in 1890, a year before joining the Football Combination.

First Football League game: 1 September, 1900, Division 2, v Leicester Fosse (a) D 2-2 – Moores; Earp, Wainwright; Pickford, Limond, Harvey; Stansfield, Smith (1), Patterson, Foster, Betteley (1).

Did you know: On 19 April 1994 Kevin Francis scored his 100th first class goal for Stockport County in three seasons. It was a 39th minute effort from an acrobatic overhead kick.

Managers (and Secretary-Managers)
Fred Stewart 1894–1911, Harry Lewis 1911–14, David Ashworth 1914–19, Albert Williams 1919–24, Fred Scotchbrook 1924–26, Lincoln Hyde 1926–31, Andrew Wilson 1932–33, Fred Westgarth 1934–36, Bob Kelly 1936–38, George Hunt 1938–39, Bob Marshall 1939–49, Andy Beattie 1949–52, Dick Duckworth 1952–56, Billy Moir 1956–60, Reg Flewin 1960–63, Trevor Porteous 1963–65, Bert Trautmann (GM) 1965–66, Eddie Quigley (TM) 1965–66, Jimmy Meadows 1966–69, Wally Galbraith 1969–70, Matt Woods 1970–71, Brian Doyle 1972–74, Jimmy Meadows 1974–75, Roy Chapman 1975–76, Eddie Quigley 1976–77, Alan Thompson 1977–78, Mike Summerbee 1978–79, Jimmy McGuigan 1979–82, Eric Webster 1982–85, Colin Murphy 1985, Les Chapman 1985–86, Jimmy Melia 1986, Colin Murphy 1986–87, Asa Hartford 1987–89, Danny Bergara April 1989–

Player and Position	*Ht*	*Wt*	*Birth Date*	*Birth Place*	*Source*	*Clubs*	*League App*	*League Gls*
Darren Ryan*	5 10	11 00	3 7 72	Oswestry	Trainee	Shrewsbury T	4	—
						Chester C	17	2
						Stockport Co	36	6
Kieran Toal	5 8	11 01	14 12 71	Manchester	Trainee	Manchester U	—	—
						Stockport Co	—	—
Michael Wallace	5 8	10 02	5 10 70	Farnworth	Trainee	Manchester C	—	—
						Stockport Co	45	3
Forwards								
Tony Barras	6 0	12 03	29 3 71	Teesside	Trainee	Hartlepool U	12	—
						Stockport Co	99	5
						Rotherham U (loan)	5	1
Chris Beaumont	5 11	11 07	5 12 65	Sheffield	Denaby	Rochdale	34	7
						Stockport Co	177	37
Paul Daughtry*	5 8		14 2 73	Oldham	Winsford	Stockport Co	—	—
David Frain	5 8	10 05	11 10 62	Sheffield	Rowlinson YC	Sheffield U	44	5
						Rochdale	42	12
						Stockport Co	185	12
Kevin Francis	6 7	15 08	6 12 67	Moseley	Mile Oak R	Derby Co	10	—
						Stockport Co	135	76
Peter Ward	6 0	11 10	15 10 64	Durham	Chester-le-Street	Huddersfield T	37	2
						Rochdale	84	10
						Stockport Co	114	7

Trainees
Burns, Steven T; Davis, Leon; Jenkins, Nicholas; McCauley, Andrew; McGavin, Wayne K. B; Radcliffe, Robert T; Ryan, Mark D; Schofield, Steven J; Warburton, Richard J; Wright, Paul E.

STOKE CITY 1993–94 *Back row (left to right):* John Butler, Martin Carruthers, Ian Wright, Vince Overson, Dave Regis, Nigel Gleghorn, Ian Cranson.
Centre row: Steve Foley, Carl Beeston, Mark Prudhoe, Thor Orlygsson, Ronnie Sinclair, Lee Sandford, Paul Rennie.
Front row: Mark Stein, David Kevan, Ernie Tapai, Graham Shaw, Tony Kelly, Paul Ware, Graham Harbey.

Division 1 STOKE CITY

Victoria Ground, Stoke-on-Trent ST4 4EG. Telephone Stoke-on-Trent (0782) 413511. Fax: (0782) 745340. Commercial Dept: (0782) 45840. Soccerline Information: 0898 700278. Football in the Community: 0782 744347.

Ground capacity: 25,409.

Record attendance: 51,380 v Arsenal, Division 1, 29 March 1937.

Record receipts: £97,000 v Liverpool, FA Cup 3rd rd, 9 January 1988.

Pitch measurements: 116yd × 75yd.

Vice-president: J. A. M. Humphries.

Chairman: P. Coates. ***Vice-chairman:*** K. A. Humphreys.

Directors: P. J. Wright, R. D. Kenyon.

Manager: Joe Jordan. ***Assistant Manager:*** Asa Hartford.

Physio: Richard Gray.

Secretary: M. J. Potts.

Sales & Marketing Manager: M. J. Cullerton.

Year Formed: 1863 *(*see Foundation*).

Turned Professional: 1885. ***Ltd Co.:*** 1908.

Club Nickname: 'The Potters'.

Previous Name: Stoke.

Previous Grounds: 1875, Sweeting's Field; 1878, Victoria Ground (previously known as the Athletic Club Ground).

Record League Victory: 10–3 v WBA, Division 1, 4 February 1937 – Doug Westland; Brigham, Harbot; Tutin, Turner (1p), Kirton; Matthews, Antonio (2), Freddie Steele (5), Jimmy Westland, Johnson (2).

Record Cup Victory: 7–1 v Burnley, FA Cup, 2nd rd (replay), 20 February 1896 – Clawley; Clare, Eccles; Turner, Grewe, Robertson; Willie Maxwell, Dickson, A. Maxwell (3), Hyslop (4), Schofield.

Record Defeat: 0–10 v Preston NE, Division 1, 14 September 1889.

Most League Points (2 for a win): 63, Division 3 (N), 1926–27.

Most League Points (3 for a win): 93, Division 2, 1992–93.

Most League Goals: 92, Division 3 (N), 1926–27.

Highest League Scorer in Season: Freddie Steele, 33, Division 1, 1936–37.

Most League Goals in Total Aggregate: Freddie Steele, 142, 1934–49.

Most Capped Player: Gordon Banks, 36 (73), England.

Most League Appearances: Eric Skeels, 506, 1958–76.

Record Transfer Fee Received: £1,500,000 from Chelsea for Mark Stein, October 1993.

Record Transfer Fee Paid: £480,000 to Sheffield W for Ian Cranson, July 1989.

Football League Record: 1888 Founder Member of Football League; 1890 Not re-elected; 1891 Re-elected; relegated in 1907, and after one year in Division 2, resigned for financial reasons; 1919 re-elected to Division 2; 1922–23 Division 1; 1923–26 Division 2; 1926–27 Division 3 (N); 1927–33 Division 2; 1933–53 Division 1; 1953–63 Division 2; 1963–77 Division 1; 1977–79 Division 2; 1979–85 Division 1; 1985–90 Division 2; 1990–92 Division 3; 1992–93 Division 2; 1993– Division 1.

Honours: *Football League:* Division 1 best season: 4th, 1935–36, 1946–47; Division 2 – Champions 1932–33, 1962–63, 1992–93; Runners-up 1921–22; Promoted 1978–79 (3rd); Division 3 (N) – Champions 1926–27. *FA Cup:* Semi-finals 1899, 1971, 1972. *Football League Cup:* Winners 1971–72. *Autoglass Trophy:* Winners: 1992. **European Competitions:** *UEFA Cup:* 1972–73, 1974–75.

STOKE CITY 1993—94 LEAGUE RECORD

Match No.	Date	Venue	Opponents	Result		H/T Score	Lg. Pos.	Goalscorers	Attendance
1	Aug 14	H	Millwall	L	1-2	1-1	—	McCarthy (og)	18,766
2	21	A	Bolton W	D	1-1	0-0	20	Stein	11,328
3	28	H	WBA	W	1-0	0-0	16	Stein	17,948
4	Sept 4	A	Portsmouth	D	3-3	1-3	16	Stein 2, Regis	12,552
5	11	H	Tranmere R	L	1-2	1-0	21	Martindale (og)	17,296
6	14	A	Middlesbrough	W	2-1	2-1	—	Carruthers, Foley	13,189
7	19	A	Nottingham F	W	3-2	2-0	—	Regis, Stein 2 (1 pen)	20,843
8	25	H	Southend U	L	0-1	0-0	9		16,145
9	Oct 2	A	Crystal Palace	L	1-4	0-3	12	Stein	12,880
10	10	A	Oxford U	L	0-1	0-1	—		6489
11	16	H	Grimsby T	W	1-0	0-0	14	Lever (og)	14,696
12	23	A	Wolverhampton W	D	1-1	1-1	14	Stein	20,421
13	30	H	Barnsley	W	5-4	2-3	11	Fleming (og), Bishop (og), Gleghorn, Overson, Carruthers	14,679
14	Nov 3	H	Sunderland	W	1-0	0-0	—	Orlygsson	13,551
15	6	A	Watford	W	3-1	1-1	8	Orlygsson, Carruthers, Regis	7767
16	14	H	Leicester C	W	1-0	1-0	9	Gleghorn	15,984
17	20	A	Notts Co	L	0-2	0-0	8		9815
18	27	A	Luton T	L	2-6	2-3	10	Regis, Linton (og)	7384
19	Dec 4	H	Watford	W	2-0	0-0	6	Bannister, Regis	13,465
20	11	H	Middlesbrough	W	3-1	2-0	7	Bannister, Orlygsson 2	13,777
21	19	A	Millwall	L	0-2	0-0	—		8930
22	26	H	Birmingham C	W	2-1	1-0	—	Orlygsson, Sandford	16,584
23	29	A	Charlton Ath	L	0-2	0-1	10		8416
24	Jan 1	H	Derby Co	W	2-1	1-1	7	Foley, Orlygsson	20,307
25	3	A	Bristol C	D	0-0	0-0	8		11,132
26	15	A	Grimsby T	D	0-0	0-0	8		8577
27	22	H	Oxford U	D	1-1	1-0	8	Regis	14,689
28	Feb 5	H	Wolverhampton W	D	1-1	0-1	9	Overson	22,579
29	12	A	Barnsley	L	0-3	0-1	10		7561
30	19	A	Peterborough U	D	1-1	1-1	8	Gleghorn	7428
31	22	H	Bolton W	W	2-0	1-0	—	Orlygsson, Regis	14,257
32	25	H	Portsmouth	W	2-0	1-0	5	Orlygsson (pen), Carruthers	14,506
33	Mar 5	A	WBA	D	0-0	0-0	6		16,060
34	12	H	Nottingham F	L	0-1	0-1	8		20,550
35	15	A	Tranmere R	L	0-2	0-0	—		6346
36	19	A	Southend U	D	0-0	0-0	9		4542
37	26	H	Crystal Palace	L	0-2	0-0	10		18,071
38	30	H	Bristol C	W	3-0	1-0	—	Adams 2, Biggins (pen)	13,208
39	Apr 2	A	Birmingham C	L	1-3	1-1	11	Carruthers	13,568
40	4	H	Charlton Ath	W	1-0	1-0	9	Orlygsson	13,569
41	9	A	Derby Co	L	2-4	0-2	9	Biggins (pen), Adams	16,593
42	13	H	Peterborough U	W	3-0	2-0	—	Regis, Biggins, Walters	10,181
43	16	A	Sunderland	W	1-0	1-0	7	Walters	17,406
44	23	H	Notts Co	D	0-0	0-0	9		16,470
45	30	A	Leicester C	D	1-1	0-0	9	Regis	19,291
46	May 8	H	Luton T	D	2-2	2-0	10	Biggins, Regis	15,911

Final League Position: 10

GOALSCORERS

League (57): Regis 10, Orlygsson 9 (1 pen), Stein 8 (1 pen), Carruthers 5, Biggins 4 (2 pens), Adams 3, Gleghorn 3, Bannister 2, Foley 2, Overson 2, Walters 2, Sandford 1, own goals 6.
Coca-Cola Cup (7): Stein 4, Carruthers 1, Gleghorn 1, Regis 1.
FA Cup (4): Regis 2, Cranson 1, Orlygsson 1.

Prudhoe 30	Butler 34 + 1	Sandford 41 + 1	Harbey 2	Overson 39	Lowe 3 + 6	Orlygsson 42 + 3	Foley 42 + 1	Stein 12	Bannister 10 + 5	Gleghorn 38 + 2	Gynn 14 + 7	Carruthers 24 + 10	Cranson 44	Williams 2	Regis 33 + 5	Kevan 1	Clarkson 14	Sturridge 5 + 8	Cowan 14	Shaw 2 + 2	Muggleton 6	Marshall 10	Ware 1	Potter 2 + 1	Clark 12	Adams 10	Biggins 10	Walters 9	*Match No.*
1	2	3	4	5	6	*7*	8	9	*10*	11	12	14																	1
1	2	3		5	6	12	8	9		11		14	4	7	*10*														2
1	2	3		5	*6*	12	8	9		11	7	14	4		10														3
1	2	3			12	*6*	8	9		11	7	14	4	5	10														4
1	2	3				6	8	9	12	11	7	14	4		*10*	5													5
1		3	5		12	6	8	9		11		7	4		10		2												6
1		3		5	12	6	8	9		11	7		4		10		2												7
1		3		5	12	6	8	9		11	*7*	10	4				2	14											8
1				5		6	*8*	9		11	7	10	4				2	14	3	12									9
				5		6	8	9		11	7	12	4				2	10	3		1								10
				5	12	6	14	9		11	*7*	8	4				2	10	3		1								11
	12	14		5		*6*	8	9		11		7	4				2	10	3		1								12
	2			5	12	6	7			11		8	4					10	3	9	1								13
	2	3		5		6	7		12	11		8	4						10	9	1								14
	2	3		5		6	7			11		8	4		9				10		1								15
1	2	3		5		6	7			11	12	8	4		9				10										16
1	2	3		5		6	7		12	11		8	4		9				10										17
	2	3		5		6	7		12	11		8			9				10			1	4						18
		3		5		6	7		8	11			4		9		2		10			1							19
		3		5		6	7		8	11			4		9		2		10			1							20
		3		5		6	7		8	11			4		9		2		10			1							21
		3		5		6	7		8	11			4		9		2		10			1							22
	10	3		5		6	*7*		8	11	12	14	4		9		2					1							23
	10	3		5		6	7		8	11			4		9		2	12				1							24
	10	3		5		6	7		8	11	12		4		9		2					1							25
	2	3		5		6	7			11		8	4		9			12				1		10					26
	2	3		5		6	7			11	14	8	4		9			*10*		12		1							27
1	2	3		5		6	7			11		8	4		9			12						10					28
1	2	3		5		6	*7*		8	11		12	4		9									14	10				29
1	2	3		5		6	7			11		8	4		9										10				30
1	2	3		5		6	7			11		8	4		9			12							10				31
1	2	3		5		6	7			11		8	4		9										10				32
1	2	3		5		6	7			11		8	4		9										10				33
1	2	3		5		6	7		8	11			4		9			12							10				34
1	2	3		5		6	7			11		8	4		9										10				35
1	2	3				6	7			11	5	8	4		9			12							10				36
1	2	3				6	7					8	4		12										10	5	9	11	37
1	2	3				*6*	7			14		8	4		12										10	5	9	11	38
1	2	3					7			6		8	4		12										10	5	9	11	39
1	2	3		5		*6*	7				14	8	4		12											10	9	11	40
1	2	3		5		6	7				8		4		12											10	9	11	41
1	*2*	3		5		6	7				14	12	4		9											10	8	11	42
1		3		5		6				14	7	12	4		9										2	10	8	*11*	43
1	2	3		5		6	11		12		7		4		9											10	8		44
1	2	3		5		6					7		4		9											10	8	11	45
1	2	3		5		12				6	*7*		4		9											10	8	11	46

Coca-Cola Cup	First Round	Mansfield T (h)	2-2
		(a)	3-1
	Second Round	Manchester U (h)	2-1
		(a)	0-2
FA Cup	Third Round	Bath C (h)	0-0
		(a)	4-1
	Fourth Round	Oldham Ath (a)	0-0
		(h)	0-1

STOKE CITY

Player and Position	Ht	Wt	Birth Date	Birth Place	Source	Clubs	League App	League Gls
Goalkeepers								
Mark Prudhoe	6 0	13 00	8 11 63	Washington	Apprentice	Sunderland	7	—
						Hartlepool U (loan)	3	—
						Birmingham C	1	—
						Walsall	26	—
						Doncaster R (loan)	5	—
						Sheffield W (loan)	—	—
						Grimsby T (loan)	8	—
						Hartlepool U (loan)	13	—
						Bristol C (loan)	3	—
						Carlisle U	34	—
						Darlington	146	—
						Stoke C	30	—
Ron Sinclair	5 10	11 13	19 11 64	Stirling	Apprentice	Nottingham F	—	—
						Wrexham (loan)	11	—
						Derby Co (loan)	—	—
						Sheffield U (loan)	—	—
						Leeds U (loan)	—	—
						Leeds U	8	—
						Halifax T (loan)	4	—
						Halifax T (loan)	10	—
						Bristol C	44	—
						Walsall (loan)	10	—
						Stoke C	55	—
Paul Straney	5 11	12 04	7 10 75	Downpatrick	Trainee	Stoke C	—	—
Defenders								
Mick Adams	5 6	11 11	8 11 61	Sheffield	Apprentice	Gillingham	92	5
						Coventry C	90	9
						Leeds U	73	2
						Southampton	144	7
						Stoke C	10	3
Robert Brunton‡			5 9 73	Dublin	Belvedere	Stoke C	—	—
John Butler	5 11	11 07	7 2 62	Liverpool	Prescot Cables	Wigan Ath	245	15
						Stoke C	221	7
John Clark	6 0	13 01	22 9 64	Edinburgh	S Form	Dundee U	242	19
						Stoke C	12	—
Ian Clarkson	5 11	12 00	4 12 70	Birmingham	Trainee	Birmingham C	136	—
						Stoke C	14	—
Ian Cranson	6 0	13 04	2 7 64	Easington	Apprentice	Ipswich T	131	5
						Sheffield W	30	—
						Stoke C	156	7
Stephen Davies*	5 11		7 9 74	Crewe	Trainee	Stoke C	—	—
Graham Harbey‡	5 8	11 08	29 8 64	Chesterfield	Apprentice	Derby Co	40	1
						Ipswich T	59	1
						WBA	97	2
						Stoke C	19	—
Vince Overson	6 0	14 10	15 5 62	Kettering	Apprentice	Burnley	211	6
						Birmingham C	182	3
						Stoke C	117	6
Graham Potter			20 5 75	Solihull	Trainee	Birmingham C	25	2
						Wycombe W (loan)	3	—
						Stoke C	3	—
Lee Sandford	6 1	12 02	22 4 68	Basingstoke	Apprentice	Portsmouth	72	1
						Stoke C	177	7
Simon Winstone*	5 7		4 10 74	Bristol	Trainee	Stoke C	—	—
Midfield								
Carl Beeston	5 9	12 04	30 6 67	Stoke	Apprentice	Stoke C	186	12
Mark Devlin	5 10	11 04	18 1 73	Irvine	Trainee	Stoke C	24	2
Steve Foley*	5 7	11 03	4 10 62	Liverpool	Apprentice	Liverpool	—	—
						Fulham (loan)	3	—
						Grimsby T	31	2
						Sheffield U	66	14
						Swindon T	151	23
						Stoke C	107	10
Nigel Gleghorn	6 0	13 04	12 8 62	Seaham	Seaham Red Star	Ipswich T	66	11
						Manchester C	34	7
						Birmingham C	142	33
						Stoke C	74	10

STOKE CITY

Colours: Red and white striped shirts, white shorts, red stockings. **Change colours:** All purple with white trim.

Foundation: The date of the formation of this club has long been in doubt. The year 1863 was claimed, but more recent research by Wade Martin has uncovered nothing earlier than 1868, when a couple of Old Carthusians, who were apprentices at the local works of the old North Staffordshire Railway Company, met with some others from that works, to form Stoke Ramblers. It should also be noted that the old Stoke club went bankrupt in 1908 when a new club was formed.

First Football League game: 8 September, 1888, Football League, v WBA (h) L 0-2 – Rowley; Clare, Underwood; Ramsey, Shutt, Smith; Sayer, McSkimming, Staton, Edge, Tunnicliffe.

Did you know: Stoke City lost only two matches in the Football Alliance as champions during 1890–91. These were both in Birmingham, 5-2 against St George's and 5-1 at Small Heath. On each occasion they had their goalkeeper carried off.

Managers (and Secretary-Managers)
Tom Slaney 1874–83*, Walter Cox 1883–84*, Harry Lockett 1884–90, Joseph Bradshaw 1890–92, Arthur Reeves 1892–95, William Rowley 1895–97, H. D. Austerberry 1897–1908, A. J. Barker 1908–14, Peter Hodge 1914–15, Joe Schofield 1915–19, Arthur Shallcross 1919–23, John "Jock" Rutherford 1923, Tom Mather 1923–35, Bob McGrory 1935–52, Frank Taylor 1952–60, Tony Waddington 1960–77, George Eastham 1977–78, Alan A'Court 1978, Alan Durban 1978–81, Richie Barker 1981–83, Bill Asprey 1984–85, Mick Mills 1985–89, Alan Ball 1989–91, Lou Macari 1991–93, Joe Jordan November 1993–

Player and Position	Ht	Wt	Birth Date	Birth Place	Source	Clubs	League App	League Gls
Mick Gynn	5 5	10 10	19 8 61	Peterborough	Apprentice	Peterborough U	156	33
						Coventry C	241	32
						Stoke C	21	—
Keith Long‡	5 9	10 00	14 11 73	Dublin	St Josephs Boys	Stoke C	—	—
Owen Lovelock‡	5 8		21 1 75	Swindon	Trainee	Stoke C	—	—
Michael Macari‡			4 2 73	Kilwinning	Trainee	West Ham U	—	—
						Stoke C	—	—
Thorvaldur Orlygsson	5 11	10 08	2 8 66	Odense	FC Akureyri	Nottingham F	37	2
						Stoke C	45	9
Gary Pick*	5 8	11 08	9 7 71	Leicester	Leicester U	Stoke C	—	—
Ernie Tapai‡	5 7	10 05	14 2 67	Melbourne	Adelaide C	Stoke C	—	—
Paul Ware	5 9	11 05	7 11 70	Congleton	Trainee	Stoke C	115	10
Forwards								
Gary Bannister*	5 8	11 10	22 7 60	Warrington	Apprentice	Coventry C	22	3
						Sheffield W	118	55
						QPR	136	56
						Coventry C	43	11
						WBA	72	18
						Oxford U (loan)	10	2
						Nottingham F	31	8
						Stoke C	15	2
Wayne Biggins	5 10	11 00	20 11 61	Sheffield	Apprentice	Lincoln C	8	1
					Matlock Town and King's Lynn	Burnley	78	29
						Norwich C	79	16
						Manchester C	32	9
						Stoke C	122	46
						Barnsley	47	16
						Celtic	9	—
						Stoke C	10	4

Continued on Page 499

Trainees
Allerton, Daniel J; Bailey, Mark; Birch, Mark; Blair, Scott; Burke, Robert E; Callan, Aidan J; Hawkes, Marc J; Holden, Mark C; Miles, Darren L; Talbot, David A; Woods, Stephen J.

****Non-Contract**
King, Ian J.

Associated Schoolboys
Atherley, Andrew P; Brownsword, Andrew; Cornes, James; Crowe, Dean; Dickin, David A; Eldershaw, Neil D; Griffin, Andrew; Heath, Alisdair D; Knight, Richard; Leatherby, Stuart; Roberts, Stephen N; Rogers, Karl; Simpson, Andrew P; Smith, Mark D; Taaffe, Steven; Wilshaw, Antony; Woolliscroft, Ashley.

Associated Schoolboys who have accepted the Club's offer of a Traineeship/Contract
Carter, Richard; Watson, David.
**Non-Contract Players who are retained must be re-signed before they are eligible to play in League matches.

SUNDERLAND 1993–94 *Back row (left to right):* Anthony Smith, Don Goodman, Anthony Robinson, Richard Ord, Lee Howey, Gordon Armstrong, Ian Sampson, Gareth Cronin, Gary Owers. *Centre row:* Jimmy Montgomery, Ian Atkins, Ian Rogerson, Alan Harding, Sean Musgrave, Andy Melville, Alec Chamberlain, Gary Bennett, Tony Norman, David Rush, Martin Gray, Stephen Brodie, Terry Butcher, Mick Buxton.

Front row: George Herd, Martin Smith, Phil Gray, Brian Atkinson, Michael Gray, Kevin Ball, Shaun Cunnington, John Kay, Craig Russell, Derek Ferguson, Steve Smelt.

Division 1 **SUNDERLAND**

Roker Park Ground, Sunderland SR6 9SW. Telephone Sunderland 091–514 0332. Fax 091– 514 5854.

Chairman: B. E. Fearn. ***Vice-chairman:*** L. V. Pickering.
Ground capacity: 22,657.

Record attendance: 75,118 v Derby Co, FA Cup 6th rd replay, 8 March 1933.

Record receipts: £186,000 v Tottenham H, Division 1, 28 August 1990.

Pitch measurements: 113yd × 74yd.

Chairman: J. R. Featherstone.

Deputy chairman: G. S. Wood.

Directors: R. S. Murray, G. S. Wood, J. G. Wood, G. Davidson. ***Associate Director:*** Alec King.

Manager: Mick Buxton.

General Manager/Secretary: G. Davidson FCA.

Chief Coach: Trevor Hartley. ***Youth team coach: George Herd.***

Physio: Steve Smelt. ***Director of Youth:*** Jimmy Montgomery. ***Commercial Manager:*** Alec King.

Year Formed: 1879. ***Turned Professional:*** 1886. ***Ltd Co.:*** 1906.

Club Nickname: 'Rokermen'.

Previous Name: 1879–80, Sunderland and District Teacher's AFC.

Previous Grounds: 1879, Blue House Field, Hendon; 1882, Groves Field, Ashbrooke; 1883, Horatio Street; 1884, Abbs Field, Fulwell; 1886, Newcastle Road; 1898, Roker Park.

Record League Victory: 9–1 v Newcastle U (away), Division 1, 5 December 1908 – Roose; Forster, Melton; Daykin, Thomson, Low; Mordue, Hogg (4), Brown, Holley (3), Bridgett (2).

Record Cup Victory: 11–1 v Fairfield, FA Cup, 1st rd, 2 February 1895 – Doig; McNeill, Johnston; Dunlop, McCreadie (1), Wilson; Gillespie (1), Millar (5), Campbell, Hannah (3), Scott (1).

Record Defeat: 0–8 v West Ham U, Division 1, 19 October 1968 and v Watford, Division 1, 25 September 1982.

Most League Points (2 for a win): 61, Division 2, 1963–64.

Most League Points (3 for a win): 93, Division 3, 1987–88.

Most League Goals: 109, Division 1, 1935–36.

Highest League Scorer in Season: Dave Halliday, 43, Division 1, 1928–29.

Most League Goals in Total Aggregate: Charlie Buchan, 209, 1911–25.

Most Capped Player: Martin Harvey, 34, Northern Ireland.

Most League Appearances: Jim Montgomery, 537, 1962–77.

Record Transfer Fee Received: £1,500,000 from Crystal Palace for Marco Gabbiadini, September 1991.

Record Transfer Fee Paid: £900,000 to WBA for Don Goodman, December 1991.

Football League Record: 1890 Elected to Division 1; 1958–64 Division 2; 1964–70 Division 1; 1970–76 Division 2; 1976–77 Division 1; 1977–80 Division 2; 1980–85 Division 1; 1985–87 Division 2; 1987–88 Division 3; 1988–90 Division 2; 1990–91 Division 1; 1991–92 Division 2; 1992– Division 1.

Honours: *Football League:* Division 1 – Champions 1891–92, 1892–93, 1894–95, 1901–02, 1912–13, 1935–36; Runners-up 1893–94; 1897–98, 1900–01, 1922–23, 1934–35; Division 2 – Champions 1975–76; Runners-up 1963–64, 1979–80; Division 3 – Champions 1987–88. *FA Cup:* Winners 1937, 1973; Runners-up 1913, 1992. *Football League Cup:* Runners-up 1984–85. **European Competitions:** *Cup-Winners' Cup:* 1973–74.

SUNDERLAND 1993—94 LEAGUE RECORD

Match No.	Date	Venue	Opponents	Result		H/T Score	Lg. Pos.	Goalscorers	Attendance
1	Aug 14	A	Derby Co	L	0-5	0-3	—		18,027
2	21	H	Charlton Ath	W	4-0	0-0	11	Goodman, Gray Michael, Cunnington, Armstrong	17,647
3	28	A	Notts Co	L	0-1	0-0	19		9166
4	Sept 12	A	Crystal Palace	L	0-1	0-1	—		11,318
5	18	H	Wolverhampton W	L	0-2	0-1	24		18,292
6	25	A	Watford	D	1-1	1-1	24	Owers	7694
7	28	H	Grimsby T	D	2-2	0-2	—	Goodman, Ord	15,488
8	Oct 2	H	Peterborough U	W	2-0	1-0	23	Gray P, Owers	17,846
9	9	H	Birmingham C	W	1-0	1-0	17	Howey	19,265
10	17	A	Middlesbrough	L	1-4	1-3	—	Goodman	12,772
11	20	H	Luton T	W	2-0	2-0	—	Goodman, Smith M	13,760
12	23	H	WBA	W	1-0	0-0	11	Ord	19,505
13	30	A	Bristol C	L	0-2	0-0	14		8162
14	Nov 3	A	Stoke C	L	0-1	0-0	—		13,551
15	6	H	Portsmouth	L	1-2	0-2	18	Smith M	17,146
16	13	A	Tranmere R	L	1-4	1-0	19	Goodman	8497
17	20	H	Southend U	L	0-2	0-1	20		15,452
18	27	H	Nottingham F	L	2-3	1-2	22	Gray P, Smith M	16,968
19	Dec 4	A	Portsmouth	W	1-0	1-0	19	Smith M	11,891
20	18	H	Derby Co	W	1-0	1-0	18	Gray P	16,001
21	27	A	Bolton W	D	0-0	0-0	17		18,496
22	28	H	Millwall	W	2-1	1-1	16	Gray P, Russell	19,283
23	Jan 1	A	Leicester C	L	1-2	0-0	16	Gray P (pen)	19,615
24	3	H	Barnsley	W	1-0	1-0	16	Gray P	19,302
25	11	A	Oxford U	W	3-0	2-0	—	Smith M 2, Goodman	5877
26	16	H	Middlesbrough	W	2-1	0-0	—	Gray P (pen), Howey	16,473
27	22	A	Birmingham C	D	0-0	0-0	13		15,884
28	Feb 5	A	WBA	L	1-2	0-2	15	Goodman	17,089
29	12	H	Bristol C	D	0-0	0-0	15		16,816
30	22	A	Charlton Ath	D	0-0	0-0	—		7904
31	25	A	Luton T	L	1-2	0-2	17	Howey	9367
32	Mar 5	H	Notts Co	W	2-0	1-0	16	Russell, Gray P	16,269
33	16	H	Crystal Palace	W	1-0	0-0	—	Gray P	15,892
34	19	H	Watford	W	2-0	0-0	14	Russell 2	16,479
35	26	A	Peterborough U	W	3-1	2-1	12	Russell, Gray P 2	8753
36	29	A	Barnsley	L	0-4	0-2	—		10,042
37	Apr 2	H	Bolton W	W	2-0	0-0	12	Russell 2	18,574
38	6	A	Millwall	L	1-2	0-2	—	Melville	10,244
39	9	H	Leicester C	L	2-3	1-1	15	Goodman, Melville	17,198
40	12	A	Grimsby T	W	1-0	0-0	—	Smith M	4732
41	16	H	Stoke C	L	0-1	0-1	13		17,406
42	23	A	Southend U	W	1-0	0-0	12	Smith M	4734
43	26	H	Oxford U	L	2-3	2-1	—	Gray P (pen), Armstrong	14,712
44	30	H	Tranmere R	W	3-2	3-0	11	Gray P 2, Russell	15,167
45	May 3	A	Wolverhampton W	D	1-1	1-1	—	Goodman	25,079
46	8	A	Nottingham F	D	2-2	0-1	12	Goodman, Russell	27,010

Final League Position: 12

GOALSCORERS

League (54): Gray P 14 (3 pens), Goodman 10, Russell 9, Smith 8, Howey 3, Armstrong 2, Melville 2, Ord 2, Owers 2, Cunnington 1, Michael Gray 1.
Coca-Cola Cup (8): Goodman 4, Gray P 3, Power 1.
FA Cup (3): Ferguson 1, Howey 1, Smith 1.

Chamberlain 43	Kay 3	Michael Gray 16 + 6	Ferguson 41	Melville 44	Sampson 2 + 2	Owers 30	Goodman 34 + 1	Howey 7 + 7	Cunnington 11	Armstrong 22 + 4	Atkinson 21 + 8	Power 1 + 2	Smith M 27 + 2	Martin Gray 16 + 6	Bennett 37 + 1	Russell 29 + 6	Gray P 39 + 2	Brodie — + 4	Ord 24 + 4	Ball 36	Rush — + 5	Lawrence 2 + 2	Rodgerson 2 + 2	Kubicki 15	Norman 3	Smith A 1	Match No.
1	2	3	4	5	6	7	8	9	10	11	12	14															1
1	2	5		6		7	8	12	9	11		10		14	4											3	2
1				6	2	7	8		9	11	5			3	4	10	12	14									3
1			5	6		2	8			11	12	14		7	4	9	10		3								4
1			5	6		7	8	12		9				2	4	11	10		3								5
1		12	5	6		7	8			9				2	4	11	10		3								6
1		12	5	6		7	8			9				2	4	11	10		3								7
1		12	5	6		7	8			9				2	4	11	10		3								8
1	2		5			7	8	9						10	4	11			3	6	12						9
1			5	6		7	8	9		11	10				4	12			3	2		14					10
1		3	5	6	14	7	8	9			11		10			12				2		4					11
1		12	5	6		7	8			14	11		10				9		3	2		4					12
1		14		5		6	8			11	7		10	3	4	12	9			2							13
1		12		5		6	8			11	7		10	3	4		9			2							14
1		3	5	6		2	8			11			10		12		9			4			7				15
1			5			7	8	9		11			10	2	4		12		3	6			14				16
1			5	6			8		11				10	12	4		9		3	2			7				17
1			5	6		7	8	12	11				10	2	4		9		3								18
1			11	5		2	8		7		12		10		4		9		3	6							19
1			5	6		2	8		7		12		10	3	4		9			11							20
1			5	6		2	8		7		12		10	3	4		9			11							21
1			5	6		2	8		7	9				3	4	12	10			11							22
1			5	6		2			7	8				3	4	10	9		12	11	14						23
1			5	6		7				9	12			2	4	11	10		3	8	14						24
1			5	6		2	8			7	12		10		4	14	9		3	11							25
1			5	6		2		14		8	12		10		4	11	9		3	7							26
1			5	6		2	8	14	7				10		4	12	9		3	11							27
1		4		5		2	8				11		10			7	9		3	6							28
1		3	5	6		2	8				11		10			7	9			4		12					29
1		3	5	6	12	2		9			11				4	8	10			7	14						30
1		3	5	6		2		8			11		14		4	10	9		12	7							31
1			5	6			8						10		4	11	9		3	7				2			32
1			5	6			8				11				4	10	9		3	7				2			33
1			5	6			8				11		12		4	10	9		3	7	14			2			34
1			5	6							11		8	12	4	10	9		3	7				2			35
1			5	6							11		10		4	8	9	12	3	7				2			36
1			5	6							11		10		4	8	9	12	3	7				2			37
1			5	6			12			14	11		10		4	8	9		3	7				2			38
1		3	5	6			8			12			10		4	11	9			7				2			39
1		3	5	6			8			14	11		10	12		7	9			4				2			40
1		3	5	6			8						10		4	11	9			7				2			41
1		3	5	6						11	7		10		4	8	9		12					2			42
1		3	5	6				12		11			10		4	8	9	14		7				2			43
		3	5	6				12		11	7		10	14		8	9			4				2	1		44
		3	5	6			8			11	7			14		10	9		12	4				2	1		45
		3	5	6			8				11				4	10	9			7			12	2	1		46

Coca-Cola Cup	First Round	Chester C (h)	3-1
		(a)	0-0
	Second Round	Leeds U (h)	2-1
		(a)	2-1
	Third Round	Aston Villa (h)	1-4
FA Cup	Third Round	Carlisle U (h)	1-1
		(a)	1-0
	Fourth Round	Wimbledon (a)	1-2

SUNDERLAND

Player and Position	Ht	Wt	Birth Date	Birth Place	Source	Clubs	League App	League Gls
Goalkeepers								
Alec Chamberlain	6 2	13 01	20 6 64	March		Ipswich T	—	—
						Colchester U	184	—
						Everton	—	—
						Tranmere R (loan)	15	—
						Luton T	138	—
						Chelsea (loan)	—	—
						Sunderland	43	—
Sean Musgrave	5 10		27 10 74	Penshaw	Trainee	Sunderland	—	—
Tony Norman	6 2	13 10	24 2 58	Mancot	Amateur	Burnley	—	—
						Hull C	372	—
						Sunderland	169	—
Defenders								
Kevin Ball	5 9	12 00	12 11 64	Hastings	Apprentice	Portsmouth	105	4
						Sunderland	145	7
Gary Bennett	6 1	12 01	4 12 61	Manchester	Amateur	Manchester C	—	—
						Cardiff C	87	11
						Sunderland	349	23
Terry Butcher	6 4	14 00	28 12 58	Singapore	Amateur	Ipswich T	271	16
						Rangers	127	9
						Coventry C	6	—
						Sunderland	38	—
Gareth Cronin*			18 2 75	Cork	Trainee	Sunderland	—	—
						Bradford C (loan)	—	—
Shaun Cunnington	5 10	11 07	4 1 66	Bourne	Bourne T	Wrexham	199	12
						Grimsby T	182	13
						Sunderland	50	8
Michael Gray			3 8 74	Sunderland	Trainee	Sunderland	49	3
John Kay	5 10	11 06	29 1 64	Sunderland	Apprentice	Arsenal	14	—
						Wimbledon	63	2
						Middlesbrough (loan)	8	—
						Sunderland	199	—
Andy Melville	6 0	12 00	29 11 68	Swansea	School	Swansea C	175	22
						Oxford U	135	13
						Sunderland	44	2
Richard Ord	6 2	12 08	3 3 70	Easington	Trainee	Sunderland	121	4
						York C (loan)	3	—
Anthony Robinson*			5 10 73	Sunderland	Trainee	Sunderland	—	—
Ian Sampson	6 2	12 08	14 11 68	Wakefield	Goole T	Sunderland	17	1
						Northampton T (loan)	8	—
Tony Smith	5 10	11 04	21 9 71	Sunderland	Trainee	Sunderland	19	—
						Hartlepool U (loan)	5	—
Midfield								
Gordon Armstrong	6 0	11 10	15 7 67	Newcastle	Apprentice	Sunderland	333	49
Brian Atkinson	5 10	12 00	19 1 71	Darlington	Trainee	Sunderland	117	4
Derek Ferguson	5 8	10 11	31 7 67	Glasgow	Gartcosh U	Rangers	111	7
						Dundee (loan)	4	—
						Hearts	103	4
						Sunderland	41	—
Martin Gray	5 9	10 11	17 8 71	Stockton	Trainee	Sunderland	35	1
						Aldershot (loan)	5	—
Alan Harding*	5 8		20 5 75	Lincoln	Trainee	Sunderland	—	—
Gary Owers	5 10	11 10	3 10 68	Newcastle	Apprentice	Sunderland	249	24
Ian Rodgerson	5 10	10 07	9 4 66	Hereford	Pegasus Juniors	Hereford U	100	6
						Cardiff C	99	4
						Birmingham C	95	13
						Sunderland	4	—
Forwards								
Mark Angel			23 8 75	Newcastle		Sunderland	—	—
Stephen Brodie	5 10	11 00	14 1 73	Sunderland	Trainee	Sunderland	4	—
John Colquhoun (To Hearts July 1993)	5 7	11 00	14 7 63	Stirling	Grangemouth Inter	Stirling Albion	104	45
						Celtic	32	4
						Hearts	231	54
						Millwall	27	3
						Sunderland	20	—

SUNDERLAND

Colours: Red and white striped shirts, black shorts, red stockings, white turnover. **Change colours:** White shirts, blue and green sleeves, navy blue shorts, white stockings, navy blue trim.

Foundation: A Scottish schoolmaster named James Allan, working at Hendon Boarding School, took the initiative in the foundation of Sunderland in 1879 when they were formed as The Sunderland and District Teachers' Association FC at a meeting in the Adults School, Norfolk Street. Because of financial difficulties, they quickly allowed members from outside the teaching profession and so became Sunderland AFC in October 1880.

First Football League game: 13 September, 1890, Football League, v Burnley (h) L 2-3 – Kirtley; Porteous, Oliver; Wilson, Auld, Gibson; Spence (1), Miller, Campbell (1), Scott, D. Hannah.

Did you know: During Sunderland's first Division 1 championship season 1891–92, the club emulated the feat achieved earlier in the term by Preston North End of 13 consecutive wins. Sunderland achieved it from 14 November to 2 April.

Managers (and Secretary-Managers)
Tom Watson 1888–96, Bob Campbell 1896–99, Alex Mackie 1899–1905, Bob Kyle 1905–28, Johnny Cochrane 1928–39, Bill Murray 1939–57, Alan Brown 1957–64, George Hardwick 1964–65, Ian McColl 1965–68, Alan Brown 1968–72, Bob Stokoe 1972–76, Jimmy Adamson 1976–78, Ken Knighton 1979–81, Alan Durban 1981–84, Len Ashurst 1984–85, Lawrie McMenemy 1985–87, Denis Smith 1987–91, Malcolm Crosby 1992–93, Terry Butcher 1993, Mick Buxton December 1993–

Player and Position	*Ht*	*Wt*	*Birth Date*	*Place*	*Source*	*Clubs*	*League App*	*Gls*
Peter Davenport	5 10	11 06	24 3 61	Birkenhead	Everton	Nottingham F	118	54
						Manchester U	92	22
						Middlesbrough	59	7
						Sunderland	99	15
Don Goodman	5 10	11 10	9 5 66	Leeds	School	Bradford C	70	14
						WBA	158	60
						Sunderland	98	37
Philip Gray	5 10	12 03	2 10 68	Belfast	Apprentice	Tottenham H	9	—
						Barnsley (loan)	3	—
						Fulham (loan)	3	—
						Luton T	59	22
						Sunderland	41	14
Gudni Helgason			16 7 76	Iceland	Volsungur	Sunderland	—	—
Lee Howey	6 2	13 09	1 4 69	Sunderland	AC Hemptinne	Sunderland	15	3
Chris Lawless			4 10 74	Dublin	Home Farm	Sunderland	—	—
David Rush	5 11	10 10	15 5 71	Sunderland	Trainee	Sunderland	59	12
						Hartlepool U (loan)	8	2
						Peterborough U (loan)	4	1
Craig Russell			4 2 74	South Shields	Trainee	Sunderland	39	9
Martin Smith			13 11 74	Sunderland	Trainee	Sunderland	29	8

Trainees
Beary, Daniel M; Berrisford, Adrian C; Brumwell, Philip; (h) Forster, Lee C; Manners, Andrew C; Mawson, David; Pickering, Steven; Preece, David; Smith, Stephen; Stoddart, Neil M; Waldock, John A.

Associated Schoolboys
Beavers, Paul M; Bell, Russell; Greenwood, Gavin E; Hay, CHristopher; McPake, Christopher; Naisbett, Philip; Norton, Peter; Southwick, Jason A; Tate, Craig D.

Associated Schoolboys who have accepted the Club's offer of a Traineeship/Contract
Brown, Mark; Holloway, Darren; Logan, Lee; Parker, Neal; Richardson, Paul.

SWANSEA CITY 1993–94 *Back row (left to right):* Jon Brady, David Barnhouse, Martin Hayes, Shaun Chapple, Andy Cook.
Centre row: Keith Walker, John Ford, Mark Harris, Roger Freestone, Stephen Torpey, Andy McFarlane, Richard Jones.
Front row: Mark Clode, Stephen Jenkins, John Hodge, John Cornforth, Jason Bowen, Colin Pascoe, Jonathan Coates.
(Photograph: Reg Pike)

Division 2 SWANSEA CITY

Vetch Field, Swansea SA1 3SU. Telephone Swansea (0792) 474114. Fax: (0792) 646120. Club shop: 33 William St, Swansea SA1 3QS. Telephone: (0792) 462584.

Ground capacity: 16,540.

Record attendance: 32,796 v Arsenal, FA Cup 4th rd, 17 February 1968.

Record receipts: £36,477.42 v Liverpool, Division 1, 18 September 1982.

Pitch measurements: 112yd × 74yd.

President: I. C. Pursey MBE.

Chairman: D. J. Sharpe.

Directors: D. G. Hammond FCA, MBIM (Vice-chairman), M. Griffiths.

Chief Executive: Robin Sharpe.

Team Manager: Frank Burrows. ***Assistant Manager:*** Bobby Smith.

Youth Team Manager: Jimmy Rimmer. ***Physio:*** Mike Davenport.

Programme Editor: Major Reg Pike.

Year Formed: 1912. ***Turned Professional:*** 1912. ***Ltd Co.:*** 1912.

Secretary: George Taylor.

Previous Name: Swansea Town until February 1970.

Club Nickname: 'The Swans'.

Record League Victory: 8–0 v Hartlepool U, Division 4, 1 April 1978 – Barber; Evans, Bartley, Lally (1) (Morris), May, Bruton, Kevin Moore, Robbie James (3 incl. 1p), Curtis (3), Toshack (1), Chappell.

Record Cup Victory: 12–0 v Sliema W (Malta), ECWC 1st rd 1st leg, 15 September 1982 – Davies; Marustik, Hadziabdic (1), Irwin (1), Kennedy, Rajkovic (1), Loveridge (2) (Leighton James), Robbie James, Charles (2), Stevenson (1), Latchford (1) (Walsh (3)).

Record Defeat: 0–8 v Liverpool, FA Cup 3rd rd, 9 January 1990.

Most League Points (2 for a win): 62, Division 3 (S), 1948–49.

Most League Points (3 for a win): 73, Division 2, 1992–93.

Most League Goals: 90, Division 2, 1956–57.

Highest League Scorer in Season: Cyril Pearce, 35, Division 2, 1931–32.

Most League Goals in Total Aggregate: Ivor Allchurch, 166, 1949–58, 1965–68.

Most Capped Player: Ivor Allchurch, 42 (68), Wales.

Most League Appearances: Wilfred Milne, 585, 1919–37.

Record Transfer Fee Received: £375,000 from Nottingham F for Des Lyttle, July 1993.

Record Transfer Fee Paid: £340,000 to Liverpool for Colin Irwin, August 1981.

Football League Record: 1920 Original Member of Division 3; 1921–25 Division 3 (S); 1925–47 Division 2; 1947–49 Division 3 (S); 1949–65 Division 2; 1965–67 Division 3; 1967–70 Division 4; 1970–73 Division 3; 1973–78 Division 4; 1978–79 Division 3; 1979–81 Division 2; 1981–83 Division 1; 1983–84 Division 2; 1984–86 Division 3; 1986–88 Division 4; 1988–92 Division 3; 1992– Division 2.

Honours: *Football League:* Division 1 best season: 6th, 1981–82; Division 2 – Promoted 1980–81 (3rd); Division 3 (S) – Champions 1924–25, 1948–49; Division 3 – Promoted 1978–79 (3rd); Division 4 – Promoted 1969–70 (3rd), 1977–78 (3rd). *FA Cup:* Semi-finals 1926, 1964. *Football League Cup:* best season: 4th rd, 1964–65, 1976–77. *Welsh Cup:* Winners 9 times; Runners-up 8 times. **Autoglass Trophy:** Winners 1994. **European Competitions:** *European Cup-Winners' Cup:* 1961–62, 1966–67, 1981–82, 1982–83, 1983–84, 1989–90, 1991–92.

SWANSEA CITY 1993—94 LEAGUE RECORD

Match No.	Date	Venue	Opponents	Result		H/T Score	Lg. Pos.	Goalscorers	Attendance
1	Aug 14	A	York C	L	1-2	0-1	—	Hodge	4596
2	21	H	Wrexham	W	3-1	1-1	10	Harris, Pascoe, Cornforth (pen)	5383
3	28	A	Barnet	W	1-0	0-0	9	Bowen	1996
4	31	H	Huddersfield T	W	1-0	1-0	—	Hayes	4318
5	Sept 4	H	Plymouth Arg	L	0-1	0-0	7		4616
6	11	A	Brentford	D	1-1	1-0	10	Cornforth	5042
7	14	A	Cambridge U	L	0-2	0-0	—		3338
8	18	H	Bradford C	W	2-0	1-0	8	Hayes, Walker	3373
9	25	A	Exeter C	L	0-1	0-0	11		3655
10	Oct 1	H	Reading	D	1-1	0-0	—	McFarlane	4245
11	9	H	Blackpool	D	4-4	3-2	13	Pascoe, Cornforth, Hayes, Walker	3775
12	16	A	Rotherham U	D	1-1	0-1	12	McFarlane	3178
13	23	H	Hull C	W	1-0	0-0	11	McFarlane	3774
14	30	A	Stockport Co	L	0-4	0-2	14		4641
15	Nov 2	H	Burnley	W	3-1	2-1	—	Hayes, Pascoe, Bowen	3358
16	6	A	Port Vale	L	0-3	0-2	14		7854
17	20	H	Leyton Orient	D	1-1	1-0	14	Torpey	3160
18	27	A	Fulham	L	1-3	0-1	15	Chapple	3282
19	Dec 11	A	Wrexham	L	2-3	0-1	17	Torpey 2	2762
20	18	H	York C	L	1-2	0-1	17	Chapple	2749
21	22	A	Cardiff C	L	0-1	0-0	—		9815
22	Jan 1	A	Bristol R	W	2-1	0-0	17	Coates, Harris	6285
23	14	H	Rotherham U	D	0-0	0-0	—		3271
24	22	A	Blackpool	D	1-1	0-0	19	Torpey	7080
25	28	H	Hartlepool U	D	1-1	0-0	—	Jenkins	2573
26	Feb 5	A	Hull C	W	1-0	0-0	17	Chapple	4668
27	12	H	Bournemouth	D	1-1	1-0	18	Bowen	3255
28	18	H	Barnet	W	2-0	2-0	—	Bowen 2	3278
29	22	A	Huddersfield T	D	1-1	0-1	—	Cornforth	3854
30	25	A	Plymouth Arg	L	1-2	1-1	17	Torpey	8930
31	Mar 5	H	Brentford	D	1-1	1-0	18	Bowen	3187
32	8	H	Brighton & HA	W	3-0	1-0	—	Pascoe, Torpey 2	2893
33	12	A	Bradford C	L	1-2	0-0	16	Cornforth	8220
34	15	H	Cambridge U	W	4-2	3-1	—	Bowen 2, Torpey, Pascoe	2699
35	19	H	Exeter C	W	2-0	0-0	14	Bowen, Clode	2512
36	26	A	Reading	L	1-2	0-0	15	Bowen	6464
37	29	A	Hartlepool U	L	0-1	0-1	—		1354
38	Apr 2	H	Cardiff C	W	1-0	0-0	15	Penney (pen)	3711
39	6	A	Brighton & HA	L	1-4	0-2	—	Penney	9303
40	9	H	Bristol R	W	2-0	0-0	14	Ford, McLean (og)	3961
41	12	H	Stockport Co	L	1-2	0-1	—	Hodge	2483
42	16	A	Burnley	D	1-1	1-0	14	Harris	10,694
43	19	A	Bournemouth	W	1-0	1-0	—	Torpey	2465
44	26	H	Port Vale	L	0-1	0-1	—		4252
45	30	A	Leyton Orient	L	1-2	0-1	16	Cornforth	3529
46	May 7	H	Fulham	W	2-1	1-0	13	Bowen, Perrett	4355

Final League Position: 13

GOALSCORERS

League (56): Bowen 11, Torpey 9, Cornforth 6 (1 pen), Pascoe 5, Hayes 4, Chapple 3, Harris 3, McFarlane 3, Hodge 2, Penney 2 (1 pen), Walker 2, Clode 1, Coates 1, Ford 1, Jenkins 1, Perrett 1, own goal 1.
Coca-Cola Cup (4): Bowen 2, Pascoe 1, Torpey 1.
FA Cup (2): Torpey 2.

Freestone 46	Clode 26 + 2	Cook 23 + 5	Walker 27	Harris 46	Pascoe 31 + 2	Hodge 15 + 12	Bowen 39 + 2	Torpey 36 + 4	Cornforth 37 + 1	Hayes 22	Chapple 19 + 10	Ford 21 + 6	Jenkins 38 + 2	Jones 6 + 1	McFarlane 15 + 13	Barnhouse 2 + 1	Perrett 8 + 3	Aspinall 5	Coates — + 4	Burns 4	Rush 13	Ampadu 11 + 2	Penney 11	Moore — + 1	Basham 5	Match No.
1	*2*	3	4	5	6	*7*	8	9	10	11	12	14														1
1	2	*3*	4	5	6	*7*	8	9	10	11	12	14														2
1	2	14	4	5	6	12	8	9	10	*11*	7	3														3
1		14	4	5		12	8	9	10	11	*7*	3	2	6												4
1		14	4	5		12	8	9	10	11	*7*	3	2	6												5
1			4	5			8	9	10	11	7	3	2	6	12											6
1		3		5			8	9	10	11	*7*		2	6	12	4										7
1			4	5	6		8	9	10	11	7	3	2													8
1		14	4	5	6		*8*	9	10	11	*7*	3	2		12											9
1		7	4	5	6		8		10	11		3	2		9		12									10
1		8	4	5	6	14		12	*10*	11		3	2		9		*7*									11
1		3	4	5	6		12		10	11			2		9		*7*	8								12
1	2	3	4	5	6	12	*7*		10	11					9			8								13
1	2	*3*	4	5	6	7			10	11		14	12		9			8								14
1	2		4	5	6	12	7	14	10	11			3		*9*			8								15
1	2	3	4	5	6	14	7		10	11			12		*9*			8								16
1	2	3	4	5	6		8	9		11	7	12		10												17
1	2	3	4	5	6		8	9	10		7						11		12							18
1	2	3		5	6		7	9			12	10	8		14	*4*	11									19
1		3	4	5			7	9			8	12	2		*10*		11		14	6						20
1	14	3		5			7	9	10		8	4	2		12		*11*			6						21
1	12	3		5	6		7	9			*10*	4	2				11		14	8						22
1		3		5	6		7	9				4	2				11		12	10	8					23
1	3			5	6	12	7	9		11	10	4	2								8					24
1	3			5	6		7	9	10	11		4	2				12				8					25
1	3	12		5			7	9	10	11	6	4	2								8					26
1	4	3		5		12	7	*9*	10	11	6		2		14						8					27
1	3		4	5	12		7	9	10	*11*	6		2								8	14				28
1	3		4	5	12	14	7	9	10		6		2								8	*11*				29
1		3	4	5	6	*7*		9	10		12		2		14						8	11				30
1		3	4	5	6		7	9	10				2		12						8	11				31
1		3	4	5	6	12	7	9	10				2								8	11				32
1		3	4	5	6	12	*7*	9	10				2		14						8	11				33
1	3		4	5	6	11	7	9	10		12		2								8					34
1	3		4	5	6	11	7	9	10				2		12						8					35
1		3	4	5	6	11	7		*10*		12		2		9								8	14		36
1		3		5	6	11	7	*9*	10		12	4	2		14								8			37
1	3			5	6	11	7	9	10		12	4	2										8			38
1	3			5	6		7	9	10		12	4	2		14							*11*	8			39
1	3			5			*7*	9	10		6	4	2	12	14							11	8			40
1	3			5		11	7	9	10			4	2		6							12	8			41
1	3			5	6	11		9					2		10	12						7	8		4	42
1	3			5	6	11		9			12	14	*2*		7							10	8		4	43
1				5		11	12	9	14		*6*	3	2	8	10								7		4	44
1	3			5		11	7	12	10				2		9							6	8		4	45
1	*3*			5		11	7	12	10				2		9		14					6	8		4	46

Coca-Cola Cup	First Round	Bristol C (h)	0-1
		(a)	2-0
	Second Round	Oldham Ath (h)	2-1
		(a)	0-2
FA Cup	First Round	Nuneaton (h)	1-1
		(a)	1-2

SWANSEA CITY

Player and Position	Ht	Wt	Birth Date	Place	Source	Clubs	League App	Gls
Goalkeepers								
Roger Freestone	6 2	12 03	19 8 68	Newport		Newport Co	13	—
						Chelsea	42	—
						Swansea C (loan)	14	—
						Hereford U (loan)	8	—
						Swansea C	134	—
Lee Jones	6 3	14 04	9 8 70	Pontypridd	Porth	Swansea C	—	—
Defenders								
David Barnhouse	5 8	11 09	19 3 75	Swansea	Trainee	Swansea C	4	—
Andy Cook	5 9	10 12	10 8 69	Romsey	Apprentice	Southampton	16	1
						Exeter C	70	1
						Swansea C	28	—
Mark Harris	6 1	12 05	15 7 63	Reading	Wokingham	Crystal Palace	2	—
						Burnley (loan)	4	—
						Swansea C	214	14
Steve Jenkins	5 10	11 02	16 7 72	Merthyr	Trainee	Swansea C	108	1
Richard Jones	5 11	11 01	26 4 69	Pontypool		Newport Co	41	1
						Hereford U	148	9
						Swansea C	7	—
Midfield								
Mike Basham	6 2	12 08	27 9 73	Barking	Trainee	West Ham U	—	—
						Colchester U (loan)	1	—
						Swansea C	5	—
Jason Bowen	5 6	10 07	24 8 72	Merthyr	Trainee	Swansea C	93	21
Shaun Chapple	5 11	12 03	14 2 73	Swansea	Trainee	Swansea C	54	5
Mark Clode	5 6	9 06	24 2 73	Plymouth	Trainee	Plymouth Arg	—	—
						Swansea C	28	1
John Cornforth	6 1	12 08	7 10 67	Whitley Bay	Apprentice	Sunderland	32	2
						Doncaster R (loan)	7	3
						Shrewsbury T (loan)	3	—
						Lincoln C (loan)	9	1
						Swansea C	99	11
John Ford	6 1	13 01	12 4 68	Birmingham	Cradley T	Swansea C	114	4
Keith Walker	6 0	11 09	17 4 66	Edinburgh	ICI Juveniles	Stirling Albion	91	17
						St Mirren	43	6
						Swansea C	138	5
Forwards								
Kwame Ampadu	5 10	11 10	20 12 70	Bradford	Trainee	Arsenal	2	—
						Plymouth Arg (loan)	6	1
						WBA (loan)	7	1
						WBA	42	3
						Swansea C	13	—
Jon Brady*	5 10	10 06	14 1 75	Newcastle (Aus)	Adamstown R	Swansea C	—	—
Jonathan Coates	5 8	10 04	27 6 75	Swansea	Trainee	Swansea C	4	1
Martin Hayes	5 10	11 12	21 3 66	Walthamstow	Apprentice	Arsenal	102	26
						Celtic	7	—
						Wimbledon (loan)	2	—
						Swansea C	37	4
John Hodge	5 6	10 00	1 4 69	Ormskirk	Exmouth	Exeter C	65	10
						Swansea C	27	2
Andy McFarlane	6 3	12 06	30 11 66	Wolverhampton	Cradley T	Portsmouth	2	—
						Swansea C	52	8
Michael Moore†	5 10	11 01	7 10 73	Derby	Derby Co	Swansea C	1	—
Colin Pascoe	5 9	10 00	9 4 65	Port Talbot	Apprentice	Swansea C	174	39
						Sunderland	126	22
						Swansea C (loan)	48	9
Darren Perrett	5 9	11 06	29 12 69	Cardiff	Cheltenham T	Swansea C	11	1
Stephen Torpey	6 2	12 11	8 12 70	Islington	Trainee	Millwall	7	—
						Bradford C	96	22
						Swansea C	40	9

SWANSEA CITY

Colours: White shirts with red and black flashes, white shorts with red and black flash, white stockings, with red and black tops. **Change colours:** Orange shirts with white and blue flashes, blue shorts, blue stockings.

Foundation: The earliest Association Football in Wales was played in the Northern part of the country and no international took place in the South until 1894, when a local paper still thought it necessary to publish an outline of the rules and an illustration of the pitch markings. There had been an earlier Swansea club, but this has no connection with Swansea Town (now City) formed at a public meeting in June 1912.

First Football League game: 28 August, 1920, Division 3, v Portsmouth (a) L 0-3 – Crumley; Robson, Evans; Smith, Holdsworth, Williams; Hole, I. Jones, Edmundson, Rigsby, Spottiswood.

Did you know: When Swansea City carried off the Autoglass Trophy last season, they became only the second Welsh club to take a domestic cup out of England via Wembley.

Managers (and Secretary-Managers)
Walter Whittaker 1912–14, William Bartlett 1914–15, Joe Bradshaw 1919–26, Jimmy Thomson 1927–31, Neil Harris 1934–39, Haydn Green 1939–47, Bill McCandless 1947–55, Ron Burgess 1955–58, Trevor Morris 1958–65, Glyn Davies 1965–66, Billy Lucas 1967–69, Roy Bentley 1969–72, Harry Gregg 1972–75, Harry Griffiths 1975–77, John Toshack 1978–83 (resigned October re-appointed in December) 1983–84, Colin Appleton 1984, John Bond 1984–85, Tommy Hutchison 1985–86, Terry Yorath 1986–89, Ian Evans 1989–90, Terry Yorath 1990–91, Frank Burrows March 1991–

Trainees
Chapman, Paul S; Creeden, Kevin M; Edwards, Christian; Evans, Ian D; Hole, Steven T; Hopkins, Peter A; Jenkins, David M; Johnston, Michael B; Jones, Andrew P; Miles, Benjamin D; Rickard, Jamie M; Savage, Christopher J; Savage, Robert T; Spiteri, Denis; Thomas, David J; Thomas, Steven P. G; Walters, Andrew L; Watkins, Christopher M; White, Dean W.

****Non-Contract**
Moore, Michael T.

Associated Schoolboys
Casey, Ryan; Davies, Dewi O; Davies, Stephen W; Evans, Alun; Jenkins, Lee D; Jones, Matthew; Phillips, Gareth; Rosselli, Dean A; Smith, Steven P.

Associated Schoolboys who have accepted the Club's offer of a Traineeship/Contract
Cunningham, John L; Grey, Jonathan R; Harris, Gareth; Jones, Lee E; Lewis, Huw A. W; Llewellyn, Lee; O'Leary, Kristian.
**Non-Contract Players who are retained must be re-signed before they are eligible to play in League matches.

Stoke City players continued from Page 487

Martin Carruthers	5 11	11 07	7 8 72	Nottingham	Trainee	Aston Villa	4	—
						Hull C (loan)	13	6
						Stoke C	34	5
Steven Leslie			6 2 76	Dumfries		Stoke C	—	—
Paul Macari			23 8 76	Manchester		Stoke C	—	—
James Mulligan	5 7	10 12	21 4 74	Dublin	Trainee	Stoke C	—	—
						Bury (loan)	3	1
Dave Regis	6 1	13 08	3 3 64	Paddington	Barnet	Notts Co	46	15
						Plymouth Arg	31	4
						Bournemouth (loan)	6	2
						Stoke C	63	15
Graham Shaw	5 8	10 05	7 6 67	Stoke	Apprentice	Stoke C	99	18
						Preston NE	121	29
						Stoke C	33	5
Simon Sturridge	5 5	10 07	9 12 69	Birmingham	Trainee	Birmingham C	150	30
						Stoke C	13	—

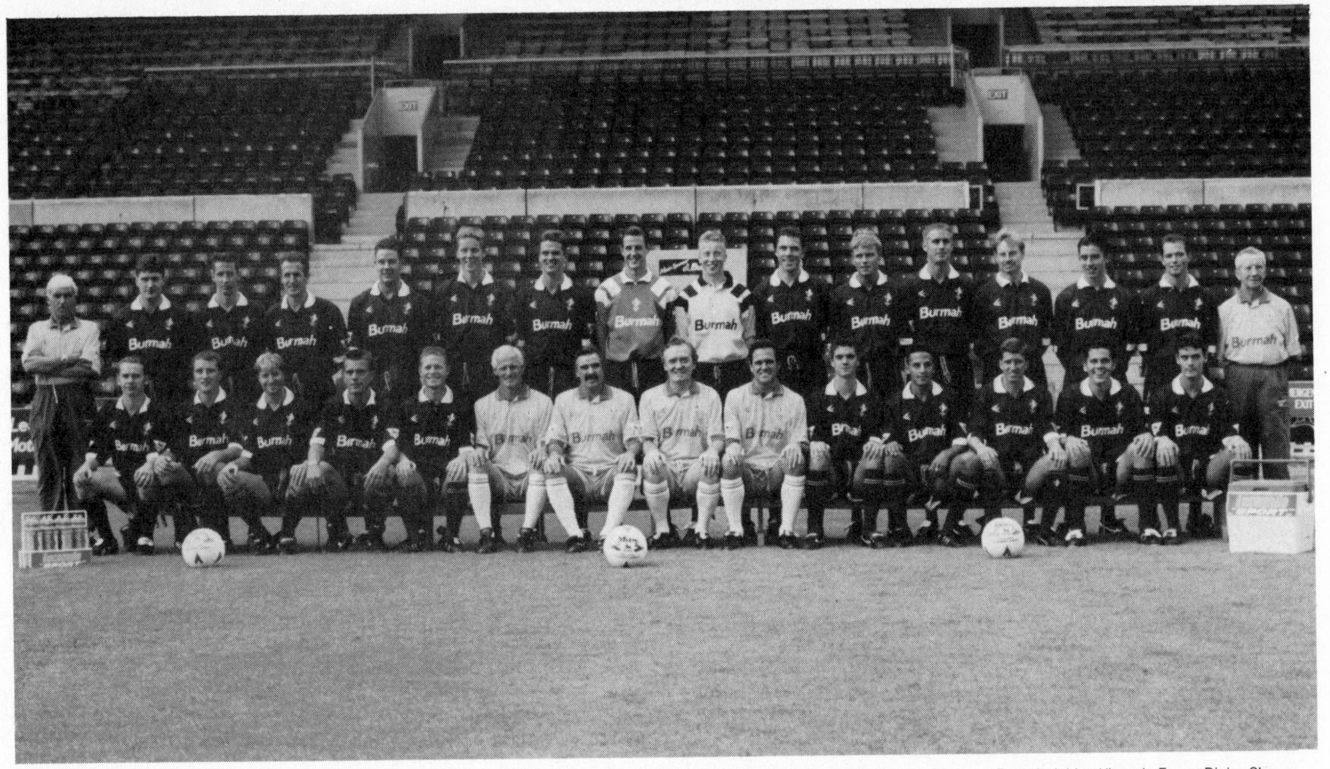

SWINDON TOWN 1993–94 *Back row (left to right):* Kevin Morris (Physio), Ross MacLaren, Steve Lane, Steve White, Adrian Whitbread, Jan Aage Fjortoft, Adrian Viveash, Fraser Digby, Shaun Taylor, Nicky Hammond, Chris Hamon, Andrew Thomson, Paul Bodin, Kevin Horlock, Craig Maskell, Eddie Buckley (Kit Manager).
Front row: Wayne O'Sullivan, Nicky Summerbee, John Moncur, Luc Nijholt, Micky Hazard, John Trollope, John Gorman (Manager), David Hay (Assistant Manager), Andy Rowland, Austin Berkley, Edwin Murray, Martin Ling, Marcus Phillips, Lee Middleton.

Division 1 SWINDON TOWN

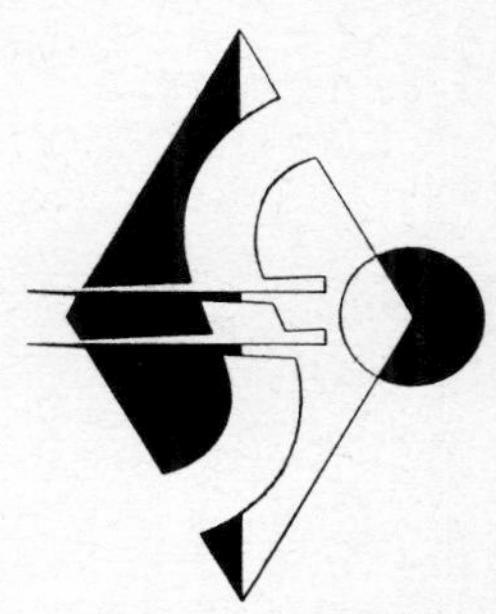

SWINDON TOWN FC

County Ground, Swindon, Wiltshire SN1 2ED. Telephone Swindon (0793) 430430. Fax: 0793 536170. Ticket Office: (0793) 529000. Clubcall: 0891 121640.

Ground capacity: 19,000 (on completion of redevelopment).

Record attendance: 32,000 v Arsenal, FA Cup 3rd rd, 15 January 1972.

Record receipts: £101,221 v Aston Villa, FA Cup 5th rd, 16 February 1992.

Pitch measurements: 114yd × 74yd.

President: C. J. Green.

Chairman: R. V. Hardman. ***Vice-chairman:*** J. M. Spearman.

Directors: P. T. Archer, Sir Seton Willis Bt, C. J. Puffett, J. R. Hunt (Associate).

Manager: John Gorman. ***Assistant. Manager:*** David Hay.

Coach: Andy Rowland. ***Physio:*** Kevin Morris.

Secretary: Jon Pollard. ***Youth Team Manager:*** John Trollope.

Commercial Manager: Janet Garrett. ***Community Officer:*** Jonathan Trigg.

Year Formed: 1881 *(*see Foundation*). ***Turned Professional:*** 1894. ***Ltd Co.:*** 1894.

Club Nickname: 'Robins'.

Previous Ground: 1881–96, The Croft.

Record League Victory: 9–1 v Luton T, Division 3 (S), 28 August 1920 – Nash; Kay, Macconachie; Langford, Hawley, Wareing; Jefferson (1), Fleming (4), Rogers, Batty (2), Davies (1). (1 og).

Record Cup Victory: 10–1 v Farnham U Breweries (away), FA Cup, 1st rd (replay), 28 November 1925 – Nash; Dickenson, Weston, Archer, Bew, Adey; Denyer (2), Wall (1), Richardson (4), Johnson (3), Davies.

Record Defeat: 1–10 v Manchester C, FA Cup 4th rd (replay), 25 January 1930.

Most League Points (2 for a win): 64, Division 3, 1968–69.

Most League Points (3 for a win): 102, Division 4, 1985–86 (League record).

Most League Goals: 100, Division 3 (S), 1926–27.

Highest League Scorer in Season: Harry Morris, 47, Division 3 (S), 1926–27.

Most League Goals in Total Aggregate: Harry Morris, 216, 1926–33.

Most Capped Player: Rod Thomas, 30 (50), Wales.

Most League Appearances: John Trollope, 770, 1960–80.

Record Transfer Fee Received: £1,000,000 from Southampton for Alan McLoughlin, December 1990.

Record Transfer Fee Paid: £500,000 to Rapid Vienna for Jan-Aage Fjortoft, July 1993.

Football League Record: 1920 Original Member of Division 3; 1921–58 Division 3 (S); 1958–63 Division 3; 1963–65 Division 2; 1965–69 Division 3; 1969–74 Division 2; 1974–82 Division 3; 1982–86 Division 4; 1986–87 Division 3; 1987–92 Division 2; 1992–93 Division 1; 1993–94 FA Premier League; 1994– Division 1.

Honours: *FA Premier League:* best season: 22nd 1993–94; *Football League* : Division 3 – Runners-up 1962–63, 1968–69; Division 4 – Champions 1985–86 (with record 102 points). *FA Cup:* Semi-finals 1910, 1912. *Football League Cup:* Winners 1968–69. *Anglo-Italian Cup:* Winners 1970.

SWINDON TOWN 1993—94 LEAGUE RECORD

Match No.	Date	Venue	Opponents	Result		H/T Score	Lg. Pos.	Goalscorers	Attendance
1	Aug 14	A	Sheffield U	L	1-3	0-1	—	Moncur	20,904
2	18	H	Oldham Ath	L	0-1	0-0	—		11,940
3	22	H	Liverpool	L	0-5	0-2	—		17,364
4	25	A	Southampton	L	1-5	0-1	—	Maskell (pen)	12,505
5	28	A	Norwich C	D	0-0	0-0	22		17,614
6	Sept 1	H	Manchester C	L	1-3	0-0	—	Summerbee	16,067
7	11	A	West Ham U	D	0-0	0-0	22		15,777
8	18	H	Newcastle U	D	2-2	0-2	22	Ling, Mutch	15,393
9	25	A	Manchester U	L	2-4	0-2	22	Mutch, Bodin (pen)	44,583
10	Oct 2	H	Blackburn R	L	1-3	1-1	22	Taylor	15,847
11	16	H	Everton	D	1-1	0-1	22	Taylor	14,437
12	23	A	Tottenham H	D	1-1	0-0	22	Bodin (pen)	31,394
13	30	H	Aston Villa	L	1-2	1-1	22	Bodin (pen)	16,322
14	Nov 6	A	Wimbledon	L	0-3	0-1	22		7758
15	20	H	Ipswich T	D	2-2	1-1	22	Scott, Bodin (pen)	13,860
16	24	H	QPR	W	1-0	1-0	—	Scott	14,674
17	27	A	Leeds U	L	0-3	0-0	22		32,630
18	Dec 4	H	Sheffield U	D	0-0	0-0	22		12,882
19	7	A	Oldham Ath	L	1-2	0-1	—	Mutch	9771
20	11	A	Liverpool	D	2-2	0-0	22	Moncur, Scott	32,739
21	18	H	Southampton	W	2-1	1-1	22	Bodin, Scott	13,565
22	27	H	Arsenal	L	0-4	0-2	22		17,214
23	29	A	Sheffield W	D	3-3	2-1	22	Mutch, Maskell 2	30,570
24	Jan 1	H	Chelsea	L	1-3	0-2	22	Mutch	16,261
25	3	A	Coventry C	D	1-1	0-0	22	Mutch	15,869
26	15	A	Everton	L	2-6	0-2	22	Moncur, Bodin	20,760
27	22	H	Tottenham H	W	2-1	1-1	22	Fjortoft, Whitbread	16,464
28	Feb 5	H	Coventry C	W	3-1	2-0	22	Fjortoft 3 (2 pens)	14,635
29	12	A	Aston Villa	L	0-5	0-1	22		27,637
30	19	H	Norwich C	D	3-3	2-2	22	Taylor, Fjortoft 2	15,341
31	25	A	Manchester C	L	1-2	1-1	22	Fjortoft	26,360
32	Mar 5	H	West Ham U	D	1-1	0-0	22	Fjortoft	15,929
33	12	A	Newcastle U	L	1-7	0-2	22	Moncur	32,219
34	19	H	Manchester U	D	2-2	1-1	22	Nijholt, Fjortoft	18,102
35	26	A	Blackburn R	L	1-3	1-2	22	Fjortoft	20,046
36	Apr 2	A	Arsenal	D	1-1	1-1	22	Bodin (pen)	31,635
37	4	H	Sheffield W	L	0-1	0-0	22		13,927
38	16	A	Ipswich T	D	1-1	1-0	22	Fjortoft	14,760
39	23	H	Wimbledon	L	2-4	0-1	22	Summerbee, Barton (og)	13,309
40	27	A	Chelsea	L	0-2	0-2	—		11,180
41	30	A	QPR	W	3-1	0-0	22	Taylor, Fjortoft, Summerbee	9875
42	May 7	H	Leeds U	L	0-5	0-2	22		17,228

Final League Position: 22

GOALSCORERS

League (47): Fjortoft 12 (2 pens), Bodin 7 (5 pens), Mutch 6, Moncur 4, Scott 4, Taylor 4, Maskell 3 (1 pen), Summerbee 3, Ling 1, Nijholt 1, Whitbread 1, own goal 1.
Coca-Cola Cup (3): Summerbee 2, Mutch 1.
FA Cup (2): Fjortoft 1, Mutch 1.

Digby 28	Summerbee 36 + 2	Nijholt 31 + 1	MacLaren 10 + 2	Whitbread 34 + 1	Taylor 42	Moncur 41	White 2 + 4	Fjortoft 26 + 10	Ling 29 + 4	Maskell 8 + 6	Horlock 32 + 6	Hazard 7 + 2	Mutch 27 + 3	Fenwick 23 + 3	Bodin 28 + 4	Scott 22 + 5	Hammond 11 + 2	Kilcline 10	Sheffield 2	McAvennie 3 + 4	Gooden 2 + 2	Hamon — + 1	Sanchez 6 + 2	Heald 1 + 1	Thomson 1	*Match No.*
1	2	3	4	5	6	7	8	9	10	11	12															1
1	2	3	8	5	6	4		9	10	11	12	7														2
1	2	3	4	5	6	*7*		9	10	12	11	14	8													3
1	2	*3*	4	5	6	7		9	10	12	11	14	8													4
1	2	3	11	5	6	4		12	10		9	7	8													5
1	2	3	11	5	6	4		14	10	12	9	*7*	*8*													6
1	2	3		5	6	4	12	9	10		*11*	7	8	14												7
1	2	4		5	6	11	12	9	*10*			7	8	14	3											8
1	2	5	14		6	*4*	12	9	10			7	8	11	3											9
1	*2*	5	14		6	4	9	12	10			7	8	11	3											10
1	2	5	4		6	7		12	10	*9*	14		8	11	3											11
1	2	5	4		6	7		9	10		12		8	11	3											12
1	2	5	4	14	6	7		9	12		10		8	*11*	3											13
1	2		4	5	6	7	14	*9*	10	12	11		8		3											14
1	2	4		5	6	7			12		9		8	11	3	10										15
1		2		5	6	7			10		4		8	11	3	9										16
1		2		5	6	7		12	10		4		8	11	3	9										17
1	14	2		5	6	7			*10*	12	4		8	11	3	9										18
1	2	4		5	6	7					10		8	11	3	9										19
1	2			5	6	*7*		14	10	12	4		8	11	3	9										20
1				5	6	7			10	9	4		8	2	3	11										21
1	12			5	6	7		14	10	9	4		*8*	2	3	11										22
1	2			5	6	7		12	10	9	4		8	3		11	14									23
	2			5	6	7		12	10	*9*	4		8	3	14	11	1									24
	2			5	6	7			10	9	4		8	11	3	12	1									25
	2	12		5	6	7		14	10		4		8	11	3	*9*	1									26
	2	3		5	6	7		9	10		11		*8*		12	14	1	4								27
	2	3		5	6	7		9	10		8				12	11	1	4								28
	2	3		5	6	7		*9*	10		8			14	12	11		4	1							29
	2	4		5	6	7		9			8				3	10	14	11	*1*	12						30
1	2	4		5	6	7		*9*	12		10		8	11	3					14						31
1	2	3		5	6	7		9	10		4		8			12				*11*	14					32
1		2			6	7		9	10		4			5	3	*8*				11	12	14				33
1	2	3		5	6	7		9	12		8					14		4		*11*			10			34
1	8	2		5	6	7		9	10						3	12		4					11			35
	8	2		5	6	7		9			14				3	*10*	1	4		12			11			36
	8	2		5	6	7		9			12				3	10	*1*	4					11	14		37
	8				6	7		9			4		12	2	3	10	1	5		14			*11*			38
	8	4			6			9			7		12	2	3	10	1	5					11			39
	8	4		5	6	7		9			11			2	3	10	1						12			40
	8			5	6	7		9			4			2	3	10	1				11					41
	8			5	6	7		9			4		12		3	10					11		14	1	*2*	42

Coca-Cola Cup	Second Round	Wolverhampton W (h)	2-0
		(a)	1-2
	Third Round	Portsmouth (a)	0-2
FA Cup	Third Round	Ipswich T (h)	1-1
		(a)	1-2

SWINDON TOWN

Player and Position	Ht	Wt	Birth Date	Birth Place	Source	Clubs	League App	League Gls
Goalkeepers								
Fraser Digby	6 1	12 12	23 4 67	Sheffield	Apprentice	Manchester U	—	—
						Oldham Ath (loan)	—	—
						Swindon T (loan)	—	—
						Swindon T	284	—
						Manchester U (loan)	—	—
Nicky Hammond	6 0	11 13	7 9 67	Hornchurch	Apprentice	Arsenal	—	—
						Bristol R (loan)	3	—
						Peterborough U (loan)	—	—
						Aberdeen (loan)	—	—
						Swindon T	60	—
Stewart Kerr (on loan from Celtic)	6 2	13 00	13 11 74	Bellshill		Swindon T	—	—
Defenders								
Terry Fenwick	5 10	11 12	17 11 59	Camden, Co. Durham	Apprentice	Crystal Palace	70	—
						QPR	256	33
						Tottenham H	93	8
						Leicester C (loan)	8	1
						Swindon T	26	—
Kevin Horlock	6 0	12 00	1 11 72	Bexley	Trainee	West Ham U	—	—
						Swindon T	52	1
Brian Kilcline	6 2	12 00	7 5 62	Nottingham	Apprentice	Notts Co	158	9
						Coventry C	173	28
						Oldham Ath	8	—
						Newcastle U	32	—
						Swindon T	10	—
Lee Middleton	5 9	11 09	10 9 70	Nuneaton	Trainee	Coventry C	2	—
						Swindon T	—	—
Edwin Murray	5 11	12 00	31 8 73	Redbridge	Trainee	Swindon T	1	—
Luc Nijholt	5 11	12 01	29 7 61	Zaandam	BSC Old Boys Basel	Motherwell	96	5
						Swindon T	32	1
Wayne O'Sullivan	5 8	10 06	25 2 74	Akrotiri	Trainee	Swindon T	—	—
Shaun Taylor	6 1	13 00	26 3 63	Plymouth	Bideford	Exeter C	200	16
						Swindon T	130	19
Andrew Thomson	6 3	13 08	28 3 74	Swindon	Trainee	Swindon T	1	—
Adrian Whitbread	6 2	11 13	22 10 71	Epping	Trainee	Leyton Orient	125	2
						Swindon T	35	1
Midfield								
Austin Berkley	5 9	10 10	28 1 73	Dartford	Trainee	Gillingham	3	—
						Swindon T	—	—
Paul Bodin	6 0	13 01	13 9 64	Cardiff	Chelsea	Newport Co	—	—
						Cardiff C	57	3
					Bath C	Newport Co	6	1
						Swindon T	93	9
						Crystal Palace	9	—
						Newcastle U (loan)	6	—
						Swindon T	88	20
Ty Gooden	5 8	12 06	23 10 72	Canvey Island	Wycombe W	Swindon T	4	—
Ross MacLaren	5 10	12 12	14 4 62	Edinburgh	Glasgow Rangers	Shrewsbury T	161	18
						Derby Co	122	4
						Swindon T	194	9
John Moncur	5 7	9 10	22 9 66	Stepney	Apprentice	Tottenham H	21	1
						Cambridge U (loan)	4	—
						Doncaster R (loan)	4	—
						Portsmouth (loan)	7	—
						Brentford (loan)	5	1
						Ipswich T (loan)	6	—
						Nottingham F (loan)	—	—
						Swindon T	58	5
Marcus Phillips	5 11	11 07	17 10 73	Bradford on Avon	Trainee	Swindon T	—	—
Lawrie Sanchez*	5 11	12 00	22 10 59	Lambeth	Thatcham	Reading	262	28
						Wimbledon	270	33
						Swindon T	8	—

SWINDON TOWN

Colours: All red. **Change colours:** Yellow shirts with green trim, sky blue shorts, white stockings.

Foundation: It is generally accepted that Swindon Town came into being in 1881, although there is no firm evidence that the club's founder, Rev. William Pitt, captain of the Spartans (an offshoot of a cricket club) changed his club's name to Swindon Town before 1883, when the Spartans amalgamated with St. Mark's Young Men's Friendly Society.

First Football League game: 28 August, 1920, Division 3, v Luton T (h) W 9-1 – Nash; Kay, Macconachie; Langford, Hawley, Wareing; Jefferson (1), Fleming (4), Rogers, Batty (2), Davies (1). 1 o.g.

Did you know: Despite being relegated from the FA Carling Premiership last season, Swindon Town became the first team to score four goals against the champions Manchester United in League matches during the campaign.

Managers (and Secretary-Managers)
Sam Allen 1902–33, Ted Vizard 1933–39, Neil Harris 1939–41, Louis Page 1945–53, Maurice Lindley 1953–55, Bert Head 1956–65, Danny Williams 1965–69, Fred Ford 1969–71, Dave Mackay 1971–72, Les Allen 1972–74, Danny Williams 1974–78, Bobby Smith 1978–80, John Trollope 1980–83, Ken Beamish 1983–84, Lou Macari 1984–89, Ossie Ardiles 1989–91, Glenn Hoddle 1991–93, John Gorman June 1993–

Player and Position	*Ht*	*Wt*	*Birth Date*	*Birth Place*	*Source*	*Clubs*	*League App*	*League Gls*
Forwards								
Jan-Aage Fjortoft	6 3	13 04	10 1 67	Aalesund	Rapid Vienna	Swindon T	36	12
Chris Hamon	6 1	13 07	27 4 70	Jersey	St Peter	Swindon T	3	—
Martin Ling	5 7	9 12	15 7 66	West Ham	Apprentice	Exeter C	116	14
						Swindon T	2	—
						Southend U	138	31
						Mansfield T (loan)	3	—
						Swindon T (loan)	1	—
						Swindon T	97	7
Frank McAvennie	5 9	11 0	22 11 59	Glasgow	Partick T	St Mirren	135	50
						West Ham U	85	33
						Celtic	55	27
						West Ham U	68	16
						Aston Villa	3	—
						Celtic	30	10
						Swindon T	7	—
Andy Mutch	5 10	11 00	28 12 63	Liverpool	Southport	Wolverhampton W	289	97
						Swindon T	30	6
Keith Scott	6 3	14 03	9 6 67	London	Leicester U	Lincoln C	16	2
					Wycombe W	Wycombe W	15	10
						Swindon T	27	4
Nicky Summerbee	5 11	11 08	26 8 71	Altrincham	Trainee	Swindon T	112	6
Adrian Viveash	6 1	11 12	30 9 69	Swindon	Trainee	Swindon T	40	1
						Reading (loan)	5	—
Steve White	5 10	11 04	2 1 59	Chipping Sodbury	Mangotsfield U	Bristol R	50	20
						Luton T	72	25
						Charlton Ath	29	12
						Lincoln C (loan)	3	—
						Luton T (loan)	4	—
						Bristol R	101	24
						Swindon T	244	83

Trainees
Cook, Shane A; Elsey, David J; Fraser, James E; Hamblin, Christopher P; Holloway, Jonathan S; James, Stuart E; Jordan, Mark J; Kearns, Andrew S; Laidlaw, Jamie D; Medcroft, Scott J; Phillips, James A; Pitman, Jamie R; Reeves, Stephen J; Thorne, Gary R; Worrall, Benjamin J.

Associated Schoolboys
Betterton, Anthony G; Bogdaniec, Simon J; Campbell, Stephen J; Coupe, Matthew W. E; Dodds, Ishmael J; Gee, David G; Godley, David C. T; Lear, Steven P; McLean, Alan; Organ, Christopher D; Payne, Jonathan D; Radcliffe, Thomas R; Rutter, Thomas; Woodman, Scott C.

Associated Schoolboys who have accepted the Club's offer of a Traineeship/Contract
Harvey, Iain D; Mildenhall, Stephen J; Souter, Ryan J; Thomas, Steven J; Wimble, Shaun.

TORQUAY UNITED 1993–94 *Back row (left to right):* Norman Medhurst (Physio), Craig Herbert, Shaun Maloney, Steve Stacey, Ellis Laight, Adrian Foster, Paul Hardy, Lee Barrow, Richard Hancox, Scott Stamps, John James (Scout).
Centre row: Chris Meyers, Darren Moore, Matthew Gardiner, Tim Thornley, Matthew Lowe, Adrian Tucker, Paul Trollope, Richard White, Duane Darby.
Front row: Mark Sale, Kevin Hodges, Tom Kelly, Paul Compton (Youth Development Officer), Don O'Riordan (Manager), Chris Curran, Ian Hathaway, Scott Colcombe.
(Photograph: Colin Bratcher)

Division 3 **TORQUAY UNITED**

Plainmoor Ground, Torquay, Devon TQ1 3PS. Telephone Torquay (0803) 328666. Clubcall: 0898 121641. Fax: 0803 323976.

Ground capacity: 6500.

Record attendance: 21,908 v Huddersfield T, FA Cup 4th rd, 29 January 1955.

Record receipts: £26,205 v Exeter C, Division 3, 1 January 1992.

Pitch measurements: 112yd × 74yd.

President: A. J. Boyce.

Chairman/Managing Director: M. Bateson. ***Directors:*** Mrs S. Bateson, D. Turner, M. Benney, M. Beer, W. Rogers, I. Hayman.

Player-Manager: Don O'Riordan. ***Physio:*** Norman Medhurst.

Company Secretary: Miss H. Kindeleit.

Secretary General Manager: D. F. Turner. ***Lottery Administrators:*** C. Munslow and A. Sandford. ***Commercial Manager:*** D. Turner.

Year Formed: 1898. ***Turned Professional:*** 1921. ***Ltd Co.:*** 1921.

Previous Name: 1910, Torquay Town; 1921, Torquay United,

Nickname: 'The Gulls'.

Previous Grounds: 1898, Teignmouth Road; 1901, Torquay Recreation Ground; 1905, Cricket Field Road; 1907–10, Torquay Cricket Ground.

Record League Victory: 9–0 v Swindon T, Division 3 (S), 8 March 1952 – George Webber; Topping, Ralph Calland; Brown, Eric Webber, Towers; Shaw (1), Marchant (1), Northcott (2), Collins (3), Edds (2).

Record Cup Victory: 7–1 v Northampton T, FA Cup, 1st rd, 14 November 1959 – Gill; Penford, Downs; Bettany, George Northcott, Rawson; Baxter, Cox, Tommy Northcott (1), Bond (3), Pym (3).

Record Defeat: 2–10 v Fulham, Division 3 (S), 7 September 1931 and v Luton T, Division 3 (S), 2 September 1933.

Most League Points (2 for a win): 60, Division 4, 1959–60.

Most League Points (3 for a win): 77, Division 4, 1987–88.

Most League Goals: 89, Division 3 (S), 1956–57.

Highest League Scorer in Season: Sammy Collins, 40, Division 3 (S), 1955–56.

Most League Goals in Total Aggregate: Sammy Collins, 204, 1948–58.

Most Capped Player: None.

Most League Appearances: Dennis Lewis, 443, 1947–59.

Record Transfer Fee Received: £180,000 from Manchester U for Lee Sharpe, May 1988.

Record Transfer Fee Paid: £60,000 to Dundee for Wes Saunders, July 1990.

Football League Record: 1927 Elected to Division 3 (S); 1958–60 Division 4; 1960–62 Division 3; 1962–66 Division 4; 1966–72 Division 3; 1972–91 Division 4; 1991– Division 3.

Honours: *Football League:* Division 3 best season: 4th, 1967–68; Division 3 (S) – Runners-up 1956–57; Division 4 – Promoted 1959–60 (3rd), 1965–66 (3rd), 1990–91 (Play-offs). *FA Cup:* best season: 4th rd, 1949, 1955, 1971, 1983, 1990. *Football League Cup:* never past 3rd rd. *Sherpa Van Trophy:* Runners-up 1989.

TORQUAY UNITED 1993—94 LEAGUE RECORD

Match No.	Date	Venue	Opponents	Result	H/T Score	Lg. Pos.	Goalscorers	Attendance
1	Aug 14	A	Walsall	W 2-1	1-0	—	Byng 2	3324
2	21	H	Wigan Ath	D 1-1	0-0	5	Moore	3465
3	28	A	Darlington	W 2-1	1-1	2	Darby, Hodges	1738
4	31	H	Carlisle U	D 1-1	1-0	—	Burton	3331
5	Sept 4	H	Colchester U	D 3-3	0-2	5	Foster 3	2989
6	11	A	Gillingham	D 2-2	0-1	7	Trollope, Foster	2927
7	18	H	Preston NE	W 4-3	1-1	5	Foster 2, Kelly, Hathaway	3912
8	25	H	Crewe Alex	D 3-3	0-2	6	Lennon (og), Darby, Trollope	4009
9	Oct 2	A	Shrewsbury T	L 2-3	1-0	7	Foster, O'Riordan	2725
10	9	H	Rochdale	D 1-1	0-1	9	Kelly	3874
11	16	A	Chesterfield	L 1-3	0-0	11	Darby	2393
12	23	H	Scunthorpe U	D 1-1	0-1	12	Foster	3241
13	30	A	Chester C	D 1-1	0-0	13	Trollope	2563
14	Nov 2	H	Northampton T	W 2-0	0-0	—	O'Riordan, Foster	2704
15	6	A	Lincoln C	L 0-1	0-0	13		3244
16	20	H	Hereford U	D 1-1	0-0	13	Trollope	2846
17	27	A	Scarborough	W 2-1	1-0	11	Foster, Hathaway	1460
18	Dec 11	A	Wigan Ath	W 3-1	3-0	8	Foster, Sale, Curran	1232
19	18	H	Walsall	L 0-1	0-0	10		2754
20	27	H	Wycombe W	D 1-1	1-0	10	Trollope	4991
21	Jan 1	H	Mansfield T	W 1-0	0-0	9	Hathaway	3496
22	3	A	Carlisle U	D 1-1	1-1	9	Foster	4872
23	8	A	Doncaster R	W 2-0	1-0	7	Sale 2	1685
24	15	H	Chesterfield	W 1-0	1-0	6	Sale	3188
25	22	A	Rochdale	L 1-4	1-1	6	Burton	2319
26	29	H	Chester C	L 1-3	1-1	7	Hathaway	2959
27	Feb 5	A	Scunthorpe U	W 3-1	1-1	7	Trollope, Darby, Foster	2755
28	12	H	Doncaster R	W 2-1	1-0	5	Foster, Buckle (pen)	3080
29	19	H	Darlington	W 2-1	0-1	3	Hathaway, Darby	3039
30	25	A	Colchester U	W 2-1	0-0	3	Hathaway, Hodges	2573
31	Mar 5	H	Gillingham	L 0-1	0-0	6		3353
32	12	A	Preston NE	L 1-3	0-1	6	Trollope	6641
33	19	A	Crewe Alex	W 3-2	2-1	6	Hathaway, Trollope 2	3484
34	26	H	Shrewsbury T	D 0-0	0-0	6		4085
35	29	A	Bury	D 1-1	1-0	—	Foster	2018
36	Apr 2	A	Wycombe W	D 1-1	0-1	6	Sale	5808
37	5	H	Bury	D 0-0	0-0	—		4111
38	9	A	Mansfield T	L 1-2	1-2	6	Goodridge	2260
39	16	A	Northampton T	W 1-0	0-0	6	Darby	3519
40	23	H	Lincoln C	W 3-2	2-0	6	Darby 2, Okorie	3270
41	30	A	Hereford U	D 2-2	1-1	6	Buckle (pen), Trollope	2726
42	May 7	H	Scarborough	W 2-0	2-0	6	Sale, Moore	3470

Final League Position: 6

GOALSCORERS

League (64): Foster 15, Trollope 10, Darby 8, Hathaway 7, Sale 6, Buckle 2 (2 pens), Burton 2, Byng 2, Hodges 2, Kelly 2, Moore 2, O'Riordan 2, Curran 1, Goodridge 1, Okorie 1, own goal 1.
Coca-Cola Cup (2): Foster 1, Trollope 1.
FA Cup (2): Moore 1, Sale 1.

Lowe 10	Barrow 19 + 1	Colcombe 27	O'Riordan 31	Moore 37	Curran 41	Trollope 42	Kelly 33 + 2	Foster 32 + 7	Byng 2 + 1	Hathaway 38 + 3	Sale 20 + 13	O'Toole 3	Hodges 26 + 3	Burton 7 + 1	Darby 21 + 15	Loram — + 1	Bayes 32	Hancox 1 + 2	Stamps 6	Myers 6	Laight — + 1	Buckle 16	Hardy — + 1	Okorie 6 + 3	Goodridge 5 + 3	Stacey 1	*Match No.*
1	2	3	4	5	6	7	8	9	10	11																	1
1	2	3	4	5	6	7	8	9	12	11	10																2
1	12		4	5	6	7	8		10	11		2	3		9												3
1	2		4		6	7	8	12		11		3	10	5	9												4
1			4	5	6	7	8	12		11		*3*	10	2	9	14											5
1	2	3	4	5	6	7	8	9		11			10		12												6
1	2	3	4	5	6	7	8	9		11	14		*10*		12												7
1	2	3	4	5	6	7	8	9		11			10		12												8
1	2	3	4	5	6	7	8	*9*		11	14		10		12												9
	2	3	4	5	6	7	8	9		11	12		10				1										10
	2	3	4	5	6	7	8	9			10		14		12		1	*11*									11
		2	4	5	6	7	8	9		14	12		*10*		11		1		3								12
		2	4	5	6	7	8	9		11					10		1		3								13
		2	4	5	6	7	8	9		11	12		14		*10*		1		3								14
		2	4	*5*	6	7	8	9		11	12		14		10		1		3								15
	2	5	4		6	7	8	9		11	10				12		1		3								16
	2	3	4	5	6	7	8	9		11	10				12		1										17
	2		4	5	6	7	3	9		11	10						1			8							18
	2		4	5	6	7	3	9		11	10				12		1	14		*8*							19
			4	5	6	7	3	9		11	10		2		12		1			8							20
			4	5	6	7	3	9		11	10		2		12		1			8							21
			4	5	6	7	3	9		*11*	10		2		12		1	14		8							22
			4	5	6	7	3	9		11	10		2				1			8							23
		3	4	5	6	7		9		11	10		2	8			1										24
		3	4	5	6	7		9		11	10		2	8	12		1										25
		3	4	5	6	7		9		11	10		*2*	8	12		1				14						26
		3	4	5	6	7		9		11			2		10		1					8					27
		3	4	5	6	7		9		11	12		2		10		1					8					28
		3	*4*	5	6	7	14	9		11	12		2		10		1					8					29
		3	4	5	6	7		9		11			2		10		1					8					30
	5	3	*4*		6	7	14	9		11	12		2		10		1					8					31
	5	3			6	7	9			11	12		2	4	10		1					8					32
	2	3		5	6	7	4			*11*	9			12	10		1					8	14				33
	2	3		5		7	4	14		11	12			6	10		1					8		*9*			34
1		3		5	6	7	4	9		11	12				10							8		*2*	14		35
		3		5	6	7	4	9		11	12				10		1					8		2	14		36
	3			5	6	7	4	*9*		11	10				12		1					8		2	14		37
				5	6	7	3	12		11	*10*				9		1					8		14	4	2	38
	5				6	7		9		*11*	10		2		12		1		3			8		14	4		39
				5	6	7	4	12		*11*	10		2		9		1					8		14	3		40
				5	6	7	4	12		14	10		2		*9*		1					8		11	3		41
				5	6	7	4	12		14	10		2		9		1					8		*11*	3		42

Coca-Cola Cup	First Round	Hereford U (a)	2-0
		(h)	0-2
FA Cup	First Round	Slough T (a)	2-1
	Second Round	Sutton U (h)	0-1

TORQUAY UNITED

Player and Position	Ht	Wt	Birth Date	Birth Place	Source	Clubs	League App	League Gls
Goalkeepers								
Ashley Bayes	6 1	13 05	19 4 72	Lincoln	Trainee	Brentford	4	—
						Torquay U	32	—
Matthew Lowe*	6 0	12 10	25 2 74	Birmingham	Trainee	Torquay U	30	—
Defenders								
Lee Barrow	5 11	13 00	1 5 73	Belper	Trainee	Notts Co	—	—
						Scarborough	11	—
						Torquay U	35	2
Nick Burton	5 11	11 12	2 10 75	Bury St Edmunds	Portsmouth	Torquay U	8	2
Chris Curran	5 11	11 09	17 9 71	Birmingham	Trainee	Torquay U	106	1
Matthew Gardiner‡	5 4	10 10	28 3 74	Birmingham	Trainee	Torquay U	7	—
Tom Kelly	5 9	12 05	28 3 64	Bellshill	Hibs	Hartlepool U	15	—
						Torquay U	120	—
						York C	35	2
						Exeter C	88	9
						Torquay U	53	5
Darren Moore	6 2	15 00	22 4 74	Birmingham	Trainee	Torquay U	73	5
Steven Stacey*			9 6 75	Bristol	Trainee	Torquay U	1	—
Scott Stamps	5 11	11 00	20 3 75	Edgbaston	Trainee	Torquay U	8	—
Midfield								
Paul Buckle	5 8	10 08	16 12 70	Hatfield	Trainee	Brentford	57	1
						Torquay U	16	2
Scott Colcombe	5 6	10 00	15 12 71	West Bromwich	Trainee	WBA	—	—
						Torquay U	79	1
Tony Ginter‡			6 11 74	Plymouth	Trainee	Torquay U	1	—
Paul Hardy	5 8	10 05	29 8 75	Plymouth	Trainee	Torquay U	1	—
Kevin Hodges	5 8	10 08	12 6 60	Bridport	Apprentice	Plymouth Arg	530	81
						Torquay U (loan)	3	—
						Torquay U	37	3
Chris Myers (on loan from Dundee U)	5 10	11 10	1 4 69	Yeovil		Torquay U	6	—
Don O'Riordan	6 0	12 08	14 5 57	Dublin	Apprentice	Derby Co	6	1
						Doncaster R (loan)	2	—
					Tulsa	Preston NE	158	8
						Carlisle U	84	18
						Middlesbrough	41	2
						Grimsby T	86	14
						Notts Co	109	5
						Mansfield T (loan)	6	—
						Torquay U	47	2
Pat O'Toole‡	5 7	11 00	2 1 65	Dublin	Shelbourne	Leicester C	—	—
						Exeter C	6	—
						Shrewsbury T	46	1
						Torquay U	3	—
Paul Trollope	6 0	12 02	3 6 72	Swindon	Trainee	Swindon T	—	—
						Torquay U (loan)	10	—
						Torquay U	78	12
Forwards								
David Byng§			9 7 77	Coventry	Trainee	Torquay U	3	2
Duane Darby	5 11	12 06	17 10 73	West Midlands	Trainee	Torquay U	84	22
Justin Fashanu (To Hearts)	6 1	13 01	19 2 61	Kensington	Apprentice	Norwich C	90	35
						Nottingham F	32	3
						Southampton	9	3
						Nottingham F	—	—
						Notts Co	64	20
						Brighton	16	2
					Edmonton	Manchester C	2	—
						West Ham U	2	—
						Leyton Orient	5	—
					Toronto B	Newcastle U	—	—
						Torquay U	41	15
						Airdrieonians	16	5
Adrian Foster	5 9	11 00	20 7 71	Kidderminster	Trainee	WBA	27	2
						Torquay U	75	24

TORQUAY UNITED

Colours: Yellow and navy hooped shirts, navy shorts, yellow stockings. **Change colours:** Riviera blue and white striped shirts, white shorts, blue stockings.

Foundation: The idea of establishing a Torquay club was agreed by old boys of Torquay College and Torbay College, while sitting in Princess Gardens listening to the band. A proper meeting was subsequently held at Tor Abbey Hotel at which officers were elected. This was in 1898 and the club's first competition was the Eastern League (later known as the East Devon League).

First Football League game: 27 August, 1927, Division 3(S), v Exeter C (h) D 1-1 – Millsom; Cook, Smith; Wellock, Wragg, Connor, Mackey, Turner (1), Jones, McGovern, Thomson.

Did you know: On 14 August 1993, David Byng became the youngest Torquay United debutant when at the age of 16 years 3 weeks he played against Walsall, scoring both goals in a 2-1 win.

Managers (and Secretary-Managers)
Percy Mackrill 1927–29, A. H. Hoskins 1929*, Frank Womack 1929–32, Frank Brown 1932–38, Alf Steward 1938–40, Billy Butler 1945–46, Jack Butler 1946–47, John McNeil 1947–50, Bob John 1950, Alex Massie 1950–51, Eric Webber 1951–65, Frank O'Farrell 1965–68, Alan Brown 1969–71, Jack Edwards 1971–73, Malcolm Musgrove 1973–76, Mike Green 1977–81, Frank O'Farrell 1981–82 (continued as GM to 1983), Bruch Rioch 1982–84, Dave Webb 1984–85, John Sims 1985, Stuart Morgan 1985–87, Cyril Knowles 1987–89, Dave Smith 1989–91, John Impey 1991–92, Ivan Golac 1992, Paul Compton 1992–93, Don O'Riordan March 1993–

Player and Position	*Ht*	*Wt*	*Birth Date*	*Birth Place*	*Source*	*Clubs*	*League App*	*League Gls*
Gregory Goodridge	5 6	10 00	10 7 71	Barbados	Lambada	Torquay U	8	1
Richard Hancox	5 10	13 00	14 10 70	Stourbridge	Stourbridge S	Torquay U	10	—
Ian Hathaway	5 6	11 04	22 8 68	Worsley	Bedworth U	Mansfield T	44	2
						Rotherham U	13	1
						Torquay U	41	7
Ellis Laight§	5 10	11 02	30 6 76	Birmingham	Trainee	Torquay U	1	—
Mark Loram‡	6 0	12 00	13 8 67	Brixham	Brixham	Torquay U	52	8
						QPR (loan)	—	—
						QPR	—	—
						Torquay U (loan)	13	4
						Torquay U	197	36
						Stockport Co (loan)	4	—
						Exeter C (loan)	3	—
Chima Okorie	5 10	12 08	8 10 68	Izomber		Peterborough U	—	—
						Grimsby T	5	—
						Torquay U	9	1
Mark Sale	6 5	13 08	27 2 72	Burton-on-Trent	Trainee	Stoke C	2	—
						Cambridge U	—	—
						Birmingham C	21	—
						Torquay U	44	8

Trainees
Brown, Michael; Byng, David G; (h) Giggs, Rhodri; Laight, Ellis S; Povey, Neil A; Setter, Lee T; Thornley, Timothy J; Tucker, Adrian J; Willis, Lee.

****Non-Contract**
Compton, Paul D.

Associated Schoolboys
Dawes, Christian L; Hapgood, Leon D; Hogg, Christopher; Nickson, Adam; Nickson, Carl; Smillie, Duncan.

Associated Schoolboys who have accepted the Club's offer of a Traineeship/Contract
Aggett, Neil R. P; Horne, Darren M; King, Robert D; Male, Neil J; Preston, Michael J; Shannon, Michael J.
**Non-Contract Players who are retained must be re-signed before they are eligible to play in League matches.

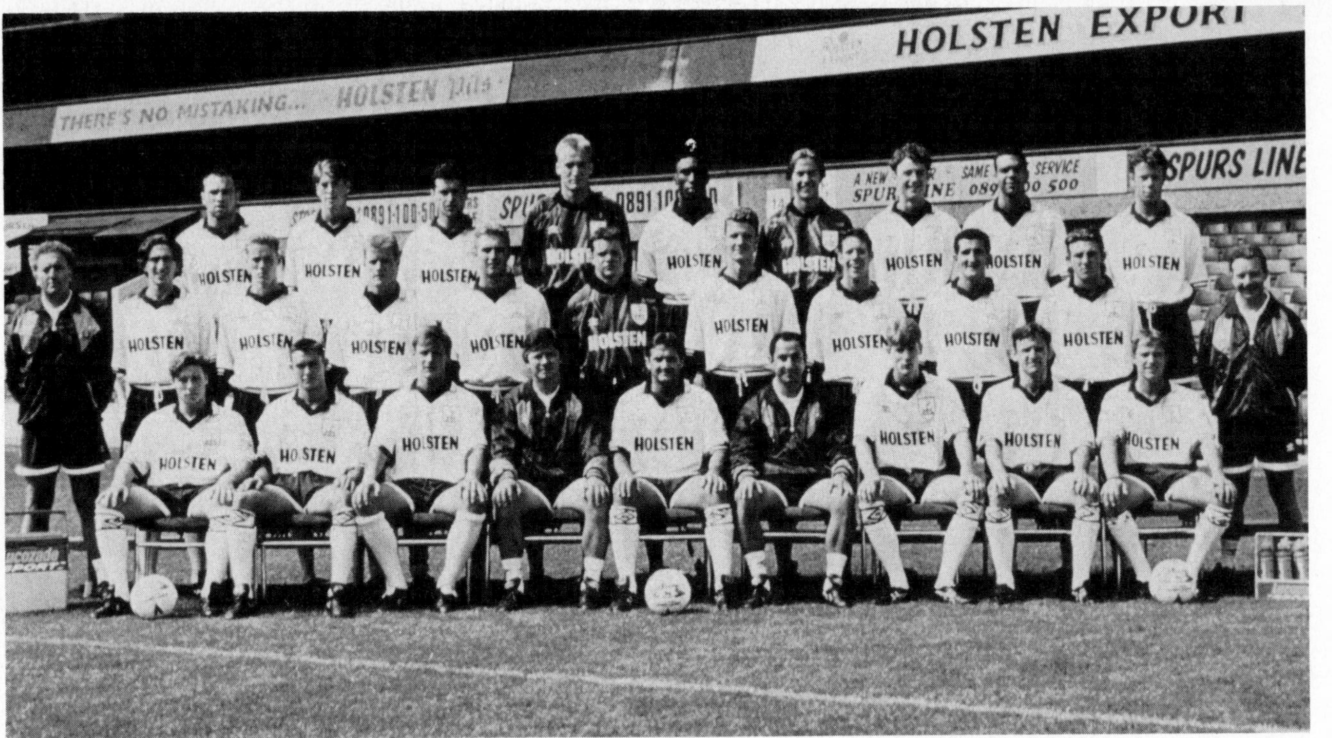

TOTTENHAM HOTSPUR 1993–94 *Back row (left to right):* Jason Cundy, Darren Anderton, Colin Calderwood, Erik Thorstvedt, Sol Campbell, Ian Walker, Steve Sedgley, Jason Dozzell, David Howells.

Centre row: Doug Livermore (First Team Coach and Chief Scout), Justin Edinburgh, John Hendry, Gordon Durie, Kevin Watson, Kevin Dearden, Gudni Bergsson, Danny Hill, Vinny Samways, Darren Caskey, Roy Reyland (Kit Manager).

Front row: Nick Barmby, Andy Turner, Teddy Sheringham, Steve Perryman (Assistant Manager), Gary Mabbutt, Ossie Ardiles (Manager), Dean Austin, Paul Allen, Paul Moran.

FA Premiership **TOTTENHAM HOTSPUR**

748 High Rd, Tottenham, London N17 0AP. Telephone 081–365 5000. Fax: 081–365 5005. Commercial Dept: 081–365 5010. Ticketline: 0891 100515. Telephone bookings: 071–396 4567. Ticket Office: 081–365 5050. Spurs Line: 0891 100500. Members Ticketline: 081–365 5100. Additional recorded information: 081–880 3377.

Ground capacity: 26,153 (until December 1994).

Record attendance: 75,038 v Sunderland, FA Cup 6th rd, 5 March 1938.

Record receipts: £336,702 v Manchester U, Division 1, 28 September 1991.

Pitch measurements: 110yd × 73yd.

Directors: A. M. Sugar (Chairman), A. G. Berry (Deputy Chairman), C. Littner (Managing), D. A. Alexiou, C. T. Sandy, I. Yawetz.

President: W. E. Nicholson OBE. ***Vice-presidents:*** F. P. Sinclair, N. Soloman.

Manager: Ossie Ardiles. ***Assistant Manager:*** Steve Perryman MBE. ***First Team Coach:*** Doug Livermore. ***Coaches:*** Chris Hughton, Pat Holland. ***Physio:*** Tony Lenaghan. ***Secretary:*** Peter Barnes. ***Commercial Manager:*** Mike Rollo. ***PRO:*** John Fennelly.

Year Formed: 1882. ***Turned Professional:*** 1895. ***Ltd Co.:*** 1898.

Club Nickname: 'Spurs'.

Previous Name: 1882–85, Hotspur Football Club.

Previous Grounds: 1882, Tottenham Marshes; 1885, Northumberland Park; 1898, White Hart Lane.

Record League Victory: 9–0 v Bristol R, Division 2, 22 October 1977 – Davies; Naylor, Holmes, Hoddle (1), McAllister, Perryman, Pratt, McNab, Morris (3), Lee (4), Taylor (1).

Record Cup Victory: 13–2 v Crewe Alex, FA Cup, 4th rd (replay), 3 February 1960 – Brown; Hills, Henry; Blanchflower, Norman, Mackay; White, Harmer (1), Smith (4), Allen (5), Jones (3 incl. 1p).

Record Defeat: 0–7 v Liverpool, Division 1, 2 September 1978.

Most League Points (2 for a win): 70, Division 2, 1919–20.

Most League Points (3 for a win): 77, Division 1, 1984–85.

Most League Goals: 115, Division 1, 1960–61.

Highest League Scorer in Season: Jimmy Greaves, 37, Division 1, 1962–63.

Most League Goals in Total Aggregate: Jimmy Greaves, 220, 1961–70.

Most Capped Player: Pat Jennings, 74 (119), Northern Ireland.

Most League Appearances: Steve Perryman, 655, 1969–86.

Record Transfer Fee Received: £5,500,000 from Lazio for Paul Gascoigne, May 1992.

Record Transfer Fee Paid: £2,200,000 to Chelsea for Gordon Durie, August 1991.

Football League Record: 1908 Elected to Division 2; 1909–15 Division 1; 1919–20 Division 2; 1920–28 Division 1; 1928–33 Division 2; 1933–35 Division 1; 1935–50 Division 2; 1950–77 Division 1; 1977–78 Division 2; 1978–92 Division 1; 1992– FA Premier League.

Honours: *Football League:* Division 1 – Champions 1950–51, 1960–61; Runners-up 1921–22, 1951–52, 1956–57, 1962–63; Division 2 – Champions 1919–20, 1949–50; Runners-up 1908–09, 1932–33; Promoted 1977–78 (3rd). *FA Cup:* Winners 1901 (as non-League club), 1921, 1961, 1962, 1967, 1981, 1982, 1991 (8 wins stands as the record); Runners-up 1986–87. *Football League Cup:* Winners 1970–71, 1972–73; Runners-up 1981–82. **European Competitions:** *European Cup:* 1961–62. *European Cup-Winners' Cup:* 1962–63 (winners), 1963–64, 1967–68, 1981–82 (runners-up), 1982–83, 1991–92. *UEFA Cup:* 1971–72 (winners), 1972–73, 1973–74 (runners-up), 1983–84 (winners), 1984–85.

TOTTENHAM HOTSPUR 1993—94 LEAGUE RECORD

Match No.	Date	Venue	Opponents	Result		H/T Score	Lg. Pos.	Goalscorers	Attendance
1	Aug 14	A	Newcastle U	W	1-0	1-0	—	Sheringham	34,565
2	16	H	Arsenal	L	0-1	0-0	—		28,355
3	21	H	Manchester C	W	1-0	0-0	8	Sedgley	24,535
4	25	A	Liverpool	W	2-1	2-1	—	Sheringham 2 (1 pen)	42,456
5	28	A	Aston Villa	L	0-1	0-0	9		32,498
6	Sept 1	H	Chelsea	D	1-1	0-1	—	Sheringham (pen)	27,567
7	11	A	Sheffield U	D	2-2	1-0	10	Sheringham 2	21,325
8	18	H	Oldham Ath	W	5-0	3-0	5	Sheringham 2, Sedgley, Durie, Dozzell	24,614
9	26	A	Ipswich T	D	2-2	1-0	—	Sheringham, Dozzell	19,437
10	Oct 3	H	Everton	W	3-2	0-1	—	Sheringham, Anderton, Caskey	27,487
11	16	A	Manchester U	L	1-2	0-0	5	Caskey	44,655
12	23	H	Swindon T	D	1-1	0-0	8	Dozzell	31,394
13	30	A	Blackburn R	L	0-1	0-1	10		17,462
14	Nov 6	A	Southampton	L	0-1	0-0	11		16,017
15	20	H	Leeds U	D	1-1	0-0	10	Anderton	31,275
16	24	H	Wimbledon	D	1-1	1-0	—	Barmby	17,744
17	27	A	QPR	D	1-1	0-1	10	Anderton	17,694
18	Dec 4	H	Newcastle U	L	1-2	0-0	14	Barmby (pen)	30,780
19	6	A	Arsenal	D	1-1	1-0	—	Anderton	35,669
20	11	A	Manchester C	W	2-0	0-0	11	Dozzell 2	21,566
21	18	H	Liverpool	D	3-3	1-0	14	Samways, Hazard (pen), Caskey	31,394
22	27	H	Norwich C	L	1-3	0-2	14	Barmby	31,130
23	28	A	West Ham U	W	3-1	2-1	11	Dozzell, Hazard, Anderton	20,787
24	Jan 1	H	Coventry C	L	1-2	1-1	12	Caskey	26,015
25	3	A	Sheffield W	L	0-1	0-1	13		32,514
26	15	H	Manchester U	L	0-1	0-0	15		31,343
27	22	A	Swindon T	L	1-2	1-1	15	Barmby	16,464
28	Feb 5	H	Sheffield W	L	1-3	0-1	16	Rosenthal	23,078
29	12	H	Blackburn R	L	0-2	0-0	16		30,236
30	27	A	Chelsea	L	3-4	2-3	—	Sedgley, Dozzell, Gray (pen)	19,398
31	Mar 2	H	Aston Villa	D	1-1	0-1	—	Rosenthal	17,452
32	5	H	Sheffield U	D	2-2	0-0	16	Scott, Dozzell	25,741
33	19	H	Ipswich T	D	1-1	0-1	17	Barmby	26,653
34	26	A	Everton	W	1-0	0-0	16	Sedgley	23,460
35	Apr 2	A	Norwich C	W	2-1	0-0	16	Sheringham, Woodthorpe (og)	21,181
36	4	H	West Ham U	L	1-4	0-1	16	Sheringham (pen)	31,502
37	9	A	Coventry C	L	0-1	0-0	18		14,487
38	17	A	Leeds U	L	0-2	0-0	—		33,658
39	23	H	Southampton	W	3-0	1-0	16	Sedgley, Samways, Anderton	25,959
40	30	A	Wimbledon	L	1-2	0-0	16	Sheringham (pen)	20,875
41	May 5	A	Oldham Ath	W	2-0	1-0	—	Samways, Howells	14,283
42	7	H	QPR	L	1-2	1-1	15	Sheringham	26,105

Final League Position: 15

GOALSCORERS

League (54): Sheringham 14 (4 pens), Dozzell 8, Anderton 6, Barmby 5 (1 pen), Sedgley 5, Caskey 4, Samways 3, Hazard 2 (1 pen), Rosenthal 2, Durie 1, Gray 1 (pen), Howells 1, Scott 1, own goal 1.
Coca-Cola Cup (6): Sheringham 2, Barmby 1, Campbell 1, Caskey 1, Howells 1.
FA Cup (2): Barmby 1, Dozzell 1.

Thorstvedt 32	Austin 20 + 3	Campbell 27 + 7	Samways 39	Calderwood 26	Mabbutt 29	Sedgley 42	Durie 10	Dozzell 28 + 4	Sheringham 17 + 2	Howells 15 + 3	Turner — + 1	Caskey 16 + 9	Anderton 35 + 2	Allen — + 1	Moran — + 5	Carr 1	Kerslake 16 + 1	Hill 1 + 2	Barmby 27	Edinburgh 24 + 1	Robinson 1 + 1	Hendry — + 3	Hazard 13 + 4	Nethercott 9 + 1	Walker 10 + 1	Mahorn 1	Scott 12	Rosenthal 11 + 4	Gray — + 2	*Match No.*
1	2	3	4	5	6	7	8	9	10	11	12																			1
1	2	3	4	5	6	7	8	9	10	11		12																		2
1	2	3	4	5	6	7	8	9	10	*11*		12	14																	3
1	2	3	4	5	6	7	8	9	10	11		12																		4
1	2	3	4	5	6	7	8	9	10	11		*12*	14																	5
1	2	3	4	5	6	7	8	9	10	12			11																	6
1	2	3	4	5	6	7	8	9	10				11	12																7
1	2	3	4	*5*	6	7	8	9	10			12	11		14															8
1		3	4	5	6	7	8	9	10			12	11			2														9
1		*3*	4	5	6	7		9	10			8	11		12		2	14												10
1		3	4		6	7		9	10	5		11			*12*		2		8	14										11
1		3	4	5	6	7		9		*10*			11		12		2	14	8											12
1		3		5	6	4		9		10			11		12				8	2	*7*	14								13
1		3	4	5	6	7		9				12	11						8	2			10							14
1		3	4	5	6	7	8			12			9						10	2			11							15
1		3	4	5	6	7				10		12	9						8	2			11							16
1		3	4	5		6				7		10	9						8	2	*12*		11	14						17
1	14	11	4	5		6		12				10	9				*2*		8	3			7							18
1	12	11	4	5		6		10				*7*	9				2			3		14	8							19
1		11	4	5		6		10				7	9				2			3			8							20
1			4	5		6		10				7	9				2		8	3			11							21
1			4	5		6		10				7	9				2		8	3			11							22
1		12	4	5		6		10				7	9				2		8	3			11							23
1		12	4	5		6		10				7	9				2		8	3			11							24
1		12	4	5		6		10				7	9				2		8	3			11							25
	12	11	4	5		6						10	9				2		*8*	3		14	7		1					26
1	2	12	4	5		6						7	9						8	3				10	14	11				27
	2		4			6						7	9						8	3				10	1		5	11	12	28
	2		4			6						7	9						8	3				10	1		5	11		29
	2	12	4		6	7		*10*					9							3				8	1		5	11	14	30
	2	3	4		6	7		10					9						8						1		5	11		31
	2	3	4		6	7		10				12	9						8						1		5	11		32
	2	3			6	4		10				7	9				12		8						1		5	11		33
		12	4		6	7		14					9				2		8	3				10	1		*5*	11		34
		3	4		6	7		10	12				9				2		8						1		5	11		35
		3	4		6	7		*10*	12	14			9				2		8						1		5	11		36
1		3	4		6	7		14	10	*11*			9				2		8								5	12		37
1	2	12			6	*4*		8	10	11			9							3			14				5	7		38
1	2		4		6	5			10	*11*			9						8	3			14	7				12		39
1	2		4		6	5			10	11			*9*						8	3			14	7				12		40
1	2		4		6	7		12	10	11										3				8			5	9		41
1	2		4		6	5			10				9					*11*	8	3			14	7				12		42

Coca-Cola Cup	Second Round	Burnley (a)	0-0
		(h)	3-1
	Third Round	Derby Co (a)	1-0
	Fourth Round	Blackburn R (h)	1-0
	Fifth Round	Aston Villa (h)	1-2
FA Cup	Third Round	Peterborough U (a)	1-1
		(h)	1-1
	Fourth Round	Ipswich T (a)	0-3

TOTTENHAM HOTSPUR

Player and Position	Ht	Wt	Birth Date	Birth Place	Source	Clubs	League App	League Gls
Goalkeepers								
Chris Day	6 0	12 00	28 7 74	Whipps Cross	Trainee	Tottenham H	—	—
Erik Thorstvedt	6 4	14 03	28 10 62	Stavanger	IFK Gothenburg	Tottenham H	172	—
Ian Walker	6 1	11 09	31 10 71	Watford	Trainee	Tottenham H	47	—
						Oxford U (loan)	2	—
						Ipswich T (loan)	—	—
Defenders								
Dean Austin	6 0	12 04	26 4 70	Hemel Hempstead	St. Albans C	Southend U	96	2
						Tottenham H	57	—
Gudni Bergsson	6 1	12 03	21 7 65	Iceland	Valur	Tottenham H	71	2
Colin Calderwood	6 0	12 00	20 1 65	Stranraer	Amateur	Mansfield T	100	1
						Swindon T	330	20
						Tottenham H	26	—
Sol Campbell	6 0	12 00	18 9 74	Newham	Trainee	Tottenham H	35	1
Stephen Carr	5 9		29 8 76	Dublin	Trainee	Tottenham H	1	—
David Culverhouse*	6 0	11 06	9 9 73	Harlow	Trainee	Tottenham H	—	—
Jason Cundy	6 1	13 07	12 11 69	Wimbledon	Trainee	Chelsea	41	1
						Tottenham H (loan)	10	—
						Tottenham H	15	1
Justin Edinburgh	5 10	11 08	18 12 69	Brentwood	Trainee	Southend U	37	—
						Tottenham H (loan)	—	—
						Tottenham H	96	1
Chris Landon‡	5 9		20 10 74	Epsom	Trainee	Tottenham H	—	—
Gary Mabbutt	5 9	12 09	23 8 61	Bristol	Apprentice	Bristol R	131	10
						Tottenham H	397	27
Stuart Nethercott	6 0	12 04	21 3 73	Chadwell Heath	Trainee	Tottenham H	15	—
						Maidstone U (loan)	13	1
						Barnet (loan)	3	—
Kevin Scott	6 2	11 06	17 12 66	Easington		Newcastle U	227	8
						Tottenham H	12	1
Neil Young	5 8	11 03	31 8 73	Harlow	Trainee	Tottenham H	—	—
Midfield								
Gary Brady	5 7		7 9 76	Glasgow	Trainee	Tottenham H	—	—
Darren Caskey	5 8	11 09	21 8 74	Basildon	Trainee	Tottenham H	25	4
Andy Gray	5 11	13 03	22 2 64	Lambeth	Dulwich H	Crystal Palace	98	27
						Aston Villa	37	4
						QPR	11	2
						Crystal Palace	90	12
						Tottenham H (loan)	14	1
						Tottenham H	19	2
						Swindon T (loan)	3	—
Darren Grogan	5 7	10 00	16 12 74	Dublin	Trainee	Tottenham H	—	—
Mike Hazard	5 7	10 05	5 2 60	Sunderland	Apprentice	Tottenham H	91	13
						Chelsea	81	9
						Portsmouth	8	1
						Swindon T	119	17
						Tottenham H	17	2
Danny Hill	5 9	11 00	1 10 74	Edmonton	Trainee	Tottenham H	7	—
David Kerslake	5 8	11 00	19 6 66	London	Apprentice	QPR	58	6
						Swindon T	135	1
						Leeds U	8	—
						Tottenham H	17	—
Nayim (Mohamed Ali Amar)	5 8	11 08	5 11 66	Morocco	Barcelona	Tottenham H	112	11
Vinny Samways	5 8	11 00	27 10 68	Bethnal Green	Apprentice	Tottenham H	193	11
Steve Sedgley	6 1	13 03	26 5 68	Enfield	Apprentice	Coventry C	84	3
						Tottenham H	164	8
Kevin Watson	5 9	12 06	3 1 74	Hackney	Trainee	Tottenham H	5	—
						Brentford (loan)	3	—
Forwards								
Darren Anderton	6 1	12 00	3 3 72	Southampton	Trainee	Portsmouth	62	7
						Tottenham H	71	12

TOTTENHAM HOTSPUR

Colours: White shirts, navy blue shorts, white stockings. **Change colours:** All navy with purple trim.

Foundation: The Hotspur Football Club was formed from an older cricket club in 1882. Most of the founders were old boys St. John's Presbyterian School and Tottenham Grammar School. The Casey brothers were well to the fore as the family provided the club's first goalposts (painted blue and white) and their first ball. They soon adopted the local YMCA as their meeing place, but after a couple of moves settled at the Red House, which is still their headquarters, although now known simply as 748 High Road.

First Football League game: 1 September, 1908, Division 2, v Wolverhampton W (h) W 3-0 – Hewitson; Coquet, Burton; Morris (1), Steel (D), Darnell; Walton, Woodward (2), Macfarlane, R. Steel, Middlemiss.

Did you know: On 18 September 1993 Tottenham Hotspur scored three goals in two minutes 34 seconds between the fifth and eighth minutes of their 5-0 win over Oldham Athletic.

Managers (and Secretary-Managers)
Frank Brettell 1898–99, John Cameron 1899–1906, Fred Kirkham 1907–08, Peter McWilliam 1912–27, Billy Minter 1927–29, Percy Smith 1930–35, Jack Tresadern 1935–38, Peter McWilliam 1938–42, Arthur Turner 1942–46, Joe Hulme 1946–49, Arthur Rowe 1949–55, Jimmy Anderson 1955–58, Bill Nicholson 1958–74, Terry Neill 1974–76, Keith Burkinshaw 1976–84, Peter Shreeves 1984–86, David Pleat 1986–87, Terry Venables 1987–91, Peter Shreeves 1991–92, Ossie Ardiles June 1993–

Player and Position	Ht	Wt	Birth Date	Birth Place	Source	Clubs	League App	League Gls
Nick Barmby	5 6	11 04	11 2 74	Hull	Trainee	Tottenham H	49	11
Peter Beadle	6 0	11 12	13 5 72	London	Trainee	Gillingham	67	14
						Tottenham H	—	—
						Bournemouth (loan)	9	2
						Southend U (loan)	8	1
Jason Dozzell	6 1	12 13	9 12 67	Ipswich	School	Ipswich T	332	52
						Tottenham H	32	8
Gordon Durie (To Rangers November 1993)	6 0	12 00	6 12 65	Paisley	Hill of Beath H	East Fife	81	26
						Hibernian	47	14
						Chelsea	123	51
						Tottenham H	58	11
John Hendry	5 11	10 06	6 1 70	Glasgow	Hillington YC	Dundee	2	—
						Forfar Ath (loan)	10	6
						Tottenham H	17	5
						Charlton Ath (loan)	5	1
Lee Hodges*	5 9	11 06	4 9 73	Epping	Trainee	Tottenham H	4	—
						Plymouth Arg (loan)	7	2
						Wycombe W (loan)	4	—
David Howells	5 11	11 10	15 12 67	Guildford	Trainee	Tottenham H	170	16
Gary Lineker	5 9	11 10	30 11 60	Leicester	Apprentice	Leicester C	194	95
						Everton	41	30
						Barcelona	99	44
						Tottenham H	105	67
Junior McDougald	5 11	10 12	12 1 75	Big Spring	Trainee	Tottenham H	—	—
Gerard McMahon	5 11	11 00	29 12 73	Belfast	Glenavon	Tottenham H	—	—
Paul Mahorn	5 8	11 06	13 8 73	Whipps Cross	Trainee	Tottenham H	1	—
						Fulham (loan)	3	—
Jeffrey Minton*	5 5	11 07	28 12 73	Hackney	Trainee	Tottenham H	2	1
Paul Moran*	5 10	11 00	22 5 68	Enfield	Trainee	Tottenham H	36	2
						Portsmouth (loan)	3	—
						Leicester C (loan)	10	1
						Newcastle U (loan)	1	—
						Southend U (loan)	1	—
						Cambridge U (loan)	—	—

Continued on Page 523

Trainees
Anderson, Ijan M; Brown, Simon J; Callcut, Dean E; Clapham, James R; Fenn, Neale M. C; Foot, Daniel F; Gain, Peter; Gosnell, Darren S; Haynes, Junior L. A; Hurst, Glynn; Knott, Gareth R; Le Bihan, Neil E. R; Maher, Kevin; Rothwell, Sam; Slade, Steven A; Spencer, Simon; Townley, Leon; Williams, Richard I; Wormull, Simon J.

Associated Schoolboys
Allen, Lee S; Dunn, James T; Chambers, Clinton H; Dobson, Stephen G; Dowling, Luke J; Ellerton, Gary J; Evans, James M; Fortune, Quinton; Gower, Mark; Jenkins, Matthew C; Mitchell, Paul R; Piercey, John W; Spencer, Ryan L; Vaughan, Wayne S. R; Warrington, Russell C; Young, Luke P.

Associated Schoolboys who have accepted the Club's offer of a Traineeship/Contract
Allen, Rory W; Arber, Mark A; Clemence, Stephen N; Davies, Darren J; Janney, Mark; McVeigh, Paul; Outram, Ross P; Shave, Arran L; Tully, Luke G; Winston, Samuel A.

TRANMERE ROVERS 1993–94 *Back row (left to right):* Alan Morgan, Mark Proctor, Dave Higgins, Mark Hughes, John McGreal, Gary Jones, Shaun Garnett, Graham Branch, Ian Nolan, John Evans, Ged Brannan.

Centre row: Norman Wilson (Secretary), Kenny Jones (Trainer), Ronnie Moore (Coach), Steve Vickers, Chris Malkin, Martin Jones, Eric Nixon, Danny Coyne, Mick Edwards, Jonathan Kenworthy, Phil Johnson, Harry McNally (Chief Scout), Warwick Rimmer (Youth Development Officer), Ray Mathias (Coach).

Front row: Dave Martindale, Tony Thomas, Ian Muir, Steve Mungall, John King (Manager), John Aldridge, Pat Nevin, Johnny Morrissey, Kenny Irons.

Division 1 **TRANMERE ROVERS**

Prenton Park, Prenton Road West, Birkenhead L42 9PN. Telephone 051–608 3677. Fax 051– 608 4294. Commercial 051–608 0371. Valley Road Training Centre: 051–652 2578. Shop: 051–608 0438. Ticket Office: 051–609 0137.

Ground capacity: 17,000 (by January 1995).

Record attendance: 24,424 v Stoke C, FA Cup 4th rd, 5 February 1972.

Record receipts: £114,150 v Aston Villa, Coca-Cola Cup semi-final 16 February 1994.

Pitch measurements: 112yd × 71yd.

President: H. B. Thomas.

Chairman and Chief Executive: F. D. Corfe.

Directors: A. J. Adams BDS, G. E. H. Jones LLB, F. J. Williams, J. J. Holsgrove FCA, G. A. Higham MSC TECH LRSC, M INST PI.

Secretary: Norman Wilson FAAI. ***Commercial Manager:*** Janet Ratcliffe.

Development Manager: Nobby Abbott.

Manager: John King. ***Trainer:*** Kenny Jones.

Youth Development Officer: Warwick Rimmer.

Coach: Ronnie Moore. ***Physios:*** Les Parry and Alex McLellan.

Year Formed: 1884. ***Turned Professional:*** 1912. ***Ltd Co.:*** 1920.

Previous Name: Belmont AFC, 1884–85.

Club Nickname: 'The Rovers'.

Previous Grounds: 1884, Steeles Field; 1887, Ravenshaws Field/Old Prenton Park; 1912, Prenton Park.

Record League Victory: 13–4 v Oldham Ath, Division 3 (N), 26 December 1935 – Gray; Platt, Fairhurst; McLaren, Newton, Spencer; Eden, MacDonald (1), Bell (9), Woodward (2), Urmson (1).

Record Cup Victory: 13–0 v Oswestry U, FA Cup 2nd pr rd, 10 October 1914 – Ashcroft; Stevenson, Bullough, Hancock, Taylor, Holden (1), Moreton (1), Cunningham (2), Smith (5), Leck (3), Gould (1).

Record Defeat: 1–9 v Tottenham H, FA Cup 3rd rd (replay), 14 January 1953.

Most League Points (2 for a win): 60, Division 4, 1964–65.

Most League Points (3 for a win): 80, Division 4, 1988–89 and Division 3, 1989–90.

Most League Goals: 111, Division 3 (N), 1930–31.

Highest League Scorer in Season: Bunny Bell, 35, Division 3 (N), 1933–34.

Most League Goals in Total Aggregate: Ian Muir, 134, 1985–94.

Most Capped Player: John Aldridge, 21 (60), Republic of Ireland.

Most League Appearances: Harold Bell, 595, 1946–64 (incl. League record 401 consecutive appearances).

Record Transfer Fee Received: £750,000 from Middlesbrough for Steve Vickers, November 1993.

Record Transfer Fee Paid: £350,000 to Celtic for Tommy Coyne, March 1993.

Football League Record: 1921 Original Member of Division 3 (N): 1938–39 Division 2; 1946–58 Division 3 (N); 1958–61 Division 3; 1961–67 Division 4; 1967–75 Division 3; 1975–76 Division 4; 1976–79 Division 3; 1979–89 Division 4; 1989–91 Division 3; 1991–92 Division 2; 1992– Division 1.

Honours: *Football League* Division 1 best season: 4th, 1992–93; Division 3 (N) – Champions 1937–38; Promotion to 3rd Division: 1966–67, 1975–76; Division 4 – Runners-up 1988–89. *FA Cup:* best season: 5th rd, 1967–68. *Football League Cup:* best season: semi-final 1994. *Welsh Cup:* Winners 1935; Runners-up 1934. *Leyland Daf Cup:* Winners 1990; Runners-up 1991.

TRANMERE ROVERS 1993—94 LEAGUE RECORD

Match No.	Date	Venue	Opponents	Result		H/T Score	Lg. Pos.	Goalscorers	Attendance
1	Aug 14	A	Crystal Palace	D	0-0	0-0	—		14,785
2	21	H	Leicester C	W	1-0	0-0	8	Malkin	8766
3	24	A	Charlton Ath	L	1-3	0-1	—	Brannan	6666
4	28	A	Grimsby T	D	0-0	0-0	9		4793
5	Sept 4	H	Notts Co	W	3-1	0-0	6	Aldridge, Kenworthy, Muir	6317
6	11	A	Stoke C	W	2-1	0-1	4	Thomas, Muir	17,296
7	14	H	Luton T	W	4-1	1-0	—	Muir, Thomas, Brannan, Aldridge	5871
8	18	H	Barnsley	L	0-3	0-1	3		6755
9	25	H	Oxford U	W	2-0	0-0	1	Nevin, Brannan	6056
10	Oct 2	A	Southend U	W	2-1	1-0	2	Kenworthy, Muir	5860
11	9	H	Bolton W	W	2-1	1-1	1	Malkin, Nevin	10,128
12	16	A	Nottingham F	L	1-2	0-1	1	Malkin	20,771
13	22	H	Bristol C	D	2-2	1-1	—	Nevin, Brannan	7123
14	30	A	Portsmouth	L	0-2	0-0	4		12,462
15	Nov 2	H	WBA	W	3-0	1-0	—	Muir 2, Nevin	7882
16	6	A	Peterborough U	D	0-0	0-0	3		5519
17	13	H	Sunderland	W	4-1	0-1	2	Aldridge, Morrissey, Nevin 2	8497
18	20	A	Millwall	L	1-3	0-2	2	Jones	8653
19	27	A	Birmingham C	W	3-0	1-0	2	Malkin, Aldridge 2	9915
20	Dec 3	H	Peterborough U	W	2-1	2-0	—	Nevin, Aldridge	6294
21	11	A	Luton T	W	1-0	0-0	1	Aldridge	7045
22	19	H	Crystal Palace	L	0-1	0-0	—		7011
23	27	H	Wolverhampton W	D	1-1	1-0	2	Irons	15,603
24	29	A	Middlesbrough	D	0-0	0-0	2		12,351
25	Jan 1	H	Watford	W	2-1	1-0	2	Malkin, Brannan	8271
26	3	A	Derby Co	L	0-4	0-3	2		16,874
27	16	H	Nottingham F	L	1-2	1-0	—	Aldridge (pen)	8500
28	23	A	Bolton W	L	1-2	0-1	—	Malkin	11,550
29	Feb 5	A	Bristol C	L	0-2	0-0	5		8171
30	11	H	Portsmouth	W	3-1	2-0	—	Aldridge, Malkin, Brannan	6914
31	23	A	Leicester C	D	1-1	1-0	—	McGreal	14,028
32	Mar 5	H	Grimsby T	L	1-2	1-2	9	Malkin	6454
33	12	A	Barnsley	L	0-1	0-0	9		6203
34	15	H	Stoke C	W	2-0	0-0	—	Aldridge 2 (1 pen)	6346
35	19	A	Oxford U	L	0-1	0-0	8		4506
36	25	H	Southend U	D	1-1	1-0	—	Aldridge	5526
37	29	H	Derby Co	W	4-0	2-0	—	O'Brien, Aldridge 2 (1 pen), Brannan	7114
38	Apr 2	A	Wolverhampton W	L	1-2	0-1	9	Aldridge	26,592
39	4	H	Middlesbrough	W	4-0	2-0	7	Brannan, Garnett, Aldridge, Nevin	8225
40	9	A	Watford	W	2-1	1-0	7	Aldridge, Jones	7347
41	12	A	Notts Co	D	0-0	0-0	—		6318
42	16	A	WBA	W	3-1	1-1	5	Garnett, Muir, Irons	15,835
43	23	H	Millwall	W	3-2	2-0	3	Aldridge 2, Irons	9141
44	26	H	Charlton Ath	W	2-0	0-0	3	Aldridge, Brannan	8170
45	30	A	Sunderland	L	2-3	0-3	3	Muir, Aldridge	15,167
46	May 8	H	Birmingham C	L	1-2	0-1	5	Muir	15,210

Final League Position: 5

GOALSCORERS

League (69): Aldridge 21 (3 pens), Brannan 9, Muir 9, Malkin 8, Nevin 8, Irons 3, Garnett 2, Jones 2, Kenworthy 2, Thomas 2, McGreal 1, Morrissey 1, O'Brien 1.
Coca-Cola Cup (20): Aldridge 7 (1 pen), Nevin 4, Brannan 2, Irons 2 (1 pen), Hughes 1, Malkin 1, Nolan 1, Thomas 1, Vickers 1.
FA Cup (0):

Nixon 42	Higgins 37	Brannan 45	Irons 29 + 5	Martindale 12 + 1	Vickers 11	Nevin 45	Aldridge 34	Malkin 27 + 1	Proctor 18	Thomas 40	Nolan 39 + 1	Kenworthy 11 + 5	Muir 10 + 6	Mungall 8 + 4	Garnett 26	Hughes 7 + 1	Branch 6 + 7	Coyne 4 + 1	Morrissey 22 + 3	Jones 2 + 4	McGreal 14 + 1	O'Brien 17	Match No.
1	2	3	4	5	6	7	8	9	10	11													1
1	2	3	4	5	6	7	8	9	10	11													2
1	2	3	4	5	6	7	8	9	10	11	12	14											3
1	2	10	4	5	6	7	8	9		11	3												4
1	2	10	4	5	6	7	8	9		11	3	14	12										5
1	2	10	4	5		7	8			11			9	3	6								6
1	2	10	4	5		7	8			11		12	9	3	6	14							7
1	2	10	4	5		7	8			11		12	9	3		6							8
1	2	4	14	5		10	8	12		11	3	7	9		6								9
1	2	4		5		10		8		11	3	7	9		6								10
1	2	4	8	5		10		9		11	3	7			6		12						11
1	2	4	8	5		10		9		11	3	7			6		12						12
1	2	4	5			10		9		11	3	7	8		6		12						13
1	2				6	10		9	4	11	3	7	8	5			12						14
1	2	5			6	10		9	4	11	3	7	8										15
	2	4	12		6	10		9	5	11	3	7	8				14	1					16
	2	4			6	10	8	9	5	11	3	7						1	12				17
1	2	4	9		6	10			5	11	3	8							7	12			18
1	2	4			6		8	9	5	11	3	10							7				19
	2	4				10	8	9	5	11	3				6			1	7				20
1	2	4				10	8	9	5	11	3				6				7				21
1	2	4	11			10	8	9	5		3			12	6		14		7				22
1	2	4	11			10	8	9	5		3				6		12		7				23
1	2	4				10		9	5	11	3				6		8		7				24
1	2	4				10		9	5	11	3				6		8		7				25
1	2	4	12			10		9	5	11	3	14			6		8		7				26
1	2	4	11	12		10	8	9			3			5		6			7		14		27
1	2	4	12			11	8	9			3			5					7		6	10	28
1	2	4				10	8	9		11				3		5		12	7			6	29
1		4	7			10	8	9		11	3					5					2	6	30
	2	4	7			10	8	9			3			12		5		1			11	6	31
1	2	4	12			10	8	9		11	3					5			14		7	6	32
1	2	4	9			10	8			11	3				7	5			14	12		6	33
1	2	4				10	8			11	3				5				7	9		6	34
1	2	4				10	8			11	3		12		5				7	9		6	35
1	2	4	9			10	8			11	3			12	5				7			6	36
1	2	4	9			10	8			11	3			12					7		5	6	37
1	2	4	9			10	8			11	3								7		5	6	38
1		4	9			10	8			11	3				5				7	12	2	6	39
1		4	9			10	8			11	3				5				7	12	2	6	40
1		4	9			10			6	11	3		8		5				7		2		41
1		4	9			10	8		6	11	3		12		5				7		2		42
1		4	9			10	8			11	3				5				7		2	6	43
1		4	9			10	8			11	3		12		5		7				2	6	44
1		4	9			10	8				3		12	11	5		7				2	6	45
1		4	9			10	8			11	3		12		5		7				2	6	46

Coca-Cola Cup	Second Round	Oxford U (h)	5-1
		(a)	1-1
	Third Round	Grimsby T (h)	4-1
	Fourth Round	Oldham Ath (h)	3-0
	Fifth Round	Nottingham F (a)	1-1
		(h)	2-0
	Semi-final	Aston Villa (h)	3-1
		(a)	1-3
FA Cup	Third Round	Oxford U (a)	0-2

TRANMERE ROVERS

Player and Position	Ht	Wt	Birth Date	Birth Place	Source	Clubs	League App	League Gls
Goalkeepers								
Danny Coyne	6 0	13 00	27 8 73	St Asaph	Trainee	Tranmere R	6	—
Martin Jones	6 1	12 00	27 3 75	Liverpool	Trainee	Tranmere R	—	—
Eric Nixon	6 2	14 03	4 10 62	Manchester	Curzon Ashton	Manchester C	58	—
						Wolverhampton W (loan)	16	—
						Bradford C (loan)	3	—
						Southampton (loan)	4	—
						Carlisle U (loan)	16	—
						Tranmere R (loan)	8	—
						Tranmere R	267	—
Defenders								
Ged Brannan	6 0	13 03	15 1 72	Liverpool	Trainee	Tranmere R	119	12
Dave Higgins	6 0	11 00	19 8 61	Liverpool	Eagle	Tranmere R	28	—
					S. Liverpool, Caernarforn	Tranmere R	264	10
Mark Hughes*	6 0	12 08	3 2 62	Port Talbot	Apprentice	Bristol R	74	3
						Torquay U (loan)	9	1
						Swansea C	12	—
						Bristol C	22	—
						Tranmere R	266	9
John McGreal	5 11	10 08	2 6 72	Birkenhead	Trainee	Tranmere R	18	1
Steve Mungall	5 8	11 05	22 5 58	Bellshill		Motherwell	20	—
						Tranmere R	480	12
Ian Nolan	6 0	11 10	9 7 70	Liverpool	Marine	Tranmere R	88	1
Tony Thomas	5 11	12 05	12 7 71	Liverpool	Trainee	Tranmere R	170	12
Midfield								
Mike Edwards	5 11	11 05	10 9 74	Bebbington	Trainee	Tranmere R	—	—
John Evans	5 10	11 00	8 9 74	Liverpool	Trainee	Tranmere R	—	—
Shaun Garnett	6 2	11 00	22 11 69	Wallasey	Trainee	Tranmere R	60	4
						Chester C (loan)	9	—
						Preston NE (loan)	10	2
						Wigan Ath (loan)	13	1
Dave Martindale*	5 11	11 10	9 4 64	Liverpool	Caernarfon	Tranmere R	166	9
John Morrissey	5 8	11 09	8 3 65	Liverpool	Apprentice	Everton	1	—
						Wolverhampton W	10	1
						Tranmere R	326	44
Liam O'Brien	6 1	13 03	5 9 64	Dublin	Shamrock R	Manchester U	31	2
						Newcastle U	151	19
						Tranmere R	17	1
Mark Proctor	5 10	11 13	30 1 61	Middlesbrough	Apprentice	Middlesbrough	109	12
						Nottingham F	64	5
						Sunderland (loan)	5	—
						Sunderland	112	19
						Sheffield W	59	4
						Middlesbrough	120	6
						Tranmere R (loan)	13	1
						Tranmere R	18	—
Forwards								
John Aldridge	5 11	11 04	18 9 58	Liverpool	South Liverpool	Newport Co	170	69
						Oxford U	114	72
						Liverpool	83	50
						Real Sociedad	63	33
						Tranmere R	107	64
Graham Branch	6 2	13 00	12 2 72	Heswall	Heswall Ath	Tranmere R	20	—
						Bury (loan)	4	1
Tommy Coyne (To Motherwell November 1993)	5 11	12 00	14 11 62	Glasgow	Hillwood BC	Clydebank	80	37
						Dundee U	52	8
						Dundee	89	51
						Celtic	105	43
						Tranmere R	12	1
Kenny Irons	5 9	11 00	4 11 70	Liverpool	Trainee	Tranmere R	154	23
Gary Jones	6 3	14 00	10 5 75	Chester	Trainee	Tranmere R	6	2
Jon Kenworthy	5 7	10 06	18 8 74	St Asaph	Trainee	Tranmere R	16	2

TRANMERE ROVERS

Colours: All white. **Change colours:** Green shirts, white shorts, green stockings.

Foundation: Formed in 1884 as Belmont they adopted their present title the following year and eventually joined their first league, the West Lancashire League in 1889–90, the same year as their first success in the Wirral Challenge Cup. The club almost folded in 1899–1900 when all the players left en bloc to join a rival club, but they survived the crisis and went from strength to strength winning the 'Combination' title in 1907–08 and the Lancashire Combination in 1913–14. They joined the Football League in 1921 from the Central League.

First Football League game: 27 August 1921, Division 3(N), v Crewe Alex (h) W 4-1 – Bradshaw; Grainger, Stuart (1); Campbell, Milnes (1), Heslop; Moreton, Groves (1), Hyam, Ford (1), Hughes.

Did you know: Of current players appearing in the Football League in 1993–94, Tranmere Rovers striker John Aldridge was the most prolific marksman, finishing the season on 255 goals in English League football.

Managers (and Secretary-Managers)
Bert Cooke 1912–35, Jackie Carr 1935–36, Jim Knowles 1936–39, Bill Ridding 1939–45, Ernie Blackburn 1946–55, Noel Kelly 1955–57, Peter Farrell 1957–60, Walter Galbraith 1961, Dave Russell 1961–69, Jackie Wright 1969–72, Ron Yeats 1972–75, John King 1975–80, Bryan Hamilton 1980–85, Frank Worthington 1985–87, Ronnie Moore 1987, John King April 1987–

Player and Position	*Ht*	*Wt*	*Birth Date*	*Place*	*Source*	*Clubs*	*League App*	*Gls*
Chris Malkin	6 0	10 12	4 6 67	Bebington	Overpool	Tranmere R	189	44
Alan Morgan	5 10	11 00	2 11 73	Aberystwyth	Trainee	Tranmere R	—	—
Ian Muir	5 8	11 00	5 5 63	Coventry	Apprentice	QPR	2	2
						Burnley (loan)	2	1
						Birmingham C	1	—
						Brighton	4	—
						Swindon T (loan)	2	—
						Tranmere R	295	134
Pat Nevin	5 6	11 09	6 9 63	Glasgow	Gartcosh U	Clyde	73	17
						Chelsea	193	36
						Everton	109	16
						Tranmere R (loan)	8	—
						Tranmere R	88	21

Trainees
Allen, Gavin; Bate, Christopher J; Cassidy, Thomas S; Davies, Philip A; Donnachie, John; Gerard, Robbie; Hammond, John E; Harland, Nicholas J; Hughes, James J; Jardine, Jamie; McKenna, David; Moore, Ian R; Parkinson, Mark R; Rogers, Alan; Rogers, David R; Smith, Stephen P; Watt, Simon C.

Associated Schoolboys
Bramwell, Aaron T; Butler, Carl W; Ellis, James; Fitzsimmons, Jamie L; Gibson, Neil D; Glover, Shaun S; Hazlehurst, Ian J; Holmes, Thomas M; Jones, Darren J; Keating, Daniel C; Lampkin, Ricky J; Lepts, Damien A; Parr, Ian J; Quayle, Mark L; Tynan, Paul S; Vaughan, Thomas; Walker, Danny; Waters, Anthony F.

Associated Schoolboys who have accepted the Club's offer of a Traineeship/Contract
Ball, David B; Black, Mark; Blundell, Greg; Jones, Paul N; Marsden, Topmmy; McIntyre, Kevin; Scott, Gary; Webster, Christopher R.

Tottenham Hotspur players continued from Page 517

Stephen Robinson	5 9	11 00	10 12 74	Crumlin	Trainee	Tottenham H	2	—
Ronny Rosenthal	5 11	12 00	11 10 63	Haifa	Standard Liege	Luton T (loan)	—	—
						Liverpool (loan)	8	7
						Liverpool	66	14
						Tottenham H	15	2
Teddy Sheringham	6 0	12 05	2 4 66	Highams Park	Apprentice	Millwall	220	93
						Aldershot (loan)	5	—
						Nottingham F	42	14
						Tottenham H	57	35
Robert Simpson	5 10		3 3 76	Luton	Trainee	Tottenham H	—	—
Andy Turner	5 9	11 00	23 3 75	Woolwich	Trainee	Tottenham H	19	3

WALSALL 1993–94 *Back row (left to right)*: Eric McManus (Youth Development Officer), Richard Knight, Kyle Lightbourne, Dean Smith, James Walker, Stephen O'Hara, Mark Gayle, Stuart Watkiss, Stuart Ryder, Steven McManus, Tom Bradley (Physio).
Front row: David Edwards, Mike Cecere, Chris Marsh, Kenny Hibbitt (Manager), Rodney McDonald, Charlie Ntamark, Martin Butler.

Division 3 **WALSALL**

Bescot Stadium, Bescot Cresent, Walsall WS1 4SA. Telephone Walsall (0922) 22791. Commercial Dept: (0922) 30696. Clubcall: 0898 121104.

Ground capacity: 9485.

Record attendance: 10,628 B International, England v Switzerland, 20 May 1991.

Record receipts: £50,926.50 v Watford, FA Cup 5th rd, 2nd replay, 2 March 1987 (at Fellows Park); £42,401 v Aston Villa, Friendly, 18 August 1990.

Pitch measurements: 113yd × 73yd.

President: .

Chairman: J. W. Bonsor.

Directors: M. N. Lloyd, K. R. Whalley, C. Welch.

Manager: Kenny Hibbitt. ***General Manager:*** Paul Taylor. ***Physio:*** T. Bradley.

Secretary/Commercial Manager: Roy Whalley.

Year Formed: 1888. ***Turned Professional:*** 1888. ***Ltd Co.:*** 1921.

Club Nickname: 'The Saddlers'.

Previous Names: Walsall Swifts (founded 1877) and Walsall Town (founded 1879) amalgamated in 1888 and were known as Walsall Town Swifts until 1895.

Previous Grounds: Fellows Park to 1990.

Record League Victory: 10–0 v Darwen, Division 2, 4 March 1899 – Tennent; E. Peers (1), Davies; Hickinbotham, Jenkyns, Taggart; Dean (3), Vail (2), Aston (4), Martin, Griffin.

Record Cup Victory: 6–1 v Leytonstone (away), FA Cup, 1st rd, 30 November 1946 – Lewis; Netley, Skidmore; Crutchley, Foulkes, Newman; Maund (1), Talbot, Darby (1), Wilshaw (2), Davies (2). 6–1 v Margate, FA Cup, 1st rd (replay), 24 November 1955 – Davies; Haddington, Vinall; Dorman, McPherson, Crook; Morris, Walsh (3), Richards (2), McLaren (1), Moore.

Record Defeat: 0–12 v Small Heath, 17 December 1892 and v Darwen, 26 December 1896, both Division 2.

Most League Points (2 for a win): 65, Division 4, 1959–60.

Most League Points (3 for a win): 82, Division 3, 1987–88.

Most League Goals: 102, Division 4, 1959–60.

Highest League Scorer in Season: Gilbert Alsop, 40, Division 3 (N), 1933–34 and 1934–35.

Most League Goals in Total Aggregate: Tony Richards, 184, 1954–63, and Colin Taylor, 184, 1958–63, 1964–68, 1969–73.

Most Capped Player: Mick Kearns, 15 (18), Republic of Ireland.

Most League Appearances: Colin Harrison, 467, 1964–82.

Record Transfer Fee Received: £600,000 from West Ham U for David Kelly, July 1988.

Record Transfer Fee Paid: £175,000 to Birmingham C for Alan Buckley, June 1979.

Football League Record: 1892 Elected to Division 2; 1895 Failed re-election; 1896–1901 Division 2; 1901 Failed re-election; 1921 Original Member of Division 3 (N); 1927–31 Division 3 (S); 1931–36 Division 3 (N); 1936–58 Division 3 (S); 1958–60 Division 4; 1960–61 Division 3; 1961–63 Division 2; 1963–79 Division 3; 1979–80 Division 4; 1980–88 Division 3; 1988–89 Division 2; 1989–90 Division 3; 1990–92 Division 4; 1992– Division 3.

Honours: *Football League:* Division 2 best season: 6th, 1898–99; Division 3 – Runners-up 1960–61; Division 4 – Champions 1959–60; Runners-up 1979–80. *FA Cup:* best season: 5th rd, 1939, 1975, 1978, and last 16 1888–89. *Football League Cup:* Semi-final 1983–84.

WALSALL 1993—94 LEAGUE RECORD

Match No.	Date	Venue	Opponents	Result		H/T Score	Lg. Pos.	Goalscorers	Attendance
1	Aug 14	H	Torquay U	L	1-2	0-1	—	McDonald	3324
2	21	A	Shrewsbury T	W	2-1	0-0	10	Gayle J, Cecere	3681
3	28	H	Doncaster R	L	1-2	0-1	13	McDonald	2965
4	31	H	Scunthorpe U	D	0-0	0-0	—		2519
5	Sept 4	A	Northampton T	W	1-0	1-0	11	McDonald	3266
6	11	H	Crewe Alex	D	2-2	2-2	12	Cecere, Wright	4404
7	18	A	Chesterfield	W	1-0	0-0	9	Wright	2800
8	25	A	Darlington	D	0-0	0-0	9		1613
9	Oct 2	H	Hereford U	D	3-3	0-0	11	Lightbourne, Wright 2	3725
10	9	H	Gillingham	W	1-0	0-0	8	Peer	4639
11	16	A	Rochdale	D	0-0	0-0	9		2923
12	23	H	Scarborough	W	1-0	0-0	6	Wright	3941
13	30	A	Carlisle U	L	1-2	1-1	8	Lightbourne	4216
14	Nov 2	H	Preston NE	W	2-0	1-0	—	Lillis 2	4446
15	6	A	Colchester U	W	1-0	1-0	4	Peer	2736
16	20	H	Lincoln C	W	5-2	3-2	4	Peer 3, Lightbourne 2	4580
17	27	A	Mansfield T	W	2-1	1-0	3	Peer, Marsh	2875
18	Dec 11	H	Shrewsbury T	L	0-1	0-1	4		4979
19	18	A	Torquay U	W	1-0	0-0	4	Keister	2754
20	27	H	Bury	L	0-1	0-0	5		6248
21	Jan 1	H	Wycombe W	W	4-2	3-1	3	McDonald, Marsh, Lightbourne, Lillis	6473
22	3	A	Scunthorpe U	L	0-5	0-0	5		3417
23	11	A	Wigan Ath	D	2-2	0-2	—	Lillis 2	1561
24	15	H	Rochdale	W	1-0	1-0	4	Lillis	4437
25	22	A	Gillingham	D	1-1	1-0	4	Smith	3211
26	29	H	Carlisle U	L	0-1	0-0	5		4833
27	Feb 5	A	Scarborough	L	0-1	0-1	6		1851
28	12	H	Chester C	D	1-1	0-1	7	Watkiss	4602
29	19	A	Doncaster R	L	0-4	0-2	8		2029
30	25	H	Northampton T	L	1-3	0-0	8	Lightbourne	4533
31	Mar 5	A	Crewe Alex	W	2-1	1-0	7	Peer, Lightbourne	4358
32	12	H	Chesterfield	L	0-1	0-1	8		4157
33	15	A	Chester C	L	1-2	0-1	—	O'Connor (pen)	3324
34	19	H	Darlington	W	3-0	2-0	8	Butler, O'Connor (pen), McDonald	2983
35	26	A	Hereford U	W	1-0	0-0	8	McDonald	2744
36	Apr 2	A	Bury	W	2-1	0-1	7	Peer, Butler	2263
37	5	H	Wigan Ath	D	1-1	0-0	—	Marsh	3815
38	9	A	Wycombe W	L	0-3	0-0	8		5512
39	16	A	Preston NE	L	0-2	0-1	8		7020
40	23	H	Colchester U	L	1-2	0-1	9	Watkiss	2980
41	30	A	Lincoln C	W	2-1	1-0	8	Marsh, Butler	2665
42	May 7	H	Mansfield T	L	0-2	0-1	10		4304

Final League Position: 10

GOALSCORERS

League (48): Peer 8, Lightbourne 7, Lillis 6, McDonald 6, Wright 5, Marsh 4, Butler 3, Cecere 2, O'Connor 2 (2 pens), Watkiss 2, Gayle J 1, Keister 1, Smith 1.
Coca-Cola Cup (1): McDonald 1.
FA Cup (4): Lightbourne 2, McDonald 1, Wright 1.

Gayle M 9 + 1	Evans 41	Marsh 39	Watkiss 38 + 1	Ryder 20 + 6	Smith 35 + 1	Ntamark 34 + 3	Tinkler 6	Cecere 4 + 2	Reece 6	McDonald 34 + 1	O'Hara 15 + 6	Gayle J 4	Wright 16 + 13	Knight 1 + 1	Peer 33	Keister 17 + 5	Lightbourne 34 + 1	Walker 31	Butler 9 + 6	Lillis 14 + 10	Byrne 5	Saunders 1 + 1	O'Connor 14	Livingstone 2 + 1	Match No.
1	2	3	4	5	6	7	8	9	10	11	12														1
1	2	3	4	5	6	7	8	14	10	11	12	9													2
1	2	3	4	5	6	7	8	12	10	11		9	14												3
1	2		4	5	3	7	8		10	11	6	9	12												4
1	2	3	4	5	6	7	8		10	11		9	12												5
1	2		4	5	6	3	8	9	10	11			7	12											6
1		3	4	5	6	7		9		11			8	2	10	12									7
1	2	3	4	5	6	7		9		11			8		10	12	14								8
1	2	3	4		6	7				11	5		9		10		8								9
14	2	3	4		6	7				11	5				10	9	8	1	12						10
	2	3	4		6	7				11	5		9		10		8	1							11
	2	3	4		6	7				11	5		9		10		8	1		12					12
	2	3	4	12	6	7				11	5		9		10		8	1		14					13
	2	3	4	5		7				11					10	6	8	1		9					14
	2	3	4	6		7				11			12		10	5	8	1		9					15
	2	3	4	6		7				11			9		10	5	8	1		12					16
	2	3	4	6		7				11			9		10	5	8	1		12					17
	2	3	4	6	12	7				11			9		10	5	8	1		14					18
	2	3		4	6	7							9		10	5	8	1		11					19
	2	3	12	4	6	7				11			14		10	5	9	1		8					20
	2	3	4		6	7				11			12		10	5	9	1		8					21
	2	3	4		6	7				11			12		10	5	9	1		8					22
	2	3	4	12	6	7					14		11		10	5	9	1		8					23
	2	3	4	12	6	7					14		11		10	5	9	1		8					24
	2	3	4		6	7					14		11		10	5	9	1	12	8					25
	2	3	4	12	6	7				11			14		10	5	9	1		8					26
	2	3	4	7	6					11	5				10		9	1	12	8					27
	2	3	4	12	6					11					10	5	9	1		8	7	14			28
	2		4	12	6						3				10	14	9	1		8	7	11	5		29
	2	3	4		6	7							12			5	9	1	14	8	11		10		30
	2	3		4	6	7					12		8		5		9	1	14		11		10		31
	2	3	6	4		7				12	5		8				9	1		14	11		10		32
	2	3	4	6		7				11	5						8	1	9				10		33
	2	3		4	6	12				11	5		14		10		9	1	8				7		34
	2	3	4		6	12				11	5				10		9	1	8	14			7		35
	2	3	4		6					11	5		12		10		9	1	8				7		36
	2	3	4		6					11	5		12		10		8	1	9				7		37
	2	3	4		6	5				11			12		10		8	1	9				7		38
	2	3	4		6	5				11					10	9	8	1	12	14			7		39
	2	3	4		6	12				11	5				10		7	1	9				8	14	40
	2	3	4		6	5				11					10	12	7		9	14			8	1	41
	2	3	4		6	5				11					10	12	7		9	14			8	1	42

Coca-Cola Cup	First Round	Exeter C (h)	0-0
		(a)	1-2
FA Cup	First Round	Wrexham (a)	1-1
		(h)	2-0
	Second Round	Scunthorpe U (h)	1-1
		(a)	0-0

WALSALL

Player and Position	Ht	Wt	Birth Date	Birth Place	Source	Clubs	League App	League Gls
Goalkeepers								
Dean Greygoose†	5 11	11 05	18 12 64	Thetford	Apprentice	Cambridge U	26	—
						Orient (loan)	—	—
						Lincoln C (loan)	6	—
						Orient	1	—
						C Palace	—	—
						Crewe Alex	205	—
					Northwich V	Walsall	—	—
Glen Livingstone‡	6 2	14 01	13 10 72	Birmingham	Trainee	Aston Villa	—	—
						York C	—	—
						Walsall	3	—
James Walker	5 11	11 00	9 7 73	Mansfield	Trainee	Notts Co	—	—
						Walsall	31	—
Defenders								
Wayne Evans	5 10	12 05	25 8 71	Welshpool	Welshpool	Walsall	41	—
Richard Knight	5 9	10 13	31 8 74	Burton	Trainee	Walsall	29	1
Steve O'Hara*	6 1	12 02	21 2 71	Lanark	Trainee	Walsall	122	4
Stuart Ryder	6 0	12 01	6 11 73	Sutton Coldfield	Trainee	Walsall	48	—
Dean Smith	6 0	12 01	19 3 71	West Bromwich	Trainee	Walsall	142	2
Stuart Watkiss	6 2	13 08	8 5 66	Wolverhampton	Apprentice	Wolverhampton W	2	—
					Rushall Olympic	Walsall	39	2
Midfield								
David Edwards	5 10	10 08	13 1 74	Bridgnorth	Trainee	Walsall	27	1
John Keister	5 8	11 00	11 11 70	Manchester	Faweh FC	Walsall	22	1
Jason Lillis*	5 11	11 10	1 10 69	Chatham	Trainee	Gillingham	29	3
						Maidstone U	75	18
						Carlisle U (loan)	4	1
					Sittingbourne	Walsall	24	6
Kevin MacDonald‡	6 1	12 06	22 12 60	Inverness	Inverness Caley	Leicester C	138	8
						Liverpool	40	1
						Leicester C (loan)	3	—
						Rangers (loan)	3	—
						Coventry C	31	—
						Cardiff C (loan)	8	—
						Walsall	53	6
Steven McManus	5 11	11 07	8 3 75	Nottingham	Trainee	Walsall	1	—
Chris Marsh	5 10	12 11	14 1 70	Dudley	Trainee	Walsall	157	10
Charlie Ntamark	5 8	11 12	22 7 64	Paddington		Walsall	161	10
Martyn O'Connor	5 8	10 08	10 12 67	Walsall	Bromsgrove R	Crystal Palace	2	—
						Walsall (loan)	10	1
						Walsall	14	2
Dean Peer	6 2	12 00	8 8 69	Dudley	Trainee	Birmingham C	120	8
						Mansfield T (loan)	10	—
						Walsall	33	8
John Tinkler	5 8	11 07	24 8 68	Trimdon		Hartlepool U	170	7
						Preston NE	24	2
						Walsall	6	—
Steven Winter‡	5 7	10 03	26 10 73	Bristol	Trainee	Walsall	18	—
Forwards								
Martin Butler	5 10	10 12	15 9 74	Wordsley	Trainee	Walsall	15	3
David Byrne (on loan from Partick T)	5 8	10 09	5 3 61	London		Walsall	5	—
Kyle Lightbourne‡	6 2	11 00	29 9 68	Bermuda		Scarborough	19	3
						Walsall	35	7
Rod McDonald	5 10	12 07	20 3 67	London	Colne Dynamoes	Walsall	149	41
Evran Wright*	5 9	11 00	17 1 64	Wolverhampton	Halesowen	Walsall	29	5

WALSALL

Colours: Red and white striped shirts with white sleeves, black shorts, red stockings. **Change colours:** Blue and black striped shirts, black shorts, blue stockings.

Foundation: Two of the leading clubs around Walsall in the 1880s were Walsall Swifts (formed 1877) and Walsall Town (formed 1879). The Swifts were winners of the Birmingham Senior Cup in 1881, while the Town reached the 4th round (5th round modern equivalent) of the FA Cup in 1883. These clubs amalgamated as Walsall Town Swifts in 1888, becoming simply Walsall in 1895.

First Football League game: 3 September, 1892, Division 2, v Darwen (h) L 1-2 – Hawkins; Withington, Pinches; Robinson, Whitrick, Forsyth; Marshall, Holmes, Turner, Gray (1), Pangbourn.

Did you know: Arguably Walsall's two most consistent seasons came in those immediately after the Second World War. They finished fifth in 1946–47 and third the following season. Yet in the two pre-war terms they had been 21st in the same Division 3 (South).

Managers (and Secretary-Managers)
H. Smallwood 1888–91*, A. G. Burton 1891–93, J. H. Robinson 1893–95, C. H. Ailso 1895–96*, A. E. Parsloe 1896–97*, L. Ford 1897–98*, G. Hughes 1898–99*, L. Ford 1899–1901*, J. E. Shutt 1908–13*, Haydn Price 1914–20, Joe Burchell 1920–26, David Ashworth 1926–27, Jack Torrance 1927–28, James Kerr 1928–29, S. Scholey 1929–30, Peter O'Rourke 1930–32, G. W. Slade 1932–34, Andy Wilson 1934–37, Tommy Lowes 1937–44, Harry Hibbs 1944–51, Tony McPhee 1951, Brough Fletcher 1952–53, Major Frank Buckley 1953–55, John Love 1955–57, Billy Moore 1957–64, Alf Wood 1964, Reg Shaw 1964–68, Dick Graham 1968, Ron Lewin 1968–69, Billy Moore 1969–72, John Smith 1972–73, Doug Fraser 1973–77, Dave Mackay 1977–78, Alan Ashman 1978, Frank Sibley 1979, Alan Buckley 1979–86, Neil Martin (joint manager with Buckley) 1981–82, Tommy Coakley 1986–88, John Barnwell 1989–90, Kenny Hibbitt May 1990–

Trainees
Baker, James A; Gardiner, Nathan; Gardner, Richard R; Jones, Mark; Lake, Stuart; Matthews, Stuart J; Pickett, James A; Power, Andrew J; Richards, David S; Rollo, James S; Roper, Ian R; Smith, Christopher G; Thomas, Matthew A; Westwood, John T.

****Non-Contract**
Green, Ronald R.

Associated Schoolboys
Bagnall, Mark G; Birthwhistle, Luke; Fairfield, Adrian; Faulconbridge, Andrew D; Fieldhouse, Mark V; Johnston, Gavin; Leeman, Kevin A; Leighton, Adam J; Peach, Richard F; Shilvock, Matthew W. G; Stanley, Darren J; Tarbuck, Wayne M; Webb, Neal; Williams, David P.

Associated Schoolboys who have accepted the Club's offer of a Traineeship/Contract
Baldwin, David J; Bentley, Gavin; Blakeley, Andrew P; Brant, Gavin J; Davies, Stuart J; Derry, Leighton W; Edwards, Gavin D; Keates, Dean S; Rowland, Stephen J; Wright, Gavin E.

**Non-Contract Players who are retained must be re-signed before they are eligible to play in League matches.

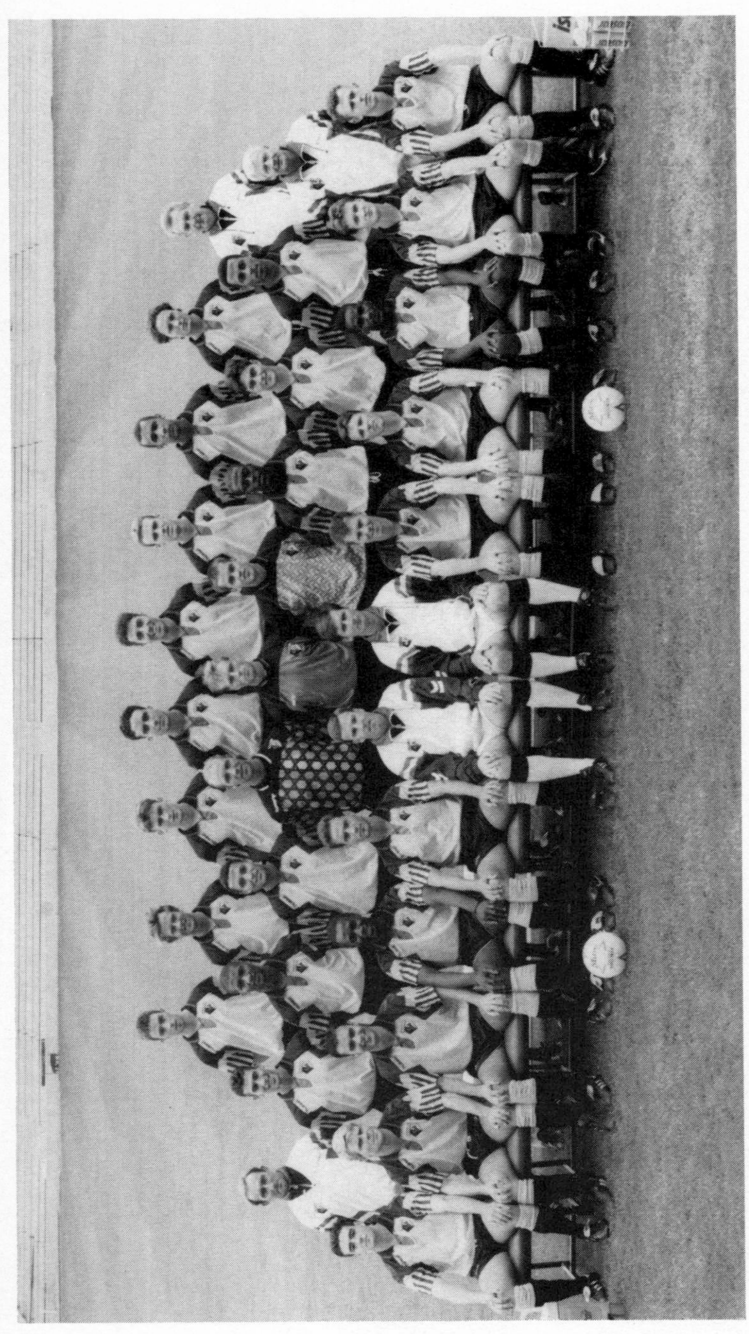

WATFORD 1993–94 *Back row (left to right):* Gerard Lavin, John White, Kevin Slinn, Julian Alsford, Barry Ashby, Robert Page, Daniel Nwaokolo, James Meara, Ken Brooks (Kit Manager). *Centre row:* Stuart Murdoch (Reserve Team Manager), Lee Nogan, Roger Willis, Jason Soloman, Simon Sheppard, Perry Suckling, Paul Wilkerson, Paul Furlong, Richard Johnson, Ken Charlery, Billy Hails (Physio).

Front row: Craig McIntosh, Andy Hessenthaler, Darren Bazeley, Keith Dublin, David Holdsworth, Kenny Jackett (Assistant Manager), Glenn Roeder (Manager), Nigel Gibbs, Gary Porter, Bruce Dyer, Alex Inglethorpe, Jason Drysdale.

Division 1 **WATFORD**

Vicarage Road Stadium, Watford WD1 8ER. Telephone Watford (0923) 230933. Fax 0923 239759. Hornet Hotline 0891 121030. Ticket Office: 220393. Club shop: 220847. Catering: 221457. Junior Hornets Club: 253836. Marketing: 225761.

Ground capacity: 20,000.

Record attendance: 34,099 v Manchester U, FA Cup 4th rd (replay), 3 February 1969.

Record receipts: £115,000 v Leeds U, Coca Cola Cup 3rd rd, 10 November 1992.

Pitch measurements: 115yd × 75yd.

Life President: Elton John.

Chairman: Dr. S. R. Timperley PHD.

Directors: G. S. Lawson Rogers, C. D. Lissack, J. Petchey, M. Winwood.

Chief Executive: Eddie Plumley FAAI.

Team Manager: Glenn Roeder. ***Assistant Manager:*** Kenny Jackett.

Reserve Team Coach: Stuart Murdoch. ***Youth Team Coach:*** Keith Waugh. ***Physio:*** Billy Hails.

Director of Marketing: Brian Blower. ***Public Relations Manager:*** Ed Coan.

Year Formed: 1891*(*see Foundation*). ***Turned Professional:*** 1897. ***Ltd Co.:*** 1909.

Club Nickname: 'The Hornets'.

Previous Name: West Herts.

Previous Ground: 1899, Cassio Road; 1922, Vicarage Road.

Record League Victory: 8–0 v Sunderland, Division 1, 25 September 1982 – Sherwood; Rice, Rostron, Taylor, Terry, Bolton, Callaghan (2), Blissett (4), Jenkins (2), Jackett, Barnes.

Record Cup Victory: 10–1 v Lowestoft T, FA Cup, 1st rd, 27 November 1926 – Yates; Prior, Fletcher (1); F. Smith, 'Bert' Smith, Strain; Stephenson, Warner (3), Edmonds (2), Swan (2), Daniels (1). (1 og).

Chairman: B. E. Fearn. ***Vice-chairman:*** L. V. Pickering.
Record Defeat: 0–10 v Wolverhampton W, FA Cup 1st rd (replay), 13 January 1912.

Most League Points (2 for a win): 71, Division 4, 1977–78.

Most League Points (3 for a win): 80, Division 2, 1981–82.

Most League Goals: 92, Division 4, 1959–60.

Highest League Scorer in Season: Cliff Holton, 42, Division 4, 1959–60.

Most League Goals in Total Aggregate: Luther Blissett, 158, 1976–83, 1984–88, 1991–92.

Most Capped Player: John Barnes, 31 (73), England and Kenny Jackett, 31, Wales.

Most League Appearances: Luther Blissett, 415, 1976–83, 1984–88, 1991–92.

Record Transfer Fee Received: £1,250,000 from Crystal Palace for Bruce Dyer, March 1994.

Record Transfer Fee Paid: £550,000 to AC Milan for Luther Blissett, August 1984.

Football League Record: 1920 Original Member of Division 3; 1921–58 Division 3 (S); 1958–60 Division 4; 1960–69 Division 3; 1969–72 Division 2; 1972–75 Division 3; 1975–78 Division 4; 1978–79 Division 3; 1979–82 Division 2; 1982–88 Division 1; 1988–92 Division 2; 1992– Division 1.

Honours: *Football League:* Division 1 – Runners-up 1982–83; Division 2 – Runners-up 1981–82; Division 3 – Champions 1968–69; Runners-up 1978–79; Division 4 – Champions 1977–78; Promoted 1959–60 (4th). *FA Cup:* Runners-up 1984. *Football League Cup:* Semi-final 1978–79. **European Competitions:** *UEFA Cup:* 1983–84.

WATFORD 1993—94 LEAGUE RECORD

Match No.	Date	Venue	Opponents	Result		H/T Score	Lg. Pos.	Goalscorers	Attendance
1	Aug 14	A	Luton T	L	1-2	0-0	—	Furlong	9149
2	21	H	Barnsley	L	0-2	0-2	23		5937
3	28	A	Oxford U	W	3-2	1-2	20	Charlery, Alsford, Porter	5159
4	Sept 4	H	Charlton Ath	D	2-2	1-1	20	Porter, Inglethorpe	6925
5	7	H	Wolverhampton W	W	1-0	1-0	—	Venus (og)	7870
6	11	A	Grimsby T	D	2-2	0-1	10	Porter, Nogan	4783
7	18	H	Notts Co	W	3-1	2-0	8	Furlong 2, Lavin	6959
8	25	H	Sunderland	D	1-1	1-1	7	Ashby	7694
9	Oct 2	A	Millwall	L	1-4	0-2	9	Nogan	7707
10	10	H	Middlesbrough	W	2-0	0-0	—	Furlong, Dyer	7582
11	16	A	Birmingham C	L	0-1	0-0	10		12,823
12	23	H	Bolton W	W	4-3	0-2	8	Porter 3 (1 pen), Charlery	7492
13	30	A	WBA	L	1-4	1-2	10	Soloman	15,299
14	Nov 3	A	Southend U	L	0-2	0-2	—		4584
15	6	H	Stoke C	L	1-3	1-1	14	Dyer	7767
16	20	H	Bristol C	D	1-1	1-0	17	Soloman	6045
17	28	H	Crystal Palace	L	1-3	0-1	—	Nogan	7485
18	Dec 4	A	Stoke C	L	0-2	0-0	22		13,465
19	7	A	Portsmouth	L	0-2	0-1	—		8242
20	11	A	Wolverhampton W	L	0-2	0-2	23		17,460
21	19	H	Luton T	D	2-2	2-0	—	Dyer 2	7567
22	27	A	Leicester C	D	4-4	0-1	21	Dyer 2, Furlong 2	21,744
23	28	H	Peterborough U	W	2-1	1-0	19	Furlong 2	7155
24	Jan 1	A	Tranmere R	L	1-2	0-1	21	Furlong	8271
25	3	H	Nottingham F	L	1-2	1-0	21	Cooper (og)	14,539
26	15	H	Birmingham C	W	5-2	3-0	18	Porter, Hessenthaler, Furlong 3 (1 pen)	7636
27	22	A	Middlesbrough	D	1-1	0-1	19	Furlong	8089
28	29	A	Derby Co	W	2-1	0-1	18	Soloman, Furlong	15,308
29	Feb 5	A	Bolton W	L	1-3	0-0	19	Inglethorpe	10,150
30	12	H	WBA	L	0-1	0-1	20		10,087
31	19	H	Derby Co	L	3-4	2-1	20	Bazeley, Ashby, Furlong	8277
32	25	A	Charlton Ath	L	1-2	0-2	20	Porter	7546
33	Mar 5	H	Oxford U	W	2-1	1-1	20	Hessenthaler, Ford M (og)	7049
34	12	A	Notts Co	L	0-1	0-1	21		6378
35	15	H	Grimsby T	L	0-3	0-1	—		5109
36	19	A	Sunderland	L	0-2	0-0	23		16,479
37	26	H	Millwall	W	2-0	1-0	21	Lavin, Hessenthaler	9036
38	30	A	Nottingham F	L	1-2	0-2	—	Porter	23,044
39	Apr 2	H	Leicester C	D	1-1	0-0	21	Bailey	8645
40	5	A	Peterborough U	W	4-3	1-1	—	Furlong, Dublin, Lavin, Bailey	7734
41	9	H	Tranmere R	L	1-2	0-1	21	Bailey	7347
42	12	A	Barnsley	W	1-0	0-0	—	Furlong	4380
43	16	H	Southend U	W	3-0	3-0	19	Bailey, Mooney, Foster	7694
44	23	A	Bristol C	D	1-1	0-1	19	Furlong	8324
45	30	H	Portsmouth	W	1-0	1-0	19	Hessenthaler	10,141
46	May 8	A	Crystal Palace	W	2-0	0-0	19	Hessenthaler, Mooney	28,749

Final League Position: 19

GOALSCORERS

League (66): Furlong 18 (1 pen), Porter 9 (1 pen), Dyer 6, Hessenthaler 5, Bailey 4, Lavin 3, Nogan 3, Soloman 3, Ashby 2, Charlery 2, Inglethorpe 2, Mooney 2, Alsford 1, Bazeley 1, Dublin 1, Foster 1, own goals 3.
Coca-Cola Cup (8): Dyer 2, Furlong 1, Hessenthaler 1, Holdsworth 1, Nogan 1, Porter 1, Soloman 1.
FA Cup (1): Porter 1 (pen).

Sheppard 18	Lavin 46	Drysdale 19	Johnson 22 + 5	Holdsworth 28	Ashby 16 + 1	Bazeley 6 + 4	Charlery 15 + 1	Furlong 38	Porter 43	Soloman 21 + 4	Nogan 21 + 5	Dublin 30 + 3	Hessenthaler 42	Dyer 29	Alsford 7 + 1	Inglethorpe 1 + 8	Page 4	Willis 2 + 2	Harding 1 + 1	Watson 17	Suckling 2	McCarthy 8 + 1	Digweed 26	Barnes 5	Ramage 11 + 2	Mooney 10	Foster 6	Millen 10	Bailey 2 + 6	Match No.
1	2	3	4	5	6	7	8	9	10	11	12	14																		1
1	2	3		5	6		8	9	10	11			4	7																2
1	2			5			8	9	10	11	12	3	4	7	6															3
1	3			5			8	9	10	11	7	2	4		6	12														4
1	3			5			8	9	10	11	7	2	4		6	12														5
1	3				5		8	9	10	11	7	2	4		6															6
1	3			5	6		8	9	10	11		2	4	7																7
1	3		11	5	6		8	9	10		12	2	4	7																8
1	3		14	5	6		8	9	10	11	12	2	4	7																9
1	3		12	5	6			9	10	11	8	2	4	7																10
1	3		12	5	6			9	10	11	8		4	7		14	2													11
1	3				6		12		10	11	8	2	4	7	5	9														12
1	3				6		8		10	11	9	2	4	7	5			12												13
1	3				6		9		10	8		2	4	7	5				11											14
1	2	3		5	12		9		10	8	11	6	4	7					14											15
	2		4	5			9		10	8		3		7				11		6	1									16
	2		4	5			9		10	8	12	3		7				11		6	1	14								17
1	2		4	5			9			8	10	3		7				12		6		11								18
1	2		10	5				9		8	11		4	7	12					6		3								19
1	2		10	5				9		8	11	6	4	7								3								20
	2		8	5				9	10		11		4	7						6		3	1							21
	2		8	5				9	10	12	11		4	7						6		3	1							22
	2		8	5				9	10		11		4	7						6		3	1							23
	2		8	5				9	10		11		4	7						6		3	1							24
	2		8	5				9	10	12	11		4	7						6		3	1							25
	2		8	5				9	10	12	11	14	4	7						6			1	3						26
	2		8	5				9	10		11		4	7						6			1	3						27
	2		8	5		11		9	10	12			4	7						6			1	3						28
	2			5		11		9	10	8		12	4	7		14				6			1	3						29
	2			5	3	11		9	10	8			4	7		12				6			1							30
	2	11			5	8		9	10				4	7		12				6			1	3						31
	2	3			6	11		9	10				4	7		12				5			1		8					32
	2	3			6	12		9	10		11	5	4	7									1		8					33
	2	3	7		6			9	10		11	5	4			12							1		8					34
	2	3	7	6		12		9	10		11	5	4										1		8					35
	2	3	7			12		9	10			5	4							6			1		8	11				36
	2	3						9	10			5	7										1		8	11	4	6	12	37
	2	3		4				9	10			5	7										1		8	11		6	12	38
	2	3						9	10			5	7				4						1		8	11		6	12	39
	2	3	14					9	10			5	7				4						1		8	11		6	12	40
	2	3						9	10			5	7				4						1		8	11		6	12	41
	2	3	12					9	10			5	7										1		8		4	6	11	42
	2	3	8			12			10			5	7										1			9	4	6	11	43
	2	3	8					9	10			5	7										1			11	4	6		44
	2	3	8					9	10			5	7										1		14	11	4	6	12	45
	2	3	8					9	10			5	7										1		12	11	4	6		46

Coca-Cola Cup	First Round	Brentford (a)	2-2
		(h)	3-1
	Second Round	Millwall (h)	0-0
		(a)	3-4
FA Cup	Third Round	West Ham U (a)	1-2

WATFORD

Player and Position	Ht	Wt	Birth Date	Birth Place	Source	Clubs	League App	League Gls
Goalkeepers								
Perry Digweed	6 0	11 04	26 10 59	London	Apprentice	Fulham	15	—
						Brighton	179	—
						WBA (loan)	—	—
						Charlton Ath (loan)	—	—
						Newcastle U (loan)	—	—
						Chelsea (loan)	3	—
						Wimbledon (loan)	—	—
						Wimbledon	—	—
						Watford	26	—
Simon Sheppard	6 4	14 03	7 8 73	Clevedon	Trainee	Watford	23	—
						Scarborough (loan)	9	—
Perry Suckling*	6 2	13 02	12 10 65	Leyton	Apprentice	Coventry C	27	—
						Manchester C	39	—
						Crystal Palace	59	—
						West Ham U (loan)	6	—
						Brentford (loan)	8	—
						Watford	39	—
Keith Waugh	6 1	13 00	27 10 56	Sunderland	Apprentice	Sunderland	—	—
						Peterborough U	195	—
						Sheffield U	99	—
						Bristol C (loan)	3	—
						Cambridge U (loan)	4	—
						Bristol C	167	—
						Coventry C	1	—
						Watford	7	—
Paul Wilkerson	6 3	13 11	11 12 74	Hertford		Watford	—	—
Defenders								
Julian Alsford	6 2	13 06	24 12 72	Poole		Watford	13	1
David Barnes	5 10	11 01	16 11 61	London	Apprentice	Coventry C	9	—
						Ipswich T	17	—
						Wolves	88	4
						Aldershot	69	1
						Sheffield U	82	1
						Watford	5	—
Jason Drysdale	5 10	12 00	17 11 70	Bristol	Trainee	Watford	145	11
Keith Dublin	6 0	12 10	29 1 66	Wycombe	Apprentice	Chelsea	51	—
						Brighton	132	5
						Watford	168	2
Colin Foster	6 4	14 01	16 7 64	Chislehurst	Apprentice	Orient	174	10
						Nottingham F	72	5
						West Ham U	93	5
						Notts Co (loan)	9	—
						Watford	6	1
Nigel Gibbs	5 7	11 01	20 11 65	St Albans	Apprentice	Watford	271	3
David Holdsworth	6 1	12 04	8 11 68	London	Trainee	Watford	192	8
Craig McIntosh*	5 8	12 04	30 6 75	Watford	Trainee	Watford	—	—
Keith Millen	6 2	12 04	26 9 66	Croydon	Juniors	Brentford	305	17
						Watford	10	—
Danny Nwaokolo*	5 11	11 10	11 10 73	London	Trainee	Watford	—	—
Robert Page	6 0	11 08	3 9 74	Llwyn	Trainee	Watford	4	—
Glenn Roeder†	6 2	13 09	13 12 55	Woodford	Apprentice	Orient	115	4
						QPR	157	17
						Notts Co (loan)	4	—
						Newcastle U	193	8
						Watford	78	2
						Leyton Orient	8	—
						Gillingham	6	—
						Watford	—	—
Jason Soloman	6 0	11 10	6 10 70	Welwyn	Trainee	Watford	98	5
Mark Watson	6 0	12 06	8 9 70	Vancouver		Watford	17	—
Midfield								
Andy Hessenthaler	5 7	11 00	17 8 65	Gravesend	Redbridge Forest	Watford	122	9
Richard Johnson	5 10	11 13	27 4 74	Kurri, Kurri	Trainee	Watford	30	—
Gerard Lavin	5 9	10 07	5 2 74	Corby	Trainee	Watford	75	3

WATFORD

Colours: Yellow shirts, black shorts, black stockings. **Change colours:** Navy/white (striped design) shirts, white shorts, white stockings.

Foundation: Tracing this club's foundation proves difficult. Nowadays it is suggested that Watford was formed as Watford Rovers in 1891. Another version is that Watford Rovers were not forerunners of the present club whose history began in 1898 with the amalgamation of West Herts and Watford St. Mary's.

First Football League game: 28 August, 1920, Division 3, v QPR (a) W 2-1 – Williams; Horseman, F. Gregory; Bacon, Toone, Wilkinson; Bassett, Ronald (1), Hoddinott, White (1), Waterall.

Did you know: Watford's first trophy for 45 years was the Football Combination Division 2 title in 1959–60. They scored 107 goals in 38 matches and John Fairbrother had 40 to his credit alone.

Managers (and Secretary-Managers)
John Goodall 1903–10, Harry Kent 1910–26, Fred Pagnam 1926–29, Neil McBain 1929–37, Bill Findlay 1938–47, Jack Bray 1947–48, Eddie Hapgood 1948–50, Ron Gray 1950–51, Haydn Green 1951–52, Len Goulden 1952–55 (GM to 1956), Johnny Paton 1955–56, Neil McBain 1956–59, Ron Burgess 1959–63, Bill McGarry 1963–64, Ken Furphy 1964–71, George Kirby 1971–73, Mike Keen 1973–77, Graham Taylor 1977–87, Dave Bassett 1987–88, Steve Harrison 1988–90, Colin Lee 1990, Steve Perryman 1990–93, Glenn Roeder July 1993–

Player and Position	*Ht*	*Wt*	*Birth Date*	*Birth Place*	*Source*	*Clubs*	*League App*	*League Gls*
Jim Meara*	5 7	10 06	7 10 72	London	Trainee	Watford	2	—
Gary Porter	5 6	10 06	6 3 66	Sunderland	Apprentice	Watford	324	43
John White	5 8	11 03	9 9 74	Honiton	Trainee	Watford	—	—
Forwards								
Darren Bazeley	5 10	11 02	5 10 72	Northampton	Trainee	Watford	74	8
Paul Furlong	6 0	12 11	1 10 68	London	Enfield	Coventry C	37	4
						Watford	79	37
Alex Inglethorpe	5 10	11 07	14 11 71	Epsom	School	Watford	12	2
Lee Nogan	5 10	11 00	21 5 69	Cardiff	Apprentice	Oxford U	64	10
						Brentford (loan)	11	2
						Southend U (loan)	6	1
						Watford	91	19
						Southend U (loan)	5	—
Craig Ramage	5 9	11 08	30 3 70	Derby	Trainee	Derby Co	42	4
						Wigan Ath (loan)	10	2
						Watford	13	—
Kevin Slinn*	5 11	11 00	2 9 74	Northampton	Trainee	Watford	—	—

Trainees
Allen, Mark J; Birch, Terry; Calderhead, Robert; Carter Martin J; Connolly, David J; Fitzgerald, Gary M; Gould, Darran; Hutchins, Neil; Kuntz, Trevor P. J; Marshall, Robert J; McGiven, Joseph C. M; Parkin, Steven C; Simpson, Colin R; Vier, Matthew P; Ward, Lee J;

****Non-Contract**
Roeder, Glenn V.

Associated Schoolboys
Alexander, Anthony; Bromley, Danny; Donkin, Jamie; Grieves, Daniel; Grime, Dominic R; Grime, Nicholas G; Harkin, Maurice P; Johnson, Andrew; Johnson, Christopher; Jones, Mark C; Mansfield, Robert C; Moore, James J; Peart, Clive A; Perpetuini, David P; Pluck, Colin I; Robinson, Dean; Robinson, Paul P; Rogers, David A; Smith, Dean W; Ward, Darran P; Williams, Gifton H.

Associated Schoolboys who have accepted the Club's offer of a Traineeship/Contract
Andrews, Wayne M; Belgrave, Kevin; Donald, Neil G. M; Easton, Clint; Rooney, Mark J; Sargent, David G.
**Non-Contract Players who are retained must be re-signed before they are eligible to play in League matches.

WEST BROMWICH ALBION 1993–94 *Back row (left to right):* John Trewick (Reserve Team Manager), Kwame Ampadu, Wayne Fereday, Scott Darton, Darryl Burgess, Paul Raven, Gary Strodder, Carl Heggs, Bob Taylor, Norman Bodell (Chief Scout).
Centre row: Danny Thomas (Physio), Gary Hackett, Stacy Coldicott, Roy Hunter, Stuart Naylor, Derek Dudley, Tony Lange, Andy Hunt, Nicky Reid, James McCue, Ronnie Allen.
Front row: Steve Lilwall, Simon Garner, Kevin Donovan, Darren Bradley, Dennis Mortimer (Assistant Manager), Keith Burkinshaw (Manager), Ian Hamilton, Micky Mellon, Bernard McNally, Kieran O'Regan.

Division 1 WEST BROMWICH ALBION

The Hawthorns, West Bromwich B71 4LF. Telephone 021–525 8888 (all Depts). Fax: 021–553 6634.

Ground capacity: 25,500 (from December 31).

Record attendance: 64,815 v Arsenal, FA Cup 6th rd, 6 March 1937.

Record receipts: £174,235.95 v Stoke C, Div 2, 23 January 1993.

Pitch measurements: 115yd × 74yd.

President: Sir F. A. Millichip. ***Vice-president:*** John G. Silk LL.B (Lond).

Chairman: T. J. Summers. ***Vice-chairman:*** A. B. Hale.

Directors: J. W. Brandrick, C. M. Stapleton, B. Hurst, T. K. Guy.

Manager: Keith Burkinshaw. ***Assistant Manager:*** Dennis Mortimer. ***Coach:*** John Trewick. ***Physio:*** Danny Thomas.

Secretary: Dr. John J. Evans BA, PHD. (Wales).

Club Statistician: Tony Matthews. ***Commercial Manager:*** Tom Cardall.

Year Formed: 1879. ***Turned Professional:*** 1885. ***Ltd Co.:*** 1892.

Previous Name: 1879–81, West Bromwich Strollers.

Club Nicknames: 'Throstles', 'Baggies', 'Albion'.

Previous Grounds: 1879, Coopers Hill; 1879, Dartmouth Park; 1881, Bunns Field, Walsall Street; 1882, Four Acres (Dartmouth Cricket Club); 1885, Stoney Lane; 1900, The Hawthorns.

Record League Victory: 12–0 v Darwen, Division 1, 4 April 1892 – Reader; Horton, McCulloch; Reynolds (2), Perry, Groves; Bassett (3), McLeod, Nicholls (1), Pearson (4), Geddes (1). (1 og).

Record Cup Victory: 10–1 v Chatham (away), FA Cup, 3rd rd, 2 March 1889 – Roberts; Horton, Green; Timmins (1), Charles Perry, Horton; Bassett (2), Perry (1), Bayliss (2), Pearson, Wilson (3). (1 og).

Record Defeat: 3–10 v Stoke C, Division 1, 4 February 1937.

Most League Points (2 for a win): 60, Division 1, 1919–20.

Most League Points (3 for a win): 85, Division 2, 1992–93.

Most League Goals: 105, Division 2, 1929–30.

Highest League Scorer in Season: William 'Ginger' Richardson, 39, Division 1, 1935–36.

Most League Goals in Total Aggregate: Tony Brown, 218, 1963–79.

Most Capped Player: Stuart Williams, 33 (43), Wales.

Most League Appearances: Tony Brown, 574, 1963–80.

Record Transfer Fee Received: £1,500,000 from Manchester U for Bryan Robson, October 1981.

Record Transfer Fee Paid: £748,000 to Manchester C for Peter Barnes, July 1979.

Football League Record: 1888 Founder Member of Football League; 1901–02 Division 2; 1902–04 Division 1; 1904–11 Division 2; 1911–27 Division 1; 1927–31 Division 2; 1931–38 Division 1; 1938–49 Division 2; 1949–73 Division 1; 1973–76 Division 2; 1976–86 Division 1; 1986–91 Division 2; 1991–92 Division 3; 1992–93 Division 2; 1933– Division 1.

Honours: *Football League:* Division 1 – Champions 1919–20; Runners-up 1924–25, 1953–54; Division 2 – Champions 1901–02, 1910–11; Runners-up 1930–31, 1948–49; Promoted to Division 1 1975–76 (3rd). *FA Cup:* Winners 1888, 1892, 1931, 1954, 1968; Runners-up 1886, 1887, 1895, 1912, 1935. *Football League Cup:* Winners 1965–66; Runners-up 1966–67, 1969–70. **European Competitions:** *European Cup-Winners' Cup:* 1968–69; *European Fairs Cup:* 1966–67; *UEFA Cup:* 1978–79, 1979–80, 1981–82.

WEST BROMWICH ALBION 1993—94 LEAGUE RECORD

Match No.	Date	Venue	Opponents	Result		H/T Score	Lg. Pos.	Goalscorers	Attendance
1	Aug 14	A	Barnsley	D	1-1	0-0	—	Donovan	12,940
2	21	H	Oxford U	W	3-1	1-1	6	Hunt, Donovan, O'Regan	17,227
3	28	A	Stoke C	L	0-1	0-0	14		17,948
4	Sept 1	H	Southend U	D	2-2	0-0	—	Taylor 2	14,482
5	5	H	Wolverhampton W	W	3-2	1-1	—	Raven, Bradley, Donovan	25,615
6	11	A	Notts Co	L	0-1	0-0	8		9870
7	18	H	Crystal Palace	L	1-4	1-0	13	Taylor	17,873
8	25	H	Middlesbrough	D	1-1	0-0	16	Taylor	15,766
9	Oct 3	A	Derby Co	L	3-5	0-0	—	Taylor, Hunt 2	13,370
10	9	A	Millwall	L	1-2	0-1	21	Bradley	11,010
11	16	H	Peterborough U	W	3-0	0-0	18	Taylor 2, Strodder	15,134
12	23	A	Sunderland	L	0-1	0-0	22		19,505
13	30	H	Watford	W	4-1	2-1	17	Hunt 2, Hamilton, Taylor	15,299
14	Nov 2	A	Tranmere R	L	0-3	0-1	—		7882
15	6	H	Bolton W	D	2-2	2-0	19	Hunt, Taylor (pen)	15,709
16	21	H	Nottingham F	L	0-2	0-2	—		15,581
17	27	H	Portsmouth	W	4-1	2-0	19	Taylor, O'Regan, Hunt 2	13,867
18	Dec 7	A	Bolton W	D	1-1	0-0	—	Hunt	9277
19	11	A	Southend U	W	3-0	0-0	16	Hamilton, Taylor, Hunt	6807
20	19	H	Barnsley	D	1-1	0-0	—	Ashcroft	16,062
21	27	H	Bristol C	L	0-1	0-1	16		22,888
22	28	A	Birmingham C	L	0-2	0-2	17		28,228
23	Jan 1	H	Luton T	D	1-1	0-1	20	Mellon	16,138
24	3	A	Charlton Ath	L	1-2	0-0	20	Hamilton	8316
25	12	A	Leicester C	L	2-4	1-2	—	Strodder, Mellon	15,640
26	15	A	Peterborough U	L	0-2	0-0	21		7757
27	22	H	Millwall	D	0-0	0-0	21		15,172
28	Feb 1	A	Grimsby T	D	2-2	0-0	—	Taylor, Fenton	4740
29	5	H	Sunderland	W	2-1	2-0	20	Donovan, Fenton	17,089
30	12	A	Watford	W	1-0	1-0	19	Burgess	10,087
31	19	H	Leicester C	L	1-2	1-1	19	Fenton	18,513
32	25	A	Wolverhampton W	W	2-1	2-1	18	Taylor, Mardon	28,039
33	Mar 5	H	Stoke C	D	0-0	0-0	19		16,060
34	12	A	Crystal Palace	L	0-1	0-1	19		16,576
35	16	H	Notts Co	W	3-0	1-0	—	Taylor 2, Hunt	14,594
36	19	A	Middlesbrough	L	0-3	0-2	19		10,516
37	26	H	Derby Co	L	1-2	0-1	20	Donovan	17,437
38	30	H	Charlton Ath	W	2-0	0-0	—	Donovan, Hunt	14,091
39	Apr 2	A	Bristol C	D	0-0	0-0	20		8624
40	12	A	Oxford U	D	1-1	1-0	—	Taylor	9028
41	16	H	Tranmere R	L	1-3	1-1	21	Nixon (og)	15,835
42	24	A	Nottingham F	L	1-2	0-1	—	Taylor	24,018
43	27	H	Birmingham C	L	2-4	1-1	—	Donovan, Burgess	20,316
44	30	H	Grimsby T	W	1-0	1-0	21	Donovan	16,870
45	May 3	A	Luton T	L	2-3	0-1	—	Taylor, Ashcroft	10,053
46	8	A	Portsmouth	W	1-0	1-0	21	Ashcroft	17,629

Final League Position: 21

GOALSCORERS

League (60): Taylor 18 (1 pen), Hunt 12, Donovan 8, Ashcroft 3, Fenton 3, Hamilton 3, Bradley 2, Burgess 2, Mellon 2, O'Regan 2, Strodder 2, Mardon 1, Raven 1, own goal 1.
Coca-Cola Cup (6): Donovan 3, Burgess 1, Hunt 1, Taylor 1.
FA Cup (1): Hunt 1.

Lange 27 + 2	Coldicott 4 + 1	Darton 6	Bradley 24	Raven 34	Burgess 43	Hunt 35	Hamilton 41 + 1	Taylor 42	O'Regan 24 + 1	Donovan 33 + 4	Garner 4 + 4	Strodder 11 + 10	Fereday 7 + 3	Lilwall 13	Ampadu 8 + 3	Parsley 19 + 1	Ashcroft 17 + 4	Mellon 18 + 3	McNally 4 + 4	Reid 3 + 2	Naylor 19 + 1	Mardon 22	Williams 5	Hunter — + 2	Heggs 3 + 3	Fenton 7	Edwards 15	Smith 18	*Match No.*
1	2	*3*	4	5	6	7	8	9	10	11	12	14																	1
1			4	5	6	7	8	9	10	11	12	14	*2*	3															2
1			4	5	6	7	8	9	10	11			2	3															3
1			4	5		7	8	9	10	11		6	2	3															4
1			4	5	6	7	8		10	11	9	14	*2*	3	12														5
1			4	5	6	7	8		10	11	9	14	*2*	3	12														6
1			4	5	6	7	8	9	10	11			2	3	12														7
1			4	5	6	7		9	10	11				3	8	2	12												8
1			4	5	6	7	8	9	10						3	2		11											9
1			4	5	6	7	8	9	2	11					3			10	12										10
1			4		6	7	8	9	11	12		5			3	2	14	*10*											11
1			4		6	7	8	9	11			5			3	2	12	10											12
1					6	7	8	9	4	11		5		3		2	10												13
1					6	7	8	9	4	11	12	5		3		*2*	10			14									14
			4		6	7	8	9	5	11			2		3		10			12	1								15
1				5		7		9	8	*11*	12	6						10		2		4	3	14					16
1				5	2	7	11	9	8								6	10				4	3		12				17
1				5	2	7	11	9	8								6	10				4	3	12					18
1				5	2	7	11	9	8								6	10				4	3						19
1				5	2	7	8	9	11								6	10				4	3		12				20
1	14			5	2		11	9	8	12				3			6	*10*				4			7				21
1	11			5	2		8	9	7	12	10			3			6					4							22
1	8			5	2		11	9			7		12	3			6	10				4							23
1	7			5	2		11	*9*	8			14	12	3			6	10				4							24
1				5	2		11					8			6			10		3		4			7	9			25
1				5	2		11			12		4			8		6	10		3	14				7	9			26
			4	5	6		8	9		11						2		10	12		1					7	3		27
			4		6		8	9		10						2					1	5				7	3	11	28
			4		6		8	9		10		12				2			14		1	5				7	3	11	29
12			4		6		8	9		10						2					1	5				7	3	11	30
1			4		6	7		9		10						2						5				8	3	11	31
			4	*6*	2	7		9		10			12			14			8		1	5					3	11	32
			4	6	2	7	12	9		10									8		1	5					3	11	33
			4	6	2	7	8	9		10											1	5			12		3	11	34
			4	6	2	7	8	9		10											1	5					3	11	35
			4	6	2	7	8	9		10							12				1	5					3	11	36
			4	6	2	7	8	9		10								12			1	5					3	11	37
				6	2	7	8	9		10						5		4			1						3	11	38
				6	2	7	8	9	4	10		12				5					1						3	11	39
				5	6	*7*	8	9	12	10		14				2		4			1						3	11	40
				5	6	7	8	9		10		12				2		4			1						3	11	41
		3		5	6	7	8	9		10							4				1	2						11	42
		3			6	7	8	9		10		12				5	4				1	2						11	43
		3			6	7	8	9		10		2				5	4		12		1							11	44
14		3			6		8	9		10		5				2	4	12	7		*1*							11	45
1		3		6		7	8	9		10		2				5	4	12	11										46

Coca-Cola Cup	First Round	Bristol R (a)	4-1
		(h)	0-0
	Second Round	Chelsea (h)	1-1
		(a)	1-2
FA Cup	First Round	Halifax T (a)	1-2

WEST BROMWICH ALBION

Player and Position	Ht	Wt	Birth Date	Birth Place	Source	Clubs	League App	League Gls
Goalkeepers								
Neil Cutler			3 9 76	Birmingham	Trainee	WBA	—	—
Derek Dudley			2 2 70	Birmingham	VS Rugby	WBA	—	—
Tony Lange	6 0	12 09	10 12 64	London	Apprentice	Charlton Ath	12	—
						Aldershot (loan)	7	—
						Aldershot	125	—
						Wolverhampton W	8	—
						Aldershot (loan)	2	—
						Torquay U (loan)	1	—
						Portsmouth (loan)	—	—
						WBA	43	—
Stuart Naylor	6 4	12 02	6 12 62	Wetherby	Yorkshire A	Lincoln C	49	—
						Peterborough U (loan)	8	—
						Crewe Alex (loan)	38	—
						Crewe Alex (loan)	17	—
						WBA	286	—
Defenders								
Darren Bradley	5 7	11 12	24 11 65	Birmingham	Apprentice	Aston Villa	20	—
						WBA	238	9
Daryl Burgess	5 11	12 03	20 4 71	Birmingham	Trainee	WBA	156	5
Stacy Coldicott	5 11	11 02	29 4 74	Worcester	Trainee	WBA	19	—
Scott Darton			27 3 75	Ipswich	Trainee	WBA	8	—
Paul R Edwards	5 11	11 00	25 12 63	Birkenhead	Altrincham	Crewe Alex	86	6
						Coventry C	36	—
						Wolverhampton W	46	—
						WBA	15	—
Craig Herbert			9 11 75	Coventry	Torquay U	WBA	—	—
Steve Lilwall	5 11	12 00	5 2 70	Solihull	Kidderminster H	WBA	57	—
Paul Mardon	6 0	11 10	14 9 69	Bristol	Trainee	Bristol C	42	—
						Doncaster R (loan)	3	—
						Birmingham C	64	1
						WBA	22	1
Neil Parsley	5 10	10 11	25 4 66	Liverpool	Witton Alb	Leeds U	—	—
						Chester C (loan)	6	—
						Huddersfield T	57	—
						Doncaster R (loan)	3	—
						WBA	20	—
Paul Raven	6 0	12 03	28 7 70	Salisbury	School	Doncaster R	52	4
						WBA	108	9
						Doncaster R (loan)	7	—
Gary Strodder	6 1	12 06	1 4 65	Leeds	Apprentice	Lincoln C	132	6
						West Ham U	65	2
						WBA	121	7
Midfield								
Roy Hunter	5 9	11 00	29 10 73	Cleveland		WBA	9	1
Bernard McNally	5 7	10 12	17 2 63	Shrewsbury	Apprentice	Shrewsbury T	282	23
						WBA	135	10
Michael Mellon	5 8	11 03	18 3 72	Paisley	Trainee	Bristol C	35	1
						WBA	38	5
Kieran O'Regan	5 8	10 12	9 11 63	Cork	Tramore Ath	Brighton	86	2
						Swindon T	26	1
						Huddersfield T	199	25
						WBA	25	2
David Smith	5 8	10 02	29 3 68	Gloucester		Coventry C	154	19
						Bournemouth (loan)	1	—
						Birmingham C	38	3
						WBA	18	—
Forwards								
Lee Ashcroft	5 10	11 00	7 9 72	Preston	Trainee	Preston NE	91	13
						WBA	21	3
Kevin Donovan	5 7	10 10	17 12 71	Halifax	Trainee	Huddersfield T	20	1
						Halifax T (loan)	6	—
						WBA	69	14

WEST BROMWICH ALBION

Colours: Navy blue and white striped shirts, white shorts, blue and white stockings. **Change colours:** Green & yellow striped shirts, green shorts, yellow stockings.

Foundation: There is a well known story that when employees of Salter's Spring Works in West Bromwich decided to form a football club in 1879, they had to send someone to the nearby Association Football stronghold of Wednesbury to purchase a football. A weekly subscription of 2d (less than 1p) was imposed and the name of the new club was West Bromwich Strollers.

First Football League game: 8 September, 1888, Football League, v Stoke (a) W 2-0 – Roberts; J. Horton, Green; E. Horton, Perry, Bayliss; Bassett, Woodhall (1), Hendry, Pearson, Wilson (1).

Did you know: On 27 December 1893 West Bromwich Albion won 8-0 at Wolves. Scorers were Billy Bassett 3, Roddy McLeod 3, Charlie Perry and Billy Williams one each. Earlier in the season they had been held 0-0 at home by Wolves.

Managers (and Secretary-Managers)
Louis Ford 1890–92*, Henry Jackson 1892–94*, Edward Stephenson 1894–95*, Clement Keys 1895–96*, Frank Heaven 1896–1902*, Fred Everiss 1902–48, Jack Smith 1948–52, Jesse Carver 1952, Vic Buckingham 1953–59, Gordon Clark 1959–61, Archie Macaulay 1961–63, Jimmy Hagan 1963–67, Alan Ashman 1967–71, Don Howe 1971–75, Johnny Giles 1975–77, Ronnie Allen 1977, Ron Atkinson 1978–81, Ronnie Allen 1981–82, Ron Wylie 1982–84, Johnny Giles 1984–85, Ron Saunders 1986–87, Ron Atkinson 1987–88, Brian Talbot 1988–91, Bobby Gould 1991–92, Ossie Ardiles 1992–93, Keith Burkinshaw June 1993–

Player and Position	*Ht*	*Wt*	*Birth Date*	*Birth Place*	*Source*	*Clubs*	*League App*	*League Gls*
Ian Hamilton	5 9	11 03	14 12 67	Stevenage	Apprentice	Southampton	—	—
						Cambridge U	24	1
						Scunthorpe U	145	18
						WBA	88	10
Carl Heggs	6 0	11 08	11 10 70	Leicester	Paget R	WBA	26	2
Andy Hunt	6 0	11 07	9 6 70	Thurrock	Kettering T	Newcastle U	43	11
						WBA (loan)	10	9
						WBA	35	12
James McCue			29 6 75	Glasgow	Trainee	WBA	—	—
William Macdonald			17 9 76	Irvine		WBA	—	—
Bob Taylor	5 10	11 09	3 2 67	Horden	Horden CW	Leeds U	42	9
						Bristol C	106	50
						WBA	107	56

Trainees
Clarke, Stuart D; Costigan, Glyn B; Cresswell, Mark A; Davies, David; Dew, Robert A; Germaine, Gary; Godfrey, Christopher P; Harnett, David R; Harris, Lee P; Hayter, Robert A; Leonard, Matthew; Love, Brett A; Marshall, Daniel P; Owen, Darren L; Simmonds, Robert J; Skitt, Craig; Taylor, Stuart G; Trigg, Simon T; Warburton, Nicholas M; West, Simon J.

Associated Schoolboys
Bradley, John N; Brock, Christopher D; Cattell, Mark P; Cunningham, Darren; Dobson, Ryan A; Eaton, Christopher; Enever, Richard; Evans, Steven J; Field, Andrew; Giles, Martin W; Gregory, Jonathan N; Jackson, David C; Jennings, Kirk; Morris, Mark; Prosser, Gareth B; Rostill, Jason K; Somerfield, Iain; Tranter, Carl; Turner, Brendon; Walwyn, Ivan; Wareham, Scott J.

Associated Schoolboys who have accepted the Club's offer of a Traineeship/Contract
Cleverley, Jay; Hughes, Andrew W; Knight, Lee K; O'Brien, Scott; Williams, Richard; Wills, James D.

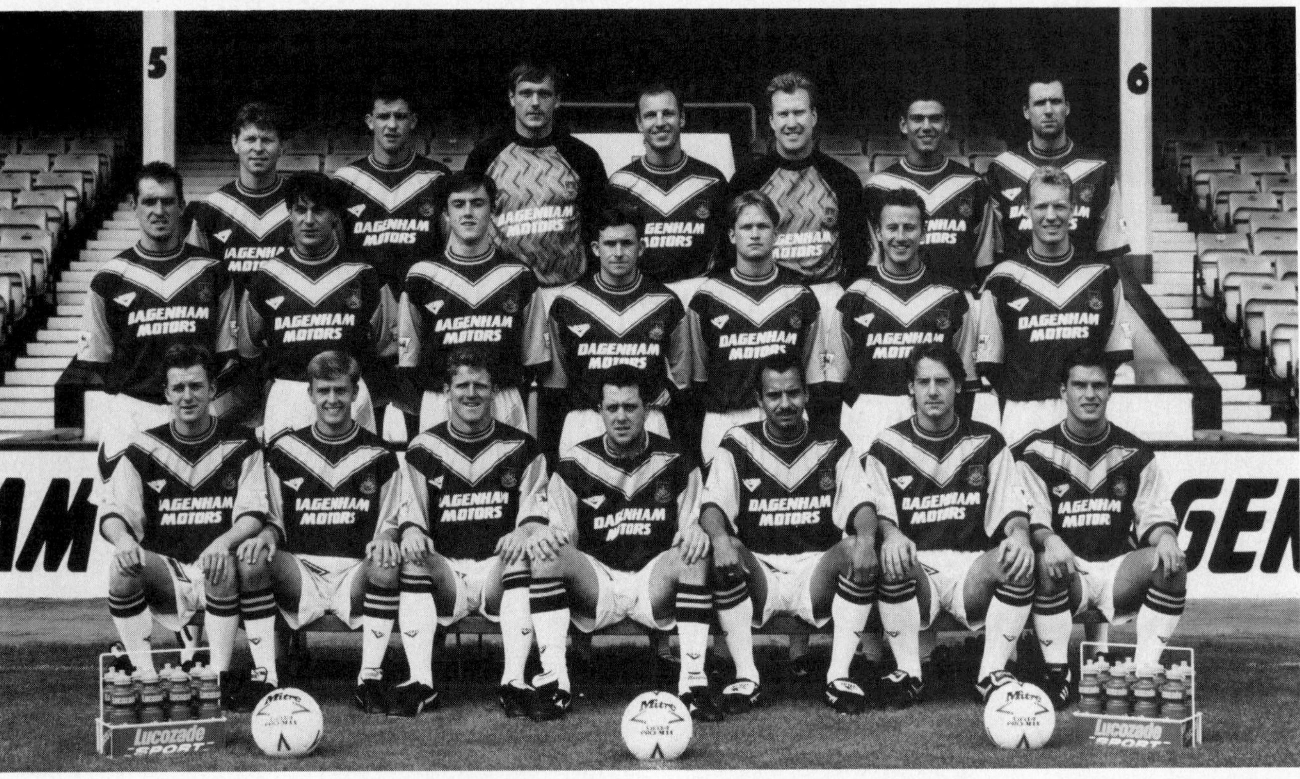

WEST HAM UNITED 1993–94 *Back row (left to right):* Tony Gale, Clive Allen, Ludek Miklosko, Alvin Martin, Gerry Peyton, Steve Jones, Colin Foster.
Centre row: Martin Allen, Trevor Morley, Danny Williamson, Matt Holmes, Paul Mitchell, Kenny Brown, Tim Breacker.
Front row: Keith Rowland, Mark Robson, Peter Butler, Julian Dicks, Dale Gordon, Ian Bishop, Steve Potts.

WEST HAM UNITED

Boleyn Ground, Green Street, Upton Park, London E13 9AZ. Telephone 081–548 2748. General: 081–472 5756. Fax 081–548 2758. Membership Office: 081–552 7640. Commercial: 081–475 0555. Hammer Line: 081 472–3322. Dial-a-seat: 081 472–2422. Football in the Community: 0898 121165 Clubcall.

Ground capacity: 20,024 (25,634 from January 1995).

Record attendance: 42,322 v Tottenham H, Division 1, 17 October 1970.

Record receipts: £146,074 v Tottenham H, League Cup 5th rd, 27 January 1987.

Pitch measurements: 112yd × 72yd.

Chairman: T. W. Brown FCIS, ATH, FCCA. ***Vice-chairman:*** M. W. Cearns ACIB.

Directors: C. J. Warner, P. J. Storrie (managing).

Manager: Billy Bonds MBE. ***Assistant Manager:*** Harry Redknapp. ***Coaches:*** Paul Hilton, Tony Carr. ***Physio:*** John Green BSC (hons) MCSP, SRP.

Secretary: Tom Finn.

Year Formed: 1895. ***Turned Professional:*** 1900. ***Ltd Co.:*** 1900.

Previous Name: Thames Ironworks FC, 1895–1900.

Club Nickname: 'The Hammers'.

Previous Ground: Memorial Recreation Ground, Canning Town: 1904 Boleyn Ground.

Record League Victory: 8–0 v Rotherham U, Division 2, 8 March 1958 – Gregory; Bond, Wright; Malcolm, Brown, Lansdowne; Grice, Smith (2), Keeble (2), Dick (4), Musgrove. 8–0 v Sunderland, Division 1, 19 October 1968 – Ferguson; Bonds, Charles; Peters, Stephenson, Moore (1); Redknapp, Boyce, Brooking (1), Hurst (6), Sissons.

Record Cup Victory: 10–0 v Bury, League Cup, 2nd rd (2nd leg), 25 October 1983 – Parkes; Stewart (1), Walford, Bonds (Orr), Martin (1), Devonshire (2), Allen, Cottee (4), Swindlehurst, Brooking (2), Pike.

Record Defeat: 2–8 v Blackburn R, Division 1, 26 December 1963.

Most League Points (2 for a win): 66, Division 2, 1980–81.

Most League Points (3 for a win): 88, Division 1, 1992–93.

Most League Goals: 101, Division 2, 1957–58.

Highest League Scorer in Season: Vic Watson, 41, Division 1, 1929–30.

Most League Goals in Total Aggregate: Vic Watson, 306, 1920–35.

Most Capped Player: Bobby Moore, 108, England.

Most League Appearances: Billy Bonds, 663, 1967–88.

Record Transfer Fee Received: £2,000,000 from Everton for Tony Cottee, July 1988.

Record Transfer Fee Paid: £1,200,000 to Celtic for Frank McAvennie, March 1989.

Football League Record: 1919 Elected to Division 2; 1923–32 Division 1; 1932–58 Division 2; 1958–78 Division 1; 1978–81 Division 2; 1981–89 Division 1; 1989–91 Division 2; 1991–93 Division 1; 1993– FA Premier League.

Honours: *Football League:* Division 1 best season: 3rd, 1985–86; Division 2 – Champions 1957–58, 1980–81; Runners-up 1922–23, 1990–91. *FA Cup:* Winners 1964, 1975, 1980; Runners-up 1922–23. *Football League Cup:* Runners-up 1966, 1981. **European Competitions:** *European Cup-Winners' Cup:* 1964–65 (winners), 1965–66, 1975–76 (runners-up), 1980–81.

WEST HAM UNITED 1993—94 LEAGUE RECORD

Match No.	Date	Venue	Opponents	Result	H/T Score	Lg. Pos.	Goalscorers	Attendance
1	Aug 14	H	Wimbledon	L 0-2	0-0	—		20,369
2	17	A	Leeds U	L 0-1	0-0	—		34,588
3	21	A	Coventry C	D 1-1	1-0	19	Gordon	12,864
4	25	H	Sheffield W	W 2-0	0-0	—	Allen C 2	19,441
5	28	H	QPR	L 0-4	0-1	17		18,084
6	Sept 1	A	Manchester U	L 0-3	0-2	—		44,613
7	11	H	Swindon T	D 0-0	0-0	19		15,777
8	18	A	Blackburn R	W 2-0	1-0	18	Chapman, Morley	14,437
9	25	A	Newcastle U	L 0-2	0-0	18		34,179
10	Oct 2	H	Chelsea	W 1-0	1-0	17	Morley	18,917
11	16	H	Aston Villa	D 0-0	0-0	17		20,416
12	23	A	Norwich C	D 0-0	0-0	17		20,175
13	Nov 1	H	Manchester C	W 3-1	2-0	—	Burrows, Chapman, Holmes	16,605
14	6	A	Liverpool	L 0-2	0-0	15		42,254
15	20	H	Oldham Ath	W 2-0	1-0	14	Martin, Morley	17,211
16	24	H	Arsenal	D 0-0	0-0	—		20,279
17	29	A	Southampton	W 2-0	2-0	—	Morley, Chapman	13,258
18	Dec 4	A	Wimbledon	W 2-1	1-0	10	Chapman 2	10,903
19	8	H	Leeds U	L 0-1	0-0	—		20,468
20	11	H	Coventry C	W 3-2	2-1	9	Breacker, Butler, Morley (pen)	17,243
21	18	A	Sheffield W	L 0-5	0-1	11		26,350
22	27	A	Ipswich T	D 1-1	0-1	12	Chapman	20,988
23	28	H	Tottenham H	L 1-3	1-2	13	Holmes	20,787
24	Jan 1	A	Everton	W 1-0	1-0	11	Breacker	19,602
25	3	H	Sheffield U	D 0-0	0-0	11		20,365
26	15	A	Aston Villa	L 1-3	1-2	24	Allen M	28,869
27	24	H	Norwich C	D 3-3	1-1	—	Sutton (og), Jones, Morley	20,738
28	Feb 12	A	Manchester C	D 0-0	0-0	12		29,118
29	25	H	Manchester U	D 2-2	0-1	12	Chapman, Morley	28,832
30	Mar 5	A	Swindon T	D 1-1	0-0	13	Morley	15,929
31	19	H	Newcastle U	L 2-4	0-1	14	Breacker, Martin	23,132
32	26	A	Chelsea	L 0-2	0-1	15		19,545
33	28	A	Sheffield U	L 2-3	2-1	—	Bishop, Holmes	13,646
34	Apr 2	H	Ipswich T	W 2-1	1-0	14	Rush, Morley	18,307
35	4	A	Tottenham H	W 4-1	1-0	13	Jones, Morley 2 (1 pen), Marsh	31,502
36	9	H	Everton	L 0-1	0-0	13		20,243
37	16	A	Oldham Ath	W 2-1	2-1	13	Allen M, Morley	11,669
38	23	H	Liverpool	L 1-2	1-1	13	Allen M	26,106
39	27	H	Blackburn R	L 1-2	0-1	—	Allen M	22,186
40	30	A	Arsenal	W 2-0	0-0	12	Morley, Allen M	33,700
41	May 3	A	QPR	D 0-0	0-0	—		10,850
42	7	H	Southampton	D 3-3	1-1	13	Williamson, Allen M, Monkou (og)	26,952

Final League Position: 13

GOALSCORERS

League (47): Morley 13 (2 pens), Chapman 7, Allen M 6, Breacker 3, Holmes 3, Allen C 2, Jones 2, Martin 2, Bishop 1, Burrows 1, Butler 1, Gordon 1, Marsh 1, Rush 1, Williamson 1, own goals 2.
Coca-Cola Cup (8): Morley 3 (1 pen), Chapman 2, Allen M 1, Boere 1, Burrows 1.
FA Cup (7): Allen M 2, Chapman 2, Bishop 1, Jones 1, Marsh 1.

Miklosko 42	Breacker 40	Dicks 7	Potts 41	Gale 31 + 1	Allen M 20 + 6	Gordon 8	Butler 26	Morley 39 + 3	Allen C 7	Holmes 33 + 1	Rowland 16 + 7	Foster 5	Robson 1 + 2	Bishop 36	Jones 3 + 5	Rush 9 + 1	Burrows 25	Chapman 26 + 4	Marsh 33	Brown 6 + 3	Boere — + 4	Martin 6 + 1	Marquis — + 1	Mitchell — + 1	Williamson 2 + 1	Match No.
1	2	3	4	5	6	7	8	9	10	11	12															1
1	2	3	*4*	6	11	7	8	9	10		12	5	14													2
1	2	3	4		6	7	8	9	10		11	5														3
1	2	3	4		6	7	8	9	10	12	11	5														4
1	2	3	4		6		8	9	10		11	5	7													5
1	2	3	4	12	6	*7*		9	10	8	11	5	14													6
1	2	3	4	5		7		9		8	11			6	10	12										7
1			4	5	12	7		11		8	2			6			3	9	10							8
1			4	5	12	7		*8*		11				6			3	9	10	2	14					9
1	2		4	5	12		7	8		11				6			3	9	10							10
1	2		4	5			7	8		11				6			3	9	10							11
1	2		4	5			7	8		11	12			6			3	9	10							12
1	2		4				7	8		11	12			6			3	9	10			5				13
1	2		4				7	8		11				6			3	9	10			5				14
1	2		4				7	8		11				6			3	9	10			5				15
1	2		4	5			7	8		11				6			3	9	10							16
1	2		4	5	10		7	8		11				6			3	9								17
1	2		4	5	10		7	8		11				6			3	9								18
1	2		4	5			7	8		11				6			3	9	10		12					19
1	2		4	5	12		7	8		11				6			3	9	10							20
1	2		4	5	12		7	8		*11*				6			3	9	10		14					21
1	2		4	5			7	8		11	12			6			3	9	10							22
1	2		4	5			7	8		11				6	12		3	9	10							23
1	2		4	5			7	8		11	12			6			3	9	10							24
1	2		4	5			7	8			11			6	12		3	9	10							25
1	2		4	5	7			8		11	3			6	12			9	10							26
1	2		4	*5*	7			12		11	3			6	8			9	10	14						27
1	2		4		7			12	10	11	3			6				9	*8*	5			14			28
1	2		4		7			8		11				6			3	9	10			5				29
1	2		4		7			8		11	12			6			3	9	10			5				30
1	2		4				7	8		11	3			6				9	10		12	5				31
1	2		4	5	*7*		8	12			11			6	14		*3*	9	10							32
1	2		4	5	12		7	8		11	3			6				9	*10*	14						33
1	2		4	5			7	9		11	3			6		8			10	12						34
1	2		4	5			7	9		11	3			6	12	8			10							35
1	2		4	5				9		11	3			6	7	8			10			12				36
1	2			5	7			9		11				6		8	3		10	4						37
1	2		4	5	7			9		11				6		8	3	12	10							38
1	2		4	5	7			9		*11*				6		8		12	10	3				14		39
1	2		4	5	7			9						6		8	3		10	11					12	40
1	2		4	5	7			9						6		8		12	10	3					11	41
1	2		4	5	7			9						6		8	3	12	10						11	42

Coca-Cola Cup	Second Round	Chesterfield (h)	5-1
		(a)	2-0
	Third Round	Nottingham F (a)	1-2
FA Cup	Third Round	Watford (h)	2-1
	Fourth Round	Notts Co (a)	1-1
		(h)	1-0
	Fifth Round	Kidderminster H (a)	1-0
	Sixth Round	Luton T (h)	0-0
		(a)	2-3

WEST HAM UNITED

Player and Position	Ht	Wt	Birth Date	Birth Place	Source	Clubs	League App	League Gls
Goalkeepers								
Tony Feuer	6 7		20 5 71	Las Vegas		West Ham U	—	—
Ludek Miklosko	6 5	14 00	9 12 61	Ostrava	Banik Ostrava	West Ham U	188	—
Gerry Peyton	6 2	13 09	20 5 56	Birmingham	Atherstone T	Burnley	30	—
						Fulham	345	—
						Southend U (loan)	10	—
						Bournemouth	202	—
						Everton	—	—
						Bolton W (loan)	1	—
						Norwich C (loan)	—	—
						Chelsea (loan)	1	—
						Brentford	19	—
						West Ham U	—	—
Defenders								
Tim Breacker	5 11	13 00	2 7 65	Bicester		Luton T	210	3
						West Ham U	137	8
Kenny Brown	5 8	11 06	11 7 67	Barking	Apprentice	Norwich C	25	—
						Plymouth Arg	126	4
						West Ham U	51	5
David Burrows	5 10	11 08	25 10 68	Dudley	Apprentice	WBA	46	1
						Liverpool	146	3
						West Ham U	25	1
Tony Gale*	6 1	13 07	19 11 59	London	Apprentice	Fulham	277	19
						West Ham U	300	5
Alvin Martin	6 1	13 07	29 7 58	Bootle	Apprentice	West Ham U	431	27
Paul Mitchell	5 10	12 00	20 10 71	Bournemouth	Trainee	Bournemouth	16	—
						West Ham U	1	—
Steven Potts	5 7	10 11	7 5 67	Hartford (USA)	Apprentice	West Ham U	236	1
Simon Webster	6 0	11 07	20 1 64	Earl Shilton	Apprentice	Tottenham H	3	—
						Exeter C (loan)	26	—
						Norwich C (loan)	—	—
						Huddersfield T	118	4
						Sheffield U	37	3
						Charlton Ath	127	7
						West Ham U	—	—
Midfield								
Martin Allen	5 10	11 00	14 8 65	Reading	School	QPR	136	16
						West Ham U	158	22
Ian Bishop	5 9	10 12	29 5 65	Liverpool	Apprentice	Everton	1	—
						Crewe Alex (loan)	4	—
						Carlisle U	132	14
						Bournemouth	44	2
						Manchester C	19	2
						West Ham U	156	9
Peter Butler	5 9	11 02	27 8 66	Halifax	Apprentice	Huddersfield T	5	—
						Cambridge U (loan)	14	1
						Bury	11	—
						Cambridge U	55	9
						Southend U	142	9
						Huddersfield T (loan)	7	—
						West Ham U	65	3
Scott Canham	5 7	11 07	5 11 74	London	Trainee	West Ham U	—	—
Darren Currie	5 9	11 07	29 11 74	Hampstead	Trainee	West Ham U	—	—
Matthew Holland	5 9	11 00	11 4 74	Bury	Trainee	West Ham U	—	—
Keith Rowland	5 10	10 00	1 9 71	Portadown	Trainee	Bournemouth	72	2
						Coventry C (loan)	2	—
						West Ham U	23	—
Matthew Rush	5 11	12 10	6 8 71	Dalston	Trainee	West Ham U	15	2
						Cambridge U (loan)	20	1
						Swansea C (loan)	13	—
Danny Williamson	5 10	11 06	5 12 73	London	Trainee	West Ham U	3	1
						Doncaster R (loan)	13	1
Forwards								
Jeroen Boere	6 3	13 05	18 11 67	Arnheim	Go Ahead	West Ham U	4	—
						Portsmouth (loan)	5	—

WEST HAM UNITED

Colours: Claret shirts, white shorts, white stockings. **Change colours:** Blue shirts, blue shorts, blue stockings.

Foundation: Thames Ironworks FC was formed by employees of this shipbuilding yard in 1895 and entered the FA Cup in their initial season at Chatham and the London League in their second. Short of funds, the club was wound up in June 1900 and relaunched a month later as West Ham United. Connection with the Ironworks was not finally broken until four years later.

First Football League game: 30 August, 1919, Division 2, v Lincoln City (h) D 1-1 – Hufton; Cope, Lee; Lane, Fenwick, McCrae; D. Smith, Moyes (1), Puddefoot, Morris, Bradshaw.

Did you know: On 26 February 1994 West Ham United were watched by their highest crowd of the season when 28,832 witnessed the 2-2 draw with Manchester United, the first competitive match to be played in front of the new Bobby Moore stand.

Managers (and Secretary-Managers)
Syd King 1902–32, Charlie Paynter 1932–50, Ted Fenton 1950–61, Ron Greenwood 1961–74 (continued as GM to 1977), John Lyall 1974–89, Lou Macari 1989–90, Billy Bonds February 1990–

Player and Position	*Ht*	*Wt*	*Birth Date*	*Birth Place*	*Source*	*Clubs*	*League App*	*League Gls*
Alex Bunbury (To Maritimo December 1993)	5 10	11 00	18 6 67	British Guyana	Montreal Supra	West Ham U	4	—
Lee Chapman	6 2	13 00	5 12 59	Lincoln	Amateur	Stoke C	99	34
						Plymouth Arg (loan)	4	—
						Arsenal	23	4
						Sunderland	15	3
						Sheffield W	149	63
					Niort	Nottingham F	48	15
						Leeds U	137	62
						Portsmouth	5	2
						West Ham U	30	7
Simon Clarke	5 11	11 02	23 9 71	Chelmsford	Trainee	West Ham U	3	—
Dale Gordon	5 10	11 08	9 1 67	Gt Yarmouth	Apprentice	Norwich C	206	31
						Rangers	45	6
						West Ham U	8	1
Matt Holmes	5 7	10 07	1 8 69	Luton	Trainee	Bournemouth	114	8
						Cardiff C (loan)	1	—
						West Ham U	52	3
Steve Jones	5 11	12 00	17 3 70	Cambridge	Billericay	West Ham U	14	4
Malcolm McPherson			9 12 74	Glasgow	Yeovil	West Ham U	—	—
Mike Marsh	5 8	11 00	21 7 69	Liverpool	Kirkby T	Liverpool	69	2
						West Ham U	33	1
Dean Martin‡	5 8	10 06	31 8 72	London	Fisher Ath	West Ham U	2	—
						Colchester U (loan)	8	2
Trevor Morley	5 11	12 01	20 3 61	Nottingham	Nuneaton	Northampton T	107	39
						Manchester C	72	18
						West Ham U	164	57
David Pratt	5 8	11 00	17 12 74	London		West Ham U	—	—
Mike Small•	6 1	13 05	2 3 62	Birmingham		Luton T	3	—
					Twente, Standard Liege	Peterborough U	4	1
					Go Ahead Eagles/PAOK Salonika	Brighton	39	15
						West Ham U	49	13
						Wolverhampton W (loan)	3	1
						Charlton Ath (loan)	2	—

Trainees
Bates, Jonathan P; Blaney, Steven D; Browne, Anthony; Geraghty, Jason W; John, Jerome L; Joscelyne, Wayne; Maeer, Darren J; Moore, Scott; Moors, Christopher A; Oakley, Warren N; Peat, Martin D; Richardson, Stuart J; Rose, CHristopher A; Shipp, Daniel A; Victory, Jamie C.

Associated Schoolboys
Boylan, Lee M; Clements, Mathew C; Evans, Christopher R; Evans, Duncan J; Ferdinand, Rio G; Fernley, Daniel P; Goodwin, Lee J; Keith, Joseph R; McFarlane, Anthony Z; Moore, Jason M; Osborne, Tommy P; Partridge, David W; Strain, Anthony M; Sweeting, Daniel B; Wells, Andrew; Wraight, Gary P.

Associated Schoolboys who have accepted the Club's offer of a Traineeship/Contract
Hodges, Lee L; Omoyimni, Emmanuel.

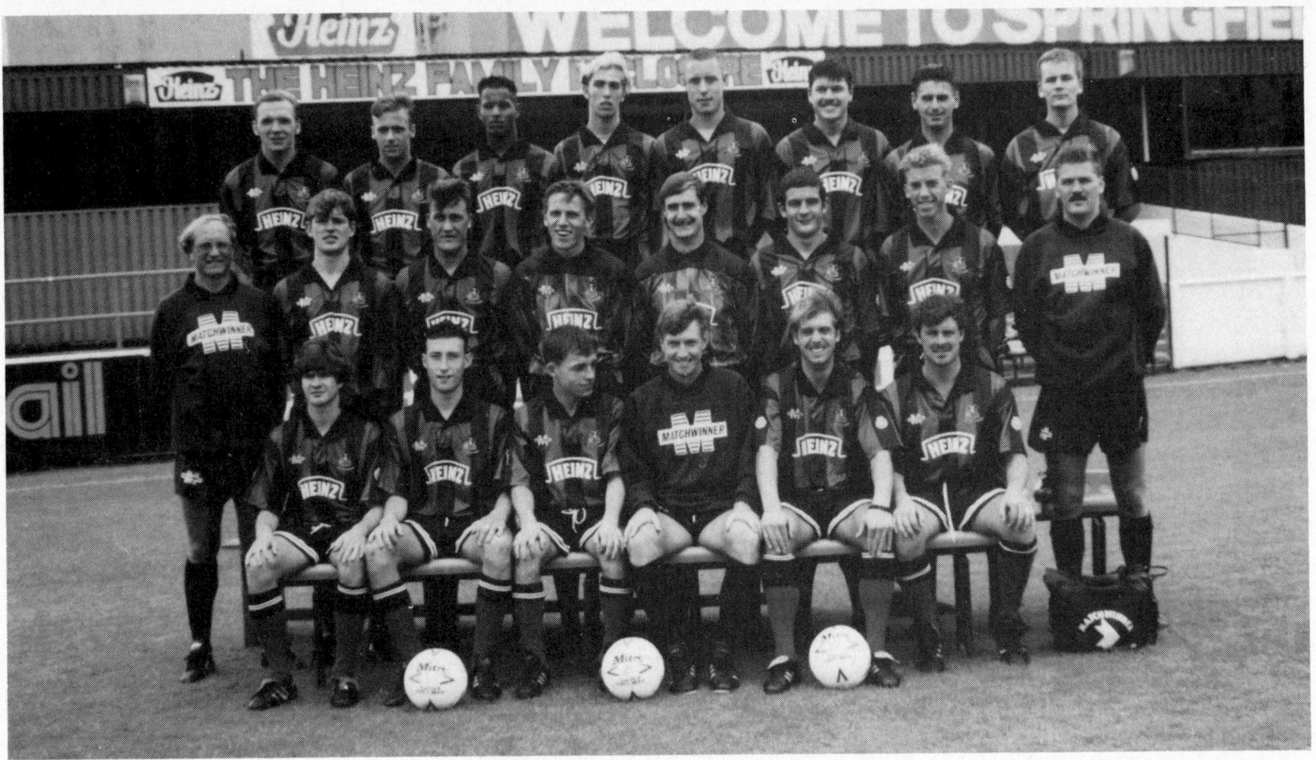

WIGAN ATHLETIC 1993–94 *Back row (left to right):* Peter Skipper, David McKearney, Julian Dowe, Greg Strong, John Robertson, Phil Daley, Mick Kennedy, John Doolan.
Centre row: David Crompton (Youth Coach), Pat Gavin, Kevin Langley, Anthony Pennock, Simon Farnworth, Alan Johnson, Chris Duffy, Alex Cribley (Coach/Physio).
Front row: Neill Rimmer, Steve Hollis, Danny Vaughan, Kenny Swain (Manager), Neil Morton, Dean Connelly.
(Photograph: Gordon Allan)

Division 3 **WIGAN ATHLETIC**

Springfield Park, Wigan WN6 7BA. Telephone Wigan (0942) 44433. Commercial Dept: (0942) 43067. Latics Clubcall 0891 121655. Fax 0942 494654.

Ground capacity: 4359 (to be increased).

Record attendance: 27,500 v Hereford U, 12 December 1953.

Record receipts: £40,577 v Leeds U, FA Cup 6th rd, 15 March 1987.

Pitch measurements: 114yd × 72yd.

President: T. Hitchen.

Chairman: S. Gage. ***Vice-chairman:***

Directors: N. Bitel, S. Jackson, J. Bennett, D. McKenzie.

Vice-president: J. H. Farrimond.

Secretary: Mrs Brenda Spencer. ***Marketing Manager:*** B. Eccles. ***Marketing Assistant:*** Gordon Allan.

Manager: Kenny Swain. ***Physio:*** Alex Cribley. ***Safety officer:*** David Johnson. ***Groundsman:*** Paul Brownsell.

Year Formed: 1932.

Club Nickname: 'The Latics'.

Record League Victory: 7–2 v Scunthorpe U (away), Division 4, 12 March 1982 – Tunks; McMahon, Glenn, Wignall, Cribley, Methven (1), O'Keefe, Barrow (1), Bradd (3), Houghton (2), Evans.

Record Cup Victory: 6–0 v Carlisle U (away), FA Cup, 1st rd, 24 November 1934 – Caunce; Robinson, Talbot; Paterson, Watson, Tufnell; Armes (2), Robson (1), Roberts (2), Felton, Scott (1).

Record Defeat: 1–6 v Bristol R, Division 3, 3 March 1990.

Most League Points (2 for a win): 55, Division 4, 1978–79 and 1979–80.

Most League Points (3 for a win): 91, Division 4, 1981–82.

Most League Goals: 80, Division 4, 1981–82.

Highest League Scorer in Season: Warren Aspinall, 21, Division 3, 1985–86.

Most League Goals in Total Aggregate: Peter Houghton, 62, 1978–84.

Most Capped Player: None.

Most League Appearances: Kevin Langley, 317, 1981–86, 1990–94.

Record Transfer Fee Received: £329,000 from Coventry C for Peter Atherton, August 1991.

Record Transfer Fee Paid: £65,000 to Everton for Eamon O'Keefe, January 1982.

Football League Record: 1978 Elected to Division 4; 1982 –92 Division 3; 1992–93 Division 2; 1993– Division 3.

Honours: Football League: Best season in Division 3: 4th, 1985–86, 1986–87; Division 4 – Promoted (3rd) 1981–82. *FA Cup:* 6th rd 1986–87. *Football League Cup:* best season: 4th rd, 1981–82. *Freight Rover Trophy:* Winners 1984–85.

WIGAN ATHLETIC 1993—94 LEAGUE RECORD

Match No.	Date	Venue	Opponents	Result		H/T Score	Lg. Pos.	Goalscorers	Attendance
1	Aug 14	H	Scunthorpe U	L	0-2	0-0	—		2353
2	21	A	Torquay U	D	1-1	0-0	17	Morton	3465
3	28	H	Wycombe W	D	1-1	1-1	18	Rennie	2388
4	31	A	Rochdale	W	2-1	0-1	—	McKearney, Langley	2628
5	Sept 4	A	Doncaster R	L	1-3	0-1	15	Strong	3075
6	11	H	Scarborough	L	1-2	0-1	16	Daley	1682
7	18	A	Northampton T	W	2-0	0-0	15	Gavin, Skipper	2235
8	25	A	Hereford U	L	0-3	0-1	17		1813
9	Oct 2	H	Chester C	W	6-3	3-1	12	Johnson, McKearney, Gavin, Gillespie 2, Rennie	1889
10	9	A	Bury	L	0-3	0-1	15		2729
11	16	H	Preston NE	D	2-2	2-2	16	McKearney 2	3741
12	23	A	Colchester U	L	1-3	1-1	17	Gillespie	2814
13	30	H	Mansfield T	W	4-1	2-0	17	Gavin 2, Gillespie, Morton	1434
14	Nov 2	A	Chesterfield	L	0-1	0-1	—		2758
15	6	H	Carlisle U	L	0-2	0-0	19		2411
16	20	A	Gillingham	D	2-2	1-1	19	Daley, Lyons	2727
17	27	H	Shrewsbury T	L	2-5	0-1	19	Williams (og), Daley	1498
18	Dec 11	H	Torquay U	L	1-3	0-3	19	Kennedy	1232
19	18	A	Scunthorpe U	L	0-1	0-0	20		2873
20	Jan 4	H	Rochdale	D	0-0	0-0	—		1912
21	11	H	Walsall	D	2-2	2-0	—	Lyons, Skipper	1561
22	15	A	Preston NE	L	0-3	0-0	21		7728
23	22	H	Bury	W	3-1	2-1	20	Kilford 2, Morton	2476
24	25	A	Darlington	D	0-0	0-0	—		1837
25	29	A	Mansfield T	W	3-2	0-0	20	Gavin, Connelly, Duffy	2285
26	Feb 5	H	Colchester U	L	0-1	0-0	20		1695
27	12	A	Lincoln C	W	1-0	0-0	19	Lyons	2534
28	19	A	Wycombe W	W	1-0	1-0	19	Lyons	4846
29	Mar 5	A	Scarborough	L	1-4	1-1	19	Furlong	1390
30	12	H	Northampton T	D	1-1	0-0	20	Wright	1855
31	19	H	Hereford U	L	3-4	1-2	20	Lyons 2, Gavin	1542
32	22	H	Doncaster R	D	0-0	0-0	—		1438
33	26	A	Chester C	L	1-2	1-2	21	Lyons	3542
34	29	H	Lincoln C	L	0-1	0-0	—		1349
35	Apr 2	H	Crewe Alex	D	2-2	1-1	20	Lyons, Kilford	2335
36	5	A	Walsall	D	1-1	0-0	—	Lyons	3815
37	9	H	Darlington	W	2-0	0-0	20	Skipper, Lyons	1709
38	16	H	Chesterfield	W	1-0	0-0	20	Robertson	1998
39	19	A	Crewe Alex	L	1-4	0-1	—	Langley	3396
40	23	A	Carlisle U	L	0-3	0-3	20		3796
41	30	H	Gillingham	W	2-0	0-0	19	Lyons (pen), Morton	1346
42	May 7	A	Shrewsbury T	D	0-0	0-0	19		7686

Final League Position: 19

GOALSCORERS

League (51): Lyons 11 (1 pen), Gavin 6, Gillespie 4, McKearney 4, Morton 4, Daley 3, Kilford 3, Skipper 3, Langley 2, Rennie 2, Connelly 1, Duffy 1, Furlong 1, Johnson 1, Kennedy 1, Robertson 1, Strong 1, Wright 1, own goal 1.
Coca-Cola Cup (2): Gavin 1, Morton 1.
FA Cup (6): Duffy 1, Gavin 1, McKearney 1 (pen), Morton 1, Skipper 1, own goal 1.

Farnworth 42	Rennie 25 + 1	Duffy 15 + 12	Robertson 34	Skipper 41	Johnson 16	Strong 16 + 2	McKearney 28	Gavin 28 + 2	Morton 32 + 7	Langley 28 + 5	Hollis — + 1	Vaughan 2 + 2	Ogden — + 2	Kennedy 15 + 2	West 1 + 1	Gillespie 8	Daley 11 + 7	Rimmer 19 + 1	Lyons 33	Carragher 27 + 5	Wright 13 + 1	Kilford 7 + 1	Connelly 8 + 5	Furlong 1 + 1	Thorne 10 + 1	Patterson 2 + 2	Match No.
1	2	3	4	5	6	7	8	9	10	11	12																1
1	2		4	5	6	7	8	9	10	11		3	12														2
1	2	12	4	5	6	7	8	9	10	11				3													3
1	2	7	4	5	6		8	9	10	11				3	12												4
1		3	4	5	6	12	8	9	10	11			14		2	7											5
1	2	6	4	5			3	9	10	11		14		8		7	12										6
1	2	6	4	5			3	9	10	11		12				7		8									7
1	2		4	5	6		3	9	10			11				7	12	8									8
1	8	2	4	5	6		3	9	10							7			11	12							9
1	6	2	4	5			3	9	10	7							12	8	11	14							10
1	2	7	4	5		6	3	9	12								10	8	11	14							11
1		14	4			5	3	9		12				6		7	10	8	11	2							12
1	4	12		5			3	9	10					6		7		8	11	2							13
1	4	12	10	5			3	9	14					6		7		8	11	2							14
1	4	2	8	5			3	9	10	7				6					11	12	14						15
1	2			5	6		8		10	12				4			9		11	7	3						16
1	2	14		5	6		8		10	12				4			9		11	7	3						17
1	2	12		5	6		8	10		4				14			9		11	7	3						18
1	2		4	5	6		8	9	10	14							12		11	7	3						19
1			4	5	6		8	9	10	7							12		11	2	3	14					20
1			4	5	6		8	12	10	7							9		11	2	3						21
1	2		4	5	6		8		10	7							9		11	12		3					22
1	3	8	4	5				12	10	7				14			9		11	2		6					23
1	3	8	4	5				9	10	7				6					11	2							24
1	3	8	4	5				9	10	7				6					11	2			12				25
1	12	8	4	5	3			9	10	7				6					11	2			14				26
1	8	12	4	5	3			9	10	7				6					11	2			14				27
1	2	12	4	5				9	10	7				6					11		3		8				28
1	2		4	5						7				6				12	11	10	3		8	9			29
1	2	12	4	5					10	7									11	6	3		8		9		30
1			4	5		14		9	12	7								6	11	2	3		8		10		31
1		14	4	5		3		9	12	7								6	11	2			8		10		32
1			4	5		3		9	8	7								10	11	2		6	12		14		33
1			4	5		3	7	9	14									10	11	2		6	12		8		34
1				5		3	7	9	12	6								10	11	2		4			8		35
1		12	4	5		3	7		8									10	11	2		6			9		36
1		12	7	5		3	4		8									10	11	2		6		14	9		37
1			7	5		3	4		8								12	10	11	2			6		9		38
1		7		5		3			8	4							12	10	11	2			6		9	14	39
1				5		6			12	14							9	10	11	2	3		7		8	4	40
1			4	5		6			8	7							9	10	11	2	3					12	41
1		11		5		6	2		8	7							9	10			3					4	42

Coca-Cola Cup	First Round	Rotherham U (h)	0-1
		(a)	2-4
FA Cup	First Round	Leek (a)	2-2
		(h)	3-0
	Second Round	Scarborough (h)	1-0
	Third Round	Grimsby T (a)	0-1

WIGAN ATHLETIC

Player and Position	Ht	Wt	Birth Date	Birth Place	Source	Clubs	League App	League Gls
Goalkeepers								
Simon Farnworth	6 0	11 13	28 10 63	Chorley	Apprentice	Bolton W	113	—
						Stockport Co (loan)	10	—
						Tranmere R (loan)	7	—
						Bury	105	—
						Preston NE	81	—
						Wigan Ath	42	—
Tony Pennock*	5 11	10 09	10 4 71	Swansea	School	Stockport Co	—	—
						Wigan Ath (loan)	2	—
						Wigan Ath	8	—
Defenders								
Steve Appleton	5 11	10 09	27 7 73	Liverpool	Trainee	Wigan Ath	48	1
Matthew Carragher	5 9	10 07	14 1 76	Liverpool	Trainee	Wigan Ath	32	—
Steve Hollis†	6 0	11 00	22 8 72	Liverpool	Liverpool	Wigan Ath	1	—
Neil Ogden	5 10	10 04	29 11 75	Billinge	Trainee	Wigan Ath	4	—
Ian Patterson	6 2	13 00	4 4 73	Chatham	Trainee	Sunderland	—	—
						Burnley	1	—
						Wigan Ath	4	—
Paul Rennie	5 9	11 04	26 10 71	Nantwich	Trainee	Crewe Alex	2	—
						Stoke C	4	—
						Wigan Ath	26	2
John Robertson	6 2	13 02	8 1 74	Liverpool	Trainee	Wigan Ath	58	2
Peter Skipper*	6 0	13 08	11 4 58	Hull	Local	Hull C	23	2
						Scunthorpe U (loan)	1	—
						Darlington	91	4
						Hull C	265	17
						Oldham Ath	27	1
						Walsall	81	2
						Wrexham	2	—
						Wigan Ath	18	—
					Stafford R	Wigan Ath	73	4
Greg Strong	6 2	11 12	5 9 75	Bolton	Trainee	Wigan Ath	18	1
Danny Vaughan‡	5 8	10 00	18 2 72	Liverpool		Crewe Alex	7	—
						Wigan Ath	4	—
Paul West	5 11	11 00	22 6 70		Alcester T	Port Vale	—	—
						Bradford C	—	—
						Wigan Ath	2	—
Mark Wright	5 11	10 12	29 1 70	Manchester	Trainee	Everton	1	—
						Blackpool (loan)	3	—
						Huddersfield T (loan)	10	1
						Huddersfield T	22	—
						Wigan Ath	14	1
Midfield								
Dino Connelly*	5 9	10 08	6 1 70	St. Helier	Celtic BC	Arsenal	—	—
						Barnsley	13	—
						Wigan Ath (loan)	12	2
						Carlisle U (loan)	3	—
						Wigan Ath	20	1
John Doolan	5 10	10 12	10 11 68	South Liverpool	Knowsley U	Wigan Ath	19	—
Chris Duffy	5 10	11 11	31 10 73	Manchester	Trainee	Crewe Alex	—	—
						Wigan Ath	27	1
Mick Kennedy*	5 9	12 00	9 4 61	Salford	Apprentice	Halifax T	76	4
						Huddersfield T	81	9
						Middlesbrough	68	5
						Portsmouth	129	4
						Bradford C	45	2
						Leicester C	9	—
						Luton T	32	—
						Stoke C	52	3
						Chesterfield	27	1
						Wigan Ath	17	1
Kevin Langley*	6 1	10 03	24 5 64	St. Helens	Apprentice	Wigan Ath	160	6
						Everton	16	2
						Manchester C (loan)	9	—
						Manchester C	—	—
						Chester C (loan)	9	—
						Birmingham C	76	2
						Wigan Ath	157	6

WIGAN ATHLETIC

Colours: Black and blue striped shirts, black shorts blue stockings. **Change colours:** Burgundy with gold trim.

Foundation: Following the demise of Wigan Borough and their resignation from the Football League in 1931, a public meeting was called in Wigan at the Queen's Hall in May 1932 at which a new club Wigan Athletic, was founded in the hope of carrying on in the Football League. With this in mind, they bought Springfield Park for £2,250, but failed to gain admission to the Football League until 46 years later.

First Football League game: 19 August, 1978, Division 4, v Hereford U (a) D 0-0 – Brown; Hinnigan, Gore, Gillibrand, Ward, Davids, Corrigan, Purdie, Houghton, Wilkie, Wright.

Did you know: On 2 October 1993 Wigan Athletic beat Chester City 6-3. It was the first time they had scored exactly six goals in a Football League game.

Managers (and Secretary-Managers)
Charlie Spencer 1932–37, Jimmy Milne 1946–47, Bob Pryde 1949–52, Ted Goodier 1952–54, Walter Crook 1954–55, Ron Suart 1955–56, Billy Cooke 1956, Sam Barkas 1957, Trevor Hitchen 1957–58, Malcolm Barrass 1958–59, Jimmy Shirley 1959, Pat Murphy 1959–60, Allenby Chilton 1960, Johnny Ball 1961–63, Allan Brown 1963–66, Alf Craig 1966–67, Harry Leyland 1967–68, Alan Saunders 1968, Ian McNeill 1968–70, Gordon Milne 1970–72, Les Rigby 1972–74, Brian Tiler 1974–76, Ian McNeill 1976–81, Larry Lloyd 1981–83, Harry McNally 1983–85, Bryan Hamilton 1985–86, Ray Mathias 1986–89, Bryan Hamilton 1989–93, Dave Philpotts 1993, Kenny Swain May 1993–

Player and Position	*Ht*	*Wt*	*Birth Date*	*Birth Place*	*Source*	*Clubs*	*League App*	*League Gls*
Neill Rimmer	5 6	10 03	13 11 67	Liverpool	Apprentice	Everton	1	—
						Ipswich T	22	3
						Wigan Ath	127	6
Forwards								
Philip Daley	6 2	12 09	12 4 67	Walton	Newton	Wigan Ath	161	39
Julian Dowe*	6 1	12 04	9 9 75	Manchester	Trainee	Wigan Ath	—	—
Carl Furlong§	5 11	12 06	18 10 76	Liverpool	Trainee	Wigan Ath	2	1
Pat Gavin	6 0	12 00	5 6 67	Hammersmith	Hanwell T	Gillingham	13	7
						Leicester C	3	—
						Gillingham (loan)	34	1
						Peterborough U	23	5
						Barnet	—	—
						Northampton T	14	4
						Wigan Ath	30	6
Andy Lyons	5 10	11 00	19 10 66	Blackpool	Fleetwood	Crewe Alex	11	2
						Wigan Ath	33	11
David McKearney	5 10	11 02	20 6 68	Crosby		Bolton W	—	—
						Crewe Alex	108	12
						Wigan Ath	28	4
Neil Morton	5 9	10 07	21 12 68	Congleton	Trainee	Crewe Alex	31	1
					Northwich Vic	Chester C	95	13
						Wigan Ath	39	4

Trainees
Dixon, Stephen; Dowds, Scott K; Furlong, Carl D; Haley, Martin A; Marshall, Phillip J; Newton, Steven J; O'Hara, Terence; Saint, Darren.

****Non-Contract**
Hollis, Stephen J; Kelsey, Andrew; Vicary, Darren C.

Associated Schoolboys
Alexander, Paul; Aspinall, Mark; Brown, Thomas M; Chisnall, Robert G; Clough, Philip; Conway, Neil; Fitzhenry, Neil; Foulds, Jason; Gallagher, Damien J; Green, Paul R; Hatton, Barry; Just, Paul G; McKie, Tony; O'Connor, Robert; O'Mara, Jonathan D; Scott, Anthony; Sing, Stephen; Standish, Paul.

Associated Schoolboys who have accepted the Club's offer of a Traineeship/Contract
Hogg, Russell S; Millett, Michael P; Salt, Daniel J; Slater, Stewart J; Tyrrell, Kevin M; Weston, Steven M.
**Non-Contract Players who are retained must be re-signed before they are eligible to play in League matches.

WIMBLEDON 1993–94 *Back row (left to right):* Joe Dillon (Assistant Kit Manager), Neal Ardley, Paul Miller, Dean Blackwell, Gary Blissett, Neil Sullivan, Hans Segers, Neil Fairbairn, Stewart Castledine, Aidan Newhouse, Brian McAllister, Marc Cable, Ron Suart (Chief Scout).

Centre row: Syd Neal (Kit Manager), Andy Clarke, Peter Fear, Greg Berry, Leighton Allen, John Scales, Lawrie Sanchez, Steve Anthrobus, Vinny Jones, Scott Fitzgerald, Dean Holdsworth, Steve Talboys, Alan Kimble, Roger Joseph, Roger Smith (Youth Development Officer).

Front row: Ernie Tippett (Youth Manager), Grant Payne, Paul McGee, Gerald Dobbs, Terry Burton (Assistant Manager), Gary Elkins, John Fashanu, Joe Kinnear (Manager), Robbie Earle, Warren Barton, Brian Sparrow (Reserve Manager), Chris Perry, Justin Skinner, Mark Thomas, Steve Allen (Physio).

FA Premiership **WIMBLEDON**

Selhurst Park, South Norwood, London SE25 6PY. Telephone 081 771 2233. Box Office 081 771 8841. Fax 081 768 0640.

Ground capacity: 17,619.

Record attendance: 30,115 v Manchester U, FA Premier League, 9 May 1993.

Record receipts: £312,024 v Manchester U, FA Premier League, 16 April 1994.

Pitch measurements: 110yd × 74yd.

Chairman: S. G. Reed. ***Vice-chairman:*** J. Lelliott.

Managing Director: S. Hammam.

Directors: P. Cork, P. R. Cooper, N. N. Hammam, P. Miller.

Chief Executive: David Barnard.

Manager: Joe Kinnear. ***Assistant manager:*** Terry Burton. ***Physio:*** Steve Allen.

Secretary: Steve Rooke. ***Commercial Manager:*** Reg Davis.

Year Formed: 1889. ***Turned Professional:*** 1964. ***Ltd Co.:*** 1964.

Previous Name: Wimbledon Old Centrals, 1899–1905.

Previous Ground: Plough Lane.

Club Nickname: 'The Dons'.

Record League Victory: 6–0 v Newport C, Division 3, 3 September 1983 – Beasant; Peters, Winterburn, Galliers, Morris, Hatter, Evans (2), Ketteridge (1), Cork (3 incl. 1p), Downes, Hodges (Driver).

Record Cup Victory: 7–2 v Windsor & Eton, FA Cup, 1st rd, 22 November 1980 – Beasant; Jones, Armstrong, Galliers, Mick Smith (2), Cunningham (1), Ketteridge, Hodges, Leslie, Cork (1), Hubbick (3).

Record Defeat: 0–8 v Everton, League Cup 2nd rd, 29 August 1978.

Most League Points (2 for a win): 61, Division 4, 1978–79.

Most League Points (3 for a win): 98, Division 4, 1982–83.

Most League Goals: 97, Division 3, 1983–84.

Highest League Scorer in Season: Alan Cork, 29, 1983–84.

Most League Goals in Total Aggregate: Alan Cork, 145, 1977–92.

Most Capped Player: Terry Phelan, 8 (25), Republic of Ireland.

Most League Appearances: Alan Cork, 430, 1977–92.

Record Transfer Fee Received: £2,500,000 from Manchester C for Keith Curle, August 1991.

Record Transfer Fee Paid: £775,000 to Port Vale for Robbie Earle, July 1991.

Football League Record: 1977 Elected to Division 4; 1979–80 Division 3; 1980–81 Division 4; 1981–82 Division 3; 1982–83 Division 4; 1983–84 Division 3; 1984–86 Division 2; 1986–92 Division 1; 1992– FA Premier League.

Honours: *FA Premier League* : best season: 6th, 1993–94; *Football League:* Division 3 – Runners-up 1983–84; Division 4 – Champions 1982–83. *FA Cup:* Winners 1987–88. *Football League Cup:* best season: 4th rd, 1979–80, 1983–84, 1988–89. *League Group Cup:* Runners-up 1981–82.

WIMBLEDON 1993—94 LEAGUE RECORD

Match No.	Date	Venue	Opponents	Result	H/T Score	Lg. Pos.	Goalscorers	Attendance
1	Aug 14	A	West Ham U	W 2-0	0-0	—	Fashanu, Sanchez	20,369
2	17	H	Chelsea	D 1-1	0-0	—	Fashanu	11,263
3	21	H	Aston Villa	D 2-2	1-1	11	Holdsworth, Fashanu	7564
4	24	A	Sheffield U	L 1-2	0-1	—	Clarke	15,555
5	28	A	Oldham Ath	D 1-1	0-1	12	Jones	9633
6	31	H	Southampton	W 1-0	1-0	—	Barton	6036
7	Sept 11	A	Norwich C	W 1-0	0-0	6	Sanchez	14,851
8	20	H	Manchester C	W 1-0	0-0	—	Earle	8533
9	27	H	QPR	D 1-1	1-1	—	Ferdinand (og)	9478
10	Oct 2	A	Leeds U	L 0-4	0-2	8		30,255
11	16	A	Sheffield W	D 2-2	0-1	9	Blissett, Jones	21,752
12	25	H	Ipswich T	L 0-2	0-0	—		7756
13	30	A	Newcastle U	L 0-4	0-1	12		33,371
14	Nov 6	H	Swindon T	W 3-0	1-0	9	Fashanu, Blissett, Holdsworth	7758
15	20	A	Manchester U	L 1-3	0-0	12	Fashanu	44,748
16	24	A	Tottenham H	D 1-1	0-1	—	Holdsworth	17,744
17	27	H	Everton	D 1-1	0-1	11	Berry	6934
18	Dec 4	H	West Ham U	L 1-2	0-1	15	Holdsworth	10,903
19	11	A	Aston Villa	W 1-0	0-0	14	Holdsworth	17,940
20	18	H	Sheffield U	W 2-0	0-0	12	Barton, Holdsworth	6728
21	26	H	Coventry C	L 1-2	1-1	—	Holdsworth	4739
22	28	A	Liverpool	D 1-1	1-1	14	Fashanu	32,232
23	Jan 1	H	Arsenal	L 0-3	0-2	15		16,584
24	15	H	Sheffield W	W 2-1	2-0	12	Ardley, Fashanu	5536
25	22	A	Ipswich T	D 0-0	0-0	12		11,849
26	Feb 5	A	Blackburn R	L 0-3	0-3	13		17,264
27	12	H	Newcastle U	W 4-2	2-0	11	Earle, Blissett, Fashanu, Holdsworth	13,358
28	25	A	Southampton	L 0-1	0-0	14		14,790
29	Mar 5	H	Norwich C	W 3-1	1-1	11	Earle 2, Holdsworth	7206
30	12	A	Manchester C	W 1-0	1-0	11	Earle	23,981
31	16	A	Chelsea	L 0-2	0-1	—		11,903
32	19	A	QPR	L 0-1	0-0	11		11,368
33	26	H	Leeds U	W 1-0	1-0	11	Fear	9035
34	29	H	Blackburn R	W 4-1	0-1	—	Fashanu, Berg (og), Holdsworth, Earle	10,537
35	Apr 2	A	Coventry C	W 2-1	2-0	8	Castledine, Holdsworth	11,312
36	4	H	Liverpool	D 1-1	0-0	8	Elkins	13,819
37	16	H	Manchester U	W 1-0	1-0	8	Fashanu	28,553
38	19	A	Arsenal	D 1-1	1-0	—	Earle	21,292
39	23	A	Swindon T	W 4-2	1-0	8	Fashanu, Earle 2, Holdsworth	13,309
40	26	H	Oldham Ath	W 3-0	1-0	—	Holdsworth 3	6766
41	30	H	Tottenham H	W 2-1	0-0	6	Holdsworth, Clarke	20,875
42	May 7	A	Everton	L 2-3	2-1	6	Holdsworth (pen), Ablett (og)	31,233

Final League Position: 6

GOALSCORERS

League (56): Holdsworth 17 (1 pen), Fashanu 11, Earle 9, Blissett 3, Barton 2, Clarke 2, Jones 2, Sanchez 2, Ardley 1, Berry 1, Castledine 1, Elkins 1, Fear 1, own goals 3.
Coca-Cola Cup (11): Holdsworth 4, Earle 3, Ardley 1, Barton 1, Clarke 1, Jones 1.
FA Cup (5): Holdsworth 3, Fashanu 1, Scales 1.

Segers 41	Joseph 13	Kimble 14	Sanchez 15	Scales 37	Fitzgerald 27 + 1	Clarke 9 + 14	Earle 42	Fashanu 35 + 1	Holdsworth 42	Fear 23	Blackwell 16 + 2	Barton 37 + 2	Talboys 6 + 1	Dobbs 3 + 7	Jones 33	Blissett 6 + 12	Ardley 14 + 2	McAllister 13	Berry 4	Elkins 18	Gayle 10	Castledine 3	Perry — + 2	Sullivan 1 + 1	*Match No.*
1	2	3	4	5	6	7	8	9	10	11	12	14													1
1	2	3	4	5		7	8	9	10		6		11												2
1	3	11	4	5		7	8	9	10		6	2		12											3
1	3	11	4	5		12	8	9	10		6	2		7											4
1	3	11	7	5	6		8	9	10			2		12	4										5
1	3	11	7	5	6	12	8	9	10			2			4										6
1	3	11	7	5	6		8	9	10			2			4										7
1	3	11	7	5	6	12	8	9	10			2			4										8
1		3	11	5	6	7	8	9	10			2			4	12	14								9
1		3	11	5	6		8	9	10		2			14	4	12	7								10
1		3	11		6	12	8		10	2					4	9	7	5							11
1		3	11		6		8	12	10	2		14			4	9	7	5							12
1		3			6	7	8	9	10	11		2		12	4			5							13
1		3			6		8	9	10			2	7		4	11	12	5							14
1	3			5	6	12	8	9	10			2	11		4			7							15
1	3			5			8	9	10			2	11		4		7		6						16
1	3			5	14	12	8	9	10			2	11		4		7		6						17
1				5	6	7	8		10			2	12		4		11	3	9						18
1				5	6		8	9	10	11		2			4		7	3							19
1				5	6		8	9	10			2	11	12	4		7	3							20
1				5	6	12	8	9	10	11		2		14	4		7	3							21
1				5	6	12	8	9	10	11		2			4		7	3							22
1					6	12	8	9	10	11	5	2			4		7			3					23
1			11	5	6		8	9	10			2			4	12	7			3					24
1	3		4	5	6		8	9	10			2				12	7			11					25
1	3		4	5	6		8	9	10			2				12	7			11					26
1				5	6	12	8	9	10	11		2			4	7				3					27
1				5	6	9	8		10		7	2		14	4	12		3		11					28
1				5	6		8	9	10	11		2			4	7		3							29
1				5	6	12	8	9	10	11		2		7	4	14		3							30
1				5	6		8	9	10	11	12	2		7	4	14				3					31
1				5	6	12	8		10	11		2			4	9			7	3					32
1				5			8	9	10	11	6	2			4					3	7				33
1				5			8	9	10	11	6	2			4					3	7				34
1				5			8	9	10	11	6	2				12				3	7	4			35
1				5			8	9	10	11	6	2				12				3	7	4	14		36
1				5			8	9	10	11	6	2			4					3	7				37
1				5			8	9	10	11	6	2								3	7	4			38
1				5		12	8	9	10	11	6	2			4					3	7			14	39
				5		12	8	9	10	11	6	2			4					3	7			1	40
1				5		7	8		10	11	6	2			4	12				3	9		14		41
1				5		7	8		10	11	6	2			4	12				3	9				42

Coca-Cola Cup	Second Round	Hereford U (a)	1-0
		(h)	4-1
	Third Round	Newcastle U (h)	2-1
	Fourth Round	Liverpool (a)	1-1
		(h)	2-2
	Fifth Round	Sheffield W (h)	1-2
FA Cup	Third Round	Scunthorpe U (h)	3-0
	Fourth Round	Sunderland (h)	2-1
	Fifth Round	Manchester U (h)	0-3

WIMBLEDON

Player and Position	Ht	Wt	Birth Date	Birth Place	Source	Clubs	League App	League Gls
Goalkeepers								
Neil Fairbairn*	5 11	11 00	4 10 74	Ashington	Trainee	Wimbledon	—	—
Hans Segers	5 11	12 12	30 10 61	Eindhoven	PSV Eindhoven	Nottingham F	58	—
						Stoke C (loan)	1	—
						Sheffield U (loan)	10	—
						Dunfermline Ath (loan)	4	—
						Wimbledon	231	—
Neil Sullivan	6 0	12 01	24 2 70	Sutton	Trainee	Wimbledon	5	—
						Crystal Palace (loan)	1	—
Defenders								
Warren Barton	5 10	11 00	19 3 69	London	Leytonstone/ Ilford	Maidstone U	42	—
						Wimbledon	141	8
Dean Blackwell	6 1	12 10	5 12 69	London	Trainee	Wimbledon	84	1
						Plymouth Arg (loan)	7	—
Marc Cable*	5 11	11 02	18 9 74	Dartford	Trainee	Wimbledon	—	—
Gerald Dobbs	5 8	11 07	24 1 71	London	Trainee	Wimbledon	33	1
Peter Fear	5 10	11 05	10 9 73	London	Trainee	Wimbledon	27	1
Scott Fitzgerald	6 0	12 02	13 8 69	London	Trainee	Wimbledon	85	1
Roger Joseph	5 11	11 10	24 12 65	Paddington	Juniors	Brentford	104	2
						Wimbledon	159	—
Alan Kimble	5 8	11 00	6 8 66	Poole		Charlton Ath	6	—
						Exeter C (loan)	1	—
						Cambridge U	299	24
						Wimbledon	14	—
Brian McAllister	5 11	12 05	30 11 70	Glasgow	Trainee	Wimbledon	53	—
						Plymouth Arg (loan)	8	—
Chris Perry	5 9	11 01	26 4 73	London	Trainee	Wimbledon	2	—
John Scales	6 2	12 07	4 7 66	Harrogate		Leeds U	—	—
						Bristol R	72	2
						Wimbledon	237	11
Justin Skinner	5 7	11 00	17 9 72	London	Trainee	Wimbledon	1	—
						Bournemouth (loan)	16	—
Midfield								
Neil Ardley	5 8	11 10	1 9 72	Epsom	Trainee	Wimbledon	51	5
Stewart Castledine	6 0	12 00	22 1 73	London	Trainee	Wimbledon	5	1
Gary Elkins	5 09	11 12	4 5 66	Wallingford	Apprentice	Fulham	104	2
						Exeter C (loan)	5	—
						Wimbledon	64	2
Marcus Gayle	6 2	12 13	27 9 70	Hammersmith	Trainee	Brentford	156	22
						Wimbledon	10	—
Vinny Jones	5 11	11 10	5 1 65	Watford	Wealdstone	Wimbledon	77	9
						Leeds U	46	5
						Sheffield U	35	2
						Chelsea	42	4
						Wimbledon	60	3
Jamie McCarthy	5 10	11 07	14 8 73	London	Trainee	Wimbledon	—	—
Aidan Newhouse	6 2	13 05	23 5 72	Wallasey	Trainee	Chester C	44	6
						Wimbledon	23	2
						Tranmere R (loan)	—	—
						Port Vale (loan)	2	—
Steve Talboys	5 11	11 10	18 9 66	Bristol	Gloucester C	Wimbledon	14	—
Mark Thomas	5 9	10 10	22 11 74	Tooting	Trainee	Wimbledon	—	—
Forwards								
Leighton Allen*	6 0	11 02	22 1 73	Brighton	Trainee	Wimbledon	—	—
Steve Anthrobus	6 0	12 02	10 11 68	Lewisham		Millwall	21	4
						Southend U (loan)	—	—
						Wimbledon	28	—
						Peterborough U (loan)	2	—

WIMBLEDON

Colours: All navy blue with gold trim. **Change colours:** White shirts, black shorts, white stockings.

Foundation: Old boys from Central School formed this club as Wimbledon Old Centrals in 1889. Their earliest successes were in the Clapham League before switching to the Southern Suburban League in 1902.

First Football League game: 20 August, 1978, Division 4, v Halifax T (h) D 3-3 – Guy; Bryant (1), Galvin, Donaldson, Aitken, Davies, Galliers, Smith, Connell (1), Holmes, Leslie (1).

Did you know: In 1934–35 Wimbledon enjoyed two firsts: reaching the second round proper of the FA Cup and the final of the Amateur Cup, where they lost 2-1 to Bishop Auckland after a goalless draw.

Managers (and Secretary-Managers)

Les Henley 1955–71, Mike Everitt 1971–73, Dick Graham 1973–74, Allen Batsford 1974–78, Dario Gradi 1978–81, Dave Bassett 1981–87, Bobby Gould 1987–90, Ray Harford 1990–91, Peter Withe 1991, Joe Kinnear January 1992–

Player and Position	*Ht*	*Wt*	*Birth Date*	*Birth Place*	*Source*	*Clubs*	*League App*	*League Gls*
Gary Blissett	6 1	11 13	29 6 64	Manchester	Altrincham	Crewe Alex	122	39
						Brentford	233	79
						Wimbledon	18	3
Andy Clarke	5 10	11 07	22 7 67	London	Barnet	Wimbledon	102	13
Robbie Earle	5 9	10 10	27 1 65	Newcastle, Staffs.	Stoke C	Port Vale	294	77
						Wimbledon	124	30
John Fashanu	6 1	11 12	18 9 63	Kensington	Cambridge U	Norwich C	7	1
						Crystal Palace (loan)	1	—
						Lincoln C	36	10
						Millwall	50	12
						Wimbledon	276	107
Dean Holdsworth	5 11	11 13	8 11 68	London	Trainee	Watford	16	3
						Carlisle U (loan)	4	1
						Port Vale (loan)	6	2
						Swansea C (loan)	5	1
						Brentford (loan)	7	1
						Brentford	110	53
						Wimbledon	78	36
Paul McGee	5 6	9 10	17 5 68	Dublin	Bohemians	Colchester U	3	—
						Wimbledon	60	9
						Peterborough U (loan)	6	—
Paul Miller	6 0	11 00	31 1 68	Bisley	Trainee	Wimbledon	80	10
						Newport Co (loan)	6	2
						Bristol C (loan)	3	—
Grant Payne	5 9	11 04	25 12 75	Woking	Trainee	Wimbledon	—	—

Trainees

Board, Kevin J. F; Brooker, Daniel P; Cobb, Simon P; Cunningham, Jason; Di Rubbo, Franco; Euell, Jason J; Fell, Gavin A; Finegan, Leon G; Fleming, Shaun A; Griffiths, Leonard W; Hodges, Daniel W; Laidlaw, Iain L; Mumford, Steven B; Owusu, Clement; Piper, Leonard H.

Associated Schoolboys

Boyle Renner, Victor D; Francis, Damien; Gardner, James; Hart, Paul; Hawkins, Peter S; Hinds, Leigh M; McCormack, Francis; Miller, Paul; O'Connor, Richard; O'Neill, Daniel H; Odlum, Gary M; Owusu, Ansah O; Petrovic, Timotije; Reynolds, Paul; Vella, Simon.

Associated Schoolboys who have accepted the Club's offer of a Traineeship/Contract

Cort, Carl E. R; Futcher, Andrew R; Longman, Luke; Lyons, Danny.

WOLVERHAMPTON WANDERERS 1993–94 *Back row (left to right):* Paul Cook, Mark Venus, Mike Stowell, Geoff Thomas, Paul Jones, Derek Mountfield, Darren Simkin.
Centre row: Steve Bull, Mark Burke, Paul Edwards, Tom Bennett, Paul Blades, David Kelly.
Front row: Mike Rankine, Kevin Keen, Garry Pendrey, Graham Turner, Paul Darby, Paul Birch, Kevin Ashley.

Division 1 **WOLVERHAMPTON WANDERERS**

Molineux Grounds, Wolverhampton WV1 4QR. Telephone Admin office: Wolverhampton (0902) 712181; lottery shop: (0902) 27524. Commercial Office: (0902) 23166. Ticket office: 0902 25899. Fax 0902 24612.

Ground capacity: 28,525.

Record attendance: 61,315 v Liverpool, FA Cup 5th rd, 11 February 1939.

Record receipts: £209,979 v Ipswich T, FA Cup 5th rd, 19 February 1994.

Pitch measurements: 116yd × 74yd.

President: Sir Jack Hayward.

Chairman: Jonathan Hayward.

Directors: Jack Harris, Billy Wright, John Harris, Nic Stones, Keith Pearson ACIS.

Team Manager: Graham Taylor.

Coaches: Chris Evans and Robert Kelly. ***Physio:*** Paul Darby.

Secretary: Keith Pearson ACIS. ***Commercial Manager:*** Gary Leaver.

Year Formed: 1877*(*see Foundation*). ***Turned Professional:*** 1888. ***Ltd Co.:*** 1982.

Club Nickname: 'Wolves'.

Previous Grounds: 1877, Goldthorn Hill; 1879, John Harper's Field; 1881, Dudley Road; 1889, Molineux.

Previous Names: 1880, St Luke's, Blakenhall combined with Blakenhall Wanderers to become Wolverhampton Wanderers (1923) Ltd until 1982.

Record League Victory: 10–1 v Leicester C, Division 1, 15 April 1938 – Sidlow; Morris, Dowen; Galley, Cullis, Gardiner; Maguire (1), Horace Wright, Westcott (4), Jones (1), Dorsett (4).

Record Cup Victory: 14–0 v Cresswell's Brewery, FA Cup, 2nd rd, 13 November 1886 – I. Griffiths; Baugh, Mason; Pearson, Allen (1), Lowder; Hunter (4), Knight (2), Brodie (4), B. Griffiths (2), Wood. Plus one goal 'scrambled through'.

Record Defeat: 1–10 v Newton Heath, Division 1, 15 October 1892.

Most League Points (2 for a win): 64, Division 1, 1957–58.

Most League Points (3 for a win): 92, Division 4, 1988–89.

Most League Goals: 115, Division 2, 1931–32.

Highest League Scorer in Season: Dennis Westcott, 38, Division 1, 1946–47.

Most League Goals in Total Aggregate: Steve Bull, 185, 1986–94.

Most Capped Player: Billy Wright, 105, England (70 consecutive).

Most League Appearances: Derek Parkin, 501, 1967–82.

Record Transfer Fee Received: £1,150,000 from Manchester C for Steve Daley, September 1979.

Record Transfer Fee Paid: £1,175,000 to Aston Villa for Andy Gray, September 1979.

Football League Record: 1888 Founder Member of Football League: 1906–23 Division 2; 1923–24 Division 3 (N); 1924–32 Division 2; 1932–65 Division 1; 1965–67 Division 2; 1967–76 Division 1; 1976–77 Division 2; 1977–82 Division 1; 1982–83 Division 2; 1983–84 Division 1; 1984–85 Division 2; 1985–86 Division 3; 1986–88 Division 4; 1988–89 Division 3; 1989–92 Division 2; 1992– Division 1.

Honours: *Football League:* Division 1 – Champions 1953–54, 1957–58, 1958–59; Runners-up 1937–38, 1938–39, 1949–50, 1954–55, 1959–60; Division 2 – Champions 1931–32, 1976–77; Runners-up 1966–67, 1982–83; Division 3 (N) – Champions 1923–24; Division 3 – Champions 1988–89; Division 4 – Champions 1987–88. *FA Cup:* Winners 1893, 1908, 1949, 1960; Runners-up 1889, 1896, 1921, 1939. *Football League Cup:* Winners 1973–74, 1979–80. *Texaco Cup:* 1970–71. *Sherpa Van Trophy:* Winners 1988. **European Competitions:** *European Cup:* 1958–59, 1959–60. *European Cup-Winners' Cup:* 1960–61. *UEFA Cup:* 1971–72 (runners-up), 1973–74, 1974–75, 1980–81.

WOLVERHAMPTON WANDERERS 1993—94 LEAGUE RECORD

Match No.	Date	Venue	Opponents	Result		H/T Score	Lg. Pos.	Goalscorers	Attendance
1	Aug 14	H	Bristol C	W	3-1	1-0	—	Bull 2, Mountfield	21,052
2	22	A	Birmingham C	D	2-2	2-0	—	Venus, Thomas	15,117
3	25	H	Millwall	W	2-0	1-0	—	Bull, Kelly D	19,570
4	28	H	Middlesbrough	L	2-3	2-1	4	Kelly D, Thomas	21,061
5	Sept 7	A	Watford	L	0-1	0-1	—		7870
6	5	A	WBA	L	2-3	1-1	—	Bull, Thomas	25,615
7	11	H	Portsmouth	D	1-1	0-0	7	Kelly D	19,019
8	18	A	Sunderland	W	2-0	1-0	6	Small, Thomas	18,292
9	25	A	Grimsby T	L	0-2	0-1	8		6310
10	Oct 2	H	Charlton Ath	D	1-1	0-0	8	Keen	16,907
11	17	A	Crystal Palace	D	1-1	1-1	—	Kelly D	13,056
12	23	H	Stoke C	D	1-1	1-1	17	Kelly D	20,421
13	30	A	Southend U	D	1-1	0-0	18	Cook (pen)	8071
14	Nov 2	H	Notts Co	W	3-0	1-0	—	Birch, Keen, Bull	15,989
15	7	A	Derby Co	W	4-0	1-0	—	Bull 3, Keen	14,310
16	10	H	Nottingham F	D	1-1	1-0	—	Kelly D	21,621
17	13	H	Barnsley	D	1-1	0-1	11	Kelly D	18,355
18	27	A	Leicester C	D	2-2	2-0	12	Bull 2	18,395
19	Dec 5	H	Derby Co	D	2-2	1-1	—	Bull, Kelly D	16,900
20	11	H	Watford	W	2-0	2-0	12	Bull, Dennison	17,460
21	18	A	Bristol C	L	1-2	0-1	12	Kelly D	15,151
22	27	A	Tranmere R	D	1-1	0-1	12	Bull	15,603
23	28	H	Oxford U	W	2-1	0-0	12	Cook (pen), Keen	25,908
24	Jan 1	A	Peterborough U	W	1-0	0-0	12	Regis	10,298
25	3	H	Bolton W	W	1-0	1-0	10	Dennison	24,053
26	15	H	Crystal Palace	W	2-0	1-0	7	Thompson (pen), Keen	23,851
27	23	A	Nottingham F	D	0-0	0-0	—		23,008
28	Feb 5	A	Stoke C	D	1-1	1-0	8	Blades	22,579
29	12	H	Southend U	L	0-1	0-0	9		22,774
30	22	H	Birmingham C	W	3-0	1-0	—	Regis, Kelly D, Keen	24,931
31	25	H	WBA	L	1-2	1-2	9	Keen	28,039
32	Mar 5	A	Middlesbrough	L	0-1	0-0	10		12,092
33	15	A	Portsmouth	L	0-3	0-1	—		7840
34	19	H	Grimsby T	D	0-0	0-0	15		20,224
35	26	A	Charlton Ath	W	1-0	1-0	13	Whittingham	8416
36	29	A	Bolton W	W	3-1	1-0	—	Whittingham 2, Thompson	12,405
37	Apr 2	H	Tranmere R	W	2-1	1-0	8	Whittingham, Mills	26,592
38	4	A	Oxford U	L	0-4	0-3	10		10,423
39	9	H	Peterborough U	D	1-1	1-1	11	Whittingham	23,676
40	12	A	Luton T	W	2-0	1-0	—	Burke, Whittingham	8545
41	16	A	Notts Co	W	2-0	0-0	9	Thompson (pen), Whittingham	13,438
42	20	A	Millwall	L	0-1	0-0	—		11,883
43	23	H	Luton T	W	1-0	1-0	8	Whittingham	25,479
44	30	A	Barnsley	L	0-2	0-0	8		11,329
45	May 3	H	Sunderland	D	1-1	1-1	—	Bull	25,079
46	8	H	Leicester C	D	1-1	0-1	8	Kelly D	27,229

Final League Position: 8

GOALSCORERS

League (60): Bull 14, Kelly D 11, Whittingham 8, Keen 7, Thomas 4, Thompson 3 (2 pens), Cook 2 (2 pens), Dennison 2, Regis 2, Birch 1, Blades 1, Burke 1, Mills 1, Mountfield 1, Small 1, Venus 1.
Coca-Cola Cup (2): Burke 1, Mountfield 1.
FA Cup (6): Kelly D 2, Blades 1, Keen 1, Mills 1, Thompson 1.

Stowell 46	Rankine 28 + 3	Venus 38 + 1	Cook 34 + 2	Mountfield 17 + 2	Blades 35	Birch 25 + 7	Thomas 8	Bull 27	Kelly D 35 + 1	Keen 36 + 5	Regis 8 + 11	Shirtliff 39	Burke 10 + 2	Thompson 36 + 1	Mills 6 + 8	Dennison 10 + 4	Small 2 + 1	Simkin 7 + 1	Kelly J 4	Edwards 10 + 1	Bennett 8 + 2	Masters 4	Marsden 8	Ferguson 12 + 2	Whittingham 13	Match No.
1	2	3	4	5	6	7	8	9	10	11	12															1
1	2	3	4	5		7	8	9	10	11	12	6														2
1	2	3	4		5	7	8	9	10	11		6	12													3
1	2		4	5	6	7	8	9	10	11				3												4
1	2	6	4	12	5	7	8			11	9		10	3	14											5
1	2	6	4		5	7	8	9	10	11	12			3												6
1	2	6	4		5	12	8		10	11	9	3	7			14										7
1	2	3		5	7	12	8		10	11		6	4				9									8
1	2	3		5	7	8		9	10	11		6	4				12									9
1		3	7	5					10	11		6	4		12		9	2	8							10
1		3	7	5	4				10		9	6				11		2	8	12						11
1		3	7	5					10	12	9	6		4		11		2	8							12
1		3	7	5				9	10	14	12	6		4		11		2	8							13
1		4	7	5		8		9	10	11		6		12				2		3						14
1	12	3	7	5		8		9	10	11		6		2						4						15
1		3	8	5		7		9	10	11		6		2						4						16
1		3	8	5		7		9	10	11		6		2						4						17
1		3	8			7		9	10	11		6		2		12		5		4						18
1		3			5	8		9	10	11	12	6		2		7		14		4						19
1		3	7		5	8		9	10			6		2		11				4	12					20
1	14	3	7			8		9	10	12				2		11		5		6	4					21
1		3	7		5	8		9	10	11		6		2								4				22
1		3	8		5			9	10	11	12	6		2		7				4						23
1	2	3	7		5	8		9	10	11	12	6								4						24
1	2	4			5	8		9	10	11	12	6		3		7					14					25
1	2	4			5			9	10	11		6		3									7	8		26
1	2	4			5			9	10	11		6		3									7	8		27
1	2	4			5				10	11	9	6		3									7	8		28
1	2	4			5				10	11	9	6	14	3		12							7	8		29
1	12	3			5				10	11	9	6		2								4	7	8		30
1		3			5				10	11	9	6		2	12	7						4		8		31
1		3	14		5				10	11		6		2	12	8						4	7		9	32
1	2	4	12	5	6	14			10	11				3									7	8	9	33
1	2	4	8		5				10	11		6		3	9								7	12		34
1	2	4	8		5	12			10	11		6		3	14									7	9	35
1	2	4	8		5	12				11		6		3	10									7	9	36
1	2	4	8		5	14				11	12	6		3	10									7	9	37
1	2	4	8	5	6	14				11	12			3	10									7	9	38
1	2		8	5	4					11	12	6		3	10	14								7	9	39
1		4	8	12	5	7						6	11	3	10						2			14	9	40
1	2		8	5		7		9				6	11	3	12						4				10	41
1	2		8		5	7		9		14		6	11	3	12						4				10	42
1	2		8		5	7		9				6	11	3							4				10	43
1	2		8		5	7		9		14		6	11	3	12						4				10	44
1	2		8		5	7		9	12	11		6		3							4				10	45
1	2	12	8		5	7		9	10	11		6		3							4					46

Coca-Cola Cup	Second Round	Swindon T (a)	0-2
		(h)	2-1
FA Cup	Third Round	Crystal Palace (h)	1-0
	Fourth Round	Port Vale (a)	2-0
	Fifth Round	Ipswich T (h)	1-1
		(a)	2-1
	Sixth Round	Chelsea (a)	0-1

WOLVERHAMPTON WANDERERS

Player and Position	Ht	Wt	Birth Date	Birth Place	Source	Clubs	League App	League Gls
Goalkeepers								
Andy Debont	6 2	15 06	7 2 74	Wolverhampton	Trainee	Wolverhampton W	—	—
Paul Jones	6 3	14 00	18 4 67	Chirk	Kidderminster H	Wolverhampton W	16	—
Mike Stowell	6 2	11 10	19 4 65	Preston	Leyland Motors	Preston NE	—	—
						Everton	—	—
						Chester C (loan)	14	—
						York C (loan)	6	—
						Manchester C (loan)	14	—
						Port Vale (loan)	7	—
						Wolverhampton W (loan)	7	—
						Preston NE (loan)	2	—
						Wolverhampton W	157	—
Defenders								
Kevin Ashley*	5 7	10 04	31 12 68	Birmingham	Apprentice	Birmingham C	57	1
						Wolverhampton W	88	1
Tom Bennett	5 11	11 08	12 12 69	Falkirk	Trainee	Aston Villa	—	—
						Wolverhampton W	107	2
Paul Blades	6 0	10 12	5 1 65	Peterborough	Apprentice	Derby Co	166	1
						Norwich C	47	—
						Wolverhampton W	75	2
Danny Collier*	6 3	12 08	15 1 74	Eccles	Trainee	Wolverhampton W	—	—
John Howard	6 2	13 02	2 4 74	Stafford	Trainee	Wolverhampton W	—	—
Neil Masters	6 1	13 03	25 5 72	Lisburn	Trainee	Bournemouth	38	2
						Wolverhampton W	4	—
Derek Mountfield*	6 1	12 07	2 11 62	Liverpool	Apprentice	Tranmere R	26	1
						Everton	106	19
						Aston Villa	90	9
						Wolverhampton W	83	4
Darren Shaw	6 0	12 02	20 12 74	Telford	Trainee	Wolverhampton W	—	—
Peter Shirtliff	6 0	13 03	6 4 61	Barnsley	Apprentice	Sheffield W	188	4
						Charlton Ath	103	7
						Sheffield W	104	4
						Wolverhampton W	39	—
Darren Simkin	6 0	12 00	24 3 70	Walsall	Blakenhall	Wolverhampton W	15	—
Mark Venus	6 0	11 08	6 4 67	Hartlepool		Hartlepool U	4	—
						Leicester C	61	1
						Wolverhampton W	186	4
Midfield								
Paul Birch	5 6	10 04	20 11 62	West Bromwich	Apprentice	Aston Villa	173	16
						Wolverhampton W	125	14
Paul Cook	5 11	10 10	22 2 67	Liverpool		Wigan Ath	83	14
						Norwich C	6	—
						Wolverhampton W	193	19
Darren Ferguson	5 10	10 04	9 2 72	Glasgow	Trainee	Manchester U	27	—
						Wolverhampton W	14	—
Kevin Keen	5 8	11 00	25 2 67	Amersham	Apprentice	West Ham U	219	21
						Wolverhampton W	41	7
Jimmy Kelly	5 7	11 10	14 2 73	Liverpool	Trainee	Wrexham	21	—
						Wolverhampton W	7	—
						Walsall (loan)	10	2
						Wrexham (loan)	9	—
Chris Marsden	5 11	10 12	3 1 69	Sheffield	Trainee	Sheffield U	16	1
						Huddersfield T	121	9
						Coventry C (loan)	7	—
						Wolverhampton W	8	—
Mark Rankine	5 10	11 01	30 9 69	Doncaster	Trainee	Doncaster R	164	20
						Wolverhampton W	73	1
Jason Smith	5 4	10 02	21 12 75	Birmingham	Trainee	Wolverhampton W	—	—
Geoff Thomas	5 10	10 07	5 8 64	Manchester	Local	Rochdale	11	1
						Crewe Alex	125	20
						Crystal Palace	195	26
						Wolverhampton W	8	4
Andy Thompson	5 4	10 06	9 11 67	Carnock	Apprentice	WBA	24	1
						Wolverhampton W	268	26
Mark Turner*	6 0	11 01	4 10 72	Bebbington	Trainee	Wolverhampton W	1	—

WOLVERHAMPTON WANDERERS

Colours: Gold shirts, black shorts, gold stockings. **Change colours:** White shirts, white shorts, white stockings.

Foundation: Another club where precise details of information are confused, due in part to the existence of an earlier Wolverhampton club which played rugby. However, it is now considered likely that it came into being in 1879 when players from St. Luke's (founded 1877) and Goldthorn (founded 1876) broke away to form Wolverhampton Wanderers Association FC.

First Football League game: 8 September, 1888, Football League, v Aston Villa (h) D 1-1 – Baynton; Baugh, Mason; Fletcher, Allen, Lowder; Hunter, Cooper, Anderson, White, Cannon. Scorer – Cox o.g.

Did you know: On 8 December 1993 against Watford, Steve Bull scored his 230th senior goal in his 350th appearance for the club in a 2-0 win.

Managers (and Secretary-Managers)
George Worrall 1877–85*, John Addenbrooke 1885–1922, George Jobey 1922–24, Albert Hoskins 1924–26 (had been secretary since 1922), Fred Scotchbrook 1926–27, Major Frank Buckley 1927–44, Ted Vizard 1944–48, Stan Cullis 1948–64, Andy Beattie 1964–65, Ronnie Allen 1966–68, Bill McGarry 1968–76, Sammy Chung 1976–78, John Barnwell 1978–81, Ian Greaves 1982, Graham Hawkins 1982–84, Tommy Docherty 1984–85, Bill McGarry 1985, Sammy Chapman 1985–86, Brian Little 1986, Graham Turner 1986–94, Graham Taylor March 1994–

Player and Position	*Ht*	*Wt*	*Birth Date*	*Birth Place*	*Source*	*Clubs*	*League App*	*League Gls*
Forwards								
Shaun Bradbury*	5 10	11 00	11 2 74	Birmingham	Trainee	Wolverhampton W	2	2
Steve Bull	5 11	11 04	28 3 65	Tipton	Apprentice	WBA	4	2
						Wolverhampton W	310	185
Mark Burke*	5 10	11 08	12 2 69	Solihull	Apprentice	Aston Villa	7	—
						Middlesbrough	57	6
						Darlington (loan)	5	1
						Ipswich T (loan)	—	—
						Wolverhampton W	68	11
						Luton T (loan)	3	—
Robert Dennison	5 7	11 00	30 4 63	Banbridge	Glenavon	WBA	16	1
						Wolverhampton W	257	35
David Kelly	5 11	11 03	25 11 65	Birmingham	Alvechurch	Walsall	147	63
						West Ham U	41	7
						Leicester C	66	22
						Newcastle U	70	35
						Wolverhampton W	36	11
Lee Mills	6 1	12 11	10 7 70	Mexborough	Stocksbridge	Wolverhampton W	14	1
Stephen Piearce	5 11	10 10	29 9 74	Sutton Coldfield	Trainee	Wolverhampton W	—	—
Cyrille Regis*	6 0	13 04	9 2 58	French Guyana	Hayes	WBA	237	82
						Coventry C	238	47
						Aston Villa	52	12
						Wolverhampton W	19	2
Darren Roberts*	6 0	12 10	12 10 69	Birmingham	Burton Alb	Wolverhampton W	21	5
						Hereford U (loan)	6	5
James Smith	5 6	10 08	17 9 74	Birmingham	Trainee	Wolverhampton W	—	—
Scott Voice	6 0	11 10	12 8 74	Wolverhampton	Trainee	Wolverhampton W	—	—

Trainees
Barnett, Jason V; Bytheway, Matthew; Dale, David A; Eades, Gary J; Ellitts, Justin S; Graham, Iain J; Gregory, Alan; Hanbury, Jay P; Innes, Michael P; Macbeth, AndrewM; Mahon, Gavin A; Morris, David T; Phillips, Richard W; Robinson, Carl P; Ross, John E. G; Townsend, Quentin L; Westwood, Christopher J.

Associated Schoolboys
Churm, Richard; Coleman, Claudio; Cooper, Ian A; Deen, Robert; Hampton, Richard P; Hardle, Simon M; Hill, Daniel F; Hill, Paul D; Johnston, Craig W; Murphy, Leroy; Perry, Mark; Randle, Wesley; Ranger, Marcus A; Sawyers, Robert; Smith, Darryl C; Turpin, Jamie L.

Associated Schoolboys who have accepted the Club's offer of a Traineeship/Contract
Biddle, Steven J; Davis, Paul; Harper, Lee N; Holmes, Martin L; Leadbitter, Richard P; Wilson, Christopher L.

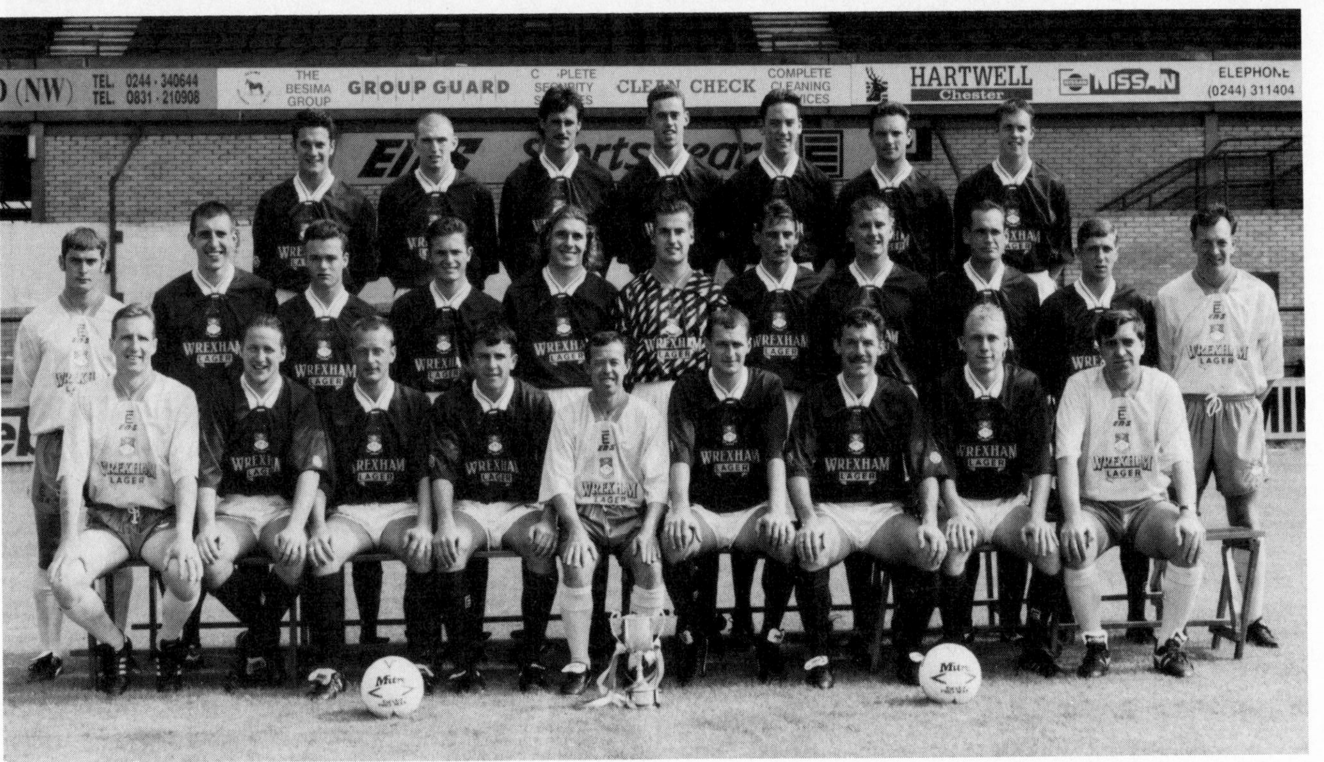

WREXHAM 1993–94 *Back row (left to right):* Kevin Jones, Karl Connolly, John Paskin, Scott Williams, Damien Roden, Gareth Owen, Phil Myddleton.
Centre row: Mike Rigg (Community Scheme Officer), Mark Sertori, Stephen Pugh, Barry Jones, Mike Lake, Mark Morris, Wayne Phillips, Craig Knight, Gary Bennett, Phil Hardy, Steve Wade (Physio).
Front row: Joey Jones (Coach), Jonathan Cross, Mark Taylor, David Brammer, Brian Flynn (Manager), Tony Humes, Mel Pejic, Steve Watkin, Kevin Reeves (Assistant Manager).

Division 2 WREXHAM

Racecourse Ground, Mold Road, Wrexham LL11 2AN. Telephone Wrexham (0978) 262129. Fax 0978 357821. Commercial Dept: (0978) 352536. Clubcall: 0891 121642.

Ground capacity: 11,881.

Record attendance: 34,445 v Manchester U, FA Cup 4th rd, 26 January 1957.

Record receipts: £126,012 v West Ham U, FA Cup 4th rd, 4 February 1992.

Pitch measurements: 111yd × 71yd.

President: G. Mytton.

Chairman: W. P. Griffiths.

Managing Director: D. L. Rhodes.

Directors: C. Griffiths, S. Mackreth, G. Paletta, B. Williams (vice-chairman).

Manager: Brian Flynn. ***Assistant Manager:*** Kevin Reeves.

Secretary: D. L. Rhodes. ***Player-coach:*** Joey Jones.

Commercial Manager: P. Stokes. ***Physio:*** Steve Wade.

Year Formed: 1873 (oldest club in Wales).

Turned Professional: 1912. ***Ltd Co.:*** 1912.

Previous Ground: Acton Park.

Club Nickname: 'Robins'.

Record League Victory: 10–1 v Hartlepools, Division 4, 3 March 1962 – Keelan; Peter Jones, McGavan; Tecwyn Jones, Fox, Ken Barnes; Ron Barnes (3), Bennion (1), Davies (3), Ambler (3), Ron Roberts.

Record Cup Victory: 6–0 v Gateshead, FA Cup, 1st rd, 20 November 1976 – Lloyd; Evans, Whittle, Davis, Roberts, Thomas (Hill), Shinton (3 incl. 1p), Sutton, Ashcroft (2), Lee (1), Griffiths. 6–0 v Charlton Ath, FA Cup, 3rd rd, 5 January 1980 – Davies; Darracott, Kenworthy, Davis, Jones (Hill), Fox, Vinter (3), Sutton, Edwards (1), McNeil (2), Carrodus.

Record Defeat: 0–9 v Brentford, Division 3, 15 October 1963.

Most League Points (2 for a win): 61, Division 4, 1969–70 and Division 3, 1977–78.

Most League Points (3 for a win): 80, Division 3, 1992–93.

Most League Goals: 106, Division 3 (N), 1932–33.

Highest League Scorer in Season: Tom Bamford, 44, Division 3 (N), 1933–34.

Most League Goals in Total Aggregate: Tom Bamford, 175, 1928–34.

Most Capped Player: Dai Davies, 28 (51), Wales.

Most League Appearances: Arfon Griffiths, 592, 1959–61, 1962–79.

Record Transfer Fee Received: £300,000 from Manchester U for Mickey Thomas, November 1978, from Manchester C for Bobby Shinton, July 1979 and from Liverpool for Lee Jones, March 1992.

Record Transfer Fee Paid: £210,000 to Liverpool for Joey Jones, October 1978.

Football League Record: 1921 Original Member of Division 3 (N); 1958–60 Division 3; 1960–62 Division 4; 1962–64 Division 3; 1964–70 Division 4; 1970–78 Division 3; 1978–82 Division 2; 1982–83 Division 3; 1983–92 Division 4; 1992–93 Division 3; 1993– Division 2.

Honours: *Football League:* Division 2 best season: 15th, 1978–79; Division 3 – Champions 1977–78; Division 3 (N) – Runners-up 1932–33; Division 4 – Runners-up 1969–70. *FA Cup:* best season: 6th rd, 1973–74, 1977–78. *Football League Cup:* best season: 5th rd, 1961, 1978. *Welsh Cup:* Winners 22 times. Runners-up 22 times. Victories equal record, but record number of final appearances. **European Competition:** *European Cup-Winners' Cup:* 1972–73, 1975–76, 1978–79, 1979–80, 1984–85, 1986–87, 1990–91.

WREXHAM 1993—94 LEAGUE RECORD

Match No.	Date	Venue	Opponents	Result		H/T Score	Lg. Pos.	Goalscorers	Attendance
1	Aug 14	H	Rotherham U	D	3-3	1-1	—	Bennett 2 (2 pens), Sertori	5570
2	21	A	Swansea C	L	1-3	1-1	18	Watkin	5383
3	28	H	Blackpool	L	2-3	1-2	22	Watkin, Bennett	4957
4	31	A	Fulham	D	0-0	0-0	—		3685
5	Sept 4	A	Stockport Co	L	0-1	0-1	23		4886
6	11	H	Reading	W	3-2	2-1	19	Phillips, Bennett, Lake	3941
7	14	H	Hull C	W	3-0	0-0	—	Bennett 3 (1 pen)	4345
8	18	A	Exeter C	L	0-5	0-3	19		3982
9	25	H	Barnet	W	4-0	1-0	16	Bennett 2 (1 pen), Cross, Jones B	3767
10	Oct 2	A	Port Vale	L	0-3	0-0	16		8722
11	9	H	Cambridge U	D	1-1	0-1	16	Bennett (pen)	4220
12	16	A	Brentford	L	1-2	0-1	18	Bennett	5801
13	23	H	Cardiff C	W	3-1	0-0	18	Taylor 2, Bennett	4245
14	30	A	Plymouth Arg	D	1-1	0-0	18	Bennett	6977
15	Nov 2	A	Brighton & HA	D	1-1	0-1	—	Watkin (pen)	5530
16	6	H	Bournemouth	W	2-1	1-0	16	Watkin, Connolly	4023
17	20	A	Hartlepool U	W	2-1	2-1	12	Watkin, Bennett	1530
18	27	H	York C	D	1-1	1-1	13	Bennett	3574
19	Dec 11	H	Swansea C	W	3-2	1-0	10	Owen, Taylor, Bennett	2762
20	17	A	Rotherham U	L	1-2	0-1	—	Bennett	2664
21	27	A	Burnley	L	1-2	1-0	14	Watkin	15,357
22	Jan 1	A	Bradford C	L	0-1	0-0	16		5829
23	3	H	Leyton Orient	W	4-2	3-1	15	Bennett 2, Taylor, Cross	3567
24	15	H	Brentford	L	1-2	1-1	15	Bennett	3701
25	22	A	Cambridge U	D	2-2	1-0	15	Bennett, Watkin	3353
26	Feb 5	A	Cardiff C	L	1-5	1-2	19	Baddeley (og)	10,847
27	12	H	Huddersfield T	W	3-1	2-0	16	Jones B, Watkin, Brammer	4011
28	19	A	Blackpool	L	1-4	1-1	17	Taylor	4069
29	22	H	Fulham	W	2-0	0-0	—	Connolly, Durkan	2094
30	Mar 5	A	Reading	W	1-0	0-0	14	Hunter	6311
31	8	H	Stockport Co	L	0-1	0-1	—		4756
32	12	H	Exeter C	D	1-1	0-0	15	Bennett	3053
33	15	A	Hull C	D	0-0	0-0	—		5749
34	19	A	Barnet	W	2-1	0-1	16	Owen, Bennett	1853
35	22	H	Bristol R	W	3-2	1-1	—	Bennett, Taylor 2	3184
36	26	H	Port Vale	W	2-1	1-0	11	Bennett 2	7202
37	29	A	Leyton Orient	D	2-2	0-1	—	Bennett (pen), Owen	2643
38	Apr 2	H	Burnley	W	1-0	0-0	11	Bennett	7253
39	4	A	Bristol R	L	1-3	0-3	12	Humes	4708
40	9	H	Bradford C	L	0-3	0-2	12		3406
41	12	A	Huddersfield T	L	0-3	0-1	—		4191
42	16	H	Brighton & HA	L	1-3	0-1	13	Brammer	2613
43	23	A	Bournemouth	W	2-1	1-0	12	Bennett 2 (1 pen)	2522
44	26	H	Plymouth Arg	L	0-3	0-2	—		2518
45	30	H	Hartlepool U	W	2-0	1-0	12	Bennett, Watkin	2013
46	May 7	A	York C	D	1-1	1-1	12	Bennett (pen)	5894

Final League Position: 12

GOALSCORERS

League (66): Bennett 32 (8 pens), Watkin 9 (1 pen), Taylor 7, Owen 3, Brammer 2, Connolly 2, Cross 2, Jones B 2, Durkan 1, Humes 1, Hunter 1, Lake 1, Phillips 1, Sertori 1, own goal 1.
Coca-Cola Cup (8): Bennett 3 (2 pens), Paskin 2, Connolly 1, Pejic 1, own goal 1.
FA Cup (1): Watkin 1.

Morris 4	Jones B 33	Hardy 25	Brammer 16 + 6	Humes 25 + 2	Sertori 15	Bennett 41	Phillips 20 + 1	Connolly 38 + 1	Watkin 39 + 1	Cross 20 + 5	Paskin 4 + 11	Williams 11 + 3	Lake 29 + 1	Taylor 28 + 2	Walton 6	Hunter 23	Pejic 40	Pugh 2 + 5	Marriott 36	Owen 24 + 3	Durkan 9 + 1	Jones K 5	Hughes 3 + 8	Kelly 9	Brace 1	Match No.
1	2	3	*4*	5	6	7	8	9	10	11	12	14														1
1	2	*3*		5	6	7	8	9	10		12	14	4	11												2
	2	3				7	8	9	10		12		4	11	1	5	6									3
	2	3			5	7	8	9	10	11			4		1		6									4
	2	3			5	7	8	9	10	11	12		4		1		6									5
	2	3			5	7	8	9	10	11	12		4		1		6									6
	2	3			5	7	8	9	10	11			4		1		6									7
	2	3		12	5	7	8	9	10	11			4		1		6									8
1	2	3			5	7	8	9		11	10		4				6									9
1	2	3	12	4	5	7	8	9		*11*	10						6	14								10
	2	3		4	5	7	8	9	10		11						6		1	12						11
	2	3		5		7	8	9	10				4	11			6		1	12						12
		3				7	2	9	10				4	11		5	6		1	8						13
		3				7	2	9	10	11			4			5	6		1	8						14
		3		14			2	9	10	12			4			*5*	6	11	1	8	7					15
		3		5			2	9	10		12		4				6	11	1	8	7					16
		3	4	5		7		9	10	11						6	2		1	8						17
		3	4	5		7		9	10	*11*			12			6	2	14	1	8						18
		3		5		7		9		10			4	11		6	2		1	8						19
		3		5		7		9		10		14	4	11		6	*2*	12	1	8						20
		3	14	5		7		9	10	12			*4*	11		6	2		1	8						21
		3		5		7			10	9			4	11		6	2	12	1	8						22
		3		5		7			10	9			4	11		6			1	8		2				23
		3				7	12		10	9	14		4	11		5	6		1	*8*		*2*				24
	2		8			7	3		10	9	14		4	*11*		5	6		1				12			25
	2		*8*			7	3		10	9	14		4	11		5	6		1				12			26
	2		12			7	8		10	3	14		4	11		5	6		1				*9*			27
	2		12				8		10	*3*	9		4	11		5	6	14	1		7					28
	2	3	8					9	10		12		4			5	6		1		7		11			29
	2		8	3				9	10				4	11		5	6		1		7					30
	2		8	3		7		9	10				4	11		5	6		1				12			31
	2		8	3		7		9	10					11		5	6		1				12	4		32
	2		8	3		7		9	10					11		5	6		1				12	4		33
	2		8	*3*		7		12	10					11		5	6		1	14			9	4		34
	2			5		7		9	10			3		11			6		1	8			12	4		35
	2		10	5		7		9				3		11			6		1	8				4		36
	2			5		7		9	10			3		11			6		1	8			12	4		37
	2			5		7		9	10			3		11			6		1	8				4		38
	2		12	5		7		9	10			3		*11*			6		1	8			14	4		39
	2		11		5	7		9	10			3					6		1	8	12			4		40
	5					7		9				3	4	11			6		1	8	10	2				41
	2		12	5		7		9	14			3	4	*11*			6		1	8	10					42
	5		4		6	7		9	10			3		11					1	8		2				43
			4		5	7		9	10	12		3		11			6		1	8		2				44
	5				6	*7*		9	10	12		3	4	14					1	8	11				2	45
	2		4	*3*	6	*7*		9	10	14				12		5			1	8	11					46

Coca-Cola Cup	First Round	Crewe Alex (a)	1-0
		(h)	3-3
	Second Round	Nottingham F (h)	3-3
		(a)	1-3
FA Cup	First Round	Walsall (h)	1-1
		(a)	0-2

WREXHAM

Player and Position	Ht	Wt	Birth Date	Birth Place	Source	Clubs	League App	League Gls
Goalkeepers								
Andrew Marriott	6 0	12 07	11 10 70	Nottingham	Trainee	Arsenal	—	—
						Nottingham F	11	—
						WBA (loan)	3	—
						Blackburn R (loan)	2	—
						Colchester U (loan)	10	—
						Burnley (loan)	15	—
						Wrexham	36	—
Mark Morris*	6 0	12 00	1 8 68	Chester		Wrexham	101	—
Defenders								
Deryn Brace†	5 9	10 03	15 3 75	Haverfordwest	Trainee	Norwich C	—	—
						Wrexham	1	—
Phil Hardy	5 8	11 00	9 4 73	Chester		Wrexham	132	—
Tony Humes	5 11	11 00	19 3 66	Blyth	Apprentice	Ipswich T	120	10
						Wrexham	73	1
Barry Hunter	6 3	12 00	18 11 68	Coleraine	Crusaders	Wrexham	23	1
Barry Jones	5 10	11 02	20 6 70	Prescot	Prescot T	Liverpool	—	—
						Wrexham	75	4
Kevin Jones*	5 10	11 00	16 2 74	Wrexham	Trainee	Wrexham	9	—
Craig Knight*	6 1	12 00	24 10 73	Wrexham	Trainee	Wrexham	1	—
Phil Myddleton*	5 8	10 12	22 12 72	St Asaph	Trainee	Wrexham	—	—
Mel Pejic	5 9	10 13	27 4 59	Chesterton	Local	Stoke C	1	—
						Hereford U	412	14
						Wrexham	86	2
Damien Roden	5 10	11 02	17 9 74	Wrexham	Trainee	Wrexham	—	—
Mark Sertori*	6 1	13 00	1 9 67	Manchester		Stockport Co	4	—
						Lincoln C	50	9
						Wrexham	110	3
Scott Williams	6 0	11 00	7 8 74	Bangor	Trainee	Wrexham	15	—
Midfield								
David Brammer	5 9	10 05	28 2 75	Bromborough	Trainee	Wrexham	24	2
Karl Connolly	5 11	11 02	9 2 70	Prescot	Napoli (Liverpool Sunday League)	Wrexham	117	19
Jonathan Cross	5 10	11 04	2 3 75	Wallasey	Trainee	Wrexham	68	9
Kieron Durkan	5 10	11 05	1 12 73	Chester	Trainee	Wrexham	12	1
Michael Lake	6 1	12 11	6 11 66	Manchester	Macclesfield T	Sheffield U	35	4
						Wrexham	56	6
Gareth Owen	5 7	11 10	21 10 71	Chester	Trainee	Wrexham	144	15
Wayne Phillips	5 10	11 00	15 12 70	Bangor	Trainee	Wrexham	99	4
Mark Taylor	5 7	11 00	20 11 64	Hartlepool	Local	Hartlepool U	47	4
						Crewe Alex (loan)	3	—
						Blackpool	100	40
						Cardiff C (loan)	6	3
						Wrexham	58	9
Forwards								
Gary Bennett	5 11	12 00	20 9 63	Liverpool	Local	Wigan Ath	20	3
						Chester C	126	36
						Southend U	42	6
						Chester C	80	15
						Wrexham	76	48
Bryan Hughes§			19 6 76	Liverpool	Trainee	Wrexham	11	—
John Paskin*	6 2	12 05	1 2 62	Capetown	Seiko	WBA	25	5
						Wolverhampton W	34	3
						Stockport Co (loan)	5	1
						Birmingham C (loan)	10	3
						Shrewsbury T (loan)	1	—
						Wrexham	51	11
Stephen Pugh	5 10	11 00	27 11 73	Bangor	Trainee	Wrexham	10	—
Steve Watkin	5 10	10 05	16 6 71	Wrexham	School	Wrexham	110	36

WREXHAM

Colours: Red shirts, white shorts, red stockings. **Change colours:** White shirts, red shorts, white stockings.

Foundation: The oldest club still in existence in Wales, Wrexham was founded in 1873 by a group of local businessmen initially to play a 17-a-side game against the Provincial Insurance team. By 1875 their team formation was reduced to 11 men and a year later they were among the founders of the Welsh FA.

First Football League game: 27 August, 1921, Division 3(N), v Hartlepools U (h) L 0-2 – Godding; Ellis, Simpson; Matthias, Foster, Griffiths; Burton, Goode, Cotton, Edwards, Lloyd.

Did you know: Gary Bennett scored in each of Wrexham's first seven home League matches in 1993–94. He failed to find the net in only another seven games at the Racecourse Ground all season.

Managers (and Secretary-Managers)
Ted Robinson 1912–25* (continued as secretary to 1930), Charlie Hewitt 1925–29, Jack Baynes 1929–31, Ernest Blackburn 1932–36, Jimmy Logan 1937–38, Arthur Cowell 1938, Tom Morgan 1938–40, Tom Williams 1940–49, Les McDowall 1949–50, Peter Jackson 1951–54, Cliff Lloyd 1954–57, John Love 1957–59, Billy Morris 1960–61, Ken Barnes 1961–65, Billy Morris 1965, Jack Rowley 1966–67, Alvan Williams 1967–68, John Neal 1968–77, Arfon Griffiths 1977–81, Mel Sutton 1981–82, Bobby Roberts 1982–85, Dixie McNeil 1985–89, Brian Flynn November 1989–

Trainees
Barnes, Richard I; Bignall, Michael; Coady, Lewis; Cody, Michael D; Dixon, Kenneth J; Edwards, Arwel R; Futcher, Stephen A; Hughes, Bryan; Jones, Paul P; Jones, Scott L; McGregor, Mark D. T; Merola, Anthony; Morgan, Steven J; Pritchard, Andrew; Rawlins, Richard P; Williams, Christopher.

****Non-Contract**
Brace, Deryn P. J; Cartwright, Mark N.

Associated Schoolboys
Davies, Andrew M; Ellison, Barry J; Griffiths, Andrew; Hooson, David J; Jones, Phillip B; Melarangi, Philip; Morris, Robert I; Nall, Darren; Pepper, Julian M; Roberts, Stephen W; Taylor, Paul A; Walsh, David; Williams, David P; Williams, Gavin P.

Associated Schoolboys who have accepted the Club's offer of a Traineeship/Contract
Owens, Robert; Roberts, Neil W; Rock, Stuart; Wilson, Gareth E.
**Non-Contract Players who are retained must be re-signed before they are eligible to play in League matches.

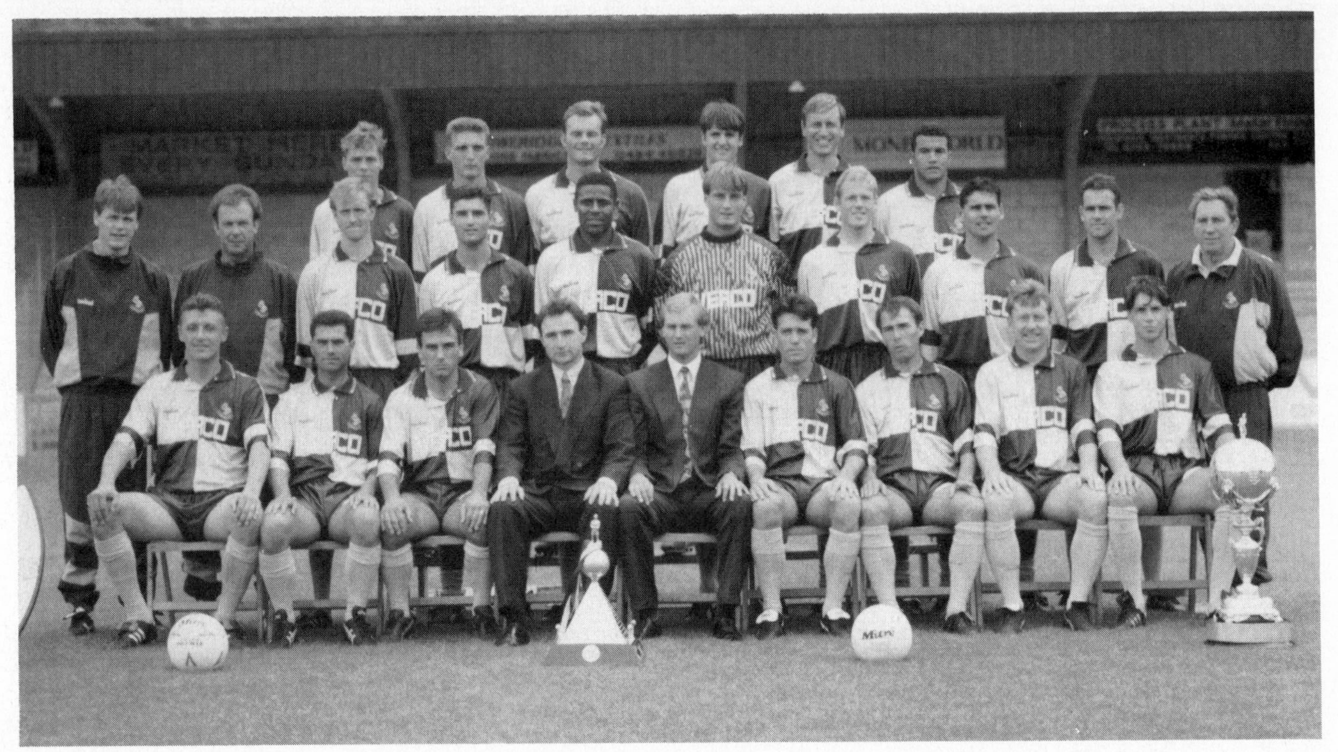

WYCOMBE WANDERERS 1993–94 *Back row (left to right):* Steve Guppy, Simon Stapleton, Keith Scott, Matt Crossley, Anton Vircavs, Hakan Hayrettin.
Centre row: Dave Jones (Physio), Jim Melvin (Youth Team Coach), Dave Carroll, Jason Cousins, Andy Kerr, Paul Hyde, Keith Ryan, Geoff Cooper, Duncan Horton, John Reardon (Kit Manager).
Front row: Glyn Creaser, Mark West, Tim Langford, Martin O'Neill (Manager), Paul Franklin (Coach), Dennis Greene, Steve Thompson, Kim Casey, Simon Hutchinson.
(Photograph: Brian Southam)

Division 2 **WYCOMBE WANDERERS**

Founded 1884

Adams Park, Hillbottom Road, Sands, High Wycombe HP12 4HJ. Telephone (0494) 472100. Fax (0494) 527633. Credit card hotline: (0494) 441118. Information Line 0891 446855.

Ground Capacity: 8864.

Record attendance: 7802 v Norwich C, FA Cup 3rd rd, 8 January 1994.

Record receipts: £46,270 v Norwich C, FA Cup 3rd rd, 8 January 1994.

Pitch measurements: 115 × 75yd.

Patron: J. Adams.

President: M. E. Seymour.

Chairman: I. L. Beeks.

Directors: G. Cox, B. R. Lee, A. Parry, G. Peart, G. Richards, A. Thibault.

Manager: Martin O'Neill MBE. ***Assistant Manager:*** Paul Franklin. ***Secretary:*** John Goldsworthy. ***Coach:*** Paul Franklin. ***Physio:*** David Jones. ***Marketing Manager:*** Mark Austin. ***Promotions Manager:*** Mike Phillips.

Year Formed: 1884. ***Turned professional:*** 1974. ***Club Nicknames:*** 'Chairboys' (after High Wycombe's tradition of furniture making), 'The Blues'.

Previous Ground: 1887 The Rye; 1893 Spring Meadow; 1895 Loakes Park, 1899 Daws Hill Park; 1901 Loakes Park; 1990 Adams Park.

Record League Victory: 4–0 v Scarborough (h), Division 3, 2 November 1993: Hyde; Cousins, Horton, Crossley (1), Evans T, Ryan, Carroll (1), Hayrettin, Thompson (Hemmings), Scott (2), Guppy.

Record Cup Victory: 4–0 v Boston U (h), FA Cup 1st rd replay, 21 November 1990: Granville; Crossley, Walford, Kerr, Creaser (1), Carroll, Blackler, Stapleton (Smith), West (2), Evans N (Ryan (1)), Hutchinson.

Most League points: 70, Division 3, 1993–94.

Most League goals: 66, Division 3, 1993–94.

Highest League goalscorer in season: Keith Scott, 10, 1993–94.

Most League appearances: Paul Hyde, Keith Ryan, 42, 1993–94.

Record Transfer Fee Received: £375,000 from Swindon T for Keith Scott, November 1993.

Record Transfer Fee Paid: £40,000 to Northampton T for Steve Brown, February 1994.

Football League Record: Promoted to Division 3 from GMVC in 1993; 1993–94 Division 3; 1994– Division 2.

Honours: FA Amateur Cup winners 1931; FA Trophy winners 1991, 1993; GM Vauxhall Conference winners 1992–93; FA Cup best season: 3rd rd 1975, 1986, 1994; Football League Cup best season: 2nd rd 1994.

WYCOMBE WANDERERS 1993—94 LEAGUE RECORD

Match No.	Date	Venue	Opponents	Result		H/T Score	Lg. Pos.	Goalscorers	Attendance
1	Aug 14	A	Carlisle U	D	2-2	1-1	—	Curran (og), Guppy	7752
2	21	H	Chester C	W	1-0	1-0	6	Scott	5607
3	28	A	Wigan Ath	D	1-1	1-1	9	Guppy	2388
4	31	A	Hereford U	W	4-3	2-2	—	Scott 2 (1 pen), Kerr 2	2847
5	Sept 4	H	Gillingham	D	1-1	0-0	6	Scott (pen)	6226
6	11	A	Bury	W	2-1	1-0	4	Kerr, Langford	2559
7	18	H	Colchester U	L	2-5	1-1	6	Scott (pen), Langford	6025
8	25	H	Doncaster R	W	1-0	0-0	4	Langford	4905
9	Oct 2	A	Chesterfield	W	3-2	1-0	4	Scott 2, Evans	2956
10	9	A	Northampton T	D	1-1	0-0	4	Guppy	5197
11	16	H	Lincoln C	L	2-3	1-3	4	Carroll, Thompson	5623
12	23	A	Darlington	D	0-0	0-0	5		2057
13	30	H	Shrewsbury T	D	1-1	1-0	5	Scott	5064
14	Nov 2	H	Scarborough	W	4-0	4-0	—	Carroll, Crossley, Scott 2	3975
15	6	A	Scunthorpe U	D	0-0	0-0	6		3604
16	20	H	Crewe Alex	W	3-1	2-1	5	Evans, Hemmings 2	6137
17	27	A	Preston NE	W	3-2	1-0	4	Langford 2, Hayrettin	9265
18	Dec 11	A	Chester C	L	1-3	0-0	5	Hemmings	3195
19	18	H	Carlisle U	W	2-0	2-0	5	Evans, Ryan	5044
20	27	A	Torquay U	D	1-1	0-1	4	Evans	4991
21	Jan 1	A	Walsall	L	2-4	1-3	6	Hemmings 2	6473
22	3	H	Hereford U	W	3-2	2-0	4	Guppy, Carroll, Evans	5528
23	15	A	Lincoln C	W	3-1	0-1	5	Langford 2, Evans	3735
24	22	H	Northampton T	W	1-0	1-0	2	Guppy	6737
25	25	H	Mansfield T	W	1-0	0-0	—	Cooper	4424
26	29	A	Shrewsbury T	L	0-1	0-0	2		5967
27	Feb 12	A	Mansfield T	L	0-3	0-1	2		3009
28	19	H	Wigan Ath	L	0-1	0-1	4		4846
29	25	A	Gillingham	W	1-0	0-0	5	Langford	4292
30	Mar 5	H	Bury	W	2-1	1-1	4	Garner, Carroll	4737
31	12	A	Colchester U	W	2-0	0-0	4	Stapleton, Titterton	3932
32	19	A	Doncaster R	W	3-0	3-0	3	Brown, Guppy 2	2358
33	26	H	Chesterfield	L	0-1	0-1	4		5752
34	29	H	Darlington	W	2-0	0-0	—	Guppy, Hemmings	4491
35	Apr 2	H	Torquay U	D	1-1	1-0	3	Crossley	5808
36	4	A	Rochdale	D	2-2	0-1	3	Carroll, Garner	2575
37	9	H	Walsall	W	3-0	0-0	3	Garner, Carroll, Hemmings	5512
38	16	A	Scarborough	L	1-3	0-2	3	Cusack	2090
39	19	H	Rochdale	D	1-1	1-0	—	Garner	5226
40	23	H	Scunthorpe U	D	2-2	0-0	3	Cousins, Creaser	5755
41	30	A	Crewe Alex	L	1-2	1-1	4	Rowbotham (og)	6182
42	May 7	H	Preston NE	D	1-1	1-1	4	Creaser	7442

Final League Position: 4

GOALSCORERS

League (67): Scott 10 (3 pens), Guppy 8, Langford 8, Hemmings 7, Carroll 6, Evans 6, Garner 4, Kerr 3, Creaser 2, Crossley 2, Brown 1, Cooper 1, Cousins 1, Cusack 1, Hayrettin 1, Ryan 1, Stapleton 1, Thompson 1, Titterton 1, own goals 2.
Coca-Cola Cup (7): Scott 2, Cousins 1, Evans 1, Langford 1, Ryan 1, Thompson 1.
FA Cup (3): Carroll 1, Hemmings 1, Langford 1.

Hyde 42	Cousins 37	Horton 15	Kerr 12 + 2	Crossley 39	Ryan 42	Carroll 41	Stapleton 21 + 1	Thompson 16 + 11	Scott 15	Guppy 41	Langford 18 + 11	Hutchinson 2 + 6	Titterton 14 + 4	Hayrettin 15 + 4	Evans 20 + 2	Hemmings 18 + 8	Potter 2 + 1	Rogers — + 1	Creaser 15	Hodges 2 + 2	Turnbull 6	Cooper — + 2	Brown 8 + 1	Garner 10 + 2	Blatherwick 2	Reid 3 + 2	Cusack 2 + 2	Cunningham 4 + 1	Match No.
1	2	3	4	5	6	7	8	9	10	*11*	12	14																	1
1	2		4	5	6	*7*	8	9	10	11	12		3	14															2
1	2		4	5	6	7			10	11	9	12	3	8															3
1	2		4	*5*	6	7			10	11	8	12	3	9	14														4
1	2		4	5	6	7			10	11		8	3	9															5
1	2		4	5	6	7			10	11	8		*3*	9	12	14													6
1	2		4	3	6	7			10	11	8			9	*5*	12	14												7
1	2		12	4	6	7			10	11	8			9	5		3												8
1			4	2	6	7			10	11				8	5	9	3												9
1		3	4	2	6	7		8	10	11				12	5	9													10
1		3	4	2	6	7		8	10	11		14		12	5	*9*													11
1	2	3		4	6	7		9	10	11		12		8	5														12
1	2	3		4	6	7		9	10	11		8			5	12													13
1	2	3		4	6	7		9	10	11				8	5	12													14
1	2	3		4	6	7		9	10		*8*			11	5	12		14											15
1	2	3		4	6	7				11	8	12		9	5	10													16
1	2	3		4	6					11	8			9	5	10			7										17
1	2			4	6	7		12		11	8		14	9	5	10			*3*										18
1	2	3		4	6	7		12		11	8			9	5	10													19
1	2	3		*4*	6	7		12		11	8		14	9	5	10													20
1	2		4		6	7	9	12		11	*8*		3		5	10				14									21
1	2				6	7	4	*9*		11	12		3	14	5	10				8									22
1	2	3	12	4	6	7	9	*8*		11	14				5					10									23
1	2	3		4	6	7	9			11	8				5					12	10								24
1	2	3		4	6	7	9			11	8				5						10	12							25
1	2	3		4	6	*7*	9	8		11	14				5						10	12							26
1	2		5	4	6	7	3	12		11	14										*9*		8	10					27
1	2			4	6	7	3	12		11	14										*9*		8	10	5				28
1	2			4	6	7	3	9		11	8										*10*		12	14	5				29
1	2			4	6	7	3	12		11	*8*		14						5					10		9			30
1	2			4	6	7	3	12		11	*8*		14						5					10		9			31
1				4	6	7	2	12		11	*8*		3			14			5				10			9			32
1	2			4	6	7				11			3			10			5				8			12	*9*	14	33
1	2			4	6	7				11	12		3			10			5				8					9	34
1	2			4	6	7	12			11			3			10			5				8					9	35
1	2			4	6	7	8			11			3			*10*			5					14			12	9	36
1	2				6	7	8	12		11			3			14			5				4	10				*9*	37
1				4	6	7	2	12		11			*3*			14			5				8	10			9		38
1	2			4	6	7	3	9		11	12					8			5					10					39
1	2			4	6	7	3	9		11	12					8			5					10					40
1	2			4	6	7	3	8		11	12					9			5					10					41
1	2			4	6	7	3	*8*		11						9			5					10		14	12		42

Coca-Cola Cup	First Round	Leyton Orient (a)	2-0
		(h)	1-0
	Second Round	Coventry C (a)	0-3
		(h)	4-2
FA Cup	First Round	Bristol R (a)	2-1
	Second Round	Cambridge U (h)	1-0
	Third Round	Norwich C (h)	0-2

WYCOMBE WANDERERS

Player and Position	Ht	Wt	Birth Date	Birth Place	Source	Clubs	League App	League Gls
Goalkeepers								
Paul Hyde	6 1	15 08	7 4 63	Hayes	Hayes	Wycombe W	42	—
Chuck Moussaddik†	5 11	12 03	23 2 70	Morocco	Wimbledon	Wycombe W	—	—
Defenders								
Jason Cousins	5 11	12 00	4 10 70	Hayes	Trainee	Brentford	21	—
					Wycombe W	Wycombe W	37	1
Glyn Creaser	6 4	15 06	1 9 59	London	Barnet	Wycombe W	15	2
Matt Crossley	6 2	13 07	18 3 68	Basingstoke	Overton U	Wycombe W	39	2
Terry Evans	6 5	15 01	12 4 65	London	Hillingdon B	Brentford	229	23
						Wycombe W	22	6
Andy Kerr*	6 0	12 07	7 4 66	West Bromwich	Telford U	Wycombe W	14	3
Steve Prindiville‡	5 9	11 07	26 12 68	Harlow	Apprentice	Leicester C	1	—
						Chesterfield	43	1
						Mansfield T	28	—
						Doncaster R	59	2
						Wycombe W	—	—
Nicky Reid*	5 10	12 00	30 10 60	Ormston	Apprentice	Manchester C	217	2
						Blackburn R	174	9
						Bristol C (loan)	4	—
						WBA	20	—
						Wycombe W	5	—
David Titterton	5 11	10 09	25 9 71	Hatton	Trainee	Coventry C	2	—
						Hereford U	51	1
						Wycombe W	18	1
Anton Vircavs‡			28 3 61	Oxford	Cheltenham T	Wycombe W	—	—
Midfield								
Dave Carroll	6 0	12 00	20 9 66	Paisley	Ruislip Manor	Wycombe W	41	6
Steve Guppy	5 11	12 00	29 3 69	Winchester	Southampton	Wycombe W	41	8
Hakan Hayrettin*	5 9	11 02	4 2 70	London	Trainee	Leyton Orient	—	—
					Barnet	Barnet	6	—
						Torquay U (loan)	4	—
						Wycombe W	19	1
Duncan Horton	5 10	11 12	18 2 67	Maidstone	Welling U	Barnet	57	3
						Wycombe W	15	—
Simon Hutchinson	5 10	13 00	24 9 69	Sheffield	Eastwood T	Wycombe W	8	—
Keith Ryan	5 11	12 07	25 6 70	Northampton	Berkhamsted T	Wycombe W	42	1
Paul Shepstone‡	5 8	10 06	8 11 70	Coventry	FA Schools	Coventry C	—	—
						Birmingham C	—	—
						Blackburn R	26	1
					Atherstone U	York C (loan)	2	—
						Motherwell	1	—
						Wycombe W	—	—
Simon Stapleton	6 0	13 00	10 12 68	Oxford	Portsmouth	Bristol R	5	—
					Wycombe W	Wycombe W	22	1
Steve Thompson†	5 7	11 09	12 1 63	Plymouth	Slough	Wycombe W	27	1
Lee Turnbull	6 0	11 09	27 9 67	Teesside	Local	Middlesbrough	16	4
						Aston Villa	—	—
						Doncaster R	123	21
						Chesterfield	87	26
						Doncaster R	11	1
						Wycombe W	6	—
Forwards								
Steve Brown	5 9	10 12	6 7 66	Northampton		Northampton T	—	—
					Irthlingborough D	Northampton T	158	19
						Wycombe W	9	2
Kim Casey‡			31 3 61	Birmingham	Cheltenham T	Wycombe W	—	—
Tony Cunningham*	6 1	13 13	12 11 57	Jamaica	Stourbridge	Lincoln C	123	32
						Barnsley	42	11
						Sheffield W	28	5
						Manchester C	18	1
						Newcastle U	47	4
						Blackpool	71	17
						Bury	58	17

WYCOMBE WANDERERS

Colours: Light & dark blue quartered shirts, dark blue shorts, dark blue stockings. **Change colours:** First: all yellow. Second: Green and white striped shirts, green shorts, white stockings.

Foundation: In 1884 a group of young furniture trade workers started playing together informally under the name of North Town Wanderers, the area of the town where they lived. They decided to better themselves by entering junior football and in 1887 Jim Ray, secretary, and Datchett Webb, captain, called a meeting at the Steam Engine public house. Wycombe Wanderers FC was formed and probably named after the famous FA Cup winners, The Wanderers, who had visited the town in 1877 for a tie with the original High Wycombe club.

First Football League game: 14 August 1993, Division 3 v Carlisle U (a), D 2-2: Hyde; Cousins, Horton (Langford), Kerr, Crossley, Ryan, Carroll, Stapleton, Thompson, Scott, Guppy (1) (Hutchinson). Wycombe's first goal was an own goal by Chris Curran.

Did you know? On 27 December 1909, Wycombe beat Staines 18-1 in the Great Western Suburban League, their all-time record score and then defeated 2nd Scots Guards 8-1 in the league on the following day.

Managers (and Secretary-Managers)
First coach appointed 1951. Prior to Brian Lee's appointment in 1969, the team was selected by a Match Committee which met every Monday evening. James McCormack 1951–52, Sid Cann 1952–61, Graham Adams 1961–62, Don Welsh 1962–64, Barry Darvill 1964–68, Brian Lee 1969–76, Ted Powell 1976–77, John Reardon 1977–78, Andy Williams 1978–80, Mike Keen 1980–84, Paul Bence 1984–86, Alan Gane 1986–87, Peter Suddaby 1987–88, Jim Kelman 1988–90, Martin O'Neill February 1990–

Player and Position	*Ht*	*Wt*	*Birth Date*	*Birth Place*	*Source*	*Clubs*	*League App*	*League Gls*
						Bolton W	9	4
						Rotherham U	69	24
						Doncaster R	25	1
						Wycombe W	5	—
Simon Garner	5 9	11 12	23 11 59	Boston	Apprentice	Blackburn R	484	168
						WBA	33	8
						Wycombe W	12	3
Dennis Greene‡			14 4 65	London	Chelmsford C	Wycombe W	—	—
Tony Hemmings	5 10	12 10	21 9 67	Burton	Northwich Vic	Wycombe W	26	7
Tim Langford	5 6	11 10	12 9 65	Kingswinford	Telford U	Wycombe W	29	8
Alec Norman†	6 1	13 00	14 2 75	Reading		Wycombe W	—	—
Mark West*			12 2 66	High Wycombe	Reading	Wycombe W	—	—

****Non-Contract**
Moussaddik, Choukri; Thompson, Steven.
****Non-Contract Players who are retained must be re-signed before they are eligible to play in League matches.**

YORK CITY 1993–94 *Back row (left to right):* Paul Barnes, Paul Atkin, Steve Tutill, Paul Stancliffe, Glen Livingstone, Ian Blackstone, Dean Kiely, Ray Warburton, Rob Ellis, Graeme Murty, Nigel Pepper.

Centre row: Ricky Sbragia (Youth Team Manager), Jon McCarthy, Scott Jordan, Wayne Hall, Tony Barratt, Andy McMillan, Alan Little (Manager), Gary Swann, Tony Canham, Steve Bushell, Mike Gosling, Glenn Naylor, Jeff Miller (Physio).

Front row: Darren Falk, Elliott Simpson, Scott Oxley, Lee Dolan, Ray Harris, Paul Vincent, Lee Medforth, Jason Cutler, Andy Warrington, Mark Watkinson, Darren Williams, Wayne Osborne, Paul Mockler, Neil McNeany, Steve Roberts, Neil Campbell.

Division 2 YORK CITY

Bootham Crescent, York YO3 7AQ. Telephone York 0904 624447. Fax 0904 631457

Ground capacity: 10,595.

Record attendance: 28,123 v Huddersfield T, FA Cup 6th rd, 5 March 1938.

Record receipts: £38,054 v Liverpool, FA Cup 5th rd, 15 February 1986.

Pitch measurements: 115yd × 74yd.

Chairman: D. M. Craig OBE, JP, BSC, fiCE, fi, MUN E, FCI ARB, M CONS E

Directors: B. A. Houghton, C. Webb, E. B. Swallow, J. E. H. Quickfall FCA.

Manager: Alan Little.

Secretary: Keith Usher. ***Commercial Manager:*** Mrs Sheila Smith.

Physio: Jeff Miller.

Hon. Orthopaedic Surgeon: Mr Peter De Boer MA, FRCS. ***Medical Officer:*** Dr R. Porter.

Year Formed: 1922. ***Turned Professional:*** 1922. ***Ltd Co.:*** 1922.

Club Nickname: 'Minstermen'.

Previous Ground: 1922, Fulfordgate; 1932, Bootham Crescent.

Record League Victory: 9–1 v Southport, Division 3 (N), 2 February 1957 – Forgan; Phillips, Howe; Brown (1), Cairney, Mollatt; Hill, Bottom (4 incl. 1p), Wilkinson (2), Wragg (1), Fenton (1).

Record Cup Victory: 6–0 v South Shields (away), FA Cup, 1st rd, 16 November 1968 – Widdowson; Baker (1p), Richardson; Carr, Jackson, Burrows; Taylor, Ross (3), MacDougall (2), Hodgson, Boyer.

Chairman: B. E. Fearn. ***Vice-chairman:*** L. V. Pickering.
Record Defeat: 0–12 v Chester, Division 3 (N), 1 February 1936.

Most League Points (2 for a win): 62, Division 4, 1964–65.

Most League Points (3 for a win): 101, Division 4, 1983–84.

Most League Goals: 96, Division 4, 1983–84.

Highest League Scorer in Season: Bill Fenton, 31, Division 3 (N), 1951–52; Arthur Bottom, 31, Division 3 (N), 1954–55 and 1955–56.

Most League Goals in Total Aggregate: Norman Wilkinson, 125, 1954–66.

Most Capped Player: Peter Scott, 7 (10), Northern Ireland.

Most League Appearances: Barry Jackson, 481, 1958–70.

Record Transfer Fee Received: £100,000 from Carlisle U for Gordon Staniforth, October 1979, and from QPR for John Byrne, October 1985.

Record Transfer Fee Paid: £50,000 to Aldershot for Dale Banton, November 1984 and £50,000 to Stoke C for Paul Barnes, July 1992.

Football League Record: 1929 Elected to Division 3 (N); 1958–59 Division 4; 1959–60 Division 3; 1960–65 Division 4; 1965–66 Division 3; 1966–71 Division 4; 1971–74 Division 3; 1974–76 Division 2; 1976–77 Division 3; 1977–84 Division 4; 1984–88 Division 3; 1988–92 Division 4; 1992–93 Division 3; 1993– Division 2.

Honours: *Football League:* Division 2 best season: 15th, 1974–75; Division 3 – Promoted 1973–74 (3rd); Division 4 – Champions 1983–84. *FA Cup:* Semi-finals 1955, when in Division 3. *Football League Cup:* best season: 5th rd, 1962.

YORK CITY 1993—94 LEAGUE RECORD

Match No.	Date	Venue	Opponents	Result		H/T Score	Lg. Pos.	Goalscorers	Attendance
1	Aug 14	H	Swansea C	W	2-1	1-0	—	Barnes 2	4596
2	21	A	Exeter C	W	2-1	1-0	4	Swann, Naylor	2807
3	28	H	Rotherham U	D	0-0	0-0	6		4674
4	31	A	Bournemouth	L	1-3	0-1	—	Canham	4113
5	Sept 4	A	Leyton Orient	L	0-2	0-1	11		3698
6	11	H	Brighton & HA	W	3-1	1-0	9	McCarthy 2, Swann	3446
7	14	H	Stockport Co	L	1-2	0-2	—	Tutill	3606
8	18	A	Fulham	W	1-0	1-0	7	Barnes	3595
9	25	A	Hartlepool U	W	2-0	1-0	6	McCarthy, Barratt	3050
10	Oct 2	H	Cardiff C	W	5-0	3-0	5	Brazil (og), Cooper, Swann, Barnes, McCarthy	3762
11	9	H	Huddersfield T	L	0-2	0-1	7		6363
12	16	A	Plymouth Arg	L	1-2	1-1	10	Barnes	5982
13	23	H	Brentford	L	0-2	0-0	10		3513
14	30	A	Bradford C	D	0-0	0-0	11		6729
15	Nov 2	H	Bristol R	L	0-1	0-0	—		3758
16	6	A	Burnley	L	1-2	0-1	17	Barnes	10,236
17	20	H	Barnet	D	1-1	1-0	17	Bushell	2966
18	27	A	Wrexham	D	1-1	1-1	17	Tutill	3574
19	Dec 11	H	Exeter C	W	3-0	3-0	14	Barnes 2 (2 pens), Cooper	2409
20	18	A	Swansea C	W	2-1	1-0	12	Cooper, Barnes	2749
21	27	H	Hull C	D	0-0	0-0	13		8481
22	28	A	Blackpool	W	5-0	2-0	11	Barnes 2, Cooper, Canham, Barratt	4501
23	Jan 1	H	Port Vale	W	1-0	0-0	9	Barnes	5903
24	3	A	Reading	L	1-2	1-1	10	Hopkins (og)	7199
25	8	A	Cambridge U	W	2-0	2-0	9	Barnes, Tutill	3534
26	15	H	Plymouth Arg	D	0-0	0-0	9		4115
27	22	A	Huddersfield T	L	2-3	1-1	9	Barnes 2	6802
28	29	H	Bradford C	D	1-1	1-1	9	Bushell	5985
29	Feb 5	A	Brentford	D	1-1	1-0	10	Barnes	5710
30	12	H	Cambridge U	W	2-0	0-0	8	Barnes 2	3334
31	19	A	Rotherham U	L	1-2	0-1	10	Blackstone	3816
32	25	H	Leyton Orient	W	3-0	2-0	9	Blackstone 2, Barnes	3414
33	Mar 5	A	Brighton & HA	L	0-2	0-1	11		8302
34	12	H	Fulham	W	2-0	0-0	10	McCarthy, Barnes (pen)	3572
35	15	A	Stockport Co	W	2-1	2-0	—	Barnes 2	3899
36	19	H	Hartlepool U	W	3-0	1-0	8	McCarthy, Barnes, Tutill	3191
37	22	H	Bournemouth	W	2-0	1-0	—	Stancliffe, Blackstone	3648
38	26	A	Cardiff C	D	0-0	0-0	5		4806
39	29	H	Reading	W	1-0	1-0	—	Swann	5558
40	Apr 2	A	Hull C	D	1-1	0-0	5	McCarthy	8190
41	4	H	Blackpool	W	2-1	2-1	5	Bushell, Blackstone	5740
42	16	A	Bristol R	W	1-0	0-0	5	Bushell	5007
43	21	A	Port Vale	L	1-2	0-1	—	Cooper	8703
44	23	H	Burnley	D	0-0	0-0	5		8642
45	30	A	Barnet	W	3-1	2-1	5	Barnes, Blackstone 2	2363
46	May 7	H	Wrexham	D	1-1	1-1	5	Canham	5894

Final League Position: 5

GOALSCORERS

League (64): Barnes 24 (3 pens), Blackstone 7, McCarthy 7, Cooper 5, Bushell 4, Swann 4, Tutill 4, Canham 3, Barratt 2, Naylor 1, Stancliffe 1, own goals 2.
Coca-Cola Cup (0):
FA Cup (2): Canham 1, McCarthy 1.

Kiely 46	McMillan 46	Hall 45	Pepper 18 + 5	Tutill 46	Atkin 13 + 1	McCarthy 44	Cooper 28 + 1	Barnes 42	Swann 44	Canham 36	Naylor 5 + 5	Barratt 5 + 14	Warburton 5 + 1	Blackstone 24 + 8	Bushell 30 + 1	Stancliffe 28	Murty 1	Match No.
1	2	3	4	5	6	7	8	9	10	11	12	14						1
1	2	3	4	5	6	7	8		10	11	9	14	12					2
1	2	3	4	5	6	7	8		10	11	9			12				3
1	2	3	4	5	6	7	8	9	10	11		12		14				4
1	2	3	4	5	6	7	8	9	10	11								5
1	2	3	4	5	6	7		9	10	11	8			12	14			6
1	2	3	4	5	6	7	8	9	10					11				7
1	2	3	4	5	6	7	8	9	10			12		11				8
1	2	3	4	5	6	7	8	9	10			11						9
1	2	3	4	5	6	7	8	9	10			11		12				10
1	2	3	4	5	6	7	8	9	10		12	11						11
1	2	3	4	5	6	7	8	9	10			11		12				12
1	2	3	4	5	6	7	8	9	10			12		11				13
1	2	3	4	5		7	8	9	10				6	11				14
1	2	3	4	5		7	8	9	10				6	11				15
1	2	3	4	5		7	8	9	10			12	6	11				16
1	2	3	4	5		7	8			11	9		6		10			17
1	2	3	4	5		7	8			11	9		6		10			18
1	2	3		5		7	8	9	4	11					10	6		19
1	2	3		5		7	8	9	4	11		12			10	6		20
1	2	3		5		7	8	9	4	11					10	6		21
1	2	3		5		7	8	9	4	11		12			10	6		22
1	2	3		5		7	8	9	4	11		12			10	6		23
1	2	3		5		7	8	9	4	11		12			10	6		24
1	2	3		5		7	8	9	4	11		12			10	6		25
1	2	3		5		7		9	4	11				8	10	6		26
1	2	3	12	5		7		9	4	11				8	10	6		27
1	2	3		5		7		9	4	11				8	10	6		28
1	2			5		7	8	9	4	3				11	10	6		29
1	2	3	14	5		7	8	9	4	11				12	10	6		30
1	2	3	12	5		7		9	4	11				8	10	6		31
1	2	3		5		7		9	4	11				8	10	6		32
1	2	3	14	5		7		9	4	11	12			8	10	6		33
1	2	3		5		7		9	4	11				8	10	6		34
1	2	3		5		7		9	4	11		12		8	10	6		35
1	2	3		5		7		9	4	11				8	10	6		36
1	2	3		5		7		9	4	11				8	10	6		37
1	2	3		5		7		9	4	11		12		8	10	6		38
1	2	3		5		7		9	4	11				8	10	6		39
1	2	3		5		7		9	4	11				8	10	6		40
1	2	3		5		7		9	4	11	12	14		8	10	6		41
1	2	3		5	14		12	9	4	11		7		8	10	6		42
1	2	3		5			8	9	4	11				12	10	6	7	43
1	2	3		5		7	8	9	4	11				12	10	6		44
1	2	3		5		7		9	4	11				8	10	6		45
1	2	3	14	5		7		9	4	11	12			8	10	6		46

Coca-Cola Cup	First Round	Rochdale (a)	0-2
		(h)	0-0
FA Cup	First Round	Burnley (a)	0-0
		(h)	2-3

YORK CITY

Player and Position	Ht	Wt	Birth Date	Birth Place	Source	Clubs	League App	League Gls
Goalkeepers								
Dean Kiely	6 0	12 08	10 10 70	Manchester	WBA	Coventry C	—	—
						Ipswich T (loan)	—	—
						York C (loan)	—	—
						York C	124	—
Defenders								
Paul Atkin	6 0	12 11	3 9 69	Nottingham	Trainee	Notts Co	—	—
						Bury	21	1
						York C	78	3
Tony Barratt	5 8	11 01	18 10 65	Salford	Billingham T	Grimsby T	22	—
					Billingham T	Hartlepool U	98	4
						York C	137	10
Robert Ellis‡	6 1	13 07	6 10 73	York	Trainee	York C	—	—
Andy McMillan	5 11	11 04	22 6 68	Bloemfontein		York C	223	2
Paul Stancliffe	6 2	13 05	5 5 58	Sheffield	Apprentice	Rotherham U	285	8
						Sheffield U	278	12
						Rotherham U (loan)	5	—
						Wolverhampton W	17	—
						York C	87	3
Steve Tutill	6 0	12 02	1 10 69	Derwent	Trainee	York C	220	6
Ray Warburton	6 0	12 09	7 10 67	Rotherham	Apprentice	Rotherham U	4	—
						York C	90	9
						Northampton T (loan)	17	1
Midfield								
Steve Bushell	5 9	11 00	28 12 72	Manchester	Trainee	York C	70	4
Tony Canham	5 8	11 05	8 6 60	Leeds	Harrogate Railway	York C	312	55
Mike Gosling‡	5 6	11 05	6 7 75	Ipswich	Trainee	York C	—	—
Craig Hall	5 7	10 00	7 5 74	Oldham	Trainee	York C	—	—
Wayne Hall	5 9	10 04	25 10 68	Rotherham	Darlington	York C	199	8
Scott Jordan	5 10	11 02	19 7 75	Newcastle	Trainee	York C	1	—
Graeme Murty	5 10	11 05	13 11 74	Middlesbrough	Trainee	York C	1	—
Nigel Pepper	5 10	11 05	25 4 68	Rotherham	Apprentice	Rotherham U	45	1
						York C	131	15
Gary Swann	5 11	11 13	11 4 62	York	Apprentice	Hull C	186	9
						Preston NE	199	37
						York C	82	4
Forwards								
Paul Barnes	5 10	12 09	16 11 67	Leicester	Apprentice	Notts Co	53	14
						Stoke C	24	3
						Chesterfield (loan)	1	—
						York C	82	45
Ian Blackstone	6 0	13 00	7 8 64	Harrogate	Harrogate T	York C	129	37
Steve Cooper	5 11	10 12	22 6 64	Birmingham		Birmingham C	—	—
						Halifax T (loan)	7	1
						Mansfield T (loan)	—	—
						Newport Co	38	11
						Plymouth Arg	73	15
						Barnsley	77	13
						Tranmere R	32	3
						Peterborough U (loan)	9	—
						Wigan Ath (loan)	4	—
						York C	29	5
Jon McCarthy	5 10	11 01	18 8 70	Middlesbrough		Hartlepool U	1	—
					Shepshed	York C	155	22
Glenn Naylor	5 11	11 02	11 8 72	York	Trainee	York C	56	14

YORK CITY

Colours: Red shirts, blue shorts, red stockings. **Change colours:** White shirts, red shorts, blue stockings.

Foundation: Although there was a York City club formed in 1903 by a soccer enthusiast from Darlington, this has no connection with the modern club because it went out of existence during World War I. Unlike many others of that period who restarted in 1919, York City did not re-form until 1922 and the tendency now is to ignore the modern club's pre-1922 existence.

First Football League game: 31 August, 1929, Division 3(N), v Wigan Borough (a) W 2-0 – Farmery; Archibald, Johnson; Beck, Davis, Thompson; Evans, Gardner, Cowie (1), Smailes, Stockhill (1).

Did you know: The first player to score a hat-trick for York City was William Bottrill on 28 December 1929 in a 4-0 home win against Wigan Borough.

Managers (and Secretary-Managers)
Bill Sherrington 1924–60 (was secretary for most of this time but virtually secretary-manager for a long pre-war spell), John Collier 1929–36, Tom Mitchell 1936–50, Dick Duckworth 1950–52, Charlie Spencer 1952–53, Jimmy McCormick 1953–54, Sam Bartram 1956–60, Tom Lockie 1960–67, Joe Shaw 1967–68, Tom Johnston 1968–75, Wilf McGuinness 1975–77, Charlie Wright 1977–80, Barry Lyons 1980–81, Denis Smith 1982–87, Bobby Saxton 1987–88, John Bird 1988–91, John Ward 1991–93, Alan Little March 1993–

Trainees
Campbell, Neil A; Cutler, Jason L; Davison, Jamie; Dolan, Lee P; Falk, Darren, L; McNeany, Neil; Medforth, Lee; Mockler, Paul F; Osborne, Wayne; Oxley, Scott; Roberts, Steven; Simpson, Elliott; Vincent, Paul R; Warrington, Andrew; Watkinson, Mark; Williams, Darren.

Associated Schoolboys
Barley, Scott L; Barnes, Liam; Boyes, Scott; Corking, Neil M; Cruddas, David A; Gamble, Crawford S; Gough, Daniel; Greening, Jonathan; Jones, Robert W; Lamb, Stephen C; Lee, Stuart; Massey, Miles G; Melville, Mark C; Pledger, Darren A; Render, Patrick; Rennison, Graham L; Siddle, James D; Thorpe, Adam.

Associated Schoolboys who have accepted the Club's offer of a Traineeship/Contract
Cresswell, Richard P. W; Culkin, Nicholas; Murr, Michael; Rich, Oliver C; Tate, Christopher.

The things they said . . .

Spurs chairman Alan Sugar, referring to his reception from demonstrators outside the High Court during his battle with Terry Venables:
"*Tottenham has a following of 29,000 - I only saw 25.*"

FA chief executive Graham Kelly, after England finish last in the four-team US Cup '93:
"*Everyone should sit tight, stay quiet, get behind the England manager and keep their fingers crossed that we get through to the [World Cup] finals.*"

Lazio doctor Claudio Bartolini, on Gascoigne's fitness level:
Paul is only 50% fit after his crazy summer. He didn't work on holiday like the others and he can't play two consecutive games because he doesn't have the strength."
World sprint gold-medallist Linford Christie, complaining about poor media coverage after Britain's successful World Championships:
"*We are good. That's the difference between us and Gazza.*"

England manager Graham Taylor, before the Poland game at Wembley:
"*This is a bloody awful job, but it's not going to turn me into a bloody awful person.*"

Stuart Hall, commentating for Radio 5 on the Manchester United v Swindon game:
"*Lee Sharpe has got dynamite in his shorts.* 25 September

Everton manager Howard Kendall, on giving 1.5m signing from Rangers Mo Johnston a free transfer:
"*All managers make mistakes. There's no guarantee, no matter how much you pay, that a player will be a success.*" 8 October

Former England manager Bobby Robson on Graham Taylor's task before the crucial World Cup qualifying match with Holland in Amsterdam:
"*Graham must appear confident at all times in front of the players. They can detect it when a manager's on edge. I put on a confident face during Italia 90 and it worked [sic].*"

Graham Taylor to a linesman after shouldn't-have-been-on-the-pitch Koeman scored for Holland against England in Rotterdam:
"*Tell your friend out there that he's just got me the sack.*"

German referee Karl Josef Assenmacher, speaking through an interpreter, on his controversial decision not to send Dutch captain Ronald Koeman off against England at Rotterdam:
"*I was 20 metres away when I saw Koeman foul Platt. It flashed through my mind 'Is this a red card or yellow?' It didn't seem a serious foul and didn't seem deliberate [sic]. . . . There was another Dutch player nearby and therefore it was only a yellow card.*"

Spurs manager Ossie Ardiles, on speculation that he might be a contender for the England job after England's defeat in Rotterdam:
"*As manager of the national team you know that, apart from the Chancellor, you'll probably be the most hated person in the country.*"

Spurs chairman Alan Sugar, who made all the club's dealing with the Inland Revenue available to the FA, on the punishment meted out by the FA for making irregular loans to players in the 1980s:
"*No doubt on the basis of the level playing field promised to me by the FA, they will be making similar requests to the other clubs.*" 14 June

Manager Kevin Keegan, on walking out of a Press conference after Newcastle's Coca-Cola Cup defeat at Wimbledon:
"*I don't want to talk about Andy Cole. I want to talk about players who want to play for the club in the right manner, week in, week out. You can make your own assumptions. If you want to talk about Andy Cole, you go and find him in London.*"

Diego Maradona, when asked in Australia what was his best ever goal:
"*The one against England.*"

The Australian Press, in one voice:
"*Which one?*"

Swansea manager Frank Burrows, sent off with captain John Cornforth by referee Kevin Lynch for allegedly abusive remarks after the dismissal of Warren Aspinall:
"*All I said was that his decision to send off Aspinall for handball was garbage. I didn't swear.*" 30 October

Referee Ian Borrett to complaining Crystal Palace manager Alan Smith at Selhurst Park during the match with Luton:
"*I'm having a crap game, and nothing you say will alter it.*" 2 November

Manager John Barton, whose side drew at Swansea in the first round of the FA Cup:
"*We are hoping to restore Nuneaton to their former greatness.*"

BBC commentator John Motson a little over 9 seconds into the San Marino-England match:
"*I don't believe it.*".

FIFA technical director Walter Gagg, after England's failure to qualify for the World Cup:
"*The English coaches have stuck too much to their own ideas and haven't looked elsewhere since the end of the European club ban. They should go to Italy, Germany, France and Spain to see how the game is developing there. They also cannot ignore South America and Africa. If they take a good look they could learn.*"

Switzerland's successful English manager Roy Hodgson:
"*It would be the biggest disaster English football has had since being beaten by Hungary 40 years ago if the FA coaching system was ripped apart because we have failed to qualify for the World Cup. Jack Charlton and myself are both products of the system, and it should not be made the whipping boy. The system is being attacked violently inside England, but outside it is still the envy of the world, certainly of Europe.*"

Norway's successful manager Egil Olsen:
"*We beat England by playing the English way, and my bible is the English coaching book, Tactics and Teamwork by Charles Hughes. We have great respect for English coaching courses.*"

Spurs manager Ossie Ardiles, after Gary Mabbutt is seriously injured in a clash with Wimbledon's John Fashanu:
"*I am very disappointed with Keith Hackett, who is one of the top referees in England. If he failed to see certain things, what chance do we have in the game?*" 24 November

Premier League chief executive Rick Parry, defending the FA's head of coaching:
"*I defy anyone to read through Charles Hughes's weighty syllabus and find mention of the long ball. And I would urge anyone to go to any of the centres of excellence around the country. If they see the long ball being coached, then I'm a Dutchman.*"

Chief executive of London club, on seeing the expenses of a referee from the north (possibly apocryphal):
"*How come we are paying someone to come from Yorkshire when we can get good refs down here?*"

Tommy Docherty:
"*John Barnes's problem is that he gets injured appearing on Question of Sport*"

Liverpool chairman David Moores, after their penalty shoot-out defeat by Wimbledon in the Coca-Cola Cup:
"*Graeme Souness is the manager of this club and his position isn't under review.*" 15 December

Ireland manager Jack Charlton, checking on the form of his Celtic players in a match against Hibs at Parkhead, explaining it was difficult to make a judgement on Pat McGinlay because the Celtic jerseys confused him:
"*Well, it wasn't easy, you know, because most of the players out there are unfamiliar to me. I kept thinking that McGinlay was Charlie Nicholas, because he looks like Nicholas - no, not Nicholas, the other one, Paul McStay.*"

FA spokesman on the decision not to charge John Fashanu over the Gary Mabbutt incident, explaining that the referee Keith Hackett had not changed his mind:
"*[The referee] merely amended his view.*" 24 December

Forest manager Frank Clark, on the possibility of Stan Collymore playing for Ireland:
"*I'd be delighted, because our agreement with Southend is that we only pay them more money if he plays for England.*"

Extract from Graham Taylor's touchline comments, among others, during England's match with Holland, as shown in a Channel 4 TV documentary:
"****. . . *****ing*. . .. ****. . . ****" January

Leeds fans, reminding the world of their reputation as prime instigators of football hate and hooliganism, throughout the one-minute silence for Sir Matt Busby at Blackburn:
"*There's only one Don Revie.*" 23 January

Chairman David Moores after accepting manager Graeme Souness's resignation:
"*Liverpool Football Club is all about winning things and being a source of pride to our fans. It has no other purpose.*" 28 January

New England coach Terry Venables:
"*We must have a system that the players understand. It's up to me to make it as simple as possible.*"

Jimmy Hill, commenting for the BBC, on Eric Cantona's off-the-ball aggression in Man United's Cup win at Norwich:
"*You need a villain in the theatre; you don't need one on the field*" 30 January

Alex Ferguson, Man United manager, on Jimmy Hill and Co:
"*If there's a prat about in this world, he's the prat. . .. The BBC are dying for us to lose. Everyone is from Liverpool with a supporter's badge. They will be at our games every week until we lose, that mob - Bob, Barry, Hansen, the lot of them. That's what will drive us on.*"
Sacked Saudi Arabia coach, Dutchman Leo Beenhakker:
"*It's because I have asked the players to train twice a day and they wanted to train three times a week.*" 22 February

Alex Ferguson, Man Utd manager, demonstrating his muddled knowledge of the laws after his keeper was sent off in the Cup tie against Charlton:
"*Schmeichel came out using his feet and the ball hit his hand. To be sent off it has to be intentional. Not only that, but he wasn't the last man. Paul Parker was behind him.*" 13 March

Ireland manager Jack Charlton, following a check-up and scan after suffering headaches:
"*At least it proves to everyone that I do have a brain.*"

Keith Pearson, Wolves secretary, on Graham Taylor's qualifications for the vacant Wolves job:
"*He did a magnificent job at Aston Villa and not a bad job with England except for a few important games.*"

Joe Kinnear, Wimbledon manager, after defeat at QPR:
"*We might have to become a long-ball team.*"

Graham Taylor, new Wolves manager:
"*If crowds start chanting 'Turnip, turnip, give us a wave, you give them a wave.*" 1 April

Doug Sharpe, Swansea chairman, on his Cardiff counterpart Rick Wright's method of keeping Cardiff fans away from trouble:
"*That idiot takes it on his back and says he's not prepared to sell tickets. That's a way of chickening out of football's problems.*" 2 April

John Motson, commentating for the BBC on FA Cup semi-final, Oldham v Man Utd:
"*Milligan hasn't scored for over a year. But he's the captain.*"

Manchester United's French star Eric Cantona, on receiving the PFA Footballer of the Year award:
"*I would like to congratulate other people from football in England, even the player who did not vote for me.*

Leeds manager Howard Wilkinson after their 1-1 draw with Chelsea at Stamford Bridge:
"*I think if they hadn't scored, we might have got a better result.*

Newcastle manager Kevin Keegan on the signing of Robert Lee from Charlton:
"*He nearly went to Middlesbrough, but I told him Newcastle was nearer London. Luckily footballers believe things like that.*

Coventry's Phil Babb, after the Man Utd v Coventry game, the last Premiership match of the season:
"*Cantona stamped on me, and something like that can end people's careers.*" 9 May

Sheff Utd manager Dave Bassett after they are relegated on the last day of the season:
"*If you continually play Russian roulette, eventually you're going to get the bullet.*"

Chelsea chairman Ken Bates on former manager John Hollins:
"*In many ways he's a nice guy. He has a very strong wife. It might have been better if I had made her manager.*"

Greek coach Alketas Panagulias, explaining heir 5-0 defeat at Wembley:
"*They [Greek players] think these players [England] are gods coming from the sky; they know the first names of your players, they know the names of their fathers and they know what cars they drive.*"

Mr Colin Mackay, Liverpool's QC in the Elliott-Saunders High Court case, in response to soccer writer Brian Glanville's remark Tot homines, tot sententiae (So many men, so many opinions):
"*Yes, in Bootle and Liverpool they talk of little else.*"

Ireland manager Jack Charlton (proving again that he has a brain) on the outrageous new FIFA edicts for World Cup officials, propagated without consultation with the national coaches:
"*It's absolutely ludicrous. They have told the referees, but nobody has told us yet. . . . I don't know what they mean when they talk about a red card for a tackle from behind. There are loads of different challenges from behind where the ball can be won cleanly. And what is the point in schooling the players to push up and clear their 18-yard area, if the opposition attackers they leave behind are not going to be penalized for offside as they should be. . . . We are talking about the World Cup here - the peak of football - and suddenly people want to make fundamental changes to some of the rules when we are playing in the finals.*" 12 June

END OF SEASON PLAY-OFFS 1993–94

Semi-finals, First Leg

15 MAY

DIVISION 1

Derby Co (1) 2 *(Cowans, Johnson)*

Millwall (0) 0 17,401

Derby Co: Taylor; Charles, Forsyth, Harkes, Short, Williams, Cowans, Johnson, Gabbiadini, Pembridge, Simpson.
Millwall: Keller; Cunningham, Huxford, Hurlock, Emblen (Kerr), Stevens, Rae, Van Den Hauwe, Goodman, Mitchell (Moralee), Barber.

Tranmere R (0) 0

Leicester C (0) 0 14,962

Tranmere R: Nixon; McGreal, Nolan, Brannan, Garnett, O'Brien, Morrissey, Aldridge, Irons (Muir), Nevin, Thomas.
Leicester C: Ward; Grayson, Gibson, Willis, Whitlow, Coatsworth, Carey, Joachim (Philpott), Blake, Gee (Oldfield), Ormondroyd.

DIVISION 2

Burnley (0) 0

Plymouth Arg (0) 0 18,794

Burnley: Beresford; Parkinson, Thompson, Davis, Pender, Joyce, McMinn (Lancashire), Deary, Heath, Francis, Eyres.
Plymouth Arg: Nicholls; Patterson, Hill, Burrows, Comyn, McCall, Barlow, Castle, Landon (Burnett), Marshall (Nugent), Dalton.

York C (0) 0

Stockport Co (0) 0 8744

York C: Kiely; McMillan, Hall, Swann, Tutill, Stancliffe, McCarthy, Blackstone (Cooper), Barnes, Bushell, Canham.
Stockport Co: Keeley; Todd, Wallace, Connelly, Flynn, Williams B, Gannon, Ward, Francis, Beaumont, Frain.

DIVISION 3

Carlisle U (0) 0

Wycombe W (1) 2 *(Thompson, Garner)* 10,862

Carlisle U: Caig; Joyce, Gallimore, Walling, Reddish, Robinson, Thomas, Rouse (Burgess), Reeves, Davey, Arnold.
Wycombe W: Hyde; Cousins, Titterton, Crossley, Creaser, Ryan, Carroll, Thompson, Reid, Garner, Guppy.

Torquay U (1) 2 *(Darby, Moore)*

Preston NE (0) 0 4440

Torquay U: Bayes; Hodges, Goodridge, Kelly, Moore, Curran, Trollope, Buckle, Darby (Hathaway), Sale, Okorie (Foster).
Preston NE: Woods; Fensome, Sulley, Cartwright, Matthewson, Moyes, Ainsworth, Lucas (Conroy), Raynor, Ellis, Bryson.

Semi-finals, Second Leg

18 MAY

DIVISION 1

Millwall (0) 1 *(Berry)*

Derby Co (3) 3 *(Gabbiadini, Johnson, Van Den Hauwe (og))* 16,470

Millwall: Keller; Cunningham, Huxford, Hurlock, Van Den Hauwe, Stevens, Rae, Allen, Moralee, Mitchell, Berry.
Derby Co: Taylor; Charles (Hayward), Forsyth, Harkes, Short, Williams (Kavanagh), Cowans, Johnson, Gabbiadini, Pembridge, Simpson.

Leicester C (1) 2 *(Ormondroyd, Speedie)*

Tranmere R (1) 1 *(Nevin)* 16,470

Leicester C: Ward; Grayson, Whitlow, Willis, Coatsworth, Carey (Speedie), Joachim, Blake, Walsh, Gibson (Thompson), Ormondroyd.
Tranmere R: Nixon; McGreal, Nolan, Brannan, Garnett, O'Brien, Morrissey, Aldridge, Irons (Muir), Nevin (Jones M), Thomas.

Dave Carroll turns away after scoring Wycombe Wanderers third goal against Preston North End at Wembley. (Action Images).

Burnley's John Deary has the height over Michael Wallace of Stockport County in the play-offs at Wembley. (Action Images).

DIVISION 2

Plymouth Arg (1) 1 *(Marshall)*

Burnley (2) 3 *(Francis 2, Joyce)* 17,515

Plymouth Arg: Nicholls; Patterson, McCall, Hill, Comyn, Burrows (Naylor), Barlow, Castle, Landon (Nugent), Marshall, Dalton.
Burnley: Beresford; Parkinson, Thompson, Davis, Pender, Joyce (Farrell), McMinn, Deary, Heath, Francis (Peel), Eyres.

Stockport Co (0) 1 *(Beaumont)*

York C (0) 0 6743

Stockport Co: Keeley; Todd, Wallace, Connelly, Flynn, Williams B, Gannon, Ward, Francis, Beaumont, Frain.
York C: Kiely; McMillan, Hall, Swann, Tutill, Stancliffe, McCarthy (Pepper), Blackstone, Barnes, Bushell, Canham.

DIVISION 3

Preston NE (2) 4 *(Ellis, Moyes, Hicks, Raynor)*

Torquay U (1) 1 *(Nevin)* 11,442

Preston NE: Woods; Fensome, Kidd, Cartwright, Hicks, Moyes, Ainsworth, Whalley, Raynor (Lucas), Ellis (Challender), Bryson.
Torquay U: Bayes; Hodges (Hathaway), O'Riordan (Foster), Kelly, Moore, Curran, Trollope, Buckle, Darby, Sale, Goodridge.

Wycombe W (1) 2 *(Carroll, Garner)*

Carlisle U (0) 1 *(Davey (pen))* 6265

Wycombe W: Hyde; Cousins, Titterton, Crossley, Creaser, Ryan, Carroll (Brown), Thompson (Hemmings), Reid, Garner, Guppy.
Carlisle U: Caig; Joyce, Gallimore, Walling, Valentine, Robinson, Thomas, Conway (Reddish), Reeves, Davey, Arnold (Burgess).

Finals at Wembley

28 MAY
DIVISION 3

Wycombe W (1) 4 *(Thompson, Garner, Carroll 2)*

Preston NE (2) 2 *(Bryson, Raynor)* 40,109

Wycombe W: Hyde; Cousins, Titterton, Crossley, Creaser, Ryan, Carroll, Thompson, Reid, Garner, Guppy.
Preston NE: Woods; Fensome, Kidd, Cartwright, Squires, Moyes, Ainsworth, Whalley, Raynor, Ellis, Bryson.

29 MAY
DIVISION 2

Burnley (1) 2 *(Eyres, Parkinson)*

Stockport Co (1) 1 *(Beaumont)* 44,806

Burnley: Beresford; Parkinson, Thompson, Davis, Pender, Joyce, McMinn, Deary, Heath, Francis (Farrell), Eyres.
Stockport Co: Keeley; Todd, Wallace, Connelly, Flynn, Williams B (Preece), Gannon (Miller), Ward, Francis, Beaumont, Frain.

30 MAY
DIVISION 1

Derby Co (1) 1 *(Johnson)*

Leicester C (1) 2 *(Walsh 2)* 73,671

Derby Co: Taylor; Charles, Forsyth (Kitson), Harkes, Short, Williams, Cowans, Johnson, Gabbiadini, Pembridge, Simpson.
Leicester C: Ward; Grayson, Whitlow, Willis, Coatsworth (Thompson), Carey, Gibson, Blake, Walsh, Roberts (Joachim), Ormondroyd.

F.A. Carling Premiership

			Home			Goals		Away			Goals			
		P	W	D	L	F	A	W	D	L	F	A	Pts	GD
1	Manchester U	42	14	6	1	39	13	13	5	3	41	25	92	+42
2	Blackburn R	42	14	5	2	31	11	11	4	6	32	25	84	+27
3	Newcastle U	42	14	4	3	51	14	9	4	8	31	27	77	+41
4	Arsenal	42	10	8	3	25	15	8	9	4	28	13	71	+25
5	Leeds U	42	13	6	2	37	18	5	10	6	28	21	70	+26
6	Wimbledon	42	12	5	4	35	21	6	6	9	21	32	65	+3
7	Sheffield W	42	10	7	4	48	24	6	9	6	28	30	64	+22
8	Liverpool	42	12	4	5	33	23	5	5	11	26	32	60	+4
9	QPR	42	8	7	6	32	29	8	5	8	30	32	60	+1
10	Aston Villa	42	8	5	8	23	18	7	7	7	23	32	57	–4
11	Coventry C	42	9	7	5	23	17	5	7	9	20	28	56	–2
12	Norwich C	42	4	9	8	26	29	8	8	5	39	32	53	+4
13	West Ham U	42	6	7	8	26	31	7	6	8	21	27	52	–11
14	Chelsea	42	11	5	5	31	20	2	7	12	18	33	51	–4
15	Tottenham H	42	4	8	9	29	33	7	4	10	25	26	45	–5
16	Manchester C	42	6	10	5	24	22	3	8	10	14	27	45	–11
17	Everton	42	8	4	9	26	30	4	4	13	16	33	44	–21
18	Southampton	42	9	2	10	30	31	3	5	13	19	35	43	–17
19	Ipswich T	42	5	8	8	21	32	4	8	9	14	26	43	–23
20	Sheffield U	42	6	10	5	24	23	2	8	11	18	37	42	–18
21	Oldham Ath	42	5	8	8	24	33	4	5	12	18	35	40	–26
22	Swindon T	42	4	7	10	25	45	1	8	12	22	55	30	–53

Endsleigh Insurance League Division 1

			Home			Goals		Away			Goals			
		P	W	D	L	F	A	W	D	L	F	A	Pts	GD
1	Crystal Palace	46	16	4	3	39	18	11	5	7	34	28	90	+27
2	Nottingham F	46	12	9	2	38	22	11	5	7	36	27	83	+25
3	Millwall	46	14	8	1	36	17	5	9	9	22	32	74	+9
4	Leicester C	46	11	9	3	45	30	8	7	8	27	29	73	+13
5	Tranmere R	46	15	3	5	48	23	6	6	11	21	30	72	+16
6	Derby C	46	15	3	5	44	25	5	8	10	29	43	71	+5
7	Notts C	46	16	3	4	43	26	4	5	14	22	43	68	–4
8	Wolverhampton W	46	10	10	3	34	19	7	7	9	26	28	68	+13
9	Middlesbrough	46	12	6	5	40	19	6	7	10	26	35	67	+12
10	Stoke C	46	14	4	5	35	19	4	9	10	22	40	67	–2
11	Charlton Ath	46	14	3	6	39	22	5	5	13	22	36	65	+3
12	Sunderland	46	14	2	7	35	22	5	6	12	19	35	65	–3
13	Bristol C	46	11	7	5	27	18	5	9	9	20	32	64	–3
14	Bolton W	46	10	8	5	40	31	5	6	12	23	33	59	–1
15	Southend U	46	10	5	8	34	28	7	3	13	29	39	59	–4
16	Grimsby T	46	7	14	2	26	16	6	6	11	26	31	59	+5
17	Portsmouth	46	10	6	7	29	22	5	7	11	23	36	58	–6
18	Barnsley	46	9	3	11	25	26	7	4	12	30	41	55	–12
19	Watford	46	10	5	8	39	35	5	4	14	27	45	54	–14
20	Luton T	46	12	4	7	38	25	2	7	14	18	35	53	–4
21	WBA	46	9	7	7	38	31	4	5	14	22	38	51	–9
22	Birmingham C	46	9	7	7	28	29	4	5	14	24	40	51	–17
23	Oxford U	46	10	5	8	33	33	3	5	15	21	42	49	–21
24	Peterborough	46	6	9	8	31	30	2	4	17	17	46	37	–28

Endsleigh Insurance League Division 2

			Home			Goals		Away			Goals			
		P	W	D	L	F	A	W	D	L	F	A	Pts	GD
1	Reading	46	15	6	2	40	16	11	5	7	41	28	89	+37
2	Port Vale	46	16	6	1	46	18	10	4	9	33	28	88	+33
3	Plymouth Arg	46	16	4	3	46	26	9	6	8	42	30	85	+32
4	Stockport Co	46	15	3	5	50	22	9	10	4	24	22	85	+30
5	York C	46	12	7	4	33	13	9	5	9	31	27	75	+24
6	Burnley	46	17	4	2	55	18	4	6	13	24	40	73	+21
7	Bradford C	46	13	5	5	34	20	6	8	9	27	33	70	+8
8	Bristol R	46	10	8	5	33	26	10	2	11	27	33	70	+1
9	Hull C	46	9	9	5	33	20	9	5	9	29	34	68	+8
10	Cambridge U	46	11	5	7	38	29	8	4	11	41	44	66	+6
11	Huddersfield T	46	9	8	6	27	26	8	6	9	31	35	65	–3
12	Wrexham	46	13	4	6	45	33	4	7	12	21	44	62	–11
13	Swansea C	46	12	7	4	37	20	4	5	14	19	38	60	–2
14	Brighton & H A	46	10	7	6	38	29	5	7	11	22	38	59	–7
15	Rotherham U	46	11	4	8	42	30	4	9	10	21	30	58	+3
16	Brentford	46	7	10	6	30	28	6	9	8	27	27	58	+2
17	Bournemouth	46	8	7	8	26	27	6	8	9	25	32	57	–8
18	Leyton Orient	46	11	9	3	38	26	3	5	15	19	45	56	–14
19	Cardiff C	46	10	7	6	39	33	3	8	12	27	46	54	–13
20	Blackpool	46	12	2	9	41	37	4	3	16	22	38	53	–12
21	Fulham	46	7	6	10	20	23	7	4	12	30	40	52	–13
22	Exeter C	46	8	7	8	38	37	3	5	15	14	46	45	–31
23	Hartlepool U	46	8	3	12	28	40	1	6	16	13	47	36	–46
24	Barnet	46	4	6	13	22	32	1	7	15	19	54	28	–45

Endsleigh Insurance League Division 3

			Home			Goals		Away			Goals			
		P	W	D	L	F	A	W	D	L	F	A	Pts	GD
1	Shrewsbury T	42	10	8	3	28	17	12	5	4	35	22	79	+24
2	Chester C	42	13	5	3	35	18	8	6	7	34	28	74	+23
3	Crewe Alex	42	12	4	5	45	30	9	6	6	35	31	73	+19
4	Wycombe W	42	11	6	4	34	21	8	7	6	33	32	70	+14
5	Preston NE	42	13	5	3	46	23	5	8	8	33	37	67	+19
6	Torquay U	42	8	10	3	30	24	9	6	6	34	32	67	+8
7	Carlisle U	42	10	4	7	35	23	8	6	7	22	19	64	+15
8	Chesterfield	42	8	8	5	32	22	8	6	7	23	26	62	+7
9	Rochdale	42	10	5	6	38	22	6	7	8	25	29	60	+12
10	Walsall	42	7	5	9	28	26	10	4	7	20	27	60	–5
11	Scunthorpe U	42	9	7	5	40	26	6	7	8	24	30	59	+8
12	Mansfield T	42	9	3	9	28	30	6	7	8	25	32	55	–9
13	Bury	42	9	6	6	33	22	5	5	11	22	34	53	–1
14	Scarborough	42	8	4	9	29	28	7	4	10	26	33	53	–6
15	Doncaster R	42	8	6	7	24	26	6	4	11	20	31	52	–13
16	Gillingham	42	8	8	5	27	23	4	7	10	17	28	51	–7
17	Colchester U	42	8	4	9	31	33	5	6	10	25	38	49	–15
18	Lincoln C	42	7	4	10	26	29	5	7	9	26	34	47	–11
19	Wigan Ath	42	6	7	8	33	33	5	5	11	18	37	45	–19
20	Hereford U	42	6	4	11	34	33	6	2	13	26	46	42	–19
21	Darlington	42	7	5	9	24	28	3	6	12	18	36	41	–22
22	Northampton T	42	6	7	8	25	23	3	4	14	19	43	38	–22

In the Endsleigh Insurance League, goals scored determine League positions where clubs are level on points. If teams still cannot be separated, the team that has conceded fewer goals is placed higher.

FOOTBALL LEAGUE 1888–89 to 1993–94

FA PREMIER LEAGUE

Maximum points: 126

	First	*Pts*	*Second*	*Pts*	*Third*	*Pts*
1992–93	Manchester U	84	Aston Villa	74	Norwich C	72
1993–94	Manchester U	92	Blackburn R	84	Newcastle U	77

FIRST DIVISION

Maximum points: 138

1992–93	Newcastle U	96	West Ham U	88	Portsmouth††	88
1993–94	Crystal Palace	90	Nottingham F	83	Millwall††	74

SECOND DIVISION

Maximum points: 138

1992–93	Stoke C	93	Bolton W	90	Port Vale††	89
1993–94	Reading	89	Port Vale	88	Plymouth Arg*††	85

THIRD DIVISION

Maximum points: 126

1992–93	Cardiff C	83	Wrexham	80	Barnet	79
1993–94	Shrewsbury T	79	Chester C	74	Crewe Alex	73

†† *Not promoted after play-offs.*

FOOTBALL LEAGUE

	First	*Pts*	*Second*	*Pts*	*Third*	*Pts*
1888–89*a*	Preston NE	40	Aston Villa	29	Wolverhampton W	28
1889–90*a*	Preston NE	33	Everton	31	Blackburn R	27
1890–91*a*	Everton	29	Preston NE	27	Notts Co	26
1891–92*b*	Sunderland	42	Preston NE	37	Bolton W	36

FIRST DIVISION to 1991–92

Maximum points: a 44; *b* 52; *c* 60; *d* 68; *e* 76; *f* 84; *g* 126; *h* 120; *k* 114.

1892–93*c*	Sunderland	48	Preston NE	37	Everton	36
1893–94*c*	Aston Villa	44	Sunderland	38	Derby Co	36
1894–95*c*	Sunderland	47	Everton	42	Aston Villa	39
1895–96*c*	Aston Villa	45	Derby Co	41	Everton	39
1896–97*c*	Aston Villa	47	Sheffield U*	36	Derby Co	36
1897–98*c*	Sheffield U	42	Sunderland	37	Wolverhampton W*	35
1898–99*d*	Aston Villa	45	Liverpool	43	Burnley	39
1899–1900*d*	Aston Villa	50	Sheffield U	48	Sunderland	41
1900–01*d*	Liverpool	45	Sunderland	43	Notts Co	40
1901–02*d*	Sunderland	44	Everton	41	Newcastle U	37
1902–03*d*	The Wednesday	42	Aston Villa*	41	Sunderland	41
1903–04*d*	The Wednesday	47	Manchester C	44	Everton	43
1904–05*d*	Newcastle U	48	Everton	47	Manchester C	46
1905–06*e*	Liverpool	51	Preston NE	47	The Wednesday	44
1906–07*e*	Newcastle U	51	Bristol C	48	Everton*	45
1907–08*e*	Manchester U	52	Aston Villa*	43	Manchester C	43
1908–09*e*	Newcastle U	53	Everton	46	Sunderland	44
1909–10*e*	Aston Villa	53	Liverpool	48	Blackburn R*	45
1910–11*e*	Manchester U	52	Aston Villa	51	Sunderland*	45
1911–12*e*	Blackburn R	49	Everton	46	Newcastle U	44
1912–13*e*	Sunderland	54	Aston Villa	50	Sheffield W	49
1913–14*e*	Blackburn R	51	Aston Villa	44	Middlesbrough*	43
1914–15*e*	Everton	46	Oldham Ath	45	Blackburn R*	43
1919–20*f*	WBA	60	Burnley	51	Chelsea	49
1920–21*f*	Burnley	59	Manchester C	54	Bolton W	52
1921–22*f*	Liverpool	57	Tottenham H	51	Burnley	49
1922–23*f*	Liverpool	60	Sunderland	54	Huddersfield T	53
1923–24*f*	Huddersfield T*	57	Cardiff C	57	Sunderland	53
1924–25*f*	Huddersfield T	58	WBA	56	Bolton W	55
1925–26*f*	Huddersfield T	57	Arsenal	52	Sunderland	48
1926–27*f*	Newcastle U	56	Huddersfield T	51	Sunderland	49
1927–28*f*	Everton	53	Huddersfield T	51	Leicester C	48
1928–29*f*	Sheffield W	52	Leicester C	51	Aston Villa	50
1929–30*f*	Sheffield W	60	Derby Co	50	Manchester C*	47
1930–31*f*	Arsenal	66	Aston Villa	59	Sheffield W	52
1931–32*f*	Everton	56	Arsenal	54	Sheffield W	50
1932–33*f*	Arsenal	58	Aston Villa	54	Sheffield W	51
1933–34*f*	Arsenal	59	Huddersfield T	56	Tottenham H	49
1934–35*f*	Arsenal	58	Sunderland	54	Sheffield W	49
1935–36*f*	Sunderland	56	Derby Co*	48	Huddersfield T	48
1936–37*f*	Manchester C	57	Charlton Ath	54	Arsenal	52
1937–38*f*	Arsenal	52	Wolverhampton W	51	Preston NE	49

* *Won or placed on goal average, goal difference or most goals scored.*

	First	Pts	Second	Pts	Third	Pts
1938–39*f*	Everton	59	Wolverhampton W	55	Charlton Ath	50
1946–47*f*	Liverpool	57	Manchester U*	56	Wolverhampton W	56
1947–48*f*	Arsenal	59	Manchester U*	52	Burnley	52
1948–49*f*	Portsmouth	58	Manchester U*	53	Derby Co	53
1949–50*f*	Portsmouth*	53	Wolverhampton W	53	Sunderland	52
1950–51*f*	Tottenham H	60	Manchester U	56	Blackpool	50
1951–52*f*	Manchester U	57	Tottenham H*	53	Arsenal	53
1952–53*f*	Arsenal*	54	Preston NE	54	Wolverhampton W	51
1953–54*f*	Wolverhampton W	57	WBA	53	Huddersfield T	51
1954–55*f*	Chelsea	52	Wolverhampton W*	48	Portsmouth*	48
1955–56*f*	Manchester U	60	Blackpool*	49	Wolverhampton W	49
1956–57*f*	Manchester U	64	Tottenham H*	56	Preston NE	56
1957–58*f*	Wolverhampton W	64	Preston NE	59	Tottenham H	51
1958–59*f*	Wolverhampton W	61	Manchester U	55	Arsenal*	50
1959–60*f*	Burnley	55	Wolverhampton W	54	Tottenham H	53
1960–61*f*	Tottenham H	66	Sheffield W	58	Wolverhampton W	57
1961–62*f*	Ipswich T	56	Burnley	53	Tottenham H	52
1962–63*f*	Everton	61	Tottenham H	55	Burnley	54
1963–64*f*	Liverpool	57	Manchester U	53	Everton	52
1964–65*f*	Manchester U*	61	Leeds U	61	Chelsea	56
1965–66*f*	Liverpool	61	Leeds U*	55	Burnley	55
1966–67*f*	Manchester U	60	Nottingham F*	56	Tottenham H	56
1967–68*f*	Manchester C	58	Manchester U	56	Liverpool	55
1968–69*f*	Leeds U	67	Liverpool	61	Everton	57
1969–70*f*	Everton	66	Leeds U	57	Chelsea	55
1970–71*f*	Arsenal	65	Leeds U	64	Tottenham H*	52
1971–72*f*	Derby Co	58	Leeds U*	57	Liverpool*	57
1972–73*f*	Liverpool	60	Arsenal	57	Leeds U	53
1973–74*f*	Leeds U	62	Liverpool	57	Derby Co	48
1974–75*f*	Derby Co	53	Liverpool*	51	Ipswich T	57
1975–76*f*	Liverpool	60	QPR	59	Manchester U	56
1976–77*f*	Liverpool	57	Manchester C	56	Ipswich T	52
1977–78*f*	Nottingham F	64	Liverpool	57	Everton	55
1978–79*f*	Liverpool	68	Nottingham F	60	WBA	59
1979–80*f*	Liverpool	60	Manchester U	58	Ipswich T	53
1980–81*f*	Aston Villa	60	Ipswich T	56	Arsenal	53
1981–82*g*	Liverpool	87	Ipswich T	83	Manchester U	78
1982–83*g*	Liverpool	82	Watford	71	Manchester U	70
1983–84*g*	Liverpool	80	Southampton	77	Nottingham F*	74
1984–85*g*	Everton	90	Liverpool*	77	Tottenham H	77
1985–86g	Liverpool	88	Everton	86	West Ham U	84
1986–87*g*	Everton	86	Liverpool	77	Tottenham H	71
1987–88*h*	Liverpool	90	Manchester U	81	Nottingham F	73
1988–89*k*	Arsenal*	76	Liverpool	76	Nottingham F	64
1989–90*k*	Liverpool	79	Aston Villa	70	Tottenham H	63
1990–91*k*	Arsenal†	83	Liverpool	76	Crystal Palace	69
1991–92*g*	Leeds U	82	Manchester U	78	Sheffield W	75

No official competition during 1915–19 and 1939–46.
† 2 pts deducted

SECOND DIVISION to 1991–92

Maximum points: a 44; *b* 56; *c* 60; *d* 68; *e* 76; *f* 84; *g* 126; *h* 132; *k* 138.

	First	Pts	Second	Pts	Third	Pts
1892–93*a*	Small Heath	36	Sheffield U	35	Darwen	30
1893–94*b*	Liverpool	50	Small Heath	42	Notts Co	39
1894–95*c*	Bury	48	Notts Co	39	Newton Heath*	38
1895–96*c*	Liverpool*	46	Manchester C	46	Grimsby T*	42
1896–97*c*	Notts Co	42	Newton Heath	39	Grimsby T	38
1897–98*c*	Burnley	48	Newcastle U	45	Manchester C	39
1898–99*d*	Manchester C	52	Glossop NE	46	Leicester Fosse	45
1899–1900*d*	The Wednesday	54	Bolton W	52	Small Heath	46
1900–01*d*	Grimsby T	49	Small Heath	48	Burnley	44
1901–02*d*	WBA	55	Middlesbrough	51	Preston NE*	42
1902–03*d*	Manchester C	54	Small Heath	51	Woolwich A	48
1903–04*d*	Preston NE	50	Woolwich A	49	Manchester U	48
1904–05*d*	Liverpool	58	Bolton W	56	Manchester U	53
1905–06*e*	Bristol C	66	Manchester U	62	Chelsea	53
1906–07*e*	Nottingham F	60	Chelsea	57	Leicester Fosse	48
1907–08*e*	Bradford C	54	Leicester Fosse	52	Oldham Ath	50
1908–09*e*	Bolton W	52	Tottenham H*	51	WBA	51
1909–10*e*	Manchester C	54	Oldham Ath*	53	Hull C*	53
1910–11*e*	WBA	53	Bolton W	51	Chelsea	49
1911–12*e*	Derby Co*	54	Chelsea	54	Burnley	52
1912–13*e*	Preston NE	53	Burnley	50	Birmingham	46
1913–14*e*	Notts Co	53	Bradford PA*	49	Woolwich A	49
1914–15*e*	Derby Co	53	Preston NE	50	Barnsley	47
1919–20*f*	Tottenham H	70	Huddersfield T	64	Birmingham	56
1920–21*f*	Birmingham*	58	Cardiff C	58	Bristol C	51
1921–22*f*	Nottingham F	56	Stoke C*	52	Barnsley	52
1922–23*f*	Notts Co	53	West Ham U*	51	Leicester C	51
1923–24*f*	Leeds U	54	Bury*	51	Derby Co	51
1924–25*f*	Leicester C	59	Manchester U	57	Derby Co	55

** Won or placed on goal average/goal difference.*

	First	Pts	Second	Pts	Third	Pts
1925–26*f*	Sheffield W	60	Derby Co	57	Chelsea	52
1926–27*f*	Middlesbrough	62	Portsmouth*	54	Manchester C	54
1927–28*f*	Manchester C	59	Leeds U	57	Chelsea	54
1928–29*f*	Middlesbrough	55	Grimsby T	53	Bradford*	48
1929–30*f*	Blackpool	58	Chelsea	55	Oldham Ath	53
1930–31*f*	Everton	61	WBA	54	Tottenham H	51
1931–32*f*	Wolverhampton W	56	Leeds U	54	Stoke C	52
1932–33*f*	Stoke C	56	Tottenham H	55	Fulham	50
1933–34*f*	Grimsby T	59	Preston NE	52	Bolton W*	51
1934–35*f*	Brentford	61	Bolton W*	56	West Ham U	56
1935–36*f*	Manchester U	56	Charlton Ath	55	Sheffield U*	52
1936–37*f*	Leicester C	56	Blackpool	55	Bury	52
1937–38*f*	Aston Villa	57	Manchester U*	53	Sheffield U	53
1938–39*f*	Blackburn R	55	Sheffield U	54	Sheffield W	53
1946–47*f*	Manchester C	62	Burnley	58	Birmingham C	55
1947–48*f*	Birmingham C	59	Newcastle U	56	Southampton	52
1948–49*f*	Fulham	57	WBA	56	Southampton	55
1949–50*f*	Tottenham H	61	Sheffield W*	52	Sheffield U*	52
1950–51*f*	Preston NE	57	Manchester C	52	Cardiff C	50
1951–52*f*	Sheffield W	53	Cardiff C*	51	Birmingham C	51
1952–53*f*	Sheffield U	60	Huddersfield T	58	Luton T	52
1953–54*f*	Leicester C*	56	Everton	56	Blackburn R	55
1954–55*f*	Birmingham C*	54	Luton T*	54	Rotherham U	54
1955–56*f*	Sheffield W	55	Leeds U	52	Liverpool*	48
1956–57*f*	Leicester C	61	Nottingham F	54	Liverpool	53
1957–58*f*	West Ham U	57	Blackburn R	56	Charlton Ath	55
1958–59*f*	Sheffield W	62	Fulham	60	Sheffield U*	53
1959–60*f*	Aston Villa	59	Cardiff C	58	Liverpool*	50
1960–61*f*	Ipswich T	59	Sheffield U	58	Liverpool	52
1961–62*f*	Liverpool	62	Leyton O	54	Sunderland	53
1962–63*f*	Stoke C	53	Chelsea*	52	Sunderland	52
1963–64*f*	Leeds U	63	Sunderland	61	Preston NE	56
1964–65*f*	Newcastle U	57	Northampton T	56	Bolton W	50
1965–66*f*	Manchester C	59	Southampton	54	Coventry C	53
1966–67*f*	Coventry C	59	Wolverhampton W	58	Carlisle U	52
1967–68*f*	Ipswich T	59	QPR*	58	Blackpool	58
1968–69*f*	Derby Co	63	Crystal Palace	56	Charlton Ath	50
1969–70*f*	Huddersfield T	60	Blackpool	53	Leicester C	51
1970–71*f*	Leicester C	59	Sheffield U	56	Cardiff C*	53
1971–72*f*	Norwich C	57	Birmingham C	56	Millwall	55
1972–73*f*	Burnley	62	QPR	61	Aston Villa	50
1973–74*f*	Middlesbrough	65	Luton T	50	Carlisle U	49
1974–75*f*	Manchester U	61	Aston Villa	58	Norwich C	53
1975–76*f*	Sunderland	56	Bristol C*	53	WBA	53
1976–77*f*	Wolverhampton W	57	Chelsea	55	Nottingham F	52
1977–78*f*	Bolton W	58	Southampton	57	Tottenham H*	56
1978–79*f*	Crystal Palace	57	Brighton*	56	Stoke C	56
1979–80*f*	Leicester C	55	Sunderland	54	Birmingham C*	53
1980–81*f*	West Ham U	66	Notts Co	53	Swansea C*	50
1981–82*g*	Luton T	88	Watford	80	Norwich C	71
1982–83*g*	QPR	85	Wolverhampton W	75	Leicester C	70
1983–84*g*	Chelsea*	88	Sheffield W	88	Newcastle U	80
1984–85*g*	Oxford U	84	Birmingham C	82	Manchester C	74
1985–86*g*	Norwich C	84	Charlton Ath	77	Wimbledon	76
1986–87*g*	Derby Co	84	Portsmouth	78	Oldham Ath††	75
1987–88*h*	Millwall	82	Aston Villa*	78	Middlesbrough	78
1988–89*k*	Chelsea	99	Manchester C	82	Crystal Palace	81
1989–90*k*	Leeds U*	85	Sheffield U	85	Newcastle U††	80
1990–91*k*	Oldham Ath	88	West Ham U	87	Sheffield W	82
1991–92*k*	Ipswich T	84	Middlesbrough	80	Derby Co	78

No competition during 1915–19 and 1939–46.
††*Not promoted after play-offs.*

THIRD DIVISION to 1991–92

Maximum points: 92; 138 from 1981–82.

	First	Pts	Second	Pts	Third	Pts
1958–59	Plymouth Arg	62	Hull C	61	Brentford*	57
1959–60	Southampton	61	Norwich C	59	Shrewsbury T*	52
1960–61	Bury	68	Walsall	62	QPR	60
1961–62	Portsmouth	65	Grimsby T	62	Bournemouth*	59
1962–63	Northampton T	62	Swindon T	58	Port Vale	54
1963–64	Coventry C*	60	Crystal Palace	60	Watford	58
1964–65	Carlisle U	60	Bristol C*	59	Mansfield T	59
1965–66	Hull C	69	Millwall	65	QPR	57
1966–67	QPR	67	Middlesbrough	55	Watford	54
1967–68	Oxford U	57	Bury	56	Shrewsbury T	55
1968–69	Watford*	64	Swindon T	64	Luton T	61
1969–70	Orient	62	Luton T	60	Bristol R	56
1970–71	Preston NE	61	Fulham	60	Halifax T	56
1971–72	Aston Villa	70	Brighton	65	Bournemouth*	62
1972–73	Bolton W	61	Notts Co	57	Blackburn R	55
1973–74	Oldham Ath	62	Bristol R*	61	York C	61
1974–75	Blackburn R	60	Plymouth Arg	59	Charlton Ath	55

** Won or placed on goal average/goal difference.*

	First	Pts	Second	Pts	Third	Pts
1975–76	Hereford U	63	Cardiff C	57	Millwall	56
1976–77	Mansfield T	64	Brighton & HA	61	Crystal Palace*	59
1977–78	Wrexham	61	Cambridge U	58	Preston NE*	56
1978–79	Shrewsbury T	61	Watford*	60	Swansea C	60
1979–80	Grimsby T	62	Blackburn R	59	Sheffield W	58
1980–81	Rotherham U	61	Barnsley*	59	Charlton Ath	59
1981–82	Burnley*	80	Carlisle U	80	Fulham	78
1982–83	Portsmouth	91	Cardiff C	86	Huddersfield T	82
1983–84	Oxford U	95	Wimbledon	87	Sheffield U*	83
1984–85	Bradford C	94	Millwall	90	Hull C	87
1985–86	Reading	94	Plymouth Arg	87	Derby Co	84
1986–87	Bournemouth	97	Middlesbrough	94	Swindon T	87
1987–88	Sunderland	93	Brighton & HA	84	Walsall	82
1988–89	Wolverhampton W	92	Sheffield U	84	Port Vale	84
1989–90	Bristol R	93	Bristol C	91	Notts Co	87
1990–91	Cambridge U	86	Southend U	85	Grimsby T*	83
1991–92	Brentford	82	Birmingham C	81	Huddersfield T	78

FOURTH DIVISION (1958–1992)

Maximum points: 92; 138 from 1981–82.

	First	Pts	Second	Pts	Third	Pts	Fourth	Pts
1958–59	Port Vale	64	Coventry C*	60	York C	60	Shrewsbury T	58
1959–60	Walsall	65	Notts Co*	60	Torquay U	60	Watford	57
1960–61	Peterborough U	66	Crystal Palace	64	Northampton T*	60	Bradford PA	60
1961–62†	Millwalh	56	Colchester U	55	Wrexham	53	Carlisle U	52
1962–63	Brentford	62	Oldham Ath*	59	Crewe Alex	59	Mansfield T*	57
1963–64	Gillingham*	60	Carlisle U	60	Workington T	59	Exeter C	58
1964–65	Brighton	63	Millwall*	62	York C	62	Oxford U	61
1965–66	Doncaster R*	59	Darlington	59	Torquay U	58	Colchester U*	56
1966–67	Stockport Co	64	Southport*	59	Barrow	59	Tranmere R	58
1967–68	Luton T	66	Barnsley	61	Hartlepools U	60	Crewe Alex	58
1968–69	Doncaster R	59	Halifax T	57	Rochdale*	56	Bradford C	56
1969–70	Chesterfield	64	Wrexham	61	Swansea C	60	Port Vale	59
1970–71	Notts Co	69	Bournemouth	60	Oldham Ath	59	York C	56
1971–72	Grimsby T	63	Southend U	60	Brentford	59	Scunthorpe U	57
1972–73	Southport	62	Hereford U	58	Cambridge U	57	Aldershot*	56
1973–74	Peterborough U	65	Gillingham	62	Colchester U	60	Bury	59
1974–75	Mansfield T	68	Shrewsbury T	62	Rotherham U	59	Chester*	57
1975–76	Lincoln C	74	Northampton T	68	Reading	60	Tranmere R	58
1976–77	Cambridge U	65	Exeter C	62	Colchester U*	59	Bradford C	59
1977–78	Watford	71	Southend U	60	Swansea C*	56	Brentford	56
1978–79	Reading	65	Grimsby T*	61	Wimbledon*	61	Barnsley	61
1979–80	Huddersfield T	66	Walsall	64	Newport Co	61	Portsmouth*	60
1980–81	Southend U	67	Lincoln C	65	Doncaster R	56	Wimbledon	55
1981–82	Sheffield U	96	Bradford C*	91	Wigan Ath	91	AFC Bournemouth	88
1982–83	Wimbledon	98	Hull C	90	Port Vale	88	Scunthorpe U	83
1983–84	York C	101	Doncaster R	85	Reading*	82	Bristol C	82
1984–85	Chesterfield	91	Blackpool	86	Darlington	85	Bury	84
1985–86	Swindon T	102	Chester C	84	Mansfield T	81	Port Vale	79
1986–87	Northampton T	99	Preston NE	90	Soqthend U	80	Wolverhampton W††	79
1987–88	Wolverhampton W	90	Cardiff C	85	Bolton W	78	Scunthorpe U††	77
1988–89	Rotherham U	82	Tranmere R	80	Crewe Alex	78	Scunthorpe U††	77
1989–90	Exeter C	89	Grimsby T	79	Southend U	75	Stockport Co††	74
1990–91	Darlington	83	Stockport Co*	82	Hartlepool U	82	Peterborough U	80
1991–92†*	Burnley	80	Rotherham U*	77	Mansfield T	77	Blackpool	76

†*Maximum points:* 88 owing to Accrington Stanley's resignation. ††*Not promoted after play-offs.*
†**Maximum points:* 126 owing to Aldershot being expelled.

THIRD DIVISION—SOUTH (1920–1958)

Maximum points: a 84; *b* 92.

	First	Pts	Second	Pts	Third	Pts
1920–21*a*	Crystal Palace	59	Southampton	54	QPR	53
1921–22*a*	Southampton*	61	Plymouth Arg	61	Portsmouth	53
1922–23*a*	Bristol C	59	Plymouth Arg*	53	Swansea T	53
1923–24*a*	Portsmouth	59	Plymouth Arg	55	Millwall	54
1924–25*a*	Swansea T	57	Plymouth Arg	56	Bristol C	53
1925–26*a*	Reading	57	Plymouth Arg	56	Millwall	53
1926–27*a*	Bristol C	62	Plymouth Arg	60	Millwall	56
1927–28*a*	Millwall	65	Northampton T	55	Plymouth Arg	53
1928–29*a*	Charlton Ath*	54	Crystal Palace	54	Northampton T*	52
1929–30*a*	Plymouth Arg	68	Brentford	61	QPR	51
1930–31*a*	Notts Co	59	Crystal Palace	51	Brentford	50
1931–32*a*	Fulham	57	Reading	55	Southend U	53
1932–33*a*	Brentford	62	Exeter C	58	Norwich C	57
1933–34*a*	Norwich C	61	Coventry C*	54	Reading*	54
1934–35*a*	Charlton Ath	61	Reading	53	Coventry C	51
1935–36*a*	Coventry C	57	Luton T	56	Reading	54
1936–37*a*	Luton T	58	Notts Co	56	Brighton	53
1937–38*a*	Millwall	56	Bristol C	55	QPR*	53
1938–39*a*	Newport Co	55	Crystal Palace	52	Brighton	49
1939–46	Competition cancelled owing to war.					

* *Won or placed on goal average/goal difference.*

	First	Pts	Second	Pts	Third	Pts
1946–47*a*	Cardiff C	66	QPR	57	Bristol C	51
1947–48*a*	QPR	61	Bournemouth	57	Walsall	51
1948–49*a*	Swansea T	62	Reading	55	Bournemouth	52
1949–50*a*	Notts Co	58	Northampton T*	51	Southend U	51
1950–51*b*	Nottingham F	70	Norwich C	64	Reading*	57
1951–52*b*	Plymouth Arg	66	Reading*	61	Norwich C	61
1952–53*b*	Bristol R	64	Millwall*	62	Northampton T	62
1953–54*b*	Ipswich T	64	Brighton	61	Bristol C	56
1954–55*b*	Bristol C	70	Leyton O	61	Southampton	59
1955–56*b*	Leyton O	66	Brighton	65	Ipswich T	64
1956–57*b*	Ipswich T*	59	Torquay U	59	Colchester U	58
1957–58*b*	Brighton	60	Brentford*	58	Plymouth Arg	58

THIRD DIVISION—NORTH (1921–1958)

Maximum points: a 76; b 84; c 80; d 92.

	First	Pts	Second	Pts	Third	Pts
1921–22*a*	Stockport Co	56	Darlington*	50	Grimsby T	50
1922–23*a*	Nelson	51	Bradford PA	47	Walsall	46
1923–24*b*	Wolverhampton W	63	Rochdale	62	Chesterfield	54
1924–25*b*	Darlington	58	Nelson*	53	New Brighton	53
1925–26*b*	Grimsby T	61	Bradford PA	60	Rochdale	59
1926–27*b*	Stoke C	63	Rochdale	58	Bradford PA	55
1927–28*b*	Bradford PA	63	Lincoln C	55	Stockport Co	54
1928–29*g*	Bradford C	63	Stockport Co	62	Wrexham	52
1929–30*b*	Port Vale	67	Stockport Co	63	Darlington*	50
1930–31*b*	Chesterfield	58	Lincoln C	57	Wrexham*	54
1931–32*c*	Lincoln C*	57	Gateshead	57	Chester	50
1932–33*b*	Hull C	59	Wrexham	57	Stockport Co	54
1933–34*b*	Barnsley	62	Chesterfield	61	Stockport Co	59
1934–35*b*	Doncaster R	57	Halifax T	55	Chester	54
1935–36*b*	Chesterfield	60	Chester*	55	Tranmere R	55
1936–37*b*	Stockport Co	60	Lincoln C	57	Chester	53
1937–38*b*	Tranmere R	56	Doncaster R	54	Hull C	53
1938–39*b*	Barnsley	67	Doncaster R	56	Bradford C	52
1939–46	Competition cancelled owing to war.					
1946–47*b*	Doncaster R	72	Rotherham U	60	Chester	56
1947–48*b*	Lincoln C	60	Rotherham U	59	Wrexham	50
1948–49*b*	Hull C	65	Rotherham U	62	Doncaster R	50
1949–50*b*	Doncaster R	55	Gateshead	53	Rochdale*	51
1950–51*d*	Rotherham U	71	Mansfield T	64	Carlisle U	62
1951–52*d*	Lincoln C	69	Grimsby T	66	Stockport Co	59
1952–53*d*	Oldham Ath	59	Port Vale	58	Wrexham	56
1953–54*d*	Port Vale	69	Barnsley	58	Scunthorpe U	57
1954–55*d*	Barnsley	65	Accrington S	61	Scunthorpe U*	58
1955–56*d*	Grimsby T	68	Derby Co	63	Accrington S	59
1956–57*d*	Derby Co	63	Hartlepool U	59	Accrington S*	58
1957–58*d*	Scunthorpe U	66	Accrington S	59	Bradford C	57

** Won or placed on goal average.*

PROMOTED AFTER PLAY-OFFS
(Not accounted for in previous section)

1986–87 Aldershot to Division 3.
1987–88 Swansea C to Divison 3.
1988–89 Leyton O to Division 3.
1989–90 Cambridge U to Division 3; Notts Co to Division 2; Sunderland to Division 1.
1990–91 Notts Co to Division 1; Tranmere R to Division 2; Torquay U to Division 3.
1991–92 Blackburn R to Premier League; Peterborough U to Division 1.
1992–93 Swindon T to Premier League; WBA to Division 1; York C to Division 2.
1993–94 Leicester C to Premier League; Burnley to Division 1; Wycombe W to Division 2

LEAGUE TITLE WINS

FA PREMIER LEAGUE – Manchester U 2.

LEAGUE DIVISION 1 – Liverpool 18, Arsenal 10, Everton 9, Manchester U 7, Aston Villa 7, Sunderland 6, Newcastle U 5, Sheffield W 4, Huddersfield T 3, Leeds U 3, Wolverhampton W 3, Blackburn R 2, Portsmouth 2, Preston NE 2, Burnley 2, Manchester C 2, Tottenham H 2, Derby Co 2, Chelsea 1, Crystal Palace 1, Sheffield U 1, WBA 1, Ipswich T 1, Nottingham F 1 each.

LEAGUE DIVISION 2 – Leicester C 6, Manchester C 6, Sheffield W 5, Birmingham C (one as Small Heath) 4, Derby Co 4, Liverpool 4, Ipswich T 3, Leeds U 3, Notts Co 3, Preston NE 3, Middlesbrough 3, Stoke C 3, Grimsby T 2, Norwich C 2, Nottingham F 2, Tottenham H 2, WBA 2, Aston Villa 2, Burnley 2, Chelsea 2, Manchester U 2, West Ham U 2, Wolverhampton W 2, Bolton W 2, Huddersfield T, Bristol C, Brentford, Bury, Bradford C, Everton, Fulham, Sheffield U, Newcastle U, Coventry C, Blackpool, Blackburn R, Sunderland, Crystal Palace, Luton T, QPR, Oxford U, Millwall, Oldham Ath, Reading 1 each.

LEAGUE DIVISION 3 – Portsmouth 2, Oxford U 2, Shrewsbury T, Plymouth Arg, Southampton, Bury, Northampton T, Coventry C, Carlisle U, Hull C, QPR, Watford, Leyton O, Preston NE, Aston Villa, Bolton W, Oldham Ath, Blackburn R, Hereford U, Mansfield T, Wrexham, Grimsby T, Rotherham U, Burnley, Bradford C, Bournemouth, Reading, Sunderland, Wolverhampton W, Bristol R, Cambridge U, Brentford, Cardiff C 1 each.

LEAGUE DIVISION 4 – Chesterfield 2, Doncaster R 2, Peterborough U 2, Port Vale, Walsall, Millwall, Brentford, Gillingham, Brighton, Stockport Co, Luton T, Notts Co, Grimsby T, Southport, Mansfield T, Lincoln C, Cambridge U, Watford, Reading, Huddersfield T, Southend U, Sheffield U, Wimbledon, York C, Swindon T, Northampton T, Wolverhampton W, Rotherham U, Exeter C, Darlington, Burnley 1 each.

To 1957–58

DIVISION 3 (South) – Bristol C 3; Charlton Ath, Ipswich T, Millwall, Notts Co, Plymouth Arg, Swansea T 2 each; Brentford, Bristol R, Cardiff C, Crystal Palace, Coventry C, Fulham, Leyton O, Luton T, Newport Co, Nottingham F, Norwich C, Portsmouth, QPR, Reading, Southampton, Brighton 1 each.

DIVISION 3 (North) – Barnsley, Doncaster R, Lincoln C 3 each; Chesterfield, Grimsby T, Hull C, Port Vale, Stockport Co 2 each; Bradford PA, Bradford C, Darlington, Derby Co, Nelson, Oldham Ath, Rotherham U, Stoke C, Tranmere R, Wolverhampton W, Scunthorpe U 1 each.

RELEGATED CLUBS

1891–92 League extended. Newton Heath, Sheffield W and Nottingham F admitted. *Second Division formed* including Darwen.
1892–93 In Test matches, Sheffield U and Darwen won promotion in place of Notts Co and Accrington S.
1893–94 In Tests, Liverpool and Small Heath won promotion. Newton Heath and Darwen relegated.
1894–95 After Tests, Bury promoted, Liverpool relegated.
1895–96 After Tests, Liverpool promoted, Small Heath relegated.
1896–97 After Tests, Notts Co promoted, Burnley relegated.
1897–98 Test system abolished after success of Stoke C and Burnley. League extended. Blackburn R and Newcastle U elected to First Division. *Automatic promotion and relegation introduced.*

FA PREMIER LEAGUE TO DIVISION 1

1992–93 Crystal Palace, Middlesbrough, Nottingham Forest
1993–94 Sheffield U, Oldham Ath, Swindon T

DIVISION 1 TO DIVISION 2

1898–99 Bolton W and Sheffield W
1899–1900 Burnley and Glossop
1900–01 Preston NE and WBA
1901–02 Small Heath and Manchester C
1902–03 Grimsby T and Bolton W
1903–04 Liverpool and WBA
1904–05 League extended. Bury and Notts Co, two bottom clubs in First Division, re-elected.
1905–06 Nottingham F and Wolverhampton W
1906–07 Derby Co and Stoke C
1907–08 Bolton W and Birmingham C
1908–09 Manchester C and Leicester Fosse
1909–10 Bolton W and Chelsea
1910–11 Bristol C and Nottingham F
1911–12 Preston NE and Bury
1912–13 Notts Co and Woolwich Arsenal
1913–14 Preston NE and Derby Co
1914–15 Tottenham H and Chelsea*
1919–20 Notts Co and Sheffield W
1920–21 Derby Co and Bradford PA
1921–22 Bradford C and Manchester U
1922–23 Stoke C and Oldham Ath
1923–24 Chelsea and Middlesbrough
1924–25 Preston NE and Nottingham F
1925–26 Manchester C and Notts Co
1926–27 Leeds U and WBA
1927–28 Tottenham H and Middlesbrough
1928–29 Bury and Cardiff C
1929–30 Burnley and Everton
1930–31 Leeds U and Manchester U
1931–32 Grimsby T and West Ham U
1932–33 Bolton W and Blackpool
1933–34 Newcastle U and Sheffield U
1934–35 Leicester C and Tottenham H
1935–36 Aston Villa and Blackburn R
1936–37 Manchester U and Sheffield W
1937–38 Manchester C and WBA
1938–39 Birmingham C and Leicester C
1946–47 Brentford and Leeds U
1947–48 Blackburn R and Grimsby T
1948–49 Preston NE and Sheffield U
1949–50 Manchester C and Birmingham C
1950–51 Sheffield W and Everton
1951–52 Huddersfield and Fulham
1952–53 Stoke C and Derby Co
1953–54 Middlesbrough and Liverpool
1954–55 Leicester C and Sheffield W
1955–56 Huddersfield and Sheffield U
1956–57 Charlton Ath and Cardiff C
1957–58 Sheffield W and Sunderland
1958–59 Portsmouth and Aston Villa
1959–60 Luton T and Leeds U
1960–61 Preston NE and Newcastle U
1961–62 Chelsea and Cardiff C
1962–63 Majchester C and Leyton O
1963–64 Bolton W and Ipswich T
1964–65 Wolverhampton W and Birmingham C
1965–66 Northampton T and Blackburn R
1966–67 Aston Villa and Blackpool
1967–68 Fulham and Sheffield U
1968–69 Leicester C and QPR
1969–70 Sunderland and Sheffield W
1970–71 Burnley and Blackpool
1971–72 Huddersfield T and Nottingham F
1972–73 Crystal Palace and WBA
1973–74 Southampton, Manchester U, Norwich C
1974–75 Luton T, Chelsea, Carlisle U
1975–76 Wolverhampton W, Burnley, Sheffield U
1976–77 Sunderland, Stoke C, Tottenham H
1977–78 West Ham U, Newcastle U, Leicester C
1978–79 QPR, Birmingham C, Chelsea
1979–80 Bristol C, Derby Co, Bolton W
1980–81 Norwich C, Leicester C, Crystal Palace
1981–82 Leeds U, Wolverhampton W, Middlesbrough
1982–83 Manchester C, Swansea C, Brighton & HA
1983–84 Birmingham C, Notts Co, Wolverhampton W
1984–85 Norwich C, Sunderland, Stoke C
1985–86 Ipswich T, Birmingham C, WBA
1986–87 Leicester C, Manchester C, Aston Villa
1987–88 Chelsea**, Portsmouth, Watford, Oxford U
1988–89 Middlesbrough, West Ham U, Newcastle U
1989–90 Sheffield W, Charlton Ath, Millwall
1990–91 Sunderland and Derby Co
1991–92 Luton T, Notts Co, West Ham U
1992–93 Brentford, Cambridge U, Bristol R
1993–94 Birmingham C, Oxford U, Peterborough U

***Relegated after play-offs.*
**Subsequently re-elected to Division 1 when League was extended after the War.*

DIVISION 2 TO DIVISION 3

1920–21 Stockport Co
1921–22 Bradford and Bristol C
1922–23 Rotherham C and Wolverhampton W
1923–24 Nelson and Bristol C
1924–25 Crystal Palace and Coventry C
1925–26 Stoke C and Stockport Co
1926–27 Darlington and Bradford C
1927–28 Fulham and South Shields
1928–29 Port Vale and Clapton O
1929–30 Hull C and Notts Co
1930–31 Reading and Cardiff C
1931–32 Barnsley and Bristol C
1932–33 Chesterfield and Charlton Ath
1933–34 Millwall and Lincoln C
1934–35 Oldham Ath and Notts Co
1935–36 Port Vale and Hull C
1936–37 Doncaster R and Bradford C
1937–38 Barnsley and Stockport Co
1938–39 Norwich C and Tranmere R
1946–47 Swansea T and Newport Co
1947–48 Doncaster R and Millwall
1948–49 Nottingham F and Lincoln C
1949–50 Plymouth Arg and Bradford
1950–51 Grimsby T and Chesterfield
1951–52 Coventry C and QPR
1952–53 Southampton and Barnsley
1953–54 Brentford and Oldham Ath
1954–55 Ipswich T and Derby Co

1955–56 Plymouth Arg and Hull C
1956–57 Port Vale and Bury
1957–58 Doncaster R and Notts Co
1958–59 Barnsley and Grimsby T
1959–60 Bristol C and Hull C
1960–61 Lincoln C and Portsmouth
1961–62 Brighton & HA and Bristol R
1962–63 Walsall and Luton T
1963–64 Grimsby T and Scunthorpe U
1964–65 Swindon T and Swansea T
1965–66 Middlesbrough and Leyton O
1966–67 Northampton T and Bury
1967–68 Plymouth Arg and Rotherham U
1968–69 Fulham and Bury
1969–70 Preston NE and Aston Villa
1970–71 Blackburn R and Bolton W
1971–72 Charlton Ath and Watford
1972–73 Huddersfield T and Brighton & HA
1973–74 Crystal Palace, Preston NE, Swindon T
1974–75 Millwall, Cardiff C, Sheffield W
1975–76 Oxford U, York C, Portsmouth
1976–77 Carlisle U, Plymouth Arg, Hereford U
1977–78 Blackpool, Mansfield T, Hull C
1978–79 Sheffield U, Millwall, Blackburn R
1979–80 Fulham, Burnley, Charlton Ath
1980–81 Preston NE, Bristol C, Bristol R
1981–82 Cardiff C, Wrexham, Orient
1982–83 Rotherham U, Burnley, Bolton W
1983–84 Derby Co, Swansea C, Cambridge U
1984–85 Notts Co, Cardiff C, Wolverhampton W
1985–86 Carlisle U, Middlesbrough, Fulham
1986–87 Sunderland**, Grimsby T, Brighton & HA
1987–88 Huddersfield T, Reading, Sheffield U**
1988–89 Shrewsbury T, Birmingham C, Walsall
1989–90 Bournemouth, Bradford, Stoke C
1990–91 WBA and Hull C
1991–92 Plymouth Arg, Brighton & HA, Port Vale
1992–93 Preston NE, Mansfield T, Wigan Ath, Chester C
1993–94 Fulham, Exeter C, Hartlepool U, Barnet

DIVISION 3 TO DIVISION 4

1958–59 Rochdale, Notts Co, Doncaster R and Stockport
1959–60 Accrington S, Wrexham, Mansfield T and York C
1960–61 Chesterfield, Colchester U, Bradford C and Tranmere R
1961–62 Newport Co, Brentford, Lincoln C and Torquay U
1962–63 Bradford PA, Brighton, Carlisle U and Halifax T
1963–64 Millwall, Crewe Alex, Wrexham and Notts Co
1964–65 Luton T, Port Vale, Colchester U and Barnsley
1965–66 Southend U, Exeter C, Brentford and York C
1966–67 Doncaster R, Workington, Darlington and Swansea T
1967–68 Scunthorpe U, Colchester U, Grimsby T and Peterborough U (demoted)
1968–69 Oldham Ath, Crewe Alex, Hartlepool and Northampton
1969–70 Bournemouth, Southport, Barrow, Stockport Co
1970–71 Reading, Bury, Doncaster R, Gillingham
1971–72 Mansfield T, Barnsley, Torquay U, Bradford C
1972–73 Rotherham U, Brentford, Swansea C, Scunthorpe U
1973–74 Cambridge U, Shrewsbury T, Southport, Rochdale
1974–75 AFC Bournemouth, Tranmere R, Watford, Huddersfield T
1975–76 Aldershot, Colchester U, Southend U, Halifax T
1976–77 Reading, Northampton T, Grimsby T, York C
1977–78 Port Vale, Bradford C, Hereford U, Portsmouth
1978–79 Peterborough U, Walsall, Tranmere R, Lincoln C
1979–80 Bury, Southend U, Mansfield T, Wimbledon
1980–81 Sheffield U, Colchester U, Blackpool, Hull C
1981–82 Wimbledon, Swindon T, Bristol C, Chester
1982–83 Reading, Wrexham, Doncaster R, Chesterfield
1983–84 Scunthorpe U, Southend U, Port Vale, Exeter C
1984–85 Burnley, Orient, Preston NE, Cambridge U
1985–86 Lincoln C, Cardiff C, Wolverhampton W, Swansea C
1986–87 Bolton W**, Carlisle U, Darlington, Newport Co
1987–88 Doncaster R, York C, Grimsby T, Rotherham U**
1988–89 Southend U, Chesterfield, Gillingham, Aldershot
1989–90 Cardiff C, Northampton T, Blackpool, Walsall
1990–91 Crewe Alex, Rotherham U, Mansfield T
1991–92 Bury, Shrewsbury T, Torquay U, Darlington

** *Relegated after play-offs.*

APPLICATIONS FOR RE-ELECTION
FOURTH DIVISION

Eleven: Hartlepool U.
Seven: Crewe Alex.
Six: Barrow (lost League place to Hereford U 1972), Halifax T, Rochdale, Southport (lost League place to Wigan Ath 1978), York C.
Five: Chester C, Darlington, Lincoln C, Stockport Co, Workington (lost League place to Wimbledon 1977).
Four: Bradford PA (lost League place to Cambridge U 1970), Newport Co, Northampton T.
Three: Doncaster R, Hereford U.
Two: Bradford C, Exeter C, Oldham Ath, Scunthorpe U, Torquay U.
One: Aldershot, Colchester U, Gateshead (lost League place to Peterborough U 1960), Grimsby T, Swansea C, Tranmere R, Wrexham, Blackpool, Cambridge U, Preston NE.
Accrington S resigned and Oxford U were elected 1962.
Port Vale were forced to re-apply following expulsion in 1968.

THIRD DIVISIONS NORTH & SOUTH

Seven: Walsall.
Six: Exeter C, Halifax T, Newport Co.
Five: Accrington S, Barrow, Gillingham, New Brighton, Southport.
Four: Rochdale, Norwich C.
Three: Crystal Palace, Crewe Alex, Darlington, Hartlepool U, Merthyr T, Swindon T.
Two: Aberdare Ath, Aldershot, Ashington, Bournemouth, Brentford, Chester, Colchester U, Durham C, Millwall, Nelson, QPR, Rotherham U, Southend U, Tranmere R, Watford, Workington.
One: Bradford C, Bradford PA, Brighton, Bristol R, Cardiff C, Carlisle U, Charlton Ath, Gateshead, Grimsby T, Mansfield T, Shrewsbury T, Torquay U, York C.

LEAGUE STATUS FROM 1986–87

	RELEGATED FROM LEAGUE	PROMOTED TO LEAGUE
1986–87	Lincoln C	Scarborough
1987–88	Newport Co	Lincoln C
1988–89	Darlington	Maidstone U
1989–90	Colchester U	Darlington
1990–91	—	Barnet
1991–92	—	Colchester U
1992–93	Halifax T	Wycombe W
1993–94	—	—

LEADING GOALSCORERS 1993–94

FA CARLING PREMIERSHIP	*League*	*FA Cup*	*Coca Cola Cup*	*Other Cups*	*Total*
Andy Cole (*Newcastle U*)	34	1	6	0	41
Alan Shearer (*Blackburn R*)	31	2	1	0	34
Chris Sutton (*Norwich C*)	25	2	1	0	28
Matthew Le Tissier (*Southampton*)	25	0	0	0	25
Ian Wright (*Arsenal*)	23	1	6	3	33
Peter Beardsley (*Newcastle U*)	21	2	1	0	24
Mark Bright (*Sheffield W*)	19	2	2	0	23
Eric Cantona (*Manchester U*)	18	4	1	2	25
Dean Holdsworth (*Wimbledon*)	17	3	4	0	24
Rodney Wallace (*Leeds U*)	17	0	0	0	17
Tony Cottee (*Everton*)	16	0	3	0	19
Les Ferdinand (*QPR*)	16	0	2	0	18
Ian Rush (*Liverpool*)	14	1	4	0	19
Kevin Campbell (*Arsenal*)	14	0	1	4	19
ENDSLEIGH INSURANCE DIVISION 1					
John McGinlay (*Bolton W*)	25	3	1	4	33
Chris Armstrong (*C Palace*)	22	0	1	1	24
John Aldridge (*Tranmere R*)	21	0	7	0	28
Stan Collymore (*Notingham F*)	19	0	5	1	25
Bob Taylor (*WBA*)	18	0	1	2	21
Paul Furlong (*Watford*)	18	0	1	0	19
Wayne Allison (*Bristol C*)	15	4	0	1	20
Paul Wilkinson (*Middlesbrough*)	15	1	1	2	19
Gary McSwegan (*Notts Co*)	15	0	1	1	17
Phil Gray (*Sunderland*)	14	0	3	0	17
Clive Mendonca (*Grimsby Town*)	14	0	2	1	17
Steve Bull (*Wolverhampton W*)	14	0	0	1	15
John Hendrie (*Middlesbrough*)	13	0	3	3	19
Tommy Johnson (*Derby Co*)	13	1	1	1	16
Paul Kitson (*Derby Co*)	13	1	0	1	15
Marco Gabbiadini (*Derby Co*)	13	0	2	0	15
DIVISION 2					
Jimmy Quinn (*Reading*)	35	2	0	3	40
Gary Bennett (*Wrexham*)	32	3	0	1	36
Kevin Francis (*Stockport Co*)	28	3	1	2	34
Paul Barnes (*York C*)	24	0	0	1	25
Dean Windass (*Hull C*)	23	1	0	0	24
John Taylor (*Bristol R*)	23	0	0	0	23
Kurt Nogan (*Brighton & HA*)	22	0	2	2	26
Andy Preece (*Stockport Co*)	21	2	0	5	28
Steve Castle (*Plymouth Arg*)	21	0	0	1	22
Steve Butler (*Cambridge U*)	21	0	0	0	21
Stuart Lovell (*Reading*)	20	0	0	1	21
David Eyres (*Burnley*)	19	4	3	1	27
Imre Varadi (*Rotherham U*)	19	1	0	1	21
Martin Foyle (*Port Vale*)	18	0	1	2	21
DIVISION 3					
Tony Ellis (*Preston NE*)	26	2	1	1	30
Mark Carter (*Bury*)	20	0	0	0	20
Steve Norris (*Chesterfield*)	19	2	0	1	22
Matt Carmichael (*Scunthorpe U*)	18	1	0	5	24
Dean Spink (*Shrewsbury T*)	18	1	0	1	20
Chris Pike (*Hereford U*)	18	1	0	0	19
Nick Forster (*Gillingham*)	18	0	0	0	18
Darren Rowbotham (*Crewe Alex*)	15	1	1	0	17
Adrian Foster (*Torquay U*)	15	0	1	0	16
Steve Whitehall (*Rochdale*)	14	1	0	0	15
Tony Naylor (*Crewe Alex*)	13	1	0	2	16
David Reeves (*Carlisle U*)	11	1	0	3	15

N.B. Players are listed in order of the League goals scored. Only those who scored in one division are included in the list. Other cup goals refer to those in European matches, Autoglass Trophy and Anglo-Italian Cup, but not in the play-offs.

FA CHARITY SHIELD WINNERS 1908–93

1908	Manchester U v QPR	4-0 after 1-1 draw	1958	Bolton W v Wolverhampton W	4-1
1909	Newcastle U v Northampton T	2-0	1959	Wolverhampton W v Nottingham F	3-1
1910	Brighton v Aston Villa	1-0	1960	Burnley v Wolverhampton W	2-2*
1911	Manchester U v Swindon T	8-4	1961	Tottenham H v FA XI	3-2
1912	Blackburn R v QPR	2-1	1962	Tottenham H v Ipswich T	5-1
1913	Professionals v Amateurs	7-2	1963	Everton v Manchester U	4-0
1920	WBA v Tottenham H	2-0	1964	Liverpool v West Ham U	2-2*
1921	Tottenham H v Burnley	2-0	1965	Manchester U v Liverpool	2-2*
1922	Huddersfield T v Liverpool	1-0	1966	Liverpool v Everton	1-0
1923	Professionals v Amateurs	2-0	1967	Manchester U v Tottenham H	3-3*
1924	Professionals v Amateurs	3-1	1968	Manchester C v WBA	6-1
1925	Amateurs v Professionals	6-1	1969	Leeds U v Manchester C	2-1
1926	Amateurs v Professionals	6-3	1970	Everton v Chelsea	2-1
1927	Cardiff C v Corinthians	2-1	1971	Leicester C v Liverpool	1-0
1928	Everton v Blackburn R	2-1	1972	Manchester C v Aston Villa	1-0
1929	Professionals v Amateurs	3-0	1973	Burnley v Manchester C	1-0
1930	Arsenal v Sheffield W	2-1	1974	Liverpool† v Leeds U	1-1
1931	Arsenal v WBA	1-0	1975	Derby Co v West Ham U	2-0
1932	Everton v Newcastle U	5-3	1976	Liverpool v Southampton	1-0
1933	Arsenal v Everton	3-0	1977	Liverpool v Manchester U	0-0*
1934	Arsenal v Manchester C	4-0	1978	Nottingham F v Ipswich T	5-0
1935	Sheffield W v Arsenal	1-0	1979	Liverpool v Arsenal	3-1
1936	Sunderland v Arsenal	2-1	1980	Liverpool v West Ham U	1-0
1937	Manchester C v Sunderland	2-0	1981	Aston Villa v Tottenham H	2-2*
1938	Arsenal v Preston NE	2-1	1982	Liverpool v Tottenham H	1-0
1948	Arsenal v Manchester U	4-3	1983	Manchester U v Liverpool	2-0
1949	Portsmouth v Wolverhampton W	1-1*	1984	Everton v Liverpool	1-0
1950	World Cup Team v Canadian Touring Team	4-2	1985	Everton v Manchester U	2-0
1951	Tottenham H v Newcastle U	2-1	1986	Everton v Liverpool	1-1*
1952	Manchester U v Newcastle U	4-2	1987	Everton v Coventry C	1-0
1953	Arsenal v Blackpool	3-1	1988	Liverpool v Wimbledon	2-1
1954	Wolverhampton W v WBA	4-4*	1989	Liverpool v Arsenal	1-0
1955	Chelsea v Newcastle U	3-0	1990	Liverpool v Manchester U	1-1*
1956	Manchester U v Manchester C	1-0	1991	Arsenal v Tottenham H	0-0*
1957	Manchester U v Aston Villa	4-0	1992	Leeds U v Liverpool	4-3

** Each club retained shield for six months.* *† Won on penalties.*

FA CHARITY SHIELD 1993

Arsenal (1) 1, Manchester U (1) 1
(*Manchester U won 5-4 on penalties*)
At Wembley, 7 August 1993, attendance 66,519

Arsenal: Seaman; Dixon (Keown), Winterburn, Davis, Linighan, Adams, Jensen, Wright, Campbell, Merson, Limpar (McGoldrick).

Scorer: Wright.

Manchester U: Schmeichel; Parker, Irwin, Bruce, Kanchelskis, Pallister, Cantona, Ince, Keane, Hughes, Giggs (Robson).

Scorer: Hughes.

TRANSFERS 1993–94

	From	To	Fee in £s
June 1993			
24 Banks, Steven	West Ham United	Gillingham	Free
1 Bradley, Russell	Halifax Town	Scunthorpe United	Free
9 Burgess, David J.	Blackpool	Carlisle United	5000
8 Charlton, Simon T.	Huddersfield Town	Southampton	250,000
7 Clough, Nigel H.	Nottingham Forest	Liverpool	2,275,000
21 Cooper, Colin T.	Millwall	Nottingham Forest	1,800,000
15 Dennis, John A.	Cambridge United	Chesterfield	20,000
24 Hannigan, Al James	Marlow	Enfield	undisclosed
18 Hunt, Andrew	Newcastle United	West Bromwich Albion	100,000
3 Jones, Gary	Boston United	Southend United	25,000
15 Keen, Mark A.	Enfield	Chelmsford City	undisclosed
23 Kelly, David T.	Newcastle United	Wolverhampton Wanderers	750,000
17 Luscombe, Lee	Brentford	Millwall	Free
18 McGoldrick, Eddie J.P.	Crystal Palace	Arsenal	1,000,000
24 Pearce, Andrew J.	Coventry City	Sheffield Wednesday	500,000
24 Prior, Spencer	Southend United	Norwich City	200,000
24 Prudhoe, Mark	Darlington	Stoke City	120,000
4 Richardson, Stephen J.	Wimborne Town	Poole Town	undisclosed
28 Russell, Kevin J.	Stoke City	Burnley	140,000
18 Thomas, Geoffrey R.	Crystal Palace	Wolverhampton Wanderers	800,000
30 Webster, Simon	Charlton Athletic	West Ham United	400,000
July 1993			
29 Baird, Ian	Heart of Midlothian	Bristol City	295,000
16 Beardsley, Peter A.	Everton	Newcastle United	1,500,000
30 Blackwood, Bevon A.	Winsford United	Witton Albion	undisclosed
23 Blissett, Gary	Brentford	Wimbledon	350,000
28 Bowling, Ian	Lincoln City	Bradford City	27,500
9 Bressington, Graham	Lincoln City	Southend United	100,000
19 Bye, Andrew G.	Farnborough Town	Yeovil Town	undisclosed
16 Carey, Brian P.	Manchester United	Leicester City	250,000
16 Carmichael, Matthew	Lincoln City	Scunthorpe United	Free
21 Carr, Darren	Crewe Alexandra	Chesterfield	30,000
9 Carruthers, Martin G.	Aston Villa	Stoke City	100,000
29 Charles, Gary A.	Nottingham Forest	Derby County	750,000
8 Clarke, Michael D.	Sutton Coldfield Town	Solihull Borough	undisclosed
19 Colgate, Mark S.	Woodford Town	Harlow Town	undisclosed
28 Collier, Darren	Blackburn Rovers	Darlington	Nominal
5 Collymore, Stanley V.	Southend United	Nottingham Forest	2,000,000
2 Cormack, Lee D.	Waterlooville	Newport (IOW)	undisclosed
1 Coyle, Owen C.	Airdrieonians	Bolton Wanderers	250,000
16 Crawshaw, Gary	Staines Town	Hendon	undisclosed
20 Curran, Christopher P.	Scarborough	Carlisle United	Free
26 Davison, Aidan J.	Millwall	Bolton Wanderers	25,000
14 Deane, Brian C.	Sheffield United	Leeds United	2,700,000
15 Durnin, John	Oxford United	Portsmouth	200,000
27 Eyres, David	Blackpool	Burnley	90,000
29 Ferguson, Derek	Heart of Midlothian	Sunderland	750,000
22 Fletcher, Gary I.	Salisbury City	Wimborne Town	undisclosed
30 Francis, Stephen S.	Reading	Huddersfield Town	150,000
13 Gallimore, Anthony	Stoke City	Carlisle United	15,000
16 Gentle, Justin	Boreham Wood	Luton Town	undisclosed
19 Gray, Philip	Luton Town	Sunderland	800,000
23 Griffiths, Bryan K.	Wigan Athletic	Blackpool	Free
19 Harford, Michael G.	Sunderland	Coventry City	200,000
16 Hava, Vassos	Woodford Town	Harlow Town	undisclosed
16 Hill, David M.	Scunthorpe United	Lincoln City	Nominal
14 Hodge, John	Exeter City	Swansea City	18,000 + exch.
15 Hoddle, Glenn	Swindon Town	Chelsea	175,000
14 Hulme, Kevin	Bury	Doncaster Rovers	42,500
9 Jeffrey, Andrew S.	Cambridge City	Cambridge United	8500
7 Joyce, Warren G.	Plymouth Argyle	Burnley	140,000
21 Keane, Roy M.	Nottingham Forest	Manchester United	3,750,000
29 Keeley, John H.	Oldham Athletic	Colchester United	Free
7 Keen, Kevin I.	West Ham United	Wolverhampton Wanderers	600,000
15 Kerr, Dylan	Leeds United	Reading	75,000
27 Kimble, Alan F.	Cambridge United	Wimbledon	150,000
23 Legg, Andrew	Swansea City	Notts County	275,000
27 Lyttle, Desmond	Swansea City	Nottingham Forest	375,000
12 Mardenborough, Stephen A.	Darlington	Lincoln City	10,000
28 McMinn, Kevin C.	Derby County	Birmingham City	115,000
14 McSwegan, Gary	Glasgow Rangers	Notts County	400,000
12 Mooney, Thomas J.	Scarborough	Southend United	100,000
19 Morgan, Stephen A.	Plymouth Argyle	Coventry City	150,000
23 Myers, Christopher	Torquay United	Dundee United	90,000
20 O'Hanlon, Kelham G.	Carlisle United	Preston North End	25,000
26 Onuorah, Chike	Bournemouth	Wimborne Town	undisclosed
8 O'Regan, Kieran	Huddersfield Town	West Bromwich Albion	25,000
9 Otto, Ricky	Leyton Orient	Southend United	100,000
21 Patterson, Mark	Derby County	Plymouth Argyle	50,000
20 Phillips, James N.	Middlesbrough	Bolton Wanderers	250,000
9 Poole, Gary J.	Plymouth Argyle	Southend United	350,000
23 Raynor, Paul J.	Cambridge United	Preston North End	36,000
22 Redman, Ian F.	Curzon Ashton	Ashton United	undisclosed
14 Robinson, Spencer L.	Bury	Bristol City	130,000
23 Rodgerson, Ian	Birmingham City	Sunderland	140,000
6 Rowbotham, Darren	Birmingham City	Crewe Alexandra	Free
22 Ruddock, Neil	Tottenham Hotspur	Liverpool	2,500,000
14 Shakespeare, Craig R.	West Bromwich Albion	Grimsby Town	120,000
16 Speedie, David R.	Southampton	Leicester City	Free
30 Sterling, Worrel R.	Peterborough United	Bristol Rovers	140,000
23 Stimson, Mark	Newcastle United	Portsmouth	100,000
26 Tankard, Allen J.	Wigan Athletic	Port Vale	87,500
19 Taverner, Neil. J.	Woodford Town	Harlow Town	undisclosed
19 Thomas, Karl	Witton Albion	Runcorn	undisclosed
26 Townsend, Andrew D.	Chelsea	Aston Villa	2,000,000

	From	To	Fee in £s
16 Ward, Gavin J.	Cardiff City	Leicester City	175,000
1 Webster, Simon	Charlton Athletic	West Ham United	400,000
30 Whitbread, Adrian R.	Leyton Orient	Swindon Town	500,000
28 Williams, Dean A.	St Albans City	Brentford	14,000
1 Williams, John M.	Newport (IOW)	Waterlooville	undisclosed
16 Wright, Evran	Stourbridge	Halesowen Harriers	undisclosed

Temporary transfers

	From	To
23 Allardyce, Craig. S	Preston North End	Macclesfield Town
26 Hargreaves, Christian	Grimsby Town	Hull City
22 Hoult, Russell	Leicester City	Kettering Town
14 Smith, Mark C.	Grimsby Town	Scunthorpe United

August 1993

	From	To	Fee in £s
20 Alford, Carl P.	Witton Albion	Macclesfield Town	1700
13 Allen, Malcolm	Millwall	Newcastle United	300,000
20 Ashby, Nicholas. R.	Aylesbury United	Kettering Town	undisclosed
11 Ashcroft, Lee	Preston North End	West Bromwich Albion	225,000
20 Barnett, Gary L.	Huddersfield Town	Leyton Orient	Nominal
11 Barrick, Dean	Rotherham United	Cambridge United	75,000
19 Benton, David	Kidderminster Harriers	Worcester City	undisclosed
5 Blake, Mark A.	Aston Villa	Portsmouth	Nominal + exch.
16 Bloomfield, Paul	Cheltenham Town	Gloucester City	undisclosed
23 Bracey, Lee	Halifax Town	Bury	25,000
27 Brown, Steven R.	Scunthorpe United	Colchester United	Free
12 Bryson, James I.C.	Sheffield United	Barnsley	20,000
9 Burnett, Wayne	Blackburn Rovers	Plymouth Argyle	exch.
13 Carter, Timothy D.	Sunderland	Hartlepool United	Free
19 Casey, Kim T.	Wycombe Wanderers	Solihull Borough	undisclosed
11 Chapman, Lee R.	Leeds United	Portsmouth	250,000
13 Chapple, Philip R.	Cambridge United	Charlton Athletic	100,000
19 Clarke, Matthew L.	Cradley Town	Halesowen Harriers	undisclosed
13 Clarke, Wayne	Walsall	Shrewsbury Town	undisclosed
11 Comyn, Andrew J.	Derby County	Plymouth Argyle	200,000
20 Conroy, Michael K.	Burnley	Preston North End	85,000
2 Cook, Andrew C.	Exeter City	Swansea City	125,000
3 Cooper, Stephen B.	Tranmere Rovers	York City	35,000
14 Cotterill, Stephen	Wimbledon	AFC Bournemouth	80,000
4 Coughlin, Russell	Swansea City	Exeter City	exch.
27 Dennis, Leonard C.	Welling United	Woking	undisclosed
1 Dozzell, Jason	Ipswich Town	Tottenham Hotspur	1,900,000
13 Falconer, William H.	Middlesbrough	Sheffield United	400,000
5 Farnworth, Simon	Preston North End	Wigan Athletic	Nominal
31 Foran, Mark J.	Millwall	Sheffield United	25,000
9 Fulton, Stephen	Celtic	Bolton Wanderers	200,000
25 Gormley, Edward J.	Doncaster Rovers	Drogheda United	undisclosed
3 Hall, Neil	Winsford United	Witton Albion	undisclosed
17 Harkes, John A.	Sheffield Wednesday	Derby County	undisclosed
20 Harrop, Mark	Dover Athletic	Gravesend & Northfleet	undisclosed
10 Helliwell, Ian	Scunthorpe United	Rotherham United	50,000
9 Hendon, Ian M.	Tottenham Hotspur	Leyton Orient	50,000
27 Hicks, Stuart J.	Doncaster Rovers	Huddersfield Town	undisclosed
13 Houghton, Scott A.	Tottenham Hotspur	Luton Town	Free
20 Hunter, Barry V.	Crusaders	Wrexham	50,000
13 Jackson, Michael J.	Crewe Alexandra	Bury	undisclosed
20 Johnson, David A.	Sheffield Wednesday	Lincoln City	undisclosed
20 Juryeff, Ian M.	Darlington	Scunthorpe United	Nominal
17 Kurila, Alan	Burton Albion	Rushden & Diamonds	undisclosed
16 Leadbitter, Christopher J.	Cambridge United	AFC Bournemouth	25,000
10 Lee, Andrew G.	Telford United	Runcorn	undisclosed
13 Leonard, Mark A.	Preston North End	Chester City	Free
20 Leworthy, David J.	Farnborough Town	Dover Athletic	50,000
9 Loveridge, Peter J.	Salisbury City	Wimborne Town	undisclosed
12 Marshall, Ian P.	Oldham Athletic	Ipswich Town	750,000
20 Matthewson, Trevor	Birmingham City	Preston North End	25,000
5 McKearney, David J.	Crewe Alexandra	Wigan Athletic	Free
9 Melville, Andrew R.	Oxford United	Sunderland	500,000 + exch.
10 Mitchell, Paul R.	AFC Bournemouth	West Ham United	40,000
17 Mooney, Simon G.	Radcliffe Borough	Mossley	undisclosed
9 Morrison, Andrew C.	Plymouth Argyle	Blackburn Rovers	150,000 + exch.
20 Mutch, Andrew T.	Wolverhampton Wanderers	Swindon Town	250,000
9 Nuttell, Michael J.	Dagenham & Redbridge	Rushden & Diamonds	7000
13 Pascoe, Colin J.	Sunderland	Swansea City	70,000
12 Peacock, Gavin K.	Newcastle United	Chelsea	1,250,000
20 Phillips, David O.	Norwich City	Nottingham Forest	500,000
2 Putney, Trevor A.	Watford	Leyton Orient	40,000
23 Pye, Mark	Harrow Borough	Enfield	undisclosed
7 Ramsey, Paul	Cardiff City	St Johnstone	undisclosed
13 Rennie, Paul A.	Stoke City	Wigan Athletic	Nominal
20 Rhodes, Jason P.	Armitage 90	Burton Albion	undisclosed
9 Richardson, Paul A.	Dagenham & Redbridge	Rushden & Diamonds	3000
6 Robinson, Ronald	Peterborough United	Exeter City	25,000
9 Rogan, Anthony G.P.	Sunderland	Oxford United	exch.
13 Ross, Michael P.	Portsmouth	Exeter City	65,000
10 Rowland, Keith	AFC Bournemouth	West Ham United	110,000
19 Scott, Robert	Sutton United	Sheffield United	20,000
5 Selby, Neil	Havant Town	Waterlooville	undisclosed
12 Sheridan, Darren S.	Winsford United	Barnsley	10,000
20 Shirtliff, Peter A.	Sheffield Wednesday	Wolverhampton Wanderers	250,000
13 Sinclair, Trevor L.	Blackpool	Queens Park Rangers	750,000
19 Sinton, Andrew	Queens Park Rangers	Sheffield Wednesday	2,750,000
13 Smith, Mark C.	Notts County	Lincoln City	undisclosed
9 Smith, Mark C.	Grimsby Town	Scunthorpe United	20,000
16 Stanborough Nicholas D.	Hinckley Athletic	Gresley Rovers	undisclosed
5 Thompson, Alan	Newcastle United	Bolton Wanderers	250,000
20 Toman, James A.	Darlington	Scunthorpe United	Nominal
6 Torpey, Stephen D.J.	Bradford City	Swansea City	80,000
9 Tuttle, David P.	Tottenham Hotspur	Sheffield United	350,000
20 Valentine, Peter	Bury	Carlisle United	undisclosed
20 Warner, Steven P.	Dover Athletic	Billericay Town	undisclosed
3 Whittingham, Guy	Portsmouth	Aston Villa	1,200,000

	From	To	Fee in £s
13 Whyte, Christopher A.	Leeds United	Birmingham City	250,000
4 Wilcox, Russell	Hull City	Doncaster Rovers	60,000
8 Williams, Dean P.	Tamworth	Brentford	2000
17 Williams, Paul R.C.	Stockport County	Coventry City	150,000
12 Wilson, Daniel J.	Sheffield Wednesday	Barnsley	200,000
2 Woods, Gordon W.	Ashton United	Curzon Ashton	undisclosed
24 Wright, Evran	Ashton United	Walsall	undisclosed
17 Yates, Steven	Bristol Rovers	Queens Park Rangers	650,000

Temporary transfers

	From	To
20 Allardyce, Craig S.	Preston North End	Macclesfield Town
27 Aspinall, Warren	Portsmouth	AFC Bournemouth
19 Austin, Kevin	Saffron Walden Town	Leyton Orient
12 Barness, Anthony	Chelsea	Middlesbrough
2 Bottomley, Paul L.	Bridlington Town	Doncaster Rovers
27 Bound, Matthew T.	Southampton	Hull City
27 Clarke, Christopher	Bolton Wanderers	Morecambe
13 Cornwell, John A.	Southend United	Cardiff City
23 Crosby, Gary	Nottingham Forest	Grimsby Town
13 Dixon, Kerry M.	Southampton	Luton Town
26 Evans, Terence W.	Brentford	Wycombe Wanderers
12 Fickling, Ashley	Sheffield United	Darlington
20 Gayle, John	Birmingham City	Walsall
12 Gormley, Edward J.	Doncaster Rovers	Drogheda United
27 Greene, Dennis B.	Wycombe Wanderers	Woking
13 Hague, Paul	Gillingham	Cork City
26 Harding, Paul J.	Notts County	Southend United
7 Harper, Stecen J.	Burnley	Doncaster Rovers
9 Heavey, Paul A.	Preston North End	Netherfield
11 Heritage, Peter M.	Doncaster Rovers	Hastings Town
20 Hicks, Stuart J.	Doncaster Rovers	Huddersfield Town
20 Jones, Gary	Southend United	Dagenham & Redbridge
2 Jones, Graeme A.	Bridlington Town	Doncaster Rovers
13 Kaminsky, Jason M.G.	Nottingham Forest	Cobh Ramblers
24 Lambert, Christopher J.P.	Reading	Blackburn Rovers
6 Lee, Jason	Lincoln City	Southend United
13 Muggleton, Carl D.	Leicester City	Stoke City
28 Mulligan, James	Stoke City	Northwich Victoria
16 Murray, Shaun	Portsmouth	Milwall
31 Payne, Christopher A.	Billericay	Brighton & Hove Albion
13 Power, Lee M.	Norwich City	Sunderland
12 Reece, Andrew J.	Bristol Rovers	Walsall
23 Shutt, Carl S.	Leeds United	Birmingham City
12 Stant, Philip	Cardiff City	Mansfield Town
27 Walton, Mark A.	Norwich City	Wrexham
27 West, Dean	Lincoln City	Boston United
20 White, Jason G.	Scunthorpe United	Darlington
27 Whitehead, Philip M.	Barnsley	Stockport County
26 Wietecha, David	Millwall	Crewe Alexandra
20 Williams, Brett	Nottingham Forest	Stoke City

September 1993

	From	To	Fee in £s
16 Allen, Paul K.	Tottenham Hotspur	Southampton	550,000
24 Benjamin, Ian T.	Luton Town	Brentford	undisclosed
6 Bullock, Martin J.	Eastwood Town	Barnsley	undisclosed
17 Burrows, David	Liverpool	West Ham United	exch.
10 Carter, Mark C.	Barnet	Bury	undisclosed
17 Chapman, Lee R.	Portsmouth	West Ham United	250,000
13 Clarkson, Ian S.	Birmingham City	Stoke City	40,000
17 Dicks, Julian A.	West Ham United	Liverpool	1,600,000 + exch.
16 Gayle, John	Birmingham City	Coventry City	undisclosed
3 Hackett, Gary S.	West Bromwich Albion	Peterborough United	40,000
29 Hargreaves, Christian	Grimsby Town	Hull City	undisclosed
24 Harper, Steven J.	Burnley	Doncaster Rovers	undisclosed
8 Hemmings, Anthony G.	Northwich Victoria	Wycombe Wanderers	25,000
3 Higginbotham, Paul A.	Stalybridge Celtic	Barrow	1000
23 Hooper, Michael D.	Liverpool	Newcastle United	550,000
21 Ironside, Ian	Middlesbrough	Stockport County	undisclosed
20 Kernaghan, Alan N.	Middlesbrough	Manchester City	1,600,000
24 Kerslake, David	Leeds United	Tottenham Hotspur	450,000
6 Lee, Jason B	Lincoln City	Southend United	150,000
17 Marsh, Michael A.	Liverpool	West Ham United	exch.
9 Martin, Dean E.	West Ham United	Kettering Town	undisclosed
16 Measham, Ian	Burnley	Doncaster Rovers	undisclosed
20 Moyes, David W.	Hamilton Academical	Preston North End	undisclosed
9 Parsley, Neil R.	Huddersfield Town	West Bromwich Albion	25,000
24 Sturridge, Simon A.	Birmingham City	Stoke City	undisclosed
9 Van Den Hauwe, Patrick W.	Tottenham Hotspur	Millwall	Free
3 Warhurst, Paul	Sheffield Wednesday	Blackburn Rovers	2,650,000
20 Westley, Graham N.	Aylesbury United	Harrow Borough	undisclosed
24 Wright, Thomas J.	Newcastle United	Nottingham Forest	450,000

Temporary transfers

	From	To
27 Allardyce, Craig S.	Preston North End	Netherfield
16 Allon, Joseph B.	Brentford	Southend United
10 Angell, Brett	Southend United	Everton
12 Barness, Anthony	Chelsea	Middlesbrough
27 Bennett, Craig	Doncaster Rovers	Bridlington Town
24 Benstead, Graham	Brentford	Kettering Town
8 Benton, Stephen	Bristol City	Clevedon Town
17 Borrows, Brian	Coventry City	Bristol City
3 Clark, Paul D.	Cambridge United	Walton & Hersham
29 Colgan, Nicholas V.	Chelsea	Crewe Alexandra
16 Cornwell, John A.	Southend United	Brentford
28 Davison, Robert	Leicester City	Sheffield United
17 Dixon, Kerry M.	Southampton	Luton Town
22 Dobson, Anthony J.	Blackburn Rovers	Portsmouth
25 Dowell, Wayne A.	Burnley	Witton Albion
17 Flitcroft, David J.	Preston North End	Lincoln City
16 Ford, Tony	Grimsby Town	Bradford City
3 Gillespie, Keith R.	Manchester United	Wigan Athletic

	From	To	Fee in £s
13 Hall, Mark A.	Southend United	Barnet	
24 Harkness, Steven	Liverpool	Huddersfield Town	
8 Harper, Steven J.	Preston North End	Doncaster Rovers	
9 Heavey, Paul A.	Preston North End	Netherfield	
3 Hine, Mark	Doncaster Rovers	Gateshead	
3 Howarth, Neil	Burnley	Macclesfield Town	
10 Jemson, Nigel B.	Sheffield Wednesday	Grimsby Town	
17 Jones, Gary	Southend United	Lincoln City	
3 Jones, Philip L.	Liverpool	Crewe Alexandra	
23 Joyce, Joseph P.	Carlisle United	Darlington	
17 Kelly, Anthony O.N.	Stoke City	Bury	
24 Knill, Alan R.	Bury	Cardiff City	
3 Livingstone, Stephen	Chelsea	Port Vale	
24 Lyne, Neil G.F.	Cambridge United	Chesterfield	
23 Mahorn, Paul G.	Tottenham Hotspur	Fulham	
13 Makin, Christopher	Oldham Athletic	Preston North End	
24 McIlhargey, Stephen	Blackpool	Chester City	
7 Milsom, Paul J.	Bristol City	Clevedon Town	
13 Muggleton, Carl D.	Leicester City	Stoke City	
17 Muir, John G.	Preston North End	Telford United	
27 Murphy, Shaun P.	Notts County	Lincoln City	
16 Painter, Peter R.	Burnley	Darlington	
24 Parkinson, Stephen	Lincoln City	Kings Lynn	
28 Peel, Nathan J.	Sheffield United	Burnley	
17 Potter, Graham S.	Birmingham City	Wycombe Wanderers	
23 Reed, John P.	Sheffield United	Mansfield Town	
17 Rioch, Gregor J.	Luton Town	Barnet	
16 Small, Michael A.	West Ham United	Wolverhampton Wanderers	
16 Tilson, Stephen B.	Southend United	Brentford	
2 Whitehead, Philip M.	Halifax Town	Stockport County	
29 Whitehead, Philip M.	Barnsley	Oxford United	
13 Williams, Andrew	Notts County	Huddersfield Town	
23 Wright, Ian M.	Stoke City	Bristol Rovers	

October 1993

	From	To	Fee in £s
14 Austin, Kevin L.	Saffron Walden Town	Leyton Orient	1000
26 Batty, David	Leeds United	Blackburn Rovers	2,700,000
8 Brien, Anthony J.	Chesterfield	Rotherham United	undisclosed
1 Carter, Richard.	Solihull Borough	Bromsgrove Rovers	2000
29 Darby, Julian T.	Bolton Wanderers	Coventry City	150,000
15 Evans, Terence W.	Brentford	Wycombe Wanderers	40,000
21 Grainger, Martin R.	Colchester United	Brentford	60,000
29 Griffiths, Carl B.	Shrewsbury Town	Manchester City	500,000
13 Hawkes, Leigh R.	Enfield	Billericay Town	undisclosed
27 Hewitt, James R.	Doncaster Rovers	Chesterfield	undisclosed
11 Holden, Richard W.	Manchester City	Oldham Athletic	450,000
4 Jeffrey, Michael R.	Doncaster Rovers	Newcastle United	60,000 + exch.
26 Judd, Robin A.	Atherstone United	Solihull Borough	undisclosed
18 Kelly, Anthony O. N.	Stoke City	Bury	30,000
12 Lambert, Colin A.	Macclesfield Town	Halifax Town	undisclosed
8 Law, Nicholas	Rotherham United	Chesterfield	undisclosed
16 Leicester, Stuart	Macclesfield Town	Stalybridge Celtic	undisclosed
8 Livett, Simon R.	Leyton Orient	Cambridge United	undisclosed
1 Lucketti, Christopher J.	Halifax Town	Bury	50,000
8 Moss, David A.	Doncaster Rovers	Chesterfield	exch.
8 Oliver, Darren	Bolton Wanderers	Rochdale	undisclosed
4 Pearce, Ian A.	Chelsea	Blackburn Rovers	300,000
25 Peel, Nathan J.	Sheffield United	Burnley	60,000
1 Pethick, Robert J.	Weymouth	Portsmouth	30,000
29 Pickering, Albert G.	Rotherham United	Coventry City	80,000
8 Power, Philip D.	Stalybridge Celtic	Macclesfield Town	undisclosed
7 Pritchard, Dean B.	Emley	Witton Albion	undisclosed
1 Roche, David	Newcastle United	Doncaster Rovers	exch.
1 Slater, Stuart	Celtic	Ipswich Town	800,000
29 Stein, Earl M. S.	Stoke City	Chelsea	1,500,000
8 Turnbull, Lee M.	Chesterfield	Doncaster Rovers	exch.
15 Wallace, David L.	Manchester United	Birmingham City	250,000
21 Whitney, John D.	Winsford United	Huddersfield Town	undisclosed
21 Williams, Andrew	Notts County	Rotherham United	undisclosed
7 Woods, Stephen G.	Clydebank	Preston North End	undisclosed
29 Wright, Ian M.	Stoke City	Bristol Rovers	undisclosed

Temporary transfers

	From	To
14 Aspinall, Warren	Portsmouth	Swansea City
29 Bailey, Dennis L.	Queens Park Rangers	Charlton Athletic
28 Benstead, Graham M.	Brentford	Kettering Town
22 Benton, Stephen	Bristol City	Cobh Ramblers
15 Blissett, Luther	Bury	Derry City
15 Boden, Christopher D.	Aston Villa	Barnsley
14 Bogie, Ian	Millwall	Leyton Orient
22 Costello, Peter	Lincoln City	Halifax Town
1 Cowan, Thomas	Sheffield United	Stoke City
4 Craddock, Jodie D.	Cambridge United	Woking
12 Crosby, Andrew K.	Doncaster Rovers	Halifax Town
28 Davison, Robert	Leicester City	Sheffield United
8 Dickov, Paul	Arsenal	Luton Town
28 Dickson, Benjamin M.	Lincoln City	Witton Albion
26 Dobson, Anthony J.	Blackburn Rovers	Portsmouth
25 Dowell, Wayne A.	Burnley	Witton Albion
15 Dumphy, Sean	Lincoln City	Doncaster Rovers
1 Esdaille, David	Bury	Witton Albion
15 Fairbairn, Neil	Wimbledon	Stevenage Borough
8 Fensome, Andrew B.	Cambridge United	Preston North End
12 Fernandes, Tamer	Brentford	Wealdstone
14 Flatts, Mark M.	Arsenal	Cambridge United
28 Flounders, Andrew J.	Rochdale	Carlisle United
12 France, Darren B.	Doncaster Rovers	Halifax Town
3 Gillespie, Keith R.	Manchester United	Wigan Athletic
8 Gray, Andrew	Reading	Woking
1 Greene, Dennis B.	Wycombe Wanderers	Enfield
1 Harriott, Marvin L.	Barnsley	Leyton Orient

	From	To	Fee in £s
11 Heavey, Paul A.	Preston North End	Netherfield	
29 Herrera, Roberto	Queens Park Rangers	Fulham	
8 Hewitt, James R.	Doncaster Rovers	Chesterfield	
3 Hine, Mark	Doncaster Rovers	Gateshead	
4 Jones, Philip L.	Liverpool	Crewe Alexandra	
12 Key, Lance W.	Sheffield Wednesday	Oldham Athletic	
22 King, Philip G.	Sheffield Wednesday	Notts County	
1 Livett, Simon R.	Leyton Orient	Cambridge United	
29 Livingstone, Stephen	Chelsea	Grimsby Town	
8 Locke, Adam S.	Southend United	Colchester United	
1 Lyons, Andrew	Crewe Alexandra	Wigan Athletic	
8 Marriott, Andrew	Nottingham Forest	Wrexham	
20 Muggleton, Carl D.	Leicester City	Stoke City	
4 Oliver, Darren	Bolton Wanderers	Peterborough United	
18 Painter, Peter R.	Burnley	Darlington	
1 Parkinson, Stephen	Lincoln City	Kings Lynn	
28 Parkinson, Stephen	Lincoln City	Witton Albion	
5 Payne, Christopher	Billericay Town	Brighton & Hove Albion	
15 Power, Lee M.	Norwich City	Portsmouth	
23 Reed, John P.	Sheffield United	Mansfield Town	
1 Reeves, David	Notts County	Carlisle United	
27 Rush, David	Sunderland	Peterborough United	
8 Whitworth, Neil A.	Manchester United	Rotherham United	
8 Williamson, Daniel A.	West Ham United	Doncaster Rovers	

November 1993

	From	To	Fee in £s
9 Bale, Kevin	Salisbury City	Newport (IOW)	undisclosed
11 Bashir, Naseem	Chesham United	Aylesbury United	undisclosed
4 Beasant, David	Chelsea	Southampton	300,000
25 Biggins, Wayne	Barnsley	Celtic	100,000 + exch.
1 Boyce, David J.	Waterlooville	Gravesend & Northfleet	undisclosed
29 Bryson, James I. C.	Barnsley	Preston North End	42,500
22 Bullock, Darren J.	Nuneaton Borough	Huddersfield Town	undisclosed
1 Byrne, John F.	Millwall	Oxford United	50,000
12 Cook, Timothy J.	Burnham	Maidenhead United	undisclosed
30 Coyne, Thomas	Tranmere Rovers	Motherwell	undisclosed
18 Cross, Paul	Hartlepool United	Darlington	undisclosed
5 Davison, Robert	Leicester City	Sheffield United	Free
5 Elliott, Matthew S.	Scunthorpe United	Oxford United	150,000
6 Emblen, Neil R.	Sittingbourne	Millwall	100,000
18 Emerson, Dean	Hartlepool United	Stockport County	undisclosed
19 Fensome, Andrew B.	Cambridge United	Preston North End	undisclosed
4 Flowers, Timothy D.	Southampton	Blackburn Rovers	2,400,000
16 Gardiner, Aaron R.	Halstead Town	Cornard United	undisclosed
6 Harle, Michael J.	Sittingbourne	Millwall	100,000
3 Hazard, Michael	Swindon Town	Tottenham Hotspur	50,000
6 King, Arthur	Hednesford Town	Dudley Town	undisclosed
5 Knill, Alan R.	Bury	Scunthorpe United	undisclosed
25 Lyons, Andrew	Crewe Alexandra	Wigan Athletic	undisclosed
19 McRobert, Lee P.	Ashford Town	Sittingbourne	undisclosed
18 Mardon, Paul J.	Birmingham City	West Bromwich Albion	undisclosed
19 Murray, Shaun	Portsmouth	Scarborough	undisclosed
17 Page, Donald R.	Rotherham United	Doncaster Rovers	undisclosed
25 Payton, Andrew P.	Celtic	Barnsley	exch.
12 Pemberton, John M.	Sheffield United	Leeds United	250,000
25 Power, John J.	Sutton United	Dulwich Hamlet	undisclosed
25 Roberts, Iwan W.	Huddersfield Town	Leicester City	300,000
17 Robson, Mark A.	West Ham United	Charlton Athletic	125,000
18 Scott, Keith	Wycombe Wanderers	Swindon Town	300,000
1 Shutt, Carl S.	Leeds United	Birmingham City	50,000
26 Sinfield, Mark R.	Enfield	Billericay Town	undisclosed
26 Southgate, Darren	Billericay Town	Ford United	undisclosed
5 Tate, Steven K.	Havant Town	Waterlooville	undisclosed
30 Vickers, Stephen	Tranmere Rovers	Middlesbrough	750,000
1 Whitehead, Philip M.	Barnsley	Oxford United	75,000
19 Whitington, Craig	Crawley Town	Scarborough	50,000
15 Wilson, Craig	Poole Town	Waterlooville	undisclosed
12 Zelem, Alan W.	Curzon Ashton	Mossley	undisclosed

Temporary transfers

	From	To	Fee in £s
12 Anders, Jason S.	Rochdale	Northwich Victoria	
26 Adebola, Bamberdele	Crewe Alexandra	Bangor City	
25 Appleby, Matthew W.	Newcastle United	Darlington	
1 Barlow, Andrew J.	Oldham Athletic	Bradford City	
18 Basham, Michael	West Ham United	Colchester United	
14 Bogie, Ian	Millwall	Leyton Orient	
30 Coleman, Simon	Derby County	Sheffield Wednesday	
1 Cowan, Thomas	Sheffield United	Stoke City	
23 Davies, Martin L.	Coventry City	Stafford Rangers	
19 Dickins, Matthew J.	Blackburn Rovers	Lincoln City	
9 Dickov, Paul	Arsenal	Luton Town	
27 Dobson, Anthony J.	Blackburn Rovers	Portsmouth	
2 Edwards, Russell J.	Crystal Palace	Slough Town	
12 Eeles, Anthony G.	Gillingham	Cork City	
22 Fairbairn, Neil	Wimbledon	Kingstonian	
8 Fensome, Andrew B.	Cambridge United	Preston North End	
15 Fernandes, Tamer	Brentford	Wealdstone	
5 Gannon, John S.	Sheffield United	Middlesbrough	
12 Goater, Leonardo S.	Rotherham United	Notts County	
29 Graham, Deiniol W. T.	Barnsley	Carlisle United	
11 Gray, Andrew	Reading	Woking	
2 Harding, Paul	Notts County	Watford	
1 Harriott, Marvin L.	Barnsley	Leyton Orient	
19 Harrison, Gerald R.	Bristol Rovers	Hereford United	
28 Herrera, Roberto	Queens Park Rangers	Fulham	
19 Hine, Mark	Doncaster Rovers	Gateshead	
18 Holden, Stephen A.	Carlisle United	Kettering Town	
3 Hoult, Russell	Leicester City	Bolton Wanderers	
1 Jenkinson, Leigh	Coventry City	Birmingham City	
22 Kabia, Jason	Lincoln City	Stafford Rangers	
29 Livingstone, Stephen	Chelsea	Grimsby Town	

	From	*To*	*Fee in £s*
19 Luscombe, Lee	Millwall	Sittingbourne	
26 McCarthy, Alan J.	Queens Park Rangers	Watford	
2 Manning, Paul J.	Millwall	Slough Town	
2 Marsden, Christopher	Huddersfield Town	Coventry City	
26 Muggleton Carl D.	Leicester City	Sheffield United	
5 Mulligan, James	Stoke City	Bury	
1 Murray, Shaun	Portsmouth	Scarborough	
26 Oakes, Michael C.	Aston Villa	Scarborough	
18 Painter, Peter R.	Burnley	Darlington	
22 Philips, Justin	Derby County	Cork City	
5 Reece, Andrew J.	Bristol Rovers	Hereford United	
23 Reed, John P.	Sheffield United	Mansfield Town	
5 Rogers, Darren J.	Birmingham City	Wycombe Wanderers	
5 Rowe, Ezekiel B.	Chelsea	Barnet	
8 Saddington, James	Millwall	Sittingbourne	
12 Thomas, Mitchell A.	West Ham United	Luton Town	
19 Trotter, Michael	Leicester City	Chesterfield	
5 Wallbridge, Andrew J.	Oxford United	Worcester City	
19 Walsh, Gary	Manchester United	Oldham Athletic	
5 Walton, David L.	Sheffield United	Shrewsbury Town	
7 Whitworth, Neil A.	Manchester United	Rotherham United	
5 Williams, Paul A.	Stockport County	Rochdale	
19 Williams, Paul R. C.	Coventry City	West Bromich Albion	
8 Williamson, Daniel A.	West Ham United	Doncaster Rovers	
December 1993			
17 Bennett, Ian M.	Peterborough United	Birmingham City	325,000
10 Blake, Noel L.	Bradford City	Dundee	undisclosed
10 Bogie, Ian	Millwall	Leyton Orient	undisclosed
9 Boothroyd, Adrian N.	Heart of Midlothian	Mansfield Town	Free
16 Charlery, Kenneth L.	Watford	Peterborough United	150,000
10 Charles, Lee	Yeading	Chertsey Town	undisclosed
17 Cooper, Gary	Peterborough United	Birmingham City	Free
21 Dobson, Anthony J.	Blackburn Rovers	Portsmouth	150,000
10 Finney, Kevin	Leek Town	Stafford Rangers	undisclosed
9 Flitcroft, David J.	Preston North End	Chester City	Free
15 Fowler, Lee E.	Preston North End	Doncaster Rovers	Free
24 Fry, Christopher D.	Hereford United	Colchester United	undisclosed
21 Gayle, Mark S. R.	Walsall	Crewe Alexandra	35,000
24 Harriott, Marvin L.	Barnsley	Bristol City	Free
10 Henderson, Damian M.	Scarborough	Scunthorpe United	Free
7 Jepson, Ronald F.	Exeter City	Huddersfield Town	80,000
7 Johnrose, Leonard	Hartlepool United	Bury	undisclosed
20 Lowe, Kenneth	Stoke City	Birmingham City	75,000 + exch.
3 McCarthy, Sean C.	Bradford City	Oldham Athletic	500,000
1 Marriott, Andrew	Nottingham Forest	Wrexham	200,000
22 Masters, Neil B.	AFC Bournemouth	Wolverhampton Wanderers	600,000
18 Mutchell, Robert D.	Oxford United	Barnet	Free
24 Painter, Peter R.	Burnley	Darlington	undisclosed
9 Patmore, Warren J.	Millwall	Northampton Town	Free
20 Potter, Graham S.	Birmingham City	Stoke City	75,000 + exch.
7 Reece, Andrew J.	Bristol Rovers	Hereford United	undisclosed
23 Reeves, David	Notts County	Carlisle United	121,000
22 Rocastle, David C.	Leeds United	Manchester City	2,000,000exch.
18 Rodwell, James	Hednesford Town	Nuneaton Borough	undisclosed
24 Ryan, John B.	Rochdale	Bury	Free
18 Simpkins, John P.	Bashley	Newport (IOW)	undisclosed
11 Taylor, Stephen C.	Rushall Olympic	Bromsgrove Rovers	undisclosed
3 Tolson, Neil	Oldham Athletic	Bradford City	50,000
10 Toman, James A.	Scunthorpe United	Scarborough	Free
17 Wallace, Matthew	Atherstone United	Hednesford Town	undisclosed
23 Walton, David L.	Sheffield United	Shrewsbury Town	undisclosed
22 White, David	Manchester City	Leeds United	2,000,000exch.
10 White, Jason G.	Scunthorpe United	Scarborough	Free
31 Willis, Roger C.	Watford	Birmingham City	150,000
30 Wilmot, Richard	Scunthorpe United	Halifax Town	undisclosed
Temporary transfers			
31 Aspinall, Warren	Portsmouth	AFC Bournemouth	
31 Barnes, Andrew J.	Crystal Palace	Carlisle United	
20 Barnett, David	Barnet	Birmingham City	
23 Blissett, Luther	Bury	Mansfield Town	
17 Burns, Christopher	Portsmouht	Swansea	
16 Clarke, Nicholas J.	Mansfield Town	Doncaster Rovers	
31 Coleman, Simon	Derby County	Sheffield Wednesday	
1 Cowan, Thomas	Sheffield United	Stoke City	
10 Croft, Brian G. A.	Queens Park Rangers	Shrewsbury Town	
7 Cross, Ryan	Hartlepool United	Bury	
17 Davies, Simon I.	Manchester United	Exeter City	
8 Dickov, Paul	Arsenal	Luton Town	
23 Fairbairn, Neil	Wimbledon	Kingstonian	
24 Finley, Alan J.	Stockport County	Rochdale	
31 Flatts, Mark M.	Arsenal	Brighton & Hove Albion	
17 Fleck, Robert	Chelsea	Bolton Wanderers	
24 Fulton, Stephen	Bolton Wanderers	Peterborough United	
7 Gannon, John S.	Sheffield United	Middlesbrough	
3 Harding, Paul J.	Notts County	Birmingham City	
9 Harriott, Marvin L.	Barnsley	Bristol City	
20 Harrison, Gerald R.	Bristol City	Hereford United	
23 Harrison, Michael	Port Vale	Stafford Rangers	
30 Herrera, Roberto	Queens Park Rangers	Fulham	
23 Hirst, Lee W.	Coventry City	Lincoln City	
31 Hodges, Lee L.	Tottenham Hotspur	Wycombe Wanderers	
18 Holden, Steven A.	Carlisle United	Kettering Town	
17 Holmes, Keith N.	Oxford United	Worcester City	
3 Hoult, Russell	Leicester City	Bolton Wanderers	
9 Humphrey, John	Crystal Palace	Reading	
10 Hyslop, Christian T.	Southend United	Northampton Town	
30 Kee, Paul	Oxford United	Ards	
23 Kilford, Ian A.	Nottingham Forest	Wigan Athletic	
17 Lowe, Kenneth	Stoke City	Birmingham City	

	From	To	Fee in £s
24 McCarthy, Alan J.	Queens Park Rangers	Watford	
8 Margetson, Martyn W.	Manchester City	Bristol Rovers	
5 Marsden, Christopher	Huddersfield Town	Coventry City	
3 Marshall, Scott R.	Arsenal	Rotherham United	
8 Myers, Christopher	Dundee United	Torquay United	
13 Newhouse, Aidan R.	Wimbledon	Tranmere Rovers	
17 Pape, Andrew M.	Barnet	Enfield	
23 Rees, Jason M.	Luton Town	Mansfield Town	
10 Roberts, Darren A.	Wolverhampton Wanderers	Telford United	
6 Rogers, Darren J.	Birmingham City	Wycome Wanderers	
5 Rowe, Ezekiel B.	Chelsea	Barnet	
7 Saddington, James	Millwall	Sittingbourne	
8 Sampson, Ian	Sunderland	Northampton Town	
23 Sheffield, Jonathan	Cambridge United	Colchester United	
31 Shutt, Carl S.	Birmingham City	Manchester City	
9 Sinnott, Lee	Crystal Palace	Bradford City	
23 Stringfellow, Ian R.	Mansfield Town	Chesterfield	
17 Thomas, Mark L.	Wimbledon	Bromley	
15 Thomas, Mitchell A.	West Ham United	Luton Town	
20 Trotter, Michael	Leicester City	Chesterfield	
4 Walton, David L.	Sheffield United	Shrewsbury Town	
10 Whitworth, Neil A.	Manchester United	Blackpool	
15 Wietecha, David	Millwall	Rotherham	
8 Williamson, Daniel A.	West Ham United	Doncaster Rovers	
10 Woods, Kenneth S.	Bury	Stalybridge Celtic	
6 Worboys, Gavin	Notts County	Exeter City	
January 1994			
21 Angell, Brett A. M.	Southend United	Everton	500,000
14 Barnes, David	Sheffield United	Watford	50,000
21 Brown, John C.	Stalybridge Celtic	Leek Town	2000
13 Cecere, Michele J.	Walsall	Exeter City	undisclosed
7 Claridge, Stephen E.	Cambridge United	Birmingham City	350,000
13 Clarke, David A.	Lincoln City	Doncaster Rovers	undisclosed
21 Coleman, Simon	Derby County	Sheffield Wednesday	250,000
14 Connor, Terence F.	Yeovil Town	Calne Town	undisclosed
11 Cross, Ryan	Hartlepool United	Bury	undisclosed
19 Edwards, Paul R.	Wolverhampton Wanderers	West Bromwich Albion	undisclosed
13 Ferguson, Darren	Manchester United	Wolverhampton Wanderers	250,000
20 Grange, Damian	Leek Town	Kidsgrove Athletic	undisclosed
28 Green, Gary	Dorchester Town	Havant Town	undisclosed
5 Harding, Paul	Notts County	Birmingham City	50,000
20 Kilcline, Brian	Newcastle United	Swindon Town	undisclosed
20 Livingstone, Stephen	Chelsea	Grimsby Town	140,000
7 McGavin, Steven J.	Colchester United	Birmingham City	100,000
4 McPherson, Malcolm	Yeovil Town	West Ham United	30,000
11 Marsden, Christopher	Huddersfield Town	Wolverhampton Wanderers	250,000
13 Mottashead, Nigel J.	Havant Town	Weymouth	undisclosed
11 Muggleton, Carl D.	Leicester City	Celtic	150,000
11 Nicholls, Danny	Witney Town	Buckingham Town	undisclosed
21 O'Brien, Liam F.	Newcastle United	Tranmere Rovers	300,000
27 Parkinson, Gary	Bolton Wanderers	Burnley	undisclosed
21 Philliskirk, Anthony	Peterborough United	Burnley	undisclosed
4 Robertson, Alexander	Rangers	Coventry City	250,000
28 Robinson, Jamie	Barnsley	Carlisle United	undisclosed
26 Rosenthal, Ronnie	Liverpool	Tottenham Hotspur	250,000
5 Shearer, Peter A.	AFC Bournemouth	Birmingham City	75,000
10 Sinnott, Lee	Crystal Palace	Bradford City	undisclosed
31 Smith, David	Birmingham City	West Bromwich Albion	90,000
21 Turnbull, Lee M.	Doncaster Rovers	Wycombe Wanderers	undisclosed
Temporary transfers			
31 Adebola, Bamberdele	Crewe Alexandra	Northwich Victoria	
21 Akinbiyi, Adeola P.	Norwich City	Hereford United	
14 Angell, Brett	Southend United	Everton	
21 Anthrobus, Stephen A.	Wimbledon	Peterborough United	
6 Appleby, Matthew W.	Newcastle United	Darlington	
6 Carter, Timothy D.	Hartlepool United	Millwall	
14 Collins, Simon	Huddersfield Town	Halifax Town	
25 Creaney, Gerard	Celtic	Portsmouth	
17 Crocker, Marcus	Plymouth Argyle	Weymouth Town	
10 Currie, David N.	Barnsley	Huddersfield Town	
10 Daish, Liam S.	Cambridge United	Birmingham City	
16 Davies, Simon I.	Manchester United	Exeter City	
27 Donowa, Brian L.	Birmingham City	Shrewsbury Town	
21 Edey, Darren	Peterborough United	Cambridge City	
31 Fairbairn, Neil	Wimbledon	Kingstonian	
7 Feeney, Mark A.	Barnsley	Coleraine	
10 Fenton, Graham A.	Aston Villa	West Bromwich Albion	
10 Foster, Colin J.	West Ham United	Notts County	
14 Gannon, James P.	Stockport County	Notts County	
12 Granville, Daniel P.	Cambridge United	Saffron Walden Town	
13 Hague, Paul	Gillingham	Sittingbourne	
26 Hirst, Lee	Coventry City	Lincoln City	
18 Holden, Steven A.	Carlisle United	Kettering Town	
5 Hoult, Russell	Leicester City	Bolton Wanderers	
10 Humphrey, John	Crystal Palace	Reading	
9 Hyslop, Christian T.	Southend United	Northampton Town	
10 Jobling, Kevin A.	Grimsby Town	Scunthorpe United	
11 Kerr, Stewart	Celtic	Swindon Town	
7 Knight, Craig	Wrexham	Crusaders	
27 Lancashire, Graham	Burnley	Chester	
28 Murphy, Matthew S.	Oxford United	Kettering Town	
21 Newhouse, Aiden R.	Wimbledon	Port Vale	
26 Peters, Robert A. A.	Brentford	Slough Town	
24 Rees, Jason	Luton Town	Mansfield Town	
9 Roberts, Darren A.	Wolverhampton Wanderers	Telford United	
13 Robinson, Ronald	Exeter City	Huddersfield Town	
5 Rowe, Ezekiel B.	Chelsea	Barnet	
10 Rush, Matthew J.	West Ham United	Swansea City	
8 Sampson, Ian	Sunderland	Northampton Town	

	From	*To*	*Fee in £s*
28 Sheffield, Johnathan	Cambridge United	Swindon Town	
7 Snowden, Trevor	Rochdale	Northwich Victoria	
14 Steele, Timothy W.	Bradford City	Hereford United	
24 Stewart, Paul A.	Liverpool	Crystal Palace	
14 Thomas, Mitchell A.	West Ham United	Luton Town	
28 Tomlinson, Michael L.	Leyton Orient	St Albans City	
31 Warren, Mark W.	Leyton Orient	West Ham United	
7 Watts, Grant S.	Crystal Palace	Colchester United	
28 West, Mark	Wycombe Wanderers	Aylesbury United	
17 Wietecha, David	Millwall	Rotherham United	
6 Williams, Gareth J.	Barnsley	Hull City	
13 Wilson, Kevin J.	Notts County	Bradford City	

February 1994

	From	*To*	*Fee in £s*
17 Adams, Neil J.	Oldham Athletic	Norwich City	250,000
16 Ampadu, Patrick K.	West Bromwich Albion	Swansea City	15,000
2 Aspinall, Warren	Portsmouth	AFC Bournemouth	20,000
21 Barnett, David	Barnet	Birmingham City	150,000
10 Beale, Dean J.	Newport (IOW)	Poole Town	undisclosed
5 Blackwood, Bevon A.	Witton Albion	Buxton	undisclosed
21 Blake, Nathan A.	Cardiff City	Sheffield United	300,000
11 Blount, Mark	Gresley Rovers	Sheffield United	undisclosed
9 Brown, Stephen	Northampton Town	Wycombe Wanderers	undisclosed
3 Buckle, Paul J.	Brentford	Torquay United	Free
10 Clark, John B.	Dundee United	Stoke City	150,000
18 Clayton, Gary	Cambridge United	Huddersfield Town	20,000
3 Cowans, Gordon S.	Aston Villa	Derby County	80,000
3 Creaney, Gerard	Celtic	Portsmouth	500,000
11 Daish, Liam S.	Cambridge United	Birmingham City	50,000
15 Daws, Anthony	Grimsby Town	Lincoln City	undisclosed
23 Endersby, Lee A.	Wembley	Harrow Borough	undisclosed
2 Fox, Ruel A.	Norwich City	Newcastle United	2,250,000
4 Garner, Simon	West Bromwich Albion	Wycome Wanderers	Free
11 Gavin, Mark W.	Bristol City	Exeter City	undisclosed
4 Hanks, Christopher	Bromsgrove Rovers	Gresley Rovers	undisclosed
17 Hyslop, Christian T.	Southend United	Colchester United	Free
15 Johnson, Alan K.	Wigan Athletic	Lincoln City	undisclosed
10 McGorry, Brian P.	AFC Bournemouth	Peterborough United	60,000
7 McKinnon, Raymond	Nottingham Forest	Aberdeen	300,000
11 Magilton, James	Oxford United	Southampton	600,000
7 Maskell, Craig D.	Swindon Town	Southampton	250,000
11 Matthew, Damian	Chelsea	Crystal Palace	150,000
21 Moody, Paul	Southampton	Oxford United	60,000
25 Pritchard, David M.	Telford United	Bristol Rovers	undisclosed
21 Ramage, Craig D.	Derby County	Watford	90,000
22 Ridings, David	Halifax Town	Lincoln City	10,000
1 Scott, Kevin W.	Newcastle United	Tottenham Hotspur	850,000
11 Smith, Eric G.	Halesowen Town	Bilston Town	undisclosed
3 Steele, Timothy W.	Bradford City	Hereford United	undisclosed
1 Thompson, David	Bristol City	Brentford	Free
4 Turner, Robert P.	Notts County	Exeter City	Free
18 Washington, Darren T.	Congleton Town	Leek Town	undisclosed
7 Williams, Paul A.	Stockport County	Rochdale	Free
28 Wood, Paul A.	AFC Bournemouth	Portsmouth	undisclosed

Temporary transfers

	From	*To*
2 Adebola, Bamberdele	Crewe Alexandra	Northwich Victoria
18 Adekola, David	Bury	Exeter City
21 Anthrobus, Stephen A.	Wimbledon	Peterborough United
5 Arnold, Ian	Carlisle United	Stalybridge Celtic
25 Barras, Anthony	Stockport County	Rotherham United
18 Blatherwick, Steven S.	Nottingham Forest	Wycombe Wanderers
25 Brock, Kevin	Newcastle United	Cardiff City
11 Byrne, David S.	Partick Thistle	Walsall
7 Campbell, David A.	Burnley	Lincoln City
18 Cornwell, John A.	Southend United	Northampton Town
2 Creaser, Glyn	Wycombe Wanderers	Yeovil Town
15 Currie, David N.	Barnsley	Huddersfield Town
4 Danzey, Michael J.	Cambridge United	Scunthorpe United
18 Dichio, Daniele S.	Queens Park Rangers	Welling United
16 Dolby, Tony C.	Millwall	Barnet
4 Edwards, Michael	Tranmere Rovers	Stalybridge Celtic
1 Flatts, Mark M.	Arsenal	Brighton & Hove Albion
7 Flounders, Andrew J.	Rochdale	Carlisle United
14 Foster, Colin J.	West Ham United	Notts County
25 Gayle, Mark S. R.	Crewe Alexandra	Liverpool
12 Granville, Daniel P.	Cambridge United	Saffron Walden Town
3 Gregory, Neil R.	Ipswich Town	Chesterfield
18 Hague, Paul	Gillingham	Sittingbourne
25 Harrison, Garry M.	Northampton Town	Bashley
21 Harrison, Gerald R.	Bristol City	Bath City
4 Hoult, Russell	Leicester City	Bolton Wanderers
4 Howarth, Neil	Burnley	Macclesfield Town
21 Huxford, Richard J.	Millwall	Birmingham City
25 Kavanagh, Graham A.	Middlesbrough	Darlington
10 Kelly, Gary A.	Bury	West Ham United
3 Kerr, Stuart P.	AFC Bournemouth	Bashley
10 Kitchen, David E.	Leyton Orient	Doncaster Rovers
4 Lakin, Barry	Leyton Orient	Woking
18 Leitch, Grant	Blackpool	Fleetwood Town
18 Lormor, Anthony	Lincoln City	Halifax Town
18 Lowe, David A.	Leicester Ciuty	Port Vale
11 McCarthy, Alan J.	Queens Park Rangers	Plymouth Argyle
25 McPherson, Malcolm	West Ham United	Dorchester Town
11 Margetson, Martyn W.	Manchester City	Bolton Wanderers
14 O'Connor, Martyn J.	Crystal Palace	Walsall
27 Peters, Robert A.	Brentford	Slough Town
7 Ramage, Andrew	Gillingham	Hastings Town
23 Rees, Jason	Luton Town	Mansfield Town
24 Rutherford, Mark R.	Shelbourne	Shrewsbury Town
11 Shelton, Gary	Bristol City	Rochdale

	From	To	Fee in £s
25 Sloan, Scott M.	Falkirk	Cambridge United	
28 Small, Michael A.	West Ham United	Charlton Athletic	
20 Snowden, Trevor	Rochdale	Northwich Victoria	
18 Stewart, Paul A.	Liverpool	Crystal Palace	
26 Sweetman, Nicholas	Leyton Orient	Baldock Town	
21 Tait, Paul R.	Birmingham City	Millwall	
2 Tomlinson, Michael	Leyton Orient	St Albans City	
4 Warburton, Raymond	York City	Northampton Town	
8 Watts, Grant	Crystal Palace	Colchester United	
28 Whittingham, Guy	Aston Villa	Wolverhampton Wanderers	
17 Wietecha, David	Millwall	Rotherham United	
4 Wilkerson, Paul S.	Watford	Stevenage Borough	
7 Williams, Gareth J.	Barnsley	Hull City	
11 Williams, Lee	Aston Villa	Peterborough United	
11 Witter, Anthony J.	Queens Park Rangers	Reading	
18 Wood, Paul A.	AFC Bournemouth	Portsmouth	
25 Wright, Dale C.	Nottingham Forest	Slough Town	

March 1994

	From	To	Fee in £s
24 Allen, Clive D.	West Ham United	Millwall	75,000
24 Allon, Joseph B.	Brentford	Port Vale	undisclosed
25 Arter, David J.	Sittingbourne	Ashford Town	undisclosed
22 Ashby, Barry J.	Watford	Brentford	exch.
24 Basham, Michael	West Ham United	Swansea City	undisclosed
24 Beagrie, Peter S.	Everton	Manchester City	1,100,000
21 Berks, Peter R.	Hednesford Town	Bilston Town	undisclosed
24 Berry, Greg J.	Wimbledon	Millwall	200,000
24 Biggins, Wayne	Celtic	Stoke City	125,000
24 Blake, Mark A.	Portsmouth	Leicester City	360,000
25 Blondrage, Andrew J.	Hastings Town	Sittingbourne	undisclosed
12 Bye, Andrew G.	Yeovil Town	Bashley	undisclosed
23 Carter, Timothy D.	Hartlepool United	Millwall	Free
8 Cox, Ian	Carlshalton Athletic	Crystal Palace	35,000
24 Cunningham, Anthony E.	Doncaster Rovers	Wycombe Wanderers	Free
1 Diaz, Jorge	Dorchester Town	Weymouth	undisclosed
10 Dyer, Bruce A.	Watford	Crystal Palace	1,250,000
11 Fereday, Wayne	West Bromwich Albion	Cardiff City	Free
24 Formby, Kevin	Burscough	Rochdale	undisclosed
23 Foster, Colin J.	West Ham United	Watford	100,000
24 Gayle, Marcus A.	Brentford	Wimbledon	250,000
24 Harrison, Gerald R.	Bristol City	Huddersfield Town	undisclosed
31 Harrison, Michael	Port Vale	Hednesford Town	undisclosed
22 Heaney, Neil	Arsenal	Southampton	300,000
24 Herrera, Roberto	Queens Park Rangers	Fulham	undisclosed
24 Hicks, Stuart J.	Huddersfield Town	Preston North End	undisclosed
23 Jones, Alexander	Rochdale	Halifax Town	undisclosed
25 Keast, Douglas W	Corby Town	Rushden & Diamonds	undisclosed
8 Kitchen, David E.	Leyton Orient	Doncaster Rovers	undisclosed
17 Lawrence, James H.	Sunderland	Doncaster Rovers	20,000
4 Lee, Jason B.	Southend United	Nottingham Forest	200,000
3 Limber, Nicholas	Manchester City	Doncaster Rovers	Free
24 Limpar, Anders	Arsenal	Everton	1,600,000
24 McHugh, Michael B.	Bradford City	Scarborough	Free
30 Marchant, Giles R.	Walton & Hersham	Sutton United	undisclosed
24 Martindale, Gary	Burscough	Bolton Wanderers	undisclosed
22 Millen, Keith D.	Brentford	Watford	65,000
24 Parkinson, Joseph S.	AFC Bournemouth	Everton	800,000
24 Patterson, Ian D.	Burnley	Wigan Athletic	Free
24 Peacock, Darren	Queens Park Rangers	Newcastle United	2,700,000
26 Peake, Jason W.	Halifax Town	Rochdale	exch.
8 Power, Lee M.	Norwich City	Bradford City	200,000
1 Rowett, Gary	Cambridge United	Everton	200,000
3 Russell, Kevin J.	Burnley	AFC Bournemouth	125,000
24 Scully, Patrick J.	Southend United	Huddersfield Town	Free
24 Taylor, Robert A.	Leyton Orient	Brentford	100,000
24 Thomas, Mitchell A.	West Ham United	Luton Town	Free
21 Tomlinson, Michael L.	Leyton Orient	Barnet	Free
11 Walsh, Paul A.	Portsmouth	Manchester City	750,000
24 Whitton, Stephen P.	Ipswich Town	Colchester United	10,000
24 Williams, Lee	Aston Villa	Peterborough United	undisclosed

Temporary transfers

	From	To
3 Adebola, Bamberdele	Crewe Alexandra	Northwich Victoria
28 Alsford, Julian	Watford	Slough Town
24 Bailey, Dennis L.	Queens Park Rangers	Watford
4 Beadle, Peter C.	Tottenham Hotspur	Southend United
24 Beckford, Jason N.	Birmingham City	Bury
26 Benton, Stephen	Bristol City	Weston Super Mare
24 Blissett, Luther	Bury	Southport
24 Boere, Jerome W.	West Ham United	Portsmouth
4 Bradbury, Shaun D.	Wolverhampton Wanderers	Telford United
22 Brown, Ian O.	Bristol City	Colchester United
4 Burke, Mark S.	Wolverhampton Wanderers	Luton Town
11 Burns, Christopher	Portsmouth	AFC Bournemouth
18 Burton, Simon P.	Preston North End	Altrincham
17 Campbell, David	Burnley	Portadown
22 Carmichael, David	Coventry City	Nuneaton Borough
23 Carter, James W. C.	Arsenal	Oxford United
7 Carter, Timothy D.	Hartlepool United	Millwall
30 Clarke, Christopher	Bolton Wanderers	Chorley
21 Clarke, Nicholas J.	Bromsgrove Rovers	Preston North End
18 Cornwell, John A.	Southend United	Northampton Town
3 Costello, Peter	Lincoln City	Kettering Town
24 Cowan, Thomas	Sheffield United	Huddersfield Town
24 Cronin, Gareth	Sunderland	Bradford City
24 Cusack, Nicholas J.	Oxford United	Wycombe Wanderers
4 Dempsey, Mark A.	Gillingham	Kettering Town
24 Dichio, Daniele S. E.	Queens Park Rangers	Barnet
23 Dickov, Paul	Arsenal	Brighton & Hove Albion
17 Dolby, Tony C.	Millwall	Barnet
18 Duffin, Stuart	Bristol City	Weymouth

	From	To	Fee in £s
28 Durbin, Gary	Bristol City	Weymouth	
31 Gonzague, Michael	Southend United	Enfield	
3 Gregory, Neil R.	Ipswich Town	Chesterfield	
24 Heald, Paul A.	Leyton Orient	Swindon Town	
18 Heavey, Paul A.	Preston North End	Fleetwood Town	
31 Holmes, Steven P.	Preston North End	Bromsgrove Rovers	
6 Howarth, Neil	Burnley	Macclesfield Town	
4 Hoyland, Jamie W.	Sheffield United	Bristol City	
18 Ireland, Simon P.	Blackburn Rovers	Mansfield Town	
23 Jones, Terence P.	Everton	Northwich Victoria	
23 Kee, Paul V.	Oxford United	Reading	
11 Kelly, Gary A.	Bury	West Ham United	
11 Kelly, James	Wolverhampton Wanderers	Wrexham	
31 Kelly, Paul	Fulham	Hendon	
24 Kerr, Paul A.	Port Vale	Leicester City	
4 Kerr, Stuart P.	AFC Bournemouth	Bashley	
24 Kilford, Ian A.	Nottingham Forest	Wigan Athletic	
4 Kubicki, Dariusz	Aston Villa	Sunderland	
8 Lakin, Barry	Leyton Orient	Woking	
24 Lancashire, Graham	Burnley	Chester City	
30 Livett, Simon R.	Cambridge United	Dagenham & Redbridge	
10 Llewellyn, Andrew D.	Bristol City	Exeter City	
3 Lormor, Anthony	Lincoln City	Halifax Town	
18 Lowe, David A.	Leicester City	Port Vale	
31 Lynch, Anthony J.	Barnet	Stevenage Borough	
24 Lyne, Neil G. F.	Cambridge United	Chesterfield	
24 McGee, Paul	Wimbledon	Peterborough United	
4 McMinn, Kevin C.	Birmingham City	Burnley	
24 Maguire, Gavin T.	Millwall	Scarborough	
23 Marshall, Scott R.	Arsenal	Oxford United	
24 Mehew, David S.	Bristol Rovers	Exeter City	
17 Mooney, Thomas J.	Southend United	Watford	
31 Morgan, Scott	Brentford	Wokingham Town	
14 Murray, Bruce E.	Millwall	Stockport County	
17 Nogan, Lee M.	Watford	Southend United	
24 Oakes, Michael C.	Aston Villa	Tranmere Rovers	
4 Parkinson, Stephen	Lincoln City	Kings Lynn	
24 Penney, David M.	Oxford United	Swansea City	
28 Peters, Robert A.	Brentford	Slough Town	
4 Quinn, Stephen J.	Blackpool	Stockport County	
24 Reid, Brian	Rangers	Newcastle United	
18 Roberts, Darren A.	Wolverhampton Wanderers	Hereford United	
9 Sertori, Mark A.	Wrexham	Preston North End	
17 Sheppard, Simon	Watford	Scarborough	
31 Skidmore, Robert J.	Bristol City	Clevedon Town	
7 Skinner, Justin J.	Wimbledon	AFC Bournemouth	
4 Small, Michael A.	West Ham United	Charleton Athletic	
31 Southon, Jamie P.	Southend United	Stevenage Borough	
30 Stewart, Paul A.	Liverpool	Crystal Palace	
24 Swales, Stephen C.	Scarborough	Millwall	
25 Sweetman, Nicholas E.	Leyton Orient	Baldock Town	
11 Thorne, Peter L.	Blackburn Rovers	Wigan Athletic	
11 Wallace, Raymond G.	Leeds United	Reading	
24 Walters, Mark	Liverpool	Stoke City	
4 Warburton, Raymond	York City	Northampton Town	
24 Ward, Mark W.	Everton	Birmingham City	
31 Ward, Richard	Huddersfield Town	Stalybridge Celtic	
24 Watson, Kevin E.	Tottenham Hotspur	Brentford	
9 Watts, Grant	Crystal Palace	Colchester United	
24 West, Mark	Wycombe Wanderers	Yeovil Town	
24 White, Christopher J.	Exeter City	Yeovil Town	
31 Whitmarsh, Paul	Doncaster Rovers	Gateshead	
27 Whittingham, Guy	Aston Villa	Wolverhampton Wanderers	
10 Williams, Gareth J.	Barnsley	Hull City	
11 Williams, Lee	Aston Villa	Peterborough United	
22 Wilson, Lee	Mansfield Town	Telford United	
24 Winnie, David	Aberdeen	Middlesbrough	
24 Woods, Raymond G.	Coventry City	Shrewsbury Town	
24 Worthington, Gary L.	Exeter City	Doncaster Rovers	
April 1994			
5 McMinn, Kevin C.	Birmingham City	Burnley	undisclosed
Temporary transfers			
5 Gonzague, Michael A.	Southend United	Enfield	
2 Harrison, Garry M.	Northampton Town	Racing Club Warwick	
May 1994			
26 Bushay, Ansil	St Albans City	Slough Town	undisclosed
26 Furlong, Paul A.	Watford	Chelsea	2,300,000
31 Hodges, Lee L.	Tottenham Hotspur	Barnet	undisclosed
12 McDougald, David E. J.	Tottenham Hotspur	Brighton & Hove Albion	undisclosed
28 Minto, Scott C.	Charlton Athletic	Chelsea	775,000
12 Morrison, David E.	Chelmsford City	Peterborough United	undisclosed
11 Munday, Mark	Herne Bay	Gravesend & Northfleet	undisclosed
17 O'Connor, Martyn J.	Crystal Palace	Walsall	undisclosed
17 Reid, Paul R.	Bradford City	Huddersfield Town	undisclosed
Temporary transfers			
1 Skidmore, Robert	Bristol City	Clevedon Town	

LEAGUE ATTENDANCES SINCE 1946–47

Season	*Matches*	*Total*	*Div. 1*	*Div. 2*	*Div. 3 (S)*	*Div. 3 (N)*
1946–47	1848	35,604,606	15,005,316	11,071,572	5,664,004	3,863,714
1947–48	1848	40,259,130	16,732,341	12,286,350	6,653,610	4,586,829
1948–49	1848	41,271,414	17,914,667	11,353,237	6,998,429	5,005,081
1949–50	1848	40,517,865	17,278,625	11,694,158	7,104,155	4,440,927
1950–51	2028	39,584,967	16,679,454	10,780,580	7,367,884	4,757,109
1951–52	2028	39,015,866	16,110,322	11,066,189	6,958,927	4,880,428
1952–53	2028	37,149,966	16,050,278	9,686,654	6,704,299	4,708,735
1953–54	2028	36,174,590	16,154,915	9,510,053	6,311,508	4,198,114
1954–55	2028	34,133,103	15,087,221	8,988,794	5,996,017	4,051,071
1955–56	2028	33,150,809	14,108,961	9,080,002	5,692,479	4,269,367
1956–57	2028	32,744,405	13,803,037	8,718,162	5,622,189	4,601,017
1957–58	2028	33,562,208	14,468,652	8,663,712	6,097,183	4,332,661
					Div. 3	*Div. 4*
1958–59	2028	33,610,985	14,727,691	8,641,997	5,946,600	4,276,697
1959–60	2028	32,538,611	14,391,227	8,399,627	5,739,707	4,008,050
1960–61	2028	28,619,754	12,926,948	7,033,936	4,784,256	3,874,614
1961–62	2015	27,979,902	12,061,194	7,453,089	5,199,106	3,266,513
1962–63	2028	28,885,852	12,490,239	7,792,770	5,341,362	3,261,481
1963–64	2028	28,535,022	12,486,626	7,594,158	5,419,157	3,035,081
1964–65	2028	27,641,168	12,708,752	6,984,104	4,436,245	3,512,067
1965–66	2028	27,206,980	12,480,644	6,914,757	4,779,150	3,032,429
1966–67	2028	28,902,596	14,242,957	7,253,819	4,421,172	2,984,648
1967–68	2028	30,107,298	15,289,410	7,450,410	4,013,087	3,354,391
1968–69	2028	29,382,172	14,584,851	7,382,390	4,339,656	3,075,275
1969–70	2028	29,600,972	14,868,754	7,581,728	4,223,761	2,926,729
1970–71	2028	28,194,146	13,954,337	7,098,265	4,377,213	2,764,331
1971–72	2028	28,700,729	14,484,603	6,769,308	4,697,392	2,749,426
1972–73	2028	25,448,642	13,998,154	5,631,730	3,737,252	2,081,506
1973–74	2027	24,982,203	13,070,991	6,326,108	3,421,624	2,163,480
1974–75	2028	25,577,977	12,613,178	6,955,970	4,086,145	1,992,684
1975–76	2028	24,896,053	13,089,861	5,798,405	3,948,449	2,059,338
1976–77	2028	26,182,800	13,647,585	6,250,597	4,152,218	2,132,400
1977–78	2028	25,392,872	13,255,677	6,474,763	3,332,042	2,330,390
1978–79	2028	24,540,627	12,704,549	6,153,223	3,374,558	2,308,297
1979–80	2028	24,623,975	12,163,002	6,112,025	3,999,328	2,349,620
1980–81	2028	21,907,569	11,392,894	5,175,442	3,637,854	1,701,379
1981–82	2028	20,006,961	10,420,793	4,750,463	2,836,915	1,998,790
1982–83	2028	18,766,158	9,295,613	4,974,937	2,943,568	1,552,040
1983–84	2028	18,358,631	8,711,448	5,359,757	2,729,942	1,557,484
1984–85	2028	17,849,835	9,761,404	4,030,823	2,667,008	1,390,600
1985–86	2028	16,488,577	9,037,854	3,551,968	2,490,481	1,408,274
1986–87	2028	17,379,218	9,144,676	4,168,131	2,350,970	1,715,441
1987–88	2030	17,959,732	8,094,571	5,341,599	2,751,275	1,772,287
1988–89	2036	18,464,192	7,809,993	5,887,805	3,035,327	1,791,067
1989–90	2036	19,445,442	7,883,039	6,867,674	2,803,551	1,891,178
1990–91	2036	19,508,202	8,618,709	6,285,068	2,835,759	1,768,666
1991–92	2064*	20,487,273	9,989,160	5,809,787	2,993,352	1,694,974
			FA Premier	*Div. 1*	*Div. 2*	*Div. 3*
1992–93	2028	20,657,327	9,759,809	5,874,017	3,483,073	1,540,428
1993–94	2028	21,683,381	10,644,551	6,487,104	2,972,702	1,579,024

This is the first time since the war that attendances have risen for seven consecutive seasons.

**Figures include matches played by Aldershot.*

LEAGUE ATTENDANCES 1993–94

FA CARLING PREMIERSHIP STATISTICS

	Average Gate			*Season 1993/94*	
	1992/93	1993/94	+/–%	Highest	Lowest
Arsenal	24,403	30,563	+25.2	36,203	21,295
Aston Villa	29,594	29,015	–2.0	45,347	16,180
Blackburn Rovers	16,246	17,721	+9.1	22,061	14,260
Chelsea	18,787	19,416	+3.3	37,064	8,923
Coventry City	14,951	13,352	–10.7	17,009	9,837
Everton	20,445	22,876	+11.9	38,157	13,265
Ipswich Town	18,223	16,382	–10.1	22,478	11,468
Leeds United	29,250	34,493	+17.9	41,127	28,717
Liverpool	37,004	38,493	+4.0	44,339	24,561
Manchester City	24,698	26,709	+8.1	35,155	20,513
Manchester United	35,152	44,244	+25.9	44,751	41,829
Newcastle United	29,018	33,679	+16.1	36,342	32,067
Norwich City	16,154	18,164	+12.4	21,181	14,851
Oldham Athletic	12,859	12,563	–2.3	16,708	9,633
Queens Park Rangers	15,015	14,228	–5.2	21,267	9,875
Sheffield United	18,801	19,562	+4.0	30,044	14,183
Sheffield Wednesday	27,263	27,191	–0.3	34,548	18,509
Southampton	15,382	14,751	–4.1	19,105	9,028
Swindon Town	10,715	15,274	+42.6	18,102	11,940
Tottenham Hotspur	27,740	27,160	–2.1	31,502	17,452
West Ham United	16,001	20,572	+28.6	28,382	15,777
Wimbledon	8,405	10,474	+24.6	28,553	5,536

ENDSLEIGH INSURANCE LEAGUE: DIVISION ONE STATISTICS

	Average Gate			*Season 1993/94*	
	1992/93	1993/94	+/–%	Highest	Lowest
Barnsley	6,415	7,610	+18.6	13,270	4,380
Birmingham City	12,328	14,506	+17.7	28,228	9,377
Bolton Wanderers	9,062	10,498	+15.8	18,496	7,058
Bristol City	11,004	8,852	–19.6	20,725	5,350
Charlton Athletic	7,005	8,056	+15.0	12,192	6,639
Crystal Palace	15,748	15,656	–0.6	28,694	10,925
Derby County	15,020	15,937	+6.1	19,300	13,370
Grimsby Town	6,088	5,989	–1.6	11,930	4,014
Leicester City	15,362	16,005	+4.2	21,744	10,366
Luton Town	8,212	7,878	–4.1	10,053	6,201
Middlesbrough	16,724	10,400	–37.8	17,056	6,286
Millwall	9,188	9,821	+6.9	16,731	5,887
Nottingham Forest	21,910	23,051	+5.2	27,010	17,584
Notts County	8,151	8,314	+2.0	17,911	5,302
Oxford United	6,356	6,877	+8.2	10,417	4,065
Peterborough United	8,064	7,412	–8.1	14,010	5,084
Portsmouth	13,706	11,692	–14.7	19,535	7,005
Southend United	5,396	6,105	+13.1	10,731	3,758
Stoke City	16,579	15,931	–3.9	22,565	10,138
Sunderland	17,258	16,934	–1.8	19,363	13,645
Tranmere Rovers	8,071	8,099	+0.3	15,603	5,526
Watford	8,275	7,907	–4.4	14,359	5,109
West Bromwich Albion	15,161	16,840	+11.1	25,615	13,867
Wolverhampton Wanderers	13,598	22,008	+61.8	28,039	15,989

ENDSLEIGH INSURANCE LEAGUE: DIVISION TWO ATTENDANCES

	Average Gate			*Season 1993/94*	
	1992/93	1993/94	+/–%	Highest	Lowest
AFC Bournemouth	4,454	4,355	–2.2	7,106	2,385
Barnet	3,429	2,431	–29.1	3,158	1,352
Blackpool	5,501	4,757	–13.5	8,969	3,121
Bradford City	6,581	6,395	–2.8	9,501	3,472
Brentford	8,476	5,611	–33.8	6,848	4,361
Brighton & Hove Albion	6,710	7,730	+ 15.2	15,423	4,518
Bristol Rovers	5,745	5,338	–7.1	7,697	3,909
Burnley	10,537	11,317	+ 7.4	18,168	8,822
Cambridge United	5,545	3,686	–33.5	4,903	2,543
Cardiff City	8,560	6,072	–29.1	10,847	3,583
Exeter City	3,275	3,320	+ 1.4	6,601	1,933
Fulham	4,736	4,655	–1.7	9,797	2,998
Hartlepool United	3,139	2,076	–33.9	3,286	1,077
Huddersfield Town	5,918	6,372	+ 7.7	16,195	3,854
Hull City	4,672	5,943	+ 27.2	11,232	3,580
Leyton Orient	5,377	4,237	–21.2	6,304	2,643
Plymouth Argyle	6,377	9,003	+ 41.2	15,609	5,657
Port Vale	8,092	8,323	+ 2.9	10,710	6,484
Reading	4,782	6,932	+ 45.4	11,840	4,971
Rotherham United	4,769	3,736	–21.7	5,543	2,643
Stockport County	5,504	5,090	–7.5	7,666	3,782
Swansea City	5,199	3,534	–32.0	5,383	2,483
Wrexham	4,987	3,961	–20.6	7,253	2,090
York City	3,946	4,633	+ 17.4	8,481	2,409

ENDSLEIGH INSURANCE LEAGUE: DIVISION THREE ATTENDANCES

	Average Gate			*Season 1993/94*	
	1992/93	1993/94	+/–%	Highest	Lowest
Bury	2,670	2,597	–2.7	4,164	1,687
Carlisle United	3,611	5,524	+ 53.0	10,279	3,796
Chester City	2,992	3,191	+ 6.7	5,638	2,195
Chesterfield	3,213	3,188	–0.8	5,285	2,110
Colchester United	3,777	2,857	–24.4	3,932	2,316
Crewe Alexandra	3,455	3,991	+ 15.5	6,494	2,700
Darlington	1,960	2,276	+ 16.1	4,831	1,613
Doncaster Rovers	2,411	2,478	+ 2.8	4,439	1,603
Gillingham	3,301	3,148	–4.6	4,573	2,453
Hereford United	2,211	2,262	+ 2.3	4,280	1,429
Lincoln City	3,331	3,179	–4.6	6,030	1,631
Mansfield Town	3,730	2,718	–27.1	4,272	1,802
Northampton Town	3,139	3,454	+ 10.0	6,432	1,866
Preston North End	5,689	7,377	+ 29.7	12,790	4,941
Rochdale	2,312	2,657	+ 14.9	4,317	1,827
Scarborough	1,929	1,681	–12.9	2,631	1,137
Scunthorpe United	3,147	3,182	+ 1.1	4,587	2,122
Shrewsbury Town	3,411	4,402	+ 29.1	7,686	2,436
Torquay United	2,695	3,437	+ 27.5	4,991	2,704
Walsall	3,628	4,237	+ 16.8	6,473	2,519
Wigan Athletic	2,598	1,897	–27.0	3,741	1,232
Wycombe Wanderers	4,602	5,448	+ 18.4	7,442	3,975

LEAGUE CUP FINALISTS 1961–94

Played as a two-leg final until 1966. All subsequent finals at Wembley.

Year	*Winners*	*Runners-up*	*Score*
1961	Aston Villa	Rotherham U	0-2, 3-0 (aet)
1962	Norwich C	Rochdale	3-0, 1-0
1963	Birmingham C	Aston Villa	3-1, 0-0
1964	Leicester C	Stoke C	1-1, 3-2
1965	Chelsea	Leicester C	3-2, 0-0
1966	WBA	West Ham U	1-2, 4-1
1967	QPR	WBA	3-2
1968	Leeds U	Arsenal	1-0
1969	Swindon T	Arsenal	3-1 (aet)
1970	Manchester C	WBA	2-1 (aet)
1971	Tottenham H	Aston Villa	2-0
1972	Stoke C	Chelsea	2-1
1973	Tottenham H	Norwich C	1-0
1974	Wolverhampton W	Manchester C	2-1
1975	Aston Villa	Norwich C	1-0
1976	Manchester C	Newcastle U	2-1
1977	Aston Villa	Everton	0-0, 1-1 (aet), 3-2 (aet)
1978	Nottingham F	Liverpool	0-0 (aet), 1-0
1979	Nottingham F	Southampton	3-2
1980	Wolverhampton W	Nottingham F	1-0
1981	Liverpool	West Ham U	1-1 (aet), 2-1
MILK CUP			
1982	Liverpool	Tottenham H	3-1 (aet)
1983	Liverpool	Manchester U	2-1 (aet)
1984	Liverpool	Everton	0-0 (aet), 1-0
1985	Norwich C	Sunderland	1-0
1986	Oxford U	QPR	3-0
LITTLEWOODS CUP			
1987	Arsenal	Liverpool	2-1
1988	Luton T	Arsenal	3-2
1989	Nottingham F	Luton T	3-1
1990	Nottingham F	Oldham Ath	1-0
RUMBELOWS LEAGUE CUP			
1991	Sheffield W	Manchester U	1-0
1992	Manchester U	Nottingham F	1-0
COCA COLA CUP			
1993	Arsenal	Sheffield W	2-1
1994	Aston Villa	Manchester U	3-1

LEAGUE CUP WINS

Aston Villa 4, Liverpool 4, Nottingham F 4, Arsenal 2, Manchester C 2, Norwich C 2, Tottenham H 2, Wolverhampton W 2, Birmingham C 1, Chelsea 1, Leeds U 1, Leicester C 1, Luton T 1, Manchester U 1, Oxford U 1, QPR 1, Sheffield W 1, Stoke C 1, Swindon T 1, WBA 1.

APPEARANCES IN FINALS

Aston Villa 6, Liverpool 6, Nottingham F 6, Arsenal 5, Manchester U 4, Norwich C 4, Manchester C 3, Tottenham H 3, WBA 3, Chelsea 2, Everton 2, Leicester C 2, Luton T 2, QPR 2, Sheffield W 2, Stoke C 2, West Ham U 2, Wolverhampton W 2, Birmingham C 1, Leeds U 1, Newcastle U 1, Oldham Ath 1, Oxford U 1, Rochdale 1, Rotherham U 1, Southampton 1, Sunderland 1, Swindon T 1.

APPEARANCES IN SEMI-FINALS

Aston Villa 9, Liverpool 8, Tottenham H 8, Arsenal 7, Manchester U 7, West Ham U 7, Nottingham F 6, Chelsea 5, Manchester C 5, Norwich C 5, Leeds U 4, WBA 4, Burnley 3, Everton 3, QPR 3, Sheffield W 3, Wolverhampton W 3, Birmingham C 2, Blackburn R 2, Bristol C 2, Coventry C 2, Ipswich T 2, Leicester C 2, Luton T 2, Middlesbrough 2, Oxford U 2, Plymouth Arg 2, Southampton 2, Stoke C 2, Sunderland 2, Swindon T 2, Blackpool 1, Bolton W 1, Bury 1, Cardiff C 1, Carlisle U 1, Chester C 1, Crystal Palace 1, Derby Co 1, Huddersfield T 1, Newcastle U 1, Oldham Ath 1, Peterborough U 1, Rochdale 1, Rotherham U 1, Shrewsbury T 1, Tranmere R 1, Walsall 1, Watford 1.

LEAGUE CUP FINALISTS 1961–93

1960–61 ROTHERHAM UNITED Ironside; Perry, Morgan, Lambert, Madden, Waterhouse, Webster, Weston, Houghton, Kirkman, Bambridge. *Scorers:* Webster, Kirkman.

2–0 ASTON VILLA Sims; Lynn, Lee, Crowe, Dugdale, Deakin, McEwan, Thomson, Brown, Wylie, McParland.

ASTON VILLA Sidebottom; Neal, Lee, Crowe, Dugdale, Deakin, McEwan, O'Neill, McParland, Thomson, Burrows. *Scorers:* O'Neill, Burrows, McParland.

3–0 aet ROTHERHAM UNITED Ironside; Perry, Morgan, Lambert, Madden, Waterhouse, Webster, Weston, Houghton, Kirkman, Bambridge. **Aston Villa won on aggregate 3–2.**

1961–62 ROCHDALE Burgin; Milburn, Winton, Bodell, Aspden, Thompson, Wragg, Hepton, Bimpson, Cairns, Whitaker.

0–3 NORWICH CITY Kennon; McCrohan, Ashman, Burton, Butler, Mullett, Mannion, Lythgoe, Scott, Hill, Punton. *Scorers:* Lythgoe 2, Punton.

NORWICH CITY Kennon; McCrohan, Ashman, Burton, Butler, Mullett, Mannion, Lythgoe, Scott, Hill, Punton. *Scorer:* Hill.

1–0 ROCHDALE Burgin; Milburn, Winton, Bodell, Aspden, Thompson, Whyke, Richardson, Bimpson, Cairns, Whitaker. **Norwich City won on aggregate 4–0.**

1962–63 BIRMINGHAM CITY Schofield; Lynn, Green, Hennessey, Smith, Beard, Hellawell, Bloomfield, Harris, Leek, Auld. *Scorers:* Leek 2, Bloomfield.

3–1 ASTON VILLA Sims; Fraser, Aitken, Crowe, Sleeuwenhoek, Lee, Baker, Graham, Thomson, Wylie, Burrows. *Scorer:* Thomson.

ASTON VILLA Chatterley took the place of Sleeuwenhoek.

0–0 BIRMINGHAM CITY No change in team. **Birmingham City won on aggregate 3–1.**

1963–64 STOKE CITY Leslie; Asprey, Allen, Palmer, Kinnell, Skeels, Dobing, Viollet, Ritchie, McIlroy, Bebbington. *Scorer:* Bebbington.

1–1 LEICESTER CITY Banks; Sjoberg, Appleton, Dougan, King, Cross, Riley, Heath, Keyworth, Gibson, Stringfellow. *Scorer:* Gibson.

LEICESTER CITY Banks; Sjoberg, Norman, Cross, King, Appleton, Riley, Gibson, Keyworth, Sweenie, Stringfellow. *Scorers:* Stringfellow, Gibson, Riley.

3–2 STOKE CITY Irvine; Asprey, Allen, Palmer, Kinnell, Skeels, Dobing, Viollet, Ritchie, McIlroy, Bebbington. *Scorers:* Viollet, Kinnell. **Leicester City won on aggregate 4–3.**

1964–65 CHELSEA Bonetti; Hinton, Harris, Hollins, Young, Boyle, Murray, Graham, McCreadie, Venables, Tambling. *Scorers:* Tambling, Venables (pen), McCreadie.

3–2 LEICESTER CITY Banks; Sjoberg, Norman, Chalmers, King, Appleton, Hodgson, Cross, Goodfellow, Gibson, Sweenie. *Scorers:* Appleton, Goodfellow.

LEICESTER CITY Banks; Walker, Norman, Roberts, Sjoberg, Appleton, Hodgson, Cross, Goodfellow, Gibson, Stringfellow.

0–0 CHELSEA Bonetti; Hinton, McCreadie, Harris, Mortimore, Upton, Murray, Boyle, Bridges, Venables, Tambling. **Chelsea won on aggregate 3–2.**

1965–66 WEST HAM UNITED Standen; Burnett, Burkett, Peters, Brown, Moore, Brabrook, Boyce, Byrne, Hurst, Dear. *Scorers:* Moore, Byrne.

2–1 WEST BROMWICH ALBION Potter; Cram, Fairfax, Fraser, Campbell, Williams, Brown, Astle, Kaye, Lovett, Clark. *Scorer:* Astle.

WEST BROMWICH ALBION Potter; Cram, Fairfax, Fraser, Campbell, Williams, Brown, Astle, Kaye, Hope, Clark. *Scorers:* Kaye, Brown, Clark, Williams.

4–1 WEST HAM UNITED Standen; Burnett, Peters, Bovington, Brown, Moore, Brabrook, Boyce, Byrne, Hurst, Sissons. *Scorer:* Peters. **West Bromwich Albion won on aggregate 5–3.**

1966–67 QUEEN'S PARK RANGERS Springett; Hazell, Langley, Sibley, Hunt, Keen, Lazarus, Sanderson, Allen, Marsh, Morgan R. *Scorers:* Morgan R, Marsh, Lazarus.

3–2 WEST BROMWICH ALBION Sheppard; Cram, Williams, Collard, Clarke D, Fraser, Brown, Astle, Kaye, Hope, Clark C. *Scorer:* C Clark 2.

1967–68 LEEDS UNITED Sprake; Reaney, Cooper, Bremner, Charlton, Hunter, Greenhoff, Lorimer, Madeley, Giles, Gray (Belfitt). *Scorer:* Cooper.

1–0 ARSENAL Furnell; Storey, McNab, McLintock, Simpson, Ure, Radford, Jenkins, Graham, Sammels, Armstrong.

1968–69 SWINDON TOWN Downsborough; Thomas, Trollope, Butler, Burrows, Harland, Heath, Smart, Smith, Noble (Penman), Rogers. *Scorers:* Smart, Rogers 2.

3–1 aet ARSENAL Wilson; Storey, McNab, McLintock, Ure, Simpson (Graham), Radford, Sammels, Court, Gould, Armstrong. *Scorer:* Gould.

1969–70 MANCHESTER CITY Corrigan; Book, Mann, Doyle, Booth, Oakes, Heslop, Bell, Summerbee (Bowyer), Lee, Pardoe. *Scorers:* Doyle, Pardoe.

2–1 aet WEST BROMWICH ALBION Osborne; Fraser, Wilson, Brown, Talbut, Kaye, Cantello, Suggett, Astle, Hartford (Krzywicki), Hope. *Scorer:* Astle.

1970–71 TOTTENHAM HOTSPUR Jennings; Kinnear, Knowles, Mullery, Collins, Beal, Gilzean, Perryman, Chivers, Peters, Neighbour. *Scorer:* Chivers 2.

2–0 ASTON VILLA Dunn; Bradley, Aitken, Godfrey, Turnbull, Tiler, McMahon, Rioch, Lochhead, Hamilton, Anderson.

1971–72 STOKE CITY Banks; Marsh, Pejic, Bernard, Smith, Bloor, Conroy, Greenhoff (Mahoney), Ritchie, Dobing, Eastham. *Scorers:* Conroy, Eastham.

2–1 CHELSEA Bonetti; Mulligan (Baldwin), Harris, Hollins, Dempsey, Webb, Cooke, Osgood, Hudson, Houseman. *Scorer:* Osgood.

1972–73 TOTTENHAM HOTSPUR Jennings; Kinnear, Knowles, Pratt (Coates), England, Beal, Gilzean, Perryman, Chivers, Peters, Pearce. *Scorer:* Coates.

1–0 NORWICH CITY Keelan; Payne, Butler, Stringer, Forbes, Briggs, Livermore, Blair (Howard), Cross, Paddon, Anderson.

1973–74 WOLVERHAMPTON WANDERERS Pierce; Palmer, Parkin, Bailey, Munro, McAlle, Sunderland, Hibbitt, Richards, Dougan, Wagstaffe (Powell). *Scorers:* Hibbitt, Richards.

2–1 MANCHESTER CITY MacRae; Pardoe, Donachie, Doyle, Booth, Towers, Summerbee, Bell, Lee, Law, Marsh. *Scorer:* Bell.

1974–75 ASTON VILLA Cumbes; Robson, Aitken, Ross, Nicholl, McDonald, Graydon, Little, Leonard, Hamilton, Carrodus. *Scorer:* Graydon.

1–0 NORWICH CITY Keelan; Machin, Sullivan, Morris, Forbes, Stringer, Miller, MacDougall, Boyer, Suggett, Powell.

1975–76 MANCHESTER CITY Corrigan; Keegan, Donachie, Doyle, Watson, Oakes, Barnes, Booth, Royle, Hartford, Tueart. *Scorers:* Barnes, Tueart.

2–1 NEWCASTLE UNITED Mahoney; Nattrass, Kennedy, Barrowclough, Keeley, Howard, Burns, Cassidy, Macdonald, Gowling, Craig. *Scorer:* Gowling.

1976–77 ASTON VILLA Burridge; Gidman, Robson, Phillips, Nicholl, Mortimer, Deehan, Little, Gray, Cropley, Carrodus.

0–0 EVERTON Lawson; Jones, Darracott, Lyons, McNaught, King, Hamilton, Dobson, Latchford, McKenzie, Goodlass.

First replay (at Hillsborough)

***R:* 1–1 aet** ASTON VILLA Burridge; Gidman, Robson, Phillips, Nicholl, Mortimer, Deehan, Little, Gray, Cowans, Carrodus. *Scorer:* Kenyon og.

EVERTON Lawson; Bernard, Darracott, Lyons, McNaught, King, Hamilton (Pearson), Kenyon, Latchford, McKenzie, Goodlass. *Scorer:* Latchford.

Second replay (at Old Trafford, Manchester)

***R:* 3–2 aet** ASTON VILLA Burridge; Gidman (Smith), Robson, Phillips, Nicholl, Mortimer, Graydon, Little, Deehan, Cropley, Cowans. *Scorers:* Little 2, Nicholl.

EVERTON Lawson; Robinson, Darracott, Lyons, McNaught, King, Hamilton, Dobson, Latchford, Pearson (Seargeant), Goodlass. *Scorers:* Latchford, Lyons.

1977–78 NOTTINGHAM FOREST Woods; Anderson, Clark, McGovern (O'Hare), Lloyd, Burns, O'Neill, Bowyer, Withe, Woodcock, Robertson.

0–0 aet LIVERPOOL Clemence; Neal, Smith, Thompson, Kennedy (Fairclough), Hughes, Dalglish, Case, Heighway, McDermott, Callaghan.

Replay (at Old Trafford, Manchester)

***R:* 1–0** NOTTINGHAM FOREST Woods; Anderson, Clark, O'Hare, Lloyd, Burns, O'Neill, Bowyer, Withe, Woodcock, Robertson. *Scorer:* Robertson (pen).

LIVERPOOL Clemence; Neal, Smith, Thompson, Kennedy, Hughes, Dalglish, Case (Fairclough), Heighway, McDermott, Callaghan.

1978–79 NOTTINGHAM FOREST Shilton; Barrett, Clark, McGovern, Lloyd, Needham, O'Neill, Gemmill, Birtles, Woodcock, Robertson. *Scorers:* Birtles 2, Woodcock.

3–2 SOUTHAMPTON Gennoe; Golac, Peach, Williams, Nicholl, Waldron, Ball, Boyer, Hayes (Sealy), Holmes, Curran. *Scorers:* Peach, Holmes.

1979–80 WOLVERHAMPTON WANDERERS Bradshaw; Palmer, Parkin, Daniel, Berry, Hughes, Carr, Hibbitt, Gray, Richards, Eves. *Scorer:* Gray.

1–0 NOTTINGHAM FOREST Shilton; Anderson, Gray, McGovern, Needham, Burns, O'Neill, Bowyer, Birtles, Francis, Robertson.

1980–81 LIVERPOOL Clemence; Neal, Kennedy A, Irwin, Kennedy R, Hansen, Dalglish, Lee, Heighway (Case), McDermott, Souness. *Scorer:* Kennedy A.

1–1 aet WEST HAM UNITED Parkes; Stewart, Lampard, Bonds, Martin, Devonshire, Neighbour, Goddard (Pearson), Cross, Brooking, Pike. *Scorer:* Stewart (pen).

Replay (at Villa Park)

***R:* 2–1** LIVERPOOL Clemence; Neal, Kennedy A, Thompson, Kennedy R, Hansen, Dalglish, Lee, Rush, McDermott, Case. *Scorers:* Dalglish, Hansen.

WEST HAM UNITED Parkes; Stewart, Lampard, Bonds, Martin, Devonshire, Neighbour, Goddard, Cross, Brooking, Pike (Pearson). *Scorer:* Goddard.

1981–82 LIVERPOOL Grobbelaar; Neal, Kennedy, Thompson A, Whelan, Lawrenson, Dalglish, Lee, Rush, McDermott (Johnson), Souness. *Scorers:* Whelan 2, Rush.

3–1 aet TOTTENHAM HOTSPUR Clemence; Hughton, Miller, Price, Hazard (Villa), Perryman, Ardiles, Archibald, Galvin, Hoddle, Crooks. *Scorer:* Archibald.

1982–83 LIVERPOOL Grobbelaar; Neal, Kennedy, Lawrenson, Whelan, Hansen, Dalglish, Lee, Rush, Johnston (Fairclough), Souness. *Scorers:* Kennedy, Whelan.

2–1 aet MANCHESTER UNITED Bailey; Duxbury, Albiston, Moses, Moran (Macari), McQueen, Wilkins, Muhren, Stapleton, Whiteside, Coppell. *Scorer:* Whiteside.

1983–84 LIVERPOOL Grobbelaar; Neal, Kennedy, Lawrenson, Whelan, Hansen, Dalglish, Lee, Rush, Johnston (Robinson), Souness.

0–0 aet EVERTON Southall; Stevens, Bailey, Ratcliffe, Mountfield, Reid, Irvine, Heath, Sharp, Richardson, Sheedy (Harper).

***R:* 1–0** LIVERPOOL Grobbelaar; Neal, Kennedy, Lawrenson, Whelan, Hansen, Dalglish, Lee, Rush, Johnston, Souness. *Scorer:* Souness.
EVERTON Southall; Stevens, Bailey, Ratcliffe, Mountfield, Reid, Irvine (King), Heath, Sharp, Richardson, Harper. *Replay (at Maine Road, Manchester)*

1984–85 NORWICH CITY Woods; Haylock, Van Wyk, Bruce, Mendham, Watson, Barham, Channon, Deehan, Hartford, Donowa. *Scorer:* Chisholm (og).
1–0 SUNDERLAND Turner; Venison, Pickering, Bennett, Chisholm, Corner (Gayle), Daniel, Wallace, Hodgson, Berry, Walker.

1985–86 OXFORD UNITED Judge; Langan, Trewick, Phillips, Briggs, Shotton, Houghton, Aldridge, Charles, Hebberd, Brock. *Scorers:* Hebberd, Houghton, Charles.
3–0 QUEEN'S PARK RANGERS Barron; McDonald, Dawes, Neill, Wicks, Fenwick, Allen (Rosenoir), James, Bannister, Byrne, Robinson.

1986–87 ARSENAL Lukic; Anderson, Sansom, Williams, O'Leary, Adams, Rocastle, Davis, Quinn (Groves), Nicholas, Hayes (Thomas). *Scorer:* Nicholas 2.
2–1 LIVERPOOL Grobbelaar; Gillespie, Venison, Spackman, Whelan, Hansen, Walsh (Dalglish), Johnston, Rush, Molby, McMahon (Wark). *Scorer:* Rush.

1987–88 LUTON TOWN Dibble; Breacker, Johnson, Hill, Foster, Donaghy, Wilson, Stein B, Harford (Stein M), Preece (Grimes). *Scorers:* Stein B 2, Wilson.
3–2 ARSENAL Lukic; Winterburn, Sansom, Thomas, Caesar, Adams, Rocastle, Davis, Smith, Groves (Hayes), Richardson. *Scorers:* Hayes, Smith.

1988–89 NOTTINGHAM FOREST Sutton; Laws, Pearce, Walker, Wilson, Hodge, Gaynor, Webb, Clough, Chapman, Parker. *Scorers:* Clough 2 (1 pen), Webb.
3–1 LUTON TOWN Sealey; Breacker, Grimes (McDonough), Preece, Foster, Beaumont, Wilson, Wegerle, Harford, Hill, Black. *Scorer:* Harford.

1989–90 NOTTINGHAM FOREST Sutton; Laws, Pearce, Walker, Chettle, Hodge, Crosby, Parker, Clough, Jemson, Carr. *Scorer:* Jemson.
1–0 OLDHAM ATHLETIC Rhodes; Irwin, Barlow, Henry, Barrett, Warhurst, Adams, Ritchie, Bunn (Palmer), Milligan, Holden R.

1990–91 SHEFFIELD WEDNESDAY Turner; Nilsson, King, Harkes (Madden), Shirtliff, Pearson, Wilson, Sheridan, Hirst, Williams, Worthington. *Scorer:* Sheridan.
1–0 MANCHESTER UNITED Sealey; Irwin, Blackmore, Bruce, Webb (Phelan), Pallister, Robson, Ince, McClair, Hughes, Sharpe.

1991–92 MANCHESTER UNITED Schmeichel; Parker, Irwin, Bruce, Phelan, Pallister, Kanchelskis (Sharpe), Ince, McClair, Hughes, Giggs. *Scorer*: McClair.
1–0 NOTTINGHAM FOREST Marriott; Charles (Laws), Williams, Walker, Wassall, Keane, Crosby, Gemmill, Clough, Sheringham, Black.

1992–93 ARSENAL Seaman; O'Leary, Winterburn, Davis, Linighan, Adams, Morrow, Wright, Campbell, Merson, Parlour. *Scorers:* Merson, Morrow.
2–1 SHEFFIELD WEDNESDAY Woods; Nilsson, King (Hyde), Palmer, Anderson, Wilson (Hirst), Harkes, Waddle, Warhurst, Bright, Sheridan. *Scorer:* Harkes.

COCA COLA CUP 1993–94

FIRST ROUND FIRST LEG

16 AUG

Doncaster R (0) 0
Blackpool (0) 1 *(Watson)* 2664
Doncaster R: Beasley; Hewitt, Freeman, Yates, Wilcox, Bottomley, Harper, Hulme, Jones (Cunningham), Jeffrey (Cullen), Moss.
Blackpool: Martin; Davies, Cook, Horner, Briggs, Stoneman, Watson, Bonner, Bamber, Gouck (Beech), Griffiths (Quinn).

17 AUG

Birmingham C (2) 3 *(Parris, Frain, Peschisolido)*
Plymouth Arg (0) 0 9304
Birmingham C: Miller; Hiley, Frain, Parris, Whyte, Dryden, Downing (Mardon), McMinn (Donowa), Peschisolido, Saville, Smith.
Plymouth Arg: Newland; Patterson, Naylor, Hill, Comyn, McCall, Garner, Castle, Evans, Marshall, Dalton (Edworthy).

Bolton W (0) 0
Bury (2) 2 *(Powell, Blissett)* 6455
Bolton W: Branagan; Brown, Phillips, Kelly, Burke, Stubbs, Lee, McAteer, Coyle, McGinlay, Thompson.
Bury: Kelly G (Nixon); Anderson, Stanislaus, Daws, Knill, Jackson, Rigby, Hughes, Blissett, Hanson, Powell.

Bournemouth (2) 3 *(Fletcher, Masters, Beardsmore)*
Cardiff C (1) 1 *(Bird)* 3054
Bournemouth: Bartram; Pennock, Masters, Morris, Watson, Parkinson, O'Connor, McGorry, Fletcher, Cotterill, Beardsmore.
Cardiff C: Kite; James, Brazil, Millar (Baddeley), Perry, Ratcliffe, Bird, Richardson, Thompson, Blake, Griffith.

Brentford (0) 2 *(Peters, Westley)*
Watford (1) 2 *(Furlong, Dyer)* 4527
Brentford: Benstead; Statham, Manuel, Bates, Westley, Ratcliffe, Stephenson, Hutchings, Bennett (Mundee), Allon, Gayle (Peters).
Watford: Sheppard; Dublin, Drysdale, Soloman, Holdsworth, Alsford, Dyer, Charlery, Furlong, Porter, Lavin.

Cambridge U (1) 1 *(Claridge)*
Luton T (0) 0 4065
Cambridge U: Filan; Jeffrey, Barrick, O'Shea, Heathcote, Daish, Middleton, Danzey, Butler, Clayton, Claridge.
Luton T: Sommer; James, Johnson, Oakes, Peake, Dreyer, Rees (Houghton), Preece, Telfer, Hughes, Benjamin.

Chesterfield (1) 3 *(Turnbull (pen), Norris, Morris)*
Carlisle U (1) 1 *(Davey)* 2841
Chesterfield: Leonard; Rogers, Carr C, Brien, Carr D, Dennis (Hebberd), Curtis (McGugan), Norris, Jules, Turnbull, Morris.
Carlisle U: Day; Burgess, Gallimore, Holden, Walling, Edmondson (Arnold), Thomas, Reddish, Oghani, Davey, Fairweather.

Crewe Alex (0) 0
Wrexham (0) 1 *(Paskin)* 3626
Crewe Alex: Smith M; Collins, Gardiner, Evans, Woodward, Lennon, Ward, Naylor, Clarkson, Whalley, Adebola (Wilson).
Wrexham: Morris; Jones B, Hardy, Lake, Humes, Sertori, Bennett, Phillips, Connolly, Watkin, Taylor (Paskin).

Darlington (1) 1 *(Juryeff)*
Bradford C (2) 5 *(McCarthy 3, Reid, Jewell)* 1979
Darlington: Collier; Gaughan, Switzer, Himsworth, Gregan, O'Shaughnessy, Shaw, Isaacs, Chapman (Ellison), Juryeff, Fickling (Ball).
Bradford C: Tomlinson P; Hoyle, Heseltine, Duxbury L, Richards, Oliver, Steele (Showler), Robson, McCarthy, Jewell (Stapleton), Reid.

Fulham (0) 2 *(Betts (og), Farrell)*
Colchester U (1) 1 *(Kinsella)* 2820
Fulham: Stannard; Morgan, Pike, Ferney, Jupp, Thomas, Hails, Cooper, Farrell (Angus), Brazil, Marshall.
Colchester U: Keeley; Betts (Allpress), Roberts, Kinsella, English, Grainger, Ball, Bennett (Abrahams), McDonough, McGavin, Smith.

Gillingham (0) 1 *(Reinelt)*
Brighton & HA (0) 0 3330
Gillingham: Barrett; Martin, Watson, Eeles, Butler, Green, Micklewhite, Smith, Reinelt, Forster (Crane), Smillie.
Brighton & HA: Rust; Munday, Chapman, Wilkins, Bissett, Pates, Edwards, Kennedy, Nogan, Codner, Wilkinson.

Hereford U (0) 0
Torquay U (2) 2 *(Trollope, Foster)* 1400
Hereford U: Judge; Downs, Anderson, Davies, Abraham, Clark H, Hall, Clements (Fry), Pike, Pickard, Nicholson.
Torquay U: Lowe; Barrow, Colcombe, O'Riordan, Moore, Curran, Trollope, Kelly, Foster, Sale, Hathaway.

Huddersfield T (0) 0
Scarborough (0) 0 2822
Huddersfield T: Francis; Trevitt, Billy, Mitchell, Dyson (Starbuck), Jackson, Dunn, Robinson P, Roberts, Onuora (Booth), Wells.
Scarborough: Evans; Thompson, Davis, Mockler, Meyer, Rockett, Charles, Knowles, Henderson, Calvert, Young.

Leyton Orient (0) 0
Wycombe W (1) 2 *(Thompson, Langford)* 4151
Leyton Orient: Turner; Hendon, Howard, Hackett, Bellamy, Ryan, Carter, Lakin (Benstock), Taylor, Tomlinson, Putney.
Wycombe W: Hyde; Cousins, Titterton, Kerr, Crossley, Ryan, Carroll, Stapleton (Hayrettin), Thompson (Langford), Scott, Guppy.

Notts Co (2) 2 *(Lund, Cox)*
Hull C (0) 0 3003

Notts Co: Catlin; Wilson, Johnson (Turner P), Williams, Cox, Walker, Devlin, Draper, McSwegan (Reeves), Lund, Legg.
Hull C: Wilson; Mitchell, Hobson, Warren, Allison, Abbott, Norton, Moran, Brown, Windass, Atkinson.

Port Vale (0) 2 *(Taylor, Slaven)*
Lincoln C (0) 2 *(Lormor 2)* 5175

Port Vale: Musselwhite; Kent, Tankard, Aspin, Billing, Glover, Slaven, Van der Laan, Foyle, Kerr, Taylor.
Lincoln C: Pollitt; Smith P, Clarke, Hill, Smith M, Dunphy, Schofield, Mardenborough (Lormor), Costello, Puttnam, Baraclough.

Preston NE (1) 1 *(Ellis)*
Burnley (1) 2 *(Eyres (pen), Davis)* 6283

Preston NE: O'Hanlon; Callaghan, Sulley, Whalley, Nebbeling, Kidd, Ainsworth, Cartwright, Norbury, Ellis, Raynor.
Burnley: Beresford; Measham, Thompson, Davis, Pender, Joyce, Francis, Deary, Farrell, Russell, Eyres.

Rochdale (0) 2 *(Stuart, Flounders (pen))*
York C (0) 0 1952

Rochdale: Hodge; Thackeray, Graham, Reid, Reeves, Butler, Stuart, Doyle, Flounders, Whitehall, Lancaster (Milner) (Bowden).
York C: Kiely; McMillan, Hall, Pepper, Tutill, Atkin, McCarthy, Cooper, Barnes (Naylor), Swann, Canham.

Shrewsbury T (1) 1 *(Evans)*
Scunthorpe U (0) 0 1939

Shrewsbury T: Edwards; Hockaday, Blake, Spink, Lynch, Evans, Summerfield, Taylor (Withe), Brown, Griffiths, Clarke.
Scunthorpe U: Samways; Thompstone, Mudd, Carmichael, Elliott, Hope, Alexander, Martin (Watson), White (Goodacre), Thornber, Smith.

Stockport Co (1) 1 *(Ryan)*
Hartlepool U (1) 1 *(West)* 2915

Stockport Co: Edwards; Miller, Wallace, Frain, Flynn, Finley, James, Ward, Francis, Ryan, Williams PA (Beaumont).
Hartlepool U: Carter; Cross R, Cross P, McGuckin, MacPhail, Nobbs, Gallagher, Wratten, West, Honour, Southall.

Sunderland (0) 3 *(Goodman 2, Power)*
Chester C (1) 1 *(Rimmer)* 9484

Sunderland: Chamberlain; Kay, Smith, Bennett, Michael Gray, Melville, Owers, Goodman, Atkinson (Martin Gray), Power, Armstrong (Howey).
Chester C: Stewart; Preece, Jakub (Jenkins), Bishop, Came, Greenall, Thompson, Lightfoot, Rimmer, Leonard, Pugh.

Swansea C (0) 0
Bristol C (0) 1 *(Robinson)* 3746

Swansea C: Freestone; Clode, Cook (Ford), Walker, Harris, Pascoe, Hodge, Bowen, Torpey, Cornforth, Hayes.
Bristol C: Welch; Munro, Scott (Osman), Aizlewood, Shail, Hewlett, Wyatt, Shelton, Baird, Robinson, Tinnion.

Walsall (0) 0
Exeter C (0) 0 2024

Walsall: Gayle M; Evans (Knight), Marsh, Watkiss, Ryder, Smith, Ntamark, Tinkler, Cecere (O'Hara), Reece, McDonald.
Exeter C: Fox; White, Robinson, Bailey, Daniels, Whiston, Storer, Coughlin, Ross, Minett (Thirlby), Wigley.

Wigan Ath (0) 0
Rotherham U (0) 1 *(Hazel)* 1531

Wigan Ath: Farnworth; Rennie, Duffy (Dowe), Robertson, Skipper, Johnson, Strong, McKearney, Gavin, Morton, Langley.
Rotherham U: Mercer; Pickering, Jacobs, Banks, Richardson, Law, Hazel, Goodwin, Helliwell, Goater, Wilder.

18 AUG

Bristol R (1) 1 *(Sterling)*
WBA (2) 4 *(Burgess, Hunt, Donovan 2)* 4562

Bristol R: Parkin; Alexander, Hardyman, Waddock, Clark, Tillson, Sterling, Taylor (Browning), Stewart, Skinner, Archer.
WBA: Lange; Coldicott, Ampadu, Bradley (Strodder), Raven, Burgess, Hunt, Hamilton, Taylor, O'Regan, Donovan.

Reading (0) 3 *(Quinn, Lovell, Parkinson)*
Northampton T (0) 0 3283

Reading: Hislop; Ranson, Kerr, McPherson, Williams, Parkinson, Gilkes, Dillon (Taylor), Quinn, Lovell, Jones.
Northampton T: Richardson; Parsons, Gillard, Phillips, Terry, Wood (Burnham), Fleming, Francis (Harmon), Gilzean, Brown, Bell.

Southend U (0) 0
Barnet (0) 2 *(Lynch, Walker)* 3249

Southend U: Sansome; Edwards, Powell, Jones K, Sussex, Bressington, Ansah (Hunt), Payne, Jones G (Mooney), Otto, Angell.
Barnet: Pape; Newson, Cooper, Smith, Walker, Barnett D, Marwood (Evans), Close, Haag, Hoddle, Lynch (Alexander).

Stoke C (1) 2 *(Gleghorn, Carruthers)*
Mansfield T (2) 2 *(Noteman, McLoughlin)* 8976

Stoke C: Prudhoe; Butler, Sandford, Kevan, Overson, Lowe, Orlygsson, Foley (Gynn), Stein, Regis (Carruthers), Gleghorn.
Mansfield T: Pearcey; Foster S (Stringfellow), Platnauer, Fairclough, Gray, Clarke, Noteman, Holland, McLoughlin, Wilkinson, Wilson.

FIRST ROUND SECOND LEG

24 AUG

Barnet (0) 1 *(Haag)*
Southend U (0) 1 *(Angell)* 2471

Barnet: Phillips; Newson, Cooper, Smith, Alexander, Barnett D, Marwood, Carter, Haag, Hoddle (Evans), Lynch.
Southend U: Sansome; Locke, Powell, Bodley, Howell, Sussex (Hunt), Ansah, Payne, Lee (Angell), Otto, Mooney.
Barnet won 3-1 on aggregate.

Blackpool (1) 3 *(Watson, Quinn, Bamber)*
Doncaster R (3) 3 *(Hulme, Harper, Wilcox)* 2490
Blackpool: Martin; Davies, Cook, Horner, Briggs, Stoneman (Beech), Watson, Bonner, Bamber, Gouck (Quinn), Griffiths.
Doncaster R: Beasley; Hewitt, Freeman, Yates, Wilcox, Bottomley, Harper, Hulme, Cunningham (Jones), Jeffrey (Prindiville), Moss.
Blackpool won 4-3 on aggregate.

Bristol C (0) 0
Swansea C (1) 2 *(Bowen 2)* 4633
Bristol C: Welch; Munro, Scott, Aizlewood, Shail, Hewlett (Osman), Wyatt (Allison), Shelton, Baird, Robinson, Tinnion.
Swansea C: Freestone; Clode, Ford, Walker, Harris, Pascoe, Chapple, Bowen, Torpey, Cornforth, Hayes.
Swansea C won 2-1 on aggregate.

Bury (0) 0
Bolton W (1) 2 *(Coyle, McGinlay)* 4528
Bury: Bracey; Anderson (Jones), Stanislaus, Daws, Knill, Jackson, Mauge, Hughes, Blissett, Hanson (Adekola), Powell.
Bolton W: Branagan; Brown, Phillips, Kelly, Burke, Stubbs, Lee, McAteer, Coyle, McGinlay, Patterson (Thompson).
aet; Bolton W won 3-0 on penalties.

Cardiff C (1) 1 *(Morris (og))*
Bournemouth (1) 1 *(Parkinson)* 4459
Cardiff C: Kite; James, Searle, Brazil, Perry, Millar, Cornwell, Richardson, Thompson, Blake, Bird.
Bournemouth: Bartram; Pennock, Mathers, Morris, Watson, Parkinson, O'Connor, McGorry (Leadbitter), Fletcher, Cotterill, Beardsmore.
Bournemouth won 4-2 on aggregate.

Carlisle U (1) 1 *(Thomas)*
Chesterfield (1) 1 *(Jules)* 4410
Carlisle U: Day; Burgess, Gallimore, Walling, Valentine, Edmondson, Thomas, Reddish (Arnold), Oghani, Davies, Fairweather (Joyce).
Chesterfield: Leonard; Rogers, Carr C, Brien, Carr D, Curtis, McGugan, Norris, Jules, Turnbull, Hebberd.
Chesterfield won 4-2 on aggregate.

Chester C (0) 0
Sunderland (0) 0 2903
Chester C: Stewart; Preece (Jenkins), Jakub, Bishop, Came, Greenall, Thompson, Lightfoot, Rimmer, Leonard, Pugh (Donnelly).
Sunderland: Chamberlain; Kay (Atkinson), Martin Gray, Bennett, Michael Gray (Howey), Melville, Owers, Goodman, Cunnington, Power, Armstrong.
Sunderland won 3-1 on aggregate.

Colchester U (1) 1 *(McDonough)*
Fulham (0) 2 *(Brazil, Farrell)* 3360
Colchester U: Keeley; Allpress, Roberts, Kinsella, English, Grainger, Ball, Bennett (Abrahams), McDonough, McGavin, Smith.
Fulham: Stannard; Morgan, Pike, Ferney (Baah), Jupp, Thomas, Hails, Cooper, Farrell (Onwere), Brazil, Marshall.
Fulham won 4-2 on aggregate.

Hartlepool U (0) 2 *(Tait, Honour)*
Stockport Co (1) 1 *(Francis)* 2273
Hartlepool U: Carter; Cross R, Cross P, McGuckin, MacPhail, Emerson, Tait, Wratten (Gilchrist), West, Honour, Southall (Peverell).
Stockport Co: Edwards; Todd, Wallace, Frain, Flynn, Finley, James (Beaumont), Ward, Francis, Gannon, Ryan.
Hartlepool U won 3-2 on aggregate.

Hull C (3) 3 *(Abbott, Atkinson, Windass)*
Notts Co (0) 1 *(Draper)* 2222
Hull C: Wilson; Mitchell, Hobson, Warren, Allison, Abbott (Hopkin), Norton, Lee, Brown, Windass, Atkinson (Mann).
Notts Co: Cherry; Wilson, Johnson, Williams, Cox, Walker, Devlin, Draper, Reeves, Turner P (Simpson), Legg (Slawson).
aet; Notts Co won on away goals.

Lincoln C (0) 0
Port Vale (0) 0 3642
Lincoln C: Pollitt; Smith P, Clarke, Hill, Dunphy, Smith M (Lormor), Schofield, Mardenborough (Johnson D), Baraclough, Costello, Puttnam.
Port Vale: Musselwhite; Kent, Tankard, Aspin, Swan, Glover, Slaven, Van der Laan, Foyle (Jeffers), Kerr, Taylor (Cross).
aet; Lincoln C won on away goals.

Luton T (0) 0
Cambridge U (0) 1 *(Claridge)* 3861
Luton T: Sommer; Williams (Hartson), Johnson, James, Peake, Dreyer, Benjamin, Hughes, Campbell (Oakes), Houghton, Preece.
Cambridge U: Filan; Jeffrey, Barrick, O'Shea, Heathcote, Daish, Fowler, Danzey, Butler, Clayton, Claridge.
Cambridge U won 2-0 on aggregate.

Mansfield T (1) 1 *(Stant)*
Stoke C (1) 3 *(Stein 2, Regis)* 4214
Mansfield T: Pearcey; Foster S, Platnauer, Fairclough, Gray, Clarke, Noteman, Holland, Stant (Stringfellow), Wilkinson (Wilson), McLoughlin.
Stoke C: Prudhoe; Butler, Sandford, Cranson, Lowe (Gynn), Overson, Gleghorn, Foley, Stein, Orlygsson, Regis.
aet; Stoke C won 5-3 on aggregate.

Plymouth Arg (0) 2 *(Barlow, Marshall)*
Birmingham C (0) 0 3659
Plymouth Arg: Nicholls; Patterson, Naylor, Hill, Comyn, McCall, Barlow, Castle, Nugent, Marshall, Dalton.
Birmingham C: Miller; Hiley, Frain, Dryden, Mardon, Whyte, Fenwick, Smith, Shutt, Saville, Moulden (Donowa).
Birmingham C won 3-2 on aggregate.

Rotherham U (3) 4 *(Banks, Gavin (og), Varadi, Law)*
Wigan Ath (1) 2 *(Gavin, Morton)* 2009
Rotherham U: Mercer; Pickering, Jacobs, Banks, Richardson, Law, Hazel (Goater), Goodwin, Helliwell, Varadi, Wilder.
Wigan Ath: Farnworth; West (Dowe), Rennie, Robertson, Skipper, Johnson, Vaughan, McKearney, Gavin, Morton, Langley.
Rotherham U won 5-2 on aggregate.

Scarborough (0) 0
Huddersfield T (1) 3 *(Dunn 2, Roberts)* 2612
Scarborough: Robinson; Thompson, Davis, Mockler (Ashdjian), Meyer, Rockett, Charles, Knowles, Henderson, Calvert, Young.
Huddersfield T: Francis; Trevitt, Billy, Starbuck, Hicks, Jackson, Dunn, Ward (Mitchell), Roberts, Onuora, Wells.
Huddersfield T won 3-0 on aggregate.

Scunthorpe U (0) 1 *(Martin)*
Shrewsbury T (1) 1 *(Griffiths)* 2320
Scunthorpe U: Samways; Alexander, Mudd, Martin, Elliott, Hope (Trebble), Thompstone, Goodacre, Watson, Toman, Smith.
Shrewsbury T: Edwards; Hockaday, Lynch, Taylor, Summerfield, Blake, Brown, Clarke, Spink, Griffiths (Williams), Evans.
Shrewsbury T won 2-1 on aggregate.

Torquay U (0) 0
Hereford U (0) 2 *(May, Hall (pen))* 2583
Torquay U: Lowe; Barrow, Colcombe, O'Riordan, Moore, Curran, Trollope, O'Toole (Loram), Foster, Darby (Byng), Hathaway.
Hereford U: Judge; Downs (Anderson), Fry, Langford, Abraham, Morris, Hall, Clark H, May (Pickard), Pike, Nicholson.
aet; Hereford U won 4-3 on penalties.

Watford (1) 3 *(Holdsworth, Soloman, Dyer)*
Brentford (1) 1 *(Westley)* 4937
Watford: Sheppard; Lavin, Drysdale, Hessenthaler, Holdsworth, Ashby, Dyer (Nogan), Charlery, Furlong, Porter, Soloman.
Brentford: Benstead; Statham, Bates, Westley, Manuel, Ratcliffe, Stephenson, Buckle (Hutchings), Bennett (Mundee), Allon, Peters.
Watford won 5-3 on aggregate.

Wrexham (2) 3 *(Connolly, Bennett (pen), Wilson (og))*
Crewe Alex (1) 3 *(Lyons, Rowbotham, Ward)* 3661
Wrexham: Morris; Jones B, Hardy, Williams, Hunter, Pejic, Bennett, Phillips, Connolly, Watkin, Taylor.
Crewe Alex: Smith M; Collins, Gardiner, Evans (Abel), Woodward, Wilson, Lennon, Clarkson, Ward, Lyons, Rowbotham.
Wrexham won 4-3 on aggregate.

Wycombe W (1) 1 *(Scott)*
Leyton Orient (0) 0 4906
Wycombe W: Hyde; Cousins, Titterton, Kerr, Crossley, Ryan, Carroll, Hayrettin, Thompson (Langford), Scott (Hutchinson), Guppy.
Leyton Orient: Turner; Hendon, Howard, Hackett, Kitchen, Lakin (Benstock), Carter, Ludden (Okai), Barnett, Tomlinson, Putney.
Wycombe W won 3-0 on aggregate.

York C (0) 0
Rochdale (0) 0 2835
York C: Kiely; McMillan, Hall, Pepper, Atkin, Tutill, McCarthy, Cooper, Naylor, Swann, Canham.
Rochdale: Hodge; Thackeray, Graham, Reid, Reeves, Butler, Stuart, Doyle, Flounders, Whitehall (Milner), Lancaster.
Rochdale won 2-0 on aggregate.

25 AUG

Bradford C (3) 6 *(Jewell 2, McCarthy 2, Steele, Showler)*
Darlington (0) 0 3062
Bradford C: Bowling; Williams, Lawford, Duxbury L, Oliver (Blake), Richards, Steele, Robson (Stapleton), McCarthy, Jewell, Showler.
Darlington: Collier; Gaughan, Switzer, Himsworth, Gregan, O'Shaughnessy, Ball (Reed), Isaacs, Ellison (Maddick), Chapman, Pearson.
Bradford C won 11-1 on aggregate.

Brighton & HA (1) 2 *(Kennedy, Nogan)*
Gillingham (0) 0 4410
Brighton & HA: Rust; Munday, Chapman, Wilkins, Bissett, Pates, Edwards, Kennedy, Nogan, Codner, Crumplin.
Gillingham: Barrett; Dunne, Watson, Eeles, Butler (Clark), Green, Micklewhite, Carpenter, Arnott, Forster (Crane), Smillie.
Brighton & HA won 2-1 on aggregate.

Burnley (1) 4 *(Russell, Eyres, Francis, Deary)*
Preston NE (0) 1 *(Cartwright)* 9346
Burnley: Beresford; Measham, Thompson, Davis, Pender, Joyce (Farrell), Francis, Deary, Heath, Russell, Eyres.
Preston NE: O'Hanlon; Masefield, Sulley, Whalley, Nebbeling, Matthewson, Ainsworth, Cartwright, Conroy (Burton), Ellis (Norbury), Raynor.
Burnley won 6-2 on aggregate.

Exeter C (1) 2 *(Jepson 2 (1 pen))*
Walsall (1) 1 *(McDonald)* 2037
Exeter C: Fox; White, Robinson, Bailey, Daniels, Whiston, Storer, Coughlin, Jepson, Ross, Taylor (Phillips).
Walsall: Gayle M; Evans, Marsh, Watkiss, Ryder, Smith, Ntamark, Tinkler, Cecere (Wright), Reece, McDonald.
Exeter C won 2-1 on aggregate.

WBA (0) 0
Bristol R (0) 0 9123
WBA: Naylor; Fereday, Lilwall, McNally, Raven, Strodder, Ashcroft, Garner (McCue), Taylor, Ampadu, Mellon (O'Regan).
Bristol R: Parkin; Channing, Maddison, Waddock, Clark, Tillson, Sterling, Taylor, Stewart, Skinner, Archer.
WBA won 4-1 on aggregate.

7 SEPT

Northampton T (0) 0
Reading (1) 2 *(Gray, Dillon)* 1631
Northampton T: Sherwood; Parsons, Burnham, Phillips, Terry, Chard, Fleming, Colkin, Gilzean (Aldridge), Brown, Bell.
Reading: Hislop; Ranson, Kerr, McPherson, Williams (Gray), Parkinson, Gilkes, Dillon, Hopkins, Lovell, Gooding (Taylor).
Reading won 5-0 on aggregate.

SECOND ROUND FIRST LEG

21 SEPT

Barnet (0) 1 *(Lynch)*
QPR (2) 2 *(Ferdinand, Barker)* 3569

Barnet: Phillips; Wilson, Rioch, Hoddle, Walker, Barnett D, Cooper, Hall (Evans), Haag, Close (Lynch), Alexander.
QPR: Stejskal; Bardsley, Wilson, Wilkins, Peacock, McDonald, Impey, Barker, Ferdinand, Penrice, Sinclair.

Barnsley (0) 1 *(Archdeacon (pen))*
Peterborough U (0) 1 *(Brissett)* 4549

Barnsley: Watson; Fleming, Bishop, Wilson, Taggart, Anderson, O'Connell, Rammell, Bryson, Redfearn, Archdeacon.
Peterborough U: Bennett; McDonald, Spearing, Bradshaw, Peters, Welsh, Iorfa (Adcock), Hackett, Philliskirk, Cooper, Brissett.

Birmingham C (0) 0
Aston Villa (0) 1 *(Richardson)* 27,815

Birmingham C: Miller; Hiley, Frain, Parris, Dryden, Whyte, Donowa, Smith, Peschisolido (McMinn), Saville, Shutt.
Aston Villa: Spink (Bosnich); Barrett, Staunton, Teale, McGrath, Richardson, Cowans, Townsend, Saunders, Atkinson, Whittingham.

Blackburn R (1) 1 *(Shearer)*
Bournemouth (0) 0 10,773

Blackburn R: Mimms; May, Le Saux, Marker, Hendry, Warhurst (Atkins), Ripley (Makel), Sherwood, Shearer, Newell, Wilcox.
Bournemouth: Bartram; Pennock, Masters, Morris, Watson, Parkinson, O'Connor, McGorry, Fletcher, Cotterill, Leadbitter.

Blackpool (2) 3 *(Bamber 2, Watson)*
Sheffield U (0) 0 6234

Blackpool: Martin; Davies, Cook, Horner, Briggs, Beech, Watson, Bonner, Bamber, Sheedy, Griffiths.
Sheffield U: Tracey; Gage, Gannon, Falconer, Wirmola (Beesley), Pemberton, Bradshaw, Hodges (Ward), Cork, Littlejohn, Whitehouse.

Bolton W (0) 1 *(Kelly (pen))*
Sheffield W (0) 1 *(Bart-Williams)* 11,590

Bolton W: Branagan; Brown, Phillips, Kelly, Darby, Stubbs, Lee, McAteer, Coyle (Green), Thompson, Patterson.
Sheffield W: Woods; Nilsson, King, Palmer, Pearce (Bart-Williams), Walker, Sheridan, Waddle, Bright, Hyde, Sinton.

Crystal Palace (1) 3 *(Gordon, Southgate, Whyte)*
Charlton Ath (0) 1 *(Leaburn)* 9615

Crystal Palace: Martyn; Humphrey, Gordon, Southgate, Young, Coleman, Shaw, Bowry, Whyte, Williams (Salako), Rodger.
Charlton Ath: Salmon; Balmer, Minto, Garland (Pardew), McLeary, Chapple, Newton (Robinson), Grant, Leaburn, Pitcher, Walsh.

Grimsby T (1) 3 *(Dobbin, Mendonca 2)*
Hartlepool U (0) 0 2353

Grimsby T: Crichton; McDermott, Croft, Agnew, Handyside (Lever), Dobbin, Watson (Shakespeare), Gilbert, Daws, Mendonca, Groves.
Hartlepool U: Carter; Cross R, Cross P, McGuckin, MacPhail, Emerson, Thompson (Johnrose), Wratten, West, Honour, Southall.

Huddersfield T (0) 0
Arsenal (2) 5 *(Wright 3, Campbell, Merson)* 14,275

Huddersfield T: Francis; Trevitt, Billy (Collins), Starbuck, Hicks, Dyson, Dunn (Onuora), Robinson P, Booth, Marsden, Wells.
Arsenal: Seaman; Keown, Winterburn, Davis, Linighan, Adams, Jensen (Hillier), Wright, Campbell, Merson (Smith), McGoldrick.

Ipswich T (1) 2 *(Milton, Whitton)*
Cambridge U (0) 1 *(Claridge (pen))* 8654

Ipswich T: Forrest; Stockwell (Goddard), Thompson N, Mason, Wark, Linighan, Williams, Milton, Whitton, Marshall, Guentchev (Yallop).
Cambridge U: Filan; Fensome (Danzey), Barrick, O'Shea, Jeffrey, Daish, Fowler, Claridge, Butler (Nyamah), Clayton, Cheetham.

Lincoln C (1) 3 *(Johnson D, Matthews, Brown)*
Everton (1) 4 *(Rideout 3, Cottee)* 9153

Lincoln C: Pollitt; Smith P, Clarke, Hill (Costello), Brown, Smith M (Flitcroft), Schofield, Baraclough, Johnson D, Matthews, Puttnam.
Everton: Kearton; Holmes, Hinchcliffe, Ebbrell, Jackson, Ablett, Ward (Radosavljevic), Horne, Cottee, Rideout, Beagrie.

Middlesbrough (4) 5 *(Hignett 4, Hendrie)*
Brighton & HA (0) 0 5651

Middlesbrough: Pears; Morris, Liburd, Pollock, Mohan, Whyte, Hendrie, Hignett, Wilkinson, Mustoe, Moore.
Brighton & HA: Rust; Myall, McCarthy, Wilkins, Bissett, Pates (Crumplin), Edwards, Kennedy (Wilkinson), Nogan, Codner, Munday.

Rochdale (1) 1 *(Carey (og))* 4499
Leicester C (1) 6 *(Whitlow, Walsh, Thompson, Oldfield, Speedie, Ormondroyd)*

Rochdale: Hodge; Thackeray, Graham, Reid, Reeves, Butler, Stuart, Doyle, Lancaster, Whitehall, Ryan (Milner).
Leicester C: Ward; Grayson, Whitlow, Carey, Walsh (Joachim), Hill, Oldfield (Gee), Thompson, Speedie, Agnew, Ormondroyd.

Rotherham U (0) 0
Portsmouth (0) 0 3866

Rotherham U: Mercer; Pickering, Jacobs, Banks, Richardson, Law, Goater (Howard), Goodwin, Helliwell, Varadi, Marginson.
Portsmouth: Knight; Gittens, Burns, McLoughlin, Symons, Awford, Butters, Powell, Durnin, Young (Doling), Kristensen.

Sunderland (1) 2 *(Goodman, Gray P)*
Leeds U (1) 1 *(Speed)* 17,101
Sunderland: Chamberlain; Martin Gray, Ord, Bennett, Ferguson, Melville, Owers, Goodman, Armstrong, Gray P, Russell (Michael Gray).
Leeds U: Beeney; Kelly, Dorigo, Hodge, Fairclough, Wetherall, Strachan, Wallace, Deane, McAllister, Speed.

Swansea C (2) 2 *(Torpey, Pascoe)*
Oldham Ath (1) 1 *(Sharp)* 5056
Swansea C: Freestone; Jenkins, Ford, Walker, Harris, Pascoe, Chapple, Bowen, Torpey, Cornforth, Hayes.
Oldham Ath: Hallworth; Fleming, Barlow, Henry, Jobson, Redmond, Adams, Olney, Sharp (Ritchie), Milligan, Bernard.

Tranmere R (1) 5 *(Aldridge 2, Nevin 3)*
Oxford U (0) 1 *(Beauchamp)* 3473
Tranmere R: Nixon; Higgins, Nolan, Brannan, Martindale, Garnett, Kenworthy, Aldridge, Muir, Nevin, Thomas.
Oxford U: Reece; Smart, Ford M, Lewis (Wanless), Robinson, Rogan, Magilton, Beauchamp, Dyer, Penney (Druce), Allen.

Watford (0) 0
Millwall (0) 0 5954
Watford: Sheppard; Dublin, Lavin, Hessenthaler, Holdsworth, Ashby, Dyer, Charlery, Furlong, Porter, Soloman.
Millwall: Keller; Cunningham, Dawes, Roberts, Van Den Hauwe, Stevens, Rae, Verveer, Moralee, Kerr (Goodman), Barber.

Wrexham (0) 3 *(Bennett 2 (1 pen), Paskin)*
Nottingham F (2) 3 *(Collymore 3)* 7860
Wrexham: Morris; Jones B, Hardy, Lake, Sertori, Pejic, Bennett, Phillips, Connolly, Watkin, Cross (Paskin).
Nottingham F: Crossley; Lyttle, Pearce, Warner (Laws), Chettle, Stone, Phillips, Gemmill, Rosario, Collymore, Woan.

22 SEPT

Bradford C (1) 2 *(McCarthy 2)*
Norwich C (0) 1 *(Fox)* 8988
Bradford C: Tomlinson P; Ford, Lawford, Duxbury L, Oliver, Richards, Jewell (McHugh), Robson, McCarthy, Stapleton (Steele), Showler.
Norwich C: Gunn; Culverhouse, Bowen, Newman, Polston, Johnson, Crook, Ekoku (Sutton), Robins, Fox, Eadie.

Burnley (0) 0
Tottenham H (0) 0 16,844
Burnley: Beresford; Farrell, Thompson, Davis, Pender, Randall, Francis, Deary, Heath, Russell, Eyres.
Tottenham H: Walker; Sedgley, Campbell, Samways, Calderwood, Mabbutt, Carr (Caskey), Durie, Dozzell, Sheringham, Anderton.

Coventry C (2) 3 *(Morgan 2, Quinn)*
Wycombe W (0) 0 9615
Coventry C: Ogrizovic; Morgan, Babb, Atherton, Rennie, Williams J (Gayle), Booty, Ndlovu, Wegerle, Quinn (Williams P), Boland.
Wycombe W: Hyde; Cousins, Potter, Crossley, Evans, Ryan, Carroll, Langford (Hemmings), Thompson (Hayrettin), Scott, Guppy.

Exeter C (1) 1 *(Storer)*
Derby Co (1) 3 *(Kitson, Simpson, Gabbiadini)* 5634
Exeter C: Fox; Minett, Robinson, Bailey, Daniels, Whiston, Storer, Coughlin, Jepson, Ross, Wigley (Worthington).
Derby Co: Taylor; Charles, Forsyth, Kuhl, Short, Wassall, Pembridge, Williams, Kitson, Gabbiadini, Simpson.

Fulham (0) 1 *(Farrell)*
Liverpool (2) 3 *(Rush, Clough, Fowler)* 13,599
Fulham: Stannard; Morgan, Pike, Ferney, Jupp, Thomas, Hails, Onwere, Eckhardt (Farrell), Brazil, Baah.
Liverpool: Grobbelaar; Jones R, Dicks, Hutchison, Wright, Ruddock, Clough, Stewart, Rush, Redknapp (McManaman), Fowler.

Hereford U (0) 0
Wimbledon (1) 1 *(Clarke)* 4872
Hereford U: Judge; Clark H (Abraham), Downs, Davies, Smith, Morris, Hall, Fry, Pike, May, Nicholson.
Wimbledon: Segers; Barton, Joseph (Clarke), Jones, Scales, Fitzgerald, Sanchez, Earle, Fashanu, Holdsworth, Kimble.

Manchester C (1) 1 *(White)*
Reading (1) 1 *(Lovell)* 9280
Manchester C: Coton; Edghill, Brightwell D, McMahon, Curle, Kernaghan, White (Mike), Sheron, Quinn, Flitcroft (Simpson), Groenendijk.
Reading: Hislop; Hopkins, Kerr, McPherson, Williams, Parkinson, Gilkes, Dillon, Quinn, Lovell, Gooding.

Newcastle U (1) 4 *(Cole 3, Bracewell)*
Notts Co (1) 1 *(Srnicek (og))* 25,887
Newcastle U: Srnicek; Venison, Beresford, Bracewell, Kilcline, Watson, Lee, Beardsley, Cole, Clark, Allen.
Notts Co: Cherry; Short, Johnson (Dijkstra), Thomas, Turner, Walker, Simpson (Devlin), Draper, McSwegan, Lund, Wilson.

Southampton (1) 1 *(Moore)*
Shrewsbury T (0) 0 5038
Southampton: Flowers; Kenna, Benali, Charlton (Banger), Moore, Wood, Bennett (Bartlett), Cockerill, Dowie, Maddison, Allen.
Shrewsbury T: Edwards; Withe, Lynch, Patterson, Williams, Blake, Spink, Brown, Summerfield (MacKenzie), Griffiths, Evans.

Stoke C (1) 2 *(Stein 2)*
Manchester U (0) 1 *(Dublin)* 23,327
Stoke C: Prudhoe; Clarkson, Sandford, Cranson, Overson, Orlygsson, Gynn, Foley, Stein, Carruthers, Gleghorn.
Manchester U: Schmeichel; Martin, Irwin, Phelan (Bruce), Kanchelskis, Pallister, Robson (Sharpe), Ferguson, McClair, Hughes, Dublin.

Swindon T (1) 2 *(Summerbee, Mutch)*
Wolverhampton W (0) 0 8649
Swindon T: Digby; Summerbee, Bodin, Moncur, Nijholt, Taylor, Hazard, Mutch, White, Ling, Fenwick.
Wolverhampton W: Stowell; Rankine, Venus, Mountfield, Blades, Shirtliff, Burke, Birch, Small, Kelly D, Keen.

WBA (1) 1 *(Donovan)*
Chelsea (0) 1 *(Shipperley)* 14,919
WBA: Lange; Parsley, Ampadu, Bradley (Mellon), Raven, Burgess, Hunt, Hamilton (Ashcroft), Taylor, O'Regan, Donovan.
Chelsea: Kharine; Clarke, Sinclair, Kjeldbjerg, Dow, Donaghy (Hall), Hoddle, Newton, Shipperley (Spencer), Peacock, Wise.

West Ham U (3) 5 *(Morley 2 (1 pen), Chapman 2, Burrows)*
Chesterfield (0) 1 *(Norris)* 12,823
West Ham U: Miklosko; Rowland, Burrows, Potts, Gale, Bishop, Gordon, Morley, Chapman, Holmes, Marsh.
Chesterfield: Leonard; Hebberd, Carr C, Brien, Carr D, McGugan, Dyche, Norris, Jules (Davies), Cash (Knowles), Curtis.

SECOND ROUND SECOND LEG

5 OCT

Arsenal (0) 1 *(Smith)*
Huddersfield T (1) 1 *(Dunn)* 18,789
Arsenal: Seaman; Dixon, Winterburn, Parlour, Linighan, Bould, McGoldrick (Heaney), Campbell, Smith, Jensen (Selley), Limpar.
Huddersfield T: Francis; Trevitt, Billy (Roberts), Starbuck (Onuora), Hicks, Jackson, Dunn, Robinson P, Booth, Dyson, Wells.
Arsenal won 6-1 on aggregate.

Bournemouth (0) 0
Blackburn R (0) 0 10,321
Bournemouth: Bartram; Pennock, Masters, Morris, Watson (O'Connor), Parkinson, Leadbitter, McGorry, Fletcher, Cotterill, Beardsmore (Wood).
Blackburn R: Mimms; Berg, Le Saux, Marker, Hendry, Moran, Ripley, Sherwood, Shearer, Gallacher (Atkins), Wilcox.
Blackburn R won 1-0 on aggregate.

Cambridge U (0) 0
Ipswich T (0) 2 *(Marshall, Kiwomya)* 6979
Cambridge U: Filan; Rowett, Barrick (Fowler), O'Shea, Jeffrey, Daish, Livett, Claridge, Danzey (Nyamah), Clayton, Hunter.
Ipswich T: Forrest; Stockwell, Thompson, Mason, Wark, Linighan, Williams, Slater, Milton, Marshall, Kiwomya.
Ipswich T won 4-1 on aggregate.

Charlton Ath (0) 0
Crystal Palace (0) 1 *(Armstrong)* 5224
Charlton Ath: Salmon; Pitcher, Minto, Balmer, Chapple, McLeary, Robinson, Newton (Grant), Leaburn, Nelson, Pardew.
Crystal Palace: Martyn; Humphrey (Gordon), Coleman, Southgate, Young, Thorn, Shaw, Bowry, Armstrong, Whyte, Rodger (Salako).
Crystal Palace won 4-1 on aggregate.

Chesterfield (0) 0
West Ham U (0) 2 *(Allen M, Boere)* 4890
Chesterfield: Marples; Hebberd, Carr C, Brien, Madden, Dennis, Dyche (Bettney), Norris (Taylor), Davies, Curtis, Jules.
West Ham U: Miklosko; Breacker, Burrows, Potts, Gale, Bishop, Butler (Allen M), Morley, Chapman (Boere), Marsh, Holmes.
West Ham U won 7-1 on aggregate.

Hartlepool U (0) 0
Grimsby T (1) 2 *(Groves, Dobbin)* 1385
Hartlepool U: Carter; Cross R, Cross P, McGuckin, MacPhail, Emerson, West (Olsson), Wratten, Houchen, Honour, Johnrose.
Grimsby T: Crichton; McDermott, Agnew, Futcher, Rodger, Dobbin, Childs, Gilbert (Jobling), Groves, Mendonca, Shakespeare.
Grimsby T won 5-0 on aggregate.

Liverpool (2) 5 *(Fowler 5)*
Fulham (0) 0 12,541
Liverpool: Grobbelaar; Jones R, Dicks, Hutchison, Wright, Ruddock, Clough, Stewart, Rush, Redknapp, Fowler.
Fulham: Stannard; Morgan, Pike, Ferney, Angus, Thomas, Eckhardt, Onwere, Farrell, Brazil, Kelly (Jupp).
Liverpool won 8-1 on aggregate.

Notts Co (0) 1 *(McSwegan)* 6068
Newcastle U (3) 7 *(Allen 2 (1 pen), Beardsley, Cole 3, Lee)*
Notts Co: Cherry; Short (Thomas), Dijkstra, Turner, Walker, Cox, Devlin, Draper, McSwegan, Agana, Legg (Lund).
Newcastle U: Hooper; Venison (Kilcline), Beresford, Bracewell (Sellars), Scott, Watson, Lee, Beardsley, Cole, Clark, Allen.
Newcastle U won 11-2 on aggregate.

Oxford U (0) 1 *(Wanless)*
Tranmere R (1) 1 *(Irons)* 2644
Oxford U: Reece; Collins, Ford M, Lewis, Robinson, Rogan, Magilton, Beauchamp, Druce (Ford R), Penney (Wanless), Allen.
Tranmere R: Nixon; Higgins, Nolan, Brannan, Martindale (Branch), Garnett, Kenworthy, Irons, Malkin, Nevin, Thomas.
Tranmere R won 6-2 on aggregate.

Peterborough U (1) 3 *(Philliskirk, McGlashan, Oliver)*
Barnsley (0) 1 *(Bryson)* 3533
Peterborough U: Bennett; McDonald, Oliver, Bradshaw, Peters, Welsh, Adcock, Hackett (Iorfa), Philliskirk, Cooper (McGlashan), Brissett.
Barnsley: Watson; Fleming, Bishop, Wilson, Taggart, Anderson, O'Connell, Liddell (Jackson), Bryson (Eaden), Redfearn, Archdeacon.
aet; Peterborough U won 4-2 on aggregate.

Portsmouth (3) 5 *(Stimson, McLoughlin, Durnin, Walsh, Burns)*
Rotherham U (0) 0 4589
Portsmouth: Knight; Gittens, Pethick, McLoughlin (Aspinall), Symons (Burns), Awford, Powell, Stimson, Durnin, Walsh, Kristensen.
Rotherham U: Mercer; Hutchings, Jacobs, Banks (Helliwell), Richardson, Law, Page, Goodwin, Goater (Kiwomya), Varadi, Wilder.
Portsmouth won 5-0 on aggregate.

Sheffield U (0) 2 *(Davison, Ward)*
Blackpool (0) 0 10,615
Sheffield U: Tracey; Bradshaw, Barnes (Ward), Falconer, Tuttle, Beesley (Hoyland), Hodges, Rogers, Flo, Davison, Whitehouse.
Blackpool: Martin; Davies, Cook, Horner, Briggs, Beech, Watson, Bonner (Gouck), Rodwell, Sheedy, Griffiths (Mitchell).
Blackpool won 3-2 on aggregate.

Wimbledon (3) 4 *(Ardley, Jones, Holdsworth, Earle)*
Hereford U (0) 1 *(Hall)* 2151
Wimbledon: Segers; Ardley, Blackwell (Blissett), Jones, Scales, Fitzgerald, Clarke, Earle, Fashanu, Holdsworth, Kimble.
Hereford U: Judge; Clark H, Downs, Davies, Smith, Morris (Brain), Hall, Fry, May (Pickard), Anderson, Nicholson.
Wimbledon won 5-1 on aggregate.

Wolverhampton W (0) 2 *(Mountfield, Burke)*
Swindon T (0) 1 *(Summerbee)* 11,756
Wolverhampton W: Stowell; Simkin, Venus, Burke, Mountfield, Shirtliff, Cook, Kelly J, Mills, Kelly D, Keen.
Swindon T: Hammond; Summerbee, Bodin, MacLaren, Nijholt, Taylor, Moncur, Mutch, Maskell (White), Hazard, Fenwick.
Swindon T won 3-2 on aggregate.

Wycombe W (1) 4 *(Ryan, Scott, Evans, Cousins)*
Coventry C (0) 2 *(Morgan, Babb)* 5933
Wycombe W: Hyde; Cousins, Crossley, Kerr, Evans, Ryan, Carroll, Hayrettin (Hutchinson), Hemmings (Horton), Scott, Guppy.
Coventry C: Ogrizovic; Morgan, Babb, Atherton, Rennie, Kruszynski, Williams J (Jenkinson), Gayle, Wegerle, Flynn (Busst), Boland.
aet; Coventry C won 5-4 on aggregate.

6 OCT

Aston Villa (0) 1 *(Saunders)*
Birmingham C (0) 0 35,856
Aston Villa: Bosnich; Cox, Staunton, Teale, McGrath, Richardson, Cowans, Townsend (Houghton), Saunders, Atkinson, Daley.
Birmingham C: Miller; Hiley (Scott), Frain, Dryden, Mardon, Whyte, Donowa (Fenwick), Tait, Hooper, Smith, Shutt.
Aston Villa won 2-0 on aggregate.

Brighton & HA (0) 1 *(Nogan)*
Middlesbrough (2) 3 *(Wilkinson, Hignett, Hendrie)* 2074
Brighton & HA: Rust; Myall, Chapman, Edwards (Geddes), Munday, Wilkinson, Funnell, Simmonds, Nogan, Codner, Tuck.
Middlesbrough: Pears; Morris (Todd), Liburd, Stamp, Mohan, Whyte, Hendrie, Hignett, Wilkinson, Mustoe, Moore (Fleming).
Middlesbrough won 8-1 on aggregate.

Chelsea (1) 2 *(Wise 2)*
WBA (1) 1 *(Taylor)* 11,959
Chelsea: Kharine; Clarke, Sinclair, Kjeldbjerg, Dow (Spencer), Donaghy, Hoddle, Newton, Shipperley, Peacock, Wise.
WBA: Lange; O'Regan, Ampadu, Bradley, Raven, Burgess, Hunt, Hamilton, Taylor, Mellon, Donovan.
Chelsea won 3-2 on aggregate.

Derby Co (1) 2 *(Gabbiadini, Johnson)*
Exeter C (0) 0 10,569
Derby Co: Taylor; Charles (Kavanagh), Forsyth, Pembridge, Short, Wassall, Harkes, Williams (Johnson), Kitson, Gabbiadini, Simpson.
Exeter C: Fox; Minett, Robinson, Bailey, Daniels, Brown, Storer, Coughlin, Jepson, Ross, Wigley.
Derby Co won 5-1 on aggregate.

Everton (1) 4 *(Rideout, Snodin, Cottee 2)*
Lincoln C (0) 2 *(Johnson D, Baraclough (pen))* 8375
Everton: Southall; Holmes, Hinchcliffe (Snodin), Ebbrell, Jackson, Ablett, Ward, Horne, Cottee, Rideout (Radosavljevic), Beagrie.
Lincoln C: Pollitt; Smith P, Clarke, Schofield, Brown, Carbon, West (Costello), Baraclough (Hill), Johnson D, Matthews, Puttnam.
Everton won 8-5 on aggregate.

Leeds U (0) 1 *(Whelan)*
Sunderland (2) 2 *(Goodman, Gray P)* 22,265
Leeds U: Beeney; Kelly, Dorigo, Newsome, Fairclough, Wetherall (Rocastle), Strachan (Strandli), Whelan, Deane, McAllister, Speed.
Sunderland: Chamberlain; Ball, Martin Gray, Bennett (Michael Gray), Ferguson, Melville, Owers, Goodman, Gray P (Howey), Ord, Armstrong.
Sunderland won 4-2 on aggregate.

Leicester C (1) 2 *(Ormondroyd, Joachim)*
Rochdale (1) 1 *(Lancaster)* 7612
Leicester C: Ward; Grayson, Lewis, Oldfield, Willis, Hill, Joachim, Thompson, Speedie (Gee), Agnew (Philpott), Ormondroyd.
Rochdale: Hodge; Thackeray, Jones, Reid (Graham), Reeves, Butler, Stuart, Doyle, Lancaster, Ryan, Milner (Flounders).
Leicester C won 8-2 on aggregate.

Manchester U (0) 2 *(Sharpe, McClair)*
Stoke C (0) 0 41,387
Manchester U: Schmeichel; Irwin, Martin (Giggs), Bruce, Sharpe, Pallister, Robson, Kanchelskis, McClair, Hughes, Keane.
Stoke C: Muggleton; Clarkson, Cowan, Cranson, Overson, Orlygsson, Gynn, Foley, Stein, Sturridge (Carruthers), Gleghorn.
Manchester U won 3-2 on aggregate.

Millwall (2) 4 *(Huxford, Murray, Moralee, Verveer)*
Watford (2) 3 *(Porter, Nogan, Hessenthaler)* 5381
Millwall: Keller; Beard (Kennedy), Cunningham, Roberts, Van Den Hauwe (Murray), Stevens, Huxford, Verveer, Dolby, Moralee, Barber.
Watford: Sheppard; Dublin, Lavin, Hessenthaler, Holdsworth, Ashby, Dyer (Johnson), Soloman, Furlong, Porter, Nogan (Inglethorpe).
aet; Millwall won 4-3 on aggregate.

Norwich C (0) 3 *(Ekoku, Fox, Sutton)*
Bradford C (0) 0 12,787
Norwich C: Gunn; Culverhouse, Bowen, Megson, Polston, Goss, Crook, Newman, Ekoku (Robins), Fox, Sutton.
Bradford C: Bowling; Ford, Lawford, Duxbury L, Oliver, Richards, Jewell (Partridge), Robson, McCarthy, Williams, Showler.
Norwich C won 4-2 on aggregate.

Nottingham F (1) 3 *(Black, Crosby, Collymore)*
Wrexham (0) 1 *(Pejic)* 11,619

Nottingham F: Wright; Laws, Lyttle, Crosby (Harvey), Chettle, Stone, Phillips, Gemmill, Howe, Collymore, Black.
Wrexham: Morris; Jones B, Hardy, Humes, Sertori, Pejic, Bennett, Phillips, Connolly, Watkin, Cross (Paskin).
Nottingham F won 6-4 on aggregate.

Oldham Ath (2) 2 *(Halle, Bernard)*
Swansea C (0) 0 6433

Oldham Ath: Gerrard; Fleming, Barlow, Milligan, Jobson (Palmer), Redmond, Halle, Bernard, Sharp, Beckford, Adams.
Swansea C: Freestone; Jenkins, Ford (Hodge), Walker, Harris, Pascoe, Perrett, Cook, McFarlane (Torpey), Cornforth, Hayes.
Oldham Ath won 3-2 on aggregate.

QPR (2) 4 *(Allen 3, Impey)*
Barnet (0) 0 6314

QPR: Stejskal; Bardsley, Wilson, Wilkins, Peacock, McDonald, Impey (Brevett), Barker, White, Allen, Sinclair.
Barnet: Phillips; Wilson (Finnigan), Rioch, Hoddle (Close), Walker, Barnett D, Marwood, Cooper, Haag, Evans, Alexander.
QPR won 6-1 on aggregate.

Reading (0) 1 *(Quinn)*
Manchester C (1) 2 *(Lomas, Quinn)* 10,052

Reading: Hislop; Ranson (Taylor), Kerr, McPherson, Williams (Gilkes), Parkinson, Hopkins, Dillon, Quinn, Lovell, Gooding.
Manchester C: Dibble; Edghill, Phelan, McMahon, Curle, Kernaghan, Simpson, Sheron, Quinn, Flitcroft, Lomas.
Manchester C won 3-2 on aggregate.

Sheffield W (0) 1 *(Bright)*
Bolton W (0) 0 16,194

Sheffield W: Woods; Nilsson, King (Pearce), Palmer, Walker, Bart-Williams, Sheridan, Waddle (Watson), Bright, Hyde, Sinton.
Bolton W: Branagan; Brown, Phillips, Kelly (Coyle), Seagraves, Stubbs, Lee, McAteer, Thompson, McGinlay, Patterson.
Sheffield W won 2-1 on aggregate.

Shrewsbury T (1) 2 *(Summerfield, Brown)*
Southampton (0) 0 5247

Shrewsbury T: Edwards; Taylor, Withe, Evans, Williams, Blake, Brown, Summerfield, Spink, Griffiths, Patterson.
Southampton: Flowers; Adams, Benali, Moore, Hall, Monkou, Moody (Wood), Reid (Cockerill), Dowie, Maddison, Allen.
Shrewsbury T won 2-1 on aggregate.

Tottenham H (1) 3 *(Sheringham 2, Howells)*
Burnley (1) 1 *(Eyres)* 20,614

Tottenham H: Thorstvedt; Kerslake, Campbell, Samways, Calderwood, Mabbutt, Sedgley, Durie (Howells) (Moran), Anderton, Sheringham, Caskey.
Burnley: Beresford; Monington, Thompson, Davis, Pender, Randall, Peel (Francis), Deary, Heath, Russell, Eyres.
Tottenham H won 3-1 on aggregate.

THIRD ROUND

26 OCT

Arsenal (0) 1 *(Wright)*
Norwich C (1) 1 *(Crook)* 24,539

Arsenal: Seaman; Dixon, Winterburn, Parlour, Linighan, Adams, Jensen, Wright, Smith, Merson (Campbell), McGoldrick (Davis).
Norwich C: Gunn; Culverhouse, Bowen, Butterworth, Prior, Goss, Crook, Newman, Eadie, Fox, Sutton.

Blackburn R (0) 0
Shrewsbury T (0) 0 10,603

Blackburn R: Mimms; Berg, Wright, Sherwood, Hendry, May, Ripley, Atkins, Shearer, Newell, Gallacher.
Shrewsbury T: Edwards; Hockaday, Withe, Taylor, Williams, Blake, Brown, MacKenzie, Summerfield, Griffiths (Spink), Patterson.

Blackpool (1) 2 *(Watson 2)*
Peterborough U (1) 2 *(Hackett, Adcock)* 4863

Blackpool: Martin; Davies, Cook, Horner, Briggs, Gouck, Watson, Bonner, Rodwell (Quinn), Sheedy (Beech), Griffiths.
Peterborough U: Bennett; McDonald, Spearing, Bradshaw, Howarth, Welsh, Adcock, Hackett, Iorfa, McGlashan, Brissett.

Everton (0) 2 *(Beagrie, Watson)*
Crystal Palace (0) 2 *(Thorn, Southgate)* 11,547

Everton: Southall; Holmes, Hinchcliffe, Ebbrell, Watson, Ablett, Stuart (Radosavljevic), Horne, Cottee, Barlow (Snodin), Beagrie.
Crystal Palace: Martyn; Humphrey, Coleman, Southgate, Young, Thorn, Shaw, Rodger, Armstrong, Whyte (Salako), Gordon.

Manchester C (0) 1 *(White)*
Chelsea (0) 0 16,713

Manchester C: Coton; Edghill, Phelan, McMahon, Curle, Kernaghan, White, Sheron (Vonk), Quinn, Flitcroft, Lomas.
Chelsea: Kharine; Clarke, Sinclair, Kjeldbjerg, Johnsen, Donaghy (Lee), Hoddle, Fleck (Shipperley), Cascarino, Newton, Barnard.

Oldham Ath (1) 2 *(Beckford, Sharp)*
Coventry C (0) 0 10,071

Oldham Ath: Gerrard; Fleming, Makin, Brennan, Halle, Redmond, Bernard, Beckford, Sharp, Milligan, Holden.
Coventry C: Ogrizovic; Borrows, Babb, Rennie, Morgan, Williams P (Gayle), McGrath, Ndlovu (Quinn), Wegerle, Flynn, Boland.

Portsmouth (0) 2 *(Durnin, Walsh)*
Swindon T (0) 0 12,554

Portsmouth: Knight; Gittens, Doling (Burns), McLoughlin, Symons, Awford, Neill, Stimson, Durnin, Walsh, Chamberlain (Pethick).
Swindon T: Digby; Summerbee, Bodin, MacLaren (Horlock), Nijholt, Taylor, Moncur, Mutch, Fjortoft, Ling (Maskell), Fenwick.

Sunderland (0) 1 *(Gray P)* 23,692
Aston Villa (2) 4 *(Atkinson 2, Richardson, Houghton)*
Sunderland: Chamberlain; Martin Gray (Lawrence), Ord (Bennett), Bell, Melville, Owers, Atkinson, Goodman, Gray P, Smith, Armstrong.
Aston Villa: Bosnich; Barrett, Small, Teale, McGrath, Richardson, Daley, Townsend, Atkinson, Parker, Whittingham (Houghton).

Tranmere R (2) 4 *(Aldridge 2, Vickers, Irons (pen))*
Grimsby T (0) 1 *(Okorie)* 5204
Tranmere R: Nixon; Higgins, Nolan, Brannan (Martindale), Irons, Vickers, Kenworthy, Aldridge (Muir), Malkin, Nevin, Thomas.
Grimsby T: Crichton; McDermott, Jobling, Futcher, Lever, Dobbin, Childs, Shakespeare (Watson), Daws (Okorie), Mendonca, Groves.

27 OCT

Derby Co (0) 0
Tottenham H (0) 1 *(Barmby)* 19,855
Derby Co: Taylor; Kavanagh (Charles), Forsyth, Kuhl (Williams), Short, Wassall, Harkes, Johnson, Kitson, Pembridge, Simpson.
Tottenham H: Thorstvedt; Edinburgh, Campbell, Samways, Calderwood, Mabbutt, Sedgley, Barmby, Dozzell, Howells, Anderton.

Liverpool (2) 3 *(Rush 3)*
Ipswich T (1) 2 *(Marshall, Mason (pen))* 19,058
Liverpool: Grobbelaar; Jones R, Dicks, Nicol, Wright, Ruddock, Stewart, Harkness (Hutchison), Rush, Matteo, Fowler.
Ipswich T: Forrest; Stockwell, Thompson, Mason, Wark, Linighan, Williams (Milton), Whelan, Marshall, Guentchev (Whitton), Slater.

Manchester U (2) 5 *(Bruce 2, McClair, Sharpe, Hughes)*
Leicester C (0) 1 *(Hill)* 41,344
Manchester U: Schmeichel; Phelan, Martin, Bruce, Sharpe (Giggs), Pallister (Irwin), Robson, Kanchelskis, McClair, Hughes, Keane.
Leicester C: Ward; Grayson, Lewis (Mills), Oldfield, Whitlow, Hill, Joachim, Thompson, Speedie, Agnew, Ormondroyd.

Middlesbrough (0) 1 *(Hendrie)*
Sheffield W (0) 1 *(Palmer)* 14,765
Middlesbrough: Pears; Morris, Liburd, Fleming, Mohan, Whyte, Hendrie, Hignett, Wilkinson, Mustoe, Moore.
Sheffield W: Pressman; Nilsson, Worthington, Palmer, Pearce, Walker (Williams), Jones (Jemson), Waddle, Bright, Hyde, Sinton.

Nottingham F (1) 2 *(Black, Collymore)*
West Ham U (0) 1 *(Morley)* 17,857
Nottingham F: Wright; Laws, Pearce, Crosby, Chettle, Stone, Phillips, Gemmill, Glover (Webb), Collymore, Black.
West Ham U: Miklosko; Breacker, Burrows, Potts, Martin, Bishop, Butler (Allen M), Morley, Chapman, Marsh, Holmes.

QPR (2) 3 *(Sinclair, Barker, Ferdinand)*
Millwall (0) 0 14,190
QPR: Stejskal; Bardsley, Wilson, Wilkins (Holloway), Peacock, McDonald, Impey, Barker, Ferdinand, Allen, Sinclair.
Millwall: Keller; Cunningham, Dolby, Roberts, Van Den Hauwe, Stevens, Rae, Verveer (Huxford), Kennedy, Moralee, Barber (Goodman).

Wimbledon (1) 2 *(Barton, Holdsworth)*
Newcastle U (1) 1 *(Sellars)* 11,531
Wimbledon: Segers; Barton, Kimble, Jones, McAllister, Fitzgerald, Clarke (Ardley), Earle, Fashanu, Holdsworth, Fear.
Newcastle U: Hooper; Venison, Beresford, Bracewell, Scott, Watson, Lee, Beardsley, Mathie, Allen (Kilcline), Sellars.

THIRD ROUND REPLAYS

9 NOV

Peterborough U (2) 2 *(Rush, Bradshaw)*
Blackpool (1) 1 *(Howarth (og))* 4418
Peterborough U: Bennett; Greenman, McDonald, Bradshaw, Howarth, Welsh, Adcock, Hackett, Rush, McGlashan, Brissett (Barnes).
Blackpool: Martin; Davies, Cook, Horner, Briggs, Gouck (Mitchell), Watson, Bonner, Rodwell, Quinn, Griffiths.

Shrewsbury T (1) 3 *(Summerfield 2, MacKenzie (pen))*
Blackburn R (1) 4 *(Newell 2 (1 pen), May, Pearce) aet* 7330
Shrewsbury T: Edwards; Hockaday, Withe, Taylor, Williams, Lynch, Brown, Smith (Clarke W), Summerfield, MacKenzie, Spink.
Blackburn R: Mimms; May, Wright, Batty, Hendry, Le Saux, Ripley, Sherwood, Newell, Gallacher (Pearce), Marker.

10 NOV

Crystal Palace (1) 1 *(Southgate)* 14,662
Everton (0) 4 *(Watson 2, Ward (pen), Young (og))*
Crystal Palace: Martyn; Humphrey, Mortimer, Southgate, Young, Coleman, Shaw, Rodger, Armstrong, Whyte, Bowry (Williams).
Everton: Southall; Holmes, Ablett, Ebbrell, Watson, Jackson, Ward, Horne, Cottee, Rideout (Barlow), Radosavljevic.

Norwich C (0) 0
Arsenal (2) 3 *(Wright 2, Merson)* 16,319
Norwich C: Gunn; Culverhouse, Bowen, Butterworth, Polston, Newman, Crook, Eadie (Sutch), Sutton, Fox, Goss.
Arsenal: Seaman; Dixon, Keown, Selley, Linighan, Bould, Jensen, Wright, Smith, Merson, Limpar.

Sheffield W (1) 2 *(Watson, Palmer)*
Middlesbrough (1) 1 *(Mustoe)* 19,482
Sheffield W: Pressman; Williams (Poric), Worthington, Palmer, Pearce, Walker, Jones, Waddle, Watson (Hyde), Jemson, Sinton.
Middlesbrough: Pears; Fleming, Liburd, Mustoe, Mohan, Barron, Kavanagh (Illman), Hignett, Stamp, Peake, Moore.

FOURTH ROUND

30 NOV

Arsenal (0) 0
Aston Villa (1) 1 *(Atkinson)* 26,453
Arsenal: Seaman; Dixon (Davis), Winterburn, Morrow, Bould, Keown, Jensen (Campbell), Wright, Smith, Merson, McGoldrick.
Aston Villa: Bosnich; Barrett, Cox, Teale, McGrath, Richardson, Houghton, Townsend, Saunders (Daley), Atkinson, Parker.

Everton (0) 0
Manchester U (1) 2 *(Hughes, Giggs)* 34,052
Everton: Southall; Jackson, Hinchcliffe, Snodin (Radosavljevic), Watson, Ablett, Ward (Barlow), Horne, Cottee, Stuart, Ebbrell.
Manchester U: Schmeichel; Parker, Irwin, Bruce, Kanchelskis, Pallister, Cantona, Ince, Robson (Ferguson), Hughes, Giggs.

Peterborough U (0) 0
Portsmouth (0) 0 6141
Peterborough U: Bennett; Greenman, Spearing, Bradshaw, Howarth, Welsh, Adcock, Hackett (Barnes), McGlashan, Ebdon, Cooper.
Portsmouth: Knight; Gittens, Kristensen, McLoughlin, Butters, Awford, Neill, Stimson, Durnin, Walsh, Dobson (Daniel).

Tranmere R (0) 3 *(Brannan 2, Aldridge)*
Oldham Ath (0) 0 9477
Tranmere R: Nixon; Higgins, Nolan, Brannan, Proctor, Vickers, Morrissey, Aldridge, Malkin, Nevin, Thomas.
Oldham Ath: Hallworth; Fleming, Makin, Halle, Jobson, Redmond, Adams, Ritchie (Palmer), Sharp, Bernard, Holden.

1 DEC

Liverpool (1) 1 *(Molby (pen))*
Wimbledon (0) 1 *(Earle)* 19,290
Liverpool: Grobbelaar; Jones R, Harkness, Redknapp, Wright, Ruddock, Matteo, Molby, Rush, Barnes (Walters), Fowler.
Wimbledon: Segers; Barton, McAllister, Jones, Scales, Fitzgerald, Ardley, Earle, Fashanu (Clarke), Holdsworth, Joseph.

Nottingham F (0) 0
Manchester C (0) 0 22,195
Nottingham F: Crossley; Lyttle, Pearce, Cooper, Chettle, Webb, Phillips, Gemmill, Bohinen, Bull (Glover), Black.
Manchester C: Coton; Vonk, Phelan, McMahon, Curle, Kernaghan, White, Sheron, Simpson, Mike, Lomas.

QPR (1) 1 *(Meaker)*
Sheffield W (1) 2 *(Jemson, Jones)* 13,253
QPR: Stejskal; Bardsley, Wilson, Wilkins, Peacock, McDonald, Impey (White), Barker, Ferdinand, Allen, Meaker.
Sheffield W: Pressman; Nilsson, Worthington, Palmer, Walker, Hyde, Jemson, Waddle, Bright, Jones, Bart-Williams (Poric).

Tottenham H (0) 1 *(Campbell)*
Blackburn R (0) 0 22,295
Tottenham H: Thorstvedt; Kerslake (Austin), Edinburgh, Samways, Calderwood, Sedgley, Caskey, Barmby, Anderton, Dozzell, Campbell.
Blackburn R: Mimms; May, Le Saux, Batty, Hendry, Berg (Pearce), Ripley, Sherwood, Shearer, Newell, Gallacher.

FOURTH ROUND REPLAYS

14 DEC

Wimbledon (1) 2 *(Holdsworth, Earle)*
Liverpool (1) 2 *(Ruddock, Segers (og))* 11,343
Wimbledon: Segers; Barton, McAllister, Jones, Scales, Fitzgerald, Ardley, Earle, Fashanu, Holdsworth, Fear (Clarke).
Liverpool: Grobbelaar; Jones R, Nicol, Redknapp, Wright (Harkness), Ruddock, McManaman, Molby (Walters), Rush, Barnes, Fowler.
aet; Wimbledon won 4-3 on penalties.

15 DEC

Manchester C (1) 1 *(Vonk)*
Nottingham F (2) 2 *(Webb, Cooper)* 14,117
Manchester C: Coton; Edghill, Phelan, McMahon, Curle, Vonk, White, Sheron, Kernaghan, Flitcroft, Lomas.
Nottingham F: Crossley; Lyttle, Pearce, Cooper, Chettle, Stone, Phillips, Gemmill (Webb), Bohinen, Collymore, Black.

Portsmouth (0) 1 *(Kristensen)*
Peterborough U (0) 0 9634
Portsmouth: Knight; Gittens (Russell), Butters, McLoughlin, Symons, Awford, Neill, Doling (Hall), Durnin, Walsh, Kristensen.
Peterborough U: Bennett; Greenman, Spearing, Bradshaw, Howarth, Welsh, Adcock, McGlashan, Furnell (Barnes), Ebdon, Halsall (Brissett).

FIFTH ROUND

11 JAN

Wimbledon (0) 1 *(Holdsworth)*
Sheffield W (0) 2 *(Watson, Bright)* 8784
Wimbledon: Segers; Barton, Elkins, Jones, Scales, Fitzgerald, Clarke (Blissett), Earle, Fashanu, Holdsworth, Ardley.
Sheffield W: Pressman; Linighan B, Coleman, Palmer, Pearce, Walker, Jones, Hyde, Watson, Bright, Sinton.

12 JAN

Manchester U (1) 2 *(Giggs, Cantona)*
Portsmouth (1) 2 *(Walsh 2)* 43,794
Manchester U: Schmeichel; Parker, Irwin, Bruce, Kanchelskis, Pallister, Cantona, Robson, McClair (Dublin), Hughes (Keane), Giggs.
Portsmouth: Knight; Dobson, Daniel, McLoughlin, Symons (Chamberlain), Awford, Stimson (Doling), Durnin, Powell, Walsh, Kristensen.

Tottenham H (0) 1 *(Caskey)*

Aston Villa (0) 2 *(Houghton, Barrett)* 31,408

Tottenham H: Thorstvedt; Kerslake, Edinburgh, Samways, Calderwood, Sedgley, Caskey, Barmby, Anderton, Dozzell, Campbell (Hendry).
Aston Villa: Bosnich; Barrett, Staunton, Teale, McGrath, Richardson, Houghton, Townsend, Saunders, Atkinson, Parker.

26 JAN

Nottingham F (0) 1 *(Gemmill)*

Tranmere R (0) 1 *(Malkin)* 20,066

Nottingham F: Crossley; Lyttle, Pearce, Cooper, Chettle, Stone (Black), Phillips, Gemmill, Bull (Webb), Glover, Woan.
Tranmere R: Nixon; Higgins, Nolan, Brannan, Hughes, O'Brien, Morrissey, Aldridge, Malkin, Nevin (Irons), Thomas.

FIFTH ROUND REPLAYS

Portsmouth (0) 0

Manchester U (1) 1 *(McClair)* 24,950

Portsmouth: Knight; Neill, Daniel, McLoughlin, Symons, Awford, Chamberlain (Powell), Creaney, Durnin, Walsh, Kristensen.
Manchester U: Schmeichel; Parker, Irwin, Bruce, Kanchelskis, Pallister, Cantona, Ince, McClair, Keane, Giggs.

29 JAN

Tranmere R (1) 2 *(Nevin, Thomas)*

Nottingham F (0) 0 12,578

Tranmere R: Nixon; Higgins (Mungall), Nolan (Irons), Brannan, Hughes, O'Brien, Morrissey, Aldridge, Malkin, Nevin, Thomas.
Nottingham F: Crossley; Lyttle, Pearce, Cooper, Chettle, Black, Phillips, Gemmill, Webb (Bohinen), Collymore (Glover), Woan.

SEMI-FINAL FIRST LEG

13 FEB

Manchester U (1) 1 *(Giggs)*

Sheffield W (0) 0 43,294

Manchester U: Schmeichel; Parker, Irwin, Bruce, Kanchelskis, Pallister, Cantona, Ince, Keane, Hughes, Giggs.
Sheffield W: Pressman; Nilsson, Coleman, Palmer, Pearce, Walker, Hyde, Waddle (Bart-Williams), Hirst, Bright, Sinton.

16 FEB

Tranmere R (2) 3 *(Nolan, Hughes, Aldridge)*

Aston Villa (0) 1 *(Atkinson)* 17,140

Tranmere R: Nixon; Garnett, Nolan, Brannan, Hughes, O'Brien, Irons, Aldridge, Malkin, Nevin, McGreal.
Aston Villa: Bosnich; Barrett, Staunton (Froggatt), Cox, McGrath, Richardson, Houghton, Townsend, Saunders, Atkinson, Daley.

SEMI-FINAL SECOND LEG

27 FEB

Aston Villa (2) 3 *(Saunders, Teale, Atkinson)*

Tranmere R (1) 1 *(Aldridge (pen))* 40,593

Aston Villa: Bosnich; Cox (Fenton), Barrett, Teale, McGrath, Richardson, Houghton (Ehiogu), Townsend, Saunders, Atkinson, Daley.
Tranmere R: Nixon; Higgins, Nolan, Brannan, Hughes (Thomas), O'Brien, Irons, Aldridge, Malkin, Nevin (Morrissey), McGreal.
Aggregate 4-4 aet; Aston Villa won 5-4 on penalties.

2 MAR

Sheffield W (1) 1 *(Hirst)* 34,878

Manchester U (3) 4 *(McClair, Kanchelskis, Hughes 2)*

Sheffield W: Pressman; Nilsson, Coleman, Palmer, Pearce, Walker, Bart-Williams, Hyde, Hirst, Bright, Sinton (Watson).
Manchester U: Schmeichel; Parker, Irwin, Bruce, Kanchelskis, Pallister, Keane, Ince, McClair, Hughes, Giggs.
Manchester U won 5-1 on aggregate.

FINAL at Wembley

27 MAR

Aston Villa (1) 3 *(Atkinson, Saunders 2 (1 pen))*

Manchester U (0) 1 *(Hughes)* 77,231

Aston Villa: Bosnich; Barrett, Staunton (Cox), Teale, McGrath, Richardson, Daley, Townsend, Saunders, Atkinson, Fenton.
Manchester U: Sealey; Parker, Irwin, Bruce (McClair), Kanchelskis, Pallister, Cantona, Ince, Keane, Hughes, Giggs (Sharpe).
Referee: K. Cooper (Pontypridd).

LEAGUE CUP ATTENDANCES

Totals

Season	*Attendances*	*Games*	*Average*
1960/61	1,204,580	112	10,755
1961/62	1,030,534	104	9,909
1962/63	1,029,893	102	10,097
1963/64	945,265	104	9,089
1964/65	962,802	98	9,825
1965/66	1,205,876	106	11,376
1966/67	1,394,553	118	11,818
1967/68	1,671,326	110	15,194
1968/69	2,064,647	118	17,497
1969/70	2,299,819	122	18,851
1970/71	2,035,315	116	17,546
1971/72	2,397,154	123	19,489
1972/73	1,935,474	120	16,129
1973/74	1,722,629	132	13,050
1974/75	1,901,094	127	14,969
1975/76	1,841,735	140	13,155
1976/77	2,236,636	147	15,215
1977/78	2,038,295	148	13,772
1978/79	1,825,643	139	13,134
1979/80	2,322,866	169	13,745
1980/81	2,051,576	161	12,743
1981/82	1,880,682	161	11,681
1982/83	1,679,756	160	10,498
1983/84	1,900,491	168	11,312
1984/85	1,876,429	167	11,236
1985/86	1,579,916	163	9,693
1986/87	1,531,498	157	9,755
1987/88	1,539,253	158	9,742
1988/89	1,552,780	162	9,585
1989/90	1,836,916	168	10,934
1990/91	1,675,496	159	10,538
1991/92	1,622,337	164	9,892
1992/93	1,558,031	161	9,677
1993/94	1,744,120	163	10,700

THE FOOTBALL TRUST
Helping the game

The Football Trust exists to help the game at all levels. It receives some £23m annually from the Government in the 1990 Budget reduction in pool betting duty and £14m from Littlewoods Spot the Ball competition.

The Trust's main task is to assist the professional game to fund capital works in line with the recommendations of the Taylor Report. Trust grants have been awarded to English and Scottish League clubs for capital works including new stadia and stands, and seating and roofing initiatives.

Schedule of Major Project Grants Offered during 1993/94

Club	Total Project Cost	Trust Grant	Finance Raised by Club	Major Project
Barnsley	2,400,000	1,000,000	1,400,000	New South Stand
Birmingham City	4,000,000	2,000,000	2,000,000	New Spion Kop & Tilton Road Stands
Blackburn Rovers	5,800,000	500,000	5,300,000	New Blackburn End Stand
Burnley	2,300,000	750,000	1,550,000	New Beehole End Stand
Bury	592,000	444,000	148,000	South Stand redevelopments
Cardiff City	563,000	250,000	313,000	Seat & cover Popular Bank & Canton Stand
Celtic	72,719	54,000	18,719	Seating in North Enclosure
Charlton Athletic	2,000,000	1,400,000	600,000	New East Stand
	783,816	450,000	333,816	New West Stand
Chelsea*	7,700,000	2,000,000	5,700,000	New North Stand
Cowdenbeath	385,000	184,000	201,000	Main Stand redevelopment
Crystal Palace*	3,100,000	1,567,882	1,532,118	New Holmesdale Road Stand
Dundee United	2,200,000	500,000	1,700,000	New East Stand
	315,000	207,000	108,000	Seating in West Stand
Grimsby Town	704,000	460,000	244,000	Seat Osmond, Findus & Pontoon Stands
Hamilton Academical*	6,000,000	1,000,000	5,000,000	New Stadium
Hartlepool United	525,000	383,000	142,000	New East Stand
Ipswich Town	19,105	7,300	11,805	Seating in Pioneer Stand
Leicester City	250,000	150,000	100,000	Seat Kop & Supporters' Enclosure
Lincoln City	1,200,000	750,000	450,000	New Sincil Bank End Stand
Luton Town	211,000	107,000	104,000	Seat Kenilworth Road End
Motherwell	1,200,000	725,000	475,000	New North Stand
Nottingham Forest*	3,900,000	400,000	3,500,000	New Trent End Stand
Oldham Athletic	471,000	215,000	256,000	Main Stand redevelopment
Peterborough United	136,000	95,000	41,000	Seat Main Stand paddock
Queens Park Rangers	1,800,000	840,000	960,000	Seat Loftus Road & Main Stand paddocks
	672,500	300,000	372,500	Seat School End
Scarborough	116,588	87,441	29,147	Cover Seamer Road End
Sheffield United*	700,000	400,000	300,000	Seat Bramall Lane Terrace
	3,100,000	427,369	2,672,631	John Street Stand redevelopment
Sheffield Wednesday	640,000	200,000	440,000	Seat Kop & north west corner
Southampton	1,600,000	1,000,000	600,000	Seat North & South Stands
St Mirren	1,430,000	1,000,000	430,000	West Stand
Stockport County*	319,069	239,302	79,767	New Barlow Stand
	1,200,000	570,000	630,000	New Cheadle End Stand
Swansea City	2,260,000	500,000	1,760,000	Seat & cover North Bank
Swindon Town	1,350,000	800,000	550,000	New Shrivenham Road Stand
Torquay United	300,000	240,000	60,000	Cover Popular End
West Bromwich Albion	3,900,000	2,000,000	1,900,000	New Birmingham Road, Halfords Lane & Smethwick End Stands
West Ham United*	4,900,000	2,000,000	2,900,000	New South Stand
	71,115,797	**26,203,294**	**44,912,503**	

* *This offer replaces an earlier offer (either in part or entirely)*

Continued overleaf

JEWSON'S FAMILY INVOLVEMENT

Walsall topped the field in the third year of the Jewson Family Football Awards and collected a cheque for £25,000 in London in April for their splendid efforts to attract families to watch soccer.

The Saddlers had boosted their facilities at their new Bescot Stadium—a far cry from the days when spectators stood braving the elements at the "laundry end" of Fellows Park—with several refinements including changing rooms, toilets and extra benefits for disabled fans.

The West Midlands club, who just missed the play-offs from the Football League's Third Division, had stiff opposition from the champions of the other two divisions, namely Bristol City and Leyton Orient. Both improved the lot of spectators at Ashton Gate and Brisbane Road respectively.

The tangible effect of the improvements is that Bristol City's average attendances in the family section were lifted by 250 percent to 1,600 per game. City also run a comprehensive programme of activities linked with the community including a women's and girls' football section.

Open days too, have proved very popular with the West Country folk in Bristol and the idea is spreading fast throughout other clubs in the League.

Facilities for disabled fans have always figured high in the quest for grants from the Jewson scheme which have totalled more than £1.3 million. Those clubs which collected cheques for their efforts in this direction, were: Middlesbrough (Div 1), Plymouth Argyle (Div 2) and Lincoln City (Div 3).

For the second year Jewsons recognized the crucial part played by groundsmen in the professional game. Their rewarding of these key men spread to the Premier League as well as the Football League so the scheme embraces the 92 clubs in England and Wales.

Forty-six-year-old John Cooper, Hull City's groundsman for the past five years, collected the top award for his work at Boothferry Park which was judged the best by referees officiating at the Humberside venue throughout the season.

The clubs were divided into three regions, Northern, Midlands and Southern, and then into divisional sections for further rewards and Cooper was adjudged the best.

The awards were: **National**—John Cooper (Hull City); Premier Steve Braddock (Arsenal), Div. 1—Steve Mulloy (Nottingham Forest), Div. 2—Cooper, Div. 3—Roger Johnson (Walsall).

Regional (Northern, Southern, Midlands): Premier—Reg Summers (Liverpool), Braddock, Tony Eden (Aston Villa). Div. 1—Steve Millard (Sunderland), John Plummer (Millwall), Mulloy; Div. 2—Cooper, Charles Hasler (Leyton Orient), Ian Darler (Cambridge United); Div. 3—Gary Kent (Chester), Bill File (Gillingham), Johnson.

Disability Awards: Div. 1—Middlesbrough. Div. 2—Plymouth Argyle; Div. 3—Lincoln City.

Progress Awards: Div. 1—Leicester City; Div. 2—Bristol Rovers; Div. 3—Bury.

TREVOR WILLIAMSON

The Trust also awards grants to enable clubs to complete important safety work and facility improvements. Initiatives include facilities for people with disabilities, family enclosures, new toilets, and anti-hooligan measures such as closed circuit television, stewarding and transport improvements.

Last season, the Trust contributed some £3.7m towards improving the safety and comfort of supporters throughout England and Scotland, bringing the Trust's total support for safety and improvement work to almost £74m. A further £1.5m was awarded to assist clubs with policing and stewarding costs, and £280,000 towards anti-hooligan measures including the installation and upgrading of CCTV at English and Scottish League grounds.

The remainder of the Trust's income is allocated to projects for the general benefit of the game in the Pyramid and at grass roots level. Grants have been made towards essential safety work at non-League clubs and the Trust has joined forces with the Football Association to provide support for pitch and changing accommodation improvements and the provision of hard surface play areas and floodlighting. Grants are also available to assist junior clubs with the purchase of kit and equipment.

ANGLO-ITALIAN CUP 1993–94

PRELIMINARY ROUND

31 AUG

Grimsby T (1) 2 *(Mendonca, Daws)*
Middlesbrough (0) 1 *(Hendrie)* 996

Grimsby T: Crichton; McDermott, Croft, Rodger, Handyside, Dobbin, Childs, Gilbert, Groves, Mendonca, Woods (Daws).
Middlesbrough: Pears; Morris (Hignett), Barness, Mustoe (Pollock), Mohan, Whyte, Fleming, Kavanagh, Wilkinson, Hendrie, Wright.

Notts Co (1) 3 *(Legg 2, Lund)*
Derby Co (0) 2 *(Harkes, Johnson)* 3276

Notts Co: Cherry; Wilson, Johnson, Short, Simpson, Walker, Devlin, Dijkstra, Lund, Slawson, Legg.
Derby Co: Taylor; Charles, Forsyth, Kuhl, Short, Wassall, Harkes, Pembridge, Kitson, Johnson, Simpson.

Peterborough U (2) 4 *(Iorfa, McGlashan, Cooper (pen), Philliskirk)*
Leicester C (1) 3 *(Oldfield (pen), Gee 2)* 3830

Peterborough U: Barber; McDonald, Spearing, McGlashan, Peters, Welsh, Iorfa, Cooper, Philliskirk, Bradshaw, Brissett.
Leicester C: Poole; Grayson, Lewis, Smith, Willis, Gibson, Lowe, Gee, Oldfield, Ormondroyd, Philpott.

Portsmouth (2) 3 *(Burns, Daniel, Powell)*
Bristol C (1) 1 *(Munro)* 2318

Portsmouth: Horne; Awford, Burns, McLoughlin, Gittens, Butters, Price, Daniel (Hall), Durnin, Walsh (Powell), Blake.
Bristol C: Welch; Munro, Scott, Aizlewood, Shail, Osman, Robinson, Brown, Baird, Martin (Allison), Shelton (Edwards).

Sunderland (0) 2 *(Goodman 2)*
Tranmere R (0) 0 6771

Sunderland: Norman; Russell, Martin Gray (Sampson), Bennett, Ferguson, Melville, Owers, Goodman, Cunnington (Atkinson), Gray P, Armstrong.
Tranmere R: Nixon; Higgins, Nolan (Kenworthy) (Muir), Irons, Martindale, Vickers, Nevin, Aldridge, Malkin, Brannan, Thomas.

Watford (1) 2 *(Dyer, Inglethorpe)*
Luton T (1) 1 *(Preece)* 2854

Watford: Sheppard; Dublin, Lavin, Hessenthaler (Johnson), Holdsworth, Alsford, Dyer, Nogan, Willis (Inglethorpe), Porter, Soloman.
Luton T: Sommer; James, Johnson, Hughes, Peake, Dreyer, Telfer, Hartson, Dixon (Williams), Houghton (Oakes), Preece.

Wolverhampton W (1) 3 *(Kelly D, Bull, Keen)*
Stoke Co (2) 3 *(Carruthers 2, Gleghorn)* 9092

Wolverhampton W: Stowell; Rankine, Thompson, Burke, Blades, Venus, Birch (Cook), Thomas, Regis (Bull), Kelly D, Keen.
Stoke C: Muggleton; Butler, Sandford, Cranson, Overson (Kevan), Orlygsson, Gynn, Foley, Stein, Carruthers (Shaw), Gleghorn.

1 SEPT

Millwall (2) 2 *(Roberts, Verveer)*
Charlton Ath (1) 2 *(Leaburn, Grant)* 4003

Millwall: Keller; Cunningham, Dawes, Roberts, Thatcher (Luscombe), Stevens, Rae, Verveer, Moralee (Murray), Kerr, Barber.
Charlton Ath: Salmon; Balmer, Pitcher, Sturgess, McLeary, Chapple, Robinson, Grant, Leaburn, Nelson (Newton), Pardew (Garland).

7 SEPT

Bristol C (1) 2 *(Allison, Rosenior)*
Oxford U (0) 1 *(Ford M)* 1515

Bristol C: Welch; Wyatt, Fowler (McIntyre), Martin, Thompson, Pennyfather, Allison, Brown, Morgan (Durbin), Rosenior, Gavin.
Oxford U: Reece; Smart, Ford M, Lewis, Cusack, Collins, Ford R (Narbett), Beauchamp, Dyer (Druce), Wanless, Allen.

Charlton Ath (2) 4 *(Balmer, Walsh, Garland, Leaburn)*
Crystal Palace (1) 1 *(Williams)* 3868

Charlton Ath: Salmon; Balmer, Sturgess, Garland, Chapple, Pardew, Grant, Pitcher, Leaburn, Nelson (Gorman), Walsh (Primus).
Crystal Palace: Martyn; Humphrey, Gordon, Southgate, Newman (Ndah), Sinnott, Shaw, O'Connor (Whyte), Armstrong, Williams, Rodger.

Luton T (0) 1 *(Dixon)*
Southend U (0) 1 *(Payne)* 1823

Luton T: Sommer; Linton, Johnson, Hughes, Peake, Dreyer (Greene), Williams, Hartson (Woolgar), Dixon, Houghton, Preece.
Southend U: Sansome; Hunt, Powell, Bodley, Scully, Harding (Ansah), Jones K, Payne, Lee, Otto, Angell.

Middlesbrough (1) 3 *(Hendrie, Wilkinson 2 (1 pen))*
Barnsley (0) 0 5173

Middlesbrough: Pears; Fleming, Liburd, Pollock, Mohan, Whyte, Hendrie, Hignett, Wilkinson, Mustoe (Stamp), Moore (Wright).
Barnsley: Butler; Eaden, Archdeacon, Wilson, Bishop, Robinson, Bullock, Rammell, Bryson, Redfearn, Williams (Sheridan).

Stoke C (1) 2 *(Cranson, Stein (pen))*
Birmingham C (0) 0 8633

Stoke C: Muggleton; Butler, Sandford, Cranson, Harbey, Lowe (Kelly), Gynn, Foley, Stein (Carruthers), Regis, Gleghorn.
Birmingham C: Miller; Scott, Rogers, Peer, Clarkson, Mardon, Fenwick, Tait, Moulden (Robinson), Morgan (Black), Potter.

Tranmere R (0) 1 *(Malkin)*
Bolton W (2) 2 *(McGinlay, Coyle)* 2786

Tranmere R: Nixon; Higgins, Nolan, Irons, Mungall, Garnett, Kenworthy, Muir, Malkin, Brannan, Branch.
Bolton W: Davison; Parkinson, Phillips, Green, Darby, Winstanley, Lee, Fulton, Coyle, McGinlay, Patterson.

8 SEPT

Derby Co (0) 3 *(Simpson, Kitson, Kuhl)*
Nottingham F (0) 2 *(Glover, Gemmill)* 6654

Derby Co: Taylor; Charles, Forsyth, Kuhl, Short, Wassall, Johnson, Williams, Kitson, Gabbiadini, Simpson.
Nottingham F: Crossley; Lyttle, Laws, Blatherwick, Chettle, Stone, Gemmill, Glover (McGregor), Rosario, Collymore, Woan.

Leicester C (0) 0
WBA (0) 0 3058

Leicester C: Ward; Smith (Coatsworth), Lewis, Oldfield, Carey, Hill, Lowe, Gee (Davison), Grayson, Philpott, Ormondroyd.
WBA: Naylor; Coldicott, Lilwall, McNally, Burgess, Strodder, Ashcroft, Mellon, Garner, Heggs, Ampadu.

14 SEPT

Barnsley (0) 2 *(Archdeacon, O'Connell)*
Grimsby T (1) 1 *(Dobbin)* 1627

Barnsley: Watson; Eaden, Robinson, Sheridan, Taggart, Bishop, O'Connell, Redfearn, Rammell (Jackson), Bryson, Archdeacon (Liddell).
Grimsby T: Crichton; McDermott, Croft, Rodger, Handyside, Dobbin, Childs (Shakespeare), Gilbert, Daws (Agnew), Jemson, Groves.

Birmingham C (0) 2 *(Wratten 2)*
Wolverhampton W (0) 2 *(Burke, Mills)* 2710

Birmingham C: Miller; Hiley, Potter, Fenwick, Whyte, Mardon, McMinn, Tait (Wratten), Black, Smith, Donowa.
Wolverhampton W: Stowell; Ashley, Venus, Burke, Blades, Shirtliff, Birch, Thomas, Mills, Rankine, Keen.

Bolton W (0) 2 *(Coyle 2)*
Sunderland (0) 0 3460

Bolton W: Davison; Parkinson, Phillips, Roscoe, Seagraves, Winstanley, Green, Fulton, Coyle, Thompson, Patterson.
Sunderland: Chamberlain; Martin Gray, Ord, Bennett, Ferguson, Melville, Owers, Goodman, Armstrong, Gray P, Russell (Howey).

Crystal Palace (2) 3 *(Williams, Armstrong (pen), Whyte)*
Millwall (0) 0 2712

Crystal Palace: Martyn; Humphrey, Gordon, Southgate, Newman, Ndah, Shaw, Massey, Armstrong (Whyte), Williams, Rodger (O'Connor).
Millwall: Emberson; Huxford, Dawes, Roberts, Van Den Hauwe, Stevens (Cunningham), Rae, Verveer (Kerr), Murray, Dolby, Luscombe.

Oxford U (0) 0
Portsmouth (2) 2 *(Durnin, Hall)* 2987

Oxford U: Kee; Smart, Ford M (Collins), Lewis, Robinson, Rogan, Magilton, Beauchamp, Dyer, Narbett (Wanless), Allen.
Portsmouth: Knight; Stimson (Walsh), Burns, McLoughlin, Symons, Awford, Blake (Powell), Hall, Chapman, Kristensen, Durnin.

15 SEPT

Nottingham F (0) 1 *(Collymore)*
Notts Co (1) 1 *(Lund)* 7347

Nottingham F: Crossley; Laws, Pearce, Blatherwick, Chettle, Stone, Phillips, Webb (Black), Rosario, Collymore, Woan.
Notts Co: Cherry; Dijkstra (Simpson), Johnson, Wilson, Turner P, Walker, Devlin, Draper, McSwegan, Slawson, Legg (Lund).

Southend U (3) 3 *(Otto, Lee, Ansah)*
Watford (0) 0 1881

Southend U: Sansome; Poole, Powell, Jones K, Howell, Bressington, Ansah (Martin), Payne, Lee, Otto, Harding (Mooney).
Watford: Sheppard; Dublin, Lavin, Hessenthaler, Ashby, Alsford, Dyer, Inglethorpe, Furlong (Charlery), Porter, Soloman.

WBA (1) 3 *(McNally, Mellon, Darton)*
Peterborough U (0) 1 *(Okorie)* 4168

WBA: Naylor; Parsley, Darton, McNally, Raven, Strodder, Ashcroft, Garner, Heggs (Taylor), Mellon, Ampadu.
Peterborough U: Barber; Bradshaw, Spearing, McGlashan, Peters, Welsh, Stanhope, Boardman, Philliskirk, Okorie (Adcock), Brissett (Hackett).

INTERNATIONAL STAGE

Group A

12 OCT

Bolton W (1) 5 *(McGinlay 2, McAteer, Thompson, Phillips)*
Ancona (0) 0 3448

Bolton W: Branagan; Brown, Phillips, Kelly, Seagraves, Stubbs, Lee, McAteer (Green), Thompson, McGinlay, Patterson.
Ancona: Armellini; Sogliano, Centofanti, Arno, Fontana, Bruniera, Turchi, Ragagnin, Bertarelli (Mazzarano), Hervatin (Pecoraro), Carruezzo.

Brescia (1) 2 *(Chapple (og), Ambrosetti)*
Charlton Ath (0) 0 3500

Brescia: Cusin; Flamigni, Mezzanotti, Bonometti, Brunetti, Ziliani, Schenardi, Di Muri, Lerda (Torchio), Borgogni (Domini), Ambrosetti.
Charlton Ath: Salmon (Vaughan); Balmer, Sturgess, Pardew, McLeary, Chapple, Newton, Pitcher, Leaburn, Nelson (Mills), Grant.

Notts Co (2) 4 *(Legg, Lund 2, Draper)*
Ascoli (0) 2 *(Spinelli, D'Ainzara)* 3756

Notts Co: Cherry; Gallagher, Thomas, Turner P, Walker, Palmer (Catlin), Devlin, Draper, McSwegan, Lund, Legg.
Ascoli: Zinetti; Mancini, Mancuso, Bosi, Fusco, Zanoncelli (Di Rocco), Cavaliere, Bugiardini, Spinelli, Troglio, Sanseverino (D'Ainzara).

Pisa (0) 3 *(Lorenzini, Rovaris, Polidori)*
Middlesbrough (0) 1 *(Hendrie)* 500

Pisa: Ambrosio; Dondo, Brandani, Baldini, Susic, Fiorentini, Rocco, Rotella, Lorenzini, Rovaris (Bombardini), Gabbriellini (Polidori).
Middlesbrough: Collett; Fleming, Liburd, Todd, Mohan, Whyte, Hignett, Kavanagh, Hendrie, Mustoe, Illmann (Taylor).

Group B

Fiorentina (1) 3 *(Batistuta 2, Orlando)*
Southend U (0) 0 2000

Fiorentina: Scalabrelli (Mareggini); Faccenda, Tosto, Zironelli, Bruno, D'Anna (Pioli), Dell'Oglio, Amerini, Batistuta, Orlando, Banchelli.
Southend U: Sansome; Poole (Lee), Powell, Jones K, Howell, Bressington, Gridelet, Payne, Mooney, Otto, Angell (Hunt).

Padova (0) 0
Portsmouth (0) 0 1117

Padova: Dal Bianco; Cuicchi, Tentoni, Ruffini, Rosa, Ottoni, Pellizzaro, Coppola, Giordano, Cardini (Nunziata), Maniero (Galderisi).
Portsmouth: Knight; Blake (Pethick), Dobson, Butters, Stimson, Hall (Chamberlain), Kristensen, Burns, Doling, Durnin, Powell.

Stoke C (1) 2 *(Carruthers, Orlygsson)*
Cosenza (0) 1 *(Fabris)* 5183

Stoke C: Prudhoe; Clarkson, Cowan, Cranson, Overson, Orlygsson, Sturridge, Lowe, Stein, Carruthers, Gleghorn.
Cosenza: Betti; Sconziano (Caramel), Matrone, Napoli, Civero, Vanigli, Fabris, Signorelli, Lemme, Fiore (Maiellaro), Rubino.

WBA (1) 1 *(Taylor)*
Pescara (2) 2 *(Borgonovo, Nobile)* 5448

WBA: Naylor; McNally, Ampadu, O'Regan, Strodder, Burgess, Garner (Ashcroft), Hamilton, Taylor, Mellon, Donovan.
Pescara: Savorani; Alfiera, Nobile, Sivebaek, Di Cara, Loseto, Palladini, Compagno (Di Marco), Borgonovo, Ceredi (De Ivliis), Massara.

Group A

9 NOV

Ancona (0) 1 *(Carruezzo)*
Charlton Ath (0) 1 *(Bailey)* 1000

Ancona: Armellini; Fontana, Cangini, Arno, Mazzarano (Vecchiola), Bruniera, Turchi, Ragagnin (De Angelis), Carruezzo, Hervatin, Caccia.
Charlton Ath: Salmon; Brown (Linger), Minto, Garland, Chapple, Balmer, Grant, Pitcher, Bailey, Nelson (Leaburn), Walsh.

Bolton W (1) 3 *(Coyle, McGinlay, Green)*
Brescia (1) 3 *(Ambrosetti 2, Hagi)* 3021

Bolton W: Davison; Parkinson, Phillips, Green, Stubbs, Winstanley, Lee (Thompson), McAteer, Coyle, McGinlay, Patterson (Fulton).
Brescia: Cusin; Mezzanotti, Marangon, Piovanelli, Baronchelli, Ziliani, Neri (Schenardi), Gallo, Ambrosetti, Hagi, Giunta (Di Muri).

Notts Co (2) 3 *(Agana, Devlin, Lund)*
Pisa (1) 2 *(Lorenzini 2)* 3253

Notts Co: Cherry; Gallagher, King, Thomas (Simpson), Johnson, Turner P, Devlin, Draper, Dijkstra (Matthews), Lund, Agana.
Pisa: Antonioli; Lampugnani, Farris, Bosco, Susic, Fasce, Mattei, Rotella, Lorenzini, Cristallini, Muzzi.

Group B

Cosenza (0) 1 *(Fabris)*
Southend U (1) 2 *(Angell 2)* 500

Cosenza: Zunico; Sconziano, Compagno (Matrone), Napoli, Napolitano, Rubino, Fabris, Caramel, Negri, Maiellaro (Fiore), Lemme.
Southend U: Sansome; Gridelet (Howell), Powell, Jones K, Edwards, Bressington, Hunt, Payne, Jones G, Otto (Lee), Angell.

Pescara (1) 2 *(Bivi, Compagno)*
Portsmouth (1) 1 *(Doling)* 2000

Pescara: Savorani, Alfieri, Nobile, Sivebaek, Di Cara, Loseto (De Ivliis), Compagno, Gaudenzi, Bivi (Ceredi), Ferretti, Massara.
Portsmouth: Horne; Pethick, Gittens, Butters (Durnin), Symons, Dobson, Blake, Doling, Hall, Power (Kristensen), Powell.

WBA (2) 3 *(Hamilton, Ottoni (og), Garner)* 2745
Padova (2) 4 *(Montrone, Giordano, Maniero, Ottoni)*

WBA: Naylor; Coldicott, Darton, McNally, Hunter, O'Regan, Garner, Hamilton, Taylor, Ashcroft (Donovan), Heggs.
Padova: Dal Bianco; Cuicchi, Tentoni, Ruffini, Ottoni, Franceschetti, Montrone, Nunziata (Coppola), Maniero (Rosa), Cardini, Giordano.

10 NOV

Stoke C (0) 0
Fiorentina (0) 0 8616

Stoke C: Prudhoe; Butler, Sandford, Cranson, Overson, Orlygsson, Foley, Carruthers, Regis, Cowan, Gleghorn.
Fiorentina: Toldo; Carnasciali, Luppi, Zironelli, Pioli, Bruno, Beltrammi, Effenberg, Batistuta, Amerini, Banchelli.

Group A

16 NOV

Brescia (2) 3 *(Schenardi, Neri 2)*
Notts Co (1) 1 *(Draper)* 2000

Brescia: Cusin; Mezzanotti (Marangon), Di Muri, Brunetti (Borgogni), Piovanelli, Ziliani, Schenardi, Gallo, Ambrosetti, Giunta, Neri.
Notts Co: Cherry; Gallagher, King, Turner P, Johnson, Robinson, Devlin, Draper, Matthews, Lund, Thomas.

Charlton Ath (0) 0
Ascoli (2) 3 *(Menolascina, Bierhoff, Troglio)* 3597

Charlton Ath: Salmon; Newton, Sturgess, Garland, McLeary, Balmer, Grant (Linger), Pitcher, Leaburn, Bailey, Walsh (Mills).
Ascoli: Zinetti; Mancini, Bugiardini, Maini, Di Rocco, Marcato, Menolascina, Bosi, Bierhoff, Troglio, Sanseverino.

Middlesbrough (0) 0
Ancona (0) 0 2985

Middlesbrough: Collett; Fleming (Oliver), Liburd, Gannon (Barron), Mohan, Whyte, Illman, Hignett, Kavanagh, Peake, Moore.
Ancona: Armellini; Fontana, Cangini, Arno (Centofanti), Lizzani, Bruniera, Vecchiola, De Angelis, Caccia, Hervatin, Bertarelli (Varini).

Pisa (1) 1 *(Mattei)*
Bolton W (1) 1 *(Phillips)* 1500
Pisa: Lazzarini; Lampugnani, Farris, Bosco, Susic, Fasce, Rocco, Mattei (Gavazzi), Lorenzini, Rovaris, Polidori (Martini).
Bolton W: Davison; Brown, Phillips, Kelly, Seagraves, Winstanley, McAteer, Stubbs, Coyle (Lee), McGinlay, Thompson.

Group B

Fiorentina (1) 2 *(Banchelli, Antonaccio)*
WBA (0) 0 5000
Fiorentina: Scalabrelli; Carnasciali, Luppi, Iachini, Pioli, D'Anna, Beltrammi (Campolo), Amerini, Banchelli (Robbiati), Zironelli, Antonaccio.
WBA: Naylor; Reid, Ampadu, Hunter, Coldicott, Burgess, Heggs, Hamilton, Taylor, Ashcroft (McNally), Donovan.

Padova (1) 3 *(Maniero 2, Giordano)*
Stoke C (0) 0 1500
Padova: Dal Bianco; Tentoni, Cardini, Ruffini, Rosa, Ottoni, Giordano, Cavezzi (Cardini), Galderisi, Coppola, Maniero.
Stoke C: Prudhoe; Butler, Sandford, Cranson, Overson, Orlygsson, Gynn, Sturridge (Bannister), Regis, Harbey, Gleghorn.

Portsmouth (0) 3 *(Kristensen, Walsh 2)*
Cosenza (0) 0 2961
Portsmouth: Knight; Gittens, Doling (Daniel), Kristensen, Russell, Pethick, Hall, Stimson, Durnin (Blake), Walsh, Dobson.
Cosenza: Betti; Sconziano, Compagno, Napoli, Napolitano, Evangelisti, Fabris, Monza, Marulla, Maiellaro, Caramel.

Southend U (0) 1 *(Lee)*
Pescara (2) 3 *(Compagno, Sivebaek, Nobile)* 3603
Southend U: Sansome; Poole, Powell, Jones K, Edwards (Howell), Bressington, Hunt (Lee), Payne, Jones G, Otto, Angell.
Pescara: Savorani; Alfieri, Nobile, Sivebaek, Di Cara, Loseto, De Ivliis, Ceredi (Palladini), Compagno, Ferretti (Di Toro), Massara.

Group A

24 NOV

Ascoli (1) 3 *(Bierhoff, Menolascina, Maini)*
Middlesbrough (0) 0 1200
Ascoli: Zinetti; Mancini, Bugiardini, Maini, Di Rocco, Marcato, Menolascina, Bosi, Bierhoff, Troglio, Sanseverino (D'Ainzara).
Middlesbrough: Collett; Fleming, Liburd, Barron, Mohan, Peake, Stamp, Hignett (Moore), Kavanagh, Mustoe, Illmann (Johnston).

22 DEC

Ancona (0) 0
Notts Co (0) 1 *(McSwegan)* 1000
Ancona: Armellini; Fontana, Sogliano, Arno, Mazzarano, Bruniera, Cangini, De Angelis (Varini), Agostini, Hervatin, Bertarelli (Bizzani).
Notts Co: Cherry; Cox, Walker, Dijkstra, Johnson, Turner P (Wilson), Devlin, Draper, Lund, McSwegan, Agana.

Ascoli (0) 1 *(Troglio)*
Bolton W (0) 1 *(Seagraves)* 1000
Ascoli: Zinetti; Di Rocco, Bugiardini, Maini (Cavaliere), Pascucci, Marcato, Pierleoni, Bosi, Bierhoff, Troglio (Menolascina), Sanseverino.
Bolton W: Hoult; Parkinson, Phillips, Kelly, Seagraves, Winstanley, McAteer, Stubbs, Coyle (Green), Fleck, Thompson.

Charlton Ath (0) 0
Pisa (2) 3 *(Muzzi 3)* 1452
Charlton Ath: Vaughan; Balmer, Sturgess, Garland (Linger), Chapple, Brown, Robinson, Pardew, Leaburn, Nelson (Grant), Robson.
Pisa: Antonioli; Flamigni, Farris, Bosco, Susic, Fasce, Gavazzi, Mattei, Lorenzini, Cristallini (Baldini), Muzzi (Rovaris).

Middlesbrough (0) 0
Brescia (0) 1 *(Ambrosetti)* 1633
Middlesbrough: Pears; Todd (Barron), Liburd, Mustoe, Mohan, Whyte, Gannon, Kavanagh, Wilkinson, Peake, Moore (Illman).
Brescia: Cusin; Marangon (Domini), Di Muri, Gallo, Baronchelli, Bonometti, Sabau, Piovanelli, Lerda (Neri), Giunta, Ambrosetti.

Group B

Cosenza (1) 2 *(Fabris, Florio)*
WBA (1) 1 *(Taylor)* 139
Cosenza: Betti; Sconziano, Compagno, Napoli, Civero, Vanigli, Fiore, Monza, Fabris, Caramel (Maiellaro), Gazzaneo (Florio).
WBA: Lange; Burgess (Hunter), Lilwall, O'Regan, Raven, Bradley, Ashcroft (Garner), Mellon, Taylor, Heggs, Hamilton.

Pescara (1) 2 *(Palladini, Mendy)*
Stoke C (1) 1 *(Regis)* 2000
Pescara: Savorani; De Ivliis, Nobile, Mendy, Di Cara, Loseto, Ceredi (Bivi), Palladini (Di Marco), Compagno, Ferretti, Massara.
Stoke C: Marshall; Butler, Sandford, Cranson, Overson (Clarkson), Orlygsson, Gynn, Carruthers (Sturridge), Regis, Cowan, Gleghorn.

Portsmouth (1) 2 *(Hall, Dobson)*
Fiorentina (0) 3 *(Banchelli, Flachi, Malusci)* 4338
Portsmouth: Knight; Russell, Dobson, McLoughlin (Aspinall), Symons, Awford, Pethick, Chamberlain (Durnin), Hall, Walsh, Kristensen.
Fiorentina: Scalabrelli; Bruno, Luppi, Tedesco (Flachi), Pioli, Malusci, Campolo (D'Anna), Amerini, Banchelli, Robbiati, Zironelli.

Southend U (0) 5 *(Lee, Edwards, Jones G 2, Otto)*
Padova (1) 2 *(Giordano, Cuicchi)* 1518
Southend U: Sansome; Poole, Powell, Jones K, Edwards, Bodley, Hunt, Payne, Mooney (Jones G), Otto, Lee.
Padova: Dal Bianco; Cuicchi, Tentoni, Ruffini, Rosa, Ottoni (Gabrieli), Giordano (Longhi), Cavezzi, Galderisi, Coppola, Maniero.

SEMI-FINAL FIRST LEG

19 JAN

Brescia (0) 1 *(Sabau)*

Pescara (0) 0 2000

Brescia: Landucci; Marangon (Piovanelli), Di Muri, Domini, Giunta, Bonometti, Schenardi, Sabau, Neri, Hagi, Ambrosetti (Gallo).
Pescara: Savorani; Alfieri, Di Cara, Sivebaek, Righetti, Loseto, De Ivliis, Di Marco (Ceredi), Compagno, Carvevale, Impallomeni (Bivi).

26 JAN

Southend U (1) 1 *(Gridelet)*

Notts Co (0) 0 3706

Southend U: Royce; Poole, Powell, Gridelet, Edwards, Bodley, Hunt, Payne, Jones G (Mooney), Otto, Lee.
Notts Co: Cherry; Johnson, Sherlock, Palmer, Foster, Turner P, Devlin, Draper, Lund, Agana, Legg.

SEMI-FINAL SECOND LEG

16 FEB

Notts Co (0) 1 *(Devlin)*

Southend U (0) 0 5485

Notts Co: Cherry; Palmer, Dijkstra, Turner P, Foster, Johnson (Sherlock), Devlin, Draper, Lund, Legg, McSwegan.
Southend U: Sansome; Poole, Powell, Gridelet, Edwards, Bressington, Hunt, Payne (Sussex), Jones G, Otto, Lee (Mooney).
aet; Notts Co won 4-3 on penalties

Pescara (1) 3 *(Sivebaek, Neri, Massara)*

Brescia (1) 2 *(Hagi, Compagno)* 3500

Pescara: Martinelli; Alfieri, De Ivliis, Di Cara, Mendy (Massara), Nobile, Ceredi, Sivebaek, Compagno, Ferretti (Loseto), Impallomeni.
Brescia: Landucci; Giunta, Di Muri, Piovanelli, Baronchelli, Ziliani, Schenardi (Bonometti), Sabau, Neri, Hagi (Consoli), Gallo.

FINAL at Wembley

20 MAR

Notts Co (0) 0

Brescia (0) 1 *(Ambrosetti)* 17,185

Notts Co: Cherry; Wilson, Dijkstra, Turner P, Johnson, Palmer, Devlin, Draper, Lund, McSwegan (Agana), Legg.
Brescia: Landucci; Marangon, Giunta, Domini, Baronchelli, Bonometti, Schenardi, Sabau, Ambrosetti (Piovanelli), Hagi, Gallo.

AUTOGLASS TROPHY 1993–94

FIRST ROUND

27 SEPT

Scarborough (2) 2 *(Cawthorn, Martin (og))*
Scunthorpe U (0) 2 *(Carmichael 2 (1 pen))* 412
Scarborough: Evans; Knowles, Swales, Calvert, Meyer, Davis, Charles, Thompson (Ashdjian), Henderson, Cawthorn (Horsfield), Young.
Scunthorpe U: Samways; Alexander, Mudd, Hope, Elliott, Bradley, Carmichael, Martin, Juryeff (Sansam), Trebble, Smith.

28 SEPT

Blackpool (1) 1 *(Watson)*
Chester C (1) 2 *(Rimmer, Lightfoot)* 2693
Blackpool: Martin; Davies, Cook, Horner, Briggs, Beech, Watson, Bonner, Bamber (Robinson), Sheedy (Mitchell), Griffiths.
Chester C: Bagnall; Preece, Jakub, Jenkins, Came, Greenall, Thompson, Lightfoot, Rimmer, Leonard, Wheeler.

Carlisle U (1) 2 *(Valentine, Edmondson)*
Preston NE (0) 0 3909
Carlisle U: Day; Burgess, Gallimore, Walling, Valentine, Edmondson, Oghani, Reddish, Thomas (Prins), Davey, Fairweather.
Preston NE: O'Hanlon; Masefield, Callaghan, Whalley, Nebbeling, Moyes, Ainsworth, Lucas, Conroy, Norbury, Raynor.

Fulham (2) 4 *(Farrell 2, Angus, Brazil)*
Brighton & HA (1) 1 *(Nogan)* 1135
Fulham: Harrison; Angus, Pike, Ferney, Jupp, Thomas, Kelly, Onwere, Farrell, Brazil, Mahorn.
Brighton & HA: Rust; Myall, Chapman, Wilkins, Munday, McCarthy (Tuck), Edwards, Crumplin, Nogan, Codner, Wilkinson.

Gillingham (0) 0
Colchester U (0) 0 1091
Gillingham: Barrett; Martin, Watson, Clark, Hague, Breen (Trott), Eeles, Reinelt, Baker, Crane, Dempsey.
Colchester U: Keeley; Betts, Roberts, Grainger, English, Cawley, Dickens, Brown S, Richardson (McDonough), McGavin, Ball.

Hartlepool U (0) 1 *(Honour)*
Darlington (0) 1 *(Painter)* 1454
Hartlepool U: Carter; Cross R, Cross P, McGuckin, MacPhail, Emerson, Peverell, Wratten, Johnrose, Honour, Olsson (West).
Darlington: Collier; Isaacs, Switzer, Himsworth (Shaw), Sunley, Madden, McNab, Gaughan, Chapman, Painter, Pearson.

Hereford U (1) 1 *(May)*
Walsall (0) 0 1044
Hereford U: Judge; Davies, Downs, Abraham, Smith, Morris, Hall, Eversham, May, Fry, Nicholson.
Walsall: Gayle M; Evans, Marsh, Watkiss, Ryder (O'Hara), Smith, Ntamark, Lightbourne, Cecere, Peer, McDonald.

Huddersfield T (1) 3 *(Starbuck, Dunn 2)*
Doncaster R (0) 1 *(Jeffrey)* 1069
Huddersfield T: Francis; Trevitt, Harkness, Starbuck, Hicks, Jackson, Dyson, Robinson P, Onuora (Roberts), Marsden (Dunn), Wells.
Doncaster R: Beasley; Measham, Freeman, Yates, Crosby, Bottomley, Harper, Hulme, Jones, Jeffrey, Prindiville (Moss).

Lincoln C (1) 1 *(Johnson)*
Mansfield T (0) 0 1449
Lincoln C: Pollitt; Clarke (Jones), Hill, Schofield, Brown, Baraclough, West, Costello, Johnson D, Matthews, Puttnam.
Mansfield T: Pearcey; Fleming (Parkin), Platnauer, Fairclough, Gray, Castledine, Noteman, Stringfellow, McLoughlin, Wilkinson, Reed (Wilson).

Plymouth Arg (0) 1 *(Castle)*
Swansea C (1) 3 *(McFarlane, Cook, Perrett)* 2664
Plymouth Arg: Nicholls; Patterson, Naylor (Edworthy), Hill, Comyn, McCall, Barlow, Castle, Nugent, Skinner (Marshall), Dalton.
Swansea C: Freestone; Jenkins, Ford, Walker, Harris, Pascoe, Perrett, Cook, McFarlane (Hodge), Cornforth, Hayes.

Stockport Co (1) 2 *(Preece, Gannon)*
Wigan Ath (0) 0 2393
Stockport Co: Edwards; Gannon, Wallace, Frain, Flynn, Connelly, Miller, Ward, Francis, Ryan, Preece.
Wigan Ath: Farnworth; Rennie, McKearney, Robertson, Skipper, Johnson, Gillespie, Rimmer (Duffy), Gavin, Morton (Carragher), Daley.

Torquay U (0) 0
Bristol R (0) 1 *(McLean)* 2445
Torquay U: Lowe; Barrow, Colcombe, O'Riordan, Moore, Stacey, Trollope, Kelly, Foster, Hodges (Sale), Hathaway.
Bristol R: Parkin; Alexander, Maddison, Browning, Wright, McLean, Sterling, Taylor (Saunders), Stewart, Waddock, Archer.

Wrexham (2) 3 *(Bennett, Cross, Paskin)*
Shrewsbury T (1) 1 *(Taylor)* 2483
Wrexham: Morris; Jones B, Hardy, Lake, Sertori, Pejic, Bennett, Phillips, Connolly, Paskin, Cross.
Shrewsbury T: Edwards; Seabury, Lynch (Withe), Taylor, Williams, Blake, Brough, Clarke, Spink, Patterson, MacKenzie.

Wycombe W (1) 1 *(Scott)*
Barnet (0) 0 2323
Wycombe W: Hyde; Crossley, Potter, Kerr, Creaser, Ryan, Hemmings (Norman), Hutchinson, Hayrettin, Scott, Guppy.
Barnet: Pape; Wilson, Rioch, Hoddle (Close), Walker, Barnett D, Hall, Cooper, Smith, Evans, Alexander.

18 OCT

Doncaster R (0) 1 *(Roche)*
Rotherham U (1) 2 *(Freeman (og), Marginson)* 1626
Doncaster R: Beasley; Measham, Freeman, Harper, Cunningham, Dunphy, Roche, Hulme, Whitmarsh (Chalmers), Turnbull, Williamson.
Rotherham U: Mercer; Pickering, Jacobs, Brien, Richardson, Whitworth, Marginson, Goodwin, Helliwell, Goater, Dolby (Kiwomya).

19 OCT

Barnet (1) 2 *(Walker, Haag (pen))*
Brentford (1) 2 *(Allon 2)* 1269
Barnet: Phillips; Wilson, Haylock, Hoddle, Walker, Barnett D, Marwood, Cooper, Haag, Close (Evans), Alexander.
Brentford: Dearden; Hutchings, Morgan, Bates, Westley, Ratcliffe, Stephenson, Smith (Mundee), Benjamin, Allon, Peters.

Chester C (1) 2 *(Greenall, Came)*
Crewe Alex (1) 2 *(Smith S (pen), Macauley)* 2370
Chester C: Felgate; Preece, Jakub, Jenkins, Came, Greenall, Thompson, Lightfoot, Rimmer, Pugh, Wheeler.
Crewe Alex: Smith M; Booty, Gardiner, Evans, Macauley, Smith S, Collins, Naylor, Walters, Whalley, Rowbotham.

Colchester U (1) 2 *(Kinsella, Brown S)*
Cambridge U (0) 2 *(Clayton, Heathcote)* 1489
Colchester U: Keeley; Locke (Ball), Allpress, Kinsella, English, Cawley, Dickens, Brown S, McDonough (Richardson), McGavin, Smith.
Cambridge U: Sheffield; Rowett, Barrick, O'Shea, Heathcote, Daish, Livett, Claridge, Jeffrey, Clayton, Nyamah (Hunter).

Darlington (0) 0
York C (1) 1 *(Barnes)* 1134
Darlington: Collier; Isaacs, Ball, Himsworth, Sunley, Grogan, Shaw (Ellison), Gaughan, Chapman, Painter, Pearson.
York C: Kiely; McMillan, Hall, Pepper, Tutill, Atkin, McCarthy, Blackstone, Barnes, Swann, Barratt.

Mansfield T (1) 3 *(Stringfellow 2, Reed)*
Chesterfield (1) 1 *(Norris)* 2291
Mansfield T: Ward; Fleming, Platnauer, Holland, Gray, Clarke, Castledine, Stringfellow, McLoughlin, Wilkinson, Reed.
Chesterfield: Marples; Hewitt, Hebberd, Dennis, Carr D, Law, Dyche, Norris, Davies, Carr C, Jules (Taylor).

Preston NE (0) 2 *(Ellis, Ainsworth)*
Burnley (0) 1 *(Eyres)* 4485
Preston NE: Woods; Fensome, Kidd, Whalley, Nebbeling, Moyes, Ainsworth (Burton), Holland, Norbury, Ellis, Raynor.
Burnley: Beresford; Monington, Thompson, Davis, Pender, Randall, Peel, Deary, Heath, Joyce (Francis), Eyres.

Scunthorpe U (0) 1 *(Carmichael)*
Hull C (1) 1 *(Abbott)* 2366
Scunthorpe U: Samways; Alexander, Mudd, Hope, Elliott, Bradley, Juryeff (Watson), Martin, Carmichael, Toman, Smith (White).
Hull C: Fettis; Mitchell, Hobson, Warren, Allison, Abbott (Lowthorpe), Norton, Moran (Hargreaves), Brown, Mann, Atkinson.

Shrewsbury T (1) 2 *(Griffiths, Spink)*
Port Vale (1) 2 *(Kerr, Taylor)* 2192
Shrewsbury T: Edwards; Hockaday, Lynch, Taylor, Williams, Blake, Brown, Spink (Gallen), Griffiths, Patterson (Smith), MacKenzie.
Port Vale: Musselwhite; Aspin, Tankard, Kerr (Kent), Swan, Glover, Jeffers, Porter, Cross, Foyle, Taylor.

Swansea C (2) 2 *(Bowen, Harris)*
Exeter C (0) 0 2071
Swansea C: Freestone; Clode, Cook, Walker, Harris, Pascoe, Bowen, Aspinall, McFarlane (Torpey), Cornforth, Hayes.
Exeter C: Veysey; Tonge (Worthington), Redwood, Darch (Taylor), Daniel, Whiston, Storer, Coughlin, Cooper D, Ross, Wigley.

Walsall (0) 0
Northampton T (0) 0 1897
Walsall: Walker; Evans, Marsh (Lillis), Watkiss, O'Hara, Smith, Ntamark, Lightbourne, Wright, Peer, McDonald.
Northampton T: Richardson; Parsons, Gillard, Phillips, Terry, Chard, Harmon, Aldridge, Gilzean, Brown, Bell.

Wigan Ath (0) 1 *(McKearney (pen))*
Bury (0) 3 *(Stevens 2, Kearney)* 983
Wigan Ath: Farnworth; Carragher, McKearney, Robertson, Strong, Langley, Gillespie, Rimmer, Daley, Morton, Duffy.
Bury: Bracey; Hughes, Stanislaus, Kearney, Jackson, Lucketti, Kelly T, Rigby, Stevens, Carter (Adekola), Mauge.

20 OCT

Brighton & HA (2) 2 *(Geddes, Nogan)*
Reading (0) 2 *(Quinn 2)* 1068
Brighton & HA: Rust; Myall, Tuck, Johnson, Foster, Geddes, Edwards (Simmonds), Farrington, Nogan, Codner, Wilkinson.
Reading: Hislop; Holzman, Kerr, McPherson, Williams, McCance (Lovell), Gilkes, Hopkins, Hartenberger (Quinn), Lambert, Taylor.

Bristol R (1) 3 *(Skinner, Stewart 2)*
Cardiff C (0) 0 2035
Bristol R: Parkin; Channing, Maddison, Browning, Wright, McLean, Sterling, Taylor (Davis), Stewart, Skinner (Clark), Archer.
Cardiff C: Kite; Perry, Searle (Bird), Brazil, Baddeley, Aizlewood, Millar, Richardson, Thompson, Blake, Griffith.

9 NOV

Brentford (0) 2 *(Ratcliffe, Smith)*
Wycombe W (2) 3 *(Scott, Creaser 2)* 3165
Brentford: Dearden; Morgan, Hutchings, Millen, Westley, Ratcliffe, Stephenson, Smith, Peters (Mundee), Allon, Metcalf (Ravenscroft).
Wycombe W: Hyde; Cousins, Horton, Creaser, Evans, Hutchinson, Rogers (Ryan), Langford, Hayrettin, Scott, Guppy (Hemmings).

Burnley (0) 1 *(Russell)*
Carlisle U (1) 2 *(Reeves, Flounders)* 4683
Burnley: Beresford; Monington, Thompson, Davis, Pender, Joyce, Francis, Deary, Heath (Peel), Russell, Eyres.
Carlisle U: Day; Burgess, Gallimore, Walling, Joyce, Edmondson (Fairweather), Thomas, Flounders, Reeves, Davey, Reddish.

Bury (1) 1 *(Kelly T)*
Stockport Co (2) 3 *(Preece 2, Francis)* 1737
Bury: Bracey; Hughes, Stanislaus, Daws, Jackson, Lucketti (Jones), Kelly T, Rigby, Adekola, Carter, Mauge (Mulligan).
Stockport Co: Edwards; Beaumont, Carstairs, Frain, Flynn, Connelly, Miller, Ward (Gannon), Francis, Ryan (James), Preece.

Cambridge U (1) 2 *(Heathcote, Rowett)*
Gillingham (0) 0 1463
Cambridge U: Sheffield; Jeffrey, Barrick (Granville), O'Shea, Heathcote, Daish, Hyde, Claridge, Fowler (Danzey), Rowett, Nyamah.
Gillingham: Banks; Martin, Palmer (Watson), Butler, Green, Hague (Clark), Carpenter, Crane, Baker, Smith, Reinelt.

Cardiff C (0) 2 *(Thompson, Stant)*
Torquay U (0) 0 1642
Cardiff C: Williams; Brazil, Searle, Millar (Wigg), Perry, Aizlewood, Bird (Thompson), Richardson, Stant, Blake, Griffith.
Torquay U: Bayes; Colcombe, Stamps, O'Riordan, Barrow, Curran, Trollope, Burton, Hodges (Foster), Sale, Hathaway.

Chesterfield (0) 1 *(Law)*
Lincoln C (0) 2 *(Hill, Loughlan)* 1475
Chesterfield: Marples; Hewitt, Cash (Carr C), Curtis, Carr D, Law, Dyche, Dennis, Davies, Hebberd, Jules.
Lincoln C: Pollitt; Smith P, Hill, Schofield, Brown, Baraclough, West, Lormor, Johnson D, Matthews (Mardenborough), Loughlan.

Exeter C (0) 1 *(Worthington)*
Plymouth Arg (0) 0 3626
Exeter C: Veysey; Minett, Robinson, Bailey, Brown, Whiston, Redwood (Phillips), Coughlin, Jepson, Ross, Worthington.
Plymouth Arg: Nicholls; Patterson, Naylor, Burrows, Comyn, McCall (Crocker), Burnett, Castle, Nugent, Skinner, Dalton.

Hull C (0) 0
Scarborough (2) 2 *(Davis, Calvert)* 1881
Hull C: Fettis; Norton, Mail, Warren, Dewhurst, Abbott, Lee (Edeson), Moran (Allison), Hargreaves, Windass, Atkinson.
Scarborough: Burridge; Knowles, Swales, Calvert, Davis (Meyer), Rockett, Charles, Murray, Henderson, Thompson, Young.

Northampton T (1) 1 *(Aldridge)*
Hereford U (1) 1 *(Pickard)* 1062
Northampton T: Sherwood; Preston, Gillard, Phillips, Terry, Chard, Harmon (Fleming), Aldridge, Gilzean, Brown, Bell.
Hereford U: Judge; Clark H, Anderson, Davies (Morris), Smith, Reece, Hall, Fry, Pickard, Pike, Nicholson.

Port Vale (0) 0
Wrexham (0) 0 4376
Port Vale: Musselwhite; Aspin, Tankard, Porter (Jeffers), Swan, Glover, Slaven, Van der Laan, Cross (Kerr), Foyle, Taylor.
Wrexham: Marriott; Williams, Hardy, Lake, Humes, Hunter, Durkan (Paskin), Owen (Brammer), Connolly, Watkin, Pugh.

Rotherham U (0) 1 *(Varadi)*
Huddersfield T (1) 1 *(Rowe)* 1598
Rotherham U: Mercer; Wilder, Jacobs, Hurst, Brien, Whitworth, Williams, Goodwin, Howard, Varadi, Hazel (Kiwomya).
Huddersfield T: Francis; Trevitt, Whitney, Mitchell, Dyson, Jackson, Rowe, Logan, Onuora, Booth (Collins), Billy.

York C (1) 2 *(Bushell, Hall)*
Hartlepool U (0) 0 1630
York C: Kiely; Barratt, Hall, Pepper, Tutill, Warburton, McCarthy, Cooper, Barnes (Canham), Bushell (Jordan), Murty.
Hartlepool U: Carter; Cross R, Cross P, McGuckin, MacPhail, Olsson (Halliday), Gilchrist, Wratten (Emerson), Houchen, Johnrose, West.

10 NOV

Reading (0) 1 *(Taylor)*
Fulham (0) 0 2034
Reading: Hislop; Ranson, Taylor, Hopkins, Williams, Gooding (Parkinson), Gilkes, Dillon, Quinn, Lovell, Hartenberger (Kerr).
Fulham: Harrison; Jupp, Ferney, Eckhardt, Angus, Baah, Hails, Bedrossian (Kelly), Farrell, Brazil, Onwere.

16 NOV

Crewe Alex (1) 2 *(Edwards, Naylor)*
Blackpool (2) 2 *(Rodwell, Smith S (og))* 2222
Crewe Alex: Smith M; Booty, Gardiner (Wilson), Evans, Macauley, Smith S, Collins, Naylor, Edwards, Lennon, Rowbotham (Tierney).
Blackpool: Martin; Davies, Cook, Horner, Briggs, Gouck, Watson, Bonner, Rodwell (Quinn), Mitchell, Griffiths.

SECOND ROUND

30 NOV

Cambridge U (1) 2 *(Daish, Rowett)*
Port Vale (1) 4 *(Foyle 2, Taylor, Cross)* 1648
Cambridge U: Filan; Jeffrey, Barrick, O'Shea, Heathcote, Daish, Livett (Hyde), Claridge, Fowler, Rowett, Nyamah (Danzey).
Port Vale: Musselwhite; Aspin, Tankard, Kerr, Swan, Glover, Jeffers, Van der Laan, Cross, Foyle, Taylor.

Carlisle U (1) 2 *(Thomas (pen), Reeves)*
Bury (1) 1 *(Hughes)* 3250
Carlisle U: Elliott; Burgess, Gallimore, Walling, Joyce, Edmondson, Thomas, Graham (Arnold), Reeves, McCreery, Reddish.
Bury: Bracey; Hughes, Stanislaus, Daws, Jackson, Reid, Kelly, Rigby, Powell (Blissett), Carter, Mauge.

Hereford U (0) 1 *(Pickard)*
Brentford (2) 2 *(Mundee 2)* 1049
Hereford U: Judge; Clark H, Anderson, Downs, Smith, Morris, Hall, Harrison, Pickard, Pike, Nicholson.
Brentford: Dearden; Statham, Hutchings, Bates, Westley, Ratcliffe, Ravenscroft (Peters), Gayle, Mundee, Smith, Harvey.

Huddersfield T (0) 0
Preston NE (0) 0 1379
Huddersfield T: Francis; Billy, Whitney, Logan, Dyson, Jackson, Rowe (Dunn), Bullock, Booth, Starbuck, Wells (Collins).
Preston NE: Woods; Fensome, Kidd, Whalley, Lucas, Moyes, Ainsworth, Challender, Conroy (Norbury), Ellis, Raynor.
aet; Huddersfield T won 5-4 on penalties

Lincoln C (0) 3 *(Loughlan, Williams, Matthews)*
Darlington (2) 2 *(Painter, Himsworth)* 1434
Lincoln C: Dickins; Smith P, Hill, Baraclough, Smith M, Brown, Schofield, Lormor, Johnson D, Loughlan (Williams), Dixon (Matthews).
Darlington: Collier; Reed, Pearson, Himsworth, Appleby, Ball, Shaw, Painter, Ellison, Ripley (Isaacs), O'Shaughnessy.

Stockport Co (1) 4 *(Beaumont 2, Frain, Preece)*
Rochdale (0) 0 2484
Stockport Co: Edwards; Beaumont, Todd, Frain, Flynn, Connelly (Barras), Miller, Wallace, Gannon, Ryan (James), Preece.
Rochdale: Hodge; Jones, Oliver (Thackeray), Graham, Reeves, Butler, Stuart, Doyle, Lancaster, Bowden, Ryan (Reid).

1 DEC

Bristol R (1) 2 *(Browning 2)*
Fulham (1) 2 *(Brazil, Maddison (og))* 2882
Bristol R: Parkin; Channing (McLean), Maddison, Browning, Clark, Wright, Sterling, Taylor, Skinner, Waddock, Archer.
Fulham: Stannard; Morgan, Herrera, Eckhardt, Angus, Jupp, Hails (Tierling), Bedrossian (Kelly), Farrell, Brazil, Baah.
aet; Fulham won 4-3 on penalties

Reading (2) 4 *(Hartenberger, Quinn, Lambert, Gooding)*
Northampton T (0) 1 *(Aldridge)* 1811
Reading: Hislop; Gooding, Kerr, Hopkins, Williams, Parkinson, Gilkes, Dillon (McPherson), Quinn, Hartenberger (Lambert), Taylor.
Northampton T: Sherwood; Parsons, Gillard, Phillips, Terry, Chard, Burnham, Aldridge, Gilzean, Brown, Bell.

Scarborough (0) 0
Scunthorpe U (0) 2 *(Carmichael 2)* 679
Scarborough: Oakes; Knowles, Swales, Calvert, Davis, Rockett, Charles, Murray, Henderson, Whitington, Young.
Scunthorpe U: Samways; Alexander, Mudd, Hope, Knill, Bradley, Thompstone, Martin, Carmichael, Thornber (White), Smith.

4 DEC

Wrexham (0) 0
Colchester U (0) 1 *(McDonough)* 1860
Wrexham: Marriott; Pejic, Hardy, Brammer, Humes, Hunter, Bennett, Lake, Connolly, Watkin, Taylor.
Colchester U: Munson; Betts, Roberts, Kinsella, English, Cawley, Ball, Brown, McDonough, McGavin, Smith.

York C (0) 1 *(McCarthy)*
Mansfield T (0) 1 *(Reed)* 1760
York C: Kiely; McMillan, Hall, Pepper, Tutill, Warburton, McCarthy, Cooper (Naylor), Barnes, Bushell, Canham.
Mansfield T: Ward; Fleming, Platnauer, Holland (Perkins), Gray, Castledine (Wilson), Fairclough, Stringfellow, Wilkinson, Parkin, Reed.
aet; Mansfield T won 5-4 on penalties

7 DEC

Chester C (1) 1 *(Lightfoot)*
Rotherham U (0) 0 1553
Chester C: Felgate; Preece, Jakub, Jenkins, Came, Greenall, Bishop, Lightfoot (Whelan), Rimmer, Leonard, Wheeler.
Rotherham U: Mercer; Wilder, Hutchings, Williams, Brien, Marshall, Hazel, Goodwin, Goater (Helliwell), Varadi, Hurst.

Bradford C (1) 2 *(Reid, Tolson)*
Crewe Alex (1) 3 *(Evans, Tierney 2)* 1724
Bradford C: Bowling; Hoyle, Williams, Duxbury L, Blake, Richards, Reid, Robson, Tolson, Duxbury M, Showler.
Crewe Alex: Smith M; Booty, Gardiner, Evans, Hughes, Wilson, Whalley (Murphy), Tierney, Collins, Lennon, Rowbotham.

Swansea C (0) 2 *(Cook, Bowen)*
Exeter C (0) 1 *(Worboys) aet* 1500
Swansea C: Freestone; Clode, Cook, Barnhouse, Harris, Pascoe, Bowen, Jenkins, Torpey (McFarlane), Cornforth (Ford), Perrett.
Exeter C: Veysey; Minett, Brown, Bailey, Daniels, Whiston, Storer, Harris (White), Worboys, Worthington (Robinson), Wigley.

14 DEC

Wycombe W (0) 3 *(Langford, Evans, Guppy)*
Cardiff C (0) 2 *(Griffith, Stant) aet* 2703

Wycombe W: Hyde; Cousins, Horton, Crossley, Evans, Ryan, Carroll, Langford, Shepstone (Thompson), Hemmings, Guppy.
Cardiff C: Grew; Evans T (Millar), Searle, Aizlewood, Baddeley, Perry, Bird (Thompson), Richardson, Stant, Blake, Griffith.

21 DEC

Bournemouth (0) 1 *(Murray)*
Leyton Orient (1) 1 *(Barnett)* 1383

Bournemouth: Bartram; Pennock, Leadbitter, Morris, Watson, Parkinson, O'Connor, McGorry, Fletcher, Cotterill, Wood (Chivers) (Murray).
Leyton Orient: Newell; Hendon, Ludden, Hackett, Bellamy, Cockerill, Carter (Kitchen), Barnett, Cooper (Gamble), West, Bogie.
aet; Leyton Orient won 5-3 on penalties

NORTHERN QUARTER-FINALS

11 JAN

Carlisle U (1) 2 *(Reeves, Thomas)*
Mansfield T (0) 1 *(Gray) aet* 8686

Carlisle U: Caig; Burgess, Gallimore, Walling, Joyce, Edmondson, Thomas, Conway (Reddish), Reeves, Davey, Arnold (Oghani).
Mansfield T: Ward; Fleming (Timons), Platnauer, Holland, Gray, Rees, Noteman (Boothroyd), McLoughlin, Wilkinson, Parkin, Fairclough.

Huddersfield T (2) 3 *(Starbuck 2, Booth)*
Crewe Alex (1) 2 *(Murphy, Naylor) aet* 2287

Huddersfield T: Francis; Billy, Whitney, Bullock, Dyson, Jackson, Rowe (Trevitt), Robinson P, Booth, Currie (Onuora), Starbuck.
Crewe Alex: Smith M; Booty, Gardiner, Evans, Hughes (Edwards), Wilson, Murphy (Abel), Naylor, Collins, Smith S, Rowbotham.

Lincoln C (1) 1 *(Brown)*
Chester C (0) 0 1733

Lincoln C: Pollitt; Smith P, Hill, Brown, Smith M, Hirst, Schofield, Baraclough, Johnson D, Matthews (Williams), Puttnam.
Chester C: Felgate; Preece, Jakub, Jenkins, Came (Bishop), Greenall, Thompson, Lightfoot, Wheeler, Leonard, Pugh (Rimmer).

Stockport Co (0) 2 *(Preece, Francis)*
Scunthorpe U (0) 0 4404

Stockport Co: Edwards; Todd, Wallace, Frain, Flynn, Barras, Miller, Ward, Francis, Beaumont, Preece.
Scunthorpe U: Samways; Alexander, Mudd, Hope, Knill, Bradley, Juryeff, Jobling, Carmichael, Bullimore (Trebble), Smith.

SOUTHERN QUARTER-FINALS

Colchester U (0) 0
Wycombe W (0) 1 *(Guppy)* 2751

Colchester U: Cheesewright; Betts, Allpress, Kinsella, English, Cawley, Ball, Dickens, Campbell (Watts), McDonough, Booty (Cook A).
Wycombe W: Hyde; Cousins, Horton, Kerr, Evans, Ryan (Shepstone), Carroll, Thompson, Stapleton, Hodges, Guppy.

Fulham (0) 1 *(Baah)*
Reading (0) 0 2864

Fulham: Stannard; Jupp, Herrera, Onwere, Angus, Thomas, Hails, Bedrossian, Farrell (Tierling), Brazil, Baah.
Reading: Hislop; Humphrey, Kerr, Hopkins, Williams, Parkinson (Gray), Gooding, Dillon, Quinn, Lovell, Taylor.

Leyton Orient (0) 1 *(Ludden)*
Brentford (0) 0 3683

Leyton Orient: Newell; Hendon, Ludden, Hackett, Bellamy, Cockerill, Carter, Barnett, Howard, West, Bogie.
Brentford: Dearden; Statham, Hutchings, Bates, Westley, Ratcliffe, Smith, Gayle, Mundee, Benjamin (Metcalf), Harvey (Manuel).

Swansea C (0) 1 *(Burns)*
Port Vale (0) 0 2630

Swansea C: Freestone; Jenkins, Cook, Ford, Harris, Pascoe, Bowen, Rush, Torpey, Burns, Perrett.
Port Vale: Musselwhite; Aspin, Stokes, Kerr, Swan, Glover, Slaven, Van der Laan (Kent), Porter, Cross (Jeffers), Taylor.

NORTHERN SEMI-FINAL

8 FEB

Carlisle U (1) 2 *(Walling, Robinson)*
Lincoln C (0) 1 *(Johnson D) aet* 6246

Carlisle U: Caig; Gallimore, Robinson, Walling, Joyce, Murray, Thomas, Flounders (Oghani), Reeves, Davey, Reddish.
Lincoln C: Pollitt; Smith P, Baraclough, Campbell, Brown, Hirst, Parkinson (Matthews), Costello, Johnson D (Dixon), Loughlan, Mardenborough.

SOUTHERN SEMI-FINALS

Fulham (1) 2 *(Brazil 2)*
Wycombe W (0) 2 *(Langford 2)* 8733

Fulham: Stannard; Jupp, Pike, Onwere (Mison), Angus, Thomas, Hails, Bedrossian (Tierling), Eckhardt, Brazil, Baah.
Wycombe W: Hyde; Cousins, Horton (Langford), Crossley, Evans (Kerr), Ryan, Carroll, Thompson, Stapleton, Garner, Guppy.
aet; Wycombe W won 4-2 on penalties

Leyton Orient (0) 0
Swansea C (2) 2 *(Chapple, Torpey)* 7010

Leyton Orient: Newell; Hendon, Ludden, Howard, Bellamy, Cockerill, Carter, Barnett (Putney), Taylor, West, Bogie (Cooper).
Swansea C: Freestone; Jenkins, Cook, Ford, Harris, Chapple, Bowen, Rush (Hodge), Torpey, Cornforth, Hayes.

NORTHERN SEMI-FINAL

1 MAR

Stockport Co (0) 0
Huddersfield T (0) 1 *(Dunn)* 4980

Stockport Co: Ironside; Connelly, Todd, Frain, Flynn, Williams B (Wallace), Gannon, Ward, Francis, Beaumont, Preece (Ryan).
Huddersfield T: Francis; Mitchell, Billy, Robinson P, Whitney, Jackson, Logan, Bullock, Booth, Dunn, Starbuck.

SOUTHERN FINAL First Leg

Swansea C (2) 3 *(Pascoe 2, Bowen)*
Wycombe W (1) 1 *(Garner)* 6335

Swansea C: Freestone; Jenkins, Cook, Walker, Harris, Pascoe, Bowen, Rush, Torpey, Cornforth, Ampadu (Hodge).
Wycombe W: Hyde; Cousins, Stapleton, Crossley, Blatherwick (Creaser), Ryan, Carroll, Langford, Thompson (Titterton), Garner, Guppy.

NORTHERN FINAL First Leg

8 MAR

Huddersfield T (1) 4 *(Jackson, Bullock, Starbuck, Dunn)*
Carlisle U (1) 1 *(Davey (pen))* 10,552

Huddersfield T: Francis; Mitchell, Billy, Robinson P, Trevitt, Jackson, Logan, Bullock, Booth, Dunn, Starbuck.
Carlisle U: Caig; Burgess, Gallimore, Walling, Joyce, Conway, Thomas, Pearson (Oghani), Reeves, Davey, Reddish.

NORTHERN FINAL Second Leg

22 MAR

Carlisle U (2) 2 *(Mitchell (og), Joyce)*
Huddersfield T (0) 0 8330

Carlisle U: Caig; Joyce, Gallimore, Walling, Valentine, Robinson, Thomas, Conway, Reeves, Davey, Reddish (Delap).
Huddersfield T: Francis; Mitchell, Billy, Robinson P, Trevitt, Jackson (Dyson), Logan, Bullock (Wells), Booth, Dunn, Starbuck.

SOUTHERN FINAL Second Leg

Wycombe W (1) 1 *(Hemmings)*
Swansea C (0) 0 6710

Wycombe W: Hyde; Cousins, Titterton, Crossley, Creaser, Ryan, Carroll, Thompson (Langford), Reid, Hemmings, Guppy.
Swansea C: Freestone; Jenkins, Clode (Cook), Walker, Harris, Pascoe, Bowen, Rush, Torpey (McFarlane), Cornforth, Hodge.

FINAL at Wembley

24 APR

Huddersfield T (0) 1 *(Logan)*
Swansea C (1) 1 *(McFarlane)* 47,733

Huddersfield T: Francis; Billy, Cowan, Starbuck, Scully, Mitchell, Logan, Robinson P, Booth, Bullock (Dunn), Baldry.
Swansea C: Freestone; Jenkins, Clode (Torpey), Basham, Harris, Pascoe, Bowen, Ampadu, McFarlane, Cornforth, Hodge (Ford).
aet; Swansea C won 3-1 on penalties

FOOTBALL LEAGUE COMPETITION ATTENDANCES

SEASON 1993–1994

ANGLO-ITALIAN CUP

(Games played in England only)

	Attendances	*Matches*	*Average*
Preliminary round	93,542	24	3,898
International stage	57,575	16	3,597
Semi-finals	9,191	2	4,596
Final	17,185	1	17,185
Totals	177,493	43	4,128

COCA-COLA CUP

	Attendances	*Matches*	*Average*
Round one	215,617	56	3,850
Round two	664,598	64	10,384
Round three	320,849	21	15,278
Round four	188,340	11	17,122
Round five	141,580	6	23,597
Semi finals	135,905	4	33,976
Final	77,231	1	77,231
Total	1,744,120	163	10,700

AUTOGLASS TROPHY

	Attendances	*Matches*	*Average*
Round one	86,554	42	2,061
Round two	29,159	16	1,822
Area quarter-finals	29,038	8	3,630
Area semi-finals	26,970	4	6,743
Area finals	31,927	4	7,928
Final	47,733	1	47,733
Total	251,381	75	3,352

FA CUP FINALS 1872–1994

1872 and 1874–92	Kennington Oval	1911	Replay at Old Trafford
1873	Lillie Bridge	1912	Replay at Bramall Lane
1886	Replay at Derby (Racecourse Ground)		
1893	Fallowfield, Manchester	1915	Old Trafford, Manchester
1894	Everton	1920–22	Stamford Bridge
1895–1914	Crystal Palace	1923 to date	Wembley
1901	Replay at Bolton	1970	Replay at Old Trafford
1910	Replay at Everton	1981	Replay at Wembley

Year	*Winners*	*Runners-up*	*Score*
1872	Wanderers	Royal Engineers	1-0
1873	Wanderers	Oxford University	2-0
1874	Oxford University	Royal Engineers	2-0
1875	Royal Engineers	Old Etonians	2-0 (after 1-1 draw aet)
1876	Wanderers	Old Etonians	3-0 (after 1-1 draw aet)
1877	Wanderers	Oxford University	2-1 (aet)
1878	Wanderers*	Royal Engineers	3-1
1879	Old Etonians	Clapham R	1-0
1880	Clapham R	Oxford University	1-0
1881	Old Carthusians	Old Etonians	3-0
1882	Old Etonians	Blackburn R	1-0
1883	Blackburn Olympic	Old Etonians	2-1 (aet)
1884	Blackburn R	Queen's Park, Glasgow	2-1
1885	Blackburn R	Queen's Park, Glasgow	2-0
1886	Blackburn R†	WBA	2-0 (after 0-0 draw)
1887	Aston Villa	WBA	2-0
1888	WBA	Preston NE	2-1
1889	Preston NE	Wolverhampton W	3-0
1890	Blackburn R	Sheffield W	6-1
1891	Blackburn R	Notts Co	3-1
1892	WBA	Aston Villa	3-0
1893	Wolverhampton W	Everton	1-0
1894	Notts Co	Bolton W	4-1
1895	Aston Villa	WBA	1-0
1896	Sheffield W	Wolverhampton W	2-1
1897	Aston Villa	Everton	3-2
1898	Nottingham F	Derby Co	3-1
1899	Sheffield U	Derby Co	4-1
1900	Bury	Southampton	4-0
1901	Tottenham H	Sheffield U	3-1 (after 2-2 draw)
1902	Sheffield U	Southampton	2-1 (after 1-1 draw)
1903	Bury	Derby Co	6-0
1904	Manchester C	Bolton W	1-0
1905	Aston Villa	Newcastle U	2-0
1906	Everton	Newcastle U	1-0
1907	Sheffield W	Everton	2-1
1908	Wolverhampton W	Newcastle U	3-1
1909	Manchester U	Bristol C	1-0
1910	Newcastle U	Barnsley	2-0 (after 1-1 draw)
1911	Bradford C	Newcastle U	1-0 (after 0-0 draw)
1912	Barnsley	WBA	1-0 (aet, after 0-0 draw)
1913	Aston Villa	Sunderland	1-0
1914	Burnley	Liverpool	1-0
1915	Sheffield U	Chelsea	3-0
1920	Aston Villa	Huddersfield T	1-0 (aet)
1921	Tottenham H	Wolverhampton W	1-0
1922	Huddersfield T	Preston NE	1-0
1923	Bolton W	West Ham U	2-0
1924	Newcastle U	Aston Villa	2-0
1925	Sheffield U	Cardiff C	1-0
1926	Bolton W	Manchester C	1-0
1927	Cardiff C	Arsenal	1-0
1928	Blackburn R	Huddersfield T	3-1
1929	Bolton W	Portsmouth	2-0
1930	Arsenal	Huddersfield T	2-0
1931	WBA	Birmingham	2-1
1932	Newcastle U	Arsenal	2-1
1933	Everton	Manchester C	3-0
1934	Manchester C	Portsmouth	2-1
1935	Sheffield W	WBA	4-2
1936	Arsenal	Sheffield U	1-0
1937	Sunderland	Preston NE	3-1
1938	Preston NE	Huddersfield T	1-0 (aet)
1939	Portsmouth	Wolverhampton W	4-1
1946	Derby Co	Charlton Ath	4-1 (aet)
1947	Charlton Ath	Burnley	1-0 (aet)
1948	Manchester U	Blackpool	4-2
1949	Wolverhampton W	Leicester C	3-1
1950	Arsenal	Liverpool	2-0
1951	Newcastle U	Blackpool	2-0
1952	Newcastle U	Arsenal	1-0

Year	Winners	Runners-up	Score
1953	Blackpool	Bolton W	4-3
1954	WBA	Preston NE	3-2
1955	Newcastle U	Manchester C	3-1
1956	Manchester C	Birmingham C	3-1
1957	Aston Villa	Manchester U	2-1
1958	Bolton W	Manchester U	2-0
1959	Nottingham F	Luton T	2-1
1960	Wolverhampton W	Blackburn R	3-0
1961	Tottenham H	Leicester C	2-0
1962	Tottenham H	Burnley	3-1
1963	Manchester U	Leicester C	3-1
1964	West Ham U	Preston NE	3-2
1965	Liverpool	Leeds U	2-1 (aet)
1966	Everton	Sheffield W	3-2
1967	Tottenham H	Chelsea	2-1
1968	WBA	Everton	1-0 (aet)
1969	Manchester C	Leicester C	1-0
1970	Chelsea	Leeds U	2-1 (aet)
	(after 2-2 draw, after extra time, at Wembley)		
1971	Arsenal	Liverpool	2-1 (aet)
1972	Leeds U	Arsenal	1-0
1973	Sunderland	Leeds U	1-0
1974	Liverpool	Newcastle U	3-0
1975	West Ham U	Fulham	2-0
1976	Southampton	Manchester U	1-0
1977	Manchester U	Liverpool	2-1
1978	Ipswich T	Arsenal	1-0
1979	Arsenal	Manchester U	3-2
1980	West Ham U	Arsenal	1-0
1981	Tottenham H	Manchester C	3-2
	(after 1-1 draw, after extra time, at Wembley)		
1982	Tottenham H	QPR	1-0
	(after 1-1 draw, after extra time, at Wembley)		
1983	Manchester U	Brighton & HA	4-0
	(after 2-2 draw, after extra time, at Wembley)		
1984	Everton	Watford	2-0
1985	Manchester U	Everton	1-0 (aet)
1986	Liverpool	Everton	3-1
1987	Coventry C	Tottenham H	3-2 (aet)
1988	Wimbledon	Liverpool	1-0
1989	Liverpool	Everton	3-2 (aet)
1990	Manchester U	Crystal Palace	1-0
	(after 3-3 draw, after extra time, at Wembley)		
1991	Tottenham H	Nottingham F	2-1 (aet)
1992	Liverpool	Sunderland	2-0
1993	Arsenal	Sheffield W	2-1 (aet)
1994	Manchester U	Chelsea	4-0
	(after 1-1 draw, after extra time, at Wembley)		

** Won outright, but restored to the Football Association.*
† A special trophy was awarded for third consecutive win.

FA CUP WINS

Manchester U 8, Tottenham H 8, Aston Villa 7, Arsenal 6, Blackburn R 6, Newcastle U 6, Liverpool 5, The Wanderers 5, WBA 5, Bolton W 4, Everton 4, Manchester C 4, Sheffield U 4, Wolverhampton W 4, Sheffield W 3, West Ham U 3, Bury 2, Nottingham F 2, Old Etonians 2, Preston NE 2, Sunderland 2, Barnsley 1, Blackburn Olympic 1, Blackpool 1, Bradford C 1, Burnley 1, Cardiff C 1, Charlton Ath 1, Chelsea 1, Clapham R 1, Coventry C 1, Derby Co 1, Huddersfield T 1, Ipswich T 1, Leeds U 1, Notts Co 1, Old Carthusians 1, Oxford University 1, Portsmouth 1, Royal Engineers 1, Southampton 1, Wimbledon 1.

APPEARANCES IN FINALS

Arsenal 12, Manchester U 12, Everton 11, Newcastle U 11, WBA 10, Liverpool 10, Aston Villa 9, Tottenham H 9, Blackburn R 8, Manchester C 8, Wolverhampton W 8, Bolton W 7, Preston NE 7, Old Etonians 6, Sheffield U 6, Sheffield W 6, Huddersfield T 5, *The Wanderers 5, Chelsea 4, Derby Co 4, Leeds U 4, Leicester C 4, Oxford University 4, Royal Engineers 4, Sunderland 4, West Ham U 4, Blackpool 3, Burnley 3, Nottingham F 3, Portsmouth 3, Southampton 3, Barnsley 2, Birmingham C 2, *Bury 2, Cardiff C 2, Charlton Ath 2, Clapham R 2, Notts Co 2, Queen's Park (Glasgow) 2, *Blackburn Olympic 1, *Bradford C 1, Brighton & HA 1, Bristol C 1, *Coventry C 1, Crystal Palace 1, Fulham 1, *Ipswich T 1, Luton 4, *Old Carthusians 1, QPR 1, Watford 1, *Wimbledon 1.

** Denotes undefeated.*

APPEARANCES IN SEMI-FINALS

Everton 22, Liverpool 19, Manchester U 19, WBA 19, Arsenal 18, Aston Villa 17, Blackburn R 16, Sheffield W 16, Tottenham H 14, Derby Co 13, Newcastle U 13, Wolverhampton W 13, Bolton W 12, Nottingham F 12, Chelsea 11, Sheffield U 11, Sunderland 11, Manchester C 10, Preston NE 10, Southampton 10, Birmingham C 9, Burnley 8, Leeds U 8, Huddersfield T 7, Leicester C 7, Old Etonians 6, Oxford University 6, West Ham U 6, Fulham 5, Notts Co 5, Portsmouth 5, The Wanderers 5, Luton T 4, Queen's Park (Glasgow) 4, Royal Engineers 4, Blackpool 3, Cardiff C 3, Clapham R 3, Ipswich T 3, Millwall 3, Norwich C 3, Old Carthusians 3, Oldham Ath 3, Stoke C 3, The Swifts 3, Watford 3, Barnsley 2, Blackburn Olympic 2, Bristol C 2, Bury 2, Charlton Ath 2, Crystal Palace (professional club) 2, Grimsby T 2, Swansea T 2, Swindon T 2, Bradford C 1, Brighton & HA 1, Cambridge University 1, Coventry C 1, Crewe Alex 1, Crystal Palace (amateur club) 1, Darwen 1, Derby Junction 1, Glasgow R 1, Hull C 1, Marlow 1, Old Harrovians 1, Orient 1, Plymouth Arg 1, Port Vale 1, QPR 1, Reading 1, Shropshire W 1, Wimbledon 1, York C 1.

FA CUP FINALISTS 1872–1993

R: replay; aet: after extra time.

1871–72 THE WANDERERS R. de C. Welch; C. W. Alcock, M. P. Betts, A. G. Bonsor, E. E. Bowen, W. P. Crake, T. C. Hooman, E. Lubbock, A. C. Thompson, R. W. S. Vidal, C. H. R. Wollaston. (In alphabetical order.) *Scorer:* 'A. H. Chequer' (M. P. Betts).

1–0 ROYAL ENGINEERS Capt. Marindin; Capt. Merriman, Lieut. Addison; Lieut. Creswell, Lieut. Mitchell, Lieut. Renny-Tailyour; Lieut. Rich, Lieut. Goodwyn, Lieut. Muirhead, Lieut. Cotter, Lieut. Bogle.

1872–73 THE WANDERERS E. E. Bowen; C. M. Thompson, R. de C. Welch; Hon. A. F. Kinnaird, L. S. Howell, C. H. R. Wollaston; J. R. Sturgiss, Rev. H. H. Stewart, W. S. Kenyon-Slaney, R. K. Kingsford, A. G. Bonsor. *Scorers:* Kinnaird, Wollaston.

2–0 OXFORD UNIVERSITY A. Kirke-Smith; A. J. Leach, C. C. Mackarness; F. H. Birley; C. J. Longman, F. B. Chappell-Maddison; H. B. Cixon, W. B. Paton, R. W. S. Vidal, W. E. Sumner, C. J. Ottaway.

1873–74 OXFORD UNIVERSITY C. E. B. Neapean; C. C. Mackarness, F. H. Birley; F. T. Green, R. W. S. Vidal, C. J. Ottaway; R. H. Benson, F. J. Patton, W. S. Rawson, F. B. Chappell-Maddison, Rev. A. H. Johnson. *Scorers:* Mackarness, Patton.

2–0 ROYAL ENGINEERS Capt. Merriman; Major Marindin, Lieut. G. W. Addison; Lieut. G. C. Onslow, Lieut. H. G. Oliver, Lieut. T. Digby; Lieut. H. W. Renny-Tailyour, Lieut. H. E. Rawson, Lieut. J. E. Blackman, Lieut. A. K. Wood, Lieut. P. G. von Donop.

1874–75 ROYAL ENGINEERS Capt. Merriman; Lieut. G. H. Sim, Lieut. G. C. Onslow; Lieut. R. M. Ruck, Lieut. P. G. von Donop, Lieut. C. K. Wood; Lieut. H. E. Rawson, Lieut. R. H. Stafford, Capt. H. W. Renny-Tailyour, Lieut. Mein, Lieut. C. Wingfield Stratford. *Scorers:* (First match) Renny-Tailyour; (Second match) Renny-Tailyour, Stafford.

1–1 aet *R:*2–0 OLD ETONIANS Capt. E. H. Drummond-Moray; M. Farrer, E. Lubbock; F. H. Wilson, Hon. A. F. Kinnaird, J. H. Stronge; F. J. Patton, C. E. Farmer, A. G. Bonsor, A. Lubbock, T. Hammond. (C. J. Ottaway, W. S. Kenyon-Slaney, R. H. Benson and A. G. Thompson took part in the first match in place of A. Lubbock, T. Hammond, M. Farrer and Capt. E. H. Drummond-Moray.) *Scorer:* Bonsor.

1875–76 THE WANDERERS W. D. O. Greig; A. Stratford, W. Lindsay; F. B. C. Maddison, F. H. Birley, C. H. R. Wollaston; H. Heron, F. Heron, J. H. Edwards, J. Kenrick, T. Hughes. *Scorers:* (First match) Edwards; (Second match) Wollaston, Hughes 2.

1-1 aet *R:*3-0 OLD ETONIANS Q. Hogg; E. Lubbock, Hon. E. Lyttelton; M. G. Faner, Hon. A. F. Kinnaird, J. H. Stronge; W. S. Kenyon-Slaney, Hon. A. Lyttelton, J. R. Sturgis, A. G. Bonsor, H. P. Allene. (C. Meysey, A. C. Thompson and J. E. C. Welldon took part in the first match in place of J. H. Stronge, M. G. Faner and E. Lubbock.) *Scorer:* Bonsor.

1876–77 THE WANDERERS Hon. A. F. Kinnaird; W. Lindsay, A. Stratford; F. H. Birley, C. A. Denton, F. T. Green; H. Heron, T. Hughes, J. Kenrick, H. Wace, C. H. R. Wollaston. *Scorers:* Heron, Kenrick.

2–1 aet OXFORD UNIVERSITY E. H. Allington; J. Bain, O. R. Dunnell; J. H. Savory, A. H. Todd, E. W. Waddington; P. H. Fernandez, A. F. Hills, H. S. Otter, E. H. Parry, W. S. Rawson. *Scorer:* Kinnaird (og).

1877–78 THE WANDERERS J. Kirkpatrick; A. Stratford, W. Lindsay; Hon. A. F. Kinnaird, F. T. Green, C. H. R. Wollaston; H. Heron, J. G. Wylie, H. Wace, C. A. Denton, J. Kenrick. *Scorers:* Kenrick 2, Kinnaird.

3-1 ROYAL ENGINEERS L. B. Friend; J. H. Cowan, W. J. Morris; C. B. Mayne, F. C. Heath, C. E. Haynes; M. Lindsay, R. B. Hedley, F. G. Bond, H. H. Barnet, O. E. Ruck. *Scorer:* unknown.

1878–79 OLD ETONIANS J. P. Hawtrey; E. Christian, L. Bury; Hon. A. F. Kinnaird, E. Lubbock, C. J. Clerke; N. Pares, H. C. Goodhart, H. Whitfield, J. B. T. Chevallier, H. Beaufoy. *Scorer:* Clerke.

1–0 CLAPHAM ROVERS R. H. Birkett; R. A. Ogilvie, E. Field; N. C. Bailey, J. F. M. Prinsep, F. L. Rawson; A. J. Stanley, S. W. Scott, H. S. Bevington, E. F. Growse, C. Keith-Falconer.

1879–80 CLAPHAM ROVERS R. H. Birkett; R. A. Ogilvie, E. Field; A. Weston, N. C. Bailey, H. Brougham; A. J. Stanley, F. Barry, F. J. Sparks, C. A. Lloyd-Jones, E. A. Ram. *Scorer:* Lloyd-Jones.

1–0 OXFORD UNIVERSITY P. C. Parr; C. W. Wilson, C. J. S. King; F. A. H. Phillips, B. Rogers, R. T. Heygate; G. B. Childs, J. Eyre, F. D. Crowdy, E. H. Hill, J. B. Lubbock.

1880–81 OLD CARTHUSIANS L. F. Gillett; W. H. Norris, E. G. Colvin; J. F. M. Prinsep, A. J. Vintcent, W. E. Hansell; L. M. Richards, W. R. Page, E. G. Wyngard, E. H. Parry, A. H. Todd. *Scorers:* Wyngard, Parry, Todd.

3-0 OLD ETONIANS J. F. P. Rawlinson; C. W. Foley, C. H. French; Hon. A. F. Kinnaird, R. B. Farrer, J. B. T. Chevallier; W. J. Anderson, H. C. Goodhart, R. H. Macaulay, H. Whitfield, P. C. Novelli.

1881–82 OLD ETONIANS J. F. P. Rawlinson; T. H. French, P. J. de Paravicini; Hon. A. F. Kinnaird, C. W. Foley, P. C. Novelli; A. T. R. Dunn, R. H. Macaulay, H. C. Goodhart, W. J. Anderson, J. B. T. Chevallier. *Scorer:* Anderson.

1–0 BLACKBURN ROVERS R. Howarth; H. McIntyre, F. Suter; H. Sharples, F. W. Hargreaves, J. Duckworth; J. Douglas, T. Strachan, J. Brown, G. Avery, J. Hargreaves.

1882–83 BLACKBURN OLYMPIC T. Hacking; J. T. Ward, S. A. Warburton; T. Gibson, W. Astley, J. Hunter; T. Dewhurst, A. Matthews, G. Wilson, J. Costley, J. Yates. *Scorers:* Costley, Matthews.

2–1 aet OLD ETONIANS J. F. P. Rawlinson, T. H. French, P. J. de Paravicini; Hon. A. F. Kinnaird, C. W. Foley, J. B. T. Chevallier; W. J. Anderson, R. H. Macaulay, H. C. Goodhart, A. T. B. Dunn, H. W. Bainbridge. *Scorer:* Goodhart.

1883–84 BLACKBURN ROVERS H. J. Arthur; J. Beverley, F. Suter; H. McIntyre, J. Hargreaves, J. H. Forrest; J. M. Lofthouse, J. Douglas, J. Sowerbutts, J. Inglis, J. Brown. *Scorers:* Brown, Forrest.

2-1 QUEEN'S PARK G. Gillespie; W. Arnott, J. MacDonald; C. Campbell, J. J. Gow, W. Anderson; W. W. Watt, Dr Smith, W. Harrower, D. S. Allan, R. M. Christie. *Scorer:* Christie.

1884–85 BLACKBURN ROVERS H. J. Arthur; R. G. Turner, F. Suter; H. McIntyre, G. Haworth, J. H. Forrest; J. M. Lofthouse, J. Douglas, J. Brown, H. E. Fecitt, J. Sowerbutts. *Scorers:* Forrest, Brown.

2–0 QUEEN'S PARK G. Gillespie; W. Arnott, W. Macleod; C. Campbell, J. MacDonald, A. Hamilton; W. Anderson, W. Sellar, W. Gray, N. McWhannel, D. S. Allan.

1885–86 BLACKBURN ROVERS H. J. Arthur; Turner, Suter; Douglas, Forrest, McIntyre; Walton, Strachan, Brown, Fecitt, J. Sowerbutts. (Heyes played in the first match at the Oval, but Walton took his place in the
0-0 replay.) *Scorers:* Brown, Sowerbutts.

***R*:2-0** WEST BROMWICH ALBION Roberts; H. Green, H. Bell; Horton, Perry, Timmins; Woodhall, T. Green, Bayliss, Loach, G. Bell.

1886–87 ASTON VILLA Warner; Coulton, Simmonds; Yates, Dawson, Burton; Davis, Brown, Hunter, Vaughton, Hodgetts. *Scorers:* Hunter, Hodgetts.

2-0 WEST BROMWICH ALBION Roberts; H. Green, Aldridge; Horton, Perry, Timmins; Woodhall, T. Green, Bayliss, Paddock, Pearson.

1887–88 WEST BROMWICH ALBION Roberts; Aldridge, Green; Horton, Perry, Timmins; Bassett, Woodhall, Bayliss, Wilson, Pearson. *Scorers:* Woodhall, Bayliss.

2-1 PRESTON NORTH END Dr R. H. Mills-Roberts; Howarth, N. J. Ross; Holmes, Russell, Graham; Gordon, J. Ross, J. Goodall, F. Dewhurst, Drummond. *Scorer:* Goodall.

1888–89 PRESTON NORTH END Dr R. H. Mills-Roberts; Howarth, Holmes; Drummond, Russell, Graham; Gordon, Ross, J. Goodall, F. Dewhurst, Thompson. *Scorers:* Dewhurst, Ross, Thompson.

3-0 WOLVERHAMPTON WANDERERS Baynton; Baugh, Mason; Fletcher, Allen, Lowder; Hunter, Wykes, Broodie, Wood, Knight.

1889–90 BLACKBURN ROVERS J. K. Horne; Southworth (Jas.), Forbes; Barton, Dewar, Forrest; Lofthouse, Campbell, Southworth (John), Walton, Townley. *Scorers:* Dewar, Southworth (John), Lofthouse, Townley 3.

6-1 SHEFFIELD WEDNESDAY Smith (J.); Brayshaw, H. Morley; Dungworth, Betts, Waller; Ingram, Woodhouse, Bennett, Mumford, Cawley. *Scorer:* Bennett.

1890–91 BLACKBURN ROVERS Pennington; Brandon, J. Forbes; Barton, Dewar, Forrest; Lofthouse, Walton, Southworth (John), Hall, Townley. *Scorers:* Dewar, Southworth, Townley.

3-1 NOTTS COUNTY Thraves; Ferguson, Hendry; H. Osborne, Calderhead, Shelton; A. McGregor, McInnes, Oswald, Locker, H. B. Daft. *Scorer:* Oswald.

1891–92 WEST BROMWICH ALBION Reader; Nicholson, McCulloch; Reynolds, Perry, Groves; Bassett, McLeod, Nicholls, Pearson, Geddes. *Scorers:* Geddes, Nicholls, Reynolds.

3-0 ASTON VILLA Warner; Evans, Cox; H. Devey, Cowan, Baird; Athersmith, J. Devey, Dickson, Campbell, Hodgetts.

1892–93 WOLVERHAMPTON WANDERERS Rose; Baugh, Swift; Malpass, Allen, Kinsey; R. Topham, Wykes, Butcher, Wood, Griffin. *Scorer:* Allen.

1-0 EVERTON Williams; Howarth, Kelso; Stewart, Holt, Boyle; Latta, Gordon, Maxwell, Chadwick, Milward.

1893–94 NOTTS COUNTY Toone; Harper, Hendry; Bramley, Calderhead, A. Shelton; Watson, Donnelly, Logan, Bruce, H. B. Daft. *Scorers:* Watson, Logan 3.

4-1 BOLTON WANDERERS Sutcliffe; Somerville, Jones; Gardiner, Paton, Hughes; Dickinson, Wilson, Tannahill, Bentley, Cassidy. *Scorer:* Cassidy.

1894–95 ASTON VILLA Wilkes; Spencer, Welford; Reynolds, Cowan (Jas.), Russell; Athersmith, Chatt, J. Devey, Hodgetts, S. Smith. *Scorer:* Devey.

1-0 WEST BROMWICH ALBION Reader; Williams, Horton; Taggart, Higgins, T. Perry; Bassett, McLeod, Richards, Hutchinson, Banks.

1895–96 SHEFFIELD WEDNESDAY Massey; Earp, Langley; H. Brandon, Crawshaw, Petrie; Brash, Brady, L. Bell, Davis, Spiksley. *Scorer:* Spiksley 2.

2-1 WOLVERHAMPTON WANDERERS Tennant; Baugh, Dunn; Owen, Malpass, Griffiths; Tonks, Henderson, Beats, Wood, Black. *Scorer:* Black.

1896–97 ASTON VILLA Whitehouse; Spencer, Evans; Reynolds, Cowan (Jas.), Crabtree; Athersmith, J. Devey, Campbell, Wheldon, Cowan (John). *Scorers:* Campbell, Wheldon, Crabtree.

3-2 EVERTON Menham; Meecham, Storrier; Boyle, Holt, Stewart; Taylor, Bell, Hartley, Chadwick, Milward. *Scorers:* Boyle, Bell.

1897–98 NOTTINGHAM FOREST Allsop; Richie, Scott; Forman (Frank), McPherson, Wragg; McInnes, Richards, Benbow, Capes, Spouncer. *Scorers:* Capes 2, McPherson.

3-1 DERBY COUNTY Fryer; Methven, Leiper; Cox, A. Goodall, Turner; J. Goodall, Bloomer. Boag, Stevenson, McOueen. *Scorer:* Bloomer.

1898–99 SHEFFIELD UNITED Foulke; Thickett, Boyle; Johnson, Morren, Needham; Bennett, Beers, Hedley, Almond, Priest. *Scorers:* Bennett, Beers, Almond, Priest.

4-1 DERBY COUNTY Fryer; Methven, Staley; Cox, Paterson, May; Arkesden, Bloomer, Boag, McDonald, Allen. *Scorer:* Boag.

1899– BURY Thompson; Darrock, Davidson; Pray, Leeming, Ross; Richards, Wood, McLuckie, Sagar, Plant.
1900 *Scorers:* McLuckie 2, Wood, Plant.

4-0 SOUTHAMPTON Robinson; Meehan, Durber; Meston, Chadwick, Petrie; Turner, Yates, Farrell, Wood, Milward.

1900–01 TOTTENHAM HOTSPUR Clawley; Erentz, Tait; Norris, Hughes, Jones; Smith, Cameron, Brown, Copeland, Kirwan. *Scorers:* (First match) Brown 2; (Second match) Cameron, Smith, Brown.

2-2 SHEFFIELD UNITED Foulke; Thickett, Boyle; Johnson, Morren, Needham; Bennett, Field, Hedley,
***R*:3-1** Priest, Lipsham. *Scorers:* (First match) Bennett, Priest; (Second match) Priest.

1901–02 SHEFFIELD UNITED Foulke; Thickett, Boyle; Needham, Wilkinson, Johnson; Barnes, Common, Hedley, Priest, Lipsham. (Bennett was injured in the first match and Barnes took his place in the replay.) *Scorers:* (First match) Common; (Second match) Hedley, Barnes.

1-1 SOUTHAMPTON Robinson; C. B. Fry, Molyneux; Meston, Bowman, Lee; A. Turner, Wood, Brown,
***R*:2-1** Chadwick, J. Turner. *Scorers:* (First match) Wood; (Second match) Brown.

1902–03 BURY Monteith; Lindsey, McEwen; Johnson, Thorpe, Ross; Richards, Wood, Sagar, Leeming, Plant. *Scorers:* Ross, Sagar, Leeming 2, Wood, Plant.

6-0 DERBY COUNTY Fryer; Methven, Morris; Warren, A. Goodall, May; Warrington, York, Boag, Richards, Davis.

1903–04 MANCHESTER CITY Hillman; McMahon, Burgess: Frost, Hynds, S. B. Ashworth; Meredith, Livingstone, Gillespie, A. Turnbull, Booth. *Scorer:* Meredith.

1-0 BOLTON WANDERERS D. Davies; Brown, Struthers; Clifford, Greenhaigh, Freebairn; Stokes, Marsh, Yenson, White, Taylor.

1904–05 ASTON VILLA George; Spencer, Miles; Pearson, Leake, Windmill; Brawn, Garratty, Hampton, Bache, Hall. *Scorer:* Hampton 2.

2-0 NEWCASTLE UNTED Lawrence; McCombie, Carr; Gardner, Aitken, McWilliam; Rutherford, Howie, Appleyard, Veitch, Gosnell.

1905–06 EVERTON Scott; W. Balmer, Crelly; Makepeace, Taylor, Abbott; Sharp, Bolton, Young, Settle, H. P. Hardman. *Scorer:* Young.
1-0 NEWCASTLE UNITED Lawrence; McCombie, Carr; Gardner, Aitken, McWilliam; Rutherford, Howie, Veitch, Orr, Gosnell.
1906–07 SHEFFIELD WEDNESDAY Lyall; Layton, Burton; Brittleton, Crawshaw, Bartlett; Chapman, Bradshaw, Wilson, Stewart, Simpson. *Scorers:* Stewart, Simpson.
2-1 EVERTON Scott; W. Balmer, R. Balmer; Makepeace, Taylor, Abbott; Sharp, Bolton, Young, Settle, H. P. Hardman. *Scorer:* Sharp.
1907–08 WOLVERHAMPTON WANDERERS Lunn; Jones, Collins; Rev. K. R. G. Hunt, Wooldridge, Bishop; Harrison, Shelton, Hedley, Radford, Pedley. *Scorers:* Hunt, Hedley, Harrison.
3-1 NEWCASTLE UNITED Lawrence; McCracken, Pudan; Gardner, Veitch, McWilliam; Rutherford, Howie, Appleyard, Speedie, Wilson. *Scorer:* Howie.
1908–09 MANCHESTER UNITED Moger; Stacey, Hayes; Duckworth, Roberts, Bell; Meredith, Halse, J. Turnbull, A. Turnbull, Wall. *Scorer:* A. Turnbull.
1-0 BRISTOL CITY Clay; Annan, Cottle; Hanlin, Wedlock, Spear; Staniforth, Hardy, Gilligan, Burton, Hilton.
1909–10 NEWCASTLE UNITED Lawrence; McCracken, Carr; Veitch, Low, McWilliam; Rutherford, Howie, Shepherd, Higgins, Wilson. (Whitson was injured in the first match and Carr took his place in the replay.) *Scorers:* (First match) Rutherford; (Second match) Shepherd 2 (1 pen).
1-1 BARNSLEY Mearns; Downs, Ness; Glendinning, Boyle, Utley; Bartrop, Gadsby, Lillycrop, Tuffnell,
***R:*2-0** Forman. *Scorer:* (First match) Tuffnell.
1910–11 BRADFORD CITY Mellors; Campbell, Taylor; Robinson, Torrance, McDonald; Logan, Spiers, O'Rourke, Devine, Thompson. (Gildea played centre-half in the first match.) *Scorer:* Spiers.
0-0 NEWCASTLE UNITED Lawrence; McCracken, Whitson; Veitch, Low, Willis; Rutherford, Jobey,
***R:*1-0** Stewart, Higgins, Wilson.
1911–12 BARNSLEY Cooper; Downs, Taylor; Glendinning, Bratley, Utley; Bartrop, Tuffnell, Lillycrop, Travers,
0-0 Moore. *Scorer:* Tuffnell.
***R:*1-0** WEST BROMWICH ALBION Pearson; Cook, Pennington; Baddeley, Buck, McNeal; Jephcott, Wright,
aet Pailor, Bowser, Shearman.
1912–13 ASTON VILLA Hardy; Lyons, Weston; Barber, Harrop, Leach; Wallace, Halse, Hampton, C. Stephenson, Bache. *Scorer:* Barber.
1-0 SUNDERLAND Butler; Gladwin, Ness; Cuggy, Thompson, Low; Mordue, Buchan, Richardson, Holley, Martin.
1913–14 BURNLEY Sewell; Bamford, Taylor; Halley, Boyle, Watson; Nesbit, Lindley, Freeman, Hodgson, Mosscrop. *Scorer:* Freeman.
1-0 LIVERPOOL Campbell; Longworth, Pursell; Fairfoul, Ferguson, McKinlay; Sheldon, Metcalf, Miller, Lacey, Nicholl.
1914–15 SHEFFIELD UNITED Gough; Cook, English; Sturgess, Brelsford, Utley; Simmons, Fazackerley, Kitchen, Masterman, Evans. *Scorers:* Simmons, Fazackerley, Kitchen.
3-0 CHELSEA Molyneux; Bettridge, Harrow; Taylor, Logan, Walker; Ford, Halse, Thompson, Croal, McNeil.
1919–20 ASTON VILLA Hardy; Smart, Weston; Ducat, Barson, Moss; Wallace, Kirton, Walker, C. Stephenson, Dorrell. *Scorer:* Kirton.
1-0 HUDDERSFIELD TOWN Mutch; Wood, Bullock; Slade, Wilson, Watson; Richardson, Mann, Taylor,
aet Swan, Islip.
1920–21 TOTTENHAM HOTSPUR Hunter; Clay, McDonald; Smith, Walters, Grimsdell; Banks, Seed, Cantrell, Bliss, Dimmock. *Scorer:* Dimmock.
1-0 WOLVERHAMPTON WANDERERS George; Woodward, Marshall; Gregory, Hodnet, Riley; Lea, Burrill, Edmonds, Potts, Brooks.
1921–22 HUDDERSFIELD TOWN Mutch; Wood, Wadsworth; Slade, Wilson, Watson; Richardson, Mann, Islip, Stephenson, W. H. Smith. *Scorer:* Smith (pen).
1-0 PRESTON NORTH END J. F. Mitchell; Hamilton, Doolan; Duxbury, McCall, Williamson; Rawlings, Jefferis, Roberts, Woodhouse, Quinn.
1922–23 BOLTON WANDERERS Pym; Haworth, Finney; Nuttall, Seddon, Jennings; Butler, Jack, J. R. Smith, J. Smith, Vizard. *Scorers:* Jack, J. R. Smith.
2-0 WEST HAM UNITED Hufton; Henderson, Young; Bishop, Kay, Tresadern, Richards, Brown, V. Watson, Moore, Ruffell.
1923–24 NEWCASTLE UNITED Bradley; Hampson, Hudspeth; Mooney, Spencer, Gibson; Low, Cowan, Harris, McDonald, Seymour. *Scorers:* Harris, Seymour.
2-0 ASTON VILLA Jackson; Smart, Mort; Moss, Dr V. E. Milne. Blackburn; York, Kirton, Capewell, Walker, Dorrell.
1924–25 SHEFFIELD UNITED Sutcliffe; Cook, Milton; Pantling, King, Green; Mercer, Boyle, Johnson, Gillespie, Tunstall. *Scorer:* Tunstall.
1-0 CARDIFF CITY Farquharson; Nelson, Blair; Wake, Keenor, Hardy; W. Davies, Gill, Nicholson, Beadles, J. Evans.
1925–26 BOLTON WANDERERS Pym; Haworth, Greenhalgh; Nuttall, Seddon, Jennings; Butler, Jack, J. R. Smith, J. Smith, Vizard. *Scorer:* Jack.
1-0 MANCHESTER CITY Goodchild; Cookson, McCloy; Pringle, Cowan, McMullan; Austin, Browell, Roberts, Johnson, Hicks.
1926–27 CARDIFF CITY Farquharson; Nelson, Watson; Keenor, Sloan, Hardy; Curtis, Irving, Ferguson, I. Davies, McLachlan. *Scorer:* Ferguson.
1-0 ARSENAL Lewis; Parker, Kennedy; Baker. Butler, John; Hulme, Buchan, Brain, Blyth, Hoar.
1927–28 BLACKBURN ROVERS Crawford; Hutton, Jones; Healless, Rankin, Campbell; Thornewell, Puddefoot, Roscamp, McLean, Rigby. *Scorers:* Roscamp 2, McLean.
3-1 HUDDERSFIELD TOWN Mercer; Goodall, Barkas; Redfern, Wilson, Steele; A. Jackson, Kelly, Brown, Stephenson, W. H. Smith. *Scorer:* Jackson.
1928–29 BOLTON WANDERERS Pym; Haworth, Finney; Kean, Seddon, Nuttall; Butler, McClelland, Blackmore, Gibson, W. Cook. *Scorers:* Butler, Blackmore.
2-0 PORTSMOUTH Gilfillan; Mackie, Bell; Nichol, McIlwaine, Thackeray; Forward, J. Smith, Weddle. Watson, F. Cook.

1929–30 ARSENAL Preedy; Parker, Hapgood; Baker, Seddon, John; Hulme, Jack, Lambert, James, Bastin. *Scorers:* James, Lambert.
2-0 HUDDERSFIELD TOWN Turner; Goodall, Spence; Naylor, Wilson, Campbell; A. Jackson, Kelly, Davies, Raw, W. H. Smith.
1930–31 WEST BROMWICH ALBION Pearson; Shaw, Trentham; Magee, W. Richardson, Edwards; Glidden, Carter, W. G. Richardson, Sandford, Wood. *Scorer:* W. G. Richardson 2.
2-1 BIRMINGHAM Hibbs; Liddell, Barkas; Cringan, Morrall, Leslie; Briggs, Crosbie, Bradford, Gregg, Curtis. *Scorer:* Bradford.
1931–32 NEWCASTLE UNITED McInroy; Nelson, Fairhurst; McKenzie, Davidson, Weaver; Boyd, Richardson, Allen, McMenemy, Lang. *Scorer:* Allen 2.
2-1 ARSENAL Moss; Parker, Hapgood; C. Jones, Roberts, Male; Hulme, Jack, Lambert, Bastin, John. *Scorer:* John.
1932–33 EVERTON Sagar; Cook, Cresswell; Britton, White, Thomson; Geldard, Dunn, Dean, Johnson, Stein. *Scorers:* Stein, Dean, Dunn.
3-0 MANCHESTER CITY Langford; Cann, Dale; Busby, Cowan, Bray; Toseland, Marshall, Herd, McMullan, Brook.
1933–34 MANCHESTER CITY Swift; Barnett, Dale; Busby, Cowan, Bray; Toseland, Marshall, Tilson, Herd, Brook. *Scorer:* Tilson 2.
2-1 PORTSMOUTH Gilfillan; Mackie, W. Smith; Nichol, Allen, Thackeray; Worrall, J. Smith, Weddle, Easson, Rutherford. *Scorer:* Rutherford.
1934–35 SHEFFIELD WEDNESDAY Brown; Nibloe, Catlin; Sharp, Millership, Burrows; Hooper, Surtees, Palethorpe, Starling, Rimmer. *Scorers:* Rimmer 2, Palethorpe, Hooper.
4-2 WEST BROMWICH ALBION Pearson; Shaw, Trentham; Murphy, W. Richardson, Edwards; Glidden, Carter, W. G. Richardson, Sandford, Boyes. *Scorers:* Boyes, Sandford.
1935–36 ARSENAL Wilson; Male, Hapgood; Crayston, Roberts, Copping; Hulme, Bowden, Drake, James, Bastin. *Scorer:* Drake.
1-0 SHEFFIELD UNITED Smith; Hooper, Wilkinson; Jackson, Johnson, McPherson; Barton, Barclay, Dodds, Pickering, Williams.
1936–37 SUNDERLAND Mapson; Gorman, Hall; Thomson, Johnson, McNab; Duns, Carter, Gurney, Gallacher, Burbanks. *Scorers:* Gurney, Carter, Burbanks.
3-1 PRESTON NORTH END Burns; Gallimore, A. Beattie; Shankly, Tremelling, Milne; Dougal, Beresford, F. O'Donnell, Fagan, H. O'Donnell. *Scorer:* F. O'Donnell.
1937–38 PRESTON NORTH END Holdcroft; Gallimore, A. Beattie; Shankly, Smith, Batey; Watmough, Mutch, Maxwell, R. Beattie, H. O'Donnell. *Scorer:* Mutch (pen).
1-0 HUDDERSFIELD TOWN Hesford; Craig, Mountford; Willingham, Young, Boot; Hulme, Isaac,
aet McFadyen, Barclay, Beasley.
1938–39 PORTSMOUTH Walker; Morgan, Rochford; Guthrie, Rowe, Wharton; Worrall, McAlinden, Anderson, Barlow, Parker. *Scorers:* Parker 2, Barlow, Anderson.
4-1 WOLVERHAMPTON WANDERERS Scott; Morris, Taylor; Galley, Cullis, Gardiner; Burton, McIntosh, Westcott, Dorsett, Maguire. *Scorer:* Dorsett.
1945–46 DERBY COUNTY Woodley; Nicholas, Howe; Bullions, Leuty, Musson; Harrison, Carter, Stamps, Doherty, Duncan. *Scorers:* H. Turner (og), Doherty, Stamps 2.
4-1 CHARLTON ATHLETIC Bartram; Phipps, Shreeve; H. Turner, Oakes, Johnson; Fell, Brown, A. A.
aet Turner, Welsh, Duffy. *Scorer:* H. Turner.
1946–47 CHARLTON ATHLETIC Bartram; Croker, Shreeve; Johnson, Phipps. Whittaker; Hurst, Dawson, W. Robinson, Welsh, Duffy. *Scorer:* Duffy.
1-0 BURNLEY Strong; Woodruff, Mather; Attwell, Brown, Bray; Chew, Morris, Harrison, Potts, F. P.
aet Kippax.
1947–48 MANCHESTER UNITED Crompton; Carey, Aston; Anderson, Chilton, Cockburn; Delaney, Morris, Rowley, Pearson, Mitten. *Scorers:* Rowley 2, Pearson, Anderson.
4-2 BLACKPOOL Robinson; Shimwell, Crosland; Johnston, Hayward, Kelly; Matthews, Munro, Mortensen, Dick, Rickett. *Scorers:* Shimwell (pen), Mortensen.
1948–49 WOLVERHAMPTON WANDERERS Williams; Pritchard, Springthorpe; W. Crook, Shorthouse, Wright; Hancock, Smyth, Pye, Dunn, Mullen. *Scorers:* Pye 2, Smyth.
3-1 LEICESTER CITY Bradley; Jelly, Scott; W. Harrison, Plummer, King; Griffiths, Lee, J. Harrison, Chisholm, Adam. *Scorer:* Griffiths.
1949–50 ARSENAL Swindin; Scott, Barnes; Forbes, L. Compton, Mercer; Cox, Logie, Goring, Lewis, D. Compton. *Scorer:* Lewis 2.
2-0 LIVERPOOL Sidlow; Lambert, Spicer; Taylor, Hughes, Jones; Payne, Baron, Stubbins, Fagan, Liddell.
1950–51 NEWCASTLE UNITED Fairbrother; Cowell, Corbett; Harvey, Brennan, Crowe; Walker, Taylor, Milburn, G. Robledo, Mitchell. *Scorer:* Milburn 2.
2-0 BLACKPOOL Farm; Shimwell, Garrett; Johnston, Hayward, Kelly; Matthews, Mudie, Mortensen; W. J. Slater, Perry.
1951–52 NEWCASTLE UNITED Simpson; Cowell, McMichael; Harvey, Brennan, E. Robledo; Walker, Foulkes, Milburn, G. Robledo, Mitchell. *Scorer:* G. Robledo.
1-0 ARSENAL Swindin; Barnes, L. Smith; Forbes, Daniel, Mercer; Cox, Logie, Holton, Lishman, Roper.
1952–53 BLACKPOOL Farm; Shimwell, Garrett; Fenton, Johnston, Robinson; Matthews, Taylor, Mortensen, Mudie, Perry. *Scorers:* Mortensen 3, Perry.
4-3 BOLTON WANDERERS Hanson; Ball, R. Banks; Wheeler, Barass, Bell; Holden, Moir, Lofthouse. Hassall, Langton. *Scorers:* Lofthouse, Moir, Bell.
1953–54 WEST BROMWICH ALBION Sanders; Kennedy, Millard; Dudley, Dugdale, Barlow; Griffin, Ryan, Allen, Nicholls, Lee. *Scorers:* Allen 2 (1 pen), Griffin.
3-2 PRESTON NORTH END Thompson; Cunningham, Walton; Docherty, Marston, Forbes; Finney, Foster, Wayman, Baxter, Morrison. *Scorers:* Morrison, Wayman.
1954–55 NEWCASTLE UNITED Simpson; Cowell, Batty; Scoular, Stokoe, Casey; White, Milburn, Keeble, Hannah, Mitchell. *Scorers:* Milburn, Mitchell, Hannah.
3-1 MANCHESTER CITY Trautmann; Meadows, Little; Barnes, Ewing, Paul; Spurdle, Hayes, Revie, Johnstone, Fagan. *Scorer:* Johnstone.

1955–56 MANCHESTER CITY Trautmann; Leivers, Little; Barnes, Ewing, Paul; Johnstone, Hayes, Revie, Dyson, Clarke. *Scorers:* Hayes, Dyson, Johnstone.
3-1 BIRMINGHAM CITY Merrick; Hall, Green; Newman, Smith, Boyd; Astall, Kinsey, Brown, Murphy, Govan. *Scorer:* Kinsey.
1956–57 ASTON VILLA Sims; Lynn, Aldis; Crowther, Dugdale, Saward; Smith, Sewell, Myerscough, Dixon, McParland. *Scorer:* McParland 2.
2-1 MANCHESTER UNITED Wood; Foulkes, Byrne; Colman, J. Blanchflower, Edwards; Berry, Whelan, T. Taylor, R. Charlton, Pegg. *Scorer:* Taylor.
1957–58 BOLTON WANDERERS Hopkinson; Hartle, Banks; Hennin, Higgins, Edwards; Birch, Stevens, Lofthouse, Parry, Holden. *Scorer:* Lofthouse 2.
2-0 MANCHESTER UNITED Gregg; Foulkes, Greaves; Goodwin, Cope, Crowther; Dawson, E. Taylor, R. Charlton, Viollet, Webster.
1958–59 NOTTINGHAM FOREST Thomson; Whare, McDonald; Whitefoot, McKinlay, Burkitt; Dwight, Quigley, Wilson, Gray, Imlach. *Scorers:* Dwight, Wilson.
2-1 LUTON TOWN Baynham; McNally, Hawkes; Groves, Owen, Pacey; Bingham, Brown, Morton, Cummins, Gregory. *Scorer:* Pacey.
1959–60 WOLVERHAMPTON WANDERERS Finlayson; Showell, Harris; Clamp, Slater, Flowers; Deeley, Stobart, Murray, Broadbent, Horne. *Scorers:* McGrath (og), Deeley 2.
3-0 BLACKBURN ROVERS Leyland; Bray, Whelan; Clayton, Woods, McGrath; Bimpson, Dobing, Dougan, Douglas, McLeod.
1960–61 TOTTENHAM HOTSPUR Brown; Baker, Henry; D. Blanchflower, Norman, Mackay; Jones, White, Smith, Allen, Dyson. *Scorers:* Smith, Dyson.
2-0 LEICESTER CITY Banks; Chalmers, Norman; McLintock, King, Appleton; Riley, Walsh, McIlmoyle, Keyworth, Cheesebrough.
1961–62 TOTTENHAM HOTSPUR Brown; Baker, Henry; D. Blanchflower, Norman, Mackay; Medwin, White, Smith, Greaves, Jones. *Scorers:* Greaves, Smith, Blanchflower (pen).
3-1 BURNLEY Blacklaw; Angus, Elder; Adamson, Cummings, Miller; Connelly, McIlroy, Pointer, Robson, Harris. *Scorer:* Robson.
1962–63 MANCHESTER UNITED Gaskell; Dunne, Cantwell; Crerand, Foulkes, Setters; Giles, Quixall, Herd, Law, R. Charlton. *Scorers:* Herd 2, Law.
3-1 LEICESTER CITY Banks; Sjoberg, Norman; McLintock, King, Appleton; Riley, Cross, Keyworth, Gibson, Stringfellow. *Scorer:* Keyworth.
1963–64 WEST HAM UNITED Standen; Bond, Burkett; Bovington, Brown, Moore; Brabrook, Boyce, Byrne, Hurst, Sissons. *Scorers:* Sissons, Hurst, Boyce.
3-2 PRESTON NORTH END Kelly; Ross, Smith; Lawton, Singleton, Kendall; Wilson, Ashworth, Dawson, Spavin, Holden. *Scorers:* Holden, Dawson.
1964–65 LIVERPOOL Lawrence; Lawler, Byrne; Strong, Yeats, Stevenson; Callaghan, Hunt, St John, Smith, Thompson. *Scorers:* Hunt, St John.
2-1 aet LEEDS UNITED Sprake; Reaney, Bell; Bremner, J. Charlton, Hunter; Giles, Storrie, Peacock, Collins, Johanneson. *Scorer:* Bremner.
1965–66 EVERTON West; Wright, Wilson; Gabriel, Labone, Harris; Scott, Trebilcock, Young, Harvey, Temple. *Scorers:* Trebilcock 2, Temple.
3-2 SHEFFIELD WEDNESDAY Springett; Smith, Megson; Eustace, Ellis, Young; Pugh, Fantham, McCalliog, Ford, Quinn. *Scorers:* McCalliog, Ford.
1966–67 TOTTENHAM HOTSPUR Jennings; Kinnear, Knowles; Mullery, England, Mackay; Robertson, Greaves, Gilzean, Venables, Saul. *Scorers:* Robertson, Saul.
2-1 CHELSEA Bonetti; A. Harris, McCreadie; Hollins, Hinton, R. Harris; Cooke, Baldwin, Hateley, Tambling, Boyle. *Scorer:* Tambling.
1967–68 WEST BROMWICH ALBION Osborne; Fraser, Williams; Brown, Talbut, Kaye (Clarke); Lovett, Collard, Astle, Hope, Clark. *Scorer:* Astle.
1-0 aet EVERTON West; Wright, Wilson; Kendall, Labone, Harvey; Husband, Ball, Royle, Hurst, Morrissey.
1968–69 MANCHESTER CITY Dowd; Book, Pardoe; Doyle, Booth, Oakes; Summerbee, Bell, Lee, Young, Coleman. *Scorer:* Young.
1-0 LEICESTER CITY Shilton; Rodrigues, Nish; Roberts, Woollett, Cross; Fern, Gibson, Lochhead, Clarke, Glover (Manley).
1969–70 CHELSEA Bonetti; Webb, McCreadie; Hollins, Dempsey, R. Harris (Hinton); Baldwin, Houseman, Osgood, Hutchinson, Cooke. *Scorers:* Houseman, Hutchinson.
2-2 aet LEEDS UNITED Sprake; Madeley, Cooper; Bremner, J. Charlton, Hunter; Lorimer, Clarke, Jones, Giles, E. Gray. *Scorers:* Charlton, Jones.
Replay (at Old Trafford, Manchester)
***R:*2-1 aet** CHELSEA Bonetti; R. Harris, McCreadie; Hollins, Dempsey, Webb; Baldwin, Cooke, Osgood (Hinton), Hutchinson, Houseman. *Scorers:* Osgood, Webb.
LEEDS UNITED Harvey; Madeley, Cooper; Bremner, J. Charlton, Hunter; Lorimer, Clarke, Jones, Giles, E. Gray. *Scorer:* Jones.
1970–71 ARSENAL Wilson; Rice, McNab; Storey (Kelly), McLintock, Simpson; Armstrong, Graham, Radford, Kennedy, George. *Scorers:* Kelly, George.
2-1 aet LIVERPOOL Clemence; Lawler, Lindsay; Smith, Lloyd, Hughes; Callaghan, Evans (Thompson), Heighway, Toshack, Hall. *Scorer:* Heighway.
1971–72 LEEDS UNITED Harvey; Reaney, Madeley; Bremner, J. Charlton, Hunter; Lorimer, Clarke, Jones, Giles, E. Gray. *Scorer:* Clarke.
1-0 ARSENAL Barnett; Rice, McNab; Storey, McLintock, Simpson; Armstrong, Ball, George, Radford (Kennedy), Graham.
1972–73 SUNDERLAND Montgomery; Malone, Guthrie; Horswill, Watson, Pitt; Kerr, Hughes, Halom, Porterfield, Tueart. *Scorer:* Porterfield.
1-0 LEEDS UNITED Harvey; Reaney, Cherry; Bremner, Madeley, Hunter; Lorimer, Clarke, Jones, Giles, E. Gray (Yorath).
1973–74 LIVERPOOL Clemence; Smith, Lindsay, Thompson, Cormack, Hughes, Keegan, Hall, Heighway,

Toshack, Callaghan. *Scorers:* Keegan 2, Heighway.

3-0 NEWCASTLE UNITED McFaul; Clark, Kennedy, McDermott, Howard, Moncur, Smith (Gibb), Cassidy, Macdonald, Tudor, Hibbitt.

1974–75 WEST HAM UNITED Day; McDowell, T. Taylor, Lock, Lampard, Bonds, Paddon, Brooking, Jennings, A. Taylor, Holland. *Scorer:* A. Taylor 2.

2-0 FULHAM Mellor; Cutbush, Lacy, Moore, Fraser, Mullery, Conway, Slough, Mitchell, Busby, Barrett.

1975–76 SOUTHAMPTON Turner; Rodrigues, Peach, Holmes, Blyth, Steele, Gilchrist, Channon, Osgood, McCalliog, Stokes. *Scorer:* Stokes.

1-0 MANCHESTER UNITED Stepney; Forsyth, Houston, Daly, Greenhoff, Buchan, Coppell, McIlroy, Pearson, Macari, Hill (McCreery).

1976–77 MANCHESTER UNITED Stepney; Nicholl, Albiston, McIlroy, B. Greenhoff, Buchan, Coppell, J. Greenhoff, Pearson, Macari, Hill (McCreery). *Scorers:* Pearson, J. Greenhoff.

2-1 LIVERPOOL Clemence; Neal, Jones, Smith, Kennedy, Hughes, Keegan, Case, Heighway, Johnson (Callaghan), McDermott. *Scorer:* Case.

1977–78 IPSWICH TOWN Cooper; Burley, Mills, Osborne (Lambert), Hunter, Beattie, Talbot, Wark, Mariner, Geddis, Woods. *Scorer:* Osborne.

1-0 ARSENAL Jennings; Rice, Nelson, Price, Young, O'Leary, Brady (Rix), Hudson, Macdonald, Stapleton, Sunderland.

1978–79 ARSENAL Jennings; Rice, Nelson, Talbot, O'Leary, Young, Brady, Sunderland, Stapleton, Price (Walford), Rix. *Scorers:* Talbot, Stapleton, Sunderland.

3-2 MANCHESTER UNITED Bailey; Nicholl, Albiston, McIlroy, McQueen. Buchan, Coppell, J. Greenhoff, Jordan, Macari, Thomas. *Scorers:* McQueen, McIlroy.

1979–80 WEST HAM UNITED Parkes; Stewart, Lampard, Bonds, Martin, Devonshire, Allen, Pearson, Cross, Brooking, Pike. *Scorer:* Brooking.

1-0 ARSENAL Jennings; Rice, Devine (Nelson), Talbot, O'Leary, Young, Brady, Sunderland, Stapleton, Price, Rix

1980–81 TOTTENHAM HOTSPUR Aleksic; Hughton, Miller, Roberts, Perryman, Villa (Brooke), Ardiles, Archibald, Galvin, Hoddle, Crooks. *Scorer:* Hutchison (og).

1-1 aet MANCHESTER CITY Corrigan; Ranson, McDonald, Reid, Power, Caton, Bennett, Gow, MacKenzie, Hutchison (Henry), Reeves. *Scorer:* Hutchison.

***R*:3-2** TOTTENHAM HOTSPUR Aleksic; Hughton, Miller, Roberts, Perryman, Villa, Ardiles, Archibald, Galvin, Hoddle, Crooks. *Scorers:* Villa 2, Crooks.

MANCHESTER CITY Corrigan; Ranson, McDonald (Tueart), Caton, Reid, Gow, Power, MacKenzie, Reeves, Bennett, Hutchison. *Scorers:* MacKenzie, Reeves (pen).

1981–82 TOTTENHAM HOTSPUR Clemence; Hughton, Miller, Price, Hazard (Brooke), Perryman, Roberts, Archibald, Galvin, Hoddle, Crooks. *Scorer:* Hoddle.

1-1 aet QPR Hucker; Fenwick, Gillard, Waddock, Hazell, Roeder, Currie, Flanagan, Allen (Micklewhite), Stainrod, Gregory. *Scorer:* Fenwick.

***R*:1-0** TOTTENHAM HOTSPUR Clemence; Hughton, Miller, Price, Hazard (Brooke), Perryman, Roberts, Archibald, Galvin, Hoddle, Crooks. *Scorer:* Hoddle (pen).

QPR Hucker; Fenwick, Gillard, Waddock, Hazell, Neill, Currie, Flanagan, Micklewhite (Burke), Stainrod, Gregory.

1982–83 MANCHESTER UNITED Bailey; Duxbury, Moran, McQueen, Albiston, Davies, Wilkins, Robson, Muhren, Stapleton, Whiteside. *Scorers:* Stapleton, Wilkins.

2-2 aet BRIGHTON & HOVE ALBION Moseley; Ramsey (Ryan), Stevens, Gatting, Pearce, Smillie, Case, Grealish, Howlett, Robinson, Smith. *Scorers:* Smith, Stevens.

***R*:4-0** MANCHESTER UNITED Bailey; Duxbury, Albiston, Wilkins, Moran, McQueen, Robson, Muhren, Stapleton, Whiteside, Davies. *Scorers:* Robson 2, Whiteside, Muhren (pen).

BRIGHTON & HOVE ALBION Moseley; Gatting, Pearce, Grealish, Foster, Stevens, Case, Howlett, Robinson, Smith, Smillie.

1983–84 EVERTON Southall; Stevens, Bailey, Ratcliffe, Mountfield, Reid, Steven, Heath, Sharp, Gray, Richardson. *Scorers:* Sharp, Gray.

2-0 WATFORD Sherwood; Bardsley, Price (Atkinson), Taylor, Terry, Sinnott, Callaghan, Johnston, Reilly, Jackett, Barnes.

1984–85 MANCHESTER UNITED Bailey; Gidman, Albiston (Duxbury), Whiteside, McGrath, Moran, Robson, Strachan, Hughes, Stapleton, Olsen. *Scorer:* Whiteside.

1-0 aet EVERTON Southall; Stevens, Van den Hauwe, Ratcliffe, Mountfield, Reid, Steven, Gray, Sharp, Bracewell, Sheedy.

1985–86 LIVERPOOL Grobbelaar; Lawrenson, Beglin, Nicol, Whelan, Hansen, Dalglish, Johnston, Rush, Molby, MacDonald. *Scorers:* Rush 2, Johnston.

3–1 EVERTON Mimms; Stevens (Heath), Van Den Hauwe, Ratcliffe, Mountfield, Reid, Steven, Lineker, Sharp, Bracewell, Sheedy. *Scorer:* Lineker.

1986–87 COVENTRY CITY Ogrizovic; Phillips, Downs, McGrath, Kilcline (Rodger), Peake, Bennett, Gynn, Regis, Houchen, Pickering. *Scorers:* Bennett, Houchen, Mabbutt (og).

3-2 aet TOTTENHAM HOTSPUR Clemence; Hughton (Claesen), M. Thomas, Hodge, Gough. Mabbutt, C. Allen, P. Allen, Waddle, Hoddle, Ardiles (Stevens). *Scorers:* C. Allen, Kilcline (og).

1987–88 WIMBLEDON Beasant; Goodyear, Phelan, Jones, Young, Thorn, Gibson (Scales), Cork (Cunningham), Fashanu, Sanchez, Wise. *Scorer:* Sanchez.

1-0 LIVERPOOL Grobbelaar; Gillespie, Ablett, Nicol, Spackman (Molby), Hansen, Beardsley, Aldridge (Johnston), Houghton, Barnes, McMahon.

1988–89 LIVERPOOL Grobbelaar; Ablett, Staunton (Venison), Nicol, Whelan, Hansen, Beardsley, Aldridge (Rush), Houghton, Barnes, McMahon. *Scorers:* Aldridge, Rush 2.

3–2 aet EVERTON Southall; McDonald, Van Den Hauwe, Ratcliffe, Watson, Bracewell (McCall), Nevin, Steven, Sharp, Cottee, Sheedy (Wilson). *Scorer:* McCall 2.

1989–90 MANCHESTER UNITED Leighton; Ince, Martin (Blackmore), Bruce, Phelan, Pallister (Robins), Robson, Webb, McClair, Hughes, Wallace. *Scorers:* Robson, Hughes 2.

3–3 aet CRYSTAL PALACE Martyn; Pemberton, Shaw, Gray (Madden), O'Reilly, Thorn, Barber (Wright), Thomas, Bright, Salako, Pardew. *Scorers:* O'Reilly, Wright 2.

R:1–0 MANCHESTER UNITED Sealey; Ince, Martin, Bruce, Phelan, Pallister, Robson, Webb, McClair, Hughes, Wallace, *Scorer:* Martin.
CRYSTAL PALACE Martyn; Pemberton, Shaw, Gray, O'Reilly, Thorn, Barber (Wright), Thomas, Bright, Salako (Madden), Pardew.

1990–91 TOTTENHAM HOTSPUR Thorstvedt; Edinburgh, Van Den Hauwe, Sedgley, Howells, Mabbutt, Stewart,
2-1 Gascoigne (Nayim), Samways (Walsh), Lineker, Allen. *Scorers:* Stewart, Walker (og).
aet NOTTINGHAM FOREST Crossley; Charles, Pearce, Walker, Chettle, Keane, Crosby, Parker, Clough, Glover (Laws), Woan (Hodge). *Scorer:* Pearce.

1991–92 LIVERPOOL Grobbelaar; Jones R, Burrows, Nicol, Molby, Wright, Saunders, Houghton, Rush, McManaman, Thomas. *Scorers:* Thomas, Rush.
2-0 SUNDERLAND Norman; Owers, Ball, Bennett, Rogan, Rush (Hardyman), Bracewell, Davenport, Armstrong, Byrne, Atkinson (Hawke).

1992–93 ARSENAL Seaman; Dixon, Winterburn, Davis, Linighan, Adams, Jensen, Wright (O'Leary), Smith, Merson, Campbell. *Scorers:* Wright, Linighan.
2–1 SHEFFIELD WEDNESDAY Woods; Nilsson (Bart-Williams), Worthington, Harkes, Palmer, Warhurst,
aet Wilson (Hyde), Waddle, Hirst, Bright, Sheridan. *Scorer:* Waddle.

Paul Ince (left disputes possession with Chelsea player-manager Glenn Hoddle during the 1994 FA Cup Final. Manchester United won 4-0. (Colorsport).

FA CUP 1993–94

PRELIMINARY AND QUALIFYING ROUNDS

Preliminary Round
Consett v Willington 5-2
Billingham Town v Alnwick Town 1-1, 2-1
Yorkshire Amateur v Brandon United 2-1
Billingham Synthonia v Darlington Cleveland Social 3-0
Harrogate Town v Peterlee Newtown 5-2
Evenwood Town v Ferryhill Athletic 3-1
Esh Winning v Gretna 0-1
Horden CW v Hebburn 4-4, 1-2
Ryhope CA v Prudhoe East End 0-3
Shildon w.o v South Shields removed
Pickering Town v Penrith 5-2
Workington v Crook Town 0-2
Tow Law Town v West Auckland Town 1-0
Lancaster City v Whickham 3-1
Murton v Durham City 3-2
Atherton LR v Blackpool (wren) Rovers 1-1, 6-1
Alfreton Town v Armthorpe Welfare 3-2
Blidworth MW v Arnold Town 1-4
Belper Town v Bamber Bridge 1-2
Caernarfon Town v Burscough 0-0, 0-2
Clitheroe v Congleton Town 1-0
Warrington Town v Bradford Park Avenue 5-0
Flixton v Farsley Celtic 2-0
Glasshoughton Welfare v Glossop North End 0-2
Eccleshill United v Denaby United 2-2, 1-2
Hucknall Town v Chadderton 4-0
Great Harwood Town v Guiseley 1-5
Ossett Town v Harworth CI 5-3
Immingham Town v Ilkeston Town 1-3
Newcastle Town v Ossett Albion 1-1, 2-1
Maine Road v Maltby MW 0-1
Lincoln United v Mossley 4-2
Oldham Town v North Ferriby United 1-3
Skelmersdale United v Thackley 0-1
Rossendale United v Rossington Main 3-0
Radcliffe Borough v Salford City 1-3
Stocksbridge Park Steels v St Helens Town 1-2
Wednesfield v Eastwood Town 1-0
West Bromwich Town v Willenhall Town 1-3
Winterton Rangers v Prescot 2-0
Bilston Town v Bridgnorth Town 0-2
Armitage v Banbury United 1-0
Chasetown v Barwell 2-1
Boldmere St Michaels v Blakenall 2-0
Halesown Harriers v Leicester United 2-4
Dudley Town v Eastwood Hanley 2-1
Desborough Town v Evesham United 1-0
Hinckley Town v Hinckley Athletic 2-1
Long Buckby v Redditch United 2-2, 1-3
Lye Town v Northampton Spencer 1-2
Daventry Town v Oldbury United 0-3
Racing Club Warwick v Pershore Town 1-2
Stewarts & Lloyds v Stratford Town 1-3
Rothwell Town v Rushall Olympic 2-0
Rocester v Rushden & Diamonds 0-1
Stourport Swifts v Stourbridge 0-0, 1-2
Brightlingsea United v Canvey Island 1-3
Bishop's Stortford v Boston 4-0
Billericay Town v Bourne Town 5-2
Bury Town v Burnham Ramblers 1-2
Haverhill Rovers v Eynesbury Rovers 1-2
Felixstowe Town v Gorleston 1-1, 2-0
(replay at Diss Town)
Fakenham Town v Great Yarmouth Town 2-2, 1-3
Histon v Heybridge Swifts 0-9
Stamford v Tiptree United 4-1
Mirrlees Blackstone v Kings Lynn 0-1
March Town United v Saffron Walden Town 3-2
Sudbury Town v Stowmarket Town 4-1
Watton United v Barking 3-1
(at Diss Town)
Wisbech Town v Brimsdown Rovers 3-1
Lowestoft Town v Tamworth 3-2
Brook House v Boreham Wood 2-1
Chatteris Town v Cornard United 2-3
Biggleswade Town v Barton Rovers 0-3
(at Letchworth Garden City)
Dunstable v Collier Row 2-2, 1-0
Edgware Town v Feltham & Hounslow Borough 3-0
Clapton v Cheshunt 1-1, 1-2
Hertford Town v Kempston Rovers 0-1
Hanwell Town v Harefield United 1-2
Ford United v Haringey Borough 1-1, 0-2
Hornchurch v Hoddesdon Town 1-1, 3-0
(replay at Ware)
Northwood v Royston Town 3-0
Langford v Leighton Town 2-1
Ruislip Manor v Letchworth Garden City 4-3
Rainham Town v Purfleet 1-5
Walthamstow Pennant v Wingate & Finchley 2-3
Tilbury v Tring Town 1-1, 4-0
Staines Town v Uxbridge 1-0
Southall v Ware 1-0
Bracknell Town v Bognor Regis Town 3-3, 0-5
Burgess Hill Town v Arundel 3-0
Bedfont w.o v Beckenham Town withdrew
Horsham YMCA v Croydon Athletic 2-2, 2-5
Eastbourne United v Egham Town 5-1
Croydon v Corinthian-Casuals 5-0
Hailsham Town v Epsom & Ewell 1-4
Faversham Town v Fisher 3-0
(Fisher awarded tie; Faversham Town used ineligible player)
Erith & Belvedere v Godalming & Guildford 2-1
Horsham v Herne Bay 1-2
Merstham v Pagham 1-4
Lewes v Littlehampton Town 3-1
Langney Sports v Malden Vale 2-1
Oakwood v Metropolitan Police 1-1, 1-3
Portfield v Steyning Town 1-0
Redhill v Ringmer 1-2
Ramsgate v Selsey 1-1, 3-3, 1-0
(tie awarded to Selsey as Ramsgate had played an ineligible player in the first match)
Southwick v Slade Green 2-1
Whyteleafe v Three Bridges 5-1
Tooting & Mitcham United v Tunbridge Wells 7-0
Tonbridge v Whitehawk 4-1
Windsor & Eton v Wick 1-4
Cove v Walton & Hersham 2-1
Bournemouth v Brockenhurst 0-1
Shoreham v Buckingham Town 0-2
Fareham Town v Eastleigh 1-1, 1-4
Newbury Town v Lancing 6-1
Gosport Borough v Hungerford Town 0-3
Peacehaven & Telscombe v Fleet Town 2-1
Oxford City v Newport (IW) 0-7
Totton v Ryde Sports 1-1, 3-1
Poole Town v Swanage Town & Herston 5-0
Petersfield United removed v Thame United w.o
Wimborne Town v Westbury United 5-0
Barnstaple Town v Exmouth Town 4-0
Bridport v Bristol Manor Farm 4-0
Bideford v Chippenham Town 2-2, 0-3
Elmore v Devizes Town 2-1
Melksham Town v Falmouth Town 1-0
Frome Town v Glastonbury 3-3, 1-0
Odd Down v Ilfracombe Town 1-1, 2-2, 1-0
Moreton Town v Minehead 2-0
Torrington v Yate Town 1-4
Shortwood United v St Blazey 3-2
Dawlish Town v Taunton Town 0-12
Weston-Super-Mare v Welton Rovers 6-1

First Qualifying Round

Billingham Town v Billingham Synthonia	0-3
Yorkshire Amateur v Dunston Fed Brewery	1-3
Gateshead v Blyth Spartans	4-0
Chester-Le-Street v Consett	2-3
Evenwood Town v Hebburn	0-0, 3-0
Gretna v Seaham Red Star	3-1
Barrow v Guisborough Town	3-1
Harrogate Railway v Harrogate Town	1-2
Shildon v Easington Colliery	0-1
Pickering Town v Northallerton Town	0-2
Bishop Auckland v Netherfield	1-4
Newcastle Blue Star v Prudhoe East End	3-2
Tow Law Town v Murton	3-3, 2-1
Lancaster City v Stockton	2-1
Whitley Bay v Spennymoor United	1-6
Whitby Town v Crook Town	5-1
Alfreton Town v Bamber Bridge	2-3
Arnold Town v Leek Town	1-3
Northwich Victoria v Emley	2-2, 0-2
Ashton United v Atherton LR	4-0
Clitheroe v Curzon Ashton	2-2, 1-0
Warrington Town v Matlock Town	3-0
Stalybridge Celtic v Fleetwood Town	6-0
Bootle v Burscough	5-1
Glossop North End v Goole Town	2-2, 0-1
Denaby United v Morecambe	0-4
Bridlington Town v Frickley Athletic	2-0
Darwen v Flixton	1-1, 0-3
Guiseley v Ilkeston Town	3-1
Ossett Town v Winsford United	1-1, 1-3
Buxton v Gainsborough Trinity	2-1
Heanor Town v Hucknall Town	1-2
Maltby MW v North Ferriby United	1-1, 2-4
Lincoln United v Nantwich Town	2-0
Chorley v Horwich RMI	3-1
Liversedge v Newcastle Town	3-2
Rossendale United v St Helens Town	1-1, 0-1
Salford City v Knowsley United	1-1, 0-6
Colwyn Bay v Hyde United	4-1
Sheffield v Thackley	1-4
Willenhall Town v West Midlands Police	1-2
Winterton Rangers v Nuneaton Borough	1-7
Droylsden v Brigg Town	1-1, 1-0
Worksop Town v Wednesfield	1-1, 2-0
Armitage 90 v Boldmere St Michaels	3-0
Chasetown v Solihull Borough	0-1
Bromsgrove Rovers v Gresley Rovers	1-1, 1-0
Bedworth United v Bridgnorth Town	2-1
Dudley Town v Hinckley Town	1-1, 3-2
Desborough Town v Raunds Town	1-3
Telford United v Halesowen Town	4-0
Grantham Town v Leicester United	3-1
Northampton Spencer v Pershore Town	0-1
Oldbury United v Pelsall Villa	1-1, 0-3
Atherstone United v Hednesford Town	2-1
Paget Rangers v Redditch United	1-1, 1-2
Rothwell Town v Stourbridge	7-1
Rushden & Diamonds v Sutton Coldfield Town	2-0
Burton Albion v Moor Green	2-1
Sandwell Borough v Stratford Town	5-0
Bishop's Stortford v Burnham Ramblers	2-0
Billericay Town v Aveley	1-1, 3-1
Boston United v Braintree Town	1-1, 2-1
Basildon United v Canvey Island	1-1, 0-1
Felixstowe Town v Heybridge Swifts	1-1, 1-5
Great Yarmouth Town v Hendon	2-2, 2-4
Cambridge City v Berkhamsted Town	4-1
Harwich & Parkeston v Eynesbury Rovers	4-1
Kings Lynn v Sudbury Town	2-1
March Town United v Wivenhoe Town	3-6
Chelmsford City v Newmarket Town	0-0, 1-1, 3-0
Spalding United v Stamford	1-2
Wisbech Town v East Thurrock United	1-1, 0-1
Lowestoft Town v Witham Town	1-0
Stevenage Borough v Wembley	2-2, 1-1, 1-0
Corby Town v Watton United	4-0
Cornard United v Halstead Town	0-1
Barton Rovers v Arlesey Town	1-0
Dagenham & Redbridge v Hitchin Town	1-0
Baldock Town v Brook House	6-0
Edgware Town v Flackwell Heath	2-0
Cheshunt v Burnham	0-2
Chesham United v St Albans City	5-0
Chalfont St Peter v Dunstable	1-0
Harefield United v Hornchurch	1-2
Haringey Borough v Hampton	0-0, 2-1
Enfield v Welling United	4-1
Hemel Hempstead v Kempston Rovers	2-1
Langford v Purfleet	1-4
Ruislip Manor v Leyton	3-1
Grays Athletic v Yeading	0-2
Kingsbury Town v Northwood	2-1
Tilbury v Southall	3-2
Staines Town v Chertsey Town	1-2
Harrow Borough v Wealdstone	3-1
Viking Sports v Wingate & Finchley	3-0
Burgess Hill Town v Chatham Town	0-1
Bedfont v Canterbury City	0-1
Kingstonian v Ashford Town	2-1
Banstead Athletic v Bognor Regis Town	0-3
Eastbourne United v Greenwich Borough	0-2
Croydon v Chipstead	4-1
Hastings Town v Molesey	1-5
Corinthian v Croydon Athletic	3-0
Fisher v Herne Bay	3-3, 2-3
Erith & Belvedere v Deal Town	4-3
Sittingbourne v Dover Athletic	1-1, 2-1
Gravesend & Northfleet v Epsom & Ewell	3-0
Lewes v Metropolitan Police	1-1, 2-3
Langney Sports v Leatherhead	3-8
Bromley v Dulwich Hamlet	3-1
Margate v Pagham	6-0
Ringmer v Southwick	1-0
Selsey v Basingstoke Town	2-3
Carshalton Athletic v Havant Town	2-0
Sheppey United v Portfield	1-1, 3-0
Tooting & Mitcham United v Wick	3-1
Tonbridge v Bemerton Heath Harlequins	3-0
Dorking v Worthing	4-1
Whitstable Town v Whyteleafe	2-1
Brockenhurst v Eastleigh	1-4
Buckingham Town v Andover	0-1
Bashley v Abingdon Town	2-1
Calne Town v Cove	5-1
Hungerford Town v Newport (IW)	0-2
Peacehaven & Telscombe v Lymington	1-1, 0-2
Dorchester Town v Wokingham Town	1-0
Maidenhead United v Newbury Town	1-2
Poole Town v Wimborne Town	0-0, 0-2
Thame United v Witney Town	1-1, 2-1
Waterlooville v Salisbury City	1-0
Thatcham Town v Totton	4-2
Bridport v Elmore	2-3
Chippenham Town v Weymouth	0-5
Gloucester City v Clevedon Town	1-2
Cinderford Town v Barnstaple Town	1-1, 1-3
Frome Town v Moreton Town	0-0, 0-1
Odd Down v Forest Green Rovers	2-2, 3-1
Trowbridge Town v Newport AFC	1-1, 5-0
Mangotsfield United v Melksham Town	3-0
Shortwood United v Weston-Super-Mare	1-3
Taunton Town v Saltash United	3-0
Worcester City v Tiverton Town	1-1, 2-4
Paulton Rovers v Yate Town	2-1

Second Qualifying Round

Dunston FB v Billingham Synthonia	1-1, 0-1
Gateshead v Consett	3-1
Gretna v Evenwood Town	8-1
Barrow v Harrogate Town	6-1
Northallerton Town v Easington Colliery	4-1
Netherfield v Newcastle Blue Star	3-2
Lancaster City v Tow Law Town	3-2
Spennymoor United v Whitby Town	2-3
Leek Town v Bamber Bridge	5-3
Emley v Ashton United	2-0
Warrington Town v Clitheroe	2-2, 2-0

Stalybridge Celtic v Bootle 2-2, 3-1
Morecambe v Goole Town 3-2
Bridlington Town v Flixton 2-1
Winsford United v Guiseley 2-1
Buxton v Hucknall Town 2-0
Lincoln United v North Ferriby United 1-5
Chorley v Liversedge 2-1
Knowsley United v St Helens Town 2-1
Colwyn Bay v Thackley 4-1
Nuneaton Borough v West Midlands Police 3-3, 3-0
Droylsden v Worksop Town 1-1, 0-3
Solihull Borough v Armitage 90 2-2, 3-2
Bromsgrove Rovers v Bedworth United 2-0
Raunds Town v Dudley Town 3-1
Telford United v Grantham Town 2-2, 3-1
Pelsall Villa v Pershore Town 1-2
Atherstone United v Redditch United 0-0, 1-1, 3-1
Rushden & Diamonds v Rothwell Town 1-1, 2-0
Burton Albion v Sandwell Borough 3-2
Billericay Town v Bishop's Stortford 1-3
Boston United v Canvey Island 2-3
Hendon v Heybridge Swifts 5-2
Cambridge City v Harwich & Parkeston 3-0
Wivenhoe Town v Kings Lynn 2-2, 4-1
Chelmsford City v Stamford AFC 5-2
Lowestoft Town v East Thurrock United 1-2
Stevenage Borough v Corby Town 4-3
Barton Rovers v Halstead Town 1-2
Dagenham & Redbridge v Baldock Town 2-1
Burnham v Edgware Town 1-3
Chesham United v Chalfont St Peter 5-0
Haringey Borough v Hornchurch 1-3
Enfield v Hemel Hempstead 1-0
Ruislip Manor v Purfleet 1-1, 0-1
Yeading v Kingsbury Town 5-2
Chertsey Town v Tilbury 2-0
Harrow Borough v Viking Sports 6-0
Canterbury City v Chatham Town 1-4
Kingstonian v Bognor Regis Town 1-1, 6-1
Croydon v Greenwich Borough 0-1
Molesey v Corinthian 2-0
Erith & Belvedere v Herne Bay 2-1
Sittingbourne v Gravesend & Northfleet 0-2
Leatherhead v Metropolitan Police 3-5
Bromley v Margate 0-3
Basingstoke Town v Ringmer 3-0
Carshalton Athletic v Sheppey United 5-1
Tonbridge v Tooting & Mitcham United 0-2
Dorking v Whitstable Town 4-0
Andover v Eastleigh 3-0
Bashley v Calne Town 3-1
Lymington v Newport (IW) 0-1
Dorchester Town v Newbury Town 0-3
Thame United v Wimborne Town 2-3
Waterlooville v Thatcham Town 3-0
Weymouth v Elmore 3-0
Clevedon Town v Barnstaple Town 2-2, 1-2
Odd Down v Moreton Town 0-2
Trowbridge Town v Mangotsfield United 0-0, 2-2, 2-3
Taunton Town v Weston-Super-Mare 2-4
Tiverton Town v Paulton Rovers 2-1

Third Qualifying Round
Billingham Synthonia v Gateshead 1-1, 1-0
Gretna v Barrow 2-1
Northallerton Town v Netherfield 4-3
Lancaster City v Whitby Town 1-2
Leek Town v Emley 1-0
Warrington Town v Stalybridge Celtic 0-1
Morecambe v Bridlington Town 2-0
Winsford United v Buxton 6-1
North Ferriby United v Chorley 1-1, 1-2
Knowsley United v Colwyn Bay 3-0
Nuneaton Borough v Worksop Town 4-1
Solihull Borough v Bromsgrove Rovers 1-2
Raunds Town v Telford United 0-4
Pershore Town v Atherstone United 1-0
Rushden & Diamonds v Burton Albion 4-0
Bishop's Stortford v Canvey Island 0-1
Hendon v Cambridge City 0-1
Wivenhoe Town v Chelmsford City 2-0
East Thurrock United v Stevenage Borough 1-5
Halstead Town v Dagenham & Redbridge 1-3
Edgware Town v Chesham United 1-2
Hornchurch v Enfield 1-4
Purfleet v Yeading 1-2
Chertsey Town v Harrow Borough 1-3
Chatham Town v Kingstonian 1-2
Greenwich Borough v Molesey 0-4
Erith & Belvedere v Gravesend & Northfleet 0-1
Metropolitan Police v Margate 5-2
Basingstoke Town v Carshalton Athletic 1-3
Tooting & Mitcham United v Dorking 2-0
Andover v Bashley 0-2
Newport (IW) v Newbury Town 4-2
Wimborne Town v Waterlooville 0-1
Weymouth v Barnstaple Town 2-1
Moreton Town v Mangotsfield United 1-1, 2-1
Weston-Super-Mare v Tiverton Town 0-0, 2-0

Fourth Qualifying Round
Witton Albion v Northallerton Town 2-1
Winsford United v Gretna 0-0, 0-5
Macclesfield Town v Southport 5-3
Altrincham v Accrington Stanley 0-2
Stalybridge Celtic v Whitby Town 0-0, 1-0
Stafford Rangers v Knowsley United 1-1, 2-2, 0-1
Billingham Synthonia v Leek Town 1-1, 1-2
Chorley v Marine 0-2
Telford United v Morecambe 2-0
Wivenhoe Town v Enfield 1-2
Hayes v Slough Town 0-2
Cambridge City v Dagenham & Redbridge 2-2, 2-0
Stevenage Borough v Nuneaton Borough 1-2
Kettering Town v Canvey Island 3-1
VS Rugby v Harrow Borough 2-2, 2-1
Aylesbury United v Marlow 1-2
Pershore Town v Yeading 1-3
Rushden & Diamonds v Bromsgrove Rovers 1-3
Chesham United v Kidderminster Harriers 1-4
Kingstonian v Metropolitan Police 0-1
Waterlooville v Gravesend & Northfleet 1-3
Crawley Town v Merthyr Tydfil 2-1
Cheltenham Town v Bath City 1-1, 2-4
Bashley v Carshalton Athletic 1-1, 2-4
Sutton United v Moreton Town 0-0, 2-0
Molesey v Tooting & Mitcham United 0-0, 2-1
Weymouth v Farnborough Town 1-4
Weston-Super-Mare v Newport (IW) 2-0

FA CUP 1993–94

COMPETITION PROPER

FIRST ROUND

12 NOV

Leek (0) 2 *(Sutton D 2)*
Wigan Ath (1) 2 *(Skipper, Morton)* 2785
Leek: Mayfield; Jones S R, Sankey, Holmes (Finney), Norris, Diskin, Wheaton (Mitchell), Somerville, Sutton D, Jones S M, Smith.
Wigan Ath: Farnworth; Carragher, Rennie, Kennedy, Skipper, Johnson, Duffy, Rimmer (Langley), Gavin, Morton (Robertson), McKearney.

13 NOV

Barnet (0) 2 *(Haag, Close)*
Carshalton (1) 1 *(Annon)* 2690
Barnet: Phillips; Wilson, Haylock (Cooper), Hoddle (Alexander), Walker, Barnett D, Marwood, Rowe, Haag, Close, Scott.
Carshalton: Cleevely; Stevens, Ritchards, Priddle, Riley, Cooper, Warden, Bowyer, Bolton, Annon (Cox), Beste.

Bournemouth (3) 4 *(McGorry, Pennock, Masters, Wood)*
Brighton & HA (1) 2 *(Kennedy 2)* 5223
Bournemouth: Bartram (Moss); Pennock, Masters, Morris, Watson, Parkinson, O'Connor, McGorry, Chivers, Leadbitter, Wood.
Brighton & HA: Rust; Munday, Chapman, Pates, Foster, McCarthy, Edwards, Kennedy, Nogan (Crumplin), Codner, Geddes.

Bradford C (0) 0
Chester C (0) 0 6204
Bradford C: Bowling; Williams, Lawford, Duxbury L, Blake (McHugh), Richards, Jewell, Robson, McCarthy, Reid, Showler.
Chester C: Felgate; Preece, Jakub, Jenkins, Whelan, Greenall, Thompson, Lightfoot, Rimmer, Pugh, Wheeler.

Burnley (0) 0
York C (0) 0 10,199
Burnley: Beresford; Monington (Randall), Thompson, Davis, Pender, Joyce, Francis, Deary, Heath, Russell (Peel), Eyres.
York C: Kiely; McMillan, Hall, Pepper, Tutill, Warburton, McCarthy, Cooper, Barratt, Bushell, Canham.

Cambridge U (0) 0
Reading (0) 0 4594
Cambridge U: Filan; Jeffrey, Barrick, O'Shea, Heathcote, Daish, Livett (Danzey), Claridge, Fowler (Hyde), Rowett, Nyamah.
Reading: Hislop; Ranson, Kerr, Hopkins, Williams, Parkinson, Gilkes, Taylor, Quinn, Lovell, Gooding.

Chesterfield (0) 0
Rochdale (0) 1 *(Stuart (pen))* 3457
Chesterfield: Marples; Hewitt, Carr C, Curtis (Jules), Carr D, Law, Dyche (Rogers), Norris, Morris, Moss, Madden.
Rochdale: Hodge; Jones, Oliver, Bowden, Reeves, Butler, Stuart, Doyle, Lancaster, Whitehall, Ryan.

Colchester U (1) 3 *(McGavin, Brown S, English)*
Sutton U (2) 4 *(Quail, Smart, Newman, Morah)* 3051
Colchester U: Keeley; Betts, Roberts, Kinsella, English, Cawley, Dickens, Brown S, McDonough, McGavin, Smith.
Sutton U: McCaulsky; Gates, Smart, Golley, Costello, Jones, Anderson, Newman (McKinnon), Morah, Quail, Byrne.

Crewe Alex (2) 4 *(Edwards, Rowbotham, Gardiner, Smith S (pen))*
Darlington (2) 2 *(Ellison, Painter)*
Crewe Alex: Smith M; Booty, Gardiner, Evans, Abel, Smith S, Collins, Naylor, Edwards (Tierney), Lennon, Rowbotham.
Darlington: Collier; Shaw, Switzer, Himsworth, Gaughan, Gregan, Isaacs (Kirkham), Painter, Ellison, Chapman, Pearson.

Enfield (0) 0
Cardiff C (0) 0 2374
Enfield: McCann; Francis, Engwell, Roberts, Heald, St Hilaire, Hobson, Pye (Bailey), Turner, Collins, Ryan.
Cardiff C. Williams; Brazil, Searle, Millar, Perry, Aizlewood, Thompson (Bird), Richardson, Stant, Blake, Griffith.

Farnborough (1) 1 *(Jones)*
Exeter C (0) 3 *(Worthington, Jepson, Ross)* 2069
Farnborough: Taylor; Stemp, Pratt, Broome, Coney, Jones, Boothe, Read, Baker, Turkington, Horton.
Exeter C: Fox; Minett, Robinson (Daniels), Bailey, Brown, Whiston, Wigley, Coughlin, Jepson, Ross, Phillips (Worthington).

Gretna (2) 2 *(Townsley, Dobie)*
Bolton W (1) 3 *(McGinlay (pen), Coyle 2)* 6447
Gretna: Priestley; Armstrong, McCartney, Gorman, Gardiner, Townsley, Halpin, Walsh, Walker (Eagling), Dobie, Potts (Monaghan).
Bolton W: Davison; Brown, Phillips, McAteer, Stubbs, Winstanley, Lee, Green (Kelly), Coyle, McGinlay, Thompson.

Kidderminster (0) 3 *(Brindley, Forsyth (pen), Davies)*
Kettering (0) 0 3775
Kidderminster: Rose; Hodson, Bancroft, Weir, Brindley, Forsyth, Cartwright, Grainger, Humphreys, Davies, Palmer.
Kettering: Benstead; Mucklebergh, Ashby, Price, Oxbrow, Taylor, Wright (Thorpe), Brown (Roderick), Martin, Donald, Clark.

Knowsley (1) 1 *(Joyce (og))*
Carlisle U (3) 4 *(Arnold 2, Davey, Reeves)* 5015
Knowsley: Johnson; Wareing, Diggle, O'Brien, Jackson, Barton (King), McMahon, Kilshaw R (Siddell), Kilshaw B, Green, Gelling.
Carlisle U: Day; Burgess, Gallimore, Walling, Joyce, Edmondson (Fairweather), Thomas, Arnold, Reeves, Davey, Reddish.

Leyton Orient (1) 2 *(Lakin, Hackett)*
Gravesend & N (1) 1 *(Portway)* 5461
Leyton Orient: Newell; Hendon, Austin, Hackett, Harriott, Okai, Tomlinson, Ryan, Cooper, West, Lakin.
Gravesend & N: Turner; Harrop, Land, Gubbins, Gibbs, Cant, Schweiso, Hunt, Graves (Coffill), Portway, Ullathorne.

Macclesfield (2) 2 *(Sorvel, Macdonald)*
Hartlepool U (0) 0 2747
Macclesfield: Farrelly; Shepherd, Bimson, Kendall, Lillis, Sorvel, Askey, Wood (Macdonald), Alford, Adams, Sharratt.
Hartlepool U: Carter; Cross R, Skedd, McGuckin, MacPhail, Olsson, Gilchrist, Wratten (Honour), Houchen, Johnrose, West (Southall).

Mansfield T (0) 1 *(Wilkinson)*
Preston NE (0) 2 *(Ellis 2 (1 pen))* 4119
Mansfield T: Ward; Fleming, Platnauer, Holland, Gray, Clarke, Noteman, Stringfellow, Wilkinson, Parkin (Fairclough), Reed.
Preston NE: O'Hanlon; Fensome, Kidd, Lucas, Nebbeling, Moyes, Masefield (Norbury), Cartwright (Whalley), Conroy, Ellis, Raynor.

Marlow (0) 0
Plymouth Arg (0) 2 *(Dalton 2)* 2700
Marlow: Mitchell K; Mitchell S, Holmes, Baron, Ferguson, Regan (Malins), Lay, Chatlin (Dell), Blackman, Buzaglo, Watkins.
Plymouth Arg: Nicholls; Patterson, Naylor, Burrows, Comyn, McCall, Burnett, Castle, Nugent, Skinner (Marshall), Dalton.

Met Police (0) 0
Crawley (0) 2 *(Whitington, Van Sittart)* 1561
Met Police: Land; Towler, Mullings (Wright), Naylor, Carrugh, Reed, Adams, Pendry, Russo, Holding, Richardson (Clarke).
Crawley: Taylor; Pearson, Turner N, Shepherd, Vessey, Jeffrey, Payne, Ford, Van Sittart (Turner L), Whittington, Dack.

Molesey (0) 0
Bath (4) 4 *(Mings, Boyle, Adcock 2)* 913
Molesey: Brace; Langley, Woods, Dodman, Boorman (Callaghan), Patullo, Wilgoss (White), McCoy, Rose, Pearson, Rattue.
Bath: Mogg; Banks, Brooks, Boyle, Crowley, Cousins (Batty), Williams, Gill, Adcock (Vernon), Mings, Chenoweth.

Northampton T (0) 1 *(Aldridge)*
Bromsgrove (1) 2 *(Shilvock, Carter)* 3382
Northampton T: Sherwood; Parsons, Gillard, Phillips, Terry, Chard, Harmon (Fleming), Aldridge, Gilzean, Burnham, Bell.
Bromsgrove: Cooksey; Webb, Brighton, Richardson, Wardle, Skelding, Shilvock, Stott, Radburn (Pearce), Crisp, Carter.

Port Vale (2) 2 *(Kerr, Foyle)*
Blackpool (0) 0 8211
Port Vale: Musselwhite; Aspin, Tankard, Kerr (Porter), Swan, Glover, Jeffers, Van der Laan, Cross, Foyle, Taylor.
Blackpool: Martin; Davies, Cook, Horner, Briggs, Gouck, Watson, Bonner, Rodwell, Quinn (Mitchell), Griffiths.

Rotherham U (0) 1 *(Wilder (pen))*
Stockport Co (0) 2 *(Todd, Preece)* 4836
Rotherham U: Mercer; Wilder, Jacobs, Todd, Richardson, Brien, Williams B, Gooding, Helliwell, Varadi, Banks.
Stockport Co: Edwards; Beaumont, Todd, Frain, Flynn, Connelly, Miller (Wallace), Gannon, Francis, Ryan, Preece.

Runcorn 0
Hull City 1 *(Atkinson)*
Match abandoned; safety reasons

Scarborough (0) 1 *(Young)*
Bury (0) 0 2194
Scarborough: Evans; Knowles, Swales, Calvert, Davis, Rockett, Charles, Murray, Henderson, Thompson, Young.
Bury: Bracey; Hughes, Stanislaus, Daws, Lucketti, Jackson, Mauge, Carter, Adekola, Rigby, Kearney.

Shrewsbury T (0) 1 *(Gallen)*
Doncaster R (0) 1 *(Williamson)* 3408
Shrewsbury T: Edwards; Hockaday, Lynch, Taylor (Gallen), Williams, Walton, Brown, Patterson, Spink, Brough, Summerfield.
Doncaster R: Beasley; Measham, Freeman, Harper, Wilcox, Cunningham, Roche, Hulme, Jones, Turnbull, Williamson.

Slough (0) 1 *(Scott)*
Torquay U (2) 2 *(Sale, Moore)* 2371
Slough: Bunting; Quamina, Hancock, Manning, Lee, Edwards, Stanley (Walker), Scott S, Scott M, Sayer, Fiore.
Torquay U: Bayes; Barrow, Colcombe, O'Riordan, Moore (Burton), Curran, Trollope, Kelly, Foster (Darby), Sale, Hathaway.

Stalybridge (1) 1 *(Aspinall)*
Marine (1) 1 *(Rowlands)* 1525
Stalybridge: Hughes; Bennett, Coathup, Dixon, Aspinall, Booth, Brown, Leicester (Kirkham), Shaughnessy, Bunn, Locke (Jackson).
Marine: Holcroft; Ward, Hanson, Roche, Draper, Gautrey, Murray, Rowlands, Ross, Camden, Dawson.

Swansea C (0) 1 *(Torpey)*
Nuneaton (0) 1 *(Shearer)* 3532
Swansea C: Freestone; Clode, Cook, Walker, Harris (Ford), Pascoe, Bowen (McFarlane), Chapple, Torpey, Perrett, Hayes.
Nuneaton: Attwood; Byrne, McGrory, Bullock, Tarry, Keogh, Simpson, Bradder, Green, Rosegreen (Shearer), Wade.

Telford (1) 1 *(Bignot)*
Huddersfield T (1) 1 *(Rowe)* 2257
Telford: Acton; Pritchard, Parrish, Niblett, Gaunt, Fergusson, Bignot, Taylor, Whitehouse, Myers, Ford.
Huddersfield T: Francis; Trevitt, Billy, Hicks, Mitchell, Jackson, Rowe, Robinson P, Roberts, Onuora, Wells.

VS Rugby (0) 0
Brentford (1) 3 *(Allon 2 (1 pen), Gayle)* 3006
VS Rugby: Batchelor; Yang, McGinty, Smithers, Statham (Magill), Smith, Mason, King, Martin, Warner, Harriman (Alsop).
Brentford: Dearden; Hutchings, Grainger, Bates, Westley, Ratcliffe, Stephenson, Smith, Gayle, Allon, Mundee.

Witton (0) 0

Lincoln C (0) 2 *(West, Lormor)* 1450

Witton: Mason; Senior, Thomas, Edey, Walker (Blackwood), Garton, Gallagher, Rose, Maynard, Burke, Hall.
Lincoln C: Pollitt; Smith P, Baraclough, Hill, Brown, Schofield, West, Loughlan (Mardenborough), Johnson D, Matthews, Lormor.

Woking (1) 2 *(Wye S, Dennis)*

Weston Super Mare (2) 2 *(Elson, Bowering)* 2766

Woking: Batty; Clement, Steele, Berry, Brown K, Wye S, Brown D, Biggins, Dennis, Fielder, Walker.
Weston Super Mare: Stevens; Holt, Chattoe, Stearnes, Bowering, Rogers, Hooker, Catherton, Withey, Elson, Tapp.

Wrexham (1) 1 *(Watkin)*

Walsall (1) 1 *(Lightbourne)* 5151

Wrexham: Marriott; Pejic, Hardy, Lake, Humes, Hunter, Bennett, Owen, Connolly, Watkin, Durkan (Pugh).
Walsall: Walker; Evans, Marsh, Watkiss, Kiester, Ryder, Ntamark, Lightbourne, Walker, Peer, McDonald.

Yeading (0) 0

Gillingham (0) 0 2285

Yeading: Mackenzie; Ardren, Dicker, Cordery, Croad, Denton, Oatway, James, Welsh (Williams), Hippolyte, Charles (Baker).
Gillingham: Banks; Martin, Palmer, Butler, Green, Dunne, Carpenter, Forster, Baker (Arnott), Smith, Reinelt.

14 NOV

Accrington S (0) 2 *(Connor, Wood)*

Scunthorpe U (1) 3 *(Toman, Goodacre 2)* 5816

Accrington S: Armfield; Wood, Cooper, Connor, Moss, Williams, Grimshaw, Hughes (Senior), Lutkevich (Lampkin), Beck, Hoskin.
Scunthorpe U: Samways; Alexander, Mudd, Hope, Knill, Carmichael, Thompstone, Martin, White (Goodacre), Toman, Smith.

Bristol R (1) 1 *(Archer)*

Wycombe W (1) 2 *(Langford, Carroll)* 6421

Bristol R: Parkin; Channing, Maddison, Browning, Clark, Wright, Sterling, Taylor, Saunders, Skinner, Archer.
Wycombe W: Hyde; Cousins, Horton, Creaser, Evans, Ryan, Carroll, Langford (Hutchinson), Hayrettin, Scott, Guppy.

Cambridge C (0) 0

Hereford U (0) 1 *(Pike)* 2325

Cambridge C: Murray; Tovey, Scott, Fallon, Beattie, Gawthorpe, Wilkins, Pincher, Ryan, Grogan, Coe.
Hereford U: Judge; Clark H, Anderson, Downs, Smith, Reece, Hall, Fry, Pickard, Pike, Nicholson.

Halifax T (2) 2 *(Peake, Saunders)*

WBA (0) 1 *(Hunt)* 4250

Halifax T: Heyes; German, Craven, Edwards, Boardman, Barr, Peake, Ridings, Lambert, Paterson (Constable), Saunders.
WBA: Lange; Coldicott, Ampadu (Reid), McNally, O'Regan, Burgess, Hunt, Hamilton, Taylor, Ashcroft, Donovan (Mellon).

15 NOV

Yeovil (0) 1 *(Wallace)*

Fulham (0) 0 6180

Yeovil: Coles; Coates, Ferns, Sherwood, Bye, Leonard, Sanderson, Wallace, Wilson, Spencer, Harrower (Cooper).
Fulham: Stannard; Jupp, Ferney, Eckhardt, Angus, Thomas, Hails, Bedrossian, Farrell, Brazil, Baah.

23 NOV

Runcorn (0) 0

Hull C (0) 2 *(Brown, Hargreaves)* 1131

Runcorn: Williams; Bates, Robertson, Brady, Lee, Anderson, Thomas, Connor, McInerny, McKenna, Carroll.
Hull C: Fettis; Allison, Miller, Warren, Dewhurst, Abbott, Norton, Hargreaves, Brown, Windass, Atkinson.

FIRST ROUND REPLAYS

Huddersfield T (0) 1 *(Jackson)*

Telford (0) 0 3517

Huddersfield T: Francis; Trevitt, Billy, Mitchell, Hicks, Jackson, Rowe, Robinson R, Roberts, Dunn, Wells.
Telford: Hughes; Pritchard, Parrish, Niblett, Mitchell (Whitehouse), Fergusson, Bignot, Taylor, Ford, Myers, Statham.

Nuneaton (0) 2 *(Simpson 2)*

Swansea C (1) 1 *(Torpey) aet* 4443

Nuneaton: Attwood; Byrne, McGorry, Keogh, Carry, Wade (Symonds), Simpson, Bradder, Green, Rosegreen, Shearer.
Swansea C: Freestone; Clode (Ford), Cook, Walker, Harris, Pascoe, Bowen, Chapple, Torpey, Cornforth, Hayes (McFarlane).

Walsall (0) 2 *(Lightbourne, McDonald)*

Wrexham (0) 0 3971

Walsall: Walker; Evans, Marsh, Watkiss, Kiester, Ryder, Ntamark, Lightbourne, Wright, Peer, McDonald.
Wrexham: Marriott; Pejic, Hardy, Brammer, Humes, Hunter, Bennett, Owen, Connolly, Watkin, Cross (Pugh).

Weston Super Mare (0) 0

Woking (0) 1 *(Clement)* 2350

Weston Super Mare: Stevens; Holt, Jones (Chattoe), Stearnes, Bowering, Rogers, Hooker, Patterson, Withey, Elson, Tapp (Banks).
Woking: Batty; Clement, Steele, Berry, Brown K, Wye S, Brown D, Biggins, Fielder, Dennis, Walker.

24 NOV

Reading (1) 1 *(Gooding)*

Cambridge U (1) 2 *(Nyamah, Heathcote)* 4725

Reading: Hislop; Ranson, Kerr, Hopkins, Williams (McPherson), Parkinson, Gilkes, Gooding, Quinn, Lovell, Taylor (Hartenberger).
Cambridge U: Filan; Jeffrey, Barrick, O'Shea, Heathcote, Daish, Livett, Claridge, Fowler, Rowett, Nyamah.

29 NOV

Marine (2) 4 *(Camden 2, Murray, Doherty (pen))*
Stalybridge (2) 4 *(Hill, Shaughnessy, Aspinall, Kirkham)* 853

Marine: Holcroft; Baines, Ward, Roche (Hanson), McBride (Doherty), Gautrey, Murray, Rowlands, Ross, Camden, Daw.
Stalybridge: Hughes; Edmonds, Coathup, Dixon, Aspinall, Booth, Brown, Bunn, Shaughnessy (Leicester), Kirkham, Hill (Bennett).
aet; Stalybridge won 4-2 on penalties

30 NOV

Cardiff C (0) 1 *(Blake)*
Enfield (0) 0 3232

Cardiff C: Grew; Brazil, Searle, Aizlewood, Baddeley, Perry (Wigg), Bird (Thompson), Millar, Stant, Blake, Griffith.
Enfield: McCann; Francis, Engwell, Rideout (Britwell), Held, Pye (Boyle), Hobson, St Hilaire, Turner, Ryan, Collins.

Chester C (1) 1 *(Lightfoot)*
Bradford C (0) 0 3707

Chester C: Felgate; Preece, Jakub, Jenkins, Came, Greenall, Thompson (Whelan), Lightfoot (Bishop), Leonard, Pugh, Wheeler.
Bradford C: Bowling; Williams (Hoyle), Lawford, Duxbury L, Blake, Richards, Showler, Robson, McHugh (Tomlinson G), Oliver, Reid.

Gillingham (3) 3 *(Smith, Micklewhite, Baker)*
Yeading (0) 1 *(James)* 3231

Gillingham: Banks; Dunne, Palmer, Clark, Butler, Carpenter, Micklewhite, Forster (Reinelt), Baker, Smith, Smillie.
Yeading: McKenzie; Ardren, Dicker, Cordery, Croad, Denton, Oatway (Williams), Welsh, James, Hippolyte, Charles (Baker).

Wigan Ath (1) 3 *(McKearney (pen), Diskin (og), Duffy)*
Leek (0) 0 1804

Wigan Ath: Farnworth; Rennie, Wright (Ogden), Langley, Skipper, Johnson, Carragher, McKearney, Daley (Furlong), Gavin, Duffy.
Leek: Sutton S; Jones S R, Banks, Norris (Jones S M), Diskin, Clowes, Beeby, Somerville, Twigg, Sutton D, Smith (Finney).

York C (1) 2 *(Canham, McCarthy)*
Burnley (2) 3 *(Heath, Joyce, Eyres)* 5720

York C: Kiely; McMillan, Hall, Pepper, Tutill, Warburton, McCarthy, Naylor (Blackstone), Barnes, Bushell, Canham.
Burnley: Beresford; Monington, Thompson, Davis, Pender, Joyce, Francis, Deary, Heath, Russell, Eyres.

1 DEC

Doncaster R (0) 1 *(Williamson)*
Shrewsbury T (0) 2 *(Spink, Walton) aet* 3524

Doncaster R: Ford; Measham, Freeman, Harper, Wilcox, Cunningham, Roche, Yates, Whitmarsh (Thew), Turnbull (Masefield), Williamson.
Shrewsbury T: Edwards; Hockaday, Withe, Taylor (Evans), Williams, Lynch, Brown, Clarke, Spink, Walton, Patterson.

SECOND ROUND

3 DEC

Port Vale (0) 1 *(Tankard)*
Huddersfield T (0) 0 8602

Port Vale: Musselwhite; Aspin, Tankard, Kerr (Porter), Swan, Glover, Jeffers, Van der Laan, Cross (Slaven), Foyle, Taylor.
Huddersfield T: Francis; Trevitt, Billy, Mitchell, Hicks, Jackson, Rowe (Onuora), Dyson, Booth, Starbuck, Wells.

4 DEC

Bournemouth (0) 1 *(Watson)*
Nuneaton (0) 1 *(Green)* 5485

Bournemouth: Bartram; Chivers, Masters, Morris, Watson, Parkinson, O'Connor, McGorry, Beardsmore (Cotterill), Wood, Leadbitter.
Nuneaton: Attwood; Byrne, McGrory, Keogh, Tarry, Wade (Symonds), Simpson, Bradder, Green, Rosegreen, Shearer.

Brentford (0) 1 *(Gayle)*
Cardiff C (1) 3 *(Westley (og), Stant, Bird)* 4845

Brentford: Dearden; Statham, Grainger, Bates, Westley, Harvey, Hutchings, Smith, Gayle, Benjamin (Stephenson), Mundee.
Cardiff C: Grew; Brazil, Searle, Aizlewood, Baddeley, Perry, Bird, Richardson, Stant, Blake, Griffith.

Burnley (2) 4 *(Ryan (og), Eyres 3)*
Rochdale (0) 1 *(Whitehall (pen))* 11,388

Burnley: Beresford; Monington, Thompson, Davis, Pender, Joyce, Francis, Deary, Heath, Russell, Eyres.
Rochdale: Hodge; Thackeray, Bowden, Graham (Jones), Reeves, Butler, Stuart (Taylor), Reid, Lancaster, Whitehall, Ryan.

Carlisle U (2) 3 *(Edmondson, Gallimore, Arnold)*
Stalybridge (0) 1 *(Kirkham)* 5546

Carlisle U: Elliott; Burgess, Gallimore, Walling, Joyce, Edmondson (Oghani), Thomas, Arnold, Reeves, McCreery, Reddish.
Stalybridge: Hughes; Edmonds, Coathup, Dixon (Locke), Aspinall, Booth, Brown, Bunn (Leicester), Shaughnessy, Kirkham, Bennett.

Chester C (2) 2 *(Preece, Leonard)*
Hull C (0) 0 4333

Chester C: Felgate; Preece, Jakub, Jenkins, Came, Greenall, Wheeler, Lightfoot, Rimmer, Leonard, Pugh (Bishop).
Hull C: Fettis; Allison, Moran, Warren, Dewhurst, Abbott, Norton, Hargreaves (Lee), Brown, Windass, Atkinson.

Crawley (0) 1 *(Ford)*
Barnet (0) 2 *(Rowe, Hoddle)* 4104

Crawley: Taylor; Pearson, Turner N, Shepherd, Vessey, Jeffrey, Payne, Ford, Van Sittart, Adam (Turner L), Dack.
Barnet: Phillips; Wilson, Newson, Hoddle, Walker, Barnett D, Marwood (Alexander), Rowe, Haag, Close, Scott.

Crewe Alex (2) 2 *(Lennon, Whalley)*
Macclesfield (0) 1 *(Askey)* 6007

Crewe Alex: Smith M: Booty, Gardiner, Evans, Hughes, Wilson, Whalley (Tierney), Naylor, Collins, Lennon, Rowbotham.
Macclesfield: Farrelly; Shepherd, Bimson, Kendall, Lillis, Sorvel, Askey, Macdonald, Alford, Adams, Sharratt.

Kidderminster (0) 1 *(Forsyth (pen))*
Woking (0) 0 4411
Kidderminster: Rose; Hodson, Bancroft, Weir, Brindley, Forsyth, Cartwright (Palmer), Grainger, Humphreys, Davies, Purdie.
Woking: Batty; Clement, Steele, Berry, Brown K, Wye S, Brown D, Biggins (Dennis), Gray, Fielder, Walker.

Leyton Orient (1) 1 *(Cooper)*
Exeter C (1) 1 *(Bailey)* 4366
Leyton Orient: Newell; Hendon, Austin, Hackett, Bellamy, Kitchen, Carter (Okai), Barnett, Cooper, West, Lakin (Howard).
Exeter C: Fox; Minett, Brown, Bailey, Daniels, Whiston, Storer, Coughlin, Jepson, Worthington, Wigley.

Lincoln C (1) 1 *(Johnson D)*
Bolton W (1) 3 *(Thompson, Brown, Coyle)* 6250
Lincoln C: Pollitt; Smith P, Baraclough, Hill, Brown, Schofield, West, Lormor (Loughlan), Johnson D (Williams), Matthews, Smith M.
Bolton W: Davison; Brown, Phillips, Kelly, Seagraves, Winstanley, McAteer, Stubbs, Coyle, McGinlay, Thompson.

Plymouth Arg (1) 2 *(Nugent 2)*
Gillingham (0) 0 6051
Plymouth Arg: Nicholls; Edworthy (Evans), Naylor, Burrows, Comyn, McCall, Burnett, Castle, Nugent, Marshall, Patterson.
Gillingham: Banks; Dunne, Palmer, Butler, Clark, Breen (Green), Reinelt, Forster, Baker, Smith, Micklewhite.

Shrewsbury T (0) 0
Preston NE (1) 1 *(Raynor)* 5018
Shrewsbury T: Edwards; Hockaday, Lynch, Taylor (Smith), Williams, Evans, Brown, Clarke, Spink, Walton, Patterson.
Preston NE: Woods; Fensome, Kidd, Whalley, Lucas, Moyes, Ainsworth (Norbury), Challender, Conroy, Ellis (Bryson), Raynor.

Stockport Co (1) 5 *(Frain, Francis 2, Beaumont, Wallace)*
Halifax T (0) 1 *(Barr (pen))* 5496
Stockport Co: Edwards; Todd, Wallace, Frain, Flynn, Gannon, Miller, Emerson, Francis (Ryan), Beaumont, Preece.
Halifax T: Heyes; German (Cameron), Craven, Edwards, Boardman (Constable), Megson, Peake, Barr, Ridings, Patterson, Saunders.

Torquay U (0) 0
Sutton U (0) 1 *(Jones)* 3414
Torquay U: Bayes; Barrow, Colcombe, O'Riordan, Moore, Curran, Trollope, Kelly (Hodges), Foster (Darby), Sale, Hathaway.
Sutton U: McCaulsky; Gates, McKinnon, Golley, Costello, Jones, Anderson, Newman, Morah, Quail (Thomas), Byrne.

Walsall (1) 1 *(Wright)*
Scunthorpe U (1) 1 *(Carmichael)* 4962
Walsall: Walker; Evans, Marsh, Watkiss, Kiester, Ryder, Ntamark, Lightbourne, Wright, Peer, McDonald (O'Hara).
Scunthorpe U: Samways; Alexander, Mudd, Hope, Knill, Bradley, Thompstone, Martin, Carmichael, Toman (White), Smith.

Wigan Ath (0) 1 *(Gavin)*
Scarborough (0) 0 1837
Wigan Ath: Farnworth; Rennie, Wright, Langley, Skipper, Johnson, Carragher, McKearney, Daley, Gavin, Lyons.
Scarborough: Evans; Knowles, Swales, Calvert, Davis, Rockett, Charles, Murray, Henderson, Horsfield (Meyer), Young.

Wycombe W (0) 1 *(Hemmings)*
Cambridge U (0) 0 6313
Wycombe W: Hyde; Cousins, Horton (Creaser), Crossley, Evans, Ryan, Carroll, Langford (Thompson), Hayrettin, Hemmings, Guppy.
Cambridge U: Filan; Jeffrey (Danzey), Barrick, O'Shea, Heathcote, Daish, Livett (Hyde), Claridge, Fowler, Rowett, Nyamah.

Yeovil (0) 0
Bromsgrove (2) 2 *(Webb, Radburn)* 5462
Yeovil: Coles; Coates, Ferns, Sherwood, Bye, Leonard (McPherson), Sanderson (Connor), Wallace, Wilson, Spencer, Harrower.
Bromsgrove: Cooksey; Webb, Brighton, Richardson, Wardle, Skelding, Shilvock, Stott, Radburn (Pearce), Crisp, Carter.

5 DEC

Bath (1) 2 *(Brooks, Batty)*
Hereford U (0) 1 *(Hall)* 3086
Bath: Mogg; Gill, Dicks, Boyle, Crowley, Cousins, Williams, Chenoweth, Adcock (Smart), Mings, Brooks (Batty).
Hereford U: Judge; Clark H, Downs, Davies, Smith (Anderson), Reece, Hall, Harrison (May), Pickard, Pike, Nicholson.

SECOND ROUND REPLAYS

14 DEC

Exeter C (0) 2 *(Storer, Harris)*
Leyton Orient (0) 2 *(Carter, Hackett)* 3628
Exeter C: Fox; Minett, Brown, Bailey, Daniels, Whiston, Storer, Harris, Worthington, Ross (Phillips), Wigley.
Leyton Orient: Newell; Hendon, Austin (Ludden), Hackett, Bellamy, Ryan, Carter, Barnett, Cooper, Howard, Kitchen.
aet; Exeter C won 5-4 on penalties

Scunthorpe U (0) 0
Walsall (0) 0 3300
Scunthorpe U: Samways; Alexander, Mudd, Hope, Knill, Bradley, Thompstone (Thornber), Martin, Carmichael, Goodacre, Juryeff (Smith).
Walsall: Walker; Evans, Marsh, Ryder, Kiester (O'Hara), Smith, Ntamark, Lightbourne, Wright, Peer, McDonald (Cecere).
aet; Scunthorpe U won 7-6 on penalties

15 DEC

Nuneaton (0) 0
Bournemouth (1) 1 *(Cotterill)* 4127
Nuneaton: Attwood; Byrne, McGrory, Keogh, Tarry, Symonds (Wade), Simpson, Bradder, Green, Rosegreen, Shearer.
Bournemouth: Bartram; Pennock, Masters, Morris, Watson, Parkinson, O'Connor, McGorry, Fletcher (Murray), Cotterill, Wood.

THIRD ROUND

8 JAN

Barnet (0) 0
Chelsea (0) 0 *at Stamford Bridge* 23,200
Barnet: Phillips; Alexander, Mutchell, Hoddle, Newson, Walker, Wilson, Lynch, Haag, Close, Scott.
Chelsea: Kharine; Clarke, Sinclair, Dow, Johnsen, Spackman (Spencer), Newton, Peacock, Stein, Shipperley, Burley.

Birmingham C (1) 1 *(Harding)*
Kidderminster (1) 2 *(Cartwright, Purdie)* 19,666
Birmingham C: Bennett; Hiley, Cooper, Parris, Dryden, Whyte, McMinn, Lowe, Saville, Donowa (Willis), Harding (Smith).
Kidderminster: Rose; Hodson, Bancroft, Weir, Brindley, Forsyth, Cartwright, Grainger, Humphreys, Deakin, Purdie.

Blackburn R (1) 3 *(Shearer, Gallacher, Sherwood)*
Portsmouth (0) 3 *(McLoughlin 3)* 17,219
Blackburn R: Flowers; May, Le Saux, Batty, Hendry, Berg, Ripley, Sherwood, Shearer, Gallacher, Wilcox.
Portsmouth: Knight; Kristensen, Dobson, McLoughlin, Symons, Awford, Doling (Durnin), Stimson (Russell), Powell, Walsh, Daniel.

Bolton W (0) 1 *(Patterson)*
Everton (1) 1 *(Rideout)* 21,702
Bolton W: Davison; Brown, Burke, McAteer, Green, Winstanley, Lee, Stubbs, Thompson, McGinlay, Patterson.
Everton: Southall; Holmes, Ablett, Horne, Jackson, Snodin, Ward, Stuart, Cottee, Rideout (Barlow), Beagrie.

Bristol C (1) 1 *(Allison)*
Liverpool (1) 1 *(Rush)* 20,617
Bristol C: Welch; Munro, Scott, Shail, Bryant, Edwards, Martin, Brown I, Robinson, Allison, Tinnion.
Liverpool: Grobbelaar; Jones, Dicks, Nicol, Ruddock, Bjornebye (McManaman), Clough, Redknapp, Rush, Barnes, Fowler.
abandoned 65 minutes; floodlight failure

Bromsgrove (1) 1 *(Crisp)*
Barnsley (0) 2 *(Rammell, Archdeacon)* 4893
Bromsgrove: Green; Webb, Brighton (Hanks), Richardson, Wardle, Skelding, Shilvock, Stott, Radburn, Crisp, Carter.
Barnsley: Butler; Eaden, Fleming, Wilson, Taggart, Bishop, O'Connell (Liddell), Redfearn, Rammell, Payton, Archdeacon.

Cardiff C (0) 2 *(Stant, Thompson)*
Middlesbrough (1) 2 *(Wilkinson, Moore)* 13,750
Cardiff C: Grew; Brazil, Searle, Aizlewood, Baddeley, Perry, Thompson, Richardson (Griffith), Stant, Blake, Millar.
Middlesbrough: Pears; Fleming, Liburd, Mustoe, Mohan, Vickers, Pollock, Stamp, Wilkinson, Peake, Moore.

Charlton Ath (1) 3 *(Pardew, Leaburn, Grant)*
Burnley (0) 0 8336
Charlton Ath: Salmon; Pitcher, Minto, Pardew (Robinson), McLeary, Chapple, Robson, Brown, Leaburn, Grant, Walsh.
Burnley: Beresford; Joyce, Thompson (Wilson), Davis, Pender, Farrell (Peel), Francis, Deary, Heath, Russell, Eyres.

Exeter C (0) 0
Aston Villa (0) 1 *(Saunders (pen))* 10,570
Exeter C: Fox; Minett, Brown, Bailey, Daniels, Whiston, Storer, Coughlin, Davies, Ross, Wigley (Phillips).
Aston Villa: Bosnich; Barrett, Staunton, Teale, Cox, Richardson, Houghton, Townsend, Saunders, Atkinson, Parker.

Grimsby T (0) 1 *(Croft)*
Wigan Ath (0) 0 4488
Grimsby T: Crichton; McDermott, Croft, Futcher, Handyside, Dobbin, Ford, Gilbert (Agnew), Rees (Shakespeare), Mendonca, Groves.
Wigan Ath: Farnworth; Carragher, Wright (Kilford), Robertson, Skipper, Johnson, Langley, McKearney, Daley, Morton (Gavin), Lyons.

Leeds U (1) 3 *(Deane, Forrester 2)*
Crewe Alex (1) 1 *(Naylor)* 23,475
Leeds U: Beeney; Kelly, Dorigo, Newsome, Fairclough, Hodge, White, Strachan, Deane, McAllister, Forrester.
Crewe Alex: Smith M; Booty, Gardiner (Whalley), Evans, Abel (Collins), Wilson, Lennon, Naylor, Walters, Smith S, Rowbotham.

Manchester C (0) 4 *(Ingebritsen 3, Kernaghan)*
Leicester C (0) 1 *(Oldfield)* 22,613
Manchester C: Coton; Edghill, Brightwell D, Kernaghan, Foster (Lomas), Groenendijk (Sheron), Rocastle, Ingebritsen, Griffiths, Vonk, Phelan.
Leicester C: Poole; Grayson, Lewis, Coatsworth (Philpott), Agnew, Hill, Joachim (Carey), Thompson, Speedie, Mills, Oldfield.

Newcastle U (1) 2 *(Cole, Beardsley)*
Coventry C (0) 0 35,444
Newcastle U: Hooper; Robinson, Beresford, Elliott, Scott, Howey, Lee, Beardsley, Cole, Clark, Sellars (Watson).
Coventry C: Ogrizovic; Borrows, Babb, Atherton, Morgan, Flynn, Williams J, Ndlovu, Wegerle (Quinn), Williams P (Rennie), Darby.

Notts Co (2) 3 *(Draper, Agana, Devlin)*
Sutton U (0) 2 *(Barrowcliffe, Smart)* 6805
Notts Co: Cherry; Wilson, Dijkstra, Cox, Johnson, Turner P, Devlin, Draper, Lund, McSwegan (Legg), Agana (Matthews).
Sutton U: McCaulsky; Gates, Smart, Golley, Costello, Jones, Anderson (Newman), Barrowcliffe, Morah, Quail, Byrne (Thomas).

Oldham Ath (0) 2 *(Beckford, Holden)*
Derby Co (1) 1 *(Johnson)* 12,810
Oldham Ath: Hallworth; Fleming, Makin, Halle, Jobson, Pedersen (Beckford), Bernard, Ritchie, Sharp, Milligan, Holden.
Derby Co: Taylor; Charles, Forsyth (Ramage), Kuhl, Short, Wassall, Simpson, Pembridge, Johnson, Gabbiadini, Williams.

Oxford U (1) 2 *(Elliott, Byrne)*
Tranmere R (0) 0 5283
Oxford U: Whitehead; Elliott, Ford M, Lewis, Robinson, Rogan, Magilton, Beauchamp, Cusack, Byrne (Allen), Dyer.
Tranmere R: Nixon; Higgins, Nolan, Brannan, Proctor (Branch), Garnett, Morrissey, Irons, Malkin, Nevin, Thomas.

Peterborough U (0) 1 *(Brissett)*
Tottenham H (0) 1 *(Dozzell)* 19,169
Peterborough U: Barber; McDonald, Carter, Bradshaw (Charlery), Greenman, Welsh, Adcock, Kruszynski, Philliskirk (Iorfa), Ebdon, Brissett.
Tottenham H: Thorstvedt; Kerslake, Edinburgh, Samways, Calderwood, Sedgley, Caskey, Barmby (Campbell), Anderton, Dozzell, Hazard.

Plymouth Arg (0) 1 *(Nugent)*
Chester C (0) 0 9170
Plymouth Arg: Nicholls; McCall, Naylor, Hill, Comyn, Burnett, Skinner, Castle, Nugent, Marshall, Dalton.
Chester C: Felgate; Preece, Jakub (Bishop), Jenkins, Came, Greenall, Thompson, Lightfoot, Wheeler (Rimmer), Leonard, Pugh.

Preston NE (0) 2 *(Moyes, Conroy)*
Bournemouth (0) 1 *(Aspinall (pen))* 8457
Preston NE: O'Hanlon; Fensome, Kidd, Lucas, Nebbeling, Moyes, Bryson (Ainsworth), Cartwright, Conroy, Ellis, Raynor.
Bournemouth: Bartram; Pennock, Leadbitter, Chivers, Watson, Parkinson, O'Connor (McGorry), Aspinall, Fletcher, Cotterill, Beardsmore (Murray).

Sheffield W (1) 1 *(Bright)*
Nottingham F (0) 1 *(Cooper)* 32,488
Sheffield W: Pressman; Nilsson (Pearce), Worthington (Watson), Palmer, Walker, Bart-Williams, Jemson, Jones, Bright, Hyde, Sinton.
Nottingham F: Crossley; Lyttle, Pearce, Cooper, Chettle, Stone, Phillips, Bohinen, Webb (Bull), Glover, Woan.

Southampton (1) 1 *(Dowie)*
Port Vale (1) 1 *(Porter)* 11,086
Southampton: Beasant; Dodd, Adams, Benali, Moore, Monkou, Le Tissier, Widdrington, Dowie, Maddison, Allen.
Port Vale: Musselwhite; Aspin, Stokes, Kerr, Swan, Glover, Jeffers, Van der Laan, Cross, Foyle (Slaven), Porter.

Stockport Co (1) 2 *(Francis, Preece)*
QPR (1) 1 *(Barker)* 7569
Stockport Co: Edwards; Todd, Wallace, Frain, Flynn, Barras, Miller, Ward, Francis, Beaumont, Preece.
QPR: Stejskal (Roberts); Bardsley, Wilson, Wilkins, Peacock, Yates, Meaker, Barker, Ferdinand, Penrice, Sinclair (Impey).

Stoke C (0) 0
Bath (0) 0 14,159
Stoke C: Marshall; Clarkson, Sandford, Cranson, Overson, Orlygsson (Sturridge), Foley, Bannister, Regis, Butler, Gleghorn.
Bath: Mogg; Gill, Dicks, Batty, Hedges, Cousins, Banks, Chenoweth (Smart), Adcock, Mings (Vernon), Brooks.

Sunderland (1) 1 *(Ferguson)*
Carlisle U (0) 1 *(Edmondson)* 23,587
Sunderland: Chamberlain; Owers, Ord, Bennett, Ferguson, Melville, Smith, Goodman, Armstrong (Martin Gray), Gray P, Ball.
Carlisle U: Caig; Burgess, Gallimore, Walling, Joyce, Edmondson, Thomas, Conway (Oghani), Reeves, Davey, McCreery (Reddish).

Swindon T (1) 1 *(Mutch)*
Ipswich T (1) 1 *(Marshall)* 12,105
Swindon T: Hammond; Summerbee, Bodin (Nijholt), Horlock, Whitbread, Taylor, Moncur, Mutch, Maskell (Fjortoft), Ling, Fenwick.
Ipswich T: Forrest; Youds, Thompson, Stockwell, Wark (Palmer), Linighan, Williams, Guentchev, Marshall, Johnson, Slater.

West Ham U (0) 2 *(Allen M, Marsh)*
Watford (1) 1 *(Porter (pen))* 19,802
West Ham U: Miklosko; Breacker, Burrows (Brown), Potts, Gale, Bishop, Allen M, Morley (Jones), Chapman, Marsh, Rowland.
Watford: Sheppard; Lavin, Dublin, Hessenthaler, Holdsworth, Watson, Dyer, Johnson, Furlong, Porter, Nogan.

Wimbledon (2) 3 *(Holdsworth 3)*
Scunthorpe U (0) 0 4944
Wimbledon: Segers; Barton, Elkins, Jones, Scales, Fitzgerald, Clarke (Blackwell), Earle, Fashanu (Blissett), Holdsworth, Ardley.
Scunthorpe U: Samways; Alexander, Mudd, Hope, Knill, Bradley, Trebble (Watson), Martin, Carmichael, Bullimore, Smith.

Wolverhampton W (0) 1 *(Kelly D)*
Crystal Palace (0) 0 25,047
Wolverhampton W: Stowell; Rankine, Thompson, Venus, Blades, Shirtliff, Dennison, Cook, Bull (Regis), Kelly D, Keen.
Crystal Palace: Martyn; Shaw, Gordon, Southgate, Young, Coleman, Rodger, Newman, Armstrong, Osborn (Whyte), Salako.

Wycombe W (0) 0
Norwich C (1) 2 *(Sutton 2)* 7802
Wycombe W: Hyde; Cousins, Stapleton, Crossley, Evans, Ryan, Carroll, Hodges (Langford), Thompson, Hemmings (Horton), Guppy.
Norwich C: Gunn; Culverhouse, Bowen, Butterworth, Woodthorpe, Megson (Smith), Crook, Newman, Ekoku (Ullathorne), Fox, Sutton.

9 JAN

Sheffield U (0) 0
Manchester U (0) 1 *(Hughes)* 22,019
Sheffield U: Kelly; Bradshaw, Beesley, Kamara, Tuttle, Hoyland (Scott), Hodges, Ward (Nilsen), Flo, Gage, Whitehouse.
Manchester U: Schmeichel; Parker, Irwin, Bruce, Kanchelskis, Pallister, Cantona, Ince, Keane, Hughes, Giggs.

10 JAN

Millwall (0) 0
Arsenal (0) 1 *(Adams)* 20,093
Millwall: Keller; Huxford, Thatcher, Roberts, Van Den Hauwe, Stevens, Rae, Verveer, Mitchell, Goodman, Barber.
Arsenal: Seaman; Dixon, Winterburn, Hillier (Jensen), Bould, Adams, Keown, Wright (Merson), Campbell, Parlour, McGoldrick.

18 JAN

Luton T (0) 1 *(Telfer)*
Southend U (0) 0 7953

Luton T: Sommer; Linton, James, Harper, Peake, Dreyer, Telfer, Oakes, Dixon (Hartson), Hughes, Preece (Campbell).
Southend U: Royce; Poole, Powell, Jones K, Edwards, Bodley, Hunt (Sussex), Payne, Jones G, Otto, Lee.

THIRD ROUND REPLAYS

Bath (0) 1 *(Chenoweth)*
Stoke C (2) 4 *(Regis 2, Cranson, Orlygsson)* 6213

Bath: Mogg; Gill, Dicks, Batty, Hedges, Cousins (Smart), Banks, Chenoweth, Adcock (Vernon), Mings, Brooks.
Stoke C: Marshall; Butler, Sandford, Cranson, Overson, Orlygsson, Foley, Carruthers (Shaw), Regis, Sturridge, Gleghorn.

Carlisle U (0) 0
Sunderland (0) 1 *(Howey) aet* 12,771

Carlisle U: Caig; Burgess, Oghani, Walling, Joyce, Edmondson (McMahon), Thomas, Conway (Arnold), Reeves, Davey, Reddish.
Sunderland: Chamberlain; Owers, Ord, Bennett, Ferguson, Melville, Ball, Howey, Gray P, Smith, Atkinson (Russell).

Ipswich T (1) 2 *(Stockwell, Marshall)*
Swindon T (0) 1 *(Fjortoft) aet* 12,796

Ipswich T: Forrest; Youds, Thompson, Mason (Whitton), Wark (Palmer), Linighan, Williams, Stockwell, Marshall, Johnson, Slater.
Swindon T: Hammond; Nijholt, Bodin, Horlock, Whitbread, Taylor, Summerbee, Mutch, Fjortoft (Maskell), Ling, Fenwick.

Port Vale (1) 1 *(Slaven)*
Southampton (0) 0 12,042

Port Vale: Musselwhite; Aspin, Stokes, Kent, Swan, Glover, Slaven, Van der Laan, Cross, Porter, Jeffers.
Southampton: Beasant; Kenna, Dodd (Banger), Charlton, Wood, Monkou, Le Tissier, Widdrington, Dowie, Maddison, Allen (Bennett).

THIRD ROUND

19 JAN

Bristol C (0) 1 *(Allison)*
Liverpool (0) 1 *(Rush)* 21,718

Bristol C: Welch; Llewellyn, Scott, Shail, Munro, Edwards, Martin, Bent, Robinson, Allison, Tinnion.
Liverpool: Grobbelaar; Jones, Dicks, Nicol, Redknapp, Ruddock, Clough, Fowler (Bjornebye), Rush, Barnes, McManaman.

THIRD ROUND REPLAYS

Chelsea (2) 4 *(Burley, Peacock, Stein, Shipperley)*
Barnet (0) 0 16,209

Chelsea: Kharine; Clarke, Sinclair, Myers (Donaghy), Johnsen, Spackman, Hopkin (Spencer), Peacock, Stein, Shipperley, Burley.
Barnet: Phillips; Alexander (Smith), Mutchell, Hoddle, Walker, Newson, Wilson, Lynch, Haag, Close, Scott.

Everton (1) 2 *(Barlow 2)*
Bolton W (0) 3 *(McGinlay, Stubbs, Coyle) aet* 34,642

Everton: Southall; Jackson, Hinchcliffe, Ebbrell, Snodin, Ablett, Ward (Stuart), Horne, Cottee, Barlow (Warzycha), Beagrie.
Bolton W: Davison; Brown, Phillips, McAteer, Green (Kelly), Winstanley, Lee, Stubbs, Coyle, McGinlay, Patterson.

Middlesbrough (0) 1 *(Kavanagh)*
Cardiff C (1) 2 *(Stant, Blake) aet* 10,769

Middlesbrough: Pears; Fleming, Liburd (Whyte), Pollock, Mohan, Vickers, Mustoe, Hignett, Wilkinson, Peake, Kavanagh.
Cardiff C: Grew; Brazil, Searle, Aizlewood, Perry, Millar, Thompson, Richardson, Stant (Griffith), Blake, Bird.

Nottingham F (0) 0
Sheffield W (0) 2 *(Pearce, Bart-Williams)* 25,268

Nottingham F: Crossley; Lyttle, Pearce, Cooper, Chettle, Stone (Crosby), Phillips, Webb, Black (Bull), Glover, Woan.
Sheffield W: Pressman; Linighan B, Sinton, Palmer, Pearce, Walker, Jones, Hyde, Watson (Jemson), Bright, Bart-Williams.

Portsmouth (0) 1 *(McLoughlin)*
Blackburn R (1) 3 *(Shearer, May, Wilcox)* 23,035

Portsmouth: Knight; Neill, Daniel, McLoughlin, Butters (Dobson), Awford, Stimson (Hall), Durnin, Powell, Walsh, Kristensen.
Blackburn R: Flowers; May, Le Saux, Batty, Hendry (Moran), Berg, Ripley, Sherwood, Shearer, Gallacher, Wilcox.

Tottenham H (1) 1 *(Barmby)*
Peterborough U (1) 1 *(Charlery)* 24,893

Tottenham H: Walker; Austin, Edinburgh, Samways, Calderwood, Sedgley, Hazard (Kerslake), Barmby, Anderton, Caskey, Campbell (Hendry).
Peterborough U: Barber; McDonald, Greenman, McGlashan (Spearing), Howarth, Welsh, Adcock, Kruszynski, Iorfa (Furnell), Charlery, Brissett.
aet; Tottenham H won 5-4 on penalties

25 JAN

Liverpool (0) 0
Bristol C (0) 1 *(Tinnion)* 36,720

Liverpool: Grobbelaar; Jones, Harkness, Nicol, Redknapp (Hutchison), Ruddock, Clough, Walters, Rush, Barnes, McManaman.
Bristol C: Welch; Llewellyn, Scott, Shail, Munro, Edwards, Martin, Bent (Pennyfather), Robinson, Allison, Tinnion.

FOURTH ROUND

29 JAN

Cardiff C (0) 1 *(Blake)*
Manchester C (0) 0 20,486

Cardiff C: Grew; Brazil, Searle, Aizlewood, Baddeley, Perry, Thompson, Richardson, Millar, Blake, Griffith.
Manchester C: Coton (Dibble); Lomas, Phelan, Kernaghan, Curle, Vonk, Rocastle, Ingebritsen (Sheron), Griffiths, Flitcroft, Groenendijk.

Charlton Ath (0) 0
Blackburn R (0) 0 8532
Charlton Ath: Salmon; Pitcher, Minto, Brown, McLeary, Chapple, Robinson (Walsh), Grant (Nelson), Leaburn, Pardew, Robson.
Blackburn R: Flowers; Berg, Le Saux, Batty, Moran, Marker, Ripley, Sherwood, Shearer, Gallacher (Pearce), Wilcox.

Chelsea (1) 1 *(Peacock)*
Sheffield W (0) 1 *(Hyde)* 26,094
Chelsea: Kharine; Clarke, Sinclair, Myers, Johnsen, Spackman, Hopkin, Peacock, Stein, Shipperley (Spencer), Burley.
Sheffield W: Pressman; Nilsson, Coleman, Palmer, Pearce, Walker, Jones (Hirst), Hyde, Watson, Jemson, Bart-Williams.

Grimsby T (0) 1 *(Groves)*
Aston Villa (1) 2 *(Houghton, Yorke)* 15,771
Grimsby T: Crichton; Ford, Croft, Futcher, Handyside (Lever), Dobbin (Shakespeare), Childs, Gilbert, Livingstone, Mendonca, Groves.
Aston Villa: Bosnich; Barrett, Staunton, Teale, McGrath, Richardson, Houghton, Townsend, Saunders (Yorke), Atkinson, Daley (Cox).

Ipswich T (0) 3 *(Marshall, Johnson, Thompson)*
Tottenham H (0) 0 22,539
Ipswich T: Forrest; Youds, Thompson, Stockwell, Wark, Linighan, Williams, Guentchev, Marshall, Johnson, Slater (Palmer).
Tottenham H: Walker; Austin, Edinburgh, Samways, Calderwood, Sedgley, Caskey, Barmby, Anderton, Dozzell (Campbell), Nethercott.

Kidderminster (0) 1 *(Humphreys)*
Preston NE (0) 0 7000
Kidderminster: Rose; Hodson, Bancroft, Weir, Brindley, Forsyth (Deakin), Cartwright, Grainger, Humphreys, Davies (Woodall), Purdie.
Preston NE: Woods; Fensome, Kidd, Lucas, Nebbeling, Moyes, Ainsworth, Cartwright, Conroy, Ellis (Norbury), Raynor.

Newcastle U (0) 1 *(Beardsley (pen))*
Luton T (1) 1 *(Thorpe)* 32,216
Newcastle U: Hooper; Venison, Beresford, Bracewell, Watson, Howey, Lee, Beardsley, Cole, Clark, Sellars.
Luton T: Sommer; Linton, James, Harper, Peake, Dreyer, Telfer, Oakes, Dixon, Thorpe (Campbell), Preece.

Notts Co (1) 1 *(Lund)*
West Ham U (1) 1 *(Jones)* 14,952
Notts Co: Cherry; Palmer, Sherlock, Turner P, Murphy, Dijkstra, Devlin, Draper (Cox), Lund, Legg (McSwegan), Agana.
West Ham U: Miklosko; Breacker, Rowland, Potts, Brown, Bishop, Allen M, Jones, Chapman, Marsh, Holmes.

Oldham Ath (0) 0
Stoke C (0) 0 14,465
Oldham Ath: Hallworth; Fleming, Makin, Pointon, Jobson, Redmond (Palmer), Adams, Bernard, Sharp, Milligan, Holden.
Stoke C: Prudhoe; Butler, Sandford, Cranson, Overson, Orlygsson, Foley, Carruthers, Regis, Potter, Gleghorn.

Oxford U (2) 2 *(Dyer, Elliott)*
Leeds U (1) 2 *(Speed, Wetherall)* 11,029
Oxford U: Whitehead; Elliott, Ford M, Lewis, Robinson, Rogan, Magilton, Beauchamp (Penney), Cusack, Byrne, Dyer (Allen).
Leeds U: Beeney; Kelly, Dorigo, White, Fairclough, Newsome (Wetherall), Strachan, Rod Wallace (Hodge), Deane, McAllister, Speed.

Plymouth Arg (0) 2 *(Marshall, Dalton)*
Barnsley (1) 2 *(Payton, Taggart)* 12,760
Plymouth Arg: Nicholls; Edworthy, Naylor, Hill, Comyn, McCall, Burnett, Castle, Nugent (Skinner), Marshall, Dalton.
Barnsley: Butler; Eaden, Fleming, Wilson, Taggart, Bishop, O'Connell, Redfearn, Rammell, Payton, Archdeacon.

Port Vale (0) 0
Wolverhampton W (1) 2 *(Blades, Keen)* 21,999
Port Vale: Musselwhite; Aspin, Stokes (Newhouse), Kent, Swan, Glover, Slaven, Van der Laan (Sandeman), Cross, Porter, Jeffers.
Wolverhampton W: Stowell; Rankine, Thompson, Venus, Blades, Shirtliff, Marsden, Ferguson, Bull (Regis), Kelly, Keen.

Wimbledon (1) 2 *(Scales, Fashanu)*
Sunderland (1) 1 *(Smith)*
Wimbledon: Segers; Barton, Joseph, Sanchez, Scales, Fitzgerald, Ardley, Earle, Fashanu, Holdsworth, Elkins.
Sunderland: Chamberlain; Owers, Ord (Howey), Bennett, Ferguson, Melville, Ball, Goodman, Gray, Smith, Atkinson (Russell).

30 JAN

Norwich C (0) 0
Manchester U (1) 2 *(Keane, Cantona)* 21,060
Norwich C: Gunn; Culverhouse, Bowen, Megson, Polston, Woodthorpe, Crook (Ekoku), Newman, Sutton, Fox, Goss.
Manchester U: Schmeichel; Parker, Irwin, Bruce, Kanchelskis, Pallister, Cantona, Ince, Keane, Hughes (McClair), Giggs.

31 JAN

Bolton W (1) 2 *(McAteer, Coyle)*
Arsenal (0) 2 *(Wright, Adams)* 18,891
Bolton W: Davison; Brown, Phillips, Kelly, McAteer, Winstanley, Lee, Stubbs, Coyle, McGinlay, Patterson.
Arsenal: Seaman; Dixon, Winterburn, Hillier, Bould, Adams, Keown, Wright, Campbell, Merson, Parlour (Smith).

FOURTH ROUND REPLAY

8 FEB

Blackburn R (0) 0
Charlton Ath (1) 1 *(Pitcher)* 15,438
Blackburn R: Flowers; Berg, Le Saux, Batty, Moran, Marker (Atkins), Ripley, Morrison, Shearer, Gallacher (Pearce), Wilcox.
Charlton Ath: Salmon; Brown, Minto, Pardew, McLeary, Balmer, Robson (Newton), Pitcher, Leaburn, Grant, Nelson.

FOURTH ROUND

9 FEB

Stockport Co (0) 0
Bristol C (1) 4 *(Shail, Allison 3)* 7691
Stockport Co: Edwards; Todd, Wallace (James), Frain, Flynn, Barras, Miller (Connelly), Ward, Francis, Beaumont, Preece.
Bristol C: Welch; Rosenior, Scott, Shail, Munro, Edwards, Martin, Pennyfather, Robinson, Allison, Tinnion.

FOURTH ROUND REPLAYS

Arsenal (1) 1 *(Smith)*
Bolton W (1) 3 *(McGinlay, McAteer, Walker) aet* 33,863
Arsenal: Seaman; Dixon, Winterburn, Hillier (Keown), Bould, Adams, Campbell, Wright (McGoldrick), Smith, Merson, Parlour.
Bolton W: Davison; Brown, Phillips, Kelly, McAteer, Seagraves, Lee, Stubbs, Coyle, McGinlay, Patterson (Walker).

Barnsley (0) 1 *(O'Connell)*
Plymouth Arg (0) 0 10,913
Barnsley: Butler; Eaden, Fleming, Wilson, Taggart, Bishop, O'Connell, Redfearn, Rammell, Payton, Archdeacon.
Plymouth Arg: Nicholls; Patterson, Taylor, Hill, Comyn, McCall, Burnett (Skinner), Castle, Evans, Marshall (Edworthy), Dalton.

Leeds U (0) 2 *(Strachan, White)*
Oxford U (0) 3 *(Byrne, Allen, Magilton) aet* 22,167
Leeds U: Beeney; Kelly, Dorigo, White, Fairclough, Newsome, Strachan, Strandli (Forrester), Deane (Wetherall), McAllister, Speed.
Oxford U: Whitehead; Elliott, Ford M, Ford R (Lewis), Robinson, Rogan, Magilton, Beauchamp, Allen, Byrne (Cusack), Dyer.

Luton T (1) 2 *(Hartson, Oakes)*
Newcastle U (0) 0 12,503
Luton T: Sommer; Linton, James, Harper, Peake, Dreyer, Telfer, Oakes (Houghton), Hartson, Campbell (Thorpe), Preece.
Newcastle U: Hooper; Venison, Beresford, Elliott, Howey, Watson, Lee, Beardsley, Cole, Clark, Sellars.

Sheffield W (1) 1 *(Bright)*
Chelsea (1) 3 *(Spencer, Peacock, Burley) aet* 26,144
Sheffield W: Pressman; Nilsson, Coleman, Palmer, Pearce, Walker, Bart-Williams, Hyde, Watson (Waddle), Bright, Sinton.
Chelsea: Kharine; Clarke, Sinclair, Barnard, Johnsen, Myers (Hopkin), Spencer (Kjeldbjerg), Newton, Stein, Peacock, Burley.

Stoke C (0) 0
Oldham Ath (1) 1 *(Beckford)* 19,871
Stoke C: Prudhoe; Butler, Sandford, Cranson, Overson, Orlygsson, Foley, Bannister, Regis, Potter (Sturridge), Gleghorn.
Oldham Ath: Hallworth; Fleming, Makin, Pointon, Jobson, McDonald, Bernard, Beckford, Sharp, Milligan, Holden.

West Ham U (0) 1 *(Chapman)*
Notts Co (0) 0 *aet* 23,373
West Ham U: Miklosko; Breacker, Rowland, Potts, Brown, Bishop, Allen M, Jones (Allen C), Chapman, Marsh, Holmes.
Notts Co: Cherry; Palmer, Sherlock, Turner P, Johnson, Dijkstra, Devlin, Draper, Lund (Matthews), Legg, McSwegan.

FIFTH ROUND

19 FEB

Bristol C (1) 1 *(Tinnion)*
Charlton Ath (0) 1 *(Robson)* 20,416
Bristol C: Welch; Munro, Scott, Shail, Bryant, Edwards, Martin, Pennyfather (Bent), Robinson, Allison, Tinnion.
Charlton Ath: Salmon; Brown, Minto, Pardew, McLeary, Balmer, Robson, Pitcher, Leaburn, Grant, Nelson.

Kidderminster (0) 0
West Ham U (0) 1 *(Chapman)* 8000
Kidderminster: Rose; Hodson, Bancroft, Weir, Brindley, Cartwright (Deakin), Grainger, Forsyth, Humphreys, Davies, Purdie.
West Ham U: Miklosko; Breacker, Rowland, Potts, Martin, Bishop, Allen M, Marsh, Chapman, Allen C (Morley), Holmes.

Oldham Ath (0) 1 *(Ritchie)*
Barnsley (0) 0 15,685
Oldham Ath: Hallworth; Fleming, Makin, Pointon (Pedersen), Jobson, McDonald (Ritchie), Bernard, Beckford, Sharp, Milligan, Holden.
Barnsley: Butler; Eaden, Fleming, Wilson, Taggart, Bishop, O'Connell, Redfearn, Rammell, Payton, Archdeacon.

Oxford U (1) 1 *(Beauchamp)*
Chelsea (2) 2 *(Spencer, Burley)* 10,787
Oxford U: Whitehead; Elliott, Ford M, Ford R, Robinson (Smart), Rogan (Cusack), Lewis, Beauchamp, Allen, Byrne, Dyer.
Chelsea: Kharine; Clarke, Myers, Kjeldbjerg, Johnsen, Burley (Hopkin), Spencer, Newton, Stein, Peacock, Wise.

Wolverhampton W (0) 1 *(Kelly)*
Ipswich T (1) 1 *(Wark)* 28,234
Wolverhampton W: Stowell; Rankine (Dennison), Thompson, Venus, Blades, Shirtliff, Marsden, Ferguson, Regis, Kelly, Keen.
Ipswich T: Forrest; Youds, Thompson, Stockwell, Wark, Linighan, Williams, Slater (Mason), Palmer, Marshall, Kiwomya (Guentchev).

20 FEB

Bolton W (0) 1 *(Stubbs)*
Aston Villa (0) 0 18,817
Bolton W: Davison; Brown, Phillips, Kelly, McAteer, Seagraves, Lee, Stubbs, Coyle, McGinlay, Patterson.
Aston Villa: Bosnich; Cox, Barrett, Townsend, McGrath, Richardson, Daley (Ehiogu), Houghton, Saunders, Atkinson (Yorke), Froggatt.

Cardiff C (0) 1 *(Stant)*
Luton T (1) 2 *(Oakes, Preece)* 17,296
Cardiff C: Grew (Kite); Brazil, Searle, Perry, Baddeley, Millar, Bird, Richardson, Thompson, Dale (Stant), Griffith.
Luton T: Sommer; Linton, James, Harper, Dreyer, Peake, Telfer, Oakes, Hartson (Dixon), Hughes, Preece.

Wimbledon (0) 0

Manchester U (1) 3 *(Cantona, Ince, Irwin)* 27,511

Wimbledon: Segers; Barton, Elkins, Jones, Scales, Fitzgerald, Fear, Earle, Fashanu, Holdsworth, Blissett.
Manchester U: Schmeichel; Parker, Irwin, Bruce, Kanchelskis, Pallister, Cantona (McClair), Ince, Keane, Hughes (Dublin), Giggs.

FIFTH ROUND REPLAYS

2 MAR

Charlton Ath (1) 2 *(Pitcher (pen), Grant)*

Bristol C (0) 0 8205

Charlton Ath: Vaughan; Brown, Minto, Pardew, Chapple, Balmer, Robson, Pitcher, Leaburn, Grant, Nelson.
Bristol C: Welch; Munro, Scott, Shail (Rosenior), Bryant, Edwards, Martin, Bent, Robinson, Allison, Tinnion.

Ipswich T (0) 1 *(Palmer)*

Wolverhampton W (2) 2 *(Mills, Thompson)* 19,385

Ipswich T: Forrest; Youds (Mason), Thompson, Stockwell, Wark, Linighan, Williams (Guentchev), Slater, Palmer, Marshall, Kiwomya.
Wolverhampton W: Stowell; Rankine, Thompson, Venus, Blades, Shirtliff, Dennison, Ferguson (Cook), Mills, Kelly D, Keen.

SIXTH ROUND

12 MAR

Bolton W (0) 0

Oldham Ath (0) 1 *(Beckford)* 20,321

Bolton W: Davison; Brown, Phillips, Kelly, Seagraves, Stubbs, Lee, McAteer, Coyle, McGinlay, Patterson (Walker).
Oldham Ath: Hallworth; Henry, Makin, Pedersen (Pointon), Jobson, Redmond, Bernard, Beckford, Sharp, Milligan, Holden.

Manchester U (0) 3 *(Hughes, Kanchelskis 2)*

Charlton Ath (0) 1 *(Leaburn)* 44,347

Manchester U: Schmeichel; Parker (Sealey), Irwin, Bruce, Kanchelskis, Pallister, Cantona, Ince, Keane, Hughes, Giggs.
Charlton Ath: Vaughan; Brown, Minto, Pardew, McLeary, Balmer, Robson, Pitcher, Leaburn, Grant (Walsh), Nelson.

13 MAR

Chelsea (0) 1 *(Peacock)*

Wolverhampton W (0) 0 29,340

Chelsea: Kharine; Clarke, Sinclair, Kjeldbjerg, Johnsen, Burley, Hopkin, Newton, Spencer (Hoddle), Peacock, Wise.
Wolverhampton W: Stowell; Rankine, Thompson, Venus, Blades, Shirtliff, Marsden, Ferguson (Cook), Whittingham, Kelly D, Keen.

14 MAR

West Ham U (0) 0

Luton T (0) 0 27,331

West Ham U: Miklosko; Breacker, Burrows, Potts, Martin, Bishop, Allen M, Morley, Chapman (Allen C), Marsh, Holmes.
Luton T: Sommer; Linton, James, Harper, Greene, Dreyer, Telfer, Oakes (Burke), Dixon (Hartson), Hughes, Preece.

SIXTH ROUND REPLAY

23 MAR

Luton T (1) 3 *(Oakes 3)*

West Ham U (1) 2 *(Allen M, Bishop)* 13,166

Luton T: Sommer; Linton, James, Harper, Peake, Dreyer, Telfer, Oakes, Dixon, Hughes, Preece.
West Ham U: Miklosko; Breacker, Burrows, Potts, Martin, Bishop, Butler, Morley, Chapman, Marsh (Jones), Allen M.

SEMI-FINALS at Wembley

9 APR

Chelsea (1) 2 *(Peacock 2)*

Luton T (0) 0 59,989

Chelsea: Kharine; Clarke, Sinclair, Kjeldbjerg, Johnsen, Burley (Barnard), Newton, Peacock, Spencer, Cascarino, Wise.
Luton T: Sommer; Linton (Hartson), James, Harper, Peake, Dreyer, Telfer, Oakes, Dixon, Hughes, Preece.

10 APR

Manchester U (0) 1 *(Hughes)*

Oldham Ath (0) 1 *(Pointon) aet* 56,399

Manchester U: Schmeichel; Parker (Butt), Irwin, Bruce, Sharpe, Pallister, McClair, Ince, Dublin (Robson), Hughes, Giggs.
Oldham Ath: Hallworth; Makin, Pointon, Henry, Jobson, Fleming, Bernard, Beckford, Sharp, Milligan, Holden.

SEMI-FINAL REPLAY at Maine Road

13 APR

Manchester U (2) 4 *(Irwin, Kanchelskis, Robson, Giggs)*

Oldham Ath (1) 1 *(Pointon)* 32,211

Manchester U: Schmeichel; Parker, Irwin, Bruce, Kanchelskis, Pallister, Robson, Ince, Keane (McClair), Hughes (Sharpe), Giggs.
Oldham Ath: Hallworth; Makin, Pointon (Redmond), Henry, Jobson, Fleming, Bernard, Beckford (Ritchie), Sharp, Milligan, Holden.

FINAL at Wembley

14 MAY

Manchester U (0) 4 *(Cantona 2 (2 pens), Hughes, McClair)*

Chelsea (0) 0 79,634

Manchester U: Schmeichel; Parker, Irwin (Sharpe), Bruce, Kanchelskis (McClair), Pallister, Cantona, Ince, Keane, Hughes, Giggs.
Chelsea: Kharine; Clarke, Sinclair, Kjeldbjerg, Johnsen, Burley (Hoddle), Spencer, Newton, Stein (Cascarino), Peacock, Wise.
Referee: D. Elleray (Harrow).

THE SCOTTISH SEASON 1993-94

Although there was disappointment in the country that we were not represented at this year's World Cup, there was also a certain amount of relief -if the truth be told. It was a long season. In many ways players, managers and staff had had enough, and the opportunity to re-charge the batteries and have a week or two without any responsibility was enough perhaps to make up for some of the disappointment.

For the fan, too, there was an opportunity to watch some football without the usual necessity for intensive support of a team. True, we all had our favourite teams in the World Cup; but that is not the same as getting behind the national team or the club team.

The national coach changed during the season, and the extent of the esteem for Andy Roxburgh abroad was shown when he was selected for a new coaching job. His successor, Craig Brown, is well used to the running of national teams, albeit at a lower level: he brings a wealth of experience to the job, and has all our good wishes as he starts his quest for a place in the next European Finals.

There is little to report on last season's international matches. There has been some success, but overall it has been a period of rebuilding, and the result of all that is to be seen soon. The Under-21s could not quite reach the heights at Toulon, but did enough over the season to suggest that there are players in the country who can do well for us in the future.

At club level it was an unrewarding season in European competition: particularly disappointing after their last year's successes was the early exit of Rangers from the European Cup, and especially when it had seemed likely that they would be able to cope with their first opponents. However, mistakes were made, and were not to be forgiven. Aberdeen and Celtic both weathered the first round, but lost in the second, not without having achieved much credit in their encounters.

And so, for most of the season, our eyes were turned on the internal matches. They were to be interesting.

With the new set-up of four divisions of ten clubs to be in place for next season, there was lively action in all parts of the three divisions. In the Premier Division, Rangers made a slow start, and Aberdeen could be forgiven for thinking that perhaps they were on their way to another League Championship; Motherwell made the running for a while, too, and whilst many of the pundits awaited their fall from the upper reaches of the table, they were confounded as the team went from strength to strength and in fact finished third in the final table, very nearly managing to eject Aberdeen from the runners-up position. In the end, it had been Rangers who again triumphed: it is perhaps a compliment to them that in this era it is almost taken for granted that they will win the league: but, as their manager says, it is up to others to come and knock them from their perch. It has been said often enough that Scottish football needs a strong Celtic, but this was another season where their boardroom and other problems overshadowed the team's actions on the pitch; Celtic's ardent fans are not the only ones to hope that a new-look staff and team will soon be challenging again for the silverware. Hibernian had a comfortable season with much to savour, though they might have been ready to sacrifice some of their success for a win against old rivals Hearts. A rather poor year for Dundee United was redeemed, as we shall see, by a glorious first elsewhere. In the lower reaches there was a battle royal for survival: six teams were involved, and though Dundee and Raith Rovers had both succumbed some weeks before the end of the season, the last relegation place was not settled until the last afternoon, and then only by the slimmest of margins: in the end St Johnstone went down, but Kilmarnock and Partick Thistle were both to heave sighs of relief, whilst Hearts were only just able to keep their heads above water. Whether the new league arrangement will be successful is open to question. At least it does mean fewer league games, and for the top clubs this could mean a great deal. There are plenty who argue for a larger league at the top, but it is difficult sometimes to differentiate between the arguments of apparent common sense and those of pure self-interest. What is certain is that the new Division 1 will be a major battle ground for some excellent teams trying to restore their top status.

In the First Division, Falkirk and Dunfermline Athletic were neck-and-neck to the post: for weeks it had been apparent that one of these clubs would obtain the single coveted place in the Premier Division. Which was it to be? With other clubs left far behind, it was first the one and then the other who topped the table. Once again, as last season, Dunfermline made a fatal slip, and Falkirk were able to gain the draw they needed in the final game to edge home by a point -with a much inferior goal difference. It was good to hear Jim Jefferies, the Falkirk manager, in his moment of triumph and relief, finding time to commiserate sincerely with the Pars who thus failed so closely for the second time running.

It was in the middle of the table that the divide was to come this season, and here the outcome was settled comparatively early: Ayr United were able to keep their place above the line without serious competition from Dumbarton or Stirling Albion, who both ran out of steam when it mattered. Noteworthy at the top end was a fine start to the season by Clyde bank who had stored up enough points to allow for a less successful period in the middle of the programme. Airdrieonians hovered near the top, and did well, but without ever threatening to displace the top two.

So to the Second Division, and at last, after many years in the lowest division, success for Stranraer. Last year they were disappointed in losing the race for promotion in the very last minute of the last game: this year they played with purpose and strength, and garnered the points regularly, building a commanding lead over other aspirants and having something in hand for the end: congratulations to them: they now find themselves in formidable company, and hopefully can acquit themselves with distinction.

The midway line was anything but clear cut towards the end of the season: Berwick Rangers, after a magnificent end of season run, swept into the runners-up spot, edging ahead of Stenhousemuir and Meadowbank Thistle. Those clubs were all safely into Division 2. Queen of the South looked to be tidily placed and so it turned out. But East Fife, with an inconsistent performance through the season, and Alloa, who had done well early but had faltered, were pressed by Forfar Athletic, East Stirlingshire and Montrose; and with two or three games left, any one of these teams could have taken the one remaining place for survival: by the last game, the situation was clearer, and by chance Alloa played East Fife, with the latter needing a draw to stay up. They managed it, but only just. It was another very close-run thing.

In mid-season, another battle had been joined for inclusion in the Scottish League. Of the four clubs who had finally emerged as contenders for the two new places, it was Ross County, former Highland League champions and doughty cup fighters, and the Inverness conglomerate Caledonian Thistle who triumphed, and they now join Division 3 of the Bell's League to seek their fortune: it will be a surprise if at least one of these clubs does not soon reach for promotion.

In the League Cup, which as usual started the season, there were the usual excitements: Meadowbank lost to Dundee only on penalties, whilst Hamilton and Stenhousemuir both took upper division teams to extra time; less usual was Partick's feat in scoring eleven goals in their second round match, whilst Arbroath, who had defeated Premier Division Raith Rovers to earn a home match with Celtic, conceded nine goals to them. The final was held at Celtic Park and Rangers beat Hibernian 2-1 in an interesting game in which Hibs had their chances; the game also saw the return from injury of Ally McCoist, who emerged as a substitute in the later stages, and almost at once scored. It was a stunning return after his long absence with a broken leg.

Falkirk won the B&Q Cup with steady progress to a final in which they were perhaps slightly flattered to win 3-0 against St Mirren.

Then to the Scottish Cup: in the first round Stranraer nearly met their match in non-League Whitehill Welfare: they survived with the skin of their teeth, won the replay easily, and went on to defeat the formidable Highland League Huntly and Falkirk before losing by the only goal to Airdrieonians at Broomfield. Ross County boosted their own hopes for league inclusion by scoring eleven goals in their first outing; they then beat Forfar 4-0 before losing to Alloa, with the chance of a tie at Ibrox hinging on the game. Alloa, though losing to Rangers, clearly enjoyed their incursion into the higher realms. Kilmarnock made their way successfully to the semi-finals, where they held Rangers in the first game at Hampden, but lost by the odd goal in the replay. The other game, Aberdeen v Dundee United, also needed a replay to settle the issue, and Dundee United, now qualifying for Europe after Rangers had settled the winning of the League, went to their eighth final, hoping that at last they might be successful. Their hopes were to be realized, and their voluble manager was clearly delighted as were the United fans. It was noted that one of the first to congratulate Mr Golac on his success was the Rangers manager.

Ace player of the season and the one who took the awards was Mark Hateley. Rangers owe much to him and his enthusiasm for the game. He was quick to applaud the rest of the team, but in truth he gave the kind of lead for which any team can hope.

There are now several new grounds and many clubs which have implemented major changes in their seating arrangements; plans are afoot everywhere; there has in some cases been a great deal of talk, but now the clubs are getting on with these changes. Pride of place must go to the refurbished national Queen's Park headquarters at Hampden. The next phase is still to come, but the improvement has been startling, and those who doubted if the Hampden Roar would ever return have been shown that it may. But it will need to have a national team worthy of it. Isn't this where we came in?

ALAN ELLIOTT

ABERDEEN Premier Division

Year Formed: 1903. *Ground & Address:* Pittodrie Stadium, Pittodrie St, Aberdeen AB2 1QH. *Telephone:* 0224 632328.
Ground Capacity: 21,634 seated: All. *Size of Pitch:* 110yd # 72yd.
Chairman: Ian R. Donald. *Secretary:* Ian J. Taggart. *Commercial Manager:* Dave Johnston.
Manager: William Miller. *Assist. Managers:* Drew Jarvie, Roy Aitken. *Physio:* David Wylie. *Coach:* Neil Cooper.
Managers since 1975: Ally MacLeod; Billy McNeill; Alex Ferguson; Ian Porterfield; Alex Smith and Jocky Scott; Willie Miller. *Club Nicknames(s):* The Dons. *Previous Grounds:* None.
Record Attendance: 45,061 v Hearts, Scottish Cup 4th rd; 13 Mar, 1954.
Record Transfer Fee received: £970,000 for David Robertson to Rangers (July 1991).
Record Transfer Fee paid: £650,000 for Hans Gillhaus from PSV Eindhoven, November 1989.
Record Victory: 13-0 v Peterhead, Scottish Cup; 9 Feb, 1923.
Record Defeat: 0-8 v Celtic, Division 1; 30 Jan, 1965.
Most Capped Players: Alex McLeish, 77, Scotland.
Most League Appearances: 556: Willie Miller, 1973-90.
Most League Goals in Season (Individual): 38: Benny Yorston, Division I; 1929-30.
Most Goals Overall (Individual): 199: Joe Harper.

ABERDEEN 1993—94 LEAGUE RECORD

Match No.	Date		Venue	Opponents	Result		H/T Score	Lg. Pos.	Goalscorers	Attendance
1	Aug	7	A	Dundee U	D	1-1	0-1	—	Booth	13,881
2		14	H	Kilmarnock	W	1-0	0-0	4	Kane	13,535
3		21	A	Dundee	D	1-1	1-0	4	Shearer	7505
4		28	H	St Johnstone	D	0-0	0-0	5		11,682
5	Sept	4	A	Celtic	W	1-0	0-0	3	Paatelainen	34,311
6		11	A	Hibernian	L	1-2	0-2	6	Shearer	8506
7		18	H	Rangers	W	2-0	2-0	3	Shearer, Pressley (og)	19,138
8		25	H	Raith R	W	4-1	1-0	1	Shearer, Jess, Richardson 2	11,472
9	Oct	2	A	Motherwell	D	0-0	0-0	1		8597
10		5	H	Hearts	D	0-0	0-0	—		13,798
11		9	A	Partick T	L	2-3	0-2	2	Paatelainen, Shearer	5600
12		16	A	Kilmarnock	D	1-1	0-0	3	Paatelainen	9108
13		23	H	Dundee U	W	2-0	2-0	2	Paatelainen, Shearer	13,566
14		30	H	Dundee	W	1-0	0-0	1	Shearer	11,885
15	Nov	6	A	St Johnstone	D	1-1	0-1	1	Booth	5757
16		9	H	Celtic	D	1-1	0-0	—	Grant (og)	19,474
17		13	H	Motherwell	D	1-1	1-1	1	Booth	12,494
18		27	H	Hibernian	W	4-0	1-0	1	Kane, Connor, Shearer, Grant	12,334
19	Dec	1	A	Rangers	L	0-2	0-2	—		45,182
20		4	A	Hearts	D	1-1	0-1	4	Shearer	9402
21		7	A	Raith R	D	1-1	1-1	—	Miller	4205
22		14	H	Partick T	W	2-1	0-0	—	Irvine, Shearer	8248
23		18	H	Kilmarnock	W	3-1	1-0	1	Miller, Shearer, Richardson	10,834
24		27	A	Dundee U	W	1-0	1-0	—	Jess	12,248
25	Jan	8	H	St Johnstone	D	1-1	0-0	2	Shearer	12,712
26		11	A	Dundee	W	1-0	0-0	—	Irvine	5219
27		19	A	Celtic	D	2-2	1-1	—	Irvine, Jess	19,083
28		22	H	Rangers	D	0-0	0-0	2		20,267
29	Feb	5	A	Hibernian	L	1-3	1-0	2	Richardson	9556
30		12	H	Raith R	W	4-0	1-0	2	Paatelainen 2, Shearer, Booth	10,553
31	Mar	5	H	Hearts	L	0-1	0-1	2		13,059
32		8	A	Motherwell	D	1-1	1-0	—	Shearer	7018
33		19	A	Kilmarnock	W	3-2	1-0	3	Miller, Shearer, Jess	8544
34		26	H	Dundee U	W	1-0	1-0	3	Shearer	12,574
35		29	H	Hibernian	L	2-3	1-1	—	Jess, Miller	10,832
36	Apr	2	A	Rangers	D	1-1	0-1	3	Kane	45,888
37		5	A	Partick T	D	1-1	1-1	—	Tierney (og)	4280
38		16	H	Motherwell	D	0-0	0-0	3		9642
39		23	H	Partick T	W	2-0	0-0	3	Jess, Grant	7827
40		27	A	Hearts	D	1-1	1-0	—	Irvine	13,811
41		30	H	Dundee	D	1-1	0-0	3	Irvine	7568
42	May	3	A	Raith R	W	2-0	1-0	—	Roddie, Shearer	2798
43		7	A	St Johnstone	W	1-0	0-0	2	Irvine	6107
44		14	H	Celtic	D	1-1	1-1	2	Irvine	16,417

Final League Position: 2

Honours
League Champions: Division I 1954-55. Premier Division 1979-80, 1983-84, 1984-85; *Runners-up:* Division I 1910-11, 1936-37, 1955-56, 1970-71, 1971-72. Premier Division 1977-78, 1980-81, 1981-82, 1988-89, 1989-90, 1990-91, 1993-94.
Scottish Cup Winners: 1947, 1970, 1982, 1983, 1984, 1986, 1990; *Runners-up:* 1937, 1953, 1954, 1959, 1967, 1978, 1993.
League Cup Winners: 1955-56, 1976-77, 1985-86, 1989-90; *Runners-up:* 1946-47, 1978-79, 1979-80, 1987-88, 1988-89, 1992-93.
Drybrough Cup Winners: 1971, 1980.
European: *European Cup* 12 matches (1980-81, 1984-85, 1985-86); *Cup Winners Cup Winners:* 1982-83. Semi-finals 1983-84. 37 matches (1967-68, 1970-71, 1978-79, 1982-83, 1983-84, 1986-87, 1990-91, 1993-94); *UEFA Cup* 34 matches (*Fairs Cup:* 1968-69. *UEFA Cup:* 1971-72, 1972-73, 1973-74, 1977-78, 1979-80, 1981-82, 1987-88, 1988-89, 1989-90, 1991-92).
Club colours: Shirt, Shorts, Stockings: Red with white trim.

Goalscorers: *League* (58): Shearer 17, Irvine 7, Jess 6, Paatelainen 6, Booth 4, Miller 4, Richardson 4, Kane 3, Grant 2, Connor 1, Roddie 1, own goals 3. *Scottish Cup* (8): Shearer 4, Booth 1, Miller 1, Richardson 1, own goal 1. *League Cup* (11): Shearer 4 (1 pen), Booth 2, Miller 2, Jess 1, McLeish 1, Richardson 1.

Snelders T 33	McKimmie S 40	Connor R 21 + 4	Grant B 26 + 4	Irvine B 42	Smith G 19 + 2	Richardson L 31 + 4	Bett J 6	Booth S 14 + 11	Jess E 38 + 3	Paatelainen M 14 + 22	Shearer D 39 + 4	Kane P 39	McLeish A 35	Miller J 24 + 3	Wright S 34 + 2	Aitken R — + 1	Ten Caat T 1 + 2	Winnie D 2 + 4	Gibson A 1 + 1	Watt M 4	Roddie A 3 + 3	Stillie D 4 + 1	Robertson H 6 + 2	Burridge J 3	McKinnon R 5	Thomson S — + 3	Match No.
1	2	3	4	5	6	7	8	9	10	11	12																1
1	2	3			6	7	8	9	14	*11*	10	4	5	12													2
1	2	14			6	7			9	11	10	4	5	*8*	3	12											3
1	2			6	3	8		9	*7*	12	10	4	5	14			11										4
1	2	3		6		7	8	9	14	12	*10*	4	5	11													5
1	2	3		6			8		*9*	11	10	4	5	7				12	14								6
1	2	11		6		8		14	9	12	*10*	4	5	7	3												7
1	2	11		6		8			9	14	10	4	*5*	7	3		12										8
1	2	*11*		6	14	8			9	12	10	4	5	7	3												9
1	2	11		6		8				14	10	4	5	7	3		12		*9*								10
	2	12		6	14		8		9	11	10	4	5	7	3					1							11
1	2	12	8	6	3	7		14	*9*	11	10	4	5														12
1	2		*8*	6	3	7			9	11	10	4	5	12	14												13
1	2	12	8	6	3	7		14	9	11	*10*	4	5														14
1	2	3	8	6		7		14	9	11	*10*	4	5		12												15
1	2	3	8	6		7		9	10		12	4		*11*	5			14									16
	2	3	8	6		7		9		11	14	4		*10*	5					1							17
1	2	11	8	6					9		10	4	5	7	3												18
	2	11	8	6		14			9	12	10	4	5	7	3					1							19
1		11	*8*	6	3	14			10	9	12	4	5	7	2												20
1		3	8	6		*11*		9	14	12	10	4	5	7	2												21
1		11	*8*	6	3			14	9	12	10	4	5	7	2												22
1		*11*		6	3	8		14	9	12	10	4	5	7	2												23
1	2	11		6				14	*9*	12	10	4	5	7	3			8									24
1	2	11	12	6				14	9		10	4	5	7	3			*8*									25
1	2	11	8	6				9	*7*		10	4	5		3			12			14						26
	2		8	6		11		14	*9*		10	4	5	*7*	3			12		1							27
1	2		8	6		11		14	9	12	10	4	5	*7*	3												28
1	2	*11*	4	6		8		9	7	14	10		5		3												29
1	2		4	6			*8*	14	7	11	10	9	5		3												30
1	2		4	6		8		9		12	10	11	5	7	3							14					31
	2		12	6	4	8		*9*	7	14	10	11	5		3							1					32
	2			6	4	8			*7*	14	10	11	5	9	3							1					33
	2		12	6		8			7	14	*10*	4	5	9	3							1	11				34
	2			6		8			7	14	10	4	*5*	9	3							1	11				35
	2		11	6		8			7	12	10	4	5		3									1	9		36
	2		11	6		8			7	10		4	5										3	1	*9*	14	37
1	2		12	6	3	8		9	7		10	4	5		11												38
1	2		8	6	5	14		9	7	12	10	4			*3*										11		39
1	2		8	6	5			9	7	12	10				3						14		11		*4*		40
1	2		4	6	5	8			7	11	*10*				3						12		9			14	41
1	2		4	6	5	8			*7*	12	10				3						*11*		9			14	42
1	2		4	6	5	12			7		10	8			3						11		14		*9*		43
	2		4	6	5	*8*			7		10	9			3						11		14	1			44

AIRDRIEONIANS Division 1

Year Formed: 1878. *Ground & Address:* Broomfield Park, Gartlea Rd, Airdrie M16 9JL. *Telephone:* 0236 62067.
Ground Capacity: 10,250, seated: 1350. *Size of Pitch:* 112yd # 67yd.
Chairman and Secretary: George W. Peat CA. *Commercial Manager:* Dorothy Martin.
Manager: Alex MacDonald. *Assistant Manager:* John McVeigh. *Physio:* Dan Young. *Coach:* Tom McAdam.
Managers since 1975: I. McMillan; J. Stewart; R. Watson; W. Munro; A. MacLeod; D. Whiteford; G. McQueen; J. Bone.
Club Nickname(s): The Diamonds or The Waysiders. *Previous Grounds:* Mavisbank.
Record Attendance: 24,000 v Hearts, Scottish Cup; 8 Mar, 1952.
Record Transfer Fee received: £200,000 for Sandy Clark to West Ham U, May 1982.
Record Transfer Fee paid: £175,000 for Owen Coyle from Clydebank, February 1990.
Record Victory: 15-1 v Dundee Wanderers, Division II; 1 Dec, 1984.
Record Defeat: 1-11 v Hibernian, Division I; 24 Oct, 1959.
Most Capped Player: Jimmy Crapnell, 9, Scotland.
Most League Appearances: 523: Paul Jonquin, 1962-79.
Most League Goals in Season (Individual): 52, Hugh Baird, Division II, 1954-55. *Most Goals Overall (Individual):* —

AIRDRIEONIANS 1993—94 LEAGUE RECORD

Match No.	Date	Venue	Opponents	Result		H/T Score	Lg. Pos.	Goalscorers	Attendance
1	Aug 7	A	St Mirren	W	1-0	1-0	—	Reid	3852
2	14	H	Brechin C	W	1-0	0-0	3	Davenport	1663
3	21	H	Hamilton A	W	4-0	0-0	2	Kirkwood, Davenport 2, Lawrence	2416
4	28	A	Dunfermline Ath	L	2-3	1-2	3	Kirkwood 2 (1 pen)	3970
5	Sept 4	H	Morton	W	2-0	2-0	2	Collins (og), Davenport	2227
6	11	A	Falkirk	L	1-2	1-0	3	Lawrence	4566
7	14	H	Clyde	W	2-1	1-0	—	Lawrence, Ferguson	1758
8	18	H	Stirling Albion	W	3-2	0-0	3	Davenport, Black, Lawrie (og)	2076
9	25	A	Clydebank	W	2-1	1-1	3	Ferguson, Lawrence	2022
10	28	A	Dumbarton	W	1-0	1-0	—	Andrew Smith	1276
11	Oct 2	H	Ayr U	D	1-1	0-0	2	Kirkwood	2140
12	9	H	St Mirren	D	1-1	0-0	2	Kirkwood	2726
13	16	A	Clyde	W	2-0	1-0	1	Andrew Smith, Ferguson	1464
14	23	H	Falkirk	D	1-1	1-0	1	Andrew Smith	5153
15	30	A	Hamilton A	L	2-3	0-1	2	Honor (pen), Lawrence	2459
16	Nov 6	H	Dunfermline Ath	D	1-1	0-1	3	Kirkwood (pen)	3368
17	9	A	Morton	D	0-0	0-0	—		1272
18	13	A	Ayr U	W	2-1	1-0	2	Davenport 2	1944
19	20	H	Dumbarton	L	0-1	0-0	3		1741
20	30	H	Clydebank	W	2-1	0-1	—	Kirkwood 2 (1 pen)	1634
21	Dec 4	A	Stirling Albion	W	4-0	4-0	1	Kirkwood (pen), Ferguson, Caesar, McKenna (og)	1401
22	11	A	Brechin C	W	2-0	0-0	1	Ferguson, Reid	682
23	18	H	Clyde	W	3-2	1-1	2	Kirkwood (pen), Ferguson, Davenport	1755
24	Jan 11	A	St Mirren	L	0-3	0-1	—		2583
25	18	H	Hamilton A	L	0-1	0-1	—		1771
26	22	H	Brechin C	L	0-1	0-0	3		1466
27	25	A	Dunfermline Ath	D	0-0	0-0	—		5419
28	Feb 1	H	Morton	D	2-2	0-2	—	Andrew Smith, Honor	1401
29	5	A	Falkirk	D	0-0	0-0	3		4484
30	12	H	Ayr U	D	0-0	0-0	3		2208
31	Mar 1	A	Dumbarton	D	0-0	0-0	—		950
32	5	H	Stirling Albion	W	3-0	1-0	3	Harvey, Boyle, Ferguson	1644
33	19	A	Clyde	W	1-0	0-0	3	Hay	2414
34	22	A	Clydebank	L	1-2	0-1	—	Jack	941
35	26	H	St Mirren	L	0-2	0-0	3		2069
36	29	A	Brechin C	W	2-0	0-0	—	Ferguson, Anthony Smith	345
37	Apr 2	H	Falkirk	D	0-0	0-0	3		3720
38	9	A	Ayr U	W	3-2	2-2	3	Andrew Smith, Davenport, Stewart	1508
39	16	H	Dumbarton	D	1-1	0-0	3	Andrew Smith	1320
40	23	A	Stirling Albion	D	1-1	1-1	3	Andrew Smith	904
41	26	H	Clydebank	D	0-0	0-0	—		994
42	30	A	Hamilton A	L	0-1	0-1	3		1612
43	May 7	H	Dunfermline Ath	W	1-0	0-0	3	Cooper (og)	6878
44	14	A	Morton	W	3-1	2-0	3	Wilson, Stewart, Ferguson	1029

Final League Position: 3

Honours
League Champions: Division II 1902-03, 1954-55, 1973-74; *Runners-up:* Division I 1922-23, 1923-24, 1924-25, 1925-26. First Division 1979-80, 1989-90, 1990-91. Division II 1900-01, 1946-47, 1949-50, 1965-66.
Scottish Cup Winners: 1924; *Runners-up:* 1975, 1992. *Scottish Spring Cup Winners:* 1976.
League Cup semi-finalists: 1991-92.
European: *UEFA Cup* 2 matches (1992-93).
Club colours: Shirt: White with Red diamond. Shorts: White. Stockings: Red.

Goalscorers: *League* (58): Kirkwood 10 (5 pens), Davenport 9, Ferguson 9, Andrew Smith 7, Lawrence 5, Honor 2 (1 pen), Reid 2, Stewart 2, Black 1, Boyle 1, Caesar 1, Harvey 1, Hay 1, Jack 1, Anthony Smith 1, Wilson 1, own goals 4. *Scottish Cup* (5): Kirkwood 4 (4 pens), Ferguson 1. *League Cup* (4): Balfour 1, Davenport 1, Kirkwood 1, Lawrence 1. *B&Q Cup* (3): Abercromby 1, Black 1, McIntyre 1.

Martin J 44	Stewart A 36	Kirkwood D 28 + 1	Sandison J 33	Caesar G 16	Reid W 14 + 4	Boyle J 17 + 10	Balfour E 18 + 7	Davenport P 35 + 3	Lawrence A 20 + 7	Smith Andr 25 + 13	Conn S — + 2	Abercromby M 1 + 6	McVicar D 20 + 1	Black K 40	Honor C 32 + 2	Jack P 32 + 3	Ferguson I 26 + 2	McIntyre J 8 + 5	Wilson M 11	Tomnay D 1	Smith Anth 4 + 2	Hay G 11	Harvey P 9 + 4	McCulloch W — + 1	Connelly G 3 + 2	Match No.
1	2	3	4	5	6	7	8	9	10	*11*	12	14														1
1	2	7	4	5	8			9	11	14		*10*	3	6												2
1	2	7	4	*5*	8		12	9	11	14			3	6	10											3
1	2	7	4	5	12		8	9	*11*	10			14	6	3											4
1		7	4	5		14	8	9	*11*	10	12			6	2	3										5
1		7	4	5	14	12	8		*11*	9			3	6	10	2										6
1		7	4	5			8	9	11	14			*3*	6	2	12	10									7
1			4	*5*		14	8	9	11	12			3	6	2	7	10									8
1		*7*	5			14	8	9	12	11			3	6	2	4	10									9
1		7	5		14	12	8	9	*11*	10			3	6	2	4										10
1		7	5			12	8	9	14	10			3	6	2	4	*11*									11
1	2	*7*	5			14	8	9	11	10			3	6		4	12									12
1	2	*7*	5				8	*9*	14	11			3	6	12	4	10									13
1	2	7	5				8	9		10			3	6	12	4	11									14
1	2	*7*				14	*8*	9	12	11			3	6	5	4	10									15
1	2	12				7	8	9	*10*	14			3	6	5	4		11								16
1	2	8				7		9	14	10		12	3		5	4	*11*		6							17
1	3	7			*10*	2		9		11					5		8		4	6	14					18
1	2				8	7		*9*		11			3	6	5		10	14	4							19
1	2	10			8	7	14	9		12			*3*	6	5	4		*11*								20
1	2	7		5	8		12	*9*		10				6	3	4	14	11								21
1	2	7		5	8		14		*10*	12			3	6		4	9	11								22
1	2	7		5	8		12	14	10				*3*	6		4	9	*11*								23
1	3	*7*		5	8	2	14	10	12	9				6		4	11									24
1	2	3	5			7	8	9	11	14				6		*4*	10	12								25
1	2	7	4	5		14			*10*	12				6		3	9	11	8							26
1	2	7	4				12	*9*		14			3	6	8		10					5	11			27
1		7	4				2	9	11	14			*3*	6	8	5							10	12		28
1	2	7		5			8	12	*11*	9		14		6	4	3							10			29
1	2	7	4		14		*8*	12		9				6	3		11					5	10			30
1	2	7	4	5					11	12				6	*8*	14	9					3	10			31
1	2		4	5	8	7		9								3	11					6	10			32
1	2		4		8	7		10		9		12		6	3		11					5				33
1	2		*4*		8	7		9		12				6	3	14	11					5	10			34
1	3		4		8	7		9	*10*			14		6	5	2		11					12			35
1	*2*		4			14				9				6	5	3	10	12	7		11		8			36
1	2		4			*7*		10		9				6	8	3	*11*	14				5	12			37
1	2		4			7		10		9				6	11	3		14				5			*8*	38
1	2		4					*10*		9		14		6		3			8		11	5			7	39
1	2		4					11		9				6	8	3			10			5			7	40
1	2		4						14	9				6	8	3	*7*	*11*	10			5	12			41
1	2		4			5		11	9					*6*	*7*	3			8		12		10		14	42
1	2		4			7		9						6	5	3	10		8		11					43
1	2		4			7		*9*						6	5	3	10		8		11		12		14	44

ALBION ROVERS Division 3

Year Formed: 1882. *Ground & Address:* Cliftonhill Stadium, Main St, Coatbridge ML5 3RB. *Telephone:* 0236 432350.
Ground capacity: total: 1238, seated: 538. *Size of Pitch:* 110yd # 70yd.
Chairman: Jack McGoogan. *Secretary:* D. Forrester CA. *Commercial Manager:* Laurie Cameron. *Managers:* Tom Spence, Sam Conn. *Assistant Manager:* —. *Physio:* Michael McBride. *Coach:* —. *Managers since 1975:* G. Caldwell; S. Goodwin; H. Hood; J. Baker; D. Whiteford; M. Ferguson; W. Wilson; B. Rooney; A. Ritchie; T. Gemmell; D. Provan; M. Oliver; B. McLaren; T. Gemmell. *Club Nickname(s):* The Wee Rovers. *Previous Grounds:* Cowheath Park, Meadow Park, Whifflet.
Record Attendance: 27,381 v Rangers, Scottish Cup 2nd rd; 8 Feb, 1936.
Record Transfer Fee received: £40,000 from Motherwell for Bruce Cleland.
Record Transfer Fee paid: £7000 for Gerry McTeague to Stirling Albion, September 1989.
Record Victory: 12-0 v Airdriehill, Scottish Cup; 3 Sept, 1887.
Record Defeat: 0-9 v St Johnstone, League Cup, 9 March 1946.
Most Capped Player: Jock White, 1 (2), Scotland.

ALBION ROVERS 1993—94 LEAGUE RECORD

Match No.	Date	Venue	Opponents	Result		H/T Score	Lg. Pos.	Goalscorers	Attendance
1	Aug 7	H	Alloa	L	0-2	0-1	—		329
2	14	A	Forfar Ath	L	0-3	0-1	13		555
3	21	H	Queen's Park	W	2-0	1-0	12	Kerrigan 2	311
4	28	A	Stranraer	L	1-2	1-1	12	Kerrigan	666
5	Sept 4	A	Berwick R	D	1-1	0-1	12	Kerrigan	434
6	11	H	Stenhousemuir	L	1-2	1-0	12	Scott	240
7	18	A	Cowdenbeath	W	1-0	0-0	11	Scott	228
8	25	H	Queen of the S	D	1-1	0-0	10	Scott	433
9	Oct 2	A	East Stirling	W	4-1	1-1	10	Scott 4 (1 pen)	343
10	9	H	Arbroath	L	0-1	0-0	10		284
11	16	H	Meadowbank T	D	0-0	0-0	10		240
12	23	A	East Fife	D	1-1	1-0	9	Cadden	721
13	30	A	Montrose	L	0-1	0-1	10		491
14	Nov 6	H	Forfar Ath	L	1-3	1-2	11	Fraser	270
15	13	H	Cowdenbeath	L	0-1	0-1	14		231
16	20	A	Queen of the S	W	2-1	0-1	12	Rowe (og), Seggie	506
17	27	A	Arbroath	D	1-1	0-0	11	Martin (og)	616
18	Dec 4	H	East Stirling	L	1-5	1-3	12	Scott	224
19	18	A	Alloa	D	1-1	1-0	12	Conn	299
20	Jan 1	A	Queen's Park	L	0-2	0-1	13		858
21	8	H	Str	L	1-2	0-0	13	Seggie	306
22	22	A	Meadowbank T	L	2-4	0-2	14	Seggie, Scott	123
23	25	H	Montrose	L	3-4	1-2	—	Scott (pen), Kerrigan 2	112
24	29	H	East Fife	D	1-1	0-0	14	Scott	273
25	Feb 5	A	Stenhousemuir	L	1-5	1-2	14	Gallagher	315
26	12	H	Berwick R	L	0-2	0-1	14		267
27	19	H	East Stirling	W	3-1	1-0	13	Scott 2, McBride M	248
28	26	A	Stranraer	L	1-2	0-0	13	Scott	784
29	Mar 5	H	Montrose	L	0-1	0-1	13		243
30	12	A	Queen of the S	W	2-1	1-1	13	McBride M, Walker	678
31	19	H	Queen's Park	D	1-1	0-0	13	Walker	358
32	26	A	Stenhousemuir	D	0-0	0-0	13		351
33	Apr 2	A	East Fife	L	1-3	1-0	13	Scott	592
34	9	H	Cowdenbeath	W	1-0	0-0	13	Scott	313
35	16	A	Berwick R	L	0-3	0-2	13		489
36	23	H	Forfar Ath	L	1-3	0-1	13	Kelly	312
37	30	H	Alloa	D	1-1	1-1	13	Scott (pen)	486
38	May 7	A	Arbroath	L	0-1	0-1	13		445
39	14	H	Meadowbank T	L	0-2	0-0	13		368

Final League Position: 13

Most League Appearances: 399, Murdy Walls, 1921-36.
Most League Goals in Season (Individual): 41: Jim Renwick, Division II; 1932-33.
Most Goals Overall (Individual): 105: Bunty Weir, 1928-31.

Honours
League Champions: Division II 1933-34, Second Division 1988-89; *Runners-up:* Division II 1913-14, 1937-38, 1947-48.
Scottish Cup Runners-up: 1920. *League Cup:* —.
Club Colours: Shirt: Yellow with red trim. Shorts: Red with yellow stripes. Stockings: Yellow.

Goalscorers: *League* (37): Scott 17 (3 pens), Kerrigan 6, Seggie 3, McBride M 2, Walker 2, Cadden 1, Conn 1, Fraser 1, Gallagher 1, Kelly 1, own goals 2. *Scottish Cup* (3): Fraser 1, McCaffrey 1, Scott 1 (pen). *League Cup* (3): Fraser 1, Kerrigan 1, Scott 1. *B&Q Cup* (2): McBride M 1, Scott 1.

McConnachie R 22 + 1	Kelly J 19	McKeown D 35 + 1	Spence T 12	Taylor G 8 + 2	Riley D 26	McBride M 24 + 8	Scott M 36 + 1	Kerrigan S 22 + 2	Fraser A 15 + 13	Gallagher J 20 + 8	Cadden S 20 + 1	Seggie D 21 + 8	Mirner E 7 + 2	Watson E 1 + 2	McCafferty T 1	Horne J 7	McCaffrey J 22	Burns R 16	Murray D 1	Conn S 31	McQuade A — + 5	Collins L 19 + 1	Friar P — + 1	Beattie J 14 + 1	Ryan M 1	Walker D 11	Lynch M 1 + 2	McDonald D 6	McBride J 8	Thompson D 3 + 2	Match No.
1	2	3	4	5	6	7	8	9	*10*	11	12	14																			1
1	*4*	3	6	5	2	7	10	9	11		8	14	12																		2
1		3	4	5		12	8	9	14		6		2	*7*	10	*11*															3
1		3	*6*	5		7	8	9	14	10			2	12		11	4														4
1		3	6	4		7	8	9		*10*		12	2	14		11	5														5
1		10	3			2	11	9		6	8	12	4			*7*	5														6
	2	10	*3*			7	8	9		14		12	6			11	5	1	4												7
	2	6	3			7	10	*9*			8	14	4			11	5	1													8
	2	3	11			7	9				10	8	6				5	1		*4*	14										9
	2	6	*3*			7	8	10		14	5		12			11	4	1		9											10
	2	6	3		*5*	7	11	10		14	8	12					4	1		9											11
12	*2*	6	3		7		10	9	11	14	8						4	1		5											12
	2	6		12	7	*11*		9	10	3	8						4	1		5	14										13
	4	6		5	2	12		9	11	3		8						1		10		*7*	14								14
	2	12			8		14	9	*11*		7	10					5	1		4		6		3							15
		3			2		11	10			4	8					5	1		9		7		6							16
		3			2		11	*10*	14		4	8					5	1		9		7		6							17
		6			2		11	10	12		4	8					5	1		9		7		3							18
		3			2	14	*10*	9		12	8	11					5	1		4		7		6							19
		6				7	10	9	12	14	8	*11*					5	1		4		2		3							20
		6				7	10	9	12		8	11					5	1		4		2		3							21
	2				11	14	10	12	9	6	8	7					5	1		4				3							22
1					2	14	9	12	8	11	10	7					5			*4*				3	6						23
1					2	11	10	9		3	6	8					5			4		7									24
1		3			2	11	10	9	12	8	6	*7*					5			4											25
1		3		12	2	11	9		*8*	6		7					5			4	14					10					26
1	2	3		5		11	9		10	6		7								4				8							27
1	2	3		*5*		11	9		10	8		7								4				6			14				28
1		5			2	11	9		*10*	6		7								4	12	8		3			14				29
1		3			2	11	9		7	6										4		14				10	*8*	5			30
1		3			2	11	*10*		7	6										4	14	8				9		5			31
1		3			2	*11*	10		14	6		12								4		8				9		5	7		32
1		3			2	11	9		12	6										4		8				10		5	*7*	14	33
1		3			2	*11*	9		8											4		6		14		10		5	7	12	34
1	2	3			7	12	9			14										4		8		*6*		10		5	11		35
1	2	5				14	9		12	*3*		8								4		6				10			11	*7*	36
1	5	3			2		9		14			8								4		6				10			11	*7*	37
	2	5			1	14	9		12	3		8								4		6				*10*			11	7	38
1	4	5			2		9		14	12		7								6		*8*		3		10			11		39

ALLOA Division 3

Year Formed: 1883. *Ground & Address:* Recreation Park, Clackmannan Rd, Alloa FK10 1RR. *Telephone:* 0259 722695.
Ground Capacity: total: 3100, seated: 180. *Size of Pitch:* 110yd # 75yd.
Chairman: Pat Lawlor. *Secretary:* E. G. Cameron. *Commercial Manager:* William McKie.
Manager: William Lamont. *Assistant Manager:* —. *Physio:* —. *Coach:* —.
Managers since 1975: H. Wilson; A. Totten; W. Garner; J. Thomson; D. Sullivan; G. Abel; B. Little; H. McCann. *Club Nickname(s):* The Wasps. *Previous Grounds:* None.
Record Attendance: 13,000 v Dunfermline Athletic, Scottish Cup 3rd rd replay; 26 Feb, 1939.
Record Transfer Fee received: £30,000 for Martin Nelson to Hamilton A (1988).
Record Transfer Fee paid: —.
Record Victory: 9-2 v Forfar Ath, Division II; 18 Mar, 1933.
Record Defeat: 0-10 v Dundee, Division II; 8 Mar, 1947: v Third Lanark, League Cup, 8 Aug, 1953.
Most Capped Player: Jock Hepburn, 1, Scotland.
Most League Appearances: —.
Most League Goals in Season (Individual): 49: William 'Wee' Crilley, Division II; 1921-22.
Most Goals Overall (Individual): —.

ALLOA 1993—94 LEAGUE RECORD

Match No.	Date	Venue	Opponents	Result		H/T Score	Lg. Pos.	Goalscorers	Attendance
1	Aug 7	A	Albion R	W	2-0	1-0	—	Newbigging (pen), Hendry	329
2	14	H	Cowdenbeath	L	0-1	0-1	5		421
3	21	H	East Stirling	D	0-0	0-0	6		415
4	28	A	East Fife	L	1-4	1-3	9	Gibson	1133
5	Sept 4	A	Stenhousemuir	D	1-1	0-1	9	Moffat	458
6	11	H	Stranraer	W	1-0	0-0	8	McAvoy	437
7	18	A	Queen of the S	W	1-0	0-0	8	Moffat	1459
8	25	H	Montrose	L	0-1	0-0	9		391
9	Oct 2	H	Meadowbank T	W	1-0	0-0	7	Newbigging (pen)	446
10	9	A	Forfar Ath	W	3-0	1-0	5	McAnenay, Gibson, Moffat	459
11	16	A	Arbroath	W	3-2	1-2	4	Ramsay 2, Willock	631
12	23	H	Berwick R	W	1-0	1-0	3	Newbigging (pen)	542
13	30	H	Queen's Park	D	1-1	0-1	3	Newbigging (pen)	545
14	Nov 6	A	Cowdenbeath	D	1-1	0-0	3	Ramsay	358
15	13	H	Queen of the S	W	1-0	1-0	3	Ramsay	477
16	20	A	Montrose	W	2-1	1-1	2	Willock, Newbigging (pen)	465
17	Dec 4	A	Meadowbank T	D	1-1	0-1	2	McCormick S	288
18	7	H	Forfar Ath	D	1-1	1-0	—	Lamont	454
19	18	H	Albion R	D	1-1	0-1	2	McCormick S	299
20	27	A	Queen's Park	L	1-2	0-1	—	Lamont	1048
21	Jan 11	A	East Stirling	W	1-0	0-0	—	McCormick S	398
22	18	H	East Fife	D	2-2	1-0	—	McCulloch, Willock	542
23	22	H	Arbroath	L	1-2	0-2	2	Moffat	578
24	Feb 1	A	Berwick R	D	1-1	1-1	—	McAvoy	558
25	5	A	Stranraer	D	1-1	0-1	2	McCormick S (pen)	1101
26	11	H	Stenhousemuir	L	1-2	0-1	4	Newbigging (pen)	856
27	Mar 2	A	Meadowbank T	L	2-3	1-1	—	McCormick S, Russell	190
28	5	H	East Stirling	L	0-1	0-0	7		449
29	12	A	Arbroath	D	0-0	0-0	7		581
30	15	H	Queen of the S	W	1-0	0-0	—	Newbigging (pen)	338
31	19	A	Berwick R	D	1-1	0-1	5	Lamont	463
32	26	H	Stranraer	D	1-1	1-1	5	Cadden	599
33	Apr 2	A	Stenhousemuir	L	0-1	0-0	6		557
34	12	H	Queen's Park	D	0-0	0-0	—		317
35	16	H	Cowdenbeath	W	1-0	0-0	7	Diver	393
36	23	A	Montrose	D	2-2	0-1	7	McCormick S, Willock	440
37	30	A	Albion R	D	1-1	1-1	6	McAnenay	486
38	May 7	H	Forfar Ath	L	1-3	1-0	7	Diver	483
39	14	H	East Fife	D	1-1	1-0	7	Kemp	1156

Final League Position: 7

Honours
League Champions: Division II 1921-22; *Runners-up:* Division II 1938-39. Second Division 1976-77, 1981-82, 1984-85, 1988-89.
Scottish Cup: —.
League Cup: —.
Club colours: Shirt: Gold with black trim. Shorts: Black. Stockings: Gold.

Goalscorers: *League* (41): Newbigging 7 (7 pens), McCormick S 6 (1 pen), Moffat 4, Ramsay 4, Willock 4, Lamont 3, Diver 2, Gibson 2, McAnenay 2, McAvoy 2, Cadden 1, Hendry 1, Kemp 1, McCulloch 1, Russell 1. *Scottish Cup* (6): Lamont 1, McAnenay 1, McAvoy 1, McCormick S 1, McCulloch 1, own goal 1. *League Cup* (1): Hendry 1. *B&Q Cup* (1): Newbigging 1.

Butter J 39	McNiven J 34 + 1	Bennett N 14 + 1	Campbell C 34 + 1	McCulloch K 36	Newbigging W 33	Gibson J 8 + 6	Ramsay S 30	Hendry M 5	Moffat B 20 + 7	McAvoy N 23 + 6	Herd W 4 + 3	McCormick S 13 + 10	Mackay J 3 + 3	Dempsey J 3	Russell G 3 + 4	Tait G 9 + 15	Lee R 13	Crombie L — + 2	McAnenay M 19 + 5	Willock A 20 + 6	Lamont P 17 + 6	McCormack J 7	Kemp B 12	Neil C 1	Nelson M 2	Lawrie D 10	Cadden S 10	Diver D 7	Match No.
1	2	3	4	5	6	7	8	9	*10*	11	12	14																	1
1	2	3	4	5	6		*8*	9	10	11	7	12	14																2
1		3	4	5	6	8		9	12	10	*11*			2	*7*	14													3
1	12	14	2	5	6	7	8		10	11		9		*4*			3												4
1	2		4	5	6	11		10	7	8	14	*9*				12	3												5
1	2	8	4	5	6	12		*9*	10	7						11	3	14											6
1	2	8	4	5	6	12			10	*11*	*7*					9	3	14											7
1	2	10	4	5	6		8		9		7	14			*11*		3												8
1	*2*	10	4	5	6	7	8		9	11	14				12		3												9
1		2	4	5	6	14	8		9				10				3		*7*	*11*	12								10
1	2	10	4	5	6	12	8		9				14				*3*			7	11								11
1	2	3	4	5	6	10	8		9							12			*7*	11	14								12
1	2		4	5	6	10	3		8				14			12			*7*	11	9								13
1	2	3	4	5	6	14	8		12	*10*									*7*	11	9								14
1	2	3	4	5	6	14	8			*7*						12	10			11	9								15
1		2	4	5	6	7	8		9	12						14	3		*10*	11									16
1		3	4	5	6		8		9	11		14				7			*10*		12	2							17
1	2		4	5	6		8		14	12		*9*				10				11	7	3							18
1	2		4	5	6		8			10		14				12	3		7	11	*9*								19
1	*2*		4	5	6		8			7		12				14	3		9		11	10							20
1	2		4	5	6		8		12			9					3		14	11	*10*	7							21
1	2		4	5	6		8			7		9				12			14	11	*10*		3						22
1	2		4	5	6		*8*		12	7		9				14			10	11			3						23
1	2			5			*8*		9	7		12	4			14			10	11			3	6					24
1	2			5			8		11	10		9	6	*4*	12	3			7	14									25
1	2		4	5	6		8		12	7		9				3			10	*11*	14								26
1	2		4	5	6					12		9			14	*3*			8	11	10				7				27
1	2		4	5	6					10		9			12	14			7	*11*					3	8			28
1	2		4	5			10			14		9							12	11	*7*		3			6	8		29
1	2			5	4		10		*11*	7		9							14		12		3			6	8		30
1	*2*		12	5	4		7					14				8			11		9		3			6	10		31
1	2		4		5		8			*7*						6			14	11	9		3				10		32
1	2			5	4		*8*		12							14				11	7		3			6	10	9	33
1	2		3	5			8			14						12			10	*11*	7					6	4	9	34
1	2		4	6					10	7						14				12	11		*3*			5	8	9	35
1	2		4	5					10	*7*		14								12	11	3				6	8	9	36
1	*2*		4		6					14		10							7	12		3	11			5	8	9	37
1	2		4		6		10								11				*7*	14	12		3			5	8	9	38
1	2		4	5	6		8		10			14							*7*	12		3	11					9	39

ARBROATH Division 3

Year Formed: 1878. *Ground & Address:* Gayfield Park, Arbroath DD11 1QB. *Telephone:* 0241 872157.
Ground Capacity: 6488. seated: 715. *Size of Pitch:* 115yd # 71yd.
President: John D. Christison. *Secretary:* Andrew Warrington. *Commercial Manager:* David Kean.
Joint Managers: George Mackie, Donald Park. *Physio:* William Shearer. *Coach:* John Martin.
Managers since 1975: A. Henderson; I. J. Stewart; G. Fleming; J. Bone; J. Young; W. Borthwick; M. Lawson, D. McGrain MBE, J. Scott.
Club Nickname(s): The Red Lichties. *Previous Grounds:* None.
Record Attendance: 13,510 v Rangers, Scottish Cup 3rd rd; 23 Feb, 1952.
Record Transfer Fee received: £120,000 for Paul Tosh to Dundee (Aug 1993).
Record Transfer Fee paid: £20,000 for Douglas Robb from Montrose (1981).
Record Victory: 36-0 v Bon Accord, Scottish Cup 1st rd; 12 Sept, 1885.
Record Defeat: 1-9 v Celtic, League Cup 3rd rd; 25 Aug 1993.
Most Capped Player: Ned Doig, 2 (5), Scotland.
Most League Appearances: 445: Tom Cargill, 1966-81.

ARBROATH 1993—94 LEAGUE RECORD

Match No.	Date		Venue	Opponents	Result		H/T Score	Lg. Pos.	Goalscorers	Attendance
1	Aug	7	H	Queen of the S	L	2-5	1-1	—	King (pen), Tindal	751
2		14	A	Montrose	D	0-0	0-0	11		1379
3		21	H	Forfar Ath	D	1-1	0-0	10	Martin	1062
4		28	A	Berwick R	L	0-2	0-1	13		492
5	Sept	4	A	Stranraer	L	1-2	1-2	13	McKinnon	658
6		11	H	Queen's Park	W	2-0	1-0	11	McKinnon, Diver	690
7		18	H	Stenhousemuir	L	1-2	1-0	12	McKinnon	633
8		25	A	Meadowbank T	L	0-3	0-1	13		273
9	Oct	2	H	Cowdenbeath	D	2-2	1-0	12	Martin, Diver	594
10		9	A	Albion R	W	1-0	0-0	11	McKinnon	284
11		16	H	Alloa	L	2-3	2-1	13	Diver, Tindal	631
12		23	A	East Stirling	W	4-2	3-0	11	Diver 3, Sorbie	393
13		30	A	East Fife	L	0-1	0-0	12		860
14	Nov	6	H	Montrose	W	2-0	2-0	10	Sorbie, Tindal	869
15		13	A	Stenhousemuir	L	0-4	0-3	11		370
16		20	H	Meadowbank T	W	3-2	2-2	10	Martin, McKinnon, Sorbie	544
17		27	H	Albion R	D	1-1	0-0	10	Sorbie	616
18	Dec	4	A	Cowdenbeath	W	1-0	0-0	10	Sorbie	290
19		18	A	Queen of the S	L	0-6	0-4	10		481
20		29	H	East Fife	W	3-2	2-0	—	Diver, King, McKinnon	839
21	Jan	11	A	Forfar Ath	W	4-1	0-1	—	Adam, Diver 2, McKinnon	801
22		22	A	Alloa	W	2-1	2-0	9	Clouston, Martin	578
23		26	H	Berwick R	L	0-4	0-2	—		585
24	Feb	2	H	East Stirling	D	1-1	0-1	—	Diver	582
25		5	A	Queen's Park	L	1-2	1-2	9	Sorbie	439
26		12	H	Stranraer	D	0-0	0-0	9		606
27		19	A	Stenhousemuir	L	0-2	0-0	9		523
28		26	H	Montrose	D	0-0	0-0	9		924
29	Mar	5	A	Forfar Ath	L	2-3	2-3	11	Feeney 2	752
30		12	H	Alloa	D	0-0	0-0	11		581
31		19	A	East Stirling	L	0-2	0-0	11		359
32		26	H	Meadowbank T	D	1-1	0-0	11	Sorbie	496
33	Apr	2	A	Cowdenbeath	L	0-1	0-0	12		219
34		9	H	Queen of the S	L	0-3	0-1	12		391
35		16	A	Stranraer	L	0-1	0-0	12		916
36		23	H	Queen's Park	W	2-1	1-0	11	Sorbie, Farnan	413
37		30	A	East Fife	W	2-1	1-0	11	Adam, Tosh	634
38	May	7	H	Albion R	W	1-0	1-0	11	Adam	445
39		14	A	Berwick R	L	0-5	0-3	12		478

Final League Position: 12

Most League Goals in Season (Individual): 45: Dave Easson, Division II; 1958-59.
Most Goals Overall (Individual): 120: Jimmy Jack; 1966-71.

Honours
League Champions Runners-up: Division II 1934-35, 1958-59, 1967-68, 1971-72.
Scottish Cup: —.
League Cup: —.
Club colours: Shirt: Maroon with sky blue trim. Shorts: White. Stockings: Maroon with sky blue hooped tops.

Goalscorers: *League* (42): Diver 10, Sorbie 8, McKinnon 7, Martin 4, Adam 3, Tindal 3, Feeney 2, King 2 (1 pen), Clouston 1, Farnan 1, Tosh 1. *Scottish Cup* (5): McKinnon 2, Adam 1, Buckley 1, Sorbie 1. *League Cup* (4): Elliot 1, Martin 1, Strachan 1, Tindal 1. *B&Q Cup* (1): Diver 1.

Harkness M 1	Hamilton J 14 + 1	Florence S 36	Mitchell B 22	Adam C 31	Martin C 22 + 3	Will B 10	King T 25 + 1	Russell R 1	Farnan C 29 + 5	Sorbie S 33 + 3	Hindson P — + 1	Tindal K 7 + 6	Jackson D 36	Elliot D 7 + 7	Strachan J 8 + 1	McKillop A 11 + 1	Clouston B 25 + 2	McKinnon C 29	Diver D 21	Buckley G 18 + 7	Scott D 6 + 14	McKeown J 1	McClelland J 2	Glennie R 11	Feeney P 6 + 2	McGregor S 3 + 4	Martin M 7	Tosh S 6 + 1	Duncan R 1	Match No.
1	2	3	4	5	6	*7*	8	9	10	11	12	14																		1
	2	3	4	5	6	7	8		10	11		12	1	*9*	14															2
	2	3	4	*5*	14	7	8		6	11		12	1	9	10															3
	2	3		9	6		*8*		4	11		12	1	14	10	5	7													4
	12	*3*	4		6		2		10	11		8	1	14		5	7	9												5
	2	3	4		14		12		8	11			1		6	5	*7*	10	9											6
	2	3	4	5	12				8	11			1		6		7	10	9											7
	2	3	4	5	*6*				8	11		14	1				7	10	9											8
	2	3	4	5	6		8		12	*11*		14	1	7				10	9											9
	2	4		5	3		8					7	1	6				10	9	11										10
	2	4		*5*	3		8		14	12		7	1	6				10	9	11										11
	2	4		5	3		8			11		7	1	6				10	9	12										12
	2		4	5	6		8			11		7	1		*3*			10	9	14	12									13
	2	3	4	5	6		8		14	11		7	1					10		9	12									14
	2	4		5	3		8		12	14		7						6	9	11	*10*	1								15
		3		5	8		7		4	11			1				2	10		9			6							16
		3		5	8		7		4	11			1	12	6		2		*10*	9	14									17
		3		5	6		7		4	11			1				2	10	9	*8*	14									18
		3		5	6		7		4	11			1	12	10		2	9		*8*	14									19
		3	4	5	6		8		2	11			1				7	10	9											20
		3	4	5			8		2	11			1		*6*		7	10	9	14										21
		3	4	5	6		*8*		2	11			1				7	10	9	12	14									22
		3	4	5	6		*8*		2				1				7	10	9	11	14									23
		3	4	5	6		8		2	*11*			1				7	10	9	14	12									24
		3	4	5	6				2	11			1	12			7	10	9	14	8									25
			6	4	10		8		5	11			1				2	3	9	7	12									26
		5		4		10	8		6	11			1				2	3	9	7	12									27
		3					7		6	11			1				2	10	9		8		4	5						28
		3	4				*8*		6	14			1	7		12	2	10	9					5	11					29
		3	4			7			6	11			1				2	10		8	12			5	9					30
		3	4			7			6	11			1	14			2			*8*	10			5	9					31
		3	4			7			6	*11*			1	14		2	12				8			5	9	10				32
			4			*7*			6				1			2	11			14	8			5	9	10	3	12		33
		8		4		*2*			6	11						5	12				14				9	10	3	7	1	34
		3		4					8	11			1			5	2			*7*	14			6		12	9	10		35
		3		4		2			12	11			1			5		*9*		7				6	14		8	10		36
		3		4					2	11			1			5		*9*		8				6		14	7	10		37
		3		4						11			1			5	2	*9*		7	12			6		14	8	10		38
		3		4						11			1			5	2	*9*		7				6	12	14	8	10		39

AYR UNITED Division 1

Year Formed: 1910. *Ground & Address:* Somerset Park, Tryfield Place, Ayr KA8 9NB. *Telephone:* 0292 263435.
Ground Capacity: 13,918. seated: 1450. *Size of Pitch:* 110yd # 72yd.
Chairman: D. M. MacIntyre. *Secretary:* J. E. Eyley. *Commercial Manager:* Sandy Kerr.
Manager: Simon Stainrod. *Assistant Manager:* Malcolm Shotton.
Managers since 1975: Alex Stuart; Ally MacLeod; Willie McLean; George Caldwell; Ally MacLeod; George Burley. *Club Nickname(s):* The Honest Men. *Previous Grounds:* None.
Record Attendance: 25,225 v Rangers, Division I; 13 Sept, 1969.
eltic*Record Transfer Fee received:* £300,000 for Steven Nicol to Liverpool (Oct 1981).
Record Transfer Fee paid: £50,000 for Peter Weir from St Mirren, June 1990.
Record Victory: 11-1 v Dumbarton, League Cup; 13 Aug, 1952.
Record Defeat: 0-9 in Division I v Rangers (1929); v Hearts (1931); v Third Lanark (1954).
Most Capped Player: Jim Nisbet, 3, Scotland.

AYR UNITED 1993—94 LEAGUE RECORD

Match No.	Date	Venue	Opponents	Result		H/T Score	Lg. Pos.	Goalscorers	Attendance
1	Aug 7	A	Clydebank	L	0-1	0-0	—		1070
2	14	H	Stirling Albion	W	2-1	0-0	7	McCormack (og), Scott	1503
3	21	A	Clyde	W	1-0	1-0	4	Bryce	920
4	28	H	Dumbarton	L	0-1	0-0	6		1675
5	Sept 4	A	St Mirren	W	1-0	0-0	5	McGivern	2578
6	11	A	Brechin C	W	2-0	1-0	5	McGlashan, Howard	565
7	14	H	Falkirk	L	0-3	0-2	—		2633
8	18	A	Hamilton A	L	1-2	0-1	6	McGivern	1529
9	25	H	Dunfermline Ath	D	1-1	0-0	6	Traynor	2012
10	28	H	Morton	D	2-2	1-1	—	Moore, Doak (og)	1659
11	Oct 2	A	Airdrieonians	D	1-1	0-0	5	McGlashan	2140
12	9	H	Clydebank	D	1-1	0-1	6	Burns	2017
13	16	A	Falkirk	L	0-2	0-1	7		3350
14	23	H	Brechin C	W	1-0	1-0	6	McGivern	1400
15	30	H	Clyde	W	1-0	0-0	6	McGivern	1765
16	Nov 6	A	Dumbarton	D	1-1	0-1	6	Bryce	918
17	9	H	St Mirren	L	0-1	0-0	—		1949
18	13	H	Airdrieonians	L	1-2	0-1	8	McGivern	1944
19	20	A	Morton	W	1-0	1-0	7	Shotton	1293
20	Dec 4	H	Hamilton A	D	1-1	0-0	7	McGivern	1508
21	11	A	Stirling Albion	D	0-0	0-0	7		786
22	14	A	Dunfermline Ath	L	1-6	0-3	—	McGivern	3206
23	18	H	Falkirk	L	0-3	0-0	8		1878
24	Jan 4	A	Clydebank	W	2-0	2-0	—	McGlashan, Hood	2015
25	8	H	Dumbarton	D	1-1	1-1	8	Hood	2084
26	11	A	Clyde	D	0-0	0-0	—		809
27	22	H	Stirling Albion	W	3-1	2-1	7	Hood, Lennox, McGivern	1780
28	25	A	St Mirren	L	1-3	1-2	—	Moore	3394
29	Feb 5	A	Brechin C	W	4-1	2-0	7	Traynor 2, Biggart 2	483
30	12	A	Airdrieonians	D	0-0	0-0	7		2208
31	Mar 1	H	Morton	W	2-1	0-1	—	Shotton, Bilsland	1752
32	5	A	Hamilton A	L	1-2	0-2	7	McGivern	1514
33	12	H	Dunfermline Ath	L	0-4	0-1	7		2336
34	19	A	Falkirk	L	0-2	0-1	7		3577
35	26	H	Clydebank	D	0-0	0-0	7		1706
36	29	A	Stirling Albion	W	3-1	2-0	—	Burns, McGivern 2	953
37	Apr 2	H	Brechin C	D	0-0	0-0	7		1521
38	9	H	Airdrieonians	L	2-3	2-2	7	Stainrod 2	1508
39	16	A	Morton	W	1-0	0-0	7	Bilsland	1169
40	23	H	Hamilton A	W	1-0	0-0	7	McGivern	1684
41	26	A	Dunfermline Ath	L	0-1	0-0	—		4006
42	30	H	Clyde	D	1-1	1-0	7	McKilligan	1696
43	May 7	A	Dumbarton	D	1-1	1-1	7	Woods	670
44	14	H	St Mirren	L	0-1	0-0	7		1919

Final League Position: 7

Most League Appearances: 371: Ian McAllister, 1977-90.
Most League Goals in Season (Individual): 66: Jimmy Smith, 1927-28.
Most Goals Overall (Individual): —.

Honours
League Champions: Division II 1911-12, 1912-13, 1927-28, 1936-37, 1958-59, 1965-66. Second Division 1987-88;
Runners-up: Division II 1910-11, 1955-56, 1968-69.
Scottish Cup: —. *League Cup:* —.
*B&Q Cup: Runners-up:*1990-91, 1991-92.
Club colours: Shirt: White with black sleeves. Shorts: Black. Stockings: White.

Goalscorers: *League* (42): McGivern 12, Hood 3, McGlashan 3, Traynor 3, Biggart 2, Bilsland 2, Bryce 2, Burns 2 (1 pen), Moore 2, Shotton 2, Stainrod 2, Howard 1, Lennox 1, McKilligan 1, Scott 1, Woods 1, own goals 2. *Scottish Cup* (1): Bryce 1. *League Cup* (0): *B&Q Cup* (8): McGivern 3, Burns 2 (1 pen), Bryce 1, McGlashan 1, own goal 1.

Duncan C 31	Burley G 12 + 1	Robertson G 20 + 1	Shotton M 38	Traynor J 34 + 8	George D 18	Mair G 25 + 1	Bryce S 12 + 5	McGivern S 38 + 2	McNab N 4	Scott B 12 + 2	Kennedy D 6 + 3	McQuilter R 7 + 1	Howard N 5	Burns H 35	Walker T 2 + 2	Beattie J 3	McGlashan C 34 + 2	Moore V 19	Lennox G 23	Jack R 14 + 4	Hood G 26 + 1	Grierson G — + 1	Spence W 13	Albiston A 1	Stainrod S 7 + 3	Biggart K 16 + 2	Woods T 3 + 8	Bilsland B 5 + 8	Connie C 2 + 4	Donaldson D 1	McVicar D 10	McKilligan N 8	Williams R — + 1	Match No.
1	2	3	4	5	6	7	8	9	10	11																								1
1		2		10			8	9	6	11	3	4	5	7	12																			2
1	2	3	4	10			8	9	6	11	14	5		*7*																				3
1		2	4	10		*7*	8	9	6	11		5			12	3																		4
1	2	3		4	6	7		9		11		5		10	8																			5
1	14	2		5	6	7		9		11			4	10		*3*	8																	6
1	2	3		5	*6*	7				11		14	4	10	9		8																	7
1	2	7		6		12		9		11		5	4	10		3	8																	8
1		2	4	7		3	12	9		11		6	5	10			8																	9
1		2	4	5		3	12	9		11		6		10			8	7																10
1	2	7	4	5		3	11	9						10			8	6																11
1		2	4	5	6	3	11							10			8		7	9														12
1	2	14	4	5	*6*	3	11	9									8	10	7	12														13
1		3	*4*	5	6		11	9			2			10			8		7		14													14
1		3	4		6		11	9			2			10			8		7		5													15
1	2	3	4	10	6		11	9									8		7	12	5													16
1			4	2	6			9			3			10			8		7	11	5													17
1	2	3	4	6				9		12				10			8		7	11	5													18
1	2	3	4				14	9			6			10			8		7	*11*	5													19
1	2	3	4	6		11	12	9						10			8		7		5													20
1		3	4	2	6	11		9			14			10			8		7	12	*5*													21
1	2	3	4	5	*6*	11		9			14			10			8		7			12												22
			4	6				9			2						8	10	7	11	5		1	3										23
			4	12	6	3				11				2			10	8	*7*	*9*	5		1		14									24
			4	12	6	3		14		*11*				2			10	8	7	9	5		1											25
			4	12	6	3	14	11						2			*10*	8	7	9	5		1											26
			4	12	6	3		9						2			14	8	7	10	5		1			*11*								27
			4	12	6	3		9						2			14	8	7	10	5		1			*11*								28
			4	8	6	3	9			14				*2*			11		7	10	5		1			12								29
			4	2		3	*8*	9									11	6		10	5		1			7	12	14						30
			4	2		3		9									11	8	6	*10*	5		1			7	12	14						31
			4	2		3		9									11	8	6	12	5		1			7		10	14					32
1				6		3		9						*2*			11		7		*5*				14	12	8	10		4				33
1			4	2		*3*		9									11	8	6	10	5				12	7		14						34
			4	6				9						2			11	8			5		1		*10*	7	14		12		3			35
			4	6				9						2			11	8			5		1		*10*	7	14		12		3			36
			4	6				9						2			11		8				1		10	7		14			3	*5*		37
1			4	6				9						2			*11*				5				10	7	12	14			3	8		38
1			4	6		11		9						2							5				*10*	7	12	14			3	8		39
1			4	6				9						2			*11*	5								7	12	10	14		3	8		40
1			4	14				9						2			11	*8*			5					7	12	10			3	6		41
1			4	12				9						2			11	8			5				*10*	*7*		14			3	6		42
1			4	12				14						2							5				10	7	9	*11*	8		3	6		43
1			4	5				9						*2*				10								7	11	12	8		3	6	14	44

BERWICK RANGERS Division 2

Year Formed: 1881. *Ground & Address:* Shielfield Park, Tweedmouth, Berwick-upon-Tweed TD15 2EF. *Telephone:* 0289 307424. Club 24 hour hotline 0891 800697. *Ground Capacity:* 4131. seated: 1366. *Size of Pitch:* 112yd # 76yd.
Chairman: Roy McDowell. *Vice-chairman:* Tom Davidson. *Company Secretary:* Colin Walker. *Club Secretary:* Dennis McCleary.
General Manager: Jim Crease. *Team Manager:* Tom Hendrie. *Physio/Coach:* Ian Oliver. *Youth Manager:* John Coughlin.
Managers since 1975: H. Melrose; G. Haig; W. Galbraith; D. Smith; F. Connor; J. McSherry; E. Tait; J. Thomson; J. Jefferies; J. Anderson.
Club Nickname(s): The Borderers. *Previous Grounds:* Bull Stob Close, Pier Field, Meadow Field, Union Park, Old Shielfield.
Record Attendance: 13,365 v Rangers, Scottish Cup 1st rd; 28 Jan, 1967.
Record Victory: 8-1 v Forfar Ath. Division II; 25 Dec, 1965: v Vale of Leithen, Scottish Cup; Dec, 1966.
Record Defeat: 1-9 v Hamilton A, First Division; 9 Aug, 1980.
Most Capped Player: —.

BERWICK RANGERS 1993—94 LEAGUE RECORD

Match No.	*Date*	*Venue*	*Opponents*	*Result*		*H/T Score*	*Lg. Pos.*	*Goalscorers*	*Attendance*
1	Aug 7	H	East Fife	L	0-1	0-1	—		518
2	14	A	East Stirling	L	1-2	0-1	12	Banks	301
3	21	A	Meadowbank T	D	1-1	1-1	13	Coughlin	311
4	28	H	Arbroath	W	2-0	1-0	7	Irvine, Kane (pen)	492
5	Sept 4	H	Albion R	D	1-1	1-0	8	Neil	434
6	11	A	Cowdenbeath	W	2-1	1-0	7	Irvine, Kane	323
7	18	H	Stranraer	W	1-0	1-0	5	Scott	435
8	25	A	Forfar Ath	D	1-1	0-1	7	Irvine	498
9	Oct 2	A	Stenhousemuir	L	1-2	0-2	9	Banks	352
10	9	H	Queen's Park	W	6-0	1-0	7	Maxwell (og), Kane 2 (1 pen), Cowan, Cunningham, Scott	406
11	16	H	Montrose	D	3-3	1-0	6	Neil 2, Graham	417
12	23	A	Alloa	L	0-1	0-1	7		542
13	30	A	Queen of the S	W	5-2	1-0	7	Hall, Neil 2, Irvine, Banks	782
14	Nov 6	H	East Stirling	D	2-2	1-1	6	Wilson, Irvine	453
15	13	A	Str	L	0-3	0-1	7		743
16	27	A	Queen's Park	D	0-0	0-0	6		587
17	30	H	Forfar Ath	L	0-2	0-0	—		297
18	Dec 4	H	Stenhousemuir	W	2-1	2-1	6	Cunningham 2	396
19	18	A	East Fife	D	1-1	0-1	8	Scott	756
20	Jan 11	H	Meadowbank T	D	2-2	2-0	—	Irvine, Hawke	431
21	18	H	Queen of the S	L	1-2	1-2	—	Hawke	457
22	22	A	Montrose	W	3-2	1-0	8	Irvine, Neil, Banks	461
23	26	A	Arbroath	W	4-0	2-0	—	Hawke 2, Graham, Cowan	585
24	Feb 1	H	Alloa	D	1-1	1-1	—	Hawke	558
25	5	H	Cowdenbeath	W	3-2	1-0	5	Cowan, Irvine 2	499
26	12	A	Albion R	W	2-0	1-0	5	Wilson, Young K	267
27	23	H	Stranraer	W	1-0	1-0	—	Irvine	567
28	Mar 1	A	Queen's Park	W	3-1	1-1	—	Hawke 2, Kane	405
29	5	H	East Fife	L	1-3	0-1	4	Neil	517
30	12	A	Montrose	L	1-3	0-1	4	Kane	636
31	19	H	Alloa	D	1-1	1-0	4	Young K	463
32	26	A	Cowdenbeath	W	5-1	3-1	4	Kane, Irvine 3, Cunningham	268
33	Apr 2	A	Queen of the S	D	0-0	0-0	4		928
34	9	H	Forfar Ath	D	2-2	0-2	4	Banks (pen), Hawke	387
35	16	H	Albion R	W	3-0	2-0	4	Kane 2, Young K	489
36	23	A	Meadowbank T	W	2-1	0-1	4	Kane, Forrester	355
37	30	H	Stenhousemuir	W	3-0	1-0	2	Hawke 2, Forrester	599
38	May 7	A	East Stirling	W	3-1	1-0	2	Hall, Banks, Forrester	438
39	14	H	Arbroath	W	5-0	3-0	2	Hawke 2, Irvine 2, Cowan	478

Final League Position: 2

Most League Appearances: 435;: Eric Tait, 1970-87.
Most League Goals in Season (Individual): 38: Ken Bowron, Division II; 1963-64.
Most Goals Overall (Individual): 115: Eric Tait, 1970-87.

Honours
League Champions: Second Division 1978-79. *Runners-up* Second Division 1993-94.
Scottish Cup: —.
League Cup: Semi-final 1963-64.
Club colours: Shirt: Black and gold stripes. Shorts: Black, gold trim. Stockings: Gold and black.

Goalscorers: *League* (75): Irvine 15, Hawke 12, Kane 10 (2 pens), Neil 7, Banks 6 (1 pen), Cowan 4, Cunningham 4, Forrester 3, Scott 3, Young K 3, Graham 2, Hall 2, Wilson 2, Coughlin 1, own goal 1. *Scottish Cup* (1): Kane 1. *League Cup* (0): *B&Q Cup* (1): Banks 1.

O'Connor G 26	Valentine C 39	Banks A 36 + 1	Hall A 28 + 3	Cowan M 37	Richardson S 17 + 5	Wilson M 23 + 3	Irvine W 37 + 1	Cunningham C 7 + 6	Scott D 11 + 7	Graham T 14 + 11	Kane K 34 + 2	Tait A 1	Gibson K 22 + 1	Coughlin J 11	Neil M 28	Romaines S 4	Gallacher S 2 + 2	Sokoluk J — + 1	Healer A 1	King T 1 + 4	Hawke W 20	Boyle L 6 + 1	Donaldson G 1 + 1	Young K 9 + 7	Kirkwood G 1	Ceccarelli P 1	Lawson O 1	Osborne M 6	Young N 3 + 1	Forrester P 2 + 3	Match No.
1	2	3	4	5	6	*7*	8	9	10	11	12																				1
	6	3	8	5			12	10	9	11	7	1	2	4																	2
1	2	3	8	5	*6*	14	10	12	9	*7*	11			4																	3
1	2	3	8	5	6		10		9	7	11			4																	4
1	2	3		5	6	14	10	12	9	*7*	11			4	8																5
1	2	3			6	7	10		14		11			4	8	5	*9*														6
1	2	3		5	6		10		9	12	11			4	7	8															7
1	2	3		5	6		10		9	14	*11*			4	7	8															8
1	2	3	8	5	6		10		*9*		11			4	7		14	12													9
1	2	3	10	5	6		7	9	12	14	*11*			4	8																10
1	2	*3*	8	5	6		10	9	12	14	11			4	7																11
1	2	3	10	5	6		11		14	12			7	4	8		*9*														12
1	2	3	4	5	6		10		9	7	11				8		12														13
1	2		4	5	6	3	10	12	9	7	11				8																14
1	2		4	5	6	*7*	8	12	14	11	10					3			9												15
1	3	14	4	5	6	12	7	*9*		11	10		2		8																16
1	4	3	8	5	6		10		*9*		11		2		7					14											17
1	6	3	4		5		10	*7*	12		11		2		8					14	9										18
1	4	3	6	5		*7*		9	12	10	11		2		8					14											19
1	4	3		5			6			*7*	11		12		8					14	9	2	10								20
1	4	3	8	5			10			14	*11*				7					6	9	2	12								21
1	4	3		5	14	*6*	10			11			7		8						9	2									22
1	4	*3*		5	14	6	10			11					8						9	2		7							23
1	4	3	14	5		6	10			11	12				8						9	2		*7*							24
1	4	3	*7*	5		6	10			14	11		2		8						9			12							25
1	4	3	7	5		6	10			14	*11*		2		8						9			12							26
1	4	3	7	5		6	9				11		2		8						10										27
	4	3	*7*	5		6	10			12	11		2		8						*9*			14	1						28
	4	*3*	7	5		6	10			14	11		2		8						9			12		1					29
	4	3		5		6	10			12	11		2		8						*9*	14		7			1				30
	4	3	12	5		6	10	14			11		7		8							*2*		9				1			31
	4	3	8	5		6	10	12			11		2								9			7				1			32
	4	3	12	5	14	6	10				11		*2*		8						9			7				1			33
	4	3	7	5		6	10				11		2		8						9			12					1		34
	4	3	8	5		*6*	10				11		2								9			7				1		14	35
	4	3	8	5		6	10				11		2								9			*7*				1		14	36
	4	3	8	5		6	10				11		2								9			*7*				1	12	14	37
	4	3	8	5	12	6	10				11		2								*9*			14					1	7	38
	4	3	8	5	12	6	10				*11*		2								9			14					1	7	39

BRECHIN CITY

Division 2

Year Formed: 1906. *Ground & Address:* Glebe Park, Trinity Rd, Brechin, Angus DD9 6BJ. *Telephone:* 0356 622856.
Ground Capacity: total: 3900. seated: 1518. *Size of Pitch:* 110yd # 67yd.
Chairman: Hugh Campbell Adamson. *Secretary:* George C. Johnston. *Commercial Manager:* —.
Manager: Ian Redford. *Assistant Manager:* John Young. *Physio:* Tom Gilmartin.
Managers since 1975: Charlie Dunn; Ian Stewart; Doug Houston; Ian Fleming; John Ritchie. *Club Nickname(s):* The City.
Previous Grounds: Nursery Park.
Record Attendance: 8122 v Aberdeen, Scottish Cup 3rd rd; 3 Feb, 1973.
Record Transfer Fee received: £100,000 for Scott Thomson to Aberdeen (1991).
Record Transfer Fee paid: £16,000 for Sandy Ross from Berwick Rangers (1991).
Record Victory: 12-1 v Thornhill, Scottish Cup 1st rd; 28 Jan, 1926.
Record Defeat: 0-10 v Airdrieonians, Albion R and Cowdenbeath, all in Division II; 1937-38.
Most Capped Player: —.

BRECHIN CITY 1993—94 LEAGUE RECORD

Match No.	Date	Venue	Opponents	Result		H/T Score	Lg. Pos.	Goalscorers	Attendance
1	Aug 7	H	Hamilton A	L	1-2	0-1	—	Miller	576
2	14	A	Airdrieonians	L	0-1	0-0	10		1663
3	21	H	Dunfermline Ath	W	1-0	0-0	8	Miller (pen)	1101
4	28	A	Morton	L	1-2	0-1	9	Miller	1312
5	Sept 4	H	Stirling Albion	L	1-2	1-0	10	Ross	610
6	11	H	Ayr U	L	0-2	0-1	11		565
7	14	A	Dumbarton	L	0-1	0-0	—		562
8	18	H	Clydebank	W	1-0	1-0	10	Redford	564
9	25	A	Clyde	D	1-1	0-1	11	Redford	565
10	28	A	St Mirren	L	0-2	0-1	—		1592
11	Oct 2	H	Falkirk	D	0-0	0-0	12		1347
12	9	A	Hamilton A	L	0-5	0-3	12		1020
13	16	H	Dumbarton	L	0-3	0-1	12		469
14	23	A	Ayr U	L	0-1	0-1	12		1400
15	30	A	Dunfermline Ath	L	0-4	0-2	12		3195
16	Nov 6	H	Morton	L	0-3	0-2	12		494
17	9	A	Stirling Albion	L	1-2	0-1	—	Brown	516
18	13	A	Falkirk	L	0-2	0-1	12		3473
19	20	H	St Mirren	L	1-4	0-0	12	Conway	840
20	30	H	Clyde	W	4-2	1-2	—	Brand 2, Christie, Scott	373
21	Dec 4	A	Clydebank	L	2-3	0-1	12	Miller, McNeill	618
22	11	H	Airdrieonians	L	0-2	0-0	12		682
23	18	A	Dumbarton	L	1-3	0-2	12	Brand	414
24	Jan 4	H	Dunfermline Ath	L	0-1	0-0	—		2120
25	8	A	Morton	D	1-1	1-0	12	Miller	1020
26	11	H	Hamilton A	D	0-0	0-0	—		383
27	15	H	Stirling Albion	W	2-0	0-0	12	Miller, McNeill	543
28	22	A	Airdrieonians	W	1-0	0-0	12	Brown	1466
29	Feb 5	H	Ayr U	L	1-4	0-2	12	Miller	483
30	12	H	Falkirk	L	0-2	0-1	12		1021
31	26	A	St Mirren	D	1-1	0-0	12	Redford	1922
32	Mar 5	H	Clydebank	L	0-1	0-0	12		424
33	12	A	Clyde	L	0-1	0-1	12		1786
34	19	H	Dumbarton	D	0-0	0-0	12		425
35	26	A	Hamilton A	L	1-9	0-3	12	Miller	1007
36	29	H	Airdrieonians	L	0-2	0-0	—		345
37	Apr 2	A	Ayr U	D	0-0	0-0	12		1521
38	9	A	Falkirk	L	2-4	1-0	12	Vannett, Nicolson	2940
39	16	H	St Mirren	L	0-1	0-0	12		682
40	23	A	Clydebank	L	1-2	0-0	12	Christie	574
41	26	H	Clyde	L	0-1	0-1	—		391
42	30	A	Dunfermline Ath	L	1-2	0-1	12	Brown	4988
43	May 7	H	Morton	L	1-2	0-1	12	Ross	444
44	14	A	Stirling Albion	W	3-0	0-0	12	Brand, Miller 2	481

Final League Position: 12

Most League Appearances: 459: David Watt, 1975-89.
Most League Goals in Season (Individual): 26: W. McIntosh, Division II; 1959-60.
Most Goals Overall (Individual): 131: Ian Campbell.

Honours
League Champions: Second Division 1982-83. C Division 1953-54. Second Division 1989-90. *Runners-up:* 1992-93.
Scottish Cup: —.
League Cup: —.
Club colours: Shirt, Shorts, Stockings: Red with white trimmings.

Goalscorers: *League* (30): Miller 10 (1 pen), Brand 4, Brown 3, Redford 3, Christie 2, McNeill 2, Ross 2, Conway 1, Nicolson 1, Scott 1, Vannett 1. *Scottish Cup* (0): *League Cup* (0): *B&Q Cup* (4): Brown 2, Miller 2.

Allan R 19	Kopel S 4	Baillie R 1	Brown R 38 + 1	Conway F 35	Redford I 40 + 3	Lees G 7 + 2	Hutt G 10	Ross A 31 + 4	Miller M 39	Brand R 25 + 1	O'Brien P 10 + 4	Bell S 7 + 3	Cairney H 28	McNeill W 19 + 11	Scott D 33	McLaren P 24 + 2	Lorimer R 4 + 1	Alexander B 13 + 1	Vannett R 24 + 1	Greig L 3 + 1	Christie G 26 + 2	Nicolson K 24	Gray B 1 + 3	Balfour D 12	Fisher D 3	Kemlo S 4 + 1	*Match No.*
1	2	3	4	5	6	*7*	8	9	10	11	12	14															1
1	2		4	5	6	11	8	9	10		7		3	12													2
1	2		4	5			6	9	10	11	8			12	3	7											3
1	2		4	5	6		8	9	10	11	7			12	3												4
1			4	5	6	12		9	10	11	8		2		3	7											5
1			4	5	6	14	3	9	10	11	*8*	7	2														6
1			4	5	6		8	9	10	11		*7*	2	12	3												7
1			4	5	*11*	8	6	9	10				2	14	3	7											8
1			4	5	11	8		9	10				2	12	3	7	6										9
1			4	5	11			9	10		8		2	14	3	7	*6*	12									10
			4	5	9	8	6		10				2	11	3	7		1									11
			4	5	*11*	8	6		10	9			2	14	3			1	7	12							12
			4	5	9	8	6		10			14	*2*	11	3			1	7								13
				2	11				10			6		8	3			1	7	9	4	5					14
			4	2	9			12	10	8					6			1	7	11	3	5					15
				6	3			9	10	11			2			7		1	8		4	5					16
			4	8	3			9		11			2	10		7		1			6	5					17
			4	8	3			9		11			2	10		7		1			6	5					18
			4	8	12			9		11			2	14	3			1	7	*10*	6	5					19
			4	2	8			9	10	11					3			1	7		5	6					20
			4		8			9	10				2	11	3			1	7		6	5					21
			4	6	8			9	10	12			2	11	3			1	7			5					22
1			4	3	8			9	11	10			2	6					*7*		14	5					23
1			4	2	8			*9*	10	11				12	6				7		3	5	14				24
1			4	2	8			12	10	9				11	6				7		3	5					25
1			4	2	8			9	10	*11*				7	6	14					3	5					26
1			4	2	8				10	9				7	6	12					3	5	11				27
1			4	2	8				10	9				11	6	7					3	5					28
1			4	2	8				10	9				11	6	7					3	5					29
1			4	2	8				10	9	12			11	6	7					3	5					30
1			4	5	8			14	10	9			2	*11*	6	7					3						31
			4	5	8				10	*9*			2	11	6	7		1	12		3		14				32
			4		8			9			11		2	*10*	3	5			7				14	1	6		33
			4		8			9		11	12		2		6	5			7		3			1	10		34
			4		8			9	10			14	2		6	5			*7*		3			1	11	12	35
					8			9	10		11	7			6	4	3		2					1		5	36
			4		6			9	10		11		2			5	8		7		3			1			37
			4	2	6			9	10		11								7		3	8		1		5	38
				4	6			9	10			7	5			2			8		3	11		1			39
				2	*6*			9	11		12	*7*	5			4	14		8		3	10		1			40
			14	*2*	12			9	10			*7*	4		6	5			8		3	11		1			41
			4		9			11	10					12	8	6			7		3	5		1		2	42
			6		14			9	11				4	8	10	2			7		3	*5*		1			43
			4		8			14	*10*	9			2	11	6				7		12	5		1		3	44

CELTIC Premier Division

Year Formed: 1888. *Ground & Address:* Celtic Park, 95 Kerrydale St, Glasgow G40 3RE. *Telephone:* 041 556 2611.
Ground Capacity: total: 51,709. *Seated:* 9000. *Size of Pitch:* 115yd # 75yd.
Managing Director Fergus McCann. *Chairman:* J. Kevin Kelly. *Secretary:* Dominic Keane. *Chief Scout* Tommy Craig. Commercial Manager: John McGuire.
Manager: Assistant Manager: Chic Bates. *Physio:* Brian Scott. *Coaches:* Frank Connor, Tom McAdam. *Managers since 1975:* Jock Stein; Billy McNeill; David Hay; Billy McNeill, Liam Brady, Lou Macari. *Club Nickname(s):* The Bhoys.
Previous Grounds: None.
Record Attendance: 92,000 v Rangers, Division I; 1 Jan, 1938.
Record Transfer Fee received: £1,400,000 for Paul Elliott to Chelsea, July 1991.
Record Transfer Fee paid: £1,500,000 for Stuart Slater from West Ham U Aug 1992.
Record Victory: 11-0 Dundee, Division I; 26 Oct, 1895.
Record Defeat: 0-8 v Motherwell, Division I; 30 Apr, 1937.
Most Capped Player: Danny McGrain, 62, Scotland.
Most League Appearances: 486: Billy McNeill 1957-75.
Most League Goals in Season (Individual): 50: James McGrory, Division I; 1935-36.
Most Goals Overall (Individual): 397: James McGrory; 1922-39.

Honours
League Champions: (35 times) Division I 1892-93, 1893-94, 1895-96, 1897-98, 1904-05, 1905-06, 1906-07, 1907-08, 1908-09,

CELTIC 1993—94 LEAGUE RECORD

Match No.	Date	Venue	Opponents	Result		H/T Score	Lg. Pos.	Goalscorers	Attendance
1	Aug 7	A	Motherwell	D	2-2	1-2	—	Slater, McAvennie	13,569
2	14	H	Hibernian	D	1-1	1-0	5	Nicholas	27,690
3	21	H	Rangers	D	0-0	0-0	6		47,942
4	28	A	Partick T	W	1-0	0-0	3	McNally	14,013
5	Sept 4	H	Aberdeen	L	0-1	0-0	8		34,311
6	11	A	Raith R	W	4-1	2-0	3	Nicholas 2, Payton 2	8114
7	18	H	Dundee U	D	1-1	0-0	5	Creaney	26,377
8	25	A	Hearts	L	0-1	0-0	8		14,761
9	Oct 2	H	Kilmarnock	D	0-0	0-0	7		23,396
10	6	A	St Johnstone	L	1-2	1-2	—	Creaney	7386
11	9	H	Dundee	W	2-1	0-0	6	Creaney, McGinlay	15,980
12	16	A	Hibernian	D	1-1	0-0	6	Creaney	14,991
13	30	A	Rangers	W	2-1	0-0	5	Collins, O'Neil	47,522
14	Nov 6	H	Partick T	W	3-0	1-0	5	McGinlay 2, Nicholas	21,642
15	9	A	Aberdeen	D	1-1	0-0	—	O'Neil	19,474
16	13	A	Kilmarnock	D	2-2	1-1	5	Nicholas, McGinlay	16,649
17	20	H	Hearts	D	0-0	0-0	5		25,990
18	24	H	Motherwell	W	2-0	1-0	—	McGinlay 2	16,654
19	27	H	Raith R	W	2-0	1-0	2	Collins 2	17,453
20	30	A	Dundee U	L	0-1	0-0	—		10,220
21	Dec 4	H	St Johnstone	W	1-0	0-0	2	McGinlay	15,941
22	11	A	Dundee	D	1-1	0-1	2	Creaney	8730
23	18	H	Hibernian	W	1-0	0-0	4	McStay	16,808
24	Jan 1	H	Rangers	L	2-4	0-3	4	Collins, Nicholas	48,506
25	8	A	Partick T	L	0-1	0-0	5		12,887
26	11	A	Motherwell	L	1-2	0-1	—	McNally	13,159
27	19	H	Aberdeen	D	2-2	1-1	—	Byrne, McStay	19,083
28	22	H	Dundee U	D	0-0	0-0	5		17,235
29	Feb 5	A	Raith R	D	0-0	0-0	5		7678
30	12	A	Hearts	W	2-0	1-0	5	Nicholas 2	14,049
31	Mar 1	H	Kilmarnock	W	1-0	0-0	—	Collins	9887
32	5	A	St Johnstone	W	1-0	1-0	5	Byrne	8622
33	19	A	Hibernian	D	0-0	0-0	5		14,639
34	26	H	Motherwell	L	0-1	0-1	5		36,199
35	30	H	Raith R	W	2-1	1-1	—	Donnelly 2	14,140
36	Apr 2	A	Dundee U	W	3-1	2-0	5	Falconer, Collins, Mowbray	9790
37	6	H	Dundee	D	1-1	1-1	—	Donnelly	16,585
38	9	H	Hearts	D	2-2	2-0	4	Vata, Collins	18,761
39	16	A	Kilmarnock	L	0-2	0-0	4		11,499
40	23	A	Dundee	W	2-0	1-0	4	McGinlay 2	5795
41	27	H	St Johnstone	D	1-1	1-0	—	Donnelly	10,602
42	30	A	Rangers	D	1-1	1-0	4	Collins	47,018
43	May 7	H	Partick T	D	1-1	0-0	4	McGinlay	16,827
44	14	A	Aberdeen	D	1-1	1-1	4	Donnelly	16,417

Final League Position: 4

1909-10, 1913-14, 1914-15, 1915-16, 1916-17, 1918-19, 1921-22, 1925-26, 1935-36, 1937-38, 1953-54, 1965-66, 1966-67, 1967-68, 1968-69, 1969-70, 1970-71, 1971-72, 1972-73, 1973-74. Premier Division 1976-77, 1978-79, 1980-81, 1981-82, 1985-86, 1987-88. *Runners-up:* 21 times.
Scottish Cup Winners: (29 times) 1892, 1899, 1900, 1904, 1907, 1908, 1911, 1912, 1914, 1923, 1925, 1927, 1931, 1933, 1937, 1951, 1954, 1965, 1967, 1969, 1971, 1972, 1974, 1975, 1977, 1980, 1985, 1988, 1989; *Runners-up:* 16 times.
League Cup Winners: (9 times) 1956-57, 1957-58, 1965-66, 1966-67, 1967-68, 1968-69, 1969-70, 1974-75, 1982-83; *Runners-up:* 9 times.
European: *European Cup Winners:* 1966-67. 78 matches (1966-67 winners, 1967-68, 1968-69, 1969-70 runners-up, 1970-71, 1971-72 semi-finals, 1972-73, 1973-74 semi-finals, 1974-75, 1977-78, 1979-80, 1981-82, 1982-83, 1986-87, 1988-89); *Cup Winners Cup:* 35 matches (1963-64 semi-finals, 1965-66 semi-finals, 1975-76, 1980-81, 1984-85, 1985-86, 1989-90); *UEFA Cup:* 28 matches (*Fairs Cup:* 1962-63, 1964-65. *UEFA Cup:* 1976-77, 1983-84, 1987-88, 1991-92, 1992-93, 1993-94).
Club colours: Shirt: Green and white hoops. Shorts: White. Stockings: White.

Goalscorers: *League* (51): McGinlay 10, Collins 8 (1 pen), Nicholas 8, Creaney 5, Donnelly 5, Byrne 2, McNally 2, McStay 2, O'Neil 2, Payton 2, Falconer 1, McAvennie 1, Mowbray 1, Slater 1, Vata 1. *Scottish Cup* (0): *League Cup* (12): McAvennie 5, Payton 3, McGinlay 2, McNally 1, Nicholas 1.

Bonner P 31	Boyd T 38	Wdowczyk D 24 + 1	Grant P 27 + 1	McNally M 30 + 2	Galloway M 16 + 6	Slater S 3 + 1	McStay P 35	McAvennie F 8 + 3	Creaney G 17 + 1	Collins J 38	Nicholas C 30 + 5	McGinlay P 39 + 2	Payton A 1 + 6	O'Neil B 14 + 14	Vata R 6 + 4	Mowbray A 20 + 2	Smith B 6 + 1	Gillespie G 25 + 2	Byrne P 18 + 4	Marshall G 1	McLaughlin B — + 8	Biggins W 4 + 5	Martin L 15	Muggleton C 12	Falconer W 14	Donnelly S 10 + 2	Hay C 2	Match No.
1	2	3	4	5	6	7	8	*9*	10	11	12	14																1
1	2	3	4	5	6		8	9		11	*10*	7	12	14														2
1	2	3	4	5	6		8	9		11	10	7	12															3
1	2	3	4	5	6		8	9		11	10	7	12															4
1	2	3	4	5	6			9		*11*	10	7	12	14	8													5
1	2	3	4	6		14		9		11	10	7	12	*8*		5												6
1	2	3	4	5	6	11	8		9		10	7		12														7
1	2	*3*	4	6		11	8	9	10			7		12		5	14											8
1	3	14	4	5	6		8		10		12	7	9				*11*	2										9
1	3		4	6			8		9		10	7		11		5		2	12									10
	3		4	5	6		8		9	*11*	10	12		14				2	7	1								11
1	3		4				8		9	11	10	6				5		2	7									12
1	3		4				8		*9*	11	10	6	14	12		5		2	7									13
1	3	2	4				8		*9*		10	6		11	12	5			7		14							14
1	3	5	4				8		*9*	11	14	6		10	12			2	7									15
1	3	2	4	5	9		8	12			10	6		11	7													16
1	3	5	4				8		9	11	10	6						2	7									17
1	3	5	4				8		*7*	11	10	6		9		12		2				14						18
1	3	5	4				8		9	11	*10*	6		7	12			2				14						19
1	3	5	4		14		8		*9*	11	10	6		7				2				12						20
1	3	5	4				8	14	*7*	11		6		9				2				10						21
1	3	5	4				8	14	*7*	11		6		9				2				10						22
1	3	5	4		14		8			11	12	6		9				2	*7*			10						23
1	3	*5*	4	12			8			11	10	6		9				2	7			14						24
1	3		4	5	6		8		*9*	11	10			14		12		2	7									25
1	3		4	6	12		8		14	10	9			11		5		2	*7*									26
1				6	14		8			11	10	4		12		5		*2*	7			9	3					27
	3			6			8			11	10	9		12		5		2	*7*				4	1				28
	3			6			8	*9*		11	4	10				5		12	*7*			14	2	1				29
	3			4			8			11	9	6		12	14	5		2	*7*					1	*10*			30
	3			6						11	9	7		8		5		*2*	12				4	1	10			31
	3			2	14		8			11	9	*6*				5		12	*7*				4	1	10			32
	3			4			8			11	*9*	6				5			7				2	1	10	14		33
	3			4			8			11	9	6		14		5		*2*	*7*					1	10	12		34
	3				*4*		8			11		6		14		5			*7*		12		2	1	10	9		35
	3			8	*4*					11		6		14	7	5					12		2	1	10	9		36
	3			4	10		8			11		6			7			5			12		2	1		9		37
	3			4	14		8			11	*6*				7			5					2	1	10	9		38
	3			4	2		8			11	12	6			*7*			5			14			1	10	9		39
1		5		4	2					11	8	6					3						7		10	9		40
1		5		4	2					11	*8*	6		14			3				12		7		10	9		41
1		7	4	6						11		*8*				5	2		12		14		3		10	9		42
1		6	12	4						11		8				5	2				14		*3*		10	9	7	43
1		4		12						11		8				5	2	6	14				3		10	9	*7*	44

CLYDE

Division 2

Year Formed: 1878. *Ground & Address:* Broadwood Stadium, Cumbernauld, G68 9NE. *Telephone:* 0236 451511.
Ground Capacity: total: 6103 all seated. *Size of Pitch:* 112yd # 76yd.
Chairman: John F. McBeth FRICS. *Secretary:* John D. Taylor. *Commercial Manager:* John Donnelly.
Manager: Alex Smith. *Assistant Manager:* John Brownlie. *Physio:* J. Watson: *Coach:* Gardner Speirs.
Managers since 1975: S. Anderson; C. Brown; J. Clark. *Club Nickname(s):* The Bully Wee. *Previous Grounds:* Barrowfield & Shawfield Stadium.
Record Attendance: 52,000 v Rangers, Division I; 21 Nov, 1908.
Record Transfer Fee received: £95,000 for Pat Nevin to Chelsea (July 1983).
Record Transfer Fee paid: £14,000 for Harry Hood from Sunderland (1966).
Record Victory: 11-1 v Cowdenbeath, Division II; 6 Oct, 1951.
Record Defeat: 0-11 v Dumbarton, Scottish Cup 4th rd, 22 Nov, 1879; v Rangers, Scottish Cup 4th rd, 13 Nov, 1880.
Most Capped Player: Tommy Ring, 12, Scotland.
Most League Appearances: 428: Brian Ahern.

CLYDE 1993—94 LEAGUE RECORD

Match No.	Date	Venue	Opponents	Result		H/T Score	Lg. Pos.	Goalscorers	Attendance
1	Aug 7	H	Morton	W	2-1	1-0	—	Fowler (og), Clarke S	1203
2	14	A	Dumbarton	L	0-3	0-2	8		1001
3	21	H	Ayr U	L	0-1	0-1	10		920
4	28	A	Clydebank	L	1-2	0-1	12	McGill	1192
5	Sept 4	H	Dunfermline Ath	L	0-2	0-2	12		1505
6	11	H	Hamilton A	W	2-0	1-0	9	Parks, Quinn	1236
7	14	A	Airdrieonians	L	1-2	0-1	—	Sludden	1758
8	18	A	St Mirren	L	1-2	1-0	11	Clarke S	2493
9	25	H	Brechin C	D	1-1	1-0	12	Sludden	565
10	29	A	Falkirk	W	1-0	0-0	—	Parks	3324
11	Oct 2	H	Stirling Albion	W	3-0	2-0	7	Knox, Parks, Thomson	777
12	9	A	Morton	D	1-1	0-1	8	Morrison (pen)	1474
13	16	H	Airdrieonians	L	0-2	0-1	9		1464
14	23	A	Hamilton A	L	0-2	0-0	10		1917
15	30	A	Ayr U	L	0-1	0-0	10		1765
16	Nov 6	H	Clydebank	D	1-1	0-1	11	Parks	891
17	9	A	Dunfermline Ath	L	0-4	0-1	—		2987
18	13	A	Stirling Albion	D	1-1	1-0	11	McConnell	943
19	23	H	Falkirk	L	0-2	0-1	—		1165
20	30	A	Brechin C	L	2-4	2-1	—	Thomson, Sludden	373
21	Dec 4	H	St Mirren	L	0-1	0-1	11		1322
22	11	H	Dumbarton	W	2-1	1-0	10	Sludden, Strain	681
23	18	A	Airdrieonians	L	2-3	1-1	10	McConnell, Tennant (pen)	1755
24	Jan 8	A	Clydebank	W	2-0	1-0	10	Strain, Parks	1151
25	11	H	Ayr U	D	0-0	0-0	—		809
26	22	A	Dumbarton	D	1-1	1-1	10	Strain	927
27	Feb 5	H	Hamilton A	L	0-2	0-1	10		5356
28	12	H	Stirling Albion	D	0-0	0-0	10		2112
29	19	H	Dunfermline Ath	L	0-1	0-0	10		4113
30	22	H	Morton	D	0-0	0-0	—		1666
31	Mar 1	A	Falkirk	L	0-2	0-1	—		2954
32	5	A	St Mirren	D	0-0	0-0	10		2080
33	12	H	Brechin C	W	1-0	1-0	10	Mackenzie	1786
34	19	H	Airdrieonians	L	0-1	0-0	10		2414
35	26	A	Morton	L	0-2	0-0	11		1190
36	29	H	Dumbarton	L	1-2	1-0	—	Tennant	789
37	Apr 2	A	Hamilton A	L	1-2	1-0	11	McConnell	1374
38	9	A	Stirling Albion	W	1-0	0-0	11	McConnell	727
39	16	H	Falkirk	D	1-1	0-0	10	Thomson	3529
40	23	H	St Mirren	W	3-0	1-0	10	O'Neill, McAulay, McGill	1901
41	26	A	Brechin C	W	1-0	1-0	—	Dickson	391
42	30	A	Ayr U	D	1-1	0-1	10	McAulay	1696
43	May 7	H	Clydebank	D	1-1	1-0	10	McConnell	1386
44	14	A	Dunfermline Ath	L	0-5	0-2	10		6163

Final League Position: 10

Most League Goals in Season (Individual): 32: Bill Boyd, 1932-33.
Most Goals Overall (Individual): —.

Honours

League Champions: Division II 1904-05, 1951-52, 1956-57, 1961-62, 1972-73. Second Division 1977-78, 1981-82, 1992-93.
Runners-up: Division II 1903-04, 1905-06, 1925-26, 1963-64.
Scottish Cup Winners: 1939, 1955, 1958; *Runners-up:* 1910, 1912, 1949.
League Cup: —
Club colours: Shirt: White with red and black trim. Shorts: Black. Stockings: Black with red and white tops.

Goalscorers: *League* (35): McConnell 5, Parks 5, Sludden 4, Strain 3, Thomson 3, Clarke S 2, McAulay 2, McGill 2, Tennant 2 (1 pen), Dickson 1, Knox 1, Mackenzie 1, Morrison 1 (pen), O'Neill 1, Quinn 1, own goal 1. *Scottish Cup* (1): McCheyne 1. *League Cup* (1): McAulay 1. *B&Q Cup* (0).

Howie S 1	McFarlane R 34	Tennant S 30 + 1	Knox K 44	Thomson J 35	Neill A 36 + 3	Ronald P 9 + 5	Bell D 13 + 5	Sludden J 16 + 1	Clarke S 16	McCarron J 26 + 5	McAulay J 21 + 6	Quinn K 3 + 10	Fridge L 42	Morrison S 13 + 7	McCheyne G 23 + 1	Dickson J 8 + 4	McGill D 4 + 12	Strain B 19 + 6	Parks G 19 + 9	Wylde G 6	McConnell I 23 + 3	Mackenzie A 18	Brown J 1 + 3	Wright A 2 + 1	Clark M 12	O'Neill M 8 + 1	Tierney P 1 + 1	Hillcoat J 1 + 1	Match No.
1	2	3	4	5	6	*7*	8	9	10	11	12	14																	1
	2	3	4	5	6		10	9		*11*	8		1	7	12	14													2
	2	3	4	5	6	7	8	*9*	10	11	12		1			14													3
	2		5	6	3		8	9		10	*4*		1	14			7	11	12										4
	2	3	5	6		14	10					12	1	4	*8*		9	11	7										5
	2	3	4	5	6	7	8	9		10	12	14	1						*11*										6
	2	*3*	4	5	6	7	8	9		10	12	14	1						11										7
	2	12	6	5	3		8	*9*	10	11		14	1					4	7										8
	2	3	5		6		8	9		*4*		12	1	14		7		11	10										9
	2	3	4	5	6		12	*9*	10				1	8		14			7	11									10
	2	3	4	5	6		14	9	*10*			12	1	8					7	11									11
	2	3	4	5	6		14	9	10			12	1	*8*					7	11									12
	2	3	4	5	6		14	9	*10*			12	1	8					7	11									13
			4	5	3		*6*		10		8	12	1	14	2	7		11	9										14
		3	5		6	7	*4*	9			8	10	1	14	2			11	12										15
		3	5		6	7				14	4	8	1	10	2			11	9		12								16
	2		5		6	7				14	4	8	1	*10*	3		12	11	9										17
	2	3	4	5	6	7		14		10			1		8			12	*11*		9								18
	2	3	4	5	6	*7*				10			1		8		12	14	11		9								19
	2		4	5	3		12	9		10	8		1	6			14	11			*7*								20
	2	3	6	5			4	9	10				1		8				12		7	*11*	14						21
	2	3	6	5			*4*	9	10				1		8	12		14			7	11							22
	2	3	4	5	6					10	8		1					11			7	9							23
	2	3	4	5	6	12				10			1					11	14		*7*	9		8					24
	2	3	4	5	6	12				10			1					11	14		*9*	7		8					25
	2		4	5	6	14				10			1		3			11	12		9	7			8				26
	2		4	5	6	12				10	8		1		3				14		*9*	7			11				27
	2		4	5	6					11	10		1		3				9		12	*7*		14	8				28
	2		4	5	6								1	12	3		14	11	10		*9*	7			8				29
	2	6	4	5						12			1	10	3		9	11			14	7			*8*				30
	2		4	5	3				10	6	12		1	8				11	14		*9*	7							31
	2		4	5	3				*10*	6	14		1	8				11	12		9	7							32
	2		4	5	14				10	12	3		1	*6*				11	8		9	7							33
	2		6	5	3				10		8		1	14			*11*	12	9	4		7							34
	2		4	5	*6*				10				1	14			12	11	9	3		7				8			35
	2	3	4	5					*10*	11	6		1		8						9	7				14			36
	2	3	4	5	14					*11*	6		1		8						9	7				10	12		37
		3	4	5	12					10	6		1		8		14				9				2	7	*11*		38
		3	4	5	10						6		1		8	11	14				*9*				2	7		12	39
		3	5		6					10	4				8	11	14	12			*9*				2	7		1	40
		3	5		6					10	4		1		8	11	14	12			9				2	*7*			41
		3	5		6					10	4		1		*8*	11	14				9		12		2	7			42
		3	5		6					12	4		1		8	11	14				9		10		2	*7*			43
		3	5		6					10	4		1		8	7	14				9	*11*	12		2				44

CLYDEBANK Division 1

Year Formed: 1965. *Ground & Address:* Kilbowie Park, Arran Place, Clydebank G81 2PB. *Telephone:* 041 952 2887.
Ground Capacity: total: 9950. seated: All. *Size of Pitch:* 110yd # 68yd.
Chairman: C. A. Steedman. *Secretary:* I. C. Steedman. *Commercial Manager:* David Curwood.
Manager and Managing Director: J. S. Steedman. *Physio:* Peter Anderson. *Coach:* Brian Wright.
Managers since 1975: William Munro; J. S. Steedman. *Club Nickname(s):* The Bankies. *Previous Grounds:* None.
Record Attendance: 14,900 v Hibernian, Scottish Cup 1st rd; 10 Feb, 1965.
Record Transfer Fee received: £175,000 for Owen Coyle from Airdrieonians, (Feb 1990).
Record Transfer Fee paid: £50,000 for Gerry McCabe from Clyde.
Record Victory: 8-1 Arbroath, First Division; 3 Jan 1977.
Record Defeat: 1-9 v Gala Fairydean, Scottish Cup qual rd; 15 Sept, 1965.
Most Capped Player: —.
Most League Appearances: 620: Jim Fallon; 1968-86.

CLYDEBANK 1993—94 LEAGUE RECORD

Match No.	*Date*	*Venue*	*Opponents*	*Result*		*H/T Score*	*Lg. Pos.*	*Goalscorers*	*Attendance*
1	Aug 7	H	Ayr U	W	1-0	0-0	—	Flannigan	1070
2	14	A	Dunfermline Ath	W	2-0	0-0	2	Flannigan, Harvey	3099
3	21	A	Dumbarton	W	4-2	2-2	3	McIntosh, Boyd (og), Jack, Eadie	1597
4	28	H	Clyde	W	2-1	1-0	1	Treanor, Eadie	1192
5	Sept 4	A	Falkirk	W	4-0	2-0	1	Flannigan 2, Treanor, Harvey	4445
6	11	H	Morton	W	3-0	2-0	1	Eadie, Henry, Flannigan	1563
7	15	A	Hamilton A	W	3-2	1-1	—	Henry, Flannigan, Eadie	1422
8	18	A	Brechin C	L	0-1	0-1	1		564
9	25	H	Airdrieonians	L	1-2	1-1	2	Eadie	2022
10	28	A	Stirling Albion	W	3-0	0-0	—	Jack, Eadie 2	985
11	Oct 2	H	St Mirren	D	1-1	1-0	1	Flannigan	2030
12	9	A	Ayr U	D	1-1	1-0	1	Jack	2017
13	16	H	Hamilton A	D	2-2	1-2	2	Harvey, Smith	819
14	23	A	Morton	D	0-0	0-0	2		1534
15	30	H	Dumbarton	W	2-1	1-0	1	Henry, Thomson (pen)	1297
16	Nov 6	A	Clyde	D	1-1	1-0	1	Crawford J	891
17	9	H	Falkirk	D	1-1	1-1	—	Jack	2079
18	13	A	St Mirren	L	0-1	0-1	4		2487
19	20	H	Stirling Albion	W	2-1	1-1	1	Smith, Lansdowne	770
20	30	A	Airdrieonians	L	1-2	1-0	—	Jack	1634
21	Dec 4	H	Brechin C	W	3-2	1-0	2	Harris, Flannigan 2	618
22	11	H	Dunfermline Ath	L	0-3	0-1	4		1900
23	18	A	Hamilton A	L	0-1	0-1	4		1202
24	Jan 4	H	Ayr U	L	0-2	0-2	—		2015
25	8	H	Clyde	L	0-2	0-1	4		1151
26	15	A	Falkirk	D	0-0	0-0	4		3900
27	18	A	Dumbarton	D	2-2	1-1	—	Flannigan, Thomson	1003
28	22	A	Dunfermline Ath	L	0-2	0-0	5		4612
29	Feb 5	H	Morton	D	0-0	0-0	6		988
30	12	H	St Mirren	L	0-3	0-0	6		1831
31	26	A	Stirling Albion	W	2-1	1-0	6	Currie, Henry	991
32	Mar 5	A	Brechin C	W	1-0	0-0	6	Smith	424
33	19	H	Hamilton A	W	3-2	0-1	5	Eadie 3	824
34	22	H	Airdrieonians	W	2-1	1-0	—	Sutherland, Henry	941
35	26	A	Ayr U	D	0-0	0-0	5		1706
36	29	H	Dunfermline Ath	L	0-1	0-0	—		1276
37	Apr 2	A	Morton	D	1-1	1-1	5	Jack	1163
38	9	A	St Mirren	L	0-2	0-0	6		1640
39	16	H	Stirling Albion	W	2-1	1-0	6	Flannigan, Eadie	732
40	23	H	Brechin C	W	2-1	0-0	5	Henry, Walker	574
41	26	A	Airdrieonians	D	0-0	0-0	—		994
42	30	H	Dumbarton	W	2-0	0-0	5	Ferguson 2	929
43	May 7	A	Clyde	D	1-1	0-1	4	Walker	1386
44	14	H	Falkirk	D	1-1	1-1	5	Henry	6616

Final League Position: 5

Most League Goals in Season (Individual): 29: Ken Eadie, First Division, 1990-91.
Most Goals Overall (Individual): 84, Blair Millar, 1977-83.

Honours
League Champions: Second Division 1975-76; *Runners-up:* First Division 1976-77, 1984-85.
Scottish Cup: Semi-finalists 1990. *League Cup:* —.
Club colours: Shirt: White with black collar and red and black shoulder flashings. Shorts: White with red and black trim. Stockings: White with red/black stripes.

Goalscorers: *League* (56): Eadie 11, Flannigan 11, Henry 7, Jack 6, Harvey 3, Smith 3, Ferguson 2, Thomson 2 (1 pen), Treanor 2, Walker 2, Crawford J 1, Currie 1, Harris 1, Lansdowne 1, McIntosh 1, Sutherland 1, own goal 1. *Scottish Cup* (2): Henry 1, Sweeney 1. *League Cup* (0): *B&Q Cup* (6): Flannigan 2, Lansdowne 1, Lee 1, Nelson 1, own goal 1.

Woods S 10	Treanor M 14	Hay G 22	Maher J 1	Sweeney S 31	McIntosh M 2 + 2	Harvey P 26	Henry J 42 + 2	Eadie K 19 + 2	Flannigan C 34 + 2	Lansdowne A 11 + 9	Crawford D 22 + 1	Murdoch S 34	Smith S 16 + 10	Jack S 33 + 1	Nelson M — + 3	Currie T 26 + 4	Crawford J 15 + 3	Lee K 3 + 2	Monaghan A 15	McQueen J 12	Thomson I 19 + 4	Ferguson G 14 + 2	Sutherland C 12 + 2	Walker J 4 + 2	Harris C 16 + 4	Cooper D 14 + 4	Quigg S 1	Elliot D — + 1	Kerrigan S 9 + 6	Matthews G 7	Bowman G — + 1	Match No.
1	2	3	4	5	6	7	8	9	10	11																						1
1	2	*6*		5	14	7	12	9	10		3	4	8	11																		2
1	2			5	6	7	12	9	10		3	4	11	8																		3
1	2	6		5	12	7	8	9	10		*3*	4		11	14																	4
1	2	6		5		7	8	9	10		3	*4*	12	11		14																5
1	2	6		5		*7*	8	9	10		3	4	12	11		14																6
1	2	6		5		*7*	8	9	10		3	4	12	11		14																7
1	2	6		5		7	8		10	12	*3*	4	9	11		14																8
1	2	6		5		*7*	8	9	10		*3*	4	12	11	14																	9
1	2	6		5		7	8	9	10			4		11			3	12														10
	2	6		5		7	8	9	10			4		11			3		1													11
				5		7	8	9	*10*			4		11	14	6	3	2	1													12
				5		7	8	9		14		4	10	11		6	3	*2*	1													13
				5		7	8		*10*	14	3	4	9	2		6	12			1	11											14
				5			7			8	3	4	9	11		6	12	2		1	10											15
		6				*7*	8			14	3	4		10		5	9	12		1	11	2										16
		6				7	8		*10*			4		11		5	9			1	3	2	14									17
		6				7	8			12		4	9	10		5	3			1	*11*	2		14								18
						7	8			11		4	9	10		5	6			1	3	2										19
		6				7	8			11		4	9	10						1	3	2			5							20
		5					7		12	8	14	4	9	10			3			1	*11*	2			6							21
		6				7	8		12	11		4	9	2		5	3			1					10							22
		6				7	8		10	11			*9*	2		5	3			1	14				4							23
		6				8	10		9			4	14	11		*5*				1	3	2			12	7						24
		3				11	8		9					6		5	12			1		2			4	7	10					25
		6		5		11	8		10		3	4				2			1		14	12			9	*7*						26
		6		5		11	8		10		3					*9*			1		12	2			4	7		14				27
		6		5		11	8		10		3								1		9	2	12		4	*7*						28
				5			8		*10*	14	3	4		2		6	*9*		1		11				12	7						29
				5			8			14	3	4	10	2		6			1		*11*				12	7			9			30
				5			8		10				12			2	3		1		11		6		4	7			9			31
				5			8		*10*		3		14			2			1		11		6	*7*	4	12			9			32
				5			8	12	10		3		*7*			2			1		11		6		4	14			9			33
				5			8	9				4		11		2	*3*		1		14		6		7	12			10			34
				5			8	9	10					11		2			1		3		6		4	*7*			12			35
				5			8	9	10			2	7						1		3		6		4	11			12			36
				5			8	9	10				*7*	11		2			1		3		6		4	14			12			37
	2			5			8	12	10			4		11			3					14	6		*7*				9	1		38
				5			8	9	10	*7*	3	4	14	11		6						2							12	1		39
							8	9	10	7	3	4				5					11	*2*		6					12	1	14	40
							8	9	10	14	3	4		11		5						2	*6*			7			12	1		41
							8		*10*	12	3	4	14			5						2	6	11		7			9	1		42
	2			5			*8*		10	3		4	12	14									6	11		7			9	1		43
	2			5			8		10	3		4		11									6	12	14	*7*			*9*	1		44

COWDENBEATH Division 3

Year Formed: 1881. *Ground & Address:* Central Park, Cowdenbeath KY4 9EY. *Telephone:* 0383 610166.
Ground Capacity: total: 4778. seated: 1072. *Size of Pitch:* 107yd # 66yd.
Chairman: Gordon McDougall. *Secretary:* Tom Ogilvie. *Commercial Director:* Ian Fraser.
Manager: Patrick Dolan.
Managers since 1975: D. McLindon; F. Connor; P. Wilson; A. Rolland; H. Wilson; W. McCulloch; J. Clark; J. Craig; R. Campbell; J. Blackley; J. Brownlie, A. Harrow, J. Reilly. *Previous Grounds:* North End Park, Cowdenbeath.
Record Attendance: 25,586 v Rangers, League Cup quarter-final; 21 Sept, 1949.
Record Transfer Fee received: £30,000 for Nicky Henderson to Falkirk, (March 1994).
Record Transfer Fee paid: —
Record Victory: 12-0 v Johnstone, Scottish Cup 1st rd; 21 Jan, 1928.
Record Defeat: 1-11 v Clyde, Division II; 6 Oct, 1951.
Most Capped Player: Jim Paterson, 3, Scotland.
Most League Appearances: —.

COWDENBEATH 1993—94 LEAGUE RECORD

Match No.	Date	Venue	Opponents	Result		H/T Score	Lg. Pos.	Goalscorers	Attendance
1	Aug 7	H	Meadowbank T	L	1-2	0-0	—	Henderson	280
2	14	A	Alloa	W	1-0	1-0	7	Henderson	421
3	21	H	East Fife	L	1-2	1-1	9	Henderson	891
4	28	A	Stenhousemuir	D	1-1	1-0	8	Henderson	367
5	Sept 4	A	Queen's Park	W	3-1	2-0	7	Callaghan 3	408
6	11	H	Berwick R	L	1-2	0-1	10	Hunter	323
7	18	H	Albion R	L	0-1	0-0	10		228
8	25	A	Stranraer	L	0-4	0-1	11		541
9	Oct 2	A	Arbroath	D	2-2	0-1	11	Herd, Hunter	594
10	9	H	East Stirling	L	1-3	1-1	13	Harris	152
11	16	H	Queen of the S	D	3-3	3-3	12	Law, Henderson, Davidson	339
12	23	A	Montrose	W	2-1	1-0	12	Henderson, Callaghan	298
13	30	A	Forfar Ath	L	2-3	1-1	11	Young, Hunter	446
14	Nov 6	H	Alloa	D	1-1	0-0	12	Callaghan	358
15	13	A	Albion R	W	1-0	1-0	10	Henderson	231
16	20	H	Stranraer	L	1-2	0-0	13	Callaghan	509
17	27	A	East Stirling	L	2-3	0-2	13	Craig (og), Herd	546
18	Dec 4	H	Arbroath	L	0-1	0-0	13		290
19	18	A	Meadowbank T	D	1-1	0-0	13	Callaghan	218
20	Jan 11	A	East Fife	L	0-2	0-1	—		789
21	18	H	Forfar Ath	L	1-2	0-0	—	Henderson	268
22	22	A	Queen of the S	W	2-1	0-0	13	Hunter, Herd (pen)	927
23	Feb 1	H	Stenhousemuir	L	1-3	1-3	—	Henderson	224
24	5	A	Berwick R	L	2-3	0-1	13	Callaghan, Hunter	499
25	12	H	Queen's Park	L	3-4	2-1	13	Herd, Callaghan, Carr	241
26	Mar 2	A	Forfar Ath	L	1-2	0-0	—	Lee	321
27	5	H	Meadowbank T	L	0-1	0-0	14		197
28	12	A	East Stirling	L	0-4	0-1	14		290
29	16	H	Stenhousemuir	D	1-1	1-1	—	Macdonald	166
30	19	A	Montrose	D	1-1	0-1	14	Callaghan	494
31	22	H	Montrose	L	0-1	0-1	—		208
32	26	H	Berwick R	L	1-5	1-3	14	Hunter	268
33	Apr 2	H	Arbroath	W	1-0	0-0	14	Callaghan	219
34	9	A	Albion R	L	0-1	0-0	14		313
35	16	A	Alloa	L	0-1	0-0	14		393
36	23	H	East Fife	L	1-2	1-1	14	McMahon B	464
37	30	H	Queen's Park	D	1-1	0-1	14	McMahon B	207
38	May 7	A	Stranraer	L	0-2	0-1	14		1531
39	14	H	Queen of the S	L	0-2	0-1	14		346

Final League Position: 14

Most League Goals in Season (Individual): 40: Willie Devlin, Division II; 1925-26.
Most Goals Overall (Individual): —.

Honours
League Champions: Division II 1913-14, 1914-15, 1938-39; *Runners-up:* Division II 1921-22, 1923-24, 1969-70. Second Division 1991-92.
Scottish Cup: —.
League Cup: —.
Club colours: Shirt: Royal blue shadow vertical stripe with white chest band. Shorts: White with blue side stripe. Stockings: Royal blue.

Goalscorers: *League* (40): Callaghan 11, Henderson 9, Hunter 6, Herd 4 (1 pen), McMahon B 2, Carr 1, Davidson 1, Harris 1, Law 1, Lee 1, Macdonald 1, Young 1, own goal 1. *Scottish Cup* (8): Callaghan 3, Henderson 3, Hunter 1, Reilly 1. *League Cup* (1): Henderson 1. *B&Q Cup* (2): Callaghan 1, Lee 1.

Filshill S 18	Thomson J 17 + 2	Bowmaker K 4 + 2	Petrie E 26 + 3	McMahon B 32 + 2	Lee I 24 + 1	Henderson N 22	Scott C 17	Callaghan W 33	Young A 7 + 2	Harris C 9 + 1	Barclay S 7 + 9	Davidson I 21 + 8	Watt D 35	Maratea D 17 + 3	Hunter P 23 + 2	Herd W 33	Stout D 5 + 5	Carr R 17 + 3	Maloney J 4	Douglas H 1	Russell R 2 + 4	Law G 1 + 1	Reilly J 10 + 3	Moffat J 17	Burke P 1	Macdonald K 10	McMahon S 2	Hamill A 9	Sim A 5	Match No.
1	2	*3*	4	5	6	7	8	9	10	11	12	14																		1
1			4	5	6	*7*	8	9		11		14	2	3	10															2
1			4	5	6	7	8	9		11			2	3	10															3
1	12		4	5	6	7	8	9		11			2		*10*	3	14													4
1			4	5	6	*7*	8	9		11			2		10	3	12													5
1			*4*	5	6	7	8	9		11	14		2		10	3														6
1			4	5	6	7	*8*	9		11	10	12	2			3		14												7
				5	7		8	9		11		4	2		10	3	12	6	1											8
1			12	5	*8*	11	3	9		14		4	2		10	6		*7*												9
			7		12		3	9		11		4	2		10	6	14	8	1	5										10
1			14	5	11	10	3					6	2	*4*		8					7	9								11
1				5	8	10	3	9				6	2	7	11	4						12								12
1	3	14	*4*		8	10		9	5			7		6	11	2														13
1				5	8	10		9	12			3	2	6	11	4		*7*					14							14
1				5	8	10		9				3	2	6	11	4		7												15
1				5	8	10		9				3	2	6	11	4		7			12									16
1					7	11	8	9	5		14	3	2	6		4							*10*							17
				5	7	11	8	9				3	2	6		4			1		12		10							18
			2	5	7	*11*	8	10				3		6	14	4			1				9							19
			8	5	7		3	9				12	2	*6*	10	4							14	1	11					20
	6		10	5	7	8					14	3	2		11	4							*9*	1						21
	11		6	5	7	8	3	9				12	2		*10*	4							14	1						22
	3		2	5	7	8		10				12			11	4		6					9	1						23
	3		5		7	8		10			14	12	2		11	4		6					*9*	1						24
	3		5	12		8		9	6			11	2		10	4		7						1						25
	3		12	5	6			10	4		*7*	8	2		14		11						9	1						26
	3		8	5					4		14	6	2	12	10		*11*	7						1		9				27
			5					10	4			3	2	6	11			14			7		9	1		8				28
	3		6	12				9				8	2		11	4		7						1		10	5			29
	3		8	5				10			14	6	2			4		7					9	1		*11*				30
			8	5				10			14		2			4		7					9	1		*11*	6	3		31
	12		8	5				9					2	6	11	4		*7*						1		10		3		32
	3		6	5				9			*7*		2			4	14							1		10		11	8	33
	3			5							*7*		2	6		4	10				14			1		9		11	8	34
	3		*6*	5				9			*7*		2	14		4					12			1		10		11	8	35
	3	6		5				9					2	12		4		7						1		10		11	8	36
1	8	3		5					12		14	7	2	9		4		6										11	*10*	37
1	3	12	2	5							9	11	6			4	10	*7*										8		38
1		3	*7*	5				10			9	12	2	6		4	*11*	14										8		39

DUMBARTON Division 2

Year Formed: 1872. *Ground & Address:* Boghead Park, Miller St, Dumbarton G82 2JA. *Telephone:* 0389 62569/67864.
Ground Capacity: total: 10,700. seated: 303. *Size of Pitch:* 110yd # 68yd.
Chairman: A. Hagen. *Secretary:* Alistair Paton.
Manager: Murdo MacLeod. *Assistant Manager:* Jim Fallon. *Physio:* Bobby McCallum. *Coach:* Alistair MacLeod.
Managers since 1975: A. Wright; D. Wilson; S. Fallon; W. Lamont; D. Wilson; D. Whiteford; A. Totten; M. Clougherty; R. Auld; J. George; W. Lamont. *Club Nickname(s):* The Sons. *Previous Grounds:* Broadmeadow, Ropework Lane.
Record Attendance: 18,000 v Raith Rovers, Scottish Cup; 2 Mar, 1957.
Record Transfer Fee received: £125,000 for Graeme Sharp to Everton (March 1982).
Record Transfer Fee paid: £50,000 for Charlie Gibson from Stirling Albion (1989).
Record Victory: 13-1 v Kirkintilloch Cl. 1st Rd; 1 Sept, 1888.
Record Defeat: 1-11 v Albion Rovers, Division II; 30 Jan, 1926: v Ayr United, League Cup; 13 Aug, 1952.

DUMBARTON 1993—94 LEAGUE RECORD

Match No.	Date	Venue	Opponents	Result		H/T Score	Lg. Pos.	Goalscorers	Attendance
1	Aug 7	A	Stirling Albion	L	0-2	0-0	—		879
2	14	H	Clyde	W	3-0	2-0	5	Boyd, Gibson 2	1001
3	21	H	Clydebank	L	2-4	2-2	6	Gibson, Meechan J	1597
4	28	A	Ayr U	W	1-0	0-0	4	Mooney	1675
5	Sept 4	H	Hamilton A	D	0-0	0-0	6		1044
6	11	A	St Mirren	W	3-0	1-0	6	Mooney 2, Gibson	2607
7	14	H	Brechin C	W	1-0	0-0	—	McConville	562
8	18	H	Falkirk	L	0-1	0-1	4		2361
9	25	A	Morton	L	1-3	0-0	5	McGarvey	1420
10	28	H	Airdrieonians	L	0-1	0-1	—		1276
11	Oct 2	A	Dunfermline Ath	L	1-4	1-0	8	Melvin	2941
12	9	H	Stirling Albion	L	1-2	1-1	10	Foster	766
13	16	A	Brechin C	W	3-0	1-0	8	Mooney pen, McDonald, Foster	469
14	23	H	St Mirren	D	3-3	0-2	8	McGarvey, Gow, McDonald	1723
15	30	A	Clydebank	L	1-2	0-1	9	Walker	1297
16	Nov 6	H	Ayr U	D	1-1	1-0	8	Gibson	918
17	10	A	Hamilton A	L	0-2	0-0	—		1182
18	13	H	Dunfermline Ath	L	1-5	0-4	9	Gibson	1437
19	20	A	Airdrieonians	W	1-0	0-0	9	Marsland	1741
20	27	H	Morton	W	2-0	1-0	9	McGarvey, Gibson	1140
21	Dec 4	A	Falkirk	D	1-1	1-0	9	Mooney	3306
22	11	A	Clyde	L	1-2	0-1	9	Mooney	681
23	18	H	Brechin C	W	3-1	2-0	9	Melvin, Mooney 2 (1 pen)	414
24	Jan 8	A	Ayr U	D	1-1	1-1	9	Meechan J	2084
25	11	A	Stirling Albion	D	0-0	0-0	—		758
26	15	H	Hamilton A	L	0-1	0-0	9		744
27	18	H	Clydebank	D	2-2	1-1	—	Gibson, Melvin	1003
28	22	H	Clyde	D	1-1	1-1	9	Gibson	927
29	Feb 5	A	St Mirren	W	3-0	1-0	9	Gibson, Meechan J, Boyd	2504
30	12	A	Dunfermline Ath	L	2-3	0-2	9	Gibson, Meechan J	3821
31	Mar 1	H	Airdrieonians	D	0-0	0-0	—		950
32	5	H	Falkirk	L	0-1	0-1	9		1815
33	12	A	Morton	D	0-0	0-0	9		1046
34	19	A	Brechin C	D	0-0	0-0	9		425
35	26	H	Stirling Albion	D	0-0	0-0	9		887
36	29	A	Clyde	W	2-1	0-1	—	Ward, MacLeod	789
37	Apr 2	H	St Mirren	L	2-3	0-2	8	Gibson, Mooney	1377
38	12	H	Dunfermline Ath	L	0-2	0-1	—		1305
39	16	A	Airdrieonians	D	1-1	0-0	8	Melvin	1320
40	23	A	Falkirk	L	0-4	0-0	8		3249
41	26	H	Morton	W	2-0	1-0	—	Cunnington, Gibson	650
42	30	A	Clydebank	L	0-2	0-0	8		929
43	May 7	H	Ayr U	D	1-1	1-1	8	Cunnington	670
44	14	A	Hamilton A	L	1-2	1-0	8	Cunnington	1451

Final League Position: 8

Most Capped Player: John Lindsay, 8, Scotland; James McAulay, 8, Scotland.
Most League Appearances: 297: Andy Jardine, 1957-67.
Most Goals in Season (Individual): 38: Kenny Wilson, Division II; 1971-72.
Most Goals Overall (Individual): 169: Hughie Gallacher, 1954-62 (including C Division 1954-55).

Honours
League Champions: Division I 1890-91 (shared with Rangers), 1891-92. Division II 1910-11, 1971-72. Second Division 1991-92; *Runners-up:* First Division 1983-84. Division II 1907-08.
Scottish Cup Winners: 1883; *Runners-up:* 1881, 1882, 1887, 1891, 1897. *League Cup:* —.
Club colours: Shirt: Gold. Shorts: Gold. Stockings: Gold and black.

Goalscorers: *League* (48): Gibson 13, Mooney 9 (2 pens), Meechan 4, Melvin 4, Cunnington 3, McGarvey 3, Boyd 2, Foster 2, McDonald 2, Gow 1, McConville 1, MacLeod 1, Marsland 1, Walker 1, Ward 1. *Scottish Cup* (1): Mooney (pen). *League Cup* (0): *B&Q Cup* (1): Foster 1.

MacFarlane I 43	Marsland J 32 + 4	Foster A 22 + 5	Melvin M 42	Meechan J 31 + 5	MacLeod M 42	Mooney M 41 + 2	McGarvey M 27 + 8	McQuade J 3	Gibson C 44	Boyd J 11 + 3	McAnenay M — + 1	Docherty R — + 1	Gow S 12 + 2	McConville R 19 + 2	Martin P 17 + 2	Fabiani R 36 + 3	McDonald J 3 + 3	Nelson M — + 3	Walker T 6 + 2	Wilson T 19	Gilmour J 1 + 5	Campbell C 12 + 2	Cunnington E 13	Ward H 7 + 3	Meechan K 1	Farrell G — + 1	*Match No.*
1	2	3	4	5	6	*7*	8	9	10	11	12	14															1
1		3	4	2	6	7		9	10	11			5	8													2
1		3	4	2	6	*7*	14	9	10	11			5	8													3
1	2	3	4	7	6	*9*	14		10	12				8	5	11											4
1	2	3	4	*7*	6	9	14		10	11				8	5												5
1	2	14	4	7	6	9			10	3				8	5	*11*											6
1	2	*11*	4		6	9	7		10	3				8	5	14											7
1	2		4	7	6	9	14		10	3				*8*	5	11	12										8
1	2	6	4	*7*		12	8		10	*3*			14		5	11	9										9
1	2	4		14	6	*7*	8		10	3					5	11	*9*	12									10
1	2	8	4		6	9	7		10	*3*				14	5	11											11
1	2	3	4	14	6	7	10		9				8		5	12			*11*								12
1	2	11	4		6	7			9				8		5	3	14		*10*								13
1	2	11	4		6	7	12		9				8		5	3	10										14
1	2	3	4		6	7	11		9				8		5		12		10								15
1	2		4		6	7	14		9				8	*11*	5	3			10								16
1	2	14	4	5	6	*7*	12		9				8	11		*3*			10								17
1	2	3	4	5		7	6		9				8	11		14			*10*								18
1	5	11	4		6	7	10		9					8		3		12		2							19
1	5	11	4		6	7	10		9					8		3				2							20
1	5	11	4	12	6	*7*	10		9					8		3			14	2							21
1	*5*	11	4	12	6	7	10		9					8		3			14	2							22
1	5	11	4	8	6	*7*	10		9							3				2	12						23
1	5		4	11	6	*7*	10		9					8		3				2	14						24
1	5		4	8	6	*7*	10		9							3		14		2	11						25
1	5		4	12	6	7	10		9	11				8		3				*2*	14						26
1	5		4	8	6	7	10		9				11			3				2							27
1	12		4	11	6	7	10		9				5	8		3				*2*	14						28
1	5	*11*	4	8	6	7	10		9	14						3				2							29
1	5	*11*	4	8	6	7	10		9	14						3				2		12					30
1	2	11	4	5	6	7	10		9							3						8					31
1	14	12	4	5	6	7	10		*9*							3				2		8	11				32
1		12	4	5	6	7	10		9							3				2		8	11				33
1	10	14	4	5	6	*7*	12		9							3				2		*8*	11				34
1			4	5	6	7			9					10		3				2		*8*	11	14			35
1	12		4	5	6	7			9					*10*		3				2		8	11	14			36
1	12			5	6	7			9				4			3				2		8	11	10			37
1	10		4	5	6	7			9						14	3				2		8	*11*	12			38
	2		4	5	6	7			9						12	3					14	8	*10*	11	1		39
1	2		4	5	6	7			9				12	14		3						*8*	10	11			40
1			4	5	6		7		9						2	3						8	10	11			41
1			4	5	6	14	7		9						2	3						8	*10*	11			42
1			4	5	6	7	8		9						2	3							10	11			43
1			4	5	6	7	*8*		9						2	3						14	10	11		12	44

DUNDEE Division 1

Year Formed: 1893. *Ground & Address:* Dens Park, Sandeman St, Dundee DD3 7JY. *Fax:* 0382 832284. *Telephone:* 0382 826104.
Ground Capacity: 16,871. seated: 11,516. *Size of Pitch:* 110yd # 70yd.
Chairman: Ron Dixon. *Secretary:* Andrew Drummond. *Marketing Manager:* George Reid.
Manager: Jim Duffy. *Coach:* John McCormack.
Managers since 1975: David White; Tommy Gemmell; Donald Mackay; Archie Knox; Jocky Scott; Dave Smith; Gordon Wallace; Iain Munro, Simon Stainrod. *Club Nickname(s):* The Dark Blues or The Dee. *Previous Grounds:* Carolina Port 1893-98.
Record Attendance: 43,024 v Rangers, Scottish Cup; 1953.
Record Transfer Fee received: £500,000 for Tommy Coyne to Celtic (March 1989).
Record Transfer Fee paid: £200,000 for Jim Leighton (Feb 1992).
Record Victory: 10-0 Division II v Alloa; 9 Mar, 1947 and v Dunfermline Ath; 22 Mar, 1947.
Record Defeat: 0-11 v Celtic, Division I; 26 Oct, 1895.
Most Capped Player: Alex Hamilton, 24, Scotland.
Most League Appearances: 341: Doug Cowie 1945-61.
Most League Goals in Season (Individual): 38: Dave Halliday, Division I; 1923-24.
Most Goals Overall (Individual): 113: Alan Gilzean.

DUNDEE 1993—94 LEAGUE RECORD

Match No.	Date	Venue	Opponents	Result		H/T Score	Lg. Pos.	Goalscorers	Attendance
1	Aug 7	A	Kilmarnock	L	0-1	0-0	—		8162
2	14	H	Motherwell	L	1-2	1-0	12	McKeown	4206
3	21	H	Aberdeen	D	1-1	0-1	12	Dodds	7505
4	28	A	Hibernian	L	0-2	0-1	12		5915
5	Sept 4	H	Rangers	D	1-1	1-0	12	Paterson	14,211
6	11	A	Dundee U	L	0-1	0-1	12		10,283
7	18	H	Raith R	L	0-1	0-0	12		4213
8	25	A	St Johnstone	L	1-2	0-2	12	Ristic	4203
9	Oct 2	H	Hearts	W	2-0	1-0	12	Paterson, Ristic	4386
10	5	H	Partick T	D	2-2	1-1	—	Dodds, Pittman	4540
11	9	A	Celtic	L	1-2	0-0	12	Dodds (pen)	15,980
12	16	A	Motherwell	L	0-1	0-1	12		5126
13	23	H	Kilmarnock	W	1-0	1-0	12	Adamczuk	4389
14	30	A	Aberdeen	L	0-1	0-0	12		11,885
15	Nov 6	H	Hibernian	W	3-2	2-1	12	Pittman, Ristic, Ritchie	4535
16	10	A	Rangers	L	1-3	0-3	—	Dodds	38,477
17	13	A	Hearts	W	2-1	1-1	12	Ritchie, Czachowski	7681
18	20	H	St Johnstone	L	0-1	0-1	12		4714
19	Dec 1	A	Raith R	L	1-2	1-2	—	Wieghorst	3609
20	4	A	Partick T	L	2-3	1-1	12	Tosh, Dodds	3312
21	7	H	Dundee U	L	1-2	0-1	—	Farningham	9256
22	11	H	Celtic	D	1-1	1-0	12	Ristic	8730
23	18	H	Motherwell	L	1-3	1-2	12	Ristic	4687
24	Jan 4	A	Kilmarnock	L	0-1	0-0	—		7406
25	8	A	Hibernian	L	0-2	0-2	12		7416
26	11	H	Aberdeen	L	0-1	0-0	—		5219
27	15	H	Rangers	D	1-1	1-0	12	Wieghorst	10,864
28	22	H	Raith R	D	2-2	1-1	12	Shaw, Blake	3784
29	Feb 5	A	Dundee U	D	1-1	0-1	12	Ristic	10,622
30	12	A	St Johnstone	D	1-1	1-1	12	Farningham	5517
31	Mar 1	H	Hearts	L	0-2	0-1	—		3965
32	5	H	Partick T	W	1-0	0-0	12	Shaw	3210
33	19	A	Motherwell	L	1-3	1-3	12	Shannon (og)	6127
34	26	H	Kilmarnock	W	3-0	3-0	12	Blake, McCann, Britton	2758
35	29	H	Dundee U	D	1-1	1-1	—	Duffy N	7645
36	Apr 2	A	Raith R	D	1-1	1-0	12	Shaw	3245
37	6	A	Celtic	D	1-1	1-1	—	Martin (og)	16,585
38	9	H	St Johnstone	L	0-1	0-1	12		2871
39	16	A	Hearts	W	2-0	0-0	11	Shaw 2	7028
40	23	H	Celtic	L	0-2	0-1	12		5795
41	26	A	Partick T	L	0-1	0-0	—		3296
42	30	A	Aberdeen	D	1-1	0-0	12	Duffy N	7568
43	May 7	H	Hibernian	W	4-0	1-0	12	McKeown, Shaw, Pittman, Anderson (pen)	2731
44	14	A	Rangers	D	0-0	0-0	12		41,620

Final League Position: 12

Honours
League Champions: Division I 1961-62. First Division 1978-79, 1991-92. Division II 1946-47; *Runners-up:* Division I 1902-03, 1906-07, 1908-09, 1948-49, 1980-81.
Scottish Cup Winners: 1910; *Runners-up:* 1925, 1952, 1964.
League Cup Winners: 1951-52, 1952-53, 1973-74; *Runners-up:* 1967-68, 1980-81.
B&Q (Centenary) Cup: Winners: 1990-91.
European: *European Cup:* 1962-63 (semi-final). *Cup Winners:* 1964-65.
UEFA Cup: (*Fairs Cup* 1967-68 semi-final), 1971-72, 1973-74, 1974-75.
Club colours: Shirt: Dark blue with red and white trim. Shorts: White. Stockings: Blue and White.

Goalscorers: *League* (42): Ristic 6, Shaw 6, Dodds 5 (1 pen), Pittman 3, Blake 2, Duffy N 2, Farningham 2, McKeown 2, Paterson 2, Ritchie 2, Wieghorst 2, Adamczuk 1, Anderson 1 (pen), Britton 1, Czachowski 1, McCann 1, Tosh 1, own goals 2. *Scottish Cup* (6): Britton 3, Shaw 2, Tosh 1. *League Cup* (2): Nielsen 1, own goal 1.

Mathers P 33	Frail S 28 + 4	Pittman S 35 + 1	Wieghorst M 21 + 3	David L 1	McGowan J 11 + 3	McMartin G 1 + 2	Vrto D 38	Ritchie P 10 + 7	Tosh P 14 + 12	Christie M 1	Paterson G 17 + 3	McQuillan J 27 + 7	McKeown G 18 + 1	Stainrod S 1	Dodds W 23 + 1	Adamczuk D 7 + 4	Duffy J 35	Armstrong L — + 1	Farningham R 20 + 4	Ristic D 16 + 2	Czachowski P 18	McCann N 20 + 2	Mobilio D — + 2	Bain K 4 + 3	Blake N 23	Dinnie A 7	Shaw G 17	Britton G 15 + 2	Pageaud M 11	Teasdale M 2 + 3	Duffy C 9	Tully C 1	Hamilton J — + 1	Anderson I — + 1	*Match No.*
1	2	3	*4*	5	6	7	8	9	10	11	12	14																							1
1	14	3	4		6		8	12	11		*5*	2	7	9	10																				2
1	12	3	4		6		8		9		5	2	11		10	*7*																			3
1	2	3	4		7			12	*9*		6		11		10	8	5	14																	4
1	2	3	4		7		8	9			6		11		10		*5*		14																5
1	2	3			7		8		9		6		11		10	12	5		4																6
1	2	3			14		8	9	12		6		11		10	7	*5*		4																7
1	2	3					8		9		6	14	7		12		5		*4*	10	11														8
1	2	3					8				5	4	*7*		10	14	6			9	11	12													9
1	2	3					8				5	4	7		10	12				9	6	*11*	14												10
1	2	3			*4*		8				5		7		10	12	6			9	11		14												11
1	2	3				14	8	12				7			10	*6*	5		4	9	11														12
1		3				14	8	12			5	2			10	7	6		4	*9*	11														13
1	2						8	7			5	12			10	3	6		4	9	11														14
1	2	3					8	7	14		5	12			10	4	6			*9*	11														15
1	2	3	*8*		14			7	12		5	4			10		6			9	11														16
1	2	3					8	7	12		5	14	*4*		10		6			9	11														17
1	2		12				8	7	14		*5*	3	4		10		6			9	11														18
1	2		*4*		14		8	12				3	*7*		10		6			9	11	5													19
1	2	3	12		6		8		7		5				10				*4*	9	11	14													20
1	2	3			4		8		7						10		6		9	12	11			5											21
1	2	14			7		8								10		6		4	9	11	*3*			5										22
1	*2*	3			7		8		14			4			10		6			9	11				5										23
1	2		14				8	7				12	6		10		3		4	9	*11*				5										24
1	2		8					7				9			10		6		14			*3*		4	5	11									25
1	2	3	8					12				4					6					11			5	10	7	9							26
1	2	3	4				*8*	14				12					6					11			5	10	7	9							27
1	2	3	4									8					6					11			5	10	7	9							28
1	2	3	10				8		*9*			4					6		12	14		11			5		7								29
1		3	10				8					2					6		11						5	4	7	9							30
	2	3	10						12			8					6					11		14	5	4	7	*9*	1						31
	12	3					8		14			2					6				10	11			5	*4*	7	9	1						32
1	*4*	3	10				8		7			2					6		12			11			5			9		14					33
	12	3	10				8		14			2							6			11			5		*7*	9	1	4					34
		3	10				8					2							6			11			5		7	9	1		4				35
		3	*10*				8		12			2							6			11		14	5		7	9	1		4				36
1		3					8		11			2					6		4					12	5		7	9			10				37
1		*3*					8		7			2					6		4			11			5			9		14	10				38
		3					8		11		12	2					6		4					10	5		7	9	1						39
							8		12				14				6		2			11		*10*	5		7	9	1		4	3			40
							8		12		14		10				3		4			11			5		7	9	1	*2*	6				41
			4				8		9			2	10				3					11			5		7	14	1	12	6				42
		3	9				8					2	10						4			11			5		7		1		6		12	14	43
		3	9				8					2	10				6					11			5		7	12	1		4				44

DUNDEE UNITED Premier Division

Year Formed: 1909 (1923). *Ground & Address:* Tannadice Park, Tannadice St, Dundee DD3 7JW. *Telephone:* 0382 833166. *Fax:* 0382 82689. *Ground Capacity:* total: 16,868, seated: south 2217; George Fox 5149.
Size of Pitch: 110yd # 74yd.
Chairman: James Y. McLean. *Company Secretary:* Miss Priti Trivedi. *Commercial Manager:* Bobby Brown.
Manager: Ivan Golac. *Physio:* —. *Coach:* Gordon Wallace.
Managers since 1975: J. McLean. *Club Nickname(s):* The Terrors. *Previous Grounds:* None.
Record Attendance: 28,000 v Barcelona, Fairs Cup; 16 Nov, 1966.
Record Transfer Fee received: £4,000,000 for Duncan Ferguson from Rangers (July 1993).
Record Transfer Fee paid: £600,000 for Gordon Petric from Partizan Belgrade (Nov 1993).
Record Victory: 14-0 v Nithsdale Wanderers, Scottish Cup 1st rd; 17 Jan, 1931.
Record Defeat: 1-12 v Motherwell, Division II; 23 Jan, 1954.
Most Capped Player: Maurice Malpas, 55, Scotland.
Most League Appearances: 612, Dave Narey; 1973-94.
Most Appearances in European Matches: 76, Dave Narey (record for Scottish player).
Most League Goals in Season (Individual): 41: John Coyle, Division II; 1955-56.
Most Goals Overall (Individual): 158: Peter McKay.

DUNDEE UNITED 1993—94 LEAGUE RECORD

Match No.	Date		Venue	Opponents	Result		H/T Score	Lg. Pos.	Goalscorers	Attendance
1	Aug	7	H	Aberdeen	D	1-1	1-0	—	McKinlay	13,881
2		14	A	Partick T	W	2-1	1-0	3	Dailly 2	4599
3		21	A	St Johnstone	D	1-1	0-0	3	McKinlay	6248
4		28	H	Hearts	D	0-0	0-0	3		8502
5	Sept	4	A	Raith R	D	1-1	1-0	5	McKinlay	5304
6		11	H	Dundee	W	1-0	1-0	2	McLaren	10,283
7		18	A	Celtic	D	1-1	0-0	4	McKinlay	26,377
8		25	H	Motherwell	D	0-0	0-0	4		6633
9	Oct	2	A	Hibernian	L	0-2	0-1	6		7556
10		5	A	Kilmarnock	D	1-1	0-0	—	McKinlay	7034
11		9	H	Rangers	L	1-3	0-3	8	Welsh	11,262
12		16	H	Partick T	D	2-2	1-1	7	Brewster, Crabbe	5750
13		23	A	Aberdeen	L	0-2	0-2	10		13,566
14		30	H	St Johnstone	W	2-0	0-0	8	Brewster, McKinlay	6275
15	Nov	6	A	Hearts	D	1-1	0-1	8	O'Neil	8362
16		9	H	Raith R	D	2-2	2-0	—	Bowman, Dailly	5775
17		13	H	Hibernian	D	2-2	2-0	6	Brewster, McKinlay	6880
18		20	A	Motherwell	L	0-2	0-1	8		5807
19		30	H	Celtic	W	1-0	0-0	—	Connolly	10,220
20	Dec	4	H	Kilmarnock	D	0-0	0-0	7		7100
21		7	A	Dundee	W	2-1	1-0	—	Brewster, Connolly	9256
22		11	A	Rangers	W	3-0	3-0	7	Bowman, Connolly, Brewster	43,058
23		18	A	Partick T	L	0-1	0-1	6		4121
24		27	H	Aberdeen	L	0-1	0-1	—		12,248
25	Jan	8	H	Hearts	W	3-0	2-0	7	Crabbe, Connolly, Brewster	8583
26		15	A	Raith R	W	2-0	1-0	6	Brewster 2	5150
27		22	A	Celtic	D	0-0	0-0	6		17,235
28		25	A	St Johnstone	D	1-1	1-0	—	Brewster	5758
29	Feb	5	H	Dundee	D	1-1	1-0	6	Connolly	10,622
30		12	H	Motherwell	L	1-2	1-2	6	Brewster	6573
31		26	A	Hibernian	W	1-0	0-0	6	Nixon	7015
32	Mar	5	A	Kilmarnock	D	1-1	1-0	6	Black (og)	7403
33		19	H	Partick T	D	2-2	2-1	6	Brewster, Cleland	6005
34		26	A	Aberdeen	L	0-1	0-1	6		12,574
35		29	A	Dundee	D	1-1	1-1	—	Brewster	7645
36	Apr	2	H	Celtic	L	1-3	0-2	6	Brewster	9790
37		5	H	Rangers	D	0-0	0-0	—		11,352
38		16	H	Hibernian	W	3-0	3-0	6	Petric, Brewster, McKinlay	6603
39		23	A	Rangers	L	1-2	0-0	6	Dailly	44,776
40		26	H	Kilmarnock	L	1-3	0-1	—	Hannah	8801
41		30	H	St Johnstone	D	0-0	0-0	6		10,635
42	May	3	A	Motherwell	W	2-1	1-1	—	Brewster, McKinlay	5208
43		7	A	Hearts	L	0-2	0-1	6		13,627
44		14	H	Raith R	L	2-3	0-3	6	Hannah, Brewster	5335

Final League Position: 6

Honours

League Champions: Premier Division 1982-83. Division II 1924-25, 1928-29; *Runners-up:* Division II 1930-31, 1959-60.
Scottish Cup Winners: 1993-94; *Runners-up:* 1974, 1981, 1985, 1987, 1988, 1991.
League Cup Winners: 1979-80, 1980-81; *Runners-up:* 1981-82, 1984-85.
Summer Cup Runners-up: 1964-65. *Scottish War Cup Runners-up:* 1939-40.
European: *European Cup:* 8 matches 1983-84 (semi-finals), 1988-89; *Cup Winners Cup:* 4 matches 1974-75; *UEFA Cup Runners-up:* 1986-87. 80 matches *Fairs Cup:* 1966-67, 1969-70, 1970-71. *UEFA Cup:* 1971-72, 1975-76, 1977-78, 1978-79, 1979-80, 1980-81, 1981-82, 1982-83, 1984-85, 1985-86, 1986-87, 1987-88, 1989-90, 1990-91, 1993-94.
Club colours: Tangerine jersey, black shorts. Change colours: White with grey/black spashes, black shorts, tangerine trim.

Goalscorers: *League* (47): Brewster 16, McKinlay 9, Connolly 5, Dailly 4, Bowman 2, Crabbe 2, Hannah 2, Cleland 1, McLaren 1, Nixon 1, O'Neil 1, Petric 1, Welsh 1, own goal 1. *Scottish Cup* (11): Brewster 4, McKinlay 2 (1 pen), Welsh 2, Crabbe 1, McInally 1, McLaren 1. *League Cup* (5): Clark 2, Connolly 1, McKinlay 1, McLaren 1.

Main A 18	Van Der Hoorn F 28	Malpas M 35	Cleland A 32 + 1	Welsh B 37	Narey D 6	Bowman D 35	McKinlay W 39	Connolly P 21 + 7	Dailly C 29 + 9	Brewster C 30 + 3	Bollan G 10 + 2	Clark J 13 + 1	Myers C 4 + 1	McLaren A 18 + 9	McInally J 29 + 2	McBain R — + 1	O'Neil J 8 + 4	Crabbe S 10 + 11	Perry M 8 + 1	Johnson G 8 + 2	Van De Kamp G 25	Petric G 27	Nixon J 7 + 8	Hannah D 6 + 4	Flies B 1	Match No.
1	2	3	4	5	6	7	8	9	10	11	12															1
1	2			5	6	7	8	9	10		3	4	*11*	12	14											2
1				5	6	7	8	9	10		3	2	*11*	4	12	14										3
1	6			5		7		9	10		3	2	*11*	8	4		12	14								4
1	6			5		7	8		10	12	*3*	2	11	9	4			14								5
1	6			5		7	8		10		3	2		9				*11*	4	14						6
1	11		2	5	6		8		10		3			9					4	7						7
1	2	6	3	5			8		10			12		9			*7*	14	4	11						8
1	2	3	6	5			8	10	14			9		12				11	*4*	7						9
1	2	3					8	10	14	12		5		9	6			*11*	4	7						10
1	2	3		5		7	8	14	10			4		9	6		12			*11*						11
1		3	6	5		7	8	14	10	*11*		2		9				12	4							12
1	4	3	6	5			8		10			2		9			11	12		7						13
1	4		3	5			8		10	7		2		9			11	12		6						14
1	4	3	6	5		7	8		10	11		2		*9*			14									15
1	4	3		5		7	8		10	11		2		9			6									16
1	4	3	2	5		7	8	14	10	*11*				9			6									17
	2	3	8	6		7			10	14				9	4		11	12			1	5				18
	2	3	11	6		7	8	9		10					4			12			1	5				19
	2	3	11	6		*7*	8	9		10					4		14	12			1	5				20
	2	3	11	6		7	8	9	12	10					4						1	5				21
	2	3	11	6		7	8	9	14	*10*					4			12			1	5				22
	2	3	11	6		7	8	9	14	*10*					4			12			1	5				23
	2	3		6		7	8	9	*11*	10				14	4						1	5				24
	2	3	12	6		7	8	*9*		10					4			11			1	5	14			25
	2	3	8	*6*		7			9	10					4			11			1	5	12	14		26
	2	3	8	6		7		9	14	10					4			*11*			1	5	12			27
	2	3	6			7	8	*9*	14	10					4			11			1	5	12			28
	2	3		6		7	8	9		10					4			11			1	5	12			29
	2	3		6		*7*	8	9	14	10					4			11			1	5	12			30
		3	2	6			8	14	7	10					4			*11*			1	5	9	12		31
		3	2	6			8		7	10					4		11					5	*9*	14	1	32
		3	2	6		7	8	*9*		10				14	4		11				1	5				33
		3	2		6	7	8		*9*	10				14	4					11	1	5				34
		3	2	6		7	8	9	11	10					4						1	5				35
		3	11	6	2	*7*	8	9		10				14	4						1	5				36
		3	2	6			8		12	10	11			*9*	4						1	5	14	*7*		37
			2			7	8	14	3	10				9	4				6	*12*	1	5		11		38
		3	2	6		7			10		8			*9*	4						1	5	14	11		39
1		3	2	6		7	8	11	10		4			14								5	*9*	12		40
		3	2			7	8		6	10				14	4						1	5	*9*	11		41
		3	2	6		7	8		11	10				14	4				12		1	5	*9*			42
			2			*7*	8	14	11	10	3		12						6		1	5	9	4		43
		3	2			7	8	14	11	10	12				4						1	5	*9*	6		44

DUNFERMLINE ATHLETIC Division 1

Year Formed: 1885. *Ground & Address:* East End Park, Halbeath Rd, Dunfermline KY12 7RB. *Telephone:* 0383 724295.
Ground Capacity: total: 18,340. seated: 4020. *Size of Pitch:* 114yd # 72yd.
Chairman: C. R. Woodrow. *Secretary:* P. A. M. D'Mello. *Commercial Manager:* Audrey Kelly.
Manager: Bert Paton. *Assistant Manager:* Dick Campbell.
Physio: Philip Yeates, MCSP.
Managers since 1975: G. Miller; H. Melrose; P. Stanton; T. Forsyth; J. Leishman; I. Munro; J. Scott. *Club Nickname(s):* The Pars. *Previous Grounds:* None.
Record Attendance: 27,816 v Celtic, Division I, 30 April, 1968.
Record Transfer Fee received: £200,000 for Ian McCall to Rangers (Aug 1987).
Record Transfer Fee paid: £540,000 for Istvan Kozma from Bordeaux (Sept 1989).
Record Victory: 11-2 v Stenhousemuir, Division II, 27 Sept, 1930.
Record Defeat: 1-11 v Hibernian, Scottish Cup, 3rd rd replay, 26 Oct, 1889.
Most Capped Player: Andy Wilson, 6 (12), Scotland.
Most League Appearances: 360: Bobby Robertson; 1977-88.
Most League Goals in Season (Individual): 55: Bobby Skinner, Division II, 1925-26.
Most Goals Overall (Individual): 154: Charles Dickson.

DUNFERMLINE ATHLETIC 1993—94 LEAGUE RECORD

Match No.	Date	Venue	Opponents	Result		H/T Score	Lg. Pos.	Goalscorers	Attendance
1	Aug 7	A	Falkirk	L	2-3	1-0	—	Den Bieman, French	5600
2	14	H	Clydebank	L	0-2	0-0	11		3099
3	21	A	Brechin C	L	0-1	0-0	12		1101
4	28	H	Airdrieonians	W	3-2	2-1	11	Preston, French, O'Boyle	3970
5	Sept 4	A	Clyde	W	2-0	2-0	8	French, O'Boyle	1505
6	11	A	Stirling Albion	L	0-2	0-0	8		2050
7	15	H	St Mirren	L	3-4	2-2	—	Robertson, Cooper, Preston (pen)	2703
8	18	H	Morton	W	4-0	2-0	8	McCathie, Preston (pen), French 2	2955
9	25	A	Ayr U	D	1-1	0-0	7	O'Boyle	2012
10	29	A	Hamilton A	W	2-0	0-0	—	Preston 2 (1 pen)	1762
11	Oct 2	H	Dumbarton	W	4-1	0-1	4	Smith, O'Boyle, McCathie, Laing	2941
12	9	H	Falkirk	W	1-0	0-0	4	Laing	6255
13	16	A	St Mirren	W	2-1	2-1	4	Den Bieman, Smith	3091
14	23	H	Stirling Albion	W	3-0	0-0	4	Robertson, O'Boyle 2	3993
15	30	H	Brechin C	W	4-0	2-0	4	Laing, Sinclair, Smith, McCathie	3195
16	Nov 6	A	Airdrieonians	D	1-1	1-0	4	Smith	3368
17	9	H	Clyde	W	4-0	1-0	—	O'Boyle, McCathie, French, Smith	2987
18	13	A	Dumbarton	W	5-1	4-0	3	French 3, Laing 2	1437
19	Dec 4	A	Morton	D	0-0	0-0	4		1591
20	7	H	Hamilton A	W	4-0	2-0	—	Laing 2, Smith, Tod	3237
21	11	A	Clydebank	W	3-0	1-0	2	McCathie, Laing, McWilliams	1900
22	14	H	Ayr U	W	6-1	3-0	—	McCathie, Smith, McWilliams, Sharp, Petrie, French	3206
23	18	H	St Mirren	W	4-2	2-1	1	French 3, Petrie	5059
24	Jan 4	A	Brechin C	W	1-0	0-0	—	Cooper	2120
25	18	A	Falkirk	L	0-2	0-0	—		8018
26	22	H	Clydebank	W	2-0	0-0	1	French, Sweeney (og)	4612
27	25	H	Airdrieonians	D	0-0	0-0	—		5419
28	Feb 5	A	Stirling Albion	L	0-1	0-1	1		1888
29	12	H	Dumbarton	W	3-2	2-0	1	Petrie, Tod 2	3821
30	19	A	Clyde	W	1-0	0-0	1	Tod	4113
31	Mar 2	A	Hamilton A	D	1-1	0-0	—	McCathie	1197
32	5	H	Morton	W	3-0	0-0	2	Tod 2, O'Boyle	3485
33	12	A	Ayr U	W	4-0	1-0	2	Den Bieman, Petrie 2, Smith	2336
34	19	A	St Mirren	W	2-0	0-0	2	Tod, O'Boyle	2603
35	26	H	Falkirk	D	1-1	1-0	2	O'Boyle	13,357
36	29	A	Clydebank	W	1-0	0-0	—	O'Boyle	1276
37	Apr 2	H	Stirling Albion	W	2-1	1-1	1	O'Boyle, Smith	4530
38	12	A	Dumbarton	W	2-0	1-0	—	Robertson, McWilliams	1305
39	16	H	Hamilton A	W	2-1	1-1	1	Tod, O'Boyle (pen)	4927
40	23	A	Morton	D	2-2	0-0	1	Tod, McCathie	2003
41	26	H	Ayr U	W	1-0	0-0	—	French	4006
42	30	H	Brechin C	W	2-1	1-0	1	Tod, Petrie	4988
43	May 7	A	Airdrieonians	L	0-1	0-0	2		6878
44	14	H	Clyde	W	5-0	2-0	2	O'Boyle 4, Tod	6163

Final League Position: 2

Honours

League Champions: First Division 1988-89. Division II 1925-26. Second Division 1985-86; *Runners-up:* First Division 1986-87, 1993-94. Division II 1912-13, 1933-34, 1954-55, 1957-58, 1972-73. Second Division 1978-79.
Scottish Cup Winners: 1961, 1968; *Runners-up:* 1965.
League Cup Runners-up: 1949-50, 1991-92.
European: *European Cup:* —. *Cup Winners Cup:* 1961-62, 1968-69 (semi-finals). *UEFA Cup:* 1962-63, 1964-65, 1965-66, 1966-67, 1969-70 (*Fairs Cup*).
Club colours: Shirt: Black and white vertical stripes, stippled with red dots. Shorts: Black with white side panel. Stockings: White with red chevrons.

Goalscorers: *League* (93): O'Boyle 17 (1 pen), French 15, Tod 11, Smith 9, Laing 8, McCathie 8, Petrie 6, Preston 5 (3 pens), Den Bieman 3, McWilliams 3, Robertson 3, Cooper 2, Sharp 1, Sinclair 1, own goal 1. *Scottish Cup* (2): Tod 2. *League Cup* (2): French 1, Robertson 1. *B&Q Cup* (7): Laing 2, O'Boyle 2, Den Bieman 1, Sharp 1, Smith 1.

Hamilton L 28	Bowes M 4 + 2	Cunnington E 7 + 2	McCathie N 43	Moyes D 1	Davies W 3 + 1	Den Bieman I 33 + 8	Smith P 43 + 1	French H 31 + 5	Robertson C 40	Preston A 20 + 6	Laing D 11 + 16	McWilliams D 12 + 8	Sharp R 30	Baillie A 14 + 1	O'Boyle G 28 + 4	Petrie S 30 + 7	McNamara J 38 + 1	Sinclair C 1 + 5	Hillcoat J 8	Cooper N 30	Tod A 19 + 3	Moore A 2 + 6	Westwater I 8	Match No.
1	2	3	4	5	6	7	8	9	10	*11*	12	14												1
1	2		4		6	*7*	12	9	8	11	14		3	5	10									2
1	2		4		10	7	6	9	8	11	12		3	5										3
1	12		4		14	7	6	8	2	11			3	5	10	*9*								4
1	2		4			*7*	6	8	3	11		14		5	10	9	12							5
1	12		4			7	6	8	3	11		10		*5*		9	2	14						6
		3	4				6	9	8	11		7				10	2		1	5				7
			4			14	6	9	8	11		7	3			*10*	2	12	1	5				8
			4				6	9	8	3	14	7			10	*11*	2		1	5				9
		3	4			14	6	*7*	8	11					10	9	2	12	1	5				10
		3	4			7	6		8	11	14				10	*9*	2	12	1	5				11
		3	4			7	6		8	11	12				10	9	2		1	5				12
		3	4			7	6		8	11	12				10	9	2		1	5				13
		3	4			7	6	14	8	11	9				10	12	2		1	*5*				14
1			4				6	*7*	8		9	12	3	5	10	14	2	11						15
1			4			12	6	7	8		9		3		10	11	2			5				16
1		14	4			12	6	7	8		*9*		3		10	11	2			5				17
1		14	4			10	6	7	8	12	9		*3*			11	2			5				18
1			4			10	6	*7*	8	12	9		3			11	2			5	14			19
1			4			10	6	7	8		*9*	12	3			11	2			5	14			20
1			4			10	6	7	8		9	12	3			11	2			5				21
1			4			*10*	6	7	8		9	11	3			12	2			5	14			22
1			4			*10*	6	7		14	9	11	3			12	2			5	8			23
1			4			7	6	9			12	11	3		*10*	14	2			5	8			24
1			4			*7*	6	9	8	14	12	11	3		10		2			5				25
1			4			*7*	6	9	8	14	12	11	3	5	10		2							26
1			4			14	6	9	8	7	12	*11*	3	5	10		2							27
1			4			14	2	9	8	7	10	*11*	3	5	12						6			28
1			4			*7*	6		8	11	14		3	5	12	9	2				10			29
1			4			7	6		8	11	14		3	5		*9*	2				10			30
1			4			*7*	6		8	11	14		3	5	12	9	2				10			31
1			4			7	6		8	*11*	12		3		14	9	2			5	10			32
1			4			*7*	6		8	14	12		3		10	9	2			5	11			33
1			4			7	6	12	8			14	3		10	*9*	2			5	11			34
1			4			7	6	12	8				3		10	*9*	2			5	11	14		35
1			4			*7*	6	12	8				3		10	9	2			5	11	14		36
			4			7	6	3	8						10	9	2			5	11		1	37
			4			*7*	6	3	*8*			14			10	9	2			5	11	12	1	38
			4			*7*	6	3				8			10	9	2	14		5	11	12	1	39
			4			7	6	3	8			14			*10*	9	2			5	11	12	1	40
			4			12	6	9	8				3		*10*	14	2			5	11	7	1	41
			4			12	6	9	*8*				3	5	10	14	2				11	7	1	42
			4			7	6	8					3	14	10	9	2			5	11		1	43
						7	6	12	8				3	4	10	9	2			5	*11*	14	1	44

EAST FIFE

Division 2

Year Formed: 1903. *Ground & Address:* Bayview Park, Methil, Fife KY8 3AG. *Telephone:* 0333 426323. *Fax:* 426376.
Ground Capacity: total: 5385. seated: 600. *Size of Pitch:* 110yd # 71yd.
Chairman: James Baxter. *Secretary:* William McPhee. *Commercial Manager:* James Bonthrone.
Manager: Alex Totten. *Assistant Manager:* Kenny Thomson. *Physio:* Bob Pender. *Coach:* David Gorman.
Managers since 1975: Frank Christie; Roy Barry; David Clarke; Gavin Murray. *Club Nickname(s):* The Fifers. *Previous Grounds:* None.
Record Attendance: 22,515 v Raith Rovers, Division I; 2 Jan, 1950.
Record Transfer Fee received: £150,000 for Paul Hunter from Hull C (March 1990).
Record Transfer Fee paid: £70,000 for John Sludden from Kilmarnock (July 1991).
Record Victory: 13-2 v Edinburgh City, Division II; 11 Dec, 1937.
Record Defeat: 0-9 v Hearts, Division I; 5 Oct, 1957.
Most Capped Player: George Aitken, 5 (8), Scotland.
Most League Appearances: 517: David Clarke, 1968-86.

EAST FIFE 1993—94 LEAGUE RECORD

Match No.	Date	Venue	Opponents	Result		H/T Score	Lg. Pos.	Goalscorers	Attendance
1	Aug 7	A	Berwick R	W	1-0	1-0	—	Reilly	518
2	14	H	Stenhousemuir	W	3-0	1-0	3	Aitken (og), Irvine, Scott	767
3	21	A	Cowdenbeath	W	2-1	1-1	1	Scott, Reilly	891
4	28	H	Alloa	W	4-1	3-1	1	Reilly, Scott 2, Beaton	1133
5	Sept 4	H	Queen of the S	L	0-2	0-0	2		1546
6	11	A	Meadowbank T	L	0-1	0-1	3		502
7	18	A	Queen's Park	L	2-4	0-2	4	Williamson, Reilly	525
8	25	H	East Stirling	L	0-1	0-0	8		775
9	Oct 2	H	Forfar Ath	W	3-2	2-1	5	Scott, Andrew, Williamson	662
10	9	A	Montrose	W	1-0	0-0	4	Reilly	655
11	16	A	Stranraer	L	2-3	2-1	7	Andrew, Williamson	644
12	23	H	Albion R	D	1-1	0-1	6	Burns (pen)	721
13	30	H	Arbroath	W	1-0	0-0	6	Scott	860
14	Nov 6	A	Stenhousemuir	W	1-0	1-0	4	Scott	493
15	13	H	Queen's Park	D	5-5	0-2	4	Irvine, Allan (pen), Hildersley, McBride, Scott	791
16	20	A	East Stirling	L	1-2	1-0	5	Sneddon	651
17	27	H	Montrose	W	5-2	3-1	4	Irvine 2, Andrew 2, Taylor	754
18	Dec 4	A	Forfar Ath	L	0-1	0-0	5		652
19	18	H	Berwick R	D	1-1	1-0	6	Scott	756
20	29	A	Arbroath	L	2-3	0-2	—	Irvine, Beaton	839
21	Jan 11	H	Cowdenbeath	W	2-0	1-0	—	Davidson (og), Beaton	789
22	18	A	Alloa	D	2-2	0-1	—	Irvine 2	542
23	25	H	Stranraer	D	1-1	1-1	—	Irvine	749
24	29	A	Albion R	D	1-1	0-0	4	McBride	273
25	Feb 5	H	Meadowbank T	L	0-2	0-0	7		681
26	12	H	Queen of the S	D	0-0	0-0	7		611
27	19	A	Montrose	L	0-3	0-1	7		723
28	26	H	Forfar Ath	D	1-1	0-0	7	Beaton	653
29	Mar 5	A	Berwick R	W	3-1	1-0	6	Allan, Hope, Dow	517
30	12	H	Queen's Park	W	1-0	0-0	5	Irvine	661
31	19	A	Stranraer	L	1-2	0-1	7	Burns (pen)	801
32	26	H	East Stirling	W	1-0	1-0	6	Burns	587
33	Apr 2	H	Albion R	W	3-1	0-1	5	Hope, Scott, Allan	592
34	9	A	Meadowbank T	D	2-2	1-1	5	Williamson, Allan	323
35	16	H	Queen of the S	L	0-1	0-0	6		716
36	23	A	Cowdenbeath	W	2-1	1-1	6	Bell, Hildersley	464
37	30	H	Arbroath	L	1-2	0-1	7	Cusick	634
38	May 7	A	Stenhousemuir	D	1-1	0-0	6	Beaton	441
39	14	A	Alloa	D	1-1	0-1	6	Sneddon	1156

Final League Position: 6

Most League Goals in Season (Individual): 41: Jock Wood, Division II; 1926-27 and Henry Morris, Division II; 1947-48.
Most Goals Overall (Individual): 196: George Dewar (149 in League).

Honours
League Champions: Division II 1947-48; *Runners-up:* Division II 1929-30, 1970-71. Second Division 1983-84.
Scottish Cup Winners: 1938; *Runners-up:* 1927, 1950.
League Cup Winners: 1947-48, 1949-50, 1953-54.
Club colours: Shirt: Amber with black collar and cuffs. Shorts: Amber with black flashes. Stockings: Amber with 3 black stripes on top.

Goalscorers: *League* (58): Scott 10, Irvine 9, Beaton 5, Reilly 5, Allan 4 (1 pen), Andrew 4, Williamson 4, Burns 3 (2 pens), Hildersley 2, Hope 2, McBride 2, Sneddon 2, Bell 1, Cusick 1, Dow 1, Taylor 1, own goals 2. *Scottish Cup* (5): Scott 3, Hildersley 1, Hope 1. *League Cup* (1): Scott 1. *B&Q Cup* (1): Allan 1.

Wilson E 19 + 1	Sneddon A 33 + 1	Williamson A 34	Barron D 20 + 2	Beaton D 38	Allan G 31 + 2	Elliott D 1	Beedie S 25	Scott R 27 + 3	Reilly J 7 + 2	McBride J 8 + 7	Taylor PH 13 + 6	Andrew B 17 + 7	Irvine AJ 22 + 8	Gowrie R — + 2	Gibb R 19 + 6	Hildersley R 21 + 4	Charles R 20	Bell G 16 + 2	Burns W 29	Yardley M 1	Jackson S — + 3	Hope D 15 + 1	Logan P — + 2	Dow C 8 + 1	Cusick J 5 + 1	Long D — + 2	*Match No.*
1	2	3	4	5	6	*7*	8	9	10	11	12	14															1
1	2	3	4	5	7		8	9	10		6		11														2
1	2	3	4	5	7		8	9	10		6		11	12													3
1	2	3	4	5	7		8	*9*	10	14	6		11	12													4
1	2	3	4	5	7		8	*9*	10	14	6		11														5
1	2	3	4	5	7		8	9	*10*	14	6	12	11														6
1	2	11	4	5	7		6	9	14		12		*10*		3	8											7
1	2	3	4	5			8	14	10		6	9	*11*		12	7											8
	2	6	4	5	7		10	9				11			3	8	1	12									9
		6	4	5	7		10	9	14			*11*			3	12	1	2	8								10
	12	6	4	5	7		10	*9*				11	14		3		1	2	8								11
	2	6		5	7		10				12	11	14		3	8	1		4	*9*							12
14	2	3		5	7		10	9		12	6		11			8	*1*		4								13
1	2			5	7		10	9		12	6	14	11		3	*8*			4								14
1	2	3	*4*	5	7		10	9		14	6		11			8											15
1	2	3		5	7		6	9		11	12		*10*		14	8			4								16
1	2	3	12	5			10			11	*6*	7	9			8			4		14						17
	2	3		5	7		10			14	6	*11*	9			8	1		4								18
	2	3		5	7		6	9			12	11			14	8	1		4			*10*					19
	2	3	12	5	7		6	9				*11*	14			8	1		4			10					20
	2	3	4	5			6			11			9		10		1	7	8		12						21
		3	4	5	7		6			11	14		9		10	12	1	2	*8*								22
		3	4	5	*7*		6			11			9		10		1	2	8				14				23
		3	4	5			6			11		7	9		10		1	*2*	8		12		14				24
		3	4	5			6	14		11		*7*	9		10	12	1	2	8								25
	2	3		5	7			14			4	8	9		10		1	12	6			*11*					26
	2	3		5				9				7	*10*		12	8	1	4	6			11		14			27
	2	*10*		5	7			9			4	14			3	8	1		6			12		11			28
1	2	3		5	7			9								8		4	6			10		11			29
1	2	3		5	7			*9*					14			8		4	6			10		11			30
1	2	3		5	*7*							14	9		12	8		4	6			10		11			31
1	2	3		5	*7*							11	14		12	8			4			10		9	6		32
1	2	3		5	14			9				11			10			4	6			8		*7*			33
1	2	3		5	7			9				*11*	14		10			4	6			8			12		34
1	2	3		5	7			9				*11*	14		10	12		4	6			8					35
	2			5	12			9							3	8	1	4	6			10		11	7		36
	2		4	5	7			9				14				8	1		6			10		*11*	3	12	37
	2		4	5	7			9				14	*10*		3		1		6			11			8	12	38
	2		4		*7*			9					14		3	8	1	5	6			11			10		39

EAST STIRLINGSHIRE Division 3

Year Formed: 1880. *Ground & Address:* Firs Park, Firs St, Falkirk FK2 7AY. *Telephone:* 0324 623583.
Ground Capacity: total: 1880. seated: 200. *Size of Pitch:* 112yd # 72yd.
Chairman: William C. White. *Secretary:* Alex Forsyth. *Commercial Manager:* Tom Kirk.
Manager: Billy Little. *Assistant Manager/Coach:* Lenny Reid. *Physio:* Sandra Togneri.
Managers since 1975: I. Ure; D. McLinden; W. P. Lamont; M. Ferguson; W. Little; D. Whiteford; D. Lawson; J. D. Connell; A. Mackin; Dom Sullivan, Bobby McCulley. *Club Nickname(s):* The Shire. *Previous Grounds:* Burnhouse, Randyford Park, Merchiston Park, New Kilbowie Park.
Record Attendance: 12,000 v Partick T, Scottish Cup 3rd rd; 19 Feb 1921.
Record Transfer Fee received: £35,000 for Jim Docherty to Chelsea (1978).
Record Transfer Fee paid: £6,000 for Colin McKinnon from Falkirk (March 1991).
Record Victory: 11-2 v Vale of Bannock, Scottish Cup 2nd rd; 22 Sept, 1888.
Record Defeat: 1-12 v Dundee United, Division II; 13 Apr, 1936.
Most Capped Player: Humphrey Jones, 5 (14), Wales.

EAST STIRLINGSHIRE 1993—94 LEAGUE RECORD

Match No.	Date		Venue	Opponents	Result		H/T Score	Lg. Pos.	Goalscorers	Attendance
1	Aug	7	A	Stenhousemuir	L	1-3	0-3	—	Craig	435
2		14	H	Berwick R	W	2-1	1-0	7	Speirs, Russell	301
3		21	A	Alloa	D	0-0	0-0	8		415
4		28	H	Meadowbank T	L	0-1	0-0	9		342
5	Sept	4	H	Montrose	L	2-3	1-1	11	McAulay, Kemp	374
6		11	A	Queen of the S	L	0-5	0-3	13		1164
7		18	H	Forfar Ath	L	1-2	0-0	14	Millar	347
8		25	A	East Fife	W	1-0	0-0	12	Macdonald	775
9	Oct	2	H	Albion R	L	1-4	1-1	14	Russell	343
10		9	A	Cowdenbeath	W	3-1	1-1	12	Yates, Herd (og), Geraghty	152
11		16	A	Queen's Park	D	1-1	0-1	11	Macdonald (pen)	417
12		23	H	Arbroath	L	2-4	0-3	13	Adam (og), Macdonald	393
13		30	H	Str	D	2-2	1-1	13	Geraghty, Macdonald	414
14	Nov	6	A	Berwick R	D	2-2	1-1	13	Crews, Kemp (pen)	453
15		13	A	Forfar Ath	D	1-1	0-1	12	Geraghty	427
16		20	H	East Fife	W	2-1	0-1	11	Kemp (pen), McCallum	651
17		27	H	Cowdenbeath	W	3-2	2-0	8	McCallum 2, Geraghty	546
18	Dec	4	A	Albion R	W	5-1	3-1	9	Robertson, Geraghty 3, Tierney	224
19		18	H	Stenhousemuir	L	0-2	0-0	9		775
20		27	A	Str	L	0-1	0-1	—		970
21	Jan	11	H	Alloa	L	0-1	0-0	—		398
22		15	A	Meadowbank T	D	1-1	0-0	10	McCallum	207
23		22	H	Queen's Park	W	2-0	1-0	10	Craig, McCallum	513
24	Feb	2	A	Arbroath	D	1-1	1-0	10	Craig	582
25		5	H	Queen of the S	D	0-0	0-0	10		403
26		12	A	Montrose	D	2-2	1-1	11	Conroy, Craig (pen)	387
27		19	A	Albion R	L	1-3	0-1	12	Macdonald (pen)	248
28	Mar	5	A	Alloa	W	1-0	0-0	10	McCallum	449
29		12	H	Cowdenbeath	W	4-0	1-0	10	Lee I, Millar, McCallum, Crews	290
30		15	H	Meadowbank T	W	1-0	0-0	—	Conroy	297
31		19	H	Arbroath	W	2-0	0-0	9	McCallum, Millar	359
32		26	A	East Fife	L	0-1	0-1	9		587
33	Apr	2	A	Montrose	W	2-0	2-0	9	McCallum, McAulay	583
34		9	H	Stenhousemuir	D	2-2	0-0	9	McCallum 2	557
35		16	A	Forfar Ath	W	2-0	1-0	8	McCallum, Millar	421
36		23	H	Stranraer	L	2-3	1-1	9	Duncan (og), Russell	862
37		30	A	Queen of the S	D	1-1	0-1	8	Lee I	2143
38	May	7	H	Berwick R	L	1-3	0-1	9	Lee I (pen)	438
39		14	A	Queen's Park	L	0-2	0-1	9		407

Final League Position: 9

Most League Appearances: 379: Gordon Simpson, 1968-80.
Most League Goals in Season (Individual): 36: Malcolm Morrison, Division II; 1938-39.
Most Goals Overall (Individual): —.

Honours
League Champions: Division II 1931-32; C Division 1947-48. *Runners-up:* Division II 1962-63. Second Division 1979-80. Division Three 1923-24.
Scottish Cup: —.
League Cup: —.
Club colours: Shirt: Black and white hoops. Shorts: Black. Stockings: Black.

Goalscorers: *League* (54): McCallum 12, Geraghty 7, Macdonald 5 (2 pens), Craig 4 (1 pen), Millar 4, Kemp 3 (2 pens), Lee I 3 (1 pen), Russell 3, Conroy 2, Crews 2, McAulay 2, Robertson 1, Speirs 1, Tierney 1, Yates 1, own goals 3. *Scottish Cup* (5): Geraghty 3, McAulay 1, Robertson 1. *League Cup* (1): Conroy 1. *B&Q Cup* (0).

McDougall G 38	Russell G 36	Kemp B 19	Craig D 38	Yates D 14 + 2	McAulay I 16 + 5	Roberts P 8 + 4	McKinnon C 3	Geraghty M 32 + 1	Robertson S 11 + 7	Conroy J 15 + 1	Speirs A 3 + 4	McInally M — + 3	Ross B 34	Crews B 24 + 5	Millar G 35 + 1	Tierney S 1 + 3	Macdonald K 11 + 3	Loney J 21 + 10	Horne J — + 1	McCallum M 16	Conway M 17 + 1	Lee R 18	Docherty A 1 + 4	Lee I 10	Lee D 4 + 3	Teasdale J 3	Imrie P 1	Match No.
1	2	3	4	5	6	7	8	*9*	10	11	12	14																1
1	2	3	6	5		10		9	8		11		4	7														2
1	2	3	6	5		7	8	9	10		11		4															3
1	2	3	6	5			8	9	10		11		4	14	*7*	12												4
1	2	3	6	*5*	8			9	11		12		4	10	7	14												5
1	2	3	6	5	12	7		11	10				4	14	*8*		9											6
1	2	3	5		8	*7*		10				14	4	6	12		9	11										7
1	2	3	5	4	8	*7*		11			12			14	10		9	6										8
1	2	3	5	4		7		11			12			8	10		9	6										9
1	2	3	5	6		12		10					4	7	8		9	11										10
1	2	3	5	6		12		10					4	7	8		9	11										11
1	2	3	5	6		14		10	*4*					7	8		9	11	12									12
1	2	3	5	6	4	12		10						7	8		9	11										13
1	2	3	5		4	9		10					6	7	8			11										14
1	2	3	5		4			10	12			14	6	7	8	*9*		11										15
1	2	3	5		4			10	12				6	7	8			11		9								16
1	2		5	12				10	7				6	3	8			11		9	4							17
1	2		5	12				10	7				6	3	8	14		11		*9*	4							18
1	2	3	5		4			10					6		8		12	11		9	7							19
1	2	3	5	*4*	14			10	7				6	12	8		9	11										20
1	2	3	5		4			10	14				6		8		12	11		9	*7*							21
1	2		5	*11*	4			10	7				6		8		12			9	14	3						22
1	2		5		4			10	12	*11*			6		8			14		9	7	3						23
1	2		5		4			10	12	11			6		8			9			7	3						24
1	2		5		*4*				12	10			6		8		9	11			7	3	14					25
1	2		5					10	12	4			6		8			11		9	7	3						26
1	2		5					10		11			6	4	8		9	12			*7*	3	14					27
1	2		5					10		11			6		8					9	*7*	3	12	4	14			28
1	2		5							11			6	14	8			12		9	*7*	3	10	4				29
1	2		5							11			6	10	8			12		9	7	3		4				30
1			5							11			6	2	8			10		9	7	3	12	4				31
1			5		12					11			6	2	8			10		9	*7*	3		4	14			32
1			5		7								6	2	8			14		9		3		4	10	*11*		33
1	2		5		.7			12					6	4	8			14		9		3			*10*	11		34
1	2		5					10		11			6	4	8			12		9	*7*	3			14			35
1	2		5		14			10		9			6	*7*	8			12				3		4		11		36
1	2				14			9		11			6	*4*	8			12			7	3		10	5			37
1	2		5					10		9			6	4	8			12				3		11	7			38
	2		5					10		12			6	4	8			11			7	3		9			1	39

FALKIRK

Premier Division

Year Formed: 1876. *Ground & Address:* Brockville Park, Hope St, Falkirk FK1 5AX. *Telephone:* 0324 624121/632487. *Fax:* 0324 612418.
Ground Capacity: total: 12,800. seated: 2661. *Size of Pitch:* 110yd # 70yd.
Chairman: G. J. Fulston. *Secretary:* A. D. Moffat. *Commercial Manager:* Jim Hendry.
Manager: Jim Jefferies. *Assistant Manager:* Billy Brown. *Physio:* John Sharp. *Coach:* Willie Wilson.
Managers since 1975: J. Prentice; G. Miller; W. Little; J. Hagart; A. Totten; G. Abel; W. Lamont; D. Clarke; J. Duffy. *Club Nickname(s):* The Bairns. *Previous Grounds:* Randyford; Blinkbonny Grounds; Hope Street.
Record Attendance: 23,100 v Celtic, Scottish Cup 3rd rd; 21 Feb, 1953.
Record Transfer Fee received: £270,000 for Gordon Marshall to Celtic (Aug 1991).
Record Transfer Fee paid: £225,000 to Chelsea for Kevin McAllister (Aug 1991).
Record Victory: 12-1 v Laurieston, Scottish Cup 2nd rd; 23 Mar, 1893.
Record Defeat: 1-11 v Airdrieonians, Division I; 28 Apr, 1951.
Most Capped Player: Alex Parker, 14 (15), Scotland.

FALKIRK 1993—94 LEAGUE RECORD

Match No.	Date	Venue	Opponents	Result		H/T Score	Lg. Pos.	Goalscorers	Attendance
1	Aug 7	H	Dunfermline Ath	W	3-2	0-1	—	Rice, Johnston, Hughes	5600
2	14	A	Morton	W	5-1	1-0	1	Cadette, Duffy 2, Taggart, Shaw	3049
3	21	H	Stirling Albion	W	2-0	1-0	1	Duffy, Cadette	4188
4	28	A	Hamilton A	D	1-1	0-0	2	Shaw	3291
5	Sept 4	H	Clydebank	L	0-4	0-2	3		4445
6	11	H	Airdrieonians	W	2-1	0-1	2	Duffy, Drinkell	4566
7	14	A	Ayr U	W	3-0	2-0	—	McLaughlin, Cadette, May (pen)	2633
8	18	A	Dumbarton	W	1-0	1-0	2	McLaughlin	2361
9	25	H	St Mirren	W	2-0	1-0	1	Drinkell 2	4633
10	29	H	Clyde	L	0-1	0-0	—		3324
11	Oct 2	A	Brechin C	D	0-0	0-0	3		1347
12	9	A	Dunfermline Ath	L	0-1	0-0	3		6255
13	16	H	Ayr U	W	2-0	1-0	3	Cadette, May	3350
14	23	A	Airdrieonians	D	1-1	0-1	3	Duffy	5153
15	30	A	Stirling Albion	W	4-3	2-1	3	Cadette, Sloan, Weir, Drinkell	2476
16	Nov 6	H	Hamilton A	D	3-3	0-1	2	Cadette 2, Drinkell	3686
17	9	A	Clydebank	D	1-1	1-1	—	Duffy	2079
18	13	H	Brechin C	W	2-0	1-0	1	Duffy, McDonald	3473
19	23	A	Clyde	W	2-0	1-0	—	Duffy 2	1165
20	Dec 4	H	Dumbarton	D	1-1	0-1	3	Hughes	3306
21	18	A	Ayr U	W	3-0	0-0	3	Weir, Cadette, Drinkell	1878
22	Jan 3	A	St Mirren	L	1-3	1-1	—	Dawson (og)	4897
23	8	A	Hamilton A	D	1-1	0-1	3	Cadette	3135
24	11	H	Morton	W	5-1	4-0	—	May, Shaw 2, Rice, Cadette	2781
25	15	H	Clydebank	D	0-0	0-0	2		3900
26	18	H	Dunfermline Ath	W	2-0	0-0	—	May, Cadette	8018
27	22	A	Morton	D	1-1	1-0	2	Sexton (og)	2087
28	Feb 5	H	Airdrieonians	D	0-0	0-0	2		4484
29	12	A	Brechin C	W	2-0	1-0	2	Cadette 2	1021
30	15	H	Stirling Albion	W	3-1	2-1	—	Shaw, Cadette, McCall	2748
31	Mar 1	H	Clyde	W	2-0	1-0	—	Weir, Shaw	2954
32	5	A	Dumbarton	W	1-0	1-0	1	Cadette	1815
33	12	H	St Mirren	W	4-0	1-0	1	Cadette, Shaw, Ristic 2	4167
34	19	H	Ayr U	W	2-0	1-0	1	Shaw, Oliver	3577
35	26	A	Dunfermline Ath	D	1-1	0-1	1	Shaw	13,357
36	29	H	Morton	W	1-0	1-0	—	May	2657
37	Apr 2	A	Airdrieonians	D	0-0	0-0	2		3720
38	9	H	Brechin C	W	4-2	0-1	1	Rice, Cadette, Oliver, Henderson	2940
39	16	A	Clyde	D	1-1	0-0	2	McCall	3529
40	23	H	Dumbarton	W	4-0	0-0	2	Ristic, Cadette, May 2	3249
41	26	A	St Mirren	W	3-0	2-0	—	Ristic, McGowan, May	2765
42	30	A	Stirling Albion	W	1-0	0-0	2	McGowan	2813
43	May 7	H	Hamilton A	W	3-0	1-0	1	Hughes, May, Shaw	4539
44	14	A	Clydebank	D	1-1	1-1	1	Henderson	6616

Final League Position: 1

Most League Appearances: (post-war): John Markie, 349.
Most League Goals in Season (Individual): 43: Evelyn Morrison, Division I; 1928-29.
Most Goals Overall (Individual): Dougie Moran, 86.

Honours
League Champions: Division II 1935-36, 1969-70, 1974-75. First Division 1990-91, 1993-94. Second Division 1979-80; *Runners-up:* Division I 1907-08, 1909-10. First Division 1985-86. Division II 1904-05, 1951-52, 1960-61.
Scottish Cup Winners: 1913, 1957. *League Cup Runners-up:* 1947-48. *B&Q Cup Winners:* 1993-94.
Club colours: Shirt: Dark blue with white flashings. Shorts: White. Stockings: Red.

Goalscorers: *League* (81): Cadette 18, Shaw 10, Duffy 9, May 9 (1 pen), Drinkell 6, Ristic 4, Hughes 3, Rice 3, Weir 3, Henderson 2, McCall 2, McGowan 2, McLaughlin 2, Oliver 2, Johnston 1, McDonald 1, Sloan 1, Taggart 1, own goals 2. *Scottish Cup* (1): Hughes 1. *League Cup* (6): Cadette 4, Duffy 1, May 1. *B&Q Cup* (15): Cadette 6, McDonald 2, May 2 (1 pen), Sloan 2, Drinkell 1, Duffy 1, Hughes 1.

Parks A 41	Duffy C 23	Johnston F 14 + 1	Weir D 37	Hughes J 28 + 1	Rice B 36 + 1	Sloan S 8 + 4	May E 34 + 4	Cadette R 39	McCall I 32 + 3	Shaw G 18 + 10	Young K — + 1	McQueen T 26	Oliver N 30 + 2	McLaughlin J 38	MacKenzie S 14 + 5	Taggart C 4 + 9	McDonald C 5 + 11	Drinkell K 18 + 2	Burley G 1	Westwater I 3	Hamilton G 7	McLaren C — + 1	Ristic D 12	McGowan J 6 + 3	Henderson N 8 + 2	Gallacher J 2 + 4	Match No.
1	2	3	4	5	*6*	7	8	9	10	11	14																1
1	2	6					7	9	10	11		3	4	*5*	8	14											2
1	6	*2*	5				7	9	10	11		3	4		8	14	12										3
1	6	2	5				7	9	10	11		3	4		8												4
1	6	2	5				7	9	*10*	11		3	4		8	14	12										5
1	6	3	4				7	9	10				2	5	11			8									6
1	*6*		4		14		7	9	10	12			2	5	11	3		*8*									7
1			4		*6*		7	9	10			3	2	5	11	14		8									8
1			4		6		7	9	10			3	2	5	11			8									9
1			4		*6*		7	9	10	12		3	2	5	11	14		8									10
1			4		6	14	7	9	*10*	12		3	2	5	11			8									11
1	10		4		6	14	7	*9*	12			3	2	5		11		8									12
1	11		4	12	6		7	9	10			3	2	5				8									13
1	11		4	6	*10*		7	9				3	2	5			14	8									14
1	11		4	5	6	10	*7*	9				3	*2*		14		12	8									15
1	*2*		4	5	6	11		9	10	14		3			7		12	8									16
1	2		4	6	10	11	7	9		14		3		5			12	*8*									17
1	2		4	6	10	11	7	*9*		14		3		5			12	8									18
1	2		4	6	10	11	7	9				3		5			12	8									19
1	2		4	6	10	*11*	7	9	14			3		5				8									20
1	2		4	6	11	14	*7*	9	*10*			3	12	5				8									21
1	2			6	10	11	12	9				3	4	5		7		8									22
1				4	6	12	*8*	9	10			3		5		7	11	14	2								23
1	2		4	6	10		8	9		*11*		3	12	5		14	7										24
	2		4	6	10		8	9	14	11			3	5		12	*7*			1							25
	2	14	4	6	10		7	9		11			*3*	5	8			12		1							26
		3	2	6	10		7	9		11				5	4		12	8		1							27
1	11	3	4	6				9	10					5	8		*7*				2	14					28
1		3	4	6	*11*			9	10	8				5	12	14	7				2						29
1	8	7	4	6				9	10	11			3	5							2						30
1		*7*	2	4	6		14	9	10	11			3	5									8				31
1			2	4	6		14	9	10	*11*		3		5									7	8			32
1			2	4	6			9	10	11		3	8	*5*	14								7				33
1			2	4	6			9	*10*	11		3	8	5	12								7		14		34
1			2	4	6		14	9	*10*	11		3	8	5									7			12	35
1			2	4	6		9		10	11		3	8	5										14	*7*	12	36
1			2	4	6		9		10	11			3	5										8	7		37
1		3			6		11	9	10	12			4	5							2		7	*8*	14		38
1		3			6		11	9	10	12			4	5							*2*		7		8	14	39
1		3			6		11	9	10				4	5							2		*7*	14	8	12	40
1					6		9		10				4	5		12	14				2		7	3	*8*	11	41
1			2	4	6		9		10	14			3	5									7	12	*8*	11	42
1			2	4	6		9		10	12			3	5			14						*7*	8	11		43
1			2	4	6		11	9	10					5	14								*7*	3	8		44

FORFAR ATHLETIC Division 3

Year Formed: 1885. *Ground & Address:* Station Park, Carseview Road, Forfar. *Telephone:* 0307 463576.
Ground Capacity: total: 8359. seated: 711. *Size of Pitch:* 115yd # 69yd.
Chairman: George Enston. *Secretary:* David McGregor.
Manager: Tommy Campbell. *Assistant Manager:* Brian McLaughlin. *Physio:* Andy Bell. *Coaches:* Stewart Kennedy, Tom McCallum.
Managers since 1975: Jerry Kerr; Archie Knox; Alex Rae; Doug Houston; Henry Hall; Bobby Glennie; Paul Hegarty. *Club Nickname(s):* Loons. *Previous Grounds:* None.
Record Attendance: 10,780 v Rangers, Scottish Cup 2nd rd; 2 Feb, 1970.
Record Transfer Fee received: £57,000 for Craig Brewster to Raith R (July 1991).
Record Transfer Fee paid: £50,000 for Ian McPhee from Airdrieonians (1991).
Record Victory: 14-1 v Lindertis, Scottish Cup 1st rd; 1 Sept 1988.
Record Defeat: 2-12 v King's Park, Division II; 2 Jan, 1930.
Most Capped Player: —.

FORFAR ATHLETIC 1993—94 LEAGUE RECORD

Match No.	Date		Venue	Opponents	Result		H/T Score	Lg. Pos.	Goalscorers	Attendance
1	Aug	7	A	Queen's Park	W	3-0	1-0	—	Petrie 3	445
2		14	H	Albion R	W	3-0	1-0	2	Bingham 3	555
3		21	A	Arbroath	D	1-1	0-0	2	Donaldson	1062
4		28	H	Queen of the S	L	1-2	0-0	4	Donaldson	579
5	Sept	4	H	Meadowbank T	L	0-2	0-0	6		489
6		11	H	Montrose	D	1-1	0-1	6	Bingham	693
7		18	A	East Stirling	W	2-1	0-0	3	Bingham, Downie	347
8		25	H	Berwick R	D	1-1	1-0	6	Downie	498
9	Oct	2	A	East Fife	L	2-3	1-2	8	Downie, Donaldson	662
10		9	H	Alloa	L	0-3	0-1	9		459
11		16	A	Stenhousemuir	L	0-2	0-1	9		380
12		23	H	Stranraer	L	0-1	0-1	10		509
13		30	H	Cowdenbeath	W	3-2	1-1	9	Heddle 2, Winter (pen)	446
14	Nov	6	A	Albion R	W	3-1	2-1	8	Archibald, Bingham, Taylor (og)	270
15		13	H	East Stirling	D	1-1	1-0	8	Bingham	427
16		30	A	Berwick R	W	2-0	0-0	—	Hamill, Kopel	297
17	Dec	4	H	East Fife	W	1-0	0-0	7	McPhee	652
18		7	A	Alloa	D	1-1	0-1	—	Bingham	454
19		18	H	Queen's Park	W	4-0	1-0	5	Winter (pen), Heddle, Kopel, Lees	472
20	Jan	11	H	Arbroath	L	1-4	1-0	—	Mann	801
21		15	A	Queen of the S	L	0-1	0-0	7		740
22		18	A	Cowdenbeath	W	2-1	0-0	—	Smith 2	268
23		22	H	Stenhousemuir	D	1-1	0-0	7	Smith	478
24	Feb	2	A	Stranraer	L	0-2	0-0	—		1010
25		5	A	Montrose	D	1-1	0-0	8	Heddle	609
26		12	A	Meadowbank T	L	2-4	1-1	8	Smith, Kopel	235
27		26	A	East Fife	D	1-1	0-0	8	Mann	653
28	Mar	2	H	Cowdenbeath	W	2-1	0-0	—	Bingham, Downie	321
29		5	H	Arbroath	W	3-2	3-2	8	Bingham, Kopel, Downie	752
30		12	A	Stenhousemuir	W	1-0	0-0	6	Downie	421
31		19	H	Queen of the S	D	4-4	1-1	6	Leddie, McPhee, Winter (pen), Heddle	486
32		26	A	Queen's Park	L	2-3	0-1	8	Heddle 2	489
33	Apr	2	H	Meadowbank T	D	0-0	0-0	8		508
34		9	A	Berwick R	D	2-2	2-0	8	Bingham, Lees	387
35		16	H	East Stirling	L	0-2	0-1	9		421
36		23	A	Albion R	W	3-1	1-0	8	Kopel 2, Smith	312
37		30	H	Stranraer	L	1-3	1-1	9	Smith	488
38	May	7	A	Alloa	W	3-1	0-1	8	Heddle, Bingham 2	483
39		14	H	Montrose	L	0-2	0-1	8		620

Final League Position: 8

Most League Appearances: 376: Alex Brash, 1974-86.
Most League Goals in Season (Individual): 45: Dave Kilgour, Division II; 1929-30.
Most Goals Overall (Individual): 124, John Clark.

Honours
League Champions: Second Division 1983-84. C Division 1948-49.
Scottish Cup: Semi-finals 1982.
League Cup: Semi-finals 1977-78.
Club colours: Shirt: Royal/sky/white geometric patterned. Shorts: White. Stockings: Royal blue.

Goalscorers: *League* (58): Bingham 13, Heddle 8, Downie 6, Kopel 6, Smith 6, Donaldson 3, Petrie 3, Winter 3 (3 pens), Lees 2, McPhee 2, Mann 2, Archibald 1, Hamill 1, Leddie 1, own goal 1. *Scottish Cup* (8): Bingham 3 (1 pen), Downie 2, Heddle 2, Kopel 1. *League Cup* (1): Hamill 1. *B&Q Cup* (2): Bingham 1, Smith 1.

Thomson S 5	Philliben R 34 + 1	McPhee I 35	Hamill A 25 + 2	Mann R 37	McIntyre S 6	Bingham D 38	Mearns G 17 + 1	Petrie S 3	Donaldson G 11	Heddle I 39	Smith R 9 + 13	Winter G 21 + 2	McCafferty A 1 + 3	Morris R 7 + 6	Leddie P 18 + 3	Arthur G 24	Downie I 22 + 11	Sheridan J — + 2	Kopel S 22 + 5	Archibald E 24	Gray B — + 1	Russell N 10	Lees G 16 + 3	Buchan S 5	Match No.
1	2	3	4	5	6	7	8	9	10	11	12														1
1	2	3	4	5	6	7	8	9	10	11	12	14													2
1	2	3	4	5	6	7	8	9	10	11		14													3
1	2	3		5	6	7	8		10	11	9	4	12												4
1	2		3	5		7	8		10	11	14	6	12	4	9										5
	2	3	4		6	7	8		10	11				5		1	9								6
	2	3	4	6		7	8		10	11			14	5		1	9								7
	2	3	4	6		7			10	11			8	5	14	1	9								8
	2	3	4	5	8	7			10	11	12	6			14	1	9								9
	2	6	3	5		11			10	8	9			4		1	7	14							10
	2	3	6	4		7			10	11	12	5				1	9		8						11
	2		3			7				11	9	6		12	8	1	10		4	5	14				12
	2	3	8	4		10				11		6			14	1	9		7	5					13
	2	3	8	4		10				11		6				1	9		7	5					14
	2	3	8	4		10				11	12	6				1	9		7	5					15
	2	3	8	4		10				11	12	6		14			9		7	5		1			16
	2	3	8	4		10				11		6				1	9		7	5					17
	2	3	8	4		10				11		6				1	9		7	5					18
	2	3	8	4		10				11		6		12		1	9		7	5			14		19
	2	3	8	4		10	5			11		6				1	12		7				9		20
	2	3	8	4		10	7			11		6				1	14		12	5			9		21
	2	8	3	4		10				11	12	6		14		1	9			5			7		22
	2	8	3	4						11	10	6		5		1	9	14					7		23
	2	3	8	4		10				11		6			5	1	9		14				7		24
	2		3	4		10	7			8	9	6			5	1	14		12				11		25
	2		3	4		10				8	9	6			7	1			12	5			11		26
	2	7		4		10				8	9				6		12		14	5		1	11	3	27
		8		4		10	2			11					6		14		7	5		1	9	3	28
		8	14	4		10	2			11	12				6		9		7	5		1		3	29
		8	12	4		10	2			11		3			6		9		7	5		1			30
		8		4		10				11	14	3			6		9		7	5		1	12	2	31
	2	8		4		10				11	14				6		9		7	5		1	12	3	32
	14	8		4		10	2			11				3	6		12		7	5		1	9		33
	3	8		4		10	2			11				12	6		14		7	5		1	9		34
	2	3		4		10	12			11	14				6		9		7	5		1	8		35
	2	3		4		10				11	9				6	1	12		7	5			8		36
	2	3		4		10				11	9				6	1	12		7	5			8		37
	2	3		4		10	8			11				12	6	1	14		7	5			9		38
	2	3		4		10	8			11	12				6	1	14		7	5			9		39

HAMILTON ACADEMICAL Division 1

Year Formed: 1874. *Ground & Address:* Douglas Park Lane, Hamilton ML3 0DF. *Telephone:* 0698 286103. *Fax:* 0698 285422.
Ground Capacity: total: 5140. seated: 642. *Size of Pitch:* 112yd # 73yd.
Chairman: James Watson. *Secretary:* Scott A. Struthers BA. *Commercial Manager:* George Miller.
Manager: Iain Munro. *Physio:* David Henderson: *Coach:* Crawford Baptie.
Managers since 1975: J. Eric Smith; Dave McParland; John Blackley; Bertie Auld; John Lambie; Jim Dempsey; John Lambie; Billy McLaren. *Club Nickname(s):* The Accies. *Previous Grounds:* Bent Farm, South Avenue, South Haugh.
Record Attendance: 28,690 v Hearts, Scottish Cup 3rd rd; 3 Mar, 1937.
Record Transfer Fee received: £225,000 for James Weir to Hearts (Aug 1993).
Record Transfer Fee paid: £60,000 for Paul Martin from Kilmarnock (Oct 1988) and for John McQuade from Dumbarton (Aug 1993).
Record Victory: 11-1 v Chryston, Lanarkshire Cup; 28 Nov, 1885.
Record Defeat: 1-11 v Hibernian, Division I; 6 Nov, 1965.
Most Capped Player: Colin Miller, 29 (40), Canada, 1988-93.

HAMILTON ACADEMICAL 1993—94 LEAGUE RECORD

Match No.	Date	Venue	Opponents	Result		H/T Score	Lg. Pos.	Goalscorers	Attendance
1	Aug 7	A	Brechin C	W	2-1	1-0	—	Chalmers, Ward	576
2	14	H	St Mirren	D	0-0	0-0	4		2599
3	21	A	Airdrieonians	L	0-4	0-0	5		2416
4	28	H	Falkirk	D	1-1	0-0	7	McLean	3291
5	Sept 4	A	Dumbarton	D	0-0	0-0	7		1044
6	11	A	Clyde	L	0-2	0-1	7		1236
7	15	H	Clydebank	L	2-3	1-1	—	Napier, McLean	1422
8	18	H	Ayr U	W	2-1	1-0	7	McLean, Clark G (pen)	1529
9	25	A	Stirling Albion	L	1-3	1-1	8	Ward	1001
10	29	H	Dunfermline Ath	L	0-2	0-0	—		1762
11	Oct 2	A	Morton	W	2-1	0-1	10	Clark G, Ward	1517
12	9	H	Brechin C	W	5-0	3-0	7	Campbell, Ward, Fitzpatrick, Clark G (pen), Duffield	1020
13	16	A	Clydebank	D	2-2	2-1	6	Ward, Duffield	819
14	23	H	Clyde	W	2-0	0-0	5	Duffield, Clark G	1917
15	30	H	Airdrieonians	W	3-2	1-0	5	Ward, Clark G 2 (1 pen)	2459
16	Nov 6	A	Falkirk	D	3-3	1-0	5	Duffield, Campbell, Napier	3686
17	10	H	Dumbarton	W	2-0	0-0	—	Duffield 2	1182
18	13	H	Morton	W	4-1	3-0	5	Duffield 2, Campbell 2	1696
19	30	A	St Mirren	L	0-1	0-1	—		2029
20	Dec 4	A	Ayr U	D	1-1	0-0	6	Campbell	1508
21	7	A	Dunfermline Ath	L	0-4	0-2	—		3237
22	18	H	Clydebank	W	1-0	1-0	5	Harris (og)	1202
23	Jan 8	H	Falkirk	D	1-1	1-0	5	Chalmers	3135
24	11	A	Brechin C	D	0-0	0-0	—		383
25	15	A	Dumbarton	W	1-0	0-0	5	Clark G	744
26	18	A	Airdrieonians	W	1-0	1-0	—	Duffield	1771
27	22	H	St Mirren	D	0-0	0-0	4		2469
28	Feb 2	H	Stirling Albion	L	0-1	0-1	—		1178
29	5	A	Clyde	W	2-0	1-0	4	Campbell, Duffield	5356
30	12	A	Morton	D	2-2	1-1	5	Baptie, McGill	1447
31	Mar 2	H	Dunfermline Ath	D	1-1	0-0	—	McGill	1197
32	5	H	Ayr U	W	2-1	2-0	4	Duffield, McGill	1514
33	12	A	Stirling Albion	D	1-1	0-1	4	Duffield (pen)	829
34	19	A	Clydebank	L	2-3	1-0	4	McLean, Sherry	824
35	26	H	Brechin C	W	9-1	3-0	4	Clark G, Ward, Baptie, McLean, McIntosh, Duffield 4 (1 pen)	1007
36	29	A	St Mirren	W	2-0	1-0	—	Chalmers, Clark G	1478
37	Apr 2	H	Clyde	W	2-1	0-1	4	McLean, Duffield	1374
38	13	H	Morton	W	3-2	0-0	—	Ward, Chalmers, McLean	1114
39	16	A	Dunfermline Ath	L	1-2	1-1	4	McIntosh	4927
40	23	A	Ayr U	L	0-1	0-0	4		1684
41	27	H	Stirling Albion	L	0-1	0-1	—		976
42	30	H	Airdrieonians	W	1-0	1-0	4	Chalmers	1612
43	May 7	A	Falkirk	L	0-3	0-1	5		4539
44	14	H	Dumbarton	W	2-1	0-1	4	Duffield 2	1451

Final League Position: 4

Most League Appearances: 447: Rikki Ferguson, 1974-88.
Most League Goals in Season (Individual): 34: David Wilson, Division I; 1936-37.
Most Goals Overall (Individual): 246: David Wilson, 1928-39.

Honours
League Champions: First Division 1985-86, 1987-88. Division II 1903-04; *Runners-up:* Division II 1952-53, 1964-65.
Scottish Cup Runners-up: 1911, 1935. *League Cup:* Semi-finalists three times.
B&Q Cup Winners: 1991-92 and 1992-93.
Club colours: Shirt: Red and white hoops. Shorts: White. Stockings: White.

Goalscorers: *League* (66): Duffield 19 (2 pens), Clark G 9 (3 pens), Ward 8, McLean 7, Campbell 6, Chalmers 5, McGill 3, Baptie 2, McIntosh 2, Napier 2, Fitzpatrick 1, Sherry 1, own goal 1. *Scottish Cup* (0): *League Cup* (0): *B&Q Cup* (1) Baptie 1.

Ferguson A 40	McKenzie P 33 + 3	Napier C 27	Reid W 30	Weir J 2	McInulty S 31 + 3	Clark G 29 + 3	Baptie C 33 + 3	Chalmers P 14 + 6	Ward K 24 + 6	Lorimer D 9 + 9	Hillcoat C 1	McEntegart S 27 + 2	Miller C 31	Moyes D 5	McLean C 9 + 9	Walsh D — + 1	McQuade J 21 + 10	McGill D 13 + 3	Fitzpatrick P 17 + 1	Duffield P 33 + 3	Campbell D 21 + 1	McIntosh M 13	Clark P 6 + 4	Sherry J 5	Powell L 2 + 3	Cormack D 4	Nicholls D 4	*Match No.*
1	2	3	4	5	6	7	8	9	10	11																		1
1	2	3	8	5	6	7			10	11	4	9																2
1	2	3	8		6	7		9	*10*	11			4	5	12	14												3
1	2	3	8		6	7		9		11		10	4	5	12													4
1	2	*3*	8		6	10		9		14		12	4	5			7	11										5
1		2	8		6	10	*9*			11			3	5	14		7		4									6
1	2	11	8		6	*10*	9		12				3	5	14		7		4									7
1	2	11	8			10	5		6	12			3		9		7		4									8
1	14	2	8			*10*	5		6				3		12		7		4	9	11							9
1	2	11	8			12	5		6				3				*7*		4	9	10							10
1		2	6		14	10	5		12	11			3				*7*		4	9	8							11
1		2	8		6	10	5		11				3		14		12		4	*9*	*7*							12
1	5	2	8		6	10			*11*				3		14		12		4	9	7							13
1	5	2	8		6	10	*7*		11			14	3				12		4	9								14
1	5	2	8		6	10	7		11				3				14		4	*9*								15
1	5	2	8							7		10	3		12		6		4	9	11							16
1	5	2	8		14				12	7		10	3				*6*		4	9	11							17
1	5	2	8		3		14		11	12		10					6		*4*	9	7							18
1	5	2	8					12	11	14		10	3				*6*		4	9	7							19
1	5	2	8			14	12		11			10	3				*6*		4	9	7							20
1	5	2	8			14	12		*11*			10	3				6		4	9	7							21
1		2	8		6	10	5	14		12			3				7		4	9	*11*							22
1		2	8		6	10	5	11					3				4		12	9	7							23
1		2	8		6	10	5	11					3				4	12		9	7							24
1		2	8		6	10	5					4	3		14		*7*	11		9	12							25
1	14	2	8		6	10	5					4	3				12	11		9	*7*							26
1		2	8		6	10	5					4	3				12	11		9	7							27
1	14		8		3	10	5					4	2				*7*	9		12	11	6						28
1	2		8			10	5		11			4	3				12	*9*		14	7	6						29
1	2		8				5		11			4	3				12	9		14	*7*	6	10					30
1	2				11		5	12	*7*			8	3				14	9		10		6	4					31
1	2				14		5	12	*7*			8	3					9		10	11	6	4					32
1	2						5	14	12	*11*		8	3				7	9		10		6	4					33
1	2				11		5	9		14			3		8			12		*10*		6	4	7				34
1	2				3	*11*	5	9	7	14		4			8					10		6	12					35
1	2				3	11	5	9	7			4			8					10		6	12					36
1	2				3	11	5	9	7			4			8					10		6	12					37
1	2				3	11	5	9	7			4			8					10		6			12			38
1	2				3		5					4			8		14	*9*		10		6	11	7	12			39
1	2				3		5	9	12	14		4					*8*	11		10		6			7			40
	2				3	11	5		12	14		4			*9*					10				8	7	1	6	41
	2				3	11	5	9				4			8					10				7		1	6	42
	2				3	*11*	5	9	8			4						14		10				7	12	1	6	43
	2				3		5	12	*11*			4					7	8		10	9		14			1	6	44

HEART OF MIDLOTHIAN Premier Division

Year Formed: 1874. *Ground & Address:* Tynecastle Park, Gorgie Rd, Edinburgh EH11 2NL. *Telephone:* 031 337 6132.
Ground Capacity: variable due to reconstruction. *Size of Pitch:* 110yd # 74yd.
Chairman: A. Wallace Mercer. *Secretary:* L. W. Porteous. *Commercial Manager:* Charles Burnett.
Manager: Tommy McLean. *Assistant Manager:* Hugh McCann.
Physio: Alan Rae. *Coach:* Walter Kidd.
Managers since 1975: J. Hagart; W. Ormond; R. Moncur; T. Ford; A. MacDonald; A. MacDonald & W. Jardine; A. MacDonald; J. Jordan, S. Clark.
Club Nickname(s): Hearts. *Previous Grounds:* The Meadows 1874, Powderhall 1878, Old Tynecastle 1881, (Tynecastle Park, 1886).
Record Attendance: 53,396 v Rangers, Scottish Cup 3rd rd; 13 Feb, 1932.
Record Transfer Fee received: £1,300,000 for Dave McPherson from Rangers (July 1992).
Record of Transfer paid: £750,000 for Derek Ferguson to Rangers (July 1990).
Record Victory: 21-0 v Anchor, EFA Cup 1880.
Record Defeat: 1-8 v Vale of Leithen, Scottish Cup, 1888.
Most Capped Player: Bobby Walker, 29, Scotland.
Most League Appearances: 458: Henry Smith, 1981-94.

HEART OF MIDLOTHIAN 1993—94 LEAGUE RECORD

Match No.	Date	Venue	Opponents	Result		H/T Score	Lg. Pos.	Goalscorers	Attendance
1	Aug 7	A	Rangers	L	1-2	0-1	—	Ferguson	42,320
2	14	H	Raith R	W	1-0	0-0	6	Robertson	8587
3	21	H	Hibernian	W	1-0	0-0	4	Johnston A	17,283
4	28	A	Dundee U	D	0-0	0-0	5		8502
5	Sept 4	H	Partick T	W	2-1	2-0	2	Levein, Fashanu	7273
6	11	A	Motherwell	L	0-2	0-0	7		7662
7	18	H	Kilmarnock	L	0-1	0-1	8		8309
8	25	H	Celtic	W	1-0	0-0	7	Robertson	14,761
9	Oct 2	A	Dundee	L	0-2	0-1	8		4386
10	5	A	Aberdeen	D	0-0	0-0	—		13,798
11	9	H	St Johnstone	D	1-1	0-0	9	Robertson	6028
12	16	A	Raith R	L	0-1	0-1	10		5278
13	23	A	Partick T	D	0-0	0-0	9		7170
14	30	A	Hibernian	W	2-0	1-0	7	Robertson 2	18,505
15	Nov 3	H	Rangers	D	2-2	0-2	—	Mackay, Colquhoun	18,370
16	6	H	Dundee U	D	1-1	1-0	6	Johnston M	8362
17	13	H	Dundee	L	1-2	1-1	9	Pittman (og)	7681
18	20	A	Celtic	D	0-0	0-0	7		25,990
19	30	A	Kilmarnock	D	0-0	0-0	—		6948
20	Dec 4	H	Aberdeen	D	1-1	1-0	9	Colquhoun	9402
21	11	A	St Johnstone	L	0-2	0-2	9		4631
22	15	H	Motherwell	L	2-3	1-1	—	Johnston M, Leitch	5531
23	18	H	Raith R	L	0-1	0-1	9		6227
24	27	A	Rangers	D	2-2	1-1	—	Millar, Robertson	45,116
25	Jan 8	A	Dundee U	L	0-3	0-2	9		8583
26	12	H	Hibernian	D	1-1	0-0	—	Millar	24,139
27	15	H	Partick T	W	1-0	1-0	9	Millar	7619
28	22	H	Kilmarnock	D	1-1	1-1	9	Robertson	9204
29	Feb 5	A	Motherwell	D	1-1	1-1	9	Robertson	7009
30	12	H	Celtic	L	0-2	0-1	10		14,049
31	Mar 1	A	Dundee	W	2-0	1-0	—	Johnston M 2 (1 pen)	3965
32	5	A	Aberdeen	W	1-0	1-0	8	Leitch	13,059
33	19	A	Raith R	D	2-2	1-1	7	Colquhoun, Levein	5697
34	26	H	Rangers	L	1-2	0-1	8	Foster	18,108
35	30	H	Motherwell	D	0-0	0-0	—		7879
36	Apr 2	A	Kilmarnock	W	1-0	1-0	7	Millar	8022
37	6	H	St Johnstone	D	2-2	2-2	—	McGowne (og), Robertson	8938
38	9	A	Celtic	D	2-2	0-2	7	Colquhoun, Frail	18,761
39	16	H	Dundee	L	0-2	0-0	7		7028
40	23	A	St Johnstone	D	0-0	0-0	7		6762
41	27	H	Aberdeen	D	1-1	0-1	—	Robertson (pen)	13,811
42	30	A	Hibernian	D	0-0	0-0	8		14,213
43	May 7	H	Dundee U	W	2-0	1-0	7	Frail, Levein	13,627
44	14	A	Partick T	W	1-0	0-0	7	McLaren	9391

Final League Position: 7

Most League Goals in Season (Individual): 44: Barney Battles.
Most Goals Overall (Individual): 206: Jimmy Wardhaugh, 1946-59.

Honours

League Champions: Division I 1894-95, 1896-97, 1957-58, 1959-60. First Division 1979-80; *Runners-up:* Division I 1893-94, 1898-99, 1903-04, 1905-06, 1914-15, 1937-38, 1953-54, 1956-57, 1958-59, 1964-65. Premier Division 1985-86, 1987-88, 1991-92. First Division 1977-78, 1982-83.
Scottish Cup Winners: 1891, 1896, 1901, 1906, 1956; *Runners-up:* 1903, 1907, 1968, 1976, 1986.
League Cup Winners: 1954-55, 1958-59, 1959-60, 1962-63; *Runners-up:* 1961-62.
European: *European Cup* 4 matches (1958-59, 1960-61). *Cup Winners Cup:* 4 matches (1976-77). *UEFA Cup:* 34 matches (*Fairs Cup:* 1961-62, 1963-64, 1965-66. *UEFA Cup:* 1984-85, 1986-87, 1988-89, 1990-91, 1992-93, 1993-94).
Club colours: Shirt: Maroon. Shorts: White. Stockings: Maroon with white tops.

Goalscorers: *League* (37): Robertson 10 (1 pen), Colquhoun 4, Johnston M 4 (1 pen), Millar 4, Levein 3, Frail 2, Leitch 2, Fashanu 1, Ferguson 1, Foster 1, Johnston A 1, Mackay 1, McLaren 1, own goals 2. *Scottish Cup* (3): Foster 1, Johnston M 1, Robertson 1. *League Cup* (2): Robertson 2.

Smith H 27	Locke G 29 + 4	McKinlay T 43	Levein C 30	Berry N 30	Van De Ven P 2	Colquhoun J 38 + 3	Mackay G 34 + 2	Fashanu J 10 + 1	Wright G 10 + 2	Robertson J 32 + 4	Ferguson I 3 + 3	Johnston A 5 + 23	Thomas K 7 + 5	Weir J 25 + 1	Hogg G 16 + 1	Leitch S 24 + 4	McLaren A 37	Walker N 17	Harrison T 1	Johnston M 31	Millar J 16 + 4	Foster W 8 + 9	Frail S 9	*Match No.*
1	2	3	4	5	6	7	8	9	10	*11*	12	14												1
1	2	3	4	5	6	7	8	*9*	10	11		12	14											2
1	2	3	4	5		7	8	9	10	*11*		12	14	6										3
1	*2*	3	4			7	8	9	10			12	11	6	5	14								4
1	2	3	4	6		*7*	8	9	10			12	11		5	14								5
1	2	3	4	5		*7*	8		10	11		12	9			14	6							6
1	2	3	4			*7*	8			11		9	14	5	12	10	6							7
1	2	3	4			7	8	*9*		11	14			12	5	10	6							8
	2	3		4		*7*		9		11	12	14		8	5	10	6	1						9
	2	3		6		12	8	9			11			7	5	10	4	1						10
	2	3		6			8	*9*		11	7	14			5	10	4	1						11
	2	3				12	8	9		*11*	7	14		6	5		4	1	10					12
		3	4			9	7					11		6	5	8	2	1		10				13
	8	3	4			9				*11*		14		2	5	7	6	1		10				14
	7		*4*			9	14		3	11		12		2	5	8	6	1		10				15
	2	3				9	8		4	11		12			5	7	6	1		10				16
	2	3				9	8		4	*11*		12	14		5	7	6	1		10				17
	8	3		6		9						11		2	5	*7*	4	1		10	14			18
	8	3				7	11			9		12	14	2	5	6	4	1		*10*				19
		3		5		*7*	8			11		14	9	2		6	4	1		10				20
	14	*3*		5		7	8	12		11			9	2		6	4	1		10				21
	10	3		5		7	11						9	2		6	4	1		8	14	12		22
	11	3		5		7	8					12	*9*	2		6	4	1		10		14		23
	6	3		2		9			14	12		*7*		5			4	1		8	10	11		24
	6	3		2		9	12			14		*7*		5		8	4	1			10	11		25
1	*2*	3	4	5		12	8			11						7	6			10	14	9		26
1	14	3	4	5		7	8			11						*9*	2			10	6			27
1	2	3	4	5		7	8			11		14				*9*	6			10		12		28
1	2	3	4	5			8		12	11						7	6			10		9		29
1	*2*	3	4				8			11		14		5		7	6			10		9		30
1		3	4	5		7	*8*							2		14	6			10	11	9		31
1	14	3	4	5		7				12				2		8	6			10	11	*9*		32
1	14	*3*	4			7				12				2	5	8	6			10	11	9		33
1	8	3	4			7				9		12		*2*	5		6			10	11	14		34
1		3	4	5		7	8		*2*	9		14					6			10	11	12		35
1		3	4	5		7	8			9							6			10	11	12	2	36
1		3	4	5		7	8			9		14					*6*			10	11		2	37
1		3	4	5		*7*	*8*			9		14					6			10	11	12	2	38
1		3	4	5		*7*	8			9		12		6						10	*11*	14	2	39
1		3	4	5		7	8			9				6						10	11		2	40
1		3	4	5		7	8			9							6			10	11		2	41
1		3	4	5		7	8			9							6			10	11		2	42
1	8	3	4	5		7				9							6			10	11	12	2	43
1	11	3	4			7	8			9				*5*			6			10	14		2	44

HIBERNIAN — Premier Division

Year Formed: 1875. *Ground & Address:* Easter Road Stadium, Albion Rd, Edinburgh EH7 5QG. *Telephone:* 031 661 2159. *Fax:* 031 659 6488.
Ground Capacity: total: 21,889. seated: 6299. *Size of Pitch:* 112yd # 74yd.
Chairman: Douglas Cromb. *Secretary:* Cecil F. Graham, FIFA, MInst CM. *Commercial Manager:* Ian Erskine.
Manager: Alex Miller. *Assistant Manager:* Andy Watson.
Physio: Stewart Collie. *Coach:* Eamonn Bannon.
Managers since 1975: Eddie Turnbull; Willie Ormond; Bertie Auld; Pat Stanton; John Blackley. *Club Nickname(s):* Hibees.
Previous Grounds: Meadows 1875-78, Powderhall 1878-79, Mayfield 1879-80, First Easter Road 1880-92, Second Easter Road 1892-.
Record Attendance: 65,860 v Hearts, Division I; 2 Jan, 1950.
Record Transfer Fee received: £1,000,000 for Andy Goram to Rangers (June 1991).
Record Transfer Fee paid: £450,000 for Keith Wright from Dundee.
Record Victory: 22-1 v 42nd Highlanders; 3 Sept, 1881.
Record Defeat: 0-10 v Rangers; 24 Dec, 1898.
Most Capped Player: Lawrie Reilly, 38, Scotland.
Most League Appearances: 446: Arthur Duncan.

HIBERNIAN 1993—94 LEAGUE RECORD

Match No.	Date	Venue	Opponents	Result		H/T Score	Lg. Pos.	Goalscorers	Attendance
1	Aug 7	H	Partick T	D	0-0	0-0	—		7452
2	14	A	Celtic	D	1-1	0-1	7	Tweed	27,690
3	21	A	Hearts	L	0-1	0-0	10		17,283
4	28	H	Dundee	W	2-0	1-0	7	Beaumont, McAllister	5915
5	Sept 4	A	Kilmarnock	D	1-1	1-0	7	Evans	7727
6	11	H	Aberdeen	W	2-1	2-0	4	McAllister, Wright	8506
7	18	A	St Johnstone	W	3-1	2-0	1	O'Neill, McAllister, Wright	5008
8	25	A	Rangers	L	1-2	1-1	5	Evans	43,200
9	Oct 2	H	Dundee U	W	2-0	1-0	2	Jackson D 2	7556
10	5	H	Raith R	W	3-2	1-1	—	Jackson D, O'Neill, McAllister	9197
11	9	A	Motherwell	W	2-0	1-0	1	Jackson D, Wright	9090
12	16	H	Celtic	D	1-1	0-0	1	Evans	14,991
13	30	H	Hearts	L	0-2	0-1	2		18,505
14	Nov 2	A	Partick T	D	0-0	0-0	—		3815
15	6	A	Dundee	L	2-3	1-2	3	Duffy (og), Wright	4535
16	9	H	Kilmarnock	W	2-1	0-1	—	Tweed, Hunter	6451
17	13	A	Dundee U	D	2-2	0-2	4	Jackson D, Hamilton	6880
18	20	H	Rangers	L	0-1	0-1	4		16,506
19	27	A	Aberdeen	L	0-4	0-1	5		12,334
20	30	H	St Johnstone	D	0-0	0-0	—		4996
21	Dec 4	A	Raith R	W	2-1	2-1	5	Wright, Findlay	4407
22	11	H	Motherwell	W	3-2	0-0	5	Wright, Findlay, Mitchell	7429
23	18	A	Celtic	L	0-1	0-0	5		16,808
24	27	H	Partick T	W	5-1	1-0	—	Hamilton, Farrell, Jackson D, McAllister, Wright	10,165
25	Jan 8	H	Dundee	W	2-0	2-0	4	McAllister, Tortolano	7416
26	12	A	Hearts	D	1-1	0-0	—	Wright	24,139
27	15	A	Kilmarnock	W	3-0	0-0	3	Farrell, Beaumont, Evans	7357
28	22	A	St Johnstone	D	2-2	0-1	3	O'Neill (pen), Jackson D	6466
29	Feb 5	H	Aberdeen	W	3-1	0-1	4	Wright 2, Lennon	9556
30	12	A	Rangers	L	0-2	0-1	4		43,265
31	26	H	Dundee U	L	0-1	0-0	4		7015
32	Mar 5	H	Raith R	W	3-0	3-0	4	Findlay, Wright 2	6042
33	12	A	Motherwell	D	0-0	0-0	4		7126
34	19	H	Celtic	D	0-0	0-0	4		14,639
35	26	A	Partick T	L	0-1	0-0	4		4632
36	29	A	Aberdeen	W	3-2	1-1	—	Wright 2, Tweed	10,832
37	Apr 2	H	St Johnstone	D	0-0	0-0	4		6628
38	16	A	Dundee U	L	0-3	0-3	5		6603
39	23	H	Motherwell	L	0-2	0-1	5		6137
40	26	A	Raith R	D	1-1	1-0	—	Wright	3040
41	30	H	Hearts	D	0-0	0-0	5		14,213
42	May 3	H	Rangers	W	1-0	1-0	—	Wright	14,517
43	7	A	Dundee	L	0-4	0-1	5		2731
44	14	H	Kilmarnock	D	0-0	0-0	5		9971

Final League Position: 5

Most League Goals in Season (Individual): 42: Joe Baker.
Most Goals Overall (Individual): 364: Gordon Smith.

Honours

League Champions: Division I 1902-03, 1947-48, 1950-51, 1951-52. First Division 1980-81. Division II 1893-94, 1894-95, 1932-33; *Runners-up:* Division I 1896-97, 1946-47, 1949-50, 1952-53, 1973-74.
Scottish Cup Winners: 1887, 1902; *Runners-up:* 1896, 1914, 1923, 1924, 1947, 1958, 1972, 1979.
League Cup Winners: 1972-73, 1991-92; *Runners-up:* 1950-51, 1968-69, 1974-75, 1993-94.
European: *European Cup:* 6 matches (1955-56 semi-finals). *Cup Winners Cup:* 6 matches (1972-73). *UEFA Cup:* 56 matches (*Fairs Cup:* 1960-61 semi-finals, 1961-62, 1962-63, 1965-66, 1967-68, 1968-69, 1970-71. *UEFA Cup:* 1973-74, 1974-75, 1975-76, 1976-77, 1978-79, 1992-93).
Club colours: Shirt: Green with white sleeves. Shorts: White. Stockings: Green with white trim.

Goalscorers: *League* (53): Wright 16, Jackson D 7, McAllister 6, Evans 4, Findlay 3, O'Neill 3 (1 pen), Tweed 3, Beaumont 2, Farrell 2, Hamilton 2, Hunter 1, Lennon 1, Mitchell 1, Tortolano 1, own goal 1. *Scottish Cup* (3): McAllister 1, O'Neill 1, Wright 1. *League Cup* (8): McAllister 2, Wright 2, Donald 1, Hunter 1, Jackson D 1, own goal 1.

Leighton J 44	Miller W 37	Tortolano J 12 + 6	McIntyre T 11	Tweed S 27 + 2	Hunter G 29	McAllister K 36	Hamilton B 40 + 2	Wright K 41 + 1	Jackson D 29 + 11	Findlay W 15 + 5	Lennon D 3 + 2	McGraw M — + 2	Beaumont D 24 + 2	Donald G 2 + 4	Farrell D 26 + 9	O'Neill M 36	Evans G 23 + 17	Mitchell G 36	Harper K 1 + 1	Jackson C 8 + 3	Love G 3 + 1	Bannon E 1	Miller G — + 1	Match No.
1	2	3	4	5	6	7	8	9	*10*	11	12	14												1
1	2		4	5	6	7	8	9	10	14			3	*11*	12									2
1	2		4		6	7	8	9	10		14		3		5	*11*	12							3
1	2		4		6	7	14	9	12	8			3		5	*11*	10							4
1	2		4	3	6	7	5	12	10	*8*					14	11	9							5
1	2			5	6	7	14	9	10	*8*					4	11	12	3						6
1	2			5	6	*7*		9	12	8					4	11	10	3	14					7
1	2			5	6	7	4	9	10						14	*11*	8	3						8
1	2	14		5		7	8	9	*10*				6		4	11	12	3						9
1	2			5		7	8	9	10				6		4	11	12	3						10
1	2			5		7	8	9	10				6		4	11	12	3						11
1	2	14			6	*7*	8	9					5		4	11	10	3						12
1	2			5	6	7	8	9	10						4	11	12	3						13
1	2	12		5	6	7	8	9	14							*11*	10	3		4				14
1	2			5	6	7	8	9	10								12	3	11	4				15
1	2			5	6	*7*	8	9	10						14	11	12	3		4				16
1	2	14		5	6		8	9	10					7	12	11		3		*4*				17
1	2	3		5	6		8	*9*	10			14			4	11	7							18
1	2	7		5	6		8		10					12	4	11	9	3						19
1	2	12		5	6		*8*	9	10	14						11	7	3		4				20
1	2	7		5	6		8	9	*10*	4						11	14	3		12				21
1	2	7		5	6		8	9	10	*4*					14	11	12	3						22
1	2	11			*6*	7	8	9	10	4			5		14		12	3						23
1	2	11		14	*6*	7	8	9	10				5		4		12	3						24
1	2	11		5		7	*8*	9	10	14			6		4		12	3						25
1	2	11			6	7	8	9	12				5			4	10	3						26
1	2	14			*6*	7	8	9					5		4	11	10	3						27
1	2	11				7	8	9	12				5		4	6	10	3						28
1	2			6		7		9			8		5		4	11	10	3						29
1	*2*			5	6	7	8				9		14	12	4	11	10	3						30
1				5		7	8	9	10		6		2		4	11	12	3						31
1			2	5		7	8	9	12	4			6			*11*	10	3			14			32
1				*5*	6	7	8	9	12	4			2		14	11	10	3						33
1					6	7	8	9	12	4			5		2	11	10	3						34
1				14	6	7	8	9	10	4			5	12	*2*	11		3						35
1				5	6	7	8	9	12						2	11	10	3		4				36
1				*5*		7	8	9	12	14			4		2	11	10	3		6				37
1	*2*	3			6	7	8	9	12				5		4	11	10			14				38
1	2	3				7	8	9	10				5		4	11	12					6		39
1	2		5				8	9	*10*	*7*					4	11	12	3		14	6			40
1	2		5				8	9	10	*7*					4	11	12	3			6			41
1	2		5			7	8	9	10	12			4			6	11	3						42
1	2		5			7	8	9	10	6			4	14	12		*11*	3						43
1	2		5			*7*	8	9	10				12				11	3		4	6		14	44

KILMARNOCK Premier Division

Year Formed: 1869. *Ground & Address:* Rugby Park, Kilmarnock KA1 2DP. *Telephone:* 0563 25184.
Ground Capacity: total: 20,230. seated: 4400. *Size of Pitch:* 115yd # 75yd.
Chairman: Robert Fleeting. *Secretary:* Kevin Collins. *Commercial Manager:* Denny Martin. *Stadium Manager:* G. Hollas.
Manager: Tommy Burns. *Assistant Manager:* Billy Stark. *Physio:* Hugh Allan.
Managers since 1975: W. Fernie; D. Sneddon; J. Clunie; E. Morrison; J. Fleeting. *Club Nickname(s):* Killie. *Previous Grounds:* Rugby Park (Dundonald Road); The Grange; Holm Quarry; Present ground since 1899.
Record Attendance: 35,995 v Rangers, Scottish Cup; 10 March, 1962.
Record Transfer Fee received: £120,000 for Davie Provan to Celtic (1978).
Record Transfer Fee paid: £100,000 for Bobby Williamson from Rotherham United (Nov 1990).
Record Victory: 11-1 v Paisley Academical, Scottish Cup; 18 Jan, 1930 (15-0 v Lanemark, Ayrshire Cup; 15 Nov, 1890).
Record Defeat: 1-9 v Celtic, Division I; 13 Aug, 1938.
Most Capped Player: Joe Nibloe, 11, Scotland.
Most League Appearances: 481: Alan Robertson, 1972-88.

KILMARNOCK 1993—94 LEAGUE RECORD

Match No.	Date	Venue	Opponents	Result		H/T Score	Lg. Pos.	Goalscorers	Attendance
1	Aug 7	H	Dundee	W	1-0	0-0	—	Brown	8162
2	14	A	Aberdeen	L	0-1	0-0	7		13,535
3	21	H	Motherwell	L	0-1	0-0	10		7555
4	28	A	Rangers	W	2-1	0-0	8	Roberts, Williamson	43,804
5	Sept 4	H	Hibernian	D	1-1	0-1	8	McCluskey	7727
6	11	H	St Johnstone	D	0-0	0-0	9		5670
7	18	A	Hearts	W	1-0	1-0	6	Skilling	8309
8	25	H	Partick T	W	3-1	1-0	3	Black (pen), McCluskey, Williamson	7411
9	Oct 2	A	Celtic	D	0-0	0-0	4		23,396
10	5	H	Dundee U	D	1-1	0-0	—	Roberts	7034
11	9	A	Raith R	D	2-2	0-2	3	Williamson, Mitchell	4482
12	16	H	Aberdeen	D	1-1	0-0	5	Mitchell	9108
13	23	A	Dundee	L	0-1	0-1	5		4389
14	30	A	Motherwell	D	2-2	1-0	4	Mitchell, Porteous	7384
15	Nov 6	H	Rangers	L	0-2	0-0	7		19,157
16	9	A	Hibernian	L	1-2	1-0	—	Brown	6451
17	13	H	Celtic	D	2-2	1-1	8	Williamson, Skilling	16,649
18	20	A	Partick T	W	1-0	0-0	6	Crainie	5876
19	27	A	St Johnstone	W	1-0	1-0	6	Williamson	4576
20	30	H	Hearts	D	0-0	0-0	—		6948
21	Dec 4	A	Dundee U	D	0-0	0-0	6		7100
22	11	H	Raith R	W	1-0	1-0	6	Brown	6012
23	18	A	Aberdeen	L	1-3	0-1	7	Skilling	10,834
24	Jan 1	H	Motherwell	D	0-0	0-0	6		10,511
25	4	H	Dundee	W	1-0	0-0	—	McSkimming	7406
26	8	A	Rangers	L	0-3	0-0	6		44,919
27	15	H	Hibernian	L	0-3	0-0	7		7357
28	22	A	Hearts	D	1-1	1-1	7	MacPherson	9204
29	Feb 5	H	St Johnstone	D	0-0	0-0	7		6345
30	12	H	Partick T	L	1-2	1-0	7	Mitchell	7511
31	Mar 1	A	Celtic	L	0-1	0-0	—		9887
32	5	H	Dundee U	D	1-1	0-1	7	Brown	7403
33	15	A	Raith R	L	2-3	0-2	—	McSkimming, Mitchell	3585
34	19	H	Aberdeen	L	2-3	0-1	8	Black, McCloy	8544
35	26	A	Dundee	L	0-3	0-3	9		2758
36	30	A	St Johnstone	W	1-0	1-0	—	MacPherson	5513
37	Apr 2	H	Hearts	L	0-1	0-1	9		8022
38	16	H	Celtic	W	2-0	0-0	10	Black (pen), Brown	11,499
39	19	A	Partick T	L	0-1	0-0	—		6981
40	23	H	Raith R	D	0-0	0-0	10		7426
41	26	A	Dundee U	W	3-1	1-0	—	Williamson 2, McSkimming	8801
42	30	A	Motherwell	L	0-1	0-0	10		8185
43	May 7	H	Rangers	W	1-0	0-0	9	Black	18,012
44	14	A	Hibernian	D	0-0	0-0	8		9971

Final League Position: 8

Most League Goals in Season (Individual): 34: Harry 'Peerie' Cunningham 1927-28 and Andy Kerr 1960-61.
Most Goals Overall (Individual): 148: W. Culley; 1912-23.

Honours
League Champions: Division I 1964-65. Division II 1897-98, 1898-99; *Runners-up:* Division I 1959-60, 1960-61, 1962-63, 1963-64. First Division 1975-76, 1978-79, 1981-82. Division II 1953-54, 1973-74. Second Division 1989-90.
Scottish Cup Winners: 1920, 1929; *Runners-up:* 1898, 1932, 1938, 1957, 1960.
League Cup Runners-up: 1952-53, 1960-61, 1962-63.
European: *European Cup:* 1965-66. *UEFA Cup (Fairs):* 1964-65 (semi-finals), 1969-70, 1970-71.
Club colours: Shirt: Blue and white vertical stripes. Shorts: Blue. Stockings: Blue.

Goalscorers: *League* (36): Williamson 7, Brown 5, Mitchell 5, Black 4 (2 pens), McSkimming 3, Skilling 3, McCluskey 2, MacPherson 2, Roberts 2, Crainie 1, McCloy 1, Porteous 1. *Scottish Cup* (5): Black 2 (1 pen), Brown 1, McSkimming 1, Williamson 1. *League Cup* (1): Mitchell 1.

Geddes R 44	MacPherson A 43	Black T 44	Montgomerie R 42	Skilling M 23	Millen A 44	Mitchell A 34	Reilly M 37 + 1	Brown T 26 + 5	McCluskey G 16 + 7	McSkimming S 40	Crainie D 6 + 8	Williamson R 36 + 2	Roberts M 7 + 6	Campbell C — + 1	Porteous I 7 + 6	Paterson C 4 + 2	Stark W 6 + 2	Burns T 12	Lauchlan J — + 1	McInally A 2 + 6	Napier C 10 + 5	McCloy S 1 + 5	Match No.
1	2	3	4	5	6	7	8	9	10	11	12												1
1	2	3	4	5	6	7	8		10	*11*	12	9	14										2
1	2	*3*	4	5	6	7	8		10	11	12	9		14									3
1	2	3	4	5	6	7		14	10	11		9	*8*		12								4
1	2	3	4	5	6	7		14	10	11		9	*8*										5
1	*2*	3	4	5	6	7			10	11		9	8		12	14							6
1	2	3	4	5	6	7	8		10	11		9			12								7
1	2	3	4	5	6	7	8		*10*	11		9	14		12								8
1	2	3	4	5	6	7	8		*10*	11		9	14										9
1	2	3	4	5	6	7	8			11		9	10										10
1	2	3	4	5	6	7	8			11		9	10										11
1	2	3	4	5	6	7	8	10	14	11		*9*											12
1	2	3		5	6	*7*	8	10	14	11		9				4							13
1	2	3	4	5	6	*7*	8	12		11		9			10								14
1	2	3	4	5	6		8	7		11		9	12		10								15
1	2	3	4	5	6		8	7		11		9	12		10								16
1	2	3	4	5	6		8	7		11		9	10		12								17
1	2	3	4	5	6		8			11	12	9			7		10						18
1	2	3	4	5	6		8	12		11	14	*9*			7		10						19
1	2	3	4	5	6		8	*7*			11	9					14	10					20
1	2	3	4	5	6		8	7		11	12	9					10						21
1	2	3	4	5	6		8	7			14	9					10	*11*					22
1	2	3	4	5	6	10	8	7		11		9											23
1	2	3	4		6	9	8			11	7		14		*10*			5					24
1	2	3	4		6	9	8	10		11	*7*				14	12		5					25
1	2	3	4		6	9	8	10		11	7		5										26
1	*2*	3	4		6	7	8		10	11	12				9		5		14				27
1	2	3			6	7	8		10	11	5	9				4							28
1	2	3	4		6	7	8	*5*	14	11		9								10	12		29
1	2	3	4		6	7	8	*5*	14	11		9								10	12		30
1	2	3	4		6	7	*8*	5				9						10		14	11		31
1	2	3	4		6	7		8	10			*9*						5		12	11	14	32
1	2	*3*	4		6	7	8	9		11		10									5	14	33
1	*2*	3	4		6		8	9	10	11		12						5			7	14	34
1		3	4		6	7		9		11		10						5		12	2	8	35
1	2	3	4		6	7	5	*10*		11		9									8	14	36
1	2	3	4		6	7	5		14	11	*10*	9									8	12	37
1	2	3	4		6	*7*	8	10	14	11		9				5					12		38
1	2	3	4		6	7	8	10	14	11		*9*				5					12		39
1	*2*	3	4		6	7	8	10	9	11		12								14	5		40
1	2	3	4		6	7	14	10		11		9						*5*		12	8		41
1	2	3	4		6	*7*		10		11		9					12	5		14	8		42
1	2	3	4		6		8	12	10	11		9					7	5					43
1	2	3	4		6	7	8	9	10	11								5			12		44

MEADOWBANK THISTLE Division 2

Year Formed: 1974. *Ground & Address:* Meadowbank Stadium, London Rd, Edinburgh EH7 6AE. *Telephone:* 031 661 5351. Head Office: 0875 812383.
Ground Capacity: total: 16,500. seated: 16,500. Main stand only used 7500. *Size of Pitch:* 105yd # 72yd.
Chairman: William L. Mill. *Secretary:* J. R. S. Renton. *Directors:* W. P. Hunter, J. Bain, R. Clark, W. Hay. *Vice-chairman:* Hugh Cowan. *Commercial Manager:* W. P. Hunter.
Manager: Michael Lawson. *Assistant Manager:* Robert Ford. *Club Doctor:* Dr M. M. Morrison. *Physio:* Arthur Duncan. *Coach:* M. McDermott.
Managers since 1975: John Bain; Alec Ness; Willie MacFarlane; Terry Christie. *Club Nickname(s):* Thistle; Wee Jags.
Previous Grounds: None.
Record Attendance: 4000 v Albion Rovers, League Cup 1st rd; 9 Sept, 1974.
Record Transfer Fee received: £115,000 for John Inglis to St Johnstone (1990).
Record Transfer Fee paid: £28,000 for Victor Kasule from Albion Rovers (1987).
Record Victory: 6-0 v Raith R, Second Division; 9 Nov, 1985.
Record Defeat: 0-8 v Hamilton A. Division II; 14 Dec, 1974.

MEADOWBANK THISTLE 1993—94 LEAGUE RECORD

Match No.	Date		Venue	Opponents	Result		H/T Score	Lg. Pos.	Goalscorers	Attendance
1	Aug	7	A	Cowdenbeath	W	2-1	0-0	—	Bailey, Rutherford	280
2		14	H	Stranraer	L	1-3	1-1	8	McLeod G	258
3		21	H	Berwick R	D	1-1	1-1	7	Price	311
4		28	A	East Stirling	W	1-0	0-0	6	Duthie	342
5	Sept	4	A	Forfar Ath	W	2-0	0-0	5	Little 2	489
6		11	H	East Fife	W	1-0	1-0	2	Little	502
7		18	A	Montrose	W	3-0	2-0	1	Little, Bailey, Duthie	547
8		25	H	Arbroath	W	3-0	1-0	1	Wilson, Little, Bailey	273
9	Oct	2	A	Alloa	L	0-1	0-0	2		446
10		9	H	Queen of the S	D	0-0	0-0	2		537
11		16	A	Albion R	D	0-0	0-0	2		240
12		23	H	Queen's Park	D	1-1	1-1	2	McLeod G	379
13		30	H	Stenhousemuir	W	3-1	0-0	1	Brock, Bailey, Little	261
14	Nov	6	A	Stranraer	L	1-3	0-2	2	McLeod G (pen)	940
15		13	H	Montrose	W	5-3	3-1	2	Smith (og), Hutchison 2, Rutherford 2	238
16		20	A	Arbroath	L	2-3	2-2	3	Wilson 2	544
17	Dec	1	A	Queen of the S	L	1-5	1-2	—	Murray	493
18		4	H	Alloa	D	1-1	1-0	3	McLeod G	288
19		18	H	Cowdenbeath	D	1-1	0-0	4	Rutherford	218
20	Jan	11	A	Berwick R	D	2-2	0-2	—	Scott, Duthie	431
21		15	H	East Stirling	D	1-1	0-0	3	Bailey	207
22		22	H	Albion R	W	4-2	2-0	3	Bailey, Little, Fleming, McLeod G	123
23		25	A	Stenhousemuir	D	1-1	1-1	—	Wilson	397
24		29	A	Queen's Park	L	2-3	1-1	3	Murray, Coyle	522
25	Feb	5	A	East Fife	W	2-0	0-0	4	Little 2	681
26		12	H	Forfar Ath	W	4-2	1-1	3	Murray 2, Little, Rutherford	235
27	Mar	2	H	Alloa	W	3-2	1-1	—	Bailey 3	190
28		5	A	Cowdenbeath	W	1-0	0-0	3	Rutherford	197
29		12	H	Stranraer	D	1-1	0-0	3	Rutherford	453
30		15	A	East Stirling	L	0-1	0-0	—		297
31		19	H	Stenhousemuir	W	1-0	0-0	3	Little	218
32		26	A	Arbroath	D	1-1	0-0	3	Graham	496
33	Apr	2	A	Forfar Ath	D	0-0	0-0	3		508
34		9	H	East Fife	D	2-2	1-1	3	McLeod G, Little	323
35		16	A	Queen's Park	W	3-1	1-1	3	Fleming, Rutherford, Bailey	448
36		23	H	Berwick R	L	1-2	1-0	3	McLeod G	355
37		30	A	Montrose	L	0-2	0-2	4		438
38	May	7	H	Queen of the S	W	2-1	0-0	4	Graham, McLeod G	562
39		14	A	Albion R	W	2-0	0-0	4	Bailey, McLeod G (pen)	368

Final League Position: 4

Most Capped Player (under 18): I. Little.
Most League Appearances: 446: Walter Boyd, 1979-89.
Most League Goals in Season (Individual): 21: John McGachie, 1986-87. *(Team):* 69; Second Division, 1986-87.
Most Goals Overall (Individual): 64: David Roseburgh, 1986-93.

Honours
League Champions: Second Division 1986-87; *Runners-up:* Second Division 1982-83. First Division 1987-88.
Scottish Cup: —. *League Cup:* Semi-finals 1984-85. *B&Q Cup:* Semi-finals 1993-94.
Club colours: Shirt: Amber with black trim. Shorts: Black. Stockings: Amber.

Goalscorers: *League* (62): Little 12, Bailey 11, McLeod G 9 (2 pens), Rutherford 8, Murray 4, Wilson 4, Duthie 3, Fleming 2, Graham 2, Hutchison 2, Brock 1, Coyle 1, Price 1, Scott 1, own goal 1. *Scottish Cup* (1): Rutherford 1. *League Cup* (1): Little 1. *B&Q Cup* (8): Brock 2, Little 2, Rutherford 2, Bailey 1, McLeod G 1 (pen).

McQueen J 11	Murray M 39	Fleming D 38	Williamson S 32	Davidson G 9	Little I 38 + 1	Price G 5 + 7	Wilson S 34 + 1	Rutherford P 32	McLeod G 35	Hutchison M 15 + 6	Bailey L 29 + 8	Duthie M 10 + 7	Elder S 3 + 3	Williamson R 2	Brock J 3 + 6	Coulston D — + 2	Ellison S 24 + 1	MacLeod I 19 + 2	Gardner L 10 + 6	Douglas R 4	Ingram N — + 3	Graham T 19 + 2	Scott S 7	Coyle M 4 + 4	McCartney C — + 3	Thorburn S 7 + 4	*Match No.*
1	2	3	4	5	6	7	8	9	10	11	12																1
1	4	3	5	2	6	12	8	9	10	11	7																2
1	4	3	5	2	6	9	8		10	11	7																3
1	4	3	5	2	6	*9*	8		10	11	7	14															4
1	4	3	5	2	6	12	8	9	10	11	7																5
1	4	3	5	2	6	12	8	9	10	*11*	7	14															6
1	4	3	5	2	6	12	8	9		*11*	7	14	10														7
1	4	3	5	2	6		8	9	10	11	7	12															8
1	4	3	5	*2*	6	14		9	10	11	7	8	12														9
1	4	3	*5*		6		8	9	10	11	7		14	2	12												10
1	4	3	5		6		8	9	10	11	*7*		2		12	14											11
	4	3	5		6		8	9	*10*	11	*7*		14	2	12		1										12
	4	3	5		6		8	9	10	14	7		*2*		11		1										13
	4	*3*	5		6		12	9	10	11	7				8	14	1	2									14
	4	3	5		6		8	9	10	11	7						1	2									15
	4	3	5		6		8	9	10	*11*	7				12		1	2	14								16
	4	3	5		6		8	9	10	12	*7*							2	11	1	14						17
	4	3			6		8	9	10	12	7							2	11	1		5					18
	4	3			*6*		8	9	10	14	7						12	2	11	1		5					19
	4	3			7	11	8		10		12	14			9		1	6				5	*2*				20
	4	3			*7*	11	8	9	10		12	14					1	6				5	2				21
	4	3			10	14	8		6		7	11					1					5	2	*9*	12		22
	4	3			10		8		6		7	11					1				12	5	2	*9*	14		23
	4	3			10		8		6		7	11					1				12	5	2	9			24
	4	3	5		9		6	10	11		*8*	7					1		12			14	2				25
	4	3	5		9		6	10		14	8	7					1	*11*	12				2				26
	4	3	5		9		6				*8*	7						11	2	1		12		14		10	27
	4	3	5		9		6	10			*8*	7					1	11	14			2				12	28
	4	3	5		9		6	10	8		12	14					1	*11*				2				7	29
	4	3	5		9		6	10	*11*		8	7					1	14				2				12	30
	4	*3*	5		9		6	10	8								1	11	14			2		12		*7*	31
	4	3	5		9		*6*	10	8								1	11	14			2		12		7	32
	4		5		9	14	6	10	8		12						1	*11*	3			2				7	33
	4	3	5		9		*6*	10	8		12						1	11	7			2				14	34
	4	3	5		9			10	8		12						1	11	7			2			14	*6*	35
	4	3	5		14			10	8		9				12		1	11	7			2				*6*	36
	4	3	5		7			10	8		*9*	6			14		1	11				2				12	37
	4	3	5		9		6	*10*	8		12						1	14	7			2		11			38
	4	3	5		*9*		6	10	8	14	11						1		7			2		12			39

MONTROSE

Division 3

Year Formed: 1879. *Ground & Address:* Links Park, Wellington St, Montrose DD10 8QD. *Telephone:* 0674 673200.
Ground Capacity: total: 4338. seated: 1398. *Size of Pitch:* 113yd # 70yd.
Chairman: Bryan Keith. *Secretary:* Malcolm J. Watters. *Commercial Manager:* Allan Paul.
Manager: John Holt. *Physio:*Neil Bryson.
Managers since 1975: A. Stuart; K. Cameron; R. Livingstone; S. Murray; D. D'Arcy; I. Stewart; C. McLelland; D. Rougvie; J. Leishman. *Club Nickname(s):* The Gable Endies. *Previous Grounds:* None.
Record Attendance: 8983 v Dundee, Scottish Cup 3rd rd; 17 Mar, 1973.
Record Transfer Fee received: £50,000 for Gary Murray to Hibernian (Dec 1980).
Record Transfer Fee paid: £17,500 for Jim Smith from Airdrieonians (Feb 1992).
Record Victory: 12-0 v Vale of Leithen, Scottish Cup 2nd rd; 4 Jan, 1975.
Record Defeat: 0-13 v Aberdeen; 17 Mar, 1951.
Most Capped Player: Alexander Keillor, 2 (6), Scotland.
Most League Appearances: 343: Martin Allan, 1983-93.

MONTROSE 1993—94 LEAGUE RECORD

Match No.	Date		Venue	Opponents	Result		H/T Score	Lg. Pos.	Goalscorers	Attendance
1	Aug	7	A	Stranraer	W	4-2	2-1	—	Grant 3, Yeats	672
2		14	H	Arbroath	D	0-0	0-0	4		1379
3		21	H	Stenhousemuir	W	2-0	0-0	3	Grant, McKenna	561
4		28	A	Queen's Park	L	1-2	0-2	5	Craib M	428
5	Sept	4	A	East Stirling	W	3-2	1-1	4	Grant 2, Craib M	374
6		11	A	Forfar Ath	D	1-1	1-0	4	Wolecki	693
7		18	H	Meadowbank T	L	0-3	0-2	6		547
8		25	A	Alloa	W	1-0	0-0	4	Yeats	391
9	Oct	2	A	Queen of the S	L	0-1	0-1	6		1009
10		9	H	East Fife	L	0-1	0-0	8		655
11		16	A	Berwick R	D	3-3	0-1	8	Grant 2, Cooper	417
12		23	H	Cowdenbeath	L	1-2	0-1	8	Grant	298
13		30	H	Albion R	W	1-0	1-0	8	Kennedy	491
14	Nov	6	A	Arbroath	L	0-2	0-2	9		869
15		13	A	Meadowbank T	L	3-5	1-3	9	Kennedy (pen), Craib M, McKenna	238
16		20	H	Alloa	L	1-2	1-1	9	Grant	465
17		27	A	East Fife	L	2-5	1-3	12	Kennedy, Yeats	754
18	Dec	4	H	Queen of the S	W	2-1	2-0	11	Kennedy 2	465
19	Jan	4	H	Stranraer	L	0-2	0-1	—		678
20		15	H	Queen's Park	L	1-2	1-1	12	Kennedy (pen)	442
21		18	A	Stenhousemuir	W	4-3	2-2	—	Wolecki 2 (1 pen), Cooper, Taylor	281
22		22	H	Berwick R	L	2-3	0-1	12	Kennedy, Taylor	461
23		25	A	Albion R	W	4-3	2-1	—	Taylor 2, Stephen, Tindal	112
24	Feb	5	H	Forfar Ath	D	1-1	0-0	12	Stephen	609
25		12	H	East Stirling	D	2-2	1-1	12	Kennedy, Stephen	387
26		19	H	East Fife	W	3-0	1-0	11	Taylor 2, Stephen	723
27		26	A	Arbroath	D	0-0	0-0	10		924
28	Mar	5	A	Albion R	W	1-0	1-0	9	Milne	243
29		12	H	Berwick R	W	3-1	1-0	9	Grant, Lavelle, McKenna	636
30		19	H	Cowdenbeath	D	1-1	1-0	10	Milne	494
31		22	A	Cowdenbeath	W	1-0	1-0	—	Milne	208
32		26	A	Queen of the S	L	0-1	0-0	10		682
33	Apr	2	H	East Stirling	L	0-2	0-2	10		583
34		13	A	Stranraer	L	0-1	0-1	—		799
35		16	A	Stenhousemuir	L	0-2	0-1	10		333
36		23	H	Alloa	D	2-2	1-0	10	Garden, Kennedy	440
37		30	H	Meadowbank T	W	2-0	2-0	10	Cooper, Kennedy	438
38	May	7	A	Queen's Park	L	2-3	0-2	10	Grant, Kennedy	395
39		14	A	Forfar Ath	W	2-0	1-0	10	Milne 2	620

Final League Position: 10

Most League Goals in Season (Individual): 28: Brian Third, Division II; 1972-73.
Most Goals Overall (Individual): —.

Honours
League Champions: Second Division 1984-85, *Runners-up:* 1990-91.
Scottish Cup: Quarter-finals 1973, 1976.
League Cup: Semi-finals 1975-76.
Club colours: Shirt: Royal Blue with white sleeves. Shorts: White with royal blue and red trim. Stockings: White with royal blue and red tops.

Goalscorers: *League* (56): Grant 12, Kennedy 11 (2 pens), Taylor 6, Milne 5, Stephen 4, Cooper 3, Craib M 3, McKenna 3, Wolecki 3 (1 pen), Yeats 3, Garden 1, Lavelle 1, Tindal 1. *Scottish Cup* (2): Kennedy 1, own goal 1. *League Cup*: (0): *B&Q Cup* (6): Kennedy 2, Yeats 2, Craib M 1, Wolecki 1.

Larter D 37	Robertson I 35	Craib M 23	Haro M 8	Smith J 31	Irvine N 22	Yeats C 16 + 2	Craib S 15 + 2	Grant D 35 + 1	Kennedy A 35 + 2	Stephen L 28 + 5	Jack R — + 3	McKenna I 9 + 11	Tosh J 26 + 1	Lavelle M 27	Wolecki E 6 + 9	Cooper C 22 + 6	Houghton G 5 + 3	Holt J — + 1	Wilkins G — + 1	Tindal K 9 + 2	Taylor D 6 + 10	Massie R 2	Milne C 16	Garden M 3 + 4	Beedie S 12	Masson P 1	Match No.
1	2	3	4	5	6	7	8	9	10	*11*	12	14															1
1	2	3	4	5	6	7	*8*	9	10	11	12	14															2
1	2	3	4	5	6	*7*	*8*	9	10	11		12	14														3
1	2	3	4	5	6	*7*	8	9	10	11		12															4
1		3	4		6	*7*	8	10		11	14	12	5	2	*9*												5
1	2	3	4				8	10		11		7	5	6	9												6
1	2	3	4			12	8	10	14	11		7	5	6	*9*												7
1	2	3		5		7	8	9	10	*11*			4	6		14											8
1	2	3		5		7	8	9	10	*11*			4	6	14		12										9
1	2	3		5		7	8	9	10	12			4	6	14	*11*											10
1	2	3		5		8	14	9	10	*11*			4	6		7											11
1	2	3		5		8		*9*	10	11		12		6	14	7	4										12
1	3	4		5	6	8	14	9	10	*11*		12				7	2										13
1	2	3		5			8		10	*11*		9	4	6		7	12	14									14
1	2	3		5			8		*10*	11		9	4	6		7	12		14								15
1		3		5				*9*	10	11		12	4	6		*7*	2			8	14						16
1		3		5	6	2	8	9	10	11			4			12				7							17
1		3		5	6	7		14	10	12		11	4				2			8	*9*						18
	2	3		5	6	7			10	12		11	4		14					8	*9*	1					19
1	2	3		5	6	7	8	9	10	11			4		12												20
	2	3		5	6		8	4	*10*	11					9	7				12	14	1					21
1	2	3		5	6			4	10	11				8	*9*	7				12	14						22
1	3			5	6			4	10	11					12	7	2			8	9						23
1	3			5		12		4	8	11			2	6		7					9		*10*	14			24
1	3			5		8		4	10	11			2	6		7							9				25
1	2	*3*		5				4	10	8		11		6		12				7	14		9				26
1	2							4	10	8			5	6		12				3	*7*		9		11		27
1	2							4	10	7		14	5	6		12				*3*	9		8		11		28
1	2				6			4	10	11		12	5	3		7					14		9		*8*		29
1	2				6			4	10			*11*	5	3		7					12		9	14	8		30
1	2			5	*6*			4	10			11	3	8	12	7							9	14			31
1	2			5	6			4	14			12	3	11	10	*7*							9		8		32
1	2		6	5	11			4	10					*7*		14							9		8	3	33
1	2			5	6			4	10				3	11	12	7							9		8		34
1	2			5	6			4	10	*11*			3		12	7							9	14	8		35
1	2			5				4	10				3	8		7					12		9	6	11		36
1	2			5	6			4	10	14				8		7					12		9	11	*3*		37
1	2			5	6			4	10	14				8		7					12		9	*11*	3		38
1	2							4	10	11			5	8		7				3	12		9		6		39

GREENOCK MORTON Division 2

Year Formed: 1874. *Ground & Address:* Cappielow Park, Sinclair St, Greenock. *Telephone:* 0475 23511.
Ground Capacity: total: 14,250. seated: 5150. *Size of Pitch:* 110yd # 71yd.
Chairman: John Wilson. *Secretary:* Mrs Jane Rankin.
Manager: Allan McGraw. *Assistant Manager:* John McMaster. *Physio:* John Tierney. *Coach:* Billy Osborne.
Managers since 1975: Joe Gilroy; Benny Rooney; Alex Miller; Tommy McLean; Willie McLean. *Club Nickname(s):* The Ton. *Previous Grounds:* Grant Street 1874, Gravel Park 1875, Cappielow Park 1879, Ladyburn Park 1882, (Cappielow Park 1883).
Record Attendance: 23,000 v Celtic; 1922.
Record Transfer Fee received: £350,000 for Neil Orr to West Ham U.
Record Transfer Fee paid: £150,000 for Allan Mahood from Nottingham Forest.
Record Victory: 11-0 v Carfin Shamrock, Scottish Cup 1st rd; 13 Nov, 1886.
Record Defeat: 1-10 v Port Glasgow Ath, Division II; 5 May, 1894 and v St Bernards, Division II; 14 Oct, 1933.
Most Capped Player: Jimmy Cowan, 25, Scotland.

GREENOCK MORTON 1993—94 LEAGUE RECORD

Match No.	Date		Venue	Opponents	Result		H/T Score	Lg. Pos.	Goalscorers	Attendance
1	Aug	7	A	Clyde	L	1-2	0-1	—	Alexander	1203
2		14	H	Falkirk	L	1-5	0-1	12	Doak	3049
3		21	A	St Mirren	D	2-2	0-1	11	Donaghy, Doak	4133
4		28	H	Brechin C	W	2-1	1-0	8	Lilley 2	1312
5	Sept	4	A	Airdrieonians	L	0-2	0-2	9		2227
6		11	A	Clydebank	L	0-3	0-2	10		1563
7		14	H	Stirling Albion	D	2-2	1-1	—	Tolmie, McCahill	1208
8		18	A	Dunfermline Ath	L	0-4	0-2	12		2955
9		25	H	Dumbarton	W	3-1	0-0	10	Collins, Doak, McEwan	1420
10		28	A	Ayr U	D	2-2	1-1	—	Scott (og), McEwan	1659
11	Oct	2	H	Hamilton A	L	1-2	1-0	11	Tolmie	1517
12		9	H	Clyde	D	1-1	1-0	11	McEwan	1474
13		16	A	Stirling Albion	D	1-1	0-1	11	McInnes	1000
14		23	H	Clydebank	D	0-0	0-0	11		1534
15		30	H	St Mirren	L	1-2	1-1	11	McWhirter (og)	3174
16	Nov	6	A	Brechin C	W	3-0	2-0	10	Alexander 3	494
17		9	H	Airdrieonians	D	0-0	0-0	—		1272
18		13	A	Hamilton A	L	1-4	0-3	10	Alexander	1696
19		20	H	Ayr U	L	0-1	0-1	10		1293
20		27	A	Dumbarton	L	0-2	0-1	10		1140
21	Dec	4	H	Dunfermline Ath	D	0-0	0-0	10		1591
22		18	H	Stirling Albion	L	0-1	0-0	11		928
23	Jan	8	H	Brechin C	D	1-1	0-1	11	Hunter	1020
24		11	A	Falkirk	L	1-5	0-4	—	Thomson	2781
25		18	A	St Mirren	L	1-5	0-4	—	McEwan	2942
26		22	H	Falkirk	D	1-1	0-1	11	Doak	2087
27	Feb	1	A	Airdrieonians	D	2-2	2-0	—	McEwan 2	1401
28		5	A	Clydebank	D	0-0	0-0	11		988
29		12	H	Hamilton A	D	2-2	1-1	11	Thomson, Anderson	1447
30		22	A	Clyde	D	0-0	0-0	—		1666
31	Mar	1	A	Ayr U	L	1-2	1-0	—	Alexander	1752
32		5	A	Dunfermline Ath	L	0-3	0-0	11		3485
33		12	H	Dumbarton	D	0-0	0-0	11		1046
34		19	A	Stirling Albion	W	3-0	1-0	11	Lilley, McArthur 2	719
35		26	H	Clyde	W	2-0	0-0	10	Mahood 2	1190
36		29	A	Falkirk	L	0-1	0-1	—		2657
37	Apr	2	H	Clydebank	D	1-1	1-1	10	Alexander	1163
38		13	A	Hamilton A	L	2-3	0-0	—	Mahood, Alexander	1114
39		16	H	Ayr U	L	0-1	0-0	11		1169
40		23	H	Dunfermline Ath	D	2-2	0-0	11	Anderson, Alexander	2003
41		26	A	Dumbarton	L	0-2	0-1	—		650
42		30	H	St Mirren	L	1-2	0-2	11	Lilley	1984
43	May	7	A	Brechin C	W	2-1	1-0	11	Alexander, Lilley	444
44		14	H	Airdrieonians	L	1-3	0-2	11	Alexander	1029

Final League Position: 11

Most League Appearances: 358: David Hayes, 1969-84.
Most League Goals in Season (Individual): 58: Allan McGraw, Division II; 1963-64.
Most Goals Overall (Individual): —.

Honours
League Champions: First Division 1977-78, 1983-84, 1986-87. Division II 1949-50, 1963-64, 1966-67.
Scottish Cup Winners: 1922; *Runners-up:* 1948. *League Cup Runners-up:* 1963-64.
B&Q Cup: Runners-up: 1992-93.
European: *UEFA Cup (Fairs):* 1968-69.
Club colours: Shirt: Royal blue tartan. Shorts: Royal blue. Stockings: Royal blue.

Goalscorers: *League* (44): Alexander 11, McEwan 6, Lilley 5, Doak 4 (1 pen), Mahood 3, Anderson 2, McArthur 2, Thomson 2, Tolmie 2, Collins 1, Donaghy 1, Hunter 1, McCahill 1, McInnes 1, own goals 2. *Scottish Cup* (4): McEwan 2, Anderson 1, Lilley 1. *League Cup* (2): Lilley 1, Tolmie 1. *B&Q Cup* (2): Alexander 1, Tolmie 1.

Wylie D 44	Collins D 35 + 2	McArthur S 35 + 5	Rafferty S 19 + 7	Doak M 15	Fowler J 34 + 4	Lilley D 34 + 4	Grace A 2 + 1	Alexander R 35 + 1	McInnes D 16	Tolmie J 35 + 1	Gahagan J 7 + 6	Thomson R 7 + 15	Pickering M 25	Donaghy M 15 + 6	McEwan A 12 + 6	McCahill S 8	Shearer N 16	Aitken S 3 + 1	McDonald I 3 + 2	Johnstone D 22	Beaton S 2	Lothian D 1	McCann M — + 1	Hunter J 21	Anderson J 19	Brown C 4	Sexton B 4	Mahood A 11 + 1	Blair P — + 1	Match No.
1	2	3	4	5	6	7	*8*	9	10	11	12	14																		1
1	2	6		5	4	7		9	10	11			3	8																2
1	2	6		5	4	*7*		9	10	11	12		3	8																3
1	2	6	14	5	4	7		9	10	*11*	12		3	8																4
1	2	6	14	5	4	*7*		9	10	11	12		3	8																5
1	2	6	12	5	4	*7*		9	10	11			3	8	14															6
1	2	6	7	5				9	10	11			3	8		4														7
1	2	3	6	5	12	8	14	*9*	10	11				7		4														8
1	2	8	*4*	5	14	7	11		10				3	12	9		6													9
1	2	8	4	5		7			10	11			3		9		6													10
1	2	8	4	5		*7*		12	10	*11*			3	14	9		6													11
1	2	8	4	5		14		*9*	10	11			3	12	7		6													12
1	2	8	4		5	12		9	10	11			3	7			6													13
1	2	6	4		3			9	10	11	14			*8*	7		5													14
1	2	8	*4*		14	12		9	10	11			3		*7*	5	6													15
1	2	3			4	*7*		9	10	11	8	14		12		5	6													16
1	2	3			4			9		11	*7*	14		10		5	6	8	12											17
1	2	10			*4*			9		11			3	8		5	6	7	14											18
1	2	10			4	7		9			11	14	3	8		5	*6*	12												19
1	2	10			4	7					11	14	3	12	*9*	5			8	6										20
1	2				4	7					11	10		8	12				6	5	3	*9*	14							21
1	2	3	12		4	10		9		*11*	7	14					6		8	5										22
1	2	10	4		8	7		9		11	*12*			14			6			5				3						23
1	2	3	4		10	7		9				11		8						5				6						24
1	2	10	4		8	7				11		12	3		14		9			*5*				6						25
1	2			5	12	7				*11*		14	3		9									6	4	8	10			26
1			4	5	10	*7*				11		14			9					8				6	2		3			27
1		12	4		8					11		7	3		*9*					5				6	2		10			28
1		14	12	4				9		11		8	3		7					5				6	2		*10*			29
1		14	4		8	12		9		11		10	3		*7*					*5*				6	2					30
1		14			4	*7*		9		11		*10*	3		12		5							6	2	8				31
1			12		4	7		9				11	3				5				10			6	2	8				32
1		3	*4*		8	*7*		9		11				10	12					5				6	2			14		33
1	12	3	4		8	7		9		11										5				6	2			10		34
1	12	3	4		8	7		9		*11*					14					5				6	2			10		35
1	8	3			4	7		*9*		11		14								5				6	2			10		36
1	8	3			4	*7*		9		11		14								5				6	2			10		37
1	8	3			4	7		9		*11*		14								5				6	2			10		38
1	8	3			4	7		9		*11*		14								5				6	2			10		39
1	8	3			4	7		9		*11*		14								5				6	2			10		40
1	8	3			4	7		9		*11*		14								5				6	2			10		41
1	8	11	14		4	7		*9*		12			3							5				6	2			10		42
1	8	14			4	7		9					*3*							5				6	2	11		10		43
1	4	6				7		9			11		3					8		5					2			10	12	44

MOTHERWELL Premier Division

Year Formed: 1886. *Ground & Address:* Fir Park, Motherwell ML1 2QN. *Telephone:* 0698 261437/8/9.
Ground Capacity: total: 15,500. seated: 11,500. *Size of Pitch:* 110yd # 75yd.
Chairman: John C. Chapman. *Secretary:* Alan C. Dick. *Commercial Manager:* John Swinburne.
Manager: —. *Assistant Manager:* Tom Forsyth. *Physio:* John Porteous. *Coach:* Cameron Murray.
Managers since 1975: Ian St. John; Willie McLean; Rodger Hynd; Ally MacLeod; David Hay; Jock Wallace; Bobby Watson, Tommy McLean. *Club Nickname(s):* The Well. *Previous Grounds:* Roman Road, Dalziel Park.
Record Attendance: 35,632 v Rangers, Scottish Cup 4th rd replay; 12 Mar, 1952.
Record Transfer Fee received: £800,000 for Tom Boyd to Chelsea (June 1991).
Record Transfer Fee paid: £175,000 for Brian Martin from St Mirren (Oct 1991).
Record Victory: 12-1 v Dundee U, Division II; 23 Jan, 1954.
Record Defeat: 0-8 v Aberdeen, Premier Division; 26 Mar, 1979.
Most Capped Player: George Stevenson, 12, Scotland.
Most League Appearances: 626: Bobby Ferrier, 1918-37.

MOTHERWELL 1993—94 LEAGUE RECORD

Match No.	Date		Venue	Opponents	Result		H/T Score	Lg. Pos.	Goalscorers	Attendance
1	Aug	7	H	Celtic	D	2-2	2-1	—	Arnott, Burns	13,569
2		14	A	Dundee	W	2-1	0-1	2	McKinnon, McGrillen	4206
3		21	A	Kilmarnock	W	1-0	0-0	1	McGrillen	7555
4		28	H	Raith R	W	4-1	2-0	1	Sinclair (og), McKinnon (pen), McGrillen, Kirk	5644
5	Sept	4	A	St Johnstone	L	0-3	0-2	1		4576
6		11	H	Hearts	W	2-0	0-0	1	O'Donnell, McGrillen	7662
7		18	A	Partick T	L	0-1	0-1	2		5947
8		25	A	Dundee U	D	0-0	0-0	2		6633
9	Oct	2	H	Aberdeen	D	0-0	0-0	3		8597
10		6	A	Rangers	W	2-1	0-0	—	Arnott 2	39,816
11		9	H	Hibernian	L	0-2	0-1	4		9090
12		16	H	Dundee	W	1-0	1-0	2	Arnott	5126
13		30	H	Kilmarnock	D	2-2	0-1	3	Kirk, Martin	7384
14	Nov	6	A	Raith R	W	3-0	1-0	2	Arnott 2, O'Donnell	4443
15		9	H	St Johnstone	W	1-0	0-0	—	Lambert	4527
16		13	A	Aberdeen	D	1-1	1-1	2	Kirk	12,494
17		20	H	Dundee U	W	2-0	1-0	1	Kirk, Arnott	5807
18		24	A	Celtic	L	0-2	0-1	—		16,654
19		30	H	Partick T	W	1-0	0-0	—	O'Donnell	5362
20	Dec	4	H	Rangers	L	0-2	0-1	3		14,069
21		11	A	Hibernian	L	2-3	0-0	4	Coyne 2	7429
22		15	A	Hearts	W	3-2	1-1	—	Coyne 2, McKinnon	5531
23		18	A	Dundee	W	3-1	2-1	3	O'Donnell 2, Coyne (pen)	4687
24	Jan	1	A	Kilmarnock	D	0-0	0-0	3		10,511
25		11	H	Celtic	W	2-1	1-0	—	O'Donnell 2	13,159
26		22	A	Partick T	D	0-0	0-0	4		5237
27		25	H	Raith R	W	3-1	1-1	—	Coyne, Kirk, McGrillen	5016
28	Feb	5	H	Hearts	D	1-1	1-1	3	McLaren (og)	7009
29		8	A	St Johnstone	L	1-2	1-2	—	Coyne	4522
30		12	A	Dundee U	W	2-1	2-1	3	Bowman (og), Van Der Hoorn (og)	6573
31	Mar	5	A	Rangers	L	1-2	0-0	3	Lambert	43,669
32		8	H	Aberdeen	D	1-1	0-1	—	McLeish (og)	7018
33		12	H	Hibernian	D	0-0	0-0	2		7126
34		19	H	Dundee	W	3-1	3-1	2	McQuillan (og), Coyne, Martin	6127
35		26	A	Celtic	W	1-0	1-0	2	Arnott	36,199
36		30	A	Hearts	D	0-0	0-0	—		7879
37	Apr	2	H	Partick T	D	2-2	1-1	2	Coyne, Philliben	6444
38		16	A	Aberdeen	D	0-0	0-0	2		9642
39		23	A	Hibernian	W	2-0	1-0	2	Coyne (pen), Krivokapic	6137
40		26	H	Rangers	W	2-1	2-1	—	Philliben, Coyne (pen)	14,050
41		30	H	Kilmarnock	W	1-0	0-0	2	Coyne	8185
42	May	3	H	Dundee U	L	1-2	1-1	—	Kirk	5208
43		7	A	Raith R	D	3-3	2-2	3	Lambert, Kirk, McKinnon	3449
44		14	H	St Johnstone	L	0-1	0-0	3		7498

Final League Position: 3

Most League Goals in Season (Individual): 52: Willie McFadyen, Division I; 1931-32.
Most Goals Overall (Individual): 283: Hugh Ferguson, 1916-25.

Honours

League Champions: Division I 1931-32. First Division 1981-82, 1984-85. Division II 1953-54, 1968-69; *Runners-up:* Division I 1926-27, 1929-30, 1932-33, 1933-34. Division II 1894-95, 1902-03. *Scottish Cup:* 1952, 1991; *Runners-up:* 1931, 1933, 1939, 1951.
League Cup: 1950-51. *Runners-up:* 1954-55 *Scottish Summer Cup:* 1944, 1965.
Club colours: Shirt: Amber with claret hoop and trimmings. Shorts: Claret. Stockings: Amber.

Goalscorers: *League* (58): Coyne 12 (3 pens), Arnott 8, Kirk 7, O'Donnell 7, McGrillen 5, McKinnon 4 (1 pen), Lambert 3, Martin 2, Philliben 2, Burns 1, Krivokapic 1, own goals 6. *Scottish Cup* (3): Coyne 1, Kirk 1, Philliben 1. *League Cup* (8): Arnott 3, McGrillen 2, Ferguson 1, Graham 1, Shannon 1.

Dykstra S 44	Shannon R 41 + 2	McKinnon R 42	Krivokapic M 42	Martin B 43	McCart C 36	Kirk S 25 + 11	Angus I 8 + 3	Arnott D 25 + 4	O'Donnell P 35	Burns A 2 + 2	McGrillen P 20 + 20	Philliben J 18 + 10	Graham A 2 + 3	Cooper D 2 + 8	Dolan J 32 + 4	Ferguson I 1	Lambert P 30 + 2	Griffin J 1 + 2	Coyne T 26	Burley G 3 + 2	Davies W 6 + 4	McMillan S — + 1	Match No.
1	2	3	4	5	6	7	8	9	10	11	12	14											1
1	2	3	4	5	6	12	8	9	10	7	11	14											2
1	2	3	4	5	6	7	8	9	10		11		12	14									3
1	2	3	4	5	6	14	8	9	10		11		12	7									4
1	2	3	4	5	6	12			10		11		14	7	8	9							5
1	2	3	4	5	6	14			10		11		9	12	8		7						6
1	2	3	4	5	6	14			10		11		9	12	8		7						7
1	2	3	4	5	6	9			10		11				8		7						8
1	2	3	4	5	6	10	14	9			11			12	8		7						9
1	2	3	4	5	6	9	10	12			11	14			8		7						10
1	2	3	4	5	6	8	12	9	10		11						7						11
1	2	3	4	5	6	11		9	10		12			14	8		7						12
1	2	3	4	5	6	11		9	10		12			14	8		7						13
1	2	3	4	5	6	8		9	10		11				12		7	14					14
1	2	3	4	5		8		9	10		12	6			11		7	14					15
1	12	3	4	5	6	8		9	10		14	2			11		7						16
1	2	3	4	5	6	8		9			11	12		14	10		7						17
1	2	3	4	5	6	8	11		10		9	12		14			7						18
1	2	3	4	5	6	7		9	10		14				8		12		11				19
1	2		4	5	6	12		9	10		14				8		7	3	11				20
1	2	3	4	5	6	9			10			14			8		7		11				21
1	2	3		5	6	12			10		9	4			8		7		11				22
1	2	3	4	5	6	9		14	10			8			12		7		11				23
1	2	3	4	5	6	9		12	10						8		7		11				24
1	2	3	4	5	6	12		9	10		14	8					7		11				25
1	2	3	4	5	6	9			10		12	8			14		7		11				26
1	2	3	4	5	6	9		7	10		12				8		14		11				27
1	2	3	4	5	6	7	14	9			12	10			8				11				28
1	2	3	4	5		7	10	12			9	6			14				11	8			29
1	2	3	4	5	6	9			10		12	8			7				11	14			30
1		3	4	5	6			9	10	12		2			8		7		11	14			31
1	12	3	4	5	6			9	10		14	2			8		7		11				32
1	2	3	4	5	6			9	10		14	12			8				11		7		33
1	2	3	4	5	6			7	10		11	12			8				9		14		34
1	2	3	4	5	6			9	10		12	14			8				11		7		35
1	2	3	4	5	6				10		11				8		7		9		12		36
1	2	3	4		6			9	10		14	5			8		7		11				37
1	2		4	5				9	10		12	6			8				11	3	7		38
1	2	3	4	5	6	14					11	12			8		7		9		10		39
1	2	3	4	5		14			10		11	6			8		7		9		12		40
1	2	3	4	5		11			10		14	6			8		7		9		12		41
1	2	3	4	5		8	11				12	6					7		9		10		42
1	2	3	4	5		12				14	11	6			8		7		9		10		43
1	2	3		5		10		11			12	6			8		7		9	4		14	44

PARTICK THISTLE Premier Division

Year Formed: 1876. *Ground & Address:* Firhill Park, 80 Firhill Rd, Glasgow G20 7BA. *Telephone:* 041 945 4811.
Ground Capacity: total: 19,336. seated: 2906. *Size of Pitch:* 110yd # 74yd.
Chairman: James Oliver. *Secretary:* Robert Reid. *General Commercial Manager:* Jez Moxey.
Manager: John Lambie. *Assistant Manager:* Gerry Collins. *Physio:* Frank Ness.
Managers since 1975: R. Auld; P. Cormack; B. Rooney; R. Auld; D. Johnstone; W. Lamont; S. Clark. *Club Nickname(s):* The Jags. *Previous Grounds:* Jordanvale Park; Muirpark; Inchview; Meadowside Park.
Record Attendance: 49,838 v Rangers, Division I; 18 Feb, 1922.
Record Transfer Fee received: £200,000 for Mo Johnston to Watford.
Record Transfer Fee paid: £85,000 for Andy Murdoch from Celtic (Feb 1991).
Record Victory: 16-0 v Royal Albert, Scottish Cup 1st rd; 17 Jan, 1931.
Record Defeat: 0-10 v Queen's Park, Scottish Cup; 3 Dec, 1881.
Most Capped Player: Alan Rough, 51 (53), Scotland.

PARTICK THISTLE 1993—94 LEAGUE RECORD

Match No.	Date	Venue	Opponents	Result		H/T Score	Lg. Pos.	Goalscorers	Attendance
1	Aug 7	A	Hibernian	D	0-0	0-0	—		7452
2	14	H	Dundee U	L	1-2	0-1	10	Craig	4599
3	21	A	Raith R	D	2-2	1-1	7	Britton, Grant	3814
4	28	H	Celtic	L	0-1	0-0	10		14,013
5	Sept 4	A	Hearts	L	1-2	0-2	11	Britton	7273
6	11	A	Rangers	D	1-1	1-1	10	Grant	40,998
7	18	H	Motherwell	W	1-0	1-0	10	Craig	5947
8	25	A	Kilmarnock	L	1-3	0-1	10	Craig	7411
9	Oct 2	H	St Johnstone	W	4-1	3-1	10	Grant 3, Taylor	3402
10	5	A	Dundee	D	2-2	1-1	—	Shaw, Taylor	4540
11	9	H	Aberdeen	W	3-2	2-0	10	Taylor, Craig, Grant	5600
12	16	A	Dundee U	D	2-2	1-1	8	Milne, Grant	5750
13	23	H	Hearts	D	0-0	0-0	7		7170
14	30	H	Raith R	D	1-1	1-0	9	Craig	4375
15	Nov 2	H	Hibernian	D	0-0	0-0	—		3815
16	6	A	Celtic	L	0-3	0-1	9		21,642
17	13	A	St Johnstone	W	3-1	1-0	7	Craig, Britton, Grant	3548
18	20	H	Kilmarnock	L	0-1	0-0	9		5876
19	27	H	Rangers	D	1-1	1-0	7	English	16,890
20	30	A	Motherwell	L	0-1	0-0	—		5362
21	Dec 4	H	Dundee	W	3-2	1-1	8	Taylor, Craig 2 (1 pen)	3312
22	14	A	Aberdeen	L	1-2	0-0	—	Craig	8248
23	18	H	Dundee U	W	1-0	1-0	8	Craig	4121
24	27	A	Hibernian	L	1-5	0-1	—	Tierney	10,165
25	Jan 8	H	Celtic	W	1-0	0-0	8	Shaw	12,887
26	12	A	Raith R	W	1-0	0-0	—	Grant	3599
27	15	A	Hearts	L	0-1	0-1	8		7619
28	22	H	Motherwell	D	0-0	0-0	8		5237
29	Feb 5	A	Rangers	L	1-5	0-2	8	Cameron	42,606
30	12	A	Kilmarnock	W	2-1	0-1	8	Craig, Grant	7511
31	Mar 5	A	Dundee	L	0-1	0-0	9		3210
32	19	A	Dundee U	D	2-2	1-2	9	Charnley (pen), Jamieson	6005
33	22	H	St Johnstone	D	0-0	0-0	—		3295
34	26	H	Hibernian	W	1-0	0-0	7	Grant	4632
35	29	H	Rangers	L	1-2	0-1	—	English	12,000
36	Apr 2	A	Motherwell	D	2-2	1-1	8	English, Grant	6444
37	5	H	Aberdeen	D	1-1	1-1	—	Grant	4280
38	16	A	St Johnstone	L	0-1	0-0	9		4933
39	19	H	Kilmarnock	W	1-0	0-0	—	Craig	6981
40	23	A	Aberdeen	L	0-2	0-0	8		7827
41	26	H	Dundee	W	1-0	0-0	—	Craig	3296
42	30	H	Raith R	D	2-2	1-2	7	English, Craig	4225
43	May 7	A	Celtic	D	1-1	0-0	8	Smith	16,827
44	14	H	Hearts	L	0-1	0-0	9		9391

Final League Position: 9

Most League Appearances: 410: Alan Rough, 1969-82.
Most League Goals in Season (Individual): 41: Alec Hair, Division I; 1926-27.
Most Goals Overall (Individual): —.

Honours
League Champions: First Division 1975-76. Division II 1896-97, 1899-1900, 1970-71; *Runners-up:* Division II 1901-02.
Scottish Cup Winners: 1921; *Runners-up:* 1930.
League Cup Winners: 1971-72; *Runners-up:* 1953-54, 1956-57, 1958-59.
European: *UEFA Cup:* 6 matches (*Fairs Cup:* 1963-64. *UEFA Cup:* 1972-73).
Club colours: Shirt: Red and yellow vertical stripes. Shorts: Black. Stockings: Black.

Goalscorers: *League* (46): Craig 14 (1 pen), Grant 13, English 4, Taylor 4, Britton 3, Shaw 2, Cameron 1, Charnley 1 (pen), Jamieson 1, Milne 1, Smith 1, Tierney 1. *Scottish Cup* (0): *League Cup* (14): Cameron 4, Craig 4, Grant 2, Britton 1, English 1, Jamieson 1, Law 1.

Nelson C 39	McKilligan N 1 + 2	Law R 25	Jamieson W 42 + 1	Tierney G 18 + 4	Clark M 10 + 1	Byrne D 21 + 2	Craig A 37 + 1	Britton G 20 + 2	Cameron I 37 + 4	English I 25 + 11	McKee K 22 + 1	Watson G 37	Kinnaird P 2 + 1	Grant R 35 + 2	Farningham R 2	Shaw G 13 + 4	McGlashan C — + 1	Milne C 29 + 2	Taylor A 27 + 5	Murdoch A 5 + 1	Smith T 3 + 5	Charnley J 25 + 1	Gibson A 6 + 5	Barnes D 3 + 4	*Match No.*
1	2	3	4	5	6	7	8	9	10	11															1
1			4	5		7	8	9	10	*6*	2	3	11	14											2
1			4	5		6		9	10		2	3	*11*	7	8	12	14								3
1	14	3	5		6	7	8	*9*	11	12	2			10	4										4
1	14		4	5	6		8	9	10		2			11		12		3	*7*						5
			4	5	6	7	8	9	12	10	2			11				*3*	14	1					6
			4	5	6	14	8	9		10	2			11				*3*	7	1					7
			4	5	*6*		8	9	12	10	2		14	11				3	7	1					8
1		2	5			6	8		10	11		4		*9*		7		3	12		14				9
1		2	5			6	8	12	10	*11*		4		9		7		3	14						10
1		2	5	12			8	10	11			4		*9*		7		3	6		14				11
1		2	5				8	10	11			4		9		7		3	6						12
1		2	5				8	10	11	12		4		9		7		3	6						13
1		2	5				8	*10*	11	14	12	4		9		7		3	6						14
1			5			7	8	10	11	12	2	4		9				3	6						15
1			5		12	*6*	8	10	11		2	4		9		7		3			14				16
1			5				8	10	11	12	2	4		9		7		3	6						17
1			5					9	10	12	2	4		*8*		7		3	6		14	11			18
1				5	6			9	8	*10*	2	4				14		3	7			11			19
1			12	5	6			*9*	11	10	2	4		14		*7*		3	8						20
1			5		6		12		10	9	2	4				7		3	8			11			21
1			5		11		8	14	10	*9*	2	4				7		3	6			12			22
1		3	5				8	9	6		2	4				14			10			11	*7*		23
1		3	5	4			8	9	6	12	2								10	14		11	7		24
1			6	5		3	8			12	2	4				7			10			11	9		25
1			6	5		3	8			12	2	4		9					10			11	7		26
1			6	5		3	8		14	12	2	4		9					10			*11*	7		27
1		2	5				8		6	9		4		7				3				11	10		28
1		2	5	12			8		14	9		4		*7*				3	*6*			10		11	29
1			5				8		11	14	2	6		*9*				3	4			10		7	30
1			5	14					11		2	6		9				3	4		8	*10*	12	7	31
1		2	5						10	8		4		9				3	6		7	11	12		32
1		2	5				6		11	8		4		9				3	7			10			33
1		3	6	5		2	7		8	10		4		9								11			34
1		3	6	5		*2*	7		8	10		4		9								11	14		35
1		2	6	5			8		*7*	10		4		9				3	14			11		12	36
1		3	6	5		2	8		7	10		4		9								11			37
1		3	6	5		2	8		7	*10*		4		9					12			11		14	38
1		2	5			3	8		7	10		4		*9*				12	6			11		14	39
1		2	5			3	8		7	10		4		9				14	*6*			11			40
1		2	5			3	8		7	*10*		4		9				6				11		14	41
1		2	5			3	8		7	10		4		9				6				11	12		42
		2	5			12	8		7	10		4		9				*3*	6	1	14	11			43
		2	5	14		3	8		7			4		9				6		1	*11*	10	12		44

QUEEN OF THE SOUTH Division 2

Year Formed: 1919. *Ground & Address:* Palmerston Park, Terregles St, Dumfries DG2 9BA. *Telephone and Fax:* 0387 54853.
Ground Capacity: total: 6750. seated: 1300. *Size of Pitch:* 112yd # 72yd.
Chairman: Norman Blount. *Secretary:* Mrs Doreen Alcorn. *Commercial Manager:* John Paterson.
Manager: William McLaren. *Physio:* Derek Kelly.
Managers since 1975: M. Jackson; G. Herd; A. Busby; R. Clark; M. Jackson; D. WIlson; W. McLaren; F. McGarvey; A. MacLeod. *Club Nickname(s):* The Doonhamers. *Previous Grounds:* None.
Record Attendance: 24,500 v Hearts, Scottish Cup 3rd rd; 23 Feb, 1952.
Record Transfer Fee received: £100,000 for K. McMinn to Rangers (1985).
Record Transfer Fee paid: —.
Record Victory: 11-1 v Stranraer, Scottish Cup 1st rd; 16 Jan, 1932.
Record Defeat: 2-10 v Dundee, Division I; 1 Dec, 1962.
Most Capped Player: Billy Houliston, 3, Scotland.

QUEEN OF THE SOUTH 1993—94 LEAGUE RECORD

Match No.	Date	Venue	Opponents	Result		H/T Score	Lg. Pos.	Goalscorers	Attendance
1	Aug 7	A	Arbroath	W	5-2	1-1	—	McFarlane, Mallan, Thomson 2, McGuire	751
2	14	H	Queen's Park	W	5-2	2-1	1	McGuire 2 (1 pen), Thomson, Mallan, Bryce	878
3	21	H	Stranraer	L	0-1	0-1	4		1650
4	28	A	Forfar Ath	W	2-1	0-0	2	Mallan 2	579
5	Sept 4	A	East Fife	W	2-0	0-0	1	Thomson 2	1546
6	11	H	East Stirling	W	5-0	3-0	1	Thomson 2, McGuire, Mallan, Bryce	1164
7	18	H	Alloa	L	0-1	0-0	2		1459
8	25	A	Albion R	D	1-1	0-0	2	Thomson	433
9	Oct 2	H	Montrose	W	1-0	1-0	1	Thomson	1009
10	9	A	Meadowbank T	D	0-0	0-0	1		537
11	16	A	Cowdenbeath	D	3-3	3-3	1	Bryce, Bell 2	339
12	23	H	Stenhousemuir	L	1-2	1-0	5	Mills	965
13	30	H	Berwick R	L	2-5	0-1	5	Thomson, McGuire	782
14	Nov 6	A	Queen's Park	L	1-3	0-1	7	Mallan	631
15	13	A	Alloa	L	0-1	0-1	6		477
16	20	H	Albion R	L	1-2	1-0	7	Thomson	506
17	Dec 1	H	Meadowbank T	W	5-1	2-1	—	Mallan 2, Bryce, Thomson, Kelly	493
18	4	A	Montrose	L	1-2	0-2	8	Thomson (pen)	465
19	18	H	Arbroath	W	6-0	4-0	7	Bryce 3, Thomson 2, McLaren	481
20	Jan 1	A	Stranraer	W	2-1	0-0	5	Thomson (pen), Mallan	1584
21	15	H	Forfar Ath	W	1-0	0-0	4	Kennedy	740
22	18	A	Berwick R	W	2-1	2-1	—	Mallan, Thomson	457
23	22	H	Cowdenbeath	L	1-2	0-0	4	Thomson	927
24	Feb 5	A	East Stirling	D	0-0	0-0	6		403
25	8	A	Stenhousemuir	L	0-3	0-2	—		387
26	12	H	East Fife	D	0-0	0-0	6		611
27	19	H	Queen's Park	W	3-0	1-0	5	McLaren, McGuire, Thomson	711
28	Mar 5	A	Stranraer	D	3-3	1-0	5	Kelly, Sermanni, Thomson	1173
29	12	H	Albion R	L	1-2	1-1	8	McGhie	678
30	15	A	Alloa	L	0-1	0-0	—		338
31	19	A	Forfar Ath	D	4-4	1-1	8	Thomson 4	486
32	26	H	Montrose	W	1-0	0-0	7	Thomson	682
33	Apr 2	H	Berwick R	D	0-0	0-0	7		928
34	9	A	Arbroath	W	3-0	1-0	6	Mallan, Thomson 2	391
35	16	A	East Fife	W	1-0	0-0	5	Kelly	716
36	23	H	Stenhousemuir	W	2-1	0-1	5	Thomson 2	1835
37	30	H	East Stirling	D	1-1	1-0	5	McGhie	2143
38	May 7	A	Meadowbank T	L	1-2	0-0	5	Kennedy	562
39	14	A	Cowdenbeath	W	2-0	1-0	5	Herd (og), Sermanni (pen)	346

Final League Position: 5

Most League Appearances: 619: Allan Ball; 1962-83.
Most League Goals in Season (Individual): 33: Jimmy Gray, Division II; 1927-28.
Most Goals Overall (Individual): 109, Andrew Thomson, 1989-94.

Honours
League Champions: Division II 1950-51; *Runners-up:* Division II 1932-33, 1961-62, 1974-75. Second Division 1980-81, 1985-86.
Scottish Cup: —.
League Cup: —.
Club colours: Shirt: Royal blue. Shorts: White. Stockings: Royal blue with white tops.

Goalscorers: *League* (69): Thomson 29 (2 pens), Mallan 11, Bryce 7, McGuire 6 (1 pen), Kelly 3, Bell 2, Kennedy 2, McGhie 2, McLaren 2, Sermanni 2 (1 pen), McFarlane 1, Mills 1, own goal 1. *Scottish Cup* (3): Thomson 2, Mills 1. *League Cup* (1): Shanks 1. *B&Q Cup* (2): Kelly 1, Thomson 1.

Davidson A 14	Mills D 30	McGhie W 30 + 1	McKeown B 35	Shanks D 13 + 1	McFarlane A 22	Jackson D 7 + 13	Sermanni P 15 + 12	Thomson A 32 + 3	McGuire D 19 + 9	Mallan S 37	Bryce T 34 + 3	Kelly P 22 + 7	Bell A 23	Rowe G 30	McLaren J 12 + 7	McColm R 6	Proudfoot K 7	Purdie D 19	Kennedy D 17	Leslie S 5 + 1	Match No.
1	2	3	4	5	6	7	8	9	10	11	12										1
1	2	3	4	5	6	*7*	*8*	9	10	11	14	12									2
1	5	*2*	4	8	6	7	14	9	10	11	12		3								3
1	2		3	5	7		12	9	10	11	8		6	4							4
1	3		4	5	6			9	10	11	8		7	2							5
1	2		4	*5*	8		14	9	*7*	11	6	12	10	3							6
1	2		4	*5*	6		14	9	*7*	11	10	12	8	3							7
1	3	14	2		10		12	9	*7*	11	6	*8*	5	4							8
1	2		4	5	8		12	9	*7*	11	6		10	3							9
1	2	3	4	5	8			9	12	11	6	*7*	10								10
1	3	2	4	*5*	7			9	14	11	*8*	12	10	6							11
1	5	2	4	*6*	8			9		11		7	10	3	12						12
1	5	*2*	4		8	14		9	7	11	10	12	6	3							13
1	2	5		*8*	10		14	9	12	11	6	7	3	4							14
		4		*5*	8	14		9		11	6	7	3	2	12	1	10				15
	2	5			6	12	14	9		11	8	7	3	4	*10*	1					16
	3	2	4		8			9		11	6	7	10	5				1			17
	3	2	4		*6*		14	9		11	8	*7*	10	5	12			1			18
		2	4		6	14	12	9		11	8		*7*	5	10		3	1			19
		2	4		6		7	9		11	10			5			3	1	8		20
		2	4		6	12	*7*	9		11	8			5		1	3		10		21
	2	5	4	14	*6*	12	*7*	9		11	10					1	3		8		22
	2	5				12	*7*	9		11	6	10		4		1	3		8		23
	5	2	4				12		7	11	10	*9*	6	3	8			1			24
	5	2	4			9	*7*		10	11		12	3		8			1		6	25
		5	4			7			14	11	6	9	3	2	*10*			1	8		26
		2	4			*7*		12	11		6	9	5	3	10			1	8		27
		2	4				7	12	14	11	10	*9*	6	5			3	1	8		28
		5	2			8	6	12	*7*	11	10	9	3		14			1	4		29
	2	5	4			14	8	9	12	11	6	7			*10*			1		3	30
	2	5	4			12		9	11		10	7			8	1			6	3	31
	2		4					9	8	11	6	7		3	12			1	5	10	32
	5	2	4			14		9	12	*11*	10	*7*		3	8			1	6		33
	5	2	4			12	8	9	*7*	11	10			3				1	6		34
	5	2	4				*8*	9	*7*	11	10	14		3	12			1	6		35
		2	4				12	9	*7*	11	10	8		3	*6*			1	5	14	36
	5	2	4				6	9	12	*11*	10	*7*		3	14			1	8		37
	2		4			14	10	9	12	11	*8*	*7*		3	6			1	5		38
	2		4			14	8			11	6	*7*		3	9			1	5	10	39

QUEEN'S PARK Division 3

Year Formed: 1867. *Ground & Address:* Hampden Park, Mount Florida, Glasgow G42 9BA. *Telephone:* 041 632 1275.
Ground Capacity: total: 38,335 all seated. *Size of Pitch:* 115yd # 75yd.
President: Malcolm D. Mackay. *Secretary:* James C. Rutherford. *Physio:* R. C. Findlay. *Coach:* Edward Hunter.
Coaches since 1975: D. McParland, J. Gilroy. *Club Nickname(s):* The Spiders. *Previous Grounds:* 1st Hampden (Recreation Ground); (Titwood Park was used as an interim measure between 1st & 2nd Hampdens); 2nd Hampden (Cathkin); 3rd Hampden.
Record Attendance: 95,772 v Rangers, Scottish Cup, 18 Jan, 1930.
Record for Ground: 149,547 Scotland v England, 1937.
Record Transfer Fee received: Not applicable due to amateur status.
Record Transfer Fee paid: Not applicable due to amateur status.
Record Victory: 16-0 v St. Peters, Scottish Cup 1st rd; 29 Aug, 1885.
Record Defeat: 0-9 v Motherwell, Division I; 26 Apr, 1930.
Most Capped Player: Walter Arnott, 15, Scotland.

QUEEN'S PARK 1993—94 LEAGUE RECORD

Match No.	Date	Venue	Opponents	Result		H/T Score	Lg. Pos.	Goalscorers	Attendance
1	Aug 7	H	Forfar Ath	L	0-3	0-1	—		445
2	14	A	Queen of the S	L	2-5	1-2	14	O'Brien, O'Neill	878
3	21	A	Albion R	L	0-2	0-1	14		311
4	28	H	Montrose	W	2-1	2-0	14	Orr G, Caven	428
5	Sept 4	H	Cowdenbeath	L	1-3	0-2	14	O'Neill (pen)	408
6	11	A	Arbroath	L	0-2	0-1	14		690
7	18	H	East Fife	W	4-2	2-0	13	McPhee 2, McCormick, Brodie	525
8	25	A	Stenhousemuir	L	0-2	0-1	14		404
9	Oct 2	H	Stranraer	D	0-0	0-0	13		518
10	9	A	Berwick R	L	0-6	0-1	14		406
11	16	H	East Stirling	D	1-1	1-0	14	Caven	417
12	23	A	Meadowbank T	D	1-1	1-1	14	McPhee	379
13	30	A	Alloa	D	1-1	1-0	14	Orr G	545
14	Nov 6	H	Queen of the S	W	3-1	1-0	14	Graham 2, McCormick	631
15	13	A	East Fife	D	5-5	2-0	13	McPhee 4, O'Neill	791
16	20	H	Stenhousemuir	L	1-2	0-0	14	O'Neill	517
17	27	H	Berwick R	D	0-0	0-0	14		587
18	Dec 4	A	Stranraer	L	0-2	0-0	14		742
19	18	A	Forfar Ath	L	0-4	0-1	14		472
20	27	H	Alloa	W	2-1	1-0	—	Rodden, O'Neill	1048
21	Jan 1	H	Albion R	W	2-0	1-0	11	O'Neill 2 (1 pen)	858
22	15	A	Montrose	W	2-1	1-1	11	Caven, O'Neill	442
23	22	A	East Stirling	L	0-2	0-1	11		513
24	29	H	Meadowbank T	W	3-2	1-1	11	Maxwell, O'Neill 2 (1 pen)	522
25	Feb 5	H	Arbroath	W	2-1	2-1	11	McCormick, O'Neill	439
26	12	A	Cowdenbeath	W	4-3	1-2	10	O'Neill 2, McCormick, Graham	241
27	19	A	Queen of the S	L	0-3	0-1	10		711
28	Mar 1	H	Berwick R	L	1-3	1-1	—	Graham	405
29	5	H	Stenhousemuir	L	2-4	1-1	12	O'Neill 2	516
30	12	A	East Fife	L	0-1	0-0	12		661
31	19	A	Albion R	D	1-1	0-0	12	McCormick	358
32	26	H	Forfar Ath	W	3-2	1-0	12	O'Neill, McCormick 2	489
33	Apr 2	H	Stranraer	D	1-1	0-1	11	Graham	920
34	12	A	Alloa	D	0-0	0-0	—		317
35	16	H	Meadowbank T	L	1-3	1-1	11	O'Neill	448
36	23	A	Arbroath	L	1-2	0-1	12	Graham	413
37	30	A	Cowdenbeath	D	1-1	1-0	12	Caven	207
38	May 7	H	Montrose	W	3-2	2-0	12	Orr G, O'Neill, Caven	395
39	14	H	East Stirling	W	2-0	1-0	11	Brodie, Caven	407

Final League Position: 11

Most League Appearances: 473: J. B. McAlpine.
Most League Goals in Season (Individual): 30: William Martin, Division I; 1937-38.
Most Goals Overall (Individual): 163: J. B. McAlpine.

Honours
League Champions: Division II 1922-23. B Division 1955-56. Second Division 1980-81.
Scottish Cup Winners: 1874, 1875, 1876, 1880, 1881, 1882, 1884, 1886, 1890, 1893; *Runners-up:* 1892, 1900.
League Cup: —.
FA Cup runners-up: 1884, 1885.
Club colours: Shirt: White and black hoops. Shorts: White. Stockings: White with black hoops.

Goalscorers: *League* (52): O'Neill 18 (3 pens), McCormick 7, McPhee 7, Caven 6, Graham 6, Orr G 3, Brodie 2, Maxwell 1, O'Brien 1, Rodden 1. *Scottish Cup* (3): McPhee 1, O'Neill 1, Rodden 1. *League Cup* (0): *B&Q Cup* (0).

Chalmers J 38	Kerr G 19 + 2	Kavanagh J 7 + 3	Fitzpatrick S 37	Sneddon S 2	Orr G 39	Elder G 30	O'Brien J 2 + 1	Black S 6 + 2	O'Neill J 39	McCormick S 29 + 7	Rodden J 10 + 6	Graham D 31 + 4	Caven R 33	Cassidy M — + 1	Orr J 19	McPhee B 14 + 5	Stevenson C 15 + 6	Maxwell I 26	Mackenzie K 2	Brodie D 12 + 13	Henrici G 4 + 1	Campbell S 5 + 2	Ferguson P 7 + 1	Moonie D 1	Moir A 2	Lynch M — + 1	Match No.
1	2	3	4	5	6	7	*8*	9	10	11	12	14															1
1	2	3	4		6	5	*9*	10	11	12		8	7	14													2
1	4	3	6		8	5		*11*	10	9		12	7		2	14											3
1	3	2	6		8	5			10	9		12	7		4	11											4
1	3	2	6		8	5			10	11		12	7		4	9											5
1		14	6		10	5	*12*		11	7			8		4	9	2	3									6
1	4	2	8		6	5			11	12						9	10	3	*7*	14							7
1	4	2	5		6				11	12			7			10	8	3	9								8
1	4	12	10		11				9	7		3	8		2		*6*	5		14							9
1	4	12	8		11				10	7		3	9					5			2	6					10
1	4		6		10	5		9	11	7		2	8			12		3									11
1	4		5		6			12	11	*7*		*10*	8			9	3			14	2						12
1			5		6	4		7	11			10	8			9	2	3			12						13
1			5		6	4		*7*	*11*	12		10	8			9	2	3		14							14
1			5		6	4			11	7		10	8			9	2	3									15
1			5		6	4			11	*7*		10	8			9	2	3		12							16
1	2		5		6	4			11	14		10	8			*9*	12	3		7							17
1			5	2	*6*	4			11	12		10	8			9	14	3		7							18
1	14		2		6	4			11	12	*7*	*10*	8			9		5					3				19
1			5		6	4			11	9	*7*	10	8				2	3		12							20
1			5		6	4			11	*9*	*7*	10	8			14	2	3		12							21
1	14		5		6	4			11	7	9	10	8				*2*	3		12							22
1	8		5		6	4			11	7	9	10					2	3		12							23
1			5		6	4			9	7	*11*	10	8		2			3		14							24
1			5		6	4			9	11	*7*	10	8		2		12	3		14							25
1			5		6	4			9	7	*11*	10	8		2			3		14							26
1			5		6	4			9	7	11	*10*	8		2		14	3		12							27
1			4		6			12	11			10	8			9	3	5		7	*2*		14				28
1			5		6	4			9			11	8				12	3		7	2	10					29
1	4		8		6	5			9	7		10	11		2	12							3				30
1	4		5		6				9	7	*11*	10			2	14	12					8	3				31
1	4		5		6				9	11		10			2					7		8	3				32
1	4		8		6	5			9	11	14	10			2					7			*3*				33
1	4		5		6				9	11		10	8		2					7			3				34
1	4		5		6				9	11	14	10	8		2					*7*			3				35
1			5		6	4			9	11		10	8		2			3		7							36
1			5		6	4			9	7	14	10	8		2			3		*11*		12					37
					6	4			9	11	12	*10*	8		2		3			*7*		14		1	5		38
1					6	4			9	*11*	14		8		2			3		7		10			5	12	39

RAITH ROVERS Division 1

Year Formed: 1883. *Ground & Address:* Stark's Park, Pratt St, Kirkcaldy KY1 1SA. *Telephone:* 0592 263514.
Ground Capacity: total: 9200. seated: 3040. *Size of Pitch:* 113yd # 67yd.
Chairman: Alex Penman. *Secretary:* Mrs S. Rankin. *Commercial Manager:* P. Rodger.
Manager: Jimmy Nicholl. *Assistant Manager and Coach:* Martin Harvey. *Physio:* Gerry Docherty. *Reserve Coach:* Derek Smith.
Managers since 1975: R. Paton; A. Matthew; W. McLean; G. Wallace; R. Wilson; F. Connor. *Club Nickname(s):* Rovers.
Previous Grounds: Robbie's Park.
Record Attendance: 31,306 v Hearts, Scottish Cup 2nd rd; 7 Feb, 1953.
Record Transfer Fee received: £250,000 for Craig Brewster to Dundee U (Aug 1993).
Record Transfer Fee paid: £100,000 for Alastair Graham from Motherwell (Sept 1993).
Record Victory: 10-1 v Coldstream, Scottish Cup 2nd rd; 13 Feb, 1954.
Record Defeat: 2-11 v Morton, Division II; 18 Mar, 1936.
Most Capped Player: David Morris, 6, Scotland.
Most League Appearances: 430: Willie McNaught.

RAITH ROVERS 1993—94 LEAGUE RECORD

Match No.	Date	Venue	Opponents	Result		H/T Score	Lg. Pos.	Goalscorers	Attendance
1	Aug 7	H	St Johnstone	D	1-1	1-1	—	Dennis	4628
2	14	A	Hearts	L	0-1	0-0	10		8587
3	21	H	Partick T	D	2-2	1-1	7	Dennis, Dalziel (pen)	3814
4	Sept 28	A	Motherwell	L	1-4	0-2	11	Coyle	5644
5	4	H	Dundee U	D	1-1	0-1	10	Nicholl	5304
6	11	H	Celtic	L	1-4	0-2	11	Crawford	8114
7	18	A	Dundee	W	1-0	0-0	11	Hetherston	4213
8	25	A	Aberdeen	L	1-4	0-1	11	Dennis	11,472
9	Oct 2	H	Rangers	D	1-1	1-1	11	McStay	8161
10	5	A	Hibernian	L	2-3	1-1	—	Dair, Rowbotham	9197
11	9	H	Kilmarnock	D	2-2	2-0	11	Graham, Dair	4482
12	16	H	Hearts	W	1-0	1-0	11	Hetherston	5278
13	23	A	St Johnstone	D	1-1	0-1	11	Dair	4411
14	30	A	Partick T	D	1-1	0-1	11	Cameron	4375
15	Nov 6	H	Motherwell	L	0-3	0-1	11		4443
16	9	A	Dundee U	D	2-2	0-2	—	Dair, Crawford	5775
17	13	A	Rangers	D	2-2	0-0	11	Dalziel (pen), Graham	42,611
18	27	A	Celtic	L	0-2	0-1	11		17,453
19	Dec 1	H	Dundee	W	2-1	2-1	—	Dalziel 2	3609
20	4	H	Hibernian	L	1-2	1-2	11	Graham	4407
21	7	H	Aberdeen	D	1-1	1-1	—	Dalziel	4205
22	11	A	Kilmarnock	L	0-1	0-1	11		6012
23	18	A	Hearts	W	1-0	1-0	11	Sinclair	6227
24	Jan 12	H	Partick T	L	0-1	0-0	—		3599
25	15	H	Dundee U	L	0-2	0-1	11		5150
26	19	H	St Johnstone	D	1-1	1-0	—	Dalziel	3693
27	22	A	Dundee	D	2-2	1-1	11	Blake (og), Dalziel	3784
28	25	A	Motherwell	L	1-3	1-1	—	Cameron	5016
29	Feb 5	H	Celtic	D	0-0	0-0	11		7678
30	12	A	Aberdeen	L	0-4	0-1	11		10,553
31	26	H	Rangers	L	1-2	1-0	11	Crawford	8988
32	Mar 5	A	Hibernian	L	0-3	0-3	11		6042
33	15	H	Kilmarnock	W	3-2	2-0	—	Graham, Cameron, Hetherston (pen)	3585
34	19	H	Hearts	D	2-2	1-1	11	McStay, Cameron	5697
35	26	A	St Johnstone	L	0-2	0-1	11		4550
36	30	A	Celtic	L	1-2	1-1	—	Crawford	14,140
37	Apr 2	H	Dundee	D	1-1	0-1	11	Crawford	3245
38	16	A	Rangers	L	0-4	0-2	12		42,545
39	23	A	Kilmarnock	D	0-0	0-0	11		7426
40	26	H	Hibernian	D	1-1	0-1	—	Cameron	3040
41	30	A	Partick T	D	2-2	2-1	11	Hetherston (pen), Cameron	4225
42	May 3	H	Aberdeen	L	0-2	0-1	—		2798
43	7	H	Motherwell	D	3-3	2-2	11	Graham, Dalziel, Hetherston	3449
44	14	A	Dundee U	W	3-2	3-0	11	Dair 2, Sinclair	5335

Final League Position: 11

Most League Goals in Season (Individual): 38: Norman Haywood, Division II; 1937-38.
Most Goals Overall (Individual): 154: Gordon Dalziel (League), 1987-94.

Honours
League Champions: First Division: 1992-93. Division II 1907-08, 1909-10 (shared), 1937-38, 1948-49; *Runners-up:* Division II 1908-09, 1926-27, 1966-67. Second Division 1975-76, 1977-78, 1986-87.
Scottish Cup Runners-up: 1913. *League Cup Runners-up:* 1948-49.
Club colours: Shirt: Navy blue, white trim. Shorts: White. Stockings: White.

Goalscorers: *League* (46): Dalziel 8 (2 pens): Cameron 6, Dair 6, Crawford 5, Graham 5, Hetherston 5 (2 pens), Dennis 3, McStay 2, Sinclair 2, Coyle 1, Nicholl 1, Rowbotham 1, own goal 1. *Scottish Cup* (2): Dair 1, McStay 1. *League Cup* (1): Cameron 1.

Carson T 8	McStay J 35 + 2	MacLeod I 3	Coyle R 41	Dennis S 43	McGeachie G 18 + 2	Nicholl J 33 + 1	Dalziel G 20 + 7	Hetherston P 34	Hawke W 1 + 1	Cameron C 30 + 11	Sinclair D 29 + 7	Rowbotham J 33 + 3	Broddle J 16 + 2	Crawford S 24 + 12	Arthur G 1	Dair J 35 + 3	Graham A 35 + 1	Thomson S 34	McAnespie S 2 + 1	Kelly N 1 + 3	Lennon D 7	Potter B 1	*Match No.*
1	2	3	4	5	6	7	8	9	10	11	12												1
1	2	3	4	5			8	9	14	10	*6*	7	11										2
1	2	3	4	5	6	7	8	9		11			14	*10*									3
	2		4	5	3	7	8	9		11	6		12	10	1								4
1	2		4	5	6	7		9		10		3		8		11							5
1	2		4	5	6	7		9		8		3		10		11							6
1	2		4	5	6	7		*9*		8	14	3		10		11							7
1	2		4	5	6	7		9		8		3		10		11	12						8
	2		4	5	6	*7*		9		12	14	3		10		11	8	1					9
	2		4	5	6	7		9		12		3		10		11	8	1					10
	2		4	5	6	*7*	8	9		12	14	3				11	10	1					11
	2		4	5	6	7	8	9		12	14	*3*				11	10	1					12
	2		4	5	6	7		9		*8*	12	3		14		11	10	1					13
	2		4	5		7		9		10	6	3				11	8	1					14
	2		4	5		7	12	9		*10*	6	3		14		11	8	1					15
	2		4		12	7	*8*	9		6	5	3		14		11	10	1					16
	2		4	5		7	*8*	9		12	6	3		14		11	10	1					17
	2		4	5		7	8	9		12	6	3				11	10	1					18
	2		4	5		7	*8*	9		12	6		3	14		11	10	1					19
	2		4	5	12	7	*8*	9			6		3	14		11	10	1					20
	2		4	5	6		8			*9*	7	14	3			11	10	1					21
	2		4	5	6		8			12	*7*	9	3	14		11	10	1					22
			4	5		7	*8*			14	6	2	3	9		11	10	1					23
			4	5		7	8			14	6	2	3	*9*		11	10	1					24
			4	5		*7*	8			9	6	2	3	14		11	10	1					25
	12		4	5	6		8			7	9	2	3			11	10	1					26
	12		4	5	6		8			7	9	2	3	14		*11*	10	1					27
			4	5	6	*7*	8			11	9	3		12			10	1	2	14			28
	2		4	5		7				10	6	3		9		11	8	1					29
	2		4	5		*7*	12			10	6	3		9		11	8	1	14				30
	2		4	5		14	12	*9*		7	6	3		10		11	8	1					31
	2			5		7	12	9		4	6	3		10		11	8	1					32
	2			5		7		9		4	6	3		10		11	8	1					33
	2			5		7		9		4	6	3		10		11	8	1					34
	2		4	5		7	12	9		6	3			10		11	8	1					35
	2		4	5		7	12	9		11	6	3		10			8	1					36
	2		4	5		7		9		6	3			10		11		1		12	8		37
	2		4	5	6	*7*		9		14		3		10		12	8	1			11		38
	2		4	5				9		7			3	10		11	8	1			6		39
	2		4	5				9		7	6	12	3	*10*		11	8	1		14			40
			4	5				9		10	6	2	3	12		14	8	1		*7*	*11*		41
			4	5		*7*		9		11		2	3	10		14	8	1			6		42
1			4	5			8	9			12	*7*	3	14		11	10		2		6		43
	2		4	5			12	9			6	14	*3*	10		11	8				7	1	44

RANGERS Premier Division

Year Formed: 1873. *Ground & Address:* Ibrox Stadium, Edminston Drive, Glasgow G51 2XD. *Telephone:* 041 427 8500.
Ground Capacity: total: 44,500. seated: 36,500. *Size of Pitch:* 115yd # 75yd.
Chairman: David Murray. *Secretary:* R. C. Ogilvie. *Commercial Manager:* Bob Reilly.
Manager: Walter Smith. *Assistant Manager:* Archie Knox. *Physio:* Bill Collins. *Coach:* Davie Dodds. *Reserve team coaches:* John McGregor, Billy Kirkwood.
Managers since 1975: Jock Wallace; John Greig; Jock Wallace; Graeme Souness. *Club Nickname(s):* The Gers. *Previous Grounds:* Burnbank, Kinning Park.
Record Attendance: 118,567 v Celtic, Division I; 2 Jan, 1939.
Record Transfer Fee received: £5,580,000 for Trevor Steven to Marseille (Aug 1991).
Record Transfer Fee paid: £2,500,000 for Alexei Mikhailichenko from Sampdoria (June 1991).
Record Victory: 14-2 v Blairgowrie, Scottish Cup 1st rd; 20 Jan, 1934.
Record Defeat: 2-10 v Airdrieonians; 1886.
Most Capped Player: George Young, 53, Scotland.
Most League Appearances: 496: John Greig, 1962-78.
Most League Goals in Season (Individual): 44: Sam English, Division I; 1931-32.
Most Goals Overall (Individual): 233: Bob McPhail; 1927-39.

Honours
League Champions: (44 times) Division I 1890-91 (shared), 1898-99, 1899-1900, 1900-01, 1901-02, 1910-11, 1911-12, 1912-13, 1917-18, 1919-20, 1920-21, 1922-23, 1923-24, 1924-25, 1926-27, 1927-28, 1928-29, 1929-30, 1930-31, 1932-33, 1933-34, 1934-35, 1936-37, 1938-39, 1946-47, 1948-49, 1949-50, 1952-53, 1955-56, 1956-57, 1958-59, 1960-61, 1962-63,

RANGERS 1993—94 LEAGUE RECORD

Match No.	Date	Venue	Opponents	Result	H/T Score	Lg. Pos.	Goalscorers	Attendance
1	Aug 7	H	Hearts	W 2-1	1-0	—	Hagen, Hateley	42,320
2	14	A	St Johnstone	W 2-1	1-1	1	Gough, Ferguson I	10,152
3	21	A	Celtic	D 0-0	0-0	2		47,942
4	28	H	Kilmarnock	L 1-2	0-0	2	Pressley	43,804
5	Sept 4	A	Dundee	D 1-1	0-1	4	Hateley	14,211
6	11	H	Partick T	D 1-1	1-1	5	Hateley	40,998
7	18	A	Aberdeen	L 0-2	0-2	7		19,138
8	25	H	Hibernian	W 2-1	1-1	6	Steven T, Hateley	43,200
9	Oct 2	A	Raith R	D 1-1	1-1	5	Hetherston (og)	8161
10	6	H	Motherwell	L 1-2	0-0	—	Ferguson I	39,816
11	9	A	Dundee U	W 3-1	3-0	5	Huistra 2, Hateley	11,262
12	16	H	St Johnstone	W 2-0	1-0	4	Huistra, Hateley	41,960
13	30	H	Celtic	L 1-2	0-0	6	McCoist	47,522
14	Nov 3	A	Hearts	D 2-2	2-0	—	Hateley 2	18,370
15	6	A	Kilmarnock	W 2-0	0-0	4	Ferguson I, Huistra	19,157
16	10	H	Dundee	W 3-1	3-0	—	Ferguson I, McCoist 2 (1 pen)	38,477
17	13	H	Raith R	D 2-2	0-0	3	Hateley 2 (1 pen)	42,611
18	20	A	Hibernian	W 1-0	1-0	2	Gough	16,506
19	27	A	Partick T	D 1-1	0-1	3	Huistra	16,890
20	Dec 1	H	Aberdeen	W 2-0	2-0	—	Hateley 2	45,182
21	4	A	Motherwell	W 2-0	1-0	1	Durie 2	14,069
22	11	H	Dundee U	L 0-3	0-3	1		43,058
23	18	A	St Johnstone	W 4-0	2-0	2	Hateley 2, Steven T, Durie	10,056
24	27	H	Hearts	D 2-2	1-1	—	Hateley 2	45,116
25	Jan 1	A	Celtic	W 4-2	3-0	1	Hateley, Mikhailichenko 2, Kuznetsov	48,506
26	8	H	Kilmarnock	W 3-0	0-0	1	Huistra, Hateley 2	44,919
27	15	A	Dundee	D 1-1	0-1	1	Durie	10,864
28	22	A	Aberdeen	D 0-0	0-0	1		20,267
29	Feb 5	H	Partick T	W 5-1	2-0	1	Durie 2, Mikhailichenko, McCall, Steven T	42,606
30	12	H	Hibernian	W 2-0	1-0	1	Durie, Steven T	43,265
31	26	A	Raith R	W 2-1	0-1	1	Ferguson I, Durie	8988
32	Mar 5	H	Motherwell	W 2-1	0-0	1	Durie, Hateley (pen)	43,669
33	19	H	St Johnstone	W 4-0	2-0	1	McCall, Hateley, McPherson, Durie	43,228
34	26	A	Hearts	W 2-1	1-0	1	McCoist, Hateley	18,108
35	29	A	Partick T	W 2-1	1-0	—	Gough, McCoist	14,706
36	Apr 2	H	Aberdeen	D 1-1	1-0	1	McCall	45,888
37	5	A	Dundee U	D 0-0	0-0	—		11,352
38	16	H	Raith R	W 4-0	2-0	1	Robertson, McCoist, Ferguson D, Mikhailichenko	42,545
39	23	H	Dundee U	W 2-1	0-0	1	Durie 2	44,776
40	26	A	Motherwell	L 1-2	1-2	—	McCoist	14,050
41	30	H	Celtic	D 1-1	0-1	1	Mikhailichenko	47,018
42	May 3	A	Hibernian	L 0-1	0-1	—		14,517
43	7	A	Kilmarnock	L 0-1	0-0	1		18,012
44	14	H	Dundee	D 0-0	0-0	1		41,620

Final League Position: 1

1963-64, 1974-75. Premier Division: 1975-76, 1977-78, 1986-87, 1988-89, 1989-90, 1990-91, 1991-92, 1992-93, 1993-94; *Runners-up:* 23 times.
Scottish Cup Winners: (26 times) 1894, 1897, 1898, 1903, 1928, 1930, 1932, 1934, 1935, 1936, 1948, 1949, 1950, 1953, 1960, 1962, 1963, 1964, 1966, 1973, 1976, 1978, 1979, 1981, 1992, 1993; *Runners-up:* 16 times.
League Cup Winners: (19 times) 1946-47, 1948-49, 1960-61, 1961-62, 1963-64, 1964-65, 1970-71, 1975-76, 1977-78, 1978-79, 1981-82, 1983-84, 1984-85, 1986-87, 1987-88, 1988-89, 1990-91, 1992-93, 1993-94; *Runners-up:* 7 times.
European: *European Cup:* 71 matches (1956-57, 1957-58, 1959-60 semi-finals, 1961-62, 1963-64, 1964-65, 1975-76, 1976-77, 1978-79, 1987-88, 1989-90, 1990-91, 1991-92, 1992-93 final pool, 1993-94).
Cup Winners Cup Winners: 1971-72. 50 matches (1960-61 runners-up, 1962-63, 1966-67 runners-up, 1969-70, 1971-72 winners, 1973-74, 1977-78, 1979-80, 1981-82, 1983-84). *UEFA Cup:* 38 matches (*Fairs Cup:* 1967-68, 1968-69 semi-finals, 1970-71 *UEFA Cup*; 1982-83, 1984-85, 1985-86, 1986-87, 1988-89).
Club colours: Shirt: Royal blue with red and white trim. Shorts: White. Stockings: Red.

Goalscorers: *League* (74): Hateley 22 (2 pens), Durie 12, McCoist 7 (1 pen), Huistra 6, Ferguson I 5, Mikhailichenko 5, Steven 4, Gough 3, McCall 3, Ferguson D 1, Hagen 1, Kuznetsov 1, MacPherson 1, Pressley 1, Robertson 1, own goal 1. *Scottish Cup* (14): Hateley 4 (1 pen), McCoist 3 (1 pen), Brown 1, Durie 1, Ferguson I 1, McPherson 1, Robertson 1, Steven 1, own goal 1. *League Cup* (8): Ferguson I 3, Hateley 2 (1 pen), Durrant 1, McCoist 1, Steven 1.

Maxwell A 31 + 1	McCall S 34	Wishart F 5	Gough R 37	Pressley S 17 + 6	Brown J 24	Murray N 20 + 2	Ferguson I 35	Hateley M 40 + 2	Hagen D 4 + 2	Mikhailichenko A 24 + 10	Durrant I 14 + 9	Huistra P 10 + 11	Steven T 32	Vinnicombe C 2 + 2	McPherson D 27 + 1	Ferguson D 7 + 3	Stevens G 28 + 1	Robertson D 32	Kuznetsov O 4 + 2	Morrow J 2	Miller C 2 + 1	McCoist A 16 + 5	Scott C 5 + 1	Durie G 23 + 1	Goram A 8	Moore C 1	Match No.
1	2	3	4	5	6	7	8	9	10	*11*	12	14															1
1		3	4	5	6	2	*8*		9	12	10	11	7	14													2
1		3	4	2		6	8	10	14		12	11	7		5	*9*											3
1			4	5		6	8	10		11	12		7			9	2	3									4
1			4	5			8	10			12	11	7			9	2	3	6								5
1			4				8	10			12		7	6	5	9	2	3		11							6
1	4			6			8	10				11	7		5	12	2	3			9						7
1		6	4			14	8	10	9	11			7		5		2	*3*									8
1			4	5		3	8	10			6	11	7				2					9	12				9
			4	5		3	8	10	9	14	6	12	7				2			*11*			1				10
1	6		4	12			8	*10*		7	9	11			5		2	3				14					11
1			4				8	10		6	12	11	7		5		2	3				9					12
1	6		4	14			8	10		12	11		7		5		*2*	3				9					13
1	2		4	14	6		8	10		7		*11*			5			3				9					14
1	2		*4*	14	6		8	10		7	11	12			5			3				9					15
1	4				6		8	10		11	7	14			5		2	3				*9*					16
1	5		4		6		8	10		7	9	*11*					2	3			14						17
1	7		4		6	2	8	10		11	9				5			3									18
1	2		4		6		8	10		*11*	9	14			5		12	3						7			19
1	2		*4*	14	6	11	8	10			12		7		5			3						9			20
1	4			6		11	8	10			12		7		5		2	3						9			21
1	6		4	14		11	8	10			12		7		*5*		2	3						9			22
1	4			5		8		10		11			7	3			2		6					9			23
1	*4*			5	6	3		10		11		12	7	14			2		8					9			24
1	8		4	5	6	*3*		10		11		12	7				2		14					9			25
1	8		4		6	5		10		11		12	7				2	3						9			26
1	8			5	6	4		10		11		12	7				*2*	3	14					9			27
1	8		4		6	5		10		11		12	7				2	3						9			28
1	8		4		6	5		10		11			7				2	3						9			29
	5		4		6		8	10		11			7				2	3				14		*9*	1		30
	4				6		8	10		14			7		5		2	3				*9*		11	1		31
	5		4		6		8	10		*11*			7		12		2	3				14		9	1		32
	2		4		6		8	10					7		5			3				9		11	1		33
	3		4		6		8	10		12			7		5		2					9		11	1		34
	3		4		6		8	10		*11*			7		5	14	2					9		12	1		35
	7		4		6	3	8	10		12					5		2					9		11	1		36
14	7		4	6		3		12		11	8				5	10								9	*1*	2	37
1	2		4		6		8	12		14	7				5	10		3				9		*11*			38
1	2		4		6		8	10					7		5			3				9		11			39
1	2		4	6			8			12			7		5	10		3				9		11			40
	2		4	6			8	10		12			7		5	14		3				*9*	1	11			41
	2		4	6		14	8	10		11	9		*7*		5			3				12	1				42
		2	4			5		10	12	11	*7*	14						3	6		8	9	1				43
	6		4				8	10		12		11	7		*5*		2	3				14	1	9			44

ST JOHNSTONE Division 1

Year Formed: 1884. *Ground & Address:* McDiarmid Park, Crieff Road, Perth PH1 2SJ. *Telephone:* 0738 26961. *Clubcall:* 0898 121559.
Ground Capacity: total: 10,721. seated: 10,721. *Size of Pitch:* 115yd # 75yd.
Chairman: G. S. Brown. *Secretary and Managing Director:* Stewart Duff.
Manager: Paul Sturrock. *Sales Executive:* —. *Physio:* J. Peacock. *Coach:* John Blackley. *Reserve Coach:* Raymond Stewart.
Managers since 1975: J. Stewart; J. Storrie; A. Stuart; A. Rennie; I. Gibson; A. Totten, J. McClelland. *Club Nickname(s):* Saints. *Previous Grounds:* Recreation Grounds, Muirton Park.
Record Attendance: (McDiarmid Park): 10,504 v Rangers, Premier Division; 20 Oct, 1990.
Record Transfer Fee received: £400,000 for Ally McCoist to Sunderland (1982).
Record Transfer Fee paid: £285,000 for Paul Wright from Hibernian (Aug 1991).
Record Victory: 9-0 v Albion R, League Cup; 9 March, 1946.
Record Defeat: 1-10 v Third Lanark, Scottish Cup; 24 January, 1903.
Most Capped Player: Sandy McLaren, 5, Scotland.

St JOHNSTONE 1993—94 LEAGUE RECORD

Match No.	Date		Venue	Opponents	Result		H/T Score	Lg. Pos.	Goalscorers	Attendance
1	Aug	7	A	Raith R	D	1-1	1-1	—	Wright	4628
2		14	H	Rangers	L	1-2	1-1	9	Wright	10,152
3		21	H	Dundee U	D	1-1	0-0	7	Torfason	6248
4		28	A	Aberdeen	D	0-0	0-0	9		11,682
5	Sept	4	H	Motherwell	W	3-0	2-0	6	Wright 2 (1 pen), Curran	4576
6		11	A	Kilmarnock	D	0-0	0-0	8		5670
7		18	H	Hibernian	L	1-3	0-2	9	Wright	5008
8		25	H	Dundee	W	2-1	2-0	9	Curran, Davies	4203
9	Oct	2	A	Partick T	L	1-4	1-3	9	Davies	3402
10		6	H	Celtic	W	2-1	2-1	—	Davies 2	7386
11		9	A	Hearts	D	1-1	0-0	7	Wright (pen)	6028
12		16	A	Rangers	L	0-2	0-1	9		41,960
13		23	H	Raith R	D	1-1	1-0	8	Torfason	4411
14		30	A	Dundee U	L	0-2	0-0	10		6275
15	Nov	6	H	Aberdeen	D	1-1	1-0	10	McGinnis	5757
16		9	A	Motherwell	L	0-1	0-0	—		4527
17		13	H	Partick T	L	1-3	0-1	10	Curran	3548
18		20	A	Dundee	W	1-0	1-0	10	Moore	4714
19		27	H	Kilmarnock	L	0-1	0-1	10		4576
20		30	A	Hibernian	D	0-0	0-0	—		4996
21	Dec	4	A	Celtic	L	0-1	0-0	10		15,941
22		11	H	Hearts	W	2-0	2-0	10	Scott, Davies	4631
23		18	H	Rangers	L	0-4	0-2	10		10,056
24	Jan	8	A	Aberdeen	D	1-1	0-0	10	Ferguson	12,712
25		19	A	Raith R	D	1-1	0-1	—	Torfason (pen)	3693
26		22	H	Hibernian	D	2-2	1-0	10	Wright, Dodds	6466
27		25	H	Dundee U	D	1-1	0-1	—	Torfason	5758
28	Feb	5	A	Kilmarnock	D	0-0	0-0	10		6345
29		8	H	Motherwell	W	2-1	2-1	—	Dodds, Ferguson	4522
30		12	H	Dundee	D	1-1	1-1	9	Dodds	5517
31	Mar	5	H	Celtic	L	0-1	0-1	10		8622
32		19	A	Rangers	L	0-4	0-2	10		43,228
33		22	A	Partick T	D	0-0	0-0	—		3295
34		26	H	Raith R	W	2-0	1-0	10	Dodds 2	4550
35		30	H	Kilmarnock	L	0-1	0-1	—		5513
36	Apr	2	A	Hibernian	D	0-0	0-0	—		6628
37		6	A	Hearts	D	2-2	2-2	—	Ferguson, Scott	8938
38		9	A	Dundee	W	1-0	1-0	9	Torfason	2871
39		16	H	Partick T	W	1-0	0-0	8	Scott	4933
40		23	H	Hearts	D	0-0	0-0	9		6762
41		27	A	Celtic	D	1-1	0-1	—	Dodds (pen)	10,602
42		30	A	Dundee U	D	0-0	0-0	9		10,635
43	May	7	H	Aberdeen	L	0-1	0-0	10		6107
44		14	A	Motherwell	W	1-0	0-0	10	Inglis	7498

Final League Position: 10

Most League Appearances: 298: Drew Rutherford.
Most League Goals in Season (Individual): 36: Jimmy Benson, Division II; 1931-32.
Most Goals Overall (Individual): 114: John Brogan, 1977-83.

Honours
League Champions: First Division 1982-83, 1989-90. Division II 1923-24, 1959-60, 1962-63; *Runners-up:* Division II 1931-32. Second Division 1987-88.
Scottish Cup: Semi-finals 1934, 1968, 1989, 1991.
League Cup Runners-up: 1969.
European: *UEFA Cup:* 1971-72.
Club colours: Shirt: Royal blue with white trim. Shorts: White. Stockings: Royal blue, white trim.

Goalscorers: *League* (35): Wright 7 (2 pens), Dodds 6 (1 pen), Davies 5, Torfason 5 (1 pen), Curran 3, Ferguson 3, Scott 3, Inglis 1, McGinnis 1, Moore 1. *Scottish Cup* (8): Dodds 4, Ferguson 2, McMartin 1, Scott 1. *League Cup* (2): Moore 1, Wright 1.

Rhodes A 44	Budden J 1 + 1	Deas P 35 + 1	McGinnis G 28	Inglis J 25	Curran H 39	Ramsey P 22	Turner T 37 + 2	Wright P 16 + 1	Torfason G 21 + 8	Buglione M 3 + 7	McGowne K 37 + 3	Davies J 30 + 2	Moore A 7 + 6	Irons D 1	McAuley S 28	Morgan A — + 3	Arkins V — + 1	Scott P 19 + 5	Cherry P 31 + 2	Cole A 1	McClelland J 1	Ferguson I 22	Dodds W 20	McMartin G — + 6	Miller C 12	Preston A 3 + 6	Maskrey S 1 + 3	Match No.
1	*2*	3	4	5	6	7	8	9	10	11	12	14																1
1		3	4	5	11	10	6	9	8	12	2		7															2
1		3	10	5	8	6	14	9	11		*2*		7	4														3
1		3	4	5	11	10	6	9			*2*	7			8	14												4
1		3	2	5	10	*8*	4	9			11	7			6		14											5
1		3	4	5	8		6	9			10	7			2			11										6
1	14	3	2		4	11	6	9	12		5	7			10			*8*										7
1		3	5		8		6	9	11		10	7	12		4			2										8
1		3	*2*		4		6	9	10		5	7	14		11			8	12									9
1		3	2	5	8		4	9	10			7			6				11									10
1		3	2	5	6		4	9	*10*	14		7			11				8									11
1		3	2	5	4		6	9	10	12		7			11				8									12
1		3	2	5	6				10	8	9	7			11	12			4									13
1		3	2	5	4				10	*9*	7	6			11	14			8									14
1		3	6	5	8			*9*	10		2	7	14		11				4									15
1		3	4	5	8		6	*9*	10		2	7	12		11				14									16
1			2	5	6		12		10		14	7	9		11				*8*	3	4							17
1			4	5	10		8		*9*	14	2	11	7		3				6									18
1		12	4	*5*	10		8		9	14	2	11	7		3				6									19
1		5			10	4	8				2	11	7		3				6			9						20
1		5			10	4	8			14	2	11	*7*		3				6			9						21
1		5			10	4	8		7	14	2	11			3			6				*9*						22
1		*5*			10	4	8		*7*		2	11	14		3			12	6			9						23
1		5			10	4	8	14	*7*		2	11			3			12	6			9						24
1		5	6		11	4	8	*9*	14		2				3							7	10					25
1		5			11	4	8	9			2				3				6			7	10	12				26
1		5			11	4	8		14		2				3			*7*	6			9	10	12				27
1		5	6		11		8				2	7			3				4			9	10					28
1		5	6	2	11	4									3			7	8			9	10	12				29
1		5	6		11	4			14		2				3			*7*	8			9	10					30
1		5		2	11	*4*	8		14		12				3			7	6			9	10					31
1		5		3	11	4	8		*9*		2		14					7	6				10	12				32
1				5	11	4	8				2							7	6			9	10	12	3			33
1				5	11	4	8				2							12	6			9	10		3	7		34
1				5	11	4	8		14		2							12	6			9	10		3	*7*		35
1		5			11	4	8				2	7						12	6			9	10		3			36
1		5			11		8				2	7						4	6			9	10		3	12		37
1		5			11		8		9		2	7						4	6				*10*		3	12	14	38
1		*5*			11		8		14		2	7						4	6			9	10		3	12		39
1		5	11				8		9		2	*7*						4	6				10		3	12	14	40
1		5	11				8				2	7						4	6			9	10		3	12		41
1			11	5			8		14		2	7						4	6			9	*10*		3			42
1			11	5			8				2	*7*						4				9	10	12	3	6	14	43
1			11	5			8				2	12						4	*6*			9	10		3	14	7	44

ST MIRREN Division 1

Year Formed: 1877. *Ground & Address:* St Mirren Park, Love St, Paisley PA3 2EJ. *Telephone:* 041 889 2558/041 840 1337. *Fax:* 041 848 6444.
Ground Capacity: total: 12,395. seated: 6380; 5920 covered, 10,275 uncovered. *Size of Pitch:* 112yd # 73yd.
Chairman: Alan W. Marshall. *Secretary:* A. R. Craig. *Commercial/Marketing Manager:* Bill Campbell.
Manager: Jimmy Bone. *General Manager:* Jack Copland. *Physio:* Andrew Binning. *Coaches* Cameron Money and Kenny McDowall.
Managers since 1975: Alex Ferguson; Jim Clunie; Rikki MacFarlane; Alex Miller; Alex Smith; Tony Fitzpatrick; David Hay.
Club Nickname(s): The Buddies. *Previous Grounds:* Short Roods 1877-79, Thistle Park Greenhill 1879-83, Westmarch 1883-94.
Record Attendance: 47,438 v Celtic, League Cup, 20 Aug, 1949.
Record Transfer Fee received: £850,000 for Ian Ferguson to Rangers (1988).
Record Transfer Fee paid: £400,000 for Thomas Stickroth from Bayer Uerdingen (1990).
Record Victory: 15-0 v Glasgow University, Scottish Cup 1st rd; 30 Jan, 1960.
Record Defeat: 0-9 v Rangers, Division I; 4 Dec, 1897.
Most Capped Player: Godmundor Torfason, 29, Iceland.

St MIRREN 1993—94 LEAGUE RECORD

Match No.	Date	Venue	Opponents	Result		H/T Score	Lg. Pos.	Goalscorers	Attendance
1	Aug 7	H	Airdrieonians	L	0-1	0-1	—		3852
2	14	A	Hamilton A	D	0-0	0-0	9		2599
3	21	H	Morton	D	2-2	1-0	8	Lavety, McWhirter	4133
4	28	A	Stirling Albion	L	0-1	0-1	10		1588
5	Sept 4	H	Ayr U	L	0-1	0-0	11		2578
6	11	H	Dumbarton	L	0-3	0-1	12		2607
7	15	A	Dunfermline Ath	W	4-3	2-2	—	Gallagher, Baker, Gardner, Lavety	2703
8	18	H	Clyde	W	2-1	0-1	9	McWhirter, McIntyre	2493
9	25	A	Falkirk	L	0-2	0-1	9		4633
10	28	H	Brechin C	W	2-0	1-0	—	Dick, McIntyre	1592
11	Oct 2	A	Clydebank	D	1-1	0-1	9	Lavety	2030
12	9	A	Airdrieonians	D	1-1	0-0	9	Gallagher	2726
13	16	H	Dunfermline Ath	L	1-2	1-2	10	McWhirter	3091
14	23	A	Dumbarton	D	3-3	2-0	9	Gallagher 3	1723
15	30	A	Morton	W	2-1	1-1	8	Lavety, Orr	3174
16	Nov 6	H	Stirling Albion	L	0-1	0-0	9		2407
17	9	A	Ayr U	W	1-0	0-0	—	McIntyre	1949
18	13	H	Clydebank	W	1-0	1-0	7	McWhirter	2487
19	20	A	Brechin C	W	4-1	0-0	6	Lavety, Elliot 2, Dawson (pen)	840
20	30	H	Hamilton A	W	1-0	0-0	—	McWhirter	2029
21	Dec 4	A	Clyde	W	1-0	1-0	5	Lavety	1322
22	18	A	Dunfermline Ath	L	2-4	1-2	6	Hewitt, McLaughlin	5059
23	Jan 3	H	Falkirk	W	3-1	1-1	—	McIntyre 2, Hewitt	4897
24	8	A	Stirling Albion	L	0-3	0-1	6		1836
25	11	H	Airdrieonians	W	3-0	1-0	—	Dawson (pen), McWhirter, Elliot	2583
26	18	H	Morton	W	5-1	4-0	—	Elliot, Dawson (pen), McIntyre, Dick, Lavety	2942
27	22	A	Hamilton A	D	0-0	0-0	6		2469
28	25	H	Ayr U	W	3-1	2-1	—	Elliot, McWhirter, Bone	3394
29	Feb 5	H	Dumbarton	L	0-3	0-1	5		2504
30	12	A	Clydebank	W	3-0	0-0	4	Bone, McIntyre, Hewitt	1831
31	26	H	Brechin C	D	1-1	0-0	4	Bone	1922
32	Mar 5	H	Clyde	D	0-0	0-0	5		2080
33	12	A	Falkirk	L	0-4	0-1	5		4167
34	19	H	Dunfermline Ath	L	0-2	0-0	6		2603
35	26	A	Airdrieonians	W	2-0	0-0	6	Bone, Hewitt	2069
36	29	H	Hamilton A	L	0-2	0-1	—		1478
37	Apr 2	A	Dumbarton	W	3-2	2-0	6	Bone, Elliot, Lavety	1377
38	9	H	Clydebank	W	2-0	0-0	5	Dick 2	1640
39	16	A	Brechin C	W	1-0	0-0	5	Lavety	682
40	23	A	Clyde	L	0-3	0-1	6		1901
41	26	H	Falkirk	L	0-3	0-2	—		2765
42	30	A	Morton	W	2-1	2-0	6	Gillies R, Lavety	1984
43	May 7	H	Stirling Albion	W	4-0	1-0	6	Elliot 2, Harvie, Gillies R	1431
44	14	A	Ayr U	W	1-0	0-0	6	McIntyre	1919

Final League Position: 6

Most League Appearances: 351: Tony Fitzpatrick, 1973-88.
Most League Goals in Season (Individual): 45: Dunky Walker, Division I; 1921-22.
Most Goals Overall (Individual): 221: David McCrae, 1923-24.

Honours
League Champions: First Division 1976-77. Division II 1967-68; *Runners-up:* 1935-36.
Scottish Cup Winners: 1926, 1959, 1987. *Runners-up* 1908, 1934, 1962.
League Cup Runners-up: 1955-56.
Victory Cup: 1919-20. *Summer Cup:* 1943-44. *Anglo-Scottish Cup:* 1979-80.
European: *Cup Winners Cup:* 1987-88. *UEFA Cup:* 1980-81, 1983-84, 1985-86.
Club colours: Shirt: Black and white halved shirts. Shorts: White. Stockings: White. Change colours: All red.

Goalscorers: *League* (61): Lavety 10, Elliot 8, McIntyre 8, McWhirter 7, Bone 5, Gallagher 5, Dick 4, Hewitt 4, Dawson 3 (3 pens), Gillies R 2, Baker 1, Gardner 1, Harvie 1, McLaughlin 1, Orr 1. *Scottish Cup* (3): Bone 1, Elliot 1, Lavety 1. *League Cup* (1): Dick 1. *B&Q Cup* (8): Gallagher 4, Lavety 2, Harvie 1, McIntyre 1.

Combe A 16	Dawson R 38	Fullarton J 37	McWhirter N 27	Taylor S 13 + 1	Orr N 24	Bone A 21 + 12	Lambert P 3	Lavety B 35 + 7	Hewitt J 27 + 4	Elliot D 34 + 2	McIntyre P 39 + 3	Gallagher E 11 + 5	Baker M 37 + 1	Dick J 31 + 4	Money C 28	Gillies R 10 + 12	Gillies K 3 + 6	Paterson A 2	McGrotty G 1	Peacock J 5 + 1	McLaughlin B 18 + 5	Gardner J 14 + 7	Farrell S 4 + 4	Harvie S 4 + 2	Hetherston B — + 3	Archdeacon P — + 2	Smith Benj 2	Smith Bria — + 2	Match No.
1	2	3	4	5	6	7	8	*9*	10	11	12	14																	1
1	2	11	*4*	5	6	14		9	10		12	7	3	8															2
		5	4		6		8	*9*	10	14	11	7	3	2	1	12													3
		5	4		6	14	8	9		*11*	2	10	3	7	1		12												4
		5	4					9		11	6		3	8	1	*10*		2	7	12	14								5
1		5		4				9	12	*11*	6	7	3	8		14		2				10							6
1	2		4		6	12		14	10		5	7	*3*	9								11	8						7
1	2	6	4			14		*9*	10		5	7	3	12								11	8						8
1	2	8	4		6			14	10	9	5	7	3	12								*11*							9
	2		4		5	*7*		9	10		12	14	3	6	1	8						11							10
	2	3	4		6	7		*9*	12		5			8	1						14	11		10					11
	2	8	4		6	7		9	12			14		10	1						5	*11*		3					12
	2		4		6	14		9	10		8		5	7	1		12					*11*		3					13
	2	8	4		6	14		9	10		5	7	3		1							*11*		12					14
	2	*11*	4		6			9	10	14	5	7	3		1						8		12						15
			4		6	14		9	10	11	5	*7*	3	12	1						2	8							16
1	2	8	4		6			9	*10*	11	5	7	3								12	14							17
	2	8	4		6	7		*9*		11	5		3		1	12					10	14							18
	2	10	4		6	7		9	14	11			3	*8*	1	12					*5*								19
	2		4		6	*7*		9	10	11	5		3	8	1						12	14							20
	2		4			7		9	10	11	5		3	8	1						6								21
	2	7	4		6	14		9	10	11	5		3	*8*	1						12								22
	2	8	4		6	14		9	10	11	5		3		1								*7*						23
	2	8	4		6	*7*		9	10	11	5		3		1	14													24
1	2	8	4	6				14	10	11	5		3	7		*9*							12						25
1	2	8	4	6				9	10	11	5		3	*7*		14							12						26
1	2	8	4		6	14		9	10	11	5		3	*7*		12													27
1	2	8	4			14		*9*	10	11	5		3	7		12					6								28
1	2	8		4		14		9	10	11	5		3	12		*7*					6								29
1	2	6		4		8		9	10	*11*	5		3	7								14	12						30
	2	6		4		8		14	10	11	5		3		1							*9*	*7*		12				31
	2	*6*				8		9	10	11	5		3	7	1	14	12				4								32
	2	6		12		8		9		11	5	14	3	*7*	1	*10*					4								33
	2	10		4		*8*		9		11	5	14	3		1		12			7	6								34
1	2	3		4		9			10	11	5			7		14				*8*	6					12			35
	2	3		*4*		9		14	10	11	5		12	7	1					8	6								36
	2	10			4	9		14		11	5		3	7	1					*8*	6	12							37
	2	10			4	*8*		9		11	5		3	7	1	14					6					12			38
	2	10			4	*8*		9		11	5			7	1	14						6					3	12	39
	2	6				10		9		3	5			*8*	1	7	14					11			12		4		40
1	2	6		4		*9*		14		11	5		3	8		10	12			7									41
	2	6						*9*		11	5		3	8	1	10	7				4	14							42
	2	6						*9*		11	5		3	8	1	10	7				4	14		12					43
1				4						11	5		3	8		10	7				*2*	9		6	14			12	44

STENHOUSEMUIR Division 2

Year Formed: 1884. *Ground & Address:* Ochilview Park, Gladstone Rd, Stenhousemuir FK5 5QL. *Telephone:* 0324 562992.
Ground Capacity: total: 3480. seated: 340. *Size of Pitch:* 113yd # 78yd.
Chairman: Greig Thomson. *Secretary:* A. T. Bulloch. *Commercial Manager:* John Sharp.
Manager: Terry Christie. *Assistant Manager:* Graeme Armstrong. *Physio:* Lee Campbell: *Coach:* Gordon Buchanan.
Managers since 1975: H. Glasgow; J. Black; A. Rose; W. Henderson; A. Rennie; J. Meakin; D. Lawson. *Club Nickname(s):* The Warriors. *Previous Grounds:* Tryst Ground 1884-86, Goschen Park 1886-90.
Record Attendance: 12,500 v East Fife, Scottish Cup 4th rd; 11 Mar, 1950.
Record Transfer Fee received: £30,000 for David Beaton to Falkirk (June 1989).
Record Transfer Fee paid: £7000 to Meadowbank T for Lee Bullen (Nov 1990).
Record Victory: 9-2 v Dundee U, Division II; 19 Apr, 1937.
Record Defeat: 2-11 v Dunfermline Ath. Division II; 27 Sept, 1930.

STENHOUSEMUIR 1993—94 LEAGUE RECORD

Match No.	Date	Venue	Opponents	Result		H/T Score	Lg. Pos.	Goalscorers	Attendance
1	Aug 7	H	East Stirling	W	3-1	3-0	—	Mathieson 2, Steel	435
2	14	A	East Fife	L	0-3	0-1	8		767
3	21	A	Montrose	L	0-2	0-0	10		561
4	28	H	Cowdenbeath	D	1-1	0-1	11	Mathieson	367
5	Sept 4	H	Alloa	D	1-1	1-0	10	Irvine	458
6	11	A	Albion R	W	2-1	0-1	9	Roseburgh, Steel	240
7	18	A	Arbroath	W	2-1	0-1	9	Mathieson, Steel	633
8	25	H	Queen's Park	W	2-0	1-0	5	Steel 2	404
9	Oct 2	H	Berwick R	W	2-1	2-0	3	Irvine 2	352
10	9	A	Stranraer	L	0-1	0-1	6		599
11	16	H	Forfar Ath	W	2-0	1-0	5	Irvine, Mathieson	380
12	23	A	Queen of the S	W	2-1	0-1	4	Roseburgh, Irvine	965
13	30	A	Meadowbank T	L	1-3	0-0	4	Roseburgh (pen)	261
14	Nov 6	H	East Fife	L	0-1	0-1	5		493
15	13	H	Arbroath	W	4-0	3-0	5	Roseburgh 2, Fisher 2	370
16	20	A	Queen's Park	W	2-1	0-0	4	Steel, Mathieson	517
17	30	H	Str	D	2-2	2-2	—	Godfrey, Roseburgh	408
18	Dec 4	A	Berwick R	L	1-2	1-2	4	Steel	396
19	18	A	East Stirling	W	2-0	0-0	3	Irvine, Swanson	775
20	Jan 18	H	Montrose	L	3-4	2-2	—	Sprott 2, Haddow	281
21	22	A	Forfar Ath	D	1-1	0-0	6	Sprott	478
22	25	H	Meadowbank T	D	1-1	1-1	—	Sludden	397
23	Feb 1	A	Cowdenbeath	W	3-1	3-1	—	Mathieson, Sludden, Sprott	224
24	5	H	Albion R	W	5-1	2-1	3	McCaffrey (og), Sprott, Sludden, Roseburgh, Mathieson	315
25	8	H	Queen of the S	W	3-0	2-0	—	Mathieson 2, Aitken	387
26	12	A	Alloa	W	2-1	1-0	2	Sludden 2	856
27	19	H	Arbroath	W	2-0	0-0	2	Sludden, Steel	523
28	Mar 5	A	Queen's Park	W	4-2	1-1	2	Sludden 2, Fisher, Mathieson	516
29	12	H	Forfar Ath	L	0-1	0-0	2		421
30	16	A	Cowdenbeath	D	1-1	1-1	—	Sludden	166
31	19	A	Meadowbank T	L	0-1	0-0	2		218
32	26	H	Albion R	D	0-0	0-0	2		351
33	Apr 2	H	Alloa	W	1-0	0-0	2	Mathieson	557
34	9	A	East Stirling	D	2-2	0-0	2	Sludden 2	557
35	16	H	Montrose	W	2-0	1-0	2	Mathieson 2	333
36	23	A	Queen of the S	L	1-2	1-0	2	Sludden	1835
37	30	A	Berwick R	L	0-3	0-1	3		599
38	May 7	H	East Fife	D	1-1	0-0	3	Sprott	441
39	14	A	Stranraer	W	1-0	1-0	3	Sludden	963

Final League Position: 3

Most Capped Player: —.
Most League Appearances: 360: Archie Rose.
Most League Goals in Season (Individual): 32: Robert Taylor, Division II; 1925-26.
Most Goals Overall (Individual): —.

Honours
League Champions: —. *Scottish Cup:* Semi-finals 1902-03. *League Cup:* Quarter-finals 1947-48, 1960-61, 1975-76.
Club colours: Shirt: Maroon with silver stripe. Shorts: White with maroon insert. Stockings: White.

Goalscorers: *League* (62): Mathieson 14, Sludden 13, Steel 8, Roseburgh 7 (1 pen), Irvine 6, Sprott 6, Fisher 3, Aitken 1, Godfrey 1, Haddow 1, Swanson 1, own goal 1. *Scottish Cup* (0): *League Cup* (4): Clouston 1, Fisher 1, Irvine 1, Mathieson 1. *B&Q Cup* (0).

Robertson S 3	Aitken N 36 + 1	Haddow L 21 + 1	Armstrong G 39	Godfrey P 29	Logan S 22 + 4	Steel T 26 + 7	Clouston B 3	Mathieson M 36	Irvine J 18 + 2	Fisher J 30	Dickov S 4 + 11	Clarke J 21 + 4	O'Neill P — + 2	Sprott A 32 + 3	Harkness M 36	Roseburgh D 28	Hallford E 10 + 1	McConnell I — + 1	Christie M 13 + 5	Donaldson E 1 + 3	Swanson D 2 + 5	Gallacher I 1	Sludden J 18	Match No.
1	2	3	4	5	6	7	8	9	10	11	12													1
1	2	3	4		6	7	8	9	*10*	11	12	5	14											2
1	2		4		6	7	8	9	*10*	11	14	5	12	3										3
		3	4		6	7		9	8	11	12	5		2	1	10								4
	5	11	4		6	12		9	8	7				2	1	10	3							5
	2	3	4		*6*	7		9	12	8	14	5		11	1	10								6
	2	3	4	5		7		9	8	*6*	12			11	1	10		14						7
	2		4	5	12	7		9	8	6	14			*11*	1	10	3							8
	2		4	5		7		9	8	6				11	1	10	3							9
	2		4	5	12	7		9	8	6		14		11	1	10	*3*							10
	2	3	4	5	10	7		9	8	6				11	1									11
	2	3	4	5	*7*	12		9	8	6				11	1	10								12
	2	*3*	4	5		7		9	8	6	12	14		11	1	10								13
	2	3	4	5		7		9	*8*	6		12		11	1	10								14
		11	4	5				9	8	6		2			1	10	*3*		7	12	14			15
	2	3	4			7		9	8	6		5		12	1	*10*			11	14				16
	2	9	4	5		7			8	6				3	1	10			11					17
	2	9	4	5		7			8	6		12		3	1	10			11					18
	2	9	4	5		7			8			10			1		*3*			14	6	11		19
	2	11	4	*5*		7		9	12		8	6		10	1					3	14			20
	2	11	4	5		7		9			8	6		10	1				14		3			21
	2	3	4	5		7		9			*8*	6		11	1				14		12		10	22
	2	3	4		*6*	7		9			8	5		11	1				14				10	23
	12	3	4	5	6	*7*		9			14	2		11	1	*8*							10	24
	7	3	4	5	6			9			12	2		11	1	8							10	25
	7		4	5	6	3		9				*2*		11	1	8					14		10	26
	2		4	5	6	7		9						11	1	8			3				10	27
	2		4	5	6	12		9		7				11	1	8			3				10	28
	2		4	5	6	12		9		7				11	1	8			3				10	29
	2		4	5	6	7		9		8				*11*	1	3			14				10	30
	2		4	5	6	*7*		9		8				11	1	3	14						10	31
	2		4		6	12		9		7		5		11	1	3			*8*		14		10	32
	2		4	5	12			9		7		6		11	1	8	3						10	33
	2		4	5	12			9		*7*		6		11	1	8	*3*		14				10	34
	2		4	5	8			9		7		6		12	1	3			11				10	35
	2		4	5	8	14		9		7		6		12	1		3		11				10	36
	2		4		8	12		9		7	14	5		*11*	1		3		6				10	37
	2		4	5	6			9		7				11	1	3			8				10	38
	2	12	4			7		9		6		5		11	1	3			8				10	39

STIRLING ALBION Division 2

Year Formed: 1945. *Ground & Address:* Forthbank Stadium, Springkerse Industrial Estate, Stirling FK7 7UJ. *Telephone:* 0786 450399.
Chairman: Peter McKenzie. *Secretary:* Marlyn Hallam. *Commercial Manager:* —.
Manager/Chief Coach: Kevin Drinkell. *Assistant Manager:* —. *Physio:* George Cameron.
Managers since 1975: A. Smith; G. Peebles; J. Fleeting, J. Brogan. *Club Nickname(s):* The Binos. *Previous Grounds:* Annfield.
Record Attendance: 26,400 v Celtic, Scottish Cup 4th rd; 14 Mar, 1959.
Record Transfer Fee received: £70,000 for John Philliben to Doncaster R (Mar 1984).
Record Transfer Fee paid: £17,000 for Douglas Lawrie from Airdrieonians (Dec 1989).
Record Victory: 20-0 v Selkirk, Scottish Cup 1st rd; 8 Dec, 1984.
Record Defeat: 0-9 v Dundee U, Division I; 30 Dec, 1967.
Most Capped Player: —.

STIRLING ALBION 1993—94 LEAGUE RECORD

Match No.	Date	Venue	Opponents	Result	H/T Score	Lg. Pos.	Goalscorers	Attendance
1	Aug 7	H	Dumbarton	W 2-0	0-0	—	Watters, Reilly	879
2	14	A	Ayr U	L 1-2	0-0	5	Callaghan	1503
3	21	A	Falkirk	L 0-2	0-1	7		4188
4	28	H	St Mirren	W 1-0	1-0	5	Flynn	1588
5	Sept 4	A	Brechin C	W 2-1	0-1	4	Armstrong, Flynn	610
6	11	H	Dunfermline Ath	W 2-0	0-0	4	Watters 2	2050
7	14	A	Morton	D 2-2	1-1	—	Tait, Armstrong	1208
8	18	A	Airdrieonians	L 2-3	0-0	5	Kerr, Callaghan	2076
9	25	H	Hamilton A	W 3-1	1-1	4	McCallum, Flynn, Watters	1001
10	28	H	Clydebank	L 0-3	0-0	—		985
11	Oct 2	A	Clyde	L 0-3	0-2	6		777
12	9	A	Dumbarton	W 2-1	1-1	5	Pew, Lawrie	766
13	16	H	Morton	D 1-1	1-0	5	Lawrie	1000
14	23	A	Dunfermline Ath	L 0-3	0-0	7		3993
15	30	H	Falkirk	L 3-4	1-2	7	Watters 2, McInnes	2476
16	Nov 6	A	St Mirren	W 1-0	0-0	7	McKenna	2407
17	9	H	Brechin C	W 2-1	1-0	—	Armstrong, Watters	516
18	13	H	Clyde	D 1-1	0-1	6	McKenna	943
19	20	A	Clydebank	L 1-2	1-1	8	Watters	770
20	Dec 4	H	Airdrieonians	L 0-4	0-4	8		1401
21	11	H	Ayr U	D 0-0	0-0	8		786
22	18	A	Morton	W 1-0	0-0	7	Watters	928
23	Jan 8	H	St Mirren	W 3-0	1-0	7	Watters Armstrong, Orr (og)	1836
24	11	H	Dumbarton	D 0-0	0-0	—		758
25	15	A	Brechin C	L 0-2	0-0	7		543
26	22	A	Ayr U	L 1-3	1-2	8	Mitchell	1780
27	Feb 2	A	Hamilton A	W 1-0	1-0	—	Watters	1178
28	5	H	Dunfermline Ath	W 1-0	1-0	8	Watters	1888
29	12	A	Clyde	D 0-0	0-0	8		2112
30	15	A	Falkirk	L 1-3	1-2	—	Gibson	2748
31	26	H	Clydebank	L 1-2	0-1	8	Armstrong	991
32	Mar 5	A	Airdrieonians	L 0-3	0-1	8		1644
33	12	H	Hamilton A	D 1-1	1-0	8	McInnes	829
34	19	H	Morton	L 0-3	0-1	8		719
35	26	A	Dumbarton	D 0-0	0-0	8		887
36	29	H	Ayr U	L 1-3	0-2	—	Drinkell	953
37	Apr 2	A	Dunfermline Ath	L 1-2	1-1	9	Mitchell	4530
38	9	H	Clyde	L 0-1	0-0	9		727
39	16	A	Clydebank	L 1-2	0-1	9	Watters	732
40	23	H	Airdrieonians	D 1-1	1-1	9	Armstrong	904
41	27	A	Hamilton A	W 1-0	1-0	—	McInnes	976
42	30	H	Falkirk	L 0-1	0-0	9		2813
43	May 7	A	St Mirren	L 0-4	0-1	9		1431
44	14	H	Brechin C	L 0-3	0-0	9		481

Final League Position: 9

Most League Appearances: 504: Matt McPhee, 1967-81.
Most League Goals in Season (Individual): 27: Joe Hughes, Division II; 1969-70.
Most Goals Overall (Individual): 129: Billy Steele, 1971-83.

Honours
League Champions: Division II 1952-53, 1957-58, 1960-61, 1964-65. Second Division 1976-77, 1990-91; *Runners-up:* Division II 1948-49, 1950-51.
Scottish Cup: —. *League Cup:* —.
Club colours: Shirt: Red with white sleeves. Shorts: White. Stockings: White.

Goalscorers: *League* (41): Watters 13, Armstrong 6, Flynn 3, McInnes 3, Callaghan 2, Lawrie 2, McKenna 2, Mitchell 2, Drinkell 1, Gibson 1, Kerr 1, McCallum 1, Pew 1, Reilly 1, Tait 1, own goal 1. *Scottish Cup* (4): Roberts 2, Armstrong 1, Pew 1. *League Cup* (0): *B&Q Cup* (0).

McGeown M 43	McCormack JT 10	Watson P 29 + 1	Tait T 42	Lawrie D 21	Mitchell C 43	Reilly R 17 + 5	Moore V 5	Watters W 29 + 11	Armstrong P 39	Flynn D 16 + 4	Kinross S — + 1	Pew D 21 + 10	Callaghan T 27 + 5	McCallum M 8 + 3	Kerr J 4	McKenna A 6 + 1	Macdonald K — + 1	Docherty A 1 + 6	McInnes I 12 + 13	McAnenay P 1	Roberts P 16 + 4	Hamilton J 21 + 1	Gibson J 16 + 5	McQuilter R 18	McLeod J 17 + 1	Reid W 11	Drinkell K 10 + 1	Monaghan M 1 + 1	Match No.
1	2	3	4	5	6	7	8	9	10	*11*	12	14																	1
1	2	3	4	5	6	7	*8*	9	10	11		14	12																2
1		3	4	5	6	7	8	*9*	10	11		14	2	12															3
1	2	3	4	5			8			*11*		7	10	9	6	12	14												4
1	2	3	4	5	6		8		10	11		9	7					12											5
1	2	3	4	5	6			14	10	*11*		7	8	9					12										6
1	*2*	3	4	5	6			11	10			7	8	9				14	12										7
1		3	4	5	2			14	10	*11*		7	8	9	6				12										8
1	2	3	4	5	6			14	10	*11*		7	8	9															9
1	2	3	4	5	6	12		14	10	*11*		7	8	9															10
1		3	4	5	2	12		9	*10*	11		7	8	14	6														11
1	2	3	4	5	6			14	10	11		*9*	8					12	7										12
1		3	4	5	6	2		14	10	11		9	*8*					12	7										13
1		3	4	5	6	9			10	11			8			2			7										14
1	2	3	4	5	6	12		9	10	*11*			8	14					7										15
1				5	6	10		9	3	14			8	*11*		2		12	7	4									16
1			4	5	6	10		9	3	14			8	*11*		2			7										17
1			4	5	6	10		9	3	14			8			2		12	7		*11*								18
1			4	5	6	3		9		*11*		14	8			2		10	7										19
1		3	4	5	6	11		9				12				*8*			7		14	2	10						20
1		3	4		6			9	10	14		7									*11*	2	12	5	8				21
1		3	4		6			9	10			7							14		*11*	2	12	5	8				22
1		3	4		6			9	10			*7*							14		11	2	12	5	8				23
1		3	4		6			9	10			*7*							14		11	2	12	5	8				24
1		3	4		6			*9*	10			7	14								11	2	12	5	8				25
1				3	6	12		14		11		*7*	4								9	2	10	5	8				26
1			4		6	14		9	3			*7*	8									2	10	5	11				27
1			4		6	7		9	3				8						12			2	10	5	11				28
1			4		6	*7*		9	3				8								14	2	10	5	11				29
1			4		6	7		9	3				8						12			2	10	5	11				30
1		3	4		6	*7*		9	8										12		14	2	10	5	11				31
1		12	4		6			14	3			7	8								*9*	2	10	5	11				32
1		3	4		6	8		14					12						7		*9*	2	10	5	11				33
1			4		6			14	3			12							7			2	10	*5*	11	8	9		34
1		5	4		6	7			3												10	2			11	8	9		35
1		5	4		6	7		12	3				14								10	*2*			11	8	9		36
		3	8		4			9	11			*7*	5		6				14				2			10	12	1	37
1		3	4		6			9	11				*5*						14		7		2		12	8	10		38
1		3	4		6			9	11			14	*5*								12	2	7			8	10		39
1		*3*	6		4			8	11			14	12								9	2		5		10	7		40
1			6		4			9	3			11	*8*						14				2	5		10	7		41
1			*6*		4			8	3			14							11		9	12	2	5		10	7		42
1			5		4			8	3			11							12		9	2	10			6	7		43
1			6		4			8	3			14									*9*	2		5	11	10	7	12	44

STRANRAER Division 1

Year Formed: 1870. *Ground & Address:* Stair Park, London Rd, Stranraer DG9 8BS. *Telephone:* 0776 3271.
Ground Capacity: total: 5000. seated: 700. *Size of Pitch:* 110yd # 70yd.
Chairman: G. F. Compton. *Secretary:* Graham Rodgers. *Commercial Manager: T. L. Sutherland.*
Manager: Alex McAnespie. *Coach:* Derek McHarg.
Managers since 1975: J. Hughes; N. Hood; G. Hamilton; D. Sneddon; J. Clark; R. Clark; A. McAnespie. *Club Nickname(s):* The Blues. *Previous Grounds:* None.
Record Attendance: 6500 v Rangers, Scottish Cup 1st rd; 24 Jan, 1948.
Record Transfer Fee received: £30,000 for Duncan George to Ayr Utd.
Record Transfer Fee paid: £15,000 for Colin Harkness from Kilmarnock (Aug 1989).
Record Victory: 7-0 v Brechin C, Division II; 6 Feb, 1965.
Record Defeat: 1-11 v Queen of the South, Scottish Cup 1st rd; 16 Jan, 1932.
Most Capped Player: —.

STRANRAER 1993—94 LEAGUE RECORD

Match No.	*Date*	*Venue*	*Opponents*	*Result*		*H/T Score*	*Lg. Pos.*	*Goalscorers*	*Atten-dance*
1	Aug 7	H	Montrose	L	2-4	1-2	—	Henderson, Diver	672
2	14	A	Meadowbank T	W	3-1	1-1	6	Sloan, Diver 2	258
3	21	A	Queen of the S	W	1-0	1-0	5	Henderson	1650
4	28	H	Albion R	W	2-1	1-1	3	Grant, Diver	666
5	Sept 4	H	Arbroath	W	2-1	2-1	3	Sloan 2	658
6	11	A	Alloa	L	0-1	0-0	5		437
7	18	A	Berwick R	L	0-1	0-1	7		435
8	25	H	Cowdenbeath	W	4-0	1-0	3	Sloan 2, Duncan, Grant	541
9	Oct 2	A	Queen's Park	D	0-0	0-0	4		518
10	9	H	Stenhousemuir	W	1-0	1-0	3	Brannigan	599
11	16	H	East Fife	W	3-2	1-2	3	Henderson, Grant, Sloan	644
12	23	A	Forfar Ath	W	1-0	1-0	1	Grant	509
13	30	A	East Stirling	D	2-2	1-1	2	Cody, Sloan	414
14	Nov 6	H	Meadowbank T	W	3-1	2-0	1	Gallagher 2, Sloan	940
15	13	H	Berwick R	W	3-0	1-0	1	Sloan 2, Duncan (pen)	743
16	20	A	Cowdenbeath	W	2-1	0-0	1	Duncan, Gallagher	509
17	30	A	Stenhousemuir	D	2-2	2-2	—	Gallagher, McIntyre	408
18	Dec 4	H	Queen's Park	W	2-0	0-0	1	Grant, Sloan	742
19	27	H	East Stirling	W	1-0	1-0	—	Ferguson	970
20	Jan 1	H	Queen of the S	L	1-2	0-0	1	Ferguson	1584
21	4	A	Montrose	W	2-0	1-0	—	Henderson, Cody	678
22	8	A	Albion R	W	2-1	0-0	1	McIntyre, Duncan (pen)	306
23	25	A	East Fife	D	1-1	1-1	—	Sloan	749
24	Feb 2	H	Forfar Ath	W	2-0	0-0	—	Sloan 2	1010
25	5	H	Alloa	D	1-1	1-0	1	Sloan	1101
26	12	A	Arbroath	D	0-0	0-0	1		606
27	23	A	Berwick R	L	0-1	0-1	—		567
28	26	H	Albion R	W	2-1	0-0	1	Henderson, Duncan (pen)	784
29	Mar 5	H	Queen of the S	D	3-3	0-1	1	Walker T, McLean, Duncan (pen)	1173
30	12	A	Meadowbank T	D	1-1	0-0	1	Henderson	453
31	19	H	East Fife	W	2-1	1-0	1	Ferguson 2	801
32	26	A	Alloa	D	1-1	1-1	1	Ferguson	599
33	Apr 2	A	Queen's Park	D	1-1	1-0	1	Walker T	920
34	13	H	Montrose	W	1-0	1-0	—	Cody	799
35	16	H	Arbroath	W	1-0	0-0	1	Gallagher	916
36	23	A	East Stirling	W	3-2	1-1	1	Grant, Duncan 2	862
37	30	A	Forfar Ath	W	3-1	1-1	1	Walker T 2, Sloan	488
38	May 7	H	Cowdenbeath	W	2-0	1-0	1	Walker T, Ferguson	1531
39	14	H	Stenhousemuir	L	0-1	0-1	1		963

Final League Position: 1

Most League Appearances: 256: Ian McDonald.
Most League Goals in Season (Individual): 27: Derek Frye, Second Division; 1977-78.
Most Goals Overall (Individual): —.

Honours
League Champions: Second Division 1993-94.
Scottish Cup: —.
League Cup: —.
Qualifying Cup Winners: 1937.
Club colours: Shirt: Royal blue with geometrical design. Shorts: White. Stockings: Royal blue.

Goalscorers: *League* (63): Sloan 16, Duncan 8 (4 pens), Ferguson 6, Grant 6, Henderson 6, Gallagher 5, Walker T 5, Diver 4, Cody 3, McIntyre 2, Brannigan 1, McLean 1. *Scottish Cup* (11): Sloan 8, Duncan 1 (pen), Ferguson 1, Henderson 1. *League Cup* (2): Henderson 2. *B&Q Cup* (2): Henderson 1, Sloan 1.

Duffy B 30 + 2	McIntyre S 16 + 8	Hughes J 24 + 1	Millar G 36	Brannigan K 36	Gallagher A 26 + 3	Sloan T 38	Grant A 32	Duncan G 35	Cody S 29	Henderson D 35	Diver D 1 + 4	McLean P 20 + 5	Spittal I 25 + 4	Ferguson W 8 + 21	Brown J 5 + 1	Walker D — + 2	Johnston S 2	Ross S 9	Walker T 12	McCaffrey J 10	McCann J — + 1	Match No.
1	*2*	3	4	5	6	7	8	9	10	11	12	14										1
1	2	3	6	5		7	8	9	10	*11*	12	14	4									2
1		2	3	5		7	8	6	10	11	9		4									3
1	2	3	*6*	5		7	8	9	10	11	12		4	14								4
1	2	3	6	5		7	8	9	10	11	12		4									5
1	2	*3*	6	5	9	7	8		10	11		14	4	12								6
1	2			5	6	7	8	9		11		10	4		3	12						7
1			2	5		7	8	9	*10*	11		6	4	12	3	14						8
1			2	5	14	7	8	*9*	10	11		6	4		3							9
1			2	5	12	*7*	8	9	10	11		6	4	14	3							10
1	14		2	*5*		7	8	9	10	11		6	4	12	3							11
1	14	3	2		5	7	8	9	10	11		*6*	4	12								12
1	14	3	2		5	7	8	9	10	11		*6*	4	12								13
1	12		2	5	10	7	8	3		11		6	4	9								14
1	3		2	5	10	7	8	11				6	4	9								15
1	3		2	5	6		8	10				11	4	9	12		7					16
1	3		2	5	6	7	8	9		11		10	4									17
1	3		2	5	6	7	8	9		11			4	12			10					18
		3	2		5	7	8	6	10	11			4	9				1				19
	14	3	2	5	6	7	8	9	10	11			*4*	12				1				20
14	4	3	2	5	6	7	8	9	10	11				12				*1*				21
1	6	3	2	5		7	8	9	10	11			4									22
1		3	2	5	6	7	8	9	10	11		4										23
1		3	2	5	6	7	8	9		11		10	4	12								24
1		3	2	5	6	7	8	9		11		10	4									25
1	8	3	2	5	6	7		10		11		12	4	9								26
1	4		2	5	6	7	8	9	10	11		3		12								27
	3		2	5	6	7		8	10	11			4	12				1	9			28
		14	2	5	6	7		3	10	11		8	*4*	12				1	9			29
1	14		2	5	6	*7*		*10*	8	11		3		12					9	4		30
1	14	3	2	*5*	6	7			10			8	12	11					9	4		31
1	14	3	2	5	6	*7*			10			8		11					9	4		32
1		3	2	5	6	7			10	11		14	12	8					*9*	4		33
1		3	2	5		7	8	6	10	11				12					9	4		34
1		3	*2*	5	14	7	8	6	10	11				12					9	4		35
		3		5	6	7	*8*	2	10	11			14	12				1	9	4		36
		3		5	*6*	7	8	2	10	11			14	12				1	9	4		37
14		3	2	5		7	8	6	10	11				12				*1*	9	4		38
	3		2	5	·	7	8	6		11		10		12				1	9	4	14	39

Scottish League 1993–94

Premier Division

		Home			*Goals*		*Away*			*Goals*			
	P	W	D	L	F	A	W	D	L	F	A	Pt	GD
Rangers	44	12	6	4	43	22	10	8	4	31	19	58	+33
Aberdeen	44	11	9	2	33	12	6	12	4	25	24	55	+22
Motherwell	44	11	7	4	31	20	9	7	6	27	23	54	+15
Celtic	44	8	11	3	25	17	7	9	6	26	21	50	+13
Hibernian	44	11	7	4	29	15	5	8	9	24	33	47	+5
Dundee U	44	5	11	6	26	25	6	9	7	21	23	42	–1
Hearts	44	6	9	7	22	24	5	11	6	15	19	42	–6
Kilmarnock	44	6	10	6	18	19	6	6	10	18	26	40	–9
Partick T	44	9	8	5	23	17	3	8	11	23	40	40	–11
St Johnstone	44	7	7	8	24	26	3	13	6	11	21	40	–12
Raith R	44	3	12	7	25	35	3	7	12	21	45	31	–34
Dundee	44	6	7	9	26	26	2	6	14	16	31	29	–15

First Division

		Home			*Goals*		*Away*			*Goals*			
	P	W	D	L	F	A	W	D	L	F	A	Pt	GD
Falkirk	44	16	4	2	47	16	10	10	2	34	16	66	+49
Dunfermline Ath	44	18	2	2	61	18	11	5	6	32	17	65	+58
Airdrieonians	44	9	9	4	28	18	11	5	6	30	20	54	+20
Hamilton A	44	13	5	4	43	20	6	7	9	23	34	50	+12
Clydebank	44	11	5	6	30	28	7	9	6	26	20	50	+8
St Mirren	44	10	3	9	30	25	11	5	6	31	30	50	+6
Ayr U	44	6	8	8	20	28	8	6	8	22	24	42	–10
Dumbarton	44	5	8	9	25	29	6	6	10	23	30	36	–11
Stirling Albion	44	7	6	9	23	30	6	3	13	18	38	35	–27
Clyde	44	6	7	9	18	20	4	5	13	17	38	32	–23
Morton	44	3	11	8	22	29	3	6	13	22	46	29	–31
Brechin C	44	4	3	15	13	34	2	4	16	17	47	19	–51

Second Division

		Home			*Goals*		*Away*			*Goals*			
	P	W	D	L	F	A	W	D	L	F	A	Pt	GD
Stranraer	39	15	2	3	38	18	8	8	3	25	17	56	+28
Berwick R	39	9	7	4	40	23	9	5	5	35	23	48	+29
Stenhousemuir	39	10	6	3	35	15	9	3	8	27	29	47	+18
Meadowbank T	39	9	8	2	36	24	8	5	7	26	24	47	+14
Queen of the S	39	9	3	7	36	20	8	6	6	33	28	43	+21
East Fife	39	9	5	5	33	23	6	6	8	25	29	41	+6
Alloa	39	6	8	6	16	17	6	9	4	25	22	41	+2
Forfar Ath	39	6	6	8	27	32	8	5	6	31	26	39	—
East Stirling	39	7	3	9	29	31	6	8	6	25	26	37	–3
Montrose	39	6	5	8	24	25	8	3	9	32	36	36	–5
Queen's Park	39	10	4	6	34	32	2	6	11	18	44	34	–24
Arbroath	39	6	8	5	24	28	6	1	13	18	39	33	–25
Albion R	39	3	5	12	18	33	4	5	10	19	33	24	–29
Cowdenbeath	39	1	4	15	19	39	5	4	10	21	33	20	–32

SCOTTISH LEAGUE 1890–91 to 1993–94

*On goal average/difference. †Held jointly after indecisive play-off. ‡Won on deciding match.
††Held jointly. ¶Two points deducted for fielding ineligible player.
Competition suspended 1940–45 during war. ‡‡Two points deducted for registration irregularities.

PREMIER DIVISION

	First	Pts	Second	Pts	Third	Pts
			Maximum points: 72			
1975–76	Rangers	54	Celtic	48	Hibernian	43
1976–77	Celtic	55	Rangers	46	Aberdeen	43
1977–78	Rangers	55	Aberdeen	53	Dundee U	40
1978–79	Celtic	48	Rangers	45	Dundee U	44
1979–80	Aberdeen	48	Celtic	47	St Mirren	42
1980–81	Celtic	56	Aberdeen	49	Rangers*	44
1981–82	Celtic	55	Aberdeen	53	Rangers	43
1982–83	Dundee U	56	Celtic*	55	Aberdeen	55
1983–84	Aberdeen	57	Celtic	50	Dundee U	47
1984–85	Aberdeen	59	Celtic	52	Dundee U	47
1985–86	Celtic*	50	Hearts	50	Dundee U	47
			Maximum points: 88			
1986–87	Rangers	69	Celtic	63	Dundee U	60
1987–88	Celtic	72	Hearts	62	Rangers	60
			Maximum points: 72			
1988–89	Rangers	56	Aberdeen	50	Celtic	46
1989–90	Rangers	51	Aberdeen*	44	Hearts	44
1990–91	Rangers	55	Aberdeen	53	Celtic*	41
			Maximum points: 88			
1991–92	Rangers	72	Hearts	63	Celtic	62
1992–93	Rangers	73	Aberdeen	64	Celtic	60
1993–94	Rangers	58	Aberdeen	55	Motherwell	54

FIRST DIVISION

	First	Pts	Second	Pts	Third	Pts
			Maximum points: 52			
1975–76	Partick T	41	Kilmarnock	35	Montrose	30
			Maximum points: 78			
1976–77	St Mirren	62	Clydebank	58	Dundee	51
1977–78	Morton*	58	Hearts	58	Dundee	57
1978–79	Dundee	55	Kilmarnock*	54	Clydebank	54
1979–80	Hearts	53	Airdrieonians	51	Ayr U	44
1980–81	Hibernian	57	Dundee	52	St Johnstone	51
1981–82	Motherwell	61	Kilmarnock	51	Hearts	50
1982–83	St Johnstone	55	Hearts	54	Clydebank	50
1983–84	Morton	54	Dumbarton	51	Partick T	46
1984–85	Motherwell	50	Clydebank	48	Falkirk	45
1985–86	Hamilton A	56	Falkirk	45	Kilmarnock	44
			Maximum points: 88			
1986–87	Morton	57	Dunfermline Ath	56	Dumbarton	53
1987–88	Hamilton A	56	Meadowbank T	52	Clydebank	49
			Maximum points: 78			
1988–89	Dunfermline Ath	54	Falkirk	52	Clydebank	48
1989–90	St Johnstone	58	Airdrieonians	54	Clydebank	44
1990–91	Falkirk	54	Airdrieonians	53	Dundee	52
			Maximum points: 88			
1991–92	Dundee	58	Partick T*	57	Hamilton A	57
1992–93	Raith R	65	Kilmarnock	54	Dunfermline Ath	52
1993–94	Falkirk	66	Dunfermline Ath	65	Airdrieonians	54

SECOND DIVISION

	First	Pts	Second	Pts	Third	Pts
			Maximum points: 52			
1975–77	Clydebank*	40	Raith R	40	Alloa	35
			Maximum points: 78			
1976–77	Stirling A	55	Alloa	51	Dunfermline Ath	50
1977–78	Clyde*	53	Raith R	53	Dunfermline Ath	48
1978–79	Berwick R	54	Dunfermline Ath	52	Falkirk	50
1979–80	Falkirk	50	East Stirling	49	Forfar Ath	46
1980–81	Queen's Park	50	Queen of the S	46	Cowdenbeath	45
1981–82	Clyde	59	Alloa*	50	Arbroath	50
1982–83	Brechin C	55	Meadowbank T	54	Arbroath	49
1983–84	Forfar Ath	63	East Fife	47	Berwick R	43
1984–85	Montrose	53	Alloa	50	Dunfermline Ath	49
1985–86	Dunfermline Ath	57	Queen of the S	55	Meadowbank T	49
1986–87	Meadowbank T	55	Raith R*	52	Stirling A	52

1987–88	Ayr U	61	St Johnstone	59	Queen's Park	51
1988–89	Albion R	50	Alloa	45	Brechin C	43
1989–90	Brechin C	49	Kilmarnock	48	Stirling A	47
1990–91	Stirling A	54	Montrose	46	Cowdenbeath	45
			Maximum points: 78			
1991–92	Dumbarton	52	Cowdenbeath	51	Alloa	50
1992–93	Clyde	54	Brechin C*	53	Stranraer	53
1993–94	Stranraer	56	Berwick R	48	Stenhousemuir*	47

FIRST DIVISION to 1974–75

Maximum points: a 36; *b* 44; *c* 40; *d* 52; *e* 60; *f* 68; g 76; *h* 84.

	First	*Pts*	*Second*	*Pts*	*Third*	*Pts*
1890–91*a*††	Dumbarton	29	Rangers	29	Celtic	24
1891–92*b*	Dumbarton	37	Celtic	35	Hearts	30
1892–93*a*	Celtic	29	Rangers	28	St Mirren	23
1893–94*a*	Celtic	29	Hearts	26	St Bernard's	22
1894–95*a*	Hearts	31	Celtic	26	Rangers	21
1895–96*a*	Celtic	30	Rangers	26	Hibernian	24
1896–97*a*	Hearts	28	Hibernian	26	Rangers	25
1897–98*a*	Celtic	33	Rangers	29	Hibernian	22
1898–99*a*	Rangers	36	Hearts	26	Celtic	24
1899–1900*a*	Rangers	32	Celtic	25	Hibernian	24
1900–01*c*	Rangers	35	Celtic	29	Hibernian	25
1901–02*a*	Rangers	28	Celtic	26	Hearts	22
1902–03*b*	Hibernian	37	Dundee	31	Rangers	29
1903–04*d*	Third Lanark	43	Hearts	39	Rangers*	38
1904–05*d*	Celtic‡	41	Rangers	41	Third Lanark	35
1905–06*e*	Celtic	49	Hearts	43	Airdrieonians	38
1906–07*f*	Celtic	55	Dundee	48	Rangers	45
1907–08*f*	Celtic	55	Falkirk	51	Rangers	50
1908–09*f*	Celtic	51	Dundee	50	Clyde	48
1909–10*f*	Celtic	54	Falkirk	52	Rangers	46
1910–11*f*	Rangers	52	Aberdeen	48	Falkirk	44
1911–12*f*	Rangers	51	Celtic	45	Clyde	42
1912–13*f*	Rangers	53	Celtic	49	Hearts*	41
1913–14*g*	Celtic	65	Rangers	59	Hearts*	54
1914–15*g*	Celtic	65	Hearts	61	Rangers	50
1915–16*g*	Celtic	67	Rangers	56	Morton	51
1916–17*g*	Celtic	64	Morton	54	Rangers	53
1917–18*f*	Rangers	56	Celtic	55	Kilmarnock	43
1918–19*f*	Celtic	58	Rangers	57	Morton	47
1919–20*h*	Rangers	71	Celtic	68	Motherwell	57
1920–21*h*	Rangers	76	Celtic	66	Hearts	56
1921–22*h*	Celtic	67	Rangers	66	Raith R	56
1922–23*g*	Rangers	55	Airdrieonians	50	Celtic	46
1923–24*g*	Rangers	59	Airdrieonians	50	Celtic	41
1924–25*g*	Rangers	60	Airdrieonians	57	Hibernian	52
1925–26*g*	Celtic	58	Airdrieonians*	50	Hearts	50
1926–27*g*	Rangers	56	Motherwell	51	Celtic	49
1927–28*g*	Rangers	60	Celtic*	55	Motherwell	55
1928–29*g*	Rangers	67	Celtic	51	Motherwell	50
1929–30*g*	Rangers	60	Motherwell	55	Aberdeen	53
1930–31*g*	Rangers	60	Celtic	58	Motherwell	56
1931–32*g*	Motherwell	66	Rangers	61	Celtic	48
1932–33*g*	Rangers	62	Motherwell	59	Hearts	50
1933–34*g*	Rangers	66	Motherwell	62	Celtic	47
1934–35*g*	Rangers	55	Celtic	52	Hearts	50
1935–36*g*	Celtic	66	Rangers*	61	Aberdeen	61
1936–37*g*	Rangers	61	Aberdeen	54	Celtic	52
1937–38*g*	Celtic	61	Hearts	58	Rangers	49
1938–39*g*	Rangers	59	Celtic	48	Aberdeen	46
1946–47*e*	Rangers	46	Hibernian	44	Aberdeen	39
1947–48*e*	Hibernian	48	Rangers	46	Partick T	36
1948–49*e*	Rangers	46	Dundee	45	Hibernian	39
1949–50*e*	Rangers	50	Hibernian	49	Hearts	43
1950–51*e*	Hibernian	48	Rangers*	38	Dundee	38
1951–52*e*	Hibernian	45	Rangers	41	East Fife	37
1952–53*e*	Rangers*	43	Hibernian	43	East Fife	39
1953–54*e*	Celtic	43	Hearts	38	Partick T	35
1954–55*e*	Aberdeen	49	Celtic	46	Rangers	41
1955–56*f*	Rangers	52	Aberdeen	46	Hearts*	45
1956–57*f*	Rangers	55	Hearts	53	Kilmarnock	42
1957–58*f*	Hearts	62	Rangers	49	Celtic	46
1958–59*f*	Rangers	50	Hearts	48	Motherwell	44

1959–60*f*	Hearts	54	Kilmarnock	50	Rangers*	42
1960–61*f*	Rangers	51	Kilmarnock	50	Third Lanark	42
1961–62*f*	Dundee	54	Rangers	51	Celtic	46
1962–63*f*	Rangers	57	Kilmarnock	48	Partick T	46
1963–64*f*	Rangers	55	Kilmarnock	49	Celtic*	47
1964–65*f*	Kilmarnock*	50	Hearts	50	Dunfermline Ath	49
1965–66*f*	Celtic	57	Rangers	55	Kilmarnock	45
1966–67*f*	Celtic	58	Rangers	55	Clyde	46
1967–68*f*	Celtic	63	Rangers	61	Hibernian	45
1968–69*f*	Celtic	54	Rangers	49	Dunfermline Ath	45
1969–70*f*	Celtic	57	Rangers	45	Hibernian	44
1970–71*f*	Celtic	56	Aberdeen	54	St Johnstone	44
1971–72*f*	Celtic	60	Aberdeen	50	Rangers	44
1972–73*f*	Celtic	57	Rangers	56	Hibernian	45
1973–74*f*	Celtic	53	Hibernian	49	Rangers	48
1974–75*f*	Rangers	56	Hibernian	49	Celtic	45

SECOND DIVISION to 1974–75

Maximum points: a 76; *b* 72; *c* 68; *d* 52; *e* 60; *f* 36; *g* 44; *h* 52.

1893–94*f*	Hibernian	29	Cowlairs	27	Clyde	24
1894–95*f*	Hibernian	30	Motherwell	22	Port Glasgow	20
1895–96*f*	Abercorn	27	Leith Ath	23	Renton	21
1896–97*f*	Partick T	31	Leith Ath	27	Kilmarnock	21
1897–98*f*	Kilmarnock	29	Port Glasgow	25	Morton	22
1898–99*f*	Kilmarnock	32	Leith Ath	27	Port Glasgow	25
1899–1900*f*	Partick T	29	Morton	26	Port Glasgow	20
1900–01*f*	St Bernard's	26	Airdrieonians	23	Abercorn	21
1901–02*g*	Port Glasgow	32	Partick T	31	Motherwell	26
1902–03*g*	Airdrieonians	35	Motherwell	28	Ayr U	27
1903–04*g*	Hamilton A	37	Clyde	29	Ayr U	28
1904–05*g*	Clyde	32	Falkirk	28	Hamilton A	27
1905–06*g*	Leith Ath	34	Clyde	31	Albion R	27
1906–07*g*	St Bernard's	32	Vale of Leven*	27	Arthurlie	27
1907–08*g*	Raith R	30	Dumbarton	‡‡27	Ayr U	27
1908–09*g*	Abercorn	31	Raith R*	28	Vale of Leven	28
1909–10*g*‡	Leith Ath	33	Raith R	33	St Bernard's	27
1910–11*g*	Dumbarton	31	Ayr U	27	Albion R	25
1911–12*g*	Ayr U	35	Abercorn	30	Dumbarton	27
1912–13*h*	Ayr U	34	Dunfarmline Ath	33	East Stirling	32
1913–14*g*	Cowdenbeath	31	Albion R	27	Dunfermline Ath	26
1914–15*h*	Cowdenbeath*	37	St Bernard's*	37	Leith Ath	37
1921–22*a*	Alloa	60	Cowdenbeath	47	Armadale	45
1922–23*a*	Queen's Park	57	Clydebank	¶50	St Johnstone	¶45
1923–24*a*	St Johnstone	56	Cowdenbeath	55	Bathgate	44
1924–25*a*	Dundee U	50	Clydebank	48	Clyde	47
1925–26*a*	Dunfermline Ath	59	Clyde	53	Ayr U	52
1926–27*a*	Bo'ness	56	Raith R	49	Clydebank	45
1927–28*a*	Ayr U	54	Third Lanark	45	King's Park	44
1928–29*b*	Dundee U	51	Morton	50	Arbroath	47
1929–30*a*	Leith Ath*	57	East Fife	57	Albion R	54
1930–31*a*	Third Lanark	61	Dundee U	50	Dunfermline Ath	47
1931–32*a*	East Stirling*	55	St Johnstone	55	Raith Rovers*	46
1932–33*c*	Hibernian	54	Queen of the S	49	Dunfermline Ath	47
1933–34*c*	Albion R	45	Dunfermline Ath*	44	Arbroath	44
1934–35*c*	Third Lanark	52	Arbroath	50	St Bernard's	47
1935–36*c*	Falkirk	59	St Mirren	52	Morton	48
1936–37*c*	Ayr U	54	Morton	51	St Bernard's	48
1937–38*c*	Raith R	59	Albion R	48	Airdrieonians	47
1938–39*c*	Cowdenbeath	60	Alloa*	48	East Fife	48
1946–47*d*	Dundee	45	Airdrieonians	42	East Fife	31
1947–48*e*	East Fife	53	Albion R	42	Hamilton A	40
1948–49*e*	Raith R*	42	Stirling Albion	42	Airdrieonians*	41
1949–50*e*	Morton	47	Airdrieonians	44	St Johnstone*	36
1950–51*e*	Queen of the S*	45	Stirling Albion	45	Ayr U	36
1951–52*e*	Clyde	44	Falkirk	43	Ayr U	39
1952–53*e*	Stirling Albion	44	Hamilton A	43	Queen's Park	37
1953–54*e*	Motherwell	45	Kilmarnock	42	Third Lanark*	36
1954–55*e*	Airdrieonians	46	Dunfermline Ath	42	Hamilton A	39
1955–56*b*	Queen's Park	54	Ayr U	51	St Johnstone	49
1956–57*b*	Clyde	64	Third Lanark	51	Cowdenbeath	45
1957–58*b*	Stirling Albion	55	Dunfermline Ath	53	Arbroath	47
1958–59*b*	Ayr U	60	Arbroath	51	Stenhousemuir	40
1959–60*b*	St Johnstone	53	Dundee U	50	Queen of the S	49
1960–61*b*	Stirling Albion	55	Falkirk	54	Stenhousemuir	50

1961–62*b*	Clyde	54	Queen of the S	53	Morton	441
1962–63*b*	St Johnstone	55	East Stirling	49	Morton	48
1963–64*b*	Morton	67	Clyde	53	Arbroath	46
1964–65*b*	Stirling Albion	59	Hamilton A	50	Queen of the S	45
1965–66*b*	Ayr U	53	Airdrieonians	50	Queen of the S	49
1966–67*b*	Morton	69	Raith R	58	Arbroath	57
1967–68*b*	St Mirren	62	Arbroath	53	East Fife	40
1968–69*b*	Motherwell	64	Ayr U	53	East Fife*	47
1969–70*b*	Falkirk	56	Cowdenbeath	55	Queen of the S	50
1970–71*b*	Partick T	56	East Fife	51	Arbroath	46
1971–72*b*	Dumbarton*	52	Arbroath	52	Stirling Albion	50
1972–73*b*	Clyde	56	Dumfermline Ath	52	Raith R*	47
1973–74*b*	Airdrieonians	60	Kilmarnock	59	Hamilton A	55
1974–75*a*	Falkirk	54	Queen of the S	53	Montrose	53

Elected to First Division: 1894 Clyde; 1897 Partick T; 1899 Kilmarnock; 1900 Partick T; 1902 Partick T; 1903 Airdrieonians; 1905 Falkirk, Aberdeen and Hamilton A; 1906 Clyde; 1910 Raith R; 1913 Ayr U.

RELEGATED FROM PREMIER DIVISION

1975–76 Dundee, St Johnstone
1976–77 Hearts, Kilmarnock
1977–78 Ayr U, Clydebank
1978–79 Hearts, Motherwell
1979–80 Dundee, Hibernian
1980–81 Kilmarnock, Hearts
1981–82 Partick T, Airdrieonians
1982–83 Morton, Kilmarnock
1983–84 St Johnstone, Motherwell
1984–85 Dumbarton, Morton
1985–86 *No relegation due to League reorganization*
1986–87 Clydebank, Hamilton A
1987–88 Falkirk, Dunfermline Ath, Morton
1988–89 Hamilton A
1989–90 Dundee
1990–91 None
1991–92 St Mirren, Dunfermline Ath
1992–93 Falkirk, Airdrieonians
1993–94 *See footnote*

RELEGATED FROM DIVISION 1

1975–76 Dunfermline Ath, Clyde
1976–77 Raith R, Falkirk
1977–78 Alloa Ath, East Fife
1978–79 Montrose, Queen of the S
1979–80 Arbroath, Clyde
1980–81 Stirling A, Berwick R
1981–82 East Stirling, Queen of the S
1982–83 Dunfermline Ath, Queen's Park
1983–84 Raith R, Alloa
1984–85 Meadowbank T, St Johnstone
1985–86 Ayr U, Alloa
1986–87 Brechin C, Montrose
1987–88 East Fife, Dumbarton
1988–89 Kilmarnock, Queen of the S
1989–90 Albion R, Alloa
1990–91 Clyde, Brechin C
1991–92 Montrose, Forfar Ath
1992–93 Meadowbank T, Cowdenbeath
1993–94 *See footnote*

RELEGATED FROM DIVISION 1 (TO 1973–74)

1921–22 *Queen's Park, Dumbarton, Clydebank
1922–23 Albion R, Alloa Ath
1923–24 Clyde, Clydebank
1924–25 Third Lanark, Ayr U
1925–26 Raith R, Clydebank
1926–27 Morton, Dundee U
1927–28 Dunfermline Ath, Bo'ness
1928–29 Third Lanark, Raith R
1929–30 St Johnstone, Dundee U
1930–31 Hibernian, East Fife
1931–32 Dundee U, Leith Ath
1932–33 Morton, East Stirling
1933–34 Third Lanark, Cowdenbeath
1934–35 St Mirren, Falkirk
1935–36 Airdrieonians, Ayr U
1936–37 Dunfermline Ath, Albion R
1937–38 Dundee, Morton
1938–39 Queen's Park, Raith R
1946–47 Kilmarnock, Hamilton A
1947–48 Airdrieonians, Queen's Park
1948–49 Morton, Albion R
1949–50 Queen of the S, Stirling Albion
1950–51 Clyde, Falkirk
1951–52 Morton, Stirling Albion
1952–53 Motherwell, Third Lanark
1953–54 Airdrieonians, Hamilton A
1954–55 No clubs relegated
1955–56 Stirling Albion, Clyde
1956–57 Dunfermline Ath, Ayr U
1957–58 East Fife, Queen's Park
1958–59 Queen of the S, Falkirk
1959–60 Arbroath, Stirling Albion
1960–61 Ayr U, Clyde
1961–62 St Johnstone, Stirling Albion
1962–63 Clyde, Raith R
1963–64 Queen of the S, East Stirling
1964–65 Airdrieonians, Third Lanark
1965–66 Morton, Hamilton A
1966–67 St Mirren, Ayr U
1967–68 Motherwell, Stirling Albion
1968–69 Falkirk, Arbroath
1969–70 Raith R, Partick T
1970–71 St Mirren, Cowdenbeath
1971–72 Clyde, Dunfermline Ath
1972–73 Kilmarnock, Airdrieonians
1973–74 East Fife, Falkirk

*Season 1921–22 – only 1 club promoted, 3 clubs relegated.

Scottish League championship wins: Rangers 44, Celtic 35, Aberdeen 4, Hearts 4, Hibernian 4, Dumbarton 2, Dundee 1, Dundee United 1, Kilmarnock 1, Motherwell 1, Third Lanark 1.

At the end of the 1993–94 four divisions were created assisted by the admission of two new clubs Ross County and Caledonian Thistle. Only one club was promoted from Division 1 and Division 2. Three relegated from the Premier joined with teams finishing second to seventh in Division 1 to form the new Division 1. Five relegated from Division 1 combined with those who finished second to sixth to form a new Division 2 and the bottom eight in Division 2 linked with the two newcomers to form a new Division 3.

SCOTTISH LEAGUE CUP FINALS 1946–94

Season	*Winners*	*Runners-up*	*Score*
1946–47	Rangers	Aberdeen	4-0
1947–48	East Fife	Falkirk	4-1 after 0-0 draw
1948–49	Rangers	Raith R	2-0
1949–50	East Fife	Dunfermline Ath	3-0
1950–51	Motherwell	Hibernian	3-0
1951–52	Dundee	Rangers	3-2
1952–53	Dundee	Kilmarnock	2-0
1953–54	East Fife	Partick T	3-2
1954–55	Hearts	Motherwell	4-2
1955–56	Aberdeen	St Mirren	2-1
1956–57	Celtic	Partick T	3-0 after 0-0 draw
1957–58	Celtic	Rangers	7-1
1958–59	Hearts	Partick T	5-1
1959–60	Hearts	Third Lanark	2-1
1960–61	Rangers	Kilmarnock	2-0
1961–62	Rangers	Hearts	3-1 after 1-1 draw
1962–63	Hearts	Kilmarnock	1-0
1963–64	Rangers	Morton	5-0
1964–65	Rangers	Celtic	2-1
1965–66	Celtic	Rangers	2-1
1966–67	Celtic	Rangers	1-0
1967–68	Celtic	Dundee	5-3
1968–69	Celtic	Hibernian	6-2
1969–70	Celtic	St Johnstone	1-0
1970–71	Rangers	Celtic	1-0
1971–72	Partick T	Celtic	4-1
1972–73	Hibernian	Celtic	2-1
1973–74	Dundee	Celtic	1-0
1974–75	Celtic	Hibernian	6-3
1975–76	Rangers	Celtic	1-0
1976–77	Aberdeen	Celtic	2-1
1977–78	Rangers	Celtic	2-1
1978–79	Rangers	Aberdeen	2-1
1979–80	Dundee U	Aberdeen	3-0 after 0-0 draw
1980–81	Dundee U	Dundee	3-0
1981–82	Rangers	Dundee U	2-1
1982–83	Celtic	Rangers	2-1
1983–84	Rangers	Celtic	3-2
1984–85	Rangers	Dundee U	1-0
1985–86	Aberdeen	Hibernian	3-0
1986–87	Rangers	Celtic	2-1
1987–88	Rangers	Aberdeen	3-3
	(Rangers won 5-3 on penalties)		
1988–89	Rangers	Aberdeen	3-2
1989–90	Aberdeen	Rangers	2-1
1990–91	Rangers	Celtic	2-1
1991–92	Hibernian	Dunfermline Ath	2-0
1992–93	Rangers	Aberdeen	2-1
1993–94	Rangers	Hibernian	2-1

SCOTTISH LEAGUE CUP WINS

Rangers 19, Celtic 9, Hearts 4, Aberdeen 4, Dundee 3, East Fife 3, Dundee U 2, Hibernian 2, Motherwell 1, Partick T 1.

APPEARANCES IN FINALS

Rangers 25, Celtic 20, Aberdeen 10, Hibernian 7, Dundee 5, Hearts 5, Dundee U 4, Partick T 4, East Fife 3, Kilmarnock 3, Dunfermline Ath 2, Motherwell 2, Falkirk 1, Morton 1, Raith R 1, St Johnstone 1, St Mirren 1, Third Lanark 1.

SCOTTISH LEAGUE CUP 1993–94

FIRST ROUND

3 AUG

Alloa (0) 1 *(Hendry)*
Berwick R (0) 0 443

Alloa: Butter; McNiven, Bennett, Campbell, McCulloch, Newbigging, Herd, Ramsay, Hendry, Smith (Russell), McAvoy.
Berwick R: O'Connor; Gibson, Valentine, Hall, Cowan, Richardson, Neil (Kane), Irvine, Cunningham (Scott), Graham, Banks.

East Fife (1) 1 *(Scott)*
Albion R (1) 2 *(Fraser, Kerrigan)* 873

East Fife: Wilson; Sneddon, Williamson, Barron, Beaton, Burns, Elliott, Beedie, Scott, Reilly, McBride.
Albion R: McConnachie; Kelly, Spence, Riley, Taylor, McKeown, McBride, Scott, Kerrigan, Fraser, Gallagher (Cadden).

Queen's Park (0) 0
Arbroath (0) 1 *(Strachan)* 554

Queen's Park: Chalmers; Kerr, Kavanagh, Fitzpatrick, Sneddon, Orr G, Elder, O'Brien (Graham), Black, O'Neill, McCormick.
Arbroath: Harkness; Hamilton, Florence, Mitchell, Adam, Martin, Will (Hindson), King, Strachan, Farnan, Sorbie.

Stenhousemuir (1) 3 *(Clouston, Irvine, Mathieson)*
Forfar Ath (1) 1 *(Hamill)* 443

Stenhousemuir: Robertson; Aitken, Haddow, Armstrong, Godfrey, Logan, Steel, Clouston, Mathieson, Irvine, Fisher (Clarke).
Forfar Ath: Thomson; Philliben, McPhee, Morris (Mearns), Mann, Hamill, Bingham, McIntyre (McCafferty), Donaldson, Petrie, Heddle.

4 AUG

Montrose (0) 0
East Stirling (1) 1 *(Conroy)* 575

Montrose: Larter; Robertson, Craib M, Haro, Smith, Yeats, McKenna (Irvine), Craib S, Jack (Grant), Kennedy, Maver.
East Stirling: McDougall; Russell, Kemp, McAulay, Craig, Speirs (Loney), Roberts, McKinnon, Geraghty, Robertson, Conroy.

Queen of the S (1) 1 *(Shanks)*
Stranraer (1) 2 *(Henderson 2)* 1317

Queen of the S: Davidson; Mills, McGhie, McKeown, Shanks, McFarlane, Jackson, Sermanni (Bryce), Thomson, McGuire D (Kelly), Mallan.
Stranraer: Duffy; McIntyre, Hughes, Millar, Brannigan, Gallagher, Sloan, Duncan (McLean), Diver (Grant), Cody, Henderson.

SECOND ROUND

10 AUG

Aberdeen (1) 5 *(Shearer 3 (1 pen), McLeish, Richardson)*
Clydebank (0) 0 11,394

Aberdeen: Snelders; Wright, Connor, Kane, McLeish, Smith, Richardson, Bett (Miller), Booth (Jess), Shearer, Paatelainen.
Clydebank: Woods; Treanor, Hay, Maher, Sweeney, McIntosh (Crawford D), Harvey, Henry, Eadie, Flannigan, Lansdowne (Jack).

Airdrieonians (2) 2 *(Davenport, Kirkwood)*
Cowdenbeath (0) 1 *(Henderson)* 1527

Airdrieonians: Martin; Stewart, Kirkwood, Sandison, Caesar, Reid, Boyle, Balfour, Davenport, Lawrence (Conn), Andrew Smith (Abercromby).
Cowdenbeath: Filshill; Watt, Thomson (Barclay), Petrie, McMahon B, Lee, Henderson, Scott (Davidson), Callaghan, Maratea, Harris.

Ayr U (0) 0
Motherwell (2) 6 *(McGrillen 2, Arnott 2, Graham, Ferguson)* 3474

Ayr U: Duncan; Burley, Robertson, Shotton, Traynor, George (Kennedy), Walker, Bryce, McGivern, McNab, Scott.
Motherwell: Dykstra; Shannon, McKinnon, Krivokapic, Martin, McCart (Dolan), Ferguson, Angus, Arnott, O'Donnell (Graham), McGrillen.

Brechin C (0) 0
St Mirren (0) 1 *(Dick)* 872

Brechin C: Allan; Kopel, Hutt, Brown, Conway, Redford, Bell, O'Brien, Ross, Miller, Lees (McNeill).
St Mirren: Combe; Dawson, Baker, McWhirter, Taylor, Orr, Bone (Lavety), Dick, Gallagher (McIntyre), Hewitt, Fullarton.

Hamilton A (0) 0
Dundee U (0) 1 *(Connolly) aet* 2743

Hamilton A: Ferguson; McKenzie, Napier, Reid, Weir, McInulty, Clark, Baptie (McEntegart), Chalmers (McLean), Ward, Lorimer.
Dundee U: Main; Van Der Hoorn, Malpas (Bollan), Cleland, Welsh, Narey, Bowman, McKinlay, Connolly, Dailly, Myers (McLaren).

Hibernian (0) 2 *(Wright, Donald)*
Alloa (0) 0 4621

Hibernian: Leighton; Miller, Tortolano, McIntyre, Tweed, Hunter, McAllister, Hamilton, Wright, Jackson D, McGraw (Donald).
Alloa: Butter; McNiven, Bennett, Campbell, McCulloch, Newbigging, Herd, Gibson (Moffat), Russell (Hendry), Ramsay, McEvoy.

Kilmarnock (1) 1 *(Mitchell)*
Morton (1) 2 *(Tolmie, Lilley)* 5112
Kilmarnock: Geddes; MacPherson, Black, Montgomerie, Skilling, Millen, Mitchell, Reilly, Crainie (Roberts), McCluskey, McSkimming.
Morton: Wylie; Collins, Pickering, Fowler, Doak, McArthur, Lilley, Donaghy, Alexander, McInnes, Tolmie (Rafferty).

Meadowbank T (1) 1 *(Little)*
Dundee (1) 1 *(Davidson (og)) aet* 811
Meadowbank T: McQueen; Murray, Fleming, Davidson, Williamson S, Little, Bailey, Wilson (Price), Rutherford (Williamson R), McLeod G, Hutchison.
Dundee: Mathers; Frail (McQuillan), Christie, Wieghorst, David (Paterson), McGowan, McMartin, Vrto, Ritchie, Dodds, Tosh.
(Dundee won 3-1 on penalties)

Stenhousemuir (1) 1 *(Fisher)*
Falkirk (1) 2 *(Cadette, Duffy) aet* 2515
Stenhousemuir: Kelly; Aitken, Haddow, Armstrong, Godfrey (Clarke), Logan, Steel, Clouston (Dickov), Mathieson, Irvine, Fisher.
Falkirk: Parks; Oliver, Johnston, Weir, Hughes, Duffy, May, Sloan (McDonald), Cadette, McCall, Shaw (McQueen).

Stirling Albion (0) 0
Celtic (0) 2 *(McGinlay, McAvennie)* 8533
Stirling Albion: McGeown; McCormack, Watson, Tait, Lawrie, Mitchell, Reilly (Kinross), Moore, Watters, Armstrong, Flynn (Pew).
Celtic: Bonner; Boyd, Wdowczyk, Grant, McNally, Galloway, Slater (McGinlay), McStay, McAvennie, Nicholas, Collins.

11 AUG

Albion R (0) 1 *(Scott)*
Partick T (2) 11 *(Craig 2, Britton, English, Jamieson, Law, Cameron 4, Grant)* 1448
Albion R: McConnachie; Kelly, Spence, Mirner, Taylor, McKeown, McBride (Seggie), Cadden, Kerrigan, Scott, Fraser (Riley).
Partick T: Nelson; McKee, Law, Jamieson, Tierney (Kinnaird), Clark, Byrne, Craig, Britton (Grant), Cameron, English.

Clyde (0) 1 *(McAulay)*
St Johnstone (1) 2 *(Wright (pen), Moore)* 1109
Clyde: Fridge; McFarlane, Tennant, Knox, Thomson, Neill, Ronald (Morrison), McAulay, Sludden (McGill), Clarke, McCarron.
St Johnstone: Rhodes; Budden, Deas, McGinnis, Inglis, Curran, Ramsey, McGowne, Wright, Torfason, Buglione (Moore).

Dunfermline Ath (0) 2 *(Robertson, French)*
East Stirling (0) 0 *aet* 2618
Dunfermline Ath: Hamilton; Bowes, Cunnington, McCathie, Baillie, Davies, Den Bieman (Smith), Robertson, French, O'Boyle (Laing), Preston.
East Stirling: McDougall; Russell, Kemp, Ross, Yates, Craig, Roberts, McKinnon, Geraghty, Robertson, Speirs (Loney).

Hearts (1) 2 *(Robertson 2)*
Stranraer (0) 0 5332
Hearts: Smith; Locke, McKinlay, Levein, Berry, Van De Ven, Colquhoun (Johnston A), Mackay, Fashanu (Thomas), Wright, Robertson.
Stranraer: Duffy; McIntyre, Hughes, Millar, Spittal, Duncan, Sloan, Grant, Diver (McLean), Cody (Walker), Henderson.

Raith R (1) 1 *(Cameron)*
Arbroath (1) 2 *(Elliot, Martin)* 1957
Raith R: Carson; McStay, MacLeod, Coyle, Dennis, McGeachie, Nicholl (Sinclair), Dalziel (Broddle), Hetherston, Hawke, Cameron.
Arbroath: Jackson; Hamilton, Florence, Mitchell, Adam, Martin, Will, King, Elliot (Hindson), Farnan, Sorbie.

Rangers (0) 1 *(Ferguson I)*
Dumbarton (0) 0 36,309
Rangers: Maxwell; Wishart, Vinnicombe, Gough, Pressley, Murray, Steven T, Ferguson I, Hagen (Huistra), Hateley, Durrant.
Dumbarton: MacFarlane; Meechan, Foster, Melvin, Gow, MacLeod, McGarvey, McConville (Marsland), McQuade (McAnenay), Gibson, Boyd.

THIRD ROUND

24 AUG

Aberdeen (1) 5 *(Shearer, Miller, Booth 2, Jess)*
Motherwell (0) 2 *(Arnott, Shannon) aet* 12,993
Aberdeen: Snelders; McKimmie, Smith, Kane, McLeish, Irvine, Jess, Bett (Connor), Booth, Shearer, Ten Caat (Miller).
Motherwell: Dykstra; Shannon, McKinnon, Krivokapic, Martin, McCart, Dolan, Angus, Arnott (McGrillen), O'Donnell, Burns (Cooper).

Dunfermline Ath (0) 0
Rangers (2) 2 *(Steven T, Ferguson I)* 12,993
Dunfermline Ath: Hamilton; Bowes, Robertson, McCathie, Baillie, Davies, Den Bieman, Smith, French (Cunnington), O'Boyle (Laing), Preston.
Rangers: Maxwell; Wishart, Robertson D, Gough, Pressley, Durrant, Steven T, Ferguson I, Ferguson D, Hateley, Mikhailichenko.

Hibernian (2) 2 *(Hunter, Wright)*
Dundee (0) 1 *(Nielsen)* 6315
Hibernian: Leighton; Miller, Beaumont, McIntyre, Farrell, Hunter, McAllister, Findlay, Wright, Evans, O'Neill (Hamilton).
Dundee: Mathers; McQuillan, Pittman, Wieghorst, Paterson, McGowan, Adamczuk, Vrto, Tosh (Nielsen), Dodds, McKeown.

Morton (0) 0
Partick T (0) 1 *(Craig)* 4124
Morton: Wylie; Collins, Pickering (Gahagan), Fowler, Doak, McArthur, Lilley, Donaghy, Alexander, McInnes, Tolmie.
Partick T: Murdoch; McKee, Watson (Kinnaird), Craig, Jamieson, Byrne, Grant, Farningham, Britton, Cameron, McKilligan.

St Mirren (0) 0
Dundee U (0) 1 *(McKinlay)* 4415

St Mirren: Money; McIntyre, Baker, McWhirter, Fullarton, Orr, Gallagher, Dick (Gillies R), Lavety, Hewitt (Gillies K), Elliot.
Dundee U: Main; Clark, Bollan, McInally, Welsh, Narey (Van Der Hoorn), Bowman, McKinlay, Connolly, Dailly, Myers (McLaren).

25 AUG

Arbroath (0) 1 *(Tindal)*
Celtic (4) 9 *(Nicholas, McGinlay, McAvennie 3, Payton 3, McNally)* 5364

Arbroath: Jackson; Hamilton, Florence, Mitchell, Adam, Farnan, Will (Tindal), King, Elliot (Hindson), Martin, Sorbie.
Celtic: Bonner; Boyd, Wdowczyk, Grant, McNally, Galloway, McGinlay, McStay (O'Neil), McAvennie, Nicholas (Payton), Collins.

Hearts (0) 0
Falkirk (0) 1 *(May)* 9583

Hearts: Smith; Locke, McKinlay, Levein, Hogg, Mauchlen (Johnston A), Colquhoun, Mackay, Fashanu (Thomas), Wright, Robertson.
Falkirk: Parks; Johnston, McQueen, Oliver, Weir, Duffy, May, MacKenzie, Cadette, McCall, Shaw.

St Johnstone (0) 0
Airdrieonians (2) 2 *(Lawrence, Balfour)* 3406

St Johnstone: Rhodes; Davies, Deas, Turner, Inglis, McGinnis (Cole), Moore (Scott), Ramsey, Wright, Curran, McGowne.
Airdrieonians: Martin; Stewart, Honor, Sandison, Caesar, Black, Kirkwood, Balfour, Davenport, Andrew Smith (Reid), Lawrence (Boyle).

QUARTER-FINALS

31 AUG

Celtic (0) 1 *(McAvennie)*
Airdrieonians (0) 0 25,738

Celtic: Bonner; Boyd, Wdowczyk, Grant, McNally, Galloway, McGinlay, McStay, McAvennie (Payton), Nicholas, Collins.
Airdrieonians: Martin; Honor, McVicar (Boyle), Sandison, Caesar, Black, Kirkwood, Balfour, Davenport, Andrew Smith, Jack (Abercromby).

Dundee U (1) 3 *(Clark 2, McLaren)*
Falkirk (0) 3 *(Cadette 3) aet* 8750

Dundee U: Main; Clark, Bollan, McInally, Welsh, Van Der Hoorn, Bowman (Crabbe), McKinlay, McLaren, Dailly, Myers (O'Neil).
Falkirk: Parks; Johnston, McQueen, Oliver, Weir, Duffy, May, MacKenzie, Cadette, McCall, Shaw.
(Dundee U won 4-2 on penalties)

Partick T (1) 2 *(Grant, Craig)*
Hibernian (0) 2 *(McAllister 2) aet* 7688

Partick T: Nelson; McKee (Kinnaird), Clark, Jamieson, Tierney, Taylor, Byrne, Craig, Grant, English (Britton), Cameron.
Hibernian: Leighton; Miller, Tweed (Hamilton), McIntyre, Farrell, Hunter, McAllister, Findlay, Wright, Evans (Jackson D), O'Neill.
(Hibernian won 3-2 on penalties)

1 SEPT

Rangers (1) 2 *(Hateley (pen), Ferguson I)*
Aberdeen (0) 1 *(Miller) aet* 44,928

Rangers: Maxwell; Stevens G, Robertson D, Gough, Pressley, Murray (Ferguson D), Steven, Ferguson I, Durrant, Hateley, Huistra (Wishart).
Aberdeen: Snelders; McKimmie, Smith (Miller), Kane, McLeish, Irvine, Richardson, Bett, Booth (Shearer), Jess, Paatelainen.

SEMI-FINALS

21 SEPT at Tynecastle Park

Dundee U (0) 0
Hibernian (1) 1 *(Jackson D)* 19,024

Dundee U: Main; Van Der Hoorn, Bollan (Cleland), Perry, Welsh, Narey, Bowman, McKinlay, McLaren, Dailly, Johnson (Clark).
Hibernian: Leighton; Miller, Mitchell, Farrell, Tweed, Hunter, McAllister, Findlay (Hamilton), Wright, Jackson D (Evans), O'Neill.

22 SEPT at Ibrox Stadium

Celtic (0) 0
Rangers (0) 1 *(Hateley)* 47,420

Celtic: Bonner; Boyd, Wdowczyk, Grant, McNally, Galloway, McGinlay, McStay, McAvennie (O'Neil), Creaney, Slater.
Rangers: Maxwell; Stevens G, Robertson D, Gough, McPherson, McCall, Steven T, Ferguson I, Durrant (Wishart), Hateley, Huistra.

FINAL at Celtic Park

24 OCT

Rangers (0) 2 *(Durrant, McCoist)*
Hibernian (0) 1 *(McPherson (og))* 47,632

Rangers: Maxwell; Stevens G, Robertson D, Gough, McPherson, McCall, Steven T, Ferguson I, Durrant, Hateley, Huistra (McCoist).
Hibernian: Leighton; Miller, Mitchell, Farrell, Tweed, Hunter, McAllister, Hamilton, Wright, Jackson D (Evans), O'Neill.
Referee: J. McCluskey (Stewarton)

SCOTTISH CUP FINALS 1874–1993

Year	*Winners*	*Runners-up*	*Score*
1874	Queen's Park	Clydesdale	2-0
1875	Queen's Park	Renton	3-0
1876	Queen's Park	Third Lanark	2-0 after 1-1 draw
1877	Vale of Leven	Rangers	3-2 after 0-0 and 1-1 draws
1878	Vale of Leven	Third Lanark	1-0
1879	Vale of Leven*	Rangers	
1880	Queen's Park	Thornlibank	3-0
1881	Queen's Park†	Dumbarton	3-1
1882	Queen's Park	Dumbarton	4-1 after 2-2 draw
1883	Dumbarton	Vale of Leven	2-1 after 2-2 draw
1884	Queen's Park‡	Vale of Leven	
1885	Renton	Vale of Leven	3-1 after 0-0 draw
1886	Queen's Park	Renton	3-1
1887	Hibernian	Dumbarton	2-1
1888	Renton	Cambuslang	6-1
1889	Third Lanark§	Celtic	2-1
1890	Queen's Park	Vale of Leven	2-1 after 1-1 draw
1891	Hearts	Dumbarton	1-0
1892	Celtic¶	Queen's Park	5-1
1893	Queen's Park	Celtic	2-1
1894	Rangers	Celtic	3-1
1895	St Bernard's	Renton	2-1
1896	Hearts	Hibernian	3-1
1897	Rangers	Dumbarton	5-1
1898	Rangers	Kilmarnock	2-0
1899	Celtic	Rangers	2-0
1900	Celtic	Queen's Park	4-3
1901	Hearts	Celtic	4-3
1902	Hibernian	Celtic	1-0
1903	Rangers	Hearts	2-0 after 1-1 and 0-0 draws
1904	Celtic	Rangers	3-2
1905	Third Lanark	Rangers	3-1 after 0-0 draw
1906	Hearts	Third Lanark	1-0
1907	Celtic	Hearts	3-0
1908	Celtic	St Mirren	5-1
1909	●●		
1910	Dundee	Clyde	2-1 after 2-2 and 0-0 draws
1911	Celtic	Hamilton A	2-0 after 0-0 draw
1912	Celtic	Clyde	2-0
1913	Falkirk	Raith R	2-0
1914	Celtic	Hibernian	4-1 after 0-0 draw
1920	Kilmarnock	Albion R	3-2
1921	Partick T	Rangers	1-0
1922	Morton	Rangers	1-0
1923	Celtic	Hibernian	1-0
1924	Airdrieonians	Hibernian	2-0
1925	Celtic	Dundee	2-1
1926	St Mirren	Celtic	2-0
1927	Celtic	East Fife	3-1
1928	Rangers	Celtic	4-0
1929	Kilmarnock	Rangers	2-0
1930	Rangers	Partick T	2-1 after 0-0 draw
1931	Celtic	Motherwell	4-2 after 2-2 draw
1932	Rangers	Kilmarnock	3-0 after 1-1 draw
1933	Celtic	Motherwell	1-0
1934	Rangers	St Mirren	5-0
1935	Rangers	Hamilton A	2-1
1936	Rangers	Third Lanark	1-0
1937	Celtic	Aberdeen	2-1
1938	East Fife	Kilmarnock	4-2 after 1-1 draw
1939	Clyde	Motherwell	4-0
1947	Aberdeen	Hibernian	2-1
1948	Rangers	Morton	1-0 after 1-1 draw
1949	Rangers	Clyde	4-1
1950	Rangers	East Fife	3-0
1951	Celtic	Motherwell	1-0
1952	Motherwell	Dundee	4-0
1953	Rangers	Aberdeen	1-0 after 1-1 draw
1954	Celtic	Aberdeen	2-1
1955	Clyde	Celtic	1-0 after 1-1 draw
1956	Hearts	Celtic	3-1
1957	Falkirk	Kilmarnock	2-1 after 1-1 draw
1958	Clyde	Hibernian	1-0
1959	St Mirren	Aberdeen	3-1
1960	Rangers	Kilmarnock	2-0
1961	Dunfermline Ath	Celtic	2-0 after 0-0 draw
1962	Rangers	St Mirren	2-0
1963	Rangers	Celtic	3-0 after 1-1 draw
1964	Rangers	Dundee	3-1

Year	Winners	Runners-up	Score
1965	Celtic	Dunfermline Ath	3-2
1966	Rangers	Celtic	1-0 after 0-0 draw
1967	Celtic	Aberdeen	2-0
1968	Dunfermline Ath	Hearts	3-1
1969	Celtic	Rangers	4-0
1970	Aberdeen	Celtic	3-1
1971	Celtic	Rangers	2-1 after 1-1 draw
1972	Celtic	Hibernian	6-1
1973	Rangers	Celtic	3-2
1974	Celtic	Dundee U	3-0
1975	Celtic	Airdrieonians	3-1
1976	Rangers	Hearts	3-1
1977	Celtic	Rangers	1-0
1978	Rangers	Aberdeen	2-1
1979	Rangers	Hibernian	3-2 after 0-0 and 0-0 draws
1980	Celtic	Rangers	1-0
1981	Rangers	Dundee U	4-1 after 0-0 draw
1982	Aberdeen	Rangers	4-1 (aet)
1983	Aberdeen	Rangers	1-0 (aet)
1984	Aberdeen	Celtic	2-1 (aet)
1985	Celtic	Dundee U	2-1
1986	Aberdeen	Hearts	3-0
1987	St Mirren	Dundee U	1-0 (aet)
1988	Celtic	Dundee U	2-1
1989	Celtic	Rangers	1-0
1990	Aberdeen	Celtic	0-0 (aet)
		(Aberdeen won 9-8 on penalties)	
1991	Motherwell	Dundee U	4-3 (aet)
1992	Rangers	Airdrieonians	2-1
1993	Rangers	Aberdeen	2-1
1994	Dundee U	Rangers	1-0

*Vale of Leven awarded cup, Rangers failing to appear for replay after 1-1 draw.
†After Dumbarton protested the first game, which Queen's Park won 2-1.
‡Queen's Park awarded cup, Vale of Leven failing to appear.
§Replay by order of Scottish FA because of playing conditions in first match, won 3-0 by Third Lanark.
¶After mutually protested game which Celtic won 1-0.
●●Owing to riot, the cup was withheld after two drawn games – Celtic 2-1, Rangers 2-1.

SCOTTISH CUP WINS

Celtic 29, Rangers 26, Queen's Park 10, Aberdeen 7, Hearts 5, Clyde 3, St Mirren 3, Vale of Leven 3, Dunfermline Ath 2, Falkirk 2, Hibernian 2, Kilmarnock 2, Motherwell 2, Renton 2, Third Lanark 2, Airdrieonians 1, Dumbarton 1, Dundee 1, Dundee U 1, East Fife 1, Morton 1, Partick Th 1, St Bernard's 1.

APPEARANCES IN FINAL

Celtic 46, Rangers 43, Aberdeen 14, Queen's Park 12, Hearts 10, Hibernian 10, Kilmarnock 7, Vale of Leven 7, Clyde 6, Dumbarton 6, St Mirren 6, Third Lanark 6, Dundee U 7, Motherwell 6, Renton 5, Dundee 4, Dunfermline Ath 3, East Fife 3, Airdrieonians 2, Falkirk 2, Hamilton A 2, Morton 2, Partick Th 2, Albion R 1, Cambuslang 1, Clydesdale 1, Raith R 1, St Bernard's 1 Thornlibank 1.

SCOTTISH CUP 1994

FIRST ROUND

11 DEC

Albion R (0) 0
Huntly (0) 0 759
Albiom R: Burns; Taylor (Gallagher), Beattie, Conn, McCaffrey, McKeown, Collins, Seggie, Kerrigan, Cadden, Scott (Fraser).
Huntly: Gardiner; McGinlay, Murphy, Walker, Rougvie, De Barros, Stewart, Copland, Thomson, Whyte (Lennox), Selbie.

Cowdenbeath (1) 1 *(Callaghan)*
Queen's Park (1) 1 *(O'Neill)* 342
Cowdenbeath: Maloney; Watt, Davidson, Herd, McMahon B, Petrie, Lee, Scott, Callaghan, Reilly (Barclay), Henderson.
Queen's Park: Chalmers; Sneddon, Maxwell, Elder, Fitzpatrick, Orr G, Stevenson (Kerr), Caven, McPhee, O'Neill, McCormick (Rodden).

East Fife (3) 5 *(Scott 3, Hope, Hildersley)*
Rothes (0) 0 987
East Fife: Charles; Sneddon, Williamson, Burns, Beaton, Beedie, Alan, Andrew, Scott, Hope (Hildersley), McBride (Irvine).
Rothes: Wallace; Madden, Winton, Esson, Henderson, Smith (Pilichos), Drews, Tulloch, Simpson, Thomson (Thain), Duncan.

Forfar Ath (4) 8 *(Downie 2, Heddle 2, Bingham 3 (1 pen), Kopel)*
Queen of the S (1) 3 *(Mills, Thomson 2)* 628
Forfar Ath: Arthur; Philliben (Morris), McPhee, Mann, Archibald, Winter, Kopel, Hamill, Downie, Bingham (Smith), Heddle.
Queen of the S: Purdie; McGhie, Mills, Rowe, Shanks (Kelly), Bell, McLaren (McFarlane), McKeown, Thomson, Bryce, Mallan.

Ross County (9) 11 *(Grant 5 (1 pen), Williamson, Duff 3, Ferries 2)*
St Cuthbert Wanderers (0) 0 1369
Ross County: Hutchison; Somerville, Reid, Williamson, Bellshaw, Alex MacLeod, Ferries, Grant, Duff (Drummond), Robertson (Ross), Wilson.
St Cuthbert Wanderers: McHendry; Kyle, Groves (Christie), McMillan, Morrison (McCreadie), Murray, Niven, Baker, Tweedie, Simpson, Adair.

Stranraer (1) 3 *(Sloan 2, Henderson)*
Whitehill Welfare (2) 3 *(Thorburn 2 (2 pens), Sneddon)* 684
Stranraer: Duffy; Millar, McIntyre, Spittal (Ferguson), Brannigan, Gallagher, Sloan, Grant, Duncan, Cody (Hughes), Henderson.
Whitehill Welfare: Ramage; Smith D, Millar, Brown, Steel, Cuthbert, Thorburn, Samuel, Sneddon (Bird), McCulloch, Tulloch.

FIRST ROUND REPLAYS

14 DEC

Queen's Park (0) 2 *(McPhee, Rodden)*
Cowdenbeath (3) 3 *(Reilly, Henderson, Callaghan)* 509
Queen's Park: Chalmers; Stevenson (McCormick), Maxwell, Kerr, Elder, Orr G, Rodden, Fitzpatrick (Ferguson), McPhee, Graham, O'Neill.
Cowdenbeath: Maloney; Petrie, Davidson, Herd, McMahon B, Maratea (Thomson), Lee, Scott, Reilly, Callaghan, Henderson.

18 DEC

Whitehill Welfare (0) 0
Stranraer (3) 4 *(Sloan 4)* 750
Whitehill Welfare: Ramage; Smith D (Richford), Millar, Brown, Steel, Cuthbert, Thorburn, Samuel, Sneddon (Smith R), McCulloch, Tulloch.
Stranraer: Ross; Millar, Hughes, Spittal, Gallagher, McCann (Cody), Sloan, Grant, Ferguson (McIntyre), Duncan, Henderson.

15 JAN

Huntly (0) 5 *(De Barros, Stewart, Lennox, Murphy, Thomson (pen))*
Albion R (1) 3 *(Fraser, Scott (pen), McCaffrey)* 2020
Huntly: Gardiner; McGinlay, Murphy, Walker, Rougvie, De Barros, Stewart, Copland (Dunsire), Thomson, Whyte (Selbie), Lennox.
Albion R: Burns; Riley, Beattie, Conn, McCaffrey,McKeown, Seggie, Cadden, Scott, Fraser, Gallagher.

SECOND ROUND

8 JAN

Berwick R (1) 1 *(Kane)*
East Fife (0) 0 742
Berwick R: Davidson; Boyle, Banks, Valentine, Cowan, Hall, Neil, Irvine, Hawke, Donaldson (Graham), Kane (Gibson).
East Fife: Charles; Sneddon, Williamson, Barron, Burns, Beedie, Allan (Taylor), Hildersley (McBride), Scott, Hope, Irvine.

East Stirling (0) 4 *(McAulay, Geraghty 2, Robertson)*
Cove R (0) 1 *(Whyte)* 867
East Stirling: McDougall; Russell, Kemp, McAulay, Craig, Ross, Conway (Robertson), Millar, McCallum, Geraghty, Loney.
Cove R: MacLean; Morrison, Whyte, Morland, Paterson, Baxter, Yule, Forbes, Stephen (Park), Murphy (Leslie), Megginson.

Forfar Ath (0) 0
Ross County (2) 4 *(Grant 3, Wilson)* 2439
Forfar Ath: Arthur; Philliben, McPhee, Mann (Smith), Archibald, Winter, Kopel, Hamill, Downie (Lees), Bingham, Heddle.
Ross County: Hutchison; Somerville, Reid (Ross), Williamson, Bellshaw, Alex MacLeod, Ferries, Grant (Robertson), Andrew MacLeod, Connelly, Wilson.

Meadowbank T (1) 1 *(Rutherford)*
Montrose (1) 2 *(Kennedy, Bailey (og))* 230
Meadowbank T: Ellison; Wilson, Scott, Murray, Graham, MacLeod I, Bailey, Little (Hutchison), Rutherford, McLeod G, Gardner (Brock).
Montrose: Larter; Robertson, Craib M, Tosh, Smith, Irvine, Tindal, Craib S, Grant (Wolecki), Kennedy, Stephen.

15 JAN

Alloa (2) 4 *(McCulloch, Wilson (og), McCormick, Lamont)*
Gala Fairydean (0) 0 805
Alloa: Butter; McNiven, McCormack J, Campbell, McCulloch, Newbigging, McAvoy, Ramsay, McCormick S, Moffat (McAnenay), Willock (Lamont).
Gala Fairydean: Cairns; Findlay, Henry, Wilson, Rae, Potts, Black, Campbell, McGovern (Simpson), Loughran (Lothian), Hunter.

Cowdenbeath (1) 1 *(Hunter)*
Stenhousemuir (0) 0 395
Cowdenbeath: Moffat; Watt, Scott, Herd, McMahon B, Petrie, Lee, Henderson (Thomson), Reilly, Callaghan, Hunter.
Stenhousemuir: Harkness; Aitken, Donaldson, Armstrong, Godfrey, Clarke, Steel, Irvine (Swanson), Mathieson, Haddow, Dickov.

Selkirk (0) 0
Arbroath (2) 3 *(McKinnon, Adam, Buckley)* 556
Selkirk: Massie; Brownlee M, Main, Scott (Ritchie), Brownlee P, Leckie, Kerr D (Wilson), Kerr A, Whitehead, Cockburn, Smith.
Arbroath: Jackson; Farnan, Florence, Mitchell, Adam, Buckley, Clouston, King, Diver, McKinnon, Sorbie.

22 JAN

Huntly (1) 1 *(De Barros)*
Stranraer (0) 2 *(Duncan (pen), Sloan)* 1862

Huntly: Gardiner; McGinlay, Murphy, Walker, Rougvie, De Barros, Stewart (Selbie), Copland, Thomson, Whyte, Lennox.
Stranraer: Duffy; Millar, Hughes, Spittal (Ferguson), Brannigan, Gallagher, Sloan, Grant, Duncan, Cody (McLean), Henderson.

THIRD ROUND

29 JAN

Airdrieonians (0) 1 *(Kirkwood (pen))*
Dunfermline Ath (0) 1 *(Tod)* 4583

Airdrieonians: Martin; Stewart, McVicar, Sandison, Jack, Black, Kirkwood, Honor, Davenport, Ferguson (Andrew Smith), Lawrence.
Dunfermline Ath: Hamilton; McNamara, Sharp, McCathie, Baillie (Tod), Smith, Preston, Robertson, French, Laing (O'Boyle), McWilliams.

Arbroath (0) 2 *(Sorbie, McKinnon)*
Dundee U (2) 3 *(Crabbe, Brewster, McKinlay (pen))* 6087

Arbroath: Jackson; Farnan, Florence, Mitchell, Adam, Martin (Scott), Clouston, King, Diver, McKinnon, Sorbie.
Dundee U: Van De Kamp; Van Der Hoorn, Malpas, McInally, Petric, Cleland, Bowman, McKinlay, Connolly, Brewster, Crabbe.

Clydebank (1) 1 *(Henry)*
Dundee (0) 1 *(Tosh)* 2170

Clydebank: Monaghan; Ferguson, Crawford D, Harris (Jack), Sweeney, Currie, Cooper, Henry (Lansdowne), Crawford J, Flannigan, Thomson.
Dundee: Mathers; Frail, Pittman, McQuillan, Blake, Duffy J (Farningham), Shaw, Vrto, Ritchie (Tosh), Wieghorst, McCann.

Hibernian (0) 2 *(O'Neill, McAllister)*
Clyde (1) 1 *(McCheyne)* 8500

Hibernian: Leighton; Miller, Mitchell, Farrell, Tweed, Beaumont, McAllister, Tortolano (Evans), Wright, Jackson D, O'Neill.
Clyde: Fridge; McFarlane, McCheyne, Knox, Thomson, Neill, Mackenzie (Parks), McAulay, McConnell, McCarron (Ronald), Strain.

Kilmarnock (1) 2 *(McSkimming, Black (pen))*
Ayr U (1) 1 *(Bryce)* 12,856

Kilmarnock: Geddes; MacPherson, Black, Montgomerie, Brown, Millen, Mitchell, Reilly, Williamson, McCluskey, McSkimming.
Ayr U: Spence; Burns, Mair, Shotton, Hood, George (Scott), Lennox (Moore), Traynor, Bryce, Jack, McGlashan.

Morton (0) 2 *(McEwan, Lilley)*
Cowdenbeath (2) 2 *(Henderson 2)* 1647

Morton: Wylie; Collins (McArthur), Pickering, Johnstone, Doak, Hunter, Lilley, Fowler (Thomson), McEwan, Sexton, Rafferty.
Cowdenbeath: Moffat; Davidson, Scott (Carr), Herd, McMahon B, Petrie, Lee, Henderson, Reilly (Barclay), Hunter, Thomson.

Motherwell (0) 1 *(Coyne)*
Celtic (0) 0 14,061

Motherwell: Dykstra; Shannon, McKinnon, Krivokapic, Martin, McCart, Lambert (Kirk), Dolan, Arnott, O'Donnell, Coyne (McGrillen).
Celtic: Muggleton; Gillespie, Boyd, O'Neil, Mowbray, McNally, Byrne (Biggins), McStay, McAvennie, McGinlay, Collins.

Partick T (0) 0
Hearts (1) 1 *(Johnston M)* 9519

Partick T: Nelson; Law, Milne, Watson, Jamieson, Cameron (Byrne), Gibson, Craig, Grant, English (Taylor), Charnley.
Hearts: Smith; McLaren, McKinlay, Levein, Berry, Locke, Colquhoun, Mackay, Leitch (Wright), Johnston M (Foster), Robertson.

Raith R (2) 2 *(Dair, McStay)*
Brechin C (0) 0 2846

Raith R: Thomson; McStay, McGeachie, Coyle, Dennis, Sinclair, Nicholl (Kelly), Dalziel, Cameron, Graham, Dair.
Brechin C: Allan; Conway, Christie, Brown, Nicolson, Scott, McLaren, Redford, Brand (O'Brien), Miller, McNeill.

Rangers (3) 4 *(Durie, Hateley (pen), Steven, Robertson)*
Dumbarton (0) 1 *(Mooney (pen))* 36,671

Rangers: Maxwell; Stevens G, Robertson, Gough, Murray, Brown, Steven T, McCall, Durie, Hateley, Mikhailichenko (McCoist).
Dumbarton: MacFarlane; Wilson, Fabiani, Melvin, Gow, MacLeod, Mooney, Meechan, Gibson, McGarvey, Foster (Boyd).

St Johnstone (0) 2 *(Dodds, McMartin)*
Hamilton A (0) 0 4331

St Johnstone: Rhodes; McGowne, McAuley, Ramsey, Deas, McGinnis, Scott, Turner (McMartin), Ferguson, Dodds (Torfason), Curran.
Hamilton A: Ferguson; Napier, Miller, McEntegart, Baptie, McInulty, McQuade, Reid, Duffield (Campbell), Clark (McKenzie), McGill.

St Mirren (1) 2 *(Elliot, Bone)*
Montrose (0) 0 3083

St Mirren: Combe; Dawson, Baker, Gillies R (Gardner), McIntyre, McLaughlin, Dick, Fullarton, Bone, Hewitt (Harvie), Elliot.
Montrose: Larter; Houghton (Yeats), Robertson, Grant, Smith, Irvine, Cooper, Tindal, Taylor, Kennedy, Stephen.

Stirling Albion (0) 1 *(Pew)*
Berwick R (0) 0 1023

Stirling Albion: McGeown; Hamilton, Watson, McAnenay (Armstrong), McQuilter, Mitchell, McInnes, Callaghan, Pew, Gibson, McLeod (Watters).
Berwick R: O'Connor; Boyle, Banks, Valentine, Cowan, Wilson, Young (Hall), Neil, Hawke, Irvine, Graham (Kane).

Stranraer (1) 2 *(Sloan, Ferguson)*
Falkirk (0) 1 *(Hughes)* 2630

Stranraer: Duffy; Millar, Hughes, McLean, Brannigan, Gallagher, Sloan, Duncan, Ferguson (McIntyre), Cody (Spittal), Henderson.
Falkirk: Westwater; Duffy, Johnston (Drinkell), Weir, McLaughlin, Hughes, May (McDonald), Sloan, Cadette, McCall, Rice.

8 FEB

Alloa (2) 2 *(McAnenay, McAvoy)*
Ross County (0) 0 4197

Alloa: Butter; McNiven, Tait, Campbell, McCulloch, Newbigging, McAnenay (Moffat), Ramsay (Mackay), McCormick, McAvoy, Willock.
Ross County: Hutchison; Somerville, Reid (Robertson), Williamson, Bellshaw, Andrew MacLeod, Ferries (Duff), Grant, Alex MacLeod, Connelly, Wilson.

East Stirling (0) 1 *(Geraghty)*
Aberdeen (0) 3 *(Craig (og), Shearer 2)* 3853

East Stirling: McDougall; Russell, Lee, McAulay (Conroy), Craig, Ross, Conway, Millar, McCallum, Geraghty, Loney.
Aberdeen: Snelders; McKimmie, Wright, Grant, McLeish, Irvine, Jess (Booth), Bett, Winnie (Miller), Shearer, Paatelainen.

THIRD ROUND REPLAYS

8 FEB

Cowdenbeath (0) 1 *(Callaghan)*
Morton (1) 2 *(Anderson, McEwan)* 729

Cowdenbeath: Moffat; Watt, Thomson (Reilly), Herd, Young, Petrie, Lee (Davidson), Henderson, Callaghan, Hunter, Carr.
Morton: Wylie; Anderson, Pickering, Rafferty, Johnstone, Hunter, Thomson, Fowler, Alexander, Sexton (McArthur), McEwan.

Dunfermline Ath (0) 1 *(Tod)*

Airdrieonians (2) 3 *(Kirkwood 2 (2 pens), Ferguson)* 6991

Dunfermline Ath: Hamilton; McNamara, Sharp, McCathie, Baillie, Smith, Den Bieman, Robertson, Petrie, O'Boyle (Tod), Preston (Laing).
Airdrieonians: Martin; Stewart, Jack (Sandison), Honor, Caesar, Black, Kirkwood, Balfour, Andrew Smith, Ferguson, Lawrence (Davenport).

9 FEB

Dundee (2) 2 *(Britton, Shaw) at Forthbank Stadium, Stirling*

Clydebank (0) 1 *(Sweeney)* 815

Dundee: Mathers; McQuillan, Pittman, Duffy J, Blake, Dinnie, Shaw, Vrto, Britton (Farningham), Wieghorst (Ristic), McCann.
Clydebank: Monaghan; Ferguson (Lansdowne), Crawford D, Murdoch, Sweeney, Currie, Cooper, Henry, Harris, Flannigan (Smith), Thomson.

FOURTH ROUND

19 FEB

Aberdeen (0) 1 *(Miller)*

Raith R (0) 0 13,740

Aberdeen: Snelders; Smith, Wright, Grant, McLeish, Irvine, Jess (Booth), Bett (Miller), Kane, Shearer, Paatelainen.
Raith R: Thomson; McStay, Rowbotham, Coyle, Dennis, Sinclair, Nicholl, Cameron, Hetherston, Crawford (Graham), Dair.

Airdrieonians (0) 1 *(Kirkwood (pen))*

Stranraer (0) 0 3269

Airdrieonians: Martin; Stewart, Hay, Sandison, Caesar, Black, Kirkwood, Honor, Ferguson, Harvey (Andrew Smith), Lawrence (Davenport).
Stranraer: Duffy; Millar, McLean (Ferguson), McIntyre, Brannigan, Gallagher, Sloan, Grant, Duncan, Cody, Henderson.

Dundee U (1) 2 *(Brewster 2)*

Motherwell (1) 2 *(Kirk, Philliben)* 12,098

Dundee U: Van De Kamp; Van Der Hoorn, Malpas, McInally, Petric, Welsh, Dailly, McKinlay, Connolly, Brewster, Crabbe (Nixon).
Motherwell: Dykstra; Shannon (Dolan), McKinnon, Krivokapic, Martin, McCart, Lambert (McGrillen), Philliben, Kirk, O'Donnell, Coyne.

Morton (0) 0

Kilmarnock (1) 1 *(Williamson)* 7255

Morton: Wylie; Anderson, Pickering, Rafferty, Johnstone, Hunter, McEwan (Lilley), Fowler, Alexander, Thomson (Sexton), Tolmie.
Kilmarnock: Geddes; MacPherson, Black, Montgomerie, Brown, Millen, Mitchell, Reilly, Williamson (Porteous), McInally, McSkimming (McCluskey).

Rangers (2) 6 *(Ferguson I, McPherson, McCoist 3 (1 pen), Newbigging (og))*

Alloa (0) 0 37,620

Rangers: Goram; Stevens G (Pressley), Robertson D, McCall, McPherson, Brown, Steven T, Ferguson I, McCoist, Hateley, Mikhailichenko.
Alloa: Butter; McNiven, Tait, Newbigging, McCulloch, McAvoy, McAnenay, Ramsay, McCormick, Lamont (Moffat), Willock (Mackay).

20 FEB

Dundee (1) 3 *(Britton, Shaw)*

St Mirren (1) 1 *(Lavety)* 6038

Dundee: Mathers; McQuillan, Pittman, Dinnie, Blake, Duffy J, Shaw, Farningham (Frail), Britton (Tosh), Wieghorst, McCann.
St Mirren: Combe; Dawson, Baker, Taylor, McIntyre, Fullarton (Gardner), Dick (Farrell), Bone, Lavety, Hewitt, Elliot.

Hibernian (1) 1 *(Wright)*

Hearts (1) 2 *(Robertson, Foster)* 20,700

Hibernian: Leighton; Miller, Beaumont, Farrell, Tweed, Lennon, McAllister, Hamilton, Wright, Jackson D (Evans), O'Neill.
Hearts: Smith; McLaren, McKinlay, Levein, Berry, Millar, Colquhoun, Mackay, Robertson (Foster), Johnston M, Leitch (Weir).

28 FEB

St Johnstone (1) 3 *(Dodds 2, Ferguson)*

Stirling Albion (2) 3 *(Roberts 2, Armstrong)* 3759

St Johnstone: Rhodes; Inglis, McAuley, Ramsey (McMartin), Deas, McGinnis, Scott, Moore (Torfason), Ferguson, Dodds, Curran.
Stirling Albion: McGeown; Hamilton, Armstrong, Tait, McQuilter, Mitchell, Roberts (Reilly), Callaghan, Watters (Pew), Gibson, McLeod.

FOURTH ROUND REPLAYS

1 MAR

Motherwell (0) 0

Dundee U (0) 1 *(Welsh)* 13,002

Motherwell: Dykstra; Philliben, McKinnon, Krivokapic, Martin, McCart, Lambert (Dolan), Kirk (McGrillen), Arnott, O'Donnell, Coyne.
Dundee U: Van De Kamp; Narey, Malpas, McInally, Petric, Welsh, Dailly, McKinlay, Nixon (Hannah), Brewster, Crabbe (Cleland).

2 MAR

Stirling Albion (0) 0

St Johnstone (2) 2 *(Scott, Ferguson)* 2452

Stirling Albion: McGeown; Pew, Armstrong, Tait, McQuilter, Mitchell, Roberts (Reilly), Callaghan, Watters (Watson), Gibson, McLeod.
St Johnstone: Rhodes; Inglis, McAuley, Ramsey, Deas, Cherry, Scott, Turner, Ferguson, Dodds, Curran.

QUARTER-FINALS

12 MAR

Airdrieonians (0) 0

Dundee U (0) 0 8440

Airdrieonians: Martin; Stewart, Honor, Sandison, Caesar, Hay, Boyle, Reid, Davenport (Anmdrew Smith), Harvey, Ferguson.
Dundee U: Van De Kamp; Narey, Malpas, McInally, Petric, Welsh, Bowman, McKinlay (Hannah), Nixon (O'Neil), Brewster, Cleland.

Kilmarnock (1) 1 *(Brown)*

Dundee (0) 0 10,446

Kilmarnock: Geddes; MacPherson, Black, Montgomerie, Burns, Millen, Mitchell, Reilly, Brown, McCluskey (Williamson), McSkimming.
Dundee: Mathers; McQuillan, Pittman, Dinnie (Tosh), Blake, Frail (Farningham), Shaw, Vrto, Britton, Wieghorst, McCann.

Rangers (0) 2 *(Brown, Hateley)*

Hearts (0) 0 41,666

Rangers: Goram; McCall, Robertson D, Gough, McPherson, Brown, Steven, Ferguson I, McCoist (Mikhailichenko), Hateley, Durie (Ferguson D).
Hearts: Smith; Weir, McKinlay, Levein, Berry (Locke), McLaren, Colquhoun (Robertson), Leitch, Foster, Johnston M, Millar.

St Johnstone (0) 1 *(Dodds)*

Aberdeen (1) 1 *(Booth)* 8447

St Johnstone: Rhodes; McGowne, Inglis, Ramsey, Deas, Cherry (Torfason), Scott, Turner, Ferguson, Dodds, Curran.
Aberdeen: Stillie; McKimmie, Wright, Smith, McLeish, Irvine, Jess (Miller), Richardson, Booth, Shearer, Kane.

QUARTER-FINAL REPLAYS

15 MAR

Aberdeen (2) 2 *(Shearer, Richardson)*
St Johnstone (0) 0 14,325

Aberdeen: Stillie; McKimmie, Wright, Smith, McLeish, Irvine, Jess, Richardson, Booth (Miller), Shearer, Kane.
St Johnstone: Rhodes; McGowne, Inglis, Ramsey (McMartin), Deas, Cherry, Scott, Turner, Ferguson, Dodds, Curran (Torfason).

Dundee U (2) 2 *(McLaren, McKinlay)*
Airdrieonians (0) 0 9335

Dundee U: Van De Kamp; Hannah, Malpas, McInally, Petric, Welsh, Bowman, McKinlay, Nixon (McLaren), Dailly, Cleland.
Airdrieonians: Martin; Stewart, Honor, Sandison, Caesar, Hay, Boyle, Reid, Davenport (Andrew Smith), Harvey (Jack), Ferguson.

SEMI-FINALS at Hampden Park

9 APR

Dundee U (0) 1 *(Welsh)*
Aberdeen (1) 1 *(Shearer)* 21,397

Dundee U: Van De Kamp; Cleland, Malpas, McInally, Petric, Welsh, Bowman, McKinlay, McLaren, Brewster, Nixon (Dailly).
Aberdeen: Burridge; McKimmie, Robertson (Miller), Kane, Smith, Irvine, Jess (Paatelainen), Richardson, McKinnon, Shearer, Grant.

10 APR

Kilmarnock (0) 0
Rangers (0) 0 35,134

Kilmarnock: Geddes; MacPherson, Black, Montgomerie, Paterson, Millen, Mitchell (McCluskey), Reilly, Williamson, Brown (McInally), McSkimming.
Rangers: Maxwell; Murray (McCoist), Robertson D, Gough, McPherson, Brown, McCall, Ferguson I, Durie, Hateley, Mikhailichenko (Ferguson D).

SEMI-FINAL REPLAYS at Hampden Park

12 APR

Dundee U (0) 1 *(McInally)*
Aberdeen (0) 0 13,936

Dundee U: Van De Kamp; Cleland, Malpas, McInally, Petric, Welsh, Bowman, McKinlay, McLaren (Nixon), Brewster (Dailly), Bollan.
Aberdeen: Snelders; McKimmie, Robertson (Booth), Kane, Smith, Irvine, Jess, Richardson, McKinnon (Miller), Shearer, Grant.

13 APR

Kilmarnock (1) 1 *(Black)*
Rangers (0) 2 *(Hateley 2)* 29,860

Kilmarnock: Geddes; MacPherson (McInally), Black, Montgomerie, Paterson, Millen, Mitchell, Reilly, Williamson, Brown (McCluskey), McSkimming.
Rangers: Maxwell; McCall, Robertson D, Gough, McPherson, Pressley, Durie, Ferguson I, McCoist, Hateley, Durrant (Huistra).

FINAL at Hampden Park

21 MAY

Dundee U (0) 1 *(Brewster)*
Rangers (0) 0 37,450

Dundee U: Van De Kamp; Cleland, Malpas, McInally, Petric, Welsh, Bowman, Hannah, McLaren (Nixon), Brewster, Dailly.
Rangers: Maxwell; Stevens G (Mikhailichenko), Robertson D, Gough, McPherson, McCall, Murray, Ferguson I, McCoist (Ferguson D), Hateley, Durie.

B & Q CUP 1993–94

FIRST ROUND

5 OCT

Albion R (0) 2 *(McBride, Scott)*
Cowdenbeath (2) 2 *(Callaghan, Lee) aet* 267

Albion R: Burns; Kelly, Spence, McCaffrey, Conn, Mirner, Seggie (McQuade), McBride, Scott, Cadden, McKeown.
Cowdenbeath: Filshill; Watt, Scott, Davidson, McMahon B, Carr (Henderson), Petrie (Harris), Herd, Callaghan, Hunter, Lee.
(Cowdenbeath won 3-2 on penalties)

Ayr U (1) 3 *(McGlashan, Burns, Bryce)*
East Fife (0) 1 *(Allan)* 1471

Ayr U: Spence; Robertson, Mair (Hood), Shotton, Traynor, Moore, Lennox, McGlashan, McGivern (Scott), Burns, Bryce.
East Fife: Charles; Bell, Gibb, Barron, Burns, Williamson, Allan (Logan), Hildersley, Scott (Reilly), Taylor, Andrew.

Dumbarton (1) 1 *(Foster)*
Stranraer (2) 2 *(Henderson, Sloan)* 446

Dumbarton: MacFarlane; Marsland, Fabiani, Melvin, Martin, Gow, Mooney, McConville, McAnenay, McDonald (Willock), Foster.
Stranraer: Duffy; Millar, Brown, Spittal, Brannigan, McLean, Sloan, Grant (Ferguson), Duncan, Cody, Henderson.

Stenhousemuir (0) 0
Clydebank (3) 5 *(Lee, Flannigan 2, Nelson, Aitken (og))* 439

Stenhousemuir: Harkness; Aitken, Hallford, Armstrong, Clarke, Logan, Steel, Dickov (Irvine), Mathieson, Roseburgh (O'Neill), Fisher.
Clydebank: Monaghan; Jack, Crawford D, Murdoch, Currie, Walker (Henry), Lee, Lansdowne (Crawford J), Smith, Flannigan, Nelson.

6 OCT

Brechin C (0) 3 *(Brand 2, Miller)*
Arbroath (0) 1 *(Diver) aet* 645

Brechin C: Alexander; Cairney, Fisher, Conway, Christie, Hutt, McLaren (Vannett), McNeill (Redford), Brand, Miller, Greig.
Arbroath: Jackson; Hamilton, Florence, Mitchell, Adam, Martin, Elliot (Will), Tindal, Diver, McKinnon, Buckley.

Clyde (0) 0
St Mirren (1) 1 *(Lavety)* 1020

Clyde: Fridge; McFarlane (Quinn), Tennant, Bell, Thomson, Neill, Parks, Prunty (Strain), McConnell, McAulay, McCarron.
St Mirren: Money; Dawson, Harvie, McWhirter, McIntyre, Orr, Bone (McGrotty), Fullarton, Lavety, Hewitt, Gardner (Hetherston).

Falkirk (1) 2 *(May (pen), Sloan)*
Alloa (0) 1 *(Newbigging)* 1966

Falkirk: Parks; Oliver, McQueen, Weir, McLaughlin, Rice, May (McDonald), Duffy, Shaw (Young), Sloan, Taggart.
Alloa: Butter; Bennett, Lee, Mackay, McCulloch, Newbigging, Herd (Russell), Campbell, McCormick S (Tait), Moffat, Ramsay.

Forfar Ath (1) 2 *(Smith, Bingham)*
Meadowbank T (1) 3 *(Bailey, Brock 2) aet* 380

Forfar Ath: Arthur; Philliben, Hamill, Morris, Mann, McPhee, Downie, Heddle, Smith, Donaldson, Bingham.
Meadowbank T: McQueen; Williamson R, Fleming, Murray, Williamson S, Coyle (Price), Bailey, Wilson, Brock, McLeod G, Duthie (McCartney).

Montrose (4) 5 *(Kennedy 2, Yeats, Craib M, Wolecki)*
East Stirling (0) 0 379

Montrose: Larter; Robertson, Craib M, Tosh, Smith, Lavelle, Yeats, Craib S (Stephen), Grant (Wolecki), Kennedy, Cooper.
East Stirling: McDougall; Russell, Kemp, Ross, Craig, Yates, Crews, Millar, Roberts, Geraghty, Loney.

Queen of the S (0) 2 *(Kelly, Thomson)*
Berwick R (1) 1 *(Banks)* 1204

Queen of the S: Davidson; Mills, Rowe, McKeown, Shanks (Kelly), Bryce, McLaren (McGuire D), McFarlane, Thomson, Bell, Mallan.
Berwick R: O'Connor; Valentine, Banks, Coughlin, Cowan, Richardson, Wilson (Sokoluk), Muir, Gallacher (Kane), Hall, Cunningham.

SECOND ROUND

19 OCT

Airdrieonians (2) 3 *(Abercromby, McIntyre, Black)*
Hamilton A (0) 1 *(Baptie)* 1907

Airdrieonians: McCulloch; Stewart, Honor, Jack, Sandison, Black, Boyle, Wilson, Abercromby, Lawrence, McIntyre (Andrew Smith).
Hamilton A: Ferguson; Napier, Miller, Fitzpatrick, McKenzie (McLean), McInulty, McQuade (Baptie), Reid, Duffield, Clark, Ward.

Ayr U (1) 2 *(McGivern 2)*
Brechin C (0) 1 *(Miller) aet* 1318

Ayr U: Duncan; Robertson, Mair, Shotton, Traynor, George, Moore (Kennedy), McGlashan, McGivern, Burns, Jack (Scott).
Brechin C: Alexander; Conway, Scott, Christie, Nicolson, Hutt (McNeill), Vannett, O'Brien, Greig, Miller, Brand.

Falkirk (2) 3 *(Sloan, McDonald 2)*
Cowdenbeath (0) 0 1732

Falkirk: Parks; Oliver, McQueen, Weir, McLaughlin, Hughes, Sloan, Duffy (May), Cadette (Taggart), McCall, McDonald.
Cowdenbeath: Filshill; Watt, Scott, McMahon B, Davidson, Russell (Maratea), Herd, Lee, Harris, Henderson, Callaghan (Carr).

Morton (0) 2 *(Alexander, Tolmie)*
St Mirren (1) 4 *(Gallagher 2, Lavety, Harvie)* 3015
Morton: Wylie; Collins, Pickering, Rafferty, Shearer, McArthur, McEwan (Lilley), Donaghy (Fowler), Alexander, McInnes, Tolmie.
St Mirren: Money; Dawson, Baker (Harvie), McWhirter, McIntyre, Orr, Gallagher, Dick, Lavety, Hewitt (Bone), Fullarton.

Queen's Park (0) 0
Clydebank (0) 1 *(Lansdowne)* 1083
Queen's Park: Chalmers; Stevenson, Maxwell, Kerr, Fitzpatrick, Orr G, McCormick, Caven, McPhee, Graham, Brodie G (Brodie D).
Clydebank: Monaghan; Jack (Crawford J), Crawford D, Murdoch, Currie, Lansdowne, Harvey, Henry, Eadie (Walker), Smith, Nelson.

20 OCT

Meadowbank T (1) 2 *(Rutherford, Little)*
Stirling Albion (0) 0 341
Meadowbank T: Ellison; Williamson R, Fleming, Murray, Williamson S, Little, Bailey, Brock (Price), Rutherford, McLeod G, Coulston (Elder).
Stirling Albion: McGeown; McKenna, Watson, Tait, Lawrie, Mitchell, McInnes (McCallum), Callaghan, Watters, Armstrong, Flynn (Reilly).

Montrose (0) 0
Stranraer (0) 0 *aet* 561
Montrose: Larter; Robertson, Craib M, Tosh, Smith, Lavelle, Cooper (Wolecki), Yeats, Grant, Kennedy, Stephen.
Stranraer: Ross; Millar, Hughes, Spittal, Gallagher, McLean, Sloan, Grant, Duncan, Cody, Henderson (Ferguson).
Montrose won 6-5 on penalties.

Queen of the S (0) 0
Dunfermline Ath (4) 6 *(Den Bieman, O'Boyle 2, Laing 2, Smith)* 2015
Queen of the S: Davidson; Mills, McGhie, McKeown, Shanks, Bell, Kelly, McFarlane, Thomson, Proudfoot (Jackson), McLaren.
Dunfermline Ath: Hillcoat; McNamara, Cunnington (Sharp), McCathie (Davies), Baillie, Robertson, Den Bieman, Smith, Laing, O'Boyle, Preston.

QUARTER-FINALS

26 OCT

Airdrieonians (0) 0
St Mirren (0) 2 *(Gallagher 2)* 2561
Airdrieonians: McCulloch; Stewart, Kirkwood, Jack, Honor, Black, Boyle, Wilson, Abercromby, Lawrence, McIntyre.
St Mirren: Money; Dawson, Baker, McWhirter, McIntyre, Orr, Gallagher, Dick, Lavety, Hewitt, Gillies R.

Ayr U (1) 2 *(Murdoch (og), Burns (pen))*
Clydebank (0) 0 1908
Ayr U: Duncan; Kennedy, Robertson, Shotton, Traynor (Hood), George, Lennox, McGlashan, McGivern, Burns, Bryce (Jack).
Clydebank: Monaghan; Jack, Thomson, Murdoch, Sweeney, Currie, Lansdowne, Henry, Lee, Walker (Crawford J), Nelson.

27 OCT

Falkirk (1) 4 *(Cadette 3, Drinkell)*
Dunfermline Ath (0) 1 *(Sharp)* 5634
Falkirk: Westwater; Oliver, McQueen, Weir, McLaughlin (Sloan), Hughes, May, Drinkell, Cadette, Rice (McDonald), Duffy.
Dunfermline Ath: Hillcoat; McNamara, Cunnington, Sharp, Baillie, Smith, Den Bieman (McWilliams), Robertson, French, Laing (Sinclair), Petrie.

Meadowbank T (1) 1 *(Rutherford)*
Montrose (1) 1 *(Yeats) aet* 385
Meadowbank T: Ellison; Elder (Hutchison), Fleming, Murray, Graham, Little, Bailey, Wilson, Rutherford, McLeod G, Brock (Coyle).
Montrose: Larter; Houghton, Robertson, Craib M, Grant, Irvine (Lavelle), Cooper (Craib S), Yeats, McKenna, Kennedy, Stephen.
(Meadowbank T won 3-1 on penalties)

SEMI-FINALS

2 NOV

Ayr U (0) 1 *(McGivern)*
St Mirren (0) 2 *(Gallagher 2)* 4309
Ayr U: Duncan; Kennedy, Robertson, Shotton, Hood, George, Lennox (Traynor), McGlashan, McGivern, Burns, Bryce (Jack).
St Mirren: Money; Dawson, Baker, McWhirter, McIntyre, Orr, Gallagher, Dick (McLaughlin), Lavety, Hewitt, Elliot.

Falkirk (0) 3 *(Cadette 2, May)*
Meadowbank T (0) 2 *(Little, McLeod G (pen))* 3936
Falkirk: Parks; Duffy, McQueen, Weir, Hughes, Rice, May (Shaw), Drinkell, Cadette, Sloan, McDonald (MacKenzie).
Meadowbank T: Ellison; MacLeod I, Fleming, Murray, Williamson S, Little, Bailey, Wilson (Coulston), Rutherford, McLeod G, Brock (Coyle).

FINAL

12 DEC at Fir Park, Motherwell

Falkirk (0) 3 *(Duffy, Cadette, Hughes)*
St Mirren (0) 0 13,763
Falkirk: Parks; Duffy, McQueen, Weir, McLaughlin, Hughes, May, Drinkell (Shaw), Cadette, McCall (Oliver), Rice.
St Mirren: Money; Dawson, Baker, McWhirter, McLaughlin, Orr, Bone (Gillies R), Dick, Lavety, Hewitt (McIntyre), Elliot.
Referee: D. Hope (Erskine)

CALEDONIAN THISTLE Division 3

Year Formed: 1994. *Ground & Address:* Telford Street Park, Inverness. *Telephone:* 0463 230274.
Ground Capacity: total: 5500. seated: 500. *Size of Pitch:* 110yd × 70yd.
Chairman: John S McDonald. *Secretary:* Scott Ayrnes (Telephone: 0463 233671).
Manager: Sergei Baltacha. *Coaches:* D. MacDonald, D. Milroy, J. Beaton, J. Sutherland, A. Young.
Club Historian: Ian Davidson.
Club colours: Shirt: Royal blue with White piping. Shorts: White. Stockings: Blue.

INVERNESS CALEDONIAN

Founded: 1886. *Ground:* Telford Street Park.

Honours
Highland League: (record 18 times) 1895–6, 1898–9, 1899–1900, 1901–2, 1910–1, 1913–4, 1925–6, 1930–1, 1950–1, 1951–2, 1963–4, 1970–1, 1976–7, 1977–8, 1981–2, 1982–3, 1983–4, 1987–8.
Scottish Qualifying Cup: (record 14 times) 1948–49, 1949–50, 1950–51, 1961–62, 1965–66, 1966–67, 1969–70, 1971–72, 1981–82, 1982–83, 1983–84, 1986–87, 1987–88, 1991–92.
North of Scotland Cup: (21 times).
Highland League Cup: 1952–53, 1969–70, 1971–72, 1976–77, 1977–78.
Inverness Cup: (19 times).
Bell's North Cup: Won outright 1979–80.

INVERNESS THISTLE

Founded: 1885. *Ground:* Kingsmills Park (the only one).

Honours
Highland League: (8 times) 1893-4, 1906-7, 1909-10, 1928-9, 1935-6, 1971-2, 1972-3, 1986-7.
Scottish Qualifying Cup: 1932-33, 1972-73, 1976-77, 1980-81, 1988-89.
North of Scotland Cup: (13 times).
Highland League Cup: 1970-71, 1972-73, 1987-88.
Inverness Charities Cup: (18 times).
Scottish North Cup: 1955-56.
Bell's North Cup: 1974-75.
Elginshire Cup: 1890-91, 1892-93, 1893-94.
Skol Cup: 1983-84.

ROSS COUNTY Division 3

Ground & Address: Victoria Park, Dingwall IV15 9QW. *Telephone:* 0349 862253. *Fax:* 0349 866277.
Ground Capacity: total: 6500. seated: 319 (including wheelchair accommodation). (under way is a three-phase reconstruction which aims for an 8000 capacity all-seated ground by the end of the century). No previous grounds.
Record Crowd: 10,000 Scottish Cup 2nd round v Rangers, 23 Feb 1966.
Manager: Bobby Wilson. *Chairman:* Hector MacLennan.
Football Secretary: Donald MacBean. *Office Secretary:* Mrs Cathie Caird.
Assistant Manager: Don Cowie.
Commerical Manager: Brian Campbell.
Physio: Douglas Sim.

Honours
Highland League Champions: 1966-67, 1990-91, 1991-92.
Highland League Cup: 1949-50, 1968-69, 1978-79, 1991-92.
Scottish Qualifying Cup: 1973-74, 1993-94.
North of Scotland Cup: 1929-30, 1969-70, 1971-72, 1991-92.
Inverness Cup: (8 times).
Club colours: Shirt: Dark Blue. Shorts: White. Stockings: White.

WELSH FOOTBALL 1993–94

KONICA LEAGUE OF WALES

		Home			Goals		Away			Goals		
	P	*W*	*D*	*L*	*F*	*A*	*W*	*D*	*L*	*F*	*A*	*Pts*
Bangor City	38	15	4	0	51	10	11	1	7	31	16	83
Inter Cardiff	38	15	1	3	46	19	11	2	6	51	25	81
Ton Pentre	38	12	5	2	35	12	9	3	7	27	25	71
Flint Town United	38	13	3	3	42	19	7	3	9	28	28	66
Holywell Town	38	13	5	1	48	19	5	5	9	26	38	64
Newtown	38	10	5	4	27	21	8	4	7	25	27	63
Connah's Quay Nomads	38	10	4	5	37	24	6	7	6	22	23	59
Cwmbran Town	38	11	5	3	31	19	5	4	10	20	27	57
Ebbw Vale	38	9	4	6	37	34	7	5	7	31	32	57
Aberystwyth Town	38	8	6	5	26	22	7	4	8	31	34	55
Porthmadog	38	7	4	8	38	28	7	3	9	52	43	49
Llanelli	38	8	1	10	44	46	6	3	10	32	54	46
Conwy United	38	7	3	9	29	29	6	3	10	26	41	45
Mold Alexandra	38	5	5	9	29	36	7	2	10	30	39	43
Haverfordwest County	38	3	5	11	17	43	7	5	7	23	38	40
Afan Lido	38	4	8	7	29	32	4	7	8	23	34	39
Caersws	38	6	4	9	23	28	3	8	8	16	28	39
Llansantffraid	38	7	3	9	26	32	2	4	13	20	45	34
Maesteg Park Athletic	38	3	4	12	17	36	5	5	9	26	35	33
Briton Ferry Athletic	38	4	4	11	32	52	4	5	10	21	32	33

THE WELSH FOOTBALL LEAGUE

		Home			Goals		Away			Goals		
Division One	*P*	*W*	*D*	*L*	*F*	*A*	*W*	*D*	*L*	*F*	*A*	*Pts*
Barry Town	34	15	0	2	50	9	12	4	1	44	19	85
Aberaman	34	9	1	7	32	24	11	3	3	39	25	64
AFC Porth	34	7	3	7	31	24	12	3	2	37	14	63
Caldicot	34	6	8	3	38	31	10	3	4	45	28	59
Pontypridd	34	8	5	4	31	19	7	3	7	22	24	52
Pembroke Boro	34	9	4	4	37	23	6	2	9	22	26	51
Cardiff Civil Service	34	10	2	5	37	20	5	4	8	22	30	51
Llanwern	34	9	2	6	30	21	4	5	8	20	32	46
Ammanford	34	7	4	6	27	24	6	2	9	25	31	45
Caerleon	34	9	4	4	33	27	3	5	9	17	32	45
Morriston	34	5	5	7	22	21	6	5	6	23	28	43
Brecon	34	6	2	9	33	37	5	6	6	24	31	41
Caerau	34	7	5	5	30	20	3	5	9	16	30	40
Abergavenny	34	7	6	4	24	21	3	3	11	16	47	39
Ferndale	34	5	6	6	22	24	2	7	8	14	38	34
Port Talbot	34	4	5	8	25	34	5	2	10	18	37	34
Blaenrhondda	34	6	3	8	28	26	2	5	10	19	38	32
Bridgend Town	34	4	4	9	26	34	2	2	13	17	47	24

		Home			Goals		Away			Goals		
Division Two	*P*	*W*	*D*	*L*	*F*	*A*	*W*	*D*	*L*	*F*	*A*	*Pts*
Taffs Wells	26	10	1	2	39	13	7	4	2	27	12	56
Treowen	26	11	2	0	31	6	6	3	4	21	19	56
Carmarthen	26	8	1	4	28	19	7	2	4	30	28	48
Risca	26	8	1	4	35	19	6	2	5	15	15	45
B.P.	26	7	2	4	26	15	5	4	4	24	22	42
Fields Park/Pont.	26	5	6	2	26	19	5	3	5	16	17	39
Garw	26	7	2	4	25	19	4	4	5	16	16	39
Skewen	26	5	6	2	20	16	5	2	6	24	27	38
Cardiff Corries	26	6	2	5	20	21	4	2	7	14	30	34
Pontyclun	26	4	4	5	21	14	3	3	7	12	23	28
Newport YMCA	26	5	3	5	21	18	2	3	8	15	32	27
Seven Sisters	26	5	0	8	17	22	2	1	10	13	32	22
Tonyrefail	26	2	2	9	19	29	4	1	8	17	25	21
Milford	26	2	4	7	15	27	1	2	10	13	45	15

		Home			Goals		Away			Goals		
Division Three	*P*	*W*	*D*	*L*	*F*	*A*	*W*	*D*	*L*	*F*	*A*	*Pts*
Penrhiwceiber	26	11	1	1	46	11	8	3	2	29	12	61
Grange Harlequins	26	11	1	1	44	14	8	2	3	48	15	60
Goytre	26	11	0	2	51	12	7	3	3	30	19	57
Porth Tywyn	26	8	1	4	31	18	7	2	4	29	16	48
Tondu Robins	26	7	2	4	25	18	7	2	4	32	20	46
Pontlottyn	26	5	5	3	25	17	7	3	3	24	19	44
Pontardawe	26	7	2	4	24	19	4	3	6	21	31	38
Treharris	26	6	2	5	33	34	5	1	7	27	28	36
Albion Rovers	26	5	2	6	31	29	3	2	8	15	28	28
Abercynon	26	3	5	5	19	27	1	5	7	14	34	22
S.W. Constabulary	26	2	3	8	18	40	3	2	8	25	41	20
Cardiff Institute	26	3	2	8	13	30	1	4	8	15	42	18
Panteg	26	2	6	5	21	29	1	2	10	13	38	17
Trelewis	26	1	1	11	10	39	4	1	8	15	48	17

KONICA LEAGUE OF WALES RESULTS 1993–94

	Aberystwyth	Afan Lido	Bangor City	Briton Ferry	Caersws	Connah's Q	Conwy United	Cwmbran Town	Ebbw Vale	Flint Town	Haverfordwest	Holywell Town	Inter Cardiff	Llanelli	Llansantfd	Maesteg Park	Mold Alex	Newtown	Porthmadog	Ton Pentre
Aberystwyth	—	2-2	0-2	0-0	1-0	0-0	0-1	0-3	1-1	2-0	0-3	5-1	1-4	1-0	1-0	1-1	3-1	3-0	4-3	0-0
Afan Lido	2-4	—	2-3	1-3	0-0	0-1	2-2	1-1	1-1	1-1	3-3	0-2	1-3	2-2	3-0	1-0	1-2	3-1	2-2	3-1
Bangor City	1-1	2-1	—	2-0	1-1	2-0	2-1	2-1	1-0	1-0	9-0	2-1	1-1	5-1	8-0	6-1	3-0	0-0	2-1	1-0
Briton Ferry	2-2	0-3	0-4	—	1-0	2-2	2-4	1-1	2-1	3-3	3-1	2-4	2-9	2-3	2-3	3-0	1-2	1-3	3-6	0-1
Caersws	4-1	2-0	0-4	1-1	—	0-0	3-2	1-1	3-0	0-1	0-1	2-1	1-2	3-3	2-3	1-0	0-2	0-1	0-2	0-3
Connah's Q	2-0	3-1	2-0	2-2	1-1	—	5-1	2-0	2-3	2-1	2-3	1-1	0-3	5-1	3-2	3-1	1-1	0-2	1-0	0-1
Conwy United	2-3	2-3	1-0	5-3	0-1	1-0	—	1-1	4-2	0-1	4-1	0-1	2-1	0-1	2-1	1-1	2-3	1-1	1-4	0-1
Cwmbran Town	1-1	1-0	1-0	3-1	4-1	1-0	0-2	—	2-2	3-2	0-3	1-1	1-1	3-1	2-1	1-1	4-0	1-0	0-1	2-1
Ebbw Vale	1-1	3-1	0-2	3-0	3-2	1-2	2-1	1-0	—	2-1	1-2	1-0	3-5	1-3	2-2	3-3	5-3	0-2	4-2	1-1
Flint Town	0-3	5-0	1-0	0-1	0-0	2-1	3-3	2-1	2-1	—	4-0	3-1	4-0	3-1	1-1	0-3	2-0	4-1	3-1	3-1
Haverfordwest	2-3	0-0	0-3	0-0	0-1	0-0	0-2	1-5	1-1	1-2	—	3-3	1-0	1-3	3-1	1-3	2-1	1-4	0-9	0-2
Holywell Town	3-1	4-0	3-0	1-3	1-1	1-1	3-1	3-1	4-2	2-2	4-0	—	1-0	6-1	0-0	2-1	1-0	2-2	3-2	4-1
Inter Cardiff	3-0	0-2	1-0	2-0	4-1	3-1	2-1	3-0	1-2	2-1	1-1	4-1	—	5-1	2-1	3-0	3-0	1-0	5-4	1-3
Llanelli	2-1	2-3	0-3	1-3	2-2	2-3	6-1	5-0	5-3	1-2	0-2	1-3	1-10	—	4-2	2-1	4-1	1-2	2-4	3-0
Llanstfd	1-2	1-1	1-2	3-1	1-1	2-2	3-0	1-0	0-2	1-0	1-2	2-0	0-1	4-0	—	2-1	0-5	1-3	1-5	1-4
Maesteg Park	1-2	1-1	0-3	1-0	2-2	0-2	1-2	0-1	1-2	0-3	0-0	2-4	0-4	1-2	1-0	—	2-4	3-2	1-1	0-1
Mold Alex	1-3	2-2	0-1	3-1	1-2	2-4	1-1	1-2	0-2	1-4	1-0	1-1	3-2	1-1	2-1	4-5	—	0-0	4-0	1-4
Newtown	2-1	0-0	1-1	2-1	1-0	1-2	2-0	1-0	0-3	3-2	0-0	1-0	0-3	3-1	3-2	0-0	2-3	—	5-2	0-0
Porthmadog	2-1	2-2	0-2	1-1	2-0	1-1	0-1	1-0	1-2	0-2	5-1	7-1	1-2	5-6	4-0	0-2	1-1	0-1	—	5-2
Ton Pentre	2-1	2-1	2-1	1-0	3-0	2-0	4-0	0-2	1-1	3-0	0-0	0-0	1-0	3-1	0-0	1-2	2-1	5-0	2-2	—

ALLBRIGHT BITTER WELSH CUP 1993–94

Preliminary Round

BP Llandarcy v South Wales Constabulary	4-0
British Aerospace v Chirk AAA	0-1
Chepstow Town v Cardiff Corinthians	3-4
Felinheli v Penmaenmawr Phoenix	2-0
Fields Park/Pontllanfraith v Pontlottyn Blast Furnace	2-4
Goytre United v Porth Tywyn Suburbs	5-2
Llanfairpwll v Llandyrnog United	3-0
Llanrwst United v Nefyn United	1-1, 1-4
Llay Welfare v Bala Town	0-4
Morda United v New Broughton	3-1
Newcastle Emlyn v Pontyclun	1-4
Newport YMCA v Trelewis Welfare	2-1
Overton/Marchwiel v Presteigne St. Andrews	6-1
Penparcau v Llangeinor	1-3
Penycae v Llay Royal British Legion	3-0
Pontardawe Athletic v Seven Sisters *(at Seven Sisters)*	2-1
Porthcawl Town v British Steel	2-1
Pwllheli Borough v Nantlle Vale	1-4
Rhydymwyn v Locomotive Llanberis	1-0
Rhyl Delta v Llangefni Town	1-4
Skewen Athletic v Milford United	5-0
Taffs Well v Panteg	2-1
Tonyrefail Welfare v Abercynon Athletic	2-3
Treowen Stars v Tredomen	3-0

First Round

Aberaman Athletic v Llanwern	3-0
Abergavenny Thursdays v Risca United	0-2
AFC Porth v Brecon Corinthians	3-1
Ammanford v Bridgend Town	1-2
Bala Town v Morda United	2-4
Barry Town v Abercynon Athletic	2-0
BP Llandarcy v Pontardawe	1-0
Buckley v Cefn Druids	2-4
Caerau v Llangeinor	1-1, 2-1
Caerleon v Ferndale Athletic	1-1, 1-3
Cardiff Corinthians v Caldicot Town	4-5
Carno v Penrhyncoch	2-1
Chirk AAA v Penley	2-0
Goytre United v Porthcawl Town	0-1
Gresford Athletic v Penycae	2-4
Llandrindod Wells v Taffs Well	2-6
Llandudno v Mostyn	2-3
Llangefni Town v Cemaes Bay	3-0
Llanidloes Town v Lex XI	1-1, 0-1
Nefyn Utd v Ruthin Town	1-4
Overton/Marchwiel v Brymbo	0-3
Pembroke Borough v Skewen Athletic	0-1
Pontlottyn BF v Cardiff Civil Services	0-2
Pontyclun v Carmarthen Town	2-1
Port Talbot Athletic v Morrison Town	0-1, 2-0
Rhos Aelwyd v Rhayader Town	0-3
Rhydymwyn v Nantlle Vale	3-0
Treowen Stars v Newport YMCA	3-0
Welshpool v Knighton Town	5-0
Y Felinheli v Llanfairpwll	0-3

Second Round

Aberaman Athletic v Ton Pentre	1-2
Afan Lido v BP Llandarcy	5-2
Bangor City v Porthmadog	2-0
Briton Ferry Athletic v Cardiff Civil Service	7-1
Caerau v Barry Town	1-1, 2-3
Caersws v Newton	1-1, 1-7
Caldicot Town v AFC Porth	2-0
Carno v Chirk AAA	6-0
Cefn Druids v Mold Alexandra	0-0, 3-2
Ebbw Vale v Bridgend Town	5-0
Ferndale Athletic v Treowen Stars	0-0, 2-3
Haverfordwest County v Maesteg Park Athletic	2-1
Lex XI v Llanfairpwll	3-4
Llanelli v Risca United	2-1
Llangefni Town v Brymbo	1-1, 1-5
Llansantffraid v Aberystwyth Town	1-1, 1-4
Morda United v Conwy United	1-0
Mostyn v Ruthin	1-0
Penycae v Holywell Town	1-5
Porthcawl Town v Pontyclun	2-2, 3-0
Rhayader Town v Flint Town United	1-5
Skewen Athletic v Port Talbot Athletic	3-2 (*aet*)
Taffs Well v Merthyr Tydfil	1-7
Welshpool v Rhydymwyn	4-3

Third Round

Bangor City v Llanfairpwll	2-0
Barry Town v Cwmbran Town	3-1
Brymbo v Connah's Quay Nomads	0-3
Cardiff City v Afan Lido	2-0
Cefn Druids v Rhyl	0-5
Ebbw Vale v Skewen Athletic	1-0
Flint Town United v Welshpool	2-1
Haverfordwest County v Briton Ferry Athletic	1-6
Hereford United v Mostyn	3-0
Holywell Town v Aberystwyth Town	3-2
Inter Cardiff v Caldicot Town	2-1
Morda United v Newton	1-7
Swansea City v Merthyr Tydfil	0-0, 2-1
Ton Pentre v Llanelli	2-1
Treowen Stars v Porthcawl Town	1-1, 3-4
Wrexham v Carno	6-1

Fourth Round

Barry Town v Holywell Town	4-0
Briton Ferry Athletic v Flint Town United	2-2, 0-3
Ebbw Vale v Connah's Quay Nomads	1-1, 2-1
Hereford United v Newton	4-0
Porthcawl Town v Inter Cardiff	1-1, 0-3
Rhyl v Swansea City	1-2
Ton Pentre v Bangor City	2-2, 0-3
Wrexham v Cardiff City	0-2

Fifth Round

Bangor City v Inter Cardiff	1-1, 1-0
Barry Town v Flint Town United	1-0
Ebbw Vale v Cardiff City	1-1, 0-3
Swansea City v Hereford United	1-0

Semi-Finals (two legs)

Bangor City v Barry Town	1-1
Barry Town v Bangor City	1-0
Swansea City v Cardiff City	2-1
Cardiff City v Swansea City	4-1

Final: Cardiff City 1, Barry Town 2

(at National Stadium, Cardiff, 15 May 1994) Att: 14,500

Cardiff City: Williams; Fereday, Perry, Aizlewood, Searle, Millar, Richardson (Adams), Brock, Griffith, Stant, Thompson (Bird), *Scorer*: Stant.

Barry Town: Morris; Hough, Griffiths, Boyle, Williams, Curtis (Smith), Wimbleton, Beattie, D'Auria, Lilygreen, Bertschin (Sanderson), *Scorers*: D'Auria, Hough.

Referee: J. Lloyd (Wrexham).

NORTHERN IRISH FOOTBALL 1993–94

"One of the most dramatic seasons in the history of Northern Ireland football" was the apt summing up of newly elected Irish FA president Sammy Walker. It was a season which was gripping from start to finish; a season which brought new life to the game in the politically troubled Province.

Internationally, the Irish FA negotiated a £280,000 four-year sponsorship from Scottish and Newcastle Breweries which covers the entire international set-up, including the managerial salary. They took over from Vauxhall, who had commercially backed the squad for four years.

Bryan Hamilton, former Linfield, Ipswich Town, Everton and Swindon forward, capped 50 times, was nominated full-time manager in succession to Billy Bingham, who retired after 14 years' distinguished service; he is now a director of Blackpool and conducting FIFA coaching courses throughout the world.

The Bingham build-up since World Cup, Mexico, 1986 has been slow and painstaking, but at last a squad – comparatively young but laced with a few experienced players - has revealed much potential. They held the Republic of Ireland to a 1–1 draw in a tension-filled World Cup qualifying match at Windsor Park in November, when a Jimmy Quinn goal almost ended Jack Charlton's hopes of making it to the USA. Alan McLaughlin's equaliser ten minutes from the end saved the day. Then came a 2–0 win over Romania in Belfast, a 4–1 defeat of Liechtenstein in the opening European Championship Group Six and a highly commendable performance in the B International with England at Hillsborough.

Linfield, who broke with tradition and signed four quality League of Ireland players, swept the boards by winning the Smirnoff Irish League, Bass Irish Cup, Budweiser Cup and the Wilkinson Sword League Cup. Their junior sides also made a decisive impact.

Drama marked the side's European Champions Cup matches. They were eliminated in the preliminary round on aggregate by Tbilisi who, however, were later expelled for alleged attempted bribery of the match officials in the home leg. Northern Ireland then defeated FC Copenhagen 3–0 in the first leg of the first round proper before losing 4–3 on aggregate after the second at the Parken Stadium, where the referee added six minutes of injury time in which period the Danes got the equaliser and went on to win in extra time.

All tournaments were sponsored, apart from the Ulster Group, while there was a spread of the other trophies with Crusaders, Distillery and Ards all picking up awards. For Glentoran, though, so long a dominant force, it was a disastrous season as they passed through one of the worst phases in club history.

Amenities continue to be improved, with Glenavon opening a magnificent all-seater stand and administrative and dressing room facilities at Mourneview Park. Distillery also have a new stand – thanks to the introduction of greyhound racing, as they diversify revenue-making activities at New Grosvenor Stadium – while Newry, under dynamic new management, have erected a superb ultra-modern dressing room complex, which is the first part of a major redevelopment over the next decade.

Promotion and relegation will be introduced by the Irish League in the 1995–96 season with a Premier Division and First Division each composed of eight clubs – the eight best-placed teams over the last two seasons will be nominated for the Premier Division. All other tournaments will operate as at present.

"We are advancing with the times. This is a revolutionary step and it will have a highly beneficial effect on the game", said League President Morton McKnight, "it will stimulate interest and prevent clubs from finding their season over in February if they've been eliminated in some of the knock-out series and are struggling in the League. Now they have to battle to avoid the drop."

MALCOLM BRODIE

SMIRNOFF IRISH LEAGUE CHAMPIONSHIP FINAL TABLE

	P	*W*	*D*	*L*	*F*	*A*	*Pts*
Linfield	30	21	7	2	63	22	70
Portadown	30	20	8	2	76	21	68
Glenavon	30	21	5	4	69	29	68
Crusaders	30	17	7	6	53	30	58
Bangor	30	14	3	13	45	49	45
Ards	30	13	2	15	59	55	41
Distillery	30	11	8	11	41	40	41
Cliftonville	30	11	10	9	40	32	40
Glentoran	30	10	7	13	46	43	37
Coleraine	30	10	7	13	41	50	37
Ballymena	30	9	6	15	38	56	33
Ballyclare	30	9	6	15	36	58	33
Carrick	30	6	7	17	42	81	25
Newry	30	5	9	16	26	52	24
Omagh T.	30	6	5	19	32	58	23
Larne	30	5	7	18	30	62	22

Note: Cliftonville deducted three points for including non-registered player.

BUDWEISER CUP FINAL

Ards 0 Linfield 3 (*at The Oval, December 21, 1993*)
Ards: Vance; Blood, Leeman, O'Neill, Jeffrey, Bustard, Beattie (Walker), McGaughey, Erskine, McCann, Bowes (Stranney).
Linfield: Lamont; Dornan, English, Doherty (McGoosh), Spiers, Beatty, Campbell, Gorman, Haylock, McIlroy, Bailie.
Scorers: Linfield—Doherty, Haylock, Campbell.
Referee: F. McDonald (Newry).
Attendance: 5000.

Semi-finals

Linfield v Distillery 3-1 (aet)
(*The Oval, December 7*)
Ards v Cliftonville 3-2
(*Windsor Park, December 8*)

Previous Winners: 1988: Glentoran, 1989: Glenavon, 1990: Glentoran, 1991: Portadown, 1992: Omagh Town, 1993: Portadown

IRISH LEAGUE CHAMPIONSHIP WINNERS

1891 Linfield
1892 Linfield
1893 Linfield
1894 Glentoran
1895 Linfield
1896 Distillery
1897 Glentoran
1898 Linfield
1899 Distillery
1900 Belfast Celtic
1901 Distillery
1902 Linfield
1903 Distillery
1904 Linfield
1905 Glentoran
1906 Cliftonville/Distillery
1907 Linfield
1908 Linfield
1909 Linfield
1910 Cliftonville
1911 Linfield
1912 Glentoran
1913 Glentoran
1914 Linfield
1915 Belfast Celtic
1920 Belfast Celtic
1921 Glentoran
1922 Linfield
1923 Linfield
1924 Queen's Island
1925 Glentoran
1926 Belfast Celtic
1927 Belfast Celtic
1928 Belfast Celtic
1929 Belfast Celtic
1930 Linfield
1931 Glentoran
1932 Linfield
1933 Belfast Celtic
1934 Linfield
1935 Linfield
1936 Belfast Celtic
1937 Belfast Celtic
1938 Belfast Celtic
1939 Belfast Celtic
1940 Belfast Celtic
1948 Belfast Celtic
1949 Linfield
1950 Linfield
1951 Glentoran
1952 Glenavon
1953 Glentoran
1954 Linfield
1955 Linfield
1956 Linfield
1957 Glentoran
1958 Ards
1959 Linfield
1960 Glenavon
1961 Linfield
1962 Linfield
1963 Distillery
1964 Glentoran
1965 Derry City
1966 Linfield
1967 Glentoran
1968 Glentoran
1969 Linfield
1970 Glentoran
1971 Linfield
1972 Glentoran
1973 Crusaders
1974 Coleraine
1975 Linfield
1976 Crusaders
1977 Glentoran
1978 Linfield
1979 Linfield
1980 Linfield
1981 Glentoran
1982 Linfield
1983 Linfield
1984 Linfield
1985 Linfield
1986 Linfield
1987 Linfield
1988 Glentoran
1989 Linfield
1990 Portadown
1991 Portadown
1992 Glentoran
1993 Linfield
1994 Linfield

ULSTER CUP

SECTIONAL TABLES

Group A	*P*	*W*	*D*	*L*	*F*	*A*	*Pts*
Linfield	3	1	2	0	6	3	5
Larne	3	1	1	1	4	4	4
Distillery	3	1	1	1	5	6	4
Carrick	3	1	0	2	5	7	3

Group B	*P*	*W*	*D*	*L*	*F*	*A*	*Pts*
Crusaders	1	2	1	0	6	3	7
Ballymena United	3	1	1	1	3	4	4
Glenavon	3	1	0	2	5	6	3
Newry Town	3	1	0	2	3	4	3

Group C	*P*	*W*	*D*	*L*	*F*	*A*	*Pts*
Bangor	3	3	0	0	6	0	9
Glentoran	3	1	1	1	3	3	4
Cliftonville	3	1	1	1	2	5	4
Coleraine	3	0	0	3	3	6	0

Group D	*P*	*W*	*D*	*L*	*F*	*A*	*Pts*
Portadown	3	3	0	0	13	0	9
Ballyclare	3	2	1	0	3	5	6
Ards	3	1	0	2	4	5	3
Omagh	3	0	0	3	0	10	0

ULSTER CUP FINAL

Bangor 0 Crusaders 1 (*at Windsor Park, Belfast, October 19, 1993*)
Bangor: Dalton; McGaffrey, Glendinning, Dornan, Brown (Woods), O'Connor, Hill, M. Kenny (Surgeon), McCallan, Magee, McEvoy.
Crusaders: McKeown; H. Kenny, Cash, Dunlop, Lawlor, Murray, Livingstone, Gardiner, Collins (McCrea), Hunter (Carroll), Burrows.
Scorers: Crusaders — Hunter.
Referee: N. Cowie (Carryduff).
Attendance: 1610

Quarter-finals

Portadown v Glentoran	3-0
Crusaders v Larne	3-0
Linfield v Ballymena United	1-0
Bangor v Ballyclare Comrades	2-0

Semi-finals

Crusaders v Portadown (*at The Oval, September 21*)	1-0
Linfield v Bangor (*at The Oval, October 12*)	1-2

Winners

1949 Linfield
1950 Larne
1951 Glentoran
1952
1953 Glentoran
1954 Crusaders
1955 Glenavon
1956 Linfield
1957 Linfield
1958 Distillery
1959 Glenavon
1960 Linfield
1961 Ballymena U
1962 Linfield
1963 Crusaders
1964 Linfield
1965 Coleraine
1966 Glentoran
1967 Linfield
1968 Coleraine
1969 Coleraine
1970 Linfield
1971 Linfield
1972 Coleraine
1973 Ards
1974 Linfield
1975 Coleraine
1976 Glentoran
1977 Linfield
1978 Linfield
1979 Linfield
1980 Ballymena U
1981 Glentoran
1982 Glentoran
1983 Glentoran
1984 Linfield
1985 Coleraine
1986 Coleraine
1987 Larne
1988 Glentoran
1989 Glentoran
1990 Portadown
1991 Bangor
1992 Linfield
1993 Crusaders

TNT GOLD CUP FINAL

SECTIONAL TABLES

Section A	*P*	*W*	*D*	*L*	*F*	*A*	*Pts*
Cliftonville	3	3	0	0	10	1	9
Linfield	3	2	0	1	5	2	6
Ards	3	0	1	2	1	7	1
Newry	3	0	1	2	1	7	1
Section B	*P*	*W*	*D*	*L*	*F*	*A*	*Pts*
Crusaders	3	2	1	0	7	1	7
Distillery	3	2	1	0	6	0	7
Omagh	3	1	0	2	3	6	3
Coleraine	3	0	0	3	1	10	0
Section C	*P*	*W*	*D*	*L*	*F*	*A*	*Pts*
Glenavon	3	3	0	0	15	3	9
Bangor	3	2	0	1	12	8	6
Carrick	3	1	0	2	5	11	3
Ballyclare	3	0	0	3	3	13	0
Section D	*P*	*W*	*D*	*L*	*F*	*A*	*Pts*
Portadown	3	3	0	0	10	3	9
Glentoran	3	2	0	1	6	2	6
Ballymena	3	1	0	2	3	6	3
Larne	3	0	0	3	1	9	0

TNT GOLD CUP FINAL

Quarter-finals

Linfield v Crusaders 5-2
Glentoran v Glenavon 3-3
(*Glentoran won 8-7 on penalties*)
Bangor v Portadown 4-0
Distillery v Cliftonville 1-1
(*Distillery won 3-1 on penalties*)

Semi-finals

Glentoran v Distillery 1-2 (aet)
(*Windsor Park, October 27*)
Bangor v Linfield 2-0
(*The Oval, October 28*)

Final

Bangor 2 Distillery 3 (aet)
(*At Windsor Park, Belfast, November 2 1993*)
Bangor: Dalton; Canning, Glendinning, Dornan, Spiers, McCafferty, Hill, Kenny, McCallan, Surgeon (Doherty), McEvoy (Crowe).
Scorers: Bangor — Glendinning, Spiers.
Distillery: Collins; Drake, Calvin, Kennedy, Irwin (Heath), Allen, Armstrong, Small (Totten), Baxter, Mitchell, Cleland.
Scorers: Distillery — Calvin, Cleland, Armstrong.
Referee: A. Snoddy (Carryduff).
Attendance: 750

IRISH CUP FINALS (from 1946–47)

1946–47 Belfast Celtic 1, Glentoran 0
1947–48 Linfield 3, Coleraine 0
1948–49 Derry City 3, Glentoran 1
1949–50 Linfield 2, Distillery 1
1950–51 Glentoran 3, Ballymena U 1
1951–52 Ards 1, Glentoran 0
1952–53 Linfield 5, Coleraine 0
1953–54 Derry City 1, Glentoran 0
1954–55 Dundela 3, Glenavon 0
1955–56 Distillery 1, Glentoran 0
1956–57 Glenavon 2, Derry City 0
1957–58 Ballymena U 2, Linfield 0
1958–59 Glenavon 2, Ballymena U 0
1959–60 Linfield 5, Ards 1
1960–61 Glenavon 5, Linfield 1
1961–62 Linfield 4, Portadown 0
1962–63 Linfield 2, Distillery 1
1963–64 Derry City 2, Glentoran 0
1964–65 Coleraine 2, Glenavon 1
1965–66 Glentoran 2, Linfield 0
1966–67 Crusaders 3, Glentoran 1
1967–68 Crusaders 2, Linfield 0
1968–69 Ards 4, Distillery 2
1969–70 Linfield 2, Ballymena U 1
1970–71 Distillery 3, Derry City 0
1971–72 Coleraine 2, Portadown 1
1972–73 Glentoran 3, Linfield 2
1973–74 Ards 2, Ballymena U 1
1974–75 Coleraine 1 : 0 : 1, Linfield 1 : 0 : 0
1975–76 Carrick Rangers 2, Linfield 1
1976–77 Coleraine 4, Linfield 1
1977–78 Linfield 3, Ballymena U 1
1978–79 Cliftonville 3, Portadown 2
1979–80 Linfield 2, Crusaders 0
1980–81 Ballymena U 1, Glenavon 0
1981–82 Linfield 2, Coleraine 1
1982–83 Glentoran 1 : 2, Linfield 1 : 1
1983–84 Ballymena U 4, Carrick Rangers 1
1984–85 Glentoran 1 : 1, Linfield 1 : 0
1985–86 Glentoran 2, Coleraine 1
1986–87 Glentoran 1, Larne 0
1987–88 Glentoran 1, Glenavon 0
1988–89 Ballymena U 1, Larne 0
1989–90 Glentoran 3, Portadown 0
1990–91 Portadown 2, Glenavon 1
1991–92 Glenavon 2, Linfield 1
1992–93 Bangor 1:1:1, Ards 1:1:0
1993–94 Linfield 2, Bangor 0

WHERE THE OTHER TROPHIES WENT

	Winners	*Runners-up*
Wilkinson Sword League Cup	Linfield	Coleraine
Ulster Cup	Crusaders	Bangor
Cawoods County Antrim Shield	Ards	Crusaders
Wilkinson Sword B Division		
Section One	Dundela	Louchcall
Section Two	Bangor Res	Glentoran II
Coca Cola Irish Youth Cup	Coleraine Colts	Ballymena Utd Youths
William Younger Intermediate Cup	Portstewart	Limavady United
Cawoods County Antrim Junior Shield	Temple Rangers Res	Lisburn Rangers
Wilkinson George Wilson Cup	Ballyclare Comrades	Distillery II
Ted Clark Mid Ulster Cup	Portadown	Duncannon Swifts
Mid Ulster Shield	Oxford United	Ballyoran
Cawoods Steel and Sons Cup	RUC	Dundela
North West Senior Cup	Limavady United	Coleraine
McEwans Sixes	Omagh Town	Glenavon
Bob Radcliff Memorial Cup	Duncannon Swifts	Louchcall
McEwans Charity Shield (Trophy Shared)	Bangor	Linfield
Stena Sealink Irish Junior Cup	Enniskillen Rangers	Oxford United
Smirnoff Knockout Cup	Duncannon Swifts	Armagh City

BASS IRISH CUP 1993–94

Fifth Round (First Round Proper)

Abbey Villa v Killyleagh YC	1-0
Ards v Glentoran	2-2, 2-3
Ballyclare Comrades v Cliftonville	1-1, 0-1
Ballymena United v Carrick Rangers	0-3
Banbridge Town v Linfield	1-3
Chimney Corner v Distillery	0-5
Donegal Celtic v Limavady United	1-0
Dundela v Drumaness Mills	2-0
Glenavon v Brantwood	2-1
Larne v Coleraine	1-4
Loughgall United v 1st Bangor	5-0
Moyola Park v Ballinamallard	1-1, 1-2 (aet)
Newry Town v Park	1-1, 1-4
Omagh Town v Coagh United	2-1
Portadown v East Belfast	3-0
Bangor v Crusaders	1-0

Sixth Round

Ballymena United v Cliftonville	0-3
Coleraine v Glenavon	2-3
Distillery v Abbey Villa	1-0
Glentoran v Dundela	4-3
Linfield v Carrick Rangers	2-0
Loughgall United v Bangor	1-2
Portadown v Donegal Celtic	4-0
Newry Town v Omagh Town	0-0, 0-1
(*Abandoned half time: snow*)	2-2 (aet)
Omagh won 6-5 on penalties	

Quarter-finals

Linfield v Cliftonville	0-0, 0-1 (aet)
Omagh Town v Portadown	1-2
Distillery v Glenavon	2-4
Glentoran v Bangor	0-2

Semi-finals

Bangor v Portadown (*Windsor Park, April 8*)	2-0
Glenavon v Linfield (*The Oval, April 9*)	0-3

Final

Bangor 0 Linfield 2 (*at The Oval, Belfast May 7 1994*)
Bangor: Dalton; Canning, Glendinning, E. Spiers, Brown, O'Connor, Hill, McCaffrey, McCallan, Magee (Surgeon), McEvoy.
Linfield: Lamont; A. Dornan, Easton, Peebles, J. Spiers (Doherty), Beatty, Campbell, Gorman, Haylock, Fenlon, Bailie.
Scorers: Linfield—Haylock, Fenlon.
Attendance: 10,000

INTERNATIONAL DIRECTORY

The latest available information has been given regarding numbers of clubs and players registered with FIFA, the world governing body. Where known, official colours are listed. With European countries, League tables show a number of signs. * indicates relegated teams, + play-offs, * + relegated after play-offs.

When provisional members are added there will be 190 FIFA countries. The four home countries, England, Scotland, Northern Ireland and Wales, are dealt with elsewhere in the Yearbook; but basic details appear in this directory.

EUROPE

ALBANIA

Federation Albanaise De Football, Rruga Dervish Hima Nr. 31, Tirana.
Founded: 1930; *Number of Clubs:* 49; *Number of Players:* 5,192; *National Colours:* Red shirts, black shorts, red stockings.
Telephone: 355–42/2 78 77; *Cable:* ALBSPORT TIRANA; *Telex:* 2228 BFSSH sb. *Fax:* 355–42/2 78 77.

International matches 1993
Northern Ireland (h) 1-2, Lithuania (a) 1-3, Latvia (a) 0-0, Republic of Ireland (h) 1-2, Denmark (a) 0-4, Denmark (h) 0-1, Spain (h) 1-5.

League Championship wins (1945–94)
Dinamo Tirana 15; Partizani Tirana 15; 17 Nentori 8; Vllaznia 7; Flamurtari 1; Labinoti 1; Teuta 1.

Cup wins (1948–94)
Partizani Tirana 13; Dinamo Tirana 12; 17 Nentori 6; Vllaznia 5; Flamurtari 2; Labinoti 1; Elbasan 1; SK Tirana 1.

Final League Table 1993–94

	P	*W*	*D*	*L*	*F*	*A*	Pts
Teuta	26	14	9	3	37	9	37
SK Tirana	26	13	7	6	36	16	33
Flamurtari	26	11	8	7	26	21	30
Vllaznia	26	11	6	9	33	28	28
Partizani	26	6	13	7	27	25	25
Dinamo	26	5	15	6	25	27	25
Apolonia	26	8	9	9	25	28	25
Elbasan	26	9	7	10	26	30	24
Albpetrol	26	8	8	10	31	31	24
Beselidhja	26	9	6	11	27	33	24
Besa	26	8	8	10	24	37	24
Laci	26	8	7	11	32	36	23
Lushnia*	26	7	9	10	20	25	23
Sopoti*	26	6	6	14	19	42	18

Top scorer: Martini (Vllaznia) 14
Cup Final: SK Tirana 0,1 Teuta 0,0

ARMENIA

Football Federation of Armenia, 9, Abovian Str. 375001 Erevan, Armenia.
Number of Clubs: 956; *Number of Players:* 12,055.
Telephone: 885–52 7582, 885–52 7014, 885–52 7974; *Telex:* 885–52 3376. *Fax:* 885–52 3376.

League Championship wins 1992–93
Shirak Gyumri 1; Ararat Erevan 1.

Cup winners 1992–93
Ararat Erevan.

Final League Table 1993

	P	*W*	*D*	*L*	*F*	*A*	Pts
Ararat Erevan	28	23	5	0	92	9	51
Shirak Guymri	28	24	1	3	101	20	49
Banants	28	23	2	3	111	21	48
Homenetmen	28	21	3	4	80	29	45
Van Erevan	28	15	2	11	71	49	32
Tsement	28	12	6	10	56	50	30
Homenmen	28	12	2	14	54	43	26
Yerazank	28	11	3	14	44	55	25
Nayrit	28	8	4	16	29	61	20
Kanaz	28	8	4	16	37	75	20
Kotaik	28	9	1	18	57	76	19
Impouls	28	8	2	18	42	89	18
Zvarnots*	28	6	4	18	42	79	16
Kassakh*	28	5	2	21	15	116	12
Malatia*	28	2	5	21	25	92	9

Top scorers: Hovepian (Banants) 26, Hovannessian (Homenetmen) 26

AUSTRIA

Oesterreichischer Fussball-Bund, Wiener Stadion, Sektor A/F, Meierestrasse, A-1020 Wien.
Founded: 1904; *Number of Clubs:* 2,081; *Number of Players:* 253,576; *National Colours:* White shirts, black shorts, black stockings.
Telephone: 0043-1-217 18; *Cable:* FOOTBALL WIEN; *Telex:* 111919 OEFB A; *Fax:* 0043-1-218 16 32.

International matches 1993
Greece (h) 2-1, France (h) 0-1, Bulgaria (h) 3-1, Finland (a) 1-3, Sweden (a) 0-1, Finland (h) 3-0, Bulgaria (a) 1-4, Israel (a) 1-1, Sweden (h) 1-1.

League Championship wins (1912–94)
Rapid Vienna 29; FK Austria 22; Admira-Energie-Wacker (prev. Sportklub Admira & Admira-Energie) 8; First Vienna 6; Tirol-Svarowski-Innsbruck (prev. Wacker Innsbruck) 7; Wiener Sportklub 3; FAC 1; Hakoah 1; Linz ASK 1; Wacker Vienna 1; WAF 1; Voest Linz 1; Austria Salzburg 1.

Cup wins (1919–94)
FK Austria 25; Rapid Vienna 13; TS Innsbruck (prev. Wacker Innsbruck) 7; Admira-Energie-Wacker (prev. Sportklub Admira & Admira-Energie) 5; First Vienna 3; Linz ASK 1; Wacker Vienna 1; WAF 1; Wiener Sportklub 1; Graz 1; Stockerau 1.

Final table 1993–94

	P	*W*	*D*	*L*	*F*	*A*	Pts
Austria Salzburg	36	21	9	6	56	18	51
FK Austria	36	22	5	9	63	39	49
Admira Wacker	36	18	8	10	51	35	44
Innsbruck	36	14	11	11	48	33	39
Rapid	36	12	11	13	38	42	35
Modling	36	12	11	13	32	49	35
Sturm Gratz	36	12	9	15	37	42	33
Vorwaerts	36	8	10	18	43	54	26
St Polten +	36	9	8	19	37	57	26
Wiener SC*	36	5	12	19	21	57	22

Top scorer: Jurcevic (Salzburg) 14
Cup Final: FK Austria 4, Linz 0

BELARUS

Football Federation of Belarus, 8–2 Kyrov Str. 220600 Minsk, Belarus.
Founded: 1992; Number of Players: 120,000.
Telephone: 172–27 2920, 172–27 2325; *Telex:* 252175 athlet su; *Fax:* 172–27 6184.

International matches 1993
Ecuador (a) 1-1, Peru (a) 1-1, Moldavia (h) 1-0.

League Championship wins 1992–93
Dynamo Minsk 2.

Cup wins 1992–93
Dynamo Minsk 1; Neman 1.

BELGIUM

Union Royale Belge Des Societes De Football; Eturl, Association, Rue De La Loi 43, Boite 1, B-1040 Bruxelles.
Founded: 1895; *Number of Clubs:* 2,120; *Number of Players:* 390,468; *National Colours:* Red shirts with tri-coloured trim, red shorts, red stockings with trim.
Telephone: 32 2 477 1211; *Cable:* UBSFA BRUXELLES; *Telex:* 23257 BVBFBF B; *Fax:* 32 2 2147 82391.

International matches 1993
Cyprus (a) 3-0, Wales (a) 0-2, Faeroes (h) 3-0, Gabon (h) 2-1, Romania (a) 1-2, RCS (h) 0-0.

League Championship wins (1896–1994)
Anderlecht 23; Union St Gilloise 11; FC Brugge 9; Standard Liege 8; Beerschot 7; RC Brussels 6; FC Liège 5; Daring Brussels 5; Antwerp 4; Mechelen 4; Lierse SK 3; SV Brugge 3; Beveren 2; RWD Molenbeek 1.

Cup wins (1954–94)
Anderlecht 8; FC Brugge 5; Standard Liege 5; Beerschot 2; Waterschei 2; Beveren 2; Gent 2; Antwerp 2; Lierse SK 1; Racing Doornik 1; Waregem 1; SV Brugge 1; Mechelen 1; FC Liège 1.

Final League Table 1993–94

	P	*W*	*D*	*L*	*F*	*A*	Pts
Anderlecht	34	24	7	3	79	31	55
FC Brugge	34	20	13	1	54	19	53
Seraing	34	15	13	6	50	27	43
Charleroi	34	18	5	11	61	49	41
Antwerp	34	14	13	7	44	38	41
Standard Liege	34	13	12	9	43	22	38
Ostend	34	10	16	8	45	41	36
Mechelen	34	11	11	12	42	40	35
Beveren	34	11	10	13	49	47	33
Ekeren	34	11	10	13	49	47	32
Lommel	34	10	10	14	41	50	30
CS Brugge	34	9	11	14	52	63	29
Liege	34	9	11	14	40	59	29
Lierse	34	7	14	13	30	42	28
Gent	34	7	13	14	43	57	27
RWD Molenbeek	34	7	11	16	32	49	25
Waregem*	34	6	7	21	32	62	19
Genk*	34	4	10	20	38	79	18

Top scorer: Weber (CS Brugge) 31
Cup Final: Anderlect 2, FC Brugge 0

BULGARIA

Bulgarian Football Union, Gotcho Gopin 19, 1000 Sofia.
Founded: 1923; *Number of Clubs:* 376; *Number of Players:* 48,240; *National Colours:* White shirts, green shorts, red stockings.
Telephone: 87 74 90; *Cable:* BULFUTBOL; *Telex:* 23145 BFS BG; *Fax:* 87 74 90.

International matches 1993
Tunisia (a) 0-3, UAE (a) 0-1, UAE (a) 3-1, Austria (a) 1-3, Finland (h) 2-0, Israel (h) 2-2, Sweden (h) 1-1, Austria (h) 4-1, France (a) 2-1.

League Championship wins (1925–94)
CSKA Sofia 27; Levski Sofia 18; Slavia Sofia 6; Vladislav Varna 3; Lokomotiv Sofia 3; Trakia Plovdiv 2; AS 23 Sofia 1; Botev Plovdiv 1; SC Sofia 1; Sokol Varna 1; Spartak Plovdiv 1; Tichka Varna 1; ZSZ Sofia 1; Beroe Stara Zagora 1; Etur 1.

Cup wins (1946–94)
Levski Sofia 18; CSKA Sofia 14; Slavia Sofia 6; Loko motiv Sofia 3; Botev Plovdiv 1; Spartak Plovdiv 1; Spartak Sofia 1; Marek Stanke 1; Trakia Plovdiv 1; Spartak Varna 1; Sliven 1.

Final League Table 1993–94

	P	*W*	*D*	*L*	*F*	*A*	Pts
Levski Sofia	28	22	5	1	78	17	71
CSKA Sofia	28	17	3	8	58	27	54
Botev Plovdiv	28	15	5	8	50	29	50
Chumen	28	14	6	8	49	34	48
Etur	28	10	10	8	42	33	40
Lokomotiv Plovdiv	28	12	4	12	38	43	40
Beroe	28	11	5	12	33	38	38
Lokomotiv Gorna	28	11	5	12	25	39	38
Slavia Sofia	28	9	9	10	30	37	36
Pirin	28	10	6	12	33	35	36
Lokomotiv Sofia	28	10	4	14	37	40	34
Dobroudja	28	8	10	10	37	42	34
Tschernomoretz*	28	8	6	14	30	36	30
Tschernomore*	28	5	6	17	24	68	21
Spartak Varna*	28	4	4	20	18	65	16

After 8 matches, Yantra were suspended from the competition and their record expunged, following an investigation concerning corruption.*
Top scorer: Sirakov (Levski Sofia) 30
Cup Final: Levski Sofia 1, Pirin 0

CROATIA

Croatian Football Federation, Illica 21/11, CRO-41000 Zagreb, Croatia.
Telephone: 841/42 46 47, 841/42 4642. *Fax:* 841/42 46 39.

International matches 1993
Ukraine (h) 3-1.

League Championship wins 1993–94
Croatia Zagreb 1; Hajduk Split 1.

Cup wins 1993–94
Hajduk Split 1, Croatia Zagreb 1.

Final League Table 1993–94

	P	W	D	L	F	A	Pts
Hajduk Split	34	22	6	6	84	36	50
Zagreb	34	20	9	5	58	30	49
Croatia Zagreb	34	20	8	6	98	34	48
Inker	34	17	8	9	48	34	42
Varteks	34	16	9	9	51	30	41
Rijeka	34	11	17	6	40	27	39
Vinkovci	34	11	13	10	37	27	35
Osijek	34	12	11	11	56	58	35
Segesta	34	12	10	12	48	44	34
Istra Pola	34	13	8	13	40	36	34
Zadar	34	8	17	9	24	36	33
Belisce	34	12	8	14	55	51	32
Sibenik	34	12	8	14	36	42	32
Primorac Stobrec	34	11	7	16	42	54	29
Pazinka Pisino*	34	8	9	17	51	67	25
Dubrovnik*	34	7	9	18	26	60	23
Dubrava*	34	7	9	18	28	63	23
Radnik*	34	3	2	29	17	109	8

Top scorer: Vlaovic (Croatia Zagreb) 28
Cup Final: Croatia Zagreb 0,2, Rijeka 1,0

CYPRUS

Cyprus Football Association, Stasinos Str. 1, Engomi 152, P.O. Box 5071, Nicosia.
Founded: 1934; *Number of Clubs:* 85; *Number of Players:* 6,000; *National Colours:* Sky blue shirts, white shorts, blue and white stockings.
Telephone: (2) 44 53 41, 44 53 42, 45 99 59; *Cable:* FOOTBALL NICOSIA; *Telex:* 3880 FOOTBALL CY; *Fax:* (2) 47 25 44.

International matches 1993
Poland (h) 0-0, Belgium (h) 0-3, RCS (h) 1-1, Romania (a) 1-2, Faeroes (h) 3-1, Israel (h) 2-2, Wales (a) 0-2, RCS (a) 0-3.

League Championship wins (1935–94)
Omonia 17; Apoel 15; Anorthosis 6; AEL 5; EPA 3; Olympiakos 3; Apollon 2; Pezoporikos 2; Chetin Kayal 1; Trast 1.

Cup wins (1935–94)
Apoel 13; Omonia 10; AEL 6; EPA 5; Anorthosis 4; Apollon 4; Trast 3; Chetin Kayal 2; Olympiakos 1; Pezoporikos 1; Salamina 1.

Final League Table 1993–94

	P	W	D	L	F	A	Pts
Apollon	26	20	3	3	675	23	63
Anorthosis	26	18	7	1	67	16	61
Apoel	26	17	5	4	64	25	56
Omonia	26	16	4	6	77	33	52
Ethnikos	26	15	2	9	45	40	47
AEL	26	12	4	10	43	47	40
Paralimni	26	9	7	10	34	34	34
Pezoporikos	26	10	4	12	34	37	34
Salamina	26	8	8	10	32	31	32
Aradippu	26	8	5	13	29	49	29
Olympiakos	26	8	3	15	36	51	27
EPA*	26	7	2	17	30	53	23
Evagoras*	26	2	5	19	15	65	11
Apep*	26	2	1	23	2	89	3

Apep 3 points deducted.
Cup Final: Omonia 1, Anorthosis 0

RCS -Representation of Czechs and Slovaks (formerly CZECHOSLOVAKIA)

Ceskoslovensky Fotbalovy Svaz, Na Porici 12, 11530 Praha 1.
Founded: 1906; *Number of Clubs:* 5,930; *Number of Players:* 375,380; *National Colours:* Red shirts, white shorts, blue stockings.
Telephone: 225836/2350065; *Cable:* SPORTSVAZ PRAHA; *Telex:* 122650 CSTV C.

International matches 1993
Cyprus (a) 1-1, Wales (h) 1-1, Romania (h) 5-2, Faeroes (a) 3-0, Wales (a) 2-2, Cyprus (h) 3-0, Belgium (a) 0-0.

League Championship wins (1926–93)
Sparta Prague 21; Slavia Prague 12; Dukla Prague (prev. UDA) 11; Slovan Bratislava 7; Spartak Trnava 5; Banik Ostrava 3; Inter-Bratislava 1; Spartak Hradec Kralove 1; Viktoria Zizkov 1; Zbrojovka Brno 1; Bohemians 1; Vitkovice 1.

Cup wins (1991–93)
Dukla Prague 8; Sparta Prague 8; Slovan Bratislava 5; Spartak Trnava 4; Banik Ostrava 3; Lokomotiv Kosice 3; TJ Gottwaldov 1; Dunajska Streda 1.
For 1993–94, there were two separate countries: the Czech Republic and Slovakia.

Final Czech Republic League Table 1993–94

	P	W	D	L	F	A	Pts
Sparta Prague	30	18	9	3	62	21	45
Slavia Prague	30	16	7	7	55	28	39
Union Cheb	30	13	10	7	31	29	36
Olpran Drnovice	30	14	7	9	41	32	35
Ceske Budejovice	30	11	13	6	33	31	35
Banik Ostrava	30	13	8	9	50	27	34
Sigma Olomouc	30	13	7	10	43	29	33
Viktoria Zizkov	30	12	9	9	40	28	33
Viktoria Plzen	30	11	11	8	32	26	33
Slovan Liberec	30	11	10	9	36	32	32
Boby Brno	30	10	7	13	38	45	27
Svit Zlin	30	9	8	13	36	48	26
Bohemians	30	9	7	14	31	52	25
Hradec Kralove	30	9	6	15	29	40	24
Vitkovice	30	3	7	20	22	64	13
Dukla Prague	30	1	8	21	21	68	10

Top scorer: Siegl (Sparta) 20
Czech Cup Final: Viktoria Zizkov 2, Sparta Praga 2
Viktoria Zizkov won 6-5 on penalties.

Final Slovakia League table 1993–94

	P	W	D	L	F	A	Pts
Slovan Bratislava	32	20	10	2	63	28	50
Inter	32	18	4	10	65	45	40
Dunajska Streda	32	13	10	9	62	47	36
Tatran Presov	32	10	14	8	47	43	34
Zilina	32	11	11	10	50	42	33
Kosice	32	8	11	13	35	54	27

Promotion/Relegation table 1993–94

	P	W	D	L	F	A	Pts
Lokomotiv Kosice	32	7	14	11	30	47	28
Trnava	32	8	12	12	25	32	28
Dukla Bystrica	32	9	9	14	31	43	27
Humenne	32	7	13	12	31	43	27
Prievidza	32	10	7	15	34	42	27
Nitra*	32	12	3	17	38	47	27

Slovak Cup Final: Slovan Bratislava 2, Tatran Presov 1.

DENMARK

Dansk Boldspil Union, Ved Amagerbanen 15, DK-2300, Copenhagen S.
Founded: 1889; *Number of Clubs:* 1,555; *Number of Players:* 268,517; *National Colours:* Red shirts, white shorts, red stockings.
Telephone: (45) 3195 0511; *Cable:* DANSKBOLDSPIL COPENHAGEN; *Telex:* 15545 DBU DK; *Fax:* (45) 3195 0588.

International matches 1993
USA (a) 2-2, El Salvador (a) 2-0, Argentina (a) 1-1, Spain (h) 1-0, Lativa (h) 2-0, Republic of Ireland (a) 1-1, Albania (h) 4-0, Lithuania (h) 4-0, Albania (a) 1-0, Northern Ireland (h) 1-0, Spain (a) 0-1.

League Championship wins (1913–94)
KB Copenhagen 15; B 93 Copenhagen 9; AB (Akademisk) 9; B 1903 Copenhagen 7; Frem 6; Esbjerg BK 5; Vejle BK 5; AGF Aarhus 5; Brondby 4; Hvidovre 3; Odense BK 3; B 1909 Odense 2; Koge BK 2; Lyngby 2; FC Copenhagen 1; Silkeborg 1.

Cup wins (1955–94)
Aarhus GF 8; Vejle BK 6; Randers Freja 3; Lyngby 3; OB Odense 3; B1909 Odense 2; Aalborg BK 2; Esbjerg BK 2; Frem 2; B 1903 Copenhagen 2; Brondby 2; B 93 Copenhagen 1; KB Copenhagen 1; Vanlose 1; Hvidovre 1; B1913 Odense 1.

Qualifying Table 1993

	P	*W*	*D*	*L*	*F*	*A*	Pts
Silkeborg	18	9	7	2	34	20	25
Odense	18	9	6	3	27	16	24
FC Copenhagen	18	10	2	6	32	22	22
Brondby	18	7	6	5	32	24	20
Lyngby	18	5	10	3	19	23	20
Aalborg	18	4	9	5	28	25	17
Ikast	18	5	7	6	31	29	17
Aarhus	18	5	5	8	30	31	15
Naestved	18	3	4	11	28	46	10
Viborg	18	3	4	11	25	50	10

Final League Table 1993–94

	P	*W*	*D*	*L*	*F*	*A*	Pts
Silkeborg	14	8	2	4	23	15	31
FC Copenhagen	14	8	2	4	37	19	29
Odense	14	5	5	4	17	16	27
Brondby	14	6	5	3	21	14	27
Aalborg	14	4	6	4	18	19	23
Lyngby	14	5	1	8	17	21	21
Ikast	14	3	5	6	16	23	20
Aarhus	14	3	2	9	11	23	16

Cup Final: Brondby 0, Naestved 0
Brondby won 3-1 on penalties.

ENGLAND

The Football Association, 16 Lancaster Gate, London W2 3LWK*Founded:* 1863; *Number of Clubs:* 42,000; *Number of Players:* 2,250,000; *National Colours:* White shirts, navy blue shorts, white stockings.
Telephone: 071/262 4542; *Cable:* FOOTBALL ASSOCIATION LONDON W2; *Telex:* 261110; *Fax:* 071/402 0486.

ESTONIA

Estonian Football Association, Refati PST 1-376, 20 0103 Tallinn.
Number of Clubs: 40; *Number of Players:* 12,000.
Telephone: 142–23 8253; *Telex:* 173236 Sport; *Fax:* 142–23 8387.

International matches 1993
Finland (a) 0-0, Latvia (a) 0-2, Slovenia (a) 0-2, Italy (a) 0-2, Malta (h) 0-1, Scotland (h) 0-3, Scotland (a) 1-3, Latvia (a) 0-2, Lithuania (h) 2-1, Portugal (h) 0-2, Italy (h) 0-3, Liechtensein (a) 2-0, Portugal (a) 0-3, Switzerland (a) 0-4.
League champions: 1992 Norma Tallinn; 1993 Norman Tallinn.

FAEROE ISLANDS

Fotboltssamband Foroya, The Faeroes' Football Assn., Gundalur, P.O. Box 1028, FR-110, Torshavn.
Founded: 1979; *Number of Clubs:* 16; *Number of Players:* 1,014.
Telephone: 298 12606; *Telex:* 81332 ITROTT FA; *Fax:* 298 12421.

International matches 1993
Cyprus (a) 1-3, Belgium (a) 0-3, Wales (h) 0-3, RCS (h) 0-3, Norway (a) 0-7, Romania (h) 0-4.

League Championship wins 1942–93
KI Klaksvik 15; HB Torshavn 14; TB Tvoroyri 7; B36 Torshavn 5; GI Gotu 4; B68 Toftir 3; SI Sorvag 1; IF Fuglafjordur 1; B71 Sandur 1.

Cup wins 1967–92
HB Torshavn 11; TB Tvoroyri 4; KI Klaksvik 2; GI Gotu 2; VB Vagur 1; NSI Runavik 1; B36 Torshavn 1.

Final League Table 1993

	P	*W*	*D*	*L*	*F*	*A*	Pts
GI	18	11	6	1	32	14	28
HB	18	9	7	2	41	20	25
KI	18	9	5	4	24	15	23
B71	18	10	3	5	30	26	23
B36	18	6	6	6	21	17	18
B68	18	5	6	7	30	28	16
TB	18	4	6	8	24	30	14
IF	18	5	3	10	27	41	13
LIF*	18	3	6	9	25	46	12
VB*	18	3	2	13	18	35	8

Cup Final: B71 2, HB 0

FINLAND

Suomen Palloliitto Finlands Bollfoerbund, Kuparitie 1, P.O. Box 29, SF-00441 Helsinki.
Founded: 1907; *Number of Clubs:* 1,135; *Number of Players:* 66,100; *National Colours:* White shirts, blue shorts, white stockings.
Telephone: 90-56 26 233; *Cable:* SUOMIFOTBOLL HELSINKI; *Telex :* 1001438 SPL SF; *Fax:* 5626413.

International matches 1993
India (a) 0-0, Cameroon (a) 0-0, India (a) 2-0, Cameroon (a) 0-2, North Korea (a) 2-3, Estonia (h) 0-0, Lithuania (h) 3-0, Poland (a) 1-2, Bulgaria (a) 0-2, Austria (h) 3-1, Israel (h) 0-0, Austria (a) 0-3, France (h) 0-2, Sweden (a) 2-3, Israel (a) 3-1.

League Championship wins (1949–93)
Helsinki JK 9; Turun Palloseura 5; Kuopion Palloseura 5; Valkeakosken Haka 4; Kuusysi 4; Lahden Reipas 3; Ilves-Kissat 2; IF Kamraterna 2; Kotkan TP 2; OPS Oulu 2; Torun Pyrkivä 1; IF Kronohagens 1; Helsinki PS 1; Kokkolan PV 1; IF Kamraterna 1; Vasa 1; Jazz Pori 1.

Cup wins (1955–93)
Valkeakosken Haka 9; Lahden Reipas 7; Kotkan TP 4; Helsinki JK 3; Mikkelin 2; Kuusysi 2; Kuopion Palloseura 2; Ilves Tampere 2; TPS Turku 2; IFK Abo 1; Drott 1; Helsinki PS 1; Pallo-Peikot 1; Rovaniemi PS 1; MyPa 1.

Final League Table 1993

	P	W	D	L	F	A	Pts
Jazz Pori	29	17	7	5	67	33	58
MyPa	29	16	6	7	47	33	54
HJK Helsinki	29	15	4	10	34	26	49
Finn Pa	29	13	7	9	46	35	46
Kuusysi	29	14	5	10	41	43	47
Tampere	29	10	8	11	37	39	38
RoPS Rovaniemi	29	11	5	13	32	35	38
TPS Turku	29	9	5	15	31	39	22

Top scorer: Sumiala (Jazz Pori) 20
Cup Final: TPS Turku 2, HJK Helsinki 1

FRANCE

Federation Francaise De Football, 60 Bis A venue D'Iena, F-75783 Paris, Cedex 16.
Founded: 1919; *Number of Clubs:* 21,629; *Number of Players:* 1,692,205; *National Colours:* Blue shirts, white shorts, red stockings.
Telephone: 44 31 73 00; *Cable:* CEFI PARIS 034; *Telex:* 640000; *Fax:* (1) 4720 8296.

International matches 1993
Israel (a) 4-0, Austria (a) 1-0, Sweden (h) 2-1, Russia (h) 3-1, Sweden (a) 1-1, Finland (a) 2-0, Israel (h) 2-3, Bulgaria (h) 1-2.

League Championship wins (1933–94)
Saint Etienne 10; Olympique Marseille 8; Stade de Reims 6; Nantes 6; AS Monaco 5; OGC Nice 4; Girondins Bordeaux 4; Lille OSC 3; Paris St Germain 2; FC Sete 2; Sochaux 2; Racing Club Paris 1 Roubaix-Tourcoing 1; Strasbourg 1.

Cup wins (1918–94)
Olympique Marseille 10; Saint Etienne 6; Lille OSC 5; Racing Club Paris 5; Red Star 5; AS Monaco 5; Olympique Lyon 4; Girondins Bordeaux 3; CAS Genereaux 2; Nancy 2; OGC Nice 2; Racing Club Strasbourg 2; Sedan 2; FC Sete 2; Stade de Reims 2; SO Montpellier 2; Stade Rennes 2; Paris St Germain 2; AS Cannes 1; Club Français 1; Excelsior Roubaix 1; Le Havre 1; Olympique de Pantin 1; CA Paris 1; Sochaux 1; Toulouse 1; Bastia 1; Nantes 1; Metz 1; Auxerre 1.

Final League Table 1993–94

	P	W	D	L	F	A	Pts
Paris St Germain	38	24	11	3	54	22	59
Marseille*	38	19	13	6	56	33	51
Auxerre	38	18	10	10	54	29	46
Bordeaux	38	19	8	11	54	37	46
Nantes	38	17	11	10	48	35	45
Cannes	38	16	12	10	50	43	44
Montpellier	38	15	13	10	41	37	43
Lyon	38	17	8	13	38	40	42
Monaco	38	14	13	11	55	37	41
Lens	38	13	13	12	49	40	39
St Etienne	38	12	13	13	38	36	37
Metz	38	12	13	13	36	35	37
Strasbourg	38	10	14	14	43	47	35
Sochaux	38	10	13	15	39	48	33
Lille	38	8	16	14	41	52	32
Caen	38	12	7	19	29	54	31
Le Havre	38	7	15	16	29	48	29
Martigues	38	5	17	16	37	58	27
Toulouse*	38	4	15	19	26	60	23
Angers*	38	4	13	21	37	63	21

Top scorer: Boli (Lens) 20, Djorkaeff (Monaco) 20, Ouedec (Nantes) 20
Cup Final: Auxerre 3, Montpellier 0

GEORGIA

Football Federation of Georgia, 5 Shota Iamanidze Str, Tbillisi 380012, Georgia.
Founded: 1992; Number of Clubs: 4050. *Number of Players:* 115,000.
Telephone: 8832–34 0744; *Telex:* 8832–96 0820. *Fax:* 00431–1602 9695 (Austria).
League Champions: 1993 Dynamo Tbilisi
Cup Final: 1992 Dynamo Tbilisi 4, Batumi 2; 1993 Dynamo Tbilisi 1, Metallurg 0.

GERMANY

Deutsche Fussball-Bund, Otto-Fleck-Schneise 6, Postfach 710265, D-6000, Frankfurt (Main) 71.
Founded: 1900; *Number of Clubs:* 26,760; *Number of Players:* 5,260,320; *National Colours:* White shirts, black shorts, white stockings.
Telephone: (069) 67 880; *Cable:* FUSSBALL FRANKFURT; *Telex:* 4 168 15; *Fax:* (69) 67 88 266.

International matches 1993
Scotland (a) 1-0, Ghana (h) 6-1, Brazil (a) 3-3, USA (a) 4-3, England (h) 2-1, Tunisia (a) 1-1, Uruguay (h) 5-0, Brazil (h) 2-1, Argentina (a) 1-2, USA (h) 3-0, Mexico (a) 0-0.

League Championship wins (1903–94)
Bayern Munich 13; IFC Nuremberg 9; Schalke 04 7; SV Hamburg 6; Borussia Moenchengladbach 5; VfB Stuttgart 4; VfB Leipzig 3; Sp Vgg Furth 3; Borussia Dortmund 3; IFC Cologne 3; IFC Kaiserslautern 3; Werder Bremen 3; Viktoria Berlin 2; Hertha Berlin 2; Hanover 96 2; Dresden SC 2; Munich 1860 1; Union Berlin 1; FC Freiburg 1; Phoenix Karlsruhe 1; Karlsruher FV 1; Holsten Kiel 1; Fortuna Dusseldorf 1; Rapid Vienna 1; VfB Mannheim 1; Rot-Weiss Essen 1; Eintracht Frankfurt 1; Eintracht Brunswick 1.

Cup wins (1935–94)
Bayern Munich 8; IFC Cologne 4; Eintracht Frankfurt 4; IFC Nuremberg 3; SV Hamburg 3; Werder Bremen 3; Dresden SC 2; Fortuna Dusseldorf 2; Karlsruhe SC 2; Munich 1860 2; Schalke 04 2; VfB Stuttgart 2; Borussia Moenchengladbach 2; Borussia Dortmund 2; First Vienna 1; VfB Leipzig 1; Kickers Offenbach 1; Rapid Vienna 1; Rot-Weiss Essen 1; SW Essen 1; Bayer Uerdingen 1; IFC Kaiserslautern 1; Hannover 96 1; Leverkusen 1.

Final League Table 1993–94

	P	W	D	L	F	A	Pts
Bayern Munich	34	17	10	7	68	37	44
Kaiserslautern	34	18	7	9	64	36	43
Leverkusen	34	14	11	9	60	47	39
Borussia Dortmund	34	15	9	10	48	45	39
Eintracht Frankfurt	34	15	8	11	57	41	38
Karlsruhe	34	14	10	10	46	43	38
Stuttgart	34	13	11	10	51	43	37
Werder Bremen	34	13	10	11	51	44	36
Duisburg	34	14	8	12	41	52	36
Moenchengladbach	34	14	7	13	65	59	35
Cologne	34	14	6	14	49	51	34
Hamburg	34	13	8	13	48	52	34
Dynamo Dresden	34	10	14	10	33	44	34
Schalke	34	10	9	15	38	50	29
Freiburg	34	10	8	16	54	57	28
Nuremberg*	34	10	8	16	41	55	28
Wattenscheid*	34	6	11	17	48	70	23
Leipzig*	34	3	11	20	32	69	17

Top scorer: Kuntz (Kaiserslautern) 18
Cup Final: Werder Bremen 3, Rot-Weiss Essen 1

GREECE

Federation Hellenique De Football, Singrou Avenue 137, Athens.
Founded: 1926; *Number of Clubs:* 4,050; *Number of Players:* 180,000; *National Colours:* White shirts, blue shorts, white stockings.
Telephone: 9338850; *Cable:* FOOTBALL ATHENES; *Telex:* 215328; *Fax:* 9359666.

International matches 1993
Luxembourg (h) 2-0, Austria (a) 1-2, Hungary (a) 1-0, Russia (a) 1-1, Luxembourg (a) 3-1, Russia (h) 1-0.

League Championship wins (1928–94)
Olympiakos 25; Panathinaikos 16; AEK Athens 11; Aris Salonika 3; PAOK Salonika 2; Larissa 1.

Cup wins (1932–94)
Olympiakos 20; Panathinaikos 15; AEK Athens 9; PAOK Salonika 2; Aris Salonika 1; Ethnikos 1; Iraklis 1; Panionios 1; Kastoria 1; Larissa 1; Ofi Crete 1.

Final League Table 1993–94

	P	*W*	*D*	*L*	*F*	*A*	Pts
AEK Athens	34	25	4	5	63	28	79
Panathinaikos	34	22	6	6	82	32	72
Olympiakos	34	18	14	2	63	27	68
Aris Salonika	34	18	9	7	55	34	63
PAOK Salonika	34	14	9	11	45	38	51
Iraklis	34	13	10	11	59	45	49
Ofi Crete	34	13	8	13	55	42	47
Xanthi	34	12	9	13	62	63	45
Panionios	34	12	7	15	49	58	43
Levakiakos	34	11	9	14	38	45	42
Larissa	34	11	9	14	45	53	42
Athinaikos	34	11	7	16	34	50	40
Apollon	34	9	13	12	30	41	40
Edessaikos	34	11	6	17	41	56	39
Doxa Drama	34	11	5	18	37	64	38
Panachaiki	34	9	10	15	36	56	37
Kalamaria*	34	8	8	18	42	66	32
Naussa*	34	5	3	26	28	76	18

Top scorers: Alexandris (AEK Athens) 24, K. Warzycha (Panathinaikos) 24
Cup Final: Panathinaikos 3, AEK Athens 3 (aet)
Panathinaikos won 4-2 on penalties

HOLLAND

Koninklijke Nederlandsche Voetbalbond, Woudenbergseweg 56, Postbus 515, NL-3700 AM, Zeist.
Founded: 1889; *Number of Clubs:* 3,097; *Number of Players:* 962,397; *National Colours:* Orange shirts, white shorts, orange stockings.
Telephone: 3429 9211/1268; *Cable:* VOETBAL ZEIST; *Telex:* 40497; *Fax:* 03439 1397.

International matches 1993
Turkey (h) 3-1, San Marino (h) 6-0, England (a) 2-2, Norway (a) 0-0, San Marino (a) 7-0, England (h) 2-0, Poland (a) 3-1.

League Championship wins (1898–94)
Ajax Amsterdam 24; Feyenoord 14; PSV Eindhoven 13; HVV The Hague 8; Sparta Rotterdam 6; Go Ahead Deventer 4; HBS The Hague 3; Willem II Tilburg 3; RCH Haarlem 2; RAP 2; Heracles 2; ADO The Hague 2; Quick The Hague 1; BVV Schiedam 1; NAC Breda 1; Eindhoven 1; Enschede 1; Volewijckers Amsterdam 1; Limburgia 1; Rapid JC Haarlem 1; DOS Utrecht 1; DWS Amsterdam 1; Haarlem 1; Be Quick Groningen 1; SVV Schiedam 1; AZ 67 Alkmaar 1.

Cup wins (1899–94)
Ajax Amsterdam 12; Feyenoord 9; PSV Eindhoven 7; Quick The Hague 4; AZ 67 Alkemaar 3; Rotterdam 3; DFC 2; Fortuna Geleen 2; Haarlem 2; HBS The Hague 2; RCH 2; VOC 2; Wageningen 2; Willem II Tilburg 2; FC Dèn Haag 2; Concordia Rotterdam 1; CVV 1; Eindhoven 1; HVV The Hague 1; Longa 1; Quick Nijmegen 1; RAP 1; Roermond 1; Schoten 1; Velocitas Breda 1; Velocitas Gr oningen 1; VSV 1; VUC 1; VVV Groningen 1; ZFC 1; NAC Breda 1; Twente Enschede 1; Utrecht 1.

Final League Table 1993–94

	P	*W*	*D*	*L*	*F*	*A*	Pts
Ajax	34	26	2	6	86	26	54
Feyenoord	34	19	13	2	61	27	51
PSV Eindhoven	34	17	10	7	60	36	44
Vitesse	34	17	6	11	63	37	40
Twente	34	15	9	10	57	43	39
Roda	34	15	8	11	55	40	38
NAC Breda	34	14	19	19	61	52	38
Willem II	34	15	7	12	48	42	37
Sparta	34	12	8	14	58	57	32
Maastricht	34	11	10	13	49	58	32
Volendam	34	13	4	17	46	55	30
Go Ahead	34	10	8	16	44	57	28
Heerenveen	34	9	10	15	35	61	28
Groningen	34	9	8	17	42	65	26
Utrecht	34	9	8	17	40	63	26
RKC Waalwijk +	34	8	9	17	38	56	25
VVV Venlo +	34	7	11	16	30	62	25
Cambuur*	34	6	7	21	28	64	19

Top scorer: Litmanen (Ajax) 26
Cup Final: Feyenoord 2, NEC Nijmegen 1

HUNGARY

Magyar Labdarugo Szovetseg, Hungarian Football Federation, Nepkoztarsasag Utja 47, H-1061 Budapest VI.
Founded: 1901; *Number of Clubs:* 1944; *Number of Players* 95,986; *National Colours:* Red shirts, white shorts, green stockings.
Telephone: 36-1-1255 817, 36-1-1420 704; 36-1-1425 103, 36-1-1421 556; *Cable:* MLSZ BUDAPEST; *Telex:* 225782 MLSZ H; *Fax:* 36-1-1425 103.

International matches 1993
Japan (a) 1-0, USA (h) 0-0, Greece (h) 0-1, Sweden (a) 0-2, Russia (a) 0-3, Republic of Ireland (a) 4-2, Iceland (a) 0-2, Russia (h) 1-3, Luxembourg (h) 1-0.

League Championship wins (1901–94)
Ferencvaros (prev. FRC) 24; MTK-VM Budapest (prev. Hungaria, Bastay and Vörös Lobogo) 19; Ujpest Dozsa 19; Honved 13; Vasas Budapest 6; Csepel 3; Raba Györ (prev. Vasas Györ) 3; BTC 2; Nagyvarad 1; Vac 1.

Cup wins (1910–94)
Farencvaros (prev. FRC) 16; MTK-VM Budapest (prev. Hungaria, Bastay and Vörös Lobogo) 9; Ujpest Dozsa 8; Raba Györ (prev. Vasas Györ) 4; Vasas Budapest 3; Honved 3; Diósgyör 2; Bocskai 1; III Ker 1; Kispesti AC 1; Soroksar 1; Szolnoki MAV 1; Siofok Banyasz 1; Bekescsaba 1; Pecs 1.
Cup not regularly held until 1964

Final League Table 1993–94

	P	*W*	*D*	*L*	*F*	*A*	Pts
Vac	30	19	8	3	58	29	46
Honved Kispest	30	18	7	5	66	33	43
Bekescsaba	30	19	3	8	68	29	41
Ferencvaros	30	16	5	9	50	32	37
Raba Gyor	30	15	7	8	51	37	37
Ujpest Dozsa	30	13	8	9	44	35	34
Debrecen	30	12	9	9	40	33	33
Csepel	30	12	8	10	36	44	32
Parmalat	30	8	9	13	33	46	25
Vasas	30	8	8	14	36	43	24
Pecs	30	7	10	13	23	39	24
BVSC	30	7	10	13	32	52	24
Siofok	30	6	10	14	33	49	22
Sopron	30	8	6	16	31	52	22
Haladas	30	5	9	16	28	48	19
MTK	30	4	9	17	30	58	17

Top scorer; Illes (Kispet) 17
Cup Final: Ferencvaros 3,2 Kispest Honved 0,1

ICELAND

Knattspyrnusamband Island, P.O. Box 8511, 128 Reykjavik.
Founded: 1929; *Number of Clubs:* 73; *Number of Players:* 23,673; *National Colours;* Blue shirts, white shorts, blue stockings.
Telephone: 84 444; *Cable* KSI REYKJAVIK; *Telex:* 2314 ISI IS; *Fax:* 1 68 97 66.

International matches 1993
USA (a) 1-1, Luxembourg (a) 1-1, Russia (h) 1-1, Hungary (h) 0-2, USA (h) 0-1, Luxembourg (h) 1-0, Tunisia (a) 1-3.

League Championship wins (1912–93)
KR 20; Valur 19; Fram 18; IA Akranes 14; Vikingur 5; IBK Keflavik 3; IBV Vestmann 2; KA Akureyri 1.

Cup wins (1960–93)
Valur 8; KR 7; Fram 7; IA Akranes 5; IBV Vestmann 3; IBA Akureyri 1; Vikingur 1; IBK Keflavik 1.

Final League Table 1993

	P	*W*	*D*	*L*	*F*	*A*	Pts
IA Akranes	18	16	1	1	62	16	49
FH	18	12	4	2	39	21	40
IBK	18	8	3	7	31	31	27
Fram	18	8	1	9	38	37	25
KR	18	7	3	8	37	34	24
Valur	18	6	4	8	25	24	22
Thor	18	5	5	8	20	30	20
IBV	18	5	4	9	26	41	19
Fylkir*	18	6	1	11	22	35	19
Vikingur*	18	3	2	13	23	54	11

Top scorer: Gudjohnson (IA Akranes) 15
Cup Final: IA Akranes 2, IBK 1

REPUBLIC OF IRELAND

The Football Association of Ireland, (Cumann Peile Na H-Eireann), 80 Merrion Square, South Dublin 2.
Founded: 1921; *Number of Clubs:* 3,190; *Number of Players:* 124,615; *National Colours:* Green shirts, white shorts, green stockings.
Telephone: 76 68 64; *Cable:* SOCCER DUBLIN; *Telex:* 913967 FAI EI; *Fax:* (01) 610 931.

International matches 1993
Wales (h) 2-1, Northern Ireland (h) 3-0, Denmark (h) 1-1, Albania (a) 2-1, Hungary (h) 2-4, Latvia (a) 2-0, Lithuania (a) 1-0, Lithuania (h) 2-0, Spain (h) 1-3, Northern Ireland (a) 1-1.

League Championship wins (1922–94)
Shamrock Rovers 15; Dundalk 8; Shelbourne 8; Bohemians 7; Waterford 6; Cork United 5; Drumcondra 5; St Patrick's Athletic 4; St James's Gate 2; Cork Athletic 2; Sligo Rovers 2; Limerick 2; Athlone Town 2; Dolphin 1; Cork Hibernians 1; Cork Celtic 1; Derry City 1, Cork City 1.

Cup wins (1922–94)
Shamrock Rovers 24; Dundalk 8; Drumcondra 5; Bohemians 5; Shelbourne 3; Cork Athletic 2; Cork United 2; St James's Gate 2; St Patrick's Athletic 2; Cork Hibernians 2; Limerick 2; Waterford 2; Alton United 1; Athlone Town 2; Sligo 2; Cork 1; Fordsons 1; Transport 1; Finn Harps 1; Home Farm 1; UCD 1; Derry City 1; Bray Wanderers 1; Galway United 1.

Qualifying Table 1993–94

	P	*W*	*D*	*L*	*F*	*A*	Pts
Shamrock Rovers	22	15	3	4	43	16	48
Cork City	22	12	5	5	43	24	41
Shelbourne	22	10	6	6	33	27	36
Galway U	22	9	7	6	30	26	34
Bohemians	22	8	7	7	23	17	31
Derry City	22	8	7	7	21	21	31
Dundalk	22	7	8	7	25	20	29
St Patrick's Ath	22	6	9	7	24	24	27
Monaghan U	22	9	3	10	27	27	30
Cobh Ramblers	22	5	4	13	20	34	19
Limerick City	22	3	8	11	15	40	17
Drogheda U	22	4	5	13	16	44	17

Final Round

	P	*W*	*D*	*L*	*F*	*A*	Pts
Shamrock Rovers	32	21	3	8	62	30	66
Cork City	32	17	8	7	60	36	59
Galway U	32	14	8	10	47	42	50
Derry City	32	12	10	10	37	35	46
Shelbourne	32	11	10	11	42	42	43
Bohemians	32	11	8	12	34	35	41

Promotion/Relegation

	P	*W*	*D*	*L*	*F*	*A*	Pts
Monaghan U	32	13	8	11	41	38	47
Dundalk	32	10	13	9	37	27	43
St Patrick's Ath	32	9	12	11	32	38	39
Cobh Ramblers	32	8	8	16	31	41	32
Limerick City*	32	6	11	15	23	50	29
Drogheda U*	32	7	7	18	26	58	28

Top scorer: Geogheau (Shamrock Rovers) 23
Cup Final: Sligo Rovers 1, Derry City 0

ISRAEL

Israel Football Association, 12 Carlibach Street, P.O. Box 20188, Tel Aviv 61201.
Founded: 1928; *Number of Clubs:* 544; *Number of Players:* 30,449; *National Colours:* White shirts, blue shorts, white stockings.
Telephone: 56 10 888; *Cable:* CADUREGEL TEL AVIV; *Telex:* 361353 FA; *Fax:* 03 5610838.

International matches 1993
Poland (h) 0-0, France (h) 0-4, Russia (h) 2-2, Ukraine (a) 1-1, Bulgaria (a) 2-2, Sweden (a) 0-5, Finland (a) 0-0, Romania (a) 0-1, Cyprus (a) 2-2, France (a) 3-2, Austria (h) 1-1, Finland (h) 1-3.

ITALY

Federazione Italiana Giuoco Calcio, Via Gregorio Allegri 14, C.P. 2450, 1-00198, Roma.
Founded: 1898; *Number of Clubs:* 20,961; *Number of Players:* 1,420,160; *National Colours:* Blue shirts, white shorts, blue stockings, white trim.
Telephone: 84 911; *Cable:* FEDERCALCIO ROMA; *Telex:* 611438 CALCIO; *Fax:* 06 849 1239.

International matches 1993
Mexico (h) 2-0, Portugal (a) 3-1, Malta (h) 6-1, Estonia (h) 2-0, Switzerland (a) 0-1, Estonia (a) 3-0, Scotland (h) 3-1, Portugal (h) 1-0.

League Championship wins (1898–1994)
Juventus 22; AC Milan 14; Inter-Milan 13; Genoa 9; Torino 8; Pro Vercelli 7; Bologna 7; Fiorentina 2; Napoli 2; AS Roma 2; Casale 1; Novese 1; Cagliari 1; Lazio 1; Verona 1; Sampdoria 1.

Cup wins (1922–94)
Juventus 8; AS Roma 8; Torino 4; Fiorentina 4; AC Milan 4; Sampdoria 4; Inter-Milan 3; Napoli 3; Bologna 2; Atalanta 1; Genoa 1; Lazio 1; Vado 1; Venezia 1; Parma 1.

Final League Table 1993–94

	P	*W*	*D*	*L*	*F*	*A*	Pts
AC Milan	34	19	12	3	36	15	50
Juventus	34	17	13	4	58	25	47
Sampdoria	34	18	8	8	64	39	44
Lazio	34	7	10	7	55	40	44
Parma	34	17	7	10	59	35	41
Napoli	34	12	12	10	41	35	36
AS Roma	34	10	15	9	35	30	35
Torino	34	11	12	11	39	37	34
Foggia	34	10	13	11	46	46	33
Cremonese	34	9	14	11	41	41	32
Genoa	34	8	16	10	32	40	32
Cagliari	34	10	12	12	39	48	32
Internazionale	34	11	9	14	46	45	31
Reggiana	34	10	11	13	29	37	31
Piacenza*	34	8	14	12	32	43	30
Udinese*	34	7	14	13	35	48	28
Atalanta*	34	5	11	18	35	65	21
Lecce*	34	3	5	26	28	72	11

Top scorer: Signori (Lazio) 23
Cup Final: Sampdoria 0,6 Ancona 0,1

LATVIA

Latvian Football Federation, Augsiela, 1, LV-1009, Riga.
Founded: 1921; *Number of Clubs:* 50; *Number of Players:*12,000.
National Colours: Carmine red shirts, white shorts, carmine red stockings.
Telephone: (371–2) 292988; *Telex:* 161183 ritm su; *Fax:* (371) 8828331.
Cable: Augsiela 1, LV–1009, Riga.

International matches 1993
Lithuania (a) 1-2, Estonia (h) 2-0, Denmark (a) 0-2, Albania (h) 0-0, Northern Ireland (h) 1-2, Republic of Ireland (h) 0-2, Estonia (h) 2-0, Lithuania (h) 0-0, Northern Ireland (a) 0-2.

League Championship wins (1922–93)
ASK Riga 9; RFK Riga 8; Olympia Liepaya 7; Sarkanais Metalurgs Liepaya 7; VEF Riga 6; Energija Riga 4; Elektrons Riga 3; Torpedo Riga 3; Skonto Riga 3; Daugava Liepaya 2; ODO Riga 2; Khimikis Daugavpils 2; RAF Yelgava 2; Keisermezhs Riga 2; Dinamo Riga 1; Zhmilyeva Team 1; Darba Rezervi 1; REZ Riga 1; Start Brotseni 1; Venta Ventspils 1; Yurnieks Riga 1; Alfa Riga 1; Gauya Valmiera 1.

Cup wins (1937–93)
Elektrons Riga 7; Sarkanais Metalurgs Liepaya 5; ODO Riga 3; VEF Riga 3; ASK Riga 3; Tseltnieks Riga 3; RFK Riga 2; Daugava Liepaya 2; Start Brotseni 2; Selmash Liepaya 2; Yurnieks Riga 2; Khimikis Daugavpils 2; RAF Yelgava 2; Rigas Vilki 1; Dinamo Liepaya 1; Dinamo Riga 1; REZ Riga 1; Voulkan Kouldiga 1; Baltija Liepaya 1; Venta Ventspils 1; Pilot Riga 1; Lielupe Yurmala 1; Energija Riga 1; Torpedo Riga 1; Daugava SKIF Riga 1; Tseltnieks Daugavpils 1; Skonto Riga 1.

Final League Table 1993

	P	*W*	*D*	*L*	*F*	*A*	Pts
Skonto Riga	18	17	0	1	63	7	34
Olympia Riga	18	12	2	4	31	17	26
RAF Yelgava	18	12	2	4	34	11	26
Pardaugava Riga	18	10	4	4	29	13	24
Auseklis Daugavplis	18	7	5	6	22	17	19
Vidus Riga	18	6	7	5	19	13	19
Olympia Liepaya	18	3	6	9	24	46	12
FC DA Riga	18	3	4	11	15	29	10
Variogs Rezekne	18	3	3	12	12	36	9
Gauya Valmiera*	18	0	1	17	14	74	1

Top scorer; Yeliseyev (Skonto) 20
Cup Final: RAF 1, Pardaugava 0

LIECHTENSTEIN

Liechtensteiner Fussball-Verband, Am schragen Weg 17, Postfach 165, 9490 Vaduz.
Founded: 1933; *Number of Clubs:* 7; *Number of Players:* 1,247; *National Colours:* Blue & red shirts, red shorts, blue stockings.
Telephone: 41–75/233 24 28; *Cable:* FUSSBALLVERBAND VADUZ; *Telex:* 889 261; *Fax:* 41–75/233 24 30.

International matches 1993
Estonia (h) 0-2.
Liechtenstein has no national league. Teams compete in Swiss regional leagues.

LITHUANIA

Lithuanian Football Federation, 6, Zemaites Street, 232675 Vilnius. Championship of 14 teams.
Number of Clubs: 20; *Number of Players:* 16,600.
Telephone: 22-261713; *Telex:* 261118 LSK SU; *Fax:* 122-661223.

International matches 1993
Latvia (h) 2-1, Finland (a) 0-3, Spain (a) 0-5, Poland (a) 1-1, Albania (h) 3-1, Ukraine (h) 1-2, Northern Ireland (h) 0-1, Spain (h) 0-2, Repbulic of Ireland (h) 0-1, Latvia (a) 0-0, Estonia (a) 1-2, Denmark (a) 0-4, Republic of Ireland (a) 0-2.

League Championship wins 1922–94
Kovas Kaunas 6; KSS Klaipeda 6; LFLS Kaunas 4; LGSF Kaunas 2; Zalgiris Vilnius 2; MSK Kaunas 1; Ekranas Panevezys 1; Romar Mazeikiai 1.

Cup wins 1992–93

Zalgiris Vilnius 2.

Final League Table 1994

	P	*W*	*D*	*L*	*F*	*A*	Pts
Romar	22	17	4	1	53	10	38
Zalgiris	22	17	3	2	57	13	37
Ekranas	22	13	5	4	48	12	31
Panerys	22	12	5	5	35	17	29
Kaunas	22	12	4	6	31	18	28
Aras	22	7	8	7	31	27	22
Sirius	22	7	5	10	25	31	19
Inkaras	22	4	7	11	22	34	15
Sakalas	22	6	3	13	22	50	15
Vilkas	22	3	7	12	14	50	13
Zydrius	22	1	7	14	12	46	9
Karchouva	22	2	4	16	13	55	8

Top scorer; Slekys (Ekranas) 16.
Cup Final: Zalgiris 1, Sirius 0

LUXEMBOURG

Federation Luxembourgeoise De Football, (F.L.F.), 50, Rue De Strasbourg, L-2560, Luxembourg.
Founded: 1908; *Number of Clubs:* 126; *Number of Players:* 21,684; *National Colours:* Red shirts, white shorts, blue stockings.
Telephone: 48 86 65; *Cable:* FOOTBALL LUXEMBOURG; *Telex:* 2426 FLF LU; *Fax:* 400 201.

International matches 1993
Greece (a) 0-2, Russia (h) 0-4, Iceland (h) 1-1, Iceland (a) 0-1, Greece (h) 1-3, Hungary (a) 0-1.

League Championship wins (1910–94)
Jeunesse Esch 21; Spora Luxembourg 11; Stade Dudelange 10; Avenir Beggen 7; Red Boys Differdange 6; US Hollerich-Bonnevoie 5; Fola Esch 5; US Luxembourg 5; Aris Bonnevoie 3; Progres Niedercor 3.

Cup wins (1922–94)
Red Boys Differdange 16; Jeunesse Esch 9; US Luxembourg 9; Spora Luxembourg 8; Avenir Beggen 6; Stade Dudelange 4; Progres Niedercorn 4; Fola Esch 3; Alliance Dudelange 2; US Rumelange 2; Aris Bonnevoie 1; US Dudelange 1; Jeunesse Hautcharage 1; National Schiffige 1; Racing Luxembourg 1; SC Tetange 1; Hesperange 1.

Qualifying positions and points 1993–94
Avenir Beggen 27; Grevenmacher 26; Jeunesse Esch 24; Union 22; Dudelange 19; Aris 15; Petange 14; Fola 13; Spora 12; Red Boys 8.
Half points total taken into top six teams play-off for final phase.

Final Table 1993–94

	P	*W*	*D*	*L*	*F*	*A*	Pts
Avenir Beggen	10	7	1	2	28	12	28.5
Grevenmacher	10	5	1	4	11	13	24
Union	10	5	2	3	12	11	23
Jeunesse Esch	10	2	2	6	12	15	18
Aris	10	4	1	5	12	17	16.5
Dudelange	10	3	1	6	14	21	16.5

Top scorer: Danelli (Dudelange) 19

MALTA

Malta Football Association, 280 St. Paul Street, Valletta.
Founded: 1900; *Number of Clubs:* 252; *Number of Players:* 5,544; *National Colours:* Red shirts, white shorts, red stockings.
Telephone: 22 26 97; *Cable:* FOOTBALL MALTA VALLETTA; *Telex:* 1752 MALFA MW; *Fax:* 24 51 36.

International matches 1993
Portugal (h) 0-1, Scotland (a) 0-3, Italy (a) 1-6, Switzerland (h) 0-2, Estonia (a) 1-0, Portugal (a) 0-4, Egypt (a) 0-3, Scotland (h) 0-2.

League Championship wins (1910–94)
Floriana 25; Sliema Wanderers 22; Valletta 14; Hibernians 7; Hamrun Spartans 6; Rabat Ajax 2; St George's 1; KOMR 1.

Cup wins (1935–94)
Floriana 18; Sliema Wanderers 17; Valletta 6; Hamrun Spartans 6; Hibernians 5; Gzira United 1; Melita 1; Zurrieq 1; Rabat Ajax 1.

Final League Table 1993–94

	P	*W*	*D*	*L*	*F*	*A*	Pts
Hibernians	18	14	3	1	48	15	31
Valletta	18	12	3	3	42	17	27
Floriana	18	11	4	3	26	10	26
Hamrun Spartans	18	8	9	1	35	10	25
Sliema Wanderers	18	8	5	5	26	11	21
Zurrieq	18	5	4	9	18	29	14
St Andrew's	18	5	3	10	18	30	13
Birkirkaba	18	6	0	12	19	36	12
Rabat Ajax*	18	2	6	10	16	38	10
Mqabba*	18	0	1	17	3	55	1

Cup Final: Floriana 2, Valletta 1

MOLDOVA

Moldavian Football Federation, Bd Stefan cel Mare 73, 2777001 Chisinau, Moldavia. *Telephone:* 3732/22 44 98, 22 12 95, *Fax:* 3732/22 22 44.
League champions 1993–94: Zimbru Chisinau.
Top scorer: Cosse (Tiligul) 24
Cup Final: Tiligul Tiraspol 1, Nistru Otaci 0.

NORTHERN IRELAND

Irish Football Association Ltd, 20 Windsor Avenue, Belfast BT9 6EG.
Founded: 1880; *Number of Clubs:* 1,555; *Number of Players:* 24,558; *National Colours:* Green shirts, white shorts, green stockings.
Telephone: (0232) 66 94 58; *Cable:* FOOTBALL BELFAST; *Telex:* 747317; *Fax:* (0232) 667620.

NORWAY

Norges Fotballforbund Ullevaal Stadion, Postboks 3823, Ulleval Hageby, 0805 Oslo 8.
Founded: 1902; *Number of Clubs:* 1,810; *Number of Players:* 300,000; *National Colours:* Red shirts, white shorts, blue & white stockings.
Telephone: 47–22/95 10 00; *Cable* FOTBALLFORBUND OSLO; *Telex:* 71722 NFF N; *Fax:* 47–22/95 10 10.

International matches 1993
Portugal (a) 1-1, Qatar (a) 6-1, Turkey (h) 3-1, England (h) 2-0, Holland (a) 0-0, Faeroes (h) 7-0, USA (a) 1-0, Poland (h) 1-0, Poland (a) 3-0, Turkey (a) 1-2.

League Championship wins (1938–93)
Fredrikstad 9; Viking Stavanger 8; Rosenborg Trondheim 7; Lillestroem 6; Valerengen 4; Larvik Turn 3; Brann Bergen 2; Lyn Oslo 2; IK Start 2; Friedig 1; Fram 1; Skeid Oslo 1; Strömsgodset Drammen 1; Moss 1.

Cup wins (1902–93)
Odds Bk, Skien 11; Fredrikstad 10; Lyn Oslo 8; Skeid Oslo 8; Sarpsborg FK 6; Brann Bergen 5; Rosenborg Trondheim 5; Orn F Horten 4; Lillestroem 4; Viking Stavanger 4; Strömsgodset Drammen 4; Frigg 3; Mjondalens F 3; Bodo Glimt 2; Mercantile 2; Grane Nordstrand 1; Kvik Halden 1; Sparta 1; Gjovik 1; Valerengen 1; Moss 1; Tromso 1; Byrne 1.
(Until 1937 the cup-winners were regarded as champions.)

Final League Table 1993

	P	*W*	*D*	*L*	*F*	*A*	Pts
Rosenborg	22	14	5	3	47	30	47
Bodo Glimt	22	14	3	5	51	21	45
Illestrom	22	13	3	6	47	26	42
Viking	22	13	2	7	38	27	41
Hamark	22	10	3	9	42	39	33
Tromso	22	6	8	8	25	25	26
Brann	22	7	5	10	31	38	26
Kongsvinger	22	7	4	11	33	41	25
Start	22	6	5	11	26	29	23
Molde*	22	5	7	10	23	36	22
Lyn*	22	6	4	12	39	53	22
Fyllingen*	22	4	5	13	21	55	17

Cup Final: Bodo Glimt 2, Stromsgodset 0

POLAND

Federation Polonaise De Foot-Ball, Al. Ujazdowskie 22, 00-478 Warszawa.
Founded: 1923; *Number of Clubs:* 5,881; *Number of Players:* 317,442; *National Colours:* White shirts, red shorts, white & red stockings.
Telephone: 48-22-28 93 44; 48-22-28 58 21; *Cable:* PEZETPEEN WARSZAWA; *Telex:* 825320 PZPN PL; *Fax:* 48 22 219175.

International matches 1993
Cyprus (a) 0-0, Israel (a) 0-0, Brazil (a) 2-2, Lithuania (h) 1-1, Finland (h) 2-1, San Marino (h) 1-0, San Marino (a) 3-0, England (h) 1-1, England (a) 0-3, Norway (a) 0-1, Norway (h) 0-3, Turkey (a) 1-2, Holland (h) 1-3.

League Championship wins (1921–94)
Gornik Zabrze 14; Ruch Chorzow 13; Wisla Krakow 6; Lech Poznan 5; Legia Warsaw 5; Pogon Lwow 4; Cracovia 3; Warta Poznan 2; Polonia Bytom 2; Stal Mielec 2; Widzew Lodz 2; Garbarnia Krakow 1; Polonia Warsaw 1; LKS Lodz 1; Slask Wroclaw 1; Szombierki Bytom 1; Zaglebie Lubin 1.

Cup wins (1951–94)
Legia Warsaw 10; Gornik Zabrze 6; Zaglebie Sosnowiec 4; Lech Poznan 3; GKS Katowice 3: Ruch Chorzow 2; Slask Wroclaw 2; Gwardia Warsaw 1; LKS Lodz 1; Polonia Warsaw 1; Wisla Krakow 1; Stal Rzeszow 1; Arka Gdynia 1; Lechia Gdansk 1; Widzew Lodz 1; Miedz Legnica 1.

Final League Table 1993–94

	P	*W*	*D*	*L*	*F*	*A*	Pts
Legia	34	19	13	2	72	24	48
Katowice	34	18	12	4	52	28	48
Gornik Zabrze	34	17	12	5	56	32	46
LKS Lodz	34	17	11	6	49	24	42
Pogon	34	11	19	4	39	24	41
Hutnik	34	12	15	7	34	28	38
Widzew	34	11	15	8	43	34	38
Ruch	34	13	10	11	48	41	36
Lech	34	12	11	11	39	32	35
Milliader	34	11	11	12	41	40	33
Stal	34	11	10	13	32	45	32
Wola	34	8	15	11	25	37	31
Zaglebie Lubin	34	9	12	13	40	47	30
Warta	34	11	8	15	32	45	30
Wisla	34	6	13	15	30	46	22
Polonia*	34	4	11	19	28	61	19
Siarka*	34	4	10	20	25	57	18
Bydgoszcz*	34	3	10	21	30	70	16

Legia, LKS Lodz and Wisla each deducted three points.
Top scorer: Burzawa (Millader) 21
Cup Final: Legia 2, LKS Lodz 0
Katowice won 5-4 on penalties.

PORTUGAL

Federacao Portuguesa De Futebol, Praca De Alegria N.25, Apartado 21.100, P-1128, Lisboa Codex.
Founded: 1914; *Number of Clubs:* 204; *Number of Players:* 79,235; *National Colours:* Red shirts, white shorts, red stockings.
Telephone: 328207/08/09; *Cable:* FUTEBOL LISBOA; *Telex:* 13489 FPF P; *Fax:* 346 7231.

International matches 1993
Malta (a) 1-0, Norway (h) 1-1, Italy (h) 1-3, Switzerland (a) 1-1, Scotland (h) 5-0, Malta (h) 4-0, Estonia (a) 2-0, Switzerland (h) 1-0, Estonia (h) 3-0, Italy (a) 0-1.

League Championship wins (1935–94)
Benfica 30; Sporting Lisbon 16; FC Porto 13; Belenenses 1.

Cup wins (1939–94)
Benfica 22; Sporting Lisbon 11; FC Porto 8; Boavista 4; Belenenses 3; Vitoria Setubal 2; Academica Coimbra 1; Leixoes Porto 1; Sporting Braga 1; Amadora 1.

Final League Table 1993–94

	P	*W*	*D*	*L*	*F*	*A*	Pts
Benfica	34	23	8	3	73	25	54
Porto	34	21	10	3	56	15	52
Sporting Lisbon	34	23	5	6	71	29	51
Boavista	34	16	6	12	46	31	38
Maritimo	34	13	12	9	45	40	38
Setubal	34	14	6	14	56	42	34
Farense	34	13	7	14	44	46	33
Estrela	34	9	15	10	39	36	33
Guimaraes	34	11	11	12	30	31	33
Uniao	34	11	9	14	36	42	31
Gil Vicente	34	10	11	13	27	47	31
Salgueiros	34	14	3	17	48	56	31
Belenenses	34	12	6	16	39	51	30
Beira Mar	34	9	11	14	28	38	29
Braga	34	9	10	15	33	43	28
Pacos*	34	7	12	15	31	49	26
Famalicao*	34	7	8	19	26	72	22
Estoril*	34	5	8	21	22	57	18

Top scorer: Yekini (Setubal) 21
Cup Final: Sporting Lisbon 0,1, Porto 0,2

ROMANIA

Federatia Romana De Fotbal, Vasile Conta 16, Bucharest 70130.
Founded: 1908; *Number of Clubs:* 414; *Number of Players:* 22,920; *National Colours:* Yellow shirts, blue shorts, red stockings.
Telephone: 10 70 90; *Cable:* SPORTROM BUCURESTI-FOTBAL; *Telex:* 11180; *Fax:* 11 70 75 and 11 98 69

International matches 1993
Ecuador (a) 0-3, Mexico (a) 0-2, Peru (a) 2-0, USA (a) 1-1, Cyprus (h) 2-1, RCS (a) 2-5, Faeroes (a) 4-0, Israel (h) 1-0, Belgium (h) 2-1, Wales (a) 2-1.

League Championship wins (1910–94)
Steaua Bucharest (prev. CCA) 16; Dinamo Bucharest 14; Venus Bucharest 8, Chinezul Timisoara 6; UT Arad 6; Ripensia Temesvar 4; Uni Craiova 4; Petrolul Ploesti 3; Olimpia Bucharest 2; Colentina Bucharest 2; Arges Pitesti 2; ICO Oradea 2; Soc RA Bucharest 1; Prahova Ploesti 1; Coltea Brasov 1; Juventus Bucharest 1; Metalochimia Resita 1; Ploesti United 1; Unirea Tricolor 1; Rapid Bucharest 1.

Cup wins (1934–94)
Steaua Bucharest (prev. CCA) 17; Rapid Bucharest 9; Dinamo Bucharest 7; Uni Craiova 6; UT Arad 2; Ripensia Temesvar 2; Politehnica Timisoara 2; ICO Oradeo 1; Metalochimia Resita 1; Petrolul Ploesti 1; Stinta Cluj 1; CFR Turnu Severin 1; Chimia Rannicu Vilcea 1; Jiul Petroseni 1; Progresul Bucharest 1; Progresul Oradea 1; Gloria Bistrita 1.

Final League Table 1993–94

	P	*W*	*D*	*L*	*F*	*A*	Pts
Steaua	34	22	9	3	63	19	53
Dinamo	34	16	7	11	65	40	39
Uni Craiova	34	16	8	10	64	46	40
Rapid Bucharest	34	16	6	12	43	32	38
Farul	34	15	7	12	42	38	37
Petrolul	34	14	10	10	34	30	38
Gloria	34	16	3	15	47	43	35
Inter Sibiu	34	13	8	13	40	41	34
Piatra	34	11	10	13	27	40	32
UT Arad	34	12	8	14	35	49	32
Progresul Bucharest	34	14	4	16	44	42	32
Cluj	34	11	9	14	39	42	31
Brasov	34	13	5	16	38	52	31
Elect. Craiova	34	10	10	14	25	34	30
Sportul	34	11	7	16	30	45	29
Otelul	34	12	5	17	38	47	29
Timisoara*	34	11	6	17	39	53	28
Brailia*	34	9	6	19	33	53	24

Top scorer: Gh. Craioveanu (Uni Craiova) 21
Cup Final: Bistrita 1, Uni Craiova 0

RUSSIA (formerly USSR)

Football Union of Russia; Luzhnetskaya Naberezyhnaja, 8. SU-119270 Moscow. Telephone: 952–01 0834; *Telex:* 411 287 priz su; *Fax:* 952–01 1303; New space up-link fax: 7–502/220 2037.
Founded: 1992; *Number of Clubs:* 43,700; *Number of Players:* 2,170,000.

International matches 1993
USA (a) 1-0, El Salvador (h) 2-1, USA (a) 0-0, Israel (a) 2-2, Luxembourg (a) 4-0, Hungary (h) 3-0, Greece (h) 1-1, Iceland (a) 1-1, France (a) 1-3, Hungary (a) 3-1, Saudi Arabia (a) 2-4, Greece (a) 0-1.

League Championship wins (1945–94)
Dynamo Kiev 13; Spartak Moscow 13; Dynamo Moscow 11; CSKA Moscow 7; Torpedo Moscow 3; Dynamo Tbilisi 2; Dnepr Dnepropetrovsk 2; Saria Voroshilovgrad 1; Ararat Erevan 1; Dynamo Minsk 1; Zenit Leningrad 1.

Cup wins (1936–94)
Spartak Moscow 11; Dynamo Kiev 10; Torpedo Moscow 7; Dynamo Moscow 6; CSKA Moscow 5; Donetsk Shaktyor 4; Lokomotiv Moscow 2; Dynamo Tbilisi 2; Ararat Erevan 2; Karpaty Lvov 1; SKA Rostov 1; Zenit Leningrad 1; Metallist Kharkov 1; Dnepr 1.

Qualifying Table 1993

	P	*W*	*D*	*L*	*F*	*A*	Pts
Spartak Moscow	34	21	11	2	81	18	53
Volgograd	34	17	8	9	56	35	42
Dynamo Moscow	34	16	10	8	65	38	42
Tekstilchik	34	14	11	9	45	34	39
Lokomotiv Moscow	34	14	11	9	45	29	39
Vladikavkaz	34	16	6	12	49	45	38
Torpedo Moscow	34	15	8	11	35	40	38
Ouralmach	34	16	4	14	51	52	36
CSKA Moscow	34	12	6	16	43	45	30
Kamaz	34	12	6	16	45	53	30
Novgorod	34	12	6	16	34	49	30
Stavropol	43	11	8	16	39	49	30
Zhemchonzhina	34	10	10	14	52	62	30
Sovekov	34	9	12	13	37	47	30
Vladivostok	34	11	7	16	29	56	29
Nakhodka	34	10	8	16	28	40	28
Rostselmach*	34	8	12	14	35	52	28
Asmaral Moscow*	34	7	6	21	28	53	20

Top scorer: Poutchenko (Kamaz) 21
Cup Final: Spartak Moscow 2, CSKA Moscow 2
Spartak Moscow won 4-2 on penalties

SAN MARINO

Federazione Sammarinese Giuoco Calcio, Viale Campo dei Giudei, 14; 47031-Rep. San Marino.
Founded: 1931; *Number of Clubs:* 17; *Number of Players:* 1,033; *Colours:* Blue and white.
Telephone: 549–99 05 15/99 05 40; *Cable:* FEDERCALCIO SAN MARINO; *Telex:* 0505 284 cosmar so; *Fax:* 549 992348.

International matches 1993
England (a) 0-6, Turkey (h) 0-0, Holland (a) 0-6, Poland (a) 0-1, Poland (h) 0-3, Holland (h) 0-7, England (h) 1-7.
League Champions 1993–94: Tre Fiori.

SCOTLAND

The Scottish Football Association Ltd, 6 Park Gardens, Glasgow G3 7YF.
Founded: 1873; *Number of Clubs:* 6,148; *Number of Players:* 135,474; *National Colours:* Dark blue shirts, white shorts, red stockings.
Telephone: 41 332 6372; *Cable:* EXECUTIVE GLASGOW; *Telex:* 778904 SFA G; *Fax:* 41 332 7559.

SLOVENIA

Nogometna Zveza Slovenije, dunajska 47/V, P.P. 90, 61109 Ljubljana, Slovenia.
Founded: 1992; *Number of Clubs:* 232; *Number of Players:* 15,048.
Telephone: 861–31 1888. *Fax:* 861–30 2337.

International matches 1993
Estonia (h) 2-0, Macedonia (h) 1-4.

League Championship wins 1992–94
SCT Olimpija 3.

Cup wins 1992–94
Branik Maribor 2; SCT Olimpija 1.

Final League Table 1993–94

	P	*W*	*D*	*L*	*F*	*A*	Pts
Olimpija	30	23	5	2	95	20	51
Mura	30	19	7	4	59	23	45
Branik Maribor	30	16	10	4	55	24	42
Publikum	30	14	10	6	50	34	38
Gorica	30	12	11	7	40	38	35
Potrosnik	30	13	6	11	57	40	32
Koper	30	11	10	9	43	38	32
Zivila Naklo	30	11	7	12	32	40	29
Rudar	30	10	7	13	37	49	27
Isola	30	9	8	13	45	51	26
Cosmos	30	8	9	13	29	44	25
Primorje	30	8	8	14	46	55	24
Optimizem	30	9	5	16	31	59	23
Istragas	30	7	7	16	25	50	21
Mavrica	30	5	8	17	35	70	18
Krka	30	2	8	20	14	58	12

Cup Final: Maribor 0,3 Mura 1,1

SPAIN

Real Federacion Espanola De Futbol, Calle Alberto Bosch 13, Apartado Postal 347, E-28014 Madrid.
Founded: 1913; *Number of Clubs:* 10,240; *Number of Players:* 408,135; *National Colours:* Red shirts, dark blue shorts, black stockings, yellow trim.
Telephone: 420 13 62; *Cable:* FUTBOL MADRID; *Telex:* 42420 RFEF; *Fax:* 420 20 94.

International matches 1993
Mexico (h) 1-1, Lithuania (h) 5-0, Denmark (a) 0-1, Northern Ireland (h) 3-1, Lithuania (a) 2-0, Chile (h) 2-0, Albania (a) 5-1, Republic of Ireland (a) 3-1, Denmark (h) 1-0.

League Championship wins (1945–94)
Real Madrid 25; Barcelona 14; Atletico Madrid 8; Athletic Bilbao 8; Valencia 4; Real Sociedad 2; Real Betis 1; Seville 1.

Cup wins (1902–94)
Athletic Bilbao 23; Barcelona 22; Real Madrid 17; Atletico Madrid 8; Valencia 5; Real Zaragoza 4; Real Union de Irun 3; Seville 3; Espanol 2; Arenas 1; Ciclista Sebastian 1; Racing de Irun 1; Vizcaya Bilbao 1; Real Betis 1; Real Sociedad 1;

Final League Table 1993–94

	P	W	D	L	F	A	Pts
Barcelona	38	25	6	7	91	42	56
La Coruna	38	22	12	4	54	18	56
Zaragoza	38	19	8	11	71	47	46
Real Madrid	38	19	7	12	61	50	45
Athletic Bilbao	38	16	11	11	61	47	43
Sevilla	38	15	12	11	56	42	42
Valencia	38	14	12	12	55	50	40
Santander	38	15	8	15	44	42	38
Oviedo	38	12	13	13	43	49	37
Tenerife	38	15	6	17	50	57	36
Real Sociedad	38	12	12	14	39	47	36
Atletico Madrid	38	13	9	16	54	54	35
Albacete	38	10	15	13	49	58	35
Sporting Gijon	38	15	5	18	42	57	35
Celta	38	11	11	16	41	51	33
Logrones	38	9	15	14	47	58	33
Rayo Vallecano +	38	9	13	16	40	58	31
Valladolid +	38	8	14	16	28	51	30
Lerida*	38	7	13	18	29	48	27
Osasuna*	38	8	10	20	34	63	26

Top scorer: Romario (Barcelona) 30
Cup Final: Zaragoza 0, Celta 0
Zaragoza won 5-4 on penalties

SWEDEN

Svenska Fotbollfoerbundet, Box 1216, S-17123 Solna.
Founded: 1904; *Number of Clubs:* 3,250; *Number of Players:* 485,000; *National Colours:* Yellow shirts, blue shorts, yellow and blue stockings.
Telephone: 8-735 0900; *Cable:* FOOTBALL-S; *Telex:* 17711 FOTBOLL S; *Fax:* 8-27 51 47.

International matches 1993
Hungary (h) 2-0, France (a) 1-2, Austria (h) 1-0, Israel (h) 5-0, Switzerland (h) 1-2, France (h) 1-1, Bulgaria (a) 1-1, Finland (h) 3-2, Austria (a) 1-1.

League Championship wins (1896–1993)
Oergryte IS Gothenburg 14; IFK Gothenburg 14; Malmo FF 14; IFK Norrköping 12; AIK Stockholm 9; Djurgaarden 8; GAIS Gothenburg 6; IF Halsingborg 5; Boras IF Elfsborg 4; Oster Vaxjo 4; Halmstad 2; Atvidaberg 2; IFK Ekilstune 1; IF Gavic Brynas 1; IF Gothenburg 1; Fassbergs 1; Norrköping IK Sleipner 1.

Cup wins (1941–93)
Malmo FF 13; IFK Norrköping 6; AIK Stockholm 4; IFK Gothenburg 4; Atvidaberg 2; Kalmar 2; GAIS Gothenburg 1; IF Halsingborg 1; Raa 1; Landskrona 1; Oster Vaxjo 1; Djurgaarden 1; Degerfors 1.

Final Table 1993

	P	W	D	L	F	A	Pts
IFK Gothenburg	26	18	5	3	48	17	59
Norrkoping	26	17	3	6	56	23	54
AIK	26	14	4	8	49	43	46
Trelleborg	26	12	6	8	46	39	42
Halmstad	26	11	5	10	50	41	38
Hacken	26	11	4	11	44	49	37
Frolunda	26	11	4	11	38	45	37
Osters	26	10	6	10	43	34	36
Helsingborg	26	10	6	10	43	46	36
Malmo	26	10	5	11	43	38	35
Orebro	26	10	3	13	35	38	33
Degefors	26	6	5	15	32	54	23
Orgryte*	26	5	6	15	26	44	21
Brage*	26	4	4	18	26	68	16

Top scorer: Bertilsson (Halmstad) 18
Cup Final: Norrkoping 4, Helsingborg 3 (aet)

SWITZERLAND

Schweizerisher Fussballverband. Haus des Schweizer Fussballs, Worbstrasse 48, 3074 Muri/BE. Mailing Address: PO Box 3000 Bern 15.
Founded: 1895; *Number of Clubs:* 1,473; *Number of Players:* 185,286; *National Colours:* Red shirts, white shorts, red stockings.
Telephone: 41–31/950 81 11; *Cable:* SWISSFOOT BERNE; *Telex:* 912910; *Fax:* 41–31/950 81 81.

International matches 1993
Japan (h) 1-1, Tunisia (a) 1-0, Portugal (h) 1-1, Malta (a) 2-0, Italy (h) 1-0, Sweden (a) 2-1, Scotland (a) 1-1, Portugal (a) 0-1, Estonia (h) 4-0.

League Championship wins (1898–1994)
Grasshoppers 22; Servette 16; Young Boys Berne 11; FC Zurich 9; FC Basle 8; Lausanne 7; La Chaux-de-Fonds 3; FC Lugano 3; Winterthur 3; FX Aarau 3; Neuchatel Xamax 2; FC Anglo-American 1; St Gallen 1; FC Brühl 1; Cantonal-Neuchatel 1; Biel 1; Bellinzona 1; FC Etoile Le Chaux-de-Fonds 1; Lucerne 1; Sion 1.

Cup wins (1926–94)
Grasshoppers 18; Lausanne 7; La Chaux-de-Fonds 6; Young Boys Berne 6; Servette 6; FC Sion 6; FC Basle 5; FC Zurich 5; Lucerne 2; FC Lugano 2; FC Granges 1; St Gallen 1; Urania Geneva 1; Young Fellows Zurich 1; Aarau.

Qualifying Table 1993–94

	P	W	D	L	F	A	Pts
Grasshoppers	22	12	7	3	37	15	31
FC Sion	22	11	9	2	34	14	31
Young Boys Berne	22	9	7	6	37	25	25
Servette	22	9	7	6	38	37	25
Lausanne	22	9	6	7	28	27	24
Lugano	22	7	8	7	23	27	22
Lucerne	22	8	5	9	26	32	21
Aarau	22	8	5	9	24	31	21
Zurich	22	6	8	8	25	22	20
Neuchatel Xamax	22	4	9	9	24	31	17
Yverdon	22	3	8	11	19	33	14
Kriens	22	3	7	12	17	38	13

Final Table 1993

	P	W	D	L	F	A	Pts
Servette	14	8	5	1	29	14	34
Grasshoppers	14	6	5	3	28	17	33
FC Sion	14	5	5	4	21	15	31
Aarau	14	7	4	3	23	16	29
Lugano	14	5	5	4	21	19	26
Young Boys Berne	14	2	6	6	13	23	23
Lausanne	14	4	1	9	14	28	21
Lucerne	14	2	3	9	15	32	18

Top scorer: Elber (Grasshoppers) 21
Cup Final: Grasshoppers 4, Schaffhausen 0

TURKEY

Federation Turque De Football, Konur Sokak No. 10, Ankara Kizilay.
Founded: 1923; *Number of Clubs:* 230; *Number of Players:* 64,521; *National Colours:* White shirts, white shorts, red and white stockings.
Telephone: 1259182/1259189; *Cable:* FUTBOLSPOR ANKARA; *Telex:* 46308; *Fax:* (4) 117 1090.

International matches 1993
Holland (a) 1-3, San Marino (a) 0-0, England (h) 0-2, Norway (a) 1-3, Poland (h) 2-1, Norway (h) 2-1.

League Championship wins (1960–94)
Fenerbahce 12; Galatasaray 10; Besiktas 9; Trabzonspor 6.

Cup wins (1963–94)
Galatasaray 10; Besiktas 5; Fenerbahce 4; Trabzonspor 4; Goztepe Izmir 2; Atay Ismir 2; Ankaragucu 2; Eskisehirspor 1; Bursapor 1; Genclerbirligi 1; Sakaryaspor 1.

Final League Table 1993–94

	P	*W*	*D*	*L*	*F*	*A*	Pts
Galatasaray	30	22	4	4	67	28	70
Fenerbahce	30	21	6	3	69	26	69
Trabzonspor	30	17	8	5	67	28	59
Besiktas	30	16	6	8	58	30	54
Samsun	30	15	5	10	53	47	50
Kocaeli	30	13	7	10	44	47	46
Genclerbirligi	30	13	5	12	51	51	44
Gaziantep	30	10	5	15	49	54	35
Bursa	30	9	8	13	26	39	35
Altay	30	8	8	14	33	45	32
Ankaragucu	30	8	8	14	39	52	32
Kayseri	30	8	7	15	31	49	31
Zeytinburnu	30	8	6	16	33	51	30
Karabuk*	30	7	7	16	35	62	28
Karsiyaka*	30	7	6	17	19	43	27
Sariyer*	30	6	8	16	28	50	26

Top scorers: Buleut (Fenerbahce) 22, Kona (Genclerbirligi) 22
Cup Final: Galatasaray 0,2 Besiktas 0,3

UKRAINE

Football Federation of Ukraine, 42, Kuybysheva Street, 252023 Kiev 23, Ukraine.
Founded: 1992; *Number of Teams:* 30,460; *Number of Players:* 757,758.
Telephone: 044/220 1344, 044/220 1300; *Telex:* 161866. *Fax:* 044/220 1294, 044/220 1344; 044/228 4135 (Dynamo Kiev).

International matches 1993
Israel (h) 1-1, Lithuania (a) 2-1, Croatia (a) 1-3, USA (a) 2-1, Mexico (a) 1-2, USA (a) 1-0.
League Champions: 1993 Dynamo Kiev
Cup Final: 1993 Dynamo Kiev 2, Karpaty Lvov 1; 1994 Odessa 1, Tavria 0 (aet)

WALES

The Football Association of Wales Limited, Plymouth Chambers, 3 Westgate Street, Cardiff.
Founded: 1876; *Number of Clubs:* 2,326; *Number of Players:* 53,926; *National Colours:* All red. *Telephone:* 0222 372325; *Telex:* 497 363 FAW G.

YUGOSLAVIA

Yugoslav Football Association, P.O. Box 263, Terazije 35, 11000 Beograd.
Founded: 1919; *Number of Clubs:* 6,532; *Number of Players:* 229,024; *National Colours:* Blue shirts, white shorts, red stockings.
Telephone: 333-433 and 11/334-253; *Cable:* JUGOFUDBAL BEOGRAD; *Telex:* 11666 FSJ YU; *Fax:* 0038-11-33 34 33.

League Championship wins (1923–94)
Red Star Belgrade 19; Partizan Belgrade 13; Hajduk Split 9; Gradjanski Zagreb; BSK Belgrade 5; Dynamo Zagreb 4; Jugoslavija Belgrade 2; Concordia Zagreb 2; FC Sarajevo 2; Vojvodina Novi Sad 2; HASK Zagreb 1; Zeljeznicar 1.

Cup wins (1947–94)
Red Star Belgrade 13; Hajduk Split 9; Dynamo Zagreb 8; Partizan Belgrade 7; BSK Belgrade 2; OFK Belgrade 2; Rejeka 2; Velez Mostar 2; Vardar Skopje 1; Borac Banjaluka 1.

Final League Table 1993–94
Group A

	P	*W*	*D*	*L*	*F*	*A*	Pts
Partizan Belgrade	18	13	3	2	47	10	42
Red Star Belgrade	18	12	2	4	40	18	37
Vojvodina	18	8	5	5	29	19	31
Spartak	18	6	5	7	22	26	24
OFK Belgrade	18	7	3	8	21	29	24
Zemun	18	6	3	9	19	25	23
Buducnost&	18	7	2	9	21	33	23
Radnicki Belgrade*	18	5	5	8	15	28	19
Proleter*	18	4	3	11	8	28	18
Becej*	18	6	1	11	22	28	17

Group B

	P	*W*	*D*	*L*	*F*	*A*	Pts
Rad	18	9	7	2	28	10	32
Napredak	18	10	4	4	23	16	27
Rudar	18	7	6	5	20	21	27
Radnicki Nis	17	8	4	5	27	12	26
Hajduk Kula	18	8	4	6	22	16	23
Kikinda	18	5	7	6	17	23	20
Sloboda	18	6	2	10	13	22	18
Jastrebac	18	6	3	9	14	16	17
Mogren	18	4	3	11	12	25	17
Sutjeska	17	4	4	9	17	32	16

Top scorer: Milosevic (Partizan) 21
Cup Final: Partizan Belgrade 3,6, Spartak Subotica 2,1

New provisional members of FIFA: Azerbaijan, Macedonia, Moldova.

SOUTH AMERICA

ARGENTINA

Asociacion Del Futbol Argentina, Viamonte 1366/76, 1053 Buenos Aires.
Founded: 1893; *Number of Clubs:* 3,035; *Number of Players:* 306,365; *National Colours:* Blue & white shirts, black shorts, white stockings.
Telephone: 40-4276; *Cable:* FUTBOL BUENOS AIRES; *Telex:* 17848 AFA AR; *Fax:* 54-1/3729696.

BRAZIL

Confederacao Brasileira De Futebol, Rua Da Alfandega, 70, P.O. Box 1078, 20.070 Rio De Janeiro.
Founded: 1914; *Number of Clubs:* 12,987; *Number of Players:* 551,358; *National Colours:* Yellow shirts, blue shorts, white stockings, green trim.
Telephone: 221/5937; *Cable:* DESPORTOS RIO DE JANEIRO; *Telex:* 2121509 CBDS BR; *Fax:* (021) 252 9294.

BOLIVIA

Federacion Boliviana De Futbol, Av. 16 De Julio No. N. 0782, Casilla Postal No. 474, Cochabamba.
Founded: 1925; *Number of Clubs:* 305; *Number of Players:* 15,290; *National Colours:* Green shirts, white shorts, green stockings.
Telephone: 59142/55895, 55896; *Cable:* FEDFUTBOL COCHABAMBA; *Telex:* 6239 FEDBOL; *Fax:* 54-1/3729696.

CHILE

Federacion De Futbol De Chile, Calle Erasmo Escala No. 1822, Casilla No. 3733, Santiago De Chile.
Founded: 1895; *Number of Clubs:* 4,598; *Number of Players:* 609,724; *National Colours:* Red shirts, blue shorts, white stockings.
Telephone: 696 5381; *Cable:* FEDFUTBOL SANTIAGO DE CHILE; *Telex:* 440474 FEBOL CZ; *Fax:* 698 7082.

COLOMBIA

Presidencia: Federacion Colombiana De Futbol, Calle 20 Norte No. 4 N-56, Barrio Versalles, Cali.
Founded: 1925; *Number of Clubs:* 3,685; *Number of Players:* 188,050; *National Colours:* Red shirts, blue shorts, tricolour stockings.
Telephone: 923/614 697 and 616 258; *Fax:* 923/689 599.

ECUADOR

Federacion Ecuatoriana De Futbol, Calle Jose Mascote 1.103 (Piso 2), Luque, Casilla 7447, Guayaquil.
Founded: 1925; *Number of Clubs:* 170; *Number of Players:* 15,700; *National Colours:* Yellow shirts, blue shorts, red stockings.
Telephone: 37 16 74; *Cable:* ECUAFUTBOL GUAYAQUIL; *Telex:* 42970 FEECFU ED; *Fax:* (593-4) 373-320.

PARAGUAY

Liga Paraguaya De Futbol, Estadio De Sajonia, Calles Mayor Martinez Y Alejo Garcia, Asuncion.
Founded: 1906; *Number of Clubs:* 1,500; *Number of Players:* 140,000; *National Colours:* Red & white shirts, blue shorts, blue stockings.
Telephone: 81743; *Telex:* 627 PY FUTBOL; *Fax:* 595 21 81743.

PERU

Federacion Peruana De Futbol, Estadio Nacional/Puerto No. 4, Calle Jose Diaz, Lima.
Founded: 1922; *Number of Clubs:* 10,000; *Number of Players:* 325,650; *National Colours:* White shirts, red trim, white shorts, white stockings.
Telephone: 32 05 17; *Cable* FEPEFUTBOL LIMA; *Telex:* 20066 FEPEFUT PE.

URUGUAY

Asociacion Uruguaya De Futbol, Guayabo 1531, Montevideo.
Founded: 1900; *Number of Clubs:* 1,091; *Number of Players:* 134,310; *National Colours:* Light blue shirts, black shorts, black stockings.
Telephone: 40 71 01/06; *Cable:* FUTBOL MONTEVIDEO; *Telex:* AUF UY 22607.

VENEZUELA

Federacion Venezolana De Futbol, Avda Este Estadio Nacional, El Paraiso Apdo. Postal 14160, Candelaria, Caracas.
Founded: 1926; *Number of Clubs:* 1,753; *Number of Players:* 63,175; *National Colours:* Magenta shirts, white shorts, white stockings.
Telephone: 461 80 10; *Cable:* FEVEFUTBOL CARACAS; *Telex:* 26 140 FVFCS VC.

ASIA

AFGHANISTAN

The Football Federation of National Olympic Committee, Kabul.
Founded: 1922; *Number of Clubs:* 30; *Number of Players:* 3,300; *National Colours:* White shirts, white shorts, white stockings.
Telephone: 20579; *Cable:* OLYMPIC KABUL.

BAHRAIN

Bahrain Football Association, P.O. Box 5464, Bahrain.
Founded: 1951; *Number of Clubs:* 25; *Number of Players:* 2,030; *National Colours:* White shirts, red shorts, white stockings.
Telephone: 72 95 63; *Cable:* BAHKORA BAHRAIN; *Telex:* 9040 FAB BN; *Fax:* 729361.

BANGLADESH

Bangladesh Football Federation, Stadium, Dhaka 2.
Founded: 1972; *Number of Clubs:* 1,265; *Number of Players:* 30,385; *National Colours:* Orange shirts, white shorts, green stockings.
Telephone: 23 60 72/23 59 28; *Cable:* FOOTBALFED DHAKA; *Telex:* 642460 BHL BJ. *Fax:* 880–2/86 47 69.

BRUNEI

Brunei Amateur Football Association, P.O. Box 2010, Bandar Seri Begawan 1920, Brunei Darussalam.
Founded: 1959; *Number of Clubs:* 22; *Number of Players:* 830; *National Colours:* Gold shirts, black shorts, gold stockings.
Telephone: 673-02-24 22 83, 24 31 71; *Cable:* BAFA BRUNEI; *Telex:* dirwyas BU 2575 Attn: BAFA; *Fax:* 673-02-24 23 00.

BURMA (now Myanmar)

Myanmar Football Federation, Aung San Memorial Stadium, Kandawgalay Post Office, Yangon.
Founded: 1947; *Number of Clubs:* 600; *Number of Players:* 21,000; *National Colours:* Red shirts, white shorts, red stockings.
Telephone: 75 249; *Cable:* YANGON MYANMAR; *Telex:* 21218 BRCROS BRN.

CHINA PR

Football Association of The People's Republic of China, 9 Tiyuguan Road, Beijing.
Founded: 1924; *Number of Clubs:* 1,045; *Number of Players:* 2,250,000; *National Colours:* Red shirts, white shorts, red stockings.
Telephone: 01/701 70 18; *Cable:* SPORTSCHINE BEIJING; *Telex:* 22034 ACSF CN; *Fax:* 01/511 25 33.

HONG KONG

The Hong Kong Football Association Ltd, 55 Fat Kwong Street, Homantin, Kowloon, Hong Kong.
Founded: 1914; *Number of Clubs:* 69; *Number of Players:* 3,274; *National Colours:* Red shirts, white shorts, red stockings.
Telephone: 3-712 9122-5; *Cable:* FOOTBALL HONG KONG; *Telex:* 40518 FAHKG HX; *Fax:* 3-760 4303.

INDIA

All India Football Federation, Netaji Indoor Stadium, Eden Gardens, Calcutta 700 021.
Founded: 1937; *Number of Clubs:* 2,000; *Number of Players:* 56,000; *National Colours:* Light blue shirts, white shorts, dark blue stockings.
Telephone: 91-497/500199; *Cable:* SOCCER CALCUTTA; *Telex:* 212216 MCPL IN.

INDONESIA

All Indonesia Football Federation, Main Stadium Senayan, Gate VII, P.O. Box 2305, Jakarta.
Founded: 1930; *Number of Clubs:* 2,880; *Number of Players:* 97,000; *National Colours:* Red shirts, white shorts, red stockings.
Telephone: 581541/584386; *Cable:* PSSI JAKARTA; *Telex:* 65739 as; *Fax:* (021) 584386.

IRAN

Football Federation of The Islamic Republic of Iran, Ave Varzandeh No. 10, P.O. Box 11/1642, Tehran.
Founded: 1920; *Number of Clubs:* 6,326; *Number of Players:* 306,000; *National Colours:* Green shirts, white shorts, red stockings.
Telephone: (021) 825534; *Cable:* FOOTBALL IRAN _ TEHRAN; *Telex:* 212691 VARZ IR.

IRAQ

Iraqi Football Association, Youth City, P.O. Box 484, Baghdad.
Founded: 1948; *Number of Clubs:* 155; *Number of Players:* 4,400; *National Colours:* White shirts, white shorts, white stockings.
Telephone: 772 8430; *Cable:* BALL BAGHDAD; *Telex:* 214074 IRFA IK; *Fax:* 772 84 24.

JAPAN

The Football Association of Japan, 2nd Floor, Gotoh Ikueikai Bldg, 1-10-7 Dogenzaka, Shibuya-Ku, Tokyo 150, Japan.
Founded: 1921; *Number of Clubs:* 13,047; *Number of Players:* 358,989; *National Colours:* Blue shirts, white shorts, blue stockings.
Telephone: 81-3-3476-2011; *Cable:* SOCCERJAPAN TOKYO; *Telex:* 2422975 FOTJPN J; *Fax:* 81 3 3476 2291.

JORDAN

Jordan Football Association, P.O. Box 1954, Amman.
Founded: 1949; *Number of Clubs:* 98; *Number of Players:* 4,305; *National Colours:* White shirts, white shorts, white stockings.
Telephone: 009626-62 4481, or 62 59 93; *Cable:* JORDAN FOOTBALL ASSOCIATION AM; *Telex:* 22415 FOBALL JO. *Fax:* 009626-62 4454.

KAMPUCHEA

Federation Khmere De Football Association, C.P. 101, Complex Sportif National, Phnom-Penh.
Founded: 1933; *Number of Clubs:* 30; *Number of Players:* 650; *National Colours:* Red shirts, white shorts, red stockings.
Telephone: 22 469; *Cable:* FKFA PHNOMPENH.

KOREA, NORTH

Football Association of The Democratic People's Rep. of Korea, Munsin-Dong 2, Dongdaewon Distr, Pyongyang.
Founded: 1928; *Number of Clubs:* 90; *Number of Players:* 3,420; *National Colours:* Red shirts, white shorts, red stockings.
Telephone: 6-3998; *Cable:* DPR KOREA FOOTBALL PYONGYANG; *Telex:* 5472 KP; *Fax:* 850-2/81 4 4 03.

KOREA, SOUTH

Korea Football Association, 110-39, Kyeonji-Dong, Chongro-Ku, Seoul.
Founded: 1928; *Number of Clubs:* 476; *Number of Players:* 2,047; *National Colours:* Red shirts, red shorts, red stockings.
Telephone: 02-733-6764; *Cable:* FOOTBALLKOREA SEOUL; *Telex:* KFASEL K 25373; *Fax:* 02 735 2755.

KUWAIT

Kuwait Football Association, Udailiyya, BL. 4, Al-Ittihad St, P.O. Box 2029 (Safat), 13021 Safat.
Founded: 1952; *Number of Clubs:* 14 (senior); *Number of Players:* 1,526; *National Colours:* Blue shirts, white shorts, blue stockings.
Telephone: 00965/255 58 51 or 255 58 39; *Cable:* FOOTKUWAIT; *Telex:* FOOTKUW 22600 KT; *Fax:* 00965/256 37 37.

LAOS

Federation De Foot-Ball Lao, c/o Dir. Des Sports, Education, Physique Et Artistique, Vientiane.
Founded: 1951; *Number of Clubs:* 76; *Number of Players:* 2,060; *National Colours:* Red shirts, white shorts, blue stockings.
Telephone: 27 41; *Cable:* FOOTBALL VIENTIANE.

LEBANON

Federation Libanaise De Football Association, P.O. Box 4732, Omar Ibn Khattab Street, Beirut.
Founded: 1933; *Number of Clubs:* 105; *Number of Players:* 8,125; *National Colours:* Red shirts, white shorts, red stockings.
Telephone: (1) 30 07 60; *Cable:* FOOTBALL BEIRUT; *Telex:* 23001 ALABAL.

MACAO

Associacao De Futebol De Macau (AFM), P.O. Box 920, Macau.
Founded: 1939; *Number of Clubs:* 52; *Number of Players:* 800; *National Colours:* Green shirts, white shorts, green and white stockings.
Telephone: 71 996 (559315); *Cable:* FOOTBALL MACAU.

MALDIVES REPUBLIC

Football Association of Maldives, Attn. Mr. Bandhu Ahamed Saleem, Sports Division, Male.
Founded: 1986; *Number of Clubs: Number of Players: National Colours:* Green shirts, white shorts, green and white stockings.
Telephone: 3432; *Telex:* 77039 MINHOM MF; *Fax:* (960) 32 47 39.

MALAYSIA

Football Association of Malaysia, Wisma Fam, Tingkat 4, Jalan SS5A/9, Kelana Jaya, 47301 Petaling, Jaya Selangor.
Founded: 1933; *Number of Clubs:* 450; *Number of Players:* 11,250; *National Colours:* Black and gold shirts, white shorts, black and gold stockings.
Telephone: 03-776 3766; *Cable:* FOOTBALL PETALING JAYA SELANGO; *Telex:* FAM PJ MA 36701; *Fax:* 03-775 7984.

NEPAL

All-Nepal Football Association, Dasharath Rangashala, Tripureshwor, Kathmandu.
Founded: 1951; *Number of Clubs:* 85; *Number of Players:* 2,550; *National Colours:* Red shirts, blue shorts, blue and white stockings.
Telephone: 2-15 703; *Cable:* ANFA KATHMANDU; *Telex:* 2390 NSC NP.

OMAN

Oman Football Association, P.O. Box 6462, Ruwi-Muscat.
Founded: 1978; *Number of Clubs:* 47; *Number of Players:* 2,340; *National Colours:* White shirts, red shorts, white stockings.
Telephone: 70 78 85; *Cable:* FOOTBALL MUSCAT; *Telex:* 3760 FOOTBALL ON; *Fax:* 707829.

PAKISTAN

Pakistan Football Federation, General Secretary, 43 Rettigon Road, Lahore, Pakistan.
Founded: 1948; *Number of Clubs:* 882; *Number of Players:* 21,000; *National Colours:* Green shirts, white shorts, green stockings.
Telephone: 92 42/210638, 7242858; *Cable:* FOOTBALL-QUETTA; *Telex:* 47643 PFF PK; *Fax:* 92 42/7237297.

PHILIPPINES

Philippine Football Federation, Room 207, Administration Building, Rizal Memorial Sports Complex, Vito Cruz, Metro Manila.
Founded: 1907; *Number of Clubs:* 650; *Number of Players:* 45,000; *National Colours:* Blue shirts, white shorts, blue stockings.
Telephone: 58 83 17; *Cable:* FOOTBALL MANILA; Telex: 63539 ANSCOR PN.

QATAR

Qatar Football Association, P.O. Box 5333, Doha.
Founded: 1960; *Number of Clubs:* 8 (senior); *Number of Players:* 1,380; *National Colours:* White shirts, maroon shorts, white stockings.
Telephone: 351641, 454444; *Cable:* FOOTQATAR DOHA; *Telex:* 47 49 QATFOT DH; *Fax:* (0974) 411660.

SAUDI ARABIA

Saudi Arabian Football Federation, Al Mather Quarter (Olympic Complex), P.O. Box 5844, Riyadh 11432.
Founded: 1959; *Number of Clubs:* 120; *Number of Players:* 9,600; *National Colours:* White shirts, white shorts, white stockings.
Telephone: 966-1/482 22 40; *Cable:* KORA RIYADH; *Telex:* 404300 SAFOTB SJ; *Fax:* 966-1/482 12 15.

SINGAPORE

Football Association of Singapore, Jalan Besar Stadium, Tyrwhitt Road, Singapore 0820.
Founded: 1892; *Number of Clubs:* 250; *Number of Players:* 8,000; *National Colours:* Sky blue shirts, sky blue shorts, sky blue stockings.
Telephone: 293 1477; *Cable:* SOCCER SINGAPORE; *Telex:* SINFA RS 37683.

SRI LANKA

Football Federation of Sri Lanka, No. 2, Old Grand Stand, Race Course _ Reid Avenue, Colombo 7.
Founded: 1939; *Number of Clubs:* 600; *Number of Players:* 18,825; *National Colours:* Maroon shirts, white shorts, white stockings.
Telephone: 596179; *Cable:* SOCCER COLOMBO; *Telex:* 21537 METALIX CE; *Fax:* 94-1-580721.

SYRIA

Association Arabe Syrienne De Football, General Sport Fed. Building, October Stadium, Damascus, Baremke.
Founded: 1936; *Number of Clubs:* 102; *Number of Players:* 30,600; *National Colours:* White shirts, white shorts, white stockings.
Telephone: 33 15 11; *Cable:* FOOTBALL DAMASCUS; *Telex:* HOTECH 41 19 35.

THAILAND

The Football Association of Thailand, c/o National Stadium, Rama I Road, Bangkok.
Founded: 1916; *Number of Clubs:* 168; *Number of Players:* 15,000; *National Colours:* Crimson shirts, white shorts, crimson stockings.
Telephone: 02 214 1058; *Cable:* FOOTBALL BANGKOK; *Telex:* 20211 FAT TH; *Fax:* 2154494.

UNITED ARAB EMIRATES

United Arab Emirates Football Association, Post Box 5458, Dubai.
Founded: 1971; *Number of Clubs:* 23 (senior); *Number of Players:* 1,787; *National Colours:* White shirts, white shorts, white stockings.
Telephone: 245 636; *Cable:* FOOTBALL EMIRATES DUBAI; *Telex:* 47623 UAEFA EM; *Fax:* 245 559.

VIETNAM

Association De Football De La Republique Du Viet-Nam, No. 36, Boulevard Tran-Phu, Hanoi. *Founded:* 1962; *Number of Clubs:* 55 (senior); *Number of Players:* 16,000; *National Colours:* Red shirts, white shorts, red stockings.
Telephone: 5/48 67; *Cable:* AFBVN, 36, TRAN-PHU-HANOI.

YEMEN

Yemen Football Association, P.O. Box 908, Sana'a.
Founded: 1962; *Number of Clubs:* 26; *Number of Players:* 1750; *National Colours:* Green.
Telephone: 00967/2/215720. *Telex:* 2710 YOUTH YE
Provisional members: Kazakhstan, Kyrgystan, Tajikistan, Turkmenistan, Uzbekistan.

CONCACAF

ANTIGUA

The Antigua Football Association, P.O. Box 773, St. Johns.
Founded: 1928; *Number of Clubs:* 60; *Number of Players:* 1,008; *National Colours:* Gold shirts, black shorts, black stockings.
Telephone: 809 462 3945; *Cable:* AFA ANTIGUA; *Telex:* 2177 SIDAN AK; *Fax:* 809 462 2649.

BAHAMAS

Bahamas Football Association, P.O. Box N 8434, Nassau, N.P.
Founded: 1967; *Number of Clubs:* 14; *Number of Players:* 700; *National Colours:* Yellow shirts, black shorts, yellow stockings.
Telephone: 809 32 47099; *Cable:* BAHSOCA NASSAU; *Fax:* 809 324 6484.

BARBADOS

Barbados Football Association, P.O. Box 833E, Bridgetown.
Founded: 1910; *Number of Clubs:* 92; *Number of Players:* 1,100; *National Colours;* Royal blue shirts, gold shorts, royal blue stockings.
Telphone: 809 424 4413; *Cable:* FOOTBALL BRIDGE-TOWN; *Telex:* 2306 SHAMROCK WB; *Fax:* (809) 436 0130.

BELIZE

Belize National Football Association, P.O. Box 1742, Belize City.
Founded: 1986; *National Colours:* Blue shirts, red & white trim, white shorts, blue stockings.
Telephone: 08-2609 or 08 2637; 02 77031 32; 08-2200; *Telex:* 102 FOREIGN BZ.

BERMUDA

The Bermuda Football Association, P.O. Box HM 745, Hamilton 5 HM CX.
Founded: 1928; *Number of Clubs:* 30; *Number of Players:* 1,947; *National Colours:* Blue shirts, white shorts, white stockings.
Telephone: (809) 295 2199; *Cable:* FOOTBALL BERMUDA; *Telex:* 3441 BFA BA; *Fax:* (809) 295 0773.

CANADA

The Canadian Soccer Association, 1600 James Naismith Drive, Gloucester, Ont. K1B 5N4.
Founded: 1912; *Number of Clubs:* 1,600; *Number of Players:* 224,290; *National Colours:* Red shirts, red shorts, red stockings.
Telephone: (613) 748-5667; *Cable:* SOCCANADA OTTAWA; *Telex:* 053-3350; *Fax:* (613) 745-1938.

CAYMAN ISLANDS

Cayman Islands Football Association, PO Box 178, Georgetown, Grand Cayman, Cayman Islands W1.
Number of Clubs: 25; *Number of Players:* 875.
Telephone: 809–949 4733, 809–949 8228. *Fax:* 809–949 8738.

COSTA RICA

Federacion Costarricense De Futbol, Calle 40-Ave, CTLI, San Jose.
Founded: 1921; *Number of Clubs:* 431; *Number of Players:* 12,429; *National Colours:* Red shirts, blue shorts, white stockings.
Telephone: 506-2/221544; *Cable:* FEDEFUTBOL SAN JOSE; *Telex:* 3394 DIDER CR; Fax: 506-2/552674.

CUBA

Asociacion De Futbol De Cuba, c/o Comite Olimpico Cubano, Calle 13 No. 601, Esq. C. Vedado, La Habana, ZP 4.
Founded: 1924; *Number of Clubs:* 70; *Number of Players:* 12,900; *National Colours:* White shirts, blue shorts, white stockings.
Telephone: 40 35 81; *Cable:* FOOTBALL HABANA; *Telex:* 511332 INDER CU.

DOMINICAN REPUBLIC

Federacion Dominicana de Futbol, Apartado De Correos No. 1953, Santo Domingo.
Founded: 1953; *Number of Clubs:* 128; *Number of Players:* 10,706; *National Colours:* Blue shirts, white shorts, red stockings.
Telephone: 542-6923. *Cable:* FEDOFUTBOL SANTO DOMINGO.

EL SALVADOR

Federacion Salvadorena De Futbol, Av. Jm. Delgado, Col. Escalon, Centro Espanol, Apartado 1029, San Salvador.
Founded: 1936; *Number of Clubs:* 944; *Number of Players:* 21,294; *National Colours:* Blue shirts, blue shorts, blue stockings.
Telephone: 23 73 62; *Cable:* FESFUT SAN SALVADOR; *Telex:* 20484 FESFUT SAL.

GRENADA

Grenada Football Association, P.O. Box 326, St. Juilles Street St. George's.
Founded: 1924; *Number of Clubs:* 15; *Number of Players:* 200; *National Colours:* Green & yellow shirts, red shorts, green & yellow stockings.
Telephone: 1-809/440 1986; *Cable:* GRENBALL GRENADA; *Telex:* 3431 CW BUR; *Fax:* 1-809/440 1986.

GUATEMALA

Federacion Nacional De Futbol De Guatemala C.A., Apartado Postal No. 1809, Guatemala C.A.
Founded: 1933; *Number of Clubs:* 1,611; *Number of Players:* 43,516; *National Colours:* White/blue diagonal striped shirts, blue shorts, white stockings.
Telephone: 362211; *Cable:* FEDFUTBOL GUATEMALA.

GUYANA

Guyana Football Association, P.O. Box 10727 Georgetown.
Founded: 1902; *Number of Clubs:* 103; *Number of Players:* 1,665; *National Colours:* Green & yellow shirts, black shorts, white & green stockings.
Telephone: 02-59458/9; *Cable:* FOOTBALL GUYANA; *Telex:* 2266 RICEBRD GY; *Fax:* (005922) 52169.

HAITI

Federation Haitienne De Football, Stade Sylvio-Cator, Port-Au-Prince.
Founded: 1904; *Number of Clubs:* 40; *Number of Players:* 4,000; *National Colours:* Red shirts, black shorts, red stockings.
Telephone: 2/3237; *Cable:* FEDHAFOOB PORT-AU-PRINCE.

HONDURAS

Federacion Nacional Autonoma De Futbol De Honduras, Apartado Postal 827, Costa Oeste Del Est. Nac, Tegucigalpa, De. C.
Founded: 1951; *Number of Clubs:* 1,050; *Number of Players:* 15,300; *National Colours:* Blue shirts, blue shorts, blue stockings.
Telephone: 32-1897; *Cable* FENAFUTH TEGUCIGALPA; *Telex:* 1209 FENEFUTH; *Fax:* 31 14 28.

JAMAICA

Jamaica Football Federation, Room 9, National Stadium, Kingston 6.
Founded: 1910; *Number of Clubs:* 266; *Number of Players:* 45,200; *National Colours:* Green shirts, black shorts, green & gold stockings.
Cable: FOOTBALL JAMAICA KINGSTON.

MEXICO

Federacion Mexicana De Futbol Asociacion, A.C., Abraham Gonzales 74, C.P. 06600, Col. Juarez, Mexico 6, D.F.
Founded: 1927; *Number of Clubs:* 77 (senior); *Number of Players:* 1,402,270; *National Colours:* Green shirts, white shorts, green stockings.
Telephone: 566 21 55; *Cable:* MEXFUTBOL MEXICO; *Telex:* 1771678 MSUTME; *Fax:* (915) 566 7580.

NETHERLANDS ANTILLES

Nederlands Antiliaanse Voetbal Unie, P.O. Box 341, Curacao, N.A.
Founded: 1921; *Number of Clubs:* 85; *Number of Players:* 4,500; *National Colours:* white shirts, white shorts, red stockings.
Telephone:Cable: NAVU CURACAO; *Telex:* 1046 ENNIA NA; *Fax:* (599-9) 611173.

NICARAGUA

Federacion Nicaraguense De Futbol, Inst. Nicaraguense De Deportes, Apartado Postal 976 0 383, Managua.
Founded: 1968; *Number of Clubs:* 31; *Number of Players:* 160 (senior); *National Colours:* Blue shirts, blue shorts, blue stockings.
Telephone: 505 2/66 41 34; *Cable:* FEDEFOOT MANAGUA; *Telex:* 2156 IND NK.

PANAMA

Federacion Nacional De Futbol De Panama, Apdo 1436, Balboa, Ancon., Panama.
Founded: 1937; *Number of Clubs:* 65; *Number of Players:* 4,225; *National Colours:* Red & white shirts, blue shorts, red stockings.
Telephone: 27–0454, 27–0448; *Cable:* PANAOLIMPIC PANAMA; *Telex:* 2534 INDE PG; *Fax:* 27–0460.

PUERTO RICO

Federacion Puertorriquena De Futbol, Coliseo Roberto Clemente, P.O. Box 4355, Hato Rey, 00919-4355.
Founded: 1940; *Number of Clubs:* 175; *Number of Players:* 4,200; *National Colurs:* White & red shirts, blue shorts, white & blue stockings.
Telephone: 766 1461; *Cable:* BORIKENFPF; *Telex:* 3450296; *Fax:* 8660489, 764-2025.

ST KITTS AND NEVIS

St Kitts and Nevis Football Association, P.O. Box 465, Basseterre, St Kitts, West Indies.
Number of Clubs: 36; *Number of Players:* 600.
Telephone: 809–465 2521, 809–465 4086; *Fax:* 809–465 550/1042.

SURINAM

Surinaamse Voetbal Bond, Cultuuruinlaan 7, P.O. Box 1223, Paramaribo.
Founded: 1920; *Number of Clubs:* 168; *Number of Players:* 4,430; *National Colours:* Red shirts, white shorts, white stockings.
Telephone: 73112; *Cable:* SVB Paramaribo.

TRINIDAD AND TOBAGO

Trinidad & Tobago Football Association, Cor. Duke & Scott-Bushe Street, Port of Spain, Trinidad, P.O. Box 400.
Founded: 1906; *Number of Clubs:* 124; *Number of Players:* 5,050; *National Colours:* Red shirts, black shorts, red stockings.
Telephone: 624 5183. *Cable:* TRAFA PORT OF SPAIN; *Telex:* 22652 TRAFA; *Fax:* 627-7661.

USA

United States Soccer Federation, 1750 East Boulder Street, Colorado Springs, CO 80909.
Founded: 1913; *Number of Clubs:* 7,000; *Number of Players:* 1,411,500; *National Colours:* White shirts, blue shorts, red stockings.
Telephone: (719) 578-4678; *Cable:* SOCCERUSA COLORADOSPRINGS; *Telex:* 450024 US SOCCER FED; *Fax:* (719) 578-4636.
Recent additions; ARUBA, SANTA LUCIA, ST. VINCENT and the GRENADINES.
New provisional member of FIFA: Dominica.

OCEANIA

AUSTRALIA

Australian Soccer Federation, First Floor, 2325 Frederick Street, Rockdale, NSW 2216.
Founded: 1961; *Number of Clubs:* 6,816; *Number of Players:* 433,957; *National Colours:* Gold shirts, green shorts, white stockings.
Telephone: 29 7026; *Cable:* FOOTBALL SYDNEY; *Telex:* AA 170512; *Fax:* 02 296 556.

FIJI

Fiji Football Association, Mr. J.D. Maharaj, Hon. Secretary Government Bldgs, P.O.B. 2514 Suva.
Founded: 1946; *Number of Clubs;* 140: *Number of Players:* 21,300; *National Colours:* White shirts, black shorts, black stockings.
Telephone: 300453; *Cable:* FOOTSOCCER SUVA; *Telex:* 2366 FJ; *Fax:* 304642.

NEW ZEALAND

New Zealand Football Association, Inc., P.O. Box 62-532, Central Park, Green Lane, Auckland 6.
Founded: 1891; *Number of Clubs:* 312; *Number of Players:* 52,969; *National Colours:* White shirts, black shorts, white stockings.
Telephone: 0-9-525-6120; *Fax:* 0-9-525-6123.

PAPUA-NEW-GUINEA

Papua New Guinea Football (Soccer) Association Inc., P.O. Box 1716, Boroko.
Founded: 1962; *Number of Clubs:* 350; *Number of Players:* 8,250; *National Colours:* Red shirts, black shorts, red stockings.
Telephone: 25 41 09; *Telex:* TOTOTRA NE 23436.

WESTERN SAMOA

Western Samoa Football (Soccer) Association, Min. of Youth, Sports Culture, Private Bag, Apia.
Founded: 1986; *National Colours:* Blue shirts, white shorts, blue and white stockings.
Telephone: 23315; *Telex:* 230 SAMGAMES SX.
Recent additions: SOLOMON ISLANDS, TAHITI and VANUATU. The Solomon Islands are situated in the South Pacific to the south-east of Papua New Guinea. There are 4,000 registered players. Vanuatu was formerly known as the New Hebrides and is a double chain of islands to the south-east of the Solomons. *Colours:* Gold and black.
New provisional members of FIFA: Cook Islands, Tonga.

AFRICA

ALGERIA

Federation Algerienne De Futbol, Route Ahmed Ouaked, Boite Postale No. 39, Alger _ Dely Ibrahim.
Founded: 1962; *Number of Clubs:* 780; *Number of Players:* 58,567; *National Colours:* Green shirts, white shorts, red stockings.
Telephone: 213/365 947 and 365 948; *Cable:* FAFOOT ALGER; *Telex:* 61378. *Fax:* 213/366 181.

ANGOLA

Federation Angolaise De Football, B.P. 3449, Luanda.
Founded: 1977; *Number of Clubs:* 276; *Number of Players:* 4,269; *National Colours:* Red shirts, black shorts, red stockings.
Telephone: 338635/338233; *Cable:* FUTANGOLA; *Telex:* 4072 CIAM AN.

BENIN

Federation Beninoise De Football, B.P. 965, Cotonou.
Founded: 1968; *Number of Clubs:* 117; *Number of Players:* 6,700; *National Colours:* Green shirts, green shorts, green stockings.
Telephone: 33 05 37; *Cable:* FEBEFOOT COTONOU;K-*Telex:* 5033 BIMEX COTONOU; *Fax:* 30 02 14.

BOTSWANA

Botswana Football Association, P.O. Box 1396, Gabarone.
Founded: 1976; *National Colours:* Sky blue shirts, white shorts, sky blue stockings. *Cable:* BOTSBALL GABARONE; *Telex:* 2977 BD; *Fax:* (267) 372 911.

BURKINA FASO

Federation Burkinabe De Foot-Ball, B.P. 57, Ouagadougou.
Founded: 1960; *Number of Clubs:* 57; *Number of Players:* 4,672; *National Colours:* Black shirts, white shorts, red stockings.
Telephone: 33 58 20; *Cable:* FEDEFOOT OUAGADOUGOU.

BURUNDI

Federation De Football Du Burundi, B.P. 3426, Bujumbura.
Founded: 1948; *Number of Clubs:* 132; *Number of Players:* 3,930; *National Colours:* Red shirts, white shorts, green stockings.
Telephone: 2 3078; *Cable:* FFB BUJA.

CAMEROON

Federation Camerounaise De Football, B.P. 1116, Yaounde.
Founded: 1960; *Number of Clubs:* 200; *Number of Players:* 9,328; *National Colours:* Green shirts, red shorts, yellow stockings.
Telephone: 22 25 38; *Cable:* FECAFOOT YAOUNDE; *Telex:* JEUNESPO 8568 KNK

CAPE VERDE ISLANDS

Federacao Cabo-Verdiana De Futebol, C.P. 234, PRAIA.
Founded: 1986; *National Colours:* Green shirts, green shorts, green stockings.
Telephone: 611362; *Cable:* FCF-CV; *Telex:* 6030 MICDE-CV.

CENTRAL AFRICAN REPUBLIC

Federation Centrafricaine De Football, B.P. 344, Bangui.
Founded: 1937; *Number of Clubs:* 256; *Number of Players:* 7,200; *National Colours:* Grey & blue shirts, white shorts, red stockings.
Telephone: 2141; *Cable:* FOOTBANGUI BANGUI.

CONGO

Federation Congolaise De Football, B.P. 4041, Brazzaville.
Founded: 1962; *Number of Clubs:* 250; *Number of Players:* 5,940; *National Colours:* Red shirts, red shorts, white stockings.
Telephone: 81 51 01; *Cable:* FECOFOOT BRAZZAVILLE; *Telex:* 5210 KG.

EGYPT

Egyptian Football Association, 5, Shareh Gabalaya, Guezira, Al Borg Post Office, Cairo.
Founded: 1921; *Number of Clubs:* 247; *Number of Players:* 19,735; *National Colours:* Red shirts, white shorts, black stockings.
Telephone: 340 1793; *Cable:* KORA CAIRO; *Telex:* 23504 KORA.

ETHIOPIA

Ethiopia Football Federation, Addis Ababa Stadium, P.O. Box 1080, Addis Ababa.
Founded: 1943; *Number of Clubs:* 767; *Number of Players:* 20,594; *National Colours:* Green shirts, yellow shorts, red stockings.
Telephone: 51 44 53 and 51 43 21. *Cable:* FOOTBALL ADDIS ABABA; *Telex:* 21377 NESCO ET.

GABON

Federation Gabonaise De Football, B.P. 181, Libreville.
Founded: 1962; *Number of Clubs:* 320; *Number of Players:* 10,000; *National Colours:* Blue shirts, white shorts, white stockings.
Telephone: 72 22 37; *Cable:* FEGAFOOT LIBREVILLE; *Telex:* 5642 GO.

GAMBIA

Gambia Football Association, P.O. Box 523, Banjul.
Founded: 1952; *Number of Clubs:* 30; *Number of Players:* 860; *National Colours:* White & red shirts, white shorts, white stockings.
Telephone: 958 35; *Cable:* SPORTS GAMBIA BANJUL; *Fax:* GNOSC 220/96270.

GHANA

Ghana Football Association, P.O. Box 1272, Accra.
Founded: 1957; *Number of Clubs:* 347; *Number of Players:* 11,275; *National Colours:* White shirts, white shorts, white stockings.
Telephone: 63 924/7; *Cable:* GFA, ACCRA; *Telex:* 2519 SPORTS GH.

GUINEA

Federation Guineenne De Football, P.O. Box 3645, Conakry.
Founded: 1959; *Number of Clubs:* 351; *Number of Players:* 10,000; *National Colours:* Red shirts, yellow shorts, green stockings.
Telephone: 445041; *Cable:* GUINEFOOT CONAKRY; *Telex:* 22302 MJ; Fax: 224/442781.

GUINEA-BISSAU

Federacao De Football Da Guinea-Bissau, Apartado 375, 1035 Bissau-Codex, Rua 4 no 10c.
Founded: 1986; *National Colours: Green shirts, green shorts, green stockings.*
Telephone: 21 25 45; *Cable:* FUTEBOL BISSAU; *Telex:* PAIGC 230 BI.

GUINEA, EQUATORIAL

Federacion Ecuatoguineana De Futbol, Malabo.
Founded: 1986; *National Colours:* All red.
Telephone: 2732; *Cable:* FEGUIFUT/MALABO.

IVORY COAST

Federation Ivoirienne De Football, Stade Felix Houphouet Boigny, B.P. 1202, Abidjan.
Founded: 1960; *Number of Clubs:* 84 (senior); *Number of Players:* 3,655; *National Colours:* Orange shirts, white shorts, green stockings.
Telephone: 22 22 82; *Cable:* FIF ABIDJAN; *Telex:* 22722 FIF CI.

KENYA

Kenya Football Federation, Nyayo National Stadium, P.O. Box 40234, Nairobi.
Founded: 1960; *Number of Clubs:* 351; *Number of Players:* 8,880; *National Colours:* Red shirts, red shorts, red stockings.
Telephone: 340382/339761/9;*Cable:* KEFF NAIROBI; *Telex:* 25784 KFF.

LESOTHO

Lesotho Sports Council, P.O. Box 1879, Maseru Lesotho.
Founded: 1932; *Number of Clubs:* 88; *Number of Players:* 2,076; *National Colours:* Blue shirts, green shorts, white stockings.
Telephone: 311 291 MASERU; *Cable:* LIPAPALI MASERU; *Telex:* 4493.

LIBERIA

The Liberia Football Association, P.O. Box 1066, Monrovia.
Founded: 1962; *National Colours:* Blue & white shirts, white shorts, blue & white stockings.
Telephone: 22 21 77; *Cable:* LIBFOTASS MONROVIA; *Telex:* 44220 EXM LBR. *Fax:* 231–735 003.

LIBYA

Libyan Arab Jamahiriya Football Federation, P.O. Box 5137, Tripoli.
Founded: 1963; *Number of Clubs:* 89; *Number of Players:* 2,941; *National Colours:* Green shirts, white shorts, green stockings.
Telephone: 46 610; *Telex:* 20896 KURATP LY. *Fax:* 218-21/607 016.

MADAGASCAR

Federation Malagasy De Football, c/o Comite Nat. De Coordination De Football, B.P. 4409, Antananarivo 101.
Founded: 1961; *Number of Clubs:* 775; *Number of Players:* 23,536; *National Colours:* Red shirts, white shorts, green stockings.
Telephone: 21373; *Telex:* 22264.

MALAWI

Football Association of Malawi, P.O. Box 865, Blantyre.
Founded: 1966; *Number of Clubs:* 465; *Number of Players:* 12,500; *National Colours:* Red shirts, red shorts, red stockings.
Telephone: 636686; *Cable:* FOOTBALL BLANTYRE; *Telex:* 4526 SPORTS MI. *Fax:* 265/63 69 41.

MALI

Federation Malienne De Football, Stade Mamdou Konate, B.P. 1020, Bamako.
Founded: 1960; *Number of Clubs:* 128; *Number of Players:* 5,480; *National Colours:* Green shirts, yellow shorts, red stockings.
Telephone: 22 41 52; *Cable:* MALIFOOT BAMAKO; Telex: 0985 1200/1202.

MAURITANIA

Federation De Foot-Ball De La Rep. Isl. De Mauritanie, B.P. 566, Nouakshott.
Founded: 1961; *Number of Clubs:* 59; *Number of Players:* 1,930; *National Colours:* Green and yellow shirts, blue shorts, green stockings.
Telephone: 536 09; *Cable:* FOOTRIM NOUAKSHOTT.

MAURITIUS

Mauritius Football Association, Chancery House, 14 Lislet Geoffroy Street, (2nd Floor, Nos. 303.305), Port Louis.
Founded: 1952; *Number of Clubs:* 397; *Number of Players:* 29,375; *National Colours:* Red shirts, white shorts, red stockings.
Telephone: 212 1418, 212 5771; *Cable:* MFA PORT LOUIS; *Telex:* 4427 MSA IW; *Fax:* (230) 208 41 00.

MOROCCO

Federation Royale Marocaine De Football, Av. Ibn Sina, C.N.S. Bellevue, B.P. 51, Rabat.
Founded: 1955; *Number of Clubs:* 350; *Number of Players:* 19,768; *National Colours:* Red shirts, green shorts, red stockings.
Telephone: 67 27 06/08 or 67 26 07; *Cable:* FERMAFOOT RABAT; *Telex:* 32940 FERMFOOT M. *Fax:* 67 10 70

MOZAMBIQUE

Federacao Mocambicana De Futebol, Av. Samora Machel, 11-2, Caixa Postal 1467, Maputo.
Founded: 1978; *Number of Clubs:* 144; *National Colours:* Red shirts, red shorts, red stockings.
Telephone: 26 475; *Cable:* MOCAMBOLA MAPUTO; *Telex:* 6-221/2.

NAMIBIA

Namibia Football Federation, 18 Curt von Francois Str. PO Box 1345, Windhoek 2000; Namibia. *Fax:* 061–22 4454.
Number of Clubs: 244; *Number of Players:* 7320.

NIGER

Federation Nigerienne De Football, Stade National Niamey, B.P. 10299, Niamey.
Founded: 1967; *Number of Clubs:* 64; *Number of Players:* 1,525; *National Colours:* Orange shirts, white shorts, green stockings.
Telephone: 73 31 97; *Cable:* FEDERFOOT NIGER NIAMEY.
Telex: (975) 5527 or 5349. *Fax:* (00227) 73 55 12.

NIGERIA

Nigeria Football Association National Sports Commission, National Stadium, P.O. Box 466, Lagos.
Founded: 1945; *Number of Clubs:* 326; *Number of Players:* 80,190; *National Colours:* Green shirts, white shorts, green stockings.
Telephone: 234-1-83 52 65; *Cable:* FOOTBALL LAGOS; *Telex:* 26570 NFA NG; *Fax:* 63 22 39.

RWANDA

Federation Rwandaise De Foot-Ball Amateur, B.P. 2000, Kigali.
Founded: 1972; *Number of Clubs:* 167; *National Colours:* Red shirts, red shorts, red stockings.
Telephone: 75811 ext. 223; *Cable:* MIJENCOOP KIGALI; *Telex:* 22504 PUBLIC RW; *Fax:* (250) 76574.

SENEGAL

Federation Senegalaise De Football, Stade De L'Amitie, Route De L'Aeroport De Yoff, Dakar.
Founded: 1960; *Number of Clubs:* 75 (senior); *Number of Players:* 3,977; *National Colours:* Green shirts, yellow shorts, red stockings.
Telephone: 25 00 57; *Cable:* SENEFOOT DAKAR.

SEYCHELLES

Seychelles Football Federation, P.O. Box 580, Mont Fleuri, Victoria.
Founded: 1986; *National Colours:* Green shirts, yellow shorts, red stockings.
Telephone: 24 126; *Telex:* 2271 SZ; *Fax:* 23 518.

ST. THOMAS AND PRINCIPE

Federation Santomense De Fut., P.O. Box 42, Sao Tome.
Founded: 1986; *National Colours:* Green shirts, green shorts, green stockings.
Telephone: 22320; *Telex:* 213 PUBLICO STP.

SIERRA LEONE

Sierra Leone Amateur Football Association, S. Stevens Stadium, Brookfields, P.O. Box 672, Freetown.
Founded: 1967; *Number of Clubs:* 104; *Number of Players:* 8,120; *National Colours:* Green shirts, white shorts, blue stockings.
Telephone: 41872; *Cable:* SLAFA FREETOWN; *Telex:* 3210 BOOTH SL.

SOMALIA

Somali Football Federation, Ministry of Sports, C.P. 247, Mogadishu.
Founded: 1951; *Number of Clubs:* 46 (senior); *Number of Players:* 1,150; *National Colours:* Sky blue shirts, white shorts, white stockings.
Telephone: 22 273; *Cable:* SOMALIA FOOTBALL MOGADISHU; *Telex:* 3061 SONOC SM.

SOUTH AFRICA

South African Football Association, First National Bank Stadium, Nasrec; PO Box 910, Johannesburg 2000; South Africa.
Number of Teams: 51,944; *Number of Players:* 1,039,880.
Telephone: 011–494 3522; Fax: 011–494 3447.

SUDAN

Sudan Football Association, P.O. Box 437, Khartoum.
Founded: 1936; *Number of Clubs:* 750; *Number of Players:* 42,200; *National Colours:* White shirts, white shorts, white stockings.
Telephone: 76 633; *Cable:* ALKOURA, KHARTOUM; *Telex:* 23007 KOR SD.

SWAZILAND

National Football Association of Swaziland, P.O. Box 641, Mbabane.
Founded: 1976; *Number of Clubs:* 136; *National Colours:* Blue and gold shirts, white shorts, blue and gold stockings.
Telephone: 46 852; *Telex:* 2245 EXP WD.

TANZANIA

Football Association of Tanzania, P.O. Box 1574, Dar Es Salaam.
Founded: 1930; *Number of Clubs:* 51; *National Colours:* Yellow shirts, yellow shorts, yellow stockings.
Telephone: 32 334; *Cable:* FAT DAR ES SALAAM.

TOGO

Federation Togolaise De Football, C.P. 5, Lome.
Founded: 1960; *Number of Clubs:* 144; *Number of Players:* 4,346; *National Colours:* Red shirts, white shorts, red stockings.

Telephone: 21 26 98; *Cable:* TOGOFOOT LOME; *Telex:* 5015 CNOT TG. *Fax:* (228) 221 314.

TUNISIA

Federation Tunisienne De Football, 20 Rue Bilal, El-Menzah VI, Tunis 1004.
Founded: 1957; *Number of Clubs:* 215; *Number of Players:* 18,300; *National Colours:* Red shirts, white shorts, red stockings.
Telephone: 23 33 03, 23 35 44; *Cable:* FOOTBALL TUNIS; *Telex:* 14783 FTFOOT TN.

UGANDA

Federation of Uganda Football Associations, P.O. Box 10475, Kampala.
Founded: 1924; *Number of Clubs:* 400; *Number of Players:* 1,518; *National Colours:* Yellow shirts, black shorts, yellow stockings.
Telephone: 256 41/25 6021; *Cable:* FUFA KAMPALA; *Telex:* 61272; *Fax:* 256 41/24 55 80.

ZAIRE

Federation Zairoise De Football-Association, Via Agence Zairoise de Presse, Brussels.
Founded: 1919; *Number of Clubs:* 3,800; *Number of Players:* 64,627; *National Colours:* Green shirts, yellow shorts, yellow stockings. *Cable:* FEZAFA KINSHASA; *Telex:* 63915. *Fax:* 87–11/5065 55.

ZAMBIA

Football Association of Zambia, P.O. Box 33474, Lusaka.
Founded: 1929; *Number of Clubs:* 20 (senior); *Number of Players:* 4,100; *National Colours:* Green shirts, white shorts, black stockings.
Telephone: 21 11 45; *Cable:* FOOTBALL LUSAKA; *Telex:* 40204; Fax: 260-1/225046.

ZIMBABWE

Zimbabwe Football Association, P.O. Box 8343, Causeway, Harare.
Founded: 1965; *National Colours:* White shirts, black shorts, black stockings.
Telephone: 514038; *Cable:* SOCCER HARARE; *Telex:* 22299 SOCCER ZW; *Fax:* 793 320.
Other addition: CHAD (readmitted).

EUROPEAN FOOTBALL CHAMPIONSHIP

(formerly EUROPEAN NATIONS' CUP)

Year	*Winners*		*Runners-up*		*Venue*	*Attendance*
1960	USSR	2	Yugoslavia	1	Paris	17,966
1964	Spain	2	USSR	1	Madrid	120,000
1968	Italy	2	Yugoslavia	0	Rome	60,000
	After 1-1 draw					75,000
1972	West Germany	3	USSR	0	Brussels	43,437
1976	Czechoslovakia	2	West Germany	2	Belgrade	45,000
	(*Czechoslovakia won on penalties*)					
1980	West Germany	2	Belgium	1	Rome	47,864
1984	France	2	Spain	0	Paris	48,000
1988	Holland	2	USSR	0	Munich	72,308
1992	Denmark	2	Germany	0	Gothenburg	37,800

OLYMPIC FOOTBALL

Previous medallists

Games	Medallists
1896 Athens*	1 Denmark 2 Greece
1990 Paris*	1 Great Britain 2 France
1904 St Louis**	1 Canada 2 USA
1908 London	1 Great Britain 2 Denmark 3 Holland
1912 Stockholm	1 England 2 Denmark 3 Holland
1920 Antwerp	1 Belgium 2 Spain 3 Holland
1924 Paris	1 Uruguay 2 Switzerland 3 Sweden
1928 Amsterdam	1 Uruguay 2 Argentina 3 Italy
1932 Los Angeles	no tournament
1936 Berlin	1 Italy 2 Austria 3 Norway
1948 London	1 Sweden 2 Yugoslavia 3 Denmark
1952 Helsinki	1 Hungary 2 Yugoslavia 3 Sweden
1956 Melbourne	1 USSR 2 Yugoslavia 3 Bulgaria
1960 Rome	1 Yugoslavia 2 Denmark 3 Hungary
1964 Tokyo	1 Hungary 2 Czechoslovakia 3 East Germany
1968 Mexico City	1 Hungary 2 Bulgaria 3 Japan
1972 Munich	1 Poland 2 Hungary 3 E Germany/USSR
1976 Montreal	1 East Germany 2 Poland 3 USSR
1980 Moscow	1 Czechoslovakia 2 East Germany 3 USSR
1984 Los Angeles	1 France 2 Brazil 3 Yugoslavia
1988 Seoul	1 USSR 2 Brazil 3 West Germany
1992 Barcelona	1 Spain 2 Poland 3 Ghana

* No official tournament
** No official tournament but gold medal later awarded by IOC

EUROPEAN CHAMPIONSHIP 1996

QUALIFYING TOURNAMENT

Group 1
(France, Romania, Poland, Israel, Slovakia, Azerbaijan)

7. 9.94 Slovakia–France
7. 9.94 Romania–Azerbaijan
8.10.94 France–Romania
12.10.94 Israel–Romania
12.10.94 Poland–Azerbaijan
12.11.94 Romania–Slovakia
16.11.94 Poland–France
16.11.94 Azerbaijan–Israel
14.12.94 Azerbaijan–France
14.12.94 Israel–Romania
. 2.95* Israel–Poland
29. 3.95 Romania–Poland
29. 3.95 Israel–France
29. 3.95 Slovakia–Azerbaijan
26. 4.95 France–Slovakia
26. 4.95 Poland–Israel
26. 4.95 Azerbaijan–Romania
7. 6.95 Poland–Slovakia
7. 6.95 Romania–Israel
16. 8.95 France–Poland
16. 8.95 Azerbaijan–Slovakia
6. 9.95 France–Azerbaijan
6. 9.95 Slovakia–Israel
6. 9.95 Poland–Romania
11.10.95 Romania–France
11.10.95 Israel–Azerbaijan
11.10.95 Slovakia–Poland
15.11.95 Slovakia–Romania
15.11.95 Azerbaijan–Poland
15.11.95 France–Israel

Group 2
(Denmark, Spain, Belgium, F.Y.R. Macedonia, Cyprus, Armenia)

7. 9.94 Cyprus–Spain
7. 9.94 F.Y.R. Macedonia–Denmark
7. 9.94 Belgium–Armenia
8.10.94 Armenia–Cyprus
12.10.94 Denmark–Belgium
12.10.94 F.Y.R. Macedonia–Spain
16.11.94 Belgium–F.Y.R. Macedonia
16.11.94 Spain–Denmark
16.11.94 Cyprus–Armenia
17.12.94 Belgium–Spain
17.12.94 F.Y.R. Macedonia–Cyprus
25. 3.95* Armenia–F.Y.R. Macedonia
29. 3.95 Spain–Belgium
29. 3.95 Cyprus–Denmark
26. 4.95 Armenia–Spain
26. 4.95 Belgium–Cyprus
26. 4.95 Denmark–F.Y.R. Macedonia
7. 6.95 Denmark–Cyprus
7. 6.95 F.Y.R. Macedonia–Belgium
7. 6.95 Spain–Armenia
16. 8.95 Armenia–Denmark
6. 9.95 Belgium–Denmark
6. 9.95 Spain–Cyprus
6. 9.95 F.Y.R. Macedonia–Armenia
7.10.95 Armenia–Belgium
11.10.95 Denmark–Spain
11.10.95 Cyprus–F.Y.R. Macedonia
15.11.95 Spain–F.Y.R. Macedonia
15.11.95 Cyprus–Belgium
15.11.95 Denmark–Armenia

Group 3
(Sweden, Switzerland, Hungary, Iceland, Turkey)

7. 9.94 Iceland–Sweden
7. 9.94 Hungary–Turkey
12.10.94 Turkey–Iceland
12.10.94 Switzerland–Sweden
16.11.94 Switzerland–Iceland
16.11.94 Sweden–Hungary
14.12.94 Turkey–Switzerland
29. 3.95 Turkey–Sweden
29. 3.95 Hungary–Switzerland
26. 4.95 Hungary–Sweden
26. 4.95 Switzerland–Turkey
1. 6.95 Sweden–Iceland
11. 6.95* Iceland–Hungary
16. 8.95 Iceland–Switzerland
6. 9.95 Sweden–Switzerland
6. 9.95 Turkey–Hungary
11.10.95 Switzerland–Hungary
11.10.95 Iceland–Turkey
11.11.95 Hungary–Iceland
15.11.95 Sweden–YTurkey

Group 4
(Italy, Ukraine, Croatia, Lithuania, Estonia, Slovenia)

4. 9.94 Estonia–Croatia
7. 9.94 Slovenia–Italy
7. 9.94 Ukraine–Lithuania
9.10.94 Croatia–Lithuania
12.10.94 Estonia–Italy
12.10.94 Ukraine–Slovenia
13.11.94 Ukraine–Estonia
16.11.94 Slovenia–Lithuania
16.11.94 Italy–Croatia
25. 3.95 Italy–Estonia
25. 3.95 Croatia–Ukraine
29. 3.95 Slovenia–Estonia
29. 3.95 Ukraine–Italy
29. 3.95 Lithuania–Croatia
26. 4.95 Lithuania–Italy
26. 4.95 Croatia–Slovenia
26. 4.95 Estonia–Ukraine
7. 6.95 Lithuania–Slovenia
11. 6.95 Estonia–Slovenia
11. 6.95 Ukraine–Croatia
16. 8.95 Estonia–Lithuania
3. 9.95 Croatia–Estonia
6. 9.95 Italy–Slovenia
6. 9.95 Lithuania–Ukraine
8.10.95 Croatia–Italy
11.10.95 Slovenia–Ukraine
11.10.95 Lithuania–Estonia
11.11.95 Italy–Ukraine
15.11.95 Slovenia–Croatia
15.11.95 Italy–Lithuania

Group 5
(Netherlands, Norway, Czech Republic, Belarus, Malta, Luxembourg)

6. 9.94 Czech Republic–Malta
7. 9.94 Luxembourg–Netherlands
7. 9.94 Norway–Belarus
12.10.94 Malta–Czech Republic
12.10.94 Belarus–Luxembourg
12.10.94 Norway–Netherlands
16.11.94 Belarus–Norway
16.11.94 Netherlands–Czech Republic
14.12.94 Malta–Norway
14.12.94 Netherlands–Luxembourg
22. 2.95* Malta–Luxembourg
29. 3.95 Czech Republic–Belarus
29. 3.95 Luxembourg–Norway
29. 3.95 Netherlands–Malta
26. 4.95 Belarus–Malta
26. 4.95 Czech Republic–Netherlands
26. 4.95 Norway–Luxembourg
7. 6.95 Belarus–Netherlands
7. 6.95 Luxembourg–Czech Republic
7.6 6.95 Norway–Malta
16. 8.95 Norway–Czech Republic
6. 9.95 Czech Republic–Norway
6. 9.95 Luxembourg–Malta
6. 9.95 Netherlands–Belarus
7.10.95 Belarus–Czech Republic
8.10.95 Malta–Netherlands
11.10.95 Luxembourg–Belarus
12.11.95 Malta–Belarus
15.11.95 Czech Republic–Luxembourg
15.11.95 Netherlands–Norway

Group 6
(Rep. of Ireland, Portugal, Northern Ireland, Austria, Latvia, Liechtenstein)

20. 4.94* Northern Ireland–Liechtenstein
7. 9.94 Liechtenstein–Austria
7. 9.94 Northern Ireland–Portugal
7. 9.94 Latvia–Rep. of Ireland
9.10.94 Latvia–Portugal
12.10.94 Austria–Northern Ireland
12.10.94 Rep. of Ireland–Liechtenstein
13.11.94 Portugal–Austria
15.11.94 Liechtenstein–Latvia
16.11.94 Northern Ireland–Rep. of Ireland
18.12.94 Portugal–Liechtenstein
29. 3.95 Rep. of Ireland–Northern Ireland
29. 3.95 Austria–Latvia
26. 4.95 Rep. of Ireland–Portugal
26. 4.95 Latvia–Northern Ireland
26. 4.95 Austria–Liechtenstein
3. 6.95* Portugal–Latvia
7. 6.95 Northern Ireland–Latvia
11. 6.95 Rep. of Ireland–Austria
15. 8.95 Liechtenstein–Portugal
16. 8.95 Latvia–Austria
3. 9.95 Portugal–Northern Ireland
6. 9.95 Austria–Rep. of Ireland
6. 9.95 Latvia–Liechtenstein
11.10.95 Rep. of Ireland–Latvia
11.10.95 Austria–Portugal
11.10.95 Liechtenstein–Northern Ireland
15.11.95 Portugal–Rep. of Ireland
15.11.95 Northern Ireland–Austria

continued on page 895

WORLD CUP 1994

Qualifying competition

Europe

Germany qualified as holders

Group 1

Tallinn, 16 August 1992, 3000

Estonia (0) 0

Switzerland (2) 6 *(Chapuisat 23, 68, Bregy 29, Knup 46, Ohrel 66, Sforza 84)*

Estonia: Poom; Hepner, Kaljen, Kallaste T, Lindmaa (Veensalu 78), Kristal, Olumets, Linnumae, Kallaste R, Reim, Pushtov (Kirs 64).
Switzerland: Pascolo; Egli, Geiger, Hottiger, Rothenbuhler, Bregy, Sutter B (Bonvin 79), Ohrel, Sforza, Chapuisat, Knup.

Berne, 9 September 1992, 10,000

Switzerland (1) 3 *(Knup 2, 71, Bregy 81)*

Scotland (1) 1 *(McCoist)*

Switzerland: Pascolo; Hottiger, Quentin, Egli, Geiger, Bregy (Piffaretti 89), Sutter A, Ohrel, Knup (Sutter B 86), Sforza, Chapuisat.
Scotland: Goram; Gough, Malpas, McCall, Boyd (Gallacher 75), McPherson, Durie, McAllister, McCoist, McStay, McClair (Durrant 57).

Cagliari, 14 October 1992, 34,000

Italy (0) 2 *(Roberto Baggio 83, Eranio 89)*

Switzerland (2) 2 *(Ohrel 17, Chapuisat 21)*

Italy: Marchegiani; Tassotti, Di Chiara, Eranio, Costacurta, Lanna, Lentini, Donadoni (Albertini 71), Vialli, Roberto Baggio, Evani (Bianchi 48).
Switzerland: Pascolo; Hottiger, Quentin, Egli, Geiger, Bregy, Sutter A, Ohrel (Piffaretti 56), Knup, Sforza, Chapuisat (Sutter B 89).

Ibrox, 14 October 1992, 22,583

Scotland (0) 0

Portugal (0) 0

Scotland: Goram; Malpas, Boyd, McCall, Whyte, Levein, Gallacher (McClair 33), McStay, McCoist, McAllister, Collins (Durrant 71).
Portugal: Vitor Baia; Joao Pinto I, Helder, Veloso, Fernando Couto, Oceano, Vitor Paneira, Semedo (Figo 53), Domingos, Futre, Andre.

Valletta, 25 October 1992, 8000

Malta (0) 0

Estonia (0) 0

Malta: Cluett; Gregory (Suda 78), Vella S, Galea, Brincat, Buttigieg, Busuttil, Vella R, Zerafa (Saliba 78), Laferla, Sultana.
Estonia: Poom; Kaljend, Hepner, Prins, Kallaste T, Ratnikov, Olumets, Pushtov (Rajala 75), Kirs (Kristal 81), Reim, Kallaste R.

Ibrox, 18 November 1992, 33,029

Scotland (0) 0

Italy (0) 0

Scotland: Goram; McPherson, Malpas, McStay, McLaren, Whyte, Durie (Jess 71), McAllister, McCoist, Durrant (Robertson 88), Boyd.
Italy: Pagliuca; Mannini, Di Chiara (Costacurta 7), Maldini, Baresi, Lentini, Albertini, Eranio, Bianchi, Signori (Donadoni 65), Roberto Baggio.

Berne, 18 November 1992, 14,200

Switzerland (2) 3 *(Bickel 2, Sforza 42, Chapuisat 89)*

Malta (0) 0

Switzerland: Pascolo; Hottiger, Geiger, Egli, Rothenbuhler, Bickel (Bonvin 82), Bregy, Sforza, Sutter A, Knup (Turkyilmaz 75), Chapuisat.
Malta: Cluett; Buttigieg, Buhagiar, Galea (Camilleri E 17), Vella S, Brincat, Gregory, Camilleri J, Saliba, Vella R (Scerri 75), Busuttil.

Valletta, 19 December 1992, 15,000

Malta (0) 1 *(Gregory 85)*

Italy (0) 2 *(Vialli 59, Signori 62)*

Malta: Cluett; Vella S, Buhagiar (Camilleri J 46), Galea, Brincat, Buttigieg, Busuttil, Saliba (Vella R 73), Gregory, Laferla, Scerri.
Italy: Pagliuca; Maldini, Di Chiara (Bianchi 46), Baresi, Costacurta, Eranio, Albertini, Donadoni (Simone 58), Evani, Vialli, Signori.

Valletta, 24 January 1993, 10,000

Malta (0) 0

Portugal (0) 1 *(Rui Aguas 56)*

Malta: Cluett; Vella S, Galea, Brincat, Buhagiar, Buttigieg, Vella R (Suda 75), Busuttil, Gregory, Laferla, Scerri (Degiorgio 65).
Portugal: Vitor Baia; Joao Pinto I, Veloso, Fernando Couto, Helder, Oceano, Vitor Paneira (Joao Pinto II 56), Samedo (Jaime Magalhaes 75), Domingos, Rui Aguas, Figo.

Ibrox, 17 February 1993, 35,490

Scotland (1) 3 *(McCoist 15, 68, Nevin 84)*

Malta (0) 0

Scotland: Goram; McPherson (Robertson 64), Boyd, McStay, McLeish, McLaren, Nevin, McAllister (Ferguson 73), McCoist, Collins, Jess.
Malta: Cluett; Vella S, Buhagiar (Camilleri E 83), Galea, Brincat, Buttigieg, Busuttil, Saliba, Camilleri J, Laferla, Sultana (Vella R 74).

Oporto, 24 February 1993, 70,000

Portugal (0) 1 *(Couto 57)*

Italy (2) 3 *(Roberto Baggio 2, Casiraghi 24, Dino Baggio 75)*

Portugal: Vitor Baia; Joao Pinto I, Helder (Rui Barros 35), Fernando Mendes, Fernando Couto, Oceano, Semedo, Figo, Domingos, Futre, Carlos Xavier (Rui Aguas 46).
Italy: Pagliuca; Tassotti, Maldini, Dino Baggio, Costacurta, Vierchowod, Fuser, Albertini, Casiraghi (Lentini 26), Roberto Baggio (Mancini 85), Signori.

Palermo, 24 March 1993, 35,000

Italy (2) 6 *(Dino Baggio 19, Signori 38, Vierchowod 48, Mancini 59, 89, Maldini 73)*
Malta (0) 1 *(Busuttil 68 (pen))*
Italy: Pagliuca (Marchegiani 80); Porrini, Maldini, Dino Baggio, Vierchowod, Baresi, Fuser, Albertini, Melli, Mancini, Signori.
Malta: Cluett; Vella S, Zerafa, Galea, Saliba, Laferla, Busuttil, Vella R, Gregory (Delia 57), Degiorgio (Suda 73), Scerri.

Berne, 31 March 1993, 31,200

Switzerland (1) 1 *(Chapuisat 39)*
Portugal (1) 1 *(Semedo 44)*
Switzerland: Pascolo; Hottiger, Herr, Geiger, Rothenbuhler, Ohrel, Bregy, Sforza, Sutter A, Knup (Bonvin 46), Chapuisat.
Portugal: Vitor Baia; Peixe, Oceano, Jorge Costa, Semedo (Fernando Mendes 50), Abel Xavier, Rui Costa, Paulo Sousa, Figo (Rui Barros 68), Futre, Rui Aguas.

Trieste, 14 April 1993, 33,000

Italy (1) 2 *(Roberto Baggio 21, Signori 86)*
Estonia (0) 0
Italy: Pagliuca; Porrini (Mannini 46), Di Chiara, Dino Baggio (Di Mauro 68), Vierchowod, Baresi, Fuser, Albertini, Melli, Roberto Baggio, Signori.
Estonia: Poom; Kallaste R, Lemsalu, Prins, Kaljend, Kallaste T, Borisov, Kristal, Reim (Olumets 89), Ratnikov, Pushtov (Rajala 83).

Valletta, 17 April 1993, 8000

Malta (0) 0
Switzerland (1) 2 *(Ohrel 31, Turkyilmaz 89)*
Malta: Cluett; Vella S, Brincat, Galea, Buhagiar, Busuttil, Buttigieg, Camilleri J (Delia 74), Saliba (Carabott 55), Laferla, Scerri.
Switzerland: Pascolo; Hottiger, Herr, Geiger, Rothenbuhler (Sylvestre 50), Henchoz, Sforza, Sutter A, Ohrel, Grassi, Bonvin (Turkyilmaz 60).

Lisbon, 28 April 1993, 28,000

Portugal (2) 5 *(Rui Barros 5, 70, Cadete 45, 72, Futre 67)*
Scotland (0) 0
Portugal: Vitor Baia; Abel Xavier, Jorge Costa, Rui Costa (Veloso 53), Fernando Couto, Oceano, Rui Barros, Paulo Sousa, Semedo, Futre, Cadete (Domingos 81).
Scotland: Goram; Gough, McInally, McPherson, McKimmie, Levein (Nevin 60), McStay, McCall, McCoist, Collins (Durrant 75), Gallacher.

Berne, 1 May 1993, 31,000

Switzerland (0) 1 *(Hottiger 55)*
Italy (0) 0
Switzerland: Pascolo; Hottiger, Geiger, Herr, Quentin, Bregy, Ohrel, Sforza, Sutter A, Knup (Grassi 76), Chapuisat.
Italy: Pagliuca; Mannini, Baresi, Vierchowod, Maldini, Fuser, Zoratto (Lentini 64), Dino Baggio, Signori, Mancini (Di Mauro 46), Roberto Baggio.

Tallinn, 12 May 1993, 14,000

Estonia (0) 0
Malta (1) 1 *(Laferla 16)*
Estonia: Poom; Kallaste R (Bragin 75), Lemsalu, Prins, Kaljend, Kallaste T, Borisov, Kristal, Reim, Ratnikov (Olumets 20), Pushtov.
Malta: Cluett; Vella S, Buhagiar, Saliba, Brincat, Buttigieg, Gregory (Delia 77), Vella R, Carabott (Sultana 46), Laferla, Camilleri J.

Tallinn, 19 May 1993, 5100

Estonia (0) 0
Scotland (1) 3 *(Gallacher 43, Collins 59, Booth 73)*
Estonia: Poom; Kallaste R, Lemsalu, Prins, Kaljend, Kallaste T, Borisov, Kristal (Hepner 46), Reim, Veensalu (Pushtov 76), Bragin.
Scotland: Gunn; Wright (McLaren 80), Boyd, McStay, Hendry, Irvine, Gallacher, Bowman, Robertson (Booth 61), McClair, Collins.

Aberdeen, 2 June 1993, 14,309

Scotland (2) 3 *(McClair 16, Nevin 27, 72 (pen))*
Estonia (0) 1 *(Bragin 57)*
Scotland: Gunn; McLaren (McKimmie 72), Boyd, McStay, Hendry, Irvine, Gallacher, Ferguson (Booth 55), McClair, Collins, Nevin.
Estonia: Poom; Kallaste R, Lemsalu (Bragin 46), Prins, Kaljend, Kallaste T, Borisov, Kristal, Reim, Olumets (Veensalu 73), Rajala.

Oporto, 19 June 1993, 7000

Portugal (3) 4 *(Nogueira 2, Rui Costa 9, Joao Pinto II 23, Cadete 87)*
Malta (0) 0
Portugal: Vitor Baia; Nogueira (Figo 70), Fernando Couto, Oceano, Abel Xavier, Semedo, Paulo Sousa, Rui Costa, Joao Pinto II, Cadete, Domingos (Rui Aguas 46).
Malta: Cluett; Vella S, Buhagiar, Delia, Cauchi, Buttigieg, Saliba, Gregory, Camilleri J (Scerri 66), Laferla, Zerafa (Vella R 41).

Tallinn, 5 September 1993, 2750

Estonia (0) 0
Portugal (0) 2 *(Rui Costa 61, Folha 76)*
Estonia: Poom; Alonen, Prins, Hepner, Kallaste T, Kallaste R, Kristal (Vilderson 72), Bregin, Klavan (Olumets 88), Borisov, Reim.
Portugal: Vitor Baia; Abel Xavier, Fernando Couto, Oceano, Nogueira, Rui Costa (Joao Pinto I 74), Paulo Sousa, Folha, Joao Pinto II, Futre, Cadete (Cesar Brito 72).

Aberdeen, 8 September 1993, 24,000

Scotland (0) 1 *(Collins 50)*
Switzerland (0) 1 *(Bregy 69 (pen))*
Scotland: Gunn; McKimmie, Robertson D, Bowman (O'Donnell 75), Irvine, McAllister, Levein, Collins, Booth (Jess 69), Durie, Nevin.
Switzerland: Pascolo; Quentin, Geiger, Herr, Rothenbuhler (Grassi 61), Bregy (Rueda 87), Sutter A, Ohrel, Sforza, Knup, Chapuisat.

Tallinn, 22 September 1993, 6000

Estonia (0) 0

Italy (1) 3 *(Roberto Baggio 18 (pen), 73, Mancini 59)*

Estonia: Poom; Hepner, Kallaste R, Bragin (Olumets 56), Prins, Alonen, Kallaste T, Borisov, Kristal, Reim, Klavan (Ratnikov 88).
Italy: Pagliuca; Baresi, Benarrivo, Costacurta, Fortunato, Lombardo (Mancini 46), Albertini, Manicone, Eranio, Casiraghi, Roberto Baggio.

Rome, 13 October 1993, 61,178

Italy (2) 3 *(Donadoni 3, Casiraghi 16, Eranio 81)*

Scotland (1) 1 *(Gallacher 16)*

Italy: Pagliuca; Mussi (Lanna 69), Baresi, Costacurta, Benarrivo, Eranio, Dino Baggio, Donadoni, Roberto Baggio, Stroppa (Zola 89), Casiraghi.
Scotland: Gunn; McKimmie, McLaren, Irvine, Boyd, Bowman (McStay 71), Jess (Durrant 46), McAllister, Gallacher, Durie, McCall.

Oporto, 13 October 1993, 48,000

Portugal (1) 1 *(Joao Pinto II 9)*

Switzerland (0) 0

Portugal: Vitor Baia; Joao Pinto I, Jorge Costa, Oceano, Paulo Sousa, Peixe, Semedo (Vitor Paneira 82), Rui Costa, Joao Pinto II, Futre, Cadete (Nogueira 57).
Switzerland: Pascolo; Hottiger, Geiger, Quentin, Herr, Bregy, Sutter A, Ohrel, Sforza, Knup (Grassi 82), Chapuisat.

Lisbon, 10 November 1993, 100,000

Portugal (2) 3 *(Futre 4, Oceano 40 (pen), Rui Aguas 85)*

Estonia (0) 0

Portugal: Vitor Baia; Joao Pinto I, Oceano, Fernando Couto, Nogueira (Folha 75), Paulo Sousa, Rui Barros, Rui Costa (Vitor Paneira 60), Joao Pinto II, Futre, Rui Aguas.
Estonia: Poom; Kallaste R, Prins, Kaljend, Hepner, Ratnikov, Bragin, Borisov, Klavan (Linnumae 70), Rajala (Pushtov 46), Reim.

Milan, 17 November 1993, 71,531

Italy (0) 1 *(Dino Baggio 83)*

Portugal (0) 0

Italy: Pagliuca; Benarrivo, Costacurta, Baresi, Maldini, Stroppa (Albertini 61), Dino Baggio, Signori (Mancini 76), Casiraghi, Donadoni, Roberto Baggio.
Portugal: Vitor Baia; Fernando Couto, Peixe, Jorge Costa, Joao Pinto I (Rui Aguas 76), Rui Costa (Domingos 68), Paulo Sousa, Rui Barros, Veloso, Joao Pinto II, Futre.

Ta Quali, 17 November 1993, 8000

Malta (0) 0

Scotland (1) 2 *(McKinlay 16, Hendry 73)*

Malta: Cluett; Brincat, Galea, Buttigieg, Buhagiar (Saliba 46), Vella S, Busuttil, Spiteri, Laferla, Gregory, Suda (Scerri 68).
Scotland: Leighton; McLaren, Hendry, McKinnon, Irvine, Durrant (Boyd 68), McAllister, McKinlay (Booth 46), Nevin, Ferguson, Gallacher.

Zurich, 17 November 1993, 20,000

Switzerland (3) 4 *(Knup 31, Herr 34, Ohrel 45, Chapuisat 61)*

Estonia (0) 0

Switzerland: Pascolo; Hottiger, Herr, Geiger, Quentin (Turkyilmaz 63), Ohrel (Rueda 46), Bregy, Bickel, Sutter A, Knup, Chapuisat.
Estonia: Poom; Hepner, Kaljend, Prins, Kallaste R, Borisov, Olumets, Bragin, Klavan (Pushtov 78), Reim, Rajala.

Group 1

	P	*W*	*D*	*L*	*F*	*A*	*Pts*
Italy	10	7	2	1	22	7	16
Switzerland	10	6	3	1	23	6	15
Portugal	10	6	2	2	18	5	14
Scotland	10	4	3	3	14	13	11
Malta	10	1	1	8	3	23	3
Estonia	10	0	1	9	1	27	1

Italy and Switzerland qualified

Group 2

Oslo, 9 September 1992, 6511

Norway (4) 10 *(Rekdal 5, 79, Halle 6, 51, 69, Sorloth 15, 21, Nilsen 46, 67, Mykland 74)*

San Marino (0) 0

Norway: Thorstvedt; Pedersen T, Bratseth, Nilsen R, Halle, Mykland, Rekdal, Leonhardsen (Ingebrigtsen 57), Jakobsen JI, Sorloth (Fjortoft 75), Flo.
San Marino: Benedettini; Guerra, Gobbi, Canti, Gennari, Mazza M, Bonini, Francini (Matteoni 70), Manzaroli, Mazza P, Pasolini O (Muccioli B 46).

Oslo, 23 September 1992, 19,998

Norway (1) 2 *(Rekdal 9 (pen), Sorloth 78)*

Holland (1) 1 *(Bergkamp 10)*

Norway: Thorstvedt; Nilsen R, Pedersen T, Bratseth, Bjornebye, Halle (Strandli 60), Mykland, Ingebrigtsen, Rekdal, Sorloth (Flo 81), Jakobsen JI.
Holland: Menzo; Koeman R, Blind, Silooy, De Boer F, Van't Schip (Taument 81), Wouters (Kieft 85), Rijkaard, Rob Witschge, Bergkamp, Van Basten.

Poznan, 23 September 1992, 11,000

Poland (1) 1 *(Waldoch 33)*

Turkey (0) 0

Poland: Bako; Rzepka, Szewczyk, Lesiak, Waldoch, Czachowski, Brzeczek, Warzycha R, Araszkiewicz (Kowalczyk 61), Kosecki (Fedoruk 64), Juskowiak.
Turkey: Hayrettin; Recep (Aykut 74), Bulent, Gokhan, Ogun, Tugay, Hami, Riza, Hakan, Oguz (Mehmet 64), Orhan.

Serravalle, 7 October 1992, 1187

San Marino (0) 0

Norway (2) 2 *(Jakobsen JI 7, Flo 19)*

San Marino: Benedettini; Guerra, Gobbi, Gennari, Bonini, Francini (Muccioli B 84), Manzaroli, Mazza M, Matteoni, Zanotti, Mazza P (Bacciocchi 25).
Norway: Thorstvedt; Bratseth, Nilsen R, Pedersen T, Halle (Bjornebye 46), Jakobsen JI, Leonhardsen (Ingebrigtsen 68), Mykland, Rekdal, Flo, Sorloth.

Wembley, 14 October 1992, 51,441

England (0) 1 *(Platt 55)*

Norway (0) 1 *(Rekdal 76)*

England: Woods; Dixon (Palmer 89), Walker, Adams, Pearce, Batty, Ince, Platt, Gascoigne, Wright I (Merson 69), Shearer.
Norway: Thorstvedt; Nilsen R, Bratseth, Pedersen T (Berg 19), Bjornebye, Halle, Jakobsen JI, Ingebrigtsen, Mykland (Flo 78), Rekdal, Sorloth.

Rotterdam, 14 October 1992, 13,000

Holland (1) 2 *(Van Vossen 43, 46)*

Poland (2) 2 *(Kosecki 18, Kowalczyk 20)*

Holland: Menzo; Van Aerle, Koeman R, Rijkaard (Fraser 80), Jonk, Wouters, Numan (Vanenburg 39), Rob Witschge, Bergkamp, Van Basten, Van Vossen.
Poland: Bako; Lesiak, Szewczyk, Kozminski, Adamczuk, Czachowski (Rzepka 39), Brzeczek, Kowalczyk (Smolarek 67), Warzycha R, Kosecki, Ziober.

Ankara, 28 October 1992, 35,000

Turkey (1) 4 *(Hakan 37, 89, Orhan 87, Hami 90)*

San Marino (0) 1 *(Bacciocchi 53)*

Turkey: Hayrettin; Riza (Mehmet 73), Bulent, Gokhan, Ogun, Orhan, Okan, Ridvan, Hakan, Oguz, Aykut (Hami 46).
San Marino: Benedettini; Gobbi, Gennari, Della Valle (Bizzocchi 84), Matteoni, Guerra, Manzaroli, Mazza P, Bacciocchi, Bonini, Francini (Zanotti 65).

Wembley, 18 November 1992, 42,984

England (2) 4 *(Gascoigne 16, 61, Shearer 28, Pearce 60)*

Turkey (0) 0

England: Woods; Dixon, Pearce, Palmer, Walker, Adams, Platt, Gascoigne, Shearer, Wright I, Ince.
Turkey: Hayrettin; Recep, Bulent, Gokhan, Ogun, Orhan, Hami (Riza 69), Unal, Mehmet (Ugur 46), Oguz, Hakan.

Istanbul, 16 December 1992, 15,000

Turkey (0) 1 *(Feyyaz 60)*

Holland (0) 3 *(Van Vossen 57, 87, Gullit 59)*

Turkey: Hayrettin; Recep, Bulent, Gokhan, Ogun, Unal (Hami 77), Oguz, Tugay, Orhan, Saffet (Feyyaz 46), Hakan.
Holland: De Goey; Silooy, Koeman R, Jonk (De Boer F 65), Rijkaard, Wouters, Rob Witschge, Gullit, Viscaal, Winter (Numan 76), Van Vossen.

Wembley, 17 February 1993, 51,154

England (2) 6 *(Platt 13, 24, 67, 83, Palmer 76, Ferdinand 86)*

San Marino (0) 0

England: Woods; Dixon, Walker, Adams, Dorigo, Gascoigne, Batty, Platt, Palmer, Ferdinand, Barnes.
San Marino: Benedettini; Muccioli B, Zanotti, Mazza M, Gennari, Canti, Guerra, Manzaroli, Bacciocchi (Mazza P 63), Bonini, Francini (Matteoni 80).

Utrecht, 24 February 1993, 14,000

Holland (2) 3 *(Overmars 4, Rob Witschge 37, 57)*

Turkey (1) 1 *(Feyyaz 36 (pen))*

Holland: De Goey; Silooy, De Kock, Koeman R, Rob Witschge, Wouters (Winter 74), Jonk, Bergkamp, Van Vossen (De Boer F 46), Gullit, Overmars.
Turkey: Engin; Recep, Bulent, Gokhan, Ali Nail, Tugay (Serhat 78), Feyyaz (Saffet 61), Unal, Hakan, Oguz, Orhan.

Serravalle, 10 March 1993, 957

San Marino (0) 0

Turkey (0) 0

San Marino: Benedettini (Muccioli S 9); Canti, Gennari, Zanotti, Valentini, Guerra, Manzaroli, Mazza M (Matteoni 61), Mazza P, Bacciocchi, Francini.
Turkey: Engin; Serhat (Hami 62), Bulent, Ali Nail, Ogun, Tugay, Aykut, Unal, Mehmet, Saffet, Orhan.

Utrecht, 24 March 1993, 17,000

Holland (2) 6 *(Van Den Brom 2, Canti (og) 29, De Wolf 52, 85, De Boer R 68 (pen), Van Vossen 78)*

San Marino (0) 0

Holland: De Goey; De Wolf, De Boer F, Winter, Rob Witschge, Wouters, Overmars, Meyer, Eykelkamp (De Boer R 46), Van Den Brom, Blinker (Van Vossen 67).
San Marino: Muccioli S; Canti, Gennari, Matteoni (Zanotti 22), Valentini, Guerra, Manzaroli, Mazza M, Bacciocchi, Bonini, Francini.

Izmir, 31 March 1993, 60,000

Turkey (0) 0

England (2) 2 *(Platt 6, Gascoigne 44)*

Turkey: Engin (Hayrettin 42); Recep (Hami 69), Ogun, Ali Nail, Tugay, Bulent, Feyyaz, Unal, Mehmet, Oguz, Orhan.
England: Woods; Dixon (Clough 46), Sinton, Palmer, Walker, Adams, Platt, Gascoigne, Barnes, Wright I (Sharpe 84), Ince.

Wembley, 28 April 1993, 73,163

England (2) 2 *(Barnes 2, Platt 23)*

Holland (1) 2 *(Bergkamp 34, Van Vossen 85 (pen))*

England: Woods; Dixon, Walker, Adams, Keown, Ince, Gascoigne (Merson 46), Palmer, Barnes, Platt, Ferdinand.
Holland: De Goey; Blind, De Boer F, Rijkaard, Winter, Wouters, Rob Witschge, Gullit (Van Vossen 69), Bergkamp, Bosman (De Wolf 46), Overmars.

Oslo, 28 April 1993, 21,530

Norway (2) 3 *(Rekdal 14, Fjortoft 17, Jakobsen JI 55)*

Turkey (0) 1 *(Feyyaz 57)*

Norway: Rossbach; Halle, Pedersen T, Bratseth, Bjornebye, Flo, Mykland (Nilsen R 82), Rekdal, Leonhardsen (Ingebrigtsen 30), Jakobsen JI, Fjortoft.
Turkey: Hayrettin; Recep, Ogun, Sedat, Serhat, Bulent, Feyyaz, Unal, Mehmet (Hamza 81), Hakan (Hami 66), Orhan.

Lodz, 28 April 1993, 10,000

Poland (0) 1 *(Furtok 68)*

San Marino (0) 0

Poland: Klak; Czachowski, Szewczyk, Kozminski, Waldoch, Brzeczek, Pisz, Juskowiak (Staniek 66), Furtok, Kosecki, Ziober.
San Marino: Benedettini; Canti, Gennari, Zanotti (Francini 79), Gobbi, Valentini, Manzaroli, Della Valle, Mazza M, Bonini (Mazza P 70), Bacciocchi.

Serravalle, 19 May 1993, 1500

San Marino (0) 0

Poland (0) 3 *(Lesniak 52, 80, Warzycha K 56)*

San Marino: Benedettini; Canti, Gennari, Zanotti, Gobbi, Valentini, Manzaroli, Francini (Muccioli B 60), Mazza M, Bonini, Bacciocchi (Mazza P 72).
Poland: Matysek; Czachowski, Brzeczek, Szewczyk, Rudy, Lesniak, Swierczewski, Warzycha K, Furtok (Staniek 82), Kosecki, Ziober.

Chorzow, 29 May 1993, 60,000

Poland (1) 1 *(Adamczuk 34)*

England (0) 1 *(Wright I 84)*

Poland: Bako; Czachowski, Szewczyk, Kozminski, Lesiak, Brzeczek (Jalocha 84), Swierczewski, Adamczuk, Furtok, Kosecki, Lesniak (Wegrzyn 75).
England: Woods; Bardsley, Dorigo, Palmer (Wright I 72), Walker, Adams, Platt, Gascoigne (Clough 79), Sheringham, Barnes, Ince.

Oslo, 2 June 1993, 22,250

Norway (1) 2 *(Leonhardsen 42, Bohinen 48)*

England (0) 0

Norway: Thorstvedt; Halle, Pedersen T, Bratseth (Nilsen R 82), Bjornebye, Flo, Mykland, Leonhardsen, Fjortoft (Sorloth 57), Rekdal, Bohinen.
England: Woods; Dixon, Pallister, Palmer, Walker (Clough 63), Adams, Platt, Gascoigne, Ferdinand, Sheringham (Wright I 46), Sharpe.

Rotterdam, 9 June 1993, 40,000

Holland (0) 0

Norway (0) 0

Holland: De Goey; Van Gobbel (Winter 81), Rijkaard, Koeman R, De Boer F, Wouters, Overmars, Jonk, Bosman (Van Vossen 46), Bergkamp, Blinker.
Norway: Thorstvedt; Johnsen (Brandsaether 85), Pedersen T, Bratseth, Bjornebye (Nilsen R 46), Flo, Mykland, Leonhardsen, Fjortoft, Rekdal, Bohinen.

Wembley, 8 September 1993, 71,220

England (1) 3 *(Ferdinand 5, Gascoigne 49, Pearce 53)*

Poland (0) 0

England: Seaman; Jones, Pearce, Ince, Pallister, Adams, Platt, Gascoigne, Ferdinand, Wright I, Sharpe.
Poland: Bako; Czachowski, Brzeczek, Kozminski, Lesiak, Warzycha R, Swierczewski, Adamczuk (Bak 77), Kosecki, Furtok (Ziober 46), Lesniak.

Oslo, 22 September 1993, 23,000

Norway (0) 1 *(Flo 55)*

Poland (0) 0

Norway: Thorstvedt; Bratseth, Halle, Pedersen T, Bjornebye (Nilsen 46), Flo, Berg, Ingebrigtsen (Grodas 56), Rekdal, Bohinen, Fjortoft.
Poland: Bako; Bak, Szewczyk, Wegrzyn, Swierczewski, Rudy, Kosecki, Warzycha R (Brzeczek 85), Kozminski, Lesniak, Ziober.

Bologna, 22 September 1993, 1000

San Marino (0) 0

Holland (3) 7 *(Bosman 1, 66, 77, Jonk 21, 44, Koeman R 52, 79 (pen))*

San Marino: Benedettini; Gobbi, Conti, Gennari, Valentini, Della Valle, Toccaceli, Mazza M, Mazza P (Matteoni 76), Bonini, Bacciocchi (Gualtieri 58).
Holland: De Goey; De Boer F, Koeman R, Wouters, Jonk, Overmars, Rijkaard, Kieft (De Boer R 56), Bergkamp, Bosman, Roy.

Rotterdam, 13 October 1993, 48,000

Holland (0) 2 *(Koeman R 62, Bergkamp 68)*

England (0) 0

Holland: De Goey; De Wolf, Koeman R, De Boer F, Rijkaard, Wouters, Bergkamp, Koeman E, Overmars (Winter 75), De Boer R (Van Gobbel 90), Roy.
England: Seaman; Parker, Dorigo, Palmer (Sinton 46), Adams, Pallister, Platt, Ince, Shearer, Merson (Wright I 69), Sharpe.

Poznan, 13 October 1993, 50,000

Poland (0) 0

Norway (0) 3 *(Flo 68, Fjortoft 70, Johnsen 89)*

Poland: Bako; Bak, Wegrzyn, Kozminski, Swierczewski, Rudy, Waldoch, Ziober, Kosecki (Brzeczek 25), Lesniak, Warzycha R.
Norway: Grodaas; Bratseth, Halle, Pedersen T, Bjornebye, Flo, Berg, Mykland, Rekdal, Bohinen, Fjortoft.

Istanbul, 27 October 1993, 15,000

Turkey (0) 2 *(Hakan 53, Bulent K 67)*

Poland (1) 1 *(Kowalczyk 18)*

Turkey: Engin; Bulent, Gokhan, Emre, Recep, Tugay, Bulent K, Oguz, Abdullah (Mehmet 80), Hakan, Orhan (Ertugrul 73).
Poland: Matysek; Lewandovski, Michalski, Kruszankin, Waldoch, Jalocha, Pisz, Adamczuk, Staniek, Kowalczyk, Juskowiak (Ziober 50).

Istanbul, 10 November 1993, 10,500

Turkey (2) 2 *(Ertugrul 5, 26)*

Norway (0) 1 *(Bohinen 47)*

Turkey: Hayrettin; Ogun (Emre 55), Gokhan, Bulent, Yusuf, Suat (Mehmet 80), Oguz, Tugay, Abdullah, Ertugrul, Orhan.
Norway: Thorstvedt; Berg, Bratseth, Pedersen T, Bjornebye, Halle, Mykland (Hardelsen 55), Rekdal, Bohinen, Johnsen (Aage 71), Jakobsen JI.

Bologna, 17 November 1993, 2378

San Marino (1) 1 *(Gualtieri 1)*

England (3) 7 *(Ince 21, 73, Wright I 32, 46, 78, 88, Ferdinand 37)*

San Marino: Benedettini; Valentini (Gobby 47), Zanotti, Canti, Gennari, Guerra, Manzaroli, Della Valle, Bacciocchi (Mazza P 61), Bonini, Gualtieri.
England: Seaman; Dixon, Pearce, Ince, Walker, Pallister, Ripley, Wright I, Ferdinand, Platt, Sinton.

Poznan, 17 November 1993, 20,000

Poland (1) 1 *(Lesniak 13)*

Holland (1) 3 *(Bergkamp 10, 56, De Boer R 88)*

Poland: Matysek; Waldoch, Michalski, Kozminski, Jalocha (Czerwiec 79), Kruszankin, Warzycha R (Celuba 70), Lewandowski, Adamczuk, Kowalczyk, Lesniak.
Holland: De Goey; Van Gobbel, Koeman R, De Boer F, Winter, Wouters, Bergkamp, Koeman E, Overmars, De Boer R, Roy.

Group 2

	P	*W*	*D*	*L*	*F*	*A*	*Pts*
Norway	10	7	2	1	25	5	16
Holland	10	6	3	1	29	9	15
England	10	5	3	2	26	9	13
Poland	10	3	2	5	10	15	8
Turkey	10	3	1	6	11	19	7
San Marino	10	0	1	9	2	46	1

Norway and Holland qualified

Group 3

Seville, 22 April 1992, 10,000

Spain (1) 3 *(Michel 2, 66 (pen), Hierro 87)*

Albania (0) 0

Spain: Zubizarreta; Abelardo, Nando, Giner, Michel (Eusebio 85), Amor, Hierro, Vizcaino, Manolo (Bakero 53), Butragueno, Goicoechea.
Albania: Strakosha (Dani 69); Josa (Peqini 55), Kola B, Lekbello, Aya, Abazi, Kushta, Barballushi, Millo, Kola A, Demollari.

Windsor Park, 28 April 1992, 4500

Northern Ireland (2) 2 *(Wilson 13, Taggart 16)*

Lithuania (1) 2 *(Narberkovas 41, Fridrikas 48)*

Northern Ireland: Fettis; Donaghy (Fleming 46), Taggart, McDonald, Worthington, Black, Magilton, Wilson, Hughes, Quinn, Dowie (Rogan 80).
Lithuania: Martinkenas; Buzmakovas, Mika, Janonis, Mazeikis, Tautkas, Urbanas, Fridrikas (Zuta 90), Narbekovas, Baranauskas, Ivanauskas (Danisevicius 89).

Dublin, 26 May 1992, 29,727

Republic of Ireland (0) 2 *(Aldridge 60, McGrath 80)*

Albania (0) 0

Republic of Ireland: Bonner; Irwin, Staunton, O'Leary, McGrath, Townsend, Keane, Houghton, Quinn, Aldridge (Coyne 83), Sheedy (McCarthy 52).
Albania: Dani; Zmijani, Qendro (Pali 71), Peqini, Vata, Abazi, Kushta, Vasi, Rraklli, Zola A (Sokoll 80), Demollari.

Tirana, 3 June 1992, 15,000

Albania (0) 1 *(Abazi 77)*

Lithuania (0) 0

Albania: Dani; Zmijani, Peqini, Lekbello, Vata, Abazi, Kushta, Milori (Rrafi 46), Millo (Fortuzi 89), Vasi, Demollari.
Lithuania: Martinkenas; Buzmakovas, Sukristovas, Mazeikis, Ziukas, Danisevicius, Baranauskas, Tautkas (Zuta 82), Urbanas, Ramelis (Zdancius 52), Kvitkauskas.

Riga, 12 August 1992, 2000

Latvia (1) 1 *(Linards 15)*

Lithuania (0) 2 *(Poderis 65, Tereskinas 86)*

Latvia: Karavayev; Ivanovs, Sprogis (Zemniskis 65), Gnedois, Glazovs (Sitik 46), Popkovs, Shevljakovs, Alexeyenko, Semionovs, Linards, Stradins.
Lithuania: Martinkenas; Buzmakovas, Janonis, Sukristovas (Poderis 56), Vainoras, Mazeikis, Baltusnikas, Baranauskas, Narbekovas (Tereskinas 2), Fridrikas, Ivanauskas.

Riga, 26 August 1992, 10,000

Latvia (0) 0

Denmark (0) 0

Latvia: Karavayev; Shevljakovs, Alexeyenko, Ivanovs, Gnedois, Popkovs (Astafjevs 65), Sprogis, Stradins, Yeliseyevs, Linards (Bulders 86), Glazovs.
Denmark: Schmeichel; Sivebaek (Elstrup 46), Olsen, Piechnik, Christofte, Heintze, Vilfort, Jensen, Laudrup B, Povlsen, Christensen.

Dublin, 9 September 1992, 32,000

Republic of Ireland (1) 4 *(Sheedy 30, Aldridge 59, 82 (pen), 86)*

Latvia (0) 0

Republic of Ireland: Bonner; Irwin, Staunton, Kernaghan, McGrath, Townsend, Keane, Whelan, Quinn (Coyne 61), Aldridge, Sheedy (Phelan 76).
Latvia: Igoshin; Astafjevs, Alexeyenko, Bulders, Gnedois, Popkovs (Semionovs 63), Sprogis, Abzinovs (Sidorovs 36), Yeliseyevs, Linards, Glazovs.

Windsor Park, 9 September 1992, 8000

Northern Ireland (3) 3 *(Clarke, Wilson, Magilton)*

Albania (0) 0

Northern Ireland: Wright; Fleming, Worthington, Taggart, McDonald, Donaghy, Wilson, Magilton, Clarke (O'Neill M 77), Dowie, Hughes.
Albania: Strakosha; Zmijani, Peqini, Lekbello, Vata, Abazi, Kushta, Milori (Bilali 69), Millo, Kepa, Rraklli.

Riga, 23 September 1992, 60,000

Latvia (0) 0

Spain (0) 0

Latvia: Karavayev; Shevljakovs, Alexeyenko, Ivanovs, Gnedois, Popkovs (Astafjevs 70), Sprogis, Stradins, Bulders (Gilis 81), Linards, Glazovs.
Spain: Zubizarreta; Ferrer, Toni, Solazabal, Lopez, Vizcaino, Goicoechea, Fonseca (Alfonso 72), Bakero, Martin Vazquez, Alvaro (Amor 59).

Vilnius, 23 September 1992, 9500

Lithuania (0) 0

Denmark (0) 0

Lithuania: Martinkenas; Mazeikis, Sukristovas, Baltusnikas, Buzmakovas, Pankratjevas, Zuta (Poderis 87), Zdancius, Tereskinas, Baranauskas, Olsanskis.
Denmark: Schmeichel; Olsen, Piechnik, Sivebaek, Christofte, Larsen, Jensen, Vilfort, Laudrup B, Elstrup, Christensen (Moller 80).

Copenhagen, 14 October 1992, 40,100

Denmark (0) 0

Republic of Ireland (0) 0

Denmark: Schmeichel; Olsen, Piechnik, Sivebaek, Heintze, Rieper, Jensen, Vilfort, Larsen, Laudrup B, Povlsen (Christensen 77).
Republic of Ireland: Bonner; Irwin, Phelan, Moran, Kernaghan, Keane, Townsend, Houghton (Kelly 73), Quinn, Aldridge, McGoldrick.

Windsor Park, 14 October 1992, 9500

Northern Ireland (0) 0

Spain (0) 0

Northern Ireland: Wright; Fleming, Worthington, Taggart, McDonald, Donaghy, Black (Morrow 61), Wilson, Clarke, Quinn, Hughes.
Spain: Zubizarreta; Ferrer, Toni, Solazabal, Lopez, Hierro, Amor, Michel, Claudio (Guardiola 63), Martin Vazquez, Manolo (Alfonso 60).

Vilnius, 28 October 1992, 5000

Lithuania (0) 1 *(Fridrikas 85)*

Latvia (1) 1 *(Linards 44)*

Lithuania: Martinkenas; Buzmakovas, Baltusnikas, Tumasonis (Zuta 61), Tereskinas, Sukristovas, Baranauskas, Ivanauskas, Pankratjevas, Fridrikas, Zdancius (Vainoras 68).
Latvia: Karavayev; Astafjevs, Alexeyenko, Ivanovs, Gnedois, Popkovs (Jemeljanovs 74), Sprogis, Stradins, Bulders, Linards, Glazovs.

Tirana, 11 November 1992, 3500

Albania (0) 1 *(Kepa 67)*

Latvia (1) 1 *(Alexeyenko 3)*

Albania: Strakosha; Zmijani, Lekbello, Vata, Peqini, Demollari, Fortuzi, Kacaj, Rraklli, Kushta (Prenja 67) (Bisha 74), Kepa.
Latvia: Karavayev; Gnedois, Sprogis, Bulders, Ivanovs, Glazovs (Popkovs 46), Shevljakovs, Alexeyenko, Stradins, Linards, Astafjevs.

Windsor Park, 18 November 1992, 11,000

Northern Ireland (0) 0

Denmark (0) 1 *(Larsen 51)*

Northern Ireland: Fettis; Fleming, Taggart, McDonald, Worthington, Donaghy, Magilton, Wilson (Black), Hughes, Clarke (Gray), Quinn.
Denmark: Schmeichel; Sivebaek (Kjeldbjerg 46), Rieper, Olsen, Heintze, Vilfort, Jensen, Larsen (Goldbaek 73), Povlsen, Laudrup B, Elstrup.

Seville, 18 November 1992, 33,000

Spain (0) 0

Republic of Ireland (0) 0

Spain: Zubizarreta; Ferrer, Goicoechea, Solazabal, Lopez, Hierro, Salinas (Bakero 52), Michel, Butragueno (Beguiristain 60), Martin Vazquez, Amor.
Republic of Ireland: Bonner; Irwin, Phelan, Moran, Keane, Townsend, McGrath, Houghton, Staunton, Aldridge, Quinn.

Seville, 16 December 1992, 24,500

Spain (0) 5 *(Bakero 49, Guardiola 51, Alfonso 79, Beguiristain 81, 82)*

Latvia (0) 0

Spain: Zubizarreta; Ferrer, Toni, Solazabal, Vizcaino, Amor, Claudio (Alfonso 55), Guardiola, Bakero (Martin Vazquez 62), Quico, Beguiristain.
Latvia: Karavayev; Erglis, Alexeyendo, Ivanovs, Astafjevs, Popkovs, Gilis, Stradins, Bulders, Linards, Glazovs.

Tirana, 17 February 1993, 12,000

Albania (0) 1 *(Rraklli 89)*

Northern Ireland (0) 2 *(Magilton 14, McDonald 38)*

Albania: Kapilani; Zmijani (Peqini 46), Kacaj, Bano, Vata, Bazgo, Lekbello (Shulku 46), Fortuzi, Abazi, Rraklli, Demollari.
Northern Ireland: Wright; Fleming, Morrow, Taggart, Magilton, McDonald, Donaghy, Gray, Dowie (Quinn 73), O'Neill, Black.

Seville, 24 February 1993, 21,000

Spain (3) 5 *(Cristobal 5, Bakero 13, Beguiristain 18, Christiansen 86, Aldana 89)*

Lithuania (0) 0

Spain: Zubizarreta; Ferrer, Lasa, Alcorta, Giner, Cristobal, Guardiola, Guerrero (Aldana 59), Salinas (Christiansen 69), Bakero, Beguiristain.
Lithuania: Martinkenas; Buzmakovas, Vainoras, Mazeikis, Janonis, Sukristovas, Baranauskas, Ivanauskas, Tereskinas (Zuta 69), Fridrikas, Zdancius.

Copenhagen, 31 March 1993, 40,272

Denmark (1) 1 *(Povlsen 20)*

Spain (0) 0

Denmark: Schmeichel; Olsen, Rieper, Kjeldbjerg, Vilfort, Jensen, Larsen (Hansen 76), Nielsen B, Laudrup B (Tofting 86), Elstrup, Povlsen.
Spain: Zubizarreta; Cristobal, Ferrer, Giner, Alcorta, Toni (Goicoechea 55), Amor, Guardiola (Nadal 46), Beguiristain, Aldana, Salinas.

Dublin, 31 March 1993, 33,000

Republic of Ireland (3) 3 *(Townsend 20, Quinn 22, Staunton 28)*

Northern Ireland (0) 0

Republic of Ireland: Bonner; Irwin, Phelan, McGrath, Moran, Keane, Townsend, Houghton, Quinn (McGoldrick 84), Coyne (Cascarino 78), Staunton.
Northern Ireland: Wright; Donaghy, Worthington, Taggart, McDonald, Morrow, Magilton (Quinn 51), O'Neill M (Black 74), Dowie, Gray, Hughes.

Copenhagen, 14 April 1993, 29,088

Denmark (1) 2 *(Vilfort 23, Strudal 76)*

Latvia (0) 0

Denmark: Schmeichel; Nielsen S, Rieper, Olsen, Kjeldbjerg, Goldbaek, Jensen (Larsen 61), Vilfort, Pingel (Strudal 70), Elstrup, Laudrup B.
Latvia: Karavayev; Gnedois, Shevljakovs, Ivanovs, Zeminskis, Erglis, Glazovs, Astafjevs, Zelberlins (Gilis 46), Linards, Stradins (Bulders 64).

Vilnius, 14 April 1993, 12,000

Lithuania (2) 3 *(Baltusnikas 20, Sukristovas 25, Baranauskas 63)*

Albania (0) 1 *(Demollari 86)*

Lithuania: Martinkenas (Stauce 60); Ziukas, Baltusnikas, Mazeikis, Kalvaitis, Apanavicius (Slekys 63), Baranauskas, Sukristovas, Poderis, Kirilovas, Zdancius.
Albania: Kapilani; Dema, Shulku, Bano, Taho, Ocelli, Kushta, Peqini, Dalipi (Dosti 46), Fortuzi, Demollari.

Dublin, 28 April 1993, 33,000

Republic of Ireland (0) 1 *(Quinn 75)*

Denmark (1) 1 *(Vilfort 27)*

Republic of Ireland: Bonner; Irwin, McGoldrick, McGrath, Kernaghan, Keane, Townsend, Houghton, Quinn, Aldridge (Cascarino 62), Staunton.
Denmark: Schmeichel; Nielsen S, Rieper, Olsen, Kjeldbjerg, Hansen F, Jensen, Vilfort, Pingel (Kristensen 60), Elstrup, Laudrup B.

Seville, 28 April 1993, 20,000

Spain (3) 3 *(Salinas 21, 26, Hierro 41)*

Northern Ireland (1) 1 *(Wilson 11)*

Spain: Zubizarreta; Ferrer, Giner, Toni, Alcorta, Hierro, Guerrero, Aldana, Beguiristain (Bakero 76), Salinas, Claudio (Quico 59).
Northern Ireland: Wright; Fleming, Worthington, Donaghy, Taggart, McDonald, Black (Dennison 73), Wilson, O'Neill M (Dowie 73), Gray, Hughes.

Riga, 15 May 1993, 1810

Latvia (0) 0

Albania (0) 0

Latvia: Lajzans; Ergils, Shevljakovs, Ivanovs, Gnedois, Popkovs, Troickis, Astafjevs (Semionovs 46), Zelberlins (Sarando 62), Linards, Gorjacilovs.
Albania: Nailbani; Ocelli, Bano, Shala, Vata, Skulku, Kushta, Zalla (Kapidani 88), Peqini, Milori, Fortuzi (Dalipi 77).

Vilnius, 25 May 1993, 4000

Lithuania (0) 0

Northern Ireland (1) 1 *(Dowie 8)*

Lithuania: Martinkenas; Baltusnikas, Buzmakovas (Bicka 68), Mazeikis, Ziukas, Olsanskis (Sleyks 46), Baranauskas, Sukristovas, Kirilovas, Fridrikas, Zdancius.
Northern Ireland: Wright; Fleming, Taggart, McDonald, Worthington, Donaghy, Magilton, O'Neill, Wilson, Hughes, Dowie.

Tirana, 26 May 1993, 10,000

Albania (1) 1 *(Kushta 7)*

Republic of Ireland (1) 2 *(Staunton 13, Cascarino 77)*

Albania: Musta; Zmijani (Fortuzi 58), Shulku, Shala, Vata, Lekbello, Kushta, Peqini, Rraklli (Bozgo 76), Milori, Demollari.
Republic of Ireland: Bonner, Irwin, Phelan, Kernaghan, Moran, Keane, Townsend, Houghton, Quinn, Aldridge (Cascarino 76), Staunton.

Vilnius, 2 June 1993, 7000

Lithuania (0) 0

Spain (0) 2 *(Guerrero 73, 77)*

Lithuania: Martinkenas; Ziukas, Baltusnikas, Mazeikis, Buzmakovas, Olsanskis, Baranauskas, Sukristovas, Kirilovas, Fridrikas (Zdancius 54), Skarbalius.
Spain: Zubizarreta; Ferrer, Lasa (Beguiristain 62), Alcorta, Giner, Hierro, Salinas (Quique 54), Nadal, Claudio, Guerrero, Amor.

Copenhagen, 2 June 1993, 39,504

Denmark (4) 4 *(Jensen 11, Pingel 20, 40, Moller 28)*

Albania (0) 0

Denmark: Schmeichel; Nielsen S, Rieper, Olsen, Kjeldbjerg, Larsen M, Jensen (Goldbaek 83), Vilfort, Pingel, Moller (Johansen 64), Laudrup B.
Albania: Musta; Fortuzi (Zala 83), Zmijani, Shulku, Ocelli, Pequini, Bano, Demollari (Bozgo 17), Kushta, Vata, Rraklli.

Riga, 2 June 1993, 2000

Latvia (0) 1 *(Linards 55)*

Northern Ireland (2) 2 *(Magilton 4, Taggart 15)*

Latvia: Karavayev; Erglis, Shevljakovs, Ivanovs, Gnedois, Popkovs, Sarando (Yeliseyevs 46), Astafjevs, Zelberlins (Babicevs 63), Linards, Gorjacilovs.
Northern Ireland: Wright; Fleming, McDonald, Taggart, Worthington, O'Neill (Quinn 85), Magilton, Donaghy, Wilson, Hughes, Dowie.

Riga, 9 June 1993, 7000

Latvia (0) 0

Republic of Ireland (2) 2 *(Aldridge 14, McGrath 42)*

Latvia: Karavayev; Erglis, Shevljakovs, Astafjevs, Ivanovs, Gnedois, Popkovs, Bulders, Babicevs (Yeliseyevs 46), Sarando (Gorjacilovs 54), Linards.
Republic of Ireland: Bonner; Irwin, Kernaghan, McGrath, Phelan, Houghton, Townsend, Keane, Staunton, Aldridge (Sheridan 80), Quinn (Cascarino 74).

Vilnius, 16 June 1993, 6000

Lithuania (0) 0

Republic of Ireland (1) 1 *(Staunton 38)*

Lithuania: Martinkenas; Ziukas, Baltusnikas, Mazeikis, Buzmakovas, Skarbalius (Zdancius 46), Baranauskas, Urbanas (Ramelis 67), Stumbrys, Kirilovas, Slekys.
Republic of Ireland: Bonner; Irwin, Phelan, McGrath, Kernaghan, Keane, Townsend, Houghton, Quinn, Aldridge (Whelan 76), Staunton.

Copenhagen, 25 August 1993, 40,300

Denmark (2) 4 *(Olsen 13, Pingel 43, Laudrup B 63, Baltusnikas (og) 70)*

Lithuania (0) 0

Denmark: Schmeichel; Olsen, Kjeldbjerg, Rieper, Hansen, Jensen (Hogh 80), Vilfort, Laudrup M, Nielsen, Laudrup B, Pingel.
Lithuania: Stauce; Ziukas, Baltusnikas, Mazeikis, Teresnikas, Olsanskis, Baranauskas, Skarbalius, Stumbrys (Apalonikas 56), Kirilovas, Slekys (Chadancus 70).

Windsor Park, 8 September 1993, 6400

Northern Ireland (1) 2 *(Quinn 35, Gray 80)*

Latvia (0) 0

Northern Ireland: Wright; Fleming, Worthington, Taggart, Donaghy, Magilton, Wilson, Gray, Quinn, Dowie, Hughes.
Latvia: Karavayev; Troickis, Alexeyenko, Ivanovs, Gnedois, Popkovs, Sarando, Shevljakovs, Babicevs, Linards, Elisevs.

Dublin, 8 September 1993, 33,000

Republic of Ireland (2) 2 *(Aldridge 4, Kernaghan 25)*

Lithuania (0) 0

Republic of Ireland: Bonner; Irwin, Phelan, Moran, Kernaghan, Keane, Houghton, Townsend (Whelan 68), Quinn (Cascarino 74), Aldridge, Staunton.
Lithuania: Stauce; Ziukas, Baltusnikas, Kalvaitis, Tereskinas, Skarbalius (Sakalinas 84), Stumbrys, Kirilovas (Maciuvicis 69), Apanavicius, Baranauskas, Slekys.

Tirana, 8 September 1993, 8000

Albania (0) 0

Denmark (0) 1 *(Pingel 64)*

Albania: Strakosha; Lekbello, Zmijani, Abazo, Millo, Shulku, Bano, Vata, Kushta, Fortuzi, Demollari.
Denmark: Schmeichel; Rieper, Olsen, Kjeldbjerg, Nielsen (Larsen 70), Hansen (Hogh 60), Vilfort, Jensen, Laudrup M, Pingel, Laudrup B.

Tirana, 22 September 1993, 8000

Albania (1) 1 *(Kushta 41)*

Spain (3) 5 *(Salinas 4, 30, 61, Toni 19, Caminero 67)*

Albania: Strakosha; Abazi, Dashi, Vata, Shulku, Kacaj, Kepa (Dalipi 79), Kushta, Shehu, Millo, Fortuzi.
Spain: Zubizarreta; Alcorta, Nadal, Camarasa, Toni, Goicoechea, Hierro, Caminero, Guerrero, Alfonso (Quique 67), Salinas.

Copenhagen, 13 October 1993, 40,200

Denmark (0) 1 *(Laudrup B 81)*

Northern Ireland (0) 0

Denmark: Schmeichel; Rieper, Olsen, Kjeldbjerg, Vilfort, Jensen, Nielsen, Laudrup M, Laudrup B, Povlsen, Pingel (Larsen H 62).
Northern Ireland: Wright; Fleming, Worthington, Taggart, McDonald, Donaghy, Magilton, Wilson (Black 61), Dowie (Quinn 83), Gray, Hughes.

Dublin, 13 October 1993, 33,000

Republic of Ireland (0) 1 *(Sheridan 74)*

Spain (3) 3 *(Caminero 12, Salinas 15, 26)*

Republic of Ireland: Bonner; Irwin, Phelan, Moran (Sheridan 22), Kernaghan, Keane, McGrath, Houghton, Quinn, Whelan, Staunton (Cascarino 46).
Spain: Zubizarreta; Ferrer, Voro, Nadal, Giner, Hierro, Goicoechea, Camarasa, Luis Enrique, Salinas (Guardiola 72), Caminero (Bakero 30).

Windsor Park, 17 November 1993, 10,500

Northern Ireland (0) 1 *(Quinn 73)*

Republic of Ireland (0) 1 *(McLoughlin 76)*

Northern Ireland: Wright; Fleming, Worthington, Taggart, McDonald, Donaghy, Magilton, Wilson (Black 83), Quinn, Gray (Dowie 73), Hughes.
Republic of Ireland: Bonner; Irwin, Phelan, Kernaghan, McGrath, Keane, Houghton (McLoughlin 66), Townsend, Quinn, Aldridge (Cascarino 81), McGoldrick.

Seville, 17 November 1993, 50,000

Spain (0) 1 *(Hierro 62)*

Denmark (0) 0

Spain: Zubizarreta; Ferrer, Giner, Alcorta, Nadal, Hierro, Goicoechea, Camarasa (Canizares 11), Bakero, Salinas (Quique 53), Luis Enrique.
Denmark: Schmeichel; Hansen, Olsen, Rieper, Nielsen (Hogh 46), Jensen, Larsen, Vilfort, Laudrup M, Povlsen (Christensen 71), Laudrup B.

Group 3

	P	*W*	*D*	*L*	*F*	*A*	*Pts*
Spain	12	8	3	1	27	4	19
Republic of Ireland	12	7	4	1	19	6	18
Denmark	12	7	4	1	15	2	18
Northern Ireland	12	5	3	4	14	13	13
Lithuania	12	2	3	7	8	21	7
Latvia	12	0	5	7	4	21	5
Albania	12	1	2	9	6	26	4

Spain and Republic of Ireland qualified

Group 4

Brussels, 22 April 1992, 18,000

Belgium (1) 1 *(Wilmots 24)*

Cyprus (0) 0

Belgium: Preud'homme; Albert, Grun, Van der Elst, Emmers, Scifo, Walem, Boffin (Borkelmans 82), Wilmots (Hofmans 75), Degryse, Oliveira.
Cyprus: Christofi M; Costa, Pittas, Constantinou C, Nicolau, Yiangudakis, Ioannou D, Larku (Constantinou G 88), Sotiriou, Papavasiliou, Hadjilukas (Panayi 70).

Bucharest, 6 May 1992, 10,000

Romania (5) 7 *(Balint 4, 40, 78, Hagi 14, Lacatus 28 (pen), Lupescu 44, Pana 55)*

Faeroes (0) 0

Romania: Stelea; Petrescu, Mihali, Popescu, Munteanu, Pana, Balint, Lupescu (Cheregi 78), Hagi, Lacatus (Gane 63), Rotariu.
Faeroes: Knudsen; Jakobsen, Hansen T, Danielsen, Justinussen, Morkore A, Jarnskor (Nielsen T 50), Dam (Jonsson 60), Hansen A, Reynheim, Muller.

Bucharest, 20 May 1992, 23,000

Romania (5) 5 *(Hagi 5, 35, Lupescu 7, 24, Balint 31)*

Wales (0) 1 *(Rush 50)*

Romania: Stelea; Petrescu, Mihali, Belodedici, Munteanu, Sabau (Timofte I 80), Popescu, Lupescu, Hagi (Gerstenmaier 71), Lacatus, Balint.
Wales: Southall; Phillips, Bowen (Blackmore 71), Aizlewood, Melville, Horne, Speed, Pembridge (Giggs 59), Hughes, Rush, Saunders.

Toftir, 3 June 1992, 5156

Faeroes (0) 0

Belgium (1) 3 *(Albert 30, Wilmots 65, 71)*

Faeroes: Johannesen; Jakobsen, Hansen T, Danielsen, Jonsson T (Jensen 71), Morkore A (Justinussen 83), Nielsen T, Dam, Hansen A, Reynheim, Muller.
Belgium: Preud'homme: Staelens, Grun, Albert, Emmers, Boffin (Versavel 75), Van der Elst, Denil, Degryse, Scifo, Oliveira (Wilmots 65).

Toftir, 16 June 1992, 4500

Faeroes (0) 0

Cyprus (1) 2 *(Sotiriou 30, Papavasiliou 58)*

Faeroes: Johannesen; Jakobsen, Hansen T, Danielsen, Jonsson, Morkore A, Hansen A, Nielsen (Jarnskor 62), Rasmussen, Reynheim, Muller (Jensen 66).
Cyprus: Christofi M; Costa (Larku 46), Pittas, Constantinou C, Nicolau, Yiangudakis, Ioannou D, Charalambous, Savidis, Sotiriou (Panayi 84), Papavasiliou.

Prague, 2 September 1992, 9000

Czechoslovakia (0) 1 *(Kadlec 77)*

Belgium (1) 2 *(Chovanec (og) 44, Czerniatynski 83)*

Czechoslovakia: Stejskal; Chovanec, Glonek, Kadlec, Mistr, Nemecek, Kubik (Hapal 65), Nemec, Kula K (Dubovsky 77), Skuhravy, Moravcik.
Belgium: Preud'homme; Emmers, Medved, Albert, Smidts, Grun, Scifo, Van der Elst, Staelens (Dauwen 87), Czerniatynski, Degryse (Wilmots 66).

Cardiff, 9 September 1992, 7000

Wales (3) 6 *(Rush 5, 64, 89, Saunders 28, Bowen 37, Blackmore 71)*

Faeroes (0) 0

Wales: Southall; Phillips, Bowen (Giggs 66), Symons, Young, Blackmore, Horne, Saunders, Rush, Hughes, Speed.
Faeroes: Knudsen; Jakobsen, Hansen T, Danielsen, Hansen O, Morkore A, Simonsen, Dam (Justinussen 56), Jonsson, Reynheim, Muller.

Kosice, 23 September 1992, 17,000

Czechoslovakia (1) 4 *(Nemecek 24, Kuka 85, 87, Dubovsky 89 (pen))*

Faeroes (0) 0

Czechoslovakia: Stejskal; Glonek, Suchoparek, Novotny, Mistr (Latal 82), Moravcik, Nemecek, Dubovsky, Nemec, Hapal (Timko 68), Kuka.
Faeroes: Knudsen; Jakobsen, Johannesen, Hansen T, Justinussen, Simonsen, Dam, Hansen O (Morkore A 58), Jonsson, Reynheim, Muller (Arge 81).

Brussels, 14 October 1992, 21,000

Belgium (1) 1 *(Smidts 27)*

Romania (0) 0

Belgium: Preud'homme; Medved, Albert, Grun, Smidts, Boffin, Staelens, Van der Elst, Scifo, Degryse, Czerniatynski (Wilmots 69).
Romania: Stelea; Petrescu, Selymes, Mihali, Lupescu, Belodedici, Munteanu, Sabau, Dumitrescu (Badea 78), Lacatus, Hagi.

Nicosia, 14 October 1992, 15,000

Cyprus (0) 0

Wales (0) 1 *(Hughes 51)*

Cyprus: Christofi M; Costa, Pittas (Hadjilukas 71), Constantinou C, Nicolau, Yiangudakis, Ioannou D, Charalambous, Sotiriou (Yiannos Ioannou 59), Papavasiliou, Savidis.
Wales: Southall; Phillips, Bowen, Blackmore, Young, Symons, Horne, Saunders, Rush, Hughes, Speed.

Bucharest, 14 November 1992, 30,000

Romania (0) 1 *(Dumitrescu 48)*

Czechoslovakia (0) 1 *(Nemecek 79 (pen))*

Romania: Stelea; Petrescu, Belodedici, Mihali, Munteanu, Sabau, Lupescu (Timofte D 78), Hagi, Dumitrescu, Lacatus, Hanganu (Vladoiu 66).
Czechoslovakia: Kouba; Novotny, Glonek, Suchoparek, Hapal, Latal, Nemecek, Moravcik, Nemec (Frydek 15), Siegl, Skuhravy (Kuka 37).

Brussels, 18 November 1992, 21,000

Belgium (0) 2 *(Staelens 53, Degryse 58)*

Wales (0) 0

Belgium: Preud'homme; Medved, Grun, Albert, Smidts, Staelens (Wilmots 82), Van der Elst, Boffin, Degryse, Scifo, Czerniatynski (Nilis 46).
Wales: Southall; Phillips, Bowen (Giggs 60), Blackmore, Young, Symons, Horne, Saunders, Rush, Hughes, Speed (Pembridge 80).

Larnaca, 29 November 1992, 3000

Cyprus (1) 1 *(Pittas 39 (pen))*

Romania (2) 4 *(Popescu 4, Raducioiu 36, Hagi 73, Hanganu 86)*

Cyprus: Christofi M; Kalotheu, Pittas, Constantinou C, Ioannou D, Yiangudakis, Andreou (Hadjilukas 25), Christofi P, Yiannos Ioannou (Sotiriou 62), Papavasiliou, Savidis.
Romania: Stelea; Petrescu, Belodedici, Mihali, Lupescu, Popescu, Lacatus, Dumitrescu, Raducioiu (Hanganu 58), Hagi, Munteanu.

Nicosia, 13 February 1993, 3000

Cyprus (0) 0

Belgium (2) 3 *(Scifo 2, 4, Albert 87)*

Cyprus: Onisferou; Costa, Yiannos Ioannou, Constantinou C, Kalotheu (Sotiriou 70), Pittas, Savidis, Yiangudakis (Charalambous 60), Papavasiliou, Christofi P, Ioannou D.
Belgium: Preud'homme; Medved, Grun, Albert, Smidts, Staelens, Scifo (Goossens 87), Van der Elst, Boffin, Degryse, Nilis (Czerniatynski 75).

Limassol, 24 March 1993, 3000

Cyprus (0) 1 *(Sotiriou 47)*

Czechoslovakia (1) 1 *(Moravcik 33)*

Cyprus: Yiannakis Ioannou; Costa, Pittas, Ioannou D, Christofi E, Yiangudakis, Xiuruppas (Panayi 86), Charalambous, Sotiriou, Papavasiliou (Larku 71), Savidis.
Czechoslovakia: Kouba; Novotny, Suchoparek (Berger 74), Vrabec, Glonek, Nemecek, Nemec, Hapal (Latal 46), Kuka, Skuhravy, Moravcik.

Cardiff, 31 March 1993, 27,002

Wales (2) 2 *(Giggs 18, Rush 39)*

Belgium (0) 0

Wales: Southall; Horne, Bodin, Aizlewood, Young, Ratcliffe, Saunders, Speed (Phillips 88), Rush, Hughes, Giggs (Bowen 89).
Belgium: Preud'homme; Medved (Oliveira 46), Grun, Albert, Smidts, Staelens, Van der Elst, Boffin, Degryse, Scifo, Czerniatynski (Severeyns 67).

Bucharest, 14 April 1993, 30,000

Romania (1) 2 *(Dumitrescu 33, 55)*

Cyprus (1) 1 *(Sotiriou 23)*

Romania: Stelea; Petrescu, Selymes, Sandoi, Belodedici, Munteanu, Lacatus (Stinga 78), Sabau, Ceausila (Predatu 64), Hagi, Dumitrescu.
Cyprus: Petridis; Kalotheu, Pittas, Constantinou C, Christofi E, Yiangudakis, Charalambous (Xiuruppas 78), Larku, Sotiriou, Papavasiliou, Savidis (Panayi 89).

Limassol, 25 April 1993, 4000

Cyprus (2) 3 *(Xiuruppas 7, Sotiriou 43, Yiannos Ioannou 75)*

Faeroes (0) 1 *(Arge 82)*

Cyprus: Petridis; Charalambous, Christofi E, Pittas, Constantinou C, Yiangudakis, Larku, Xiuruppas (Yiannos Ioannou 65), Papavasiliou, Sotiriou (Hadjilukas 76), Savidis.
Faeroes: Knudsen; Jakobsen, Johannesen, Morkore K, Justinussen, Morkore A, Faero (Nielsen 46), Olsen, Reynheim (Arge 54), Hansen A, Jonsson.

Ostrava, 28 April 1993, 16,000

Czechoslovakia (1) 1 *(Latal 41)*

Wales (1) 1 *(Hughes 31)*

Czechoslovakia: Kouba; Glonek (Bejbl 66), Kadlec, Novotny, Vrabec, Latal, Nemec (Dubovsky 79), Kubik, Nemecek, Kuka , Luhovy.
Wales: Southall; Phillips, Bodin (Bowen 52), Melville, Symons, Blackmore, Horne, Saunders, Rush, Hughes, Giggs.

Brussels, 22 May 1993, 20,641

Belgium (1) 3 *(Wilmots 32, 75, Scifo 50 (pen))*

Faeroes (0) 0

Belgium: Preud'homme; Smidts (Oliveira 76), Emmers, Grun, Staelens, Boffin, Van der Elst, Degryse, Wilmots, Scifo, Nilis.
Faeroes: Knudsen; Jakobsen, Olsen, Morkore K (Reynatugvu 89), Justinussen, Morkore A, Dam, Hansen A, Nielsen T, Arge (Rasmussen 87), Reynheim.

Kosice, 2 June 1993, 15,000

Czechoslovakia (2) 5 *(Vrabec 13, Latal 37, Dubovsky 58, 83, 89)*

Romania (1) 2 *(Raducioiu 26, 55)*

Czechoslovakia: Kouba; Suchoparek, Novotny, Vrabec, Latal, Moravcik, Nemecek, Kubik (Nemec 46), Dubovsky, Kuka (Glonek 81), Skuhravy.
Romania: Lung; Belodedici, Prodan (Hanganu 77), Popescu, Munteanu, Sabau, Hagi, Lupescu, Dumitrescu, Lacatus (Panduru 65), Raducioiu.

Toftir, 6 June 1993, 4209

Faeroes (0) 0

Wales (2) 3 *(Saunders 22, Young 31, Rush 69)*

Faeroes: Knudsen; Jakobsen, Hansen T, Johannesen, Justinussen, Reynatugvu (Rasmussen 49), Nielsen T, Dam, Hansen A, Reynheim (Mohr 59), Arge.
Wales: Southall; Phillips, Bodin, Aizlewood, Young (Melville 49), Symons, Horne, Saunders, Rush, Hughes (Speed 75), Giggs.

Toftir, 16 June 1993, 1000

Faeroes (0) 0

Czechoslovakia (3) 3 *(Hasek 3, Postulka 38, 44)*

Faeroes: Knudsen; Justinussen R (Rasmussen 68), Johannesen, Jakobsen (Hansen T 70), Morkore K, Justinussen A, Morkore A, Reynatugvu, Hansen A, Dam, Nielsen.
Czechoslovakia: Kouba; Suchoparek, Hasek, Repka, Latal, Nemecek, Dubovsky, Postulka, Berger, Kuka (Kinder 54), Moravcik (Kubik 81).

Toftir, 8 September 1993, 2500

Faeroes (0) 0

Romania (1) 4 *(Raducioiu 24, 58, 60, 77)*

Faeroes: Knudsen; Johannesen, Jakobsen, Morkore K, Justinussen, Hansen A, Dam, Jarnskor, Morkore A (Nolsee 78), Reynheim, Hansen O (Reynatugvu 78).
Romania: Prunea; Petrescu (Panduru 77), Prodan, Popescu, Selymes, Sabau, Lupescu, Hagi, Munteanu, Vladoiu (Craioveanu 68), Raducioiu.

Cardiff, 8 September 1993, 37,558

Wales (2) 2 *(Giggs 21, Rush 35)*

Czechoslovakia (1) 2 *(Kuka 16, Dubovsky 67)*

Wales: Southall; Phillips, Symons, Aizlewood (Melville 78), Young, Bowen (Speed 75), Horne, Saunders, Rush, Hughes, Giggs.
Czechoslovakia: Kouba; Latal (Skuhravy 59), Kadlec, Nemecek, Novotny, Suchoparek, Hapal, Hasek, Moravcik, Kuka, Dubovsky.

Bucharest, 13 October 1993, 25,000

Romania (0) 2 *(Radicioiu 67 (pen), Dumitrescu 84)*

Belgium (0) 1 *(Scifo 87 (pen))*

Romania: Prunea; Belodedici, Petrescu, Prodan, Munteanu, Sabau (Selymes 27), Popescu, Lupescu, Hagi (Vladoiu 86), Dumitrescu, Raducioiu.
Belgium: Preud'homme; Medved, Grun, Albert, Smidts, Borkelmans (Oliveira 70), Scifo, Staelens, Van der Elst, Boffin, Wilmots (Czerniatynski 78).

Cardiff, 13 October 1993, 10,000

Wales (0) 2 *(Saunders 70, Rush 82)*

Cyprus (0) 0

Wales: Southall; Phillips, Horne, Aizlewood, Young, Symons (Goss 70), Giggs, Rush, Saunders, Hughes, Speed.
Cyprus: Petridis; Constantinou G, Pittas, Ioannou D (Panayi 71), Evagoras, Yargoudakis (Xiuruppas 75), Charalambous, Kosta, Sotiriou, Larku, Papavasiliou.

Kosice, 27 October 1993, 15,600

Czechoslovakia (2) 3 *(Dubovsky 12, Hapal 23, Skuhravy 77)*

Cyprus (0) 0

Czechoslovakia: Molnar; Suchoparek, Kadlec, Novotny, Moravcik, Nemecek, Dubovsky, Hapal, Smicer (Timko 72), Skuhravy, Kuka (Postulka 80).
Cyprus: Petridis; Constantinou G, Andreou (Kalotheu 69), Constantinou C, Panayi, Kleanthous, Larku, Papavasiliou, Chatsiloukas, Sotiriou, Xiuruppas (Stephani 62).

Brussels, 17 November 1993, 30,000

Belgium (0) 0

Czechoslovakia (0) 0

Belgium: De Wilde; Medved, De Wolf, Albert, Smidts, Staelens, Van der Elst, Scifo, Versavel, Nilis (Czerniatynski 78), Oliveira (Boffin 52).
Czechoslovakia: Kouba; Novotny, Kadlec, Suchoparek (Timko 80), Moravcik, Hazek, Hapal (Latal 70), Dubovsky, Nemecek, Skuhravy, Kuka.

Cardiff, 17 November 1993, 40,000

Wales (0) 1 *(Saunders 60)*

Romania (1) 2 *(Hagi 33, Radicioiu 83)*

Wales: Southall; Phillips, Young, Melville, Bodin (Allen 69), Symons (Goss 53), Giggs, Horne, Rush, Saunders, Speed.
Romania: Prunea; Belodedici, Petrescu, Prodan, Selymes (Munteanu 53), Sabau, Popescu, Lupescu, Hagi, Raducioiu, Dumitrescu (Mihali 89).

Group 4

	P	*W*	*D*	*L*	*F*	*A*	*Pts*
Romania	10	7	1	2	29	12	15
Belgium	10	7	1	2	16	5	15
Czechoslovakia	10	4	5	1	21	9	13
Wales	10	5	2	3	19	12	12
Cyprus	10	2	1	7	8	18	5
Faeroes	10	0	0	10	1	38	0

Romania and Belgium qualified

Group 5

Yugoslavia excluded due to UN sanctions.

Athens, 13 May 1992, 10,000

Greece (1) 1 *(Sofanidis 28)*

Iceland (0) 0

Greece: Papadopoulos; Apostolakis, Kalitzakis, Manolas, Mitsibonas, Tsaluhidis Y, Tsaluhidis P, Sofiandis, Tursunidis (Nioblias 77), Alexandria, Tsiantakis (Borbokis 60).
Iceland: Kristinsson B; Jonsson Kr, Marteinsson (Magnusson 74), Vaisson, Bergsson, Jonsson K, Gudjohnsen, Bjarnasson, Gretarsson, Sverrisson, Kristinsson R.

Budapest, 3 June 1992, 10,000

Hungary (1) 1 *(Kiprich 3)*

Iceland (0) 2 *(Orlygsson 51, Magnusson 73)*

Hungary: Petry; Telek, Kovacs E, Lorincz, Simon, Limperger, Pisont (Balog 78), Vincze (Eszenyi 54), Keller, Kiprich, Kovacs K.
Iceland: Kristinsson B; Gretarsson S (Magnusson 64), Bergsson, Orlygsson, Kristinsson R, Gretarsson A, Valsson, Jonsson Kr, Jonsson K (Bragason 80), Bjarnasson, Marteinsson.

Luxembourg, 9 September 1992, 3000

Luxembourg (0) 0

Hungary (1) 3 *(Detari 16, Kovacs K 52, 79)*

Luxembourg: Van Rijswijck; Bossi, Wolf, Petry, Birsens, Girres, Hellers, Weis, Salbene (Holtz 58), Langers, Malget (Thill 80).
Hungary: Petry; Nagy T, Disztl L, Keller, Lorincz, Limperger (Telek 65), Kiprich, Balog, Pisont (Bognar G 81), Detari, Kovacs K.

Reykjavik, 7 October 1992, 6350

Iceland (0) 0

Greece (0) 1 *(Tsaluhidis P 61)*

Iceland: Kristinsson B; Bergsson, Jonsson Kr, Gudjohnsen, Marteinsson (Margeirsson 29), Kristinsson R, Bjarnasson (Hakonarsson 71), Gretarsson A, Orlygsson, Gretarsson S, Sverrisson.
Greece: Mirtsos; Apostolakis, Kalitsodakis, Manolas, Kalitzakis, Papaioannou (Mitropoulos 55), Tsiantakis, Tsaluhidis P, Dimitriadis (Franceskos 69), Nioblias, Donis.

Moscow, 14 October 1992, 13,000

Russia (0) 1 *(Yuran 64)*

Iceland (0) 0

Russia: Cherchesov; Khlestov, Onopko, Kulkov, Kolotovkin, Shalimov, Dobrovolski, Karpin, Lediakhov (Tatarchuk 46), Yuran (Kolivanov 76), Kiriakov.
Iceland: Kristinsson B; Marteinsson, Jonsson Kr, Valsson, Gretarsson A, Kristinsson R (Hakonarsson 88), Bergsson, Orlygsson, Margeirsson, Gudjohnsen (Bjarnasson 76), Gretarsson S.

Moscow, 28 October 1992, 1750

Russia (2) 2 *(Yuran 4, Radchenko 23)*

Luxembourg (0) 0

Russia: Cherchesov; Khlestov, Onopko, Kulkov, Karpin, Shalimov, Dobrovolski, Mostovoi, Radchenko (Tatarchuk 80), Kiriakov (Borodyuk 63), Yuran.
Luxembourg: Van Rijswijck; Birsens, Bossi, Wolf, Hellers, Girres, Salbene (Thill 77), Weis, Holtz (Groff 53), Langers, Malget.

Salonika, 11 November 1992, 40,000

Greece (0) 0

Hungary (0) 0

Greece: Mirtsos; Apostolakis, Pahaturidis, Manolas, Kolitsidakis, Tsaluhidis P, Mitropoulos, Nioblias, Dimitriadis (Valtsis 46), Tursunidis, Tsiantakis (Franceskos 63).
Hungary: Petry; Disztl L, Limperger, Lorincz, Nagy, Urban, Lipcsei, Kiprich (Salloi 32), Meszaros (Paling 78), Balog, Kovacs K.

Athens, 17 February 1993, 40,000

Greece (1) 2 *(Dimitriadis 30 (pen), Mitropoulos 65)*

Luxembourg (0) 0

Greece: Minou; Manolas, Apostolakis, Kalitzakis, Tsaluhidis P, Nioblias, Tsiantakis, Dimitriadis, Donis (Mitropoulos 58), Franceskos (Karapialis 56), Karataidis.
Luxembourg: Koch; Petry, Wolf, Bossi, Birsens, Salbene, Hellers, Weis, Groff (Scuto 67), Malget, Langers.

Budapest, 31 March 1993, 30,000

Hungary (0) 0

Greece (0) 1 *(Apostolakis 70)*

Hungary: Petry; Telek, Csabo, Disztl L (Nagy T 36), Pisont (Balog 71), Urban, Detari, Eszenyi, Duro, Kiprich, Kovacs K.
Greece: Minou; Manolas, Kalitzakis, Kolitsidakis, Tsiantakis, Apostolakis, Mitropoulos, Nioblias, Tsaluhidis P, Maragos (Antoniou 63), Machlas (Franceskos 82).

Luxembourg, 14 April 1993, 3000

Luxembourg (0) 0

Russia (1) 4 *(Kiriakov 12, 46, Shalimov 57, Kulkov 90)*

Luxembourg: Koch; Petry, Bossi, Birsens, Wolf, Salbene (Scuto 80), Hellers, Weis, Groff, Malget, Morocutti (Thill 60).
Russia: Cherchesov; Onopko, Gorlukovich, Ivanov, Shalimov, Kolivanov, Dobrovolski, Korneyev (Kulkov 60), Kanchelskis, Yuran, Kiriakov (Popov 75).

Moscow, 28 April 1993, 30,000

Russia (0) 3 *(Kanchelskis 55, Kolivanov 60, Yuran 86)*

Hungary (0) 0

Russia: Kharine; Gorlukovich, Ivanov A, Onopko, Kanchelskis, Shalimov, Dobrovolski, Korneyev (Kulkov 57), Kolivanov, Yuran, Kiriakov (Mostovoi 72).
Hungary: Petry; Telek, Nagy T, Lorincz, Pisont, Marton, Detari, Balog (Vincze 64), Duro (Banfi 64), Kovacs K, Csabi.

Luxembourg, 20 May 1993, 2000

Luxembourg (0) 1 *(Birgison (og) 70)*

Iceland (1) 1 *(Gudjohnsen 40)*

Luxembourg: Van Rijswijck; Ferron (Carboni 64), Petry, Birsens, Wolf, Holtz, Salbene, Hellers, Groff (Scuto 50), Langers, Malget.
Iceland: Kristinsson B; Birgison, Bergsson, Jonsson Kr, Orlygsson, Kristinsson R, Gretarsson A, Ingolfsson (Martinsson 82), Gudjohnsen, Gunnlaugsson (Thordarsson 56), Sverrisson.

Moscow, 23 May 1993, 40,000

Russia (0) 1 *(Dobrovolski 75 (pen))*

Greece (1) 1 *(Mitropoulos 45)*

Russia: Kharine; Gorlukovich, Onopko, Ivanov A, Kanchelskis, Shalimov, Dobrovolski, Kulkov (Tatarchuk 62), Kolivanov, Yuran, Kiriakov.
Greece: Minou; Apostolakis, Kolitsidakis, Manolas, Kalitzakis, Tsaluhidis P, Marangos, Nioblias, Machlas (Antoniou 82), Mitropoulos (Karapialis 64), Tsiantakis.

Reykjavik, 2 June 1993, 3096

Iceland (1) 1 *(Sverrisson 26)*

Russia (1) 1 *(Kiriakov 38)*

Iceland: Kristinsson B; Bergsson, Birgison, Jonsson Kr, Dervic, Stefansson, Thordarsson, Kristinsson R (Gretarsson A 78), Gudjohnsen, Sverrisson (Ingolfsson 83), Gunnlaugsson.
Russia: Kharine; Gorlukovich, Onopko, Kulkov, Ivanov, Kanchelskis, Dobrovolski, Tatarchuk (Korneyev 63), Kolivanov, Yuran (Lediakhov 75), Kiriakov.

Reykjavik, 16 June 1993, 5000

Iceland (1) 2 *(Sverrisson 13, Gudjohnsen 77)*

Hungary (0) 0

Iceland: Kristinsson B; Bjarnsson, Bergsson, Jonsson Kr, Dervic, Thordarsson, Kristinsson R, Stefansson (Gretarsson A 64), Gunnlaugsson, Gudjohnsen, Sverrisson.
Hungary: Petry; Simon, Telek, Lorincz, Urban, Pisont, Marton, Balog, Kerezturi, Orosz (Hamori 64), Hamar (Salloi 80).

Budapest, 8 September 1993, 5000

Hungary (1) 1 *(Nikiforov 21 (og))*

Russia (1) 3 *(Piatnicki 15, Kiriakov 53, Borodyuk 90)*

Hungary: Vegh; Banfi, Bordas, Puglits, Kuttor, Lipczei (Halmai 69), Vincze, Detari, Albert (Kovacs 64), Klausz, Csertoi.
Russia: Kharine; Gorlukovich, Onopko, Ivanov, Nikiforov, Kanchelskis, Shalimov, Piatnicki (Dobrovolski 71), Kolivanov, Yuran (Borodyuk 56), Kiriakov.

Reykjavik, 8 September 1993, 3969

Iceland (0) 1 *(Ingolfsson 54 (pen))*

Luxembourg (0) 0

Iceland: Kristinsson B; Birgison, Bergsson, Jonsson Kr, Thordarsson, Jonsson S, Ingolfsson, Kristinsson R, Gudjohnsen, Gudjonsson, Gunnlaugsson.
Luxembourg: Koch; Bossi, Petry, Birsens, Wolf, Holtz, Hellers, Salbene, Groff, Langers (Morocutti 65), Malget (Cardoni 82).

Luxembourg, 12 October 1993, 2558

Luxembourg (0) 1 *(Fanelli 83)*

Greece (1) 3 *(Machlas 31, Apostolakis 65, Saravakos 73)*

Luxembourg: Koch; Ferron, Petry, Strasser, Wolf, Holtz, Birsens, Cardoni (Malget 46), Groff, Morocutti (Fanelli 69), Langers.
Greece: Minou; Apostolakis, Machlas, Manolas, Kalitzakis, Tsaluhidis P, Saravakos, Nioblias, Mitropoulos (Alexandris 78), Dimitriadis (Maragos 46), Tsiantakis.

Budapest, 27 October 1993, 1500

Hungary (1) 1 *(Detari 20)*

Luxembourg (0) 0

Hungary: Vegh; Banfi, Mracko, Kuttor, Bordas, Csertai, Detari, Lipcsei, Fule (Orosz 46), Klausz, Vincze (Puglits 23).
Luxembourg: Koch; Bossi, Petry, Wolf, Strasser, Hellers, Saibane, Birsens, Groff (Malget 75), Langers, Fanello (Morocutti 76).

Athens, 17 November 1993, 60,000

Greece (0) 1 *(Machlas 68)*

Russia (0) *6*

Greece: Minou; Apostolakis, Ioannidis, Manolas, Karataidis, Tsaluhidis P, Saravakos (Alexandris 77), Nioblias, Machlas, Mitropoulos (Marangos 33), Tsiantakis.
Russia: Cherchesov; Khlestov, Onopko, Popov (Mostovoi 80), Kulkov, Nikiforov, Shalimov, Kolivanov, Dobrovolski, Kiriakov, Yuran (Salenko 46).

Group 5

	P	*W*	*D*	*L*	*F*	*A*	*Pts*
Greece	8	6	2	0	10	2	14
Russia	8	5	2	1	15	4	12
Iceland	8	3	2	3	7	6	8
Hungary	8	2	1	5	6	11	5
Luxembourg	8	0	1	7	2	17	1

Russia and Greece qualified

Group 6

Helsinki, 14 May 1992, 10,000

Finland (0) 0

Bulgaria (2) 3 *(Balakov 16, Kostadinov 25, 85)*

Finland: Huttunen; Petaja, Holmgren, Heikkinen, Eriksson, Rinne (Huhtamaki 76), Litmanen, Myyry, Jarvinen, Vanhala (Tegelberg 60), Tarkkio.
Bulgaria: Mikhailov; Ivanov, Tzvetanov, Iliev, Houbchev, Sirakov, Yankov, Stoichkov (Yordanov 69), Penev, Balakov, Kostadinov.

Sofia, 9 September 1992, 45,000

Bulgaria (2) 2 *(Stoichkov 21 (pen), Balakov 29)*

France (0) 0

Bulgaria: Mikhailov; Kiriakov, Ivanov, Tzvetanov, Iliev, Yankov, Kostadinov (Yordanov 75), Stoichkov, Penev (Stoilov 76), Sirakov, Balakov.
France: Martini; Fournier, Petit, Boli, Roche, Casoni, Deschamps, Sauzee, Papin, Ginola, Vahirua (Durand 61).

Helsinki, 9 September 1992, 13,617

Finland (0) 0

Sweden (0) 1 *(Ingesson 77 (pen))*

Finland: Laukkanen; Hjelm, Tarkkio (Tauriainen 72), Ukkonen, Litmanen, Myyry (Vanhala 85), Paatelainen, Jarvinen, Holmgren, Kanerva, Remes.
Sweden: Ravelli (Eriksson L 88); Andersson P, Bjorklund, Erlingmark, Ljung, Ingesson, Limpar, Pettersson (Ekstrom 62), Schwarz, Thern, Dahlin.

Stockholm, 7 October 1992, 20,625

Sweden (0) 2 *(Dahlin 56, Pettersson 76)*

Bulgaria (0) 0

Sweden: Eriksson L; Erlingmark, Andersson P, Bjorklund, Ljung, Limpar, Thern, Schwarz, Pettersson, Ingesson, Dahlin (Andersson K 87).
Bulgaria: Mikhailov; Mladenov, Kiriakov, Ivanov, Tzvetanov, Kostadinov (Yordanov 83), Sirakov, Stoilov, Yankov, Balakov, Penev.

Paris, 14 October 1992, 39,186

France (1) 2 *(Papin 3, Cantona 77)*

Austria (0) 0

France: Martini; Sauzee, Boli, Casoni, Deschamps, Sassus, Fournier (Gnako 63), Durand, Gravelaine (Vahirua 73), Papin, Cantona.
Austria: Wohlfahrt; Feiersinger, Streiter, Zsak, Wazinger, Stoger (Pfeifenberger 84), Artner, Herzog, Baur, Schinkels (Ogris 46), Polster.

Vienna, 28 October 1992, 20,000

Austria (2) 5 *(Herzog 41, 46, Polster 49, Stoger 56, Ogris 87)*

Israel (0) 2 *(Zohar 57, 77)*

Austria: Wohlfahrt; Zsak, Streiter (Baur 71), Wazinger, Prosenik, Stoger, Artner, Herzog, Schinkels (Flogel 76), Ogris, Polster.
Israel: Ginzburg; Ben-Shimon, Yeuda, Harazi A, Avi Cohen (Berkovich 52), Zohar, Klinger, Hazan, Nimny, Rosenthal, Tikva (Drieks 78).

Tel Aviv, 11 November 1992, 40,000

Israel (1) 1 *(Banin 42)*

Sweden (1) 3 *(Limpar 37, Dahlin 58, Ingesson 74)*

Israel: Ginzburg; Avi Cohen, Harazi (Berkovich 61), Hazan, Ben-Shimon, Klinger, Banin, Nimny, Revivo (Tikva 70), Zohar, Rosenthal.
Sweden: Ravelli; Nilsson R, Andersson P, Bjorklund, Ljung, Limpar, Rehn, Ingesson, Thern, Dahlin (Ekstrom 82), Brolin (Landberg 87).

Paris, 14 November 1992, 30,000

France (2) 2 *(Papin 17, Cantona 31)*

Finland (0) 1 *(Jarvinen 54)*

France: Martini; Roche, Boli, Casoni, Durand (Karembeu 71), Sauzee, Deschamps, Lizarazu, Papin, Cantona, Gravelaine (Vahirua 78).
Finland: Laukkanen; Holmgren, Kanerva, Ukkonen, Petaja (Kinnunen 85), Hjelm, Litmanen, Myyry, Jarvinen, Tarkkio, Paatelainen (Tauriainen 23).

Tel Aviv, 2 December 1992, 15,000

Israel (0) 0

Bulgaria (0) 2 *(Sirakov 55, Penev 83)*

Israel: Ginzburg; Halfon, Hilel, Shelach, Ben-Shimon, Klinger, Banin, Mizrahi (Hazan 80), Berkovich (Harazi R 84), Revivo, Rosenthal.
Bulgaria: Mikhailov; Kiriakov, Ivanov, Bezinski, Iliev, Yankov, Kostadinov, Stoichkov, Penev, Sirakov, Yordanov (Iskrenov 89).

Tel Aviv, 17 February 1993, 29,000

Israel (0) 0

France (1) 4 *(Cantona 28, Blanc 62, 84, Roche 89)*

Israel: Ginzburg; Klinger, Halfon, Hazan, Harazi A, Hilel, Atar (Drieks 56), Banin, Nimny, Harazi R, Rosenthal.
France: Lama; Boli, Roche, Blanc, Lizarazu (Loko 82), Deschamps, Sauzee, Le Guen, Ginola (Petit 63), Papin, Cantona.

Vienna, 27 March 1993, 37,500

Austria (0) 0

France (0) 1 *(Papin 58)*

Austria: Wohlfahrt; Pecl, Zsak, Artner, Feiersinger, Cerny, Kuhbauer, Schinkels (Ogris 71), Herzog, Polster, Pfeifenberger.
France: Lama; Angloma, Roche, Blanc, Petit, Lizarazu, Deschamps, Le Guen, Sauzee (Martins 87), Papin, Gravelaine (Loko 71).

Vienna, 14 April 1993, 19,500

Austria (2) 3 *(Pfeifenberger 11, Kuhbauer 25, Polster 89)*

Bulgaria (0) 1 *(Ivanov 54)*

Austria: Wohlfahrt; Streiter, Pecl, Zsak, Feiersinger, Kuhbauer (Cerny 86), Lainer, Baur, Polster, Herzog, Pfeifenberger (Ogris 68).
Bulgaria: Mikhailov; Dochev (Lechkov 73), Ivanov, Iliev, Bezinski (Iskrenov 82), Yankov, Kostadinov, Kiriakov, Balakov, Stoichkov, Penev.

Paris, 28 April 1993, 43,000

France (1) 2 *(Cantona 42 (pen), 82)*

Sweden (1) 1 *(Dahlin 14)*

France: Lama; Angloma, Petit, Boli, Blanc, Le Guen, Deschamps, Sauzee, Ginola (Vahirua 46), Martins (Lizarazu 89), Cantona.
Sweden: Ravelli; Nilsson R, Andersson P, Bjorklund, Ljung, Rehn, Thern (Kamark 27), Brolin, Schwarz, Ingesson, Dahlin (Pettersson 65).

Sofia, 28 April 1993, 35,000

Bulgaria (2) 2 *(Stoichkov 14, Yankov 43)*

Finland (0) 0

Bulgaria: Mikhailov; Kiriakov, Rakov, Markov (Besinski 89), Yankov, Lechkov, Kostadinov (Iskrenov 56), Stoichkov, Penev, Sirakov, Balakov.
Finland: Jakonen; Kinnunen, Kanerva, Heikkinen, Holmgren, Suominen, Litmanen, Lindberg, Hjelm, Paatelainen, Petaja (Rajamaki 62).

Sofia, 12 May 1993, 25,000

Bulgaria (1) 2 *(Stoichkov 35 (pen), Sirakov 60)*

Israel (0) 2 *(Harazi R 52, Rosenthal 53)*

Bulgaria: Mikhailov; Kiriakov, Ratkov, Markov, Ivanov, Lechkov (Borimirov 65), Balakov, Sirakov, Iskrenov (Yankov 37), Penev, Stoichkov.
Israel: Ginzburg; Halfon, Hilel, Hazan, Shelach, Klinger, Banin, Schwarz, Rosenthal, Harazi R (Atar 88), Ohana (Harazi A 89).

Pori, 13 May 1993, 13,682

Finland (2) 3 *(Paatelainen 17, Rajamaki 20, Hjelm 50)*

Austria (0) 1 *(Zisser 89)*

Finland: Jakonen; Heikkinen, Kanerva, Holmgren (Lindberg 60), Kinnunen, Petaja, Rajamaki, Hjelm, Suominen, Litmanen, Paatelainen (Gronholm 76).
Austria: Wohlfahrt; Streiter, Zsak (Cerny 60), Zisser, Baur, Kuhbauer, Herzog, Artner, Lainer, Ogris, Polster (Stoger 58).

Stockholm, 19 May 1993, 27,800

Sweden (0) 1 *(Eriksson J 50)*

Austria (0) 0

Sweden: Ravelli; Nilsson R, Eriksson J, Bjorklund, Ljung, Rehn, Schwarz, Brolin, Ingesson, Ekstrom (Zetterberg 80), Dahlin (Eklund 87).
Austria: Wohlfahrt; Streiter, Pecl, Lainer, Stoger, Baur, Herzog (Janeschitz 62), Artner, Feiersinger, Ogris, Pfeifenberger.

Stockholm, 2 June 1993, 22,000

Sweden (2) 5 *(Brolin 17, 41, 65, Zetterberg 55, Landberg 89)*

Israel (0) 0

Sweden: Ravelli; Nilsson R, Eriksson J, Bjorklund, Ljung, Rehn (Landberg 74), Andersson P, Zetterberg, Ingesson, Brolin, Dahlin.
Israel: Ginzburg; Halfon, Hilel, Klinger, Shelach, Bromer, Ohana (Revivo 65), Hazan, Schwarz, Harazi R, Rosenthal (Harazi A 46).

Lahti, 16 June 1993, 4620

Finland (0) 0

Israel (0) 0

Finland: Jakonen; Kinnunen (Lindberg 84), Holmgren, Kanerva, Heikkinen, Petaja, Suominen, Litmanen, Rajamaki, Paatelainen, Gronholm (Ruhanan 75).
Israel: Ginzburg; Klinger, Halfon, Bromer, Shelach, Amsalem, Hazan, Schwarz, Banin, Harazi R (Atar 89), Ohana.

Stockholm, 22 August 1993, 30,530

Sweden (0) 1 *(Dahlin 87)*

France (0) 1 *(Sauzee 76)*

Sweden: Ravelli; Nilsson R, Eriksson J, Andersson P, Ljung, Ingesson, Thern, Zetterberg (Rehn 68), Landberg (Limpar 79), Brolin, Dahlin.
France: Lama; Desailly, Blanc, Roche, Lizarazu, Deschamps, Le Guen, Sauzee, Pedros (Vahirua 79), Papin, Cantona.

Vienna, 25 August 1993, 21,000

Austria (2) 3 *(Kuhbauer 28, Pfeifenberger 41, Herzog 90 (pen))*

Finland (0) 0

Austria: Wohlfahrt; Streiter, Kogler, Pfeffer, Feiersinger (Flogel 83), Stoger, Artner, Herzog, Kuhbauer (Baur 85), Ogris, Pfeifenberger.
Finland: Jakonen; Kinnunen, Heikkinen, Kanerva, Petaja, Suominen, Litmanen (Gronholm 76), Lindberg (Ruhanen 69), Hjelm, Rajamaki, Paatelainen.

Sofia, 8 September 1993, 38,000

Bulgaria (1) 1 *(Stoichkov 21 (pen))*

Sweden (1) 1 *(Dahlin 26)*

Bulgaria: Ananiev; Kremenliev, Ivanov, Zvetanov, Rakov, Yankov, Kostadinov (Yordanov 75), Stoichkov, Alexandrov (Donkov 53), Lechkov, Balakov.
Sweden: Ravelli; Nilsson R, Andersson P, Eriksson J, Ljung, Ingesson, Thern, Limpar, Schwarz, Dahlin (Rehn 75), Brolin (Ekstrom 77).

Tampere, 8 September 1993, 10,000

Finland (0) 0

France (0) 2 *(Blanc 47, Papin 55 (pen))*

Finland: Jakonen; Kinnunen, Petaja, Kanerva, Eriksson, Suominen (Paavola 75), Hjelm, Lindberg, Litmanen, Rajamaki (Ruhanen 76), Paatelainen.
France: Lama; Desailly, Roche, Blanc, Petit, Deschamps (Guerin 87), Le Guen, Martins (Pedros 73), Sauzee, Papin, Cantona.

Sofia, 13 October 1993, 25,000

Bulgaria (2) 4 *(Penev 6, 76, Stoichkov 33 (pen), Lechkov 87)*

Austria (0) 1 *(Herzog 51)*

Bulgaria: Mikhailov; Houbchev, Ivanov, Yankov (Todorov 83), Zvetvanov, Lechkov, Balakov, Stoichkov, Kremenliev, Kostadinov (Borimirov 63), Penev.
Austria: Wohlfahrt; Baur, Streiter, Flogel, Pfeffer, Artner, Herzog, Stoger, Kogler, Polster, Ogris.

Paris, 13 October 1993, 32,741

France (2) 2 *(Sauzee 30, Ginola 40)*

Israel (1) 3 *(Harazi R 21, Berkovich 85, Atar 89)*

France: Lama; Desailly, Blanc, Roche (Lizarazu 22), Petit, Le Guen, Deschamps, Sauzee, Ginola (Djorkaeff 87), Papin, Cantona.
Israel: Ginzburg; Halfon, Hazan, Harazi A, Glam, Klinger, Levi, Nimny (Berkovich 65), Atar, Harazi R, Rosenthal.

Stockholm, 13 October 1993, 30,177

Sweden (3) 3 *(Dahlin 27, 45, Larsson H 40)*

Finland (1) 2 *(Suominen 15, Litmanen 60)*

Sweden: Ravelli; Nilsson R, Eriksson J, Ljung, Kamark, Ingesson (Landberg 8), Zetterberg, Schwarz, Dahlin, Larsson H (Martinsson 80), Limpar.
Finland: Jakonen; Kinnunen, Heikkinen, Eriksson (Jarvinen 46), Kanerva, Suominen, Lindberg, Aaltonen, Petaja, Hjelm, Litmanen.

Tel Aviv, 27 October 1993, 27,000

Israel (1) 1 *(Rosenthal 3)*

Austria (1) 1 *(Reinmayr 15)*

Israel: Ginzburg; Halfon, Hazan, Harazi A, Glam, Klinger, Levi, Berkovich (Schwartz 78), Atar (Ohan 65), Rosenthal, Harazi R.
Austria: Wohlfahrt; Kogler, Streiter, Pfeffer, Winklhofer, Feiersinger, Artner, Stoger, Reinmayr, Ogris, Polster (Pfeifenberger 65).

Vienna, 10 November 1993, 25,000

Austria (0) 1 *(Herzog 70)*

Sweden (0) 1 *(Mild 67)*

Austria: Wohlfahrt; Winklhofer, Lainer, Kogler, Feiersinger, Stoger, Artner, Herzog, Reinmayr, Polster, Pacult (Westerhaler 71).
Sweden: Ravelli; Nilsson R, Andersson P, Kamark, Ljung, Landberg (Alexandersson 80), Zetterberg, Mild, Jansson, Schwarz, Larsson (Lilienberg 73).

Tel Aviv, 10 November 1993, 10,000

Israel (0) 1 *(Harazi R 90)*

Finland (0) 3 *(Hyrylainen 53, Paavola 72, Hjelm 84)*

Israel: Ginzburg; Harazi A, Klinger, Shelach, Glam, Hazan, Levi, Nimny, Rosenthal, Harazi R, Ohana.
Finland: Jakonen; Kinnunen, Heikkinen, Petaja, Hyrylainen, Suominen, Litmanen, Lindberg, Hjelm, Aaltonen, Paavola.

Paris, 17 November 1993, 48,402

France (1) 1 *(Cantona 33)*

Bulgaria (1) 2 *(Kostadinov 36, 90)*

France: Lama; Blanc, Desailly, Roche, Petit, Le Guen, Deschamps, Sauzee (Guerin 85), Pedros, Papin (Ginola 75), Cantona.
Bulgaria: Mikhailov; Kremenliev, Houbchev, Zvetanov (Borimirov 86), Ivanov, Yankov, Balakov, Lechkov (Alexandrov 86), Kostadinov, Penev, Stoichkov.

Group 6

	P	*W*	*D*	*L*	*F*	*A*	*Pts*
Sweden	10	6	3	1	19	8	15
Bulgaria	10	6	2	2	19	10	14
France	10	6	1	3	17	10	13
Austria	10	3	2	5	15	16	8
Finland	10	2	1	7	9	18	5
Israel	10	1	3	6	10	27	5

Sweden and Bulgaria qualified

South America

Group A

Barranquilla, 2 August 1993, 70,000

Colombia (0) 0

Paraguay (0) 0

Colombia: Cordoba; Herrera, Perea, Mendoza, Wilson Perez, Alvarez, Gomez G (Garcia A 46), Rincon, Valderrama, Asprilla, Trellez (Valenciano 67).
Paraguay: Chilavert; Duarte, Rivarola, Ayala, Suarez, Acuna, Struway, Gonzalez, Monzon (Nunes 56), Cabanas, Mendoza (Gamarra 74).

Lima, 2 August 1993, 45,000

Peru (0) 0

Argentina (1) 1 *(Batistuta 29)*

Peru: Miranda; Reynoso, Jorge Soto, Barco, Olivares, Carranza, Martinez (Muchotrigo 60), Del Solar, Palacios, Gonzalez (Maestri 60), Rivera.
Argentina: Goycochea; Basualdo F, Borelli, Ruggeri, Altamirano, Zapata, Redondo, Simeone, Leo Rodriguez (Basualdo JH 68), Batistuta, Acosta (Garcia C 79).

Lima, 8 August 1993, 18,000

Peru (0) 0

Colombia (1) 1 *(Rincon 44)*

Peru: Miranda; Rivera (Charun 14), Jose Soto, Barco, Olivares, Carranza, Palacios, Del Solar, Zegarra (Saenz 65), Muchotrigo, Maestri.
Colombia: Cordoba; Herrera, Perea, Mendoza, Wilson Perez, Gomez, Lozanco, Rincon, Valderrama, Asprilla, Trellez (Aristizabal 62).

Asuncion, 8 August 1993, 25,000

Paraguay (1) 1 *(Struway 44)*

Argentina (1) 3 *(Medina Bello l5, 78, Redondo 65)*

Paraguay: Chilavert; Duarte, Rivarola, Ayala, Suarez, Struway, Acuna, Nunes (Ferreira 63), Gonzalez (Monzon 65), Cabanas, Mendoza.
Argentina: Goycochea; Basualdo F, Borelli, Ruggeri, Altamirano, Villarreal (Basualdo JH 46), Redondo, Simeone, Leo Rodriguez (Caceres 46), Medina Bello, Batistuta.

Asuncion, 15 August 1993, 20,000

Paraguay (2) 2 *(Mendoza 14, Chilavert 30 (pen))*

Peru (1) 1 *(Del Solar 44)*

Paraguay: Chilavert; Duarte, Sanabria R, Gamarra, Suarez, Cabanas, Struway, Monzon (Sanabria V 83), Gonzalez, Torres, Mendoza (Acuna 53).
Peru: Miranda; Charun (Valencia 63), Barco, Jose Soto, Olivares, Carranza, Zegarra, Del Solar, Reynoso, Baroni (Muchotrigo 60), Carty.

Barranquilla, 15 August 1993, 60,000

Colombia (1) 2 *(Valenciano 2, Valencia 52)*

Argentina (0) 1 *(Medina Bello 67)*

Colombia: Cordoba; Herrera, Perea, Mendoza, Wilson Perez, Gaviria, Lozano, Rincon, Valderrama, Valenciano (Asprilla 76), Valencia.
Argentina: Goycochea; Basualdo F, Borelli, Caceres, Altamirano, Redondo, Zapata, Basualdo JH (Zamora 46), Simeone, Medina Bello, Acosta (Leo Rodriguez 81).

Buenos Aires, 22 August 1993, 60,000

Argentina (2) 2 *(Batistuta 32, Medina Bello 37)*

Peru (0) 1 *(Palacios 66)*

Argentina: Goycochea; Craviotto, Ruggeri, Borelli, Caceres (Altamirano 27), Zapata, Redondo, Gorosito, Leo Rodriguez (Basualdo JH 70), Medina Bello, Batistuta.
Peru: Miranda; Carranza, Reynoso, Barco, Olivares, Jose Soto, Del Solar, Palacios, Zegarra, Gonzalez (Muchotrigo 65), Baroni (Maestri 86).

Asuncion, 22 August 1993, 20,000

Paraguay (0) 1 *(Rivarola 54)*

Colombia (1) 1 *(Rincon 22)*

Paraguay: Chilavert; Duarte (Barrios 46), Rivarola, Ayala, Suarez, Acuna, Struway, Cabanas, Gonzalez, Torres, Mendoza.
Colombia: Cordoba; Herrera, Perea (Gaviria 71), Mendoza, Wilson Perez, Gomez, Alvarez, Valderrama, Rincon, Valenciano (Asprilla 46), Valencia.

Barranquilla, 29 August 1993, 70,000

Colombia (2) 4 *(Valenciano 40, Rincon 45, Mendoza 66, Wilson Perez 76)*

Peru (0) 0

Colombia: Cordoba; Cabrera, Perea, Mendoza, Wilson Perez, Alvarez, Gomez, Rincon, Valderrama, Valenciano, Asprilla.
Peru: Miranda; Carranza, Reynoso, Jorge Soto, Olivares (Charun 74), Barco, Del Solar, Jose Soto, Zegarra, Gonzalez (Muchotrigo 46), Baroni.

Buenos Aires, 29 August 1993, 60,000

Argentina (0) 0

Paraguay (0) 0

Argentina: Goycochea; Basualdo F, Borelli, Ruggeri, Altamirano, Zapata, Redondo (Leo Rodriguez 63), Simeone, Gorosito (Zamora 70), Medina Bello, Batistuta.
Paraguay: Chilavert; Barrios, Rivarola, Suarez, Ayala, Struway, Gonzalez (Monzon 85), Sanabria V, Acuna, Torres, Mendoza (Ferreira 63).

Lima, 5 September 1993, 2000

Peru (1) 2 *(Muchotrigo 22, Jorge Soto 77)*

Paraguay (0) 2 *(Mendoza 61, 81)*

Peru: Miranda; Jorge Soto, Reynoso, Jose Soto, Olivares, Barco, Del Solar, Zegarra, Valencia, Muchotrigo, Baroni.
Paraguay: Chilavert; Barrios (Ferreira 81), Rivarola, Ayala, Suarez, Sanabria V (Monzon 81), Struway, Acuna, Torres, Cabanas, Mendoza.

Buenos Aires, 5 September 1993, 60,000

Argentina (0) 0

Colombia (1) 5 *(Asprilla 41, 50, 76, Rincon 74, Valencia 85)*

Argentina: Goycochea; Saldana, Ruggeri, Borelli, Altamirano, Zapata, Redondo (Garcia 54), Simeone, Leo Rodriguez (Acosta 71), Medina Bello, Batistuta.
Colombia: Cordoba; Herrera, Perea, Mendoza, Wilson Perez, Gomez, Alvarez, Rincon, Valderrama, Asprilla, Valencia.

Group A

	P	*W*	*D*	*L*	*F*	*A*	*Pts*
Colombia	6	4	2	0	13	2	10
Argentina	6	3	1	2	7	9	7
Paraguay	6	1	4	1	6	7	6
Peru	6	0	1	5	4	12	1

Colombia qualified; Argentina in play-off v Australia

Group B

Cuidad Guyana, 18 July 1993, 12,500

Venezuela (1) 1 *(Palencia 14)*

Bolivia (4) 7 *(Sanchez E 27, 39, 54, Ramallo 39, 61, 68, Cristaldo 40)*

Venezuela: Gomez; Garcia C, Mathias (Rivas H 46), Echenique (Milillo 31), Morales, Hernandez, Rodriguez, Palencia, Camacho, Echenausi, Dolgetta.
Bolivia: Rojas; Rimba, Sandy, Borja, Cristaldo, Quinteros, Melgar, Baldivieso, Etcheverry (Castillo 85), Ramallo (Alvaro Pena 76), Sanchez E.

Guayaquil, 18 July 1993, 40,000

Ecuador (0) 0

Brazil (0) 0

Ecuador: Espinoza; Coronel, Tenorio B, Noriega, Capurro, Tenorio M, Carcelen, Carabali (Hurtado I 65), Aguinaga, Chala (Hurtado E 67), Munoz.
Brazil: Taffarel; Jorginho, Marcio Santos, Valber, Branco, Luis Henrique (Evair 70), Mauro Silva, Zinho, Rai, Bebeto, Careca (Dunga 70).

San Cristobal, 25 July 1993, 12,000

Venezuela (0) 0

Uruguay (0) 1 *(Herrera 59)*

Venezuela: Gomez; Echenausi, Mathias (Garcia 80), Gonzalez, Filosa, Hernandez, Palencia, Dolgetta, Rodriguez, Rivas S, Rivas H.
Uruguay: Siboldi; Herrera (De los Santos 71), Sanchez, Kanapkis, Cabrera, Moran, Ostolaza, Zalazar, Francescoli, Fonseca, Ruben Sosa (Aguilera 85).

La Paz, 25 July 1993, 45,000

Bolivia (0) 2 *(Etcheverry 88, Pena 89)*

Brazil (0) 0

Bolivia: Trucco; Borja, Rimba, Quinteros, Cristaldo, Sandy, Melgar, Baldivieso, Etcheverry, Ramallo (Alvaro Pena 73), Sanchez E (Castillo 81).
Brazil: Taffarel; Cafu, Marcio Santos, Valber, Leonardo, Luis Henrique (Jorginho 42), Mauro Silva, Zinho, Rai (Palinha 63), Bebeto, Muller.

Montevideo, 1 August 1993, 55,000

Uruguay (0) 0

Ecuador (0) 0

Uruguay: Siboldi; Herrera, Sanchez, Kanapkis, Cabrera, Moran (Da Silva J 80), Ostolaza, Zalazar, Francescoli, Fonseca (Aguilera 46), Ruben Sosa.
Ecuador: Espinoza; Noriega, Capurro, Tenorio B (Carabali 80), Carcelen, Tenorio M, Hurtado I, Coronel, Aguinaga (Chala 40), Munoz, Hurtado E.

San Cristobal, 1 August 1993, 26,000

Venezuela (0) 1 *(Garcia J 84)*

Brazil (1) 5 *(Rai 34 (pen), Bebeto 70, 79, Branco 71, Palinha 88)*

Venezuela: Gomez; Filosa, Echenausi, Gonzalez, Mathias, Hernandez, Rivas H, Chacon, Rivas S (Contreras 80), Dolgetta (Garcia J 72), Rodriguez.
Brazil: Taffarel; Jorginho, Antonio Carlos, Elivelton, Valber, Marcio Santos, Branco, Mauro Silva, Dunga, Rai (Palinha 64), Bebeto, Careca (Evair 64).

La Paz, 8 August 1993, 45,000

Bolivia (0) 3 *(Sanchez E 71, Etcheverry 81, Melgar 86)*

Uruguay (0) 1 *(Francescoli 89)*

Bolivia: Trucco; Borja, Quinteros, Rimba, Sandy, Cristaldo, Baldivieso, Melgar, Castillo (Etcheverry 53), Sanchez E, Ramallo (Alvaro Pena 84).
Uruguay: Siboldi; Herrera, Sanchez, Kanapkis, Cabrera, Moran, Gutierrez, Zalazar, Francescoli, Fonseca (Moas 66), Ruben Sosa (Aguilera 59).

Guayaquil, 8 August 1993, 30,000

Ecuador (2) 5 *(Munoz 23, Hurtado E 40, 50, 75, Chala 60)*

Venezuela (0) 0

Ecuador: Espinoza; Coronel (Zambrano 69), Capurro, Montanero, Hurtado I, Carcelen, Carabali, Munoz, Fernandez, Hurtado E, Chala (Aviles 69).
Venezuela: Gomez; Filosa, Gonzalez, Rivas H, Mathias, Milillo, Morales (Garcia C 54), Chacon (Contreras 88), Rivas S, Dolgetta, Garcia J.

Montevideo, 15 August 1993, 55,000

Uruguay (0) 1 *(Fonseca 79)*

Brazil (1) 1 *(Marcio Santos 28)*

Uruguay: Siboldi; Sanguinetti, Kanapkis, Sanchez, Cabrera, Ostolaza (Zalazar 71), Moran, Francescoli, Fonseca, Aguilera, Ruben Sosa (Adrian Paz 59).
Brazil: Taffarel; Jorginho, Marcio Santos, Ricardo Rocha, Branco, Dunga, Mauro Silva, Zinho, Rai, Bebeto (Antonio Carlos 71), Muller (Valdeir 84).

La Paz, 15 August 1993, 35,000

Bolivia (1) 1 *(Ramallo 18)*

Ecuador (0) 0

Bolivia: Trucco; Borja, Sandy, Quinteros, Rimba, Cristaldo, Melgar, Sanchez E, Baldivieso, Etcheverry (Villarroel 82), Ramallo (Alvaro Pena 70).
Ecuador: Espinoza; Noriega, Tenorio B, Capurro, Carabali, Hurtado I, Carcelen, Coronel, Aguinaga (Fernandez 65), Munoz (Chala 60), Hurtado E.

Sao Paulo, 22 August 1993, 77,916

Brazil (1) 2 *(Bebeto 34, Dunga 54)*

Ecuador (0) 0

Brazil: Taffarel; Jorginho, Marcio Santos, Ricardo Gomes, Branco (Cafu 75), Dunga, Mauro Silva, Zinho, Rai (Palinha 81), Bebeto, Muller.
Ecuador: Espinoza; Tenorio M, Hurtado I, Capurro, Coronel, Carcelen, Carabali, Fernandez (Gavica 77), Munoz (Aviles 65), Chala, Hurtado E.

La Paz, 22 August 1993, 35,000

Bolivia (1) 7 *(Ramallo 8, Melgar 58, 90, Sanchez E 69, Sandy 75, Etcheverry 78, 82)*

Venezuela (0) 0

Bolivia: Trucco; Borja, Sandy, Quinteros, Rimba, Villarroel (Castillo 70), Cristaldo, Melgar, Etcheverry, Sanchez E, Ramallo (Alvaro Pena 70).
Venezuela: Gomez; Filosa, Garcia J (Garcia C 30), Tortolero, Echenausi, Contreras, Hernandez, Rodriguez, Gonzalez, Rivas S (Morales 46), Paezpumar.

Montevideo, 29 August 1993, 60,000

Uruguay (3) 4 *(Kanapkis 7, 31, Cedres 41, Ruben Sosa 64)*

Venezuela (0) 0

Uruguay: Siboldi; Mendez, Herrera, Kanapkis, Soca (De los Santos 34), Dorta, Gutierrez, Francescoli, Aguilera (Adrian Paz 65), Cedres, Ruben Sosa.
Venezuela: Gomez; Rivas H, Gonzalez, Garcia C, Filosa, Echenausi (Contreras 78), Mathias, Paezpumar, Chacon, Rivas S, Garcia J (Rodriguez 46).

Recife, 29 August 1993, 76,636

Brazil (5) 6 *(Rai 12, Muller 18, Bebeto 22, 60, Branco 36, Ricardo Gomes 44)*

Bolivia (0) 0

Brazil: Taffarel; Jorginho, Ricardo Rocha, Ricardo Gomes, Branco, Mauro Silva, Dunga, Rai, Zinho (Palinha 55), Bebeto (Evair 71), Muller.
Bolivia: Trucco; Rimba, Borja, Sandy, Quinteros, Cristaldo, Melgar, Baldivieso, Sanchez E, Etcheverry (Juan Pena 41), Ramallo (Alvaro Pena 71).

Guayaquil, 5 September 1993, 60,000

Ecuador (0) 0

Uruguay (1) 1 *(Ruben Sosa 9)*

Ecuador: Espinoza; Capurro, Tenorio B, Noriega, Hurtado I (Aviles 63), Carcelen (Chala 75), Carabali, Aguinaga, Gavica, Hurtado E, Munoz.
Uruguay: Siboldi; Canals, Mendez, Herrera, Kanapkis, Batista, Dorta, Gutierrez, Francescoli (Fonseca 66), Aguilera (Saralegui 63), Ruben Sosa.

Belo Horizonte, 5 September 1993, 64,000

Brazil (3) 4 *(Ricardo Gomes 27, 90, Palinha 29, Evair 31)*

Venezuela (0) 0

Brazil: Taffarel; Jorginho, Ricardo Rocha, Ricardo Gomes, Branco, Mauro Silva, Palinha, Rai, Zinho, Valdeir (Luis Henrique 75), Evair.
Venezuela: Gomez; Filosa, Tortolero, Rivas H, Garcia C, Rodriguez, Chacon (Hernandez 83), Echenausi, Paezpumar (Milillo 75), Garcia J, Morales.

Montevideo, 12 September 1993, 65,000

Uruguay (1) 2 *(Francescoli 3 (pen), Fonseca 51)*

Bolivia (1) 1 *(Ramallo 22)*

Uruguay: Siboldi; Mendez, Herrera, Canals, Batista, Dorta, Gutierrez (Zalazar 46), Francescoli, Aguilera, Fonseca (Saralegui 73), Cedres.
Bolivia: Trucco; Quinteros, Rimba, Rivero, Juan Pena, Cristaldo, Melgar, Borja, Baldivieso (Pinedo 80), Sanchez E , Ramallo (Alvaro Pena 62).

Ciudad Guyana, 12 September 1993, 2000

Venezuela (1) 2 *(Garcia J 1, Morales 47)*

Ecuador (1) 1 *(Tenorio B 5)*

Venezuela: Gomez; Filosa, Tortolero, Morales, Gonzalez, Paezpumar, Echenausi, Rivas H, Rivas S, Garcia J (Contreras 46), Camacho (Rodriguez 80).
Ecuador: Espinoza; Munoz (Aviles 58), Noriega, Capurro, Hurtado I, Carcelen, Coronel, Tenorio B, Fernandez, Hurtado E, Chala (Gavica 58).

Rio, 19 September 1993, 101,500

Brazil (0) 2 *(Romario 72, 82)*

Uruguay (0) 0

Brazil: Taffarel; Jorginho, Ricardo Rocha, Ricardo Gomes, Branco, Mauro Silva, Dunga, Rai, Zinho, Bebeto, Romario.
Uruguay: Siboldi; Herrera, Canals (Adrian Paz 68), Mendez, Kanapkis, Batista, Gutierrez, Dorta, Francescoli (Zalazar 68), Ruben Sosa, Fonseca.

Guayaquil, 19 September 1993, 5000

Ecuador (0) 1 *(Noriega 72)*

Bolivia (1) 1 *(Ramallo 45)*

Ecuador: Espinoza; Coronel, Noriega, Hurtado I, Capurro, Fernandez, Chala (Carcelen 54), Tenorio M, Aguinaga, Aviles, Munoz (Gavica 43).
Bolivia: Trucco; Soruco (Pinedo 78), Sandy, Quinteros, Cristaldo, Rivero, Borja, Melgar, Baldivieso, Sanchez E, Ramallo (Etcheverry 58).

Group B

	P	*W*	*D*	*L*	*F*	*A*	*Pts*
Brazil	8	5	2	1	20	4	12
Bolivia	8	5	1	2	22	11	11
Uruguay	8	4	2	2	10	7	10
Ecuador	8	1	3	4	7	7	5
Venezuela	8	1	0	7	4	34	2

Brazil and Bolivia qualified

Concacaf

USA qualified as hosts

Pre-preliminary round

Dominican Republic 1, Puerto Rico 2
Puerto Rico 1, Dominican Republic 1
St Lucia 1, St Vincent 0
St Vincent 3, St Lucia 1

Preliminary round

Bermuda 1, Haiti 0
Haiti 2, Bermuda 1
Jamaica 2, Puerto Rico 1
Puerto Rico 0, Jamaica 1
Cuba withdrew, St Vincent w.o
Netherlands Antilles 1, Antigua 1
Antigua 3, Netherlands Antilles 0
Guyana 1, Surinam 2
Surinam 1, Guyana 1
Barbados 1, Trinidad & Tobago 2
Trinidad & Tobago 3, Barbados 0

First round

Central Region

Guatemala 0, Honduras 0
Honduras 2, Guatemala 0
Panama 1, Costa Rica 0
Costa Rica 5, Panama 1
Nicaragua 0, El Salvador 5
El Salvador 5, Nicaragua 1

Caribbean Region

Surinam 0, St Vincent 0
St Vincent 2, Surinam 1
Antigua 0, Bermuda 3
Bermuda 2, Antigua 1
Trinidad & Tobago 1, Jamaica 2
Jamaica 1, Trinidad & Tobago 1

Second round

Group A

Costa Rica 2, Honduras 3
St Vincent 0, Mexico 4
Mexico 2, Honduras 0
St Vincent 0, Costa Rica 1
Mexico 4, Costa Rica 0
St Vincent 0, Honduras 4
Honduras 4, St Vincent 0
Costa Rica 2, Mexico 0
Honduras 2, Costa Rica 1
Mexico 11, St Vincent 0
Costa Rica 5, St Vincent 0
Honduras 1, Mexico 1

Group B

Bermuda 1, El Salvador 0
Jamaica 1, Canada 1
Bermuda 1, Jamaica 1
El Salvador 1, Canada 1
Canada 1, Jamaica 0
El Salvador 4, Bermuda 1
Canada 2, El Salvador 3
Jamaica 3, Bermuda 2
Canada 4, Bermuda 2
Jamaica 0, El Salvador 2
Bermuda 0, Canada 0
El Salvador 2, Jamaica 1

Third Round

Honduras 2, Canada 2
El Salvador 2, Mexico 1
Canada 2, El Salvador 0
Mexico 3, Honduras 0
Canada 3, Honduras 1
Mexico 3, El Salvador 1
Honduras 2, El Salvador 0
Mexico 4, Canada 0
Honduras 1, Mexico 4
El Salvador 1, Canada 2
Canada 1, Mexico 2
El Salvador 2, Honduras 1

Mexico qualified

Oceania

Group 1

Solomon Islands 1, Tahiti 1
Solomon Islands 1, Australia 2
Tahiti 0, Australia 3
Australia 2, Tahiti 0
Australia 6, Solomon Islands 1
Tahiti 4, Solomon Islands 2

Group 2

New Zealand 3, Fiji 0
Vanuatu 1, New Zealand 4
New Zealand 8, Vanuatu 0
Fiji 3, Vanuatu 0
Fiji 0, New Zealand 0
Vanuatu 0, Fiji 3

Second Round

New Zealand 0, Australia 1
Australia 3, New Zealand 0

Winner Oceania v Second Concacaf

Canada 2, Australia 1
Australia 2, Canada 1
Australia won 4-1 on penalties

Winner Oceania/Concacaf v 4th South America

Sydney, 31 October 1993, 43,967

Australia (1) 1 *(Aurelio Vidmar 42)*

Argentina (1) 1 *(Balbo 37)*

Australia: Bosnich; Tony Vidmar (Mitchell 72), Tobin, Zelic, Van Bierk, Durakovic, Ivanovic, Wade, Slater, Aurelio Vidmar, Arnold.
Argentina: Goycochea; Chamot, Borelli, Vazquez, MacAlister, Perez, Redondo, Basualdo JH (Zapata 70), Maradona, Balbo (Caceres 88), Batistuta.

Buenos Aires, 17 November 1993, 60,000

Argentina (0) 1 *(Batistuta 60)*

Australia (0) 0

Argentina: Goycochea; Chamot, Vazquez, Ruggeri, MacAlister, Simeone, Perez, Redondo, Maradona, Balbo (Zapata 68), Batistuta.
Australia: Zabica; Ivanovic, Tony Vidmar (Veart 63), Durakovic, Tobin, Van Bierk, Slater, Wade, Aurelio Vidmar, Arnold, Farina.

Argentina qualified

Africa

First Round

Group A

Algeria 3, Burundi 1
Burundi 1, Ghana 0
Ghana 2, Algeria 0
Burundi 0, Algeria 0
Ghana 1, Burundi 0
Algeria 2, Ghana 1
Uganda withdrew

Group B

Zaire 4, Liberia 2
Cameroon 5, Swaziland 0
Swaziland 1, Zaire 0
Zaire 1, Cameroon 2
Swaziland 0, Cameroon 0
Zaire v Swaziland not played
Cameroon 0, Zaire 0
Liberia withdrew

Group C

Zimbabwe 1, Togo 0
Egypt 1, Angola 0
Togo 1, Egypt 4
Zimbabwe 2, Egypt 1
Angola 1, Zimbabwe 1
Togo 1, Zimbabwe 2
Angola 0, Egypt 0
Egypt 3, Togo 0
Zimbabwe 2, Angola 1
Angola v Togo not played
Egypt 0, Zimbabwe 0 (after 2-1 win declared null and void due to crowd trouble)
Togo 0, Angola 1

Group D

Nigeria 4, South Africa 0
South Africa 1, Congo 0
Congo 0, Nigeria 1
South Africa 0, Nigeria 0
Congo 0, South Africa 1
Nigeria 2, Congo 0
Libya withdrew

Group E

Ivory Coast 6, Botswana 0
Niger 0, Ivory Coast 0
Botswana 0, Niger 1
Botswana 0, Ivory Coast 0
Ivory Coast 1, Niger 0
Niger 2, Botswana 1
Sudan withdrew

Group F

Morocco 5, Ethiopia 0
Tunisia 5, Benin 1
Benin 0, Morocco 1
Ethiopia 0, Tunisia 0
Ethiopia 3, Benin 1
Tunisia 1, Morocco 1
Benin 0, Tunisia 5
Ethiopia 0, Morocco 1
Morocco 5, Benin 0
Tunisia 3, Ethiopia 0
Benin 1, Ethiopia 0
Morocco 0, Tunisia 0

Group G

Gabon 3, Mozambique 1
Mozambique 0, Senegal 1
Gabon 3, Senegal 2
Mozambique 1, Gabon 1
Senegal 6, Mozambique 1
Senegal 1, Gabon 0
Mauritania withdrew

Group H

Madagascar 3, Namibia 0
Zambia 2, Tanzania 0
Tanzania 0, Madagascar 0
Namibia 0, Zambia 4
Tanzania 2, Namibia 0
Madagascar 2, Zambia 0
Tanzania 1, Zambia 3
Namibia 0, Madagascar 1
Zambia 4, Namibia 0
Zambia 3, Madagascar 1
Tanzania withdrew

Group I

Guinea 4, Kenya 0
Kenya 2, Guinea 0
Mali and Gambia withdrew

Second round

Group A

Algeria 1, Ivory Coast 1
Ivory Coast 2, Nigeria 1
Nigeria 4, Algeria 1
Ivory Coast 1, Algeria 0
Nigeria 4, Ivory Coast 1
Algeria 1, Nigeria 1

Nigeria qualified

Group B

Morocco 1, Senegal 0
Zambia 2, Morocco 1
Senegal 1, Morocco 3
Senegal 0, Zambia 0
Zambia 4, Senegal 0
Morocco 1, Zambia 0

Morocco qualified

Group C

Cameroon 3, Guinea 1
Guinea 3, Zimbabwe 0
Zimbabwe 1, Cameroon 0
Guinea 0, Cameroon 1
Zimbabwe 1, Guinea 0
Cameroon 3, Zimbabwe 1

Cameroon qualified

Asia

First round

Group A (in Jordan)

Jordan 1, Yemen 1
Pakistan 0, China 5
Jordan 1, Iraq 1
Yemen 5, Pakistan 1
Iraq 6, Yemen 1
Jordan 0, China 3
Iraq 8, Pakistan 0
Yemen 1, China 0
Iraq 1, China 0
Jordan 3, Pakistan 1
(in China)
China 3, Pakistan 0
Yemen 1, Jordan 1
Iraq 4, Jordan 0
Pakistan 0, Yemen 3
China 4, Jordan 1
Yemen 0, Iraq 3
Pakistan 0, Iraq 4
China 1, Yemen 0
Pakistan 5, Jordan 0
China 2, Iraq 1

Group B (in Iran)

Syria 2, Taiwan 0
Iran 0, Oman 0
Iran 6, Taiwan 0
Oman 0, Syria 0
Iran 1, Syria 1
Oman 2, Taiwan 1
(in Syria)
Oman 0, Iran 1
Taiwan 1, Syria 8
Taiwan 0, Iran 6
Syria 2, Oman 1
Taiwan 1, Oman 7
Syria 1, Iran 1

Myanmar withdrew

Group C (in Qatar)

Korea DPR 3, Vietnam 0
Qatar 3, Indonesia 1
Korea DPR 2, Singapore 1
Qatar 4, Vietnam 0
Korea DPR 4, Indonesia 0
Vietnam 2, Singapore 3
Qatar 4, Singapore 1
Vietnam 1, Indonesia 0
Indonesia 0, Singapore 2
Qatar 1, Korea DPR 2
(in Singapore)
Indonesia 1, Qatar 4
Vietnam 0, Korea DPR 1
Singapore 1, Korea DPR 3
Vietnam 0, Qatar 4
Indonesia 1, Korea DPR 2
Singapore 1, Vietnam 0
Indonesia 2, Vietnam 1
Singapore 1, Qatar 0
Korea DPR 2, Qatar 2
Singapore 2, Indonesia 1

Group D (in Lebanon)

Hong Kong 2, Bahrain 1
Lebanon 2, India 2
Bahrain 0, Korea Rep 0
Lebanon 2, Hong Kong 2
India 1, Hong Kong 2
Lebanon 0, Korea Rep 1
India 0, Korea Rep 3
Lebanon 0, Bahrain 0
Bahrain 2, India 1
Hong Kong 0, Korea Rep 3
(in Korea Rep)
Bahrain 0, Lebanon 0
Korea Rep 4, Hong Kong 1
India 0, Bahrain 3
Korea Rep 2, Lebanon 0
Korea Rep 7, India 0
Hong Kong 1, Lebanon 2
India 1, Lebanon 2
Bahrain 3, Hong Kong 0
Korea Rep 3, Bahrain 0
Hong Kong 1, India 3

Group E (in Malaysia)

Macao 0, Saudi Arabia 6
Malaysia 1, Kuwait 1
Macao 1, Kuwait 10
Malaysia 1, Saudi Arabia 1
Kuwait 0, Saudi Arabia 0
Malaysia 9, Macao 0
(in Saudi Arabia)
Kuwait 2, Malaysia 0
Saudi Arabia 8, Macao 0
Kuwait 8, Macao 0
Saudi Arabia 3, Malaysia 0
Macao 0, Malaysia 5
Saudi Arabia 2, Kuwait 0

Group F (in Japan)

Japan 1, Thailand 0
Sri Lanka 0, UAE 4
Japan 8, Bangladesh 0
Thailand 1, Sri Lanka 0
Sri Lanka 0, Bangladesh 1
UAE 1, Thailand 0
Japan 5, Sri Lanka 0
UAE 1, Bangladesh 0

Japan 2, UAE 0
Thailand 4, Bangladesh 1
(in UAE)
Thailand 0, Japan 1
UAE 3, Sri Lanka 0
Bangladesh 1, Japan 4
Thailand 1, UAE 2
Bangladesh 0, UAE 7
Sri Lanka 0, Thailand 3
Bangladesh 1, Thailand 4
Sri Lanka 0, Japan 6
Bangladesh 3, Sri Lanka 0
UAE 1, Japan 1

Second Round (in Qatar)

Korea DPR 3, Iraq 2
Saudi Arabia 0, Japan 0
Iran 0, Korea Rep 3
Korea DPR 1, Saudi Arabia 2
Japan 1, Iran 2
Iraq 2, Korea Rep 2
Korea DPR 0, Japan 3
Iran 1, Iraq 2
Korea Rep 1, Saudi Arabia 1
Iraq 1, Saudi Arabia 1
Japan 1, Korea Rep 0
Iran 2, Korea DPR 1
Korea Rep 3, Korea DPR 0
Saudi Arabia 4, Iran 3
Iraq 2, Japan 2

Saudi Arabia and Korea Rep qualified

THE WORLD CUP 1930–94

Year	Winners	Runners-up	Venue	Attendance	Referee
1930	Uruguay 4	Argentina 2	Montevideo	90,000	Langenus (B)
1934	Italy 2 *(after extra time)*	Czechoslovakia 1	Rome	50,000	Eklind (Se)
1938	Italy 4	Hungary 2	Paris	45,000	Capdeville (F)
1950	Uruguay 2	Brazil 1	Rio de Janeiro	199,854	Reader (E)
1954	West Germany 3	Hungary 2	Berne	60,000	Ling (E)
1958	Brazil 5	Sweden 2	Stockholm	49,737	Guigue (F)
1962	Brazil 3	Czechoslovakia 1	Santiago	68,679	Latychev (USSR)
1966	England 4 *(after extra time)*	West Germany 2	Wembley	93,802	Dienst (Sw)
1970	Brazil 4	Italy 1	Mexico City	107,412	Glockner (EG)
1974	West Germany 2	Holland 1	Munich	77,833	Taylor (E)
1978	Argentina 3 *(after extra time)*	Holland 1	Buenos Aires	77,000	Gonella (1)
1982	Italy 3	West Germany 1	Madrid	90,080	Coelho (Br)
1986	Argentina 3	West Germany 2	Mexico City	114,580	Filho (Br)
1990	West Germany 1	Argentina 0	Rome	73,603	Codesal (Mex)
1994	Brazil 0 *(Brazil won 3-2 on penalties act)*	Italy 0	Los Angeles	94,194	Puhl (Hungary)

GOALSCORING AND ATTENDANCES IN WORLD CUP FINAL ROUNDS

Venue	*Matches*	*Goals (avge)*	*Attendance (avge)*
1930, Uruguay	18	70 (3.9)	434,500 (24,138)
1934, Italy	17	70 (4.1)	395,000 (23,235)
1938, France	18	84 (4.6)	483,000 (26,833)
1950, Brazil	22	88 (4.0)	1,337,000 (60,772)
1954, Switzerland	26	140 (5.4)	943,000 (36,270)
1958, Sweden	35	126 (3.6)	868,000 (24,800)
1962, Chile	32	89 (2.8)	776,000 (24,250)
1966, England	32	89 (2.8)	1,614,677 (50,458)
1970, Mexico	32	95 (2.9)	1,673,975 (52,311)
1974, West Germany	38	97 (2.5)	1,774,022 (46,684)
1978, Argentina	38	102 (2.7)	1,610,215 (42,374)
1982, Spain	52	146 (2.8)	2,064,364 (38,816)
1986, Mexico	52	132 (2.5)	2,441,731 (46,956)
1990, Italy	52	115 (2.2)	2,515,168 (48,368)
1994, USA	52	141 (2.71)	3,567,415 (68,604)

WORLD CUP USA 1994

Final Tournament

Once the dust settled in LA, the overall impression from the 1994 World Cup finals was more positive than negative. This might appear damming with faint praise, but the pre-tournament noises had been far from encouraging.

Media attention had been focused on the Americans who were supposed not to know anything about the world's greatest sporting event which was about to take off on their doorsteps. Yet the kind of people interviewed are those who think quite seriously that Europe is a country. What does one expect from a nation which holds a World Series Baseball competition confined solely to North America?

The ending of the World Cup was disappointing because of the penalty shoot-out. This has to be removed from future tournaments. The only sensible way is to play on until one team scores a goal. If they can drag themselves into the nervous-tension draining of spot kicks, they can certainly carry on playing.

All that said, Brazil deserved their success, albeit in the unsatisfactory method with which it was obtained. Italy were always second best in the final. Moreover on the statistics from the game Brazil had more goal attempts 22 to eight; gained more corners five to three and were offside more times nine to three!

However, of all the 24 teams involved in the tournament, Brazil arguably completed more passes than any of their rivals and kept the ball on the ground when so doing. The long ball game was not in evidence not wholly because of the chasing required in the extreme heat.

There was understandably much talk about the number of yellow cards flashed – 227 in all and the accompanying red version – 15. This was as a result of FIFA's pressure on the referees to implement the laws of the game as they have stood for some time concerning the so-called 'tackle from behind'. This nonsense that it was a new directive should be squashed for the last time. What was being outlawed was one player kicking another player.

The other move to allow players standing in an offside position but not interfering with the game, produced a variety of odd interpretations and led to the increase in goalscoring to some small extent. That goals were more freely available was something which was to be applauded anyway, though the manner of them was not always as one would have liked.

The 141 goals scored in open play represented a 2.71 average. This compared with only 2.21 in 1990, but was below the 2.8 achieved in 1982 in Spain. The halcyon days of goalscoring will never return and the figure of 5.3 from 1954 seems unbelievable now, though it was perfectly acceptable in those days.

As to the teams and their performances, there were the favourites who fell by the wayside and the outsiders who did better than expected. This has always been true of all World Cup final competitions. Among the teams who failed to cause the ripples predicted for them were Germany, Colombia, Argentina and Bolivia.

The Germans are feared because it is dangerous to underestimate their potential in such circumstances. A better indication of their pending demise should have been taken from that pre-tournament friendly when they were beaten 2-0 by the Republic of Ireland. They had an old, tired look about them. Colombia managed the impossible: peaking before the tournament, lapsing during it and recovering their best form after being knocked-out. Argentina suffered from the Maradona incident and lacked character as a result of the upset. Bolivia simply did not live up to their billing and clearly can only operate at high altitude when everyone else is suffering.

The surprises were Sweden, who would have done even better had they not adopted negative tactics in too many important matches, the Saudis, Romania and to some extent, Nigeria. The Swedes showed that the European Championship in 1992 was not an isolated incident of improvement. The Romanians were fluent and enterprising and only a naive approach to the match against an Italian team reduced to ten men, spoiled a commendable contribution. The Saudis will benefit from more contact with first-class opposition and scored the best goal of the finals through Saeed Owairan against Belgium.

Taking the ball inside his own half, he beat one player, side-stepped another, caused a third to off-balance himself and beat a fourth before scoring.

Bulgaria were something of an enigma. They deservedly beat the Germans, but how much of this was down to the excellent performance in midfield of Yordan Lechkov, who plays in the Bundesliga and knows most of their players' habits. They also caught Argentina immediately after the Maradona episode.

As to individuals, Romario was probably the most technically gifted player in the tournament, but he, too, was not on top form in the final.

Consistent performances also came from Paolo Maldini (Italy), Gheorghe Hagi (Romania), Kennet Andersson (Sweden) and Franco Baresi (Italy) who returned from a 23 day absence during which he was recovering from an operation to be outstanding in the final. Among the disappointments were Faustino Asprilla and Carlos Valderrama (both Colombia), Rai (Brazil), Bodo Illgner (Germany) and Josip Weber (Belgium).

In addition there were surprisingly fine displays from Alexi Lalas (USA), Ilie Dumitrescu (Romania) and the virtual second choice Brazilian central defenders Marcio Santos and Aldair.

The great sadness of the competition came from the killing of Andreas Escobar, the Colombian player who was the only one to put through his own goal during the finals. He was shot on his return home. Escobar had scored Colombia's goal against England at Wembley six years earlier.

Roberto Baggio, the Italian who was European and World Player of the Year, had a curious tournament. He flitted only momentarily into his most penetrating pose and clearly unfit in the final, might have cost Italy a possible victory.

Comparisons with this Brazil and those of 1970 are not entirely valid. For all his expertise and skill Romario would not have replaced any of the front players, though Jorginho and Leonardo might have challenged the flank defenders and the twin centre-backs also had a case for inclusion. In goal Taffarel was an improvement on Felix, but almost anyone would have been!

Attendances were as predicted the best ever in the finals. There were 3,567,415 spectators for the 52 matches for an average of 68,604. The highest was in Pasadena for the Brazil v Italy final which attracted 94,194.

The fastest goal was scored by Batistuta (Argentina) after two minutes against Greece. Two Bulgarians scored the latest goals in normal time: three minutes of injury time in fact, Borimirov also against Greece and Sirakov against Argentina.

Among the firsts were: 1. An indoor game USA v Switzerland in the Pontiace Silverdome, Detroit; 2. Five goals by one player in a match: Salenko (Russia); 3. Three substitutes in a match: When Italian goalkeeper Pagliuca was sent off and replaced.

Matthaus (Germany) and Maradona (Argentina) equalled Seeler (Germany) and Zmuda (Yugoslavia) by playing in their 21st final match.

The 15 players dismissed were: Vladiou (Romania) v Switzerland, Etchverry (Bolivia) v Germany, Nadal (Spain) v South Korea, Pagliuca (Italy) v Norway, Cristaldo (Bolivia) v South Korea, Song (Cameroon) v Brazil, Gorlukovich (Russia) v Sweden, Tzvetanov (Bulgaria) v Argentina, Zola (Italy) v Nigeria, Luis Garcia (Mexico) v Bulgaria, Kremenliev (Bulgaria) v Mexico, Leonardo (Brazil) v USA, Clavijo (USA) v Brazil, Schwarz (Sweden) v Romania and Thern (Sweden) v Brazil.

Sweden were top scorers with 15 goals, Brazil conceded only three.

All 15 penalties were converted, 65 goals were scored in the first half, 73 in the second half and three in extra time. Greece failed to score a goal. A European team has yet to win the World Cup outside its own continent.

WORLD CUP 1994

Final tournament

First Round

Group A

Detroit, 18 June 1994, 77,557

USA (1) 1 *(Wynalda 45)*

Switzerland (1) 1 *(Bregy 40)*

USA: Meola; Kooiman, Balboa, Lalas, Caligiuri, Ramos, Dooley, Sorber, Wynalda (Wegerle 59), Harkes, Stewart (Cobi Jones 81).
Switzerland: Pascolo; Hottiger, Herr, Geiger, Quentin, Ohrel, Bregy, Sforza (Wyss 77), Sutter, Bickel (Subiat 73), Chapuisat.
Referee: Lamolina (Argentina)

Los Angeles, 18 June 1994, 91,856

Colombia (1) 1 *(Valencia 42)*

Romania (2) 3 *(Raducioiu 15, 87, Hagi 33)*

Colombia: Cordoba; Herrera, Perea, Escobar, Perez, Alvarez, Valderrama, Rincon, Gomez, Asprilla, Valencia.
Romania: Stelea; Belodedici, Prodan, Mihali, Petrescu, Lupescu, Popescu, Hagi, Munteanu, Dumitrescu (Selymes 63), Raducioiu (Papura 90).
Referee: Al Sharif (Syria).

Detroit, 22 June 1994, 61,428

Romania (1) 1 *(Hagi 36)*

Switzerland (1) 4 *(Sutter 16, Chapuisat 53, Knup 66, 73)*

Romania: Stelea; Belodedici, Prodan, Mihali, Petrescu, Lupescu (Panduru 85), Popescu, Munteanu, Hagi, Dumitrescu (Vladiou 71), Raducioiu.
Switzerland: Pascolo; Hottiger, Herr, Geiger, Quentin, Ohrel (Sylvestre 84), Bregy, Sforza, Sutter (Bickel 71), Knup, Chapuisat.
Referee: Jouini (Tunisia).

Los Angeles, 23 June 1994, 93,194

USA (1) 2 *(Escobar (og) 35, Stewart 53)*

Colombia (0) 1 *(Valencia 90)*

USA: Meola; Balboa, Clavijo, Lalas, Caligiuri, Ramos, Harkes, Dooley, Sorber, Stewart (Cobi Jones 76), Wynalda (Wegerle 61).
Colombia: Cordoba; Perez, Perea, Escobar, Herrera, Alvarez, Valderrama, Rincon, Gaviria, Asprilla (Valencia 46), De Avila (Valenciano 46).
Referee: Baldas (Italy).

Los Angeles, 26 June 1994, 93,869

USA (0) 0

Romania (1) 1 *(Petrescu 17)*

USA: Meola; Clavijo, Balboa, Lalas, Caligiuri, Harkes, Dooley, Ramos (Cobi Jones 64), Sorber (Wegerle 75), Stewart, Wynalda.
Romania: Prunea; Belodedici (Mihali 89), Petrescu, Selymes, Lupescu, Prodan, Hagi, Popescu, Munteanu, Dumitrescu, Raducioiu (Galca 84).
Referee: Van der Ende (Holland).

San Francisco, 26 June 1994, 83,769

Switzerland (0) 0

Colombia (1) 2 *(Gaviria 44, Lozano 90)*

Switzerland: Pascolo; Hottiger, Herr, Geiger, Quentin, Ohrel, Bregy, Sforza, Sutter (Subiat 82), Knup (Grassi 82), Chapuisat.
Colombia: Cordoba; Herrera, Mendoza, Escobar, Perez, Gaviria (Lozano 79), Alvarez, Valderrama, Rincon, Valencia (De Avila 64), Asprilla.
Referee: Mikkelsen (Denmark).

Group A

	P	*W*	*D*	*L*	*F*	*A*	*Pts*
Romania	3	2	0	1	5	5	6
Switzerland	3	1	1	1	5	4	4
USA	3	1	1	1	3	3	4
Colombia	3	1	0	2	4	5	3

Group B

Los Angeles, 20 June 1994, 83,959

Cameroon (1) 2 *(Embe 32, Omam-Biyik 47)*

Sweden (1) 2 *(Ljung 8, Dahlin 75)*

Cameroon: Bell; Song-Bahanag, MBouh, Kalla-Nkongo, Tataw, Libiih, MFede (Maboang-Kessack 87), Foe, Agbo, Omam-Biyik, Embe (Mouyeme 80).
Sweden: Ravelli; Nilsson, Patrik Andersson, Bjorklund, Ljung, Ingesson (Kennet Andersson 75), Thern, Schwarz, Blomqvist (Larsson 61), Brolin, Dahlin.
Referee: Tejada (Peru).

San Francisco, 20 June 1994, 81,061

Brazil (1) 2 *(Romario 26, Rai (pen) 53)*

Russia (0) 0

Brazil: Taffarel; Jorginho, Ricardo Rocha (Aldair 75), Marcio Santos, Leonardo, Dunga (Mazinho 84), Rai, Mauro Silva, Zinho, Bebeto, Romario.
Russia: Kharine; Nikiforov, Khlestov, Ternavski, Gorlukovich, Karpin, Kuznetsov, Piatnitski, Radchenko (Borodyuk 78), Tsymbalar, Yuran (Salenko 56).
Referee: Lim Kee Chon (Mauritius).

San Francisco, 24 June 1994, 83,410

Brazil (1) 3 *(Romario 39, Marcio Santos 65, Bebeto 73)*

Cameroon (0) 0

Brazil: Taffarel; Jorginho, Aldair, Marcio Santos, Leonardo, Rai (Muller 82), Mauro Silva, Dunga, Zinho (Paulo Sergio 75), Bebeto, Romario.
Cameroon: Bell; Song-Bahanag, Kalla-Nkono, MBouh, Tataw, Libiih, MFede (Maboang-Kessack 72), Foe, Agbo, Embe (Milla 64), Omam-Biyik.
Referee: Arturo Brizio Carter (Mexico).

Detroit, 25 June 1994, 71,528

Sweden (1) 3 *(Brolin 39 (pen), Dahlin 60, 82)*

Russia (1) 1 *(Salenko (pen) 4)*

:*Sweden:* Ravelli; Nilsson, Patrik Andersson, Bjorklund (Erlingmark 89), Ljung, Brolin, Schwarz, Thern, Ingesson, Dahlin, Kennet Andersson (Larsson 84).
Russia: Kharine; Nikiforov, Gorlukovich, Kuznetsov, Mostovoi, Khlestov, Onopko, Borodyuk (Galjamin 51), Popov (Karpin 41), Radchenko, Salenko.
Referee: Quiniou (France).

Detroit, 28 June 1994, 77,217

Brazil (0) 1 *(Romario 47)*

Sweden (1) 1 *(Kennet Andersson 24)*

Brazil: Taffarel; Jorginho, Aldair, Marcio Santos, Leonardo, Dunga, Mauro Silva (Mazinho 46), Rai (Paulo Sergio 73), Zinho, Romario, Bebeto.
Sweden: Ravelli; Nilsson, Patrik Andersson, Kamark, Ljung, Larsson (Blomqvist 65), Schwarz (Mild 75), Thern, Ingesson, Kennet Andersson, Brolin.
Referee: Puhl (Hungary).

San Francisco, 28 June 1994, 74,914

Russia (3) 6 *(Salenko l6, 41, 44 (pen), 72, 75, Radchenko 82)*

Cameroon (0) 1 *(Milla 47)*

Russia: Cherchesov; Nikiforov, Ternavski, Khlestov, Tetradze, Onopko, Korneyev (Radchenko 66), Karpin, Lediakhov (Beschastnykh 78), Tsymbalar, Salenko.
Cameroon: Songoo; Tataw, Kalla-Nkongo, Ndip-Akem, Agbo, Libiih, Kana-Biyik, MFede (Milla 46), Foe, Omam-Biyik, Embe (Tchami 49).
Referee: Al Sharif (Syria).

Group B

	P	*W*	*D*	*L*	*F*	*A*	*Pts*
Brazil	3	2	1	0	6	1	7
Sweden	3	1	2	0	6	4	5
Russia	3	1	0	2	7	6	3
Cameroon	3	0	1	2	3	11	1

Group C

Chicago, 17 June 1994, 63,117

Germany (1) 1 *(Klinsmann 61)*

Bolivia (0) 0

Germany: Illgner; Matthaus, Kohler, Berthold, Effenberg, Hassler (Strunz 83), Sammer, Moller, Brehme, Riedle (Basler 60), Klinsmann.
Bolivia: Trucco; Quinteros, Rimba, Sandy, Borja, Soria, Erwin Sanchez, Melgar, Cristaldo, Romallo (Etcheverry 79), Baldivieso (Moreno 66).
Referee: Arturo Brizio Carter (Mexico).

Dallas, 18 June 1994, 56,247

Spain (0) 2 *(Salinas 50, Goicoechea 55)*

South Korea (0) 2 *(Hong Myung-Bo 84, Seo Jung-Won 90)*

Spain: Canizares; Nadal, Ferrer, Sergi, Fernandez, Alkorta, Goicoechea, Hierro, Guerrero (Caminero 46), Luis Enrique, Salinas (Felipe 63).
South Korea: Choi In-Young; Hong-Gi, Kim Pan-Keun, Park Jung-Bae, Lee Young-Jin, Noh Jung-Yoon (Ha Seok-Ju 72), Kim Joo-Sung (Seo Jung-Won 59), Ko Jeong-Woon, Choi Young-Il, Hong Myong-Bo, Hwang Sun-Hong.
Referee: Mikkelsen (Denmark).

Chicago, 21 June 1994, 63,113

Germany (0) 1 *(Klinsmann 48)*

Spain (1) 1 *(Goicoechea 14)*

Germany: Illgner; Matthaus, Kohler, Berthold, Strunz, Hassler, Effenberg, Sammer, Brehme, Moller (Voller 62), Klinsmann.
Spain: Zubizarreta; Ferrer, Abelardo, Alkorta, Sergi, Goicoechea (Bakero 65), Hierro, Caminero, Guardiola (Camarasa 78), Luis Enrique, Salinas.
Referee: Ernesto Filippi Cavani (Uruguay).

Boston, 24 June 1994, 53,000

South Korea (0) 0

Bolivia (0) 0

South Korea: Choi In-Young; Hong Myung-Bo, Kim Pan-Keun, Shin Hong-Gi, Noh Jung-Yoon (Choi Young-Il 71), Park Jung-Bae, Ko Jeong-Woon, Lee Young-Jin, Kim Joo-Sung, Hwang Sun-Hong, Seo Jung-Won (Ha Seok-Ju 65).
Bolivia: Trucco; Rimba, Quinteros, Sandy, Cristaldo, Borja, Melgar, Soria, Erwin Sanchez, Baldivieso, Ramallo (Pena 66).
Referee: Mottram (Scotland).

Chicago, 27 June 1994, 63,089

Bolivia (0) 1 *(Erwin Sanchez 67)*

Spain (1) 3 *(Guardiola 20 (pen), Caminero 66, 71)*

Bolivia: Trucco; Rimba, Pena, Sandy, Soruco, Borja, Erwin Sanchez, Soria (Castillo 63), Melgar, Ramallo, Ramos (Morena 46).
Spain: Zubizarreta; Ferrer, Voro, Abelardo, Sergi, Goicoechea, Guardiola, Guerrero, Caminero, Felipe (Hierro 46), Salinas.
Referee: Badilla (Costa Rica).

Dallas, 27 June 1994, 63,998

Germany (3) 3 *(Klinsmann 12, 37, Riedle 20)*

South Korea (0) 2 *(Hwang Sun-Hong 52, Hong Myung-Bo 63)*

Germany: Illgner; Matthaus (Moller 64), Kohler, Berthold, Effenberg (Helmer 75), Hassler, Buchwald, Sammer, Brehme, Riedle, Klinsmann.
South Korea: Choi In-Young (Lee Won-Jae 46); Hong Myung-Bo, Kim Pan-Keun, Choi Young-Il, Park Jung-Bae, Cho Jin-Ho (Seo Jung-Won 46), Lee Young-Jin (Chung Jong-Son 40), Kim Joo-Sung, Shin Hong-Gi, Ko Jeong-Woon, Hwang Sun-Hong.
Referee: Quiniou (France).

Group C

	P	*W*	*D*	*L*	*F*	*A*	*Pts*
Germany	3	2	1	0	5	3	7
Spain	3	1	2	0	6	4	5
South Korea	3	0	2	1	4	5	2
Bolivia	3	0	1	2	1	4	1

Group D

Boston, 21 June 1994, 53,644

Argentina (2) 4 *(Batistuta 2, 45, 90 (pen), Maradona 60)*

Greece (0) 0

Argentina: Islas; Ruggeri, Sensini, Caceres, Chamot, Simeone, Redondo, Maradona (Ortega 84), Balbo (Mancuso 81), Caniggia, Batistuta.
Greece: Minou; Manolas, Apostolakis, Kolitsidakis, Kalitzakis, Tsiantakis (Marangos 46), Tsalouchidis, Nioplias, Koifidis, Saravakos, Machlas (Mistropoulos 59).
Referee: Angeles (USA).

Dallas, 22 June 1994, 44,932

Bulgaria (0) 0

Nigeria (2) 3 *(Yekini 21, Amokachi 43, Amunike 54)*

Bulgaria: Mikhailov; Hubchev, Kremenliev, Ivanov, Tzvetanov, Borimirov (Yordanov 71), Lechkov (Sirakov 57), Balakov, Jankov, Kostadinov, Stoichkov.
Nigeria: Rufai; Nwanu, Eguavoen, Uche, Iroha, Siasia (Adepoju 67), Finidi (Ezeugo 76), Oliseh, Amunike, Amokachi, Yekini.
Referee: Badilla (Costa Rica).

Boston, 25 June 1994, 54,453

Argentina (2) 2 *(Caniggia 22, 29)*

Nigeria (1) 1 *(Siasia 9)*

Argentina: Islas; Sinisi (Diaz 87), Caceres, Ruggeri, Chamot, Balbo (Mancuso 71), Simeone, Maradona, Redondo, Batistuta, Caniggia.
Nigeria: Rufai; Nwanu, Eguavoen, Okechukwu, Finidi, Siasia (Adepoju 57), Emenalo, Oliseh (Okocha 87), Amokachi, Yekini, Amunike.
Referee: Karlsson (Sweden).

Chicago, 26 June 1994, 63,160

Bulgaria (1) 4 *(Stoichkov 5 (pen), 56 (pen), Lechkov 66, Borimirov 90)*

Greece (0) 0

Bulgaria: Mikhailov; Hubchev, Kremenliev, Ivanov, Tzvetanov (Kiriakov 77), Yankov, Lechkov, Balakov, Kostadinov (Borimirov 82), Sirakov, Stoichkov.
Greece: Atmatzidis; Apostolakis, Karataidis, Karagiannis, Kalitzakis, Marangos, Nioplias, Hantzidis (Mistropoulos 46), Kofidis, Machlas, Alexoudis (Dimitriadis 59).
Referee: Bujsaim (UAE).

Boston, 1 July 1994, 53,001

Greece (0) 0

Nigeria (1) 2 *(Finidi 45, Amokachi 90)*

Greece: Karkamanis; Alexiou, Hantzidis, Karagiannis, Kofidis (Dimitriadis 79), Nioplias, Kalitzakis, Tsalouchidis, Alexandris, Machlas, Mitropoulos (Tsiantakis 73).
Nigeria: Rufai; Keshi, Okechukwu, Nwanu, Siasia, Amokachi, Oliseh, Finidi (Adepoju 83), Emenalo, Yekini (Okocha 79), Amunike.
Referee: Mottram (Scotland).

Dallas, 1 July 1994, 63,998

Argentina (0) 0

Bulgaria (0) 2 *(Stoichkov 61, Sirakov 90)*

Argentina: Islas; Caceres, Ruggeri, Chamot, Diaz, Rodriguez (Medina 66), Simeone, Redondo, Balbo, Batistuta, Caniggia (Ortega 27).
Bulgaria: Mikhailov; Hubchev, Kremenliev, Ivanov, Kostadinov (Kiriakov 74), Lechkov (Borimirov 76), Yankov, Balakov, Tzvetanov, Sirakov, Stoichkov.
Referee: Jouini (Tunisia).

Group D

	P	*W*	*D*	*L*	*F*	*A*	*Pts*
Nigeria	3	2	0	1	6	2	4
Bulgaria	3	2	0	1	6	3	6
Argentina	3	2	0	1	6	3	6
Greece	3	0	0	3	0	10	0

Group E

New York, 18 June 1994, 73,511

Italy (0) 0

Republic of Ireland (1) 1 *(Houghton 12)*

Italy: Pagliuca; Tassotti, Baresi, Costacurta, Maldini, Donadoni, Dino Baggio, Albertini, Evani (Massaro 46), Roberto Baggio, Signori (Berti 84).
Republic of Ireland: Bonner; Irwin, McGrath, Babb, Phelan, Houghton (McAteer 68), Keane, Sheridan, Townsend, Staunton, Coyne (Aldridge 90).
Referee: Van der Ende (Holland).

Washington, 19 June 1994, 52,359

Norway (0) 1 *(Rekdal 85)*

Mexico (0) 0

Norway: Thorstvedt; Haaland, Bratseth, Berg, Bjornebye, Flo, Bohinen, Mykland (Rekdal 79), Leonhardsen, Jakobsen (Halle 46), Fjortoft.
Mexico: Campos; Gutierrez (Bernal 70), Suarez, Juan de Dios Ramirez, Jesus Ramirez, Ambriz, Del Olmo, Valdez (Galdino 46), Luis Garcia, Zague, Sanchez.
Referee: Puhl (Hungary).

New York, 23 June 1994, 74,624

Italy (0) 1 *(Dino Baggio 68)*

Norway (0) 0

Italy: Pagliuca; Benarrivo, Costacurta, Baresi (Apolloni 48), Maldini, Berti, Albertini, Dino Baggio, Signori, Casiraghi (Massaro 67), Roberto Baggio (Marchegiani 21).
Norway: Thorstvedt; Haaland, Berg, Bratseth, Bjornebye, Rushfeldt (Jakobsen 46), Leonhardsen, Mykland (Rekdal 80), Bohinen, Flo, Fjortoft.
Referee: Krug (Germany).

Florida, 24 June 1994, 61,219

Mexico (1) 2 *(Luis Garcia 44, 66)*

Republic of Ireland (0) 1 *(Aldridge 84)*

Mexico: Campos; Del Olmo, Suarez, Juan de Dios Ramirez, Rodriguez (Salvador 80), Bernal, Ambriz, Luis Garcia, Garcia Aspe, Hermosillo (Gutierrez 80), Zague.
Republic of Ireland: Bonner; Irwin, McGrath, Babb, Phelan, Houghton, Keane, Sheridan, Townsend, Staunton (Aldridge 69), Coyne (McAteer 66).
Referee: Rothlisberger (Switzerland).

New York, 28 June 1994, 76,332

Republic of Ireland (0) 0

Norway (0) 0

Republic of Ireland: Bonner; Kelly G, McGrath, Babb, Staunton, Keane, McAteer, Sheridan, Townsend (Whelan 74), Houghton, Aldridge (Kelly D 64).
Norway: Thorstvedt; Berg, Bratseth, Johnsen, Halle (Jakobsen 35), Flo, Mykland, Leonhardsen (Bohinen 68), Rekdal, Bjornebye, Sorloth.
Referee: Torres Cadena (Colombia).

Washington, 28 June 1994, 53,186

Italy (0) 1 *(Massaro 48)*

Mexico (0) 1 *(Bernal 58)*

Italy: Marchegiani; Benarrivo, Apolloni, Costacurta, Maldini, Berti, Albertini, Dino Baggio (Donadoni 66), Signori, Roberto Baggio, Casiraghi (Massaro 46).
Mexico: Campos; Rodriguez, Suarez, Juan de Dios Ramirez, Del Olmo, Bernal, Ambriz, Luis Garcia (Chabaz 83), Garcia Aspe, Hermosillo, Zague.
Referee: Lamolina (Argentina).

Group E

	P	W	D	L	F	A	Pts
Mexico	3	1	1	1	3	3	4
Republic of Ireland	3	1	1	1	2	2	4
Italy	3	1	1	1	2	2	4
Norway	3	1	1	1	1	1	4

Group F

Florida, 19 June 1994, 60,790

Belgium (1) 1 *(Degryse 11)*

Morocco (0) 0

Belgium: Preud'homme; De Wolf, Grun, Smidts, Staelens, Van der Elst, Scifo, Boffin (Borkelmans 85), Degryse, Weber, Nilis (Emmers 54).
Morocco: Azmi (Alaoui El Achraf 88); Naybet, Abdella, Triki, El Hadrioui, Hababi, Azzouzi, El Haddaoui (Bahja 68), Daoudi, Hadji, Chaouch (Samadi 81).
Referee: Torres Cadena (Colombia).

Washington, 21 June 1994, 52,535

Holland (0) 2 *(Jonk 50, Taument 87)*

Saudi Arabia (1) 1 *(Amin 19)*

Holland: De Goey; Koeman, Van Gobbel, Frank de Boer, Rijkaard, Jonk, Wouters, Bergkamp, Overmars (Taument 59), Ronald de Boer, Roy (Van Vossen 82).
Saudi Arabia: Al Deayea; Al Dosari, Al Khlaiwi, Madani, Al Jawad, Al Bishi, Owairan (Saleh 69), Amin, Jebreen, Al Muwallid, Majed Mohammed (Falatah 46).
Referee: Vega Diaz (Spain).

Florida, 25 June 1994, 61,219

Belgium (0) 1 *(Albert 66)*

Holland (0) 0

Belgium: Preud'homme; De Wolf, Grun, Albert, Emmers (Medved 78), Scifo, Van der Elst, Staelens, Borkelmans (Smidts 60), Weber, Degryse.
Holland: De Goey; Koeman, Valckx, Frank de Boer, Taument (Overmars 64), Rijkaard, Bergkamp, Jonk, Wouters, Roy, Ronald de Boer (Witschge 46).
Referee: Marsiglia (Brazil).

New York, 25 June 1994, 72,404

Saudi Arabia (1) 2 *(Al Jaber 8 (pen), Amin 46)*

Morocco (1) 1 *(Chaouch 28)*

Saudi Arabia: Al Deayea; Al Jawad, Al Anazi (Zebermawi 30), Madani, Al Khlaiwi, Al Bishi, Amin, Jebreen, Al Muwallid, Al Jaber (Al Ghesheyan 81), Owairan.
Morocco: Azmi; Naybet, Abdellah (El Ghrissi 57), Triki, El Hadrioui, Hababi (Hadji 74), Azzouzi, El Khalej, Daoudi, Bahja, Chaouch.
Referee: Don (England).

Orlando, 29 June 1994, 60,578

Morocco (0) 1 *(Nader 47)*

Holland (1) 2 *(Bergkamp 43, Roy 78)*

Morocco: Alaoui; El Khalej, Neqrouz, Triki, El Hadrioui, Samadi, Azzouzi (Daoudi 60), Hababi, Nader, Bahja, Bouyboud (Hadji 46).
Holland: De Goey; Koeman, Frank de Boer, Valckx, Winter, Jonk, Wouters, Witschge, Overmars (Taument 55), Bergkamp, Van Vossen (Roy 66).
Referee: Tejada (Peru).

Washington, 29 June 1994, 52,959

Belgium (0) 0

Saudi Arabia (1) 1 *(Owairan 5)*

Belgium: Preud'homme; De Wolf, Smidts, Albert, Medved, Staelens, Van der Elst, Scifo, Boffin, Degryse (Nilis 24), Wilmots (Weber 54).
Saudi Arabia: Al Deayea; Zebermawi, Madani, Al Khaiwi, Al Jawad, Al Bishi, Saleh, Owairan (Al Dosari 63), Jebreen, Mohammed (Al Muwallid 46), Falatah.
Referee: Krug (Germany).

Group F

	P	W	D	L	F	A	Pts
Holland	3	2	0	1	4	3	6
Saudi Arabia	3	2	0	1	4	3	6
Belgium	3	2	0	1	2	1	6
Morocco	3	0	0	3	2	5	0

Second Round

Chicago, 2 July 1994, 60,246

Germany (3) 3 *(Voller 6, 39, Klinsmann 11)*

Belgium (1) 2 *(Grun 8, Albert 90)*

Germany: Illgner; Matthaus (Brehme 46), Helmer, Kohler, Berthold, Hassler, Buchwald, Sammer, Wagner, Voller, Klinsmann (Kuntz 86).
Belgium: Preud'homme; De Wolf, Grun, Albert, Emmers, Van der Elst, Scifo, Staelens, Smidts (Bovin 66), Weber, Nilis (Czerniatynski 77).
Referee: Rothlisberger (Switzerland).

Washington, 2 July 1994, 53,141

Spain (1) 3 *(Hierro 15, Luis Enrique 74, Beguiristain 86 (pen)*

Switzerland (0) 0

Spain: Zubizarreta; Alkorta, Nadal, Abelardo, Ferrer, Hierro (Otero 76), Camarasa, Goicoechea (Beguiristain 62), Bakero, Sergi, Luis Enrique.
Switzerland: Pascolo; Hottiger, Herr, Geiger, Quentin (Studer 58), Ohrel (Subiat 73), Bregy, Sforza, Bickel, Knup, Chapuisat.
Referee: Van der Ende (Holland).

Dallas, 3 July 1994, 60,277

Saudi Arabia (0) 1 *(Al Ghesheyan 85)*

Sweden (1) 3 *(Dahlin 6, Kennet Andersson 51, 88)*

Saudi Arabia: Al Deayea; Madani, Zebermawi, Al Khlaiwi, Al Jawad (Al Ghesheyan 55), Al Bishi (Al Muwallid 61), Amin, Owairan, Saleh, Al Jaber, Falatah.
Sweden: Ravelli; Nilsson, Patrik Andersson, Bjorklund (Kamark 55), Ljung, Brolin, Schwarz, Thern (Mild 69), Ingesson, Kennet Andersson, Dahlin.
Referee: Marsiglia (Brazil).

Los Angeles, 3 July 1994, 90,469

Romania (2) 3 *(Dumitrescu 11, 18, Hagi 58)*

Argentina (1) 2 *(Batistuta 16 (pen), Balbo 75)*

Romania: Prunea; Belodedici, Petrescu, Prodan, Munteanu, Mihali, Hagi (Galca 86), Lupescu, Popescu, Selymes, Dumitrescu (Papura 89).
Argentina: Islas; Sensini (Medina Bello 63), Caceres, Ruggeri, Chamot, Simeone, Basualdo, Redondo, Ortega, Balboa, Batistuta.
Referee: Parietto (Italy).

Orlando, 4 July 1994, 61,355

Holland (2) 2 *(Bergkamp 12, Jonk 41)*

Republic of Ireland (0) 0

Holland: De Goey; Koeman, Valckx, Frank de Boer, Rijkaard, Winter, Jonk, Witschge (Numan 79), Overmars, Bergkamp, Van Vossen (Roy 70).
Republic of Ireland: Bonner; Kelly G, McGrath, Babb, Phelan, Houghton, Keane, Sheridan, Townsend, Staunton (McAteer 64), Coyne (Cascarino 74).
Referee: Mikkelsen (Denmark).

San Francisco, 4 July 1994, 84,147

Brazil (0) 1 *(Bebeto 74)*

USA (0) 0

Brazil: Taffarel; Jorginho, Aldair, Marcio Santos, Leonardo, Mazinho, Dunga, Mauro Silva, Zinho (Cafu 69), Romario, Bebeto.
USA: Meola; Clavijo, Balboa, Lalas, Caligiuri, Ramos (Wynalda 46), Sorber, Dooley, Perez (Wegerle 66), Cobi Jones, Stewart.
Referee: Quiniou (France).

Boston, 5 July 1994, 54,367

Nigeria (1) 1 *(Amunike 26)*

Italy (0) 2 *(Roberto Baggio 87, 103 (pen)) aet*

Nigeria: Rufai; Nwanu, Eguavoen, Okechukwu, Emenalo, Finidi, Okocha, Oliseh, Amunike (Oliha 57), Amokachi (Adepoju 36), Yekini.
Italy: Marchigiani; Mussi, Costacurta, Maldini, Benarrivo, Berti (Dino Baggio 46), Albertini, Donadoni, Signori (Zola 63), Roberto Baggio, Massaro.
Referee: Arturo Brizio Carter (Mexico).

New York, 5 July 1994, 71,030

Mexico (1) 1 *(Garcia Aspe (pen) 18)*

Bulgaria (1) 1 *(Stoichkov 7) aet*

Mexico: Campos; Rodriguez, Juan de Dios Ramirez, Suarez, Jesus Ramirez, Bernal, Ambriz, Luis Garcia, Garcia Aspe, Zague, Galindo.
Bulgaria: Mikhailov; Hubchev, Yordanov, Kremenliev, Kiriakov, Sirakov (Guentchev 104), Borimirov, Lechkov, Balakov, Stoichkov, Kostadinov (Mitarski 120).
Bulgaria won 3-1 on penalties
Referee: Al Sharif (Syria).

Quarter-finals

Boston, 9 July 1994, 53,644

Italy (1) 2 *(Dino Baggio 26, Roberto Baggio 88)*

Spain (0) 1 *(Caminero 59)*

Italy: Pagliuca; Tassotti, Costacurta, Maldini, Benarrivo, Conte (Berti 66), Dino Baggio, Albertini (Signori 46), Donadoni, Roberto Baggio, Massaro.
Spain: Zubizarreta; Nadal, Ferrer, Abelardo, Alkorta, Otero, Goicoechea, Bakero (Hierro 65), Caminero, Sergi (Salinas 60), Luis Enrique.
Referee: Puhl (Hungary).

Dallas, 9 July 1994, 63,998

Holland (0) 2 *(Bergkamp 63, Winter 76)*

Brazil (0) 3 *(Romario 52, Bebeto 61, Branco 81)*

Holland: De Goey; Koeman, Valckx, Wouters, Winter, Rijkaard (Ronald de Boer 65), Jonk, Witschge, Overmars, Bergkamp, Van Vossen (Roy 54).
Brazil: Taffarel; Jorginho, Aldair, Marcio Santos, Branco (Cafu 90), Mazinho (Rai 81), Dunga, Mauro Silva, Zinho, Bebeto, Romario.
Referee: Badilla (Costa Rica).

New York, 10 July 1994, 72,416

Bulgaria (0) 2 *(Stoichkov 75, Lechkov 79)*

Germany (0) 1 *(Matthaus 48 (pen))*

Bulgaria: Mikhailov; Hubchev, Ivanov, Yankov, Kiriakov, Lechkov, Sirakov, Balakov, Tzvetanov, Kostadinov (Guentchev 90), Stoichkov (Yordanov 84).
Germany: Illgner; Matthaus, Kohler, Helmer, Berthold, Hassler (Brehme 83), Buchwald, Moller, Wagner (Strunz 58), Voller, Klinsmann.
Referee: Torres Cadena (Colombia).

San Francisco, 10 July 1994, 81,715

Sweden (0) 2 *(Brolin 79, Kennet Andersson 115)*

Romania (0) 2 *(Raducioiu 89, 101) aet*

Sweden: Ravelli; Nilsson, Patrik Andersson, Bjorklund (Kamark 84), Ljung, Brolin, Schwarz, Mild, Ingesson, Kennet Andersson, Dahlin (Larsson).
Romania: Prunea; Belodedici, Prodan, Popescu, Lupescu, Petrescu, Selymes, Hagi, Munteanu (Panduru 84), Dumitrescu, Raducioiu.
Referee: Don (England).
Sweden won 5-4 on penalties

Semi-finals

New York, 13 July 1994, 77,094

Italy (2) 2 *(Roberto Baggio 21, 26)*

Bulgaria (1) 1 *(Stoichkov 44 (pen))*

Italy: Pagliuca; Mussi, Costacurta, Maldini, Benarrivo, Berti, Albertini, Dino Baggio (Conte 56), Donadoni, Casiraghi, Roberto Baggio (Signori 71).
Bulgaria: Mikhailov; Kiriakov, Ivanov, Hubchev, Tzvetanov, Yankov, Lechkov, Balakov, Sirakov, Kostadinov (Yordanov 72), Stoichkov (Guentchev 79).
Referee: Quiniou (France).

Los Angeles, 13 July 1994, 84,569

Brazil (0) 1 *(Romario 80)*

Sweden (0) 0

Brazil: Taffarel; Jorginho, Aldair, Marcio Santos, Branco, Dunga, Mauro Silva, Mazinho (Rai 46), Zinho, Bebeto, Romario.
Sweden: Ravelli; Nilsson, Patrik Andersson, Bjorklund, Ljung, Mild, Brolin, Thern, Ingesson, Dahlin (Rehn), Kennet Andersson.
Referee: Torres Cadena (Colombia).

Third/Fourth place match

Los Angeles, 16 July 1994, 83,716

Sweden (4) 4 *(Brolin 8, Mild 30, Larsson 37, Kennet Andersson 39)*

Bulgaria (0) 0

Sweden: Ravelli; Nilsson, Patrik Andersson, Bjorklund, Kamark, Brolin, Schwarz, Mild, Ingesson, Kennet Andersson, Larsson (Limpar 79).
Bulgaria: Mikhailov (Nikolov 46); Kiriakov, Ivanov (Kremenliev 42), Hubchev, Tzvetanov, Yankov, Lechkov, Sirakov (Yordanov 46), Balakov, Stoichkov, Kostadinov.
Referee: Bujsaim (UAE).

Final

Los Angeles, 17 July 1994, 94,194

Brazil (0) 0

Italy (0) 0 *aet*

Brazil: Taffarel; Jorginho (Cafu 21), Marcio Santos, Aldair, Branco, Mazinho, Mauro Silva, Dunga, Zinho (Viola 109), Bebeto, Romario.
Italy: Pagliuca; Mussi (Apolloni 34), Maldini, Baresi, Benarrivo, Donadoni, Albertini, Dino Baggio (Evani 101), Berti, Roberto Baggio, Massaro.
Brazil won 3-2 on penalties
Referee: Puhl (Hungary).
Penalty sequence: Baresi (shot over); Marcio Santos (saved); Albertini (scored); Romario (scored off upright); Evani (scored); Branco (scored); Massaro (saved); Dunga (scored), Roberto Baggio (shot over).

BRITISH AND IRISH INTERNATIONAL RESULTS 1872–1994

BRITISH INTERNATIONAL CHAMPIONSHIP 1883–1984

Year	Champions	Pts
1883–84	Scotland	6
1884–85	Scotland	5
1885–86	England	5
	Scotland	5
1886–87	Scotland	6
1887–88	England	6
1888–89	Scotland	5
1889–90	Scotland	5
	England	5
1890–91	England	6
1891–92	England	6
1892–93	England	6
1893–94	Scotland	5
1894–95	England	5
1895–96	Scotland	5
1896–97	Scotland	5
1897–98	England	6
1898–99	England	6
1899–1900	Scotland	6
1900–01	England	5
1901–02	Scotland	5
1902–03	England	4
	Ireland	4
	Scotland	4
1903–04	England	5
1904–05	England	5
1905–06	England	4
	Scotland	4
1906–07	Wales	5
1907–08	Scotland	5
	England	5
1908–09	England	6
1909–10	Scotland	4
1910–11	England	5
1911–12	England	5
	Scotland	5
1912–13	England	4
1913–14	Ireland	5
1919–20	Wales	4
1920–21	Scotland	6
1921–22	Scotland	4
1922–23	Scotland	5
1923–24	Wales	6
1924–25	Scotland	6
1925–26	Scotland	6
1926–27	Scotland	4
	England	4
1927–28	Wales	5
1928–29	Scotland	6
1929–30	England	6
1930–31	Scotland	4
	England	4
1931–32	England	6
1932–33	Wales	5
1933–34	Wales	5
1934–35	England	4
	Scotland	4
1935–36	Scotland	4
1936–37	Wales	6
1937–38	England	4
1938–39	England	4
	Scotland	4
	Wales	4
1946–47	England	5
1947–48	England	5
1948–49	Scotland	6
1949–50	England	6
1950–51	Scotland	6
1951–52	Wales	5
	England	5
1952–53	England	4
	Scotland	4
1953–54	England	6
1954–55	England	6
1955–56	England	3
	Scotland	3
	Wales	3
	N. Ireland	3
1956–57	England	5
1957–58	England	4
	N. Ireland	4
1958–59	N. Ireland	4
	England	4
1959–60	England	4
	Scotland	4
	Wales	4
1960–61	England	6
1961–62	Scotland	6
1962–63	Scotland	6
1963–64	Scotland	4
	England	4
	N. Ireland	4
1964–65	England	5
1965–66	England	5
1966–67	Scotland	5
1967–68	England	5
1968–69	England	6
1969–70	England	4
	Scotland	4
	Wales	4
1970–71	England	5
1971–72	England	4
	Scotland	4
1972–73	England	6
1973–74	England	4
	Scotland	4
1974–75	England	4
1975–76	Scotland	6
1976–77	Scotland	5
1977–78	England	6
1978–79	England	5
1979–80	N. Ireland	5
1980–81	*Not completed*	
1981–82	England	6
1982–83	England	5
1983–84	N. Ireland	3

Note: In the results that follow, WC = World Cup, EC = European Championship. For Ireland, read Northern Ireland from 1921.

ENGLAND v SCOTLAND

Played: 107; England won 43, Scotland won 40, Drawn 24. *Goals:* England 188, Scotland 168.

		E	*S*
1872	Glasgow	0	0
1873	Kennington Oval	4	2
1874	Glasgow	1	2
1875	Kennington Oval	2	2
1876	Glasgow	0	3
1877	Kennington Oval	1	3
1878	Glasgow	2	7
1879	Kennington Oval	5	4
1880	Glasgow	4	5
1881	Kennington Oval	1	6
1882	Glasgow	1	5
1883	Sheffield	2	3
1884	Glasgow	0	1
1885	Kennington Oval	1	1
1886	Glasgow	1	1
1887	Blackburn	2	3
1888	Glasgow	5	0
1889	Kennington Oval	2	3
1890	Glasgow	1	1
1891	Blackburn	2	1
1892	Glasgow	4	1

		E	S
1893	Richmond	5	2
1894	Glasgow	2	2
1895	Everton	3	0
1896	Glasgow	1	2
1897	Crystal Palace	1	2
1898	Glasgow	3	1
1899	Birmingham	2	1
1900	Glasgow	1	4
1901	Crystal Palace	2	2
1902	Birmingham	2	2
1903	Sheffield	1	2
1904	Glasgow	1	0
1905	Crystal Palace	1	0
1906	Glasgow	1	2
1907	Newcastle	1	1
1908	Glasgow	1	1
1909	Crystal Palace	2	0
1910	Glasgow	0	2
1911	Everton	1	1
1912	Glasgow	1	1
1913	Chelsea	1	0
1914	Glasgow	1	3
1920	Sheffield	5	4
1921	Glasgow	0	3
1922	Aston Villa	0	1
1923	Glasgow	2	2
1924	Wembley	1	1
1925	Glasgow	0	2
1926	Manchester	0	1
1927	Glasgow	2	1
1928	Wembley	1	5
1929	Glasgow	0	1
1930	Wembley	5	2
1931	Glasgow	0	2
1932	Wembley	3	0
1933	Glasgow	1	2
1934	Wembley	3	0
1935	Glasgow	0	2
1936	Wembley	1	1
1937	Glasgow	1	3
1938	Wembley	0	1
1939	Glasgow	2	1
1947	Wembley	1	1
1948	Glasgow	2	0
1949	Wembley	1	3
WC1950	Glasgow	1	0
1951	Wembley	2	3
1952	Glasgow	2	1
1953	Wembley	2	2
WC1954	Glasgow	4	2
1955	Wembley	7	2
1956	Glasgow	1	1
1957	Wembley	2	1
1958	Glasgow	4	0
1959	Wembley	1	0
1960	Glasgow	1	1
1961	Wembley	9	3
1962	Glasgow	0	2
1963	Wembley	1	2
1964	Glasgow	0	1
1965	Wembley	2	2
1966	Glasgow	4	3
EC1967	Wembley	2	3
EC1968	Glasgow	1	1
1969	Wembley	4	1
1970	Glasgow	0	0
1971	Wembley	3	1
1972	Glasgow	1	0
1973	Glasgow	5	0
1974	Wembley	0	2
1975	Wembley	5	1
1976	Glasgow	1	2
1977	Wembley	1	2
1978	Glasgow	1	0
1979	Wembley	3	1
1980	Glasgow	2	0
1981	Wembley	0	1
1982	Glasgow	1	0
1983	Wembley	2	0
1984	Glasgow	1	1
1985	Glasgow	0	1
1986	Wembley	2	1
1987	Glasgow	0	0
1988	Wembley	1	0
1989	Glasgow	2	0

ENGLAND v WALES

Played: 97; England won 62, Wales won 14, Drawn 21. *Goals:* England 239, Scotland 90.

		E	W
1879	Kennington Oval	2	1
1880	Wrexham	3	2
1881	Blackburn	0	1
1882	Wrexham	3	5
1883	Kennington Oval	5	0
1884	Wrexham	4	0
1885	Blackburn	1	1
1886	Wrexham	3	1
1887	Kennington Oval	4	0
1888	Crewe	5	1
1889	Stoke	4	1
1890	Wrexham	3	1
1891	Sunderland	4	1
1892	Wrexham	2	0
1893	Stoke	6	0
1894	Wrexham	5	1
1894	Queen's Club, Kensington	1	1
1896	Cardiff	9	1
1897	Sheffield	4	0
1898	Wrexham	3	0
1899	Bristol	4	0
1900	Cardiff	1	1
1901	Newcastle	6	0
1902	Wrexham	0	0
1903	Portsmouth	2	1
1904	Wrexham	2	2
1905	Liverpool	3	1
1906	Cardiff	1	0
1907	Fulham	1	1
1908	Wrexham	7	1
1909	Nottingham	2	0
1910	Cardiff	1	0
1911	Millwall	3	0
1912	Wrexham	2	0
1913	Bristol	4	3
1914	Cardiff	2	0
1920	Highbury	1	2
1921	Cardiff	0	0
1922	Liverpool	1	0
1923	Cardiff	2	2
1924	Blackburn	1	2
1925	Swansea	2	1
1926	Crystal Palace	1	3
1927	Wrexham	3	3
1927	Burnley	1	2
1928	Swansea	3	2
1929	Chelsea	6	0
1930	Wrexham	4	0
1931	Liverpool	3	1
1932	Wrexham	0	0
1933	Newcastle	1	2
1934	Cardiff	4	0
1935	Wolverhampton	1	2
1936	Cardiff	1	2
1937	Middlesbrough	2	1
1938	Cardiff	2	4
1946	Manchester	3	0
1947	Cardiff	3	0
1948	Aston Villa	1	0
WC1949	Cardiff	4	1
1950	Sunderland	4	2
1951	Cardiff	1	1
1952	Wembley	5	2
WC1953	Cardiff	4	1
1954	Wembley	3	2
1955	Cardiff	1	2
1956	Wembley	3	1
1957	Cardiff	4	0
1958	Aston Villa	2	2
1959	Cardiff	1	1
1960	Wembley	5	1
1961	Cardiff	1	1
1962	Wembley	4	0
1963	Cardiff	4	0
1964	Wembley	2	1
1965	Cardiff	0	0
EC1966	Wembley	5	1
EC1967	Cardiff	3	0
1969	Wembley	2	1
1970	Cardiff	1	1
1971	Wembley	0	0
1972	Cardiff	3	0
WC1972	Cardiff	1	0
WC1973	Wembley	1	1
1973	Wembley	3	0
1974	Cardiff	2	0
1975	Wembley	2	2
1976	Wrexham	2	1
1976	Cardiff	1	0
1977	Wembley	0	1
1978	Cardiff	3	1
1979	Wembley	0	0
1980	Wrexham	1	4
1981	Wembley	0	0
1982	Cardiff	1	0
1983	Wembley	2	1
1984	Wrexham	0	1

ENGLAND v IRELAND

Played: 96; England won 74, Ireland won 6, Drawn 16. *Goals:* England 319, Ireland 80.

Year	Venue	*E*	*I*
1882	Belfast	13	0
1883	Liverpool	7	0
1884	Belfast	8	1
1885	Manchester	4	0
1886	Belfast	6	1
1887	Sheffield	7	0
1888	Belfast	5	1
1889	Everton	6	1
1890	Belfast	9	1
1891	Wolverhampton	6	1
1892	Belfast	2	0
1893	Birmingham	6	1
1894	Belfast	2	2
1895	Derby	9	0
1896	Belfast	2	0
1897	Nottingham	6	0
1898	Belfast	3	2
1899	Sunderland	13	2
1900	Dublin	2	0
1901	Southampton	3	0
1902	Belfast	1	0
1903	Wolverhampton	4	0
1904	Belfast	3	1
1905	Middlesbrough	1	1
1906	Belfast	5	0
1907	Everton	1	0
1908	Belfast	3	1
1909	Bradford	4	0
1910	Belfast	1	1
1911	Derby	2	1
1912	Dublin	6	1
1913	Belfast	1	2
1914	Middlesbrough	0	3
1919	Belfast	1	1
1920	Sunderland	2	0
1921	Belfast	1	1
1922	West Bromwich	2	0
1923	Belfast	1	2
1924	Everton	3	1
1925	Belfast	0	0
1926	Liverpool	3	3
1927	Belfast	0	2
1928	Everton	2	1
1929	Belfast	3	0
1930	Sheffield	5	1
1931	Belfast	6	2
1932	Blackpool	1	0
1933	Belfast	3	0
1935	Everton	2	1
1935	Belfast	3	1
1936	Stoke	3	1
1937	Belfast	5	1
1938	Manchester	7	0
1946	Belfast	7	2
1947	Everton	2	2
1948	Belfast	6	2
WC1949	Manchester	9	2
1950	Belfast	4	1
1951	Aston Villa	2	0
1952	Belfast	2	2
WC1953	Everton	3	1
1954	Belfast	2	0
1955	Wembley	3	0
1956	Belfast	1	1
1957	Wembley	2	3
1958	Belfast	3	3
1959	Wembley	2	1
1960	Belfast	5	2
1961	Wembley	1	1
1962	Belfast	3	1
1963	Wembley	8	3
1964	Belfast	4	3
1965	Wembley	2	1
EC1966	Belfast	2	0
EC1967	Wembley	2	0
1969	Belfast	3	1
1970	Wembley	3	1
1971	Belfast	1	0
1972	Wembley	0	1
1973	Everton	2	1
1974	Wembley	1	0
1975	Belfast	0	0
1976	Wembley	4	0
1977	Belfast	2	1
1978	Wembley	1	0
EC1979	Wembley	4	0
1979	Belfast	2	0
EC1979	Belfast	5	1
1980	Wembley	1	1
1982	Wembley	4	0
1983	Belfast	0	0
1984	Wembley	1	0
WC1985	Belfast	1	0
WC1985	Wembley	0	0
EC1986	Wembley	3	0
EC1987	Belfast	2	0

SCOTLAND v WALES

Played: 101; Scotland won 60, Wales won 18, Drawn 23. *Goals:* Scotland 238, Wales 111.

Year	Venue	*S*	*W*
1876	Glasgow	4	0
1877	Wrexham	2	0
1878	Glasgow	9	0
1879	Wrexham	3	0
1880	Glasgow	5	1
1881	Wrexham	5	1
1882	Glasgow	5	0
1883	Wrexham	4	1
1884	Glasgow	4	1
1885	Wrexham	8	1
1886	Glasgow	4	1
1887	Wrexham	2	0
1888	Edinburgh	5	1
1889	Wrexham	0	0
1890	Paisley	5	0
1891	Wrexham	4	3
1892	Edinburgh	6	1
1893	Wrexham	8	0
1894	Kilmarnock	5	2
1895	Wrexham	2	2
1896	Dundee	4	0
1897	Wrexham	2	2
1898	Motherwell	5	2
1899	Wrexham	6	0
1900	Aberdeen	5	2
1901	Wrexham	1	1
1902	Greenock	5	1
1903	Cardiff	1	0
1904	Dundee	1	1
1905	Wrexham	1	3
1906	Edinburgh	0	2
1907	Wrexham	0	1
1908	Dundee	2	1
1909	Wrexham	2	3
1910	Kilmarnock	1	0
1911	Cardiff	2	2
1912	Tynecastle	1	0
1913	Wrexham	0	0
1914	Glasgow	0	0
1920	Cardiff	1	1
1921	Aberdeen	2	1
1922	Wrexham	1	2
1923	Paisley	2	0
1924	Cardiff	0	2
1925	Tynecastle	3	1
1926	Cardiff	3	0
1927	Glasgow	3	0
1928	Wrexham	2	2
1929	Glasgow	4	2
1930	Cardiff	4	2
1931	Glasgow	1	1
1932	Wrexham	3	2
1933	Edinburgh	2	5
1934	Cardiff	2	3
1935	Aberdeen	3	2
1936	Cardiff	1	1
1937	Dundee	1	2
1938	Cardiff	1	2
1939	Edinburgh	3	2
1946	Wrexham	1	3
1947	Glasgow	1	2
WC1948	Cardiff	3	1
1949	Glasgow	2	0
1950	Cardiff	3	1
1951	Glasgow	0	1
WC1952	Cardiff	2	1
1953	Glasgow	3	3
1954	Cardiff	1	0
1955	Glasgow	2	0
1956	Cardiff	2	2
1957	Glasgow	1	1
1958	Cardiff	3	0
1959	Glasgow	1	1
1960	Cardiff	0	2
1961	Glasgow	2	0
1962	Cardiff	3	2
1963	Glasgow	2	1
1964	Cardiff	2	3
EC1965	Glasgow	4	1
EC1966	Cardiff	1	1
1967	Glasgow	3	2
1969	Wrexham	5	3
1970	Glasgow	0	0
1971	Cardiff	0	0
1972	Glasgow	1	0
1973	Wrexham	2	0
1974	Glasgow	2	0
1975	Cardiff	2	2
1976	Glasgow	3	1
WC1977	Glasgow	1	0
1977	Wrexham	0	0
WC1977	Liverpool	2	0
1978	Glasgow	1	1
1979	Cardiff	0	3
1980	Glasgow	1	0
1981	Swansea	0	2
1982	Glasgow	1	0
1983	Cardiff	2	0
1984	Glasgow	2	1
WC1985	Glasgow	0	1
WC1985	Cardiff	1	1

SCOTLAND v IRELAND

Played: 91; Scotland won 60, Ireland won 15, Drawn 16. *Goals:* Scotland 253, Ireland 81.

		S	*I*			*S*	*I*			*S*	*I*
1884	Belfast	5	0	1920	Glasgow	3	0	1957	Belfast	1	1
1885	Glasgow	8	2	1921	Belfast	2	0	1958	Glasgow	2	2
1886	Belfast	7	2	1922	Glasgow	2	1	1959	Belfast	4	0
1887	Glasgow	4	1	1923	Belfast	1	0	1960	Glasgow	5	2
1888	Belfast	10	2	1924	Glasgow	2	0	1961	Belfast	6	1
1889	Glasgow	7	0	1925	Belfast	3	0	1962	Glasgow	5	1
1890	Belfast	4	1	1926	Glasgow	4	0	1963	Belfast	1	2
1891	Glasgow	2	1	1927	Belfast	2	0	1964	Glasgow	3	2
1892	Belfast	3	2	1928	Glasgow	0	1	1965	Belfast	2	3
1893	Glasgow	6	1	1929	Belfast	7	3	1966	Glasgow	2	1
1894	Belfast	2	1	1930	Glasgow	3	1	1967	Belfast	0	1
1895	Glasgow	3	1	1931	Belfast	0	0	1969	Glasgow	1	1
1896	Belfast	3	3	1932	Glasgow	3	1	1970	Belfast	1	0
1897	Glasgow	5	1	1933	Belfast	4	0	1971	Glasgow	0	1
1898	Belfast	3	0	1934	Glasgow	1	2	1972	Glasgow	2	0
1899	Glasgow	9	1	1935	Belfast	1	2	1973	Glasgow	1	2
1900	Belfast	3	0	1936	Edinburgh	2	1	1974	Glasgow	0	1
1901	Glasgow	11	0	1937	Belfast	3	1	1975	Glasgow	3	0
1902	Belfast	5	1	1938	Aberdeen	1	1	1976	Glasgow	3	0
1903	Glasgow	0	2	1939	Belfast	2	0	1977	Glasgow	3	0
1904	Dublin	1	1	1946	Glasgow	0	0	1978	Glasgow	1	1
1905	Glasgow	4	0	1947	Belfast	0	2	1979	Glasgow	1	0
1906	Dublin	1	0	1948	Glasgow	3	2	1980	Belfast	0	1
1907	Glasgow	3	0	1949	Belfast	8	2	WC1981	Glasgow	1	1
1908	Dublin	5	0	1950	Glasgow	6	1	1981	Glasgow	2	0
1909	Glasgow	5	0	1951	Belfast	3	0	WC1981	Belfast	0	0
1910	Belfast	0	1	1952	Glasgow	1	1	1982	Belfast	1	1
1911	Glasgow	2	0	1953	Belfast	3	1	1983	Glasgow	0	0
1912	Belfast	4	1	1954	Glasgow	2	2	1984	Belfast	0	2
1913	Dublin	2	1	1955	Belfast	1	2	1992	Glasgow	1	0
1914	Belfast	1	1	1956	Glasgow	1	0				

WALES v IRELAND

Played: 90; Wales won 42, Ireland won 27, Drawn 21. *Goals:* Wales 181, Ireland 126.

		W	*I*			*W*	*I*			*W*	*I*
1882	Wrexham	7	1	1912	Cardiff	2	3	WC1954	Wrexham	1	2
1883	Belfast	1	1	1913	Belfast	1	0	1955	Belfast	3	2
1884	Wrexham	6	0	1914	Wrexham	1	2	1956	Cardiff	1	1
1885	Belfast	8	2	1920	Belfast	2	2	1957	Belfast	0	0
1886	Wrexham	5	0	1921	Swansea	2	1	1958	Cardiff	1	1
1887	Belfast	1	4	1922	Belfast	1	1	1959	Belfast	1	4
1888	Wrexham	11	0	1923	Wrexham	0	3	1960	Wrexham	3	2
1889	Belfast	3	1	1924	Belfast	1	0	1961	Belfast	5	1
1890	Shrewsbury	5	2	1925	Wrexham	0	0	1962	Cardiff	4	0
1891	Belfast	2	7	1926	Belfast	0	3	1963	Belfast	4	1
1892	Bangor	1	1	1927	Cardiff	2	2	1964	Cardiff	2	3
1893	Belfast	3	4	1928	Belfast	2	1	1965	Belfast	5	0
1894	Swansea	4	1	1929	Wrexham	2	2	1966	Cardiff	1	4
1895	Belfast	2	2	1930	Belfast	0	7	EC1967	Belfast	0	0
1896	Wrexham	6	1	1931	Wrexham	3	2	EC1968	Wrexham	2	0
1897	Belfast	3	4	1932	Belfast	0	4	1969	Belfast	0	0
1898	Llandudno	0	1	1933	Wrexham	4	1	1970	Swansea	1	0
1899	Belfast	0	1	1934	Belfast	1	1	1971	Belfast	0	1
1900	Llandudno	2	0	1935	Wrexham	3	1	1972	Wrexham	0	0
1901	Belfast	1	0	1936	Belfast	2	3	1973	Everton	0	1
1902	Cardiff	0	3	1937	Wrexham	4	1	1974	Wrexham	1	0
1903	Belfast	0	2	1938	Belfast	0	1	1975	Belfast	0	1
1904	Bangor	0	1	1939	Wrexham	3	1	1976	Swansea	1	0
1905	Belfast	2	2	1947	Belfast	1	2	1977	Belfast	1	1
1906	Wrexham	4	4	1948	Wrexham	2	0	1978	Wrexham	1	0
1907	Belfast	3	2	1949	Belfast	2	0	1979	Belfast	1	1
1908	Aberdare	0	1	WC1950	Wrexham	0	0	1980	Cardiff	0	1
1909	Belfast	3	2	1951	Belfast	2	1	1982	Wrexham	3	0
1910	Wrexham	4	1	1952	Swansea	3	0	1983	Belfast	1	0
1911	Belfast	2	1	1953	Belfast	3	2	1984	Swansea	1	1

OTHER BRITISH INTERNATIONAL RESULTS 1908–1994

ENGLAND

		v ALBANIA	E	A
WC1989	8 Mar	Tirana	2	0
WC1989	26 Apr	Wembley	5	0

		v ARGENTINA	E	A
1951	9 May	Wembley	2	1
1953	17 May	Buenos Aires	0	0
(abandoned after 21 mins)				
WC1962	2 June	Rancagua	3	1
1964	6 June	Rio de Janeiro	0	1
WC1966	23 July	Wembley	1	0
1974	22 May	Wembley	2	2
1977	12 June	Buenos Aires	1	1
1980	13 May	Wembley	3	1
WC1986	22 June	Mexico City	1	2
1991	25 May	Wembley	2	2

		v AUSTRALIA	E	A
1980	31 May	Sydney	2	1
1983	11 June	Sydney	0	0
1983	15 June	Brisbane	1	0
1983	18 June	Melbourne	1	1
1991	1 June	Sydney	1	0

		v AUSTRIA	E	A
1908	6 June	Vienna	6	1
1908	8 June	Vienna	11	1
1909	1 June	Vienna	8	1
1930	14 May	Vienna	0	0
1932	7 Dec	Chelsea	4	3
1936	6 May	Vienna	1	2
1951	28 Nov	Wembley	2	2
1952	25 May	Vienna	3	2
WC1958	15 June	Boras	2	2
1961	27 May	Vienna	1	3
1962	4 Apr	Wembley	3	1
1965	20 Oct	Wembley	2	3
1967	27 May	Vienna	1	0
1973	26 Sept	Wembley	7	0
1979	13 June	Vienna	3	4

		v BELGIUM	E	B
1921	21 May	Brussels	2	0
1923	19 Mar	Highbury	6	1
1923	1 Nov	Antwerp	2	2
1924	8 Dec	West Bromwich	4	0
1926	24 May	Antwerp	5	3
1927	11 May	Brussels	9	1
1928	19 May	Antwerp	3	1
1929	11 May	Brussels	5	1
1931	16 May	Brussels	4	1
1936	9 May	Brussels	2	3
1947	21 Sept	Brussels	5	2
1950	18 May	Brussels	4	1
1952	26 Nov	Wembley	5	0
WC1954	17 June	Basle	4	4*
1964	21 Oct	Wembley	2	2
1970	25 Feb	Brussels	3	1
EC1980	12 June	Turin	1	1
WC1990	27 June	Bologna	1	0*

**After extra time*

		v BOHEMIA	E	B
1908	13 June	Prague	4	0

		v BRAZIL	E	B
1956	9 May	Wembley	4	2
WC1958	11 June	Gothenburg	0	0
1959	13 May	Rio de Janeiro	0	2
WC1962	10 June	Vina del Mar	1	3
1963	8 May	Wembley	1	1
1964	30 May	Rio de Janeiro	1	5
1969	12 June	Rio de Janeiro	1	2
WC1970	7 June	Guadalajara	0	1
1976	23 May	Los Angeles	0	1
1977	8 June	Rio de Janeiro	0	0
1978	19 Apr	Wembley	1	1
1981	12 May	Wembley	0	1
1984	10 June	Rio de Janeiro	2	0
1987	19 May	Wembley	1	1
1990	28 Mar	Wembley	1	0
1992	17 May	Wembley	1	1
1993	13 June	Washington	1	1

		v BULGARIA	E	B
WC1962	7 June	Rancagua	0	0
1968	11 Dec	Wembley	1	1
1974	1 June	Sofia	1	0
EC1979	6 June	Sofia	3	0
EC1979	22 Nov	Wembley	2	0

		v CAMEROON	E	C
WC1990	1 July	Naples	3	2*
1991	6 Feb	Wembley	2	0

		v CANADA	E	C
1986	24 May	Burnaby	1	0

		v CHILE	E	C
WC1950	25 June	Rio de Janeiro	2	0
1953	24 May	Santiago	2	1
1984	17 June	Santiago	0	0
1989	23 May	Wembley	0	0

		v CIS	E	C
1992	29 Apr	Moscow	2	2

		v COLOMBIA	E	C
1970	20 May	Bogota	4	0
1988	24 May	Wembley	1	1

		v CYPRUS	E	C
EC1975	16 Apr	Wembley	5	0
EC1975	11 May	Limassol	1	0

		v CZECHOSLOVAKIA	E	C
1934	16 May	Prague	1	2
1937	1 Dec	Tottenham	5	4
1963	29 May	Bratislava	4	2
1966	2 Nov	Wembley	0	0
WC1970	11 June	Guadalajara	1	0
1973	27 May	Prague	1	1
EC1974	30 Oct	Wembley	3	0
EC1975	30 Oct	Bratislava	1	2
1978	29 Nov	Wembley	1	0
WC1982	20 June	Bilbao	2	0
1990	25 Apr	Wembley	4	2
1992	25 Mar	Prague	2	2

		v DENMARK	E	D
1948	26 Sept	Copenhagen	0	0
1955	2 Oct	Copenhagen	5	1
WC1956	5 Dec	Wolverhampton	5	2
WC1957	15 May	Copenhagen	4	1
1966	3 July	Copenhagen	2	0
EC1978	20 Sept	Copenhagen	4	3
EC1979	12 Sept	Wembley	1	0
EC1982	22 Sept	Copenhagen	2	2
EC1983	21 Sept	Wembley	0	1
1988	14 Sept	Wembley	1	0
1989	7 June	Copenhagen	1	1

			E	D
1990	15 May	Wembley	1	0
EC1992	11 June	Malmo	0	0
1994	9 Mar	Wembley	1	0

		v ECUADOR	E	Ec
1970	24 May	Quito	2	0

		v EGYPT	E	Eg
1986	29 Jan	Cairo	4	0
WC1990	21 June	Cagliari	1	0

		v FIFA	E	FIFA
1938	26 Oct	Highbury	3	0
1953	21 Oct	Wembley	4	4
1963	23 Oct	Wembley	2	1

		v FINLAND	E	F
1937	20 May	Helsinki	8	0
1956	20 May	Helsinki	5	1
1966	26 June	Helsinki	3	0
WC1976	13 Juje	Helsinki	4	1
WC1976	13 Oct	Wembley	2	1
1982	3 June	Helsinki	4	1
WC1984	17 Oct	Wembley	5	0
WC1985	22 May	Helsinki	1	1
1992	3 June	Helsinki	2	1

		v FRANCE	E	F
1923	10 May	Paris	4	1
1924	17 May	Paris	3	1
1925	21 May	Paris	3	2
1927	26 May	Paris	6	0
1928	17 May	Paris	5	1
1929	9 May	Paris	4	1
1931	14 May	Paris	2	5
1933	6 Dec	Tottenham	4	1
1938	26 May	Paris	4	2
1947	3 May	Highbury	3	0
1949	22 May	Paris	3	1
1951	3 Oct	Highbury	2	2
1955	15 May	Paris	0	1
1957	27 Nov	Wembley	4	0
EC1962	3 Oct	Sheffield	1	1
EC1963	27 Feb	Paris	2	5
WC1966	20 July	Wembley	2	0
1969	12 Mar	Wembley	5	0
WC1982	16 June	Bilbao	3	1
1984	29 Feb	Paris	0	2
1992	19 Feb	Wembley	2	0
EC1992	14 June	Malmo	0	0

		v GERMANY	E	G
1930	10 May	Berlin	3	3
1935	4 Dec	Tottenham	3	0
1938	14 May	Berlin	6	3
1991	11 Sept	Wembley	0	1
1993	19 June	Detroit	1	2

		v EAST GERMANY	E	EG
1963	2 June	Leipzig	2	1
1970	25 Nov	Wembley	3	1
1974	29 May	Leipzig	1	1
1984	12 Sept	Wembley	1	0

		v WEST GERMANY	E	WG
1954	1 Dec	Wembley	3	1
1956	26 May	Berlin	3	1
1965	12 May	Nuremberg	1	0
1966	23 Feb	Wembley	1	0
WC1966	30 July	Wembley	4	2*
1968	1 June	Hanover	0	1
WC1970	14 June	Leon	2	3*
EC1972	29 Apr	Wembley	1	3
EC1972	13 May	Berlin	0	0
1975	12 Mar	Wembley	2	0
1978	22 Feb	Munich	1	2
WC1982	29 June	Madrid	0	0
1982	13 Oct	Wembley	1	2
1985	12 June	Mexico City	3	0
1987	9 Sept	Dusseldorf	1	3
WC1990	4 July	Turin	1	1*

**After extra time*

		v GREECE	E	G
EC1971	21 Apr	Wembley	3	0
EC1971	1 Dec	Athens	2	0
EC1982	17 Nov	Athens	3	0
EC1983	30 Mar	Wembhey	0	0
1989	8 Feb	Athens	2	1
1994	17 May	Wembley	5	0

		v HOLLAND	E	N
1935	18 May	Amsterdam	1	0
1946	27 Nov	Huddersfield	8	2
1964	9 Dec	Amsterdam	1	1
1969	5 Nov	Amsterdam	1	0
1970	14 Jun	Wembley	0	0
1977	9 Feb	Wembley	0	2
1982	25 May	Wembley	2	0
1988	23 Mar	Wembley	2	2
EC1988	15 June	Dusseldorf	1	3
WC1990	16 June	Cagliari	0	0
WC1993	28 Apr	Wembley	2	2
WC1993	13 Oct	Rotterdam	0	2

		v HUNGARY	E	H
1908	10 June	Budapest	7	0
1909	29 May	Budapest	4	2
1909	31 May	Budapest	8	2
1934	10 May	Budapest	1	2
1936	2 Dec	Highbury	6	2
1953	25 Nov	Wembley	3	6
1954	23 May	Budapest	1	7
1960	22 May	Budapest	0	2
WC1962	31 May	Rancagua	1	2
1965	5 May	Wembley	1	0
1978	24 May	Wembley	4	1
WC1981	6 June	Budapest	3	1
WC1982	18 Nov	Wembley	1	0
EC1983	27 Apr	Wembley	2	0
EC1983	12 Oct	Budapest	3	0
1988	27 Apr	Budapest	0	0
1990	12 Sept	Wembley	1	0
1992	12 May	Budapest	1	0

		v ICELAND	E	I
1982	2 June	Reykjavik	1	1

		v REPUBLIC OF IRELAND	E	RI
1946	30 Sept	Dublin	1	0
1949	21 Sept	Everton	0	2
WC1957	8 May	Wembley	5	1
WC1957	19 May	Dublin	1	1
1964	24 May	Dublin	3	1
1976	8 Sept	Wembley	1	1
EC1978	25 Oct	Dublin	1	1
EC1980	6 Feb	Wembley	2	0
1985	26 Mar	Wembley	2	1
EC1988	12 June	Stuttgart	0	1
WC1990	11 June	Cagliari	1	1
EC1990	14 Nov	Dublin	1	1
EC1991	27 Mar	Wembley	1	1

		v ISRAEL	E	I
1986	26 Feb	Ramat Gan	2	1
1988	17 Feb	Tel Aviv	0	0

		v ITALY	E	I
1933	13 May	Rome	1	1
1934	14 Nov	Highbury	3	2
1939	13 May	Milan	2	2

			E	I
1948	16 May	Turin	4	0
1949	30 Nov	Tottenham	2	0
1952	18 May	Florence	1	1
1959	6 May	Wembley	2	2
1961	24 May	Rome	3	2
1973	14 June	Turin	0	2
1973	14 Nov	Wembley	0	1
1976	28 May	New York	3	2
WC1976	17 Nov	Rome	0	2
WC1977	16 Nov	Wembley	2	0
EC1980	15 June	Turin	0	1
1985	6 June	Mexico City	1	2
1989	15 Nov	Wembley	0	0
WC1990	7 July	Bari	1	2

		v KUWAIT	E	K
WC1982	25 June	Bilbao	1	0

		v LUXEMBOURG	E	L
1927	21 May	Luxembourg	5	2
WC1960	19 Oct	Luxembourg	9	0
WC1961	28 Sept	Highbury	4	1
WC1977	30 Mar	Wembley	5	0
WC1977	12 Oct	Luxembourg	2	0
EC1982	15 Dec	Wembley	9	0
EC1983	16 Nov	Luxembourg	4	0

		v MALAYSIA	E	M
1991	12 June	Kuala Lumpur	4	2

		v MALTA	E	M
EC1971	3 Feb	Valletta	1	0
EC1971	12 May	Wembley	5	0

		v MEXICO	E	M
1959	24 May	Mexico City	1	2
1961	10 May	Wembley	8	0
WC1966	16 July	Wembley	2	0
1969	1 June	Mexico City	0	0
1985	9 June	Mexico City	0	1
1986	17 May	Los Angeles	3	0

		v MOROCCO	E	M
WC1986	6 June	Monterrey	0	0

		v NEW ZEALAND	E	NZ
1991	3 June	Auckland	1	0
1991	8 June	Wellington	2	0

		v NORWAY	E	N
1937	14 May	Oslo	6	0
1938	9 Nov	Newcastle	4	0
1949	18 May	Oslo	4	1
1966	29 June	Oslo	6	1
WC1980	10 Sept	Wembley	4	0
WC1981	9 Sept	Oslo	1	2
WC1992	14 Oct	Wembley	1	1
WC1993	2 June	Oslo	0	2
1994	22 May	Wembley	0	0

		v PARAGUAY	E	P
WC1986	18 June	Mexico City	3	0

		v PERU	E	P
1959	17 May	Lima	1	4
1962	20 May	Lima	4	0

		v POLAND	E	P
1966	5 Jan	Everton	1	1
1966	5 July	Chorzow	1	0
WC1973	6 Jqne	Chorzow	0	2
WC1973	17 Oct	Wembley	1	1
WC1986	11 June	Monterrey	3	0
WC1989	3 June	Wembley	3	0
WC1989	11 Oct	Katowice	0	0
EC1990	17 Oct	Wembley	2	0
WC1991	13 Nov	Poznan	1	1
WC1993	29 May	Katowice	1	1
WC1993	8 Sept	Wembley	3	0

		v PORTUGAL	E	P
1947	25 May	Lisbon	10	0
1950	14 May	Lisbon	5	3
1951	19 May	Everton	5	2
1955	22 May	Oporto	1	3
1958	7 May	Wembley	2	1
WC1961	21 May	Lisbon	1	1
WC1961	25 Oct	Wembley	2	0
1964	17 May	Lisbon	4	3
1964	4 June	São Paulo	1	1
WC1966	26 July	Wembley	2	1
1969	10 Dec	Wembley	1	0
1974	3 Apr	Lisbon	0	0
EC1974	20 Nov	Wembley	0	0
EC1975	19 Nov	Lisbon	1	1
WC1986	3 June	Monterrey	0	1

		v ROMANIA	E	R
1939	24 May	Bucharest	2	0
1968	6 Nov	Bucharest	0	0
1969	15 Jan	Wembley	1	1
WC1970	2 June	Guadalajara	1	0
WC1980	15 Oct	Bucharest	1	2
WC1981	29 April	Wembley	0	0
WC1985	1 May	Bucharest	0	0
WC1985	11 Sept	Wembley	1	1

		v SAN MARINO	E	SM
WC1992	17 Feb	Wembley	6	0
WC1993	17 Nov	Bologna	7	1

		v SAUDI ARABIA	E	SA
1988	16 Nov	Riyadh	1	1

		v SPAIN	E	S
1929	15 May	Madrid	3	4
1931	9 Dec	Highbury	7	1
WC1950	2 July	Rio de Janeiro	0	1
1955	18 May	Madrid	1	1
1955	30 Nov	Wembley	4	1
1960	15 May	Madrid	0	3
1960	26 Oct	Wembley	4	2
1965	8 Dec	Madrid	2	0
1967	24 May	Wembley	2	0
EC1968	3 Apr	Wembley	1	0
EC1968	8 May	Madrid	2	1
1980	26 Mar	Barcelona	2	0
EC1980	18 June	Naples	2	1
1981	25 Mar	Wembley	1	2
WC1982	5 July	Madrid	0	0
1987	18 Feb	Madrid	4	2
1992	9 Sept	Santander	0	1

		v SWEDEN	E	S
1923	21 May	Stockholm	4	2
1923	24 May	Stockholm	3	1
1937	17 May	Stockholm	4	0
1947	19 Nov	Highbury	4	2
1949	13 May	Stockholm	1	3
1956	16 May	Stockholm	0	0
1959	28 Oct	Wembley	2	3
1965	16 May	Gothenburg	2	1
1968	22 May	Wembley	3	1
1979	10 June	Stockholm	0	0
1986	10 Sept	Stockholm	0	1
WC1988	19 Oct	Wembley	0	0
WC1989	6 Sept	Stockholm	0	0
EC1992	17 June	Stockholm	1	2

		v SWITZERLAND	E	S
1933	20 May	Berne	4	0
1938	21 May	Zurich	1	2
1947	18 May	Zurich	0	1
1948	2 Dec	Highbury	6	0
1952	28 May	Zurich	3	0
WC1954	20 June	Berne	2	0
1962	9 May	Wembley	3	1
1963	5 June	Basle	8	1
EC1971	13 Oct	Basle	3	2
EC1971	10 Nov	Wembley	1	1
1975	3 Sept	Basle	2	1
1977	7 Sept	Wembley	0	0
WC1980	19 Nov	Wembley	2	1
WC1981	30 May	Basle	1	2
1988	28 May	Lausanne	1	0

		v TUNISIA	E	T
1990	2 June	Tunis	1	1

		v TURKEY	E	T
WC1984	14 Nov	Istanbul	8	0
WC1985	16 Oct	Wembley	5	0
EC1987	29 Apr	Izmir	0	0
EC1987	14 Oct	Wembley	8	0
EC1991	1 May	Izmir	1	0
EC1991	16 Oct	Wembley	1	0
WC1992	18 Nov	Wembley	4	0
WC1993	31 Mar	Izmir	2	0

		v URUGUAY	E	U
1953	31 May	Montevideo	1	2
WC1954	26 June	Basle	2	4
1964	6 May	Wembley	2	1
WC1966	11 July	Wembley	0	0
1969	8 June	Montevideo	2	1
1977	15 June	Montevideo	0	0
1984	13 June	Montevideo	0	2
1990	22 May	Wembley	1	2

		v USA	E	USA
WC1950	29 June	Belo Horizonte	0	1
1953	8 June	New York	6	3
1959	28 May	Los Angeles	8	1
1964	27 May	New York	10	0
1985	16 Juje	Los Angeles	5	0
1993	9 June	Foxboro	0	2

		v USSR	E	USSR
1958	18 May	Moscow	1	1
WC1958	8 June	Gothenburg	2	2
WC1958	17 June	Gothenburg	0	1
1958	22 Oct	Wembley	5	0
1967	6 Dec	Wembley	2	2
EC1968	8 June	Rome	2	0
1973	10 June	Moscow	2	1
1984	2 June	Wembley	0	2
1986	26 Mar	Tbilisi	1	0
EC1988	18 June	Frankfurt	1	3
1991	21 May	Wembley	3	1

		v YUGOSLAVIA	E	Y
1939	18 May	Belgrade	1	2
1950	22 Nov	Highbury	2	2
1954	16 May	Belgrade	0	1
1956	28 Nov	Wembley	3	0
1958	11 May	Belgrade	0	5
1960	11 May	Wembley	3	3
1965	9 May	Belgrade	1	1
1966	4 May	Wembley	2	0
EC1968	5 June	Florence	0	1
1972	11 Oct	Wembley	1	1
1974	5 June	Belgrade	2	2
EC1986	12 Nov	Wembley	2	0
EC1987	11 Nov	Belgrade	4	1
1989	13 Dec	Wembley	2	1

SCOTLAND

		v ARGENTINA	S	A
1977	18 June	Buenos Aires	1	1
1979	2 June	Glasgow	1	3
1990	28 Mar	Glasgow	1	0

		v AUSTRALIA	S	A
WC1985	20 Nov	Glasgow	2	0
WC1985	4 Dec	Melbourne	0	0

		v AUSTRIA	S	A
1931	16 May	Vienna	0	5
1933	29 Nov	Glasgow	2	2
1937	9 May	Vienna	1	1
1950	13 Dec	Glasgow	0	1
1951	27 May	Vienna	0	4
WC1954	16 June	Zurich	0	1
1955	19 May	Vienna	4	1
1956	2 May	Glasgow	1	1
1960	29 May	Vienna	1	4
1963	8 May	Glasgow	4	1
(abandoned after 79 mins)				
WC1968	6 Nov	Glasgow	2	1
WC1969	5 Nov	Vienna	0	2
EC1978	20 Sept	Vienna	2	3
EC1979	17 Oct	Glasgow	1	1
1994	20 Apr	Vienna	2	1

		v BELGIUM	S	B
1947	18 May	Brussels	1	2
1948	28 Apr	Glasgow	2	0
1951	20 May	Brussels	5	0
EC1971	3 Feb	Liège	0	3
EC1971	10 Nov	Aberdeen	1	0
1974	2 June	Brussels	1	2
EC1979	21 Nov	Brussels	0	2
EC1979	19 Dec	Glasgow	1	3
EC1982	15 Dec	Brussels	2	3
EC1983	12 Oct	Glasgow	1	1
EC1987	1 Apr	Brussels	1	4
EC1987	14 Oct	Glasgow	2	0

		v BRAZIL	S	B
1966	25 June	Glasgow	1	1
1972	5 July	Rio de Janeiro	0	1
1973	30 June	Glasgow	0	1
WC1974	18 June	Frankfurt	0	0
1977	23 June	Rio de Janeiro	0	2
WC1982	18 June	Seville	1	4
1987	26 May	Glasgow	0	2
WC1990	20 June	Turin	0	1

		v BULGARIA	S	B
1978	22 Feb	Glasgow	2	1
EC1986	10 Sept	Glasgow	0	0
EC1987	11 Nov	Sofia	1	0
EC1990	14 Nov	Sofia	1	1
EC1991	27 Mar	Glasgow	1	1

		v CANADA	S	C
1983	12 June	Vancouver	2	0
1983	16 June	Edmonton	3	0
1983	20 June	Toronto	2	0
1992	21 May	Toronto	3	1

		v CHILE	S	C
1977	15 June	Santiago	4	2
1989	30 May	Glasgow	2	0

		v CIS	S	C
EC1992	18 June	Norrkoping	3	0

		v COLOMBIA	S	C
1988	17 May	Glasgow	0	0

		v COSTA RICA	S	CR
WC1990	11 June	Genoa	0	1

		v CYPRUS	S	C
WC1968	17 Dec	Nicosia	5	0
WC1969	11 May	Glasgow	8	0
WC1989	8 Feb	Limassol	3	2
WC1989	26 Apr	Glasgow	2	1

		v CZECHOSLOVAKIA	S	C
1937	22 May	Prague	3	1
1937	8 Dec	Glasgow	5	0
WC1961	14 May	Bratislava	0	4
WC1961	26 Sept	Glasgow	3	2
WC1961	29 Nov	Brussels	2	4*
1972	2 July	Porto Alegre	0	0
WC1973	26 Sept	Glasgow	2	1
WC1973	17 Oct	Prague	0	1
WC1976	13 Oct	Prague	0	2
WC1977	21 Sept	Glasgow	3	1

*After extra time

		v DENMARK	S	D
1951	12 May	Glasgow	3	1
1952	25 May	Copenhagen	2	1
1968	16 Oct	Copenhagen	1	0
EC1970	11 Nov	Glasgow	1	0
EC1971	9 June	Copenhagen	0	1
WC1972	18 Oct	Copenhagen	4	1
WC1972	15 Nov	Glasgow	2	0
EC1975	3 Sept	Copenhagen	1	0
EC1975	29 Oct	Glasgow	3	1
WC1986	4 June	Nezahualcayotl	0	1

		v EGYPT	S	E
1990	16 May	Aberdeen	1	3

		v ESTONIA	S	E
WC1993	19 May	Tallinn	3	0
WC1993	2 June	Aberdeen	3	1

		v FINLAND	S	F
1954	25 May	Helsinki	2	1
WC1964	21 Oct	Glasgow	3	1
WC1965	27 May	Helsinki	2	1
1976	8 Sept	Glasgow	6	0
1992	25 Mar	Glasgow	1	1

		v FRANCE	S	F
1930	18 May	Paris	2	0
1932	8 May	Paris	3	1
1948	23 May	Paris	0	3
1949	27 Apr	Glasgow	2	0
1950	27 May	Paris	1	0
1951	16 May	Glasgow	1	0
WC1958	15 June	Orebro	1	2
1984	1 June	Marseilles	0	2
WC1989	8 Mar	Glasgow	2	0
WC1989	11 Oct	Paris	0	3

		v GERMANY	S	G
1929	1 June	Berlin	1	1
1936	14 Oct	Glasgow	2	0
EC1992	15 June	Norrkoping	0	2
1993	24 Mar	Glasgow	0	1

		v EAST GERMANY	S	EG
1974	30 Oct	Glasgow	3	0
1977	7 Sept	East Berlin	0	1
EC1982	13 Oct	Glasgow	2	0
EC1983	16 Nov	Halle	1	2
1985	16 Oct	Glasgow	0	0
1990	25 Apr	Glasgow	0	1

		v WEST GERMANY	S	WG
1957	22 May	Stuttgart	3	1
1959	6 May	Glasgow	3	2
1964	12 May	Hanover	2	2
WC1969	16 Apr	Glasgow	1	1
WC1969	22 Oct	Hamburg	2	3
1973	14 Nov	Glasgow	1	1
1974	27 Mar	Frankfurt	1	2
WC1986	8 June	Queretaro	1	2

		v HOLLAND	S	N
1929	4 June	Amsterdam	2	0
1938	21 May	Amsterdam	3	1
1959	27 May	Amsterdam	2	1
1966	11 May	Glasgow	0	3
1968	30 May	Amsterdam	0	0
1971	1 Dec	Rotterdam	1	2
WC1978	11 June	Mendoza	3	2
1982	23 Mar	Glasgow	2	1
1986	29 Apr	Eindhoven	0	0
EC1992	12 June	Gothenburg	0	1
1994	23 Mar	Glasgow	0	1
1994	27 May	Utrecht	1	3

		v HUNGARY	S	H
1938	7 Dec	Glasgow	3	1
1954	8 Dec	Glasgow	2	4
1955	29 May	Budapest	1	3
1958	7 May	Glasgow	1	1
1960	5 June	Budapest	3	3
1980	31 May	Budapest	1	3
1987	9 Sept	Glasgow	2	0

		v ICELAND	S	I
WC1984	17 Oct	Glasgow	3	0
WC1985	28 May	Reykjavik	1	0

		v IRAN	S	I
WC1978	7 June	Cordoba	1	1

		v REPUBLIC OF IRELAND	S	RI
WC1961	3 May	Glasgow	4	1
WC1961	7 May	Dublin	3	0
1963	9 June	Dublin	0	1
1969	21 Sept	Dublin	1	1
EC1986	15 Oct	Dublin	0	0
EC1987	18 Feb	Glasgow	0	1

		v ISRAEL	S	I
WC1981	25 Feb	Tel Aviv	1	0
WC1981	28 Apr	Glasgow	3	1
1986	28 Jan	Tel Aviv	1	0

		v ITALY	S	I
1931	20 May	Rome	0	3
WC1965	9 Nov	Glasgow	1	0
WC1965	7 Dec	Naples	0	3
1988	22 Dec	Perugia	0	2
WC1992	18 Nov	Glasgow	0	0
WC1993	13 Oct	Rome	1	3

		v LUXEMBOURG	S	L
1947	24 May	Luxembourg	6	0
EC1986	12 Nov	Glasgow	3	0
EC1987	2 Dec	Esch	0	0

		v MALTA	S	M
1988	22 Mar	Valletta	1	1
1990	28 May	Valletta	2	1

			S	M
WC1993	17 Feb	Glasgow	3	0
WC1993	17 Nov	Valletta	2	0

		NEW ZEALAND	S	NZ
WC1982	15 June	Malaga	5	2

		v NORWAY	S	N
1929	28 May	Oslo	7	3
1954	5 May	Glasgow	1	0
1954	19 May	Oslo	1	1
1963	4 June	Bergen	3	4
1963	7 Nov	Glasgow	6	1
1974	6 June	Oslo	2	1
EC1978	25 Oct	Glasgow	3	2
EC1979	7 June	Oslo	4	0
WC1988	14 Sept	Oslo	2	1
WC1989	15 Nov	Glasgow	1	1
1992	3 June	Oslo	0	0

		v PARAGUAY	S	P
WC1958	11 June	Norrkoping	2	3

		v PERU	S	P
1972	26 Apr	Glasgow	2	0
WC1978	3 June	Cordoba	1	3
1979	12 Sept	Glasgow	1	1

		v POLAND	S	P
1958	1 June	Warsaw	2	1
1960	4 June	Glasgow	2	3
WC1965	23 May	Chorzow	1	1
WC1965	13 Oct	Glasgow	1	2
1980	28 May	Poznan	0	1
1990	19 May	Glasgow	1	1

		v PORTUGAL	S	P
1950	21 May	Lisbon	2	2
1955	4 May	Glasgow	3	0
1959	3 June	Lisbon	0	1
1966	18 June	Glasgow	0	1
EC1971	21 Apr	Lisbon	0	2
EC1971	13 Oct	Glasgow	2	1
1975	13 May	Glasgow	1	0
EC1978	29 Nov	Lisbon	0	1
EC1980	26 Mar	Glasgow	4	1
WC1980	15 Oct	Glasgow	0	0
WC1981	18 Nov	Lisbon	1	2
WC1992	14 Oct	Glasgow	0	0
WC1993	28 Apr	Lisbon	0	5

		v ROMANIA	S	R
EC1975	1 June	Bucharest	1	1
EC1975	17 Dec	Glasgow	1	1
1986	26 Mar	Glasgow	3	0
EC1990	12 Sept	Glasgow	2	1
EC1991	16 Oct	Bucharest	0	1

		v SAN MARINO	S	S
EC1991	1 May	Serravalle	2	0
EC1991	13 Nov	Glasgow	4	0

		v SAUDI ARABIA	S	SA
1988	17 Feb	Riyadh	2	2

		v SPAIN	S	Sp
WC1957	8 May	Glasgow	4	2
WC1957	26 May	Madrid	1	4
1963	13 June	Madrid	6	2
1965	8 May	Glasgow	0	0
EC1974	20 Nov	Glasgow	1	2
EC1975	5 Feb	Valencia	1	1
1982	24 Feb	Valencia	0	3
WC1984	14 Nov	Glasgow	3	1
WC1985	27 Feb	Seville	0	1
1988	27 Apr	Madrid	0	0

		v SWEDEN	S	Sw
1952	30 May	Stockholm	1	3
1953	6 May	Glasgow	1	2
1975	16 Apr	Gothenburg	1	1
1977	27 Apr	Glasgow	3	1
WC1980	10 Sept	Stockholm	1	0
WC1981	9 Sept	Glasgow	2	0
WC1990	16 June	Genoa	2	1

		v SWITZERLAND	S	Sw
1931	24 May	Geneva	3	2
1948	17 May	Berne	1	2
1950	26 Apr	Glasgow	3	1
WC1957	19 May	Basle	2	1
WC1957	6 Nov	Glasgow	3	2
1973	22 June	Berne	0	1
1976	7 Apr	Glasgow	1	0
EC1982	17 Nov	Berne	0	2
EC1983	30 May	Glasgow	2	2
EC1990	17 Oct	Glasgow	2	1
EC1991	11 Sept	Berne	2	2
WC1992	9 Sept	Berne	1	3
WC1993	8 Sept	Aberdeen	1	1

		v TURKEY	S	T
1960	8 June	Ankara	2	4

		v URUGUAY	S	U
WC1954	19 June	Basle	0	7
1962	2 May	Glasgow	2	3
1983	21 Sept	Glasgow	2	0
WC1986	13 June	Nezahualcoyotl	0	0

		v USA	S	USA
1952	30 Apr	Glasgow	6	0
1992	17 May	Denver	1	0

		v USSR	S	USSR
1967	10 May	Glasgow	0	2
1971	14 June	Moscow	0	1
WC1982	22 June	Malaga	2	2
1991	6 Feb	Glasgow	0	1

		v YUGOSLAVIA	S	Y
1955	15 May	Belgrade	2	2
1956	21 Nov	Glasgow	2	0
WC1958	8 June	Vasteras	1	1
1972	29 June	Belo Horizonte	2	2
WC1974	22 June	Frankfurt	1	1
1984	12 Sept	Glasgow	6	1
WC1988	19 Oct	Glasgow	1	1
WC1989	6 Sept	Zagreb	1	3

		v ZAIRE	S	Z
WC1974	14 June	Dortmund	2	0

WALES

		v ARGENTINA	W	A
1992	3 June	Tokyo	0	1

		v AUSTRIA	W	A
1954	9 May	Vienna	0	2
EC1955	23 Nov	Wrexham	1	2
EC1974	4 Sept	Vienna	1	2
1975	19 Nov	Wrexham	1	0
1992	29 Apr	Vienna	1	1

		v BELGIUM	W	B
1949	22 May	Liège	1	3
1949	23 Nov	Cardiff	5	1

			W	B
EC1990	17 Oct	Cardiff	3	1
EC1991	27 Mar	Brussels	1	1
WC1992	18 Nov	Brussels	0	2
WC1993	31 Mar	Cardiff	2	0

		v BRAZIL	*W*	*B*
WC1958	19 June	Gothenburg	0	1
1962	12 May	Rio de Janeiro	1	3
1962	16 May	São Paulo	1	3
1966	14 May	Rio de Janeiro	1	3
1966	18 May	Belo Horizonte	0	1
1983	12 June	Cardiff	1	1
1991	11 Sept	Cardiff	1	0

		v BULGARIA	*W*	*B*
EC1983	27 Apr	Wrexham	1	0
EC1983	16 Nov	Sofia	0	1

		v CANADA	*W*	*C*
1986	10 May	Toronto	0	2
1986	20 May	Vancouver	3	0

		v CHILE	*W*	*C*
1966	22 May	Santiago	0	2

		v COSTA RICA	*W*	*CR*
1990	20 May	Cardiff	1	0

		v CYPRUS	*W*	*C*
WC1992	14 Oct	Limassol	1	0
WC1993	13 Oct	Cardiff	2	0

		v CZECHOSLOVAKIA	*W*	*C*
WC1957	1 May	Cardiff	1	0
WC1957	26 May	Prague	0	2
EC1971	21 Apr	Swansea	1	3
EC1971	27 Oct	Prague	0	1
WC1977	30 Mar	Wrexham	3	0
WC1977	16 Nov	Prague	0	1
WC1980	19 Nov	Cardiff	1	0
WC1981	9 Sept	Prague	0	2
EC1987	29 Apr	Wrexham	1	1
EC1987	11 Nov	Prague	0	2
WC1993	28 Apr	Ostrava†	1	1
WC1993	8 Sept	Cardiff†	2	2

† *Czechoslovakia played as RCS (Republic of Czechs and Slovaks)*

		v DENMARK	*W*	*D*
WC1964	21 Oct	Copenhagen	0	1
WC1965	1 Dec	Wrexham	4	2
EC1987	9 Sept	Cardiff	1	0
EC1987	14 Oct	Copenhagen	0	1
1990	11 Sept	Copenhagen	0	1

		v ESTONIA	*W*	*E*
1994	23 May	Tallinn	2	1

		v FINLAND	*W*	*F*
EC1971	26 May	Helsinki	1	0
EC1971	13 Oct	Swansea	3	0
EC1987	10 Sept	Helsinki	1	1
EC1987	1 Apr	Wrexham	4	0
WC1988	19 Oct	Swansea	2	2
WC1989	6 Sept	Helsinki	0	1

		v FAEROES	*W*	*F*
WC1992	9 Sept	Cardiff	6	0
WC1993	6 June	Toftir	3	0

		v FRANCE	*W*	*F*
1933	25 May	Paris	1	1
1939	20 May	Paris	1	2
1953	14 May	Paris	1	6
1982	2 June	Toulouse	1	0

		v EAST GERMANY	*W*	*EG*
WC1957	19 May	Leipzig	1	2
WC1957	25 Sept	Cardiff	4	1
WC1969	16 Apr	Dresden	1	2
WC1969	22 Oct	Cardiff	1	3

		v WEST GERMANY	*W*	*WG*
1968	8 May	Cardiff	1	1
1969	26 Mar	Frankfurt	1	1
1976	6 Oct	Cardiff	0	2
1977	14 Dec	Dortmund	1	1
EC1979	2 May	Wrexham	0	2
EC1979	17 Oct	Cologne	1	5
WC1989	31 May	Cardiff	0	0
WC1989	15 Nov	Cologne	1	2
EC1991	5 June	Cardiff	1	0
EC1991	16 Oct	Nuremberg	1	4

		v GREECE	*W*	*G*
WC1964	9 Dec	Athens	0	2
WC1965	17 Mar	Cardiff	4	1

		v HOLLAND	*W*	*N*
WC1988	14 Sept	Amsterdam	0	1
WC1989	11 Oct	Wrexham	1	2
1992	30 May	Utrecht	0	4

		v HUNGARY	*W*	*H*
WC1958	8 June	Sanviken	1	1
WC1958	17 June	Stockholm	2	1
1961	28 May	Budapest	2	3
EC1962	7 Nov	Budapesp	1	3
EC1963	20 Mar	Cardiff	1	1
EC1974	30 Oct	Cardiff	2	0
EC1975	16 Apr	Budapest	2	1
1985	16 Oct	Cardiff	0	3

		v ICELAND	*W*	*I*
WC1980	2 June	Reykjavik	4	0
WC1981	14 Oct	Swansea	2	2
WC1984	12 Sept	Reykjavik	0	1
WC1984	14 Nov	Cardiff	2	1
1991	1 May	Cardiff	1	0

		v IRAN	*W*	*I*
1978	18 Apr	Teheran	1	0

		v REPUBLIC OF IRELAND	*W*	*RI*
1960	28 Sept	Dublin	3	2
1979	11 Sept	Swansea	2	1
1981	24 Feb	Dublin	3	1
1986	26 Mar	Dublin	1	0
1990	28 Mar	Dublin	0	1
1991	6 Feb	Wrexham	0	3
1992	19 Feb	Dublin	1	0
1993	17 Feb	Dublin	1	2

		v ISRAEL	*W*	*I*
WC1958	15 Jan	Tel Aviv	2	0
WC1958	5 Feb	Cardiff	2	0
1984	10 June	Tel Aviv	0	0
1989	8 Feb	Tel Aviv	3	3

		v ITALY	*W*	*I*
1965	1 May	Florence	1	4
WC1968	23 Oct	Cardiff	0	1
WC1969	4 Nov	Rome	1	4
1988	4 June	Brescia	1	0

		v JAPAN	*W*	*J*
1992	7 June	Matsuyama	1	0

		v KUWAIT	*W*	*K*
1977	6 Sept	Wrexham	0	0
1977	20 Sept	Kuwait	0	0

		v LUXEMBOURG	W	L
EC1974	20 Nov	Swansea	5	0
EC1975	1 May	Luxembourg	3	1
EC1990	14 Nov	Luxembourg	1	0
EC1991	13 Nov	Cardiff	1	0

		v MALTA	W	M
EC1978	25 Oct	Wrexham	7	0
EC1979	2 June	Valletta	2	0
1988	1 June	Valletta	3	2

		v MEXICO	W	M
WC1958	11 June	Stockholm	1	1
1962	22 May	Mexico City	1	2

		v NORWAY	W	M
EC1982	22 Sept	Swansea	1	0
EC1983	21 Sept	Oslo	0	0
1984	6 June	Trondheim	0	1
1985	26 Feb	Wrexham	1	1
1985	5 June	Bergen	2	4
1994	9 Mar	Cardiff	1	3

		v POLAND	W	P
WC1973	28 Mar	Cardiff	2	0
WC1973	26 Sept	Katowice	0	3
1991	29 May	Radom	0	0

		v PORTUGAL	W	P
1949	15 May	Lisbon	2	3
1951	12 May	Cardiff	2	1

		v ROMANIA	W	R
EC1970	11 Nov	Cardiff	0	0
EC1971	24 Nov	Bucharest	0	2
1983	12 Oct	Wrexham	5	0
WC1992	20 May	Bucharest	1	5
WC1993	17 Nov	Cardiff	1	2

		v SAUDI ARABIA	W	SA
1986	25 Feb	Dahran	2	1

		v SPAIN	W	S
WC1961	19 Apr	Cardiff	1	2
WC1961	18 May	Madrid	1	1
1982	24 Mar	Valencia	1	1
WC1984	17 Oct	Seville	0	3
WC1985	30 Apr	Wrexham	3	0

		v SWEDEN	W	S
WC1958	15 June	Stockholm	0	0
1988	27 Apr	Stockholm	1	4
1989	26 Apr	Wrexham	0	2
1990	25 Apr	Stockholm	2	4
1994	20 Apr	Wrexham	0	2

		v SWITZERLAND	W	S
1949	26 May	Berne	0	4
1951	16 May	Wrexham	3	2

		v TURKEY	W	T
EC1978	29 Nov	Wrexham	1	0
EC1979	21 Nov	Izmir	0	1
WC1980	15 Oct	Cardiff	4	0
WC1981	25 Mar	Ankara	1	0

		v REST OF UNITED KINGDOM	W	UK
1951	5 Dec	Cardiff	3	2
1969	28 July	Cardiff	0	1

		v URUGUAY	W	U
1986	21 Apr	Wrexham	0	0

		v USSR	W	USSR
WC1965	30 May	Moscow	1	2
WC1965	27 Oct	Cardiff	2	1
WC1981	30 May	Wrexham	0	0
WC1981	18 Nov	Tbilisi	0	3
1987	18 Feb	Swansea	0	0

		v YUGOSLAVIA	W	Y
1953	21 May	Belgrade	2	5
1954	22 Nov	Cardiff	1	3
EC1976	24 Apr	Zagreb	0	2
EC1976	22 May	Cardiff	1	1
EC1982	15 Dec	Titograd	4	4
EC1983	14 Dec	Cardiff	1	1
1988	23 Mar	Swansea	1	2

NORTHERN IRELAND

		v ALBANIA	NI	A
WC1965	7 May	Belfast	4	1
WC1965	24 Nov	Tirana	1	1
EC1982	15 Dec	Tirana	0	0
EC1983	27 Apr	Belfast	1	0
WC1992	9 Sept	Belfast	3	0
WC1993	17 Feb	Tirana	2	1

		v ALGERIA	NI	A
WC1986	3 June	Guadalajara	1	1

		v ARGENTINA	NI	A
WC1958	11 June	Halmstad	1	3

		v AUSTRALIA	NI	A
1980	11 June	Sydney	2	1
1980	15 June	Melbourne	1	1
1980	18 June	Adelaide	2	1

		v AUSTRIA	NI	A
WC1982	1 July	Madrid	2	2
EC1982	13 Oct	Vienna	0	2
EC1983	21 Sept	Belfast	3	1
EC1990	14 Nov	Vienna	0	0
EC1991	16 Oct	Belfast	2	1

		v BELGIUM	NI	B
WC1976	10 Nov	Liège	0	2
WC1977	16 Nov	Belfast	3	0

		v BRAZIL	NI	B
WC1986	12 June	Guadalajara	0	3

		v BULGARIA	NI	B
WC1972	18 Oct	Sofia	0	3
WC1973	26 Sept	Sheffield	0	0
EC1978	29 Nov	Sofia	2	0
EC1979	2 May	Belfast	2	0

		v CHILE	NI	C
1989	26 May	Belfast	0	1

		v COLOMBIA	NI	C
1994	4 June	Boston	0	2

		v CYPRUS	NI	C
EC1971	3 Feb	Nicosia	3	0
EC1971	21 Apr	Belfast	5	0
WC1973	14 Feb	Nicosia	0	1
WC1973	8 May	London	3	0

		v CZECHOSLOVAKIA	NI	C
WC1958	8 June	Halmstad	1	0
WC1958	17 June	Malmo	2	1*

**After extra time*

		v DENMARK	*NI*	*D*
EC1978	25 Oct	Belfast	2	1
EC1979	6 June	Copenhagen	0	4
1986	26 Mar	Belfast	1	1
EC1990	17 Oct	Belfast	1	1
EC1991	13 Nov	Odense	1	2
WC1992	18 Nov	Belfast	0	1
WC1993	13 Oct	Copenhagen	0	1

		v FAEROES	*NI*	*F*
EC1991	1 May	Belfast	1	1
EC1991	11 Sept	Landsrona	5	0

		v FINLAND	*NI*	*F*
WC1984	27 May	Pori	0	1
WC1984	14 Nov	Belfast	2	1

		v FRANCE	*NI*	*F*
1951	12 May	Belfast	2	2
1952	11 Nov	Paris	1	3
WC1958	19 June	Norrkoping	0	4
1982	24 Mar	Paris	0	4
WC1982	4 July	Madrid	1	4
1986	26 Feb	Paris	0	0
1988	27 Apr	Belfast	0	0

		v GERMANY	*NI*	*G*
1992	2 June	Bremen	1	1

		v WEST GERMANY	*NI*	*WG*
WC1918	15 June	Malmo	2	2
WC1960	26 Oct	Belfast	3	4
WC1961	10 May	Hamburg	1	2
1966	7 May	Belfast	0	2
1977	27 Apr	Cologne	0	5
EC1982	17 Nov	Belfast	1	0
EC1983	16 Nov	Hamburg	1 0	

		v GREECE	*NI*	*G*
WC1961	3 May	Athens	1	2
WC1961	17 Oct	Belfast	2	0
1988	17 Feb	Athens	2	3

		v HOLLAND	*NI*	*N*
1962	9 May	Rotterdam	0	4
WC1965	17 Mar	Belfast	2	1
WC1965	7 Apr	Rotterdam	0	0
WC1976	13 Oct	Rotterdam	2	2
WC1977	12 Oct	Belfast	0	1

		v HONDURAS	*NI*	*H*
WC1982	21 June	Zaragoza	1	1

		v HUNGARY	*NI*	*H*
WC1988	19 Oct	Budapest	0	1
WC1989	6 Sept	Belfast	1	2

		v ICELAND	*NI*	*I*
WC1977	11 June	Reykjavik	0	1
WC1977	21 Sept	Belfast	2	0

		v REPUBLIC OF IRELAND	*NI*	*RI*
EC1978	20 Sept	Bublin	0	0
EC1979	21 Nov	Belfast	1	0
WC1988	14 Sept	Belfast	0	0
WC1989	11 Oct	Dublin	0	3
WC1993	31 Mar	Dublin	0	3
WC1993	17 Nov	Belfast	1	1

		v ISRAEL	*NI*	*I*
1968	10 Sept	Jaffa	3	2
1976	3 Mar	Tel Aviv	1	1
WC1980	26 Mar	Tel Aviv	0	0
WC1981	18 Nov	Belfast	1	0
1984	16 Oct	Belfast	3	0
1987	18 Feb	Tel Aviv	1	1

		v ITALY	*NI*	*I*
WC1957	25 Apr	Rome	0	1
1957	4 Dec	Belfast	2	2
WC1958	15 Jan	Belfast	2	1
1961	25 Apr	Bologna	2	3

		v LATVIA	*NI*	*L*
WC1993	2 June	Riga	2	1
WC1993	8 Sept	Belfast	2	0

		v LIECHTENSTEIN	*NI*	*L*
EC1994	20 Apr	Belfast	4	1

		v LITHUANIA	*NI*	*L*
WC1992	28 Apr	Belfast	2	2
WC1993	25 May	Vilnius	1	0

		v MALTA	*NI*	*M*
1988	21 May	Belfast	3	0
WC1989	26 Apr	Valletta	2	0

		v MEXICO	*NI*	*M*
1966	22 June	Belfast	4	1
1994	11 June	Miami	0	3

		v MOROCCO	*NI*	*M*
1986	23 Apr	Belfast	2	1

		v NORWAY	*NI*	*N*
EC1974	4 Sept	Oslo	1	2
EC1975	29 Oct	Belfast	3	0
1990	27 Mar	Belfast	2	3

		v POLAND	*NI*	*P*
EC1962	10 Oct	Katowice	2	0
EC1962	28 Nov	Belfast	2	0
1988	23 Mar	Belfast	1	1
1991	5 Feb	Belfast	3	1

		v PORTUGAL	*NI*	*P*
WC1957	16 Jan	Lisbon	1	1
WC1957	1 May	Belfast	3	0
WC1973	28 Mar	Coventry	1	1
WC1973	14 Nov	Lisbon	1	1
WC1980	19 Nov	Lisbon	0	1
WC1981	29 Apr	Belfast	1	0

		v ROMANIA	*NI*	*R*
WC1984	12 Sept	Belfast	3	2
WC1985	16 Oct	Bucharest	1	0
1994	23 Mar	Belfast	2	0

		v SPAIN	*NI*	*S*
1958	15 Oct	Madrid	2	6
1963	30 May	Bilbao	1	1
1963	30 Oct	Belfast	0	1
EC1970	11 Nov	Seville	0	3
EC1972	16 Feb	Hull	1	1
WC1982	25 June	Valencia	1	0
1985	27 Mar	Palma	0	0
WC1986	7 June	Guadalajara	1	2
WC1988	21 Dec	Seville	0	4
WC1989	8 Feb	Belfast	0	2
WC1992	14 Oct	Belfast	0	0
WC1993	28 Apr	Seville	1	3

		v SWEDEN	*NI*	*S*
EC1974	30 Oct	Solna	2	0
EC1975	3 Sept	Belfast	1	2
WC1980	15 Oct	Belfast	3	0
WC1981	3 June	Solna	0	1

		v SWITZERLAND	*NI*	*S*
WC1964	14 Oct	Belfast	1	0
WC1964	14 Nov	Lausanne	1	2

		v TURKEY	NI	T
WC1968	23 Oct	Belfast	4	1
WC1968	11 Dec	Istanbul	3	0
EC1983	30 Mar	Belfast	2	1
EC1983	12 Oct	Ankara	0	1
WC1985	1 May	Belfast	2	0
WC1985	11 Sept	Izmir	0	0
EC1986	12 Nov	Izmir	0	0
EC1987	11 Nov	Belfast	1	0

		v URUGUAY	NI	U
1964	29 Apr	Belfast	3	0
1990	18 May	Belfast	1	0

		v USSR	NI	USSR
WC1969	19 Sept	Belfast	0	0
WC1969	22 Oct	Moscow	0	2
EC1971	22 Sept	Moscow	0	1
EC1971	13 Oct	Belfast	1	1

		v YUGOSLAVIA	NI	Y
EC1975	16 Mar	Belfast	1	0
EC1975	19 Nov	Belgrade	0	1
WC1982	17 June	Zaragoza	0	0
EC1987	29 Apr	Belfast	1	2
EC1987	14 Oct	Sarajevo	0	3
EC1990	12 Sept	Belfast	0	2
EC1991	27 Mar	Belgrade	1	4

REPUBLIC OF IRELAND

		v ALBANIA	RI	A
WC1992	26 May	Dublin	2	0
WC1993	26 May	Tirana	2	1

		v ALGERIA	RI	A
1982	28 Apr	Algiers	0	2

		v ARGENTINA	RI	A
1951	13 May	Dublin	0	1
1979	29 May	Dublin	0	0*
1980	16 May	Dublin	0	1

* Not considered a full international

		v AUSTRIA	RI	A
1952	7 May	Vienna	0	6
1953	25 Mar	Dublin	4	0
1958	14 Mar	Vienna	1	3
1962	8 Apr	Dublin	2	3
EC1963	25 Sept	Vienna	0	0
EC1963	13 Oct	Dublin	3	2
1966	22 May	Vienna	0	1
1968	10 Nov	Dublin	2	2
EC1971	30 May	Dublin	1	4
EC1971	10 Oct	Linz	0	6

		v BELGIUM	RI	B
1928	12 Feb	Liège	4	2
1929	30 Apr	Dublin	4	0
1930	11 May	Brussels	3	1
WC1934	25 Feb	Dublin	4	4
1949	24 Apr	Dublin	0	2
1950	10 May	Brussels	1	5
1965	24 Mar	Dublin	0	2
1966	25 May	Liège	3	2
WC1980	15 Oct	Dublin	1	1
WC1981	25 Mar	Brussels	0	1
EC1986	10 Sept	Brussels	2	2
EC1987	29 Apr	Dublin	0	0

		v BOLIVIA	RI	B
1994	24 May	Dublin	1	0

		v BRAZIL	RI	B
1974	5 May	Rio de Janeiro	1	2
1982	27 May	Uberlandia	0	7
1987	23 May	Dublin	1	0

		v BULGARIA	RI	B
WC1977	1 June	Sofia	1	2
WC1977	12 Oct	Dublin	0	0
EC1979	19 May	Sofia	0	1
EC1979	17 Oct	Dublin	3	0
EC1987	1 Apr	Sofia	1	2
WC1987	14 Oct	Dublin	2	0

		v CHILE	RI	C
1960	30 Mar	Dublin	2	0
1972	21 June	Recife	1	2
1974	12 May	Santiago	2	1
1982	22 May	Santiago	0	1
1991	22 May	Dublin	1	1

		v CHINA	RI	C
1984	3 June	Sapporo	1	0

		v CYPRUS	RI	C
WC1980	26 Mar	Nicosia	3	2
WC1980	19 Nov	Dublin	6	0

		v CZECHOSLOVAKIA	RI	C
1938	18 May	Prague	2	2
EC1959	5 Apr	Dublin	2	0
EC1959	10 May	Bratislava	0	4
WC1961	8 Oct	Dublin	1	3
WC1961	29 Oct	Prague	1	7
EC1967	21 May	Dublin	0	2
EC1967	22 Nov	Prague	2	1
WC1969	4 May	Dublin	1	2
WC1969	7 Oct	Prague	0	3
1979	26 Sept	Prague	1	4
1981	29 Apr	Dublin	3	1
1986	27 May	Reykjavik	1	0

		v CZECH REPUBLIC	RI	C
1994	5 June	Dublin	1	3

		v DENMARK	RI	D
WC1956	3 Oct	Dublin	2	1
WC1957	2 Oct	Copenhagen	2	0
WC1968	4 Dec	Dublin	1	1
	(abandoned after 51 mins)			
WC1969	27 May	Copenhagen	0	2
WC1969	15 Oct	Dublin	1	1
EC1978	24 May	Copenhagen	3	3
EC1979	2 May	Dublin	2	0
WC1984	14 Nov	Copenhagen	0	3
WC1985	13 Nov	Dublin	1	4
WC1992	14 Oct	Copenhagen	0	0
WC1993	28 Apr	Dublin	1	1

		v ECUADOR	RI	E
1972	19 June	Natal	3	2

		v EGYPT	RI	E
WC1990	17 June	Palermo	0	0

		v ENGLAND	RI	E
1946	30 Sept	Dublin	0	1
1949	21 Sept	Everton	2	0
WC1957	8 May	Wembley	1	5
WC1957	19 May	Dublin	1	1
1964	24 May	Dublin	1	3
1976	8 Sept	Wembley	1	1
EC1978	25 Oct	Dublin	1	1
EC1980	6 Feb	Wembley	0	2

			RI	E
1985	26 Mar	Wembley	1	2
EC1988	12 June	Stuttgart	1	0
WC1990	11 June	Cagliari	1	1
EC1990	14 Nov	Dublin	1	1
EC1991	27 Mar	Wembley	1	1

		v FINLAND	RI	F
WC1949	8 Sept	Dublin	3	0
WC1949	9 Oct	Helsinki	1	1
1990	16 May	Dublin	1	1

		v FRANCE	RI	F
1937	23 May	Paris	2	0
1952	16 Nov	Dublin	1	1
WC1953	4 Oct	Dublin	3	5
WC1953	25 Nov	Paris	0	1
WC1972	15 Nov	Dublin	2	1
WC1973	19 May	Paris	1	1
WC1976	17 Nov	Paris	0	2
WC1977	30 Mar	Dublin	1	0
WC1980	28 Oct	Paris	0	2
WC1981	14 Oct	Dublin	3	2
1989	7 Feb	Dublin	0	0

		v GERMANY	RI	G
1935	8 May	Dortmund	1	3
1936	17 Oct	Dublin	5	2
1939	23 May	Bremen	1	1
1994	29 May	Hanover	2	0

		v WEST GERMANY	RI	WG
1951	17 Oct	Dublin	3	2
1952	4 May	Cologne	0	3
1955	28 May	Hamburg	1	2
1956	25 Nov	Dublin	3	0
1960	11 May	Dusseldorf	1	0
1966	4 May	Dublin	0	4
1970	9 May	Berlin	1	2
1975	1 Mar	Dublin	1	0†
1979	22 May	Dublin	1	3
1981	21 May	Bremen	0	3†
1989	6 Sept	Dublin	1	1

†*v West Germany 'B'*

		v HOLLAND	RI	N
1932	8 May	Amsterdam	2	0
1934	8 Apr	Amsterdam	2	5
1935	8 Dec	Dublin	3	5
1955	1 May	Dublin	1	0
1956	10 May	Rotterdam	4	1
WC1980	10 Sept	Dublin	2	1
WC1981	9 Sept	Rotterdam	2	2
EC1982	22 Sept	Rotterdam	1	2
EC1983	12 Oct	Dublin	2	3
EC1988	18 June	Gelsenkirchen	0	1
WC1990	21 June	Palermo	1	1
1991	11 Sept	Gyor	2	1
1994	20 Apr	Tilburg	1	0
WC1994	4 July	Orlando	0	2

		v HUNGARY	RI	H
1934	15 Dec	Dublin	2	4
1936	3 May	Budapest	3	3
1936	6 Dec	Dublin	2	3
1939	19 Mar	Cork	2	2
1939	18 May	Budapest	2	2
WC1969	8 June	Dublin	1	2
WC1969	5 Nov	Budapest	0	4
WC1989	8 Mar	Budapest	0	2
WC1989	4 June	Dublin	2	0
1991	11 Sept	Gyor	2	1

		v ICELAND	RI	I
EC1962	12 Aug	Dublin	4	2
EC1962	2 Sept	Reykjavik	1	1
EC1982	13 Oct	Dublin	2	0
EC1983	21 Sept	Reykjavik	3	0
1986	25 May	Reykjavik	2	1

		v IRAN	RI	I
1972	18 June	Recife	2	1

		v N. IRELAND	RI	NI
EC1978	20 Sept	Dublin	0	0
EC1979	21 Nov	Belfast	0	1
WC1988	14 Sept	Balfast	0	0
WC1989	11 Oct	Dublin	3	0
WC1993	31 Mar	Dublin	3	0
WC1993	17 Nov	Belfast	1	1

		v ISRAEL	RI	I
1984	4 Apr	Tel Aviv	0	3
1985	27 May	Tel Aviv	0	0
1987	10 Nov	Dublin	5	0

		v ITALY	RI	I
1926	21 Mar	Turin	0	3
1927	23 Apr	Dublin	1	2
EC1970	8 Dec	Rome	0	3
EC1971	10 May	Dublin	1	2
1985	5 Feb	Dublin	1	2
WC1990	30 June	Rome	0	1
1992	4 June	Foxboro	0	2
WC1994	18 June	New York	1	0

		v LATVIA	RI	L
WC1992	9 Sept	Dublin	4	0
WC1993	2 June	Riga	2	1

		v LITHUANIA	RI	L
WC1993	16 June	Vilnius	1	0
WC1993	8 Sept	Dublin	2	0

		v LUXEMBOURG	RI	I
1936	9 May	Luxembourg	5	1
WC1953	28 Oct	Dublin	4	0
WC1954	7 Mar	Luxembourg	1	0
EC1987	28 May	Luxembourg	2	0
EC1987	9 Sept	Dublin	2	1

		v MALTA	RI	M
EC1983	30 Mar	Valletta	1	0
EC1983	16 Nov	Dublin	8	0
WC1989	28 May	Dublin	2	0
WC1989	15 Nov	Valletta	2	0
1990	2 June	Valletta	3	0

		v MEXICO	RI	M
1984	8 Aug	Dublin	0	0
WC1994	24 June	Orlando	1	2

		v MOROCCO	RI	M
1990	12 Sept	Dublin	1	0

		v NORWAY	RI	N
WC1937	10 Oct	Oslo	2	3
WC1937	7 Nov	Dublin	3	3
1950	26 Nov	Dublin	2	2
1951	30 May	Oslo	3	2
1954	8 Nov	Dublin	2	1
1955	25 May	Oslo	3	1
1960	6 Nov	Dublin	3	1
1964	13 May	Oslo	4	1
1973	6 June	Oslo	1	1
1976	24 Mar	Dublin	3	0
1978	21 May	Oslo	0	0
WC1984	17 Oct	Oslo	0	1
WC1985	1 May	Dublin	0	0

			RI	N
1988	1 June	Oslo	0	0
WC1994	28 June	New York	0	0

		v POLAND	RI	P
1938	22 May	Warsaw	0	6
1938	13 Nov	Dublin	3	2
1958	11 May	Katowice	2	2
1958	5 Oct	Dublin	2	2
1964	10 May	Cracow	1	3
1964	25 Oct	Dublin	3	2
1968	15 May	Dublin	2	2
1968	30 Oct	Katowice	0	1
1970	6 May	Dublin	1	2
1970	23 Sept	Dublin	0	2
1973	16 May	Wroclaw	0	2
1973	21 Oct	Dublin	1	0
1976	26 May	Posjan	2	0
1977	24 Apr	Dublin	0	0
1978	12 Apr	Lodz	0	3
1981	23 May	Bydgoszcz	0	3
1984	23 May	Dublin	0	0
1986	12 Nov	Warsaw	0	1
1988	22 May	Dublin	3	1
EC1991	1 May	Dublin	0	0
EC1991	16 Oct	Poznan	3	3

		v PORTUGAL	RI	P
1946	16 June	Lisbon	1	3
1947	4 May	Dublin	0	2
1948	23 May	Lisbon	0	2
1949	22 May	Dublin	1	0
1972	25 June	Recife	1	2
1992	7 June	Boston	2	0

		v ROMANIA	RI	R
1988	23 Mar	Dublin	2	0
WC1990	25 June	Genoa	0	0*

		v RUSSIA	RI	R
1994	23 Mar	Dublin	0	0

		v SCOTLAND	RI	S
WC1961	3 May	Glasgow	1	4
WC1961	7 May	Dublin	0	3
1963	9 June	Dublin	1	0
1969	21 Sept	Dublin	1	1
EC1986	15 Oct	Dublin	0	0
EC1987	18 Feb	Glasgow	1	0

		v SPAIN	RI	S
1931	26 Apr	Barcelona	1	1
1931	13 Dec	Dublin	0	5
1946	23 June	Madrid	1	0
1947	2 Mar	Dublin	3	2
1948	30 May	Barcelona	1	2
1949	12 June	Dublin	1	4
1952	1 June	Madrid	0	6
1955	27 Nov	Dublin	2	2
EC1964	11 Mar	Seville	1	5
EC1964	8 Apr	Dublin	0	2
WC1965	5 May	Dublin	1	0
WC1965	27 Oct	Seville	1	4
WC1965	10 Nov	Paris	0	1
EC1966	23 Oct	Dublin	0	0
EC1966	7 Dec	Valencia	0	2
1977	9 Feb	Dublin	0	1
EC1982	17 Nov	Dublin	3	3
EC1983	27 Apr	Zaragoza	0	2
WC1985	26 May	Cork	0	0
WC1988	16 Nov	Seville	0	2
WC1989	26 Apr	Dublin	1	0
WC1992	18 Nov	Seville	0	0
WC1993	13 Oct	Dublin	1	3

		v SWEDEN	RI	S
WC1949	2 June	Stockholm	1	3
WC1949	13 Nov	Dublin	1	3
1959	1 Nov	Dublin	3	2
1960	18 May	Malmo	1	4
EC1970	14 Oct	Dublin	1	1
EC1970	28 Oct	Malmo	0	1

		v SWITZERLAND	RI	S
1935	5 May	Basle	0	1
1936	17 Mar	Dublin	1	0
1937	17 May	Berne	1	0
1938	18 Sept	Dublin	4	0
1948	5 Dec	Dublin	0	1
EC1975	11 May	Dublin	2	1
EC1975	21 May	Berne	0	1
1980	30 Apr	Dublin	2	0
WC1985	2 June	Dublin	3	0
WC1985	11 Sept	Berne	0	0
1992	25 Mar	Dublin	2	1

		v TRINIDAD & TOBAGO	RI	TT
1982	30 May	Port of Spain	1	2

		v TUNISIA	RI	T
1988	19 Oct	Dublin	4	0

		v TURKEY	RI	T
EC1966	16 Nov	Dublin	2	1
EC1967	22 Feb	Ankara	1	2
EC1974	20 Nov	Izmir	1	1
EC1975	29 Oct	Dublin	4	0
1976	13 Oct	Ankara	3	3
1978	5 Apr	Dublin	4	2
1990	26 May	Izmir	0	0
EC1990	17 Oct	Dublin	5	0
EC1991	13 Nov	Istanbul	3	1

		v URUGUAY	RI	U
1974	8 May	Montevideo	0	2
1986	23 Apr	Dublin	1	1

		v USA	RI	USA
1979	29 Oct	Dublin	3	2
1991	1 June	Boston	1	1
1992	29 Apr	Dublin	4	1
1992	30 May	Washington	1	3

		v USSR	RI	USSR
WC1972	18 Oct	Dublin	1	2
WC1973	13 May	Moscow	0	1
EC1974	30 Oct	Dublin	3	0
EC1975	18 May	Kiev	1	2
WC1984	12 Sept	Dublin	1	0
WC1985	16 Oct	Moscow	0	2
EC1988	15 June	Hanover	1	1
1990	25 Apr	Dublin	1	0

		v WALES	RI	W
1960	28 Sept	Dublin	2	3
1979	11 Sept	Swansea	1	2
1981	24 Feb	Dublin	1	3
1986	26 Mar	Dublin	0	1
1990	28 Mar	Dublin	1	0
1991	6 Feb	Wrexham	3	0
1992	19 Feb	Dublin	0	1
1993	17 Feb	Dublin	2	1

		v YUGOSLAVIA	RI	Y
1955	19 Sept	Dublin	1	4
1988	27 Apr	Dublin	2	0

OTHER BRITISH AND IRISH INTERNATIONAL MATCHES 1993–94

Wembley, 9 March 1994, 71,970

England (1) 1 *(Platt)*
Denmark (0) 0

England: Seaman; Parker, Adams, Pallister, Le Saux, Anderton, Platt, Ince (Batty), Gascoigne (Le Tissier), Beardsley, Shearer.
Denmark: Schmeichel; Kjeldbjerg, Olsen, Rieper, Vilfort (Hoegh), Laudrup B, Laudrup M, Larsen, Jensen, Dethlefsen, Christensen (Fredrikson).

Cardiff, 9 March 1994, 10,000

Wales (0) 1 *(Coleman)*
Norway (1) 3 *(Flo, Mykland, Jakobsen)*

Wales: Southall; Melville, Young, Coleman, Perry, Horne, Phillips, Blake (Pembridge), Rush, Speed (Saunders), Hughes M (Hughes C).
Norway: Grodas; Loken, Berg, Pedersen, Bjornebye, Flo, Mykland, Rekdal (Solbakken), Bohinen, Jakobsen, Fjortoft (Frigaard).

Windsor Park, 23 March 1994, 5500

Northern Ireland (1) 2 *(Morrow, Gray)*
Romania (0) 0

Northern Ireland: Wright; Fleming, Donaghy, Taggart, Morrow, Wilson, Lomas, Magilton, Hughes (Black), Gray, Quinn (Dowie).
Romania: Prunea (Stelea); Petrescu, Lupescu (Mihali), Belodedici, Prodan, Munteanu, Sabau, Popescu (Gilca), Hagi, Dumitrescu, Raducioiu (Panduru).

Dublin, 23 March 1994, 34,000

Republic of Ireland (0) 0
Russia (0) 0

Republic of Ireland: Bonner (Kelly A); Kelly G, Carey, Babb, McGoldrick, McAteer, O'Brien, Whelan, McLoughlin, Kelly D (Coyne), Cascarino.
Russia: Kharine; Rakhimov, Gorlukovich, Kovtoun, Tetradze, Popov, Komeev (Tchertshev), Radchenko (Kossolapov), Borodyuk, Kuznetsov, Salenko.

Hampden Park, 23 March 1994, 36,809

Scotland (0) 0
Holland (0) 1 *(Roy)*

Scotland: Goram; McKimmie, McLaren, Hendry, Levein (Boyd), Robertson (Collins), McCall, McStay (McKinlay), McAllister, Durie, Nevin (Jess).
Holland: De Goey; Van Gobbel, Blind, Frank De Boer, Witschge, Jonk, Rijkaard, Bosman (Winter), Taument (Overmars), Bergkamp (Gillhaus), Roy.

Windsor Park, 20 April 1994, 7000

Northern Ireland (3) 4 *(Quinn 2, Lomas, Dowie)*
Liechtenstein (0) 1 *(Hasler)*

Northern Ireland: Wright; Fleming, Taggart, Donaghy, Worthington, Magilton (O'Neill), Wilson, Lomas, Hughes, Quinn, Dowie (Gray).
Liechtenstein: Oehry; Stocker, Frick C, Ospelt, Moser, Quaderer, Ritter, Zech, Telser, Matt (Hasler), Frick M.
European Championship Group 6.

Vienna, 20 April 1994, 35,000

Austria (1) 1 *(Hutter)*
Scotland (1) 2 *(McGinlay, McKinlay)*

Austria: Wohlfahrt; Prosenik (Kuhbauer), Kogler, Schottel, Hochmaier, Hutter, Stoger, Herzog, Baur, Polster (Weissenberger), Cerny.
Scotland: Leighton; McKimmie, McLaren, Hendry, Irvine, Boyd (Ferguson I), McKinlay, McAllister, Collins (McCall), McGinlay (Shearer), Jess (Nevin).

Tilburg, 20 April 1994, 30,000

Holland (0) 0
Republic of Ireland (0) 1 *(Coyne)*

Holland: De Goey; Valckx, Koeman (De Wolf), Frank de Boer, Rijkaard, Jonk (Winter), Overmars, Bergkamp (Taument), Roy, Ronald de Boer.
Republic of Ireland: Bonner; Kelly G, Moran, Babb, Phelan (McLoughlin), Whelan, McGoldrick (McAteer), Sheridan, Townsend, Staunton, Coyne (O'Coyle).

Wrexham, 20 April 1994, 4694

Wales (0) 0
Sweden (0) 2 *(Larsson, Brolin)*

Wales: Southall; Horne, Melville, Neilson, Bodin, Bowen (Blackmore), Goss (Blake), Phillips, Speed, Roberts (Hughes C), Rush.
Sweden: Ravelli; Nilsson R (Nilsson M), Andersson P, Bjorklund, Ljung, Larsson, Ingesson (Rehn), Schwarz, Limpar (Blomqvist), Andersson K, Brolin.

Wembley, 17 May 1994, 23,659

England (3) 5 *(Anderton, Beardsley, Platt 2 (1 pen), Shearer)*
Greece (0) 0

England: Flowers; Jones (Pearce), Adams, Bould, Le Saux, Anderton (Le Tissier), Richardson, Merson, Beardsley (Wright), Platt, Shearer.
Greece: Karkamanis; Apostolakis, Kalitzakis, Kolitsidakis (Karataidis), Karagiannis, Tsalouchidis, Nioplias, Hantzidis (Saravakos), Kofidis (Kostis), Tsiantakis, Machlas (Mitropoulos).

Wembley, 22 May 1994, 64,327

England (0) 0
Norway (0) 0

England: Seaman; Jones, Bould, Adams, Le Saux, Anderton (Le Tissier), Ince (Wright), Wise, Platt, Beardsley, Shearer.
Norway: Thorstvedt (By Rise); Berg H, Johnsen, Bratseth, Nilsen (Haaland), Flo, Berg O (Ingebrigtsen), Rekdal, Bohinen, Jakobsen, Fjortoft (Sorloth).

Tallinn, 23 May 1994, 3500

Estonia (0) 1 *(Reim (pen))*
Wales (0) 2 *(Rush, Phillips)*

Estonia: Poom; Kallaste, Lemsalu, Prins, Kaljend, Koauan, Olumets (Pari), Linnumae, Kristal, Reim, Lindmaa.
Wales: Southall; Williams, Melville (Bodin), Neilson, Coleman, Phillips, Horne, Jones R, Hughes, Rush, Bowen J.

Dublin, 24 May 1994, 32,500

Republic of Ireland (0) 1 *(Sheridan)*
Bolivia (0) 0

Republic of Ireland: Bonner; Irwin (Kelly G), Moran (Kernaghan), Babb, Phelan, Houghton (McAteer), Keane, Townsend, Sheridan, Staunton, Coyne (Cascarino).
Bolivia: Trucco; Rimba, Quinteros, Sandy, Sporuco (Pena J), Baldivieso, Melgar, Cristaldo, Pinedo (Borja), Pena A (Castillo), Ramos (Moreno).

Utrecht, 27 May 1994, 17,500

Holland (1) 3 *(Roy, Van Vossen, Irvine (og))*
Scotland (0) 1 *(Shearer)*

Holland: De Goey; Valckx, Jonk, Frank de Boer, Winter, Wouters, Witschge, Ronald de Boer (Numan), Overmars, Gullit (Van Vossen), Roy (Taument).
Scotland: Leighton (Gunn); Clarke, Hendry, Irvine, McKimmie, McCall, McKinlay (Nevin), McAllister, Collins (Ferguson I), McGinlay (Shearer), Durie (Jess).

Hannover, 29 May 1994, 50,000

Germany (0) 0
Republic of Ireland (1) 2 *(Cascarino, Kelly G)*

Germany: Illgner; Kohler (Effenberg), Buchwald (Berthold), Strunz, Basler, Sammer, Wagner, Moller (Hassler), Klinsmann, Riedle (Voller).
Republic of Ireland: Kelly A; Irwin (Kelly G), McGrath, Babb, Phelan, Keane, McAteer (Houghton), Sheridan (Whelan), Townsend, Staunton, Cascarino (Coyne).

Boston, 4 June 1994, 21,153

Colombia (2) 2 *(Perez, Valencia)*
Northern Ireland (0) 0

Colombia: Cordoba; Escobar, Herrera, Gomez, Valderrama, Valencia (De Avila), Alvarez, Perea, Asprilla (Aristizabal), Perez, Rincon.
Northern Ireland: Wright; Fleming, Worthington, Taggart, Donaghy, Magilton (Dennison), Wilson (Lomas), Morrow, Quinn (O'Boyle), Dowie (Patterson), Hughes.

Dublin, 5 June 1994, 43,465

Republic of Ireland (1) 1 *(Townsend)*
Czech Republic (1) 3 *(Kuka 2 (1 pen), Suchoparek)*

Republic of Ireland: Bonner; Kelly G, McGrath (Babb), Kernaghan, Phelan, McGoldrick (McAteer), Sheridan, Townsend, Staunton, Aldridge (Keane), Cascarino (Coyne).
Czech Republic: Kouba; Kubik, Kotulek, Repka, Suchoparek, Nemec, Novotny, Oborsky, Smejkal (Nedved), Frydek (Samec), Kuka.

Miami, 11 June 1994, 8418

Mexico (2) 3 *(Garcia 2 (1 pen), Hermosillo)*
Northern Ireland (0) 0

Mexico: Campos; Gutierrez, Perales, Suarez, Ambriz, Ramirez, Valdes, Del Olmo, Sanchez (Hermosillo 70), Garcia (Galindo) (Espinoza), Zague.
Northern Ireland: Fettis (Wright); Fleming (Morrow), Donaghy, Taggart, Worthington, Wilson (Lennon), Lomas, Magilton (Patterson), Hughes, O'Boyle, Quinn (Dowie).

Eric Cantona (right) in delight after scoring for Manchester United, with Roy Keane in attendance. (Action Images).

INTERNATIONAL APPEARANCES

This is a list of full international appearances by Englishmen, Irishmen, Scotsmen and Welshmen in matches against the Home Countries and against foreign nations. It does not include unofficial matches against Commonwealth and Empire countries. The year indicated refers to the season; ie 1993 is the 1992-93 season. Explanatory code for matches played by all five countries: A represents Austria; Alb, Albania; Alg, Algeria; Arg, Argentina; Aus, Australia; B, Bohemia; Bel, Belgium; Bol, Bolivia; Br, Brazil; Bul, Bulgaria; C,CIS; Ca, Canada; Cam, Cameroon; Ch, Chile; Chn, China; Co, Colombia; Cr, Costa Rica; Cy, Cyprus; Cz, Czechoslovakia; CzR, Czech Republic; D, Denmark; E, England; Ec, Ecuador; Ei, Republic of Ireland; EG, East Germany; Eg, Egypt; Es, Estonia; F, France; Fa, Faeroes; Fi, Finland; G, Germany; Gr, Greece; H, Hungary; Ho, Holland; Hon, Honduras; I, Italy; Ic, Iceland; Ir, Iran; Is, Israel; J,Japan; K, Kuwait; L, Luxembourg; La, Latvia; Li, Lithuania; Lie, Liechtenstein; M, Mexico; Ma, Malta; Mal, Malaysia; Mor, Morocco; N, Norway; Ni, Northern Ireland; Nz, New Zealand; P, Portugal; Para, Paraguay; Pe, Peru; Pol, Poland; R, Romania; RCS, Republic of Czechs and Slovaks; R of E, Rest of Europe; R of UK, Rest of United Kingdom; R of W, Rest of World; Ru, Russia; S.Ar, Saudi Arabia; S, Scotland; Se, Sweden; Sm, San Marino; Sp, Spain; Sw, Switzerland; T, Turkey; Tr, Trinidad & Tobago; Tun, Tunisia; U, Uruguay; US, United States of America; USSR, Soviet Union; W, Wales; WG, West Germany; Y, Yugoslavia; Z, Zaire.

As at June 1994.

ENGLAND

Abbott, W. (Everton), 1902 v W (1)
A'Court, A. (Liverpool), 1958 v Ni, Br, A, USSR; 1959 v W (5)
Adams, T. A. (Arsenal), 1987 v Sp, T, Br; 1988 v WG, T, Y, Ho, H, S, Co, Sw, Ei, Ho, USSR; 1989 v D, Se, S.Ar.; 1991 v Ei (2); 1993 v N, T, Sm, T, Ho, Pol, N; 1994 v Pol, Ho, D, Gr, N (31)
Adcock, H. (Leicester C), 1929 v F, Bel, Sp; 1930 v Ni, W (5)
Alcock, C. W. (Wanderers), 1875 v S (1)
Alderson, J. T. (C Palace), 1923 v F (1)
Aldridge, A. (WBA), 1888 v Ni; (with Walsall Town Swifts), 1889 v Ni (2)
Allen, A. (Stoke C) 1960 v Se, W, Ni (3)
Allen, A. (Aston Villa), 1888 v Ni (1)
Allen, C. (QPR), 1984 v Br (sub), U, Ch; (with Tottenham H), 1987 v T; 1988 v Is (5)
Allen, H. (Wolverhampton W), 1888 v S, W, Ni; 1889 v S; 1890 v S (5)
Allen, J. P. (Portsmouth), 1934 v Ni, W (2)
Allen, R. (WBA), 1952 v Sw; 1954 v Y, S; 1955 v WG, W (5)
Alsford, W. J. (Tottenham H), 1935 v S (1)
Amos, A. (Old Carthusians), 1885 v S; 1886 v W (2)
Anderson, R. D. (Old Etonians), 1879 v W (1)
Anderson, S. (Sunderland), 1962 v A, S (2)
Anderson, V. (Nottingham F), 1979 v Cz, Se; 1980 v Bul, Sp; 1981 v N, R, W, S; 1982 v Ni, Ic; 1984 v Ni; (with Arsenal), 1985 v T, Ni, Ei, R, Fi, S, M, US; 1986 v USSR, M; 1987 v Se, Ni (2), Y, Sp, T; (with Manchester U), 1988 v WG, H, Co (30)
Anderton, D. R. (Tottenham H), 1994 v D, Gr, N (3)
Angus, J. (Burnley), 1961 v A (1)
Armfield, J. C. (Blackpool), 1959 v Br, Pe, M, US; 1960 v Y, Sp, H, S; 1961 v L, P, Sp, M, I, A, W, Ni, S; 1962 v A, Sw, Pe, W, Ni, S, L, P, H, Arg, Bul, Br; 1963 v F (2), Br, EG, Sw, Ni, W, S; 1964 v R of W, W, Ni, S; 1966 v Y, Fi (43)
Armitage, G. H. (Charlton Ath), 1926 v Ni (1)
Armstrong, D. (Middlesbrough), 1980 v Aus; (with Southampton), 1983 v WG; 1984 v W (3)
Armstrong, K. (Chelsea), 1955 v S (1)
Arnold, J. (Fulham), 1933 v S (1)
Arthur, J. W. H. (Blackburn R), 1885 v S, W, Ni; 1886 v S, W; 1887 v W, Ni (7)
Ashcroft, J. (Woolwich Arsenal), 1906 v Ni, W, S (3)
Ashmore, G. S. (WBA), 1926 v Bel (1)
Ashton, C. T. (Corinthians), 1926 v Ni (1)
Ashurst, W. (Notts Co), 1923 v Se (2); 1925 v S, W, Bel (5)
Astall, G. (Birmingham C), 1956 v Fi, WG (2)
Astle, J. (WBA), 1969 v W; 1970 v S, P, Br (sub), Cz (5)
Aston, J. (Manchester U), 1949 v S, W, D, Sw, Se, N, F; 1950 v S, W, Ni, Ei, I, P, Bel, Ch, US; 1951 v Ni (17)
Athersmith, W. C. (Aston Villa), 1892 v Ni, 1897 v S, W, Ni; 1898 v S, W, Ni; 1899 v S, W, Ni; 1900 v S, W (12)
Atyeo, P. J. W. (Bristol C), 1956 v Br, Se, Sp; 1957 v D, Ei (2) (6)
Austin, S. W. (Manchester C), 1926 v Ni (1)

Bach, P. (Sunderland), 1899 v Ni (1)
Bache, J. W. (Aston Villa), 1903 v W; 1904 v W, Ni; 1905 v S; 1907 v Ni; 1910 v Ni; 1911 v S (7)
Baddeley, T. (Wolverhampton W), 1903 v S, Ni; 1904 v S, W, Ni (5)
Bagshaw, J. J. (Derby Co), 1920 v Ni (1)
Bailey, G. R. (Manchester U), 1985 v Ei, M (2)
Bailey, H. P. (Leicester Fosse), 1908 v W, A (2), H, B (5)
Bailey, M. A. (Charlton Ath), 1964 v US; 1965 v W (2)
Bailey, N. C. (Clapham Rovers), 1878 v S; 1879 v S, W; 1880 v S; 1881 v S; 1882 v S, W; 1883 v S, W; 1884 v S, W, Ni; 1885 v S, W, Ni; 1886 v S, W; 1887 v S, W (19)
Baily, E. F. (Tottenham H), 1950 v Sp; 1951 v Y, Ni, W; 1952 v A (2), Sw, W; 1953 v Ni (9)
Bain, J. (Oxford University), 1887 v S (1)
Baker, A. (Arsenal), 1928 v W (1)
Baker, B. H. (Everton), 1921 v Bel; (with Chelsea), 1926 v Ni (2)
Baker, J. H. (Hibernian), 1960 v Y, Sp, H, Ni, S; (with Arsenal) 1966 v Sp, Pol, Ni (8)
Ball, A. J. (Blackpool), 1965 v Y, WG, Se; 1966 v S, Sp, Fi, D, U, Arg, P, WG (2), Pol (2); (with Everton), 1967 v W, S, Ni, A, Cz, Sp; 1968 v W, S, USSR, Sp (2), Y, WG; 1969 v Ni, W, S, R (2), M, Br, U; 1970 v P, Co, Ec, R, Br, Cz (sub), WG, W, S, Bel; 1971 v Ma, EG, Gr, Ma (sub), Ni, S; 1972 v Sw, Gr; (with Arsenal) WG (2), S; 1973 v W (3), Y, S (2), Cz, Ni, Pol; 1974 v P (sub); 1975 v WG, Cy (2), Ni, W, S (72)
Ball, J. (Bury), 1928 v Ni (1)
Balmer, W. (Everton), 1905 v Ni (1)
Bamber, J. (Liverpool), 1921 v W (1)
Bambridge, A. L. (Swifts), 1881 v W; 1883 v W; 1884 v Ni (3)
Bambridge, E. C. (Swifts), 1879 v S; 1880 v S; 1881 v S; 1882 v S, W, Ni; 1883 v W; 1884 v S, W, Ni; 1885 v S, W, Ni; 1886 v S, W; 1887 v S, W, Ni (18)
Bambridge, E. H. (Swifts), 1876 v S (1)
Banks, G. (Leicester C), 1963 v S, Br, Cz, EG; 1964 v W, Ni, S, R of W, U, P (2), US, Arg; 1965 v Ni, S, H, Y, WG, Se; 1966 v Ni, S, Sp, Pol (2), WG (2), Y, Fi, U, M, F, Arg, P; 1967 v Ni, W, S, Cz; (with Stoke C), 1968 v W, Ni, S, USSR (2), Sp, WG, Y; 1969 v Ni, S, R (2), F, U, Br; 1970

v W, Ni, S, Ho, Bel, Co, Ec, R, Br, Cz; 1971 v Gr, Ma (2), Ni, S; 1972 v Sw, Gr, WG (2), W, S (73)
Banks, H. E. (Millwall), 1901 v Ni (1)
Banks, T. (Bolton W), 1958 v USSR (3), Br, A; 1959 v Ni (6)
Bannister, W. (Burnley), 1901 v W; (with Bolton W), 1902 v Ni (2)
Barclay, R. (Sheffield U), 1932 v S; 1933 v Ni; 1936 v S (3)
Bardsley, D. J. (QPR), 1993 v Sp (sub), Pol (2)
Barham, M. (Norwich C), 1983 v Aus (2) (2)
Barkas, S. (Manchester C), 1936 v Bel; 1937 v S; 1938 v W, Ni, Cz (5)
Barker, J. (Derby Co), 1935 v I, Ho, S, W, Ni; 1936 v G, A, S, W, Ni; 1937 v W (11)
Barker, R. (Herts Rangers), 1872 v S (1)
Barker, R. R. (Casuals), 1895 v W (1)
Barlow, R. J. (WBA), 1955 v Ni (1)
Barnes, J. (Watford), 1983 v Ni (sub), Aus (sub), Aus (2); 1984 v D, L (sub), F (sub), S, USSR, Br, U, Ch; 1985 v EG, Fi, T, Ni, R, Fi, S, I (sub), M, WG (sub), US (sub); 1986 v R (sub), Is (sub), M (sub), Ca (sub), Arg (sub); 1987 v Se, T (sub), Br; (with Liverpool), 1988 v WG, T, Y, Is, Ho, S, Co, Sw, Ei, Ho, USSR; 1989 v Se, Gr, Alb, Pol, D; 1990 v Se, I, Br, D, U, Tun, Ei, Ho, Eg, Bel, Cam; 1991 v H, Pol, Cam, Ei, T, USSR, Arg; 1992 v Cz, Fi; 1993 v Sm, T, Ho, Pol, US, G (73)
Barnes, P. S. (Manchester C), 1978 v I, WG, Br, W, S, H; 1979 v D, Ei, Cz, Ni (2), S, Bul, A; (with WBA), 1980 v D, W; 1981 v Sp (sub), Br, W, Sw (sub); (with Leeds U), 1982 v N (sub), Ho (sub) (22)
Barnet, H. H. (Royal Engineers), 1882 v Ni (1)
Barrass, M. W. (Bolton W), 1952 v W, Ni; 1953 v S (3)
Barrett, A. F. (Fulham), 1930 v Ni (1)
Barrett, E. D. (Oldham Ath), 1991 v Nz; 1993 v Br, G (3)
Barrett, J. W. (West Ham U), 1929 v Ni (1)
Barry, L. (Leicester C), 1928 v F, Bel; 1929 v F, Bel, Sp (5)
Barson, F. (Aston Villa), 1920 v W (1)
Barton, J. (Blackburn R), 1890 v Ni (1)
Barton, P. H. (Birmingham), 1921 v Bel; 1922 v Ni; 1923 v F; 1924 v Bel, S, W; 1925 v Ni (7)
Bassett, W. I. (WBA), 1888 v Ni, 1889 v S, W; 1890 v S, W; 1891 v S, Ni; 1892 v S; 1893 v S, W; 1894 v S; 1895 v S, Ni; 1896 v S, W, Ni (16)
Bastard, S. R. (Upton Park), 1880 v S (1)
Bastin, C. S. (Arsenal), 1932 v W; 1933 v I, Sw; 1934 v S, Ni, W, H, Cz; 1935 v S, Ni, I; 1936 v S, W, G, A; 1937 v W, Ni; 1938 v S, G, Sw, F (21)
Batty, D. (Leeds U), 1991 v USSR (sub), Arg, Aus, Nz, Mal; 1992 v G, T, H (sub), F, Se; 1993 v N, Sm, US, Br; (with Blackburn R), 1994 v D (sub) (15)
Baugh, R. (Stafford Road), 1886 v Ni; (with Wolverhampton W) 1890 v Ni (2)
Bayliss, A. E. J. M. (WBA), 1891 v Ni (1)
Baynham, R. L. (Luton T), 1956 v Ni, D, Sp (3)
Beardsley, P. A. (Newcastle U), 1986 v Eg (sub), Is, USSR, M, Ca (sub), P (sub), Pol, Para, Arg; 1987 v Ni (2), Y, Sp, Br, S; (with Liverpool), 1988 v WG, T, Y, Is, Ho, H, S, Co, Sw, Ei, Ho; 1989 v D, Se, S.Ar, Gr (sub), Alb (sub + 1), Pol, D; 1990 v Se, Pol, I, Br, U (sub), Tun (sub), Ei, Eg (sub), Cam (sub), WG, I; 1991 v Pol (sub), Ei (2), USSR (sub); (with Newcastle U), 1994 v D, Gr, N (52)
Beasant, D. J. (Chelsea), 1990 v I (sub), Y (sub) (2)
Beasley, A. (Huddersfield T), 1939 v S (1)
Beats, W. E. (Wolverhampton W), 1901 v W; 1902 v S (2)
Beattie, T. K. (Ipswich T), 1975 v Cy (2), S; 1976 v Sw, P; 1977 v Fi, I (sub), Ho; 1978 v L (sub) (9)
Becton, F. (Preston NE), 1895 v Ni; (with Liverpool), 1897 v W (2)
Bedford, H. (Blackpool), 1923 v Se; 1925 v Ni (2)
Bell, C. (Manchester C), 1968 v Se, WG; 1969 v W, Bul, F, U, Br; 1970 v Ni (sub), Ho (2), P, Br (sub), Cz, WG (sub); 1972 v Gr, WG (2), W, Ni, S; 1973 v W (3), Y, S (2), Ni, Cz, Pol; 1974 v A, Pol, I, W, Ni, S, Arg, EG, Bul, Y; 1975 v Cz, P, WG, Cy (2), Ni, S; 1976 v Sw, Cy (48)
Bennett, W. (Sheffield U), 1901 v S, W (2)
Benson, R. W. (Sheffield U), 1913 v Ni (1)
Bentley, R. T. F. (Chelsea), 1949 v Se; 1950 v S, P, Bel, Ch, USA; 1953 v W, Bel; 1955 v W, WG, Sp, P (12)
Beresford, J. (Aston Villa), 1934 v Cz (1)
Berry, A. (Oxford University), 1909 v Ni (1)
Berry, J. J. (Manchester U), 1953 v Arg, Ch, U; 1956 v Se (4)
Bestall, J. G. (Grimsby T), 1935 v Ni (1)
Betmead, H. A. (Grimsby T), 1937 v Fi (1)
Betts, M. P. (Old Harrovians), 1877 v S (1)
Betts, W. (Sheffield W), 1889 v W (1)
Beverley, J. (Blackburn R), 1884 v S, W, Ni (3)
Birkett, R. H. (Clapham Rovers), 1879 v S (1)
Birkett, R. J. E. (Middlesbrough), 1936 v Ni (1)
Birley, F. H. (Oxford University), 1874 v S; (with Wanderers), 1875 v S (2)
Birtles, G. (Nottingham F), 1980 v Arg (sub), I; 1981 v R (3)
Bishop, S. M. (Leicester C), 1927 v S, Bel, L, F (4)
Blackburn, F. (Blackburn R), 1901 v S; 1902 v Ni; 1904 v S (3)
Blackburn, G. F. (Aston Villa), 1924 v F (1)
Blenkinsop, E. (Sheffield W), 1928 v F, Bel; 1929 v S, W, Ni, F, Bel, Sp; 1930 v S, W, Ni, G, A; 1931 v S, W, Ni, F, Bel; 1932 v S, W, Ni, Sp; 1933 v S, W, Ni, A (26)
Bliss, H. (Tottenham H), 1921 v S (1)
Blissett, L. (Watford), 1983 v WG (sub), L, W, Gr (sub), H, Ni, S (sub), Aus (1 + 1 sub); (with AC Milan), 1984 v D (sub), H, W (sub), S, USSR (14)
Blockley, J. P. (Arsenal), 1973 v Y (1)
Bloomer, S. (Derby Co), 1895 v S, Ni; 1896 v W, Ni; 1897 v S, W, Ni; 1898 v S; 1899 v S, W, Ni; 1900 v S; 1901 v S, W; 1902 v S, W, Ni; 1904 v S; 1905 v S, W, Ni; (with Middlesbrough), 1907 v S, W (23)
Blunstone, F. (Chelsea), 1955 v W, S, F, P; 1957 v Y (5)
Bond, R. (Preston NE), 1905 v Ni, W; 1906 v S, W, Ni; (with Bradford C), 1910 v S, W, Ni (8)
Bonetti, P. P. (Chelsea), 1966 v D; 1967 v Sp, A; 1968 v Sp; 1970 v Ho, P, WG (7)
Bonsor, A. G. (Wanderers), 1873 v S; 1875 v S (2)
Booth, F. (Manchester C), 1905 v Ni (1)
Booth, T. (Blackburn R), 1898 v W; (with Everton), 1903 v S (2)
Bould, S. A. (Arsenal), 1994 v Gr, N (2)
Bowden, E. R. (Arsenal), 1935 v W, I; 1936 v W, Ni, A; 1937 v H (6)
Bower, A. G. (Corinthians), 1924 v Ni, Bel; 1925 v W, Bel; 1927 v W (5)
Bowers, J. W. (Derby Co), 1934 v S, Ni, W (3)
Bowles, S. (QPR), 1974 v P, W, Ni; 1977 v I, Ho (5)
Bowser, S. (WBA), 1920 v Ni (1)
Boyer, P. J. (Norwich C), 1976 v W (1)
Boyes, W. (WBA), 1935 v Ho; (with Everton), 1939 v W, R of E (3)
Boyle, T. W. (Burnley), 1913 v Ni (1)
Brabrook, P. (Chelsea), 1958 v USSR; 1959 v Ni; 1960 v Sp (3)
Bracewell, P. W. (Everton), 1985 v WG (sub), US; 1986 v Ni (3)
Bradford, G. R. W. (Bristol R), 1956 v D (1)
Bradford, J. (Birmingham), 1924 v Ni; 1925 v Bel; 1928 v S; 1929 v Ni, W, F, Sp; 1930 v S, Ni, G, A; 1931 v W (12)
Bradley, W. (Manchester U), 1959 v I, US, M (sub) (3)
Bradshaw, F. (Sheffield W), 1908 v A (1)
Bradshaw, T. H. (Liverpool), 1897 v Ni (1)

Bradshaw, W. (Blackburn R), 1910 v W, Ni; 1912 v Ni; 1913 v W (4)
Brann, G. (Swifts), 1886 v S, W; 1891 v W (3)
Brawn, W. F. (Aston Villa), 1904 v W, Ni (2)
Bray, J. (Manchester C), 1935 v W; 1936 v S, W, Ni, G; 1937 v S (6)
Brayshaw, E. (Sheffield W), 1887 v Ni (1)
Bridges, B. J. (Chelsea), 1965 v S, H, Y; 1966 v A (4)
Bridgett, A. (Sunderland), 1905 v S; 1908 v S, A (2), H, B; 1909 v Ni, W, H (2), A (11)
Brindle, T. (Darwen), 1880 v S, W (2)
Brittleton, J. T. (Sheffield W), 1912 v S, W, Ni; 1913 v S; 1914 v W (5)
Britton, C. S. (Everton), 1935 v S, W, Ni, I; 1937 v S, Ni, H, N, Se (9)
Broadbent, P. F. (Wolverhampton W), 1958 v USSR; 1959 v S, W, Ni, I, Br; 1960 v S (7)
Broadis, I. A. (Manchester C), 1952 v S, A, I; 1953 v S, Arg, Ch, U, US; (with Newcastle U), 1954 v S, H, Y, Bel, Sw, U (14)
Brockbank, J. (Cambridge University), 1872 v S (1)
Brodie, J. B. (Wolverhampton W), 1889 v S, Ni; 1891 v Ni (3)
Bromilow, T. G. (Liverpool), 1921 v W; 1922 v S, W; 1923 v Bel; 1926 v Ni (5)
Bromley-Davenport, W. E. (Oxford University), 1884 v S, W (2)
Brook, E. F. (Manchester C), 1930 v Ni; 1933 v Sw: 1934 v S, W, Ni, F, H, Cz; 1935 v S, W, Ni, I; 1936 v S, W, Ni; 1937 v H; 1938 v W, Ni (18)
Brooking, T. D. (West Ham U), 1974 v P, Arg, EG, Bul, Y; 1975 v Cz (sub), P; 1976 v P, W, Br, I, Fi; 1977 v Ei, Fi, I, Ho, Ni, W; 1978 v I, WG, W, S (sub), H; 1979 v D, Ei, Ni, W (sub), S, Bul, Se (sub), A; 1980 v D, Ni, Arg (sub), W, Ni, S, Bel, Sp; 1981 v Sw, Sp, R, H; 1982 v H, S, Fi, Sp (sub) (47)
Brooks, J. (Tottenham H), 1957 v W, Y, D (3)
Broome, F. H. (Aston Villa), 1938 v G, Sw, F; 1939 v N, I, R, Y (7)
Brown, A. (Aston Villa), 1882 v S, W, Ni (3)
Brown, A. S. (Sheffield U), 1904 v W; 1906 v Ni (2)
Brown, A. (WBA), 1971 v W (1)
Brown, G. (Huddersfield T), 1927 v S, W, Ni, Bel, L, F; 1928 v W; 1929 v S; (with Aston Villa), 1933 v W (9)
Brown, J. (Blackburn R), 1881 v W; 1882 v Ni; 1885 v S, W, Ni (5)
Brown, J. H. (Sheffield W), 1927 v S, W, Bel, L, F; 1930 v Ni (6)
Brown, K. (West Ham U), 1960 v Ni (1)
Brown, W. (West Ham U), 1924 v Bel (1)
Bruton, J. (Burnley), 1928 v F, Bel; 1929 v S (3)
Bryant, W. I. (Clapton), 1925 v F (1)
Buchan, C. M. (Sunderland), 1913 v Ni; 1920 v W; 1921 v W, Bel; 1923 v F; 1924 v S (6)
Buchanan, W. S. (Clapham R), 1876 v S (1)
Buckley, F. C. (Derby Co), 1914 v Ni (1)
Bull, S. G. (Wolverhampton W), 1989 v S (sub), D (sub); 1990 v Y, Cz, D (sub), U (sub), Tun (sub), Ei (sub), Ho (sub), Eg, Bel (sub); 1991 v H, Pol (13)
Bullock, F. E. (Huddersfield T), 1921 v Ni (1)
Bullock, N. (Bury), 1923 v Bel; 1926 v W; 1927 v Ni (3)
Burgess, H. (Manchester C), 1904 v S, W, Ni; 1906 v S (4)
Burgess, H. (Sheffield W), 1931 v S, Ni, F, Bel (4)
Burnup, C. J. (Cambridge University), 1896 v S (1)
Burrows, H. (Sheffield W), 1934 v H, Cz; 1935 v Ho (3)
Burton, F. E. (Nottingham F), 1889 v Ni (1)
Bury, L. (Cambridge University), 1877 v S; (with Old Etonians), 1879 v W (2)
Butcher, T. (Ipswich T), 1980 v Aus; 1981 v Sp; 1982 v W, S, F, Cz, WG, Sp; 1983 v D, WG, L, W, Gr, H, Ni, S, Aus (3); 1984 v D, H, L, F, Ni; 1985 v EG, Fi, T, Ni, Ei, R, Fi, S, I, WG, US; 1986 v Is, USSR, S, M, Ca, P, Mor, Pol, Para, Arg; (with Rangers), 1987 v Se, Ni (2), Y, Sp, Br, S; 1988 v T, Y; 1989 v D, Se, Gr, Alb (2), Ch, S, Pol, D; 1990 v Se, Pol, I, Y, Br, Cz, D, U, Tun, Ei, Ho, Bel, Cam, WG (77)
Butler, J. D. (Arsenal), 1925 v Bel (1)
Butler, W. (Bolton W), 1924 v S (1)
Byrne, G. (Liverpool), 1963 v S; 1966 v N (2)
Byrne, J. J. (C Palace), 1962 v Ni; (with West Ham U), 1963 v Sw; 1964 v S, U, P (2), Ei, Br, Arg; 1965 v W, S (11)
Byrne, R. W. (Manchester U), 1954 v S, H, Y, Bel, Sw, U; 1955 v S, W, Ni, WG, F, Sp, P; 1956 v S, W, Ni, Br, Se, Fi, WG, D, Sp; 1957 v S, W, Ni, Y, D (2), Ei (2); 1958 v W, Ni, F (33)

Callaghan, I. R. (Liverpool), 1966 v Fi, F; 1978 v Sw, L (4)
Calvey, J. (Nottingham F), 1902 v Ni (1)
Campbell, A. F. (Blackburn R), 1929 v W, Ni; (with Huddersfield T), 1931 v W, S, Ni; 1932 v W, Ni, Sp (8)
Camsell, G. H. (Middlesbrough), 1929 v F, Bel; 1930 v Ni, W; 1934 v F; 1936 v S, G, A, Bel (9)
Capes, A. J. (Stoke C), 1903 v S (1)
Carr, J. (Middlesbrough), 1920 v Ni; 1923 v W (2)
Carr, J. (Newcastle U), 1905 v Ni; 1907 v Ni (2)
Carr, W. H. (Owlerton, Sheffield), 1875 v S (1)
Carter, H. S. (Sunderland), 1934 v S, H; 1936 v G; 1937 v S, Ni, H; (with Derby Co), 1947 v S, W, Ni, Ei, Ho, F, Sw (13)
Carter, J. H. (WBA), 1926 v Bel; 1929 v Bel, Sp (3)
Catlin, A. E. (Sheffield W), 1937 v W, Ni, H, N, Se (5)
Chadwick, A. (Southampton), 1900 v S, W (2)
Chadwick, E. (Everton), 1891 v S, W; 1892 v S; 1893 v S; 1894 v S; 1896 v Ni; 1897 v S (7)
Chamberlain, M (Stoke C), 1983 v L (sub); 1984 v D (sub), S, USSR, Br, U, Ch; 1985 v Fi (sub) (8)
Chambers, H. (Liverpool), 1921 v S, W, Bel; 1923 v S, W, Ni, Bel; 1924 v Ni (8)
Channon, M. R. (Southampton), 1973 v Y, S (2), Ni, W, Cz, USSR, I; 1974 v A, Pol, I, P, W, Ni, S, Arg, EG, Bul, Y; 1975 v Cz, P, WG, Cy (2), Ni (sub), W, S; 1976 v Sw, Cz, P, W, Ni, S, Br, I, Fi; 1977 v Fi, I, L, Ni, W, S, Br (sub), Arg, U; (with Manchester C), 1978 v Sw (46)
Charles, G. A. (Nottingham F), 1991 v Nz, Mal (2)
Charlton, J. (Leeds U), 1965 v S, H, Y, WG, Se; 1966 v W, Ni, S, A, Sp, Pol (2), WG (2), Y, Fi, D, U, M, F, Arg, P; 1967 v W, S, Ni, Cz; 1968 v W, Sp; 1969 v W, R, F; 1970 v Ho (2), P, Cz (35)
Charlton, R. (Manchester U), 1958 v S, P, Y; 1959 v S, W, Ni, USSR, I, Br, Pe, M, US; 1960 v W, S, Se, Y, Sp, H; 1961 v Ni, W, S, L, P, Sp, M, I, A; 1962 v W, Ni, S, A, Sw, Pe, L, P, H, Arg, Bul, Br; 1963 v S, F, Br, Cz, EG, Sw; 1964 v S, W, Ni, R of W, U, P, Ei, Br, Arg, US (sub); 1965 v Ni, S, Ho; 1966 v W, Ni, S, A, Sp, WG (2), Y, Fi, N, Pol, U, M, F, Arg, P; 1967 v Ni, W, S, Cz; 1968 v W, Ni, S, USSR (2), Sp (2), Se, Y; 1969 v S, W, Ni, R (2), Bul, M, Br; 1970 v W, Ni, Ho (2), P, Co, Ec, Cz, R, Br, WG (106)
Charnley, R. O. (Blackpool), 1963 v F (1)
Charsley, C. C. (Small Heath), 1893 v Ni (1)
Chedgzoy, S. (Everton), 1920 v W; 1921 v W, S, Ni; 1922 v Ni; 1923 v S; 1924 v W; 1925 v Ni (8)
Chenery, C. J. (C Palace), 1872 v S; 1873 v S; 1874 v S (3)
Cherry, T. J. (Leeds U), 1976 v W, S (sub), Br, Fi; 1977 v Ei, I, L, Ni, S (sub), Br, Arg, U; 1978 v Sw, L, I, Br, W; 1979 v Cz, W, Se; 1980 v Ei, Arg (sub), W, Ni, S, Aus, Sp (sub) (27)
Chilton, A. (Manchester U), 1951 v Ni; 1952 v F (2)
Chippendale, H. (Blackburn R), 1894 v Ni (1)
Chivers, M. (Tottenham H), 1971 v Ma (2), Gr, Ni, S; 1972 v Sw (1 + 1 sub), Gr, WG (2), Ni (sub), S; 1973 v W (3), S (2), Ni, Cz, Pol, USSR, I; 1974 v A, Pol (24)
Christian, E. (Old Etonians), 1879 v S (1)

Clamp, E. (Wolverhampton W), 1958 v USSR (2), Br, A (4)

Clapton, D. R. (Arsenal), 1959 v W (1)

Clare, T. (Stoke C), 1889 v Ni; 1892 v Ni; 1893 v W; 1894 v S (4)

Clarke, A. J. (Leeds U), 1970 v Cz; 1971 v EG, Ma, Ni, W (sub), S (sub); 1973 v S (2), W, Cz, Pol, USSR, I; 1974 v A, Pol, I; 1975 v P; 1976 v Cz, P (sub) (19)

Clarke, H. A. (Tottenham H), 1954 v S (1)

Clay, T. (Tottenham H), 1920 v W; 1922 v W, S, Ni (4)

Clayton, R. (Blackburn R), 1956 v Ni, Br, Se, Fi, WG, Sp; 1957 v S, W, Ni, Y, D (2), Ei (2); 1958 v S, W, Ni, F, P, Y, USSR; 1959 v S, W, Ni, USSR, I, Br, Pe, M, US; 1960 v W, Ni, S, Se, Y (35)

Clegg, J. C. (Sheffield W), 1872 v S (1)

Clegg, W. E. (Sheffield W), 1873 v S; (with Sheffield Albion), 1879 v W (2)

Clemence, R. N. (Liverpool), 1973 v W (2); 1974 v EG, Bul, Y; 1975 v Cz, P, WG, Cy, Ni, W, S; 1976 v Sw, Cz, P, W (2), Ni, S, Br, Fi; 1977 v Ei, Fi, I, Ho, L, S, Br, Arg, U; 1978 v Sw, L, I, WG, Ni, S; 1979 v D, Ei, Ni (2), S, Bul, A (sub); 1980 v D, Bul, Ei, Arg, W, S, Bel, Sp; 1981 v R, Sp, Br, Sw, H; (with Tottenham H), 1982 v N, Ni, Fi; 1983 v L; 1984 v L (61)

Clement, D. T. (QPR), 1976 v W (sub + 1), I; 1977 v I, Ho (5)

Clough, B. H. (Middlesbrough), 1960 v W, Se (2)

Clough, N. H. (Nottingham F), 1989 v Ch; 1991 v Arg (sub), Aus, Mal; 1992 v F, Cz, C; 1993 v Sp, T (sub), Pol (sub), N (sub), US, Br, G (14)

Coates, R. (Burnley), 1970 v Ni; 1971 v Gr (sub); (with Tottenham H), Ma, W (4)

Cobbold, W. N. (Cambridge University), 1883 v S, Ni; 1885 v S, Ni; 1886 v S, W; (with Old Carthusians), 1887 v S, W, Ni (9)

Cock, J. G. (Huddersfield T), 1920 v Ni; (with Chelsea), v S (2)

Cockburn, H. (Manchester U), 1947 v W, Ni, Ei; 1948 v S, I; 1949 v S, Ni, D, Sw, Se; 1951 v Arg, P; 1952 v F (13)

Cohen, G. R. (Fulham), 1964 v U, P, Ei, US, Br; 1965 v W, S, Ni, Bel, H, Ho, Y, WG, Se; 1966 v W, S, Ni, A, Sp, Pol (2), WG (2), N, D, U, M, F, Arg, P; 1967 v W, S, Ni, Cz, Sp; 1968 v W, Ni (37)

Coleclough, H. (C Palace), 1914 v W (1)

Coleman, E. H. (Dulwich Hamlet), 1921 v W (1)

Coleman, J. (Woolwich Arsenal), 1907 v Ni (1)

Common, A. (Sheffield U), 1904 v W, Ni; (with Middlesbrough), 1906 v W (3)

Compton, L. H. (Arsenal), 1951 v W, Y (2)

Conlin, J. (Bradford C), 1906 v S (1)

Connelly, J. M. (Burnley), 1960 v W, N, S, Se; 1962 v W, A, Sw, P; 1963 v W, F; (with Manchester U), 1965 v H, Y, Se; 1966 v W, Ni, S, A, N, D, U (20)

Cook, T. E. R. (Brighton), 1925 v W (1)

Cooper, N. C. (Cambridge University), 1893 v Ni (1)

Cooper, T. (Derby Co), 1928 v Ni; 1929 v W, Ni, S, F, Bel, Sp; 1931 v F; 1932 v W, Sp; 1933 v S; 1934 v S, H, Cz; 1935 v W (15)

Cooper, T. (Leeds U), 1969 v W, S, F, M; 1970 v Ho, Bel, Co, Ec, R, Cz, Br, WG; 1971 v EG, Ma, Ni, W, S; 1972 v Sw (2); 1975 v P (20)

Coppell, S. J. (Manchester U), 1978 v I, WG, Br, W, Ni, S, H; 1979 v D, Ei, Cz, Ni (2), W (sub), S, Bul, A; 1980 v D, Ni, Ei (sub), Sp, Arg, W, S, Bel, I; 1981 v R (sub), Sw, R, Br, W, S, Sw, H; 1982 v H, S, Fi, F, Cz, K, WG; 1983 v L, Gr (42)

Copping, W. (Leeds U), 1933 v I, Sw; 1934 v S, Ni, W, F; (with Arsenal), 1935 v Ni, I; 1936 v A, Bel; 1937 v N, Se, Fi; 1938 v S, W, Ni, Cz; 1939 v W, R of E; (with Leeds U), R (20)

Corbett, B. O. (Corinthians), 1901 v W (1)

Corbett, R. (Old Malvernians), 1903 v W (1)

Corbett, W. S. (Birmingham), 1908 v A, H, B (3)

Corrigan, J. T. (Manchester C), 1978 v I (sub), Br; 1979 v W; 1980 v Ni, Aus; 1981 v W, S; 1982 v W, Ic (9)

Cottee, A. R. (West Ham U), 1987 v Se (sub), Ni (sub); 1988 v H (sub); (with Everton) 1989 v D (sub), Se (sub), Ch (sub), S (7)

Cotterill, G. H. (Cambridge University), 1891 v Ni; (with Old Brightonians), 1892 v W; 1893 v S, Ni (4)

Cottle, J. R. (Bristol C), 1909 v Ni (1)

Cowan, S. (Manchester C), 1926 v Bel; 1930 v A; 1931 v Bel (3)

Cowans, G. (Aston Villa), 1983 v W, H, Ni, S, Aus (3); (with Bari), 1986 v Eg, USSR; (with Aston Villa), 1991 v Ei (10)

Cowell, A. (Blackburn R), 1910 v Ni (1)

Cox, J. (Liverpool), 1901 v Ni; 1902 v S; 1903 v S (3)

Cox, J. D. (Derby Co), 1892 v Ni (1)

Crabtree, J. W. (Burnley), 1894 v Ni; 1895 v Ni, S; (with Aston Villa), 1896 v W, S, Ni; 1899 v S, W, Ni; 1900 v S, W, Ni; 1901 v W; 1902 v W (14)

Crawford, J. F. (Chelsea), 1931 v S (1)

Crawford, R. (Ipswich T), 1962 v Ni, A (2)

Crawshaw, T. H. (Sheffield W), 1895 v Ni; 1896 v S, W, Ni; 1897 v S, W, Ni; 1901 v Ni; 1904 v W, Ni (10)

Crayston, W. J. (Arsenal), 1936 v S, W, G, A, Bel; 1938 v W, Ni, Cz (8)

Creek, F. N. S. (Corinthians), 1923 v F (1)

Cresswell, W. (South Shields), 1921 v W; (with Sunderland), 1923 v F; 1924 v Bel; 1925 v Ni; 1926 v W; 1927 v Ni; (with Everton), 1930 v Ni (7)

Crompton, R. (Blackburn R), 1902 v S, W, Ni; 1903 v S, W; 1904 v S, W, Ni; 1906 v S, W, Ni; 1907 v S, W, Ni; 1908 v S, W, Ni, A (2), H, B; 1909 v S, W, Ni, H (2), A; 1910 v S, W; 1911 v S, W, Ni; 1912 v S, W, Ni; 1913 v S, W, Ni; 1914 v S, W, Ni (41)

Crooks, S. D. (Derby Co), 1930 v S, G, A; 1931 v S, W, Ni, F, Bel; 1932 v S, W, Ni, Sp; 1933 v Ni, W, A; 1934 v S, Ni, W, F, H, Cz; 1935 v Ni; 1936 v S, W; 1937 v W, H (26)

Crowe, C. (Wolverhampton W), 1963 v F (1)

Cuggy, F. (Sunderland), 1913 v Ni; 1914 v Ni (2)

Cullis, S. (Wolverhampton W), 1938 v S, W, Ni, F, Cz; 1939 v S, Ni, R of E, N, I, R, Y (12)

Cunliffe, A. (Blackburn R), 1933 v Ni, W (2)

Cunliffe, D. (Portsmouth), 1900 v Ni (1)

Cunliffe, J. N. (Everton), 1936 v Bel (1)

Cunningham, L. (WBA), 1979 v W, Se, A (sub); (with Real Madrid), 1980 v Ei, Sp (sub); 1981 v R (sub) (6)

Curle, K. (Manchester C), 1992 v C (sub), H, D (3)

Currey, E. S. (Oxford University), 1890 v S, W (2)

Currie, A. W. (Sheffield U), 1972 v Ni; 1973 v USSR, I; 1974 v A, Pol, I; 1976 v Sw; (with Leeds U), 1978 v Br, W (sub), Ni, S, H (sub); 1979 v Cz, Ni (2), W, Se (17)

Cursham, A. W. (Notts Co), 1876 v S; 1877 v S; 1878 v S; 1879 v W; 1883 v S, W (6)

Cursham, H. A. (Notts Co), 1880 v W; 1882 v S, W, Ni; 1883 v S, W, Ni; 1884 v Ni (8)

Daft, H. B. (Notts Co), 1889 v Ni; 1890 v S, W; 1891 v Ni; 1892 v Ni (5)

Daley, A. M. (Aston Villa), 1992 v Pol (sub), C, H, Br, Fi (sub), D (sub), Se (7)

Danks, T. (Nottingham F), 1885 v S (1)

Davenport, P. (Nottingham F), 1985 v Ei (sub) (1)

Davenport, J. K. (Bolton W), 1885 v W; 1890 v Ni (2)

Davis, G. (Derby Co), 1904 v W, Ni (2)

Davis, H. (Sheffield W), 1903 v S, W, Ni (3)

Davison, J. E. (Sheffield W), 1922 v W (1)

Dawson, J. (Burnley), 1922 v S, Ni (2)

Day, S. H. (Old Malvernians), 1906 v Ni, W, S (3)

Dean, W. R. (Everton), 1927 v S, W, F, Bel, L; 1928 v S, W, Ni, F, Bel; 1929 v S, W, Ni; 1931 v S; 1932 v Sp; 1933 v Ni (16)

Deane, B. C. (Sheffield U), 1991 v Nz (sub + 1); 1993 v Sp (sub) (3)
Deeley, N. V. (Wolverhampton W), 1959 v Br, Pe (2)
Devey, J. H. G. (Aston Villa), 1892 v Ni; 1894 v Ni (2)
Devonshire, A. (West Ham U), 1980 v Aus (sub), Ni; 1982 v Ho, Ic; 1983 v WG, W, Gr; 1984 v L (8)
Dewhurst, F. (Preston NE), 1886 v W, Ni; 1887 v S, W, Ni; 1888 v S, W, Ni; 1889 v W (9)
Dewhurst, G. P. (Liverpool Ramblers), 1895 v W (1)
Dickinson, J. W. (Portsmouth), 1949 v N, F; 1950 v S, W, Ei, P, Bel, Ch, US, Sp; 1951 v Ni, W, Y; 1952 v W, Ni, S, A (2), I, Sw; 1953 v W, Ni, S, Bel, Arg, Ch, U, US; 1954 v W, Ni, S, R of E, H (2), Y, Bel, Sw, U; 1955 v Sp, P; 1956 v W, Ni, S, D, Sp; 1957 v W, Y, D (48)
Dimmock, J. H. (Tottenham H), 1921 v S; 1926 v W, Bel (3)
Ditchburn, E. G. (Tottenham H), 1949 v Sw, Se; 1953 v US; 1957 v W, Y, D (6)
Dix, R. W. (Derby Co), 1939 v N (1)
Dixon, J. A. (Notts Co), 1885 v W (1)
Dixon, K. M. (Chelsea), 1985 v M (sub), WG, US; 1986 v Ni, Is, M (sub), Pol (sub); 1987 v Se (8)
Dixon, L. M. (Arsenal), 1990 v Cz; 1991 v H, Pol, Ei (2), Cam, T, Arg; 1992 v G, T, Pol, Cz (sub); 1993 v Sp, N, T, Sm, T, Ho, N, US; 1994 v Sm (21)
Dobson, A. T. C. (Notts Co), 1882 v Ni; 1884 v S, W, Ni (4)
Dobson, C. F. (Notts Co), 1886 v Ni (1)
Dobson, J. M. (Burnley), 1974 v P, EG, Bul, Y; (with Everton), 1975 v Cz (5)
Doggart, A. G. (Corinthians), 1924 v Bel (1)
Dorigo, A. R. (Chelsea), 1990 v Y (sub), Cz (sub), D (sub), I; 1991 v H (sub), USSR; (with Leeds U), 1992 v G, Cz (sub), H, Br; 1993 v Sm, Pol, US, Br; 1994 v H (15)
Dorrell, A. R. (Aston Villa), 1925 v W, Bel, F; 1926 v Ni (4)
Douglas, B. (Blackburn R), 1958 v S, W, Ni, F, P, Y, USSR (2), Br, A; 1959 v S, USSR; 1960 v Y, H; 1961 v Ni, W, S, L, P, Sp, M, I, A; 1962 v W, Ni, S, Pe, L, P, H, Arg, Bul, Br; 1963 v S, Br, Sw (36)
Downs, R. W. (Everton), 1921 v Ni (1)
Doyle, M. (Manchester C), 1976 v W, S (sub), Br, I; 1977 v Ho (5)
Drake, E. J. (Arsenal), 1935 v Ni, I; 1936 v W; 1937 v H; 1938 v F (5)
Ducat, A. (Woolwich Arsenal), 1910 v S, W, Ni; (with Aston Villa), 1920 v S, W; 1921 v Ni (6)
Dunn, A. T. B. (Cambridge University), 1883 v Ni; 1884 v Ni; (with Old Etonians), 1892 v S, W (4)
Duxbury, M. (Manchester U), 1984 v L, F, W, S, USSR, Br, U, Ch; 1985 v EG, Fi (10)

Earle, S. G. J. (Clapton), 1924 v F; (with West Ham U), 1928 v Ni (2)
Eastham, G. (Arsenal), 1963 v Br, Cz, EG; 1964 v W, Ni, S, R of W, U, P, Ei, US, Br, Arg; 1965 v H, WG, Se; 1966 v Sp, Pol, D (19)
Eastham, G. R. (Bolton W), 1935 v Ho (1)
Eckersley, W. (Blackburn R), 1950 v Sp; 1951 v S, Y, Arg, P; 1952 v A (2), Sw; 1953 v Ni, Arg, Ch, U, US; 1954 v W, Ni, R of E, H (17)
Edwards, D. (Manchester U), 1955 v S, F, Sp, P; 1956 v S, Br, Se, Fi, WG; 1957 v S, Ni, Ei (2), D (2); 1958 v W, Ni, F (18)
Edwards, J. H. (Shropshire Wanderers), 1874 v S (1)
Edwards, W. (Leeds U), 1926 v S, W; 1927 v W, Ni, S, F, Bel, L; 1928 v S, F, Bel; 1929 v S, W, Ni; 1930 v W, Ni (16)
Ellerington, W. (Southampton), 1949 v N, F (2)
Elliott, G. W. (Middlesbrough), 1913 v Ni; 1914 v Ni; 1920 v W (3)
Elliott, W. H. (Burnley), 1952 v I, A; 1953 v Ni, W, Bel (5)

Evans, R. E. (Sheffield U), 1911 v S, W, Ni; 1912 v W (4)
Ewer, F. H. (Casuals), 1924 v F; 1925 v Bel (2)

Fairclough, P. (Old Foresters), 1878 v S (1)
Fairhurst, D. (Newcastle U), 1934 v F (1)
Fantham, J. (Sheffield W), 1962 v L (1)
Fashanu, J. (Wimbledon), 1989 v Ch, S (2)
Felton, W. (Sheffield W), 1925 v F (1)
Fenton, M. (Middlesbrough), 1938 v S (1)
Fenwick, T. (QPR), 1984 v W (sub), S, USSR, Br, U, Ch; 1985 v Fi, S, M, US; 1986 v R, T, Ni, Eg, M, P, Mor, Pol, Arg; (with Tottenham H), 1988 v Is (sub) (20)
Ferdinand, L. (QPR), 1993 v Sm, Ho, N, US; 1994 v Pol, Sm (6)
Field, E. (Clapham Rovers), 1876 v S; 1881 v S (2)
Finney, T. (Preston NE), 1947 v W, Ni, Ei, Ho, F, P; 1948 v S, W, Ni, Bel, Se, I; 1949 v S, W, Ni, Se, N, F; 1950 v S, W, Ni, Ei, I, P, Bel, Ch, US, Sp; 1951 v W, S, Arg, P; 1952 v W, Ni, S, F, I, Sw, A; 1953 v W, Ni, S, Bel, Arg, Ch, U, US; 1954 v W, S, Bel, Sw, U, H, Y; 1955 v WG; 1956 v S, W, Ni, D, Sp; 1957 v S, W, Y, D (2), Ei (2); 1958 v W, S, F, P, Y, USSR (2); 1959 v Ni, USSR (76)
Fleming, H. J. (Swindon T), 1909 v S, H (2); 1910 v W, Ni; 1911 v W, Ni; 1912 v Ni; 1913 v S, W; 1914 v S (11)
Fletcher, A. (Wolverhampton W), 1889 v W; 1890 v W (2)
Flowers, R. (Wolverhampton W), 1955 v F; 1959 v S, W, I, Br, Pe, US, M (sub); 1960 v W, Ni, S, Se, Y, Sp, H; 1961 v Ni, W, S, L, P, Sp, M, I, A; 1962 v W, Ni, S, A, Sw, Pe, L, P, H, Arg, Bul, Br; 1963 v Ni, W, S, F (2), Sw; 1964 v Ei, US, P; 1965 v W, Ho, WG; 1966 v N (49)
Flowers, T. D. (Southampton), 1993 v Br; (with Blackburn R), 1994 v Gr (2)
Forman, Frank (Nottingham F), 1898 v S, Ni; 1899 v S, W, Ni; 1901 v S; 1902 v S, Ni; 1903 v W (9)
Forman, F. R. (Nottingham F), 1899 v S, W, Ni (3)
Forrest, J. H. (Blackburn R), 1884 v W; 1885 v S, W, Ni; 1886 v S, W; 1887 v S, W, Ni; 1889 v S; 1890 v Ni (11)
Fort, J. (Millwall), 1921 v Bel (1)
Foster, R. E. (Oxford University), 1900 v W; (with Corinthians), 1901 v W, Ni, S; 1902 v W (5)
Foster, S. (Brighton & HA), 1982 v Ni, Ho, K (3)
Foulke, W. J. (Sheffield U), 1897 v W (1)
Foulkes, W. A. (Manchester U), 1955 v Ni (1)
Fox, F. S. (Millwall), 1925 v F (1)
Francis, G. C. J. (QPR), 1975 v Cz, P, W, S; 1976 v Sw, Cz, P, W, Ni, S, Br, Fi (12)
Francis, T. (Birmingham C), 1977 v Ho, L, S, Br; 1978 v Sw, L, I (sub), WG (sub), Br, W, S, H; (with Nottingham F), 1979 v Bul (sub), Se, A (sub); 1980 v Ni, Bul, Sp; 1981 v Sp, R, S (sub), Sw; (with Manchester C), 1982 v N, Ni, W, S (sub), Fi (sub), F, Cz, K, WG, Sp; (with Sampdoria), 1983 v D, Gr, H, Ni, S, Aus (3); 1984 v D, Ni, USSR; 1985 v EG (sub), T (sub), Ni (sub), R, Fi, S, I, M; 1986 v S (52)
Franklin, C. F. (Stoke C), 1947 v S, W, Ni, Ei, Ho, F, Sw, P; 1948 v S, W, Ni, Bel, Se, I; 1949 v S, W, Ni, D, Sw, N, F, Se; 1950 v W, S, Ni, Ei, I (27)
Freeman, B. C. (Everton), 1909 v S, W; (with Burnley), 1912 v S, W, Ni (5)
Froggatt, J. (Portsmouth), 1950 v Ni, I; 1951 v S; 1952 v S, A (2), I, Sw; 1953 v Ni, W, S, Bel, US (13)
Froggatt, R. (Sheffield W), 1953 v W, S, Bel, US (4)
Fry, C. B. (Corinthians), 1901 v Ni (1)
Furness, W. I. (Leeds U), 1933 v I (1)

Galley, T. (Wolverhampton W), 1937 v N, Se (2)
Gardner, T. (Aston Villa), 1934 v Cz; 1935 v Ho (2)
Garfield, B. (WBA), 1898 v Ni (1)
Garratty, W. (Aston Villa), 1903 v W (1)
Garrett, T. (Blackpool), 1952 v S, I; 1954 v W (3)
Gascoigne, P. J. (Tottenham H), 1989 v D (sub), S.Ar (sub), Alb (sub), Ch, S (sub); 1990 v Se (sub), Br (sub), Cz, D,

U, Tun, Ei, Ho, Eg, Bel, Cam, WG; 1991 v H, Pol, Cam; (with Lazio), 1993 v N, T, Sm, T, Ho, Pol, N; 1994 v Pol, D (29)
Gates, E. (Ipswich T), 1981 v N, R (2)
Gay, L. H. (Cambridge University), 1893 v S; (with Old Brightonians), 1894 v S, W (3)
Geary, F. (Everton), 1890 v Ni; 1891 v S (2)
Geaves, R. L. (Clapham Rovers), 1875 v S (1)
Gee, C. W. (Everton), 1932 v W, Sp; 1937 v Ni (3)
Geldard, A. (Everton), 1933 v I, Sw; 1935 v S; 1938 v Ni (4)
George, C. (Derby Co), 1977 v Ei (1)
George, W. (Aston Villa), 1902 v S, W, Ni (3)
Gibbins, W. V. T. (Clapton), 1924 v F; 1925 v F (2)
Gidman, J. (Aston Villa), 1977 v L (1)
Gillard, I. T. (QPR), 1975 v WG, W; 1976 v Cz (3)
Gilliat, W. E. (Old Carthusians), 1893 v Ni (1)
Goddard, P. (West Ham U), 1982 v Ic (sub) (1)
Goodall, F. R. (Huddersfield T), 1926 v S; 1927 v S, F, Bel, L; 1928 v S, W, F, Bel; 1930 v S, G, A; 1931 v S, W, Ni, Bel; 1932 v Ni; 1933 v W, Ni, A, I, Sw; 1934 v W, Ni, F (25)
Goodall, J. (Preston NE), 1888 v S, W; 1889 v S, W; (with Derby Co), 1891 v S, W; 1892 v S; 1893 v W; 1894 v S; 1895 v S, Ni; 1896 v S, W; 1898 v W (14)
Goodhart, H. C. (Old Etonians), 1883 v S, W, Ni (3)
Goodwyn, A. G. (Royal Engineers), 1873 v S (1)
Goodyer, A. C. (Nottingham F), 1879 v S (1)
Gosling, R. C. (Old Etonians), 1892 v W; 1893 v S; 1894 v W; 1895 v W, S (5)
Gosnell, A. A. (Newcastle U), 1906 v Ni (1)
Gough, H. C. (Sheffield U), 1921 v S (1)
Goulden, L. A. (West Ham U), 1937 v Se, N; 1938 v W, Ni, Cz, G, Sw, F; 1939 v S, W, R of E, I, R, Y (14)
Graham, L. (Millwall), 1925 v S, W (2)
Graham, T. (Nottingham F), 1931 v F; 1932 v Ni (2)
Grainger, C. (Sheffield U), 1956 v Br, Se, Fi, WG; 1957 v W, Ni; (with Sunderland), 1957 v S (7)
Gray, A. A. (C Palace), 1992 v Pol (1)
Greaves, J. (Chelsea), 1959 v Pe, M, US; 1960 v W, Se, Y, Sp; 1961 v Ni, W, S, L, P, Sp, I, A; (with Tottenham H), 1962 v S, Sw, Pe, H, Arg, Bul, Br; 1963 v Ni, W, S, F (2), Br, Cz, Sw; 1964 v W, Ni, R of W, P (2), Ei, Br, U, Arg; 1965 v Ni, S, Bel, Ho, H, Y; 1966 v W, A, Y, N, D, Pol, U, M, F; 1967 v S, Sp, A (57)
Green, F. T. (Wanderers), 1876 v S (1)
Green, G. H. (Sheffield U), 1925 v F; 1926 v S, Bel, W; 1927 v W, Ni; 1928 v F, Bel (8)
Greenhalgh, E. H. (Notts Co), 1872 v S; 1873 v S (2)
Greenhoff, B. (Manchester U), 1976 v W, Ni; 1977 v Ei, Fi, I, Ho, Ni, W, S, Br, Arg, U; 1978 v Br, W, Ni, S (sub), H (sub); (with Leeds U), 1980 v Aus (sub) (18)
Greenwood, D. H. (Blackburn R), 1882 v S, Ni (2)
Gregory, J. (QPR), 1983 v Aus (3); 1984 v D, H, W (6)
Grimsdell, A. (Tottenham H), 1920 v S, W; 1921 v S, Ni; 1923 v W, Ni (6)
Grosvenor, A. T. (Birmingham), 1934 v Ni, W, F (3)
Gunn, W. (Notts Co), 1884 v S, W (2)
Gurney, R. (Sunderland), 1935 v S (1)

Hacking, J. (Oldham Ath), 1929 v S, W, Ni (3)
Hadley, N. (WBA), 1903 v Ni (1)
Hagan, J. (Sheffield U), 1949 v D (1)
Haines, J. T. W. (WBA), 1949 v Sw (1)
Hall, A. E. (Aston Villa), 1910 v Ni (1)
Hall, G. W. (Tottenham H), 1934 v F; 1938 v S, W, Ni, Cz; 1939 v S, Ni, R of E, I, Y (10)
Hall, J. (Birmingham C), 1956 v S, W, Ni, Br, Se, Fi, WG, D, Sp; 1957 v S, W, Ni, Y, D (2), Ei (2) (17)
Halse, H. J. (Manchester U), 1909 v A (1)
Hammond, H. E. D. (Oxford University), 1889 v S (1)
Hampson, J. (Blackpool), 1931 v Ni, W; 1933 v A (3)
Hampton, H. (Aston Villa), 1913 v S, W; 1914 v S, W (4)
Hancocks, J. (Wolverhampton W), 1949 v Sw; 1950 v W; 1951 v Y (3)
Hapgood, E. (Arsenal), 1933 v I, Sw; 1934 v S, Ni, W, H, Cz; 1935 v S, Ni, W, I, Ho; 1936 v S, Ni, W, G, A, Bel; 1937 v Fi; 1938 v S, G, Sw, F; 1939 v S, W, Ni, R of E, N, I, Y (30)
Hardinge, H. T. W. (Sheffield U), 1910 v S (1)
Hardman, H. P. (Everton), 1905 v W; 1907 v S, Ni; 1908 v W (4)
Hardwick, G. F. M. (Middlesbrough), 1947 v S, W, Ni, Ei, Ho, F, Sw, P; 1948 v S, W, Ni, Bel, Se (13)
Hardy, H. (Stockport Co), 1925 v Bel (1)
Hardy, S. (Liverpool), 1907 v S, W, Ni; 1908 v S; 1909 v S, W, Ni, H (2), A; 1910 v S, W, Ni; 1912 v Ni; (with Aston Villa), 1913 v S; 1914 v Ni, W, S; 1920 v S, W, Ni (21)
Harford, M. G. (Luton T), 1988 v Is (sub); 1989 v D (2)
Hargreaves, F. W. (Blackburn R), 1880 v W; 1881 v W; 1882 v Ni (3)
Hargreaves, J. (Blackburn R), 1881 v S, W (2)
Harper, E. C. (Blackburn R), 1926 v S (1)
Harris, G. (Burnley), 1966 v Pol (1)
Harris, P. P. (Portsmouth), 1950 v Ei; 1954 v H (2)
Harris, S. S. (Cambridge University), 1904 v S; (with Old Westminsters), 1905 v Ni, W; 1906 v S, W, Ni (6)
Harrison, A. H. (Old Westminsters), 1893 v S, Ni (2)
Harrison, G. (Everton), 1921 v Bel; 1922 v Ni (2)
Harrow, J. H. (Chelsea), 1923 v Ni, Se (2)
Hart, E. (Leeds U), 1929 v W; 1930 v W, Ni; 1933 v S, A; 1934 v S, H, Cz (8)
Hartley, F. (Oxford C), 1923 v F (1)
Harvey, A. (Wednesbury Strollers), 1881 v W (1)
Harvey, J. C. (Everton), 1971 v Ma (1)
Hassall, H. W. (Huddersfield T), 1951 v S, Arg, P; 1952 v F; (with Bolton W), 1954 v Ni (5)
Hateley, M. (Portsmouth), 1984 v USSR (sub), Br, U, Ch; (with AC Milan), 1985 v EG (sub), Fi, Ni, Ei, Fi, S, I, M; 1986 v R, T, Eg, S, M, Ca, P, Mor, Para (sub); 1987 v T (sub), Br (sub), S; (with Monaco), 1988 v WG (sub), Ho (sub), H (sub), Co (sub), Ei (sub), Ho (sub), USSR (sub); (with Rangers), 1992 v Cz (32)
Haworth, G. (Accrington), 1887 v Ni, W, S; 1888 v S; 1890 v S (5)
Hawtrey, J. P. (Old Etonians), 1881 v S, W (2)
Hawkes, R. M. (Luton T), 1907 v Ni; 1908 v A (2), H, B (5)
Haygarth, E. B. (Swifts), 1875 v S (1)
Haynes, J. N. (Fulham), 1955 v Ni; 1956 v S, Ni, Br, Se, Fi, WG, Sp; 1957 v W, Y, D, Ei (2); 1958 v W, Ni, S, F, P, Y, USSR (3), Br, A; 1959 v S, Ni, USSR, I, Br, Pe, M, US; 1960 v Ni, Y, Sp, H; 1961 v Ni, W, S, L, P, Sp, M, I, A; 1962 v W, Ni, S, A, Sw, Pe, P, H, Arg, Bul, Br (56)
Healless, H. (Blackburn R), 1925 v Ni; 1928 v S (2)
Hector, K. J. (Derby Co), 1974 v Pol (sub), I (sub) (2)
Hedley, G. A. (Sheffield U), 1901 v Ni (1)
Hegan, K. E. (Corinthians), 1923 v Bel, F; 1924 v Ni, Bel (4)
Hellawell, M. S. (Birmingham C), 1963 v Ni, F (2)
Henfrey, A. G. (Cambridge University), 1891 v Ni; (with Corinthians), 1892 v W; 1895 v W; 1896 v S, W (5)
Henry, R. P. (Tottenham H), 1963 v F (1)
Heron, F. (Wanderers), 1876 v S (1)
Heron, G. H. H. (Uxbridge), 1873 v S; 1874 v S; (with Wanderers), 1875 v S; 1876 v S; 1878 v S (5)
Hibbert, W. (Bury), 1910 v S (1)
Hibbs, H. E. (Birmingham), 1930 v S, W, A, G; 1931 v S, W, Ni; 1932 v W, Ni, Sp; 1933 v S, W, Ni, A, I, Sw; 1934 v Ni, W, F; 1935 v S, W, Ni, Ho; 1936 v G, W (25)
Hill, F. (Bolton W), 1963 v Ni, W (2)
Hill, G. A. (Manchester U), 1976 v I; 1977 v Ei (sub), Fi (sub), L; 1978 v Sw (sub), L (6)
Hill, J. H. (Burnley), 1925 v W; 1926 v S; 1927 v S, Ni, Bel, F; 1928 v Ni, W; (with Newcastle U), 1929 v F, Bel, Sp (11)

Hill, R. (Luton T), 1983 v D (sub), WG; 1986 v Eg (sub) (3)
Hill, R. H. (Millwall), 1926 v Bel (1)
Hillman, J. (Burnley), 1899 v Ni (1)
Hills, A. F. (Old Harrovians), 1879 v S (1)
Hilsdon, G. R. (Chelsea), 1907 v Ni; 1908 v S, W, Ni, A, H, B; 1909 v Ni (8)
Hine, E. W. (Leicester C), 1929 v W, Ni; 1930 v W, Ni; 1932 v W, Ni (6)
Hinton, A. T. (Wolverhampton W), 1963 v F; (with Nottingham F), 1965 v W, Bel (3)
Hirst, D. E. (Sheffield W), 1991 v Aus, Nz (sub); 1992 v F (3)
Hitchens, G. A. (Aston Villa), 1961 v M, I, A; (with Inter-Milan), 1962 v Sw, Pe, H, Br (7)
Hobbis, H. H. F. (Charlton Ath), 1936 v A, Bel (2)
Hoddle, G. (Tottenham H), 1980 v Bul, W, Aus, Sp; 1981 v Sp, W, S; 1982 v N, Ni, W, Ic, Cz (sub), K; 1983 v L (sub), Ni, S; 1984 v H, L, F; 1985 v Ei (sub), S, I (sub), M, WG, US; 1986 v R, T, Ni, Is, USSR, S, M, Ca, P, Mor, Pol, Para, Arg; 1987 v Se, Ni, Y, Sp, T, S; (with Monaco), 1988 v WG, T (sub), Y (sub), Ho (sub), H (sub), Co (sub), Ei (sub), Ho, USSR (53)
Hodge, S. B. (Aston Villa), 1986 v USSR (sub), S, Ca, P (sub), Mor (sub), Pol, Para, Arg; 1987 v Se, Ni, Y; (with Tottenham H), Sp. Ni, T, S; (with Nottingham F), 1989 v D; 1990 v I (sub), Y (sub), Cz, D, U, Tun; 1991 v Cam (sub), T (sub) (24)
Hodgetts, D. (Aston Villa), 1888 v S, W, Ni; 1892 v S, Ni; 1894 v Ni (6)
Hodgkinson, A. (Sheffield U), 1957 v S, Ei (2), D; 1961 v W (5)
Hodgson, G. (Liverpool), 1931 v S, Ni, W (3)
Hodkinson, J. (Blackburn R), 1913 v W, S; 1920 v Ni (3)
Hogg, W. (Sunderland), 1902 v S, W, Ni (3)
Holdcroft, G. H. (Preston NE), 1937 v W, Ni (2)
Holden, A. D. (Bolton W), 1959 v S, I, Br, Pe, M (5)
Holden, G. H. (Wednesbury OA), 1881 v S; 1884 v S, W, Ni (4)
Holden-White, C. (Corinthians), 1888 v W, S (2)
Holford, T. (Stoke), 1903 v Ni (1)
Holley, G. H. (Sunderland), 1909 v S, W, H (2), A; 1910 v W; 1912 v S, W, NI; 1913 v S (10)
Holliday, E. (Middlesbrough), 1960 v W, Ni, Se (3)
Hollins, J. W. (Chelsea), 1967 v Sp (1)
Holmes, R. (Preston NE), 1888 v Ni; 1891 v S; 1892 v S; 1893 v S, W; 1894 v Ni; 1895 v Ni (7)
Holt, J. (Everton), 1890 v W; 1891 v S, W; 1892 v S, Ni; 1893 v S; 1894 v S, Ni; 1895 v S; (with Reading), 1900 v Ni (10)
Hopkinson, E. (Bolton W), 1958 v W, Ni, S, F, P, Y; 1959 v S, I, Br, Pe, M, US; 1960 v W, Se (14)
Hossack, A. H. (Corinthians), 1892 v W; 1894 v W (2)
Houghton, W. E. (Aston Villa), 1931 v Ni, W, F, Bel; 1932 v S, Ni; 1933 v A (7)
Houlker, A. E. (Blackburn R), 1902 v S; (with Portsmouth), 1903 v S, W; (with Southampton), 1906 v W, Ni (5)
Howarth, R. H. (Preston NE), 1887 v Ni; 1888 v S, W; 1891 v S; (with Everton), 1894 v Ni (5)
Howe, D. (WBA), 1958 v S, W, Ni, F, P, Y, USSR (3), Br, A; 1959 v S, W, Ni, USSR, I, Br, Pe, M, US; 1960 v W, Ni, Se (23)
Howe, J. R. (Derby Co), 1948 v I; 1949 v S, Ni (3)
Howell, L. S. (Wanderers), 1873 v S (1)
Howell, R. (Sheffield U), 1895 v Ni; (with Liverpool) 1899 v S (2)
Hudson, A. A. (Stoke C), 1975 v WG, Cy (2)
Hudson, J. (Sheffield), 1883 v Ni (1)
Hudspeth, F. C. (Newcastle U), 1926 v Ni (1)
Hufton, A. E. (West Ham U), 1924 v Bel; 1928 v S, Ni; 1929 v F, Bel, Sp (6)
Hughes, E. W. (Liverpool), 1970 v W, Ni, S, Ho, P, Bel; 1971 v EG, Ma (2), Gr, W; 1972 v Sw, Gr, WG (2), W, Ni, S; 1973 v W (3), S (2), Pol, USSR, I; 1974 v A, Pol, I, W, Ni, S, Arg, EG, Bul, Y; 1975 v Cz, P, Cy (sub), Ni; 1977 v I, L, W, S, Br, Arg, U; 1978 v Sw, L, I, WG, Ni, S, H; 1979 v D, Ei, Ni, W, Se; (with Wolverhampton W), 1980 v Sp (sub), Ni, S (sub) (62)
Hughes, L. (Liverpool), 1950 v Ch, US, Sp (3)
Hulme, J. H. A. (Arsenal), 1927 v S, Bel, F; 1928 v S, Ni, W; 1929 v Ni, W; 1933 v S (9)
Humphreys, P. (Notts Co), 1903 v S (1)
Hunt, G. S. (Tottenham H), 1933 v I, Sw, S (3)
Hunt, Rev K. R. G. (Leyton), 1911 v S, W (2)
Hunt, R. (Liverpool), 1962 v A; 1963 v EG; 1964 v S, US, P; 1965 v W; 1966 v S, Sp, Pol (2), WG (2), Fi, N, U, M, F, Arg, P; 1967 v Ni, W, Cz, Sp, A; 1968 v W, Ni, USSR (2), Sp (2), Se, Y; 1969 v R (2) (34)
Hunt, S. (WBA), 1984 v S (sub), USSR (sub) (2)
Hunter, J. (Sheffield Heeley), 1878 v S; 1880 v S, W; 1881 v S, W; 1882 v S, W (7)
Hunter, N. (Leeds U), 1966 v WG, Y, Fi, Sp (sub); 1967 v A; 1968 v Sp, Se, Y, WG, USSR; 1969 v R, W; 1970 v Ho, WG (sub); 1971 v Ma; 1972 v WG (2), W, Ni, S; 1973 v W (2) USSR (sub); 1974 v A, Pol, Ni (sub), S; 1975 v Cz (28)
Hurst, G. C. (West Ham U), 1966 v S, WG (2), Y, Fi, D, Arg, P; 1967 v Ni, W, S, Cz, Sp, A; 1968 v W, Ni, S, Se (sub), WG, USSR (2); 1969 v Ni, S, R (2), Bul, F, M, U, Br; 1970 v W, Ni, S, Ho (1 + 1 sub), Bel, Co, Ec, R, Br, WG; 1971 v EG, Gr, W, S; 1972 v Sw (2), Gr, WG (49)

Ince, P. E. C. (Manchester U), 1993 v Sp, N, T (2), Ho, Pol, US, Br, G; 1994 v Pol, Ho, Sm, D, N (14)
Iremonger, J. (Nottingham F), 1901 v S; 1902 v Ni (2)

Jack, D. N. B. (Bolton W), 1924 v S, W; 1928 v F, Bel; (with Arsenal), 1930 v S, G, A; 1933 v W, A (9)
Jackson, E. (Oxford University), 1891 v W (1)
Jarrett, B. G. (Cambridge University), 1876 v S; 1877 v S; 1878 v S (3)
Jefferis, F. (Everton), 1912 v S, W (2)
Jezzard, B. A. G. (Fulham), 1954 v H; 1956 v Ni (2)
Johnson, D. E. (Ipswich T), 1975 v W, S; 1976 v Sw; (with Liverpool), 1980 v Ei, Arg, Ni, S, Bel (8)
Johnson, E. (Saltley College), 1880 v W; (with Stoke C), 1884 v Ni (2)
Johnson, J. A. (Stoke C), 1937 v N, Se, Fi, S, Ni (5)
Johnson, T. C. F. (Manchester C), 1926 v Bel; 1930 v W; (with Everton), 1932 v S, Sp; 1933 v Ni (5)
Johnson, W. H. (Sheffield U), 1900 v S, W, Ni; 1903 v S, W, Ni (6)
Johnston, H. (Blackpool), 1947 v S, Ho; 1951 v S; 1953 v Arg, Ch, U, US; 1954 v W, Ni, H (10)
Jones, A. (Walsall Swifts), 1882 v S, W; (with Great Lever), 1883 v S (3)
Jones, H. (Blackburn R), 1927 v S, Bel, L, F; 1928 v S, Ni (6)
Jones, H. (Nottingham F), 1923 v F (1)
Jones, M. D. (Sheffield U), 1965 v WG, Se; (with Leeds U), 1970 v Ho (3)
Jones, R. (Liverpool), 1992 v F; 1994 v Pol, Gr, N (4)
Jones, W. (Bristol C), 1901 v Ni (1)
Jones, W. H. (Liverpool), 1950 v P, Bel (2)
Joy, B. (Casuals), 1936 v Bel (1)

Kail, E. I. L. (Dulwich Hamlet), 1929 v F, Bel, Sp (3)
Kay, A. H. (Everton), 1963 v Sw (1)
Kean, F. W. (Sheffield W), 1923 v S, Bel; 1924 v W; 1925 v Ni; 1926 v Ni, Bel; 1927 v L; (with Bolton W), 1929 v F, Sp (9)
Keegan, J. K. (Liverpool), 1973 v W (2); 1974 v W, Ni, Arg, EG, Bul, Y; 1975 v Cz, WG, Cy (2), Ni, S; 1976 v Sw, Cz,

P, W (2), Ni, S, Br, Fi; 1977 v Ei, Fi, I, Ho, L; (with SV Hamburg), W, Br, Arg, U; 1978 v Sw, I, WG, Br, H; 1979 v D, Ei, Cz, Ni, W, S, Bul, Se, A; 1980 v D, Ni, Ei, Sp (2), Arg, Bel, I; (with Southampton), 1981 v Sp, Sw, H; 1982 v N, H, Ni, S, Fi, Sp (sub) (63)

Keen, E. R. L. (Derby Co), 1933 v A; 1937 v W, Ni, H (4)

Kelly, R. (Burnley), 1920 v S; 1921 v S, W, Ni; 1922 v S, W; 1923 v S; 1924 v Ni; 1925 v W, Ni, S; (with Sunderland), 1926 v W; (with Huddersfield T), 1927 v L; 1928 v S (14)

Kennedy, A. (Liverpool), 1984 v Ni, W (2)

Kennedy, R. (Liverpool), 1976 v W (2), Ni, S; 1977 v L, W, S, Br (sub), Arg (sub); 1978 v Sw, L; 1980 v Bul, Sp, Arg, W, Bel (sub), I (17)

Kenyon-Slaney, W. S. (Wanderers), 1873 v S (1)

Keown, M. R. (Everton), 1992 v F, Cz, C, H, Br, Fi, D, Fe, Se; (with Arsenal), 1993 v Ho, G (sub) (11)

Kevan, D. T. (WBA), 1957 v S; 1958 v W, Ni, S, P, Y, USSR (3), Br, A; 1959 v M, US; 1961 v M (14)

Kidd, B. (Manchester U), 1970 v Ni, Ec (sub) (2)

King, R. S. (Oxford University), 1882 v Ni (1)

Kingsford, R. K. (Wanderers), 1874 v S (1)

Kingsley, M. (Newcastle U), 1901 v W (1)

Kinsey, G. (Wolverhampton W), 1892 v W; 1893 v S; (with Derby Co), 1896 v W, Ni (4)

Kirchen, A. J. (Arsenal), 1937 v N, Se, Fi (3)

Kirton, W. J. (Aston Villa), 1922 v Ni (1)

Knight, A. E. (Portsmouth), 1920 v Ni (1)

Knowles, C. (Tottenham H), 1968 v USSR, Sp, Se, WG (4)

Labone, B. L. (Everton), 1963 v Ni, W, F; 1967 v Sp, A; 1968 v S, Sp, Se, Y, USSR, WG; 1969 v Ni, S, R, Bul, M, U, Br; 1970 v S, W, Bel, Co, Ec, R, Br, WG (26)

Lampard, F. R. G. (West Ham U), 1973 v Y; 1980 v Aus (2)

Langley, E. J. (Fulham), 1958 v S, P, Y (3)

Langton, R. (Blackburn R), 1947 v W, Ni, Ei, Ho, F, Sw; 1948 v Se; (with Preston NE), 1949 v D, Se; (with Bolton W), 1950 v S; 1951 v Ni (11)

Latchford, R. D. (Everton), 1978 v I, Br, W; 1979 v D, Ei, Cz (sub), Ni (2), W, S, Bul, A (12)

Latheron, E. G. (Blackburn R), 1913 v W; 1914 v Ni (2)

Lawler, C. (Liverpool), 1971 v Ma, W, S; 1972 v Sw (4)

Lawton, T. (Everton), 1939 v S, W, Ni, R of E, N, I, R, Y; (with Chelsea), 1947 v S, W, Ni, Ei, Ho, F, Sw, P; 1948 v W, Ni, Bel; (with Notts Co), 1948 v S, Se, I; 1949 v D (23)

Leach, T. (Sheffield W), 1931 v W, Ni (2)

Leake, A. (Aston Villa), 1904 v S, Ni; 1905 v S, W, Ni (5)

Lee, E. A. (Southampton), 1904 v W (1)

Lee, F. H. (Manchester C), 1969 v Ni, W, S, Bul, F, M, U; 1970 v W, Ho (2), P, Bel, Co, Ec, R, Br, WG; 1971 v EG, Gr, Ma, Ni, W, S; 1972 v Sw (2), Gr, WG (27)

Lee, J. (Derby Co), 1951 v Ni (1)

Lee, S. (Liverpool), 1983 v Gr, L, W, Gr, H, S, Aus; 1984 v D, H, L, F, Ni, W, Ch (sub) (14)

Leighton, J. E. (Nottingham F), 1886 v Ni (1)

Le Saux, G. P. (Blackburn R), 1994 v D, Gr, N (3)

Le Tissier, M. P. (Southampton), 1994 v D (sub), Gr (sub), N (sub) (3)

Lilley, H. E. (Sheffield U), 1892 v W (1)

Linacre, H. J. (Nottingham F), 1905 v W, S (2)

Lindley, T. (Cambridge University), 1886 v S, W, Ni; 1887 v S, W, Ni; 1888 v S, W, Ni; (with Nottingham F), 1889 v S; 1890 v S, W; 1891 v Ni (13)

Lindsay, A. (Liverpool), 1974 v Arg, EG, Bul, Y (4)

Lindsay, W. (Wanderers), 1877 v S (1)

Lineker, G. (Leicester C), 1984 v S (sub); 1985 v Ei, R (sub), S (sub), I (sub), WG, US; (with Everton), 1986 v R, T, Ni, Eg, USSR, Ca, P, Mor, Pol, Para, Arg; (with Barcelona), 1987 v Ni (2), Y, Sp, T, Br; 1988 v WG, T, Y, Ho, H, S, Co, Sw, Ei, Ho, USSR; 1989 v Se, S.Ar, Gr, Alb (2), Pol, D; (with Tottenham H) 1990 v Se, Pol, I, Y, Br, Cz, D, U, Tun, Ei, Ho, Eg, Bel, Cam, WG, I; 1991 v H, Pol, Ei (2), Cam, T, Arg, Aus, Nz, Mal; 1992 v G, T, Pol, F (sub), Cz (sub), C, H, Br, Fi, D, F, Se (80)

Lintott, E. H. (QPR), 1908 v S, W, Ni; (with Bradford C), 1909 v S, Ni, H (2) (7)

Lipsham, H. B. (Sheffield U), 1902 v W (1)

Little, B. (Aston Villa), 1975 v W (sub) (1)

Lloyd, L. V. (Liverpool), 1971 v W; 1972 v Sw, Ni; (with Nottingham F), 1980 v W (4)

Lockett, A. (Stoke C), 1903 v Ni (1)

Lodge, L. V. (Cambridge University), 1894 v W; 1895 v S, W; (with Corinthians), 1896 v S, Ni (5)

Lofthouse, J. M. (Blackburn R), 1885 v S, W, Ni; 1887 v S, W; (with Accrington), 1889 v Ni; (with Blackburn R), 1890 v Ni (7)

Lofthouse, N. (Bolton W), 1951 v Y; 1952 v W, Ni, S, A (2), I, Sw; 1953 v W, Ni, S, Bel, Arg, Ch, U, US; 1954 v W, Ni, R of E, Bel, U; 1955 v Ni, S, F, Sp, P; 1956 v W, S, Sp, D, Fi (sub); 1959 v W, USSR (33)

Longworth, E. (Liverpool), 1920 v S; 1921 v Bel; 1923 v S, W, Bel (5)

Lowder, A. (Wolverhampton W), 1889 v W (1)

Lowe, E. (Aston Villa), 1947 v F, Sw, P (3)

Lucas, T. (Liverpool), 1922 v Ni; 1924 v F; 1926 v Bel (3)

Luntley, E. (Nottingham F), 1880 v S, W (2)

Lyttelton, Hon. A. (Cambridge University), 1877 v S (1)

Lyttelton, Hon. E. (Cambridge University), 1878 v S (1)

McCall, J. (Preston NE), 1913 v S, W; 1914 v S; 1920 v S; 1921 v Ni (5)

McDermott, T. (Liverpool), 1978 v Sw, L; 1979 v Ni, W, Se; 1980 v D, Ni (sub), Ei, Ni, S, Bel (sub), Sp; 1981 v N, R, Sw, R (sub), Br, Sw (sub), H; 1982 v N, H, W (sub), Ho, S (sub), Ic (25)

McDonald, C. A. (Burnley), 1958 v USSR (3), Br, A; 1959 v W, Ni, USSR (8)

McFarland, R. L. (Derby Co), 1971 v Gr, Ma (2), Ni, S; 1972 v Sw, Gr, WG, W, S; 1973 v W (3), Ni, S, Cz, Pol, USSR, I; 1974 v A, Pol, I, W, Ni; 1976 v Cz, S; 1977 v Ei, I (28)

McGarry, W. H. (Huddersfield T), 1954 v Sw, U; 1956 v W, D (4)

McGuinness, W. (Manchester U), 1959 v Ni, M (2)

McInroy, A. (Sunderland), 1927 v Ni (1)

McMahon, S. (Liverpool), 1988 v Is, H, Co, USSR; 1989 v D (sub); 1990 v Se, Pol, I, Y (sub), Br, Cz (sub), D, Ei (sub), Eg, Bel, I; 1991 v Ei (17)

McNab, R. (Arsenal), 1969 v Ni, Bul, R (1 + 1 sub) (4)

McNeal, R. (WBA), 1914 v S, W (2)

McNeil, M. (Middlesbrough), 1961 v W, Ni, S, L, P, Sp, M, I; 1962 v L (9)

Mabbutt, G. (Tottenham H), 1983 v WG, Gr, L, W, Gr, H, Ni, S (sub); 1984 v H; 1987 v Y, Ni, T; 1988 v WG; 1992 v T, Pol, Cz (16)

Macaulay, R. H. (Cambridge University), 1881 v S (1)

Macdonald, M. (Newcastle U), 1972 v W, Ni, S (sub); 1973 v USSR (sub); 1974 v P, S (sub), Y (sub); 1975 v WG, Cy (2), Ni; 1976 v Sw (sub), Cz, P (14)

Macrae, S. (Notts Co), 1883 v S, W, Ni; 1884 v S, W, Ni (6)

Maddison, F. B. (Oxford University), 1872 v S (1)

Madeley, P. E. (Leeds U), 1971 v Ni; 1972 v Sw (2), Gr, WG (2), W, S; 1973 v S, Cz, Pol, USSR, I; 1974 v A, Pol, I; 1975 v Cz, P, Cy; 1976 v Cz, P, Fi; 1977 v Ei, Ho (24)

Magee, T. P. (WBA), 1923 v W, Se; 1925 v S, Bel, F (5)

Makepeace, H. (Everton), 1906 v S; 1910 v S; 1912 v S, W (4)

Male, C. G. (Arsenal), 1935 v S, Ni, I, Ho; 1936 v S, W, Ni, G, A, Bel; 1937 v S, Ni, H, N, Se, Fi; 1939 v I, R, Y (19)

Mannion, W. J. (Middlesbrough), 1947 v S, W, Ni, Ei, Ho, F, Sw, P; 1948 v W, Ni, Bel, Se, I; 1949 v N, F; 1950 v S, Ei, P, Bel, Ch, US; 1951 v Ni, W, S, Y; 1952 v F (26)
Mariner, P. (Ipswich T), 1977 v L (sub), Ni; 1978 v L, W (sub), S; 1980 v W, Ni (sub), S, Aus, I (sub), Sp (sub); 1981 v N, Sw, Sp, Sw, H; 1982 v N, H, Ho, S, Fi, F, Cz, K, WG, Sp; 1983 v D, WG, Gr, W; 1984 v D, H, L; (with Arsenal), 1985 v EG, R (35)
Marsden, J. T. (Darwen), 1891 v Ni (1)
Marsden, W. (Sheffield W), 1930 v W, S, G (3)
Marsh, R. W. (QPR), 1972 v Sw (sub); (with Manchester C), WG (sub + 1), W, Ni, S; 1973 v W (2), Y (9)
Marshall, T. (Darwen), 1880 v W; 1881 v W (2)
Martin, A. (West Ham U), 1981 v Br, S (sub); 1982 v H, Fi; 1983 v Gr, L, W, Gr, H; 1984 v H, L, W; 1985 v Ni; 1986 v Is, Ca, Para; 1987 v Se (17)
Martin, H. (Sunderland), 1914 v Ni (1)
Martyn, A. N. (C Palace), 1992 v C (sub), H; 1993 v G (3)
Marwood, B. (Arsenal), 1989 v S.Ar (sub) (1)
Maskrey, H. M. (Derby Co), 1908 v Ni (1)
Mason, C. (Wolverhampton W), 1887 v Ni; 1888 v W; 1890 v Ni (3)
Matthews, R. D. (Coventry C), 1956 v S, Br, Se, WG; 1957 v Ni (5)
Matthews, S. (Stoke C), 1935 v W, I; 1936 v G; 1937 v S; 1938 v S, W, Cz, G, Sw, F; 1939 v S, W, Ni, R of E, N, I, Y; 1947 v S; (with Blackpool), 1947 v Sw, P; 1948 v S, W, Ni, Bel, I; 1949 v S, W, Ni, D, Sw; 1950 v Sp; 1951 v Ni, S; 1954 v Ni, R of E, H, Bel, U; 1955 v Ni, W, S, F, WG, Sp, P; 1956 v W, Br; 1957 v S, W, Ni, Y, D (2), Ei (54)
Matthews, V. (Sheffield U), 1928 v F, Bel (2)
Maynard, W. J. (1st Surrey Rifles), 1872 v S; 1876 v S (2)
Meadows, J. (Manchester C), 1955 v S (1)
Medley, L. D. (Tottenham H), 1951 v Y, W; 1952 v F, A, W, Ni (6)
Meehan, T. (Chelsea), 1924 v Ni (1)
Melia, J. (Liverpool), 1963 v S, Sw (2)
Mercer, D. W. (Sheffield U), 1923 v Ni, Bel (2)
Mercer, J. (Everton), 1939 v S, Ni, I, R, Y (5)
Merrick, G. H. (Birmingham C), 1952 v Ni, S, A (2), I, Sw; 1953 v Ni, W, S, Bel, Arg, Ch, U; 1954 v W, Ni, S, R of E, H (2), Y, Bel, Sw, U (23)
Merson, P. C. (Arsenal), 1992 v G (sub), Cz, H, Br (sub), Fi (sub), D, Se (sub); 1993 v Sp (sub), N (sub), Ho (sub), Br (sub), G; 1994 v Ho, Gr (14)
Metcalfe, V. (Huddersfield T), 1951 v Arg, P (2)
Mew, J. W. (Manchester U), 1921 v Ni (1)
Middleditch, B. (Corinthians), 1897 v Ni (1)
Milburn, J. E. T. (Newcastle U), 1949 v S, W, Ni, Sw; 1950 v W, P, Bel, Sp; 1951 v W, Arg, P; 1952 v F; 1956 v D (13)
Miller, B. G. (Burnley), 1961 v A (1)
Miller, H. S. (Charlton Ath), 1923 v Se (1)
Mills, G. R. (Chelsea), 1938 v W, Ni, Cz (3)
Mills, M. D. (Ipswich T), 1973 v Y; 1976 v W (2), Ni, S, Br, I (sub), Fi; 1977 v Fi (sub), I, Ni, W, S; 1978 v WG, Br, W, Ni, S, H; 1979 v D, Ei, Ni (2), S, Bul, A; 1980 v D, Ni, Sp (2); 1981 v Sw (2), H; 1982 v N, H, S, Fi, F, Cz, K, WG, Sp (42)
Milne, G. (Liverpool), 1963 v Br, Cz, EG; 1964 v W, Ni, S, R of W, U, P, Ei, Br, Arg; 1965 v Ni, Bel (14)
Milton, C. A. (Arsenal), 1952 v A (1)
Milward, A. (Everton), 1891 v S, W; 1897 v S, W (4)
Mitchell, C. (Upton Park), 1880 v W; 1881 v S; 1883 v S, W; 1885 v W (5)
Mitchell, J. F. (Manchester C), 1925 v Ni (1)
Moffat, H. (Oldham Ath), 1913 v W (1)
Molyneux, G. (Southampton), 1902 v S; 1903 v S, W, Ni (4)
Moon, W. R. (Old Westminsters), 1888 v S, W; 1889 v S, W; 1890 v S, W; 1891 v S (7)
Moore, H. T. (Notts Co), 1883 v Ni; 1885 v W (2)
Moore, J. (Derby Co), 1923 v Se (1)
Moore, R. F. (West Ham U), 1962 v Pe, H, Arg, Bul, Br; 1963 v W, Ni, S, F (2), Br, Cz, EG, Sw; 1964 v W, Ni, S, R of W, U, P (2), Ei, Br, Arg; 1965 v Ni, S, Bel, H, Y, WG, Se; 1966 v W, Ni, S, A, Sp, Pol (2), WG (2), N, D, U, M, F, Arg, P; 1967 v W, Ni, S, Cz, Sp, A; 1968 v W, Ni, S, USSR (2), Sp (2), Se, Y, WG; 1969 v Ni, W, S, R, Bul, F, M, U, Br; 1970 v W, Ni, S, Ho, P, Bel, Co, Ec, R, Br, Cz, WG; 1971 v EG, Gr, Ma, Ni, S; 1972 v Sw (2), Gr, WG (2), W, S; 1973 v W (3), Y, S (2), Ni, Cz, Pol, USSR, I; 1974 v I (108)
Moore, W. G. B. (West Ham U), 1923 v Se (1)
Mordue, J. (Sunderland), 1912 v Ni; 1913 v Ni (2)
Morice, C. J. (Barnes), 1872 v S (1)
Morley, A. (Aston Villa), 1982 v H (sub), Ni, W, Ic; 1983 v D, Gr (6)
Morley, H. (Notts Co), 1910 v Ni (1)
Morren, T. (Sheffield U), 1898 v Ni (1)
Morris, F. (WBA), 1920 v S; 1921 v Ni (2)
Morris, J. (Derby Co), 1949 v N, F; 1950 v Ei (3)
Morris, W. W. (Wolverhampton W), 1939 v S, Ni, R (3)
Morse, H. (Notts Co), 1879 v S (1)
Mort, T. (Aston Villa), 1924 v W, F; 1926 v S (3)
Morten, A. (C Palace), 1873 v S (1)
Mortensen, S. H. (Blackpool), 1947 v P; 1948 v W, S, Ni, Bel, Se, I; 1949 v S, W, Ni, Se, N; 1950 v S, W, Ni, I, P, Bel, Ch, US, Sp; 1951 v S, Arg; 1954 v R of E, H (25)
Morton, J. R. (West Ham U), 1938 v Cz (1)
Mosforth, W. (Sheffield W), 1877 v S; (with Sheffield Albion), 1878 v S; 1879 v S, W; 1880 v S, W; (with Sheffield W), 1881 v W; 1882 v S, W (9)
Moss, F. (Arsenal), 1934 v S, H, Cz; 1935 v I (4)
Moss, F. (Aston Villa), 1922 v S, Ni; 1923 v Ni; 1924 v S, Bel (5)
Mosscrop, E. (Burnley), 1914 v S, W (2)
Mozley, B. (Derby Co), 1950 v W, Ni, Ei (3)
Mullen, J. (Wolverhampton W), 1947 v S; 1949 v N, F; 1950 v Bel (sub), Ch, US; 1954 v W, Ni, S, R of E, Y, Sw (12)
Mullery, A. P. (Tottenham H), 1965 v Ho; 1967 v Sp, A; 1968 v W, Ni, S, USSR, Sp (2), Se, Y; 1969 v Ni, S, R, Bul, F, M, U, Br; 1970 v W, Ni, S (sub), Ho (sub), Bel, P, Co, Ec, R, Cz, WG, Br; 1971 v Ma, EG, Gr; 1972 v Sw (35)

Neal, P. G. (Liverpool), 1976 v W, I; 1977 v W, S, Br, Arg, U; 1978 v Sw, I, WG, Ni, S, H; 1979 v D, Ei, Ni (2), S, Bul, A; 1980 v D, Ni, Sp, Arg, W, Bel, I; 1981 v R, Sw, Sp, Br, H; 1982 v N, H, W, Ho, Ic, F (sub), K; 1983 v D, Gr, L, W, Gr, H, Ni, S, Aus (2); 1984 v D (50)
Needham, E. (Sheffield U), 1894 v S; 1895 v S; 1897 v S, W, Ni; 1898 v S, W; 1899 v S, W, Ni; 1900 v S, Ni; 1901 v S, W, Ni; 1902 v W (16)
Newton, K. R. (Blackburn R), 1966 v S, WG; 1967 v Sp, A; 1968 v W, S, Sp, Se, Y, WG; 1969 v Ni, W, S, R, Bul, M, U, Br, F; (with Everton), 1970 v Ni, S, Ho, Co, Ec, R, Cz, WG (27)
Nicholls, J. (WBA), 1954 v S, Y (2)
Nicholson, W. E. (Tottenham H), 1951 v P (1)
Nish, D. J. (Derby Co), 1973 v Ni; 1974 v P, W, Ni, S (5)
Norman, M. (Tottenham H), 1962 v Pe, H, Arg, Bul, Br; 1963 v S, F, Br, Cz, EG; 1964 v W, Ni, S, R of W, U, P (2), US, Br, Arg; 1965 v Ni, Bel, Ho (23)
Nuttall, H. (Bolton W), 1928 v W, Ni; 1929 v S (3)

Oakley, W. J. (Oxford University), 1895 v W; 1896 v S, W, Ni; (with Corinthians), 1897 v S, W, Ni; 1898 v S, W, Ni; 1900 v S, W, Ni; 1901 v S, W, Ni (16)
O'Dowd, J. P. (Chelsea), 1932 v S; 1933 v Ni, Sw (3)
O'Grady, M. (Huddersfield T), 1963 v Ni; (with Leeds U), 1969 v F (2)
Ogilvie, R. A. M. M. (Clapham R), 1874 v S (1)

Oliver, L. F. (Fulham), 1929 v Bel (1)
Olney, B. A. (Aston Villa), 1928 v F, Bel (2)
Osborne, F. R. (Fulham), 1923 v Ni, F; (with Tottenham H), 1925 v Bel; 1926 v Bel (4)
Osborne, R. (Leicester C), 1928 v W (1)
Osgood, P. L. (Chelsea), 1970 v Bel, R (sub), Cz (sub); 1974 v I (4)
Osman, R. (Ipswich T), 1980 v Aus; 1981 v Sp, R, Sw; 1982 v N, Ic; 1983 v D, Aus (3); 1984 v D (11)
Ottaway, C. J. (Oxford University), 1872 v S; 1874 v S (2)
Owen, J. R. B. (Sheffield), 1874 v S (1)
Owen, S. W. (Luton T), 1954 v H, Y, Bel (3)

Page, L. A. (Burnley), 1927 v S, W, Bel, L, F; 1928 v W, Ni (7)
Paine, T. L. (Southampton), 1963 v Cz, EG; 1964 v W, Ni, S, R of W, U, US, P; 1965 v Ni, H, Y, WG, Se; 1966 v W, A, Y, N, M (19)
Pallister, G. A. (Middlesbrough), 1988 v H; 1989 v S.Ar; (with Manchester U), 1991 v Cam (sub), T; 1992 v G; 1993 v N, US, Br, G; 1994 v Pol, Ho, Sm, D (13)
Palmer, C. L. (Sheffield W), 1992 v C, H, Br, Fi (sub), D, F, Se; 1993 v Sp (sub), N (sub), T, Sm, T, Ho, Pol, N, US, Br (sub); 1994 v Ho (18)
Pantling, H. H. (Sheffield U), 1924 v Ni (1)
Paravacini, P. J. de (Cambridge University), 1883 v S, W, Ni (3)
Parker, P. A. (QPR), 1989 v Alb (sub), Ch, D; 1990 v Y, U, Ho, Eg, Bel, Cam, WG, I; 1991 v H, Pol, USSR, Aus, Nz; (with Manchester U), 1992 v G; 1994 v Ho, D (19)
Parker, T. R. (Southampton), 1925 v F (1)
Parkes, P. B. (QPR), 1974 v P (1)
Parkinson, J. (Liverpool), 1910 v S, W (2)
Parr, P. C. (Oxford University), 1882 v W (1)
Parry, E. H. (Old Carthusians), 1879 v W; 1882 v W, S (3)
Parry, R. A. (Bolton W), 1960 v Ni, S (2)
Patchitt, B. C. A. (Corinthians), 1923 v Se (2) (2)
Pawson, F. W. (Cambridge University), 1883 v Ni; (with Swifts), 1885 v Ni (2)
Payne, J. (Luton T), 1937 v Fi (1)
Peacock, A. (Middlesbrough), 1962 v Arg, Bul; 1963 v Ni, W; (with Leeds U), 1966 v W, Ni (6)
Peacock, J. (Middlesbrough), 1929 v F, Bel, Sp (3)
Pearce, S. (Nottingham F), 1987 v Br, S; 1988 v WG (sub), Is, H; 1989 v D, Se, S.Ar, Gr, Alb (2), Ch, S, Pol, D; 1990 v Pol, I, Y, Br, Cz, D, U, Tun, Ei, Ho, Eg, Bel, Cam, WG; 1991 v H, Pol, Ei (2), Cam, T, Arg, Aus, Nz (2), Mal; 1992 v T, Pol, F, Cz, Br (sub), Fi, D, F, Se; 1993 v Sp, N, T; 1994 v Pol, Sm, Gr (sub) (56)
Pearson, H. F. (WBA), 1932 v S (1)
Pearson, J. H. (Crewe Alex), 1892 v Ni (1)
Pearson, J. S. (Manchester U), 1976 v W, Ni, S, Br, Fi; 1977 v Ei, Ho (sub), W, S, Br, Arg, U; 1978 v I (sub), WG, Ni (15)
Pearson, S. C. (Manchester U), 1948 v S; 1949 v S, Ni; 1950 v Ni, I; 1951 v P; 1952 v S, I (8)
Pease, W. H. (Middlesbrough), 1927 v W (1)
Pegg, D. (Manchester U), 1957 v Ei (1)
Pejic, M. (Stoke C), 1974 v P, W, Ni, S (4)
Pelly, F. R. (Old Foresters), 1893 v Ni; 1894 v S, W (3)
Pennington, J. (WBA), 1907 v S, W; 1908 v S, W, Ni, A; 1909 v S, W, H (2), A; 1910 v S, W; 1911 v S, W, Ni; 1912 v S, W, Ni; 1913 v S, W; 1914 v S, Ni; 1920 v S, W (25)
Pentland, F. B. (Middlesbrough), 1909 v S, W, H (2), A (5)
Perry, C. (WBA), 1890 v Ni; 1891 v Ni; 1893 v W (3)
Perry, T. (WBA), 1898 v W (1)
Perry, W. (Blackpool), 1956 v Ni, S, Sp (3)
Perryman, S. (Tottenham H), 1982 v Ic (sub) (1)
Peters, M. (West Ham U), 1966 v Y, Fi, Pol, M, F, Arg, P, WG; 1967 v Ni, W, S, Cz; 1968 v W, Ni, S, USSR (2), Sp (2), Se, Y; 1969 v Ni, S, R, Bul, F, M, U, Br; 1970 v Ho (2), P (sub), Bel; (with Tottenham H), W, Ni, S, Co, Ec, R, Br, Cz, WG; 1971 v EG, Gr, Ma (2), Ni, W, S; 1972 v Sw, Gr, WG (1 + 1 sub), Ni (sub); 1973 v S (2), Ni, W, Cz, Pol, USSR, I; 1974 v A, Pol, I, P, S (67)
Phelan, M. C. (Manchester U), 1990 v I (sub) (1)
Phillips, L. H. (Portsmouth), 1952 v Ni; 1955 v W, WG (3)
Pickering, F. (Everton), 1964 v US; 1965 v Ni, Bel (3)
Pickering, J. (Sheffield U), 1933 v S (1)
Pickering, N. (Sunderland), 1983 v Aus (1)
Pike, T. M. (Cambridge University), 1886 v Ni (1)
Pilkington, B. (Burnley), 1955 v Ni (1)
Plant, J. (Bury), 1900 v S (1)
Platt, D. (Aston Villa), 1990 v I (sub), Y (sub), Br, D (sub), Tun (sub), Ho (sub), Eg (sub), Bel (sub), Cam, WG, I; 1991 v H, Pol, Ei (2), T, USSR, Arg, Aus, Nz (2), Mal; (with Bari), 1992 v G, T, Pol, Cz, C, Br, Fi, D, F, Se; (with Juventus), 1993 v Sp, N, T, Sm, T, Ho, Pol, N, Br (sub), G; (with Sampdoria), 1994 v Pol, Ho, Sm, D, Gr, N (48)
Plum, S. L. (Charlton Ath), 1923 v F (1)
Pointer, R. (Burnley), 1962 v W, L, P (3)
Porteous, T. S. (Sunderland), 1891 v W (1)
Priest, A. E. (Sheffield U), 1900 v Ni (1)
Prinsep, J. F. M. (Clapham Rovers), 1879 v S (1)
Puddefoot, S. C. (Blackburn R), 1926 v S, Ni (2)
Pye, J. (Wolverhampton W), 1950 v Ei (1)
Pym, R. H. (Bolton W), 1925 v S, W; 1926 v W (3)

Quantrill, A. (Derby Co), 1920 v S, W; 1921 v W, Ni (4)
Quixall, A. (Sheffield W), 1954 v W, Ni, R of E; 1955 v Sp, P (sub) (5)

Radford, J. (Arsenal), 1969 v R; 1972 v Sw (sub) (2)
Raikes, G. B. (Oxford University), 1895 v W; 1896 v W, Ni, S (4)
Ramsey, A. E. (Southampton), 1949 v Sw; (with Tottenham H), 1950 v S, I, P, Bel, Ch, US, Sp; 1951 v S, Ni, W, Y, Arg, P; 1952 v S, W, Ni, F, A (2), I, Sw; 1953 v Ni, W, S, Bel, Arg, Ch, U, US; 1954 v R of E, H (32)
Rawlings, A. (Preston NE), 1921 v Bel (1)
Rawlings, W. E. (Southampton), 1922 v S, W (2)
Rawlinson, J. F. P. (Cambridge University), 1882 v Ni (1)
Rawson, H. E. (Royal Engineers), 1875 v S (1)
Rawson, W. S. (Oxford University), 1875 v S; 1877 v S (2)
Read, A. (Tufnell Park), 1921 v Bel (1)
Reader, J. (WBA), 1894 v Ni (1)
Reaney, P. (Leeds U), 1969 v Bul (sub); 1970 v P; 1971 v Ma (3)
Reeves, K. (Norwich C), 1980 v Bul; (with Manchester C), Ni (2)
Regis, C. (WBA), 1982 v Ni (sub), W (sub), Ic; 1983 v WG; (with Coventry C), 1988 v T (sub) (5)
Reid, P. (Everton), 1985 v M (sub), WG, US (sub); 1986 v R, S (sub), Ca (sub), Pol, Para, Arg; 1987 v Br; 1988 v WG, Y (sub), Sw (sub) (13)
Revie, D. G. (Manchester C), 1955 v Ni, S, F; 1956 v W, D; 1957 v Ni (6)
Reynolds, J. (WBA), 1892 v S; 1893 v S, W; (with Aston Villa), 1894 v S, Ni; 1895 v S; 1897 v S, W (8)
Richards, C. H. (Nottingham F), 1898 v Ni (1)
Richards, G. H. (Derby Co), 1909 v A (1)
Richards, J. P. (Wolverhampton W), 1973 v Ni (1)
Richardson, J. R. (Newcastle U), 1933 v I, Sw (2)
Richardson, K. (Aston Villa), 1994 v Gr (1)
Richardson, W. G. (WBA), 1935 v Ho (1)
Rickaby, S. (WBA), 1954 v Ni (1)
Rigby, A. (Blackburn R), 1927 v S, Bel, L, F; 1928 v W (5)
Rimmer, E. J. (Sheffield W), 1930 v S, G, A; 1932 v Sp (4)

Rimmer, J. J. (Arsenal), 1976 v I (1)
Ripley, S. E. (Blackburn R), 1994 v Sm (1)
Rix, G. (Arsenal), 1981 v N, R, Sw (sub), Br, W, S; 1982 v Ho (sub), Fi (sub), F, Cz, K, WG, Sp; 1983 v D, WG (sub), Gr (sub); 1984 v Ni (17)
Robb, G. (Tottenham H), 1954 v H (1)
Roberts, C. (Manchester U), 1905 v Ni, W, S (3)
Roberts, F. (Manchester C), 1925 v S, W, Bel, F (4)
Roberts, G. (Tottenham H), 1983 v Ni, S; 1984 v F, Ni, S, USSR (6)
Roberts, H. (Arsenal), 1931 v S (1)
Roberts, H. (Millwall), 1931 v Bel (1)
Roberts, R. (WBA), 1887 v S; 1888 v Ni; 1890 v Ni (3)
Roberts, W. T. (Preston NE), 1924 v W, Bel (2)
Robinson, J. (Sheffield W), 1937 v Fi; 1938 v G, Sw; 1939 v W (4)
Robinson, J. W. (Derby Co), 1897 v S, Ni; (with New Brighton Tower), 1898 v S, W, Ni; (with Southampton), 1899 v W, S; 1900 v S, W, Ni; 1901 v Ni (11)
Robson, B. (WBA), 1980 v Ei, Aus; 1981 v N, R, Sw, Sp, R, Br, W, S, Sw, H; 1982 v N; (with Manchester U), H, Ni, W, Ho, S, Fi, F, Cz, WG, Sp; 1983 v D, Gr, L, S; 1984 v H, L, F, Ni, S, USSR, Br, U, Ch; 1985 v EG, Fi, T, Ei, R, Fi, S, M, I, WG, US; 1986 v R, T, Is, M, P, Mor; 1987 v Ni (2), Sp, T, Br, S; 1988 v T, Y, Ho, H, S, Co, Sw, Ei, Ho, USSR; 1989 v S, Se, S.Ar, Gr, Alb (2), Ch, S, Pol, D; 1990 v Pol, I, Y, Cz, U, Tun, Ei, Ho; 1991 v Cam, Ei; 1992 v T (90)
Robson, R. (WBA), 1958 v F, USSR (2), Br, A; 1960 v Sp, H; 1961 v Ni, W, S, L, P, Sp, M, I; 1962 v W, Ni, Sw, L, P (20)
Rocastle, D. (Arsenal), 1989 v D, S.Ar, Gr, Alb (2), Pol (sub), D; 1990 v Se (sub), Pol, Y, D (sub); 1992 v Pol, Cz, Br (sub) (14)
Rose, W. C. (Wolverhampton W), 1884 v S, W, Ni; (with Preston NE), 1886 v Ni; (with Wolverhampton W), 1891 v Ni (5)
Rostron, T. (Darwen), 1881 v S, W (2)
Rowe, A. (Tottenham H), 1934 v F (1)
Rowley, J. F. (Manchester U), 1949 v Sw, Se, F; 1950 v Ni, I; 1952 v S (6)
Rowley, W. (Stoke C), 1889 v Ni; 1892 v Ni (2)
Royle, J. (Everton), 1971 v Ma; 1973 v Y; (with Manchester C), 1976 v Ni (sub), I; 1977 v Fi, L (6)
Ruddlesdin, H. (Sheffield W), 1904 v W, Ni; 1905 v S (3)
Ruffell, J. W. (West Ham U), 1926 v S; 1927 v Ni; 1929 v S, W, Ni; 1930 v W (6)
Russell, B. B. (Royal Engineers), 1883 v W (1)
Rutherford, J. (Newcastle U), 1904 v S; 1907 v S, Ni, W; 1908 v S, Ni, W, A (2), H, B (11)

Sadler, D. (Manchester U), 1968 v Ni, USSR; 1970 v Ec (sub); 1971 v EG (4)
Sagar, C. (Bury), 1900 v Ni; 1902 v W (2)
Sagar, E. (Everton), 1936 v S, Ni, A, Bel (4)
Salako, J. A. (C Palace), 1991 v Aus (sub), Nz (sub + 1), Mal; 1992 v G (5)
Sandford, E. A. (WBA), 1933 v W (1)
Sandilands, R. R. (Old Westminsters), 1892 v W; 1893 v Ni; 1894 v W; 1895 v W; 1896 v W (5)
Sands, J. (Nottingham F), 1880 v W (1)
Sansom, K. (C Palace), 1979 v W; 1980 v Bul, Ei, Arg, W (sub), Ni, S, Bel, I; (with Arsenal), 1981 v N, R, Sw, Sp, R, Br, W, S, Sw; 1982 v Ni, W, Ho, S, Fi, F, Cz, WG, Sp; 1983 v D, WG, Gr, L, Gr, H, Ni, S; 1984 v D, H, L, F, S, USSR, Br, U, Ch; 1985 v EG, Fi, T, Ni, Ei, R, Fi, S, I, M, WG, US; 1986 v R, T, Ni, Eg, Is, USSR, S, M, Ca, P, Mor, Pol, Para, Arg; 1987 v Se, Ni (2), Y, Sp, T; 1988 v WG, T, Y, Ho, S, Co, Sw, Ei, Ho, USSR (86)
Saunders, F. E. (Swifts), 1888 v W (1)
Savage, A. H. (C Palace), 1876 v S (1)
Sayer, J. (Stoke C), 1887 v Ni (1)
Scattergood, E. (Derby Co), 1913 v W (1)
Schofield, J. (Stoke C), 1892 v W; 1893 v W; 1895 v Ni (3)
Scott, L. (Arsenal), 1947 v S, W, Ni, Ei, Ho, F, Sw, P; 1948 v S, W, Ni, Bel, Se, I; 1949 v W, Ni, D (17)
Scott, W. R. (Brentford), 1937 v W (1)
Seaman, D. A. (QPR), 1989 v S.Ar, D (sub); 1990 v Cz (sub); (with Arsenal), 1991 v Cam, Ei, T, Arg; 1992 v Cz, H (sub); 1994 v Pol, Ho, Sm, D, N (14)
Seddon, J. (Bolton W), 1923 v F, Se (2); 1924 v Bel; 1927 v W; 1929 v S (6)
Seed, J. M. (Tottenham H), 1921 v Bel: 1923 v W, Ni, Bel; 1925 v S (5)
Settle, J. (Bury), 1899 v S, W, Ni; (with Everton), 1902 v S, Ni; 1903 v Ni (6)
Sewell, J. (Sheffield W), 1952 v Ni, A, Sw; 1953 v Ni; 1954 v H (2) (6)
Sewell, W. R. (Blackburn R), 1924 v W (1)
Shackleton, L. F. (Sunderland), 1949 v W, D; 1950 v W; 1955 v W, WG (5)
Sharp, J. (Everton), 1903 v Ni; 1905 v S (2)
Sharpe, L. S. (Manchester U), 1991 v Ei (sub); 1993 v T (sub), N, US, Br, G; 1994 v Pol, Ho (8)
Shaw, G. E. (WBA), 1932 v S (1)
Shaw, G. L. (Sheffield U), 1959 v S, W, USSR, I; 1963 v W (5)
Shea, D. (Blackburn R), 1914 v W, Ni (2)
Shearer, A. (Southampton), 1992 v F, C, F; (with Blackburn R), 1993 v Sp, N, T; 1994 v Ho, D, Gr, N (10)
Shellito, K. J. (Chelsea), 1963 v Cz (1)
Shelton A. (Notts Co), 1889 v Ni; 1890 v S, W; 1891 v S, W; 1892 v S (6)
Shelton, C. (Notts Rangers), 1888 v Ni (1)
Shepherd, A. (Bolton W), 1906 v S; (with Newcastle U), 1911 v Ni (2)
Sheringham, E. P. (Tottenham H), 1993 v Pol, N (2)
Shilton, P. L. (Leicester C), 1971 v EG, W; 1972 v Sw, Ni; 1973 v Y, S (2), Ni, W, Cz, Pol, USSR, I; 1974 v A, Pol, I, W, Ni, S, Arg; (with Stoke C), 1975 v Cy; 1977 v Ni, W; (with Nottingham F), 1978 v W, H; 1979 v Cz, Se, A; 1980 v Ni, Sp, I; 1981 v N, Sw, R; 1982 v H, Ho, S, F, Cz, K, WG, Sp; (with Southampton), 1983 v D, WG, Gr, W, Gr, H, Ni, S, Aus (3); 1984 v D, H, F, Ni, W, S, USSR, Br, U, Ch; 1985 v EG, Fi, T, Ni, R, Fi, S, I, WG; 1986 v R, T, Ni, Eg, Is, USSR, S, M, Ca, P, Mor, Pol, Para, Arg; 1987 v Se, Ni (2), Sp, Br; (with Derby Co), 1988 v WG, T, Y, Ho, S, Co, Sw, Ei, Ho; 1989 v D, Se, Gr, Alb (2), Ch, S, Pol, D; 1990 v Se, Pol, I, Y, Br, Cz, D, U, Tun, Ei, Ho, Eg, Bel, Cam, WG, I (125)
Shimwell, E. (Blackpool), 1949 v Se (1)
Shutt, G. (Stoke C), 1886 v Ni (1)
Silcock, J. (Manchester U), 1921 v S, W; 1923 v Se (3)
Sillett, R. P. (Chelsea), 1955 v F, Sp, P (3)
Simms, E. (Luton T), 1922 v Ni (1)
Simpson, J. (Blackburn R), 1911 v S, W, Ni; 1912 v S, W, Ni; 1913 v S; 1914 v W (8)
Sinton, A. (QPR), 1992 v Pol, C, H (sub), Br, F, Se; 1993 v Sp, T, Br, G; (with Sheffield W), 1994 v Ho (sub), Sm (12)
Slater, W. J. (Wolverhampton W), 1955 v W, WG; 1958 v S, P, Y, USSR (3), Br, A; 1959 v USSR; 1960 v S (12)
Smalley, T. (Wolverhampton W), 1937 v W (1)
Smart, T. (Aston Villa), 1921 v S; 1924 v S, W; 1926 v Ni; 1930 v W (5)
Smith, A. (Nottingham F), 1891 v S, W; 1893 v Ni (3)
Smith, A. K. (Oxford University), 1872 v S (1)
Smith, A. M. (Arsenal), 1989 v S.Ar (sub), Gr, Alb (sub), Pol (sub); 1991 v T, USSR, Arg; 1992 v G, T, Pol (sub), H (sub), D, Se (sub) (13)
Smith, B. (Tottenham H), 1921 v S; 1922 v W (2)
Smith, C. E. (C Palace), 1876 v S (1)
Smith, G. O. (Oxford University), 1893 v Ni; 1894 v W, S; 1895 v W; 1896 v Ni, W, S; (with Old Carthusians), 1897

v Ni, W, S; 1898 v Ni, W, S; (with Corinthians), 1899 v Ni, W, S; 1899 v Ni, W, S; 1901 v S (20)
Smith, H. (Reading), 1905 v W, S; 1906 v W, Ni (4)
Smith, J. (WBA), 1920 v Ni; 1923 v Ni (2)
Smith, Joe (Bolton W), 1913 v Ni; 1914 v S, W; 1920 v W, Ni (5)
Smith, J. C. R. (Millwall), 1939 v Ni, N (2)
Smith, J. W. (Portsmouth), 1932 v Ni, W, Sp (3)
Smith, Leslie (Brentford), 1939 v R (1)
Smith, Lionel (Arsenal), 1951 v W; 1952 v W, Ni; 1953 v W, S, Bel (6)
Smith, R. A. (Tottenham H), 1961 v Ni, W, S, L, P, Sp; 1962 v S; 1963 v S, F, Br, Cz, EG; 1964 v W, Ni, R of W (15)
Smith, S. (Aston Villa), 1895 v S (1)
Smith, S. C. (Leicester C), 1936 v Ni (1)
Smith, T. (Birmingham C), 1960 v W, Se (2)
Smith, T. (Liverpool), 1971 v W (1)
Smith, W. H. (Huddersfield T), 1922 v W, S; 1928 v S (3)
Sorby, T. H. (Thursday Wanderers, Sheffield), 1879 v W (1)
Southworth, J. (Blackburn R), 1889 v W; 1891 v W; 1892 v S (3)
Sparks, F. J. (Herts Rangers), 1879 v S; (with Clapham Rovers), 1880 v S, W (3)
Spence, J. W. (Manchester U), 1926 v Bel; 1927 v Ni (2)
Spence, R. (Chelsea), 1936 v A, Bel (2)
Spencer, C. W. (Newcastle U), 1924 v S; 1925 v W (2)
Spencer, H. (Aston Villa), 1897 v S, W; 1900 v W; 1903 v Ni; 1905 v W, S (6)
Spiksley, F. (Sheffield W), 1893 v S, W; 1894 v S, Ni; 1896 v Ni; 1898 v S, W (7)
Spilsbury, B. W. (Cambridge University), 1885 v Ni; 1886 v Ni, S (3)
Spink, N. (Aston Villa), 1983 v Aus (sub) (1)
Spouncer, W. A. (Nottingham F), 1900 v W (1)
Springett, R. D. G. (Sheffield W), 1960 v Ni, S, Y, Sp, H; 1961 v Ni, S, L, P, Sp, M, I, A; 1962 v W, Ni, S, A, Sw, Pe, L, P, H, Arg, Bul, Br; 1963 v Ni, W, F (2), Sw; 1966 v W, A, N (33)
Sproston, B. (Leeds U), 1937 v W; 1938 v S, W, Ni, Cz, G, Sw, F; (with Tottenham H), 1939 v W, R of E; (with Manchester C), N (11)
Squire, R. T. (Cambridge University), 1886 v S, W, Ni (3)
Stanbrough, M. H. (Old Carthusians), 1895 v W (1)
Staniforth, R. (Huddersfield T), 1954 v S, H, Y, Bel, Sw, U; 1955 v W, WG (8)
Starling, R. W. (Sheffield W), 1933 v S; (with Aston Villa), 1937 v S (2)
Statham, D. (WBA), 1983 v W, Aus (2) (3)
Steele, F. C. (Stoke C), 1937 v S, W, Ni, N, Se, Fi (6)
Stein, B. (Luton T), 1984 v F (1)
Stephenson, C. (Huddersfield T), 1924 v W (1)
Stephenson, G. T. (Derby Co), 1928 v F, Bel; (with Sheffield W), 1931 v F (3)
Stephenson, J. E. (Leeds U), 1938 v S; 1939 v Ni (2)
Stepney, A. C. (Manchester U), 1968 v Se (1)
Sterland, M. (Sheffield W), 1989 v S.Ar (1)
Steven, T. M. (Everton), 1985 v Ni, Ei, R, Fi, I, US (sub); 1986 v T (sub), Eg, USSR (sub), M (sub), Pol, Para, Arg; 1987 v Se, Y (sub), Sp (sub); 1988 v T, Y, Ho, H, S, Sw, Ho, USSR; 1989 v S; (with Rangers), 1990 v Cz, Cam (sub), WG (sub), I; 1991 v Cam; (with Marseille), 1992 v G, C, Br, Fi, D, F (36)
Stevens, G. A. (Tottenham H), 1985 v Fi (sub), T (sub), Ni; 1986 v S (sub), M (sub), Mor (sub), Para (sub) (7)
Stevens, M. G. (Everton), 1985 v I, WG; 1986 v R, T, Ni, Eg, Is, S, Ca, P, Mor, Pol, Para, Arg; 1987 v Br, S; 1988 v T, Y, Is, Ho, H (sub), S, Sw, Ei, Ho, USSR; (with Rangers), 1989 v D, Se, Gr, Alb (2), S, Pol; 1990 v Se, Pol, I, Br, D, Tun, Ei, I; 1991 v USSR; 1992 v C, H, Br, Fi (46)
Stewart, J. (Sheffield W), 1907 v S, W; (with Newcastle U), 1911 v S (3)
Stewart, P. A. (Tottenham H), 1992 v G (sub), Cz (sub), C (sub) (3)
Stiles, N. P. (Manchester U), 1965 v S, H, Y, Se; 1966 v W, Ni, S, A, Sp, Pol (2), WG (2), N, D, U, M, F, Arg, P; 1967 v Ni, W, S, Cz; 1968 v USSR; 1969 v R; 1970 v Ni, S (28)
Stoker, J. (Birmingham), 1933 v W; 1934 v S, H (3)
Storer, H. (Derby Co), 1924 v F; 1928 v Ni (2)
Storey, P. E. (Arsenal), 1971 v Gr, Ni, S; 1972 v Sw, WG, W, Ni, S; 1973 v W (3), Y, S (2), Ni, Cz, Pol, USSR, I (19)
Storey-Moore, I. (Nottingham F), 1970 v Ho (1)
Strange, A. H. (Sheffield W), 1930 v S, A, G; 1931 v S, W, Ni, F, Bel; 1932 v S, W, Ni, Sp; 1933 v S, Ni, A, I, Sw; 1934 v Ni, W, F (20)
Stratford, A. H. (Wanderers), 1874 v S (1)
Streten, B. (Luton T), 1950 v Ni (1)
Sturgess, A. (Sheffield U), 1911 v Ni; 1914 v S (2)
Summerbee, M. G. (Manchester C), 1968 v S, Sp, WG; 1972 v Sw, WG (sub), W, Ni; 1973 v USSR (sub) (8)
Sunderland, A. (Arsenal), 1980 v Aus (1)
Sutcliffe, J. W. (Bolton W), 1893 v W; 1895 v S, Ni; 1901 v S; (with Millwall), 1903 v W (5)
Swan, P. (Sheffield W), 1960 v Y, Sp, H; 1961 v Ni, W, S, L, P, Sp, M, I, A; 1962 v W, Ni, S, A, Sw, L, P (19)
Swepstone, H. A. (Pilgrims), 1880 v S; 1882 v S, W; 1883 v S, W, Ni (6)
Swift, F. V. (Manchester C), 1947 v S, W, Ni, Ei, Ho, F, Sw, P; 1948 v S, W, Ni, Bel, Se, I; 1949 v S, W, Ni, D, N (19)

Tait, G. (Birmingham Excelsior), 1881 v W (1)
Talbot, B. (Ipswich T), 1977 v Ni (sub), S, Br, Arg, U; (with Arsenal), 1980 v Aus (6)
Tambling, R. V. (Chelsea), 1963 v W, F; 1966 v Y (3)
Tate, J. T. (Aston Villa), 1931 v F, Bel; 1933 v W (3)
Taylor, E. (Blackpool), 1954 v H (1)
Taylor, E. H. (Huddersfield T), 1923 v S, W, Ni, Bel; 1924 v S, Ni, F; 1926 v S (8)
Taylor, J. G. (Fulham), 1951 v Arg, P (2)
Taylor, P. H. (Liverpool), 1948 v W, Ni, Se (3)
Taylor, P. J. (C Palace), 1976 v W (sub + 1), Ni, S (4)
Taylor, T. (Manchester U), 1953 v Arg, Ch, U; 1954 v Bel, Sw; 1956 v S, Br, Se, Fi, WG; 1957 v Ni, Y (sub), D (2), Ei (2); 1958 v W, Ni, F (19)
Temple, D. W. (Everton), 1965 v WG (1)
Thickett, H. (Sheffield U), 1899 v S, W (2)
Thomas, D. (Coventry C), 1983 v Aus (1 + 1 sub) (2)
Thomas, D. (QPR), 1975 v Cz (sub), P, Cy (sub + 1), W, S (sub); 1976 v Cz (sub), P (sub) (8)
Thomas, G. R. (C Palace), 1991 v T, USSR, Arg, Aus, Nz (2), Mal; 1992 v Pol, F (9)
Thomas, M. L. (Arsenal), 1989 v S.Ar; 1990 v Y (2)
Thompson, P. (Liverpool), 1964 v P (2), Ei, US, Br, Arg; 1965 v Ni, W, S, Bel, Ho; 1966 v Ni; 1968 v Ni, WG; 1970 v S, Ho (sub) (16)
Thompson, P. B. (Liverpool), 1976 v W (2), Ni, S, Br, I, Fi; 1977 v Fi; 1979 v Ei (sub), Cz, Ni, S, Bul, Se (sub), A; 1980 v D, Ni, Bul, Ei, Sp (2), Arg, W, S, Bel, I; 1981 v N, R, H; 1982 v N, H, W, Ho, S, Fi, F, Cz, K, WG, Sp; 1983 v WG, Gr (42)
Thompson T. (Aston Villa), 1952 v W; (with Preston NE), 1957 v S (2)
Thomson, R. A. (Wolverhampton W), 1964 v Ni, US, P, Arg; 1965 v Bel, Ho, Ni, W (8)
Thornewell, G. (Derby Co), 1923 v Se (2); 1924 v F; 1925 v F (4)
Thornley, I. (Manchester C), 1907 v W (1)
Tilson, S. F. (Manchester C), 1934 v H, Cz; 1935 v W; 1936 v Ni (4)
Titmuss, F. (Southampton), 1922 v W; 1923 v W (2)

Todd, C. (Derby Co), 1972 v Ni; 1974 v P, W, Ni, S, Arg, EG, Bul, Y; 1975 v P (sub), WG, Cy (2), Ni, W, S; 1976 v Sw, Cz, P, Ni, S, Br, Fi; 1977 v Ei, Fi, Ho (sub), Ni (27)
Toone, G. (Notts Co), 1892 v S, W (2)
Topham, A. G. (Casuals), 1894 v W (1)
Topham, R. (Wolverhampton W), 1893 v Ni; (with Casuals) 1894 v W (2)
Towers, M. A. (Sunderland), 1976 v W, Ni (sub), I (3)
Townley, W. J. (Blackburn R), 1889 v W; 1890 v Ni (2)
Townrow, J. E. (Clapton Orient), 1925 v S; 1926 v W (2)
Tremelling, D. R. (Birmingham), 1928 v W (1)
Tresadern, J. (West Ham U), 1923 v S, Se (2)
Tueart, D. (Manchester C), 1975 v Cy (sub), Ni; 1977 v Fi, Ni, W (sub), S (sub) (6)
Tunstall, F. E. (Sheffield U), 1923 v S; 1924 v S, W, Ni, F; 1925 v Ni, S (7)
Turnbull, R. J. (Bradford), 1920 v Ni (1)
Turner, A. (Southampton), 1900 v Ni; 1901 v Ni (2)
Turner, H. (Huddersfield T), 1931 v F, Bel (2)
Turner, J. A. (Bolton W), 1893 v W; (with Stoke C) 1895 v Ni; (with Derby Co) 1898 v Ni (3)
Tweedy, G. J. (Grimsby T), 1937 v H (1)

Ufton, D. G. (Charlton Ath), 1954 v R of E (1)
Underwood A. (Stoke C), 1891 v Ni; 1892 v Ni (2)
Urwin, T. (Middlesbrough), 1923 v Se (2); 1924 v Bel; (with Newcastle U), 1926 v W (4)
Utley, G. (Barnsley), 1913 v Ni (1)

Vaughton, O. H. (Aston Villa), 1882 v S, W, Ni; 1884 v S, W (5)
Veitch, C. C. M. (Newcastle U), 1906 v S, W, Ni; 1907 v S, W; 1909 v W (6)
Veitch, J. G. (Old Westminsters), 1894 v W (1)
Venables, T. F. (Chelsea), 1965 v Ho, Bel (2)
Vidal, R. W. S. (Oxford University), 1873 v S (1)
Viljoen, C. (Ipswich T), 1975 v Ni, W (2)
Viollet, D. S. (Manchester U), 1960 v H; 1962 v L (2)
Von Donop (Royal Engineers), 1873 v S; 1875 v S (2)

Wace, H. (Wanderers), 1878 v S; 1879 v S, W (3)
Waddle, C. R. (Newcastle U), 1985 v Ei, R (sub), Fi (sub), S (sub), I, M (sub), WG, US; (with Tottenham H), 1986 v R, T, Ni, Is, USSR, S, M, Ca, P, Mor, Pol (sub), Arg (sub); 1987 v Se (sub), Ni (2), Y, Sp, T, Br, S; 1988 v WG, Is, H, S (sub), Co, Sw (sub), Ei, Ho (sub); 1989 v Se, S.Ar, Alb (2), Ch, S, Pol, D (sub); (with Marseille), 1990 v Se, Pol, I, Y, Br, D, U, Tun, Ei, Ho, Eg, Bel, Cam, WG, I (sub); 1991 v H (sub), Pol (sub); 1992 v T (62)
Wadsworth, S. J. (Huddersfield T), 1922 v S; 1923 v S, Bel; 1924 v S, Ni; 1925 v S, Ni; 1926 v W; 1927 v Ni (9)
Wainscoat, W. R. (Leeds U), 1929 v S (1)
Waiters, A. K. (Blackpool), 1964 v Ei, Br; 1965 v W, Bel, Ho (5)
Walker, D. S. (Nottingham F), 1989 v D (sub), Se (sub), Gr, Alb (2), Ch, S, Pol, D; 1990 v Se, Pol, I, Y, Br, Cz, D, U, Tun, Ei, Ho, Eg, Bel, Cam, WG, I; 1991 v H, Pol, Ei (2), Cam, T, Arg, Aus, Nz (2), Mal; 1992 v T, Pol, F, Cz, C, H, Br, Fi, D, F, Se; (with Sampdoria), 1993 v Sp, N, T, Sm, T, Ho, Pol, N, US (sub), Br, G; (with Sheffield W), 1994 v Sm (59)
Walden, F. I. (Tottenham H), 1914 v S; 1922 v W (2)
Walker, W. H. (Aston Villa), 1921 v Ni; 1922 v Ni, W, S; 1923 v Se (2); 1924 v S; 1925 v Ni, W, S, Bel, F; 1926 v Ni, W, S; 1927 v Ni, W; 1933 v A (18)
Wall, G. (Manchester U), 1907 v W; 1908 v Ni; 1909 v S; 1910 v W, S; 1912 v S; 1913 v Ni (7)
Wallace, C. W. (Aston Villa), 1913 v W; 1914 v Ni; 1920 v S (3)
Wallace, D. L. (Southampton), 1986 v Eg (1)
Walsh, P. (Luton T), 1983 v Aus (2 + 1 sub); 1984 v F, W (5)
Walters, A. M. (Cambridge University), 1885 v S, N; 1886 v S; 1887 v S, W; (with Old Carthusians), 1889 v S, W; 1890 v S, W (9)
Walters, K. M. (Rangers), 1991 v Nz (1)
Walters, P. M. (Oxford University), 1885 v S, Ni; (with Old Carthusians), 1886 v S, W, Ni; 1887 v S, W; 1888 v S, Ni; 1889 v S, W; 1890 v S, W (13)
Walton, N. (Blackburn R), 1890 v Ni (1)
Ward, J. T. (Blackburn Olympic), 1885 v W (1)
Ward, P. (Brighton & HA), 1980 v Aus (sub) (1)
Ward, T. V. (Derby Co), 1948 v Bel; 1949 v W (2)
Waring, T. (Aston Villa), 1931 v F, Bel; 1932 v S, W, Ni (5)
Warner, C. (Upton Park), 1878 v S (1)
Warren, B. (Derby Co), 1906 v S, W, Ni; 1907 v S, W, Ni; 1908 v S, W, Ni, A (2), H, B; (with Chelsea), 1909 v S, Ni, W, H (2), A; 1911 v S, Ni, W (22)
Waterfield, G. S. (Burnley), 1927 v W (1)
Watson, D. (Norwich C), 1984 v Br, U, Ch; 1985 v M, US (sub); 1986 v S; (with Everton), 1987 v Ni; 1988 v Is, Ho, S, Sw (sub), USSR (12)
Watson, D. V. (Sunderland), 1974 v P, S (sub), Arg, EG, Bul, Y; 1975 v Cz, P, WG, Cy (2), Ni, W, S; (with Manchester C), 1976 v Sw, Cz (sub), P; 1977 v Ho, L, Ni, W, S, Br, Arg, U; 1978 v Sw, L, I, WG, Br, W, Ni, S, H; 1979 v D, Ei, Cz, Ni (2), W, S, Bul, Se, A; (with Werder Bremen), 1980 v D; (with Southampton), Ni, Bul, Ei, Sp (2), Arg, Ni, S, Bel, I; 1981 v N, R, Sw, R, W, S, Sw, H; (with Stoke C), 1982 v Ni, Ic (65)
Watson, V. M. (West Ham U), 1923 v W, S; 1930 v S, G, A (5)
Watson, W. (Burnley), 1913 v S; 1914 v Ni; 1920 v Ni (3)
Watson, W. (Sunderland), 1950 v Ni, I; 1951 v W, Y (4)
Weaver, S. (Newcastle U), 1932 v S, 1933 v S, Ni (3)
Webb, G. W. (West Ham U), 1911 v S, W (2)
Webb, N. J. (Nottingham F), 1988 v WG (sub), T, Y, Is, Ho, S, Sw, Ei, USSR (sub); 1989 v D, Se, Gr, Alb (2), Ch, S, Pol, D; (with Manchester U), 1990 v Se, I (sub); 1992 v F, H, Br (sub), Fi, D (sub), Se (26)
Webster, M. (Middlesbrough), 1930 v S, A, G (3)
Wedlock, W. J. (Bristol C), 1907 v S, Ni, W; 1908 v S, Ni, W, A (2), H, B; 1909 v S, W, Ni, H (2), A; 1910 v S, W, Ni; 1911 v S, W, Ni; 1912 v S, W, Ni; 1914 v W (26)
Weir, D. (Bolton W), 1889 v S, Ni (2)
Welch, R. de C. (Wanderers), 1872 v S; (with Harrow Chequers), 1874 v S (2)
Weller, K. (Leicester C), 1974 v W, Ni, S, Arg (4)
Welsh, D. (Charlton Ath), 1938 v G, Sw; 1939 v R (3)
West, G. (Everton), 1969 v W, Bul, M (3)
Westwood, R. W. (Bolton W), 1935 v S, W, Ho; 1936 v Ni, G; 1937 v W (6)
Whateley, O. (Aston Villa), 1883 v S, Ni (2)
Wheeler, J. E. (Bolton W), 1955 v Ni (1)
Wheldon, G. F. (Aston Villa), 1897 v Ni; 1898 v S, W, Ni (4)
White, D. (Manchester C), 1993 v Sp (1)
White, T. A. (Everton), 1933 v I (1)
Whitehead, J. (Accrington), 1893 v W; (with Blackburn R), 1894 v Ni (2)
Whitfeld, H. (Old Etonians), 1879 v W (1)
Whitham, M. (Sheffield U), 1892 v Ni (1)
Whitworth, S. (Leicester C), 1975 v WG, Cy, Ni, W, S; 1976 v Sw, P (7)
Whymark, T. J. (Ipswich T), 1978 v L (sub) (1)
Widdowson, S. W. (Nottingham F), 1880 v S (1)
Wignall, F. (Nottingham F), 1965 v W, Ho (2)
Wilkes, A. (Aston Villa), 1901 v S, W; 1902 v S, W, Ni (5)
Wilkins, R. G. (Chelsea), 1976 v I; 1977 v Ei, Fi, Ni, Br, Arg, U; 1978 v Sw (sub), L, I, WG, W, Ni, S, H; 1979 v D, Ei, Cz, Ni, W, S, Bul, Se (sub), A; (with Manchester

U), 1980 v D, Ni, Bul, Sp (2), Arg, W (sub), Ni, S, Bel, I; 1981 v Sp (sub), R, Br, W, S, Sw, H (sub); 1982 v Ni, W, Ho, S, Fi, F, Cz, K, WG, Sp; 1983 v D, WG; 1984 v D, Ni, W, S, USSR, Br, U, Ch; (with AC Milan), 1985 v EG, Fi, T, Ni, Ei, R, Fi, S, I, M; 1986 v T, Ni, Is, Eg, USSR, S, M, Ca, P, Mor; 1987 v Se, Y (sub) (84)

Wilkinson, B. (Sheffield U), 1904 v S (1)

Wilkinson, L. R. (Oxford University), 1891 v W (1)

Williams, B. F. (Wolverhampton W), 1949 v F; 1950 v S, W, Ei, I, P, Bel, Ch, US, Sp; 1951 v Ni, W, S, Y, Arg, P; 1952 v W, F; 1955 v S, WG, F, Sp, P; 1956 v W (24)

Williams, O. (Clapton Orient), 1923 v W, Ni (2)

Williams, S. (Southampton), 1983 v Aus (1 + 1 sub); 1984 v F; 1985 v EG, Fi, T (6)

Williams, W. (WBA), 1897 v Ni; 1898 v W, Ni, S; 1899 v W, Ni (6)

Williamson, E. C. (Arsenal), 1923 v Se (2) (2)

Williamson, R. G. (Middlesbrough), 1905 v Ni; 1911 v Ni, S, W; 1912 v S, W; 1913 v Ni (7)

Willingham, C. K. (Huddersfield T), 1937 v Fi; 1938 v S, G, Sw, F; 1939 v S, W, Ni, R of E, N, I, Y (12)

Willis, A. (Tottenham H), 1952 v F (1)

Wilshaw, D. J. (Wolverhampton W), 1954 v W, Sw, U; 1955 v S, F, Sp, P; 1956 v W, Ni, Fi, WG; 1957 v Ni (12)

Wilson, C. P. (Hendon), 1884 v S, W (2)

Wilson, C. W. (Oxford University), 1879 v W; 1881 v S (2)

Wilson, G. (Sheffield W), 1921 v S, W, Bel; 1922 v S, Ni; 1923 v S, W, Ni, Bel; 1924 v W, Ni, F (12)

Wilson, G. P. (Corinthians), 1900 v S, W (2)

Wilson, R. (Huddersfield T), 1960 v S, Y, Sp, H; 1962 v W, Ni, S, A, Sw, Pe, P, H, Arg, Bul, Br; 1963 v Ni, F, Br, Cz, EG, Sw; 1964 v W, S, R of W, U, P (2), Ei, Br, Arg; (with Everton), 1965 v S, H, Y, WG, Se; 1966 v WG (sub), W, Ni, A, Sp, Pol (2), Y, Fi, D, U, M, F, Arg, P, WG; 1967 v Ni, W, S, Cz, A; 1968 v Ni, S, USSR (2), Sp (2), Y (63)

Wilson, T. (Huddersfield T), 1928 v S (1)

Winckworth, W. N. (Old Westminsters), 1892 v W; 1893 v Ni (2)

Windridge, J. E. (Chelsea), 1908 v S, W, Ni, A (2), H, B; 1909 v Ni (8)

Wingfield-Stratford, C. V. (Royal Engineers), 1877 v S (1)

Winterburn, N. (Arsenal), 1990 v I (sub); 1993 v G (sub) (2)

Wise, D. F. (Chelsea), 1991 v T, USSR, Aus (sub), Nz (2); 1994 v N (6)

Withe, P. (Aston Villa), 1981 v Br, W, S; 1982 v N (sub), W, Ic; 1983 v H, Ni, S; 1984 v H (sub); 1985 v T (11)

Wollaston, C. H. R. (Wanderers), 1874 v S; 1875 v S; 1877 v S; 1880 v S (4)

Wolstenholme, S. (Everton), 1904 v S; (with Blackburn R), 1905 v W, Ni (3)

Wood, H. (Wolverhampton W), 1890 v S, W; 1896 v S (3)

Wood, R. E. (Manchester U), 1955 v Ni, W; 1956 v Fi (3)

Woodcock, A. S. (Nottingham F), 1978 v Ni; 1979 v Ei (sub), Cz, Bul (sub), Se; 1980 v Ni; (with Cologne), Bul, Ei, Sp (2), Arg, Bel, I; 1981 v N, R, Sw, R, W (sub), S; 1982 v Ni (sub), Ho, Fi (sub), WG (sub), Sp; (with Arsenal), 1983 v WG (sub), Gr, L, Gr; 1984 v L, F (sub), Ni, W, S, Br, U (sub); 1985 v EG, Fi, T, Ni; 1986 v R (sub), T (sub), Is (sub) (42)

Woodger, G. (Oldham Ath), 1911 v Ni (1)

Woodhall, G. (WBA), 1888 v S, W (2)

Woodley, V. R. (Chelsea), 1937 v S, N, Se, Fi; 1938 v S, W, Ni, Cz, G, Sw, F; 1939 v S, W, Ni, R of E, N, I, R, Y (19)

Woods, C. C. E. (Norwich C), 1985 v US; 1986 v Eg (sub), Is (sub), Ca (sub); (with Rangers), 1987 v Y, Sp (sub), Ni (sub), T, S; 1988 v Is, H, Sw (sub), USSR; 1989 v D (sub); 1990 v Br (sub), D (sub); 1991 v H, Pol, Ei, USSR, Aus, Nz (2), Mal; (with Sheffield W), 1992 v G, T, Pol, F, C, Br, Fi, D, F, Se; 1993 v Sp, N, T, Sm, T, Ho, Pol, N, US (43)

Woodward, V. J. (Tottenham H), 1903 v S, W, Ni; 1904 v S, Ni; 1905 v S, W, Ni; 1907 v S; 1908 v S, W, Ni, A (2), H, B; 1909 v W, Ni, H (2), A; (with Chelsea), 1910 v Ni; 1911 v W (23)

Woosnam, M. (Manchester C), 1922 v W (1)

Worrall, F. (Portsmouth), 1935 v Ho; 1937 v Ni (2)

Worthington, F. S. (Leicester C), 1974 v Ni (sub), S, Arg, EG, Bul, Y; 1975 v Cz, P (sub) (8)

Wreford-Brown, C. (Oxford University), 1889 v Ni; (with Old Carthusians), 1894 v W; 1895 v W; 1898 v S (4)

Wright, E, G. D. (Cambridge University), 1906 v W (1)

Wright, I. E. (C Palace), 1991 v Cam, Ei (sub), USSR, Nz; (with Arsenal), 1992 v H (sub); 1993 v N, T (2), Pol (sub), N (sub), US (sub), Br, G (sub); 1994 v Pol, Ho (sub), Sm, Gr (sub), N (sub) (18)

Wright, J. D. (Newcastle U), 1939 v N (1)

Wright, M. (Southampton), 1984 v W; 1985 v EG, Fi, T, Ei, R, I, WG; 1986 v R, T, Ni, Eg, USSR; 1987 v Y, Ni, S; (with Derby Co), 1988 v Is, Ho (sub), Co, Sw, Ei, Ho; 1990 v Cz (sub), Tun (sub), Ho, Eg, Bel, Cam, WG, I; 1991 v H, Pol, Ei (2), Cam, USSR, Arg, Aus, Nz, Mal; (with Liverpool), 1992 v F, Fi; 1993 v Sp (43)

Wright, T. J. (Everton), 1968 v USSR; 1969 v R (2), M (sub), U, Br; 1970 v W, Ho, Bel, R (sub), Br (11)

Wright, W. A. (Wolverhampton W), 1947 v S, W, Ni, Ei, Ho, F, Sw, P; 1948 v S, W, Ni, Bel, Se, I; 1949 v S, W, Ni, D, Sw, Se, N, F; 1950 v S, W, Ni, Ei, I, P, Bel, Ch, US, Sp; 1951 v Ni, S, Arg; 1952 v W, Ni, S, F, A (2), I, Sw; 1953 v Ni, W, S, Bel, Arg, Ch, U, US; 1954 v W, Ni, S, R of E, H (2), Y, Bel, Sw, U; 1955 v W, Ni, S, WG, F, Sp, P; 1956 v Ni, W, S, Br, Se, Fi, WG, D, Sp; 1957 v S, W, Ni, Y, D (2), Ei (2); 1958 v W, Ni, S, P, Y, USSR (3), Br, A, F; 1959 v W, Ni, S, USSR, I, Br, Pe, M, US (105)

Wylie, J. G. (Wanderers), 1878 v S (1)

Yates, J. (Burnley), 1889 v Ni (1)

York, R. E. (Aston Villa), 1922 v S; 1926 v S (2)

Young, A. (Huddersfield T), 1933 v W; 1937 v S, H, N, Se; 1938 v G, Sw, F; 1939 v W (9)

Young, G. M. (Sheffield W), 1965 v W (1)

R. E. Evans also played for Wales against E, Ni, S; J. Reynolds also played for Ireland against E, W, S.

NORTHERN IRELAND

Aherne, T. (Belfast C), 1947 v E; 1948 v S; 1949 v W; (with Luton T), 1950 v W (4)

Alexander, A. (Cliftonville), 1895 v S (1)

Allen, C. A. (Cliftonville), 1936 v E (1)

Allen, J. (Limavady), 1887 v E (1)

Anderson, T. (Manchester U), 1973 v Cy, E, S, W; 1974 v Bul, P; (with Swindon T), 1975 v S (sub); 1976 v Is; 1977 v Ho, Bel, WG, E, S, W, Ic; 1978 v Ic, Ho, Bel; (with Peterborough U), S, E, W; 1979 v D (sub) (22)

Anderson, W. (Linfield), 1898 v W, E, S; 1899 v S (4)

Andrews, W. (Glentoran), 1908 v S; (with Grimsby T), 1913 v E, S (3)
Armstrong, G. (Tottenham H), 1977 v WG, E, W (sub), Ic (sub); 1978 v Bel, S, E, W; 1979 v Ei, D, Bul, E, Bul, E, S, W, D; 1980 v E, Ei, Is, S, E, W, Aus (3); 1981 v Se; (with Watford), P, S, P, S, Se; 1982 v S, Is, E, F, W, Y, Hon, Sp, A, F; 1983 v A, T, Alb, S, E, W; (with Real Mallorca), 1984 v A, WG, E, W, Fi; 1985 v R, Fi, E, Sp; (with WBA), 1986 v T, R (sub), E (sub), F (sub); (with Chesterfield), D (sub), Br (sub) (63)

Baird, G. (Distillery), 1896 v S, E, W (3)
Baird, H. (Huddersfield T), 1939 v E (1)
Balfe, J. (Shelbourne), 1909 v E; 1910 v W (2)
Bambrick, J. (Linfield), 1929 v W, S, E; 1930 v W, S, E; 1932 v W; (with Chelsea), 1935 v W; 1936 v E, S; 1938 v W (11)
Banks, S. J. (Cliftonville), 1937 v W (1)
Barr, H. H. (Linfield), 1962 v E; (with Coventry C), 1963 v E, Pol (3)
Barron, H. (Cliftonville), 1894 v E, W, S; 1895 v S; 1896 v S; 1897 v E, W (7)
Barry, H. (Bohemians), 1900 v S (1)
Baxter, R. A. (Cliftonville), 1887 v S, W (2)
Bennett, L. V. (Dublin University), 1889 v W (1)
Berry, J. (Cliftonville), 1888 v S, W; 1889 v E (3)
Best, G. (Manchester U), 1964 v W, U; 1965 v E, Ho (2), S, Sw (2), Alb; 1966 v S, E, Alb; 1967 v E; 1968 v S; 1969 v E, S, W, T; 1970 v S, E, W, USSR; 1971 v Cy (2), Sp, E, S, W; 1972 v USSR, Sp; 1973 v Bul; 1974 v P; (with Fulham), 1977 v Ho, Bel, WG; 1978 v Ic, Ho (37)
Bingham, W. L. (Sunderland), 1951 v F; 1952 v E, S, W; 1953 v E, S, F, W; 1954 v E, S, W; 1955 v E, S, W; 1956 v E, S, W; 1957 v E, S, W, P (2), I; 1958 v S, E, W, I (2), Arg, Cz (2), WG, F; (with Luton T), 1959 v E, S, W, Sp; 1960 v S, E, W; (with Everton), 1961 v E, S, WG (2), Gr, I; 1962 v E, Gr; 1963 v E, S, Pol (2), Sp; (with Port Vale), 1964 v S, E, Sp (56)
Black, J. (Glentoran), 1901 v E (1)
Black, K. (Luton T), 1988 v Fr (sub), Ma (sub); 1989 v Ei, H, Sp (2), Ch (sub); 1990 v H, N, U; 1991 v Y (2), D, A, Pol, Fa; (with Nottingham F), 1992 v Fa, A, D, S, Li, G; 1993 v Sp, D (sub), Alb, Ei (sub), Sp; 1994 v D (sub), Ei (sub), R (sub) (30)
Blair, H. (Portadown), 1931 v S; 1932 v S; (with Swansea), 1934 v S (3)
Blair, J. (Cliftonville), 1907 v W, E, S; 1908 v E, S (5)
Blair, R. V. (Oldham Ath), 1975 v Se (sub), S (sub), W; 1976 v Se, Is (5)
Blanchflower, R. D. (Barnsley), 1950 v S, W; 1951 v E, S; (with Aston Villa), F; 1952 v W; 1953 v E, S, W, F; 1954 v E, S, W; 1955 v E, S (with Tottenham H), W; 1956 v E, S, W; 1957 v E, S, W, I, P (2); 1958 v E, S, W, I (2), Cz (2), Arg, F, WG; 1959 v E, S, W, Sp; 1960 v E, S, W; 1961 v E, S, W, WG (2); 1962 v E, S, W, Gr, Ho; 1963 v E, S, Pol (2) (56)
Blanchflower, J. (Manchester U), 1954 v W; 1955 v E, S; 1956 v S, W; 1957 v S, E, P; 1958 v S, E, I (2) (12)
Bookman, L. O. (Bradford C), 1914 v W; (with Luton T), 1921 v S, W; 1922 v E (4)
Bothwell, A. W. (Ards), 1926 v S, E, W; 1927 v E, W (5)
Bowler, G. C. (Hull C), 1950 v E, S, W (3)
Boyle, P. (Sheffield U), 1901 v E; 1902 v E; 1903 v S, W; 1904 v E (5)
Braithwaite, R. S. (Linfield), 1962 v W; 1963 v P, Sp; (with Middlesbrough), 1964 v W, U; 1965 v E, S, Sw (2), Ho (10)
Breen, T. (Belfast C), 1935 v E, W; 1937 v E, S; (with Manchester U), 1937 v W; 1938 v E, S; 1939 v W, S (9)
Brennan, B. (Bohemians), 1912 v W (1)
Brennan, R. A. (Luton T), 1949 v W; (with Birmingham C), 1950 v E, S, W; (with Fulham), 1951 v E (5)
Briggs, W. R. (Manchester U), 1962 v W; (with Swansea T), 1965 v Ho (2)
Brisby, D. (Distillery), 1891 v S (1)
Brolly, T. (Millwall), 1937 v W; 1938 v W; 1939 v E, W (4)
Brookes, E. A. (Shelbourne), 1920 v S (1)
Brotherston, N. (Blackburn R), 1980 v S, E, W, Aus (3); 1981 v Se, P; 1982 v S, Is, E, F, S, W, Hon (sub), A (sub); 1983 v A (sub), WG, Alb, T, Alb, S (sub), E (sub), W; 1984 v T; 1985 v Is (sub), T (27)
Brown, J. (Glenavon), 1921 v W; (with Tranmere R), 1924 v E, W (3)
Brown, J. (Wolverhampton W), 1935 v E, W; 1936 v E; (with Coventry C), 1937 v E, W; 1938 v S, W; (with Birmingham C), 1939 v E, S, W (10)
Brown, W. G. (Glenavon), 1926 v W (1)
Brown, W. M. (Limavady), 1887 v E (1)
Browne, F. (Cliftonville), 1887 v E, S, W; 1888 v E, S (5)
Browne, R. J. (Leeds U), 1936 v E, W; 1938 v E, W; 1939 v E, S (6)
Bruce, W. (Glentoran), 1961 v S; 1967 v W (2)
Buckle, H. (Cliftonville), 1882 v E (1)
Buckle, H. R. (Sunderland), 1904 v E; (with Bristol R), 1908 v W (2)
Burnett, J. (Distillery), 1894 v E, W, S; (with Glentoran), 1895 v E, W (5)
Burnison, J. (Distillery), 1901 v E, W (2)
Burnison, S. (Distillery), 1908 v E; 1910 v E, S; (with Bradford), 1911 v E, S, W; (with Distillery), 1912 v E; 1913 v W (8)
Burns, J. (Glenavon), 1923 v E (1)
Butler, M. P. (Blackpool), 1939 v W (1)

Campbell, A. C. (Crusaders), 1963 v W; 1965 v Sw (2)
Campbell, D. A. (Nottingham F), 1986 v Mor (sub), Br; 1987 v E (2), T, Y; (with Charlton Ath), 1988 v Y, T (sub), Gr (sub), Pol (sub) (10)
Campbell, J. (Cliftonville), 1896 v W; 1897 v E, S, W; (with Distillery), 1898 v E, S, W; (with Cliftonville), 1899 v E; 1900 v E, S; 1901 v S, W; 1902 v S; 1903 v E; 1904 v S (15)
Campbell, J. P. (Fulham), 1951 v E, S (2)
Campbell, R. (Bradford C), 1982 v S, W (sub) (2)
Campbell, W. G. (Dundee), 1968 v S, E; 1969 v T; 1970 v S, W, USSR (6)
Carey, J. J. (Manchester U), 1947 v E, S, W; 1948 v E; 1949 v E, S, W (7)
Carroll, E. (Glenavon), 1925 v S (1)
Casey, T. (Newcastle U), 1955 v W; 1956 v W; 1957 v E, S, W, I, P (2); 1958 v WG, F; (with Portsmouth), 1959 v E, Sp (12)
Cashin, M. (Cliftonville), 1898 v S (1)
Caskey, W. (Derby Co), 1979 v Bul, E, Bul, E, D (sub); 1980 v E (sub); (with Tulsa R), 1982 v F (sub) (7)
Cassidy, T. (Newcastle U), 1971 v E (sub); 1972 v USSR (sub); 1974 v Bul (sub), S, E, W; 1975 v N; 1976 v S, E, W; 1977 v WG (sub); 1980 v E, Ei (sub), Is, S, E, W, Aus (3); (with Burnley), 1981 v Se, P; 1982 v Is, Sp (sub) (24)
Caughey, M. (Linfield), 1986 v F (sub), D (sub) (2)
Chambers, J. (Distillery), 1921 v W; (with Bury), 1928 v E, S, W; 1929 v E, S, W; 1930 v S, W; (with Nottingham F), 1932 v E, S, W (12)
Chatton, H. A. (Partick T), 1925 v E, S; 1926 v E (3)
Christian, J. (Linfield), 1889 v S (1)
Clarke, C. J. (Bournemouth), 1986 v F, D, Mor, Alg (sub), Sp, Br; (with Southampton), 1987 v E, T, Y; 1988 v Y, T, Gr, Pol, F, Ma; 1989 v Ei, H, Sp (1 + 1 sub); (with QPR), Ma, Ch; 1990 v H, Ei, N; (with Portsmouth), 1991 v Y (sub), D, A, Pol, Y (sub), Fa; 1992 v Fa, D, S, G; 1993 v Alb, Sp, D (38)
Clarke, R. (Belfast C), 1901 v E, S (2)

Cleary, J. (Glentoran), 1982 v S, W; 1983 v W (sub); 1984 v T (sub); 1985 v Is (5)

Clements, D. (Coventry C), 1965 v W, Ho; 1966 v M; 1967 v S, W; 1968 v S, E; 1969 v T (2), S, W; 1970 v S, E, W, USSR (2); 1971 v Sp, E, S, W, Cy; (with Sheffield W), 1972 v USSR (2), Sp, E, S, W; 1973 v Bul, Cy (2), P, E, S, W; (with Everton), 1974 v Bul, P, S, E, W; 1975 v N, Y, E, S, W; 1976 v Se, Y; (with New York Cosmos), E, W (48)

Clugston, J. (Cliftonville), 1888 v W; 1889 v W, S, E; 1890 v E, S; 1891 v E, W; 1892 v E, S, W; 1893 v E, S, W (14)

Cochrane, D. (Leeds U), 1939 v E, W; 1947 v E, S, W; 1948 v E, S, W; 1949 v S, W; 1950 v S, E (12)

Cochrane, M. (Distillery), 1898 v S, W, E; 1899 v E; 1900 v E, S, W; (with Leicester Fosse), 1901 v S (8)

Cochrane, T. (Coleraine), 1976 v N (sub); (with Burnley), 1978 v S (sub), E (sub), W (sub); 1979 v Ei (sub); (with Middlesbrough), D, Bul, E, Bul, E; 1980 v Is, E (sub), W (sub), Aus (1 + 2 sub); 1981 v Se (sub), P (sub), S, P, S, Se; 1982 v E (sub), F; (with Gillingham), 1984 v S, Fi (sub) (26)

Collins, F. (Celtic), 1922 v S (1)

Condy, J. (Distillery), 1882 v W; 1886 v E, S (3)

Connell, T. (Coleraine), 1978 v W (sub) (1)

Connor, J. (Glentoran), 1901 v S, E; (with Belfast C), 1905 v E, S, W; 1907 v E, S; 1908 v E, S; 1909 v W; 1911 v S, E, W (13)

Connor, M. J. (Brentford), 1903 v S, W; (with Fulham), 1904 v E (3)

Cook, W. (Celtic), 1933 v E, W, S; (with Everton), 1935 v E; 1936 v S, W; 1937 v E, S, W; 1938 v E, S, W; 1939 v E, S, W (15)

Cooke, S. (Belfast YMCA), 1889 v E; (with Cliftonville), 1890 v E, S (3)

Coulter, J. (Belfast C), 1934 v E, S, W; (with Everton), 1935 v E, S, W; 1937 v S, W; (with Grimsby T), 1938 v S, W; (with Chelmsford C), 1939 v S (11)

Cowan, J. (Newcastle U), 1970 v E (sub) (1)

Cowan, T. S. (Queen's Island), 1925 v W (1)

Coyle, F. (Coleraine), 1956 v E, S; 1957 v P; (with Nottingham F), 1958 v Arg (4)

Coyle, L. (Derry C), 1989 v Ch (sub) (1)

Coyle, R. I. (Sheffield W), 1973 v P, Cy (sub), W (sub); 1974 v Bul (sub), P (sub) (5)

Craig, A. B. (Rangers), 1908 v E, S, W; 1909 v S; (with Morton), 1912 v S, W; 1914 v E, S, W (9)

Craig, D. J. (Newcastle U), 1967 v W; 1968 v W; 1969 v T (2), E, S, W; 1970 v E, S, W, USSR; 1971 v Cy (2), Sp, S (sub); 1972 v USSR, S (sub); 1973 v Cy (2), E, S, W; 1974 v Bul, P; 1975 v N (25)

Crawford, S. (Distillery), 1889 v E, W; (with Cliftonville), 1891 v E, S, W; 1893 v E, W (7)

Croft, T. (Queen's Island), 1924 v E (1)

Crone, R. (Distillery), 1889 v S; 1890 v E, S, W (4)

Crone, W. (Distillery), 1882 v W; 1884 v E, S, W; 1886 v E, S, W; 1887 v E; 1888 v E, W; 1889 v S; 1890 v W (12)

Crooks, W. (Manchester U), 1922 v W (1)

Crossan, E. (Blackburn R), 1950 v S; 1951 v E; 1955 v W (3)

Crossan, J. A. (Sparta-Rotterdam), 1960 v E; (with Sunderland), 1963 v W, P, Sp; 1964 v E, S, W, U, Sp; 1965 v E, S, Sw (2); (with Manchester C), W, Ho (2), Alb; 1966 v S, E, Alb, WG; 1967 v E, S; (with Middlesbrough), 1968 v S (24)

Crothers, C. (Distillery), 1907 v W (1)

Cumming, L. (Huddersfield T), 1929 v W, S; (with Oldham Ath), 1930 v E (3)

Cunningham, R. (Ulster), 1892 v S, E, W; 1893 v E (4)

Cunningham, W. E. (St Mirren), 1951 v W; 1953 v E; 1954 v S; 1955 v S; (with Leicester C), 1956 v E, S, W; 1957 v E, S, W, I, P (2); 1958 v S, W, I, Cz (2), Arg, WG, F; 1959 v E, S, W; 1960 v E, S, W; (with Dunfermline Ath), 1961 v W; 1962 v W, Ho (30)

Curran, S. (Belfast C), 1926 v S, W; 1928 v S (3)

Curran, J. J. (Glenavon), 1922 v W; (with Pontypridd), 1923 v E, S; (with Glenavon), 1924 v E (4)

Cush, W. W. (Glenavon), 1951 v E, S; 1954 v S, E; 1957 v W, I, P (2); (with Leeds U), 1958 v I (2), W, Cz (2), Arg, WG, F; 1959 v E, S, W, Sp; 1960 v E, S, W; (with Portadown), 1961 v WG, Gr; 1962 v Gr (26)

Dalton, W. (YMCA), 1888 v S; (with Linfield), 1890 v S, W; 1891 v S, W; 1892 v E, S, W; 1894 v E, S, W (11)

D'Arcy, S. D. (Chelsea), 1952 v W; 1953 v E; (with Brentford), 1953 v S, W, F (5)

Darling, J. (Linfield), 1897 v E, S; 1900 v S; 1902 v E, S, W; 1903 v E, S, W; 1905 v E, S, W; 1906 v E, S, W; 1908 v W; 1909 v E; 1910 v E, S, W; 1912 v S (21)

Davey, H. H. (Reading), 1926 v E; 1927 v E, S; 1928 v E; (with Portsmouth), 1928 v W (5)

Davis, T. L. (Oldham Ath), 1937 v E (1)

Davison, J. R. (Cliftonville), 1882 v E, W; 1883 v E, W; 1884 v E, W, S; 1885 v E (8)

Dennison, R. (Wolverhampton W), 1988 v F, Ma; 1989 v H, Sp Ch (sub); 1990 v Ei, U; 1991 v Y (2), A. Pol, Fa (sub); 1992 v Fa, A, D (sub); 1993 v Sp (sub); 1994 v Co (sub) (17)

Devine, J. (Glentoran), 1990 v U (sub) (1)

Devine, W. (Limavady), 1886 v E, W; 1887 v W; 1888 v W (4)

Dickson, D. (Coleraine), 1970 v S (sub), W; 1973 v Cy, P (4)

Dickson, T. A. (Linfield), 1957 v S (1)

Dickson, W. (Chelsea), 1951 v W, F; 1952 v E, S, W; 1953 v E, S, W, F; (with Arsenal), 1954 v E, W; 1955 v E (12)

Diffin, W. (Belfast C), 1931 v W (1)

Dill, A. H. (Knock and Down Ath), 1882 v E, W; (with Cliftonville), 1883 v W; 1884 v E, S, W; 1885 v E, S, W (9)

Doherty, I. (Belfast C), 1901 v E (1)

Doherty, J. (Cliftonville), 1933 v E, W (2)

Doherty, L. (Linfield), 1985 v Is; 1988 v T (sub) (2)

Doherty, M. (Derry C), 1938 v S (1)

Doherty, P. D. (Blackpool), 1935 v E, W; 1936 v E, S; (with Manchester C), 1937 v E, W; 1938 v E, S; 1939 v E, W; (with Derby Co), 1947 v E; (with Huddersfield T), 1947 v W; 1948 v E, W; 1949 v S; (with Doncaster R), 1951 v S (16)

Donaghy, M. (Luton T), 1980 v S, E, W; 1981 v Se, P, S (sub); 1982 v S, Is, E, F, S, W, Y, Hon, Sp, F; 1983 v A, WG, Alb, T, Alb, S, E, W; 1984 v A, T, WG, S, E, W, Fi; 1985 v R, Fi, E, Sp, T; 1986 v T, R, E, F, D, Mor, Alg, Sp, Br; 1987 v E (2), T, Is, Y; 1988 v Y, T, Gr, Pol, F, Ma; 1989 v Ei, H; (with Manchester U), Sp (2), Ma, Ch; 1990 v Ei, N; 1991 v Y (2), D, A, Pol, Fa; 1992 v Fa, A, D, S, Li, G; (with Chelsea), 1993 v Alb, Sp, D, Alb, Ei, Sp, Li, La; 1994 v La, D, Ei, R, Lie, Co, M (91)

Donnelly, L. (Distillery), 1913 v W (1)

Doran, J. F. (Brighton), 1921 v E; 1922 v E, W (3)

Dougan, A. D. (Portsmouth), 1958 v Cz; (with Blackburn R), 1960 v S; 1961 v E, W, I, Gr; (with Aston Villa), 1963 v S, Pol (2); (with Leicester C), 1966 v S, E, W, M, Alb, WG; 1967 v E, S; (with Wolverhampton W), 1967 v W; 1968 v S, W, Is; 1969 v T (2), E, S, W; 1970 v S, E, USSR (2); 1971 v Cy (2), Sp, E, S, W; 1972 v USSR (2), E, S, W; 1973 v Bul, Cy (43)

Douglas, J. P. (Belfast C), 1947 v E (1)

Dowd, H. O. (Glenavon), 1974 v W; (with Sheffield W), 1975 v N (sub), Se (3)

Dowie, I. (Luton T), 1990 v N (sub), U; 1991 v Y, D, A (sub), (with West Ham U), Y, Fa; (with Southampton) 1992 v Fa, A, D (sub), S (sub), Li; 1993 v Alb (2), Ei, Sp

(sub), Li, La; La, D, Ei (sub), R (sub), Lie, Co, M (sub) (25)
Duggan, H. A. (Leeds U), 1930 v E; 1931 v E, W; 1933 v E; 1934 v E; 1935 v S, W; 1936 v S (8)
Dunlop, G. (Linfield), 1985 v Is; 1987 v E, Y; 1990 v Ei (4)
Dunne, J. (Sheffield U), 1928 v W; 1931 v W, E; 1932 v E, S; 1933 v E, W (7)

Eames, W. L. E. (Dublin U), 1885 v E, S, W (3)
Eglington, T. J. (Everton), 1947 v S, W; 1948 v E, S, W; 1949 v E (6)
Elder, A. R. (Burnley), 1960 v W; 1961 v S, E, W, WG (2), Gr; 1962 v E, S, Gr; 1963 v E, S, W, P (2), Sp; 1964 v W, U; 1965 v E, S, W, Sw (2), Ho (2), Alb; 1966 v E, S, W, M, Alb; 1967 v E, S, W; (with Stoke C), 1968 v E, W; 1969 v E (sub), S, W; 1970 v USSR (40)
Elleman, A. R. (Cliftonville), 1889 v W; 1890 v E (2)
Elwood, J. H. (Bradford), 1929 v W; 1930 v E (2)
Emerson, W. (Glentoran), 1920 v E, S, W; 1921 v E; 1922 v E, S; (with Burnley), 1922 v W; 1923 v E, S, W; 1924 v E (11)
English, S. (Rangers), 1933 v W, S (2)
Enright, J. (Leeds C), 1912 v S (1)

Falloon, E. (Aberdeen), 1931 v S; 1933 v S (2)
Farquharson, T. G. (Cardiff C), 1923 v S, W; 1924 v E, S, W; 1925 v E, S (7)
Farrell, P. (Distillery), 1901 v S, W (2)
Farrell, P. (Hibernian), 1938 v W (1)
Farrell, P. D. (Everton), 1947 v S, W; 1948 v E, S, W; 1949 v E, W (7)
Feeney, J. M. (Linfield), 1947 v S; (with Swansea T), 1950 v E (2)
Feeney, W. (Glentoran), 1976 v Is (1)
Ferguson, W. (Linfield), 1966 v M; 1967 v E (2)
Ferris, J. (Belfast C), 1920 v E, W; (with Chelsea), 1921 v S, E; (with Belfast C), 1928 v S (5)
Ferris, R. O. (Birmingham C), 1950 v S; 1951 v F; 1952 v S (3)
Fettis, A. (Hull C), 1992 v D, Li; 1993 v D; 1994 v M (4)
Finney, T. (Sunderland), 1975 v N, E (sub), S, W; 1976 v N, Y, S; (with Cambridge U), 1980 v E, Is, S, E, W, Aus (2) (14)
Fitzpatrick, J. C. (Bohemians), 1896 v E, S (2)
Flack, H. (Burnley), 1929 v S (1)
Fleming, J. G. (Nottingham F), 1987 v E (2), Is, Y; 1988 v T, Gr, Pol; 1989 v Ma, Ch; (with Manchester C), 1990 v H, Ei; (with Barnsley), 1991 v Y; 1992 v Li (sub), G; 1993 v Alb, Sp, D, Alb, Sp, Li, La; 1994 v La, D, Ei, R, Lie, Co, M (28)
Forbes, G. (Limavady), 1888 v W; (with Distillery), 1891 v E, S (3)
Forde, J. T. (Ards), 1959 v Sp; 1961 v E, S, WG (4)
Foreman, T. A. (Cliftonville), 1899 v S (1)
Forsyth, J. (YMCA), 1888 v E, S (2)
Fox, W. (Ulster), 1887 v E, S (2)
Fulton, R. P. (Belfast C), 1930 v W; 1931 v E, S, W; 1932 v W, E; 1933 v E, S; 1934 v E, W, S; 1935 v E, W, S; 1936 v S, W; 1937 v E, S, W; 1938 v W (20)

Gaffikin, J. (Linfield Ath), 1890 v S, W; 1891 v S, W; 1892 v E, S, W; 1893 v E, S, W; 1894 v E, S, W; 1895 v E, W (15)
Galbraith, W. (Distillery), 1890 v W (1)
Gallagher, P. (Celtic), 1920 v E, S; 1922 v S; 1923 v S, W; 1924 v S, W; 1925 v S, W, E; (with Falkirk), 1927 v S (11)
Gallogly, C. (Huddersfield T), 1951 v E, S (2)
Gara, A. (Preston NE), 1902 v E, S, W (3)
Gardiner, A. (Cliftonville), 1930 v S, W; 1931 v S; 1932 v E, S (5)
Garrett, J. (Distillery), 1925 v W (1)
Gaston, R. (Oxford U), 1969 v Is (sub) (1)
Gaukrodger, G. (Linfield), 1895 v W (1)
Gaussen, A. W. (Moyola Park), 1884 v E, S; 1888 v E, W; 1889 v E, W (6)
Geary, J. (Glentoran), 1931 v S; 1932 v S (2)
Gibb, J. T. (Wellington Park) 1884 v S, W; 1885 v S, E, W; 1886 v S; 1887 v S, E, W; 1889 v S (10)
Gibb, T. J. (Cliftonville), 1936 v W (1)
Gibson W. K. (Cliftonville), 1894 v S, W, E; 1895 v S; 1897 v W; 1898 v S, W, E; 1901 v S, W, E; 1902 v S, W (13)
Gillespie, R. (Hertford), 1886 v E, S, W; 1887 v E, S, W (6)
Gillespie, W. (Sheffield U), 1913 v E, S; 1914 v E, W; 1920 v S, W; 1921 v E; 1922 v E, S, W; 1923 v E, S, W; 1924 v E, S, W; 1925 v E, S; 1926 v S, W; 1927 v E, W; 1928 v E; 1929 v E; 1931 v E (25)
Gillespie, W. (West Down), 1889 v W (1)
Goodall, A. L. (Derby Co), 1899 v S, W; 1900 v E, W; 1901 v E; 1902 v S; 1903 v E, W; (with Glossop), 1904 v E, W (10)
Goodbody, M. F. (Dublin University), 1889 v E; 1891 v W (2)
Gordon, H. (Linfield), 1891 v S; 1892 v E, S, W; 1893 v E, S, W; 1895 v E, W; 1896 v E, S (11)
Gordon, T. (Linfield), 1894 v W; 1895 v E (2)
Gorman, W. C. (Brentford), 1947 v E, S, W; 1948 v W (4)
Gowdy, J. (Glentoran), 1920 v E; (with Queen's Island), 1924 v W; (with Falkirk), 1926 v E, S; 1927 v E, S (6)
Gowdy, W. A. (Hull C), 1932 v S; (with Sheffield W), 1933 v S; (with Linfield), 1935 v E, S, W; (with Hibernian), 1936 v W (6)
Graham, W. G. L. (Doncaster R), 1951 v W, F; 1952 v E, S, W; 1953 v S, F; 1954 v E, W; 1955 v S, W; 1956 v E, S; 1959 v E (14)
Gray, P. (Luton T), 1993 v D (sub), Alb, Ei, Sp; (with Sunderland), 1994 v La, D, Ei, R, Lie (sub) (9)
Greer, W. (QPR), 1909 v E, S, W (3)
Gregg, H. (Doncaster R), 1954 v W; 1957 v E, S, W, I, P (2); 1958 v E, I; (with Manchester U), 1958 v Cz, Arg, WG, F, W; 1959 v E, W; 1960 v S, E, W; 1961 v E, S; 1962 v S, Gr; 1964 v S, E (25)

Hall, G. (Distillery), 1897 v E (1)
Halligan, W. (Derby Co), 1911 v W; (with Wolverhampton W), 1912 v E (2)
Hamill, M. (Manchester U), 1912 v E; 1914 v E, S; (with Belfast C), 1920 v E, S, W; (with Manchester C), 1921 v S (7)
Hamilton, B. (Linfield), 1969 v T; 1971 v Cy (2), E, S, W; (with Ipswich T), 1972 v USSR (1 + 1 sub), Sp; 1973 v Bul, Cy (2), P, E, S, W; 1974 v Bul, S, E, W; 1975 v N, Se, Y, E; 1976 v Se, N, Y; (with Everton), Is, S, E, W; 1977 v Ho, Bel, WG, E, S, W, Ic; (with Millwall), 1978 v S, E, W; 1979 v Ei (sub); (with Swindon T), Bul (2), E, S, W, D; 1980 v Aus (2 sub) (50)
Hamilton, J. (Knock), 1882 v E, W (2)
Hamilton, R. (Distillery), 1908 v W (1)
Hamilton, R. (Rangers), 1928 v S; 1929 v E; 1930 v S, E; 1932 v S (5)
Hamilton, W. (QPR), 1978 v S (sub); (with Burnley), 1980 v S, E, W, Aus (2); 1981 v Se, P, S, P, S, Se; 1982 v S, Is, E, W, Y, Hon, Sp, A, F; 1983 v A, WG, Alb (2), S, E, W; 1984 v A, T, WG, S, E, W, Fi; (with Oxford U), 1985 v R, Sp; 1986 v Mor (sub), Alg, Sp (sub), Br (sub) (41)
Hamilton, W. D. (Dublin Association), 1885 v W (1)
Hamilton, W. J. (Dublin Association), 1885 v W (1)
Hampton, H. (Bradford C), 1911 v E, S, W; 1912 v E, W; 1913 v E, S, W; 1914 v E (9)
Hanna, D. R. A. (Portsmouth), 1899 v W (1)
Hanna, J. (Nottingham F), 1912 v S, W (2)

Hannon, D. J. (Bohemians), 1908 v E, S; 1911 v E, S; 1912 v W; 1913 v E (6)
Harkin, J. T. (Southport), 1968 v W; 1969 v T; (with Shrewsbury T), W (sub); 1970 v USSR; 1971 v Sp (5)
Harland, A. I. (Linfield), 1923 v E (1)
Harris, J. (Cliftonville), 1921 v W (1)
Harris, V. (Shelbourne), 1906 v E; 1907 v E, W; 1908 v E, W, S; (with Everton), 1909 v E, W, S; 1910 v E, S, W; 1911 v E, S, W; 1912 v E; 1913 v E, S; 1914 v S, W (20)
Harvey, M. (Sunderland), 1961 v I; 1962 v Ho; 1963 v W, Sp; 1964 v S, E, W, U, Sp; 1965 v E, S, W, Sw (2), Ho (2), Alb; 1966 v S, E, W, M, Alb, WG; 1967 v E, S; 1968 v E, W; 1969 v Is, T (2), E; 1970 v USSR; 1971 v Cy, W (sub) (34)
Hastings, J. (Knock), 1882 v E, W; (with Ulster), 1883 v W; 1884 v E, S; 1886 v E, S (7)
Hatton, S. (Linfield), 1963 v S, Pol (2)
Hayes, W. E. (Huddersfield T), 1938 v E, S; 1939 v E, S (4)
Healy, F. (Coleraine), 1982 v S, W, Hon (sub); (with Glentoran), 1983 v A (sub) (4)
Hegan, D. (WBA), 1970 v USSR; (with Wolverhampton W), 1972 v USSR, E, S, W; 1973 v Bul, Cy (7)
Henderson, A. W. (Ulster), 1885 v E, S, W (3)
Hewison, G. (Moyola Park), 1885 v E, S (2)
Hill, C. F. (Sheffield U), 1990 v N, U; 1991 v Pol, Y; 1992 v A, D (6)
Hill, M. J. (Norwich C), 1959 v W; 1960 v W; 1961 v WG; 1962 v S; (with Everton), 1964 v S, E, Sp (7)
Hinton, E. (Fulham), 1947 v S, W; 1948 v S, E, W; (with Millwall), 1951 v W, F (7)
Hopkins, J. (Brighton), 1926 v E (1)
Houston, J. (Linfield), 1912 v S, W; 1913 v W; (with Everton), 1913 v E, S; 1914 v S (6)
Houston, W. (Linfield), 1933 v W (1)
Houston, W. G. (Moyola Park), 1885 v E, S (2)
Hughes, M. E. (Manchester C), 1992 v D, S, Li, G; (with Strasbourg), 1993 v Alb, Sp, D, Ei, Sp, Li, La; 1994 v La, D, Ei, R, Lie, Co, M (18)
Hughes, P. (Bury), 1987 v E, T, Is (3)
Hughes, W. (Bolton W), 1951 v W (1)
Humphries, W. (Ards), 1962 v W; (with Coventry C), 1962 v Ho; 1963 v E, S, W, Pol, Sp; 1964 v S, E, Sp; 1965 v S; (with Swansea T), 1965 v W, Ho, Alb (14)
Hunter, A. (Distillery), 1905 v W; 1906 v W, E, S; (with Belfast C), 1908 v W; 1909 v W, E, S (8)
Hunter, A. (Blackburn R), 1970 v USSR; 1971 v Cy (2), E, S, W; (with Ipswich T), 1972 v USSR (2), Sp, E, S, W; 1973 v Bul, Cy (2), P, E, S, W; 1974 v Bul, S, E, W; 1975 v N, Se, Y, E, S, W; 1976 v Se, N, Y, Is, S, E, W; 1977 v Ho, Bel, WG, E, S, W, Ic; 1978 v Ic, Ho, Bel; 1979 v Ei, D, S, W, D; 1980 v E, Ei (53)
Hunter, R. J. (Cliftonville), 1884 v E, S, W (3)
Hunter, V. (Coleraine), 1962 v E; 1964 v Sp (2)

Irvine, R. J. (Linfield), 1962 v Ho; 1963 v E, S, W, Pol (2), Sp; (with Stoke C), 1965 v W (8)
Irvine, R. W. (Everton), 1922 v S; 1923 v E, W; 1924 v E, S; 1925 v E; 1926 v E; 1927 v E, W; 1928 v E, S; (with Portsmouth), 1929 v E; 1930 v S; (with Connah's Quay), 1931 v E; (with Derry C), 1932 v W (15)
Irvine, W. J. (Burnley), 1963 v W, Sp; 1965 v S, W, Sw, Ho (2), Alb; 1966 v S, E, W, M, Alb; 1967 v E, S; 1968 v E, W; (with Preston NE), 1969 v Is, T, E; (with Brighton), 1972 v E, S, W (23)
Irving, S. J. (Dundee), 1923 v S, W; 1924 v S, E, W; 1925 v S, E, W; 1926 v S, W; (with Cardiff C), 1927 v S, E, W; 1928 v S, E, W; (with Chelsea), 1929 v E; 1931 v W (18)

Jackson, T. (Everton), 1969 v Is, E, S, W; 1970 v USSR (1 + 1 sub); (with Nottingham F), 1971 v Sp; 1972 v E, S, W; 1973 v Cy, E, S, W; 1974 v Bul, P, S (sub), E (sub), W (sub); 1975 v N (sub), Se, Y, E, S, W; (with Manchester U); 1976 v Se, N, Y; 1977 v Ho, Bel, WG, E, S, W, Ic (35)
Jamison, J. (Glentoran), 1976 v N (1)
Jennings, P. A. (Watford), 1964 v W, U; (with Tottenham H), 1965 v E, S, Sw (2), Ho, Alb; 1966 v S, E, W, Alb, WG; 1967 v E, S; 1968 v S, E, W; 1969 v Is, T (2), E, S, W; 1970 v S, E, USSR (2); 1971 v Cy (2), E, S, W; 1972 v USSR, Sp, S, E, W; 1973 v Bul, Cy, P, E, S, W; 1974 v P, S, E, W; 1975 v N, Se, Y, E, S, W; 1976 v Se, N, Y, Is, S, E, W; 1977 v Ho, Bel, WG, E, S, W, Ic; (with Arsenal), 1978 v Ic, Ho, Bel; 1979 v Ei, D, Bul, E, Bul, E, S, W, D; 1980 v E, Ei, Is; 1981 v S, P, S, Se; 1982 v S, Is, E, W, Y, Hon, Sp, F; 1983 v Alb, S, E, W; 1984 v A, T, WG, S, W, Fi; 1985 v R, Fi, E, Sp, T; (with Tottenham H), 1986 v T, R, E, F, D; (with Everton), Mor; (with Tottenham H), Alg, Sp, Br (119)
Johnston, H. (Portadown), 1927 v W (1)
Johnston, R. (Old Park), 1885 v S, W (2)
Johnston, S. (Distillery), 1882 v W; 1884 v E; 1886 v E, S (4)
Johnston, S. (Linfield), 1890 v W; 1893 v S, W; 1894 v E (4)
Johnston, S. (Distillery), 1905 v W (1)
Johnston, W. C. (Glenavon), 1962 v W; (with Oldham Ath), 1966 v M (sub) (2)
Jones, J. (Linfield), 1930 v S, W; 1931 v S, W, E; 1932 v S, E; 1933 v S, E, W; 1934 v S, E, W; 1935 v S, E, W; 1936 v E, S; (with Hibernian), 1936 v W; 1937 v E, W, S; (with Glenavon), 1938 v E (23)
Jones, J. (Glenavon), 1956 v W; 1957 v E, W (3)
Jones, S. (Distillery), 1934 v E; (with Blackpool), 1934 v W (2)
Jordan, T. (Linfield), 1895 v E, W (2)

Kavanagh, P. J. (Celtic), 1930 v E (1)
Keane, T. R. (Swansea T), 1949 v S (1)
Kearns, A. (Distillery), 1900 v E, S, W; 1902 v E, S, W (6)
Kee, P. V. (Oxford U), 1990 v N; 1991 v Y (2), D, A, Pol, Fa (7)
Keith, R. M. (Newcastle U), 1958 v E, W, Cz (2), Arg, I, WG, F; 1959 v E, S, W, Sp; 1960 v S, E; 1961 v S, E, W, I, WG (2), Gr; 1962 v W, Ho (23)
Kelly, H. R. (Fulham), 1950 v E, W; (with Southampton), 1951 v E, S (4)
Kelly, J. (Glentoran), 1896 v E (1)
Kelly, J. (Derry C), 1932 v E, W; 1933 v E, W, S; 1934 v W; 1936 v E, S, W; 1937 v S, E (11)
Kelly, P. (Manchester C), 1921 v E (1)
Kelly, P. M. (Barnsley), 1950 v S (1)
Kennedy, A. L. (Arsenal), 1923 v W; 1925 v E (2)
Kernaghan, N. (Belfast C), 1936 v W; 1937 v S; 1938 v E (3)
Kirkwood, H. (Cliftonville), 1904 v W (1)
Kirwan, J. (Tottenham H), 1900 v W; 1902 v E, W; 1903 v E, S, W; 1904 v E, S, W; 1905 v E, S, W; (with Chelsea), 1906 v E, S, W; 1907 v W; (with Clyde), 1909 v S (17)

Lacey, W. (Everton), 1909 v E, S, W; 1910 v E, S, W; 1911 v E, S, W; 1912 v E; (with Liverpool), 1913 v W; 1914 v E, S, W; 1920 v E, S, W; 1921 v E, S, W; 1922 v E, S; (with New Brighton), 1925 v E (23)
Lawther, W. I. (Sunderland), 1960 v W; 1961 v I; (with Blackburn R), 1962 v S, Ho (4)
Leatham, J. (Belfast C), 1939 v W (1)
Ledwidge, J. J. (Shelbourne), 1906 v S, W (2)
Lemon, J. (Glentoran), 1886 v W; 1888 v S; (with Belfast YMCA), 1889 v W (3)
Lennon, N. F. (Crewe Alex), 1994 v M (sub) (1)
Leslie, W. (YMCA), 1887 v E (1)

Lewis, J. (Glentoran), 1899 v S, E, W; (with Distillery), 1900 v S (4)
Little, J. (Glentoran), 1898 v W (1)
Lockhart, H. (Rossall School), 1884 v W (1)
Lockhart, N. (Linfield), 1947 v E; (with Coventry C), 1950 v W; 1951 v W; 1952 v W; (with Aston Villa), 1954 v S, E; 1955 v W; 1956 v W (8)
Lomas, S. M. (Manchester C), 1994 v R, Lie, Co (sub), M (sub) (4)
Lowther, R. (Glentoran), 1888 v E, S (2)
Loyal, J. (Clarence), 1891 v S (1)
Lutton, R. J. (Wolverhampton W), 1970 v S, E; (with West Ham U), 1973 v Cy (sub), S (sub), W (sub); 1974 v P (6)
Lyner, D. (Glentoran), 1920 v E, W; 1922 v S, W; (with Manchester U), 1923 v E; (with Kilmarnock), 1923 v W (6)

McAdams, W. J. (Manchester C), 1954 v W; 1955 v S; 1957 v E; 1958 v S, I; (with Bolton W), 1961 v E, S, W, I, WG (2), Gr; 1962 v E, Gr; (with Leeds U), Ho (15)
McAlery, J. M. (Cliftonville), 1882 v E, W (2)
McAlinden, J. (Belfast C), 1938 v S; 1939 v S; (with Portsmouth), 1947 v E; (with Southend U), 1949 v E (4)
McAllen, J. (Linfield), 1898 v E; 1899 v E, S, W; 1900 v E, S, W; 1901 v W; 1902 v S (9)
McAlpine, W. J. (Cliftonville), 1901 v S (1)
McArthur, A. (Distillery), 1886 v W (1)
McAuley, J. L. (Huddersfield T), 1911 v E, W; 1912 v E, S; 1913 v E, S (6)
McAuley, P. (Belfast C), 1900 v S (1)
McBride, S. (Glenavon), 1991 v D (sub), Pol (sub); 1992 v Fa (sub), D (4)
McCabe, J. J. (Leeds U), 1949 v S, W; 1950 v E; 1951 v W; 1953 v W; 1954 v S (6)
McCabe, W. (Ulster), 1891 v E (1)
McCambridge, J. (Ballymena), 1930 v S, W; (with Cardiff C), 1931 v W; 1932 v E (4)
McCandless, J. (Bradford), 1912 v W; 1913 v W; 1920 v W, S; 1921 v E (5)
McCandless, W. (Linfield), 1920 v E, W; 1921 v E; (with Rangers), 1921 v W; 1922 v S; 1924 v W, S; 1925 v S; 1929 v W (9)
McCann, P. (Belfast C), 1910 v E, S, W; 1911 v E; (with Glentoran), 1911 v S; 1912 v E; 1913 v W (7)
McCashin, J. (Cliftonville), 1896 v W; 1898 v S, W; 1899 v S (4)
McCavana, W. T. (Coleraine), 1955 v S; 1956 v E, S (3)
McCaw, D. (Distillery), 1882 v E (1)
McCaw, J. H. (Linfield), 1927 v W; 1930 v S; 1931 v E, S, W (5)
McClatchey, J. (Distillery), 1886 v E, S, W (3)
McClatchey, R. (Distillery), 1895 v S (1)
McCleary, J. W. (Cliftonville), 1955 v W (1)
McCleery, W. (Linfield), 1930 v E, W; 1931 v E, S, W; 1932 v S, W; 1933 v E, W (9)
McClelland, J. (Arsenal), 1961 v W, I, WG (2), Gr; (with Fulham), 1966 v M (6)
McClelland, J. (Mansfield T), 1980 v S (sub), Aus (3); 1981 v Se, S; (with Rangers), S, Se (sub); 1982 v S, W, Y, Hon, Sp, A, F; 1983 v A, WG, Alb, T, Alb, S, E, W; 1984 v A, T, WG, S, E, W, Fi; 1985 v R, Is; (with Watford), Fi, E, Sp, T; 1986 v T, F (sub); 1987 v E (2), T, Is, Y; 1988 v T, Gr, F, Ma; 1989 v Ei, H, Sp (2), Ma; (with Leeds U), 1990 v N (53)
McCluggage, A. (Bradford), 1924 v E; (with Burnley), 1927 v S, W; 1928 v S, E, W; 1929 v S, E, W; 1930 v W; 1931 v E, W (12)
McClure, G. (Cliftonville), 1907 v S, W; 1908 v E; (with Distillery), 1909 v E (4)
McConnell, E. (Cliftonville), 1904 v S, W; (with Glentoran), 1905 v S; (with Sunderland), 1906 v E; 1907 v E; 1908 v S, W; (with Sheffield W), 1909 v S, W; 1910 v S, W, E (12)
McConnell, P. (Doncaster R), 1928 v W; (with Southport), 1932 v E (2)
McConnell, W. G. (Bohemians), 1912 v W; 1913 v E, S; 1914 v E, S, W (6)
McConnell, W. H. (Reading), 1925 v W; 1926 v E, W; 1927 v E, S, W; 1928 v E, W (8)
McCourt, F. J. (Manchester C), 1952 v E, W; 1953 v E, S, W, F (6)
McCoy, J. (Distillery), 1896 v W (1)
McCoy, R. (Coleraine), 1987 v Y (sub) (1)
McCracken, R. (C Palace), 1921 v E; 1922 v E, S, W (4)
McCracken, W. (Distillery), 1902 v E, W; 1903 v E; 1904 v E, S, W; (with Newcastle U), 1905 v E, S, W; 1907 v E; 1920 v E; 1922 v E, S, W; (with Hull C), 1923 v S (15)
McCreery, D. (Manchester U), 1976 v S (sub), E, W; 1977 v Ho, Bel, WG, E, S, W, Ic; 1978 v Ic, Ho, Bel, S, E, W; 1979 v Ei, D, Bul, E, Bul, W, D; (with QPR), 1980 v E, Ei, S (sub), E (sub), W (sub), Aus (1 + 1 sub); 1981 v Se (sub), P (sub); (with Tulsa R), S, P, Se; 1982 v S, Is, E (sub), F, Y, Hon, Sp, A, F; (with Newcastle U), 1983 v A; 1984 v T (sub); 1985 v R, Sp (sub); 1986 v T (sub), R, E, F, D, Alg, Sp, Br; 1987 v T, E, Y; 1988 v Y; 1989 v Sp, Ma, Ch; (with Hearts), 1990 v H, Ei, N, U (sub) (67)
McCrory, S. (Southend U), 1958 v E (1)
McCullough, K. (Belfast C), 1935 v W; 1936 v E; (with Manchester C), 1936 v S; 1937 v E, S (5)
McCullough, W. J. (Arsenal), 1961 v I; 1963 v Sp; 1964 v S, E, W, U, Sp; 1965 v E, Sw; (with Millwall), 1967 v E (10)
McCurdy, C. (Linfield), 1980 v Aus (sub) (1)
McDonald, A. (QPR), 1986 v R, E, F, D, Mor, Alg, Sp, Br; 1987 v E (2), T, Is, Y; 1988 v Y, T, Pol, F, Ma; 1989 v Ei, H, Sp, Ch; 1990 v H, Ei, U; 1991 v Y, D, A, Fa; 1992 v Fa, S, Li, G; 1993 v Alb, Sp, D, Alb, Ei, Sp, Li, La; 1994 v D, Ei (43)
McDonald, R. (Rangers), 1930 v S; 1932 v E (2)
McDonnell, J. (Bohemians), 1911 v E, S; 1912 v W; 1913 v W (4)
McElhinney, G. (Bolton W), 1984 v WG, S, E, W, Fi; 1985 v R (6)
McFaul, W. S. (Linfield), 1967 v E (sub); (with Newcastle U), 1970 v W; 1971 v Sp; 1972 v USSR; 1973 v Cy; 1974 v Bul (6)
McGarry, J. K. (Cliftonville), 1951 v W, F, S (3)
McGaughey, M. (Linfield), 1985 v Is (sub) (1)
McGee, G. (Wellington Park), 1885 v E, S, W (3)
McGrath, R. C. (Tottenham H), 1974 v S, E, W; 1975 v N; 1976 v Is (sub); 1977 v Ho; (with Manchester U), Bel, WG, E, S, W, Ic; 1978 v Ic, Ho, Bel, S, E, W; 1979 v Bul (sub), E (2 sub) (21)
McGregor, S. (Glentoran), 1921 v S (1)
McGrillen, J. (Clyde), 1924 v S; (with Belfast C), 1927 v S (2)
McGuire, E. (Distillery), 1907 v S (1)
McIlroy, H. (Cliftonville), 1906 v E (1)
McIlroy, J. (Burnley), 1952 v E, S, W; 1953 v E, S, W; 1954 v E, S, W; 1955 v E, S, W; 1956 v E, S, W; 1957 v E, S, W, I, P (2); 1958 v E, S, W, I (2), Cz (2), Arg, WG, F; 1959 v E, S, W, Sp; 1960 v E, S, W; 1961 v E, W, WG (2), Gr; 1962 v E, S, Gr, Ho; 1963 v E, S, Pol (2); (with Stoke C), 1963 v W; 1966 v S, E, Alb (55)
McIlroy, S. B. (Manchester U), 1972 v Sp, S (sub); 1974 v S, E, W; 1975 v N, Se, Y, E, S, W; 1976 v Se, N, Y, S, E, W; 1977 v Ho, Bel, E, S, W, Ic; 1978 v Ic, Ho, Bel, S, E, W; 1979 v Ei, D, Bul, E, Bul, E, S, W, D; 1980 v E, Ei, Is, S, E, W; 1981 v Se, P, S, P, S, Se; 1982 v S, Is; (with Stoke C), E, F, S, W, Y, Hon, Sp, A, F; 1983 v A, WG, Alb, T, Alb, S, E, W; 1984 v A, T, S, E, W, Fi; 1985 v Fi, E, T; (with Manchester C), 1986 v T, R, E, F, D, Mor, Alg, Sp, Br; 1987 v E (sub) (88)
McIlvenny, J. (Distillery), 1890 v E; 1891 v E (2)

McIlvenny, P. (Distillery), 1924 v W (1)
McKeag, W. (Glentoran), 1968 v S, W (2)
McKee, F. W. (Cliftonville), 1906 v S, W; (with Belfast C), 1914 v E, S, W (5)
McKelvie, H. (Glentoran), 1901 v W (1)
McKenna, J. (Huddersfield), 1950 v E, S, W; 1951 v E, S, F; 1952 v E (7)
McKenzie, H. (Distillery), 1923 v S (1)
McKenzie, R. (Airdrie), 1967 v W (1)
McKeown, H. (Linfield), 1892 v E, S, W; 1893 v S, W; 1894 v S, W (7)
McKie, H. (Cliftonville), 1895 v E, S, W (3)
McKinney, D. (Hull C), 1921 v S; (with Bradford C), 1924 v S (2)
McKinney, V. J. (Falkirk), 1966 v WG (1)
McKnight, A. (Celtic), 1988 v Y, T, Gr, Pol, F, Ma; (with West Ham U) 1989 v Ei, H, Sp (2) (10)
McKnight, J. (Preston NE), 1912 v S; (with Glentoran), 1913 v S (2)
McLaughlin, J. C. (Shrewsbury T), 1962 v E, S, W, Gr; 1963 v W; (with Swansea T), 1964 v W, U; 1965 v E, W, Sw (2); 1966 v W (12)
McLean, T. (Limavady), 1885 v S (1)
McMahon, J. (Bohemians), 1934 v S (1)
McMaster, G. (Glentoran), 1897 v E, S, W (3)
McMichael, A. (Newcastle U), 1950 v E, S; 1951 v E, S, F; 1952 v E, S, W; 1953 v E, S, W, F; 1954 v E, S, W; 1955 v E, W; 1956 v W; 1957 v E, S, W, I, P (2); 1958 v E, S, W, I (2), Cz (2), Arg, WG, F; 1959 v S, W, Sp; 1960 v E, S, W (40)
McMillan, G. (Distillery), 1903 v E; 1905 v W (2)
McMillan, S. (Manchester U), 1963 v E, S (2)
McMillen, W. S. (Manchester U), 1934 v E; 1935 v S; 1937 v S; (with Chesterfield), 1938 v S, W; 1939 v E, S (7)
McMordie, A. S. (Middlesbrough), 1969 v Is, T (2), E, S, W; 1970 v E, S, W, USSR; 1971 v Cy (2), E, S, W; 1972 v USSR, Sp, E, S, W; 1973 v Bul (21)
McMorran, E. J. (Belfast C), 1947 v E; (with Barnsley), 1951 v E, S, W; 1952 v E, S, W; 1953 v E, S, F; (with Doncaster R), 1953 v W; 1954 v E; 1956 v W; 1957 v I, P (15)
McMullan, D. (Liverpool), 1926 v E, W; 1927 v S (3)
McNally, B. A. (Shrewsbury T), 1986 v Mor; 1987 v T (sub); 1988 v Y, Gr, Ma (sub) (5)
McNinch, J. (Ballymena), 1931 v S; 1932 v S, W (3)
McParland, P. J. (Aston Villa), 1954 v W; 1955 v E, S; 1956 v E, S; 1957 v E, S, W, P; 1958 v E, S, W, I (2), Cz (2), Arg, WG, F; 1959 v E, S, W, Sp; 1960 v E, S, W; 1961 v E, S, W, I, WG (2), Gr; (with Wolverhampton W), 1962 v Ho (34)
McShane, J. (Cliftonville), 1899 v S; 1900 v E, S, W (4)
McVickers, J. (Glentoran), 1888 v E; 1889 v S (2)
McWha, W. B. R. (Knock), 1882 v E, W; (with Cliftonville), 1883 v E, W; 1884 v E; 1885 v E, W (7)
Macartney, A. (Ulster), 1903 v S, W; (with Linfield), 1904 v S, W; (with Everton), 1905 v E, S; (with Belfast C), 1907 v E, S, W; 1908 v E, S, W; (with Glentoran), 1909 v E, S, W (15)
Mackie, J. (Arsenal), 1923 v W; (with Portsmouth), 1935 v S, W (3)
Madden, O. (Norwich C), 1938 v E (1)
Magill, E. J. (Arsenal), 1962 v E, S, Gr; 1963 v E, S, W, Pol (2), Sp; 1964 v E, S, W, U, Sp; 1965 v E, S, Sw (2), Ho, Alb; 1966 v S, (with Brighton), E, Alb, W, WG, M (26)
Magilton, J. (Oxford U), 1991 v Pol, Y, Fa; 1992 v Fa, A, D, S, Li, G; 1993 v Alb, D, Alb, Ei, Li, La; 1994 v La, D, Ei; (with Southampton), R, Lie, Co, M (22)
Maginnis, H. (Linfield), 1900 v E, S, W; 1903 v S, W; 1904 v E, S, W (8)
Maguire, E. (Distillery), 1907 v S (1)
Mahood, J. (Belfast C), 1926 v S; 1928 v E, S, W; 1929 v E, S, W; 1930 v W; (with Ballymena), 1934 v S (9)
Manderson, R. (Rangers), 1920 v W, S; 1925 v S, E; 1926 v S (5)
Mansfield, J. (Dublin Freebooters), 1901 v E (1)
Martin, C. J. (Glentoran), 1947 v S; (with Leeds U), 1948 v E, S, W; (with Aston Villa), 1949 v E; 1950 v W (6)
Martin, D. (Bo'ness), 1925 v S (1)
Martin, D. C. (Cliftonville), 1882 v E, W; 1883 v E (3)
Martin, D. K. (Belfast C), 1934 v E, S, W; 1935 v S; (with Wolverhampton W), 1935 v E; 1936 v W; (with Nottingham F), 1937 v S; 1938 v E, S; 1939 v S (10)
Mathieson, A. (Luton T), 1921 v W; 1922 v E (2)
Maxwell, J. (Linfield), 1902 v W; 1903 v W, E; (with Glentoran), 1905 v W, S; (with Belfast C), 1906 v W; 1907 v S (7)
Meek, H. L. (Glentoran), 1925 v W (1)
Mehaffy, J. A. C. (Queen's Island), 1922 v W (1)
Meldon, J. (Dublin Freebooters), 1899 v S, W (2)
Mercer, H. V. A. (Linfield), 1908 v E (1)
Mercer, J. T. (Distillery), 1898 v E, S, W; 1899 v E; (with Linfield), 1902 v E, W; (with Distillery), 1903 v S, W; (with Derby Co), 1904 v E, W; 1905 v S (11)
Millar, W. (Barrow), 1932 v W; 1933 v S (2)
Miller, J. (Middlesbrough), 1929 v W, S; 1930 v E (3)
Milligan, D. (Chesterfield), 1939 v W (1)
Milne, R. G. (Linfield), 1894 v E, S, W; 1895 v E, W; 1896 v E, S, W; 1897 v E, S; 1898 v E, S, W; 1899 v E, W; 1901 v W; 1902 v E, S, W; 1903 v E, S; 1904 v E, S, W; 1906 v E, S, W (27)
Mitchell, E. J. (Cliftonville), 1933 v S; (with Glentoran), 1934 v W (2)
Mitchell, W. (Distillery), 1932 v E, W; 1933 v E, W; (with Chelsea), 1934 v W, S; 1935 v S, E; 1936 v S, E; 1937 v E, S, W; 1938 v E, S (15)
Molyneux, T. B. (Ligoniel), 1883 v E, W; (with Cliftonville), 1884 v E, W, S; 1885 v E, W; 1886 v E, W, S; 1888 v S (11)
Montgomery, F. J. (Coleraine), 1955 v E (1)
Moore, C. (Glentoran), 1949 v W (1)
Moore, J. (Linfield Ath), 1891 v E, S, W (3)
Moore, P. (Aberdeen), 1933 v E (1)
Moore, T. (Ulster), 1887 v S, W (2)
Moore, W. (Falkirk), 1923 v S (1)
Moorhead, F. W. (Dublin University), 1885 v E (1)
Moorhead, G. (Linfield), 1923 v S; 1928 v S; 1929 v S (3)
Moran, J. (Leeds C), 1912 v S (1)
Moreland, V. (Derby Co), 1979 v Bul (2 sub), E, S; 1980 v E, Ei (6)
Morgan, F. G. (Linfield), 1923 v E; (with Nottingham F), 1924 v S; 1927 v E; 1928 v E, S, W; 1929 v E (7)
Morgan, S. (Port Vale), 1972 v Sp; 1973 v Bul (sub), P, Cy, E, S, W; (with Aston Villa), 1974 v Bul, P, S, E; 1975 v Se; 1976 v Se (sub), N, Y; (with Brighton & HA), S, W (sub); (with Sparta Rotterdam), 1979 v D (18)
Morrison, J. (Linfield Ath), 1891 v E, W (2)
Morrison, T. (Glentoran), 1895 v E, S, W; (with Burnley), 1899 v W; 1900 v W; 1902 v E, S (7)
Morrogh, E. (Bohemians), 1896 v S (1)
Morrow, S. J. (Arsenal), 1990 v U (sub); 1991 v A (sub), Pol, Y; 1992 v Fa, S (sub), G (sub); 1993 v Sp (sub), Alb, Ei; 1994 v R, Co, M (sub) (13)
Morrow, W. J. (Moyola Park), 1883 v E, W; 1884 v S (3)
Muir, R. (Oldpark), 1885 v S, W (2)
Mullan, G. (Glentoran), 1983 v S, E, W, Alb (sub) (4)
Mulholland, S. (Celtic), 1906 v S, E (2)
Mulligan, J. (Manchester C), 1921 v S (1)
Murphy, J. (Bradford C), 1910 v E, S, W (3)
Murphy, N. (QPR), 1905 v E, S, W (3)
Murray, J. M. (Motherwell), 1910 v E, S; (with Sheffield W), 1910 v W (3)

Napier, R. J. (Bolton W), 1966 v WG (1)
Neill, W. J. T. (Arsenal), 1961 v I, Gr, WG; 1962 v E, S, W, Gr; 1963 v E, W, Pol, Sp; 1964 v S, E, W, U, Sp; 1965 v

E, S, W, Sw, Ho (2), Alb; 1966 v S, E, W, Alb, WG, M; 1967 v S, W; 1968 v S, E; 1969 v E, S, W, Is, T (2); 1970 v S, E, W, USSR (2); (with Hull C), 1971 v Cy, Sp; 1972 v USSR (2), Sp, S, E, W; 1973 v Bul, Cy (2), P, E, S, W (59)

Nelis, P. (Nottingham F), 1923 v E (1)

Nelson, S. (Arsenal), 1970 v W, E (sub); 1971 v Cy, Sp, E, S, W; 1972 v USSR (2), Sp, E, S, W; 1973 v Bul, Cy, P; 1974 v S, E; 1975 v Se, Y; 1976 v Se, N, Is, E; 1977 v Bel (sub), WG, W, Ic; 1978 v Ic, Ho, Bel; 1979 v Ei, D, Bul, E, Bul, E, S, W, D; 1980 v E, Ei, Is; 1981 v S, P, S, Se; (with Brighton & HA), 1982 v E, S, Sp (sub), A (51)

Nicholl, C. J. (Aston Villa), 1975 v Se, Y, E, S, W; 1976 v Se, N, Y, S, E, W; 1977 v W; (with Southampton), 1978 v Bel (sub), S, E, W; 1979 v Ei, Bul, E, Bul, E, W; 1980 v Ei, Is, S, E, W, Aus (3); 1981 v Se, P, S, P, S, Se; 1982 v S, Is, E, F, W, Y, Hon, Sp, A, F; 1983 v S (sub), E, W; (with Grimsby T), 1984 v A, T (51)

Nicholl, H. (Belfast C), 1902 v E, W; 1905 v E (3)

Nicholl, J. M. (Manchester U), 1976 v Is, W (sub); 1977 v Ho, Bel, E, S, W, Ic; 1978 v Ic, Ho, Bel, S, E, W; 1979 v Ei, D, Bul, E, Bul, E, S, W, D; 1980 v E, Ei, Is, S, E, W, Aus (3); 1981 v Se, P, S, P, S, Se; 1982 v S, Is, E; (with Toronto B), F, W, Y, Hon, Sp, A, F; (with Sunderland), 1983 v A, WG, Alb, T, Alb; (with Toronto B), S, E, W; 1984 v T; (with Rangers), WG, S, E; (with Toronto B), Fi; 1985 v R; (with WBA), Fi, E, Sp, T; 1986 v T, R, E, F, Alg, Sp, Br (73)

Nicholson, J. J. (Manchester U), 1961 v S, W; 1962 v E, W, Gr, Ho; 1963 v E, S, Pol (2); (with Huddersfield T), 1965 v W, Ho (2), Alb; 1966 v S, E, W, Alb, M; 1967 v S, W; 1968 v S, E, W; 1969 v S, E, W, T (2); 1970 v S, E, W, USSR (2); 1971 v Cy (2), E, S, W; 1972 v USSR (2) (41)

Nixon, R. (Linfield), 1914 v S (1)

Nolan-Whelan, J. V. (Dublin Freebooters), 1901 v E, W; 1902 v S, W (4)

O'Boyle, G. (Dunfermline Ath), 1994 v Co (sub), M (2)

O'Brien, M. T. (QPR), 1921 v S; (with Leicester C), 1922 v S, W; 1924 v S, W; (with Hull C), 1925 v S, E, W; 1926 v W; (with Derby Co), 1927 v W (10)

O'Connell, P. (Sheffield W), 1912 v E, S; (with Hull C), 1914 v E, S, W (5)

O'Doherty, A. (Coleraine), 1970 v E, W (sub) (2)

O'Driscoll, J. F. (Swansea T), 1949 v E, S, W (3)

O'Hagan, C. (Tottenham H), 1905 v S, W; 1906 v S, W, E; (with Aberdeen), 1907 v E, S, W; 1908 v S, W; 1909 v E (11)

O'Hagan, W. (St Mirren), 1920 v E, W (2)

O'Hehir, J. C. (Bohemians), 1910 v W (1)

O'Kane, W. J. (Nottingham F), 1970 v E, W, S (sub); 1971 v Sp, E, S, W; 1972 v USSR (2); 1973 v P, Cy; 1974 v Bul, P, S, E, W; 1975 v N, Se, E, S (20)

O'Mahoney, M. T. (Bristol R), 1939 v S (1)

O'Neill, C. (Motherwell), 1989 v Ch (sub); 1990 v Ei (sub); 1991 v D (3)

O'Neill, J. (Leicester C), 1980 v Is, S, E, W, Aus (3); 1981 v P, S, P, S, Se; 1982 v S, Is, E, F, S, F (sub); 1983 v A, WG, Alb, T, Alb, S; 1984 v S (sub); 1985 v Is, Fi, E, Sp, T; 1986 v T, R, E, F, D, Mor, Alg, Sp, Br (39)

O'Neill, J. (Sunderland), 1962 v W (1)

O'Neill, M. A. (Newcastle U), 1988 v Gr, Pol, F, Ma; 1989 v Ei, H, Sp (sub), Sp (sub), Ma (sub), Ch; (with Dundee U), 1990 v H (sub), Ei; 1991 v Pol; 1992 v Fa (sub), S (sub), G (sub); 1993 v Alb (sub + 1), Ei, Sp, Li, La; (with Hibernian), 1994 v Lie (sub) (23)

O'Neill, M. H. (Distillery), 1972 v USSR (sub), (with Nottingham F), Sp (sub), W (sub); 1973 v P, Cy, E, S, W; 1974 v Bul, P, E (sub), W; 1975 v Se, Y, E, S; 1976 v Y (sub); 1977 v E (sub), S; 1978 v Ic, Ho, S, E, W; 1979 v Ei, D, Bul, E, Bul, D; 1980 v Ei, Is, Aus (3); 1981 v Se, P; (with Norwich C), P, S, Se; (with Manchester C), 1982 v S; (with Norwich C), E, F, S, Y, Hon, Sp, A, F; 1983 v A, WG, Alb, T, Alb, S, E; (with Notts Co), 1984 v A, T, WG, E, W, Fi; 1985 v R, Fi (64)

O'Reilly, H. (Dublin Freebooters), 1901 v S, W; 1904 v S (3)

Parke, J. (Linfield), 1964 v S; (with Hibernian), 1964 v E, Sp; (with Sunderland), 1965 v Sw, S, W, Ho (2), Alb; 1966 v WG; 1967 v E, S; 1968 v S, E (14)

Patterson, D. J. (C Palace), 1994 v Co (sub), M (sub) (2)

Peacock, R. (Celtic), 1952 v S; 1953 v F; 1954 v W; 1955 v E, S; 1956 v E, S; 1957 v W, I, P; 1958 v S, E, W, I (2), Arg, Cz (2), WG; 1959 v E, S, W; 1960 v S, E; 1961 v E, S, I, WG (2), Gr; (with Coleraine), 1962 v S (31)

Peden, J. (Linfield), 1887 v S, W; 1888 v W, E; 1889 v S, E; 1890 v W, S; 1891 v W, E; 1892 v W, E; 1893 v E, S, W; (with Distillery), 1896 v W, E, S; 1897 v W, S; 1898 v W, E, S; (with Linfield), 1899 v W (24)

Penney, S. (Brighton & HA), 1985 v Is; 1986 v T, R, E, F, D, Mor, Alg, Sp; 1987 v E, T, Is; 1988 v Pol, F, Ma; 1989 v Ei, Sp (17)

Percy, J. C. (Belfast YMCA), 1889 v W (1)

Platt, J. A. (Middlesbrough), 1976 v Is (sub); 1978 v S, E, W; 1980 v S, E, W, Aus (3); 1981 v Se, P; 1982 v F, S, W (sub), A; 1983 v A, WG, Alb, T; (with Ballymena U), 1984 v E, W (sub); (with Coleraine), 1986 v Mor (sub) (23)

Ponsonby, J. (Distillery), 1895 v S; 1896 v E, S, W; 1897 v E, S, W; 1899 v E (8)

Potts, R. M. C. (Cliftonville), 1883 v E, W (2)

Priestley, T. J. (Coleraine), 1933 v S; (with Chelsea), 1934 v E (2)

Pyper, Jas. (Cliftonville), 1897 v S, W; 1898 v S, E, W; 1899 v S; 1900 v E (7)

Pyper, John (Cliftonville), 1897 v E, S, W; 1899 v E, W; 1900 v E, W, S; 1902 v S (9)

Pyper, M. (Linfield), 1932 v W (1)

Quinn, J. M. (Blackburn R), 1985 v Is, Fi, E, Sp, T; 1986 v T, R, E, F, D (sub), Mor (sub); 1987 v E (sub), T; (with Swindon T), 1988 v Y (sub), T, Gr, Pol, F (sub), Ma; (with Leicester C), 1989 v Ei, H (sub), Sp (sub + 1); (with Bradford C), Ma, Ch; 1990 v H, (with West Ham U), N; 1991 v Y (sub); (with Bournemouth), 1992 v Li; (with Reading), 1993 v Sp, D, Alb (sub), Ei (sub), La (sub); 1994 v La, D (sub), Ei, R, Lie, Co, M (41)

Rafferty, P. (Linfield), 1980 v E (sub) (1)

Ramsey, P. (Leicester C), 1984 v A, WG, S; 1985 v Is, E, Sp, T; 1986 v T, Mor; 1987 v Is, E, Y (sub); 1988 v Y; 1989 v Sp (14)

Rankine, J. (Alexander), 1883 v E, W (2)

Raper, E. O. (Dublin University), 1886 v W (1)

Rattray, D. (Avoniel), 1882 v E; 1883 v E, W (3)

Rea, B. (Glentoran), 1901 v E (1)

Redmond, J. (Cliftonville), 1884 v W (1)

Reid, G. H. (Cardiff C), 1923 v S (1)

Reid, J. (Ulster), 1883 v E; 1884 v W; 1887 v S; 1889 v W; 1890 v S, W (6)

Reid, S. E. (Derby Co), 1934 v E, W; 1936 v E (3)

Reid, W. (Hearts), 1931 v E (1)

Reilly, J. (Portsmouth), 1900 v E; 1902 v E (2)

Renneville, W. T. (Leyton), 1910 v S, E, W; (with Aston Villa), 1911 v W (4)

Reynolds, J. (Distillery), 1890 v E, W; (with Ulster), 1891 v E, S, W (5)

Reynolds, R. (Bohemians), 1905 v W (1)

Rice, P. J. (Arsenal), 1969 v Is; 1970 v USSR; 1971 v E, S, W; 1972 v USSR, Sp, E, S, W; 1973 v Bul, Cy, E, S, W; 1974 v Bul, P, S, E, W; 1975 v N, Y, E, S, W; 1976 v Se, N, Y, Is, S, E, W; 1977 v Ho, Bel, WG, E, S, Ic; 1978 v Ic, Ho, Bel; 1979 v Ei, D, E (2), S, W, D; 1980 v E (49)

Roberts, F. C. (Glentoran), 1931 v S (1)
Robinson, P. (Distillery), 1920 v S; (with Blackburn R), 1921 v W (2)
Rogan, A. (Celtic), 1988 v Y (sub), Gr, Pol (sub); 1989 v Ei (sub), H, Sp (2), Ma (sub), Ch; 1990 v H, N (sub), U; 1991 v Y (2), D, A; (with Sunderland), 1992 v Li (sub) (17)
Rollo, D. (Linfield), 1912 v W; 1913 v W; 1914 v W, E; (with Blackburn R), 1920 v S, W; 1921 v E, S, W; 1922 v E; 1923 v E; 1924 v S, W; 1925 v W; 1926 v E; 1927 v E (16)
Rosbotham, A. (Cliftonville), 1887 v E, S, W; 1888 v E, S, W; 1889 v E (7)
Ross, W. E. (Newcastle U), 1969 v Is (1)
Rowley, R. W. M. (Southampton), 1929 v S, W; 1930 v W, E; (with Tottenham H), 1931 v W; 1932 v S (6)
Russell, A. (Linfield), 1947 v E (1)
Russell, S. R. (Bradford C), 1930 v E, S; (with Derry C), 1932 v E (3)
Ryan, R. A. (WBA), 1950 v W (1)

Sanchez, L. P. (Wimbledon), 1987 v T (sub); 1989 v Sp, Ma (3)
Scott, E. (Liverpool), 1920 v S; 1921 v E, S, W; 1922 v E; 1925 v W; 1926 v E, S, W; 1927 v E, S, W; 1928 v E, S, W; 1929 v E, S, W; 1930 v E; 1931 v E; 1932 v W; 1933 v E, S, W; 1934 v E, S, W; (with Belfast C), 1935 v S; 1936 v E, S, W (31)
Scott, J. (Grimsby), 1958 v Cz, F (2)
Scott, J. E. (Cliftonville), 1901 v S (1)
Scott, L. J. (Dublin University), 1895 v S, W (2)
Scott, P. W. (Everton), 1975 v W; 1976 v Y; (with York C), Is, S, E (sub), W; 1978 v S, E, W; (with Aldershot), 1979 v S (sub) (10)
Scott, T. (Cliftonville), 1894 v E, S; 1895 v S, W; 1896 v S, E, W; 1897 v E, W; 1898 v E, S, W; 1900 v W (13)
Scott, W. (Linfield), 1903 v E, S, W; 1904 v E, S, W; (with Everton), 1905 v E, S; 1907 v E, S; 1908 v E, S, W; 1909 v E, S, W; 1910 v E, S; 1911 v E, S, W; 1912 v E; (with Leeds City), 1913 v E, S, W (25)
Scraggs, M. J. (Glentoran), 1921 v W; 1922 v E (2)
Seymour, H. C. (Bohemians), 1914 v W (1)
Seymour, J. (Cliftonville), 1907 v W; 1909 v W (2)
Shanks, T. (Woolwich Arsenal), 1903 v S; 1904 v W; (with Brentford), 1905 v E (3)
Sharkey, P. (Ipswich T), 1976 v S (1)
Sheehan, Dr G. (Bohemians), 1899 v S; 1900 v E, W (3)
Sheridan, J. (Everton), 1903 v W, E, S; 1904 v E, S; (with Stoke C), 1905 v E (6)
Sherrard, J. (Limavady), 1885 v S; 1887 v W; 1888 v W (3)
Sherrard, W. (Cliftonville), 1895 v E, W, S (3)
Sherry, J. J. (Bohemians), 1906 v E; 1907 v W (2)
Shields, J. (Southampton), 1957 v S (1)
Silo, M. (Belfast YMCA), 1888 v E (1)
Simpson, W. J. (Rangers), 1951 v W, F; 1954 v E, S; 1955 v E; 1957 v I, P; 1958 v S, E, W, I; 1959 v S (12)
Sinclair, J. (Knock), 1882 v E, W (2)
Slemin, J. C. (Bohemians), 1909 v W (1)
Sloan, A. S. (London Caledonians), 1925 v W (1)
Sloan, D. (Oxford U), 1969 v Is; 1971 v Sp (2)
Sloan, H. A. de B. (Bohemians), 1903 v E; 1904 v S; 1905 v E; 1906 v W; 1907 v E, W; 1908 v W; 1909 v S (8)
Sloan, J. W. (Arsenal), 1947 v W (1)
Sloan, T. (Cardiff C), 1926 v S, W, E; 1927 v W, S; 1928 v E, W; 1929 v E; (with Linfield), 1930 v W, S; 1931 v S (11)
Sloan, T. (Manchester U), 1979 v S, W (sub), D (sub) (3)
Small, J. (Clarence), 1887 v E (1)
Small, J. M. (Cliftonville), 1893 v E, S, W (3)
Smith, E. E. (Cardiff C), 1921 v S; 1923 v W, E; 1924 v E (4)
Smith, J. (Distillery), 1901 v S, W (2)
Smyth, R. H. (Dublin University), 1886 v W (1)
Smyth, S. (Wolverhampton W), 1948 v E, S, W; 1949 v S, W; 1950 v E, S, W; (with Stoke C), 1952 v E (9)
Smyth, W. (Distillery), 1949 v E, S; 1954 v S, E (4)
Snape, A. (Airdrie), 1920 v E (1)
Spence, D. W. (Bury), 1975 v Y, E, S, W; 1976 v Se, Is, E, W, S (sub); (with Blackpool), 1977 v Ho (sub), WG (sub), E (sub), S (sub), W (sub), Ic (sub); 1979 v Ei, D (sub), E (sub), Bul (sub), E (sub), S, W, D; 1980 v Ei; (with Southend U), Is (sub), Aus (sub); 1981 v S (sub), Se (sub); 1982 v F (sub) (29)
Spencer, S. (Distillery), 1890 v E, S; 1892 v E, S, W; 1893 v E (6)
Spiller, E. A. (Cliftonville), 1883 v E, W; 1884 v E, W, S (5)
Stanfield, O. M. (Distillery), 1887 v E, S, W; 1888 v E, S, W; 1889 v E, S, W; 1890 v E, S; 1891 v E, S, W; 1892 v E, S, W; 1893 v E, W; 1894 v E, S, W; 1895 v E, S; 1896 v E, S, W; 1897 v E, S, W (30)
Steele, A. (Charlton Ath), 1926 v W, S; (with Fulham), 1929 v W, S (4)
Stevenson, A. E. (Rangers), 1934 v E, S, W; (with Everton), 1935 v E, S; 1936 v S, W; 1937 v E, W; 1938 v E, W; 1939 v E, S, W; 1947 v S, W; 1948 v S (17)
Stewart, A. (Glentoran), 1967 v W; 1968 v S, E; (with Derby Co), 1968 v W; 1969 v Is, T (1 + 1 sub) (7)
Stewart, D. C. (Hull C), 1978 v Bel (1)
Stewart, I. (QPR), 1982 v F (sub); 1983 v A, WG, Alb, T, Alb, S, E, W; 1984 v A, T, WG, S, E, W, Fi; 1985 v R, Fi, Is, E, Sp, T; (with Newcastle U), 1986 v R, E, D, Mor, Alg (sub), Sp (sub), Br; 1987 v E, Is (sub) (31)
Stewart, R. H. (St Columb's Court), 1890 v E, S, W; (with Cliftonville), 1892 v E, S, W; 1893 v E, W; 1894 v E, S, W (11)
Stewart, T. C. (Linfield), 1961 v W (1)
Swan, S. (Linfield), 1899 v S (1)

Taggart, G. P. (Barnsley), 1990 v N, U; 1991 v Y, D, A, Pol, Fa; 1992 v Fa, A, D, S, Li, G; 1993 v Alb, Sp, D, Alb, Ei, Sp, Li, La; 1994 v La, D, Ei, R, Lie, Co, M (28)
Taggart, J. (Walsall), 1899 v W (1)
Thompson, F. W. (Cliftonville), 1910 v E, S, W; (with Bradford C), 1911 v E; (with Linfield), v W; 1912 v E, W; 1913 v E, S, W; (with Clyde), 1914 v E, S (12)
Thompson, J. (Belfast Ath), 1889 v S (1)
Thompson, J. (Distillery), 1897 v S (1)
Thunder, P. J. (Bohemians), 1911 v W (1)
Todd, S. J. (Burnley), 1966 v M (sub); 1967 v E; 1968 v W; 1969 v E, S, W; 1970 v S, USSR; (with Sheffield W), 1971 v Cy (2), Sp (sub) (11)
Toner, J. (Arsenal), 1922 v W; 1923 v W; 1924 v W, E; 1925 v E, S; (with St Johnstone), 1927 v E, S (8)
Torrans, R. (Linfield), 1893 v S (1)
Torrans, S. (Linfield), 1889 v S; 1890 v S, W; 1891 v S, W; 1892 v E, S, W; 1893 v E, S; 1894 v E, S, W; 1895 v E; 1896 v E, S, W; 1897 v E, S, W; 1898 v E, S; 1899 v E, W; 1901 v S, W (26)
Trainor, D. (Crusaders), 1967 v W (1)
Tully, C. P. (Celtic), 1949 v E; 1950 v E; 1952 v S; 1953 v E, S, W, F; 1954 v S; 1956 v E; 1959 v Sp (10)
Turner, E. (Cliftonville), 1896 v E, W (2)
Turner, W. (Cliftonville), 1886 v E; 1886 v S; 1888 v S (3)
Twoomey, J. F. (Leeds U), 1938 v W; 1939 v E (2)

Uprichard, W. N. M. C. (Swindon T), 1952 v E, S, W; 1953 v E, S; (with Portsmouth), 1953 v W, F; 1955 v E, S, W; 1956 v E, S, W; 1958 v S, I, Cz; 1959 v S, Sp (18)

Vernon, J. (Belfast C), 1947 v E, S; (with WBA), 1947 v W; 1948 v E, S, W; 1949 v E, S, W; 1950 v E, S; 1951 v E, S, W, F; 1952 v S, E (17)

Waddell, T. M. R. (Cliftonville), 1906 v S (1)
Walker, J. (Doncaster R), 1955 v W (1)
Walker, T. (Bury), 1911 v S (1)
Walsh, D. J. (WBA), 1947 v S, W; 1948 v E, S, W; 1949 v E, S, W; 1950 v W (9)
Walsh, W. (Manchester C), 1948 v E, S, W; 1949 v E, S (5)
Waring, R. (Distillery), 1899 v E (1)
Warren, P. (Shelbourne), 1913 v E, S (2)
Watson, J. (Ulster), 1883 v E, W; 1886 v E, S, W; 1887 v S, W; 1889 v E, W (9)
Watson, P. (Distillery), 1971 v Cy (sub) (1)
Watson, T. (Cardiff C), 1926 v S (1)
Wattle, J. (Distillery), 1899 v E (1)
Webb, C. G. (Brighton), 1909 v S, W; 1911 v S (3)
Weir, E. (Clyde), 1939 v W (1)
Welsh, E. (Carlisle U), 1966 v W, WG, M; 1967 v W (4)
Whiteside, N. (Manchester U), 1982 v Y, Hon, Sp, A, F; 1983 v WG, Alb, T; 1984 v A, T, WG, S, E, W, Fi; 1985 v R, Fi, Is, E, Sp, T; 1986 v R, E, F, D, Mor, Alg, Sp, Br; 1987 v E (2), Is, Y; 1988 v T, Pol, F; (with Everton), 1990 v H, Ei (38)
Whiteside, T. (Distillery), 1891 v E (1)
Whitfield, E. R. (Dublin University), 1886 v W (1)
Williams, J. R. (Ulster), 1886 v E, S (2)
Williams, P. A. (WBA), 1991 v Fa (sub) (1)
Williamson, J. (Cliftonville), 1890 v E; 1892 v S; 1893 v S (3)
Willigham, T. (Burnley), 1933 v W; 1934 v S (2)
Willis, G. (Linfield), 1906 v S, W; 1907 v S; 1912 v S (4)
Wilson, D. J. (Brighton & HA), 1987 v T, Is, E (sub); (with Luton T), 1988 v Y, T, Gr, Pol, F, Ma; 1989 v Ei, H, Sp, Ma, Ch; 1990 v H, Ei, N, U; (with Sheffield W), 1991 v Y, D, A, Fa; 1992 v A (sub), S (24)
Wilson, H. (Linfield), 1925 v W (1)
Wilson, K. J. (Ipswich T), 1987 v Is, E, Y; (with Chelsea), 1988 v Y, T, Gr (sub), Pol (sub), F (sub); 1989 v H (sub), Sp (2), Ma, Ch; 1990 v Ei (sub), N, U; 1991 v Y (2), A, Pol, Fa; 1992 v Fa, A, D, S; (with Notts Co), Li, G; 1993 v Alb, Sp, D, Sp, Li, La; 1994 v La, D, Ei, R, Lie, Co, M (40)
Wilson, M. (Distillery), 1884 v E, S, W (3)
Wilson, R. (Cliftonville), 1888 v S (1)
Wilson, S. J. (Glenavon), 1962 v S; 1964 v S; (with Falkirk), 1964 v E, W, U, Sp; 1965 v E, Sw; (with Dundee), 1966 v W, WG; 1967 v S; 1968 v E (12)
Wilton, J. M. (St Columb's Court), 1888 v E, W; 1889 v S, E; (with Cliftonville), 1890 v E; (with St Columb's Court), 1892 v W; 1893 v S (7)
Worthington, N. (Sheffield W), 1984 v W, Fi (sub); 1985 v Is, Sp (sub); 1986 v T, R (sub), E (sub), D, Alg, Sp; 1987 v E (2), T, Is, Y; 1988 v Y, T, Gr, Pol, F, Ma; 1989 v Ei, H, Sp, Ma; 1990 v H, Ei, U; 1991 v Y, D, A, Fa; 1992 v A, D, S, Li, G; 1993 v Alb, Sp, D, Ei, Sp, Li, La; 1994 v La, D, Ei, Lie, Co, M (50)
Wright, J. (Cliftonville), 1906 v E, S, W; 1907 v E, S, W (6)
Wright, T. J. (Newcastle U), 1989 v Ma, Ch; 1990 v H, U; 1992 v Fa, A, S, G; 1993 v Alb, Sp, Alb, Ei, Sp, Li, La; 1994 v La; (with Nottingham F), D, Ei, R, Lie, Co, M (sub) (22)
Young, S. (Linfield), 1907 v E, S; 1908 v E, S; (with Airdrie), 1909 v E; 1912 v S; (with Linfield), 1914 v E, S, W (9)

SCOTLAND

Adams, J. (Hearts), 1889 v Ni; 1892 v W; 1893 v Ni (3)
Agnew, W. B. (Kilmarnock), 1907 v Ni; 1908 v W, Ni (3)
Aird, J. (Burnley), 1954 v N (2), A, U (4)
Aitken, A. (Newcastle U), 1901 v E; 1902 v E; 1903 v E, W; 1904 v E; 1905 v E, W; 1906 v E; (with Middlesbrough), 1907 v E, W; 1908 v E; (with Leicester Fosse), 1910 v E; 1911 v E, Ni (14)
Aitken, G. G. (East Fife), 1949 v E, F; 1950 v W, Ni, Sw; (with Sunderland), 1953 v W, Ni; 1954 v E (8)
Aitken, R. (Dumbarton), 1886 v E; 1888 v Ni (2)
Aitken, R. (Celtic), 1980 v Pe (sub), Bel, W (sub), E, Pol; 1983 v Bel, Ca (1 + 1 sub); 1984 v Bel (sub), Ni, W (sub); 1985 v E, Ic; 1986 v W, EG, Aus (2), Is, R, E, D, WG, U; 1987 v Bul, Ei (2), L, Bel, E, Br; 1988 v H, Bel, Bul, L, S.Ar, Ma, Sp, Co, E; 1989 v N, Y, I, Cy, F, Cy, E, Ch; 1990 v Y, F, N; (with Newcastle U), Arg (sub), Pol, Ma, Cr, Se, Br; (with St Mirren), 1992 v R (sub) (57)
Aitkenhead, W. A. C. (Blackburn R), 1912 v Ni (1)
Albiston, A. (Manchester U), 1982 v Ni; 1984 v U, Bel, EG, W, E; 1985 v Y, Ic, Sp (2), W; 1986 v EG, Ho, U (14)
Alexander, D. (East Stirlingshire), 1894 v W, Ni (2)
Allan, D. S. (Queen's Park), 1885 v E, W; 1886 v W (3)
Allan, G. (Liverpool), 1897 v E (1)
Allan, H. (Hearts), 1902 v W (1)
Allan, J. (Queen's Park), 1887 v E, W (2)
Allan, T. (Dundee), 1974 v WG, N (2)
Ancell, R. F. D. (Newcastle U), 1937 v W, Ni (2)
Anderson, A. (Hearts), 1933 v E; 1934 v A, E, W, Ni; 1935 v E, W, Ni; 1936 v E, W, Ni; 1937 v G, E, W, Ni, A; 1938 v E, W, Ni, Cz, Ho; 1939 v W, H (23)
Anderson, F. (Clydesdale), 1874 v E (1)
Anderson, G. (Kilmarnock), 1901 v Ni (1)
Anderson, H. A. (Raith R), 1914 v W (1)
Anderson, J. (Leicester C), 1954 v Fi (1)
Anderson, K. (Queen's Park), 1896 v Ni; 1898 v E, Ni (3)
Anderson, W. (Queen's Park), 1882 v E; 1883 v E, W; 1884 v E; 1885 v E, W (6)
Andrews, P. (Eastern), 1875 v E (1)
Archibald, A. (Rangers), 1921 v W; 1922 v W, E; 1923 v Ni; 1924 v E, W; 1931 v E; 1932 v E (8)
Archibald, S. (Aberdeen), 1980 v P (sub); (with Tottenham H), Ni, Pol, H; 1981 v Se (sub), Is, Ni, Is, Ni, E; 1982 v Ni, P, Sp (sub), Ho, Nz (sub), Br, USSR; 1983 v EG, Sw (sub), Bel; 1984 v EG, E, F; (with Barcelona), 1985 v Sp, E, Ic (sub); 1986 v WG (27)
Armstrong, M. W. (Aberdeen), 1936 v W, Ni; 1937 v G (3)
Arnott, W. (Queen's Park), 1883 v W; 1884 v E, Ni; 1885 v E, W; 1886 v E; 1887 v E, W; 1888 v E; 1889 v E; 1890 v E; 1891 v E; 1892 v E; 1893 v E (14)
Auld, J. R. (Third Lanark), 1887 v E, W; 1889 v W (3)
Auld, R. (Celtic), 1959 v H, P; 1960 v W (3)

Baird, A. (Queen's Park), 1892 v Ni; 1894 v W (2)
Baird, D. (Hearts), 1890 v Ni; 1891 v E; 1892 v W (3)
Baird, H. (Airdrieonians), 1956 v A (1)
Baird, J. C. (Vale of Leven), 1876 v E; 1878 v W; 1880 v E (3)
Baird, S. (Rangers), 1957 v Y, Sp (2), Sw, WG; 1958 v F, Ni (7)
Baird, W. U. (St Bernard), 1897 v Ni (1)
Bannon, E. (Dundee U), 1980 v Bel; 1983 v Ni, W, E, Ca; 1984 v EG; 1986 v Is, R, E, D (sub), WG (11)
Barbour, A. (Renton), 1885 v Ni (1)
Barker, J. B. (Rangers), 1893 v W; 1894 v W (2)
Barrett, F. (Dundee), 1894 v Ni; 1895 v W (2)
Battles, B. (Celtic), 1901 v E, W, Ni (3)

Battles, B. jun. (Hearts), 1931 v W (1)
Bauld, W. (Hearts), 1950 v E, Sw, P (3)
Baxter, J. C. (Rangers), 1961 v Ni, Ei (2), Cz; 1962 v Ni, W, E, Cz (2), U; 1963 v W, Ni, E, A, N, Ei, Sp; 1964 v W, E, N, WG; 1965 v W, Ni, Fi; (with Sunderland), 1966 v P, Br, Ni, W, E, I; 1967 v W, E, USSR; 1968 v W (34)
Baxter, R. D. (Middlesbrough), 1939 v E, W, H (3)
Beattie, A. (Preston NE), 1937 v E, A, Cz; 1938 v E; 1939 v W, Ni, H (7)
Beattie, R. (Preston NE), 1939 v W (1)
Begbie, I. (Hearts), 1890 v Ni; 1891 v E; 1892 v W; 1894 v E (4)
Bell, A. (Manchester U), 1912 v Ni (1)
Bell, J. (Dumbarton), 1890 v Ni; 1892 v E; (with Everton), 1896 v E; 1897 v E; 1898 v E; (with Celtic), 1899 v E, W, Ni; 1900 v E, W (10)
Bell, M. (Hearts), 1901 v W (1)
Bell, W. J. (Leeds U), 1966 v P, Br (2)
Bennett, A. (Celtic), 1904 v W; 1907 v Ni; 1908 v W; (with Rangers), 1909 v W, Ni, E; 1910 v E, W; 1911 v E, W; 1913 v Ni (11)
Bennie, R. (Airdrieonians), 1925 v W, Ni; 1926 v Ni (3)
Berry, D. (Queen's Park), 1894 v W; 1899 v W, Ni (3)
Berry, W. H. (Queen's Park), 1888 v E; 1889 v E; 1890 v E; 1891 v E (4)
Bett, J. (Rangers), 1982 v Ho; 1983 v Bel; (with Lokeren), 1984 v Bel, W, E, F; 1985 v Y, Ic, Sp (2), W, E, Ic; (with Aberdeen), 1986 v W, Is, Ho; 1987 v Bel; 1988 v H (sub); 1989 v Y; 1990 v F (sub), N, Arg, Eg, Ma, Cr (25)
Beveridge, W. W. (Glasgow University), 1879 v E, W; 1880 v W (3)
Black, A. (Hearts), 1938 v Cz, Ho; 1939 v H (3)
Black, D. (Hurlford), 1889 v Ni (1)
Black, E. (Metz), 1988 v H (sub), L (sub) (2)
Black, I. H. (Southampton), 1948 v E (1)
Blackburn, J. E. (Royal Engineers), 1873 v E (1)
Blacklaw, A. S. (Burnley), 1963 v N, Sp; 1966 v I (3)
Blackley, J. (Hibernian), 1974 v Cz, E, Bel, Z; 1976 v Sw; 1977 v W, Se (7)
Blair, D. (Clyde), 1929 v W, Ni; 1931 v E, A, I; 1932 v W, Ni; (with Aston Villa), 1933 v W (8)
Blair, J. (Sheffield W), 1920 v E, Ni; (with Cardiff C), 1921 v E; 1922 v E; 1923 v E, W, Ni; 1924 v W (8)
Blair, J. (Motherwell), 1934 v W (1)
Blair, J. A. (Blackpool), 1947 v W (1)
Blair, W. (Third Lanark), 1896 v W (1)
Blessington, J. (Celtic), 1894 v E, Ni; 1896 v E, Ni (4)
Blyth, J. A. (Coventry C), 1978 v Bul, W (2)
Bone, J. (Norwich C), 1972 v Y (sub); 1973 v D (2)
Booth, S. (Aberdeen), 1993 v G (sub), Es (2 subs); 1994 v Sw, Ma (sub) (5)
Bowie, J. (Rangers), 1920 v E, Ni (2)
Bowie, W. (Linthouse), 1891 v Ni (1)
Bowman, D. (Dundee U), 1992 v Fi, US (sub); 1993 v G, Es; 1994 v Sw, I (6)
Bowman, G. A. (Montrose), 1892 v Ni (1)
Boyd, J. M. (Newcastle U), 1934 v Ni (1)
Boyd, R. (Mossend Swifts), 1889 v Ni; 1891 v W (2)
Boyd, T. (Motherwell), 1991 v R (sub), Sw, Bul, USSR; (with Chelsea), 1992 v Sw, R; (with Celtic), Fi, Ca, N, C; 1993 v Sw, P, I, Ma, G, Es (2); 1994 v I, Ma (sub), Ho (sub), A (21)
Boyd, W. G. (Clyde), 1931 v I, Sw (2)
Brackenbridge, T. (Hearts), 1888 v Ni (1)
Bradshaw, T. (Bury), 1928 v E (1)
Brand, R. (Rangers), 1961 v Ni, Cz, Ei (2); 1962 v Ni, W, Cz, U (8)
Branden, T. (Blackburn R), 1896 v E (1)
Brazil, A. (Ipswich T), 1980 v Pol (sub), H; 1982 v Sp, Ho (sub), Ni, W, E, Nz, USSR (sub); 1983 v EG, Sw, W, E (sub) (13)
Bremner, D. (Hibernian), 1976 v Sw (sub) (1)
Bremner, W. J. (Leeds U), 1965 v Sp; 1966 v E, Pol, P, Br, I (2); 1967 v W, Ni, E; 1968 v W, E; 1969 v W, E, Ni, D, A, WG, Cy (2); 1970 v Ei, WG, A; 1971 v W, E; 1972 v P, Bel, Ho, Ni, W, E, Y, Cz, Br; 1973 v D (2), E (2), Ni (sub), Sw, Br; 1974 v Cz, WG, Ni, W, E, Bel, N, Z, Br, Y; 1975 v Sp (2); 1976 v D (54)
Brennan, F. (Newcastle U), 1947 v W, Ni; 1953 v W, Ni, E; 1954 v Ni, E (7)
Breslin, B. (Hibernian), 1897 v W (1)
Brewster, G. (Everton), 1921 v E (1)
Brogan, J. (Celtic), 1971 v W, Ni, P, E (4)
Brown, A. (Middlesbrough), 1904 v E (1)
Brown, A. (St Mirren), 1890 v W; 1891 v W (2)
Brown, A. D. (East Fife), 1950 v Sw, P, F; (with Blackpool), 1952 v USA, D, Se; 1953 v W; 1954 v W, E, N (2), Fi, A, U (14)
Brown, G. C. P. (Rangers), 1931 v W; 1932 v E, W, Ni; 1933 v E; 1934 v A; 1935 v E, W; 1936 v E, W; 1937 v G, E, W, Ni, Cz; 1938 v E, W, Cz, Ho (19)
Brown, H. (Partick T), 1947 v W, Bel, L (3)
Brown, J. (Cambuslang), 1890 v W (1)
Brown, J. B. (Clyde), 1939 v W (1)
Brown, J. G. (Sheffield U), 1975 v R (1)
Brown, R. (Dumbarton), 1884 v W, Ni (2)
Brown, R. (Rangers), 1947 v Ni; 1949 v Ni; 1952 v E (3)
Brown, R. jun. (Dumbarton), 1885 v W (1)
Brown, W. D. F. (Dundee), 1958 v F; 1959 v E, W, Ni; (with Tottenham H), 1960 v W, Ni, Pol, A, H, T; 1962 v Ni, W, E, Cz; 1963 v W, Ni, E, A; 1964 v Ni, W, N; 1965 v E, Fi, Pol, Sp; 1966 v Ni, Pol, I (28)
Browning, J. (Celtic), 1914 v W (1)
Brownlie, J. (Hibernian), 1971 v USSR; 1972 v Pe, Ni, E; 1973 v D (2); 1976 v R (7)
Brownlie, J. (Third Lanark), 1909 v E, Ni; 1910 v E, W, Ni; 1911 v W, Ni; 1912 v W, Ni, E; 1913 v W, Ni, E; 1914 v W, Ni, E (16)
Bruce, D. (Vale of Leven), 1890 v W (1)
Bruce, R. F. (Middlesbrough), 1934 v A (1)
Buchan, M. M. (Aberdeen), 1972 v P (sub), Bel; (with Manchester U), W, Y, Cz, Br; 1973 v D (2), E; 1974 v WG, Ni, W, N, Br, Y; 1975 v EG, Sp, P; 1976 v D, R; 1977 v Fi, Cz, Ch, Arg, Br; 1978 v EG, W (sub), Ni, Pe, Ir, Ho; 1979 v A, N, P (34)
Buchanan, J. (Cambuslang), 1889 v Ni (1)
Buchanan, J. (Rangers), 1929 v E; 1930 v E (2)
Buchanan, P. S. (Chelsea), 1938 v Cz (1)
Buchanan, R. (Abercorn), 1891 v W (1)
Buckley, P. (Aberdeen), 1954 v N; 1955 v W, Ni (3)
Buick, A. (Hearts), 1902 v W, Ni (2)
Burley, G. (Ipswich T), 1979 v W, Ni, E, Arg, N; 1980 v P, Ni, E (sub), Pol; 1982 v W (sub), E (11)
Burns, F. (Manchester U), 1970 v A (1)
Burns, K. (Birmingham C), 1974 v WG; 1975 v EG (sub), Sp (2); 1977 v Cz (sub), W, Se, W (sub); (with Nottingham F), 1978 v Ni (sub), W, E, Pe, Ir; 1979 v N; 1980 v Pe, A, Bel; 1981 v Is, Ni, W (20)
Burns, T. (Celtic), 1981 v Ni; 1982 v Ho (sub), W; 1983 v Bel (sub), Ni, Ca (1 + 1 sub); 1988 v E (sub) (8)
Busby, M. W. (Manchester C), 1934 v W (1)

Cairns, T. (Rangers), 1920 v W; 1922 v E; 1923 v E, W; 1924 v Ni; 1925 v W, E, Ni (8)
Calderhead, D. (Queen of the South), 1889 v Ni (1)
Calderwood, R. (Cartvale), 1885 v Ni, E, W (3)
Caldow, E. (Rangers), 1957 v Sp (2), Sw, WG, E; 1958 v Ni, W, Sw, Par, H, Pol, Y, F; 1959 v E, W, Ni, WG, Ho, P; 1960 v E, W, Ni, A, H, T; 1961 v E, W, Ni, Ei (2), Cz; 1962 v Ni, W, E, Cz (2), U; 1963 v W, Ni, E (40)
Callaghan, P. (Hibernian), 1900 v Ni (1)
Callaghan, W. (Dunfermline Ath), 1970 v Ei (sub), W (2)
Cameron, J. (Rangers), 1886 v Ni (1)
Cameron, J. (Queen's Park), 1896 v Ni (1)

Cameron, J. (St Mirren), 1904 v Ni; (with Chelsea), 1909 v E (2)
Campbell, C. (Queen's Park), 1874 v E; 1876 v W; 1877 v E, W; 1878 v E; 1879 v E; 1880 v E; 1881 v E; 1882 v E, W; 1884 v E; 1885 v E; 1886 v E (13)
Campbell, H. (Renton), 1889 v W (1)
Campbell, Jas (Sheffield W), 1913 v W (1)
Campbell, J. (South Western), 1880 v W (1)
Campbell, J. (Kilmarnock), 1891 v Ni; 1892 v W (2)
Campbell, John (Celtic), 1893 v E, Ni; 1898 v E, Ni; 1900 v E, Ni; 1901 v E, W, Ni; 1902 v W, Ni; 1903 v W (12)
Campbell, John (Rangers), 1899 v E, W, Ni; 1901 v Ni (4)
Campbell, K. (Liverpool), 1920 v E, W, Ni; (with Partick T), 1921 v W, Ni; 1922 v W, Ni, E (8)
Campbell, P. (Rangers), 1878 v W; 1879 v W (2)
Campbell, P. (Morton), 1898 v W (1)
Campbell, R. (Falkirk), 1947 v Bel, L; (with Chelsea), 1950 v Sw, P, F (5)
Campbell, W. (Morton), 1947 v Ni; 1948 v E, Bel, Sw, F (5)
Carabine, J. (Third Lanark), 1938 v Ho; 1939 v E, Ni (3)
Carr, W. M. (Coventry C), 1970 v Ni, W, E; 1971 v D; 1972 v Pe; 1973 v D (sub) (6)
Cassidy, J. (Celtic), 1921 v W, Ni; 1923 v Ni; 1924 v W (4)
Chalmers, S. (Celtic), 1965 v W, Fi; 1966 v P (sub), Br; 1967 v Ni (5)
Chalmers, W. (Rangers), 1885 v Ni (1)
Chalmers, W. S. (Queen's Park), 1929 v Ni (1)
Chambers, T. (Hearts), 1894 v W (1)
Chaplin, G. D. (Dundee), 1908 v W (1)
Cheyne, A. G. (Aberdeen), 1929 v E, N, G, Ho; 1930 v F (5)
Christie, A. J. (Queen's Park), 1898 v W; 1899 v E, Ni (3)
Christie, R. M. (Queen's Park), 1884 v E (1)
Clark, J. (Celtic), 1966 v Br; 1967 v W, Ni, USSR (4)
Clark, R. B. (Aberdeen), 1968 v W, Ho; 1970 v Ni; 1971 v W, Ni, E, D, P, USSR; 1972 v Bel, Ni, W, E, Cz, Br; 1973 v D, E (17)
Clarke, S. (Chelsea), 1988 v H, Bel, Bul, S.Ar, Ma; 1994 v Ho (6)
Cleland, J. (Royal Albert), 1891 v Ni (1)
Clements, R. (Leith Ath), 1891 v Ni (1)
Clunas, W. L. (Sunderland), 1924 v E; 1926 v W (2)
Collier, W. (Raith R), 1922 v W (1)
Collins, J. (Hibernian), 1988 v S.Ar; 1990 v EG, Pol (sub), Ma (sub); (with Celtic), 1991 v Sw (sub), Bul (sub); 1992 v Ni (sub), Fi; 1993 v P, Ma, G, P, Es (2); 1994 v Sw, Ho (sub), A, Ho (18)
Collins, R. Y. (Celtic), 1951 v W, Ni, A; 1955 v Y, A, H; 1956 v Ni, W; 1957 v E, W, Sp (2), Sw, WG; 1958 v Ni, W, Sw, H, Pol, Y, F, Par; (with Everton), 1959 v E, W, Ni, WG, Ho, P; (with Leeds U), 1965 v E, Pol, Sp (31)
Collins, T. (Hearts), 1909 v W (1)
Colman, D. (Aberdeen), 1911 v E, W, Ni; 1913 v Ni (4)
Colquhoun, E. P. (Sheffield U), 1972 v P, Ho, Pe, Y, Cz, Br; 1973 v D (2), E (9)
Colquhoun, J. (Hearts), 1988 v S.Ar (sub) (1)
Combe, J. R. (Hibernian), 1948 v E, Bel, Sw (3)
Conn, A. (Hearts), 1956 v A (1)
Conn, A. (Tottenham H), 1975 v Ni (sub), E (2)
Connachan, E. D. (Dunfermline Ath), 1962 v Cz, U (2)
Connelly, G. (Celtic), 1974 v Cz, WG (2)
Connolly, J. (Everton), 1973 v Sw (1)
Connor, J. (Airdrieonians), 1886 v Ni (1)
Connor, J. (Sunderland), 1930 v F; 1932 v Ni; 1934 v E; 1935 v Ni (4)
Connor, R. (Dundee), 1986 v Ho; (with Aberdeen), 1988 v S.Ar (sub); 1989 v E; 1991 v R (4)
Cook, W. L. (Bolton W), 1934 v E; 1935 v W, Ni (3)
Cooke, C. (Dundee), 1966 v W, I; (with Chelsea), P, Br; 1968 v E, Ho; 1969 v W, Ni, A, WG (sub), Cy (2); 1970 v A; 1971 v Bel; 1975 v Sp, P (16)
Cooper, D. (Rangers), 1980 v Pe, A (sub); 1984 v W, E; 1985 v Y, Ic, Sp (2), W; 1986 v W (sub), EG, Aus (2), Ho, WG (sub), U (sub); 1987 v Bul, L, Ei, Br; (with Motherwell), 1990 v N, Eg (22)
Cormack, P. B. (Hibernian), 1966 v Br; 1969 v D (sub); 1970 v Ei, WG; (with Nottingham F), 1971 v D (sub), W, P, E; 1972 v Ho (sub) (9)
Cowan, J. (Aston Villa), 1896 v E; 1897 v E; 1898 v E (3)
Cowan, J. (Morton), 1948 v Bel, Sw; F; 1949 v E, W, F; 1950 v E, W, Ni, Sw, P, F; 1951 v E, W, Ni, A (2), D, F, Bel; 1952 v Ni, W, USA, D, Se (25)
Cowan, W. D. (Newcastle U), 1924 v E (1)
Cowie, D. (Dundee), 1953 v E, Se; 1954 v Ni, W, Fi, N, A, U; 1955 v W, Ni, A, H; 1956 v W, A; 1957 v Ni, W; 1958 v H, Pol, Y, Par (20)
Cox, C. J. (Hearts), 1948 v F (1)
Cox, S. (Rangers), 1949 v E, F; 1950 v E, F, W, Ni, Sw, P; 1951 v E, D, F, Bel, A; 1952 v Ni, W, USA, D, Se; 1953 v W, Ni, E; 1954 v W, Ni, E (24)
Craig, A. (Motherwell), 1929 v N, Ho; 1932 v E (3)
Craig, J. (Celtic), 1977 v Se (sub) (1)
Craig, J. P. (Celtic), 1968 v W (1)
Craig, T. (Rangers), 1927 v Ni; 1928 v Ni; 1929 v N, G, Ho; 1930 v Ni, E, W (8)
Craig, T. B. (Newcastle U), 1976 v Sw (1)
Crapnell, J. (Airdrieonians), 1929 v E, N, G; 1930 v F; 1931 v Ni, Sw; 1932 v E, F; 1933 v Ni (9)
Crawford, D. (St Mirren), 1894 v W, Ni; 1900 v W (3)
Crawford, J. (Queen's Park), 1932 v F, Ni; 1933 v E, W, Ni (5)
Crerand, P. T. (Celtic), 1961 v Ei (2), Cz; 1962 v Ni, W, E, Cz (2), U; 1963 v W, Ni; (with Manchester U), 1964 v Ni; 1965 v E, Pol, Fi; 1966 v Pol (16)
Cringan, W. (Celtic), 1920 v W; 1922 v E, Ni; 1923 v W, E (5)
Crosbie, J. A. (Ayr U), 1920 v W; (with Birmingham), 1922 v E (2)
Croal, J. A. (Falkirk), 1913 v Ni; 1914 v E, W (3)
Cropley, A. J. (Hibernian), 1972 v P, Bel (2)
Cross, J. H. (Third Lanark), 1903 v Ni (1)
Cruickshank, J. (Hearts), 1964 v WG; 1970 v W, E; 1971 v D, Bel; 1976 v R (6)
Crum, J. (Celtic), 1936 v E; 1939 v Ni (2)
Cullen, M. J. (Luton T), 1956 v A (1)
Cumming, D. S. (Middlesbrough), 1938 v E (1)
Cumming, J. (Hearts), 1955 v E, H, P, Y; 1960 v E, Pol, A, H, T (9)
Cummings, G. (Partick T), 1935 v E; 1936 v W, Ni; (with Aston Villa), E; 1937 v G; 1938 v W, Ni, Cz; 1939 v E (9)
Cunningham, A. N. (Rangers), 1920 v Ni; 1921 v W, E; 1922 v Ni; 1923 v E, W; 1924 v E, Ni; 1926 v E, Ni; 1927 v E, W (12)
Cunningham, W. C. (Preston NE), 1954 v N (2), U, Fi, A; 1955 v W, E, H (8)
Curran, H. P. (Wolverhampton W), 1970 v A; 1971 v Ni, E, D, USSR (sub) (5)

Dalglish, K. (Celtic), 1972 v Bel (sub), Ho; 1973 v D (1 + 1 sub), E (2), W, Ni, Sw, Br; 1974 v Cz (2), WG (2), Ni, W, E, Bel, N (sub), Z, Br, Y; 1975 v EG, Sp (sub + 1), Se, P, W, Ni, E, R; 1976 v D (2), R, Sw, Ni, E; 1977 v Fi, Cz, W (2), Se, Ni, E, Ch, Arg, Br; (with Liverpool), 1978 v EG, Cz, W, Bul, Ni (sub), W, E, Pe, Ir, Ho; 1979 v A, N, P, W, Ni, E, Arg, N; 1980 v Pe, A, Bel (2), P, Ni, W, E, Pol, H; 1981 v Se, P, Is; 1982 v Se, Ni, P (sub), Sp, Ho, Ni, W, E, Nz, Br (sub); 1983 v Bel, Sw; 1984 v U, Bel, EG; 1985 v Y, Ic, Sp, W; 1986 v EG, Aus, R; 1987 v Bul (sub), L (102)

Davidson, D. (Queen's Park), 1878 v W; 1879 v W; 1880 v W; 1881 v E, W (5)
Davidson, J. A. (Partick T), 1954 v N (2), A, U; 1955 v W, Ni, E, H (8)
Davidson, S. (Middlesbrough), 1921 v E (1)
Dawson, A. (Rangers), 1980 v Pol (sub), H; 1983 v Ni, Ca (2) (5)
Dawson, J. (Rangers), 1935 v Ni; 1936 v E; 1937 v G, E, W, Ni, A, Cz; 1938 v W, Ho, Ni; 1939 v E, Ni, H (14)
Deans, J. (Celtic), 1975 v EG, Sp (2)
Delaney, J. (Celtic), 1936 v W, Ni; 1937 v G, E, A, Cz; 1938 v Ni; 1939 v W, Ni; (with Manchester U), 1947 v E; 1948 v E, W, Ni (13)
Devine, A. (Falkirk), 1910 v W (1)
Dewar, G. (Dumbarton), 1888 v Ni; 1889 v E (2)
Dewar, N. (Third Lanark), 1932 v E, F; 1933 v W (3)
Dick, J. (West Ham U), 1959 v E (1)
Dickie, M. (Rangers), 1897 v Ni; 1899 v Ni; 1900 v W (3)
Dickson, W. (Dumbarton), 1888 v Ni (1)
Dickson, W. (Kilmarnock), 1970 v Ni, W, E; 1971 v D, USSR (5)
Divers, J. (Celtic), 1895 v W (1)
Divers, J. (Celtic), 1939 v Ni (1)
Docherty, T. H, (Preston NE), 1952 v W; 1953 v E, Se; 1954 v N (2), A, U; 1955 v W, E, H (2), A; 1957 v E, Y, Sp (2), Sw, WG; 1958 v Ni, W, E, Sw; (with Arsenal), 1959 v W, E, Ni (25)
Dodds, D. (Dundee U), 1984 v U (sub), Ni (2)
Dodds, J. (Celtic), 1914 v E, W, Ni (3)
Doig, J. E. (Arbroath), 1887 v Ni; 1889 v Ni; (with Sunderland), 1896 v E; 1899 v E; 1903 v E (5)
Donachie, W. (Manchester C), 1972 v Pe, Ni, E, Y, Cz, Br; 1973 v D, E, W, Ni; 1974 v Ni; 1976 v R, Ni, W, E; 1977 v Fi, Cz, W (2), Se, Ni, E, Ch, Arg, Br; 1978 v EG, W, Bul, W, E, Ir, Ho; 1979 v A, N, P (sub) (35)
Donaldson, A. (Bolton W), 1914 v E, Ni, W; 1920 v E, Ni; 1922 v Ni (6)
Donnachie, J. (Oldham Ath), 1913 v E; 1914 v E, Ni (3)
Dougall, C. (Birmingham C), 1947 v W (1)
Dougall, J. (Preston NE), 1939 v E (1)
Dougan, R. (Hearts), 1950 v Sw (1)
Douglas, A. (Chelsea), 1911 v Ni (1)
Douglas, J. (Renfrew), 1880 v W (1)
Dowds, P. (Celtic), 1892 v Ni (1)
Downie, R. (Third Lanark), 1892 v W (1)
Doyle, D. (Celtic), 1892 v E; 1893 v W; 1894 v E; 1895 v E, Ni; 1897 v E; 1898 v E, Ni (8)
Doyle, J. (Ayr U), 1976 v R (1)
Drummond, J. (Falkirk), 1892 v Ni; (with Rangers), 1894 v Ni; 1895 v Ni, E; 1896 v E, Ni; 1897 v Ni; 1898 v E; 1900 v E; 1901 v E; 1902 v E, W, Ni; 1903 v Ni (14)
Dunbar, M. (Cartvale), 1886 v Ni (1)
Duncan, A. (Hibernian), 1975 v P (sub), W, Ni, E, R; 1976 v D (sub) (6)
Duncan, D. (Derby Co), 1933 v E, W; 1934 v A, W; 1935 v E, W; 1936 v E, W, Ni; 1937 v G, E, W, Ni; 1938 v W (14)
Duncan, D. M. (East Fife), 1948 v Bel, Sw, F (3)
Duncan, J. (Alexandra Ath), 1878 v W; 1882 v W (2)
Duncan, J. (Leicester C), 1926 v W (1)
Duncanson, J. (Rangers), 1947 v Ni (1)
Dunlop, J. (St Mirren), 1890 v W (1)
Dunlop, W. (Liverpool), 1906 v E (1)
Dunn, J. (Hibernian), 1925 v W, Ni; 1927 v Ni; 1928 v Ni, E; (with Everton), 1929 v W (6)
Durie, G. S. (Chelsea), 1988 v Bul (sub); 1989 v I (sub), Cy; 1990 v Y, EG, Eg, Se; 1991 v Sw (sub), Bul (2), USSR (sub), Sm; (with Tottenham H), 1992 v Sw, R, Sm, Ni (sub), Fi, Ca, N (sub), Ho, G; 1993 v Sw, I; 1994 v Sw, I; (with Rangers), Ho (2) (27)
Durrant, I. (Rangers), 1988 v H, Bel, Ma, Sp; 1989 v N (sub); 1993 v Sw (sub), P (sub), I, P (sub); 1994 v I (sub), Ma (11)
Dykes, J. (Hearts), 1938 v Ho; 1939 v Ni (2)

Easson, J. F. (Portsmouth), 1931 v A, Sw; 1934 v W (3)
Ellis, J. (Mossend Swifts), 1892 v Ni (1)
Evans, A. (Aston Villa), 1982 v Ho, Ni, E, Nz (4)
Evans, R. (Celtic), 1949 v E, W, Ni, F; 1950 v W, Ni, Sw, P; 1951 v E, A; 1952 v Ni; 1953 v Se; 1954 v Ni, W, E, N, Fi; 1955 v Ni, P, Y, A, H; 1956 v E, Ni, W, A; 1957 v WG, Sp; 1958 v Ni, W, E, Sw, H, Pol, Y, Par, F; 1959 v E, WG, Ho, P; 1960 v E, Ni, W, Pol; (with Chelsea), 1960 v A, H, T (48)
Ewart, J. (Bradford C), 1921 v E (1)
Ewing, T. (Partick T), 1958 v W, E (2)

Farm, G. N. (Blackpool), 1953 v W, Ni, E, Se; 1954 v Ni, W, E; 1959 v WG, Ho, P (10)
Ferguson, D. (Rangers), 1988 v Ma, Co (sub) (2)
Ferguson, D. (Dundee U), 1992 v US (sub), Ca, Ho (sub); 1993 v G (4)
Ferguson, I. (Rangers), 1989 v I, Cy (sub), F; 1993 v Ma (sub), Es; 1994 v Ma, A (sub), Ho (sub) (8)
Ferguson, J. (Vale of Leven), 1874 v E; 1876 v E, W; 1877 v E, W; 1878 v W (6)
Ferguson, R. (Kilmarnock), 1966 v W, E, Ho, P, Br; 1967 v W, Ni (7)
Fernie, W. (Celtic), 1954 v Fi, A, U; 1955 v W, Ni; 1957 v E, Ni, W, Y; 1958 v W, Sw, Par (12)
Findlay, R. (Kilmarnock), 1898 v W (1)
Fitchie, T. T. (Woolwich Arsenal), 1905 v W; 1906 v W, Ni; (with Queen's Park), 1907 v W (4)
Flavell, R. (Airdrieonians), 1947 v Bel, L (2)
Fleck, R. (Norwich C), 1990 v Arg, Se, Br (sub); 1991 v USSR (4)
Fleming, C. (East Fife), 1954 v Ni (1)
Fleming, J. W. (Rangers), 1929 v G, Ho; 1930 v E (3)
Fleming, R. (Morton), 1886 v Ni (1)
Forbes, A. R. (Sheffield U), 1947 v Bel, L, E; 1948 v W, Ni; (with Arsenal), 1950 v E, P, F; 1951 v W, Ni, A; 1952 v W, D, Se (14)
Forbes, J. (Vale of Leven), 1884 v E, W, Ni; 1887 v W, E (5)
Ford, D. (Hearts), 1974 v Cz (sub), WG (sub), W (3)
Forrest, J. (Rangers), 1966 v W, I; (with Aberdeen), 1971 v Bel (sub), D, USSR (5)
Forrest, J. (Motherwell), 1958 v E (1)
Forsyth, A. (Partick T), 1972 v Y, Cz, Br; 1973 v D; (with Manchester U), E; 1975 v Sp, Ni (sub), R, EG; 1976 v D (10)
Forsyth, C. (Kilmarnock), 1964 v E; 1965 v W, Ni, Fi (4)
Forsyth, T. (Motherwell), 1971 v D; (with Rangers), 1974 v Cz; 1976 v Sw, Ni, W, E; 1977 v Fi, Se, W, Ni, E, Ch, Arg, Br; 1978 v Cz, W, Ni, W (sub), E, Pe, Ir (sub), Ho (22)
Foyers, R. (St Bernards), 1893 v W; 1894 v W (2)
Fraser, D. M. (WBA), 1968 v Ho; 1969 v Cy (2)
Fraser, J. (Moffat), 1891 v Ni (1)
Fraser, M. J. E. (Queen's Park), 1880 v W; 1882 v W, E; 1883 v W, E (5)
Fraser, J. (Dundee), 1907 v Ni (1)
Fraser, W. (Sunderland), 1955 v W, Ni (2)
Fulton, W. (Abercorn), 1884 v Ni (1)
Fyfe, J. H. (Third Lanark), 1895 v W (1)

Gabriel, J. (Everton), 1961 v W; 1964 v N (sub) (2)
Gallacher, H. K. (Airdrieonians), 1924 v Ni; 1925 v E, W, Ni; 1926 v W; (with Newcastle U), 1926 v E, Ni; 1927 v E, W, Ni; 1928 v E, W; 1929 v E, W, Ni; 1930 v W, Ni, F; (with Chelsea), 1934 v E; (with Derby Co), 1935 v E (20)

Gallacher, K. W. (Dundee U), 1988 v Co, E (sub); 1989 v N, I; (with Coventry C), 1991 v Sm; 1992 v R (sub), Sm (sub), Ni (sub), N (sub), Ho (sub), G (sub), C; 1993 v Sw (sub), P; (with Blackburn R), P, Es (2); 1994 v I, Ma (19)
Gallacher, P. (Sunderland), 1935 v Ni (1)
Galloway, M. (Celtic), 1992 v R (1)
Galt, J. H. (Rangers), 1908 v W, Ni (2)
Gardiner, I. (Motherwell), 1958 v W (1)
Gardner, D. R. (Third Lanark), 1897 v W (1)
Gardner, R. (Queen's Park), 1872 v E; 1873 v E; (with Clydesdale), 1874 v E; 1875 v E; 1878 v E (5)
Gemmell, T. (St Mirren), 1955 v P, Y (2)
Gemmell, T. (Celtic), 1966 v E; 1967 v W, Ni, E, USSR; 1968 v Ni, E; 1969 v W, Ni, E, D, A, WG, Cy; 1970 v E, Ei, WG; 1971 v Bel (18)
Gemmill, A. (Derby Co), 1971 v Bel; 1972 v P, Ho, Pe, Ni, W, E; 1976 v D, R, Ni, W, E; 1977 v Fi, Cz, W (2), Ni (sub), E (sub), Ch (sub), Arg, Br; 1978 v EG (sub); (with Nottingham F), Bul, Ni, W, E (sub), Pe (sub), Ir, Ho; 1979 v A, N, P, N; (with Birmingham C), 1980 v A, P, Ni, W, E, H; 1981 v Se, P, Is, Ni (43)
Gibb, W. (Clydesdale), 1873 v E (1)
Gibson, D. W. (Leicester C), 1963 v A, N, Ei, Sp; 1964 v Ni; 1965 v W, Fi (7)
Gibson, J. D. (Partick T), 1926 v E; 1927 v E, W, Ni; (with Aston Villa), 1928 v E, W; 1930 v W, Ni (8)
Gibson, N. (Rangers), 1895 v E, Ni; 1896 v E, Ni; 1897 v E, Ni; 1898 v E; 1899 v E, W, Ni; 1900 v E, Ni; 1901 v W; (with Partick T), 1905 v Ni (14)
Gilchrist, J. E. (Celtic), 1922 v E (1)
Gilhooley, M. (Hull C), 1922 v W (1)
Gillespie, G. (Rangers), 1880 v W; 1881 v E, W; 1882 v E; (with Queen's Park), 1886 v W; 1890 v W; 1891 v Ni (7)
Gillespie, G. T. (Liverpool), 1988 v Bel, Bul, Sp; 1989 v N, F, Ch; 1990 v Y, EG, Eg, Pol, Ma, Br (sub); 1991 v Bul (13)
Gillespie, Jas (Third Lanark), 1898 v W (1)
Gillespie, John (Queen's Park), 1896 v W (1)
Gillespie, R. (Queen's Park), 1927 v W; 1931 v W; 1932 v F; 1933 v E (4)
Gillick, T. (Everton), 1937 v A, Cz; 1939 v W, Ni, H (5)
Gilmour, J. (Dundee), 1931 v W (1)
Gilzean, A. J. (Dundee), 1964 v W, E, N, WG; 1965 v Ni, (with Tottenham H), Sp; 1966 v Ni, W, Pol, I; 1968 v W; 1969 v W, E, WG, Cy (2), A (sub); 1970 v Ni, E (sub), WG, A; 1971 v P (22)
Glavin, R. (Celtic), 1977 v Se (1)
Glen, A. (Aberdeen), 1956 v E, Ni (2)
Glen, R. (Renton), 1895 v W; 1896 v W; (with Hibernian), 1900 v Ni (3)
Goram, A. L. (Oldham Ath), 1986 v EG (sub), R, Ho; 1987 v Br; (with Hibernian) 1989 v Y, I; 1990 v EG, Pol, Ma; 1991 v R, Sw, Bul (2), USSR, Sm; (with Rangers), 1992 v Sw, R, Sm, Fi, N, Ho, G, C; 1993 v Sw, P, I, Ma, P; 1994 v Ho (29)
Gordon, J. E. (Rangers), 1912 v E, Ni; 1913 v E, Ni, W; 1914 v E, Ni; 1920 v W, E, Ni (10)
Gossland, J. (Rangers), 1884 v Ni (1)
Goudle, J. (Abercorn), 1884 v Ni (1)
Gough, C. R. (Dundee U), 1983 v Sw, Ni, W, E, Ca (3); 1984 v U, Bel, EG, Ni, W, E, F; 1985 v Sp, E, Ic; 1986 v W, EG, Aus, Is, R, E, D, WG, U; (with Tottenham H), 1987 v Bul, L, Ei (2), Bel, E, Br; 1988 v H; (with Rangers), S.Ar, Sp, Co, E; 1989 v Y, I, Cy, F, Cy; 1990 v F, Arg, EG, Eg, Pol, Ma, Cr; 1991 v USSR, Bul; 1992 v Sm, Ni, Ca, N, Ho, G, C; 1993 v Sw, P (61)
Gourlay, J. (Cambuslang), 1886 v Ni; 1888 v W (2)
Govan, J. (Hibernian), 1948 v E, W, Bel, Sw, F; 1949 v Ni (6)
Gow, D. R. (Rangers), 1888 v E (1)
Gow, J. J. (Queen's Park), 1885 v E (1)
Gow, J. R. (Rangers), 1888 v Ni (1)
Graham, A. (Leeds U), 1978 v EG (sub); 1979 v A (sub), N, W, Ni, E, Arg, N; 1980 v A; 1981 v W (10)
Graham, G. (Arsenal), 1972 v P, Ho, Ni, Y, Cz, Br; 1973 v D (2); (with Manchester U), E, W, Ni, Br (sub) (12)
Graham, J. (Annbank), 1884 v Ni (1)
Graham, J. A. (Arsenal), 1921 v Ni (1)
Grant, J. (Hibernian), 1959 v W, Ni (2)
Grant, P. (Celtic), 1989 v E (sub), Ch (2)
Gray, A. (Hibernian), 1903 v Ni (1)
Gray, A. M. (Aston Villa), 1976 v R, Sw; 1977 v Fi, Cz; 1979 v A, N; (with Wolverhampton W), 1980 v P, E (sub); 1981 v Se, P, Is (sub), Ni; 1982 v Se (sub), Ni (sub); 1983 v Ni, W, E, Ca (1 + 1 sub); (with Everton), 1985 v Ic (20)
Gray, D. (Rangers), 1929 v W, Ni, G, Ho; 1930 v W, E, Ni; 1931 v W; 1933 v W, Ni (10)
Gray, E. (Leeds U), 1969 v E, Cy; 1970 v WG, A; 1971 v W, Ni; 1972 v Bel, Ho; 1976 v W, E; 1977 v Fi, W (12)
Gray, F. T. (Leeds U), 1976 v Sw; 1979 v N, P, W, Ni, E, Arg (sub); (with Nottingham F), 1980 v Bel (sub); 1981 v Se, P, Is, Ni, Is, W; (with Leeds U), Ni, E; 1982 v Se, Ni, P, Sp, Ho, W, Nz, Br, USSR; 1983 v EG, Sw, Bel, Sw, W, E, Ca (32)
Gray, W. (Pollokshields Ath), 1886 v E (1)
Green, A. (Blackpool), 1971 v Bel (sub), P (sub), Ni, E; (with Newcastle U), 1972 v W, E (sub) (6)
Greig, J. (Rangers), 1964 v E, WG; 1965 v W, Ni, E, Fi (2), Sp, Pol; 1966 v Ni, W, E, Pol, I (2), P, Ho, Br; 1967 v W, Ni, E; 1968 v Ni, W, E, Ho; 1969 v W, Ni, E, D, A, WG, Cy (2); 1970 v W, E, Ei, WG, A; 1971 v D, Bel, W (sub), Ni, E; 1976 v D (44)
Groves, W. (Hibernian), 1888 v W; (with Celtic), 1889 v Ni; 1890 v E (3)
Guilliland, W. (Queen's Park), 1891 v W; 1892 v Ni; 1894 v E; 1895 v E (4)
Gunn, B. (Norwich C), 1990 v Eg; 1993 v Es (2); 1994 v Sw, I, Ho (sub) (6)

Haddock, H. (Clyde), 1955 v E, H (2), P, Y; 1958 v E (6)
Haddow, D. (Rangers), 1894 v E (1)
Haffey, F. (Celtic), 1960 v E; 1961 v E (2)
Hamilton, A. (Queen's Park), 1885 v E, W; 1886 v E; 1888 v E (4)
Hamilton, A. W. (Dundee), 1962 v Cz, U, W, E; 1963 v W, Ni, E, A, N, Ei; 1964 v Ni, W, E, N, WG; 1965 v Ni, W, E, Fi (2), Pol, Sp; 1966 v Pol, Ni (24)
Hamilton, G. (Aberdeen), 1947 v Ni; 1951 v Bel, A; 1954 v N (2) (5)
Hamilton, G. (Port Glasgow Ath), 1906 v Ni (1)
Hamilton, J. (Queen's Park), 1892 v W; 1893 v E, Ni (3)
Hamilton, J. (St Mirren), 1924 v Ni (1)
Hamilton, R. C. (Rangers), 1899 v E, W, Ni; 1900 v W; 1901 v E, Ni; 1902 v W, Ni; 1903 v E; 1904 v Ni; (with Dundee), 1911 v W (11)
Hamilton, T. (Hurlford), 1891 v Ni (1)
Hamilton, T. (Rangers), 1932 v E (1)
Hamilton, W. M. (Hibernian), 1965 v Fi (1)
Hannah, A. B. (Renton), 1888 v W (1)
Hannah, J. (Third Lanark), 1889 v W (1)
Hansen, A. D. (Liverpool), 1979 v W, Arg; 1980 v Bel, P; 1981 v Se, P, Is; 1982 v Se, Ni, P, Sp, Ni (sub), W, E, Nz, Br, USSR; 1983 v EG, Sw, Bel, Sw; 1985 v W (sub); 1986 v R (sub); 1987 v Ei (2), L (26)
Hansen, J. (Partick T), 1972 v Bel (sub), Y (sub) (2)
Harkness, J. D. (Queen's Park), 1927 v E, Ni; 1928 v E; (with Hearts), 1929 v W, E, Ni; 1930 v E, W; 1932 v W, F; 1934 v Ni, W (12)
Harper, J. M. (Aberdeen), 1973 v D (1 + 1 sub); (with Hibernian), 1976 v D; (with Aberdeen), 1978 v Ir (sub) (4)
Harper, W. (Hibernian), 1923 v E, Ni, W; 1924 v E, Ni, W; 1925 v E, Ni, W; (with Arsenal), 1926 v E, Ni (11)

Harris, J. (Partick T), 1921 v W, Ni (2)
Harris, N. (Newcastle U), 1924 v E (1)
Harrower, W. (Queen's Park), 1882 v E; 1884 v Ni; 1886 v W (3)
Hartford, R. A. (WBA), 1972 v Pe, W (sub), E, Y, Cz, Br; (with Manchester C), 1976 v D, R, Ni (sub); 1977 v Cz (sub), W (sub), Se, W, Ni, E, Ch, Arg, Br; 1978 v EG, Cz, W, Bul, W, E, Pe, Ir, Ho; 1979 v A, N, P, W, Ni, E, Arg, N; (with Everton), 1980 v Pe, Bel; 1981 v Ni (sub), Is, W, Ni, E; 1982 v Se; (with Manchester C), Ni, P, Sp, Ni, W, E, Br (50)
Harvey, D. (Leeds U), 1973 v D; 1974 v Cz, WG, Ni, W, E, Bel, Z, Br, Y; 1975 v EG, Sp (2); 1976 v D (2); 1977 v Fi (sub) (16)
Hastings, A. C. (Sunderland), 1936 v Ni; 1938 v Ni (2)
Haughney, M. (Celtic), 1954 v E (1)
Hay, D. (Celtic), 1970 v Ni, W, E; 1971 v D, Bel, W, P, Ni; 1972 v P, Bel, Ho; 1973 v W, Ni, E, Sw, Br; 1974 v Cz (2), WG, Ni, W, E, Bel, N, Z, Br, Y (27)
Hay, J. (Celtic), 1905 v Ni; 1909 v Ni; 1910 v W, Ni, E; 1911 v Ni, E; (with Newcastle U), 1912 v E, W; 1914 v E, Ni (11)
Hegarty, P. (Dundee U), 1979 v W, Ni, E, Arg, N (sub); 1980 v W, E; 1983 v Ni (8)
Heggie, C. (Rangers), 1886 v Ni (1)
Henderson, G. H. (Rangers), 1904 v Ni (1)
Henderson, J. G. (Portsmouth), 1953 v Se; 1954 v Ni, E, N; 1956 v W; (with Arsenal), 1959 v W, Ni (7)
Henderson, W. (Rangers), 1963 v W, Ni, E, A, N, Ei, Sp; 1964 v W, Ni, E, N, WG; 1965 v Fi, Pol, E, Sp; 1966 v Ni, W, Pol, I, Ho; 1967 v W, Ni; 1968 v Ho; 1969 v Ni, E, Cy; 1970 v Ei; 1971 v P (29)
Hendry, E. C. J. (Blackburn R), 1993 v Es (2); 1994 v Ma, Ho, A, Ho (6)
Hepburn, J. (Alloa Ath), 1891 v W (1)
Hepburn, R. (Ayr U), 1932 v Ni (1)
Herd, A. C. (Hearts), 1935 v Ni (1)
Herd, D. G. (Arsenal), 1959 v E, W, Ni; 1961 v E, Cz (5)
Herd, G. (Clyde), 1958 v E; 1960 v H, T; 1961 v W, Ni (5)
Herriot, J. (Birmingham C), 1969 v Ni, E, D, Cy (2), W (sub); 1970 v Ei (sub), WG (8)
Hewie, J. D. (Charlton Ath), 1956 v E, A; 1957 v E, Ni, W, Y, Sp (2), Sw, WG; 1958 v H, Pol, Y, F; 1959 v Ho, P; 1960 v Ni, W, Pol (19)
Higgins, A. (Kilmarnock), 1885 v Ni (1)
Higgins, A. (Newcastle U), 1910 v E, Ni; 1911 v E, Ni (4)
Highet, T. C. (Queen's Park), 1875 v E; 1876 v E, W; 1878 v E (4)
Hill, D. (Rangers), 1881 v E, W; 1882 v W (3)
Hill, D. A. (Third Lanark), 1906 v Ni (1)
Hill, F. R. (Aberdeen), 1930 v F; 1931 v W, Ni (3)
Hill, J. (Hearts), 1891 v E; 1892 v W (2)
Hogg, G (Hearts), 1896 v E, Ni (2)
Hogg, J. (Ayr U), 1922 v Ni (1)
Hogg, R. M. (Celtic), 1937 v Cz (1)
Holm, A. H. (Queen's Park), 1882 v W; 1883 v E, W (3)
Holt, D. D. (Hearts), 1963 v A, N, Ei, Sp; 1964 v WG (sub) (5)
Holton, J. A. (Manchester U), 1973 v W, Ni, E, Sw, Br; 1974 v Cz, WG, Ni, W, E, N, Z, Br, Y; 1975 v EG (15)
Hope, R. (WBA), 1968 v Ho; 1969 v D (2)
Houliston, W. (Queen of the South), 1949 v E, Ni, F (3)
Houston, S. M. (Manchester U), 1976 v D (1)
Howden, W. (Partick T), 1905 v Ni (1)
Howe, R. (Hamilton A), 1929 v N, Ho (2)
Howie, J. (Newcastle U), 1905 v E; 1906 v E; 1908 v E (3)
Howie, H. (Hibernian), 1949 v W (1)
Howieson, J. (St Mirren), 1927 v Ni (1)
Hughes, J. (Celtic), 1965 v Pol, Sp; 1966 v Ni, I (2); 1968 v E; 1969 v A; 1970 v Ei (8)
Hughes, W. (Sunderland), 1975 v Se (sub) (1)
Humphries, W. (Motherwell), 1952 v Se (1)
Hunter, A. (Kilmarnock), 1972 v Pe, Y; (with Celtic), 1973 v E; 1974 v Cz (4)
Hunter, J. (Dundee), 1909 v W (1)
Hunter, J. (Third Lanark), 1874 v E; (with Eastern), 1875 v E; (with Third Lanark), 1876 v E; 1877 v W (4)
Hunter, R. (St Mirren), 1890 v Ni (1)
Hunter, W. (Motherwell), 1960 v H, T; 1961 v W (3)
Husband, J. (Partick T), 1947 v W (1)
Hutchison, T. (Coventry C), 1974 v Cz (2), WG (2), Ni, W, Bel (sub), N, Z (sub), Y (sub); 1975 v EG, Sp (2), P, E (sub), R (sub); 1976 v D (17)
Hutton, J. (Aberdeen), 1923 v E, W, Ni; 1924 v Ni; 1926 v W, E, Ni; (with Blackburn R), 1927 v Ni; 1928 v W, Ni (10)
Hutton, J. (St Bernards), 1887 v Ni (1)
Hyslop, T. (Stoke C), 1896 v E; (with Rangers), 1897 v E (2)

Imlach, J. J. S. (Nottingham F), 1958 v H, Pol, Y, F (4)
Imrie, W. N. (St Johnstone), 1929 v N, G (2)
Inglis, J. (Kilmarnock Ath), 1884 v Ni (1)
Inglis, J. (Rangers), 1883 v E, W (2)
Irons, J. H. (Queen's Park), 1900 v W (1)
Irvine, B. (Aberdeen), 1991 v R; 1993 v G, Es (2); 1994 v Sw, I, Ma, A, Ho (9)

Jackson, A. (Cambuslang), 1886 v W; 1888 v Ni (2)
Jackson, A. (Aberdeen), 1925 v E, W, Ni; (with Huddersfield T), 1926 v E, W, Ni; 1927 v W, Ni; 1928 v E, W; 1929 v E, W, Ni; 1930 v E, W, Ni, F (17)
Jackson, C. (Rangers), 1975 v Se, P (sub), W; 1976 v D, R, Ni, W, E (8)
Jackson, J. (Partick T), 1931 v A, I, Sw; 1933 v E; (with Chelsea), 1934 v E; 1935 v E; 1936 v W, Ni (8)
Jackson, T. A. (St Mirren), 1904 v W, E, Ni; 1905 v W; 1907 v W, Ni (6)
James, A. W. (Preston NE), 1926 v W; 1928 v E; 1929 v E, Ni; (with Arsenal), 1930 v E, W, Ni; 1933 v W (8)
Jardine, A. (Rangers), 1971 v D (sub); 1972 v P, Bel, Ho; 1973 v E, Sw, Br; 1974 v Cz (2), WG (2), Ni, W, E, Bel, N, Z, Br, Y; 1975 v EG, Sp (2), Se, P, W, Ni, E; 1977 v Se (sub), Ch (sub), Br (sub); 1978 v Cz, W, Ni, Ir; 1980 v Pe, A, Bel (2) (38)
Jarvie, A. (Airdrieonians), 1971 v P (sub), Ni (sub), E (sub) (3)
Jenkinson, T. (Hearts), 1887 v Ni (1)
Jess, E. (Aberdeen), 1993 v I (sub), Ma; 1994 v Sw (sub), I, Ho (sub), A, Ho (sub) (7)
Johnston, L. H. (Clyde), 1948 v Bel, Sw (2)
Johnston, M. (Watford), 1984 v W (sub), E (sub), F; 1985 v Y; (with Celtic), Ic, Sp (2), W; 1986 v EG; 1987 v Bul, Ei (2), L; (with Nantes), 1988 v H, Bel, L, S.Ar, Sp, Co, E; 1989 v N, Y, I, Cy, F, Cy, E, Ch (sub); (with Rangers), 1990 v F, N, EG, Pol, Ma, Cr, Se, Br; 1992 v Sw, Sm (sub) (38)
Johnston, R. (Sunderland), 1938 v Cz (1)
Johnston, W. (Rangers), 1966 v W, E, Pol, Ho; 1968 v W, E; 1969 v Ni (sub); 1970 v Ni; 1971 v D; (with WBA), 1977 v Se, W (sub), Ni, E, Ch, Arg, Br; 1978 v EG, Cz, W (2), E, Pe (22)
Johnstone, D. (Rangers), 1973 v W, Ni, E, Sw, Br; 1975 v EG (sub), Se (sub); 1976 v Sw, Ni (sub), E (sub); 1978 v Bul (sub), Ni, W; 1980 v Bel (14)
Johnstone, J. (Abercorn), 1888 v W (1)
Johnstone, J. (Celtic), 1965 v W, Fi; 1966 v E; 1967 v W, USSR; 1968 v W; 1969 v A, WG; 1970 v E, WG; 1971 v D, E; 1972 v P, Bel, Ho, Ni, E (sub); 1974 v W, E, Bel, N; 1975 v EG, Sp (23)
Johnstone, Jas (Kilmarnock), 1894 v W (1)
Johnstone, J. A. (Hearts), 1930 v W; 1933 v W, Ni (3)

Johnstone, R. (Hibernian), 1951 v E, D, F; 1952 v Ni, E; 1953 v E, Se; 1954 v W, E, N, Fi; 1955 v Ni, H; (with Manchester C), 1955 v E; 1956 v E, Ni, W (17)
Johnstone, W. (Third Lanark), 1887 v Ni; 1889 v W; 1890 v E (3)
Jordan, J. (Leeds U), 1973 v E (sub), Sw (sub), Br; 1974 v Cz (sub + 1), WG (sub), Ni (sub), W, E, Bel, N, Z, Br, Y; 1975 v EG, Sp (2); 1976 v Ni, W, E; 1977 v Cz, W, Ni, E; 1978 v EG, Cz, W; (with Manchester U), Bul, Ni, E, Pe, Ir, Ho; 1979 v A, P, W (sub), Ni, E, N; 1980 v Bel, Ni (sub), W, E, Pol; 1981 v Is, W, E; (with AC Milan), 1982 v Se, Ho, W, E, USSR (52)

Kay, J. L. (Queen's Park), 1880 v E; 1882 v E, W; 1883 v E, W; 1884 v W (6)
Keillor, A. (Montrose), 1891 v W; 1892 v Ni; (with Dundee), 1894 v Ni; 1895 v W; 1896 v W; 1897 v W (6)
Keir, L. (Dumbarton), 1885 v W; 1886 v Ni; 1887 v E, W; 1888 v E (5)
Kelly, H. T. (Blackpool), 1952 v USA (1)
Kelly, J. (Renton), 1888 v E; (with Celtic), 1889 v E; 1890 v E; 1892 v E; 1893 v E, Ni; 1894 v W; 1896 v Ni (8)
Kelly, J. C. (Barnsley), 1949 v W, Ni (2)
Kelso, R. (Renton), 1885 v W, Ni; 1886 v W; 1887 v E, W; 1888 v E, Ni; (with Dundee), 1898 v Ni (8)
Kelso, T. (Dundee), 1914 v W (1)
Kennaway, J. (Celtic), 1934 v A (1)
Kennedy, A. (Eastern), 1875 v E; 1876 v E, W; (with Third Lanark), 1878 v E; 1882 v W; 1884 v W (6)
Kennedy, J. (Celtic), 1964 v W, E, WG; 1965 v W, Ni, Fi (6)
Kennedy, J. (Hibernian), 1897 v W (1)
Kennedy, S. (Aberdeen), 1978 v Bul, W, E, Pe, Ho; 1979 v A, P; 1982 v P (sub) (8)
Kennedy, S. (Partick T), 1905 v W (1)
Kennedy, S. (Rangers), 1975 v Se, P, W, Ni, E (5)
Ker, G. (Queen's Park), 1880 v E; 1881 v E, W; 1882 v W, E (5)
Ker, W. (Granville), 1872 v E; (with Queen's Park), 1873 v E (2)
Kerr, A. (Partick T), 1955 v A, H (2)
Kerr, P. (Hibernian), 1924 v Ni (1)
Key, G. (Hearts), 1902 v Ni (1)
Key, W. (Queen's Park), 1907 v Ni (1)
King, A. (Hearts), 1896 v E, W; (with Celtic), 1897 v Ni; 1898 v Ni; 1899 v Ni, W (6)
King, J. (Hamilton A), 1933 v Ni; 1934 v Ni (2)
King, W. S. (Queen's Park), 1929 v W (1)
Kinloch, J. D. (Partick T), 1922 v Ni (1)
Kinnaird, A. F. (Wanderers), 1873 v E (1)
Kinnear, D. (Rangers), 1938 v Cz (1)

Lambie, J. A. (Queen's Park), 1886 v Ni; 1887 v Ni; 1888 v E (3)
Lambie, W. A. (Queen's Park), 1892 v Ni; 1893 v W; 1894 v E; 1895 v E, Ni; 1896 v E, Ni; 1897 v E, Ni (9)
Lamont, D. (Pilgrims), 1885 v Ni (1)
Lang, A. (Dumbarton), 1880 v W (1)
Lang, J. J. (Clydesdale), 1876 v W; (with Third Lanark), 1878 v W (2)
Latta, A. (Dumbarton), 1888 v W; 1889 v E (2)
Law, D. (Huddersfield T), 1959 v W, Ni, Ho, P; 1960 v Ni, W; (with Manchester C), 1960 v E, Pol, A; 1961 v E, Ni; (with Torino), 1962 v Cz (2), E; (with Manchester U), 1963 v W, Ni, E, A, N, Ei, Sp; 1964 v W, E, N, WG; 1965 v W, Ni, E, Fi (2), Pol, Sp; 1966 v Ni, E, Pol; 1967 v W, E, USSR; 1968 v Ni; 1969 v Ni, A, WG; 1972 v Pe, Ni, W, E, Y, Cz, Br; (with Manchester C), 1974 v Cz (2), WG (2), Ni, Z (55)
Law, G. (Rangers), 1910 v E, Ni, W (3)
Law, T. (Chelsea), 1928 v E; 1930 v E (2)

Lawrence, J. (Newcastle U), 1911 v E (1)
Lawrence, T. (Liverpool), 1963 v Ei; 1969 v W, WG (3)
Lawson, D. (St Mirren), 1923 v E (1)
Leckie, R. (Queen's Park), 1872 v E (1)
Leggat, G. (Aberdeen), 1956 v E; 1957 v W; 1958 v Ni, H, Pol, Y, Par; (with Fulham), 1959 v E, W, Ni, WG, Ho; 1960 v E, Ni, W, Pol, A, H (18)
Leighton, J. (Aberdeen), 1983 v EG, Sw, Bel, Sw, W, E, Ca (2); 1984 v U, Bel, Ni, W, E, F; 1985 v Y, Ic, Sp (2), W, E, Ic; 1986 v W, EG, Aus (2), Is, D, WG, U; 1987 v Bul, Ei (2), L, Bel, E; 1988 v H, Bel, Bul, L, S.Ar, Ma, Sp; (with Manchester U), Co, E; 1989 v N, Cy, F, Cy, E, Ch; 1990 v Y, F, N, Arg, Ma (sub, Cr, Se, Br; (with Hibernian), 1994 v Ma, A, Ho (61)
Lennie, W. (Aberdeen), 1908 v W, Ni (2)
Lennox, R. (Celtic), 1967 v Ni, E, USSR; 1968 v W, L; 1969 v D, A, WG, Cy (sub); 1970 v W (sub) (10)
Leslie, L. G. (Airdrieonians), 1961 v W, Ni, Ei (2), Cz (5)
Levein, C. (Hearts), 1990 v Arg, EG, Eg (sub), Pol, Ma (sub), Se; 1992 v R, Sm; 1993 v P, G, P; 1994 v Sw, Ho (13)
Liddell, W. (Liverpool), 1947 v W, Ni; 1948 v E, W, Ni; 1950 v E, W, P, F; 1951 v W, Ni, E, A; 1952 v W, Ni, E, USA, D, Se; 1953 v W, Ni, E; 1954 v W; 1955 v P, Y, A, H; 1956 v Ni (28)
Liddle, D. (East Fife), 1931 v A, I, Sw (3)
Lindsay, D. (St Mirren), 1903 v Ni (1)
Lindsay, J. (Dumbarton), 1880 v W; 1881 v W, E; 1884 v W, E; 1885 v W, E; 1886 v E (8)
Lindsay, J. (Renton), 1888 v E; 1893 v E, Ni (3)
Linwood, A. B. (Clyde), 1950 v W (1)
Little, R. J. (Rangers), 1953 v Se (1)
Livingstone, G. T. (Manchester C), 1906 v E; (with Rangers), 1907 v W (2)
Lochhead, A. (Third Lanark), 1889 v W (1)
Logan, J. (Ayr U), 1891 v W (1)
Logan, T. (Falkirk), 1913 v Ni (1)
Logie, J. T. (Arsenal), 1953 v Ni (1)
Loney, W. (Celtic), 1910 v W, Ni (2)
Long, H. (Clyde), 1947 v Ni (1)
Longair, W. (Dundee), 1894 v Ni (1)
Lorimer, P. (Leeds U), 1970 v A (sub); 1971 v W, Ni; 1972 v Ni (sub), W, E; 1973 v D (2), E (2); 1974 v WG (sub), E, Bel, N, Z, Br, Y; 1975 v Sp (sub); 1976 v D (2), R (sub) (21)
Love, A. (Aberdeen), 1931 v A, I, Sw (3)
Low, A. (Falkirk), 1934 v Ni (1)
Low, T. P. (Rangers), 1897 v Ni (1)
Low, W. L. (Newcastle U), 1911 v E, W; 1912 v Ni; 1920 v E, Ni (5)
Lowe, J. (Cambuslang), 1891 v Ni (1)
Lowe, J. (St Bernards), 1887 v Ni (1)
Lundie, J. (Hibernian), 1886 v W (1)
Lyall, J. (Sheffield W), 1905 v E (1)

McAdam, J. (Third Lanark), 1880 v W (1)
McAllister, G. (Leicester C), 1990 v EG, Pol, Ma (sub); (with Leeds U), 1991 v R, Sw, Bul, USSR (sub), Sm; 1992 v Sw (sub), Sm, Ni, Fi (sub), US, Ca, N, Ho, G, C; 1993 v Sw, P, I, Ma; 1994 v Sw, I, Ma, Ho, A, Ho (28)
McArthur, D. (Celtic), 1895 v E, Ni; 1899 v W (3)
McAtee, A. (Celtic), 1913 v W (1)
McAulay, J. (Dumbarton), 1882 v W; (with Arthurlie), 1884 v Ni (2)
McAulay, J. (Dumbarton), 1883 v E, W; 1884 v E; 1885 v E, W; 1886 v E; 1887 v E, W (8)
McAuley, R. (Rangers), 1932 v Ni, W (2)
McAvennie, F. (West Ham U), 1986 v Aus (2), D (sub), WG (sub); (with Celtic), 1988 v S.Ar (5)
McBain, E. (St Mirren), 1894 v W (1)
McBain, N. (Manchester U), 1922 v E; (with Everton), 1923 v Ni; 1924 v W (3)
McBride, J. (Celtic), 1967 v W, Ni (2)

McBride, P. (Preston NE), 1904 v E; 1906 v E; 1907 v E, W; 1908 v E; 1909 v W (6)
McCall, J. (Renton), 1886 v W; 1887 v E, W; 1888 v E; 1890 v E (5)
McCall, S. M. (Everton), 1990 v Arg, EG, Eg (sub), Pol, Ma, Cr, Se, Br; 1991 v Sw, USSR, Sm; (with Rangers), 1992 v Sw, R, Sm, US, Ca, N, Ho, G, C; 1993 v Sw, P (2); 1994 v I, Ho, A (sub), Ho (27)
McCalliog, J. (Sheffield W), 1967 v E, USSR; 1968 v Ni; 1969 v D; (with Wolverhampton W), 1971 v P (5)
McCallum, N. (Renton), 1888 v Ni (1)
McCann, R. J. (Motherwell), 1959 v WG; 1960 v E, Ni, W; 1961 v E (5)
McCartney, W. (Hibernian), 1902 v Ni (1)
McClair, B. (Celtic), 1987 v L, Ei, E, Br (sub); (with Manchester U), 1988 v Bul, Ma (sub), Sp (sub); 1989 v N, Y, I (sub), Cy, F (sub); 1990 v N (sub), Arg (sub); 1991 v Bul (2), Sm; 1992 v Sw (sub), R, Ni, US, Ca (sub), N, Ho, G, C; 1993 v Sw, P (sub), Es (2) (30)
McClory, A. (Motherwell), 1927 v W; 1928 v Ni; 1935 v W (3)
McCloy, P. (Ayr U), 1924 v E; 1925 v E (2)
McCloy, P. (Rangers), 1973 v W, Ni, Sw, Br (4)
McCoist, A. (Rangers), 1986 v Ho; 1987 v L (sub), Ei (sub), Bel, E, Br; 1988 v H, Bel, Ma, Sp, Co, E; 1989 v Y (sub), F, Cy, E; 1990 v Y, F, N, EG (sub), Eg, Pol, Ma (sub), Cr (sub), Se (sub), Br; 1991 v R, Sw, Bul (2), USSR; 1992 v Sw, Sm, Ni, Fi (sub), US, Ca, N, Ho, G, C; 1993 v Sw, P, I, Ma, P (46)
McColl, A. (Renton), 1888 v Ni (1)
McColl, I. M. (Rangers), 1950 v E, F; 1951 v W, Ni, Bel; 1957 v E, Ni, W, Y, Sp, Sw, WG; 1958 v Ni, E (14)
McColl, R. S. (Queen's Park), 1896 v W, Ni; 1897 v Ni; 1898 v Ni; 1899 v Ni, E, W; 1900 v E, W; 1901 v E, W; (with Newcastle U), 1902 v E; (with Queen's Park), 1908 v Ni (13)
McColl, W. (Renton), 1895 v W (1)
McCombie, A. (Sunderland), 1903 v E, W; (with Newcastle U), 1905 v E, W (4)
McCorkindale, J. (Partick T), 1891 v W (1)
McCormick, R. (Abercorn), 1886 v W (1)
McCrae, D. (St Mirren), 1929 v N, G (2)
McCreadie, A. (Rangers), 1893 v W; 1894 v E (2)
McCreadie, E. G. (Chelsea), 1965 v E, Sp, Fi, Pol; 1966 v P, Ni, W, Pol, I; 1967 v E, USSR; 1968 v Ni, W, E, Ho; 1969 v W, Ni, E, D, A, WG, Cy (2) (23)
McCulloch, D. (Hearts), 1935 v W; (with Brentford), 1936 v E; 1937 v W, Ni; 1938 v Cz; (with Derby Co), 1939 v H, W (7)
MacDonald, A. (Rangers), 1976 v Sw (1)
McDonald, J. (Edinburgh University), 1886 v E (1)
McDonald, J. (Sunderland), 1956 v W, Ni (2)
MacDougall, E. J. (Norwich C) 1975 v Se, P, W, Ni, E; 1976 v D, R (sub) (7)
McDougall, J. (Liverpool), 1931 v I, A (2)
McDougall, J. (Airdrieonians), 1926 v Ni (1)
McDougall, J. (Vale of Leven), 1877 v E, W; 1878 v E; 1879 v E, W (5)
McFadyen, W. (Motherwell), 1934 v A, W (2)
Macfarlane, A. (Dundee), 1904 v W; 1906 v W; 1908 v W; 1909 v Ni; 1911 v W (5)
McFarlane, R. (Greenock Morton), 1896 v W (1)
Macfarlane, W. (Hearts), 1947 v L (1)
McGarr, E. (Aberdeen), 1970 v Ei, A (2)
McGarvey, F. P. (Liverpool), 1979 v Ni (sub), Arg; (with Celtic), 1984 v U, Bel (sub), EG (sub), Ni, W (7)
McGeoch, A. (Dumbreck), 1876 v E, W; 1877 v E, W (4)
McGhee, J. (Hibernian), 1886 v W (1)
McGhee, M. (Aberdeen), 1983 v Ca (1 + 1 sub); 1984 v Ni (sub), E (4)
McGinlay, J. (Bolton W), 1994 v A, Ho (2)
McGonagle, W. (Celtic), 1933 v E; 1934 v A, E, Ni; 1935 v Ni, W (6)
McGrain, D. (Celtic), 1973 v W, Ni, E, Sw, Br; 1974 v Cz (2), WG, W (sub), E, Bel, N, Z, Br, Y; 1975 v Sp, Se, P, W, Ni, E, R; 1976 v D (2), Sw, Ni, W, E; 1977 v Fi, Cz, W (2), Se, Ni, E, Ch, Arg, Br; 1978 v EG, Cz; 1980 v Bel, P, Ni, W, E, Pol, H; 1981 v Se, P, Is, Ni, Is, W (sub), Ni, E; 1982 v Se, Sp, Ho, Ni, E, Nz, USSR (sub) (62)
McGregor, J. C. (Vale of Leven), 1877 v E, W; 1878 v E; 1880 v E (4)
McGrory, J. E. (Kilmarnock), 1965 v Ni, Fi; 1966 v P (3)
McGrory, J. (Celtic), 1928 v Ni; 1931 v E; 1932 v Ni, W; 1933 v E, Ni; 1934 v Ni (7)
McGuire, W. (Beith), 1881 v E, W (2)
McGurk, F. (Birmingham), 1934 v W (1)
McHardy, H. (Rangers), 1885 v Ni (1)
McInally, A. (Aston Villa), 1989 v Cy (sub), Ch; (with Bayern Munich), 1990 v Y (sub), F (sub), Arg, Pol (sub), Ma, Cr (8)
McInally, J. (Dundee U), 1987 v Bel, Br; 1988 v Ma (sub); 1991 v Bul (2); 1992 v US (sub), N (sub), C (sub); 1993 v G, P (10)
McInally, T. B. (Celtic), 1926 v Ni; 1927 v W (2)
McInnes, T. (Cowlairs), 1889 v Ni (1)
McIntosh, W. (Third Lanark), 1905 v Ni (1)
McIntyre, A. (Vale of Leven), 1878 v E; 1882 v E (2)
McIntyre, H. (Rangers), 1880 v W (1)
McIntyre, J. (Rangers), 1884 v W (1)
McKay, D. (Celtic), 1959 v E, WG, Ho, P; 1960 v E, Pol, A, H, T; 1961 v W, Ni; 1962 v Ni, Cz, U (sub) (14)
Mackay, D. C. (Hearts), 1957 v Sp; 1958 v F; 1959 v W, Ni; (with Tottenham H), 1959 v WG, E; 1960 v W, Ni, A, Pol, H, T; 1961 v W, Ni, E; 1963 v E, A, N; 1964 v Ni, W, N; 1966 v Ni (22)
Mackay, G. (Hearts), 1988 v Bul (sub), L (sub), S.Ar (sub), Ma (4)
McKay, J. (Blackburn R), 1924 v W (1)
McKay, R. (Newcastle U), 1928 v W (1)
McKean, R. (Rangers), 1976 v Sw (sub) (1)
McKenzie, D. (Brentford), 1938 v Ni (1)
Mackenzie, J. A. (Partick T), 1954 v W, E, N, Fi, A, U; 1955 v E, H; 1956 v A (9)
McKeown, M. (Celtic), 1889 v Ni; 1890 v E (2)
McKie, J. (East Stirling), 1898 v W (1)
McKillop, T. R. (Rangers), 1938 v Ho (1)
McKimmie, S. (Aberdeen), 1989 v E, Ch; 1990 v Arg, Eg, Cr (sub), Br; 1991 v R, Sw, Bul, Sm; 1992 v Sw, R, Ni, Fi, US, Ca (sub), N (sub), Ho, G, C; 1993 v P, Es (sub); 1994 v Sw, I, Ho, A, Ho (27)
McKinlay, D. (Liverpool), 1922 v W, Ni (2)
McKinlay, W. (Dundee U), 1994 v Ma, Ho (sub), A, Ho (4)
McKinnon, A. (Queen's Park), 1874 v E (1)
McKinnon, R. (Rangers), 1966 v W, E, I (2), Ho, Br; 1967 v W, Ni, E; 1968 v Ni, W, E, Ho; 1969 v D, A, WG, Cy; 1970 v Ni, W, E, Ei, WG, A; 1971 v D, Bel, P, USSR, D (28)
McKinnon, R. (Motherwell), 1994 v Ma (1)
MacKinnon, W. (Dumbarton), 1883 v E, W; 1884 v E, W (4)
McKinnon, W. W. (Queen's Park), 1872 v E; 1873 v E; 1874 v E; 1875 v E; 1876 v E, W; 1877 v E; 1878 v E; 1879 v E (9)
McLaren, A. (St Johnstone), 1929 v N, G, Ho; 1933 v W, Ni (5)
McLaren, A. (Preston NE), 1947 v E, Bel, L; 1948 v W (4)
McLaren, A. (Hearts), 1992 v US, Ca, N; 1993 v I, Ma, G, Es (sub + 1); 1994 v I, Ma, Ho, A (12)
McLaren, J. (Hibernian), 1888 v W; (with Celtic), 1889 v E; 1890 v E (3)
McLean, A. (Celtic), 1926 v W, Ni; 1927 v W, E (4)
McLean, D. (St Bernards), 1896 v W; 1897 v Ni (2)
McLean, D. (Sheffield W), 1912 v E (1)
McLean, G. (Dundee), 1968 v Ho (1)

McLean, T. (Kilmarnock), 1969 v D, Cy, W; 1970 v Ni, W; 1971 v D (6)

McLeish, A. (Aberdeen), 1980 v F, Ni, W, E, Pol, H; 1981 v Se, Is, Ni, Is, Ni, E; 1982 v Se, Sp, Ni, Br (sub); 1983 v Bel, Sw (sub), W, E, Ca (3); 1984 v U, Bel, EG, Ni, W, E, F; 1985 v Y, Ic, Sp (2), W, E, Ic; 1986 v W, EG, Aus (2), E, Ho, D; 1987 v Bel, E, Br; 1988 v Bel, Bul, L, S.Ar (sub), Ma, Sp, Co, E; 1989 v N, Y, I, Cy, F, Cy, E, Ch; 1990 v Y, F, N, Arg, EG, Eg, Cr, Se, Br; 1991 v R, Sw, USSR, Bul; 1993 v Ma (77)

McLeod, D. (Celtic), 1905 v Ni; 1906 v E, W, Ni (4)

McLeod, J. (Dumbarton), 1888 v Ni; 1889 v W; 1890 v Ni; 1892 v E; 1893 v W (5)

MacLeod, J. M. (Hibernian), 1961 v E, Ei (2), Cz (4)

MacLeod, M. (Celtic), 1985 v E (sub); 1987 v Ei, L, E, Br; (with Borussia Dortmund), 1988 v Co, E; 1989 v I, Ch; 1990 v Y, F, N (sub), Arg, EG, Pol, Se Br; (with Hibernian), 1991 v R, Sw, USSR (sub) (20)

McLeod, W. (Cowlairs), 1886 v Ni (1)

McLintock, A. (Vale of Leven), 1875 v E; 1876 v E; 1880 v E (3)

McLintock, F. (Leicester C), 1963 v N (sub), Ei, Sp; (with Arsenal), 1965 v Ni; 1967 v USSR; 1970 v Ni; 1971 v W, Ni, E (9)

McLuckie, J. S. (Manchester C), 1934 v W (1)

McMahon, A. (Celtic), 1892 v E; 1893 v E, Ni; 1894 v E; 1901 v Ni; 1902 v W (6)

McMenemy, J. (Celtic), 1905 v Ni; 1909 v Ni; 1910 v E, W; 1911 v Ni, W, E; 1912 v W; 1914 v W, Ni, E; 1920 v Ni (12)

McMenemy, J. (Motherwell), 1934 v W (1)

McMillan, J. (St Bernards), 1897 v W (1)

McMillan, I. L. (Airdrieonians), 1952 v E, USA, D; 1955 v E; 1956 v E; (with Rangers), 1961 v Cz (6)

McMillan, T. (Dumbarton), 1887 v Ni (1)

McMullan, J. (Partick T), 1920 v W; 1921 v W, Ni, E; 1924 v E, Ni; 1925 v E; 1926 v W; (with Manchester C), 1926 v E; 1927 v E, W; 1928 v E, W; 1929 v W, E, Ni (16)

McNab, A. (Morton), 1921 v E, Ni (2)

McNab, A. (Sunderland), 1937 v A; (with WBA), 1939 v E (2)

McNab, C. D. (Dundee), 1931 v E, W, A, I, Sw; 1932 v E (6)

McNab, J. S. (Liverpool), 1923 v W (1)

McNair, A. (Celtic), 1906 v W; 1907 v Ni; 1908 v E, W; 1909 v E; 1910 v W; 1912 v E, W, Ni; 1913 v E; 1914 v E, Ni; 1920 v E, W, Ni (15)

McNaught, W. (Raith R), 1951 v A, W, Ni; 1952 v E; 1955 v Ni (5)

McNeil, H. (Queen's Park), 1874 v E; 1875 v E; 1876 v E, W; 1877 v W; 1878 v E; 1879 v E, W; 1881 v E, W (10)

McNeil, M. (Rangers), 1876 v W; 1880 v E (2)

McNeill, W. (Celtic), 1961 v E, Ei (2), Cz; 1962 v Ni, E, Cz, U; 1963 v Ei, Sp; 1964 v W, E, WG; 1965 v E, Fi, Pol, Sp; 1966 v Ni, Pol; 1967 v USSR; 1968 v E; 1969 v Cy, W, E, Cy (sub); 1970 v WG; 1972 v Ni, W, E (29)

McPhail, J. (Celtic), 1950 v W; 1951 v W, Ni, A; 1954 v Ni (5)

McPhail, R. (Airdrieonians), 1927 v E; (with Rangers), 1929 v W; 1931 v E, Ni; 1932 v W, Ni, F; 1933 v E, Ni; 1934 v A, Ni; 1935 v E; 1937 v G, E, Cz; 1938 v W, Ni (17)

McPherson, D. (Kilmarnock), 1892 v Ni (1)

McPherson, D. (Hearts), 1989 v Cy, E; 1990 v N, Ma, Cr, Se, Br; 1991 v Sw, Bul (2), USSR (sub), Sm; 1992 v Sw, R, Sm, Ni, Fi, US, Ca, N, Ho, G, C; (with Rangers), 1993 v Sw, I, Ma, P (27)

McPherson, J. (Clydesdale), 1875 v E (1)

McPherson, J. (Vale of Leven), 1879 v E, W; 1880 v E; 1881 v W; 1883 v E, W; 1884 v E; 1885 v Ni (8)

McPherson, J. (Kilmarnock), 1888 v W; (with Cowlairs), 1889 v E; 1890 v Ni, E; (with Rangers), 1892 v W; 1894 v E; 1895 v E, Ni; 1897 v Ni (9)

McPherson, J. (Hearts), 1891 v E (1)

McPherson, R. (Arthurlie), 1882 v E (1)

McQueen, G. (Leeds U), 1974 v Bel; 1975 v Sp (2), P, W, Ni, E, R; 1976 v D; 1977 v Cz, W (2), Ni, E; 1978 v EG, Cz, W; (with Manchester U), Bul, Ni, W; 1979 v A, N, P, Ni, E, N; 1980 v Pe, A, Bel; 1981 v W (30)

McQueen, M. (Leith Ath), 1890 v W; 1891 v W (2)

McRorie, D. M. (Morton), 1931 v W (1)

McSpadyen, A. (Partick T), 1939 v E, H (2)

McStay, P. (Celtic), 1984 v U, Bel, EG, Ni, W, E (sub); 1985 v Y, Ic, Sp (2), W; 1986 v EG (sub), Aus, Is, U; 1987 v Bul, Ei (1 + 1 sub), L (sub), Bel, E, Br; 1988 v H, Bel, Bul, L, S.Ar, Sp, Co, E; 1989 v N, Y, I, Cy, F, Cy, E, Ch; 1990 v Y, F, N, Arg, EG (sub), Eg, Pol (sub), Ma, Cr, Se (sub), Br; 1991 v R, USSR, Bul; 1992 v Sm, Fi, US, Ca, N, Ho, G, C; 1993 v Sw, P, I, Ma, P, Es (2); 1994 v I (sub), Ho (69)

McStay, W. (Celtic), 1921 v W, Ni; 1925 v E, Ni, W; 1926 v E, Ni, W; 1927 v E, Ni, W; 1928 v W, Ni (13)

McTavish, J. (Falkirk), 1910 v Ni (1)

McWhattie, G. C. (Queen's Park), 1901 v W, Ni (2)

McWilliam, P. (Newcastle U), 1905 v E; 1906 v E; 1907 v E, W; 1909 v E, W; 1910 v E; 1911 v W (8)

Macari, L. (Celtic), 1972 v W (sub), E, Y, Cz, Br; 1973 v D; (with Manchester U), E (2), W (sub), Ni (sub); 1975 v Se, P (sub), W, E (sub), R; 1977 v Ni (sub), E (sub), Ch, Arg; 1978 v EG, W, Bul, Pe (sub), Ir (24)

Macauley, A. R. (Brentford), 1947 v E; (with Arsenal), 1948 v E, W, Ni, Bel, Sw, F (7)

Madden, J. (Celtic), 1893 v W; 1895 v W (2)

Main, F. R. (Rangers), 1938 v W (1)

Main, J. (Hibernian), 1909 v Ni (1)

Maley, W. (Celtic), 1893 v E, Ni (2)

Malpas, M. (Dundee U), 1984 v F; 1985 v E, Ic; 1986 v W, Aus (2), Is, R, E, Ho, D, WG; 1987 v Bul, Ei, Bel; 1988 v Bel, Bul, L, S.Ar, Ma; 1989 v N, Y, I, Cy, F, Cy, E, Ch; 1990 v Y, F, N, Eg, Pol, Ma, Cr, Se, Br; 1991 v R, Bul (2), USSR, Sm; 1992 v Sw, R, Sm, Ni, Fi, US, Ca (sub), N, Ho, G; 1993 v Sw, P, I (55)

Marshall, G. (Celtic), 1992 v US (1)

Marshall, H. (Celtic), 1899 v W; 1900 v Ni (2)

Marshall, J. (Middlesbrough), 1921 v E, W, Ni; 1922 v E, W, Ni; (with Llanelly), 1924 v W (7)

Marshall, J. (Third Lanark), 1885 v Ni; 1886 v W; 1887 v E, W (4)

Marshall, J. (Rangers), 1932 v E; 1933 v E; 1934 v E (3)

Marshall, R. W. (Rangers), 1892 v Ni; 1894 v Ni (2)

Martin, F. (Aberdeen), 1954 v N (2), A, U; 1955 v E, H (6)

Martin, N. (Hibernian), 1965 v Fi, Pol; (with Sunderland), 1966 v I (3)

Martis, J. (Motherwell), 1961 v W (1)

Mason, J. (Third Lanark), 1949 v E, W, Ni; 1950 v Ni; 1951 v Ni, Bel, A (7)

Massie, A. (Hearts), 1932 v Ni, W, F; 1933 v Ni; 1934 v E, Ni; 1935 v E, Ni, W; 1936 v W, Ni; (with Aston Villa), 1936 v E; 1937 v G, E, W, Ni, A; 1938 v W (18)

Masson, D. S. (QPR), 1976 v Ni, W, E; 1977 v Fi, Cz, W, Ni, E, Ch, Arg, Br; 1978 v EG, Cz, W; (with Derby Co), Ni, E, Pe (17)

Mathers, D. (Partick T), 1954 v Fi (1)

Maxwell, W. S. (Stoke C), 1898 v E (1)

May, J. (Rangers), 1906 v W, Ni; 1908 v E, Ni; 1909 v W (5)

Meechan, P. (Celtic), 1896 v Ni (1)

Meiklejohn, D. D. (Rangers), 1922 v W; 1924 v W; 1925 v W, Ni, E; 1928 v W, Ni; 1929 v E, Ni; 1930 v E, Ni; 1931 v E; 1932 v W, Ni; 1934 v A (15)

Menzies, A. (Hearts), 1906 v E (1)

Mercer, R. (Hearts), 1912 v W; 1913 v Ni (2)

Middleton, R. (Cowdenbeath), 1930 v Ni (1)
Millar, A. (Hearts), 1939 v W (1)
Millar, J. (Rangers), 1897 v E; 1898 v E, W (3)
Millar, J. (Rangers), 1963 v A, Ei (2)
Miller, J. (St Mirren), 1931 v E, I, Sw; 1932 v F; 1934 v E (5)
Miller, P. (Dumbarton), 1882 v E; 1883 v E, W (3)
Miller, T. (Liverpool), 1920 v E; (with Manchester U), 1921 v E, Ni (3)
Miller, W. (Third Lanark), 1876 v E (1)
Miller, W. (Celtic), 1947 v E, W, Bel, L; 1948 v W, Ni (6)
Miller, W. (Aberdeen), 1975 v R; 1978 v Bul; 1980 v Bel, W, E, Pol, H; 1981 v Se, P, Is (sub), Ni, W, Ni, E; 1982 v Ni, P, Ho, Br, USSR; 1983 v EG, Sw (2), W, E, Ca (3); 1984 v U, Bel, EG, W, E, F; 1985 v Y, Ic, Sp (2), W, E, Ic; 1986 v W, EG, Aus (2), Is, R, E, Ho, D, WG, U; 1987 v Bul, E, Br; 1988 v H, L, S.Ar, Ma, Sp, Co, E; 1989 v N, Y; 1990 v Y, N (65)
Mills, W. (Aberdeen), 1936 v W, Ni; 1937 v W (3)
Milne, J. V. (Middlesbrough), 1938 v E; 1939 v E (2)
Mitchell, D. (Rangers), 1890 v Ni; 1892 v E; 1893 v E, Ni; 1894 v E (5)
Mitchell, J. (Kilmarnock), 1908 v Ni; 1910 v Ni, W (3)
Mitchell, R. C. (Newcastle U), 1951 v D, F (2)
Mochan, N. (Celtic), 1954 v N, A, U (3)
Moir, W. (Bolton W), 1950 v E (1)
Moncur, R. (Newcastle U), 1968 v Ho; 1970 v Ni, W, E, Ei; 1971 v D, Bel, W, P, Ni, E, D; 1972 v Pe, Ni, W, E (16)
Morgan, H. (St Mirren), 1898 v W; (with Liverpool), 1899 v E (2)
Morgan, W. (Burnley), 1968 v Ni; (with Manchester U), 1972 v Pe, Y, Cz, Br; 1973 v D (2), E (2), W, Ni, Sw, Br; 1974 v Cz (2), WG (2), Ni, Bel (sub), Br, Y (21)
Morris, D. (Raith R), 1923 v Ni; 1924 v E, Ni; 1925 v E, W, Ni (6)
Morris, H. (East Fife), 1950 v Ni (1)
Morrison, T. (St Mirren), 1927 v E (1)
Morton, A. L. (Queen's Park), 1920 v W, Ni; (with Rangers), 1921 v E; 1922 v E, W; 1923 v E, W, Ni; 1924 v E, W, Ni; 1925 v E, W, Ni; 1927 v E, Ni; 1928 v E, W, Ni; 1929 v E, W, Ni; 1930 v E, W, Ni; 1931 v E, W, Ni; 1932 v E, W, F (31)
Morton, H. A. (Kilmarnock), 1929 v G, Ho (2)
Mudie, J. K. (Blackpool), 1957 v W, Ni, E, Y, Sw, Sp (2), WG; 1958 v Ni, E, W, Sw, H, Pol, Y, Par, F (17)
Muir, W. (Dundee), 1907 v Ni (1)
Muirhead, T. A. (Rangers), 1922 v Ni; 1923 v E; 1924 v W; 1927 v Ni; 1928 v Ni; 1929 v W, Ni; 1930 v W (8)
Mulhall, G. (Aberdeen), 1960 v Ni; (with Sunderland), 1963 v Ni; 1964 v Ni (3)
Munro, A. D. (Hearts), 1937 v W, Ni; (with Blackpool), 1938 v Ho (3)
Munro, F. M. (Wolverhampton W), 1971 v Ni (sub), E (sub), D, USSR; 1975 v Se, W (sub), Ni, E, R (9)
Munro, I. (St Mirren), 1979 v Arg, N; 1980 v Pe, A, Bel, W, E (7)
Munro, N. (Abercorn), 1888 v W; 1889 v E (2)
Murdoch, J. (Motherwell), 1931 v Ni (1)
Murdoch, R. (Celtic), 1966 v W, E, I (2); 1967 v Ni; 1968 v Ni; 1969 v W, Ni, E, WG, Cy; 1970 v A (12)
Murphy, F. (Celtic), 1938 v Ho (1)
Murray, J. (Renton), 1895 v W (1)
Murray, J. (Hearts), 1958 v E, H, Pol, Y, F (5)
Murray, J. W. (Vale of Leven), 1890 v W (1)
Murray, P. (Hibernian), 1896 v Ni; 1897 v W (2)
Murray, S. (Aberdeen), 1972 v Bel (1)
Mutch, G. (Preston NE), 1938 v E (1)

Napier, C. E. (Celtic), 1932 v E; 1935 v E, W; (with Derby Co), 1937 v Ni, A (5)
Narey, D. (Dundee U), 1977 v Se (sub); 1979 v P, Ni (sub), Arg; 1980 v P, Ni, Pol, H; 1981 v W, E (sub); 1982 v Ho, W, E, Nz (sub), Br, USSR; 1983 v EG, Sw, Bel, Ni, W, E, Ca (3); 1986 v Is, R, Ho, WG, U; 1987 v Bul, E, Bel; 1989 v I, Cy (35)
Neil, R. G. (Hibernian), 1896 v W; (with Rangers), 1900 v W (2)
Neill, R. W. (Queen's Park), 1876 v W; 1877 v E, W; 1878 v W; 1880 v E (5)
Neilles, P. (Hearts), 1914 v W, Ni (2)
Nelson, J. (Cardiff C), 1925 v W, Ni; 1928 v E; 1930 v F (4)
Nevin, P. K. F. (Chelsea), 1986 v R (sub), E (sub); 1987 v L, Ei, Bel (sub); 1988 v L; (with Everton), 1989 v Cy, E; 1991 v R (sub), Bul (sub), Sm (sub); 1992 v US, G (sub), C (sub); (with Tranmere R), 1993 v Ma, P (sub), Es; 1994 v Sw, Ma, Ho, A (sub), Ho (22)
Niblo, T. D. (Aston Villa), 1904 v E (1)
Nibloe, J. (Kilmarnock), 1929 v E, N, Ho; 1930 v W; 1931 v E, Ni, A, I, Sw; 1932 v E, F (11)
Nicholas, C. (Celtic), 1983 v Sw, Ni, E, Ca (3); (with Arsenal), 1984 v Bel, F (sub); 1985 v Y (sub), Ic (sub), Sp (sub), W (sub); 1986 v Is, R (sub), E, D, U (sub); 1987 v Bul, E (sub); (with Aberdeen), 1989 v Cy (sub) (20)
Nicol, S. (Liverpool), 1985 v Y, Ic, Sp, W; 1986 v W, EG, Aus, E, D, WG, U; 1988 v H, Bul, S.Ar, Sp, Co, E; 1989 v N, Y, Cy, F; 1990 v Y, F; 1991 v Sw, USSR, Sm; 1992 v Sw (27)
Nisbet, J. (Ayr U), 1929 v N, G, Ho (3)
Niven, J. B. (Moffatt), 1885 v Ni (1)

O'Donnell, F. (Preston NE), 1937 v E, A, Cz; 1938 v W; (with Blackpool), E, Ho (6)
O'Donnell, P. (Motherwell), 1994 v Sw (sub) (1)
Ogilvie, D. H. (Motherwell), 1934 v A (1)
O'Hare, J. (Derby Co), 1970 v W, Ni, E; 1971 v D, Bel, W, Ni; 1972 v P, Bel, Ho (sub), Pe, Ni, W (13)
Ormond, W. E. (Hibernian), 1954 v E, N, Fi, A, U; 1959 v E (6)
O'Rourke, F. (Airdrieonians), 1907 v Ni (1)
Orr, J. (Kilmarnock), 1892 v W (1)
Orr, R. (Newcastle U), 1902 v E; 1904 v E (2)
Orr, T. (Morton), 1952 v Ni, W (2)
Orr, W. (Celtic), 1900 v Ni; 1903 v Ni; 1904 v W (3)
Orrock, R. (Falkirk), 1913 v W (1)
Oswald, J. (Third Lanark), 1889 v E; (with St Bernards), 1895 v E; (with Rangers), 1897 v W (3)

Parker, A. H. (Falkirk), 1955 v P, Y, A; 1956 v E, Ni, W, A; 1957 v Ni, W, Y; 1958 v Ni, W, E, Sw; (with Everton), Par (15)
Parlane, D. (Rangers), 1973 v W, Sw, Br; 1975 v Sp (sub), Se, P, W, Ni, E, R; 1976 v D (sub); 1977 v W (12)
Parlane, R. (Vale of Leven), 1878 v W; 1879 v E, W (3)
Paterson, G. D. (Celtic), 1939 v Ni (1)
Paterson, J. (Leicester C), 1920 v E (1)
Paterson, J. (Cowdenbeath), 1931 v A, I, Sw (3)
Paton, A. (Motherwell), 1952 v D, Se (2)
Paton, D. (St Bernards), 1896 v W (1)
Paton, M. (Dumbarton), 1883 v E; 1884 v W; 1885 v W, E; 1886 v E (5)
Paton, R. (Vale of Leven), 1879 v E, W (2)
Patrick, J. (St Mirren), 1897 v E, W (2)
Paul, H. McD. (Queen's Park), 1909 v E, W, Ni (3)
Paul, W. (Partick T), 1888 v W; 1889 v W; 1890 v W (3)
Paul, W. (Dykebar), 1891 v Ni (1)
Pearson, T. (Newcastle U), 1947 v E, Bel (2)
Penman, A. (Dundee), 1966 v Ho (1)
Pettigrew, W. (Motherwell), 1976 v Sw, Ni, W; 1977 v W (sub), Se (5)
Phillips, J. (Queen's Park), 1877 v E, W; 1878 v W (3)
Plenderleith, J. B. (Manchester C), 1961 v Ni (1)
Porteous, W. (Hearts), 1903 v Ni (1)
Pringle, C. (St Mirren), 1921 v W (1)

Provan, D. (Rangers), 1964 v Ni, N; 1966 v I (2), Ho (5)
Provan, D. (Celtic), 1980 v Bel (2 sub), P (sub), Ni (sub); 1981 v Is, W, E; 1982 v Se, P, Ni (10)
Pursell, P. (Queen's Park), 1914 v W (1)

Quinn, J. (Celtic), 1905 v Ni; 1906 v Ni, W; 1908 v Ni, E; 1909 v E; 1910 v E, Ni, W; 1912 v E, W (11)
Quinn, P. (Motherwell), 1961 v E, Ei (2); 1962 v U (4)

Rae, J. (Third Lanark), 1889 v W; 1890 v Ni (2)
Raeside, J. S. (Third Lanark), 1906 v W (1)
Raisbeck, A. G. (Liverpool), 1900 v E; 1901 v E; 1902 v E; 1903 v E, W; 1904 v E; 1906 v E; 1907 v E (8)
Rankin, G. (Vale of Leven), 1890 v Ni; 1891 v E (2)
Rankin, R. (St Mirren), 1929 v N, G, Ho (3)
Redpath, W. (Motherwell), 1949 v W, Ni; 1951 v E, D, F, Bel, A; 1952 v Ni, E (9)
Reid, J. G. (Airdrieonians), 1914 v W; 1920 v W; 1924 v Ni (3)
Reid, R. (Brentford), 1938 v E, Ni (2)
Reid, W. (Rangers), 1911 v E, W, Ni; 1912 v Ni; 1913 v E, W, Ni; 1914 v E, Ni (9)
Reilly, L. (Hibernian), 1949 v E, W, F; 1950 v W, Ni, Sw, F; 1951 v W, E, D, F, Bel, A; 1952 v Ni, W, E, USA, D, Se; 1953 v Ni, W, E, Se; 1954 v W; 1955 v H (2), P, Y, A, E; 1956 v E, W, Ni, A; 1957 v E, Ni, W, Y (38)
Rennie, H. G. (Hearts), 1900 v E, Ni; (with Hibernian), 1901 v E; 1902 v E, Ni, W; 1903 v Ni, W; 1904 v Ni; 1905 v W; 1906 v Ni; 1908 v Ni, W (13)
Renny-Tailyour, H. W. (Royal Engineers), 1873 v E (1)
Rhind, A. (Queen's Park), 1872 v E (1)
Richmond, A. (Queen's Park), 1906 v W (1)
Richmond, J. T. (Clydesdale), 1877 v E; (with Queen's Park), 1878 v E; 1882 v W (3)
Ring, T. (Clyde), 1953 v Se; 1955 v W, Ni, E, H; 1957 v E, Sp (2), Sw, WG; 1958 v Ni, Sw (12)
Rioch, B. D. (Derby Co), 1975 v P, W, Ni, E, R; 1976 v D (2), R, Ni, W, E; 1977 v Fi, Cz, W; (with Everton), W, Ni, E, Ch, Br; 1978 v Cz; (with Derby Co), Ni, E, Pe, Ho (24)
Ritchie, A. (East Stirlingshire), 1891 v W (1)
Ritchie, H. (Hibernian), 1923 v W; 1928 v Ni (2)
Ritchie, J. (Queen's Park), 1897 v W (1)
Ritchie, W. (Rangers), 1962 v U (sub) (1)
Robb, D. T. (Aberdeen), 1971 v W, E, P, D (sub), USSR (5)
Robb, W. (Rangers), 1926 v W; (with Hibernian), 1928 v W (2)
Robertson, A. (Clyde), 1955 v P, A, H; 1958 v Sw, Par (5)
Robertson, D. (Rangers), 1992 v Ni; 1994 v Sw, Ho (3)
Robertson, G. (Motherwell), 1910 v W; (with Sheffield W), 1912 v W; 1913 v E, Ni (4)
Robertson, G. (Kilmarnock), 1938 v Cz (1)
Robertson, H. (Dundee), 1962 v Cz (1)
Robertson, J. (Dundee), 1931 v A, I (2)
Robertson, J. (Hearts), 1991 v R, Sw, Bul (sub), Sm (sub); 1992 v Sm, Ni (sub), Fi; 1993 v I (sub), Ma (sub), G, Es (11)
Robertson, J. N. (Nottingham F), 1978 v Ni, W (sub), Ir; 1979 v P, N; 1980 v Pe, A, Bel (2), P; 1981 v Se, P, Is, Ni, Is, Ni, E; 1982 v Se, Ni (2), E (sub), Nz, Br, USSR; 1983 v EG, Sw; (with Derby Co), 1984 v U, Bel (28)
Robertson, J. G. (Tottenham H), 1965 v W (1)
Robertson, J. T. (Everton), 1898 v E; (with Southampton), 1899 v E; (with Rangers), 1900 v E, W; 1901 v W, Ni, E; 1902 v W, Ni, E; 1903 v E, W; 1904 v E, W, Ni; 1905 v W (16)
Robertson, P. (Dundee), 1903 v Ni (1)
Robertson, T. (Queen's Park), 1889 v Ni; 1890 v E; 1891 v W; 1892 v Ni (4)
Robertson, T. (Hearts), 1898 v Ni (1)
Robertson, W. (Dumbarton), 1887 v E, W (2)
Robinson, R. (Dundee), 1974 v WG (sub); 1975 v Se, Ni, R (sub) (4)
Rough, A. (Partick T), 1976 v Sw, Ni, W, E; 1977 v Fi, Cz, W (2), Se, Ni, E, Ch, Arg, Br; 1978 v Cz, W, Ni, E, Pe, Ir, Ho; 1979 v A, P, W, Arg, N; 1980 v Pe, A, Bel (2), P, W, E, Pol, H; 1981 v Se, P, Is, Ni, Is, W, E; 1982 v Se, Ni, Sp, Ho, W, E, Nz, Br, USSR; (with Hibernian), 1986 v W (sub), E (53)
Rougvie, D. (Aberdeen), 1984 v Ni (1)
Rowan, A. (Caledonian), 1880 v E; (with Queen's Park), 1882 v W (2)
Russell, D. (Hearts), 1895 v E, Ni; (with Celtic), 1897 v W; 1898 v Ni; 1901 v W, Ni (6)
Russell, J. (Cambuslang), 1890 v Ni (1)
Russell, W. F. (Airdrieonians), 1924 v W; 1925 v E (2)
Rutherford, E. (Rangers), 1948 v F (1)

St John, I. (Motherwell), 1959 v WG; 1960 v E, Ni, W, Pol, A; 1961 v E; (with Liverpool), 1962 v Ni, W, E, Cz (2), U; 1963 v W, Ni, E, N, Ei (sub), Sp; 1964 v Ni; 1965 v E (21)
Sawers, W. (Dundee), 1895 v W (1)
Scarff, P. (Celtic), 1931 v Ni (1)
Schaedler, E. (Hibernian), 1974 v WG (1)
Scott, A. S. (Rangers), 1957 v Ni, Y, WG; 1958 v W, Sw; 1959 v P; 1962 v Ni, W, E, Cz, U; (with Everton), 1964 v W, N; 1965 v Fi; 1966 v P, Br (16)
Scott, J. (Hibernian), 1966 v Ho (1)
Scott, J. (Dundee), 1971 v D (sub), USSR (2)
Scott, M. (Airdrieonians), 1898 v W (1)
Scott, R. (Airdrieonians), 1894 v Ni (1)
Scoular, J. (Portsmouth), 1951 v D, F, A; 1952 v E, USA, D, Se; 1953 v W, Ni (9)
Sellar, W. (Battlefield), 1885 v E; 1886 v E; 1887 v E, W; 1888 v E; (with Queen's Park), 1891 v E; 1892 v E; 1893 v E, Ni (9)
Semple, W. (Cambuslang), 1886 v W (1)
Shankly, W. (Preston NE), 1938 v E; 1939 v E, W, Ni, H (5)
Sharp, G. M. (Everton), 1985 v Ic; 1986 v W, Aus (2 sub), Is, R, U; 1987 v Ei; 1988 v Bel (sub), Bul, L, Ma (12)
Sharp, J. (Dundee), 1904 v W; (with Woolwich Arsenal), 1907 v W, E; 1908 v E; (with Fulham), 1909 v W (5)
Shaw, D. (Hibernian), 1947 v W, Ni; 1948 v E, Bel, Sw, F; 1949 v W, Ni (8)
Shaw, F. W. (Pollokshields Ath), 1884 v E, W (2)
Shaw, J. (Rangers), 1947 v E, Bel, L; 1948 v Ni (4)
Shearer, D. (Aberdeen), 1994 v A (sub), Ho (sub) (2)
Shearer, R. (Rangers), 1961 v E, Ei (2), Cz (4)
Sillars, D. C. (Queen's Park), 1891 v Ni; 1892 v E; 1893 v W; 1894 v E; 1895 v W (5)
Simpson, J. (Third Lanark), 1895 v E, W, Ni (3)
Simpson, J. (Rangers), 1935 v E, W, Ni; 1936 v E, W, Ni; 1937 v G, E, W, Ni, A, Cz; 1938 v W, Ni (14)
Simpson, N. (Aberdeen), 1983 v Ni; 1984 v F (sub); 1987 v E; 1988 v E (4)
Simpson, R. C. (Celtic), 1967 v E, USSR; 1968 v Ni, E; 1969 v A (5)
Sinclair, G. L. (Hearts), 1910 v Ni; 1912 v W, Ni (3)
Sinclair, J. W. E. (Leicester C), 1966 v P (1)
Skene, L. H. (Queen's Park), 1904 v W (1)
Sloan, T. (Third Lanark), 1904 v W (1)
Smellie, R. (Queen's Park), 1887 v Ni; 1888 v W; 1889 v E; 1891 v E; 1893 v E, Ni (6)
Smith, A. (Rangers), 1898 v E; 1900 v E, Ni, W; 1901 v E, Ni, W; 1902 v E, Ni, W; 1903 v E, Ni, W; 1904 v Ni; 1905 v W; 1906 v E, Ni; 1907 v W; 1911 v E, Ni (20)
Smith, D. (Aberdeen), 1966 v Ho; (with Rangers), 1968 v Ho (2)
Smith, G. (Hibernian), 1947 v E, Ni; 1948 v W, Bel, Sw, F; 1952 v E, USA; 1955 v P, Y, A, H; 1956 v E, Ni, W; 1957 v Sp (2), Sw (18)

Smith, H. G. (Hearts), 1988 v S.Ar (sub); 1992 v Ni, Ca (3)
Smith, J. (Rangers), 1935 v Ni; 1938 v Ni (2)
Smith, J. (Ayr U), 1924 v E (1)
Smith, J. (Aberdeen), 1968 v Ho (sub); (with Newcastle U), 1974 v WG, Ni (sub), W (sub) (4)
Smith, J. E. (Celtic), 1959 v H, P (2)
Smith, Jas (Queen's Park), 1872 v E (1)
Smith, John (Mauchline), 1877 v E, W; 1879 v E, W; (with Edinburgh University), 1880 v E; (with Queen's Park), 1881 v W, E; 1883 v E, W; 1884 v E (10)
Smith, N. (Rangers), 1897 v E; 1898 v W; 1899 v E, W, Ni; 1900 v E, W, Ni; 1901 v Ni, W; 1902 v E, Ni (12)
Smith, R. (Queen's Park), 1872 v E; 1873 v E (2)
Smith, T. M. (Kilmarnock), 1934 v E; (with Preston NE), 1938 v E (2)
Somers, P. (Celtic), 1905 v E, Ni; 1907 v Ni; 1909 v W (4)
Somers, W. S. (Third Lanark), 1879 v E, W; (with Queen's Park), 1880 v W (3)
Somerville, G. (Queen's Park), 1886 v E (1)
Souness, G. J. (Middlesbrough), 1975 v EG, Sp, Se; (with Liverpool), 1978 v Bul, W, E (sub), Ho; 1979 v A, N, W, Ni, E; 1980 v Pe, A, Bel, P, Ni; 1981 v P, Is (2); 1982 v Ni, P, Sp, W, E, Nz, Br, USSR; 1983 v EG, Sw, Bel, Sw, W, E, Ca (2 + 1 sub); 1984 v U, Ni, W; (with Sampdoria), 1985 v Y, Ic, Sp (2), W, E, Ic; 1986 v EG, Aus (2), R, E, D, WG (54)
Speedie, D. R. (Chelsea), 1985 v E; 1986 v W, EG (sub), Aus, E; (with Coventry C), 1989 v Y (sub), I (sub), Cy (1 + 1 sub), Ch (10)
Speedie, F. (Rangers), 1903 v E, W, Ni (3)
Speirs, J. H. (Rangers), 1908 v W (1)
Stanton, P. (Hibernian), 1966 v Ho; 1969 v Ni; 1970 v Ei, A; 1971 v D, Bel, P, USSR, D; 1972 v P, Bel, Ho, W; 1973 v W, Ni; 1974 v WG (16)
Stark, J. (Rangers), 1909 v E, Ni (2)
Steel, W. (Morton), 1947 v E, Bel, L; (with Derby Co), 1948 v F, E, W, Ni; 1949 v E, W, Ni, F; 1950 v E, W, Ni, Sw, P, F; (with Dundee), 1951 v W, Ni, E, A (2), D, F, Bel; 1952 v W; 1953 v W, E, Ni, Se (30)
Steele, D. M. (Huddersfield), 1923 v E, W, Ni (3)
Stein, C. (Rangers), 1969 v W, Ni, D, E, Cy (2); 1970 v A (sub), Ni (sub), W, E, Ei, WG; 1971 v D, USSR, Bel, D; 1972 v Cz (sub); (with Coventry C), 1973 v E (2 sub), W (sub), Ni (21)
Stephen, J. F. (Bradford), 1947 v W; 1948 v W (2)
Stevenson, G. (Motherwell), 1928 v W, Ni; 1930 v Ni, E, F; 1931 v E, W; 1932 v W, Ni; 1933 v Ni; 1934 v E; 1935 v Ni (12)
Stewart, A. (Queen's Park), 1888 v Ni; 1889 v W (2)
Stewart, A. (Third Lanark), 1894 v W (1)
Stewart, D. (Dumbarton), 1888 v Ni (1)
Stewart, D. (Queen's Park), 1893 v W; 1894 v Ni; 1897 v Ni (3)
Stewart, D. S. (Leeds U), 1978 v EG (1)
Stewart, G. (Hibernian), 1906 v W, E; (with Manchester C), 1907 v E, W (4)
Stewart, J. (Kilmarnock), 1977 v Ch (sub); (with Middlesbrough), 1979 v N (2)
Stewart, R. (West Ham U), 1981 v W, Ni, E; 1982 v Ni, P, W; 1984 v F; 1987 v Ei (2), L (10)
Stewart, W. E. (Queen's Park), 1898 v Ni; 1900 v Ni (2)
Storrier, D. (Celtic), 1899 v E, W, Ni (3)
Strachan, G. (Aberdeen), 1980 v Ni, W, E, Pol, H (sub); 1981 v Se, P; 1982 v Ni, P, Sp, Ho (sub), Nz, Br, USSR; 1983 v EG, Sw, Bel, Sw, Ni (sub), W, E, Ca (2 + 1 sub); 1984 v EG, Ni, E, F; (with Manchester U), 1985 v Sp (sub), E, Ic; 1986 v W, Aus, R, D, WG, U; 1987 v Bul, Ei (2); 1988 v H; 1989 v F (sub); (with Leeds U), 1990 v F; 1991 v USSR, Bul, Sm; 1992 v Sw, R, Ni, Fi (50)
Sturrock, P. (Dundee U), 1981 v W (sub), Ni, E (sub); 1982 v P, Ni (sub), W (sub), E (sub); 1983 v EG (sub), Sw, Bel (sub), Ca (3); 1984 v W; 1985 v Y (sub); 1986 v Is (sub), Ho, D, U; 1987 v Bel (20)
Summers, W. (St Mirren), 1926 v E (1)
Symon, J. S. (Rangers), 1939 v H (1)

Tait, T. S. (Sunderland), 1911 v W (1)
Taylor, J. (Queen's Park), 1872 v E; 1873 v E; 1874 v E; 1875 v E; 1876 v E, W (6)
Taylor, J. D. (Dumbarton), 1892 v W; 1893 v W; 1894 v Ni; (with St Mirren), 1895 v Ni (4)
Taylor, W. (Hearts), 1892 v E (1)
Telfer, W. (Motherwell), 1933 v Ni; 1934 v Ni (2)
Telfer, W. D. (St Mirren), 1954 v W (1)
Templeton, R. (Aston Villa), 1902 v E; (with Newcastle U), 1903 v E, W; 1904 v E; (with Woolwich Arsenal), 1905 v W; (with Kilmarnock), 1908 v Ni; 1910 v E, Ni; 1912 v E, Ni; 1913 v W (11)
Thomson, A. (Arthurlie), 1886 v Ni (1)
Thomson, A. (Third Lanark), 1889 v W (1)
Thomson, A. (Airdrieonians), 1909 v Ni (1)
Thomson, A. (Celtic), 1926 v E; 1932 v F; 1933 v W (3)
Thomson, C. (Hearts), 1904 v Ni; 1905 v E, Ni, W; 1906 v W, Ni; 1907 v E, W, Ni; 1908 v E, W, Ni; (with Sunderland), 1909 v W; 1910 v E; 1911 v Ni; 1912 v E, W; 1913 v E, W; 1914 v E, Ni (21)
Thomson, C. (Sunderland), 1937 v Cz (1)
Thomson, D. (Dundee), 1920 v W (1)
Thomson, J. (Celtic), 1930 v F; 1931 v E, W, Ni (4)
Thomson, J. J. (Queen's Park), 1872 v E; 1873 v E; 1874 v E (3)
Thomson, J. R. (Everton), 1933 v W (1)
Thomson, R. (Celtic), 1932 v W (1)
Thomson, R. W. (Falkirk), 1927 v E (1)
Thomson, S. (Rangers), 1884 v W, Ni (2)
Thomson, W. (Dumbarton), 1892 v W; 1893 v W; 1898 v Ni, W (4)
Thomson, W. (Dundee), 1896 v W (1)
Thornton, W. (Rangers), 1947 v W, Ni; 1948 v E, Ni; 1949 v F; 1952 v D, Se (7)
Thomson, W. (St Mirren), 1980 v Ni; 1981 v Ni (sub + 1) 1982 v P; 1983 v Ni, Ca; 1984 v EG (7)
Toner, W. (Kilmarnock), 1959 v W, Ni (2)
Townsley, T. (Falkirk), 1926 v W (1)
Troup, A. (Dundee), 1920 v E; 1921 v W, Ni; 1922 v Ni; (with Everton), 1926 v E (5)
Turnbull, E. (Hibernian), 1948 v Bel, Sw; 1951 v A; 1958 v H, Pol, Y, Par, F (8)
Turner, T. (Arthurlie), 1884 v W (1)
Turner, W. (Pollokshields Ath), 1885 v Ni; 1886 v Ni (2)

Ure, J. F. (Dundee), 1962 v W, Cz; 1963 v W, Ni, E, A, N, Sp; (with Arsenal), 1964 v Ni, N; 1968 v Ni (11)
Urquhart, D. (Hibernian), 1934 v W (1)

Vallance, T. (Rangers), 1877 v E, W; 1878 v E; 1879 v E, W; 1881 v E, W (7)
Venters, A. (Cowdenbeath), 1934 v Ni; (with Rangers), 1936 v E; 1939 v E (3)

Waddell, T. S. (Queen's Park), 1891 v Ni; 1892 v E; 1893 v E, Ni; 1895 v E, Ni (6)
Waddell, W. (Rangers), 1947 v W; 1949 v E, W, Ni, F; 1950 v E, Ni; 1951 v E, D, F, Bel, A; 1952 v Ni, W; 1954 v Ni; 1955 v W, Ni (17)
Wales, H. M. (Motherwell), 1933 v W (1)
Walker, A. (Celtic), 1988 v Co (sub) (1)
Walker, F. (Third Lanark), 1922 v W (1)
Walker, G. (St Mirren), 1930 v F; 1931 v Ni, A, Sw (4)
Walker, J. (Hearts), 1895 v Ni; 1897 v W; 1898 v Ni; (with Rangers), 1904 v W, Ni (5)

Walker, J. (Swindon T), 1911 v E, W, Ni; 1912 v E, W, Ni; 1913 v E, W, Ni (9)
Walker, N. (Hearts), 1993 v G (1)
Walker, R. (Hearts), 1900 v E, Ni; 1901 v E, W; 1902 v E, W, Ni; 1903 v E, W, Ni; 1904 v E, W, Ni; 1905 v E, W, Ni; 1906 v Ni; 1907 v E, Ni; 1908 v E, W, Ni; 1909 v E, W; 1912 v E, W, Ni; 1913 v E, W (29)
Walker, T. (Hearts), 1935 v E, W; 1936 v E, W, Ni; 1937 v G, E, W, Ni, A, Cz; 1938 v E, W, Ni, Cz, Ho; 1939 v E, W, Ni, H (20)
Walker, W. (Clyde), 1909 v Ni; 1910 v Ni (2)
Wallace, I. A. (Coventry C), 1978 v Bul (sub); 1979 v P (sub), W (3)
Wallace, W. S. B. (Hearts), 1965 v Ni; 1966 v E, Ho; (with Celtic), 1967 v E, USSR (sub); 1968 v Ni; 1969 v E (sub) (7)
Wardhaugh, J. (Hearts), 1955 v H; 1957 v Ni (2)
Wark, J. (Ipswich T), 1979 v W, Ni, E, Arg, N (sub); 1980 v Pe, A, Bel (2); 1981 v Is, Ni; 1982 v Se, Sp, Ho, Ni, Nz, Br, USSR; 1983 v EG, Sw (2), Ni, E (sub); 1984 v U, Bel, EG; (with Liverpool), E, F; 1985 v Y (29)
Watson, A. (Queen's Park), 1881 v E, W; 1882 v E (3)
Watson, J. (Sunderland), 1903 v E, W; 1904 v E; 1905 v E; (with Middlesbrough), 1909 v E, Ni (6)
Watson, J. (Motherwell), 1948 v Ni; (with Huddersfield T), 1954 v Ni (2)
Watson, J. A. K. (Rangers), 1878 v W (1)
Watson, P. R. (Blackpool), 1934 v A (1)
Watson, R. (Motherwell), 1971 v USSR (1)
Watson, W. (Falkirk), 1898 v W (1)
Watt, F. (Kilbirnie), 1889 v W, Ni; 1890 v W; 1891 v E (4)
Watt, W. W. (Queen's Park), 1887 v Ni (1)
Waugh, W. (Hearts), 1938 v Cz (1)
Weir, A. (Motherwell), 1959 v WG; 1960 v E, P, A, H, T (6)
Weir, J. (Third Lanark), 1887 v Ni (1)
Weir, J. B. (Queen's Park), 1872 v E; 1874 v E; 1875 v E; 1878 v W (4)
Weir, P. (St Mirren), 1980 v Ni, W, Pol (sub), H; (with Aberdeen), 1983 v Sw; 1984 v Ni (6)
White, John (Albion R), 1922 v W; (with Hearts), 1923 v Ni (2)
White, J. A. (Falkirk), 1959 v WG, Ho, P; 1960 v Ni; (with Tottenham H), 1960 v W, Pol, A, T; 1961 v W; 1962 v Ni, W, E, Cz (2); 1963 v W, Ni, E; 1964 v Ni, W, E, N, WG (22)
White, W. (Bolton W), 1907 v E; 1908 v E (2)
Whitelaw, A. (Vale of Leven), 1887 v Ni; 1890 v W (2)
Whyte, D. (Celtic), 1988 v Bel (sub), L; 1989 v Ch (sub); 1992 v US (sub); (with Middlesbrough), 1993 v P, I (6)
Wilson, A. (Sheffield W), 1907 v E; 1908 v E; 1912 v E; 1913 v E, W; 1914 v Ni (6)
Wilson, A. (Portsmouth), 1954 v Fi (1)
Wilson, A. N. (Dunfermline), 1920 v E, W, Ni; 1921 v E, W, Ni; (with Middlesbrough), 1922 v E, W, Ni; 1923 v E, W, Ni (12)
Wilson, D. (Queen's Park), 1900 v W (1)
Wilson, D. (Oldham Ath), 1913 v E (1)
Wilson, D. (Rangers), 1961 v E, W, Ni, Ei (2), Cz; 1962 v Ni, W, E, Cz, U; 1963 v W, E, A, N, Ei, Sp; 1964 v E, WG; 1965 v Ni, E, Fi (22)
Wilson, G. W. (Hearts), 1904 v W; 1905 v E, Ni; 1906 v W; (with Everton), 1907 v E; (with Newcastle U), 1909 v E (6)
Wilson, Hugh, (Newmilns), 1890 v W; (with Sunderland), 1897 v E; (with Third Lanark), 1902 v W; 1904 v Ni (4)
Wilson, I. A. (Leicester C), 1987 v E, Br; (with Everton), 1988 v Bel, Bul, L (5)
Wilson, J. (Vale of Leven), 1888 v W; 1889 v E; 1890 v E; 1891 v E (4)
Wilson, P. (Celtic), 1926 v Ni; 1930 v F; 1931 v Ni; 1933 v E (4)
Wilson, P. (Celtic), 1975 v Sp (sub) (1)
Wilson, R. P. (Arsenal), 1972 v P, Ho (2)
Wiseman, W. (Queen's Park), 1927 v W; 1930 v Ni (2)
Wood, G. (Everton), 1979 v Ni, E, Arg (sub); (with Arsenal), 1982 v Ni (4)
Woodburn, W. A. (Rangers), 1947 v E, Bel, L; 1948 v W, Ni; 1949 v E, F; 1950 v E, W, Ni, P, F; 1951 v E, W, Ni, A (2), D, F, Bel; 1952 v E, W, Ni, USA (24)
Wotherspoon, D. N. (Queen's Park), 1872 v E; 1873 v E (2)
Wright, K. (Hibernian), 1992 v Ni (1)
Wright, S. (Aberdeen), 1993 v G, Es (2)
Wright, T. (Sunderland), 1953 v W, Ni, E (3)
Wylie, T. G. (Rangers), 1890 v Ni (1)

Yeats, R. (Liverpool), 1965 v W; 1966 v I (2)
Yorston, B. C. (Aberdeen), 1931 v Ni (1)
Yorston, H. (Aberdeen), 1955 v W (1)
Young, A. (Hearts), 1960 v E, A (sub), H, T; 1961 v W, Ni; (with Everton), Ei; 1966 v P (8)
Young, A. (Everton), 1905 v E; 1907 v W (2)
Young, G. L. (Rangers), 1947 v E, Ni, Bel, L; 1948 v E, Ni, Bel, Sw, F; 1949 v E, W, Ni, F; 1950 v E, W, Ni, Sw, P, F; 1951 v E, W, Ni, A (2), D, F, Bel; 1952 v E, W, Ni, USA, D, Se; 1953 v W, E, Ni, Se; 1954 v Ni, W; 1955 v W, Ni, P, Y; 1956 v Ni, W, E, A; 1957 v E, Ni, W, Y, Sp, Sw (53)
Young, J. (Celtic), 1906 v Ni (1)
Younger, T. (Hibernian), 1955 v P, Y, A, H; 1956 v E, Ni, W, A; (with Liverpool), 1957 v E, Ni, W, Y, Sp (2), Sw, WG; 1958 v Ni, W, E, Sw, H, Pol, Y, Par (24)

WALES

Adams, H. (Berwyn R), 1882 v Ni, E; (with Druids), 1883 v Ni, E (4)
Aizlewood, M. (Charlton Ath), 1986 v S.Ar, Ca (2); 1987 v Fi; (with Leeds U), USSR, Fi (sub); 1988 v D (sub), Se, Ma, I; 1989 v Ho, Se (sub), WG; (with Bradford C), 1990 v Fi, WG, Ei, Cr; (with Bristol C), 1991 v D, Bel (2), L, Ei, Ic, Pol, WG; 1992 v Br, L, Ei, A, R, Ho, Arg, J; 1993 v Ei, Bel, Fa; 1994 v RCS, Cy (38)
Allchurch, I. J. (Swansea T), 1951 v E, Ni, P, Sw; 1952 v E, S, Ni, R of UK; 1953 v S, E, Ni, F, Y; 1954 v S, E, Ni, A; 1955 v S, E, Ni, Y; 1956 v E, S, Ni, A; 1957 v E, S; 1958 v Ni, Is (2), H (2), M, Sw, Br; (with Newcastle U), 1959 v E, S, Ni; 1960 v E, S; 1961 v Ni, H, Sp (2); 1962 v E, S, Br (2), M; (with Cardiff C), 1963 v S, E, Ni, H (2); 1964 v E; 1965 v S, E, Ni, Gr, I, USSR; (with Swansea T), 1966 v USSR, E, S, D, Br (2), Ch (68)
Allchurch, L. (Swansea T), 1955 v Ni; 1956 v A; 1958 v S, Ni, EG, Is; 1959 v S; (with Sheffield U), 1962 v S, Ni, Br; 1964 v E (11)
Allen, B. W. (Coventry C), 1951 v S, E (2)
Allen, M. (Watford), 1986 v S.Ar (sub), Ca (1 + 1 sub); (with Norwich C), 1989 v Is (sub); 1990 v Ho, WG; (with Millwall), Ei, Se, Cr (sub); 1991 v L (sub), Ei (sub); 1992 v A; 1993 v Ei (sub); (with Newcastle U), 1994 v R (sub) (14)

Arridge, S. (Bootle), 1892 v S, Ni; (with Everton), 1894 v Ni; 1895 v Ni; 1896 v E; (with New Brighton Tower), 1898 v E, Ni; 1899 v E (8)
Astley, D. J. (Charlton Ath), 1931 v Ni; (with Aston Villa), 1932 v E; 1933 v E, S, Ni; 1934 v E, S; 1935 v S; 1936 v E, Ni; (with Derby Co), 1939 v E, S; (with Blackpool), F (13)
Atherton, R. W. (Hibernian), 1899 v E, Ni; 1903 v E, S, Ni; (with Middlesbrough), 1904 v E, S, Ni; 1905 v Ni (9)

Bailiff, W. E. (Llanelly), 1913 v E, S, Ni; 1920 v Ni (4)
Baker, C. W. (Cardiff C), 1958 v M; 1960 v S, Ni; 1961 v S, E, Ei; 1962 v S (7)
Baker, W. G. (Cardiff C), 1948 v Ni (1)
Bamford, T. (Wrexham), 1931 v E, S, Ni; 1932 v Ni; 1933 v F (5)
Barnes, W. (Arsenal), 1948 v E, S, Ni; 1949 v E, S, Ni; 1950 v E, S, Ni, Bel; 1951 v E, S, Ni, P; 1952 v E, S, Ni, R of UK; 1954 v E, S; 1955 v S, Y (22)
Bartley, T. (Glossop NE), 1898 v E (1)
Bastock, A. M. (Shrewsbury), 1892 v Ni (1)
Beadles, G. H. (Cardiff C), 1925 v E, S (2)
Bell, W. S. (Shrewsbury Engineers), 1881 v E, S; (with Crewe Alex), 1886 v E, S, Ni (5)
Bennion, S. R. (Manchester U), 1926 v S; 1927 v S; 1928 v S, E, Ni; 1929 v S, E, Ni; 1930 v S; 1932 v Ni (10)
Berry, G. F. (Wolverhampton W), 1979 v WG; 1980 v Ei, WG (sub), T; (with Stoke C), 1983 v E (sub) (5)
Blackmore, C. G. (Manchester U), 1985 v N (sub); 1986 v S (sub), H (sub), S.Ar, Ei, U; 1987 v Fi (2), USSR, Cz; 1988 v D (2), Cz, Y, Se, Ma, I; 1989 v Ho, Fi, Is, WG; 1990 v F; Ho, WG, Cr; 1991 v Bel, L; 1992 v Ei (sub), A, R (sub), Ho, Arg, J; 1993 v Fa, Cy, Bel, RCS; 1994 v Se (sub) (38)
Blake, N. A. (Sheffield U), 1994 v N, Se (sub) (2)
Blew, H. (Wrexham), 1899 v E, S, Ni; 1902 v S, Ni; 1903 v E, S; 1904 v E, S, Ni; 1905 v S, Ni; 1906 v E, S, Ni; 1907 v S; 1908 v E, S, Ni; 1909 v E, S; 1910 v E (22)
Boden, T. (Wrexham), 1880 v E (1)
Bodin, P. J. (Swindon T), 1990 v Cr; 1991 v D, Bel, L, Ei; (with C Palace), Bel, Ic, Pol, WG; 1992 v Br, G, L (sub); (with Swindon T), Ei (sub), Ho, Arg; 1993 v Ei, Bel, RCS, Fa; 1994 v R, Se, Es (sub) (22)
Boulter, L. M. (Brentford), 1939 v Ni (1)
Bowdler, H. E. (Shrewsbury), 1893 v S (1)
Bowdler, J. C. H. (Shrewsbury), 1890 v Ni; (with Wolverhampton W), 1891 v S; 1892 v Ni; (with Shrewsbury), 1894 v E (4)
Bowen, D. L. (Arsenal), 1955 v S, Y; 1957 v Ni, Cz, EG; 1958 v E, S, Ni, EG, Is (2), H (2), M, Se, Br; 1959 v E, S, Ni (19)
Bowen, E. (Druids), 1880 v S; 1883 v S (2)
Bowen, J. P. (Swansea C), 1994 v Es (1)
Bowen, M. R. (Tottenham H), 1986 v Ca (2 sub); (with Norwich C), 1988 v Y (sub); 1989 v Fi (sub), Is, Se, WG (sub); 1990 v Fi (sub), Ho, WG, Se; 1992 v Br (sub), G, L, Ei, A, R, Ho (sub), J; 1993 v Fa, Cy, Bel (1 + sub), RCS (sub); 1994 v RCS, Se (26)
Bowsher, S. J. (Burnley), 1929 v Ni (1)
Boyle, T. (C Palace), 1981 v Ei, S (sub) (2)
Britten, T. J. (Parkgrove), 1878 v S; (with Presteigne), 1880 v S (2)
Brookes, S. J. (Llandudno), 1900 v E, Ni (2)
Brown, A. I. (Aberdare Ath), 1926 v Ni (1)
Bryan, T. (Oswestry), 1886 v E, Ni (2)
Buckland, T. (Bangor), 1899 v E (1)
Burgess, W. A. R. (Tottenham H), 1947 v E, S, Ni; 1948 v E, S; 1949 v E, S, Ni, P, Bel, Sw; 1950 v E, S, Ni, Bel; 1951 v S, Ni, P, Sw; 1952 v E, S, Ni, R of UK; 1953 v S, E, Ni, F, Y; 1954 v S, E, Ni, A (32)
Burke, T. (Wrexham), 1883 v E; 1884 v S; 1885 v E, S, Ni; (with Newton Heath), 1887 v E, S; 1888 v S (8)
Burnett, T. B. (Ruabon), 1877 v S (1)
Burton, A. D. (Norwich C), 1963 v Ni, H; (with Newcastle U), 1964 v E; 1969 v S, E, Ni, I, EG; 1972 v Cz (9)
Butler, J. (Chirk), 1893 v E, S, Ni (3)
Butler, W. T. (Druids), 1900 v S, Ni (2)

Cartwright, L. (Coventry C), 1974 v E (sub), S, Ni; 1976 v S (sub); 1977 v WG (sub); (with Wrexham), 1978 v Ir (sub); 1979 v Ma (7)
Carty, T. – See McCarthy – (Wrexham).
Challen, J. B. (Corinthians), 1887 v E, S; 1888 v E; (with Wellingborough GS), 1890 v E (4)
Chapman, T. (Newtown), 1894 v E, S, Ni; 1895 v S, Ni; (with Manchester C), 1896 v E; 1897 v E (7)
Charles, J. M. (Swansea C), 1981 v Cz, T (sub), S (sub), USSR (sub); 1982 v Ic; 1983 v N (sub), Y (sub), Bul (sub), S, Ni, Br; 1984 v Bul (sub); (with QPR), Y (sub), S; (with Oxford U), 1985 v Ic (sub), Sp, Ic; 1986 v Ei; 1987 v Fi (19)
Charles, M. (Swansea T), 1955 v Ni; 1956 v E, S, A; 1957 v E, Ni, Cz (2), EG; 1958 v E, S, EG, Is (2), H (2), M, Se, Br; 1959 v E, S; (with Arsenal), 1961 v Ni, H, Sp (2); 1962 v E, S; (with Cardiff C), 1962 v Br, Ni; 1963 v S, H (31)
Charles, W. J. (Leeds U), 1950 v Ni; 1951 v Sw; 1953 v Ni, F, Y; 1954 v E, S, Ni, A; 1955 v S, E, Ni, Y; 1956 v E, S, A, Ni; 1957 v E, S, Ni, Cz (2), EG; (with Juventus), 1958 v Is (2), H (2) M, Se; 1960 v S; 1962 v E, Br (2), M; (with Leeds U), 1963 v S; (with Cardiff C), 1964 v S; 1965 v S, USSR (38)
Clarke, R. J. (Manchester C), 1949 v E; 1950 v S, Ni, Bel; 1951 v E, S, Ni, P, Sw; 1952 v S, E, Ni, R of UK; 1953 v S, E; 1954 v E, S, Ni; 1955 v Y, S, E; 1956 v Ni (22)
Coleman, C. (C Palace), 1992 v A (sub); 1993 v Ei (sub); 1994 v N, Es (4)
Collier, D. J. (Grimsby T), 1921 v S (1)
Collins, W. S. (Llanelly), 1931 v S (1)
Conde, C. (Chirk), 1884 v E, S, Ni (3)
Cook, F. C. (Newport Co), 1925 v E, S; (with Portsmouth), 1928 v E, S; 1930 v E, S, Ni; 1932 v E (8)
Crompton, W. (Wrexham), 1931 v E, S, Ni (3)
Cross, E. A. (Wrexham), 1876 v S; 1877 v S (2)
Cross, K. (Druids), 1879 v S; 1881 v E, S (3)
Crowe, V. H. (Aston Villa), 1959 v E, Ni; 1960 v E, Ni; 1961 v S, E, Ni, Ei, H, Sp (2); 1962 v E, S, Br, M; 1963 v H (16)
Cumner, R. H. (Arsenal), 1939 v E, S, Ni (3)
Curtis, A. (Swansea C), 1976 v E, Y (sub), S, Ni, Y (sub), E; 1977 v WG, S (sub), Ni (sub); 1978 v WG, E, S; 1979 v WG, S; (with Leeds U), E, Ni, Ma; 1980 v Ei, WG, T; (with Swansea C), 1982 v Cz, Ic, USSR, Sp, E, S, Ni; 1983 v N; 1984 v R (sub); (with Southampton), S; 1985 v Sp, N (1 + 1 sub); 1986 v H; (with Cardiff C), 1987 v USSR (35)
Curtis, E. R. (Cardiff C), 1928 v S; (with Birmingham), 1932 v S; 1934 v Ni (3)

Daniel, R. W. (Arsenal), 1951 v E, Ni, P; 1952 v E, S, Ni, R of UK; 1953 v S, E, Ni, F, Y; (with Sunderland), 1954 v E, S, Ni; 1955 v E, Ni; 1957 v S, E, Ni, Cz (21)
Darvell, S. (Oxford University), 1897 v S, Ni (2)
Davies, A. (Manchester U), 1983 v Ni, Br; 1984 v E, Ni; 1985 v Ic; (with Newcastle U), 1986 v H; (with Swansea C), 1988 v Ma, I; 1989 v Ho; (with Bradford C), 1990 v Fi, Ei (11)
Davies, A. (Wrexham), 1876 v S; 1877 v S (2)
Davies, A. (Druids), 1904 v S; (with Middlesbrough), 1905 v S (2)
Davies, A. O. (Barmouth), 1885 v Ni; 1886 v E, S; (with Swifts), 1887 v E, S; 1888 v E, Ni; (with Wrexham), 1889 v S; (with Crewe Alex), 1890 v E (9)
Davies, A. T. (Shrewsbury), 1891 v Ni (1)
Davies, C. (Brecon), 1899 v Ni; (with Hereford), 1900 v Ni (2)

Davies, C. (Charlton Ath), 1972 v R (sub) (1)
Davies, D. (Bolton W), 1904 v S, Ni; 1908 v E (sub) (3)
Davies, D. C. (Brecon), 1899 v Ni; (with Hereford); 1900 v Ni (2)
Davies, D. W. (Treharris), 1912 v Ni; (with Oldham Ath), 1913 v Ni (2)
Davies, E. Lloyd (Stoke C), 1904 v E; 1907 v E, S, Ni; (with Northampton T), 1908 v S; 1909 v Ni; 1910 v Ni; 1911 v E, S; 1912 v E, S; 1913 v E, S; 1914 v Ni, E, S (16)
Davies, E. R. (Newcastle U), 1953 v S, E; 1954 v E, S; 1958 v E, EG (6)
Davies, G. (Fulham), 1980 v T, Ic; 1982 v Sp (sub), F (sub); 1983 v E, Bul, S, Ni, Br; 1984 v R (sub), S (sub), E, Ni; 1985 v Ic; (with Manchester C), 1986 v S.Ar, Ei (16)
Davies, Rev. H. (Wrexham), 1928 v Ni (1)
Davies, Idwal (Liverpool Marine), 1923 v S (1)
Davies, J. E. (Oswestry), 1885 v E (1)
Davies, Jas (Wrexham), 1878 v S (1)
Davies, John (Wrexham), 1879 v S (1)
Davies, Jos (Newton Heath), 1888 v E, S, Ni; 1889 v S; 1890 v E; (with Wolverhampton W), 1892 v E; 1893 v E (7)
Davies, Jos (Everton), 1889 v S, Ni; (with Chirk), 1891 v Ni; (with Ardwick), v E, S; (with Sheffield U), 1895 v E, S, Ni; (with Manchester C), 1896 v E; (with Millwall), 1897 v E; (with Reading), 1900 v E (11)
Davies, J. P. (Druids), 1883 v E, Ni (2)
Davies, Ll. (Wrexham), 1907 v Ni; 1910 v Ni, S, E; (with Everton), 1911 v S, Ni; 1912 v Ni, S, E; 1913 v Ni, S, E; 1914 v Ni (13)
Davies, L. S. (Cardiff C), 1922 v E, S, Ni; 1923 v E, S, Ni; 1924 v E, S, Ni; 1925 v S, Ni; 1926 v E, Ni; 1927 v E, Ni; 1928 v S, Ni, E; 1929 v S, Ni, E; 1930 v E, S (23)
Davies, O. (Wrexham), 1890 v S (1)
Davies, R. (Wrexham), 1883 v Ni; 1884 v Ni; 1885 v Ni (3)
Davies, R. (Druids), 1885 v E (1)
Davies, R. O. (Wrexham), 1892 v Ni, E (2)
Davies, R. T. (Norwich C), 1964 v Ni; 1965 v E; 1966 v Br (2), Ch; (with Southampton), 1967 v S, E, Ni; 1968 v S, Ni, WG; 1969 v S, E, Ni, I, WG, R of UK; 1970 v E, S, Ni; 1971 v Cz, S, E, Ni; 1972 v R, E, S, N; (with Portsmouth), 1974 v E (29)
Davies, R. W. (Bolton W), 1964 v E; 1965 v E, S, Ni, D, Gr, USSR; 1966 v E, S, Ni, USSR, D, Br (2), Ch (sub); 1967 v S; (with Newcastle U), E; 1968 v S, Ni, WG; 1969 v S, E, Ni, I; 1970 v EG; 1971 v R, Cz; (with Manchester C), 1972 v E, S, Ni; (with Manchester U), 1973 v E, S (sub), Ni; (with Blackpool), 1974 v Pol (34)
Davies, Stanley (Preston NE), 1920 v E, S, Ni; (with Everton), 1921 v E, S, Ni; (with WBA), 1922 v E, S, Ni; 1923 v S; 1925 v S, Ni; 1926 v S, E, Ni; 1927 v S; 1928 v S; (with Rotherham U), 1930 v Ni (18)
Davies, T. (Oswestry), 1886 v E (1)
Davies, T. (Druids), 1903 v E, Ni, S; 1904 v S (4)
Davies, W. (Wrexham), 1884 v Ni (1)
Davies, W. (Swansea T), 1924 v E, S, Ni; (with Cardiff C), 1925 v E, S, Ni; 1926 v E, S, Ni; 1927 v S; 1928 v Ni; (with Notts Co), 1929 v E, S, Ni; 1930 v E, S, Ni (17)
Davies, William (Wrexham), 1903 v Ni; 1905 v Ni; (with Blackburn R), 1908 v E, S; 1909 v E, S, Ni; 1911 v E, S, Ni; 1912 v Ni (11)
Davies, W. C. (C Palace), 1908 v S; (with WBA), 1909 v E; 1910 v S; (with C Palace), 1914 v E (4)
Davies, W. D. (Everton), 1975 v H, L, S, E, Ni; 1976 v Y (2), E, Ni; 1977 v WG, S (2), Cz, E, Ni; 1978 v K; (with Wrexham), S, Cz, WG, Ir, E, S, Ni; 1979 v Ma, T, WG, S, E, Ni, Ma; 1980 v Ei, WG, T, E, S, Ni, Ic; 1981 v T, Cz, Ei, T, S, E, USSR; (with Swansea C), 1982 v Cz, Ic, USSR, Sp, E, S, F; 1983 v Y (52)
Davies, W. H. (Oswestry), 1876 v S; 1877 v S; 1879 v E; 1880 v E (4)
Davies, W. O. (Millwall Ath), 1913 v E, S, Ni; 1914 v S, Ni (5)
Davis, G. (Wrexham), 1978 v Ir, E (sub), Ni (3)
Day, A. (Tottenham H), 1934 v Ni (1)
Deacy, N. (PSV Eindhoven), 1977 v Cz, S, E, Ni; 1978 v K (sub), S (sub), Cz (sub), WG, Ir, S (sub), Ni; (with Beringen), 1979 v T (12)
Dearson, D. J. (Birmingham), 1939 v S, Ni, F (3)
Derrett, S. C. (Cardiff C), 1969 v S, WG; 1970 v I; 1971 v Fi (4)
Dewey, F. T. (Cardiff Corinthians), 1931 v E, S (2)
Dibble, A. (Luton T), 1986 v Ca (1 + 1 sub); (with Manchester C), 1989 v Is (3)
Doughty, J. (Druids), 1886 v S; (with Newton Heath), 1887 v S, Ni; 1888 v E, S, Ni; 1889 v S; 1890 v E (8)
Doughty, R. (Newton Heath and Druids), 1888 v S, Ni (2)
Durban, A. (Derby Co), 1966 v Br (sub); 1967 v Ni; 1968 v E, S, Ni, WG; 1969 v EG, S, E, Ni, WG; 1970 v E, S, Ni, EG, I; 1971 v R, S, E, Ni, Cz, Fi; 1972 v Fi, Cz, E, S, Ni (27)
Dwyer, P. (Cardiff C), 1978 v Ir, E, S, Ni; 1979 v T, S, E, Ni, Ma (sub); 1980 v WG (10)

Edwards, C. (Wrexham), 1878 v S (1)
Edwards, G. (Birmingham C), 1947 v E, S, Ni; 1948 v E, S, Ni; (with Cardiff C), 1949 v Ni, P, Bel, Sw; 1950 v E, S (12)
Edwards, H. (Wrexham Civil Service), 1878 v S; 1880 v E; 1882 v E, S; 1883 v S; 1884 v Ni; 1887 v Ni (7)
Edwards, J. H. (Wanderers), 1876 v S (1)
Edwards, J. H. (Oswestry), 1895 v Ni; 1897 v E, Ni (3)
Edwards, J. H. (Aberystwyth), 1898 v Ni (1)
Edwards, L. T. (Charlton Ath), 1957 v Ni, EG (2)
Edwards, R. I. (Chester), 1978 v K (sub); 1979 v Ma, WG; (with Wrexham), 1980 v T (sub) (4)
Edwards, T. (Linfield), 1932 v S (1)
Egan, W. (Chirk), 1892 v S (1)
Ellis, B. (Motherwell), 1932 v E; 1933 v E, S; 1934 v S; 1936 v E; 1937 v S (6)
Ellis, E. (Nunhead), 1931 v S; (with Oswestry), E; 1932 v Ni (3)
Emanuel, W. J. (Bristol C), 1973 v E (sub), Ni (sub) (2)
England, H. M. (Blackburn R), 1962 v Ni, Br, M; 1963 v Ni, H; 1964 v E, S, Ni; 1965 v E, D, Gr (2), USSR, Ni, I; 1966 v E, S, Ni, USSR, D; (with Tottenham H), 1967 v S, E; 1968 v E, Ni, WG; 1969 v EG; 1970 v R of UK, EG, E, S, Ni, I; 1971 v R; 1972 v Fi, E, S, Ni; 1973 v E (3), S; 1974 v Pol; 1975 v H, L (44)
Evans, B. C. (Swansea C), 1972 v Fi, Cz; 1973 v E (2), Pol, S; (with Hereford U), 1974 v Pol (7)
Evans, D. G. (Reading), 1926 v Ni; 1927 v Ni, E; (with Huddersfield T), 1929 v S (4)
Evans, H. P. (Cardiff C), 1922 v E, S, Ni; 1924 v E, S, Ni (6)
Evans, I. (C Palace), 1976 v A, E, Y (2), E, Ni; 1977 v WG, S (2), Cz, E, Ni; 1978 v K (13)
Evans, J. (Oswestry), 1893 v Ni; 1894 v E, Ni (3)
Evans, J. (Cardiff C), 1912 v Ni; 1913 v Ni; 1914 v S; 1920 v S, Ni; 1922 v Ni; 1923 v E, Ni (8)
Evans, J. H. (Southend U), 1922 v E, S, Ni; 1923 v S (4)
Evans, Len (Aberdare Ath), 1927 v Ni; (with Cardiff C), 1931 v E, S; (with Birmingham), 1934 v Ni (4)
Evans, M. (Oswestry), 1884 v E (1)
Evans, R. (Clapton), 1902 v Ni (1)
Evans, R. E. (Wrexham), 1906 v E, S; (with Aston Villa), Ni; 1907 v E; 1908 v E, S; (with Sheffield U), 1909 v S; 1910 v E, S, Ni (10)
Evans, R. O. (Wrexham), 1902 v Ni; 1903 v E, S, Ni; (with Blackburn R), 1908 v Ni; (with Coventry C), 1911 v E, Ni; 1912 v E, S, Ni (10)
Evans, R. S. (Swansea T), 1964 v Ni (1)
Evans, T. J. (Clapton Orient), 1927 v S; 1928 v E, S; (with Newcastle U), Ni (4)

Evans, W. (Tottenham H), 1933 v Ni; 1934 v E, S; 1935 v E; 1936 v E, Ni (6)
Evans, W. A. W. (Oxford University), 1876 v S; 1877 v S (2)
Evans, W. G. (Bootle), 1890 v E; 1891 v E; (with Aston Villa), 1892 v E (3)
Evelyn, E. C. (Crusaders), 1887 v E (1)
Eyton-Jones, J. A. (Wrexham), 1883 v Ni; 1884 v Ni, E, S (4)

Farmer, G. (Oswestry), 1885 v E, S (2)
Felgate, D. (Lincoln C), 1984 v R (sub) (1)
Finnigan, R. J. (Wrexham), 1930 v Ni (1)
Flynn, B. (Burnley), 1975 v L (2 sub), H (sub), S, E, Ni; 1976 v A, E, Y (2), E, Ni; 1977 v WG (sub), S (2), Cz, E, Ni; 1978 v K (2), S; (with Leeds U), Cz, WG, Ir (sub), E, S, Ni; 1979 v Ma, T, S, E, Ni, Ma; 1980 v Ei, WG, E, S, Ni, Ic; 1981 v T, Cz, Ei, T, S, E, USSR; 1982 v Cz, USSR, E, S, Ni, F; 1983 v N; (with Burnley), Y, E, Bul, S, Ni, Br; 1984 v N, R, Bul, Y, S, N, Is (66)
Ford, T. (Swansea T), 1947 v S; (with Aston Villa), 1947 v Ni; 1948 v S, Ni; 1949 v E, S, Ni, P, Bel, Sw; 1950 v E, S, Ni, Bel; 1951 v S; (with Sunderland), 1951 v E, Ni, P, Sw; 1952 v E, S, Ni, R of UK; 1953 v S, E, Ni, F, Y; (with Cardiff C), 1954 v A; 1955 v S, E, Ni, Y; 1956 v S, Ni, E, A; 1957 v S (38)
Foulkes, H. E. (WBA), 1932 v Ni (1)
Foulkes, W. I. (Newcastle U), 1952 v E, S, Ni, R of UK; 1953 v E, S, F, Y; 1954 v E, S, Ni (11)
Foulkes, W. T. (Oswestry), 1884 v Ni; 1885 v S (2)
Fowler, J. (Swansea T), 1925 v E; 1926 v E, Ni; 1927 v S; 1928 v S; 1929 v E (6)

Garner, J. (Aberystwyth), 1896 v S (1)
Giggs, R. J. (Manchester U), 1992 v G (sub), L (sub), R (sub); 1993 v Fa (sub), Bel (sub + 1), RCS, Fa; 1994 v RCS, Cy, R (11)
Giles, D. (Swansea C), 1980 v E, S, Ni, Ic; 1981 v T, Cz, T (sub), E (sub), USSR (sub); (with C Palace), 1982 v Sp (sub); 1983 v Ni (sub), Br (12)
Gillam, S. G. (Wrexham), 1889 v S (sub), Ni; (with Shrewsbury), 1890 v E, Ni; (with Clapton), 1894 v S (5)
Glascodine, G. (Wrexham), 1879 v E (1)
Glover, E. M. (Grimsby T), 1932 v S; 1934 v Ni; 1936 v S; 1937 v E, S, Ni; 1939 v Ni (7)
Godding, G. (Wrexham), 1923 v S, Ni (2)
Godfrey, B. C. (Preston NE), 1964 v Ni; 1965 v D, I (3)
Goodwin, U. (Ruthin), 1881 v E (1)
Goss, J. (Norwich C), 1991 v Ic, Pol (sub); 1992 v A; 1994 v Cy (sub), R (sub), Se (6)
Gough, R. T. (Oswestry White Star), 1883 v S (1)
Gray, A. (Oldham Ath), 1924 v E, S, Ni; 1925 v E, S, Ni; 1926 v E, S; 1927 v S; (with Manchester C), 1928 v E, S; 1929 v E, S, Ni; (with Manchester Central), 1930 v S; (with Tranmere R), 1932 v E, S, Ni; (with Chester), 1937 v E, S, Ni; 1938 v E, S, Ni (24)
Green, A. W. (Aston Villa), 1901 v Ni; (with Notts Co), 1903 v E; 1904 v S, Ni; 1906 v Ni, E; (with Nottingham F), 1907 v E; 1908 v S (8)
Green, C. R. (Birmingham C), 1965 v USSR, I; 1966 v E, S, USSR, Br (2); 1967 v E; 1968 v E, S, Ni, WG; 1969 v S, I, Ni (sub) (15)
Green, G. H. (Charlton Ath), 1938 v Ni; 1939 v E, Ni, F (4)
Grey, Dr W. (Druids), 1876 v S; 1878 v S (2)
Griffiths, A. T. (Wrexham), 1971 v Cz (sub); 1975 v A, H (2), L (2), E, Ni; 1976 v A, E, S, E (sub), Ni, Y (2); 1977 v WG, S (17)
Griffiths, F. J. (Blackpool), 1900 v E, S (2)
Griffiths, G. (Chirk), 1887 v Ni (1)
Griffiths, J. H. (Swansea T), 1953 v Ni (1)
Griffiths, L. (Wrexham), 1902 v S (1)
Griffiths, M. W. (Leicester C), 1947 v Ni; 1949 v P, Bel; 1950 v E, S, Bel; 1951 v E, Ni, P, Sw; 1954 v A (11)
Griffiths, P. (Chirk), 1884 v E, Ni; 1888 v E; 1890 v S, Ni; 1891 v Ni (6)
Griffiths, P. H. (Everton), 1932 v S (1)
Griffiths, S. (Wrexham), 1902 v S (1)
Griffiths, T. P. (Everton), 1927 v E, Ni; 1929 v E; 1930 v E; 1931 v Ni; 1932 v Ni, S, E; (with Bolton W), 1933 v E, S, Ni; (with Middlesbrough), F; 1934 v E, S; 1935 v E, Ni; 1936 v S; (with Aston Villa), Ni; 1937 v E, S, Ni (21)

Hall, G. D. (Chelsea), 1988 v Y (sub), Ma, I; 1989 v Ho, Fi, Is; 1990 v Ei; 1991 v Ei; 1992 v A (sub) (9)
Hallam, J. (Oswestry), 1889 v E (1)
Hanford, H. (Swansea T), 1934 v Ni; 1935 v S; 1936 v E; (with Sheffield W), 1936 v Ni; 1938 v E, S; 1939 v F (7)
Harrington, A. C. (Cardiff C), 1956 v Ni; 1957 v E, S; 1958 v S, Ni, Is (2); 1961 v S, E; 1962 v E, S (11)
Harris, C. S. (Leeds U), 1976 v E, S; 1978 v WG, Ir, E, S, Ni; 1979 v Ma, T, WG, E (sub), Ma; 1980 v Ni (sub), Ic (sub); 1981 v T, Cz (sub), Ei, T, S, E, USSR; 1982 v Cz, Ic, E (sub) (24)
Harris, W. C. (Middlesbrough), 1954 v A; 1957 v EG, Cz; 1958 v E, S, EG (6)
Harrison, W. C. (Wrexham), 1899 v E; 1900 v E, S, Ni; 1901 v Ni (5)
Hayes, A. (Wrexham), 1890 v Ni; 1894 v Ni (2)
Hennessey, W. T. (Birmingham C), 1962 v Ni, Br (2); 1963 v S, E, H (2); 1964 v E, S; 1965 v S, E, D, Gr, USSR; 1966 v E, USSR; (with Nottingham F), 1966 v S, Ni, D, Br (2), Ch; 1967 v S, E; 1968 v E, S, Ni; 1969 v WG, EG, R of UK; 1970 v EG; (with Derby Co), E, S, Ni; 1972 v Fi, Cz, E, S; 1973 v E (39)
Hersee, A. M. (Bangor), 1886 v S, Ni (2)
Hersee, R. (Llandudno), 1886 v Ni (1)
Hewitt, R. (Cardiff C), 1958 v Ni, Is, Se, H, Br (5)
Hewitt, T. J. (Wrexham), 1911 v E, S, Ni; (with Chelsea), 1913 v E, S, Ni; (with South Liverpool), 1914 v E, S (8)
Heywood, D. (Druids), 1879 v E (1)
Hibbott, H. (Newtown Excelsior), 1880 v E, S; (with Newtown), 1885 v S (3)
Higham, G. G. (Oswestry), 1878 v S; 1879 v E (2)
Hill, M. R. (Ipswich T), 1972 v Cz, R (2)
Hockey, T. (Sheffield U), 1972 v Fi, R; 1973 v E (2); (with Norwich C), Pol, S, E, Ni; (with Aston Villa), 1974 v Pol (9)
Hoddinott, T. F. (Watford), 1921 v E, S (2)
Hodges, G. (Wimbledon), 1984 v N (sub), Is (sub); 1987 v USSR, Fi, Cz; (with Newcastle U), 1988 v D; (with Watford), D (sub), Cz (sub), Se, Ma (sub), I (sub); 1990 v Se, Cr; (with Sheffield U), 1992 v Br (sub), Ei (sub), A (16)
Hodgkinson, A. V. (Southampton), 1908 v Ni (1)
Holden, A. (Chester C), 1984 v Is (sub) (1)
Hole, B. G. (Cardiff C), 1963 v Ni; 1964 v Ni; 1965 v S, E, Ni, D, Gr (2), USSR, I; 1966 v E, S, Ni, USSR, D, Br (2), Ch; (with Blackburn R), 1967 v S, E, Ni; 1968 v E, S, Ni, WG; (with Aston Villa), 1969 v I, WG, EG; 1970 v I; (with Swansea C), 1971 v R (30)
Hole, W. J. (Swansea T), 1921 v Ni; 1922 v E; 1923 v E, Ni; 1928 v E, S, Ni; 1929 v E, S (9)
Hollins, D. M. (Newcastle U), 1962 v Br (sub), M; 1963 v Ni, H; 1964 v E; 1965 v Ni, Gr, I; 1966 v S, D, Br (11)
Hopkins, I. J. (Brentford), 1935 v S, Ni; 1936 v E, Ni; 1937 v E, S, Ni; 1938 v E, Ni; 1939 v E, S, Ni (12)
Hopkins, J. (Fulham), 1983 v Ni, Br; 1984 v N, R, Bul, Y, S, E, Ni, N, Is; 1985 v Ic (1 + 1 sub), N; (with C Palace), 1990 v Ho, Cr (16)
Hopkins, M. (Tottenham H), 1956 v Ni; 1957 v Ni, S, E, Cz (2), EG; 1958 v E, S, Ni, EG, Is (2), H (2), M, Se, Br;

1959 v E, S, Ni; 1960 v E, S; 1961 v Ni, H, Sp (2); 1962 v Ni, Br (2), M; 1963 v S, Ni, H (34)
Horne, B. (Portsmouth), 1988 v D (sub), Y, Se (sub), Ma, I; 1989 v Ho, Fi, Is; (with Southampton), Se, WG; 1990 v WG (sub), Ei, Se, Cr; 1991 v D, Bel (2), L, Ei, Ic, Pol, WG; 1992 v Br, G, L, Ei, A, R, Ho, Arg, J; (with Everton), 1993 v Fa, Cy, Bel, Ei, Bel, RCS, Fa; 1994 v RCS, Cy, R, N, Se, Es (44)
Howell, E. G. (Builth), 1888 v Ni; 1890 v E; 1891 v E (3)
Howells, R. G. (Cardiff C), 1954 v E, S (2)
Hugh, A. R. (Newport Co), 1930 v Ni (1)
Hughes, A. (Rhos), 1894 v E, S (2)
Hughes, A. (Chirk), 1907 v Ni (1)
Hughes, C. M. (Luton T), 1992 v Ho (sub); 1994 v N (sub), Se (sub), Es (4)
Hughes, E. (Everton), 1899 v S, Ni; (with Tottenham H), 1901 v E, S; 1902 v Ni; 1904 v E, Ni, S; 1905 v E, Ni, S; 1906 v E, Ni; 1907 v E (14)
Hughes, E. (Wrexham), 1906 v S; (with Nottingham F), 1906 v Ni; 1908 v S, E; 1910 v Ni, E, S; 1911 v Ni, E, S; (with Wrexham), 1912 v Ni, E, S; (with Manchester C), 1913 v E, S; 1914 v N (16)
Hughes, F. W. (Northwich Victoria), 1882 v E, Ni; 1883 v E, Ni, S; 1884 v S (6)
Hughes, I. (Luton T), 1951 v E, Ni, P, Sw (4)
Hughes, J. (Cambridge University), 1877 v S; (with Aberystwyth), 1879 v S (2)
Hughes, J. (Liverpool), 1905 v E, S, Ni (3)
Hughes, J. I. (Blackburn R), 1935 v Ni (1)
Hughes, L. M. (Manchester U), 1984 v E, Ni; 1985 v Ic, Sp, Ic, N, S, Sp, N; 1986 v S, H, U; (with Barcelona), 1987 v USSR, Cz; 1988 v D (2), Cz, Se, Ma, I; (with Manchester U), 1989 v Ho, Fi, Is, Se, WG; 1990 v Fi, WG, Cr; 1991 v D, Bel (2), L, Ic, Pol, WG; 1992 v Br, G, L, Ei, R, Ho, Arg, J; 1993 v Fa, Cy, Bel, Ei, Bel, RCS, Fa; 1994 v RCS, Cy, N (53)
Hughes, P. W. (Bangor), 1887 v Ni; 1889 v Ni, E (3)
Hughes, W. (Bootle), 1891 v E; 1892 v S, Ni (3)
Hughes, W. A. (Blackburn R), 1949 v E, Ni, P, Bel, Sw (5)
Hughes, W. M. (Birmingham), 1938 v E, Ni, S; 1939 v E, Ni, S, F; 1947 v E, S, Ni (10)
Humphreys, J. V. (Everton), 1947 v Ni (1)
Humphreys, R. (Druids), 1888 v Ni (1)
Hunter, A. H. (FA of Wales Secretary), 1887 v Ni (1)

Jackett, K. (Watford), 1983 v N, Y, E, Bul, S; 1984 v N, R, Y, S, Ni, N, Is; 1985 v Ic, Sp, Ic, N, S, Sp, N; 1986 v S, H, S.Ar, Ei, Ca (2); 1987 v Fi (2); 1988 v D, Cz, Y, Se (31)
Jackson, W. (St Helens Rec), 1899 v Ni (1)
James, E. (Chirk), 1893 v E, Ni; 1894 v E, S, Ni; 1898 v S, E; 1899 v Ni (8)
James, E. G. (Blackpool), 1966 v Br (2), Ch; 1967 v Ni; 1968 v S; 1971 v Cz, S, E, Ni (9)
James, L. (Burnley), 1972 v Cz, R, S (sub); 1973 v E (3), Pol, S, Ni; 1974 v Pol, E, S, Ni; 1975 v A, H (2), L (2), S, E, Ni; 1976 v A; (with Derby Co), S, E, Y (2), Ni; 1977 v WG, S (2), Cz, E, Ni; 1978 v K (2); (with QPR), WG; (with Burnley), 1979 v T; (with Swansea C), 1980 v E, S, Ni, Ic; 1981 v T, Ei, T, S, E; 1982 v Cz, Ic, USSR, E (sub), S, Ni, F; (with Sunderland), 1983 v E (sub) (54)
James, R. M. (Swansea C), 1979 v Ma, WG (sub), S, E, Ni, Ma; 1980 v WG; 1982 v Cz (sub), Ic, Sp, E, S, Ni, F; 1983 v N, Y, E, Bul; (with Stoke C), 1984 v N, R, Bul, Y, S, E, Ni, N, Is; 1985 v Ic, Sp, Ic; (with QPR), N, S, Sp, N; 1986 v S, S.Ar, Ei, U, Ca (2); 1987 v Fi (2), USSR, Cz; (with Leicester C), 1988 v D (2); (with Swansea C), Y (47)
James, W. (West Ham U), 1931 v Ni; 1932 v Ni (2)
Jarrett, R. H. (Ruthin), 1889 v Ni; 1890 v S (2)
Jarvis, A. L. (Hull C), 1967 v S, E, Ni (3)
Jenkins, E. (Lovell's Ath), 1925 v E (1)
Jenkins, J. (Brighton), 1924 v Ni, E, S; 1925 v S, Ni; 1926 v E, S; 1927 v S (8)
Jenkins, R. W. (Rhyl), 1902 v Ni (1)
Jenkyns, C. A. L. (Small Heath), 1892 v E, S, Ni; 1895 v E; (with Woolwich Arsenal), 1896 v S; (with Newton Heath), 1897 v Ni; (with Walsall), 1898 v S, E (8)
Jennings, W. (Bolton W), 1914 v E, S; 1920 v S; 1923 v Ni, E; 1924 v E, S, Ni; 1927 v S, Ni; 1929 v S (11)
John, R. F. (Arsenal), 1923 v S, Ni; 1925 v Ni; 1926 v E; 1927 v E; 1928 v E, Ni; 1930 v E, S; 1932 v E; 1933 v F, Ni; 1935 v Ni; 1936 v S; 1937 v E (15)
John, W. R. (Walsall), 1931 v Ni; (with Stoke C), 1933 v E, S, Ni, F; 1934 v E, S; (with Preston NE), 1935 v E, S; (with Sheffield U), 1936 v E, S, Ni; (with Swansea T), 1939 v E, S (14)
Johnson, M. G. (Swansea T), 1964 v Ni (1)
Jones, A. (Port Vale), 1987 v Fi, Cz (sub); 1988 v D, (with Charlton Ath), D (sub), Cz (sub); 1990 v Hol (sub) (6)
Jones, A. F. (Oxford University), 1877 v S (1)
Jones, A. T. (Nottingham F), 1905 v E; (with Notts Co), 1906 v E (2)
Jones, Bryn (Wolverhampton W), 1935 v Ni; 1936 v E, S, Ni; 1937 v E, S, Ni; 1938 v E, S, Ni; (with Arsenal), 1939 v E, S, Ni; 1947 v S, Ni; 1948 v E; 1949 v S (17)
Jones, B. S. (Swansea T), 1963 v S, E, Ni, H (2); 1964 v S, Ni; (with Plymouth Arg), 1965 v D; (with Cardiff C), 1969 v S, E, Ni, I (sub), WG, EG, R of UK (15)
Jones, Charlie (Nottingham F), 1926 v E; 1927 v S, Ni; 1928 v E; (with Arsenal), 1930 v E, S; 1932 v E; 1933 v F (8)
Jones, Cliff (Swansea T), 1954 v A; 1956 v E, Ni, S, A; 1957 v E, S, Ni, Cz (2), EG; 1958 v EG, E, S, Is (2); (with Tottenham H), 1958 v Ni, H (2), M, Se, Br; 1959 v Ni; 1960 v E, S, Ni; 1961 v S, E, Ni, Sp, H, Ei; 1962 v E, Ni, S, Br (2), M; 1963 v S, Ni, H; 1964 v E, S, Ni; 1965 v E, S, Ni, D, Gr (2), USSR, I; 1967 v S, E; 1968 v E, S, WG; (with Fulham), 1969 v I, R of UK (59)
Jones, C. W. (Birmingham), 1935 v Ni; 1939 v F (2)
Jones, D. (Chirk), 1888 v S, Ni; (with Bolton W), 1889 v E, S, Ni; 1890 v E; 1891 v S; 1892 v Ni; 1893 v E; 1894 v E; 1895 v E; 1898 v S; (with Manchester C), 1900 v E, Ni (14)
Jones, D. E. (Norwich C), 1976 v S, E (sub); 1978 v S, Cz, WG, Ir, E; 1980 v E (8)
Jones, D. O. (Leicester C), 1934 v E, Ni; 1935 v E, S; 1936 v E, Ni; 1937 v Ni (7)
Jones, Evan (Chelsea), 1910 v S, Ni; (with Oldham Ath), 1911 v E, S; 1912 v E, S; (with Bolton W), 1914 v Ni (7)
Jones, F. R. (Bangor), 1885 v E, Ni; 1886 v S (3)
Jones, F. W. (Small Heath), 1893 v S (1)
Jones, G. P. (Wrexham), 1907 v S, Ni (2)
Jones, H. (Aberaman), 1902 v Ni (1)
Jones, Humphrey (Bangor), 1885 v E, Ni, S; 1886 v E, Ni, S; (with Queen's Park), 1887 v E; (with East Stirlingshire), 1889 v E, Ni; 1890 v E, S, Ni; (with Queen's Park), 1891 v E, S (14)
Jones, Ivor (Swansea T), 1920 v S, Ni; 1921 v Ni, E; 1922 v S, Ni; (with WBA), 1923 v E, Ni; 1924 v S; 1926 v Ni (10)
Jones, Jeffrey (Llandrindod Wells), 1908 v Ni; 1909 v Ni; 1910 v S (3)
Jones, J. (Druids), 1876 v S (1)
Jones, J. (Berwyn Rangers), 1883 v S, Ni; 1884 v S (3)
Jones, J. (Wrexham), 1925 v Ni (1)
Jones, J. L. (Sheffield U), 1895 v E, S, Ni; 1896 v Ni, S, E; 1897 v Ni, S, E; (with Tottenham H), 1898 v Ni, E, S; 1899 v S, Ni; 1900 v S; 1902 v E, S, Ni; 1904 v E, S, Ni (21)
Jones, J. Love (Stoke C), 1906 v S; (with Middlesbrough), 1910 v Ni (2)
Jones, J. O. (Bangor), 1901 v S, Ni (2)

Jones, J. P. (Liverpool), 1976 v A, E, S; 1977 v WG, S (2), Cz, E, Ni; 1978 v K (2), S, Cz, WG, Ir, E, S, Ni; (with Wrexham), 1979 v Ma, T, WG, S, E, Ni, Ma; 1980 v Ei, WG, T, E, S, Ni, Ic; 1981 v T, Ei, T, S, E, USSR; 1982 v Cz, Ic, USSR, Sp, E, S, Ni, F; 1983 v N; (with Chelsea), Y, E, Bul, S, Ni, Br; 1984 v N, R, Bul, Y, S, E, Ni, N, Is; 1985 v Ic, N, S, N; (with Huddersfield T), 1986 v S, H, Ei, U, Ca (2) (72)

Jones, J. T. (Stoke C), 1912 v E, S, Ni; 1913 v E, Ni; 1914 v S, Ni; 1920 v E, S, Ni; (with C Palace), 1921 v E, S; 1922 v E, S, Ni (15)

Jones, K. (Aston Villa), 1950 v S (1)

Jones, Leslie J. (Cardiff C), 1933 v F; (with Coventry C), 1935 v Ni; 1936 v S; 1937 v E, S, Ni; (with Arsenal), 1938 v E, S, Ni; 1939 v E, S (11)

Jones, P. W. (Bristol R), 1971 v Fi (1)

Jones, R. (Bangor), 1887 v S; 1889 v E; (with Crewe Alex), 1890 v E (3)

Jones, R. (Leicester Fosse), 1898 v S (1)

Jones, R. (Druids), 1899 v S (1)

Jones, R. (Bangor), 1900 v S, Ni (2)

Jones, R. (Millwall), 1906 v S, Ni (2)

Jones, R. A. (Druids), 1884 v E, Ni, S; 1885 v S (4)

Jones, R. A. (Sheffield W), 1994 v Es (1)

Jones, R. S. (Everton), 1894 v Ni (1)

Jones, S. (Wrexham), 1887 v Ni; (with Chester), 1890 v S (2)

Jones, S. (Wrexham), 1893 v S, Ni; (with Burton Swifts), 1895 v S; 1896 v E, Ni; (with Druids), 1899 v E (6)

Jones, T. (Manchester U), 1926 v Ni; 1927 v E, Ni; 1930 v Ni (4)

Jones, T. D. (Aberdare), 1908 v Ni (1)

Jones, T. G. (Everton), 1938 v Ni; 1939 v E, S, Ni; 1947 v E, S; 1948 v E, S, Ni; 1949 v E, Ni, P, Bel, Sw; 1950 v E, S, Bel (17)

Jones, T. J. (Sheffield W), 1932 v Ni; 1933 v F (2)

Jones, W. E. A. (Swansea T), 1947 v E, S; (with Tottenham H), 1949 v E, S (4)

Jones, W. J. (Aberdare), 1901 v E, S; (with West Ham U), 1902 v E, S (4)

Jones, W. Lot (Manchester C), 1905 v E, Ni; 1906 v E, S, Ni; 1907 v E, S, Ni; 1908 v S; 1909 v E, S, Ni; 1910 v E; 1911 v E; 1913 v E, S; 1914 v S, Ni; (with Southend U), 1920 v E, Ni (20)

Jones, W. P. (Druids), 1889 v E, Ni; (with Wynstay), 1890 v S, Ni (4)

Jones, W. R. (Aberystwyth), 1897 v S (1)

Keenor, F. C. (Cardiff C), 1920 v E, Ni; 1921 v E, Ni, S; 1922 v Ni; 1923 v E, Ni, S; 1924 v E, Ni, S; 1925 v E, Ni, S; 1926 v S; 1927 v E, Ni, S; 1928 v E, Ni, S; 1929 v E, Ni, S; 1930 v E, Ni, S; 1931 v E, Ni, S; (with Crewe Alex), 1933 v S (32)

Kelly, F. C. (Wrexham), 1899 v S, Ni; (with Druids), 1902 v Ni (3)

Kelsey, A. J. (Arsenal), 1954 v Ni, A; 1955 v S, Ni, Y; 1956 v E, Ni, S, A; 1957 v E, Ni, S, Cz (2), EG; 1958 v E, S, Ni, Is (2), H (2), M, Se, Br; 1959 v E, S; 1960 v E, Ni, S; 1961 v E, Ni, S, H, Sp (2); 1962 v E, S, Ni, Br (2) (41)

Kenrick, S. L. (Druids), 1876 v S; 1877 v S; (with Oswestry), 1879 v E, S; (with Shropshire Wanderers), 1881 v E (5)

Ketley, C. F. (Druids), 1882 v Ni (1)

King, J. (Swansea T), 1955 v E (1)

Kinsey, N. (Norwich C), 1951 v Ni, P, Sw; 1952 v E; (with Birmingham C), 1954 v Ni; 1956 v E, S (7)

Knill, A. R. (Swansea C), 1989 v Ho (1)

Krzywicki, R. L. (WBA), 1970 v EG, I; (with Huddersfield T), Ni, E, S; 1971 v R, Fi; 1972 v Cz (sub) (8)

Lambert, R. (Liverpool), 1947 v S; 1948 v E; 1949 v P, Bel, Sw (5)

Latham, G. (Liverpool), 1905 v E, S; 1906 v S; 1907 v E, S, Ni; 1908 v E; 1909 v Ni; (with Southport Central), 1910 v E; (with Cardiff C), 1913 v Ni (10)

Law, B. J. (QPR), 1990 v Se (1)

Lawrence, E. (Clapton Orient), 1930 v Ni; (with Notts Co), 1932 v S (2)

Lawrence, S. (Swansea T), 1932 v Ni; 1933 v F; 1934 v S, E, Ni; 1935 v E, S; 1936 v S (8)

Lea, A. (Wrexham), 1889 v E; 1891 v S, Ni; 1893 v Ni (4)

Lea, C. (Ipswich T), 1965 v Ni, I (2)

Leary, P. (Bangor), 1889 v Ni (1)

Leek, K. (Leicester C), 1961 v S, E, Ni, H, Sp (2); (with Newcastle U), 1962 v S; (with Birmingham C), v Br (sub), M; 1963 v E; 1965 v S, Gr; (with Northampton T), 1965 v Gr (13)

Lever, A. R. (Leicester C), 1953 v S (1)

Lewis, B. (Chester), 1891 v Ni; (with Wrexham), 1892 v S, E, Ni; (with Middlesbrough), 1893 v S, E; (with Wrexham), 1894 v S, E, Ni; 1895 v S (10)

Lewis, D. (Arsenal), 1927 v E; 1928 v Ni; 1930 v E (3)

Lewis, D. (Swansea C), 1983 v Br (sub) (1)

Lewis, D. J. (Swansea T), 1933 v E, S (2)

Lewis, D. M. (Bangor), 1890 v Ni, S (2)

Lewis, J. (Bristol R), 1906 v E (1)

Lewis, J. (Cardiff C), 1926 v S (1)

Lewis, T. (Wrexham), 1881 v E, S (2)

Lewis, W. (Bangor), 1885 v E; 1886 v E, S; 1887 v E, S; 1888 v E; 1889 v E, Ni, S; (with Crewe Alex), 1890 v E; 1891 v E, S; 1892 v E, S, Ni; 1894 v E, S, Ni; (with Chester), 1895 v S, Ni, E; 1896 v E, S, Ni; (with Manchester C), 1897 v E, S; (with Chester), 1898 v Ni (27)

Lewis, W. L. (Swansea T), 1927 v E, Ni; 1928 v E, Ni; 1929 v S; (with Huddersfield T), 1930 v E (6)

Lloyd, B. W. (Wrexham), 1976 v A, E, S (3)

Lloyd, J. W. (Wrexham), 1879 v S; (with Newtown), 1885 v S (2)

Lloyd, R. A. (Ruthin), 1891 v Ni; 1895 v S (2)

Lockley, A. (Chirk), 1898 v Ni (1)

Lovell, S. (C Palace), 1982 v USSR (sub); (with Millwall), 1985 v N; 1986 v S (sub), H (sub), Ca (1 + 1 sub) (6)

Lowrie, G. (Coventry C), 1948 v E, S, Ni; (with Newcastle U), 1949 v P (4)

Lowndes, S. (Newport Co), 1983 v S (sub), Br (sub); (with Millwall), 1985 v N (sub); 1986 v S.Ar (sub), Ei, U, Ca (2); (with Barnsley), 1987 v Fi (sub); 1988 v Se (sub) (10)

Lucas, P. M. (Leyton Orient), 1962 v Ni, M; 1963 v S, E (4)

Lucas, W. H. (Swansea T), 1949 v S, Ni, P, Bel, Sw; 1950 v E; 1951 v E (7)

Lumberg, A. (Wrexham), 1929 v Ni; 1930 v E, S; (with Wolverhampton W), 1932 v S (4)

McCarthy, T. P. (Wrexham), 1899 v Ni (1)

McMillan, R. (Shrewsbury Engineers), 1881 v E, S (2)

Maguire, G. T. (Portsmouth), 1990 v Fi (sub), Ho, WG, Ei, Se; 1992 v Br (sub), G (7)

Mahoney, J. F. (Stoke C), 1968 v E; 1969 v EG; 1971 v Cz; 1973 v E (3), Pol, S, Ni; 1974 v Pol, E, S, Ni; 1975 v A, H (2), L (2), S, E, Ni; 1976 v A, Y (2), E, Ni; 1977 v WG, Cz, S, E, Ni; (with Middlesbrough), 1978 v K (2), S, Cz, Ir, E (sub), S, Ni; 1979 v WG, S, E, Ni, Ma; (with Swansea C), 1980 v Ei, WG, T (sub); 1982 v Ic, USSR; 1983 v Y, E (51)

Martin, T. J. (Newport Co), 1930 v Ni (1)

Marustik, C. (Swansea C), 1982 v Sp, E, S, Ni, F; 1983 v N (6)

Mates, J. (Chirk), 1891 v Ni; 1897 v E, S (3)

Mathews, R. W. (Liverpool), 1921 v Ni; (with Bristol C), 1923 v E; (with Bradford), 1926 v Ni (3)

Matthews, W. (Chester), 1905 v Ni; 1908 v E (2)

Matthias, J. S. (Brymbo), 1896 v S, Ni; (with Shrewsbury), 1897 v E, S; (with Wolverhampton W), 1899 v S (5)
Matthias, T. J. (Wrexham), 1914 v S, E; 1920 v Ni, S, E; 1921 v S, E, Ni; 1922 v S, E, Ni; 1923 v S (12)
Mays, A. W. (Wrexham), 1929 v Ni (1)
Medwin, T. C. (Swansea T), 1953 v Ni, F, Y; (with Tottenham H), 1957 v E, S, Ni, Cz (2), EG; 1958 v E, S, Ni, Is (2), H (2), M, Br; 1959 v E, S, Ni; 1960 v E, S, Ni; 1961 v S, Ei, E, Sp; 1963 v E, H (30)
Melville, A. K. (Swansea C), 1990 v WG, Ei, Se, Cr (sub); (with Oxford U), 1991 v Ic, Pol, WG; 1992 v Br, G, L, R, Ho, J (sub); 1993 v RCS, Fa (sub); (with Sunderland), 1994 v RCS (sub), R, N, Se, Es (20)
Meredith, S. (Chirk), 1900 v S; 1901 v S, E, Ni; (with Stoke C), 1902 v E; 1903 v Ni; 1904 v E; (with Leyton), 1907 v E (8)
Meredith, W. H. (Manchester C), 1895 v E, Ni; 1896 v E, Ni; 1897 v E, Ni, S; 1898 v E, Ni; 1899 v E; 1900 v E, Ni; 1901 v E, Ni; 1902 v E, S; 1903 v E, S, Ni; 1904 v E; 1905 v E, S; (with Manchester U), 1907 v E, S, Ni; 1908 v E, Ni; 1909 v E, S, Ni; 1910 v E, S, Ni; 1911 v E, S, Ni; 1912 v E, S, Ni; 1913 v E, S, Ni; 1914 v E, S, Ni; 1920 v E, S, Ni (48)
Mielczarek, R. (Rotherham U), 1971 v Fi (1)
Millership, H. (Rotherham Co), 1920 v E, S, Ni; 1921 v E, S, Ni (6)
Millington, A. H. (WBA), 1963 v S, E, H; (with C Palace), 1965 v E, USSR; (with Peterborough U), 1966 v Ch, Br; 1967 v E, Ni; 1968 v Ni, WG; 1969 v I, EG; (with Swansea T), 1970 v E, S, Ni; 1971 v Cz, Fi; 1972 v Fi (sub), Cz, R (21)
Mills, T. J. (Clapton Orient), 1934 v E, Ni; (with Leicester C), 1935 v E, S (4)
Mills-Roberts, R. H. (St Thomas' Hospital), 1885 v E, S, Ni; 1886 v E; 1887 v E; (with Preston NE), 1888 v E, Ni; (with Llanberis), 1892 v E (8)
Moore, G. (Cardiff C), 1960 v E, S, Ni; 1961 v Ei, Sp; (with Chelsea), 1962 v Br; 1963 v Ni, H; (with Manchester U), 1964 v S, Ni; (with Northampton T), 1966 v Ni, Ch; (with Charlton Ath), 1969 v S, E, Ni, R of UK; 1970 v E, S, Ni, I; 1971 v R (21)
Morgan, J. R. (Cambridge University), 1877 v S; (with Swansea T), 1879 v S; (with Derby School Staff), 1880 v E, S; 1881 v E, S; 1882 v E, S, Ni; (with Swansea T), 1883 v E (10)
Morgan, J. T. (Wrexham), 1905 v Ni (1)
Morgan-Owen, H. (Oxford University), 1901 v E; 1902 v S; 1906 v E, Ni; (with Welshpool), 1907 v S (5)
Morgan-Owen, M. M. (Oxford University), 1897 v S, Ni; 1898 v E, S; 1899 v S; 1900 v E, S; (with Corinthians), 1903 v S; 1906 v S, E, Ni; 1907 v E (12)
Morley, E. J. (Swansea T), 1925 v E; (with Clapton Orient), 1929 v E, S, Ni (4)
Morris, A. G. (Aberystwyth), 1896 v E, Ni, S; (with Swindon T), 1897 v E; 1898 v S; (with Nottingham F), 1899 v E, S; 1903 v E, S; 1905 v E, S; 1907 v E, S; 1908 v E; 1910 v E, S, Ni; 1911 v E, S, Ni; 1912 v E (21)
Morris, C. (Chirk), 1900 v E, S, Ni; (with Derby Co), 1901 v E, S, Ni; 1902 v E, S; 1903 v E, S, Ni; 1904 v Ni; 1905 v E, S, Ni; 1906 v S; 1907 v S; 1908 v E, S; 1909 v E, S, Ni; 1910 v E, S, Ni; (with Huddersfield T), 1911 v E, S, Ni (28)
Morris, E. (Chirk), 1893 v E, S, Ni (3)
Morris, H. (Sheffield U), 1894 v S; (with Manchester C), 1896 v E; (with Grimsby T), 1897 v E (3)
Morris, J. (Oswestry), 1887 v S (1)
Morris, J. (Chirk), 1898 v Ni (1)
Morris, R. (Chirk), 1900 v E, Ni; 1901 v Ni; 1902 v S; (with Shrewsbury T), 1903 v E, Ni (6)
Morris, R. (Druids), 1902 v E, S; (with Newtown), Ni; (with Liverpool), 1903 v S, Ni; 1904 v E, S, Ni; (with Leeds C), 1906 v S; (with Grimsby T), 1907 v Ni; (with Plymouth Arg), 1908 v Ni (11)
Morris, S. (Birmingham), 1937 v E, S; 1938 v E, S; 1939 v F (5)
Morris, W. (Burnley), 1947 v Ni; 1949 v E; 1952 v S, Ni, R of UK (5)
Moulsdale, J. R. B. (Corinthians), 1925 v Ni (1)
Murphy, J. P. (WBA), 1933 v F, E, Ni; 1934 v E, S; 1935 v E, S, Ni; 1936 v E, S, Ni; 1937 v S, Ni; 1938 v E, S (15)

Nardiello, D. (Coventry C), 1978 v Cz, WG (sub) (2)
Neal, J. E. (Colwyn Bay), 1931 v E, S (2)
Neilson, A. B. (Newcastle U), 1992 v Ei; 1994 v Se, Es (3)
Newnes, J. (Nelson), 1926 v Ni (1)
Newton, L. F. (Cardiff Corinthians), 1912 v Ni (1)
Nicholas, D. S. (Stoke C), 1923 v S; (with Swansea T), 1927 v E, Ni (3)
Nicholas, P. (C Palace), 1979 v S (sub), Ni (sub), Ma; 1980 v Ei, WG, T, E, S, Ni, Ic; 1981 v T, Cz, E; (with Arsenal), T, S, E, USSR; 1982 v Cz, Ic, USSR, Sp, E, S, Ni, F; 1983 v Y, Bul, S, Ni; 1984 v N, Bul, N, Is; (with C Palace), 1985 v Sp; (with Luton T), N, S, Sp, N; 1986 v S, H, S.Ar, Ei, U, Ca (2); 1987 v Fi (2) USSR, Cz; (with Aberdeen), 1988 v D (2), Cz, Y, Se; (with Chelsea), 1989 v Ho, Fi, Is, Se, WG; 1990 v Fi, Ho, WG, Ei, Se, Cr; 1991 v D (sub), Bel, L, Ei; (with Watford), Bel, Pol, WG; 1992 v L (73)
Nicholls, J. (Newport Co), 1924 v E, Ni; (with Cardiff C), 1925 v E, S (4)
Niedzwiecki, E. A. (Chelsea), 1985 v N (sub); 1988 v D (2)
Nock, W. (Newtown), 1897 v Ni (1)
Nogan, L. M. (Watford), 1992 v A (sub) (1)
Norman, A. J. (Hull C), 1986 v Ei (sub), U, Ca; 1988 v Ma, I (5)
Nurse, M. T. G. (Swansea T), 1960 v E, Ni; 1961 v S, E, H, Ni, Ei, Sp (2); (with Middlesbrough), 1963 v E, H; 1964 v S (12)

O'Callaghan, E. (Tottenham H), 1929 v Ni; 1930 v S; 1932 v S, E; 1933 v Ni, S, E; 1934 v Ni, S, E; 1935 v E (11)
Oliver, A. (Blackburn R), 1905 v E; (with Bangor), S (2)
O'Sullivan, P. A. (Brighton), 1973 v S (sub); 1976 v S; 1979 v Ma (sub) (3)
Owen, D. (Oswestry), 1879 v E (1)
Owen, E. (Ruthin Grammar School), 1884 v E, Ni, S (3)
Owen, G. (Chirk), 1888 v S; (with Newton Heath), 1889 v S, Ni; 1893 v Ni (4)
Owen, J. (Newton Heath), 1892 v E (1)
Owen, Trevor (Crewe Alex), 1899 v E, S (2)
Owen, T. (Oswestry), 1879 v E (1)
Owen, W. (Chirk), 1884 v E; 1885 v Ni; 1887 v E; 1888 v E; 1889 v E, Ni, S; 1890 v S, Ni; 1891 v E, S, Ni; 1892 v E, S; 1893 v S, Ni (16)
Owen, W. P. (Ruthin), 1880 v E, S; 1881 v E, S; 1882 v E, S, Ni; 1883 v E, S; 1884 v E, S, Ni (12)
Owens, J. (Wrexham), 1902 v S (1)

Page, M. E. (Birmingham C), 1971 v Fi; 1972 v S, Ni; 1973 v E (1 + 1 sub), Ni; 1974 v S, Ni; 1975 v H, L, S, E, Ni; 1976 v E, Y (2), E, Ni; 1977 v WG, S; 1978 v K (sub + 1), WG, Ir, E, S; 1979 v Ma, WG (28)
Palmer, D. (Swansea T), 1957 v Cz; 1958 v E, EG (3)
Parris, J. E. (Bradford), 1932 v Ni (1)
Parry, B. J. (Swansea T), 1951 v S (1)
Parry, C. (Everton), 1891 v E, S; 1893 v E; 1894 v E; 1895 v E, S; (with Newtown), 1896 v E, S, Ni; 1897 v Ni; 1898 v E, S, Ni (13)
Parry, E. (Liverpool), 1922 v S; 1923 v E, Ni; 1925 v Ni; 1926 v Ni (5)
Parry, M. (Liverpool), 1901 v E, S, Ni; 1902 v E, S, Ni; 1903 v E, S; 1904 v E, Ni; 1906 v E; 1908 v E, S, Ni; 1909 v E, S (16)

Parry, T. D. (Oswestry), 1900 v E, S, Ni; 1901 v E, S, Ni; 1902 v E (7)
Parry, W. (Newtown), 1895 v Ni (1)
Pascoe, C. (Swansea C), 1984 v N, Is; (with Sunderland), 1989 v Fi, Is, WG (sub); 1990 v Ho (sub), WG (sub); 1991 v Ei, Ic (sub); 1992 v Br (10)
Paul, R. (Swansea T), 1949 v E, S, Ni, P, Sw; 1950 v E, S, Ni, Bel; (with Manchester C), 1951 v S, E, Ni, P, Sw; 1952 v E, S, Ni, R of UK; 1953 v S, E, Ni, F, Y; 1954 v E, S, Ni; 1955 v S, E, Y; 1956 v E, Ni, S, A (33)
Peake, E. (Aberystwyth), 1908 v Ni; (with Liverpool), 1909 v Ni, S, E; 1910 v S, Ni; 1911 v Ni; 1912 v E; 1913 v E, Ni; 1914 v Ni (11)
Peers, E. J. (Wolverhampton W), 1914 v Ni, S, E; 1920 v E, S; 1921 v S, Ni, E; (with Port Vale), 1922 v E, S, Ni; 1923 v E (12)
Pembridge, M. A. (Luton T), 1992 v Br, Ei, R, Ho, J (sub); (with Derby Co), Bel (sub), Ei; 1994 v N (sub) (8)
Perry, E. (Doncaster R), 1938 v E, S, Ni (3)
Perry, J. (Cardiff C), 1994 v N (1)
Phennah, E. (Civil Service), 1878 v S (1)
Phillips, C. (Wolverhampton W), 1931 v Ni; 1932 v E; 1933 v S; 1934 v E, S, Ni; 1935 v E, S, Ni; 1936 v S; (with Aston Villa), 1936 v E, Ni; 1938 v S (13)
Phillips, D. (Plymouth Arg), 1984 v E, Ni, N; (with Manchester C), 1985 v Sp, Ic, S, Sp, N; 1986 v S, H, S.Ar, Ei, U; (with Coventry C), 1987 v Fi, Cz; 1988 v D (2), Cz, Y, Se; 1989 v Se, WG; (with Norwich C), 1990 v Fi, Ho, WG, Ei, Se; 1991 v D, Bel, Ic, Pol, WG; 1992 v L, Ei, A, R, Ho (sub), Arg, J; 1993 v Fa, Cy, Bel, Ei, Bel, RCS, Fa; (with Nottingham F), 1994 v RCS, Cy, R, N, Se, Es (52)
Phillips, L. (Cardiff C), 1971 v Cz, S, E, Ni; 1972 v Cz, R, S, Ni; 1973 v E; 1974 v Pol (sub), Ni; 1975 v A; (with Aston Villa), H (2), L (2), S, E, Ni; 1976 v A, E, Y (2), E, Ni; 1977 v WG, S (2), Cz, E; 1978 v K (2), S, Cz, WG, E, S; 1979 v Ma; (with Swansea C), T, WG, S, E, Ni, Ma; 1980 v Ei, WG, T, S (sub), Ni, Ic; 1981 v T, Cz, T, S, E, USSR; (with Charlton Ath), 1982 v Cz, USSR (58)
Phillips, T. J. S. (Chelsea), 1973 v E; 1974 v E; 1975 v H (sub); 1978 v K (4)
Phoenix, H. (Wrexham), 1882 v S (1)
Poland, G. (Wrexham), 1939 v Ni, F (2)
Pontin, K. (Cardiff C), 1980 v E (sub), S (2)
Powell, A. (Leeds U), 1947 v E, S; 1948 v E, S, Ni; (with Everton), 1949 v E; 1950 v Bel; (with Birmingham C), 1951 v S (8)
Powell, D. (Wrexham), 1968 v WG; (with Sheffield U), 1969 v S, E, Ni, I, WG; 1970 v E, S, Ni, EG; 1971 v R (11)
Powell, I. V. (QPR), 1947 v E; 1948 v E, S, Ni; (with Aston Villa), 1949 v Bel; 1950 v S, Bel; 1951 v S (8)
Powell, J. (Druids), 1878 v S; 1880 v E, S; 1882 v E, S, Ni; 1883 v E, S, Ni; (with Bolton W), 1884 v E; (with Newton Heath), 1887 v E, S; 1888 v E, S, Ni (15)
Powell, Seth (WBA), 1885 v S; 1886 v E, Ni; 1891 v E, S; 1892 v E, S (7)
Price, H. (Aston Villa), 1907 v S; (with Burton U), 1908 v Ni; (with Wrexham), 1909 v S, E, Ni (5)
Price, J. (Wrexham), 1877 v S; 1878 v S; 1879 v E; 1880 v E, S; 1881 v E, S; (with Druids), 1882 v S, E, Ni; 1883 v S, Ni (12)
Price, P. (Luton T), 1980 v E, S, Ni, Ic; 1981 v T, Cz, Ei, T, S, E, USSR; (with Tottenham H), 1982 v USSR, Sp, F; 1983 v N, Y, E, Bul, S, Ni; 1984 v N, R, Bul, Y, S (sub) (25)
Pring, K. D. (Rotherham U), 1966 v Ch, D; 1967 v Ni (3)
Pritchard, H. K. (Bristol C), 1985 v N (sub) (1)
Pryce-Jones, A. W. (Newtown), 1895 v E (1)
Pryce-Jones, W. E. (Cambridge University), 1887 v S; 1888 v S, E, Ni; 1890 v Ni (5)
Pugh, A. (Rhostyllen), 1889 v S (1)
Pugh, D. H. (Wrexham), 1896 v S, Ni; 1897 v S, Ni; (with Lincoln C), 1900 v S; 1901 v S, E (7)
Pugsley, J. (Charlton Ath), 1930 v Ni (1)
Pullen, W. J. (Plymouth Arg), 1926 v E (1)

Rankmore, F. E. J. (Peterborough), 1966 v Ch (sub) (1)
Ratcliffe, K. (Everton), 1981 v Cz, Ei, T, S, E, USSR; 1982 v Cz, Ic, USSR, Sp, E; 1983 v Y, E, Bul, S, Ni, Br; 1984 v N, R, Bul, Y, S, E, Ni, N, Is; 1985 v Ic, Sp, Ic, N, S, Sp; 1986 v S, H, S.Ar, U; 1987 v Fi (2), USSR, Cz; 1988 v D (2), Cz; 1989 v Fi, Is, Se, WG; 1990 v Fi; 1991 v D, Bel (2), L, Ei, Ic, Pol, WG; 1992 v Br, G; (with Cardiff C), 1993 v Bel (59)
Rea, J. C. (Aberystwyth), 1894 v Ni, S, E; 1895 v S; 1896 v S, Ni; 1897 v S, Ni; 1898 v Ni (9)
Reece, G. I. (Sheffield U), 1966 v E, S, Ni, USSR; 1967 v S; 1969 v R of UK (sub); 1970 v I (sub); 1971 v S, E, Ni, Fi; 1972 v Fi, R, E (sub), S, Ni; (with Cardiff C), 1973 v E (sub), Ni; 1974 v Pol (sub), E, S, Ni; 1975 v A, H (2), L (2), S, Ni (29)
Reed, W. G. (Ipswich T), 1955 v S, Y (2)
Rees, A. (Birmingham C), 1984 v N (sub) (1)
Rees, J. M. (Luton T), 1992 v A (sub) (1)
Rees, R. R. (Coventry C), 1965 v S, E, Ni, D, Gr (2), I, R; 1966 v E, S, Ni, R, D, Br (2), Ch; 1967 v E, Ni; 1968 v E, S, Ni; (with WBA), WG; 1969 v I; (with Nottingham F), 1969 v WG, EG, S (sub), R of UK; 1970 v E, S, Ni, EG, I; 1971 v Cz, R, E (sub), Ni (sub), Fi; 1972 v Cz (sub), R (39)
Rees, W. (Cardiff C), 1949 v Ni, Bel, Sw; (with Tottenham H), 1950 v Ni (4)
Richards, A. (Barnsley), 1932 v S (1)
Richards, D. (Wolverhampton W), 1931 v Ni; 1933 v E, S, Ni; 1934 v E, S, Ni; 1935 v E, S, Ni; 1936 v S; (with Brentford), 1936 v E, Ni; 1937 v S, E; (with Birmingham), Ni; 1938 v E, S, Ni; 1939 v E, S (21)
Richards, G. (Druids), 1899 v E, S, Ni; (with Oswestry), 1903 v Ni; (with Shrewsbury), 1904 v S; 1905 v Ni (6)
Richards, R. W. (Wolverhampton W), 1920 v E, S; 1921 v Ni; 1922 v E, S; (with West Ham U), 1924 v E, S, Ni; (with Mold), 1926 v S (9)
Richards, S. V. (Cardiff C), 1947 v E (1)
Richards, W. E. (Fulham), 1933 v Ni (1)
Roach, J. (Oswestry), 1885 v Ni (1)
Robbins, W. W. (Cardiff C), 1931 v E, S; 1932 v Ni, E, S; (with WBA), 1933 v F, E, S, Ni; 1934 v S; 1936 v S (11)
Roberts, A. M. (QPR), 1993 v Ei (sub) (1)
Roberts, D. F. (Oxford U), 1973 v Pol, E (sub), Ni; 1974 v E, S; 1975 v A; (with Hull C), L, Ni; 1976 v S, Ni, Y; 1977 v E (sub), Ni; 1978 v K (1 + 1 sub), S, Ni (17)
Roberts, I. W. (Watford), 1990 v Ho; (with Huddersfield T), 1992 v A, Arg, J; (with Leicester C), 1994 v Se (5)
Roberts, Jas (Chirk), 1898 v S (1)
Roberts, Jas (Wrexham), 1913 v S, Ni (2)
Roberts, J. (Corwen), 1879 v S; 1880 v E, S; 1882 v E, S, Ni; (with Berwyn R), 1883 v E (7)
Roberts, J. (Ruthin), 1881 v S; 1882 v S (2)
Roberts, J. (Bradford C), 1906 v Ni; 1907 v Ni (2)
Roberts, J. G. (Arsenal), 1971 v S, E, Ni, Fi; 1972 v Fi, E, Ni; (with Birmingham C), 1973 v E (2), Pol, S, Ni; 1974 v Pol, E, S, Ni; 1975 v A, H, S, E; 1976 v E, S (22)
Roberts, J. H. (Bolton), 1949 v Bel (1)
Roberts, P. S. (Portsmouth), 1974 v E; 1975 v A, H, L (4)
Roberts, R. (Druids), 1884 v S; (with Bolton W), 1887 v S; 1888 v S, E; 1889 v S, E; 1890 v S; 1892 v Ni; (with Preston NE), S (9)
Roberts, R. (Wrexham), 1886 v Ni; 1887 v Ni (2)
Roberts, R. (Rhos), 1891 v Ni; (with Crewe Alex), 1893 v E (2)
Roberts, W. (Llangollen), 1879 v E, S; 1880 v E, S; (with Berwyn R), 1881 v S; 1883 v S (6)
Roberts, W. (Wrexham), 1886 v E, S, Ni; 1887 v Ni (4)

Roberts, W. H. (Ruthin), 1882 v E, S; 1883 v E, S, Ni; (with Rhyl), 1884 v S (6)
Rodrigues, P. J. (Cardiff C), 1965 v Ni, Gr (2); 1966 v USSR, E, S, D; (with Leicester C), Ni, Br (2), Ch; 1967 v S; 1968 v E, S, Ni; 1969 v E, Ni, EG, R of UK; 1970 v E, S, Ni, EG; (with Sheffield W), 1971 v R, E, S, Cz, Ni; 1972 v Fi, Cz, R, E, Ni (sub); 1973 v E (3), Pol, S, Ni; 1974 v Pol (40)
Rogers, J. P. (Wrexham), 1896 v E, S, Ni (3)
Rogers, W. (Wrexham), 1931 v E, S (2)
Roose, L. R. (Aberystwyth), 1900 v Ni; (with London Welsh), 1901 v E, S, Ni; (with Stoke C), 1902 v E, S; 1904 v E; (with Everton), 1905 v S, E; (with Stoke C), 1906 v E, S, Ni; 1907 v E, S, Ni; (with Sunderland), 1908 v E, S; 1909 v E, S, Ni; 1910 v E, S, Ni; 1911 v S (24)
Rouse, R. V. (C Palace), 1959 v Ni (1)
Rowlands, A. C. (Tranmere R), 1914 v E (1)
Rowley, T. (Tranmere R), 1959 v Ni (1)
Rush, I. (Liverpool), 1980 v S (sub), Ni; 1981 v E (sub); 1982 v Ic (sub), USSR, E, S, Ni, F; 1983 v N, Y, E, Bul; 1984 v N, R, Bul, Y, S, E, Ni; 1985 v Ic, N, S, Sp; 1986 v S, S.Ar, Ei, U; 1987 v Fi (2), USSR, Cz; (with Juventus), 1988 v D, Cz, Y, Se, Ma, I; (with Liverpool), 1989 v Ho, Fi, Se, WG; 1990 v Fi, Ei; 1991 v D, Bel (2), L, Ei, Pol, WG; 1992 v G, L, R; 1993 v Fa, Cy, Bel (2), RCS, Fa; 1994 v RCS, Cy, R, N, Se, Es (66)
Russell, M. R. (Merthyr T), 1912 v S, Ni; 1914 v E; (with Plymouth Arg), 1920 v E, S, Ni; 1921 v E, S, Ni; 1922 v E, Ni; 1923 v E, S, Ni; 1924 v E, S, Ni; 1925 v E, S; 1926 v E, S; 1928 v S; 1929 v E (23)

Sabine, H. W. (Oswestry), 1887 v Ni (1)
Saunders, D. (Brighton & HA), 1986 v Ei (sub), Ca (2); 1987 v Fi, USSR (sub); (with Oxford U), 1988 v Y, Se, Ma, I (sub); 1989 v Ho (sub), Fi; (with Derby Co), Is, Se, WG; 1990 v Fi, Ho, WG, Se, Cr; 1991 v D, Bel (2), L, Ei, Ic, Pol, WG; 1992 v Br, G, Ei, R, Ho, Arg, J; 1993 v Fa; (with Aston Villa), Cy, Bel (2), RCS, Fa; 1994 v RCS, Cy, R, N (sub) (44)
Savin, G. (Oswestry), 1878 v S (1)
Sayer, P. (Cardiff C), 1977 v Cz, S, E, Ni; 1978 v K (2), S (7)
Scrine, F. H. (Swansea T), 1950 v E, Ni (2)
Sear, C. R. (Manchester C), 1963 v E (1)
Shaw, E. G. (Oswestry), 1882 v Ni; 1884 v S, Ni (3)
Sherwood, A. T. (Cardiff C), 1947 v E, Ni; 1948 v S, Ni; 1949 v E, S, Ni, P, Sw; 1950 v E, S, Ni, Bel; 1951 v E, S, Ni, P, Sw; 1952 v E, S, Ni, R of UK; 1953 v S, E, Ni, F, Y; 1954 v E, S, Ni, A; 1955 v S, E, Y, Ni; 1956 v E, S, Ni, A; (with Newport Co), 1957 v E, S (41)
Shone, W. W. (Oswestry), 1879 v E (1)
Shortt, W. W. (Plymouth Arg), 1947 v Ni; 1950 v Ni, Bel; 1952 v E, S, Ni, R of UK; 1953 v S, E, Ni, F, Y (12)
Showers, D. (Cardiff C), 1975 v E (sub), Ni (2)
Sidlow, C. (Liverpool), 1947 v E, S; 1948 v E, S, Ni; 1949 v S; 1950 v E (7)
Sisson, H. (Wrexham Olympic), 1885 v Ni; 1886 v S, Ni (3)
Slatter, N. (Bristol R), 1983 v S; 1984 v N (sub), Is; 1985 v Ic, Sp, Ic, N, S, Sp, N; (with Oxford U), 1986 v H (sub), S.Ar, Ca (2); 1987 v Fi (sub), Cz; 1988 v D (2), Cz, Ma, I; 1989 v Is (sub) (22)
Smallman, D. P. (Wrexham), 1974 v E (sub), S (sub), Ni; (with Everton), 1975 v H (sub), E, Ni (sub); 1976 v A (7)
Southall, N. (Everton), 1982 v Ni; 1983 v N, E, Bul, S, Ni, Br; 1984 v N, R, Bul, Y, S, E, Ni, N, Is; 1985 v Ic, Sp, Ic, N, S, Sp, N; 1986 v S, H, S.Ar, Ei; 1987 v USSR, Fi, Cz; 1988 v D, Cz, Y, Se; 1989 v Ho, Fi, Se, WG; 1990 v Fi, Ho, WG, Ei, Se, Cr; 1991 v D, Bel (2), L, Ei, Ic, Pol, WG; 1992 v Br, G, L, Ei, A, R, Ho, Arg, J; 1993 v Fa, Cy, Bel, Ei, Bel, RCS, Fa; 1994 v RCS, Cy, R, N, Se, Es (74)
Speed, G. A. (Leeds U), 1990 v Cr (sub); 1991 v D, L (sub), Ei (sub), Ic, WG (sub); 1992 v Br, G (sub), L, Ei, R, Ho, Arg, J; 1993 v Fa, Cy, Bel, Ei, Bel, Fa (sub); 1994 v RCS (sub), Cy, R, N, Se (25)
Sprake, G. (Leeds U), 1964 v S, Ni; 1965 v S, D, Gr; 1966 v E, Ni, USSR; 1967 v S; 1968 v E, S; 1969 v S, E, Ni, WG, R of UK; 1970 v EG, I; 1971 v R, S, E, Ni; 1972 v Fi, E, S, Ni; 1973 v E (2), Pol, S, Ni; 1974 v Pol; (with Birmingham C), S, Ni; 1975 v A, H, L (37)
Stansfield, F. (Cardiff C), 1949 v S (1)
Stevenson, B. (Leeds U), 1978 v Ni; 1979 v Ma, T, S, E, Ni, Ma; 1980 v WG, T, Ic (sub); 1982 v Cz; (with Birmingham C), Sp, S, Ni, F (15)
Stevenson, N. (Swansea C), 1982 v E, S, Ni; 1983 v N (4)
Stitfall, R. F. (Cardiff C), 1953 v E; 1957 v Cz (2)
Sullivan, D. (Cardiff C), 1953 v Ni, F, Y; 1954 v Ni; 1955 v E, Ni; 1957 v E, S; 1958 v Ni, H (2), Se, Br; 1959 v S, Ni; 1960 v E, S (17)
Symons, C. J. (Portsmouth), 1992 v Ei, Ho, Arg, J; 1993 v Fa, Cy, Bel, Ei, RCS, Fa; 1994 v RCS, Cy, R (13)

Tapscott, D. R. (Arsenal), 1954 v A; 1955 v S, E, Ni, Y; 1956 v E, Ni, S, A; 1957 v Ni, Cz, EG; (with Cardiff C), 1959 v E, Ni (14)
Taylor, J. (Wrexham), 1898 v E (1)
Taylor, O. D. S. (Newtown), 1893 v S, Ni; 1894 v S, Ni (4)
Thomas, C. (Druids), 1899 v Ni; 1900 v S (2)
Thomas, D. A. (Swansea T), 1957 v Cz; 1958 v EG (2)
Thomas, D. S. (Fulham), 1948 v E, S, Ni; 1949 v S (4)
Thomas, E. (Cardiff Corinthians), 1925 v E (1)
Thomas, G. (Wrexham), 1885 v E, S (2)
Thomas, H. (Manchester U), 1927 v E (1)
Thomas, M. (Wrexham), 1977 v WG, S (1 + 1 sub), Ni (sub); 1978 v K (sub), S, Cz, Ir, E, Ni (sub); 1979 v Ma; (with Manchester U), T, WG, Ma (sub); 1980 v Ei, WG (sub), T, E, S, Ni; 1981 v Cz, S, E, USSR; (with Everton), 1982 v Cz; (with Brighton & HA), USSR (sub), Sp, E, S (sub), Ni (sub); 1983 (with Stoke C), v N, Y, E, Bul, S, Ni, Br; 1984 v R, Bul, Y; (with Chelsea), S, E; 1985 v Ic, Sp, Ic, S, Sp, N; 1986 v S; (with WBA), H, S.Ar (sub) (51)
Thomas, M. R. (Newcastle U), 1987 v Fi (1)
Thomas, R. J. (Swindon T), 1967 v Ni; 1968 v WG; 1969 v E, Ni, I, WG, R of UK; 1970 v E, S, Ni, EG, I; 1971 v S, E, Ni, R, Cz; 1972 v Fi, Cz, R, E, S, Ni; 1973 v E (3), Pol, S, Ni; 1974 v Pol; (with Derby Co), E, S, Ni; 1975 v H (2), L (2), S, E, Ni; 1976 v A, Y, E; 1977 v Cz, S, E, Ni; 1978 v K, S; (with Cardiff C), Cz (50)
Thomas, T. (Bangor), 1898 v S, Ni (2)
Thomas, W. R. (Newport Co), 1931 v E, S (2)
Thomson, D. (Druids), 1876 v S (1)
Thomson, G. F. (Druids), 1876 v S; 1877 v S (2)
Toshack, J. B. (Cardiff C), 1969 v S, E, Ni, WG, EG, R of UK; 1970 v EG, I; (with Liverpool), 1971 v S, E, Ni, Fi; 1972 v Fi, E; 1973 v E (3), Pol, S; 1975 v A, H (2), L (2), S, E; 1976 v Y (2), E; 1977 v S; 1978 v K (2), S, Cz; (with Swansea C), 1979 v WG (sub), S, E, Ni, Ma; 1980 v WG (40)
Townsend, W. (Newtown), 1887 v Ni; 1893 v Ni (2)
Trainer, H. (Wrexham), 1895 v E, S, Ni (3)
Trainer, J. (Bolton W), 1887 v S; (with Preston NE), 1888 v S; 1889 v E; 1890 v S; 1891 v S; 1892 v Ni, S; 1893 v E; 1894 v Ni, E; 1895 v Ni, E; 1896 v S; 1897 v Ni, S, E; 1898 v S, E; 1899 v Ni, S (20)
Turner, H. G. (Charlton Ath), 1937 v E, S, Ni; 1938 v E, S, Ni; 1939 v Ni, F (8)
Turner, J. (Wrexham), 1892 v E (1)
Turner, R. E. (Wrexham), 1891 v E, Ni (2)
Turner, W. H. (Wrexham), 1887 v E, Ni; 1890 v S; 1891 v E, S (5)

Van Den Hauwe, P. W. R. (Everton), 1985 v Sp; 1986 v S, H; 1987 v USSR, Fi, Cz; 1988 v D (2), Cz, Y, I; 1989 v Fi, Se (13)
Vaughan, Jas (Druids), 1893 v E, S, Ni; 1899 v E (4)
Vaughan, John (Oswestry), 1879 v S; 1880 v S; 1881 v E, S; 1882 v E, S, Ni; 1883 v E, S, Ni; (with Bolton W), 1884 v E (11)
Vaughan, J. O. (Rhyl), 1885 v Ni; 1886 v Ni, E, S (4)
Vaughan, N. (Newport Co), 1983 v Y (sub), Br; 1984 v N; (with Cardiff C), R, Bul, Y, Ni (sub), N, Is; 1985 v Sp (sub) (10)
Vaughan, T. (Rhyl), 1885 v E (1)
Vearncombe, G. (Cardiff C), 1958 v EG; 1961 v Ei (2)
Vernon, T. R. (Blackburn R), 1957 v Ni, Cz (2), EG; 1958 v E, S, EG, Se; 1959 v S; (with Everton), 1960 v Ni; 1961 v S, E, Ei; 1962 v Ni, Br (2), M; 1963 v S, E, H; 1964 v E, S; (with Stoke C), 1965 v Ni, Gr, I; 1966 v E, S, Ni, USSR, D; 1967 v Ni; 1968 v E (32)
Villars, A. K. (Cardiff C), 1974 v E, S, Ni (sub) (3)
Vizard, E. T. (Bolton W), 1911 v E, S, Ni; 1912 v E, S; 1913 v S; 1914 v E, Ni; 1920 v E; 1921 v E, S, Ni; 1922 v E, S; 1923 v E, Ni; 1924 v E, S, Ni; 1926 v E, S; 1927 v S (22)

Walley, J. T. (Watford), 1971 v Cz (1)
Walsh, I. (C Palace), 1980 v Ei, T, E, S, Ic; 1981 v T, Cz, Ei, T, S, E, USSR; 1982 v Cz (sub), Ic; (with Swansea C), Sp, S (sub), Ni (sub), F (18)
Ward, D. (Bristol R), 1959 v E; (with Cardiff C), 1962 v E (2)
Warner, J. (Swansea T), 1937 v E; (with Manchester U), 1939 v F (2)
Warren, F. W. (Cardiff C), 1929 v Ni; (with Middlesbrough), 1931 v Ni; 1933 v F, E; (with Hearts), 1937 v Ni; 1938 v Ni (6)
Watkins, A. E. (Leicester Fosse), 1898 v E, S; (with Aston Villa), 1900 v E, S; (with Millwall), 1904 v Ni (5)
Watkins, W. M. (Stoke C), 1902 v E; 1903 v E, S; (with Aston Villa); 1904 v E, S, Ni; (with Sunderland), 1905 v E, S, Ni; (with Stoke C), 1908 v Ni (10)
Webster, C (Manchester U), 1957 v Cz; 1958 v H, M, Br (4)
Whatley, W. J. (Tottenham H), 1939 v E, S (2)
White, P. F. (London Welsh), 1896 v Ni (1)
Wilcocks, A. R. (Oswestry), 1890 v Ni (1)
Wilding, J. (Wrexham Olympians), 1885 v E, S, Ni; 1886 v E, Ni; (with Bootle), 1887 v E; 1888 v S, Ni; (with Wrexham), 1892 v S (9)
Williams, A. (Reading), 1994 v Es (1)
Williams, A. L. (Wrexham), 1931 v E (1)
Williams, B. (Bristol C), 1930 v Ni (1)
Williams, B. D. (Swansea T), 1928 v Ni, E; 1930 v E, S; (with Everton), 1931 v Ni; 1932 v E; 1933 v E, S, Ni; 1935 v Ni (10)
Williams, D. G. (Derby Co), 1988 v Cz, Y, Se, Ma, I; 1989 v Ho, Is, Se, WG; 1990 v Fi, Ho; (with Ipswich T), 1993 v Ei (12)
Williams, D. M. (Norwich C), 1986 v S.Ar (sub), U, Ca (2); 1987 v Fi (5)
Williams, D. R. (Merthyr T), 1921 v E, S; (with Sheffield W), 1923 v S; 1926 v S; 1927 v E, Ni; (with Manchester U), 1929 v E, S (8)
Williams, E. (Crewe Alex), 1893 v E, S (2)
Williams, E. (Druids), 1901 v E, Ni, S; 1902 v E, Ni (5)
Williams, G. (Chirk), 1893 v S; 1894 v S; 1895 v E, S, Ni; 1898 v Ni (6)
Williams, G. E. (WBA), 1960 v Ni; 1961 v S, E, Ei; 1963 v Ni, H; 1964 v E, S, Ni; 1965 v S, E, Ni, D, Gr (2), USSR, I; 1966 v Ni, Br (2), Ch; 1967 v S, E, Ni; 1968 v Ni; 1969 v I (26)
Williams, G. G. (Swansea T), 1961 v Ni, H, Sp (2); 1962 v E (5)
Williams, G. J. J. (Cardiff C), 1951 v Sw (1)
Williams, G. O. (Wrexham), 1907 v Ni (1)
Williams, H. J. (Swansea), 1965 v Gr (2); 1972 v R (3)
Williams, H. T. (Newport Co), 1949 v Ni, Sw; (with Leeds U), 1950 v Ni; 1951 v S (4)
Williams, J. H. (Oswestry), 1884 v E (1)
Williams, J. J. (Wrexham), 1939 v F (1)
Williams, J. T. (Middlesbrough), 1925 v Ni (1)
Williams, J. W. (C Palace), 1912 v S, Ni (2)
Williams, R. (Newcastle U), 1935 v S, E (2)
Williams, R. P. (Caernarvon), 1886 v S (1)
Williams, S. G. (WBA), 1954 v A; 1955 v E, Ni; 1956 v E, S, A; 1958 v E, S, Ni, Is (2), H (2), M, Se, Br; 1959 v E, S, Ni; 1960 v E, S, Ni; 1961 v Ni, Ei, H, Sp (2); 1962 v E, S, Ni, Br (2), M; (with Southampton), 1963 v S, E, H (2); 1964 v E, S; 1965 v S, E, D; 1966 v D (43)
Williams, W. (Druids), 1876 v S; 1878 v S; (with Oswestry), 1879 v E, S; (with Druids), 1880 v E; 1881 v E, S; 1882 v E, S, Ni; 1883 v Ni (11)
Williams, W. (Northampton T), 1925 v S (1)
Witcomb, D. F. (WBA), 1947 v E, S; (with Sheffield W), 1947 v Ni (3)
Woosnam, A. P. (Leyton Orient), 1959 v S; (with West Ham U), E; 1960 v E, S, Ni; 1961 v S, E, Ni, Ei, Sp, H; 1962 v E, S, Ni, Br; (with Aston Villa), 1963 v Ni, H (17)
Woosnam, G. (Newton White Star), 1879 v S (1)
Worthington, T. (Newtown), 1894 v S (1)
Wynn, G. A. (Wrexham), 1909 v E, S, Ni; (with Manchester C), 1910 v E; 1911 v Ni; 1912 v E, S; 1913 v E, S; 1914 v E, S (11)
Wynn, W. (Chirk), 1903 v Ni (1)

Yorath, T. C. (Leeds U), 1970 v I; 1971 v S, E, Ni; 1972 v Cz, E, S, Ni; 1973 v E, Pol, S; 1974 v Pol, E, S, Ni; 1975 v A, H (2), L (2), S; 1976 v A, E, S, Y (2), E, Ni; (with Coventry C), 1977 v WG, S (2), Cz, E, Ni; 1978 v K (2), S, Cz, WG, Ir, E, S, Ni; 1979 v T, WG, S, E, Ni; (with Tottenham H), 1980 v Ei, T, E, S, Ni, Ic; 1981 v T, Cz; (with Vancouver W), Ei, T, USSR (59)
Young, E. (Wimbledon), 1990 v Cr; (with C Palace), 1991 v D, Bel (2), L, Ei; 1992 v G, L, Ei, A; 1993 v Fa, Cy, Bel, Ei, Bel, Fa; 1994 v RCS, Cy, R, N (20)

REPUBLIC OF IRELAND

Aherne, T. (Belfast C), 1946 v P, Sp; (with Luton T), 1950 v Fi, E, Fi, Se, Bel; 1951 v N, Arg, N; 1952 v WG (2), A, Sp; 1953 v F; 1954 v F (16)
Aldridge, J. W. (Oxford U), 1986 v W, U, Ic, Cz; 1987 v Bel, S, Pol; (with Liverpool), S, Bul, Bel, Br, L; 1988 v Bul, Pol, N, E, USSR, Ho; 1989 v Ni, Tun, Sp, F (sub), H, Ma (sub), H; 1990 v WG; (with Real Sociedad), Ni, Ma, Fi (sub), T, E, Eg, Ho, R, I; 1991 v T, E (2), Pol; (with Tranmere R), 1992 v H (sub), T, W (sub), Sw (sub), US (sub), Alb, I, P (sub); 1993 v La, D, Sp, D, Alb, La, Li; 1994 v Li, Ni, CzR, I (sub), M (sub), N (60)
Ambrose, P. (Shamrock R), 1955 v N, Ho; 1964 v Pol, N, E (5)
Anderson, J. (Preston NE), 1980 v Cz (sub), US (sub); 1982 v Ch, Br, Tr; (with Newcastle U), 1984 v Chn; 1986 v W, Ic, Cz; 1987 v Bul, Bel, Br, L; 1988 v R (sub), Y (sub); 1989 v Tun (16)
Andrews, P. (Bohemians), 1936 v Ho (1)
Arrigan, T. (Waterford), 1938 v N (1)

Babb, P. A. (Coventry C), 1994 v Ru, Ho, Bol, G, CzR (sub), I, M, N, Ho (9)
Bailham, E. (Shamrock R), 1964 v E (1)
Barber, E. (Shelbourne), 1966 v Sp; (with Birmingham C), 1966 v Bel (2)
Barry, P. (Fordsons), 1928 v Bel; 1929 v Bel (2)
Beglin, J. (Liverpool), 1984 v Chn; 1985 v M, D, I, Is, E, N, Sw; 1986 v Sw, USSR, D, W; 1987 v Bel (sub), S, Pol (15)
Bermingham, J. (Bohemians), 1929 v Bel (1)
Bermingham, P. (St James' Gate), 1935 v H (1)
Braddish, S. (Dundalk), 1978 v Pol (1)
Bonner, P. (Celtic), 1981 v Pol; 1982 v Alg; 1984 v Ma, Is, Chn; 1985 v I, Is, E, N; 1986 v U, Ic; 1987 v Bel (2), S (2), Pol, Bul, Br, L; 1988 v Bul, R, Y, N, E, USSR, Ho; 1989 v Sp, F, H, Sp, Ma, H; 1990 v WG, Ni, Ma, W, Fi, T, E, Eg, Ho, R, I; 1991 v Mor, T, E (2), W, Pol, US; 1992 v H, Pol, T, W, Sw, Alb, I; 1993 v La, D, Sp, W, Ni, D, Alb, La, Li; 1994 v Li, Sp, Ni, Ru, Ho, Bol, CzR, I, M, N, Ho (77)
Bradshaw, P. (St James' Gate), 1939 v Sw, Pol, H (2), G (5)
Brady, F. (Fordsons), 1926 v I; 1927 v I (2)
Brady, T. R. (QPR), 1964 v A (2), Sp (2), Pol, N (6)
Brady, W. L. (Arsenal), 1975 v USSR, T, Sw, USSR, Sw, WG; 1976 v T, N, Pol; 1977 v E, T, F (2), Sp, Bul; 1978 v Bul, N; 1979 v Ni, E, D, Bul, WG; 1980 v W, Bul, E, Cy; (with Juventus), 1981 v Ho, Bel, F, Cy, Bel; 1982 v Ho, F, Ch, Br, Tr; (with Sampdoria), 1983 v Ho, Sp, Ic, Ma; 1984 v Ic, Ho, Ma, Pol, Is; (with Internazionale), 1985 v USSR, N, D, I, E, N, Sp, Sw; 1986 v Sw, USSR, D, W; (with Ascoli), 1987 v Bel, S (2), Pol; (with West Ham U), Bul, Bel, Br, L; 1988 v L, Bul; 1989 v F, H (sub), H (sub); 1990 v WG, Fi (72)
Breen, T. (Manchester U), 1937 v Sw, F; (with Shamrock R), 1947 v E, Sp, P (5)
Brennan, F. (Drumcondra), 1965 v Bel (1)
Brennan, S. A. (Manchester U), 1965 v Sp; 1966 v Sp, A, Bel; 1967 v Sp, T, Sp; 1969 v Cz, D, H; 1970 v S, Cz, D, H, Pol (sub), WG; (with Waterford), 1971 v Pol, Se, I (19)
Brown, J. (Coventry C), 1937 v Sw, F (2)
Browne, W. (Bohemians), 1964 v A, Sp, E (3)
Buckley, L. (Shamrock R), 1984 v Pol (sub); (with Waregem), 1985 v M (2)
Burke, F. (Cork), 1934 v Bel (1)
Burke, F. (Cork Ath), 1952 v WG (1)
Burke, J. (Shamrock R), 1929 v Bel (1)
Byrne, A. B. (Southampton), 1970 v D, Pol, WG; 1971 v Pol, Se (2), I (2), A; 1973 v F, USSR (sub), F, N; 1974 v Pol (14)
Byrne, D. (Shelbourne), 1929 v Bel; (with Shamrock R), 1932 v Sp; (with Coleraine), 1934 v Bel (3)
Byrne, J. (Bray Unknowns), 1928 v Bel (1)
Byrne, J. (QPR), 1985 v I, Is (sub), E (sub), Sp (sub); 1987 v S (sub), Bel (sub), Br, L (sub); 1988 v L, Bul (sub), Is, R, Y (sub), Pol (sub); (with Le Havre), 1990 v WG (sub), W, Fi, T (sub), Ma; (with Brighton & HA), 1991 v W; (with Sunderland), 1992 v T, W; (with Millwall), 1993 v W (23)
Byrne, P. (Shamrock R), 1984 v Pol, Chn; 1985 v M; 1986 v D (sub), W (sub), U (sub), Ic (sub), Cz (8)
Byrne, P. (Shelbourne), 1931 v Sp; 1932 v Ho; (with Drumcondra), 1934 v Ho (3)
Byrne, S. (Bohemians), 1931 v Sp (1)

Campbell, A. (Santander), 1985 v I (sub), Is, Sp (3)
Campbell, N. (St Patrick's Ath), 1971 v A (sub); (with Fortuna, Cologne), 1972 v Ir, Ec, Ch, P; 1973 v USSR, F (sub); 1975 v WG; 1976 v N; 1977 v Sp, Bul (sub) (11)
Cannon, H. (Bohemians), 1926 v I; 1928 v Bel (2)
Cantwell, N. (West Ham U), 1954 v L; 1956 v Sp, Ho; 1957 v D, WG, E (2); 1958 v D, Pol, A; 1959 v Pol, Cz (2); 1960 v Se, Ch, Se; 1961 v N; (with Manchester U), S (2); 1962 v Cz (2), A; 1963 v Ic (2), S; 1964 v A, Sp, E; 1965 v Pol, Sp; 1966 v Sp (2), A, Bel; 1967 v Sp, T (36)
Carey, B. P. (Manchester U), 1992 v US (sub); 1993 v W; (with Leicester C), 1994 v Ru (3)
Carey, J. J. (Manchester U), 1938 v N, Cz, Pol; 1939 v Sw, Pol, H (2), G; 1946 v P, Sp; 1947 v E, Sp, P; 1948 v P, Sp; 1949 v Sw, Bel, P, Se, Sp; 1950 v Fi, E, Fi, Se; 1951 v N, Arg, N; 1953 v F, A (29)
Carolan, J. (Manchester U), 1960 v Se, Ch (2)
Carroll, B. (Shelbourne), 1949 v Bel; 1950 v Fi (2)
Carroll, T. R. (Ipswich T), 1968 v Pol; 1969 v Pol, A, D; 1970 v Cz, Pol, WG; 1971 v Se; (with Birmingham C), 1972 v Ir, Ec, Ch, P; 1973 v USSR (2), Pol, F, N (17)
Cascarino, A. G. (Gillingham), 1986 v Sw, USSR, D; (with Millwall), 1988 v Pol, N (sub), USSR (sub), Ho (sub); 1989 v Ni, Tun, Sp, F, H, Sp, Ma, H; 1990 v WG (sub), Ni, Ma; (with Aston Villa), W, Fi, T, E, Eg, Ho (sub), R (sub), I (sub); 1991 v Mor (sub), T (sub), E (2 sub), Pol (sub), Ch (sub), US; (with Celtic), 1992 v Pol, T; (with Chelsea), W, Sw, US (sub); 1993 v W, Ni (sub), D (sub), Alb (sub), La (sub); 1994 v Li (sub), Sp (sub), Ni (sub), Ru, Bol (sub), G, CzR, Ho (sub) (51)
Chandler, J. (Leeds U), 1980 v Cz (sub), US (2)
Chatton, H. A. (Shelbourne), 1931 v Sp; (with Dumbarton), 1932 v Sp; (with Cork), 1934 v Ho (3)
Clarke, J. (Drogheda U), 1978 v Pol (sub) (1)
Clarke, K. (Drumcondra), 1948 v P, Sp (2)
Clarke, M. (Shamrock R), 1950 v Bel (1)
Clinton, T. J. (Everton), 1951 v N; 1954 v F, L (3)
Coad, P. (Shamrock R), 1947 v E, Sp, P; 1948 v P, Sp; 1949 v Sw, Bel, P, Se; 1951 v N (sub); 1952 v Sp (11)
Coffey, T. (Drumcondra), 1950 v Fi (1)
Colfer, M. D. (Shelbourne), 1950 v Bel; 1951 v N (2)
Collins, F. (Jacobs), 1927 v I (1)
Conmy, O. M. (Peterborough U), 1965 v Bel; 1967 v Cz; 1968 v Cz, Pol; 1970 v Cz (5)
Connolly, J. (Fordsons), 1926 v I (1)
Connolly, N. (Cork), 1937 v G (1)
Conroy, G. A. (Stoke C), 1970 v Cz, D, H, Pol, WG; 1971 v Pol, Se (2), I; 1973 v USSR, F, USSR, N; 1974 v Pol, Br, U, Ch; 1975 v T, Sw, USSR, Sw, WG (sub); 1976 v T (sub), Pol; 1977 v E, T, Pol (27)
Conway, J. P. (Fulham), 1967 v Sp, T, Sp; 1968 v Cz; 1969 v A (sub), H; 1970 v S, Cz, D, H, Pol, WG; 1971 v I, A; 1974 v U, Ch; 1975 v WG (sub); 1976 v N, Pol; (with Manchester C), 1977 v Pol (20)
Corr, P. J. (Everton), 1949 v P, Sp; 1950 v E, Se (4)
Courtney, E. (Cork U), 1946 v P (1)
Coyle, O. C. (Bolton W), 1994 v Ho (sub) (1)
Coyne, T. (Celtic), 1992 v Sw, US, Alb (sub), US (sub), I (sub), P (sub); 1993 v La (sub); (with Tranmere R), Ni; (with Motherwell), 1994 v Ru (sub), Ho, Bol, G (sub), CzR (sub), I, M, Ho (16)
Cummins, G. P. (Luton T), 1954 v L (2); 1955 v N (2), WG; 1956 v Y, Sp; 1958 v D, Pol, A; 1959 v Pol, Cz (2); 1960 v Se, Ch, WG, Se; 1961 v S (2) (19)
Cuneen, T. (Limerick), 1951 v N (1)
Curtis, D. P. (Shelbourne), 1957 v D, WG; (with Bristol C), 1957 v E (2); 1958 v D, Pol, A; (with Ipswich T), 1959 v Pol; 1960 v Se, Ch, WG, Se; 1961 v N, S; 1962 v A; 1963 v Ic; (with Exeter C), 1964 v A (17)
Cusack, S. (Limerick), 1953 v F (1)

Daish, L. S. (Cambridge U), 1992 v W (1)
Daly, G. A. (Manchester U), 1973 v Pol (sub), N; 1974 v Br (sub), U (sub); 1975 v Sw (sub), WG; 1977 v E, T, F; (with Derby Co), F, Bul; 1978 v Bul, T, D; 1979 v Ni, E, D, Bul; 1980 v Ni, E, Cy, Sw, Arg; (with Coventry C), 1981 v Ho, Bel, Cy, W, Bel, Cz, Pol (sub); 1982 v Alg, Ch, Br, Tr; 1983 v Ho, Sp (sub), Ma (sub); 1984 v Is (sub), Ma; (with Birmingham C), 1985 v M (sub), N, Sp, Sw;

1986 v Sw; (with Shrewsbury T), U, Ic (sub), Cz (sub); 1987 v S (sub) (48)

Daly, J. (Shamrock R), 1932 v Ho; 1935 v Sw (2)

Daly, M. (Wolverhampton W), 1978 v T, Pol (2)

Daly, P. (Shamrock R), 1950 v Fi (sub) (1)

Davis, T. L. (Oldham Ath), 1937 v G, H; (with Tranmere R), 1938 v Cz, Pol (4)

Deacy, E. (Aston Villa), 1982 v Alg (sub), Ch, Br, Tr (4)

De Mange, K. J. P. P. (Liverpool), 1987 v Br (sub); (with Hull C), 1989 v Tun (sub) (2)

Dempsey, J. T. (Fulham), 1967 v Sp, Cz; 1968 v Cz, Pol; 1969 v Pol, A, D; (with Chelsea), 1969 v Cz, D; 1970 v H, WG; 1971 v Pol, Se (2), I; 1972 v Ir, Ec, Ch, P (19)

Dennehy, J. (Cork Hibernians), 1972 v Ec (sub), Ch; (with Nottingham F), 1973 v USSR (sub), Pol, F, N; 1974 v Pol (sub); 1975 v T (sub), WG (sub); (with Walsall), 1976 v Pol (sub); 1977 v Pol (sub) (11)

Desmond, P. (Middlesbrough), 1950 v Fi, E, Fi, Se (4)

Devine, J. (Arsenal), 1980 v Cz, Ni; 1981 v Cz; 1982 v Ho, Alg; 1983 v Sp, Ma; (with Norwich C), 1984 v Ic, Ho, Is; 1985 v USSR, N (12)

Donnelly, J. (Dundalk), 1935 v H, Sw, G; 1936 v Ho, Sw, H, L; 1937 v G, H; 1938 v N (10)

Donnelly, T. (Drumcondra), 1938 v N; (Shamrock R), 1939 v Sw (2)

Donovan, D. C. (Everton), 1955 v N, Ho, N, WG; 1957 v E (5)

Donovan, T. (Aston Villa), 1980 v Cz (1)

Dowdall, C. (Fordsons), 1928 v Bel; (with Barnsley), 1929 v Bel; (with Cork), 1931 v Sp (3)

Doyle, C. (Shelbourne), 1959 v Cz (1)

Doyle, D. (Shamrock R), 1926 v I (1)

Doyle, L. (Dolphin), 1932 v Sp (1)

Duffy, B. (Shamrock R), 1950 v Bel (1)

Duggan, H. A. (Leeds U), 1927 v I; 1930 v Bel; 1936 v H, L; (with Newport Co), 1938 v N (5)

Dunne, A. P. (Manchester U), 1962 v A; 1963 v Ic, S; 1964 v A, Sp, Pol, N, E; 1965 v Pol, Sp; 1966 v Sp (2), A, Bel; 1967 v Sp, T, Sp; 1969 v Pol, D, H; 1970 v H; 1971 v Se, I, A; (with Bolton W), 1974 v Br (sub), U, Ch; 1975 v T, Sw, USSR, Sw, WG; 1976 v T (33)

Dunne, J. (Sheffield U), 1930 v Bel; (with Arsenal), 1936 v Sw, H, L; (with Southampton), 1937 v Sw, F; (with Shamrock R), 1938 v N (2), Cz, Pol; 1939 v Sw, Pol, H (2), G (15)

Dunne, J. C. (Fulham), 1971 v A (1)

Dunne, L. (Manchester C), 1935 v Sw, G (2)

Dunne, P. A. J. (Manchester U), 1965 v Sp; 1966 v Sp (2), WG; 1967 v T (5)

Dunne, S. (Luton T), 1953 v F, A; 1954 v F, L; 1956 v Sp, Ho; 1957 v D, WG, E; 1958 v D, Pol, A; 1959 v Pol; 1960 v WG, Se (15)

Dunne, T. (St Patrick's Ath), 1956 v Ho; 1957 v D, WG (3)

Dunning, P. (Shelbourne), 1971 v Se, I (2)

Dunphy, E. M. (York C), 1966 v Sp; (with Millwall), 1966 v WG; 1967 v T, Sp, T, Cz; 1968 v Cz, Pol; 1969 v Pol, A, D (2), H; 1970 v D, H, Pol, WG (sub); 1971 v Pol, Se (2), I (2), A (23)

Dwyer, N. M. (West Ham U), 1960 v Se, Ch, WG, Se; (with Swansea T), 1961 v W, N, S (2); 1962 v Cz (2); 1964 v Pol (sub), N, E; 1965 v Pol (14)

Eccles, P. (Shamrock R), 1986 v U (sub) (1)

Egan, R. (Dundalk), 1929 v Bel (1)

Eglington, T. J. (Shamrock R), 1946 v P, Sp; (with Everton), 1947 v E, Sp, P; 1948 v P; 1949 v Sw, P, Se; 1951 v N, Arg; 1952 v WG (2), A, Sp; 1953 v F, A; 1954 v F, L, F; 1955 v N, Ho, WG; 1956 v Sp (24)

Ellis, P. (Bohemians), 1935 v Sw, G; 1936 v Ho, Sw, L; 1937 v G, H (7)

Fagan, E. (Shamrock R), 1973 v N (sub) (1)

Fagan, F. (Manchester C), 1955 v N; 1960 v Se; (with Derby Co), 1960 v Ch, WG, Se; 1961 v W, N, S (8)

Fagan, K. (Shamrock R), 1926 v I (1)

Fairclough, M. (Dundalk), 1982 v Ch (sub), Tr (sub) (2)

Fallon, S. (Celtic), 1951 v N; 1952 v WG (2), A, Sp; 1953 v F; 1955 v N, WG (8)

Fallon, W. J. (Notts Co), 1935 v H; 1936 v H; 1937 v H, Sw, F; 1939 v Sw, Pol; (with Sheffield W), 1939 v H, G (9)

Farquharson, T. G. (Cardiff C), 1929 v Bel; 1930 v Bel; 1931 v Sp; 1932 v Sp (4)

Farrell, P. (Hibernian), 1937 v Sw, F (2)

Farrell, P. D. (Shamrock R), 1946 v P, Sp; (with Everton), 1947 v Sp, P; 1948 v P, Sp; 1949 v Sw, P (sub), Sp; 1950 v E, Fi, Se; 1951 v Arg, N; 1952 v WG (2), A, Sp; 1953 v F, A; 1954 v F (2); 1955 v N, Ho, WG; 1956 v Y, Sp; 1957 v E (28)

Feenan, J. J. (Sunderland), 1937 v Sw, F (2)

Finucane, A. (Limerick), 1967 v T, Cz; 1969 v Cz, D, H; 1970 v S, Cz; 1971 v Se, I (1 + 1 sub); 1972 v A (11)

Fitzgerald, F. J. (Waterford), 1955 v Ho; 1956 v Ho (2)

Fitzgerald, P. J. (Leeds U), 1961 v W, N, S; (with Chester), 1962 v Cz (2) (5)

Fitzpatrick, K. (Limerick), 1970 v Cz (1)

Fitzsimons, A. G. (Middlesbrough), 1950 v Fi, Bel; 1952 v WG (2), A, Sp; 1953 v F, A; 1954 v F, L, F; 1955 v Ho, N, WG; 1956 v Y, Sp, Ho; 1957 v D, WG, E (2); 1958 v D, Pol, A; 1959 v Pol; (with Lincoln C), 1959 v Cz (26)

Flood, J. J. (Shamrock R), 1926 v I; 1929 v Bel; 1930 v Bel; 1931 v Sp; 1932 v Sp (5)

Fogarty, A. (Sunderland), 1960 v WG, Se; 1961 v S; 1962 v Cz (2); 1963 v Ic (2), S (sub); 1964 v A (2); (with Hartlepools U), Sp (11)

Foley, J. (Cork), 1934 v Bel, Ho; (with Celtic), 1935 v H, Sw, G; 1937 v G, H (7)

Foley, M. (Shelbourne), 1926 v I (1)

Foley, T. C. (Northampton T), 1964 v Sp, Pol, N; 1965 v Pol, Bel; 1966 v Sp (2), WG; 1967 v Cz (9)

Foy, T. (Shamrock R), 1938 v N; 1939 v H (2)

Fullam, J. (Preston NE), 1961 v N; (with Shamrock R), 1964 v Sp, Pol, N; 1966 v A, Bel; 1968 v Pol; 1969 v Pol, A, D; 1970 v Cz (sub) (11)

Fullam, R. (Shamrock R), 1926 v I; 1927 v I (2)

Gallagher, C. (Celtic), 1967 v T, Cz (2)

Gallagher, M. (Hibernian), 1954 v L (1)

Gallagher, P. (Falkirk), 1932 v Sp (1)

Galvin, A. (Tottenham H), 1983 v Ho, Ma; 1984 v Ho (sub), Is (sub); 1985 v M, USSR, N, D, I, N, Sp; 1986 v U, Ic, Cz; 1987 v Bel (2), S, Bul, L; (with Sheffield W), 1988 v L, Bul, R, Pol, N, E, USSR, Ho; 1989 v Sp; (with Swindon T), 1990 v WG (29)

Gannon, E. (Notts Co), 1949 v Sw; (with Sheffield W), 1949 v Bel, P, Se, Sp; 1950 v Fi; 1951 v N; 1952 v WG, A; 1954 v L, F; 1955 v N; (with Shelbourne), 1955 v N, WG (14)

Gannon, M. (Shelbourne), 1972 v A (1)

Gaskins, P. (Shamrock R), 1934 v Bel, Ho; 1935 v H, Sw, G; (with St James' Gate), 1938 v Cz, Pol (7)

Gavin, J. T. (Norwich C), 1950 v Fi (2); 1953 v F; 1954 v L; (with Tottenham H), 1955 v Ho, WG; (with Norwich C), 1957 v D (7)

Geoghegan, M. (St James' Gate), 1937 v G; 1938 v N (2)

Gibbons, A. (St Patrick's Ath), 1952 v WG; 1954 v L; 1956 v Y, Sp (4)

Gilbert, R. (Shamrock R), 1966 v WG (1)

Giles, C. (Doncaster R), 1951 v N (1)

Giles, M. J. (Manchester U), 1960 v Se, Ch; 1961 v W, N, S (2); 1962 v Cz (2), A; 1963 v Ic, S; (with Leeds U), 1964 v A (2), Sp (2), Pol, N, E; 1965 v Sp; 1966 v Sp (2), A, Bel; 1967 v Sp, T (2); 1969 v A, D, Cz; 1970 v S, Pol, WG; 1971 v I; 1973 v F, USSR; 1974 v Br, U, Ch; 1975 v USSR, T, Sw, USSR, Sw; (with WBA), 1976 v T; 1977 v

E, T, F (2), Pol, Bul; (with Shamrock R), 1978 v Bul, T, Pol, N, D; 1979 v Ni, D, Bul, WG (59)

Givens, D. J. (Manchester U), 1969 v D, H; 1970 v S, Cz, D, H; (with Luton T), 1970 v Pol, WG; 1971 v Se, I (2), A; 1972 v Ir, Ec, P; (with QPR), 1973 v F, USSR, Pol, F, N; 1974 v Pol, Br, U, Ch; 1975 v USSR, T, Sw, USSR, Sw, WG; 1976 v T, N, Pol; 1977 v E, T, F (2), Sp, Bul; 1978 v Bul, N, D; (with Birmingham C), 1979 v Ni (sub), E, D, Bul, WG; 1980 v US (sub), Ni (sub), Sw, Arg; 1981 v Ho, Bel, Cy (sub), W; (with Neuchatel X), 1982 v F (sub) (56)

Glen, W. (Shamrock R), 1927 v I; 1929 v Bel; 1930 v Bel; 1932 v Sp; 1936 v Ho, Sw, H, L (8)

Glynn, D. (Drumcondra), 1952 v WG; 1955 v N (2)

Godwin, T. F. (Shamrock R), 1949 v P, Se, Sp; 1950 v Fi, E; (with Leicester C), 1950 v Fi, Se, Bel; 1951 v N; (with Bournemouth), 1956 v Ho; 1957 v E; 1958 v D, Pol (13)

Golding, L. (Shamrock R), 1928 v Bel; 1930 v Bel (2)

Gorman, W. C. (Bury), 1936 v Sw, H, L; 1937 v G, H; 1938 v N, Cz, Pol; 1939 v Sw, Pol, H; (with Brentford), 1947 v E, P (13)

Grace, J. (Drumcondra), 1926 v I (1)

Grealish, A. (Orient), 1976 v N, Pol; 1978 v N, D; 1979 v Ni, E, WG; (with Luton T), 1980 v W, Cz, Bul, US, Ni, E, Cy, Sw, Arg; 1981 v Ho, Bel, F, Cy, W, Bel, Pol; (with Brighton & HA), 1982 v Ho, Alg, Ch, Br, Tr; 1983 v Ho, Sp, Ic, Sp; 1984 v Ic, Ho; (with WBA), Pol, Chn; 1985 v M, USSR, N, D, Sp (sub), Sw; 1986 v USSR, D (44)

Gregg, E. (Bohemians), 1978 v Pol, D (sub); 1979 v E (sub), D, Bul, WG; 1980 v W, Cz (8)

Griffith, R. (Walsall), 1935 v H (1)

Grimes, A. A. (Manchester U), 1978 v T, Pol, N (sub); 1980 v Bul, US, Ni, E, Cy; 1981 v Cz, Pol; 1982 v Alg; 1983 v Sp (2); (with Coventry C), 1984 v Pol, Is; (with Luton T), 1988 v L, R (17)

Hale, A. (Aston Villa), 1962 v A; (with Doncaster R), 1963 v Ic; 1964 v Sp (2); (with Waterford), 1967 v Sp; 1968 v Pol (sub); 1969 v Pol, A, D; 1970 v S, Cz; 1971 v Pol (sub); 1972 v A (sub) (13)

Hamilton, T. (Shamrock R), 1959 v Cz (2) (2)

Hand, E. K. (Portsmouth), 1969 v Cz (sub); 1970 v Pol, WG; 1971 v Pol, A; 1973 v USSR, F, USSR, Pol, F; 1974 v Pol, Br, U, Ch; 1975 v T, Sw, USSR, Sw, WG; 1976 v T (20)

Harrington, W. (Cork), 1936 v Ho, Sw, H, L (4)

Hartnett, J. B. (Middlesbrough), 1949 v Sp; 1954 v L (2)

Haverty, J. (Arsenal), 1956 v Ho; 1957 v D, WG, E (2); 1958 v D, Pol, A; 1959 v Pol; 1960 v Se, Ch; 1961 v W, N, S (2); (with Blackburn R), 1962 v Cz (2); (with Millwall), 1963 v S; 1964 v A, Sp, Pol, N, E; (with Celtic), 1965 v Pol; (with Bristol R), 1965 v Sp; (with Shelbourne), 1966 v Sp (2), WG, A, Bel; 1967 v T, Sp (32)

Hayes, A. W. P. (Southampton), 1979 v D (1)

Hayes, W. E. (Huddersfield T), 1947 v E, P (2)

Hayes, W. J. (Limerick), 1949 v Bel (1)

Healey, R. (Cardiff C), 1977 v Pol; 1980 v E (sub) (2)

Heighway, S. D. (Liverpool), 1971 v Pol, Se (2), I, A; 1973 v USSR; 1975 v USSR, T, USSR, WG; 1976 v T, N; 1977 v E, F (2), Sp, Bul; 1978 v Bul, N, D; 1979 v Ni, Bul; 1980 v Bul, US, Ni, E, Cy, Arg; 1981 v Bel, F, Cy, W, Bel; (with Minnesota K), 1982 v Ho (34)

Henderson, B. (Drumcondra), 1948 v P, Sp (2)

Hennessy, J. (Shelbourne), 1965 v Pol, Bel, Sp; 1966 v WG; (with St Patrick's Ath), 1969 v A (5)

Herrick, J. (Cork Hibernians), 1972 v A, Ch (sub); (with Shamrock R), 1973 v F (sub) (3)

Higgins, J. (Birmingham C), 1951 v Arg (1)

Holmes, J. (Coventry C), 1971 v A (sub); 1973 v F, USSR, Pol, F, N; 1974 v Pol, Br; 1975 v USSR, Sw; 1976 v T, N, Pol; 1977 v E, T, F, Sp; (with Tottenham H), F, Pol, Bul; 1978 v Bul, T, Pol, N, D; 1979 v Ni, E, D, Bul; (with Vancouver W), 1981 v W (30)

Horlacher, A. F. (Bohemians), 1930 v Bel; 1932 v Sp, Ho; 1934 v Ho (sub); 1935 v H; 1936 v Ho, Sw (7)

Houghton, R. J. (Oxford U), 1986 v W, U, Ic, Cz; 1987 v Bel (2), S (2), Pol, L; 1988 v L, Bul; (with Liverpool), Is, Y, N, E, USSR, Ho; 1989 v Ni, Tun, Sp, F, H, Sp, Ma, H; 1990 v Ni, Ma, Fi, E, Eg, Ho, R, I; 1991 v Mor, T, E (2), Pol, Ch, US; 1992 v H, Alb, US, I, P; (with Aston Villa), 1993 v D, Sp, Ni, D, Alb, La, Li; 1994 v Li, Sp, Ni, Bol, G (sub), I, M, N, Ho (62)

Howlett, G. (Brighton & HA), 1984 v Chn (sub) (1)

Hoy, M. (Dundalk), 1938 v N; 1939 v Sw, Pol, H (2), G (6)

Hughton, C. (Tottenham H), 1980 v US, E, Sw, Arg; 1981 v Ho, Bel, F, Cy, W, Bel, Pol; 1982 v F; 1983 v Ho, Sp, Ma, Sp; 1984 v Ic, Ho, Ma; 1985 v M (sub), USSR, N, I, Is, E, Sp; 1986 v Sw, USSR, U, Ic; 1987 v Bel, Bul; 1988 v Is, Y, Pol, N, E, USSR, Ho; 1989 v Ni, F, H, Sp, Ma, H; 1990 v W (sub), USSR (sub), Fi, T (sub), Ma; 1991 v T; (with West Ham U), Ch; 1992 v T (53)

Hurley, C. J. (Millwall), 1957 v E; (with Sunderland), 1958 v D, Pol, A; 1959 v Cz (2); 1960 v Se, Ch, WG, Se; 1961 v W, N, S (2); 1962 v Cz (2), A; 1963 v Ic (2), S; 1964 v A (2), Sp (2), Pol, N; 1965 v Sp; 1966 v WG, A, Bel; 1967 v T, Sp, T, Cz; 1968 v Cz, Pol; 1969 v Pol, D, Cz, (with Bolton W), H (40)

Hutchinson, F. (Drumcondra), 1935 v Sw, G (2)

Irwin, D. J. (Manchester U), 1991 v Mor, T, W, E, Pol, US; 1992 v H, Pol, W, US, Alb, US (sub), I; 1993 v La, D, Sp, Ni, D, Alb, La, Li; 1994 v Li, Sp, Ni, Bol, G, I, M (28)

Jordan, D. (Wolverhampton W), 1937 v Sw, F (2)

Jordan, W. (Bohemians), 1934 v Ho; 1938 v N (2)

Kavanagh, P. J. (Celtic), 1931 v Sp; 1932 v Sp (2)

Keane, R. M. (Nottingham F), 1991 v Ch; 1992 v H, Pol, W, Sw, Alb, US; 1993 v La, D, Sp, W, Ni, D, Alb, La, Li; (with Manchester U), 1994 v Li, Sp, Ni, Bol, G, CzR (sub), I, M, N, Ho (26)

Keane, T. R. (Swansea T), 1949 v Sw, P, Se, Sp (4)

Kearin, M. (Shamrock R), 1972 v A (1)

Kearns, F. T. (West Ham U), 1954 v L (1)

Kearns, M. (Oxford U), 1970 v Pol (sub); (with Walsall), 1974 v Pol (sub), U, Ch; 1976 v N, Pol; 1977 v E, T, F (2), Sp, Bul; 1978 v N, D; 1979 v Ni, E; (with Wolverhampton W), 1980 v US, Ni (18)

Kelly, A. T. (Sheffield U), 1993 v W (sub); 1994 v Ru (sub), G (3)

Kelly, D. T. (Walsall), 1988 v Is, R, Y; (with West Ham U), 1989 v Tun (sub); (with Leicester C), 1990 v USSR, Ma; 1991 v Mor, W (sub), Ch, US; 1992 v H; (with Newcastle U), I (sub), P; 1993 v Sp (sub), Ni; (with Wolverhampton W), 1994 v Ru, N (sub) (17)

Kelly, G. (Leeds U), 1994 v Ru, Ho, Bol (sub), G (sub), CzR, N, Ho (7)

Kelly, J. (Derry C), 1932 v Ho; 1934 v Bel; 1936 v Sw, L (4)

Kelly, J. A. (Drumcondra), 1957 v WG, E; (with Preston NE), 1962 v A; 1963 v Ic (2), S; 1964 v A (2), Sp (2), Pol; 1965 v Bel; 1966 v A, Bel; 1967 v Sp (2), T, Cz, Pol; 1968 v Pol, Cz; 1969 v Pol, A, D, Cz, D, H; 1970 v S, D, H, Pol, WG; 1971 v Pol, Se (2), I (2), A; 1972 v Ir, Ec, Ch, P; 1973 v USSR, F, USSR, Pol, F, N (48)

Kelly, J. P. V. (Wolverhampton W), 1961 v W, N, S; 1962 v Cz (2) (5)

Kelly, M. J. (Portsmouth), 1988 v Y, Pol (sub); 1989 v Tun; 1991 v Mor (4)

Kelly, N. (Nottingham F), 1954 v L (1)

Kendrick, J. (Everton), 1927 v I; 1934 v Bel, Ho; 1936 v Ho (4)
Kennedy, M. F. (Portsmouth), 1986 v Ic, Cz (sub) (2)
Kennedy, W. (St James' Gate), 1932 v Ho; 1934 v Bel, Ho (3)
Keogh, J. (Shamrock R), 1966 v WG (sub) (1)
Keogh, S. (Shamrock R), 1959 v Pol (1)
Kernaghan, A. N. (Middlesbrough), 1993 v La, D (2), Alb, La, Li; 1994 v Li; (with Manchester C), Sp, Ni, Bol (sub), CzR (11)
Kiernan, F. W. (Shamrock R), 1951 v Arg, N; (with Southampton), 1952 v WG (2), A (5)
Kinnear, J. P. (Tottenham H), 1967 v T; 1968 v Cz, Pol; 1969 v A; 1970 v Cz, D, H, Pol; 1971 v Se (sub), I; 1972 v Ir, Ec, Ch, P; 1973 v USSR, F; 1974 v Pol, Br, U, Ch; 1975 v USSR, T, Sw, USSR, WG; (with Brighton & HA), 1976 v T (sub) (26)
Kinsella, J. (Shelbourne), 1928 v Bel (1)
Kinsella, P. (Shamrock R), 1932 v Ho; 1938 v N (2)
Kirkland, A. (Shamrock R), 1927 v I (1)

Lacey, W. (Shelbourne), 1927 v I; 1928 v Bel; 1930 v Bel (3)
Langan, D. (Derby Co), 1978 v T, N; 1980 v Sw, Arg; (with Birmingham C), 1981 v Ho, Bel, F, Cy, W, Bel, Cz, Pol; 1982 v Ho, F; (with Oxford U), 1985 v N, Sp, Sw; 1986 v W, U; 1987 v Bel, S, Pol, Br (sub), L (sub); 1988 v L (25)
Lawler, J. F. (Fulham), 1953 v A; 1954 v L, F; 1955 v N, H, N, WG; 1956 v Y (8)
Lawlor, J. C. (Drumcondra), 1949 v Bel; (with Doncaster R), 1951 v N, Arg (3)
Lawlor, M. (Shamrock R), 1971 v Pol, Se (2), I (sub); 1973 v Pol (5)
Lawrenson, M. (Preston NE), 1977 v Pol; (with Brighton), 1978 v Bul, Pol, N (sub); 1979 v Ni, E; 1980 v E, Cy, Sw; 1981 v Ho, Bel, F, Cy, Pol; (with Liverpool), 1982 v Ho, F; 1983 v Ho, Sp, Ic, Ma, Sp; 1984 v Ic, Ho, Ma, Is; 1985 v USSR, N, D, I, E, N; 1986 v Sw, USSR, D; 1987 v Bel, S; 1988 v Bul, Is (38)
Leech, M. (Shamrock R), 1969 v Cz, D, H; 1972 v A, Ir, Ec, P; 1973 v USSR (sub) (8)
Lennon, C. (St James' Gate), 1935 v H, Sw, G (3)
Lennox, G. (Dolphin), 1931 v Sp; 1932 v Sp (2)
Lowry, D. (St Patrick's Ath), 1962 v A (sub) (1)
Lunn, R. (Dundalk), 1939 v Sw, Pol (2)
Lynch, J. (Cork Bohemians), 1934 v Bel (1)

McAlinden, J. (Portsmouth), 1946 v P, Sp (2)
McAteer, J. W. (Bolton W), 1994 v Ru, Ho (sub), Bol (sub), G, CzR (sub), I (sub), M (sub), N, Ho (sub) (9)
McCann, J. (Shamrock R), 1957 v WG (1)
McCarthy, J. (Bohemians), 1926 v I; 1928 v Bel; 1930 v Bel (3)
McCarthy, M. (Manchester C), 1984 v Pol, Chn; 1985 v M, D, I, Is, E, Sp, Sw; 1986 v Sw, USSR, W (sub), U, Ic, Cz; 1987 v S (2), Pol, Bul, Bel, Br, L; (with Celtic), 1988 v Bul, Is, R, Y, N, E, USSR, Ho; 1989 v Ni, Tun, Sp, F, H, Sp; (with Lyon), 1990 v WG, Ni, W, USSR; (with Millwall) Fi, T, E, Eg, Ho, R, I; 1991 v Mor, T, E, US; 1992 v H, T, Alb (sub), US, I, P (57)
McCarthy, M. (Shamrock R), 1932 v Ho (1)
McConville, T. (Dundalk), 1972 v A; (with Waterford), 1973 v USSR, F, USSR, Pol, F (6)
McDonagh, Joe (Shamrock R), 1984 v Pol (sub), Ma (sub); 1985 v M (sub) (3)
McDonagh, J. (Everton), 1981 v W, Bel, Cz; (with Bolton W), 1982 v Ho, F, Ch, Br; 1983 v Ho, Sp, Ic, Ma, Sp; (with Notts Co), 1984 v Ic, Ho, Pol; 1985 v M, USSR, N, D, Sp, Sw; 1986 v Sw, USSR, D (24)
McEvoy, M. A. (Blackburn R), 1961 v S (2); 1963 v S; 1964 v A, Sp (2), Pol, N, E; 1965 v Pol, Bel, Sp; 1966 v Sp (2); 1967 v Sp, T, Cz (17)
McGee, P. (QPR), 1978 v T, N (sub), D (sub); 1979 v Ni, E, D (sub), Bul (sub); 1980 v Cz, Bul; (with Preston NE), US, Ni, Cy, Sw, Arg; 1981 v Bel (sub) (15)
McGoldrick, E. J. (C Palace), 1992 v Sw, US, I, P (sub); 1993 v D, W, Ni (sub), D; (with Arsenal), 1994 v Ni, Ru, Ho, CzR (12)
McGowan, D. (West Ham U), 1949 v P, Se, Sp (3)
McGowan, J. (Cork U), 1947 v Sp (1)
McGrath, M. (Blackburn R), 1958 v A; 1959 v Pol, Cz (2); 1960 v Se, WG, Se; 1961 v W; 1962 v Cz (2); 1963 v S; 1964 v A (2), E; 1965 v Pol, Bel, Sp; 1966 v Sp; (with Bradford), 1966 v WG, A, Bel; 1967 v T (22)
McGrath, P. (Manchester U), 1985 v I (sub), Is, E, N (sub), Sw (sub); 1986 v Sw (sub), D, W, Ic, Cz; 1987 v Bel (2), S (2), Pol, Bul, Br, L; 1988 v L, Bul, Y, Pol, N, E, Ho; 1989 v Ni, F, H, Sp, Ma, H; (with Aston Villa), 1990 v WG, Ma, USSR, Fi, T, E, Eg, Ho, R, I; 1991 v E (2), W, Pol, Ch (sub), US; 1992 v Pol, T, Sw, US, Alb, US, I, P; 1993 v La, Sp, Ni, D, La, Li; 1994 v Sp, Ni, G, CzR, I, M, N, Ho (69)
McGuire, W. (Bohemians), 1936 v Ho (1)
McKenzie, G. (Southend U), 1938 v N (2), Cz, Pol; 1939 v Sw, Pol, H (2), G (9)
Mackey, G. (Shamrock R), 1957 v D, WG, E (3)
McLoughlin, A. F. (Swindon T), 1990 v Ma, E (sub), Eg (sub); 1991 v Mor (sub), E (sub); (with Southampton), W, Ch (sub); 1992 v H (sub), W (sub); (with Portsmouth), US, I (sub), P; 1993 v W; 1994 v Ni (sub), Ru, Ho (sub) (16)
McLoughlin, F. (Fordsons), 1930 v Bel; (with Cork), 1932 v Sp (2)
McMillan, W. (Belfast Celtic), 1946 v P, Sp (2)
McNally, J. B. (Luton T), 1959 v Cz; 1961 v S; 1963 v Ic (3)
Macken, A. (Derby Co), 1977 v Sp (1)
Madden, O. (Cork), 1936 v H (1)
Maguire, J. (Shamrock R), 1929 v Bel (1)
Malone, G. (Shelbourne), 1949 v Bel (1)
Mancini, T. J. (QPR), 1974 v Pol, Br, U, Ch; (with Arsenal), 1975 v USSR (5)
Martin, C. (Bo'ness), 1927 v I (1)
Martin, C. J. (Glentoran), 1946 v P (sub), Sp; 1947 v E; (with Leeds U), 1947 v Sp; 1948 v P, Sp; (with Aston Villa), 1949 v Sw, Bel, P, Se, Sp; 1950 v Fi, E, Fi, Se, Bel; 1951 v Arg; 1952 v WG, A, Sp; 1954 v F (2), L; 1955 v N, Ho, N, WG; 1956 v Y, Sp, Ho (30)
Martin, M. P. (Bohemians), 1972 v A, Ir, Ec, Ch, P; 1973 v USSR; (with Manchester U), 1973 v USSR, Pol, F, N; 1974 v Pol, Br, U, Ch; 1975 v USSR, T, Sw, USSR, Sw, WG; (with WBA), 1976 v T, N, Pol; 1977 v E, T, F (2), Sp, Pol, Bul; (with Newcastle U), 1979 v D, Bul, WG; 1980 v W, Cz, Bul, US, Ni; 1981 v F, Bel, Cz; 1982 v Ho, F, Alg, Ch, Br, Tr; 1983 v Ho, Sp, Ma, Sp (51)
Meagan, M. K. (Everton), 1961 v S; 1962 v A; 1963 v Ic; 1964 v Sp; (with Huddersfield T), 1965 v Bel; 1966 v Sp (2), A, Bel; 1967 v Sp, T, Sp, T, Cz; 1968 v Cz, Pol; (with Drogheda), 1970 v S (17)
Meehan, P. (Drumcondra), 1934 v Ho (1)
Milligan, M. J. (Oldham Ath), 1992 v US (sub) (1)
Monahan, P. (Sligo R), 1935 v Sw, G (2)
Mooney, J. (Shamrock R), 1965 v Pol, Bel (2)
Moore, P. (Shamrock R), 1931 v Sp; 1932 v Ho; (with Aberdeen), 1934 v Bel, Ho; 1935 v H, G; (with Shamrock R), 1936 v Ho; 1937 v G, H (9)
Moran, K. (Manchester U), 1980 v Sw, Arg; 1981 v Bel, F, Cy, W (sub), Bel, Cz, Pol; 1982 v F, Alg; 1983 v Ic; 1984 v Ic, Ho, Ma, Is; 1985 v M; 1986 v D, Ic, Cz; 1987 v Bel (2), S (2), Pol, Bul, Br, L; 1988 v L, Bul, Is, R, Y, Pol, N, E, USSR, Ho; (with Sporting Gijon), 1989 v Ni, Sp, H, Sp, Ma, H; 1990 v Ni, Ma; (with Blackburn R), W, USSR (sub), Ma, E, Eg, Ho, R, I; 1991 v T (sub), W, E, Pol, Ch, US; 1992 v Pol, US; 1993 v D, Sp, Ni, Alb; 1994 v Li, Sp, Ho, Bol (70)

Moroney, T. (West Ham U), 1948 v Sp; 1949 v P, Se, Sp; 1950 v Fi, E, Fi, Bel; 1951 v N (2); 1952 v WG; (with Evergreen U), 1954 v F (12)
Morris, C. B. (Celtic), 1988 v Is, R, Y, Pol, N, E, USSR, Ho; 1989 v Ni, Tun, Sp, F, H (1 + 1 sub); 1990 v WG, Ni, Ma (sub), W, USSR, Fi (sub), T, E, Eg, Ho, R, I; 1991 v E; 1992 v H (sub), Pol, W, Sw, US (2), P; (with Middlesbrough), 1993 v W (35)
Moulson, C. (Lincoln C), 1936 v H, L; (with Notts Co), 1937 v H, Sw, F (5)
Moulson, G. B. (Lincoln C), 1948 v P, Sp; 1949 v Sw (3)
Mucklan, C. (Drogheda U), 1978 v Pol (1)
Muldoon, T. (Aston Villa), 1927 v I (1)
Mulligan, P. M. (Shamrock R), 1969 v Cz, D, H; 1970 v S, Cz, D; (with Chelsea), 1970 v H, Pol, WG; 1971 v Pol, Se, I; 1972 v A, Ir, Ec, Ch, P; (with C Palace), 1973 v F, USSR, Pol, F, N; 1974 v Pol, Br, U, Ch; 1975 v USSR, T, Sw, USSR, Sw; (with WBA), 1976 v T, Pol; 1977 v E, T, F (2), Pol, Bul; 1978 v Bul, N, D; 1979 v E, D, Bul (sub), WG; (with Shamrock R), 1980 v W, Cz, Bul, US (sub) (50)
Munroe, L. (Shamrock R), 1954 v L (1)
Murphy, A. (Clyde), 1956 v Y (1)
Murphy, B. (Bohemians), 1986 v U (1)
Murphy, J. (C Palace), 1980 v W, US, Cy (3)
Murray, T. (Dundalk), 1950 v Bel (1)

Newman, W. (Shelbourne), 1969 v D (1)
Nolan, R. (Shamrock R), 1957 v D, WG, E; 1958 v Pol; 1960 v Ch, WG, Se; 1962 v Cz (2); 1963 v Ic (10)

O'Brien, F. (Philadelphia F), 1980 v Cz, E, Cy (sub), Arg (sub) (4)
O'Brien, L. (Shamrock R), 1986 v U; (with Manchester U), 1987 v Br; 1988 v Is (sub), R (sub), Y (sub), Pol (sub); 1989 v Tun; (with Newcastle U), Sp (sub); 1992 v Sw (sub); 1993 v W; (with Tranmere R), 1994 v Ru (11)
O'Brien, M. T. (Derby Co), 1927 v I; (with Walsall), 1929 v Bel; (with Norwich C), 1930 v Bel; (with Watford), 1932 v Ho (4)
O'Brien, R. (Notts Co), 1976 v N, Pol; 1977 v Sp, Pol (4)
O'Byrne, L. B. (Shamrock R), 1949 v Bel (1)
O'Callaghan, B. R. (Stoke C), 1979 v WG (sub); 1980 v W, US; 1981 v W; 1982 v Br, Tr (6)
O'Callaghan, K. (Ipswich T), 1981 v Cz, Pol; 1982 v Alg, Ch, Br, Tr (sub); 1983 v Sp, Ic (sub), Ma (sub), Sp (sub); 1984 v Ic, Ho, Ma; 1985 v M (sub), N (sub), D (sub), E (sub); (with Portsmouth), 1986 v Sw (sub), USSR (sub); 1987 v Br (20)
O'Connell, A. (Dundalk), 1967 v Sp; (with Bohemians), 1971 v Pol (sub) (2)
O'Connor, T. (Shamrock R), 1950 v Fi, E, Fi, Se (4)
O'Connor, T. (Fulham), 1968 v Cz; (with Dundalk), 1972 v A, Ir (sub), Ec (sub), Ch; (with Bohemians), 1973 v F (sub), Pol (sub) (7)
O'Driscoll, J. F. (Swansea T), 1949 v Sw, Bel, Se (3)
O'Driscoll, S. (Fulham), 1982 v Ch, Br, Tr (sub) (3)
O'Farrell, F. (West Ham U), 1952 v A; 1953 v A; 1954 v F; 1955 v Ho, N; 1956 v Y, Ho; (with Preston NE), 1958 v D; 1959 v Cz (9)
O'Flanagan, K. P. (Bohemians), 1938 v N, Cz, Pol; 1939 v Pol, H (2), G; (with Arsenal), 1947 v E, Sp, P (10)
O'Flanagan, M. (Bohemians), 1947 v E (1)
O'Hanlon, K. G. (Rotherham U), 1988 v Is (1)
O'Kane, P. (Bohemians), 1935 v H, Sw, G (3)
O'Keefe, E. (Everton), 1981 v W; (with Port Vale), 1984 v Chn; 1985 v M, USSR (sub), E (5)
O'Keefe, T. (Cork), 1934 v Bel; (with Waterford), 1938 v Cz, Pol (3)
O'Leary, D. (Arsenal), 1977 v E, F (2), Sp, Bul; 1978 v Bul, N, D; 1979 v E, Bul, WG; 1980 v W, Bul, Ni, E, Cy; 1981 v Ho, Cz, Pol; 1982 v Ho, F; 1983 v Ho, Ic, Sp; 1984 v Pol, Is, Chn; 1985 v USSR, N, D, Is, E (sub), N, Sp, Sw; 1986 v Sw, USSR, D, W; 1989 v Sp, Ma, H; 1990 v WG, Ni (sub), Ma, W (sub), USSR, Fi, T, Ma, R (sub); 1991 v Mor, T, E (2), Pol, Ch; 1992 v H, Pol, T, W, Sw, US, Alb, I, P; 1993 v W (67)
O'Leary, P. (Shamrock R), 1980 v Bul, US, Ni, E (sub), Cz, Arg; 1981 v Ho (7)
O'Mahoney, M. T. (Bristol R), 1938 v Cz, Pol; 1939 v Sw, Pol, H, G (6)
O'Neill, F. S. (Shamrock R), 1962 v Cz (2); 1965 v Pol, Bel, Sp; 1966 v Sp (2), WG, A; 1967 v Sp, T, Sp, T; 1969 v Pol, A, D, Cz, D (sub), H (sub); 1972 v A (20)
O'Neill, J. (Everton), 1952 v Sp; 1953 v F, A; 1954 v F, L, F; 1955 v N, Ho, N, WG; 1956 v Y, Sp; 1957 v D; 1958 v A; 1959 v Pol, Cz (2) (17)
O'Neill, J. (Preston NE), 1961 v W (1)
O'Neill, W. (Dundalk), 1936 v Ho, Sw, H, L; 1937 v G, H, Sw, F; 1938 v N; 1939 v H, G (11)
O'Regan, K. (Brighton & HA), 1984 v Ma, Pol; 1985 v M, Sp (sub) (4)
O'Reilly, J. (Brideville), 1932 v Ho; (with Aberdeen), 1934 v Bel, Ho; (with Brideville), 1936 v Ho; Sw, H, L; (with St James' Gate), 1937 v G, H, Sw, F; 1938 v N (2), Cz, Pol; 1939 v Sw, Pol, H (2), G (20)
O'Reilly, J. (Cork U), 1946 v P, Sp (2)

Peyton, G. (Fulham), 1977 v Sp (sub); 1978 v Bul, T, Pol; 1979 v D, Bul, WG; 1980 v W, Cz, Bul, E, Cy, Sw, Arg; 1981 v Ho, Bel, F, Cy; 1982 v Tr; 1985 v M (sub); 1986 v W, Cz; (with Bournemouth), 1988 v L, Pol; 1989 v Ni, Tun; 1990 v USSR, Ma; 1991 v Ch; 1992 v US (2), I (sub), P (33)
Peyton, N. (Shamrock R), 1957 v WG; (with Leeds U), 1960 v WG, Se (sub); 1961 v W; 1963 v Ic, S (6)
Phelan, T. (Wimbledon), 1992 v H, Pol (sub), T, W, Sw, US, I (sub), P; (with Manchester C), 1993 v La (sub), D, Sp, Ni, Alb, La, Li; 1994 v Li, Sp, Ni, Ho, Bol, G, CzR, I, M, Ho (25)

Quinn, N. J. (Arsenal), 1986 v Ic (sub), Cz; 1987 v Bul (sub); 1988 v L (sub), Bul (sub), Is, R (sub), Pol (sub), E (sub); 1989 v Tun (sub), Sp (sub), H (sub); (with Manchester C), 1990 v USSR, Ma, Eg (sub), Ho, R, I; 1991 v Mor, T, E (2) W, Pol; 1992 v H, W (sub), US, Alb, US, I (sub), P; 1993 v La, D, Sp, Ni, D, Alb, La, Li; 1994 v Li, Sp, Ni (42)

Reid, C. (Brideville), 1931 v Sp (1)
Richardson, D. J. (Shamrock R), 1972 v A (sub); (with Gillingham), 1973 v N (sub); 1980 v Cz (3)
Rigby, A. (St James' Gate), 1935 v H, Sw, G (3)
Ringstead, A. (Sheffield U), 1951 v Arg, N; 1952 v WG (2), A, Sp; 1953 v A; 1954 v F; 1955 v N; 1956 v Y, Sp, Ho; 1957 v E (2); 1958 v D, Pol, A; 1959 v Pol, Cz (2) (20)
Robinson, J. (Bohemians), 1928 v Bel; (with Dolphin), 1931 v Sp (2)
Robinson, M. (Brighton & HA), 1981 v F, Cy, Bel, Pol; 1982 v Ho, F, Alg, Ch; 1983 v Ho, Sp, Ic, Ma; (with Liverpool), 1984 v Ic, Ho, Is; 1985 v USSR, N; (with QPR), N, Sp, Sw; 1986 v D (sub), W, Cz (23)
Roche, P. J. (Shelbourne), 1972 v A; (with Manchester U), 1975 v USSR, T, Sw, USSR, Sw, WG; 1976 v T (8)
Rogers, E. (Blackburn R), 1968 v Cz, Pol; 1969 v Pol, A, D, Cz, D, H; 1970 v S, D, H; 1971 v I (2), A; (with Charlton Ath), 1972 v Ir, Ec, Ch, P; 1973 v USSR (19)
Ryan, G. (Derby Co), 1978 v T; (with Brighton & HA), 1979 v E, WG; 1980 v W, Cy (sub), Sw, Arg (sub); 1981 v F (sub), Pol (sub); 1982 v Ho (sub), Alg (sub), Ch (sub), Tr; 1984 v Pol, Chn; 1985 v M (16)
Ryan, R. A. (WBA), 1950 v Se, Bel; 1951 v N, Arg, N; 1952 v WG (2), A, Sp; 1953 v F, A; 1954 v F, L, F; 1955 v N; (with Derby Co), 1956 v Sp (16)

Saward, P. (Millwall), 1954 v L; (with Aston Villa), 1957 v E (2); 1958 v D, Pol, A; 1959 v Pol, Cz; 1960 v Se, Ch, WG, Se; 1961 v W, N; (with Huddersfield T), 1961 v S; 1962 v A; 1963 v Ic (2) (18)

Scannell, T. (Southend U), 1954 v L (1)

Scully, P. J. (Arsenal), 1989 v Tun (sub) (1)

Sheedy, K. (Everton), 1984 v Ho (sub), Ma; 1985 v D, I, Is, Sw; 1986 v Sw, D; 1987 v S, Pol; 1988 v Is, R, Pol, E (sub), USSR; 1989 v Ni, Tun, H, Sp, Ma, H; 1990 v Ni, Ma, W (sub), USSR, Fi (sub), T, E, Eg, Ho, R, I; 1991 v W, E, Pol, Ch, US; 1992 v H, Pol, T, W; (with Newcastle U), Sw (sub), Alb; 1993 v La, W (sub) (45)

Sheridan, J. J. (Leeds U), 1988 v R, Y, Pol, N (sub); 1989 v Sp; (with Sheffield W), 1990 v W, T (sub), Ma, I (sub); 1991 v Mor (sub), T, Ch, US (sub); 1992 v H; 1993 v La; 1994 v Sp (sub), Ho, Bol, G, CzR, I, M, N, Ho (24)

Slaven, B. (Middlesbrough), 1990 v W, Fi, T (sub), Ma; 1991 v W, Pol (sub); 1993 v W (7)

Sloan, J. W. (Arsenal), 1946 v P, Sp (2)

Smyth, M. (Shamrock R), 1969 v Pol (sub) (1)

Squires, J. (Shelbourne), 1934 v Ho (1)

Stapleton, F. (Arsenal), 1977 v T, F, Sp, Bul; 1978 v Bul, N, D; 1979 v Ni, E (sub), D, WG; 1980 v W, Bul, Ni, E, Cy; 1981 v Ho, Bel, F, Cy, Bel, Cz, Pol; (with Manchester U), 1982 v Ho, F, Alg; 1983 v Ho, Sp, Ic, Ma, Sp; 1984 v Ic, Ho, Ma, Pol, Is, Chn; 1985 v N, D, I, Is, E, N, Sw; 1986 v Sw, USSR, D, U, Ic, Cz (sub); 1987 v Bel (2), S (2), Pol, Bul, L; (with Ajax), 1988 v L, Bul; (with Derby Co), R, Y, N, E, USSR, Ho; (with Le Havre), 1989 v F, Sp, Ma; (with Blackburn R), 1990 v WG, Ma (sub) (70)

Staunton, S. (Liverpool), 1989 v Tun, Sp (2), Ma, H; 1990 v WG, Ni, Ma, W, USSR, Fi, T, Ma, E, Eg, Ho, R, I; 1991 v Mor, T, E (2), W, Pol, Ch, US; (with Aston Villa), 1992 v Pol, T, Sw, US, Alb, US, I, P; 1993 v La, Sp, Ni, D, Alb, La, Li; 1994 v Li, Sp, Ho, Bol, G, CzR, I, M, N, Ho (51)

Stevenson, A. E. (Dolphin), 1932 v Ho; (with Everton), 1947 v E, Sp, P; 1948 v P, Sp; 1949 v Sw (7)

Strahan, F. (Shelbourne), 1964 v Pol, N, E; 1965 v Pol; 1966 v WG (5)

Sullivan, J. (Fordsons), 1928 v Bel (1)

Swan, M. M. G. (Drumcondra), 1960 v Se (sub) (1)

Synnott, N. (Shamrock R), 1978 v T, Pol; 1979 v Ni (3)

Thomas, P. (Waterford), 1974 v Pol, Br (2)

Townsend, A. D. (Norwich C), 1989 v F, Sp (sub), Ma (sub), H; 1990 v WG (sub), Ni, Ma, W, USSR, Fi (sub), T, Ma (sub), E, Eg, Ho, R, I; (with Chelsea), 1991 v Mor, T, E (2), W, Pol, Ch, US; 1992 v Pol, W, US, Alb, US, I; 1993 v La, D, Sp, Ni, D, Alb, La, Li; (with Aston Villa), 1994 v Li, Ni, Ho, Bol, G, CzR, I, M, N, Ho (49)

Traynor, T. J. (Southampton), 1954 v L; 1962 v A; 1963 v Ic (2), S; 1964 v A (2), Sp (8)

Treacy, R. C. P. (WBA), 1966 v WG; 1967 v Sp, Cz; 1968 v Cz; (with Charlton Ath), 1968 v Pol; 1969 v Pol, Cz, D; 1970 v S, D, H (sub), Pol (sub), WG (sub); 1971 v Pol, Se (sub + 1), I, A; (with Swindon T), 1972 v Ir, Ec, Ch, P; 1973 v USSR, F, USSR, Pol, F, N; 1974 v Pol; (with Preston NE), Br; 1975 v USSR, Sw (2), WG; 1976 v T, N (sub), Pol (sub); (with WBA), 1977 v F, Pol; (with Shamrock R), 1978 v T, Pol; 1980 v Cz (sub) (42)

Tuohy, L. (Shamrock R), 1956 v Y; 1959 v Cz (2); (with Newcastle U), 1962 v A; 1963 v Ic (2); (with Shamrock R), 1964 v A; 1965 v Bel (8)

Turner, A. (Celtic), 1963 v S; 1964 v Sp (2)

Turner, C. J. (Southend U), 1936 v Sw; 1937 v G, H, Sw, F; (with West Ham U), 1938 v N (2), Cz, Pol; 1939 v H (10)

Vernon, J. (Belfast C), 1946 v P, Sp (2)

Waddock, G. (QPR), 1980 v Sw, Arg; 1981 v W, Pol (sub); 1982 v Alg; 1983 v Ic, Ma, Sp, Ho (sub); 1984 v Ic, Ho, Is; 1985 v I, Is, E, N, Sp; 1986 v USSR; (with Millwall), 1990 v USSR, T (20)

Walsh, D. J. (Linfield), 1946 v P, Sp; (with WBA), 1947 v Sp, P; 1948 v P, Sp; 1949 v Sw, P, Se, Sp; 1950 v E, Fi, Se; 1951 v N; (with Aston Villa), Arg, N; 1952 v Sp; 1953 v A; 1954 v F (2) (20)

Walsh, J. (Limerick), 1982 v Tr (1)

Walsh, M. (Blackpool), 1976 v N, Pol; 1977 v F (sub), Pol; (with Everton), 1979 v Ni (sub); (with QPR), D (sub), Bul, WG (sub); (with Porto), 1981 v Bel (sub), Cz; 1982 v Alg (sub); 1983 v Sp, Ho (sub), Sp (sub); 1984 v Ic (sub), Ma, Pol, Chn; 1985 v USSR, N (sub), D (21)

Walsh, M. (Everton), 1982 v Ch, Br, Tr; 1983 v Ic (4)

Walsh, W. (Manchester C), 1947 v E, Sp, P; 1948 v P, Sp; 1949 v Bel; 1950 v E, Se, Bel (9)

Waters, J. (Grimsby T), 1977 v T; 1980 v Ni (sub) (2)

Watters, F. (Shelbourne), 1926 v I (1)

Weir, E. (Clyde), 1939 v H (2), G (3)

Whelan, R. (St Patrick's Ath), 1964 v A, E (sub) (2)

Whelan, R. (Liverpool), 1981 v Cz (sub); 1982 v Ho (sub), F; 1983 v Ic, Ma, Sp; 1984 v Is; 1985 v USSR, N, I (sub), Is, E, N (sub), Sw (sub); 1986 v USSR (sub), W; 1987 v Bel (sub), S, Bul, Bel, Br, L; 1988 v L, Bul, Pol, N, E, USSR, Ho; 1989 v Ni, F, H, Sp, Ma; 1990 v WG, Ni, Ma, W, Ho (sub); 1991 v Mor, E; 1992 v Sw; 1993 v La, W (sub), Li (sub); 1994 v Li (sub), Sp, Ru, Ho, G (sub), N (sub) (51)

Whelan, W. (Manchester U), 1956 v Ho; 1957 v D, E (2) (4)

White, J. J. (Bohemians), 1928 v Bel (1)

Whittaker, R. (Chelsea), 1959 v Cz (1)

Williams, J. (Shamrock R), 1938 v N (1)

BRITISH AND IRISH INTERNATIONAL GOALSCORERS SINCE 1872

Where two players with the same surname and initials have appeared for the same country, and one or both have scored, they have been distinguished by reference to the club which appears *first* against their name in the international appearances section (pages 812–859). Unfortunately, four of the scorers in Scotland's 10-2 victory v Ireland in 1888 are unknown, as is the scorer of one of their nine goals v Wales in March 1878.

ENGLAND

Player	Goals
A'Court, A.	1
Adams, T. A.	4
Adcock, H.	1
Alcock, C. W.	1
Allen, A.	3
Allen, R.	2
Anderson, V.	2
Anderton, D. R.	1
Astall, G.	1
Athersmith, W. C.	3
Atyeo, P. J. W.	5
Bache, J. W.	4
Bailey, N. C.	2
Baily, E. F.	5
Baker, J. H.	3
Ball, A. J.	8
Bambridge, A. L.	1
Bambridge, E. C.	12
Barclay, R.	2
Barnes, J.	11
Barnes, P. S.	4
Barton, J.	1
Bassett, W. I.	7
Bastin, C. S.	12
Beardsley, P. A.	9
Beasley, A.	1
Beattie, T. K.	1
Becton, F.	2
Bedford, H.	1
Bell, C.	9
Bentley, R. T. F.	9
Bishop, S. M.	1
Blackburn, F.	1
Blissett, L.	3
Bloomer, S.	28
Bond, R.	2
Bonsor, A. G.	1
Bowden, E. R.	1
Bowers, J. W.	2
Bowles, S.	1
Bradford, G. R. W.	1
Bradford, J.	7
Bradley, W.	2
Bradshaw, F.	3
Bridges, B. J.	1
Bridgett, A.	3
Brindle, T.	1
Britton, C. S.	1
Broadbent, P. F.	2
Broadis, I. A.	8
Brodie, J. B.	1
Bromley-Davenport, W.	2
Brook, E. F.	10
Brooking, T. D.	5
Brooks, J.	2
Broome, F. H.	3
Brown, A.	4
Brown, A. S.	1
Brown, G.	5
Brown, J.	3
Brown, W.	1
Buchan, C. M.	4
Bull, S. G.	4
Bullock, N.	2
Burgess, H.	4
Butcher, T.	3
Byrne, J. J.	8
Camsell, G. H.	18
Carter, H. S.	7
Carter, J. H.	4
Chadwick, E.	3
Chamberlain, M.	1
Chambers, H.	5
Channon, M. R.	21
Charlton, J.	6
Charlton, R.	49
Chenery, C. J.	1
Chivers, M.	13
Clarke, A. J.	10
Cobbold, W. N.	7
Cock, J. G.	2
Common, A.	2
Connelly, J. M.	7
Coppell, S. J.	7
Cotterill, G. H.	2
Cowans, G.	2
Crawford, R.	1
Crawshaw, T. H.	1
Crayston, W. J.	1
Creek, F. N. S.	1
Crooks, S. D.	7
Currey, E. S.	2
Currie, A. W.	3
Cursham, A. W.	2
Cursham, H. A.	5
Daft, H. B.	3
Davenport, J. K.	2
Davis, G.	1
Davis, H.	1
Day, S. H.	2
Dean, W. R.	18
Devey, J. H. G.	1
Dewhurst, F.	11
Dix, W. R.	1
Dixon, K. M.	4
Dixon, L. M.	1
Douglas, B.	11
Drake, E. J.	6
Ducat, A.	1
Dunn, A. T. B.	2
Eastham, G.	2
Edwards, D.	5
Elliott, W. H.	3
Evans, R. E.	1
Ferdinand, L.	3
Finney, T.	30
Fleming, H. J.	9
Flowers, R.	10
Forman, Frank	1
Forman, Fred	3
Foster, R. E.	3
Francis, G. C. J.	3
Francis, T.	12
Freeman, B. C.	3
Froggatt, J.	2
Froggatt, R.	2
Galley, T.	1
Gascoigne, P. J.	6
Geary, F.	3
Gibbins, W. V. T.	3
Gilliatt, W. E.	3
Goddard, P.	1
Goodall, J.	12
Goodyer, A. C.	1
Gosling, R. C.	2
Goulden, L. A.	4
Grainger, C.	3
Greaves, J.	44
Grovesnor, A. T.	2
Gunn, W.	1
Haines, J. T. W.	2
Hall, G. W.	9
Halse, H. J.	2
Hampson, J.	5
Hampton, H.	2
Hancocks, J.	2
Hardman, H. P.	1
Harris, S. S.	2
Hassall, H. W.	4
Hateley, M.	9
Haynes, J. N.	18
Hegan, K. E.	4
Henfrey, A. G.	2
Hilsdon, G. R.	14
Hine, E. W.	4
Hirst, D. E.	1
Hitchens, G. A.	5
Hobbis, H. H. F.	1
Hoddle, G.	8
Hodgetts, D.	1
Hodgson, G.	1
Holley, G. H.	8
Houghton, W. E.	5
Howell, R.	1
Hughes, E. W.	1
Hulme, J. H. A.	4
Hunt, G. S.	1
Hunt, R.	18
Hunter, N.	2
Hurst, G. C.	24
Ince, P. E. C.	2
Jack, D. N. B.	3
Johnson, D. E.	6
Johnson, E.	2
Johnson, J. A.	2
Johnson, T. C. F.	5
Johnson, W. H.	1
Kail, E. I. L.	2
Kay, A. H.	1
Keegan, J. K.	21
Kelly, R.	8
Kennedy, R.	3
Kenyon-Slaney, W. S.	2
Keown, M. R.	3
Kevan, D. T.	8
Kidd, B.	1
Kingsford, R. K.	1
Kirchen, A. J.	2
Kirton, W. J.	1
Langton, R.	1
Latchford, R. D.	5
Latherton, E. G.	1
Lawler, C.	1
Lawton, T.	22
Lee, F.	10
Lee, J.	1
Lee, S.	2
Lindley, T.	15
Lineker, G.	48
Lofthouse, J. M.	3
Lofthouse, N.	30
Hon. A. Lyttelton	1
Mabbutt, G.	1
Macdonald, M.	6
Mannion, W. J.	11
Mariner, P.	13
Marsh, R. W.	1
Matthews, S.	11
Matthews, V.	1
McCall, J.	1
McDermott, T.	3
Medley, L. D.	1
Melia, J.	1
Mercer, D. W.	1
Metson, P. C.	1
Milburn, J. E. T.	10
Miller, H. S.	1
Mills, G. R.	3
Milward, A.	3
Mitchell, C.	5
Moore, J.	1
Moore, R. F.	2
Moore, W. G. B.	2
Morren, T.	1
Morris, F.	1
Morris, J.	3
Mortensen, S. H.	23
Morton, J. R.	1
Mosforth, W.	3
Mullen, J.	6
Mullery, A. P.	1
Neal, P. G.	5
Needham, E.	3
Nicholls, J.	1
Nicholson, W. E.	1
O'Grady, M.	3
Osborne, F. R.	3
Own goals	22
Page, L. A.	1
Paine, T. L.	7
Palmer, C. L.	1
Parry, E. H.	1
Parry, R. A.	1
Pawson, F. W.	1
Payne, J.	2
Peacock, A.	3
Pearce, S.	4
Pearson, J. S.	5
Pearson, S. C.	5
Perry, W.	2
Peters, M.	20
Pickering, F.	5
Platt, D.	23
Pointer, R.	2
Quantrill, A.	1
Ramsay, A. E.	3
Revie, D. G.	4
Reynolds, J.	3
Richardson, J. R.	2
Rigby, A.	3
Rimmer, E. J.	2
Roberts, H.	1
Roberts, W. T.	4
Robinson, J.	3
Robson, B.	26
Robson, R.	4
Rowley, J. F.	6
Royle, J.	2
Rutherford, J.	3

Sagar, C.	1
Sandilands, R. R.	2
Sansom, K.	1
Schofield, J.	1
Seed, J. M.	1
Settle, J.	6
Sewell, J.	3
Shackleton, L. F.	1
Sharp, J.	1
Shearer, A.	3
Shepherd, A.	2
Simpson, J.	1
Smith, A. M.	2
Smith, G. O.	12
Smith, Joe	1
Smith, J. R.	2
Smith, J. W.	4
Smith, R.	13
Smith, S.	1
Sorby, T. H.	1
Southworth, J.	3
Sparks, F. J.	3
Spence, J. W.	1
Spiksley, F.	5
Spilsbury, B. W.	5
Steele, F. C.	8
Stephenson, G. T.	2
Steven, T. M.	4
Stewart, J.	2
Stiles, N. P.	1
Storer, H.	1
Summerbee, M. G.	1
Tambling, R. V.	1
Taylor, P. J.	2
Taylor, T.	16
Thompson, P. B.	1
Thornewell, G.	1
Tilson, S. F.	6
Townley, W. J.	2
Tueart, D.	2
Vaughton, O. H.	6
Veitch, J. G.	3
Violett, D. S.	1
Waddle, C. R.	6
Walker, W. H.	9
Wall, G.	2
Wallace, D.	1
Walsh, P.	1
Waring, T.	4
Warren, B.	2
Watson, D. V.	4
Watson, V. M.	4
Webb, G. W.	1
Webb, N.	4
Wedlock, W. J.	2
Weir, D.	2
Weller, K.	1
Welsh, D.	1
Whateley, O.	2
Wheldon, G. F.	6
Whitfield, H.	1
Wignall, F.	2
Wilkes, A.	1
Wilkins, R. G.	3
Willingham, C. K.	1
Wilshaw, D. J.	10
Wilson, D.	1
Wilson, G. P.	1
Winckworth, W. N.	1
Windridge, J. E.	7
Wise, D. F.	1
Withe, P.	1
Wollaston, C. H. R.	1
Wood, H.	1
Woodcock, T.	16
Woodhall, G.	1
Woodward, V. J.	29
Worrall, F.	2
Worthington, F. S.	2
Wright, I. E.	5
Wright, M.	1
Wright, W. A.	3
Wylie, J. G.	1
Yates, J.	3

NORTHERN IRELAND

Anderson, T.	4
Armstrong, G.	12
Bambrick, J.	12
Barr, H. H.	1
Barron, H.	3
Best, G.	9
Bingham, W. L.	10
Black, K.	1
Blanchflower, D.	2
Blanchflower, J.	1
Brennan, B.	1
Brennan, R. A.	1
Brotherston, N.	3
Brown, J.	1
Browne, F.	2
Campbell, J.	1
Campbell, W. G.	1
Casey, T.	2
Caskey, W.	1
Cassidy, T.	1
Chambers, J.	3
Clarke, C. J.	13
Clements, D.	2
Cochrane, T.	1
Condy, J.	1
Connor, M. J.	1
Coulter, J.	1
Croft, T.	1
Crone, W.	1
Crossan, E.	1
Crossan, J. A.	10
Curran, S.	2
Cush, W. W.	5
Dalton, W.	6
D'Arcy, S. D.	1
Darling, J.	1
Davey, H. H.	1
Davis, T. L.	1
Dill, A. H.	1
Doherty, L.	1
Doherty, P. D.	3
Dougan, A. D.	8
Dowie, I.	3
Dunne, J.	4
Elder, A. R.	1
Emerson, W.	1
English, S.	1
Ferguson, W.	1
Ferris, J.	1
Ferris, R. O.	1
Finney, T.	2
Gaffkin, J.	5
Gara, A.	3
Gawkrodger, G.	1
Gibb, J. T.	2
Gibb, T. J.	1
Gibson, W. K.	1
Gillespie, W.	12
Goodall, A. L.	2
Gray, P.	2
Halligan, W.	1
Hamill, M.	1
Hamilton, B.	4
Hamilton, W.	5
Hannon, D. J.	1
Harkin, J. T.	2
Harvey, M.	3
Hill, C. F.	1
Hughes, M.	1
Humphries, W.	1
Hunter, A. (*Distillery*)	1
Hunter, A. (*Blackburn R*)	1
Irvine, R. W.	3
Irvine, W. J.	8
Johnston, H.	2
Johnston, S.	2
Johnston, W. C.	1
Jones, S.	1
Jones, J.	1
Kelly, J.	4
Kernaghan, N.	2
Kirwan, J.	2
Lacey, W.	3
Lemon, J.	2
Lockhart, N.	3
Lomas, S. M.	1
Magilton, J.	4
Mahood, J.	2
Martin, D. K.	3
Maxwell, J.	7
McAdams, W. J.	7
McAllen, J.	1
McAuley, J. L.	1
McCandless, J.	3
McCaw, J. H.	1
McClelland, J.	1
McCluggage, A.	2
McCracken, W.	1
McCrory, S.	1
McCurdy, C.	1
McDonald, A.	3
McGarry, J. K.	1
McGrath, R. C.	4
McIlroy, J.	10
McIlroy, S. B.	5
McKnight, J.	2
McLaughlin, J. C.	6
McMordie, A. S.	3
McMorran, E. J.	4
McParland, P. J.	10
McWha, W. B. R.	1
Meldon, J.	1
Mercar, J.	1
Mercer, J. T.	1
Millar, W.	1
Milligan, D.	1
Milne, R. G.	2
Molyneux, T. B.	1
Moreland, V.	1
Morgan, S.	3
Morrow, S. J.	1
Morrow, W. J.	1
Murphy, N.	1
Neill, W. J. T.	2
Nelson, S.	1
Nicholl, C. J.	3
Nicholl, J. M.	2
Nicholson, J. J.	6
O'Hagan, C.	2
O'Kane, W. J.	1
O'Neill, J.	1
O'Neill, M. A.	1
O'Neill, M. H.	8
Own goals	5
Peacock, R.	2
Peden, J.	7
Penney, S.	2
Pyper, James	2
Pyper, John	1
Quinn, J. M.	10
Reynolds, J.	1
Rowley, R. W. M.	2
Sheridan, J.	2
Sherrard, J.	1
Simpson, W. J.	5
Sloan, H. A. de B.	4
Smyth, S.	5
Spence, D. W.	3
Stanfield, O. M.	9
Stevenson, A. E.	5
Stewart, I.	2
Taggart, G. P.	5
Thompson, F. W.	2
Tully, C. P.	3
Turner, E.	1
Walker, J.	1
Walsh, D. J.	5
Welsh, E.	1
Whiteside, N.	9
Whiteside, T.	1
Williams, J. R.	1
Williamson, J.	1
Wilson, D. J.	1
Wilson, K. J.	6
Wilson, S. J.	7
Wilton, J. M.	2
Young, S.	2

SCOTLAND

Aitken, R.	1
Aitkenhead, W. A. C.	2
Alexander, D.	1
Allan, D. S.	4
Allan, J.	2
Anderson, F.	1
Anderson, W.	4
Andrews, P.	1
Archibald, A.	1
Archibald, S.	4
Baird, D.	2
Baird, J. C.	2
Baird, S.	2
Bannon, E.	1
Barbour, A.	1
Barker, J. B.	4
Battles, B. Jr	1
Bauld, W.	2
Baxter, J. C.	3
Bell, J.	5
Bennett, A.	2
Berry, D.	1
Bett, J.	1
Beveridge, W. W.	1
Black, A.	3
Black, D.	1
Bone, J.	1
Booth, S.	1
Boyd, R.	2
Boyd, W. G.	1
Brackenridge, T.	1
Brand, R.	8
Brazil, A.	1
Bremner, W. J.	3
Brown, A. D.	6
Buchanan, P. S.	1
Buchanan, R.	1
Buckley, P.	1
Buick, A.	2
Burns, K.	1
Cairns, T.	1
Calderwood, R.	2
Caldow, E.	4
Campbell, C.	1
Campbell, John (*Celtic*)	5
Campbell, John (*Rangers*)	4
Campbell, P.	2
Campbell, R.	1
Cassidy, J.	1
Chalmers, S.	3
Chambers, T.	1
Cheyne, A. G.	4
Christie, A. J.	1
Clunas, W. L.	1
Collins, J.	4
Collins, R. Y.	10

Combe, J. R. 1
Conn, A. 1
Cooper, D. 6
Craig, J. 1
Craig, T. 1
Cunningham, A. N. 5
Curran, H. P. 1

Dalglish, K. 30
Davidson, D. 1
Davidson, J. A. 1
Delaney, J. 3
Devine, A. 1
Dewar, G. 1
Dewar, N. 4
Dickson, W. 4
Divers, J. 1
Docherty, T. H. 1
Dodds, D. 1
Donaldson, A. 1
Donnachie, J. 1
Dougall, J. 1
Drummond, J. 2
Dunbar, M. 1
Duncan, D. 7
Duncan, D. M. 1
Duncan, J. 1
Dunn, J. 2
Durie, G. S. 4

Easson, J. F. 1
Ellis, J. 1

Ferguson, J. 6
Fernie, W. 1
Fitchie, T. T. 1
Flavell, R. 2
Fleming, C. 2
Fleming, J. W. 3
Fraser, M. J. E. 4

Gallacher, H. K. 23
Gallacher, K. W. 2
Gallacher, P. 1
Galt, J. H. 1
Gemmell, T. (*St Mirren*) 1
Gemmell, T. (*Celtic*) 1
Gemmill, A. 8
Gibb, W. 1
Gibson, D. W. 3
Gibson, J. D. 2
Gibson, N. 1
Gillespie, Jas. 3
Gillick, T. 3
Gilzean, A. J. 12
Gossland, J. 2
Goudie, J. 1
Gough, C. R. 6
Gourlay, J. 1
Graham, A. 2
Graham, G. 3
Gray, A. 7
Gray, E. 3
Gray, F. 1
Greig, J. 3
Groves, W. 5

Hamilton, G. 4
Hamilton, J. (*Queen's Park*) 3
Hamilton, R. C. 14
Harper, J. M. 2
Harrower, W. 5
Hartford, R. A. 4
Heggie, C. 5
Henderson, J. G. 1
Henderson, W. 5
Hendry, E. C. J. 1
Herd, D. G. 4
Hewie, J. D. 2
Higgins, A. (*Newcastle U*) 1
Higgins, A. (*Kilmarnock*) 4
Highet, T. C. 1
Holton, J. A. 2
Houliston, W. 2

Howie, H. 1
Howie, J. 2
Hughes, J. 1
Hunter, W. 1
Hutchison, T. 1
Hutton, J. 1
Hyslop, T. 1

Imrie, W. N. 1

Jackson, A. 8
Jackson, C. 1
James, A. W. 3
Jardine, A. 1
Jenkinson, T. 1
Johnston, L. H. 1
Johnston, M. 14
Johnstone, D. 2
Johnstone, J. 4
Johnstone, Jas. 1
Johnstone, R. 9
Johnstone, W. 1
Jordan, J. 11

Kay, J. L. 5
Keillor, A. 3
Kelly, J. 1
Kelso, J. 1
Ker, G. 10
King, A. 1
King, J. 1
Kinnear, D. 1

Lambie, W. A. 5
Lang, J. J. 1
Law, D. 30
Leggat, G. 8
Lennie, W. 1
Lennnox, R. 3
Liddell, W. 6
Lindsay, J. 6
Linwood, A. B. 1
Logan, J. 1
Lorimer, P. 4
Love, A. 1
Lowe, J. (*Cambuslang*) 1
Lowe, J. (*St Bernards*) 1

Macari, L. 5
MacDougall, E. J. 3
MacLeod, M. 1
Mackay, D. C. 4
Mackay, G. 1
MacKenzie, J. A. 1
Madden, J. 5
Marshall, H. 1
Marshall, J. 1
Mason, J. 4
Massie, A. 1
Masson, D. S. 5
McAdam, J. 1
McAllister, G. 4
McAulay, J. 1
McAvennie, F. 1
McCall, J. 1
McCall, S. M. 1
McCalliog, J. 1
McCallum, N. 1
McClair, B. J. 2
McCoist, A. 15
McColl, R. S. 13
McCulloch, D. 3
McDougall, J. 4
McFarlane, A. 1
McFadyen, W. 2
McGhee, M. 2
McGinlay, J. 1
McGregor, J. C. 1
McGrory, J. 6
McGuire, W. 1
McInally, A. 3
McInnes, T. 2
McKie, J. 2
McKimmie, S. 1
McKinlay, W. 2
McKinnon, A. 1

McKinnon, R. 1
McKinnon, W. W. 5
McLaren, A. 4
McLaren, J. 1
McLean, A. 1
McLean, T. 1
McLintock, F. 1
McMahon, A. 6
McMenemy, J. 5
McMillan, I. L. 2
McNeil, H. 5
McNeill, W. 3
McPhail, J. 3
McPhail, R. 7
McPherson, J. 8
McPherson, R. 1
McQueen, G. 5
McStay, P. 9
Meiklejohn, D. D. 3
Millar, J. 2
Miller, T. 2
Miller, W. 1
Mitchell, R. C. 1
Morgan, W. 1
Morris, D. 1
Morris, H. 3
Morton, A. L. 5
Mudie, J. K. 9
Mulhall, G. 1
Munro, A. D. 1
Munro, N. 1
Murdoch, R. 5
Murphy, F. 1
Murray, J. 1

Napier, C. E. 3
Narey, D. 1
Neil, R. G. 2
Nevin, P. K. F. 4
Nicholas, C. 5
Nisbet, J. 2

O'Donnell, F. 2
O'Hare, J. 5
Ormond, W. E. 1
O'Rourke, F. 1
Orr, R. 1
Orr, T. 1
Oswald, J. 1
Own goals 14

Parlane, D. 1
Paul, H. McD. 2
Paul, W. 6
Pettigrew, W. 2
Provan, D. 1

Quinn, J. 7
Quinn, P. 1

Rankin, G. 2
Rankin, R. 2
Reid, W. 4
Reilly, L. 22
Renny-Tailyour, H. W. 1
Richmond, J. T. 1
Ring, T. 2
Rioch, B. D. 6
Ritchie, J. 1
Robertson, A. 2
Robertson, J. 2
Robertson, J. N. 8
Robertson, J. T. 2
Robertson, T. 1
Robertson, W. 1
Russell, D. 1

Scott, A. S. 5
Sellar, W. 4
Sharp, G. 1
Shaw, F. W. 1
Shearer, D. 1
Simpson, J. 1
Smith, A. 5
Smith, G. 4
Smith, J. 1

Smith, John 12
Somerville, G. 1
Souness, G. J. 3
Speedie, F. 2
St John, I. 9
Steel, W. 12
Stein, C. 10
Stevenson, G. 4
Stewart, R. 1
Stewart, W. E. 1
Strachan, G. 5
Sturrock, P. 3

Taylor, J. D. 1
Templeton, R. 1
Thomson, A. 1
Thomson, C. 4
Thomson, R. 1
Thomson, W. 1
Thornton, W. 1

Waddell, T. S. 1
Waddell, W. 6
Walker, J. 2
Walker, R. 7
Walker, T. 9
Wallace, I. A. 1
Wark, J. 7
Watson, J. A. K. 1
Watt, F. 2
Watt, W. W. 1
Weir, A. 1
Weir, J. B. 2
White, J. A. 3
Wilson, A. 2
Wilson, A. N. 13
Wilson, D. (*Queen's Park*) 2
Wilson, D. (*Rangers*) 9
Wilson, H. 1
Wylie, T. G. 1

Young, A. 5

WALES

Allchurch, I. J. 23
Allen, M. 3
Astley, D. J. 12
Atherton, R. W. 2

Bamford, T. 1
Barnes, W. 1
Blackmore, C. G. 1
Bodin, P. J. 3
Boulter, L. M. 1
Bowdler, J. C. H. 3
Bowen, D. L. 1
Bowen, M. 3
Boyle, T. 1
Bryan, T. 1
Burgess, W. A. R. 1
Burke, T. 1
Butler, A. 1

Chapman, T. 2
Charles, J. 1
Charles, M. 6
Charles, W. J. 15
Clarke, R. J. 5
Coleman, C. 2
Collier, D. J. 1
Cross, K. 1
Cumner, R. H. 1
Curtis, A. 6
Curtis, E. R. 3

Davies, D. W. 1
Davies, E. Lloyd 1
Davies, G. 2
Davies, L. S. 6
Davies, R. T. 8
Davies, R. W. 7
Davies, S. 5
Davies, W. 6
Davies, W. H. 1

Davies, William	5
Davies, W. O.	1
Deacy, N.	4
Doughty, J.	6
Doughty, R.	2
Durban, A.	2
Dwyer, P.	2
Edwards, G.	2
Edwards, R. I.	4
England, H. M.	3
Evans, I.	1
Evans, J.	1
Evans, R. E.	2
Evans, W.	1
Eyton-Jones, J. A.	1
Flynn, B.	7
Ford, T.	23
Foulkes, W. I.	1
Fowler, J.	3
Giles, D.	2
Giggs, R. J.	2
Glover, E. M.	7
Godfrey, B. C.	2
Green, A. W.	3
Griffiths, A. T.	6
Griffiths, M. W.	2
Griffiths, T. P.	3
Harris, C. S.	1
Hersee, R.	1
Hewitt, R.	1
Hockey, T.	1
Hodges, G.	2
Hole, W. J.	1
Hopkins, I. J.	2
Horne, B.	2
Howell, E. G.	3
Hughes, L. M.	12
James, E.	2
James, L.	10
James, R.	8
Jarrett, R. H.	3
Jenkyns, C. A.	1
Jones, A.	1
Jones, Bryn	6
Jones, B. S.	2
Jones, Cliff	15
Jones, C. W.	1
Jones, D. E.	1
Jones, Evan	1
Jones, H.	1
Jones, I.	1
Jones, J. O.	1
Jones, J. P.	1
Jones, Leslie J.	1
Jones, R. A.	2
Jones, W. L.	6
Keenor, F. C.	2
Krzywicki, R. L.	1
Leek, K.	5
Lewis, B.	3
Lewis, J.	1
Lewis, W.	10
Lewis, W. L.	2
Lovell, S.	1
Lowrie, G.	2
Mahoney, J. F.	1
Mays, A. W.	1
Medwin, T. C.	6
Meredith, W. H.	11
Mills, T. J.	1
Moore, G.	1
Morgan, J. R.	2
Morgan-Owen, H.	1
Morgan-Owen, M. M.	2
Morris, A. G.	9
Morris, H.	2
Morris, R.	1
Nicholas, P.	2
O'Callaghan, E.	3
O'Sullivan, P. A.	1
Owen, G.	2
Owen, W.	4
Owen, W. P.	6
Own goals	12
Palmer, D.	3
Parry, T. D.	3
Paul, R.	1
Peake, E.	1
Pembridge, M.	1
Perry, E.	1
Phillips, C.	5
Phillips, D.	2
Powell, A.	1
Powell, D.	1
Price, J.	4
Price, P.	1
Pryce-Jones, W. E.	3
Pugh, D. H.	2
Reece, G. I.	2
Rees, R. R.	3
Richards, R. W.	1
Roach, J.	2
Robbins, W. W.	4
Roberts, J. (*Corwen*)	1
Roberts, Jas.	1
Roberts, P. S.	1
Roberts, R. (*Druids*)	1
Roberts, W. (*Llangollen*)	2
Roberts, W. (*Wrexham*)	1
Roberts, W. H.	1
Rush, I.	28
Russell, M. R.	1
Sabine, H. W.	1
Saunders, D.	14
Shaw, E. G.	2
Sisson, H.	4
Slatter, N.	2
Smallman, D. P.	1
Tapscott, D. R.	4
Thomas, M.	4
Thomas, T.	1
Toshack, J. B.	13
Trainer, H.	2
Vaughan, John	2
Vernon, T. R.	8
Vizard, E. T.	1
Walsh, I.	7
Warren, F. W.	3
Watkins, W. M.	4
Wilding, J.	4
Williams, G. E.	1
Williams, G. G.	1
Williams, W.	1
Woosnam, A. P.	4
Wynn, G. A.	1
Yorath, T. C.	2
Young, E.	1

EIRE

Aldridge, J.	14
Ambrose, P.	1
Anderson, J.	1
Bermingham, P.	1
Bradshaw, P.	4
Brady, L.	9
Brown, D.	1
Byrne, J. (*Bray*)	1
Byrne, J. (*QPR*)	4
Cantwell, J.	14
Carey, J.	3
Carroll, T.	1
Cascarino, A.	12
Coad, P.	3
Conroy, T.	2
Conway, J.	3
Coyne, T.	4
Cummings, G.	5
Curtis, D.	8
Daly, G.	13
Davis, T.	4
Dempsey, J.	1
Dennehy, M.	2
Donnelly, J.	3
Donnelly, T.	1
Duffy, B.	1
Duggan, H.	1
Dunne, J.	12
Dunne, L.	1
Eglington, T.	2
Ellis, P.	1
Fagan, F.	5
Fallon, S.	2
Fallon, W.	2
Farrell, P.	3
Fitzgerald, P.	2
Fitzgerald, J.	1
Fitzsimmons, A.	7
Flood, J. J.	4
Fogarty, A.	3
Fullam, J.	1
Fullam, R.	1
Galvin, A.	1
Gavin, J.	2
Geoghegan, M.	2
Giles, J.	5
Givens, D.	19
Glynn, D.	1
Grealish, T.	8
Grimes, A. A.	1
Hale, A.	2
Hand, E.	2
Haverty, J.	3
Holmes, J.	1
Horlacher, A.	2
Houghton, R.	4
Hughton, C.	1
Hurley, C.	2
Irwin, D.	1
Jordan, D.	1
Kelly, D.	7
Kelly, G.	1
Kelly, J.	2
Kernaghan, A. N.	1
Lacey, W.	1
Lawrenson, M.	5
Leech, M.	2
McCann, J.	1
McCarthy, M.	2
McEvoy, A.	6
McGee, P.	4
McGrath, P.	7
McLoughlin, A. F.	1
Madden, O.	1
Mancini, T.	1
Martin, C.	6
Martin, M.	4
Mooney, J.	1
Moore, P.	7
Moran, K.	6
Moroney, T.	1
Mulligan, P.	1
O'Callaghan, K.	1
O'Connor, T.	2
O'Farrell, F.	2
O'Flanagan, K.	3
O'Keefe, E.	1
O'Leary, D. A.	1
O'Neill, F.	1
O'Reilly, J.	2
O'Reilly, J.	1
Own goals	6
Quinn, N.	10
Ringstead, A.	7
Robinson, M.	4
Rogers, E.	5
Ryan, G.	1
Ryan, R.	3
Sheedy, K.	9
Sheridan, J.	3
Slaven, B.	1
Sloan, W.	1
Squires, J.	1
Stapleton, F.	20
Staunton, S.	5
Strahan, J.	1
Sullivan, J.	1
Townsend, A. D.	5
Treacy, R.	5
Touhy, L.	4
Waddock, G.	3
Walsh, D.	5
Walsh, M.	3
Waters, J.	1
White, J. J.	2
Whelan, R.	3

OTHER INTERNATIONAL MATCHES 1993

January

Tunisia (2) 3, Bulgaria (0) 0
Italy (0) 2, Mexico (0) 0
Ghana (0) 4, Nigeria (0) 0
Venezuela 0, Peru 0
Ecuador (1) 1, Belarus (0) 1
Peru (1) 1, Honduras (0) 1
Spain (0) 1, Mexico (1) 1
Peru (1) 1, Belarus (1) 1
USA (0) 2, Denmark (1) 2
Ecuador (2) 3, Romania (0) 0

February

Cyprus 0, Poland 0
Israel 0, Poland 0
Peru (0) 0, Romania (1) 2
El Salvador (0) 0, Denmark (1) 2
USA (1) 1, Romania (1) 1
Mexico (1) 2, Romania (0) 0
Portugal (0) 1, Norway (0) 1
USA (0) 0, Russia (1) 1
Republic of Ireland (0) 2, Wales (1) 1
Russia (0) 2, El Salvador (0) 1
Argentina (1) 1, Brazil (0) 1
Finland (0) 4, Estonia (0) 3
Latvia (0) 1, Lithuania (0) 2
Finland (1) 3, Lithuania (0) 0
USA 0, Russia 0
Estonia (0) 0, Latvia (2) 2
Argentina (1) 4, Denmark (1) 4
Venezuela 0, Colombia 0

March

Jordan (0) 1, Syria (1) 1
Paraguay (0) 1, Bolivia (0) 0
USA (1) 2, Canada (2) 2
Austria (2) 2, Greece (1) 1
Qatar (0) 1, Jordan (0) 2
Peru (1) 1, Bolivia (0) 0
Honduras 0, Bolivia 0
Brazil (2) 2, Poland (1) 2
Tunisia (0) 0, Switzerland (0) 1
El Salvador (1) 2, USA (0) 2
Costa Rica (0) 0, Canada (0) 1
Israel (0) 2, Russia (0) 2
Scotland (0) 0, Germany (1) 1
Honduras (0) 1, USA (0) 4
Malawi (1) 1, Zambia (0) 0
Qatar (0) 1, Norway (3) 6
Slovakia (1) 2, Lithuania (1) 2
Chile (0) 2, Bolivia (0) 1
Colombia (2) 4, Costa Rica (1) 1
Poland (1) 1, Lithuania (1) 1

April

Slovenia (2) 2, Estonia (0) 0
Oman (1) 1, Malaysia (0) 0
Saudi Arabia (0) 0, USA (0) 2
Poland (1) 2, Finland (0) 1
Germany (0) 6, Ghana (1) 1
Hungary (0) 0, Sweden (0) 2
USA (0) 1, Iceland (1) 1
Kuwait (0) 3, Australia (1) 1
Singapore (0) 0, Saudi Arabia (0) 3
Korea Rep (0) 1, Iraq (0) 1
Ukraine (0) 1, Israel (0) 1
Korea Rep (1) 2, Iraq (1) 2

May

USA (1) 1, Colombia (1) 2
Lithuania (0) 0, Ukraine (0) 1
Colombia (1) 1, Venezuela (1) 1
New Zealand (2) 2, Fiji (0) 0
USA 0, Bolivia 0
New Zealand (3) 5, Fiji (0) 0
USA 0, Peru 0
Bolivia (1) 2, Paraguay (0) 1
Rep of Ireland (2) 2, Hungary (0) 4
Chile (0) 1, Colombia (0) 1

June

Colombia (0) 1, Chile (0) 0
Peru (1) 1, Bolivia (0) 0
France (0) 2, Venezuela (0) 0
Ecuador (0) 1, Chile (0) 2
France (0) 1, Colombia (0) 3
Peru (2) 3, Venezuela (0) 1
Bolivia (0) 1, Chile (2) 3
USA (2) 3, Canada (0) 0
Croatia (2) 3, Ukraine (0) 1

July

Malawi (2) 3, Swaziland (0) 1
Ivory Coast (0) 3, Nigeria (0) 2
Malawi (1) 1, Swaziland (0) 1
Malawi (0) 0, Swaziland (0) 1
Peru (0) 1, Uruguay (1) 2
Brazil (0) 2, Paraguay (0) 0
Uruguay (3) 3, Peru (0) 0
France (3) 3, Russia (1) 1

August

Brazil (0) 1, Mexico (0) 1
Guinea (1) 4, Sierra Leone (0) 0
Sweden (1) 1, Switzerland (1) 2
Faeroes (0) 0, Norway (4) 7
Fiji (0) 2, New Zealand (0) 1
Fiji (0) 1, New Zealand (0) 1
Fiji 0, New Zealand 0
Iceland (0) 0, USA (0) 1

September

Swaziland (0) 0, Zimbabwe (1) 1
Norway (1) 1, USA (0) 0
Spain (0) 2, Chile (0) 0
Morocco (2) 3, Mali (0) 0
Saudi Arabia (1) 4, Thailand (0) 0
Zimbabwe (1) 2, Senegal (0) 0
Saudi Arabia (1) 3, Thailand (0) 0
Mexico (0) 1, Cameroon (0) 0
Romania (0) 1, Israel (0) 0
Tunisia (0) 1, Germany (0) 1
Saudi Arabia (1) 1, Costa Rica (0) 2
Korea Rep (1) 1, Australia (0) 1
Korea Rep (0) 1, Australia (0) 0
Saudi Arabia (2) 3, Costa Rica (1) 2
Mexico (0) 0, Poland (0) 1

October

Japan (0) 1, Ivory Coast (0) 0
Cyprus (1) 2, Israel (1) 2
Belgium (0) 2, Gabon (0) 1
Mexico (0) 4, South Africa (0) 0
Saudi Arabia (1) 4, Russia (1) 2
Germany (3) 5, Uruguay (0) 0
USA (0) 1, Mexico (0) 1
USA (1) 1, Ukraine (2) 2
Iceland (1) 1, Tunisia (1) 3
Mexico (2) 2, Ukraine (1) 1
USA (0) 0, Ukraine (1) 1
Liechtenstein (0) 0, Estonia (0) 2
UAE (1) 2, Jordan (1) 1
UAE (0) 0, Jordan (0) 2

November

Mexico (2) 3, China PR (0) 0
Egypt 1 (3), Malta (0) 0
Tunisia (2) 4, Gabon (0) 0
Malta (2) 2, Gabon (0) 1
Tunisia (1) 2, Egypt (0) 0
USA (1) 1, Jamaica (0) 0
Antigua (2) 3, St. Kitts & Nevis (0) 0
USA (4) 8, Cayman (0) 1
Germany (2) 2, Brazil (1) 1

December

USA (0) 7, El Salvador (0) 0
Bangladesh (0) 3, Myanmar (0) 1
Uganda (0) 0, Tanzania (0) 1
Germany (1) 1, Argentina (1) 2
Mexico (0) 0, Brazil (1) 1
USA (0) 0, Germany (1) 3
Mexico 0, Germany 0
Ghana 0, Egypt 0

UEFA UNDER-21 CHAMPIONSHIP 1992–94

Group 1
Scotland 0, Portugal 0
Italy 1, Switzerland 0
Switzerland 4, Malta 0
Malta 0, Italy 1
Malta 0, Portugal 2
Scotland 3, Malta 0
Portugal 2, Italy 0
Italy 3, Malta 0
Switzerland 1, Portugal 1
Malta 1, Switzerland 4
Portugal 7, Malta 0
Switzerland 2, Scotland 0
Scotland 0, Switzerland 0
Portugal 2, Scotland 1
Switzerland 0, Italy 2
Scotland 1, Italy 2
Italy 5, Scotland 2
Malta 0, Scotland 1
Italy 2, Portugal 1
Portugal 3, Switzerland 0

Group 2
San Marino 0, Norway 3
Holland 1, Poland 3
England 0, Norway 2
Turkey 4, San Marino 0
England 0, Turkey 1
Turkey 1, Holland 1
England 6, San Marino 0
Holland 0, Turkey 1
San Marino 0, Turkey 2
Holland 3, San Marino 0
Turkey 0, England 0
San Marino 0, Poland 5
Poland 1, England 4
Norway 1, England 1
Holland 2, Norway 1
Norway 3, San Marino 2
Norway 1, Holland 0
Poland 3, Turkey 0
Turkey 1, Poland 0
Poland 2, Holland 0
San Marino 0, England 4
San Marino 1, Holland 3
Norway 3, Turkey 2
Turkey 3, Norway 1
England 3, Holland 0
Holland 1, England 1
Poland 3, San Marino 0
England 1, Poland 2
Norway 3, Poland 1
Poland 2, Norway 0

Group 3
Denmark 3, Republic of Ireland 2
Albania 0, Germany 1
Spain 2, Republic of Ireland 1
Germany 1, Spain 2
Germany 4, Albania 1
Republic of Ireland 0, Germany 1
Germany 8, Republic of Ireland 0
Denmark 0, Spain 1
Denmark 1, Germany 4
Albania 1, Republic of Ireland 1
Denmark 5, Albania 0
Spain 1, Albania 1
Albania 0, Spain 3
Rep of Ireland 3, Albania 1
Rep of Ireland 0, Denmark 2
Republic of Ireland 0, Spain 2
Spain 1, Denmark 0
Germany 0, Denmark 1
Albania 1, Denmark 0
Spain 3, Germany 1

Group 4
Belgium 1, Romania 0
Cyprus 2, Wales 4
Romania 1, Czechoslovakia 0
Belgium 3, Wales 1
Cyprus 0, Romania 2
Cyprus 0, Czechoslovakia 2
Wales 0, Belgium 0
Romania 1, Cyprus 0
Czechoslovakia 4, Romania 2
Belgium 3, Cyprus 0
Cyprus 0, Belgium 1
Romania 2, Wales 3
Wales 1, Romania 2
Czechoslovakia 1, Belgium 0
Belgium 0, Czechoslovakia 2
Romania 3, Belgium 1
Wales 6, Cyprus 2
Czechoslovakia 2, Cyprus 0
Czechslovakia 1, Wales 1
Wales 0, Czechoslovakia 4

Group 5
Iceland 1, Greece 3
Russia 5, Iceland 0
Russia 2, Luxembourg 1
Greece 2, Hungary 1
Romania 1, Czechoslovakia 0
Greece 6, Luxembourg 0
Hungary 1, Greece 2
Luxembourg 0, Russia 6
Luxembourgg 1, Iceland 3
Russia 1, Greece 1
Iceland 0, Russia 1
Iceland 2, Hungary 1
Greece 3, Iceland 0
Hungary 3, Iceland 2
Luxembourg 0, Hungary 0
Hungary 2, Luxembourg 0
Luxembourg 0, Greece 4
Russia 2, Hungary 0
Hungary 0, Russia 6
Iceland 3, Luxembourg 0
Greece 2, Russia 2

Group 6
Sweden 6, Bulgaria 0
France 6, Austria 1
Austria 1, Israel 5
Israel 1, Sweden 1
Israel 1, Bulgaria 2
Israel 1, France 2
Austria 0, France 1
Austria 2, Bulgaria 0
Bulgaria 1, Israel 0
Sweden 1, Austria 1
Sweden 4, Israel 1
Finland 1, Israel 0
Finland 0, Bulgaria 0
Bulgaria 3, Finland 1
Bulgaria 0, France 1
France 2, Bulgaria 0
Finland 1, Sweden 0
Sweden 4, Finland 0
Bulgaria 0, Sweden 0
Israel 6, Austria 0
France 1, Finland 2
Finland 0, France 1
France 3, Israel 0
Bulgaria 3, Austria 0
France 2, Sweden 1
Sweden 1, France 1
Finland 2, Austria 0
Austria 2, Finland 2

Quarter-finals, first leg
France 2, Russia 0
Italy 3, Czechoslovakia 0
Poland 1, Portugal 3
Spain 0, Greece 0

Quarter-finals, second leg
Czechoslovakia 1, Italy 1
Greece 2, Spain 4
Russia 0, France 1
Portugal 2, Poland 0

Semi-finals (tournament in France)
Portugal 2, Spain 0
France 0, Italy 0
(*Italy won 5-3 on penalties*)

Third place
Spain 2, France 1

Final
Italy 1, Portugal 0 (*sudden death extra time*)

10th UEFA UNDER-18 CHAMPIONSHIP 1993–94

Group 1
Latvia (0) 0, Finland (1) 2
Latvia (0) 0, Russia (2) 3
Finland (1) 2, Russia (1) 2
Finland (1) 2, Latvia (0) 0
Russia (1) 2, Finland (0) 0
Russia (2) 5, Latvia (0) 1

Group 2
Wales (1) 1, Iceland (0) 2
Iceland (1) 7, Estonia (0) 0
Estonia (0) 0, Wales (0) 1

Group 3
Northern Ireland (1) 1, Belarus (0) 1
Northern Ireland 0, Lithuania 0
Belarus (0) 1, Lithuania (1) 1

Group 4
Malta (1) 2, San Marino (0) 0
Malta (0) 0, Croatia (3) 4
San Marino (0) 1, Croatia (4) 8

Group 5
Cyprus (0) 0, Belgium (0) 2
Belgium (0) 1, Cyprus (0) 1

Group 6
Israel (0) 2, Ukraine (0) 0
Israel (0) 0, Georgia (0) 1
Ukraine (0) 5, Georgia (0) 1

Group 7
Turkey (2) 5, Armenia (0) 0
Turkey (0) 1, Switzerland (0) 1
Armenia (0) 0, Switzerland (5) 9

Group 8
Bulgaria 0, Slovenia 0
Slovenia (2) 3, Italy (5) 6
Italy (2) 3, Bulgaria (0) 2
Slovenia (0) 1, Bulgaria (1) 2
Italy (1) 3, Slovenia (0) 0
Bulgaria (0) 1, Italy (0) 0

Group 9
Norway (0) 0, Denmark (0) 2
Norway (1) 1, Holland (1) 2
Denmark (0) 1, Norway (1) 1
Holland (2) 4, Norway (0) 1
Denmark (0) 0, Holland (0) 1
Holland (0) 1, Denmark (2) 2

Group 10
Czechoslovakia (0) 1, Poland (0) 0
Poland (1) 3, Czechoslovakia (1) 1
Poland (0) 0, Portugal (0) 1
Czechoslovakia 0, Portugal 0
Portugal (1) 2, Poland (0) 1
Portugal (0) 2, Czechoslovakia (2) 2

Group 11
Republic of Ireland (0) 1, Sweden (1) 2
Republic of Ireland (1) 2, Scotland (2) 2
Sweden (1) 4, Scotland (1) 2

Group 12
England (0) 1, Rumania (0) 1
Rumania (0) 0, France (0) 1
Rumania (1) 1, England (1) 1
France (0) 2, England (0) 0
England (2) 3, France (1) 3

Group 13
Luxembourg (0) 0, Hungary (2) 4
Austria (0) 0, Hungary (2) 2
Hungary (0) 2, Austria (1) 2
Hungary (2) 4, Luxembourg (0) 0
Austria (2) 3, Luxembourg (0) 0
Luxembourg (2) 3, Austria (0) 1

Group 14
Germany (1) 4, Greece (1) 2
Greece (1) 2, Germany (1) 2

Second Round
Group 1
Iceland (0) 0, Portugal (3) 7
Portugal (1) 3, Iceland (1) 1

Group 2
Russia (1) 2, Italy (0) 0
Italy (0) 0, Russia (0) 1

Group 3
Hungary (1) 1, Belarus (2) 2
Belarus 0, Hungary 0

Group 4
Sweden 0, Switzerland 0
Switzerland (0) 1, Sweden (2) 2

Group 5
Germany 0, Belgium 0
Belgium 0, Germany 0

Group 6
Ukraine (1) 2, Holland (1) 2
Holland 0, Ukraine 0

Group 7
Croatia 0, France 0
France (1) 3, Croatia (0) 0
(*Final Tournament in Spain July 1994*)

12th UEFA UNDER-16 CHAMPIONSHIP 1994

FINAL TOURNAMENT IN REPUBLIC OF IRELAND

Group A
Austria 1, Albania 0
Spain 0, Belarus 1
Spain 1, Austria 1
Albania 1, Belarus 1
Albania 0, Spain 4
Belarus 1, Austria 1

Group B
Czech Republic 1, Republic of Ireland 0
England 1, Portugal 0
England 1, Republic of Ireland 1
Portugal 2, Czech Republic 0
England 2, Czech Republic 1
Republic of Ireland 0, Portugal 3

Group C
Germany 0, Russia 2
Switzerland 3, Denmark 4
Denmark 3, Russia 2
Switzerland 1, Germany 5
Denmark 3, Germany 4
Russia 5, Switzerland 1

Group D
Turkey 2, Iceland 1
Ukraine 2, Belgium 1
Iceland 1, Belgium 2
Turkey 1, Ukraine 1
Belgium 0, Turkey 4
Iceland 1, Ukraine 2

Quarter-finals
England 2, Ukraine 2 *(Ukraine won on penalties)*
Turkey 0, Portugal 0 *(Turkey won on penalties)*
Belarus 1, Denmark 3
Russia 0, Austria 2

Semi-finals
Austria 0, Turkey 1
Denmark 2, Ukraine 2 *(Denmark won on penalties)*

Match for third place
Ukraine 2, Austria 0

Final
Turkey 1, Denmark 0

Group 7
(Germany, Wales, Bulgaria, Georgia, Albania, Moldova)

7. 9.94	Wales–Albania
7. 9.94	Germany–Moldova
12.10.94	Moldova–Wales
12.10.94	Bulgaria–Georgia
16.11.94	Albania–Germany
16.11.94	Georgia–Wales
16.11.94	Bulgaria–Moldova
14.12.94	Wales–Bulgaria
14.12.94	Moldova–Germany
14.12.94	Albania–Georgia
18.12.94	Germany–Albania
29. 3.95	Georgia–Germany
29. 3.95	Bulgaria–Wales
29. 3.95	Albania–Moldova
26. 4.95	Germany–Wales
26. 4.95	Moldova–Bulgaria
26. 4.95	Georgia–Albania
7. 6.95	Bulgaria–Germany
7. 6.95	Wales–Georgia
7. 6.95	Moldova–Albania
6. 9.95	Germany–Georgia
6. 9.95	Wales–Moldova
6. 9.95	Albania–Bulgaria
7.10.95	Bulgaria–Albania
8.10.95	Germany–Moldova
11.10.95	Wales–Germany
11.10.95	Georgia–Bulgaria
15.11.95	Germany–Bulgaria
15.11.95	Albania–Wales
15.11.95	Moldova–Georgia

Group 8
(Russia, Greece, Scotland, Finland, Faroe Islands, San Marino)

7. 9.94	Finland–Scotland
7. 9.94	Faroe Islands–Greece
12.10.94	Scotland–Faroe Islands
12.10.94	Greece–Finland
12.10.94	Russia–San Marino
16.11.94	Scotland–Russia
16.11.94	Greece–San Marino
16.11.94	Finland–Faroe Islands
14.12.94	Finland–San Marino
18.12.94	Greece–Scotland
29. 3.95	Russia–Scotland
29. 3.95	San Marino–Finland
26. 4.95	San Marino–Scotland
26. 4.95	Greece–Russia
26. 4.95	Faroe Islands–Finland
6. 5.95*	Russia–Faroe Islands
7. 6.95	Faroe Islands–Scotland
7. 6.95	San Marino–Russia
11. 6.95	Finland–Greece
16. 8.95	Scotland–Greece
16. 8.95	Finland–Russia
16. 8.95	Faroe Islands–San Marino
6. 9.95	Scotland–Finland
6. 9.95	Faroe Islands–Russia
6. 9.95	San Marino–Greece
11.10.95	Russia–Greece
11.10.95	Scotland–Faroe Islands
15.11.95	Scotland–San Marino
15.11.95	Russia–Finland
15.11.95	Greece–Faroe Islands

* to be confirmed

ENGLAND UNDER-21 RESULTS 1976–94

EC UEFA Competition for Under-21 Teams

v ALBANIA

Year	Date		Venue	Eng	Alb
EC1989	Mar	7	Shkroda	2	1
EC1989	April	25	Ipswich	2	0

v BELGIUM

Year	Date		Venue	Eng	Bel
1994	June	5	Marseille	2	1

v BRAZIL

Year	Date		Venue	Eng	B
1993	June	11	Toulon	0	0

v BULGARIA

Year	Date		Venue	Eng	Bulg
EC1979	June	5	Pernik	3	1
EC1979	Nov	20	Leicester	5	0
1989	June	5	Toulon	2	3

v CZECHOSLOVAKIA

Year	Date		Venue	Eng	Cz
1990	May	28	Toulon	2	1
1993	June	9	Toulon	1	1

v DENMARK

Year	Date		Venue	Eng	Den
EC1978	Sept	19	Hvidovre	2	1
EC1979	Sept	11	Watford	1	0
EC1982	Sept	21	Hvidovre	4	1
EC1983	Sept	20	Norwich	4	1
EC1986	Mar	12	Copenhagen	1	0
EC1986	Mar	26	Manchester	1	1
1988	Sept	13	Watford	0	0
1994	Mar	8	Brentford	1	0

v EAST GERMANY

Year	Date		Venue	Eng	EG
EC1980	April	16	Sheffield	1	2
EC1980	April	23	Jena	0	1

v FINLAND

Year	Date		Venue	Eng	Fin
EC1977	May	26	Helsinki	1	0
EC1977	Oct	12	Hull	8	1
EC1984	Oct	16	Southampton	2	0
EC1985	May	21	Mikkeli	1	3

v FRANCE

Year	Date		Venue	Eng	Fra
EC1984	Feb	28	Sheffield	6	1
EC1984	Mar	28	Rouen	1	0
1987	June	11	Toulon	0	2
EC1988	April	13	Besancon	2	4
EC1988	April	27	Highbury	2	2
1988	June	12	Toulon	2	4
1990	May	23	Toulon	7	3
1991	June	3	Toulon	1	0
1993	June	15	Toulon	1	0
1993	May	31	Aubagne	0	3

v GERMANY

Year	Date		Venue	Eng	G
1991	Sept	10	Scunthorpe	2	1

v GREECE

Year	Date		Venue	Eng	Gre
EC1982	Nov	16	Piraeus	0	1
EC1983	Mar	29	Portsmouth	2	1
1989	Feb	7	Patras	0	1

v HOLLAND

Year	Date		Venue	Eng	H
EC1993	Apr	27	Portsmouth	3	0
EC1993	Oct	12	Utrecht	1	1

v HUNGARY

Year	Date		Venue	Eng	Hun
EC1981	June	5	Keszthely	2	1
EC1981	Nov	17	Nottingham	2	0
EC1983	April	26	Newcastle	1	0
EC1983	Oct	11	Nyiregyhaza	2	0
1990	Sept	11	Southampton	3	1

v ITALY

Year	Date		Venue	Eng	Italy
EC1978	Mar	8	Manchester	2	1
EC1978	April	5	Rome	0	0
EC1984	April	18	Manchester	3	1
EC1984	May	2	Florence	0	1
EC1986	April	9	Pisa	0	2
EC1986	April	23	Swindon	1	1

v ISRAEL

Year	Date		Venue	Eng	Isr
1985	Feb	27	Tel Aviv	2	1

v MEXICO

Year	Date		Venue	Eng	Mex
1988	June	5	Toulon	2	1
1991	May	29	Toulon	6	0

v MOROCCO

Year	Date		Venue	Eng	Mor
1987	June	7	Toulon	2	0
1988	June	9	Toulon	1	0

v NORWAY

Year	Date		Venue	Eng	Nor
EC1977	June	1	Bergen	2	1
EC1977	Sept	6	Brighton	6	0
1980	Sept	9	Southampton	3	0
1981	Sept	8	Drammen	0	0
EC1992	Oct	13	Peterborough	0	2
EC1993	June	1	Stavanger	1	1

v POLAND

				Eng	Pol
EC1982	Mar	17	Warsaw	2	1
EC1982	April	7	West Ham	2	2
EC1989	June	2	Plymouth	2	1
EC1989	Oct	10	Jastrzebie	3	1
EC1990	Oct	16	Tottenham	0	1
EC1993	May	28	Zdroj	4	1
EC1993	Sept	7	Millwall	1	2

v PORTUGAL

Year	Date		Venue	Eng	Por
1987	June	13	Toulon	0	0
1990	May	21	Toulon	0	1
1993	June	7	Toulon	2	0
1994	June	7	Toulon	2	0

v REPUBLIC OF IRELAND

Year	Date		Venue	Eng	Rep Ire
1981	Feb	25	Liverpool	1	0
1985	Mar	25	Portsmouth	3	2
1989	June	9	Toulon	0	0
EC1990	Nov	13	Cork	3	0
EC1991	Mar	26	Brentford	3	0

v RUSSIA

Year	Date		Venue	Eng	Rus
1994	May	30	Bandol	2	0

v ROMANIA

Year	Date		Venue	Eng	Rom
EC1980	Oct	14	Ploesti	0	4
EC1981	April	28	Swindon	3	0
EC1985	April	30	Brasov	0	0
EC1985	Sept	10	Ipswich	3	0

v SAN MARINO

Year	Date		Venue	Eng	SM
EC1993	Feb	16	Luton	6	0
EC1993	Nov	17	San Marino	4	0

v SENEGAL

Year	Date		Venue	Eng	Sen
1989	June	7	Toulon	6	1
1991	May	27	Toulon	2	1

v SCOTLAND

Year	Date		Venue	Eng	Scot
1977	April	27	Sheffield	1	0
EC1980	Feb	12	Coventry	2	1
EC1980	Mar	4	Aberdeen	0	0
EC1982	April	19	Glasgow	1	0
EC1982	April	28	Manchester	1	1
EC1988	Feb	16	Aberdeen	1	0
EC1988	Mar	22	Nottingham	1	0
1993	June	13	Toulon	1	0

v SPAIN

Year	Date		Venue	Eng	Spa
EC1984	May	17	Seville	1	0
EC1984	May	24	Sheffield	2	0
1987	Feb	18	Burgos	2	1
1992	Sept	8	Burgos	1	0

v SWEDEN

Year	Date		Venue	Eng	Swe
1979	June	9	Vasteras	2	1
1986	Sept	9	Ostersund	1	1
EC1988	Oct	18	Coventry	1	1
EC1989	Sept	5	Uppsala	0	1

v SWITZERLAND

Year	Date		Venue	Eng	Swit
EC1980	Nov	18	Ipswich	5	0
EC1981	May	31	Neuenburg	0	0
1988	May	28	Lausanne	1	1

v USA

Year	Date		Venue	Eng	USA
1989	June	11	Toulon	0	2
1994	June	2	Toulon	3	0

v TURKEY

Year	Date		Venue	Eng	Tur
EC1984	Nov	13	Bursa	0	0
EC1985	Oct	15	Bristol	3	0
EC1987	April	28	Izmir	0	0
EC1987	Oct	13	Sheffield	1	1
EC1991	April	30	Izmir	2	2
EC1992	Nov	17	Orient	0	1
EC1993	Mar	30	Izmir	0	0

			v USSR	Eng	USSR
1987	June	9	Toulon	0	0
1988	June	7	Toulon	1	0
1990	May	25	Toulon	2	1
1991	May	31	Toulon	2	1

			v WALES	Eng	Wales
1976	Dec	15	Wolverhampton	0	0
1979	Feb	6	Swansea	1	0
1990	Dec	5	Tranmere	0	0

			v WEST GERMANY	Eng	WG
EC1982	Sept	21	Sheffield	3	1
EC1982	Oct	12	Bremen	2	3
1987	Sept	8	Ludenscheid	0	2

			v YUGOSLAVIA	Eng	Yugo
EC1978	April	19	Novi Sad	1	2
EC1978	May	2	Manchester	1	1
EC1986	Nov	11	Peterborough	1	1
EC1987	Nov	10	Zemun	5	1

ENGLAND B RESULTS 1949–94

Year	*Date*		*Venue*		
			v ALGIERS	Eng	Alg
1990	Dec	11	Algiers	0	0
			v AUSTRALIA	Eng	Aust
1980	Nov	17	Birmingham	1	0
			v CIS	Eng	CIS
1992	April	28	Moscow	1	1
			v CZECHOSLOVAKIA	Eng	Cz
1978	Nov	28	Prague	1	0
1990	April	24	Sunderland	2	0
1992	Mar	24	Budejovice	1	0
			v FINLAND	Eng	Fin
1949	May	15	Helsinki	4	0
			v FRANCE	Eng	Fra
1952	May	22	Le Havre	1	7
1992	Feb	18	Loftus Road	3	0
			v WEST GERMANY	Eng	WG
1954	Mar	24	Gelsenkirchen	4	0
1955	Mar	23	Sheffield	1	1
1978	Feb	21	Augsburg	2	1
			v HOLLAND	Eng	Hol
1949	May	18	Amsterdam	4	0
1950	Feb	22	Newcastle	1	0
1952	Mar	26	Amsterdam	1	0
			v ICELAND	Eng	Ice
1989	May	19	Reykjavik	2	0
1991	April	27	Watford	1	0
			v ITALY	Eng	It
1950	May	11	Milan	0	5
1989	Nov	14	Brighton	1	1
			v LUXEMBOURG	Eng	Lux
1950	May	21	Luxembourg	2	1
			v MALAYSIA	Eng	Mal
1978	May	30	Kuala Lumpur	1	1
			v MALTA	Eng	Mal
1987	Oct	14	Ta'Qali	2	0
			v NEW ZEALAND	Eng	NZ
1978	June	7	Christchurch	4	0
1978	June	11	Wellington	3	1
1978	June	14	Auckland	4	0
1979	Oct	15	Leyton	4	1
1984	Nov	13	Nottingham	2	0
			v NORTHERN IRELAND	Eng	NI
1994	May	10	Sheffield	4	2
			v NORWAY	Eng	Nor
1989	May	22	Stavanger	1	0
			v REPUBLIC OF IRELAND	Eng	RoI
1990	Mar	27	Cork	1	4
			v SCOTLAND	Eng	Scot
1953	Mar	11	Edinburgh	2	2
1954	Mar	3	Sunderland	1	1
1956	Feb	29	Dundee	2	2
1957	Feb	6	Birmingham	4	1
			v SINGAPORE	Eng	Sin
1978	June	18	Singapore	8	0
			v SPAIN	Eng	Sp
1980	Mar	26	Sunderland	1	0
1981	Mar	25	Granada	2	3
1991*	Dec	18	Castellon	1	0

*Spanish Olympic IX

			v SWITZERLAND	Eng	Sw
1950	Jan	18	Sheffield	5	0
1954	May	22	Basle	0	2
1956	Mar	21	Southampton	4	1
1989	May	16	Winterthur	2	0
1991	May	20	Walsall	2	1
			v USA	Eng	USA
1980	Oct	14	Manchester	1	0
			v WALES	Eng	Wal
1991	Feb	5	Swansea	1	0
			v YUGOSLAVIA	Eng	Yug
1954	May	16	Ljubljana	1	2
1955	Oct	19	Manchester	5	1
1989	Dec	12	Millwall	2	1

BRITISH AND IRISH UNDER–21 INTERNATIONALS 1993–94

England Under–21 internationals

7 Sept

England (0) 1 *(Ehiogu)*
Poland (1) 2 5390

England: Walker; Jackson, Ehiogu, Cox, Small, Anderton (Sheron), Flitcroft, Redknapp (Ardley), McManaman, Cole, Sutton.

12 Oct

Holland (0) 1
England (0) 1 *(Flitcroft)* 3330

England: Watson D; Ardley, Minto, Sutton, Ehiogu, Awford, Flitcroft, Sheron, Cole, Clark (Redknapp), Sinclair.

17 Nov

San Marino (0) 0
England (3) 4 (*Fowler, Anderton, Sutton, Sheron*) 200

England: Watson D; Ardley, Small, Newton, Ehiogu, Cox, Anderton, Sheron, Sutton, Fowler (Shipperley), Sinclair (Watson S).

8 Mar

England (0) 1 (*Sinclair*)
Denmark (0) 0 11,553

England: Gerrard (Oakes); Watson S, Edghill, Campbell, Nethercott, Parlour, Redknapp, Barmby (Joachim), Sutton, Bart-Williams, Sinclair.

30 May

Russia (0) 0
England (1) 2 (*Sinclair, Bart-Williams (pen)*)

Endgland: Gerrard; Edghill (Makin), Nethercott, Campbell, Gordon, Parlour (Selley), Redknapp, Bart-Williams, Sinclair, Fear, Dyer (Fowler).

31 May

France (1) 3
England (0) 0

England: Nicholls (Oakes); Makin, Nethercott, Campbell, Gordon (Matteo), Sinclair, Fear (Eadie), Redknapp, Bart-Williams (Selley), Dyer, Fowler.

2 June

USA (0) 0
England (1) 3 (*Dyer, Fowler, Redknapp (pen)*)

England: Oakes; Makin, Nethercott, Campbell, Gordon, Sinclair, Selley, Redknapp, Eadie, Dyer, Fowler (Fear).

5 June

Belgium (0) 1
England (1) 2 (*Campbell, Dyer*)

England: Oakes; Makin, Nethercott, Campbell, Gordon, Sinclair, Parlour, Redknapp, Matteo, Bart-Williams, Dyer.

7 June

Portugal (0) 0
England (0) 2 (*Sinclair, Dyer*)

England: Oakes; Makin, Nethercott, Campbell, Gordon, Sinclair, Parlour, Redknapp, Matteo, Bart-Williams, Dyer.

Scotland Under–21 internationals

7 Sept

Scotland (0) 0
Switzerland (0) 0 3059

Scotland: Howie; Burley, Bollan, Pressley, O'Neil, Tweed, Telfer, Murray N, Thomas, Dailly, McLaren (McGrillen).

13 Oct

Italy (3) 5
Scotland (0) 2 (*Bernard, Dailly*) 10,000

Scotland: Howie; Wright, Dow, Murray N, Pressley, Tweed (McLaren), Skilling, Bernard, McGrillen, Dailly (Burley), Darren Ferguson.

16 Nov

Malta (0) 0
Scotland (1) 1 (*Thomas*) 1400

Scotland: Kerr; Lavin, Baker, Wright, Pressley, Fullarton, Thomas, Bernard, Lavety (Liddell), Dailly, Locke.

19 Apr

Austria (1) 2
Scotland (0) 1 (*Dailly (pen)*) 497

Scotland: Kerr; McNamara, Baker, Fullarton, Pressley, Hood, Locke (Lavety), Hannah, Crawford (Scott), Dailly, McCann.

30 May

Egypt (0) 1
Scotland (1) 1 (*Donnelly*)

Scotland: Kerr; Lavin, Pressley, Dailly, Robertson, Hannah, Locke (Lavety), Fullarton, McCann, Donnelly (Scott), Crawford.

1 June

Portugal (0) 0
Scotland (1) 2 (*Lavin, Hannah*)

Scotland: Kerr; Lavin, Pressley, Dailly, Fullarton, Hannah, Scott, Locke, McCann, Crawford, Donnelly.

3 June

Belgium (2) 2
Scotland (0) 0

Scotland: Kerr, Lavin (Johnston), Pressley, Dailly, Fullarton, Hannah, McNamara (Lavety), Scott, Crawford, Donnelly, McCann.

Wales Under–21 internationals

7 Sept

Wales (0) 0
RCS (0) 4 1500
Wales: Margetson; Neilson, Searle (Meaker), Chapple, Ready, McCarthy, Powell (Jones L), Edwards, Blake, Bowen, Robinson.

13 Oct

Wales (4) 6 (*Jones L 3, Hartson 2, Ready*)
Cyprus (1) 2 658
Wales: Margetson (Coyne); Hughes, Robinson, McCarthy, Ready, Neilson, Kenworthy, Owen, Hartson, Jones L (Bird), Edwards.

16 Nov

Wales (0) 1 (*Hartson*)
Romania (0) 2 1600
Wales: Coyne; Robinson, Edwards, McCarthy, Hughes, Neilson, Ready, Owen (Meaker), Jones R, Hartson, Jones L (Brown).

Republic of Ireland Under–21 internationals

12 Oct

Republic of Ireland (0) 0
Spain (1) 2
Republic of Ireland: Colgan; Kelly, McCarthy, Greene, Hardy, Buckley, Kinsella, Boland (Sheridan), Turner, Gallen J (Power), O'Connor.

B International

10 May

England (3) 4 (*Holdsworth, Merson, Bould, Scales*)
Northern Ireland (2) 2 (*O'Boyle, Quinn*) 8281
England: Pressman (Martyn); Barton (Edghill), Scales, Bould, Beresford, Fox (Summerbee), Lee, Bart-Williams (Stubbs), Merson, Holdsworth, Sutton (Armstrong).
Northern Ireland: Fettis; Lomas, McGibbon (Hunter), Patterson, Horlock, Dennison, Lennon (McMahon), O'Neill M (Robinson), Black, O'Boyle, Quinn (Millar).

Semi-Professional International/FA Representative Matches 1993–94

29 Sept

FA XI 6 *Herefordshire FA 2*
FA XI: Cooksey, Bloomfield, Vickers, Richardson, Clark, Webb, Purdie, Hodges, Davies, Cook, Smith G.
Subs: Preedy for Hodges, Watkins A for Cooksey, Watkins J for Purdie.
Scorers: Cook 2, Purdie 2, Webb, Preedy.

19 Oct

FA XI 1 *Western League 4*
FA XI: Teasdale, Bowles, Meacham, Thorpe, Kilgour, Gillard, Knight, Batty, McPherson, Dann, Harrower.
Subs: Bush for Teasdale, Rutter for Dann.
Scorer: Batty.

3 Nov

FA XI 1 *Southern League 4*
FA XI: Cooksey, Hodson, Parrish, Weir and Brindley, Butterworth, Williams, Bignot, Burr, Davies and Purdie.
Subs: Bodkin for Bignot, Pritchard for Hodson, Carrington for Cooksey.
Scorer: Burr.

16 Nov

FA XI 0 *Northern Premier League 2*
FA XI: Mason, Shepherd and Bimson, Butler and Parker, Mooney, Constable, Alford and Askey, Burke, Gamble.
Subs: Brabin for Gamble, Hughes for Mason, Dove for Mooney.

7 Dec

FA XI 1 *Isthmian League 4*
FA XI: Williams, Stebbing and Watts, Hone, Conner, Biggins, Jackson, Broom, Abbott, Leworthy, Fiore.
Subs: Keen for Stebbing, Batty for Williams, Fielder for Abbott, Milton for Biggins.
Scorer: Broom.

11 Jan

FA XI 2 *Combined Services 2*
FA XI: Popple, Atkinson, O'Brien, Ainsley, Wrightson, Alcide, Farrey, Ord, Lamb, Suddick, Saunders.
Subs: Race for Popple, Peattie for Saunders, Parkinson for Ainsley, Saunders for O'Brien.
Scorers: Lamb, Ord.

22 Sept

Wales 1 England 2
England: Benstead, Hodson, Brighton and Richardson, Holden, Brabin, Humphreys, Webb, Robbins, Leworthy, Collins.
Subs: Hone for Hodson, Ross for Leworthy, Venables for Collins.
Scorers: Webb, Humphreys.

14 Mar

Guernsey 1 England 3
England: Rose, Simpson, Brighton, Hone, Richardson, Brabin, Venables, Brown D, Robbins, Browne C, Milton.
Subs: Hodson for Richardson, Williams for Rose, Webb for Brabin, Bartlett for Brighton.
Scorers: Browne 2, Venables.

30 May

Finland U-21 2 England 0
England: Benstead, Simpson, Ashby and Holden, Richardson and Webb, Milton, Humphreys, Robbins, Collins, Brabin.
Subs: Hodson for Simpson, Rose for Benstead, Hone for Holden, Browne C for Webb, Brown D for Robbins.

1 June

Norway U-21 2 England 1
England: Rose and Hodson, Ashby, Hone, Richardson, Brown D, Milton, Humphreys, Robbins, Collins, Brabin.
Subs: Holden for Hone, Browne C for Robbins, Simpson for Milton, Benstead for Rose, Webb for Collins.
Scorer: Browne C.

UNDER-21 APPEARANCES 1976–1993

ENGLAND

Ablett, G. (Liverpool), 1988 v Fr (1)
Adams, A. (Arsenal). 1985 v Ei, Fi; 1986 v D; 1987 v Se, Y (5)
Adams, N. (Everton), 1987 v Se (1)
Allen, B. (QPR), 1992 v H, M, Cz, F; 1993 v N (sub), T (6)
Allen, C. (QPR), 1980 v EG (sub); (with C Palace), 1981 v N, R (3)
Allen, M. (QPR), 1987 v Se (sub); 1988 v Y (sub) (2)
Allen, P. (West Ham U), 1985 v Ei, R; (with Tottenham H, 1986 v R (3)
Anderson, V. A. (Nottingham F), 1978 v I (1)
Anderton, D. R. (Tottenham H), 1993 v Sp, Sm, Ho, Pol, N; 1994 v Pol, Sm (7)
Andrews, I. (Leicester C), 1987 v Se (1)
Ardley, N. C. (Wimbledon), 1994 v Pol (sub), Ho, Sm (3)
Ashcroft, L. (Preston NE), 1992 v (sub) (1)
Atherton, P. (Coventry C), 1992 v T (1)
Atkinson, B. (Sunderland), 1991 v W (sub), Sen, M, USSR (sub), F; 1992 v Pol (sub) (6)
Awford, A. T. (Portsmouth), 1993 v Sp, N, T; 1994 v Ho (4)

Bailey, G. R. (Manchester U), 1979 v W, Bul; 1980 v D, S (2), EG; 1982 v N; 1983 v D, Gr; 1984 v H, F (2), I, Sp (14)
Baker, G. E. (Southampton), 1981 v N, R (2)
Barker, S. (Blackburn R), 1985 v Is (sub), Ei, R; 1986 v I (4)
Barmby, N. J. (Tottenham H), 1994 v D (1)
Bannister, G. (Sheffield W), 1982 v Pol (1)
Barnes, J. (Watford), 1983 v D, Gr (2)
Barnes, P. S. (Manchester C), 1977 v W (sub), S, Fi, N; 1978 v N, Fi, I (2), Y (9)
Barrett, E. D. (Oldham Ath), 1990 v P, F, USSR, Cz (4)
Bart-Williams, C. G. (Sheffield W), 1993 v Sp, N, T; 1994 v D, Ru, F, Bel, P (8)
Batty, D. (Leeds U), 1988 v Sw (sub); 1989 v Gr (sub), Bul, Sen, Ei, US; 1990 v Pol (7)
Beazeley, D. S. (Watford), 1992 v H (sub) (1)
Beagrie, P. (Sheffield U), 1988 v WG, T (2)
Beardsmore, R. (Manchester U), 1989 v Gr, Alb (sub), Pol, Bul, USA (5)
Beeston, C (Stoke C), 1988 v USSR (1)
Bertschin, K. E. (Birmingham C), 1977 v S; 1978 v Y (2)H(3)
Birtles, G. (Nottingham F), 1980 v Bul, EG (sub) (2)
Blackwell, D. R. (Wimbledon), 1991 v W, T, Sen (sub), M, USSR, F (6)
Blake, M. A. (Aston Villa), 1990 v F (sub), Cz (sub); 1991 v H, Pol, Ei (2), W; 1992 v Pol (8)
Blissett, L. L. (Watford), 1979 v W, Bul (sub), Se; 1980 v D (4)
Bracewell, P. (Stoke C), 1983 v D, Gr (1 pl 1 sub), H; 1984 v D, H, F (2), I (2), Sp (2); 1985 v T (13)
Bradshaw, P. W. (Wolverhampton W), 1977 v W, S; 1978 v Fi, Y (4)
Breacker, T. (Luton T), 1986 v I (2) (2)
Brennan, M. (Ipswich T), 1987 v Y, Sp, T, Mor, F (5)
Brightwell, I. (Manchester C), 1989 v D, Alb; 1990 v Se (sub), Pol (4)
Brock, K. (Oxford U), 1984 v I, Sp (2); 1986 v I (4)
Bull, S. G. (Wolverhampton W), 1989 v Alb (2) Pol; 1990 v Se, Pol (5)
Burrows, D. (WBA), 1989 v Se (sub); (with Liverpool), Gr, Alb (2) Pol; 1990 v Se, Pol (7)
Butcher, T. I. (Ipswich T), 1979 v Se; 1980 v D, Bul, S (2), EG (2) (7)
Butters, G. (Tottenham H), 1989 v Bul, Sen (sub), Ei (sub) (3)
Butterworth, I. (Coventry C), 1985 v T, R; (with Nottingham F), 1986 v R, T, D (2), I (2) (8)

Caesar, G. (Arsenal), 1987 v Mor, USSR (sub), F (3)
Callaghan, N. (Watford), 1983 v D, Gr (sub), H (sub); 1984 v D, H, F (2), I, Sp (9)
Campbell, K. J. (Arsenal), 1991 v H, T (sub); 1992 v G, T (4)
Campbell, S. (Tottenham), 1994 v D, Ru, F, US, Bel, P (6)
Carr, C. (Fulham), 1985 v Ei (sub) (1)
Carr, F. (Nottingham F), 1987 v Se, Y, Sp (sub), Mor, USSR; 1988 v WG (sub), T, Y, F (9)
Caton, T. (Manchester C), 1982 v N, H (sub), Pol (2), S; 1983 v WG (2), Gr; 1984 v D, H, F (2), I (2) (14)
Chamberlain, M. (Stoke C), 1983 v Gr; 1984 v F (sub), I, Sp (4)
Chapman, L. (Stoke C), 1981 v Ei (1)
Charles, G. A. (Nottingham F), 1991 v H, W (sub), Ei; 1992 v T (4)
Chettle, S. (Nottingham F), 1988 v M, USSR, Mor, F; 1989 v D, Se, Gr, Alb (2), Bul; 1990 v Se, Pol (12)
Clark, L. R. (Newcastle U), 1992 v Cz, F; 1993 v Sp, N, T, Ho (sub), Pol (sub); 1994 v Ho (8)
Clough, N. (Nottingham F), 1986 v D (sub); 1987 v Se, Y, T, USSR, F (sub). P; 1988 v WG, T, Y, S (2), M, Mor, F (15)
Cole, A. A. (Arsenal), 1992 v H, Cz (sub), F (sub); (with Bristol C) 1993 v Sm, (with Newcastle U) Pol, N; 1994 v Pol, Ho (8)
Coney, D. (Fulham), 1985 v T (sub); 1986 v R; 1988 v T, WG (8)
Connor, T. (Brighton & H A), 1987 v Y (1)
Cooke, R. (Tottenham H), 1986 v D (sub) (1)
Cooper, C. (Middlesbrough), 1988 v F (2), M, USSR, Mor; 1989 v D, Se, Gr (8)
Corrigan, J. T. (Manchester C), 1978 v I (2), Y (3)
Cottee, A. (West Ham U), 1985 v Fi (sub), Is (sub), Ei, R, Fi; 1987 v Sp, P; 1988 v WG (8)
Cowans, G. S. (Aston Villa), 1979 v W, Se; 1980 v Bul, EG; 1981 v R (5)
Cox, N. J. (Aston Villa), 1993 v T, Ho, Pol, N; 1994 v Pol, Sm (6)
Cranson, I. (Ipswich T), 1985 v Fi, Is, R; 1986 v R, I (5)
Crooks, G. (Stoke C), 1980 v Bul, S (2), EG (sub) (4)
Crossley, M. G. (Nottingham F), 1990 v P, USSR, Cz (3)
Cundy, J. V. (Chelsea), 1991 v Ei (2); 1992 v Pol (3)
Cunningham, L. (WBA), 1977 v S, Fi, N (sub); 1978 v N, Fi, I (6)
Curbishley, L. C. (Birmingham C), 1981 v Sw (1)

Daniel, P. W. (Hull C), 1977 v S, Fi, N; 1978 v Fi, I, Y (2) (7)
Davis, P. (Arsenal), 1982 v Pol, S; 1983 v D, Gr (1 pl 1 sub), H (sub); 1987 v T; 1988 v WG, T, Y, Fr (11)
D'Avray, M. (Ipswich T), 1984 v I, Sp (sub) (2)
Deehan, J. M. (Aston Villa), 1977 v N; 1978 v N, Fi, I; 1979 v Bul, Se (sub); 1980 v D (7)
Dennis, M. E. (Birmingham C), 1980 v Bul; 1981 v N, R (3)
Dickens, A. (West Ham U), 1985 v Fi (sub) (1)
Dicks, J. (West Ham U), 1988 v Sw (sub), M, Mor, F (4)
Digby, F. (Swindon T), 1987 v Sp (sub), USSR, P; 1988 v T; 1990 v Pol (5)
Dillon, K. P. (Birmingham C), 1981 v R (1)
Dixon, K. (Chelsea), 1985 v Fi (1)
Dobson, A. (Coventry C), 1989 v Bul, Sen, Ei, US (4)

Dodd, J. R. (Southampton), 1991 v Pol, Ei, T, Sen, M, F; 1992 v G, Pol (8)
Donowa, L. (Norwich C), 1985 v Is, R (sub), Fi (sub) (3)
Dorigo, A. (Aston Villa), 1987 v Se, Sp, T, Mor, USSR, F, P; 1988 v WG, Y, S (2) (11)
Dozzell, J. (Ipswich T), 1987 v Se, Y (sub), Sp, USSR, F, P; 1989 v Se, Gr (sub); 1990 v Se (sub) (9)
Draper, M. A. (Notts Co), 1991 v Ei (sub); 1992 v G, Pol (3)
Duxbury, M. (Manchester U), 1981 v Sw (sub), Ei (sub), R (sub), Sw; 1982 v N; 1983 v WG (2) (7)
Dyer, B. A. (Crystal Palace), 1994 v Ru, F, US, Bel, P (5)
Dyson, P. I. (Coventry C), 1981 v N, R, Sw, Ei (4)

Eadie, D. M. (Norwich C), 1994 v F (sub), US (2)
Ebbrell, J. (Everton), 1989 v Sen, Ei, US (sub); 1990 v P, F, USSR, Cz; 1991 v H, Pol, Ei, W, T; 1992 v G, T (14)
Edghill, R. A. (Manchester C), 1994 v D, Ru (2)
Ehiogu, U. (Aston Villa), 1992 v H, M, Cz, F; 1993 v Sp, N, T, Sm, T, Ho, Pol, N; 1994 v Pol, Ho, Sm (15)
Elliott, P. (Luton T), 1985 v Fi; 1986 v T, D (3)

Fairclough, C. (Nottingham F), 1985 v T, Is, Ei; 1987 v Sp, T; (with Tottenham H), 1988 v Y, F (7)
Fairclough, D. (Liverpool), 1977 v W (1)
Fashanu, J. (Norwich C), 1980 v EG; 1981 v N (sub), R, Sw, Ei (sub), H; (with Nottingham F), 1982 v N, H, Pol. S; 1983 v WG (sub) (11)
Fear, P. (Wimbledon), 1994 v Ru, F, US (sub) (3)
Fenwick, T. W. (C Palace), 1981 v N, R, Sw, Ei; (with QPR), R; 1982 v N, H, S (2); 1983 v WG (2) (11)
Fereday, W. (QPR), 198.5 v T, Ei (sub). Fi; 1986 v T (sub), I (5)
Flitcroft, G. W. (Manchester C), 1993 v Sm, Hol, N; 1994 v Pol, Ho (5)
Flowers, T. (Southampton), 1987 v Mor, F; 1988 v WG (sub) (3)
Forsyth, M. (Derby Co), 1988 v Sw (1)
Foster, S. (Brighton & HA), 1980 v EG (sub) (1)
Fowler, R. B. (Liverpool), 1994 v Sm, Ru (sub), F, US (4)
Froggatt, S. J. (Aston Villa), 1993 v Sp, Sm (sub) (2)
Futcher, P. (Luton T), 1977 v W, S, Fi, N; (with Manchester C), 1978 v N, Fi, I (2), Y (2); 1979 v D (11)

Gabbiadini, M. (Sunderland), 1989 v Bul, USA (2)
Gale, A. (Fulham), 1982 v Pol (1)
Gascoigne, P. (Newcastle U), 1987 v Mo, USSR, P; 1988 v WG, Y, S (2), F (2), Sw, M, USSR (sub), Mor (13)
Gayle, H. (Birmingham C), 1984 v I, Sp (2) (3)
Gernon, T. (Ipswich T), 1983 v Gr (1)
Gerrard, P. W. (Oldham Ath), 1993 v T, Ho, Pol, N; 1994 v D, Ru (6)
Gibbs, N. (Watford), 1987 v Mor, USSR, F, P; 1988 v T (5)
Gibson, C. (Aston Villa), 1982 v N (1)
Gilbert, W. A. (C Palace), 1979 v W, Bul; 1980 v Bul; 1981 v N, R, Sw, R, Sw, H; 1982 v N (sub), H (11)
Goddard, P. (West Ham U), 1981 v N, Sw, Ei (sub); 1982 v N (sub), Pol, S; 1983 v WG (2) (8)
Gordon, D. (Norwich C), 1987 v T (sub), Mor (sub), F, P (4)
Gordon, D. D. (Crystal Palace), 1994 v Ru, F, US, Bel, P (5)
Gray, A. (Aston Villa), 1988 v S, F (2)

Haigh, P. (Hull C), 1977 v N (sub) (1)
Hall, R. A. (Southampton), 1992 v H (sub), F; 1993 v Sm, T, Ho, Pol (6)
Hardyman, P. (Portsmouth), 1985 v Ei; 1986 v D (2)
Hateley, M. (Coventry C), 1982 v Pol, S; 1983 v Gr (2), H; (with Portsmouth), 1984 v F (2), I, Sp (2) (10)
Hayes, M. (Arsenal), 1987 v Sp, T; 1988 v F (sub) (3)
Hazell, R. J. (Wolverhampton W), 1979 v D (1)
Heaney, N. A. (Arsenal), 1992 v H, M, Cz, F; 1993 v N, T (6)
Heath, A. (Stoke C), 1981 v R, Sw, H; 1982 v N, H; (with Everton), Pol, S; 1983 v WG (8)
Hendon, I. M. (Tottenham H), 1992 v H, M, Cz, F; 1993 v Sp, N, T (7)
Hesford, I. (Blackpool), 1981 v Ei (sub), Pol (2), S (2); 1983 v WG (2) (7)
Hilaire, V. (C Palace), 1980 v Bul, S (1 + 1 sub), EG (2); 1981 v N, R, Sw (sub); 1982 v Pol (sub) (9)
Hillier, D. (Arsenal), 1991 v T (1)
Hinchcliffe, A. (Manchester C), 1989 v D (1)
Hinshelwood, P. A. (C Palace), 1978 v N; 1980 v EG (2)
Hirst, D. (Sheffield W), 1988 v USSR, F; 1989 v D, Bul (sub), Sen, Ei, US (7)
Hoddle, G. (Tottenham H), 1977 v W (sub); 1978 v Fi (sub), I (2), Y; 1979 v D, W, Bul; 1980 v S (2), EG (2)H(12)
Hodge, S. (Nottingham F), 1983 v Gr (sub); 1984 v D, F, I, Sp (2); (with Aston Villa), 1986 v R, T (8)
Hodgson, D. J. (Middlesbrough), 1981 v N, R (sub), Sw, Ei; 1982 v Pol; 1983 v WG (6)
Holdsworth, D. (Watford), 1989 v Gr (sub) (1)
Horne, B. (Millwall), 1989 v Gr (sub), Pol, Bul, Ei, US (5)
Hucker, P. (QPR), 1984 v I, Sp (2)

Impey, A. R. (QPR), 1993 v T (1)
Ince, P. (West Ham U), 1989 v Alb; 1990 v Se (2)

Jackson, M. A. (Everton), 1992 v H, M, Cz, F; 1993 v Sm (sub), T, Ho, Pol, N; 1994 v Pol (10)
James, D. (Watford), 1991 v Ei (2), T, Sen, M, USSR, F; 1992 v G, T, Pol (10)
James, J. C. (Luton T), 1990 v F, USSR (2)
Jemson, N. B. (Nottingham F), 1991 v W (1)
Joachim, J. K. (Leicester C), 1994 v D (sub) (1)
Johnson, T. (Notts Co), 1991 v H (sub), Ei (sub); 1992 v G, T, Pol; (with Derby Co), M, Cz (sub) (7)
Johnston, C. P. (Middlesbrough), 1981 v N, Ei (2)
Jones, D. R. (Everton, 1977 v W (1)
Jones, C. H. (Tottenham H), 1978 v Y (sub) (1)
Jones, R. (Liverpool), 1993 v Sm, Ho (2)

Keegan, G. A. (Manchester C), 1977 v W (1)
Kenny, W. (Everton), 1993 v T (1)
Keown, M. (Aston Villa), 1987 v Sp, Mor, USSR, P; 1988 v T, S, F (2) (8)
Kerslake, D. (QPR), 1986 v T (1)
Kilcline, B. (Notts C), 1983 v D, Gr (2)
King, A. E. (Everton), 1977 v W; 1978 v Y (2)
Kitson, P. (Leicester C), 1991 v Sen (sub), M, F; 1992 v Pol; (with Derby Co), M, Cz, F (7)
Knight, A. (Portsmouth), 1983 v Gr, H (2)
Knight, I. (Sheffield W), 1987 v Se (sub), Y (2)

Lake, P. (Manchester C), 1989 v D, Alb (2), Pol; 1990 v Pol (5)
Langley, T. W. (Chelsea), 1978 v I (sub) (1)
Lee, D. J. (Chelsea), 1990 v F; 1991 v H, Pol, Ei (2), T, Sen, USSR, F; 1992 v Pol (10)
Lee, R. (Charlton Ath), 1986 v I (sub); 1987 v Se (sub) (2)
Lee, S. (Liverpool), 1981 v R, Sw, H; 1982 v S; 1983 v WG (2) (6)
Le Saux, G. (Chelsea), 1990 v P, F, USSR, Cz (4)
Lowe, D. (Ipswich T), 1988 v F, Sw (sub) (2)
Lukic, J. (Leeds U), 1981 v N, R, Ei, R, Sw, H; 1982 v H (7)
Lund, G. (Grimsby T), 1985 v T; 1986 v R, T (3)

McCall, S. H. (Ipswich T), 1981 v Sw, H; 1982 v H, S; 1983 v WG (2) (6)

McDonald, N. (Newcastle U), 1987 v Se (sub), Sp, T; 1988 v WG, Y (sub) (5)
McGrath, L. (Coventry C), 1986 v D (1)
MacKenzie, S. (WBA), 1982 v N, S (2) (3)
McLeary, A. (Millwall), 1988 v Sw (1)
McMahon, S. (Everton), 1981 v Ei; 1982 v Pol; 1983 v D, Gr (2); (with Aston Villa), 1984 v H (6)
McManaman, S. (Liverpool), 1991 v W, M (sub); 1993 v N, T, Sm, T; 1994 v Pol (7)
Mabbutt, G. (Bristol R), 1982 v Pol (2), S; (with Tottenham H), 1983 v D; 1984 v F; 1986 v D, I (7)
Makin, C. (Oldham Ath), 1994 v Ru (sub), F, US, Bel, P (5)
Marriott, A. (Nottingham F), 1992 v M (1)
Martin, L. (Manchester U), 1989 v Gr (sub), Alb (sub) (2)
Martyn, N. (Bristol R), 1988 v S (sub), M, USSR, Mor, F; 1989 v D, Se, Gr, Alb (2); 1990 v Se (11)
Matteo, D. (Liverpool), 1994 v F (sub), Bel, P (3)
Matthew, D. (Chelsea), 1990 v P, USSR (sub), Cz; 1991 v Ei, M, USSR, F; 1992 v G (sub), T (9)
May, A. (Manchester C), 1986 v I (sub) (1)
Merson, P. (Arsenal), 1989 v D, Gr, Pol (sub); 1990 v Pol (4)
Middleton, J. (Nottingham F), 1977 v Fi, N; (with Derby Co), 1978 v N (3)
Miller, A. (Arsenal), 1988 v Mor (sub); 1989 v Sen; 1991 v H, Pol (4)
Mills, G. R. (Nottingham F), 1981 v R; 1982 v N (2)
Mimms, R. (Rotherham U), 1985 v Is (sub), Ei (sub); (with Everton), 1986 v I (3)
Minto, S. C. (Charlton Ath), 1991 v W; 1992 v H, M, Cz; 1993 v T; 1994 v Ho (6)
Moran, S. (Southampton), 1982 v N (sub); 1984 v F (2)
Morgan, S. (Leicester C), 1987 v Se, Y (2)
Mortimer, P. (Charlton Ath), 1989 v Sen, Ei (2)
Moses, R. M. (WBA), 1981 v N (sub), Sw, Ei, R, Sw, H; 1982 v N (sub); (with Manchester U), H (8)
Mountfield, D. (Everton), 1984 v Sp (1)
Muggleton, C. D. (Leicester C), 1990 v F (1)
Mutch, A. (Wolverhampton W), 1989 v Pol (1)

Nethercott, S. (Tottenham), 1994 v D, Ru, F, US, Bel, P (6)
Newell, M. (Luton T), 1986 v D (1 + sub), I (1 + sub) (4)
Newton, E. J. I. (Chelsea), 1993 v T (sub); 1994 v Sm (2)
Nicholls, A. (Plymouth Arg), 1994 v F (1)

Oakes, M. C. (Aston Villa), 1994 v D (sub), F (sub), US, Bel, P (5)
Oldfield, D. (Luton T), 1989 v Se (1)
Olney, I. A. (Aston Villa), 1990 v P, F, USSR, Cz; 1991 v H, Pol, Ei (2), T; 1992 v Pol (sub) (10)
Ord, R. J. (Sunderland), 1991 v W, M, USSR (3)
Osman, R. C. (Ipswich T), 1979 v W (sub), Se; 1980 v D, S (2), EG (2) (7)
Owen, G. A. (Manchester C), 1977 v S, Fi, N; 1978 v N, Fi, I (2), Y; 1979 v D, W; (with WBA), Bul, Se (sub); 1980 v D, S (2), EG; 1981 v Sw, R; 1982 v N (sub), H; 1983 v WG (2) (22)

Painter, I. (Stoke C), 1986 v I (1)
Palmer, C. (Sheffield W), 1989 v Bul, Sen, Ei, US (4)
Parker, G. (Hull C), 1986 v I (2); (with Nottingham F), v F; 1987 v Se, Y (sub), Sp (6)
Parker, P. (Fulham), 1985 v Fi, T, Is (sub), Ei, R, Fi; 1986 v T, D (8)
Parkes, P. B. F. (QPR), 1979 v D (1)
Parkin, S. (Stoke C), 1987 v Sp (sub); 1988 v WG (sub), T, S (sub), F (5)
Parlour, R. (Arsenal), 1992 v H, M, Cz, F; 1993 v Sp, N, T; 1994 v D, Ru, Bel, P (11)

Peach, D. S. (Southampton), 1977 v S, Fi, N; 1978 v N, I (2) (6)
Peake, A. (Leicester C), 1982 v Pol (1)
Pearce, S. (Nottingham F), 1987 v Y (1)
Pickering N. (Sunderland), 1983 v D (sub), Gr, H; 1984 v F (sub), F, I (2), Sp; 1985 v Is, R, Fi; 1986 v R, T; (with Coventry C), D, I (15)
Platt, D. (Aston Villa), 1988 v M, Mor, F (3)
Porter, G. (Watford), 1987 v Sp (sub), T, Mor, USSR, F, P (sub); 1988 v T (sub), Y, S (2), F, Sw (12)
Pressman, K. (Sheffield W), 1989 v D (sub) (1)
Proctor, M. (Middlesbrough), 1981 v Ei (sub), Sw; 1982 (with Nottingham F), v N, Pol (4)

Ramage, C. D. (Derby Co), 1991 v Pol (sub), W; 1992 v Fr (sub) (3)
Ranson, R. (Manchester C), 1980 v Bul, EG; 1981 v R (sub), R, Sw, (1 + sub), H, Pol (2), S (10)
Redknapp, J. F. (Liverpool), 1993 v Sm, Pol, N; 1994 v Pol, Ho (sub), D, Ru, F, US, Bel, P (11)
Redmond, S. (Manchester C), 1988 v F (2), M, USSR, Mor, F; 1989 v D, Se, Gr, Alb (2), Pol; 1990 v Se, Pol (14)
Reeves, K. P. (Norwich C), 1978 v I, Y (2); 1979 v N, W, Bul, Sw; 1980 v D, S; (with Manchester C), EG (10)
Regis, C. (WBA), 1979 v D, Bul, Se; 1980 v S, EG; 1983 v D (6)
Reid, N. S. (Manchester C), 1981 v H (sub); 1982 v H, Pol (2), S (2) (6)
Reid, P. (Bolton W), 1977 v S, Fi, N; 1978 v Fi, I, Y (6)
Richards, J. P. (Wolverhampton W), 1977 v Fi, N (2)
Rideout, P. (Aston Villa), 1985 v Fi, Is, Ei (sub), R; (with Bari), 1986 v D (5)
Ripley, S. (Middlesbrough), 1988 v USSR, F (sub); 1989 v D (sub), Se, Gr, Alb (2); 1990 v Se (8)
Ritchie, A. (Brighton & HA), 1982 v Pol (1)
Rix, G. (Arsenal), 1978 v Fi (sub), Y; 1979 v D, Se; 1980 v D (sub), Bul, S (7)
Robins, M. G. (Manchester U), 1990 v P, F, USSR, Cz; 1991 v H (sub), Pol (6)
Robson, B. (WBA), 1979 v W, Bul (sub), Se; 1980 v D, Bul, S (2) (7)
Robson, S. (Arsenal), 1984 v I; 1985 v Fi, Is, Fi; 1986 v R, I (6)
Robson, S. (West Ham U), 1988 v S, Sw (2)
Rocastle, D. (Arsenal), 1987 v Se, Y, Sp, T; 1988 v WG, T, Y, S (2), F (2 subs), M, USSR, Mor (14)
Rodger, G. (Coventry C), 1987 v USSR, F, P; 1988 v WG (4)
Rosario, R. (Norwich C), 1987 v T (sub), Mor, F, P (sub)jy(4)
Rowell, G. (Sunderland), 1977 v Fi (1)
Ruddock, N. (Southampton), 1989 v Bul (sub), Sen, Ei, US (4)
Ryan, J. (Oldham Ath), 1983 v H (1)

Samways, V. (Tottenham H), 1988 v Sw (sub); USSR, F; 1989 v D, Se (5)
Sansom, K. G. (C Palace), 1979 v D, W, Bul, Se; 1980 v S (2), EG (2) (8)
Seaman, D. (Birmingham C), 1985 v Fi, T, Is, Ei, R, Fi; 1986 v R, F, D, I (10)
Sedgley, S. (Coventry C), 1987 v USSR, F (sub), P; 1988 v F; 1989 v D (sub), Se, Gr, Alb (2), Pol; (with Tottenham H), 1990 v Se (11)
Sellars, S. (Blackburn R), 1988 v S (sub), F, Sw (3)
Selley, I. (Arsenal), 1994 v Ru (sub), F (sub), US (3)
Sharpe, L. (Manchester U), 1989 v Gr; 1990 v P (sub), F, USSR, Cz; 1991 v H, Pol (sub), Ei (8)
Shaw, G. R. (Aston Villa), 1981 v Ei, Sw, H; 1982 v H, S; 1983 v WG (2) (7)
Shearer, A. (Southampton), 1991 v Ei (2), W, T, Sen, M, USSR, F; 1992 v G, T, Pol (11)

Shelton, G. (Sheffield W), 1985 v Fi (1)
Sheringham, T. (Millwall), 1988 v Sw (1)
Sheron, M. N. (Manchester C), 1992 v H, F; 1993 v N (sub), T (sub), Sm, Ho, Pol, N; 1994 v Pol (sub), Ho, Sm (11)
Sherwood, T. A. (Norwich C), 1990 v P, F, USSR, Cz (4)
Shipperley, N. J. (Chelsea), 1994 v Sm (sub) (1)
Simpson, P. (Manchester C), 1986 v D (sub); 1987 v Y, Mor, F, P (5)
Sims, S. (Leicester C), 1977 v W, S, Fi, N; 1978 v N, Fi, I (2), Y (2) (10)
Sinclair, F. M. (Chelsea), 1994 v Ho, Sm, D, Ru, F, US, Bel, P (8)
Sinnott, L. (Watford), 1985 v Is (sub) (1)
Slater, S. I. (West Ham U), 1990 v P, USSR (sub), Cz (sub) (3)
Small, B. (Aston Villa), 1993 v Sm, T, Ho, Pol, N; 1994 v Pol, Sm (7)
Smith, D. (Coventry C), 1988 v M, USSR (sub), Mor; 1989 v D, Se, Alb (2), Pol; 1990 v Se, Pol (10)
Smith, M. (Sheffield W), 1981 v Ei, R, Sw, H; 1982 v Pol (sub) (5)
Snodin, I. (Doncaster R), 1985 v T, Is, R, Fi (4)
Statham, B. (Tottenham H), 1988 v Sw; 1989 v D (sub), Se (3)
Statham, D. J. (WBA), 1978 v Fi, 1979 v W, Bul, Se; 1980 v D; 1983 v D (6)
Stein, B. (Luton T), 1984 v D, H, I (3)
Sterland, M. (Sheffield W), 1984 v D, H, F (2), I. Sp (2) (7)
Steven, T. (Everton), 1985 v Fi, T (2)
Stevens, G. (Brighton & HA), 1983 v H; (with Tottenham H), 1984 v H, F (1 + 1 sub), I (sub), Sp (1 + 1 sub); 1986 v I (8)
Stewart, P. (Manchester C), 1988 v F (1)
Stuart, G. C. (Chelsea), 1990 v P (sub), F, USSR, Cz; 1991 v T (sub) (5)
Suckling, P. (Coventry C), 1986 v D; (with Manchester C), 1987 v Se (sub), Y, Sp, T; (with C Palace), 1988 v S (2), F (2), Sw (10)
Sunderland, A. (Wolverhampton W), 1977 v W (1)
Sutton, C. R. (Norwich), 1993 v Sp (sub), T (sub), T, Ho; 1994 v Pol, Ho, Sm, D (8)
Swindlehurst, D. (C Palace), 1977 v W (1)
Sutch, D. (Norwich C), 1992 v H, M, Cz; 1993 v T (4)

Talbot, B. (Ipswich T), 1977 v W (1)
Thomas, D. (Coventry C), 1981 v Ei; 1983 v WG (2), Gr, H; (with Tottenham H), v I, Sp (7)
Thomas, M. (Luton T), 1986 v T, D, I (3)
Thomas, M. (Arsenal), 1988 v Y, S, F (2), M, USSR, Mor; 1989 v Gr, Alb (2), Pol; 1990 v Se (12)
Thomas, R. E. (Watford), 1990 v P (1)
Thompson, G. L. (Coventry C), 1981 v R, Sw, H; 1982 v N, H, S (6)
Thorn, A. (Wimbledon), 1988 v WG (sub). Y, S, F, Sw (5)
Tiler, C. (Barnsley), 1990 v P, USSR, Cz; 1991 v H, Pol, Ei (2), T, Sen, USSR, F; (with Nottingham F), 1992 v G, T (13)

Venison, B. (Sunderland), 1983 v D, Gr; 1985 v Fi, T, Is, Fi; 1986 v R, T, D (2) (10)
Vinnicombe, C. (Rangers), 1991 v H (sub), Pol, Ei (2), T, Sen, M, USSR (sub), F; 1992 v G, T, Pol (12)

Waddle, C. (Newcastle U), 1985 v Fi (1)
Wallace, D. (Southampton), 1983 v Gr, H; 1984 v D, H, F (2), I, Sp (sub); 1985 v Fi, T, Is; 1986 v R, D, I (14)
Wallace, Ray (Southampton), 1989 v Bul, Sen (sub), Ei; 1990 v Se (4)
Wallace, Rod (Southampton), 1989 v Bul, Ei (sub), US; 1991 v H, Pol, Ei, T, Sen, M, USSR, F (11)
Walker, D. (Nottingham F), 1985 v Fi; 1987 v Se, T; 1988 v WG, T, S (2) (7)
Walker, I. M. (Tottenham H), 1991 v W; 1992 v H, Cz, F; 1993 v Sp, N, T, Sm; 1994 v Pol (9)
Walsh, G. (Manchester U), 1988 v WG, Y (2)
Walsh, P. M. (Luton T), 1983 v D (sub), Gr (2), H (4)
Walters, K. (Aston Villa), 1984 v D (sub). H (sub); 1985 v Is, Ei, R; 1986 v R, T, D, I (sub) (9)
Ward, P. D. (Brighton & HA), 1978 v N; 1980 v EG (2)
Warhurst, P. (Oldham Ath), 1991 v H, Pol, W, Sen, M (sub), USSR, F (sub); (with Sheffield W), 1992 v G (8)
Watson, D. (Norwich C), 1984 v D, F (2), I (2), Sp (2) (7)
Watson, D. N. (Barnsley), 1994 v Ho, Sm (2)
Watson, G. (Sheffield W), 1991 v Sen, USSR (2)
Watson, S. C. (Newcastle U), 1993 v Sp (sub), N; 1994 v Sm (sub), D (4)
Webb, N. (Portsmouth), 1985 v Ei; (with Nottingham F), 1986 v D (2) (3)
Whelan, P. J. (Ipswich T), 1993 v Sp, T (sub) (2)
White, D. (Manchester C), 1988 v S (2), F, USSR; 1989 v Se; 1990 v Pol (6)
Whyte, C. (Arsenal), 1982 v S (1 + 1 sub); 1983 v D, Gr (4)
Wicks, S. (QPR), 1982 v S (1)
Wilkins, R. C. (Chelsea), 1977 v W (1)
Wilkinson, P. (Grimsby T), 1985 v Ei, R (sub); (with Everton), 1986 v R (sub), I (4)
Williams, P. (Charlton Ath), 1989 v Bul, Sen, Ei, US (sub) (4)
Williams, P. D. (Derby Co), 1991 v Sen, M, USSR; 1992 v G, T, Pol (6)
Williams, S. C. (Southampton); 1977 v S, Fi, N; 1978 v N, I (1 pl sub), Y (2); 1979 v D, Bul, Se (sub); 1980 v D, EG (2) (14)
Winterburn, N. (Wimbledon), 1986 v I (1)
Wise, D. (Wimbledon), 1988 v Sw (1)
Woodcook, A. S. (Nottingham F), 1978 v Fi, I (2)
Woods, C. C. E. (Nottingham F), 1979 v W (sub). Se; (with QPR), 1980 v Bul, EG; 1981 v Sw; (with Norwich C), 1984 v D (6)
Wright, A. G. (Blackburn), 1993 v Sp, N (2)
Wright, M. (Southampton), 1983 v Gr, H; 1984 v D, H (4)
Wright, W. (Everton), 1979 v D, W, Bul; 1980 v D, S (2) (6)

Yates, D. (Notts Co), 1989 v D (sub), Bul, Sen, Ei, US (5)

SCOTLAND

Aitken, R. (Celtic), 1977 v Cz, W, Sw; 1978 v Cz, W; 1979 v P, N (2); 1980 v Bel, E; 1984 v EG, Y (2); 1985 v WG, Ic, Sp (16)
Albiston, A. (Manchester U), 1977 v Cz, W, Sw; 1978 v Sw, Cz (5)
Archdeacon, O. (Celtic), 1987 v WG (sub) (1)
Archibald, S. (Aberdeen), 1980 v B, E (2), WG; (with Tottenham H), 1981 v D (5)

Bain, K. (Dundee), 1993 v P, I, Ma, P (4)
Baker, M. (St. Mirren), 1993 v F, M, E; 1994 v Ma, A (5)
Bannon, E. J. P. (Hearts), 1979 v US, (with Chelsea), P, N (2); (with Dundee U), 1980 v Bel, WG, E (7)
Beattie, J. (St Mirren), 1992 v D, US, P, Y (4)
Beaumont, D. (Dundee U), 1985 v Ic (1)
Bell, D. (Aberdeen), 1981 v D; 1984 v Y (2)
Bernard, P. R. J. (Oldham Ath), 1992 v R (sub), D, Se (sub), US; 1993 v Sw, P, I, Ma, P, F, Bul, M, E; 1994 v I, Ma (15)
Bett, J. (Rangers), 1981 v Se, D; 1982 v Se, D, I, E (2) (7)

Black, E. (Aberdeen), 1983 v EG, Sw (2), Bel; 1985 v Ic, Sp (2), Ic (8)
Blair, A. (Coventry C), 1980 v E; 1981 v Se; (with Aston Villa), 1982 v Se, D, I (5)
Bollan, G. (Dundee U), 1992 v D, G (sub), US, P, Y; 1993 v Sw, P, I, P, F, Bul, M, E; 1994 v Sw (14)
Booth, S. (Aberdeen), 1991 v R (sub), Bul (sub pl 1), Pol, F (sub); 1992 v Sw, R, D, Se, US, P, Y; 1993 v Ma, P (14)
Bowes, M. J. (Dunfermline Ath), 1992 v D (sub) (1)
Bowman, D. (Hearts), 1985 v WG (sub) (1)
Boyd, T. (Motherwell), 1987 v WG, Ei (2), Bel; 1988 v Bel (5)
Brazil, A. (Hibernian), 1978 v W (1)
Brazil, A. (Ipswich T), 1979 v N; 1980 v Bel (2), E (2), WG; 1981 v Se; 1982 v Se (8)
Brough, J. (Hearts), 1981 v D (1)
Burley, G. E. (Ipswich T), 1977 v Cz, W, Sw; 1978 v Sw, Cz (5)
Burley, C. (Chelsea), 1992 v D; 1993 v Sw, P, I, P; 1994 v Sw, I (sub) (7)
Burns, H. (Rangers), 1985 v Sp, Ic (sub) (2)
Burns, T. (Celtic), 1977 v Cz, W, E; 1978 v Sw; 1982 v E (5)

Campbell, S. (Dundee), 1989 v N (sub), Y, F (3)
Casey, J. (Celtic), 1978 v W (1)
Christie, M. (Dundee), 1992 v D, P (sub), Y (3)
Clark, R. (Aberdeen), 1977 v Cz, W, Sw (3)
Clarke, S. (St Mirren), 1984 v Bel, EG, Y; 1985 v WG, Ic, Sp (2), Ic (8)
Cleland, A. (Dundee U), 1990 v F, N (2); 1991 v R, Sw, Bul; 1992 v Sw, R, G, Se (2) (11)
Collins, J. (Hibernian), 1988 v Bel, E; 1989 v N, Y, F; 1990 v Y, F, N (8)
Connolly, P. (Dundee U), 1991 v R (sub), Sw, Bul (3)
Connor, R. (Ayr U), 1981 v Se; 1982 v Se (2)
Cooper, D. (Clydebank), 1977 v Cz, W, Sw, E; (with Rangers), 1978 v Sw, Cz (6)
Cooper, N. (Aberdeen), 1982 v D, E (2); 1983 v Bel, EG, Sw (2); 1984 v Bel, EG, Y; 1985 v Ic, Sp, Ic (13)
Crabbe, S. (Hearts), 1990 v Y (sub), F (2)
Craig, T. (Newcastle U), 1977 v E (1)
Crainie, D. (Celtic), 1983 v Sw (sub) (1)
Crawford, S. (Raith R), 1994 v A, Eg, P, Bel (4)
Creaney, G. (Celtic), 1991 v Sw, Bul (2), Pol, F; 1992 v Sw, R, G (2), Se (2) (11)

Dailly, C. (Dundee U), 1991 v R; 1992 v US, R; 1993 v Sw, P, I, Ic, P, F, Bul, M, E; 1994 v Sw, I, Ma, A, Eg, P, Bel (19)
Dawson, A. (Rangers), 1979 v P, N (2); 1980 v B (2), E (2) WG (8)
Deas, P. A. (St Johnstone), 1992 v D (sub); 1993 v Ma (2)
Dennis, S. (Raith R), 1992 v Sw (1)
Dickov, P. (Arsenal), 1992 v Y; 1993 v F, M, E (4)
Dodds, D. (Dundee U), 1978 v W (1)
Donald, G. S. (Hibernian), 1992 v US (sub), P, Y (sub) (3)
Donnelly, S. (Celtic), 1994 v Eg, P, Bel (3)
Dow, A. (Dundee), 1993 v Ma (sub), Ic; (with Chelsea) 1994 v I (3)
Duffy, J. (Dundee), 1987 v Ei (1)
Durie, G. S. (Chelsea), 1987 v WG, Ei, Bel; 1988 v Bel (4)
Durrant, I. (Rangers), 1987 v WG, Ei, Bel; 1988 v E (4)
Doyle, J. (Partick Th), 1981 v D, I (sub) (2)

Ferguson, D. (Rangers), 1987 v WG, Ei, Bel; 1988 v E; 1990 v Y (5)
Ferguson, D. (Dundee U), 1992 v D, G, Se (2); 1993 v Sw, I, Ma (7)
Ferguson, D. (Manchester U), 1992 v US, P (sub), Y; 1993 v Sw, Ma (5)
Ferguson, I. (Dundee), 1983 v EG (sub), Sw (sub); 1984 v Bel (sub), EG (4)
Ferguson, I. (Clyde), 1987 v WG (sub), Ei (with St Mirren), Ei, Bel; 1988 v Bel; (with Rangers), E (sub) (6)
Ferguson, R. (Hamilton A), 1977 v E (1)
Findlay, W. (Hibernian), 1991 v R, Pol, Bul (2), Pol (5)
Fitzpatrick, A. (St Mirren), 1977 v W (sub), Sw (sub), E; 1978 v Sw, Cz (5)
Flannigan, C. (Clydebank), 1993 v Ic (sub) (1)
Fleck, R. (Rangers), 1987 v WG (sub), Ei, Bel; (with Norwich C), 1988 v E (2); 1989 v Y (6)
Fridge, L. (St Mirren), 1989 v F; 1990 v Y (2)
Fullarton, J. (St. Mirren), 1993 v F, Bul; 1994 v Ma, A, Eg, P, Bel (7)
Fulton, M. (St Mirren), 1980 v Bel, WG, E; 1981 v Se, D (sub)
Fulton, S. (Celtic), 1991 v R, Sw, Bul, Pol, F; 1992 v G (2) (7)

Gallacher, K. (Dundee U), 1987 v WG, Ei (2), Bel (sub); 1988 v E (2); 1990 v Y (7)
Galloway, M. (Hearts), 1989 v F; (with Celtic), 1990 v N (2)
Gardiner, J. (Hibernian), 1993 v F (1)
Geddes, R. (Dundee), 1982 v Se, D, E (2); 1988 v E (5)
Gemmill, S. (Nottingham F), 1992 v Sw, R (sub), G (sub), Se (sub) (4)
Gillespie, G. (Coventry C), 1979 v US; 1980 v E; 1981 v D; 1982 v Se, D, I (2), E (8)
Glover, L. (Nottingham F), 1988 v Bel (sub); 1989 v N; 1990 v Y (3)
Goram, A. (Oldham Ath), 1987 v Ei (1)
Gough, C. R. (Dundee U), 1983 v EG, Sw, Bel; 1984 v Y (2) (5)
Grant, P. (Celtic), 1985 v WG, Ic, Sp; 1987 v WG, Ei (2), Bel; 1988 v Bel, E (2) (10)
Gunn, B. (Aberdeen), 1984 v EG, Y (2); 1985 v WG, Ic, Sp (2), Ic; 1990 v F (9)
Gray, S. (Aberdeen), 1987 v WG (1)

Hagen, D. (Rangers), 1992 v D (sub), US (sub), P, Y; 1993 v Sw (sub), P, Ic, P (8)
Hamilton, B. (St Mirren), 1989 v Y, F (sub); 1990 v F, N (4)
Handyside, P. (Grimsby T), 1993 V Ic (sub), Bul, M, E (4)
Hannagh, D. (Dundee U), 1993 v F (sub), Bul, M; 1994 v A, Eg, P, Bel (7)
Hartford, R. A. (Manchester C), 1977 v Sw (1)
Hegarty, P. (Dundee U), 1987 v WG, Bel; 1988 v E (2); 1990 v F, N (4)
Hendry, J. (Tottenham H), 1992 v D (sub) (1)
Hewitt, J. (Aberdeen), 1982 v I; 1983 v EG, Sw (2); 1984 v Bel, Y (sub) (6)
Hogg, G. (Manchester U), 1984 v Y; 1985 v WG, Ic, Sp (4)
Hood, G. (Ayr U), 1993 v F, E (sub); 1994 v A (3)
Howie, S. (Cowdenbeath), 1993 v Ma, Ic, P; 1994 v Sw, I (5)
Hunter, G. (Hibernian), 1987 v Ei (sub); 1988 v Bel, E (3)
Hunter, P. (East Fife), 1989 v N (sub), F (sub); 1990 v F (sub) (3)

Jardine, I. (Kilmarnock), 1979 v US (1)
Jess, E. (Aberdeen), 1990 v F (sub), N (sub); 1991 v R, Sw, Bul (2), Pol, F; 1992 v Sw, R, G (2), Se (1 + sub) (14)
Johnson, G. I. (Dundee U), 1992 v US, P, Y (3)
Johnson, I (Dundee U), 1993 v Sw, P, Ma (3)
Johnston, A. (Hearts), 1994 v Bel (1)
Johnston, F. (Falkirk), 1993 v Ic (1)

Johnston, M. (Partick Th), 1984 v EG (sub); (with Watford), Y (2) (3)

Kirkwood, D. (Hearts), 1990 v Y (1)
Kerr, S. (Celtic), 1993 v Bul, M, E; 1994 v Ma, A, Eg, P, Bel (8)

Lambert, P. (St Mirren), 1991 v R, Sw, Bul (2), Pol, F; 1992 v Sw, R, G (2), Se (11)
Lavety, B. (St. Mirren), 1993 v Ic, Bul (sub), M (sub), E; 1994 v Ma, A (sub), Eg (sub), Bel (sub) (8)
Lavin, G. (Watford), 1993 v F, Bul, M; 1994 v Ma, Eg, P, Bel (7)
Leighton, J. (Aberdeen), 1982 v I (1)
Levein, C. (Hearts), 1985 v Sp, Ic (2)
Liddell, A. M. (Barnsley), 1994 v Ma (sub) (1)
Lindsey, J. (Motherwell), 1979 v US (1)
Locke, G. (Hearts), 1994 v Ma, A, Eg, P (4)

McAllister, G. (Leicester C), 1990 v N (1)
McAlpine, H. (Dundee U), 1983 v EG, Sw (2), Bel; 1984 v Bel (5)
McAuley, S. (St. Johnstone), 1993 v P (sub) (1)
McAvennie, F. (St Mirren), 1982 v I, E; 1985 v Is, Ei, R (5)
McBride, J. (Everton), 1981 v D (1)
McCall, S. (Bradford C), 1988 v E; (with Everton), 1990 v F (2)
McCann, N. (Dundee), 1994 v A, Eg, P, Bel (4)
McClair, B. (Celtic), 1984 v Bel (sub), EG, Y (1 pl sub); 1985 v WG, Ic, Sp, Ic (8)
McCluskey, G. (Celtic), 1979 v US, P; 1980 v Bel, (2); 1982 vD,I(6)
McCoist, A. (Rangers), 1984 v Bel (1)
McCulloch, A. (Kilmarnock); 1981 v Se (1)
McCulloch, I. (Notts Co), 1982 v E (2)
MacDonald, J. (Rangers), 1980 v WG (sub); 1981 v Se; 1982 v Se (sub), L, I (2), E (2 sub) (8)
McGarvey, F. (St Mirren), 1977 v E; 1978 v Cz; (with Celtic), 1982 v D (3)
McGarvey, S. (Manchester U), 1982 v E (sub); 1983 v Bel, Sw; 1984 v Bel (4)
McGhee, M. (Aberdeen), 1981 v D (1)
McGinnis, G. (Dundee U), 1985 v Sp (1)
McGrillen, P. (Motherwell), 1994 v Sw (sub), I (2)
McInally, J. (Dundee U), 1989 v F (1)
McKimmie, S. (Aberdeen), 1985 v WG, Ic (2) (3)
McKinlay, T. (Dundee), 1984 v EG (sub); 1985 v WG, Ic, Sp (2), Ic (6)
McKinlay, W. (Dundee U), 1989 v N, Y (sub), F; 1990 v Y, F, N (6)
McKinnon, R. (Dundee U), 1991 v R, Pol (sub); 1992 v G (2), Se (2) (6)
McLaren, A, (Hearts), 1989 v F; 1990 v Y, N; 1991 v Sw, Bul, Pol, F; 1992 v R, G, Se (2) (11)
McLaren, A. (Dundee U), 1993 v I, Ma (sub); 1994 v Sw, I (sub) (4)
McLaughlin, J. (Morton), 1981 v D; 1982 v Se, D, I, E (2); 1983 v EG, Sw (2), Bel (10)
McLeish, A. (Aberdeen), 1978 v W; 1979 v US; 1980 v Bel, E (2); 1987 v Ei (6)
MacLeod, A. (Hibernian), 1979 v P, N (2) (3)
McLeod, J. (Dundee U), 1989 v N; 1990 v F (2)
MacLeod, M. (Dumbarton), 1979 v US; (with Celtic), P (sub), N (2); 1980 v Bel (5)
McNab, N. (Tottenham H), 1978 v W (1)
McNally, M. (Celtic), 1991 v Bul; 1993 v Ic (2)
McNamara, J. (Dunfermline Ath), 1994 v A, Bel (2)
McNichol, J. (Brentford), 1979 v P. N (2); 1980 v Bel (2), WG, E (7)
McNiven, D. (Leeds U), 1977 v Cz, W (sub), Sw (sub) (3)

McPherson, D. (Rangers), 1984 v Bel; 1985 v Sp; (with Hearts), 1989 v N, Y (4)
McQuilken, J. (Celtic), 1993 v Bul, E (2)
McStay, P. (Celtic), 1983 v EG, Sw (2); 1984 v Y (2) (5)
McWhirter, N. (St Mirren), 1991 v Bul (sub) (1)
Main, A. (Dundee U), 1988 v E; 1989 v Y; 1990 v N (3)
Malpas, M. (Dundee U), 1983 v Bel, Sw (1 + 1 sub); 1984 v Bel, EG, Y (2); 1985 v Sp (8)
May, E. (Hibernian), 1989 v Y (sub), F (2)
Melrose, J. (Partick Th), 1977 v Sw; 1979 v US, P, N (2); 1980 v Bel (sub), WG, E (8)
Miller J. (Aberdeen, 1987 v Ei (sub); 1988 v Bel; (with Celtic) E; 1989 v N, Y; 1990 v F, N (7)
Miller, W. (Aberdeen), 1978 v Sw, Cz (2)
Miller, W. (Hibernian), 1991 v R, Sw, Bul, Pol, F; 1992 v R, G (sub) (7)
Milne, R. (Dundee U), 1982 v Se (sub); 1984 v Bel, EG (3)
Money, I. C. (St Mirren), 1987 v Ei; 1988 v Bel; 1989 v N (3)
Muir, L. (Hibernian), 1977 v Cz (sub) (1)
Murray, N. (Rangers), 1993 v P (sub), Ma, Ic, P; 1994 v Sw, I (6)
Murray, R. (Bournemouth), 1993 v Ic (sub) (1)

Narey, D. (Dundee U), 1977 v Cz, Sw; 1978 v Sw, Cz (4)
Nevin, P. (Chelsea), 1985 v WG, Ic, Sp (2), Ic (5)
Nicholas, C. (Celtic), 1981 v Se; 1982 v Se; 1983 v EG, Sw, Bel; (with Arsenal), 1984 v Y (6)
Nicol, S. (Ayr U), 1981 v Se; 1982 v Se, D; (with Liverpool), 1982 v I (2), E (2); 1983 v EG, Sw (2), Bel; 1984 v Bel, EG, Y (14)
Nisbet, S. (Rangers), 1989 v N, Y, F; 1990 v Y, F (5)

O'Donnell, P. (Motherwell), 1992 v Sw (sub), R, D, G (2), Se (1 + sub); 1993 v P (8)
O'Neil, B. (Celtic), 1992 v D, G, Se (2); 1993 v Sw, P, I (7)
O'Neil, J. (Dundee U), 1991 v Bul (sub) (1)
Orr, N. (Morton), 1978 v W (sub); 1979 v US, P, N (2); 1980 v Bel, E (7)

Parlane, D. (Rangers), 1977 v W (1)
Paterson, C. (Hibernian), 1981 v Se; 1982 v I (2)
Payne, G. (Dundee U), 1978 v Sw, Cz, W (3)
Pressley, S. (Rangers), 1993 v Ic, F, Bul, M, E; 1994 v Sw, I, M, A, Eg, P, Bel (12)
Provan, D. (Kilmarnock), 1977 v Cz (sub) (1)

Rae, A. (Millwall), 1991 v Bul (sub pl 1), F (sub); 1992 v Sw, R, G (sub), Se (2) (8)
Redford, I. (Rangers), 1981 v Se (sub); 1982 v Se, D, I (2), E (6)
Reid, B. (Rangers), 1991 v F; 1992 v D, US, P (4)
Reid, C. (Hibernian), 1993 v Sw, P, I (3)
Reid, M. (Celtic), 1982 v E; 1984 v Y (2)
Reid, R. (St Mirren), 1977 v W, Sw, E (3)
Rice, B. (Hibernian), 1985 v WG (1)
Richardson, L. (St Mirren), 1980 v WG, E (sub) (2)
Ritchie, A. (Morton), 1980 v Bel (1)
Robertson, A. (Rangers) 1991 v F (1)
Robertson, C. (Rangers), 1977 v E (sub) (1)
Robertson, D. (Aberdeen), 1987 v Ei (sub); 1988 v E (2); 1989 v N, Y; 1990 v Y, N (7)
Robertson, H. (Aberdeen), 1994 v Eg (1)
Robertson, J. (Hearts), 1985 v WG, Ic (sub) (2)
Robertson, L. (Rangers), 1993 v F, M (sub), E (sub) (3)
Roddie, A. (Aberdeen), 1992 v US, P; 1993 v Sw (sub), P, Ic (5)
Ross, T. W. (Arsenal), 1977 v W (1)
Russell, R. (Rangers), 1978 v W; 1980 v Bel; 1984 v Y (3)

Salton, D. B. (Luton T), 1992 v D, US, P, Y; 1993 v Sw, I (6)
Scott, P. (St Johnstone), 1994 v A (sub), Eg (sub), P, Bel (4)
Shannon, R. (Dundee), 1987 v WG, Ei (2), Bel; 1988 v Bel, E (2) (7)
Sharp, G. (Everton), 1982 v E (1)
Sharp, R. (Dunfermline Ath), 1990 v N (sub); 1991 v R, Sw, Bul (4)
Simpson, N. (Aberdeen), 1982 v I (2), E; 1983 v EG, Sw (2), Bel; 1984 v Bel, EG, Y; 1985 v Sp (11)
Sinclair, G. (Dumbarton), 1977 v E (1)
Skilling, M. (Kilmarnock), 1993 v Ic (sub); 1994 v I (2)
Smith, B. M. (Celtic), 1992 v G (2), US, P, Y (5)
Smith, G. (Rangers), 1978 v W (1)
Smith, H. G. (Hearts), 1987 v WG, Bel (2)
Sneddon, A. (Celtic), 1979 v US (1)
Speedie, D. (Chelsea), 1985 v Sp (1)
Spencer, J. (Rangers), 1991 v Sw (sub), F; 1992 v Sw (3)
Stanton, P. (Hibernian), 1977 v Cz (1)
Stark, W. (Aberdeen), 1985 v Ic (1)
Stephen, R. (Dundee), 1983 v Bel (sub) (1)
Stevens, G. (Motherwell), 1977 v E (1)
Stewart, J. (Kilmarnock), 1978 v Sw, Cz; (with Middlesbrough), 1979 v P (3)
Stewart, R. (Dundee U), 1979 v P, N (2); (with West Ham U), 1980 v Bel (2), E (2), WG; 1981 v D; 1982 v I (2), E (12)
Strachan, G. (Aberdeen), 1980 v Bel (1)
Sturrock, P. (Dundee U), 1977 v Cz, W, Sw, E; 1978 v Sw, Cz; 1982 v Se, I, E (9)
Sweeney, S. (Clydebank), 1991 v R, Sw (sub), Bul (2), Pol; 1992 v Sw, R (7)

Telfer, P. (Luton T), 1993 v Ma, P; 1994 v Sw (3)
Thomas, K. (Hearts), 1993 v F (sub), Bul, M, E; 1994 v Sw, Ma (6)
Thomson, W. (Partick Th), 1977 v E (sub); 1978 v W; (with St Mirren), 1979 v US, N (2); 1980 v Bel (2), E (2), WG (10)
Tolmie, J. (Morton), 1980 v Bel (sub) (1)
Tortolano, J. (Hibernian), 1987 v WG, Ei (2)
Tweed, S. (Hibernian), 1993 v Ic; 1994 v Sw, I (3)

Walker, A. (Celtic), 1988 v Bel (1)
Wallace, I. (Coventry C), 1978 v Sw (1)
Walsh, C. (Nottingham F), 1984 v EG, Sw (2). Bel; 1984 v EG (5)
Wark, J. (Ipswich T), 1977 v Cz, W, Sw; 1978 v W; 1979 v P; 1980 v E (2), WG (8)
Watson, A. (Aberdeen), 1981 v Se, D; 1982 v D, I (sub) (4)
Watson, K. (Rangers), 1977 v E; 1978 v Sw (sub) (2)
Watt, M. (Aberdeen), 1991 v R, Sw, Bul (2), Pol, F; 1992 v Sw, R, G (2), Se (2) (12)
Whyte, D. (Celtic), 1987 v Ei (2), Bel; 1988 v E (2); 1989 v N, Y; 1990 v Y, N (9)
Will, J. A. (Arsenal), 1992 v D (sub), Y; 1993 v Ic (sub) (3)
Wilson, T. (St Mirren), 1983 v Sw (sub) (1)
Wilson, T. (Nottingham F), 1988 v E; 1989 v N, Y; 1990 v F (4)
Winnie, D. (St Mirren), 1988 v Bel (1)
Wright, P. (Aberdeen), 1989 v Y, F; (with QPR), 1990 v Y (sub) (3)
Wright, S. (Aberdeen), 1991 v Bul, Pol, F; 1992 v Sw, G (2), Se (2); 1993 v Sw, P, I, Ma; 1994 v I, Ma (14)
Wright, T. (Oldham Ath), 1987 v Bel (sub) (1)

WALES

Aizlewood, M. (Luton T), 1979 v E; 1981 v Ho (2)

Balcombe, S. (Leeds Y), 1982 v F (sub) (1)
Bater, P. T. (Bristol R), 1977 v E, S (2)
Bird, A. (Cardiff C), 1993 v Cy (sub); 1994 v Cy (sub) (2)
Blackmore, C. (Manchester U), 1984 v N, Bul, Y (3)
Blake, N. (Cardiff C), 1991 v Pol (sub); 1993 v Cy, Bel, RCS; 1994 v RCS (5)
Bodin, P. (Cardiff C), 1983 v Y (1)
Bowen, J. P. (Swansea C), 1993 v Cy, Bel (2); 1994 v RCS, R (sub) (5)
Bowen, M. (Tottenham H), 1983 v N; 1984 v Bul, Y (3)
Boyle, T. (C Palace), 1982 v F (1)

Cegielski, W. (Wrexham), 1977 v E (sub), S (2)
Chapple, S. R. (Swansea C), 1992 v R; 1993 v Cy, Bel (2), RCS; 1994 v RCS (6)
Charles, J. M. (Swansea C), 1979 v E; 1981 v Ho (2)
Clark, J. (Manchester U), 1978 v S; (with Derby Co), 1979 v E (2)
Coleman, C. (Swansea C); 1990 v Pol; 1991 v E, Pol (3)
Coyne, D. (Tranmere R), 1992 v R; 1994 v Cy (sub), R (3)
Curtis, A. T. (Swansea C), 1977 v E (1)

Davies, A. (Manchester U), 1982 v F (2) Ho; 1983 v N, Y, Bul (6)
Davies, G. M. (Hereford U), 1993 v Bel, RCS (2)
Davies, I. C. (Norwich C), 1978 v S (sub) (1)
Deacy, N. (PSV Eindhoven), 1977 v S (1)
Dibble, A. (Cardiff C), 1983 v Bul; 1984 v N, Bul (3)
Doyle, S. C. (Preston NE), 1979 v E (sub); (with Huddersfield T), 1984 v N (2)
Dwyer, P. J. (Cardiff C), 1979 v E (1)

Ebdon, M. (Everton), 1990 v Pol; 1991 v E (2)
Edwards, R. (Bristol C.), 1991 v Pol; 1992 v R (2)
Edwards, R. I. (Chester), 1977 v S; 1978 v W (2)
Edwards, R. W. (Bristol C), 1993 v Cy, Bel (2), RCS; 1994 v RCS, Cy, R (7)
Evans, A. (Bristol R), 1977 v E (1)

Foster, M. G. (Tranmere R), 1993 v RCS (1)
Freestone, R. (Chelsea), 1990 v Pol (1)

Gale, D. (Swansea C), 1983 v Bul; 1984 v N (sub) (2)
Giggs, R. (Manchester U), 1991 v Pol (1)
Giles, D. C. (Cardiff C), 1977 v S; 1978 v S; (with Swansea C), 1981 v Ho; (with C. Palace), 1983 v Y (4)
Giles, P. (Cardiff C), 1982 v F (2), Ho (3)
Graham, D. (Manchester U.), 1991 v E (1)
Griffith, C. (Cardiff C), 1990 v Pol (1)
Griffiths, C. (Shrewsbury T), 1991 v Pol (sub) (1)

Hall, G. D. (Chelsea), 1990 v Pol (1)
Hartson, J. (Luton T), 1994 v Cy, R (2)
Hodges, G. (Wimbledon), 1983 v Y (sub), Bul (sub); 1984 v N, Bul, Y (5)
Holden, A. (Chester C), 1984 v Y (sub) (1)
Hopkins, J. (Fulham), 1982 v F (sub), Ho; 1983 v N, Y, Bul (5)
Hughes, D. R. (Southampton), 1994 v R (1)
Hughes, I. (Bury), 1992 v R; 1993 v Cy, Bel (sub), RCS; 1994 v Cy, R (6)
Hughes, M. (Manchester U), 1983 v N, Y; 1984 v N. Bul, Y (5)
Hughes, W. (WBA), 1977 v E, S; 1978 v S (3)

Jackett, K. (Watford), 1981 v Ho; 1982 v F (2)
James, R. M. (Swansea C), 1977 v E, S; 1978 v S (3)
Jenkins, S. R. (Swansea C), 1993 v Cy (sub), Bel (2)
Jones, F. (Wrexham), 1981 v Ho (1)
Jones, L. (Cardiff C), 1982 v F (2), Ho (3)
Jones, P. L. (Liverpool), 1992 v R; 1993 v Cy, Bel (2), RCS; 1994 v RCS (sub), Cy, R (8)

Jones, R. (Sheffield W), 1994 v R (1)
Jones, V. (Bristol R), 1979 v E; 1981 v Ho (2)

Kendall, M. (Tottenham H), 1978 v S (1)
Kenworthy, J. R. (Tranmere R), 1994 v Cy (1)

Law, B. J. (QPR), 1990 v Pol; 1991 v E (2)
Letheran, G. (Leeds U), 1977 v E, S (2)
Lewis, D. (Swansea C), 1982 v F (2), Ho; 1983 v N, Y, Bul; 1984 v N, Bul, Y (9)
Lewis, J. (Cardiff C), 1983 v N (1)
Loveridge, J. (Swansea C), 1982 v Ho; 1983 v N, Bul (3)
Lowndes, S. R. (Newport Co), 1979 v E; 1981 v Ho; (with Millwall), 1984 v Bul, Y (4)

McCarthy, A. J. (QPR), 1994 v RCS, Cy, R (3)
Maddy, P. (Cardiff C), 1982 v Ho; 1983 v N (sub) (2)
Margetson, M. W. (Manchester C), 1992 v R; 1993 v Cy, Bel (2), RCS; 1994 v RCS, Cy (7)
Marustik, C. (Swansea C), 1982 v F (2); 1983 v Y, Bul; 1984 v N, Bul, Y (7)
Meaker, M. J. (QPR), 1994 v RCS (sub), R (sub) (2)
Melville, A. K. (Swansea C), 1990 v Pol; (with Oxford U), 1991 v E (2)
Micallef, C. (Cardiff C), 1982 v F, Ho; 1983 v N (3)

Nardiello, D. (Coventry C), 1978 v S (1)
Neilson, A. B. (Newcastle U), 1993 v Cy, Bel (2), RCS; 1994 v RCS, Cy, R (7)
Nicholas, P. (C Palace), 1978 v S; 1979 v E; (with Arsenal), 1982 v F (3)
Nogan, K. (Luton T), 1990 v Pol; 1991 v E (2)
Nogan, L. (Oxford U.) 1991 v E (1)

Owen, G. (Wrexham), 1991 v E (sub), Pol; 1992 v R; 1993 v Cy, Bel (2); 1994 v Cy, R (8)

Pascoe, C. (Swansea C), 1983 v Bul (sub); 1984 v N (sub), Bul, Y (4)
Pembridge, M. (Luton T), 1991 v Pol (1)
Perry, J. (Cardiff C), 1990 v Pol; 1991 v E, Pol (3)
Peters, M. (Manchester C), 1992 v R; (with Norwich C), 1993 v Cy, RCS (3)
Phillips, D. (Plymouth Arg), 1984 v N, Bul, Y (3)
Phillips, L. (Swansea C), 1979 v E; (with Charlton Ath), 1983 v N (2)
Pontin, K. (Cardiff C), 1978 v S (1)
Powell, L. (Southampton), 1991 v Pol (sub); 1992 v R (sub); 1993 v Bel (sub); 1994 v RCS (4)
Price, P. (Luton T), 1981 v Ho (1)
Pugh, D. (Doncaster R), 1982 v F (2) (2)
Pugh, S. (Wrexham), 1993 v Bel (2 subs) (2)

Ratcliffe, K. (Everton), 1981 v Ho; 1982 v F (2)
Ready, K. (QPR), 1992 v R; 1993 v Bel (2); 1994 v RCS, Cy (5)
Rees, A. (Birmingham C), 1984 v N (1)
Rees, J. (Luton T), 1990 v Pol; 1991 v E, Pol (3)
Roberts, A. (QPR), 1991 v E, Pol (2)
Roberts, G. (Hull C), 1983 v Bul (1)
Roberts, J. G. (Wrexham), 1977 v E (1)
Robinson, J. (Brighton & HA), 1992 v R; (with Charlton Ath), 1993 v Bel; 1994 v RCS, Cy, R (5)
Rush, I. (Liverpool), 1981 v Ho; 1982 v F (2)

Sayer, P. A. (Cardiff C), 1977 v E, S (2)
Searle, D. (Cardiff C), 1991 v Pol (sub); 1992 v R; 1993 v Cy, Bel (2), RCS; 1994 v RCS (6)
Slatter, N. (Bristol R), 1983 v N, Y, Bul; 1984 v N, Bul, Y (6)
Speed, G. A. (Leeds U), 1990 v Pol; 1991 v E, Pol (3)
Stevenson, N. (Swansea C), 1982 v F, Ho (2)
Stevenson, W. B. (Leeds U), 1977 v E, S; 1978 v S (3)
Symons, K. (Portsmouth), 1991 v E, Pol (2)

Thomas, Martin R. (Bristol R), 1979 v E; 1981 v Ho (2)
Thomas, Mickey R. (Wrexham), 1977 v E; 1978 v S (2)
Thomas, D. G. (Leeds U), 1977 v E; 1979 v E; 1984 v N (3)
Tibbott, L. (Ipswich T), 1977 v E, S (2)

Vaughan, N. (Newport Co), 1982 v F, Ho (2)

Walsh, I. P. (C Palace), 1979 v E; (with Swansea C), 1983 v Bul (2)
Walton, M. (Norwich C.), 1991 v Pol (sub) (1)
Williams, D. (Bristol R), 1983 v Y (1)
Williams, G. (Bristol R), 1983 v Y, Bul (2)
Wilmot, R. (Arsenal), 1982 v F (2), Ho; 1983 v N, Y; 1984 v Y (6)

International Records

MOST GOALS IN AN INTERNATIONAL

England	Malcolm Macdonald (Newcastle U) 5 goals v Cyprus, at Wembley	16.4.1975
	Willie Hall (Tottenham H) 5 goals v Ireland, at Old Trafford	16.11.1938
	G. O. Smith (Corinthians) 5 goals v Ireland, at Sunderland	18.2.1899
	Steve Bloomer (Derby Co) 5 goals* v Wales, at Cardiff	16.3.1896
	Oliver Vaughton (Aston Villa) 5 goals v Ireland, at Belfast	18.2.82
Scotland	Charles Heggie (Rangers) 5 goals v Ireland, at Belfast	20.3.1886
Ireland	Joe Bambrick (Linfield) 6 goals v Wales, at Belfast	1.2.1930
Wales	James Price (Wrexham) 4 goals v Ireland, at Wrexham	25.2.1882
	Mel Charles (Cardiff C) 4 goals v Ireland, at Cardiff	11.4.1962
	Ian Edwards (Chester) 4 goals v Malta, at Wrexham	25.10.1978

* There are conflicting reports which make it uncertain whether Bloomer scored four or five goals in this game.

MOST GOALS IN AN INTERNATIONAL CAREER

		Goals	*Games*
England	Bobby Charlton (Manchester U)	49	106
Scotland	Denis Law (Huddersfield T, Manchester C, Torino, Manchester U)	30	55
	Kenny Dalglish (Celtic, Liverpool)	30	102
Ireland	Colin Clarke (Bournemouth, Southampton, QPR, Portsmouth	13	38
Wales	Ian Rush (Liverpool, Juventus)	28	66
	Ivor Allchurch (Swansea T, Newcastle U, Cardiff C)	23	68
Republic of Ireland	Frank Stapleton (Arsenal, Manchester U, Ajax, Derby Co, Le Havre, Blackburn R)	20	70

HIGHEST SCORES

World Cup Match	New Zealand	13	Fiji	0	1981
European Championship	Spain	12	Malta	1	1983
Olympic Games	Denmark	17	France	1	1908
	Germany	16	USSR	0	1912
International Match	Germany	13	Finland	0	1940
	Spain	13	Bulgaria	0	1933
European Cup	Feyenoord	12	K R Reykjavik	2	1969
European Cup-Winners' Cup	Sporting Lisbon	16	Apoel Nicosia	1	1963
Fairs & UEFA Cups	Ajax	14	Red Boys	0	1984

GOALSCORING RECORDS

World Cup Final	Geoff Hurst (England) 3 goals v West Germany	1966
World Cup Final tournament	Just Fontaine (France) 13 goals	1958
Major European Cup game	Lothar Emmerich (Borussia Dortmund) v Floriana in Cup-Winners' Cup – 6 goals	1965
Career	Arthur Friedenreich (Brazil) 1329 goals	1910–30
	Pelé (Brazil) 1281 goals	*1956–78
	Franz 'Bimbo' Binder (Austria, Germany) 1006 goals	1930–50

**Pelé subsequently scored two goals in Testimonial matches making his total 1283.*

MOST CAPPED INTERNATIONALS IN BRITISH ISLES

England	Bobby Moore	108 appearances	1962–73
Northern Ireland	Pat Jennings	119 appearances	1964–86
Scotland	Kenny Dalglish	102 appearances	1971–86
Wales	Neville Southall	74 appearances	1982–94
Republic of Ireland	Paddy Bonner	77 appearances	1981–94

TRANSFERS

Record British moves (UK only)

£5,000,000 Chris Sutton, Norwich to Blackburn R, July 1994
£4,000,000 Duncan Ferguson, Dundee U to Rangers, July 1993
£3,750,000 Roy Keane, Nottingham F to Manchester U, July 1993
£3,300,000 Alan Shearer, Southampton to Blackburn R, June 1992
£2,900,000 Dean Saunders, Derby Co to Liverpool, July 1991
£2,750,000 Brian Deane, Sheffield U to Leeds U, June 1993
£2,700,000 Basile Boli, Marseille to Rangers, July 1994
£2,600,000 Carlton Palmer, Sheffield W to Leeds U, July 1994.
£2,500,000 Keith Curle, Wimbledon to Manchester C, July 1991
£2,500,000 Ian Wright, Crystal Palace to Arsenal, September 1991
£2,500,000 Terry Phelan, Wimbledon to Manchester C, August 1992

Other British moves

£6,500,000 David Platt, Bari to Juventus, May 1992
£5,500,000 David Platt, Aston Villa to Bari, July 1991
£5,500,000 Paul Gascoigne, Tottenham H to Lazio, May 1992
£5,200,000 David Platt, Juventus to Sampdoria, July 1993
£5,000,000 Trevor Steven, Rangers to Marseille, August 1991
£4,500,000 Chris Waddle, Tottenham H to Marseille, July 1989
£3,200,000 Ian Rush, Liverpool to Juventus, June 1987
£2,800,000 Ian Rush, Juventus to Liverpool, August 1988
£2,750,000 Gary Lineker, Everton to Barcelona, June 1986
£2,700,000 Des Walker, Sampdoria to Sheffield W, July 1993
£2,300,000 Mark Hughes, Manchester U to Barcelona, May 1986

World records

£13,000,000 Gianluigi Lentini, Torino to AC Milan, June 1992
£12,000,000 Gianluca Vialli, Sampdoria to Juventus, June 1992
£10,000,000 Jean-Pierre Papin, Marseille to AC Milan, June 1992
£8,000,000 Igor Shalimov, Foggia to Internazionalle, June 1992

FA SCHOOLS AND YOUTH GAMES 1993–94

ENGLAND UNDER–16

4 Aug

England 4 (*Cassidy 2, Richardson, Wallwork*)
Denmark 2

England: Moore, Harrison, Broomes, Hilton, Shore, Teather, Clemence, Cassidy, Richardson, Carragher, Wallwork. (subs used: Futcher, Crooks, Ducros, McCann).

5 Aug

England 1 (*Teather*)
Norway 2

England: Darnborough, Futcher, Wallwork, Broomes, Hilton, Crooks, McGann, Clemence, Ducros, Richardson, Cassidy. (subs used: Harrison, Teather, Shore, Carragher).

7 Aug

England 2 (*Shore, Ducros*)
Sweden 2

England: Moore, Harrison, Broomes, Wallwork, Hilton, Shore, Teather, Clemence, Richardson, Cassidy, Carragher.

8 Aug

England 1 (*Shore*)
Finland 1

England: Darnborough, Futcher, Broomes, Wallwork, Hilton, Crooks, McGann, Clemence, Carragher, Cassidy, Ducros.

30 Oct

England 2 (*Broomes, Ducros*)
Eire 0

England: Wright (Moore), Millett, Hilton, Curtis, Wallwork (Futcher), Broomes, Quashie (Thompson), Clemence (Atkinson), Richardson (Carragher), Ducros, Cassidy.

24 Nov

Holland 1
England 1 (*Thompson*)

England: Wright, Millett, Hilton, Broomes, Wallwork, Thompson, Richardson (Carragher), Curtis, Ducros (Quashie), Clemence, Cassidy.

8 DEC

Italy 0
England 2 (*Carragher, Ducros*)

England: Wright, Millett, Hilton, Broomes, Wallwork, Thompson (Rankin), Richardson (Curtis), Clemence, Ducros, Carragher, Cassidy.

2 Feb

England 0
Italy 0

England: Darnborough, Millett, Hilton, Wallwork, Thompson, Richardson, Clemence, Ducros, Carragher, Cassidy (Quashie).

8 Mar

England 1 (*Cassidy*)
Holland 0

England: Wright, Millett, Hilton, Broomes, Wallwork, Thompson (Quashie), Richardson, Clemence, Ducros, Carragher (Rankin), Cassidy.

26 Apr

Portugal 0
England 1 (*Cassidy*)

England: Wright, Millett, Hilton, Broomes, Wallwork, Richardson, Clemence, Carragher (Heskey), Ducros, Cassidy (Quashie), Shore.

26 Apr

England 1 (*Clemence*)
Eire 1

England: Wright, Millett, Hilton, Broomes, Wallwork, Quashie (Shore), Richardson, Clemence, Ducros (Heath), Cassidy, Heskey.

30 Apr

England 2 (*Cassidy, Richardson*)
RCS 0

England: Wright, Millett, Hilton, Broomes, Richardson, Clemence, Carragher, Cassidy, Heath (Quashie), Shore, Crooks (Heskey).

3 May

England 2 (*Carragher, Ducros*)
Ukraine 2

England: Wright, Millett, Hilton, Broomes, Wallwork, Richardson, Clemence, Carragher (Quashie), Ducros (Heskey), Cassidy, Shore.

UNDER–17

13 Mar

Combined Services 1
FA Youth 5 (*Clarke 3, Mahoney-Johnson, Burton*)

FA Youth: Hurst (Tyler), Griggs, Boxall, Clarke, Purse, Mills, Mahoney-Johnson, Gaine, Burton, Harris, Parmenter.

22 Mar

South West Counties 1
FA Youth 6 (*Preedy, Povey, Carey 4*)

FA Youth: Flahaven, Law, Hayfield, Preedy, Ayres, Thorne (James), Stowell, Setter (Povey), Povey, Licata, Phillips.

6 Apr

ESFA XI 1
FA Youth 5 (*Cooke 2, Vine 3*)

FA Youth: Willetts (Oakes), Ward (Ludlun), Neville, O'Connor, Allen, Blunt (Petchey), Cooke, Vine, Johnson, Wharton, Beresford.

UNDER–18

24 Aug

England 2 (*Cureton, Holland*)

Eire 2

England: Pettinger, Hinshlewood (Stamp), Strong (Worrall), Ford, Bowman, Thatcher, Holland, Walker, Irving, Gallen, Cureton.

7 Sept

England 1 (*Faulkner*)

Romania 1

England: Pettinger, Hinshlewood, Challis, Ford, Faulkner, Thatcher, Holland, Appleby (Bennett), Irving, Gallen, Cureton.

13 Oct

Romania 1

England 1 (*Gallen*)

England: Pettinger, Hinshlewood, Challis, Ford, Bowman, O'Connor, Hewlett (Holland), McGowan, Jackson (Irving), Gallen, Stamp.

27 Oct

France 2

England 0

England: Pettinger, Hinshlewood, Burrows (Cureton), Ford, Bowman, O'Connor, Holland, Stamp, Jackson, Gallen, McGowan (Irving).

16 Nov

England 3 (*Gallen 2, Simpson*)

France 3

England: Pettinger, Neville, Holland, Worrall (Ford), O'Connor, Thatcher, Stamp, Frodsham, Simpson, Gallen, Cureton (Wright).

UNDER–17 WORLD YOUTH CHAMPIONSHIP

Group A
Japan (0) 0, Ghana (1) 1
Italy (0) 1, Mexico (1) 2
Ghana (1) 4, Mexico (0) 1
Japan 0, Italy 0
Ghana (3) 4, Italy (0) 0
Japan (1) 2, Mexico (1) 1

Group B
Australia (2) 2, Argentina (1) 2
Canada (0) 0, Nigeria (3) 8
Australia (2) 5, Canada (0) 0
Argentina (0) 0, Nigeria (0) 4
Australia (0) 0, Nigeria (0) 2
Argentina (3) 5, Canada (0) 0

Group C
Colombia (0) 0, Qatar (1) 2
USA (1) 2, RCS (1) 2
Colombia (1) 2, USA (0) 1
Qatar (0) 0, RCS (1) 2
Colombia (0) 1, RCS (1) 3
Qatar (0) 1, USA (2) 5

Group D
Chile (0) 2, China PR (1) 2
Tunisia (0) 1, Poland (1) 3
Chile (1) 2, Tunisia (0) 0
China PR (0) 0, Poland (0) 2
Chile (1) 3, Poland (2) 3
China PR (0) 0, Tunisia (1) 1

Quarter-finals
Ghana 0, Australia 0
Ghana won 1-0 (aet)
Nigeria (2) 2, Japan (0) 1
RCS (1) 1, Chile (2) 4
Poland (1) 3, USA (0) 0

Semi-finals
Ghana (1) 3, Chile (0) 0
Nigeria (0) 2, Poland (0) 1

Match for third place
Chile (0) 1, Poland (1) 1
Chile won 4-2 on penalties

Final
Ghana (0) 1, Nigeria (1) 2

WFA NATIONAL LEAGUE

Premier Division

		Home			Goals		Away			Goals			
	P	*W*	*D*	*L*	*F*	*A*	*W*	*D*	*L*	*F*	*A*	*GD*	*Pts*
Doncaster B	18	8	1	0	60	6	8	0	1	50	10	+94	49
Arsenal	18	6	2	1	36	11	8	1	0	49	4	+70	45
Knowsley U	18	7	0	2	39	16	6	2	1	24	14	+33	41
Wembley	18	4	1	4	17	20	5	1	3	18	14	+1	29
MillwallL	18	5	0	4	24	29	4	1	4	18	17	–4	28
Leasowe P	18	3	2	4	17	16	4	0	5	25	32	–6	23
Stanton R	18	4	1	4	14	20	2	4	3	18	18	–6	23
Red Star S	18	1	2	6	12	36	1	1	7	13	34	–45	6*
Ipswich T	18	1	2	6	11	38	0	1	8	3	48	–72	6
Wimbledon	18	1	0	8	5	37	1	0	8	11	44	–65	3*

Ipswich Town and Wimbledon relegated from the Premier Division

Division 1 North

		Home			Goals		Away			Goals			
	P	*W*	*D*	*L*	*F*	*A*	*W*	*D*	*L*	*F*	*A*	*GD*	*Pts*
Wolverhampton	18	9	0	0	43	7	3	4	2	18	21	+33	40
Sheffield W	18	6	1	2	24	10	7	0	2	22	10	+26	40
Abbeydale	18	5	1	3	23	12	4	1	4	15	19	+7	29
Bronte	18	5	2	2	22	11	3	2	4	24	15	+20	28
Cowgate K	18	4	1	4	19	18	5	0	4	19	23	–3	28
Villa A	18	4	2	3	26	18	4	1	4	11	16	+3	27
St Helens	18	4	0	5	20	23	3	1	5	16	34	–21	22
Langford	18	4	1	4	14	15	1	1	7	11	26	–16	17
Nottingham A	18	3	1	5	13	22	2	0	7	12	27	–24	16
Kidderminster	18	2	2	5	14	22	1	1	7	10	27	–25	12

Wolverhampton Wanderers promoted to the Premier Division.

Kidderminster Harriers elected to compete in the playoffs, and retained their place in Division 1 North by beating Manchester Belle Vue in the Northern playoff final.

Division 1 South

		Home			Goals		Away			Goals			
	P	*W*	*D*	*L*	*F*	*A*	*W*	*D*	*L*	*F*	*A*	*GD*	*Pts*
Bromley B	18	7	1	1	27	7	7	2	0	41	9	+52	45
Town & Co	18	6	1	2	33	18	5	1	3	18	11	+22	35
Bristol	18	5	0	4	25	18	6	1	2	25	16	+16	34
Epsom & E	18	5	2	2	19	13	5	0	4	18	13	+11	32
Brighton & H	18	3	3	3	12	10	6	1	2	24	13	+13	31
Maidstone T	18	4	3	2	17	13	4	2	3	20	15	+9	29
Hemel H	18	4	1	4	24	18	0	5	4	9	26	–11	18
Horsham	18	2	2	5	15	22	2	2	5	9	11	–9	16
Oxford U	18	1	2	6	6	18	2	2	5	11	19	–20	13
Hassocks	18	0	1	8	6	39	0	0	9	1	51	–83	1

Bromley Borough promoted to the Premier Division

Hassocks elected not to compete in the playoffs, and are replaced by Brentford, from the Greater London region, who beat Whitehawk (previously known as Saltdean) in the Southern playoff final.

WFA NATIONAL LEAGUE CUP 1993–94

First Round
Horsham 0, Arsenal 6
Nottingham A 1, Red Star 7
Leasowe 2, Cowgate 1
Langford 3, Hemel Hempstead 5
Villa 0, Wolves 5
Epsom & Ewell 1, Bromley 2
Ipswich 1, Knowsley 4
Wembley 5, Hassocks 0
Millwall 4, Oxford 0
Doncaster 10, Maidstone 0
Bronte 0, Sheffield Wed 4

Second Round
Kidderminster 0, Arsenal 6
Town & Country 1, Red Star 3
Brighton 2, Leasowe 6
Hemel Hempstead 3, Wimbledon 4
Wolves 1, Bromley 3
Knowsley 3, Wembley 1
Milklwall 6, Stanton 5
Doncaster 9, Sheffield Wed 0

Third Round
Arsenal 9, Red Star 1
Leasowe 2, Wimbledon 2
(*Leasowe won on penalties*)
Bromley 1, Knowsley 5
Millwall 1, Doncaster 6

Semi-finals
Arsenal 4, Leasowe 1
Knowsley 0, Doncaster 4

Final
Arsenal v Doncaster
(*held over until start of 1994–95 season*)

WFA NATIONAL LEAGUE 1993–94

Premier Division

	Arsenal	Doncaster B	Ipswich T	Knowsley U	Leasowe P	Millwall L	Red Star S	Stanton R	Wembley	Wimbledon
Arsenal	—	3-1	7-0	2-2	4-0	3-1	4-0	2-2	2-3	9-2
Doncaster B	2-2	—	10-0	7-0	11-0	6-1	9-3	3-0	2-0	10-0
Ipswich T	1-11	0-3	—	1-1	2-8	2-5	1-1	0-4	2-4	2-1
Knowsley U	0-5	1-7	15-0	—	4-1	2-1	7-0	3-2	2-0	5-0
Leasowe P	1-2	1-3	4-0	0-2	—	2-3	2-1	2-2	1-1	4-2
Millwall L	0-6	1-6	4-1	2-5	2-6	—	5-2	6-2	2-1	2-0
Red Star S	0-7	1-10	1-1	2-5	2-0	0-3	—	2-2	1-4	3-4
Stanton R	0-4	1-5	3-0	0-5	3-2	1-1	3-0	—	1-3	2-0
Wembley	0-5	1-5	2-1	0-1	3-4	1-0	3-2	0-0	—	7-2
Wimbledon	0-7	1-10	2-0	0-3	1-4	0-3	0-4	0-4	1-2	—

Division 1 North

	Abbeydale	Bronte	Cowgate K	Kidderminster H	Langford	Nottingham A	St Helens	Sheffield W	Villa A	Wolverhampton W
Abbeydale	—	2-2	0-2	3-2	3-0	5-3	7-0	0-1	2-0	1-2
Bronte	5-2	—	2-0	5-2	3-0	3-0	1-2	0-2	1-1	2-2
Cowgate K	1-3	4-1	—	2-1	3-2	1-3	2-2	0-4	5-0	1-2
Kidderminster H	0-3	3-2	1-2	—	1-1	1-0	3-4	2-4	1-4	2-2
Langford	2-1	0-1	1-2	2-0	—	0-4	2-1	3-1	1-2	3-3
Nottingham A	3-3	1-6	2-5	0-2	1-0	—	3-0	1-5	0-1	2-0
St Helens	0-1	0.10	3-0	4-2	2-5	4-1	—	0-1	1-2	6-1
Sheffield W	0-2	1-0	7-1	4-0	4-2	3-0	1-2	—	2-1	2-2
Villa A	3-0	2-2	2-3	1-1	2-0	4-1	8-3	2-4	—	2-4
Wolverhampton W	5-0	2-0	5-4	6-0	7-1	6-0	7-2	2-0	3-0	—

Division 1 South

	Brighton & H	Bristol	Bromley B	Epsom & E	Hassocks	Hemel H	Horsham	Maidstone T	Oxford	Town & Co
Brighton & H	—	3-0	1-1	0-2	4-0	1-1	1-0	1-1	0-2	1-3
Bristol	1-2	—	3-4	3-2	9-0	3-0	?-0	1-4	3-1	2-5
Bromley B	1-1	0-1	—	2-1	4-0	7-0	2-0	3-1	5-3	3-0
Epsom & E	1-5	2-2	0-5	—	5-0	4-1	0-0	3-0	3-0	1-0
Hassocks	0-6	3-6	1-10	0-6	—	1-1	0-2	0-2	0-1	1-5
Hemel H	1-2	0-5	0-2	3-0	10-1	—	2-2	2-5	4-1	2-0
Horsham	2-3	2-4	2-6	1-3	4-0	1-1	—	1-4	2-1	0-0
Maidstone T	1-0	0-4	1-1	3-1	5-0	3-3	2-1	—	1-1	1-2
Oxford	1-4	1-2	0-5	0-1	2-0	1-1	1-2	0-0	—	0-3
Town & Co	5-1	5-1	1-7	1-2	8-0	5-1	3-2	4-3	1-1	—

FA WOMEN'S CHALLENGE CUP

First Round

Ashington East North v Newcastle	0-5
City Roses v Wigginton Grasshoppers	3-0
Barnsley v Cleveland	2-3
Bradford City v Sheffield United & Hallam University	11-1
Wakefield v Brighouse	10-3
Huddersfield Town v Grimsby	22-0
Wigan v Liverpool Feds	10-0
Broadoak v Bolton	12-1
Runcorn v Newsham	1-7
Bury v Warrington Town	6-4
Haslingden v Vernon-Carus	2-0
Bangor City Girls v Preston Rangers	0-5
Tranmere Rovers v Stockport	8-2
Oldham Athletic v Manchester Belle Vue	3-4
Manchester City v Manchester United	2-0
Nottingham Forest v Birmingham City	1-9
Worcester City v Stratford	16-0
Rugby v Rainworth Miners Welfare	1-7
TNT Ladies v Derby City	3-1
Nettleham v Derby County	1-3
Leicester City v Highfield Rangers	3-2
St Germaine v Peterborough Pythons	2-0
Dunstable v Stevenage Town	9-0
Welwyn Garden City v Colchester Royals	1-10
Colchester United v Pye	0-5
Sutton Athletic v Abbey Rangers	1-2
Leyton Orient v Tonbridge Angels	23-0
Crowborough Athletic v Palace Eagles	2-5
Gillingham Girls v Brentford	2-17
Walton & Hersham v Teynham Gunners	4-0
Winchester All Stars v Charlton	0-7
Collier Row v Enfield	3-0
Tottenham Hotspur v Chislehurst United	4-0
Edenbridge Town v SE Rangers	0-4
Lambeth v Barnet	5-3
Carterton v Havant	0-3
Farnborough v Launton	0-1
Isle of Wight v Binfield	0-9
Portsmouth v Gosport Borough	1-2
Paghem v Corematch	1-9
Bournemouth v Aylesbury United	3-2
Whitehawk v Reading	17-0
Reading Royals v Newbury	0-1
Swansea v Bristol City	4-6
Cheltenham YMCA v Truro City	3-3, 4-4
Truro City won 4-4 on penalties	
Tongwynlais v Swindon Spitfires	2-1
Cardiff Institute removed, Yate Town w.o	
Plymouth Pilgrims v Clevedon Town	2-0
Inter Cardiff v Frome	2-1

Second Round

Amble Town v Sheffield Wednesday	0-6
Cowgate Kestrels v Newcastle	2-1
Cleveland v Wakefield	0-9
Bronte v Bradford City	4-2
City Roses v Kilnhurst	0-4
Huddersfield Town v Middlesbrough	14-1
Manchester Belle Vue v Broadoak	1-2
Preston Rangers v Leek Town	3-2
Liverpool District v Wigan	0-5
Haslingden v Tranmere Rovers	1-5
Bury v Manchester City	4-1
St Helens v Newsham	5-1
Stockport County v Rochdale	1-0
Abbeydale/Alvechurch v Wolverhampton	0-5
Nottingham Argyle v Birmingham City	3-2
Rainworth Miners Welfare v Derby County	5-0
Chesterfield v TNT Ladies	3-1
Kidderminster Harriers v Sporting Kesteven	13-0
Leicester City v Villa Aztecs	1-7
Colchester Royals v St Germaine	2-6
Town & County v Bedford Belles	9-0
Dunstable v Langford	4-1
Pye v Leighton Linslade	5-0
Collier Row v Sittingbourne	4-0
Lambeth v Palace Eagles	9-2
Abbey Rangers v Queens Park Rangers	1-7
Maidstone Tigresses v Epsom & Ewell	1-2
Leyton Orient v Drayton Wanderers	3-2
Walton & Hersham v Charlton	2-3
Hackney v Bromley Borough	2-3
SE Rangers v Tottenham Hotspur	1-13
Hemel Hempstead v Brentford	3-0
Newbury v Launton	5-2
Bournemouth v Chailey Mavericks	10-0
Havant withdrew, Hassocks w.o	
Corematch v Whitehawk	0-6
Gosport Borough v Brighton & Hoven Albion	1-2
Oxford United v Binfield	3-0
Shoreham v Horsham	0-5
Inter Cardiff v Bristol City	3-1
Bristol v Bristol Rovers	13-0
Yate Town v Tongwynlais	0-6
Torquay United v Truro City	2-5
Plymouth Pilgrims v Worcester City	4-5

Third Round

Stockport County v Nottingham Argyle	2-1
Cowgate Kestrels v Kilnhurst	4-1
Bronte v Villa Aztecs	1-2
Broadoak v Wakefield	0-2
St Helens v Wolverhampton	2-10
Tranmere Rovers v Sheffield Wednesday	2-4
Wigan v Preston Rangers	2-5
Chesterfield v Bury	2-1
Rainworth Miners Welfare v Huddersfield Town	2-4
Pye v Dunstable	0-3
Town & County v Hemel Hempstead	5-4
Tottenham Hotspur v St Germaine	0-0, 3-1
Bromley Borough v Collier Row	7-0
Leyton Orient v Queens Park Rangers	16-0
Lambeth v Charlton	0-1
Worcester City v Kidderminster Harriers	1-6
Newbury v Brighton & Hove Albion	1-2
Oxford United v Inter Cardiff	2-4
Horsham v Bristol	3-2
Tongwynlais v Truro City	2-5
Epsom & Ewell v Bournemouth	2-1
Whitehawk v Hassocks	8-2

Fourth Round

Doncaster Belles v Millwall Lionesses	9-0
Truro City v Stockport County	1-0
Tottenham Hotspur v Inter Cardiff	1-3
Chesterfield v Wakefield	1-2
Red Star Southampton v Bromley Borough	1-3
Horsham v Brighton & Hove Albion	0-2
Huddersfield Town v Whitehawk	6-0
Arsenal v Sheffield Wednesday	8-0
Kidderminster Harriers v Cowgate Kestrels	2-1
Charlton v Leasowe Pacific	0-7
Town & County v Ipswich Town	4-1
Leyton Orient v Knowsley United	2-7
Wembley v Wolverhampton	2-0
Epsom & Ewell v Wimbledon	0-0, 2-1
Preston Rangers v Villa Aztecs	6-2
Stanton Rangers v Dunstable	6-0

Fifth Round

Leasowe Pacific v Town & County	9-0
Epsom & Ewell v Inter Cardiff	7-0
Brighton & Hove Albion v Truro City	1-0
Doncaster Belles v Bromley Borough	10-1

Wembley v Arsenal	2-4
Wakefield v Stanton Rangers	1-3
Knowsley United v Huddersfield Town	5-2
Kidderminster Harriers v Preston Rangers	0-6

Sixth Round

Preston Rangers v Stanton Rangers	2-3
Arsenal v Knowsley United	0-1
Doncaster Belles v Brighton & Hove Albion	5-1
Epsom & Ewell v Leasowe Pacific	2-3

Semi-finals

Stanton Rangers v Knowsley United	0-1
Leasowe Pacific v Doncaster Belles	0-6

Final (at Scunthorpe)

Doncaster Belles v Knowsley United	1-0

EUROPEAN CUP

EUROPEAN CUP FINALS 1956–93

Year	Winners	Runners-up	Venue	Attendance	Referee
1956	Real Madrid 4	Reims 3	Paris	38,000	Ellis (E)
1957	Real Madrid 2	Fiorentina 0	Madrid	124,000	Horn (Ho)
1958	Real Madrid 3	AC Milan 2 *(aet)*	Brussels	67,000	Alsteen (Bel)
1959	Real Madrid 2	Reims 0	Stuttgart	80,000	Dutsch (WG)
1960	Real Madrid 7	Eintracht Frankfurt 3	Glasgow	135,000	Mowat (S)
1961	Benfica 3	Barcelona 2	Berne	28,000	Dienst (Sw)
1962	Benfica 5	Real Madrid 3	Amsterdam	65,000	Horn (Ho)
1963	AC Milan 2	Benfica 1	Wembley	45,000	Holland (E)
1964	Internazionale 3	Real Madrid 1	Vienna	74,000	Stoll (A)
1965	Internazionale 1	Benfica 0	Milan	80,000	Dienst (Sw)
1966	Real Madrid 2	Partizan Belgrade 1	Brussels	55,000	Kreitlein (WG)
1967	Celtic 2	Internazionale 1	Lisbon	56,000	Tschenscher (WG)
1968	Manchester U 4	Benfica 1 *(aet)*	Wembley	100,000	Lo Bello (I)
1969	AC Milan 4	Ajax 1	Madrid	50,000	Ortiz (Sp)
1970	Feyenoord 2	Celtic 1 *(aet)*	Milan	50,000	Lo Bello (I)
1971	Ajax 2	Panathinaikos 0	Wembley	90,000	Taylor (E)
1972	Ajax 2	Internazionale 0	Rotterdam	67,000	Helies (F)
1973	Ajax 1	Juventus 0	Belgrade	93,500	Guglovic (Y)
1974	Bayern Munich 1	Atletico Madrid 1	Brussels	65,000	Loraux (Bel)
Replay	Bayern Munich 4	Atletico Madrid 0	Brussels	65,000	Delcourt (Bel)
1975	Bayern Munich 2	Leeds U 0	Paris	50,000	Kitabdjian (F)
1976	Bayern Munich 1	St Etienne 0	Glasgow	54,864	Palotai (H)
1977	Liverpool 3	Moenchengladbach 1	Rome	57,000	Wurtz (F)
1978	Liverpool 1	FC Brugge 0	Wembley	92,000	Corver (Ho)
1979	Nottingham F 1	Malmo 0	Munich	57,500	Linemayr (A)
1980	Nottingham F 1	Hamburg 0	Madrid	50,000	Garrido (P)
1981	Liverpool 1	Real Madrid 0	Paris	48,360	Palotai (H)
1982	Aston Villa 1	Bayern Munich 0	Rotterdam	46,000	Konrath (F)
1983	Hamburg 1	Juventus 0	Athens	75,000	Rainea (R)
1984	Liverpool 1	Roma 1	Rome	69,693	Fredriksson (Se)
	(aet; Liverpool won 4–2 on penalties)				
1985	Juventus 1	Liverpool 0	Brussels	58,000	Daina (Sw)
1986	Steaua Bucharest 0	Barcelona 0	Seville	70,000	Vautrot (F)
	(aet; Steaua won 2–0 on penalties)				
1987	Porto 2	Bayern Munich 1	Vienna	59,000	Ponnet (Bel)
1988	PSV Eindhoven 0	Benfica 0	Stuttgart	70,000	Agnolin (I)
	(aet; PSV won 6–5 on penalties)				
1989	AC Milan 4	Steaua Bucharest 0	Barcelona	97,000	Tritschler (WG)
1990	AC Milan 1	Benfica 0	Vienna	57,500	Kohl (A)
1991	Red Star Belgrade 0	Marseille 0	Bari	56,000	Lanese (I)
	(aet; Red Star won 5–3 on penalties				
1992	Barcelona 1	Sampdoria 0 *(aet)*	Wembley	70,827	Schmidhuber (G)
1993	Marseille* 1	AC Milan 0	Munich	64,400	Rothlisberger (Sw)

**Subsequently stripped of title.*

Daniele Massaro celebrates his first goal for AC Milan in the European Cup Final. (Action Images).

EUROPEAN CUP 1993–94

Preliminary Round, First Leg

B68 Toftir (0) 0, Croatia Zagreb (3) 5 *(Cvitanovic 15, Leshak 32, Vlaovic 44, Turkovic 84, Adzic 89)* 1000
Cwmbran Town (3) 3 *(King 4 (pen), Ford 25, 27)*, Cork City (0) 2 *(Caulfield 62, Buckley 75)* 3582
Ekranas (0) 0, Floriana (0) 1 *(Buttigieg) 1000*
HJK Helsinki (1) 1 *(Heinola 15)*, Norma Tallinn (1) 1 *(Borisov 16)* 2000
Omonia (1) 2 *(Shilikashvili 15, 61)*, Aarau (0) 1 *(Ratinho 62)* 5000
Rosenborg (1) 2 *(Bragstad 9, Loken 54)*, Avenir Beggen (0) 0 789
Skonto Riga (0) 0, Olimpija Ljubljana (1) 1 *(Milinovic 16)* 3000
Tbilisi Dynamo (1) 2 *(Arveladze S 9, Inalishvili 66)*, Linfield (0) 1 *(Johnston 56)* 60,000
Zimbrul (0) 1 *(Revda 83)*, Beitar Jerusalem (1) 1 *(Harazi 10)* 10,000
Partizani Tirana (0) 0, IA Akranes (0) 0 8000

Preliminary Round, Second Leg

Aarau (2) 2 *Stiel 6, Heldmann 38)*, Omonia (0) 0 4000
IA Akranes (0) 3 *(Hognasson 70, Gudjohnsson 74, 81)*, Partizani Tirana (0) 0 1200
Beitar Jerusalem (1) 2 *(Harazi 5, Greshnayev 72 (pen))*, Zimbrul (0) 0 5000
Cork City (0) 2 *(Morley 74, Glynn 85)*, Cwmbran Town (1) 1 *(McNeil 7)* 5250
Croatia Zagreb (1) 6 *(Zivkovic 17, Vlaovic 53, 84, 88, 89, Hailovic 74)*, B68 Toftir (0) 0 8000
Floriana (0) 1 *(Buttigieg 60)*, Ekranas (0) 0 4000
Linfield (0) 1 *(Haylock 71)*, Tbilisi Dynamo (0) 1 *(Arveladze S 46)* 5000
Norma Tallinn (0) 0, HJK Helsinki (0) 1 *(Belokhovostov (og) 81)* 200
Olimpija Ljubljana (0) 0, Skonto Riga (0) 1 *(Proitski 68)* 1000 *Skonto Riga won 12-10 on penalties*
Rosenborg (0) 1 *(Skammelsrud 70)*, Avenir Beggen (0) 0 4481

First Round, First Leg

Aarau (0) 0, AC Milan (0) 1 *(Papin 54)* 12,000
AIK Stockholm (1) 1 *(Lidman 36)*, Sparta Prague (0) 0 5854
IA Akranes (0) 1 *(Thordarson 75)*, Feyenoord (0) 0 6327
Galatasaray (1) 2 *(Turkyilmaz 31, Arif 51)*, Cork City (0) 1 *(Barry 62)* 18,000
HJK Helsinki (0) 0, Anderlecht (0) 3 *(Bosman 49, Versavel 74, Boffin 80)* 1500
Dynamo Kiev (2) 3 *(Shkapenko 6, Leonerko 45 (pen), 56)*, Barcelona (1) 1 *(Koeman 28 (pen))* 60,000
Kispest Honved (1) 2 *(Szabados 40, Stefanov 70)*, Manchester United (3) 3 *(Keane 9, 43, Cantona 44)* 9000
Lech Poznan (2) 3 *(Moskai 6, Podbrozny 32 (pen), Trzeciak 60)*, Beitar Jerusalem (0) 0 7000
Linfield (2) 3 *(Haylock 38, McConnell 42, Johnston 60)*, FC Copenhagen (0) 0 6400
Monaco (0) 1 *(Vlahos (og) 81)*, AEK Athens (0) 0 8000
Porto (1) 2 *(Kostadinov 8, Semedo 78)*, Floriana (0) 0 7000
Rangers (1) 3 *(McPherson 45, Hateley 56, 79)*, Levski Sofia (0) 2 *(Borimirov 77, Todorov 83)* 37,013
Rosenborg (3) 3 *(Tangen 29 (pen), Leonhardsen 35, Loeken 42)*, FK Austria (1) 1 *(Zsak 33 (pen))* 9619
Skonto Riga (0) 0, Moscow Spartak (4) 5 *(Pogodin 2, 39, Rodionov 7, 41, Bestchastnykh 67)* 2900
Steaua (1) 1 *(Panduru 35)*, Croatia Zagreb (1) 2 *(Cvitanovic 19, Jelicic 62)* 12,000
Werder Bremen (2) 5 *(Hobsch 26, 32, 60, Rufer 55, 90)*, Dynamo Minsk (0) 2 *(Gerassimez 52, Velichko 77)* 10,274

First Round, Second Leg

AEK Athens (1) 1 *(Siskovic 12)*, Monaco (1) 1 *(Djorkaeff 5)* 31,500
Anderlecht (3) 3 *(Nilis 16, 21, 42)*, HJK Helsinki (0) 0 11,500
Barcelona (2) 4 *(Laudrup 8, Bakero 16, 47, Koeman 67)*, Dynamo Kiev (1) 1 *(Rebrov 28)* 88,600
Beitar Jerusalem (1) 2 *(Ohana 11, Schwartz 72)*, Lech Poznan (3) 4 *(Wilkashik 4, Scheczik 23, Brojana 31, Tapinski 70)* 5000
FC Copenhagen (2) 4 *(Moller 2, Michael Johansen 26, Hojer 90, Mikkelsen 96) aet,* Linfield (0) 0 7051
Cork City (0) 0, Galatasaray (0) 1 *(Turkyilmaz 76)* 6500
Croatia Zagreb (1) 2 *(Vlaovic 7, Adziz 71)*, Steaua (1) 3 *(Panduru 14, Vladoiu 49, 61)* 10,000
Feyenoord (1) 3 *(Refos 25, Obiku 65, Blinker 83)*, IA Akranes (0) 0 23,000
FK Austria (1) 4 *(Nabekovas 12, Schmid 50, Zsak 74, Kogler 81)*, Rosenborg (1) 1 *(Dahlum 32)* 6500
Floriana (0) 0, Porto (0) 0 5000
Levski Sofia (1) 2 *(Sirakov 36, Todorov 90)*, Rangers (1) 1 *(Durrant 44)* 50,000
Manchester United (0) 2 *(Bruce 55, 64)*, Kispest Honved (0) 1 *(Salloi 78)* 35,781
AC Milan (0) 0, Aarau (0) 0 40,000
Dynamo Minsk (1) 1 *(Byelkevich 41)*, Werder Bremen (0) 1 *(Rufer 80 (pen))* 7500
Moscow Spartak (3) 4 *(Tsymbalar 4, 40, Pisarev 15, Onopko 87)*, Skonto Riga (0) 0 3500
Sparta Prague (1) 2 *(Siegl 15, 80)*, AIK Stockholm (0) 0 16,654

Second Round, First Leg

Barcelona (1) 3 *(Koeman 37 (pen), 68, Quique 89)*, FK Austria (0) 0 87,600
FC Copenhagen (0) 0, AC Milan (3) 6 *(Papin 1, 71, Simone 5, 14, Laudrup 43, Orlando 60)* 34,285
Lech Poznan (1) 1 *(Podbrozny 44)*, Moscow Spartak (3) 5 *(Pisarev 8, 62, Karpin 10, Onopko 30, 53)* 8762
Levski Sofia (0) 2 *(Yankov 75, Ginchev 90)*, Werder Bremen (0) 2 *(Bode 50, Rufer 52)* 46,500
Manchester United (2) 3 *(Robson 3, Hakan (og) 13, Cantona 81)*, Galatasaray (2) 3 *(Arif 16, Turkyilmaz 31, 63)* 39,396
Monaco (0) 4 *(Ikpeba 50, 75, Klinsmann 52, 64)*, Steaua (1) 1 *(Dumitrescu 22 (pen))* 11,000
Porto (0) 1 *(Domingos Oliveira 90)*, Feyenoord (0) 0 40,000
Sparta Prague (0) 0, Anderlecht (0) 1 *(Nilis 74)* 25,621

Second Round, Second Leg

Anderlecht (1) 4 *(Bosman 2, Nilis 47, 71, Versavel 89)*, Sparta Prague (1) 2 *(Dvirnik 18, Vonasek 60)* 19,000
Feyenoord (0) 0, Porto (0) 0 43,000
FK Austria (1) 1 *(Ogris 39)*, Barcelona (1) 2 *(Stoichkov 6, 78)* 22,500
AC Milan (1) 1 *(Papin 45)*, FC Copenhagen (0) 0 6786
Moscow Spartak (1) 2 *(Karpin 6, Khlestov 81)*, Lech Poznan (1) 1 *(Dembilski 28)* 10,000
Steaua (0) 1 *(Dumitrescu 84)*, Monaco (0) 0 21,000
Werder Bremen (0) 1 *(Basler 75)*, Levski Sofia (0) 0 28,000
Galatasaray (0) 0, Manchester United (0) 0 40,000

Champions League

Group A

Monaco (2) 4 *(Klinsmann 17, Ikpeba 41, Djorkaeff 62 (pen), Thuram 89)*, Spartak Moscow (0) 1 *(Pisarev)* 16,000

Galatasaray (0) 0, Barcelona (0) 0 30,000

Barcelona (2) 2 *(Beguiristain 16, 27)*, Monaco (0) 0 89,000

Spartak Moscow (0) 0, Galatasaray (0) 0 40,000

Monaco (2) 2 *(Scifo 36, Djorkaeff 41, Klinsmann 52)*, Galatasaray (0) 0 20,000

Spartak Moscow (0) 2 *(Rodionov 77, Karpin 88)*, Barcelona (1) 2 *(Stoichkov 10, Romario 66)* 60,000

Barcelona (1) 5 *(Stoichkov 34, Amor 75, Koeman 78, 80, Romario 86 (pen))*, Spartak Moscow (1) 1 *(Karpin 3)* 78,400

Galatasaray (0) 0, Monaco (0) 2 *(Scifo 54, Gnako 90)* 35,000

Barcelona (1) 3 *(Amor 22, Koeman 71 (pen), Eusebio 77)*, Galatasaray (0) 0 80,000

Spartak Moscow (0) 0, Monaco (0) 0 40,000

Galatasaray (0) 1 *(Cihat 86)*, Spartak Moscow (0) 2 *(Onopko 55, Karpin 83)* 25,000

Monaco (0) 0, Barcelona (1) 1 *(Stoichkov 13)* 16,000

Final table

	P	*W*	*D*	*L*	*F*	*A*	*Pts*
Barcelona	6	4	2	0	13	3	10
Monaco	6	3	1	2	9	4	7
Spartak Moscow	6	1	3	2	6	12	5
Galatasaray	6	0	2	4	1	10	2

Group B

Anderlecht (0) 0, AC Milan (0) 0 28,000

Porto (2) 3 *(Domingos 7, Rui Jorge 34, Jose Carlos 82)*, Werder Bremen (0) 2 *(Hobsch 85, Rufer 86)* 45,000

Werder Bremen (0) 5 *(Rufer 66, 89, Bratseth 72, Hobsch 81, Bode 83)*, Anderlecht (3) 3 *(Albert 16, Boffin 18, 33)* 32,000

AC Milan (2) 3 *(Raducioiu 16, Panucci 39, Massaro 63)*, Porto (0) 0 35,000

AC Milan (0) 2 *(Maldini 48, Savicevic 68)*, Werder Bremen (0) 1 *(Basler 54)* 41,239

Anderlecht (0) 1 *(Nilis 88)*, Porto (0) 0 17,000

Werder Bremen (0) 1 *(Rufer 52 (pen))*, AC Milan (0) 1 *(Savicevic 74)* 31,000

Porto (1) 2 *(Drulovic 10, Secretario 90)*, Anderlecht (0) 0 38,000

AC Milan (0) 0, Anderlecht (0) 0 65,000

Werder Bremen (0) 0, Porto (2) 5 *(Rui Filipe 11, Kostadinov 35, Secretario 70, Domingos 74, Timofte 90 (pen))* 32,000

Anderlecht (1) 1 *(Bosman 45)*, Werder Bremen (1) 2 *(Bode 33, 65)*, 13,000

Porto (0) 0, AC Milan (0) 0 50,000

Final table

	P	*W*	*D*	*L*	*F*	*A*	*Pts*
AC Milan	6	2	4	0	6	2	8
Porto	6	3	1	2	10	6	7
Werder Bremen	6	2	1	3	11	15	5
Anderlecht	6	1	2	3	5	9	4

Semi-finals

Barcelona (2) 3 *(Stoichkov 10, 35, Koeman 72)*, Porto (0) 0 98,000

AC Milan (1) 3 *(Desailly 14, Albertini 48, Massaro 66)*, Monaco (0) 0 78,650

Final: AC Milan (2) 4, Barcelona (0) 0

(in Athens, 18 May 1994, 70,000)

AC Milan: Rossi; Tassotti, Galli, Maldini (Nava 85), Panucci, Boban, Albertini, Desailly, Donadoni, Savicevic, Massaro.
Scorers: Massaro 22, 45, Savicevic 47, Desailly 58.
Barcelona: Zubizarreta; Ferrer, Koeman, Nadal, Beguiristain (Eusebio 51), Bakero, Guardiola, Amor, Sergi (Quique), Stoichkov, Romero.

EUROPEAN CUP 1993–94 -BRITISH AND IRISH CLUBS

Preliminary Round, First Leg

18 AUG

Cwmbran (3) 3 *(King (pen), Ford 2)*
Cork City (0) 2 *(Caulfield, Buckley)* 3582

Cwmbran: O'Hagan; Burrows, King, Dicks, Blackie, Copeman, Parselle, Goodridge, Ford, Wharton, Powell.
Cork City: Harrington; Daly, Napier, O'Donoghue, Hague, Roche, Barry, Hyde, Gaynor, Morley, Glynn.

Dynamo Tbilisi (1) 2 *(Arveladze S, Inalishvili)*
Linfield (0) 1 *(Johnston)* 60,000

Dynamo Tbilisi: Zoidze; Nemsade, Lobjanidze, Shelia, Inalishvili, Kavelashvili (Anchabadze), Arveladze A, Djamaduli, Arveladze R, Kinkladze, Arveladze S.
Linfield: Lamont; Dornan, Easton, Doherty, McConnell, Peebles, McCoosh, Gorman, Johnston, Haylock (Beatty), Bailie.

Preliminary Round, Second Leg

1 SEPT

Cork City (0) 2 *(Morley, Glynn)*
Cwmbran (1) 1 *(McNeil)* 5250

Cork City: Harrington; Daly, Hague, O'Donoghue, Napier, Buckley, Roche (Glynn), Hyde (Murphy), Gaynor, Morley, Caulfield.
Cwmbran: O'Hagan; Burrows, Blackie, Copeman, King, Dicks, McNeil, Goodridge, Payne, Ford, Wharton (Smith).

Linfield (0) 1 *(Haylock)*
Dynamo Tbilisi (0) 1 *(Arveladze S)* 5000

Linfield: Lamont; Dornan, Easton, Doherty, McConnell, Beatty (Anderson) (Gorman), Johnston, Haylock, Peebles, Bailie.
Dynamo Tbilisi: Zoidze; Nemsade, Chikovani, Shelia, Inalishvili, Kavelashvili, Arveladze A (Anchabadze), Djamaduli (Beradze), Arveladze R, Kinkladze, Arveladze S.
Dynamo Tbilisi were expelled for offering a bribe to the Turkish referee and match officials; Linfield reinstated.

First Round, First Leg

15 SEPT

Galatasaray (1) 2 *(Turkyilmaz, Arif)*
Cork City (0) 1 *(Barry)* 18,000

Galatasaray: Hayrettin; Stumpf, Bulent, Yusuf, Falko, Tugay, Arif (Mustafa), Hamza, Hakan, Suat, Turkyilmaz.
Cork City: Harrington; Cotter, Daly, O'Donoghue, Napier, Buckley, Barry (Roche), Hyde, Murphy, Gaynor, Morley (Caulfield).

Kispest Honved (1) 2 *(Szabados, Stefanov)*
Manchester U (3) 3 *(Keane 2, Cantona)* 9000

Kispest Honved: Brockhauser, Szabados, Plokal, Halmai, Banfi, Csehi, Illes, Stefanov, Duro (Orosz), Vincze, Hamar.
Manchester U: Schmeichel; Parker, Irwin, Bruce, Sharpe, Pallister, Robson, Ince, Cantona, Keane, Giggs (Phelan).

Rangers (1) 3 *(McPherson, Hateley 2)*
Levski Sofia (0) 2 *(Borimirov, Todorov)* 37,013

Rangers: Maxwell; Stevens, McPherson, Pressley, Robertson, Steven, Ferguson I, McCall, Durrant (Morrow), Hateley, Ferguson D.
Levski Sofia: Morgun; Kremenilev, Slavchev, Houbtchev, Markov, Tzvetanov, Yankov, Todorov, Grigorach (Ivanov), Borimirov, Trendafilov.

16 SEPT

Linfield (2) 3 *(Haylock, McConnell, Johnston)*
FC Copenhagen (0) 0 6400

Linfield: Lamont; Dornan, Easton, Doherty, McConnell, Beatty, Gorman (Knell), Johnston, Haylock, Peebles, Bailie.
FC Copenhagen: Petersen; Wegner, Tur, Lykke (Nielsen), Hojer, Falch, Juul, Uldbjerg, Manniche, Martin Johansen (Moller), Kaus.

First Round, Second Leg

29 SEPT

Cork City (0) 0
Galatasaray (0) 1 *(Turkyilmaz)* 6500

Cork City: Harrington; Cotter (Glynn), Daly, O'Donoghue, Napier, Buckley, Barry (Roche), Hyde, Murphy, Morley, Gaynor.
Galatasaray: Hayrettin; Stumpf, Bulent, Yusuf, Falko, Tugay, Erdal (Arif), Hamza, Hakan, Suat, Turkyilmaz.

FC Copenhagen (2) 4 *(Moller, Michael Johansen, Hojer, Mikkelsen)*
Linfield (0) 0 7051

FC Copenhagen: Petersen; Lonstrup, Tur (Lykke), Kaus, Hojer, Nielsen (Mikkelsen), Moller, Uldbjerg, Manniche, Martin Johansen, Michael Johansen.
Linfield: Lamont; Spiers, Easton, Doherty, McConnell, Beatty, Campbell (Knell), Gorman, Haylock, Peebles, Bailie.

Levski Sofia (1) 2 *(Sirakov, Todorov)*
Rangers (1) *(Durrant)* 50,000

Levski Sofia: Nikolov; Kremenliev, Houbtchev, Tzvetanov, Markov, Yankov, Borimirov, Sirakov, Slavchev, Todorov, Ivanov (Grigorach).
Rangers: Maxwell; Stevens, Gough, McPherson, Wishart, Steven, McCall, Ferguson I, Durrant, Hagen, Hateley.

Manchester U (0) 2 *(Bruce 2)*
Kispest Honved (0) 1 *(Salloi)* 35,781

Manchester U: Schmeichel; Parker, Irwin (Martin), Bruce, Sharpe, Pallister, Robson, Ince (Phelan), Cantona, Hughes, Giggs.
Kispest Honved: Brockhauser; Csabi, Plokai, Halmai, Banfi, Csehi (Duro), Szabados, Vincze, Illes, Salloi, Hamar (Orosz).

Second Round, First Leg

20 OCT

Manchester U (2) 3 *(Robson, Hakan (og), Cantona)*
Galatasaray (2) 3 *(Arif, Turkyilmaz 2)* 39,396

Manchester U: Schmeichel; Martin, Sharpe, Bruce, Keane, Pallister, Robson (Phelan), Ince, Cantona, Hughes, Giggs.
Galatasaray: Hayrettin; Stumpf, Bulent, Ugur, Gotz, Tugay, Arif, Hamza, Hakan, Suat (Yusuf), Turkyilmaz (Erdal).

Second Round, Second Leg

3 NOV

Galatasaray (0) 0
Manchester U (0) 0 40,000

Galatasaray: Hayrettin; Yusuf, Gotz, Stumpf, Hamza, Arif (Ugur), Suat, Tugay, Bulent, Turkyilmaz, Hakan.
Manchester U: Schmeichel; Phelan (Neville), Irwin, Bruce, Parker, Sharpe, Robson, Ince, Cantona, Keane (Dublin), Giggs.

Mark Hateley, hair flowing in characteristic fashion, keeps his eye on the ball for Glasgow Rangers. (Colorsport).

EUROPEAN CUP-WINNERS' CUP

EUROPEAN CUP-WINNERS' CUP FINALS 1961–93

Year	Winners	Runners-up	Venue	Attendance	Referee
1961	Fiorentina 2	Rangers 0 *(1st Leg)*	Glasgow	80,000	Steiner (A)
	Fiorentina 2	Rangers 1 *(2nd Leg)*	Florence	50,000	Hernadi (H)
1962	Atletico Madrid 1	Fiorentina 1	Glasgow	27,389	Wharton (S)
Replay	Atletico Madrid 3	Fiorentina 0	Stuttgart	45,000	Tschenscher (WG)
1963	Tottenham Hotspur 5	Atletico Madrid 1	Rotterdam	25,000	Van Leuwen (Ho)
1964	Sporting Lisbon 3	MTK Budapest 3 *(aet)*	Brussels	9000	Van Nuffel (Bel)
Replay	Sporting Lisbon 1	MTK Budapest 0	Antwerp	18,000	Versyp (Bel)
1965	West Ham U 2	Munich 1860 0	Wembley	100,000	Szolt (H)
1966	Borussia Dortmund 2	Liverpool 1 *(aet)*	Glasgow	41,657	Schwinte (F)
1967	Bayern Munich 1	Rangers 0 *(aet)*	Nuremberg	69,480	Lo Bello (I)
1968	AC Milan 2	Hamburg 0	Rotterdam	60,000	Ortiz (Sp)
1969	Slovan Bratislava 3	Barcelona 2	Basle	40,000	Van Ravens (Ho)
1970	Manchester C 2	Gornik Zabrze 1	Vienna	10,000	Schiller (A)
1971	Chelsea 1	Real Madrid 1 *(aet)*	Athens	42,000	Scheurer (Sw)
Replay	Chelsea 2	Real Madrid 1 *(aet)*	Athens	24,000	Bucheli (Sw)
1972	Rangers 3	Moscow Dynamo 2	Barcelona	35,000	Ortiz (Sp)
1973	AC Milan 1	Leeds U 0	Salonika	45,000	Mihas (Gr)
1974	Magdeburg 2	AC Milan 0	Rotterdam	5000	Van Gemert (Ho)
1975	Dynamo Kiev 3	Ferencvaros 0	Basle	13,000	Davidson (S)
1976	Anderlecht 4	West Ham U 2	Brussels	58,000	Wurtz (F)
1977	Hamburg 2	Anderlecht 0	Amsterdam	65,000	Partridge (E)
1978	Anderlecht 4	Austria/WAC 0	Paris	48,679	Adlinger (WG)
1979	Barcelona 4	Fortuna Dusseldorf 3 *(aet)*	Basle	58,000	Palotai (H)
1980	Valencia 0	Arsenal 0	Brussels	40,000	Christov (Cz)
	(aet; Valencia won 5-4 on penalties)				
1981	Dynamo Tbilisi 2	Carl Zeiss Jena 1	Dusseldorf	9000	Lattanzi (I)
1982	Barcelona 2	Standard Liege 1	Barcelona	100,000	Eschweiler (WG)
1983	Aberdeen 2	Real Madrid 1 *(aet)*	Gothenburg	17,804	Menegali (I)
1984	Juventus 2	Porto 1	Basle	60,000	Prokop (EG)
1985	Everton 3	Rapid Vienna 1	Rotterdam	30,000	Casarin (I)
1986	Dynamo Kiev 3	Atletico Madrid 0	Lyon	39,300	Wohrer (A)
1987	Ajax 1	Lokomotiv Leipzig 0	Athens	35,000	Agnolin (I)
1988	Mechelen 1	Ajax 0	Strasbourg	39,446	Pauly (WG)
1989	Barcelona 2	Sampdoria 0	Berne	45,000	Courtney (E)
1990	Sampdoria 2	Anderlecht 0	Gothenburg	20,103	Galler (Sw)
1991	Manchester U 2	Barcelona 1	Rotterdam	45,000	Karlsson (Se)
1992	Werder Bremen 2	Monaco 0	Lisbon	16,000	D'Elia (I)
1993	Parma 3	Antwerp 1	Wembley	37,393	Assenmacher (G)

Arsenal's European Cup-Winners Cup marksman Alan Smith in upright pose against the Italian club Parma. (Colorsport).

EUROPEAN CUP-WINNERS'CUP 1993–94

Preliminary Round, First Leg

Balzers 3 *(Nushar, Frick 2)*, Albpetrol 1 *(Poci)* 500
RAF Jelgava 0, Havnar Boltfelag 1 *(Kozlav)* 1000
Dudelange (0) 0, Maccabi Haifa (1) 1 *(Mizrahi 39)*, 1363
Lugano (1) 5 *(Andrioli 37, 83, Subiat 59, Fink 68, Penzavali 87)*, Neman Grodno (0) 0 4000
Valur (0) 3 *(Gregory 52, 59, Larusson 70)*, MyPa (1) 1 *(Rajamaky 34)* 2000
Sliema Wanderers (0) 1 *(Gregory 67)*, Degerfors (2) 3 *(Octosson 6, 30, Froberg 52)* 4000
Bangor (1) 1 *(McAvoy 24)*, Apoel (1) 1 *(Sotirou 45)* 3000
Nikol Tallinn (0) 0, Lillestrom (4) 4 *(Karlsson 4, Gulbrandsen 8, Schiller 37, Bjarmann 42)* 7500
Kosice (2) 2 *(Danko 20, Podegayve 40)*, Zalgiris (0) 0 6000
Karpaty Lvov (0) 1 *(Yevtushok)*, Shelbourne (0) 0 25,000
Publikum Celje (0) 0, Odense (0) 1 *(Nedergaard 82)* 2000

Preliminary Round, Second Leg

Albpetrol 0, Balzers 0 2500
Degerfors (2) 3 *(Ottosson 3, Froberg 15, Eriksson 63 (pen))*, Sliema Wanderers (0) 0 4019
Havnar Boltfelag w.o. RAF Jelgava failed to fulfill fixture.
Apoel (1) 2 *(Mihaijlovic 15, Pounas 69)*, Bangor (1) 1 *(Glendinning 4)* 16,000
Lillestrom (3) 4 *(Gulbrandsen 35, Bergdolmo 38, Mjelde 40, MacManus 71)*, Nikol Tallinn (0) 1 *(Arendas 70)* 1120
Maccabi Haifa (2) 6 *(Mizrahi 25, 51 (pen), Kondoroav 32, Atar 56, Holzman 74, Harazi 77)*, Dudelange (0) 1 *(Olhausen 89)* 3500
MyPa (0) 0, Valur (0) 1 *(Larusson 68)* 3000
Neman Grodno (0) 2 *(Solodobvnikov 61, Mazurchik 70)*, Lugano (1) 1 *(Subiat 29)* 4000
Odense (0) 0, Publikum Celje (0) 0 2525
Shelbourne (1) 3 *(Costello 9, Mooney 67, Lizzi 76)*, Karpaty Lvov (0) 1 *(Masur 88)* 5000
Zalgiris (0) 0, Kosice (1) 1 *(Durasa 13)* 3000

First Round, First Leg

Apoel (0) 0, Paris St Germain (0) 1 *(Sassus 78)* 13,000
Bayer Leverkusen (1) 2 *(Hapal 32, Thom 66)*, Boby Brno (0) 0 6100
Degerfors (0) 1 *(Berger 72)*, Parma (0) 2 *(Asprilla 87, 88)* 10,482
Valur (0) 0, Aberdeen (2) 3 *(Shearer 9, Jess 28, 56)* 656
Benfica (0) 1 *(Rui Aguas 88)*, Katowice (0) 0 30,000
CSKA Sofia (3) 8 *(Shishkov 12, 21, 57, 69, Andenov 41, 52, Nankov 67 (pen), 80)*, Balzers (0) 0 35,000
Hajduk Split (1) 1 *(Mornar 44)*, Ajax (0) 0 10,000
Innsbruck (0) 3 *(Danek 48, Westerthaler 58, Carracedo 65)*, Ferencvaros (0) 0 7500
Kosice (0) 2 *(Danko 70 (pen), 79)*, Besiktas (1) 1 *(Sergen 2)*, 6000
Lillestrom (0) 0, Torino (1) 2 *(Silenzi 26, Jarni 58)* 5056
Moscow Torpedo (0) 1 *(Borisov 88)*, Maccabi Haifa (0) 0 10,000
Odense (1) 1 *(Keown (og) 18)*, Arsenal (1) 2 *(Wright 35, Merson 68)* 9580
Panathinaikos (2) 3 *(Donis 13, Saravakos 37, Warzycha 48)*, Shelbourne (0) 0 30,000
Real Madrid (1) 3 *(Djubovsky 44, Michel 66 (pen), Fernandez (og) 70)*, Lugano (0) 0 37,600
Standard Liege (1) 5 *(Bisconti 13, Wilmots 63, 84, Andre Cruz 71 (pen), Asselman 76)*, Cardiff City (1) 2 *(Bird 39, 62)* 25,000
Uni Craiova (0) 4 *(Craioveanu 47, Gane 58, 71, Calin 82)*, Havnar Boltfelag (0) 0 9000

First Round, Second Leg

Cardiff City (0) 1 *(James 59)*, Standard Liege (2) 3 *(Wilmots 14, Lashaf 36, Bisconti 50)* 6096
Maccabi Haifa (1) 3 *(Mizrahi 6, Petz 71, Holzman 85)*, Moscow Torpedo (1) 1 *(Kalaychev 12)* 13,000
Paris St Germain (2) 2 *(Le Guen 1, Gravelaine 32)*, Apoel (0) 0 13,500
Parma (1) 2 *(Balleri 2, Brolin 67)*, Degerfors (0) 0 17,000
Aberdeen (0) 4 *(Miller 51, Jess 60, 69, Irvine 65)*, Valur (0) 0 10,000
Ajax (2) 6 *(Ronald de Boer 11, Davids 36, 76, Litmanen 57, Frank de Boer 61, Pettersson 71)*, Hajduk Split (0) 0 40,000
Arsenal (0) 1 *(Campbell 52)*, Odense (0) 1 *(Nielsen 86)*, 25,689
Balzers (0) 1 *(Kuster 63)*, CSKA Sofia (1) 3 *(Andenov 31, Tanev 54, Ciric 90)*, 1200
Besiktas (1) 2 *(Metin 44, 72)*, Kosice (0) 0 27,000
Boby Brno (0) 0, Bayer Leverkusen (1) 3 *(Kirsten 16, Fischer 57, Worns 75)*, 10,105
Ferencvaros (0) 1 *(Detari 50)*, Innsbruck (1) 2 *(Westerthaler 19, 90)* 12,000
Katowice (0) 1 *(Kucz 46)*, Benfica (0) 1 *(Vitor Paneira 70)* 7000
Havnar Boltfelag (0) 0, Uni Craiova (2) 3 *(Gane 27, 33, Vase 76)* 276
Lugano (0) 1 *(Subiat 62)*, Real Madrid (1) 3 *(Hierro 40, Zamorano 78, 87)* 8000
Shelbourne (0) 1 *(Mooney 86)*, Panathinaikos (1) 2 *(Georgiadis 26, Saravakos 57)* 2000
Torino (1) 1 *(Silenzi 45)*, Lillestrom (0) 2 *(Sinigaglia (og) 48, Mjielde 58)* 25,000

Second Round, First Leg

Ajax (0) 2 *(Rijkaard 60, Ronald de Boer 81)*, Besiktas (1) 1 *(Mehmet 41)* 42,000
Arsenal (1) 3 *(Wright 39, 63, Merson 50)*, Standard Liege (0) 0 25,258
Benfica (2) 3 *(Babunski (og) 26, Rui Costa 37, Schwarz 90)*, CSKA Sofia (0) 1 *(Andenov 60)* 40,000
Innsbruck (0) 1 *(Streiter 69 (pen))*, Real Madrid (1) 1 *(Alfonso 50)* 10,000
Maccabi Haifa (0) 0, Parma (0) 1 *(Brolin 90)* 13,000
Panathinaikos (1) 1 *(Warzycha 44)*, Bayer Leverkusen (1) 4 *(Paulo Sergio 42, Thom 52, Kirsten 59, Hapal 72)* 60,000
Paris St Germain (2) 4 *(Guerin 12, Ginola 17 (pen), Bita (og) 58, Valdo 71)*, Uni Craiova (0) 0 20,000
Torino (1) 3 *(Sergio 45, Fortunato 51, Aguilera 88)*, Aberdeen (2) 2 *(Paatelainen 9, Jess 24)* 30,000

Second Round, Second Leg

Aberdeen (1) 1 *(Richardson 12)*, Torino (1) 2 *(Carbone 39, Silenzi 53)* 21,655
CSKA Sofia (0) 1 *(Andenov 56)*, Benfica (1) 3 *(Rui Costa 37, Joao Pinto 73, Yuran 89)* 25,000
Parma (0) 0, Maccabi Haifa (0) 1 *(Mizrahi 51)* 9312
Parma won 3-1 on penalties
Real Madrid (1) 3 *(Michel 6, Butragueno 46, Alfonso 65)*, Innsbruck (0) 0 19,300
Uni Craiova (0) 0, Paris St Germain (1) 2 *(Guerin 29, 48)* 20,000
Standard Liege (0) 0, Arsenal (4) 7 *(Smith 2, Selley 20, Adams 36, Campbell 41, 80, Merson 72, McGoldrick 82)* 15,000
Bayer Leverkusen (0) 1 *(Kirsten 83)*, Panathinaikos (1) 2 *(Saravakos 6 (pen), Georgiadis 66)* 15,000
Besiktas (0) 0, Ajax (1) 4 *(Litmanen 19, 71, 74, Pettersson 77)* 27,000

Quarter-finals, First Leg

Benfica (0) 1 *(Isaias 89)*, Bayer Leverkusen (0) 1 *(Happe 64)* 85,000
Torino (0) 0, Arsenal (0) 0 32,480
Ajax (0) 0, Parma (0) 0 40,000
Real Madrid (0) 0, Paris St Germain (1) 1 *(Weah 32)* 62,000

Quarter-finals, Second Leg

Arsenal (0) 1 *(Adams 66)*, Torino (0) 0 34,678
Bayer Leverkusen (1) 4 *(Kirsten 24, 80, Schuster 58, Hapal 80)*, Benfica (0) 4 *(Xavier 59, Joao Pinto 60, Kulkov 78, 86)* 20,500
Paris St Germain (0) 1 *(Ricardo 51)*, Real Madrid (1) 1 *(Butragueno 20)* 45,000
Parma (1) 2 *(Minotti 15, Brolin 48)*, Ajax (0) 0 25,000

Semi-finals, First Leg

Paris St Germain (0) 1 *(Ginola 50)*, Arsenal (1) 1 *(Wright 35)* 46,000
Benfica (1) 2 *(Isaias 7, Rui Costa 60)*, Parma (1) 1 *(Zola 13)* 70,000

Semi-finals, Second Leg

Arsenal (1) 1 *(Campbell 6)*, Paris St Germanin (0) 0 34,212
Parma (0) 1 *(Sensini 77)*, Benfica (0) 0 25,000

Final: Arsenal (0) 1, Parma (0) 0

(in Copenhagen, 4 May 1994, 33,765)

Arsenal: Seaman; Dixon, Winterburn, Davis, Bould, Adams, Campbell, Morrow, Smith, Merson (McGoldrick 86), Selley.
Scorer: Smith.
Parma: Bucci; Benarrivo, Di Chiara, Minotti, Apolloni, Sensini, Brolin, Pin (Melli 70), Crippa, Zola, Asprilla.
Referee: Krondl (Czech Republic).

EUROPEAN CUP-WINNERS' CUP 1993–94 -BRITISH AND IRISH CLUBS

Preliminary Round, First Leg

18 AUG

Bangor (1) 1 *(McEvoy)*
Apoel (1) 1 *(Sotirou)* 3000
Bangor: Eachus; Canning, Glendinning, McGuinness, Brown, O'Connor, Hill, Kenny, McCallan (Surgeon), McCreadie (Magee), McEvoy.
Apoel: Petrides; Pounas, Kleanthous, Charalambous, Gudinov, Aristocleus (Magnitis), Mihajlovic, Sotirou, Gunev, Ioannou (Nwakama).

Karpaty Lvov (0) 1 *(Yevtoushok)*
Shelbourne (0) 0 25,000
Karpaty Lvov: Stronsitsky; Yevtoushok, Tchychevsky, Shyn, Makrytsky, Petrik, Pokladok, Kardash, Rafaltshouk (Shobiagytsky), Plotko, Stelmach.
Shelbourne: Byrne; Neville, Whelan, Brady, Dunne, Mooney, Doolin, Rutherford, Costello, Atkins (Browne), O'Doherty.

Preliminary Round, Second Leg

1 SEPT

Apoel (1) 2 *(Mihajlovic, Pounas)*
Bangor (1) 1 *(Glendinning)* 16,000
Apoel: Petrides; Costa, Klleanthous, Pounas, Gudinov, Aristocleus (Magnitis), Mihajlovic, Sotirou, Nwakama (Phasoyliotis), Ioannou, Hadjilucas.
Bangor: Eachus; Canning, Glendinning, McGuinness, Brown, O'Connor, Hill, Kenny, McCallan (Surgeon), Crowe (Dornan), McEvoy.

Shelbourne (1) 3 *(Costello, Mooney, Lizzi)*
Karpaty Lvov (0) 1 *(Masur)* 4200
Shelbourne: Byrne; Flood, Whelan, Neville, Brady, Mooney, Costello, Doolin, Rutherford, Duffy, O'Doherty (Lizzi).
Karpaty Lvov: Stronsitsky; Moknitsky, Tchychevsky, Evu, Mazur, Riznik, Stelmach, Petrik, Plotko, Kardash, Pokladok.

First Round, First Leg

14 SEPT

Valur (0) 0
Aberdeen (2) 3 *(Shearer, Jess 2)* 656
Valur: Sigurdsson; Stefansson, Jonsson J (Valsson), Davidsson, Helgason, Jonsson E, Gylfason, Adolfsson, Gregory (Hreidarsson), Larusson, Magnusson.
Aberdeen: Snelders; McKimmie, McLeish, Irvine, Wright, Kane, Miller (Aitken), Bett (Winnie), Connor, Jess, Shearer.

15 SEPT

Odense (1) 1 *(Keown (og))*
Arsenal (1) 2 *(Wright, Merson)* 9580
Odense: Hogh; Helveg, Hemmingsen, Sanglid (Hjorth), Nedergaard, Nielsen A, Steen-Nielsen, Skaarup, Thorup, Dethlefsen, Tchami.
Arsenal: Seaman; McGoldrick, Winterburn, Davis, Linighan, Keown, Jensen, Wright (Smith), Campbell, Merson, Selley.

Panathinaikos (2) 3 *(Donis, Saravakos, Warzycha)*
Shelbourne (0) 0 30,000
Panathinaikos: Wandzyk; Mavridis, Kalitszakis, Georgiadis, Apostolakis, Donis, Christodiou (Markou), Fratzeskos, Maragos (Giotas), Saravakos, Warzycha.
Shelbourne: Byrne; Flood, Whelan, Brady, Wilson (Browne), Mooney, Costello, Doolin, Rutherford, Cooney, O'Doherty.

Standard Liege (1) 5 *(Bisconti, Wilmots 2, Cruz (pen), Asselman)*
Cardiff C (1) 2 *(Bird 2)* 25,000
Standard Liege: Bodart; Smeets, Leonard, Bisconti, Cruz, Pister, Hellers, Asselman, Bettagno, Rychkov, Wilmots.
Cardiff C: Kite; James, Searle, Baddeley, Perry, Ratcliffe, Bird, Richardson, Stant, Blake, Griffith.

First Round, Second Leg

28 SEPT

Cardiff C (0) 1 *(James)*
Standard Liege (2) 3 *(Wilmots, Lashaf, Bisconti)* 6096
Cardiff C: Williams; James, Searle, Baddeley, Perry, Ratcliffe, Bird (Wigg), Miller (Bartley), Stant, Thompson, Griffith.
Standard Liege: Bodart (Munaron); Bisconti, Leonard, Vervoort (Smeets), Cruz, Pister, Hellers, Asselman, Lashaf, Van Rooy, Wilmots.

29 SEPT

Aberdeen (0) 4 *(Miller, Jess 2, Irvine)*
Valur (0) 0 10,000
Aberdeen: Snelders; McKimmie (Winnie), Irvine, Smith, Wright, Kane, Bett, Richardson, Miller (Gibson), Jess, Paatelainen.
Valur: Sigurdsson; Gajic, Helgason, Jonsson J, Davidsson (Petursson), Jonsson S, Gylfason, Adolfsson (Hreidarsson), Gregory, Larusson, Magnusson.

Arsenal (0) 1 *(Campbell)*
Odense (0) 1 *(Nielsen)* 25,689
Arsenal: Seaman; Dixon, Winterburn, Davis, Keown, Adams, Jensen, Wright (Smith), Campbell, Merson, McGoldrick.
Odense: Hogh; Nedergaard, Hemmingsen, Steen-Nielsen, Helveg, Nielsen A, Hjorth (Melvang), Dethlefsen, Thorup, Tchami, Skaarup (Damsted).

Shelbourne (0) 1 *(Mooney)*
Panathinaikos (1) 2 *(Georgiadis, Saravakos)* 2000

Shelbourne: Byrne; Flood, Neville, Whelan, Brady, Mooney, Costello, Doolin, Rutherford, O'Doherty, Duffy (Cooney).
Panathinaikos: Wandzyk; Apostolakis, Mavridis, Antoniou, Kalitzakis, Donis (Giotas), Noblias, Maragos, Georgiadis (Fratzeskos), Warzycha, Saravakos.

Second Round, First Leg

20 OCT

Arsenal (1) 3 *(Wright 2, Merson)*
Standard Liege (0) 0 25,258

Arsenal: Seaman; Dixon, Winterburn, Davis, Keown (Linighan), Adams, Jensen, Wright (Campbell), Smith, Merson, McGoldrick.
Standard Liege: Munaron; Genaux, Hellers, Rednic, Leonard, Vervoort, Wilmots, Pister, Van Rooy, Asselman (Goossens), Lashaf.

Torino (1) 3 *(Sergio, Fortunato, Aguilera)*
Aberdeen (2) 2 *(Paatelainen, Jess)* 30,000

Torino: Galli; Mussi, Sergio, Gregucci (Osio), Annoni, Fusi, Francescoli, Fortunato, Silenzi, Carbone (Aguilera), Venturin.
Aberdeen: Snelders; McKimmie, Smith, Kane, McLeish, Irvine, Richardson, Grant, Jess (Wright), Connor, Paatelainen.

Second Round, Second Leg

3 NOV

Aberdeen (1) 1 *(Richardson)*
Torino (1) 2 *(Carbone, Silenzi)* 21,655

Aberdeen: Snelders; McKimmie, McLeish, Irvine, Smith (Connor), Grant (Miller), Richardson, Kane, Jess, Shearer, Paatelainen.
Torino: Galli; Mussi (Cois), Gregucci (Falcone), Dellicari, Sergio, Fusi, Fortunato, Sinigaglia, Venturin, Silenzi, Carbone.

Standard Liege (0) 0 15,000
Arsenal (4) 7 *(Smith, Selley, Adams, Campbell 2, Merson, McGoldrick)*

Standard Liege: Munaron; Genaux, Hellers, Cruz, Leonard, Van Rooy, Pister, Wilmots, Bisconti, Goossens, Asselman.
Arsenal: Seaman; Dixon, Winterburn, Davis, Keown (Bould), Adams, Jensen, Campbell, Smith (McGoldrick), Merson, Selley.

Quarter-finals, First Leg

2 MAR

Torino (0) 0
Arsenal (0) 0 32,480

Torino: Galli; Fusi, Gregucci, Sottil (Sinigaglia), Cois, Mussi, Fortunato, Venturin, Jarni, Francescoli, Silenzi (Carbone).
Arsenal: Seaman; Dixon, Winterburn, Davis (Selley), Bould, Adams, Jensen, Campbell, Smith, Merson, Hillier.

Quarter-finals, Second Leg

15 MAR

Arsenal (0) 1 *(Adams)*
Torino (0) 0 34,678

Arsenal: Seaman; Dixon, Winterburn, Davis, Bould, Adams, Jensen (Keown), Wright, Smith, Merson, Hillier (Selley).
Torino: Galli; Annoni, Mussi, Cois, Gregucci, Fusi, Sinigaglia (Poggi), Fortunato, Silenzi, Francescoli, Venturin (Jarni).

Semi-finals, First Leg

29 MAR

Paris St Germain (0) 1 *(Ginola)*
Arsenal (1) 1 *(Wright)* 46,000

Paris St Germain: Lama; Lalcer (Bravo), Sassus, Ricardo, Colleter, Le Guen, Fournier, Guerin, Valdo, Ginola, Weah.
Arsenal: Seaman; Dixon, Winterburn, Davis (Keown), Bould, Adams, Jensen, Wright, Smith (Campbell), Selley.

Semi-finals, Second Leg

12 APR

Arsenal (1) 1 *(Campbell)*
Paris St Germain (0) 0 34,212

Arsenal: Seaman; Dixon, Winterburn (Keown), Davis (Hillier), Bould, Adams, Jensen, Wright, Smith, Campbell, Selley.
Paris St Germain: Lama; Sassus (Lalcer), Colleter, Ricardo, Roche, Le Guen, Fournier, Guerin, Rai (Gravelaine), Valdo, Ginola.

INTER-CITIES FAIRS & UEFA CUP

FAIRS CUP FINALS 1958–71

(Winners in italics)

Year	First Leg	Attendance	Second Leg	Attendance
1958	London 2 Barcelona 2	45,466	*Barcelona* 6 London 0	62,000
1960	Birmingham C 0 Barcelona 0	40,500	*Barcelona* 4 Birmingham C 1	70,000
1961	Birmingham C 2 Roma 2	21,005	*Roma* 2 Birmingham C 0	60,000
1962	Valencia 6 Barcelona 2	65,000	Barcelona 1 *Valencia* 1	60,000
1963	Dynamo Zagreb 1 Valencia 2	40,000	*Valencia* 2 Dynamo Zagreb 0	55,000
1964	*Zaragoza* 2 Valencia 1	50,000	(in Barcelona)	
1965	*Ferencvaros* 1 Juventus 0	25,000	(in Turin)	
1966	Barcelona 0 Zaragoza 1	70,000	Zaragoza 2 *Barcelona* 4	70,000
1967	Dynamo Zagreb 2 Leeds U 0	40,000	Leeds U 0 *Dynamo Zagreb* 0	35,604
1968	Leeds U 1 Ferencvaros 0	25,368	Ferencvaros 0 *Leeds U* 0	70,000
1969	Newcastle U 3 Ujpest Dozsa 0	60,000	Ujpest Dozsa 2 *Newcastle U* 3	37,000
1970	Anderlecht 3 Arsenal 1	37,000	*Arsenal* 3 Anderlecht 0	51,612
1971	Juventus 0 Leeds U 0 *(abandoned 51 minutes)*	42,000		
	Juventus 2 Leeds U 2	42,000	*Leeds U* 1* Juventus 1	42,483

UEFA CUP FINALS 1972–93

(Winners in italics)

Year	First Leg	Attendance	Second Leg	Attendance
1972	Wolverhampton W 1 Tottenham H 2	45,000	*Tottenham H* 1 Wolverhampton W 1	48,000
1973	Liverpool 0 Moenchengladbach 0 *(abandoned 27 minutes)*	44,967		
	Liverpool 3 Moenchengladbach 0	41,169	Moenchengladbach 0 *Liverpool* 2	35,000
1974	Tottenham H 2 Feyenoord 2	46,281	*Feyenoord* 2 Tottenham 0	68,000
1975	Moenchengladbach 0 Twente 0	45,000	Twente 1 *Moenchengladbach* 5	24,500
1976	Liverpool 3 FC Brugge 2	56,000	FC Brugge 1 *Liverpool* 1	32,000
1977	Juventus 1 Athletic Bilbao 0	75,000	Athletic Bilbao 2 *Juventus* 1*	43,000
1978	Bastia 0 PSV Eindhoven 0	15,000	*PSV Eindhoven* 3 Bastia 0	27,000
1979	Red Star Belgrade 1 Moenchengladbach 1	87,500	*Moenchengladbach* 1 Red Star Belgrade 0	45,000
1980	Moenchengladbach 3 Eintracht Frankfurt 2	25,000	*Eintracht Frankfurt* 1* Moenchengladbach 0	60,000
1981	Ipswich T 3 AZ 67 Alkmaar 0	27,532	AZ 67 Alkmaar 4 *Ipswich T* 2	28,500
1982	Gothenburg 1 Hamburg 0	42,548	Hamburg 0 *Gothenburg* 3	60,000
1983	Anderlecht 1 Benfica 0	45,000	Benfica 1 *Anderlecht* 1	80,000
1984	Anderlecht 1 Tottenham H 1	40,000	*Tottenham H* 1[1] Anderlecht 1	46,258
1985	Videoton 0 Real Madrid 3	30,000	*Real Madrid* 0 Videoton 1	98,300
1986	Real Madrid 5 Cologne 1	80,000	Cologne 2 *Real Madrid* 0	15,000
1987	Gothenburg 1 Dundee U 0	50,023	Dundee U 1 *Gothenburg* 1	20,911
1988	Espanol 3 Bayer Leverkusen 0	42,000	*Bayer Leverkusen* 3[2] Espanol 0	22,000
1989	Napoli 2 Stuttgart 1	83,000	Stuttgart 3 *Napoli* 3	67,000
1990	Juventus 3 Fiorentina 1	45,000	Fiorentina 0 *Juventus* 0	32,000
1991	Internazionale 2 Roma 0	68,887	Roma 1 *Internazionale* 0	70,901
1992	Torino 2 Ajax 2	65,377	*Ajax** 0 Torino 0	40,000
1993	Borussia Dortmund 1 Juventus 3	37,000	*Juventus* 3 Borussia Dortmund 0	62,781

* *won on away goals* [1] *Tottenham H won 4-3 on penalties aet* [2] *Bayer Leverkusen won 3-2 on penalties aet*

Internazionale players in carefree mood after clinching the UEFA Cup. (Colorsport).

UEFA CUP 1993–94

First Round, First Leg

Aalborg (0) 1 *(Thorst 66)*, La Coruna (0) 0 8100
Antwerp (0) 2 *(Severyns 57, Bursac 90)*, Maritimo (0) 0 7000
Salzburg (1) 2 *(Amerhauser 40, Pfeifenberger 85)*, Dunajska Streda (0) 0 6500
Bohemians (0) 0, Bordeaux (1) 1 *(Dugarry 16)* 5500
Crusaders (0) 0, Servette (0) 0 3400
Dnepr (0) 1 *(Maximov 77)*, Admira Wacker (0) 0 12,000
Hearts (0) 2 *(Robertson 70, Colquhoun 75)*, Atletico Madrid (0) 1 *(Kosecki 77)* 15,596
Karlsruhe (2) 2 *(Schmitt 20, Kiriakov 29)*, PSV Eindhoven (1) 1 *(Popescu 35 (pen))* 25,000
Kuusysi (3) 4 *(Annunen 17, Lius 19, 75, Lehtinen 25)*, Waregem (0) 0 2000
Dynamo Moscow (0) 0, Eintracht Frankfurt (3) 6 *(Gaudino 9, Weber 25, Furtok 45, Bein 48, Okocha 81, Yeboah 89)* 17,000
Union Luxembourg (0) 0, Boavista (1) 1 *(Casaca 40)* 1067
Vac (1) 2 *(Szediacsek 43, Nyilas 78)*, Apollon (0) 0 4000
Young Boys (0) 0, Celtic (0) 0 7300
Borussia Dortmund (0) 0, Vladikavkaz (0) 0 34,539
Botev Plovdiv (1) 2 *(Balakov 15, Hvoinev 88)*, Olympiakos (1) 3 *(Amanasidis 12, Tsiantakis 59, Batista 87)* 25,000
Brondby (1) 2 *(Vilfort 20, Kristensen 46)*, Dundee United (0) 0 5756
Gloria Bistrita (0) 0, Branik Maribor (0) 0 3800
Internazionale (1) 3 *(Bergkamp 11 (pen), 74, 78)*, Rapid Bucharest (0) 1 *(Andrasi 52)* 22,500
Juventus (0) 3 *(Roberto Baggio 49, 87, Ravanelli 70)*, Lokomotiv Moscow (0) 0 27,500 in Bologna
Kocaelispor (0) 0, Sporting Lisbon (0) 0 15,000
Lazio (1) 2 *(Casiraghi 22, Cravero 55)*, Lokomotiv Plovdiv (0) 0 39,500
Norrkoping (0) 0, Mechelen (1) 1 *(Czerniatynski 45)* 5557
Norwich City (0) 3 *(Ekoku 51, Goss 68, Polston 71)*, Vitesse (0) 0 16,818
Osters (1) 1 *(Persson 36)*, Kongsvinger (1) 3 *(Engerbakk 33, Francis 57, Frigard 59)* 1956
Slavia Prague (0) 1 *(Berger 52)*, Ofi Crete (0) 1 *(Georgamis 64)* 4106
Slovan Bratislava (0) 0, Aston Villa (0) 0 10,886
Tenerife (1) 2 *(Pinilla 19 (pen), Minambres 70)*, Auxerre (2) 2 *(Vahirua 16, Saib 21)* 20,000
Trabzonspor (3) 3 *(Ogun 28, 39, Hami 29)*, Valletta (1) 1 *(Zarb 25)* 20,000
Twente (0) 2 *(Boerebach 64, Prine Polley 70, Vurens 75)*, Bayern Munich (2) 2 *(Nerlinger 11, Ziege 27, 90, Scholl 65)* 18,000
Dinamo Bucharest (2) 3 *(Moldovan 5, 30, Pana 87 (pen))*, Cagliari (2) 2 *(Prunea (og) 13, Dely Valdes 38)* 5000
FC Reykjavik (0) 1 *(Ingimundarson 89)*, MTK Budapest (1) 2 *(Hamori 34, Zsivotzky 68)* 600
Nantes (1) 1 *(Oudec 12)*, Valencia (1) 1 *(Mijatovic 15)* 14,766

First Round, Second Leg

Admira Wacker (1) 2 *(Bacher 45, Ljung 90)*, Dnepr (1) 3 *(Bezhanar 43, Pokhlebaev 50, Mikaylenko 68)* 7300
Atletico Madrid (1) 3 *(Gonzalez 34, Manolo 72, Luis Garcia 76)*, Hearts (0) 0 35,000
Boavista (3) 4 *(Oliveira 18, 26, Marlon Brandao 30 (pen), Owubokiri 88)*, Union Luxembourg (0) 0 4000
Bordeaux (2) 5 *(Zidane 22, Vercruysse 25, 72, Paille 60, Fofana 67)*, Bohemians (0) 0 15,000
Dunajska Streda (0) 0, Salzburg (1) 2 *(Stadler 19, Pfeifenberger 58)* 8000
Dundee United (0) 3 *(McKinlay 67, Crabbe 79, Clark 119)*, Brondby (0) 1 *(Kristensen 91)* 8514
Eintracht Frankfurt (0) 1 *(Furtok 65)*, Moscow Dynamo (1) 2 *(Simutenkov 22, Dobrovolski 54)* 4900
La Coruna (1) 5 *(Bebeto 18, 51, 71, Barragan 66, 86)*, Aalborg (0) 0 20,000
Lokomotiv Moscow (0) 0, Juventus (0) 1 *(Marocchi 54)* 5000
Maritimo (0) 2 *(Heitor Junior 66, Vado 77)*, Antwerp (2) 2 *(Severeyns 37, Segers 42)*, 8000
Mechelen (0) 1 *(Eszenyi 113)*, Norrkoping (1) 1 *(Biohm 33)* 6500
PSV Eindhoven (0) 0, Karlsruhe (0) 0 24,000
Servette (0) 4 *(Anderson 57, Sinval 58, 60, Giallanza 63)*, Crusaders (0) 0 5200
Vladikavkaz (0) 0, Borussia Dortmund (0) 1 *(Chapuisat 62)* 31,500
Apollon (1) 4 *(Scepovic 40, 65, Spolarec 111 (pen), Kricmarevic 118)*, Vac (0) 0 8000
Aston Villa (2) 2 *(Atkinson 15, Townsend 22)*, Slovan Bratislava (0) 1 *(Tittel 86)* 24,461
Auxerre (0) 0, Tenerife (0) 1 *(Felipe 68)* 14,000
Bayern Munich (2) 3 *(Matthaus 18 (pen), Karnebeek (og) 45, Ziege 62)*, Twente (0) 0 24,000
Branik Maribor (1) 2 *(Stanic 5, 80)*, Gloria Bistrita (0) 0 6000
Cagliari (1) 2 *(Matteoli 6, Oliveira 63)*, Dinamo Bucharest (0) 0 37,500
Celtic (0) 1 *(Baumann (og) 106)*, Young Boys (0) 0 21,500
Kongsvinger (2) 4 *(Frigard 36, 82, 89, Engerback 45)*, Osters (1) 1 *(Landberg 41 (pen))* 3759
Lokomotiv Plovdiv (0) 0, Lazio (1) 2 *(Luzardi 22, Cravero 66)* 23,000
MTK Budapest (0) 0, FC Reykjavik (0) 0 1000
Ofi Crete (1) 1 *(Mahlas 42)*, Slavia Prague (0) 0 10,000
Olympiakos (1) 5 *(Christensen 38, 78, Tsiantakis 73, Mtsibonas 77 (pen), Batista 85)*, Botev Plovdiv (0) 1 *(Dimitrov 67 (pen))* 19,000
Rapid Bucharest (0) 0, Internazionale (0) 2 *(Battistini 75, Jonk 63)* 23,000
Sporting Lisbon (1) 2 *(Cadete 6, Pacheco 57)*, Kocaelispor (0) 0 45,000
Valletta (1) 1 *(Zarb 8)*, Trabzonspor (2) 3 *(Hani 11, Ogun 43, Unal 66)* 2000
Vitesse (0) 0, Norwich City (0) 0 9133
Waregem (0) 1 *(De Kneef 54)*, Kuusysi (0) 2 *(Annunen 84, Lius 88)* 5000
Valencia (0) 3 *(Penev 72 (pen), Galvez 104)*, *Gomez 112)*, Nantes (0) 1 *(Pedros 50)* 46,700

Second Round, First Leg

Branik Maribor 0, Borussia Dortmund 0 14,000
Celtic (1) 1 *(Creaney 9)*, Sporting Lisbon (0) 0 31,321
Internazionale (1) 1 *(Bergkamp 6)*, Apollon (0) 0 15,000
Kongsvinger (0) 1 *(Frigaard 89)*, Juventus (0) 1 *(Kohler 61)* 10,213
Lazio (0) 1 *(Winter 74)*, Boavista (0) 0 40,000
Mechelen (1) 5 *(Eszenyi 44, 80, 83, De Boeck 59, Leen 72)*, MTK Budapest (0) 0 7000
Trabzonspor (1) 1 *(Orhan 27)*, Cagliari (0) 1 *(Dely Valdes 89)* 21,500
Valencia (1) 3 *(Mijatovic 35, Penev 47, 74)*, Karlsruhe (0) 1 *(Schmitt 79)* 42,900

Atletico Madrid (0) 1 *(Luis Garcia 58)*, Ofi Crete (0) 0 11,600
Salzburg (0) 1 *(Jurcevic 67)*, Antwerp (0) 0 11,000
Bayern Munich (1) 1 *(Nerlinger 41)*, Norwich City (2) 2 *(Goss 13, Bowen 30)* 28,500
Bordeaux (1) 2 *(Paille 35, Vercruysse 56)*, Servette (0) 1 *(Anderson 55)* 15,000
Eintracht Frankfurt (0) 2 *(Furtok 65, Okocha 77)*, Dnepr (0) 0 6900
Kuusysi (1) 1 *(Lius 13)*, Brondby (1) 4 *(Okechukwu 1, Vilfort 59, Strudal 64, 84)* 5000
La Coruna (0) 1 *(Riesco 87)*, Aston Villa (0) 1 *(Saunders 80)* 26,800
Tenerife (1) 2 *(Julio Llorente 38, Del Solar 49)*, Olympiakos (1) 1 *(Christensen 10)* 20,000

Second Round, Second Leg

Antwerp (0) 0, Salzburg (0) 1 *(Feiersinger 84)* 7500
Juventus (1) 2 *(Moller 27, Ravanelli 68)*, Kongsvinger (0) 0 14,000
Karlsruhe (3) 7 *(Schmitt 29, 34, 59, 63), Schutterle 37, Schmarov 46, Bilic 90)*, Valencia (0) 0 25,000
MTK Budapest (0) 1 *(Kovacs 59)*, Mechelen (1) 1 *(Carlos Pereira 10)* 1500
Ofi Crete (0) 2 *(Mahlas 51, Tsifoutis 64)*, Atletico Madrid (0) 0 13,000
Apollon (2) 3 *(Spolijiarec 11, Cepovic 32, Iosephides 85)*, Internazionale (3) 3 *(Shalimov 6, Bergkamp 8, Fontalan 38)* 12,000
Aston Villa (0) 0, La Coruna (1) 1 *(Manjarin 36)* 26,737
Borussia Dortmund (0) 2 *(Chapuisat 48, 52)*, Branik Maribor (1) 1 *(Bozgo 21)* 25,000
Brondby (1) 3 *(Kristensen 39, Madsen 68, Hoegh 85 (pen))*, Kuusysi (1) 1 *(Annunen 6)* 5834
Caligari 0, Trabzonspor 0 30,000
Dnepr (1) 1 *(Chukhliba 43)*, Eintracht Frankfurt (0) 0 25,000
Norwich City (0) 1 *(Goss 50)*, Bayern Munich (1) 1 *(Valencia 4)* 20,829
Servette (0) 0, Bordeaux (0) 1 *(Schepul (og) 66)* 18,000
Sporting Lisbon (1) 2 *(Cadete 18, 60)*, Celtic (0) 0 60,000
Boavista (1) 2 *(Owubokiri 20, 52)*, Lazio (0) 0 10,000
Olympiakos (2) 4 *(Christensen 13, 34, 84, Ioannides 58)*, Tenerife (1) 3 *(Minambres 23, Chano 49 (pen), Amanatides 68 (og))* 28,000

Third Round, First Leg

Bordeaux (0) 1 *(Zidane 77)*, Karlsruhe (0) 0 32,000
Eintracht Frankfurt (0) 1 *(Dickhaut 89)*, La Coruna (0) 0 12,000
Ofi Crete (0) 1 *(Velic 89)*, Boavista (3) 4 *(Artur Oliveira 4, 22, 54, Owubokiri 42)* 10,000
Brondby (1) 1 *(Kristensen 19)*, Borussia Dortmund (0) 1 *(Chapuisat 61)* 16,817
Juventus (1) 3 *(Moller 3, Roberto Baggio 69 (pen), Ravanelli 75)*, Tenerife (0) 0 10,000
Norwich City (0) 0, Internazionale (0) 1 *(Bergkamp (pen))* 20,805
Sporting Lisbon (1) 2 *(Cherbakov 24, Cadete 63)*, Salzburg (0) 0 42,500
Mechelen (1) 1 *(Czerniatynski 38)*, Cagliari (1) 3 *(Matteoli 33, Oliviera 82, Pusceddu 87)* 7000

Third Round, Second Leg

Salzburg (0) 3 *(Lainer 47, Huetter 90, Amerhauser 113)*, Sporting Lisbon (0) 0 10,500
Boavista (1) 2 *(Nelson 24, Nogueira 77)*, Ofi Crete (0) 0 7000
Karlsruhe (1) 3 *(Schmitt 16, 75, Kiriakov 65)*, Bordeaux (0) 0 25,000
La Coruna (0) 0, Eintracht Frankfurt (1) 1 *(Gaudino 15)* 33,000
Borussia Dortmund (1) 1 *(Zorc 29)*, Brondby (0) 0 35,000
Cagliari (1) 2 *(Firicano 14, Allegri 79)*, Mechelen (0) 0 32,000
Internazionale (0) 1 *(Bergkamp 88)*, Norwich City (0) 0 30,000
Tenerife (1) 2 *(Aguilera 37, Del Solar 86)*, Juventus (0) 1 *(Moller 85)* 21,000

Quarter-finals, First Leg

Boavista (1) 1 *(Owubokiri 38)*, Karlsruhe (0) 1 *(Wittwer 77)* 18,500
Borussia Dortmund (0) 1 *(Schulz 83)*, Internazionale (2) 3 *(Jonk 33, 36, Shalimov 89)* 35,800
Cagliari (0) 1 *(Dely Valdes 59)*, Juventus (0) 0 25,000
Salzburg (1) 1 *(Huetter 30)*, Eintracht Frankfurt (0) 0 47,000

Quarter-finals, Second Leg

Eintracht Frankfurt (1) 1 *(Gaudino 21)*, Salzburg (0) 0 28,500
Juventus (1) 1 *(Dino Baggio 23)*, Cagliari (1) 2 *(Firicano 34, Oliveira 61)* 45,000
Karlsruhe (1) 1 *(Santos (og) 35)*, Boavista (0) 0 21,000
Internazionale (0) 1 *(Manicone 81)*, Borussia Dortmund (1) 2 *(Zorc 38, Zelic 46)* 20,000

Semi-finals, First Leg

Salzburg 0, Karlsruhe 0 30,000
Cagliari (1) 3 *(Oliveira 11, Criniti 81, Pancaro 86)*, Internazionale (1) 2 *(Fontalan 6, Sosa 61)* 30,000

Semi-finals, Second Leg

Internazionale (1) 3 *(Bergkamp 38 (pen), Berti 54, Jonk 63)*, Cagliari (0) 0 58,848
Karlsruhe (0) 1 *(Krieg 54)*, Salzburg (1) 1 *(Stadler 12)* 23,000

Final, First Leg: Salzburg (0) 0, Internazionale (1) 1

(in Vienna, 26 April 1994, 47,500)

Salzburg: Konrad; Lainer, Weber, Winklhofer (Steiner 61), Furstaller, Aigner, Amerhauser (Muzek 46), Artner, Marquinho, Pfeifenberger, Stadler.
Internazionale: Zenga; Paganin A, Orlando, Jonk, Bergomi, Battistini, Bianchi, Manicone, Berti, Bergkamp (Dell'Anno 89), Sosa (Ferri 74).
Scorer: Berti 35.
Referee: Nielsen (Denmark).

Final, Second Leg: Internazionale (0) 1, Salzburg (0) 0

(in Milan, 11 May 1994, 80,326)

Internazionale: Zenga; Paganin A, Fontolan (Ferri 67), Jonk, Bergomi, Battistini, Orlando, Manicone, Berti, Bergkamp (Paganin M 89), Sosa.
Scorer: Jonk 62.
Salzburg: Konrad; Lainer, Weber, Winklhofer (Amerhauser 67), Furstaller, Aigner, Jurcevic, Artner (Steiner 75), Marquinho, Feiersinger, Hutter.
Referee: McCluskey (Scotland).

EUROPEAN CUP DRAWS 1994–95

Champions Cup Preliminary Round
Paris St Germain v VAC Samsung (Hungary), Legia Warsaw v Hajduk Split, Steaua Bucharest v Servette (Switzerland), Sparta Prague v IFK Gothenburg, AEK Athens v Rangers, Maccabi Haifa (Israel) v Casino Salzburg, Silkeborg (Denmark) v Dynamo Kiev (Ukraine), Avenir Beggen (Luxembroug) v Galatasaray.

Champions League Draw
Group 1: Avenir Beggen or Galatasaray, Manchester United, Sparta Prague or IFK Gothenburg, Barcelona.
Group 2: Bayern Munich, Silkeborg or Dynamo Kiev, Spartak Moscow, Paris St Germain or VAC FC Samsung.
Group 3: Steaua Bucharest or Servette, Legia Warsaw or Hajduk Split, Benfica, Anderlecht.
Group 4: AC Milan, Maccabi Haifa or Salzburg, AEK Athens or Rangers, Ajax Amsterdam.

Cup-Winners' Cup Preliminary Round
FC Pirin (Bulgaria) v Schaan (Liechtenstein), Norma Tallinn (Estonia) v Maribor Branik (Slovenia), Fandok Bobruisk (Belarus) v Tirana (Albania), Tiligul Tiraspol (Moldova) v Omonia Nicosia (Cyprus), Ferencvaros (Hungary) v F91 Dudelange (Luxembourg), Floriana (Malta) v Sligo Rovers, Barry Town v Zalgiris Vilnius (Lithuania), Bodo Glimt (Norway) v Olimpija Riga (Latvia), Viktoria Zizkov (Czech Republic) v IFK Noorkoping (Sweden), Sandoyar Itrottarfelag (Faeroes) v HJK Helsinki, IBK Keflavik (Iceland) v Maccabi Tel-Aviv (Israel), Bangor (Northern Ireland) v Tatran Presov (Slovakia).

UEFA Cup Preliminary Round
Slavia Prague v Cork City, Motherwell v Havnar Boltfelag (Faeroes), FC Copenhagen v FC Jazz (Finland), Portadown v Slovan Bratislava, Bangor (Wales) v Akranes (Iceland), Anjalankoski (Finland) v Inter Bratislava, Odense BK v Flora Tallinn (Estonia), Lillestrom v Shakhter Donetsk (Ukraine), Gotu Itrottarfelag (Faeroes) v Trelleboras (Sweden), Gornik Zabrze (Poland) v Shamrock Rovers.
FC Romar (Lithuania) v AIK Solna (Sweden), Hafnarfjordur (Iceland) v Linfield, Skonto Riga (Latvia) v Aberdeen, Inter Cardiff v GKS Katowice, Rosenborg BK (Norway) v CS Grevenmacher (Luxembourg), Aarau (Switzerland) v FC Mura (Slovenia), Anorthosis Famagusta (Cyprus) v FC Chumen (Blugaria), Dynamo Tbilisi (Georgia) v Universitatae Craiova (Romania), FC Badar (Macedonia) v Bekescsabai (Hungary), SCT Olimpija (Slovenia) v Levski Sofia (Bulgaria), Fenerbahce (Turkey) v Touran (Azerbaijan).
Valletta (Malta) v Rapid Bucuresti (Romania), Kispest Honved (Hungary) v Zimbru Chisinau (Moldova), Ararat Erevan (Armenia) v CSKA Sofia, Dynamo Minsk (Belarus) v Hibernians (Malta), Teuta (Albania) v Apollon (Cyprus), Aris Thessaloniki (Greece) v Hapoel Beer Sheva (Israel).

UEFA CUP 1993–94 -BRITISH AND IRISH CLUBS

First Round, First Leg

14 SEPT

Bohemians (0) 0
Bordeaux (1) 1 *(Dugarry)* 5500
Bohemians: Henderson; O'Connor, Best, O'Driscoll, Kelch, Tilson, Moody, Fenlon, Dunne, Cousins (Geoghegan), Fitzgerald (King H).
Bordeaux: Horg; Croci, Lizarazu, Senac, Dogon, Lucas, Zidane (Witschge), Guerit, Daniel, Vercruysse, Dugarry (Fofana).

Crusaders (0) 0
Servette (0) 0 3400
Crusaders: McKeown; Lawlor, Cash (Lynch), Dunlop, Walker (Mallon), Hunter K, Livingstone, Gardiner, Murray, Hunter G, Burrows.
Servette: Pascolo; Barberis, Sauthier, Schepull, Djurovski, Duchosal, Sinval, Ohrel, Anderson, Aeby, Neuville.

Hearts (0) 2 *(Robertson, Colquhoun)*
Atletico Madrid (0) 1 *(Kosecki)* 15,596
Hearts: Smith; Locke, Levein, Weir, McKinlay, Mackay, McLaren, Leitch, Colquhoun, Robertson (Thomas), Fashanu.
Atletico Madrid: Diego; Gonzalez, Perez, Lopez, Gomez, Moacir, Manolo (Huerpos), Quevedo, Luis Garcia (Koseki), Mori, Kiko.

Young Boys (0) 0
Celtic (0) 0 7300
Young Boys: Kobel; Rotzetter, Reich, Weber, Moser, Baumann, Bregy, Sutter (Agostino), Kunz, Nowak, Ippoliti (Perfido).
Celtic: Bonner; Boyd, McNally, Galloway, Wdowczyk, Grant, McGinlay, McStay, Collins (O'Neil), Nicholas, Payton (Creaney).

15 SEPT

Brondby (1) 2 *(Vilfort, Kristensen)*
Dundee U (0) 0 5756
Brondby: Krogh; Bjur (Madsen), Okechukwu, Hogh, Risaser, Rieper, Jensen, Kristensen, Strudal, Thogersen, Vilfort.
Dundee U: Main; Clark, Welsh, Van Der Hoorn, Bollan, Perry, McKinlay (Johnson), Bowman, McLaren, Dailly, Crabbe (Connolly).

Norwich C (0) 3 *(Ekoku, Goss, Polston)*
Vitesse (0) 0 16,818
Norwich C: Gunn; Culverhouse, Bowen, Newman, Polston, Goss, Crook, Megson (Eadie), Ekoku, Fox, Sutton (Robins).
Vitesse: Van der Gouw; Straal, Van der Looi, Bos, Vermeulen, Lammers, Cocu, Loeffen, Latuheru, Gillhaus, Helder.

Slovan Bratislava (0) 0
Aston Villa (0) 0 10,886
Slovan Bratislava: Vencel; Stupala, Zeman, Tittel, Lancz (Pecko), Kristofik, Tomaschek, Kinder, Timko (Gostic), Maixner, Nigro.
Aston Villa: Spink; Barrett, Staunton, Teale, McGrath, Richardson, Houghton, Townsend, Saunders, Atkinson, Cowans.

First Round, Second Leg

28 SEPT

Atletico Madrid (1) 3 *(Gonzalez, Manolo, Garcia)*
Hearts (0) 0 35,000
Atletico Madrid: Diego; Bizo, Gomez, Pedro Gonzalez, Caminero, Lopez, Moacir, Manolo, Quevedo, Kosecki, Pirri.
Hearts: Smith; Locke, Levein, McLaren, McKinlay, Hogg, Mackay, Leitch, Colquhoun (Thomas), Fashanu (Ferguson), Robertson.

Bordeaux (2) 5 *(Zidane, Vercruysse 2, Paille, Fofana)*
Bohemians (0) 0 15,000
Bordeaux: Huard; Croci, Lizarazu, Santos, Senac, Dib (Daniel), Zidane, Guerit, Paille (Grenet), Vercruysse, Fofana.
Bohemians: Henderson; Broughan (Crawford), Kelch, Best, O'Driscoll, Dunne, Moody, O'Connor, Cousins (Fitzgerald), Fenlon, Tilson.

Dundee U (0) 3 *(McKinlay, Crabbe, Clark)*
Brondby (0) 1 *(Kristensen) aet* 8514
Dundee U: Main; Van Der Hoorn (O'Neil), Cleland, Malpas, Narey, Welsh, Bowman, McKinlay, Clark, Dailly (Connolly), Crabbe.
Brondby: Krogh; Eggen, Okechukwu, Hogh, Madsen, Rieper, Jensen (Bjur), Kristensen, Strudal (Raun), Thogersen, Vilfort.

Servette (0) 4 *(Anderson, Sinval 2, Giallanza)*
Crusaders (0) 0 5200
Servette: Pascolo; Barberis, Sauthier, Schepull, Djurovski, Duchosal (Gerble), Sinval, Ohrel, Anderson, Neuville (Barea), Giallanza.
Crusaders: McKeown; Lawlor, Stewart, Dunlop, Walker, Hunter K (Lynch), Livingstone, Gardiner (McCrae), Murray, Cash, Burrows.

29 SEPT

Aston Villa (2) 2 *(Atkinson, Townsend)*
Slovan Bratislava (0) 1 *(Tittel)* 24,461
Aston Villa: Spink; Cox, Staunton, Teale, McGrath, Richardson, Cowans, Townsend, Saunders, Atkinson, Whittingham.
Slovan Bratislava: Vencel; Stupala, Zeman, Kristofik (Lancz), Kinder, Tittel, Pecko, Tomaschek, Chvila, Nigro, Timko (Gostic).

Celtic (0) 1 *(Baumann (og))*

Young Boys (0) 0 *aet* 21,500

Celtic: Bonner; McNally, Gillespie (Wdowczyk), Galloway, Boyd, McGinlay (Nicholas), Grant, McStay, O'Neil, Payton, Creaney.
Young Boys: Kobel; Reich, Streun, Weber, Rotzetter, Bregy, Baumann, Moser, Ippoliti, Kunz (Greber), Agostino (Perfido).

Vitesse (0) 0

Norwich C (0) 0 9133

Vitesse: Van der Gouw; Sturing, Bos, Van de Looi, Vermeulen, Laamers, Cocu, Straal (Pothuizen), Latuheru, Gillhaus, Helder.
Norwich C: Gunn; Culverhouse, Bowen, Butterworth, Polston, Goss, Crook, Newman, Ekoku (Megson), Fox, Sutton.

Second Round, First Leg

19 OCT

Bayern Munich (1) 1 *(Nerlinger)*

Norwich C (2) 2 *(Goss, Bowen)* 28,500

Bayern Munich: Aumann; Jorginho, Kreuzer, Matthaus, Helmer, Scholl (Labbadia), Wouters, Nerlinger, Ziege (Sternkopf), Valencia, Witeczek.
Norwich C: Gunn; Culverhouse, Bowen, Butterworth, Prior, Goss, Crook, Newman, Robins (Sutch), Fox, Sutton.

La Coruna (0) 1 *(Riesco)*

Aston Villa (0) 1 *(Saunders)* 26,800

La Coruna: Liano; Nando, Djukic, Rivera, Voro (Vales), Mauro Silva, Donat, Fran, Lopez Rekarte, Bebeto, Manjarin (Riesco).
Aston Villa: Bosnich; Barrett, Small, Teale, McGrath, Richardson, Cowans, Townsend, Saunders, Atkinson, Daley.

20 OCT

Celtic (1) 1 *(Creaney)*

Sporting Lisbon (0) 0 31,321

Celtic: Bonner; Gillespie, Grant, Mowbray, Boyd, McGinlay, Byrne (O'Neil), McStay, Collins, Creaney, Nicholas.
Sporting Lisbon: Costinha; Nelson, Torres, Peixe, Valckx, Sousa, Capucho (Figo), Pacheco, Cherbakov, Balakov, Cadete.

Second Round, Second Leg

3 NOV

Aston Villa (0) 0

La Coruna (1) 1 *(Manjarin)* 26,737

Aston Villa: Bosnich; Barrett, Small, Teale, McGrath, Richardson, Cowans (Houghton), Townsend, Saunders, Atkinson, Daley.
La Coruna: Liano; Voro, Nando, Ribera, Djukic, Mauro Silva, Lopez Rekarte, Donato, Manjarin (Reisco), Fran, Bebeto (Vales).

Norwich C (0) 1 *(Goss)*

Bayern Munich (1) 1 *(Valencia)* 20,829

Norwich C: Gunn; Culverhouse, Bowen, Butterworth, Polston, Goss, Crook, Newman, Eadie (Akinbiyi), Fox (Sutch), Sutton.
Bayern Munich: Aumann; Jorginho, Ziege, Kreuzer, Helmer, Nerlinger, Wouters (Sternkopf), Witeczek (Scholl), Matthaus, Valencia.

Sporting Lisbon (1) 2 *(Cadete 2)*

Celtic (0) 0 60,000

Sporting Lisbon: Costinha; Nelson, Peixe, Valckx, Torres, Sousa, Figo, Filipe (Capucho), Cherbakov, Balakov, Cadete (Leal).
Celtic: Bonner; Grant, Gillespie, Mowbray, Boyd, Byrne, McStay, McGinlay, Collins, Creaney, Nicholas (O'Neil).

Third Round, First Leg

24 NOV

Norwich C (0) 0

Internazionale (0) 1 *(Bergkamp (pen))* 20,805

Norwich C: Gunn; Culverhouse, Bowen, Butterworth, Polston, Goss, Crook, Newman, Sutton, Fox, Sutch (Power).
Internazionale: Zenga; Bergomi, Orlando, Paganin M, Paganin A, Battistini, Dell'Anno, Jonk, Fontalan (Schillaci), Bergkamp, Sosa (Ferri).

Third Round, Second Leg

8 DEC

Internazionale (0) 1 *(Bergkamp)*

Norwich C (0) 0 30,000

Internazionale: Zenga; Bergomi, Orlando, Shalimov, Paganin M, Battistini, Paganin A, Dell'Anno, Fontalan, Bergkamp, Sosa.
Norwich C: Gunn; Woodthorpe, Bowen, Newman, Prior (Power), Ullathorne, Megson, Ekoku (Sutch), Sutton, Fox, Goss.

Summary of Appearances

EUROPEAN CUP (1955–94)

English clubs
12 Liverpool
6 Manchester U
3 Nottingham F, Leeds U
2 Derby Co, Wolverhampton W, Everton, Aston Villa, Arsenal
1 Burnley, Tottenham H, Ipswich T, Manchester C

Scottish clubs
15 Celtic, Rangers
3 Aberdeen
2 Hearts
1 Dundee, Dundee U, Kilmarnock, Hibernian

Welsh clubs
1 Cwmbran

Clubs for Northern Ireland
18 Linfield
8 Glentoran
2 Crusaders, Portadown
1 Glenavon, Ards, Distillery, Derry C, Coleraine

Clubs for Eire
7 Shamrock R, Dundalk
6 Waterford
3 Drumcondra
2 Bohemians, Limerick, Athlone T, Shelbourne
1 Cork Hibs, Cork Celtic, Cork City, Derry C*, Sligo Rovers, St Patrick's Ath

Winners: Celtic 1966–67; Manchester U 1967–68; Liverpool 1976–77, 1977–78, 1980–81, 1983–84; Nottingham F 1978–79, 1979–80; Aston Villa 1981–82

Finalists: Celtic 1969–70; Leeds U 1974–75; Liverpool 1984–85

EUROPEAN CUP-WINNERS' CUP (1960–94)

English clubs
6 Tottenham H
5 Manchester U
4 West Ham U, Liverpool
2 Arsenal, Chelsea, Everton, Manchester C
1 Wolverhampton W, Leicester C, WBA, Leeds U, Sunderland, Southampton, Ipswich T

Scottish clubs
10 Rangers
8 Aberdeen
7 Celtic
2 Dunfermline Ath, Dundee U
1 Dundee, Hibernian, Hearts, St Mirren, Motherwell, Airdrie

Welsh clubs
14 Cardiff C
7 Wrexham, Swansea C
2 Bangor C
1 Borough U, Newport Co, Merthyr Tydfil

Clubs from Northern Ireland
7 Glentoran
4 Ballymena U, Coleraine, Glenavon
3 Crusaders
2 Ards, Linfield
1 Bangor, Derry C, Distillery, Portadown, Carrick Rangers, Cliftonville

Clubs from Eire
6 Shamrock R
3 Limerick, Waterford, Dundalk, Bohemians
2 Cork Hibs, Galway U, Shelbourne
1 Cork Celtic, St Patrick's Ath, Finn Harps, Home Farm, Sligo Rovers, University College Dublin, Derry C*, Cork City, Bray Wanderers

Winners: Tottenham H 1962–63; West Ham U 1964–65; Manchester C 1969–70; Chelsea 1970–71; Rangers 1971–72; Aberdeen 1982–83; Everton 1984–85; Manchester U 1990-91; Arsenal 1993–94

Finalists: Rangers 1960–61, 1966–67; Liverpool 1965–66; Leeds U 1972–73; West Ham U 1975–76; Arsenal 1979–80

EUROPEAN FAIRS CUP & UEFA CUP (1955–94)

English clubs
8 Leeds U, Ipswich T
7 Liverpool
6 Everton, Arsenal, Manchester U
5 Aston Villa, Southampton, Tottenham H
4 Manchester C, Birmingham C, Newcastle U, Nottingham F, Wolverhampton W, WBA
3 Chelsea, Sheffield W
2 Stoke C, Derby Co, QPR
1 Burnley, Coventry C, Norwich C, London Rep XI, Watford

Scottish clubs
17 Dundee U
14 Hibernian
10 Aberdeen
9 Celtic, Hearts
8 Rangers
5 Dunfermline Ath
4 Dundee
3 St Mirren, Kilmarnock
2 Partick Th
1 Morton, St Johnstone

Clubs from Northern Ireland
11 Glentoran
6 Coleraine
4 Linfield
3 Glenavon
2 Portadown
1 Ards, Ballymena U, Bangor, Crusaders

Clubs from Eire
8 Bohemians
4 Dundalk
3 Finn Harps, Shamrock R
2 Shelbourne, Drumcondra, St Patrick's Ath, Derry C*
1 Cork Hibs, Athlone T, Limerick, Drogheda U, Galway U, Cork City

Winners: Leeds U 1967–68, 1970–71; Newcastle U 1968–69; Arsenal 1969–70; Tottenham H 1971–72, 1983–84; Liverpool 1972–73, 1975–76; Ipswich T 1980–81

Finalists: London 1955–58, Birmingham C 1958–60, 1960–61; Leeds U 1966–67; Wolverhampton W 1971–72; Tottenham H 1973–74; Dundee U 1986–87

** Now play in League of Ireland.*

WORLD CLUB CHAMPIONSHIP

Played annually up to 1974 and intermittently since then between the winners of the European Cup and the winners of the South American Champions Cup — known as the Copa Libertadores. In 1980 the winners were decided by one match arranged in Tokyo in February 1981 and the venue has been the same since. AC Milan replaced Marseille who had been stripped of their European Cup title in 1993.

1960 Real Madrid beat Penarol 0-0, 5-1
1961 Penarol beat Benfica 0-1, 5-0, 2-1
1962 Santos beat Benfica 3-2, 5-2
1963 Santos beat AC Milan 2-4, 4-2, 1-0
1964 Inter-Milan beat Independiente 0-1, 2-0, 1-0
1965 Inter-Milan beat Independiente 3-0, 0-0
1966 Penarol beat Real Madrid 2-0, 2-0
1967 Racing Club beat Celtic 0-1, 2-1, 1-0
1968 Estudiantes beat Manchester United 1-0, 1-1
1969 AC Milan beat Estudiantes 3-0, 1-2
1970 Feyenoord beat Estudiantes 2-2, 1-0
1971 Nacional beat Panathinaikos* 1-1, 2-1
1972 Ajax beat Independiente 1-1, 3-0
1973 Independiente beat Juventus* 1-0
1974 Atlético Madrid* beat Independiente 0-1, 2-0
1975 Independiente and Bayern Munich could not agree dates; no matches.
1976 Bayern Munich beat Cruzeiro 2-0, 0-0
1977 Boca Juniors beat Borussia Moenchengladbach* 2-2, 3-0
1978 Not contested
1979 Olimpia beat Malmö* 1-0, 2-1
1980 Nacional beat Nottingham Forest 1-0
1981 Flamengo beat Liverpool 3-0
1982 Penarol beat Aston Villa 2-0
1983 Gremio Porto Alegre beat SV Hamburg 2-1
1984 Independiente beat Liverpool 1-0
1985 Juventus beat Argentinos Juniors 4-2 on penalties after a 2-2 draw
1986 River Plate beat Steaua Bucharest 1-0
1987 FC Porto beat Penarol 2-1 after extra time
1988 Nacional (Uru) beat PSV Eindhoven 7-6 on penalties after 1-1 draw
1989 AC Milan beat Atletico Nacional (Col) 1-0 after extra time
1990 AC Milan beat Olimpia 3-0
1991 Red Star Belgrade beat Colo Colo 3-0
1992 Sao Paulo beat Barcelona 2-1

*European Cup runners-up; winners declined to take part.

1993

12 December in Tokyo

AC Milan (0) 2 *(Massaro 48, Papin 81)*

Sao Paulo (1) 3 *(Palinha 19, Cerezo 60, Muller 87)* 80,000

AC Milan: Rossi; Panucci, Maldini, Albertini (Orlando 80), Costacurta, Baresi, Donadoni, Desailly, Papin, Massaro, Raducioiu (Tassotti 80).

Sao Paulo: Zetti; Cafu, Valber, Ronaldo, Doriva, Andre, Muller, Dinho, Palinha (Juninho 75), Leonardo, Cerezo.
Referee: Quiniou (France).

EUROPEAN SUPER CUP

Played annually between the winners of the European Champions' Cup and the European Cup-Winners' Cup. AC Milan replaced Marseille in 1993–94.

Previous Matches

1972 Ajax beat Rangers 3-1, 3-2
1973 Ajax beat AC Milan 0-1, 6-0
1974 Not contested
1975 Dynamo Kiev beat Bayern Munich 1-0, 2-0
1976 Anderlecht beat Bayern Munich 4-1, 1-2
1977 Liverpool beat Hamburg 1-1, 6-0
1978 Anderlecht beat Liverpool 3-1, 1-2
1979 Nottingham F beat Barcelona 1-0, 1-1
1980 Valencia beat Nottingham F 1-0, 1-2
1981 Not contested
1982 Aston Villa beat Barcelona 0-1, 3-0
1983 Aberdeen beat Hamburg 0-0, 2-0
1984 Juventus beat Liverpool 2-0
1985 Juventus v Everton not contested due to UEFA ban on English clubs
1986 Steaua Bucharest beat Dynamo Kiev 1-0
1987 FC Porto beat Ajax 1-0, 1-0
1988 KV Mechelen beat PSV Eindhoven 3-0, 0-1
1989 AC Milan beat Barcelona 1-1, 1-0
1990 AC Milan beat Sampdoria 1-1, 2-0
1991 Manchester U beat Red Star Belgrade 1-0
1992 Barcelona beat Werder Bremen 1-1, 2-1

1993-94

First Leg, 12 January 1994, Parma

Parma (0) 0

AC Milan (1) 1 *(Papin 43)* 8083

Parma: Ballotta; Balleri, Benarrivo (Di Chiara 77), Minotti, Apolloni, Sensini, Brolin, Pin, Crippa, Zola, Asprilla.
AC Milan: Rossi; Tassotti, Maldini, Albertini (Massaro 70), Costacurta, Baresi, Eranio, Desailly, Papin, Savicevic (Panucci 87), Donadoni.
Referee: Diaz Vega (Spain).

Second Leg, 2 February 1994, Milan

AC Milan (0) 0

Parma (1) 2 *(Sensini 23, Crippa 95)* aet 24,074

AC Milan: Rossi; Panucci, Maldini, Albertini (Lentini 64), Costacurta, Baresi, Laudrup (Carbone 76), Desailly, Papin, Donadoni, Massaro.
Parma: Ballotta; Benarrivo, Di Chiara, Minotti, Matrecano, Sensini, Brolin, Pin, Crippa, Zola (Zoratto 104), Asprilla.
Referee: Rothlisberger (Switzerland).

SOUTH AMERICA

COPA LIBERTADORES 1994

First Round

Group 1

	P	W	D	L	F	A	Pts
Indep Medellin (Col)	6	3	2	1	6	1	8
Olimpia (Par)	6	3	2	1	5	3	8
Jun. Barranqilla (Col)	6	2	1	3	4	5	5
Cerro Porteno (Par)	6	1	1	4	4	10	3

Group 2

	P	W	D	L	F	A	Pts
Velez Sarfield (Arg)	6	3	2	1	8	7	8
Cruzeiro (Br)	6	3	1	2	7	8	7
Palmeiras (Br)	6	3	0	3	14	7	6
Boca Juniors (Arg)	6	1	1	4	7	14	3

Group 3

	P	W	D	L	F	A	Pts
Emelec (Ecu)	6	3	1	2	9	4	7
Universitario (Per)	6	2	2	2	4	5	6
Barcelona (Ecu)	6	2	2	2	5	3	6
Alianza (Per)	6	2	1	3	6	11	5

Group 4

	P	W	D	L	F	A	Pts
Colo Colo (Chi)	6	4	1	1	11	6	9
Union Espanola (Chi)	6	3	1	2	6	6	7
Defensor (Uru)	6	1	3	2	3	5	5
Nacional (Urg)	6	1	1	4	5	8	3

Group 5

	P	W	D	L	F	A	Pts
Bolivar (Bol)	6	3	3	0	9	2	9
The Strongest (Bol)	6	2	3	1	13	7	7
Minerven (Ven)	6	2	1	3	10	17	5
Maritimo (Ven)	6	1	1	4	7	13	3

Second Round, First Leg
Bolivar 2, The Strongest 1
Junior 1, Colo Colo 1
Universitario 2, Indep Medellin 1
Minerven 2, Emelec 0
Barcelona 0, Olimpia 1
Union Espanola 1, Cruzeiro 0
Defensor 1, Velez Sarsfield 1
Palmeiros 0, Sao Paulo 0
Sao Paulo qualified as holders

Second Leg
The Strongest 0, Bolivar 4
Colo Colo 2, Junior 2
(*Colo Colo won 4-3 on penalties*)
Indep Medellin 2, Universitario 0
Emelec 3, Minerven 1
Olimpia 2, Barcelona 1
Velez Sarsfield 0, Defensor 0
(*Velez won 4-3 on penalties*)
Cruzeiro 0, Union Espanola 0
Sao Paulo v Palmeiras not yet played
(*Tournament still running*)

SOUTH AMERICAN SUPER CUP

First Round, First Leg
River Plate 2, Argentinos Juniors 1
Estudiantes 2, Boca Juniors 0
Santos 0, Nacional 0
Cruzeiro 6, Colo Colo 1
Sao Paulo 2, Independiente 0
Olimpia 1, Flamengo 0
Nacional 1, Racing Club 1
Penarol 1, Gremio 0

First Round, Second Leg
Colo Colo 3, Cruzeiro 3
Nacional 1, Santos 0
Argentinos Juniors 1, River Plate 2
Independiente 1, Sao Paulo 1
Boca Juniors 1, Estudiantes 3
Flamengo 3, Olimpia 1
Racing Club 1, Nacional 3
Gremio 2, Penarol 0

Second Round, First Leg
Cruzeiro 1, Nacional 2
Sao Paulo 2, Gremio 2
Nacional 1, Estudiantes 0
River Plate 2, Flamengo 1

Second Round, Second Leg
Flamengo 1, River Plate 0
Gremio 0, Sao Paulo 1
Estudiantes 0, Nacional 1
Nacional 2, Cruzeiro 3

Semi-Finals, First Leg
Sao Paulo 1, Nacional 0
Flamengo 2, Nacional 1

Semi-Finals, Second Leg
Nacional 0, Flamengo 3
Nacional 2, Sao Paulo 1

Final First Leg
Flamengo 2, Sao Paulo 2

Final Second Leg
Sao Paulo 2 Flamengo 2
(*Sao Paulo won 5-3 on penalties*)

AFRICA

1994 AFRICAN NATIONS CUP

Group A
Tunisia (0) 0, Mali (2) 2
Zaire (0) 1, Mali (0) 0
Tunisia (1) 1, Zaire (0) 1

	P	*W*	*D*	*L*	*F*	*A*	*Pts*
Zaire	2	1	1	0	2	1	3
Mali	2	1	0	1	2	1	2
Tunisia	2	0	1	1	1	3	1

Group B
Nigeria (1) 3, Gabon (0) 0
Egypt (2) 4, Gabon (0) 0
Nigeria 0, Egypt 0

	P	*W*	*D*	*L*	*F*	*A*	*Pts*
Egypt	2	1	1	0	4	0	3
Nigeria	2	1	1	0	3	0	3
Gabon	2	0	0	2	0	7	0

Group C
Ivory Coast (2) 4, Sierra Leone (0) 0
Zambia 0, Sierra Leone 0
Ivory Coast (0) 0, Zambia (0) 1

	P	*W*	*D*	*L*	*F*	*A*	*Pts*
Zambia	2	1	1	0	1	0	3
Ivory Coast	2	1	0	1	4	1	2
Sierra Leone	2	0	1	1	0	4	1

Group D
Ghana (0) 1, Guinea (0) 0
Senegal (0) 2, Guinea (1) 1
Ghana (0) 1, Senegal (0) 0

	P	*W*	*D*	*L*	*F*	*A*	*Pts*
Ghana	2	2	0	0	2	0	4
Senegal	2	1	0	1	2	2	2
Guinea	2	0	0	2	1	3	0

Final round—Quarter finals
Zaire (0) 0, Nigeria (0) 2
Egypt (0) 0, Mali (0) 1
Zambia (1) 1, Senegal (0) 0
Ghana (0) 1, Ivory Coast (1) 2

Semi finals
Nigeria (0) 2, Ivory Coast (0) 2
(0,0) after penalties
Mali (0) 0, Zambia (3) 4

Match for 3rd place
Mali (0) 1, Ivory Coast (1) 3

Final
Nigeria (1) 2, Zambia (1) 1

International matches 1993

Argentina
Brazil (h) 1-1; Denmark (h) 1-1; Bolivia (h) 0-1; Mexico (a) 1-1; Colombia (h) 1-1; Brazil (h) 1-1; Colombia (h) 0-0; Mexico (h) 0-0; Peru (a) 1-0; Paraguay (a) 3-1; Colombia (a) 1-2; Peru (h) 2-1; Paraguay (h) 0-0; Colombia (h) 0-5; Australia (a) 1-1; Australia (h) 1-0; Germany (h) 2-1.

Bolivia
Honduras (h) 3-1; Paraguay (a) 0-1; Paraguay (h) 2-1; Salvador (a) 2-2; Honduras (a) 0-0; Honduras (a) 0-0; Chile (a) 1-2; USA (a) 0-0; Peru (a) 0-1; Chile (a) 1-3; Argentina (a) 0-1; Colombia (h) 1-1; Mexico (a) 0-0; Venezuela (a) 7-1; Brazil (h) 2-0; Uruguay (h) 3-1; Ecuador (h) 1-0; Venezuela (h) 7-0; Brazil (a) 0-6; Uruguay (a) 1-2; Ecuador (a) 1-1.

Brazil
Argentina (a) 1-1; Poland (h) 2-2; Germany (h) 3-3; England (h) 1-1; Peru (h) 0-0; Chile (a) 2-3; Paraguay (h) 3-0; Argentina (a) 1-1; Paraguay (h) 2-0; Ecuador (a) 0-0; Bolivia (a) 0-2; Venezuela (a) 5-1; Mexico (h) 1-1; Uruguay (a) 1-1; Ecuador (h) 2-0; Bolivia (h) 6-0; Venezuela (h) 4-0; Uruguay (h) 2-0; Germany (a) 1-2; Mexico (a) 10-0.

Chile
Bolivia (h) 2-1; Colombia (h) 1-1; Chile (a) 0-1; Bolivia (h) 3-1; Paraguay (a) 0-1; Brazil (h) 3-2; Peru (a) 0-1; Spain (a) 0-2.

Colombia
Venezuela (a) 0-0; Costa Rica (h) 4-2; USA (h) 2-1; Venezuela (h) 1-1; Chile (a) 1-1; Chile (h) 1-0; Mexico (h) 2-1; Bolivia (a) 1-1; Argentina (a) 1-1; Uruguay (h) 1-1; Argentina (a) 0-0; Ecuador (h) 1-0; Paraguay (h) 0-0; Peru (a) 1-0; Argentina (h) 2-1; Paraguay (a) 1-1; Peru (h) 4-0; Argentina (a) 5-0.

Ecuador
Belarus (h) 1-1; Romania (h) 3-0; Peru (h) 1-0; Venezuela (h) 6-1; USA (h) 2-0; Uruguay (h) 2-1; Paraguay (h) 3-0; Mexico (a) 0-2; Colombia (a) 0-1; Brazil (h) 0-0; Uruguay (a) 0-0; Venezuela (h) 5-0; Bolivia (a) 0-1; Brazil (a) 0-2; Uruguay (h) 0-1; Venezuela (a) 1-2; Bolivia (h) 1-1.

Paraguay
Bolivia (h) 1-0; Paraguay (a) 1-2; Mexico (a) 1-3; Chile (h) 1-0; Peru (h) 1-1; Brazil (a) 0-3; Ecuador (a) 0-3; Brazil (a) 0-2; Colombia (a) 0-0; Argentina (h) 1-3; Peru (h) 2-1; Colombia (h) 1-1; Argentina (a) 0-0; Peru (a) 2-2.

Peru
Venezuela (a) 0-0; Honduras (h) 1-1; Belarus (h) 1-1; Rumania (a) 0-2; USA (a) 0-0; Ecuador (a) 0-1; Bolivia (a) 0-1; Venezuela (h) 3-1; Brazil (a) 0-0; Paraguay (a) 1-1; Chile (h) 1-0; Mexico (a) 2-4; Uruguay (a) 0-3; Argentina (h) 0-1; Colombia (h) 0-1; Paraguay (a) 1-2; Argentina (a) 1-2; Colombia (a) 0-4; Paraguay (h) 2-2.

Uruguay
USA (h) 1-0; Venezuela (a) 2-2; Ecuador (a) 1-2; Colombia (a) 1-1; Peru (h) 3-0; Venezuela (a) 1-0; Ecuador (h) 0-0; Bolivia (a) 1-3; Brazil (h) 1-1; Venezuela (h) 4-0; Ecuador (a) 1-0; Bolivia (h) 2-1; Brazil (a) 0-2; Germany (a) 0-5.

Venezuela
Peru (h) 0-0; Colombia (h) 0-0; Colombia (a) 1-1; Peru (a) 1-3; Ecuador (a) 1-6; Uruguay (h) 2-2; USA (a) 3-3; Bolivia (h) 1-7; Uruguay (h) 0-1; Brazil (h) 1-5; Bolivia (a) 0-7; Uruguay (a) 0-4; Brazil (a) 0-4; Ecuador (h) 2-1.

Champions
Argentina: Velez Sarsfield
Bolivia: The Strongest
Brazil: Palmeiras
Chile: Colo Colo
Colombia: Junior
Ecuador: Emelec
Paraguay: Olimpia
Peru: Universitario
Uruguay: Penarol
Venezuela: Sport Maritimo

GM VAUXHALL CONFERENCE 1993-94

GM VAUXHALL CONFERENCE TABLE 1993–94

		Home			*Goals*		*Away*			*Goals*		
	Pl	W	D	L	F	A	W	D	L	F	A	Pts
Kidderminster Harriers	42	13	5	3	31	12	9	4	8	32	23	75
Kettering Town	42	9	7	5	23	14	10	8	3	23	10	72
Woking	42	12	5	4	35	25	6	8	7	23	33	67
Southport	42	10	7	4	26	21	8	5	8	31	30	66
Runcorn	42	12	6	3	41	26	2	13	6	22	31	61
Dagenham & Redbridge	42	12	5	4	41	23	3	9	9	21	31	59
Macclesfield Town	42	7	8	6	24	18	9	3	9	24	31	59
Dover Athletic	42	9	3	9	28	24	8	4	9	20	25	58
Stafford Rangers	42	10	7	4	39	22	4	8	9	17	30	57
Altrincham	42	8	5	8	23	22	8	4	9	18	20	57
Gateshead	42	10	6	5	23	18	5	6	10	22	35	57
Bath City	42	6	8	7	28	21	7	9	5	19	17	56
Halifax Town	42	7	9	5	28	18	6	7	8	27	31	55
Stalybridge Celtic	42	6	6	9	27	30	8	6	7	27	25	54
Northwich Victoria	42	7	9	5	26	19	4	10	7	18	26	52
Welling United	42	7	7	7	25	23	6	5	10	22	26	51
Telford United	42	8	7	6	24	22	5	5	11	17	27	51
Bromsgrove Rovers	42	5	8	8	26	32	7	7	7	28	34	51
Yeovil Town	42	7	4	10	23	26	7	5	9	26	36	51
Merthyr Tydfil	42	8	7	6	34	26	4	8	9	26	35	49
Slough Town	42	8	8	5	30	24	3	6	12	14	34	47
Witton Albion	42	4	8	9	18	30	3	5	13	19	33	34

Note : Merthyr Tydfil deducted 2 points

ATTENDANCES BY CLUB 1993–94

Club	Aggregate Attendance 1993-94	Average Attendance 1993-94	Average Attendance 1992-93	% Change
Altrincham	15,778	751	809	–7
Bath City	14,339	683	642	+6
Bromsgrove Rovers	23,911	1,139	1,429	–20
Dagenham & Redbridge	19,999	952	1,201	–21
Dover Athletic	28,293	1,347	1,425	–5
Gateshead	10,016	477	420	+14
Halifax Town	21,742	1,035	2,225	–53
Kettering Town	42,535	2,025	1,454	+39
Kidderminster Harriers	47,260	2,250	1,439	+56
Macclesfield Town	17,921	853	658	+30
Merthyr Tydfil	12,201	581	602	–3
Northwich Victoria	19,593	933	815	+14
Runcorn	12,465	594	615	–3
Slough Town	18,475	880	1,242	–29
Southport	27,143	1,293	1,025	+26
Stafford Rangers	19,923	949	945	+1
Stalybridge Celtic	12,910	615	809	–24
Telford United	19,507	929	1,023	–9
Welling United	20,310	967	947	+2
Witton Albion	15,967	760	909	–16
Woking	35,950	1,712	1,987	–14
Yeovil Town	52,394	2,495	2,615	–5

HIGHEST ATTENDANCES 1993-94

4,438 Kidderminster Harriers v Bromsgrove Rovers 5.4.94
4,358 Kidderminster Harriers v Dagenham & Redbridge 5.2.94
4,114 Kidderminster Harriers v Altrincham 7.5.94
3,938 Bromsgrove Rovers v Kidderminster Harriers 27.12.93
3,877 Kidderminster Harriers v Southport 12.3.94
3,812 Kidderminster Harriers v Yeovil Town 15.1.94
3,371 Yeovil Town v Bath City 27.12.93
3,349 Yeovil Town v Dagenham & Redbridge 24.8.93
3,130 Woking v Kettering Town 3.1.94
3,120 Kettering Town v Telford United 1.1.94
3,102 Yeovil Town v Stalybridge Celtic 28.8.93
3,083 Yeovil Town v Welling United 14.9.93

VAUXHALL CONFERENCE LEADING GOALSCORERS 1993–94

Conf.			*FAC*	*FAT*	*DC*
25	Paul Dobson (Gateshead)	+	3	4	2
23	Karl Thomas (Runcorn)	+	–	5	2
17	Paul Adcock (Bath City)	+	4	1	–
	Terry Robbins (Welling United)	+	–	2	2
16	Mickey Spencer (Yeovil Town)	+	–	1	1
	Clive Walker (Woking)	+	-	3	–
15	David Gamble (Southport)	+	2	2	–
	David Leworthy (Dover Athletic)	+	1	1	3
14	Carl Alford (Macclesfield Town)	+	3	2	6
	Paul Davies (Kidderminster Harriers)	+	1	–	3
	Morrys Scott (Slough Town)	+	2	1	–
13	Recky Carter (Bromsgrove Rovers)	+	3	2	–
	Jamie Paterson (Halifax Town)	+	–	2	1
	Delwyn Humphreys (Kidderminster H.)	+	3	–	1

FAC; FA Cup. FAT; FA Trophy. DC; Drinkwise Cup.

HIGHEST SCORER

4 Danny Dichio WELLING UNITED v Slough Town (Vauxhall Conference 19.2.94)

HIGHEST AGGREGATE SCORES

1-8 Woking v Dagenham & Redbridge 19.4.94
2-6 Woking v Halifax Town 25.9.93
6-2 Welling United v Slough Town 19.2.94
4-3 Macclesfield Town v Bromsgrove Rovers 24.8.93
5-2 Slough Town v Yeovil Town 21.9.93
6-1 Macclesfield Town v Gateshead 6.11.93
4-3 Dover Athletic v Bromsgrove Rovers 1.1.94
3-4 Dagenham & Redbridge v Woking 8.3.94
4-3 Merthyr Tydfil v Witton Albion 7.5.94

LARGEST HOME WINS

6-0 Halifax Town v Telford United 2.10.93
6-1 Macclesfield Town v Gateshead 6.11.93
5-0 Dover Athletic v Woking 30.8.93
5-0 Runcorn v Halifax Town 11.9.93
5-0 Merthyr Tydfil v Northwich Victoria 30.10.93
5-0 Stalybridge Celtic v Dagenham & Redbridge 1.5.94

LARGEST AWAY WINS

1-8 Woking v Dagenham & Redbridge 19.4.94
0-5 Runcorn v Kidderminster Harriers 20.4.94
0-5 Bromsgrove Rovers v Telford United 29.3.94
0-5 Witton Albion v Welling United 12.3.94

MATCHES WITHOUT DEFEAT

15 Runcorn
14 Woking
13 Kidderminster Harriers
11 Northwich Victoria, Southport

MATCHES WITHOUT SUCCESS

13 Bromsgrove Rovers
12 Telford United
9 Dagenham & Redbridge, Merthyr Tydfil, Stalybridge Celtic, Witton Albion

CONSECUTIVE CONFERENCE VICTORIES

8 Kidderminster Harriers
6 Southport
5 Telford United
4 Altrincham, Dover Athletic

CONSECUTIVE CONFERENCE DEFEATS

5 Welling United, Yeovil Town
4 Altrincham, Dover Athletic, Gateshead
3 Bath City, Bromsgrove Rovers (×2), Halifax Town, Kidderminster Harriers, Merthyr Tydfil, Northwich Victoria, Runcorn (×2), Slough Town (×2), Stafford Rangers, Stalybridge Celtic, Telford United, Witton Albion (×3)

GM VAUXHALL CONFERENCE 1993–94

APPEARANCES AND GOALSCORERS

Altrincham
Vauxhall Appearances: Baker, W. 2; Bell, W. 6; Burton, S. 2; Butler, B. 1; Carmody, M. 38; Clarke, T. 12; Cockram, D. 8; Collings, P. 26; Cross, S. 29; Dempsey, M. 13; Doherty, M. 8; Esdaille, D. 4; France, P. 41; Gorton, A. 2; Green, A. 15; Green, R. 27; Harris, R. 38; Hayde, M. 22; Heesom, D. 18; Hughes, M. 4; Jones, P. 3; MacFadzean, J. 1; May, L. 3; Mellish, S. 17; Ogley, M. 17; Pennington, S. 5; Powell, G. 11; Raymond, S. 3; Reid, A. 25; Richards, A. 6; Rowlands, P. 6; Saunders, S. 5; Sharratt, C. 10; Smith, A. 2; Smith, J. 14; Strange, A. 7; Strange, S. 4; Terry, S. 29; Tunnacliffe, I. 9; Woodhead, S. 21; Wright, M. 3.
Goals(41): Harris 7, Green A. 5, Terry 5, France 3, Sharratt 3, Bell 2, Cross 2, Green R. 2, Ogley 2, Richards 2, Strange A 2, Cockram 1, Doherty 1, Pennington 1, Powell 1, OG 2.

Bath City
Vauxhall Appearances: Adcock, P. 40; Banks, C. 33; Batty, P. 31; Boyle, M. 27; Brooks, N. 22; Chenoweth, P. 39; Cousins, R. 42; Crowley, R. 31; Dicks, G. 31; Gill, J. 37; Harrison, G. 3; Hedges, I. 22; Lucas, J. 5; Mings, A. 26; Mogg, D. 37; Noble, W. 12; Rudgley, S. 2; Smart, G. 36; Thaws, K. 8; Torres, R. 3; Vernon, D. 24; Weston, I. 2; Williams, G. 1.
Goals(47): Adcock 17, Cousins 5, Chenoweth 4, Crowley 4, Smart 4, Batty 3, Boyle 3, Gill 2, Mings 2, Brooks 1, Noble 1, OG 1.

Bromsgrove Rovers
Vauxhall Appearances: Brighton, S. 34; Burgher, S. 13; Carter, R. 27; Carty, p. 12; Clarke, N. 5; Cooksey, S. 17; Crane, S. 1; Crisp, M. 33; Devery, B. 13; Gaunt, C. 12; Gray, M. 1; Gray, R, 18; Green, H. 25; Hanks, C. 15; Hodges, D. 1; Holmes, S. 9; Masefield, P. 14; McKeever, S. 1; O'Meara, S. 21; Pearce, C. 21; Pitcher, S. 1; Radburn, C. 27; Richardson, K. 31; Scandrett, R. 2; Shilvock, R. ; Skelding, J. 42; Stott, S. 37; Taylor, S. 16; Wardle, P. 27; Webb, P. 38; Young, L. 4.
Goals(54): Carter 13, Stott 10, Webb 5, Crisp 5, Radburn 4, Hanks 3, Shilvock 2, Skelding 2, Taylor 2, Brighton 1, Burgher 1, Clarke 1, Devery 1, Gray 1, O'Meara 1, Richardson1, Wardle 1.

Dagenham & Redbridge
Vauxhall Appearances: Bacon, P. 4; Blackford, G. 37; Broom, J. 17; Butterworth, G. 42; Cavell, P. 24; Conner, S. 36; Crown, D. 33; DeSouza, J. 18; Double, L. 4; Filson, M. 5; Foster, K. 1; Fowler, L. 8; Greene, D. 18; Greaves, S. 7; Jones, G. 5; Livett, S. 12; Martin, E. 4; McKenna, J. 41; Mettioui, A. 2; Owers, A. 13; Parratt, D. 6; Payne, C. 7; Pearson, R. 1; Ramage, A. 1; Reed, P. 9; Richardson, I. 37; Sorrell, T. 14; Stebbing, G. 42; Stimson, J. 1; Walsh, M. 4; Watts, P. 41; Wordsworth, D. 10.
Goals(62): Crown 9, Greene 8, Richardson 8, Cavell 7, Desouza 7, Broom 4, Conner 4, Livett 4, Blackford 2, Butterworth 2, Wordsworth 2, Jones 1, Owers 1, Payne 1, Sorrell 1, Watts1.

Dover Athletic
Vauxhall Appearances: Bartlett, J. 41; Blewden, C. 35; Browne, C. 29; Chivers, S. 4; Darlington, J. 16; Dixon, Tim. 18; Dixon, Tony. 37; Donn, N. 34; Grayburn, M. 1; Hambley, T. 10; Jackson, J. 37; Lewis, J. 24; Leworthy, D. 40; Milton, R. 38; Munden, M. 38; O'Brien, P. 18; O'Connell, I. 40; Scott, D. 40; Walker, D. 42; Walsh, M. 4.
Goals(48): Leworthy 15, Browne 11, Milton 5, Blewden 4, O'Connell 3, Bartlett 2, Lewis, 2 Dixon Tim 1, Donn 1, Jackson 1, Scott 1, Walker 1, Walsh 1.

Gateshead
Vauxhall Appearances: Adams, S. 2; Armstrong, S. 1; Askew, B. 2; Borthwick, J. 8; Cole, A. 11; Corner, D. 32; Cullen, T. 2; Dalziel, I. 11; Dobson, P. 40; Farrey, M. 19; Gibson, T. 4; Guthrie, P. 8; Harvey, L. 5; Higgins, S. 26; Hine, M. 32; Lamb, A. 35; McDonald, G. 3; Nicholls, D. 14; Nicholson, G. 3; Nobbs, K. 41; Parkinson, G. 27; Payne, L. 1; Proudlock, P. 40; Rowe, B. 29; Sharpe, P. 15; Shirtliff, P. 15; Smith, S. 33; Sweeney, P. 15; Tinkler, J. 9; Watson, J. 19; Whitmarsh, P. 7; Wrightson, J. 35.
Goals(45): Dobson 25, Lamb 4, Farrey 3, Proudlock 3, Rowe 3, Hine 2, Sharpe 2, Nobbs1, Parkinson 1, Whitmarsh 1.

Halifax Town
Vauxhall Appearances: Barr, B. 39; Boardman, C. 28; Bracey, L. 1; Brown, N. 3; Burr, S. 8; Cameron, D. 3; Collins, S. 3; Constable, S. 29; Costello, P. 2; Craven, P. 26; Crosby, A. 1; Edwards, E. 26; Filson, M. 13; France, D. 2; German, D. 28; Gray, R. 1; Gregory, T. 6; Greenwood, N. 3; Hanson, D. 13; Hardy, J. 8; Heyes, D. 18; Higgins, D. 5; Hook, S. 2; Horsfield, J. 9; Jones, A. 12; Lambert, C. 20; Lormor, T. 7; Lucketti, C. 8; Megson, K. 32; O'Toole, P. 7; Paterson, J. 42; Peake, J. 27; Prindiville, S. 17; Rathbone, M. 2; Ridings, D. 15; Saunders, S. 14; Smith, N. 7; Wilmot, R. 20.
Goals(55): Paterson 13, Lambert 7, Peake 6, Saunders 6, Barr 4, Hanson 4, Ridings 4, Megson 3, Smith 2, Edwards 1, Filson 1, Lormor 1, Lucketti 1, OG 2.

Kettering Town
Vauxhall Appearances: Ashby, N. 42; Ashdjian, J. 9; Benstead, G. 33; Brown, P. 39; Clarke, S. 24; Costello, P. 6; Dempsey, M. 12; Donald, W. 41; Donovan, N. 8; Graham, J. 26; Holden, S. 29; Loughlan, T. 5; Martin, D. 31; Martin, M. 1; Muckleberg, T. 2; Murphy, M. 5; Oxbrow, D. 40; Price, G. 36; Reed, G. 32; Roderick, M. 13; Stringfellow, I. 14; Taylor, R. 37; Thorpe, A. 12; Whitehouse, M. 6; Wright, O. 28.
Goals(46): Brown 8, Graham 6, Taylor 5, Costello 4, Martin 4, Clarke 2, Dempsey 2, Oxbrow 2, Price 2, Reed 2, Roderick 2, Thorpe 2, Whitehouse 2, Ashby 1, Donald 1, Loughlan1.

Kidderminster Harriers
Vauxhall Appearances: Bancroft, P. 36; Brindley, C. 42; Cartwright, N. 36; Davies, P. 35; Deakin, J. 21; Forsyth, R. 40; Gillett, C. 4; Gordon, C. 5; Grainger, P. 42; Hadley, D. 6; Hodson, S. 42; Humphreys, D. 30; Palmer, L. 33; Purdie, J. 38; Rose, K. 43; Weir, M. 40; West, M. 1; Williams, W. 8; Wolsey, M. 2; Woodall, M. 14.
Goals(63): Davies 14, Humphreys 13, Cartwright 8, Purdie 8, Forsyth 4, Palmer 4, Weir3, Brindley 2, Grainger 2, Bancroft 1, Deakin 1, Gordon 1, OG 2.

Macclesfield Town
Vauxhall Appearances: Adams, S. 28; Alford, C. 34; Allardyce, C. 2; Askey, J. 30; Bimson, S. 35; Brown, G. 1; Dempsey, S. 10; Farrelly, S. 35; Green, R. 5; Heron, D. 3; Howarth, N. 23; Kendall, P. 25; Leicester, S. 6; Lennon, P. 3; Lillis, M. 36; Locke, S. 7; Lyons, D. 17; McDonald, M. 24; Mitchell, R. 8; Powell, G. 7; Power, P. 27; Roberts, G. 11; Sharratt, C. 24; Shepherd, G. 35; Sorvel, N. 42; Sutton, S. 1; Thorpe, A. 5; Walker, G. 3; Wood, S. 15.
Goals(48): Alford 14, Power 9, Sorvel 5, Sharratt 4, Askey 3, Howarth 3, Green 2, Powell 2, Adams 1, Farrelly 1, Lyons 1, McDonald 1, Roberts 1, Wood 1.

Merthyr Tydfil
Vauxhall Appearances: Benbow, I. 36; Coates, M. 25; David, R. 5; Davies, M. 39; Drewitt, I. 40; Dyer, S. 17; Gorman, A. 7; Holtham, M. 32; Hutchison, T. 13; James, Robbie. 15; James, Ryan. 37; Jones, M. 10; Jones, N. 30; Lewis, A. 11; Lewis, D. 34; Owen, C. 8; Rogers, K. 40; Tucker, M. 40; Twose, G. 2; Wager, G. 38; Williams, C. 13; Williams, Mark. 34; Williams, Morgan. 4.
Goals(60): Dyer 10, Drewitt 8, Rogers 8, Coates 7, Benbow 5, Williams C. 5, Tucker 4, Holtham 3, James 3, Williams M. 3, Davies 2, James 2.

Northwich Victoria

Vauxhall Appearances: Abercrombie, S. 3; Adebola, D. 18; Anders, J. 3; Berks, J. 1; Birchall, M. 4; Boyd, G. 39; Bullock, T. 31; Butler, B. 35; Bunter, S. 24; Christie, D. 6; Donnelly, P. 19; Greygoose, D. 11; Hancock, M. 36; Hardy, N. 39; Hemmings, T. 5; Jones, M. 39; Jones, T. 5; Lewin, C. 10; Lloyd, T. 3; McGee, T. 2; Mulligan, J. 2; Norman, D. 27; O'Connor, M. 31; Parker, J. 30; Paxton, D. 1; Sewell, J. 3; Simms, M. 33; Smith, B. 5; Snowden, T. 7; Tinson, D. 21; Westray, K. 30.
Goals(44): Hardy 8, Adebola 7, Bunter 7, O'Connor 6, Butler 3, Snowden 3, Donnelly2, Parker 2, Anders 1, Birchall 1, Hancock 1, Hemmings 1, Lewin 1, Westray 1.

Runcorn

Vauxhall Appearances: Anderson, G. 30; Baldwin, M. 1; Bates, J. 41; Brabin, G. 34; Brady, I. 34; Brown, J. 5; Carroll, J. 7; Connor, J. 38; Gallagher, M. 1; Hill, G. 26; Lee, A. 27; McInerny, I. 36; McKenna, K. 35; O'Brien, S. 3; Parker, N. 9; Robertson, P. 38; Rowlands, P. 3; Shaw, N. 8; Smith, M. 11; Thomas, K. 41; Wall, J. 5; Williams, A. 42.
Goals(63): Thomas 23, McKenna 9, McInerny 7, Connor 6, Brabin 3, Brady 3, Anderson2, Shaw 2, Hill 1, Lee 1, Parker 1, Robertson 1, Smith 1, OG 3.

Slough Town

Vauxhall Appearances: Alsford, J. 5; Book, S. 2; Briley, L. 23; Bunting, T. 40; Dowson, A. 39; Edwards, R. 4; Fiore, M. 40; Hancock, D. 26; Hazel, I. 35. ; Lee, B. 36; Mackay, P. 4; Macpherson, G. 2; Manning, P. 27; Margerison, L. 4; Peters, R. 14; Quamina, M. 36; Sayer, A. 34; Scott, M. 38; Scott, S. 30; Smith, B. 6; Stanley, N. 31; Walker, L. 7; Whitby, S. 14; Wright, D. 4.
Goals(44): Scott M. 14, Sayer 7, Hazel 5, Stanley 4, Fiore 3, Peters 3, Alsford 1, Hancock 1, Lee 1, Manning 1, Scott 1, Walker 1, OG 2.

Southport

Vauxhall Appearances: Appleton, S. 1; Blackhurst, J. 2; Blissett, L. 5; Brennan, M. 5; Chadwick, D. 1; Comstive, P. 32; Dove, L. 35; Edwards, E. 10; Farley, A. 5; Fuller, D. 39; Gamble, D. 39; Goulding, D. 29; Halliday, M. 5; Harvey, J. 7; Haw, S. 40; Lodge, P. 26; Lyons, D. 15; McDonald, A. 38; Mitchell, R. 10; Mooney, K. 25; Moore, P. 42; Mullen, P. 6; Pilling, A. 5; Quinlan, P. 24; Todhunter, S. 1; Walmsley, C. 37; Williams, L. 8; Withers, P. 37.
Goals(57): Gamble 15, Haw 10, Withers 10, Quinlan 6, Walmsley 4, Blissett 2, Comstive2, Goulding 2, McDonald 2, Lodge 1, Mitchell 1, OG 2.

Stafford Rangers

Vauxhall Appearances Berry, G. 20; Bodkin, M. 23; Boughey, D. 41; Bradshaw, M. 42; Burr, S. 18; Burton, C. 6; Clayton, P. 16; Davies, M. 2; Essex, S. 35; Finney, K. 9; Foy, D. 25; Griffiths, T. 20; Hanlon, S. 13; Harrison, M. 1; Hemming, C. 22; Hope, M. 18; Kabia, J. 3; Luby, S. 5; Massey, A. 6; May, L. 8; Mee, A. 16; Mettioui, A. 29; Palgrave, B. 5; Price, R. 40; Shepstone, P. 15; Simpson, P. 38; Vickers, I. 1; Williams, D. 38; Wood, F. 4.
Goals(56): Mettioui 11, May 8, Simpson 7, Burr 7, Clayton 4, Bodkin 2, Boughey 2, Foy2, Shepstone 2, Williams 2, Berry 1, Bradshaw 1, Burton 1, Essex 1, Finney 1, Hanlon 1, Mee1, Palgrave 1, Wood 1.

Stalybridge Celtic

Vauxhall Appearances Allen, P. 2; Anderson, S. 38; Arnold, I. 22; Aspinall, J. 34; Bennett, P. 30; Blain, C. 10; Booth, K. 25; Boyle, G. 5; Brown, J. 13; Brown, J. 8; Bunn, F. 15; Clayton, P. 17; Coathup, L. 35; Dixon, P. 29; Dulson, C. 1; Edmonds, N. 16; Edwards, M. 3; Harold, I. 15; Hill, J. 3; Hughes, R. 42; Jackson, R. 22; Kirkham, P. 25; Leicester, S. 32; Locke, S. 15; Lutkevitch, M. 10; Ogley, M. 25; Power, P. 7; Prokas, R. 1; Richards, A. 2; Shaughnessy, S. 22; Ward, R. 1; Woods, K. 3.
Goals(54): Kirkham 10, Arnold 7, Clayton 6, Anderson 5, Jackson 4, Edmonds 3, Shaughnessy 3, Brown 2, Bunn 2, Dixon 2, Leicester 2, Aspinall 1, Brown 1, Blain 1, Edwards1, Harold 1, Power 1, OG 2.

Telford United

Vauxhall Appearances Acton, D. 17; Bignot, M. 42; Bowen, S. 2; Bradbury, S. 5; Davidson, J. 9; Fergusson, S. 35; Ford, G. 24; Foster, G. 2; Foster, S. 19; Frisby, S. 2; Gaunt, C. 9; Gernon, I. 17; Hindmarch, R. 1; Holmes, M. 12; Hughes, K. 25; Hunter, P. 3; Joseph, A. 2; Lemon, P. 3; Miller, C. 2; Mitchell, I. 9; Muir, J. 2; Myers, M. 36; Niblett, N. 48; Parrish, S. 41; Pritchard, D. 25; Roberts, D. 10; Sleeuvenhoek, K. 11; Statham, D. 34; Taylor, C. 40; Whitehouse, M. 28; Wilson, L. 12.
Goals(41): Taylor 11, Whitehouse 6, Roberts 5, Bignot 4, Wilson 4, Fergusson 3, Ford2, Parrish 2, Sleeuvenhoek 2, Mitchell 1, Niblett 1.

Welling United

Vauxhall Appearances Abbott, G. 37; Barnes, S. 13; Brown, W. 29; Burgess, R. 3; Clemmence, N. 21; Collins, P. 6; Copley, P. 33; Dennis, L. 2; Dichio, D. 3; Finnan, S. 22; Hales, K. 29; Hone, M. 41; O'Keefe, S. 1; Ransom, N. 35; Reynolds, T. 37; Robbins, T. 40; Robinson, S. 42; Rutherford, M. 12; Smith, D. 11; Steffe, P. 4; White, S. 42; Williams, D. 42.
Goals(47): Robbins 17, Dichio 6, Abbott 5, Reynolds 5, White 4, Hone 3, Copley 2, Brown 1, Rutherford 1, OG 3.

Witton Albion

Vauxhall Appearances Allison, M. 13; Bennett, M. 1; Blackwood, B. 19; Bondswell, A. 3; Burke, B. 39; Cunningham, H. 8; Dixon, B. 4; Dowell, W. 6; Edey, C. 42; Esdaille, D. 5; Gallagher, J. 40; Garton, W. 23; Godfrey, W. 2; Grayson, S. 12; Haddon, G. 6; Hall, N. 14; Henry, A. 19; Holmes, C. 2; Holt, M. 2; Mason, K. 26; Maynard, D. 18; McCarty, D. 9; McNab, N. 12; McNeilis, S. 9; Parkinson, S. 2; Pritchard, D. 22; Richardson, D. 7; Rose, C. 33; Savage, M. 3; Senior, S. 23; Shaw, C. 11; Thomas, G. 32; Thorpe, A. 11; Timmons, J. 9; Toal, K. 6; Tobin, S. 18; Walker, G. 8; Williams, L. 1; Williams, O. 8.
Goals(37): Burke 11, Shaw 3, Hall 2, Maynard 2, Cunningham 2, Pritchard 2, Edey 2, Blackwood 2, Tobin 2, Rose 2, Walker 1, Gallagher 1, Timmons 1, McNeilis 1, Grayson 1, OG2.

Woking

Vauxhall Appearances Agboola, R. 6; Batty, L. 38; Bennett, G. 3; Berry, G. 40; Biggins, M. 14; Brown, D. 41; Brown, Del. 5; Brown, K. 41; Clement, A. 32; Craddock, J. 7; Dennis, L. 17; Fielder, C. 27; Fleming, D. 2; Gray, A. 7; Greene, D. 3; Hay, D. 8; Haylock, P. 1; Heritage, P. 3; Hislop, C. 3; Hutchinson, G. 1; Lakin, B. 11; Morah, O. 1; Puckett, D. 25; Rattray, K. 27; Read, T. 4; Steele, S. 35; Swift, K. 4; Tucker, M. 28; Walker, C. 37; Wye, L. 25; Wye, S. 9.
Goals(58): Walker 16, Dennis 6, Puckett 5, Hay 4, Rattray 4, Brown 3, Clement 3, Craddock 2, Gray 2, Lakin 2, Steele 2, Wye L. 2, Bennett 1, Biggins 1, Brown 1, Tucker 1, WyeS. 1, OG 2.

Yeovil Town

Vauxhall Appearances Burke, R. 1; Bye, A. 23; Coates, N. 28; Coates, M. 14; Coles, D. 31; Connor, T. 14; Cooper, R. 23; Cordice, N. 17; Creaser, G. 4; Dobbins, W. 18; Ferns, P. 31; Gorman, A. 3; Harrower, S. 26; Knight, K. 4; Leonard, D. 32; Mason, P. 11; McClelland, J. 8; McPherson, M. 13; Nevin, P. 8; Rutter, S. 5; Sanderson, P. 24; Sherwood, J. 42; Spencer, M. 38; Taylor, T. 4; Wallace, A. 32; West, M. 11; White, C. 10; Wilson, P. 30; Willmott, I. 8.
Goals(49): Spencer 16, Wilson 9, Sanderson 5, Wallace 5, Coates 2, Ferns 2, Leonard2, McPherson 2, West 2, Cooper 1, Cordice 1, Rutter 1, Sherwood 1.

VAUXHALL CONFERENCE: MEMBER CLUBS SEASON 1993–1994

Club: ALTRINCHAM
Colours: Red and white striped shirts, black shorts
Ground: Moss Lane, Altrincham, Cheshire WA15 8AP
Tel: 061-928 1045
Year Formed: 1903
Record Gate: 10,275 (1925 v Sunderland Boys)
Nickname: The Robins
Manager: John King
Secretary: pending

Club: BATH CITY
Colours: Black and white striped shirts, black shorts
Ground: Twerton Park, Bath BA2 1DB
Telephone: 0225 423087 and 313247
Year Formed: 1889
Record Gate: 18,020 (1960 v Brighton)
Nickname: City
Manager: Tony Ricketts
Secretary: Paul Britton

Club: BROMSGROVE ROVERS
Colours: Green and white striped shirts, black shorts
Ground: Victoria Ground, Birmingham Road, Bromsgrove, Worcs. B61 0DR
Tel: 0527 876949
Year Formed: 1885
Record Gate: 7563 (1957-58 v Worcester City)
Nickname: Rovers
Manager: Bobby Hope
Secretary: Brian Hewings

Club: DAGENHAM & REDBRIDGE
Colours: Red shirts, red shorts
Ground: Victoria Road Ground, Victoria Road, Dagenham, Essex RM10 7XL
Tel: 081-592 7194
Year formed: 1992
Record gate: 5300 v Leyton Orient (1992)
Nickname: The Daggers
Manager: David Cusack
Secretary: Derek Almond

Club: DOVER ATHLETIC
Colours: White shirts, black shorts
Ground: Crabble Athletic Ground, Lewisham Road, River, Dover, Kent CT17 0PB
Tel: 0304 822373
Year formed: 1983
Record gate: 4035 versus Bromsgrove Rovers (1992)
Nickname: The Lilywhites
Manager: Chris Kinnear
Secretary: John Durrant

Club: FARNBOROUGH TOWN
Colours: Yellow and royal blue shirts, royal blue shorts
Ground: Cherrywood Road, Farnborough, Hampshire GU14 8UD
Tel: 0252 541469
Year formed: 1967
Record gate: 3069 (1991 v Colchester U)
Nickname: Boro
Manager: Alan Taylor
Secretary: Terry Parr

Club: GATESHEAD
Colours: Black and white halved shirts, black shorts
Ground: International Stadium, Neilson Road, Gateshead NE10 0EF
Telephone: 091-487 3883
Year Formed: 1977 (Reformed)
Record Gate: 20,752 (1937 v Lincoln C)
Nickname: Tynesiders
Manager: Colin Richardson
Secretary: Clare Tierney

Club: HALIFAX TOWN
Colours: Blue shirts with red trim, white shorts
Ground: Shay Ground, Halifax HX1 2YS
Tel: 0422 353423
Year formed: 1911
Record gate: 36,885 versus Tottenham Hotspur (1953)
Nickname: The Shaymen
Manager: John Bird
Secretary: Ian Steward

Club: KETTERING TOWN
Colours: Red shirts, red shorts
Ground: Rockingham Road, Kettering, Northants NN16 9AW
Tel: 0536 83028/410815
Year Formed: 1875
Record Gate: 11,536 (1947 v Peterborough)
Nickname: The Poppies
Manager: Graham Carr
Secretary: Gerry Knowles

Club: KIDDERMINSTER HARRIERS
Colours: Red and white shirts, red shorts
Ground: Aggborough, Hoo Road, Kidderminster DY10 1NB
Tel: 0562 823931
Year Formed: 1886
Record Gate: 9155 (1948 v Hereford)
Nickname: The Harriers
Manager: Graham Allner
Secretary: Ray Mercer

Club: MACCLESFIELD TOWN
Colours: Royal blue shirts, white shorts
Ground: Moss Rose Ground, London Road, Macclesfield, Cheshire SK10 3JH
Tel: 0625 424324/511113
Year Formed: 1875
Record Gate: 8900 (1968 v Stockport Co)
Nickname: The Silkmen
Manager: Sammy McIlroy
Secretary: Colin Garlick

Club: MERTHYR TYDFIL
Colours: White shirts, black shorts
Ground: Penydarren Park, Merthyr Tydfil, Mid Glam CF47 8RF
Tel: 0685 384102
Year Formed: 1945
Record Gate: 21,000 (1949 v Reading)
Nickname: The Martyrs
Manager: Gerald Aplin
Secretary: Howard King

Club: NORTHWICH VICTORIA
Colours: Green and white shirts, green and white shorts
Ground: The Drill Field, Northwich, Cheshire CW9 5HN
Tel: 0606 41450
Year Formed: 1874
Record Gate: 11,290 (1949 v Witton A) 12,000 (1977 v Watford FAC4)
Nickname: The Vics
Manager: John Williams
Secretary: Derek Nuttall

Club: RUNCORN
Colours: Yellow shirts, green shorts
Ground: Canal Street, Runcorn, Cheshire WA7 1RZ
Tel: 0928 560076
Year Formed: 1919
Record Gate: 10,011 (1939 v Preston NE)
Nickname: The Linnets
Manager: John Carroll
Secretary: Graham Ost

Club: SOUTHPORT
Colours: Old gold and black shirts, black/old gold shorts
Ground: Haig Avenue, Southport PR8 6JZ
Tel: 0704 533422
Year formed: 1881
Record gate: 20,010 (1932 v Newcastle United)
Nickname: The Sandgrounders
Manager: Brian Kettle
Secretary: Roy Morris

Club: STAFFORD RANGERS
Colours: Black and white shirts, black shorts
Ground: Marston Road, Stafford ST16 3BX
Tel: 0785 42750
Year Formed: 1876
Record Gate: 8536 (1975 v Rotherham)
Nickname: The Boro
Manager: Brendan Phillips
Secretary: Mike Hughes

Club: STALYBRIDGE CELTIC
Colours: Blue and white quartered shirts, blue shorts
Ground: Bower Ford, Mottram Road, Stalybridge, Cheshire SK15 2RT
Tel: 061-338 2828
Year Formed: 1911
Record Gate: 9753 (1922-23 v West Bromwich Albion)
Nickname: Celtic
Manager: Peter Wragg
Secretary: Martyn Torr

Club: STEVENAGE BOROUGH
Colours: Red and white shirts, white shorts
Ground: Broadhall Way, Stevenage, Herts SG2 8RH
Tel: 0438 743322
Year formed: 1976
Record gate: 3005 (1994 v Harrow Borough)
Nickname: The Boro
Manager: Paul Fairclough
Secretary: John Jackson

Club: TELFORD UNITED
Colours: White shirts, blue shorts
Ground: Bucks Head, Watling Street, Telford TF1 2NJ
Tel: 0952 223838
Year Formed: 1877
Record Gate: 13,000 (1935 v Shrewsbury)
Nickname: The Lillywhites
Manager: George Foster
Secretary: Mike Ferriday

Club: WELLING UNITED
Colours: Red shirts, red shorts
Ground: Park View Road Ground, Welling, Kent DA16 1SY
Tel: 081-301 1196
Year Formed: 1963
Record Gate: 4020 (1989 v Gillingham)
Nickname: The Wings
Manager: Terry Robbins
Secretary: Barrie Hobbins

Club: WOKING
Colours: Red and white halved shirts, black shorts
Ground: Kingfield Sports Ground, Kingfield, Woking, Surrey GU22 9AA
Tel: 0483 772470
Year Formed: 1889
Record Gate: 6000 (1978-79 v Swansea)
Nickname: The Cardinals
Manager: Geoff Chapple
Secretary: Phil Ledger, JP

Club: YEOVIL TOWN
Colours: Green/white striped shirts, white shorts
Ground: Huish Park, Lufton Way, Yeovil BA22 8YF
Tel: 0935 23662
Year Formed: 1923
Record Gate: 17,200 (1949 v Sunderland)
Nickname: The Glovers
Manager: Brian Hall
Secretary: Roger Brinsford

VAUXHALL CONFERENCE RESULTS GRID 1993-94

	Altrincham	Bath City	Bromsgrove Rovers	Dagenham & Redbridge	Dover Athletic	Gateshead	Halifax Town	Kettering Town	Kidderminster Harriers	Macclesfield Town	Merthyr Tydfil	Northwich Victoria	Runcorn	Slough Town	Southport	Stafford Rangers	Stalybridge Celtic	Telford United	Welling United	Witton Albion	Woking	Yeovil Town
Altrincham	—	0-2	2-3	1-2	2-0	0-3	0-0	1-1	1-0	0-1	3-0	2-2	2-1	2-0	1-2	0-0	0-0	2-0	2-0	1-3	0-2	1-0
Bath City	0-1	—	0-1	0-0	0-0	2-3	2-2	0-3	4-0	5-1	0-3	0-0	0-0	3-0	2-1	2-3	1-1	3-0	0-0	1-1	0-1	3-0
Bromsgrove Rovers	1-2	0-1	—	2-0	1-2	3-0	1-0	0-4	0-3	3-0	3-3	0-0	0-0	0-1	2-2	3-3	2-0	0-5	1-1	3-3	0-0	1-2
Dagenham & Redbridge	3-0	3-0	4-2	—	2-1	1-1	3-0	2-3	1-1	1-1	0-1	1-1	2-1	1-0	3-3	1-0	0-1	4-1	2-0	2-1	3-4	2-1
Dover Athletic	1-0	0-3	4-3	1-1	—	3-1	1-2	0-1	3-1	1-2	1-0	2-0	2-3	0-0	0-2	2-0	1-1	0-1	0-1	1-0	5-0	0-2
Gateshead	2-1	1-0	0-1	3-1	1-2	—	2-1	0-0	0-2	1-0	0-0	1-0	2-2	0-0	1-3	0-0	2-1	0-2	1-0	3-0	1-1	2-1
Halifax Town	0-0	0-0	3-0	0-1	0-1	3-1	—	0-0	1-0	1-2	2-1	1-2	1-1	1-0	2-2	1-1	2-1	6-0	1-1	0-0	2-3	1-1
Kettering Town	1-0	0-1	0-1	1-1	1-0	0-0	0-1	—	1-1	0-1	0-0	0-0	2-2	2-0	2-0	2-0	3-2	1-2	2-2	1-0	3-0	1-0
Kidderminster Harriers	0-1	0-0	1-1	2-1	3-0	1-1	2-1	0-2	—	2-1	2-0	2-0	3-0	0-0	2-0	2-0	1-0	2-0	1-0	0-0	3-1	2-3
Macclesfield Town	1-0	0-0	4-3	3-0	0-2	6-1	0-1	0-0	0-0	—	1-2	0-0	0-0	2-2	0-1	0-0	1-3	1-0	1-0	2-0	1-1	1-2
Merthyr Tydfil	0-0	1-1	2-1	0-0	0-0	3-0	2-1	0-1	1-4	2-1	—	5-0	1-1	5-1	2-2	2-0	1-2	0-3	0-1	4-3	2-3	1-1
Northwich Victoria	2-0	3-1	1-1	2-2	0-1	1-2	0-2	1-1	3-0	1-1	1-2	—	1-1	1-1	2-1	0-0	2-0	1-0	3-1	0-1	0-0	1-1
Runcorn	2-1	0-0	4-1	2-1	2-1	1-1	5-0	0-0	0-5	2-1	1-1	1-2	—	3-2	3-0	2-2	1-1	3-2	2-4	1-0	2-1	4-0
Slough Town	0-2	0-0	1-1	3-1	1-0	2-1	2-0	0-2	1-5	1-1	3-2	2-2	3-0	—	0-0	3-0	2-3	0-0	1-1	0-1	0-0	5-2
Southport	3-1	1-1	1-2	0-0	3-2	1-1	2-2	0-1	1-1	1-0	3-2	0-0	1-0	1-0	—	0-2	0-2	1-0	2-1	2-1	2-1	1-1
Stafford Rangers	0-1	2-0	0-0	2-0	2-2	3-1	1-1	1-0	2-3	2-3	5-1	3-1	2-2	0-0	0-2	—	2-2	1-1	3-0	1-0	3-0	4-2
Stalybridge Celtic	1-3	1-3	0-2	5-0	0-0	2-1	1-1	1-1	0-2	0-2	2-2	1-1	1-2	0-1	3-1	1-2	—	1-0	2-1	2-1	2-2	1-2
Telford United	0-2	0-0	0-0	0-0	0-1	0-0	3-2	1-2	1-0	1-3	1-0	2-1	1-1	4-1	1-3	2-1	0-2	—	2-0	2-2	2-0	1-1
Welling United	2-1	0-0	1-1	0-0	2-0	1-2	0-2	2-0	0-3	0-1	1-1	0-1	1-1	6-2	0-2	2-1	1-2	0-0	—	2-1	2-2	2-0
Witton Albion	0-1	0-3	4-1	1-1	1-2	1-0	2-2	0-1	2-0	0-2	2-2	1-1	1-1	1-0	0-2	1-1	0-3	0-0	0-5	—	0-0	1-2
Woking	1-1	4-1	0-0	1-8	3-0	1-0	2-6	0-0	1-0	3-0	2-1	2-1	1-1	2-1	1-0	4-0	3-0	0-0	0-2	3-1	—	1-2
Yeovil Town	0-0	1-2	2-3	2-1	1-3	0-2	0-0	1-0	0-1	4-0	2-2	0-3	4-2	0-2	3-2	0-1	0-0	1-0	0-1	2-0	0-1	—

DRINKWISE CUP 1993-94

First Round *(two legs)*
Altrincham 1 (Richards)
Gateshead 3 (Farrey, Proudlock, Dobson) 378
Gateshead 3 (Dobson, Lamb, Proudlock)
Altrincham 1 (og) 251
Kettering Town 0
Welling United 0 961
Welling United 2 (Robbins 2)
Kettering Town 1 (Thorpe) 457
Merthyr Tydfil 0
Dover Athletic 2 (O'Connell, Browne) 303
Dover Athletic 2 (Leworthy 2)
Merthyr Tydfil 0 967
Southport 1 (Dove)
Runcorn 4 (Brady 2, McKenna, Thomas) 912
Runcorn 2 (Lee, Thomas)
Southport 1 (Quinlan) 509
Stalybridge Celtic 2 (Locke, Jackson)
Telford United 0 352
Telford United 2 (Whitehouse 2)
Stalybridge Celtic 1 (Locke) 408
Witton Albion 1 (Senior)
Macclesfield Town 2 (Alford, Roberts) 826
Macclesfield Town 4 (Alford (pen), Askey 2, Sharratt)
Witton Albion 1 (Burke) 466

Byes to Second Round
Bath City, Bromsgrove Rovers, Dagenham & Redbridge, Halifax Town, Kidderminster Harriers, Northwich Victoria, Slough Town, Stafford Rangers, Woking, Yeovil Town

Second Round
Bath City 0
Yeovil Town 1 (Spencer) 584
Bromsgrove Rovers 2 (Webb (pen), Hanks)
Slough Town 1 (Stanley) 692
Dover Athletic 1 (Leworthy)
Dagenham & Redbridge 2 (Broom 2) 749
Halifax Town 3 (Costello, Ridings, Paterson)
Gateshead 0 749
Kidderminster Harriers 3 (Humphreys, Davies 2)
Stafford Rangers 0 774
Northwich Victoria 1 (Boyd)
Stalybridge Celtic 0 521
Runcorn 0
Macclesfield Town 4 (Wood, Askey 2, Shepherd) 471
Welling United 1 (Abbott)
Woking 0 616

Quarter-Finals
Dagenham & Redbridge 1 (Crown)
Yeovil Town 2 (Wilson, McPherson) 466
Halifax Town 1 (Saunders)
Macclesfield Town 2 (Lillis, Alford) 621
Northwich Victoria 3 (Bunter, O'Connor, Hardy)
Kidderminster Harriers 2 (Deakin, Davies) 474
Welling United 1 (Abbott)
Bromsgrove Rovers 2 (Stott, Radburn) 320

Semi-Finals *(two legs)*
Bromsgrove Rovers 1 (Webb (pen))
Yeovil Town 2 (Wilson, Sanderson) 1,175
Yeovil Town 0
Bromsgrove Rovers 1 (Gray) 1,922
aggregate 2-2, Yeovil win on away goals
Macclesfield Town 2 (Alford, Lyons)
Northwich Victoria 1 (Snowdon) 578
Northwich Victoria 0
Macclesfield Town 1 (Alford) 1,008

Final *(two legs)*
Macclesfield Town 4 (McDonald, Alford, Lyons 2)
Yeovil Town 1 (McClelland) 651
Yeovil Town 0
Macclesfield Town 0 1,241
Macclesfield Town won 4-1 on aggregate

NORTHERN PREMIER FOOTBALL LEAGUE

PREMIER DIVISION

		Home					Away					Total
	P	W	D	L	F	A	W	D	L	F	A	Pts
Marine	42	15	6	0	56	24	12	3	6	50	38	90
Leek Town	42	18	1	2	41	17	9	7	5	38	33	89
Boston United	42	13	5	3	57	20	10	4	7	33	23	78
Bishop Auckland	42	14	4	3	40	25	9	5	7	33	33	78
Frickley Athletic	42	14	4	3	55	19	7	8	6	35	32	75
Colwyn Bay	42	10	7	4	39	17	8	7	6	35	34	68
Morecambe	42	9	5	7	47	22	11	2	8	43	34	67
Barrow	42	9	4	8	31	28	9	6	6	28	23	64
Hyde United	42	12	5	4	52	25	5	5	11	28	46	61
Chorley	42	10	6	5	45	31	7	4	10	25	36	61
Whitley Bay	42	12	4	5	37	30	5	5	11	24	42	60
Gainsborough Trinity	42	7	6	8	36	30	8	5	8	28	36	56
Emley	42	7	11	3	39	33	5	5	11	24	38	52
Matlock Town	42	9	6	6	44	34	4	6	11	27	42	51
Buxton	42	10	4	7	44	35	3	6	12	23	38	49
Accrington Stanley	42	9	2	10	37	43	5	5	11	26	42	49
Droylsden	42	8	7	6	33	35	3	7	11	24	47	47
Knowsley United	42	7	8	6	26	22	4	3	14	26	44	44
Winsford United	42	7	4	10	28	36	2	7	12	22	38	38
Horwich RMI (1)	42	3	6	12	25	41	5	6	10	25	34	35
Bridlington Tn (3)	42	4	6	11	24	34	3	4	14	17	57	28
Fleetwood Town	42	4	3	14	24	44	3	4	14	31	70	28

FIRST DIVISION

		Home					Away					Total
	P	W	D	L	F	A	W	D	L	F	A	Pts
Guiseley	40	16	4	0	47	13	13	2	5	40	24	93
Spennymoor United	40	12	4	4	50	27	13	2	5	45	23	81
Ashton United	40	13	5	2	51	22	11	2	7	34	19	79
Lancaster City	40	12	4	4	41	18	8	6	6	33	28	70
Netherfield	40	11	3	6	33	23	9	3	8	35	37	65
Alfreton Town	40	11	3	6	52	38	7	7	6	31	32	64
Warrington Town	40	10	5	5	30	25	7	6	7	22	23	62
Goole Town	40	8	6	6	31	22	8	5	7	41	36	59
Great Harwood Town	40	8	7	5	29	27	7	7	6	27	33	59
Gretna	40	11	3	6	38	26	5	4	11	26	39	55
Workington	40	9	5	6	40	38	5	5	10	30	36	52
Worksop Town	40	8	4	8	42	38	6	5	9	37	49	51
Bamber Bridge	40	9	8	3	42	27	4	3	13	20	32	50
Curzon Ashton	40	9	4	7	33	28	4	4	12	29	43	47
Congleton Town	40	9	2	9	25	27	3	7	10	28	41	45
Radcliffe Borough	40	8	6	6	33	30	2	8	10	29	45	44
Mossley (3)	40	5	6	9	21	33	5	6	9	23	35	39
Caernarfon Town	40	7	8	5	33	37	2	3	15	21	51	38
Farsley Celtic	40	4	6	10	24	40	2	10	8	18	37	34
Harrogate Town	40	4	4	12	19	46	4	5	11	21	40	33
Eastwood Town	40	4	7	9	23	29	3	4	13	24	34	32

Leading goalscorers

Premier Division

Lge	*Cup*	*Tot.*	
24	16	40	Darren Twigg (Leek Town)
26	8	34	Andy Hayward (Frickley Athletic)
21	13	34	Steve Jones (Colwyn Bay)
31	2	33	Tony McDonald (Chorley)
26	6	32	Chris Camden (Marine)
21	11	32	Jim McCluskie (Morecambe)
26	3	29	Brian Ross (Marine)
25	4	29	Neil Grayson (Boston United)

First Division

Lge	*Cup*	*Tot.*	
32	11	43	Kenny Clark (Worksop Town)
29	9	38	Andy Whittaker (Ashton United 33 for Netherfield)
21	16	37	Mark Dobie (Gretna)
19	16	35	Mark Edwards (Ashton United)
17	14	31	Billy Roberts (Guiseley)
22	8	30	Phil Stafford (Alfreton Town)
18	12	30	Mark Rookyard (Goole Town)
16	14	30	Andy Shaw (Spennymoor United)

NORTHERN PREMIER LEAGUE CHALLENGE CUP

Qualifying Round
Radcliffe Borough 1, Curzon Ashton 2
Great Harwood Town 4, Worksop Town 1

First Round
Alfreton Town 4, Harrogate Town 2
Ashton United 5, Goole Town 3 (*after 2-2 draw*)
Bamber Bridge 1, Spennymoor United 3
Curzon Ashton 0, Guiseley 1
Farsley Celtic 3, Congleton Town 0 (*after 1-1 draw*)
Great Harwood Town 1, Netherfield 0
Gretna 4, Mossley 3 (*after 1-1 draw*)
Warrington Town 2, Lancaster City 4 (*after 1-1 draw*)
Workington 1, Eastwood Town 2

Second Round
Accrington Stanley 6, Guiseley 4
Alfreton Town 0, Droylsden 1
Ashton United 5, Farsley Celtic 2
Barrow 2, Buxton 3
Boston United 6, Fleetwood Town 0
Bridlington Town 4, Bishop Auckland 7
Emley 3, Lancaster City 0
Frickley Athletic 0, Gretna 1
Gainsborough Trinity 0, Colwyn Bay 2
Great Harwood Town 2, Horwich RMI 1 (*after 1-1 draw*)
Hyde United 4, Matlock Town 0
Knowsley United 2, Eastwood Town 0 (*aet and a 1-1 draw*)
Leek Town 3, Caernarfon Town 1
Morecambe 5, Chorley 2
Spennymoor United 3, Marine 0
Whitley Bay 2, Winsford United 0

Third Round
Ashton United 0, Accrington Stanley 0
(*after 2-2 draw, Accrington Stanley won on penalties*)
Bishop Auckland 2, Gretna 2
(*after 1-1 draw, aet, Bishop Auckland won on penalties*)
Boston United 1, Buxton 0
Emley 1, Droylsden 0
Hyde United 2, Colwyn Bay 1
Leek Town 2, Knowsley United 1
Morecambe 0, Great Harwood Town 2
Spennymoor United 2, Whitley Bay 1

Fourth Round
Accrington Stanley 3, Emley 1
(*after 0-0 draw and aet*)
Bishop Auckland 1, Spennymoor United 2
Boston United 0, Leek Town 1
Hyde United 5, Great Harwood Town 2

Semi-finals (two legs)
Hyde United 3, Leek Town 1
Leek Town 3, Hyde United 2
Spennymoor United 3, Accrington Stanley 1
Accrington Stanley 1, Spennymoor United 4

Final
Hyde United 1, Spennymoor United (*at Harrogate Town*)

NORTHERN PREMIER LEAGUE PRESIDENT'S CUP

First Round
Barrow 3, Warrington Town 1
Bridlington Town 0, Frickley Athletic 3
Curzon Ashton 0, Morecambe 3
Great Harwood Town 2, Accrington Stanley 3 (*after 2-2 draw*)
Guiseley 1, Marine 0 (*after 1-1 draw*)
Hyde United 3, Knowsley United 1
Leek Town 4, Gretna 0 (*after 0-0 draw*)
Winsford United 0, Ashton United 3

Second Round
Barrow 0, Accrington Stanley 1
Guiseley 3, Frickley Athletic 0
Leek Town 5, Hyde United 0 (*after 0-0 draw*)
Ashton United 4, Morecambe 3 (*after 1-1 draw*)

Semi-finals (two legs)
Guiseley 0, Ashton United 0
Ashton United 0, Guiseley 1
Leek Town 3, Accrington Stanley 1
Accrington Stanley 1, Leek Town 1

Final (two legs)
Guiseley 3, Leek Town 1
Leek Town 1, Guiseley 2

NORTHERN PREMIER LEAGUE FIRST DIVISION CUP

First Round
Caernarfon Town 1, Spennymoor United 4
Congleton Town 2, Radcliffe Borough 0
Curzon Ashton 3, Netherfield 2 (*after 0-0 draw*)
Farsley Celtic 4, Mossley 0
Workington 2, Eastwood Town 1

Second Round
Alfreton Town 1, Curzon Ashton 0 (*after 2-2 draw*)
Ashton United 2, Workington 1
Bamber Bridge 1, Congleton Town 0
Farsley Celtic 4, Gretna 2
Great Harwood Town 2, Worksop Town 3
Harrogate Town 2, Goole Town 5 (*after 0-0 draw*)
Guiseley 1, Lancaster City 1
(*Guiseley won 5-4 on penalties after two 1-1 draws*)
Warrington Town 1, Spennymoor United 2

Third Round
Ashton United 3, Spennymoor United 2
Bamber Bridge 3, Farsley Celtic 0
Goole Town 1, Worksop Town 0 (*after 0-0 draw*)
Guiseley 1, Alfreton Town 2

Semi-finals (two legs)
Bamber Bridge 4, Alfreton Town 3
Alfreton Town 0, Bamber Bridge 0
Ashton United 0, Goole Town 1
Goole Town 0, Ashton United 2

Final
Bamber Bridge 1, Ashton United 3

NORTHERN PREMIER LEAGUE—PREMIER DIVISION RESULTS 1993–94

	Accrington Stanley	Barrow	Bishop Auckland	Boston United	Bridlington Town	Buxton	Chorley	Colwyn Bay	Droylsden	Emley	Fleetwood Town	Frickley Athletic	Gainsborough Trinity	Horwich RMI	Hyde United	Knowsley United	Leek Town	Marine	Matlock Town	Morecambe	Whitley Bay	Winsford United
Accrington Stanley	—	0-5	1-2	1-3	2-1	3-1	1-1	5-5	2-0	1-2	3-1	2-4	2-4	1-0	4-1	2-1	0-3	0-2	0-2	3-2	0-1	4-2
Barrow	1-0	—	0-2	0-2	4-0	4-0	3-1	0-2	2-2	1-2	1-1	1-3	1-1	0-2	1-4	2-1	3-0	2-1	2-1	1-2	1-0	1-1
Bishop Auckland	0-0	2-1	—	1-1	1-1	2-1	3-1	3-2	3-1	2-1	3-2	3-1	1-0	1-0	1-2	1-2	2-2	1-4	2-0	2-1	2-0	4-2
Boston United	0-1	0-0	1-2	—	5-0	2-2	4-0	6-1	2-0	4-0	4-1	2-2	6-1	2-1	3-1	4-1	3-3	4-2	2-0	2-0	0-1	1-1
Bridlington Town	1-1	1-2	0-4	0-1	—	2-3	0-1	2-0	1-1	1-2	4-1	0-3	0-0	0-2	4-0	0-1	1-1	1-2	2-2	0-4	1-1	3-2
Buxton	3-0	3-0	0-2	0-1	3-1	—	2-3	1-0	0-3	2-2	4-1	1-1	2-5	4-4	3-0	3-1	1-2	2-2	4-1	0-2	5-4	1-0
Chorley	4-1	3-0	2-5	2-0	1-2	0-0	—	2-2	6-1	1-1	5-2	2-1	1-1	1-1	4-2	4-1	3-1	0-4	1-2	2-2	0-2	1-0
Colwyn Bay	2-2	2-3	6-0	1-1	5-0	3-1	2-0	—	4-0	1-0	2-2	1-1	1-2	1-0	2-1	0-0	0-1	0-0	3-0	2-3	1-0	0-0
Droylsden	2-1	0-0	4-2	0-2	1-0	2-1	3-1	0-0	—	3-3	1-1	2-2	1-4	1-2	3-3	2-1	1-3	2-0	2-4	0-3	3-2	0-0
Emley	4-2	0-0	2-2	1-1	1-1	1-4	0-3	3-3	1-1	—	3-2	0-0	0-2	1-1	2-2	2-1	1-1	6-2	4-4	2-0	3-1	2-0
Fleetwood Town	1-2	2-3	1-2	1-3	1-0	1-2	1-2	0-3	1-1	2-2	—	1-1	1-2	2-3	1-0	0-3	2-1	2-3	3-1	0-6	0-1	1-3
Frickley Athletic	2-0	0-0	5-0	0-1	5-0	3-1	5-0	0-1	3-0	1-0	2-2	—	1-0	5-2	4-1	1-0	1-3	5-2	1-0	3-3	6-1	2-2
Gainsborough Trinity	0-1	2-1	0-0	2-2	3-1	1-1	1-1	0-1	1-2	2-0	5-1	2-3	—	4-0	1-1	2-1	3-5	1-2	2-2	0-1	1-3	3-1
Horwich RMI	2-4	0-2	2-1	0-5	0-1	1-0	2-2	2-3	2-2	1-1	2-3	1-1	1-2	—	0-1	3-0	0-1	3-5	1-1	1-3	1-1	0-2
Hyde United	1-4	2-1	1-1	2-1	6-1	1-1	2-1	1-2	4-2	2-1	5-2	4-0	4-0	1-1	—	0-0	5-0	1-3	1-0	2-3	6-0	1-1
Knowsley United	0-0	2-0	1-1	1-2	0-0	1-1	0-1	1-5	2-0	2-0	0-1	0-2	1-1	1-0	2-1	—	0-0	1-1	5-1	2-3	1-1	3-1
Leek Town	2-1	0-0	2-1	2-1	0-2	2-1	1-0	2-0	4-2	2-0	3-0	1-0	2-0	2-0	3-0	3-2	—	1-4	2-1	2-0	2-1	3-1
Marine	2-1	2-2	3-1	3-2	3-0	1-0	4-1	1-1	2-1	4-1	4-0	4-1	3-0	1-1	1-1	3-2	3-2	—	0-0	4-2	6-3	2-2
Matlock Town	3-3	0-2	0-2	2-1	3-0	1-1	2-1	3-1	1-1	2-3	6-1	1-5	5-2	1-0	1-2	2-2	3-3	1-2	—	3-1	1-1	3-0
Morecambe	5-0	1-2	0-2	1-2	7-1	4-1	0-1	1-1	1-2	1-0	8-0	1-2	3-0	1-1	2-3	5-0	0-0	3-2	2-2	—	0-0	1-0
Whitley Bay	4-1	0-2	2-1	2-1	4-3	1-0	0-0	1-1	1-1	2-0	4-3	2-2	0-1	3-1	2-0	1-3	0-4	0-4	3-0	3-1	—	2-1
Winsford United	3-1	1-2	0-0	1-0	2-2	2-1	0-4	0-1	4-1	1-3	1-4	1-0	0-0	1-3	2-2	4-3	1-2	2-3	0-3	0-1	2-0	—

NORTHERN PREMIER LEAGUE—FIRST DIVISION RESULTS 1993–94

	Alfreton Town	Ashton United	Bamber Bridge	Caernarfon Town	Congleton Town	Curzon Ashton	Eastwood Town	Farsley Celtic	Goole Town	Great Harwood Town	Gretna	Guiseley	Harrogate Town	Lancaster City	Mossley	Netherfield	Radcliffe Borough	Spennymoor United	Warrington Town	Workington	Worksop Town
Alfreton Town	—	0-3	2-0	3-3	4-0	4-3	4-1	4-0	1-4	4-1	5-3	3-1	2-2	3-0	2-3	2-5	2-0	2-2	1-4	1-2	3-1
Ashton United	3-2	—	2-0	4-2	2-0	4-1	3-0	5-2	4-2	2-2	2-1	0-2	4-1	1-1	1-1	4-0	2-2	1-2	1-0	1-1	5-0
Bamber Bridge	2-2	1-2	—	2-0	1-1	3-1	0-0	1-1	2-2	3-2	1-1	3-2	1-0	0-3	7-1	3-2	2-2	0-2	1-1	3-2	6-0
Caernarfon Town	0-0	2-1	1-1	—	2-0	2-2	4-4	2-1	2-2	1-4	2-2	0-5	2-0	2-2	0-0	1-2	4-1	3-5	1-0	2-1	0-4
Congleton Town	2-1	0-5	3-0	4-2	—	1-1	2-1	2-0	1-3	1-2	1-2	0-2	0-2	0-2	1-0	2-1	3-1	0-1	0-0	2-0	0-1
Curzon Ashton	0-2	1-3	5-1	2-1	5-2	—	1-0	1-0	1-1	1-1	1-0	0-2	3-2	4-2	4-2	1-2	0-0	1-2	0-1	1-1	1-3
Eastwood Town	1-3	1-2	0-2	1-1	0-3	3-0	—	1-1	0-1	1-1	2-0	0-2	3-0	0-2	0-0	1-2	2-2	0-2	1-1	2-0	4-4
Farsley Celtic	2-3	0-2	1-1	1-0	1-1	0-3	0-5	—	0-3	2-2	2-0	0-2	1-2	1-2	2-1	4-5	2-2	1-3	0-0	1-0	3-3
Goole Town	1-1	0-1	1-0	6-1	2-2	2-0	0-0	0-1	—	0-1	2-1	1-2	2-2	2-0	1-3	2-0	4-0	2-1	2-2	1-4	0-0
Great Harwood Town	2-2	1-1	1-1	2-0	2-1	3-2	2-1	0-0	0-2	—	4-2	1-2	0-1	1-1	2-1	4-1	0-0	0-6	0-0	3-1	1-2
Gretna	1-2	1-4	1-0	4-1	2-1	3-1	1-0	2-0	2-1	2-1	—	1-2	1-1	2-2	3-1	1-1	4-0	1-2	4-1	1-2	1-3
Guiseley	3-1	1-0	3-2	4-0	2-2	2-0	1-0	4-0	2-0	1-1	1-0	—	2-0	1-1	3-2	4-0	2-0	2-1	2-0	6-2	1-1
Harrogate Town	1-3	1-0	0-4	1-1	1-1	0-3	4-2	1-1	1-4	0-1	2-0	0-1	—	0-4	0-0	1-5	2-6	2-5	0-1	1-4	1-0
Lancaster City	5-0	0-1	1-0	2-1	3-0	5-2	2-1	0-0	1-2	3-0	1-2	1-2	4-1	—	2-0	1-1	2-2	1-0	1-0	1-1	5-2
Mossley	1-1	2-2	0-2	2-0	1-0	1-2	3-2	2-2	1-1	0-1	1-3	1-6	1-1	0-2	—	1-3	1-0	0-2	0-2	1-1	2-0
Netherfield	3-0	1-0	4-3	2-1	3-5	1-1	0-1	1-2	2-1	1-2	2-0	3-0	0-0	4-1	0-1	—	0-3	1-0	3-2	0-0	2-0
Radcliffe Borough	0-0	2-1	1-0	2-1	2-2	1-1	0-2	1-1	2-1	1-1	2-3	2-2	3-0	0-2	2-4	2-0	—	4-2	1-2	0-3	5-2
Spennymoor United	2-2	3-1	2-1	1-3	0-0	2-1	2-1	1-1	5-3	4-0	4-0	1-2	5-0	1-0	3-0	1-3	4-1	—	1-2	5-3	3-3
Warrington Town	0-2	1-0	2-0	2-0	2-1	1-3	1-0	1-1	1-2	2-2	1-3	1-1	3-2	1-1	0-1	1-0	2-1	2-2	—	2-1	4-2
Workington	1-3	1-2	1-0	2-3	5-2	2-1	2-1	2-2	4-2	0-2	1-1	3-0	3-1	4-3	1-1	1-1	2-2	0-4	3-1	—	2-6
Worksop Town	2-1	0-3	1-2	4-0	1-4	3-1	2-2	6-2	4-4	4-0	2-2	3-2	0-3	1-2	1-1	0-1	5-4	0-1	1-2	2-1	—

BEAZER HOMES LEAGUE 1993–94

Premier Division

	P	W	D	L	F	A	Pts
Farnborough Town	42	25	7	10	74	44	82
Cheltenham Town	42	21	12	9	67	38	75
Halesowen Town	42	21	11	10	69	46	74
Atherstone United	42	22	7	13	57	43	73
Crawley Town	42	21	10	11	56	42	73
Chelmsford City	42	21	7	14	74	59	70
Trowbridge Town	42	16	17	9	52	41	65
Sittingbourne	42	17	13	12	65	48	64
Corby Town	42	17	8	17	52	56	59
Gloucester City	42	17	6	19	55	60	57
Burton Albion	42	15	11	16	57	49	56
Hastings Town	42	16	7	19	51	60	55
Hednesford Town	41	15	9	18	67	66	54
Gresley Rovers	41	14	11	17	61	72	53
Worcester City	42	14	9	19	61	70	51
Solihull Borough	42	13	11	18	52	57	50
Cambridge City	42	13	11	18	50	60	50
Dorchester Town	42	12	11	19	38	51	47
Moor Green	42	11	10	21	49	66	43
Waterlooville	42	11	10	21	47	69	43
Bashley	42	11	10	21	47	80	43
Nuneaton Borough	42	11	8	23	42	66	41

Midland Division

	P	W	D	L	F	A	Pts
Rushden & Diamonds	42	29	11	2	109	37	98
VS Rugby	42	28	8	6	98	41	92
Weston Super Mare	42	27	10	5	94	39	91
Newport AFC	42	26	9	7	84	37	87
Clevedon Town	42	24	10	8	75	46	82
Redditch United	42	19	11	12	79	62	68
Tamworth	42	19	7	16	82	68	64
Bilston Town	42	16	10	16	65	73	58
Stourbridge	42	17	6	19	71	75	57
Evesham United	42	16	8	18	50	60	56
Grantham Town	42	16	6	20	77	73	54
Bridgnorth Town	42	15	6	21	56	68	51
Racing Club Warwick	42	13	12	17	53	66	51
Dudley Town	42	13	10	19	64	61	49
Forest Green Rovers	42	12	12	18	61	84	48
Sutton Coldfield Tn	42	12	8	22	53	75	44
Bedworth United	42	12	7	23	62	81	43
Hinckley Town	42	11	10	21	44	71	43
Leicester United	42	11	9	22	34	73	42
King's Lynn	42	9	11	22	47	72	38
Yate Town	42	10	6	26	48	86	36
Armitage	42	8	11	23	45	103	35

Southern Division

	P	W	D	L	F	A	Pts
Gravesend & Northft	42	27	11	4	87	24	92
Sudbury Town	42	27	11	7	98	47	89
Witney Town	42	27	8	7	69	36	89
Salisbury City	42	26	10	6	90	39	88
Havant Town	42	27	4	11	101	41	85
Ashford Town	42	24	13	5	93	46	85
Baldock Town	42	26	7	9	76	40	85
Newport IOW	42	22	8	12	74	51	74
Margate	42	20	8	14	76	58	68
Weymouth	42	18	9	15	71	65	63
Tonbridge	42	19	5	18	59	62	62
Buckingham Town	42	14	14	14	43	42	56
Braintree Town	42	16	7	19	72	84	55
Fareham Town	42	12	12	18	54	75	48
Poole Town	42	13	6	23	54	86	45
Burnham	42	10	9	23	53	92	39
Fisher 93	42	9	10	23	52	81	37
Dunstable	42	9	7	26	50	91	34
Erith & Belvedere	42	9	5	28	40	72	32
Canterbury City	42	8	7	27	35	80	31
Wealdstone	42	6	7	29	45	95	25
Bury Town	42	3	5	34	36	121	14

LEADING GOALSCORERS
(League and Cup)

Premier Division

L. Ryan (Cambridge City)	28
T. Senior (Farnborough Town)	26
C. Boothe (Farnborough Town)	24
P. Joinson (Halesowen Town)	22
L. McRobert (Sittingbourne)	21
S. Restarick (Chelmsford City)	21

Midland Division

A. Warner (VS Rugby)	33
M. Nuttell (Rushden & Diamonds)	32
D. Watkins (Rushden & Diamonds)	26
P. McBean (Tamworth)	24
C. Moss (Redditch United)	23
I. King (VS Rugby)	22

Southern Division

S. Portway (Gravesend & North)	41
P. Odey (Salisbury City)	34
A. Jones (Havant Town)	31
K. Phillips (Baldock Town)	29
D. Fosbury (Havant Town)	25
S. Sanders (Salisbury City)	23
M. Stanton (Ashford Town)	23
S. Parnell (Sudbury Town)	23
G. Bennett (Braintree Town)	22
M. Dent (Ashford Town)	22

BEAZER HOMES SOUTHERN LEAGUE PREMIER DIVISION RESULTS 1993–94

	Atherstone United	Bashley	Burton Albion	Cambridge City	Chelmsford City	Cheltenham Town	Corby Town	Crawley Town	Dorchester Town	Farnborough Town	Gloucester City	Gresley Rovers	Halesowen Town	Hastings Town	Hednesford Town	Moor Green	Nuneaton Borough	Sittingbourne	Solihull Borough	Trowbridge Town	Waterlooville	Worcester City
Atherstone United	—	4-0	3-1	0-1	3-0	3-2	2-0	2-0	1-0	2-0	2-1	3-0	1-2	1-1	0-2	0-1	1-0	0-1	4-1	0-1	1-0	2-1
Bashley	1-2	—	1-0	0-2	1-5	2-1	2-1	1-1	0-1	5-0	4-5	2-0	2-1	1-5	1-1	2-0	1-0	0-3	2-3	1-1	2-1	2-2
Burton Albion	1-2	2-1	—	1-1	0-0	1-1	1-0	0-1	0-0	2-1	4-1	1-0	0-2	2-0	3-0	1-0	6-1	1-2	2-1	1-1	1-0	2-1
Cambridge City	0-0	1-1	0-0	—	1-3	1-1	1-1	0-1	1-2	1-5	2-0	1-0	3-2	1-0	4-1	1-3	3-0	2-2	0-2	2-0	3-0	4-3
Chelmsford City	0-0	4-0	3-1	2-0	—	0-1	2-3	1-2	3-0	1-0	2-1	2-1	0-1	0-2	4-1	1-1	1-1	3-2	3-1	3-1	3-2	2-1
Cheltenham Town	5-1	2-0	1-0	2-1	5-0	—	4-1	1-3	0-1	1-1	0-1	1-1	3-1	1-0	3-0	3-1	1-0	0-0	1-2	0-1	1-0	1-0
Corby Town	1-0	1-2	2-1	0-0	0-0	1-1	—	5-1	0-0	0-6	2-1	2-1	2-1	0-1	4-2	2-1	1-0	3-2	1-0	1-0	0-1	3-2
Crawley Town	0-1	6-2	1-1	2-1	0-2	0-1	0-0	—	1-1	1-0	0-0	0-1	0-1	3-0	3-1	2-0	1-0	1-1	3-0	1-1	2-1	2-0
Dorchester Town	2-2	1-3	2-1	3-1	1-0	0-2	0-0	1-2	—	0-1	1-2	1-2	1-1	0-0	1-4	1-1	1-0	1-3	1-1	0-1	1-2	0-3
Farnborough Town	1-0	3-1	2-0	2-2	7-6	1-1	1-0	1-2	0-0	—	1-0	5-0	3-0	3-1	1-0	1-0	1-2	2-1	1-1	1-0	3-0	3-1
Gloucester City	3-0	1-0	4-2	2-1	2-5	1-3	2-4	3-0	1-0	0-1	—	1-1	0-0	2-1	2-0	2-1	2-1	0-1	3-1	0-1	2-1	1-2
Gresley Rovers	1-1	1-1	0-4	2-1	2-1	1-1	1-0	1-1	0-2	4-0	2-0	—	1-1	3-0	0-2	3-3	5-3	1-1	2-1	1-3	2-1	3-4
Halesowen Town	0-0	2-0	2-2	3-0	3-1	1-1	2-0	2-2	2-0	2-3	1-0	2-1	—	2-1	2-1	0-1	3-1	2-1	1-3	1-1	4-0	2-1
Hastings Town	1-2	1-0	3-2	1-0	3-1	1-1	2-0	0-1	1-0	1-0	1-0	2-1	1-1	—	0-3	1-3	2-3	0-3	1-2	2-2	2-0	3-2
Hednesford Town	1-2	6-0	2-2	4-1	1-2	2-0	3-1	2-1	2-4	0-2	1-1	3-1	1-1	1-2	—	0-0	4-1	1-1	2-1	0-1	3-2	4-2
Moor Green	2-2	0-0	2-0	0-1	3-1	1-2	0-4	0-2	1-3	1-2	3-0	2-4	0-3	1-0	2-4	—	1-0	0-1	1-1	3-1	2-0	0-2
Nuneaton Borough	0-1	1-1	1-2	0-1	1-1	2-1	2-1	2-1	0-2	2-1	1-3	2-3	1-1	0-2	0-0	1-0	—	2-1	0-3	2-0	3-0	1-1
Sittingbourne	2-0	1-1	0-0	3-2	1-2	1-3	2-0	2-3	1-2	1-3	0-0	1-2	3-2	2-1	3-0	5-2	2-2	—	1-0	1-0	0-0	4-0
Solihull Borough	0-2	2-0	0-0	2-0	0-1	1-2	1-2	0-1	1-1	0-0	2-4	4-2	0-2	2-2	0-0	2-1	1-0	1-0	—	0-2	1-1	0-1
Trowbridge Town	4-1	3-0	3-2	0-0	2-1	2-2	1-1	0-0	1-0	0-0	2-0	2-0	3-1	1-1	3-2	2-2	0-0	0-0	2-2	—	0-0	2-2
Waterlooville	0-3	1-1	1-0	2-2	0-1	0-3	2-1	1-2	2-0	2-3	1-1	2-2	1-4	4-1	2-0	0-0	3-2	2-2	2-2	2-0	—	3-2
Worcester City	3-0	2-0	0-4	2-0	1-1	1-1	2-1	2-0	1-0	0-2	2-0	2-2	0-2	3-1	0-0	3-3	0-1	1-1	0-4	2-1	1-2	—

BEAZER HOMES SOUTHERN LEAGUE MIDLAND DIVISION RESULTS 1993–94

	Armitage	Bedworth United	Bilston Town	Bridgnorth Town	Clevedon Town	Dudley Town	Evesham United	Forest Green Rovers	Grantham Town	Hinckley Town	King's Lynn	Leicester United	Newport AFC	Racing Club Warwick	Redditch United	Rushden & Diamonds	Stourbridge	Sutton Coldfield Town	Tamworth	VS Rugby	Weston-Super-Mare	Yate Town
Armitage	—	0-1	1-0	2-7	0-2	0-0	1-3	0-2	4-3	0-1	3-3	2-1	2-1	4-1	0-2	0-3	2-2	1-2	2-11	0-1	0-2	0-3
Bedworth United	5-3	—	4-2	1-3	1-3	0-3	0-1	4-1	0-2	1-2	1-1	1-1	0-2	1-2	2-1	1-2	3-1	1-2	1-2	2-5	0-1	2-1
Bilston Town	1-2	1-0	—	2-0	2-1	1-2	3-2	3-2	2-4	6-1	0-1	1-1	1-5	0-0	2-2	0-1	1-3	2-0	2-0	0-3	0-6	2-0
Bridgnorth Town	5-0	0-2	0-2	—	0-0	1-0	0-1	0-1	3-2	4-0	2-0	0-3	1-0	3-1	2-2	0-2	1-4	1-2	1-0	0-4	2-2	0-1
Clevedon Town	1-1	3-2	2-2	3-0	—	1-0	2-1	1-0	4-2	2-2	3-0	0-0	0-2	2-0	3-3	0-0	3-1	0-1	1-1	4-0	1-3	2-1
Dudley Town	4-0	1-1	1-2	3-4	0-1	—	2-0	0-1	3-6	0-0	1-4	5-0	2-2	0-2	0-3	2-2	0-3	2-4	3-3	2-0	1-1	1-1
Evesham United	3-2	2-1	0-3	1-1	0-2	0-3	—	4-2	3-0	0-1	2-0	1-0	2-4	3-3	1-0	1-4	2-0	1-0	1-2	1-5	0-2	0-0
Forest Green Rovers	5-2	1-1	2-2	0-0	2-1	2-1	0-4	—	0-2	1-1	1-0	0-1	3-8	1-0	0-0	3-5	4-2	2-5	2-4	0-5	0-2	5-0
Grantham Town	2-2	2-4	0-3	4-1	2-3	0-1	1-1	1-1	—	1-1	2-1	0-2	0-2	1-2	2-1	0-1	4-0	1-0	2-0	2-3	0-1	3-2
Hinckley Town	3-0	3-3	0-1	1-1	4-1	0-0	0-0	1-0	2-4	—	1-2	1-0	2-3	0-1	0-2	0-4	2-0	2-2	1-2	0-1	2-2	0-3
King's Lynn	0-0	0-1	0-1	2-3	0-1	1-1	0-1	1-1	1-0	3-2	—	3-0	1-1	1-2	2-3	1-1	3-2	0-0	0-0	2-4	1-4	3-2
Leicester United	2-2	3-0	0-0	0-2	0-4	0-5	1-1	1-1	1-3	0-2	1-0	—	1-2	1-2	2-1	0-2	3-2	0-0	3-1	0-3	0-6	0-1
Newport AFC	0-0	3-1	1-0	2-1	2-0	2-1	3-1	0-1	1-0	2-0	3-0	5-0	—	2-1	3-1	0-2	4-0	3-0	3-1	2-0	0-1	2-3
Racing Club Warwick	1-1	2-2	2-2	2-3	0-1	1-2	0-2	1-1	1-4	2-0	2-1	0-2	0-0	—	1-0	2-2	0-2	3-2	1-2	0-2	2-1	4-2
Redditch United	1-1	3-1	0-0	4-0	2-3	1-2	2-0	4-1	2-1	2-0	1-1	1-0	2-1	1-1	—	1-2	1-3	3-2	5-0	2-0	0-0	3-2
Rushden & Diamonds	4-0	3-1	5-1	2-0	2-0	2-1	1-0	5-0	3-3	2-3	6-0	4-0	1-1	1-1	7-0	—	3-3	2-0	5-1	1-1	3-2	3-0
Stourbridge	5-0	1-3	2-6	1-0	2-3	3-1	1-1	1-5	3-1	3-1	2-0	4-1	0-0	1-1	2-2	0-1	—	1-2	2-0	3-1	0-3	0-2
Sutton Coldfield Town	1-3	2-2	3-1	2-1	0-1	0-3	1-1	3-3	2-4	0-1	2-3	0-1	1-1	4-1	1-5	1-2	0-2	—	0-1	0-3	0-3	2-2
Tamworth	0-0	2-0	9-2	1-0	3-3	2-1	1-2	4-1	3-1	4-0	2-2	2-1	0-1	0-2	3-4	1-1	1-0	2-0	—	1-4	1-2	6-0
VS Rugby	6-1	5-2	2-0	2-1	2-2	2-1	1-0	1-1	3-0	3-0	3-1	0-0	1-1	2-1	4-1	2-2	2-0	0-1	1-0	—	4-1	1-1
Weston-Super-Mare	3-0	2-1	1-1	4-1	0-1	2-1	4-0	1-1	0-0	1-0	3-2	3-0	3-3	2-0	3-3	2-1	1-2	2-0	5-1	1-1	—	4-2
Yate Town	0-1	1-2	2-2	0-1	0-4	0-2	1-0	2-1	0-5	2-1	1-0	0-1	0-1	2-2	1-2	2-4	1-2	2-3	0-2	1-5	1-2	—

BEAZER HOMES SOUTHERN LEAGUE SOUTHERN DIVISION RESULTS 1993–94

	Ashford Town	Baldock Town	Braintree Town	Buckingham Town	Burnham	Bury Town	Canterbury City	Dunstable	Erith & Belvedere	Fareham Town	Fisher	Gravesend & Northfleet	Havant Town	Margate	Newport IOW	Poole Town	Salisbury City	Sudbury Town	Tonbridge	Wealdstone	Weymouth	Witney Town
Ashford Town	—	2-0	3-2	3-0	4-0	6-1	1-1	6-3	3-1	2-3	2-0	2-2	4-2	1-0	3-2	3-0	1-1	2-2	1-0	2-0	3-1	1-2
Baldock Town	1-1	—	1-0	2-1	4-0	2-1	2-0	0-0	2-2	2-0	3-2	1-2	4-2	1-1	3-2	3-1	2-0	1-3	0-2	1-0	1-1	2-0
Braintree Town	1-3	2-1	—	1-3	5-0	1-1	4-1	1-1	4-1	3-0	3-1	1-4	0-1	1-1	0-2	5-1	0-1	1-3	2-1	2-2	1-1	1-2
Buckingham Town	0-0	1-0	0-2	—	2-2	1-0	2-0	0-1	2-2	0-0	0-0	0-2	0-0	0-2	1-1	1-0	0-1	0-0	2-1	0-0	1-1	0-1
Burnham	1-1	1-4	6-1	1-1	—	4-2	1-1	3-2	0-3	1-2	0-0	1-1	1-0	0-2	0-2	3-1	1-2	1-4	1-0	3-0	1-3	1-2
Bury Town	0-4	0-4	0-2	0-3	1-4	—	2-1	3-3	1-2	0-3	2-3	2-5	1-3	0-2	0-3	0-0	1-5	1-5	0-2	4-0	1-1	0-1
Canterbury City	0-4	0-3	1-4	0-1	3-2	3-2	—	1-3	3-0	0-2	2-3	0-5	0-3	0-2	0-4	1-1	0-2	3-0	1-2	1-2	3-1	0-1
Dunstable	3-2	1-2	2-1	0-2	2-2	0-3	0-2	—	0-3	3-2	2-1	1-4	0-1	1-1	0-4	1-2	1-1	0-1	1-4	1-0	2-4	1-2
Erith & Belvedere	1-1	0-1	0-3	0-2	1-0	5-1	2-0	0-1	—	2-1	1-2	0-1	0-2	2-3	0-2	1-3	0-2	0-1	1-3	2-0	0-3	1-4
Fareham Town	2-3	0-3	1-0	4-2	0-1	3-1	1-1	2-2	1-0	—	3-3	0-0	0-5	4-2	1-4	1-4	1-1	0-2	1-0	1-0	3-2	1-2
Fisher	0-2	0-4	2-2	0-3	1-1	6-0	3-1	1-3	3-1	1-1	—	0-2	0-4	0-1	0-1	2-0	0-2	2-2	2-1	1-1	1-1	1-2
Gravesend & Northfleet	0-0	1-2	4-0	0-0	6-0	3-0	1-0	1-0	0-0	2-0	1-0	—	3-1	4-1	0-1	4-0	0-0	2-2	0-0	4-1	4-1	1-0
Havant Town	3-3	3-1	1-2	0-1	3-0	3-0	3-0	2-1	5-2	4-1	3-2	2-1	—	1-1	3-0	10-0	1-0	2-1	2-1	2-0	2-0	1-2
Margate	3-2	0-2	6-0	2-1	4-0	2-2	2-0	2-1	1-0	0-0	1-3	0-2	1-0	—	0-1	5-0	1-4	2-1	5-1	4-1	3-1	0-3
Newport IOW	2-1	0-2	1-0	1-1	0-0	3-0	0-0	4-1	1-0	0-0	3-0	0-2	3-2	3-2	—	1-0	3-3	1-3	1-3	1-1	1-3	1-3
Poole Town	0-0	1-2	2-3	1-2	2-0	3-0	0-1	3-1	2-1	1-1	5-4	1-1	1-2	3-2	1-2	—	1-0	0-4	0-1	5-1	0-2	1-1
Salisbury City	1-2	2-0	5-1	2-1	5-2	6-1	1-1	2-0	1-0	3-2	6-0	1-4	1-0	2-2	1-1	3-2	—	1-0	2-0	4-0	3-1	1-1
Sudbury Town	4-5	2-1	9-0	2-0	5-1	4-1	3-1	5-2	2-0	2-1	2-0	1-0	0-0	3-0	2-1	1-2	1-3	—	2-1	3-2	2-0	2-1
Tonbridge	1-2	0-0	0-3	0-0	5-3	2-0	2-0	1-0	0-2	3-3	2-1	1-3	0-8	2-1	4-1	2-0	0-5	3-3	—	3-0	2-0	0-1
Wealdstone	0-0	1-2	3-4	2-5	0-3	5-1	1-2	4-0	1-1	2-2	3-0	0-3	0-4	1-3	0-6	1-2	2-3	0-1	1-2	—	3-0	1-4
Weymouth	0-2	2-2	4-1	3-1	2-1	2-0	2-0	3-2	3-0	4-0	1-0	1-1	0-3	3-2	1-4	2-1	1-1	2-2	1-0	1-3	—	6-1
Witney Town	0-0	0-2	2-2	2-0	3-0	1-0	0-0	3-1	1-0	2-0	1-1	0-1	3-2	1-1	4-0	5-1	1-0	1-1	0-1	2-0	1-0	—

DR. MARTENS CUP

Preliminary Round
Chelmsford City 2, Buckingham Town 1
Buckingham Town 2, Chelmsford City 1
(*Buckingham Town won 4-2 on penalties*)
Grantham Town 1, Rushden & Diamonds 3
Rushden & Diamonds 3, Grantham Town 2

First Round First Leg
Sudbury Town 1, Baldock Town 0
Buckingham Town 0, Braintree Town 2
Gravesend & Northfleet 5, Crawley Town 1
Burnham 5, Bury Town 0
Hastings Town 0, Erith & Belvedere 0
Tonbridge 3, Sittingbourne 2
Ashford Town 4, Canterbury City 2
Margate 0, Fisher 0
Poole Town 1, Salisbury City 5
Weymouth 1, Newport IOW 0
Weston-Super-Mare 3, Cheltenham Town 1
Trowbridge Town 2, Worcester City 1
Wealdstone 1, Dunstable 0
Waterlooville 2, Farnborough Town 2
Fareham Town 2, Dorchester Town 3
Havant Town 3, Bashley 0
Gresley Rovers 4, Hinckley Town 0
Forest Green Rovers 2, Bridgnorth Town 4
Clevedon Town 5, Halesowen Town 2
Redditch United 0, Dudley Town 0
Bilston Town 1, Leicester United 2
Atherstone United 1, Corby Town 1
Rushden & Diamonds 2, Bedworth United 0
Cambridge City 4, Kings Lynn 1
VS Rugby 2, Hednesford Town 1
Nuneaton Borough 4, Solihull Borough 1
Evesham United 1, Yate Town 0
Gloucester City 2, Witney Town 1
Sutton Coldfield 1, Racing Club Warwick 1
Moor Green 3, Tamworth 2
Burton Albion 3, Armitage 0
Newport AFC 1, Stourbridge 3

First Round Second Leg
Baldock Town 0, Sudbury Town 1
Braintree Town 1, Buckingham Town 1
Crawley Town 1, Gravesend & Northfleet 0
Bury Town 2, Burnham 1
Erith & Belvedere 0, Hastings Town 6
Sittingbourne 0, Tonbridge 2
Canterbury City 0, Ashford Town 7
Fisher 1, Margate 1
(*Margate won on away goals*)
Salisbury City 0, Poole Town 1
Newport IOW 0, Weymouth 0
Cheltenham Town 4, Weston-Super-Mare 1
Worcester City 0, Trowbridge Town 0
Dunstable 3, Wealdstone 3
Farnborough Town 2, Waterlooville 4
Dorchester Town 2, Fareham Town 2
Bashley 1, Havant Town 1
Hinckley Town 0, Gresley Rovers 6
Bridgnorth Town 1, Forest Green Rovers 2
Halesowen Town 4, Clevedon Town 0
Dudley Town 3, Redditch United 0
Leicester United 0, Bilston Town 5
Corby Town 1, Atherstone United 0
Bedworth United 0, Rushden & Diamonds 0
Kings Lynn 0, Cambridge City 3
Hednesford Town 4, VS Rugby 0
Solihull Borough 1, Nuneaton Borough 2
Yate Town 0, Evesham United 0
Witney Town 1, Gloucester City 1
Racing Club Warwick 0, Sutton Coldfield 1
Tamworth 2, Moor Green 2
Armitage 0, Burton Albion 6
Stourbridge 1, Newport AFC 2

Second Round
Sudbury Town 3, Braintree Town 1
Gravesend & Northfllet 3, Burnham 0
Hastings Town 0, Tonbridge 2
Ashford Town 0, Margate 2
Salisbury City 2, Weymouth 2
Replay: Weymouth 1, Salisbury City 3
Cheltenham Town 2, Trowbridge Town 3
Wealdstone 0, Waterlooville 2
Dorchester Town 2, Havant Town 1
Gresley Rovers 4, Bridgnorth Town 0
Halesowen Town 2, Dudley Town 1
Bilston Town 1, Corby Town 3
Rushden & Diamonds 2, Cambridge City 2
Replay: Cambridge City 3, Rushden & Diamonds 1
Hednesford Town 1, Nuneaton Borough 1
Replay: Nuneaton Borough 3, Hednesford Town 1
Evesham Town 1, Gloucester City 3
Sutton Coldfield 1, Moor Green 3
Burton Albion 2, Stourbridge 1

Third Round
Sudbury Town 0, Gravesend & Northfleet 1
(*Gravesend & Northfleet expelled from competition; ineligible player*)
Tonbridge 4, Margate 1
Salisbury City 1, Trowbridge Town 0
Waterlooville 1, Dorchester Town 2
Gresley Rovers 3, Halesowen Town 2
Corby Town 2, Cambridge City 1
Hednesford Town 0, Gloucester City 1
Moor Green 0, Burton Albion 3

Fourth Round
Sudbury Town 2, Tonbridge 0
Salisbury City 4, Dorchester Town 0
Gresley Rovers 0, Corby Town 0
Replay: Corby Town 1, Gresley Rovers 3
Gloucester City 0, Burton Albion 1

Semi-final (two legs)
Sudbury Town 2, Salisbury City 2
Salisbury City 1, Sudbury Town 4
Gresley Rovers 1, Burton Albion 0
Burton Albion 0, Gresley Rovers 1

Final (two legs)
Sudbury Town 2, Gresley Rovers 1
Gresley Rovers 0, Sudbury Town 3

DIADORA FOOTBALL LEAGUE 1993–94

Premier Division

		Home			Away			Totals			Goals		
	P	*W*	*D*	*L*	*W*	*D*	*L*	*W*	*D*	*L*	*F*	*A*	*Pts*
Stevenage Borough	42	15	2	4	16	2	3	31	4	7	88	39	97
Enfield	42	14	4	3	14	4	3	28	8	6	80	28	92
Marlow	42	14	3	4	11	4	6	25	7	10	90	67	82
Chesham United	42	13	1	7	11	7	3	24	8	10	73	45	80
Sutton United	42	13	5	3	10	5	6	23	10	9	77	31	79
Carshalton Athletic	42	12	2	7	10	5	6	22	7	13	81	53	73
St. Albans City	42	12	5	4	9	5	7	21	10	11	81	54	73
Hitchin Town	42	11	2	8	10	5	6	21	7	14	81	56	70
Harrow Borough	42	9	8	4	9	3	9	18	11	13	54	56	65
Kingstonian	42	9	3	9	9	6	6	18	9	15	101	64	63
Hendon	42	8	4	9	10	5	6	18	9	15	61	51	63
Aylesbury United	42	8	3	10	9	4	8	17	7	18	64	67	58
Hayes	42	7	6	8	8	2	11	15	8	19	63	72	53
Grays Athletic	42	8	1	12	7	4	10	15	5	22	56	69	50
Bromley	42	7	5	9	7	2	12	14	7	21	56	69	49
Dulwich Hamlet	42	4	6	11	9	2	10	13	8	21	52	74	47
Yeading	42	7	5	9	4	8	9	11	13	18	58	66	46
Molesey	42	5	8	8	6	3	12	11	11	20	44	62	44
Wokingham Town	42	6	3	12	5	3	13	11	6	25	38	67	39
Dorking	42	6	1	14	3	3	15	9	4	29	58	104	31
Basingstoke Town	42	2	7	12	3	5	13	5	12	25	v38	v86	27
Wivenhow Town	42	2	3	16	3	0	18	5	3	34	v38	152	18

Division

		Home			Away			Totals			Goals		
	P	*W*	*D*	*L*	*W*	*D*	*L*	*W*	*D*	*L*	*F*	*A*	*Pts*
Bishop's Stortford	42	14	4	3	10	9	2	24	13	5	83	31	85
Purfleet	42	11	5	5	11	7	3	22	12	8	70	44	78
Walton & Hersham	42	12	6	3	10	5	6	22	11	9	81	53	77
Tooting & Mitcham	42	12	6	3	9	6	6	21	12	9	66	37	75
Heybridge Swifts	42	11	5	5	9	6	6	20	11	11	72	45	71
Billericay Town	42	8	5	8	12	6	3	20	11	11	70	51	71
Abingdon Town	42	10	6	5	10	4	7	20	10	12	61	50	70
Worthing	42	12	4	5	7	7	7	19	11	12	79	46	68
Leyton	42	10	4	7	10	4	7	20	8	14	88	66	68
Boreham Wood	42	8	9	4	9	6	6	17	15	10	69	50	66
Staines Town	42	11	5	5	7	4	10	18	9	15	85	56	63
Bognor Regis Town	42	10	5	6	5	9	7	15	14	13	57	48	59
Wembley	42	8	3	10	8	7	6	16	10	16	66	52	58
Barking	42	7	6	8	8	5	8	15	11	16	63	69	56
Uxbridge	42	7	6	8	8	2	11	15	8	19	57	58	53
Whyteleafe	42	8	4	9	7	2	12	15	6	21	71	90	51
Maidenhead United	42	7	6	8	5	7	9	12	13	17	52	48	49
Berkhamstead Town	42	7	5	9	5	4	12	12	9	21	65	77	45
Ruislip Manor	42	6	5	10	4	3	14	10	8	24	42	79	38
Chalfont St.Peter	42	4	6	11	3	4	14	7	10	25	40	79	31
Windsor & Eton	42	4	4	13	4	3	14	8	7	27	47	94	31
Croydon	42	1	2	18	2	1	18	3	3	36	37	198	12

Division Two

		Home			Away			Totals			Goals		
	P	*W*	*D*	*L*	*W*	*D*	*L*	*W*	*D*	*L*	*F*	*A*	*Pts*
Newbury Town	42	19	1	1	13	6	2	32	7	3	115	36	103
Chertsey Town	42	19	2	0	14	1	6	33	3	6	121	48	102
Aldershot Town	42	17	2	2	13	5	3	30	7	5	78	27	97
Barton Rovers	42	13	4	4	12	4	5	25	8	9	68	37	83
Witham Town	42	11	5	5	10	5	6	21	10	11	68	51	73
Maiden Vale	42	10	5	6	10	5	6	20	10	12	70	49	70
Thame United	42	10	4	7	9	8	4	19	12	11	87	51	69
Metropolitan Police	42	8	7	6	12	2	7	20	9	13	75	54	69
Banstead Athletic	42	11	5	5	8	4	9	19	9	14	56	53	66
Aveley	42	11	2	8	8	3	10	19	5	18	60	66	62
Edgware Town	42	6	6	9	10	4	7	16	10	16	88	76	58
Saffron Walden T	42	10	6	5	7	1	13	17	7	18	61	62	58
Hemel Hempstead	42	8	4	9	6	7	8	14	11	17	47	43	53
Egham Town	42	7	6	8	7	2	12	14	8	20	48	65	50
Ware	42	10	3	8	4	4	13	14	7	21	48	76	49
Hungerford Town	42	10	3	8	3	4	14	13	7	22	56	66	46
Tilbury	42	8	2	11	5	1	15	13	3	26	59	81	42
Hampton	42	6	3	12	6	2	13	12	5	25	42	70	41
Leatherhead	42	7	1	13	3	5	13	10	6	26	46	92	36
Lewes	42	6	5	10	2	5	14	8	10	24	38	85	34
Collier Row	42	5	4	12	2	4	15	7	8	27	37	88	29
Rainham Town	42	2	2	17	2	0	19	4	2	36	24	116	14

Division Three

		Home			Away			Totals			Goals		
	P	*W*	*D*	*L*	*W*	*D*	*L*	*W*	*D*	*L*	*F*	*A*	*Pts*
Bracknell Town	40	14	4	2	11	4	5	25	8	7	78	29	83
Cheshunt	40	10	7	3	13	5	2	23	12	5	62	34	81
Oxford City	40	15	3	2	9	3	8	24	6	10	94	55	78
Harlow Town	40	11	5	4	11	6	3	22	11	7	61	36	77
Southall	40	9	7	4	8	5	7	17	12	11	66	53	63
Camberley Town	40	13	5	2	5	2	13	18	7	15	56	50	61
Hertford Town	40	11	2	7	7	4	9	18	6	16	67	65	60
Royston Town	40	10	5	5	5	6	9	15	11	14	44	41	56
Northwood	40	10	4	6	5	7	8	15	11	14	78	77	56
Epsom & Ewell	40	9	4	7	6	5	9	15	9	16	63	62	54
Harefield United	40	5	8	7	7	7	6	12	15	13	45	55	51
Cove	40	11	3	6	4	3	13	15	6	19	59	74	51
Kingsbury Town	40	6	6	8	6	8	6	12	14	14	57	54	50
Feltham & Hounslow	40	9	3	8	5	4	11	14	7	19	60	63	49
Leighton Town	40	9	5	6	3	6	11	12	11	17	51	64	47
East Thurrock Utd.	40	5	10	5	5	5	10	10	15	15	65	64	45
Clapton	40	10	4	6	2	5	13	12	9	19	51	65	45
Hornchurch	40	7	4	9	5	4	11	12	8	20	42	60	44
Tring Town	40	5	5	10	5	6	9	10	11	19	48	64	41
Flackwell Heath	40	3	6	11	6	5	9	9	11	20	44	83	38
Horsham	40	5	4	11	1	4	15	6	8	26	43	86	26

LEADING GOALSCORERS

		Lge	*Lge Cup*	*Carlsberg*
Premier Division				
35	Jimmy Bolton (Carshalton Athletic)	29	5	1
27	Martin Gittings (Stevenage Borough)	27		
	David Lay (Marlow)	21	6	
Division One				
28	Leo Fortune-West (Bishop's Stortford)	23	4	1
27	Justin Mitchell (Walton & Hersham)	27		
24	Barry Popplewell (Leyton)	19	1	4
Division Two				
42	Matthew McDonnell (Newbury)	40	1	1
32	Mario Russo (Metropolitan Police)	30	2	
28	Scott McGleish (Edgware Town)	27		1
	Mark Butler (Aldershot Town)	26	1	1
	Lee Charles (Chertsey Town)	20	5	3
	(including goals for Yeading)	*2)*		
Division Three				
33	Tony Wood (Bracknell Town)	30	2	1
	(including goals at Flackwell Heath	*12*	*2*	*1)*
24	Mark Randall (Northwood)	21	3	
23	David Whitehead (Hertford Town)	22	1	

DIADORA LEAGUE PREMIER DIVISION

	Aylesbury Utd	Basingstoke	Bromley	Carshalton Ath	Chesham Utd	Dorking	Dulwich Hamlet	Enfield	Grays Athletic	Harrow Borough	Hayes	Hendon	Hitchin Town	Kingstonian	Marlow	Molesey	St. Albans	Stevenage Boro	Sutton Utd	Wivenhoe Town	Wokingham	Yeading
Aylesbury Utd	—	4-4	2-1	3-0	0-2	2-0	1-3	1-0	0-1	0-1	1-0	2-3	1-1	3-6	1-5	2-1	1-2	0-1	1-2	3-0	3-0	1-1
Basingstoke	2-3	—	1-3	0-2	3-3	0-0	0-1	1-2	0-0	1-1	4-1	0-1	1-3	1-1	1-3	1-2	0-1	1-2	0-0	6-2	1-2	1-1
Bromley	0-0	3-0	—	0-2	1-2	2-1	3-2	1-2	0-2	0-3	0-0	3-3	0-0	2-2	2-3	0-1	2-0	1-2	1-4	6-0	1-0	2-1
Carshalton Ath	1-3	2-0	2-1	—	1-1	1-2	0-1	0-3	3-0	2-1	2-0	3-0	1-4	1-4	2-1	0-1	3-3	2-0	1-0	4-3	1-0	2-0
Chesham Utd	1-4	2-1	5-0	2-1	—	3-0	2-1	2-3	2-1	3-0	0-1	2-1	0-3	1-0	1-3	0-1	0-0	1-2	1-0	5-1	3-0	3-2
Dorking	1-4	1-2	0-3	1-4	3-4	—	0-1	1-3	3-3	4-3	0-1	1-2	3-1	2-0	2-3	3-1	1-2	1-5	1-3	4-1	1-3	4-3
Dulwich Hamlet	2-0	1-1	1-2	2-1	0-2	1-1	—	2-2	2-3	1-2	3-2	0-1	0-0	1-7	2-3	1-0	1-2	0-2	0-3	0-1	2-2	1-1
Enfield	4-0	0-1	2-0	1-1	0-1	6-0	3-0	—	1-0	2-0	2-0	1-0	0-3	3-0	0-0	—	1-1	3-0	1-0	8-0	1-0	0-0
Grays Athletic	0-2	2-0	3-2	1-1	0-2	4-0	4-0	1-4	—	0-1	0-1	0-3	0-2	0-3	4-7	1-2	0-1	1-2	1-0	1-0	0-3	2-1
Harrow Borough	0-1	4-0	0-0	3-0	0-4	3-2	2-1	1-1	1-1	—	3-3	2-1	1-1	2-4	2-0	1-1	0-0	1-0	0-1	3-0	1-1	1-0
Hayes	0-0	4-0	3-1	3-3	1-1	3-2	1-2	0-1	1-3	1-1	—	1-1	2-2	2-1	2-0	3-0	2-1	1-3	1-8	0-2	1-2	0-1
Hendon	2-2	6-0	2-1	1-1	0-1	3-1	2-1	0-2	2-1	0-2	0-2	—	2-4	0-0	0-1	2-0	1-0	1-2	0-1	0-2	1-1	5-2
Hitchin Town	5-1	1-0	1-0	1-0	2-1	2-3	2-3	2-3	2-3	0-1	3-2	0-0	—	1-3	2-1	2-0	1-3	1-3	0-0	6-2	1-0	4-2
Kingstonian	2-1	5-0	3-0	0-2	1-2	2-2	3-0	1-2	3-0	7-0	4-1	1-3	3-5	—	1-1	0-0	0-1	3-5	0-2	8-1	5-0	1-2
Marlow	1-0	2-0	3-4	0-6	0-2	2-1	4-2	2-1	3-1	0-1	4-3	2-1	1-0	3-3	—	2-1	4-2	0-0	3-2	3-1	3-1	1-1
Molesey	1-2	0-0	2-3	0-1	1-1	3-0	0-0	0-1	0-2	0-0	3-2	2-3	1-2	1-1	1-1	—	2-1	1-2	0-0	4-0	2-0	0-0
St. Albans	1-1	6-1	2-0	1-3	1-1	3-0	4-3	2-1	5-3	3-1	4-0	0-0	2-1	1-4	1-2	4-1	—	1-2	0-0	9-1	2-0	1-1
Stevenage Boro	4-0	0-0	0-1	2-4	0-0	4-3	2-0	0-1	1-0	3-0	2-1	3-0	1-2	4-1	4-2	4-2	3-0	—	3-2	6-0	1-0	4-1
Sutton Utd	3-1	5-0	3-0	2-2	3-1	3-0	0-3	1-1	1-0	3-1	0-1	0-1	2-0	2-1	2-2	4-1	4-1	0-0	—	5-0	1-0	1-1
Wivenhoe Town	0-4	1-2	0-0	0-8	1-1	1-0	3-4	1-2	0-4	2-3	0-6	0-4	0-7	1-1	2-3	3-4	0-3	0-1	0-3	—	3-2	2-4
Wokingham	0-3	0-0	2-1	0-4	2-0	3-1	0-1	1-1	3-0	0-1	0-1	0-2	2-0	1-3	0-6	1-1	1-3	0-1	0-1	1-0	—	1-2
Yeading	1-2	3-1	2-3	2-1	0-2	1-2	0-0	1-2	1-1	2-0	2-3	1-1	2-1	2-3	2-0	3-0	1-1	0-2	0-0	4-1	1-3	—

DIADORA LEAGUE DIVISION ONE

	Abingdon Town	Barking	Berkhamsted T	Billericay T	Bishops Stort	Bognor Regis T	Boreham Wood	Chalfont St P.	Croydon	Heybridge Swts	Leyton	Maidenhead Utd	Purfleet	Ruislip Manor	Staines Town	Tooting & M	Uxbridge	Walton & Hersh	Wembley	Whyteleafe	Windsor & Eton	Worthing
Abingdon Town	—	0-1	1-0	0-3	1-0	1-1	3-1	1-1	2-1	0-0	2-1	3-1	1-1	3-0	2-1	0-1	1-0	0-3	3-3	1-2	1-0	3-3
Barking	1-1	—	0-0	2-2	3-2	0-0	0-2	1-0	0-2	3-2	1-2	1-1	0-3	1-1	3-2	1-2	0-3	4-2	0-1	5-0	3-0	0-1
Berkhamsted T	3-2	0-0	—	0-2	0-1	1-1	3-2	2-1	14-1	3-3	1-1	0-2	1-5	0-1	4-1	0-4	3-4	2-3	1-3	2-2	2-1	2-0
Billericay T	2-0	1-0	1-1	—	0-0	1-0	0-1	3-4	3-0	0-4	3-4	3-2	2-2	6-1	0-5	0-1	2-0	3-1	0-1	3-4	1-1	0-0
Bishops Stort	2-0	4-0	3-0	1-2	—	1-0	5-2	4-0	9-1	0-0	2-2	1-1	2-3	3-0	3-1	2-2	1-2	1-0	3-1	5-1	5-0	2-0
Bognor Regis T	1-0	1-2	4-2	0-1	0-0	—	2-2	4-1	8-0	1-2	3-2	2-1	2-2	1-0	3-1	1-1	1-0	0-1	0-4	4-1	0-1	0-0
Boreham Wood	1-1	2-3	0-0	1-1	0-0	0-0	—	0-1	10-0	2-1	1-2	2-0	0-2	3-1	1-1	2-1	1-0	0-0	0-0	1-0	2-2	3-1
Chalfont St P.	0-1	1-1	0-2	1-3	1-1	0-0	1-1	—	4-0	1-1	0-6	0-2	1-2	0-2	0-5	2-1	1-2	1-1	2-1	0-1	3-0	0-3
Croydon	0-9	4-1	0-4	0-1	1-4	1-2	1-5	2-2	—	0-0	1-3	0-3	1-4	2-7	0-14	0-7	1-4	1-4	1-2	3-7	1-2	0-7
Heybridge Swts	0-0	2-3	4-1	3-1	2-3	2-0	1-2	4-1	6-0	—	3-2	2-1	0-0	0-0	0-0	0-1	4-2	1-2	2-2	3-0	1-0	2-1
Leyton	2-3	0-2	1-3	0-2	0-1	2-1	1-1	3-2	3-1	1-2	—	1-1	2-1	2-0	5-3	0-1	4-0	5-1	4-1	6-1	3-3	1-1
Maidenhead Utd	0-1	3-2	1-0	0-2	1-1	1-1	0-2	3-1	4-0	1-0	0-1	—	1-1	1-2	0-1	1-1	0-0	0-1	0-0	4-0	4-1	1-2
Purfleet	4-0	2-1	1-1	3-2	0-2	2-0	0-2	1-0	2-4	0-0	1-0	1-0	—	2-1	4-0	1-0	0-3	0-0	0-0	0-1	3-1	1-1
Ruislip Manor	0-2	2-2	1-2	1-1	1-1	2-0	1-2	1-2	0-0	1-2	1-0	3-1	2-3	—	0-6	3-0	0-0	0-1	2-0	0-2	1-2	2-1
Staines Town	0-0	1-3	2-0	1-1	0-0	0-2	1-1	2-0	3-0	0-1	2-3	3-1	0-1	4-0	—	3-0	4-1	0-0	3-2	1-0	2-0	2-1
Tooting & M	3-0	3-1	3-0	1-1	0-1	0-1	3-3	0-0	6-0	2-0	2-2	0-0	3-1	1-0	4-2	—	1-0	1-0	1-4	1-0	2-0	1-1
Uxbridge	1-0	2-2	6-0	0-1	0-1	2-2	4-2	2-1	3-1	0-1	1-2	0-0	1-2	0-0	2-0	0-2	—	2-3	0-3	0-0	2-1	1-1
Walton & Hersh	1-3	3-3	2-1	1-2	2-2	3-0	3-1	1-0	6-2	2-1	5-2	2-2	2-2	5-0	1-1	1-1	1-0	—	2-1	2-1	3-1	1-2
Wembley	4-5	3-0	3-0	3-2	0-1	0-1	1-2	1-0	7-0	0-1	1-1	0-2	1-1	2-0	2-0	0-1	2-0	1-1	—	1-4	0-1	2-4
Whyteleafe	0-1	1-4	2-1	0-0	1-1	2-4	1-2	3-2	6-1	3-2	1-2	1-3	0-1	6-2	3-3	2-0	0-2	1-4	1-1	—	3-1	3-2
Windsor & Eton	1-2	2-3	1-3	0-4	0-1	2-2	0-0	1-1	5-3	1-4	2-3	1-0	1-4	1-0	2-3	1-1	1-4	1-4	0-2	4-3	—	2-3
Worthing	0-1	3-0	1-0	1-2	0-1	1-1	2-1	4-1	5-0	2-3	2-1	2-2	2-1	6-0	0-1	0-0	5-1	1-0	0-0	5-1	2-0	—

DIADORA LEAGUE DIVISION TWO

	Aldershot Town	Aveley	Banstead Ath	Barton Rovers	Chertsey Town	Collier Row	Edgware Town	Egham Town	Hampton	Hemel Hempstead	Hungerford Town	Leatherhead	Lewes	Malden Vale	Met Police	Newbury Town	Rainham Town	Saffron Walden	Thame Utd	Tilbury	Ware	Witham Town
Aldershot Town	—	2-1	1-2	1-0	1-1	1-0	3-0	3-2	3-0	2-0	3-1	1-0	4-0	1-2	3-1	1-0	2-0	1-0	0-0	2-0	4-0	1-0
Aveley	1-0	—	1-0	2-2	2-3	2-1	1-2	4-0	1-0	0-3	3-2	0-2	2-1	1-0	0-1	1-2	6-2	0-0	1-5	2-1	4-1	0-1
Banstead Ath	0-0	2-2	—	0-3	4-3	2-0	1-3	1-0	2-0	0-0	3-2	3-0	1-0	1-1	0-1	0-1	4-1	0-2	3-1	3-1	1-0	1-1
Barton Rovers	0-1	2-0	1-0	—	1-0	3-0	5-4	4-1	1-1	0-0	2-0	1-0	4-0	0-2	1-0	0-0	3-0	0-1	2-2	2-0	3-2	0-3
Chertsey Town	3-2	3-2	4-0	3-2	—	10-2	1-1	0-0	2-0	5-1	4-2	6-2	5-0	3-0	5-1	3-2	4-0	5-2	5-0	1-0	3-0	5-1
Collier Row	1-3	1-2	2-3	1-0	2-3	—	2-2	3-1	0-1	0-1	1-1	2-1	0-0	0-3	2-2	0-3	0-2	3-2	3-2	0-3	1-3	0-2
Edgware Town	0-2	2-2	1-1	0-1	2-3	5-1	—	3-4	1-1	3-1	2-2	1-1	2-3	1-2	1-3	1-3	4-1	4-1	2-2	3-1	3-0	3-4
Egham Town	0-0	1-0	0-1	1-1	1-2	0-0	2-7	—	0-2	1-0	0-5	1-1	4-0	0-1	2-1	0-0	3-0	0-3	0-2	3-0	1-1	3-1
Hampton	0-3	4-0	2-1	0-1	0-2	2-1	1-2	0-1	—	1-1	1-0	2-3	1-1	1-4	0-1	1-1	2-0	0-3	0-3	1-2	3-1	0-5
Hemel Hempstead	0-1	0-1	2-3	0-3	2-0	2-1	1-1	0-2	0-1	—	5-0	1-1	2-1	1-1	1-3	0-3	2-0	3-1	0-1	2-0	3-0	1-1
Hungerford Town	0-0	3-1	1-0	2-3	2-1	3-1	2-1	0-1	2-0	0-3	—	4-0	3-1	1-2	1-4	0-1	1-0	0-2	1-1	4-0	0-0	0-1
Leatherhead	0-5	2-3	1-2	0-2	1-5	0-1	0-2	2-0	1-0	0-1	2-0	—	1-0	1-0	2-1	3-6	6-0	0-1	0-8	0-0	0-2	1-2
Lewes	1-3	1-2	0-0	0-1	1-3	1-0	1-1	2-1	0-4	0-0	1-0	1-1	—	1-1	1-3	1-4	2-0	2-0	0-2	3-2	1-2	2-3
Malden Vale	1-2	1-1	1-1	0-1	2-0	0-2	0-2	1-0	2-0	0-0	2-0	2-1	6-1	—	2-2	1-2	5-1	3-2	2-1	3-4	3-1	1-1
Met Police	1-3	5-1	1-3	1-1	0-1	2-0	0-2	0-3	2-1	0-0	5-1	5-0	4-2	1-1	—	1-1	0-1	2-1	0-0	4-1	0-0	1-1
Newbury Town	0-3	4-1	2-0	3-0	5-2	6-0	3-1	4-1	4-2	1-0	2-1	6-0	2-1	2-0	2-0	—	7-0	6-1	3-3	4-2	4-0	5-1
Rainham Town	1-2	0-1	1-4	0-4	0-3	1-1	1-2	0-3	0-3	1-0	0-3	0-4	0-0	1-7	1-2	1-2	—	3-0	1-6	2-3	0-5	0-1
Saffron Walden	2-2	0-1	3-0	0-1	0-1	1-1	0-4	5-1	2-0	1-0	2-2	3-2	7-1	0-0	1-5	0-0	1-0	—	2-2	3-1	3-0	2-1
Thame Utd	3-0	0-1	0-1	3-2	1-3	3-0	7-0	0-0	5-0	2-2	2-1	3-0	1-0	1-2	1-3	1-2	2-1	2-0	—	0-1	2-2	1-1
Tilbury	1-2	2-1	3-0	3-4	1-2	2-0	1-5	1-2	0-2	1-0	1-2	5-2	1-2	1-2	2-3	1-1	2-1	0-1	2-2	—	5-1	1-0
Ware	0-2	1-0	3-1	0-1	0-2	0-0	2-1	3-2	2-1	0-3	1-1	4-2	1-1	2-1	0-3	0-1	2-0	1-0	1-2	2-1	—	0-2
Witham Town	2-2	1-3	1-1	0-0	0-1	2-1	3-1	1-0	4-1	0-3	1-0	0-0	1-1	4-0	2-0	1-5	2-0	2-0	1-2	2-0	5-2	—

DIADORA LEAGUE DIVISION THREE

	Bracknell Town	Camberley Town	Cheshunt	Clapton	Cove	East Thurrock U	Epsom & Ewell	Felt & Hounslow	Flackwell Hth	Harefield Utd	Harlow Town	Hertford Town	Hornchurch	Horsham	Kingsbury Town	Leighton Town	Northwood	Oxford City	Royston Town	Southall	Tring Town
Bracknell Town	—	1-1	2-0	1-0	3-1	4-2	3-2	0-1	2-2	3-2	2-3	6-0	3-0	3-0	2-2	2-0	1-1	4-0	2-0	2-1	2-0
Camberley Town	0-1	—	1-1	2-0	5-1	4-0	0-0	2-0	2-0	1-1	0-1	3-1	3-0	3-1	1-1	0-0	1-0	2-1	1-0	3-1	3-1
Cheshunt	0-0	1-0	—	0-0	0-1	1-3	1-0	2-0	1-1	0-1	0-0	2-2	2-1	4-3	1-1	2-0	4-1	2-0	1-0	2-1	1-1
Clapton	1-0	2-0	1-3	—	1-1	3-2	2-0	4-2	1-1	1-1	2-3	3-1	0-2	2-1	1-1	3-0	0-1	1-3	3-0	0-1	4-0
Cove	0-3	1-0	0-2	4-3	—	2-1	2-5	2-2	5-1	0-0	2-0	1-2	4-1	2-1	1-4	5-2	3-3	1-2	2-0	5-2	1-0
East Thurrock U	1-1	1-2	1-1	1-1	5-0	—	2-4	2-3	1-3	1-2	0-0	1-1	2-0	3-0	2-2	5-0	4-4	1-1	1-1	2-2	2-0
Epsom & Ewell	0-1	3-1	0-1	1-0	3-1	2-2	—	0-2	4-0	3-2	1-1	3-1	2-1	1-0	1-1	1-2	2-5	2-3	2-0	0-3	1-1
Felt & Hounslow	1-2	3-0	1-3	3-0	1-1	5-1	2-1	—	0-1	0-1	0-0	3-2	1-2	5-0	1-2	0-3	5-2	3-1	0-0	1-2	2-1
Flackwell Hth	1-0	1-0	0-0	1-1	0-0	1-5	2-2	2-1	—	1-4	1-2	1-2	0-1	1-1	1-4	1-1	1-5	1-4	1-2	0-2	1-4
Harefield Utd	0-1	1-0	1-3	1-1	1-0	0-0	0-1	2-2	1-1	—	2-3	0-0	2-0	1-0	1-0	0-1	2-2	1-5	1-1	1-1	1-3
Harlow Town	3-0	2-0	0-1	2-1	1-0	1-0	2-0	3-0	3-0	1-1	—	1-0	0-1	1-1	2-3	4-2	1-1	1-2	1-0	2-2	1-1
Hertford Town	1-0	2-1	0-2	5-1	1-2	3-2	4-2	3-0	3-1	1-2	2-3	—	0-2	4-2	2-3	1-1	1-0	2-1	0-2	1-1	1-0
Hornchurch	0-0	0-0	0-2	0-1	2-1	0-1	2-0	3-1	1-2	1-1	0-3	1-2	—	3-2	3-1	1-1	2-1	2-1	1-2	0-1	3-4
Horsham	0-6	0-5	1-1	3-0	3-1	3-1	2-5	1-3	1-3	0-1	0-2	0-1	1-1	—	0-0	3-2	3-1	1-2	0-0	1-3	1-2
Kingsbury Town	0-0	1-4	1-3	2-3	1-2	1-0	2-3	1-0	4-1	3-0	0-0	0-1	1-0	1-1	—	0-0	2-0	1-1	1-2	1-2	1-1
Leighton Town	1-2	4-0	1-4	2-1	4-0	2-3	2-1	2-1	1-3	5-0	1-3	2-0	0-0	2-0	1-0	—	2-2	1-3	0-0	1-1	1-1
Northwood	0-5	5-1	2-2	4-0	2-1	1-1	2-4	1-1	0-1	3-3	2-1	0-6	2-1	3-1	2-3	2-0	—	3-2	1-2	2-1	1-0
Oxford City	1-0	4-1	1-2	5-0	2-3	2-0	3-0	1-1	4-0	0-0	3-0	6-4	3-1	3-1	2-1	2-0	4-4	—	3-2	3-0	5-0
Royston Town	0-1	0-1	3-0	1-0	1-0	0-2	0-0	3-1	2-0	4-1	0-1	1-1	1-1	2-1	2-2	1-1	2-0	3-1	—	1-0	1-2
Southall	1-6	6-0	0-1	3-3	2-0	0-0	1-1	3-0	4-3	2-1	1-1	2-1	1-1	0-0	2-1	3-0	1-2	1-2	4-2	—	0-0
Tring Town	0-1	1-2	2-3	1-0	2-0	1-1	0-0	1-2	2-2	0-2	1-2	1-2	5-1	2-3	2-1	3-0	0-5	2-2	0-0	0-2	—

DIADORA FOOTBALL LEAGUE CUP 1993–94

Preliminary Round
Epsom & Ewell 1, Hungerford Town 0
Chertsey Town 1, Royston Town 0
Horsham 2, East Thurrock Utd 1
Worthing 3, Hemel Hempstead 2 (*aet*)
Newbury Town 2, Kingsbury Town 0
Leatherhead 1, Hornchurch 0
Aldershot Town 5, Clapton 1
Feltham & Hounslow 2, Thame Utd 3
Aveley 0, Ruislip Manor 0
Hertford 1, Lewes 3
Harefield Utd 0, Collier Row 1
Banstead Ath 1, Edgware Town 0
Metropolitan Police 3, Rainham Town 0
Hampton 0, Berkhamsted Town 1
Bracknell Town 1, Chestnut 2
Malden Vale 2, Tilbury 1
Oxford City 3, Egham Town 0
Barton Rovers 1, Harlow Town 2
Cove 5, Flackwell Heath 3 (*aet*)
Saffron Walden Town 4, Southall 2
Northwood 1, Witham Town 1
Leighton Town 0, Tring Town 1
Ware 0, Camberley Town 2

Preliminary Round replays
Ruislip Manor 3, Aveley 1
Witham Town 1, Northwood 2

First Round
Hendon 2, Boreham Wood 3 (*aet*)
Epsom & Ewell 1, Chertsey Town 2 (*aet*)
Walton & Hersham 2, Abingdon Town 1
Horsham 2, Worthing 3
Molesey 1, Newbury Town 1
Leatherhead 1, Staines Town 3
Chalfont St Peter 1, Leyton 5
St Albans City 2, Bromley 1 (*aet*)
Aldershot Town 0, Kingstonian 4
Hitchin Town 4, Uxbridge 3
Croydon 1, Thame Utd 2
Ruislip Manor 1, Harrow Borough 3
Tooting & Mitcham 2, Lewes 1
Carshalton Athletic 5, Wivenhoe Town 1
Collier Row 1, Whyteleafe 2
Banstead Ath 0, Bishop's Stortford 6
Metropolitan Police 3, Wokingham Town 4
Berkhamsted Town 1, Chesham Utd 4
Aylesbury Utd 2, Cheshunt 1 (*aet*)
Grays Ath 4, Dulwich Hamlet 2
Malden Vale 2, Oxford City 3
Heybridge Swifts 1, Basingstoke Town 2
Barking 1, Wembley 3
Marlow 2, Yeading 0
Sutton Utd 2, Purfleet 0
Bognor Regis Town 2, Hayes 0
Harlow Town 1, Dorking 2 (*aet*)
Cove 1, Enfield 5
Saffron Walden Town 2, Stevenage Borough 0
Northwood 1, Windsor & Eton 3
Billericay Town 3, Tring Town 0
Camberley Town 1, Maidenhead Utd 3

Second Round
Boreham Wood 2, Chertsey Town 3
Walton & Hersham 0, Worthing 1
Molesey 0, Staines Town 1
Leyton 3, St Albans City 4
Kingstonian 4, Hitchin Town 3 (*aet*)
Thame Utd 4, Harrow Borough 4
Tooting & Mitcham 0, Carshalton Ath 3
Whyteleafe 2, Bishop's Stortford 7
Wokingham Town 2, Chesham Utd 1
Wokingham Town removed from competition; playing ineligible player
Aylesbury Utd 1, Greys Ath 4
Oxford City 1, Basingstoke Town 3
Wembley 2, Marlow 2
Sutton Utd 1, Bognor Regis Town 3
Dorking 1, Enfield 4
Saffron Walden Town 2, Windsor & Eton 1
Billericay Town 1, Maidenhead Utd 1 (*aet*)

Second Round replays
Harrow Borough 3, Thame Utd 3
(*Harrow Borough won 5-4 on penalty kicks*)
Marlow 2, Wembley 1
Maidenhead Utd 0, Billericay Town 1

Third Round
Chertsey Town 3, Worthing 0
Staines Town 0, St Albans City 1
Kingstonian 6, Harrow Borough 1
Carshalton Ath 1, Bishop's Stortford 0
Chesham Utd 3, Grays Ath 2
Basingstoke Town 1, Marlow 1
Bognor Regis Town 2, Enfield 3
Saffron Walden Town 3, Maidenhead Utd 1

Third Round replay
Marlow 3, Basingstoke Town 2 (*aet*)

Fourth Round
Chertsey Town 5, St Albans City 0
Kingstonian 0, Carshalton Ath 1
Chesham Utd 0, Marlow 3
Enfield 3, Saffron Walden Town 1 (*aet*)

Semi-finals, first leg
Carshalton Ath 0, Chertsey Town 3
Marlow 1, Enfield 1

Semi-finals, second leg
Chertsey Town 2, Carshalton Ath 1
Enfield 2, Marlow 1 (*aet*)

Final
Chertsey Town 3, Enfield 0
(*at Hayes*)

CARLSBERG CUP 1993–94

First Round
Berkhamstead Town 1, Yeading 2
Bishop's Stortford 3, Hayes 0
Boreham Wood 1, Hitchin Town 3
Dulwich Hamlst 2, Tooting & Mitcham 1
Chesham Utd 0, St Albans City 2
Barking 0, Leyton 2
Chalfont St Peter 1, Maidenhead Utd 1
Whyteleafe 3, Croydon 4 (*aet*)
Marlow 2, Ruislip Manor 1
Bognor Regis Town 2, Carshalton Ath 2 (*aet*)
(*Carshalton Ath won 4-1 on penalties*)
Sutton Utd 5, Worthing 1
Staines Town 1, Basingstoke Town 3

Second Round
Wivenhoe Town 1, Yeading 3
Billericay Town 1, Bishop's Stortford 2
Enfield 0, Hendon 1
Wembley 1, Uxbridge 2 (*aet*)
Harrow Borough 2, Aylesbury Utd 1 (*aet*)
Grays Ath 2, Hitchin Town 1
Dulwich Hamlet 2, Walton & Hersham 0
Kingstonian 4, Abingdon Town 0
St Albans City 5, Leyton 3
Stevenage Borough 1, Heybridge Swifts 3
Molesey 3, Maidenhead Utd 2 (*aet*)
Bromley 3, Croydon 1
Marlow 0, Purfleet 1
Carshalton Ath 3, Sutton Utd 1
Basingstoke Town 1, Wokingham Town 1
(*Wokingham Town won 4-3 on penalties*)
Windsor & Eton 0, Dorking 2

Third Round
Yeading 0, Bishop's Stortford 1
Hendon 1, Uxbridge 0
Harrow Borough 1, Grays Ath 4

Dulwich Hamlet 1, Kingstonian 0
St Albans City 3, Heybridge Swifts 3 (*aet*)
(*St Albans City won 4-3 on penalties*)
Molesey 2, Bromley 1
Purfleet 2, Carshalton Ath 2 (*aet*)
(*Purfleet won 8-7 on penalties*)
Wokingham Town 2, Dorking 1

Fourth Round
Bishop's Stortford 1, Hendon 1
(*Hendon won 3-1 on penalties*)
Grays Ath 1, Dulwich Hamlet 2
St Albans City 2, Molesey 1
Purfleet 1, Wokingham Town 1 (*aet*)
(*Wokingham Town won 5-4 on penalties*)

Semi-finals
Hendon 2, Dulwich Hamlet 1 (*aet*)
St Albans City 0, Wokingham Town 2

Final
Hendon 2, Wokingham Town 1
(*at Marlow*)

CARLSBERG TROPHY

First Round
Horsham 1, Feltham & Hounslow 5
Saffron Walden Town 2, Northwood 1
Flackwell Heath 5, Southall 2
Harefield United 1, Camberley Town 0
Hungerford Town 0, Newbury Town 1
Bracknell Town 1, Leatherhead 1
(*Leatherhead won 5-4 on penalties*)
Tring Town 1, Hemel Hempstead 4
Cheshunt 2, East Thurrock United 1
Barton Rovers 0, Leighton Town 1
Kingsbury Town 1, Hornchurch 2 (*aet*)
Collier Row 1, Rainham Town 1 (*aet*)
(*Rainham Town won 4-2 on penalties*)

Second Round
Aldershot Town 2, Malden Vale 0
Feltham & Hounslow 1, Epsom & Ewell 3
Chertsey Town 4, Metropolitan Police 0
Thame United 2, Oxford City 0
Saffron Walden Town 2, Tilbury 1
Witham Town 5, Flackwell Heath 1
Harefield United 0, Cove 2 (*aet*)
Banstead Athletic 2, Lewes 0
Egham Town 0, Newbury Town 1
Hampton 1, Leatherhead 0
Hemel Hempstead 2, Royston Town 0 (*aet*)
Cheshunt 5, Ware 2
Aveley 3, Clapton 2
Leighton Town 1, Hornchurch 3
Edgware Town 2, Rainham Town 1
Hertford Town 0, Harlow Town 2

Third Round
Aldershot Town 0, Epsom & Ewell 2
Chertsey Town 7, Thame United 3
Saffron Walden Town 1, Witham Town 2
Cove 1, Banstead Athletic 5
Newbury Town 5, Hampton 1
Hemel Hempstead 2, Cheshunt 1
Aveley 0, Hornchurch 2 (*aet*)
Edgware Town 3, Harlow Town 0

Fourth Round
Epsom & Ewell 0, Chertsey Town 7
Witham Town 0, Banstead Athletic 1
Newbury Town 2, Hemel Hempstead 1
Hornchurch 5, Edgware Town 0

Semi-finals
Chertsey Town 1, Banstead Athletic 0
Newbury Town 0, Hornchurch 2 (*aet*)

Final
Chertsey Town 1, Hornchurch 0
(*at Horsham*)

ENDSLEIGH INSURANCE LEAGUE MANAGERS OF THE MONTH

SEPTEMBER
Division 1 – **John King** (Tranmere Rovers); *Division 2* – **Alan Ball** (Exeter City); *Division 3* – **Dave Sutton** (Rochdale).
OCTOBER
Division 1 – **Steve Gritt/Alan Curbishley** (Charlton Athletic); *Division 2* – **Mark McGhee** (Reading); *Division 3* – **John Beck** (Preston North End).
NOVEMBER
Division 1 – **Barry Fry** (Birmingham City); *Division 2* – **John Ward** (Bristol Rovers); *Division 3* – **Kenny Hibbitt** (Walsall).
DECEMBER
Division 1 – **Alan Smith** (Crystal Palace); *Division 2* – **Peter Shilton** (Plymouth Argyle); *Division 3* – **Dario Gradi** (Crewe Alexandra).
JANUARY
Division 1 – **Graham Turner** (Wolverhampton Wanderers); *Division 2* – **John Ward** (Bristol Rovers); *Division 3* – **Steve Wicks** (Scarborough).
FEBRUARY
Division 1 – **Mick Walker** (Notts County); *Division 2* – **Liam Brady** (Brighton & Hove Albion); *Division 3* – **Don O'Riordan** (Torquay United).
MARCH
Division 1 – **Frank Clark** (Nottingham Forest); *Division 2* – **Alan Little** (York City); *Division 3* – **John Duncan** (Chesterfield).
APRIL
Division 1 – **Alan Smith** (Crystal Palace); *Division 2* – **John Rudge** (Port Vale); *Division 3* – **Fred Davies** (Shrewsbury Town).
Managers of the Year: *Division 1* – **Alan Smith** (Crystal Palace); *Division 2* – **Mark McGhee** (Reading); *Division 3* – **Fred Davies** (Shrewsbury Town).

FA CHALLENGE TROPHY 1993–94

First Qualifying Round

Bridlington Town v Ferryhill Athletic 4-0
Peterlee Newton v Workington 0-2
Ashton United v Chester-Le-Street Town 1-2
Dunston Federation Brewery v Easington Colliery 3-0
Fleetwood Town v Great Harwood Town 0-6
Durham City v Tow Law Town 0-1
Whitley Bay v Chorley 1-1, 1-3
Shildon v Harrogate Town 1-1, 2-4
Consett v Hebburn 2-2, 2-1
Brandon United v Seaham Red Star 0-2
Matlock Town v Knowsley United 0-0, 1-1, 3-0
Tamworth v Worksop Town 3-2
Buxton v Curzon Ashton 0-0, 4-2
Dudley Town v Mossley 3-2
Grantham Town v Bedworth United 5-2
Burton Albion v Caernarfon Town 3-0
Horwich RMI v Congleton Town 0-2
Gainsborough Trinity v Eastwood Town 5-3
Gresley Rovers v Goole Town 1-2
Sutton Coldfield Town v Colwyn Bay 1-1, 0-4
Atherstone United v Redditch United 1-1, 0-2
Leicester United v Moor Green 0-2
Droylsden v Solihull Borough 2-0
Barking v Billericay Town 0-1
Bishop's Stortford v Braintree Town 1-0
Hitchin Town v Boreham Wood 0-2
Hendon v Marlow 1-2
Ruislip Manor v Chelmsford City 1-4
Sudbury Town v Purfleet 3-3, 0-3
Leyton v Chalfont St Peter 6-4
Berkhamsted Town v Yeading 1-1, 0-2
Uxbridge v Harrow Borough 1-2
Ashford Town v Windsor & Eton 3-1
Bromley v Molesey 0-2
Gravesend & Northfleet v Bognor Regis Town 3-0
Tooting & Mitcham United v Whyteleafe 3-1
Dorking v Sittingbourne 1-5
Margate v Worthing 0-2
Fisher 93 v Walton & Hersham 1-0
Croydon v Canterbury City 3-0
Dulwich Hamlet v Hastings Town 2-1
Wokingham Town v Maidenhead United 1-0
Fareham Town v Weston-Super-Mare 1-2
Salisbury City v Poole Town 1-3
Newport AFC v Havant Town 1-0
Basingstoke Town v Abingdon Town 0-2
Weymouth v Witney Town 0-2

Second Qualifying Round

Guiseley v Tow Law Town 4-3
Dunston Federation Brewery v Newcastle Blue Star 2-1
Harrogate Town v Chorley 3-1
Stockton v Great Harwood Town 2-1
Workington v Bridlington Town 0-2
Seaham Red Star v West Auckland Town 3-1
Consett v Chester-Le-Street Town 3-0
Gainsborough Trinity v Matlock Town 1-2
Goole Town v Dudley Town 3-1
Alfreton Town v Congleton Town 2-0
Redditch United v Moor Green 2-1
Stourbridge v Halesowen Town 0-1
Grantham Town v Droylsden 3-2
Buxton v Colwyn Bay 1-6
Rushden & Diamonds v Burton Albion 0-1
Tamworth v Emley 2-2, 0-4
Baldock Town v Purfleet 2-3
Marlow v Hayes 1-1, 3-2
Yeading v Leyton 1-1, 3-1
Cambridge City v Chelmsford City 1-1, 2-3
Bishop's Stortford v Billericay Town 1-2
Wembley v Staines Town 1-1, 0-1
Harrow Borough v Boreham Wood 0-0, 2-1
Tooting & Mitcham United v Erith & Belvedere 1-2
Molesey v Sittingbourne 0-4
Ashford Town v Gravesend & Northfleet 1-1, 0-2
Croydon v Worthing 1-7
Fisher 93 v Dulwich Hamlet 0-2
Witney Town v Dorchester Town 0-1
Weston-Super-Mare v Newport AFC 2-0
Abingdon Town v Wokingham Town 1-1, 1-2
Poole Town v Waterlooville 1-1, 0-2

Third Qualifying Round

Harrogate Town v Guiseley 3-4
Consett v Billingham Synthonia 1-3
Bishop Auckland v Murton 2-2, 4-1
Stockton v Spennymoor United 0-3
Seaham Red Star v Gretna 0-3
Alfreton Town v Bridlington Town 4-1
Goole Town v Northallerton Town 1-1, 0-1
Colwyn Bay v Guisborough Town 2-2, 3-2
Hyde United v Accrington Stanley 2-0
Matlock Town v Blyth Spartans 1-3
Dunston Federation Brewery v Frickley Athletic 1-5
Barrow v Emley 2-2, 1-2
Enfield v Corby Town 2-1
Billericay Town v Yeading 2-0
Purfleet v Heybridge Swifts 3-2
VS Rugby v Chelmsford City 0-3
Staines Town v St Albans City 0-3
Nuneaton Borough v Aylesbury United 2-2, 2-1
Wivenhoe Town v Grantham Town 1-2
Burton Albion v Halesowen Town 1-2
Redditch United v Hednesford Town 1-1, 0-1
Leek Town v Stevenage Borough 0-2
Wealdstone v Harrow Borough 2-2, 0-3
Erith & Belvedere v Weston-Super-Mare 1-4
Dulwich Hamlet v Gloucester City 2-1
Dorchester Town v Bashley 0-0, 0-3
Sittingbourne v Kingstonian 1-2
Worcester City v Crawley Town 1-1, 2-1
Waterlooville v Wokingham Town 3-0
Trowbridge Town v Cheltenham Town 1-1, 0-1
Worthing v Carshalton Athletic 3-0
Gravesend & Northfleet v Marlow 1-4

First Round

Alfreton Town v Runcorn 0-5
Gretna v Warrington Town 1-1, 3-2
Halifax Town v Emley 2-1
Halesowen Town v Gateshead 0-2
Stalybridge Celtic v Colwyn Bay 1-1, 2-2, 1-2
Winsford United v Guiseley 0-1
Grantham Town v Witton Albion 3-2
Billingham Synthonia v Frickley Athletic 2-1
Spennymoor United v Hyde United 2-1
Blyth Spartans v Bishop Auckland 1-3
Hednesford Town v Whitby Town 1-0
Boston United v Macclesfield Town 1-1, 0-1
Morecambe v Northwich Victoria 2-1
Telford United v Northallerton Town 2-1
Marine v Southport 0-0, 1-3
Altrincham v Stafford Rangers 0-2
Cheltenham Town v Nuneaton Borough 1-0
Dulwich Hamlet v Kingstonian 1-2
Welling United v Chelmsford City 6-1
Kettering Town v Stevenage Borough 2-1
St Albans City v Merthyr Tydfil 4-5
Billericay Town v Slough Town 0-2
Kidderminster Harriers v Dagenham & Redbridge 0-2
Waterlooville v Bromsgrove Rovers 1-1, 1-2
Farnborough Town v Grays Athletic 1-1, 0-2
Bashley v Woking 2-4
Weston-Super-Mare v Dover Athletic 0-2
Yeovil Town v Bath City 3-3, 0-4
Sutton United v Chesham United 2-0
Enfield v Purfleet 2-0

Harrow Borough v Worcester City	3-3, 3-5
Worthing v Marlow	3-0

Second Round

Runcorn v Telford United	2-1
Grantham Town v Bishop Auckland	1-2
Colwyn Bay v Southport	0-3
Dagenham & Redbridge v Woking	1-2
Worcester City v Macclesfield Town	0-0, 2-3
Worthing v Enfield	1-1, 0-2
Spennymoor United v Halifax Town	1-2
Kettering Town v Billingham Synthonia	2-2, 1-3
Guiseley v Stafford Rangers	3-2
Kingstonian v Merthyr Tydfil	0-2
Sutton United v Bath City	6-1
Grays Athletic v Bromsgrove Rovers	1-2
Welling United v Dover Athletic	1-3
Gateshead v Gretna	0-0, 1-0
Cheltenham Town v Hednesford Town	1-0
Morecambe v Slough Town	1-0

Third Round

Macclesfield Town v Billingham Synthonia	0-1
Cheltenham Town v Guiseley	0-0, 0-1
Gateshead v Merthyr Tydfil	3-2
Sutton United v Dover Athletic	0-0, 3-2
Runcorn v Halifax Town	1-1, 2-0
Bishop Auckland v Enfield	2-2, 1-2
Woking v Bromsgrove Rovers	3-2
Morecambe v Southport	2-1

Fourth Round

Gateshead v Runcorn	0-3
Sutton United v Enfield	1-1, 0-1
Woking v Billingham Synthonia	1-1, 2-1
Guiseley v Morecambe	3-2

Semi-finals (two legs)

Woking v Enfield	1-1, 0-0, 3-0 (at Wycombe)
Runcorn v Guiseley	1-1 (at Chester), 1-0

Trophy Final at Wembley

21 May

Woking (2) 2 *(Brown D, Hay)*

Runcorn (0) 1 *(Shaw (pen))* 15,818

Woking: Batty; Berry, Brown K, Tucker, Wye, Clement, Brown D (Rattray), Steele, Fielder, Hay (Puckett), Walker.

Runcorn: Williams; Bates, Lee, Brabin, Robertson, Shaw, Anderson, Connor, McKenna, McInerney (Hill), Thomas.

Referee: P. Durkin (Portland).

FA CHALLENGE VASE 1993–94

Extra Preliminary Round

Shotton Comrades v Ponteland United	0-5
Heaton Stannington v Cleator Moor Celtic	1-6
West Allotment Celtic v Bedlington Terriers	4-1
Sunderland Kennet Roker v Walker	2-4
Marske United v Holker Old Boys	0-2
Wolviston v Seaton Delaval Amateurs	2-6
Seaton Delaval Terriers v Newton Aycliffe	1-3
Mickleover RBL v North Trafford	0-5
(at North Trafford)	
Hall Road Rangers v Heswall	2-1
Clipstone Welfare v Westhoughton Town	5-0
Priory (Eastwood) v Ayone	5-2
Christleton v Waterloo Dock	1-3
(at Upton AA FC)	
Poulton Victoria v Rainworth MW	3-3, 2-1
Maghull v General Chemicals	1-1, 3-1
Nettleham v Merseyside Police	2-3
Borrowash Victoria v Wythenshawe Amateur	1-0
Grove United v Ashfield United	0-1
Kimberley Town v Worsbro Bridge MW	3-2
Shirebrook Town v Hallam	1-5
RES Parkgate v Cheadle Town	3-1
St Dominics v Vauxhall	1-4
Lucas Sports v Ashville	5-1
(at Ashville)	
Louth United v Castleton Gabriels	1-0
Atherton Collieries v Liversedge	1-2
Blackpool Mechanics v Ellesmere Port Town	1-4
Walsall Wood v Lutterworth Town	1-0
Holwell Sports v Barwell	3-1
Alvechurch v Meir KA	3-0
St Andrews v Bolehall Swifts	0-0, 4-0
Pegasus Juniors v Westfields	2-2, 2-5
(at Hereford United)	
Dunkirk v Cradley Town	6-1
Stapenhill v Brierley Hill Town	2-1
Knowle v Kings Heath	4-1
Oadby Town v Anstey Nomads	1-1, 3-1
Gedling Town v Birstall United	2-1
Sawbridgeworth Town v Hadleigh United	5-3
Clacton Town v Brightlingsea United	1-0
Warboys Town v Brantham Athletic	1-2
Somersham Town v Stanway Rovers	1-0
Ely City v Downham Town	7-0
Woodbridge Town v Ipswich Wanderers	0-3
Long Sutton Athletic v Great Wakering Rovers	1-5
Beaconsfield United v Brook House	1-3
St Margaretsbury v London Colney	1-2
(at Hertford Town)	
Wootton Blue Cross v Tower Hamlets	1-5
Concord Rangers v Bowers United	3-0
Totternhoe v Luton Old Boys	2-0
Hillingdon Borough v Welwyn Garden City	3-1
Stansted v East Ham United	0-2
Romford v Potton United	1-2
(at East Ham United)	
Leverstock Green v Potters Bar Town	3-1
Barkingside v Cockfosters	3-1
Rayners Lane v Harpenden Town	2-1
Slade Green v Eastbourne United	2-1
Cray Wanderers v Ashford Town (Middx)	2-3
Furness v Cranleigh	1-0
Broadbridge Heath v Hartley Wintney	3-1
Newhaven v St Andrews (London)	4-2
Crowborough Athletic v Worthing United	3-1
West Wickham v Alma Swanley	1-4
Farleigh Rovers v Eastbourne Town	2-0
Folkestone Invicta v Ash United	3-2
Shoreham v Cobham	0-3
Arundel v Ditton	2-1
Thamesmead Town v Beckenham Town	4-0
Petersfield United removed, Christchurch w.o	
Swindon Supermarine v Clanfield	5-1
Sandhurst Town v Flight Refuelling	1-1, 1-0
Bat Sports v Sherborne Town	1-2
Sholing Sports withdrew, North Leigh w.o	
Whitchurch United v Peppard	1-3
Tuffley Rovers v Keynsham Town	1-4
DRG v Bishop Sutton	0-1
Almondsbury Town v Larkhall Athletic	1-3
Patchway v Brislington	0-5
Old Georgians v Wotton Rovers	1-0
Clyst Rovers v Cirencester Town	0-1
Porthleven v Newquay	0-2
Hallen v Ellwood	2-1
Moreton Town v Backwell United	1-0
Crediton United v Bridgwater Town	2-0

Preliminary Round

Walker v Eppleton CW	1-3
Horden CW v Penrith	0-3
Darlington Cleveland Social v Evenwood Town	1-2
Pickering Town v Holker Old Boys	7-3
Billingham Town v Cleator Moor Celtic	4-0
Newton Aycliffe v Crook Town	1-4
Whickham v Netherfield	1-0
Prudhoe East End v Norton & Stockton Amateurs	4-3
Ponteland United v Alnwick Town	2-0
Harrogate Railway v West Allotment Celtic	3-0
Annfield Plain v Seaton Delaval Amateurs	0-2
Langley Park S&S United v Willington	0-1
Esh Winning v Ryhope CA	2-1
Nantwich Town v Ossett Town	2-0
Clitheroe v Maine Road	1-0
Tadcaster Albion v Louth United	1-3
Chadderton v Ossett Albion	0-4
Blidworth MW v Kimberley Town	2-4
Lincoln United v Skelmersdale United	3-2
Belper Town v Bradford Park Avenue	1-0
Armthorpe Welfare v Harworth CI	4-1
Hallam v St Helens Town	2-0
Lancaster City v Ilkeston Town	0-1
Garforth Town v Maghull	1-1, 1-2
Selby Town v Bacup Borough	2-4
Prescot AFC v Hucknall Town	3-1
Thackley v Clipstone Welfare	3-0
Salford City v Poulton Victoria	2-0
Heanor Town v Stocksbridge Park Steels	1-3
Priory (Eastwood) v Rossendale United	2-5
Merseyside Police v Farsley Celtic	2-1
Glossop North End v Hatfield Main	2-1
Borrowash Victoria v Eccleshill United	1-2
Immingham Town v Maltby MW	2-6
Liversedge v Winterton Rangers	3-0
North Trafford v Lucas Sports	2-1
Sheffield v Hall Road Rangers	2-0
Bootle v Ellesmere Port Town	3-1
Waterloo Dock v RES Parkgate	0-2
Rossington Main v Pontefract Collieries	0-1
Oldham Town v Darwen	1-3
Formby v Radcliffe Borough	1-2
Ashfield United v Vauxhall	0-4
Yorkshire Amateur v Blackpool (wren) Rovers	2-0
Glasshoughton Welfare v Denaby United	2-3
St Andrews v Boldmere St Michaels	0-1
Northampton Spencer v Banbury United	3-2
Gedling Town v Walsall Wood	3-3, 0-3
Stapenhill v Pershore Town	3-1
Long Buckby v Knowle	3-1
Rushall Olympic v Sandwell Borough	1-0
Alvechurch v Halesowen Harriers	4-2
Chasetown v Stourport Swifts	4-1
Highgate United v Holwell Sports	1-2
Daventry Town v Dunkirk	0-3
Racing Club Warwick v Wellingborough Town	3-0
Raunds Town v Wednesfield	4-2
Lye Town v Stratford Town	1-0
Willenhall Town v West Bromwich Town	0-3
Westfields v Mile Oak Rovers & Youth	4-2
Cogenhoe United v Northfield Town	6-1
Paget Rangers v Desborough Town	3-2

Blakenall v Oadby Town 1-1, 0-6
Hinckley Town v Stewarts & Lloyds 5-1
Rocester v Newport Pagnell Town 4-0
Watton United v Witham Town 1-3
Sawbridgeworth Town v Bury Town 2-1
Fakenham Town v Boston 5-5, 1-2
Halstead Town v Norwich United 4-0
Spalding United v Holbeach United 1-1, 4-3
Great Wakering Rovers v Gorleston 4-1
Cornard United v Felixstowe Town 1-1, 2-0
Brantham Athletic v Ely City 5-4
Histon v Tiptree United 3-0
Soham Town Rangers v Basildon United 5-3
Mirrlees Blackstone v Sudbury Wanderers (abandoned at 0-1 after 45 minutes; waterlogged pitch), 3-1
March Town United v Bourne Town 1-0
Kings Lynn v Clacton Town 1-0
Stowmarket Town v Ipswich Wanderers 5-2
Chatteris Town v Stamford 2-2, 2-1
Eynesbury Rovers v Haverhill Rovers 2-3
Newmarket Town v Somersham Town 4-0
Arlesey Town v Flackwell Heath 2-0
Hornchurch v East Ham United 2-0
Hemel Hempstead v Haringey Borough 4-2
Kingsbury Town v Cheshunt 1-2
East Thurrock United v Concord Rangers 2-4
Ware v Tower Hamlets 3-2
Kempston Rovers v Ford United 0-2
Wingate & Finchley v Hatfield Town 2-10
Brook House v Royston Town 2-4
Viking Sports v Leverstock Green 3-4
Letchworth Garden City v Hertford Town 4-0
Hillingdon Borough v Potton United 1-1, 0-1
London Colney v Feltham & Hounslow Borough 1-2
Stotfold v Barkingside 6-2
Biggleswade Town v Rayners Lane 1-3
Leighton Town v Totternhoe 2-0
Southall v Burnham Ramblers 1-5
(at Burnham Ramblers)
Rainham Town v Hanwell Town 2-5
Shillington v Langford 2-1
Hampton v Collier Row 0-1
Clapton v Dunstable 2-1
Three Bridges v Horsham YMCA 2-2
(tie awarded to Horsham YMCA as Three Bridges played an ineligible player)
Burgess Hill Town v Pagham 3-1
Bracknell Town v Steyning Town 6-0
Bedfont v Egham Town 2-1
Merstham v Arundel 1-1, 1-3
Leatherhead v Whitehawk 0-1
(at Whitehawk)
Epsom & Ewell v Ashford Town (Middx) 1-1, 1-3
Newhaven v Furness 2-1
Farleigh Rovers v Corinthian 0-3
Cobham v Crowborough Athletic 0-2
Chipstead v Chichester City 1-0
Lancing v Horsham 2-1
Faversham Town v Croydon Athletic 1-3
Chatham Town v Southwick 2-1
Greenwich Borough v Alma Swanley 1-4
Corinthian-Casuals v Broadbridge Heath 4-0
Redhill v Godalming & Guildford 1-3
Portfield v Ramsgate 3-1
Whitstable Town v Wick 2-3
Selsey v Herne Bay 0-1
Slade Green v Ringmer 3-2
Thamesmead Town v Folkestone Invicta 2-4
Sheppey United v Langney Sports 8-0
Oakwood v Deal Town 3-0
Swindon Supermarine v Eastleigh 1-2
Sandhurst Town v Totton 1-0
Swanage Town & Herston v North Leigh 1-3
Bournemouth v First Tower United 0-1
Newbury Town v Westbury United 4-1
Thatcham Town v Brockenhurst 1-1, 1-1, 3-0
Aldershot Town v Gosport Borough 7-0
Thame United v Kintbury Rangers 9-0
Sherborne Town v Horndean 2-2, 3-1
Calne Town v Bicester Town 1-0
Bemerton Heath Harlequins v Christchurch 1-2
Abingdon United v Cove 2-5
Hamworthy United v Ryde Sports 1-5
Milton United v Wantage Town 1-0
Peppard v Fleet Town 5-2
Frome Town v Ilfracombe Town 3-1
Chard Town v Cinderford Town 2-1
Crediton United v Torpoint Athletic 1-2
Mangotsfield United v Brislington 3-0
Moreton Town v Taunton Town 0-2
Liskeard Athletic v Melksham Town 1-2
Fairford Town v Bridport 1-2
Glastonbury v Falmouth Town 1-3
Cirencester Town v Wellington Town 3-1
Bristol Manor Farm v Keynsham Town 0-2
Dawlish Town v Torrington 1-5
Odd Down v Chippenham Town 2-2, 1-2
Minehead v Hallen 5-2
Shortwood United v St Blazey 1-2
Exmouth Town v Bishop Sutton 0-2
Elmore v Newquay 4-3
Larkhall Athletic v Devizes Town 2-0
Old Georgians v Barnstaple Town 0-2

First Round

Whickham v Billingham Town 3-2
Harrogate Railway v Pickering Town 1-4
Penrith v Eppleton CW 2-1
Esh Winning v South Shields 2-7
Willington v Prudhoe East End 0-1
Ponteland United v Seaton Delaval Amateurs 2-1
Crook Town v Evenwood Town 1-0
Eccleshill United v Belper Town 1-2
Prescot AFC v Hallam 2-0
Rossendale United v Bootle 2-4
Vauxhall v Denaby United 2-1
Salford City v RES Parkgate 0-0, 1-4
Liversedge v North Ferriby United 4-1
Thackley v Stocksbridge Park Steels 0-0, 2-0
Pontefract Collieries v Maltby MW 2-4
Merseyside Police v Louth United 4-5
Ossett Albion v Sheffield 1-1, 0-4
Bacup Borough v Clitheroe 1-1, 2-1
Lincoln United v Darwen 2-0
Kimberley Town v Nantwich Town 1-2
Yorkshire Amateur v Armthorpe Welfare 1-0
Newcastle Town v Glossop North End 3-4
Radcliffe Borough v North Trafford 2-0
Maghull v Ilkeston Town 0-1
Friar Lane OB v Cogenhoe United 1-1, 0-2
Northampton Spencer v Walsall Wood 3-0
Arnold Town v Boldmere St Michaels 3-0
Bridgnorth Town v Lye Town 1-0
Westfields v Racing Club Warwick 1-0
Armitage 90 v Chatteris Town 1-2
Raunds Town v Stapenhill 5-2
Chasetown v Long Buckby 3-1
Dunkirk v Rushall Olympic 4-4, 3-2
Rocester v West Bromwich Town 4-2
Hinckley Town v Oadby Town 0-3
Holwell Sports v Paget Rangers 1-1, 4-2
Oldbury United v Alvechurch 3-3, 0-1
March Town United v Witham Town 4-0
Spalding United v Sawbridgeworth Town 1-4
Lowestoft Town v Brantham Athletic 10-1
Harwich & Parkeston v Newmarket Town 2-3
Boston v Mirrlees Blackstone 2-1
Haverhill Rovers v Tilbury 2-1
Kings Lynn v Great Yarmouth Town 2-1
Stowmarket Town v Soham Town Rangers 2-5
Halstead Town v Histon 5-0
Great Wakering Rovers v Cornard United 4-1
Edgware Town v Feltham & Hounslow Borough 1-0
Tring Town v Hatfield Town 5-2
Leverstock Green v Brimsdown Rovers 1-2
Burnham v Hemel Hempstead 0-1

Concord Rangers v Letchworth Garden City 0-2
Ware v Arlesey Town 0-1
Cheshunt v Royston Town 1-1, 2-0
Hornchurch v Leighton Town 4-0
Harefield United v Aveley 0-3
Shillington v Burnham Ramblers 2-0
Clapton v Barton Rovers 0-1
Northwood v Stotfold 1-0
Collier Row v Rayners Lane 4-1
Potton United v Ford United 0-0, 1-1, 0-1
Ashford Town (Middx) v Bedfont 0-2
Burgess Hill Town v Chatham Town 2-0
Newhaven v Tonbridge 2-3
Croydon Athletic v Littlehampton Town 3-1
Arundel v Lewes 0-3
Sheppey United v Corinthian-Casuals 0-2
Portfield v Oakwood 2-0
Alma Swanley v Tunbridge Wells 0-1
Crowborough Athletic v Slade Green 2-0
Hanwell Town v Lancing 2-3
Corinthian v Whitehawk 0-3
Wick v Hailsham Town 3-1
Godalming & Guildford v Chipstead 2-2, 3-2
Bracknell Town v Folkestone Invicta 3-0
Herne Bay v Horsham YMCA 3-0
Cove v Eastleigh 1-3
Newbury Town v Sandhurst Town 2-0
Lymington v Thame United 0-2
Hungerford Town v Melksham Town 2-3
North Leigh v Christchurch 3-1
Peppard v Oxford City 1-0
After protest from Oxford City over pitch dimensions, Peppard were removed from competition and Oxford went through
Ryde Sports v Andover 0-3
Milton United v Calne Town 4-2
First Tower United v Sherborne Town 1-0
Thatcham Town v Aldershot Town 0-1
St Blazey v Chard Town 3-1
Chippenham Town v Torpoint Athletic 2-2, 0-3
Yate Town v Cirencester Town 2-1
Saltash United v Barnstaple Town 1-1,1-2
Mangotsfield United v Minehead 3-1
Larkhall Athletic v Frome Town 0-1
Bishop Sutton v Bideford 1-2
Elmore v Torrington 2-1
Taunton Town v Keynsham Town 2-0
Bridport v Falmouth Town 1-2

Second Round
Atherton LR v Prudhoe East End 3-0
Ponteland United v Liversedge 3-1
Yorkshire Amateur v Sheffield 3-2
Burscough v Penrith 2-3
Cammell Laird v Bootle 6-2
Brigg Town v Flixton 3-1
Bamber Bridge v Vauxhall 4-2
South Shields v Maltby MW 2-3
Thackley v Prescot AFC 2-1
Pickering Town v Bacup Borough 0-1
RES Parkgate v Whickham 0-3
Radcliffe Borough v Crook Town 3-1
Chasetown v Oadby Town 3-4
Arnold Town v Lincoln United 1-2
Cogenhoe United v Evesham United 0-0, 2-1
Belper Town v Ilkeston Town 1-0
Dunkirk v Louth United 4-2
Pelsall Villa v Alvechurch 1-1, 3-2
Bridgnorth Town v Chatteris Town 5-1
Westfields v Northampton Spencer 1-1, 0-3
Holwell Sports v Nantwich Town 1-6
Rothwell Town v Eastwood Hanley 1-1, 1-2
Hinckley Athletic v West Midlands Police 2-1
Rocester v Glossop North End 1-2
Bilston Town v Raunds Town 2-2, 0-4
Walthamstow Pennant v Saffron Walden Town 1-4
Arlesey Town v Haverhill Rovers 2-1
Brimsdown Rovers v Shillington 2-1
Edgware Town v Wisbech Town 1-2
Tring Town v Diss Town 0-0, 0-2
Collier Row v Newmarket Town 3-2
Lowestoft Town v Buckingham Town 0-2
Letchworth Garden City v Soham Town Rangers 2-3
Hoddesdon Town v Cheshunt 1-4
Hemel Hempstead v Ford United 0-1
Kings Lynn v Hornchurch 7-1
Halstead Town v Sawbridgeworth Town 3-1
Boston v Barton Rovers 3-1
March Town United v Great Wakering Rovers 0-2
Aveley v Canvey Island 2-4
Godalming & Guildford v Bracknell Town 2-4
Wick v Malden Vale 0-1
Burgess Hill Town v Metropolitan Police 0-3
Thame United v North Leigh 2-1
Aldershot Town v Herne Bay 2-1
Whitehawk v Portfield 4-1
Eastleigh v Peacehaven & Telscombe 1-2
Crowborough Athletic v Corinthian-Casuals 1-4
Chertsey Town v Newbury Town 0-3
Tunbridge Wells v Lewes 2-0
Bedfont v Northwood 1-1, 2-1
Newport (IW) v Banstead Athletic 2-2, 0-0, 1-1, 1-6
Lancing v Tonbridge 3-4
Croydon Athletic v Oxford City 2-0
Forest Green Rovers v Barnstaple Town 0-0
Forest Green Rovers removed from competition after fielding an ineligible player
Torpoint Athletic v First Tower United 2-0
Melksham Town v Taunton Town 0-6
Welton Rovers v Wimborne Town 0-1
Mangotsfield United v Tiverton Town 0-5
Yate Town v Elmore 1-2
Andover v Bideford 6-2
Milton United v Falmouth Town 1-4
Clevedon Town v St Blazey 4-0
Paulton Rovers v Frome Town 2-1

Third Round
Thackley v Lincoln United 2-1
Cammell Laird v Glossop North End 2-3
Oadby Town v Ponteland United 2-0
Nantwich Town v Bacup Borough 2-0
Belper Town v Brigg Town 2-1
Radcliffe Borough v Yorkshire Amateur 2-0
Penrith v Atherton LR 0-1
Whickham v Bamber Bridge 1-0
Dunkirk v Maltby MW 2-1
Wisbech Town v Collier Row 1-2
Great Wakering Rovers v Hinckley Athletic 3-3, 1-2
Northampton Spencer v Cogenhoe United 1-2
Boston v Bedfont 6-1
Ford United v Diss Town 1-2
Saffron Walden Town v Raunds Town 1-4
Bridgnorth Town v Cheshunt 3-1
Soham Town Rangers v Brimsdown Rovers 3-0
Buckingham Town v Kings Lynn 1-2
Pelsall Villa v Halstead Town
(abandoned at 0-0 after 57 minutes; waterlogged pitch), 2-4
Eastwood Hanley v Arlesey Town 1-2
Canvey Island v Corinthian-Casuals 2-1
Taunton Town v Barnstaple Town 2-0
Elmore v Thame United 1-2
Croydon Athletic v Paulton Rovers 0-2
Tonbridge v Tiverton Town 0-1
Aldershot Town v Malden Vale 1-0
Tunbridge Wells v Torpoint Athletic 2-6
Clevedon Town v Wimborne Town 3-4
Bracknell Town v Newbury Town 1-2
Banstead Athletic v Peacehaven & Telscombe 1-0
Falmouth Town v Andover 3-1
Whitehawk v Metropolitan Police 3-2

Fourth Round

Radcliffe Borough v Boston	3-3, 1-2
Atherton LR v Thackley	0-0, 3-2
Raunds Town v Belper Town	1-2
Whickham v Dunkirk	0-0, 0-1
Kings Lynn v Nantwich Town	1-0
Bridgnorth Town v Glossop North End	3-2
Oadby Town v Cogenhoe United	5-1
Halstead Town v Wimborne Town	1-5
Canvey Island v Newbury Town	1-2
Taunton Town v Banstead Athletic	1-1, 2-0
Whitehawk v Thame United	3-2
Torpoint Athletic v Diss Town	0-3
Aldershot Town v Soham Town Rangers	5-0
Tiverton Town v Paulton Rovers	5-0
Hinckley Athletic v Collier Row	4-2
Arlesey Town v Falmouth Town	5-3

Fifth Round

Hinckley Athletic v Newbury Town	0-3
Atherton LR v Bridgnorth Town	1-0
Oadby Town v Arlesey Town	1-2
Dunkirk v Tiverton Town	0-2
Diss Town v Kings Lynn	2-0
Whitehawk v Boston	2-3
Aldershot Town v Wimborne Town	1-0
Belper Town v Taunton Town	1-3

Sixth Round

Aldershot Town v Atherton LR	0-0, 0-0, 0-2
Arlesey Town v Boston	2-3
Diss Town v Tiverton Town	1-0
Taunton Town v Newbury Town	2-0

Semi-finals (two legs)

Taunton Town v Boston	1-0, 1-0
Diss Town v Atherton LR	3-1, 0-2, 2-1 (at Rugby)

Vase Final at Wembley

7 May

Diss Town (0) 2 *(Gibbs (pen), Mendham)*
Taunton Town (1) 1 *(Fowler) aet* 13,450

Diss Town: Woodcock; Carter, Hartle, Smith, Wolsey (Musgrave), Casey (Bugg), Mendham, Barth, Warne, Miles, Gibbs.
Taunton Town: Maloy; Morris, Graddon, Palfrey, Walsh, Ewens, West (Hendy), Perett (Ward), Fowler, Durham, Jarvis.
Referee: K. Morton (Bury St Edmunds).

FA COUNTY YOUTH CHALLENGE CUP 1993–94

First Round

Nottinghamshire v Manchester	2-3
Derbyshire v West Riding	0-5
Birmingham v Cheshire	1-2
Staffordshire v Westmorland	9-1
Shropshire v Northamptonshire	3-6
Oxfordshire v Herefordshire	4-1
Berks & Bucks v Cambridgeshire	1-0
Bedfordshire v Kent	0-2
Surrey v Hampshire	7-2
Dorset v Royal Navy	1-0
Somerset & Avon v Army	3-1
Gloucestershire v Devon	0-3
Sussex v Wiltshire	4-0

Second Round

Cumberland v Manchester	0-2
Lincolnshire v Durham	0-4
East Riding v Liverpool	3-4
Northumberland v West Riding	3-5
North Riding v Cheshire	3-2
Lancashire v Staffordshire	2-3
Sheffield & Hallamshire v Northamptonshire	3-2
Leicestershire & Rutland v Oxfordshire	2-0
Worcestershire v Berks & Bucks	1-1, 2-0
Norfolk v Kent	0-3
Hertfordshire v Suffolk	1-1, 3-5
Essex v Surrey	2-4
London v Dorset	1-0
Huntingdonshire v Somerset & Avon	1-3
Middlesex v Devon	3-3, 3-1
Cornwall v Sussex	0-2

Third Round

Liverpool v North Riding	4-2
Durham v Manchester	0-1
Sheffield & Hallamshire v West Riding	1-3
Leicestershire & Rutland v Staffordshire	0-3
Suffolk v London	1-2
Kent v Worcestershire	1-0
Middlesex v Surrey	0-3
Sussex v Somerset & Avon	1-0

Fourth Round

Surrey v West Riding	0-1
Staffordshire v Manchester	2-1
Kent v London	2-2, 2-1
Sussex v Liverpool	3-2

Semi-finals

Sussex v Kent	2-1
Staffordshire v West Riding	0-4

Final

West Riding v Sussex	3-1

FA SUNDAY CUP 1993–94

First Round

Croxteth & Gilmoss RBL v Bedini Altone 3-0
Baildon Athletic v Newfield 2-3
Carnforth v Almithak 1-0
Humbledon Plains Farm v Clubmoor Nalgo 1-1, 2-1
Dudley & Weetslade v Framwellgate Moor & Pity Me 4-5
East Levenshulme v East Bowling Unity 4-0
Littlewoods Athletic v Mitre 3-2
Green Man 88 v Lion Hotel 0-2
Moorlands Hotel v Allerton 1-2
Hartlepool Lion Hotel v Iron Bridge 5-0
Woodlands 84 v BRNESC 0-3
Royal Oak v Bolton Woods 0-1
Waterloo Social Club Blyth v Northwood 1-4
Sandon v Western Approaches 2-4
Cork & Bottle v Berner United 2-1
Bourneville Warriors v Broad Plain House (Sunday) 1-2
Dulwich v Sawston Keys 2-3
Brookvale Athletic v Clifton Albion 2-0
Poringland Wanderers v Ford Basildon 2-4
Kenwick Dynamo v Courage 0-1
Olton Royale v Inter Volante 1-1, 2-0
Leicester City Bus v St Clements Hospital 2-3
Hobbies v Continental 1-0
Elliott Bull & Tiger v AD Bulwell 1-1, 4-2
Corby Phoenix v Ansells Stockland Star 4-1
BRSC Aidan v Ford United Supporters 1-1, 1-2
Caversham Park v Chapel United 2-0
Lebeq Tavern v Olympic Star 5-0
Hammer v Sandwell 3-0
Inter Royalle v Fryerns Community 2-2, 2-3
Hanham Sunday v Kerria Sports 2-4
S&N Fairway v Leavesden Sports & Social 0-3
Oakwood Sports v Sheerness Steel United 4-0
Oxford Road Social v Northfield Rangers 1-2
Ouzavich v Poole Town Special 8-1
Tottenham Wine v Vosper 1-3
Somerset Ambury V&E v Thorn Walk Tavern 3-0
Slade Celtic v London Boys 4-0
St Joseph's (Sth Oxley) v St Joseph's AFC (Bristol) 2-0

Second Round

Newfield v Croxteth & Gilmoss RBL 4-3
Allerton v Western Approaches 4-0
Golden Eagle v Carnforth 1-3
Oakenshaw v Northwood 3-0
East Levenshulme v A3 3-0
Albion Sports v Hartlepool Lion Hotel 1-5
B&A Scaffolding v Bolton Woods 4-0
Dock v BRNESC 2-2, 2-1
Lobster v Nicosia 1-2
Nenthead v Lion Hotel 2-5
Marston Sports v Gibraltar 1-1, 3-6
Seymour v Manfast Kirkby 2-1
Framwellgate Moor & Pity Me v Littlewoods Athletic 3-1
Etnaward v Humbledon Plains Farm 0-1
St Joseph's (Luton) v Olton Royale 2-1
Elliott Bull & Tiger v Corby Phoenix 1-0
St Clements Hospital v Sawston Keys 9-1
Hobbies v Courage 5-3
Forest Athletic v Ford Basildon 2-1
Heathfield v Brookvale Athletic 3-1
Lodge Cottrell v Broad Plain House (Sunday) 3-3

After protest by Lodge Cottrell, Broad Plain House removed from competition for fielding a contract player

Cork & Bottle v Hundred Acre 5-1
Bedfont Sunday v Lebeq Tavern 0-4
Hammer v Bly Spartans 3-2
Oakwood Sports v Northfield Rangers 2-0
St Joseph's (Sth Oxley) v Fryerns Community 0-2
Marine v Ouzavich 0-1
Vosper v Kerria Sports 1-0
Slade Celtic v Leavesden Sports & Social 2-1
Reading Borough v Theale 0-1
Somerset Ambury V&E v Ranelagh Sports 1-4
Caversham Park v Ford United Supporters 1-2

Third Round

Seymour v Carnforth 5-1
Oakenshaw v Nicosia 1-0
East Levenshulme v Newfield 1-0
B&A Scaffolding v Gibraltar 5-3
Hartlepool Lion Hotel v Humbledon Plains Farm 1-0
Allerton v Framwellgate Moor & Pity Me 2-1
Dock v Lion Hotel 1-2
Hammer v St Clements Hospital 3-5
Slade Celtic v Ranelagh Sports 1-2
St Joseph's (Luton) v Vosper 2-0
Ouzavich v Forest Athletic 2-1
Ford United Supporters v Hobbies 2-1
Oakwood Sports v Lodge Cottrell 1-3
Elliott Bull & Tiger v Theale 1-4
Cork & Bottle v Lebeq Tavern 1-3
Fryerns Community v Heathfield 1-2

Fourth Round

Seymour v Allerton 0-0, 2-3
Hartlepool Lion Hotel v Oakenshaw 2-0
Lion Hotel v East Levenshulme 5-1
Lodge Cottrell v B&A Scaffolding 1-3
St Joseph's (Luton) v Heathfield 2-0
St Clements Hospital v Lebeq Tavern 3-2
Ranelagh Sports v Theale 4-3
Ford United Supporters v Ouzavich 2-3

Fifth Round

Lion Hotel v Hartlepool Lion Hotel 0-1
B&A Scaffolding v Ranelagh Sports 2-3
Allerton v Ouzavich 0-1
St Clements Hospital v St Joseph's (Luton) 2-3

Semi-finals

St Joseph's (Luton) v Hartlepool Lion Hotel 1-1, 1-4
Ranelagh Sports v Ouzavich 3-1

Final

Ranelagh Sports v Hartlepool Lion Hotel 2-0

FA YOUTH CHALLENGE CUP 1993–94

Extra Preliminary Round
Sutton Coldfield Town v Bedworth United 4-0
Petersfield United removed, Woking w.o

Preliminary Round
Darlington v Blackpool Mechanics 7-1
Guisborough Town v Huddersfield Town 1-5
Prudhoe East End v Atherton LR 3-2
Hartlepool United v Carlisle United 1-3
Bolton Wanderers v Marine 3-1
Burscough v Grimsby Town 0-5
Chadderton v Rochdale 1-4
(at Rochdale)
Bury v Altrincham 7-1
Wrexham v Southport 7-1
Wigan Athletic v Prescot AFC 5-2
Stockport County v Warrington Town 2-3
Stalybridge Celtic v Lincoln City 1-6
Mansfield Town v Hinckley Athletic 9-1
Port Vale v Hednesford Town 3-2
Burton Albion v Lutterworth Town 6-1
Bridgnorth Town v Worksop Town 0-3
Stratford Town v Corby Town 4-0
Boldmere St Michaels v Hinckley Town 3-5
Chasetown v Rothwell Town 0-1
Bromsgrove Rovers v Sutton Coldfield Town 2-1
Nuneaton Borough v Wednesfield 4-1
Brierley Hill Town v Redditch United 2-4
Pershore Town v Willenhall Town 3-1
Pelsall Villa v Lye Town 2-5
Stewart & Lloyds v Leighton Town 0-1
Banbury United v Dunstable 3-0
Baldock Town v Kempston Rovers 1-2
Eynesbury Rovers v Rushden & Diamonds 1-6
Braintree Town v Peterborough United 2-8
Canvey Island v March Town United 1-7
Kings Lynn v Saffron Walden Town 1-2
Great Yarmouth Town v Bishop's Stortford 2-1
Wivenhoe Town v Stevenage Borough 1-2
Barkingside v Leyton 5-1
Grays Athletic v Waltham Abbey 1-3
East Thurrock United v Wisbech Town 4-0
Brook House v Wingate & Finchley 1-1, 3-4
Edgware Town v Uxbridge 4-0
Royston Town v Northwood 5-0
Enfield v Beaconsfield United 10-0
Hanwell Town v Ruislip Manor 3-4
Harefield United v Marlow 5-0
Kingsbury Town v Staines Town 1-1, 4-3
Hillingdon Borough v Hampton 1-3
Dover Athletic v Herne Bay 5-0
Newhaven v Faversham Town 3-0
Corinthian v Gillingham 0-7
Ringmer v Ashford Town 2-3
Peacehaven & Telscombe removed, Bracknell Town w.o
Chatham Town v Egham Town 2-0
Croydon Athletic v Thamesmead Town 7-1
Chipstead v Bedfont 3-2
Kingstonian v Whitehawk 10-0
Malden Vale v Three Bridges 2-4
Oakwood v Whitstable Town 1-6
Molesey removed, Farnborough Town w.o
Shoreham removed, Welling United w.o
Slough Town v Worthing 0-1
Walton & Hersham removed, Whyteleafe w.o
Steyning Town v Redhill 5-1
Wick v Thatcham Town 2-1
Fleet Town v Maidenhead United 3-5
Basingstoke Town v Wokingham Town 1-4
Aldershot Town v Woking 6-1
Havant Town v Frome Town 3-0
Newbury Town v Chippenham Town 2-4
Romsey Town v Yate Town 3-5
Oxford City v Dorchester Town 1-1, 3-1
Cheltenham Town v Worcester City 1-1, 2-4
Gloucester City v Weston-Super-Mare 3-0
Torquay United v Yeovil Town 2-1
Hereford United v Bristol Rovers 1-1, 3-5

First Qualifying Round
Huddersfield Town v Carlisle United 2-1
Darlington v Prudhoe East End 9-0
Grimsby Town v Bury 4-1
Bolton Wanderers v Rochdale 1-2
Wigan Athletic v Lincoln City 3-4
Wrexham v Warrington Town 1-2
Port Vale v Worksop Town 5-0
Mansfield Town v Burton Albion 1-1, 1-2
Hinckley Town v Bromsgrove Rovers 1-1, 2-0
Stratford Town v Rothwell Town 3-1
Redditch United v Lye Town 0-1
Nuneaton Borough v Pershore Town 6-3
Banbury United v Rushden & Diamonds 2-1
Leighton Town v Kempston Rovers 5-0
March Town United v Great Yarmouth Town 0-0, 1-5
Peterborough United v Saffron Walden Town 6-1
Barkingside v East Thurrock United 0-5
Stevenage Borough v Waltham Abbey 3-1
Edgware Town v Enfield 1-2
Wingate & Finchley v Royston Town 0-4
Harefield United v Hampton 4-1
Ruislip Manor v Kingsbury Town 1-2
Newhaven v Ashford Town
(abandoned at 3-2 after 45 minutes; waterlogged pitch), 3-1
Dover Athletic v Gillingham 0-5
Chatham Town v Chipstead
(abandoned at 0-3 after 45 minutes; waterlogged pitch), 1-3
Bracknell Town v Croydon Athletic 1-3
Three Bridges v Farnborough Town 3-1
Kingstonian v Whitstable Town 4-1
Worthing v Steyning Town 3-1
Welling United v Whyteleafe 3-0
Maidenhead United v Aldershot Town 4-4, 0-4
Wick v Wokingham Town 2-5
Chippenham Town v Oxford City 4-3
Havant Town v Yate Town 1-0
Gloucester City v Bristol Rovers 1-6
Worcester City v Torquay United 1-2

Second Qualifying Round
Huddersfield Town v Darlington 5-1
Grimsby Town v Rochdale 1-0
Lincoln City v Warrington Town 2-2, 3-1
Port Vale v Burton Albion 1-1, 2-0
Hinckley Town v Stratford Town 0-2
Lye Town v Nuneaton Borough 0-1
Banbury United v Leighton Town 1-3
Great Yarmouth Town v Peterborough United 2-2, 0-8
East Thurrock United v Stevenage Borough 1-1, 2-1
Enfield v Royston Town 4-3
Harefield United v Kingsbury Town 5-0
Newhaven v Gillingham 0-4
Chipstead v Croydon Athletic 1-4
Three Bridges v Kingstonian 1-5
Worthing v Welling United 1-2
Aldershot Town v Wokingham Town 0-2
Chippenham Town v Havant Town 0-1
Bristol Rovers v Torquay United 0-0, 1-3

First Round
Tranmere Rovers v Huddersfield Town 1-1, 1-3
Doncaster Rovers v Lincoln City 2-0
Rotherham United v Preston North End 2-1
Bradford City v Barnsley 2-1
Blackburn Rovers v Sheffield Wednesday 1-0

Newcastle United v Burnley 1-1, 0-3
Oldham Athletic v Hull City 3-2
Blackpool v Grimsby Town 0-1
Scunthorpe United v Sunderland 0-3
Stratford Town v Nuneaton Borough 2-2, 1-2
Kidderminster Harriers v Peterborough United 0-2
Stoke City v Shrewsbury Town 3-1
Cambridge United v Aston Villa 1-4
Birmingham City v Wolverhampton Wanderers 4-1
Luton Town v Derby County 1-1, 1-1, 0-1
Northampton Town v Leicester City 1-3
Cambridge City v Leighton Town 3-3, 0-1
Walsall v Port Vale 0-1
Ipswich Town v Carshalton Athletic 8-0
Gillingham v Lewes 3-0
Dulwich Hamlet v East Thurrock United 2-2, 4-2
Brighton & Hove Albion v Fulham 3-1
Harefield United v St Albans City 1-1, 1-0
Boreham Wood v Enfield 1-2
Croydon Athletic v Epsom & Ewell 3-1
Sutton United v Wycombe Wanderers 0-2
Reading v Charlton Athletic 2-2, 3-2
Kingstonian v Welling United 2-5
Portsmouth v Bashley 4-0
Southampton v Bournemouth 1-0
Torquay United v Oxford United 3-2
Cardiff City v Witney Town 5-0
Havant Town v Wokingham Town 0-0, 1-2
Exeter City v Swansea City 4-2

Second Round
Middlesbrough v Oldham Athletic 2-0
Burnley v Leeds United 3-0
Bradford City v Manchester United 2-0
Crewe Alexandra v Huddersfield Town 4-2
York City v Blackburn Rovers 0-0, 1-1, 1-2
Doncaster Rovers v Manchester City 1-4
Everton v Grimsby Town 0-2
Rotherham United v Sunderland 2-4
Sheffield United v Liverpool 1-2
Coventry City v Leicester City 2-1
Ipswich Town v Queens Park Rangers 3-1
Tottenham Hotspur v Stoke City 1-2
West Bromwich Albion v Leighton Town 2-1
West Ham United v Leyton Orient 6-0
Watford v Aston Villa 1-3
Birmingham City v Peterborough United 1-1
(penalty kicks taken aet contrary to rules of competition), 1-2
Port Vale v Southend United 1-3
Chelsea v Norwich City 1-1, 0-1
Nottingham Forest v Nuneaton Borough 3-1
Notts County v Derby County 0-3
Colchester United v Arsenal 2-3
Southampton v Wimbledon 2-6
Torquay United v Enfield 3-1
Croydon Athletic v Wycombe Wanderers 2-3
Reading v Bristol City 0-1
Gillingham v Swindon Town 1-2
Dulwich Hamlet v Crystal Palace 0-5
Cardiff City v Harefield United 2-0
Welling United v Portsmouth 4-6
Brighton & Hove Albion v Wokingham Town 1-0
Brentford v Exeter City 5-1
Plymouth Argyle v Millwall 3-3, 1-2

Third Round
Manchester City v Norwich City 0-2
Bristol City v Aston Villa 1-4
Middlesbrough v Nottingham Forest 2-2, 3-3, 2-1
Blackburn Rovers v Bradford City 1-1, 1-1, 0-4
Wimbledon v Burnley 3-4
Ipswich Town v Peterborough United 1-1, 0-0, 1-0
Grimsby Town v Torquay United 3-1
West Bromwich Albion v Crewe Alexandra 2-1
Liverpool v West Ham United 2-2, 2-3
Brentford v Arsenal 1-1, 1-3
Swindon Town v Brighton & Hove Albion 0-1
Sunderland v Derby County 0-1
Cardiff City v Coventry City 1-2
Millwall v Wycombe Wanderers 2-2, 5-0
Southend United v Stoke City 0-4
Portsmouth v Crystal Palace 2-0

Fourth Round
Coventry City v Norwich City 0-2
Brighton & Hove Albion v Millwall 3-4
Middlesbrough v West Bromwich Albion 2-0
Ipswich Town v Portsmouth 2-4
Grimsby Town v Bradford City 0-0, 1-1, 0-2
Aston Villa v West Ham United 1-2
Stoke City v Derby County 3-1
Burnley v Arsenal 0-1

Fifth Round
Arsenal v Stoke City 3-1
West Ham United v Bradford City 0-1
Middlesbrough v Portsmouth 5-0
Millwall v Norwich City 2-0

Semi-finals (two legs)
Middlesbrough v Millwall 2-2, 1-3
Bradford City v Arsenal 0-1, 0-1

FA Youth Cup Final, first leg

6 May

Millwall (1) 3 *(Gordon, Kennedy, own goal)*
Arsenal (0) 2 *(Rawlins, McGowan)* 6098

Millwall: Cronin; Irving, Luckett, Mulraney, Thatcher, Francis, Pitcher (O'Neil), Gordon, Kennedy, Williams, Wright.
Arsenal: Imber; Griggs, Taylor, Howell, Hall, McDonald, Black, Rose, Rawlins, McGowan, Hughes.

FA Youth Cup Final, second leg

12 May

Arsenal (1) 3 *(Clarke, Rawlins, Hughes)*
Millwall (0) 0 4750

Arsenal: Imber; Griggs, Taylor, Clarke, McDonald, Hall, Black, Rose (Howell), Rawlins (Drake), McGowan, Hughes.
Millwall: Cronin; Irving, Luckett, Mulraney, Thatcher, Francis, Pitcher, Gordon, Kennedy, Williams, Wright.

SCHOOLS FOOTBALL 1993–94

ESFA BRITISH GAS TROPHY 1993–94

FOURTH ROUND

Manchester v Wigan	1-0
Tameside v Nottingham	2-1
West Kent v Basildon	1-5
Swansea v Barnet	2-2, 3-1
Reading v Aldershot	2-1
Blackheath v West Cornwall	4-1
Huntingdon v Southampton	3-2
Cambridge v Lea Valley	3-2
Watford v East Berks	1-3
Woking v Exeter	1-1, 0-1
Sefton v Cannock	0-1
Bradford v Wolverhampton	6-0
West Tyne v Sheffield	0-6
Nuneaton v E. Northumberland	1-2
Bolton v Derby	2-2, 0-1
Leeds v N. Leicester	1-1, 2-3

FIFTH ROUND

Manchester v Tameside	0-3
Basildon v Swansea	1-0
Reading v Blackheath	1-1, 1-5
Huntingdon v Cambridge	1-3
East Berks v Exeter	4-1
Cannock v Bradford	0-2
Sheffield v E. Northumberland	4-3
Derby v N. Leicester	2-2, 1-2

SIXTH ROUND

Tameside v Basildon	1-1, 3-2
Blackheath v Cambridge	0-1
East Berks v Bradford	0-0, 0-1
Sheffield v N. Leicester	5-0

SEMI-FINALS

Tameside v Cambridge	1-0
Bradford v Sheffield	0-1

FINAL

Tameside v Sheffield	1-0, 1-3

ESFA MARS U.19 INDIVIDUAL SCHOOLS CHAMPIONSHIP 1993–94

SECOND ROUND

Cambridgeshire A v Derbyshire	2-4
W. Midlands v Shropshire	1-4
Norfolk v Nottinghamshire	5-2
Merseyside B v Gt Manchester A	3-0
Durham v Cleveland	1-3
Merseyside A v West Yorkshire A	1-2
South Yorkshire B v W. Midlands B	7-0
Northumberland B v Humberside	1-0
Bedfordshire v Hertfordshire A	2-2, 9-8*
Essex A v Inner London A (disqual.)	
Oxfordshire v Surrey A	0-2
Hertfordshire B v Essex B	0-3
S. Glamorgan v Warwickshire	5-2
Dorset v Sussex A	1-4
Avon B v Sussex B	0-1
Devon v Wiltshire	5-2

THIRD ROUND

Derbyshire v Shropshire	2-0
Norfolk v Merseyside B	0-2
Cleveland v West Yorkshire A	1-0
South Yorkshire B v Northumberland B	2-1
Bedfordshire v Essex A	2-2+
Surrey A v Essex B	2-5
S. Glamorgan v Sussex A	0-4
Sussex B v Devon	4-1

FOURTH ROUND

Derbyshire v Merseyside B	0-0, 4-3
Cleveland v South Yorkshire B	1-0
Bedfordshire v Essex B	1-3
Sussex A v Sussex B	3-1

SEMI-FINALS

Derbyshire v Cleveland	2-2, 6-4
Essex B v Sussex A	2-0

FINAL

Derbyshire (Chesterfield College) v Essex B (S.E. Essex 6th Form College)	1-1

* Bedfordshire won on penalties
\+ Bedfordshire won 4-2 on penalties

ESFA U.16 INDIVIDUAL SCHOOLS CHAMPIONSHIP 1993–94

SECOND ROUND

Berkshire v Middlesex	1-1, 3-1
Norfolk v Essex A	0-3
Wiltshire v Sussex	1-1, 0-1
Gloucestershire v Somerset	3-1
Hertfordshire B v Essex B	0-2
Bedfordshire v Warwickshire B	3-3*
Dorset v Devon A	1-0
Kent B v Oxfordshire	0-2
Humberside A v West Yorkshire A	3-1
South Yorkshire A v W. Midlands A	2-5
North Yorkshire v Cleveland A	2-4
Cheshire B v Merseyside A	6-5
Merseyside B v Cheshire A	3-1
Leicestershire v Derbyshire	1-0
Lancashire B v Durham B	2-0
West Yorkshire B v South Yorkshire B	1-4

THIRD ROUND

Berkshire v Essex A	0-4
Sussex v Gloucestershire	2-0
Essex B v Bedfordshire	6-0
Dorset v Oxfordshire	2-2, 3-2
Humberside A v W. Midlands A	0-3
Cleveland A v Cheshire B	1-1, 1-2
Merseyside B v Leicestershire	4-2
Lancashire B v South Yorkshire B	2-1

FOURTH ROUND

Essex A v Sussex	2-0
Essex B v Dorset	5-1
W. Midlands A v Cheshire B	7-1
Merseyside B v Lancashire B	2-2, 1-1+

SEMI-FINALS

Essex A v Essex B	3-2
W. Midlands A v Lancashire B	1-2

FINAL

Essex A (Barking Abbey School) v Lancashire B (St Theodore's School, Burnley)	2-0

* Bedfordshire won on penalties
\+ Lancashire B won on penalties

ESFA ADIDAS U.16 COUNTY CHAMPIONSHIP 1993–94

SEMI-FINALS

Devon v Nottinghamshire	0-2
Essex v Merseyside	4-2

FINAL

Essex v Nottinghamshire	2-1

ESFA ADIDAS U.19 COUNTY CHAMPIONSHIP 1993–94

SEMI-FINALS
Middlesex v West Midlands 3-1
Merseyside v Devon 1-0

FINAL
Merseyside v Middlesex 0-2

McDONALD'S 5-A-SIDE CUP

SEMI-FINALS
St Wilfrid's School v Windsor High School 5-2
Hadrian Park Middle School v St Augustine's School 4-1

FINAL
Hadrian Park Middle School v St Wilfrid's School 4-1

THE MONSTER MUNCH SEVENS

SEMI-FINALS
Newbury v Derby 3-0
Liverpool v Tower Hamlets 3-0

3RD AND 4TH PLACE PLAY-OFFS
Derby v Tower Hamlets 1-0

FINAL
Liverpool v Newbury 1-0

THE MONSTER MUNCH SIX-A-SIDE CUP

SEMI-FINALS
Howard Middle School (Bury St Edmunds) v Courthouse Junior School (Maidenhead) 1-0
Cavendish Primary School (Hull) v Thorpe Hesley Junior School (Rotherham) 5-0

3RD AND 4TH PLACE PLAY-OFFS
Courthouse Junior School v Thorpe Hesley Junior School 2-1

FINAL
Cavendish Primary School v Howard Middle School 4-1

INTERNATIONAL SEASON 1993–94

UNDER 15
England 2, Wales 0 – Coventry City, 11 February*
England 5, Northern Ireland 1 – Sunderland F.C., 25 February*
England 3, Switzerland 0 – Wembley, 12 March +
Holland 0, England 1 – Appingedam, 9 April
Scotland 0, England 1 – Cumbernauld, 5 May*
Germany 2, England 3 – Berlin, 17 May
Germany 1, England 3 – Cottbus, 19 May
England 2, France 1 – Wembley, 11 June + +

** Denotes matches in Soccerpal Victory Shield*
+ For the Walkers Crisps Challenge Cup
+ + For the Walkers Crisps International Shield

SOCCERPAL VICTORY SHIELD FINAL TABLE 1993–94

	P	*W*	*D*	*L*	*F*	*A*	*Pts*
England	3	3	0	0	8	1	6
Northern Ireland	3	2	0	0	4	6	4
Scotland	3	1	0	2	3	3	2
Wales	3	0	0	3	0	5	0

Scorers....Branch 5, Gower 5, Wilson 5, Bunn 3, Marshall, Platts
Overall Record...Played 8, Won 8, Drawn 0, Lost 0, Goals For 20 Goals Against 5
This is the first time that an England Schools' team has ever had a 100% season's record since an eight match programme began in the late 1950s.

UNDER 18
England 1, France 2 – Gillingham F.C., 2 March
England 3, Wales 0 – Berne, 27 March*
Switzerland 0, England 3 – Berne, 31 March*
Austria 1, England 1 – Gloggnitz, 19 April
Slovakia 4, England 0 – Bratislava, 21 April
England 2, Holland 1 – Carrow Road, 3 May

** Denotes match in Centenary Shield*
Scorers: Lester (4), Stevens 3 (Penalties), Bates (2), Smith
Overall Record: Played 6 Won 3 Drawn 1 Lost 2 Goals For 10 Goals Against 8

CENTENARY SHIELD FINAL TABLE 1993–94

	P	*W*	*D*	*L*	*F*	*A*	*Pts*
England	2	2	0	0	6	0	4
Wales	2	1	0	1	1	3	2
Switzerland	2	0	0	2	0	4	0

BOODLE & DUNTHORNE INDEPENDENT SCHOOLS FA CUP 1993–94

FIRST ROUND
Bye – Forest.
Bye – Repton.
Bye – Ardingly.
QEGS, Blackburn 1, Eton 2 *aet*
Wolverhampton GS 0, St. Bede's 6
Alleyn's 0, Bolton 4
Malvern 2, Latymer Upper 1
Aldenham 1, King's, Chester 3
Wellingborough 2, Westminster 1 *aet*
Bury GS 1, Brentwood 4
Shrewsbury 5, KES, Witley 0
Lancing 3, Manchester GS 2
Hulme GS 3, Batley GS 2
Chigwell 4, Highgate 2 *aet*
Kimbolton 1, Charterhouse 4
John Lyon 2, Bradfield 4

SECOND ROUND
Repton 1, Charterhouse 2
Lancing 0, Hulme GS 1
Bradfield 6, Wellingborough 0
Ardingly 3, Bolton 0
Eton 1, King's, Chester 1 *aet*
(*King's won 7-6 on penalties*
St. Bede's 1, Shrewsbury 0 *aet)*
Chigwell 1, Brentwood 2
Malvern 2, Forest 0

THIRD ROUND
Charterhouse 0, Ardingly 3
Bradfield 2, St. Bede's 2 *aet*
(*Bradfield won 7-6 on penalties*)
King's, Chester 4, Hulme GS 2
Brentwood 2, Malvern 0

SEMI-FINALS
King's, Chester 1, Brentwood 1 *aet*
(*King's won 4-2 on penalties*)
Ardingly 1, Bradfield 0 *aet*

FINAL
Ardingly 1, Kings' School, Chester 3
(*at Craven Cottage*)

THE NEVILLE OVENDEN FOOTBALL COMBINATION

Division One

	P	W	D	L	F	A	Pts
Chelsea	38	24	8	6	79	41	80
Ipswich Town	38	19	8	11	71	52	65
Tottenham	38	19	6	13	69	47	63
Crystal Palace	38	17	11	10	63	40	62
Norwich City	38	18	7	13	68	54	61
Wimbledon	38	16	13	9	53	48	61
QPR	38	17	8	13	58	49	59
West Ham United	38	16	10	12	59	45	58
Swindon Town	38	18	4	16	54	53	58
Bristol Rovers	38	15	12	11	50	52	57
Southampton	38	15	10	13	62	66	55
Millwall	38	12	11	15	57	67	47
Charlton Athletic	38	13	7	18	61	62	46
Luton Town	38	12	9	17	64	70	45
Arsenal	38	13	6	19	67	76	45
Oxford United	38	11	10	17	53	66	43
Portsmouth	38	10	11	17	43	60	41
Brighton & Hove Albion	38	9	10	19	38	58	37
Watford	38	9	8	21	49	75	35
Bristol City	38	8	9	21	47	84	33

Division Two

	P	W	D	L	F	A	Pts
Birmingham City	18	13	1	4	53	17	40
Plymouth Argyle	18	12	2	4	63	18	38
Swansea City	18	11	4	3	47	26	37
Torquay United	18	11	2	5	33	18	35
AFC Bournemouth	18	9	3	6	36	38	30
Exeter City	18	7	2	9	40	41	23
Hereford United	18	6	1	11	36	52	19
Cardiff City	18	4	4	10	28	44	16
Yeovil Town	18	4	2	12	21	47	14
Cheltenham Town	18	2	1	15	16	72	7

League Cup Table
Group "A"

	P	W	D	L	F	A	Pts
Torquay United	8	5	2	1	17	9	17
AFC Bournemouth	8	4	1	3	10	11	13
Exeter City	8	3	2	3	15	17	11
Plymouth Argyle	8	3	1	4	15	14	10
Yeovil Town	8	2	1	6	11	18	6

Group "B"

	P	W	D	L	F	A	Pts
Birmingham City	8	6	2	0	22	10	20
Cardiff City	8	4	1	3	8	10	13
Swansea City	8	3	3	2	20	9	12
Cheltenham Town	8	1	2	5	9	18	5
Hereford United	8	1	2	5	15	27	5

THE PONTIN'S LEAGUE

Division One

	P	W	D	L	F	A	Pts
Manchester United	34	22	7	5	77	38	73
Aston Villa	34	18	9	7	61	29	63
Bolton Wanderers	34	15	10	9	88	65	55
Wolverhampton Wanderers	34	15	9	10	45	38	54
Derby County	34	14	8	12	55	51	50
Nottingham Forest	34	14	8	12	55	51	50
Sunderland	34	12	13	9	47	53	49
Blackburn Rovers	34	14	7	13	40	47	49
Leeds United	34	13	8	13	42	48	47
Coventry City	34	13	7	14	42	41	46
Sheffield United	34	12	9	13	57	60	45
Notts County	34	12	8	14	43	50	44
Everton	34	12	7	15	54	50	43
Liverpool	34	10	11	13	42	51	41
Newcastle United	34	10	8	16	46	53	38
Sheffield Wednesday	34	7	12	15	46	63	33
Leicester City	34	8	7	19	37	58	31
York City	34	6	10	18	36	67	28

Division Two

	P	W	D	L	F	A	Pts
Tranmere Rovers	34	25	4	5	77	36	79
West Bromwich Albion	34	20	7	7	64	38	67
Stoke City	34	21	3	10	54	41	66
Rotherham United	34	18	8	8	61	35	62
Manchester City	34	18	8	8	57	31	62
Oldham Athletic	34	17	5	12	61	46	56
Burnley	34	16	4	14	55	49	52
Huddersfield Town	34	15	6	13	69	56	51
Port Vale	34	11	14	9	43	40	47
Preston North End	34	14	5	15	54	54	47
Bradford City	34	12	7	15	47	52	43
Grimsby Town	34	11	7	16	48	61	40
Barnsley	34	11	7	16	38	54	40
Middlesbrough	34	8	11	15	39	55	35
Hull City	34	10	4	20	36	62	34
Blackpool	34	7	7	20	33	61	28
Mansfield Town	34	6	7	21	33	60	25
Scunthorpe United	34	7	4	23	41	79	25

FEDERATION BREWERY NORTHERN LEAGUE

Division One

	P	W	D	L	F	A	Pts
Durham City	38	23	11	4	88	39	80
Blyth Spartans	38	22	7	9	81	37	73
Seaham Red Star	38	20	10	8	70	40	70
Whitby Town	38	17	14	7	90	57	65
Guisborough Town	38	17	12	9	71	41	63
Northallerton Town	38	18	7	13	68	39	61
Tow Law Town	38	18	6	14	70	58	60
Murton	38	17	8	13	63	65	59
Shildon	38	17	6	15	59	54	57
Billingham Synthonia	38	15	9	14	57	45	54
Dunston Federation	38	15	9	14	72	69	54
Consett*	38	15	6	17	67	70	48
Ferryhill Athletic	38	11	8	19	61	81	41
Newcastle Blue Star	38	11	8	19	44	65	41
Hebburn	38	12	5	21	55	93	41
Eppleton CW	38	11	7	20	52	76	40
Chester Le Street**	38	13	5	20	64	74	38
West Auckland	38	10	8	20	49	89	38
Brandon United*	38	9	6	23	45	94	33
Stockton*	38	9	8	21	46	86	32

* 3 points deducted
** 6 points deducted

Division Two

	P	W	D	L	F	A	Pts
Bedlington Terriers	36	28	5	3	114	36	89
Peterlee Newtown	36	23	9	4	77	27	78
Prudhoe East End	36	21	9	6	72	36	72
Evenwood Town	36	22	4	10	78	47	70
Easington Colliery	36	20	7	9	77	40	67
Billingham Town	36	21	3	12	88	49	66
Crook Town	36	18	8	10	80	58	62
Norton & SA	36	18	7	11	72	70	61
Darlington CS	36	18	2	16	65	68	56
Whickham*	36	16	7	13	71	64	52
Washington	36	14	5	17	67	72	47
Esh Winning	36	12	7	17	50	72	43
Langley Park SSC	36	12	5	19	55	67	41
Shotton Comrades	36	9	9	18	61	84	36
Alnwick Town*	36	10	7	19	50	69	34
Willington	36	9	3	24	48	90	30
Ashington*	36	8	3	25	46	100	24
Ryhope CA**	36	7	3	26	37	94	18
Horden	36	3	3	30	35	100	12

* 3 points deducted
** 6 points deducted

SKOL MIDLAND FOOTBALL COMBINATION

Premier Division

	P	W	D	L	F	A	Pts
Pershore Town	42	25	13	4	84	35	88
West Midlands Police	42	25	10	7	95	49	85
Shifnal Town	42	25	8	9	112	35	83
Shepshed Albion	42	23	10	9	87	47	79
Boldmere St. Michaels	42	22	7	13	74	54	73
Northfield Town	42	20	9	13	83	65	69
Studley BKL	42	19	11	12	91	76	68
Wellesbourne	42	18	11	13	78	60	65
Stratford Town	42	19	8	15	73	56	65
Meir KA	42	17	11	14	101	78	62
Stapenhill	42	17	11	14	77	55	62
Barwell	42	18	8	16	69	61	62
Sandwell Borough	42	15	14	13	82	71	59
Bolehall Swifts	42	17	7	18	61	77	58
Knowle	42	12	13	17	63	67	49
Bloxwich Town	42	14	6	22	65	108	48
Coleshill Town	42	10	15	17	53	72	45
Kings Heath	42	11	9	22	65	99	42
Highgate United	42	12	6	24	58	98	42
Chelmsley Town	42	8	9	25	55	94	33
Ansells	42	5	11	26	43	109	26
Mile Oak Rovers	42	2	9	31	32	135	15

LANCASHIRE LEAGUE

Division One

	P	W	D	L	F	A	Pts
Burnley A	28	19	6	3	79	24	63
Crewe Alexandra Reserve	28	19	3	6	71	27	60
Everton A	28	16	8	4	61	30	56
Manchester United A	28	15	7	6	58	34	52
Blackburn Rovers A	28	14	3	11	44	52	45
Liverpool A	28	14	2	12	66	42	44
Oldham Athletic A	28	13	4	11	61	49	43
Tranmere Rovers A	28	12	6	10	44	41	42
Manchester City A	28	9	8	11	42	45	35
Bury Reserve	28	10	5	13	55	61	35
Rochdale Reserve	28	9	2	17	60	90	29
Chester City A	28	8	3	17	39	72	27
Marine Reserve	28	7	4	17	29	53	25
Blackpool A	28	4	10	14	34	58	22
Morecambe Reserves	28	5	1	22	20	85	16

Division Two

	P	W	L	D	F	A	Pts
Preston North End B	34	22	7	5	89	42	73
Manchester United B	34	20	8	6	111	44	68
Liverpool B	34	20	7	7	92	48	67
Everton B	34	19	6	9	70	49	63
Carlisle United A	34	19	5	10	83	54	62
Wigan Athletic A	34	17	6	11	67	62	57
Burnley B	34	15	11	8	67	41	56
Tranmere Rovers B	34	17	5	12	65	56	56
Oldham Athletic B	34	14	8	12	65	73	50
Bolton Wanderers A	34	12	9	13	51	55	45
Crewe Alexandra A	34	12	5	17	64	67	41
Manchester City B	34	11	7	16	59	66	40
Blackpool B	34	10	9	15	59	77	39
Blackburn Rovers B	34	9	11	14	50	48	38
Stockport County A	34	9	7	18	59	87	34
Rochdale A	34	7	8	19	58	111	29
Bury A	34	6	6	22	39	75	24
Marine Youth	34	2	5	27	28	121	11

CARLING NORTH WEST COUNTIES LEAGUE

Division One

	P	W	D	L	F	A	Pts
Atherton LR	42	25	13	4	83	34	88
Rossendale United	42	25	9	8	76	46	84
Burscough	42	22	13	7	107	50	79
Nantwich Town	42	22	11	9	80	54	77
Eastwood Hanley	42	22	11	9	75	52	77
Bootle	42	21	10	11	77	61	73
Penrith	42	20	11	11	62	44	71
Blackpool Rovers	42	19	10	13	64	57	67
Clitheroe	42	19	9	14	75	58	66
Kidsgrove Athletic	42	16	10	16	70	61	58
St Helens Town	42	14	13	15	60	55	55
Prescot	42	14	13	15	46	47	55
Maine Road	42	14	13	15	58	64	55
Newcastle Town	42	14	10	18	66	67	52
Bradford Park Avenue	42	12	12	18	54	79	48
Darwen	42	12	8	22	38	61	44
Glossop North End	42	12	8	22	58	86	44
Salford City	42	11	10	21	50	67	43
Chadderton	42	10	8	24	49	85	38
Bacup Borough	42	9	9	24	57	85	36
Skelmersdale United	42	8	8	26	55	92	32
Flixton	42	9	5	28	35	90	32

Division Two

	P	W	D	L	F	A	Pts
Haslingden	34	26	5	3	117	39	83
North Trafford	34	24	2	8	95	36	74
Holker Old Boys	34	23	3	8	75	40	72
Stantondale	34	20	8	6	88	45	68
Castleton Gabriels	34	19	6	9	55	46	63
Nelson	34	16	8	10	75	52	56
Atherton Collieries	34	15	9	10	58	40	54
Maghull	34	15	8	11	70	46	53
Ellesmere Port Town	34	14	8	12	62	63	50
Formby	34	12	11	11	59	50	47
Oldham Town	34	13	6	15	61	68	45
Cheadle Town	34	11	9	14	69	62	42
Blackpool Mechanics	34	10	5	19	50	69	35
Westhoughton Town	34	9	3	22	53	100	30
Ashton Town	34	7	8	19	42	91	29
Irlam Town	34	8	4	22	41	73	28
K Chell	34	4	6	24	35	97	18
Squires Gate	34	1	9	24	20	108	12

VAUX WEARSIDE LEAGUE

Division One

	P	W	D	L	F	A	Pts
Hartlepool Town	32	23	6	3	93	27	75
Marske United	32	25	2	5	97	25	74
Jarrow Roofing	32	20	7	5	79	34	67
South Shields	31	17	7	7	75	43	58
Silksworth	32	16	3	13	53	50	51
Kennek Roker	32	14	8	10	55	49	50
Ryhope CW	32	12	6	14	55	74	42
Windscale	30	11	7	12	71	66	40
Cleadon SC	32	11	7	14	47	68	40
Herrington CW	32	11	5	16	68	72	38
Hartlepool BWOB	32	11	5	16	56	64	38
Annfield Plain	32	10	8	14	47	57	38
North Shields	32	11	5	16	61	80	38
Cleator Moor	32	10	4	18	49	85	34
Boldon CA	32	8	6	18	43	70	30
Wolviston	32	6	8	18	46	82	26
Jarrow	31	5	4	22	36	85	19

* 3 points deducted

Division Two

	P	W	D	L	F	A	Pts
Nissan	31	27	2	2	88	31	83
North Ormesby	32	25	6	1	102	15	81
Hebburn DT	30	20	4	6	74	34	64
Birtley Town	32	19	6	7	74	34	63
Washington Glebe	31	18	6	7	82	49	60
Stanley United	32	18	5	9	66	46	59
SS County Kitchens	32	16	5	11	70	53	53
Northallerton TS	32	16	3	13	69	61	51
Marchon	32	15	5	12	73	42	50
Guisborough Priory*	32	12	4	16	68	63	37
Murton Inter	32	10	6	16	54	71	36
Fulwell Myers	32	9	4	19	41	71	31
Wingate Mall	32	7	6	19	46	76	27
Tradelink	32	7	4	21	48	95	25
Newcastle City	32	6	7	19	40	91	25
Usworth Vill	32	2	6	24	24	94	12
Esh Albion	32	1	5	26	29	122	8

* 3 points deducted

THE JEWSON SOUTH-WESTERN FOOTBALL LEAGUE

	P	W	D	L	F	A	Pts
Bodmin Town	34	26	2	6	103	27	80
Newquay	34	24	8	2	92	33	80
Truro City	34	25	4	5	98	31	79
Falmouth Town	34	20	10	4	75	43	70
Launceston	34	19	7	8	86	43	64
Porthleven	34	16	6	12	71	66	54
Torpoint Athletic	34	14	10	10	67	59	52
St Austell	34	14	6	14	72	57	48
Holsworthy	34	13	9	12	44	50	48
Tavistock	34	13	7	14	71	70	46
St Blazey	34	12	9	13	76	59	45
Mullion	34	11	6	17	56	77	39
Devon/Cornwall Police	34	8	10	16	54	70	34
Appledore/BAAC	34	8	8	18	44	75	32
Millbrook	34	6	7	21	48	86	25
Wadebridge Town	34	6	5	23	34	94	23
Penzance	34	5	6	23	54	107	21
Okehampton Argyle	34	3	6	25	19	116	15

COURAGE BEST SCOTCH NORTHERN ALLIANCE

Premier Division

	P	W	D	L	F	A	Pts
Morpeth Town	30	25	2	3	86	27	77
Carlisle City	30	22	3	5	73	33	69
Ponteland United	30	18	5	7	80	43	59
Seaton Delaval Amateurs	30	16	7	7	61	37	55
West Allotment Celtic	30	17	3	10	74	48	54
Carlisle Gillford Park	30	13	7	10	56	31	46
Walker	30	14	3	13	64	57	45
Spittal Rovers	30	13	5	12	40	44	44
Winlaton Hallgarth	30	12	6	12	58	50	42
Seaton Terrace	30	12	6	12	49	47	42
Longbenton	30	11	6	13	60	53	39
Westerhope	30	11	3	16	40	55	36
Blyth Kitty Brewster	30	8	3	19	39	76	27
Haltwhistle Crown Paints*	30	6	5	19	38	51	20
Heaton Stannington	30	4	4	22	38	117	16
Wark	30	2	4	24	31	118	10

* 3 points deducted

Division One

	P	W	D	L	F	A	Pts
Amble Town	28	21	4	3	100	29	67
Benfield Park	28	19	6	3	84	20	63
NEI Reyrolle	28	20	3	5	84	34	63
Swalwell	28	16	6	6	67	40	54
Dudley Welfare	28	12	7	9	51	55	43
Ryton	28	13	4	11	45	52	43
North Shields St Columbas*	28	13	6	9	62	47	42
Hexham Swinton	28	10	7	11	48	46	37
Newbiggin Central Welfare	28	9	9	10	57	49	36
Percy Main Amateurs	28	11	2	15	53	80	35
Gosforth Bohemians	28	9	4	15	51	66	31
Proctor and Gamble	28	7	4	17	34	76	25
Northern Counties*	28	7	4	17	45	72	22
Wylam	28	6	1	21	35	86	19
Forest Hall	28	2	3	23	20	83	9

* 3 points deducted

Division Two

	P	W	D	L	F	A	Pts
Ashington Hirst	28	23	4	1	126	38	73
Orwin NW	28	20	4	4	91	49	64
Shankhouse	28	18	4	6	93	25	58
Heddon Institute	28	17	2	9	73	41	53
Newcastle University	28	15	2	11	56	58	47
Marden Athletic	28	16	1	11	70	56	46
Highfields United	28	14	3	11	67	47	45
Stobswood Welfare	28	14	2	12	68	48	44
DHSS†	28	14	5	9	60	62	44
Norgas United	28	11	2	15	52	83	35
Monkseaton Kosa	28	7	6	15	45	59	27
Durham Ranger	28	8	3	17	53	83	27
Shilbottle Colliery Welfare	28	6	4	18	32	62	22
Northern Electric†	28	5	1	22	36	82	16
Wallsend Rising Sun†	28	0	1	27	19	148	1

** 3 points deducted

† Resigned from league

WEST MIDLANDS (REGIONAL) LEAGUE

Premier Division

	P	W	D	L	F	A	Pts
Ilkeston Town	38	25	6	7	102	43	81
Stourport Swifts	38	24	7	7	83	37	79
Oldbury United	38	23	9	6	85	42	78
Blakenall	38	23	8	7	78	45	77
Paget Rangers	38	21	5	12	79	43	68
Knypersley Victoria	38	19	8	11	75	60	65
Rocester	38	20	4	14	83	63	64
Hinckley Athletic	38	18	7	13	77	58	61
Chasetown	38	18	6	14	51	57	60
Pelsall Villa	38	16	8	14	70	78	56
Willenhall Town	38	15	8	15	73	60	53
Wednesfield	38	13	11	14	65	63	50
Halesowen Harriers	38	15	5	18	63	66	50
Darlaston	38	12	12	14	61	74	48
Lye Town	38	10	10	18	43	67	40
Brierley Hill Town	38	11	5	22	56	83	38
Rushall Olympic*	38	10	7	21	53	76	34
Westfields	38	7	7	24	58	92	28
Cradley Town	38	4	10	24	42	104	22
West Bromwich Town	38	3	3	32	37	123	12

* 3 points deducted

Division One

	P	W	D	L	F	A	Pts
Stafford Town	40	32	2	6	109	52	98
Gornal Athletic	40	30	4	6	92	35	94
Tividale	40	26	5	9	96	48	83
Ludlow Town	40	21	7	12	70	39	70
Walsall Wood	40	19	10	11	71	40	67
Bloxwich Strollers	40	20	3	17	101	68	63
Wolverhampton United	40	18	8	14	89	70	62
Tipton Town	40	19	5	16	68	67	62
Malvern Town	40	18	8	14	73	74	62
Ettingshall HT	40	16	10	14	70	71	58
Wolverhampton Casuals	40	17	5	18	73	63	56
Hill Top Rangers	40	14	11	15	66	72	53
Lichfield**	40	14	12	14	66	60	50
Great Wyrley	40	13	9	18	63	85	48
Cannock Chase	40	12	11	17	60	84	47
Donnington Wood	40	11	10	19	50	54	43
Manders	40	11	10	19	54	70	43
Bilston United	40	11	10	19	54	91	43
Moxley Rangers	40	8	5	27	47	81	29
Wem Town	40	8	5	27	46	116	29
Cheslyn Hay	40	5	4	31	32	110	19

** 4 points deducted

WINSTONLEAD KENT LEAGUE

Division One

	P	W	D	L	F	A	Pts
Herne Bay	40	33	4	3	102	26	103
Furness	40	23	9	8	94	37	78
Chatham Town	40	23	9	8	86	50	78
Thamesmead Town	40	21	11	8	93	47	74
Alma Swanley	40	22	8	10	90	50	74
Dartford	40	21	11	8	70	44	74
Beckenham Town	40	22	4	14	85	59	70
Corinthian	40	21	6	13	91	51	69
Ramsgate	40	20	6	14	90	67	66
Deal Town	40	18	8	14	102	73	62
Sheppey United	40	17	10	13	69	67	61
Folkestone Invicta	40	17	6	17	83	73	57
Faversham Town	40	14	6	20	68	80	48
Greenwich Borough	40	14	5	21	72	85	47
Whitstable Town	40	12	9	19	68	72	45
Tunbridge Wells	40	11	10	19	54	71	43
Cray Wanderers	40	11	9	20	37	65	42
Crockenhill*	40	8	10	22	55	99	33
Slade Green	40	8	7	25	42	87	31
Darenth Heathside	40	5	4	31	38	128	19
Kent Police	40	1	4	35	30	188	7

* 1 point deducted

REFUGE ASSURANCE MIDLAND LEAGUE

	P	W	D	L	F	A	Pts
Redgate Clayton	32	21	6	5	101	30	69
Ball Haye Green	32	19	7	6	68	30	64
Leek CSOB	32	16	7	9	62	39	55
Norton United	32	14	10	8	61	46	52
Parkway Clayton	32	15	7	10	52	41	52
Brocton	32	14	7	11	52	47	49
Audley	32	14	7	11	50	46	49
Rists United	32	16	1	15	45	56	49
Staffs Police	32	12	8	12	61	59	44
Eccleshall	32	12	8	12	59	61	44
Milton United	32	11	10	11	44	55	43
Goldenhill W	32	11	9	12	42	43	42
Congleton Hornets	32	11	8	13	44	50	41
Cannock Town	32	9	3	20	50	78	30
Hanford	32	7	7	18	37	59	28
Heath Hayes	32	6	9	17	34	81	27
Brereton Social	32	3	8	21	34	75	17

GREAT MILLS LEAGUE

Premier Division

	P	W	D	L	F	A	Pts
Tiverton Town	34	31	3	0	125	22	96
Taunton Town	34	26	2	6	98	38	80
Mangotsfield United	34	19	6	9	75	40	63
Paulton Rovers	34	18	7	9	55	42	61
Saltash United	34	18	6	10	67	36	60
Torrington	34	16	10	8	66	46	58
Liskeard Athletic	34	16	5	13	66	46	53
Chippenham Town	34	14	7	13	58	51	49
Bideford**	34	13	8	13	60	69	44
Odd Down	34	10	12	12	59	58	42
Crediton United	34	10	8	16	42	65	38
Westbury United	34	9	9	16	40	61	36
Bristol Manor Farm	34	11	3	20	51	77	36
Calne Town	34	8	9	17	50	76	33
Frome Town	34	9	6	19	33	61	33
Elmore	34	8	8	18	51	83	32
Exmouth Town	34	6	4	24	35	93	22
Minehead**	34	6	3	25	38	105	15

** 6 points deducted

First Division

	P	W	D	L	F	A	Pts
Barnstaple Town	38	27	8	3	107	39	89
Bridport	38	24	7	7	90	46	79
Brislington	38	23	8	7	73	35	77
Pewsey Vale	38	20	11	7	84	47	71
Keynsham Town	38	21	7	10	80	50	70
Clyst Rovers	38	16	15	7	68	50	63
Backwell United	38	18	8	12	64	45	62
Welton Rovers	38	16	10	12	73	53	58
Devizes Town	38	16	10	12	64	61	58
Chard Town	38	16	9	13	48	51	57
Ilfracombe Town	38	16	8	14	70	42	56
Bishop Sutton	38	12	14	12	58	48	50
Glastonbury	38	14	8	16	68	66	50
Larkhall Athletic	38	12	7	19	52	69	43
Warminster Town	38	8	11	19	47	57	35
Wellington	38	9	6	23	51	92	33
Dawlish Town	38	9	5	24	46	125	32
Heavitree United	38	8	7	23	47	90	31
Radstock Town	38	8	6	24	44	73	30
Ottery St Mary	38	2	5	31	37	132	11

JEWSON (EASTERN COUNTIES) LEAGUE

Premier Division

	P	W	D	L	F	A	Pts
Wroxham	42	28	7	7	92	41	91
Halstead Town	41	27	6	8	109	48	87
Newmarket Town	39	25	8	6	77	41	83
Diss Town	39	21	10	8	83	45	73
Wisbech Town	42	19	11	12	61	44	68
Felixstowe Town	42	18	12	12	65	47	66
Stowmarket Town	41	20	6	15	67	57	66
Sudbury Wanderers	42	18	10	14	75	59	64
Lowestoft Town	42	19	7	16	62	62	64
Haverhill Rovers	42	18	9	15	71	61	63
Harwich & Parkeston	40	15	13	12	69	60	58
Cornard United	42	15	10	17	68	70	55
Chatteris Town	39	16	7	16	49	59	55
Tiptree United	40	14	9	17	62	64	51
Watton United	42	13	8	21	47	75	47
Great Yarmouth Town	41	12	8	21	49	59	44
Fakenham Town	42	10	13	19	51	81	43
Soham Town Rangers	42	10	10	22	68	102	40
March Town United	41	9	11	21	39	69	38
Histon	41	8	11	22	46	86	35
Gorleston	42	8	9	25	43	77	33
Norwich United	42	8	7	27	49	94	31

Division One

	P	W	D	L	F	A	Pts
Hadleigh United	31	25	4	2	91	27	79
Woodbridge Town	32	24	5	3	97	26	77
Warboys Town	33	21	5	7	54	31	68
Sudbury Town Reserves	30	19	3	8	90	41	60
Mildenhall Town	34	16	4	14	69	58	52
Downham Town	34	15	7	12	52	43	52
Somersham Town	32	14	8	10	65	51	50
Ipswich Wanderers	33	14	5	14	64	54	47
Brightlingsea United	32	14	4	14	49	49	46
Ely City	34	11	12	11	49	51	45
Stanway Rovers	31	12	6	13	50	54	42
Cambridge City Res	33	12	4	17	60	66	40
Clacton Town	32	10	8	14	42	56	38
Bury Town Reserves	34	10	7	17	58	91	37
Brantham Athletic	34	9	6	19	59	90	33
Long Sutton Athletic	33	6	10	17	46	75	28
Swaffham Town	34	6	5	23	33	91	23
Thetford Town	34	3	5	26	28	102	14

JOHN SMITH'S BITTER CENTRAL MIDLANDS LEAGUE

Supreme Division

	P	W	D	L	F	A	Pts
Glapwell	32	22	7	3	75	25	73
Oakham United	32	20	4	8	62	39	64
Kiveton Park	32	17	10	5	71	34	61
Staveley Miners Welfare	32	16	9	7	76	39	57
Gedling Town	32	16	8	8	61	41	56
Priory (Eastwood)	32	13	12	7	51	38	51
Blidworth Welfare	32	15	3	14	51	39	48
Borrowash Victoria	32	11	12	9	51	43	45
Heanor Town	32	12	7	13	49	54	43
Shirebrook Town	32	12	5	15	51	57	41
Rossington	32	12	4	16	56	76	40
Sheffield Aurora	32	9	8	15	50	61	35
Long Eaton United	32	7	11	14	40	57	32
Harworth Colliery Institute	32	8	8	16	49	85	32
Nettleham	32	9	4	19	28	63	31
Sandiacre Town	32	8	4	20	49	73	28
Kimberley Town	32	4	6	22	34	80	18

Premier Division

	P	W	D	L	F	A	Pts
Nuthall	28	20	4	4	63	27	64
South Normanton Athletic	28	20	1	7	84	31	61
Norton Woodseats	28	18	5	5	72	37	59
Thorne Colliery	28	16	4	8	59	34	52
Askern Welfare	28	16	3	9	73	43	51
Mickleover Sports	28	15	4	9	54	38	49
Derby Carriage & Wagon (Reckitts)	28	11	8	9	51	39	41
Radford	28	11	8	9	50	43	41
Newhall United	28	9	8	11	42	50	35
Biwater	28	9	5	14	48	54	32
Derby Rolls Royce	28	8	6	14	53	57	30
Mickleover Royal British Legion	28	8	6	14	28	40	30
Stanton Ilkeston	28	5	3	20	29	65	18
Blackwell Miners Welfare	28	4	5	19	29	64	17
Shardlow St James	28	3	4	21	17	130	13

The record of Kingston FC has been expunged

SPARTAN FOOTBALL LEAGUE

Premier Division

	P	W	D	L	F	A	Pts
Willesden (Hawk)	36	26	7	3	77	25	85
Croydon Athletic	36	26	5	5	118	37	83
St Margaretsbury	36	23	5	8	77	48	74
Hillingdon Borough	36	21	7	8	86	45	70
Tower Hamlets	36	22	3	11	91	59	69
Corinthian Casuals	36	19	6	11	82	44	63
Walthamstow Pennant	36	17	7	12	69	60	58
Brook House	35	16	3	16	64	66	51
Waltham Abbey	35	15	5	15	48	51	50
Cockfosters	36	13	9	14	55	52	48
Hanwell Town	34	14	3	17	58	56	45
Haringey Borough**	36	14	6	16	45	58	42
Barkingside	36	11	8	17	65	87	41
Brimsdown Rovers	36	11	4	21	37	50	37
Beaconsfield United	36	9	9	18	49	89	36
N Greenford United	36	10	4	22	40	71	34
Beckton United**	36	9	5	22	60	116	26
Southgate Athletic	36	6	5	25	47	90	23
Amersham Town	36	5	5	26	42	106	20

** 6 points deducted

St Andrews record expunged

ESSEX SENIOR LEAGUE

	P	W	D	L	F	A	Pts
Basildon United	30	21	7	2	64	18	70
Ford United	30	20	6	4	64	16	66
Canvey Island	30	19	5	6	50	22	62
Romford	30	16	6	8	52	37	54
Great Wakering Rovers	30	16	5	9	69	40	53
Bowers United	30	14	6	10	40	44	48
Brentwood	30	13	6	11	49	43	45
Sawbridgeworth Town	30	13	6	11	46	40	45
Concord Rangers	30	11	7	12	50	41	40
East Ham United	30	10	8	12	46	54	38
Maldon Town	30	11	3	16	38	46	36
Eton Manor	30	8	2	20	37	74	26
Southend Manor	30	6	7	17	42	65	25
Burnham Ramblers	30	7	4	19	32	55	25
Hullbridge Sports	30	5	7	18	30	74	22
Stansted	30	4	7	19	28	68	19

NORTHERN COUNTIES EAST LEAGUE

Premier Division

	P	W	D	L	F	A	Pts
Stocksbridge PS	38	23	5	10	82	39	74
Thackley	38	21	11	6	57	32	74
Lincoln United	38	21	9	8	82	44	72
Sheffield	38	22	5	11	69	49	71
Brigg Town	38	18	8	12	77	54	62
Pickering Town	38	17	10	11	76	61	61
Maltby MW	38	18	6	14	77	52	60
Ossett Albion	38	16	12	10	73	59	60
North Ferriby United	38	18	5	15	57	43	59
Armthorpe Welfare	38	14	15	9	55	42	57
Liversedge	38	17	4	17	63	65	55
Glasshoughton Welfare	38	13	11	14	51	58	50
Denaby United	38	13	7	18	66	66	46
Hucknall Town	38	13	5	20	48	65	44
Belper Town	38	12	7	19	57	75	43
Ossett Town	38	10	11	17	43	71	41
Pontefract Collieries	38	10	10	18	52	71	40
Ashfield United	38	9	8	21	50	85	35
Eccleshill United	38	8	9	21	44	75	33
Winterton Rangers	38	6	4	28	40	103	22

Division One

	P	W	D	L	F	A	Pts
Arnold Town	28	20	1	7	88	34	61
Hallam	28	18	5	5	64	26	59
Louth United	28	17	4	7	72	38	55
Hatfield Main	28	17	4	7	61	33	55
Yorkshire Amateurs	28	16	4	8	51	25	52
Garforth Town	28	15	6	7	39	28	51
Rossington Main	28	12	4	12	43	47	40
Worsbrough Bridge	28	11	3	14	49	47	36
Harrogate Railway	28	10	5	13	47	56	35
Hall Road Rangers	28	9	6	13	57	63	33
Selby Town**	28	10	5	13	44	66	29
Tadcaster Albion	28	8	2	18	38	73	26
RES Parkgate	28	6	5	17	43	69	23
Immingham Town	28	6	5	17	33	76	23
Brodsworth MW	28	3	5	20	26	74	14

** 6 points deducted

SOUTH EAST COUNTIES LEAGUE

Division One

	P	W	D	L	F	A	Pts
Queens Park Rangers	30	24	2	4	121	49	50
Tottenham Hotspur	30	20	4	6	85	40	44
West Ham United	30	19	5	6	78	44	43
Chelsea	30	19	3	8	67	39	41
Millwall	30	18	4	8	86	59	40
Fulham	30	19	2	9	59	46	40
Arsenal	30	15	7	8	66	42	37
Ipswich Town	30	11	8	11	50	49	30
Watford	30	11	5	14	52	63	27
Norwich City	30	11	2	17	42	60	24
Cambridge United	30	6	9	15	40	69	21
Portsmouth	30	7	5	18	44	76	19
Southend United	30	8	3	19	40	78	19
Leyton Orient	30	6	6	18	32	65	18
Charlton Athletic	30	6	3	21	46	87	15
Gillingham	30	4	4	22	30	72	12

Division Two

	P	W	D	L	F	A	Pts
Crystal Palace	26	15	5	6	56	32	35
Swindon Town	26	14	6	6	49	26	34
Wimbledon	26	15	1	10	61	44	31
Reading	26	10	9	7	39	36	29
Oxford United	26	11	6	9	46	38	28
Brentford	26	10	8	8	40	34	28
Luton Town	26	11	4	11	40	47	26
Brighton & Hove Albion	26	10	6	10	37	44	26
Southampton	26	8	7	11	29	30	23
Bristol Rovers	26	9	5	12	40	48	23
Bristol City	26	8	6	12	35	44	22
AFC Bournemouth	26	9	2	15	40	53	20
Tottenham Hotspur	26	8	4	14	35	49	20
Colchester United	26	6	7	13	33	55	19

HELLENIC LEAGUE

Premier Division

	P	W	D	L	F	A	Pts
Moreton Town	34	25	6	3	74	21	81
Shortwood United	34	21	6	7	66	48	69
Banbury United†	34	18	9	7	74	44	63
Wantage Town†	34	18	9	7	68	38	63
Fairford Town	34	18	7	9	76	51	61
Cinderford Town	34	17	6	11	57	39	57
Bicester Town	34	17	6	11	64	48	57
Swindon Supermarine*	34	16	6	12	64	42	51
Rayners Lane	34	13	7	14	64	53	46
Tuffley Rovers	34	14	4	16	60	53	46
Milton United	34	13	6	15	59	58	45
Abingdon United	34	12	8	14	60	57	44
Cirencester Town	34	12	4	18	53	62	40
North Leigh	34	10	9	15	60	58	39
Almondsbury Town	34	10	7	17	38	61	37
Headington Amateurs	34	7	11	16	43	77	32
Wollen Sports	34	4	6	24	34	95	18
Kintbury Rangers	34	2	1	31	17	126	17

* 3 points deducted
† Level on points and goal difference

Division One

	P	W	D	L	F	A	Pts
Carterton Town	34	21	8	5	82	27	71
Pegasus Juniors	34	21	6	7	86	44	69
Highworth Town	34	20	8	6	58	30	68
Lambourn Sports	34	17	10	7	65	38	61
Bishops Cleeve	34	17	8	9	79	54	59
Hallen	34	16	10	8	62	50	58
Easington Sports	34	15	9	10	66	49	54
Wallingford Town	34	14	11	9	74	54	53
Wootton Bassett	34	15	8	11	65	57	53
Cheltenham Saracens	34	14	9	11	63	50	51
Ardley United	34	12	11	11	59	50	47
Kidlington	34	10	8	16	52	68	38
Purton	34	10	7	17	52	74	37
Cirencester United	34	8	7	19	50	81	31
Didcot Town	34	9	2	23	49	97	29
Yarnton**	34	8	4	22	43	85	26
Clanfield	34	4	9	21	32	75	21
Letcombe	34	6	3	25	26	80	21

** 2 points deducted

Reserve Division

	P	W	D	L	F	A	Pts
Swindon Supermarine	24	18	3	3	90	27	57
Carterton Town	24	18	2	4	68	32	56
Fairford Town	24	17	3	4	63	23	54
Headington Amateurs	24	17	3	4	73	39	54
Highworth Town	24	14	5	5	60	34	47
Cheltenham Saracens	24	15	1	8	59	38	46
Bicester Town	24	12	7	5	67	37	43
Abingdon United	24	12	6	6	62	42	42
North Leigh	24	13	2	9	55	36	41
Easington Sports	24	11	5	8	40	30	38
Cirencester Town	24	11	4	9	42	29	37
Almondsbury Town	24	9	6	9	47	43	33
Wallingford Town	24	8	8	8	59	45	32
Wantage Town	24	9	3	12	52	49	30
Kidlington	24	9	3	12	40	44	30
Cirencester United	24	8	6	10	43	54	30
Wollen Sports	24	9	3	12	49	61	30
Banbury United	24	8	3	13	39	47	27
Milton United	24	8	3	13	44	63	27
Letcombe	24	6	5	13	36	64	23
Kintbury Rangers	24	5	6	13	42	69	21
Ardley United	24	3	5	16	22	78	14
Yarnton	24	3	4	17	27	99	13
Clanfield	24	3	3	18	32	71	12
Didcot Town	24	2	5	17	24	81	11

Moreton Town and Witney Town records expunged

SOUTH MIDLANDS LEAGUE

Premier Division

	P	W	D	L	F	A	Pts
Bedford Town	30	22	5	3	94	26	71
Luton Old Boys	30	19	2	9	61	47	59
Biggleswade Town	30	16	5	9	48	36	53
Welwyn GC	30	14	5	11	43	44	47
Brache Sparta	30	13	7	10	47	36	46
Arlesey Town	30	12	8	10	54	49	44
Wingate & Finchley	30	13	5	12	45	44	44
Hoddesdon Town	30	11	10	9	42	33	43
Langford	30	12	7	11	54	50	43
Hatfield Town	30	13	4	13	57	54	43
Harpenden Town	30	11	7	12	38	38	40
Shillington	30	10	5	15	42	47	35
Buckingham Athletic	30	9	2	19	51	76	29
Potters Bar Town	30	7	7	16	35	60	28
Letchworth GC	30	8	4	18	39	75	28
Milton Keynes	30	5	7	18	31	66	22

continued on page 981

AMATEUR FOOTBALL ALLIANCE 1993–94

AFA SENIOR CUP

1st Round Proper
O. Foresters 1, O. Suttonians 2
O. Owens 5, O. Malvernian 0
Hadley 0, Ulysses 2
Winchmore Hill 2*:0*, O. Esthameians 2*:1*
Bank of England 4, O. Westhamians 0
West Wickham 3, Latymer O. Boys 0
O. Chigwellians 5, O. Salesians 0
O. Latymerians 4*, O. Tollingtonian 2*
Norsemen 5, O. Isleworthians 2
Midland Bank 1, Parkfield 2
Fulham Crompton O. Boys 1, Cardinal Manning O. Boys 6
Ealing Association 8, Brentham 0
Bourneside 2*scr, O. Kingsburians 2*w/o
Crouch End Vampires 3, Broomfield 1
Merton 2, Wake Green 3
Civil Service 4, Lensbury 1
National Westminster Bank 6, Cuaco 1
O. Parkonians 3*, O. Finchleians 1*
South Bank Polytechnic 11, Royal Bank of Scotland 0
Nottinghamshire 1*:1, O. Stationers 1*:3
O. Woodhouseians 4, B.B.C. 2
O. Grammarians 1, O. Parmiterians 0
Baltic Exchange 0, O. Colfeians 5
Lancing O. Boys 0, O. Ignatians 7
O. Addeyans 0, Glyn O. Boys 6
O. Southallians 0, Silhill 6
O. Hamptonians 1, Nottsborough 4
O. Actonians Assn 3, O. Vaughanians 0
Albanian 4, O. Minchendenians 5
O. Tenisonians 2, Alleyn O. Boys 0
O. Bealonians 1, O. Aloysians 2
O. Meadonians 0, Polytechnic 4

2nd Round Proper
O. Stationers 2, Parkfield 1
Crouch End Vampires 2, O. Kingsburians 1
Bank of England 4, O. Colfeians 0
O. Grammarians 3*, Silhill 2*
O. Latymerians 2, Ulysses 0
O. Aloysians 4, O. Owens 0
West Wickham 2*, O. Minchendenians 1*
O. Chigwellians 0*:0*:1p, O. Parkonians 0*:0*:3p
Ealing Assn 4, Cardinal Manning O. Boys 3
National Westminster Bank 2, Polytechnic 3
Wake Green 2*, Glyn O. Boys 0*
O. Actonians Assn 1, O. Suttonians 2
South Bank Polytechnic 3, O. Esthameians 0
Norsemen 0, O. Ignatians 2
Nottsborough 3*:0, Civil Service 3*:1
O. Woodhouseians 2, O. Tenisonians 1

3rd Round Proper
O. Suttonians 0, O. Ignatians 2
Polytechnic 3, Bank of England 1
Crouch End Vampires 4, O. Grammarians 1
Ealing Assn 0, O. Latymerians 1
O. Woodhouseians 1, South Bank Polytechnic 4
O. Parkonians 2, Wake Green 1
West Wickham 3, O. Aloysians 1
O. Stationers 1, Civil Service 3

4th Round Proper
Polytechnic 2, O. Parkonians 0
West Wickham 0, South Bank Polytechnic 1
Civil Service 0, O. Ignatians 1
Crouch End Vampires 1, O. Latymerians 0

Semi-finals
O. Ignatians 2*, South Bank Polytechnic 1*
Crouch End Vampires 2, Polytechnic 0

* *after extra time*
p *decided on penalties*

OTHER AFA CUP RESULTS

Intermediate
Old Hamptonians Res. 0, Carshalton Res. 1

Junior
Civil Service 3rd 3, Winchmore Hill 3rd 0

Minor
Old Esthameians 4th 3, Polytechnic 4th 0

Senior Novets
Lloyds Bank 5th 1, Old Suttonians 5th 0

Intermediate Novets
Norsemen 6th 2, Old Salvatorians 6th 4

Junior Novets
Old Parmiterians 10th 3, National Westminster Bank "B" 2

Veterans
Old Chigwellians Vets 3, Winchmore Hill Vets 5

Open Veterans
Toby Veterans 0, Port of London Authority Vets 1

AFA Essex Senior
Old Chigwellians 2, Old Parkonians 1

AFA Middlesex Senior
Civil Service 1, E. Barnet Old Grammarians 0

AFA Surrey Senior
National Westminster Bank 2*, South Bank Polytechnic 1*

AFA Essex Intermediate
Old Highburians Res. 1, Old Parmiterians Res. 4

AFA Kent Intermediate
Lloyds Bank Res. 2, Colonial Mutual 1st 0

AFA Middlesex Intermediate
Old Ignatians Res. 4, Polytechnic Res. 0

AFA Surrey Intermediate
National Westminster Bank Res. 5*, Temple Bar 1st 2*

W E Greenland Memorial
Hill Samuel 1, Old Etonians 2

* *after extra time*

LONDON OLD BOYS' CUPS

Senior Cup–Old Hamptonians 1, Old Meadonians 2
Intermediate Cup–Latymer Old Boys Res. 3, 1, Old Parmiterians Res. 3, 2
Junior Cup–Old Meadonians 3rd 2, Old Parmiterians 3rd 1
Minor Cup–Old Minchendenians 4th 0, Old Salvatorians 4th 1
Novets Cup–Albanian 5th 3, Old Parmiterians 5th 4
Drummond Cup–Old Salvatorians 6th 4, Old Actonians Association 6th 0
Nemean Cup–Old Salvatorians 7th 2, Old Vaughanians 8th 3
Veterans' Cup–Old Owens Veterans 0, Old Woodvillians Veterans 2

SOUTHERN OLYMPIAN LEAGUE

Senior Section

Division One	P	W	D	L	F	A	Pts
Parkfield	18	11	4	3	56	30	26
Witan	18	11	3	4	45	25	25
Old Owens	18	11	3	4	44	27	25
Nottsborough	18	8	5	5	34	22	21
Old Grammarians	18	9	2	7	46	33	20
Wandsworth Borough	18	7	1	10	34	37	15
Mill Hill Village	18	6	3	9	26	41	15
St Mary's College	18	5	4	9	27	46	14
Old Bealonians	18	5	3	10	27	44	13
Old Finchleians	18	2	2	14	27	61	6

Division Two	P	W	D	L	F	A	Pts
Southgate County	20	15	3	2	56	18	33
Ulysses	20	11	6	3	44	20	28
UCL Academicals	20	11	5	4	59	27	27
Albanian	20	10	4	6	51	36	24
Hadley	20	11	1	8	41	28	23
Duncombe Sports	20	8	5	7	43	35	21
Old Fairlopians	20	10	1	9	40	54	21
Ealing Association	20	6	2	12	53	60	14
Corinthian-Casuals "A"	20	6	2	12	40	54	14
Pollygons	20	5	4	11	46	61	14
Old Monovians	20	0	1	19	13	93	1

Division Three	P	W	D	L	F	A	Pts
Hale End Athletic	20	15	4	1	54	20	34
Honourable Artillery Company	19	13	3	3	53	21	29
Old Woodhouseians	20	9	7	4	51	31	25
Bourneside	16	10	2	4	49	43	22
BBC	19	8	5	6	43	27	19*
Old Colfeians	20	8	2	10	39	45	18
City of London	20	5	8	7	34	40	18
Westerns	20	5	5	10	43	57	15
Birkbeck College	20	6	3	11	27	43	13
Pegasus (Inner Temple)	20	2	5	13	29	55	9
Hampstead Heathens	19	3	2	14	25	65	8

Division Four	P	W	D	L	F	A	Pts
London Welsh	14	12	0	2	60	14	28
Brent	14	9	2	3	50	18	20
Fulham Compton Old Boys	14	10	0	4	48	26	20
Centymca	14	4	4	6	34	21	25
Inland Revenue	20	8	2	10	39	40	18
Mayfield Athletic	20	8	2	10	48	49	18
London Airways	20	7	3	10	42	52	17
Economicals	14	1	0	13	15	77	2

** 2 points deducted for breach of rule*

Intermediate Section
Division One–10 Teams–won by Albanian Res.
Division Two–11 Teams–won by Witan Res.
Division Three–10 Teams–won by Hale End Athletic Res.
Division Four–11 Teams–won by London Airways 1st

Junior Section
Division One–10 Teams–won by Old Finchleians 3rd
Division Two–10 Teams–won by Mill Hill Village 3rd
Division Three–9 Teams–won by Mill Hill Village 4th
Division Four–10 Teams–won by Albanian 5th

Minor Section
Division "A"–10 Teams–won by UCL Academicals 4th
Division "B"–10 Teams–won by Albanian 6th
Division "C"–9 Teams–won by London Welsh 3rd
Division "D"–10 Teams–won by Mayfield Athletic 4th
Division "E"–6 Teams–won by Old Finchleians 8th
Division "F"–8 Teams–won by Fulham Compton Old Boys 5th
Veterans Division–6 Teams–won by Tansley Veterans
Senior Challenge Bowl–won by Parkfield
Senior Challenge Shield–won by Old Owens
Intermediate Challenge Cup–won by Old Owens Res.
Intermediate Challenge Shield–won by Nottsborough Res.
Junior Challenge Cup–won by Old Owens 3rd
Junior Challenge Shield–won by BBC 3rd
Mander Cup–won by UCL Academicals 4th
Mander Shield– City of London 4th
Burntwood Trophy–won by Old Finchleians 5th
Burntwood Shield–won by BBC 5th
Thomas Parmiter Cup–won by City of London 6th
Thomas Parmiter Shield–won by Parkfield 8th
Veterans' Challenge Cup–won by Albanian Veterans
Veterans' Challenge Shield–won by Old Finchleians Veterans

ARTHUR DUNN CUP

Final
Old Chigwellians 2, 5, Old Salopians 2, 2

ARTHURIAN LEAGUE

Premier Division	P	W	D	L	F	A	Pts
Lancing Old Boys	16	9	6	1	38	19	24
Old Chigwellians	16	10	3	3	41	18	23
Old Carthusians	16	10	2	4	41	24	22
Old Brentwoods	16	8	1	7	34	37	17
Old Etonians	16	6	3	7	22	22	15
Old Malvernians	16	4	6	6	24	29	14
Old Reptonians	16	6	1	9	27	35	13
Old Cholmeleians	16	5	3	8	27	34	11*
Old Salopians	16	0	3	13	25	61	3

Division One	P	W	D	L	F	A	Pts
Old Wellingburians	18	14	1	3	70	19	29
Old Aldenhamians	18	14	1	3	67	26	29
Old Foresters	18	14	2	2	61	25	28*
Old Bradfieldians	18	9	2	7	43	44	20
Old Harrovians	18	9	1	8	59	42	19
Old Haileyburians	18	8	1	9	38	40	17
Old Witleians	18	6	2	10	40	52	14
Old Wykehamists	18	5	0	13	37	53	10
Old Ardinians	18	3	1	14	23	89	10
Old Westminsters	18	1	3	14	29	77	5

Division Two	P	W	D	L	F	A	Pts
Old Cholmeleians Res.	16	12	3	1	50	21	27
Old Carthusians Res.	16	10	3	3	38	29	23
Old Chigwellians Res.	16	7	5	4	53	37	19
Old Chigwellians 3rd	16	6	4	6	35	40	16
Old Reptonians Res.	16	4	5	7	29	34	13
Old Etonians Res.	16	5	2	9	44	43	12
Old Foresters Res.	16	6	2	8	36	46	12*
Old Salopians Res.	16	4	3	9	21	39	11
Old Brentwoods Res.	16	4	1	11	28	45	9

Division Three	P	W	D	L	F	A	Pts
Old Aldenhamians Res.	16	11	1	4	57	36	23
Lancing Old Boys Res.	16	10	2	4	46	27	22
Old Wellingburians Res.	16	6	6	4	28	30	18
Old Harrovians Res.	16	7	3	6	32	27	17
Old Malvernians Res.	16	7	3	6	36	34	17
Old Cholmeleians 3rd	16	6	4	6	31	30	16
Old Westminsters Res.	16	5	4	7	33	39	14
Old Cholmeleians 4th	16	5	3	8	35	37	13
Old Eastbournians	16	0	4	12	20	58	4

Division Four–8 Teams–won by Old Etonians 3rd
Division Five–7 Teams–won by Old Brentwoods 4th
Junior League Cup–Old Carthusians Res. 1, Old Harrovians Res. 0
Derrik Moore Veterans' Cup–Old Brentwoods Vets 2, Old Carthusians Vets 1

** 2 points deductions for breaches of rule*

LONDON LEGAL LEAGUE

Division One	P	W	D	L	F	A	Pts
Wilde Sapte	18	10	8	0	43	24	28
Slaughter & May	18	12	2	4	51	31	26
Gray's Inn	18	11	2	5	59	31	24
Pegasus (Inner Temple)	18	8	5	5	47	31	21
Herbert Smith	18	8	1	9	39	39	17
Freshfields	18	7	2	9	37	46	16
Linklaters & Paines	18	6	4	8	35	54	16
Cameron Markby Hewitt	18	5	4	9	45	44	14
Clifford Chance	18	4	4	10	28	33	12
Allen & Overy	18	2	2	14	31	82	6

Division Two	P	W	D	L	F	A	Pts
Nabarro Nathanson	18	15	1	2	53	17	31
D.J. Freeman & Co	18	11	4	3	44	30	26
Lovell White Durrant	18	11	1	6	42	28	23
Gouldens	18	6	6	6	39	39	18
Stephenson Harwood	18	8	1	9	39	39	17
Taylor Joynson Garrett	18	7	2	9	29	29	16
Simmons & Simmons	18	6	2	10	39	41	14
Norton Rose	18	6	2	10	20	35	14
Macfarlanes	18	4	3	11	20	39	11
Titmuss Sainer & Webb	18	5	0	13	26	54	10

Division Three	P	W	D	L	F	A	Pts
Watson Farley & Williams	18	14	3	1	61	18	31
S.J. Berwin	18	12	3	3	71	38	27
Rosling King	18	12	1	5	59	39	25
Baker & McKenzie	18	9	5	4	55	30	23
Denton Hall	18	10	3	5	44	26	23
Beachcroft Stanleys	18	8	2	8	44	22	18
McKenna & Co	18	6	3	9	37	47	15
Richards Butler	18	5	2	11	28	56	12
Mishcon de Reya	18	1	1	16	21	69	3
Rowe & Maw	18	1	1	16	24	79	3

League Challenge Cup–Gray's Inn 3, Watson Farley & Williams 0
Weavers Arms Cup–Gouldens 0, Nabarro Nathanson 3

LONDON FINANCIAL F.A.

Senior Section

Division One	P	W	D	L	F	A	Pts
Coutts	18	15	1	2	92	18	31
Liverpool Victoria	18	13	1	4	76	28	27
Credit Suisse	18	11	3	4	47	27	25
Temple Bar	18	8	3	7	51	33	19
Kleinwort Benson	18	7	3	8	50	57	17
Hill Samuel Investment Management	18	7	3	8	34	42	17
Sun Alliance	18	6	2	10	32	48	14
Colonial Mutual	18	5	2	11	27	52	12
Granby	18	3	3	12	30	69	9
Salomon Brothers	18	2	5	11	23	88	9

Division Two	P	W	D	L	F	A	Pts
Bank America	18	14	2	2	55	14	30
Hong Kong Bank	18	13	2	3	60	25	28
Chemical Bank	18	13	1	4	76	29	27
Citibank	18	12	2	4	50	26	26
Eagle Star	18	8	3	7	48	49	19
Bardhill	18	6	3	9	32	33	15
Allied Irish Bank	18	4	4	10	29	49	12
Noble Lowndes	18	2	5	11	22	51	9
Bowring	18	3	2	13	26	69	8
Temple Bar Res.	18	2	2	14	46	61	6

Division Three	P	W	D	L	F	A	Pts
Morgan Stanley International	20	17	2	1	109	28	36
Sedgwick	20	16	2	2	95	25	34
Coutts Res.	20	13	1	6	60	42	27
Polytechnic "A"	20	10	4	6	66	49	24
National Westminster Bank "A"	20	10	1	9	59	49	21
Union Bank of Switzerland	20	9	2	9	48	47	20
Gaflac	20	8	2	10	35	57	18
Goldman Sachs	20	7	1	12	29	24	15
Granby Res.	20	5	2	13	37	105	12
Liverpool Victoria Res.	20	4	3	13	41	84	11
Temple Bar 3rd	20	0	2	18	25	94	2

Division Four–11 Teams–won by Morgan Guaranty
Division Five–10 Teams–won by ANZ Banking Group
Division Six–9 Teams–won by British Gas Bromley
Sportsmanship Trophy–won by ANZ Banking

LONDON INSURANCE F.A.

League Merged in London Financial F.A.
Challenge Cup–Liverpool Victoria 5*, Temple Bar 3*
Charity Cup–Liverpool Victoria 1, Granby 0
Junior Cup–Sedgwick 9, Sun Alliance Res. 2
Minor Cup–Cuaco 5th 2, Temple Bar 5th 1
W A Jewell Memorial Trophy (5-a-side)–Winners–Temple Bar, Runners-up–Granby

Representative Matches
London Insurance F.A. 2, Southern Olympian League 2
London Insurance F.A. 1, Bristol Insurance Institute 4
Southern Amateur League "B" 3, London Insurance F.A. 1
United Hospitals 1, London Insurance F.A. 3
Old Boys' League 2, London Insurance F.A. 1
London Banks League 2, London Insurance F.A. "B" 2

LONDON BANKS F.A.

Challenge Cup–Lensbury Res 2, Lloyds Bank 0
Senior Cup–Coutts 1, Morgan Guaranty 0
Senior Plate–Goldman Sachs 5, Salomon Brothers 1
Minor Cup–National Westminster Bank 6th 2, Lloyds Bank 5th
Junior Cup–National Westminster Bank "A" 2, Citibank Res. 1
Junior Plate–Union Bank of Switzerland 3, Chase Manhattan Bank 0
Veterans' Cup–Midland Bank 3, Lensbury 1
Sportsman Cup–Morgan Guaranty 3, Kleinwort Benson 0

Representative Team Results
United Banks

v Stock Exchange	Won 3–1
v Royal Marines	Lost 1–2
v Old Boys' League	Won 2–1

London Banks

v Royal Marines	Lost 2–4
v London Insurance F.A. "B"	Drawn 2-2

STOCK EXCHANGE F.A.

Representative Matches
Stock Exchange F.A. 0, Essex Sunday Corinthians 2
Stock Exchange F.A. 4, United Hospitals 1
United Banks 3, Stock Exchange F.A. 1
Stock Exchange F.A. 4, Independent Sunday League 4
Stock Exchange F.A. 0, London Legal League 2
Southern Amateur League "B" 3, Stock Exchange F.A. 0
Stock Exchange F.A. 1, South Essex Sunday League 6

Annual European Tournament–Amsterdam 1994
Stock Exchange F.A. 0, Paris Bourse 1
Stock Exchange F.A. 4, Dusseldorf Bourse 5

OLD BOYS' LEAGUE

Premier Division	P	W	D	L	F	A	Pts
Old Ignatians	20	14	4	2	54	19	32
Cardinal Manning Old Boys	20	13	3	4	50	26	29
Old Meadonians	20	13	2	5	45	16	28
Glyn Old Boys	20	9	5	6	38	28	23
Old Aloysians	20	7	6	7	34	28	20
Old Hamptonians	20	8	4	8	35	41	20
Chertsey Old Salesians	20	9	2	9	32	41	20
Old Tenisonians	20	6	4	10	21	32	16
Old Danes	20	4	5	11	28	49	13
Old Wilsonians	20	4	2	14	20	46	10
Old Tiffinians	20	4	1	15	21	52	9

Senior Division One	P	W	D	L	F	A	Pts
Old Tenisonians Res.	18	13	2	3	33	16	28
Clapham Old Xaverians	18	12	2	4	47	32	26
Phoenix Old Boys	18	9	6	3	43	27	24
Old Isleworthians	18	9	2	7	38	35	20
Old Edmontonians	18	6	5	7	37	39	17
Latymer Old Boys	18	7	2	9	36	34	16
Old Salvatorians	18	6	3	9	25	25	15
Old Suttonians	18	6	3	9	35	37	15
Old Wokingians	18	5	4	9	25	35	14
Enfield Old Grammarians	18	2	1	15	17	56	5

Senior Division Two	P	W	D	L	F	A	Pts
Old Kingsburians	20	14	2	4	70	20	30
Shene Old Grammarians	20	14	2	4	55	30	30
Old Vaughanians	20	12	3	5	58	30	27
Mill Hill County Old Boys	20	11	4	5	59	39	26
Old Tollingtonians	20	9	2	9	45	35	20
Old Minchendenians	20	8	3	9	38	47	19
Old Ignatians Res.	20	8	1	11	41	54	17
Old Meadonians Res.	20	7	3	10	31	44	17
Old Southallians	20	5	4	11	44	63	14
John Fisher Old Boys	20	4	3	13	32	68	11
Leyton County Old Boy	20	4	1	15	29	72	7*

Senior Division Three	P	W	D	L	F	A	Pts
Old Manorians	20	16	4	0	62	15	36
Old Camdenians	20	12	6	2	39	20	30
Old Highburians	20	7	6	7	46	39	20
Chorley Wood Danes Old Boys	20	6	8	6	44	39	20
Old Hamptonians Res.	20	9	2	9	30	32	20
Phoenix Old Boys Res.	20	6	7	7	46	42	19
Old Greenfordians	20	7	3	10	37	46	17
Old Alpertonians	20	6	5	9	29	49	17
Old Addeyans	20	6	4	10	47	46	16
Old Dorkinians	20	6	3	11	29	49	15
Old Aloysians Res.	20	3	4	13	25	57	10

** 2 points deducted for breach of rule*

Intermediate Division North–12 Teams–won by Latymer Old Boys Res.
Intermediate Division South–12 Teams–won by Glyn Old Boys Res.
Division One North–10 Teams–won by Old Camdenians Res.
Division One South–11 Teams–won by Old Tiffinians Res.
Division One West–11 Teams–won by Mill Hill County Old Boys Res.
Division Two North–8 Teams–won by London Hospital Old Boys
Division Two South–11 Teams–won by Old Sedcopians Res.
Division Two West–11 Teams–won by Old Vaughanians 3rd
Division Three North–9 Teams–won by Latymer Old Boys 4th
Division Three South–11 Teams–won by Old Strandians
Division Three West–10 Teams–won by Old Magdalenians
Division Four North–9 Teams–won by Old Edmontonians 4th
Division Four South–11 Teams–won by Clapham Old Xaverians 4th
Division Four West–11 Teams–won by Old Southallians 3rd
Division Five North–9 Teams–won by Davenant Wanderers Old Boys
Division Five South–9 Teams–won by Old St. Mary's Res.
Division Five West–9 Teams–won by Old Salvatorians 6th
Division Six North–9 Teams–won by Old Egbertians 3rd
Division Six South–9 Teams–won by Old Tiffinians 5th
Division Six West–10 Teams–won by Old Southallians 4th Boys 4th
Division Seven North–9 Teams–won by Old Wood Green Old Boys 4th
Division Seven South–10 Teams–won by Old Addeyans 4th
Division Seven West–10 Teams–won by Phoenix Old Boys 5th
Division Eight North–9 Teams–won by Q. Mary College Old Boys Res.
Division Eight South–10 Teams–won by Chertsey Old Salesians 6th
Division Eight West–9 Teams–won by Phoenix Old Boys 6th
Division Nine South–8 Teams–won by Old Wilsonians 7th
Division Nine West–7 Teams–won by Old Salvatorians 10th

SOUTHERN AMATEUR LEAGUE

Senior Section

First Division	P	W	D	L	F	A	Pts
South Bank Polytechnic	22	15	4	3	49	23	34
Crouch End Vampires	22	9	11	2	39	24	29
Norsemen	22	9	6	7	40	30	24
Civil Service	22	10	4	8	36	41	24
National Westminster Bank	22	9	5	8	42	28	23
Old Actonians Association	22	11	1	10	35	32	23
Old Esthameians	22	7	8	7	38	34	22
Winchmore Hill	22	8	4	10	31	34	20
Midland Bank	22	8	4	10	32	44	20
West Wickham	22	4	10	8	34	40	18
Carshalton	22	7	4	11	37	49	18
Lensbury	22	4	1	17	30	64	9

Second Division	P	W	D	L	F	A	Pts
East Barnet Old Grammarians	22	16	4	2	59	22	36
Old Latymerians	22	14	4	4	48	27	32
Polytechnic	22	12	4	6	54	30	28
Old Stationers	22	12	3	7	50	36	27
Alexandra Park	22	9	8	5	61	38	26
Lloyds Bank	22	9	6	7	34	31	24
Old Parkonians	22	8	5	9	35	33	21
Old Bromleians	22	8	5	9	41	47	21
Kew Association	22	8	3	11	44	46	19
Broomfield	22	7	5	10	41	46	19
Southgate Olympic	22	2	2	18	24	93	6
Ibis	22	0	5	17	22	64	5

Third Division	P	W	D	L	F	A	Pts
Old Parmiterians	22	14	5	3	58	17	33
Old Westminster Citizens	22	14	5	3	56	29	33
Cuaco	22	14	3	5	68	33	31
Bank of England	22	12	6	4	50	28	30
Barclays Bank	22	12	5	5	52	27	29
Brentham	22	9	5	8	49	49	23
Old Lyonians	22	9	4	9	51	41	22
Alleyn Old Boys	22	7	5	10	40	55	19
Old Salesians	22	6	6	10	43	45	18
Merton	22	5	3	14	36	56	13
Reigate Priory	22	2	3	17	27	80	7
Royal Bank of Scotland	22	2	2	18	19	89	6

Reserve Teams Section
First Division–12 Teams–won by Old Esthameians Res.
Second Division–12 Teams–won by Old Parmiterians Res.
Third Division–12 Teams–won by Old Salesians Res.
3rd Teams Section
First Division–12 Teams–won by National Westminster Bank 3rd
Second Division–12 Teams–won by Old Parmiterians 3rd
Third Division–12 Teams–won by Crouch End Vampires 3rd
4th Teams Section
First Division–12 Teams–won by Old Stationers 4th
Second Division–12 Teams–won by Old Parmiterians 4th
Third Division–12 Teams–won by Old Parkonians 4th
5th Teams Section
First Division–10 Teams–won by National Westminster Bank 5th
Second Division–10 Teams–won by Old Parmiterians 5th
Third Division–10 Teams–won by Old Westminster Citizens 5th
6th Teams Section
First Division–10 Teams–won by Civil Service 6th
Second Division–9 Teams–won by West Wickham 6th
Third Division–8 Teams–won by Lloyds Bank 6th
7th Teams Section
First Division–9 Teams–won by Winchmore Hill 7th
Second Division–9 Teams–won by Old Stationers 7th
8th Teams Section
First Division–7 Teams–won by Old Parmiterians 8th
Second Division–6 Teams–won by Barclays Bank 8th
9th and 10th Teams Section
First Division–12 Teams–won by Old Parmiterians 9th

MIDLAND AMATEUR LEAGUE

Division One	*P*	*W*	*D*	*L*	*F*	*A*	*Pts*
Sherwood Amateurs	20	15	5	0	73	22	35
Lady Bay	20	14	3	4	89	30	31
Old Elizabethans	20	11	4	5	62	19	26
Magdala Amateurs	20	11	4	5	57	43	26
Derbyshire Amateurs	20	8	3	8	39	50	19
Bassingfield	20	6	6	8	49	53	18
Peoples College	20	7	3	10	35	51	17
Brunts Old Boys	20	8	1	11	36	54	17
Old Bemrosians	20	4	4	12	34	60	12
Kirton B. W.	20	3	4	13	27	79	10
Nottinghamshire	20	2	5	13	20	60	9

Division Two	*P*	*W*	*D*	*L*	*F*	*A*	*Pts*
F.C. Toton	20	13	3	4	48	28	29
Magdala Amateurs Res.	20	12	4	4	48	29	28
Ilkeston Electric	20	12	3	5	54	42	27
Chilwell	20	10	4	6	46	39	24
Old Elizabethans Res.	20	8	7	5	61	46	23
Nottingham Univ. Postgraduates	20	9	5	6	46	46	23
Woodborough United	20	7	3	10	49	51	17
Sherwood Amateurs Res.	20	5	6	9	48	48	16
Tibshelf Old Boys	20	7	1	12	38	61	15
County Nalgo	20	3	5	12	32	48	11
Beeston Old Boys Assn.	20	2	3	15	51	83	7

Division Three–12 Teams–won by–Keyworth A.F.C.
Division Four–10 Teams–won by–Derbyshire Amateurs 3rd.
Senior Cup—won by–Old Bemrosians
Intermediate Cup—won by–Sherwood Amateurs 3rd.
Minor Cup—won by–Old Elizabethans 3rd.
Challenge Trophy—won by–Old Elizabethans
Division Two Challenge Cup—won by–Magdala Amateurs Res.
Division Three Challenge Cup—won by–Keyworth A.F.C.
Division Four Challenge Cup—won by–Derbyshire Amateurs 3rd.
Supplementary Cup—won by–Tibshelf Old Boys Res.
H.B. Poole Trophy—won by–Sherwood Amateurs

HEREWARD SPORTS UNITED COUNTIES FOOTBALL LEAGUE

	P	*W*	*D*	*L*	*F*	*A*	*Pts*
Rothwell	42	34	3	5	114	38	105
Stotfold	42	31	5	6	114	48	98
Northampton Spencer	42	26	8	8	99	55	86
Cogenhoe	42	25	6	11	93	55	81
Raunds	42	24	8	10	93	55	80
Mirrless Blackstone	42	21	8	13	83	60	71
Long Buckby	42	19	13	10	83	56	70
Boston	42	21	6	15	89	56	69
Eynesbury	42	18	13	11	104	63	67
Holbeach	42	18	8	16	80	81	62
S & L Corby	42	18	7	17	67	80	61
Potton	42	16	9	17	74	65	57
Bourne	42	16	9	17	87	81	57
Spalding	42	15	10	17	71	68	55
Newport Pagnell	42	14	11	17	52	64	53
Wellingborough	42	10	11	21	62	95	41
Desborough	42	12	5	25	70	105	41
Wootton	42	11	7	24	65	86	40
Stamford	42	11	6	25	56	80	39
Daventry	42	10	5	27	47	95	35
Kempston	42	4	10	28	39	81	22
Brackley	42	2	4	36	41	216	10

JEWSON WESSEX LEAGUE

	P	*W*	*D*	*L*	*F*	*A*	*Pts*
Wimborne Town	42	34	5	3	126	41	107
Andover	42	27	8	7	137	48	89
AFC Lymington	42	27	5	10	83	33	86
Thatcham Town	42	25	7	10	96	51	82
Gosport Borough	42	23	10	9	87	55	79
Fleet Town	42	21	9	12	82	48	72
Bemerton Heath Har	42	19	11	12	72	56	68
Brockenhurst	42	17	12	13	70	64	63
BAT	42	17	10	15	66	66	61
Christchurch	42	15	13	14	55	58	58
Bournemouth	42	16	6	20	67	78	54
Ryde Sports	42	14	10	18	61	77	52
Portsmouth RN	42	13	10	19	59	78	49
East Cowes Vics	42	14	7	21	78	114	49
Eastleigh	42	12	12	18	47	54	48
Downton	42	12	10	20	59	82	46
Horndean	42	13	6	23	56	95	45
Petersfield Town	42	11	7	24	64	96	40
Aerostructures S&S	42	11	6	25	41	84	39
Swanage & Herston	42	10	7	25	53	89	37
AFC Totton	42	9	9	24	43	90	36
Whitchurch United	42	11	2	29	51	96	35

HIGHLAND LEAGUE

	P	*W*	*D*	*L*	*F*	*A*	*Pts*
Huntly	34	27	4	3	95	21	85
Caledonian	34	20	7	7	80	44	67
Ross County	34	21	4	9	80	51	67
Cove Rangers	34	20	4	10	89	46	64
Lossiemouth	34	19	6	9	74	45	63
Elgin City	34	19	6	9	60	33	63
Keith	34	16	6	12	57	40	54
Buckie Thistle	34	16	6	12	54	48	54
Fraserburgh	34	15	8	11	52	36	53
Brora Rangers	34	13	9	12	60	61	48
Peterhead	34	12	8	14	55	56	44
Clachnacuddin	34	11	7	16	49	60	40
Forres Mechanics	34	11	6	17	56	67	39
Deveronvale	34	7	8	19	46	84	29
Inverness Thistle	34	6	9	19	38	62	27
Fort William	34	8	3	23	26	78	27
Nairn County	34	6	3	25	30	114	21
Rothes	34	4	6	24	42	97	18

UNIVERSITY FOOTBALL 1993–94

UNIVERSITY MATCH

(26 March 1994, at Craven Cottage, Fulham)
Oxford 5, Cambridge 0

Oxford: P. Hazlewood; J. Dunning, S. Smith, A. Smith, H. Campbell, D. Willis, E. Ellidge (C. Mills), G. Box, M. Sherrell, C. Hollins (H. Kraft), A. Dechet. *Scorers*: Dechet 2, Hollins, Ellidge, A. Smith.
Cambridge: J. Park; I. Ball, J. McCullough, M. Hargreaves, P. Collins, R. Luke, S. Oestmann, M. Deckers, A. Miller (G. Potts), I. Riggs, R. Taylor (D. Walker).
Referee: P. Vosper.
Oxford won the 100th Varsity match in convincing style. Chris Hollins, son of John Hollins the former Chelsea Player, was outstanding in their attack. Cambridge have won 45 matches, Oxford 40 with 25 drawn.

UNIVERSITY OF LONDON INTER-COLLEGIATE LEAGUE

Premier Division

	P	*W*	*D*	*F*	*L*	*A*	Pts
Royal Holloway College	14	10	1	3	51	23	21
Goldsmiths' College	14	9	2	3	32	22	20
University College	14	9	0	5	44	18	18
King's College	14	8	0	6	24	20	16
London School of Economics	14	6	1	7	27	33	13
Queen Mary Westfield College	14	5	2	7	28	27	12
Imperial College	14	4	2	8	25	46	10
St George's Hospital Medical School	14	0	2	12	15	57	2

Division One

	P	*W*	*D*	*F*	*L*	*A*	Pts
University College Res.	18	15	3	0	52	12	33
Royal Free Hosp. Sch. Med.	18	11	2	5	43	23	24
R. Holloway College Res.	18	10	2	6	50	28	22
Ch. Cross & W'minster Hosp. Med. Sch.	18	8	2	8	31	35	18
U.M.D.S.	18	8	1	9	29	30	17
King's College Hosp. Med. Sch.	18	8	1	9	32	37	17
St. Bartholomew's Hosp. Med. Sch.	18	7	1	10	31	37	15
Univ. Coll. & Middx. Hosp. Med. Sch.	18	6	2	10	24	36	14
Imperial College Res.	18	4	2	12	28	52	10
St Mary's Hospital Med. Sch.	18	4	2	12	19	49	10

Division Two

	P	*W*	*D*	*L*	*F*	*A*	Pts
Queen Mary Westfield College Res.	16	11	4	1	68	29	26
London Sch. Economics Res.	16	12	1	3	56	20	25
University College 3rd	16	8	5	3	38	34	21
R. Holloway College 3rd	16	8	4	4	31	17	20
The R. London Hosp. Med. College	16	8	2	6	52	41	18
King's College Res.	16	5	2	9	40	37	12
Sch. Slavonic & E. Europ'n Studies	16	4	4	8	28	37	12
R. School of Mines	16	3	0	13	13	66	6
King's College 3rd	16	1	2	13	18	63	4

Division Three

	P	*W*	*D*	*L*	*F*	*A*	Pts
Goldsmiths' College Res.	17	13	3	1	51	21	29
Imperial College 3rd	18	11	3	4	69	40	25
University College 4th	18	8	4	6	50	31	20
Queen Mary Westfield College 3rd	18	7	4	7	46	42	18
Royal Veterinary College	18	7	3	8	49	53	17
St George's Hospital Medical School Res.	17	7	2	8	22	40	16
London School of Economic 3rd	18	6	3	9	42	48	15
Goldsmiths' College 3rd	17	4	6	7	28	43	14
R. Free Hospital School of Medicine Res.	17	5	2	10	36	53	12
Imperial College 4th	18	5	0	13	36	58	10

Division Four–10 Teams–won by R. Holloway College 4th
Division Five–9 Teams–won by Queen Mary Westfield College 5th
Division Six–8 Teams–won by R. Holloway College 5th
Challenge Cup Final: R. Holloway College 1 King's College 0

UAU COMMERCIAL UNION CHAMPIONSHIP 1993–94

First XI
First play-off
Northumbria 5, Humber 7
Huddersfield w.o. Liverpool Institute scr.
Liverpool JM 2, Crewe & Alsager 1
Liverpool 2, New College, Durham 3
Leeds Metro 2, Manchester Metro 0
Chester 3, Leeds 2
Teesside 1, Newcastle 5
Loughborough 5, De Mont (Leics) 0
Oxford Brookes 2, Worcester 1
Nottingham 3, Wolves (Wal) 1
Central England 1, Sheffield Hall 2
Swansea Institute 1, Wolves (St Peter) 0
Warwick 1, UWCC 2
Cardiff Institute 5, Trinity College 2
Derby 3, Aberystwyth 6
Bedford 5, Westminster 0
Surrey 0, Bristol 3
London Hospital 3, Cranfield (SHR) 1
Exeter 6, Essex 0
De Mont (MK) 1, Reading 5
Kings 1, Hertfordshire 0
Roehampton 3, Southampton 1
St Mary's Hospital 1, QMW 2
Bournemouth 4, MarJohns 1
Royal Free scr, West Sussex w.o.
Brighton 0, St Mary's College 3
East Anglia w.o. St. Barts scr
West London 6, Goldsmiths 2

SEcond play-off
Humberside 5, Huddersfield 3
Liverpool JM 5, New College, Durham 1
Leeds Metro 1, Chester 3
Newcastle 0, Loughborough 2
Oxford Brookes 0, Nottingham 1
Sheffield Hall 4, Swansea Institute 1
UWCC 3, Cardiff Institute 1
Aberystwyth 4, Bedford 2
Bristol 4, London Hospital 1
Exeter 4, Reading 3
Kings 0, Roehampton 4
QMW 1, Bournemouth 4

QMW 1, Bournemouth 4
West Sussex 5, St Mary's College 0
East Anglia 3, West London Institute 0

Third play-off
Humberside 2, Edinburgh 7
Liverpool JM 3, Strathclyde 1
Chester 2, Loughborough 1
Nottingham 3, Sheffield Hall 1
UWCC 2, Aberystwyth 1
Bristol 2, Exeter 1
Roehampton 0, Bournemouth 1
West Sussex 4, East Anglia 1

Quarter-finals
Edinburgh 4, Liverpool JM 0
Chester 1, Nottingham 0
UWCC 5, Bristol 3
Bournemouth 5, West Sussex 8

Semi-finals
West Sussex 1, UWCC 2
Edinburgh 3, Chester 0

Final
UWCC 1, Edinburgh 2
(*after 3-3 draw*)

Second XI
Final
Cardiff Institute 3, Chester 2 *aet*

Third XI
Final
Birmingham 4, Crewe & Alsager 1

Fourth XI
Final
Liverpool 4, Leeds 4
(*Leeds won 4-3 on penalties*)

WOMEN'S CHAMPIONSHIP

First play-off
Univ Coll Hopsital 1, Essex 8
Westminster 0, RHBNC 19
Cambridge w.o. Kingston scr
Kings 3, Kent 4
Greenwich 1, Exeter 2
Marjohn 0, Brighton 2
Sheffield 9, UWCC 3
Newman 0, Warwick 15
Cheltenham & Gloucester 11, Oxford Brookes 2
Birmingham 8, Wolves (Wal) 0
Cardiff Institute 1, Sheffield Hall 2
Trinity Wales 3, Worcester 2
Bedford 8, UCNW 0
Loughborough w.o. Nene scr
North Cheshire 5, Newcastle 0
Liverpool 4, Hull 0
Leeds Metro w.o. Teesside scr
Ripon York 3, Liverpool Institute 5
Leeds 0, Manchester 7
Crewe & Alsager 6, Liverpool JM 0
Sunderland w.o. Central Lancashire scr.

Second play-off
Essex 0, West of England 8
Roehampton 2, RHBNC 3
Kent 3, Exeter 2
Southampton 1, West London Institute 6
Brighton 22, North London 1
East Anglia 0, Sheffield 22
Warwick 4, Cheltenham & Gloucester 0
Birmingham 3, Sheffield Hall 1
Trinity 1, Bedford 9
Loughborough 4, North Cheshire 0
Liverpool 5, Leeds Metro 3
Liverpool Institute 2, Manchester 4
Crewe & Alsager 7, Sunderland 0

Third play-off
West of England 6, RHBNC 7
Cambridge 4, Kent 3
West London 2, Brighton 7
Sheffield 3, Warwick 2
Birmingham 3, Bedford 2
Loughborough 2, Liverpool 0
(*after 1-1 draw*)
Aberdeen 4, Manchester 3
Crewe & Alsager 3, Glasgow 1

Quarter-finals
RHBNC 0, Cambridge 9
Brighton 6, Sheffield 0
Birmingham 1, Loughborough 4
Aberdeen 1, Crewe & Alsager 7

Semi-finals
Cambridge 2, Crewe & Alsager 5
Brighton 0, Loughborough 3

Final
Loughborough 2, Crewe & Alsager 0

UNIVERSITY OF LONDON F.A. 1993–94

Representative XI Results

Ulysses	Lost	1-4
Old Boys' League	Lost	0-3
Southern Amateur League	Lost	2-4
United Hospitals	Drawn	2-2
Royal Navy XI	Lost	0-5
Arthurian League	Drawn	1-1
Royal Air Force XI	Drawn	2-2
London Legal League	Won	3-2
Army Crusaders	Won	2-1
Southern Olympian League	Lost	1-2
Metropolitan Police	Lost	1-3
Cambridge University	Won	3-1
Middlesex County FA XI	Drawn	1-1
A.F.A.	Won	4-1
Crystal Palace XI	Lost	0-2
Oxford University	Lost	0-2

ADDRESSES

The Football Association: R. H. G. Kelly, F.C.I.S., 16 Lancaster Gate, London W2 3LW

Scotland: J. Farry, 6 Park Gardens, Glasgow G3 7YE. *041-332 6372*

Northern Ireland (Irish FA): D. I. Bowen, 20 Windsor Avenue, Belfast BT9 6EG. *0232-669458*

Wales: A. Evans, 3 Westgate Street, Cardiff, South Glamorgan CF1 1JF. *0222-372325*

Republic of Ireland (FA of Ireland): S. Connolly, 80 Merrion Square South, Dublin 2. *0001-766864*

International Federation (FIFA): S. Blatter, FIFA House, Hitzigweg 11, CH-8032 Zurich, Switzerland. *1-384-9595. Fax: 1-384-9696*

Union of European Football Associations: G. Aigner, Jupiter Strasse 33, PO Box 16, CH-3000 Berne 15, Switzerland. *031-321735. Fax: 031-321838.*

THE LEAGUES

The Premier League: R. N. Parry, 16 Lancaster Gate London, W2 3LW. *071-262 4542*

The Football League: J. D. Dent, F.C.I.S., The Football League, Lytham St Annes, Lancs FY8 1JG. *0253-729421. Telex 67675*

The Scottish League: P. Donald, 188 West Regent Street, Glasgow G2 4RY. *041-248 384415*

The Irish League: H. Wallace, 87 University Street, Belfast BT7 1HP. *0232-242888*

Football League of Ireland: E. Morris, 80 Merrion Square South, Dublin 2. *0001-765120*

GM Vauxhall Conference: P. D. Hunter, 24 Barnehurst Road, Bexleyheath, Kent DA7 6EZ. *0322-521116*

Central League: D. J. Grimshaw, 118 St Stephens Road, Deepdale, Preston, Lancs PR1 6TD. *0772-795386*

North West Counties League: M. Darby, 87 Hillary Road, Hyde, Cheshire SK14 4EB.

Eastern Counties League: C. Lamb, 26 Dunthorpe Road, Clacton, Essex CO16 8UJ. *0255 436398*

Football Combination: N. Chamberlain, 2 Vicarage Close, Old Costessey, Norwich NR8 5DL. *0603-743998*

Hellenic League: M. J. Jenkins, 3 Leamington Drive, Faringdon, Oxon SN7 7JZ. *0367 240042*

Kent League: R. Vintner, The Thatched Barn, Catt's Wood Road, Lower Hardres, Canterbury, Kent CT4 5PG

Lancashire Amateur League: R. G. Bowker, 13 Shores Green Drive, Wincham, Northwich, Cheshire CW9 6EE. *061-480 7723*

Lancashire Football League: J. W. Howarth, 465 Whalley Road, Clapton-le-Moors, Accrington, Lancs BB5 5RP. *0254-398957*

Leicestershire Senior League: D. Jamieson, 48 King Georges Road, Loughborough, Leics LE11 2PA. *0509 263411*

London Spartan: D. Cordell, 44 Greenleas, Waltham Abbey, Essex. *Lea Valley 712428*

Manchester League: F. J. Fitzpatrick, 102 Victoria Road, Stretford, Manchester. *061-865 2726*

Midland Combination: L. W. James, 175 Barnet Lane, Kingswinford, Brierley Hill, West Midlands. *Kingswinford 3459*

Mid-Week Football League: N. A. S. Matthews, Cedar Court, Steeple Aston, Oxford. *0869-40347*

Northern Premier: R. D. Bayley, 22 Woburn Drive, Hale, Altrincham, Cheshire. *061-980 7007*

Northern Intermediate League: G. Thompson, Clegg House, 253 Pitsmoor Road, Sheffield S3 9AQ. *0742-27817*

Northern League: T. Golightly, 85 Park Road North, Chester-le-Street, Co Durham D43 3SA. *091-388-2056*

North Midlands League: G. Thompson, 7 Wren Park Close, Ridgway, Sheffield.

Peterborough and District League: M. J. Croson, 44 Storrington Way, Werrington, Peterborough, Cambs PE4 6QP.

Vauxhall League: N. Robinson, 226 Rye Lane, Peckham SE15 4NL. *081-653 3903*

Southern Amateur League: S. J. Lucas, 23 Beaufort Close, North Weald Bassett, Epping, Essex CM16 6JZ. *037882-3932*

South-East Counties League: A. Leather, 66 Green Acres, Chichester Road, Croydon, Surrey CR0 5UX. *081-681 7100*

Southern League: D. J. Strudwick, 11 Welland Close, Durrington, Worthing, West Sussex BN13 3NR. *0903-67788*

South Midlands League: M. Mitchell, 26 Leighton Court, Dunstable, Beds LU6 1EW. *0582-67291*

South Western League:

United Counties League: R. Gamble, 8 Bostock Avenue, Northampton. *0604-37766*

Wearside League: B. Robson, 12 Deneside, Howden-le-Wear, Crook, Co. Durham DL15 8JR. *0388-762034*

Western League: M. E. Washer, 16 Heathfield Road, Nailsea, Bristol BS19 1EB.

The Welsh League: K. J. Tucker, 16 The Parade, Merthyr Tydfil, Mid Glamorgan CF47 0ET. *0685-723884*

West Midlands Regional League: N. R. Juggins, 14 Badger Way, Blackwell, Bromsgrove, Worcs B60 1EX.

West Yorkshire League: W. Keyworth, 2 Hill Court Grove, Bramley, Yorks L13 2AP. *Pudsey 74465*

Northern Counties (East): B. Wood, 6 Restmore Avenue, Guiseley, Nr Leeds LS20 9DG. *0943-874558 (home); Bradford 29595 (9 a.m. to 5 p.m.)*

COUNTY FOOTBALL ASSOCIATIONS

Bedfordshire: P. D. Brown, 19 Lambs Close, Dunstable, LU5 4QA *0582-668013*

Berks and Bucks: W. S. Gosling, 15a London Street, Faringdon, Oxon SN7 8AG. *0367-242099*

Birmingham County: M. Pennick, County FA Offices, Rayhall Lane, Great Barr, Birmingham B43 6JE. *021-357 4278*

Cambridgeshire: R. E. Rogers, 20 Aingers Road, Histon, Cambridge CB4 4JP. *022023-2803*

Cheshire: A. Collins, The Cottage, Hartford Moss Rec Centre, Winnington, Northwich CW8 4BG.

Cornwall: J. M. Ryder, Penare, 16 Gloweth View, Truro, Cornwall TR1 3JZ.

Cumberland: R. Johnson, 72 Victoria Road, Workington, Cumbria CA14 2QT. *0900-3979*

Derbyshire: K. Compton, The Grandstand, Moorways Stadium, Moor Lane, Derby DE2 8FB. *0332-361422*

Devon County: C. Squirrel, 51a Wolborough Street, Newton Abbot, Devon TQ12 IJQ. *0626 332077*

Dorset County: P. Hough, County Ground, Blandford Close, Hamworthy, Poole, Dorset BH15 4BF. *0202-682375*

Durham: J. R. Walsh, 'Codeslaw', Ferens Park, Durham DH1 1JZ. *0385-48653*

East Riding County: D. R. Johnson, 52 Bethune Ave, Hull HU4 7EJ. *0482-641458*

Essex County: T. Alexander, 31 Mildmay Road, Chelmsford, Essex CM2 0DN. *0245-357727*

Gloucestershire: E. J. Marsh, 46 Douglas Road, Horfield, Bristol BS7 0JD. *0272-519435*

Guernsey: D. Dorey, Haut Regard, St. Clair Hill, St. Sampson's, Guernsey, GY2 4DT, CI. *0481-46231*

Hampshire: R. G. Barnes, 8 Ashwood Gardens, off Winchester Road, Southampton SO9 2UA. *0703-766884*

Herefordshire: E. R. Prescott, 7 Kirkland Close, Hampton Park, Hereford HR1 1XP. *0432-51134*

Hertfordshire: R. G. Kibble, 4 The Wayside, Leverstock Green, Hemel Hempstead, Herts HP3 8NR. *0442-255918*

Huntingdonshire: M. M. Armstrong, 1 Chapel End, Great Giddings, Huntingdon. Cambs PE17 5NP. *08323-262*
Isle of Man: Mrs A. Garrett, 60 Ballagarey Road, Glen Vale, IOM. *0624-676349*
Jersey: C. Tostevin, Wellesley, Greve Dazette St Clement, Jersey JE2 6SA. *0534-24929*
Kent County: K. T. Masters, 69 Maidstone Road, Chatham, Kent ME4 6DT. *0634-43824*
Lancashire: J. Kenyon, 31a Wellington St, St John's, Blackburn, Lancs BB1 8AU. *0254-64333*
Leicestershire and Rutland: R. E. Barston, Holmes Park, Dog and Gun Lane, Whetstone, Leicester LE8 3LJ. *0533-867828*
Lincolnshire: F. S. Richardson, PO Box 26, 12 Dean Road, Lincoln LN2 4DP. *0522-24917*
Liverpool County: F. L. J. Hunter, 23 Greenfield Road, Old Swann, Liverpool L13 3EN. *051-526-9515*
London: R. S. Ashford, Aldworth Grove, London SE13 6HY. *081-690 9626*
Manchester County: F. Brocklehurst, Sports Complex, Brantingham Road, Chorlton, Manchester M21 1TG. *061-881 0299*
Middlesex County: P. J. Clayton, 39 Roxborough Road, Harrow, Middx HA1 1NS. *081-424 8524*
Norfolk County: R. Kiddell, 153 Middletons Lane, Hellesdon, Norwich, Norfolk NR6 5SF. *0603 488222*
Northamptonshire: B. Walden, 2 Duncan Close, Red House Road, Moulton Park, Northampton NN3 1WL. *0604-670741*
North Riding County: P. Kirby, 284 Linthorpe Road, Middlesbrough TS1 3QU. *0642-224585*
Northumberland: R. E. Maughan, Seymour House, 10 Brenkley Way, Blezard Bus Park, Seaton Burn, Newcastle upon Tyne NE13 6DT. *091-297 0101*
Nottinghamshire: W. T. Annable, 7 Clarendon Street, Nottingham NG1 5HS. *0602-418954*
Oxfordshire: P. J. Ladbrook, 3 Wilkins Road, Cowley, Oxford OX4 2HY. *0865-775432*
Sheffield and Hallamshire: G. Thompson, Clegg House, 5 Onslow Road, Sheffield S11 7AF. *0742-670068*
Shropshire: A. W. Brett, 5 Ebnal Road, Shrewsbury SY2 6PW. *0743-56066*
Somerset & Avon (South): Mrs H. Marchment, 30 North Road, Midsomer Norton, Bath BA3 2QQ. *0761-413176*
Staffordshire: G. S. Brookes, County Showground, Weston Road, Stafford ST18 0DB. *0785-56994*
Suffolk County: W. M. Steward, 2 Millfields, Haughley, Suffolk IP14 3PU. *0449-673481*
Surrey County: A. P. Adams, 321 Kingston Road, Leatherhead, Surrey KT22 7TU. *0372 373543*
Sussex County: D. M. Worsfold, County Office, Culver Road, Lancing, Sussex BN15 9AX. *0903-753547*
Westmorland: J. B. Fleming, Beezon Chambers, off Sandes Avenue, Kendal, Cumbria. *0539-730946*
West Riding County: R. Carter, Unit 3, Low Mills Road, Wortley, Leeds LS12 4UY. *0532-310101*
Wiltshire: E. M. Parry, 44 Kennet Avenue, Swindon SN2 3LG. *0793-29036*
Worcestershire: M. R. Leggett Fermain, 12 Worcester Road, Eyesham, Worcs WR11 4JV. *0905-612336*

OTHER USEFUL ADDRESSES

Amateur Football Alliance: W. P. Goss, 55 Islington Park Street, London N1 1QB. *071-359 3493*
English Schools FA: M. R. Berry, 4a Eastgate Street, Stafford ST16 2NN. *0785-51142*
Oxford University: M. H. Matthews, University College, Oxford OX1 4BH.
Cambridge University: Dr A. J. Little, St Catherine's College, Cambridge CB2 1RL.
Army: Major T. C. Knight, Clayton Barracks, Aldershot, Hants GU11 2BG. *0252-24431 Ext 3571*
Royal Air Force: Group Capt P. W. Hilton, 15 Western Court, Western Road, Cheltenham, Glos GL50 3RH. *0242 255215*
Royal Navy: Lt-Cdr J. Danks, R.N. Sports Office, H.M.S. Temeraire, Portsmouth, Hants PO1 4QS. *0705-822351 Ext 22671*
Universities Athletic Union: G. Gregory-Jones, Suite 36, London Fruit Exchange, Brushfield Street, London E1 6EU. *071-247 3066*
Central Council of Physical Recreation: General Secretary, 70 Brompton Road, London SW3 1HE. *071-584 6651*
British Olympic Association: 6 John Prince's Street, London W1M 0DH. *071-408 2029*
National Federation of Football Supporters' Clubs: Chairman: Tony Kershaw, 87 Brookfield Avenue, Loughborough, Leicestershire LE11 3LN. *01509 267643 (and fax)*. Hon Secretary: Mark Agate, "The Stadium", 14 Coombe Close, Lordswood, Chatham, Kent ME5 8NU. *01634 863520 (and fax)*
National Playing Fields Association: Col R. Satterthwaite, O.B.E., 578b Catherine Place, London, SW1.
The Scottish Football Commercial Managers Association: J. E. Hillier (Chairman), c/o Keith FC Promotions Office, 60 Union Street, Keith, Banffshire, Scotland.
Professional Footballers' Association: G. Taylor, 2 Oxford Court, Bishopsgate, Off Lower Mosley Street, Manchester M2 3W2. *061-236 0575*
Referees' Association: W. J. Taylor, Cross Offices, Summerhill, Kingswinford, West Midlands DY6 9JE. *0384-288386*
Women's Football Alliance: Miss H. Jeavons, 9 Wyllyotts Place, Potters Bar, Herts EN6 2JB. *0707 651840*
The Association of Football League Commercial Managers: G. H. Dimbleby, Secretary WBA FC, The Hawthorns, Halford Lane, West Bromwich B71 4LF.
The Association of Football Statisticians: R. J. Spiller, 22 Bretons, Basildon, Essex SS15 5BY. *0268-416020*
The Football Programme Directory: David Stacey, 'The Beeches', 66 Southend Road, Wickford, Essex SS11 8EN.
England Football Supporters Association: Publicity Officer, David Stacey, 66 Southend Road, Wickford, Essex SS11 8EN.
The Football League Executive Staffs Association: PO Box 52, Leamington Spa, Warwickshire.
The Ninety-Two Club: 104 Gilda Crescent, Whitchurch, Bristol BS14 9LD.
Scottish 38 Club: Mark Byatt, 6 Greenfields Close, Loughton, Essex IG10 3HG. *081-508 6088*
The Football Trust: Second Floor, Walkden House, 10 Melton Street, London NW1 2EJ. *071-388 4504*
The Football Supporters Association: PO Box 11, Liverpool L26 1XP. *051-709-2594.*
Association of Provincial Football Supporters' Clubs in London: Tina A. Robertson, 45 Durham Avenue, Heston, Middlesex TW5 0HG. *081-843-9854*
World Association of Friends of English Football: PO Box 2221, D-30022 Hannover, Germany. *0511-885616*

FOOTBALL AND THE LAW

Football and the Law throughout 1993–94 carried on from where it left off in the close season, with Tottenham Hotspur either in court or shadowed by the wings of the legal eagles. A final curtain call came after the season and commercial ball were over, in an FA Tribunal council chamber.

Furthermore, no greater contrast to all this surfaced when death scythed away two creators of the romance that once was Spurs. Arthur Rowe, push and run inventor of the simple game; coach to the Oxbridge Pegasus and the no less immortal Danny Blanchflower, the great Bill Nicholson's counterpoint for the glory game double, which has receded into time after more than 30 years.

In Parliament, the government ministers who double up sport and physical recreation with a jigsaw of other portfolios, extended the Taylor Report deadline for all-seater stadia to high profile clubs, but upset the likes of battling Barnsley, left to squeeze their die-hard Tykes into a 9000 pint pot. In France, the Football Federation sustained a Marseille saga by withdrawing for an unspecified period the club President Bernard Tapie's director's licence, and banned for life its general manager, Jean-Pierre Bernès. Off the field, after a spectator at the World Cup qualifier between Wales and Romania had been killed by a rocket at Cardiff Arms Park in November, two offenders were sentenced to three-year prison sentences for manslaughter.

On the field activities resulted in out of court settlements in Scotland reported in legal journals as *Murray v Dolan and Motherwell FC* and *Durrant v Simpson and Aberdeen FC*; and the Procurator-Fiscal decided to put the boot in against the record transfer fee holder Duncan Ferguson—Dundee United to Rangers. This for allegedly head-butting a Raith Rovers opponent, a case yet to be tried at the time of writing during the World Cup.

FIFA's elimination from the World Cup of the criminal violence which destroyed Pele's participation during the 1966 competition for which no offender was punished, stemmed from a little publicised in legal form set of Specific Instructions for Referees after directions from the International Football Association Board (the game's Parliament), as distinct from amendments to the Laws of the Game, after its AGM at FIFA House, Zurich, Switzerland on 5 March 1994. These concerned details of the *reckless challenges* about elbows and *kicking an opponent* based on *tackling from behind* with little or no attempt to play the ball.

They became binding throughout the world as *from 1 July 1994*; but the said International Football Association Board gave FIFA permission to implement them as from the first World Cup match on 17 June 1994.

In the last week of the same competition, a *Guardian* newspaper American report from John Duncan recorded how a Bangladeshi fan of Diego Maradona, a lawyer Anwarul Wadud, was suing the FIFA President Joao Havelange in the Dacca courts, claiming that he had banned illegally the Argentine as a decision which was "undesirable and an undescribable sad news", of which the *Guardian* commented, "an opinion not widely held outside Argentina and Bangladesh".

Nearer home, I must declare an interest as one of Paul Elliott's barristers to record how the namesake of one of England's greatest centre-forwards in the Corinthian and cricketing G.O. Smith tradition, known to Arsenal and Hampshire cricket fans as Ted Drake, Mr Justice Drake, rejected his claim for *negligence* against Dean Saunders and Liverpool FC for injuries suffered from a tussle for the ball at Liverpool on 5 September 1992. In a near 90-minutes judgment now in 40 typescript pages he explained, consistent with the Scottish reported cases settled out of court,

> *"Unless and until some workable alternative is devised, it would be wholly wrong to prevent an injured player from claiming compensation in the courts."*

Indeed, the Criminal Injuries Compensation Board encourages victims of alleged criminal foul play (which was *never* alleged against Saunders or Liverpool) to report such misconduct to the police; and if FIFA's Instructions do not work, violent offenders, as in the World Cup, should beware. The Procurator-Fiscal in Scotland and Crown Prosecution Service are on the red card alert.

EDWARD GRAYSON

President, British Association for Sport and Law

OTHER AWARDS 1993–94

FOOTBALLER OF THE YEAR

The Football Writers' Association Award for the Footballer of the Year went to Alan Shearer of Blackburn Rovers and England.

Past Winners
1947–48 Stanley Matthews (Blackpool), 1948–49 Johnny Carey (Manchester U), 1949–50 Joe Mercer (Arsenal), 1950–51 Harry Johnston (Blackpool), 1951–52 Billy Wright (Wolverhampton W), 1952–53 Nat Lofthouse (Bolton W), 1953–54 Tom Finney (Preston NE), 1954–55 Don Revie (Manchester C), 1955–56 Bert Trautmann (Manchester C), 1956–57 Tom Finney (Preston NE), 1957–58 Danny Blanchflower (Tottenham H), 1958–59 Syd Owen (Luton T), 1959–60 Bill Slater (Wolverhampton W), 1960–61 Danny Blanchflower (Tottenham H), 1961–62 Jimmy Adamson (Burnley), 1962–63 Stanley Matthews (Stoke C), 1963–64 Bobby Moore (West Ham U), 1964–65 Bobby Collins (Leeds U), 1965–66 Bobby Charlton (Manchester U), 1966–67 Jackie Charlton (Leeds U), 1967–68 George Best (Manchester U), 1968–69 Dave Mackay (Derby Co) shared with Tony Book (Manchester C), 1969–70 Billy Bremner (Leeds U), 1970–71 Frank McLintock (Arsenal), 1971–72 Gordon Banks (Stoke C), 1972–73 Pat Jennings (Tottenham H), 1973–74 Ian Callaghan (Liverpool), 1974–75 Alan Mullery (Fulham), 1975–76 Kevin Keegan (Liverpool), 1976–77 Emlyn Hughes (Liverpool), 1977–78 Kenny Burns (Nottingham F), 1978–79 Kenny Dalglish (Liverpool), 1979–80 Terry McDermott (Liverpool), 1980–81 Frans Thijssen (Ipswich T), 1981–82 Steve Perryman (Tottenham H), 1982–83 Kenny Dalglish (Liverpool), 1983–84 Ian Rush (Liverpool), 1984–85 Neville Southall (Everton), 1985–86 Gary Lineker (Everton), 1986–87 Clive Allen (Tottenham H), 1987–88 John Barnes (Liverpool), 1988–89 Steve Nicol (Liverpool), 1989–90 John Barnes (Liverpool), 1990–91 Gordon Strachan (Leeds U), 1991–92 Gary Lineker (Tottenham H), 1992–93 Chris Waddle (Sheffield W).

THE PFA AWARDS 1994

Player of the Year: Eric Cantona (Manchester U).
Previous Winners: 1974 Norman Hunter (Leeds U); 1975 Colin Todd (Derby Co); 1976 Pat Jennings (Tottenham H); 1977 Andy Gray (Aston Villa); 1978 Peter Shilton (Nottingham F); 1979 Liam Brady (Arsenal); 1980 Terry McDermott (Liverpool); 1981 John Wark (Ipswich T); 1982 Kevin Keegan (Southampton); 1983 Kenny Dalglish (Liverpool); 1984 Ian Rush (Liverpool); 1985 Peter Reid (Everton); 1986 Gary Lineker (Everton); 1987 Clive Allen (Tottenham H); 1988 John Barnes (Liverpool); 1989 Mark Hughes (Manchester U); 1990 David Platt (Aston Villa); 1991 Mark Hughes (Manchester U); 1992 Gary Pallister (Manchester U); Paul McGrath (Aston Villa).

Young Player of the Year: Andy Cole (Newcastle U).
Previous Winners: 1974 Kevin Beattie (Ipswich T); 1975 Mervyn Day (West Ham U); 1976 Peter Barnes (Manchester C); 1977 Andy Gray (Aston Villa); 1978 Tony Woodcock (Nottingham F); 1979 Cyrille Regis (WBA); 1980 Glenn Hoddle (Tottenham H); 1981 Gary Shaw (Aston Villa); 1982 Steve Moran (Southampton); 1983 Ian Rush (Liverpool); 1984 Paul Walsh (Luton T); 1985 Mark Hughes (Manchester U); 1986 Tony Cottee (West Ham U); 1987 Tony Adams (Arsenal); 1988 Paul Gascoigne (Tottenham H); 1989 Paul Merson (Arsenal); 1990 Matthew Le Tissier (Southampton); 1991 Lee Sharpe (Manchester U); 1992 Ryan Giggs (Manchester U); 1993 Ryan Giggs (Manchester U).

Merit Award: Billy Bingham.
Previous Winners: 1974 Bobby Charlton CBE, Cliff Lloyd OBE; 1975 Denis Law; 1976 George Eastham OBE; 1977 Jack Taylor OBE; 1978 Bill Shankly OBE; 1979 Tom Finney OBE; 1980 Sir Matt Busby CBE; 1981 John Trollope MBE; 1982 Joe Mercer OBE; 1983 Bob Paisley OBE; 1984 Bill Nicholson; 1985 Ron Greenwood; 1986 The 1966 England World Cup team, Sir Alf Ramsey, Harold Shepherdson; 1987 Sir Stanley Matthews; 1988 Billy Bonds MBE; 1989 Nat Lofthouse; 1990 Peter Shilton; 1991 Tommy Hutchison; 1992 Brian Clough; 1993 the 1968 Manchester United team.

THE SCOTTISH PFA AWARDS 1994

Player of the Year: Premier Division: Mark Hateley (Rangers); First Division: Richard Cadette (Falkirk); Second Division: Andy Thomson (QoS).

Previous Winners: 1978 Derek Johnstone (Rangers); 1979 Paul Hegarty (Dundee U); 1980 Davie Provan (Celtic); 1981 Sandy Clark (Airdrieonians); 1982 Mark McGhee (Aberdeen); 1983 Charlie Nicholas (Celtic); 1984 Willie Miller (Aberdeen); 1985 Jim Duffy (Morton); 1986 Richard Gough (Dundee U); 1987 Brian McClair (Celtic); 1988 Paul McStay (Celtic); 1989 Theo Snelders (Aberdeen); 1990 Jim Bett (Aberdeen); 1991 Paul Elliott (Celtic); 1993 Ally McCoist (Rangers); 1993 Andy Goram (Rangers).

Young Player of the Year: Phil O'Donnell (Motherwell).

Previous Winners: 1978 Graeme Payne (Dundee U); 1979 Graham Stewart (Dundee U); 1980 John MacDonald (Rangers); 1981 Francis McAvennie (St Mirren); 1982 Charlie Nicholas (Celtic); 1983 Pat Nevin (Clyde); 1984 John Robertson (Hearts); 1985 Craig Levein (Hearts); 1986 Craig Levein (Hearts); 1987 Robert Fleck (Rangers); 1988 John Collins (Hibernian); 1989 Bill McKinlay (Dundee U); 1990 Scott Crabbe (Hearts); 1991 Eoin Jess (Aberdeen); 1992 Phil O'Donnell (Motherwell); 1993 Eoin Jess (Aberdeen).

SCOTTISH FOOTBALL WRITERS' ASSOCIATION

Player of the Year 1994 – Mark Hateley (Rangers)

1965 **Billy McNeill** (Celtic)
1966 **John Greig** (Rangers)
1967 **Ronnie Simpson** (Celtic)
1968 **Gordon Wallace** (Raith R)
1969 **Bobby Murdoch** (Celtic)
1970 **Pat Stanton** (Hibernian)
1971 **Martin Buchan** (Aberdeen)
1972 **Dave Smith** (Rangers)
1973 **George Connelly** (Celtic)
1974 **Scotland's World Cup Squad**
1975 **Sandy Jardine** (Rangers)
1976 **John Greig** (Rangers)
1977 **Danny McGrain** (Celtic)
1978 **Derek Johnstone** (Rangers)
1979 **Andy Ritchie** (Morton)
1980 **Gordon Strachan** (Aberdeen)
1981 **Alan Rough** (Partick Th)
1982 **Paul Sturrock** (Dundee U)
1983 **Charlie Nicholas** (Celtic)
1984 **Willie Miller** (Aberdeen)
1985 **Hamish McAlpine** (Dundee U)
1986 **Sandy Jardine** (Hearts)
1987 **Brian McClair** (Celtic)
1988 **Paul McStay** (Celtic)
1989 **Richard Gough** (Rangers)
1990 **Alex McLeish** (Aberdeen)
1991 **Maurice Malpas** (Dundee U)
1992 **Ally McCoist** (Rangers)
1993 **Andy Goram** (Rangers)

EUROPEAN FOOTBALLER OF THE YEAR 1993

Roberto Baggio of Juventus and Italy received the annual *France Football* award for European Football of the Year and thus won the honour for the first time. Players with Italian clubs have dominated the competition winning the accolade for six of the last seven years and with ten from twelve since 1982. Baggio was also honoured as FIFA World Player of the Year.

Past winners
1956 **Stanley Matthews** (Blackpool
1957 **Alfredo Di Stefano** (Real Madrid)
1958 **Raymond Kopa** (Real Madrid)
1959 **Alfredo Di Stefano** (Real Madrid)
1960 **Luis Suarez** (Barcelona)
1961 **Omar Sivori** (Juventus)
1962 **Josef Masopust** (Dukla Prague)
1963 **Lev Yashin** (Moscow Dynamo)
1964 **Denis Law** (Manchester United)
1965 **Eusebio** (Benfica)
1966 **Bobby Charlton** (Manchester United)
1967 **Florian Albert** (Ferencvaros)
1968 **George Best** (Manchester United)
1969 **Gianni Rivera** (AC Milan)
1970 **Gerd Muller** (Bayern Munich)
1971 **Johan Cruyff** (Ajax)
1972 **Franz Beckenbauer** (Bayern Munich)
1973 **Johan Cruyff** (Barcelona)
1974 **Johan Cruyff** (Barcelona)
1975 **Oleg Blokhin** (Dynamo Kiev)
1976 **Franz Beckenbauer** (Bayern Munich)
1977 **Allan Simonsen** (Borussia Moenchengladbach)
1978 **Kevin Keegan** (SV Hamburg)
1979 **Kevin Keegan** (SV Hamburg)
1980 **Karl-Heinz Rummenigge** (Bayern Munich)
1981 **Karl-Heinz Rummenigge** (Bayern Munich)
1982 **Paolo Rossi** (Juventus)
1983 **Michel Platini** (Juventus)
1984 **Michel Platini** (Juventus)
1985 **Michel Platini** (Juventus)
1986 **Igor Belanov** (Dynamo Kiev)
1987 **Ruud Gullit** (AC Milan)
1988 **Marco Van Basten** (AC Milan)
1989 **Marco Van Basten** (AC Milan)
1990 **Lothar Matthaus** (Inter-Milan)
1991 **Jean-Pierre Papin** (Marseille)
1992 **Marco Van Basten** (AC Milan)

FA Carling Premiership

Carling Manager of the Month Award Winners 1993/94

The Carling Manager of the Month Award is judged by a panel formed by Carling and representing all sides of the game. It consists of: **Graham Kelly**, chief executive of the FA; **Rick Parry**, chief executive of the FA Carling Premiership; **Steve Coppell**, chief executive of the League Managers Association; **Gordon Taylor**, chief executive of the Professional Footballers Association; **Brian Barwick**, football editor, BBC Sport; **Vic Wakeling**, Head of Football, BSkyB; **Tony Kershaw**, National Federation of Supporters Clubs; **David Lee**, Football Supporters Association; **Alex Montgomery**, chairman of the Football Writers Association; **Trevor East**, deputy controller, sport ITV; and **Neil Midgley**, Referees Association.

August	Alex Ferguson	Manchester United
Setpember	Joe Kinnear	Wimbledon
October	Mike Walker	Norwich City
November	Kevin Keegan	Newcastle United
December	Trevor Francis	Sheffield Wednesday
January	Kenny Dalglish	Blackburn Rovers
February	Joe Royle	Oldham Athletic
March	Joe Kinnear	Wimbledon
April	Joe Kinnear	Wimbledon

Each winner receives a Carling Manager of the Month trophy, a cheque for £750 and a magnum of champagne.

Carling Manager of the Year **Alex Ferguson** **Manchester United**

Joe Kinnear received a special award from his fellow managers in the LMA in recognition of his achievements during the season at Wimbledon.

Carling No.1 Award

The same panel also vote for the winner of the Carling No.1 Award. This is given to the person who has made the greatest contribution to the FA Carling Premiership. The award is open to anyone connected with the FA Carling Premiership.

Pre-season **Steve Bruce** Manchester United
Leading Manchester United to their first title in over 25 years.

August **David Elleray** Referee
Expert handling of Manchester United's thrilling 2-1 victory at Aston Villa.

September **Efan Ekoku** Norwich City
Scoring four goals in Norwich City's 5-1 victory at Everton.

October **Matthew Le Tissier** Southampton
Superb performances in the games against Newcastle United and Liverpool, scoring four outstanding goals.

November **Newcastle United Fans**
In recognition of the club's huge and passionate support.

December **Gary Mabbutt** Tottenham Hotspur
Outstanding professionalism in the face of diabetes and serious injury.

January **Everton Fans**
Exemplary behaviour at Old Trafford during the minute's silence in memory of Sir Matt Busby.

February **Aileen Turton** Sheffield Wednesday Fan
Acting as a football commentator at every Sheffield Wednesday game for 15 years for her blind son Mark.

March **Ian Wright** Arsenal
Scoting hat-tricks in the away wins at Ipswich Town and Southampton.

April **Andy Cole** Newcastle United
Breaking Newcastle United's 39-year goalscoring record.

RECORDS

Major British Records

HIGHEST WINS

First-Class Match		Arbroath (*Scottish Cup 1st Round*)	36	Bon Accord	0	12 Sept 1885
International Match		England	13	Ireland	0	18 Feb 1882
FA Cup		Preston NE (*1st Round*)	26	Hyde U	0	15 Oct 1887
League Cup		West Ham U (*2nd Round, 2nd Leg*)	10	Bury	0	25 Oct 1983
		Liverpool (*2nd Round, 1st Leg*)	10	Fulham	0	23 Sept 1986
FA PREMIER LEAGUE						
	(*Home*)	Blackburn R	7	Norwich C	1	3 Oct 1992
		Newcastle U	7	Swindon T	1	12 March 1994
FOOTBALL LEAGUE						
Division 1	(*Home*)	WBA	12	Darwen	0	4 April 1892
		Nottingham F	12	Leicester Fosse	0	21 April 1909
	(*Away*)	Newcastle U	1	Sunderland	9	5 Dec 1908
		Cardiff C	1	Wolverhampton W	9	3 Sept 1955
Division 2	(*Home*)	Newcastle U	13	Newport Co	0	5 Oct 1946
	(*Away*)	Burslem PV	0	Sheffield U	10	10 Dec 1892
Division 3	(*Home*)	Gillingham	10	Chesterfield	0	5 Sept 1987
	(*Away*)	Halifax T	0	Fulham	8	16 Sept 1969
Division 3(S)	(*Home*)	Luton T	12	Bristol R	0	13 April 1936
	(*Away*)	Northampton T	0	Walsall	8	2 Feb 1947
Division 3(N)	(*Home*)	Stockport Co	13	Halifax T	0	6 Jan 1934
	(*Away*)	Accrington S	0	Barnsley	9	3 Feb 1934
Division 4	(*Home*)	Oldham Ath	11	Southport	0	26 Dec 1962
	(*Away*)	Crewe Alex	1	Rotherham U	8	8 Sept 1973
Aggregate Division 3(N)		Tranmere R	13	Oldham Ath	4	26 Dec 1935
SCOTTISH LEAGUE						
Premier Division	(*Home*)	Aberdeen	8	Motherwell	0	26 March 1979
	(*Away*)	Hamilton A	0	Celtic	8	5 Nov 1988
Division 1	(*Home*)	Celtic	11	Dundee	0	26 Oct 1895
	(*Away*)	Airdrieonians	1	Hibernian	11	24 Oct 1950
Division 2	(*Home*)	Airdrieonians	15	Dundee Wanderers	1	1 Dec 1894
	(*Away*)	Alloa Ath	0	Dundee	10	8 March 1947

LEAGUE CHAMPIONSHIP HAT-TRICKS

Huddersfield T	1923–24 to 1925–26
Arsenal	1932–33 to 1934–35
Liverpool	1981–82 to 1983–84

MOST GOALS FOR IN A SEASON

		Goals	Games	*Season*
FA PREMIER LEAGUE				
	Newcastle U	82	42	1993–94
FOOTBALL LEAGUE				
Division 1	Aston V	128	42	**1930–31**
Division 2	Middlesbrough	122	42	**1926–27**
Division 3(S)	Millwall	127	42	**1927–28**
Division 3(N)	Bradford C	128	42	**1928–29**
Division 3	QPR	111	46	**1961–62**
Division 4	Peterborough U	134	46	**1960–61**
SCOTTISH LEAGUE				
Premier Division	Rangers	101	44	**1991–92**
	Dundee U	90	36	**1982–83**
	Celtic	90	36	**1982–83**
	Celtic	90	44	**1986–87**
Division 1	Hearts	132	34	**1957–58**
Division 2	Raith R	142	34	**1937–38**
New Division 1	Dunfermline Ath	93	44	**1993–94**
	Motherwell	92	39	**1981–82**
New Division 2	Ayr U	95	39	**1987–88**

FEWEST GOALS FOR IN A SEASON

		Goals	Games	Season
FA PREMIER LEAGUE				
	Ipswich T	35	42	1993–94
FOOTBALL LEAGUE	(minimum 42 games)			
Division 1	Stoke C	24	42	**1984–85**
Division 2	Watford	24	42	**1971–72**
	Birmingham C	31	46	**1988–89**
Division 3(S)	Crystal Palace	33	42	**1950–51**
Division 3(N)	Crewe Alex	32	42	**1923–24**
Division 3	Stockport Co	27	46	**1969–70**
Division 4	Crewe Alex	29	46	**1981–82**
SCOTTISH LEAGUE	(minimum 30 games)			
Premier Division	Hamilton A	19	36	**1988–89**
	Dunfermline Ath	22	44	**1991–92**
Division 1	Brechin C	30	44	**1993–94**
	Ayr U	20	34	**1966–67**
Division 2	Lochgelly U	20	38	**1923–24**
New Division 1	Stirling Alb	18	39	**1980–81**
New Division 2	Berwick R	32	39	**1987–88**

MOST GOALS AGAINST IN A SEASON

		Goals	Games	Season
FA PREMIER LEAGUE				
	Swindon T	100	42	1993–94
FOOTBALL LEAGUE				
Division 1	Blackpool	125	42	**1930–31**
Division 2	Darwen	141	34	**1898–99**
Division 3(S)	Merthyr T	135	42	**1929–30**
Division 3(N)	Nelson	136	42	**1927–28**
Division 3	Accrington S	123	46	**1959–60**
Division 4	Hartlepools U	109	46	**1959–60**
SCOTTISH LEAGUE				
Premier Division	Morton	100	36	**1984–85**
	Morton	100	44	**1987–88**
Division 1	Leith Ath	137	38	**1931–32**
Division 2	Edinburgh C	146	38	**1931–32**
New Division 1	Queen of the S	99	39	**1988–89**
	Cowdenbeath	109	44	**1992–93**
New Division 2	Meadowbank T	89	39	**1977–78**

FEWEST GOALS AGAINST IN A SEASON

		Goals	Games	Season
FA PREMIER LEAGUE				
	Arsenal	28	42	1993–94
FOOTBALL LEAGUE	(minimum 42 games)			
Division 1	Liverpool	16	42	**1978–79**
Division 2	Manchester U	23	42	**1924–25**
	West Ham U	34	46	1990–91
Division 3(S)	Southampton	21	42	**1921–22**
Division 3(N)	Port Vale	21	46	**1953–54**
Division 3	Middlesbrough	30	46	**1986–87**
Division 4	Lincoln C	25	46	**1980–81**
SCOTTISH LEAGUE	(minimum 30 games)			
Premier Division	Rangers	19	36	**1989–90**
	Rangers	23	44	**1986–87**
	Celtic	23	44	**1987–88**
Division 1	Celtic	14	38	**1913–14**
Division 2	Morton	20	38	**1966–67**
New Division 1	Hibernian	24	39	**1980–81**
	Falkirk	32	44	**1993–94**
New Division 2	St Johnstone	24	39	**1987–88**
	Stirling Alb	24	39	**1990–91**

MOST POINTS IN A SEASON

		Points	Games	Season
FOOTBALL LEAGUE	(under old system of two points for a win)			
Division 1	Liverpool	68	42	**1978–79**
Division 2	Tottenham H	70	42	**1919–20**
Division 3	Aston V	70	46	**1971–72**
Division 3(S)	Nottingham F	70	46	**1950–51**
	Bristol C	70	46	**1954–55**
Division 3(N)	Doncaster R	72	42	**1946–47**
Division 4	Lincoln C	74	46	**1975–76**

FA PREMIER LEAGUE	(three points for a win)			
	Manchester U	92	42	1993–94
FOOTBALL LEAGUE				
Division 1	Everton	90	42	**1984–85**
	Liverpool	90	40	**1987–88**
Division 2	Chelsea	99	46	**1988–89**
Division 3	Bournemouth	97	46	**1986–87**
Division 4	Swindon T	102	46	**1985–86**
SCOTTISH LEAGUE				
Premier Division	Aberdeen	59	36	1984–85
	Rangers	73	44	1992–93
Division 1	Rangers	76	42	**1920–21**
Division 2	Morton	69	38	**1966–67**
New Division 1	St Mirren	62	39	**1976–77**
	Falkirk	66	44	**1993–94**
New Division 2	Forfar Ath	63	39	**1983–84**

FEWEST POINTS IN A SEASON

FA PREMIER LEAGUE		*Points*	Games	*Season*
	Swindon T	30	42	1993–94
FOOTBALL LEAGUE	(minimum 34 games)			
Division 1	Stoke C	17	42	**1984–85**
Division 2	Doncaster R	8	34	**1904–05**
	Loughborough T	8	34	**1899–1900**
	Walsall	31	46	**1988–89**
Division 3	Rochdale	21	46	**1973–74**
	Cambridge U	21	46	**1984–85**
Division 3(S)	Merthyr T	21	42	**1924–25 & 1929–30**
	QPR	21	42	**1925–26**
Division 3(N)	Rochdale	11	40	**1931–32**
Division 4	Workington	19	46	**1976–77**
SCOTTISH LEAGUE	(minimum 30 games)			
Premier Division	St Johnstone	11	36	**1975–76**
	Morton	16	44	**1987–88**
Division 1	Stirling Alb	6	30	**1954–55**
Division 2	Edinburgh C	7	34	**1936–37**
New Division 1	Queen of the S	10	39	**1988–89**
	Cowdenbeath	13	44	**1992–93**
New Division 2	Berwick R	16	39	**1987–88**
	Stranraer	16	39	**1987–88**

MOST WINS IN A SEASON

FA PREMIER LEAGUE		*Wins*	Games	*Season*
	Manchester U	27	42	1993–94
FOOTBALL LEAGUE				
Division 1	Tottenham H	31	42	**1960–61**
Division 2	Tottenham H	32	42	**1919–20**
Division 3(S)	Millwall	30	42	**1927–28**
	Plymouth Arg	30	42	**1929–30**
	Cardiff C	30	42	**1946–47**
	Nottingham F	30	46	**1950–51**
	Bristol C	30	46	**1954–55**
Division 3(N)	Doncaster R	33	42	**1946–47**
Division 3	Aston Villa	32	46	**1971–72**
Division 4	Lincoln C	32	46	**1975–76**
	Swindon T	32	46	**1985–86**
SCOTTISH LEAGUE				
Premier Division	Aberdeen	27	36	**1984–85**
	Rangers	33	44	**1991–92**
	Rangers	33	44	**1992–93**
Division 1	Rangers	35	42	**1920–21**
Division 2	Morton	33	38	**1966–67**
New Division 1	Motherwell	26	39	**1981–82**
New Division 2	Forfar Ath	27	39	**1983–84**
	Ayr U	27	39	**1987–88**

RECORD HOME WINS IN A SEASON

Brentford won all 21 games in Division 3(S), 1929–30

UNDEFEATED AT HOME

Liverpool 85 games (63 League, 9 League Cup, 7 European, 6 FA Cup), Jan 1978–Jan 1981

RECORD AWAY WINS IN A SEASON

Doncaster R won 18 of 21 games in Division 3(N), 1946–47

FEWEST WINS IN A SEASON

		Wins	Games	*Season*
FA PREMIER LEAGUE				
	Swindon T	5	42	1993–94
FOOTBALL LEAGUE				
Division 1	Stoke C	3	22	**1889–90**
	Woolwich Arsenal	3	38	**1912–13**
	Stoke C	3	42	**1984–85**
Division 2	Loughborough T	1	34	**1899–1900**
	Walsall	5	46	**1988–89**
Division 3(S)	Merthyr T	6	42	**1929–30**
	QPR	6	42	**1925–26**
Division 3(N)	Rochdale	4	40	**1931–32**
Division 3	Rochdale	2	46	**1973–74**
Division 4	Southport	3	46	**1976–77**
SCOTTISH LEAGUE				
Premier Division	St Johnstone	3	36	**1975–76**
	Kilmarnock	3	36	**1982–83**
	Morton	3	44	**1987–88**
Division 1	Vale of Leven	0	22	**1891–92**
Division 2	East Stirlingshire	1	22	**1905–06**
	Forfar Ath	1	38	**1974–75**
New Division 1	Queen of the S	2	39	**1988–89**
	Cowdenbeath	3	44	**1992–93**
New Division 2	Forfar Ath	4	26	**1975–76**
	Stranraer	4	39	**1987–88**

MOST DEFEATS IN A SEASON

		Defeats	Games	*Season*
FA PREMIER LEAGUE				
	Southampton	23	42	1993–94
FOOTBALL LEAGUE				
Division 1	Stoke C	31	42	**1984–85**
Division 2	Tranmere R	31	42	**1938–39**
	Chester C	33	46	**1992–93**
Division 3	Cambridge U	33	46	**1984–85**
Division 3(S)	Merthyr T	29	42	**1924–25**
	Walsall	29	46	**1952–53**
	Walsall	29	46	**1953–54**
Division 3(N)	Rochdale	33	40	**1931–32**
Division 4	Newport Co	33	46	**1987–88**
SCOTTISH LEAGUE				
Premier Division	Morton	29	36	**1984–85**
Division 1	St Mirren	31	42	**1920–21**
Division 2	Brechin C	30	36	**1962–63**
	Lochgelly	30	38	**1923–24**
New Division 1	Queen of the S	29	39	**1988–89**
	Cowdenbeath	34	44	**1992–93**
New Division 2	Berwick R	29	39	**1987–88**

HAT-TRICKS

Career 34 Dixie Dean (Tranmere R, Everton, Notts Co, England)
Division 1 (one season post-war) 6 Jimmy Greaves (Chelsea), 1960–61
Three for one team one match
West, Spouncer, Hooper, Nottingham F v Leicester Fosse, Division 1, 21 April 1909
Barnes, Ambler, Davies, Wrexham v Hartlepools U, Division 4, 3 March 1962
Adcock, Stewart, White, Manchester C v Huddersfield T, Division 2, 7 Nov 1987
Loasby, Smith, Wells, Northampton T v Walsall, Division 3S, 5 Nov 1927
Bowater, Hoyland, Readman, Mansfield T v Rotherham U, Division 3N, 27 Dec 1932

FEWEST DEFEATS IN A SEASON
(Minimum 20 games)

		Defeats	Games	*Season*
FA PREMIER LEAGUE				
	Manchester U	4	42	1993–94
FOOTBALL LEAGUE				
Division 1	Preston NE	0	22	**1888–89**
	Arsenal	1	38	**1990–91**
	Liverpool	2	40	**1987–88**
	Leeds U	2	42	**1968–69**
Division 2	Liverpool	0	28	**1893–94**
	Burnley	2	30	**1897–98**
	Bristol C	2	38	**1905–06**
	Leeds U	3	42	**1963–64**
	Chelsea	5	46	**1988–89**
Division 3	QPR	5	46	**1966–67**
	Bristol R	5	46	**1989–90**
Division 3(S)	Southampton	4	42	**1921–22**
	Plymouth Arg	4	42	**1929–30**
Division 3(N)	Port Vale	3	46	**1953–54**
	Doncaster R	3	42	**1946–47**
	Wolverhampton W	3	42	**1923–24**
Division 4	Lincoln C	4	46	**1975–76**
	Sheffield U	4	46	**1981–82**
	Bournemouth	4	46	**1981–82**
SCOTTISH LEAGUE				
Premier Division	Celtic	3	44	**1987–88**
Division 1	Rangers	0	18	**1898–99**
	Rangers	1	42	**1920–21**
Division 2	Clyde	1	36	**1956–57**
	Morton	1	36	**1962–63**
	St Mirren	1	36	**1967–68**
New Division 1	Partick T	2	26	**1975–76**
	St Mirren	2	39	**1976–77**
	Raith R	4	44	**1992–93**
	Falkirk	4	44	**1993–94**
New Division 2	Raith R	1	26	**1975–76**
	Clydebank	3	26	**1975–76**
	Forfar Ath	3	39	**1983–84**
	Raith R	3	39	**1986–87**

MOST DRAWN GAMES IN A SEASON

		Draws	Games	*Season*
FA PREMIER LEAGUE				
	Manchester C	18	42	1993–94
	Sheffield U	18	42	1993–94
FOOTBALL LEAGUE				
Division 1	Norwich C	23	42	**1978–79**
Division 4	Exeter C	23	46	**1986–87**
SCOTTISH LEAGUE				
Premier Division	Aberdeen	21	44	**1993–94**
New Division 1	East Fife	21	44	1986–87

MOST GOALS IN A GAME

FA PREMIER LEAGUE	Efan Ekoku (Norwich C) 4 goals v Everton	25 Sept 1993
FOOTBALL LEAGUE		
Division 1	Ted Drake (Arsenal) 7 goals v Aston Villa	14 Dec 1935
	James Ross (Preston NE) 7 goals v Stoke	6 Oct 1888
Division 2	Tommy Briggs (Blackburn R) 7 goals v Bristol R	5 Feb 1955
	Neville Coleman (Stoke C) 7 goals v Lincoln C (away)	23 Feb 1957
Division 3(S)	Joe Payne (Luton T) 10 goals v Bristol R	13 April 1936
Division 3(N)	Bunny Bell (Tranmere R) 9 goals v Oldham Ath	26 Dec 1935
Division 3	Steve Earle (Fulham) 5 goals v Halifax T	16 Sept 1969
	Barrie Thomas (Scunthorpe U) 5 goals v Luton T	24 April 1965
	Keith East (Swindon T) 5 goals v Mansfield T	20 Nov 1965
	Alf Wood (Shrewsbury T) 5 goals v Blackburn R	2 Oct 1971
	Tony Caldwell (Bolton W) 5 goals v Walsall	10 Sept 1983
	Andy Jones (Port Vale) 5 goals v Newport Co	4 May 1987
	Steve Wilkinson (Mansfield T) 5 goals v Birmingham C	3 April 1990
Division 4	Bert Lister (Oldham Ath) 6 goals v Southport	26 Dec 1962
FA CUP	Ted MacDougall (Bournemouth) 9 goals v Margate (*1st Round*)	20 Nov 1971
LEAGUE CUP	Frankie Bunn (Oldham Ath) 6 goals v Scarborough	25 Oct 1989
SCOTTISH LEAGUE CUP	Jim Fraser (Ayr U) 5 goals v Dumbarton	13 Aug 1952

SCOTTISH LEAGUE

Premier Division	Paul Sturrock (Dundee U) 5 goals v Morton	17 Nov 1984
Division 1	Jimmy McGrory (Celtic) 8 goals v Dunfermline Ath	14 Sept 1928
Division 2	Owen McNally (Arthurlie) 8 goals v Armadale	1 Oct 1927
	Jim Dyet (King's Park) 8 goals v Forfar Ath	2 Jan 1930
	John Calder (Morton) 8 goals v Raith R	18 April 1936
	Norman Hayward (Raith R) 8 goals v Brechin C	20 Aug 1937
SCOTTISH CUP	John Petrie (Arbroath) 13 goals v Bon Accord (*1st Round*)	12 Sept 1885

MOST LEAGUE GOALS IN A SEASON

		Goals	Games	Season
FA PREMIER LEAGUE	Andy Cole (Newcastle U)	34	40	1993–94
Division 1	Dixie Dean (Everton)	60	39	1927–28
Division 2	George Camsell (Middlesbrough)	59	37	1926–27
Division 3(S)	Joe Payne (Luton T)	55	39	1936–37
Division 3(N)	Ted Harston (Mansfield T)	55	41	1936–37
Division 3	Derek Reeves (Southampton)	39	46	1959–60
Division 4	Terry Bly (Peterborough U)	52	46	1960–61
FA CUP	Sandy Brown (Tottenham H)	15		1900–01
LEAGUE CUP	Clive Allen (Tottenham H)	12		1986–87
SCOTTISH LEAGUE				
Division 1	William McFadyen (Motherwell)	52	34	1931–32
Division 2	Jim Smith (Ayr U)	66	38	1927–28

MOST LEAGUE GOALS IN A CAREER

FOOTBALL LEAGUE		*Goals*	Games	Season
Arthur Rowley	WBA	4	24	1946–48
	Fulham	27	56	1948–50
	Leicester C	251	303	1950–58
	Shrewsbury T	152	236	1958–65
		434	619	
SCOTTISH LEAGUE				
Jimmy McGrory	Celtic	1	3	1922–23
	Clydebank	13	30	1923–24
	Celtic	396	375	1924–38
		410	408	

MOST CUP GOALS IN A CAREER

FA CUP (post-war)

Pre-war: Henry Cursham 48 (Notts Co)
Denis Law 41 (Huddersfield T, Manchester C, Manchester U)

A CENTURY OF LEAGUE AND CUP GOALS IN CONSECUTIVE SEASONS

George Camsell	Middlesbrough	59 Lge	5 Cup	1926–27
(101 goals)		33	4	1927–28
Steve Bull	Wolverhampton W	34 Lge	18 Cup	1987–88
(102 goals)		37	13	1988–89

(Camsell's cup goals were all scored in the FA Cup; Bull had 12 in the Sherpa Van Trophy, 3 Littlewoods Cup, 3 FA Cup in 1987–88; 11 Sherpa Van Trophy, 2 Littlewoods Cup in 1988–89.)

LONGEST SEQUENCE OF CONSECUTIVE SCORING (Individual)

FA PREMIER LEAGUE		
Mark Stein (Chelsea)	9 in 7 games	1993–94
FOOTBALL LEAGUE RECORD		
Bill Pendergast (Chester)	15 in 12 games	1938–39

LONGEST WINNING SEQUENCE

FOOTBALL LEAGUE		*Games*	Season
Division 1	Everton	12	1893–94 (4) and 1894–95 (8)
Division 2	Manchester U	14	1904–05
	Bristol C	14	1905–06
	Preston NE	14	1950–51
Division 3	Reading	13	1985–86
From season's start			
Division 1	Tottenham H	11	1960–61
Division 3	Reading	13	1985–86

LONGEST WINNING SEQUENCE IN A SEASON

FOOTBALL LEAGUE		*Games*	Season
Division 1	Tottenham H	11	1960–61
Division 2	Manchester U	14	1904–05
Division 2	Bristol C	14	1905–06
Division 2	Preston NE	14	1950–51
SCOTTISH LEAGUE			
Division 2	Morton	23	1963–64

LONGEST UNBEATEN SEQUENCE

FOOTBALL LEAGUE		Games	Seasons
Division 1	Nottingham F	42	Nov 1977–Dec 1978

LONGEST UNBEATEN CUP SEQUENCE

Liverpool 25 rounds League/Milk Cup 1980–84

LONGEST UNBEATEN SEQUENCE IN A SEASON

FOOTBALL LEAGUE		*Games*	*Season*
Division 1	Burnley	30	**1920–21**

LONGEST UNBEATEN START TO A SEASON

FOOTBALL LEAGUE		Games	*Season*
Division 1	Leeds U	29	**1973–74**
Division 1	Liverpool	29	**1987–88**

LONGEST SEQUENCE WITHOUT A WIN IN A SEASON

FOOTBALL LEAGUE		Games	*Season*
Division 2	Cambridge U	31	**1983–84**

LONGEST SEQUENCE WITHOUT A WIN FROM SEASON'S START

Division 1	Manchester U	12	**1930–31**

LONGEST SEQUENCE OF CONSECUTIVE DEFEATS

FOOTBALL LEAGUE		Games	*Season*
Division 2	Darwen	18	1898–99

GOALKEEPING RECORDS (without conceding a goal)

British record (all competitive games)
Chris Woods, Rangers, in 1196 minutes from 26 November 1986 to 31 January 1987.

Football League
Steve Death, Reading, 1103 minutes from 24 March to 18 August 1979.

PENALTIES

Most in a season (individual)		*Goals*	Season
Division 1	Francis Lee (Manchester C)	13	1971–72
Most awarded in one game			
Five	Crystal Palace (4 – 1 scored, 3 missed) v Brighton & HA (1 scored), Div 2		1988–89
Most saved in a season			
Division 1	Paul Cooper (Ipswich T)	8 (of 10)	1979–80

MOST LEAGUE APPEARANCES

995 Peter Shilton (286 Leicester City, 110 Stoke City, 202 Nottingham Forest, 188 Southampton, 175 Derby County, 34 Plymouth Argyle) 1966–94
824 Terry Paine (713 Southampton, 111 Hereford United) 1957–77
795 Tommy Hutchison (165 Blackpool, 314 Coventry City, 46 Manchester City, 92 Burnley 178 Swansea City, also 68 Alloa 1965–68) 1968–91
777 Alan Oakes (565 Manchester City, 211 Chester City, 1 Port Vale) 1959–84
770 John Trollope (all for Swindon Town) 1960–80†
764 Jimmy Dickinson (all for Portsmouth) 1946–65
761 Roy Sproson (all for Port Vale) 1950–72
758 Ray Clemence (48 Scunthorpe United, 470 Liverpool, 240 Tottenham Hotspur) 1966–87
757 Pat Jennings (48 Watford, 472 Tottenham Hotspur, 237 Arsenal) 1963–86
752 John Burridge (27 Workington, 134 Blackpool, 65 Aston Villa, 6 Southend U (loan), 88 Crystal Palace, 39 QPR, 74 Wolverhampton W, 6 Derby Co (loan), 109 Sheffield U, 62 Southampton, 67 Newcastle U, 65 Hibernian, 3 Scarborough, 4 Lincoln C, 3 Aberdeen) 1968–94
† record for one club

Consecutive
401 Harold Bell (401 Tranmere R; 459 in all games) 1946–55

FA CUP
88 Ian Callaghan (79 Liverpool, 7 Swansea C, 2 Crewe Alex)

Most Senior Matches
1378 Peter Shilton (995 League, 86 FA Cup, 102 League Cup, 125 Internationals, 13 Under-23, 4 Football League XI, 53 others including European Cup, UEFA Cup, World Club Championship, various domestic cup competitions)

MOST FA CUP FINAL GOALS

Ian Rush (Liverpool) 5: 1986(2), 1989(2), 1992(1)

MOST LEAGUE MEDALS

Phil Neal (Liverpool) 8: 1976, 1977, 1979, 1980, 1982, 1983, 1984, 1986

OTHER RECORDS

YOUNGEST PLAYERS
FA Premier League Andy Turner, 17 years 145 days, Tottenham H v Southampton, 15.8.92
FA Premier League Scorer Andy Turner, 17 years 166 days, Tottenham H v Everton, 5.9.92.
Football League Albert Geldard, 15 years 158 days, Bradford Park Avenue v Millwall, Division 2, 16.9.29; and Ken Roberts, 15 years 158 days, Wrexham v Bradford Park Avenue, Division 3N, 1.9.51
Football League scorer
Ronnie Dix, 15 years 180 days, Bristol Rovers v Norwich City, Division 3S, 3.3.28.
Division 1
Derek Forster, 15 years 185 days, Sunderland v Leicester City, 22.8.84.
Division 1 scorer
Jason Dozzell, 16 years 57 days as substitute Ipswich Town v Coventry City, 4.2.84
Division 1 hat-tricks
Alan Shearer, 17 years 240 days, Southampton v Arsenal, 9.4.88
Jimmy Greaves, 17 years 10 months, Chelsea v Portsmouth, 25.12.57
FA Cup (any round)
Andy Awford, 15 years 88 days as substitute Worcester City v Borehamwood, 3rd Qual. rd, 10.10.87
FA Cup proper
Scott Endersby, 15 years 288 days, Kettering v Tilbury, 1st rd, 26.11.77
FA Cup Final
James Prinsep, 17 years 245 days, Clapham Rovers v Old Etonians, 1879
FA Cup Final scorer
Norman Whiteside, 18 years 18 days, Manchester United v Brighton & Hove Albion, 1983
FA Cup Final captain
David Nish, 21 years 212 days, Leicester City v Manchester City, 1969
League Cup Final scorer
Norman Whiteside, 17 years 324 days, Manchester United v Liverpool, 1983
League Cup Final captain
Barry Venison, 20 years 7 months 8 days, Sunderland v Norwich City, 1985

OLDEST PLAYERS
Football League
Neil McBain, 52 years 4 months, New Brighton v Hartlepools United, Div 3N, 15.3.47 (McBain was New Brighton's manager and had to play in an emergency)
Division 1
Stanley Matthews, 50 years 5 days, Stoke City v Fulham, 6.2.65
FA Cup Final
Walter Hampson, 41 years 8 months, Newcastle United v Aston Villa, 1924
FA Cup
Billy Meredith, 49 years 8 months, Manchester City v Newcastle United, 29.3.24
International debutant
Leslie Compton, 38 years 2 months, England v Wales, 15.11.50
International
Billy Meredith, 45 years 229 days, Wales v England, 15.3.20

SENDINGS-OFF

Season	294 (League, cup etc.)	1993–94
Day	15 (3 League, 12 FA Cup*)	20 Nov 1982
	**worst overall FA Cup total*	
League	13	14 Dec 1985
Weekend	15	22/23 Dec 1990
FA Cup Final	Kevin Moran, Manchester U v Everton	1985
Wembley	Boris Stankovic, Yugoslavia v Sweden (Olympics)	1948
	Antonio Rattin, Argentina v England (World Cup)	1966
	Billy Bremner (Leeds U) and Kevin Keegan (Liverpool), Charity Shield	1974
	Gilbert Dresch, Luxembourg v England (World Cup)	1977
	Mike Henry, Sudbury T v Tamworth (FA Vase)	1989
	Lee Dixon, Arsenal v Tottenham H (FA Cup semi-final)	1993
	Peter Swan, Port Vale v WBA (play-offs)	1993
	Michael Wallace and Chris Beaumont (both Stockport Co) v Burnley (play-offs)	1994
Quickest	Mark Smith, Crewe Alex v Darlington (away) Div 3: 19 secs	12 March 1994
Division 1	Liam O'Brien, Manchester U v Southampton (away): 85 secs	3 Jan 1987
World Cup	Jose Batista, Uruguay v Scotland, Neza, Mexico (World Cup): 55 secs	13 June 1986
Most one game	Four: Northampton T (0) v Hereford U (4) Div 3	11 Nov 1992
	Four: Crewe Alex (2) v Bradford PA (2) Div 3N	8 Jan 1955
	Four: Sheffield U (1) v Portsmouth (3) Div 2	13 Dec 1986
	Four: Port Vale (2) v Northampton T (2) Littlewoods Cup	18 Aug 1987
	Four: Brentford (2) v Mansfield T (2) Div 3	12 Dec 1987

RECORD ATTENDANCES

FA Premier League	45,347	Aston Villa v Liverpool, Villa Park	7.5.1994
Football League	83,260	Manchester U v Arsenal, Maine Road	17.1.1948
Scottish League	118,567	Rangers v Celtic, Ibrox Stadium	2.1.1939
FA Cup Final	126,047*	Bolton W v West Ham U, Wembley	28.4.1923
European Cup	135,826	Celtic v Leeds U, semi-final at Hampden Park	15.4.1970
Scottish Cup	146,433	Celtic v Aberdeen, Hampden Park	24.4.37
World Cup	199,854†	Brazil v Uruguay, Maracana, Rio	16.7.50

* It has been estimated that as many as 70,000 more broke in without paying.
† 173,830 paid.

Brazilian captain Dunga carries the World Cup trophy with colleagues accompanying him, after the success at the 1994 tournament in the USA.

FOOTBALL CLUB CHAPLAINCY

With the concept of football club chaplaincy now well established in our sport at Premiership and Football League level, and with chaplains operating at nearly half the English clubs featured in this Yearbook, it is inevitable that there will be occasions when there is no great increase to report in the number of chaplains. However, those who support the notion of the football chaplain, who value his ministry and are eager to see it extend to the vast majority of our clubs, need have no anxieties, for there is no way that the chaplaincy involvement has lost its momentum. Indeed, this has been a season of consolidation for us.

The number of chaplains may not have grown hugely, but we have held several regional conferences which have demonstrated to us all just what supremely high-quality men are ministering in our football clubs. This has always been the case of course, but as our numbers have grown to the level they now are, so it has increasingly been worthwhile to meet together locally as well as at our two-yearly national conference. Thus men who might feel unable to attend a home-counties location for two days (even with the lure of watching England play at Wembley!) are glad to devote a morning and afternoon to meeting their colleagues, exchanging news and views and spending some time in fellowship and prayer for their footballing ministry.

The best-attended regional conference was, inevitably, that which was hosted by Manchester United at Old Trafford, but during last summer and autumn several smaller meetings were held in other areas of the country.

The football chaplains also have a confidence about them. Of course they are confident about their ministry and the One whom they proclaim and represent, but they are also sure of the integrity of its extension into football clubs. Chaplains have long been an accepted part of many areas of life such as schools, theatres, industry, the armed forces etc., and in one sense it is surprising that it took so long for them to become established in football, particularly when it is remembered that about a quarter of the English League clubs have their origins in Churches, Chapels or Sunday Schools.

Our confidence is enhanced, too, by the fact that several times each year there is mention of chaplaincy in the sports pages or colour supplements of the national newspapers and, while never sought, the coverage is at least appreciative and sometimes laudatory.

It would be a mistake to think that the football chaplains are a totally recent innovation, for we've had chaplains at some clubs since before England won the World Cup. When the chaplains of two First Division outfits watched a match together last season, for example, they aggregated almost fifty years of football chaplaincy service at their clubs. Not a bad record, is it?

Cohesion is another word that now aptly describes the football chaplaincy movement. The chaplains have always had the support of Christians in Sport, an organization to which most of them belong and value its work in sport in general and football in particular, but, thanks to the vision of one of the major denominations, there is now a clergyman who devotes his time fully to sports ministry with a particular emphasis on football. He is Rev John Boyers, honorary chaplain at Manchester United, who keeps in contact with all the chaplains. He's also in touch with several clubs who are interested in exploring the possibility of appointing a chaplain, and assists them in finding the right man for that particular place.

Further information about football chaplaincy for clergymen who would be interested in serving in this way, or for clubs who might wish to consider such an appointment, may be obtained from Christians in Sport, PO Box 93, Oxford OX2 7YP, or from Rev John Boyers, 19 Chestnut Drive, Sale, Cheshire M33 4HJ.

OFFICIAL CHAPLAINS TO FA PREMIERSHIP AND FOOTBALL LEAGUE CLUBS

Rev John Bingham—Chesterfield
Rev Richard Chewter—Exeter C
Rev Michael Lowe—Bournemouth
Rev Andrew Taggart—Torquay U
Rev David Jeans—Sheffield W
Rev Nigel Sands—Crystal Palace
Rev Graham Spencer—Leicester C
Rev Phillip Miller—Ipswich T
Rev Allen Bagshawe—Hull C
Rev David Tully—Newcastle U
Rev Derek Cleave—Bristol C
Rev Brian Rice—Hartlepool U
Rev Ken Sykes—Watford
Rev Michael Chantry—Oxford U
Rev Michael Futens—Derby C
Very Rev Brandon Jackson—Lincoln C
Rev Paul Bennett—Swindon T
Rev Ken Hawkins—Birmingham C
Rev Simon Stevenette—Bristol R
Rev Kevin McIlhennie—Gillingham
Rev Michael Hunter—Grimsby T
Rev Dick Syms—York City
Rev Dennis Hall—Wigan Ath
Rev William Hall—Middlesbrough
Rev Canon John Hestor—Bright & HA
Rev Mervyn Terrett—Luton T
Rev Jim Rushton—Carlisle U
Rev Robert de Berry—Queen's Park Rangers
Rev Gary Piper—Fulham
Rev Charlie Mackenzie—Barnsley
Rev Barry Kirk—Reading
Rev Martin Short—Bradford C
Rev John Boyers—Manchester U
Rev Martin Butt—Walsall
Rev Kevin Tugwell—Cardiff C
Rev Steve Riley—Leeds U
Revs Alan Poulter and Gerald Courell—Tranmere R
Rev Mark Kichenside—Charlton Ath
Rev Owen Beament—Millwall
Rev Elwin Cockett—West Ham U
Rev Mike Woodhead—Sheffield U
Rev Jim Pearce—Southampton

The chaplains hope that those who read this article will see the value and benefit of chaplaincy work in sport, and will take appropriate steps to spread the word where this is possible. They would also like to thank the editor of the Rothmans Yearbook for his continued support for this specialist and growing area of work.

STOP PRESS

Jack Charlton calls for a Gunga Din* approach to water supplies at the World Cup...No England in the USA and our table soccer team is knocked out in the first round by Belgium...FIFA say water will be administered only off the pitch...Tottenham have 12 points deducted from 1994–95, are fined a record £600,000 and banned from the FA Cup for next season, plus ordered to pay the costs of the inquiry...Lou Macari is sacked by Celtic...World Cup opens to a disappointing game, five bookings and a dismissal, one scrappy goal...Hearts axe manager Sandy Clark...Tom McLean ex-Motherwell takes over...Charlton is fined £10,000 and banned from the touchline after an incident when trying to put on a substitute...TV ratings for the World Cup surprise the Yanks...Basile Boli joins Rangers from Marseille for £2.7 million...Millwall escape closure, but have a two-match home ban and fine of £100,000 both suspended sentences and three points to be deducted if there is further fan trouble...Carlton Palmer moves from Sheffield Wednesday to Leeds for £2.6 million...Maradona is banned after taking a banned substance...Good and bad news for Tottenham. They save six points for next season but find their fine raised to £1.5 million...FA Premier clubs open their hearts and accounts to the Inland Revenue...Tommy Burns becomes Celtic manager after leaving Kilmarnock with assistant Billy Stark...Alex McLeish is lined up for Motherwell...Chris Sutton breaks the British transfer record in a £5 million move from Norwich to Blackburn...TV viewing figures for the World Cup final: 18.6 Britons watched, 13.3 on BBC, 5.3 on ITV...Mike Pejic replaces Graham Barrow as Chester manager with Kevin Ratcliffe as player-coach...Sam Allardyce is confirmed as Blackpool boss...England will play the USA at Wembley on 7 September...and also hope to meet World Champions Brazil...Spurs buy World Cup stars Ilie Dumitrescu from Steaua for £2.6 million and Jurgen Klinsmann for £2 million from Monaco.

Pick of the other major summer moves:

Paul Furlong, Watford to Chelsea £2.3 million; Stefan Schwarz, Benfica to Arsenal £1.75m; Tony Daley, Aston Villa to Wolves £1.25m; Bryan Roy, Foggia to Nottingham Forest £2.25m; Brian Laudrup, Fiorentina to Rangers £2.25m; Nicky Summerbee, Swindon to Manchester City £1.5m.

*Rudyard Kipling's immortal water-carrier.

Live Television coverage by BSKYB

The following matches have been selected for live TV coverage:

Sunday 21 August: Leicester C v Newcastle U; Monday 22 August: Nottingham F v Manchester U; Sunday 28 August: Liverpool v Arsenal; Monday 29 August: Coventry C v Aston Villa; Sunday 11 September: Leeds U v Manchester U; Monday 12 September: Tottenham H v Southampton; Sunday 18 September: Chelsea v Blackburn R; Sunday 25 September: West Ham U v Arsenal; Monday 26 September: Sheffield W v Leeds U; Sunday 2 October: Nottingham F v QPR; Sunday 9 October: Newcastle U v Blackburn R; Monday 10 October: West Ham U v Crystal Palace; Sunday 16 October: Ipswich T v Sheffield W; Monday 17 October: Nottingham F v Wimbledon; Sunday 23 October: Blackburn R v Manchester U; Sunday 30 October: Wimbledon v Norwich C; Monday 31 October; QPR v Liverpool; Sunday 6 November: Aston Villa v Manchester U; Thursday 10 November: Manchester U v Manchester C (subject to either club being involved in a Coca-Cola Cup third round replay); Sunday 20 November: Leicester C v Manchester C; Monday 21 November: Everton v Liverpool; Monday 5 December: Everton v Leeds U; Monday 12 December: Tottenham H v Sheffield W.

BBC selections for the first two weeks:

Saturday 20 August: Manchester U v QPR; Crystal Palace v Liverpool; Saturday 27 August: Leeds U v Chelsea; Tottenham H v Manchester U.

OBITUARIES

Andrew, George (b. Glasgow 24.11.45; d. 7.93). A wing-half who joined West Ham in 1963 but, after only two League appearances for the Hammers in a central defensive position, he signed for Crystal Palace in July, 1967. He was unable to break into the first team at Selhurst Park, so he stepped down to Southern League Romford where he made 157 League appearances.

Argue, Jim (b. 1949; d. 8.93). A fine full-back who played under Willie Ormond at St. Johnstone and helped the Saints reach the Scottish League Cup Final in 1969, although he did not play in the final itself. In all he played 200 games for the Perth club until a serious leg injury terminated his career.

Banks, Ralph (b. Farnworth 28.6.20; d. 10.93). The brother of Tommy Banks, who eventually took his left-back spot, Ralph gave valuable service to Bolton Wanderers during his 107 League match career. He played in the 1953 F.A. Cup Final against Blackpool and had the unenviable task of marking Stanley Matthews. In January, 1954, he left Burnden Park for Aldershot, where he made 43 League appearances, before ending his playing days at Weymouth.

Barton, Tony (b. Sutton 8.4.37; d. 20.8.93). An orthodox right-winger, who played for England Schoolboys and Youth teams. He signed for Fulham in 1954 for whom he made 51 League appearances and scored eight goals. Also at Craven Cottage during his stay were Johnny Haynes and Bobby Robson. In 1959, he joined Nottingham Forest, but in December, 1961, after 22 League games, he was off to Portsmouth. Six months later, Tony had won a Third Division Championship medal in a forward line containing the prolific centre-forward, Ron Saunders, a man he was to succeed in later years as manager at Aston Villa. Tony made 130 League appearances and scored 34 goals for Pompey, until a knee injury forced his premature retirement in 1967. A year later, he was appointed chief scout at Fratton Park where he stayed for 14 years. He then accepted an offer from Ron Saunders to become assistant manager at Aston Villa. When Saunders was sacked, Tony took Villa to victory in the 1982 European Cup Final, but two years later, he too was dismissed and joined Northampton. A heart attack kept him out of the game until he joined Southampton as assistant to Chris Nicholl. Tony rejoined Pompey as chief scout in 1989 and then took over reserve team duties. When boss Frank Burrows was fired in 1991, he assumed temporary control of the first team. With many people expecting him to keep the job full-time, Jim Smith was appointed in his place. Before his death, Tony had been assisting former Brighton, Spurs and Pompey defender Gary Stevens at Petersfield United.

Birkett, Wilf (b. Warrington 26.6.22; d. 24.12.93). Former Everton, Shrewsbury and Southport goalkeeper, who made 11 wartime appearances for Everton, before joining Southport, first as a guest, then permanently in November, 1946. He left briefly to have a short spell with Shrewsbury, making 20 appearances between July, 1952 and July, 1953, before rejoining Southport. After a total of 177 games, Wilf retired to become assistant trainer.

Bean, Alf 'Billy' (b. Lincoln 25.8.15; d. 23.11.93). Alf signed for his local club, Lincoln City, in 1934 as an amateur and went on to make 174 League appearances before retiring in 1949. He operated as a half-back in the Red Imps side of 1948 that won the Third Division North Championship..

Blanchflower, Danny (b. Belfast 10.2.26; d. 9.12.93). A superbly gifted wing-half with a wonderful presence on the ball, Danny was able to change the course of a match with his astute passing ability. He won 56 caps for Northern Ireland, represented the Irish and Football Leagues and was Footballer of the Year in 1958 and again in 1961, when he also skippered Totenham Hotspur to the League and F.A. Cup double. Danny guested for Swindon Town during the war, joined Glentoran after hostilities as an amateur and signed professionally in 1946. In April, 1949, he was transferred to Barnsley for £6,500 where he played 68 League games and scored two goals. In 1951, he joined Aston Villa for £15,000 and amassed 148 League appearances, scoring on ten occasions. In December, 1954 came the move that was to transform his career and trigger Tottenham to the most successful period in their history. Following a £30,000 fee, he made 337 League appearances for Spurs, scoring 15 times. Apart from the double in 1961, Danny skippered Spurs to F.A. Cup success in 1962 and to a European Cup-Winners' Cup triumph a year later. He also captained

Harry Brooks, leading goalscorer in the FA Cup during 1945-46 with 13 goals. (JR).

Danny Blanchflower, leading out Tottenham Hotspur in his heyday at White Hart Lane. (N. S. Barrett Collection).

Sir Matt Busby, forever synonymous with Manchester United. (N.S. Barrett Collection).

Northern Ireland to the quarter-finals of the 1958 World Cup tournament. After his retirement from the first class game, Danny became a sports journalist with The Sunday Express and then had spells in management with Northern Ireland between June 1976 and November, 1978, followed in December of that year by a nine month period in charge at Chelsea.

Brooks, Harry (b. Tibshelf 2.6.15; d. 2.94). Prolific scoring centre-forward who joined Aldershot from Doncaster Rovers in 1939. Established himself in wartime football and also guested with distinction for Bristol City, Aberaman Athletic, Cardiff City, Norwich City, Chester and Manchester City for whom he scored in a 1-1 draw at Bolton on 17 May 1941, Was top scorer in the FA Cup during 1945–46 with 13 goals including five in successive ties. Retired in 1948 after scoring 98 goals for Aldershot alone.

Buck, Teddy (b. Dipton 29.10.04; d. 3.8.93). A half-back who began with Leeds United in 1927, but after only eight League outings, moved to Grimsby Town for £2,000 in 1929. Teddy made 354 League appearances, a further 32 in F.A. Cup, had 208 war-time outings and won a Second Division championship medal with Grimsby in 1933–34, for whom he played until 1946.

Busby, Sir Matt (b. Orbiston 26.5.09; d. 20.1.94). One of the great football managers—who took charge of Manchester United In 1945—and remained at the Old Trafford helm until 1969. His Football League playing career began in February, 1928, when he signed for Manchester City from Denny Hibernian. He began as an inside-forward, but successfully converted to an excellent half-back, strong in the tackle and with good vision. He won an F.A. Cup winners' medal in 1934 when City beat Pompey two-one and that same year he won a Scotland cap against Wales. In 1936, an £8,000 move took Matt to Liverpool, but after the war he retired from the playing side when the approach to manage United was offered. During his reign, the club won the League Championship in 1952, 1956, 1957, 1965 and 1967, plus the F.A. Cup in 1949 and 1963. In 1958, he received a CBE, the year of the horrific Munich air disaster, when the team was decimated and Matt himself was also injured. But with the great man's guidance, United did recover and another superb side was built. Ten years after the Munich tragedy, Matt was celebrating victory in the European Champions' Cup—a spendid 4-1 win over Benfica—which meant a first success for an English club in Europe's premier club competition. The side containing Charlton, Law and Best that he presided over was one of the finest in English football and is remembered not only in Britain, but throughout the world. He was knighted in 1968. The following year he decided it was time to hand over the reins to Wilf McGuinness. Sir Matt became general manager and then joined the United board before becoming club president in 1980.

Chapman, Neville (b. Cockfield 15.9.41; d. 14.10.93). A half-back who made 52 League appearances for Middlesbrough between 1961 and 1967. He moved to Darlington in September of that year and had 32 League outings for the Feethams club.

Cheadle, Tom (b. Stoke 8.4.19; d. 4.9.93). Tom signed for Port Vale in 1946 and made 332 League appearances before joining Crewe Alexandra in 1957. It was at Gresty Road that he finished his full-time career, having 37 outings, before becoming a coach with the club.

Cockroft, Joe (b. Barnsley 20.6.11; d. 2.94). Signed for Rotherham in 1931, but after only three League outings, he joined Gainsborough Trinity. Joe moved on to West Ham in 1933, for whom he made 251 League appearances. During the war he guested for Sheffield Wednesday, making 199 appearances before joining the Owls permanently in 1946. He played 87 times for the Hillsborough club and then, in 1948, the half-back was the subject of a £4,000 transfer to neighbours Sheffield United. There, approaching 38 years of age, he finally saw out his first class playing career, before taking over the reins of Wisbech Town as player-manager.

Cookson, Jim (b. Liverpool 22.8.27; d. 24.1.93). A full-back, who had just one war-time outing for Everton before he moved up the coast to Southport in 1949. He was at Haig Avenue until 1951, making 55 League appearances.

Donald, Richard 'Dick' (b. Aberdeen 20.2.11; d. 31.12.93). Played for his local club in the thirties, making 19 League appearances, before joining the Aberdeen board of directors in 1949. He became Chairman of the Dons in 1970 and saw the club have numerous League, Cup and European Cup Winners Cup successes. He has a stand named in his honour at the wonderfully appointed Pittodrie, Britain's first all-seater stadium.

Ellis, John 'Jack' (b. Tyldsley 25.1.08; d. 1.94). A former Wolves, Bristol Rovers, Hull City and Clapton Orient goalkeeper in the thirties before hostilities interrupted his career. During the war, he made guest appearances for Rochdale, York and Wrexham.

Emery, Don (b. Cardiff 11.6.20; d. 11.93). Formerly an inside-forward who converted to a full-back. Don began with Cardiff City and then had ten years at Swindon Town whom he left in the 1947–48 season to join Aberdeen. Famed for a 'rocket' shot, Don scored 25 goals in 125 games before being snapped up by East Fife in 1952. Two years later, he was celebrating a Scottish League Cup Final victory over Partick Thistle.

Finch, John 'Jack' (b. West Ham 3.2.09; d. 15.11.93). Joined Fulham in 1930 and played at centre, inside-forward and on the wing. He made 295 appearances, scoring 51 times for the Cottagers before the war, then hit a further 11 goals in 71 games during hostilities. He also guested for Crystal Palace before becoming player-manager of Sittingbourne United. In 1946, he signed for Colchester United, but later took coaching posts in Nigeria and Iceland.

Fisher, Fred (b. Wednesbury 14.1.20; d. 6.93). A full-back who joined Grimsby Town in 1937 and stayed until 1951, when he left the Mariners to sign for Rochdale. Fred returned to Grimsby in 1964 to take up a scouting post and also served Nottingham Forest in a similar position.

Fox, Geoff (b. Bristol 19.1.25; d. 1.1.94). A full-back who started out with Ipswich, but after 11 League appearances he returned 'home' to sign for Bristol Rovers for whom he played 306 games between 1947 and 1955. Geoff won a Third Division South Championship medal in 1953 and saw out his full-time playing career with Swindon Town, making 48 League appearances between 1955 and 1957.

Geidmintis, Tony (b. Stepney 30.7.49; d. 16.4.93). Tony was a marvellous servant to Workington, for whom he made 328 League appearances, scoring 37 times, between 1965 and 1976. He became Workington's youngest ever player when, in April, 1965, at the age of 15, he made his debut. In 1976, he was transferred to Watford, but 48 League games later, he was off to Northampton Town, where he had 63 outings. In July, 1979, Tony moved to Halifax Town and then returned briefly to Workington in 1980–81 to play in the Northern Premier League.

Gibson, Henry 'Harry' (b. Newcastle-upon-Tyne 17.4.30; d. 6.11.93). Signed for Fulham in 1952 and made one League appearance, before departing for Aldershot in August, 1956, where he had three League outings at half-back.

Graham, Doug (b. Morpeth 15.7.21; d. 11.93). Doug made 90 war-time appearances for Newcastle United, for whom he signed in 1940; then, after hostilities, he went on to play a further 71 League games between 1946 and 1950. In November of that year, the full-back joined Preston but, after being unable to make the first team, he signed for Lincoln City in December 1951. There he had 182 League outings before retiring from the game.

Hamilton, Alex (b. Bo'ness 1939; d. 7.93). A full-back who won a Scottish League Championship medal with Dundee in 1962 and was a member of the side that reached the semi-finals of the European Cup a year later. Alex joined Dundee in 1957 and stayed until the late sixties before heading for South Africa, where he played for Durban United and East London United. He took a coaching post after his playing career finished, then returned to Dundee in 1988 to take an administrative job. He still remains Dundee's most capped player, with 24 appearances for Scotland.

Hancocks, Johnny (b. Oakengates 30.4.19; d. 2.94). Only 5 feet 4 inches, this speedy right-winger started out with Walsall, then joined Wolves for £4,000 in May, 1946. He had an explosive shot and, in 343 League games for Wolverhampton, notched an amazing 158 goals. Johnny represented England three times and also played for the Football League. He won a League Championship medal in 1954 and had F.A. Cup Final success in 1949 when Wanderers beat Leicester City in the Final.

Holton, Jim (b. Lesmahagow 11.4.51; d. 4.10.93). A towering central defender who started out with West Bromwich Albion in 1968, but was unable to break into the first team. In June, 1971, he signed for Shrewsbury where he made 67 League appearances. In January, 1973, came a move to Manchester United. Jim was immediately rewarded with a Scottish Under 23 cap and went on to make 15 full appearances in the dark blue shirt. With United he won a Second Division Championship medal in 1975, but his career at Old Trafford was unfortunately punctuated by injuries. In 1976, he was off to Sunderland, where he made 15 League appearances, then he had a productive spell at Coventry with 91 League games between 1977 and 1979. He signed for Sheffield Wednesday in August, 1981, but was forced to retire without making any League appearances.

Jancovic, Bosco (b. Yugoslavia 22.5.51; d. 10.93). A striker who joined Middlesbrough for £140,000 in July, 1979, following great success with Zeljeznicar of Sarajevo, whom he helped win the Yugoslav Championship. Bosco won five caps for his country and was twice Yugoslavia's leading scorer before his move to Britain. With the 'Boro he scored 16 goals in 50 League games before leaving for Metz in 1981. He eventually returned to Yugoslavia, but was forced to leave war-stricken Bosnia in 1993 to seek refuge in Kotor, Montenegro, where he died prematurely from cancer.

Jennings, Wally (b. 1909; d. 4.11.93). A defender who played either in the centre of defence or full-back for Bristol City. He made 122 League appearances for the Ashton Gate club between 1929 and 1934 before moving on to Cardiff City, where he had 30 League outings. Wally finished his playing career with Cheltenham and then had scouting appointments with Everton, Bristol Rovers and Bath City.

Julians, Len (b. Tottenham 19.6.33; d. 17.12.93). Len began his League career with Leyton Orient in 1955 staying until 1958, when, after hitting 35 goals in 67 games, he was transferred to Arsenal. A further 7 goals in 18 matches followed, then the centre-forward was off to Nottingham Forest in June, 1960. At The City Ground, he amassed another 24 goals in 59 League appearances, which prompted Millwall to sign him in January, 1964. Len did The Lions proud, notching 58 times in 125 League games, which was an important factor in Millwall's rise from the Fourth to Second Division in successive seasons.

Knight, Frank (b. Hucknall 26.10.21; d. 18.12.93). A wing-half for Nottingham Forest between 1946 and 1949, where he made 48 League appearances for his local club. After his playing career,Frank spent a further 22 years at The City Ground, as a member of the backroom staff.

McAlinden, Jimmy (b. Belfast 31.12.17; d. 11.93). Started out with Belfast Celtic, with whom he won an Irish Cup winners medal in 1938. He then joined Portsmouth and a year later was celebrating Pompey's triumphant F.A. Cup victory over Wolves. When war broke out he returned to Belfast Celtic and won further Irish Cup medals in 1941 and 1944. Following hostilities, he went back to Pompey, but after a total of 60 League games (27 pre-war) and 15 goals, he was tranferred to Stoke City in September, 1947. Following 33 games and two goals, Jimmy was off to Southend in 1948, where he amassed 218 League appearances and scored 12 times. The talented inside-forward also had the distinction of being capped four times by Northern Ireland and twice by Eire. Jimmy also achieved great success as a manager. In 1956–57 he was at Glenavon's helm when they won the Irish League and Cup double. He was later in charge of Distillery when two goals by current Wycombe Wanderers boss, Martin O'Neill, paved the way for a three-nil win over Derry City in the 1971 Irish Cup Final. He also had a spell in the managerial chair at Drogheda United.

McGettigan, Larry (b. Hackney 25.12.52; d. 12.1.94). Watford winger who made 50 League appearances after turning professional in November 1970. Joined Barnsley on a free transfer in July 1975 but left immediately and had a trial with Brentford before drifting out of the game.

McGowan, Danny (b. Dublin 8.11.24; d. 3.94). Joined West Ham in May, 1948 from Shelborne and stayed until 1953, making 82 League appearances for the Hammers. A wing-half, Danny won three caps for Ireland in the late forties.

Macauley, Archie (b. Falkirk 30.7.15; d. 6.93). Began with Rangers and won a Scottish League Championship medal in the 1934–35 season. He joined West Ham in 1937 for £6,000 and, but for the war, would have made many more appearances for the Hammers. In 1946, he left Upton Park for Brentford, where he played 26 times and scored twice from his half-back position. In July, 1947, Archie signed for Arsenal, for whom he made 103 appearances and won a Championship medal. His League career finished at Fulham and between 1950 and 1952 he had 49 outings. He made seven international appearances for Scotland and also represented Great Britain in a match against the Rest of Europe. A long managerial career followed, with Guildford City, Dundee (trainer-coach), Norwich City, West Bromwich Albion and Brighton and Hove Albion.

Meadows, Jimmy (b. Bolton 21.7.31; d. 1.94). A winger who converted to full-back, Jimmy began with Southport in 1949 and scored seven times in 60 League matches for the Haig Avenue outfit. In March, 1951, he moved to Manchester City and had made 130 League appearances, scoring 30 goals, when a injury received in the 1956 F.A. Cup Final, brought a premature end to his career. He joined the City training staff in the late fifties and stayed at Maine Road until the mid-sixties when he left to join Stockport County, eventually as manager. They won the Fourth Division Championship under his guidance in 1967. Jimmy then went to Bury as assistant manager in 1969, becoming assistant manager at Blackpool a year later. He then had spells in charge of Bolton Wanderers and Southport, whom he took to Fourth Division title in 1973. He returned to Stockport in 1974 and briefly to Blackpool in 1978, before finishing with spells in Kuwait and Sweden. In 1955, he won his sole England cap, gained in the 7-2 victory over Scotland.

Mills, Don (b. Rotherham 17.8.26; d. 2.94). An inside-forward who started out with Queens Park Rangers in 1946 and made 43 appearances before leaving for Torquay United in 1949. After 13 goals in 34 games for 'the Gulls' he rejoined QPR in 1950, but a year later was off to Cardiff City where he made only one League appearance. A move to Leeds followed in September, 1951, where he bagged nine goals in 34 matches. In December, 1952, he returned to Torquay, where he stayed until 1961, amassing 310 League appearances and scoring 68 goals.

Mills, James (b. Dalton 30.9.15; d. 14.1.94). Began with Rotherham United in the late thirties and made 53 League appearances before the outbreak of the war and played 219 games during hostilities. In October, 1946, he left Millmoor and went to Hull City, turning out for 'The Tigers' in 42 League games. In December, 1947, he was transferred to Halifax, for whom he made 19 League appearances, before moving on to Gainsborough Trinity in 1948.

Molloy, Peter (b. Rossendale 4.11; d. 16.2.93). A half-back, whose League career largely spanned a ten year period before the war, during which time he played for Fulham, Bristol Rovers, Cardiff City, Queens Park Rangers, Stockport County, Carlisle United and Bradford City. During the war he played for Distillery then, in 1948, he made his sole appearance for Notts County, having signed for the Magpies in April of that year. Peter also represented the Irish Football League.

Moore, Sam (b. Birmingham 6.9.34; d. 1.3.94). A forward who joined Wolves in November, 1954, but after being unable to break into the first team, Sam moved to Walsall, where he made 64 League appearances, scoring 12 times. In June, 1958, he signed for Gillingham, where he stayed for a season, scoring eight goals in 33 League games.

Morgan, Billy (b. Burnley 16.12.06; d. 4.11.93). Signed for Burnley 1920 after wartime service in the Navy. A wing-half, his career was cut short by injury in March 1924 when his right leg was broken in two places just above the ankle. Debut October 1921 v Bradford City, made 34 League and Cup appearances.

Morgan, William (b. Ryton-on-Tyne 1914; d. 2.94). A goalkeeper who played 150 pre-war League games for Coventry City, having signed for the Highfield Road club in 1932. He continued to play for City during the war and also made guest appearances for Nottingham Forest and Leicester City.

Oliver, Harry (b. Sunderland 16.2.21; d. 14.1.94). Watford full-back and captain who later switched to centre-half. Pre-war with Hartlepool United was transferred to Brentford for £1,500 at 17 and moved to Vicarage Road in May 1948 for £2,000. Former schoolboy international, he made over 100 League appearances for Watford.

Oxford, Ken (b. Manchester 14.11.29; d. 6.8.93). A former England Youth international goalkeeper, who signed for Manchester City in 1947, but only had one League game for the Maine Road club before spells with Derby County in 1949 and Chesterfield a year later. Ken made no League appearances for either club and in July, 1951, he moved on to Norwich City, where he amassed 128 League games between making his debut in 1953 and leaving for Derby in 1957. At £4,000, Ken proved a sound acquisition and he totalled 151 League matches for the Rams' before moves to Doncaster Rovers (16 games) in 1964 and Port Vale (three appearances) the following year completed his League career. He later played for and managed Boston United.

Richards, Gordon (b. Rhos 23.10.33; d. 17.11.93). Played for his local club, Wrexham, between 1952 and 1957, making 96 League appearances and scoring 24 goals—a tremendous ratio for an outside-left. In January, 1958, he left The Racecourse to join Chester and in 74 games scored 16 goals. In 1960, a serious knee injury brought a premature end to his League career.

Robinson, John (b. Blackburn 23.4.18; d. 4.93). A goalkeeper who began with Accrington Stanley, where he made 16 appearances before moving on to Manchester City in 1937 two years later. War interrupted his career at Maine Road and he made only two League appearances before signing for Bury in 1946. At Gigg Lane he had 12 outings, then moved to Southend in 1947 where, after only six games, he was forced to retire with a shoulder injury.

Rodgers, Arnold (b. Wickersley 5.12.23; d. 6.10.93). Arnold started his Football League career with Huddersfield Town for whom he made 28 appearances, scoring 17 goals. In October, 1949, he joined Bristol City for £5,000 and was a prolific scorer, with 106 goals in 195 League games. In 1954–55 he won a Third Division South Championship medal in a City side who equalled the record points total of 70, set for that League by Nottingham Forest in 1951. In June, 1956, Arnold was signed by Shrewsbury, but he only had 13 outings, scoring on three occasions, before he retired from the professional game.

Rowe, Arthur (b. Tottenham 1.9.06; d. 8.11.93). A centre-half with Spurs between May, 1929 and May, 1939. Arthur played a total of 201 games for Tottenham and made one international appearance for England in 1933 before his retirement from the game in 1939. He took up a brief coaching appointment in Hungary and, when war broke out, Arthur returned to Britain to serve in the Army as a PTI. He also ran the Army football team, which was the prelude to a wonderful managerial career. After the war, he became Secretary/Manager of Chelmsford City befoe moving on to manage Tottenham Hotspur in 1949. Arthur had immediate success, steering Spurs to the Championships of Division Two in 1950, followed by the First Division title a year later. In the mid-fifties his health deteriorated and a nervous breakdown forced a complete break from football. He handed over temporary control to Jimmy Anderson in 1955 and eventually Anderson took over full-time in January, 1956. Arthur had a brief spell as coach at West Bromwich Albion then, in 1958, he became assistant manager at Crystal Palace before taking overall control in 1960. Following promotion to the Third Division in 1961, he suffered a relapse of ill health in 1962 and resigned the same year. In 1966 Arthur took up a post as assistant manager at Selhurst Park, which he held until 1971. He later took consultancy posts with Orient and Millwall.

Selkirk, Jack (b. Doncaster 20.1.23; d. 11.8.93). Signed for Rotherham United in 1944 and gave wonderful service to his one and only club, making 427 League appearances between 1946 and 1957. Jack was an ever present full-back during United's Third Division North Championship winning season of 1950–51. He scored his first-ever goal for 'the Millers' in the final game of that particular campaign, with a direct free-kick! He was also a star of the Rotherham side that reached the Fifth Round of the F.A. Cup in 1953 and was an invaluable member of the team that secured Rotherham's highest ever League position—third in the Second Division—in 1955.

Simpson, John (b. Kendal 5.10.33; d. 7.12.93). After spending just three months on Lincoln City's books, during which time he made five League appearances, this commanding goalkeeper joined Gillingham in June, 1957. John went on to play 571 League matches for the Gills—a club record—giving magnificent service until 1972. He won a Fourth Division Championship medal in 1964, conceding only 30 goals.

Smith, Henry (b. Newburn 11.10.08; d. 1993). A full-back who signed for Nottingham Forest in 1928, and had 156 outings before a move to Darlington in 1937. At Feethams, he played 65 times, then was transferred to Bristol Rovers in August, 1939. Although he played war-time football with Rovers, as well as guesting for City, Henry had to wait until after the war to make his Football League debut, by which time he was approaching his 39th birthday. He made four League appearances before becoming groundsman at Eastville in 1956.

Steele, Joe (b. Blackridge 4.10.28; d. 11.93). An outside left who started out with Newcastle United in 1948, but after being unable to break into the first team, Joe joined Bury in 1950. There he made 18 League appearances, scoring once. In 1951, he signed for Leyton Orient, but made no appearances for the first team.

Taylor, Brian (b. Gateshead 2.7.49; 10.12.93). Brian signed for Coventry in July, 1970, but left the following year for Walsall, where he amassed 216 League appearances and scored 25 goals. He stayed at Fellows Park until 1977, then came a move to Plymouth, where he scored for Argyle on his debut against Pompey. However, the following year, after 35 League games and five goals, he was off to Preston North End, where he remained until

March, 1982. Brian had 99 League outings for the Deepdale club, scoring once, before a move to Wigan Athletic. His first class playing career terminated at the end of the 1981–82 season, having made eight League appearances for Athletic.

Turner, Arthur (b. Chesterton 1.4.09; d. 12.1.94). Joined Stoke City in 1930 and won a Second Division Championship medal in 1933. In 1939, after more than 300 games for Stoke, the powerful centre-half signed for Birmingham City for £6,000 and made 186 appearances for the Blues during the war. In February, 1948, he left St. Andrews to join Southport, but he only had 28 outings for them before going to Crewe Alexandra as player-manager in October of that year. Arthur retired from playing in 1949, then became assistant boss at Stoke in 1952 before taking over the helm at Birmingham in 1954. He guided City to the Second Division Championship in 1955. In 1959 came the most significant move of his carerer, when he took over at Oxford United. At The Manor he achieved wonders, taking the club from the Southern League to the Second Division. Promotion from the Fourth Division was achieved in 1965, then the Third Division title followed in 1968—by a team costing a mere £14,500! He became general manager of the club in 1969 but, in 1972, due to financial restrictions, United could no longer afford his services, so he left the club. In the early seventies he took scouting posts at Rotherham and Sheffield United.

Vernon, Roy (b. Ffynngroew 14.4.37; d. 4.12.93). A Welsh International inside-forward who won 32 caps for his country. Roy was one of the most skilful players of his generation and a prolific goalscorer. He began his career with Blackburn Rovers, hitting 49 goals in 131 League games between 1955 and 1960. In February of that year he joined Everton for £27,000 plus Eddie Thomas in part exchange. It proved an inspired purchase by the Goodison club. Roy netted 101 goals in 176 League outings, helped secure the title for Everton in 1963, and topped the club goalscoring charts four seasons in succession. In March, 1965, he was snapped up by Stoke City and again proved an invaluable aquisition, notching 22 times in 87 games. His first class playing career was completed at Halifax, whom he joined in 1969–70. But he didn't stay beyond the end of that season, spending a brief period in Cape Town, before returning to join former Blackburn team-mates Ronnie Clayton and Bryan Douglas at Great Harwood in the Northern Premier League.

Waddington, Tony (b. Manchester 9.11.24; d. 21.1.94). A wing-half for Crewe Alexandra, who made 172 appearances scoring seven goals, between 1946 and 1952. He was then forced to retire through injury and became coach at Stoke City. He took over the Potters helm in 1960 and remained in charge until 1977. Tony was adept at signing experienced professionals and the likes of Jimmy McIlroy, George Eastham, Stanley Matthews and Dennis Viollet all achieved success at the club. Tony guided City to the Second Division Championship in 1963 and a splendid League Cup triumph over Chelsea in 1972. After his departure from The Victoria Ground in 1977, he had a spell out of the game, but returned to manage Crewe from 1979 until 1981.

Wallace, Joe (b. Glasgow 28.12.33; d. 1993). A wing-half, who made 337 League appearances for Shrewsbury Town between 1954 and 1962, before he joined Southport. There he played 79 League games before retiring in 1965.

Ward, Gerry (b. London 5.10.36; d. 1.94). A wing-half, who played for England at Schoolboy, Youth and Amateur level. He signed for Arsenal in October, 1953 and, at 16 years and 321 days, is still the youngest player to represent Arsenal. He made 95 League appearances for Arsenal, scoring on ten occasions, before leaving for Leyton Orient in July, 1963. He had 43 outings for the Brisbane Road club, then left the League to play for Cambridge City and later Barnet.

Wilson, Charlie (b. Cleethorpes 10.2.04; d. 22.2.94). A great servant to Grimsby Town making 273 League appearances between 1923 and 1933. A wing-half converted to a full-back, Charlie was a key member of the Third Division North title winning team of 1925–26 and the successful 1928–29 side, who finished runners-up in the Second Division. In 1933, he joined Bournemouth and ended his League career at Peterborough United.

Withers, Edward 'osh' (b. Ower 8.9.15; d. 7.1.94). Joined Southampton in 1934, he made only a handful of appearances before a transfer to Bristol Rovers in 1937. The inside forward made 17 appearances in the '37–38 season, but then suddenly retired from the first class game, returning to Hampshire to play non-league football.

THE FA CARLING PREMIERSHIP and ENDSLEIGH INSURANCE LEAGUE FIXTURES 1994–95

Saturday 13 August 1994

Endsleigh League Division 1
Barnsley v Derby Co
Bristol C v Sunderland
Grimsby T v Bolton W
Luton T v WBA
Middlesbrough v Burnley
Millwall v Southend U
Oldham Ath v Charlton Ath
Portsmouth v Notts Co
Sheffield U v Watford
Stoke C v Tranmere R
Wolverhampton W v Reading

Endsleigh League Division 2
Blackpool v Huddersfield T
Chester C v Bradford C
Leyton O v Birmingham C
Oxford U v Hull C
Peterborough U v Bristol R
Plymouth Arg v Brentford
Rotherham U v Shrewsbury T
Stockport Co v Cardiff C
Swansea C v Brighton & HA
Wrexham v AFC Bournemouth
Wycombe W v Cambridge U
York C v Crewe Alex

Endsleigh League Division 3
Barnet v Scunthorpe U
Bury v Rochdale
Carlisle U v Wigan Ath
Chesterfield v Scarborough
Colchester U v Torquay U
Darlington v Preston NE
Fulham v Walsall
Gillingham v Hartlepool U
Hereford U v Doncaster R
Lincoln C v Exeter C

Sunday 14 August 1994

Endsleigh League Division 1
Swindon T v Port Vale

Saturday 20 August 1994

FA Carling Premiership
Arsenal v Manchester C
Chelsea v Norwich C
Coventry C v Wimbledon
Crystal Palace v Liverpool
Everton v Aston Villa
Ipswich T v Nottingham F
Manchester U v QPR
Sheffield W v Tottenham H
Southampton v Blackburn R
West Ham U v Leeds U

Endsleigh League Division 1
Bolton W v Bristol C
Burnley v Stoke C
Charlton Ath v Barnsley
Derby Co v Luton T
Port Vale v Oldham Ath
Reading v Portsmouth
Southend U v Middlesbrough
Sunderland v Millwall
Tranmere R v Swindon T
Watford v Grimsby T
WBA v Sheffield U

Endsleigh League Division 2
AFC Bournemouth v Blackpool
Birmingham C v Chester C
Bradford C v Leyton O
Brentford v Peterborough U
Brighton & HA v Plymouth Arg
Bristol R v York C
Cambridge U v Stockport Co
Cardiff C v Oxford U
Crewe Alex v Rotherham U
Huddersfield T v Wycombe W
Hull C v Swansea C
Shrewsbury T v Wrexham

Endsleigh League Division 3
Doncaster R v Northampton T
Exeter C v Bury
Hartlepool U v Darlington
Hereford U v Preston NE
Mansfield T v Colchester U
Rochdale v Chesterfield
Scarborough v Barnet
Scunthorpe U v Fulham
Torquay U v Carlisle U
Walsall v Lincoln C
Wigan Ath v Gillingham

Sunday 21 August 1994

FA Carling Premiership
Leicester C v Newcastle U

Endsleigh League Division 1
Notts Co v Wolverhampton W

Monday 22 August 1994

FA Carling Premiership
Nottingham F v Manchester U

Tuesday 23 August 1994

FA Carling Premiership
Blackburn R v Leicester C
Leeds U v Arsenal
Wimbledon v Ipswich T

Wednesday 24 August 1994

FA Carling Premiership
Aston Villa v Southampton
Manchester C v West Ham U
Newcastle U v Coventry C
Norwich C v Crystal Palace
QPR v Sheffield W
Tottenham H v Everton

Saturday 27 August 1994

FA Carling Premiership
Aston Villa v Crystal Palace
Blackburn R v Coventry C
Leeds U v Chelsea
Manchester C v Everton
Newcastle U v Southampton
Norwich C v West Ham U
Nottingham F v Leicester C
QPR v Ipswich T
Tottenham H v Manchester U
Wimbledon v Sheffield W

Endsleigh League Division 1
Barnsley v Reading
Bristol C v Port Vale
Grimsby T v Tranmere R
Luton T v Southend U
Middlesbrough v Bolton W
Millwall v Derby Co
Oldham Ath v Burnley
Portsmouth v Charlton Ath
Sheffield U v Notts Co
Stoke C v Sunderland
Swindon T v Watford

Endsleigh League Division 2
Blackpool v Shrewsbury T
Chester C v Huddersfield T
Leyton O v Hull C
Oxford U v Cambridge U
Peterborough U v Crewe Alex
Plymouth Arg v Bradford C
Rotherham U v AFC Bournemouth
Stockport Co v Brentford
Swansea C v Birmingham C
Wrexham v Brighton & HA
Wycombe W v Bristol R
York C v Cardiff C

Endsleigh League Division 3
Barnet v Preston NE
Bury v Hartlepool U
Carlisle U v Scarborough
Chesterfield v Mansfield T
Colchester U v Doncaster R
Darlington v Exeter C
Fulham v Wigan Ath
Gillingham v Rochdale
Hereford U v Walsall
Lincoln C v Torquay U
Scunthorpe U v Northampton T

Sunday 28 August 1994

FA Carling Premiership
Liverpool v Arsenal

Endsleigh League Division 1
Wolverhampton W v WBA

Monday 29 August 1994

FA Carling Premiership
Coventry C v Aston Villa

Tuesday 30 August 1994

FA Carling Premiership
Crystal Palace v Leeds U
Everton v Nottingham F
Ipswich T v Tottenham H

Endsleigh League Division 1
Bolton W v Millwall
Burnley v Bristol C
Charlton Ath v Sheffield U
Notts Co v Oldham Ath
Port Vale v Barnsley
Reading v Stoke C
Southend U v Portsmouth
Sunderland v Grimsby T
Tranmere R v Luton T
Watford v Wolverhampton W

Endsleigh League Division 2
AFC Bournemouth v Peterborough U
Birmingham C v Wycombe W
Bradford C v Oxford U
Brentford v Rotherham U
Cambridge U v Chester C

Cardiff C v Wrexham
Crewe Alex v Stockport Co
Huddersfield T v Leyton O
Hull C v Plymouth Arg
Shrewsbury T v Swansea C

Endsleigh League Division 3
Bury v Preston NE
Doncaster R v Fulham
Exeter C v Colchester U
Hartlepool U v Barnet
Mansfield T v Darlington
Rochdale v Lincoln C
Scarborough v Hereford U
Scunthorpe U v Gillingham
Torquay U v Northampton T
Walsall v Carlisle U
Wigan Ath v Chesterfield

Wednesday 31 August 1994

FA Carling Premiership
Arsenal v Blackburn R
Chelsea v Manchester C
Leicester C v QPR
Manchester U v Wimbledon
Sheffield W v Norwich C
Southampton v Liverpool
West Ham U v Newcastle U

Endsleigh League Division 1
Derby Co v Middlesbrough
WBA v Swindon T

Endsleigh League Division 2
Brighton & HA v York C
Bristol R v Blackpool

Saturday 3 September 1994

FA Carling Premiership
Bolton W v Stoke C
Burnley v Barnsley
Charlton Ath v Bristol C
Derby Co v Grimsby T
Notts Co v Swindon T
Port Vale v Luton T
Reading v Millwall
Southend U v Oldham Ath
Sunderland v Wolverhampton W
Tranmere R v Sheffield U
Watford v Middlesbrough
WBA v Portsmouth

Endsleigh League Division 2
AFC Bournemouth v York C
Birmingham C v Plymouth Arg
Bradford C v Wycombe W
Brentford v Wrexham
Brighton & HA v Leyton O
Bristol R v Stockport Co
Cambridge U v Rotherham U
Cardiff C v Swansea C
Crewe Alex v Blackpool
Huddersfield T v Oxford U
Hull C v Chester C
Shrewsbury T v Peterborough U

Endsleigh League Division 3
Doncaster R v Darlington
Exeter C v Gillingham
Hartlepool U v Chesterfield
Mansfield T v Bury
Preston NE v Lincoln C
Rochdale v Hereford U
Scarborough v Colchester U
Scunthorpe U v Carlisle U
Torquay U v Fulham
Walsall v Northampton T
Wigan Ath v Barnet

Saturday 10 September 1994

FA Carling Premiership
Aston Villa v Ipswich T
Blackburn R v Everton
Liverpool v West Ham U
Manchester C v Crystal Palace
Newcastle U v Chelsea
Norwich C v Arsenal
Nottingham F v Sheffield W
QPR v Coventry C
Wimbledon v Leicester C

Endsleigh League Division 1
Barnsley v Watford
Bristol C v Notts Co
Grimsby T v Charlton Ath
Luton T v Burnley
Middlesbrough v Sunderland
Millwall v WBA
Oldham Ath v Reading
Portsmouth v Port Vale
Sheffield U v Bolton W
Stoke C v Southend U
Swindon T v Derby Co
Wolverhampton W v Tranmere R

Endsleigh League Division 2
Blackpool v Cardiff C
Chester C v Brighton & HA
Leyton O v Cambridge U
Oxford U v Birmingham C
Peterborough U v Hull C
Plymouth Arg v Huddersfield T
Rotherham U v Bristol R
Stockport Co v AFC Bournemouth
Swansea C v Bradford C
Wrexham v Crewe Alex
Wycombe W v Brentford
York C v Shrewsbury T

Endsleigh League Division 3
Barnet v Doncaster R
Bury v Scunthorpe U
Carlisle U v Exeter C
Chesterfield v Walsall
Colchester U v Hartlepool U
Darlington v Torquay U
Fulham v Preston NE
Gillingham v Scarborough
Hereford U v Wigan Ath
Lincoln C v Mansfield T
Northampton T v Rochdale

Sunday 11 September 1994

FA Carling Premiership
Leeds U v Manchester U

Monday 12 September 1994

FA Carling Premiership
Tottenham H v Southampton

Tuesday 13 September 1994

Endsleigh League Division 1
Barnsley v Notts Co
Bristol C v Derby Co
Grimsby T v Port Vale
Luton T v Bolton W
Middlesbrough v WBA
Oldham Ath v Watford
Sheffield U v Sunderland
Wolverhampton W v Southend U

Endsleigh League Division 2
Blackpool v Brighton & HA
Chester C v Cardiff C
Leyton O v AFC Bournemouth
Oxford U v Crewe Alex
Peterborough U v Huddersfield T
Plymouth Arg v Cambridge U
Rotherham U v Birmingham C
Stockport Co v Shrewsbury T
Swansea C v Bristol R
Wrexham v Bradford C
Wycombe W v Hull C
York C v Brentford

Endsleigh League Division 3
Barnet v Rochdale
Bury v Doncaster R
Carlisle U v Mansfield T
Chesterfield v Exeter C
Colchester U v Walsall
Darlington v Scunthorpe U
Fulham v Scarborough
Gillingham v Preston NE
Hereford U v Torquay U
Lincoln C v Wigan Ath
Northampton T v Hartlepool U

Wednesday 14 September 1994

Endsleigh League Division 1
Millwall v Burnley
Portsmouth v Tranmere R
Stoke C v Charlton Ath
Swindon T v Reading

Friday 16 September 1994

Endsleigh League Division 3
Doncaster R v Hereford U

Saturday 17 September 1994

FA Carling Premiership
Coventry C v Leeds U
Crystal Palace v Wimbledon
Everton v QPR
Leicester C v Tottenham H
Manchester U v Liverpool
Sheffield W v Manchester C
Southampton v Nottingham F
West Ham U v Aston Villa

Endsleigh League Division 1
Bolton W v Portsmouth
Burnley v Wolverhampton W
Charlton Ath v Swindon T
Derby Co v Oldham Ath
Notts Co v Stoke C
Port Vale v Middlesbrough
Reading v Sheffield U
Southend U v Bristol C
Sunderland v Barnsley
Tranmere R v Millwall
Watford v Luton T
WBA v Grimsby T

Endsleigh League Division 2
AFC Bournemouth v Chester C
Birmingham C v Peterborough U
Bradford C v York C
Brentford v Blackpool
Brighton & HA v Oxford U
Bristol R v Wrexham
Cambridge U v Swansea C
Cardiff C v Plymouth Arg
Crewe Alex v Wycombe W
Huddersfield T v Stockport Co
Hull C v Rotherham U
Shrewsbury T v Leyton O

Endsleigh League Division 3
Exeter C v Lincoln C
Hartlepool U v Gillingham
Mansfield T v Northampton T
Preston NE v Darlington
Rochdale v Bury
Scarborough v Chesterfield
Scunthorpe U v Barnet
Torquay U v Colchester U
Walsall v Fulham
Wigan Ath v Carlisle U

Sunday 18 September 1994

FA Carling Premiership
Arsenal v Newcastle U
Chelsea v Blackburn R

Monday 19 September 1994

FA Carling Premiership
Ipswich T v Norwich C

Saturday 24 September 1994

FA Carling Premiership
Blackburn R v Aston Villa
Coventry C v Southampton
Crystal Palace v Chelsea
Everton v Leicester C
Ipswich T v Manchester U
Manchester C v Norwich C
Newcastle U v Liverpool
QPR v Wimbledon
Tottenham H v Nottingham F

Endsleigh League Division 1
Bristol C v Middlesbrough
Derby Co v Stoke C
Millwall v Luton T
Notts Co v Charlton Ath
Oldham Ath v Barnsley
Port Vale v Sheffield U
Portsmouth v Wolverhampton W
Southend U v Bolton W
Swindon T v Grimsby T
Tranmere R v Sunderland
Watford v Reading
WBA v Burnley

Endsleigh League Division 2
AFC Bournemouth v Cardiff C
Birmingham C v Hull C
Blackpool v Wrexham
Bradford C v Huddersfield T
Brighton & HA v Cambridge U
Crewe Alex v Brentford
Oxford U v Leyton O
Peterborough U v Rotherham U
Plymouth Arg v Chester C
Shrewsbury T v Bristol R
Stockport Co v Wycombe W
Swansea C v York C

Endsleigh League Division 3
Bury v Chesterfield
Darlington v Colchester U
Doncaster R v Preston NE
Fulham v Hereford U
Hartlepool U v Lincoln C
Mansfield T v Exeter C
Northampton T v Carlisle U
Scarborough v Rochdale
Scunthorpe U v Wigan Ath
Torquay U v Barnet
Walsall v Gillingham

Sunday 25 September 1994

FA Carling Premiership
West Ham U v Arsenal

Monday 26 September 1994

FA Carling Premiership
Sheffield W v Leeds U

Saturday 1 October 1994

FA Carling Premiership
Arsenal v Crystal Palace
Aston Villa v Newcastle U
Leeds U v Manchester C
Liverpool v Sheffield W
Manchester U v Everton
Norwich C v Blackburn R
Southampton v Ipswich T
Wimbledon v Tottenham H

Endsleigh League Division 1
Barnsley v Swindon T
Bolton W v Derby Co
Burnley v Tranmere R
Charlton Ath v Watford
Grimsby T v Portsmouth
Luton T v Bristol C
Middlesbrough v Millwall
Reading v Notts Co
Sheffield U v Oldham Ath
Stoke C v WBA
Sunderland v Southend U
Wolverhampton W v Port Vale

Endsleigh League Division 2
Brentford v Shrewsbury T
Bristol R v Crewe Alex
Cambridge U v Bradford C
Cardiff C v Peterborough U
Chester C v Oxford U
Huddersfield T v Brighton & HA
Hull C v AFC Bournemouth
Leyton O v Plymouth Arg
Rotherham U v Blackpool
Wrexham v Birmingham C
Wycombe W v Swansea C
York C v Stockport Co

Endsleigh League Division 3
Barnet v Fulham
Carlisle U v Darlington
Chesterfield v Torquay U
Colchester U v Bury
Exeter C v Hartlepool U
Gillingham v Mansfield T
Hereford U v Scunthorpe U
Lincoln C v Northampton T
Preston NE v Walsall
Rochdale v Doncaster R
Wigan Ath v Scarborough

Sunday 2 October 1994

FA Carling Premiership
Chelsea v West Ham U
Nottingham F v QPR

Monday 3 Octber 1994

FA Carling Premiership
Leicester C v Coventry C

Saturday 8 October 1994

FA Carling Premiership
Chelsea v Leicester C
Coventry C v Ipswich T
Liverpool v Aston Villa
Manchester C v Nottingham F
Norwich C v Leeds U
Sheffield W v Manchester U
Southampton v Everton
Tottenham H v QPR
Wimbledon v Arsenal

Endsleigh League Division 1
Barnsley v Southend U
Bristol C v Millwall
Burnley v Bolton W
Charlton Ath v Reading
Derby Co v Watford
Grimsby T v Sheffield U
Middlesbrough v Tranmere R
Notts Co v Port Vale
Oldham Ath v Portsmouth
Stoke C v Luton T
Swindon T v Wolverhampton W
WBA v Sunderland

Endsleigh League Division 2
Birmingham C v Huddersfield T
Bradford C v Brighton & HA
Brentford v Bristol R
Cambridge U v Wrexham
Cardiff C v Crewe Alex
Chester C v Swansea C
Hull C v Blackpool
Oxford U v Plymouth Arg
Shrewsbury T v AFC Bournemouth
Stockport Co v Rotherham U
Wycombe W v Leyton O
York C v Peterborough U

Endsleigh League Division 3
Barnet v Hereford U
Colchester U v Chesterfield
Darlington v Bury
Doncaster R v Wigan Ath
Exeter C v Northampton T
Gillingham v Torquay U
Lincoln C v Carlisle U
Mansfield T v Hartlepool U
Preston NE v Scunthorpe U
Rochdale v Fulham
Walsall v Scarborough

Sunday 9 October 1994

FA Carling Premiership
Newcastle U v Blackburn R

Monday 10 October 1994

FA Carling Premiership
West Ham U v Crystal Palace

Tuesday 11 October 1994

Endsleigh League Division 3
Northampton T v Mansfield T

Saturday 15 October 1994

FA Carling Premiership
Arsenal v Chelsea
Aston Villa v Norwich C
Blackburn R v Liverpool
Crystal Palace v Newcastle U
Everton v Coventry C
Leeds U v Tottenham H
Leicester C v Southampton
Manchester U v West Ham U
QPR v Manchester C

Endsleigh League Division 1
Bolton W v Oldham Ath
Luton T v Middlesbrough
Millwall v Stoke C
Port Vale v Charlton Ath
Portsmouth v Swindon T
Reading v Bristol C
Sheffield U v Barnsley
Southend U v Derby Co
Sunderland v Burnley
Tranmere R v WBA
Watford v Notts Co
Wolverhampton W v Grimsby T

Endsleigh League Division 2
AFC Bournemouth v Brentford
Blackpool v Bradford C
Brighton & HA v Birmingham C
Bristol R v Cardiff C
Crewe Alex v Shrewsbury T
Huddersfield T v Cambridge U
Leyton O v Chester C
Peterborough U v Stockport Co
Plymouth Arg v Wycombe W
Rotherham U v York C
Swansea C v Oxford U
Wrexham v Hull C

Endsleigh League Division 3
Bury v Lincoln C
Carlisle U v Colchester U
Chesterfield v Darlington
Fulham v Exeter C
Hartlepool U v Preston NE
Hereford U v Gillingham
Northampton T v Barnet
Scarborough v Doncaster R
Scunthorpe U v Walsall
Torquay U v Mansfield T
Wigan Ath v Rochdale

Sunday 16 October 1994

FA Carling Premiership
Ipswich T v Sheffield W

Monday 17 October 1994

FA Carling Premiership
Nottingham F v Wimbledon

Saturday 22 October 1994

FA Carling Premiership
Arsenal v Coventry C
Aston Villa v Nottingham F
Chelsea v Ipswich T
Crystal Palace v Everton
Leeds U v Leicester C
Liverpool v Wimbledon
Manchester C v Tottenham H
Newcastle U v Sheffield W
Norwich C v QPR
West Ham U v Southampton

Endsleigh League Division 1
Barnsley v WBA
Charlton Ath v Burnley
Grimsby T v Bristol C
Notts Co v Derby Co
Oldham Ath v Stoke C
Port Vale v Bolton W
Portsmouth v Middlesbrough
Reading v Sunderland
Sheffield U v Luton T
Swindon T v Southend U
Watford v Tranmere R
Wolverhampton W v Millwall

Endsleigh League Division 2
AFC Bournemouth v Bradford C
Blackpool v Swansea C
Brentford v Birmingham C
Bristol R v Brighton & HA
Cardiff C v Cambridge U
Crewe Alex v Huddersfield T
Peterborough U v Wycombe W
Rotherham U v Leyton O
Shrewsbury T v Hull C
Stockport Co v Plymouth Arg
Wrexham v Oxford U
York C v Chester C

Endsleigh League Division 3
Bury v Gillingham
Carlisle U v Barnet
Chesterfield v Fulham
Colchester U v Preston NE
Darlington v Hereford U
Exeter C v Scunthorpe U
Hartlepool U v Walsall
Lincoln C v Scarborough
Mansfield T v Doncaster R
Northampton T v Wigan Ath
Torquay U v Rochdale

Sunday 23 October 1994

FA Carling Premiership
Blackburn R v Manchester U

Saturday 29 October 1994

FA Carling Premiership
Coventry C v Manchester C
Everton v Arsenal
Ipswich T v Liverpool
Leicester C v Crystal Palace
Manchester U v Newcastle U
Nottingham F v Blackburn R
QPR v Aston Villa
Sheffield W v Chelsea
Southampton v Leeds U
Tottenham H v West Ham U

Endsleigh League Division 1
Bolton W v Watford
Bristol C v Portsmouth
Burnley v Notts Co
Derby Co v Charlton Ath
Luton T v Barnsley
Middlesbrough v Swindon T
Millwall v Sheffield U
Southend U v Grimsby T
Stoke C v Wolverhampton W
Sunderland v Oldham Ath
Tranmere R v Port Vale
WBA v Reading

Endsleigh League Division 2
Birmingham C v Bristol R
Bradford C v Cardiff C
Brighton & HA v Rotherham U
Cambridge U v Brentford
Huddersfield T v AFC Bournemouth
Hull C v Crewe Alex
Leyton O v Stockport Co
Oxford U v Shrewsbury T
Plymouth Arg v Blackpool
Swansea C v Peterborough U
Wycombe W v York C

Endsleigh League Division 3
Barnet v Chesterfield
Doncaster R v Torquay U
Fulham v Carlisle U
Gillingham v Darlington
Hereford U v Lincoln C
Preston NE v Exeter C
Rochdale v Mansfield T
Scarborough v Northampton T
Scunthorpe U v Hartlepool U
Walsall v Bury
Wigan Ath v Colchester U

Sunday 30 October 1994

FA Carling Premiership
Wimbledon v Norwich C

Endsleigh League Division 2
Chester C v Wrexham

Monday 31 October 1994

FA Carling Premiership
QPR v Liverpool

Tuesday 1 November 1994

FA Carling Premiership
Everton v West Ham U
Ipswich T v Leeds U

Endsleigh League Division 1
Bolton W v Swindon T
Bristol C v Wolverhampton W
Burnley v Watford
Luton T v Grimsby T
Middlesbrough v Oldham Ath
Southend U v Notts Co
Sunderland v Charlton Ath
Tranmere R v Barnsley

Endsleigh League Division 2
Birmingham C v Crewe Alex
Bradford C v Brentford
Cambridge U v Bristol R
Huddersfield T v Wrexham
Hull C v York C
Leyton O v Cardiff C
Oxford U v Blackpool
Plymouth Arg v Peterborough U
Swansea C v Rotherham U
Wycombe W v Shrewsbury T

Wednesday 2 November 1994

FA Carling Premiership
Coventry C v Crystal Palace
Nottingham F v Newcastle U
Sheffield W v Blackburn R
Southampton v Norwich C
Wimbledon v Aston Villa

Endsleigh League Division 1
Derby Co v Reading
Millwall v Portsmouth
Stoke C v Sheffield U
WBA v Port Vale

Endsleigh League Division 2
Brighton & HA v AFC Bournemouth
Chester C v Stockport Co

Saturday 5 November 1994

FA Carling Premiership
Blackburn R v Tottenham H
Chelsea v Coventry C
Crystal Palace v Ipswich T
Leeds U v Wimbledon
Liverpool v Nottingham F
Manchester C v Southampton
Newcastle U v QPR
Norwich C v Everton
West Ham U v Leicester C

Endsleigh League Division 1
Barnsley v Stoke C
Charlton Ath v Bolton W
Grimsby T v Middlesbrough
Notts Co v Sunderland
Oldham Ath v Tranmere R
Port Vale v Southend U
Portsmouth v Derby Co
Reading v Burnley
Sheffield U v Bristol C
Swindon T v Millwall
Watford v WBA
Wolverhampton W v Luton T

Endsleigh League Division 2
AFC Bournemouth v Cambridge U
Blackpool v Leyton O
Brentford v Hull C
Bristol R v Bradford C
Cardiff C v Brighton & HA
Crewe Alex v Swansea C
Peterborough U v Chester C
Rotherham U v Plymouth Arg
Shrewsbury T v Birmingham C
Stockport Co v Oxford U
Wrexham v Wycombe W
York C v Huddersfield T

Endsleigh League Division 3
Bury v Scarborough
Carlisle U v Rochdale
Chesterfield v Hereford U
Colchester U v Gillingham
Darlington v Walsall
Exeter C v Doncaster R
Hartlepool U v Wigan Ath
Lincoln C v Barnet
Mansfield T v Preston NE
Northampton T v Fulham
Torquay U v Scunthorpe U

Sunday 6 November 1994

FA Carling Premiership
Arsenal v Sheffield W
Aston Villa v Manchester U

Wednesday 9 November 1994

FA Carling Premiership
Liverpool v Chelsea

Thursday 10 November 1994

FA Carling Premiership
Manchester U v Manchester C

Saturday 12 November 1994

Endsleigh League Division 1
Barnsley v Bristol C
Charlton Ath v WBA
Grimsby T v Millwall

Notts Co v Tranmere R
Oldham Ath v Luton T
Portsmouth v Stoke C
Reading v Middlesbrough
Sheffield U v Derby Co
Watford v Southend U
Wolverhampton W v Bolton W

Saturday 19 November 1994

FA Carling Premiership
Coventry C v Norwich C
Ipswich T v Blackburn R
Manchester U v Crystal Palace
Nottingham F v Chelsea
QPR v Leeds U
Sheffield W v West Ham U
Southampton v Arsenal
Tottenham H v Aston Villa
Wimbledon v Newcastle U

Endsleigh League Division 1
Bolton W v Notts Co
Bristol C v Swindon T
Burnley v Sheffield U
Derby Co v Port Vale
Luton T v Portsmouth
Middlesbrough v Wolverhampton W
Millwall v Barnsley
Southend U v Reading
Stoke C v Grimsby T
Sunderland v Watford
Tranmere R v Charlton Ath
WBA v Oldham Ath

Endsleigh League Division 2
Birmingham C v AFC Bournemouth
Bradford C v Crewe Alex
Brighton & HA v Peterborough U
Cambridge U v Shrewsbury T
Chester C v Blackpool
Huddersfield T v Brentford
Hull C v Bristol R
Leyton O v York C
Oxford U v Rotherham U
Plymouth Arg v Wrexham
Swansea C v Stockport Co
Wycombe W v Cardiff C

Endsleigh League Division 3
Barnet v Bury
Doncaster R v Hartlepool U
Fulham v Lincoln C
Gillingham v Chesterfield
Hereford U v Carlisle U
Preston NE v Northampton T
Rochdale v Colchester U
Scarborough v Torquay U
Scunthorpe U v Mansfield T
Walsall v Exeter C
Wigan Ath v Darlington

Sunday 20 November 1994

FA Carling Premiership
Leicester C v Manchester C

Monday 21 November 1994

FA Carling Premiership
Everton v Liverpool

Wednesday 23 November 1994

FA Carling Premiership
Leicester C v Arsenal
Tottenham H v Chelsea

Endsleigh League Division 1
Swindon T v Burnley

Friday 25 November 1994

Endsleigh League Division 2
Cardiff C v Hull C

Saturday 26 November 1994

FA Carling Premiership
Arsenal v Manchester U
Aston Villa v Sheffield W
Blackburn R v QPR
Chelsea v Everton
Crystal Palace v Southampton
Leeds U v Nottingham F
Liverpool v Tottenham H
Manchester C v Wimbledon
Newcastle U v Ipswich T
Norwich C v Leicester C
West Ham U v Coventry C

Endsleigh League Division 1
Barnsley v Bolton W
Charlton Ath v Middlesbrough
Grimsby T v Burnley
Notts Co v WBA
Oldham Ath v Bristol C
Port Vale v Millwall
Portsmouth v Sunderland
Reading v Tranmere R
Sheffield U v Southend U
Swindon T v Luton T
Watford v Stoke C
Wolverhampton W v Derby Co

Endsleigh League Division 2
AFC Bournemouth v Oxford U
Blackpool v Wycombe W
Brentford v Brighton & HA
Bristol R v Huddersfield T
Crewe Alex v Cambridge U
Peterborough U v Leyton O
Rotherham U v Chester C
Shrewsbury T v Bradford C
Stockport Co v Birmingham C
Wrexham v Swansea C
York C v Plymouth Arg

Endsleigh League Division 3
Bury v Fulham
Carlisle U v Doncaster R
Chesterfield v Preston NE
Colchester U v Scunthorpe U
Darlington v Barnet
Exeter C v Scarborough
Hartlepool U v Rochdale
Lincoln C v Gillingham
Mansfield T v Walsall
Northampton T v Hereford U
Torquay U v Wigan Ath

Tuesday 29 November 1994

Endsleigh League Division 1
Port Vale v Sunderland

Saturday 3 December 1994

FA Carling Premiership
Coventry C v Liverpool
Ipswich T v Manchester C
Leicester C v Aston Villa
Manchester U v Norwich C
Nottingham F v Arsenal
QPR v West Ham U
Sheffield W v Crystal Palace
Southampton v Chelsea
Tottenham H v Newcastle U
Wimbledon v Blackburn R

Endsleigh League Division 1
Bolton W v Port Vale
Bristol C v Grimsby T
Burnley v Charlton Ath
Derby Co v Notts Co
Luton T v Sheffield U
Middlesbrough v Portsmouth
Millwall v Wolverhampton W
Southend U v Swindon T
Stoke C v Oldham Ath
Sunderland v Reading
Tranmere R v Watford
WBA v Barnsley

Monday 5 December 1994

FA Carling Premiership
Everton v Leeds U

Saturday 10 December 1994

FA Carling Premiership
Aston Villa v Everton
Blackburn R v Southampton
Leeds U v West Ham U
Liverpool v Crystal Palace
Manchester C v Arsenal
Newcastle U v Leicester C
Norwich C v Chelsea
Nottingham F v Ipswich T
QPR v Manchester U
Wimbledon v Coventry C

Endsleigh League Division 1
Barnsley v Charlton Ath
Bristol C v Bolton W
Grimsby T v Watford
Luton T v Derby Co
Middlesbrough v Southend U
Millwall v Sunderland
Oldham Ath v Port Vale
Portsmouth v Reading
Sheffield U v WBA
Stoke C v Burnley
Swindon T v Tranmere R
Wolverhampton W v Notts Co

Endsleigh League Division 2
Blackpool v AFC Bournemouth
Chester C v Birmingham C
Leyton O v Bradford C
Oxford U v Cardiff C
Peterborough U v Brentford
Plymouth Arg v Brighton & HA
Rotherham U v Crewe Alex
Stockport Co v Cambridge U
Swansea C v Hull C
Wrexham v Shrewsbury T
Wycombe W v Huddersfield T
York C v Bristol R

Endsleigh League Division 3
Barnet v Scarborough
Bury v Exeter C
Carlisle U v Torquay U
Chesterfield v Rochdale
Colchester U v Mansfield T
Darlington v Hartlepool U
Fulham v Scunthorpe U
Gillingham v Wigan Ath
Lincoln C v Walsall
Northampton T v Doncaster R
Preston NE v Hereford U

Monday 12 December 1994

FA Carling Premiership
Tottenham H v Sheffield W

Friday 16 December 1994

FA Carling Premiership
Ipswich T v Wimbledon

Endsleigh League Division 2
AFC Bournemouth v Wrexham
Cambridge U v Wycombe W
Crewe Alex v York C

Endsleigh League Division 3
Doncaster R v Colchester U
Northampton T v Scunthorpe U

Saturday 17 December 1994

FA Carling Premiership
Arsenal v Leeds U

Chelsea v Liverpool
Coventry C v Newcastle U
Crystal Palace v Norwich C
Everton v Tottenham H
Leicester C v Blackburn R
Manchester U v Nottingham F
Sheffield W v QPR
Southampton v Aston Villa
West Ham U v Manchester C

Endsleigh League Division 1
Bolton W v Grimsby T
Burnley v Middlesbrough
Charlton Ath v Oldham Ath
Derby Co v Barnsley
Notts Co v Portsmouth
Port Vale v Swindon T
Reading v Wolverhampton W
Southend U v Millwall
Sunderland v Bristol C
Tranmere R v Stoke C
Watford v Sheffield U

Endsleigh League Division 2
Birmingham C v Leyton O
Bradford C v Chester C
Brentford v Plymouth Arg
Brighton & HA v Swansea C
Bristol R v Peterborough U
Cardiff C v Stockport Co
Huddersfield T v Blackpool
Hull C v Oxford U
Shrewsbury T v Rotherham U

Endsleigh League Division 3
Exeter C v Darlington
Hartlepool U v Bury
Preston NE v Barnet
Rochdale v Gillingham
Scarborough v Carlisle U
Torquay U v Lincoln C
Walsall v Hereford U
Wigan Ath v Fulham

Sunday 18 December 1994

Endsleigh League Division 1
WBA v Luton T

Endsleigh League Division 3
Mansfield T v Chesterfield

Wednesday 21 December 1994

FA Carling Premiership
Newcastle U v Everton

Monday 26 December 1994

FA Carling Premiership
Arsenal v Aston Villa
Chelsea v Manchester U
Coventry C v Nottingham F
Crystal Palace v QPR
Everton v Sheffield W
Leeds U v Newcastle U
Leicester C v Liverpool
Manchester C v Blackburn R
Norwich C v Tottenham H
Southampton v Wimbledon
West Ham U v Ipswich T

Endsleigh League Division 1
Barnsley v Grimsby T
Burnley v Port Vale
Charlton Ath v Southend U
Notts Co v Millwall
Oldham Ath v Wolverhampton W
Reading v Luton T
Sheffield U v Middlesbrough
Stoke C v Swindon T
Sunderland v Bolton W
Tranmere R v Derby Co
Watford v Portsmouth
WBA v Bristol C

Endsleigh League Division 2
Birmingham C v Cambridge U
Brentford v Leyton O
Bristol R v AFC Bournemouth
Crewe Alex v Chester C
Hull C v Huddersfield T
Peterborough U v Oxford U
Rotherham U v Bradford C
Shrewsbury T v Cardiff C
Stockport Co v Wrexham
Swansea C v Plymouth Arg
Wycombe W v Brighton & HA
York C v Blackpool

Endsleigh League Division 3
Bury v Wigan Ath
Chesterfield v Doncaster R
Colchester U v Northampton T
Darlington v Scarborough
Exeter C v Torquay U
Gillingham v Fulham
Hartlepool U v Carlisle U
Mansfield T v Hereford U
Preston NE v Rochdale
Scunthorpe U v Lincoln C
Walsall v Barnet

Tuesday 27 December 1994

FA Carling Premiership
Nottingham F v Norwich C
Tottenham H v Crystal Palace

Endsleigh League Division 1
Bolton W v Tranmere R
Bristol C v Stoke C
Derby Co v Burnley
Grimsby T v Oldham Ath
Luton T v Sunderland
Millwall v Watford
Port Vale v Reading
Portsmouth v Barnsley
Southend U v WBA
Swindon T v Sheffield U

Endsleigh League Division 2
AFC Bournemouth v Crewe Alex
Blackpool v Stockport Co
Brighton & HA v Shrewsbury T
Chester C v Brentford
Huddersfield T v Rotherham U
Leyton O v Swansea C
Oxford U v Wycombe W
Plymouth Arg v Bristol R
Wrexham v Peterborough U

Endsleigh League Division 3
Barnet v Gillingham
Carlisle U v Bury
Doncaster R v Scunthorpe U
Fulham v Colchester U
Hereford U v Exeter C
Lincoln C v Darlington
Northampton T v Chesterfield
Rochdale v Walsall
Scarborough v Mansfield T
Torquay U v Hartlepool U

Wednesday 28 December 1994

FA Carling Premiership
Aston Villa v Chelsea
Blackburn R v Leeds U
Ipswich T v Arsenal
Liverpool v Manchester C
Manchester U v Leicester C
QPR v Southampton
Sheffield W v Coventry C
Wimbledon v West Ham U

Endsleigh League Division 1
Middlesbrough v Notts Co
Wolverhampton W v Charlton Ath

Endsleigh League Division 2
Bradford C v Hull C
Cambridge U v York C
Cardiff C v Birmingham C

Endsleigh League Division 3
Wigan Ath v Preston NE

Saturday 31 December 1994

FA Carling Premiership
Arsenal v QPR
Chelsea v Wimbledon
Coventry C v Tottenham H
Crystal Palace v Blackburn R
Everton v Ipswich T
Leeds U v Liverpool
Leicester C v Sheffield W
Manchester C v Aston Villa
Norwich C v Newcastle U
Southampton v Manchester U
West Ham U v Nottingham F

Endsleigh League Division 1
Barnsley v Wolverhampton W
Burnley v Southend U
Charlton Ath v Millwall
Notts Co v Luton T
Oldham Ath v Swindon T
Reading v Grimsby T
Sheffield U v Portsmouth
Stoke C v Middlesbrough
Sunderland v Derby Co
Tranmere R v Bristol C
Watford v Port Vale
WBA v Bolton W

Endsleigh League Division 2
Birmingham C v Blackpool
Brentford v Oxford U
Bristol R v Chester C
Crewe Alex v Leyton O
Hull C v Brighton & HA
Peterborough U v Cambridge U
Rotherham U v Cardiff C
Shrewsbury T v Plymouth Arg
Stockport Co v Bradford C
Swansea C v Huddersfield T
Wycombe W v AFC Bournemouth
York C v Wrexham

Endsleigh League Division 3
Bury v Torquay U
Chesterfield v Lincoln C
Colchester U v Hereford U
Darlington v Northampton T
Exeter C v Wigan Ath
Gillingham v Carlisle U
Hartlepool U v Fulham
Mansfield T v Barnet
Preston NE v Scarborough
Scunthorpe U v Rochdale
Walsall v Doncaster R

Monday 2 January 1995

FA Carling Premiership
Aston Villa v Leeds U
Blackburn R v West Ham U
Ipswich T v Leicester C
Liverpool v Norwich C
Newcastle U v Manchester C
Nottingham F v Crystal Palace
Sheffield W v Southampton
Tottenham H v Arsenal
Wimbledon v Everton

Endsleigh League Division 1
Bolton W v Reading
Bristol C v Watford
Derby Co v WBA
Grimsby T v Notts Co
Luton T v Charlton Ath
Middlesbrough v Barnsley
Millwall v Oldham Ath
Port Vale v Stoke C

Portsmouth v Burnley
Southend U v Tranmere R
Swindon T v Sunderland
Wolverhampton W v Sheffield U

Endsleigh League Division 2
AFC Bournemouth v Swansea C
Blackpool v Peterborough U
Bradford C v Birmingham C
Brighton & HA v Stockport Co
Cambridge U v Hull C
Cardiff C v Brentford
Chester C v Wycombe W
Huddersfield T v Shrewsbury T
Leyton O v Bristol R
Oxford U v York C
Plymouth Arg v Crewe Alex
Wrexham v Rotherham U

Endsleigh League Division 3
Barnet v Exeter C
Carlisle U v Chesterfield
Doncaster R v Gillingham
Fulham v Mansfield T
Hereford U v Hartlepool U
Lincoln C v Colchester U
Northampton T v Bury
Rochdale v Darlington
Scarborough v Scunthorpe U
Torquay U v Preston NE
Wigan Ath v Walsall

Tuesday 3 January 1995

FA Carling Premiership
Manchester U v Coventry C
QPR v Chelsea

Saturday 7 January 1995

Endsleigh League Division 2
Birmingham C v Brentford
Bradford C v AFC Bournemouth
Brighton & HA v Bristol R
Cambridge U v Cardiff C
Chester C v York C
Huddersfield T v Crewe Alex
Hull C v Shrewsbury T
Leyton O v Rotherham U
Oxford U v Wrexham
Plymouth Arg v Stockport Co
Swansea C v Blackpool
Wycombe W v Peterborough U

Endsleigh League Division 3
Barnet v Carlisle U
Doncaster R v Mansfield T
Fulham v Chesterfield
Gillingham v Bury
Hereford U v Darlington
Preston NE v Colchester U
Rochdale v Torquay U
Scarborough v Lincoln C
Scunthorpe U v Exeter C
Walsall v Hartlepool U
Wigan Ath v Northampton T

Saturday 14 January 1995

FA Carling Premiership
Arsenal v Everton
Aston Villa v QPR
Blackburn R v Nottingham F
Chelsea v Sheffield W
Crystal Palace v Leicester C
Leeds U v Southampton
Liverpool v Ipswich T
Manchester C v Coventry C
Newcastle U v Manchester U
Norwich C v Wimbledon
West Ham U v Tottenham H

Endsleigh League Division 1
Barnsley v Luton T
Charlton Ath v Derby Co
Grimsby T v Southend U
Notts Co v Burnley
Oldham Ath v Sunderland
Port Vale v Tranmere R
Portsmouth v Bristol C
Reading v WBA
Sheffield U v Millwall
Swindon T v Middlesbrough
Watford v Bolton W
Wolverhampton W v Stoke C

Endsleigh League Division 2
AFC Bournemouth v Plymouth Arg
Blackpool v Cambridge U
Brentford v Swansea C
Bristol R v Oxford U
Cardiff C v Huddersfield T
Crewe Alex v Brighton & HA
Peterborough U v Bradford C
Rotherham U v Wycombe W
Shrewsbury T v Chester C
Stockport Co v Hull C
Wrexham v Leyton O
York C v Birmingham C

Endsleigh League Division 3
Bury v Hereford U
Carlisle U v Preston NE
Chesterfield v Scunthorpe U
Colchester U v Barnet
Darlington v Fulham
Exeter C v Rochdale
Hartlepool U v Scarborough
Lincoln C v Doncaster R
Mansfield T v Wigan Ath
Northampton T v Gillingham
Torquay U v Walsall

Saturday 21 January 1995

FA Carling Premiership
Coventry C v Arsenal
Everton v Crystal Palace
Ipswich T v Chelsea
Leicester C v Leeds U
Manchester U v Blackburn R
Nottingham F v Aston Villa
QPR v Norwich C
Sheffield W v Newcastle U
Southampton v West Ham U
Tottenham H v Manchester C
Wimbledon v Liverpool

Endsleigh League Division 1
Bolton W v Charlton Ath
Bristol C v Sheffield U
Burnley v Reading
Derby Co v Portsmouth
Luton T v Wolverhampton W
Middlesbrough v Grimsby T
Millwall v Swindon T
Southend U v Port Vale
Stoke C v Barnsley
Sunderland v Notts Co
Tranmere R v Oldham Ath
WBA v Watford

Endsleigh League Division 2
Birmingham C v Shrewsbury T
Bradford C v Bristol R
Brighton & HA v Cardiff C
Cambridge U v AFC Bournemouth
Chester C v Peterborough U
Huddersfield T v York C
Hull C v Brentford
Leyton O v Blackpool
Oxford U v Stockport Co
Plymouth Arg v Rotherham U
Swansea C v Crewe Alex
Wycombe W v Wrexham

Endsleigh League Division 3
Barnet v Lincoln C
Doncaster R v Exeter C
Fulham v Northampton T
Gillingham v Colchester U
Hereford U v Chesterfield
Preston NE v Mansfield T
Rochdale v Carlisle U
Scarborough v Bury
Scunthorpe U v Torquay U
Walsall v Darlington
Wigan Ath v Hartlepool U

Tuesday 24 January 1995

FA Carling Premiership
Arsenal v Southampton
Blackburn R v Ipswich T
Crystal Palace v Manchester U
Leeds U v QPR
Liverpool v Everton

Wednesday 25 January 1995

FA Carling Premiership
Aston Villa v Tottenham H
Chelsea v Nottingham F
Manchester C v Leicester C
Newcastle U v Wimbledon
Norwich C v Coventry C
West Ham U v Sheffield W

Saturday 28 January 1995

Endsleigh League Division 2
AFC Bournemouth v Huddersfield T
Blackpool v Plymouth Arg
Brentford v Cambridge U
Bristol R v Birmingham C
Cardiff C v Bradford C
Crewe Alex v Hull C
Peterborough U v Swansea C
Rotherham U v Brighton & HA
Shrewsbury T v Oxford U
Stockport Co v Leyton O
Wrexham v Chester C
York C v Wycombe W

Endsleigh League Division 3
Bury v Walsall
Carlisle U v Fulham
Chesterfield v Barnet
Colchester U v Wigan Ath
Darlington v Gillingham
Exeter C v Preston NE
Hartlepool U v Scunthorpe U
Lincoln C v Hereford U
Mansfield T v Rochdale
Northampton T v Scarborough
Torquay U v Doncaster R

Saturday 4 February 1995

FA Carling Premiership
Coventry C v Chelsea
Everton v Norwich C
Ipswich T v Crystal Palace
Leicester C v West Ham U
Manchester U v Aston Villa
Nottingham F v Liverpool
QPR v Newcastle U
Sheffield W v Arsenal
Southampton v Manchester C
Tottenham H v Blackburn R
Wimbledon v Leeds U

Endsleigh League Division 1
Bolton W v Wolverhampton W
Bristol C v Barnsley
Burnley v Swindon T
Derby Co v Sheffield U
Luton T v Oldham Ath
Middlesbrough v Reading
Millwall v Grimsby T
Southend U v Watford
Stoke C v Portsmouth
Sunderland v Port Vale
Tranmere R v Notts Co
WBA v Charlton Ath

Endsleigh League Division 2
Birmingham C v Stockport Co
Bradford C v Shrewsbury T
Brighton & HA v Brentford
Cambridge U v Crewe Alex
Chester C v Rotherham U
Huddersfield T v Bristol R
Hull C v Cardiff C
Leyton O v Peterborough U
Oxford U v AFC Bournemouth
Plymouth Arg v York C
Swansea C v Wrexham
Wycombe W v Blackpool

Endsleigh League Division 3
Barnet v Darlington
Doncaster R v Carlisle U
Fulham v Bury
Gillingham v Lincoln C
Hereford U v Northampton T
Preston NE v Chesterfield
Rochdale v Hartlepool U
Scarborough v Exeter C
Scunthorpe U v Colchester U
Walsall v Mansfield T
Wigan Ath v Torquay U

Saturday 11 February 1995

FA Carling Premiership
Arsenal v Leicester C
Aston Villa v Wimbledon
Blackburn R v Sheffield W
Chelsea v Tottenham H
Crystal Palace v Coventry C
Leeds U v Ipswich T
Liverpool v QPR
Manchester C v Manchester U
Newcastle U v Nottingham F
Norwich C v Southampton
West Ham U v Everton

Endsleigh League Division 1
Barnsley v Tranmere R
Charlton Ath v Sunderland
Grimsby T v Luton T
Notts Co v Southend U
Oldham Ath v Middlesbrough
Port Vale v WBA
Portsmouth v Millwall
Reading v Derby Co
Sheffield U v Stoke C
Swindon T v Bolton W
Watford v Burnley
Wolverhampton W v Bristol C

Endsleigh League Division 2
AFC Bournemouth v Brighton & HA
Blackpool v Oxford U
Brentford v Bradford C
Bristol R v Cambridge U
Cardiff C v Leyton O
Crewe Alex v Birmingham C
Peterborough U v Plymouth Arg
Rotherham U v Swansea C
Shrewsbury T v Wycombe W
Stockport Co v Chester C
Wrexham v Huddersfield T
York C v Hull C

Endsleigh League Division 3
Bury v Barnet
Carlisle U v Hereford U
Chesterfield v Gillingham
Colchester U v Rochdale
Darlington v Wigan Ath
Exeter C v Walsall
Hartlepool U v Doncaster R
Lincoln C v Fulham
Mansfield T v Scunthorpe U
Northampton T v Preston NE
Torquay U v Scarborough

Friday 17 February 1995

Endsleigh League Division 2
Swansea C v Brentford

Saturday 18 February 1995

FA Carling Premiership
Coventry C v West Ham U
Everton v Chelsea
Ipswich T v Newcastle U
Leicester C v Norwich C
Manchester U v Arsenal
Nottingham F v Leeds U
QPR v Blackburn R
Sheffield W v Aston Villa
Southampton v Crystal Palace
Tottenham H v Liverpool
Wimbledon v Manchester C

Endsleigh League Division 1
Bolton W v Barnsley
Bristol C v Oldham Ath
Burnley v Grimsby T
Derby Co v Wolverhampton W
Luton T v Swindon T
Middlesbrough v Charlton Ath
Millwall v Port Vale
Southend U v Sheffield U
Stoke C v Watford
Sunderland v Portsmouth
Tranmere R v Reading
WBA v Notts Co

Endsleigh League Division 2
Birmingham C v York C
Bradford C v Peterborough U
Brighton & HA v Crewe Alex
Cambridge U v Blackpool
Chester C v Shrewsbury T
Huddersfield T v Cardiff C
Hull C v Stockport Co
Leyton O v Wrexham
Oxford U v Bristol R
Plymouth Arg v AFC Bournemouth
Wycombe W v Rotherham U

Endsleigh League Division 3
Barnet v Colchester U
Doncaster R v Lincoln C
Fulham v Darlington
Gillingham v Northampton T
Hereford U v Bury
Preston NE v Carlisle U
Rochdale v Exeter C
Scarborough v Hartlepool U
Scunthorpe U v Chesterfield
Walsall v Torquay U
Wigan Ath v Mansfield T

Tuesday 21 February 1995

FA Carling Premiership
Arsenal v Nottingham F
Blackburn R v Wimbledon
Crystal Palace v Sheffield W
Leeds U v Everton

Endsleigh League Division 1
Barnsley v Millwall
Charlton Ath v Tranmere R
Grimsby T v Stoke C
Notts Co v Bolton W
Oldham Ath v WBA
Port Vale v Derby Co
Reading v Southend U
Sheffield U v Burnley
Watford v Sunderland
Wolverhampton W v Middlesbrough

Endsleigh League Division 2
AFC Bournemouth v Birmingham C
Blackpool v Chester C
Brentford v Huddersfield T
Cardiff C v Wycombe W
Crewe Alex v Bradford C
Peterborough U v Brighton & HA
Rotherham U v Oxford U
Shrewsbury T v Cambridge U
Stockport Co v Swansea C
Wrexham v Plymouth Arg
York C v Leyton O

Wednesday 22 February 1995

FA Carling Premiership
Aston Villa v Leicester C
Chelsea v Southampton
Liverpool v Coventry C
Manchester C v Ipswich T
Newcastle U v Tottenham H
Norwich C v Manchester U
West Ham U v QPR

Endsleigh League Division 1
Portsmouth v Luton T
Swindon T v Bristol C

Endsleigh League Division 2
Bristol R v Hull C

Saturday 25 February 1995

FA Carling Premiership
Blackburn R v Norwich C
Coventry C v Leicester C
Crystal Palace v Arsenal
Everton v Manchester U
Ipswich T v Southampton
Manchester C v Leeds U
Newcastle U v Aston Villa
QPR v Nottingham F
Sheffield W v Liverpool
Tottenham H v Wimbledon
West Ham U v Chelsea

Endsleigh League Division 1
Bristol C v Luton T
Derby Co v Bolton W
Millwall v Middlesbrough
Notts Co v Reading
Oldham Ath v Sheffield U
Port Vale v Wolverhampton W
Portsmouth v Grimsby T
Southend U v Sunderland
Swindon T v Barnsley
Tranmere R v Burnley
Watford v Charlton Ath
WBA v Stoke C

Endsleigh League Division 2
AFC Bournemouth v Hull C
Birmingham C v Wrexham
Blackpool v Rotherham U
Bradford C v Cambridge U
Brighton & HA v Huddersfield T
Crewe Alex v Bristol R
Oxford U v Chester C
Peterborough U v Cardiff C
Plymouth Arg v Leyton O
Shrewsbury T v Brentford
Stockport Co v York C
Swansea C v Wycombe W

Endsleigh League Division 3
Bury v Colchester U
Darlington v Carlisle U
Doncaster R v Rochdale
Fulham v Barnet
Hartlepool U v Exeter C
Mansfield T v Gillingham
Northampton T v Lincoln C
Scarborough v Wigan Ath
Scunthorpe U v Hereford U
Torquay U v Chesterfield
Walsall v Preston NE

Saturday 4 March 1995

FA Carling Premiership
Aston Villa v Blackburn R
Chelsea v Crystal Palace
Leeds U v Sheffield W
Leicester C v Everton
Liverpool v Newcastle U
Manchester U v Ipswich T
Norwich C v Manchester C
Nottingham F v Tottenham H
Southampton v Coventry C
Wimbledon v QPR

Endsleigh League Division 1
Barnsley v Oldham Ath
Bolton W v Southend U
Burnley v WBA
Charlton Ath v Notts Co
Grimsby T v Swindon T
Luton T v Millwall
Middlesbrough v Bristol C
Reading v Watford
Sheffield U v Port Vale
Stoke C v Derby Co
Sunderland v Tranmere R
Wolverhampton W v Portsmouth

Endsleigh League Division 2
Brentford v Crewe Alex
Bristol R v Shrewsbury T
Cambridge U v Brighton & HA
Cardiff C v AFC Bournemouth
Chester C v Plymouth Arg
Huddersfield T v Bradford C
Hull C v Birmingham C
Leyton O v Oxford U
Rotherham U v Peterborough U
Wrexham v Blackpool
Wycombe W v Stockport Co
York C v Swansea C

Endsleigh League Division 3
Barnet v Torquay U
Carlisle U v Northampton T
Chesterfield v Bury
Colchester U v Darlington
Exeter C v Mansfield T
Gillingham v Walsall
Hereford U v Fulham
Lincoln C v Hartlepool U
Preston NE v Doncaster R
Rochdale v Scarborough
Wigan Ath v Scunthorpe U

Sunday 5 March 1995

FA Carling Premiership
Arsenal v West Ham U

Tuesday 7 March 1995

FA Carling Premiership
Blackburn R v Arsenal
Leeds U v Crystal Palace
Wimbledon v Manchester U

Endsleigh League Division 1
Barnsley v Burnley
Bristol C v Charlton Ath
Grimsby T v Derby Co
Luton T v Port Vale
Middlesbrough v Watford
Oldham Ath v Southend U
Sheffield U v Tranmere R
Wolverhampton W v Sunderland

Endsleigh League Division 2
Blackpool v Crewe Alex
Chester C v Hull C
Leyton O v Brighton & HA
Oxford U v Huddersfield T
Peterborough U v Shrewsbury T
Plymouth Arg v Birmingham C
Rotherham U v Cambridge U
Stockport Co v Bristol R
Swansea C v Cardiff C
Wrexham v Brentford
Wycombe W v Bradford C
York C v AFC Bournemouth

Wednesday 8 March 1995

FA Carling Premiership
Aston Villa v Coventry C
Liverpool v Southampton
Manchester C v Chelsea
Newcastle U v West Ham U
Norwich C v Sheffield W
Nottingham F v Everton
QPR v Leicester C
Tottenham H v Ipswich T

Endsleigh League Division 1
Millwall v Reading
Portsmouth v WBA
Stoke C v Bolton W
Swindon T v Notts Co

Saturday 11 March 1995

FA Carling Premiership
Arsenal v Liverpool
Chelsea v Leeds U
Coventry C v Blackburn R
Crystal Palace v Aston Villa
Everton v Manchester C
Ipswich T v QPR
Leicester C v Nottingham F
Manchester U v Tottenham H
Sheffield W v Wimbledon
Southampton v Newcastle U
West Ham U v Norwich C

Endsleigh League Division 1
Bolton W v Middlesbrough
Burnley v Oldham Ath
Charlton Ath v Portsmouth
Derby Co v Millwall
Notts Co v Sheffield U
Port Vale v Bristol C
Reading v Barnsley
Southend U v Luton T
Sunderland v Stoke C
Tranmere R v Grimsby T
Watford v Swindon T
WBA v Wolverhampton W

Endsleigh League Division 2
AFC Bournemouth v Rotherham U
Birmingham C v Swansea C
Bradford C v Plymouth Arg
Brentford v Stockport Co
Brighton & HA v Wrexham
Bristol R v Wycombe W
Cambridge U v Oxford U
Cardiff C v York C
Crewe Alex v Peterborough U
Huddersfield T v Chester C
Hull C v Leyton O
Shrewsbury T v Blackpool

Endsleigh League Division 3
Doncaster R v Barnet
Exeter C v Carlisle U
Hartlepool U v Colchester U
Mansfield T v Lincoln C
Preston NE v Fulham
Rochdale v Northampton T
Scarborough v Gillingham
Scunthorpe U v Bury
Torquay U v Darlington
Walsall v Chesterfield
Wigan Ath v Hereford U

Friday 17 March 1995

Endsleigh League Division 2
Swansea C v Shrewsbury T

Saturday 18 March 1995

FA Carling Premiership
Aston Villa v West Ham U
Blackburn R v Chelsea
Leeds U v Coventry C
Liverpool v Manchester U
Manchester C v Sheffield W
Newcastle U v Arsenal
Norwich C v Ipswich T
Nottingham F v Southampton
QPR v Everton
Tottenham H v Leicester C
Wimbledon v Crystal Palace

Endsleigh League Division 1
Barnsley v Port Vale
Bristol C v Burnley
Grimsby T v Sunderland
Luton T v Tranmere R
Middlesbrough v Derby Co
Millwall v Bolton W
Oldham Ath v Notts Co
Portsmouth v Southend U
Sheffield U v Charlton Ath
Stoke C v Reading
Swindon T v WBA
Wolverhampton W v Watford

Endsleigh League Division 2
Blackpool v Bristol R
Chester C v Cambridge U
Leyton O v Huddersfield T
Oxford U v Bradford C
Peterborough U v AFC Bournemouth
Plymouth Arg v Hull C
Rotherham U v Brentford
Stockport Co v Crewe Alex
Wrexham v Cardiff C
Wycombe W v Birmingham C
York C v Brighton & HA

Endsleigh League Division 3
Barnet v Hartlepool U
Carlisle U v Walsall
Chesterfield v Wigan Ath
Colchester U v Exeter C
Darlington v Mansfield T
Fulham v Doncaster R
Gillingham v Scunthorpe U
Hereford U v Scarborough
Lincoln C v Rochdale
Northampton T v Torquay U
Preston NE v Bury

Tuesday 21 March 1995

Endsleigh League Division 1
Bolton W v Sheffield U
Burnley v Luton T
Charlton Ath v Grimsby T
Notts Co v Bristol C
Port Vale v Portsmouth
Reading v Oldham Ath
Southend U v Stoke C
Sunderland v Middlesbrough
Tranmere R v Wolverhampton W
Watford v Barnsley

Endsleigh League Division 2
AFC Bournemouth v Stockport Co
Birmingham C v Oxford U
Bradford C v Swansea C
Brentford v Wycombe W
Cambridge U v Leyton O
Cardiff C v Blackpool
Crewe Alex v Wrexham
Huddersfield T v Plymouth Arg
Hull C v Peterborough U
Shrewsbury T v York C

Wednesday 22 March 1995

Endsleigh League Division 1
Derby Co v Swindon T
WBA v Millwall

Endsleigh League Division 2
Brighton & HA v Chester C
Bristol R v Rotherham U

Saturday 25 March 1995

Endsleigh League Division 1
Barnsley v Sunderland
Bristol C v Southend U
Grimsby T v WBA
Luton T v Watford
Middlesbrough v Port Vale
Millwall v Tranmere R
Oldham Ath v Derby Co
Portsmouth v Bolton W
Sheffield U v Reading
Stoke C v Notts Co
Swindon T v Charlton Ath
Wolverhampton W v Burnley

Endsleigh League Division 2
Blackpool v Brentford
Chester C v AFC Bournemouth
Leyton O v Shrewsbury T
Oxford U v Brighton & HA
Peterborough U v Birmingham C
Plymouth Arg v Cardiff C
Rotherham U v Hull C
Stockport Co v Huddersfield T
Swansea C v Cambridge U
Wrexham v Bristol R
Wycombe W v Crewe Alex
York C v Bradford C

Endsleigh League Division 3
Barnet v Wigan Ath
Bury v Mansfield T
Carlisle U v Scunthorpe U
Chesterfield v Hartlepool U
Colchester U v Scarborough
Darlington v Doncaster R
Fulham v Torquay U
Gillingham v Exeter C
Hereford U v Rochdale
Lincoln C v Preston NE
Northampton T v Walsall

Saturday 1 April 1995

FA Carling Premiership
Arsenal v Norwich C
Chelsea v Newcastle U
Coventry C v QPR
Crystal Palace v Manchester C
Everton v Blackburn R
Ipswich T v Aston Villa
Leicester C v Wimbledon
Manchester U v Leeds U
Sheffield W v Nottingham F
Southampton v Tottenham H
West Ham U v Liverpool

Endsleigh League Division 1
Bolton W v Luton T
Burnley v Millwall
Charlton Ath v Stoke C
Derby Co v Bristol C
Notts Co v Barnsley
Port Vale v Grimsby T
Reading v Swindon T
Southend U v Wolverhampton W
Sunderland v Sheffield U
Tranmere R v Portsmouth
Watford v Oldham Ath
WBA v Middlesbrough

Endsleigh League Division 2
AFC Bournemouth v Leyton O
Birmingham C v Rotherham U
Bradford C v Wrexham
Brentford v York C
Brighton & HA v Blackpool
Bristol R v Swansea C
Cambridge U v Plymouth Arg
Cardiff C v Chester C
Crewe Alex v Oxford U
Huddersfield T v Peterborough U
Hull C v Wycombe W
Shrewsbury T v Stockport Co

Endsleigh League Division 3
Doncaster R v Bury
Exeter C v Chesterfield
Hartlepool U v Northampton T
Mansfield T v Carlisle U
Preston NE v Gillingham
Rochdale v Barnet
Scarborough v Fulham
Scunthorpe U v Darlington
Torquay U v Hereford U
Walsall v Colchester U
Wigan Ath v Lincoln C

Tuesday 4 April 1995

Endsleigh League Division 2
Blackpool v Birmingham C

Saturday 8 April 1995

FA Carling Premiership
Aston Villa v Manchester C
Blackburn R v Crystal Palace
Ipswich T v Everton
Liverpool v Leeds U
Manchester U v Southampton
Newcastle U v Norwich C
Nottingham F v West Ham U
QPR v Arsenal
Sheffield W v Leicester C
Tottenham H v Coventry C
Wimbledon v Chelsea

Endsleigh League Division 1
Bolton W v WBA
Bristol C v Tranmere R
Derby Co v Sunderland
Grimsby T v Reading
Luton T v Notts Co
Middlesbrough v Stoke C
Millwall v Charlton Ath
Port Vale v Watford
Portsmouth v Sheffield U
Southend U v Burnley
Swindon T v Oldham Ath
Wolverhampton W v Barnsley

Endsleigh League Division 2
AFC Bournemouth v Wycombe W
Bradford C v Stockport Co
Brighton & HA v Hull C
Cambridge U v Peterborough U
Cardiff C v Rotherham U
Chester C v Bristol R
Huddersfield T v Swansea C
Leyton O v Crewe Alex
Oxford U v Brentford
Plymouth Arg v Shrewsbury T
Wrexham v York C

Endsleigh League Division 3
Barnet v Mansfield T
Carlisle U v Gillingham
Doncaster R v Walsall
Fulham v Hartlepool U
Hereford U v Colchester U
Lincoln C v Chesterfield
Northampton T v Darlington
Rochdale v Scunthorpe U
Scarborough v Preston NE
Torquay U v Bury
Wigan Ath v Exeter C

Saturday 15 April 1995

FA Carling Premiership
Arsenal v Ipswich T
Chelsea v Aston Villa
Coventry C v Sheffield W
Crystal Palace v Tottenham H
Everton v Newcastle U
Leeds U v Blackburn R
Leicester C v Manchester U
Manchester C v Liverpool
Norwich C v Nottingham F
Southampton v QPR
West Ham U v Wimbledon

Endsleigh League Division 1
Barnsley v Portsmouth
Burnley v Derby Co
Charlton Ath v Wolverhampton W
Notts Co v Middlesbrough
Oldham Ath v Grimsby T
Reading v Port Vale
Sheffield U v Swindon T
Stoke C v Bristol C
Sunderland v Luton T
Tranmere R v Bolton W
Watford v Millwall
WBA v Southend U

Endsleigh League Division 2
Birmingham C v Cardiff C
Brentford v Chester C
Bristol R v Plymouth Arg
Crewe Alex v AFC Bournemouth
Hull C v Bradford C
Peterborough U v Wrexham
Rotherham U v Huddersfield T
Shrewsbury T v Brighton & HA
Stockport Co v Blackpool
Swansea C v Leyton O
Wycombe W v Oxford U
York C v Cambridge U

Endsleigh League Division 3
Bury v Carlisle U
Chesterfield v Northampton T
Colchester U v Fulham
Darlington v Lincoln C
Exeter C v Hereford U
Gillingham v Barnet
Hartlepool U v Torquay U
Mansfield T v Scarborough
Preston NE v Wigan Ath
Scunthorpe U v Doncaster R
Walsall v Rochdale

Monday 17 April 1995

FA Carling Premiership
Aston Villa v Arsenal
Blackburn R v Manchester C
Ipswich T v West Ham U
Liverpool v Leicester C
Manchester U v Chelsea
Newcastle U v Leeds U
Nottingham F v Coventry C
QPR v Crystal Palace
Sheffield W v Everton
Tottenham H v Norwich C
Wimbledon v Southampton

Endsleigh League Division 1
Bolton W v Sunderland
Bristol C v WBA
Derby Co v Tranmere R
Grimsby T v Barnsley
Luton T v Reading
Middlesbrough v Sheffield U
Port Vale v Burnley
Portsmouth v Watford
Swindon T v Stoke C
Wolverhampton W v Oldham Ath

Endsleigh League Division 2
Bradford C v Rotherham U
Cambridge U v Birmingham C
Cardiff C v Shrewsbury T
Chester C v Crewe Alex
Huddersfield T v Hull C
Leyton O v Brentford
Oxford U v Peterborough U

Plymouth Arg v Swansea C
Wrexham v Stockport Co

Endsleigh League Division 3
Barnet v Walsall
Carlisle U v Hartlepool U
Doncaster R v Chesterfield
Fulham v Gillingham
Hereford U v Mansfield T
Lincoln C v Scunthorpe U
Northampton T v Colchester U
Rochdale v Preston NE

Tuesday 18 April 1995

Endsleigh League Division 1
Southend U v Charlton Ath

Endsleigh League Division 2
AFC Bournemouth v Bristol R
Blackpool v York C

Endsleigh League Division 3
Scarborough v Darlington
Torquay U v Exeter C
Wigan Ath v Bury

Wednesday 19 April 1995

Endsleigh League Division 1
Millwall v Notts Co

Endsleigh League Division 2
Brighton & HA v Wycombe W

Saturday 22 April 1995

Endsleigh League Division 1
Barnsley v Middlesbrough
Burnley v Portsmouth
Charlton Ath v Luton T
Notts Co v Grimsby T
Oldham Ath v Millwall
Reading v Bolton W
Sheffield U v Wolverhampton W
Stoke C v Port Vale
Sunderland v Swindon T
Tranmere R v Southend U
Watford v Bristol C
WBA v Derby Co

Endsleigh League Division 2
Birmingham C v Bradford C
Brentford v Cardiff C
Bristol R v Leyton O
Crewe Alex v Plymouth Arg
Hull C v Cambridge U
Peterborough U v Blackpool
Rotherham U v Wrexham
Shrewsbury T v Huddersfield T
Stockport Co v Brighton & HA
Swansea C v AFC Bournemouth
Wycombe W v Chester C
York C v Oxford U

Endsleigh League Division 3
Bury v Northampton T
Chesterfield v Carlisle U
Colchester U v Lincoln C
Darlington v Rochdale
Exeter C v Barnet
Gillingham v Doncaster R
Hartlepool U v Hereford U
Mansfield T v Fulham
Preston NE v Torquay U
Scunthorpe U v Scarborough
Walsall v Wigan Ath

Saturday 29 April 1995

FA Carling Premiership
Arsenal v Tottenham H
Chelsea v QPR
Coventry C v Manchester U
Crystal Palace v Nottingham F
Everton v Wimbledon
Leeds U v Aston Villa
Leicester C v Ipswich T
Manchester C v Newcastle U
Norwich C v Liverpool
Southampton v Sheffield W
West Ham U v Blackburn R

Endsleigh League Division 1
Barnsley v Sheffield U
Bristol C v Reading
Burnley v Sunderland
Charlton Ath v Port Vale
Derby Co v Southend U
Grimsby T v Wolverhampton W
Middlesbrough v Luton T
Notts Co v Watford
Oldham Ath v Bolton W
Stoke C v Millwall
Swindon T v Portsmouth
WBA v Tranmere R

Endsleigh League Division 2
Birmingham C v Brighton & HA
Bradford C v Blackpool
Brentford v AFC Bournemouth
Cambridge U v Huddersfield T
Cardiff C v Bristol R
Chester C v Leyton O
Hull C v Wrexham
Oxford U v Swansea C
Shrewsbury T v Crewe Alex
Stockport Co v Peterborough U
Wycombe W v Plymouth Arg
York C v Rotherham U

Endsleigh League Division 3
Barnet v Northampton T
Colchester U v Carlisle U
Darlington v Chesterfield
Doncaster R v Scarborough
Exeter C v Fulham
Gillingham v Hereford U
Lincoln C v Bury
Mansfield T v Torquay U
Preston NE v Hartlepool U
Rochdale v Wigan Ath
Walsall v Scunthorpe U

Saturday 6 May 1995

FA Carling Premiership
Arsenal v Wimbledon
Aston Villa v Liverpool
Blackburn R v Newcastle U
Crystal Palace v West Ham U
Everton v Southampton
Ipswich T v Coventry C
Leeds U v Norwich C
Leicester C v Chelsea
Manchester U v Sheffield W
Nottingham F v Manchester C
QPR v Tottenham H

Endsleigh League Division 1
Bolton W v Burnley
Luton T v Stoke C
Millwall v Bristol C
Port Vale v Notts Co
Portsmouth v Oldham Ath
Reading v Charlton Ath
Sheffield U v Grimsby T
Southend U v Barnsley
Sunderland v WBA
Tranmere R v Middlesbrough
Watford v Derby Co
Wolverhampton W v Swindon T

Endsleigh League Division 2
AFC Bournemouth v Shrewsbury T
Blackpool v Hull C
Brighton & HA v Bradford C
Bristol R v Brentford
Crewe Alex v Cardiff C
Huddersfield T v Birmingham C
Leyton O v Wycombe W
Peterborough U v York C
Plymouth Arg v Oxford U
Rotherham U v Stockport Co
Swansea C v Chester C
Wrexham v Cambridge U

Endsleigh League Division 3
Bury v Darlington
Carlisle U v Lincoln C
Chesterfield v Colchester U
Fulham v Rochdale
Hartlepool U v Mansfield T
Hereford U v Barnet
Northampton T v Exeter C
Scarborough v Walsall
Scunthorpe U v Preston NE
Torquay U v Gillingham
Wigan Ath v Doncaster R

Saturday 13 May 1995

FA Carling Premiership
Chelsea v Arsenal
Coventry C v Everton
Liverpool v Blackburn R
Manchester C v QPR
Newcastle U v Crystal Palace
Norwich C v Aston Villa
Sheffield W v Ipswich T
Southampton v Leicester C
Tottenham H v Leeds U
West Ham U v Manchester U
Wimbledon v Nottingham F

FA CARLING PREMIERSHIP FIXTURES 1993–94

	Arsenal	Aston Villa	Blackburn R	Chelsea	Coventry C	Crystal Palace	Everton	Ipswich T	Leeds U	Leicester C	Liverpool	Manchester C	Manchester U	Newcastle U	Norwich C	Nottingham F	QPR	Sheffield W	Southampton	Tottenham H	West Ham U	Wimbledon
Arsenal	—	26.12	31.8	15.10	22.10	1.10	14.1	15.4	17.12	11.2	11.3	20.8	26.11	18.9	1.4	21.2	31.12	6.11	24.1	29.4	5.3	6.5
Aston Villa	17.4	—	4.3	23.12	8.3	27.8	10.12	10.9	2.1	22.2	6.5	8.4	6.11	1.10	15.10	22.10	14.1	26.11	24.8	25.1	18.3	11.2
Blackburn R	7.3	24.9	—	18.3	27.8	8.4	10.9	24.1	28.12	23.8	15.10	17.4	23.10	6.5	25.2	14.1	26.11	11.2	10.12	5.11	2.1	21.2
Chelsea	13.5	15.4	18.9	—	5.11	4.3	26.11	22.10	11.3	8.10	17.12	31.8	26.12	1.4	20.8	25.1	29.4	14.1	22.2	11.2	2.10	31.12
Coventry C	21.1	29.8	11.3	4.2	—	2.11	13.5	8.10	17.9	25.2	3.12	29.10	29.4	17.12	19.11	26.12	1.4	15.4	24.9	31.12	18.2	20.8
Crystal Palace	25.2	11.3	31.12	24.9	11.2	—	22.10	5.11	30.8	14.1	20.8	1.4	24.1	15.10	17.12	29.4	26.12	21.2	26.11	15.4	6.5	17.9
Everton	29.10	20.8	1.4	18.2	15.10	21.1	—	31.12	5.12	24.9	21.11	11.3	25.2	15.4	4.2	30.8	17.9	26.12	6.5	17.12	1.11	29.4
Ipswich T	28.2	1.4	19.11	21.1	6.5	4.2	8.4	—	1.11	2.1	29.10	3.12	24.9	18.2	19.9	20.8	11.3	16.10	25.2	30.8	17.4	16.12
Leeds U	28.8	29.4	15.4	27.8	18.3	7.3	21.2	11.2	—	22.10	31.12	1.10	11.9	26.12	6.5	26.11	24.1	4.3	14.1	15.10	10.12	5.11
Leicester C	23.11	3.12	17.12	6.5	3.10	29.10	4.3	29.4	21.1	—	26.12	20.11	15.4	21.8	18.2	11.3	31.8	31.12	15.10	17.9	4.2	1.4
Liverpool	28.8	8.10	13.5	9.11	22.2	10.12	24.1	14.1	8.4	17.4	—	28.12	18.3	4.3	2.1	5.11	11.2	1.10	8.3	26.11	10.9	22.10
Manchester C	10.12	31.12	26.12	8.3	14.1	10.9	27.8	22.2	25.2	25.1	15.4	—	11.2	29.4	24.9	8.10	13.5	18.3	5.11	22.10	24.8	26.11
Manchester U	18.2	4.2	21.1	17.4	3.1	19.11	1.10	4.3	1.4	28.12	17.9	10.11	—	29.10	3.12	17.12	20.8	6.5	8.4	11.3	15.10	31.8
Newcastle U	18.3	25.2	9.10	10.9	24.8	13.5	21.12	26.11	17.4	10.12	24.9	2.1	14.1	—	8.4	11.2	5.11	22.10	27.8	22.2	8.3	25.1
Norwich C	10.9	13.5	1.10	10.12	25.1	24.8	5.11	18.3	8.10	26.11	29.4	4.3	22.2	31.12	—	15.4	22.10	8.3	11.2	26.12	27.8	14.1
Nottingham F	3.12	21.1	29.10	19.11	17.4	2.1	8.3	10.12	18.2	27.8	4.2	6.5	22.8	2.11	27.12	—	2.10	10.9	18.3	4.3	8.4	17.10
QPR	8.4	29.10	18.2	3.1	10.9	17.4	18.3	27.8	19.11	8.3	31.10	15.10	10.12	4.2	21.1	25.2	—	24.8—	28.12	6.5	3.12	24.9
Sheffield W	4.2	18.2	2.11	29.10	28.12	3.12	17.4	13.5	26.9	8.4	25.2	17.9	8.10	21.1	31.8	1.4	17.12	—	2.1	20.8	19.11	11.3
Southampton	19.11	17.12	20.8	3.12	4.3	18.2	8.10	1.10	29.10	13.5	31.8	4.2	31.12	11.3	2.11	17.9	15.4	29.4	—	1.4	21.1	26.12
Tottenham H	2.1	19.11	4.2	28.11	8.4	27.12	24.8	8.3	13.5	18.3	18.2	21.1	27.8	3.12	17.4	24.9	8.10	12.12	12.9	—	29.10	25.2
West Ham U	25.9	17.9	29.4	25.2	26.11	10.10	11.2	26.12	20.8	5.11	1.4	17.12	13.5	31.8	11.3	31.12	22.2	25.1	22.10	14.1	—	15.4
Wimbledon	8.10	2.11	3.12	8.4	10.12	18.3	2.1	23.8	4.2	10.9	21.1	18.2	7.3	19.11	30.10	13.5	4.3	27.8	17.4	1.10	28.12	—

ENDSLEIGH INSURANCE FIXTURES 1993–94

DIVISION ONE

	Barnsley	Bolton W	Bristol C	Burnley	Charlton Ath	Derby Co	Grimsby T	Luton T	Middlesbrough	Millwall	Notts Co	Oldham Ath	Port Vale	Portsmouth	Reading	Sheffield U	Southend U	Stoke C	Sunderland	Swindon T	Tranmere R	Watford	WBA	Wolverhampton
Barnsley	—	26.11	12.11	7.3	10.12	13.8	26.12	14.1	22.4	21.2	13.9	4.3	18.3	15.4	27.8	29.4	8.10	5.11	25.3	1.10	11.2	10.9	22.10	31.12
Bolton W	18.2	—	20.8	6.5	21.1	1.10	17.12	1.4	11.3	30.8	19.11	15.10	3.12	17.9	2.1	21.3	4.3	3.9	17.4	1.11	27.12	29.10	8.4	4.2
Bristol C	4.2	10.12	—	18.3	7.3	13.9	3.12	25.2	24.9	8.10	10.9	18.2	27.8	29.10	29.4	21.1	25.3	27.12	13.8	19.11	8.4	2.1	17.4	1.11
Burnley	3.9	8.10	30.8	—	3.12	15.4	18.2	21.3	17.12	1.4	29.10	11.3	26.12	22.4	21.1	19.11	31.12	20.8	29.4	4.2	1.10	1.11	4.3	17.9
Charlton Ath	20.8	5.11	3.9	22.10	—	14.1	21.3	22.4	26.11	31.12	4.3	17.12	29.4	11.3	8.10	30.8	26.12	1.4	11.2	17.9	21.2	1.10	12.11	15.4
Derby Co	17.12	25.2	1.4	27.12	29.10	—	3.9	20.8	31.8	11.3	3.12	17.9	19.11	21.1	2.11	4.2	29.4	24.9	8.4	22.3	17.4	8.10	2.1	18.2
Grimsby T	17.4	13.8	22.10	26.11	10.9	7.3	—	11.2	5.11	12.11	2.1	27.12	13.9	1.10	8.4	8.10	14.1	21.2	18.3	4.3	27.8	10.12	25.3	29.4
Luton T	29.10	13.9	1.10	10.9	2.1	10.12	1.11	—	15.10	4.3	8.4	4.2	7.3	19.11	17.4	3.12	27.8	6.5	27.12	18.2	18.3	25.3	13.8	21.1
Middlesbrough	2.1	27.8	4.3	13.8	18.2	18.3	21.1	29.4	—	1.10	28.12	1.11	25.3	3.12	4.2	17.4	10.12	8.4	10.9	29.10	8.10	7.3	13.9	19.11
Millwall	19.11	18.3	6.5	14.9	8.4	27.8	4.2	24.9	25.2	—	19.4	2.1	18.2	2.11	8.3	29.10	13.8	15.10	10.12	21.1	25.3	27.12	10.9	3.12
Notts Co	1.4	21.2	21.3	14.1	24.9	22.10	22.4	31.12	15.4	26.12	—	30.8	8.10	17.12	25.2	11.3	11.2	17.9	5.11	3.9	12.11	29.4	26.11	21.8
Oldham Ath	24.9	29.4	26.11	27.8	13.8	25.3	15.4	12.11	11.2	22.4	18.3	—	10.12	8.10	10.9	25.2	7.3	22.10	14.1	31.12	5.11	13.9	21.2	26.12
Port Vale	30.8	22.10	11.3	17.4	15.10	21.2	2.1	4.39	17.9	26.11	6.5	20.8	—	21.3	27.12	24.9	5.11	2.1	29.11	17.12	14.1	8.4	11.2	25.2
Portsmouth	27.12	25.3	14.1	2.1	27.8	5.11	25.2	22.2	22.10	11.2	13.8	6.5	10.9	—	10.12	8.4	18.3	12.11	26.11	15.10	14.9	17.4	8.3	24.9
Reading	11.3	22.4	15.10	5.11	6.5	11.2	31.12	26.12	12.11	3.9	1.10	21.3	15.4	20.8	—	17.9	21.2	30.8	22.10	1.4	26.11	4.3	14.1	17.12
Sheffield U	15.10	10.9	5.11	21.2	18.3	12.11	6.5	22.10	26.12	14.1	27.8	1.10	4.3	31.12	25.3	—	26.11	11.2	13.9	15.4	7.3	13.8	10.12	22.4
Southend U	6.5	24.9	17.9	8.4	18.4	15.10	29.10	11.3	20.8	17.12	1.11	3.9	21.1	30.8	19.11	18.2	—	21.3	25.2	3.12	2.1	4.2	27.12	1.4
Stoke C	21.1	8.3	15.4	10.12	14.9	4.3	19.11	8.10	31.12	29.4	25.3	3.12	22.4	4.2	18.3	2.11	10.9	—	27.8	26.12	13.8	18.2	1.10	29.10
Sunderland	17.9	26.12	17.12	15.10	1.11	31.12	30.8	15.4	21.3	20.8	21.1	29.10	4.2	18.2	3.12	1.4	1.10	11.3	—	22.4	4.3	19.11	6.5	3.9
Swindon T	25.2	11.2	22.2	23.11	25.3	10.9	24.9	26.11	14.1	5.11	8.3	8.4	14.8	29.4	14.9	27.12	22.10	17.4	2.1	—	10.12	27.8	18.3	8.10
Tranmere R	1.11	15.4	31.12	25.2	19.11	26.12	11.3	30.8	6.5	17.9	4.2	21.1	29.10	1.4	18.2	3.9	22.4	17.12	24.9	20.8	—	3.12	15.10	21.3
Watford	21.3	14.1	22.4	11.2	25.2	6.5	20.8	17.9	3.9	15.4	15.10	1.4	31.12	26.12	24.9	17.12	12.11	26.11	21.2	11.3	22.10	—	5.11	30.8
WBA	3.12	31.12	26.12	24.9	4.2	22.4	17.9	18.12	1.4	22.3	18.2	9.11	2.11	3.9	29.10	20.8	15.4	25.2	8.10	31.8	29.4	21.1	—	11.3
Wolverhampton	8.4	12.11	11.2	25.3	28.12	26.11	15.10	5.11	21.2	22.10	10.2	17.4	1.10	4.3	13.8	2.1	13.9	14.1	7.3	6.5	10.9	18.3	28.8	—

ENDSLEIGH INSURANCE FIXTURES 1993–94

DIVISION TWO

	Birmingham C	Blackpool	Bournemouth	Bradford C	Brentford	Brighton & HA	Bristol R	Cambridge U	Cardiff C	Chester C	Crewe Alex	Huddersfield T	Hull C	Leyton O	Oxford U	Peterborough U	Plymouth Arg	Rotherham U	Shrewsbury T	Stockport Co	Swansea C	Wrexham	Wycombe W	York City
Birmingham C	—	31.12	19.11	22.4	7.1	29.4	29.10	26.12	15.4	20.8	1.11	8.10	24.9	17.12	21.3	17.9	3.9	1.4	21.1	4.2	11.3	25.2	30.8	18.2
Blackpool	4.4	—	10.12	15.10	25.3	13.9	18.3	14.1	10.9	21.2	7.3	13.8	6.5	5.11	11.2	2.1	28.1	25.2	27.8	27.12	22.10	24.9	26.11	18.4
Bournemouth	21.2	20.8	—	22.10	15.10	11.2	18.4	5.11	24.9	17.9	27.12	28.1	25.2	1.4	26.11	30.8	14.1	11.3	6.5	21.3	2.1	16.12	8.4	3.9
Bradford C	2.1	29.4	7.1	—	1.11	8.10	21.1	25.2	29.10	17.12	19.11	24.9	28.12	20.8	30.8	18.2	11.3	17.4	4.2	8.4	21.3	1.4	3.9	17.9
Brentford	22.10	17.9	29.4	11.2	—	26.11	8.10	28.1	22.4	15.4	4.3	21.2	5.11	26.12	31.12	20.8	17.12	30.8	1.10	11.3	14.1	3.9	21.3	1.4
Brighton & HA	15.10	1.4	2.11	6.5	4.2	—	7.1	24.9	21.1	22.3	18.2	25.2	8.4	3.9	17.9	19.11	20.8	29.10	27.12	2.1	17.12	11.3	19.4	31.8
Bristol R	28.1	31.8	26.12	5.11	6.5	22.10	—	11.2	15.10	31.12	1.10	26.11	22.2	22.4	14.1	17.12	15.4	22.3	4.3	3.9	1.4	17.9	11.3	20.8
Cambridge U	17.4	18.2	21.1	1.10	29.10	4.3	1.11	—	7.1	30.8	4.2	29.4	2.1	21.3	11.3	8.4	1.4	3.9	19.11	20.8	17.9	8.10	16.12	28.12
Cardiff C	28.12	21.3	4.3	28.1	2.1	5.11	29.4	22.10	—	1.4	8.10	14.1	25.11	11.2	20.8	1.10	17.9	8.4	17.4	17.12	3.9	30.8	21.2	11.3
Chester C	10.12	19.11	25.3	13.8	27.12	10.9	8.4	18.3	13.9		17.4	27.8	7.3	29.4	1.10	21.1	4.3	4.2	18.2	2.11	8.10	10.30	2.1	7.1
Crewe Alex	11.2	3.9	15.4	21.2	24.9	14.1	25.2	26.11	6.5	26.12	—	22.10	28.1	31.12	1.4	11.3	22.4	20.8	15.10	30.8	5.11	21.3	17.9	16.12
Huddersfield T	6.5	17.12	29.10	4.3	19.11	1.10	4.2	15.10	18.2	11.3	7.1	—	17.4	30.8	3.9	1.4	21.3	27.12	2.1	17.9	8.4	1.11	20.8	21.1
Hull C	4.3	8.10	1.10	15.4	21.1	31.12	19.11	22.4	4.2	3.9	29.10	26.12	—	11.3	17.12	21.3	30.8	17.9	7.1	18.2	20.8	29.4	1.4	1.11
Leyton O	13.8	21.1	13.9	10.12	17.4	7.3	2.1	10.9	1.11	15.10	8.4	18.3	27.8	—	4.3	4.2	1.10	7.1	25.3	29.10	27.12	18.2	6.5	19.11
Oxford U	10.9	1.11	4.2	18.3	8.4	25.3	18.2	27.8	10.12	25.2	13.9	7.3	13.8	24.9	—	17.4	8.10	19.11	29.10	21.1	29.4	7.1	27.12	2.1
Peterborough U	25.3	22.4	18.3	14.1	10.12	21.2	13.8	31.12	25.2	5.11	27.8	13.9	10.9	26.11	26.12	—	11.2	24.9	7.3	15.10	28.1	15.4	22.10	6.5
Plymouth Arg	7.3	29.10	18.2	27.8	13.8	10.12	27.12	13.9	25.3	24.9	2.1	10.9	18.3	25.2	6.5	1.11	—	21.1	8.4	7.1	17.4	19.11	15.10	4.2
Rotherham U	13.9	1.10	27.8	26.12	18.3	28.1	10.9	7.3	31.12	26.11	10.12	15.4	25.3	22.10	21.2	4.3	5.11	—	13.8	6.5	11.2	22.4	14.1	15.10
Shrewsbury T	5.11	11.3	8.10	26.11	25.2	15.4	24.9	21.2	26.12	14.1	29.4	22.4	22.10	17.9	28.1	3.9	31.12	17.12	—	1.4	30.8	20.8	11.2	21.3
Stockport Co	26.11	15.4	10.9	31.12	27.8	22.4	7.3	10.12	13.8	11.2	18.3	25.3	14.1	28.1	5.11	29.4	22.10	8.10	13.9	—	21.2	26.12	24.9	25.2
Swansea C	27.8	7.1	22.4	10.9	17.2	13.8	13.9	25.3	7.3	6.5	21.1	31.12	10.12	15.4	15.10	29.10	26.12	1.11	17.3	19.11	—	4.2	25.2	24.9
Wrexham	1.10	4.3	13.8	13.9	7.3	27.8	25.3	6.5	18.3	28.1	10.9	11.2	15.10	14.1	22.10	27.12	21.2	2.1	10.12	17.4	26.11	—	5.11	8.4
Wycombe W	18.3	4.2	31.12	7.3	10.9	26.12	27.8	13.8	19.11	22.4	25.3	10.12	13.9	8.10	15.4	7.1	29.4	18.2	1.11	4.3	1.10	21.1	—	29.10
York City	14.1	26.12	7.3	25.3	13.9	18.3	10.12	15.4	27.8	22.10	13.8	5.11	11.2	21.2	22.4	8.10	26.11	29.4	10.9	1.10	4.3	31.12	28.1	—

ENDSLEIGH INSURANCE FIXTURES 1993–94

DIVISION THREE

	Barnet	Bury	Carlisle U		Colchester U	Darlington	Doncaster R	Exeter C	Fulham	Gillingham	Hartlepool U	Hereford U	Lincoln C	Mansfield T	Northampton T	Preston N.E.	Rochdale	Scarborough	Scunthorpe U	Torquay U	Walsall	Wigan Ath
Barnet	—	19.11	7.1	29.10	18.2	4.2	10.9	2.1	1.10	27.12	18.3	8.10	21.1	8.4	29.4	27.8	13.9	10.12	13.8	4.3	17.4	25.3
Bury	11.2	—	15.4	24.9	25.2	6.5	13.9	10.12	26.11	22.10	27.8	14.1	15.10	25.3	22.4	30.8	13.8	5.11	10.9	31.12	28.1	26.12
Carlisle U	22.10	27.12	—	2.1	15.10	1.10	26.11	10.9	28.1	8.4	17.4	11.2	6.5	13.9	4.3	14.1	5.11	27.8	25.3	10.12	18.3	13.8
Chesterfield	28.1	4.3	22.4	—	6.5	15.10	26.12	13.9	22.10	11.2	25.3	5.11	31.12	21.8	15.4	26.11	10.12	13.8	14.1	1.10	10.9	18.3
Colchester U	14.1	1.10	29.4	8.10	—	4.3	27.8	18.3	15.4	5.11	10.9	31.12	22.4	10.12	26.12	22.10	11.2	25.3	26.11	13.8	13.9	28.1
Darlington	26.11	8.10	25.2	29.4	24.9	—	25.3	27.8	14.1	28.1	10.12	22.10	15.4	18.3	31.12	13.8	22.4	26.12	13.9	10.9	5.11	11.2
Doncaster R	11.3	1.4	4.2	17.4	16.12	3.9	—	21.1	30.8	2.1	19.11	16.9	18.2	7.1	20.8	24.9	25.2	29.4	27.12	29.10	8.4	8.10
Exeter C	22.4	20.8	11.3	1.4	30.8	17.12	5.11	—	29.4	3.9	1.10	15.4	17.9	4.3	8.10	28.1	14.1	26.11	22.10	26.12	11.2	31.12
Fulham	25.2	4.2	29.10	7.1	27.12	18.2	18.3	15.10	—	17.4	8.4	24.9	19.11	2.1	21.1	10.9	6.5	13.9	10.12	25.3	13.8	27.8
Gillingham	15.4	7.1	31.12	19.11	21.1	29.10	22.4	25.3	26.12	—	13.8	29.4	4.2	1.10	18.2	13.9	27.8	10.9	18.3	8.10	4.3	10.12
Hartlepool U	30.8	17.12	26.12	3.9	11.3	20.8	11.2	25.2	31.12	17.9	—	22.4	24.9	6.5	1.4	15.10	26.11	14.1	28.1	15.4	22.10	5.11
Hereford U	6.5	18.2	19.11	21.1	8.4	7.1	13.8	27.12	4.3	15.10	2.1	—	29.10	17.4	4.2	20.8	25.3	18.3	1.10	13.9	27.8	10.9
Lincoln C	5.11	29.4	8.10	8.4	2.1	27.12	14.1	13.8	11.2	26.11	4.3	28.1	—	10.9	1.10	25.3	18.3	22.10	17.4	27.8	10.12	13.9
Mansfield T	31.12	3.9	1.4	18.12	20.8	30.8	22.10	24.9	22.4	25.2	8.10	26.12	11.3	—	17.9	5.11	28.1	15.4	11.2	29.4	26.11	14.1
Northampton T	15.10	2.1	24.9	27.12	17.4	8.4	10.12	6.5	5.11	14.1	13.9	26.11	25.2	11.10	—	11.2	10.9	28.1	16.12	18.3	25.3	22.10
Preston N.E.	17.12	18.3	18.2	4.2	7.1	17.9	4.3	29.10	11.3	1.4	29.4	10.12	3.9	21.1	19.11	—	26.12	31.12	8.10	22.4	1.10	15.4
Rochdale	1.4	17.9	21.1	20.8	19.11	2.1	1.10	18.2	8.10	17.12	4.2	3.9	30.8	29.10	11.3	17.4	—	4.3	8.4	7.1	27.12	29.4
Scarborough	20.8	21.1	17.12	17.9	3.9	18.4	15.10	4.2	1.4	11.3	18.2	30.8	7.1	27.12	29.10	8.4	24.9	—	2.1	19.11	6.5	25.2
Scunthorpe U	17.9	11.3	3.9	18.2	4.2	1.4	15.4	7.1	20.8	30.8	29.10	25.2	26.12	19.11	27.8	6.5	31.12	22.4	—	21.1	15.10	24.9
Torquay U	24.9	8.4	20.8	25.2	17.9	11.3	28.1	18.4	3.9	6.5	27.12	1.4	17.12	15.10	30.8	2.1	22.10	11.2	5.11	—	14.1	26.11
Walsall	26.12	29.10	30.8	11.3	1.4	21.1	31.12	19.11	17.9	24.9	7.1	17.12	20.8	4.2	3.9	25.2	15.4	8.10	29.4	18.2	—	22.4
Wigan Ath	3.9	18.4	17.9	30.8	29.10	19.11	6.5	8.5	17.12	20.8	21.1	11.3	1.4	18.2	7.1	28.12	15.10	1.10	4.3	4.2	2.1	—

OTHER FIXTURES—SEASON 1994–95

July
16 Sat Pre Season Commences

August
10 Wed Euro Comps Prel - 1st Leg
13 Sat Football League Season Commences
14 Sun FA Charity Shield
20 Sat FA Premier League Season Commences
24 Wed Euro Comps Prel - 2nd Leg
27 Sat FA Challenge Cup Preliminary Rd
29 Mon Bank Holiday

September
3 Sat FA Vase Extra Preliminary Rd
FA Youth Challenge Cup Extra Preliminary Rd*
7 Wed International Date
10 Sat FA Challenge Cup 1st Rd Qualifying
FA Youth Challenge Cup Preliminary Rd*
14 Wed Euro Comps 1st Rd - 1st Leg
17 Sat FA Challenge Trophy 1st Rd Qualifying
18 Sun FA Women's Rd (*prov*)
24 Sat FA Challenge Cup 2nd Rd Qualifying
25 Sun FA Sunday Cup Preliminary Rd (*if required*)
28 Wed Euro Comps 1st Rd - 2nd Leg

October
1 Sat FA Challenge Vase Preliminary Rd
FA Youth Challenge Cup 1st Rd Qualifying*
8 Sat FA Challenge Cup 3rd Rd Qualifying
12 Wed International Date
15 Sat FA Challenge Trophy 2nd Rd Qualifying
FA Youth Challenge Cup 2nd Rd Qualifying*
FA County Youth Challenge Cup 1st Rd*
16 Sun FA Women's Cup 2nd Rd (*prov*)
19 Wed Euro Comps 2nd Rd - 1st Leg
22 Sat FA Challenge Cup 4th Rd Qualifying
29 Sat FA Challenge Vase 1st Rd
30 Sun FA Sunday Cup 1st Rd

November
2 Wed Euro Comps 2nd Rd - 2nd Leg
12 Sat FA Challenge Cup 1st Rd Proper
FA Youth Challenge Cup 1st Rd Proper*
13 Sun FA Women's Cup 3rd Rd (*prov*)
16 Wed International Date
19 Sat FA Challenge Vase 2nd Rd
20 Sun FA Sunday Cup 2nd Rd
23 Wed Euro Comps 3rd Rd - 1st Leg
26 Sat FA Challenge Trophy 3rd Rd Qualifying
FA County Youth Challenge Cup 2nd Rd*

December
3 Sat FA Challenge 2nd Rd Proper
4 Sun FA Women's Cup 4th Rd (*prov*)
7 Wed Euro Comps 3rd Rd - 2nd Leg
10 Sat FA Challenge Vase 3rd Rd
FA Youth Challenge Cup 2nd Rd Proper*
11 Sun FA Sunday Cup 3rd Rd
14 Wed International Date
25 Sun Christmas Day
26 Mon Boxing Day
27 Tue Bank Holiday

* = closing date of round.

January
1 Sun New Years Day
2 Mon Bank Holiday
7 Sat FA Challenge Cup 3rd Rd Proper
14 Sat FA Challenge Vase 4th Rd
FA Youth Challenge Cup 3rd Rd Proper*
FA County Youth Challenge Cup 3rd Rd*
15 Sun FA Women's Cup 5th Rd (*prov*)
21 Sat FA Challenge Trophy 1st Rd Proper
22 Sun FA Sunday Cup 4th Rd
28 Sat FA Challenge Cup 4th Rd Proper

February
4 Sat FA Challenge Vase 5th Rd
FA Youth Challenge Cup 4th Rd Proper*
11 Sat FA Challenge Trophy 2nd Rd Proper
12 Sun FA Women's Cup 6th Rd (*prov*)
18 Sat FA Challenge Cup 5th Rd Proper
FA County Youth Challenge Cup 4th Rd*
19 Sun FA Sunday Cup 5th Rd
25 Sat FA Challenge Vase 6th Rd

March
1 Wed Euro Comps Quarter Finals - 1st leg
4 Sat FA Challenge Trophy 3rd Rd Proper
FA Youth Challenge Cup 5th Rd Proper*
11 Sat FA Challenge Cup 6th Rd Proper
15 Wed Euro Comps Quarter Finals - 2nd Leg
18 Sat FA Challenge Vase Semi-Final 1st Leg
FA County Youth Challenge Cup Semi-Final*
19 Sun FA Women's Cup Semi-Final (*prov*)
25 Sat FA Challenge Trophy 4th Rd Proper
FA Challenge Vase Semi-Final 2nd Leg
29 Wed International Date

April
1 Sat FA Youth Challenge Cup Semi-Finals*
2 Sun FA Sunday Cup Semi-Final
5 Wed Euro Comps Semi Finals - 1st Leg
8 Sat FA Challenge Trophy Semi-Finals - 1st Leg
9 Sun FA Challenge Cup Semi-Finals
14 Fri Good Friday
15 Sat FA Challenge Trophy Semi-Finals - 2nd Leg
17 Mon Easter Monday
19 Wed Euro Comps Semi Finals - 2nd Leg
26 Wed International Date
29 Sat FA County Youth Final (*fixed date*)
30 Sun FA Women's Cup Final (*prov*)

May
1 Mon Bank Holiday
3 Wed European Final
6 Sat FA Youth Challenge Cup Final*
7 Sun FA Sunday Cup Final
10 Wed European Final
13 Sat FA Challenge Vase Final - Wembley Stadium
14 Sun FA Challenge Trophy Final - Wembley Stadium
17 Wed European Final
20 Sat FA Challenge Cup Final - Wembley Stadium
24 Wed European Final
25 Thu FA Challenge Cup Final Possible Replay - Wembley Stadium
29 Mon Bank Holiday

continued from page 26
fait accompli relegation are strongly denied. Ray Wilkins joins newly promoted Crystal Palace. In the High Court, Dean Saunders, giving his version of the challenge in question, says he lifted his feet instinctively to avoid getting seriously hurt.

28 Wycombe twice go behind but beat Preston 4-2 in the Div 3 play-off at Wembley to earn promotion in their first season in the League.

29 Ireland inflict Germany's first home defeat for 6 years with a somewhat sensational 2-0 victory in Hanover. In the Division 2 play-off final at Wembley, Stockport take a 2-minute lead, but Michael Wallace and then scorer Chris Beaumont are sent off and Burnley, who finished 12 points behind their opponents in the League, win 2-1. Archie Gemmill is sacked after 7 years on Nottm Forest's coaching staff.

30 It's 3rd time lucky for Leicester at Wembley as they need some good fortune to beat Derby 2-1 in the Div 1 play-off final, Steve Walsh scoring both goals, the first-half equalizer in controversial circumstances after keeper Martin Taylor appears to be fouled. Ruud Gullit walks out on the Dutch World Cup squad, apparently after further disagreements with coach Dick Advocaat.

31 Wolves complete the £1.25m signing of winger Tony Daley from Villa on a 4-year contract. The Scottish League make it 3 points for a win next season.

June

England win Toulon Under-21s ... Forest sign £2.5m Roy ... Bobby Charlton knighted ... FA Cup to be sponsored ... Dean Saunders cleared ... FIFA tampers with the laws

1 Arsenal sign Swedish World Cup midfielder Stefan Schwarz from Benfica for £1.75m. Former Ipswich back George Burley, Ayr manager for the last 5 years, takes over at Colchester. Further punishment for Marseille - they are barred from signing new players.

2 Danny Wilson becomes player-manager of Barnsley, taking over from Viv Anderson, who has joined Bryan Robson as assistant at Middlesbrough.

3 The FA nominate Newcastle, 3rd in the Premiership, for an extra English club place in next season's UEFA Cup (after Villa and Blackburn) as a replacement for an entry from the former Yugoslavia. Liverpool announce a planned new rights issue to raise £9.8m for improvements and new players.

4 Colombia register an impressive 2-0 win over N.Ireland in Boston.

5 Ireland are brought down to earth in Dublin, where the Czechs beat them 3-1 in their farewell performance before setting out for the United States. The USA enjoy an encouraging result in their last warm-up match, beating Mexico 1-0 in Pasadena, where most of the 91,000 crowd are Mexicans, with a goal from Coventry's Roy Wegerle. Croatian Josip Weber, who became a Belgian citizen in March, scores 5 in Brussels on his début for Belgium in their 9-0 thrashing of Zambia, who are reduced to 10 men after half an hour.

7 England Under-21s beat Portugal 2-0 to win the Toulon tournament for the 4th time in 5 years. Italian club Foggia's Dutch international winger Bryan Roy agrees to sign for newly promoted Nottm Forest in a deal worth around £2.5m.

8 The unpopular squad numbering in the Premiership is to stay.

9 The Football League will allow clubs to have team numbers on their shorts (and shirts without numbers) if they wish, and squad numbers too - the choice is up to each club. Brazil hit form at the right time, beating Honduras 8-2 in San Diego, but their victory does not satisfy the media critics at home.

10 Bobby Charlton is knighted in the Birthday Honours list, the 4th footballer to be so honoured - after Sir Stanley, Sir Alf and the late Sir Matt. Rangers striker Ally McCoist receives the MBE. The FA Cup is to be part of a big sponsorship deal to be called Total Football in which the FA and Wembley Stadium will pool certain commercial rights to allow up to a dozen companies to associate themselves with the FA Cup, England internationals, and other important games. The 9-day High Court hearing finishes with Dean Saunders cleared of making a reckless challenge and Paul Elliott, who loses his claim for compensation, is left with a bill for costs estimated at £500,000. Mr Justice Drake, while emphasising that players have every right to seek redress in the courts for career-wrecking injuries resulting from foul play, accepted in this instance that Saunders had made an honest attempt to play the ball.

11 Ireland manager Jack Charlton blows his top as he accuses FIFA of risking World Cup chaos by tampering with the laws at the last moment, referring to strict directives to World Cup referees and linesmen to treat the tackle from behind (whatever that is) as a red-card offence and to not give offside for attackers coming back from an offside position. The justifiably indignant Charlton's main gripe is the lack of consultation with and explanation afforded to coaches and the suddenness of the edicts.

12 FIFA's 'crazy gang' strikes again, with a new edict to referees to prevent players being supplied with drinks during matches, prompting Ireland's chief medical officer Michael Walsh to warn of possible fatal consequences if the ban is not lifted. Kevin Moran and David Kelly are injured and will not be available for selection for Ireland's World Cup opener with Italy on Saturday. Jack Charlton denies newspaper rumours that Roy Keane and assistant manager Maurice Setters were involved in a row during training, and threatens to end co-operation with the media if certain members of the press continue to try to undermine the Irish party. Former Liverpool chairman Noel White is elected unopposed as chairman of the FA's international committee, replacing the retired Peter Swales. Swindon chairman Ray Hardman insists Spurs should be demoted, as Swindon were in 1990, if they are found guilty of wrongful payments to players. England Schoolboys beat France 2-1 to complete their first ever 100% season, having won all 8 matches.

REFEREEING AND THE REFEREES

The spotlight has fallen on referees more than ever over the last two seasons, as FIFA seeks to impose fresh rulings into the Seventeen Laws in order to make the game cleaner, to keep the ball in play more often and to encourage attacking football. Originally the Four Home Countries of England, Ireland, Scotland and Wales formed the International Board who had the Law-making powers within their control. Nowadays FIFA representatives have an equal number of four votes with the Home Countries and six out of eight votes are needed for a change in the Laws or their sub-text.

The International Board meets annually and changes are published at the end of one season for implementation at the start of the next.

The referees, as arbitrators and enforcers of the Laws on the field of play, have been required to apply new instructions for the start of the 1994–95 season, although it is emphasized that Law Twelve relating to misconduct has not been amended. FIFA now requires referees to be stricter on the tackle from behind in which players are frequently kicked. Linesmen will be asked to follow the system adopted in World Cup '94 and give the benefit of the doubt to attacking players in possible off-side positions; whilst the Laws will provide for a substitute goalkeeper to be used as well as the two normal outfield players, even though the original goalkeeper may have been sent off for misconduct. Domestically in England control of referees is supervised by the Football Association Referees' Committee and their Instructional Committee is responsible for the Referee Instructors Course held annually. The Referees Association deals with the practical side producing kits, manuals and details of in-service training and also supplies an Insurance Scheme.

Each County has a County Football Association which in turn has a Referees' Secretary and the County Football Association finances courses and seminars for referees, also appointing a Disciplinary Committee which exacts fines from errant players.

In view of the change which saw the Football League having four Divisions reduced to three, with the Football Association controlling the Premier League, it was decided to introduce a National Panel of referees prior to that stage. This is administered by the National Director of Refereeing, Ken Ridden at the Football Association, 16 Lancaster Gate, London W2 3LW. He is responsible for appointing referees to Premiership games but the Football League have their own Committee who appoint their referees. For the 1994–95 season the Premiership Referees will not referee in the Endsleigh Insurance League. Colin Downey of the Football Association makes the various FA Cup appointments.

The age for National Referees to retire is 48 but subject to fitness and successful markings, referees can be invited to remain on the Panel longer. Referees are constantly assessed either by officially appointed assessors or in the Premiership also by the clubs themselves.

Three former FIFA referees retired last season namely Roger Milford, Keith Hackett and Alan Gunn. New referees added to the list this term include last season's two FA Cup linesmen Graham Barber and Paul Rejer and they are supplemented by A. N. Butler; A. P. D'Urso; R. D. Furnandiz; R. J. Harris; S. W. Mathieson; U. D. Rennie; P. R. Richards; and M. A. Riley. The three over age referees are Terry Holbrook, Kelvin Morton and Joe Worrall.

KEN GOLDMAN

The full current list of National Referees is as follows:-

LIST OF REFEREES FOR SEASON 1994–95

Paul Alcock, (S. Merstham, Surrey)
David Allison, (Lancaster)
Gerald Ashby, (Worcester)
Mike Bailey, (Impington, Cambridge)
Graham Barber, (Guildford)
Neil Barry, (Scunthorpe)
Ray Bigger, (Croydon)
Martin Bodenham, (Looe, Cornwall)
John Brandwood, (Lichfield, Staffs.)
Kevin Breen, (Liverpool)
Keith Burge, (Tonypandy)
Billy Burns, (Scarborough)
Alan Butler, (Sutton-in-Ashfield)
George Cain, (Bootle)
Keith Cooper, (Pontypridd)
Keith Cooper, (Swindon)
Ian Cruikshanks, (Hartlepool)
Paul Danson, (Leicester)
Alan Dawson, (Jarrow)
Roger Dilkes, (Mossley, Lancs.)
Phil Don, (Hanworth Park, Middlesex)
Steve Dunn, (Bristol)
Paul Durkin, (Portland, Dorset)
Andy D'Urso, (Wickford, Essex)
David Elleray, (Harrow)
Alan Flood, (Stockport)
Peter Foakes, (Clacton-on-Sea)
Roger Furnandiz, (Doncaster)
Dermot Gallagher, (Banbury, Oxon)
Rodger Giffod, (Llanbradach, Mid Glam.)
Bob Harris, (Oxford)
Paul Harrison, (Oldham)
Robert Hart, (Darlington)
Terry Heilbron, (Newton Aycliff)
Ian Hemley, (Ampthill, Beds.)
Brian Hill, (Kettering)
John Holbrook, (Ludlow)
Terry Holbrook, (Walsall)*
Peter Jones, (Loughborough)
John Kirkby, (Sheffield)
Ken Leach, (Wolverhampton)
John Lloyd, (Wrexham)
Stephen Lodge, (Barnsley)
Eddie Lomas, (Manchester)
Terry Lunt, (Ashton-in-Makerfield, Lancs)
Ken Lupton, (Stockton-on-Tees)
Kevin Lynch, (Lincoln)
Scott Mathieson, (Stockport)
Kelvin Morton, (Bury St. Edmunds)*
David Orr, (Iver)
Jim Parker, (Preston)
Micky Pierce, (Portsmouth)
Graham Poll, (Berkhamsted)
Graham Pooley, (Bishops Stortford)
Richard Poulain, (Huddersfield)
Mike Reed, (Birmingham)
Paul Rejer, (Tipton)
Uriah Rennie, (Sheffield)
Phil Richards, (Preston)
Mike Riley, (Leeds)
Jim Rushton, (Stoke-on-Trent)
Gurnam Singh, (Wolverhampton)
Paul Vanes, (Warley, West Midlands)
John Watson, (Whitley Bay)
Trevor West, (Hull)
Clive Wilkes, (Gloucester)
Alan Wilkie, (Chester-le-Street)
Gary Willard, (Worthing, W. Sussex)
Jeff Winter, (Middlesbrough)
Eddie Wolstenholme, (Blackburn)
Joe Worrall, (Warrington)*
Philip Wright, (Northwich)

* Over 48.